The ENCYCLOPEDIA
of CHRISTIANITY

Volume 2
E–I

The
of

Volume 2

editors

translator and English-language editor

statistical editor

WILLIAM B. EERDMANS PUBLISHING COMPANY
BRILL

ENCYCLOPEDIA CHRISTIANITY

E–I

Erwin Fahlbusch
Jan Milič Lochman
John Mbiti
Jaroslav Pelikan
Lukas Vischer

Geoffrey W. Bromiley

David B. Barrett

GRAND RAPIDS, MICHIGAN / CAMBRIDGE, U.K.
LEIDEN / BOSTON / KÖLN

Originally published in German as
Evangelisches Kirchenlexikon, Dritte Auflage (Neufassung)
© 1986, 1989, 1992, 1996, 1997
Vandenhoeck & Ruprecht, Göttingen, Germany

English translation © 2001 by
Wm. B. Eerdmans Publishing Company

Published 2001 by
Wm. B. Eerdmans Publishing Company
255 Jefferson Ave. S.E., Grand Rapids, Michigan 49503

Printed in the United States of America

05 04 03 02 01   10 9 8 7 6 5 4 3 2 1

Library of Congress Cataloging-in-Publication Data

Evangelisches Kirchenlexikon. English.
    The encyclopedia of Christianity / editors, Erwin Fahlbusch . . . [et al.];
translator and English-language editor, Geoffrey W. Bromiley;
statistical editor, David B. Barrett; foreword, Jaroslav Pelikan.
        p.   cm.
    Includes index.
    Contents: v. 2. E–I.
    ISBN 0-8028-2414-5 (cloth: v. 2.: alk. paper)
    1. Christianity — Encyclopedias.   I. Fahlbusch, Erwin.
II. Bromiley, Geoffrey William.   III. Title.
BR95.E8913   2001
230′.003 — DC21   98-45953
                                            CIP

Brill ISBN 90 04 11695 8

Contents

List of Entries

This list does not include headings that simply refer the reader to a cross-reference.

Publishers' Note to Volume Two

The William B. Eerdmans Publishing Company and E. J. Brill are pleased to publish this second volume of the *Encyclopedia of Christianity*. As in the first volume, so here the articles reflect the commitment of the original *Evangelisches Kirchenlexikon* to describe Christianity both broadly and deeply, taking full account of its varied global, ecumenical, sociocultural, and historical contexts.

The task of shaping the *EC* for an English-language audience has been considerably eased by the addition to the editorial staff of Norman A. Hjelm and Roger S. Boraas. They have, respectively, assigned new articles or additions to articles where needed for the sake of an English readership, and anglicized and updated the bibliographies that accompany each article. Thanks are due these two, as well as the various editors and advisers mentioned in the Publishers' Preface to volume 1, for helping move this entire project one step nearer to completion.

Introduction

This introduction provides a brief guide to the editorial conventions followed throughout the *Encyclopedia of Christianity,* as well as to the statistical information specially prepared for the *EC* by David Barrett.

ALPHABETIZATION

Articles are arranged alphabetically word by word (not letter by letter), with hyphens and apostrophes counted as continuing the single word; all commas are ignored. For example:

Antiochian Theology
Anti-Semitism, Anti-Judaism
. . .
Augsburg Confession
Augsburg, Peace of
. . .
Calvin, John
Calvinism
Calvin's Theology
. . .
Church Year
Churches of Christ

STATISTICS

The *EC* includes separate articles for each of the six major areas (formerly "continents") currently recognized by the United Nations (i.e., Africa, Asia, Europe, Latin America and the Caribbean, Northern America, and Oceania). It also presents separate articles for all independent countries of the world, omitting only those whose population, according to U.N. estimates for 1995, is less than 200,000 (e.g., Andorra, Nauru).

Accompanying each country article is a standard statistical box with the following format:

Argentina

	1960	1980	2000
Population (1,000s):	20,616	28,094	37,032
Annual growth rate (%):	1.55	1.51	1.19

Area: 2,780,400 sq. km. (1,073,518 sq. mi.)

A.D. *2000*

Population density: 13/sq. km. (34/sq. mi.)
Births / deaths: 1.90 / 0.78 per 100 population
Fertility rate: 2.44 per woman
Infant mortality rate: 20 per 1,000 live births
Life expectancy: 74.2 years (m: 70.6, f: 77.7)
Religious affiliation (%): Christians 92.9 (Roman Catholics 90.2, Protestants 5.9, indigenous 5.4, marginal 1.4, unaffiliated 1.1, other Christians 0.6), nonreligious 2.2, Muslims 2.0, Jews 1.5, other 1.4.

The demographic information in these boxes is taken from the *World Population Prospects: The 1996 Revision* (New York [United Nations], 1998). Depending on the presentation in U.N. tables, figures for 1960, 1980, and 2000 are either for that year alone or for a five-year period beginning with that year. In each case where the United Nations provides three estimates, the medium variant estimates are cited. Information on country area is taken from the *1996 Britannica Book of the Year* (Chicago, 1996). For countries like Argentina, where the birth rate minus the death rate (1.12 per 100 population) does not equal the annual growth rate (1.19), the difference is due to migration — in this case, *into* the country.

David Barrett, editor of the *World Christian Encyclopedia* (New York, 1982; 3-vol. rev. ed., forthcoming) and president of Global Evangelization Movement, Richmond, Virginia, has provided all the information on religious affiliation in the statistical boxes. In the first place, the boxes present the breakdown of overall religious affiliation for each country, using the following 16 categories:

atheists — persons professing atheism, skepticism, or disbelief, including antireligious (opposed to all religion)

Baha'is — followers of the Baha'i World Faith, founded in the 19th century by Bahā' Allāh

Buddhists — followers of any of the branches of Buddhism; worldwide, 56 percent are Mahayana (northern), 38 percent Theravada (Hinayana, or southern), 6 percent Tantrayana (Lamaism)

Chinese folk religionists — followers of the traditional Chinese religion, which includes local deities, ancestor veneration, Confucian ethics, Taoism, divination, and some Buddhist elements

Christians — followers of Jesus Christ, either affiliated with churches or simply identifying themselves as such in censuses or polls

Confucianists — non-Chinese followers of Confucius and Confucianism, mostly Koreans in Korea

Hindus — followers of the main Hindu traditions; worldwide, 70 percent are Vaishnavas, 25 percent Saivas, 3 percent Saktas, 2 percent neo-Hindus and reform Hindus

Jews — adherents of Judaism

Muslims — followers of Islam; worldwide, 83 percent are Sunnites, 16 percent Shiites, 1 percent other schools

new religionists — followers of Asian 20th-century new religions, new religious movements, radical new crisis religions, and non-Christian syncretistic mass religions, all founded since 1800 and most since 1945

nonreligious — persons professing no religion, nonbelievers, agnostics, freethinkers, dereligionized secularists indifferent to all religion

Shintoists — Japanese who profess Shinto as their first or major religion

Sikhs — followers of the Sikh reform movement arising out of Hinduism

spiritists — non-Christian spiritists, spiritualists, thaumaturgists, medium-religionists

Taoists — followers of the religion developed from the Taoist philosophy and from folk religion and Buddhism

tribal religionists — primal or primitive religionists, animists, spirit-worshipers, shamanists, ancestor-venerators, polytheists, pantheists, traditionalists, local or tribal folk-religionists

The country boxes list each religious group that numbers at least 1.0 percent of the population of that county; any groups that number 0.9 percent or less of the population are grouped together under "other." Because of rounding, the totals of all the religious groups in a country may not equal 100.0 percent.

Second, for the category "Christians," the infor-

mation in the boxes shows in parentheses the breakdown by ecclesiastical bloc, using the following seven categories:

Anglicans — persons in a church that is in fellowship with the archbishop of Canterbury, especially through its participation in the Lambeth Conference; Episcopalians

indigenous — Christians in denominations, churches, or movements who regard themselves as outside of mainline Anglican/Orthodox/ Protestant/Roman Catholic Christianity; autonomous bodies independent of foreign origin or control (e.g., Independent Charismatic Churches [Braz.], house church movement [China], isolated radio believers [Saudi Arabia], Zion Christian Church [S.Af.], Vineyard Christian Fellowship [U.S.])

marginal — followers of para-Christian or quasi-Christian Western movements or deviations out of mainline Protestantism, not professing Christian doctrine according to the classic Trinitarian creeds (i.e., Apostles', Nicene) but often claiming a second or supplementary or ongoing source of divine revelation in addition to the Bible (e.g., Christian Scientists, Jehovah's Witnesses, Mormons, Unitarians)

Orthodox — Eastern (Chalcedonian), Oriental (Pre-Chalcedonian, Non-Chalcedonian, Monophysite), Nestorian (Assyrian), and nonhistorical Orthodox

Protestants — persons in churches that trace their origin or formulation to the 16th-century Reformation and thus typically emphasize justification by faith alone and the Bible as the supreme authority, including (1) churches in the Lutheran, Calvinistic, and Zwinglian traditions; and (2) other groups arising before, during, or after the Reformation (e.g., Waldenses, Bohemian Brethren, Baptists, Friends, Congregationalists, Methodists, Adventists, Pentecostals, Assemblies of God)

Roman Catholics — persons in a church that recognizes the pope, the bishop of Rome (with the associated hierarchy), as its spiritual head

unaffiliated — professing Christians not associated with any church

As with the different religions, so for the different types of Christians, any group that numbers at least 1.0 percent of the population of the country is listed. Any groups of Christians that number 0.9 percent or less of the population are included together under "other Christians." Because of rounding, the totals of all the individual Christian groups may not equal the total percentage of Christians. Furthermore, where persons affiliate themselves with, or are claimed by, two Christian groups at once, the total of the percentages of the individual Christian groups in a country may exceed the countrywide percentage of Christians. This problem of double counting (evident, for example, in the Argentina box on p. xi) is left unresolved in the *EC*.

Accompanying each major area article are three tables that list most of the information appearing in the individual country statistical boxes. The first table displays demographic information; the second, data on overall religious affiliation; the third, data on church affiliation. The religion tables list separately the 12 most popular religions worldwide (i.e., the above list of 16 minus Baha'is, Confucianists, Shintoists, and Taoists), with all the others accounted for under "Other." In the tables showing ecclesiastical breakdown, all Christians are counted in one of the seven categories (or, in cases of double counting, in more than one category). The tables of religion and of Christianity report country by country all adherents of a religious position or Christian grouping that total at least 0.1 percent of the population. In addition, all tables present totals for the major area as a whole, as well as for each region that U.N. statistics distinguish within the major area. (The tables accompanying "Africa," for example, show totals for the whole continent; for the regions of eastern, middle, northern, southern, and western Africa; and also for each country that has a separate article in the *EC*.) Finally, for purposes of comparison, relevant figures for the whole world appear as the top row of each major area table.

CROSS-REFERENCES

A variety of cross-references aid the reader in locating articles or specific sections of articles. One type appears as a main title, either (1) making clear where a subject is treated or (2) indicating the exact article title. For example:

(1) **Aid** → Christian Development Services; Development 1.4

Anathema → Confessions and Creeds

(2) **Ancient Church** → Early Church

Ancient Oriental Churches → Oriental Orthodox Churches

Other cross-references appear within the text of articles. Those referring to other sections of the present article have the form "(see 1)," "(see 3.2)."

Cross-references to other articles cited as such appear (3) within parentheses in the text, following a cross-reference arrow and using the exact spelling and capitalization of the article title, and (4) on a separate line after the text proper and before the bibliography. In both cases, multiple cross-references are separated by semicolons, and only a single, initial arrow is used. Items cross-referenced within the text of an article normally do not also appear following the text of the article.

(3) In the latter part of the 20th century some churches in the United States and Europe have tried to revive the right of church asylum for some refugees whom the government refused to recognize as political refugees (→ Sanctuary 1; Resistance, Right of, 2).

As such, dance rejects an antibiblical dualism (→ Anthropology 2.3 and 3.2; Soul).

The Roman Catholic Church reacted negatively, placing Beccaria's book on the Index (→ Censorship; Inquisition 2). Then in the 19th century F. D. E. Schleiermacher (1768-1834; → Schleiermacher's Theology) criticized theologically the theory of retribution.

(4) → Anglican Communion 4; Clergy and Laity; Consensus 4; Councils of the Church

→ Catholicism (Roman); Church 3.2; Lay Movements

→ Communities, Spiritual; Ethics 2; Monasticism 3.2.2; Property, esp. 3.2-3

Finally (5), cross-references also appear within the flow of the text, with an arrow appearing before a word or phrase that points clearly (but not necessarily exactly) to the title of another article. Specific sections referred to are indicated by section marks and numbers in parentheses. Normally (6), the exact name of an article is used if a specific section is cited.

(5) The extension of the problem to political matters makes it necessary to define the re-

lations between the obedience of → faith (§3), → freedom (§2), and → reason.

In the controversy with the → Pelagians Augustine's main concern was to show that grace is not limited to external aids like the → law (§§3.1-2) or the teaching and example of Christ.

Jewish → proselyte baptism incorporates the baptized not only into the religious fellowship but also into God's → covenant → people. This matter is relevant in the dialogue between Israel and the → church (§§1.4.1.3, 2.1, 5.5.3).

(6) . . . the 19th-century → apocalyptic movement in the United States.

vs. . . . the 19th-century apocalyptic movement (→ Apocalypticism 3) in the United States.

BIBLIOGRAPHIES

Within a bibliography (or separate section of a bibliography), entries are ordered first by author, then by title (disregarding an initial article in any language). Successive articles by the same author(s) are separated by semicolons.

In individual bibliographic entries, the names of series are included only if the title is omitted (typically only for biblical commentaries). For works appearing both in a non-English language and in English translation, normally only the English title is cited.

Consulting Editors

Ulrich Becker *Education*
Eugene L. Brand *Liturgy; Worship*
Faith E. Burgess *Women's Studies/Issues*
Carsten Colpe *Religious Studies*
Hans-Werner Gensichen† *Asia; Mission Studies*
Martin Greschat *Biographies; Church History*
Heimo Hofmeister *Philosophy*
Hubertus G. Hubbeling† *Philosophy*
Anastasios Kallis *Orthodoxy*
Leo Laeyendecker *Sociology*

Ekkehard Mühlenberg *Church History*
Hans-Jürgen Prien *Latin America*
Dietrich Ritschl *Systematic Theology; Ethics*
Jürgen Roloff *New Testament*
Joachim Scharfenberg† *Practical Theology; Psychology*
Traugott Schöfthaler *Sociology*
Rudolf Smend *Old Testament*
Albert Stein† *Law; Church Law*

Contributors

K. C. Abraham, *Bangalore, India*
Ecumenical Association of Third World Theologians
Edwin Aguiluz, *Heredia, C.R.*
Honduras
Ruth Albrecht, *Hamburg*
Hesychasm; Hussites
Richard E. Allison, *Ashland, Ohio*
Foot Washing
Constantin Andronikof†, *Paris*
Eucharistic Ecclesiology; God 6
Helga Anschütz, *Reinbek, Ger.*
Iran
Dirk van Arkel, *Oegstgeest, Neth.*
Ghetto
Jan Assmann, *Heidelberg, Ger.*
Egyptian Religion

Marianne Awerbuch, *Berlin*
Israel 2
Robert Bach, *Wuppertal, Ger.*
Ezra and Nehemiah, Books of
Dieter Baltzer, *Beckum, Ger.*
Ezekiel, Book of
James Barr, *Oxford*
Fundamentalism
Ecumenical Patriarch Bartholomew, *Istanbul*
Economy (Orthodox Theology)
Christian Bartsch, *Düsseldorf, Ger.*
Early Catholicism
Arno Baruzzi, *Augsburg, Ger.*
Future
Paul Bassett, *Kansas City, Mo.*
Holiness Movement

CONTRIBUTORS

JÖRG BAUR, *Göttingen, Ger.*
Independent Churches

JOHANNES BERGER, *Mannheim, Ger.*
Industrial Society

KLAUS BERGER, *Heidelberg, Ger.*
Gentiles, Gentile Christianity

WILHELM BERGER, *Klagenfurt, Aus.*
Ideology

ULRICH BERNER, *Bayreuth, Ger.*
Incarnation 1

REINHOLD BERNHARDT, *Heidelberg, Ger.*
God 7

HELMUT BERNSMEIER, *Bad Zwesten, Ger.*
Impressionism

PETER BEYERHAUS, *Tübingen, Ger.*
Evangelical Missions; Faith Missions

KARL-HEINRICH BIERITZ, *Rostock, Ger.*
Eucharist, Overview, 1, 4

HANS BIETENHARD, *Steffisburg, Switz.*
Hope 1

ANDRÉ BIRMELÉ, *Strasbourg, Fr.*
France

RENÉ BLANC, *Paris*
French Missions

HANS JOCHEN BOECKER, *Wuppertal, Ger.*
Holiness Code

JONATHAN J. BONK, *New Haven, Conn.*
Ethiopia; Ethiopian Orthodox Church

HARTMUT BOOCKMANN, *Göttingen, Ger.*
Feudalism; Flagellants

ROGER S. BORAAS, *Elkins Park, Pa.*
Ethics 2; Hermeneutics 1

SUSANNE BOSSE, *Göttingen, Ger.*
Gestalt Psychology

STEVEN BOUMA-PREDIGER, *Holland, Mich.*
Ecology; Environment; Environmental Ethics

BERNHARD BRON, *Siegen, Ger.*
Guilt

GRAEME BROWN, *Edinburgh*
Iona Community

ROBERT F. BROWN, *Newark, Del.*
Epistemology 1; Idealism

DON S. BROWNING, *Chicago*
Ego Psychology; Identity

MICHAEL VON BRÜCK, *Munich*
Hinduism; Hinduism and Christianity; India

WOLF-DIETRICH BUKOW, *Cologne*
Everyday Life 2

CHRISTOPH BURCHARD, *Heidelberg, Ger.*
Golden Rule

JAMES R. BUTTS, *Sonoma, Calif.*
Genizah

TED A. CAMPBELL, *Washington, D.C.*
Ecumenical Symbols; Ecumenical Theology 4;
Episcopacy 6

RODOLFO CARDENAL, S.J., *San Salvador, E.S.*
El Salvador

SUSANNA BEDE CAROSELLI, S.S.G., *Grantham, Pa.*
Iconography

EMILIO CASTRO, *Geneva*
Evangelism

DAN-ILIE CIOBOTEA, *Celigny, Switz.*
Eschatology 4

ANNE L. CLARK, *Burlington, Vt.*
Hildegard of Bingen

CARSTEN COLPE, *Berlin*
Ecstasy; Egypt; Fire; God 1-3; Hell 1;
History of Religion; Iranian Religions

JOHN S. CONWAY, *Vancouver, B.C.*
Germany

JOHN W. COOPER, *Grand Rapids*
Immortality

JAMES L. CRENSHAW, *Durham, N.C.*
Ecclesiastes, Book of

PAUL A. CROW JR., *Indianapolis*
Faith and Order Movement

RONALD S. CUNSOLO, *Ormond Beach, Fla.*
Italy

KARL-FRITZ DAIBER, *Hannover, Ger.*
Foreigners, Aliens 1

INGOLF U. DALFERTH, *Tübingen, Ger.*
Faith 3

JOSEF DERBOLAV, *Bonn*
Ethics 1

WALTER DIETRICH, *Bern, Switz.*
Isaiah, Book of

JAMES DONOHUE, C.R., *Emmitsburg, Md.*
Funeral 2.2-3, 5.1

MARY ANN DONOVAN, S.C., *Berkeley, Calif.*
Irenaeus of Lyons

SILKE DORER-GOMMERMANN, *Hofheim, Ger.*
Erasmus

ANGELIKA DÖRFLER-DIERKEN, *Grosshansdorf, Ger.*
Eckhart, Meister

BERND T. DRÖSSLER, *Erfurt, Ger.*
Immunity

SIEGFRIED RUDOLF DUNDE, *Bonn*
Humility

HELMUT DÜRBECK, *Nürnberg, Ger.*
Greek Language

MARKUS EHAM, *Munich*
Gregorian Chant

CHRISTOPH ELSAS, *Berlin*
Hellenistic-Roman Religion; Henotheism;
Initiation Rites 1

GEORG ELWERT, *Berlin*
Ethnology; Hunger
HARRY ESKEW, *New Orleans*
Hymnology
ERWIN FAHLBUSCH, *Montouliers, Fr.*
Eschatology, Overview; European Theology
(Modern Period) 2; Everyday Life 1, 3-4;
Grace, Overview; Hierarchy 2; Incarnation 3
ALAN D. FALCONER, *Geneva*
Ireland
WOLFGANG FAUTH, *Göttingen, Ger.*
Greek Religion
GÜNTER FIGAL, *Stuttgart*
Historicism
BALTHASAR FISCHER, *Trier, Ger.*
Holy Year; Initiation Rites 2
HERMANN FISCHER, *Hamburg*
Encyclopedia
THOMAS FITZGERALD, *Brookline, Mass.*
Ecumenical Patriarchate
WALLACE N. FLETCHER, *Philadelphia*
Group and Group Dynamics
CHARLES W. FORMAN, *New Haven, Conn.*
Fiji
DENNIS W. FRADO, *New York*
Foreigners, Aliens
DEAN FREIDAY, *Manasquan, N.J.*
Friends, Society of
CHRISTOFER FREY, *Bochum, Ger.*
Humanity
HERBERT FROST, *Cologne*
Elder
THOMAS GANDOW, *Berlin*
EST
ADRIAAN GEENSE†, *Geneva*
Ecumenical Theology 1-3
ERICH GELDBACH, *Bochum, Ger.*
Evangelical Movement; Free Church; Hutterites
CHRISTOF GESTRICH, *Berlin*
Forgiveness
BERNHARD GIESEN, *Giessen, Ger.*
Functionalism
EVA GIESSLER-WIRSIG, *Freiburg, Ger.*
History, Auxiliary Sciences to
DAVID GILL, *Sydney, Austral.*
Force, Violence, Nonviolence 2
KAREN GLOY, *Luzern, Switz.*
Irrationalism
WINFRIED GLÜER, *Metzingen, Ger.*
Hong Kong and Macao
J. F. GERHARD GOETERS†, *Bonn*
Heidelberg Catechism; Helvetic Confession

FELICITAS D. GOODMAN, *Columbus, Ohio*
Exorcism 1
ANDREAS GRAESER, *Bern, Switz.*
Greek Philosophy
CARLOS GRANJA RODRÍGUEZ, *Quito, Ecua.*
Ecuador
HANS-HERMANN GROOTHOFF,
Bergisch Gladbach, Ger.
Education 1
HEINER GROTE†, *Bensheim, Ger.*
Encyclicals; Exemption; Filiation
ANSELM GRÜN, *Münsterschwarzach, Ger.*
Fasting
JOHANNES GRÜNDEL, *Munich*
Ethics 4
BERNHARÐUR GUÐMUNDSSON, *Reykjavik, Ice.*
Iceland
ALLEN C. GUELZO, *St. Davids, Pa.*
Edwards, Jonathan
ANTONIUS H. J. GUNNEWEG†, *Bonn*
Genesis, Book of; Israel 1
ROBIN F. GURNEY, *Geneva*
Europe
GERT HAENDLER, *Bad Doberan, Ger.*
Germanic Mission
HERMANN HAFNER, *Marburg, Ger.*
Edification
HEINZ HALM, *Tübingen, Ger.*
Islam 1-9
CHARLES E. HAMBRICK-STOWE, *Lancaster, Pa.*
Finney, Charles Grandison
ERNST HAMMERSCHMIDT†, *Vienna*
Ethiopian Orthodox Church
ROBERT HANHART, *Göttingen, Ger.*
Esther, Book of
HERBERT HANREICH, *Heidelberg, Ger.*
Immanence and Transcendence
GUNNAR HASSELBLATT†, *Berlin*
Ethiopia
PHILIP HEFNER, *Chicago*
Evolution
S. MARK HEIM, *Newton Centre, Mass.*
Free Church
HANS-GÜNTER HEIMBROCK, *Frankfurt*
Godparent
HERIBERT HEINEMANN, *Bochum, Ger.*
Hierarchy 1
ARMIN HEINEN, *Aachen, Ger.*
Fascism
ERICH HEINTEL, *Ottenschlag, Aus.*
God 3
PETER HEINTEL, *Klagenfurt, Aus.*
Ideology

CONTRIBUTORS

ANDREAS HEINZ, *Trier, Ger.*
Eucharistic Spirituality
REINHARD HENKEL, *Heidelberg, Ger.*
Geography of Religion
ALASDAIR I. C. HERON, *Erlangen, Ger.*
Extra calvinisticum; Filioque; Grace 4; Hell 2
NORMAN A. HJELM, *Wynnewood, Pa.*
Evangelical Catholicity; Grundtvig, Nikolai
Fredrik Severin
RALPH HJELM, *Peterborough, N.H.*
God Is Dead Theology
WOLFGANG HOFFMAN, S.J., *Bonn*
Equatorial Guinea
HEIMO HOFMEISTER, *Heidelberg, Ger.*
Freedom 1
KARL HOHEISEL, *Bonn*
Esotericism
TRAUGOTT HOLTZ, *Halle, Ger.*
Easter; Historiography 2
HEINRICH HOLZE, *Rostock, Ger.*
False Decretals
BRITTA HÜBENER, *Heidelberg, Ger.*
Fatima
WOLFGANG HUBER, *Berlin*
Enemy
JÜRGEN HÜBNER, *Heidelberg, Ger.*
Eugenics; Genetic Counseling
LAËNNEC HURBON, *Santo Domingo, D.R.*
Haiti
ALFRED JÄGER, *Bielefeld, Ger.*
Gospel 2
GOTTHARD JASPER, *Erlangen, Ger.*
Emancipation
GERT JEREMIAS, *Tübingen, Ger.*
Hymn 2
CHERYL BRIDGES JOHNS, *Cleveland, Tenn.*
Glossolalia
THEODOR JØRGENSEN, *Copenhaven*
Grundtvig, Nikolai Fredrik Severin
FRANK OTFRIED JULY, *Schwäbisch Hall, Ger.*
Illusion; Intuition
ANASTASIOS KALLIS, *Münster, Ger.*
Icon
KONSTANTINOS D. KALOKYRIS, *Thessaloníki, Gr.*
Iconostasis
PETER KAMPITS, *Vienna*
Humanism
ISOLDE KARLE, *Heidelberg, Ger.*
Father
MARTIN KARRER, *Wuppertal, Ger.*
Emperor Worship; Eschatology 2
DIETER KARTSCHOKE, *Berlin*
Heliand

JAMES KEEGAN, *Bethany, W.Va.*
Information
KLAUS KIESOW, *Münster, Ger.*
Elijah; Elisha
CHARLES A. KIMBALL, *Winston-Salem, N.C.*
Israel 3
OTTO KIMMINICH, *Regensburg, Ger.*
International Law
STEFFEN KJELDGAARD-PEDERSEN, *Copenhagen*
Gnesio-Lutherans
KARL-HEINZ KOHL, *Mainz, Ger.*
Fetishism
EVANGELOS KONSTANTINOU, *Würzburg, Ger.*
Epanagoge
KLAUS KOSCHORKE, *Munich*
Historiography 3
THOMAS KOSZINOWSKI, *Hamburg*
Iraq
RICHARD P. KRENZER, *Rodgau, Ger.*
Education 2
MANFRED KROPP, *Mainz, Ger.*
Islamic Philosophy 4.6
AARNO LAHTINEN, *Helsinki, Fin.*
Estonia
PETER LANDAU, *Munich*
Investiture
CAMERON LEE, *Pasadena, Calif.*
Family 3
DANIEL E. LEE, *Rock Island, Ill.*
Euthanasia
RISTO LEHTONEN, *Helsinki, Fin.*
Finland
WOLFGANG LIENEMANN, *Basel, Switz.*
Force, Violence, Nonviolence 1
SILVANO LILLI, *Rome*
International Evangelical Church
ANDREAS LINDEMANN, *Bielefeld, Ger.*
Ephesians, Epistle to the
CHRISTIAN LINK, *Bochum, Ger.*
Innocence, State of
GERHARD LINN, *Berlin*
Evangelism
JAN MILIČ LOCHMAN, *Basel, Switz.*
Eschatology 3, 7; Evil; Glory; Hope 3
ILSE VON LOEWENCLAU, *Berlin*
Faith 1
PAUL LÖFFLER, *Lauenburg, Ger.*
Islam and Christianity
WINRICH A. LÖHR, *Bonn*
Francis of Assisi
KONRAD LÜBBERT†, *Wedel, Ger.*
International Fellowship of Reconciliation

DIETER LÜHRMANN, *Marburg, Ger.*
Faith 2; Galatians, Epistle to the
WARNER LUOMA, *Wadena, Minn.*
Indonesia
TERRY MACARTHUR, *Geneva*
Hymnal 3
FRANK MACCHIA, *Costa Mesa, Calif.*
Glossolalia
WILLIAM MCKANE, *St. Andrews, Scot.*
Isaac
MIHÁLY MÁRKUS, *Tata, Hung.*
Hungary
PAUL V. MARSHALL, *Bethlehem, Pa.*
Eucharistic Prayer
PETER MASER, *Münster, Ger.*
Fish
ALBERT MAUDER†, *Bad Kleinkirchheim, Aus.*
Exequies
MELANIE A. MAY, *Rochester, N.Y.*
Feminism; Feminist Theology; Homosexuality
JOHN MBITI, *Burgdorf, Switz.*
Eschatology 6; Funeral 4; Gabon; Guinea
VIOREL MEHEDINŢU, *Neckargemünd, Ger.*
Funeral 3; Grace 2
ROBERT MELSON, *West Lafayette, Ind.*
Genocide
OTTO MERK, *Erlangen, Ger.*
Ethics 3
HELMUT MERKEL, *Osnabrück, Ger.*
Ebionites; Hellenism
HARDING MEYER, *Strasbourg, Fr.*
Ecumenical Dialogue
CESARE MILANESCHI, *Cosenza, It.*
Italy
DAVID W. MILLER, *Princeton*
Economic Ethics
BERND MOELLER, *Göttingen, Ger.*
Empire and Papacy
JEAN-PIERRE MONSARRAT†, *Paris*
France
SCOTT H. MOORE, *Waco, Tex.*
Existential Theology; Existentialism
KARL-HEINZ ZUR MÜHLEN, *Meckenheim, Ger.*
Indulgence
EKKEHARD MÜHLENBERG, *Göttingen, Ger.*
Early Church; Heresies and Schisms
KENNETH MULHOLLAND, *Columbia, S.C.*
Honduras
HUBERTUS MYNAREK, *Odernheim, Ger.*
Free Religion (Freireligiöse); International Association for Religious Freedom
SAMUEL NAFZGER, *St. Louis, Mo.*
International Lutheran Council

PETER NAGEL, *Halle, Ger.*
Gnosis, Gnosticism
WOLFGANG NETHÖFEL, *Hamburg*
Existential Theology
WOLFGANG NIKOLAUS, *Vienna*
Good, The
BRANKO NIKOLITSCH, *Berlin*
Guatemala
HANS G. NUTZINGER, *Kassel, Ger.*
Economy
BERND OBERDORFER, *Augsburg, Ger.*
Francke, August Hermann
JÖRG OHLEMACHER, *Griefswald, Ger.*
Fellowship Movement
KLAUS OTTE, *Mehren, Ger.*
Happiness
GEORGE C. PAPADEMETRIOU, *Brookline, Mass.*
Greece
G. KEITH PARKER, *Brevard, N.C.*
Electronic Church; House Church
WINSTON D. PERSAUD, *Dubuque, Iowa*
Guyana
CRAIG A. PHILLIPS, *Narberth, Pa.*
Fundamental Theology; Hermeneutics 2-3; Interpretation
FRIEDHELM PIEPER, *Heppenheim, Ger.*
International Council of Christians and Jews
RICHARD V. PIERARD, *Terre Haute, Ind.*
Fellowship Movement; German Christians; German Missions; Inner Mission
JOHN S. POBEE, *Accra, Ghana*
Equatorial Guinea; Ghana; Guinea-Bissau; Ivory Coast
HEINRICH POMPEY, *Freiburg, Ger.*
Exorcism 2
STEPHEN G. POST, *Cleveland, Ohio*
Family 1
HERMANN J. POTTMEYER, *Bochum, Ger.*
Infallibility
WILHELM PRATSCHER, *Vienna*
Holy Spirit 1
HORST DIETRICH PREUSS†, *Neuendettelsau, Ger.*
Eschatology 1; God 4
HANS-JÜRGEN PRIEN, *Cologne*
Guyana; Haiti; Honduras
WAYNE PROUDFOOT, *New York*
Experience
MICHAEL PYE, *Marburg, Ger.*
Fatalism
MURIEL M. RADTKE, *Wenham, Mass.*
Education 2
KONRAD RAISER, *Geneva*
Ecumenical Mission

CONTRIBUTORS

J. PAUL RAJASHEKAR, *Philadelphia*
Hinduism; Hinduism and Christianity; India

NORBERT RATH, *Münster, Ger.*
Enlightenment

ULRICH RATSCH, *Heidelberg, Ger.*
Energy

BRUCE R. REICHENBACH, *Minneapolis*
Epistemology 2; God 3; God, Arguments
for the Existence of

HELMUT REINALTER, *Innsbruck, Aus.*
Freethinkers

JOHN D. REMPEL, *New York*
Force, Violence, Nonviolence 2

HAROLD REMUS, *Waterloo, Ont.*
Health and Illness

GUENTHER C. RIMBACH, *Riverside, Calif.*
Expressionism

DIETRICH RITSCHL, *Reigoldswil, Switz.*
Ethics, Overview; Faith, Overview; Fear; God 7;
Golden Age; Healing; Holy Spirit 2

ADOLF MARTIN RITTER, *Heidelberg, Ger.*
Ephesus, Council of

HANS ROLLMANN, *St. John's, Nfld.*
History of Religions School

JÜRGEN ROLOFF, *Erlangen, Ger.*
Eucharist 2; Exegesis, Biblical 2; God 5; Grace 1

WILLY RORDORF, *Peseux, Switz.*
Heretical Baptism

ROSETTA E. ROSS, *New Brighton, Minn.*
Ethics 5

LUDWIG ROTT, *Bergneustadt, Ger.*
International Council of Christian Churches

WILLIAM G. RUSCH, *New York*
Ecumenism, Ecumenical Movement; Gregory I;
Gregory VII; Innocent III

LAMIN SANNEH, *New Haven, Conn.*
Gambia

GERHARD SAUTER, *Bonn*
Hermeneutics 3

DEMOSTHENES SAVRAMIS†, *Bonn*
Greece

WALTER SAWATSKY, *Elkhart, Ind.*
Georgia

THOMAS F. SCHAEFFER, *Chicago*
Hong Kong and Macao

PETER SCHÄFER, *Berlin*
Hasidism

ROLF SCHÄFER, *Oldenburg, Ger.*
Fundamental Theology

CARL SCHALK, *Melrose Park, Ill.*
Gospel Song; Gradual; Hymnal 2

BERNDT SCHALLER, *Göttingen, Ger.*
Enoch; Hasmonaeans; Herod, Herodians;
High Priest

JOACHIM SCHARFENBERG†, *Kiel, Ger.*
Empathy

WOLFGANG SCHEFFLER, *Berlin*
Holocaust

JAMES A. SCHERER, *Oak Park, Ill.*
International Missionary Council

ALFRED SCHINDLER, *Zurich*
Historiography 3

WERNER H. SCHMIDT, *Bonn*
Exodus, Book of

HANS-CHRISTOPH SCHMIDT-LAUBER, *Vienna*
Emergency Baptism

PHILIPP SCHMITZ, *Frankfurt*
Faithfulness

HANS SCHNEIDER, *Marburg, Ger.*
Gallicanism; Huguenots

WOLFGANG SCHNEIDER, *Giessen, Ger.*
Functionalism

ERNST L. SCHNELLBÄCHER, *Neckargemünd, Ger.*
International Ecumenical Fellowship

THADDEUS A. SCHNITKER, *Münster, Ger.*
Easter; Ecumenical Symbols; Eulogia;
Harvest Festivals; Hours, Canonical

GÜNTHER SCHNURR, *Heidelberg, Ger.*
Eucharist 3

LOTHAR SCHREINER, *Wuppertal, Ger.*
Indonesia

TOM SCHWANDA, *Grand Rapids*
Hus, Jan; Hussites

WERNER SCHWARTZ, *Frankenthal, Ger.*
Envy; Epistemology 2; Hedonism

HANS SCHWARZ, *Regensburg, Ger.*
European Theology (Modern Period) 1

KURT-VICTOR SELGE, *Berlin*
Franciscans; Ignatius of Loyola; Inquisition

FRANK C. SENN, *Evanston, Ill.*
Easter; Funeral 5.2; Holy Week; Incense

KLAUS SEYBOLD, *Basel, Switz.*
Hymn 1

NOTGER SLENCZKA, *Göttingen, Ger.*
International Council of Community Churches

RUDOLF SMEND, *Göttingen, Ger.*
Exegesis, Biblical 1; Historiography 1

JANE I. SMITH, *Hartford, Conn.*
Islam 10

REINER SÖRRIES, *Erlangen, Ger.*
Images

HERMANN SPIECKERMANN, *Hannover, Ger.*
Hammurabi, Code of; Hebrews

MAX L. STACKHOUSE, *Princeton*
Economic Ethics

HANS-PETER STÄHLI, *Bielefeld, Ger.*
Hebrew Language

JOACHIM STALMANN, *Hannover, Ger.*
Hymnal 1

EKKEHARD STARKE, *Duisburg, Ger.*
Human Dignity

KONRAD STAUSS, *Grönenbach, Ger.*
Humanistic Psychology

WOLFGANG STECK, *Munich*
Funeral 1, 2.1, 2.4-5

JOHANN ANSELM STEIGER, *Heidelberg, Ger.*
Herder, Johann Gottfried

ALBERT STEIN†, *Brühl, Ger.*
Ephor

JÜRGEN STEIN, *Bremen, Ger.*
Excommunication

HEINZ-GÜNTHER STOBBE, *Münster, Ger.*
Institution

ALEX STOCK, *Frechen, Ger.*
Images of Christ

KONRAD STOCK, *Giessen, Ger.*
Hope 2

FRITZ STOLZ, *Männedorf, Switz.*
Holy War

GEORG STRECKER†, *Göttingen, Ger.*
Household Rules

PETER STUHLMACHER, *Tübingen, Ger.*
Gospel 1; Hermeneutics 2

DARLIS J. SWAN, *Chicago*
Ecumenical Learning

MARK N. SWANSON, *St. Paul, Minn.*
Egypt; Islam and Christianity

YAKOB TESFAY, *Asmara, Erit.*
Eritrea

WINFRIED THIEL, *Bochum, Ger.*
Habakkuk, Book of; Haggai, Book of; Hosea, Book of

HEINZ EDUARD TÖDT†, *Heidelberg, Ger.*
Equality; Freedom 2

SIEGBERT UHLIG, *Norderstedt, Ger.*
Ethiopian Orthodox Church

HANS G. ULRICH, *Erlangen, Ger.*
Ethics 6-7

RUURD VELDHUIS, *Groningen, Neth.*
Emanation

LUKAS VISCHER, *Geneva*
Evangelical

SAMIR VOUWZEE, *Delft, Neth.*
Islamic Philosophy 1-4.5

HARALD WAGNER, *Recklinghausen, Ger.*
Grace 3

ULRIKE WAGNER-RAU, *Preetz, Ger.*
Grief

GEOFFREY WAINWRIGHT, *Durham, N.C.*
Eucharist 5

CLARENCE WALHOUT, *Grand Rapids*
Imagination

EDWIN S. WALKER, *Columbia, S.C.*
Haiti

HANS-FRIEDRICH WEISS, *Rostock, Ger.*
Hebrews, Epistle to the

MICHAEL WELKER, *Heidelberg, Ger.*
Heaven

TIMOTHY J. WENGERT, *Philadelphia*
Formula of Concord

GERD A. WEWERS†, *Salzgitter, Ger.*
Haggadah; Halakah

DIETRICH WIEDERKEHR, *Luzern, Switz.*
Eschatology 5

ROWAN D. WILLIAMS, *Newport, Gwent, Wales*
Incarnation 2; Inspiration

KLAUS WINKLER†, *Hannover, Ger.*
Friendship; Humor

WOLFGANG WISCHMEYER, *Erlangen, Ger.*
Ephesus

JOHN WITTE JR., *Atlanta*
Family 2

SUSAN K. WOOD, *Collegeville, Minn.*
Episcopacy 1-5

CARLTON R. YOUNG, *Nashville*
Hymnody

JOACHIM ZEHNER, *Berlin*
Forgiveness

ELISABETH ZEIL-FAHLBUSCH, *Harare, Zim.*
Education 3

WALTHER C. ZIMMERLI, *Brunswick, Ger.*
Empiricism; Hegelianism; Individualism

HARTMUT ZINSER, *Berlin*
Human Sacrifice

EKKEHARD ZIPSER, *Hamburg*
Guatemala

Abbreviations

Abbreviations generally follow those given in the *Journal of Biblical Literature* "Instructions for Contributors." For those not listed there, the abbreviations in the second edition of S. M. Schwertner's *Internationales Abkürzungsverzeichnis für Theologie und Grenzgebiete* (Berlin, 1992) are used; for works of theology or related fields not listed in either source, new abbreviations have been formed.

Writings listed below under the section "Early Church Writings" include those of writers through Augustine.

BIBLICAL BOOKS, WITH THE APOCRYPHA

Gen.	Genesis	Hab.	Habakkuk
Exod.	Exodus	Zeph.	Zephaniah
Lev.	Leviticus	Hag.	Haggai
Num.	Numbers	Zech.	Zechariah
Deut.	Deuteronomy	Mal.	Malachi
Josh.	Joshua	Add. Est.	Additions to Esther
Judg.	Judges	Bar.	Baruch
Ruth	Ruth	Bel	Bel and the Dragon
1-2 Sam.	1-2 Samuel	1-2 Esdr.	1-2 Esdras
1-2 Kgs.	1-2 Kings	4 Ezra	4 Ezra
1-2-3-4 Kgdms.	1-2-3-4 Kingdoms	Jdt.	Judith
1-2 Chr.	1-2 Chronicles	Ep. Jer.	Epistle of Jeremiah
Ezra	Ezra	1-2-3-4 Macc.	1-2-3-4 Maccabees
Neh.	Nehemiah	Pr. Azar.	Prayer of Azariah
Esth.	Esther	Pr. Man.	Prayer of Manasseh
Job	Job	Sir.	Sirach / Ecclesiasticus / Wisdom of Jesus, Son of Sirach
Ps.	Psalms		
Prov.	Proverbs	Sus.	Susanna
Eccl.	Ecclesiastes	Tob.	Tobit
Cant.	Canticles / Song of Solomon / Song of Songs	Wis.	Wisdom of Solomon
		Matt.	Matthew
Isa.	Isaiah	Mark	Mark
Jer.	Jeremiah	Luke	Luke
Lam.	Lamentations	John	John
Ezek.	Ezekiel	Acts	Acts of the Apostles
Dan.	Daniel	Rom.	Romans
Hos.	Hosea	1-2 Cor.	1-2 Corinthians
Joel	Joel	Gal.	Galatians
Amos	Amos	Eph.	Ephesians
Obad.	Obadiah	Phil.	Philippians
Jonah	Jonah	Col.	Colossians
Mic.	Micah	1-2 Thess.	1-2 Thessalonians
Nah.	Nahum	1-2 Tim.	1-2 Timothy

Titus	Titus	1-2 Pet.	1-2 Peter
Phlm.	Philemon	1-2-3 John	1-2-3 John
Heb.	Hebrews	Jude	Jude
Jas.	James	Rev.	Revelation

OLD TESTAMENT PSEUDEPIGRAPHA

| *1-2-3 Enoch* | Ethiopic, Slavonic, Hebrew | *Jub.* | *Jubilees* |
| | *Enoch* | *Pss. Sol.* | *Psalms of Solomon* |

EARLY CHURCH WRITINGS, WITH NAG HAMMADI TRACTATES

2 Ap. Jas.	*2 Apocryphon of James*	Eusebius	
Ap. John	*Apocryphon of John*	*Hist. eccl.*	*Historia ecclesiastica*
Apos. Const.	*Apostolic Constitutions*	*Gos. Phil.*	*Gospel of Philip*
Athanasius		*Gos. Thom.*	*Gospel of Thomas*
Contra Arian.	*Apologia contra Arianas*	Gregory of Nazianzus	
De incar.	*De incarnatione Dei Verbi*	*Or. theol.*	*Orationes theologicae*
Ep. Serap.	*Epistulae ad Serapionem*	Gregory of Nyssa	
Augustine		*De beat.*	*Orationes de beatitudinibus*
Conf.	*Confessions*	Ign. [Ignatius]	
De bapt.	*De baptismo contra Donatistas*	*Eph.*	*Letter to the Ephesians*
De doc. christ.	*De doctrina christiana*	*Magn.*	*Letter to the Magnesians*
De Gen. ad litt.	*De Genesi ad litteram*	*Phld.*	*Letter to the Philadelphians*
De lib. arb.	*De libero arbitrio*	*Pol.*	*Letter to Polycarp*
De nat. boni	*De natura boni*	*Smyrn.*	*Letter to the Smyrnaeans*
De Trin.	*De Trinitate libri quindecim*	*Trall.*	*Letter to the Trallians*
In Evang. Iohan.	*In Evangelium Iohannis Tractatus*	Irenaeus	
Barn.	*Barnabas*	*Adv. haer.*	*Adversus omnes haereses*
Basil the Great		Justin Martyr	
De Spir. S.	*De Spiritu Sancto*	*Apol.*	*Apologia*
Chrys. [Chrysostom]		*Dial.*	*Dialogue with Trypho*
Cat.	*Cathecheses*	*Mart. Pol.*	*Martyrdom of Polycarp*
In Heb. hom.	*In epistulam ad Hebraeos homiliae*	*Orig. World*	*On the Origin of the World*
In Joh. hom.	*In Ioannem homiliae*	Origen	
In 1 Tim. hom.	*In epistulam primum ad Timotheum homiliae*	*C. Cels.*	*Contra Celsum*
		In Gen. hom.	*In Genesim homiliae*
1-2 Clem.	*1-2 Clement*	Pol. [Polycarp]	
Clement of Alexandria		*Phil.*	*Letter to the Philippians*
Exc. Theod.	*Excerpta ex Theodoto*	Serapion	
Paed.	*Paedagogus*	*Sacra.*	*Sacramentary* (or *Euchologion*)
Cyril of Alexandria		*Soph. Jes. Chr.*	*Sophia of Jesus Christ*
Dial. Trin.	*De Trinitate dialogi*	Tatian	
Cyril of Jerusalem		*Orat.*	*Oratio ad Graecos*
Cat.	*Catecheses*	Tertullian	
Did.	*Didache*	*Ad Scap.*	*Ad Scapulam*
Did. apos.	*Didascalia apostolorum*	*Apol.*	*Apologeticus pro Christianis*
Epiphanius		*De bapt.*	*De baptismo*
Pan.	*Panarion*	*De cor.*	*De corona*
		De pud.	*De pudicitia*
		De res. car.	*De resurrectione carnis*

ABBREVIATIONS

DEAD SEA SCROLLS AND RELATED TEXTS
("1Q" indicates a document found in Qumran Cave 1, etc.)

CD	Cairo (Genizah text of the) Damascus (Document)		Community, Manual of Discipline)
1QH	*Hôdāyōt (Thanksgiving Hymns)*	1QSa	Appendix A *(Rule of the Congregation)* to 1QS
1QM	*Milḥāmāh (War Scroll)*		
1QpHab	*Pesher on Habakkuk*	4QMessApoc	*Messianic Apocalypse*
1QS	*Serek hayyaḥad (Rule of the*	11QMelch	*Melchizedek* text

CLASSICAL TARGUMS AND RABBINIC WRITINGS

b.	Babylonian Talmud	*Midr. Ps.*	*Midrash of Psalms*
m.	Mishnah	*Pesaḥ*	*Pesaḥim*
t.	Tosefta	*Soṭa*	*Soṭa*
y.	Jerusalem Talmud	*Tg. Isa.*	*Targum of Isaiah*
Lev. Rab.	*Leviticus Rabbah*		

OTHER ANCIENT, MEDIEVAL, AND EARLY MODERN WRITINGS

Alcherus Claraevallensis
   De spir. et an.   *De spiritu et anima*
Anselm
   Pros.   *Proslogium*
Aristotle
   De cae.   *De caelo*
   Eth. Nic.   *Ethica Nicomachea*
   Metaph.   *Metaphysica*
   Ph.   *Physica*
   Pol.   *Politica*
Augs. Conf.   Augsburg Confession
Calvin, J.
   Inst.   *Institutes of the Christian Religion*
Descartes, R.
   Med.   *Meditationes de prima philosophia*
Hesiod
   Cat.   *Catalogs of Women*
   Theog.   *Theogony*
Hume, D.
   Dialogues   *Dialogues concerning Natural Religion*
Josephus
   Ant.   *Jewish Antiquities*
   J.W.   *Jewish War*
   Life   *Life of Flavius Josephus*
Kant, I.
   Grundlegung   *Grundlegung zur Metaphysik der Sitten*

   Prol.   *Prolegomena zu einer jeden zukünftigen Metaphysik*
Melanchthon, P.
   Treatise   *Treatise on the Power and Primacy of the Pope*
Philo
   De opif. mun.   *De opificio mundi*
   Decal.   *De Decalogo*
Pindar
   Pyth.   *Pythion*
Plato
   Grg.   *Gorgias*
   Leg.   *Leges*
   Phdr.   *Phaedrus*
   Phlb.   *Philebus*
   Rep.   *Republic*
   Ti.   *Timaeus*
Plotinus
   Enn.   *Enneades*
Polybius
   Hist.   *Historia*
Porphyry
   Plot.   *Vita Plotini*
Schmalk. Art.   Schmalkaldic Articles
Theodoret of Cyrrhus
   Comm. Isa.   *Commentaria in Isaiam*
Thomas Aquinas
   Summa theol.   *Summa theologiae*
Thucydides
   Hist.   *History of the Pelopennesian War*

MODERN PUBLICATIONS AND EDITIONS

AA	I. Kant, *Gesammelte Schriften* (Berlin Akademie Ausgabe)
AAS	*Acta apostolicae sedis*
AB	Anchor Bible
ABD	*Anchor Bible Dictionary*
AbNTC	Abingdon NT Commentaries
ACO	*Acta conciliorum oecumenicorum*
ACW	Ancient Christian Writers
AfER	*African Ecclesiastical Review*
AHP	*Archivum historiae pontificiae*
AHR	*American Historical Review*
AJA	*American Journal of Archaeology*
AmA	*American Anthropologist*
ANESTP	*Ancient Near Eastern Supplementary Texts and Pictures*
ANET	*Ancient Near Eastern Texts*
ANRW	*Aufstieg und Niedergang der römischen Welt*
AOB	*Altorientalische Bilder zum Alten Testament*
AOT	*Altorientalische Texte zum Alten Testament*
ARG	*Archiv für Reformationsgeschichte*
ARW	*Archiv für Religionswissenschaft*
ASR	*American Sociological Review*
ATD	Das Alte Testament Deutsch
ATR	*Anglican Theological Review*
BA	*Biblical Archaeologist*
BASOR	*Bulletin of the American Schools of Oriental Research*
BBR	*Bulletin for Biblical Research*
BE(E)	*Boletín eclesiástico* (Ecua.)
Bib	*Biblica*
BibRev	*Bible Review*
BJRL	*Bulletin of the John Rylands University Library of Manchester*
BKAT	Biblischer Kommentar: Altes Testament
BMCL	*Bulletin of Medieval Canon Law*
BoJ.B	*Bonner Jahrbücher — Beihefte*
BoTr	*Bogoslovskie trudy. Theological Works. Travaux théologiques*
BSAW	*Berichte der Sächsischen Akademie der Wissenschaften*
BSLK	*Bekenntnisschriften der evangelisch-lutherischen Kirche*
BSRK	*Bekenntnisschriften der reformierten Kirche*
BT	*Bible Translator*
BThA	*Bulletin de théologie africaine*
BTZ	*Berliner theologische Zeitschrift*
CA	*Current Anthropology*
CanCR	*Canadian Catholic Review*
Cath.	*Catholicisme. Hier, aujourd'hui, demain*
CBC	Cambridge Bible Commentary
CBQ	*Catholic Biblical Quarterly*
CCen	*Christian Century*
CChr.CM	Corpus Christianorum, Continuatio mediaevalis
CD	K. Barth, *Church Dogmatics*
CDCWM	*Concise Dictionary of the Christian World Mission*
CDP	*Cambridge Dictionary of Philosophy*
CDT	*Catholic Dictionary of Theology*
CEurH	*Central European History*
CGG	*Christlicher Glaube in moderner Gesellschaft*
CHIs	*Cambridge History of Islam*
ChrTo	*Christianity Today*
CIC	Codex Iuris Canonici
CleR	*Clergy Review*
Com.	*Commentary: A Jewish Review*
CPG	*Clavis patrum Graecorum*
CR.BS	*Currents in Research: Biblical Studies*
CRE	*Christus und die Religionen der Erde. Handbuch der Religionsgeschichte*
CRef	Corpus Reformatorum
CScR	*Christian Scholar's Review*
CSEL	Corpus scriptorum ecclesiasticorum latinorum
CSSH	*Comparative Studies in Society and History*
CuSoc	*Current Sociology*
CV	*Communio viatorum*
DBSup	*Dictionnaire de la Bible, Supplément*
DCE	*Dictionary of Christian Ethics*
DEM	*Dictionary of the Ecumenical Movement*
DH	Denzinger-Hünermann, *Enchiridion symbolorum* (37th ed., 1991)
DHGE	*Dictionnaire d'histoire et de géographie ecclésiastiques*
DSp	*Dictionnaire de spiritualité, ascétique et mystique*
DTC	*Dictionnaire de théologie catholique*
EAR	*Encyclopedia of American Religions*
EC	*Enciclopedia cattolica*
ECR	*Eastern Churches Review*
EcTr	*Ecumenical Trends*
EDNT	*Exegetical Dictionary of the New Testament*
EI²	*Encyclopaedia of Islam* (new ed.)
EJ	*Encyclopaedia Judaica*

ABBREVIATIONS

EKKNT	Evangelisch-katholischer Kommentar zum Neuen Testament	HPhG	Handbuch philosophischer Grundbegriffe
EKO	Evangelische Kirchenordnungen des XVI. Jahrhunderts	HPTh	Handbuch der Pastoraltheologie
		HR	History of Religions
EncA	Encyclopedia of Aesthetics	HRG	Handbuch der Religionsgeschichte
EncAE	Encyclopedia of Applied Ethics	HRGem	Handbuch Religiöse Gemeinschaften
EncBio	Encyclopedia of Bioethics (rev. ed.)	HST	Handbuch systematischer Theologie
EncJud	Encyclopaedia Judaica	HTKNT	Herders theologischer Kommentar zum Neuen Testament
EncPh	Encyclopedia of Philosophy		
EncPR	Encyclopedia of Politics and Religion	HTR	Harvard Theological Review
EncRel(E)	Encyclopedia of Religion (ed. M. Eliade)	HUCA	Hebrew Union College Annual
EncRS	Encyclopedia of Religion and Society	HWP	Historisches Wörterbuch der Philosophie
ER	Ecumenical Review	IB	Interpreter's Bible
ERE	Encyclopaedia of Religion and Ethics	IBC	Interpretation: A Bible Commentary for Teaching and Preaching
ERT	Evangelical Review of Theology		
ETL	Ephemerides theologicae Lovanienses	IBMR	International Bulletin of Missionary Research
EvT	Evangelische Theologie		
ExAu	Ex auditu	ICC	International Critical Commentary
ExpTim	Expository Times	IDB	Interpreter's Dictionary of the Bible
FC	Fathers of the Church	IDZ	Internationale Dialog Zeitschrift
FiHi	Fides et historia	IKZ	Internationale kirchliche Zeitschrift
FOTL	Forms of the Old Testament Literature	Imm.	Immanuel: Ecumenical Theological Research Fraternity in Israel
FQS	Franziskanische Quellenschriften		
FS	Franziskanische Studien	Int	Interpretation: A Journal of Bible and Theology
FZPhTh	Freiburger Zeitschrift für Philosophie und Theologie		
		IoR	Iconography of Religions (Leiden)
GGB	Geschichtliche Grundbegriffe	IRM	International Review of Missions
GRel	Geographia religionum	ISBE	International Standard Bible Encyclopedia (rev. ed.)
GuL	Geist und Leben. Zeitschrift für Aszese und Mystik		
		JAAR	Journal of the American Academy of Religion
HAR	Hebrew Annual Review		
HAT	Handbuch zum Alten Testament	JAMS	Journal of the American Musicological Society
HBD	Harper's Bible Dictionary		
HBT	Horizons in Biblical Theology	JAOS	Journal of the American Oriental Society
HCE	Handbuch der christlichen Ethik	JBQ	Jewish Bible Quarterly
HCOT	Historical Commentary on the Old Testament	JChS	Journal of Church and State
		Jdm	Judaism: A Quarterly Journal of Jewish Life and Thought
HDG	Handbuch der Dogmengeschichte		
HDRG	Handwörterbuch zur deutschen Rechtsgeschichte	JES	Journal of Ecumenical Studies
		JETS	Journal of the Evangelical Theological Society
HDThG	Handbuch der Dogmen- und Theologiegeschichte		
		JHPs	Journal of Humanistic Psychology
HFTh	Handbuch der Fundamentaltheologie	JJS	Journal of Jewish Studies
HKAT	Handkommentar zum Alten Testament	JL	Jüdisches Lexikon
HKG(J)	Handbuch der Kirchengeschichte (ed. H. Jedin)	JLH	Jahrbuch für Liturgik und Hymnologie
		JLW	Jahrbuch für Liturgiewissenschaft
HKKR	Handbuch des katholischen Kirchenrechts	JMLB	Jahrbuch des Martin-Luther-Bundes
HlD	Heiliger Dienst	JMRS	Journal of Medieval and Renaissance Studies
HNT	Handbuch zum Neuen Testament		
HO	Handbuch der Orientalistik	JNES	Journal of Near Eastern Studies
HÖ	Handbuch der Ökumenik	JNSL	Journal of Northwest Semitic Languages
HPG	Handbuch pädagogischer Grundbegriffe	JPentT	Journal of Pentecostal Theology
HPh	Handbuch der Philosophie	JPh	Journal of Philosophy
		JPsT	Journal of Psychology and Theology

JPSV	Jewish Publication Society Version	NCBC	New Century Bible Commentary
JQR	Jewish Quarterly Review	NCE	New Catholic Encyclopedia
JR	Journal of Religion	NDSW	New Dictionary of Sacramental Worship
JSGVK	Jahresbericht der Schlesischen Gesellschaft für Vaterländische Kultur	NEB	New English Bible
		NEBrit	New Encyclopaedia Britannica
JSHRZ	Jüdische Schriften aus hellenistisch-römischer Zeit	NEchtB	Neue Echter Bibel
		NGDMM	New Grove Dictionary of Music and Musicians
JSJ	Journal for the Study of Judaism in the Persian, Hellenistic, and Roman Period	NHC	Nag Hammadi Codices
JSOT	Journal for the Study of the Old Testament	NHThG	Neues Handbuch theologischer Grandbegriffe
JSP	Journal for the Study of the Pseudepigrapha	NIB	New Interpreter's Bible
		NICNT	New International Commentary on the New Testament
JTS	Journal of Theological Studies		
KAT	Kommentar zum Alten Testament	NICOT	New International Commentary on the Old Testament
KEK	Kritisch-exegetischer Kommentar über das Neue Testament	NIGTC	New International Greek Testament Commentary
KJV	King James Version		
KM	Die Katholischen Missionen	NPNF	A Select Library of (the) Nicene and Post-Nicene Fathers of the Christian Church
KuD	Kerygma und Dogma		
KZSS	Kölner Zeitschrift für Soziologie und Sozialpsychologie		
		NRSV	New Revised Standard Version
LCI	Lexikon der christlichen Ikonographie	NRT	La nouvelle revue théologique
Leit.	Leiturgia. Handbuch des evangelischen Gottesdienstes	NSchol	New Scholasticism
		NSHE	New Schaff-Herzog Encyclopedia of Religious Knowledge
LJ	Liturgisches Jahrbuch		
LM	Lutherische Monatshefte	NTD	Das Neue Testament Deutsch
LPGL	G. W. H. Lampe, Patristic Greek Lexicon	NTS	New Testament Studies
LTK	Lexicon für Theologie und Kirche	Numen	Numen: International Review for the History of Religions
LW	Luther's Works, "American Edition" (55 vols.; St. Louis and Philadelphia, 1955-76)		
		NWDLW	New Westminster Dictionary of Liturgy and Worship
MÂ	Moyen-âge. Revue d'histoire et de philologie	NZSTh	Neue Zeitschrift für systematische Theologie
MBM	Münchener Beiträge zur Mediävistik und Renaissance-Forschung	ODB	Oxford Dictionary of Byzantium
		ODCC	Oxford Dictionary of the Christian Church (3d ed.)
MCE	Modern Catholic Encyclopedia		
MdKI	Materialdienst des Konfessionskundlichen Instituts	OF	Orate fratres
		ÖL	Ökumenelexikon
MDÖC	Materialdienst der Ökumenischen Centrale	ÖR	Ökumenische Rundschau
		OR(E)	L'osservatore romano (Eng. ed.)
MECW	Karl Marx, Friedrich Engels: Collected Works	OrthFor	Orthodoxes Forum
		OS	Ostkirchliche Studien
MGG	Musik in Geschichte und Gegenwart	ÖTBK	Ökumenischer Taschenbuchkommentar zum Neuen Testament
MisSt	Mission Studies		
MJTh	Marburger Jahrbuch Theologie	OTL	Old Testament Library
MQ	Musical Quarterly	OTP	Old Testament Pseudepigrapha
MuK	Musik und Kirche	PAPS	Proceedings of the American Philosophical Society
MW	Muslim World		
MySal	Mysterium salutis	ParMiss	Parole et mission
NAB	Nederlands archievenblad	PG	Patrologia Graeca
NAC	New American Commentary	PL	Patrologia Latina
NBLi	National Bulletin on Liturgy	PRSt	Perspectives in Religious Studies

ABBREVIATIONS

PsRev	*Psychological Review*	StPatr	*Studia patristica: Papers Presented to the International Conference on Patristic Studies*
PW	Pauly-Wissowa, *Real-Encyclopädie der classischen Altertumswissenschaft*		
PWSup	Supplement to PW	Str-B	H. L Strack and P. Billerbeck, *Kommentar zum Neuen Testament aus Talmud und Midrasch*
QGPRK	*Quelle zur Geschichte des Papsttums und des römischen Katholizismus*		
Quat.	*Quatember. Evangelische Jahresbriefe*	StTh	*Studia theologica*
RAC	*Reallexikon für Antike und Christentum*	SVSQ	*St. Vladimir's Seminary Quarterly*
RB	*Revue biblique*	SWJA	*Southwestern Journal of Anthropology*
RBén	*Revue bénédictine de critique, d'histoire et de littérature religieuses*	SyR	*Symbolik der Religionen*
		TBLNT	*Theologisches Begriffslexikon zum Neuen Testament*
RBK	*Reallexikon zur byzantinischen Kunst*		
RCL	*Religion in Communist Lands*	TDNT	*Theological Dictionary of the New Testament*
RDC	*Revue de droit canonique*		
Rdgs	Readings — A New Biblical Commentary	TDOT	*Theological Dictionary of the Old Testament*
RE	*Realencyklopädie für protestantische Theologie und Kirche*	TF	*Theologische Forschung*
		TGI	*Textbuch zur Geschichte Israels*
REEu	*Religion in Eastern Europe*	THAT	*Theologisches Handwörterbuch zum Alten Testament*
RefW	*Reformed Worship*		
RevExp	*Review and Expositor*	ThBeitr	*Theologische Beiträge*
RevQ	*Revue de Qumran*	Theol(A)	*Theologia (Athens)*
RFE/RL	Radio Free Europe/Radio Liberty	ThPP	*Theology and Public Policy*
RGG	*Religion in Geschichte und Gegenwart* (3d ed.)	TLZ	*Theologische Literaturzeitung*
		TRE	*Theologische Realenzyklopädie*
RLA	*Reallexikon der Assyriologie*	TRT	*Taschenlexikon Religion und Theologie*
RM	*Die Religionen der Menschheit*	TRu	*Theologische Rundschau*
RNT	Regensburger Neues Testament	TUAT	*Texte aus der Umwelt des Alten Testaments*
RSPT	*Revue des sciences philosophiques et théologiques*		
		TynBul	*Tyndale Bulletin*
RSV	Revised Standard Version	TZ	*Theologische Zeitschrift*
SAnM	*St. Anthony Messenger*	UH	*Unsere Heimat. Zeitschrift des Vereins für Landeskunde von Niederösterreich und Wien*
SBLSP	*Society of Biblical Literature Seminar Papers*		
SBO	*Studia biblica et orientalia*	US	*Una Sancta. Rundbriefe für interkonfessionelle Begegnung*
SBT	*Studies in Biblical Theology*		
SCJ	*Sixteenth Century Journal: A Journal for Renaissance and Reformation Students and Scholars*	USQR	*Union Seminary Quarterly Review*
		VFTW	*Voices from the Third World*
		VisRel	*Visible Religion: Annual for Religious Iconography*
SecCent	*Second Century*		
SEv	Studies in Evangelicalism	VL	*Vetus Latina*
SJT	*Scottish Journal of Theology*	VT	*Vetus Testamentum*
SJudA	*Studia Judaica Austriaca*	VTSup	*Vetus Testamentum Supplements*
SM	*Sacramentum mundi. Theologisches Lexikon für die Praxis*	WA	M. Luther, *Werke. Kritische Gesamtausgabe* (Weimarer Ausgabe)
SM(E)	*Sacramentum mundi* (Eng. ed.)	WBC	Word Biblical Commentary
SozW	*Soziale Welt*	WCE	*World Christian Encyclopedia*
Spec.	*Speculum: A Journal of Mediaeval Studies*	WD	*Wort und Dienst*
SQAW	*Schriften und Quellen der alten Welt*	WiWei	*Wissenschaft und Weisheit: Zeitschrift für augustinisch-franziskanische Theologie und Philosophie in der Gegenwart*
SR	*Studies in Religion / Sciences religieuses*		
StEv	*Studia evangelica*		
StGen	*Studium generale*	WJP	*Wiener Jahrbuch für Philosophie*
StLi	*Studia liturgica*	WM	*Wörterbuch der Mythologie*

WW	*Word and World*	ZBK	*Zürcher Bibelkommentar*
WZ(H).GS	*Wissenschaftliche Zeitschrift der Martin-Luther-Universität Halle-Wittenberg. Gesellschafts- und sprachwissenschaftliche Reihe*	ZDW	*Zeitschrift für deutsche Wortforschung*
		ZEE	*Zeitschrift für evangelische Ethik*
		ZHF	*Zeitschrift für historische Forschung*
		ZKG	*Zeitschrift für Kirchengeschichte*
WZ(L).GS	*Wissenschaftliche Zeitschrift der Karl-Marx-Universität Leipzig. Gesellschafts- und sprachwissenschaftliche Reihe*	ZKT	*Zeitschrift für katholische Theologie*
		ZM	*Zeitschrift für Missionswissenschaft*
		ZNW	*Zeitschrift für die neutestamentliche Wissenschaft*
WzM	*Wege zum Menschen*		
YACC	*Yearbook of American and Canadian Churches*	ZRGG	*Zeitschrift für Religions- und Geistesgeschichte*
ZAM	*Zeitschrift für Aszese und Mystik*	ZTK	*Zeitschrift für Theologie und Kirche*
ZAW	*Zeitschrift für die alttestamentliche Wissenschaft*	*Zwing.*	*Zwingliana*

STATES AND PROVINCES

Ala.	Alabama	Mont.	Montana
B.C.	British Columbia	N.C.	North Carolina
Calif.	California	Nebr.	Nebraska
Colo.	Colorado	Nfld.	Newfoundland
Conn.	Connecticut	N.H.	New Hampshire
D.C.	District of Columbia	N.J.	New Jersey
Del.	Delaware	N.Y.	New York
Fla.	Florida	Okla.	Oklahoma
Ga.	Georgia	Ont.	Ontario
Ill.	Illinois	Oreg.	Oregon
Ind.	Indiana	Pa.	Pennsylvania
Kans.	Kansas	S.C.	South Carolina
Ky.	Kentucky	Tenn.	Tennessee
Mass.	Massachusetts	Tex.	Texas
Md.	Maryland	Va.	Virginia
Mich.	Michigan	Vt.	Vermont
Minn.	Minnesota	Wis.	Wisconsin
Mo.	Missouri	W.Va.	West Virginia

GENERAL

A.D.	*anno Domini,* in the year of [our] Lord	chap(s).	chapter(s)
Arab.	Arabic	comm.	comment
Aram.	Aramaic	comp.	compiler
art(s).	article(s)	C.R.	Costa Rica
Aus.	Austria	D	Deuteronomic source
Austral.	Australia	d.	died
b.	born	diss.	dissertation
B.C.	before Christ	D.R.	Dominican Republic
bk(s).	book(s)	E	Elohistic source
Braz.	Brazil	Ecua.	Ecuador
ca.	circa	ed(s).	edited (by), edition, editor(s)
can(s).	canon(s)	e.g.	*exempli gratia,* for example
cent.	century	EKD	Evangelische Kirche in Deutschland
cf.	*confer,* compare	Eng.	England, English

ABBREVIATIONS

ep.	*epistulae,* letters		no.	number
Erit.	Eritrea		n.p.	no place
E.S.	El Salvador		NT	New Testament
esp.	especially		orig.	originally, original
est.	estimated		OT	Old Testament
ET	English translation		P	Priestly source
et al.	*et alii,* and others		p(p).	page(s)
etc.	*et cetera,* and so forth		par.	parallel(s), parallel to
exp.	expanded		par(s).	paragraph(s)
f	females		pass.	passive
ff.	and following		Pers.	Persian
Fin.	Finland		Pi.	Piel
fl.	*floruit,* flourished		pl.	plural
Fr.	France, French		P.N.G.	Papua New Guinea
frg.	fragment		pt.	part
FS	Festschrift		pub.	published, publication
ft.	foot, feet		Q	hypothetical source of material common to Matthew and Luke but not found in Mark
Ger.	Germany, German			
Gk.	Greek		q(q).	question(s)
Gr.	Greece		repr.	reprinted
ha.	hectare(s)		rev.	revised (by, in), revision
Heb.	Hebrew		Russ.	Russian
Hiph.	Hiphil		S.Af.	South Africa
Hithp.	Hithpael		Scot.	Scotland
Hung.	Hungary		ser.	series
ibid.	*ibidem,* in the same place		sess.	session
Ice.	Iceland, Icelandic		sing.	singular
i.e.	*id est,* that is		Sp.	Spanish
It.	Italy, Italian		sq.	square
J	Yahwist source		St.	Saint
km.	kilometer(s)		supp.	supplement
κτλ.	καὶ τὰ λοίπα, etc.		*SW*	*Sämtliche Werke,* complete works
L	material in Luke not found in Matthew or Mark		Swed.	Swedish
			Switz.	Switzerland
Lat.	Latin		text. em.	textual emendation
lect.	lecture		trans.	translated by, translator(s), translation
lit.	literally		Turk.	Turkish
log.	logion		U.K.	United Kingdom
LXX	Septuagint		U.N.	United Nations
M	material in Matthew not found in Mark or Luke		UNESCO	United Nations Educational, Scientific, and Cultural Organization
m	males		U.S.	United States
m.	meter(s)		USSR	Union of Soviet Socialist Republics
MEng.	Middle English		v(v).	verse(s)
MFr.	Middle French		var.	variant (reading)
mi.	mile(s)		Vg	(Latin) Vulgate
mid.	middle		vol(s).	volume(s)
MS(S)	manuscript(s)		vs.	versus
MT	Masoretic Text		YMCA	Young Men's Christian Association
Myc.	Mycenaean		YWCA	Young Women's Christian Association
n(n).	note(s)		Zim.	Zimbabwe
n.d.	no date		→	cross-reference to another article
Neth.	Netherlands		<	derived from

The ENCYCLOPEDIA
of CHRISTIANITY

Volume 2
E–I

E

Early Catholicism

1. Modern studies in church history and especially NT studies use the term "early Catholicism" to refer to the attempt on the part of the → Reformation and → Protestantism to understand and explicate their own manifest divergence from → Catholicism also as a difference in history, that is, as a difference manifesting itself already during the first centuries of Christianity. Because Reformational Christianity had broken loose from what had hitherto been its own history, it had to answer for itself the question of its material and historical continuity as a → church. (See S. Franck, *Chronica* [1531]; M. Luther, *Wider Hans Worst* [1541]; and the *Historia ecclesiae Christi* [1559-74] of the Magdeburg Centuriators.)

2. The term "early Catholicism" was itself decisively shaped by the particular form in which the Reformational question of the church was discussed during the 19th and early 20th century (esp. by R. Rothe, F. C. Baur, A. Schwegler, A. Ritschl, E. Troeltsch, and A. von Harnack). At that time the "social character" (Troeltsch) of the Lutheran and Reformed churches became a debated issue and was consciously contrasted, on the one hand (and both within and across denominations), with "Catholic" or "catholicizing" orthodoxy and restoration and, on the other, with "Gnostic speculation" (Baur), as well as with historical

→ materialism and → socialism (Harnack). Thus Baur (1792-1860) explicitly regarded the task of understanding early Christianity historically as a contemporary issue, as "self-comprehension of the present out of the past." The conscious goal and determinative notion here is to understand "Catholicism," which claims to be "substantial truth," in all its forms merely as a "moment in the development of → truth." Out of this situation of the early church as merely a moment in the development of truth, the antithesis arose between "Paulinism" and "Judaism"; in its own turn, that antithesis led to the early Catholic church.

Similar ideas were articulated by Harnack (1851-1930), whose work on historical ecclesiology sought to preserve "the continuity of conditions amidst the forces of change and dissolution" against tendencies of the age, which could be suspected of socialism. Thus he sought in the medium of culture and learning *(Bildung)*, which necessarily includes historicocritical research, to mediate and resolve the experienced "antitheses of the age" into a higher unity of "spirit" and "life." To this end he drew the antitheses into a uniform and unified worldview *(Weltanschauung)* that was informed by full-fledged ecclesiastical, dogmatic, and secular historical knowledge. Here, in the sphere of the history of ideas, we can locate Harnack's thesis on the development of early Catholicism, in which he sees the dialectic of the Christianizing of antique culture and the Hellenizing of Christianity.

1

3. In the wake of the growing radicalization of Pauline interpretation, the present debate has not maintained the term "early Catholicism" along the lines of the history of philosophy discussed above but has tried to give contours to early Christianity by describing individual historical characteristics (esp. E. Käsemann, H. Conzelmann, P. Vielhauer, L. Goppelt, S. Schulz, and U. Luz) and by including the fields of ecclesiastical and dogmatic history (esp. C. Andresen). Thus the term "early Catholicism" can still be used as an equivalent of "early Catholic Church," "postapostolic age," or "pre-Catholic age." Still, although the term has indeed been historically productive for articulating or understanding certain phenomena, its capacity to do so does not really go beyond what earlier terminology could do as well. The only new aspects were that the "expansion of the time" (after a period of "imminent expectation") was now seen to be decisive for early Catholicism and that a sequence of early Catholic characteristics (interpretation of history, constitution, sacraments, law, etc.) was established. Theologically, the term was productive in that it sharpened anew the Reformation principle of *sola Scriptura* (revolving around the canonical question: Is there a → canon within the canon? Can we regard the deuterocanonicals as early Catholic writings within the canon? What is the center of Scripture?), but without reaching a consensus (esp. in the debate that Käsemann and Schulz led).

In contrast, Roman Catholic theology took up the task of applying the term "early Catholicism" as a historicotheological category and phenomenon of the first Christian centuries, trying to weave it into the → historiography and history of the → Roman Catholic Church (H. Küng, K. H. Neufeld, H. Wagner, H. Schürmann, et al.).

It is still indispensable for the churches of the Reformation — by including new insights from the science of early history, historical sociology (→ Social History), and → anti-Semitism/anti-Judaism, and by taking into account the dialectical concept of history proper to the term "early Catholicism" — to find historicotheological criteria for the course and understanding of the first two centuries of the Christian era.

→ Apostolic Fathers; Church Fathers; Dogma, History of; Early Church; Offices, Ecclesiastical; Tradition

Bibliography: C. BARTSCH, *"Frühkatholizismus" als Kategorie historisch-kritischer Theologie* (Berlin, 1980) bibliography • F. C. BAUR, *Ausgewählte Werke* (3 vols.; Stuttgart, 1963-66); idem, *Die christliche Gnosis oder die christliche Religionsphilosophie in ihrer geschichtlichen Entwicklung* (Tübingen, 1835); idem, *Die Tübinger Schule und ihre Stellung zur Gegenwart* (2d ed.; Tübingen, 1860) • J. BECKER, ed., *Christian Beginnings: Word and Community from Jerusalem to Postapostolic Times* (Louisville, Ky., 1987) • N. BROX, *A History of the Early Church* (London, 1994) • H. CONZELMANN, *An Outline of the Theology of the NT* (London, 1969); idem, *Theologie als Schriftauslegung* (Munich, 1974) • L. GOPPELT, *Theology of the NT* (2 vols.; Grand Rapids, 1981-82) • A. VON HARNACK, *Entstehung und Entwicklung der Kirchenverfassung und des Kirchenrechts in den zwei ersten Jahrhunderten . . .* (Leipzig, 1910); idem, *The Expansion of Christianity in the First Three Centuries* (2 vols.; Salem, N.H., 1972; orig. pub., 1902) • E. KÄSEMANN, *Exegetische Versuchen und Besinnungen* (2 vols.; 6th ed.; Göttingen, 1970) • U. LUZ, "Erwägungen zur Entstehung des 'Frühkatholizismus,'" *ZNW* 65 (1974) 88-111 • N. NAGLER, *Frühkatholizismus. Zur Methodologie einer kritischen Debatte* (Frankfurt, 1994) • K. H. NEUFELD, "'Frühkatholizismus'–Idee und Begriff," *ZKT* 94 (1972) 1-28; idem, "Frühkatholizismus–woher?" ibid. 96 (1974) 353-84 • J. PELIKAN, *The Christian Tradition: A History of the Development of Doctrine* (5 vols.; Chicago, 1971-89) • A. RITSCHL, *Die Entstehung der altkatholischen Kirche* (2d ed.; Bonn, 1857) • S. SCHULZ, *Die Mitte der Schrift. Der Frühkatholizismus im Neuen Testament als Herausforderung an den Protestantismus* (Stuttgart, 1976) • F. A. SULLIVAN, *Salvation outside the Church? Tracing the History of Catholic Response* (New York, 1992) • E. TROELTSCH, "Die Soziallehren der christlichen Kirchen und Gruppen," *Gesammelte Schriften* (vol. 1; Tübingen, 1912) • H. WAGNER, *An den Ursprüngen des frühkatholischen Problems. Die Ortsbestimmung des Katholizismus im älteren Luthertum* (Frankfurt, 1973) bibliography • W. R. WAGNER, *After the Apostles? Christianity in the Second Century* (Minneapolis, 1994).

CHRISTIAN BARTSCH

Early Church

1. Term
2. Historical Survey
    2.1. Christian Congregations
    2.2. Catholic Church
    2.3. Later Imperial Church

1. Term

In church history the idea of the early church has theological as well as historical significance. A theological evaluation sees in it the true → church, whose teaching and forms have an authoritative character. Agreement with it guaranteed not only one's own orthodoxy but also the catholicity of one's church. Since the church did not remain unchanged through the centuries, the question of the limits of the early church as the true church unavoidably arises. The → Roman Catholic Church is least disturbed by such questions, since it itself claims to be the bearer of the continuous tradition of faith and doctrine up to the present day. The Greek Orthodox Church extends the normative age of the early church and → church fathers up to the end of the Iconoclastic Controversy (→ Images; Iconography) at the seventh ecumenical council (→ Nicaea, 787). It considered the necessity of an image of Christ to be an interpretation of the dogma of the → incarnation (→ Christology). Other Eastern churches had already taken an independent course on account of the Christological definition of → Chalcedon (451). In the West the Carolingians saw that the church in the Frankish empire had to accredit itself by agreement with the Fathers and especially with the Roman fathers up to Gregory I (590-604).

In the Reformation period the new churches delimited themselves confessionally from the form of faith assumed by the papal church. They adopted the humanistic principles (→ Renaissance) that the truth may be purely drawn only from the sources and that subsequent tradition must be set aside as obscure history. But they took seriously the charge that they had arbitrarily fallen away from ancient, unchanging truth and because of their ahistorical character were thus no longer catholic. Thus the Church of England appealed to the early church of the first six centuries as witness to its own catholicity in doctrine and especially in → liturgy and the episcopal system (→ Episcopacy). The Lutherans and Reformed argued in terms of *sola Scriptura* (→ Reformation Principles) but rejected the notion that the truth falls nonhistorically from heaven, for truth of this kind would be open to the suspicion of sectarian → subjectivism. Hence they appealed to the early church in defending their catholicity. The → Reformers M. → Luther (1483-1546), U. → Zwingli (1484-1531), and J. → Calvin (1509-64) found it enough at first to appeal to the binding authority of the three creeds of the early church and to the first four ecumenical councils. Reformation theologians then gave a special position to all the first six centuries, but they did not credit this whole period with unspotted purity, assessing it rather according to agreement with the apostolic church and therefore with the Bible. They attached importance to a continuous chain of witnesses to the true

church, even through the time of papal dominion and on to the present. Counter-Reformation polemics stressed afresh that religious truth is always old and challenged the Protestants to demonstrate their allegiance to the early church of the Fathers (→ Catholic Reform and Counterreformation). The Lutheran Johann Gerhard (1582-1637) and especially the Calvinists attempted along these lines to establish the → orthodoxy of their faith historically. But they rejected the proposal of Georg Calixtus (1586-1656) to derive theology from the early church fathers, as though they could be a basis for the unity of the church's faith on account of their pre-confessional character.

In the → modern period the historiographical term "early church" has become more or less completely detached from theological assessment. It fits into the secular division of historical epochs and, on the basis of political and cultural upheaval, delimits a "church of antiquity." Study of the early church thus became study of the history of Christendom during late antiquity. The Roman Empire and the culture and society of late antiquity provide the external framework. Various estimates of its length, ranging from around 395 to 600 as the terminus ad quem, are based especially on political changes — for example, the division of the empire or the final triumph of the barbarian kingdoms. The forced superannuation of the Roman emperor in the West in 467 forms a reference point.

A comprehensive inner arrangement of the history of the early church cannot rely solely on social and political changes, for they relate only to the Constantinian turning point around 312-13, which obviously affected the church, whereas the division of the empire in 395 and the appearance of barbarian groups at the beginning of the fifth century had only a tentative influence on the church. More important were differences in the appearance of the church itself, especially as they related to a different ecclesiological and theological self-understanding. Such distinctions can thus help us to put events and phenomena in a coherent nexus.

2. Historical Survey

2.1. *Christian Congregations*

Up to the end of the second century the church consisted of individual congregations. Except in → Palestine, they existed in cities on imperial lines of communication, with larger groupings at major trading centers (e.g., → Antioch or the Aegean coast of Asia Minor). The size of the Roman Empire was no obstacle to expansion. Greek culture (→ Greek Language) facilitated what might be called the worldwide propagation of the message of the one Lord of life. A Christian congregation would style itself "the church in . . ." (note the formula in the → Catholic Epistles and the → Apostolic Fathers). In addition to letters, itinerant prophets and teachers helped to maintain contact during the postapostolic period.

The churches viewed themselves as aliens in this world. They shared with the Jews the experience of the dispersion (→ Diaspora), which helps us to understand why Christians of the Jewish diaspora adopted a presbyterian type of constitution, and also why their → piety was primarily oriented to → fasting, prayer, and almsgiving. They used the Greek Bible of the Jews (→ Bible Versions), but the → law had for them only → allegorical significance (→ Hermeneutics). Special religious rules of life thus did not distinguish them from people around them. Their cultic forms were → baptism and the Lord's Supper (→ Eucharist). The former initiated persons into the church's fellowship. The latter, which at first took the form of a meal of fellowship and love, increasingly took on a sacramental character (→ Sacrament) and, in so doing, became the core of Sunday → worship.

The alien status of Christians meant that they were not at home in the empire. Confessing Christ as Lord, they rejected the gods of → Hellenistic-Roman religion. Their → monotheism had a political character, for it excluded them from public life and led society to view them as fanatic enemies of the human race. The situation was one of latent persecution. Occasional outbreaks of popular hatred and denunciations demanded a readiness for discipleship in → martyrdom. The → apologists, it is true, emphasized the blameless lives that Christians led because of their faith, whereas pagan philosophers allegedly demanded such lives only in words. But they also equated the gods of pagan myths with the wicked demonic powers, whose tools the emperors had become. With consistent rigorism Tertullian (d. ca. 225) interpreted the culture as a whole religiously and warned Christians to steer clear of it in a way that was hardly possible in real life. This approach was the fruit of a heightened expectation of the end, which → Montanism had kindled.

→ Gnosticism reflected human alienation in a cosmological → myth. In contrast to → Platonism, it regarded the creator of the world as a fallen demiurge. If it was thus disparaging the biblical Creator in opposition to the church's belief, a break became inevitable when Marcion (d. ca. 160) equated the creator with the God of the servile law of the Jews and rejected the Jewish Bible (→ Marcionites).

The apologists did not have the resources to engage in theological controversy, but their recourse to the philosophical tradition of antiquity showed how a Christian → theology could be constructed with a philosophical claim to truth. The theology of Irenaeus of Lyons (d. ca. 200), with its orientation to → salvation history, formed a transition (→ Theology of History). It confessed the one God, who both creates and consummates. From Gen. 1:26 it derived the creation destiny of humanity, presenting to humanity this likeness as the goal revealed in Christ. This step opened the door to philosophical and theological development.

2.2. Catholic Church

As represented by the → bishop and episcopal collegiality, the church conferred on the churches a catholic (i.e., ecumenical) and thus also orthodox unity. Episcopal synods, letters, and consecrations, accompanied by the participation of neighboring bishops, gave visibility to this unity. Various factors contributed to the development of an exclusively episcopal form. Ignatius of Antioch (d. ca. 107) had already based his metropolitan situation on the metaphor that the bishop, like God, gives unity to the congregation as its father. The sacramental view of the Lord's Supper gave the "shepherd" of the church a priestly task. The establishment of a penitential system conferred on episcopal office the additional priestly authority to remit sins (→ Penitence). External influences helped to make sense of these theological developments. The defeat of theological Gnosticism and of the prophetic spirit of Montanism demanded an apostolic teaching authority. The bishop met this demand better than a presbytery (→ Elder), especially since succession was manifested in individuals back to the → apostles. In the persecutions, which sought to destroy the church, the episcopal constitution authenticated itself in the steadfastness of those who held the episcopal office (→ Persecution of Christians).

As catholicity became institutionalized, doctrinal norms were clarified. The church listed the Scriptures in which alone, but completely, the doctrine that Christ had entrusted to the apostles had taken written form. As the NT, these enjoyed the same canonical authority as the Jewish Bible, so that now in two parts the Christian Bible revealed salvation history from its commencement up to the → parousia of Christ (→ Canon). At the very least, the truth of Christian belief had to show itself by its derivation from scriptural → revelation. Along with this unequivocal norm, reference began to be made to a second one — the canon of truth, or rule of faith. This norm had its root in the baptismal confession but received formulation and the intended → authority only in the creed of Nicaea (→ Niceno-Constantinopolitan Creed).

Theology blossomed in cosmopolitan → Alexandria. In debate with Gnostic theology Clement (d. ca. 215) and especially Origen (ca. 185-ca. 254) sought the higher but scriptural knowledge, which would make us like God. Questions about the nature of God, the human situation, and divine providence were subordinate to this goal, which was in agreement with Platonism. Such theology, which sought to lead the faith of the community beyond formal moralism and material expectations for the future life, ran into resistance (→ Origenism).

2.3. Later Imperial Church

The church now became institutionalized → religion, which the empire needed to retain divine favor. Constantine (306-37) ascribed his victory over imperial rivals to the Christian God and thus, in one stroke, altered the church's situation in the empire. Even before the end of the fourth century, imperial law not only gave the church a religious monopoly but enforced orthodoxy within it (→ Arianism). Along the lines of imperial government, the church organized itself in metropolitan areas. Bishops assumed legal duties. They were elected by the clergy and people, but their position was similar to that of privileged state officials. The church expressed itself publicly in its own cultic buildings (→ Basilica), with paradigmatic representative structures in → Rome, → Jerusalem, and Constantinople (→ Byzantium). The official calendar of feasts showed Christian influence. Preachers tried to adorn their sermons with the elegant rhetoric of the schools. The sign of the cross denoted triumph over the demonism of → polytheism and thus also over the powers of death. When Rome lost its political leadership, the bishop of Rome claimed universal spiritual lordship over believers (→ Pope, Papacy).

Monasticism checked the trend toward → secularization. Externally, by its flight from culture, it gave evidence of earthly homelessness, changing the desert, the haunt of demons, into a place of residence. The → asceticism of the → anchorites embodied the ideal Christian lifestyle. They held this ideal before the people, and the clergy at least could not evade it. More far-reaching was the inner experience, after separation from the world of temptation, of finding evil powers in the → self and taking up the battle of faith against them without falling victim to the primal enemy of arrogance. Eastern monasticism in particular came in this way to see in → humility the supreme Christian → virtue, to which → obedience and asceticism can finally be no more than means. If few at-

tained this character, for many it was at least the goal of their pilgrimage.

The battle with Arianism made orthodoxy a matter on which → salvation depended. → Athanasius of Alexandria (bishop 328-73) established the theological concept that Christ as the Redeemer from death cannot himself be subject to it as a created being. Christ, then, is coessential with God. The → Cappadocians then found the theological terms for this truth, and the doctrine of the → Trinity became a → dogma. Apollinaris of Laodicea (d. ca. 390) drew theological inferences from Athanasius regarding the incarnate Son of God that continued in the → Monophysitism of → Cyril of Alexandria (bishop 412-44). Greek Orthodoxy reflected in its Christology the divine appropriation of salvation to us; the dogmatic formulas offered only the delimiting outward aspect. In the Latin West Augustine (354-430) was led by his reading of the apostle → Paul to present the appropriation of salvation as a doctrine of grace. In the interplay of the doctrine of → God and → anthropology, he achieved a fundamental insight whose validity has not yet been set in full dialogue with the theology of the Eastern churches. In distinction from the East, Augustine recognized the dubious nature of the imperial church of later antiquity. He thus prepared the church for future experiences, though the papal church of the Middle Ages wrongly appealed to his notion of the city of God.

Bibliography: C. ANDRESEN, *Geschichte der alten Christenheit* (Stuttgart, 1971); idem, ed., *HDThG* vol. 1 • H. VON CAMPENHAUSEN, *Ecclesiastical Authority and Spiritual Power in the Church of the First Three Centuries* (Stanford, Calif., 1969; orig. pub., 1953) • H. CHADWICK, *The Early Church* (Harmondsworth, 1984; orig. pub., 1967) • B. DALEY, *The Hope of the Early Church: A Handbook of Patristic Eschatology* (Cambridge, 1991) • A. DI BERARDINO, ed., *Encyclopedia of the Early Church* (2 vols.; New York, 1992) • A. FAIVRE, *The Emergence of the Laity in the Early Church* (New York, 1990) • R. L. FOX, *Pagans and Christians* (New York, 1987) • W. H. C. FREND, *The Rise of Christianity* (London, 1986) • S. G. HALL, *Doctrine and Practice in the Early Church* (Grand Rapids, 1992) • A. VON HARNACK, *The Expansion of Christianity in the First Three Centuries* (2 vols.; Salem, N.H., 1972; orig. pub., 1902); idem, *History of Dogma* (7 vols.; New York, 1961; orig. pub., 1886-90) vols. 1-2 • H. JEDIN and J. P. DOLAN, eds., *History of the Church*, vol. 1, *From the Apostolic Community to Constantine;* vol. 2, *The Imperial Church from Constantine to the Early Middle Ages* (New York, 1980) • J. N. D. KELLY, *Early Christian Doctrines*

(5th ed.; London, 1984) • H. Rahner, *Church and State in Early Christianity* (San Francisco, 1992) • M. Simonetti, *Biblical Interpretation in the Early Church: An Historical Introduction to Patristic Exegesis* (Edinburgh, 1994) • C. A. Volz, *Pastoral Life and Practice in the Early Church* (Minneapolis, 1990) • M. J. Watkins and T. Paige, eds., *Worship, Theology, and Ministry in the Early Church* (Sheffield, 1992).

Ekkehard Mühlenberg

Early Jerusalem Church → Primitive Christian Community

Easter

1. Term
2. Relation to Passover
3. Forms of Observance
4. Debate over the Date

1. Term

The origin of the English word "Easter" is uncertain. In the eighth century the Venerable Bede (ca. 673-735) proposed that it derived from Eostre, the Anglo-Saxon goddess of spring. Modern English-language dictionaries suggest that it comes ultimately from a Germanic stem meaning "east."

In Romance and other languages, the word for Easter (e.g., Fr. *Pâques;* Sp. *Pascua;* Russ. *Paskhar*) comes from the Heb. *pesaḥ* through the Gk. *pascha.* Recent liturgical usage has employed the noun "Pasch" and the adjective "paschal" in speaking of this Christian celebration.

2. Relation to Passover

Easter is the Christian feast that is closest to Jewish roots. It is also the center and high point of the → church year.

For Jews the night of the → passover commemorated four salvation nights: those of → creation (§2; Genesis 1), the sacrifice of Isaac (Genesis 22), the exodus (Exodus 14–15), and the coming of the Messiah. On this night of celebration God's saving acts were a living reality for all participants: "[Yahweh] brought us forth from slavery to freedom, anguish to joy, mourning to festival, darkness to great light, subjugation to redemption, so we should say before him, Hallelujah" (*m. Pesaḥ.* 10:5).

Easter developed out of the Jewish passover, as the Gk. *pascha* shows. Whether the NT presupposes a Christian passover is uncertain (see 1 Cor. 5:7-8;

Acts 20:6; John 2:13, etc.). In any case, 1 Cor. 5:7-8 offers a profound Christian interpretation of the passover.

3. Forms of Observance

Universally observed by the middle of the second century, Easter was at first a single service (→ worship) held overnight until cockcrow. It consisted of a vigil with readings, followed by a joyous agape feast with the → Eucharist. The readings included Exodus 12 and 14 and the accounts of the → passion and → resurrection. This was a night of watching and rejoicing, the night of transition from → death to → life, from → grief to → joy. The → suffering, death, and resurrection of Jesus were seen as a saving unit. His transition from death to new life meant transition for Christians from the bondage of → sin to a life of freedom with God. Another emphasis in Asia Minor was on expectation of the Lord's return (→ Parousia).

Easter night was greatly enriched in two ways in the fourth century. First, it became the great baptismal night (transition from death to life; → Baptism). Second, a light ritual inaugurated the celebration (transition from darkness to light). Everywhere in the East, and in most places in the West, Genesis 1 and 22 and Exodus 12–14 were the readings (see 2).

In the fifth century the night service had become very lengthy, but it gradually began to be reduced. By the early sixth century it ended by midnight, and a second eucharistic celebration followed on → Sunday morning with the full congregation. From the middle of the eighth century, the vigil was moved progressively earlier, so that its ancient character was lost. By the time of the → Reformation, the night service was often held on Saturday morning, with almost none of the → congregation present.

Liturgical reforms in the 16th century either put the first celebration on Saturday and kept the main feast on Easter Sunday (Rome) or abandoned the vigil altogether (→ Reformers). The → Orthodox churches, however, retained the all-night vigil as the true celebration and viewed it as the climax of the church year.

Since the 1930s, → liturgical movements in various churches have directed more and more attention to the vigil. The → Roman Catholic Church promoted its return in 1951, prescribed it in 1955, and gave it a place in its new calendar in 1970. It has also been reintroduced in other churches. The form is everywhere more or less the same: the paschal candle, long readings, baptism, and a festal Eucharist. This return to common origins is an instance of liturgical → oikoumene of the first rank. The vigil, however, is still mostly eclipsed by the well-attended eucharistic celebrations of Easter Sunday morning.

Easter has received considerable emphasis in American Protestant churches. Outdoor sunrise services are popular and are frequently ecumenical. This custom has clashed with efforts in some Protestant churches to restore the vigil.

4. Debate over the Date

The death and resurrection of Jesus Christ occurred during the Jewish passover. There was a concern in the → early church to keep the annual Christian celebration of the resurrection in proximity to the Jewish festival.

Ecclesiastical debate centered on whether the annual commemoration of the paschal mystery should be on the 14th of Nisan (cf. Lev. 23:5 etc.), the first day of the full moon of spring, no matter what day of the week this fell on, or whether it should be on the Sunday after the 14th of Nisan, in keeping with the weekly celebration of Christ's resurrection on the "Lord's Day." The first alternative was defended by the so-called Quartodecimans in Asia Minor, who were concerned to celebrate the Lord's passion on the very day of his crucifixion. Rome and most other local churches, however, celebrated Easter on a Sunday, the day of the Lord's resurrection.

The Quartodeciman celebration of *pascha* probably had its roots in Palestine and reflects the oldest observance of Easter. On the eve of the 14th of Nisan, when the Jews were eating the passover, Christians kept a → fast until dawn (see 3). Like Jews, Christians awaited the Redeemer's coming on this night. Christ obviously took the place of the paschal lamb. His presence was experienced in the Eucharist, which represented the resurrection, and his parousia was joyfully awaited.

The Sunday celebration of Easter clearly developed out of this early observance. Perhaps it first arose in Jerusalem and Palestine after the year 135 with the new → Gentile Christian congregations. Under the Roman bishop Soter it was introduced about 165 into Rome (K. Holl), but it might well have arisen there independently about 115 under Sixtus I (B. Lohse). It can hardly go back to the first century (W. Rordorf). Sunday was the day of the Lord's resurrection (1 Cor. 16:2; Acts 20:7; Rev. 1:10). It thus attracted the celebration to itself, especially as Nisan 14 came on different days of the week. The separation from → Judaism also favored this development. Commemoration of the resurrection now received more emphasis as the content of Easter.

Bishop Polycrates of Ephesus (2d cent.) wrote a letter to Bishop Victor I of Rome (189-98) in defense of quartodeciman practice. Upon receipt of this letter, Victor issued letters to all the churches, excommunicating the churches of Asia Minor. Other bishops opposed Victor's reaction, including → Irenaeus of Lyons (d. ca. 200), who had presided over a Gallican synod that declared in favor of the Sunday Easter.

By the third century a Sunday celebration of Easter was fairly generally accepted, but the proper date was still a subject of debate. In 325 the First Council of → Nicaea settled the issue by decreeing that the date of Easter should be the first Sunday after the first full moon of spring. The intention of the council was to celebrate Easter after the Jewish passover, since if the 14th of Nisan fell on a Sunday, Easter would be the following Sunday. Since this arrangement was based on phases of the moon rather than on the solar calendar, thus maintaining the relation of Easter to the Jewish passover, the date of Easter could vary between March 22 and April 25.

Only in the sixth century did the Alexandrian 19-year cycle of calculating the date of the "paschal moon" finally prevail over an older, 84-year cycle followed by Rome. This difference was settled when Rome adopted an Easter cycle prepared in 525 by the monk Dionysius Exiguus.

The changing date of Easter was made known by paschal letters. Of these, the ones from Alexandria (e.g., from Dionysius the Great [d. ca. 265] and → Athanasius [d. 373]) were especially important, since they dealt with what were at times thorny theological and ecclesiastical issues of the day.

The Julian calendar was revised in 1582 under the authority of Pope Gregory XIII (1572-85), a change that non–Roman Catholic countries accepted only hesitantly. The 1923 Pan-Orthodox Council (→ Pan-Orthodox Conferences), meeting in Istanbul, accepted the Gregorian calendar but excepted the calculation of Easter.

In modern times there has been a growing desire to fix the date of Easter, something argued much earlier by Martin → Luther (1483-1546; → Luther's Theology). → Vatican II did not oppose such a move if the non–Roman Catholic churches would give their assent. In Nairobi in 1975 the Fifth Assembly of the → World Council of Churches proposed the second Sunday of April but gave up this effort when it became clear that the Orthodox churches were not prepared to accept it. In 1997 in Aleppo, Syria, a consultation sponsored by the WCC and the Middle East Council of Churches, "Towards a Common Date for Easter," proposed specific recommendations for resolving the issue. Initial strong support for this proposal came from the North American Orthodox-Catholic Theological Consultation (meeting in November 1998).

→ Soteriology

Bibliography: A. ADAM, *The Liturgical Year: Its History and Its Meaning after the Reform of the Liturgy* (New York, 1981) • G. BERTONIÈRE, *The Historical Development of the Easter Vigil and Related Services in the Greek Church* (Rome, 1972) • K. H. BIERITZ, *Das Kirchenjahr* (Berlin, 1986) • P. F. BRADSHAW and L. A. HOFFMAN, eds., *Passover and Easter: Two Liturgical Traditions* (Notre Dame, Ind., 1999) • R. CANTALAMESSA, ed., *Easter in the Early Church: An Anthology of Jewish and Early Christian Texts* (Collegeville, Minn., 1993) • O. CASEL, "Art und Sinn der ältesten christlichen Osterfeier," *JLW* 14 (1938) 1-78 • K. HOLL, "Ein Bruchstück aus einem bisher unbekannten Brief des Epiphanius," *Gesammelte Aufsätze* (Tübingen, 1928) 2.204-24 • W. HUBER, *Passa und Ostern* (Berlin, 1969) • B. LOHSE, *Das Passafest der Quartadecimaner* (Gütersloh, 1953) • A. A. MCARTHUR, *The Evolution of the Christian Year* (London, 1953) • H. AUF DER MAUR, "Feiern im Rhythmus der Zeit I," *Handbuch der Liturgiewissenschaft* (pt. 5; Regensburg, 1983) • W. RORDORF, "Zum Ursprung des Osterfestes am Sonntag," *TZ* 18 (1962) 167-89 • T. J. TALLEY, *The Origins of the Liturgical Year* (New York, 1986) 1-57. See also the bibliography in "Church Year."

TRAUGOTT HOLTZ, FRANK C. SENN,
and THADDEUS A. SCHNITKER

Eastern Orthodox Churches, Eastern Orthodoxy → Orthodox Church; Orthodoxy 3

EATWOT → Ecumenical Association of Third World Theologians

Ebionites

From the time of Irenaeus (d. ca. 200), "Ebionites" was the term used for → Jewish Christians in the lists of heretics drawn up by the → church fathers. Originally it was the self-designation of a specific group that, adopting OT and postbiblical ideas, gave itself the title "the poor" (Heb. *'ebyônîm*). From the time of Hippolytus (d. ca. 236) the Hebrew word was taken to refer to a supposed founder of the sect called Ebion. Besides the judgments of the Fathers, seven fragments of an Ebionite gospel have been

preserved, which show similarity to the → Synoptics. According to critical reconstruction some of the sources of the Pseudo-Clementines might also be of Ebionite origin.

Ebionites could be found up to the fifth century in Syria, Asia Minor, Egypt, and east of the Jordan. Since the → primitive Christian community supposedly emigrated to east of the Jordan after the destruction of → Jerusalem, some have tried to see in the Ebionites the descendants of this community and also to explain the name accordingly (see Gal. 2:10; Rom. 15:26). All such speculation, however, is uncertain.

In spite of our incomplete knowledge of developments within this group of Greek-speaking Jewish Christians, we can list five features as characteristic of the Ebionites' thought.

1. The Ebionites confessed → monotheism and emphasized observance of the Mosaic → law (§2), especially the sanctifying of the → Sabbath, the rules of cultic cleanness, and the feasts. A related feature was their stress on the Lord's brother → James (§2) and their rejection of → Paul and his epistles.
2. They rejected the → sacrificial system. References in the Pentateuch to this system they regarded as post-Mosaic falsifications, as they did the positive statements about the → monarchy.
3. They considered → Jesus, who they believed taught them to recognize "falsified pericopes," to be an embodiment of the true prophet, who from the beginning has been going through the world. They viewed → Moses as an earlier embodiment of this prophet.
4. They held that, alongside the true prophet, there is an opposing "female prophecy," which includes the OT → prophets (§2). → Gnostic → dualism lies behind this idea.
5. They also had a Gnostic → Christology. They taught that the Holy Spirit came into the man Jesus at his → baptism. Some Ebionites rejected the → virgin birth. Others, though, were closer to the main church in this and other matters.

Bibliography: J. H. CREHAN, "Ebionites," *CDT* 2.204-6 • S. GORANSON, "Ebionites," *ABD* 2.260-61 • A. F. J. KLIJN and G. J. REININK, *Patristic Evidence for Jewish Christian Sects* (Leiden, 1973) 19-43 • H. J. SCHOEPS, *Jewish Christianity: Factional Disputes in the Early Church* (Philadelphia, 1969) • G. STRECKER, *Das Judenchristentum in den Pseudoklementinen* (2d ed.; Berlin, 1981); idem, "Judenchristentum und Gnosis," *Altes Testament, Frühjudentum, Gnosis* (ed. K.-W. Tröger; Gütersloh, 1980) 261-82 • P. VIELHAUER, "The Gospel of the Ebionites," *NT Apocrypha* (E. Hennecke; ed. W. Schneemelcher and R. M. Wilson; Philadelphia, 1963) 1.153-58.

HELMUT MERKEL

Ecclesiastes, Book of

1. Name
2. Origin
3. Structure
4. Content

1. Name

The Hebrew name of the Book of Ecclesiastes, Qoheleth, derives from *qhl* (call, assemble). The feminine ending suggests an office, according to which the author would have been responsible for an assembly of persons or a collection of sayings. The Greek form *Ekklēsiastēs* (assembly leader) led to "the preacher." The name "Qoheleth" was influenced by the Solomonic legend, according to which the king assembled the people for the dedication of the → temple. The author adopted the literary fiction of → Solomonic authorship, albeit only for the first two chapters, whereas the epilogue identifies the author as a *ḥākām* (teacher).

2. Origin

Both the language and the syntax of this book exhibit later linguistic peculiarities, and the presence of two Persian loanwords — *pardēs* (park, 2:5) and *pitgām* (sentence, judgment, 8:11) — supports this dating. The author uses the shortened form of personal and relative pronouns, frequently the participles instead of finite verbs, and a wide array of Aramaisms; elsewhere this vocabulary occurs on the whole only in Esther, Daniel, Ezra, and the → Mishnah. Ecclesiastes was probably composed in Palestine during the middle of the third century. Several fragments (from 5:13-17; 6:3-8; 7:7-9) found in → Qumran have been dated a century later.

3. Structure

No clear structure is discernible, despite regular refrains and stereotypical expressions defining smaller units. Collections of aphorisms have been inserted into a discussion resembling a treatise. Although the basic literary genre is that of reflection, other forms are also present, including royal testament, aphorism, lament, admonition, numerical saying, and the saying about being or not being. The book begins with a thematic assertion and a poem (1:2, 3-11) and ends with a poem and a thematic assertion (11:7–12:7; 12:8). A foreword (1:1) and either one or two afterwords (12:9-14), which frame the book, were appended later.

4. Content

Qoheleth's view of things does not correspond to the biblical context. Despite being schooled in the Wisdom tradition, he rejects the premise that rational thinking and moral action elicit tangible forms of divine favor. Whereas his teachers presuppose a beneficent Creator (→ Creation), Qoheleth sees impartial → chance as the factor governing life. The shadow of → death affects all creatures equally. Qoheleth represents the view that in death, human beings and animals are equal and that the only meaningful course is to enjoy the pleasures of life while one is still young. Because of his inclination to present contradictory views, usually without identifying them as such, Qoheleth's own views at central points cannot be discerned. Was he an optimist or pessimist (→ Optimism and Pessimism)? Was he hostile toward women? Was he a guardian of divine → freedom or a representative of divine despotism?

Regardless of how these questions are answered, one thing seems certain: → Wisdom literature brought about a spiritual and intellectual crisis in ancient → Israel (§1) and produced the poetic masterpiece Job and the remarkably modern book of Ecclesiastes. Qoheleth dared to doubt the wisdom of the schools from his own angle of vision by rejecting every basis of perception or wisdom except his own observation, an epistemological principle leading him to the sobering conclusion that everything under the sun is vain. Various parallels can be adduced for this crisis and the literature it generated (the Gilgamesh epic, the "Dialogue of Pessimism" [*ANET* 600-601], the *Songs of the Harper,* the Insinger Papyrus, Greek popular philosophy; → Greek philosophy). Qoheleth's teachings were easily misinterpreted (see the Wisdom of Solomon), and although the successors of Shammai (1st cent.) objected to its canonization (→ Canon), the opposing view of the students of Hillel (ca. 50 B.C.–A.D. 10) was able to assert itself. As a text of the → Megilloth, Ecclesiastes was read during the Feast of Tabernacles (→ Jewish Practices 2.2).

Bibliography: Commentaries: J. L. CRENSHAW (OTL; Philadelphia, 1987) • K. GALLING (HAT; 2d ed.; Tübingen, 1969) • H. W. HERTZBERG (KAT; Gütersloh, 1963) • R. KROEBER (SQAW; Berlin, 1963) • A. LAUHA (BKAT; Neukirchen, 1978) • N. LOHFINK (NEchtB; Würzburg, 1980) • R. E. MURPHY (WBC; Dallas, 1992) • G. S. OGDEN (Rdgs; Sheffield, 1987) • E. PODECHARD

(Ebib; Paris, 1912) • C.-L. SEOW (AB; Garden City, N.Y., 1997) • R. N. WHYBRAY (NCBC; Grand Rapids, 1989) • W. ZIMMERLI (ATD; 3d ed.; Göttingen, 1980).

Other works: A. BARUCQ, *Ecclésiaste* (Paris, 1968); idem, "Qohelet," *DBSup* 9.609-74 • J. BLENKINSOPP, "Ecclesiastes 3:1-15: Another Interpretation," *JSOT* 66 (1995) 55-64 • R. BRAUN, *Kohelet und die frühhellenistische Popularphilosophie* (Berlin, 1973) • J. L. CRENSHAW, "Qohelet in Current Research," *HAR* 7 (1983) 41-56; idem, *Urgent Advice and Probing Questions: Collected Writings on OT Wisdom* (Macon, Ga., 1995) 499-585 • F. ELLERMEIER, *Qohelet* (2d ed.; Herzberg, 1970) • M. V. Fox, *Qohelet and His Contradictions* (Sheffield, 1989); idem, *A Time to Tear Down and a Time to Build Up: A Rereading of Ecclesiastes* (Grand Rapids, 1999) • H. L. GINSBERG, *Studies in Kohelet* (New York, 1950) • R. GORDIS, *Koheleth–the Man and His World* (New York, 1951) • O. KAISER, "Die Botschaft des Buches Kohelet," *ETL* 71 (1995) 48-70 • C. KLEIN, *Kohelet und die Weisheit Israels. Eine Formgeschichtliche Studie* (Stuttgart, 1994) • J. A. LOADER, *Polar Structures in the Book of Qohelet* (Berlin, 1979) • O. LORETZ, *Qoheleth und der alte Orient* (Freiburg, 1964) • D. LYS, *L'Ecclésiaste ou que vaut la vie?* (Paris, 1977) • D. MICHEL, *Qohelet* (Darmstadt, 1988) • T. A. PERRY, *Dialogues with Kohelet* (University Park, Pa., 1993) • A. SCHOORS, *The Preacher Sought to Find Pleasing Words: A Study of the Language of Qoheleth* (Louvain, 1992); idem, ed., *Qohelet in the Context of Wisdom* (Louvain, 1998) • C. F. WHITLEY, *Kohelet* (Grand Rapids, 1979).

JAMES L. CRENSHAW

Ecclesiology → Church

Eckhart, Meister

Meister Eckhart (ca. 1260-ca. 1328), a → Dominican mystic, was born in Hochheim (near Gotha or Erfurt) in Thuringia. Eckhart entered the Erfurt Dominican monastery around 1275. After completing the usual training, he studied theology at the Dominican Studium Generale at Cologne, probably under Albertus Magnus (d. 1280), and from 1293 at Paris. In 1294 he became the prior of Erfurt and representative of the provincial Dietrich von Freiberg. In 1302 Eckhart was promoted to master in Paris. From 1303 to 1311 he was active as the first provincial of the newly created Saxon Province of his order. Although Eckhart was elected provincial of Teutonia Province in 1310, the general sent him to Paris in 1311, where he taught till 1313. From 1314 to about 1323 Eckhart engaged in pastoral care, preaching, and visitations at the convents in Strasbourg, during which time he wrote numerous exegetical pieces and German sermons. Eckhart also oversaw convents in Cologne, where, at the earliest beginning in 1323, he taught at the Studium Generale (→ Orders and Congregations).

In 1326 the archbishop of Cologne, Heinrich II of Virneburg, initiated a → heresy investigation against Eckhart, even though the Dominicans had defended him against any suspicion of heresy. He was accused of having obscured the distinction between → God and human beings by emphasizing too strongly the notion of the *unio mystica.* The two → Franciscans charged with leading the investigation highlighted suspicious statements primarily from Eckhart's German writings. For his own part, Eckhart appealed to Pope John XXII in Avignon. Eckhart died, however, before being able to go to Avignon to defend himself. On March 27, 1329, the pope produced the bull *In agro dominico,* which cited 28 propositions from Eckhart's teachings. Of these, 17 were declared heretical, the others "extremely bold" and "suspected of heresy."

Almost all of Eckhart's Latin writings belong to his main work, the *Opus tripartitum,* extant portions of which include prologues (incomplete); commentaries on Genesis, Exodus, Wisdom, and John; sermon drafts; and various other writings (incomplete). Although only a few of his Latin works have been preserved, the collection of his German works is much broader, including especially his "Discourse on Distinguishing" and "On Disinterest," delivered to young brothers in the Erfurt order. Around 1318 Eckhart dedicated his *Liber benedictus* with the *Book of Divine Comfort* and *The Aristocrat* to the widowed Queen Agnes of Hungary. Of the approximately 150 sermons ascribed to him, 86 are considered genuine today. Eckhart's German writings were circulated throughout the German-Dutch linguistic region until about 1500, albeit frequently anonymously or pseudonymously. Despite being condemned, Eckhart's teachings enjoyed widespread distribution and even exerted an influence within → Protestantism.

The center of Eckhart's teaching is the formula *esse est Deus* (being is God), which expresses the identity of these two entities: God is true being, and all other being exists only insofar as it is being from God. Eckhart expresses this idea, for example, with the image of the mirror in water, which reflects the sun's rays such that it itself shines as the sun. Philosophical cognition, on the one hand, and Christian faith as the expression of the new being revealed in

Christ, on the other, do not refer to two different truths. Rather, the *philosophus* (i.e., Aristotle), → Moses, and Christ all teach the same thing, manifested in Moses in the mode of → faith *(credibile)*, in Aristotle in that of probability *(probabile)*, and in Christ in that of truth *(veritas)*.

God's → incarnation takes place in the "little spark of the soul" in every person when that person, in a state of *Abgeschiedenheit* (disinterest, abstractedness), divests himself or herself of the world. Eckhart's teaching encourages preaching and pastoral care, and it criticizes several forms of feminine → mysticism for lacking interiority. For him, self-mortification through asceticism is of less value than self-annihilation in surrender to God; common → prayer is to be preferred to private prayer; "being in love with God" is not the same as "loving God"; and love of God manifests itself externally as love of one's neighbor.

Bibliography: Primary source: J. QUINT et al., eds., *Meister Eckhart. Die deutschen und lateinischen Werke* (5 vols.; Stuttgart, 1936-63).

Secondary works: W. CORDUAN, "A Hair's Breadth from Pantheism: Meister Eckhart's God-Centered Spirituality," *JETS* 37 (1994) 265-74 • O. DAVIS, *Meister Eckhart, Mystical Theologian* (London, 1991) • A. M. HOLLYWOOD, *The Soul as Virgin Wife: Mechthild of Magdeburg, Marguerite Porete, and Meister Eckhart* (Notre Dame, Ind., 1995) • F. IOHN, *Die Predigt Meister Eckharts. Seelsorge und Häresie* (Heidelberg, 1993) • C. F. KELLEY, *Meister Eckhart on Divine Knowledge* (New Haven, 1977) • B. MCGUINN, *Meister Eckhart and the Beguine Mystics* (New York, 1997) • R. MANSTETTEN, *Esse est Deus. Meister Eckharts christologische Versöhnung von Philosophie und Religion und ihre Ursprünge in der Tradition des Abendlandes* (Freiburg, 1993).

ANGELIKA DÖRFLER-DIERKEN

Ecology

1. Term
2. Modern Issues
3. Church Positions

1. Term

The term "ecology" refers to the earth and its communities of life, particularly as they interact in complex and dynamic ways. The science of ecology studies the interrelationships of organisms and their → environments. Derived from the Greek terms *oikos* and *logos*, ecology is the study of the (worldwide) household; as such, it is related etymologically to economics (the law of the household).

2. Modern Issues

The zoologist Ernst Haeckel (1834-1919) introduced the term "ecology" in 1866. He used it to describe what then was called the economy of nature. In coining this term and using it in this way, Haeckel helped to found a new biological discipline that would attempt to describe the relationships in the natural world without reference to humanity. Ecology in this biological sense did not necessarily imply the protection of nature. In the last decades of the 20th century, however, with the growing awareness of various forms of ecological degradation and with the rise of new subdisciplines like conservation biology, ecology has been linked to the care of creation.

This extension of the meaning of ecology began in earnest with the publication in 1962 of *Silent Spring* by the American biologist Rachel Carson. The book described in considerable detail the chemical poisoning of the earth's ecosystems. By the early 1970s ecological degradations of various kinds had become increasingly a matter of global analysis and concern. For example, the first Club of Rome Report (1972) concluded that at the then current rates of growth, there would be severe ecological problems by the middle of the 21st century, especially given the pressures of exponentially increasing human population. This report spawned other global analyses, including the Global 2000 Report (1980) and, more recently, the Agenda 21 document produced in 1992 by the Rio Earth Summit. The upshot of these many gatherings and reports is that the limits of the earth's resources must be respected so as to leave enough water, air, soil, forest, and the like for future generations, and this stewardship must be done in ways that are equitable. In short, our human economies must be sustainable and just.

The deepening of ecological awareness after 1970 posed a challenge in politics, economics, and science (→ Economic Ethics). In Europe, for example, political groups like the Green Party were formed and have wielded some influence. In the United States, Vice-President Al Gore wrote a best-selling book, *Earth in the Balance* (1992), about the need to protect and preserve the natural world. In economics, various critiques of traditional neoclassical economics have been made and numerous proposals put forward that more accurately reflect the actual ecological costs of market transactions (e.g., the index for sustainable economic welfare developed by Herman Daly and John Cobb). In science many areas of research — from solar technology to organic farming — have taken an ecological turn. Despite these developments, many argue that the earth is in even greater peril now than in the recent past. Indeed, one widely read book argues that we have reached "the end of nature" — that there is no place left on earth unaffected by human action — since we have changed the very chemistry of the atmosphere. As Bill McKibben puts it: "The rain bore a brand: it was a steer, not a deer."

3. Church Positions

The churches have entered into the issue in a variety of ways. For example, the World Council of Churches (WCC) convened an ecumenical gathering in Seoul, Korea, in 1990 with the theme "Justice, Peace, and the Integrity of Creation." This conjunction of biblical motifs makes clear the churches' concern to see social justice, international peace, and ecological harmony as aspects of a single vision of God's good future. In the United States, the National Religious Partnership for the Environment (NRPE), formed in 1993, is a coalition of mainline Protestant, evangelical Protestant, Catholic, and Jewish groups united by their common concern that religious folk see care for creation as integral to their faith. In addition to joint endeavors like the NRPE, many denominations have instituted programs and published books and curricula on Christian responsibility to protect and nurture the earth and its nonhuman creatures.

Reasons given by the churches for caring for creation vary. Often emphasis is given to various aspects of the doctrine of creation, as in the WCC reference to the integrity of creation. In this view, there is an ecological integrity or wholeness to the earth that must be preserved if human life is to endure and if nonhuman life is to flourish. One of the basic laws of ecology is that everything is connected to everything else, often in intricate webs of interdependence. Disruptions of this web of life, for example, by the human-caused extinction of keystone species, affect the entire biosphere. The doctrine of creation, among other things, fosters respect for the integrity of creation — in whole and in part.

Other arguments for a Christian concern for creation focus on incarnation and redemption — for example, by emphasizing the goodness of the human body and material world and by stressing Christ's cosmic redemption (Colossians 1) and the future renewal of all things (Revelation 21–22). In taking on human flesh and living among us (John 1:14), Christ transfigured the material world, as the Orthodox put it, and will bring this work of redemption to completion. Whatever specific argu-

ments are adduced, many within the church are calling into question both the reigning anthropocentrism of Western culture and common antiecological patterns of living.

→ City; Philosophy of Nature; Science and Theology; Technology

Bibliography: A. LEOPOLD, *A Sand County Almanac* (New York, 1987) • B. MCKIBBEN, *The End of Nature* (New York, 1989) • G. T. MILLER JR., *Living in the Environment: Principles, Connections, and the Solutions* (Belmont, Calif., 1997) • E. ODUM, *Fundamentals of Ecology* (Philadelphia, 1971; orig. pub., 1953) • D. ORR, *Ecological Literacy: Education and the Transition to a Postmodern World* (Albany, N.Y., 1992) • H. ROLSTON III, *Environmental Ethics: Duties to and Values in the Natural World* (Philadelphia, 1988) • E. O. WILSON, *The Diversity of Life* (New York, 1993) • D. WORSTER, *Nature's Economy: A History of Ecological Ideas* (Cambridge, 1994).

STEVEN BOUMA-PREDIGER

Economic Ethics

1. Ethics, the Economy, and the Corporation
   1.1. Biblical and Greek Roots
   1.2. Oikos and Polis
   1.3. The Corporation
2. Earlier Christian Approaches
   to Economic Ethics
   2.1. The Early Tradition
   2.2. Reformation and Scholasticism
   2.3. The Enlightenment
3. Twentieth-Century Economic Ethics
   and Christianity
   3.1. Max Weber
   3.2. The Social Gospel and Christian Realism
   3.3. The Roman Catholic Church
   3.4. The World Council of Churches
   3.5. Other Perspectives
4. Economic Ethics Entering
   the Twenty-first Century
   4.1. Globalization
   4.2. Questions and Issues

1. Ethics, the Economy, and the Corporation

The question of how to organize the economic life of society has occupied the world's leaders and thinkers since at least the time of the patriarch Joseph in Egypt. It appears as a primary concern of Moses, Solomon, and Socrates, much as it was of the sages of other traditions elsewhere. After all, the production, distribution, exchange, ownership, and use of goods and services have been a part of → society for as long as recorded history.

A central dimension of biblical teaching has been the question of how faith should inform the ordering of economic life and how morals should shape behavior and attitudes. Over the centuries, biblical themes have shaped, if not fully determined, the development of Western ideas of fair weights and measures, just price, → usury, property, → stewardship, → vocation, → charity, and a host of other motifs that, with notable modifications, have set the context for the development of modern Western → industrial society. This complex has, in turn, influenced contemporary business activity around the world, even where other religious traditions are dominant or where people consciously resist → modernity or Christianity.

Modern economics, however — from Adam Smith through Karl Marx to the current Chicago school — has tended to separate religious and ethical theory from the "sciences" dealing with economic laws and economic relations. Such laws are largely descriptive, secular, and abstract. Even when business administration programs include business ethics, they seldom treat the religious roots of moral norms or the sources of the operating values that are implicit in business activity. Closer inspection, however, reveals that economic life is neither devoid of religious influence nor feasible without a network of operating values and norms.

A challenge facing contemporary Christian ethicists in economic matters is to rediscover the deeply religious roots of modern economic life and to discern anew how to apply articulate, theologically informed ethical thought to today's increasingly complex economic life at home and in the global marketplace.

1.1. Biblical and Greek Roots

The ethical aspects of the → economy from a Christian perspective find their roots firmly planted in the Bible and in the subsequent trajectory of theological thought and application over the centuries. The Hebrew Scriptures introduce the notions of honest representation of goods, restitution for injury, and nonexploitation of the poor or the needy, especially for economic gain. The → Torah and the prophetic writings demand fair trade and labor policies that, while distinguishing between Jew and Gentile ("citizen member" and "resident alien"), call for treating the → foreigner and the migrant worker with decency and basic → human rights.

In the NT the emphasis on economic matters continues, often in the form of artfully crafted case studies, or → parables, told by Jesus. Indeed, Jesus talked about → money, possessions, and wealth with a frequency second only to that of his discourse on the → kingdom of God. Over half of Jesus' parables contain direct reference to economic life or are situated in a marketplace context. Overall, the biblical teachings on → poverty, wealth, property, trade, production, distribution, and labor practices are numerous, wide-ranging, and resistant to simple ideological distinctions or codification. Common threads, however, link Mosaic teachings, prophetic voices, → Wisdom literature, Jesus' teaching, and apostolic writings. All of these writings treat the question of economic justice, namely, how to determine what is right, good, and fitting in regard to the economic life of the community and the rights of persons (→ Righteousness, Justice).

Parallel to these distinct biblical developments, ancient empires from at least Alexander the Great through Rome established wider ranges of relative peace that allowed international trade to flourish. This experience evidently influenced Greek philosophers, among them the → Stoics and the Neoplatonists, who sought to understand how relative degrees of justice could be practiced beyond the boundaries of ethnicity or religious solidarity. Substantial degrees of trust and fairness were necessary in view of the established wider networks of trade and the broad range of marketplace dealings. Themes of lex naturalis (natural law) and lex gentium (the law of nations) were wedded to biblical themes very early in the tradition, thus forming what is referred to as Christian ethics.

→ Ethics (from Gk. ethos) seeks not only to describe what is done in an established moral habitat or in common practice but to state what ought to be done and why. The issue of "why" may lead to one or more of three widely accepted modes of doing ethics. The first focuses on the definitions of what is right and wrong. How one makes these definitions and argues for them is studied by deontological theories of ethics — biblical sources frequently refer to "the laws of God." The second focuses on the striving for what is good and the avoidance of what is evil. How one determines that difference and makes the case for it is studied by teleological ethics — biblical texts often speak of the promises or purposes of God, and of hope for the kingdom of God. The third focuses on what is fitting or unfitting to a particular activity, practice, situation, or context; how one discerns such fitness is studied by contextual or ethological ethics — biblical authors sometimes appeal to the mercies or providence of God.

Humans experience these three modes of doing ethics in tension, for what is right does not seem to lead to what is good in all cases, and what is held to be right and good does not seem to fit the actual experiences of mercy that people report. Every ethical judgment and policy, however, likely includes some relative synthesis or integration of them. Christian ethics, in its various modes, claims that a theological account offers what is, in principle, a compelling and necessary way of accounting for what is right, good, and fitting, and not wrong, evil, or unfitting. It also seeks to account for the deepest reasons why they cannot so easily be integrated and why we can still make relative human judgments and develop corrigible policies. It knows that the limitations of sin often require contrition, repentance, justification, and reform. For this reason, the work of ethics is never done — perhaps especially with regard to economics, where the right and the → good ever seem to contradict the play of those interests that are fitting to economic behavior. Furthermore, the social change carried by economic forces seems to alter our views of the rules and goals of life.

1.2. *Oikos and Polis*

The economy (from Gk. *oikonomia,* in turn from *oikos,* "house," and *nemō,* "manage") concerns the management of a household. Economics, the study of how to do that task well, was historically seen as a branch of ethics, one that asks how we ought to organize, manage, and control the economic life and behave in economic production, distribution, and → consumption. Generally, there have been three major organized centers of economic activity: the household, the state, and the corporation. The nature and character of these characteristic organizations and control of the economic life are not always mutually exclusive; they often coexist in combinations and variations.

The earliest economic life, as envisaged in Plato's *Republic,* was located in and controlled by the → family or household *(oikos).* In most cultures the oikos was understood to include both nuclear family and wider kinship relations, such as clan, tribe, or caste. This extended family was the primary center of production, distribution, and consumption — even more, of economic loyalty. What served the welfare of that unit was considered right and good. Strict customs and practices were developed to control this process.

Over time, and in some cultures, however, the center of economic activity shifted from the familial unit to the → state *(polis),* whether the governmental regime was royal, imperial, republican, or democratic. This movement is not always clear-cut, for household and regime have often been combined, as one sees in all dynasties and patriarchies East and West, ancient and modern. Aristotle especially influenced the philosophical and theological morality of the West by championing the role of the state as the primary center of controlling economic life for the good of the people (see his *Eth. Nic.* and *Pol.*). When the nation-state became the main unit controlling economic life, one sees the origins of modern forms of statist economies.

1.3. *The Corporation*

In the late Middle Ages, the religious and legal concept of a corporation, a *persona ficta,* was developed on the basis of arguments concerning the corporate nature of the → church with its many members, which was held to be independent of both family and regime. Each corpus was given attendant rights and responsibilities. Participation in these independent corporate forms, especially the monastic → orders, forever altered the economic roles of the oikos and the polis. Membership and standing in this new community was less dependent on inherited status or fixed class (noble or base). This new unit did not have familial ties or political duties as its central value, but it did accent an ascetic work ethic that generated efficient production, a limited consumption, justice in dealings, and service to God and humanity. Drawing also on laws governing the reality of "collective individuals" such as free cities, universities, and guilds, the corporation model was gradually secularized and became the chief unit of production and distribution. Its success was measured by profits and/or share of the market. "Family firms" adopted it, as did state-chartered monopolies, such as the Spanish, Portuguese, English, and Dutch "trading companies," which were so influential in colonializing much of the world. The corporation, however, also gradually reordered the values of the family and modulated governmental policies through direct and indirect channels.

Over time, the corporation proved to be more than an institutional entity or an organizational mechanism, although it is also these. Its nature derives from its deep ecclesial roots, largely forgotten today by noted critics of the corporation such as D. Korten and U. Duchrow, but amply documented by O. Gierke, E. Barker, and H. Berman, among others. It may be necessary to recall this history if one is to discern the nature of this current reality, see the actual shape of the ethos in which it is embedded, and discover how to reshape it and guide its future in relation to basic principles of the right, the good, and the fitting.

The deepest roots of the corporation are in the → synagogues and burial or mystery cults (→ Mystery Religions), which determined the organizational models that the early Christians took over, modified, and turned into the church. These institutions established a range of organizational activity outside the family and the state as centers of meaning. People could join the church irrespective of birth or citizenship or (as determined by these two factors) socioeconomic status. The church rejected family and state as sovereign authorities, especially in matters of relationship to the divine. Members lived under a covenant *(testamentum)* and understood themselves to be the *corpus Christi,* just as the life of Jesus transcended both family and state.

For the first time in human history, an enduring model of a third center of organization — what sociologists today call voluntary associations or, less elegantly, nongovernmental organizations (NGOs) — was formed. The model came into being in this way: gradually the church spawned religious orders, hospitals, and schools, all managing to secure a right to exist, own property, buy and sell goods and services, and develop capital, while denying connections with the family (through → celibacy) or with the state (by obedience to religious authority only) and promising to ignore wealth (in taking the vow of poverty). The nature and character of these relations has not been uniform or without dispute within the Christian tradition, but they are historically decisive.

Medieval Scholastics such as Thomas Aquinas and Duns Scotus addressed questions concerning private property, private groups holding property, and contract law within a Christian context. Over time, the idea that property is personal yet best administered in a communal mode by agreements under law came to be accepted by family and state, leading to modern concepts of private property, corporate management, and common law. The church, in other words, became the first "transethnic," "transnational" corporation able to establish, potentially for all, an alternative model for human community.

Still other dimensions of the formation of the ethos of modern corporations are revealed by Max Weber, whose social analysis confirmed the power of religion as an independent variable in the formation of modern social and economic structures. In addition to his much-debated concept of the → Puritan work ethic, Weber also argued that pre-Reformation forms of Christianity decisively influenced the development of modern economic life. The growth of the → city, Weber argued, is rooted in a kind of fellowship that was formed by the secular appropriation of egalitarian principles communicated by the Roman Mass, the religious service at which people ate and drank at the table together as equals. The city is where the new middle class is formed and where "stations in life" are left behind as new occupations are created and the opportunity blooms to form new, self-governing associations.

When these religious roots are forgotten, however, the city and the civilization revert to tribal, feudal, or garrison centers of high-density population, with much mutual exploitation. If the historians and Weber are correct that at least some kinds of religious expression helped create the preconditions for modernization, then it can be argued that ethical attempts to use purely secular theories of the nature and character of the corporation will fail and that a deeper theological ethics is necessary to ensure the corporation's healthy reform and development.

2. Earlier Christian Approaches to Economic Ethics
2.1. *The Early Tradition*

It is difficult, if not impossible, to identify a single orthodox position of Christianity regarding the ethics of the economy. Over the centuries, various schools of thought developed, each of which formed syntheses of biblical insight and philosophical theory, and each of which tended to emphasize certain modes of ethical analysis. Some traditions, drawing on Platonic, Neoplatonic, and Stoic lines of thought, emphasize the laws of God and are → deontological in nature. Plato was pessimistic about economic life and thought that it needed to be controlled by politics, which in turn was to be guided by philosophers, who could discover in the moral logic of thought what was true and just, and thus what was necessary for the common good. Another strand, drawing on the Aristotelian tradition, stressed the natural aims or goals of life and was → teleological in nature. Aristotle and his Christian heirs stressed the discovery of truth by empirical observation and held optimistic views of human nature.

The teachings from these traditions interacted with the social history produced by the formation of the corporation in the context of changing forms of the oikos and the polis. Few aspects of modern philosophy, theology, and ethics are without precedents in these lines of thought. Guidance has been given on many topics over the centuries, including poverty and wealth, interest and usury, wages and working conditions, and private and communally owned property — usually spelled out in terms of basic theories of commutative justice (honesty and basic fairness in dealings), distributive justice (basic equities in opportunity and proper regard for contribution and need), and productive justice (protections of the requisites and due rewards for generating wealth or aiding the well-being of a commonwealth).

Christian appropriations of the philosophical traditions, ancient and modern, are often rooted in theological assessments of the material world. Many held that the physical world was fallen, or inferior to the spiritual realm. The authors of the NT and members of the early church breathed much of the same moral air as the Greek philosophers who probed questions about the ontological nature of materiality and spirituality. These tensions are evident in the Scriptures, particularly in the writings of the four Gospels, Paul, and James. They framed a basic struggle whose legacy is still evident in modern time: the material versus the spiritual. There is, to be sure, strong biblical support for the Hebraic view, which celebrates the earth and all creation as good, and which holds that the purpose of creation is to provide for humanity's needs in responsible ways. Many early Christian thinkers, however, took a different path, and their influence is still felt. They held that poverty, asceticism, and the denial of material comfort were more holy and spiritually superior to any other alternatives.

The biblical texts commending "evangelical simplicity" have often been used to imply the sacralization of poverty. Those who joined the monasteries vowing poverty, chastity, and obedience, as mentioned above, were seen as the true community of faith. Somewhat ironically, the formation of cooperative and disciplined communities of production in monasteries often resulted in the creation of extraordinary wealth. The subsequent reassertion of the ideals of poverty on the basis of the → gospel, in turn, brought vast mendicant systems of institutionalized begging.

2.2. Reformation and Scholasticism

The → Reformers, on the basis of a new reading of the biblical texts and an analysis of their context, reacted against both fat orders and thin mendicants. Martin Luther and John Calvin desacralized poverty, banned beggars, and dissolved monastic orders. Preoccupation with wealth is indeed a spiritual and social peril, but poverty is not a mark of holiness. Poverty is to be overcome by hard → work, organized benevolence for those unable to work, removal of barriers to access to and participation in the economy, and elimination of whatever artificial obstacles to new forms of economic behavior that limit productivity.

The concept of calling (vocatio) was reinterpreted to apply not just to ordained priests and consecrated nuns but to all baptized Christians. Daily work, even as a scullery maid or a laborer, could be a calling and a way to honor God and serve one's neighbor. Today, the covert values of many modern industrial societies are derivative of these Protestant theological premises. Even if today's workers or managers do not use the word "vocation" for their "career," they are morally and socially driven to find meaning in their work, to become "professional," and to train their children to be active, independent, economic agents, finding a productive place in the common life.

The theological trajectory of sacralizing poverty, however, is also still present in theological ethics. Many → liberation theologians, such as Gustavo Gutiérrez or Leonardo Boff, have effectively resacralized poverty, charging that those not in poverty must be responsible for others being in it, or beneficiaries of the fact that others are in it. And some, such as John Cobb, Larry Rasmussen, and Dan Maguire, who focus on → ecological issues, recommend policies that would in other ways demand the resacralization of poverty.

Another signature of the Reformers, especially the Calvinist and Puritan strands, was to stress the cocreative aspects of humanity. Calvinism opened the door to legitimize, if not compel, the work of ordinary people in nonreligious occupations as theologically significant (see Calvin Inst. 3.10). The Reformers viewed diligent labor as honorable and an important part of the work of the kingdom. People were called to reform not only the church, their morals, and the common piety but the fallen world in ways pleasing to God. Nature was no longer deified, and the use of → technology in business became a vehicle also to serve God and neighbor.

This struggle between the productive nature of the economy and the spiritual nature of faith is also evidenced in the Aristotelian traditions as adopted by several streams of thought, including the one deriving from Thomas Aquinas. More widely, Aristotle's classic writings on money and interest also influenced Jewish and Islamic teaching for centuries. Aristotle held a generally negative or suspicious view of money and trade, one that continues to be the ethical emphasis of many strands of church teaching. Aristotle argued that since money was not able to reproduce itself, interest was unnatural and morally wrong. Thomas adopted and amplified this view, coupling it with traditional Pentateuch teachings forbidding the taking of usury among "one's own kind." This prohibition led theological thought to resist efforts to organize complex financing based on the charging of interest. Luther's *Trade and Usury* (1524; *LW* 45) reflects persistent Aristotelian and Thomistic views, while also expressing the popular folk sentiment of his times, which was in favor of protectionism and critical of international trade, luxury items, and pricing for profit.

The major theological breakthrough on the question of interest, as B. Nelson has shown, came with the new exegetical insights of Calvin, who reinterpreted the context and purpose of biblical prohibitions as limits on excessive or exploitative rates. He also redefined the ancient idea of a "communal brotherhood" toward a "universal fellowship," made fresh distinctions between interest and usury, and stressed the concept of just price. Theologically and ethically, he thus generally legitimized the use of interest and credit. The economic ramifications of increasingly available credit and the related concept of just price, while often forgotten today, were enormous and far-reaching.

2.3. *The Enlightenment*

During the → Enlightenment, Christian thinkers began to move away from moral influence founded in ancient authorities and special revelation, in its place stressing human → reason, → experience, and nontheological "scientific objectivity" to guide state and economic life. Many philosophers opposed the idea of a divine order or purpose in the world. They signaled a shift from → faith to reason, from → creation to → nature, from → providence to → progress, and from → ontology to → epistemology. John Locke is a transitional figure, arguing that private property is a positive good, reasonable to the mind, necessary to a civil society that protects natural rights, and intended by God (see his *On Property*). His views are still under debate, with some accusing him of celebrating "possessive individualism," while others see him as a "principled liberal" who saw the implications of the work ethic and covenant for a theory of property rights and just contract.

In his wake, Adam Smith, economist and moral philosopher of seminal proportions, sought to find the operative principles that turned poor nations into wealthy ones and to discern how those principles could be cultivated to achieve desirable results. He is especially remembered for his concept of the invisible hand, a secularized view of providence whereby the prudent division of labor increased productivity and the creation of wealth, if not sabotaged by either physiocratic policies of laissez-faire economics or statist policies of mercantilism. Smith believed that government should allow the free invention of things and social forms beyond what is "natural," but it also had the responsibility to abolish monopolies, encourage international trade, and support education for the common good. To support his case, he introduced a → utilitarian element (a form of teleology) into economic ethics, which had the longer-term effect of reducing other views of ethics and much of theology.

Almost simultaneously, the industrial revolution — drawing on new technologies and the expanded role of the corporation in society, which was due to developing ideas of limited liability and trusteeship (which Smith never adequately treated) — forever changed the basic unit of production from household and state. This shift created new ethical issues for economic life in society and began to uproot rural populations. In the wake of this revolution, thinkers such as John Stuart Mill and Karl Marx developed sharp critiques of → capitalism and the new divisions of labor and capital, workers and owners. Although much social and scientific thought of this period rejected revelation as a source of guidance for economic life, one still sees the effects of the long history of theological and philosophical debate regarding the material versus the spiritual, and the degree to which human society should try to follow, or transform, nature.

3. Twentieth-Century Economic Ethics and Christianity

Much of 20th-century economic ethics is a response to the influence and presuppositions of Smith and Marx, the one presuming that the logic of capitalism would increase human well-being, the other presuming that capitalism was dehumanizing and would, by both the determinations of history and the intentional actions of the workers (who by bitter experience were stripped of illusions about that history), be replaced by more communitarian forms of life. Virtually all 20th-century ethicists have had to respond to basic Marxist ideas about reality: the presumption that the past is a history of oppression that needs to be left behind; the drive to mobilize the oppressed to transform society; the conviction that moral, spiritual, and religious ideas are a product of the social location in which they are developed; and the view that capitalist lifestyles have destroyed community and are built on a foundation of exploitation. In many ways Marx was the culmination of the Enlightenment. No one else stated quite so forcefully the view that society in all its aspects is an artifact constructed out of human interests and intelligence, as shaped by the quest for liberation.

Marx offered a critique of religion as an opiate for the masses, while ironically becoming an icon in what many consider to be a new "secular religion," a center of loyalty and dogma regarding economy, → philosophy, and → politics for at least half the world's people — at least for a time. The history of the 20th century could be written in terms of its various responses to Marxism, culminating with its ultimate rejection of Marxist social analysis with the fall of the Berlin Wall in 1989 and the subsequent reemergence of democratic capitalism, religious impulse, and private corporations as the dominant economic and ethical model.

3.1. *Max Weber*

Perhaps the most important post-Marxist voice early in the 20th century was the sociologist Max Weber. As noted earlier, Weber rejected Marx's material-based analysis of class and society. Weber observed, after exhaustive if not always fully accurate cross-cultural research, that religion was not a product of society but, rather, that it existed independently and exerted distinct influences on the economy and society. Weber concluded that we cannot understand modern sciences, political and legal systems, or modern capitalism without reference to religion. Indeed, the particular Calvinist and Puritan type of religion, which stressed a religiously motivated inner → asceticism, rational behavior, and work as a calling, coupled with the advent of → bureaucracy, prepared the conditions for the development and flourishing of modern rational capitalism.

Weber's findings, while not without challenge, were developed further by his colleague and friend Ernst Troeltsch. Troeltsch developed a socio-historical approach to Christian ethics. His monumental cross-cultural research helped illuminate the power that religious ideas have in shaping society and, conversely, how historical forces also influence religion. He concluded that the institutional form of the church, as it is adopted in theory and in practice, was itself an expression of the social ethic of the Christian community. His three types (church, → sect, and → mysticism) each articulated a lived response to, and a social ethic for, the issues of their times.

3.2. *The Social Gospel and Christian Realism*

Many Protestant responses to Marx in the 20th century rejected Marx's → atheism but embraced his recognition of class struggle and economic inequities in the wake of the industrial revolution. Modern theologians developed the "Social Gospel," "Christian realism," and various "liberation theologies" in order to engage the elements of liberalism or of socialism they thought were valid but ignored by their traditions. The → Social Gospel, while having some roots in the theology of Albrecht Ritschl, became identified with the teachings of Richard Ely, an economist who founded the American Economic Association, and Walter Rauschenbusch, a Protestant pastor during the decades before World War I. Rauschenbusch, also influenced by Troeltsch, combined evangelical enthusiasm with a concern for the social condition of the poor and downtrodden, especially those victimized by the negative dimensions of industrialization on laborers. He recognized that the gospel had a social as well as a salvific purpose and that it was a Christian's duty to strive to make this world reflect the coming kingdom as a social reality.

The Social Gospel movement was a turning point for Protestant → social ethics, and it influenced subsequent Christian responses. However, the optimism of the Social Gospel movement faded in the aftermath of World War I and the ensuing global economic depression. Some theologians responded by endorsing Christian socialism, which again located economic authority and ownership largely in the polis. This popular path was taken by many influential Protestants, including Paul Tillich, Karl Barth, H. Richard Niebuhr, and Jürgen Moltmann, although some of these figures later modified their views, distancing themselves from the dogmas of → socialism.

Another response to the Social Gospel was Christian realism, a reaction by Reinhold Niebuhr to the overly optimistic hopes of the Social Gospel, which, in its popular forms, held that goodness and evil are environmentally determined — that is, that if the environment could be improved, evil would disappear. Niebuhr, writing during and after the devastation of World War I and the despair of the Great Depression, concluded that the reality of → sin and → evil in society was not to be underestimated and was independent of environmental conditions. Niebuhr saw at first hand the problems of industrialization during his years as a pastor in Detroit. Thus, he sought to combine the idealism of the Social Gospel with a tough-minded realism about the dynamics of power and the prevalence of sin, particularly in institutional and group settings. Furthermore, Niebuhr also linked love and justice as necessary to ethics, giving justice a practical priority over love in human affairs, since love without justice is not love, even if love remains as an "impossible possibility," a regulative principle for justice. An unloving, unmerciful justice is not finally just.

Niebuhr's brother, H. Richard, also made lasting contributions to ethical thinking in the 20th century. H. R. Niebuhr built further on the analysis of Troeltsch to develop five possible typologies for Christian action in the world, modeled on Christological perspectives. After reviewing four types — Christ against culture, the Christ of culture, Christ above culture, and Christ and culture in paradox, each of which can be valid in particular circumstances — Niebuhr concluded that the central insight is that Christ can effectively enter into and transform culture.

3.3. *The Roman Catholic Church*

The Roman Catholic tradition developed through a series of → social encyclicals that paralleled what is here traced in the Protestant traditions. The official Roman Catholic response to economic ethics in the 20th century was also a response to industrialization and the Marxist challenge, beginning with Leo XIII's *Rerum novarum* (1891), which bears some similarities to the Social Gospel. It too sought to dignify labor and stop the exploitation of workers. Pius XI extended this accent in *Quadragesimo anno* (1931), as did John XXIII in his remarkable *Pacem in terris* (1963), which also addressed issues confronting the world during the cold war.

At the time of → Vatican II, Paul VI was instrumental in issuing both *Dignitatis humanae* (1965) and *Populorum progressio* (1967). John Paul II then added extensively to that tradition with four encyclicals: *Laborem exercens* (1981), *Sollicitudo rei socialis* (1987), *Centesimus annus* (1991), and *Veritatis splendor* (1993). Influenced by his life in Poland under Communist rule, John Paul II stressed the importance of religious freedom and the rights and responsibilities of → democracy and also celebrated the moral purpose of work, while warning against the uncritical appropriation of → Marxism. Similarly, he warned against the excesses of unbridled capitalism and stressed the moral obligation to find a "third way" to leverage the creativity and productivity of democratic capitalism, wanting to ensure that all have access to the system and benefit from it. Other Catholic initiatives, such as those by the dissident theologian Hans Küng, work with political and interfaith organizations to develop a common "global ethic" that stresses human responsibility in the economic and political spheres and supplements current accents on human rights.

Another essentially Catholic response (embraced quickly also by many liberal Protestants) to the economic issues of the 20th century, one drawing heavily on Marxist social analysis, was so-called liberation theology. It emerged in Latin America during the 1960s and still enjoys a loyal, albeit waning, following. Seeking to overcome the oppression of systemic poverty, mercantilist economies, and uncomfortably close ties between church and state, liberation theology seeks to do theology "from below" and stresses "God's preferential option for the poor" as its organizing principle. The Peruvian Roman Catholic priest Gustavo Gutiérrez was one of the first and most articulate advocates of this theology. Other Latin American Roman Catholic theologians

contributed to the movement, such as the Brazilians Hugo Assman and Leonardo Boff. They have together also influenced the Presbyterian Rubem Alves in Brazil and the Methodist José Míguez Bonino in Argentina.

Liberation theology stresses that theology, and therefore economic ethics, must be done from the perspective of the poor and the oppressed. Its primary goal is liberation from oppression, with less attention paid to developing a vision of a just and ordered economy. It sharply critiques modern business and often uses utilitarian methods to seek its aims of liberation. Liberation theology stresses the independence of the national economy from international influences and the building of → base communities, which seek to be self-sufficient and self-governing. Many liberal Protestants, Catholics, and oppressed people around the world, including strong voices within formerly apartheid South Africa, have become allies of this theology of liberation.

3.4. *The World Council of Churches*

In many ways, these various developments were adopted by Protestant and Eastern Orthodox leaders between the 1960s and the 1980s, especially as can be seen in the official documents of the → World Council of Churches (WCC). Strongly influenced by the Social Gospel as it had shaped aspects of the missionary movement, more recently by Christian socialism, and then notably by liberation theology, this body has developed an economic ethics that has focused on issues of distributive justice, ecological ethics, sustainable development, and, more recently, debt forgiveness for → Third World countries (esp. Ulrich Duchrow, Martin Robra, and Jürgen Moltmann), although WCC leaders earlier were among the most active advocates of loans to the emerging governments of the now-indebted lands. The extended participation in the WCC and its programs of representatives from newly independent nations, many having participated in the struggles against → colonialism and → racism and for development and modernization, has been significant. The newly established states were often more extensively aided in these struggles by socialist lands than by capitalist ones.

The WCC tends to take a suspicious view of capitalism, particularly large-scale global business and free trade, preferring instead more government involvement, taxation, and regulation of trade affairs. In contrast, a voice generally not represented by the WCC and one that has grown in influence and effectiveness in the late 20th century, is the → evangelical arm of the church (largely → Protestant but to some extent also → Roman Catholic).

3.5. *Other Perspectives*

Many evangelical groups, long associated with personal salvation as the primary theological focus, have taken the lead in faith-based initiatives of economic empowerment. These evangelical groups stress the economic themes of discipline, asceticism, stewardship, productive justice, open markets, minimal regulation, reduced trade barriers, and democratic governments, while also rejecting or modulating the neoliberal presuppositions of the Chicago school, which has "natural laws" of evolutionary psychology as its principal frame of reference. International groups such as World Vision, World Harvest, and Habitat for Humanity, along with regional faith-based initiatives and inner-city churches, are stressing themes uncannily reminiscent of Weber, as religious teachings again mix with and influence participation in economic initiatives ($\rightarrow$ Relief and Development Organizations).

The late 20th century brought a new range of voices on, and approaches to, economic ethics. Christian ethicists and sociologists have moved beyond, even if they are still influenced by, the socialist-capitalist debate. With the dramatic collapse of Communism, the turn of Maoist China to a "social market" economy, the fiscal disarray of those nations where liberation movements were strongest, and the revisionist policies of labor-oriented parties in Europe, many Christian socialists and liberationists are revising their approach to economic matters. The theories of Max Weber, obscured for a time by the rebirth of Marxist analysis in the 1960s, are being reconsidered in fresh ways. Today there are various responses to Weber's enduring question about the role that religion plays in forming and guiding the economic life.

One outspoken Catholic voice is that of Michael Novak, who argues for democratic capitalism as the form in which the economic life should be lived, urging that business be seen as a calling. He grounds his ethics in the Catholic social encyclicals. In contrast to Novak, David Korten argues that global corporations now have unbridled power, are beyond governmental control, and are destroying both humanity and the environment. While Korten's data are often incomplete, and although he omits examples of any positive effects of business, he raises valid questions about a number of particular cases.

The British sociologist David Martin recently made a strong case that a revised version of Weber's Puritan work ethic is being played out in Latin America, where in many places communities are religiously inspired by $\rightarrow$ Pentecostal movements to engage in economic life with renewed vigor and discipline. Meanwhile, Peter Berger offers a bold social analysis and an optimistic vision of capitalism to counter Marxist criticism. He has encouraged a new generation of scholars to inquire into the questions of whether $\rightarrow$ Confucianism (e.g., in Singapore and Korea) or specific forms of $\rightarrow$ Buddhism (e.g., in Japan) play comparable roles to that of traditional Protestantism. Robert Wuthnow, however, argues that religion in the West today plays less of a guiding role and more of a therapeutic role, as people increasingly compartmentalize faith and work; Miroslav Volf wants to move beyond work as a "calling" to align work and gifts more deliberately in harmony with economic needs. David Tracy (drawing on Catholic and postmodern thought), Robert Benne (using a Lutheran understanding of $\rightarrow$ law and gospel), and Max L. Stackhouse (grounded in a covenantal theology of justice), however, represent initiatives that affirm the validity of, and need for, a public theology that engages the economic life in order to sustain what is good and reform what is incompatible with Christian ethics.

In the governmental sphere, one sees increasing attempts to normalize legal systems and monetary policies in the economic sphere. While not without critics, some old and several new internationally recognized treaties and organizations are changing the face of global business, including the North American Free Trade Agreement, the World Trade Organization, the International Labor Organization, the World Bank and International Monetary Fund, the "Group of Seven" (G7), the European Union, and several international law courts plus U.N. bodies that oversee development, health, ecological, and educational programs with great economic implications.

Moreover, an increasing number of quasi-governmental bodies and voluntary associations are influencing the economic ethics of our times. Groups such as Transparency International (fighting corruption), the Caux Roundtable (mobilizing business to reduce social and economic threats to world peace), and a host of ethics centers are active in setting standards and policies for ethics in the economic sphere. In addition, one observes the impact of mission and parachurch organizations, including World Vision, Opportunity International, Women's World Bank, and other faith-based micro–lending institutions.

Internal to contemporary financial institutions and policies, a variety of actions and movements have developed. Once ignored, the socially responsible investing movement (SRI) is now a serious voice on Wall Street and in the investment community. Furthermore, most industry associations have developed self-regulatory bodies that try to ferret out abuse and establish standards of practice. Business schools and boardrooms are now aware of the moral imperative and claim long-term financial benefits for sound environmental policies. They also listen to stakeholder views in addition to those of shareholders. Abuse and ethical breaches still occur in the economic sphere, just as they do in church, politics, family life, and other spheres of life, yet the 20th century ended with increasing corporate debate as to whether the bottom line is not to be measured in more than just monetary terms.

4. Economic Ethics Entering the Twenty-first Century

4.1. *Globalization*

The most remarkable economic development as we enter a new century is globalization. While this development involves legal, political, technological, and social changes of many kinds, it often first affects people economically. Many peoples in eastern Europe, Asia, and increasingly in Latin America are seeking to create vibrant new economies, often with little direct support from overtly religious institutions, doctrines, or leaders. Outside of North America the question of economic ethics, as well as the impact of historical and present religious traditions, is in great transition. In Africa and parts of other continents where decolonialization has occurred, many leaders have opted for nationalization of the economy and the assertion of local and sometimes tribal or ethnic values. Often this approach has resulted in marked initial gains but at the cost of longer-term development and innovation. Increasingly, Third World countries must decide how — or whether — to compete on a global basis. A combination of irresponsible lending, misguided macroeconomic projects, and internal corruption has left dozens of Third World countries saddled with crippling debt. Church-based movements such as Jubilee 2000 urge massive debt forgiveness, which, while appealing in many ways, has not been combined with much evidence that the original problems causing the overindebtedness will be solved.

Another strategy adopted by some countries is to try to opt out of the global economy and its externally imposed ways and to build self-contained economies. Present evidence, however, from four countries that have tried this approach — Afghanistan, Cuba, Myanmar, and North Korea — suggests that such a strategy is unlikely to be successful. Meanwhile, western Europe, much of eastern Europe, North America, parts of Latin America, and the "Confucian Rim" have a different response to globalization. These economies actively engage in policies that support globalization and are increasingly adopting one or another form of democratic capitalism. Several factors have combined to develop new forms and increased levels of global trade and economic and political interdependence among trading partners, including mobility of capital, labor, and production; reduction of foreign exchange barriers; increased wealth, savings, and access to credit; technology transfers; and large-scale transoceanic oil and container shipping. Moreover, the Internet, e-commerce, and the low cost of advanced technology are redefining how business is conducted as barriers to entry drop in virtually every sector of industry.

Such trends do not mean, however, that capitalism, in its range of forms, is beyond critique or without need of theologically informed ethical challenge and guidance. Despite the breathtaking advances of modern science, technology, telecommunications, medicine, transportation, manufacturing, finance, and global trade, ethicists cannot ignore the associated costs or abuses. Corruption continues to drain many economies, crony capitalism and mercantilism still masquerade as democratic capitalism, environmental damage occurs, and highly exploitative uses of child, female, prison, and even slave labor are practiced. Furthermore, regional unemployment often becomes chronic, as skill mismatches occur between new hi-tech knowledge workers and traditional unskilled or semiskilled labor. Communities are disrupted as manufacturers relocate to low-cost centers. Most evidence suggests, however, that the use of low-skilled labor in developing economies is usually transitory, for greater efficiency can be gained by technological transfer. Indeed, few countries in the world today do not want increased investment and more labor-intensive factories, even if the conditions under which some workers operate scandalize those who know wider humane standards. Nevertheless, economies based in a traditional oikos are threatened, and in many cases the polis is simply not able to control transnational corporate power. Countries are essentially compelled to join the new economic order, which they must do from the bottom, or be left further behind.

4.2. *Questions and Issues*

As the 21st century unfolds, it remains to be seen whether the global economy will devour itself and destroy the very conditions that have allowed it to flourish, or whether ethically informed economic leaders will endorse principles of the right, the good, and the fitting and bring them into some feasible integration that serves wider ranges of humanity.

Indeed, additional ethical issues lurk in the background. What is the long-term carrying capacity of the earth, or will new technologies emerge to produce more without damaging or depleting the → environment? What is the impact of the population explosion in some countries and the steady-state or declining birth rates in others? Who or what is to become the custodian of capital if the nation-state is no longer the primary agent? Does our situation imply a new economic feudalism of the kings of finance, with increasing gaps of wealth between the top and the bottom of the economic scales? Or will Simon Kuznets be proved right, that over time the middle classes will grow into a significant majority? Will something like a world federation be required, a world government, implying that economic issues will require a political solution after all? And, most important, will Christian theology, some forms of which are arguably as responsible for the "hypermodernization" of the global situation as any other set of values, or "religion in general" provide the moral vision for just and global economic institutions?

Economic leaders and ethicists might find some answers by reflecting on the moral underpinnings of the modern corporate enterprise and, within that context, on how religion might freshly and positively influence the organization of the economic life. Several issues ought to be considered:

First, social justice must be operative and provide the space for relationships to function between buyer and seller, owner and worker, producer and consumer, and shareholder and stakeholder. Furthermore, insights into the ancient biblical concept of covenantal justice may well offer a compelling model of a just polity with an inner moral and spiritual architecture suited to our → pluralistic, global era.

Second, corporate ethics must take into consideration a balance between the classic forms of commutative justice and distributive justice, and a more recently emphasized concept of productive justice, as David Krueger and others have argued.

Third, the religious roots of attitudes toward work should be explored, irrespective of religion or sect, as they influence humanity's approaches to work. It matters to the economy and ethics whether work is seen as a calling with this-worldly spiritual possibilities, as a curse, as merely a temporal necessity to keep body and soul together, or as a mark of the class struggle.

Fourth, we all still wrestle with the ancient question of the material versus the spiritual, and what humanity's attitude toward nature is. It matters whether nature is to be preserved and not altered, or whether humanity might seek to alter and control the environment for the betterment of society.

Fifth, theological and ethical reflection on these economic issues must be undertaken in a context of religious and ethnographic plurality and diversity. As Hans Küng suggests, however, there is common ground and a *Weltethik,* even among a multiplicity of religions, an argument that is also recognized among those who argue for a "public theology" to engage social and economic discussions about polity and policy.

Finally, theological ethics must offer new paradigms of ethical guidance and spiritual nurture to support business professionals as they seek to integrate the teachings of their faith with the demands of the marketplace. Many Christians compartmentalize their work and faith and seldom turn to the church for ethical guidance or spiritual nurture in work-related matters.

As we enter the 21st century, the question of how to organize the economic life of society is as important if not more important than it was to the ancient sages. Humanity's technological capacity to create and destroy has reached historic proportions, bringing benefits and costs that are unprecedented. We have argued here that the oikos, the polis, and the corporation are all vital organizational centers that will deeply shape any market. Today, the most critical issues have to do with the moral core of the corporation, the ethos that produced it, and the new shape that capitalism is taking. All these factors derive substantially from profoundly theological and historical roots.

The guidance of modern economic systems, the character of the individuals who participate in and lead businesses, and the moral fabric of the 21st century will depend in substantial measure on whether society can grasp and refresh the theological foundations upon which its institutions, each with its own ethos and practices, rest — especially since they have now become nearly universally secular in form, with no consciousness of their moral and spiritual roots. Without this consciousness the roots dry up. The challenge for contemporary economic ethics is to recover and recast the moral and spiritual foundations for ethical business practice and to articulate effectively a just and holy pattern of guidance in a pluralistic world.

Bibliography: General: D. LANDIS, *The Wealth and Poverty of Nations* (New York, 1998) • M. L. STACKHOUSE, D. P. McCANN, and S. J. ROELS, eds., *On Moral Business: Classical and Contemporary Resources for Ethics in Economic Life* (Grand Rapids, 1995) • M. L. STACKHOUSE, P. PARIS, D. BROWNING, and D. OBENCHAIN, eds., *God and Globalization* (4 vols.; Harrisburg, Pa., 2000-2001) • E. TROELTSCH, *The Social Teaching of the Christian Churches* (Louisville, Ky., 1992; orig. pub., 1912) • M. WEBER, *Economy and Society: An Outline of Interpretive Sociology* (2 vols.; Berkeley, Calif., 1978; orig. pub., 1922).

On 1: H. BERMAN, *Law and Revolution* (Cambridge, Mass., 1983) • O. VON GIERKE, *Das deutsche Genossenschaftsrecht* (Berlin, 1861; partial ET *Natural Law and the Theory of Society, 1500-1800* [Boston, 1957]) • D. KORTEN, *When Corporations Rule the World* (San Francisco, 1996) • B. NELSON, *The Idea of Usury: From Tribal Brotherhood to Universal Otherhood* (Princeton, 1957) • M. L. STACKHOUSE, "The Moral Roots of the Corporation," *ThPP* 5 (1993) 29-39.

On 2: J. COBB, *Sustainability: Economics, Ecology, and Justice* (Maryknoll, N.Y., 1992) • U. DUCHROW, *Alternatives to Global Capitalism: Drawn from Biblical History, Designed for Political Action* (Utrecht, 1996) • D. MAGUIRE, L. RASMUSSEN, and R. R. REUTHER, *Ethics for a Small Planet* (Albany, N.Y., 1998) • K. MARX, *The Communist Manifesto* (New York, 1992; orig. pub., 1848).

On 3: R. BENNE, *The Ethic of Democratic Capitalism: A Moral Reassessment* (Philadelphia, 1981) • P. BERGER, *The Capitalist Revolution* (New York, 1986) • G. GUTIÉRREZ, *A Theology of Liberation: History, Politics, and Salvation* (Maryknoll, N.Y., 1973) • R. HÜTTER and T. DIETER, eds., *Ecumenical Ventures in Ethics: Protestants Engage Pope John Paul II's Moral Encyclicals* (Grand Rapids, 1998) • D. MARTIN, *Tongues of Fire: The Explosion of Protestantism in Latin America* (Oxford, 1990) • J. MÍGUEZ BONINO, *Doing Theology in a Revolutionary Situation* (Philadelphia, 1975); idem, *Toward a Christian Political Ethics* (Philadelphia, 1983) • J. MOLTMANN, *God in Creation: A New Theology of Creation and the Spirit of God* (New York, 1985) • H. R. NIEBUHR, *Christ and Culture* (New York, 1951) • R. NIEBUHR, *An Interpretation of Christian Ethics* (2d ed.; San Francisco, 1963; orig. pub., 1935); idem, *Moral Man and Immoral Society: A Study in Ethics and Politics* (New York, 1960; orig. pub., 1932) • M. NOVAK, *The Capitalist Ethic and the Spirit of Catholicism* (New York, 1993) • R. PRESTON, *Confusions in Christian Social Ethics: Problems for Geneva and Rome* (Grand Rapids, 1995) • W. RAUSCHENBUSCH, *A Theology for the Social Gospel* (Louisville, Ky., 1997; orig. pub., 1916) • A. RITSCHL, *The Christian Doctrine of Justification and Reconciliation* (Clifton, N.J., 1966; orig. pub., 1870-74) • M. ROBRA, *Ökumenische Sozialethik* (Gütersloh, 1994) • D. TRACY, *The Analogical Imagination: Christian Theology and the Culture of Pluralism* (New York, 1981) • E. TROELTSCH, *Protestantism and Progress: The Significance of Protestantism for the Rise of the Modern World* (Philadelphia, 1986; orig. pub., 1906) • M. VOLF, *Work in the Spirit: Toward a Theology of Work* (New York, 1991) • M. WEBER, *The Protestant Ethic and the Spirit of Capitalism* (Los Angeles, 1998; orig. pub., 1904-5) • G. WEIGEL and R. ROYAL, eds., *A Century of Catholic Social Thought: Essays on "Rerum Novarum" and Nine Other Key Documents* (Washington, D.C., 1991) • R. WUTHNOW, *God and Mammon in America* (New York, 1994).

On 4: R. BENNE, *The Paradoxical Vision: A Public Theology for the Twenty-first Century* (Minneapolis, 1995) • D. A. KRUEGER et al., *The Business Corporation and Productive Justice* (Nashville, 1997) • H. KÜNG, *A Global Ethic for Global Politics and Economics* (New York, 1998) • M. L. STACKHOUSE, *Covenant and Commitments: Faith, Family, and Economic Life* (Louisville, Ky., 1997); idem, *Public Theology and Political Economy* (Washington, D.C., 1991).

MAX L. STACKHOUSE and DAVID W. MILLER

Economy

1. Definition
2. Historical Forms
3. Present-Day Forms
4. North and South Problems
5. The State and Economy

1. Definition

"Economy" may be defined in two different — even opposite — ways. A *phenomenological and historical view* understands it as a branch of human and social life, as a specific human means of satisfying basic needs, namely, of providing for a life and increasing security, of individual enrichment, of development for both individuals and society as a whole (A. Rich, 22). Historically, especially in the 19th century, different economic stages were perceived that, from the standpoint of → Marxism, were linked to different social formations. Usually today we view these differences much more simply, contrasting, for example, a preindustrial economy with an industrial economy, often in conjunction with an emerging postindustrial → service society. The distinctions commonly made refer to present-day forms of economy (see 3) and involve comparison of various practical and/or theoretical subdivisions of the prototypical "market" and "planned" economies.

A wholly different point of view arises out of the common use of the verb "economize," which generally no longer denotes human activity in the economic sphere but, rather, a sparing but intentional handling of limited resources in order to achieve predetermined goals (e.g., the satisfying of needs), whether such activity occurs in the traditional field of economics or in another area of life. Economic imperialism has put this view to the forefront by making analysis of economizing the central, if not the only, theme of sociological study and in principle subjecting all the spheres of life to economics. Historically connected with this view (though, initially, to be distinguished from it conceptually) is the fact that in the course of historical development, forms of economic thought and values (esp. cost-benefit analysis) and → money have permeated the most diverse spheres of human life and continue to do so, in what J. Habermas has criticized as a colonializing of the world. Advocates of economic imperialism as a rule do not think it makes sense to accept a limited view of the economy, for in principle all areas of life are open to, and require, economic analysis.

In general we might regard the economy as the part of human activity that seeks to meet human needs by offering goods and services. Three closely related questions arise simultaneously: What kinds of goods are to be produced? How are they to be produced? For whom are they to be produced? Response to these questions depends essentially upon who owns the property, who has the capabilities of production, and how the decisions of individuals and enterprises are coordinated. For practical as well as normative reasons, not all goods and services can or should be provided by coordinated individual decisions as the market demands, and so the question arises of the role and scope of → state involvement (see 5).

Economics uses methodological presuppositions in analyzing the economy. In this regard it is at a distance from, and even in conflict with, other social sciences and the humanities, making a strict differentiation between questions of the appropriate use of means (i.e., of allocation and efficiency) and questions of the distribution of resources, capacity, income, and so forth (i.e., having to do with distribution). This distinction has enabled economics to make considerable progress in the last two centuries, though exposing it also to the charge of justifying or disguising existing economic injustices (esp. the North-South conflict; see 4).

2. Historical Forms

2.1. Since the forms of economy throughout history are so many, any attempt to classify them, even if limited to Europe and North America (as is customary), will immediately come under considerable suspicion. Such attempts cannot do justice to the concreteness or uniqueness of individual economies. Well-known efforts to categorize economies include the theories of economic stages propounded in the last half of the 19th century by the earlier and later branches of the so-called historical school of economics. B. Hildebrand, for example, in 1864 distinguished between an initial, essentially moneyless barter economy, which was followed by a money economy using coins, which then increasingly changed into a general credit economy. K. Bücher (1893) differentiated the closed, household economy of antiquity and the early Middle Ages from the city economy (lasting up to the 18th cent.), which then became a national economy. (Later, a global economy was sometimes added as a fourth stage.) Similarly, G. Schmoller (1894) distinguished village, city, territorial, and national economies.

These stages, which were far too automatic, were abandoned in the early 20th century in favor of theories that stressed comprehensive economic styles (A. Spiethoff, W. Sombart). Later classifications put more emphasis on the process of industrialization. W. G. Hoffmann, for example, in 1931 pointed to the earlier dominance of the consumer goods industries, followed by a relative growth of capital goods industries. These two are now reaching an equilibrium, with capital accumulation now of central significance. W. W. Rostow (1960) divided the industrialization process into five stages of growth: (1) a traditional society with limited productivity, (2) an initial period of growth through the formation of the nation, (3) a "take-off" phase of continuous development, (4) a period of steady growth with a high rate of investment, and (5) the stage of mass → consumption. Attempts to adjust → Third World countries to this European and North American schema have thus far been largely unsuccessful for various reasons (see 4).

2.2. Official Soviet Marxism turned some hints of K. Marx (1818-83) about the historical relations between the forces and the relations of production into a doctrine of historical necessity. It differentiated five basic means of production that in principle, though not in detail, ought to coincide with historical periods.

First there is *primitive society*, with small social groupings and a subsistence economy. At this stage simple means of production are possessed and used jointly, mostly for tilling the soil.

Then comes → *slavery* (Marx's "slave-owning society"), in which the means of production and some of the people are the property of others. This stage emerges when the forces of production generate a surplus over the subsistence level, thus making the use of slaves profitable. The societies of ancient Greece and Rome (→ Roman Empire) in particular serve as historical examples of this stage.

Following the upheavals of migrations, → *feudalism* then develops, which involves a layered society (M. Bloch, 1961). Prototypically, however, there is a twofold division between feudal lords and feudal dependents (serfs, smallholders, etc.). Private ownership on the part of feudal lords now becomes dominant, and production of the society increases as the dependents do direct work beyond their subsistence (e.g., the corvée) or as they pay tribute — in kind or, later, in currency — to the feudal lords.

In the later Middle Ages commercial enterprises gradually led on to → *capitalism,* which is characterized, technologically, by the introduction of machinery and heavy industry and, socioeconomically, by the use of wage labor. The paid laborers, though freed from feudal obligations, do not own any property and thus, according to Marx, are forced to submit to the command of capital (though they are legally equal contractually with their employer). In the production process such laborers produce a surplus value for the capitalists, who then realize it in the marketplace (Marx's "sphere of circulation").

The inner contradictions of capitalism, especially its tendency to concentrate and centralize the means of production in the hands of fewer and fewer capitalists, necessarily produce its dissolution by *socialism.* This system is characterized by social ownership of the means of production, deliberate planning of the process of production, and an orientation of production to the needs of all members of the society instead of only to the exploitative interests of the capitalists (see 3). Marx and F. Engels (1820-95), to be sure, did not provide us with any systematic theory of socialism. Textbook depictions of "historical materialism" can thus be based only on an unsystematic collection of cursory comments by these authors, taken from the most varied contexts.

The socialist mode of production is of dubious inevitability. In fact, the various stages sketched out in Marxist history are also vulnerable to the criticism that they are based on a strongly Eurocentric pattern of development that can hardly be applied to Third World countries (see 4).

3. Present-Day Forms

3.1. After the collapse of the socialist economies, the traditional theoretical and practical classification of actual economies according to their coordination by the market or by planning — a distinction oriented to W. Eucken's polar distinction between a *centrally planned economy* and a (free) *market economy* — proved to be of little value. Almost all planned economies have now entered upon the difficult process of transition to market economies in what some have called transformation societies. Even the special Yugoslav model of market-oriented workers' management has been broken off as the country has disintegrated. The actual planned economies of socialism were fundamentally weakened by the fact that there was no definitive theory of socialist planning. They depended instead on the superficial observations of Marxist theoreticians, who set over against the obvious shortcomings of early capitalism only the intellectual counterutopia of an "association of direct producers," without bothering to address the concrete problems of incentives, information, and coordination that must be solved if an economy is to be based on division of labor. The attempt to implement ethically based concepts (concerning joint production, just distribution, self-determination in the workplace, etc.) in the course of developing a planned socialist economy (of whatever type) is open to criticism because it fails to connect the goal with the reality ("normativist fallacy").

Real market economies, for their part, are characterized by the coexistence of various individual plans that do not all fall under the jurisdiction of the market, for many decisions in enterprises and organizations are made hierarchically. The relations between the state and the economy (see 5) also leave room for direct coordination in decision making, and financing apart from the market also plays a central role. It is best, then, to speak of *mixed economies,* in which, on the macro level, the market mechanism dominates but which also include management based on hierarchical and democratic principles.

3.2. The central constituent of modern societies — market coordination on the basis of free contracts — derives from Adam Smith (1723-90), who in his system of natural freedom referred to the working of an invisible hand on the basis of self-love but who also took into account sympathy with others in realizing what is best for the social good. Overly simplified, from this classic liberalism two essential tendencies developed. First was the *neoliberalism* of F. A. von Hayek (1899-1992) and others that dominated especially the English-speaking world. This approach intends to lead the welfare state back to classical state functions and relies more on the self-evolution of → norms, institutions, and structures than on deliberate action by the state.

The second tendency was so-called *ordoliberalism*, as defined essentially by W. Eucken (1952). This view, drawing from historical experiences (concentration of resources, monopolies, inflation, world economic crises, and many others), helps establish those strong forces that "clamor for unrestricted competition also within an industrial economy" (p. 373). This is accomplished by means of deliberate shaping by the state and maintenance of a stable order of competition and money. Unlike both classic liberalism and neoliberalism, ordoliberalism takes the view that it is not enough to realize certain principles of law but then let the economy develop on its own. The concept of a politically ordered economy presupposes a state that is strong at least in this respect, and that may very well come into conflict with the economy in its own turn (see 5).

3.3. To achieve order in a market economy, certain constitutive principles are needed that serve to establish a functioning price system under full competition. There is also need of some regulative principles to correct situations where a market economy is defective due, for example, to externalities or to irregularities in the labor market. Finally, distributive concepts are needed such as progressive taxation.

These views of Eucken were later developed both theoretically and practically in the emerging German federal republic, for example, by A. Müller-Armack (1966), into the notion of a social market economy — a policy of social balance that would recognize achievement, efficiency, and accomplishment but that would also find a place for → solidarity and → subsidiarity. Holding the balance between a market economy and social policy is a necessary but difficult matter, for the two impinge upon one another, so that emphasis on the one at the expense of the other (whether through dismantling of the welfare state or through overburdening the economy and the state with social obligations) threatens both the theory and the practice. This model, although appealing to developed countries, is as yet only provisional and, even there, can easily break down.

3.4. A central concept in neoliberalism is self-evolution. Also it views the market process as one of seeking, learning, and discovery. Both elements can be important enhancements of an otherwise static picture of social order such as is presented by ordoliberalism. J. M. Buchanan (b. 1919) combines

the two strains in his "constitutional economics." The process of transformation presently underway in the countries of central and eastern Europe shows how important Eucken's concept of the interdependence of orders is — it means the mutual dependence of all economic decisions, values, and actions on the one hand and, on the other, an economic order in which all constituent parts interact with such other orders as those of the state, the society, and the culture. At the same time, those "framing" orders must be shaped in such a way as to leave sufficient room for innovative and evolutionary processes.

3.5. The many efforts to apply both theoretically and practically either ordoliberal or neoliberal ideas to → development (§1.2) in Third World countries have so far all been highly unsuccessful. We see from this fact how important it is to shape appropriately the various orders of life into what will be a meaningful economic order. We can see here the Eurocentricity of most of the ideas for economic development, which take as little account of the historical, cultural, and intellectual assumptions of Third World countries as they do of the enormous discrepancies between the First World and the Third World (see 4).

4. North and South Problems
Probably the most serious weak points in our economic theories and applications appear in the North-South problems — the relation between the First and Third Worlds. Theoretically, the problem is that of the Eurocentricity of our economic concepts. In practice, it is that of the enormous differences between the two areas as regards standard of living, technology, and power. An important assumption of liberal theory and policy — namely, that the participants in an exchange have a roughly equivalent rank and value — is thereby seriously violated. What should be a mutual interdependence that promotes the prosperity of all participants becomes so often instead a one-sided dependence that tends to lock in place existing deficits and inequalities within Third World countries.

The optimistic view of the 1960s — that integration of world trade and possible initial support are all that is needed to guarantee that the so-called developing nations will take off on a pattern of self-sustaining growth after the European and North American model — has now given way, both theoretically and empirically, to a thoroughgoing skepticism and even to outright rejection. In the last few decades only a very few countries, mostly in East Asia, have been able to follow the development path taken by the industrial nations, while between the rest of the Third World and the First World the gap has only increased. There are many structural causes for this discrepancy. International relations play a part, as do domestic social conditions. Enlightened goodwill on the part of all concerned cannot set these factors aside or even mitigate them. On the contrary, the majority of the developing countries have now been plunged into the crisis of international indebtedness, which has only helped to make them more dependent than ever. The credit institutions of the industrial countries have increasingly had to wrestle with the negative consequences of overindebtedness by adjustment and retrenchment.

The → dependence, in the narrower economic sense, of many developing countries on a few exports, combined with their lack of manufacturing and their reliance on foreign investors, has hardly shown any improvement. The 1994 version of *Friedensgutachten* (Peace report) calls for new guidelines for changing the world economic order, including (1) an achievement of human → rights in economic life, (2) a deliberate lessening of inequality by rejecting economic policies that are one-sidedly supply oriented, (3) a policy on alternative energy and resources, (4) a transition to long-term farming and an ecologically oriented production policy, (5) a reduction of the enormous burden of international debt by unilateral forgiveness, and (6) effective control over multinational corporations. Whether these ideas and demands can be put into practice will depend upon the adoption of binding international labor rights, the reforming of international institutions in favor of the Third World, and a shift in thinking to promote domestic production over an intensification of environmentally polluting global trade.

5. The State and Economy

For countries of both the First World and the Third, the relation between the state and the economy is a central problem. As experiences in the transformation process and in the developing countries themselves have shown, a reliable and stable state is needed that will deal with tasks beyond those that classic liberalism has defined (safeguarding of property, ensuring the performance of contracts, etc.), including handling problems of the → environment and → ecology and matters of social policy. At the same time, however, the opposite danger exists that too great activity by the state will paralyze the economic process, weaken incentives, confuse the processing of information, and distort the whole process of competition into a selfish rent-seeking that

does not help the community at large. The difficult issue is reflected in an exemplary fashion in the European and North American deregulation, understood as the abolition of many unproductive state ordinances. It is very hard to say, however, which of these were really unproductive according to any universally valid criteria. First, state ordinances must themselves be measured by their empirical results, and thus there must be a certain process of trial and error. Second, and conversely, the absence of regulations can allow undesirable and uncontrolled growth or produce bad norms (e.g., in social policy, labor market policy, matters of product security, and also the environment and ecology). Because the various orders are interdependent, it is extremely difficult to determine the right balance between standardization and flexibility. Even → labor unions take up different positions, some more cooperative, some more conflict oriented.

It is not clear that the idea of functional equivalents — equal value rather than equality — can be helpful. In general, we see that both ordo- and neoliberal ideas have so far been developed in a national context. Whether they can be transferred to greater units such as the European Union is doubtful, however, for the national orders differ widely in different states, and because of these differences it will be hard to achieve a harmony within the supranational economic order.

We can see this difficulty in the inadequate legitimation and control of these great economic units, in which inadequate intermediary institutions have been developed. Similar problems afflict other economic unions as, for example, the North American Free Trade Zone (NAFTA). It is also hard to show what global measures can be taken to protect the earth's climate or how to ensure against a global recession

→ Economic Ethics

Bibliography: L. BETHELL, *Latin America since 1930: Economy, Society, and Politics* (Cambridge, 1999) • M. BLOCH, *Feudal Society* (2 vols.; Chicago, 1961) • S. P. BURGGRAF, *The Feminine Economy and Economic Man: Reviving the Role of Family in the Post-Industrial Age* (Reading, Mass., 1997) • A. ETZIONI, *The Moral Dimension: Towards a New Economics* (London, 1986) • W. EUCKEN, *Grundsätze der Wirtschaftspolitik* (Tübingen, 1952) • R. FRIEDLAND and A. F. ROBERTSON, *Beyond the Marketplace: Rethinking Economy and Society* (New York, 1990) • W. G. HOFFMANN, *Studien und Typen der Industrialisierung* (Jena, 1931) • P. T. KROEKER, *Christian Ethics and Political Economy in North America: A Critical Analysis* (Montreal, 1995) •

K. Marx, *Capital: A Critique of Political Economy* (1867), *MECW* 35; idem, *A Contribution to the Critique of Political Economy* (1859), *MECW* 29.259-417 • V. Mortensen, ed., *A Just Africa: Ethics and the Economy* (Geneva, 1994) • A. Müller-Armack, *Wirtschaftsordnung und Wirtschaftspolitik. Studien und Konzepte zur Sozialen Marktwirtschaft und zur europäischen Integration* (2d ed., Bern, 1976; orig. pub., 1966) • H. G. Nutzinger, ed., *Liberalismus im Kreuzfeuer. Thesen und Gegenthesen zu den Grundlagen der Wirtschaftspolitik* (Frankfurt, 1986) • H.-R. Peters, *Einführung in die Theorie der Wirtschaftssysteme* (2d ed.; Munich, 1993) • A. Rich, *Wirtschaftsethik* (2 vols.; Gütersloh, 1984-90) • W. W. Rostow, *The Stages of Economic Growth* (London, 1960) • M. Sahlins, *Stone Age Economics* (London, 1974) • A. Smith, *An Inquiry into the Nature and Causes of the Wealth of Nations* (2 vols.; London, 1776; repr., New York, 1976) • S. Viljoen, *Economic Systems in World History* (London, 1974) • A. M. C. Waterman, *Revolution, Economics, and Religion: Christian Political Economy, 1798-1833* (Cambridge, 1991) • World Council of Churches, *Christian Faith and the World Economy Today* (Geneva, 1992).

          Hans G. Nutzinger

Economy (Orthodox Theology)

1. As a term of theology, "economy" denotes the nonapplication of a generally valid law in a specific case when the suspension of the law results in greater spiritual good than could be expected from applying it. Although economy in this sense has existed from the founding of the → church, it is hard to define exactly, since it is not a legal concept but an expression of → love, and therefore a reality that we can experience but not describe. Economy, at least as applied in the Orthodox Church, is not applied generally but only in special cases, thus differing from the → dispensation of Latin law, which is a legal determination applying equally to all similar cases.

2. Economy has its basis in Holy Scripture (Acts 16:3; 17:30, etc.), in the resolutions and the spirit of → councils, and in the → church fathers and writers. The mystical authority for actions of this kind derives from the redeeming → Word of God and the → Holy Spirit, who is at work in the church. It makes possible the intervention of the → bishop as *oikonomos* (administrator) both in his own diocese and in cooperation with others at councils.

Such intervention seems to be demanded when the claims of the → law clash with those of the Christian spirit. The model of this economy is the divine economy itself (→ Order of Salvation), along with human love (see Patriarch Nicholas I ["the Mystic," d. 925], *PG* 111.213A). What is promoted is the smooth functioning of the church body and especially the salvation of souls.

Economy is especially characteristic of the Eastern tradition and the → Orthodox Church, in which it has played a role for centuries. On the path of the Orthodox Church to its high and holy Pan-Orthodox council (→ Pan-Orthodox Conferences), a text was prepared in 1971 that expresses the agreed position of → Orthodoxy (§3) about economy (for Ger. trans., see *US* 28 [1973] 93-102).

3. The theme of economy has great ecumenical relevance. The above-mentioned text aroused the interest of other churches, especially the → Roman Catholic Church, since it touched on the relations of Orthodoxy to the non-Orthodox. The ontological existence of all Christian churches and → denominations was recognized, and the position was taken that the Orthodox Church has considerable freedom in applying economy to other believers in Christ, and that this principle will govern future relations with other churches and denominations.

    → Church 3.1; Church Law

Bibliography: M. Foyas, *Peri tēn ekklēsiastikēn oikonomian. Apantēsis eis Kathēgētas tēs Theologias* (Athens, 1976) • H. Kotsonis, *Problèmes de l'économie ecclésiastique* (Gembloux, 1971) • Maximos, Metropolitan of Sardes, *The Oecumenical Patriarchate in the Orthodox Church: A Study in the History and Canons of the Church* (Thessaloníki, 1976) • "Oikonomia," *Kanon* 6 (1983) 13-83 • J. H. P. Reumann, "The Use of Oikonomia and Related Terms in Greek Sources to about A.D. 100, as a Background for Patristic Applications" (Diss., University of Pennsylvania, 1957) • E. J. Storman, *Towards the Healing of Schism: The Sees of Rome and Constantinople* (New York, 1987) • F. Thomsen, "Economy: An Examination of the Various Theories of Economy Held within the Orthodox Church, with Special Reference to the Economical Recognition of the Validity of Non-Orthodox Sacraments," *JTS* 16 (1965) 368-420.

    Ecumenical Patriarch Bartholomew

Ecstasy

1. Scope of the Term
2. Profane and Sacred
3. In Religions and Religious Philosophies

1. Scope of the Term

The broadest usage of "ecstasy" encompasses several semantic domains. Ethologically, the moment when the earliest hunter and his prey first met was probably one of united concentration on the encounter, of holding of breath and silence, of tense quiet along with the ability to spring very quickly into action.

1.1. On the human side the continuation and development of this basic attitude is a history of self-interpretation, with new social contexts and anthropologies as inalterable presuppositions. This was first the case probably in → shamanism, and it still is so where it survives. In the Gk. term *ekstasis* the idea came in that we are able to get "outside ourselves," and from the fifth century B.C. or even earlier this meant leaving the normal bodily state, while from the first century B.C. it also meant that the most essential part — the → soul or → self or organ of perception — can be taken out of the person or the body.

1.2. Semasiologically, a trance (MEng., by way of MFr. *transe,* from Lat. *transeo,* "pass [over]") means the same, though it is often defined as the psychological opposite of ecstasy. A trance is a sleeplike state in which → spiritist media are the presupposition for the materialization of spirits or the dead (or the consequence of this materialization, according to their own understanding). The trance is thus close to possession, and the hyperkinetic form of this state resembles ecstasy. If that with which one is possessed or, more mildly, inspired is regarded as a god that replaces the extinguished consciousness (not the soul), then we have the meaning of the classical Gk. term *enthousiasmos.*

2. Profane and Sacred

Ecstasy occurs throughout spiritual and cultural history. It may be profane as well as holy (→ Sacred and Profane). Phenomena like rapture and → glossolalia, → visions and auditions, as well as hyperesthesia, anesthesia, and paresthesia often coincide with it. It may befall people without their knowing the reason for it, but it can also be induced by inner means (meditation, autohypnosis, hunger), outer means (drugs, objects on which to focus in order to exclude thought), or means that move from outer to inner (prolonged ritualized repetitions, dancing).

2.1. In technologically less advanced cultures profane ecstasy may accompany → initiations, rites of passages, and preparations for war, or it may be a reaction to certain failures or social reverses. In literate cultures we find ecstasy among the Corybants and Maenads of Greece, the dancers and → flagellants after the Black Death in the 14th century (→

Dance Macabre), the Shakers, the Quakers (→ Society of Friends), some psychopaths, and also social dropouts. In profane ecstasy there may be knowledge of events at a distance or in the future (clairvoyance, → divination).

2.2. Religiously, ecstasy occurs only in connection with a historical → religion that arose in some other way; that is, it itself is not pure religion, or the original core of a religion or of all religion. It may be experienced as the basic impulse toward the development of → mysticism.

3. In Religions and Religious Philosophies

In religions, ecstasy may influence whole social areas, as it may affect whole structures of thought in religious philosophies (→ Philosophy of Religion).

3.1. We may single out especially the customs centered on the soma drinks of the Veda, the erotic, orgiastic practices of the Shakti cults, and the breathing practices of → Hinduism that derived from the blowing of the fire-god Agni (→ fire). We may also mention the presumably cataleptic character of preclassical → prophecy (1 Sam. 10:5-13; 19:18-24; 21:11-15; 1 Kgs. 18:28-29; 2 Kgs. 3:15-16) and of prophecy in Ezekiel in ancient → Israel (§1), the widespread capacity for visions in Jewish and Christian → apocalyptic, and glossolalia and certain forms of → prayer in the → primitive Christian community and in → Paul. We may refer also to the howling and dancing dervishes in Anatolia (the site of the earlier Cybele Attis cult and → Montanism; → Mystery Religions); to the heavenly communions of the 13th-century → cabala; to "meditating," "hearing," "states," and the "reversing of becoming" on the "path" in → Sufism; and to the piety of monastic mysticism among the Victorines, Carmelites, and → Franciscans (→ Orders and Congregations).

Jewish, Christian, and Islamic ecstatics had to consider whether their experiences and utterances were in keeping with their scriptures. The cabalists were masters of this art. The Sufis could lose their freedom or even their lives if they failed. On the basis of extensive scholarly work, Pope Benedict XIV (1740-58) developed solid criteria for distinguishing legitimate ecstasy from illegitimate; → Protestantism, however, did not find it so easy.

3.2. In very different ways ecstasy may be seen behind → metaphysics and → epistemological processes when induction, speculation, and generalization are overtaken by → intuition, vision, and experience of identity or the like. This process occurs in Philo of Alexandria, Plotinus, Porphyry, Dionysius the Pseudo-Areopagite, several medieval → Scholastics, and modern → theosophists.

Bibliography: M. BUBER, *Ecstatic Confessions* (San Francisco, 1985) • H. CANCIK, ed., *Rausch–Ekstase–Mystik* (Düsseldorf, 1978) • E. ENSLEY, *Sounds of Wonder: Speaking in Tongues in the Catholic Tradition* (New York, 1977) • A. M. GREELY, *Ecstasy: A Way of Knowing* (Englewood Cliffs, N.J., 1974) • N. G. HOLM, ed., *Religious Ecstasy* (Uppsala, 1982) • M. LASKI, *Ecstasy: A Study of Some Secular and Religious Experiences* (New York, 1968) • J. G. LAWLER, "Ecstasy: Towards a General Field Theory," *JAAR* 42 (1974) 605-13 • C. MAZZONI, *Saint Hysteria: Neuroses, Mysticism, and Gender in European Culture* (Ithaca, N.Y., 1996) • J. STITZIEL, "God, the Devil, Medicine, and the Word: A Controversy over Ecstatic Women in Protestant Middle Germany, 1691-1693," *CEurH* 29 (1996) 309-38. Also much material and extensive bibliographies appear under "Ekstase" or "Ecstasy" in *ERE, HWP, JL, LTK, RAC, RE* (under "Verzückung"), *RGG, TDNT,* and *TRE.*

CARSTEN COLPE

Ecuador

	1960	*1980*	*2000*
Population (1,000s):	4,439	7,961	12,646
Annual growth rate (%):	2.95	2.67	1.74
Area: 272,045 sq. km. (105,037 sq. mi.)			

A.D. *2000*

Population density: 46/sq. km. (120/sq. mi.)
Births / deaths: 2.32 / 0.58 per 100 population
Fertility rate: 2.76 per woman
Infant mortality rate: 41 per 1,000 live births
Life expectancy: 70.8 years (m: 68.3, f: 73.5)
Religious affiliation (%): Christians 97.5 (Roman Catholics 94.5, indigenous 2.1, Protestants 2.1, marginal 2.0, other Christians 0.3), nonreligious 1.5, other 1.0.

1. General
2. History of the Christian Churches
3. Church-State Relations
4. Other Religious Groups

1. General

The population of the Republic of Ecuador is divided between the coastal plains (40 percent), the sierra, or Andes, region (58 percent), and the eastern lowlands, the primeval Amazon forest, which is increasingly being opened up (2 percent). The ethnic makeup of society reflects the postcolonial situation, with approximately 55 percent mestizo (mixed Amerindian and Spanish), 25 percent Amerindian (mostly Quechua), 10 percent Spanish, and 10 percent black. The Indians of Ecuador are mostly illit-erate and are socially, politically, and economically → marginalized.

The overall socioeconomic situation in Ecuador is one of great inequality in landowning and economic resources. The so-called banana period ended around 1960. The oil period began in the 1970s, a new emphasis that has led to neglect of agriculture, to higher imports, and to galloping inflation. The socioeconomic tensions have led to frequent shifts between oligarchic, popularist, neoconservative, and military regimes. In the late 1990s a slump in oil prices, exacerbated by some ill-conceived fiscal stabilization measures on the part of the government, environmental crises (deforestation, soil erosion, desertification, water pollution, and pollution from oil production wastes), and natural disasters (frequent earthquakes, landslides, periodic droughts, and, in 1998, Hurricane Georges, which caused extensive property damage), led to a situation of national economic crisis.

Besides the → Roman Catholic Church, there are now some 80 other churches and denominations in Ecuador. Because of their ineffective missionary efforts, the churches of historic → Protestantism are weakly rooted. The many free denominations stand aloof from the → ecumenical movement, so that the establishment of an office of the Catholic Bishops' Conference for ecumenical concerns has made little difference.

In 1985 a pastoral letter from the bishops' conference charged the various non–Roman Catholic religious groups with separatist and isolationist tendencies. In the face of a militant proselytism, seemingly little can be done economically, culturally, or politically to bring the Christian churches together.

In Ecuador the non–Roman Catholic denominations consist of minority groups that have sometimes been unsteady and intolerant and that seek to gain influence in more important churches. In this respect, groups such as the → Pentecostal churches and → Adventists, as well as → Jehovah's Witnesses and → Mormons, pose a problem for the Roman Catholic Church and also for the other confessions. They differ among themselves spiritually, morally, and in social commitment and political interests. There is also a variety of other groups, from those that are connected with the drug scene to those that have formed separate societies. They manifest and propagate themselves by Bible reading, individual witness, lay education, training, and division.

The Roman Catholic Church regards the main reasons for the growth of these groups as economic. The free denominations, especially those of North American origin, have large economic resources.

Lack of religious instruction also plays a part. Religious ignorance among the people is the source of disorientation and confusion. Important, too, is the role of the laity. In Protestantism the laity plays a key role in the congregation and in the organization itself. The whole situation poses a salutary challenge to Roman Catholicism, with its central → hierarchical structures. It has admitted to an overblown clericalism and conceded to the laity the right of active participation in church affairs (→ Clergy and Laity).

2. History of the Christian Churches

The first church to arrive in Ecuador was the Roman Catholic Church, in 1534. It brought with it the "militantly anti-Protestant Catholicism of the Counter-Reformation, or → Catholic reform, of the 16th century" (W. Padilla). The 300-year colonial period stood wholly under the sign of the Roman Catholic Church (→ Colonialism; Colonialism and Mission). It adopted all the rulings of → Trent, which banned Bible reading in the language of the people and forbade non-Catholics to emigrate to the Spanish colonies. An ideological and religious monopoly was set up in all the Spanish colonies in America, supported by the → Inquisition in 1569, all of which had the sole aim of keeping Roman Catholic doctrine pure.

Cracks in this monolithic block began to appear at the beginning of the 19th century, when the colonies achieved independence from Spain. English and Dutch smugglers and pirates brought the peoples of Latin America into their first contact with Protestant thought. Young Creoles, however, were exposed to strong Protestant influence when, as future leaders of the American nations, they went to England and France to study. The formation of the republic in 1830 opened the door to other denominations. Their acceptance was vigorously promoted when Vicente Rocafuerte took over the government in 1835. As he saw it, religious intolerance was incompatible with the interests of a developing young state. His bold step furthered a development for which the way had been prepared as early as 1822, namely, the spread of the Bible by the American → Bible Society and the missionary work of the first Protestant in Ecuador, the Scot James Thompson of the British Bible Society.

With the sanctioning of new denominations in Ecuador, Rocafuerte also sought reform of the educational system, which had thus far been a Roman Catholic monopoly. Thus, for example, he introduced the Lancasterian system, in which the Bible served as a textbook. Up to 1896 individuals rather than organizations, with moderate success, tried to prepare the way for Protestantism.

The rise of → liberalism as a political force in 1895 finally opened the country's doors to non–Roman Catholic Christian churches. At this time the first Protestant missions established themselves in Ecuador. They represented a → fundamentalist theology within Anglo-American Protestantism. The year 1895 marked the beginning of the work of the Alliance Mission, the United Evangelical Mission, and the American Bible Society, whose members included two Ecuadorians converted in Peru.

Until 1908 the Methodists (→ Methodism) devoted themselves to basic educational work in Quito and Cuenca. Educating children and young people is a key part of the work of all the churches. In 1909 the Methodist mission broke off its work for more than 60 years. The Seventh-day Adventists came to the country in 1904, and by 1912 they had a church building in Quito.

In 1918 the Alliance Mission began a new sphere of activity among the Quechua Indians. From 1922 the Adventists worked among the Colta Indians. In 1931, after initial failures, the fruits of these efforts appeared with the largest Protestant mission in Ecuador, the radio station HCJB, Voice of the Andes (World Radio Missionary Fellowship), begun by R. E. Larson and C. W. Jones. This was the first missionary radio station in all of Latin America. As of 1995 it sponsored broadcasts in 23 Quechua dialects and around the world in 47 languages.

As a result of North American influence the Plymouth Brethren (originally from Ireland) came to Ecuador in 1945 under the name Hermanos Libres (Free Brethren). The same year saw the formation of the first national Protestant Church and the Protestant Ecuadorian church Alianza Cristiana y Misionera (Christian Missionary Alliance). This was no longer an exotic plant but a tree with roots in the soil of Ecuador. All its members were nationals. It united 14 local congregations from the three geographic regions of the land: coast, Andean highlands, and tropical lowlands. Its organization rested on the three principles of autonomy, autarky, and self-responsible instruction. It was a first attempt to unite all Protestant denominations for more effective → evangelism. It was less clear, however, regarding work on behalf of the underprivileged people of Ecuador.

The years 1945 to 1962 marked a period of stabilization for the Protestant churches. The renewal resulting from → Vatican II helped to soften the polemical and hostile attitude of the Roman Catholic Church toward the Protestant groups. Thus far, however, there has not been any true ecumenical movement in Ecuador.

After World War II 14 new Protestant missions and organizations entered the country, thus complicating even further the overall ecclesiastical and theological picture. The churches range from the Episcopal Church, of North American and Anglican origin (→ Episcopacy), to Pentecostal groups like the Church of the Foursquare Gospel and the United Pentecostal Church. The → Unitarians are also present in Ecuador.

The period after the war was also one of paternalistic social involvement, a problem that had not yet been faced. From now on we find many new forms of Christian work: ministry in hospitals, programs to educate the rural population, work in secondary schools, care for the territory to the east, using airplanes. These new forms did not mean any neglect of evangelism. In 1949 the Association of Evangelical Churches came into being, to which three national churches belong.

The martyrdom of five Protestant missionaries by the Waorani (Auca) tribe in 1956 attracted worldwide attention to pioneer work among small jungle tribes. Most of these tribes now have churches, as well as the Scriptures in their own language.

The period from 1962 to 1984 was one of expansion, and also one when the Christian groups began to rethink their program of evangelism and social work. In general, the main Protestant emphasis was on the Quechua Mission, on the indigenous population, a sector where the Roman Catholic Church was also active, especially Bishop Leonidas Proaño, who worked intensively in → base communities. Protestants and Roman Catholics work more in rivalry than in support of Indian self-help organizations like the Federation of Shuar Centers (*Jivaro*) in the eastern lowlands.

In 2000 the largest non–Roman Catholic churches were the Association of Indian Evangelical Churches (related to the Gospel Missionary Union, with over 60,000 members), the Church of God (Cleveland, Tenn.), plus smaller groups of Baptists, Christian and Missionary Alliance, Foursquare Gospel, and Assemblies of God. Counting more members than all but the first group are the Jehovah's Witnesses and Mormons.

3. Church-State Relations
Before the rise of liberalism, power lay in the hand of conservative forces in the Andean highlands — namely, the great landowners as well as the state, army, and church. After 1895 and the religious statute of 1907, which is still in force, all religious groups gained recognition. The Roman Catholic Church was no longer the state church, and → reli-

gious liberty was introduced. In 1937 the Catholic Church reached an agreement with the government on relations between → church and state.

4. Other Religious Groups
Non-Christian religions have recently succeeded in gaining a foothold in Ecuador. These include Hare → Krishna, → Children of God, → Baha'i, and the Moon sects (→ Unification Church).

Bibliography: R. ANDRADE, *Historia del Ecuador* (vol. 2; Quito, 1983) • D. B. BARRETT, *WCE* 270-73 • CONFERENCIA EPISCOPAL ECUATORIANA, "El Protestantismo en el Ecuador, análisis y conclusiones," *BE(E)*, nos. 5-6 (1985) • A. M. GOFFIN, *The Rise of Protestant Evangelism in Ecuador, 1895-1990* (Gainesville, Fla., 1994) • A. ISAACS, *Military Rule and Transition in Ecuador, 1972-92* (Pittsburgh, 1993) • W. PADILLA, *Breve reseña histórica del Protestantismo en el Ecuador* (Quito, 1984) • S. RADCLIFFE and S. WESTWOOD, *Remaking the Nation: Place, Identity, and Politics in Latin America* (London, 1996) • D. W. SCHODT, *Ecuador: An Andean Enigma* (Boulder, Colo., 1987) • J. SWANSON, *Echoes of the Call: Identity and Ideology among American Missionaries in Ecuador* (New York, 1995).

CARLOS GRANJA RODRÍGUEZ

Ecumene → Oikoumene

Ecumenical Association of Third World Theologians

The Ecumenical Association of Third World Theologians (EATWOT) is a network of theologians from Asia, Africa, and Latin America, as well as some from North American → minority groups. They have made a commitment to pursue their vocation as theologians from the perspective of the poor and → marginalized sectors of their societies.

The origin of this network is often traced to the conversations of some African students in Louvain, Belgium, in the 1970s. Together they determined to hold a colloquium of Asian, African, and Latin American theologians in order to learn from each other and to develop theologies rooted in their experiences of oppression and struggle for liberation. Preliminary discussions were held by theologians from these continents who had attended the Fifth Assembly of the World Council of Churches in Nairobi (1975), where an agreement was reached to call a tricontinental meeting in Dar es Salaam, Tanzania, in 1976. From these three continents 22 theologians gathered for what is now regarded as the meeting that led directly to the formation of EATWOT.

It was commonly recognized at the Dar es Salaam meeting that theologies originating in the West and, as it were, imposed on the South do not necessarily speak relevantly to the emerging → Third World consciousness. Participants were convinced of the need for a new approach, a method of doing theology that is grounded in the struggles of Third World people for freedom and justice. Moreover, they were aware of attempts toward the same end being made by theologians both from Latin America and among African Americans in the United States. They became convinced that a clear and comprehensive methodology for such theology could be developed only when theologians from all Third World countries engaged in serious dialogue. In order to bring about and maintain such ongoing dialogue, EATWOT was formed.

Several international and continental meetings of EATWOT have been held: an African conference in Ghana (1977), an Asian conference at Colombo, Sri Lanka (1979), and a Latin American conference at São Paulo, Brazil (1980). The published conference reports provide both an analysis of the forces of oppression peculiar to each continent and a delineation of ensuing implications for the theological task.

Following these continental dialogues, the first assembly of EATWOT was held in Delhi, India, in 1981. Under the theme "The Irruption of the Third World: Challenges to Theology," the assembly endeavored both to synthesize the continental → dialogues and to chart future directions for EATWOT. → Poverty as found in the three continents and differing perceptions of that poverty became the focal point of the Delhi assembly. For Asians, the irruption of the Third World was also that of "the non-Christian world." The interrelation between poverty and religiosity in Asia was the main point of this consideration. The African contribution to the discussion centered on perceptions, from that continent, of poverty as anthropological poverty, the deprivation of people of their dignity, → culture, creativity, and → faith. Latin American theologians offered a clear class analysis of poverty and its link to → colonialism.

The dialogue at Delhi was mutually enriching, but there was no → consensus concerning a methodology for theology or for its future. EATWOT, however, was firmly established; African American theologians from the United States were also now entering into the discussion.

Although the main focus of EATWOT is dialogue between partners from the Third World, the association is also determined to respond to theologians from the North (the so-called First World) who also seek ways of responding to the cries of the poor. Thus in January 1983 a dialogue between First and Third World theologians was organized in Geneva. The theme of this meeting was "Doing Theology in a Divided World." Apart from a common commitment to struggle against all forms of oppression, this conference did not result in concrete action or network building.

Through a special working commission EATWOT sought to develop new perspectives in church historiography. Several consultations were held to call into question traditional Eurocentric patterns of church history, in particular, the periodization derived from events in Europe and the United States (L. Vischer).

The second international assembly of EATWOT was held in December 1986 in Oaxtepec, Mexico, under the rubric "The Commonalities and Divergencies among Third World Theologies." As indicated by this theme, the conference envisaged a threefold process: (1) to identify concerns common to theologies from different continents, (2) to consider how these theologies differ from each other, and (3) to begin a process of cross-fertilization between them. While the first two steps proved relatively easy, the third was exceedingly difficult. Differences still stood out, not least since nontheological factors persisted in preventing the realization of common frameworks and a meaningful unity.

In this situation it was nevertheless significant that all partners realized that an exclusive dependence on → Marxist analysis for understanding Third World realities was far too limited. Despite the usefulness of such analysis, partners acknowledged a need to integrate other dimensions — primarily religion, culture, and → racism — if this understanding was to be reached. Ultimately it was seen that human beings and their experience provide the basic data for such an understanding.

In the early years of its existence, EATWOT was a male enterprise. At the urging of some women who participated in the 1981 Delhi assembly and at subsequent meetings, a women's commission on theology was formed in 1983. This women's commission organized several continental dialogues, and before the Oaxtepec assembly, 26 women theologians gathered to share the results of these dialogues. Women members of EATWOT not only have deepened the organization's awareness of gender violence but also have demonstrated the richness of women's unique experience as a resource for doing theology.

EATWOT's third assembly was held in January 1992 in Nairobi, Kenya. A distinct emphasis in this conference was provided, both in preparatory work and in plenary papers and discussions, by a concentration on the → spirituality and struggles of indigenous peoples. The theme at Nairobi was "Cry for Life: The Spirituality of the Third World." It was firmly declared that Third World theology should be decisively shaped by the spirituality of marginalized people — women, indigenous people, minjung, Dalits, and others. This "eco-spirituality" is rooted in the experience of people whose life is close to the earth. At Nairobi the focus of discussion significantly shifted from theology to creative forms of spirituality that were dynamic and life giving.

"The Search for a New Just World Order: Challenges to Theology" was the theme of the fourth assembly of EATWOT, held in December 1996 at Tagaytay, Philippines. This conference was conscious that a new world situation had arisen in which even the term "Third World" had become a misnomer. As a consequence of the end of the cold war, the collapse of → socialism, and the emergence of the worldwide market as the dominant economic force (→ Economic Ethics), there is now a new Third World situation. The spiritual and cultural impact of the process of globalization has brought new challenges to theology, for in this changed world situation, vast masses of people in the poorer nations have become redundant. That fact alone is justification for continuing the kind of theological project that EATWOT has initiated.

The main work of the Ecumenical Association of Third World Theologians is done through conferences and network building. Dialogue between partners occupies the center of the association's activities. The enduring significance of EATWOT's consistently held theological methodology was sharply stated at the Dar es Salaam conference of 1976: "We reject as irrelevant an academic type of theology that is divorced from action. We are prepared for a radical break in → epistemology which makes commitment the first act of theology and engages in critical reflection on the praxis of the reality of the Third World" (*VFTW* 11/1 [1988] 16). And from the Oaxtepec assembly of 1986: "Our aim is not new doctrines, but new relationships and lifestyles. Method implies a direction, and liberation is the direction" (ibid., 129).

Bibliography: K. C. ABRAHAM, ed., *Third World Theologies: Commonalities and Divergencies* (Maryknoll, N.Y., 1993) • K. C. ABRAHAM and B. MBUY-BEYA, eds., *Spirituality of the Third World: A Cry for Life* (Maryknoll, N.Y., 1994) • J. H. CONE, "Ecumenical Association of Third-World Theologians," *DEM* 322-24 • V. FABELLA, *Beyond Bonding: A Third World Woman's Theological Journey* (Manila, 1993) • V. FABELLA and M. ODUYOYE, eds., *With Passion and Compassion: Third World Women Doing Theology* (Maryknoll, N.Y., 1988) • V. FABELLA and S. TORRES, eds., *Doing Theology in a Divided World* (Maryknoll, N.Y., 1985); idem, eds., *Irruption of the Third World: Challenge to Theology* (Maryknoll, N.Y., 1983). • O. U. KALU, ed., *African Church Historiography: An Ecumenical Perspective* (Geneva, 1986) • L. VISCHER, ed., *Towards a History of the Church in the Third World: Papers and Reports of a Consultation on the Issue of Periodisation, Convened by the Commission on Church History of EATWOT* (Geneva, 1983). See also three issues of *VFTW: Emerging Concerns of Third World Theology* (16/1 [1993]), *Search for a New Just World Order: Challenges to Theology* (22/2 [1999]), and *Statements up to Mexico 1986* (11/1 [1988]).

K. C. ABRAHAM

Ecumenical Dialogue

1. Term
2. Formal Features
3. Levels
4. Goals
5. Themes and Results
6. Dialogues and Reception

1. Term

In a broad sense "ecumenical dialogue" may denote any conversation between different churches and Christians that promotes fellowship with each other or common understanding of Christian responsibility to the world. In the customary narrower sense the phrase refers to discussions held primarily by official representatives of two or more churches on controversial theological issues with the goal of stating and clarifying these issues so as to eliminate their divisive character. The adjective "ecumenical" distinguishes these dialogues within Christianity from dialogues between → religions. The many discussions of → union in different countries do not usually count as ecumenical dialogues in the narrower sense because they represent a form of attempted unification between churches.

2. Formal Features

As in all → dialogue, so in ecumenical dialogue the parity (→ Equality) of the partners is an essential prerequisite. Dialogue requires a mutual recognition that both sides are Christian, though not necessarily of the other's status as a church. Another vital feature of ecumenical dialogue, as of any dialogue, is the tension that exists between the faithfulness of each party to its own convictions and each party's readiness to accept the convictions of the other as a question put to itself.

The aim of ecumenical dialogue is that there be understanding and fellowship between the churches. Preferably, the dialogue should be conducted by officially commissioned representatives of the parties and not simply by individual Christians or theologians. In most cases, then, churches or church authorities conduct these dialogues and accept their results, though the official character of an ecumenical dialogue does not necessarily mean that the results are binding on the churches.

The dialogues may be bilateral or multilateral. Each form has its own special possibilities and limits. Bilateral dialogue, usually conducted by the larger denominational groups, can focus on specific differences. It normally holds out greater possibilities of mutual understanding, yet it also runs the risk of not doing justice to the interdependence of ecumenical dialogues and the indivisibility of the → ecumenical movement. Multilateral dialogues, usually conducted by the → World Council of Churches (WCC) and its Faith and Order Commission or within regional or national councils or groupings, can safeguard the coherence of ecumenical concern and thus accord with the biblical petition "that they may all be one" (John 17:21). Yet such dialogues tend not to take sufficiently into account the distinctiveness and identity of individual churches and traditions. Today, then, the two forms are seen as interrelated and complementary.

3. Levels

Ecumenical dialogues take place for the most part on two levels: (1) the international and global and (2) the national and regional. Since → faith and the → church are both universal and contextual, marked by both historical continuity and variability, the two levels are interrelated. The WCC or the → Christian World Communions conduct the global dialogues; the national or provincial churches or, less frequently, ecumenical bodies like → national Christian councils or → national councils of churches conduct the national dialogues.

During and after the 1960s a whole network of bilateral ecumenical dialogues developed that involved most of the churches. Some churches like the → Roman Catholic Church (→ Ecumenism, Ecumenical Movement), the → Anglican Communion, the → Lutheran churches, and the → Orthodox

Church play a bigger role, others a smaller role, but there are often structural, financial, or personal reasons for the smaller participation; it is not necessarily a sign of ecumenical reservations. Again, ecumenical dialogue as a form of ecumenical effort is more in keeping with some traditions than others.

3.1. It is hard to speak definitively about national or regional dialogues, since some last only for a short time and the results are often not published (→ Local Ecumenism). In the latter part of the 20th century there were as many as 50 such dialogues. Some were more important than others. In Europe, for instance, dialogue beginning in 1964 between the Lutheran, Reformed, and Union churches resulted in the → Leuenberg Agreement (1973). In Germany there has been dialogue between Protestants and the Roman Catholics (from 1946), discussion between the Evangelical Church in Germany and various Orthodox churches (from 1959) and the Church of England (from 1964), also between Roman Catholics and Lutherans (from 1976). In France the Groupe des Dombes began dialogue among Roman Catholics, Reformed, and Lutherans in 1937. In the United States dialogue began between Lutherans and the Reformed in 1963 (concluded by the Formula of Agreement, officially adopted by the churches in 1997), between Lutherans and Roman Catholics in 1965, between Roman Catholics and the Reformed in 1965, and between Anglicans and Lutherans in 1969.

3.2. On the global level it is easier to summarize the dialogues and their results. Multilateral conversations sponsored by the Faith and Order Commission are especially important. Additionally, by the year 1998 altogether 27 bilateral dialogues of different types had taken place (dates refer to the year of publication of the first document from the respective dialogue): Adventist and Lutheran (1998), Anglican and Lutheran (1972), Anglican and Methodist (1996), Anglican and Oriental Orthodox (1987), Anglican and Orthodox (1976), Anglican and Reformed (1984), Anglican and Roman Catholic (1971), Assyrian Church of the East and Roman Catholic (1994), Baptist and Lutheran (1990), Baptist and Reformed (1977), Baptist and Roman Catholic (1988), Disciples of Christ and Reformed (1987), Disciples of Christ and Roman Catholic (1981), Evangelical and Roman Catholic (1984), Lutheran and Methodist (1984), Lutheran and Orthodox (1985), Lutheran and Reformed (1989), Lutheran and Roman Catholic (1972), Methodist and Reformed (1987), Methodist and Roman Catholic (1971), Old Catholic and Orthodox (1975), Oriental Orthodox and Orthodox (1985), Oriental Orthodox and Roman Catholic (1970), Orthodox and Reformed (1988), Orthodox and Roman Catholic (1964), Pentecostal and Roman Catholic (1976), and Reformed and Roman Catholic (1977).

4. Goals

In character, most of today's ecumenical dialogues are doctrinal. They deal primarily with theological and ecclesiological differences between the churches in dialogue. In the new historical situation they have resumed the tradition of the religious colloquies of the → Reformation period. They are characterized by the conviction that traditional distinctions are still critical and must be explored if sustainable and durable fellowship is to be achieved.

Different dialogues may have different goals, but the overall aim of all of them is → consensus. Consensus does not have to mean a common agreement that removes every difference, but it does involve an agreement that overcomes the differences in the sense of robbing them of their church-dividing character and making possible agreement in disagreement. This type of consensus may be called convergence, nuanced consensus, fundamental agreement, or basic consensus.

5. Themes and Results

The nature and goal of ecumenical dialogue determine its themes. Though variations may be seen in this regard, the themes are for the most part theological or doctrinal. Questions of Christian → ethics, world responsibility (→ Social Ethics), and the duty of mission have been marginal in ecumenical dialogue in the narrower sense, arising only sporadically. Only in the later 20th century did they begin to figure more prominently. The same applies to issues of → spirituality or → piety and to liturgical questions, which play a role only as supplementary problems of common life and practical fellowship. Insofar as theological consensus developed and differences lost their divisive character, the possibilities of gradual and partial fellowship (intercommunion, mutual recognition of ministries) came under discussion, including even the possible form and structure of the church fellowship that is sought.

The five leading topics of ecumenical dialogues in the later 20th century were (1) the understanding and practice of the → Eucharist; (2) the ordained ministry (→ Offices, Ecclesiastical), usually a question of → bishops and the → pope; (3) → authority in the church, which directly involves Scripture (→ Canon), → confessions, → councils and their rulings, → dogmas, and church → tradition, and which is closely related to the previous issue of lead-

ership; (4) the doctrine of the church (ecclesiology); and (5) the doctrine of → justification, which particularly concerns Lutherans.

It is too early to say that the resolving of all controversial issues between churches is now in sight. The results of ecumenical dialogues do not support such a view. This is especially true of dialogues between Reformation and post-Reformation churches on the one hand, and Roman Catholics and Orthodox on the other. As regards the five main themes, the chief problems are those of authority and the ministry, especially church leadership. Ecumenical dialogue has yet to explore more fully the issue of the papacy in regard to both primacy and → infallibility, also → Mariology, veneration of → Mary and the → saints, the binding nature of church tradition, and the understanding of the church itself. Progress has been made on issues of → marriage and → mixed marriage, but here too there are remaining points of controversy. Women's → ordination became an increasingly urgent theme of ecumenical dialogue toward the end of the 20th century.

6. Dialogues and Reception

The ecumenical dialogue that aims at consensus in faith and doctrine is not the only form of ecumenical effort, but it is certainly a vital form, for the unity of the church demands fellowship in faith, and visible unity demands a clear articulation of this fellowship. Any disparagement of the attempt to achieve the consensus at which ecumenical dialogue aims must be firmly resisted. Ecumenical dialogue can contribute to the unity of the church, however, only to the degree that the churches "receive" the results into their thinking and practice, that is, only insofar as they evaluate them and appropriate them. This process of ecumenical → reception is difficult and burdensome, even though essential. There is thus a need more fully to relate ecumenical dialogue to ecumenical reception, to link them together, and in this way to avoid a mere dialogic formulating and accumulating of declarations of consensus.

Bibliography: J. A. Burgess and J. Gros, eds., *Building Unity: Ecumenical Dialogues with Roman Catholic Participation in the United States* (New York, 1989); idem, eds., *Growing Consensus: Church Dialogues in the United States, 1962-1991* (New York, 1995) • N. Ehrenström and G. Gassmann, *Confessions in Dialogue: A Survey of Bilateral Conversations among World Confessional Families, 1959-1974* (Geneva, 1975) • M. Kinnamon and B. E. Cope, eds., *The Ecumenical Movement: An Anthology of Key Texts and Voices* (Grand

Rapids and Geneva, 1997) • H. Meyer, *That All May Be One: Perceptions and Models of Ecumenicity* (Grand Rapids, 1999) • H. Meyer, D. Papandreou, J. Urban, and L. Vischer, eds., *Dokumente wachsender Übereinstimmung. Sämtliche Berichte und Konsenstexte interkonfessioneller Gespräche auf Weltebene,* vol. 2, *1982-1990* (Frankfurt, 1992) • H. Meyer and L. Vischer, eds., *Growth in Agreement: Reports and Agreed Statements of Ecumenical Conversations on a World Level* (New York, 1984) for the years 1931-82 J. F. Puglisi, *A Workbook of Bibliographies for the Study of Interchurch Dialogues* (Rome, 1978) • W. G. Rusch and J. Gros, *Deepening Communion: International Ecumenical Documents with Roman Catholic Participation* (Washington, D.C., 1998) • E. J. Stormon, ed., *Towards the Healing of Schism: The Sees of Rome and Constantinople–Public Statements and Correspondence between the Holy See and the Ecumenical Patriarchate, 1958-1984* (New York, 1987) • T. F. Stransky and J. B. Sheerin, eds., *Doing the Truth in Charity: Statements of Popes Paul VI, John Paul I, John Paul II, and the Secretariat for Promoting Christian Unity, 1964-1980* (New York, 1982).

HARDING MEYER

Ecumenical Learning

Learning has always been important for the → ecumenical movement, for in a world rampant with → secularization and globalization, where Christianity appears to be no more than one option among many religious pluralities, learning is essential for survival. Ecumenical learning had its beginnings as early as 1910, when the ecumenical movement was born. At the World Missionary Conference that year in Edinburgh, one of the topics discussed was "Education in Relation to the Christianization of National Life." More recently the concept has been housed within the → World Council of Churches (WCC) in a formal sense, although the idea of learning as part of the → oikoumene predates the advent of any structures.

In 1957 the Central Committee of the WCC described ecumenical learning as "fostering understanding of, commitment to and informed participation in, this whole ecumenical process. The vision of the one missionary church in process of renewal when it is apprehended by Christians, leads them to an ecumenical commitment, i.e. to participation in the process of letting the churches be more truly the church." Ecumenical learning officially became part of the ecumenical movement at the fifth WCC assembly, at Nairobi in 1975, when education issues first appeared on the assembly agenda. Ecumenists then defined ecumenical learning, or "education for ecumenism," as the imparting of information about the ecumenical movement, and it was seen as a separate task and program in the church.

After the Nairobi assembly, church leaders gave ecumenical learning a more comprehensive meaning involving action, participation, and → partnership. As described in WCC documents after 1957, the characteristics of ecumenical learning seem especially relevant for today's focus on ecumenical learning, along with the larger issue of ecumenical formation. Those characteristics include at least the following seven:

An *emphasis on relationships* rather than exclusive attention to structural and doctrinal agreement. The phrase "liturgy over legislation," coined by John Bluck in *Canberra Take-Aways* (published after the 1991 Canberra Assembly), makes the point succinctly.

A focus on the *full participation of men and women,* lay and ordained, in the life of the Christian community. This goal was aided by the WCC study "The Community of Women and Men in the Church," carried out from 1978 to 1982.

Attention to *contextual learning.* Ecumenical learning, recognizing the danger in making exclusively universal approaches, advocates the interpretation of learning in a local context. This idea is similar to that of the need to bring the gospel message to bear on the particular culture of the learners. "Context" in ecumenical learning has been described as "all that is included in the human environment — social, political, religious and physical — understood from both contemporary and historical perspectives" ("Education in a Context of Change"). Being sensitive to context in learning also suggests greater awareness of the importance of the learner's experience.

A commitment to *lifelong learning in community.* The idea of the learner as a participant in community (including family, congregation, or school) connotes a sense of continuity with all learning and highlights the importance of nurture and respect for the dignity of the individual. It also brings the obligation to listen to the story of the learner's own journey.

A recognition of the need for *ecumenical memory building.* One of the crises currently facing the ecumenical movement is a lack of memory of events, people, and places that constitute the history of the movement. In order to keep memory alive, those who will carry the torch into the future need to catch the vision of telling the story, of mentoring others to lead the movement well into the new millennium.

Acknowledging the *importance of globalization* and its impact on learning in an ecumenical setting. The Brazilian educator Paulo Freire (1921-97) contributed to ecumenical learning in the context of globalized relations between the technological (the so-called First and Second) and the developing (the Third) worlds. → Technology is rapidly making persons into objects, a process Freire resisted through his view of authentic education as the creation of subjects capable of acting upon and transforming the world. This approach contrasts with hierarchical models, which sometimes lose sight of needs.

An intentional focus on *models of integrative theological education.* Ecumenical learning presumes a desire for synthesis as well as a holistic approach to education and transformation. This framework has implications for how information is shared and by what model or process. The concept of ecumenically teaching → systematic theology, church history, biblical studies, and related subjects was introduced by the WCC as early as 1986 at the global consultation "The Teaching of Ecumenics," held at the Ecumenical Institute of Bossey, near Geneva (S. Amirtham and C. H. S. Moon). This model, which integrates subjects into an ecumenical framework, remains viable but relatively untested today. The process of integration is demonstrated by a case study conducted by the group Partnership for Theological Education, in Manchester, England. The partnership describes itself as an ecumenical body that seeks to express in educational terms what it means to be part of the mission of God to the world. The organization comprises six theological colleges, in addition to educational units of ten denominations (see "Education in a Context of Change").

A good example of ecumenical learning occurred in December 1998 at the Eighth Assembly of the WCC, in Harare, Zimbabwe. A model for discussion, dialogue, and education called *padare* was chosen as a reflection of the African culture in which the assembly was held. The padare, derived from an ancient Shona term growing out of Zimbabwean tradition, describes a special meeting place. Those planning the assembly hoped that the meetings so designated could function as "open spaces" where people from widely different backgrounds could discuss a variety of issues, from the meaning of → koinonia to the church's response to HIV/AIDS (→ Public Health). Providing such a meeting place to discuss common issues was an experiment in ecu-

menical learning at the global level. No written reports were expected at the padare, but they were designed to enhance the work of the delegates and perhaps help to determine future agendas for the WCC. Many participants thought that more interesting developments took place in the padare than in the formal proceedings.

Wherever ecumenical learning takes place — in formal discussion or in a context of worship and celebration — it is an essential part of the response to the prayer of Jesus Christ that all may be one so that the world may believe.

Bibliography: Alive Together: A Practical Guide to Ecumenical Learning (Geneva, 1989) • S. AMIRTHAM and C. H. S. MOON, eds., *The Teaching of Ecumenics* (Geneva, 1987) • U. BECKER, "Ecumenical Learning," *DEM* 341-42; idem, "The History of Education in the World Council of Churches: A Brief Survey," *Education Newsletter 1998* (Geneva), no. 2 • J. BLUCK, "What the Assembly Offers a Congregation," *Canberra Take-Aways* (Geneva, 1991) • *Education Newsletter 1985*, no. 1 • P. FREIRE, *Pedagogy of the Oppressed* (New York, 1972) • C. F. PARVEY, ed., *The Community of Women and Men in the Church: The Sheffield Report* (Philadelphia and Geneva, 1983) • E. STIMSON, ed., *Together on Holy Ground* (Geneva, 1999) popular report on the Harare assembly.

DARLIS J. SWAN

Ecumenical Mission

1. The term "ecumenical mission" denotes an understanding of Christian → mission according to which witness to the one → gospel is the comprehensive task of the worldwide church. Ecumenical mission views itself against the background of the divine sending to the whole world (*missio Dei;* → Missiology) and is oriented to the ultimate unifying of all things under the rule of God (→ Eschatology).

2. This understanding brings together insights from almost a century of ecumenical missionary discussion. Between the Edinburgh Missionary Conference (1910) and the end of World War II, the International Missionary Council (IMC, founded 1921) took the lead. In many countries, especially in Asia (India, Burma, Ceylon, Japan, and China), national missionary councils or Christian councils (→ National Christian Councils) were also formed. After the founding of the → World Council of Churches (WCC) in 1948, close relations developed between the IMC and the WCC, which among other things

led to the formation of regional ecumenical organizations (→ Ecumenism, Ecumenical Movement). After lengthy preparations the Third Assembly of the WCC, at New Delhi in 1961, united the two bodies, and the IMC continued its work as the WCC Commission for World Mission and Evangelization.

3. The beginning of cooperative global mission at the end of the 19th century had been under the slogan "The evangelization of the world in this generation." World War I dampened this early enthusiasm. The → missionary conferences in Jerusalem (1928) and Tambaram, India (1938), took a self-critical look at the enterprise in the light of the new challenges of → secularism, political → ideologies, and the social consequences of worldwide industrialization (→ Industrial Society). They stressed the common Christian message (Jerusalem: "Our message is Jesus Christ") and the churches' inalienable responsibility for mission (Tambaram).

A new impulse came after the destruction of World War II. The slogans now were → "hope" (§3) and → "partnership" (from the IMC meeting in Whitby, Canada, in 1947), also the inseparability of → unity and mission in the church's ecumenical calling (meeting of the WCC Central Committee in Rolle, Switzerland, 1951). The 1952 IMC conference in Willingen, West Germany, gave voice to the new perspective, stating that the movement of mission in which the IMC was participating had its origin in the triune God, and that to do this work God sends his church to the ends of the earth, to all nations, as long as time shall last. In his *Missio Dei* (1957), G. F. Vicedom (1903-74) formulated the results of this new understanding of mission (note the theological studies of evangelization in 1959 and of mission in 1961) when he claimed that we must overcome the old distinctions between mission and evangelization (→ Evangelism) and between home and foreign mission (→ Inner Mission). The uniting of the IMC and the WCC followed, along with the integrating of church and mission in many countries. Since the church is fully the church only in mission, it follows that the churches "in six continents" are summoned to partnership in mission (Commission on World Mission and Evangelism [CWME], Mexico City, 1963).

In the last part of the 20th century, discussion of ecumenical mission has focused on the missionary renewal of the churches, → salvation in the context of the modern world (CWME, Bangkok, 1972), the gospel of the → kingdom of God as good news for the poor (Melbourne mission conference, 1980), and mission in discipleship of Christ (mission con-

ference in San Antonio, Tex., 1989). The most important results were summed up in *Mission and Evangelism: An Ecumenical Affirmation* (1982). Following the guidelines for dialogue set up in 1979, → ecumenical dialogue with those of other beliefs (begun in 1967) produced controversy regarding the relation between mission and → dialogue. After 1983 the theme of gospel and → culture also became a highly relevant one (esp. at a mission conference in Salvador, Brazil, in 1996).

4. In practice, ecumenical mission is not limited to cooperation among the predominantly Protestant member churches of the WCC. Important gains followed from the more vigorous discussions begun with the Orthodox in 1969 on the missionary perspectives of their tradition (mission as → "liturgy after the Liturgy," the Eucharist as "food for → missionaries"; → Eucharistic Ecclesiology; Orthodox Church; Orthodox Missionary Societies).

After 1965 close cooperation also developed with the → Roman Catholic Church. For example, representatives of Catholic missionary → orders took part as consultants in the work of the WCC Commission for World Mission (→ Catholic Missions). A result of a prolonged exchange on the understanding and practice of ecumenical mission was the document *Common Witness* (1982).

Relations with evangelical churches and missions (→ Evangelical Movement 3; Evangelical Missions) have been more difficult. When the IMC was integrated into the WCC, evangelicals saw themselves as the true heirs of the Edinburgh tradition and tended to distance themselves from the approaches of ecumenical mission, a position they expressed at world congresses in Wheaton (Ill.) and Berlin (both 1966), as well as in Lausanne (1974) and Manila (1989). In spite of many meetings and consultations after 1968 and a general theological approximation (e.g., on evangelism, → conversion, → proclamation, and social → responsibility), thus far there has been no express partnership.

→ Ecumenical Theology; Mission 3; Third World

Bibliography: D. J. Bosch, *Transforming Mission: Paradigm Shifts in Theology of Mission* (Maryknoll, N.Y., 1996) • I. Bria, *Go Forth in Peace: Orthodox Perspectives on Mission* (Geneva, 1986); idem, *The Liturgy after the Liturgy: Mission and Witness from an Orthodox Perspective* (Geneva, 1996) • E. Castro, *Sent Free: Mission and Unity in the Perspective of the Kingdom* (Geneva, 1985) • W. Günther, *Von Edinburgh nach Mexiko City* (Stuttgart, 1970) • W. R. Hogg, *Ecumenical Founda-*

tions: A History of the International Missionary Council and Its Nineteenth-Century Background (New York, 1952); idem, One World, One Mission (New York, 1960) • H. J. MARGULL, Hope in Action: The Church's Task in the World (Philadelphia, 1962); idem, ed., Zur Sendung der Kirche. Material der ökumenischen Bewegung (Munich, 1963) reports of previous mission conferences and other ecumenical documents • K. MÜLLER, T. SUNDERMEIER, S. B. BEVANS, and R. H. BLIESE, eds., Dictionary of Mission: Theology, History, Perspectives (Maryknoll, N.Y., 1997) • L. NEWBIGIN, The Gospel in a Pluralist Society (Grand Rapids, 1989) • J. M. PHILLIPS and R. T. COOTE, eds., Toward the Twenty-first Century in Christian Mission (Grand Rapids, 1993) • J. A. SCHERER, Gospel, Church, and Kingdom: Comparative Studies in World Mission Theology (Minneapolis, 1987) • J. A. SCHERER and S. B. BEVANS, eds., New Directions in Mission and Evangelization, vol. 1, Basic Statements, 1974-1991; vol. 2, Theological Foundations (Maryknoll, N.Y., 1992-94) • G. F. VICEDOM, The Mission of God: An Introduction to a Theology of Mission (St. Louis, 1965; orig. pub., 1957) • WORLD COUNCIL OF CHURCHES, Common Witness (Geneva, 1982); idem, Mission and Evangelism: An Ecumenical Affirmation (Geneva, 1983) • T. YATES, Christian Mission in the Twentieth Century (Cambridge, 1994).

KONRAD RAISER

Ecumenical Patriarchate

The Ecumenical Patriarchate of Constantinople is the ranking church within the communion of the 14 → autocephalous and 2 autonomous churches that presently compose Orthodox Christianity (→ Orthodox Church). The → patriarch of Constantinople, present-day Istanbul, is regarded as the "first among equals" within the hierarchy of Orthodox → bishops. His full title is "Archbishop of Constantinople–New Rome and Ecumenical Patriarch." The patriarchate includes episcopal sees — metropolitanates, archdioceses, and dioceses — not only in Turkey and Greece but also in other regions, including the Americas and western Europe.

Early Christian tradition identifies Andrew the apostle as one of the evangelizers in the region of → Byzantium, the strategic ancient Greek trading city on the Bosporus. This was the site selected in 324 by Emperor Constantine for the new capital of the → Roman Empire; it was dedicated as such in 330. By the middle of the fourth century, the role of the bishop of "New Rome," or Constantinople, was increasingly recognized. The Council of Constantinople in 381 affirmed that the bishop of the new capital would "enjoy the privileges of honor after the bishop of Rome" (can. 3). The Council of → Chalcedon in 451 identified the See of Constantinople as a place of appeal and spoke of its bishop as having "equal prerogatives" (cans. 9, 17) with the bishop of old Rome (can. 28). The same canon also placed the civil dioceses of Pontus, Asia, and Thrace within Constantinople's jurisdiction. The bishop of Constantinople was also granted the → authority to provide bishops for the so-called barbarian lands, then understood as regions beyond the boundaries of both church and empire.

These conciliar decisions established the Church of Constantinople as an ecclesiastical → jurisdiction similar to those of → Rome, → Alexandria, and → Antioch. In the ordering of these ancient episcopal sees, known as the pentarchy, Constantinople was always ranked after Rome and before Alexandria, Antioch, and Jerusalem. By the fifth century, the bishops of these sees were generally recognized as → "patriarchs." The patriarch of Constantinople was regarded as the "ecumenical patriarch" from the late sixth century. Initially, this title reflected the importance of the patriarch not only within the life of the church but also within Roman-Byzantine society.

Between the 4th and 15th centuries, the activities of the patriarchate took place within the context of an empire that not only was Christian but also was committed to the defense of the faith. Although Byzantine theologians spoke about the cooperation between → church and state, relations were sometimes strained, as the case of Patriarch John → Chrysostom (398-404) demonstrates. He was deposed and exiled because of his criticism of the immorality of many clerics and members of the royal family. Relations between the patriarch and the emperor often were affected by the theological debates that served as the impetus for the "general" or "ecumenical" → councils that met in or near Constantinople. With the church divisions that followed the Council of Chalcedon as well as the Muslim political conquests of Palestine, Syria, and Egypt in the 7th century, the influence of the other eastern patriarchates was reduced, thus further strengthening the role of the Ecumenical Patriarchate both within the Byzantine Empire and beyond its political borders.

Within a society that honored learning, the Ecumenical Patriarchate guided the Patriarchal Academy, a center for advanced theological studies that complemented the activities of the University of Constantinople. The architecture of the church buildings of Constantinople provided inspiration for those subsequently erected in Italy, Ukraine, and Russia. The → worship within the patriarchal cathedral of Hagia Sophia (Holy Wisdom), known as the Great Church, had a profound influence upon liturgical developments throughout the Christian East. In addition, following the victory over iconoclasm, the patriarchate nurtured a dramatic renewal of → iconography.

Under the direction of Patriarch Photios (858-67, 877-86), a new → missionary initiative was launched in the 9th century in Moravia by Cyril and Methodius, and in Bulgaria under their disciples (→ Mission; Slavic Mission). Other missionaries went to the Caucasus in the early 12th century. As a result of contacts with missionaries from Constantinople, Princess Olga of Kiev was converted in 957, which led ultimately to the conversion of Prince Vladimir in 998. From that time Christianity, expressed through the Constantinopolitan tradition, became the official religion of the regions around Kiev and Novgorod.

Tensions between the Church of Rome and the Ecumenical Patriarchate can be traced back at least to the fifth century, when Rome refused to accept canon 28 of the Council of Chalcedon. During the subsequent debates over → Christology, a break in communion known as the Acacian schism (→ Heresies and Schisms) lasted from 484 to 519. At the time of the Monothelite controversy in the seventh century, communion was again briefly broken between the two patriarchates. In the ninth century, Patriarch Photios became embroiled in controversy with Pope Nicholas I, chiefly over the addition of the → filioque to the creed, missionary conflicts, and the papal claims. A council in 879 restored relations. While formal → excommunications were exchanged in 1054, a genuine schism was not in place until much later. Constantinople consistently rejected the growing claims of papal jurisdiction throughout the church. The tragic sack of Constantinople in 1204 by Western → crusaders only compounded differences in church polity and liturgical practice. The brief establishment by Rome of a Western hierarchy in Constantinople may have marked a formal schism. While Constantinople had representatives at both the Council of Lyon in 1274 and that of Ferrara-Florence in 1438-39, it subsequently rejected the decisions of both, thereby deepening the schism between Catholicism centered at Rome and Orthodoxy centered at Constantinople.

The city of Constantinople fell to the Muslim Turks in 1453, and shortly thereafter all vestiges of the Roman-Byzantine Empire came to an end. The Ecumenical Patriarchate and the Church of Constantinople, however, continued to function in the new political reality. Beginning in 1454 under Sul-

tan Mehmet II the Conqueror, the authority of the patriarchate over all Orthodox Christians in the sultan's political domain was recognized. While the other patriarchates continued to exist, they became somewhat subordinate to Constantinople. The authority of the Ecumenical Patriarchate also came to be more restricted. Moreover, as time went on, it was not always in a position to minister properly to a flock that was multiethnic and multilingual. In 1589 the patriarchate granted autocephalous status to the Church of Russia.

The patriarchate was not always in a position to reply properly to the theological issues raised by the Protestant Reformation of the 16th century. While the correspondence from 1573 between Patriarch Jeremiah and Lutheran theologians at Tübingen was noteworthy, it did not lead to a genuine dialogue (→ Ecumenical Dialogue). Similarly, the Confessio Fidei of Patriarch Cyril Lucaris in 1629, with its Calvinistic perspectives, was forcefully repudiated between 1638 and 1691 by no less than six local councils of Orthodox bishops. Anglican Nonjurors also maintained correspondence with Constantinople and other Orthodox patriarchates, especially between 1716 and 1725.

With the breakup of the Ottoman Empire and the creation of new nation-states in the Balkans during the 19th century, the Ecumenical Patriarchate granted autocephalous status to the churches of Greece (1850), Serbia (1879), Romania (1885), Albania (1937), Bulgaria (1945), and, most recently, the Czech Republic and Slovakia (1999).

Since the beginning of the 20th century, the Ecumenical Patriarchate has expressed its primatial ministry within the Orthodox Church in four significant areas. First, it has advocated greater unity among the Orthodox churches and has taken the initiative in proposing common issues and concerns needing attention by the entire church. Second, the Ecumenical Patriarchate has continued to be a center of appeal through which it serves as an arbitrator in disputes involving other regional churches. Third, it has coordinated Orthodox participation in the various global expressions of the contemporary → ecumenical movement. Finally, the Ecumenical Patriarchate has exercised a special responsibility for overseeing and guiding the development of new regional churches that are beyond the boundaries of other autocephalous churches. As a result of both missions and immigration, the growth of Orthodox Christianity in the so-called → diaspora of the Americas, western Europe, Australia, and the Far East is a complex one that is unique in the entire history of Orthodoxy. In being attentive to these areas today, the Ecumenical Patriarchate exercises its primacy in a manner that does not diminish the integrity of the other autocephalous churches or the need for genuine → conciliarity among them.

→ Church Government; Early Church; Nicaea, Councils of; Pan-Orthodox Conferences; Uniate Churches

Bibliography: F. Dvornik, *Byzantium and the Roman Primacy* (rev. ed.; New York, 1979) • G. Every, *The Byzantine Patriarchate* (London, 1962) • T. FitzGerald, *The Ecumenical Patriarchate and Christian Unity* (Brookline, Mass., 1997) • D. J. Geanakopoulos, *A Short History of the Ecumenical Patriarchate, 330-1990* (Brookline, Mass., 1990) • J. M. Hussey, *The Orthodox Church in the Byzantine Empire* (Oxford, 1986) • Maximos of Sardis, *The Ecumenical Patriarchate in the Orthodox Church* (Thessaloníki, 1976) • J. Meyendorff, *The Byzantine Legacy in the Orthodox Church* (New York, 1982) • R. Potz, *Patriarch und Synode in Konstantinopel. Das Verfassungsrecht des ökumenischen Patriarchates* (Vienna, 1971) • S. Runciman, *The Great Church in Captivity* (Cambridge, 1968) • A-E. Tachiaos, *Cyril and Methodius* (Thessaloníki, 1989) • T. Ware, *The Orthodox Church* (rev. ed.; London, 1993).

Thomas FitzGerald

Ecumenical Symbols

The term "ecumenical symbols" is sometimes used to describe Christian confessions of faith that have been affirmed across the boundaries of confessional traditions. Most specifically, the term refers to the use of the → Apostles' Creed and the Nicene (or → Niceno-Constantinopolitan) Creed, and less commonly to the → Athanasian Creed (or, from its opening words, the *Quicunque Vult*), the three creeds affirmed in the Lutheran Book of Concord and the Anglican Articles of Religion. Although these creeds were affirmed in both Roman Catholic and Protestant bodies at the time of the Reformation, the Apostles' Creed and Athanasian Creed have not been utilized in the Christian East. Though the term might not always be used, what it signifies plays an important role in → ecumenical dialogues (→ Dialogue 2), for example, when acceptance of the first two creeds figures as a condition of church unity (e.g., in the Chicago Lambeth Quadrilateral of 1888).

These → symbols became important because they were used in the basic → worship services of → baptism and the → Eucharist. They bear witness to the essentially → Trinitarian structure of the Christian faith and are in keeping with the celebration of the → liturgy. Again, since many churches have historically used them, they are well adapted to express the church's basic confession of its Lord to others. Their terminology does need interpretation today, however, and therefore the Commission on → Faith and Order of the → World Council of Churches invited the churches to express their faith in the study document *Confessing the One Faith,* which is meant as an interpretation of the ecumenical symbols, not as their replacement.

→ Confessions and Creeds; Ecumenism, Ecumenical Movement; Ecumenical Theology; Oikoumene

Bibliography: T. E. Best, ed., *Faith and Renewal* (Geneva, 1986) • T. A. Campbell, *Christian Confessions: A Historical Introduction* (Louisville, Ky., 1996) • T. Hopko, "Towards the Common Expression of the Apostolic Faith Today," Best, *Faith and Renewal,* 115-26 • J. N. D. Kelly, *Early Christian Creeds* (5th ed.; Reading, Mass., 1982) • J. Leith, *Creeds of the Churches* (3d ed.; Atlanta, 1982) • H. G. Link, "Auf dem Weg zum gemeinsamen Glauben," *ÖR* 33 (1984) 495-510; idem, ed., *Apostolic Faith Today: A Handbook for Study* (Geneva, 1985) • R. Mumm, "Zur Frage des Ökumenischen Rates 'Was heißt apostolischer Glaube?' *Quat.* 50 (1986) 4-14 • D. Ritschl, "Wege ökumenischer Entscheidungsfindung," *Ökumenische Existenz heute* (ed. W. Huber, D. Ritschl, and T. Sundermaier; Munich, 1986) 11-48 • World Council of Churches, *Confessing the One Faith* (rev. ed.; Geneva, 1996).

Thaddeus A. Schnitker and Ted A. Campbell

Ecumenical Theology

1. Term and Agencies
2. Tasks and Concepts
3. Possibilities and Limits
4. Comparative Study of Denominations
   4.1. Field and Task
   4.2. History

1. Term and Agencies

1.1. The practice of ecumenical theology is much older than the term itself. It began with → Paul's arguments concerning the unity of churches of Jews and → Gentiles (→ Jewish Christians; Judaism) and their many groups and → charismata and continued as theology developed with a common concern for → truth. It prepared the way for the decisions of the ecumenical → councils and accompanied the → reception of these rulings. In a paradoxical way it was also the driving force behind the polemical writings of the → Reformers, whose aim was to reform the one → church, not to split it.

1.2. As an explicit discipline, ecumenical theology arose in opposition to the polemical theology (→ Polemics) that justifies division and as a theoretical component of the → ecumenical movement (→ Denomination 3.2). It takes place on various theoretical levels and under the aegis of various institutions. Thus we find the Ecumenical Institute of Bossey, the Ecumenical College of the → World Council of Churches and the University of Geneva, and various ecumenical institutes and chairs at universities (e.g., Heidelberg, Bonn, Bochum). The Dutch theological faculties together support the Ecumenical Institute in Utrecht. Many denominations (Roman Catholics, Anglicans, Presbyterians, and Methodists) are united in supporting the Irish School of Ecumenics at Dublin. The Institute for Ecumenical Research at Strasbourg is a foundation of the → Lutheran World Federation, the → Evangelical Alliance has a similar institute at Bensheim, and the Roman Catholic University of Lublin set up an Ecumenical Institute in 1983. In the United States several denominations participate in the Washington Institute of Ecumenics, and the larger church councils also have study programs. In Latin America the churches support the Departamento Ecuménico de Investigación in Costa Rica.

In these programs research and teaching supplement the classic academic theological courses. Along with such common ecumenical themes as the ministry (→ Offices, Ecclesiastical), the → sacraments, and → authority in the church, work is increasingly being done on social and political topics. As the study of mission interacts with that of religion, dialogue with the → religions also plays a part (esp. in the departments of religion in U.S. universities). The breadth of meaning of the term "ecumenical" (→ Oikoumene) is naturally reflected in the diversity of topics addressed in ecumenical theology. In what follows we consider ecumenical theology only as specific methodological reflection on the resolving of ecumenical conflicts.

2. Tasks and Concepts

The most important issue is whether controversial positions are truly controversial in the light of modern exegetical (→ Exegesis, Biblical) and systematic research. Unity in faith is not necessarily the same as unity in doctrinal formulation. Dogmatic → hermeneutics studies the motifs in the development of doctrine, its structure, and possible shifts of struc-

ture. The older method of comparative dogmatics built on the homogeneity of language and concepts and did not reckon with the possible convergence of controversial theological concepts as they are translated into other linguistic structures (→ Language). E. Schlink (1903-84) wrote his great ecumenical dogmatics from this angle and made fruitful application to many ecumenical themes.

G. Lindbeck enlarged this perspective in a promising way for → ecumenical dialogue by distinguishing dogmatic statements as *propositional truths* (which can be compared materially and positionally) from dogmatic statements as *regulative theories* (which control the → identity and life of a given confessional group). This cultural-linguistic method, which thus takes into account sociological criteria (→ Sociology), yields remarkable results, even with such classic ecumenical problems as those posed by → Chalcedon, → Mariology (§1), and papal → infallibility.

A further task of ecumenical theology is to investigate controversies that provisionally cannot be bridged by either of the above methods. The aim now is to fix their place in the total life of faith in such a manner that they no longer justify the separation of the churches. On the Roman Catholic side H. Fries and K. → Rahner published their theses under the title *Unity of the Churches: An Actual Possibility* (1983). On the common basis of Scripture (→ Canon) and the creed (→ Confession of Faith), the rule that would make further conversation possible is that no church may say definitively what is binding → dogma in another church. Proposals were also made to overcome remaining obstacles (e.g., recognition of ministries and the church's infallible teaching office). On the Protestant side E. Herms doubted any real possibility of reunion in view of a basic difference in ecclesiology, and O. Cullmann made a plea for unity through diversity on the basis of Paul's doctrine of charismata.

Ecumenical theology also has the task of reflecting continuously on the meaning of church → unity as the goal of the ecumenical movement (→ Denomination 3). There is insufficient clarity or agreement, however, as to the content of the term. Only the Roman Catholic conception of ecumenical theology has a clear understanding, namely, that the unity that is sought is institutional reunion with the visible → Roman Catholic Church. This unity does not rule out diversity, for example, in liturgical forms. In every other form of ecumenical theology, discussion of the models of unity is incomplete. One may ask whether ecumenical discussion is not wrong to let itself be governed too much by the ideal of unity. Should it not perhaps replace the paradigm of unity by that of → koinonia, of communion, notwithstanding the remaining differences?

The term "theology" itself is controversial as well. As an academic discipline, it tends to create divisions rather than heal them. → Third World theologies orient themselves more to contextual experiences than to the dogmatic tradition of the universal church (→ Contextual Theology). Could we not say that → spirituality, joint prayer, singing, believing, serving, eating, and conviviality are more important than common theorizing? If so, ecumenical theology might then be the dialogue of different contextual theologies (→ Culture and Christianity 4; Ecumenical Association of Third World Theologians). In the process one need not fear the loss of Christian identity that the dogmatic tradition of the universal church has seen it as its task to protect. If with such relations there is a weakening of the confessional identity that has thus far been the starting point of all → ecumenical dialogue (→ Confession of Faith 5), a new ecumenical theology might forge its content out of reflection on the Christian faith of specific individuals in new historical circumstances. In place of the ecumenical problem of a true and visible church, we would then be inquiring into the universally intended message of Jesus as it shows, proves, and verifies itself in human faith and action at specific times and places (E. Fahlbusch). Ecumenical theology would not then be an isolated discipline but would again be part of general theological reflection on the truth that unites (see 1.1). With regard to its future, it would also be conceivable only as *intercultural* theology (→ Theology of Religions).

Within the theoretical work of ecumenical theology, nontheological and nontheoretical factors in continuing divisions of the churches are also important. The theoretical achievement of a convergence or doctrinal consensus in no way guarantees the achievement of church unity. The collusion theory of P. Lengsfeld (which highlights the interplay of various factors) tries to take these nontheoretical factors into theoretical account. It thus enlarges considerably the traditional field of work in ecumenical theology.

3. Possibilities and Limits

With enlargement, however, the limits of the possibilities of ecumenical theology also come to light. They are a result of the shifting place of the subject. They are also technical. The agencies change frequently or are not readily identifiable in the church. Their findings, which are often experimental, are not binding. What has been achieved may not be remembered. Typical ecumenical "conference theology" is in many cases a product of compromise. It lacks the unifying force of a single author or an authoritative church body.

Nevertheless, the fact that ecumenical theology goes on is more important than the reaching of a fixed → consensus that still awaits reception. In the long run, ecumenical theology has the same task as all theology, namely, that of building up local → congregations in their constantly changing historical, cultural, and social conditions.

Bibliography: O. CULLMANN, *Unity through Diversity: Its Foundation, and a Contribution to the Discussion concerning the Possibilities of Its Actualization* (Philadelphia, 1988) • G. R. EVANS, *Method in Ecumenical Theology: The Lessons So Far* (Cambridge, 1996) • H. FRIES and K. RAHNER, *Unity of the Churches: An Actual Possibility* (Philadelphia, 1983) • A. GEENSE, "Teaching Systematic Theology Ecumenically," *The Teaching of Ecumenics* (ed. S. Amirtham; Geneva, 1987) 54-68 • R. JENSON, *Unbaptized God: The Basic Flaw in Ecumenical Theology* (Minneapolis, 1992) • P. LENGSFELD, *Ökumenische Theologie* (Stuttgart, 1980) • G. LINDBECK, *The Nature of Doctrine: Religion and Theology in a Postliberal Age* (Philadelphia, 1984) • C. LINK, U. LUZ, and L. VISCHER, *Sie aber hielten fest an die Gemeinschaft. Einheit der Kirche als Prozeß im Neuen Testament und heute* (Zurich, 1988) • K. RAISER, *Ecumenism in Transition: A Paradigm Shift for the Ecumenical Movement?* (Geneva, 1991) • E. SCHLINK, *Ökumenische Dogmatik* (Göttingen, 1983) • R. SLENCZKA, "Dogma und Kircheneinheit," *HDThG* 3.426-603 • WORLD COUNCIL OF CHURCHES, *A Treasure in Earthen Vessels: An Instrument for an Ecumenical Reflection on Hermeneutics* (Geneva, 1998).

ADRIAAN GEENSE†

4. Comparative Study of Denominations

4.1. *Field and Task*

The comparative study of → denominations is an area of theology belonging partly to church history and partly to → systematic theology. It covers the doctrine and life of the various Christian churches, groups, and movements and their relation to one another. F. Kattenbusch (1851-1935), whose *Lehrbuch der vergleichenden Confessionskunde* (Textbook of the comparative study of denominations, 1892) popularized the concept, described the task of this discipline as being to present and compare present-day churches as vital historic entities along with their many unconscious factors. Under the influence of the → ecumenical movement, its aim is to promote understanding among separated churches by better acquaintance with similarities and differences in their life and teaching.

4.2. History

The history of the study reflects the shifting understanding of denominational relations, theological controversies and trends in the churches' histories, and relevant links to political events and sociocultural changes. In modern church history, it begins with the conditions of the 16th-century divisions resulting from the → Reformation, when the justification and form of competing denominational churches, called religious or church parties up to the 18th century, raised the question of the true church and the legitimacy of the church bodies that had developed. At first it was a matter of → polemics as churches pressed their own claims and condemned or tried to convince others; a famous example is French archbishop Jacques B. Bossuet's *Exposition de la doctrine de l'église catholique sur les matières de controverse* (Exposition of the doctrine of the Catholic Church on controversial subjects, 1680).

→ Spiritualist, → pietistic, and → evangelical movements of the 17th century stressed the spiritual unity of Christians and consequently deemphasized the differences between the various Christian denominations. Gottfried Arnold's *Unparteiische Kirchen- und Ketzerhistorie* (Nonpartisan history of churches and sects, 1699), for example, attempted to present a common Christian history, stressing the spirituality that united believers. This view could also be expressed in some visionary schemes for Christian unity, for instance, that of the Moravian organizer Count N. L. von → Zinzendorf. Combined with the → Enlightenment's skepticism regarding traditional beliefs, the culture of the late 17th century and the 18th century saw the rise of various forms of religious → toleration, represented, for instance, in the British Act of Toleration of 1689, which allowed for toleration of dissenting Protestants under certain controlled conditions.

Despite these irenic moves, however, the literature comparing denominational teachings, through the early 20th century, was overwhelmingly directed toward demonstrating the truth of a particular denominational tradition over against others, and this literature often involved significant distortions of the teachings and practices of other churches. This denominationally conservative emphasis was bolstered in the 19th century by a series of European and American movements emphasizing traditional teachings against the encroachments of modernity

(specifically, the → Oxford or Tractarian movement in Britain, the "New Lutheranism" and "Old Lutheran" churches of Prussia, and the "Mercersburg theology" among Reformed Christians in the United States). The 19th-century literature of "comparative symbolics" (comparing the historic teachings of Christian traditions) generally held this defensive character and was particularly important among Lutherans, an example of such literature in English being Charles Augustus Briggs's *Theological Symbolics* (1914).

The 20th-century ecumenical movement brought about a significantly renewed commitment to the mutual understanding of Christian traditions. The → Faith and Order movement, in particular, sought "to draw churches out of isolation into conference"; a central element in their conferring together, through the decade of the 1950s, was a mutual study and understanding of each other's denominational teachings and practices. From the time of the Lund meeting of Faith and Order in 1952, however, it was recognized that the work of "comparative ecclesiologies" alone could not lead to a workable basis for the visible unity of the churches. Since → Vatican II and the intensifying of bilateral and multilateral → dialogue between the churches, the dominant concern has been for an ecumenical theology. The task of comparative studies, however, remains important as a groundwork for proposals for deeper unity and also as an initial step in engaging new ecumenical partners (e.g., in bringing → Pentecostal Christians into dialogue with the ecumenical movement).

Bibliography: T. A. CAMPBELL, *Christian Confessions: A Historical Introduction* (Louisville, Ky., 1996) • E. CLARK, *The Small Sects in America* (rev. ed.; Nashville, 1965; orig. pub., 1937) • E. FAHLBUSCH, *Einheit der Kirche–eine kritische Betrachtung des ökumenischen Dialogs* (Munich, 1983) • *HÖ* • F. MEAD and S. S. HILL, *Handbook of Denominations in the United States* (10th ed.; Nashville, 1995) • J. G. MELTON, ed., *Encyclopedia of American Religions* (6th ed.; Detroit, 1999) • A. C. PIEPKORN, *Profiles in Belief: The Religious Bodies of the United States and Canada* (4 vols.; New York, 1977-79) • *YACC.*

TED A. CAMPBELL

Ecumenicity → Local Ecumenism

Ecumenism, Ecumenical Movement

The concept "ecumenism" has had different meanings over the history of the church. It has become firmly attached now to the modern movement, begun in 1910 in Edinburgh, concerned with the unity of Christians for the sake of the mission of the church to the world. At the turn of the 21st century, both "ecumenism" and "ecumenical movement" refer primarily to the multidimensional movement of churches and Christians whose goal is both the visi- ble → unity of the churches and an integration of mission, service, and renewal.

1. Concept

1.1. *Early and Biblical Usage*

The root of "ecumenism" derives from Gk. *oikoumenē*, a passive participle of *oikeō*, "inhabit." As early as the fifth century B.C. the participle was used to designate the inhabited world. The word occurs in the Septuagint, especially in the Psalms, where it means "world" or "earth." The word is not common in the NT, where it most often has a secular meaning (e.g., referring to the whole world [Matt. 24:14] or the Roman Empire [Luke 2:1]). Hebrews connects *oikoumenē* with eschatology (2:5); in Revelation it denotes the sphere of the devil's working (12:9).

1.2. *Usage in Church History*

In early patristic literature the word *oikoumenē* is employed sometimes in the sense "world" (*1 Clem.* 60:1), at other times in the sense "empire" (Theodoret of Cyrrhus, *Comm. Isa.* 13.9.) In the second century it was used for the first time in connection with the church (*Mart. Pol.* 5.1). The word first became part of official ecclesiastical usage when the Council of Constantinople (381) referred to the Council of → Nicaea (325) as an ecumenical synod. Here "ecumenical" has the special meaning of that which is accepted as authoritative and universally valid; a council is ecumenical when it is received as speaking on behalf of the whole church.

During the sixth century the word "ecumenical" was at the center of heated debates and conflicts between Rome and Constantinople as the See of Constantinople began to claim exclusive use of the title "ecumenical patriarch." By this time "ecumenical" was also being applied to three writers and theologians — Basil the Great, Gregory Nazianzus, and John → Chrysostom, the so-called ecumenical doctors of the church. Their writings were accepted as a norm and standard for the entire church.

With the fall of the Byzantine Empire in the 15th century, the word "ecumenical" lost all secular political accents. It continued only in the ecclesiastical vocabulary. The → *oikoumenē* is the universal → church, conveying what is universal, valid, and authoritative for the whole church.

In the 16th century a new application of the word appeared. For the first time the phrase "catholic and ecumenical" was used (by Nikolaus Selnecker, a professor of theology in Leipzig) to describe the → Apostles', → Nicene, and → Athanasian Creeds. This terminology is utilized in the Book of Concord of 1580, where these three creeds appear under the designation *triasymbola catholica et oecumenica.*

In the 17th and 18th centuries the word "ecumenical" was employed in relation to councils, creeds, and the patriarch of Constantinople. In the 19th century the word again took on a new accent. In efforts to establish the Evangelical Alliance in 1846 (→ World Evangelical Fellowship), "ecumenical" was used to indicate an attitude rather than a fact, namely, the sense of belonging to the worldwide unity of the church of Jesus Christ, a community that transcends national and confessional limits. By the end of the 19th century, the word sometimes conveyed an awareness of the essential unity, in spite of divisions, of the "church universal."

In the 20th century, and especially through the thought of Nathan Söderblom, the meaning became firmly fixed as that which covers the life of the church as a whole. By 1920 there were frequent references to "ecumenical" as representing the whole church of Christ. The word was becoming irrevocably attached to the movement, begun in Edinburgh in 1910, of churches toward unity. At the Oxford Conference on → Life and Work, in 1937, it was stated, "The term 'ecumenical' refers to the expression within history of the given unity of the Church. The thought and action of the Church are ecumenical, in so far as they attempt to realize the *una sancta,* the fellowship of Christians who acknowledge the one Lord."

In 1951 the Central Committee of the → World Council of Churches defined "ecumenical" as describing everything that relates to "the whole task of the whole church to bring the Gospel to the whole world. It therefore covers equally the missionary movement and the movement toward unity."

The various nuances of "ecumenism" are noted in the introduction to the *Dictionary of the Ecumenical Movement:* ecumenism as a search for unity in the truth found in Jesus; as a search for the will of God in every area of life and work; as a search to discern, proclaim, and participate in the triune God's purpose for humankind; and as the mission of God to the world. In contemporary literature and thought, "ecumenism" and "ecumenical movement" refer to a multidimensional movement, including mission, social concerns, and ethical questions, whose center and goal is the unity of the churches. This movement has never been a unified and homogeneous phenomenon, for it is always embedded in the changing contexts of history.

1.3. *Common Basis*

All ecumenical thought and action is founded on the fundamental conviction that the message of the NT, in continuity with themes in the Hebrew Scriptures, is that unity belongs to the nature of the church. The unity of the church is a matter of Christian faith and confession, and not mere utility (Eph. 4:15). Thus the church in its unity is indestructible. This insight is part of Christian faith and confession. The unity of the church is viewed as God's gift. Every effort for Christian unity presupposes an essential unity of the church that already exists. The task of ecumenism, then, is to allow this God-given unity to become visible. Other terminology besides visibility has been used in ecumenical thought, but the intention is the same: to preserve the distinction between God's action as a gift and human action as response, the difference between the unity given and the unity sought.

1.4. *Differing Interpretations*
1.4.1. *Anglican Communion*

The Anglican understanding of ecumenism is found in the Chicago-Lambeth Quadrilateral, developed by W. R. Huntington in 1870 and adopted by the Lambeth Conference of 1888 (→ Anglican Communion 4.1) in a slightly modified form. The unity of the church is to be based on the Holy Scriptures, the Apostles' and Nicene Creeds, the two sacraments of → baptism and the Lord's Supper (→ Eucharist, esp. 3.3), and the historic episcopate, locally adapted (→ Bishop, Episcopate; Episcopacy). The last point, which was largely the result of developments within Anglicanism, has assumed a central position in all ecumenical efforts involving Anglican churches.

1.4.2. *Free Churches*

In their ecumenical understanding → free churches have stressed the personal → faith of individual Christians, the spiritual and free nature of the church, the priesthood of all believers in local congregations, and an unwillingness to see Christian unity merely in terms of common → church orders and structures or through theological → consensus. For these churches the purpose of ecumenism is to glorify Christ together in witness and service.

1.4.3. *Orthodox Church*

In 1920 the Church of Constantinople issued an encyclical inviting "all the churches of Christ everywhere" to form a league of churches. Orthodox participation in ecumenical efforts since that time has been marked by certain views: the unity of the church was lost because churches have not maintained the → tradition of the ancient and undivided church, which includes the apostolic faith, sacramental life, and the ministry of the episcopate. These constitutive elements coming from the early and undivided church are an indivisible whole. Only in the → Orthodox Church is this tradition preserved. Orthodoxy rejects the notion of an equality of → confessions. Unity among churches thus cannot simply be the result of theological agreement, but it must be lived out in → mystery and tradition as found in Orthodoxy.

1.4.4. *Churches of the Reformation*

The churches arising from the → Reformation can relate their ecumenical efforts to basic assertions about unity that come from their own origins in the 16th century, including the → Augsburg Confession (art. 7) and the Second → Helvetic Confession (art. 17). According to these documents, two elements are particularly important for unity: agreement in the proclamation of the → gospel, and freedom in ecclesiastical customs and traditions. The fundamental focus of unity is the church's public proclamation of the gospel through → Word and → sacrament. There is therefore need for agreement in the → proclamation of the faith. This consensus is doctrinal and must be formulated in a binding manner. Along with this insistence is an equal stress on freedom in ecclesiastical customs and traditions; the unity of the church is not dependent on uniformity of ceremonies or rites. For these Reformation churches, communion in ecclesiastical office cannot be a matter of indifference, but the question of that communion is secondary to agreement and sharing in the proclamation of the gospel in Word and sacrament.

1.4.5. *Roman Catholic Church*

Apart from the participation of individual members, the → Roman Catholic Church did not play any significant role in the ecumenical movement before 1960. In 1928 Pius XI issued the encyclical *Mortalium animos,* which rejected Roman Catholic involvement in the ecumenical movement. This situation changed with the Second → Vatican Council and the promulgation in 1964 of the Dogmatic Constitution on the Church *(Lumen gentium)* and the Decree on Ecumenism *(Unitatis redintegratio).*

The concept of unity is placed by Roman Catholicism in a Trinitarian and → salvation-history framework with a strong stress on the work of the → Holy Spirit, who is the principle of the church's unity. Two constitutive elements for the unity of the church coincide with Anglican and Reformation views: agreement in the true faith and in the administration of the sacraments. The Roman Catholic position, like the Anglican, also explicitly includes the ministry and specifically the office of bishops. Bishops have a ministry for communion, and they are the visible source and foundation of unity for their local churches. From this unifying role of bishops the role of the papal office for the unity of the

church must be understood (→ Pope, Papacy). The bishop of Rome belongs to the college of bishops and, as its head, guarantees its indivisibility. For Roman Catholic thought the papacy, viewed as a continuation of the Petrine office, together with the episcopate is essential for the church's unity. In the Catholic view, all necessary bonds of visible communion are completely present in the Roman Catholic Church. *Unitatis redintegratio* indicates that this unity "subsists" *(subsistit)* in the Catholic Church. Yet the council wished by its Constitution on the Church and its Decree on Ecumenism to indicate that many important elements for the unity of the church exist in other Christian communities.

In 1995 John Paul II issued his encyclical *Ut unum sint.* For the first time a papal document addressed the ecumenical movement in a positive and supportive manner, revealing commitment to → ecumenical dialogue even on such topics as the papal office itself.

Two documents released in September 2000 by the Congregation for the Doctrine of the Faith reflect the ongoing debate within the Roman Catholic Church about its relation to the ecumenical movement. It remains to be seen how much influence such documents will have, in light of the commitments of the Second Vatican Council and *Ut unum sint.*

1.5. *Goal*

The goal of ecumenism is the communion of all who believe in Christ — that is, the unity of Christians. The ecumenical movement is thus essentially a movement toward Christian unity, although not a movement of ecclesiastical self-centeredness. The ecumenical movement has from its earliest days been concerned with common service in response to war, poverty, and social injustice, common witness in mission and evangelism, and common renewal of the churches.

This integration of unity, service, mission, and renewal within one movement has not always been easy. Tensions and disputes have often arisen within the ecumenical movement concerning the place and relative weight of these several components, disagreements that continue into the present. Yet at the same time there has been the insistence that the ecumenical movement is one, that it calls all Christians to visible unity, variously understood, and that it calls renewed Christians and churches to common mission and service in God's creation.

1.6. *Relation to Interfaith Efforts*

In view of the general understanding of ecumenism presented here, a distinction should be made between ecumenism as an enterprise among Christians and interfaith efforts, which seek better understanding and cooperation between the major world religions. Both efforts are important, but they are distinct. The term "interreligious ecumenism" is occasionally used, but it is an imprecise collective phrase, covering relations between various religions, mutual efforts at joint learning, and programs of practical cooperation. Its focus is on the relation between religions and not on any notion of unity.

1.7. Forms

Ecumenism exists at global, regional, and local levels. It is practiced in a variety of forms: in councils of churches; in bilateral conversations (dialogues) between two churches; in multilateral theological conversations among several churches or confessions; as spiritual ecumenism, where Christians join in an appropriate manner in common prayer and worship, especially for the unity of the church; and in engagement with the world, sometimes referred to as secular ecumenism, where there is a participation of Christians for the reconciliation and renewal of humanity.

2. History

Most authorities identify the beginnings of ecumenism with the ecumenical movement of the last hundred years. R. Rouse and S. Neill, however, begin their account of the movement's history in 1517. It is clear, however, that consciousness of the unity of the church antedates both 1910 and 1517. In fact, it can be traced back to the NT church itself.

2.1. NT and the Early Church

The texts of the NT speak about the church and its unity in specific historical situations. Rather than offering one timeless picture of the church, they present a number of ecclesiastical images. The Gospels portray → Jesus making fellowship *(koinōnia)* a reality among those who followed him. Other texts offer the picture of a fellowship in the Holy Spirit in the confession of Jesus the Christ, a fellowship in worship and love. The rule of Christ under the Spirit is the source of unity, but it is a unity that assumes diversity. Tensions and differences, even contradictions, are evident in the NT with its different theologies; the NT nevertheless proclaims one church, a fellowship of local churches with a mutual recognition of confession, baptism, and the Lord's Supper (→ Confession of Faith).

Unity is at the center of the thought and theology of the apostle → Paul. Closely connecting the unity of the church with → Christology, Paul employs unitary images such as "the people of God," "the temple of God," and "the body of Christ." He also recognized much diversity that did not threaten the fundamental unity of the church. Organizational patterns or differing Christological formulations did not affect this unity. The Gospel of Mark, although not using the word *ekklēsia* (church), presents a view of the true community of the elect. The Gospel of Matthew reflects an ecclesiology of the body of the elect versus the nonelect; the unity of the former is in constant danger. Both the Gospel of Luke and Acts give considerable attention to the unity of the church (esp. Acts 2; 4; 15). Here is presented an idyllic situation of correct belief, → community of goods, and unity of heart and soul. The Johannine literature is much interested in unity (e.g., John 17). In this gospel, unity with Christ leads to unity of believers; unity of the latter reproduces the unity of believers with the Father and the Son.

With its considerable diversity the NT maintains a remarkable unanimity on many aspects of unity. The unity of the church is not merely a desirable feature of the life of the church but is a condition of the church's very existence. This unity derives from its one Lord. The NT does not know → denominations or opposing churches; it recognizes diversity, but not divisions. Its church knows tensions and disputes, but divisions and large numbers of Christians separated from fellowship with one another are not to be found.

The unity and diversity of the church affirmed in Scripture was largely maintained for centuries, in spite of controversy and theological dispute. In the second century → Irenaeus stressed unity as a unity of teaching, or orthodoxy. In the fourth century the unity of the church received a new dimension when Christianity became the state religion of the Roman Empire. The ecumenical councils of → Nicaea (325), Constantinople (381), → Ephesus (431), and → Chalcedon (451) demanded universal recognition with a definition of belief. The earlier unity maintained by the first four councils was broken after the Council of Chalcedon in 451, when churches that did not accept this council's Christological formulations established themselves in Egypt and Syria. By the fifth century the patriarchal structure formed an organizational principle of unity for the churches accepting the decisions of Chalcedon.

Another break in unity occurred in 1054 between the Latin patriarch and the Eastern patriarchates (→ Heresies and Schisms 3). Cultural and political as well as theological factors were the cause of this rupture, and one of its results was the creation of two views of unity. In Eastern Orthodoxy the patriarchal model with sister → autocephalous churches prevailed, while in the West Roman primacy was so strengthened that the Roman Catholic

Church came to understand itself as the universal church of Christ, from which the Eastern churches had separated themselves.

2.2. Medieval Church

As the result of the Fourth Crusade, a Latin kingdom (ultimately short-lived) was established in Constantinople in 1204 with a Latin patriarch. This development seriously damaged relationships between the Eastern and Western churches. The Second Council of Lyons (1274), greatly motivated by political concerns, sought to bring about a union between the Greek and Roman churches. The Greek legates at the council generally accepted the demands of the Roman church, but the union achieved by the council was ephemeral, lasting only 15 years. The Council of Florence (1438-ca. 1445) was a continuation of councils that had met earlier in Basel and then in Ferrara. In 1439 it issued the Union of Florence, a statement with obvious political motivations. Based on a principle of unity in faith with a diversity of liturgical rites, this document sought to bring about a union between the Greek and Roman churches, and between Rome and the Chaldeans, Maronites, and Syrians. None of these unions was long-lasting. Popular reaction in Constantinople against such a union with the Roman church was strong. When Constantinople fell in 1453, the union of Eastern and Western churches ended.

In the medieval period the Western church largely maintained its unity through the ever-increasing primacy of the bishop of Rome, by the persecution of heretics, and by active support of emerging civil states. Tensions were present in Western Christianity; popular figures started movements of renewal, and there were calls for a council to renew the church. Despite various pressures, however, the Western church remained intact until the 16th century.

2.3. The Reformation

Before the 16th century, groups such as the English Lollards, originally followers of John → Wycliffe, and the → Hussites, disciples of John → Hus, attacked the hierarchical structure of the Western church, clerical → celibacy, the doctrine of transubstantiation, and the practice of → indulgences. They never succeeded in accomplishing a reformation of the church, but in many ways they set the context for the 16th-century division of the Western church.

Martin → Luther and other reformers like Ulrich → Zwingli, Martin → Bucer, and Guillaume Farel sought to call the church of their day to an evangelical reform. Luther and his followers were clear that their intention was neither to establish a new church

nor to divide the Western church. Contrary to their purpose, however, their efforts at reform resulted in divisions in the church of the West. Political, economic, and social factors were clearly involved in the debates. Luther's appearance at the Diet in Worms in 1521 brought no agreement. The attempt at the Diet in Augsburg in 1530 to preserve the unity of the church did not succeed. The discussions at Regensburg in 1541 and the Augsburg Interim of 1548, when, with the protection of the emperor and princes, theologians of the Roman and Reformation sides sought to articulate a common basic position of faith, did not bring success. The Peace of Augsburg (1555; → Augsburg, Peace of) acknowledged the existence of Catholicism and → Lutheranism, providing that in each land subjects should follow the faith of their ruler (→ Cuius regio eius religio).

As these events were unfolding, confessions being produced by Lutheran and other reformers (e.g., the Book of Concord, 1580) stressed that the teaching of the reformers should not be conceived as the dogma of a new church but simply as the correct teaching of the one, holy, catholic, and apostolic church, to which the reformers belonged. These views were found also in the writings of John → Calvin, expressed through several editions of his *Institutes of the Christian Religion* (1536 to 1559), and in writings of the leaders of the English Reformation. Such commitments were less true of Anabaptist and spiritualistic groups, the so-called left wing of the Reformation.

In spite of the desires of leading reformers, the unity of the Western church was now split. Four main groups arose from the Reformation: Lutherans, mainly in Germany and the Nordic countries; Reformed (→ Reformed and Presbyterian Churches), mainly in Switzerland, Germany, and Great Britain, where they were known as Presbyterians and → Congregationalists; Anglicans, originally in Great Britain, but eventually a worldwide communion; and → Anabaptists and spiritualistic groups, mainly in Germany, England, and the Low Countries. All these groups at various times settled in North America, where further divisions among the churches resulted in numerous independent denominations. In the course of mission activities in the 19th century, these groups established churches in Africa and Asia.

2.4. Sixteenth–Eighteenth Centuries

At the close of the 16th century, Eastern Christianity was split between Chalcedonian (Orthodox, or Eastern Orthodox) and non-Chalcedonian (→ Oriental Orthodox) churches; Western Christianity was divided among the Roman Catholic Church and various Protestant groups and churches.

In the 17th century a part of the Russian Orthodox Church refused to accept the liturgical reforms of Patriarch Nikon. Called → Old Believers, they were → excommunicated in 1667. In the next century a new schism occurred in the Roman Catholic Church when the church of Utrecht refused to accept the condemnation of Jansenism and separated from Rome. Late in the 18th century the Anglican Church experienced a break when, under John → Wesley (though against his express wish), → Methodism was born as a separate denomination.

During the 17th and 18th centuries many individual Christians had a vision of peace or even unity among the churches, although there were no official conversations between them. Francis de Sales developed a dialogue with Gerard Wolter von Meulen, a Lutheran from Loccum. Individuals such as C. R. de Spinola, G. W. Molanus, G. W. Leibniz, and J.-B. Bossuet were concerned with efforts for unity. The influence of → humanism was felt in the thought of Georg Calixtus, who stressed recognition of the "consensus of the first five centuries" (consensus quinquesaecularis). An evangelical-biblical humanism concentrated on "in essentials, unity; in nonessentials, liberty; in all things, charity" — an irenic expression originating with the 17th-century Lutheran scholar Peter Meiderlin. Other individuals working for unity included the English Benedictine John Barnes, Obadiah Walker of Oxford, the French Benedictine Leandrede Saint Martin, and the Italian Gregorio Panzani. In the 17th century, ecumenism was almost exclusively an issue of unity in doctrine. An exception was the left wing of the Reformation with its stress on Christian unity as a given, accompanied necessarily by → conversion (§1) and genuine → discipleship.

In the 18th century the → Enlightenment and → Pietism tended to relativize the confessionalism prevalent in the previous century. The Enlightenment taught that all differences are merely historical; Pietism, that doctrine is not decisive, especially in comparison to what can be experienced and what is practical.

William Wake, archbishop of Canterbury, corresponded with theologian L. E. Dupin of the Sorbonne with a view to a union between the Anglican and Gallican churches. Wake wished to distinguish between fundamentals and nonfundamentals. Count Nicolaus Ludwig von → Zinzendorf was an ardent missionary of Pietism and, in contact with Cardinal de Noailles of Paris, sought to promote the unity of the church. The last half of the 18th century witnessed a revival of → preaching. This movement, the evangelical awakening, stressed personal conver-

sion and missionary enthusiasm. It also brought an awareness of the divisions among the churches.

2.5. Nineteenth Century

At the start of the 19th century Christianity was split both by confessions and by many national churches that experienced little fellowship together. In theological thought there was much polemic and self-affirmation. The Roman Catholic Church led its own life as a global church, making no efforts for church unity with the Orthodox churches. Protestant churches also tended to live only within their own sphere.

The 19th-century missionary movement gave the churches their first sense of global consciousness. As a result of a growing internationalism, as well as of the pressures of an increasingly secular environment, the churches gained an ecumenical perspective. One effect of such internationalism was the establishment of world conferences and organizations, a development that influenced the churches in the coming years.

The missionary enterprise had resulted in the founding of the British and Foreign Bible Society in 1804, an agency that brought together Protestants, Roman Catholics, and Orthodox in its work. In 1805 the Baptist missionary William Carey proposed the calling of a missionary conference of all denominations, to meet in 1810. The German Christian Fellowship at Basel developed numerous contacts in the churches. In 1846 the Evangelical Alliance was formed in London. This alliance, comprising persons from 52 different churches, was the only ecumenical organization that arose out of the evangelical revival of the 19th century. About this time the → Young Men's Christian Association (1844) and the → Young Women's Christian Association (1854) were established. Anglicans, Roman Catholics, and Orthodox Christians joined in London in the foundation of the Association for the Promotion of the Union of Christendom (1857). In 1867 the Anglican Communion began to hold its Lambeth Conferences, and in 1875 the → World Alliance of Reformed Churches came into existence, followed in 1881 by the Ecumenical Methodist Conferences and the Union of Utrecht, and in 1891 by the International Congregational Council. In 1895 John R. Mott founded the → World Student Christian Federation, an organization where future leaders in the ecumenical movement would form friendships and develop common commitments and agendas.

During this century such individuals as Alexander Campbell of the Disciples of Christ, the Lutheran Samuel Schmucker, the Episcopalian William Reed Huntington, and later the Congregationalist Elias B. Sanford pioneered ecumenical thinking, especially in North America, paving the way to the next century.

2.6. Twentieth Century

As the 20th century opened, there were increasing signs that the isolation and sectarianism of the churches were coming to an end. Secular influences and the development of, and reflection about, → mission and global responsibility influenced the churches. In 1905 both the Baptist World Congress and the Federal Council of Churches in the United States were formed. In 1908 Paul Wattson, an Episcopalian clergyman who later became Roman Catholic, proposed a Week of Prayer for Christian Unity, which has persisted as a major ecumenical influence in the churches.

2.6.1. World Missionary Conference (Edinburgh, 1910)

The World Missionary Conference, held in Edinburgh in 1910, is usually described as the beginning of the modern ecumenical movement. In a real sense this claim is true, but the conference must also be seen in perspective as summing up and bringing into focus the movement throughout the 19th century for uniting Christians to share the gospel with the world. The two key figures at Edinburgh were John R. Mott and Joseph H. Oldham, both products of the student Christian movement. The Edinburgh Conference was a consultative gathering, made up of members of Protestant mission societies; Orthodox and Roman Catholics were not present. Still, Edinburgh marked a new sense of fellowship among Christians, trained future leaders of the ecumenical movement, and contributed to future ecumenical work.

The conference emphasized enduring ecumenical concerns: the evangelization of the world, where a divided and competing Christianity was a great hindrance; a commitment to → peace and social justice; and a specific inner-ecclesiastical motive — to seek the unity of the church because, on the basis of a confession of faith, the church is essentially one. The conference established continuation committees, and its momentum was not lost.

2.6.2. 1910-48

The ecumenical movement after the Edinburgh Conference developed along four main lines.

2.6.2.1. Mission. In 1920 an international mission conference was held in Crans, Switzerland, and in the next year Mott and Oldham presided at the founding of the → International Missionary Council (IMC), which was designed to promote study, coordination, and organization for mission. The council held enlarged meetings at Jerusalem in 1928, where the main concern was → secularization, and at Tambaram (Madras) in 1938, where the relation of Christianity and world religions was discussed. In 1946 the IMC and the Provisional Committee of the World Council of Churches together established the → Commission for Churches on International Affairs. At the 1947 meeting of the IMC in Whitby, Ontario, older and younger churches affirmed their partnership together and summed up their work in the slogan "One World, One Christ." In 1948, at the inauguration of the World Council of Churches (WCC), the IMC was in fraternal association.

In 1952 the IMC met in Willingen, Germany, under the theme "Mission under the Cross." In 1958 the council decided to integrate into the WCC as its Division for World Mission and Evangelism, a shift that took place in 1961 at the New Delhi assembly.

2.6.2.2. Peace. As a result of the Edinburgh Conference, an international group of Protestants assembled in 1914 in Constance to form the World Alliance for Promoting International Friendship. One year later the name was changed to World Alliance for Promoting International Friendship through the Churches. In 1919 several members of the World Alliance created the → International Fellowship of Reconciliation, a group that included Roman Catholics. The World Alliance held a peace conference in Prague in 1928 and subsequently worked closely with the Life and Work movement, but it decided in 1938 that it wished to remain a distinct movement. The alliance was dissolved in 1948 with the establishment of the WCC; its concerns were taken up in a new organization founded that same year, the World Alliance for International Friendship through Religion.

2.6.2.3. Life and Work. The idea of establishing a worldwide movement of churches to work for peace and justice was discussed before 1914, with World War I heightening interest in such a movement. With Archbishop Nathan Söderblom of Sweden a leading figure, a preparatory conference was held in Geneva in 1920. It aimed to help work for a just and lasting peace and to formulate a Christian response to the postwar economic, social, and moral issues.

The first Life and Work conference met in Stockholm in 1925, with representation by the Orthodox, but not by Roman Catholics. The conference, which deliberately avoided addressing theological issues, was deeply divided about how to relate Christian hope to the churches' responsibility for the world. A continuation committee from the conference, led by Bishop G. K. A. Bell of the Church of England, became a permanent body in 1930. It sponsored the

Second Life and Work Conference, held in Oxford in 1937. The conference report on its theme, "Church, Community, and State," represents the 20th century's first theologically formulated statement on the Christian task in the modern world.

The Life and Work movement became a dynamic element in the formation of the new WCC. It contributed contemporary ecumenical concerns on such topics as international relations, → racism, economic justice, human → rights, and → religious liberty.

2.6.2.4. *Faith and Order.* While no disputed theological questions were allowed at Edinburgh in 1910, it was even then acknowledged that the true unity of the church would require doctrinal agreement on the faith and ordering of the church. Two American Episcopalians — Bishop Charles H. Brent and layman Robert Gardener — promoted the idea of a world conference, the prerequisites of which would be confession of Jesus Christ as God and Savior, and recognition of the need to overcome differences in belief and church order between the individual churches. A preliminary meeting was held in Geneva (1920), which led to the first World Conference on → Faith and Order, in 1927 in Lausanne, Switzerland. The conference received reports on the nature of the church, a common confession of faith, ministry, and the sacraments.

The second World Conference met in Edinburgh in 1937 and reached an important consensus on the doctrine of grace. Along with Life and Work, the conference agreed to form a world council of churches. Subsequent Faith and Order conferences were held in Lund, Sweden (1952), Montreal (1963), and Santiago de Compostela, Spain (1993). As a result of the Second Vatican Council, Roman Catholics participated in Montreal as observers; after 1968 the Roman Catholic Church became an official member of Faith and Order.

Since 1948 Faith and Order has functioned as a commission of 120 members within the structure of the WCC. It has dealt with a broad spectrum of theological issues, including the church and concepts of unity, Scripture and tradition, the significance of creeds and confessions, the → ordination of women, as well as baptism, Eucharist, and ordained ministry. It periodically conducts forums on bilateral dialogues and regularly publishes a survey of church union negotiations. In 1982 it published *Baptism, Eucharist, and Ministry,* probably the best-known ecumenical text of the 20th century (→ Baptism 2.3).

2.6.3. *World Council of Churches (1948-)*
Plans in process during the 1930s to form a world council of churches were interrupted by the Second

World War. A provisional committee for the council continued to function in Geneva during the war, however, under the leadership of Willem A. → Visser 't Hooft from the Netherlands, who became the council's first general secretary. Soon after the conclusion of the war, plans were put in place for the first and constituting assembly of the WCC. Initiatives begun in 1938 in Utrecht reached their conclusion in Amsterdam in 1948.

2.6.3.1. *First assembly (Amsterdam, 1948).* A total of 351 delegates from 147 churches gathered in Amsterdam under the theme "Man's Disorder and God's Design." Attention was given to theological accord and to the need for mission. Adopting the basic formula of Faith and Order, the WCC defined itself as "a fellowship of churches which accept our Lord Jesus Christ as God and Saviour." As the council began its life with the motto "staying together," it brought together two of the mainstreams of the ecumenical movement: Faith and Order, and Life and Work.

Headquartered in Geneva, the council experienced an increasing, and increasingly diverse, membership of churches through the years. Initially it was largely North Atlantic and Protestant in membership, but it has come to include a variety of Protestant and Orthodox churches from around the world. About every seven years the WCC holds an assembly, the most authoritative expression of its life. Between assemblies, the Central Committee, elected by the assembly, meets regularly.

Implications of membership in the WCC were more clearly worked out after Amsterdam at the meeting of the Central Committee in Toronto in 1950. There it was stated that the WCC was not based upon any one particular conception of the church or of the unity of the church. Its role was to be instrumental in helping the churches enter into relation with one another.

2.6.3.2. *Second assembly (Evanston, Ill., 1954).* This assembly took as its theme "Christ — the Hope of the World." This theme set the tone of the assembly, at which the churches committed themselves to live out the motto "growing together." Younger churches were better represented than in Amsterdam. Although there were sharp differences over the Christian concept of → hope, the assembly agreed in affirming Christian responsibility for peace and justice and urged the banning of → weapons of mass destruction. There were statements on religious liberty and racial equality, and the assembly encouraged the missionary task of the laity (→ Clergy and Laity). Evanston was much aware of its context in a world divided between Communist and non-Communist nations.

2.6.3.3. *Third assembly (New Delhi, 1961).* The theme of the third assembly was "Jesus Christ, the Light of the World." At New Delhi the basis of the WCC was revised and expanded to the following: "The World Council of Churches is a fellowship of churches which confess the Lord Jesus Christ as God and Saviour according to the Scriptures and therefore seek to fulfill together their common calling to the glory of the one God, Father, Son and Holy Spirit."

The integration of the International Missionary Council was achieved in New Delhi. And four Orthodox churches — the churches of Romania, Poland, and Bulgaria, as well as the Patriarchate of Moscow — were admitted as members. The New Delhi Declaration on Unity, from section 2 of its report, became a benchmark for ecumenical work. Here for the first time the various ecumenical intentions and particular concerns were compressed into a common, almost confessional, statement that described the unity being sought. The declaration stressed the multidimensional nature of this unity, which became one of its enduring features. This unity will include agreement in confession of the faith, mutuality in sacraments and ministry, commitment to worship and prayer, common witness and service, the ability to act and to speak together, the local and universal dimensions, and unity as well as diversity.

2.6.3.4. *Fourth assembly (Uppsala, Sweden, 1968).* Meeting under the theme "Behold, I Make All Things New," the fourth assembly devoted much energy to the rapidly changing world situation. Global economic and social development, the need to strongly condemn racism, and the financial responsibility of Christians to developing countries were all stressed (→ Third World). The assembly was one-third larger than its three predecessors; delegates were present from 235 churches in 84 countries, with one-third of the participants coming from Africa, Asia, and Latin America. Although it was the most activist and politically oriented assembly, it also addressed the issues of unity and catholicity.

In the assembly's "Appeal to the Churches of the World," some have seen an optimistic → theology of revolution that played a part in the rise of → liberation theology in Latin America after 1970. As a result of decisions at Uppsala, the WCC in ensuing years added its controversial → Program to Combat Racism and created the Commission on the Churches' Participation in Development, the Christian Medical Commission, and its unit Dialogue with People of Living Faiths and Ideologies.

2.6.3.5. *Fifth assembly (Nairobi, Kenya, 1975).* This assembly was attended by delegates from 285 churches, who examined the theme "Jesus Christ Frees and Unites." In many ways Nairobi was an assembly of consolidation, seeking to provide a theological basis for much that surfaced in Uppsala. The assembly declared that faith in the triune God and sociopolitical engagement belong together, as do conversion to Christ and active participation in changing economic and social structures. Items on the agenda included "What Unity Requires," which offered a vision of conciliar fellowship to the churches. → Evangelism was discussed; interfaith → dialogue, the subject of contentious debate, was encouraged. The issues of racism, → sexism, and human rights were also on the agenda. Concern for the sharing of resources by the churches entered ecumenical discussions at Nairobi.

2.6.3.6. *Sixth assembly (Vancouver, Canada, 1983).* The theme of this assembly was "Jesus Christ — the Life of the World." It was the most representative assembly to date, with 30 percent women, 13 percent youth (persons under 30), and 46 percent laypeople. Worship was a major feature of the assembly, especially a celebration of the Lord's Supper according to the Lima Liturgy, which was based on the text of *Baptism, Eucharist, and Ministry.* The assembly asked the churches to respond to this ecumenical convergence text by 1987. A priority of the WCC was to be the engagement of member churches in a conciliar process for "justice, peace, and the integrity of creation." The foundations of this process were established as the confession of Christ as the life of the world and Christian resistance to racism, sexism, → caste oppression, economic exploitation, militarism, violations of human rights, and the misuse of science and → technology.

The Vancouver assembly gathered different socioethical studies, activities, and programs into a conciliar process of mutual commitment for justice, peace, and the integrity of creation. This process became a kind of movement within the larger ecumenical movement. "Conciliar assemblies" were part of this continuing process of mutual commitment. Notable among these assemblies was a 1989 conference at Basel, Switzerland, sponsored by the Conference of European Churches together with the Roman Catholic Church. A world convocation on justice, peace, and the integrity of creation gathered in Seoul, Korea, in 1990, issuing a final document with common commitments and covenants. On occasion the process was criticized for its lack of theological content and its indifference to the question of the visible unity of the churches. Nevertheless, a broad spectrum of Orthodox and Protestant churches, together with the Roman Catholic Church, participated in the conciliar process. (The Roman Catholic Church, however, did not take part in the Seoul meeting.)

2.6.3.7. *Seventh assembly (Canberra, Australia, 1991).* The theme of the seventh assembly was "Come, Holy Spirit — Renew the Whole Creation." This focus on the Holy Spirit was a departure from the themes of earlier assemblies, and it raised questions about how to maintain the link between the Spirit and Christ. Meeting in the context of the Gulf War, the assembly in its discussions revealed deep differences about the justification both of that war and of all → war. The assembly disclosed how many obstacles to visible unity remained on such topics as the Eucharist, ministry, and the nature of the church. There were difficult discussions about the mandated balances of participation, for member churches fell short of the goal of 20 percent youth. The assembly approved a declaration, "The Unity of the Church as Koinonia: Gift and Calling," which built on the formula of unity from New Delhi. This declaration indicates the usefulness and integrative power of the concept of → koinonia in the process of seeking visible unity.

The China Christian Council, considered a united church in formation, was welcomed as a new member. It was the first time in more than 30 years that Christians from mainland China attended an assembly of the World Council of Churches. The location of the assembly gave high visibility to indigenous peoples, and an assembly statement committed the WCC to support and monitor a treaty process between the Aborigines and the Australian government.

2.6.3.8. *Eighth assembly (Harare, Zimbabwe, 1998).* Marking the 50th anniversary of the formation of the WCC, the eighth assembly took as its theme "Turn to God — Rejoice in Hope." The assembly was the largest to date, with 966 voting delegates from 336 member churches. More than one-third were women, and 134 youth were present. The assembly reflected on the policy statement "Towards a Common Understanding and Vision of the World Council of Churches," which had been adopted by the Central Committee in 1997. A new feature of the assembly was the *padare,* meeting places separate from the official deliberations that gave opportunity for exchange of ideas, listening, and sharing. Many people at Harare found these occasions more compelling than the regular sessions. The assembly message, "Being Together under the Cross in Africa," endeavored to speak to the present social setting to the churches, not least in respect to the effects of globalization and HIV/AIDS (→ Public Health). A conspicuous feature of this assembly was its almost total lack (apart from the hearings of the assembly) of attention to the topic of the visible unity of the church.

2.7. *Ecumenism in the Churches*
The ecumenical movement has at times been perceived as an endeavor only of mainline Protestant churches. A review of the history of other Christian communities, however, shows such a conclusion to be false.

2.7.1. *Roman Catholic Church*
The Roman Catholic Church declined invitations in 1919 and 1921 to attend the first conferences of Faith and Order and of Life and Work because of its view of church unity. In *Mortalium animos* Pius rejected all ecumenical activities, urging only a return of non-Catholics to the Roman Catholic Church. This document was uncompromising. Nevertheless, there were also efforts within the church that sought to understand the ecumenical movement, even while not repudiating this encyclical.

In 1949 the letter *Ecclesia sancta* represented a more positive evaluation of the ecumenical movement. At the same time, theologians such as Max Pribella and Y. M. J. Congar made serious scholarly efforts to articulate a Roman Catholic understanding of ecumenism. In 1960 → John XXIII created the Secretariat for Promoting Christian Unity, which in 1988 became the Pontifical Council for Promoting Christian Unity. Regular contact on an official level between the Roman Catholic Church and the World Council of Churches became possible. Cardinal Augustin Bea, first president of the secretariat, and his successors, Cardinal Johannes Willebrands and Cardinal Edward Cassidy, facilitated ecumenical relations in a variety of ways. Roman Catholic observers, designated by the Vatican, attended the WCC's New Delhi Assembly in 1961.

In 1964 the Second Vatican Council adopted a decree on ecumenism. This text acknowledges that there is one ecumenical movement and speaks of the ecumenical aim as the restoration of unity *(redintegratio unitatis),* not as a return to the Roman Catholic Church. In 1965 a Joint Working Group, an official consultative forum for the Vatican and the WCC, was established to meet annually and submit reports to its two sponsoring bodies. In 1968 the Roman Catholic Church joined the Commission on Faith and Order of the WCC. From 1968 to 1980 it took part in → SODEPAX, a joint committee with the WCC on society, development, and peace.

Since the Second Vatican Council the Roman

Catholic Church has joined numerous regional, national, and local councils of churches. It has participated in many theological dialogues on the national and international levels. In 1967 and 1968 the Secretariat for Promoting Christian Unity issued *The Ecumenical Directory,* a series of guidelines for ecumenical understanding and participation. Further materials on eucharistic participation and local ecumenical work were released in 1972 and 1975 ($\rightarrow$ Local Ecumenism). A new edition of *The Ecumenical Directory,* published in 1993, developed the notion of unity as subsisting in the Roman Catholic Church, a notion expressed in *Lumen gentium,* the constitution on the church issued by the Second Vatican Council. It also affirms that many significant elements of the church and its unity exist in other Christian faith communities.

2.7.2. *Orthodox Church*

The Greek Orthodox Church has been a longtime participant in the ecumenical movement. In 1902 Joachim III, patriarch of Constantinople, sent an encyclical to all Orthodox churches to deal with the question of a possible rapprochement with all those who believe in the triune God so that the day of the union of all Christians might come. In 1920 the Church of Constantinople became the first church to call for a permanent organ of fellowship and co-operation among the churches. Until 1948 the Orthodox churches, with the exception of the Russian Orthodox Church, took part in all the early meetings of both Life and Work and Faith and Order. At the establishment of the WCC that year, the $\rightarrow$ Ecumenical Patriarchate, the $\rightarrow$ Ethiopian Orthodox Church, and the $\rightarrow$ Syrian Orthodox Church of India were founding members, although a number of other Orthodox churches declined membership. In 1961 four others joined, followed later in the 1960s by other Eastern and Oriental Orthodox churches.

Without compromising its ecclesiological claims to be the one true church of Christ, Eastern Orthodoxy now almost unanimously takes part in the ecumenical movement. Orthodoxy has much to offer the movement in its understanding of dogma, liturgical life, the patristic spirit, and concepts of Christian experience. The relationship, however, has not always been easy for Orthodoxy (nor indeed for other churches).

2.7.3. *Evangelicals and Fundamentalists*

The word "evangelical" has a history at least back to the 16th century. In the modern period the English term "evangelical" has come to mean a person who confesses the $\rightarrow$ infallibility of the Bible, the $\rightarrow$ Trinity, the deity of Christ, vicarious $\rightarrow$ atonement, the personality and work of the Holy Spirit, and the

personal return of Christ, while at the same time emphasizing the missionary mandate to evangelize the world. Many $\rightarrow$ evangelicals reject the name "fundamentalist," which they see reflecting an extreme conservatism and having a different theological basis and a separatistic ethos. Evangelicals have established such institutions as the World Evangelical Fellowship and the Lausanne Committee for World Evangelization. Evangelical churches are found among the member churches of the WCC.

Fundamentalists established the American Council of Christian Churches in opposition to the Federal Council of Churches and, after 1950, to the National Council of the Churches of Christ in the U.S.A. In 1948 the $\rightarrow$ International Council of Christian Churches, a small fundamentalist group, held its first assembly in Amsterdam to counter the establishment of the WCC.

Differing views of the uniqueness and finality of Christ for salvation, the role of interfaith conversations, and views of Scriptural $\rightarrow$ inspiration have kept most evangelicals and $\rightarrow$ fundamentalists from participation in the ecumenical movement, and especially the WCC. Recently some evangelicals have been open to a more active role in ecumenism, especially in the work of Faith and Order. This has not been true of fundamentalists. In 2000 the $\rightarrow$ National Association of Evangelicals in the United States dropped its restriction that members could not also belong to the $\rightarrow$ National Council of the Churches of Christ or the WCC.

2.8. *Dialogues*

Dialogues have become a valuable tool aiding divided churches to move toward the ecumenical goal of visible unity. In the early years of the 20th century theological dialogues did occur, although they were most often unofficial and were promoted by individuals rather than church bodies. In the 1940s and early 1950s dialogues receded in importance, but stimulated by the Second Vatican Council, the entrance of the Roman Catholic Church into the ecumenical movement, and the ongoing work of Faith and Order, an explosion of bilateral dialogues on the national and international levels took place. Almost every church or confession in the ecumenical movement became involved.

These dialogues share three characteristics: they are official (i.e., the churches appoint the representatives), they report to their sponsoring churches, and they are generally concerned with doctrinal issues. The mandates of these dialogues have ranged from better understanding to enabling the churches to enter into full communion with each other. Anglican-Lutheran, Anglican–Old Catholic, and Lutheran-Reformed dialogues have enabled the churches in several places to enter into full communion with each other. Eastern and Oriental Orthodox dialogue has recommended the overcoming of the Christological disputes of the early church. Anglican–Roman Catholic, Lutheran–Roman Catholic, and Orthodox–Roman Catholic dialogues have done significant work and are marks of progress toward full communion. "The Joint Declaration on the Doctrine of Justification," signed in 1999 in Augsburg, Germany, by representatives of the Roman Catholic Church and the → Lutheran World Federation, is a signal accomplishment of an international bilateral dialogue and represents an almost unprecedented ecumenical advance. The largely unanswered question coming from many of these dialogues, however, is that of ecumenical → reception. That is, how are the churches to receive the fruits of dialogue into their faith and lives?

Multilateral dialogues, involving several partners, have existed side by side with bilateral conversations. On the national or regional level such dialogues have resulted in such new expressions of Christian unity as the → Church of South India (1947), the Church of North India (1970), and the ongoing process in the United States of the Consultation on Church Union (The Churches of Christ Uniting). In particular, Faith and Order has offered itself as the locus for multilateral dialogue.

Bilateral and multilateral dialogues must each be distinguished from interfaith dialogue, in which the goal is not unity. Interfaith dialogue has been a controversial issue in the ecumenical movement because some have feared syncretism and the loss of the uniqueness and finality of God's revelation in Christ.

2.9. *Regional and Local Groups*

Ecumenism as a movement exists not only internationally (i.e., as the World Council of Churches) but in regional, national, and local settings, including the → All Africa Conference of Churches, Canadian Council of Churches, → Caribbean Conference of Churches, → Christian Conference of Asia, Churches Together in England, → Conference of European Churches, → Latin America Council of Churches, → Middle East Council of Churches, National Council of the Churches of Christ in the U.S.A. (NCC), and → Pacific Conference of Churches. Many of these councils are in contact with each other and coordinate their efforts and work. The Roman Catholic Church has membership in a number of these councils, although not in the NCC or the WCC. All these councils face questions about the nature of their relation to member churches, their ecclesiological signifi-

cance, and maintaining an adequate form and structure. Still, they are an essential expression of the ecumenical movement. They allow divided churches in their own settings to work cooperatively and to discuss divisive issues.

In addition to councils, a number of international and national ecumenical organizations such as → Bible societies, missionary societies, the Christian Literature Fund, the → Christian Peace Conference, the World Student Christian Federation, and the World Association for Christian Communication have promoted ecumenical work in the past or continue it in the present.

2.10. *Christian World Communions*

Since the rise of an awareness of Christian division, especially in the 19th and 20th centuries, a number of Christian churches and confessions have established international organizations, in part to conduct their ecumenical work. These include Seventh-day → Adventists (1863), Anglicans (1867), the World Alliance of Reformed Churches (1875), the → Baptist World Alliance (1905), and the Lutheran World Federation (1947). The description of these organizations as World Confessional Families proved not to be satisfactory, since several did not understand themselves as a particular confession; it was replaced in 1979 by the term → "Christian World Communions."

3. Evaluation

Any evaluation of the modern ecumenical movement as it enters the second century of its existence must be positive. There is no doubt that this movement was a — if not *the* — major feature of the church history of the 20th century. Its influence was apparent in virtually every area of the churches' action and thinking. In a relatively short period of time, many churches and their members have moved from attitudes of hostility and mistrust to a much more open position. Many old walls of division have been torn down, and caricatures have been removed. Many of the historical disagreements between Christians have been softened, if not removed. Far from being the result of indifference, the reason for this progress has to do with solid achievements in theological reflection, created by new insights from the study of Scripture, church history, and the significance of cultural differences. New understandings of a Christian faith liberated from the controversies of the past is a possibility for the 21st century. To a degree that would been difficult to imagine in 1910, most of the churches in the ecumenical movement are now comfortable with each other. Large areas where cooperation in mission and service to the world are possible have been identified, and the churches increasingly act together in these areas. Life has been shared in councils of churches, and ecumenism is increasingly seen neither as an option nor as a matter of expediency. Rather, ecumenism and its call to visible unity are seen as integral to the nature of the church.

Ecumenism not only has made possible considerable practical cooperation and better understanding. In the course of the last century, it also has created, largely through Faith and Order and the bilateral dialogues, an ecumenical theology of great potential. This theology stands as a resource for the churches to discover and tap.

As the 20th century closed, there were increasing signs — after decades of work — that the dialogues could influence the lives of churches and change their relations. Virtually every church in the ecumenical movement has had the occasion to alter old relationships and enter into new ones that are harbingers of full communion. In particular, the 1982 Faith and Order agreement *Baptism, Eucharist, and Ministry* has positively influenced the churches and challenged their work.

Yet with all this success and possibility for the future, there were a number of deep concerns as the ecumenical movement entered the new century. Can all this ecumenical work be *received*, owned by the churches, so that it affects faith and life in such a way that the oneness of the church can more visibly be made manifest? Will the ecumenical movement remain merely a means of social cooperation? What influence will the considerable theological achievement of the ecumenical movement have? Will theological consensus be secured between the churches, or will it be jeopardized, as many feel happened in the conciliar process Justice, Peace, and the Integrity of Creation?

At least three factors give rise to these questions: (1) a general tendency to be comfortable with the present level of ecumenical accomplishment and to remain content with a peaceful and cooperative coexistence among the churches, (2) a tendency to abandon the quest for doctrinal consensus as simply too difficult, and (3) a continuing polarization between Life and Work (the struggle for communion in life and action) and Faith and Order (the struggle for communion in faith).

Beyond these questions seems to lie a more basic concern: what is the goal of the ecumenical movement at the present time? Is it full communion, visible unity (however these terms are defined), based on theological consensus? Or is the goal something else? The lack of a precisely articulated goal is caus-

ing a crisis for the movement at the opening of the 21st century.

This present crisis in ecumenical urgency is one of simultaneous progress and retreat. Along with the considerable ecumenical success now visible, there is an obvious decrease in interest in ecumenical themes, events, and publications. In some quarters there is apparent disdain for ecumenical achievement and uncertainty about ecumenical orientation, a reserve — if not resistance — toward things ecumenical.

This situation is fed by the continuing challenge of ecumenical reception in the churches, by an erosion of conviction concerning the meaning and authority of both Scripture and tradition, and by the pressures of → secularism. Councils of churches struggle with their goal and nature. They debate their purpose and their constituency. Indeed, how are they to function in a context that is more and more postdenominational, perhaps even postecumenical? While the ecumenical movement has always lived in crisis, the present dilemma appears to transcend the normal crises through which movements by their very nature pass. This present precariousness is caused precisely by a continuing lack of clarity about the goal of the ecumenical movement. Will the movement be able to recover its primary concern for visible unity in one faith and in one eucharistic fellowship expressed in worship and in common life in Christ? On this question hang the future of the movement and its character. The question will finally be answered as the ecumenical movement grapples with a number of emerging issues.

4. Emerging Issues
4.1. *Goal*
As the previous section has made clear, the ecumenical movement must give immediate attention to its goal. It must secure from its members an agreement that this multidimensional movement has one central goal: the visible unity of divided churches. If this common goal, defined by the WCC in 1961 at New Delhi, cannot be reaffirmed, the present fragmentation of the movement can be expected to continue.

4.2. *Concepts of Unity and Models of Union*
More attention must be given in the ecumenical movement to concepts of unity and models of union, to the church's essential characteristics and marks, to its constitutive elements, and to the forms by which ecclesial unity might be manifested. In short, more clarity and specificity are required concerning the church that in the future will embody the visible unity of Christians.

4.3. *Ecumenical Reception*

This topic is now a major challenge. While at one time theological dialogue itself was deemed the more difficult task, today the process by which the churches make the results of dialogue part of their faith and life is viewed as more challenging and harder to achieve. Without an authentic reception of the results of ecumenical dialogue, the movement will flounder in the future.

4.4. *Councils of Churches*

The emerging roles of councils of churches will be a major issue in the future. Are such councils only the servants of their member churches? Do the councils have a prophetic role to confront the churches? Do such councils have an emerging ecclesial character? Such questions will influence the future course of the movement.

4.5. *Life and Work, Faith and Order*

Tensions between these two streams of the movement have been evident throughout the history of modern ecumenism. All present signs suggest that this tension will continue, although recent attempts have been made, especially in the WCC, to find greater coordination and understanding. The degree to which the oneness of the ecumenical movement can be confirmed will facilitate ecumenical progress in the future.

4.6. *Other Churches*

Evangelical, charismatic (→ Charismatic Movement), and → Pentecostal churches have until now been distant from the ecumenical movement. To be true to itself and its goal, the movement must find ways that these churches can, with integrity, become involved in the movement. This task is all the more urgent in that many of these churches are the fastest-growing Christian communities.

4.7. *New Issues*

The perennial, unresolved issues facing the ecumenical movement include ecclesiology, authority, and ministry. Additional issues, however, have arisen in the churches since the historic divisions of the 5th, 11th, and 16th centuries. Some of these topics are of a social or ethical nature (e.g., racism and human → sexuality), others are theological (e.g., the Marian dogmas of the Roman Catholic Church, papal infallibility, and the ordination of women). The ecumenical movement will not succeed in calling the churches to greater unity until these subjects — old and new — are addressed fully and satisfactorily. Some of these issues may have a church-dividing potential that has not previously been recognized. The slogan of yesteryear "doctrine divides, but service unities" is no longer self-evident.

4.8. *The Next Generation*

The formation of the next generation of ecumenical leaders will be a key factor for the future of the ecumenical movement. The generation of leaders who started their active ecumenical careers in the 1950s through the 1960s is passing. Whether enough has been done to encourage a new generation to grasp the importance and urgency of the ecumenical vision is an open question. The commitment of new leadership in all the churches is a decisive factor in the determination of the ecumenical future. Will the leaders of the next generation be ecumenically active? Or will they be largely preoccupied with the internal problems of their own churches?

Bibliography: History and primary studies: J. Briggs, M. Oduyoye, and G. Tsetsis, eds., *A History of the Ecumenical Movement* (vol. 3; Geneva, forthcoming) • J. A. Burgess and J. Gros, eds., *Building Unity* (New York, 1989); idem, eds., *Growing Consensus* (New York, 1995) • H. E. Fey, ed., *A History of the Ecumenical Movement*, vol. 2, *The Ecumenical Advance, 1948-1968* (2d ed.; Geneva, 1986; orig. pub., 1970) • G. Gassmann, ed., *Documentary History of Faith and Order, 1963-1993* (Geneva, 1993) • M. Kinnamon and B. E. Cope, eds., *The Ecumenical Movement: An Anthology of Key Texts and Voices* (Grand Rapids, 1997) • H. Krüger, W. Löser, and W. Müller-Römheld, eds., *ÖL* • G. Limouris, ed., *Orthodox Visions of Ecumenism: Statements, Messages, and Reports on the Ecumenical Movement, 1902-1992* (Geneva, 1994) • N. Lossky et al., eds., *Dictionary of the Ecumenical Movement* (Geneva, 1991) • H. Meyer and L. Vischer, eds., *Growth in Agreement* (Ramsey, N.J., 1984) • O. Michel, "Οἰκουμένη," *TDNT* 5.157-59 • Pontifical Council for Promoting Christian Unity, *Directory for the Application of Principles and Norms on Ecumenism* (Vatican City, 1993) • R. Rouse and S. C. Neill, eds., *A History of the Ecumenical Movement*, vol. 1, *1517-1948* (3d ed.; Geneva, 1986; orig. pub., 1954) • W. G. Rusch and J. Gros, eds., *Deepening Communion: International Ecumenical Documents with Roman Catholic Participation* (Washington, D.C., 1998) • W. G. Rusch, J. Gros, and H. Meyer, eds., *Growth in Agreement* (vol. 2; Geneva, 2000) • E. J. Stormon, ed., *Towards the Healing of Schism* (New York, 1987) • T. F. Stransky and J. B. Sheerin, eds., *Doing the Truth in Charity* (Ramsey, N.J., 1982) • H. J. Urban and H. Wagner, eds., *HÖ* • L. Vischer, ed., *A Documentary History of the Faith and Order Movement, 1927-1963* (St. Louis, 1963).

Secondary studies: J. A. Burgess, ed., *In Search of Christian Unity: Basic Consensus, Basic Differences* (Minneapolis, 1991) • H. Fries and K. Rahner, *Unity of the Churches: An Actual Possibility* (Philadelphia,

1985) • Groupe des Dombes, *For the Conversion of the Churches* (Geneva, 1993) • Institute for Ecumenical Research, Strasbourg, *Crisis and Challenge of the Ecumenical Movement: Integrity and Indivisibility* (Geneva, 1994) • R. W. Jenson, *Unbaptized God: The Basic Flaw in Ecumenical Theology* (Minneapolis, 1992) • H. Meyer, *That All May Be One: Perceptions and Models of Ecumenicity* (Grand Rapids, 1999) • K. Raiser, *Ecumenism in Transition: A Paradigm Shift in the Ecumenical Movement?* (Geneva, 1991) • W. G. Rusch, *Reception: An Ecumenical Challenge* (Philadelphia, 1987) • T. Sabev, *The Orthodox Churches in the World Council of Churches: Towards the Future* (Geneva, 1996).

William G. Rusch

Edification

1. Biblical
2. In Church History
3. Present-Day

1. Biblical

In the OT we find God's promised work of salvation, and the prophetic proclamation that addresses it, described metaphorically as a "building" of the "house of Israel" (Jer. 1:10; 18:9; 24:6; 31:28; 42:10; 45:4; Ezek. 36:36; Ps. 28:5). This is the root of the NT use of the concept, which is developed especially in → Paul and his circle. We find five essential variations or components.

1.1. Edification is the apostolic work (→ Apostle, Apostolate) of founding and directing the → congregation (1 Cor. 3:10-15; 2 Cor. 12:19; Eph. 2:20-22). As in the OT, its opposite is "tearing down" (2 Cor. 10:8; 13:10).

1.2. Edification is the mutual encouragement of church members (1 Thess. 5:11).

1.3. Edification is a term for the orientation of gifts (→ Charisma) and ministries (1 Corinthians 12–14; Eph. 4:12) or of personal conduct (1 Cor. 8:1; 10:23; Rom. 14:19; 15:2) for the benefit of others or the whole congregation.

1.4. The unity and totality of the congregation are always in view, even when it is a matter of the edification of an individual (Eph. 4:16; 1 Pet. 2:5).

1.5. Edification is always a work of the Spirit, and its achievement is thus seen as the work of God or of Christ (Eph. 2:20-22; 4:7-16).

2. In Church History

In the following centuries a development of the thoughts of Paul soon led to a focusing of edification on individuals. The Middle Ages used the term in various ways, including a reference to the task and shaping of → theology. M. → Luther (1483-1546) employed the word only sparingly, possibly through reservations about its mystical and spiritualized use (G. Krause).

→ Pietism, which viewed edification in terms of the improvement of church members in personal → faith, the appropriation of biblical truth, and Christian life, regarded it as a task that should be promoted through → preaching, devotional meetings (P. Spener's *collegia pietatis,* "pious meetings"), and family and individual reading of the Bible and other devotional writings. F. D. E. → Schleiermacher (1768-1834), who saw in edification the awakening and quickening of the pious consciousness, made it a leading concept of practical theology. Already before Pietism there were tendencies toward a subjective and psychological use of the term. By way of Pietism and the → Enlightenment, the final result was that the term has become weak and shallow in common usage.

3. Present-Day

Related to the crisis in the concept of edification is a crisis in its substance. With the dissolution of a responsible form of → piety that involves communication of the contents of faith, the striving for edification has lost its goal, its material basis, and its focus. A renewal of the concept and of the substance can come only with a clear orientation to the total framework of the NT. Aspects that relate to the whole congregation are now often called simply "(spiritual) edification of the congregation." In fact, the various practices of personal edification (Bible reading, → devotions, → meditation, the reading of → devotional literature) need to be embedded in the total context of the life of the church in the world and its witness to the truth of the → gospel. Only in this context can personal, mutual edification gain new power in the sense of personal encouragement.

→ Spirituality

Bibliography: E. C. Achelis, "Edification," *NSHE* 4.76-77 • K. Barth, *CD* IV/2 • E. E. Ellis, *Pauline Theology: Ministry and Society* (Grand Rapids, 1959) • G. Friedrich and G. Krause, "Erbauung," *TRE* 10.18-28 • O. Michel, "Οἶκος κτλ.," *TDNT* 5.119-59 • R. Schaeffler, *Glaubensreflexion und Wissenschaftslehre* (Freiburg, 1980) 36-41 • F. Schwarz and C. A. Schwarz, *Theologie des Gemeindeaufbaus* (Wuppertal, 1984) • B. H. Throckmorton Jr., "Edification," *IDB* 2.24 • P. Vielhauer, *Oikodome* (2d ed.; Karlsruhe, 1979).

Hermann Hafner

Education

1. Europe

1.1. *Definition*

The popular term "education" — as also, from the 18th century, "culture" — defies comprehensive definition. It receives its concrete sense from the context in which it is used. Historically it derives from *educatio,* and there is a relation also to *eruditio.* It thus has an underlying sense that becomes clear when we relate it to other cultures. As a "function of society" (W. Dilthey), education cannot be abstracted from social → development and treated in isolation. Thus in liberal democratic industrial countries its development differs from that in → socialist lands. There is in the former some → autonomy for (inter)personal existence and political → democracy, albeit with increasing competitiveness and a concern for careers. In the latter it is highly instrumentalized.

In the Western industrial countries the original unity of church, community, and the social classes has now broken down, having been replaced by a certain → pluralism of basic convictions, a neutral → state, and a separation of vocation and personal life. There thus arises the question of conditions for the possibility of humanizing such a → society and its education, the problem of relating education to → work being particularly prominent.

The situation is similar but also different in the so-called developing countries (→ Third World). These cannot ignore their history and must find their own concepts, for which there are hardly any models (see 3).

1.2. *History and Problems*

"Education" might be used as a general term for all that is done directly or indirectly to lead → youth to social maturity. Yet it can also denote the imparting of modes of conduct that serve the end of social intercourse and of dispositions on the basis of which these modes of conduct are not just used instrumentally but can even be revised innovatively. (Note I. Kant's thesis that politeness is the outward form of morality.) Whereas the pre-Christian → Golden Rule could be viewed as a kind of rule for (private) intercourse, the Christian command of love of neighbor relates to an inner attitude to the other as a child of God. It demands identification with this other and thus initiates a movement into the "depths of subjectivity" (Kant) such as one finds nowhere else.

→ Ethics of the Christian or Kantian type ultimately is beyond education, which has led to the question whether one can do anything indirectly to advance Christianity or morality. Three answers have been given to this question in the course of history. The first is the Christian answer that by nature we are bad and that our evil will must be broken (→ Augustine). The second is the revised Christian and also pedagogical answer that it is a matter of knowing the self and achieving the art of living with others, since only interpersonal relations educate us for personal existence. The third answer is that an evolution in the art of perception must precede a revolution in the art of thinking (*metanoia;* Kant and others). The inherent problems here have continually been overlooked, which has led to alienated (instrumental) concepts of education. With this understanding of life and education, a development of very great significance has been initiated that constitutes both the potential strength and the potential weakness of our world. All are early referred to their inner history and therewith to their relation to their fellow human beings and to the world, and also to God. On the one hand, this approach makes possible high personal and moral achievements; on the other hand, it can degenerate into → individualism and a → hedonistic understanding of self-fulfillment.

In connection with the increasingly rational organization of the social system, including education, and the corresponding privatizing of religion, morality, and culture, as well as the liberalizing of private life and at times even of public life, education in the traditional sense, in spite of many significant opposing movements, has for the first time been totally called into question. This development has naturally strengthened the need for a theory of education (→ Pedagogy). By the nature of the case, abstract theories, grounded in theology or philosophy, have arisen on the one side (A. H. Niemeyer, F. H. C. Schwarz, J. F. Herbart, etc.), while practically oriented but still abstract theories have arisen on the other. As J.-J. Rousseau first saw, and after him J. H. Pestalozzi and W. Humboldt, only a study of the genesis of the person, of education as a life-historical process, can rescue us from this dilemma.

1.3. *Further History and Problems*

Several traditions have helped to shape our understanding of culture, especially the humanistic Roman tradition of erudition, or *cultura animi* (mental culture), and the Greek tradition of *enkyklios paideia* (general education), which dominated European thinking and schooling well into the 18th century (G. Dolch, E. Lichtenstein, C. Menze).

Three developments in the 18th century challenged this view. The first was the growth of national literatures, which made necessary a reinterpretation of Latin and Greek teaching and led in Germany to a new humanism with its theory of ancient and modern languages and a capacity for thought and expression oriented to the future. The second was the autonomous → philosophy and science of the → Enlightenment and its culture, which could not be united with the older hermeneutical-practical learning of the scholastic disciplines (apart from mathematics) but had to be given a place in the schools — a didactic dilemma that still exists today. The third was universal academic and vocational education for all boys and girls as a result of the French → Revolution, industrialization, and Reformation ideals, a goal thus far unrealized.

1.4. *Theory*

In the meantime another understanding of education has developed that incorporates not only the tradition of erudition but the motifs of the doctrine of the *imago Dei* (→ Anthropology), of → mysticism, of modern → aesthetics, and of specifically modern insights into the historicity of the world and into human individuality. Humboldt (1767-1835) was the first to develop this theory in terms of an interaction of the (developing) I and the (self-disclosing) world. Here Christian thinking about salvation, on the one side, and, on the other, life and conversion link up with a modern historical and social self-understanding. In this context the question of how and under what conditions we can acquire both historical and social and personal → identity assumed central significance.

Dilthey (1833-1911) described this process of a differentiation of the spiritual life by adjustment to social life in the historical world, and of an integration of this spiritual life into the identity of a rich self, referring expressly to the importance of the emotional life in disclosure of life and the world. In spite of what Dilthey called its teleological structure, education of this kind is always a gift (Menze).

Dilthey certainly delineated in this way aesthetic (moral) education, but he always regarded education as also religious and scientific, for he had reached the conviction that as a result of the modern process of evolution as differentiation, original religious and metaphysical → truth had split up into independent religious, artistic, and scientific truth.

Many writers tried to develop this theory as an → anthropological theory, but after Dilthey it could not become a theory of humanity in general but only of "developed humanity" in "developed [i.e., European] society." Likewise the scientific thinking of the time came into the theory, with the paradigms and findings of educational and developmental psychology, of psychoanalysis, of socialization research (→ Socialization; Biography, Biographical Research), of research into small groups and families, and so forth. All such approaches helped to give much better knowledge of false developments and difficulties.

The increased use of science, however, also led to corrections of some widespread theories, such as the insight that early influences in no way rule out a later revolution in the manner of thinking, or recognition that as we are a product of society and the self (Pestalozzi), we are also a product of nature; we come into the world with a differentiated genetic disposition with which we must come to terms.

The humanities and social sciences have criticized the theory of education as nonoperable, but the questions put by all these disciplines are specific ones. If they are posed absolutely, they remove the → freedom and possibility of an innovative, humane structuring of life. If they are incorporated into the concept of education, they can work in favor of → humanity.

From the *Pampaedia* of J. A. Comenius (1592-1670), by way of A. W. Schlegel's (1767-1845) equation of criticism of the age with the theory of education, to Dilthey's linking of this theory to the epochal crisis of our history, the theory of education and the theory of the present age have necessarily presupposed one another.

1.5. *Present Situation*

The task of educating in terms of our history remains. Talk of negative (antiauthoritarian) education, which has cropped up constantly since the time of Rousseau, does not mean in any sense that young people are to be left on their own, though education can still make inappropriate demands on them. Education, though, including Christian and religious education, certainly needs to be rethought as a whole. → Moral education and schools for general education are possible only if they are oriented to modern theory. In this regard linguistic education and a concern to give expression to life and to teach people how to live it are of central importance.

Our world has undergone a change, however, that has brought pedagogical traditions and institutions into question and initiated broad public discussion (witness talk of "the generation gap"). Our society is increasingly becoming an "organized society" that leaves less room for interpersonal life but urgently needs the cooperation of persons in shaping it. This process has changed the nature of education and much reduced its influence. We also must consider that our horizon is now global, which taxes our possibilities of identification, posing an educational as well as a moral problem. This situation, which we understand only conditionally, underlies the fact that in spite of many movements of opposition and renewal, we have not been able to work out any convincing or consistent theory of education.

The task of education, including the development of academic institutions, is posed for Christians and non-Christians alike. Yet even and precisely in a global world that is increasingly shaped by a technical civilization and filled with new anxiety about the future, the biblical message is the basis of a → hope for which secular thought can provide no basis.

Bibliography: History: G. Dolch, Lehrplan des Abendlandes (Ratingen, 1959) bibliography • C. S. Jaeger, The Envy of Angels: Cathedral Schools and Social Ideals in Medieval Europe, 950-1200 (Philadelphia, 1994) • S. Kusukawa, The Transformation of Natural Philosophy: The Case of Philip Melanchthon (Cambridge, 1995) • P. H. Labalme, Beyond Their Sex: Learned Women of the European Past (New York, 1980) • E. Lichtenstein, Zur Entwicklung des Bildungsbegriffs von Meister Eckhart bis Hegel (Heidelberg, 1966) • A. Maierù, University Training in Medieval Europe (Leiden, 1994) • L. W. Spitz, The Reformation: Education and History (Brookfield, Vt., 1998).

General: W. Boyd and E. J. King, The History of Western Education (11th ed.; London, 1975) • W. Brezinka, Erziehungsziele, Erziehungsmittel, Erziehungserfolg (3d ed.; Munich, 1995) • B. Finkelstein, Regulated Children/Liberated Children: Education in Psychohistorical Perspective (New York, 1979) • H.-H. Groothoff, Wilhelm Dilthey–Zur Erneuerung der Theorie der Bildung und des Bildungswesens (Hannover, 1981) bibliography • H.-H. Groothoff and U. Herrmann, eds., Wilhelm Dilthey, Schriften zur Pädagogik (Paderborn, 1971) • C. Menze, "Bildung," HPG 1.134-84

(bibliography); idem, Die Bildungsreform Wilhelm von Humboldts (Hannover, 1975); idem, Wilhelm von Humboldts Lehre und Bild vom Menschen (Ratingen, 1965); idem, ed., Wilhelm von Humboldt, Bildung und Sprache (Paderborn, 1959) bibliography.

Present situation: T. W. Adorno, "Education after Auschwitz," Never Again: The Holocaust's Challenge for Education (ed. H. Schreier and M. Heyl; Hamburg, 1997); idem, Erziehung zur Mündigkeit (14th ed.; Frankfurt, 1993) • J. Boli, "Education," EncPR 1.224-29 • A. Fischer, ed., Jugend '97. Zukunftsperspektiven, gesellschaftliches Engagement, politische Orientierungen (Opladen, 1997).

Hans-Hermann Groothoff

2. United States
2.1. Public Education

In the United States a first move toward public education came after the War of Independence (1776-83) with mostly private initiatives. Around 1800 several individuals produced plans of education that formulated a goal of legally guaranteed free education for all children, one that would develop all their abilities (→ Childhood). Such an education was considered the rock of "political salvation" (R. Coram) by means of → democracy. The public school system developed first especially in New England and New York; it rested on the district school system that had begun in Massachusetts and then was adopted by other states. A law passed in Massachusetts in 1647 for the establishment of fee-paying and subsidized reading and writing schools and Latin grammar schools was the basis of the district school system. Largely independent school committees were integrated in 1837 with a board of education embracing districts and the state with a view to coordinating developments. The first public high school was founded in Boston in 1821. The University of Virginia, essentially the idea of Thomas Jefferson (1743-1826), received its charter in 1819 and opened in 1825. It was the first of such establishments, forming the final stage of the system of public education after elementary schools and high schools.

2.2. Didactic and Methodological Structure

The structure of public education reflects social demands. The American Federation of Labor (founded 1866), for example, has wanted the public schools to include vocational education. Others have advocated a curriculum closer to life. This emphasis led to the so-called Oswego Method (promoted by E. A. Sheldon, head of the Oswego [N.Y.] State Normal School), a kind of American Pestalozzianism, which emphasized observing and describing physical objects. Others have highlighted projects, or "units of instruction," under the influence of statements in American Herbartianism (championed particular by C. De Garmo, president [1895-99] of the National Herbart Society) on the concentration of departments and materials. → Pragmatism (testing theories by their results in actual situations; reality as a process of constant change; direction by → experience, the conditions of which we can shape by intelligence) led John Dewey (1859-1952) to think through more deeply than others the meaning of public education. His key concept was "anticipatory interaction" (*Experience and Nature* [1925]), according to which one person understands the concern of the other by approaching it from the other's standpoint. This is → communication, which must be practiced in a democratic community and which can be learned by practice in public education as a minicommunity.

2.3. *Dissatisfaction with Public Education*

Dissatisfaction with public education led to the demand for, and the debate about, parochial education, which was implicitly allowed by the Fourteenth Amendment (1868), prohibiting the restriction of civil → rights. This dissatisfaction was fueled, on the one hand, by the conviction that public education — which had been shaped at first by a basic Protestant mood — should not violate the "laws of → conscience" and should not be sectarian (H. Mann) and, on the other, by the increasing → secularization of its goals through external social changes (e.g., industrial development; → Industrial Society) and intellectual debates (e.g., regarding evolutionary and pragmatic thought). Reform Judaism, which was gaining influence within → Judaism in the 19th century, demanded non-Christian → moral education in a climate of racial toleration as part of public education. In response to what was perceived as the public schools' support of Protestant views of Christianity and believing strongly that the family and church are directly responsible for the education of the children, the → Roman Catholic Church sponsored what has become the largest parochial school system in the United States. Some in → Protestantism wanted general Christian education in the public schools to be free from denominational distinctives, but others with strong basic objections to the philosophical constriction of public education — particularly Lutherans (→ Lutheranism), Calvinists, and Seventh-day → Adventists — provided religious education in their own schools.

The legal right of parochial schools to exist was affirmed by the U.S. Supreme Court in 1925, when it ruled unconstitutional an Oregon law requiring all children to attend public schools. In subsequent decisions, the Court has overruled efforts to provide direct federal and state aid to support parochial schools.

Beginning in the 1960s, as the public schools became more secular and less Protestant, many Roman Catholic parents chose to send their children back to local public schools, thus precipitating a sharp decline in overall parochial enrollment figures. Conversely, some Protestant parents became increasingly concerned by the growing secularization of the schools and chose to enroll their children in privately funded Christian day schools, causing a growth spurt in this sector of education at the same time. Ironically, although the public school came to symbolize the great American experiment in democracy (U.S. schools would bring all children together, providing equal educational opportunity for all), the schools have not operated in this fashion (C. L. Glenn, *Myth*)

It is notable that, also fearing increasing assimilation, the Jewish day-school movement experienced unusual growth in the latter years of the 1990s. These full-time day schools combine the teaching of general subject matter with a full curriculum of Orthodox Jewish studies, although the most impressive growth has been attributed to other branches of American Judaism. The establishment of these grassroots schools, however, remains controversial among leading national Jewish organizations, since the religious diversity of the homes from which the students come creates pressure for a broader curriculum than might be desired in an institution designed to inculcate particular religious values along with a general curriculum of studies (J. Wertheimer)

The home school movement, another response to parental dissatisfaction with the public schools, continued to gain momentum in the 1990s. Despite a series of legal challenges, home schooling is now permitted in every state. Although parents have chosen to home-school their children for a variety of reasons (e.g., to remove children from the socially destructive behaviors reported at many public schools or to give special attention to their gifted youngsters), many of the home-schooling parents are → conservative Christians who choose to remove their children from the daily influence of contemporary values of American society evident in the public schools. Although specific enrollment figures are difficult to verify, enrollment nationwide appeared to hover at more than a million students in grades K-12 in the 1999-2000 school year, according to the National Home Education Research Institute.

Parents (primarily mothers) who school their own children at home include both certified teachers and those who are not. Two states, Iowa and Michigan, require that all teachers in homes be state certified. Using a loosely organized support network of other parents, curriculum materials developed for individual instruction (including correspondence courses such as the Calvert School in Baltimore and videotaped lessons), and the Internet, many home-schooled students have benefited significantly from an individualized educational program. Despite the general public's perception that children schooled at home may not be ready for higher education or the work world or may lack → socialization skills, evidence has been forthcoming to the contrary.

Other attempts in the late 20th century to accommodate decentralized decision-making and provide more parental choice in schooling included charter schools and a program of school vouchers. The number of charter schools (i.e., publicly funded schools created and governed by interested parties in local communities to foster unique learning environments or philosophies, largely independent of most state laws and regulations) has grown phenomenally in the 1990s. The first charter school began in Minnesota in 1992; by the end of 1999, close to 1,770 charter schools were operating nationwide with about 350,000 students. It is estimated that during the 2000-2001 school year, more than 500 new charter schools will open. Many of the charter schools that have a religious base have been challenged by the courts and may be unable to sustain public support for their schooling efforts (N. Gillespie).

Another evidence of dissatisfaction with the public system of education in America is the often-discussed program of educational vouchers. Such a voucher would be issued to parents and be redeemable for schooling. An unrestricted voucher could be used in any school, along with additional funds from the parents. A restricted voucher, in contrast, would be redeemable only in approved schools, and parents would not be allowed to subsidize the tuition voucher in order to enroll in a more desirable school. Under this plan, all schools — both public and private — would be supported by public monies. This idea, first proposed by John Stuart Mill in 1859, has yet to meet with widespread public acceptance.

Bibliography: R. F. BUTTS, *Public Education in the United States: From Revolution to Reform* (New York, 1978) • M. ENGEL, *The Struggle for Control of Public Ed-*ucation: Market Ideology vs. Democratic Values (Philadelphia, 2000) • N. GILLESPIE, "Charter Course," *Reason,* March 2000 • C. L. GLENN, *The Myth of the Common School* (Amherst, Mass., 1988); idem, "What Would Equal Treatment Mean for Public Education?" *Equal Treatment of Religion in a Pluralistic Society* (ed. S. V. Monsma and J. C. Soper; Grand Rapids, 1998) 75-100 • J. A. JOHNSON et al., *Introduction to the Foundations of American Education* (11th ed.; Boston, 1999) • R. P. KRENZER, *Erziehungsdenken in den Vereinigten Staaten von Amerika* (Frankfurt, 1984) • C. J. LUCAS, *Teacher Education in America: Reform Agendas for the Twenty-first Century* (New York, 1997) • N. G. MC-CLUSKEY, *Public Schools and Moral Education: The Influence of Horace Mann, William Torrey Harris, and John Dewey* (New York, 1975) • G. F. MADAUS, T. KELLAGHAN, and R. L. SCHWAB, *Teach Them Well: An Introduction to Education* (New York, 1989) • J. NATHAN, *Charter Schools: Creating Hope and Opportunity for American Education* (San Francisco, 1996) • G. G. STRONKS and D. BLOMBERG, *A Vision with a Task: Christian Schooling for Responsive Discipleship* (Grand Rapids, 1993) • J. P. VITERITTI, *Choosing Equality: School Choice, the Constitution, and Civil Society* (Washington, D.C., 1999) • J. WERTHEIMER, "Who's Afraid of Jewish Day Schools?" *Com.,* December 1999, 49-53.

RICHARD P. KRENZER and MURIEL M. RADTKE

3. Third World (Africa)

3.1. Traditional Education

According to the educational tradition of precolonial Africa, character formation and the learning of specific skills are inseparably related (in what has been called a multivalent orientation). The relevance of education arises out of the needs of → society and its order, the sharing and passing on of collective spiritual and moral values, and the close relation between education and → work (a "functional" orientation). For individuals, education represents an integrated → experience. It includes physical and recreational training (e.g., dancing and music), intellectual and moral training (e.g., local history, geography, mythology, and oral literature), and gender-specific vocational and manual training (e.g., agriculture, hunting, handicrafts, home economics, and child raising). Education, which involves observation, imitation, and participation, is both formal and informal. Adult society as a whole is responsible for the instruction of the young. Education follows the physical, emotional, and mental development of the → child and adolescent, culminating in a ceremony of initiation into adulthood (the so-called rites of passage).

→ Initiation rites preserve the accumulated wisdom of society in its understanding of religion, → magic, law, hygiene, and medicine. The rites vary in timing, length, and procedure, but the elements are much the same among all peoples, generally signifying a kind of → regeneration. Some of the rites are secret and open only to the participants. They are very ceremonial, and it is expected that all will submit to them, since they are important for the unity and purity of the society. Often participants of a given year form a class and receive a collective name, which strengthens group solidarity and readiness for cooperation.

Alongside and above this general system, some groups maintain institutions of more specialized training, such as the secret societies (e.g., the men's Poro Society and the women's Sande Society of West Africa). Other institutions train blacksmiths, doctors, priests, and political leaders. The systems are in general more strongly differentiated the greater the social stratification and the division of labor in the relevant society.

In the Asian and Arab spheres, we might mention in this regard the Buddhist monastic schools, as well as Hindu, temple, and Koranic schools.

3.2. *Islam, Christian Mission, and Colonialism*
Wherever → Islam advanced from Arab North Africa — to western, central, or eastern Africa — Islamic schools were set up long before Christian → missions and European → colonialism arrived. The curriculum, however, was limited to the study of the → Koran and of Arabic. (Higher education was available in the universities of North Africa.)

Along with European exploration, trade, conquest, and colonial rule, Christian mission began in the course of the 19th century in all areas south of the Sahara. From the very first, this presence brought a certain measure of rudimentary formal education in reading, writing, and arithmetic, with a view to the training of local teachers, assistant pastors, subordinate workers, and translators who could help in spreading the gospel (→ Evangelism) and serve the missions — and later the colonial governments. Thus the formal, linear school system of the West entered with Christian missions, even though it was alien to the African context. In the ensuing years it largely overlaid and even in many cases totally replaced traditional educational systems. The resultant problems are still matters of discussion.

The colonial governments at first mostly left education to the missions. Only in the 1920s and 1930s did a process of rethinking begin that, in the interests of the colonial powers, moved in the direction of a semisecular education. The spread and penetration of Western schools were closely bound up with the nature, aggressiveness, and nationalistic coloring of colonialism. French policy aimed at the assimilation and institutionalizing of a centralized system similar to that at home (for the producing of a Frenchified local elite). English policy tended toward decentralization, racial segregation, and a measure of accommodation. In general, the education offered in all the colonies varied widely between city and countryside. It was adequate neither in quantity nor in quality because of a lack of interest in the masses, as well as a lack of commitment to vocational and higher education (except in Latin America and India, where higher institutions existed already in the 19th cent.).

Radical criticism of colonialism denounces education that is oriented to the home countries as a competitive and elite system (with capitalist and individualistic criteria of success) and also as one that is alien to African tradition and identity (since it uses the language and culture of the colonial power). Such education serves only to foster and prolong dependence (see A. Memmi and F. Fanon; for Latin America, P. Freire, I. Illich, and others).

3.3. *Developments after Independence*
In spite of some exemplary new beginnings, the system inherited from the colonial period has persisted in most countries, untouched in either form or content. Formal education was regarded as a means to strengthen national political awareness and as the key to modernization and economic development. To satisfy widespread popular demands for more education, and to meet the great need for labor in all sectors of public administration, the school system was greatly expanded.

Along with elementary schools, which aim to eliminate social and regional inequalities by giving a basic education, secondary schools and universities were established to hasten political and economic autonomy. This achievement should not be underestimated. Quantitative expansion, however, often brought with it problems of quality and relevance (e.g., continuing dependence on foreign teachers, financial support, and materials). Substantive reforms often came only hesitantly, marginally, and unsystematically. Curricula remained academic and therefore remote from the daily life and experience of the students, who have mostly come from rural areas. Such programs have been oriented to bureaucratic careers and thus arouse expectations that often cannot be fulfilled. Training colleges for technical and scientific work, for → adult education, and for rural → development (e.g., improvement of agricultural methods) have been thus far neglected.

3.4. *Perspectives and Problems Today*

The tension between a Western academic system, which favors the minority employed by government and industry in the modern sector, and practicable alternatives that will meet the needs of the majority is the central theme of discussion of present-day education in many countries of the Third World. Bound up with it are general ideological questions such as those raised by P. Freire and others (→ Literacy). Freire has developed for Latin America a humanistic concept of education as a vehicle for radical social change. Its goal is maturity, dignity, freedom, dialogue, and the end of oppression and alienation by the rebellion of the oppressed (→ Third World 1.5).

Given the presuppositions of the global economic and political system, radical changes in the educational system are not likely. Many models available today, however, reflect a growing sense of national history, cultural identity, and direction of development and try to take into account the economic situation, including financial crises and → unemployment. Thus since about 1970 there have been revisions in the plans for teaching, learning, and testing in the elementary and secondary schools (e.g., the introduction of more practical and vocationally relevant subjects). Educational materials in integrated science, history, political education, and other fields have also been adapted to the national context. Nonformal programs of education and training have also been established to enhance the quality of life in rural areas and among disadvantaged classes (e.g., in literacy, extension services, agricultural cooperatives, village polytechnics and cooperatives, and training through self-financing). Tanzania offers an example of far-reaching changes in educational policy with its adoption of an independent African → socialism at the end of the 1960s. Turning back to traditional communal forms of organization *(ujamaa)*, it aims at a system that will reintegrate school and commune, and school and work. Though few new models have been fully implemented in Africa (or the so-called developing countries as a group), it is wrong to assume that no steps have been taken in this direction. Paying closer attention to them would in turn aid evaluation of Western systems.

→ Acculturation; Colonialism and Mission; Dependence; Development Education

Bibliography: D. W. CHAPMAN and C. A. CARRIER, eds., *Improving Educational Quality: A Global Perspective* (New York, 1990) • P. ERNY, *The Child and His Environ-* *ment in Black Africa: An Essay on Traditional Education* (Nairobi, 1981) • A. B. FAFUNWA and J. U. AISIKU, eds., *Education in Africa: A Comparative Survey* (London, 1982) • F. FANON, *The Wretched of the Earth* (Harmondsworth, 1991; orig. pub., 1969) • P. FREIRE, *Pedagogy of the Oppressed* (New York, 1997; orig. pub., 1972) • I. ILLICH, *Deschooling Society* (New York, 1983) • G. LUND, ed., *Theological Education in Africa: An Annotated Bibliography* (Wheaton, Ill., 1992) • J. LYNCH, C. MODGIL, and S. MODGIL, eds., *Education and Development: Tradition and Innovation* (5 vols.; London, 1997) • A. MEMMI, *The Colonizer and the Colonized* (3d ed.; Boston, 1995) • T. REAGAN, *Non-Western Educational Traditions: Alternative Approaches to Educational Thought and Practice* (Mahwah, N.J., 1996) • D. G. SCANLON, ed., *Church, State, and Education in Africa* (New York, 1966) • S. SNOOK, *Developing Leaders through Theological Education by Extension: Case Studies from Africa* (Wheaton, Ill., 1992) • A. R. THOMPSON, *Education and Development in Africa* (London, 1981) • UNESCO, *Educational Reforms and Innovations in Africa* (Paris, 1978); idem, *Final Report: Conference of Ministers of Education of African Member States, Lagos 1976* (Paris, 1976) • P. VAN RENSBURG, *The Serowe Brigades–Alternative Education in Botswana* (London, 1979) • K. WATSON, ed., *Education in the Third World* (Kent, 1982) • A. R. WELCH, ed., *Third World Education: Quality and Equality* (New York, 2000).

ELISABETH ZEIL-FAHLBUSCH

Edwards, Jonathan

1. Early Interests and Calling
2. Role in the Great Awakening
3. Later Writings, Assessment

Jonathan Edwards (1703-58) was the most influential American-born theologian of the 18th century, and his writings continued to exert significant influence in English-speaking evangelical Protestant circles through much of the 19th century. Edwards's popularity waned in the early part of the 20th century, as his theology was condemned by Progressive intellectuals and historians as antimodern and redolent of the → fundamentalism they bitterly criticized as repressive and irrational. However, Edwards's reputation was also refashioned by 20th-century neoorthodox theological thinkers, who appreciated Edwards for his sober comprehension of the evil in human nature and for being a brave critic of → liberalism, in terms of both liberalism's unthinking → empiricism and its preoccupation with → individualism. Evangelical Protestant thinkers in the 20th century saw in Edwards a model of intellectual inquiry and integrity who would encourage American evangelicals to slough off anti-intellectual attitudes inherited from the fundamentalist movement. He was a fourth-generation descendant of the original English → Puritan migration to Britain's New England colonies; as such, his career as a thinker and philosopher represented in all its complexity the struggle of conservative Calvinist scholasticism to shore up its intellectual integrity in the face of the new challenges of the → Enlightenment, using a strategy that involved coming to terms with the Enlightenment by formulating an evangelical sentimentality strongly related to the 18th-century Pietist counter-Enlightenment.

1. Early Interests and Calling

Edwards was born on October 5, 1703, the son of Timothy Edwards, the pastor of the Congregationalist parish of East Windsor, Connecticut, and Esther Stoddard Edwards, whose father, Solomon Stoddard, was the pastor of the church of Northampton, Massachusetts, and the most powerful ecclesiastical figure in western New England. Edwards entered Connecticut's Collegiate School (subsequently renamed Yale College) in 1716, graduating in 1720. His education had rested on the English and Dutch Protestant scholastics — William Ames, Francis Burgersdycke, Adrian Heereboord, and Peter Maastricht — but he had also dipped into the "new philosophy" of Isaac Newton, Antoine Arnauld, and John Locke. He began keeping commonplace books with his own speculations on → epistemology and natural science.

In 1722 Edwards briefly served as pastor of a small congregation in New York City, where he also began keeping notebooks on biblical subjects. He left New York in 1723, probably to seek out a larger pastorate in Connecticut, but instead chose to accept an invitation in 1724 from Yale to return as a junior instructor (or tutor). He spent the next three years working out more deeply his explorations into epistemology and pursuing "a clearer and more immediate view of . . . God's exerting himself, with respect to spirits and mind, as I have of his operations concerning matter and bodies" (H. Stout [hereafter *WJE*], 6.114). Rather than embracing an outright Lockean naturalism (i.e., all substance is material) or a synthetic → Cartesian → dualism (i.e., material and spiritual substances coexist), Edwards felt pulled to an immaterialism similar to that of Bishop Berkeley or Nicholas Malebranche, in which "that which truly is the substance of all bodies is the infinitely exact and precise and perfectly stable idea in God's mind" (6.344).

There was, however, little future for junior tutors, and in November 1726 the Northampton church called Edwards to become the assistant pastor of his grandfather Stoddard. Edwards was ordained by the Northampton church (in keeping with Puritan Congregational polity, which located the power of ordination to ministry in the local congregation) in February 1727. Five months later he married Sarah Pierrepont of New Haven.

Solomon Stoddard died in 1729, and Edwards succeeded him as pastor of the Northampton church. Stoddard had long enjoyed a reputation for stand-pat orthodoxy against the softening concessions to the Enlightenment being made by the New England elite in Boston and Cambridge, while at the same time reaching for experiential innovations similar to the Continental Pietists to excite the religious fervor of the Northampton church. (He abolished the inherited Congregational dogma that banned from the Lord's Supper all but those church members who could give an acceptable "relation" of a saving experience of divine grace, but he did so because he was convinced that opening the Lord's Supper to his entire parish would actually promote conversions.) Edwards showed that he intended to subtract nothing from Stoddard's purposes. Invited in 1731 to deliver the Boston Public Lecture, Edwards warned against the tendency of "man . . . to exalt himself and depend on his own power or goodness," when in fact God acts, in immaterialist fashion, as "an extrinsic occasional agent" on the mind, and not on the reason or "ratiocination" but upon a "sense of the heart" which "immediately perceives" a beauty, "a divine, and transcendent, and most evidently distinguishing glory" in God (J. E. Smith, H. S. Stout, and K. P. Minkema, 105-24). Edwards thus made immaterialist philosophy serve the interests of Calvinist → piety.

2. Role in the Great Awakening

The promotion of piety became Edwards's particular burden in the 1730s, especially when in 1734 "a very remarkable blessing of heaven" fell on the Northampton congregation in a communal revival of experiential religion. This was a new religious phenomenon in New England. Religious experience in the Puritan past had been largely a matter of individual spiritual renewal, under the careful direction of → pastors and family elders. Stoddard had provoked several small communal renewals of piety in Northampton during his pastorate, however, and now Edwards's 1734 revival (which continued into 1735) saw "more than 300 souls . . . savingly brought home to Christ in this town." Not only the numbers, but the character of the revived was unprecedented: it involved not only males and females alike, but children as young as four years old, and outbursts of enthusiasm in worship, "some weeping with sorrow and distress, others with joy and love, others with pity and concern for the souls of their neighbors" (*WJE* 4.157-58).

Edwards struggled to both defend and analyze this eruption in *A Faithful Narrative of the Surprising Work of God,* which originated as an explanatory letter to Benjamin Colman and which was expanded for publication in England in 1737. A second wave of revival came to Northampton in 1740, led this time by the celebrated English preacher George → Whitefield, who was nearing the close of a preaching circuit through the British North American colonies that had touched off even larger → revivals of religion (later known as the Great Awakening) in Philadelphia, New York, and Boston. Whitefield preached for Edwards in Northampton, and soon a fresh outbreak of revivals consumed much of western New England.

Whitefield's preaching also generated angry criticism, both from the Boston elite who spurned revivals as raw enthusiasm and from nervous country parsons who feared the destabilizing effect of mass revivals on the peace of their flocks. By 1742 the New England clergy had become polarized into an "Old Light" faction, which condemned the revivals, and a "New Light" group, who encouraged them and who found in Edwards their principal theorist of revivals and religious → experience. Edwards not only participated fully as a preacher in promoting revivals (delivering in Enfield, Connecticut, his most famous sermon, "Sinners in the Hands of an Angry God") but published three important defenses of New Light revivalism: *Distinguishing Marks of a Work of the Spirit of God* (1741), *Some Thoughts concerning the Present Revival of Religion* (1742), and *A Treatise concerning the Religious Affections* (1746).

Distinguishing Marks, originally preached as the 1741 Yale commencement address, dealt with Old Light critics directly by enumerating nine major charges leveled at the New Lights and then (without denying their abstract validity) denying that they proved anything against the New England revivals. To the contrary, he highlighted five "sure, distinguishing, Scripture evidences and marks of a work of the Spirit of God," all of which demonstrated that "that extraordinary influence that has lately appeared on the minds of the people . . . is undoubtedly . . . from the Spirit of God" (*WJE* 4.260). *Some Thoughts* saw Edwards go on the offensive, insisting

that the revivals were the proof that human nature was a unitary composite of reasoning and willing, so that movements of God on "the sense of the heart" moved the whole person together. Even more, Edwards insisted, the revivals were themselves the fulfillment of prophecy, so that Old Light resistance was cast, not as the voice of restraint, but of unbelief. *The Religious Affections* was Edwards's most profound effort, laying out in 12 signs the distinction between true and false religion and the right place of the emotions, or "affections" (avoiding the pejorative term "passions"), in religious experience.

Both *Some Thoughts* and *The Religious Affections,* however, show signs of stress in Edwards, since the aftermath of the Great Awakening in Northampton proved to be a severe disappointment to Edwards, as many of the awakened gradually subsided into religious listlessness. In 1744 Edwards reimposed the communion test, abandoned by Solomon Stoddard, which had required profession of an experience of saving grace. The Northampton church, which had been bred to "esteem" Stoddard's teachings "all as oracles," rose in revolt against Edwards. They discerned, in the reinstated test, an effort by Edwards to add to simple good intentions and acceptable outward qualifications a new attempt to judge people's inner sanctity, and to use the sacrament as a warning that mere blamelessness of life was not enough to merit sacramental participation. Edwards protested that he had no intention of "pretending to a discriminating judgment of men's spiritual state, so as infallibly to determine who are true converts and who are not" (*WJE* 16.343). But new applications for admission to communion evaporated, influential families stepped away from supporting Edwards, and by 1749 it was clear even to Edwards that his days were numbered in Northampton. A council of local churches and clergy was called by the Northampton church in June 1750, and on June 22 he was formally dismissed from the office of pastor in Northampton.

3. Later Writings, Assessment

"Thrown upon the wide ocean of the world" (*WJE* 16.355), Edwards accepted an offer of the Boston Commissioners of the Society for Propagating the Gospel in New England to take charge of the Mohegan Indian mission at Stockbridge, Massachusetts, 60 miles west of Northampton. He was an indifferent missionary, but the → mission work gave him time to turn back to his philosophical notebooks, and between 1751 and 1757 he produced two manuscript "dissertations" on ontology and ethics (*Concerning the End for Which God Created the*

World and *On the Nature of True Virtue*), plus two major treatises (*Freedom of the Will* [1754] and *Original Sin* [1758]). *Freedom of the Will* was his magnum opus, and the greatest work of theological philosophy in America before the writings of William James. In it Edwards directly addressed the capture by Hobbesian → materialism of determinist notions of human volition and condemned the subsequent flight of Edwards's Calvinist contemporaries into various forms of free-willism. Edwards insisted that determinism (and, through it, → Calvinism) had to be embraced, Hobbes or not, as the only workable basis for a viable theism. Determinism, Edwards argued, not only secured a doctrine of → providence, without which any notion of God would be worthless, but left more than sufficient room for human action without inducing → fatalism.

Edwards was at work on *History of Redemption* in 1757 when the trustees of the College of New Jersey (Princeton), which had been founded to train New Light clergy in the mid-Atlantic British colonies, offered Edwards its presidency. He accepted and arrived to take up his duties in late January 1758. On February 23 he was inoculated against smallpox as a precaution, but adverse complications from the inoculations set in, and he died on March 22. He was buried at Princeton.

Edwards never lost the sense he had acquired in the 1720s of the all-encompassing sovereignty of God and of how God's ideas were constitutive of all reality. This conviction, so similar to → Pascal and → Pietism as well as immaterialism, locates Edwards within the two intellectual movements in the 18th century most critical of the Enlightenment. At the same time, his practical writings (esp. the revival treatises and his edition of the journal of the missionary David Brainerd) and preaching established him as a complex theological thinker and the single most influential practical activist in shaping the contours of American evangelicalism (→ Evangelical).

Bibliography: Primary sources: J. E. SMITH, H. S. STOUT, and K. P. MINKEMA, eds., *A Jonathan Edwards Reader* (New Haven, 1995) • H. STOUT, ed., *The Works of Jonathan Edwards* (New Haven, 1957-).

Secondary works: T. ERDT, *Jonathan Edwards: Art and the Sense of the Heart* (Amherst, Mass., 1980) • N. FIERING, *Jonathan Edwards's Moral Thought and Its British Context* (Chapel Hill, N.C., 1981) • A. C. GUELZO, *Edwards on the Will: A Century of American Theological Debate, 1750-1850* (Middletown, Conn., 1989) • C. HOLBROOK, *The Ethics of Jonathan Edwards: Morality and Aesthetics* (Ann Arbor, Mich., 1973) • W. S. MORRIS, *The Young Jonathan Edwards: A Reconstruction* (Brooklyn, N.Y., 1991) • P. TRACY, *Jonathan Edwards, Pastor: Religion and Society in Eighteenth-Century Northampton* (New York, 1979) • O. E. WINSLOW, *Jonathan Edwards, 1703-1758: A Biography* (New York, 1940).

ALLEN C. GUELZO

Ego Psychology

Ego psychology is a movement within → psychoanalytic psychology. It is associated with the names of Anna Freud (1895-1982), Heinz Hartmann, David Rapaport, Robert White, and Erik Erikson. The common feature of this school is its increased emphasis, in contrast to Sigmund Freud (1856-1939), upon the ego as the central organizing agency of the personality. This school saw the ego as somewhat more independent of the id than did Freud. In addition, it saw the ego as crucial for mental health, treating it as an agency of the mind, and believed that, along with the vicissitudes of the id, it is worthy of study with the tools of psychoanalysis. Psychoanalytic ego psychology should be distinguished from the neo-Freudian school of psychoanalysis associated with the names of Karen Horney, Erich Fromm, and Harry Stack Sullivan. It should also be distinguished from the British school of object relations theory associated with the names of W. R. D. Fairbairn, D. W. Winnicott, and Harry Guntrip. And finally, it can be distinguished from the American school of self-psychology originated by Heinz Kohut.

Although Freud's late structural theory of the personality, which distinguished between the superego, ego, and id, did indeed give a prominent role to the ego as the executive center of the personality and the agency most involved in the signaling of → anxiety, Freud still tended to see the ego as relatively powerless in relation to the libidinal forces of the id. For instance, he believed the energies of the ego were totally derived, through complex processes of neutralization, from the id.

Anna Freud's work *The Ego and the Mechanisms of Defense* (1936) took a step toward a more mature ego psychology by presenting a brilliant description of the basic defense maneuvers that the ego performs in warding off frightening sources of anxiety from the id, the superego, or the external world. The major figure in psychoanalytic ego psychology, however, was Heinz Hartmann. In his seminal *Ego Psychology and the Problem of Adaptation* (1939), Hartmann advanced the theory that the ego had its own structures that grounded the processes of thinking, perceiving, remembering, and motility. Not all psychic structure evolved, as Freud had taught, out of → conflict between libidinal impulse (→ Libido) and the renunciations forced by the external world. Hence Hartmann spoke of a "conflict-free" sphere of the ego that developed alongside of, and indeed sometimes supported, the part of the ego that was more directly a result of libidinal conflict. Although Hartmann posited a fund of psychobiological structures supporting the functions of the ego's thinking, perceiving, remembering, and motility, he did retain Freud's belief that the energies of the ego were derived from the neutralized energies of the id, both the sexual or life energies called eros and those energies that Freud in his later theories associated with death and destructiveness.

Robert White, in his *Ego and Reality in Psychoanalytic Theory* (1963), took a step further in arguing that the ego had both energies and structures independent of the id. He spoke of the ego's "need for effectance" and of "independent ego energies." For White, → health was significantly associated with the ego's sense of being a center of → causality.

Erikson is the most widely known and respected of the psychoanalytic ego psychologists. Although he was not as theoretically oriented as either Hartmann or White, he still made enormous conceptual contributions to psychoanalysis. He, like Hartmann and White, saw the ego as an important agency of the personality. His major contribution involved charting the stages of ego development. Erikson argued that development centers on a series of nuclear conflicts within the ego that must be favorably resolved for development to move forward toward maturity. Erikson is also famous for introducing the concept of → identity into psychoanalytic theory. The ego, according to Erikson, develops a psychosocial identity, which gives it a sense of self-definition, self-cohesion, and self-esteem. Social attitudes on the part of others, → ideologies, and the great historic symbols and traditions all enter into individual styles of ego synthesis to play a part in establishing individual and social ego-identity.

Psychoanalytic ego psychology is a fundamental source for the clinical practice of a variety of helping disciplines, especially in the United States. It has also been a major source for the → psychotherapeutic theories informing American pastoral psychotherapy and → counseling (→ Pastoral Care).

→ Development 2; Narcissism; Psychology; Self

Bibliography: E. Erikson, *Childhood and Society* (New York, 1950); idem, *Identity, Youth, and Crisis* (New York, 1963) • A. Freud, *The Ego and the Mechanisms of Defense* (1936; rev. ed., New York, 1967) • H. Hart-mann, *Ego Psychology and the Problem of Adaptation* (New York, 1939, 1964) • R. White, *Ego and Reality in Psychoanalytic Theory* (New York, 1963).

Don S. Browning

Egypt

	1960	1980	2000
Population (1,000s):	27,840	43,749	68,119
Annual growth rate (%):	2.51	2.57	1.73

Area: 997,739 sq. km. (385,229 sq. mi.)

A.D. 2000

Population density: 68/sq. km. (177/sq. mi.)
Births / deaths: 2.40 / 0.65 per 100 population
Fertility rate: 2.97 per woman
Infant mortality rate: 43 per 1,000 live births
Life expectancy: 68.1 years (m: 66.6, f: 69.6)
Religious affiliation (%): Muslims 83.4, Christians 16.0 (Orthodox 14.4, other Christians 1.6), other 0.6.

1. Data
2. Christian Churches
3. Islam
4. Church Relations to the State and Islam

1. Data

Egypt is the most populous Arab country, even though the Nile makes only 4 percent of its land mass suitable for habitation and cultivation. The foundation of the modern Arab Republic of Egypt (Jumhūrīyat Miṣr al-ʿArabīyah), as it has been called since 1971, was laid in July 1952, when the reforming Free Officers under Colonel Gamal Abdel Nasser (1918-70) seized power. Egypt had previously been a constitutional monarchy, set up in 1923 after the defeat of the Ottoman Empire in World War I. It had also been an Ottoman province from 1517, although it came to occupy a special position under the Albanian adventurer Muḥammad ʿAlī (ruled 1805-49), who established a dynasty that lasted until the revolution of 1952. He and his successors wrested effective power in Egypt from the Ottomans until 1882, when the country in all but name became a British protectorate (a status formalized in 1914). From 1958 until 1961 Egypt joined with Syria to form the United Arab Republic, renewing a relationship that had been a fairly constant feature of Islamic history up to the 16th century except for interruption by the → Crusades.

The current president, Hosni Mubarak (in office

since 1981), continues many of the policies of his predecessor, Anwar Sadat (in office from 1970 until his assassination in 1981): moving toward a free-market economy instead of the Arab socialism of Nasser; looking to the West for help in confronting numerous problems in agriculture, urbanization, and industrialization; and working toward normalization of Arab-Israeli relationships. He favors a liberal multiparty system under state control and state dialogue with religious groups.

2. Christian Churches

Christianity is important in Egypt as the oldest religious group in the country. → Judaism, which has seen the emigration of the vast majority of its 75,000 members since 1950, has little current influence. The beginnings of Christianity in Egypt are shrouded in mystery. While Western historians strive to take account of a complex diversity of literary and papyrological evidence for early Christian Egypt, including the → Nag Hammadi Gnostic library (→ Heresies and Schisms), Egyptian Christians proudly recall the itinerary of the Holy Family during their flight into Egypt (Matt. 2:13-15) and recite the account of Egypt's evangelization by St. Mark the Evangelist. In any event, Christianity quickly became a significant force in Egypt, and at the time of the Arab conquest in 641 it had long been in a position of cultural dominance. During these early centuries Egyptian Christianity made critical contributions to early Christian literature, dogmatic formulation, and forms of life. It may be sufficient here to mention the names of → church fathers and founders of the great → Alexandrian theology such as → Clement (ca. 150-ca. 215) and → Origen (ca. 185-ca. 254), patriarchs who took a leading role in the church's dogmatic definitions such as → Athanasius (patriarch 328-73) and → Cyril (patriarch 412-44), and founders of anchoritic and cenobitic monasticism such as (respectively) Anthony (251?-356) and Pachomius (ca. 290-346). Ancient Christian Egypt was a magnet for visitors, whether to the monasteries and hermitages of the desert fathers or to shrines such as that of St. Menas, which especially in the fourth and fifth centuries drew pilgrims from throughout the Christian world.

Most Egyptian Christians supported the anti-Chalcedonian position of Patriarch Dioscoros (patriarch 444-51, d. 454), who was deposed and exiled by the Council of → Chalcedon in 451. Byzantine attempts to impose the official imperial theology came to an end with the Arab Muslim conquest of the eastern Byzantine provinces and the separation

from the Byzantine heartland of the Christian communities that were pejoratively labeled Monophysite. The Muslim rulers of Egypt for the most part permitted the free exercise of Christian faith, although Christians came to experience a variety of social, cultural, and economic pressures toward the adoption of the Arabic language and the embracing of Islamic faith. The Egyptian church eventually responded to pressures of Arabization with a program of translation of crucial texts and the use of Arabic in the liturgy, culminating in a brilliant flowering of Arabic-language Christian literature in the 13th century, evoked, for example, by mention of the Awlād al-ʿAssāl, three brothers who made extraordinary contributions in theology, biblical study and translation, apologetics, and canon law.

With the passage of time, however, many Egyptian Christians converted to Islam, particularly in the Delta, leading to the current situation in which only a minority of Egypt's population is Christian. The general decadence *(inḥiṭāṭ)* that characterized cultural life in the Arab world during the Ottoman period did not leave the Egyptian church unaffected. Modernizing trends in the 19th century, as well as competition from Roman Catholic and Protestant groups, contributed to a reawakening of the → Coptic Orthodox Church, one that accelerated with the "Sunday School movement" that thrived during the 1940s and 1950s and the monastic revival that this movement inspired.

The Coptic Orthodox Church regards itself as the guardian of a rich theological, liturgical, ecclesiastical, legal, artistic, and literary heritage, a church that has been faithful in its Christian life without interruption, despite → persecution under the Romans (the Coptic "calendar of the martyrs" begins with the accession in A.D. 284 of the persecuting Emperor Diocletian) and the vicissitudes of life under Muslim rule. It is led by "the patriarch of Alexandria and all the See of St. Mark," who enjoys the title "pope" and whose cathedral is now located in Cairo. There are no reliable statistics as to the number of members, though estimates range as high as nine million (in Egypt), which would make this church the largest Christian community in the Middle East. A very considerable Coptic emigration from Egypt over the past three decades has led to the founding of Coptic Orthodox churches throughout the world, especially in North America, Europe, and Australia. Bishops — of whom there are now more than 60 — are celibate monks recruited from the monasteries, while congregational priests are mostly married.

An extraordinary monastic revival since about

1960 has led to a tremendous expansion of some monasteries, the repopulation of deserted ones, and the building of new ones. Some of the most important monasteries are those of Wadi an-Naṭrūn between Cairo and Alexandria, the newly reestablished monastery of St. Menas, the monasteries of St. Anthony and St. Paul near the Gulf of Suez, and al-Muḥarraq Monastery near Asyūṭ. A number of convents for nuns, in Cairo and elsewhere, also deserve mention.

Coptic Orthodox churches, including many new ones, preserve the ancient Coptic language of the liturgy (alongside Arabic) and are actively involved in providing → religious education for members of all ages. A theological seminary located at the patriarchate in Cairo, in addition to a number of seminaries throughout Egypt and the Coptic Institute for Higher Studies in Cairo, provides training for → priests and lay leaders in the churches. In the last few years a number of monasteries, independent publishing houses, and organizations such as the Patristic Centre of the St. Antonius Foundation have contributed to a noteworthy upsurge in the publication of Coptic Orthodox literature, including medieval Arabic theology and good Arabic translations of patristic texts.

Other → Oriental (i.e., non-Chalcedonian) Orthodox communities are represented in Egypt, including the Armenian, the Ethiopian, and the Syrian Orthodox churches. Christian communities that recognize the Council of Chalcedon are also present. There is a small Chalcedonian Orthodox community under their patriarch of Alexandria, as well as a → Melchite (Greek Catholic) community. Through → union with → Rome, a Coptic Catholic community came into being in the 18th century, and today Catholics play a very significant role in education and — with their theological institutes, specialized libraries, and highly trained leadership — in the spiritual and intellectual life of Egyptian Christians. In addition to the Coptic Catholics, Syrian, Armenian, Maronite, Chaldean, and Latin Catholics have settled in Egypt.

Beginning with the arrival of three American missionaries in 1854, an evangelical synod associated with the United Presbyterian Church of North America took shape, made up mostly of former Coptic Orthodox. In 1958 the Evangelical Synod of the Nile, with seven presbyteries, achieved full independence. It has an ambitious program of medical, educational, and development activity; noteworthy is the work of the Coptic Evangelical Organization for Social Services, a leading Egyptian non-governmental organization. The Evangelical Synod

has a seminary in Cairo for the training of pastors and lay leaders. Other smaller denominations and missions are also present in Egypt, including an Anglican Church (founded through the work of the Church Missionary Society, esp. from 1882), and a number of small Protestant denominations (including Wesleyan, Pentecostal, Baptist, Adventist, and Plymouth Brethren).

Many of the churches in Egypt cooperate through the → World Council of Churches and the → Middle East Council of Churches. The latter brings theological institutions from throughout the Middle East together in the Association for Theological Education in the Middle East. Other independent ecumenically based organizations, such as the Bible Society of Egypt, carry on a wide range of activities.

3. Islam

Islam established itself in Egypt in the seventh century, and today Sunni Muslims compose some 85 percent of the population. According to article 2 of the Egyptian constitution (as amended in 1980), Islam is the religion of the state and the Islamic Shariʿa is the (before 1980: "a") chief source of legislation. This last point has been controversial, given the mixed nature of Egypt's European- and Ottoman-influenced law codes. While the governing authorities have taken the position that this constitutional provision means that future legislation should not come into conflict with clear provisions of the Islamic Shariʿa, Islamic revivalists have called for the immediate implementation of the Islamic Shariʿa to the exclusion of other codes. The battle over the Shariʿa is fought in a variety of ways, for example, over periodic attempts since 1979 to reform personal-status laws in such a way as to protect the rights of women in matters of divorce and multiple marriages. Christians, it might be noted, have followed debates concerning the place of the Shariʿa in Egyptian society with unease, sensing that one question to be resolved is whether, in the revivalists' vision of an authentically Islamic state, Christians will be full co-citizens with Muslims, or whether they will be merely *dhimmiyūn* (protected people).

The center of Islamic theology and law is al-Azhar University in Cairo (founded in 970), which claims and provides leadership throughout the Sunni Islamic world. Its head, the *shaykh al-Azhar,* like the mufti of the republic (the senior scholar qualified to issue Islamic legal opinions) and the minister of religious foundations (responsible esp. for government-supported mosques), is appointed by the government. Sufi piety has always been a part of the Egyptian Islamic mosaic, and the annual celebrations at the shrines of particular holy men (e.g., the *mawlid,* or feast, of Sayyid al-Badawī in Ṭanṭa) may attract participants numbering in the millions. About 70 Sufi orders are now grouped into a Sufi Council, which regulates their organization and their integration into officially sanctioned Islam.

Some Sufi orders, as well as other Islamic organizations, do their best to avoid co-option or control by the state. The Muslim Brotherhood *(al-Ikhwān al-Muslimūn)* must be mentioned here. Founded in Egypt in 1928, it evolved into a movement working for an authentically Islamic society capable of meeting the challenges of modernity and of resisting ongoing forms of Western → colonialism. Its success as a mass organization and its political activities have brought it into frequent clashes with state power. Although initially allied to Nasser's Free Officers, the Nasserist regime soon turned against the Brotherhood and brutally repressed it. Repeated imprisonment and torture of its members contributed to the development within the movement of militant ideologies, largely indebted to the thought of Sayyid Quṭb, a member imprisoned for the first time in 1954 and executed in 1966. The governments of Sadat (in the 1970s) and Mubarak (in the 1980s) made conciliatory gestures toward the moderate Brothers who sought to work "within the system" and to establish the Brotherhood as a serious force in Egyptian social and political life. At the same time, however, militant movements proliferated, including those responsible for the murder of Sadat in 1981 and for a number of highly publicized attacks in the 1990s on public officials, Copts, and foreign tourists. Recent government policy has wavered between making concessions to the moderate Islamists and considering them as cover for militant elements.

4. Church Relations to the State and Islam

The official vision of Christian-Muslim relations in Egypt is summed up under the slogan *al-waḥdah al-waṭanīyah* (national unity), referring to harmonious Christian-Muslim relations in the one Egyptian homeland. There is considerable substance to the slogan: from the seventh century, Christians and Muslims have lived together in Egypt, normally with a high degree of mutual tolerance and cooperation. Frequently related stories include those of the friendly meeting between the conqueror and first Islamic governor of Egypt, ʿAmr ibn al-ʿĀṣ (642-44), with the Coptic patriarch Benjamin; of Copts and Muslims preaching in one another's houses of wor-

ship during the struggle for independence from the British; and of the very significant Christian participation in the Wafd party, which after World War I led Egypt to independence and the establishment of a liberal constitutional monarchy.

Throughout the 20th century, however, the relationships of the Christian community to the state and to the Islamic community were in flux. Article 40 of the Egyptian constitution guarantees the equality of citizens before the law without distinction of race, origin, language, or religion, and article 46 guarantees freedom of belief and religious practice. The building and repair of churches, however, have been governed by the Ottoman "Ḥamayūnī Line," requiring a decree from the head of state (or, since 1998, the provincial governor), and open proselytization of Muslims, or conversion of Muslims to Christianity, is in effect forbidden. (In 1977, however, the Coptic Church was successful in its opposition to a proposed law that would have made leaving Islam punishable by death.) Complaints about a variety of problems, including discrimination against Christians in certain sectors of Egyptian life, a near absence of Christian programming in the media, and a strongly Islamic bias in educational curricula may be heard from human → rights activists (including many Muslims), ordinary Copts in Egypt, and members of the growing (and increasingly vocal) Coptic diaspora throughout the world.

The Christian reawakening mentioned earlier ran parallel to an Islamic upsurge inaugurated by the Muslim Brotherhood, and by the 1970s there was great potential for conflict not merely between the two communities but also between each and the state. Just before his assassination in 1981, Sadat had ordered the arrest of hundreds of Islamic and Christian activists and had exiled Coptic Orthodox Pope Shenouda (patriarch since 1971) to his desert monastery. In the Mubarak era church officials have been careful to display their loyalty to a government that has democratic and secular commitments and that represents a bulwark against militant tendencies, and they have nurtured ties of friendship and cooperation with moderate Islamic leaders. The current system is not entirely stable, however, and periodic episodes of terrorist attacks against Copts (as at the Church of St. George in Abu Qurqās in February 1997) or of sectarian violence (as in the town of al-Kushḥ in January 2000) put considerable stress on Christian-Muslim relations and the ideology of *al-waḥdah al-waṭanīyah.* A great challenge of the new century will be to give renewed substance to this venerable slogan.

Bibliography: N. ABDEL-FATTAH and D. RASHWAN, eds., *The State of Religion in Egypt Report, 1995* (Cairo, 1997) • A. S. ATIYA, *A History of Eastern Christianity* (London, 1968); idem, ed., *The Coptic Encyclopedia* (8 vols.; New York, 1991) • M. W. DALY, ed., *The Cambridge History of Egypt,* vol. 2, *Modern Egypt from 1517 to the End of the Twentieth Century* (Cambridge, 1998) • N. VAN DOORN-HARDER and K. VOGT, eds., *Between Desert and City: The Coptic Orthodox Church Today* (Oslo, 1997) • D. FRANKFURTER, *Pilgrimage and Holy Space in Late Antique Egypt* (Leiden, 1998) • S. E. IBRAHIM et al., *The Copts of Egypt* (London, 1996) • G. KRÄMER, "Dhimmi or Citizen? Muslim-Christian Relations in Egypt," *The Christian-Muslim Frontier: Chaos, Clash, or Dialogue?* (ed. J. S. Nielsen; London, 1998) 33-49 • O. F. A. MEINARDUS, *Christian Egypt, Ancient and Modern* (Cairo, 1977); idem, *Christian Egypt, Faith and Life* (Cairo, 1970); idem, *Monks and Monasteries of the Egyptian Deserts* (Cairo, 1992); idem, *Two Thousand Years of Coptic Christianity* (Cairo, 1999) • T. H. PARTRICK, *Traditional Egyptian Christianity: A History of the Coptic Orthodox Church* (GREENSBORO, N.C., 1996) • B. A. PEARSON and J. E. GOEHRING, eds., *The Roots of Egyptian Christianity* (Philadelphia, 1986) • C. F. PETRY, ed., *The Cambridge History of Egypt,* vol. 1, *Islamic Egypt, 640-1517* (Cambridge, 1998) • C. H. ROBERTS, *Manuscript, Society, and Belief in Early Christian Egypt* (London, 1979) • P. J. VATIKIOTIS, *The History of Egypt: From Muhammad Ali to Mubarak* (Baltimore, 1985).

CARSTEN COLPE and MARK N. SWANSON

Egyptian Religion

1. The Gods and Mythology
   1.1. Names and Forms
   1.2. Divine Nearness and Transcendence
   1.3. Explicit Theology
2. Cult of the Dead
   2.1. The Hereafter
   2.2. Immortality
   2.3. Passage of the Dead

1. The Gods and Mythology
1.1. *Names and Forms*
In Egyptian religion the combination of a theistic idea of God with a theriomorphic form (also with mixed forms) is typical. In the construction of the divine identity, there is thus a multiplicity that comes to expression in many names and forms. Splitting the major gods into local forms and fusing the gods together (→ Syncretism) are contradictory tendencies.

Alongside 25-30 major deities, among whom the sun god and the equally ranked state god Amon-Re are always chief, there are a large but indefinite number of lesser deities. With the polytheistic concept of a god as a member of the divine world, there developed from as early as the wisdom literature (from 2000 B.C.) the concept of God as a transcendent Creator and Sustainer who embraces the world of human and divine beings. Countergods are Seth (the enemy of Osiris, who appears also as the partner of Horus and is integrated into the pantheon as the helper of the sun god) and Apepi (the enemy of the sun god, who threatens to stop the sun in its course).

1.2. *Divine Nearness and Transcendence*
Religion, understood as intercourse with the gods, implies ideas of possible contact (receiving divine attention, undergoing religious experience), which can be viewed as dimensions of divine nearness. In the sphere of religious action and experience in Egypt, three dimensions are dominant.

1.2.1. The first is the *cultic* dimension, which has both a local and a political aspect. The cult rests on the idea of the gods dwelling at fixed locations on earth. The temples of local gods are also geographic centers and points of reference for a sense of belonging and political identity. The city god represents the city, the community god the state. The Old Kingdom (2750-2250 B.C.) included both a state and a local cult. The local cult (confirmed archaeologically in only a few cases) took place in modest brick chapels. The state cult took place in monumental buildings, first as the cult of dead kings at the pyramids, then in the fifth dynasty (2400-2250 B.C.) as the cult of the sun at the royal sanctuaries of the sun.

Only with the restoration of the central monarchy after the first intermediate period (2250-2050 B.C.) do we have the typical state monopoly of cultic sites. Now the king was in charge of all buildings, cults, and sacrifices throughout the land. He everywhere built stone temples, delegated the local cults and offerings to priestly guilds, and participated in significant feasts (especially the Osiris mysteries at Abydos). The cults were unified after the model of the royal cult of the dead, regional traditions being restricted to festivals.

In the New Kingdom (1550-1070 B.C.) the state character of local cults found manifestation in a host of monumental new temples. The most important feasts developed in the typical form of processions (oracles also from the 13th cent.) which attracted pilgrims from other regions. The priesthood became a new professional class that eventually became more and more a separate caste.

With the fresh collapse of centralized rule in the third intermediate period (1070-650 B.C.) and the later period (663-525 B.C.), the idea of the earthly rule of God took → theocratic forms. The temples, as divine strongholds, had strong walls around them and were leading intellectual, economic, and administrative centers. The dominance of the cultic dimension culminated in Egypt being honored as the dwelling place of the gods, or *templum totius mundi* (sanctuary of the whole world).

1.2.2. The second dimension is the *cosmic* dimension, which rests on the idea of the divinity of the world, expressed most sharply in the cosmic gods (the earth god Geb, husband of the sky goddess Nut; Shu, the god of light and air, son of the sun god Re) and in the concept of the course of the sun. This concept is distinctively polytheistic, for all the major gods have a hand in this work, which keeps the world going. As a model of the world, the idea of the course of the sun colors the Egyptian view of the world, which is more one of time than of space, as that of a pulsating life process in the rhythm of the two eternities Djet and Neheh. The sun's course is a continuous creation, an order that is achieved afresh each day out of chaos. This order is *ma'at* (order, justice, truth), the Egyptian term for the meaningful fullness of creation that the Creator intended but that is achieved only approximately in reality. Cooperating with the sun's course, the king is under obligation to establish this order.

1.2.3. The third dimension is the *mythological* dimension, which relates to the presence of the gods in what is told about them, with language becoming in effect a temple. Egypt had no canon of sacred writings, but it had many liturgical recitations that expound ritual action in terms of divine events in the world. When these elements developed into narrative compositions, the result was → myth in the narrower sense. The process of development began in the Old Kingdom and lasted to the final stages of Egyptian religion.

The central myth (which in a sense is a state myth) was that of Osiris. Osiris here is more the dead father than the god of the cycles of vegetation and of the cosmos (esp. the moon and the Nile) who dies and rises again, which is how the cult and theology knew him. As such, he was the mythical model for the monarchy (in the role of the son Horus) and for beliefs concerning death and afterlife. The state myth was also the myth of the birth of the divine king, which developed the divine sonship of the king with reference to the sun god or Amon. This myth exerted a de-

cisive influence on the theology of the king in the OT and also on the → Christology of the NT.

The myth of the heavenly cow, as a myth of original guilt, set the present situation in the light of a history that expounded it as the reversal of an original but lost unity when gods and humans lived together on earth under the rule of the sun god. Of the many cosmogonic myths, the most important was the one from Heliopolis, which has the world emanate from the original god Atum as a secretion (seed, phlegm, spittle, sweat, or speech). A rival view was the Memphis doctrine of conception by the heart and tongue of Ptah (i.e., involving the word, not as emanation, but as the expression of conscious planning). In Egypt, however, cosmogony was less a theme of myth than it was of theology.

1.3. *Explicit Theology*

In diametric opposition to the implicit theology of living practice was the explicit theology of the nature of deity, which stemmed about 2000 B.C. from the problem of → theodicy. In the New Kingdom this discussion led to a hymnology that had as its theme, not the personality of the deity as part of a constellation of deities within a polytheistic social sphere, but the transcendent unity of a god beyond the world of the gods. This movement of opposition culminated about 1360 B.C. in the revolutionary religious action of Akhenaton (Amenhotep IV), who closed down the traditional cults and replaced them with the new cult of Aton, god of light. This Amarna religion espoused a militant → monotheism. It replaced the polytheistic view of the divinity of the world with one in which God and the world were juxtaposed. Deprived of its own divine life, the de-divinized world became a mere object of the sustaining energy of the light of the sun. The hymns that developed this view of reality came into OT monotheism by way of Canaanite sources. Parts of the so-called Great Hymn (ÄHG no. 92) find parallels in Psalm 104. On the other side, Amarna religion meant a restoration and enhancement of the royal monopoly of religion. The king was the only priest of the new God. He alone had personal access to the deity, which was revealed to all other living creatures only as cosmic energy. Only the king was the authority for personal devotion. This framework may be seen as a reaction to profound changes in the view of God, which later made a full breakthrough with the failure of Amarna religion.

The idea of God in the period of the Ramses (beginning ca. 1300 B.C.) rested on a new concept of the personality of God, according to which God is not part of a constellation, integrated into the polytheistic social sphere of the divine world, but an inner unity with a single will and ability to plan. Reality comes from the planning will of God, whether as the history of the country or as individual destiny. God makes himself known in oracles. All people are immediate to him in their acts and must decide whether to live in fear of God or in forgetfulness of him. Destiny and history, as a new dimension of the nearness of God, come preponderantly to the fore. The God from whose will reality springs is transcendent and hidden as the one God. The polytheistic world of the gods is simply his form of appearing in the world. The gods are aspects of God, and the cosmos is his body. This concept of God has strong pantheistic features, linking the experience of transcendence in the Amarna period to the divinity of the world. This Ramesside pantheism lived on, especially in magic (Bes Pantheos [a dwarflike Egyptian demon who assumed pantheistic traits in late Egyptian and Greek texts] and Agathos Daimōn [Good spirit]) and the mysteries (Isis religion). From these it passed on into the West by way of hermetism, → gnosis, and → alchemy.

2. Cult of the Dead

2.1. *The Hereafter*

According to the Egyptian view, the pharaoh is a god who after death mounts up to heaven. Royal tombs actualized this ascent, in the Old Kingdom by the clear emphasis on verticality in the symbol of the pyramids, and in the New Kingdom in the form of a system of underground passages and chambers mirroring the passage of the sun through heaven and the underworld.

2.2. *Immortality*

Belief in the dead gained the upper hand only at the end of the Old Kingdom. Previously individual immortality depended on the degree of proximity to the king in this world, originally by burial with him, later by a grave in the royal necropolis. During the Middle Kingdom (2050-1780 B.C.) there emerged the idea of the *ba* as an immortal soul, in the form of which the dead could command transition to the hereafter either into heaven or into the underworld. To do so they had to undergo a series of tests, success in which would open up access for them to eternal nourishment in the bulrush fields and also to the barque of the sun. Later these concepts took the more solid form of an all-powerful idea of the judgment of the dead.

2.3. *Passage of the Dead*

The books of the dead provided support for the passage of the dead to existence in the hereafter, as did various rites. Embalming and washing the dead, along with the associated recitations, accompanied the dead into the divine world. Interment and the "opening the mouth" ceremony inaugurated the sacrificial cult at the grave. In spite of the growing significance of the idea of transition, the identity secured in this life remained decisively intact. The mummy and the monuments preserved and objectified this identity. Similarly, along with the idea of divine pardon at the judgment of the dead, living on in human memory was always a central concern.

Bibliography: J. ASSMANN, *Moses the Egyptian: The Memory of Egypt in Western Monotheism* (Cambridge, Mass., 1997) • S. GRAF, *Books of the Dead: Manuals for Living and Dying* (London, 1994) • G. HART, *A Dictionary of Egyptian Gods and Goddesses* (London, 1990) • K. KOCH, *Geschichte der ägyptischen Religion. Von den Pyramiden bis zu den Mysterien der Isis* (Stuttgart, 1993) • S. MORENZ, *Ägyptische Religion* (2d ed.; Stuttgart, 1977); idem, *Gott und Mensch im alten Ägypten* (2d ed.; Leipzig, 1984) • W. J. MURNAME, *Texts from the Amarna Period in Egypt* (Atlanta, 1995) • E. F. WENTE, trans., *Letters from Ancient Egypt* (Atlanta, 1990).

JAN ASSMANN

El Salvador

	1960	1980	2000
Population (1,000s):	2,578	4,547	6,319
Annual growth rate (%):	3.11	0.56	1.92
Area: 21,041 sq. km. (8,124 sq. mi.)			

A.D. *2000*

Population density: 300/sq. km. (778/sq. mi.)
Births / deaths: 2.50 / 0.58 per 100 population
Fertility rate: 2.76 per woman
Infant mortality rate: 35 per 1,000 live births
Life expectancy: 70.7 years (m: 67.7, f: 73.7)
Religious affiliation (%): Christians 97.6 (Roman Catholics 91.0, indigenous 11.1, Protestants 10.3, marginal 2.5, other Christians 0.5), nonreligious 1.4, other 1.0.

1. General
2. History
3. Protestants

1. General

The Central American republic of El Salvador has by far the highest population density of any country in Central or South America. This factor, along with an inequitable distribution of resources, results in a grinding → poverty for most of the people. After 1932 there was also an ongoing policy of government repression, so that the situation of the poor is clearly bleak.

From 1980 to 1992 the country suffered a bloody and destructive civil war. Explosive outbreaks, reactions to extreme poverty, were initiated by paramilitary organizations, leading to armed conflict with the government, which enjoyed the backing of the United States. During the war some 75,000 people lost their lives. The terms of the peace treaty permitted the incorporation of the guerrillas into political life and opened the door for democratization. The transitional period after the war, however, has been characterized by an increase in violence and in the widening breach between rich and poor. These two problems, plus the legacy of authoritarianism, have hindered the democratization of El Salvador.

Christian faith is the basis of the people's outlook. Up to the recent past, however, there was no direct link between faith and the demands for justice (→ Righteousness, Justice) and liberation. Only after → Vatican II and the 1968 Medellín bishops' conference (→ Latin American Council of Bishops) has faith matured and come to have a connection with the process of liberation. A true church of the poor has been gradually emerging, for the poor are seeing that they are the main and favored subject of the church. Oscar A. Romero, archbishop of San Salvador from 1977 to 1980, is indissolubly bound up with this development. Yet even his clear policy did not carry all the bishops with it, and it could not be sustained after his assassination on March 24, 1980.

Romero's successor, Arturo Rivera (who had different talents and was under various pressures), insisted more on the ethical dimension of faith. Even so, he kept alive the → base communities' flame of hope. Changes in the bishops' conference and the distrust toward the base communities and → liberation theology have considerably reduced his leadership in ecclesiastical life. Since the end of the 1980s, the Salvadoran church has been characterized more by charismatic and Pentecostal movements, which have shown little interest in the country's current situation.

Faith tested in persecution and martyrdom are broad characteristics of the Salvadoran church (→ Persecution of Christians 4.2). Thousands of catechists, delegates of the Word, 5 nuns, 11 priests (most of them parish → pastors), 1 archbishop, and thousands of other Christians have been murdered because of their advocacy of faith and justice. In actuality, despite the surge of conservatism, the Salvadoran church affectionately preserves this martyr tradition.

2. History

El Salvador was evangelized at the same time as the rest of Central America, beginning in 1540, after the military conquest (→ Mission 3). The mode of → evangelism was also the same, namely, the system of forced Indian settlements, or → reductions, where the subjected native population was gathered to provide labor. In the reductions the members of the orders tried to establish the faith of the conquerors. They met with stiff resistance from the natives, who did not want spiritual subjection but who viewed the new faith from their own perspective and developed a → syncretism that for centuries was the basis of a specific popular religion (→ Popular Religion).

In the struggle for independence from Spain (1811-21), various Creole priests emerged who defended their own interests against the demands of the Spaniards, which by now had become intolerable. Their strivings for autonomy went as far as to insist on religious freedom from Guatemala and the establishment by civil law of a separate → diocese, which previously neither crown nor papacy had been willing to grant. A decade of schism and unrest resulted. Only in 1843 did the church set up the Diocese of El Salvador, the papacy being opposed to conceding the rights of patronage to the Salvadoran state.

The first canonical → bishop was himself involved directly in the regional power struggles of the epoch and ended his term in exile. The faith of the people remained constant, based on a traditionalism that resisted both time and the march of history.

Toward the end of the 19th century coffee was the country's only export, a situation that led to → secularization and the first real struggle for power with the church. The disputes were violent, including the exile of church leaders, but soon came to an end. The institutional church sought to preserve various privileges that the secular state was not prepared to grant. In the hierarchy the view prevailed that it could not fulfill its religious task without these rights. The persecution the church received was not a true Christian persecution, for it arose over the privileges it enjoyed, not because of its faith.

In a surprisingly short time the two sides reached agreement, but the church remained subordinate to the state (→ Church and State). It accepted the hegemony of both the state and the coffee oligarchy, hoping in vain to eventually regain some of its lost privileges. In the process, however, it neglected the prophetic dimension of its work. The state granted the church some freedom but kept it under control, even as the hierarchy placed its moral authority in the service of the state and the dominant groups. This situation prevailed up to the mid-1960s, but then some groups had begun to question the established order. This process culminated in a formal break made by Archbishop Romero, who opposed the state in the name of the oppressed people, now increasingly organized in church base communities as "the church of the people."

The Christian base communities and liberation theology had a conspicuous role in the early 1980s, when the faith and social commitment of many Christians sprang to life. In the mid-1980s, however, the movement began to feel the destructive effects of the war and of the distrust of ecclesiastical authorities. The end of the war heightened this crisis. The base communities survived into the new millennium with faith and hope, although in much smaller numbers. These communities are now concentrated in rural and in marginal urban zones, accompanied by some priests and a few nuns.

3. Protestants

In 1897 the Misión Centroamericana (Central American Mission) was founded with the coming of the first → missionary from North America, who visited the villages and brought Bibles to each home. This mission soon gained influence both in the capital and in the provinces. In 1990 there were Salvadoran pastors in most of the 250 congregations, most of them in the center of the country and the western districts.

The work of the → Baptists began in 1911 under the direction of the U.S. American Baptist Home Mission Society. Originally limited to the interior and the west, this work later spread to the east. In 1990 this group had 58 congregations and 11 mission schools. Along with the preaching of the Word, this mission also gives aid in the communes. These are two of the larger and more representative Protestant groups.

The Missouri Synod Lutherans (→ Lutheran Churches) began work in the 1950s and by 1990 had formed an indigenous church with some 10,000 members in 76 congregations under a bishop, various pastors, and a dozen lay pastors (deacons). The Lutherans cooperate with the Baptists and Episcopalians in diakonia to provide the personal and material help of the → Lutheran World Federation for refugees. In 1984 this work led to the assassination of Pastor David Fernández of San Miguel.

The number of Protestants rose from 1.2 percent of the population in 1949 to 5.3 percent in 1980, to almost double that figure in 2000. Of these Protestants, 60-70 percent are Pentecostals (→ Pentecostal Churches), whose numbers increased significantly beginning around 1965, as did the numbers of smaller evangelical groups and fundamentalist sects (→ Evan-

gelical Movement; Fundamentalism). Only 20 percent of the Protestants belong to churches in the → ecumenical movement. The growth of Protestantism is linked to the poverty of the people and the general uncertainty of life, though also to the policy of the United States, which since Medellín has tried to limit the social influence of the → Roman Catholic Church.

The poverty of the greatest part of the people, along with the war, has brought the historic Protestant churches and Roman Catholics closer together. This ecumenism, however, is less the result of dogmatic agreement than it is of the common need to proclaim the good news in a country ravaged by war and poverty. The clearest ecumenical manifestations occurred during the time of Archbishop Romero. After the war, ecumenical relations began slowly dissolving, so that little activity is visible in 2000. More prominent is the church's ability to capture the attention of the → masses through the use of radio, television, and large rallies.

Bibliography: P. BERRYMAN, *The Religious Roots of Rebellion* (London, 1984) • P. BORGES, *Historia de la Iglesia en Hispanoamérica y Filipinas* (2 vols.; Madrid, 1992) • J. BROCKMAN, *La palabra queda. Vida de Mons. Oscar A. Romero* (San Salvador, 1985) • R. CARDENAL, *Historia de una esperanza. Vida de Rutilio Grande* (San Salvador, 1985); idem, *El poder eclesiástico en El Salvador, 1871-1931* (San Salvador, 1980); idem, ed., *América Central*, vol. 6, *Historia general de la iglesia en América Latina* (Salamanca, 1985) • R. CARDENAL, I. MARTÍN BARÓ, and J. SOBRINO, *La voz de los sin voz. La palabra viva de Mons. Romero* (San Salvador, 1980) • M. DOGGET, *Death Foretold: The Jesuit Murderers in El Salvador* (New York, 1993) • P. GALDÁMEZ, *The Faith of People: The Life of a Basic Christian Community in El Salvador* (New York, 1986) • D. KEOGH, *Church and Politics in Latin America* (London, 1990) • P. LERNOUX, *Cry of the People: The Struggle for Human Rights in Latin America. The Catholic Church in Conflict with U.S. Policy* (New York, 1980); idem, *People of God: The Struggle for World Catholicism* (New York, 1989) • T. S. MONTGOMERY, *Revolution in El Salvador: From Civil Strife to Civil Peace* (Boulder, Colo., 1995) • A. L. PETERSON, *Martyrdom and the Politics of Religion: Progressive Catholicism in El Salvador's Civil War* (Albany, N.Y., 1997) • H. J. PRIEN, *Historia del cristianismo en América Latina* (Salamanca, 1985) • H. SCHÄFER, "'¡Oh Señor de los cielos, danos poder en la tierra!' El fundamentalismo y los carismas: La reconquista del campo de acción en América Latina," *Mesoamérica* 33 (1997) 125-46 • A. WHITE, *El Salvador* (London, 1973).

RODOLFO CARDENAL, S.J.

Elder

Elders, or presbyters (Gk. *presbyteroi*), are members of Christian congregations entrusted with special ministries in leadership, → liturgy, → church discipline, and → diakonia.

1. The organization of the → early church shows plainly the influence of the Jewish synagogue and the Greek laws pertaining to societies, though there is no direct continuity. In the NT we see various → charismata, from which the offices of → bishop, elder, and → deacon soon arose. For the most part, the elders had collegial functions. Already in the → Pastoral Epistles and the → Apostolic Fathers, a tendency is apparent to subordinate the elder as a → priest hierarchically to the bishop, as in the canon law of the → Roman Catholic Church, and partly so also in the → Orthodox Church and the → Anglican Communion.

2. In spite of some beginnings in the early M. → Luther (1483-1546), the congregation did not achieve a legal coresponsibility in the German → Reformation. U. → Zwingli (1484-1531) and some German city-states followed up certain later medieval innovations and gave a share in church leadership to communal boards.

Influenced by Lambert of Avignon (1486-1530) and M. → Bucer (1491-1551), J. → Calvin (1509-64) developed a doctrine of four offices, entrusting leadership and church discipline to elders as well as pastors, teachers, and deacons. By way of France, Holland, and the Lower Rhine, this scheme later became a basic element in the presbyterial-synodal constitution of Reformed and Presbyterian churches. Elders also have a role in Congregational, independent, and Baptist churches.

In the 19th century many Protestant churches shared leadership with selected organs of the congregation, though partly under the influence of ideas of democracy and self-government. It was the → church struggle that first brought to the office a new consideration of its spiritual nature.

3. Most → Reformed, → Lutheran, and → union churches today have elders who are elected (more rarely appointed) and who serve without salary. They must usually be between 18 and 75 years of age. In many churches women may also be elected. Liturgical installation is customary, and sometimes → ordination. Elders share in leadership, administration, liturgy, and diakonia, but with less emphasis today on discipline. Lutherans stress their task of advising the → pastor. They normally play a part in → synods and to some extent also in → church government.

4. Since → Vatican II and the 1983 → Codex Iuris Canonici, the Roman Catholic Church has stressed more strongly the importance of consultative lay boards (congregational councils, etc.) in addition to the official → hierarchy.

→ Starets

Bibliography: G. BERGHOEF and L. DE KOSTER, *The Elders Handbook: A Practical Guide for Church Leaders* (Grand Rapids, 1979) • R. A. CAMPBELL, *The Elders: Seniority within Earliest Christianity* (Edinburgh, 1994) • H. VON CAMPENHAUSEN, *Ecclesiastical Authority and Spiritual Power in the Church of the First Three Centuries* (Stanford, Calif., 1969) • H. FROST, *Strukturprobleme evangelischer Kirchenverfassung* (Göttingen, 1972) • M. M. GARIJO-GUEMBE, *Communion of the Saints: Foundation, Nature, and Structure of the Church* (Collegeville, Minn., 1994) • S. HARTMANN et al., "Amt / Ämter / Amtsverständnis," *TRE* 2.500-622 • E. SCHWEIZER, *Gemeinde und Gemeindeordnung im Neuen Testament* (2d ed.; Zurich, 1962) • H. SCHWENDENWEIN, *Das neue Kirchenrecht* (Graz, 1983) • C. J. SETZER, "Tradition of the Elders," *ABD* 6.638-39 • A. STEIN, *Evangelisches Kirchenrecht* (Neuwied, 1980) • L. VISCHER, *Eldership in the Reformed Churches Today* (Geneva, 1991).

HERBERT FROST

Election → Predestination

Electronic Church

"Electronic church" is a euphemism for radio and television religious programming (→ Mass Media) that applies modern high → technology (in computers and marketing) to media use. With much diversity in ideology, the major electronic churches usually share common characteristics: (1) strong charismatic leaders with clear and simple answers; (2) a divine success story with a miraculous mythology around their beginnings; (3) a distinctive style that identifies a unique package for the gospel (e.g., Jerry Falwell's "Old Time Gospel"); (4) a quest for an audience; (5) a tendency toward big problems, mostly financial but also moral; (6) in some cases also active participation in the New Religious Right. Few electronic churches are connected with traditional churches or have active congregations of their own.

→ Anglicans began religious broadcasting in the United States in 1921. In 1934 the government gave free "public service" time to mainline Protestant groups, forcing conservatives and independents to buy air time. A few strong political personalities such as the fascist Roman Catholic priest Father Coughlin were negative precursors of the electronic church. More positive transition figures were the Roman Catholic archbishop Fulton J. Sheen, Baptist Billy Graham, and Pentecostal Oral Roberts. Sheen's pastoral talk/entertainment show, Graham's revival style, and Roberts's "theology" for television finance became models to be refined, adapted, and expanded by the modern electronic church.

The electronic church as a marketing success depends upon rapidly expanding computer technology. Mailing lists have millions of names, reducing costs of appeals as well as filling databases of information about prayer requests and personal problems by those who telephone or write. "Personalized" computer letters can thus be programmed for emotional appeals. Cash flow of all electronic churches exceeds half a billion dollars yearly. Scientific studies put the total audience at 20 million people. Upwards of three-quarters of these are 50 years old and older; most are women and live in the eastern and southern United States. The pseudo-intimacy of the electronic church speaks to loneliness, fear, and alienation; such parasocial interaction, however, leads only to parapersonal → communication via technology.

Most electronic church theology includes (1) biblical literalism; (2) God as a deus ex machina; (3) sin and Satan (→ Devil) as behind all problems; (4) an emotional → conversion (§1), whereby the Holy Spirit brings good feelings and harmony in relationships; (5) a triumph of divine experience in → healing, → miracles, or financial success (but only with a faith that is strong enough); (6) a very personal and familiar Jesus; and (7) criticism of, and opposition to, the electronic church as a sign of unbelief.

The future of the electronic church holds increasing competition for money and audience, expansion overseas, and economic failure for some. In the United States, moreover, the immoral behavior, fraudulent business practices, and even imprisonment of some televangelists have seriously compromised the overall credibility and impact of the electronic church.

Bibliography: R. ABELMAN and S. M. HOOVER, eds., *Religious Television: Controversies and Conclusions* (Norwood, N.J., 1990) • "The Emerging Electronic Church," *YACC* 1999, 204-26 (list of websites of religious groups) • W. HENDRICKS, "The Theology of the Electronic Church," *RevExp* (1984) 59-76 • S. S. HILL and D. E. OWEN, *The New Religious Right in America* (Nashville, 1982) • S. M. HOOVER, *The Electronic Giant* (Elgin, Ill., 1982); idem, *Mass Media Religion: The Social Sources of the Electronic Church* (Beverly Hills, Calif., 1988) • J. PECK, *The Gods of Televangelism: The Crisis of Meaning and the Appeal of Religious Television* (Cresskill, N.J., 1993) • Q. J. SCHULTZE, *Televangelism and American Culture: The Business of Popular Religion* (Grand Rapids, 1991) • D. A. STOUT and J. M. BUDDENBAUM, eds., *Religion and the Mass Media: Audiences and Adaptations* (Thousand Oaks, Calif., 1996) • K. M. WOLFE, "Television, the 'Bartered Bride'; Broadcasting, Commerce, and Religion: Transatlantic Perspectives," *Religion: Contemporary Issues* (ed. B. R. Wilson; London, 1992).

G. KEITH PARKER

Elevation → Eucharistic Spirituality

Elijah

1. Elijah's name (Heb. *'ēliyyāhû* [less often *'ēliyyâ*] = "my God is Yahweh") intimates his program, and the story of his ministry goes hand in hand with his historical figure. He was a champion of exclusive Yahweh worship in the time of Ahab (871-852 B.C.) and Ahaziah (852-851) of Israel. According to 1 Kgs. 17:1 he was from Tishbe in Gilead (site uncertain). The secret of his person and the very threatening nature of his appearance made him the crystallization point for an increasingly legendary literary and theological tradition, whose development has not been fully explained. It probably arose out of the trial by sacrifice in 1 Kgs. 18:21-39 and the story of the death of Ahaziah in 2 Kgs. 1:2-17.

Elijah was an uncompromising worshiper of Yahweh. He opposed the religious policy of the house of Omri both in foreign affairs (the marriage with the Phoenician Jezebel) and in domestic affairs (in relation to Canaanite sections of the population). He posed the sharp alternative of → Yahweh or Baal. Over against the functional → polytheism of Ahaziah, he set the claim of Yahweh to every sphere of life in → Israel (§1).

2. The tradition and present form of the stories is primarily → Deuteronomistic, except for the post-Deuteronomistic addenda that include the story of raising the dead boy in 1 Kgs. 17:17-24, the miracle of fire in 2 Kgs. 1:10-14, and possibly the Horeb →

theophany in 1 Kgs. 19:11-14. Some scholars think that materials come from an older Elijah collection (1 Kgs. 17:1–19:18) along with individual stories (2 Kgs. 1:2 and vv. 5-8[?]) and a Naboth story in which Elijah did not originally appear (1 Kgs. 21:1-16). On this view the Elijah collection was a planned work in opposition to Baal worship (1 Kgs. 17:1–18:46), with the trial by sacrifice on Carmel as the oldest piece (18:21-39). It originally ended in 18:46 at the "entrance of Jezreel" (cf. 2 Kgs. 9:21) and exhibited features that suggest dating it to the time of Jehu (cf. 18:40 with 2 Kings 10). Presumably during the dangerous wars with the Arameans, the foreboding chap. 19 was added as an interpretation of the new situation. Only the Deuteronomistic inclusion of the story of Naboth lends to the portrayal of Elijah an element of social criticism, bringing it more in line with what is encountered in written prophecy.

The story of the rapture of Elijah is part of the → Elisha tradition (2 Kgs. 2:1, 7-18). It forms a basis (together with the Horeb theophany?) for the later exaltation of Elijah (see Mal. 4:5-6; Sir. 48:1-12; Matt. 17:3), in which he becomes the eschatological forerunner of the Messiah (Matt. 17:12), the mysterious helper of the Jews in time of need, and the mediator of mystical secrets.

Bibliography: L. BRONNER, *The Stories of Elijah and Elisha as Polemics against Baal Worship* (Leiden, 1968) • R. B. COOTE, ed., *Elijah and Elisha in Socioliterary Perspectives* (Atlanta, 1992) • G. FOHRER, *Elia* (2d ed.; Zurich, 1968) • A. J. HAUSER and R. GREGORY, *From Carmel to Horeb: Elijah in Crisis* (Sheffield, 1990) with Hauser, "Yahweh versus Death: The Real Struggle in 1 Kings 17–19," 8-89, and Gregory, "Irony and the Unmasking of Elijah," 91-175 • G. HENTSCHEL, *Die Elija-Erzählungen* (Leipzig, 1977) • N. KINCHI, "Elijah's Self-Offering: 1 Kings 17.21," *Bib* 75 (1994) 74-79 • P. J. KISSLING, *Reliable Characters in the Primary History: Profiles of Moses, Joshua, Elijah, and Elisha* (Sheffield, 1996) • N. OSWALD and H. SEEBASS, "Elia," *TRE* 9.498-504 (bibliography) • B. P. ROBINSON, "Elijah at Horeb; 1 Kings 19:1-18; A Coherent Narrative," *RB* 98 (1991) 513-36 • O. H. STECK, *Überlieferung und Zeitgeschichte in der Elia-Erzählungen* (Neukirchen, 1968) • E. R. WENDLAND, "Elijah and Elisha: Sorcerers or Witch Doctors?" *BT* 43 (1992) 213-23.

KLAUS KIESOW

Elisha

Elisha (Heb. *ʾĕlîšāʿ*, i.e., *ʾēlyāšāʿ* = "God has helped"), who came from Abel-mehola (= Tell Abû Ṣûṣ, on the west bank of the middle Jordan?) and was at work in the second half of the ninth century B.C., was a leader of the community of prophets centered at Gilgal near Jericho. Some scholars view his link with → Elijah as a later construction (1 Kgs. 19:19b-21; 2 Kgs. 2:1-18). He had dealings with kings of the dynasty of Jehu, whom he supported in wars against the → Arameans and to whom he owed the title "the chariots of Israel and its horsemen" (2 Kgs. 13:14). His role as initiator of the Jehu revolution (2 Kgs. 9:1-13) has been contested; only here does he fight against the Baal cult. The stories of his magical and mantic powers give a vivid picture of the life of a prophetic group.

According to some hypotheses, many if not all of the Elisha stories came into the → Deuteronomistic history later (1 Kgs. 19:19b-21; 2 Kgs. 2; 3:4–8:15; 13:14-21; but cf. 2 Kgs. 9:1-13). Three collections are thought to come from prophetic circles: miracle stories (2 Kgs. 4:1-44; 6:1-23; 8:1-6), the Aramean narratives (2 Kgs. 5:1-14; 8:7-15; 13:14-17), and the stories that present Elisha as Elijah's successor (1 Kgs. 19:19b-21; 2 Kgs. 2:1-14), each of which presents different aspects of Elisha.

Bibliography: L. BRONNER, *The Stories of Elijah and Elisha as Polemics against Baal Worship* (Leiden, 1968) • R. B. COOTE, ed., *Elijah and Elisha in Socioliterary Perspectives* (Atlanta, 1992) • B. O. LONG, "The Shunammite Woman: In the Shadow of the Prophet?" *BibRev* 7 (1991) 12-19 • R. D. MOORE, *God Saves: Lessons from the Elisha Stories* (Sheffield, 1990) • H.-C. SCHMITT, *Elisa* (Gütersloh, 1972) • H. SCHWEIZER, *Elischa in den Kriegen* (Munich, 1974) • H. SEEBASS, "Elisa," *TRE* 9.506-9 (bibliography) • E. R. WENDLAND, "Elijah and Elisha: Sorcerers or Witch Doctors?" *BT* 43 (1992) 213-23.

KLAUS KIESOW

Emanation

"Emanation," from the Lat. *emano* (flow out), occurs in certain → metaphysical conceptions of the structure and origin of the world. In these systems, reality consists of a hierarchy of being in which lower forms develop out of higher forms, and the multiplicity of the world ultimately derives from the unity of a first principle.

The idea occurs only rarely in classical → Greek

philosophy (Gk. *aporroia,* "outflow, emanation"), and then mostly in an epistemological connection (e.g., in Empedocles). Only in → Gnosticism does it become significant metaphysically. Here with the help of rich mythological materials (→ Myth) and complicated schemes, descriptions are given of the emanation of various hypostases from the original divine principle, and the beginning of the material world is ascribed to an evil demiurge (→ Dualism). The idea of emanation became philosophically important in the Neoplatonism (→ Platonism) of Plotinus (ca. 205-70) and his successors. Everything real arises in a timeless process from the superabundant riches of a perfect, transcendent, and ineffable principle (*to hen,* "the one"): first nous (cf. Plato's ideas), then psyche (the world soul), and finally, on the outer edge of emanation, matter. To explain the process Plotinus used → metaphors like light, tree, and source. What emanated seems at first to be different, but it maintains its identity through → contemplation, the return to its origin. We can achieve the restoration of original unity only by the long path of reflection, purgation, and liberation from everything sensory and particular. In our earthly lives we can hope to attain it only in a few moments of mystical experience (→ Mysticism).

We also find the idea of emanation in Dionysius the Pseudo-Areopagite (ca. 500), Duns Scotus (ca. 1265-1308; → Scotism), Thomas Aquinas (ca. 1225-74; → Thomism), the Jewish → cabala, G. W. Leibniz (1646-1716), and the later F. W. J. von Schelling (1775-1854). Emanation can be viewed as the opposite of → evolution. If we assume an element of will in emanation from a higher principle, it can come close to the Christian doctrine of → creation. If we see in it a necessary event in which lesser hypostases belong essentially to the unfolding of deity, we are not far from → pantheism or → Spinozism.

Bibliography: A. F. HOLMES, "Christian Philosophy," *NEBrit* (1986) 16.336-42, esp. 337 • K. KREMER, "Emanation," *HWP* 2.445-48 • P. MERLAN, "Emanation," *EncPh* 2.473-74; idem, "Plotinus," ibid. 5.351-59 • D. RATZINGER, "Emanation," *RAC* 1219-28.

RUURD VELDHUIS

Emancipation

1. Meaning and History
2. Institutional and Group Use
3. Modern Usage
4. Emancipation and Redemption

1. Meaning and History

Originally in Roman law emancipation was a legal act by which a paterfamilias released a child from parental control (*emancipo = e manu capio,* "let go of the hand," "release," "free"). This act had implications for civil law. Nonemancipated sons had political rights and could engage in trade or marry, but they had no → property rights. In other languages the term has lost the idea of achieving → adulthood, although in the Napoleonic Code it follows the Roman tradition and denotes the achieving of independence in civil law.

The social and political expansion of usage came by way of a more reflexive use of the verb "emancipate," which was originally transitive. The legal act thus gave way to a process of achieving self-mastery, which in the 18th century still bore the more negative sense of adjusting to unsuitable freedoms. The French → Revolution introduced a positive use, while from the standpoint of the → philosophy of history, liberation for → autonomy came with I. Kant's (1724-1804) famous definition of the → Enlightenment as "man's release from his self-incurred tutelage" (p. 85; → Kantianism). Kant did not use the term "emancipation," for he still viewed it in terms of Roman law, but the idea of a gradual progress to maturity soon came to be called emancipation, now understood as a general process with freedom as the goal. The once-for-all act of a declaration of adulthood faded into the background.

As a political slogan, "emancipation" came to be used with reference to specific groups at the beginning of the 19th century and to take on political significance. Around 1840 it became a leading concept to describe all history, both past and future. K. → Marx (1818-83) in his writing on the Jewish question distinguished between political and general human emancipation. By establishing civil equality over against → feudalism, political emancipation had made → progress, but it had not banished alienation. Only general human emancipation championed by the → proletariat would bring self-liberation (→ Marxism), by abolishing private ownership of the means of production in the classless society. From a legal act of declaring adulthood, emancipation had now become a revolutionary restructuring of society and the goal of human history.

2. Institutional and Group Use

As social structures weakened, the term "emancipation" from the end of the 18th century came to denote many movements aiming at → freedom and → equality. The term could denote both the legal act and the temporal movement.

Institutionally, one could speak of the emancipation of the → church from the → state (→ Church and State), the school from the church, the university from the state, the press from → censorship, the community from state oversight, trade from concessions, or colonies from the motherland (→ Colonialism).

Emancipation as the demand for equality on the part of certain groups has a primary legal connotation and thus links up with the ancient use, though embracing broad social and political programs for the future that take into account social, economic, religious, and natural obstacles or consequences that cannot be overcome legally. In this sense E. Burke in 1797 demanded the emancipation of Irish Roman Catholics, that is, the granting of their civil equality. Very quickly this usage came to be applied generally to all religious dissenters, and a demand arose for the emancipation of the Jews. The demand for the emancipation of → women has been affected from the very first, as regards its extent or limitation, by various views of "nature," depending finally on different attitudes to → marriage, → family, → society, and the state (→ Feminism). As the press became politically conscious, it demanded the emancipation of the working class (→ Labor Movement), which it would have to achieve for itself. The emancipation of → slaves in the United States, declared on January 1, 1863, by President Abraham Lincoln, was more of a matter of manumission than of full emancipation.

The 20th century has met many of the 19th-century demands for emancipation on the legal level, but fewer in terms of social conditions. At the same time, with the massive denial of rights to racial or political-ideological → minorities, this century has seen reverses of emancipation, and there are many new and unsolved problems regarding the demands for emancipation raised in the → Third World (→ Dependence).

3. Modern Usage

On a traditional philosophical basis, and with the support of the use in the work of J. Habermas, "emancipation" since the 1960s has become a key term in modern social-scientific → pedagogy, with some regard also to emancipatory → psychology (i.e., emancipation as liberation from impulse). As an educational goal (→ Education), emancipation has gained official status. In K. Mollenhauer it is defined as the overthrow of irrational control and the defense against it. It is liberation from the forces not merely of material → power but of → prejudices and → ideologies. Emancipatory educational theory becomes a permanent criticism of society, with the result that conservatives accuse it of destroying all commitment to beliefs, → norms, and → institutions. Insofar as the concept derives from the Enlightenment, it shares in philosophical → optimism and the belief in progress. Even if more pessimistic perspectives have now replaced these notions, enlightenment supposedly goes on, and with it progressive emancipation from forces that are not understood or willingly accepted. Emancipation becomes simultaneously destiny and task (M. Greiffenhagen, 39).

4. Emancipation and Redemption

With regard to → theology, E. → Troeltsch (1865-1923) considered → secularism as the emancipation of → culture from Christianity. On a Marxist view emancipation replaces the Christian hope of redemption. In contrast to a mistaken contrasting of immanent emancipation and transcendent redemption (→ Soteriology), Christian expectation of redemption finds its point, not in emancipation from suffering, but in emancipation as the solidarity of sufferers (H. N. Janowski, in Greiffenhagen, 467). This understanding makes possible new contacts with modern demands for emancipation, as formulated, for example, in → liberation theology.

Bibliography: P. L. BERGER, R. D. GASTIL, and G. WEIGEL, *The Structure of Freedom: Correlations, Causes, and Cautions* (Grand Rapids, 1991) • K. M. GRASS and R. KOSELLECK, "Emanzipation," *GGB* 2.153-97 • M. GREIFFENHAGEN, ed., *Emanzipation* (Hamburg, 1973) with extensive bibliography and interdisciplinary contributions • I. KANT, "What Is Enlightenment?" (1783), *Foundations of the Metaphysics of Morals and What Is Enlightenment?* (trans. L. W. Beck; Indianapolis, 1959) 85-92 • J. MARITAIN and D. A. GALLAGHER, *Christianity and Democracy; and, The Rights of Man and Natural Law* (San Francisco, 1986) • K. MOLLENHAUER, *Erziehung und Emanzipation* (Munich, 1968) • F. SCHLEIERMACHER, *On Freedom* (trans. A. L. Blackwell; Lewiston, N.Y., 1992) • A. K. SEN, *Inequality Reexamined* (New York, 1992) • W. A. VISSER 'T HOOFT, *The Fatherhood of God in an Age of Emancipation* (Geneva, 1982).

GOTTHARD JASPER

Emergency Baptism

Since the early church saw → baptism not merely as a rite of → initiation but as a means of conferring → salvation, as early as the second century it could be administered by laymen as well as clergy when there was danger of death (so-called clinical baptism). Tertullian and the Fourth Council of Carthage, however, would not allow women to administer it. Because of the → consecration of the water and the → anointing, which were reserved for → priests, the East hesitated to allow emergency baptism by laymen (*Apos. Const.* 3.10.1-2). In the West the → bishop would subsequently lay on hands (3d cent., Africa; → Laying on of Hands).

→ Thomas Aquinas (ca. 1225-74; → Thomism) defended the practice of the West by distinguishing between what is absolutely essential to the sacrament and what pertains to its solemn observance. In his view, even the unbaptized might give baptism in case of need (*Summa theol.* III, q. 66, art. 10; q. 67, art. 5).

The 15th century went as far as to allow baptism of the unborn, or uterine baptism. The → Reformation rejected this practice on the ground that "only those who have been born once can be born again" (e.g., Church Order of Hoya, 1581 [*EKO* 6.1159]). The 16th-century Lutheran church orders gave instruction, especially to midwives, on how to administer emergency baptism, since baptism was a means of grace (Apology of Augs. Conf. 9). Emergency baptism was then to be followed up in church with a reading (Mark 10) and → prayer.

Most of the → Reformed churches follow J. → Calvin (1509-64) in rejecting emergency baptism on the ground that God "adopts our babies as his own before they are born" (*Inst.* 4.15.20; → Calvin's Theology). The issue became fiercely contested in England, where the Elizabethan Prayer Book of 1559 allowed emergency baptism (mostly given by midwives), but the → Puritans opposed it. In a revision sponsored by James I in 1604, emergency baptism remained but was to be administered only by the clergy. The Anglicans agreed with the Reformed that there is no absolute necessity of baptism, rejecting the medieval view that unbaptized infants are condemned to hell, or at least to limbo. They differed from the Reformed, however, by giving precedence to the necessity of precept over regularity, thus preserving a place for emergency baptism by an ordained minister and not necessarily at public worship.

→ Clergy and Laity

Bibliography: P. Cramer, *Baptism and Change in the Early Middle Ages, c. 200–c. 1150* (Cambridge, 1993) • J. Jeremias, *Infant Baptism in the First Four Centuries* (London, 1960) 87-97 • R. McDonnell and G. T. Montague, *Christian Initiation and Baptism in the Holy Spirit: Evidence from the First Eight Centuries* (Collegeville, Minn., 1991) • L. L. Mitchell, *Worship: Initiation and the Churches* (Washington, D.C., 1991) • "Taufe," *Leit.* 5 • J. Warns, *Baptism: Studies in the Original Christian Baptism, Its History and Conflicts, Its Relation to a State or National Church, and Its Significance for the Present Time* (London, 1957) 73-101.

Hans-Christoph Schmidt-Lauber

Emigration → Refugees

Empathy

Although the Eng. term "empathy" was coined only in the early 20th century, the Ger. equivalent *Einfühling* was developed much earlier by J. G. Herder (1744-1803). It played a great role in the metaphysical-aesthetic speculations of → Romanticism. In 1903 T. Lipps subjected it to an incisive description and analysis. In the United States it was taken up in a sociopsychological context as a method of sensitivity training. From S. Freud (1856-1939) by way of F. T. Vischer, it made its way into psychoanalysis. H. Kohut made it into a scientifically valid → psychotherapeutic method resting on the reactivation of human capacities that are ontogenetically much earlier, as these are expressed in the forms and changes of → narcissism. The concept has been integral also to the → counseling theories of U.S. psychotherapist Carl Rogers (→ Rogerian Psychotherapy).

As the central concept of Herder, empathy played a decisive role in liberal → pastoral care, especially in O. Baumgarten (1858-1934). The very different concerns of → dialectical theology, however, pushed it into the background. As a hermeneutical limiting concept, it has been rediscovered in the movement of pastoral care in a combination of its functions in the spheres of social psychology, depth psychology, and aesthetic hermeneutics. Empathetic treatment of texts is important in the total understanding of phylogenetically earlier items, such as myths and symbols, and also in the spontaneous understanding of human living documents. Both spheres, urged Anton Boisen, the founder of the movement, must be brought together in a pastoral-psychological circle of understanding. This synthesis takes place mainly in pastoral "Balint groups" (so named after British psychoanalyst Michael Balint), preachers' discussion groups, and bibliodramatic self-experience groups.

Bibliography: O. BAUMGARTEN, *Protestantische Seelsorge* (Tübingen, 1931) • A. T. BOISEN, *The Exploration of the Inner World* (Philadelphia, 1971; orig. pub., 1936) • R. KATZ, *Empathy* (London, 1963) • H. KOHUT, *Die Heilung des Selbst* (Frankfurt, 1979) • K. F. MORRISON, *I Am You: The Hermeneutics of Empathy in Western Literature, Theology, and Art* (Princeton, 1988) • D. M. OWENS, *Hospitality to Strangers: Empathy in the Physician-Patient Relationship* (Atlanta, 1993) • E. SCHUCHARDT, *Why Is This Happening to Me? Guidance and Hope for Those Who Suffer* (Minneapolis, 1989) • R. L. UNDERWOOD, *Empathy and Confrontation in Pastoral Care* (Philadelphia, 1985) • L. M. ZUNIN and H. S. ZUNIN, *The Art of Condolence: What to Write, What to Say, What to Do at a Time of Loss* (New York: 1992).

JOACHIM SCHARFENBERG†

Emperor Worship

1. In early antiquity an idea of charismatic kingship was widespread from Mesopotamia to Germany. This notion ascribed a divine origin to rulers in their responsibility for the cult, which was the basis of public well-being. In Egypt this impulse resulted in the divine monarchy of the pharaoh, who was regarded as the son of Amon-Re and who was venerated, usually after death, only on the basis of his beneficence. Under Ramses II, however, there is evidence for actual worship of a statue of the living ruler. In view of its critical orientation to → Yahweh, traces of this notion are rare in the OT (see Ps. 45:6).

2. In Greek cities the attributing of outstanding deeds to divine working led to the founding of cults of benefactors from 404 B.C. (Lysander). Tied to this practice was the veneration of Alexander the Great (336-323), who promoted this concept politically and thus laid the foundation on which the Ptolemies and Seleucids, following earlier traditions, developed an official emperor worship.

3. Up to the late republic the Romans developed no tradition of their own in this area, but with their conquests from the time of Titus Quinctius Flamininus (191 B.C.), they were honored with benefactor cults. Though Augustus (27 B.C.–A.D. 14) was depicted as divine in the provinces (e.g., see his Kalabsha Gate of Egypt, now in Berlin) and temples for him were built (e.g., by → Herod, Josephus *J.W.* 1.403-4), in Rome he respected the criterion developed there of an apotheosis only after death and only on the basis of outstanding achievements on behalf of the state. He thus acknowledged traditional Roman antipathy against emperor worship, as reflected in the case of Caesar, who had been assassinated after the decision in 44 B.C. that he be deified in Rome. Even though the cult of the emperor did become widespread in the provinces, this criterion did form the basis of a criticism of the divine claims of his successors (Caligula, Domitian). In the principate, the cult of the living emperor thus developed in Rome primarily in connection with that of the state. Only in the dominate, or absolute rule, beginning with Aurelian (269/70-75), did the living emperor have himself worshiped throughout as "lord and god" (→ Roman Empire; Roman Religion).

4. The importance of emperor worship in the → persecution of Christians has often been exaggerated, stimulated by Revelation 13. We read of compulsory sacrifice to the emperor only from the time of Pliny the Younger, in about 110. This practice was not authorized by Trajan (Pliny *Ep.* 10.96-97), and there was no more trace of it for a long time.

In the great persecutions compulsory sacrifice to the emperor does not seem to have been specially used to obtain convictions but was integrated into the general recognition of pagan gods and the authority of the state. The → apologists, who cooperated as much as possible, opposed only the worship of a ruler, but they did not reject paying him supreme honor above all gods and praying for him, inasmuch as, in their view, he received his position from God (→ Tertullian *Apol.* 30ff. and *Ad Scap.* 2.7ff.). They thus prepared the ground for the idea of the divine right of kings, which permitted a continuation of essential motifs of emperor worship — prostration and divine titles — even after this practice ended under Constantine (306-37, who also proscribed it at the newly erected Temple of Flavius in Hispellum [modern-day Spello, in Italian Umbria]).

The final witness to Christian opposition is perhaps the development of the Feast of the Ascension in answer to the revival of the pagan idea of apotheosis under Julian (360-63). Honoring of at least the good rulers continued to modern times (e.g., see Luther WA 31/1.198), but without reestablishment of emperor worship in the true sense.

→ Hellenism; Hellenistic-Roman Religion

Bibliography: Le culte des souverains dans l'Empire Romain (Geneva, 1973) • J. R. FEARS, "Herrscherkult," RAC 14.1047-93 • S. J. FRIESEN, *Twice Neokoros: Ephesus, Asia, and the Cult of the Flavian Imperial Fam-*

ily (Leiden, 1993) • J. N. KRAYBILL, *Imperial Cult and Commerce in John's Apocalypse* (Sheffield, 1996) • S. R. F. PRICE, *Rituals and Power: The Roman Imperial Cult in Asia Minor* (Cambridge, 1984) • D. SVENSON, *Darstellung hellenistischer Könige mit Götterattributen* (Frankfurt, 1995) • F. TAEGER, *Charisma. Studien zur Geschichte des antiken Herrscherkultes* (2 vols.; Stuttgart, 1957-60) • L. L. THOMPSON, *The Book of Revelation: Apocalypse and Empire* (New York, 1990) • A. WLOSOK, ed., *Römischer Kaiserkult* (Darmstadt, 1978) • D. ZELLER, *Menschwerdung Gottes–Vergöttlichung von Menschen* (Göttingen, 1988). See also numerous articles in *ANRW* 2.16.2 and 2.23.2.

MARTIN KARRER

Empire and Papacy

1. Significance in the Middle Ages
2. Development to Charlemagne
3. Emperor as World Ruler to 1046
4. Rise of Papal Power and Climax under Innocent III
5. Decline
6. Reformation Period

1. Significance in the Middle Ages

The relation between empire and papacy, their interplay and fundamental rivalry, was basic to both secular and ecclesiastical history in the → Middle Ages (§2). The social thinking of Latin Christendom was characterized by the idea that the secular world is ruled by two heads. It differed essentially from that of the Christian East, with its tendencies toward caesaropapism (the emperor ruling the church). In historical reality the idea contributed to the closed nature of the medieval *corpus Christianum,* but it also resulted in a significant historical dynamic. Medieval society was united by it both ideally and legally. Yet it also hampered the evolution of a universal social order after the manner of the → Roman or → Byzantine Empires.

2. Development to Charlemagne

There were certain presuppositions for this development in antiquity (→ Early Church). Already in the NT we find some relation between the Roman Empire and the Christian church. The relation took various forms after the Christianizing of the empire under Constantine (306-37). Constantine himself established a first political basis for the medieval order when he moved his capital from → Rome to Constantinople and thus decisively established the

older claims of the Roman bishop to primacy, at least in the Latin West. By no means accidentally it was thus a pope, Gelasius I (492-96), who in 494, in a work that later became famous, set alongside one another the *regalis potestas* (royal power) of the emperor (in the East) and the *sacrata auctoritas* (sacred authority) of the pope, relating the two to each other and thus formulating for the first time the medieval doctrine of two heads, or two powers.

The most important stage in further development came with events in the mid-eighth century. Between 749 and 754 a momentous pact was made between the Frankish mayor of the palace Pepin III (741-68) and the popes. The three main terms were as follows. By papal decree Pepin was made king. A new form of Christian legitimacy was thus conferred, with anointing of the king as its sacramental form. Next, the new king was designated defender of the pope, with the title *patricius Romanorum,* which had thus far been held by the Byzantine emperor. Finally, lands then under the control of the Byzantines were to be given to the pope (the so-called Patrimony of St. Peter), which would give him a kind of secular base in Italy (→ Donation of Constantine; Papal States). The idea of a Christian Western society now began to take shape. It would be a body with two heads that were related and essentially referred to one another, though widely separated.

Legally and politically, the crowning of Charlemagne (768-814) on Christmas Day 800 simply completed the earlier development. Yet it was still a central event in the Middle Ages, for Charlemagne was the model of the medieval ruler inasmuch as he understood and ruled his enormous kingdom sacrally and thus provided future emperors with a very important ideological model. Leo III (795-816), however, who crowned Charlemagne, opened the door to the idea that the Roman Empire had been revived and continued in the Latin West, doing so on his own papal initiative. In many ways, the path ahead was thus the same for empire and papacy.

3. Emperor as World Ruler to 1046

After Charlemagne a century and a half passed before the relation between empire and papacy took any significantly new turn. It came above all with Otto the Great (936-73), who brought to its height the *regnum Teutonicorum,* which had been developing during the ninth century, and who could thus lay claim to the imperial dignity and legacy of Charlemagne. Otto formally followed Charlemagne in every respect, even to the point of believing that he was responsible for the church and for the salvation of his subjects. He made this view plain both in his acts and in the liturgy of coronation, which made him regent of the state church. His coronation in 962 was thus of supreme importance. He was given primacy over "all other kings of the world." Throughout the Middle Ages the emperor, as an ideal prince at the head of all other princes, would have the task of representing the unity of the world, just as the pope represented the unity of the church. Since 962 it was also decided that only the pope could confer this dignity on the emperor. The medieval German Empire was thus supremely exalted. At the same time, however, it was also perilously entangled.

Already under the successors of Otto it was plain that there was little chance of establishing the universality of the empire or of asserting its supremacy over the other kingdoms of Europe. Only in Rome, where the papacy was hampered by many local difficulties, could the emperors assert themselves as world rulers. One of them, Otto III (983-1002), even took up residence for a time in the holy city and was buried in St. Peter's Church. All of them claimed a right to have a say in papal elections (→ Pope, Papacy). For a time the emperor, as also the pope, could be addressed as the vicar of Christ. The relation between emperor and pope seemed to have achieved complete harmony in terms of the two swords of Luke 22:35-38 (cf. Matt. 26:51-56).

4. Rise of Papal Power and Climax under Innocent III

4.1. In truth, however, the empire was not really sovereign over the papacy. This fact was shown after the Synod of Sutri (1046), when on the zealous initiative of an emperor, Henry III (1039-56), the → curia reorganized itself in the spirit of monastic reform (→ Monasticism). The ground was fairly quickly cut from under imperial cocontrol in the church when Cardinal Humbert of Silva Candida (d. 1061) extended the canonical prohibition of simony to lay → investiture of church officeholders.

Thirty years after Sutri, → Gregory VII (1073-85) completely reversed earlier relations by claiming supreme authority not only over the church but also over the world, and by conferring on himself the right to dethrone kings and to release their subjects from oaths of loyalty (highlighted in 1077 by his treatment of Henry IV at Canossa). The church was now challenging the amalgamation of secular and spiritual government and the sacral nature of secular rule, suspecting the sin of pride in such rule. Rivalry and strife had arisen between empire and papacy.

4.2. A compromise was reached early in the 12th century with the Concordat of Worms (1122), which ended the Investiture Controversy. The first Hohenstaufens, especially Frederick Barbarossa (1152-90), could to a certain extent neutralize their ideological losses by increases in power in other respects. When Henry VI (1190-97) in 1194 secured control of Sicily by marriage, the popes for a short time could even see their own position in Italy threatened.

4.3. The popes, however, still had the stronger weapons. With the development of imperial law in the 12th century came that of the superior → canon law. The → Crusades, the → Cistercian reform, and early → Scholasticism established a period of church supremacy, and the imperial dignity was still dependent on the papacy. As earlier, empire and papacy still had some important common interests. They thus quickly joined ranks when the rise of the heretical poverty movement (→ Heresies and Schisms) threatened the unity of Christendom, and together they imposed a strict heresy law (for the first time in 1184).

4.4. The supremacy of the papacy came to its clearest expression under → Innocent III (1198-1216), the greatest and certainly the most successful of the medieval popes. Innocent offered the clearest formulation of the papal claim to world dominion — and was also able to make it good. By his success in the struggle for the German throne, his reducing of many kings to → feudal subjection, and the establishment of a Latin kingdom in Constantinople, he could entertain almost eschatological expectations. God himself seemed gloriously to have confirmed his claim to be the vicar of Christ, though on the basis of his power of the → keys he saw himself as the true emperor and as justified in intervening with power whenever it was a matter of sin *(ratione peccati)*. For him the two-lights theory had replaced the two-swords, or two-kingdoms, theory. As God has related the sun and the moon in the natural order, so he has related pope and emperor in the Christian order. The emperor is lesser than the pope, and he also receives his light from the pope, for the spiritual rule of the soul is superior to the secular rule of the body. The expansion of papal rule had found a justification as elegant as it was unlimited.

5. Decline

5.1. The papacy could not maintain the position that it reached under Innocent III. Immediately after his death, his life's work came under challenge when the young Hohenstaufen Frederick II (1215-50) adopted the same course as his predecessors and began forcefully and energetically to rule both Sicily and the empire. The period of papal supremacy under Innocent was thus followed by that of the bitterest struggles between empire and papacy that the Middle Ages had ever seen. Yet the two institutions were still closely entwined. Frederick II advanced his own claims to supremacy and became a dangerous neighbor for the pope. The popes again used spiritual weapons against him. He was excommunicated and declared to be deposed in 1245, his subjects being released from their oaths of loyalty. He died a defeated man. In this case, the papacy carried the day against the empire.

5.2. Nevertheless the papacy, which by no means could establish a world rule on its own, was compelled to look for new defenders. It thus came into oppressive dependence on Anjou and France. At the same time, as it felt compelled to use secular weapons and to secularize spiritual weapons, it clearly suffered in its moral and Christian character.

It was not just an isolated incident, then, when disaster ended the pontificate of Boniface VIII (1294-1303), a pope who, in conflict with French king Philip IV the Fair (1285-1314), reasserted with great precision the claim of the curia to universal dominion. Quoting → Thomas Aquinas (ca. 1225-74), Boniface claimed in the → bull *Unam sanctam* (1302) that subjection to the Roman pontiff is necessary for salvation (*subesse Romano pontifici esse de necessitate salutis*). With the failure of Boniface, the popes that followed found themselves largely subject instead to the policies of France.

5.3. There was now no longer any consistent relation between empire and papacy. The empire was regionalized, and the papacy fell into a series of existential crises (exile in Avignon, the Great Schism, the conciliar movement, and the Renaissance papacy). Only occasionally were there more lasting contacts. The conflict between John XXII (1316-34) and Louis IV the Bavarian (1314-47) showed that the spiritual weapons of the curia had begun to lose their earlier power. A century later, at the Council of Constance (1414-18; → Councils of the Church), it was mostly an emperor, Sigismund (king of the Romans, 1410-37), who was able to put an end to the decades-long schism between the papacy and Latin Christendom.

6. Reformation Period

A century later came the last significant cooperation between empire and papacy. In the person of Charles V (1519-56) a strong emperor came to the throne, the first in a long time. The curia, which found itself threatened by his rule over much of Italy, had worked against his election. Yet in the controversy with M. → Luther (1483-1546), who as never before criticized the papacy, dismembering it theologically (→ Luther's Theology), Charles resolutely took the side of the curia, and in the long run an astonishing measure of harmony was achieved between empire and papacy in this crucial situation. For example, the imperial ban quickly followed the papal excommunication of Luther in 1521.

As earlier, however, the empire could not fully overcome papal mistrust. Particularly the emperor's desire for a council to check heresy led to a bitter, decades-long debate with the curia, which lasted until the actual start of the Council of → Trent. Even then, constant political problems stood in the way of the full cooperation that was needed to arrest the → Reformation. The common goal of a united Christendom was thus neither achieved nor restored. With the peace of Augsburg in 1555 (→ Augsburg, Peace of), both of Christendom's heads lost their function.

→ Church and State

Bibliography: H. BEUMANN, *Kaisergestalten des Mittelalters* (3d ed.; Munich, 1991) • U.-R. BLUMENTHAL, *Der Investiturstreit* (Stuttgart, 1982) • W. BRANDMÜLLER, *Das Konzil von Konstanz, 1414-1418* (2 vols.; Paderborn, 1991-97) • J. FLECKENSTEIN, *Die Hofkapelle der deutschen Könige (und Kaiser)* (2 vols.; Stuttgart, 1959-66); idem, ed., *Probleme um Friedrich II.* (Sigmaringen, 1974) • R. FOREVILLE, *Le pape Innocent III et la France* (Stuttgart, 1992) • M. GRESCHAT, ed., *Das Papsttum* (2 vols.; Stuttgart, 1984) • *Histoire du Christianisme* (vols. 4-7; Paris, 1990-94) • H. JEDIN, *Geschichte des Konzils von Trient* (vol. 1; 3d ed.; Freiburg, 1977) • H. LUTZ, *Politik, Kultur und Religion im Werdeprozeß der frühen Neuzeit* (Klagenfurt, 1982) • J. MIETHKE, "Kaiser und Papst im Spätmittelalter. Zu den Ausgleichsbemühungen zwischen Ludwig dem Bayern und der Kurie in Avignon," *ZHF* 10 (1983) 421-46 • B. MOELLER, "Papst Innocenz III und die Wende des Mittelalters," *Die Reformation und das Mittelalter* (ed. B. Moeller; Göttingen, 1991) 21-34 • C. MORRIS, *The Papal Monarchy: The Western Church from 1050 to 1250* (Oxford, 1992) • K. PENNINGTON, *Pope and Bishops: A Study of the Papal Monarchy in the Twelfth and Thirteenth Centuries* (Philadelphia, 1984) • P. RASSOW, *Die Kaiser-Idee Karls V.* (Berlin, 1932) • Y. RENOUARD, *La papauté à Avignon* (2d ed.; Paris, 1962) • J. RICHARDS, *The Popes and the Papacy in the Early Middle Ages, 476-752* (London, 1979) • P. RICHÉ, *Les Carolingiens* (2d ed.; Paris, 1992) • L. SANTIFALLER, *Zur Geschichte des ottonisch-salischen Reichskirchensystems* (2d ed.; Vienna, 1964) • R. SCHIEFFER, *Die Entstehung des päpstlichen Investiturverbots für den deutschen König* (Stuttgart, 1981) • T. SCHMIDT, *Der Bonifaz-Prozeß* (Cologne, 1989) • P. E. SCHRAMM, "Sacerdotium und Regnum im Austausch ihrer Vorrechte," *Kaiser, Könige und Päpste* (vol. 4/1; Stuttgart, 1970) 57-106 • R. W. SOUTHERN, *Western Society and Church in the Middle Ages* (2 vols.; New York and Grand Rapids, 1970-72) • G. TELLENBACH, *Libertas. Kirche und Weltordnung im Zeitalter des Investiturstreites* (Stuttgart, 1936); idem, *Die westliche Kirche vom 10. bis zum frühen 12. Jahrhundert* (Göttingen, 1988) • B. TIERNEY, *The Crisis of Church and State, 1050-1300* (Toronto, 1988) • W. ULLMANN, *A Short History of the Papacy in the Middle Ages* (New York, 1972) • S. WEINFURTER, ed., *Die Salier und das Reich* (vol. 2; Sigmaringen, 1991) • G. WOLF, ed., *Zum Kaisertum Karls des Grossen* (Darmstadt, 1972). For additional bibliographies, see *AHP* 1ff. (1963-).

BERND MOELLER

Empiricism

The term "empiricism" (from Gk. *empeiria*, "experience") received its present meaning toward the end of the 18th century. Previously it was used to distinguish medicine based on practical experience *(medicina empirica)* from academic medicine *(medicina rationalis)*. Immanuel Kant (1724-1804) used the term in 1781 to denote the philosophical trend that deduces even the knowledge of "pure reason" from experience. Since then the concept has made its way into philosophical lexica and histories of → philosophy.

We must distinguish between a use that serves philosophical classification and one that expresses a philosophical program. One may note the following model of development: (1) emergence of philosophical positions, (2) classification in the history of philosophy, and (3) programmatic refinement. Only in the 19th century did the term come to describe a program of theoretical and practical philosophy, and then in the 20th century an epistemological theory. In general, "empiricism" designates any philosophical position whose theoretical and practical content derives ultimately not from reason (→ Rationalism) but from → experience.

As a classificatory concept in the history of philosophy, "empiricism" embraces in a broader sense the theoretical elements in all philosophies to which this characterization applies. Thus Kant could call Aristotle (384-322 B.C.) an empiricist. In the narrower sense, however, it denotes a trend in modern philosophy. The problem of the → modern period

was to make the fact of → knowledge and morality conceivable without finding in God a transcendent guarantee, and without sinking into skepticism. In the 17th and 18th centuries there were two fundamental solutions of this problem: the human spontaneity of reason (rationalism) and the human receptivity of sensory experience (empiricism). Since British philosophers tended to favor the latter, it came to be known as English empiricism (in contrast to French rationalism). The boundaries, however, were fluid. One can also distinguish between a radical empiricism that traces both sensory data and their logical connections to experience and a modified empiricism that explains only the former and not the latter empirically.

Francis Bacon (1561-1626) has been called the father of modern empiricism. His epistemological program opposed the → scholastic method of deduction from supreme metaphysical principles. In its place he put a differentiated concept of induction. Laws and general principles were to be derived inductively from experimentally achieved data and organized as "natural history."

The main representatives of classic British empiricism were John Locke (1632-1704), George Berkeley (1685-1753), and David Hume (1711-76), with Thomas Hobbes (1588-1679) as a pioneer and mediator. Hobbes formulated the basic empirical principle that there is nothing in the understanding that was not previously in the senses. Locke sharpened this concept, opposing strongly the rationalistic notion of innate ideas and viewing the human mind as a tabula rasa on which all concepts (ideas) are impressed by either inner or outer experience. Berkeley's position shows finally that empiricism may be combined with the most diverse → ontologies. He himself combined it with "immaterialism," or idealism, as his basic principle — *esse est percipi* — demonstrates.

Undoubtedly the most consistent, and for Kant the most striking, development of this position was to be found in Hume. Any idea may be traced back directly or indirectly to impressions, the connection between which is simply a matter of habit induced by constant repetition. Thus empirically grounded skepticism is called for over against such classical concepts as substance and → causality. This step brought matters full circle. English empiricism, which was designed to overcome modern skepticism, had itself become a form of → skepticism. Principles of common sense were then adduced as a means to overcome the skepticism in English empiricism. Under Thomas Reid, James Beattie, and George Oswald, the Scottish school made these ideas into separate philosophical principles, which led to the great tradition of Anglo-Saxon → pragmatism.

The practical, and especially the political, philosophy of classic English empiricism is very significant, although hard to bring under a single common denominator. The most important figure in this regard is incontestably John Locke, whose concept of → tolerance lies behind the economic-liberal ethic of → utilitarianism.

Kant attempted to make a Solomonic decision to resolve the conflict between rationalism and empiricism by dividing the fields in such a way that a priori elements remain in epistemology, but the true function of delimitation is ascribed to a posteriori experience, and only moral action (→ Ethics) obeys the laws of the intelligibly free ego. This attempt founded a philosophical empiricism. In contrast, John Stuart Mill (1806-73) sharpened epistemological empiricism by inductively deriving the laws of logic and mathematics from experience and becoming the classic proponent of psychologism in → logic. His ethics represented a further development of utilitarianism.

Against this background at the turn to the 20th century the "empirio-criticism" of Richard Avenarius (1843-96) and Ernst Mach (1838-1916), which proposed a view of the world reduced to experiential elements, led to neopositivism, which opposed Mills's psychologistic concept of logic, tried to build scientific knowledge on modern logic and experience, and thus called itself logical empiricism. The Vienna Circle, led by Moritz Schlick (1882-1936) and Rudolf Carnap (1891-1970), aimed to overthrow the older metaphysical tradition by recognizing as meaningful only statements that are logically or empirically verifiable.

Criticism of the implied delimiting criterion of verifiability, especially by Karl Popper (1902-94), showed that statements of a lawlike nature can never be verified on logical grounds, which according to the criterion of verifiability leads to the absurd conclusion that they are meaningless. Popper's own "critical rationalism" represents one of the reduced forms in which empiricism still exists. "Modified realism" is an associated position (defended by Paul Feyerabend, Hilary Putnam, and others). Modern epistemological theory has no place for a strict empiricism. Epistemologists do not doubt that the basis of experience is itself dependent on theory.

It is an open question how far at the metalevel empirical elements still enter into the discussion of theory within the critical realism of evolutionary epistemology. On the level of daily practice, and the implied self-understanding of many sciences, empiricism is still the view of things by which people live.

Bibliography: R. L. ARMSTRONG, *Metaphysics and British Empiricism* (Lincoln, Nebr., 1970) • P. K. FEYERABEND, *Problems of Empiricism* (Cambridge, 1981) • D. W. HANLYN, "Empiricism," *EncPh* 2.499-505 • J. HOUSTON, *Reported Miracles: A Critique of Hume* (Cambridge, 1994) • J. C. KEMP, *Ethical Naturalism: Hobbes and Hume* (London, 1970) • A. QUINTON, *Utilitarian Ethics* (London, 1973) • H. SCHNÄDELBACH, *Erfahrung, Begründung und Reflexion. Versuch über den Positivismus* (Frankfurt, 1979) • G. VESEY, ed., *Impression of Empiricism* (London, 1976) • G. VOLLMER, *Evolutionäre Erkenntnistheorie* (2d ed.; Stuttgart, 1980) • N. WOLTERSTORFF, *John Locke and the Ethics of Belief* (Cambridge, 1996) • K. E. YANDELL, *Hume's "Inexplicable Mystery": His Views on Religion* (Philadelphia, 1990).

WALTHER C. ZIMMERLI

Encyclicals

Encyclicals are circular letters issued by the → pope. As *litterae encyclicae,* they are sent to all → bishops who live in peace and fellowship with the apostolic see, or to all Roman Catholics, or to all people of good will. As *epistolae encyclicae,* they are addressed only to bishops and believers in a particular area. Written in either Latin or the vernacular, they deal with a wide range of matters of doctrine and church order, → faith, piety and life, social order (→ Social Encyclicals), → mission, and → ecumenism. They are mostly concrete and time-bound and make no → infallible pronouncements. Yet → Vatican II's dogmatic constitution on the church demands obedience to the authentic teaching office of the Roman bishop, "even when he does not speak *ex cathedra*" (*Lumen gentium* 25). The significance of encyclicals may be summed up in the formula that they are binding but may be superseded.

Next in rank and authority to encyclicals are apostolic admonitions or instructions, which contain the findings of Roman episcopal → synods published in revised form by the pope. These circular letters and pronouncements are cited by the first words of the text *(Arenga)* and are recorded in the *Acta apostolicae sedis.*

→ Constitution; Motu proprio; Teaching Office

Bibliography: C. CARLEN, comp., *The Papal Encyclicals* (5 vols.; Wilmington, N.C., 1981); idem, comp., *Papal Pronouncements: A Guide, 1740-1978* (2 vols.: Ann Arbor, Mich., 1990) • A. J. FREEMANTLE, *The Papal Encyc-*

licals in Their Historical Context (exp. ed.; New York, 1963) • J. M. MILLER, "Interior Intelligibility: The Use of Scripture in Papal and Conciliar Documents," *CanCR* 11 (1993) 9-18 • G. WEIGEL and R. ROYAL, *Building Free Society: Democracy, Capitalism, and Catholic Social Teaching* (Grand Rapids, 1993).

HEINER GROTE†

Encyclopedia

1. General
  1.1. Term
  1.2. History of the Term
2. Theological
  2.1. Theological Encyclopedia
  2.2. Theological Theory

1. General

The term "encyclopedia" denotes the total body of knowledge either of → science as a whole or of a particular science, and it proclaims the unity of a science in its various disciplines.

1.1. Term

The original Greek term was *enkyklios paideia* (circular, or general, education). For the Greek Sophists (→ Greek Philosophy), this phrase denoted the compass and measure of knowledge that all free Greeks had to attain before receiving specialized training or entering into practical life.

1.2. History of the Term

Out of the idea of a canon of knowledge there developed various summary groupings of the knowledge of the time, such as those of the → Middle Ages (§1) — most notably, the *Speculum majus* of Vincent of Beauvais (ca. 1190-1264). Increasingly the outer interrelating of knowledge gave way to a demonstration of its inner unity or organism, as symbolized by the tree. The first instance of the term itself is in G. Budé (1540).

A classic example of the interconnecting of all learning and of science is the great French *Encyclopédie, ou dictionnaire raisonné des sciences, des arts et des métiers* (1751-80). In Hegel's *Enzyklopädie der philosophischen Wissenschaften* (1817; 3d ed., 1830; ET *Encyclopedia of the Philosophical Sciences in Outline* [New York, 1990]), an attempt is made to develop speculatively the unity of → philosophy.

2. Theological

In → theology the term "encyclopedia" expresses comprehensively the total compass of the science in lexical form, and it also serves as a theoretical category.

2.1. Theological Encyclopedia

In the German Protestant world one may refer to the various editions of *Realencyklopädie für protestantische Theologie und Kirche* (1854-66; 3d ed., 1896-1913) and of *Die Religion in Geschichte und Gegenwart* (1909-13; 3d ed., 1957-65; 4th ed., 1998ff.). One may also refer to *Theologische Realenzyklopädie,* initiated in 1977 by G. Krause and G. Müller.

The standard work in Roman Catholic theology is *Lexikon für Theologie und Kirche* (1930-38; 2d ed., 1957-68).

2.2. Theological Theory

The main point in this regard is to show the inner unity of theology in its many disciplines and to define its relation to other sciences (→ Philosophy of Science). F. → Schleiermacher (1768-1834) attempted this task in comprehensive fashion. In his programmatic sketch *Kurze Darstellung des theologischen Studiums* (1811; 3d ed., 1910, repr. 1993; ET *Brief Outline of Theology as a Field of Study* [New York, 1990]), he described theology as positive, that is, a science that is not deducible from an idea of learning, and he found the unity of the philosophical, historical, and practical divisions in the practical task of giving guidance to the church. He failed to establish his view, however, especially when he integrated → dogmatics into historical theology. Present efforts reflect more a sense of the problem than a successful attempt to develop the disciplines systematically from the essence of theology. Difficulties are the relating of theology to the humanities and the theoretical grounding of theology in learning as a whole, in view of the crisis in traditional cultural institutions.

Bibliography: On 1: R. COLLISON, *Encyclopaedias: Their History throughout the Ages* (2d ed.; New York, 1966) • "Encyclopaedias," *NEBrit* (15th ed., 1998) 18.258-77 • F. SCHALK, "Enzyklopädie" and "Enzyklopädismus," *HWP* 2.573-77 bibliography • S. P. WALSH, *Anglo-American General Encyclopedias, 1703-1967: A Historical Bibliography* (New York, 1968) • J. M. WELLS, ed., *The Circle of Knowledge: Encyclopedias Past and Present* (Chicago, 1968).

On 2: F. BÖCKLE et al., eds., *Christlicher Glaube in moderner Gesellschaft. Enzyklopädische Bibliothek in 30 Bänden* (Freiburg, 1980ff.) • R. BULTMANN, *Theologische Enzyklopädie* (ed. E. Jüngel and K. W. Müller; Tübingen, 1984) • *DTC* • G. EBELING, *The Study of Theology* (London, 1979) • *EncRel(E)* • *ERE* • G. HUMMEL, "Enzyklopädie," *TRE* 9.716-42 • *NCE* • W. PANNENBERG, *Theology and the Philosophy of Science* (London, 1976) • *RE* • D. RITSCHL, *The Logic of Theology* (Philadelphia, 1987).

HERMANN FISCHER

End Times → Eschatology

Enemy

1. Concept
2. Love of Enemy
3. Love of Enemy and Politics

Enmity is a basic experience of individual and collective life. Confronting this basic experience is the extreme form that → Jesus gives to the command of love of neighbor when, in the → Sermon on the Mount, he includes in it → love of one's enemies. Theology, however, has typically devoted very little discussion to the concept and problem of the enemy.

1. Concept
An enemy is one who hates and pursues us. A sense of threat always goes hand in hand with the term. As seen most clearly in Greek tragedy, however, the experience of enmity is a necessary stage in human life. The recognition of enmity as a source of knowledge is an insight that → psychoanalysis has taken up in our time.

In most languages (e.g., in what the OT says about the enemy), personal enmity and collective enmity are closely related. A basic distinction was first made in Roman law. There the enemy *(hostis)* was one who was in a state of → war with the Roman people. This enemy was to be distinguished from one's personal enemy *(inimicus)*, as also from a robber or bandit. The linking of enmity to a political subject had far-reaching consequences. It came into the classical doctrine of the just war developed by → Augustine (→ Augustine's Theology). One of the marks of this teaching is that only the lawful government may define an enemy and declare war. This view stands behind medieval attempts to limit private feuds and to achieve a state monopoly of power. The goal — realized at best only partially — was to limit enmity conceptually and politically. I. Kant's (1724-1804) definition gives it classical formulation. For him an enemy is one whose publicly expressed will (whether by word or deed) gives evidence of a maxim that, if it became a general rule, would make peace among nations impossible and perpetuate the natural state.

Such attempts to restrain enmity were defied by peoples' wars in the 19th century and world wars in the 20th century. Enmity between nations was now ideologized in the supposed interests of higher ideals (→ Ideology). The combination of ideological nationalism (→ Nation, Nationalism) with the explosion of weapons technology (→ Disarmament and Armament) has made it extremely doubtful whether legal attempts to restrict enmity can succeed. Finally, the invention and development of nuclear → weapons have produced attitudes and forms of thought according to which absolute weapons seem to demand absolute enemies.

2. Love of Enemy
The command to love one's enemy (Matt. 5:38-48; Luke 6:27-38) is not exclusive to the Christian tradition. Jesus' command forcefully summarizes, rather, a → hope that has been common in many traditions from the wisdom of Babylon onward, namely, that hatred and revenge can be overcome. In Jesus, as in → Greek philosophy, the aim is not a gradual overcoming of the idea of revenge but its elimination in principle. Already in Jesus' own proclamation this radicalism has its basis in a reference to God's turning in love to the world and humanity. In the Christian confession (→ Confession of Faith) this insight continues in the perception that God's love for a hostile world, demonstrated by the → cross and → resurrection of Jesus, is the basis of all love of the enemy.

Since the proclamation of Jesus Christ aims to overcome revenge, it directly links love of enemy with renunciation of → force. Jesus advocates herewith not only an ethos of mutual interaction but also a demand for a unilateral approach. The persuasive power of this demand lies primarily in the realism with which it applies to the situation of his hearers. Those of whom he demands love of enemy are first confronted with the fact that they have enemies. At the time of its formulation the demand can thus relate to the experience of the Jewish people, who were pursuing very effectively a strategy of nonviolent → conflict resolution in their relations with Rome as an occupying power. The hyperbolic examples given by Jesus link such experience to the opportunities for freedom from force. Yet the demand of Jesus goes beyond this experience. Formulated in the most general way, it refers to the coming of the dominion of God (→ Kingdom of God). All enmity will then be at an end. This reference shows, however, that the experience of enmity and violence belongs to the old and passing world. Those who become followers of Jesus (→ Discipleship) have a share in overcoming this world.

The radical nature of the law of love of enemy does not lie in the extension of the circle of → friendship to those whom one would normally regard as enemies. This application would simply be an invitation to render enmity innocuous. The point is that the enemy is now defined as one to be loved. The scope of the command is the religious and national enemy, as well as one's personal enemies.

The Christian tradition has continually evaded the radicalness of this love of one's enemy. The reduction of the commands of the Sermon on the Mount to *consilia evangelica* (evangelical counsels) works just as much in this direction as does their restriction to the area of private enmity.

3. Love of Enemy and Politics

The question of the political rationality (→ Reason) of love of enemy has reached its climax in the atomic age, thus revealing how dubious is the concept of a → politics that regards the distinction between friend and enemy as normal (C. Schmitt). Expressing political enmity by the weapons of mass destruction makes it obvious that the attempt to gain one's own security by increasing the risk of destruction for one's enemy (the policy of deterrence) is bound to fail in the long run because it increases the danger of collective self-destruction rather than improving security. For a humanity that has now achieved destructive power over its own history, there is security only *with* the enemy, not *against* the enemy.

Such a policy of collective security is an insight of political reason; it forces us to see the political situation through the eyes of the enemy. This approach requires us to revise our picture of the enemy, the accomplishment of which must be a priority for the churches. The political form of loving one's enemy does not consist in an illusionary denial of conflicts and clashes of interest but in an → empathy that views these conflicts soberly and looks beyond them to find a sphere of common interests and possibilities of cooperation for the sake of → peace.

→ Aggression; Pacifism; Peace Movement

Bibliography: J. BLANK, *Im Dienst der Versöhnung. Friedenpraxis aus christlicher Sicht* (Munich, 1984) • P. HOFFMANN, "Tradition und Situation. Zur 'Verbindlichkeit' des Gebots der Feindesliebe in der synoptischen Überlieferung und in die gegenwärtigen Friedensdiskussion," *Ethik im Neuen Testament* (ed. K. Kertelge; Freiburg, 1984) 50-188 • W. HUBER, "Feindschaft und Feindesliebe," *ZEE* 26 (1982) 128-58 • S. KEEN, *Faces of the Enemy: Reflections of the Hostile Imagination* (San Francisco, 1986) • P. LAPIDE, *Die Bergpredigt–Utopie oder Programm?* (Mainz, 1982) • D. PETERS, *Surviving Church Conflict* (Scottdale, Pa., 1997) • H. E. RICHTER, *Zur Psychologie des Friedens* (Reinbek, 1982) • U. SCHMIDHÄUSER, *Entfeindung. Entwurf eines Denkens jenseits der Feindbilder* (Stuttgart, 1983) • C. SCHMITT, *Der Begriff des Politischen* (2d ed.; Berlin, 1963); idem, *Theorie der Partisanen. Zwischenbemerkung zum Begriff des Politischen* (Berlin, 1963) • R. J. STOLLER, *Perversion: The Erotic Form of Hatred* (New York, 1976) • W. M. SWARTLEY, *The Love of Enemy and Nonretaliation in the NT* (Louisville, Ky., 1992) • C. F. VON WEIZSÄCKER, "Die intelligente Feindesliebe," *Der bedrohte Friede* (Munich, 1981) 533-38 • H. ZEHR, *Changing Lenses: A New Focus for Crime and Justice* (Scottdale, Pa., 1990).

WOLFGANG HUBER

Energy

Energy (Gk. *energeia*, "efficacy, reality, activity") is a measure of the capacity for → work. All processes in → nature, and thus also all human activities, involve the exchange, delivery, and transformation of energy. It comes in various forms (mechanical energy, heat, light, chemical changes, electrical energy, etc.), which to some extent may be transformed into one another. In all these processes the total energy remains constant (the law of conservation of energy); it is neither used up nor generated. The most important carriers or sources can be divided into those that are exhaustible and those that are renewable.

The *exhaustible sources* of energy — fossil fuels such as coal, oil, and natural gas, or the raw materials of fission such as uranium and thorium — can no longer be increased today; sooner or later, these sources will be exhausted. Reserves of coal will probably last some 300 years; those of oil and natural gas, some 50 years. Estimates for uranium and thorium are imprecise. According to their use in present-day reactors, they should last some decades until materials are available for nuclear fusion. If the process of fusion can be controlled in reactors in a way that is socially and economically acceptable, then a source of energy will be available for centuries to come.

Renewable sources of energy come from ongoing or constantly repeated natural processes. The most important of these originate in the energy of the sun; others are geothermal energy and tidal energy. The energy radiated by the sun each year on the earth's surface exceeds all human use by about 15,000 times. Of this direct energy, 0.5 percent is changed into the forces of wind, wave, and water, while by photosynthesis 0.15 percent is changed into organic matter, the so-called biomass (esp.

wood). Finally, the work capacity of humans and animals is dependent on the sun. This energy is available in reduced intensity and with variations according to time and place. Large surfaces are needed to collect it (solar collector systems, open countryside for windmills, forests, areas for plants, etc.), and so too are storage facilities. These restrictions limit its use and greatly increase the cost.

Fossil fuels provide 80 percent of the world's consumption of energy, but in industrial countries the figure is over 90 percent. Oil dominates; it surpassed coal at the end of the 1950s. Most oil resources are in the hands of a few countries, which have thus gained in economic importance. Some of them have joined forces in the Organization of Petroleum Exporting Countries (OPEC), which in 1999 included 11 members. The OPEC nations set oil prices not merely for the industrial states but especially for countries of the → Third World.

In the developing countries wood and other forms of biomass have been readily available as noncommercial sources of energy. On average these provide 45 percent of the energy used and, in some cases (e.g., Nepal and Tanzania), over 90 percent. As industrialization increases, however, so does the proportion of fossil fuels used. Wood is becoming scarcer with deforestation, the clearing of land for agriculture, and increased usage. The increase in oil prices has also increased that of wood in city markets of the Third World. The impoverished → masses find it increasingly difficult to meet their need for wood.

The use of energy always has an impact on the → environment. As a rule, the effects of exhaustible sources cause more damage (e.g., wastes, increase of carbon dioxide, radioactivity, pollution of the atmosphere and water), but the use of renewable sources also does harm (e.g., deforestation, destabilization of water tables by the creation of large reservoirs).

Up to the 20th century the availability of energy resources was limited by the rate of exploration and the technology of exploitation. The global use of energy, however, has now reached a point where it is coming up against natural limits. The finite nature of nonrenewable energy sources, the limited intensity and the long period needed for the growth of renewable fuels, and the ability of the environment to absorb greater usage are all important factors. A comparison of the rate of consumption shows how serious is the problem. People in industrial states use on average ten times as much energy as those in developing countries. If the per capita usage in the Third World were to rise to the level of that found today in → industrial societies, the global output would go up three or four times. The limits of available resources and of what the environment would sustain would then be reached all the faster. To ward off the threatened crisis, global energy politics must set itself two goals.

First, total energy use must be stabilized — achieving, if possible, a level lower than it now is. The industrial states in particular must be less profligate in their use. All technological possibilities of rational energy use must be exploited. In the long run, changes in consumer attitudes (→ Consumption) will also have to be achieved.

Second, remaining needs must be increasingly met from renewable energy sources, which over the years will be the only ones available and which cause less environmental damage. The total amount of direct or indirect energy from the sun will be enough for the purpose. Yet there will still be the task of selecting the techniques appropriate to local resources and making the best possible use of them.

→ Ecology

Bibliography: L. R. Brown, *State of the World 2000* (New York, 2000) • G. T. Miller, *Living in the Environment: Principles, Connections, and Solutions* (11th ed.; Pacific Grove, Calif., 2000) • United Nations, *Energy Statistics Yearbook* (New York, 1992).

Ulrich Ratsch

Enlightenment

1. Term
2. Interpretations
3. Criticisms
4. Dialectic

1. Term

The term "enlightenment" (Fr. *les lumières, siècle des lumières;* Ger. *Aufklärung*) is used to refer to the movement originating in French → rationalism and English → empiricism that decisively affected intellectual life in Europe from the end of the 17th century to the end of the 18th. It criticized → revelation and → religion; developed new methods and new ways of thinking in philosophy, history, and science; evoked new themes, forms, and media in literature; and to a large extent shaped the face of the modern world, especially by establishing new views and institutions in education, law, government, and politics. The same word also denotes (1) the century before the French Revolution, when a middle-class movement of liberation arose against the system of feudal absolutism; (2) rationalizing processes in other cultures, such as the Greek Enlightenment of the sixth and fifth centuries B.C.; and (3) the general process of rationalizing in European culture (as in M. Horkheimer and T. W. Adorno's "dialectic of enlightenment").

As an intellectual movement, the Enlightenment began in Britain (F. Bacon and T. Hobbes, and then esp. J. Locke, J. Toland, B. Mandeville, the third earl of Shaftesbury, G. Berkeley, and D. Hume). France became the main center in the 18th century (esp. P. Bayle, Voltaire, Montesquieu, D. Diderot, J. d'Alembert, J. O. La Mettrie, C.-A. Helvétius, P.-H.-D. Holbach, É. Condillac, and Condorcet), from which it spread out across the whole of Europe. The German Enlightenment began later. Starting with the rationalism of C. Thomasius, G. W. Leibniz, and C. Wolff, it reached its peak in about 1780 with H. S. Reimarus, G. E. Lessing, M. Mendelssohn, C. F. Nicolai, C. Wieland, G. C. Lichtenberg, G. Forster, and especially I. Kant (→ Kantianism). Only in the 1780s did "enlightenment" establish itself as the term for the corresponding intellectual and social movement and also for the epoch. Along with the self-designation of the epoch as the age of the Enlightenment or the enlightened age, we find such characterizations as the age of criticism, and — most important in self-understanding — the age of → reason. Among the various ideas suggested by the term, we might mention especially the ideal of clear and distinct knowledge, which stems from the → epistemology of R. Descartes (→ Cartesianism) and the metaphor of illuminating or enlightening.

2. Interpretations

In his essay "What Is Enlightenment?" (1784), Kant (1724-1804) defined the concept as "man's release from his self-incurred tutelage. Tutelage is man's incapacity to make use of his understanding without direction from another. Self-incurred is this tutelage when its cause lies not in lack of reason but in lack of resolution and courage to use it without direction from another. *Sapere aude!* 'Have courage to use your own reason!' — that is the motto of enlightenment" (p. 85).

For Kant, public criticism was the most important condition of the self-enlightenment of educated people. He saw the freedom "to make public use of one's reason at every point" (p. 87), as well as → tolerance in religious matters, as both the presupposition and the result of enlightenment. Kant regarded enlightenment as an ongoing process: "If we are asked, 'Do we live in an *enlightened age?*' the answer is, 'No,' but we

live in an *age of enlightenment*" (90). His critical view of it as a process of gradual emergence from "barbarity" and "tutelage" came at the end of the age of enlightenment. But Kant did not primarily think of "enlightenment" as the term for an epoch. It was for him the theoretical self-confirmation of an emancipated reason that was no longer subject to dogmatic guardians, with all the practical implications. For him the path of enlightenment led by way of self-reflection to → autonomy.

Around 1790 Lichtenberg (1742-99) formulated the practical reference point of the Enlightenment in terms of a right understanding of essential needs. The French Revolution was a test whether the great concepts of the Enlightenment — such as → freedom, human dignity, tolerance, autonomy, → progress, justice, reason, and → virtue — could be expressed in an institutional order, whether a constitutional state could be set up in accordance with these ideals. Assessment of the Enlightenment has ever since been linked to assessment of the French Revolution.

G. W. F. Hegel (1770-1831) constantly related enlightenment to → revolution. He pointed out that the source of the French Revolution had been found in philosophy, stating that not without reason people had equated philosophy with practical wisdom, since it is not just truth in and for itself, as pure essence, but also truth as it is lived in the world. Thus we cannot oppose the thesis that revolution received its first stimulus from philosophy (*Lectures on the Philosophy of History*). Even earlier, in his *Phenomenology of the Spirit* (1807), Hegel had viewed the Enlightenment philosophically from the same perspective, speaking of its fight against → superstition, with special reference to the French Revolution and its battle against → Catholicism and the related feudal system. Enlightenment that leads on to revolution, however, is allegedly more a negative action. No positive work or act can thus produce universal freedom; it needs a negative act. It is "the fury of dissolution." For Hegel the danger of the Enlightenment was that with the radicalizing of its criticism, it would cut the ground from under its own feet.

Even before Hegel, several — including Lessing, Mendelssohn, and Wieland — had referred to the ambivalence of enlightenment. Lessing (1729-81), in the context of contemporary criticism of revelation and religion, criticized the various theological trends (i.e., → neology, → deism, → orthodoxy, and → Pietism) from what seemed to be a paradoxical position. On the one hand, he demanded the adoption of the results of modern critical → hermeneutics, of a historical understanding of revelation and

Christianity; on the other hand, he would not simply abandon the perceived significance of → revelation and → religion. At the price of contradictions, he refused to make a radical break with the intellectual position from and against which he was arguing. The age of Enlightenment itself was already anticipating its criticism with Kant and Lessing, as with J. G. Hamann, J. G. Herder, and F. von Schiller.

3. Criticisms

From the time of the French Revolution, the Enlightenment was often regarded as politically dangerous. Its friends and foes polarized into "progressives" and "reactionaries." The intellectual movements at the beginning of the 19th century, in direct or indirect criticism, became movements of opposition to rationalistic enlightenment. This characterization was true of → idealism, → historicism, and → Romanticism.

Hegel's philosophy sought to retain the intellectual substance of Enlightenment philosophy in a different and more reflective way. Idealism was the Enlightenment come to itself. The debate of K. Marx (1818-83) and F. Engels (1820-95) with the Enlightenment, especially the French materialists, led to its adoption and development, but also to criticism of the purely "mechanical" → materialism of the French rationalists and to the discovery of the class character of the Enlightenment as it could be seen in the French Revolution and its consequences (→ Marxism). A historicizing and neutralizing of the concept marked the later 19th century.

4. Dialectic

The work of F. Nietzsche (1844-1900) reveals a mixture of Enlightenment and anti-Enlightenment traits. He was radically for the Enlightenment and radically against it. In his influence the radical opposition was dominant. In his criticism of Christianity and of the basic concepts of the older Enlightenment (reason, truth, morality, tolerance, → equality), he wanted to unmask the unacknowledged implications and consequences of the morality that had developed on the soil of Christianity and of rationalism. Shrill though his criticism of the foundations of contemporary morality and philosophy might sound, he was following an impulse consistent with the Enlightenment itself, as M. Foucault (1926-84) and J. Derrida (b. 1930) later did in the 20th century. He was seeking new sources of strength by way of dissolution.

M. Horkheimer (1895-1973) and T. W. Adorno (1903-69) interpreted Nietzsche, as they did also Marx and Freud, against the foil of a "dialectic of en-

lightenment" (1947), that is, in the sense of the necessary self-reflection of enlightenment. As they saw it, the aim of enlightenment in the sense of progressive thinking had always been to relieve humans of fear and set them up as masters. A fully enlightened earth, however, shines under the sign of triumphant disaster. The linking of enlightenment with mastery over nature from the very beginnings of European civilization led, for Horkheimer and Adorno, to a triumphal march of instrumental reason, which is now giving evidence of its catastrophic consequences: the destruction of nature (→ Ecology), the possibility of fascism and → war, and the emptying out of cultural meaning by an industrial → culture that swallows up everything. Simply put, the Enlightenment is totalitarian. Hegel's "fury of dissolution" seems to have become the fate of the rational process. Mythology itself has brought into play the endless process of enlightenment, in which every theoretical outlook inevitably falls victim to the destructive criticism of being only a belief, until even the concepts of spirit, truth, and indeed enlightenment itself become no more than animistic magic. The demanded self-reflection of the Enlightenment ought to contribute, not to the discrediting of the call of the 18th-century philosophers of the Enlightenment for freedom, autonomy, and human dignity, but to their swifter actualization (→ Rights, Human and Civil). Along these lines the later Adorno stated that he found Kant's definition of Enlightenment still extraordinarily relevant (*Erziehung zur Mündigkeit* [1969]). In the perspective of critical theory, an enlightenment that reflects on its own conditions, consequences, and limits is not something that is historically ended or self-encapsulated. It is still needed, not as a finished concept, but as a relevant task of critical philosophy.

In the course of establishing a functional system-theory, N. Luhmann called for a "reflective enlightenment" in a step from rational enlightenment by way of an "unmasking enlightenment" to a "sociological enlightenment" (*Soziologische Aufklärung* [1967]; → Social Systems). Rejecting such a formal view, J. Habermas (b. 1929) defined enlightenment materially as → emancipation linked to the structures of linguistic understanding (*Theorie des kommunikativen Handelns* [1981]). Taking issue with both, W. Oelmüller (1930-99) viewed the Enlightenment historically as a process of both criticizing and conserving tradition (*Die unbefriedigte Aufklärung*). O. Negt and A. Kluge investigated present-day possibilities of furthering the processes of enlightenment and emancipation with the help of categories like self-regulation and "enlightenment work" (*Geschichte und Eigensinn* [1981]).

There is still debate as to what enlightenment is or should be. In the two centuries since Kant's classic definition, the term has always had both a theoretical and a practical, normative, and sociopolitical character. It is no accident, then, that it will continue to be contested as long as enlightenment itself remains possible and necessary.

Bibliography: C. J. Berry, *The Social Theory of the Scottish Enlightenment* (Edinburgh, 1997), an introductory survey • E. Breuer, *The Limits of Enlightenment: Jews, Germans, and the Eighteenth-Century Study of Scripture* (Cambridge, Mass., 1996) • M. Horkheimer and T. W. Adorno, *Dialectic of Enlightenment* (New York, 1972; orig. pub., 1947) • I. Kant, "What Is Enlightenment?" (1783), *Foundations of the Metaphysics of Morals and What Is Enlightenment?* (trans. L. W. Beck; Indianapolis, 1959) 85-92 • W. Oelmüller, *Die unbefriedigte Aufklärung. Beiträge zu einer Theorie der Moderne von Lessing, Kant und Hegel* (2d ed.; Frankfurt, 1979); idem, *Was ist heute Aufklärung?* (Düsseldorf, 1972) • R. Piepmeier, M. Schmidt, and H. Greive, "Aufklärung," *TRE* 4.575-615 • M. B. Prince, *Philosophical Dialogue in the British Enlightenment: Theology, Aesthetics, and the Novel* (Cambridge, 1996) • P. Pütz, *Die deutsche Aufklärung* (2d ed.; 1979), history of research; idem, ed., *Erforschung der deutschen Aufklärung* (Königstein, 1980), collection of texts • T. Rendtorff, ed., *Religion als Problem der Aufklärung* (Göttingen 1981) • G. A. J. Rogers, ed., *Locke's Philosophy: Content and Context* (New York, 1996) • W. A. Rusher, ed., *The Ambiguous Legacy of the Enlightenment* (Lanham, Md., 1995) • T. P. Saine, *The Problem of Being Modern; or, The German Pursuit of Enlightenment. from Christian Wolff to the French Revolution* (Detroit, 1997) • S. Tweyman, ed., *David Hume: Critical Assessments* (4 vols.; London, 1994) • J. Yolton, J. V. Price, and J. Stephens, eds., *The Dictionary of Eighteenth-Century British Philosophers* (2 vols.; Bristol, 1999).

Norbert Rath

Enoch

1. The name "Enoch" (or "Hanoch," both from Gk. *Henōch,* Heb. *ḥănôk*) is of uncertain meaning, perhaps "follower" or "initiate." It is used in the Bible for various figures in Genesis 1–11 and the story of the patriarchs: (1) the eldest son of Cain and builder of the first city, of the same name (Gen. 4:17-18); (2) the son of Jared, descendant of Seth (see 2); (3) the son of Midian, grandson of → Abraham (Gen. 25:4; 1 Chr. 1:33); and (4) the eldest son of Reuben, grandson of → Jacob (Gen. 46:9; Exod. 6:14; 1 Chr. 5:3), and founder of the family of the Hanochites (Num. 26:5).

2. Jewish piety connected many speculations with Enoch the son of Jared. Already in the oldest account (Gen. 5:21-24 P), he bears many mythical features. He lives for 365 years, the number of days in the solar year. He is distinguished by a close walk with God and by experiencing translation instead of → death. He is the seventh of the fathers of the race after → Adam. All these motifs point toward links with → Babylonian myths (H. Gunkel).

In postcanonical writings the motifs are filled out and supplemented by related legendary material. Enoch is honored as the first man versed in writing and learning (astronomy; *Jub.* 4:17-19). He is a model of pious → righteousness (Sir. 44:16; *Jub.* 10:17), reveals divine judgment (*Jub.* 4:23-24; *1 Enoch* 12:4-6), has a vision of the paradisial world (*1 Enoch* 24–26), and is a heavenly → high priest (*Jub.* 4:25; midrash of Num. 12:15). He is given the functions of the end-time Son of Man (*1 Enoch* 71:14) and is equated with → angels (*2 Enoch* 22:8-11; *3 Enoch* 4:2, where he merges with the great angel Metatron). He is mentioned only marginally in early Christian writings (Luke 3:37; Heb. 11:5; Jude 14-15). Traditions about him strongly influenced Christian → eschatology and → Christology (§1.2).

3. The role of Enoch as a leading figure, particularly in circles of Jewish → apocalypse and → mysticism, is reflected in the books dedicated or ascribed to him (→ Pseudepigrapha):

Ethiopic Enoch (or *1 Enoch*), a collection of originally independent tractates, was composed between the third century b.c. and the first century a.d. Its largest sections are the Book of the Watchers (1–36) and the Book of the Similitudes (37–71, with important witness to Jewish expectation of the Son of Man). It is preserved complete in Ethiopic, and fragments exist in Greek from an original Aramaic.

Slavonic Enoch (or *2 Enoch*), known from about 20 fragmentary manuscripts in Old Slavonic, evidently existed in a longer and a shorter recension. Of debatable origin, it is probably pre-Christian.

Hebrew Enoch (or *3 Enoch*), a compendium of Jewish *Merkabah* mysticism that probably comes from Palestine in the fifth/sixth century a.d., is part of the many-branched *Hekhalot* writings.

The *Book of Giants* is known only fragmentarily from the → Qumran discoveries. For details of other works, see S. Uhlig, 467.

Bibliography: P. S. ALEXANDER, "The Historical Setting of the Hebrew Book of Enoch," *JJS* 28 (1977) 156-80 • F. I. ANDERSEN, "Second (Slavonic Apocalype of) Enoch," *OTP* 1.91-221 • R. A. ARGALL, *1 Enoch and Sirach: A Comparative Literary Analysis of the Themes of Revelation, Creation, and Judgment* (Atlanta, 1995) • M. BLACK, "A Bibliography on 1 Enoch in the Eighties," *JSP* 5 (1989) 3-16; idem, *The Book of I Enoch* (Leiden, 1985) • T. J. COLE, "Enoch, a Man Who Walked with God," *BSac* 148/591 (1991) 288-97 • H. GUNKEL, *Genesis* (Göttingen, 1977) • H. HOFMANN, *Das sogenanntes hebräisches Henochbuch* (Bonn, 1984) • J. T. MILIK and M. BLACK, *The Books of Enoch* (Oxford, 1976) • G. W. E. NICKELSBURG, "Scripture in 1 Enoch and 1 Enoch as Scripture," *Texts and Contexts* (ed. T. Fornberg and D. Hellholm; Oslo, 1995) 333-54 • B. A. PEARSON, "1 Enoch in the Apocryphon of John," ibid. 355-67 • P. SACCHI, "Henochgestalt / Henochliteratur," *TRE* 15.42-54 (bibliography) • P. A. TILLER, *A Commentary on the Animal Apocalypse of 1 Enoch* (Atlanta, 1993) • S. UHLIG, "Das äthiopisches Henochbuch," *JSHRZ* 5.6 • J. C. VANDER KAM, *Enoch: A Man for All Generations* (Columbia, S.C., 1995).

BERNDT SCHALLER

Entrance → Liturgy 2

Environment

1. The term "environment" generally refers to the natural world. For example, people often speak of concern for the environment or of environmental policy or of environmental law. In each case the word refers to the nonhuman realm, taken in whole or in part. For example, environmental law is the section of the legal code that pertains to human duties to care for creation (e.g., to protect endangered species or to regulate production of toxic wastes). Environmental policy refers to the codes and procedures, sometimes codified in law, that provide guidelines for a government or a business in dealing with the natural world (e.g., wetlands protection or automobile emissions).

One common use of the word is in the term → "environmental ethics." As used here, "environmental" refers to the earth and its communities of → life. In contrast to traditional ethics — which has to do only with humans and their actions — environmental ethics refers to duties we humans have to creatures or systems of the nonhuman world (e.g., to sentient → animals, plants, species, and ecosystems).

The natural sciences, especially biology and more specifically the discipline of → ecology, have contributed greatly to our understanding of the environment. We know much about how the world works — from the cycling of water and nutrients to the flow of energy through various food chains.

2. While the term "environment" is for many clearly the term of choice, some argue that its use is problematic. For example, it is abstract, lacking the concreteness of marmot or mountain or meadow or earth — or even biosphere. Few people describe where they live by speaking of their environment. Furthermore, it suggests something we live in but that is apart from us, rather than the home we inhabit and of which we are an integral part. In other words, it connotes a disjunction between human and nonhuman — a → dualism between nature and culture — that many argue is simply not true to the way things are. Finally, the term "environment" is somewhat sterile. It fails to capture the blooming, buzzing confusion of creatures in dynamic interaction within the natural world. The term "environment" is, in short, too tame.

Bibliography: R. BUCHHOLZ, *Principles of Environmental Management: The Greening of Business* (Upper Saddle River, N.J., 1998) • J. DESJARDINS, *Environmental Ethics: An Introduction to Environmental Philosophy* (Belmont, Calif., 1997) • F. B. GOLLEY, *A Primer for Environmental Literacy* (New Haven, 1998) • D. ORR, *Ecological Literacy: Education and the Transition to a Postmodern World* (Albany, N.Y., 1992) • L. POJMAN, *Global Environmental Ethics: Readings in Theory and Application* (Belmont, Calif., 1997) • H. ROLSTON III, *Environmental Ethics: Duties to and Values in the Natural World* (Philadelphia, 1988) • D. WORSTER, *Nature's Economy: A History of Ecological Ideas* (Cambridge, 1994).

STEVEN BOUMA-PREDIGER

Environmental Ethics

1. Term and History
2. Anthropological Issues
3. Christian Theology and Practice

1. Term and History

While "environmental ethics" has no universally agreed upon definition, one common way of describing it is *an ethic for the earth and its communities of life.* In contrast to typical → ethics — which has to do with moral duties, rights, goods, values, and the like with respect to humans and their actions — environmental ethics, as prominent philosopher-ethicist Holmes Rolston III puts it, refers to duties to, and values in, the natural world — that is, duties we humans have to sentient animals, plants, species, and ecosystems. In this way, environmental ethics expands the scope of what counts morally to include more than merely humans. And thus it is sometimes used synonymously with the term "ecological ethics," though some prefer this latter term since it is less abstract and sterile and thus more true to the world as experienced by us — not an "environment" but an earth home (the *eco-* in "ecological" comes from Gk. *oikos*, "house, home") inhabited by marmots and Sitka spruces and tall-grass prairies. In short, environmental ethics refers to disciplined reflection on the natural world with the goal of identifying how we as humans should live.

While environmental ethics, as an academic discipline in the modern sense, is relatively new, concern for the earth and its creatures and systems is as old as the human species. No human economy can function without depending on the larger economy of nature, and hence peoples of diverse times and places have pursued knowledge of and familiarity with what we today call the → environment. The contemporary situation, however, has given urgency to the task of environmental ethics and spurred its development in the last few decades. For example, the publication in 1962 of Rachel Carson's *Silent Spring,* which described the many deleterious effects of pesticides on marine and terrestrial animals, was one of the most significant events in raising public consciousness, as was the first Earth Day celebration in April 1970. The Club of Rome Report (→ Ecology 2), published in 1972, and the Global 2000 Report, in 1980, likewise drew attention to the limits of economic growth and called into question the patterns of → consumption of the so-called developed nations, especially the United States. More recently, scientific data about global climate change, holes in the ozone layer, and extinction of species — to cite only three of the more well-known ecological degradations — add to the sense that all is not well on our home planet and make the task of environmental ethics more important than ever.

Given the complexity of the natural world, plus the difficulties associated with understanding various ecological problems, it is no surprise that environmental ethics is an interdisciplinary endeavor that takes into account not only the natural sciences, particularly biology and geology, but also various of the social sciences (e.g., economics and → politics) and also disciplines within the humanities like philosophy and religion. Environmental ethics, therefore, requires a broad knowledge across the disciplines and often in colleges and universities gives rise to and/or finds a prominent place in programs of environmental studies.

2. Anthropological Issues

A core issue in environmental ethics is anthropocentrism. Does environmental ethics have only to assure human well-being, or does it have to see to the rights and interests of nonhuman creatures and systems? For example, some argue that we ought to care for the natural world because we owe it to our children — we have obligations to posterity or future generations. Others claim that such an argument is still too human-centered, that while our obligations do indeed include humans distant from us in time, they also extend to California condors and sequoias and jack-pine forests. And while some claim that any action taken by humans must be rooted in the rights of natural objects to such care, others argue that even if there are no rights of nature, we humans have duties to care for the natural world simply because it is valuable in and of itself. Indeed, one form of nonanthropocentrism, commonly called biocentrism, argues that not only do nonhuman creatures have moral standing, they have a value equal to that of humans. In short, there is a variety of views concerning whether nonhuman creatures should be morally considered and, if so, what value such beings may have.

One of the most important insights of environmental ethics is that we humans must live in harmony with the natural world — limiting our needs and wants in such a way that other creatures may live and flourish. In this regard, environmental ethicists can and must learn more from the ecological sciences about how the world works. Similarly, experts in science and → technology who have no interest or expertise in ethics must learn from the moral philosopher and theological ethicist.

3. Christian Theology and Practice

In a number of ways Christian theology can and ought to make an essential contribution to environmental ethics. For example, it can point out how typical environmental ethics often is blind to the fact of our own creatureliness — that we are also creatures, 'ādām (man; human) from 'ădāmâ (earth, soil), humans from the humus. And Christian theology can, when necessary, also remind environmental ethics that we humans are more than merely dust; we are also created in God's image. Properly understood, there is no → dualism between human and nonhuman, culture and nature.

So too a robust Christian doctrine of the → incarnation affirms the earthliness and bodiliness of humanity. Matter matters to the God of the Bible, and so it should also to us. This bold claim is reaffirmed in the Christian view of the future, in which bodies are resurrected and all creation — human and nonhuman — flourishes in praise to God.

Finally, Christian theology and ethics ought to remind environmental ethics that there is more to the good life than respecting rules (deontology) and considering consequences (teleology). Any fully adequate moral life must include attention to the virtues (aretaics) — or settled dispositions to act excellently — that constitute the good person and the good community. As important as our conduct is our character.

The demand by the → World Council of Churches for justice, → peace, and the integrity of → creation (→ Conciliarity 3) has rightly challenged the churches of the world not to divorce environmental ethics from the question of social justice (→ Righteousness, Justice 1). Indeed, the term "environmental justice," which links concern for ecological integrity with concern for social justice, has now gained common currency and is on the agenda of many of the world's churches. As was plainly evident, for example, at the Rio Earth Summit in 1992, it is hypocritical of the richest countries of the world to demand that the poorest should subjugate their interests to the protection of the natural world as a condition for the rich countries to do the same. For example, there is no moral high ground for those in North America, who represent only 5 percent of the world's population but use 25 percent of the world's energy resources.

Bibliography: R. ATTFIELD, *The Ethics of Environmental Concern* (Athens, Ga., 1991) • J. DESJARDINS, *Environmental Ethics: An Introduction to Environmental Philosophy* (Belmont, Calif., 1997) • R. F. NASH, *The Rights of Nature: A History of Environmental Ethics* (Madison, Wis., 1989) • M. OELSCHLAEGER, *Caring for Creation: An Ecumenical Approach to the Environmental Crisis* (New Haven, 1994) • D. ORR, *Ecological Literacy: Education and the Transition to a Postmodern World* (Albany, N.Y., 1992) • L. RASMUSSEN, *Earth Community Earth Ethics* (Maryknoll, N.Y., 1996) • H. ROLSTON III, *Environmental Ethics: Duties to and Values in the Natural World* (Philadelphia, 1988) • L. WILKINSON et al., eds., *Earthkeeping in the Nineties: Stewardship of Creation* (rev. ed.; Grand Rapids, 1991).

STEVEN BOUMA-PREDIGER

Envy

1. In Scripture
2. In Human Behavior
3. Moral Theology

1. In Scripture

According to Scripture, envy is a basic negative factor in human life. In → primeval history, Cain slew Abel out of envy (Gen. 4:3-16). Envy moved → Joseph's brothers to sell him into slavery in Egypt (Gen. 37:4). Saul showed envy in his relation to → David (1 Sam. 18:6-9). Envy can express itself in the glance of an eye (1 Sam. 18:9; Sir. 14:9; 31:13-14; cf. Matt. 20:15; Mark 7:22). Later Jewish → Wisdom literature considered envy, as the opposite of wisdom and generosity, the root of a cramped attitude to life (Wis. 6:23; cf. 7:13). Warnings were issued against envying the ungodly for their undeserved good fortune (Ps. 37:1, 7; 73:2-20; Prov. 23:3-5; 24:19-20), which would not finally last. Envy is here brought into relation to the problem of → theodicy.

In the NT envy appears among the vices listed in the Epistles. Taken from similar lists in Jewish and Hellenistic → ethics (→ Hellenism; Judaism), these negative attitudes are explained as the result and expression of a fundamental rejection of God (→ Sin) that can be overcome only by the full renewing of the believer by the → Holy Spirit (→ Regeneration; cf. Rom. 1:29; Gal. 5:21; 1 Tim. 6:4; Titus 3:3; 1 Pet. 2:1).

2. In Human Behavior

2.1. Envy as a basic category of human → behavior is a term for the jealous and hostile feelings and actions of one person toward another because the other has objects of value, property, qualities, or other advantages that seem to be desirable. It is motivated by the sense of being disadvantaged as compared to the other. Stronger than the desire to have the goods and so forth is resentment, that is, the desire that the other should not have them. Envy is related to the jealousy that tries to take full possession of a loved person out of fear of losing that one. Its antithesis is the generosity that in inner freedom grants to others what is theirs, thus making possible an openness of encounter.

2.2. The writings of many cultures speak of the envy of the gods, either as a correction in the sense of compensatory justice equalizing excessive good fortune, or as a hostile reaction to human hubris (e.g., among ancient authors, see Homer, Pindar, Aeschylus, and Herodotus; among modern writers, F. von Schiller).

2.3. → Philosophy shows a concern for the danger that envy will disrupt harmonious relations in → society and for the threat that it poses to its subjects by destroying their sense of self-worth (→ Self). It proposes, in antithesis, a society that is free from envy because it is a society of perfect justice (Plato). It distinguishes among legitimate indignation at the excessive good fortune of unworthy persons, envy itself, and an eagerness to take over the goods of others (Aristotle). It stresses the damaging effect of envy when people no longer try to better their own situation (Chrysostom, B. Spinoza). When the envious repress their → aggression against others, a resentment can arise that blames the fortunate for one's own poorer circumstances (F. Nietzsche, see also M. Scheler).

Modern discussions rest on the premise that in spite of the equality of opportunity, inequalities will arise, for example, between the rich and the poor (→ Equality; Poverty). They either explain envy as a universal human phenomenon, the idea of a society free from it being → utopian (see H. Schoeck), or they regard the envious reaction of the socially underprivileged, not as a moral feeling, but as a force that essentially underlies the striving for justice (J. Rawls).

3. Moral Theology

The traditional → moral theology of → Roman Catholicism lists envy as one of the seven deadly sins. At issue is an attitude rather than a single act. A fresh approach from the standpoint of theological ethics is still awaited. It will need to take into account the psychoanthropological stress on the corrosive effects of envy on the human personality (→ Anthropology; Psychology) and the sociopolitical concern for the establishment of a just social order in which envy would no longer find a place (→ Social Ethics). It might orient itself to the individual emphasis of the NT list of vices and the OT Wisdom sayings, but with the vision of a just world that equalizes unjustifiable distinctions between individuals and → groups as far as possible and sees also the need to learn to accept unavoidable distinctions.

Bibliography: C. E. CURRAN, *The Church and Morality: An Ecumenical and Catholic Approach* (Minneapolis, 1993) • M. W. DICKIE, "Envy," *ABD* 2.528-32 • E. M. EENIGENBURG, *Biblical Foundations and a Method for Doing Christian Ethics* (Lanham, Md., 1994) • W. MARXSEN, *NT Foundations for Christian Ethics* (Edinburgh, 1991) • K.-H. NUSSER, "Neid," *HWP* 6.695-706 • J. RAWLS, *A Theory of Justice* (Oxford, 1972) 530-41 • H. SCHOECK, *Envy: A Theory of Social Behavior* (New York, 1969) • A. B. ULANOV and B. ULANOV, *Cinderella and Her Sisters: The Envied and the Envying* (Philadelphia, 1983).

WERNER SCHWARTZ

Epanagoge

Alongside the Procheiros Nomos (i.e., accessible, or additional, statute book), the Epanagoge (Gk. *epanagōgē*, "return to the [starting] point; introduction") is the second draft of what was meant to serve as an introduction to the publishing of a comprehensive legal collection planned by Emperor Basil I (867-86). The term has reference to the law books of Emperor Justinian (reigned 527-65). The Epanagoge was composed after 879, probably between 884 and 886. As compared with older collections, the Epanagoge contains new titles (e.g., two on the emperor and three on the patriarch) that offer interesting testimony to the Byzantine two-powers theory.

Modern Byzantine research suggests that the author of the Epanagoge was → Patriarch Photius (858-67, 877-86), who wanted to bring into the new code a stricter separation of power between the emperor and the patriarch so as to protect the freedom of the church against imperial interference (→ Church and State). Because this goal conflicted with the traditional emperor-ideology of → Byzantium, Basil never sanctioned the draft as law.

→ Orthodox Church; Two Kingdoms Doctrine

Bibliography: Editions: PHOTIUS, *The Homilies of Photius, Patriarch of Constantinople* (trans. C. Mango; Cambridge, Mass., 1958); idem, *On the Mystagogy of the Holy Spirit* (trans. J. P. Farrell; Brookline, Mass., 1987) • J. ZEPOS and P. ZEPOS, *Jus graecoromanum* (vol. 2; Athens, 1931) 236-368.

Secondary works: F. DVORNIK, *The Photian Schism: History and Legend* (Cambridge, 1948) • H. HUNGER, *Die hochsprachliche profane Literatur der Byzantiner* (vol. 2; Munich, 1978) 454-55 • A. SCHMINCK, "Epanagoge," *ODB* 1.703-4.

EVANGELOS KONSTANTINOU

Ephesians, Epistle to the

1. Contents
2. Composition
3. Uniqueness

1. Contents

Ephesians is a theological treatise in epistolary form. Its main theme is the → church. There are no references to the congregation addressed, nor are there any actual polemics. The first part (chaps. 1–3) develops the theology. The greeting in 1:1-2 is surprisingly similar to that in Colossians. Vv. 3-14 then praise God (cf. 2 Cor. 1:3-7) for his saving work for believers. Vv. 15-19 contain a thanksgiving to God (cf. 1 Cor. 1:4-9) that reaches a climax with a description of the saving event in vv. 20-23. The soteriological consequences are shown in 2:1-10, especially vv. 5-7, with terms from the Pauline doctrine of → justification in vv. 8-9. In 2:11-13, 19-22 we have a "once-now" schema describing the past and present of the recipients. A song is added (vv. 14-18) that hails Christ as our peace and the → reconciliation with God that he has achieved. Then in 3:1-13, by means of the revelation schema in vv. 3-5, 9-10, we are told that the church rests on the teaching of the apostle → Paul (cf. 2:20). The goal is the thanksgiving of 3:14-19, which leads on to a → doxology in vv. 20-21.

The → parenesis in the second part (beginning *parakalō . . . hymas,* "I beg you," in 4:1) reminds the recipients that they are members of the one body of Christ (vv. 1-16). Individual normative statements formulate the concrete directions (4:17–5:20), for which it is difficult to discern any actual occasions. The → household rules in 5:21–6:9 are similar to those in Col. 3:18–4:1. On a Christological basis, they tell members of their responsibilities. Then 6:10-20 uses similar speech to that of → Qumran in 1QM 4:6-8 to advise regarding the fight against satanic forces; the decisive weapon is the → Word of God (6:17). The reference to Tychicus as the bearer of personal news (6:21-22) is literally the same as in Col. 4:7-8. A wish for peace and grace forms the conclusion (6:23-24).

2. Composition

The lack of greetings and the formulation of 3:2 show that there are no personal relations between Paul and those addressed, so that Ephesians can hardly be an authentic letter of Paul to the Ephesians. Some MSS — to be sure, extremely ancient — seem not to have had the words "in Ephesus" in 1:1. Marcion, probably on the basis of Col. 4:16, canonized Ephesians as the Epistle to the Laodiceans. Some scholars think that Ephesians was a circular letter sent by Paul to various churches, with the name of the particular church added in each case. On this view the original was not sent, with only copies coming into circulation. Why in this view other place-names have not been handed down remains a puzzle.

Ephesians seems to be directly dependent on

Colossians (cf. Eph. 1:15-16 with Col. 1:4, 9; 3:2-13 with Col. 1:24-29; 4:16 with Col. 2:19). This dependence is especially true in the epistolary framework (1:1-2; 6:21-22), though personal greetings are missing (such as in Col. 4:10-14, 15-17). One theory, then, is that the author borrowed from Colossians to make his theological tractate look like a Pauline letter but actually was writing to the whole church. There is no evidence that Ephesians was written as an introduction to the whole Pauline corpus.

As regards place and time, if Colossians is post-Pauline, Ephesians can hardly have been written before A.D. 80; if not, then perhaps around 70. The dependence on Colossians and the address suggest western Asia Minor as the place, but not → Ephesus itself. If a historical experience stands behind 6:10-20, one might think of an actual → persecution, possibly, on the post-Pauline theory, in the days of Domitian (81-96).

Ephesians claims to be written from prison (3:1, 13; 4:1), but the pseudepigraphic features receive no strong emphasis. The style differs strongly from that of the Pauline letters, especially in its long series of genitives and prepositional phrases and in its complicated relative clauses (e.g., 1:3-14 is a single sentence). The author writes in almost hymnic style, though an actual → hymn fragment exists probably only in 2:14-18.

3. Uniqueness

Ephesians constantly relates the church to the event of salvation. The *ekklēsia* is not, as in Paul, the individual congregation but the universal church built on the foundation of the → apostles and (Christian) → prophets and equipped with special offices (2:20; 3:5; 4:11-12). It mediates the wisdom of God over against cosmic powers (3:10). It can almost be equated with Christ (3:21). Its relation to Christ is compared to that of a wife to her husband (5:22-33). → Eschatology is no longer structured in temporal terms. The church is the body of Christ the Head, to whom all powers are subjected already and who perfectly fulfills all things by his → resurrection and → ascension (1:20-23; the death of Jesus ocurs only within the song in 2:14-18). Believers too are thus raised already and set in → heaven (2:5-6).

It is commonly assumed that Ephesians stresses the fellowship of Jews and → Gentiles in the one church (see 2:11-22). Those addressed, however, are Gentile Christians (v. 11), and the reference to nearness and farness is to the relationship with God (2:19). The central point is that individual Christians by → baptism (4:5) have a part in Christ's worldwide body. In spite of the stress on the "already" of salvation (2:8), the book contains much exhortation that in both form and content follows the Pauline tradition (e.g., in its juxtaposing indicative and imperative ideas, as in 2:10).

The worldview of Ephesians is dualistic. Heaven and earth are hostile spheres (2:1-3, 4-7; cf. vv. 14-17); there is no underworld (→ Dualism). Incorporation into Christ's body means liberation from the earthly sphere and transposition into the reality beyond (2:5-10). This view is in direct analogy to the → soteriology of → Gnosticism. Redemption frees from the claim of the world and darkness and gives both light and a share in the world to come (note the call to wake up in 5:14). Ephesians seems to hold the soteriology, though not the later mythology, of Gnosticism and to have transmitted it on a Pauline basis. We find dualistic thinking in later → Judaism (Qumran), but the only analogies for a realized consummation of salvation seem to be in Gnosticism. Ephesians sees no discrepancy between the Gnostic and Pauline traditions, though the → Pastoral Epistles warn against "what is falsely called knowledge [gnōsis]" (1 Tim. 6:20) and the teaching that the resurrection has taken place already (2 Tim. 2:18), some think with Ephesians 2 in view.

Bibliography: Commentaries: F. F. Bruce (NICNT; Grand Rapids, 1984) 229-416 • J. Gnilka (HTKNT 10/2; 2d ed.; Freiburg, 1977) • H. Hübner (HNT; Tübingen, 1997) 129-277 • A. T. Lincoln (WBC; Dallas, 1990) • A. Lindemann (ZBK; Zurich, 1985) • U. Luz (NTD; Göttingen, 1998) 105-80 • F. Mussner (ÖTBK 10; Gütersloh, 1982) • P. Perkins (AbNTC; Nashville, 1997) • H. Schlier (7th ed.; Düsseldorf, 1971) • R. Schnackenburg (EKKNT; Neukirchen, 1982).

Other works: E. Faust, Pax Christi et Pax Caesaris. Religionsgeschichtliche, traditionsgeschichtliche und sozialgeschichtliche Studien zum Epheserbrief (Fribourg, 1993) • H. Merklein, Das kirchliche Amt nach dem Epheserbrief (Munich, 1973) • C. L. Mitton, The Epistle to the Ephesians: Its Authorship, Origin, and Purpose (Oxford, 1951) • T. A. Moritz, A Profound Mystery: The Use of the OT in Ephesians (Leiden, 1996).

Andreas Lindemann

Ephesus

1. History
2. Church History
3. Christian Buildings

1. History

Originally located on the bay of Coressus at the mouth of the Caÿster (Turk. Küçük Menderes) River, the city of Ephesus was refounded by Lysimachus, king of Thrace and Macedonia (306-281 B.C.). When it came under Roman rule in 133 B.C., it was capital of the senatorial province of Asia (29 B.C.–A.D. 297) and, even with competition from Pergamum and Smyrna, the most important and wealthiest city of Asia Minor. The sebasteion, dedicated to Rome (→ Roman Religion) and Augustus, housed the provincial archives, courts, and treasury. The → temple of Artemis, the Artemiseum, was erected on a sacred site in the sixth century B.C. and was rebuilt after a fire in the fourth century (a marble temple 110 × 55 m. [360 × 180 ft.]). The cultic statue of the Ephesian Artemis was made of wood and, after being oiled for hundreds of years, had become black. The clothing and decorations could be taken off. Especially typical was the decoration of the breast, which to date has resisted convincing explanation. The cult and devotional image were popular, and the incident in Acts 19:23-40 is true to life.

2. Church History

The apostle → Paul found a Christian sect in Ephesus, stayed over two years there, and from Ephesus organized → a mission in the surrounding area. There is a recollection of Paul in the lists of bishops, which begin with Timothy, whose bones were known and later (356) sent off to Constantinople. Much more important is the local tradition concerning "John." In the writings of the second century, this tradition is in competition with one in the Roman West, though there is doubt as to the identification of John. The Johannine writings (→ John, Gospel of; John, Epistles of; Revelation) seem in fact to be connected with Ephesus. Around 190 Bishop Polycrates boasted that his city contained the graves of one of the prophetic daughters of Philip and also of the beloved disciple John. In the middle of the third century, the graves of two different Johns were known.

The bishops of Ephesus attended all the → councils and had → jurisdiction over the 11 provinces of the imperial diocese of Asia. At the Council of → Chalcedon (451) this jurisdiction was limited to the Province of Asia (in favor of Constantinople), but by 474 it had already expanded again. Ephesus was chosen by the emperor for the councils of 431 (→ Ephesus, Council of) and 449 (the so-called robber council).

Ephesus was plundered by the Arabs (655 and

717) and destroyed by the Seljuks (1090). After achieving new importance in the Byzantine kingdom, it was finally destroyed in 1403 by Timur, after which it sank into insignificance. By the Treaty of Lausanne (1923), its Christian Greek population was exchanged for Turks.

3. Christian Buildings

The older episcopal church in the fourth century was perhaps the large three-naved → basilica to the east of the city. The councils took place in the Church of the Holy Mother of God and Ever Virgin Mary, built about 400 from the ruins of the exchange by the harbor. The tomb of John, which can be traced back to the third century, became a place of → pilgrimage under the Christian emperors. The grotto of the Seven Sleepers is an ancient one. The legend of seven holy youths killed during the Decian persecution but then awakened 200 years later arose in the fifth century, and various buildings, mosaics, paintings, and pilgrim inscriptions from the Middle Ages to modern times honor these youths. The house where → Mary died was found at the end of the 19th century on the basis of a vision of Anna Katharina of Emmerich (1774-1824).

Bibliography: L. Bürchner, "Ephesos," PW 1.5.2773-822 • J. Keil, *Führer durch Ephesos* (5th ed.; Vienna, 1964) • D. Knibbe, S. Karwiese, and W. Alzinger, "Ephesos," PWSup 12.248-364, 1588-1704 • H. Koester, *Ephesos, Metropolis of Asia: An Interdisciplinary Approach to Its Archaeology, Religion, and Culture* (Philadelphia, 1995) • F. Miltner, *Ephesos. Stadt der Artemis und des Johannes* (Vienna, 1958) • R. E. Oster, *A Bibliography of Ancient Ephesus* (Metuchen, N.J., 1987) • W. M. Ramsay, *The Seven Cities of Asia* (London, 1907) • M. Restle, "Ephesos," *RBK* 2.164-207 • G. M. Rogers, *The Sacred Identity of Ephesus: Foundation Myths of a Roman City* (London, 1991) • P. Stengel, "Ephesia," PW 1.5.2753-71.

Wolfgang Wischmeyer

Ephesus, Council of

The Third Ecumenical Council of Ephesus — the first of which we have records (published by the contending parties) — was called on Pentecost (June 7) 431 by Emperor Theodosius II (408-50), mainly to settle the doctrinal dispute between Nestorius (d. ca. 451) and → Cyril of Alexandria (bishop 412-44; → Christology 2). But it could not be opened either at the appointed time or even actually at all; there were simply separate sittings of the

majority, which supported Cyril and which was later joined by the Roman delegates, and the minority, under the leadership of John of Antioch (bishop 429-41). Cyril's party indeed held a decisive session on June 22 before John and his followers arrived in Ephesus. This session read Cyril's letter to Nestorius from early 430 (Cyril, *Ep.* 4), described it as in agreement with "the faith of → Nicaea," and declared Nestorius deposed. It never changed this view.

Ultimately, however, Cyril did not have things all his own way. Under persistent pressure from Rome and the imperial court, in early 433 he declared himself ready to sign an agreed statement proposed by John that in essentials corresponded to the formula of the "Oriental" countersynod of 431, though solemnly maintaining belief in the *theotokos* (→ Mary, Devotion to) and the unity of Christ's person as the God-man. This union text of 433 must be set alongside the resolutions of June 22, 431, in any discussion of the dogmatic findings of this council in terms of their historical influence and their recognition as normatively ecumenical (at least after → Chalcedon).

Bibliography: Primary sources: ACO 1 • CPG 4.30-69 • A. J. Festugière, *Ephèse et Chalcédoine* (Geneva, 1982-83).

Secondary works: P.-P. Camelot, *Ephesus und Chalcedon* (Mainz, 1963) • A. Grillmeier, *Christ in Christian Tradition* (2d ed.; London, 1975) 443-87 • J. Liébart, "Éphèse (Concile d')," *DHGE* (1963) 15.561-74 • J. J. O'Keefe, "A Historic-Systematic Study of the Christology of Nestorius" (Diss., Münster, 1987) • A. M. Ritter, "Der nestorianische Streit vor, auf und nach dem Konzil von Ephesus (431)," *HDThG* (2d ed.) 1.245-53 • L. R. Wickham, "Pelagianism in the East," *The Making of Orthodoxy* (ed. R. Williams; Cambridge, 1989) 200-213.

Adolf Martin Ritter

Ephor

The title "ephor" (Gk. *ephoros,* "overseer") was used — and occasionally is still used today in Catholic, Protestant, and Anglican circles — for those who supervise church institutions and for officials charged with the training of → pastors or the administration of funds. It was a title in ancient Sparta that J. → Calvin recalled in *Inst.* 4.20.31 and that stresses a biblical aspect of church leadership (2 Cor. 8:21; Col. 4:17). The extra salary that, according to German Protestant → church law, deans and others receive is sometimes called the ephor allowance.

Albert Stein†

Epiclesis → Eucharistic Prayer

Epigraphy → History, Auxiliary Sciences to, 4

Epiphany → Church Year

Episcopacy

1. NT and Patristic Periods
2. Roman Catholicism
3. Anglicanism
4. Lutheranism
5. Anglican/Lutheran Ecumenical Agreements on the Historic Episcopacy
6. Other Protestant Groups

1. NT and Patristic Periods

The history of the origin of → bishops is obscure. Recent scholarship has attempted to discover pre-Christian antecedents, both Jewish and Gentile, in such sources as the Septuagint and Philo. In the LXX version of the OT, the term *episkopos* (from which Eng. "bishop") is used of God (Job 20:29; Wis. 1:6) as well as of ordinary "overseers," but never of cultic persons. Philo uses the term once, of Moses. The → Qumran MSS have also raised again the possible Jewish origins of a position that could be described as an overseer or inspector (*mĕbaqqēr*, from *bāqar*, "look after") of the community who taught the works of God to its members, looked after those members "like a shepherd his flock," and supervised the admission of new members, the discipline of offenders, and all financial transactions (CD 13:7-23). Such pre-Christian evidence for the office of bishop is enlightening but not determinative.

Three Greek words in the NT relate to the idea of bishop: *episkopeō*, "supervise, oversee, care for" (1 Pet. 5:2); *episkopē*, "position or function of supervisor" (1 Tim. 3:1); and *episkopos*, "supervisor, overseer," which occurs only five times (Acts 20:28; Phil. 1:1; 1 Tim. 3:2; Titus 1:7; 1 Pet. 2:25). Some scholars see this last term as being interchangeable with the title *presbyteros*, → "elder," used for the same persons (Acts 20:17, 28; 1 Tim. 3:2; 5:17; Titus 1:5, 7; 1 Pet. 5:1-3). The presbyter-bishops exercised a leadership of oversight in their local churches.

Evidently the emergence of a single bishop distinct from a college of presbyter-bishops did not occur until well into the second century. The three men counted as popes after Peter — Linus, Anacletus, and Clement (collectively ca. 64-97) — were probably presbyter-bishops, but not "monarchical" bishops (a term first used only in much later times). There is no evidence in Acts that any of the → Twelve, including → Peter, were bishops or presided over a local church. There is no mention of a Roman episcopacy of Peter in the NT, although that fact alone does not mean that Peter did not exercise a position of primacy in the early church. It does imply, however, that the separate office of bishop did not exist as such in the first century. One may conclude that although the title "bishop" was not used in the earliest Christian period as it is now understood, essential elements for the episcopal office were present.

Ignatius of Antioch (ca. 35-ca. 105) is the first writer to attribute to the bishop the office of *episcopē* in the local church. In Ignatius, furthermore, the "monepiscopate" first emerged, that is, the bishop as the head of a threefold ministerial office (of bishops, presbyters, and → deacons). The bishop's primary function was to maintain the → unity of the local church in the apostolic faith (e.g., Ign. *Eph.* 5:1; *Smyrn.* 8). Thus the bishop was seen to have received from the Spirit of God the charism of truth to explain the Scriptures rightly (Irenaeus, *Adv. haer.* 4.26.4). Ministry in Ignatius's church was exercised by one bishop, several elders (*presbyteroi*), and several deacons (*diakonoi*). Within this structure, the admonition is frequently given to "do nothing without the bishop" (e.g., Ign. *Magn.* 7.1 [or the presbyters]; *Trall.* 2.2). The task of the bishop in preserving the church in unity is closely related to his unique authority with respect to → baptism and the → Eucharist.

→ Irenaeus of Lyons (ca. 130-ca. 200) viewed the bishop primarily as teacher of the apostolic faith. Because of his confrontation with the → Gnostics, he attached particular importance to the continuity of church teaching and its relationship to apostolic → tradition and → authority. While for Ignatius the bishop is primarily the one who maintins unity by gathering the people around the Eucharist, for Irenaeus he is above all the one who teaches the one apostolic faith, by which unity is preserved: "Having received this preaching and this faith, the church, although scattered in the whole world, carefully preserves it as if living in one house" (*Adv. haer.* 1.10.3).

In the early third-century *Apostolic Tradition*, attributed to Hippolytus (d. ca. 236), bishops are chosen by the people. Bishops lay hands on the chosen one while the assembly prays silently that the Spirit come upon him (2.2.4). The ordination prayer asks that he receive a "governing Spirit" (3.3.4). It asks that he feed the Holy Flock, serve as high priest, minister blamelessly day and night, propitiate God's countenance, and offer gifts of the Holy Church. The new bishop is empowered to forgive sins, to allot pastoral charges according to God's bidding, and to loose bonds.

In the *Apostolic Constitutions* (ca. 350-80), the bishop is chosen by the whole people. There is a threefold questioning as to his identity, his worthiness, and again his worthiness, including testimony to his faith. Following the norm of the Council of → Nicaea (325), at least three bishops ordain. The people then give their formal assent.

2. Roman Catholicism

Vatican I (1870) defined the universal primacy of the institution of the papacy and its → infallibility when speaking ex cathedra, that is, when the pope declares officially that a doctrine concerning faith or morals is to be held definitively and irrevocably by the whole Roman Catholic Church. Because of its premature adjournment at the outbreak of the Franco-Prussian War, however, Vatican I did not develop a theology of the episcopacy.

The Second → Vatican Council (1962-65) confirmed the teaching of Vatican I regarding the institution, permanence, nature, and import of the sacred primacy of the Roman pontiff and his infallible teaching office. The → pope is the visible source and foundation of the unity of the church, both in faith and in communion (*Lumen gentium* [*LG*] 18). The council situated this teaching, however, within a theology of the episcopacy that balances and complements the teaching on the papacy of Vatican I.

Before Vatican II it was a disputed theological question whether episcopal consecration was sacramental (i.e., part of the sacrament of orders), or whether it was a jurisdictional addition to the presbyterial order. *Lumen gentium* affirms the former, stating that "the fullness of the sacrament of Orders is conferred by episcopal consecration, that fullness, namely, which both in the liturgical tradition of the Church and in the language of the Fathers of the Church is called the high priesthood, the acme of the sacred ministry" (21). On October 30, 1963, this position carried with a vote of 2,123 in favor and only 24 against.

Bishops are considered to be the successors of the → apostles and vicars and legates of Christ. Bishops are teachers of doctrine, ministers of sacred → worship, and holders of office in government. Among their principal tasks, the → preaching of the → gospel is preeminent (*LG* 20, 25, 28).

The episcopacy is considered to be a → hierarchical office in the church instituted by God. The of-

fice of the episcopacy is thus essential to the nature of the church. By virtue of their episcopal consecration and hierarchical communion with the bishop of Rome and other bishops, the bishops as a group constitute a college or permanent assembly, whose head is the bishop of Rome. A bishop represents his own church within this college, and all the bishops, together with the pope, represent the whole church (*LG* 19-20, 22).

The college of bishops does not constitute a legislative body apart from the pope. The pope is both member and head of the college. Together with the pope and never apart from him, the bishops have supreme and full authority over the universal church. Although an individual bishop does not possess infallibility, bishops, in union with the pope, can teach infallibly in an ecumenical council. Also, they teach infallibly when "even though dispersed throughout the world but preserving for all that amongst themselves and with Peter's successor the bond of communion, in their authoritative teaching concerning matters of faith and morals, they are in agreement that a particular teaching is to be held definitively and absolutely" (*LG* 25).

Vatican II teaches that the fullness of the sacrament of orders is conferred by episcopal consecration. By virtue of this → ordination, a bishop's authority is proper, ordinary, and immediate; in other words, through his ordination a bishop possesses an authority that is not juridically delegated by the bishop of Rome. In Roman → Catholicism the basic unit of the church is a particular church, usually a → diocese, defined as an altar community "under the sacred ministry of the bishop." The bishop is responsible for the unity and communion of this church with the other churches. He exercises his pastoral office to this church and not over other churches or the church universal, although he has a responsibility to have care and solicitude for the whole church (*LG* 21, 23, 26-27).

3. Anglicanism

In → Anglicanism the office of bishop was simply part of the status quo of the English Reformation; Henry VIII (ruled 1509-47) did not alter any of the constitutional or pastoral structures of the church when he separated the church in England from papal jurisdiction and placed it under the supervision of the Crown. The Edwardian Ordinal (1550) regarded it as evident that "from the Apostles' time there have been these Orders of Ministers in Christ's church: Bishops, Priests, and Deacons." The Elizabethan Settlement of 1559 reaffirmed this position.

Under the supervision of the Crown, the bishops

were ministers for the spiritual government of the nation. Their responsibility was to see that "the pure Word of God is preached and the sacraments are duly ministered according to Christ's ordinance" (Thirty-nine Articles 19 [1571]). Because bishops remained somewhat distant from the people and were caught up in the symbols and dress of prelacy, they became the targets of the → Puritan reform. Contemporary understandings of the status and function of the episcopacy were forged in that controversy, including the equality between bishops and presbyters. For Richard Hooker (ca. 1544-1600) the difference lay in the derivation of authority, with a presbyter receiving his from the bishop.

Other issues included the relation of the episcopal to the apostolic office, the "divine right" (ius divinum) of the episcopal office, and the importance of succession in office and continuity in ordination. For Anglicans the office of a bishop represents a partial continuation of the office of an apostle. Hooker acknowledged that although the apostles, as eyewitnesses, had no successors and that their ministry of → Word and → sacrament continues in the office of presbyter, their ministry of oversight exists in the office of bishop (Of the Laws of Ecclesiastical Polity, 7.4.1-4). The analogy between apostles and bishops and the appeal to tradition in the continuous practice of the episcopacy in the church led to Hooker's conclusion that the episcopacy is of divine origin.

The legitimacy of the nonepiscopal churches of the Reformation, particularly those churches outside England ordered on the presbyterian model, was conceded, since such churches had been compelled to choose between retention of the episcopacy and reformation according to scriptural norms of doctrine and practice. Within England, however, the episcopacy was normative, and presbyterial ordination was anomalous. The Act of Uniformity of 1662, under Charles II, formally excluded those clergy who had not been episcopally ordained from pastoral office in the Church of England.

Between 1559 and 1689 it is possible to distinguish four different positions regarding episcopacy within the Church of England. Hooker and John Whitgift (ca. 1532-1604), archbishop of Canterbury, held an adiaphorist view of the episcopacy, in accordance with art. 23. They believed that although no form of church order is prescribed in Scripture, the episcopal pattern serves the best interest of the Anglican Church. Richard Bancroft (1544-1610), also archbishop of Canterbury, believed in episcopacy as a divine right but not as divinely prescribed in every situation. Archbishop William Laud (1573-1645)

held that episcopacy is of divine right and is proved by history always to be God's will for the church. Henry Dodwell (1641-1711) took the highest view of episcopacy, seeing it as the channel of sacramental → grace necessary for → salvation. Even before the 19th-century → Oxford Movement, then, Anglicanism included a few who held the necessity of episcopacy.

The episcopacy has thus acquired various meanings within the Anglican Church. Traditionally, the office of bishop is seen to continue the apostolic function of oversight; the bishop has a teaching function as guardian and promoter of the church's common faith. Episcopacy is normative for the governance of the church. Regular episcopal succession guarantees the legitimacy of the church's ministry and establishes the local church's unity, communion, and continuity with the universal church. Current debate is whether "the historic episcopate" belongs to the very definition of the church itself (esse), its well-being (bene esse), or its "full being" (plene esse). (To be sure, these Latin terms are less and less current in this increasingly ecumenical debate.)

Where formerly the church was constituted by its continuance in apostolic and scriptural teaching, now the episcopacy is seen also to ground the identity of the church. In the Chicago-Lambeth Quadrilateral (1886, 1888) the episcopal order is included as a factor belonging to the church's fullness and therefore as necessary for "the restoration of the organic unity of the Church." With regard to the episcopacy the Anglican Church seeks a middle way. On the one hand, it does not treat nonepiscopal ministries as identical in status and authority with the episcopal ministry; on the other hand, it does not declare the sacraments of nonepiscopal bodies null and void (Lambeth Conference, 1948).

The Anglican system has a bishop (acting alone) and bishops who act with their synod, with overlapping powers. Bishops are part of a synod, yet their authority transcends it. A bishop shares episcopē with his or her synod and with fellow Anglican bishops. The mode of election varies, but consecration should always be by at least three bishops. He or she exercises authority by virtue of divine commission and in synodic association with clergy and laity.

4. Lutheranism

According to traditional Lutheran teaching, the only ministry essential in the life of the church is the ministry of proclaiming the gospel and administering the sacraments (Augs. Conf. 5). An episcopal ministry of oversight in succession cannot be considered essential either for the church's identity or for the office of ministry. The Lutheran Reformation followed the view of → Jerome, for whom the terms "presbyter" and "bishop" originally referred to the same ministry. M. → Luther himself equated the two as early as 1519 (WA 2.240; see also *To the Christian Nobility of the German Nation* [1520], *LW* 44.175). The later differentiation between the two ministries occurred as a matter of human choice and not as a biblical mandate.

Lutherans desired to preserve an effective *episcopē* and to "retain the order of the church and the various ranks in the church" (Apology of Augs. Conf. 14.1). They were unable to do so, however, because of the unwillingness of bishops to ordain reformed clergy. They consequently distinguished between *episcopē*, exercised *de iure divino*, even in some of its jurisdictional aspects, and the polity of the church in its historical development, which they viewed as created by human authority (Augs. Conf. 28.21-22). At the time of the → Reformation, Lutherans regarded the episcopal office as corrupt and the sitting bishops as usurpers who had become temporal princes opposed to the proclamation of the gospel. This situation constituted a state of emergency in which the ministry of oversight had to be carried out by others (the so-called *Notbischöfe*, "emergency bishops"), including faithful princes. The → Reformers envisioned their choice as being either the historic episcopacy or the right preaching of the gospel. Since they desired to keep the ecclesiastical and canonical polity, they did not demand that bishops relinquish their status but nevertheless claimed the right themselves to ordain as a means of meeting the emergency situation (Schmalk. Art. 3.10-13; see also Formula of Concord, Solid Declaration 10.19). They intended to recall the bishops to their evangelical foundation, not to replace or circumvent the episcopal structure itself.

The rite of ordination to the ministry at Wittenberg followed the form of episcopal ordination. The ordinands were addressed as future bishops, and the ministers of ordination were the → pastors of neighboring cities (i.e., neighboring bishops, as prescribed by canon 4 of the Council of Nicaea). Those ordained entered into an apostolic succession in teaching and the orderly transmission of the gospel.

The chief responsibility and duty of the bishop is the ministry of the Word (*LW* 28.286). The bishop is to set forth the Word correctly and is to be devoted above all to the conservation of doctrine; teaching is his principal work (ibid. 29.59). In describing the responsibilities of the office of bishop, the → Augsburg Confession specifies that "according to

divine right it is the office of the bishop to preach the gospel, to forgive sin, to judge doctrine and reject doctrine that is contrary to the gospel, and to exclude from the Christian community the ungodly whose ungodly life is manifest — not with human power but with God's Word alone. That is why parishioners and churches owe obedience to bishops" (28.21-22). Whatever other power and → jurisdiction bishops may have, they have by virtue of human right.

As the German Reformation progressed, Lutheran → "superintendents" replaced canonical bishops. The former office, held by one of the leading pastors in a city, embodied Luther's linking together of the offices of presbyter and bishop and distinguished evangelical from Catholic communities. Civil authorities, however, endorsed by Luther's encouragement of "emergency bishops" who were princes, tended to co-opt the ministry of oversight.

In 1900 the majority of Lutherans in Germany and the Nordic countries belonged to national or regional churches whose leaders were called by a variety of titles, most notably bishops or superintendents. During the 20th century episcopacy, normally related to some form of synodic structure, has clearly become the most common form of church leadership in Lutheranism.

Episcopal leadership in Lutheran churches is personal, communal, and collegial, as pointed out in *Consultation on the Ordained Ministry of Women and the Episcopal Ministry* (46), a study document of the → Lutheran World Federation (LWF). Episcopacy originates from the ministry of oversight over the local → congregation gathered in worship. Consequently, bishops are pastoral ministers of Word and sacrament. They exercise regional oversight as a form of this pastoral ministry. Influenced by recent *communio* ecclesiology, emphasis has increasingly been placed within Lutheranism on the bishop's role in serving the unity of the church and witnessing for peace and justice in the wider society. Bishops "represent the larger church to congregations committed to their charge. They represent the communion of these congregations within and to the larger church," according to *Lutheran Understanding of the Episcopal Office* (18), another study of the LWF. The bishop promotes and is a symbol for the unity and cohesion of the church.

Lutherans acknowledge three types of episcopal succession: succession in apostolic mission, defined as succession in the apostolic gospel; succession within the see, defined as a succession of ongoing episcopal ministry in a particular place; and a succession of consecrations (also referred to as the historic succession of bishop), in which each bishop enters episcopal ministry through a laying on of hands by other bishops. A succession in canonical episcopal ordinations was lost in much of Continental Lutheranism during the Reformation era but was retained in Sweden and Finland and preserved with only one interruption in Denmark, Norway, and Iceland. In the 20th century the Lutheran churches in Estonia, Latvia, the United Kingdom, Tanzania, Zimbabwe, Malaysia, and El Salvador have endorsed such succession. For Lutherans episcopal succession is one sign among others of continuity in the one gospel. It serves, but does not guarantee, this continuity.

5. Anglican/Lutheran Ecumenical Agreements on the Historic Episcopacy

In 1992 representatives of British and Irish Anglican churches and of the Nordic and Baltic Lutheran churches, with the sole exception of the Church of Denmark, approved the Porvoo Common Statement and the Porvoo Agreement. Chapter 4 of that agreement, which is entitled "Episcopacy in the Service of the Apostolicity of the Church," notes that the churches of the Baltic states have not always had bishops but that they now have bishops who stand in the historic succession of the → laying on of hands. The churches of Sweden and Finland, like the Anglican churches, also have historic succession. In Denmark, Norway, and Iceland the churches preserved continuity in the episcopal office, although at the time of the Reformation they occasionally practiced presbyterial ordination. Through the agreement regarding the episcopal office, the participating churches consented to affirm together the value and use of the sign of the historic episcopal succession. Those churches in which the sign has at some time not been used are free to recognize the value of the sign and should embrace it without denying their own apostolic continuity. Those churches in which the sign has been used are free to recognize the reality of the episcopal office and should affirm the apostolic continuity of those churches in which the sign of episcopal succession has at some time not been used (4.57). In the Porvoo Declaration these churches committed themselves "to invite one another's bishops normally to participate in the laying on of hands at the ordination of bishops as a sign of the unity and continuity of the Church."

In 1999 in the United States the Churchwide Assembly of the Evangelical Lutheran Church in America (ELCA) adopted the document *Called to Common Mission: A Lutheran Proposal for a Revision of the Concordat of Agreement;* the same document was approved by the Episcopal Church at its General Convention in 2000. Through their common approval American Lutherans and Episcopalians committed themselves to a relationship of full communion, to take effect formally on January 1, 2001.

Called to Common Mission asserts that the two churches will "share an episcopal succession that is both evangelical and historic. They promise to include regularly one or more bishops of the other church to participate in the laying-on-of-hands at the ordinations / installations of their own bishops as a sign, though not a guarantee, of the unity and apostolic continuity of the whole church. With the laying-on-of-hands by other bishops, such ordinations / installations will involve prayer for the gift of the Holy Spirit. Both churches value and maintain a ministry of *episkopē* as one of the ways, in the context of ordained ministries and of the whole people of God, in which the apostolic succession of the church is visibly expressed and personally symbolized in fidelity to the gospel through the ages." All installations of bishops in the ELCA will involve prayer for the gift of the Holy Spirit and the laying on of hands by other bishops, at least three of whom are to be in the historic succession. Although freely accepting the historic episcopate, the ELCA, in conformity to article 7 of the Augsburg Confession, does not affirm that it is necessary for the unity of the church.

Comparable actions toward full communion are being taken by the Evangelical Lutheran Church in Canada and the Anglican Church of Canada. Similar agreements have been and are being pursued in other parts of the world. Most notable among the latter is perhaps the Meissen Agreement (1988) between the Evangelical Church in Germany and the Church of England; although it is far-reaching, it does not at this time propose full communion between the two churches. An Anglican-Lutheran Commission in southern Africa is also preparing steps toward full communion between the churches there.

Bibliography: On 1: P. C. BOUTENEFF and A. D. FALCONER, eds., *Episkopé and Episcopacy and the Quest for Visible Unity* (Geneva, 1999) • R. E. BROWN, *Priest and Bishop: Biblical Reflections* (New York, 1970) • J. R. WRIGHT, "The Origins of the Episcopate and Episcopal Ministry in the Early Church," *On Being a Bishop: Papers on Episcopacy from the Moscow Consultation 1992* (ed. J. R. Wright; New York, 1993) 10-32.

On 2: A. FLANNERY, ed., *Vatican Council II: The Conciliar and Post Conciliar Documents* (vol. 1; rev. ed.; Grand Rapids, 1992) esp. *Christus Dominus* (564-90) and *Lumen gentium* (350-426).

On 3: K. S. Chittleborough, "Towards a Theology and Practice of the Bishop-in-Synod," *Authority in the Anglican Communion* (ed. S. W. Sykes; Toronto, 1987) 144-62 • R. A. Norris, "Episcopacy," *The Study of Anglicanism* (rev. ed.; ed. S. Sykes, J. Booty, and J. Knight; London, 1998) 333-48.

On 4: I. Asheim and V. R. Gold, eds., *Episcopacy in the Lutheran Church? Studies in the Development and Definition of the Office of Church Leadership* (Philadelphia, 1970) • Church of Sweden, *Bishop, Priest, and Deacon in the Church of Sweden: A Letter from the Bishops concerning the Ministry of the Church* (Uppsala, 1990) • R. Kolb and T. J. Wengert, eds., *The Book of Concord: The Confessions of the Evangelical Lutheran Church* (Minneapolis, 2000) • Lutheran World Federation, *Consultation on the Ordained Ministry of Women and the Episcopal Ministry: Report of an International Consultation* (Geneva, 1993); idem, *Lutheran Understanding of the Episcopal Office* (Geneva, 1983); idem, *The Office of Bishop: Swedish Lutheran–Roman Catholic Dialogue* (Geneva, 1993).

On 5: ELCA, *Called to Common Mission: A Lutheran Proposal for a Revision of the Concordat of Agreement* (Chicago, 1999) • D. F. Martensen, ed., *Concordat of Agreement: Supporting Essays* (Minneapolis and Cincinnati, 1995) • W. A. Norgren and W. G. Rusch, eds., "Toward Full Communion" and "Concordat of Agreement," *Lutheran-Episcopal Dialogue* (series 3; Minneapolis and Cincinnati, 1991) • *Together in Mission and Ministry: The Porvoo Common Statement, with Essays on Church and Ministry in Northern Europe* (London, 1993) • *Visible Unity and the Ministry of Oversight: The Second Theological Conference Held under the Meissen Agreement between the Church of England and the Evangelical Church in Germany* (London, 1997).

Susan K. Wood

6. Other Protestant Groups

Besides some Lutheran churches (see 4), other Protestant communities adopted various forms of episcopacy. → *Mennonite churches* typically recognize bishops, preachers, and deacons, although these three are not seen as distinct orders of ministry.

The → Moravian Church has maintained an episcopacy inherited from its forebears in the late medieval Utraquist movement (→ Bohemian Brethren). Claims of an uninterrupted succession of bishops by way of → Waldensian consecrations have been challenged by historians, but the succession of bishops remains an important sign of continuity for Moravians, who have worked in recent decades to restore the office of bishop as primarily pastoral and teaching (vs. administrative).

→ Methodist Churches of the North American pattern that goes back to the Methodist Episcopal Church (founded in 1784) have historically maintained a threefold ministry of deacons, elders, and bishops, although such early American Methodist leaders as Francis Asbury maintained that the episcopacy was not a distinct order of ministry but a higher status of elders. John → Wesley's ordinations (and his consecration of Thomas Coke) in September 1784, which led to the founding of the Methodist Episcopal Church, violated Anglican canons, but Wesley reasoned that elders have an "inherent right" to ordain and could do so in cases of necessity. The African Methodist Episcopal Church, the African Methodist Episcopal Zion Church, the Christian Methodist Episcopal Church, and the United Methodist Church all follow this pattern of episcopal leadership. British Methodist churches, it should be noted, do not follow this pattern and do not utilize the terminology of bishops, although British Methodist district presidents exercise a kind of episcopal oversight in their churches.

Many other evangelical and free churches have officers variously identified as bishops or superintendents (implicitly acknowledging that the Lat. *superintendens* translates the Gk. *episkopos,* both having the sense "overseer"). For example, the → Church of the Nazarene (the largest Holiness denomination) has superintendents, and the Pentecostal Holiness Church has a single bishop for the denomination. Some historic Baptist confessional documents referred to local pastors as bishops, and in recent years there has been a tendency in very large African-American Baptist congregations (the so-called megachurches, with memberships in the thousands), with numerous clergy and (typically) multiple satellite congregations, to consecrate their founding pastor or senior pastor, sometimes in an elaborate ceremony, as bishop.

Ted A. Campbell

Epistemology

1. Philosophical

1.1. *Knowledge and Belief*

Epistemology (Gk. *epistēmē,* "knowledge") concerns what counts as knowledge and how we acquire it. Formal systems (logic and mathematics) are known a priori, apart from → experience. Philosophers disagree as to whether knowledge about the world is a posteriori (derived from experience) or is in some sense also a priori. Most discussion involves knowledge of propositions (expressed in language), although other kinds include tacit knowledge (without explicit awareness of it) and "knowing how," or skill in doing something.

Plato (427-347 B.C.) is credited with what philosophers regard as the standard analysis, namely, that knowledge is "justified true belief." A belief or conviction can be false or mistaken. To count as knowledge my belief must be true (accurate about what is the case), but not just happen to be true. To know, I must understand why it is true, the reason or evidence that, independent of my psychological state of believing, establishes its truth. For instance, my belief that an owl is in a tree is knowledge only if I understand that the features of the bird I see are indeed distinctive features of an owl.

Skeptics think knowledge is unattainable because the senses are unreliable or because we lack a defensible criterion for distinguishing → truth from error. Moderate → skepticism accepts some kinds of knowledge but restricts the domains in which it is attainable.

1.2. *Truth and Justification*

Many philosophers think truth depends upon correspondence of the object as I apprehend it with the object as it is in reality. Others take the measure of truth to be the coherence or compatibility of my belief with other things known on good grounds to be true. Still others locate truth in the belief's usefulness in pursuing worthy goals. There are disputes about justification too. What evidence or argument is germane to demonstrating the truth of a belief? Must we have certainty, or will a high probability suffice? Must the belief be verified, or is it enough to fail at all reasonable avenues for disproving it? Should scientific method be normative for assessing the truth of all sorts of beliefs? Philosophers examine such issues with great technical precision, but without unanimity in results. The various answers given potentially affect many human endeavors, including assessing the status of religious beliefs.

1.3. *Major Figures*

Plato's theory of knowledge, based on the mind's intellectual vision of the unchangeable, eternal ideas, distrusted the bodily senses and gave impetus to ra-

tionalism in philosophy and mysticism in religion (→ Platonism). Aristotle (384-322 B.C.; → Aristotelianism) restored an empirical dimension by holding that our minds construct our concepts of kinds of things by abstracting their essential features from our multiple sensory experiences of objects. This shift led later to a synthesis of the supernatural and the natural into a unified body of knowledge by → Thomas Aquinas (ca. 1225-74; → Thomism) and to a revival of empirical study of natural phenomena by Francis Bacon (1561-1626). A proponent of the correspondence theory of truth, René Descartes (1596-1650; → Cartesianism), said the clarity and distinctness of our ideas, not evidence from bodily senses, guarantees their truth. David Hume (1711-76), in contrast, attributed knowledge (other than logic and mathematics) to "impressions" received by the bodily senses and the mind's subsequent arranging of them into general concepts of objects and their interactions.

Immanuel Kant (1724-1804; → Kantianism) unified this modern → rationalism and → empiricism by holding that the mind, a priori, furnishes the structures or categories by which our sensations become synthesized into our experienced world of known objects. G. W. F. Hegel (1770-1831; → Hegelianism), an → idealist, justified the truth of beliefs not in isolated judgments but as a function of their place within a conceptual system with the greatest comprehensive explanatory power. Edmund Husserl (1859-1938) devised a → phenomenological epistemology combining meticulous description of how objects present themselves to us with analysis of the intentionality or predisposition we bring to experience; his thought influenced Martin Heidegger (1889-1976) and → existentialism. Studies of → logic and → language by Gottlob Frege (1848-1925) underlie 20th-century → analytic philosophy, also inspired by Hume, which was often critical of religious discourse and beliefs.

1.4. *Debates and Difficulties*

Epistemology in the 20th century and beyond has become increasingly complex, intersecting with diverse views of the nature of → causality, the status of inductive reasoning, traditional → philosophy of science, and the emerging field of cognitive science, with its new understanding of mind and brain operations. So-called Gettier counterexamples, named for Edmund Gettier (b. 1927), with their instances of justified true beliefs that do not count as knowledge, challenge the standard analysis, and there is no consensus on how to deal with them. Some analytic philosophers argue that beliefs must first be shown to be meaningful before addressing their truth or falsity, and that in cases such as religion this demonstration is impossible. Disciples of Ludwig Wittgenstein (1889-1951) declare that language, concepts, and beliefs have their setting within limited communities, or "forms of life," and issues of their "truth" have no applicability outside these domains. Others relativize knowledge by treating it as a social construct arising from political or power relationships among groups. Foundationalists, invoking Aristotle and Descartes, maintain two levels in knowledge: (1) basic beliefs that are starting points not subject to justification and (2) the rest of the belief structure, justified by procedures resting on the foundation of the basic beliefs.

Bibliography: L. M. ALCOFF, Epistemology: The Big Questions (Malden, Mass., 1998) • R. AUDI, A Contemporary Introduction to the Theory of Knowledge (New York, 1998) • R. CHISHOLM, Theory of Knowledge (Englewood Cliffs, N.J., 1989) • D. HAMLYN, "Epistemology, History of," EncPh 3.8-38 • P. MOSER, "Epistemology," CDP (2d ed.) 273-78 • K. SAYRE, Belief and Knowledge: Mapping the Cognitive Landscape (London, 1997).

ROBERT F. BROWN

2. Theological

2.1. Religious Knowledge

A person who has a religious experience (→ Religion) takes it to be an experience of some supernatural being or presence. The experience, understood by some as a kind of perception, may yield knowledge of a → truth, recognition of a moral demand (→ Ethics), or appreciation of an → aesthetic value. It is oriented to the grasping of one's own existence and its meaning in relation to some ultimate reality and to the shaping of life's reality in terms of this experience. To some, since the experience cannot be fully explained by natural causes, it provides a prima facie justification for beliefs about God. Religious knowledge takes many forms. Its span ranges from → wisdom rooted in → everyday experience to mystical insight arrived at in resolving the tension between subject and object.

2.2. Christian Theology

As an effort to give a methodologically controlled account of Christian → faith, Christian → theology offers a description and critical analysis of Christian talk about God and the possibility of knowledge of → God that comes to expression in it. In the process it has traditionally distinguished between natural knowledge of God and knowledge of God on the basis of → revelation.

The idea of a natural knowledge of God finds

some support in the Bible (see Rom. 1:19-20). God may be known through → conscience or through the works of → creation. The → early church used the doctrine of the Logos to make contact with the philosophy and religion of the Hellenistic world around it. Medieval philosophers like → Thomas Aquinas held that although knowledge of God is innate, it is vague and confused and thus needs the theistic arguments to be made explicit (Summa theol. I, q. 2, art. 1; → Scholasticism; God, Arguments for the Existence of). Before the criticism of I. Kant (1724-1804), the theistic arguments occupied a significant place in Protestant theology from the → Reformers to the → Enlightenment.

Another approach affirms that knowledge of God comes by revelation. God reveals himself, and people know him (Heb. yd' in the OT, Gk. ginōskō, gnōsis in the NT), acknowledge him, and, with their faith and a corresponding life, respond to his address to them in the history of → Israel (§1) and → Jesus of Nazareth. The saving event recorded in the Bible is thus normative for the knowledge of faith. Some hold that the knowledge of revelation follows on a natural and rational knowledge of God, which provides in part a knowledge of God and his attributes. Others reject all natural knowledge of God as an impermissible attempt to arrive at a knowledge of God. K. → Barth (1886-1968) argued rigorously on the basis of revelation, finding all religion unmasked as a human enterprise, as understood in the criticism of religion by L. Feuerbach (1804-72; → Religion, Criticism of). They regard knowledge of God as possible only as a reception in faith of that which God communicates in his self-revelation (i.e., his own nature, for which there is no → analogy in any other being). For still others, however, the need for continuity with the contemporary sense of truth and the need for → dialogue with the religions and religious movements suggest that we should take up again the tradition of the → liberal theology of the 19th century, for example, by stressing the point of contact in human experiences of religion (E. Brunner) or by developing the correlation between existential questions and theological answers (P. → Tillich).

2.3. Problems

Theological discussion of epistemological problems now focuses on three vital matters.

2.3.1. Theology concerns itself methodologically with the question of → hermeneutics as it tries to open up the texts of a remote age to modern understanding, or more basically as it tries to integrate the linguistic utterances of an alien ego into our own perception.

2.3.2. In epistemological theory it is a matter of

finding the *epistemological basis of theology* and hence of trying to allot theology its place in the modern theory of knowledge and scientific practice, of showing how far one can speak about knowledge in theology, and of methodologically ordering what is said about the statements on God and reality that are found throughout the Christian → tradition. For example, Nancey Murphy reconstructs theology along the lines of Imre Lakatos's research program. The method of science, seen broadly to be highly successful because at the very least it embodies critical objectivity that makes for intersubjective testing, can be adapted for religion, provided the subjective features of religion are completed with objective hypotheses to be tested and objective data in terms of which to evaluate the hypotheses.

2.3.3. Analytic → philosophy of religion expressly attempts a *critical examination of what religion says about God* (→ Speech). It asks what kind of statements religious pronouncements are, whether they are cognitive statements of fact or merely have the form of such statements, to what feelings and ideas believers feel they are committed, and what consistency and truth religious beliefs have. Questions of justification and warrant for religious beliefs, growing out of the debate over evidentialism and foundationalism (A. Plantinga and N. Wolterstorff), have replaced the former concerns about verification, which as a theory met its demise late in the 1960s and 1970s.

When the transcendental theory of → idealism and the empirical theory of → positivism are both challenged, a concept can assert itself that was developed under the influence of L. Wittgenstein and M. Polanyi, namely, that religious faith is a way of seeing God, the world, and humanity that is made possible by direct experience of the religious dimension of reality. Religious knowledge arises, then, as life is lived within a given perspective.

Bibliography: W. ALSTON, *Perceiving God: The Epistemology of Religious Experience* (Ithaca, N.Y., 1991) • C. F. DAVIES, *The Evidential Force of Religious Experience* (New York, 1989) • J. H. GILL, *The Possibility of Religious Knowledge* (Grand Rapids, 1971) • B. MITCHELL, *The Justification of Religious Belief* (New York, 1981) • N. MURPHY, *Theology in an Age of Scientific Reasoning* (Ithaca, N.Y., 1990) • A. PLANTINGA, *Warranted Christian Belief* (New York, 2000) • A. PLANTINGA and N. WOLTERSTORFF, eds., *Faith and Rationality* (Notre Dame, Ind., 1983) • M. POLANYI, *Personal Knowledge: Towards a Post-critical Philosophy* (London, 1997) • D. RITSCHL, *The Logic of Theology* (Philadelphia, 1987).

WERNER SCHWARTZ and BRUCE R. REICHENBACH

Equality

1. Term
2. History
3. Theological and Ethical Evaluation

1. Term

The term "equality" implies that things or persons are alike in one or more respects. It carries with it the philosophical and biblical connotations of the Greek *homoiotēs* and *isotēs*. It has also taken on overtones from the *égalité* of the French → Revolution (1789). → Liberation theology has adopted some of the concepts inherent in the terms "equity" and "equality," with their different nuances.

2. History

2.1. In the Athens of Pericles there was resistance to privileges and a demand for political, economic, and social equality. "Isonomy" (equality before the law) became the epitome of → democracy. After ambivalent experiences with strivings for equality, Greek and Roman philosophy (→ Greek Philosophy) differentiated the respects in which equality was to be promoted or rejected. The equal treatment of nonequals produces unjust inequality. Equality came to be centrally bound up with justice (→ Righteousness, Justice).

2.2. The OT looks with astonishment at the fact that God has no equal. It is thus surprising to hear God saying in Gen. 1:26, "Let us make humankind in our image, according to our likeness," and to learn that we share in his world rule. → Israel (§1) was aware of the fundamental human equality in birth and death: "There is for all one entrance into life, and one way out" (Wis. 7:6, see also v. 3). Israel's recollection of its own bondage in Egypt prevented it from imposing radical inequality on racial groups or aliens. Later there were added to these traditions favoring human equality Hellenistic ideas about equal civil rights (2 Macc. 8:30). When the Messiah comes, none will any longer be subject to another (*Pss. Sol.* 17:41). For Philo (b. 15-10 B.C., d. A.D. 45-50), *isotēs* is a basic principle of the cosmos and the mother of righteousness. Social equality must be proportional and geometric (see Plato *Grg.* 508A), as well as grounded in the → Torah, the will of God, and → natural law.

2.3. The central NT statement is in Phil. 2:6-7. Not ethically but soteriologically, by the Mediator, people who are so radically unlike God in their → sin are taken up into solidarity with Christ. Without any righteousness before God (Rom. 3:23-24) they are called to be children of God and are thus equal "in

Christ" (1 Cor. 12:13; Gal. 3:28). The practical result is not a program of social equality, although the message necessarily has social implications. It opens the door to ideas of equality of a different origin.

2.4. In the → early church Clement (ca. 150-ca. 215) was the first to develop theologically the traditions of the philosophy of antiquity concerning equality. The patristic teaching on → virtue accepts such ideas, not so much in social criticism, but in personal morality. The principle of equality is taught with unusual strictness in John Chrysostom (ca. 347-407), who shows that injustice is the reason for all economic inequality (→ Property) and who urges the sharing of goods (*In 1 Tim. hom.* 12.3-4), which may be achieved in → monasticism. Augustine (354-430) finds a Christological basis for equality (→ Augustine's Theology). It is sin, as *perversa imitatio Dei* and cupidity, which brings us down from the higher levels of being in this world, on which equality is possible. → Asceticism in both men and women can counteract the consequence of sin and regain equality for us. We must also try to mitigate social inequalities in the name of Christ.

The early church paid much attention to the problem of gender inequality (→ Men; Women) but found support in Gen. 2:21-24 for a certain inequality by creation. Over against the hierarchies and inequalities that were becoming stronger in late antiquity, Christians and → Stoics influenced law and custom in favor of equality, even with barbarians — though not with any revolutionary results.

2.5. In the Middle Ages hierarchical tendencies increased inequalities. → Freedom came to mean much the same as privilege, and prerogatives differed according to status. Terms like *aequitas* (Gk. *epieikeia,* "equity") preserved the traditions of antiquity. Equity was regarded as a principle of natural law and was given legal status. Equality was established among equals, within a given social class. Divine creation, however, was regarded as a hierarchical order (Thomas Aquinas *Summa theol.* I, q. 65, art. 2). It combined the principle of unity (being ordered to God) and the *praelatio,* or ladder of being. The → Golden Rule of Matt. 7:12, the epitome of natural law for Gratian and the → Corpus Iuris Canonici, acted as a counterweight to hierarchical inequality. It was regarded as a wise and comprehensive maxim of equity from the standpoint of Christian virtue, but still equality was recognized only within the same legal entity or class. Albertus Magnus (ca. 1200-1280) was the first in the Middle Ages to refer to the Athenian linking of democracy and equality.

Biblical statements favoring equality influenced

monasticism, various protest movements, Joachim of Fiore (ca. 1135-1202, who said that Christians are all equal in the age of the Spirit), the → Waldenses (who emphasized the equality of believers as a principle of the community, as well as the rule of poverty), the → Franciscans (esp. in the debate about poverty), and, more radically, the Taborites. Marsilius of Padua (ca. 1280-ca. 1343) espoused the equality of all priests in opposition to papal supremacy and church → hierarchy. John Wycliffe (ca. 1320-84) adopted this pioneering criticism of hierarchy, as did the theologians of the 15th-century conciliar movement (→ Conciliarism). This was the first great movement toward equality among medieval Christians and in older European society. Ideas of equality began to creep into law, and popular traditions enshrined the view that in former times all people had been equal as God's creatures, even from the days of → Adam and Eve.

2.6. The → Reformation under the young Martin Luther (1483-1546) at first strongly supported the idea of equality on a theological basis (→ Luther's Theology). If God alone justifies us by grace, we are all equal before him, and all believers are priests. All being equal, none can rule, but each is subject to the other (*LW* 45.117). Such ideas had an impact beyond the Christian community, and fervor for equality helped to spread the Reformation. But Luther soon attacked the misuse of Protestant statements about equality and freedom that were leading to revolt, for example, in the → Peasants' War. He reacted sharply, restricting equality to the inner life and thus robbing the Reformation of its revolutionary social force. Nevertheless, the idea of equality took organizational form among the rebellious peasants, for example, in popular assemblies for purposes of self-government. This development was wholly in line with Luther's early reforming ideas concerning equality. It is surprising that the writings of Thomas Müntzer (ca. 1489-1525) contain little argument for equality, though he regarded poverty and weakness as marks of election and pressed for a changed form of community life.

The independent movement of the → Anabaptists achieved in small circles, as the communion of saints, mild forms of a community of goods of use rather than of acquisition. The → Bohemian Brethren proceeded more strictly. In the "enthusiastic," rather than strictly "Anabaptist," "kingdom of God" established in Münster in 1534 and 1535, property rights were set aside, but not power relationships and configurations. Radicals of this kind discredited the Reformation concept of equality. In a short time the clergy lost some of their privileged status, but the ruling nobility and middle class were favored. Over the long haul the idea of equality had an impact in nonchurch circles, for example, among the Levellers in England (ca. 1647) and the settlers of North America. For John Calvin (1509-64) equality was not a pressing problem (CRef 2.1093; 26.321; 49.503-4). The mature Philipp Melanchthon (1497-1560) took up a Thomistic concept of order, with the result that the biblical concept of equality soon applied only against the hierarchy in the Protestant world; it could have a broader impact only by linking up with new ideas of equality.

2.7. The modern period developed powerful doctrines of equality as the middle classes rose to power. The new Stoicism, ideas of natural law, and humanistic and early → Enlightenment → individualism all combined to transfer equality as simply an essential predicate of humanity to the political and social spheres. The model of the successful free market provided a stimulus to this development. It gave individuals the freedom to buy and sell their goods and labor under the same rules and privileges that everyone else enjoyed. The legal equality of those who thus found release from alien bondage and privilege was a condition of the dynamic growth of → capitalism, for which economic liberalism offered a theoretical and ideological superstructure, in sharp contrast to the → social ethics of the church (C. B. Macpherson, 61-86, 295-310). Running parallel was a demand for political equality, including universal suffrage, first radically discussed by the Levellers in the Putney debate of 1647 (ibid., 126ff., 138ff.) and then gradually accepted in western Europe and North America, though extended to women only in the 20th century.

Toward the end of the 18th century, along with human and civil → rights, the principle of equality found its way into constitutions and had a powerful influence on jurisprudence. For example, the Virginia Declaration of Rights (adopted June 12, 1776) affirmed, "All men are by nature equally free and independent and have certain inherent rights." Along the same lines, but in a more radical way that provoked a conservative reaction, the French Revolution proclaimed *liberté, égalité,* and *fraternité.* The first two principles were adopted into the revolutionary constitutions of, for example, Belgium in 1831 and the Frankfurt Assembly in 1848/49. T. Mommsen (1817-1903) formulated the principle of equality in his anonymous work *Die Grundrechte des deutschen Volkes* (1849), "You all know the democratic gospel, 'Equality before the law!' Pay heed to it and guard it well, for in it you have the core of freedom, the core of a happy future" (p. 16). J.-J. Rousseau (1712-78) had earlier taught that equality is the core of freedom,

though A. de Tocqueville (1805-59) in his *De la démocratie en Amérique* (Democracy in America; 1835) asked the critical question whether social equality would not level down all relations and promote a mass society and despotism.

The antinomy of equality and freedom led to the idea that one cannot have the maximum of both at the same time. One must either have one at the cost of the other or achieve a compromise by concessions on both sides. Since the 19th century this tension has found resolution in different ways in the great → ideologies. Equality was increasingly rated higher on the scales of → conservatism, nationalism (→ Nation, Nationalism), → liberalism, democracy, and → socialism. For K. Marx (1818-83) the proletarian demand for equality really meant the abolition of classes (→ Class and Social Stratum) by putting the means of production in the hands of society (→ Marxism). Only in this way, he thought, could real legal and political equality be achieved. The equality of older communism, like the purely formal middle-class equality, came under the criticism of both Marx and Lenin (1870-1924). The socialist movements of the 19th and 20th centuries did not accept this reduction to the question of class conflict but adopted some of the humanist components of the middle class and Christian views of equality.

The theology of German-speaking Protestantism for the most part viewed the French revolutions of 1789 and 1848 with a condemnatory middle-class antiegalitarianism, the only exceptions being → religious socialism, the left wing of → liberal theology, and the Christian section of the → women's movement. The religious socialist movement in the early 20th century, popularized by L. Ragaz (1868-1945) and H. Kutter (1863-1931), saw an affinity between the demands for equality in the → labor movement and the primitive Christian understanding of fellowship. The union of religious socialists that G. Dehn (1882-1970) and others founded in 1919 rejected the traditional shelving of Christian requirements in the economic and political sphere and viewed equality in the light of the basic concept of fraternity. Here, as was also the case with regard to the women's movement, ecclesiastical resonance was primarily negative.

Papal social teaching condemned doctrines of equality as a legacy of the Reformation and the revolutions. Pope Leo XIII (1878-1903), in his encyclical *Quod apostolici muneris* (1878), allowed that the gospel teaches equality in view of our common nature and our common calling to be God's children, but still argued that inequality in law and power derives from the author of nature himself. In spite of such teaching, constitutional equality of rights and treatment has established itself in democratic → industrial societies, as has also a dominant tendency in civil law to combat the passive acceptance of social inequality.

During the epoch of → fascism the ideology of inequality between the races, between leader and led, and between men and women took an extremely crude and inhuman form, but since 1945 the principle of equality has found a firm and normative place in the list of fundamental human rights. Its social achievement is hampered or promoted by dominant ideological trends and economic and political possibilities. The social ethics of the churches afffirms equality in principle, but theology, riveted to the past, shows little interest. Many people are unwilling to yield to the pressure of ideologies of → emancipation.

3. Theological and Ethical Evaluation

As regards equality in and of itself, we cannot judge. The principle is the result of long developments that have led to constitutional industrial societies that are caught up in the conflict of → ideologies and political movements and that operate in the cooperative and antinomian interplay of elementary principles like freedom, political and social participation, Western or socialist democracy, and economic and social planning. In this field, taking note of the difference between theory and fulfillment, we must recognize the effective trends and choose between them or decide on our own priorities. Christians find criteria for this choice by clarifying the orientation of their faith as they listen to the biblical message and the Christian tradition.

Theologically, God's turning to us in Christ sets us in a basic equality that is primarily spiritual and that must express itself in a practical regard for → human dignity (Gen. 1:27). To assign different value to individuals or groups is an arrogant attack on the majesty of the divine decision and on the divine will to save, which applies first and precisely to the lowly. As regards human gifts, both spiritual and natural, there is a variety that we must take note of as they unfold. Specific gifts, however, are not a private possession. They are bound together in solidarity, and they bear a constructive relationship to respect for the equality of all members of the community (→ Church Growth; Congregation).

We cannot transfer directly to the secular realm that which applies in the Christian community, yet here too Christian criteria must govern our choice of options in regard to equality. J. Rawls in his book

A Theory of Justice (1971) resolves the tension between the free development of personality and a righteous equality in a way that shows affinity to a theological assessment. Social and economic inequalities, he says, are tolerable only when they are to the benefit of all, offering the best possible prospects to those who have the least advantages. We cannot negate differences in principle (i.e., no "egalitarianism"). We must allow for the free development of gifts, yet only in such a way that they benefit all, and especially the socially deprived. Freedom, then, is understood communicatively, yet equality does not involve a program of leveling down but is the basis of the mutual → solidarity of those who give and receive in different ways, open to the commandment of a love of neighbor that is grounded in love of God.

→ Ethics; Humanity; Racism; Sexism; Society

Bibliography: R. A. Athens, *Egalitarian Community: Ethnography and Exegesis* (Tuscaloosa, Ala., 1991) • A. P. Fiske, *Structures of Social Life: The Four Elementary Forces of Human Relations: Communal Sharing, Authority Ranking, Equality Matching, Market Pricing* (New York, 1991) • K. B. Hackstaff, *Marriage in a Culture of Divorce* (Philadelphia, 1999) • W. A. Henry, *In Defense of Elitism* (New York, 1994) • Leo xiii, "Quod apostolici muneris" (1878), *The Papal Encyclicals* (5 vols.; ed. C. Carlen; Raleigh, N.C., 1981) 2.11-16 • M. Lowe, *Woman's Nature: Rationalizations of Inequality* (New York, 1983) • C. B. Macpherson, *The Political Theory of Possessive Individualism: From Hobbes to Locke* (Oxford, 1962) • K. Malik, *The Meaning of Race: Race, History, and Culture in Western Society* (New York, 1996) • G. Mikula, *Justice and Social Interaction: Experimental and Theoretical Contributions from Psychological Research* (Bern, 1980) • T. Mommsen, *Die Grundrechte des deutschen Volkes* (Leipzig, 1849; repr., Frankfurt, 1969) • J. Rawls, *A Theory of Justice* (Cambridge, Mass., 1971) • K. Thraede, "Gleichheit," *RAC* 11.122-64 • P. Westen, *Speaking of Equality: An Analysis of the Rhetorical Force of "Equality" in Moral and Legal Discourse* (Princeton, 1990).

Heinz Eduard Tödt†

Equatorial Guinea

The Republic of Equatorial Guinea was a Spanish colony until 1968, when it gained its independence. It consists of mainland Mbini (formerly Río Muni), between Cameroon to the north and Gabon to the south and east, the island Bioko (formerly Fernando

	1960	1980	2000
Population (1,000s):	252	217	452
Annual growth rate (%):	1.33	7.22	2.41

Area: 28,051 sq. km. (10,831 sq. mi.)

A.D. 2000

Population density: 16/sq. km. (42/sq. mi.)
Births / deaths: 3.87 / 1.46 per 100 population
Fertility rate: 5.13 per woman
Infant mortality rate: 98 per 1,000 live births
Life expectancy: 52.0 years (m: 50.4, f: 53.6)
Religious affiliation (%): Christians 88.3 (Roman Catholics 81.6, indigenous 4.4, Protestants 3.5, unaffiliated 1.3, other Christians 0.5), Muslims 4.1, nonreligious 3.2, atheists 1.9, tribal religionists 1.9, other 0.6.

Póo), and some smaller islands. Spanish is the national language. Petroleum, timber, and cocoa are the basic exports. In spite of good prospects at the time of independence, Equatorial Guinea has become economically depressed and is today one of the poorest countries in Africa, the gross domestic product per capita being barely $1,500 per year (1997 est.). The only bright spot is the recent discovery of large oil and gas reserves.

Almost 90 percent of the inhabitants of Equatorial Guinea are Christians. There is also a fairly high number of → atheists, attributed largely to President Macías Masie Nguema's reign of terror, which extended from 1968 to his overthrow and execution in 1979. Most of the Christians belong to the → Roman Catholic Church; there are also a few thousand → Methodists and Presbyterians (→ Reformed and Presbyterian Churches) and at least one → Independent Church. Protestant work encountered many obstacles in the colonial period under Spanish rule.

Portugal first reached Equatorial Guinea in the late 15th century, ceding the land to Spain in 1778. These initial connections ensured the presence of Roman Catholicism. A → concordat in 1853 between Spain and the Holy See declared Roman Catholicism to be the state religion of Equatorial Guinea. The same concordat made provision for Roman Catholicism's protection from competing faiths, which often led to either expulsion or nonrecognition of non–Roman Catholic Christian groups. In spite of opposition, Protestants — especially Baptist missions from the West Indies (ca. 1841), Primitive Methodists from England, Presbyterians (1850), and evangelicals with the backing of United Presbyterian Church (U.S.A.) and the Worldwide Evangelization Crusade — have also established a presence. Presbyterians were not recog-

nized until 1906, however, and Protestant schools were not permitted during the Spanish rule. All Protestant churches were closed in 1952.

Internal self-government in 1963 and full independence in 1968 brought new changes to the status of Christianity in Equatorial Guinea. The association of Roman Catholic Church with the hated colonialist history was excised by placing the Roman Catholic Church in jeopardy, even though the 1968 constitution provided for religious freedom. Article 35 of the 1973 constitution introduced an important, albeit open-ended, condition: "The exercise of any religion is free provided that it respects the law and public order. It is illegal and punishable to place faith and religious belief in opposition to the principles and purposes of the state."

The freedom that came with independence quickly perished in the terror of a systematic → persecution of all Christians. This terror involved the expulsion of foreign church workers, the closing of churches and their conversion to other uses, the prohibition of → baptism and → worship, and the torture, assassination, and — in at least two cases — public crucifixion of Christians. Tens of thousands fled Equatorial Guinea, chiefly to Gabon and Cameroon. This stage coincided with the accession to office of President Macías, who wanted to be venerated as a messiah. During his reign he managed to keep the favor of the East and toleration of the West, but in August 1979 his nephew, then chief of the palace guard, ousted him. He was tried, sentenced to death, and executed. An active opposition party abroad, however, claimed that Nguema was not dead and that his clan would rule again. It thus refused to return and work with the government.

After the persecution the church had to make a fresh start. A papal visit of a few hours in February 1982 gave a new boost to Roman Catholics. In October that year Equatorial Guinea became a Roman Catholic province with its own archbishopric of Malabo and the bishoprics of Bata and Ebebiyin. There are very few national priests. Priests, monks, and nuns from Spain are active in pastoral care and the work of development. The church must face the real danger that too great a dependence on Spain will hinder the growth of an active national church.

At the end of the 20th century Equatorial Guinea was a republic in transition to becoming a multiparty democracy, although that transition appears to have been halted. The country faces an uphill struggle to overcome the effects of gross economic corruption and mismanagement, as well as the murder and exile of virtually all its educated citizens.

Bibliography: M. CASTRO, "Equatorial Guinea," *Africa South of the Sahara, 1998* (27th ed.; London, 1998) 409-14 • R. FEGLEY, *Equatorial Guinea: An African Tragedy* (New York, 1989) • W. HOFFMANN, "Äquatorial Guinea," *KM* 96 (1977) 138ff.; 100 (1981) 201ff. • R. A. KLINTENBERG, *Equatorial Guinea, Macias Country: The Forgotten Refugees* (Geneva, 1987) • R. E. KLITGAARD, *Tropical Gangsters* (New York, 1990) • I. K. SUNDIATA, *Equatorial Guinea: Colonialism, State Terror, and the Search for Stability* (Boulder, Colo., 1990); idem, *From Slaving to Neoslavery: The Bight of Biafra and Fernando Po in the Era of Abolition, 1827-1930* (Madison, Wis., 1996).

WOLFGANG HOFFMAN, S.J., and JOHN S. POBEE

Erasmus

Desiderius Erasmus of Rotterdam (1469?-1536) was a leading humanist, theologian, and writer. He lived and conducted research in various European cities and was involved especially with publishing ancient and early Christian authors. Both his new edition of the Greek NT (→ Bible Manuscripts and Editions 3) and his advocacy of tolerance and peace are of theological significance.

Erasmus was the illegitimate child of Roger Gerard, a priest, and Margaret, a physician's daughter. He grew up in Gouda, Netherlands, became a choirboy at the cathedral school in Utrecht, and from 1478 to 1485 attended the school of the chapter of St. Lebuinus in Deventer. Influenced by the spirit of the *devotio moderna,* Erasmus spent two years with the → Brethren of the Common Life in 's Hertogenbosch. In 1486/1488 he entered the Augustinian → monastery in Steyn near Gouda and became an enthusiastic Latinist and writer. After being ordained to the priesthood in 1492, he left the monastery in 1493 and became secretary to Henry of Bergen, → bishop of Cambrai. Erasmus worked at this time on the humanistic dialogues *Antibarbari* (1520) and *Colloquia* (1518) as well as on a collection of proverbs (→ Humanism). In 1495 he began study of → theology in Paris at the Collège de Montaigu but left quite soon because of his disinclination toward the scholastic theology taught there (→ Scholasticism).

After earning his livelihood for a time through private instruction, Erasmus accompanied his pupil William Blount, Lord Mountjoy, to England in 1499, where he met Thomas More and John Colet. The latter encouraged Erasmus to spend more time with theology and especially with biblical → exegesis. For the sake of reading ancient sources, Erasmus learned Greek. Upon returning to the Continent in 1500, he published the *Adagiorum collectanea,* a collection of approximately 800 proverbs from ancient authors.

Thenceforth Erasmus moved back and forth between Paris, the Netherlands, England, and Italy, searching through libraries and continually plagued by lack of money. His *Enchiridion militis Christiani* (1503) shows Erasmus's change into a Christian humanist. In 1504 he discovered Lorenzo Valla's work *Adnotationes* on the NT in the library of the monastery at Park, near Louvain. Valla's work and various deficient editions of the Vg prompted Erasmus to publish a new edition of the Latin Bible, which was produced in 1516 by the Basel printer August Froben, as well as an annotated Latin translation of the NT. Soon thereafter he published the first of his numerous editions of the → church fathers, including Jerome (1516), Cyprian (1520), Origen (1527), and Augustine (1528-29).

In 1506 Erasmus received a doctorate of theology in Turin, worked for a year as a private instructor in Bologna, and then, with the famous Venetian printer Aldus Manutius, expanded his editions of the *Adagia* and of various Greek authors, including Plato. In 1508 he came to → Rome as tutor of Alexander Stewart, son of the Scottish king James IV; there he was offered but declined a position in the → curia. Between 1509 and 1514 Erasmus lived in England again, where in 1509 in the house of Thomas More he wrote his famous *Moriae encomium* (ET *The Praise of Folly* [1549]), gave lectures in Cambridge, wrote a pedagogical book for Colet, and composed a satire about the bellicose Pope Julius II. After a two-year stay in Basel with Froben, Erasmus spent 1517-21 largely in Louvain, the stronghold of conservative theology. He left the city to avoid getting caught in the crossfire between the → Reformers and the Roman Catholic theologians, since both sides claimed him as an ally.

Like Luther, Erasmus desired a reform of the church itself, emphasizing in his *Enchiridion* an inward and invisible → devotion over physical works. Over the course of the → Reformation, Erasmus eventually took the side of the → Roman Catholic Church, even though he initially remained neutral toward Luther: "I am neither an accuser nor a protective patron of Luther nor someone accused by him," he said in 1520. With his understanding of the → freedom of the will, as explicated in his *De libero arbitrio* (1524), Erasmus ultimately did polemicize against Luther, who countered with *De servo arbitrio* (On the bondage of the will, 1525), thereby sealing the break between the two. In his later years, Erasmus assumed a moderately conservative posture, prompting hostility from orthodox Catholics, the Reformers, and neopagan humanists alike.

Except for the years between 1529 and 1535, when he lived in Freiburg, Erasmus lived from 1521 onward in Basel. Until his death in 1536, he was involved in producing editions of the church fathers as well as revised editions of the NT and other works.

Bibliography: Primary sources: Collected Works of Erasmus (Toronto, 1974ff.) • J. LeClerc, ed., *Opera omnia* (10 vols.; Leiden, 1703-6).

Bibliography: Bibliotheca Erasmiana. Répertoire des œuvres d'Erasme (Ghent, 1893; repr., Nieuwkoop, 1961).

Secondary works: R. H. Bainton, *Erasmus of Christendom* (New York, 1969) • A. G. Dickens, *Erasmus the Reformer* (London, 1994) • L. E. Halkin, *Erasmus: A Critical Biography* (Oxford, 1993) • M. Hoffmann, *Rhetoric and Theology: The Hermeneutic of Erasmus* (Toronto, 1994) • L. Jardine, *Erasmus, Man of Letters: The Construction of Charisma in Print* (Princeton, 1993) • B. Mansfield, *Interpretations of Erasmus c. 1750-1920* (Toronto, 1992) • J. C. Olin, *Erasmus, Utopia, and the Jesuits: Essays on the Outreach of Humanism* (New York, 1994).

Silke Dorer-Gommermann

Eremites → Anchorites

Erhard Seminars Training → EST

Eritrea

1. History
2. Religions

1. History

Eritrea, located in the Horn of Africa, is bounded on the northeast by the Red Sea, on the west by Sudan, on the southeast by Djibouti, and on the south by Ethiopia. Only in 1993 did Eritrea become an independent state.

Evidence of human history in Eritrea goes back to the eighth millennium B.C. During the 3rd and 4th centuries A.D., Eritrea was part of the Ethiopian kingdom of Axum. In the 6th century that kingdom declined; between 675 and 1490 it was a small

	1960	1980	2000
Population (1,000s):	1,420	2,382	3,809
Annual growth rate (%):	2.49	2.49	2.36

Area: 117,400 sq. km. (45,300 sq. mi.)

A.D. 2000

Population density: 32/sq. km. (84/sq. mi.)
Births / deaths: 3.71 / 1.35 per 100 population
Fertility rate: 4.88 per woman
Infant mortality rate: 87 per 1,000 live births
Life expectancy: 52.1 years (m: 50.8, f: 53.5)
Religious affiliation (%): Muslims 51.0, Christians 43.8 (Orthodox 31.0, unaffiliated 8.4, Roman Catholics 3.7, other Christians 0.8), nonreligious 4.6, other 0.6.

Christian enclave in the midst of → Islam, largely cut off from the rest of the Christian world. The Ethiopian kingdom emerged in the 16th century as Abyssinia.

Subsequently, Eritrea was colonized by the Turks and then the Egyptians. The more formal colonial history of Eritrea, however, began in 1889, when Italy claimed the land as its colony (→ Colonialism). The Italians ruled the territory until 1941, when it was captured by the British. Although other former Italian colonies (e.g., Somalia and Libya) were granted independence fairly soon after World War II ended, Eritrea long remained a colony. From 1942 to 1952 it was under the mandate of the British, who administered the territory on behalf of the → United Nations. In December 1950 the General Assembly voted that Eritrea eventually be federated with Ethiopia as an autonomous entity under the Ethiopian crown. By 1962 all elements of autonomy within the federation were eliminated, however, and Ethiopia unilaterally annexed Eritrea.

Liberation movements within the country were suppressed by Ethiopia, but Eritreans who lived abroad sponsored an armed struggle to gain their country's independence. The ensuing war of liberation lasted 31 years. In 1980, when Ethiopia was itself under Communist rule, the Eritrean People's Liberation Front (EPLF) emerged as the dominant political and military force in Eritrea, effectively uniting the majority both of the combatants and of the populace at large. The EPLF ultimately led Eritrea to its independence, though at a cost of the lives of 30 percent of the country's youth. In honor of the youth who fell, June 20 is observed yearly as Martyrs' Day. Candlelight processions are held then throughout the land as a reaffirmation of the national commitment to building a free, developed, and progressive nation.

The EPLF continues to lead Eritrea as a provisional government. Much of its energy has been diverted, however, to the waging of violent border disputes with Ethiopia; only in 2000 has there been a cease-fire. Famine, which ravaged the Horn of Africa in the 1980s and 1990s, has also preoccupied this new country.

2. Religions

The majority of Eritreans adhere to either Islam or Christianity, each of which claims about half of the total population. A few thousand persons are followers of traditional African religions, most notably the Kunama-speaking → animists.

Both Christianity and Islam have long histories in Eritrea. Christianity was introduced into the territory encompassing present-day Ethiopia and Eritrea in the fourth century by two Syrians, Frumentius and Aedesius of Tyre. The first → bishop, Frumentius, was consecrated in → Alexandria by → Athanasius. This history accounts for the long and strong relationship between Eritrean and Ethiopian Christianity and the Coptic Church of Egypt, two churches within the family of → Oriental, or non-Chalcedonian, Orthodoxy (→ Ethiopian Orthodox Church). The antiquity of Orthodoxy in Eritrea is attested by the presence of many active monasteries, Debre Bizen (4th cent.) and Debre Sina (6th cent.) being the most venerable. The Orthodox churches of Eritrea and Ethiopia share a common history, liturgical language (Ge'ez), church calendar, and, until Eritrean independence, ordained leadership. There is now a patriarch of the Eritrean Orthodox Church — Abuna (lit. "our father") Philippos I (b. 1905) — who was consecrated in 1998 in Cairo by Pope Shenouda III of the → Coptic Orthodox Church of Egypt.

Other Christian churches in Eritrea include the → Roman Catholic Church, introduced to the country in the 19th century by the Italian colonialists, and a number of smaller Protestant groups established as a result of → missionary efforts in the 19th and 20th centuries. The Evangelical Church of Eritrea, founded in 1926 and with 12,000 members in 2000, is affiliated with the → Lutheran World Federation. Tracing its roots to the Swedish Evangelical Mission, which arrived in Massawa in 1866, it is now the oldest autonomous Lutheran church in Africa and the mother of the much-larger Evangelical Ethiopian Church Mekane Yesus. A smaller Lutheran Church in Eritrea, with approximately 3,500 members, was founded in 1911 by several Swedish missionaries who

resigned from their parent organization. None of the Eritrean churches has ecumenical connections.

Islam was also introduced early into Eritrea, coming in 1517 with the Turks under Selim I and, soon thereafter, in 1530 in the person of the imam of Harer — Aḥmad Grāñ, the Left-Handed. The Christians who stayed in the region were allowed to practice their religion freely. Moreover, the ethos of the area made coexistence natural and provided for healthy dialogue and mutual conversation between Christians and Muslims. This coexistence has been furthered by the common national commitment to the construction of a united Eritrean nation.

Solitude has marked the national life of Eritrea. During its struggle for independence the country was largely ignored by the rest of the world. In this solitude, Eritrea has come to rely solely on its own people, an experience that is shaping the nation's self-reliance and → development.

Bibliography: D. CONNELL, *Against All Odds: A Chronicle of the Eritrean Revolution* (Trenton, N.J., 1993) • R. IYOB, *The Eritrean Struggle for Independence: Domination, Resistance, Nationalism, 1941-1993* (New York, 1995) • T. MEDHANIE, *Eritrea and Neighbours in the "New World Order": Geopolitics, Democracy, and "Islamic Fundamentalism"* (Münster, 1994) • T. NEGASH, *Eritrea and Ethiopia: The Federal Experience* (New Brunswick, N.J., 1997) • A. TESFAI and M. DOORNBOS, eds., *Post-conflict Eritrea: Prospects for Reconstruction and Development* (Lawrenceville, N.J., 1999) • *The United Nations and the Independence of Eritrea* (New York, 1996).

YAKOB TESFAY

Eschatology

Overview
1. OT
   1.1. Concept
   1.2. History
   1.3. Origin
   1.4. Development
   1.5. Basic Convictions
2. NT
   2.1 Jesus
   2.2 Before and Alongside Paul
   2.3 Paul
   2.4 Pauline Churches
   2.5 Synoptics and Acts
   2.6 Johannine Writings
   2.7 Development
3. History of Dogma

Overview

Eschatology is traditionally the doctrine of the last things (from Gk. *eschatos,* denoting what is last in time). It is of particular interest in modern theology, which speaks of a new phase and of the "eschatologizing" of all theology. At the same time, the haziness of the term (it is also used outside theology) and its varied use seem to make it an example of linguistic confusion in theology.

The word was used first by the strict Lutheran theologian Abraham Calovius (1612-86), who, at the end of his 12-volume dogmatics, dealt with → death, → resurrection, the → last judgment, and the consummation under the title *Eschatologia sacra.* In the 19th century, though there was "something alien" about the term (F. D. E. → Schleiermacher), it was taken up and used more generally, not only for the traditional themes, but also for ideas of → heaven, the → immortality of the → soul, the perfecting of the → church, the imminent end of the world (→ Apocalypticism 4), universal reconciliation (→ Apocatastasis), a → theology of history, notions of → salvation history, the belief in → evolution, and the belief in → progress.

In the 20th century, after the shattering experiences of world wars, the anthropological and historical implications of eschatology emerged in → philosophy with the ideas of existential → anxiety and meaninglessness (J. P. Sartre), the borderline situation (K. Jaspers), being unto death (M. Heidegger), and the principle of hope (E. Bloch; → Existentialism). The Christian eschatological model may be discerned in the philosophy of history (K. Löwith), which has been exposed to criticism (J. Habermas). The Marxist utopia (→ Marxism) might be viewed as secularized eschatology.

There is today a marked sensitivity to eschatological themes. Eschatology flourishes in a climate of resignation in face of everyday experiences, the nuclear threat (→ Disarmament and Armament; War; Weapons), and the this-worldly hope of → peace. It is stimulated by reflection on → suffering, sickness, and death; by wrestling with the many scientific and technological possibilities for shaping life and the world; and by the limitations of growth (→ Creation; Ecology; Environment; Future; Poverty; Technology). It is also reflected in a diffused belief in the world to come such as is found in popular → piety and especially in eschatological groups (→ Adventists; Apostolic Churches; Jehovah's Witnesses; Mormons; Unification Church).

Modern experiences and the challenges of other religions and worldviews that also address the fate of the individual and the course and end of world history force the Christian churches to give an account of their → hope. This true theme of eschatology is rooted in the witness of the OT and NT and seeks actualization in the life of Christians. In dealing with it, theology must develop the traditional topics and take up the questions that are dealt with in → political theology and → liberation theology. Above all, however, it must offer a hermeneutics of eschatological statements if it is to succeed in communicating an experience of reality and secular hope by means of the hope that grows out of faith (→ Salvation). Eschatology has paradigmatic significance for Christian witness in the world.

ERWIN FAHLBUSCH

1. OT

1.1. *Concept*

If in terms of Christian → dogmatics we understand the concept "eschatology" only dualistically and temporally as denoting "the last things," then we can refer only to certain texts from the OT and early Jewish → apocalyptic. Such an approach, however, has not proved satisfactory in research thus far because much of the contents of NT and Christian eschatology come from other OT spheres (e.g., those of the Day of the Lord and of the kingship of God). Thus it is hard to isolate the concept from the rest of the vocabulary of OT theology. All attempts at further differentiation have thus far simply made us aware of difficulties for which there is as yet no acceptable solution.

1.2. History

In the conquest we already encounter a → future that is promised and given in history by God. If we speak of a final turn, of a radical and definitive alteration of existing relations by a new intervention of → Yahweh in history, we must ask whether the terms used are clear and whether they cover what the OT actually says. Is the reference to an absolute end of the national history of Israel? Can such an end be thought of without something following and without reflection on the relation of Yahweh to other peoples? Do texts that promise a total world change (e.g., Isa. 2:1-4; 11:6-9) always presuppose a break? Before apocalyptic, did the OT think in terms of something definitive and final? What is the relation between the end of national history and the end of an existing historical phase (H. W. Wolff)? Given the stress of the present experience of finality (→ Aporia), is a final hope transferred to the future, or is it not more in keeping with the OT to say that in no fulfillment of → promise and no situation on its historical path could → Israel (§1) be satisfied with the present state because it always expected more and greater things from its God?

1.3. Origin

Since the world around early Israel provides no clear indication concerning the origin of OT eschatology, and since it can be assumed to have had only a strengthening and substantive influence on apocalyptic, many scholars think that Israel's own concept of God and related understanding of history led to the rise of eschatology. The development of OT hopes of the future produced eschatology, and divergent judgments of literary and redactional criticism regarding individual texts do nothing to alter the total picture. Into this development went the various aspects and contents of judgment and → salvation — the Day of Yahweh and the remnant, the new exodus and conquest, the lordship of God, the new heaven and new earth, and finally even the → resurrection.

1.4. Development

Many scholars, then, use the term "eschatology" relative to the OT only in the very general sense of future expectations or expressions of hope. They include basic statements of faith in Yahweh that press for development or fulfillment (fellowship with Yahweh, promises, Yahweh's royal dominion, etc.). Hence we cannot describe eschatological prophecy (→ Prophet, Prophecy) as merely an unoriginal per-

version of preexilic prophecy that fails to do justice to the OT view of God.

We must see differences in the expectations, however, and can perhaps talk about eschatology only when the expected and promised and even already coming future salvation is described as one that comes after experienced history and has a definitive character (as portrayed in Deutero-Isaiah, Haggai, and Zechariah). Since certain texts suggest this view, and since no radical break can be established between preexilic and postexilic prophecy, we can speak of development. In this regard it should be noted that the OT itself lends no support for the argument that what is older is theologically more essential.

1.5. Basic Convictions

The basic convictions of OT eschatology and its development might be listed as follows: (1) the goal of God's ways is the establishment of his full sovereignty; (2) we alone cannot solve our own problems or those of the world; and (3) the coming kingdom of God is more than the fulfillment of humanity.

A comprehensive *bibliography*, which covers the literature until 1977, including the more important older contributions on the topic, appears in an anthology edited by H. D. Preuss, *Eschatologie im Alten Testament* (Darmstadt, 1978). See also the bibliographic information (up to 1981) in R. Smend, "Eschatologie II: Altes Testament," *TRE* 10.256-64.

Other studies: J. Barr, *The Garden of Eden* (London, 1992) • A. E. Bernstein, *The Formation of Hell: Death and Retribution in the Ancient and Early Christian Worlds* (London, 1993) • J. M. Bremmer, T. P. J. van den Hout, and R. Peters, eds., *Hidden Futures: Death and Immortality in Ancient Egypt, Anatolia, the Classical, Biblical, and Arabic-Islamic World* (Amsterdam, 1994) • A. Falaturi, W. Strolz, and S. Talmon, eds., *Das Heil und die Utopien* (Freiburg, 1983) • W. Harrelson, "Prophetic Eschatological Visions and the Kingdom of God," *FS G. E. Mendenhall* (Winona Lake, Ind., 1983) 117-26 • *Hermeneutik eschatologischer biblischer Texte* (Greifswald, 1983) • J. Jeremias, "Zur Eschatologie des Hoseabuches," *FS H. W. Wolff* (Neukirchen, 1981) 217-34 • R. Kilian, K. Funk, and P. Fassl, eds., *Eschatologie* (FS E. Neuhäusler; St. Ottilien, 1981), see esp. articles by R. Kilian and D. Kinet • I. H. Marshall, "Slippery Words I: Eschatology," *ExpTim* 89 (1978) 264-69 • J. N. Oswalt, "Recent Studies in OT Eschatology and Apocalyptic," *JETS* 24 (1981) 303-13 • R. Schnackenburg, ed., *Zukunft. Zur Eschatologie bei Juden und Christen* (Düsseldorf, 1980) see esp. article by S. Talmon • W. Werner, *Eschatologische Texte in Jesaja 1–39* (Würzburg, 1982) • H. W. Wolff, "Endzeitvorstellungen und Orientierungskrise in der alttestamentlichen Prophetie," *FS H.-J. Kraus* (Neukirchen, 1983) 75-86.

HORST DIETRICH PREUSS†

2. NT

From the beginning of the 20th century, the great importance of eschatology and its ideas associated with the imminent reign of God and the (imminent) end of things has been recognized as essential for understanding the NT, although there has been no consensus regarding its development or appraisal. The theory of "thoroughgoing eschatology" (A. Schweitzer) is that → Jesus held strong → apocalyptic expectations in which he was mistaken, and therefore we must reject them. In R. Bultmann's thought, we must expound these expectations as a summons to make a decision vis-à-vis the end. By contrast, C. H. Dodd spoke of "realized eschatology," meaning that the → kingdom of God has come already in the work of Jesus and that future expectations of the end are secondary.

Is a balance possible between these extremes through variations of an anticipatory eschatology (suggested esp. after the middle of the 20th cent.)? Or was Jesus' own thinking, itself little influenced by eschatology, then confronted by an eschatological-apocalyptic current emerging in the early church (suggested by one strand of research in the late 20th cent.)? Debate continues concerning the role of the delay of the end (E. Grässer) and also concerning the → Gnosticism that arose in the early church. Because so many issues are still open to discussion, a description of only preliminary validity can be given at this time.

2.1. Jesus

After John the Baptist provided initial impulses, Jesus then sought to collect together the eschatological Israel in his concern for the poor and the lost, in healings and exorcisms, through provocative words (esp. concerning the Law and Halakah) and actions, as well as in his calling of the Twelve. In this capacity, he understood himself as the representative and agent of the reign of God, which he anticipates as coming from heaven in the future (up to Mark 14:25) and which becomes near and even present in a spatial and temporal sense (Mark 1:14-15; Luke 11:20 and throughout). Its overwhelming earthly implementation is already commencing in small steps (Mark 4:30-32), and its powerful inbreaking is certain (*Gos. Thom.* log. 10.98 and elsewhere amplify even the daring imagery of the Gospels).

The goal of all eschatological remarks is to change a person's behavior in the present and to prompt that person to become fully engaged on be-

half of the reign of God (Matt. 13:44, 45-46, and elsewhere). Accordingly, Jesus continually shifts focus from hopes for the future to an immediate life with God (even taking a position with regard to → resurrection, Mark 12:18-27). To the extent that he does represent near expectation in the temporal sense (Mark 9:1), his position can be explained on the basis of his certainty that God's reign will indeed come (see the line leading up to Mark 14:25).

Within this framework, the lack of consensus among scholars (including the question of whether the term "eschatology" is to be applied to Jesus in the first place) also reflects problems attaching to sources and their assessment. A preference for the Synoptic tradition tends to accentuate the future; preference for the *Gospel of Thomas* and for Johannine traditions tends to focus on the immediacy of God's reign or of the life Jesus both predicted and actualized. The Son of Man sayings reflect this tension (perhaps with the old roots for its poles between Luke 9:58; 12:8; 17:24 Q; Mark 8:38).

2.2. Before and Alongside Paul

Early Christian eschatology finds a common basis as it looks back upon God's saving work in and for Jesus. The communities' own experiences, the accompanying Jewish and Hellenistic religious situation, and the historical situation at large all influenced its development, resulting in a considerable variety in eschatological thought. In part, experience of salvation and of the Spirit is linked with eager expectation, so that a Son of Man Christology develops, and sayings about the end (Mark 13:30; Matt. 10:23) are constructed anew. → Q might have been assembled in this milieu. Elsewhere, enthusiastic thinking develops that relates → baptism as much to Jesus' resurrection as to his death (corrected in Rom. 6:4-5), so that Christians now stand fully in → salvation and have nothing new to expect in the future, not even a resurrection of the dead (see 1 Cor. 15:12).

2.3. Paul

→ Paul brings with him an apocalyptic inheritance that is probably also driving his own mission forward (e.g., 1 Thess. 1:10; 4:13–5:11). Yet he is also certain that a salvation that changes life has already come (2 Cor. 5:17; 6:2). The result is a dynamic between future and present eschatology ("already" and "not yet," per Romans 6 etc.) that emerges as he deals with problems in his churches. Thus in 1 Thess 4:13-18, discussing the death of church members, he bases belief in their resurrection on the resurrection of Jesus, develops this understanding of resurrection in 1 Corinthians 15 in his debate with critics, and in 2 Cor. 5:1-10 cautiously reformulates his imagery (concerning new clothing, etc.). Paul emphasizes the future (e.g., 1 Cor.

13:12) because in his own eschatological reservations it ensures God's sovereignty and places high demands on, and simultaneously relativizes, all that takes place in the world (Rom. 13:11-14; 1 Cor. 7:29-31), yet also gives encouragement in situations of conflict (e.g., Phil. 1:6; → Temptation). The constant point of reference is a soteriological → Christology, so that the motif of deliverance even breaks through that of judgment (1 Cor. 3:13-15). In Rom. 11:25-32 (see also 15:8-13) this theme issues in hope for universal salvation that pays highest tribute to Israel.

2.4. *Pauline Churches*

Contemporaneous with Paul as well as after his ministry, a consciousness of living in an age quite close to both judgment and deliverance became widespread, and many texts that earlier had been read in the light of (or even used against) Paulinism were now read independently (e.g., 1 Peter, with its moving passages 3:18-22 and 4:5-6, and James, with its combination of wisdom and judgment-eschatology).

The question of the presence of salvation played a special role in the Pauline churches (after 2 Thess. 2:2ff.). Especially Colossians and Ephesians, influenced by baptism theology (e.g., Col. 2:12-13; Eph. 2:5), considerably expand the salvific sphere opened up in the present by Christ (whereby resonance with Gnostic thought seems somewhat weaker today than earlier). In Colossians we again find a future consummation in contrast with spatial and eschatological ideas — an orientation of thought to that which is above (3:2-4). Ephesians focuses (2:1-10 etc.) on the deliverance of Christians already accomplished. This emphasis comes closer to the idea that the resurrection has taken place already and that there is in the future neither resurrection nor judgment. The Pastoral Epistles (2 Tim. 2:16-19) and Polycarp (*Phil.* 7.1) dispute this view vigorously, from the standpoint of a conventionalized post-Pauline futurist eschatology. In Revelation an eschatological sense of salvation characteristic of Asia Minor reacts in various ways with experiences of affliction (1:9 etc.). In a sketch of the establishment of the lordship of God and of Jesus over against a last attack by ungodly powers (chaps. 4–20), a futurist eschatology receives fresh development, culminating in 20:4-6 (→ Millenarianism) and 21:1–22:5.

2.5. *Synoptics and Acts*

The → Synoptics place considerable emphasis on eschatological watchfulness (Mark 13:33-37; Matt. 25:13; Luke 21:34-36, etc.). Although such views include motifs involving the delay of the → parousia (Luke 12:42-46 and par.; Matt. 25:3-5), these motifs play a less significant role than earlier assumed, since the temporal component fluctuates as a result of the early Christians' own qualitative experience of time. Thus despite traditions of near expectation (Mark 9:1; 13:30), Mark still leaves room for an open continuation (according to 16:7, with a new beginning in Galilee). Matthew contains an intensive expectation of judgment (13:37-41, 47-50; 25:31-46) that includes the nations in the reign of the Resurrected (Matt. 28:18-20); the eschatological attitude toward Israel is a matter of dispute (23:37-39 etc.).

Luke/Acts understands the present as a time to stand fast (Luke 21:19), and the possibility of individual eschatology commencing with death begins to emerge (Luke 23:43; Acts 7:55-56). Along the path of the "light for the nations," from the turning point of the ages (Luke 16:16) to the ends of the earth (Luke 2:30-32; Acts 1:8; 13:47-48), history expands (even to a reestablishment of Israel's hopes, Luke 1:68-79; 13:34-35; 22:29-30; Acts 1:6; 3:20-21; 15:16) without, however, eliminating eschatology.

2.6. *Johannine Writings*

By contrast, John emphasizes that the Resurrected and, thanks to the Spirit, salvation are present. The present itself becomes wholly a time of salvation, and traditionally future *eschata* occur even now: judgment, resurrection and (eternal) life, and the casting out of the ruler of this world (John 3:17-18; 5:21-27; 11:25; 12:31). At the same time, however, John does not lose sight of the long interim period, of Jesus' physical absence, or of the community's many temptations (13:31–14:31; 15:18-21; 16:2-3, 19-20) and thus also the need for his addressees to be consoled. He thus also announces to them a future consummation of salvation (5:28-29; 6:39-40, 44, 54; 14:2-3) whose guarantee against this world (up to the Paraclete saying in 16:7-15) is the salvation that is present even now. In this sense, present and future eschatology belong substantively together and are not to be separated (characteristic passages include 4:23 and 5:25).

In a shift away from this view, 1 John passes on to the Johannine churches an understanding of the present in terms of the historical dynamism of the last hour between darkness and light, an hour characterized by the appearance of anti-Christians (2:8, 18, etc.; → Antichrist), in the process emphasizing more the future expectation of parousia and judgment (2:28; 4:17). Despite some common features, the eschatology of the Johannine writings is not uniform (2 John 7 being extremely unusual). Within the context of religious history, one can discern Jewish elements of intensive and dualistic eshatology preceding any contact with Gnosticism, and scholars have proposed various developmental theses to account for these connections.

2.7. *Development*

Accordingly, the development of eschatology resulted in various common features within and between the early Christian churches, though also in a simultaneity of differing views. Apocalyptic and enthusiastic elements, though also various temporal and spatial categories, assert themselves in any given situation. Time, for example, is experienced not in the quantitative linear sense but as long or short in a qualitative-existential sense. Accordingly, long sayings are constructed anew anticipating an urgent fulfillment of all previous predictions (Mark 13:30 emerges probably as a recent member of the strata in Mark 13); there is still imminent expectation in 1 Peter (4:7) and Hebrews (10:25), where, admittedly, spatial imagery is predominant (12:22-24 etc.), and in Revelation (1:3 etc.) it even becomes immediately relevant once again.

At the same time, writers are aware, albeit without succumbing to any genuinely serious doubts, that near expectation in the temporal sense has remained unfulfilled. Here the spectrum of reaction extends from a positive emphasis on the delay of the parousia against any imminent expectation (in 2 Thess. 2:1-12) to an eschatological sketch that does not need the parousia (John). The absence of the parousia, though still addressed as a theme up till the end of the NT period itself (*1 Clem.* 23; 2 Pet. 3:3-13), does not on the whole provide any key to the development of eschatology. Here one must simply acknowledge the complexity of NT eschatology. Theologically, one decisive constituent is the existential experience of salvation in Jesus Christ. This experience binds the Christian life eschatologically to Christ, no matter whether the future is something new or is simply a fulfillment of what has already begun.

Bibliography: H. Baarlink, *Die Eschatologie der synoptischen Evangelien* (Stuttgart, 1986) • V. Balabanski, *Eschatology in the Making: Mark, Matthew, and Didache* (Cambridge, 1993) • C. H. Dodd, *The Parables of the Kingdom* (rev. ed.; London, 1978; orig. pub., 1935) • K. Erlemann, *Naherwartung und Parusieverzögerung im Neuen Testament. Ein Beitrag zur Frage religiöser Zeiterfahrung* (Tübingen, 1997) • M. Evang, H. Merklein, and M. Wolter, eds., *Eschatologie und Schöpfung* (Berlin, 1997) • P. Fiedler and D. Zeller, eds., *Gegenwart und kommendes Reich* (Stuttgart, 1975) • J. Frey, *Die johanneische Eschatologie* (2 vols.; Tübingen, 1997-98) • R. W. Funk et al., eds., *The Five Gospels: The Search for the Authentic Words of Jesus. New Translation and Commentary* (New York, 1993) • H. E. Gloer, ed., *Eschatology and the NT* (Peabody, Mass., 1988) • E. Grässer, *Das Problem der Parusieverzögerung in den synoptischen Evangelien und in der Apostelgeschichte* (3d ed.; Berlin, 1977) • M. Hengel and A. M. Schwemer, eds., *Königsherrschaft Gottes und himmlischer Kult* (Tübingen, 1991) • G. Klein, "Eschatologie IV: Neues Testament," *TRE* 10.270-99 (bibliography) • B. Lannert, *Die Wiederentdeckung der neutestamentlichen Eschatologie durch Johannes Weiß* (Tübingen, 1989) • J. L. Leuba, ed., *Temps et eschatologie* (Paris, 1994) • G. S. Oegema, *Zwischen Hoffnung und Gericht. Untersuchungen zur Rezeption der Apokalyptik im frühen Christentum und Judentum* (Neukirchen, 1999) • W. H. Schmidt and J. Becker, *Zukunft und Hoffnung* (Stuttgart, 1981) • A. Schweitzer, *The Quest of the Historical Jesus: A Critical Study of Its Progress from Reimarus to Wrede* (New York, 1968; orig. pub., 1906) • A. Yarbro Collins, *Cosmology and Eschatology in Jewish and Christian Apocalypticism* (Leiden, 1996)

Martin Karrer

3. History of Dogma

3.1. *Fathers*

In the course of the history of dogma, the tensions in the motifs of biblical eschatology were quickly relaxed, and stability was achieved. NT accents still affected the church, gave the persecuted communities the courage to endure, and stimulated theologians to approach eschatology along → millenarian lines (Irenaeus, Tertullian). In the broad stream of institutional Christianity, however, we do not find repeated the eschatological intensity of the apostolic age. Here already is a feature of → patristics.

On the one hand, → Gnostic and Platonic (→ Platonism) elements exerted an influence. Eschatologically, the main interest was in the destiny of the → soul from a metaphysical and religious standpoint, for the soul must be rescued from its alienation through matter and the body. There was no positive expectation for the visible world. On the other hand, after the Constantinian revolution we find a caesaropapist attempt in the East (e.g., Eusebius) and an ecclesiocratic attempt in the West (e.g., Augustine) to claim that the victory of Christianity was the fulfillment of eschatological hopes. In the Augustinian scheme of the "world week" (→ Augustine's Theology), the sixth day represents the sixth and temporal last millennium, the age of the → church. This age will be the final historical epoch before eternity.

3.2. *Middle Ages*

In contrast, Joachim of Fiore (ca. 1135-1202) championed radical eschatological views. For him, in keeping with a → Trinitarian belief in God, history runs in three stages. The third, that of the → Holy Spirit, is just dawning; we are moving toward the great future. Any equation of a present age with the → kingdom of God is doubtful. Universal renewal is possible — and due.

These emphases fell on fruitful soil particularly in Bohemia. "The state of the world will be renewed," said Jan Želivský in 1422. The reforming postulates of the → Hussites fall within the horizon of eschatological expectation. Even in J. A. Comenius (1592-1670) the eschatological hope can still inspire a broad program of culture and action in the form of "ecumenical reformation," with "ecumenical" here embracing both church and society.

3.3. *Reformation*
Among the → Reformers the Lutherans were more restrained in this field (→ Reformation). In their view the eschatological → hope relates to our redemption from → sin and → death, not to this world. The Lutheran → confessions use surprisingly dark colors when they reflect cosmologically on eschatology ("The world is growing worse and men are becoming weaker and more infirm," Augs. Conf. 23.14). For the Reformers, though, the personal hope of Christians is strong precisely in this situation. "Eternal life is promised us, even though we are dead. We are told of a blessed resurrection, even though we are surrounded by decay. What would become of us if we did not rely on hope and if, through the darkness, our minds did not hasten beyond the present world?" (J. → Calvin, CRef 55.143-44). In Protestant → orthodoxy eschatology becomes the final chapter in → dogmatics, the concluding light in the dogmatic system. It deals mainly with the fate of the elect and the reprobate after death.

Problems mount in the age of → rationalism and → Culture Protestantism. Insofar as such central themes as the kingdom of God are dealt with, there is often uncritical equation with ideas of moral and cultural progress in the imminent historical sense. Socially engaged Pietists like Johann Christoph Blumhardt (1805-80) and his son Christoph Friedrich Blumhardt (1842-1919; → Pietism) are clear exceptions.

3.4. *Twentieth-Century Renaissance of Eschatology*
The 20th century has seen a renaissance of eschatology. NT research drew attention sharply to the prominence of eschatological motifs in the Bible (J. Weiß, A. Schweitzer), a feature that at first was felt to be alien. The crisis in Western culture, however, soon led to a deeper understanding of eschato-

logical emphases, which pioneering theological projects from → dialectical theology onward have adopted resolutely (K. Barth, R. Bultmann, J. L. Hromádka, R. Niebuhr, P. Althaus, K. Rahner, J. Moltmann, W. Pannenberg, etc.).

The developing consensus in reappraising eschatology by no means indicates substantive agreement. Bultmann understands eschatology in terms of an existential desecularizing, but for others it is an incentive to develop the theme of revelation (Pannenberg) or political responsibility (Hromádka) from the standpoint of a → theology of history. In other approaches (e.g., American → process theology), eschatological motifs are set in a cosmological framework under the influence of evolutionary thinking (→ Evolution).

3.5. *Ecumenical Movement*
Eschatology is prominent also in the → ecumenical movement. In fact, ecumenism would be hardly thinkable without an orientation to eschatological promises. The motif of the coming kingdom of God has been an essential challenge to ecumenical involvement from the very first (W. A. → Visser 't Hooft), whether along the lines of ecclesiology (eschatological relativizing of the denominational status quo) or along those of social ethics (a spur to social engagement from the standpoint of the kingdom of God). It is no accident that the basic eschatological motif has repeatedly been a central theme (e.g., the 1954 Evanston Assembly of the → World Council of Churches, "Christ — the Hope of the World"; the 1980 Melbourne WCC Conference on World Mission and Evangelism, "Your Kingdom Come"). → Faith and Order also dealt intensively with the eschatological subject of hope at conferences it sponsored in Accra, Ghana (1974), and Bangalore, India (1978).

See bibliography in §7 below.

JAN MILIČ LOCHMAN

4. Orthodox Tradition
4.1. *Dogmatics*
Many Orthodox manuals of → dogmatics deal with eschatology only in their last chapter. They understand by it the end of our earthly life, the end of the world, and eternal life. The main source of Orthodox dogmatics, however, is the Bible, expounded in the spirit of the → church fathers.

We are made in the image of the eternal God (→ Anthropology). For this reason → death, the separation of body and → soul, is unnatural. It is the result of the breach between God and → Adam. In faith in Christ, who has established an indestructible fellowship between God and humanity, death becomes a passage (through Pesach) from earthly life to eternal life.

The immortality of the soul is grounded, not in its indestructible substance, but in the creative will of God, who desires for us as his partners in dialogue an ability to remember, a sense of responsibility, and an awareness of our relation with him. Because God's → love is eternal, the life of the beings to whom he turns must also be eternal.

In individual judgment directly after death we must render an account to our Creator. The use that we have made of our → freedom determines whether we enjoy fellowship with God in paradise or suffer separation from God in → hell, a state of isolation and rejection of the divine love.

Universal judgment at the end of the world (i.e., the → resurrection of the dead and the coming of a new → heaven and a new earth) differs from individual judgment in that each person and each people will be judged publicly by the historical consequences of their deeds. The bodies of the resurrected will then share either in the joys of paradise or in the sufferings of hell.

The state of the soul between individual and universal judgment is seen in the framework of the progress of believers in fellowship with God — as the communion of the saints with one another and as communion of the earthly → church with the → saints, who pray for the salvation of all humanity, just as the church prays for all, the living and the dead. Orthodoxy believes in the duty and beneficial effect of → prayer for the dead, but it rejects the doctrine of purgatory as a place of expiation through suffering. → Apocatastasis (universal reconciliation) is not the doctrine of the church. Orthodoxy thinks it enough to pray for the → salvation of all.

The world's movement toward its end has two aspects. All humanity is summoned to prepare the way for the → kingdom of God, which is "righteousness and peace and joy in the Holy Spirit" (Rom. 14:17). There is always resistance, however, and even hostility. God alone will perfect the new creation. The new heaven and earth, incorruptible and of an indescribable beauty, will mean, not the suspension of matter, but its full "pneumaticizing" and transfiguration by the Spirit of the risen Christ.

4.2. Liturgical, Sacramental, and Ascetic Spirituality

Orthodox → spirituality has different emphases from those of manuals of dogmatics. In the first place, the eschaton, or kingdom of God, has already come with the → incarnation of the Son of God

(Heb. 1:2; 1 Cor. 10:11). This coming constitutes already the beginning of indestructible fellowship between God and us in the person of Christ. It is thus the consummation of → creation and also the judgment of the fallen world.

Second, the hidden presence of the eschaton, or the risen Christ in the world, has continued from the event of → Pentecost.

Third, the eschaton in its entire fullness and glory will come as the resurrection of the dead and the radical transfiguration of all creation (1 Corinthians 15; Rev. 21:1). On this basis the church in the → Holy Spirit experiences the tension between Christ crucified and Christ as world judge, between Christ as first risen and the resurrection of the dead, between Christ on the Mount of Transfiguration and the transfiguration of the whole world. By watchfulness and → asceticism, the church takes a critical stance against the self-absorption of the fallen world. In its love for God and his creation, it shares its Easter joy with the world, and by the saints it is at work prophetically, summoning the world to radical renewal in God. Thus eschatology is not just the last chapter in dogmatics but the basic dimension of the lived-out faith of the church.

→ Orthodoxy 3

Bibliography: P. EVDOKIMOV, L'Orthodoxie (Neuchâtel, 1965) • G. HELLAMO, Adventus Domini: Eschatological Thought in Fourth-Century Apses and Catecheses (Leiden, 1989) • C. P. ROTH, ed., Gregory of Nyssa: The Soul and the Resurrection (Crestwood, N.Y., 1993) • J. SCHAPER, Eschatology in the Greek Psalter (Tübingen, 1995) • A. SCHMEMANN, L'Eucharistie, sacrament du Royaume (Paris, 1985) • D. STANILOAE, Orthodox Dogmatics (in Romanian) (vol. 3; Bucharest, 1978) • P. TREMPELAS, Dogmatique de l'Église orthodoxe catholique (vol. 3; Chevetogne, 1968).

DAN-ILIE CIOBOTEA

5. Roman Catholic Theology

5.1. Concentration and Expansion

After a disparate listing of various biblical ideas and materials with no hermeneutical mediation or criticism, a first phase of renewal in Roman Catholic eschatology began in biblical theology and dogmatics with concentration on the gracious work of salvation, its enactment in the death and resurrection of Christ, and its fulfillment for humanity and the world. In contrast to its prior alienation from God's saving will, the → future is now the history of faith and the practice of → hope. Expansion of eschatology has overcome the truncated immortality of the

→ soul by embracing the whole person, the mere salvation of individual souls by embracing the community, and the isolation of people from the world by embracing the whole cosmos.

5.2. Convergence with Evolution

The long insulation of → Catholicism resulted in a delayed adoption of an evolutionary perspective and dynamism of the future as the active horizon of eschatological reflection. Evolution of prehuman nature was sketched by Pierre Teilhard de Chardin (1881-1955) as a vision of the future. The development of the human person was integrated into the further and higher formation of the earlier centered and complex structures. The biblical symbol was consciously employed for the hypothetical convergence point Omega, for Teilhard was fitting belief in → creation, → incarnation, and Christ's transfiguration into an evolutionary framework. The cosmic, evolutionary extension of the Christian faith and a world-related → spirituality had a marked impact but also came under official condemnation because of the naturalizing of → faith and → grace.

5.3. Hope as History of Freedom

Dialogue between → Marxism and Christianity has made clear the polemical contrast between a gracious, otherworldly consummation and social conflict within history. Liberation is a step toward a more comprehensive redemption (→ Vatican II). Correction of earlier omissions has led to some partial overemphases on the other side (e.g., neglect of the person). Such points, however, must not be condemned as Marxist falsifications, especially as Marxism also maintains an openness to the "new world" (E. Bloch). An "eschatological caveat" (J. B. Metz) rules out any totalitarian anticipation of the → kingdom of God.

The cosmological and political integration of eschatology stood in the climate of an optimistic belief in → progress. The uncertainties (→ Aporia) and antagonisms of natural science, along with political tensions, quickly destroyed this optimism. We cannot overlook the victims of history, the dead and the conquered. Disasters do not fit into naively extended curves of growth. Eschatology must oppose inhuman → anonymity and futurelessness and remember → suffering and the dead. The biblical models of → apocalyptic have taken on new relevance. Hope rests not on immanent future forces but on the resurrection of the dead.

5.4. Traditional Themes in a New Light

The regaining of dialogic relevance has made the problem of identity one of the abiding themes of eschatology. There is eternal life for individuals, yet not apart from social → responsibility, but as the recipients of promise. Links have been sought between individual death and the consummation of the race in order to overcome an anthropomorphic "intermediate state," including the individual manifoldness of the general end of the world, present → resurrection in individual death (L. Boros), and creaturely participation in God's eternity (G. Lohfink). In place of dualistic doctrines of immortality (→ Dualism), a personal core is postulated as the substratum of identity (J. Ratzinger).

The Christological center of eschatology gives priority to → heaven (salvation) over → hell (missed salvation). Even in rejection, judicial encounter with God as a possibility of salvation (→ Last Judgment) is also encompassed by pardoning → love. The → freedom that God respects does not float in a neutral sphere but is taken up into the drama of the descent and resurrection of Christ. Even the remotest resistance is transcended by the nearness of God in Jesus. Hell is not an equal possibility to the promise of salvation, which is greater. → Apocatastasis may be rejected, but it still contains the greater core of the truth of salvation.

Bibliography: H. U. von Balthasar, *Theodramatik,* vol. 4, *Das Endspiel* (Einsiedeln, 1983) • W. Breuning et al., "Die Vollendung der Heilsgeschichte," *MySal* 5.553-890 • G. Greshake and G. Lohfink, *Naherwartung–Auferstehung–Unsterblichkeit* (3d ed.; Freiburg, 1978) • J. Gustafson, *The Mystery of Death: A Catholic Perspective* (Dubuque, Iowa, 1994) • H. Küng, *Eternal Life? Life after Death as a Medical, Philosophical, and Theological Problem* (Garden City, N.Y., 1984) • J. B. Metz, *Glaube in Geschichte und Gesellschaft* (Mainz, 1977) • V. K. Owusu, *The Roman Funeral Liturgy: History, Celebration, and Theology* (Nettetal, 1993) • K. Rahner, *Zur Theologie der Zukunft* (Munich, 1971) • J. Ratzinger, *Eschatologie–Tod und ewiges Leben* (Regensburg, 1977) • A. van de Walle, *Bis zum Anbruch der Morgenröte. Grundriß einer christlichen Eschatologie* (Düsseldorf, 1983) • H. Vorgrimler, *Hoffnung auf Vollendung. Aufriß der Eschatologie* (Freiburg, 1980) • D. Wiederkehr, *Perspektiven der Eschatologie* (Zurich, 1974).

Dietrich Wiederkehr

6. African Christianity

6.1. Christian Eschatology as a New Element in African Thinking

The southern two-thirds of Africa has become predominantly Christian in the 20th century (→ Mission). Here Christianity has found many points of contact with traditional African religion. At the same time, it has introduced new religious elements, one of which is its eschatology. The consideration of time as a component of eschatology, however, poses certain problems, because in the African worldview, time has only two main dimensions: the past and the present, with a short but ever-flowing future. It has no concept of time, history, or the world either coming to an abrupt end or gradually reaching a purposeful goal, or telos. The future is endless, being experienced in the framework of a rhythm of nature (day and night, the seasons), of personal journey (birth, growth, procreation, death, and the hereafter), and of community life (festivals, planting, harvesting, hunting, rituals). In this respect, Christian eschatology has introduced a new set of ideas, and Africans have responded to them selectively, paying more attention to some than to others.

6.2. Christian Hope

The Christian → hope has become a living characteristic of African Christianity. It is expressed in two areas.

6.2.1. There is a strong expectation of an imminent return of Jesus Christ, the end of the world, the creation of new heavens and a new earth, and the establishing of the → kingdom of God, in which → suffering and death are no more (Revelation 21–22; Isa. 65:17; 1 Cor. 15:23-28, 51-55; 2 Pet. 3:10-13, etc.).

Information about the last things is taken from biblical passages and passed on in catechetical and other religious instruction, as well as in sermons, hymns, → prayers, and conversations. The eschatological understanding is characterized by a literal interpretation of the Bible (→ Exegesis, Biblical; Biblical Theology 2.3). Life situations also play a big part in shaping eschatological expectations, for example, the racial oppression associated with apartheid in South Africa (→ Racism), sickness, famine, → war, material need, and modern technological → progress.

6.2.2. Many experience Christian hope through the power of God in their lives. This hope comes in the form of healing of the sick (→ Laying on of Hands), → exorcising of evil spirits (→ Demons), and even (so it is claimed) raising of the dead. Also there are filling with the → Holy Spirit and the experience of Christ's salvation through → baptism and the → Eucharist (H.-J. Becken, K. Enang).

6.2.3. For many African Christians there is still the question of death and the hereafter. It is firmly held that when Christians die they go to → heaven (directly or via purgatory). There, while they wait for the general resurrection at the end of the world, they enjoy already the bliss of heaven. It is often asked, however, what happens in the hereafter to people who died before hearing the → gospel and thus being saved. This is a difficult question. Some Christians hold that such persons perish forever, others that they get a chance in the spirit world to hear the gospel (see 1 Pet. 3:19-20), while still others simply refer the problem to God to solve. The continuation of life after death is a strong element in African religion, and Christian eschatology is interpreted as reaffirming this belief, with the addition that the next life will be either in heaven with God or in hell with the devil. This position has obvious evangelistic implications (→ Evangelism).

6.3. Eschatological and Apocalyptic Texts

6.3.1. Many Bible passages are taken literally as pointing to eschatological promises, including those that are basically apocalyptic, since the Christians typically do not draw any distinction between them. In particular, passages about "the day of the Lord" (Joel 1:15; 2:1-11; Zeph. 1:14-18, etc.), the discourses of Jesus in Matthew 24 and parallels and in John 14, the references in the letters of Paul (e.g., 1 Corinthians 15; 1 Thess. 4:13–5:11) and Peter (2 Pet. 3:3-14), and the Book of Revelation are commonly cited.

Consequently, many Christians take natural phenomena like earthquakes and solar and lunar eclipses, as well as aspects of human history (e.g., "wars and rumors of wars" and the development of means of rapid travel), to be clear signs that the end of the world and the → parousia of the Lord are near. This teaching is repeated in many hymns. Through sermons believers are urged to be ready "to meet the Lord in the air" (1 Thess. 4:17), or sooner through death. → Funeral (§4) services are full of this hope and expectation, namely, that the Lord is near, that the departed are with him and will be resurrected, and that the living perhaps may not die before the Lord returns.

6.3.2. Certain eschatological symbols are cherished and interpreted literally. Thus, heaven has now become a concrete place, the city of God, the home prepared by Jesus for his followers (John 14:1-3). The → paradise lost in Genesis 3 is regained eschatologically in Revelation 21–22; there the water of life (Zech. 14:8; Rev. 22:1) and the tree of life (Rev. 22:2) reappear. Healing is a meaningful symbol, not only for humanity but also for the whole creation (Rom. 8:18-25; Isa. 11:4-9; 65:17-25; Rev. 21:1-4). At the same time, there is hell with its ever-burning fire, reserved for unbelievers and for Satan and Satan's consort. African peoples are very much aware of spiritual realities, which they see caught up in the eschatological drama that is unfolding and will reach a climax at the end of the world.

Christian eschatology has introduced a lengthening of future time into African thought, even if some of that dimension tends toward a form of escapism from this world to the next. Nevertheless, African Christianity is keeping alive the eschatological expectations of NT times. This eschatology is pragmatic more than it is reflective. There is indeed value in moving eschatology from the library shelves and ivory towers to the streets and fields and homes, where most of the Christians live and work.

Bibliography: H.-J. Becken, *Theologie der Heilung. Das Heilen in den Unabhängigen Kirchen in Südafrika* (Hermannsburg, 1972) • T. G. Christensen, *An African Tree of Life* (Maryknoll, N.Y., 1990) • K. Enang, *Salvation in a Nigerian Background* (Berlin, 1979) • J. S. Mbiti, "Eschatologie und Jenseits," *Theologie und Kirche in Afrika* (ed. H. Bürkle; Stuttgart, 1968) 211-35; idem, "Eschatology," *Biblical Revelation and African Beliefs* (ed. K. A. Dickson and P. Ellingworth; London, 1969) 159-84; idem, *NT Eschatology in an African Background* (Oxford, 1978) • J. I. Smith and Y. Y. Hadad, *The Islamic Understanding of Death and Resurrection* (Albany, N.Y., 1981).

JOHN MBITI

7. Dogmatics

7.1. *Theological Order*

In a Christian sense, eschatology is fundamentally more than a last chapter in the dogmatic system. "From first to last, and not merely in the epilogue, Christianity is eschatology, is → hope, forward looking and forward moving, and therefore also revolutionizing and transforming the present" (J. Moltmann, 16). Eschatology is a pervasive dimension of theology. The *theos* of biblical theology is the "eschatological → God," the God of promise, the God who comes. So too is the biblical *logos*. The biblical concept of → truth is oriented primarily, not to the disclosure or illumination of being (*alētheia*), but to the promise and to demonstrating the faithfulness (*'emet*) of the Last One. A church that sees itself in this light does not regard itself as a closed society of those who possess the truth but as a pilgrim community with a missionary task in the world (→ Mission).

7.2. *Basic Theme*

The basic theme of eschatology is "the future of him who has come" (W. Kreck). Eschatology is not free-ranging thinking but a discipline anchored in the history of Jesus Christ. This characteristic distinguishes it from its sister, → apocalyptic. Eschatology is exegesis of the present in terms of the future; apocalyptic is eisegesis of the future into the present (K. Rahner, 43). Qualifying our present, the history of Jesus is regarded by the NT as eschatological and definitive. In → Jesus Christ the OT promises are fulfilled already (Luke 4:18-19). In him the → kingdom of God has drawn near (Mark 1:15) and is indeed already "among you" (Luke 17:21). Thus the end time has now begun. It is not an open, ambivalent, or obscure matter. It is decisively characterized by the words, deeds, → suffering, and especially → resurrection of Jesus. Here is the climax of the history of God's kingdom, which in the life of Jesus is powerfully attested to be a history of God's solidarity with us in life and death. Thus at the end of the NT, from the midst of the New Jerusalem, in a summing up of eschatological hope, there rings out a clear voice that promises this consummation: the wiping away of tears, the satisfying of the thirst for → righteousness, and the overcoming of death — and thus the perfecting of fellowship, of the → covenant of God with us and us with God (Rev. 21:1-7).

7.3. *Themes and Hermeneutics*

These basic themes of eschatology are filled with tension. Fundamental to eschatological thinking is the tension between the "already" and the "not yet" of the salvation enclosed in Christ's history. As regards our situation as affected by Christ's resurrection, the NT has two emphases: "The present dawn of the kingdom of God is always spoken of so as to show that the present reveals the future as salvation and judgment, and therefore does not anticipate it. Again, the future is always spoken of as unlocking and lighting up the present, and therefore revealing today as the day of decision" (G. Bornkamm, 92). The one-sided options of a present, realized eschatology (C. H. Dodd, R. Bultmann) and of a consistently future eschatology (M. Werner, F. Buri) are simplistic. Similar attempts should be avoided in relation to specific eschatological themes. Here again we come up against tension-laden statements. Is there continuity or discontinuity between → time and eternity? Is the parousia the end or the goal of history? Is the triumph of the last day one of judgment or one of → grace (→ Last Judgment)? Is there ultimate reconciliation (→ Apocatastasis) or a twofold outcome? Biblical verses can be found to support both alternatives in each case. Does this mean that eschatology is a hermeneutical maze? Not at all, if we do not regard the statements as static but as motivating hints in the light of Christ's history. Luther's old hermeneutical principle of "what promotes Christ" might well prove to be the best in a hermeneutics of eschatological motifs.

7.4. *Eschatology and Ethics*

With its horizon of liberation and decision, biblical eschatology finds an important place for ethical demonstration (→ Ethics). The NT indicative is surprisingly closely linked to the eschatological imperative. If it enjoins an existential desecularizing, having as though we had not (see 1 Cor. 7:29), it also gives power for → discipleship (Romans 12–13). Ethics shows us what eschatology means for faith. A faith that leaves the future empty or speaks of it only negatively is in danger of leaving ethics empty as well. But a faith that reckons realistically with the fact that the life of Jesus Christ will glorify itself in our mortal bodies can see this earthly, bodily life only in the light of the Coming One and consider how our concrete acts can bear witness to this Coming One (W. Kreck, 175). This attitude is the basis, not only of the personal → responsibility of Christians, but also of their social and, finally, their cosmic responsibility. The NT expresses the eschatological hope in such images and concepts as kingdom, city, new heaven and new earth, and new creation. Clearly, then, the eschatological promise does not relate merely to the salvation of our souls. We must demonstrate and practice it in → solidarity with other people and with all our fellow creatures (Rom. 8:19-25).

Bibliography: J. BAILLIE, *And the Life Everlasting* (Oxford, 1934) • H. U. VON BALTHASAR, "Eschatologie," *Fragen der Theologie heute* (ed. J. Feiner, J. Trütsch, and F. Böckle; Zurich, 1957); idem, "Eschatologie im Umriß," *Skizzen zur Theologie* (vol. 4; Einsiedeln, 1974) • K. BARTH, *The Epistle to the Romans* (Oxford, 1933) • J. BLANCHARD, *Whatever Happened to Hell?* (Darlington, 1993) • G. BORNKAMM, *Jesus of Nazareth* (New York, 1960) • J. BOWKER, *The Meanings of Death* (Cambridge, 1991) • M. BULL, ed., *Apocalypse Theory and the Ends of the World* (Oxford, 1995) • R. BULTMANN, *History and Eschatology* (Edinburgh, 1957) • O. CULLMANN, *Christ and Time* (2d ed.; Philadelphia, 1964) • J. DAVIES, ed., *Ritual and Remembrance: Responses to Death in Human Societies* (Sheffield, 1994) • F. M. KAMM, *Morality, Mortality*, vol. 1, *Death and Whom to Save from It* (New York, 1993) • W. KRECK, *Die Zukunft des Gekommenen. Grundprobleme der Eschatologie* (2d ed.; Munich, 1966) • E. KUNZ, *Protestantische Eschatologie von der Reformation bis zur Aufklärung* (Freiburg, 1980) • J. L. KVANVIG, *The Problem of Hell* (New York, 1993) • J. B. METZ, *Glaube in Geschichte und Gesellschaft* (Mainz, 1977) • J. MOLTMANN, *Theology of Hope* (Minneapolis, 1993) • R. NIEBUHR, *The Nature and Destiny of Man* (vol. 2; New York, 1943) • K. RAHNER, *Zur Theologie der Zukunft* (Munich, 1971) • J. RATZINGER, *Eschatologie–Tod und ewiges Leben* (Regensburg, 1977) • G. J. RILEY, *Resurrection Reconsidered: Thomas and John in Controversy* (Minneapolis, 1995) • P. SCHÄFER, *Eschatologie. Trient und Gegenreformation* (Freiburg, 1984) • H. SCHWARZ, *Eschatology* (Grand Rapids, 2000) • A. SCHWEITZER, *The Quest of the Historical Jesus* (2d ed.; New York, 1968) • R. SMEND et al., "Eschatologie," *TRE* 10.254-363 (bibliography) • F. J. TIPLER, *The Physics of Immortality* (New York, 1994) • A. K. TURNER, *The History of Hell* (London, 1995) • G. WAINWRIGHT, *Eucharist and Eschatology* (London, 1971; 2d ed., 1981) • WORLD COUNCIL OF CHURCHES, *The Christian Hope and the Task of the Church* (New York, 1954) report of the 1954 Evanston Assembly.

JAN MILIČ LOCHMAN

Esotericism

In antiquity the word "esoteric" was used for knowledge that was imparted only to an inner circle of fully initiated students, while "exoteric" denoted that which in principle was accessible to everybody. In a broader sense the esoteric soon became anything that is entrusted only to a select group on the basis of certain qualities. In contrast to secret societies, whose very existence is meant to be secret, such a circle is a nonsecret order or group that guards a secret. We find such circles in all cultures in the cultic field, as well as philosophical and, increasingly, political fields.

Whereas in modern usage the adjective "esoteric" may be used for anything that is not accessible to the public at large, in practice the derived noun "esotericism" has come to be equated with → occultism, a new term for → magic without the connotation of dealings with the → devil. In the widest sense esotericism presupposes that alongside objective things that we try to explain rationally and scientifically there are hidden forces at work in us and the world that transcend normal sensory → experience and causal analytic thinking. Since the religions, especially the higher and universal religions, postulate reciprocal dealings between us and the supersensory, they must be grouped to some extent under esotericism (→ Religion).

There is the profound difference, however, insofar as although the historical religions admit the inadequacy of all concepts and ideas (→ Negative Theology), esoterics view these religions as part of the sphere of the exoteric — of letter, → allegory, and scholasticism, invoking instead the spirit as expressed in a fundamentally ambivalent → symbol, a spirit that can never be articulated exhaustively.

Through often unrestricted association and analogy they bring out the relations that supposedly obtain between things, though we may not be able to conceive of them in terms of time and space, and they seek access thereby to the deepest meaning of the world. In religions more strongly tied to dogma they also feel justified in stressing points neglected or totally ignored in the official → confessions.

Often the search for → truth beyond → dogma leads to the forming of special societies directed in many cases against exoteric groups, though even in the West esotericism involves more than sects or heresies. Distinctions in the exoteric that esotericism opposes means that esotericism is ultimately not homogeneous; it might embrace, for example, in Western esotericism and in the official Eastern confessions, transmigration of souls, divine immediacy, or the divine likeness of the → soul. The only typical thing is the striving by way of secret relations to overcome existing institutional structures and to set up an invisible fellowship of believers. The justification and danger of esotericism lie in this transcending of everyday reality and experience (→ Everyday Life) in the religious field. Only a fine line separates the desired vanquishing of rigidity and the undesired relapse into uncritical fantasizing.

Bibliography: A. Baldwin, ed., *Platonism and the English Imagination* (Cambridge, 1994) • A. Faivre, "Esotericism," *EncRel(E)* 5.156-63 • P. Kingsley, *Ancient Philosophy: Mystery and Magic* (Oxford, 1995) • H. E. Miers, *Lexikon des Geheimwissens* (3d ed.; Munich, 1980) • A. W. Price, *Mental Conflict: Issues in Ancient Philosophy* (London, 1995) • A. Tiryakian, ed., *On the Margin of the Visible: Sociology, the Esoteric, and the Occult* (New York, 1974) • P. Zauker, *The Mask of Socrates: The Image of the Intellectual in Antiquity* (Berkeley, Calif., 1995).

Karl Hoheisel

Essenes → Qumran

EST

Widespread in the United States and the German-speaking world (where, since 1985, it has been known as the Forum or Center Leadership Program), EST, or Erhard Seminars Training, was founded in 1971 by Werner Hans Erhard (Jack Rosenberg). The program and its offshoots involve intensive courses partly based on Erhard's experiences in Scientology (→ Church of Scientology)

and an experience of illumination by means of two 34-hour workshops. The aim is to stop being a victim and to become one's own boss. The procedure is to break down the participants psychologically so that they will let themselves be reconstructed by the trainers.

EST is not compatible with Christian → anthropology. Responsibility for others is rejected because each must create his or her own universe. Thus the member is his or her own god, restricted only by EST rituals. EST is an extreme example within the cults or → youth religions of an authoritarian group oriented to economic success.

Among the offshoots and organizations of EST was the hunger program, which tried to impart the idea that hunger could be banished by the end of the second millennium. Ministry Workshop and Mastery Foundation are designed to reach the clergy of the different denominations.

Bibliography: R. Bach and H. Molter, *Psychoboom* (Cologne, 1976) • S. S. Mosatche, *Searching* (New York, 1983) • M. T. Singer, with J. Lalich, *Cults in Our Midst* (San Francisco, 1995).

Thomas Gandow

Esther, Book of

The Book of Esther, whose canonicity was long contested, was one of the last writings among the five → Megilloth to be taken up into the Kethubim (writings) of the Palestinian → canon. Telling the story of the origin of the Feast of Purim (*pur* = "lot"), the book is a Jewish variation on the novel of antiquity (cf. Judith in the → Apocrypha). In content it validates the Jewish → diaspora as a guarantee of the Persian Empire.

Esther, the ward of Mordecai, who had been deported (in 598 B.C., on one reading of Esth. 2:6), comes with other virgins (her origins are unknown) to the court of Ahasuerus, or Xerxes I (486-465), as a replacement for his wife Vashti, who has been put away for disobedience. At about this time Mordecai saves the king by uncovering a plot on his life (chaps. 1-2). The opponent of Mordecai, the vizier Haman, is angered when Mordecai refuses to do obeisance to him. Haman then decides to destroy all Jewish people throughout the whole empire, choosing by lot the 13th day of the 12th month, Adar, as the time of destruction (chap. 3). Mordecai asks Esther to intervene, though this step will involve her in danger. Her intervention brings things to a head. She is permitted by the king to hold two banquets for the king and Haman. After the first, Haman determines to ask the king for the execution of Mordecai (chaps. 4–5). This decision, however, coincides with the king's recollection that he has not yet rewarded the person who saved his life. The king then orders Haman to give to Mordecai the honors that Haman expected for himself (chap. 6). At the second banquet Esther's accusation seals Haman's fate. Haman begs Esther for mercy, but the king sees Haman's behavior as an assault on his queen. The gallows that Haman had already set up for Mordecai become his own place of execution (chap. 7). Esther inherits Haman's possessions, and Mordecai his office (8:1-2). The 13th and 14th of Adar are no longer days of pogrom, as Haman had intended, but days of Israel's revenge on its enemies throughout the Persian Empire. The 14th of Adar becomes a feast day for the Israelites in the provinces, the 15th for the Israelites in Susa (chaps. 9-10).

The Book of Esther is the oldest record of hatred of the Jews in the narrower sense of dislike because the Jews are different on the basis of their → law (Esth. 3:8; → Anti-Semitism, Anti-Judaism). Whether the book comes from the Persian period is debated (cf. Ezra 4:15, 19). The terminus ante quem for "Mordecai's day" is 2 Maccabees (15:36). Accusations from outside Israel are perhaps the reason why the theologoumenon of retributive justice is presented in Esther without mention of God (note "from another quarter," 4:14). Only the Greek translation and the (originally Greek) additions interpret the text according to its original sense, introducing "God" or "Lord" several times and identifying Israel's enemy Haman with Persia's enemy the Macedonians (Add. Esth. E14).

Bibliography: Commentaries: H. BARDTKE (KAT; Leipzig, 1965) • G. GERLEMAN (BKAT; Neukirchen, 1973) • M. HALLER (HAT; Tübingen, 1940) • C. A. MOORE (AB; Garden City, N.Y., 1971) • H. RINGGREN (ATD; Göttingen, 1958; 3d ed., 1981).

Other works: A. BRUNNER, ed., *A Feminist Companion to Esther, Judith, and Susanna* (Sheffield, 1995) • D. J. A. CLINES, *The Esther Scroll: The Story of the Story* (Sheffield, 1984) • K. M. CRAIG, *Reading Esther: A Case for the Literary Carnivalesque* (Louisville, Ky., 1995) • L. DAY, *Three Faces of a Queen: Characterization in the Books of Esther* (Sheffield, 1995) • M. V. FOX, *Character and Ideology in the Book of Esther* (Columbia, S.C., 1991) • H. M. J. GEVARYAHU, "Esther Is a Story of Jewish Defense Not a Story of Jewish Revenge," *JBQ* 21 (1993) 3-12 • W. HARRELSON, "Textual and Translation Problems in the Book of Esther," *PRSt* 17/3 (1990) 197-208 • M. HELTZER, "The Book of Esther–Where Does Fiction Start and History End?" *BibRev* 8 (1992) 24-30 • R. LUBITCH, "A Feminist's Look at Esther," *Jdm* 42 (1993) 438-46 • C. A. MOORE, *Studies in the Book of Esther* (New York, 1982) • I. J. MOSALA, "The Implication of the Text of Esther for African Women's Struggle for Liberation in South Africa," *Semeia* 59 (1992) 129-37 • A. M. RODRIGUEZ, *Esther: A Theological Approach* (Berrien Springs, Mich., 1995) • B. D. WOLFISH, *Esther in Medieval Garb: Jewish Interpretation of Esther in the Middle Ages* (Albany, N.Y., 1993).

ROBERT HANHART

Estonia

	1960	1980	2000
Population (1,000s):	1,216	1,473	1,418
Annual growth rate (%):	1.20	0.62	−0.63

Area: 45,227 sq. km. (17,462 sq. mi.)

A.D. 2000

Population density: 31/sq. km. (81/sq. mi.)
Births / deaths: 0.94 / 1.35 per 100 population
Fertility rate: 1.30 per woman
Infant mortality rate: 10 per 1,000 live births
Life expectancy: 70.6 years (m: 65.3, f: 75.8)
Religious affiliation (%): Christians 63.5 (Orthodox 22.6, unaffiliated 21.8, Protestants 17.6, other Christians 1.5), nonreligious 26.1, atheists 9.9, other 0.5.

1. General Situation
2. Christian Churches
   2.1. Orthodox
   2.2. Lutheran
   2.3. Evangelical Christian and Baptist Union
   2.4. Others
3. Interchurch Relations
4. Non-Christian Religions
5. Church and State

1. General Situation

Estonia, situated on the eastern littoral of the Baltic Sea, is bordered by Latvia on the south and Russia on the east. It is a democratic, parliamentary republic, holding membership in the → United Nations, the Council of Europe, and the Organization for Security and Cooperation in Europe. Ethnically, 61.5 percent of the people in 1995 were Estonians (vs. 88.2 percent in 1934), 30.3 percent Russians (vs. 8.2 percent in 1934), 3.1 percent Ukrainians, 1.2 percent Belarusians, 1.0 percent Finns, and 2.9 other groups.

As a result of an invasion of German merchants and knights (the Knights of the Sword, later the Teutonic Order) around the turn of the 13th century, the Estonians were forcibly brought under German rule. Later, from 1629 to 1721, the Estonians were part of Sweden-Finland, then from 1721 to 1918, part of the Russian Empire. Baltic German elite, however, played a dominant role in Estonian social life till the end of the 19th century. The modern-day capital, Tallinn (*Taani linn,* "Danish castle"), opposite Helsinki on the Gulf of Finland, was established when Danes ruled the northern part of the territory in the 13th and 14th centuries. The University of Tartu was founded by Swedes in 1632.

The Estonian national awakening began in the 1860s, first with cultural emphases, later with political. Estonia achieved its independence in February 1918, soon after the October 1917 revolution in Russia, with the present borders of the country dating from 1920. In August 1939 Nazi Germany and the Soviet Union signed a treaty of nonaggression, and then in June 1940 the Soviet Union forcibly annexed Estonia. Germany occupied the country in 1941, only to lose it back to the Soviets in 1944. Finally, in August 1991, Estonia was able to declare its independence restored. Since then it has initiated democratic reforms and a shift to a market economy.

2. Christian Churches

The Christian presence in Estonia, arriving from the East via trade routes, dates from the turn of the second millennium. The most significant influences on the Christianization of the Baltic region were the German and Danish invasions and the evangelization (→ Evangelism) initiated by the Western church in 1196. In 1215 Pope → Innocent III dedicated the Baltic mission field to the Virgin → Mary, calling it Maarjamaa (the land of Mary). Until the 20th century, the ecclesiastical and social life of Estonia was influenced most heavily by relations with the German upper class.

The → Reformation spread to the Baltic area beginning in the 1520s. The → Lutheran Church was established in Livonia and Estonia under Swedish rule in the 17th century, with Swedish church law in force from 1692/94 to 1832. The first translation of the Bible into Estonian was published in 1739 (→ Bible Versions 4). In the 1730s the → Moravian Brethren traveled to the Baltic countries from Herrnhut in Germany and subsequently exercised a significant influence on the spiritual and social awakening of the Estonian peasants. This movement, which remained influential in northern Estonia until the beginning of the 20th century, remained primarily within the Lutheran Church.

The influence of the Eastern church was at first limited to the area of Setumaa in southeastern Esto-

nia, where the Setus, a people closely related to the Estonians, embraced the Orthodox faith (→ Orthodox Church). Until the 19th century, Russian immigrants represented the largest number of Estonian Orthodox believers. During the period 1840-80, however, great numbers of Estonians converted to Orthodoxy for social and political reasons (→ Conversion 2).

2.1. Orthodox

In 1996 there were 84 Orthodox congregations, divided between those under the jurisdiction of the Estonian Orthodox Church (EOC) and those under the Russian Orthodox Church (ROC). Approximately two-thirds of Estonian Orthodox identify with the ROC, one-third with the EOC.

During the period of czarist rule, the Estonian Orthodox were part of the Moscow → Patriarchate. Shortly after the beginning of the first period of independence, however, the Orthodox community in Estonia placed itself under the → jurisdiction of the Patriarchate of Constantinople, which granted the church autonomy in 1923. At that time approximately 80 percent of church members were Estonian, as were the majority of the clergy. In 1941, by order of the Soviet government, the church was reunited with the Patriarchate of Moscow. By the end of the Soviet period, over half of the Estonian Orthodox were Russians.

At the end of the 1980s some of the Estonian Orthodox began to push for a severing of ties with the Moscow Patriarchate and for a restoration of autonomy under Constantinople's jurisdiction. The situation led in early 1996 to a temporary rupture in communion between the Patriarchates of Moscow and Constantinople — Moscow viewed the Estonians as historically and rightfully related to the Church of Russia, with the tie to Constantinople since 1923 a temporary expedient only; for its part, Constantinople wished to return the Estonian church to autonomy under its oversight, the status quo ante. The patriarchates ended the ecclesiastical crisis by agreeing that each Estonian → congregation should decide for itself which jurisdiction it wished to affiliate with. Congregations that sought autonomy (i.e., alignment with Constantinople) were temporarily assigned to the care of Archbishop John of the Orthodox Church of Finland. In the spring of 1999 the Patriarchate of Constantinople nominated a metropolitan of "Tallinn and All Estonia" to lead the EOC.

2.2. Lutheran

The Lutherans, who represent over 80 percent of all Protestants in Estonia, have since 1919 been organized as the Estonian Evangelical Lutheran Church

(EELC). Previously, Estonian Lutherans were part of the Evangelical Lutheran Church in Russia, a kind of state church dominated by Germans. The new Estonian church leaders emphasized the nature of the EELC as a "free folk church in free Estonia," thus distancing themselves from the former "masters' church," led by the German elite. The EELC had German and Swedish deaneries until World War II, when the minority groups emigrated. In 1996 it had 168 congregations (190 in 1937), with approximately 170,000 members. The church order (1991) is episcopal-synodic, with the archbishop, assisted by a → bishop, the chairman of the church's executive body. Reform of the church order was begun in 1997.

The EELC has established children's and youth work, social and diaconal services, → pastoral care in hospitals and prisons, and publishing activities. Home and foreign → missions were organized in 1996. The Estonian Seamen's Mission and the Estonian Church Railroad Workers Association each have ties with the EELC. It publishes the newspaper *Eesti Kirik* (The Church of Estonia) and the children's magazine *Laste sõber* (The children's friend). It also sponsors two educational institutions in Tallinn: the Theological Institute and the Diaconal School of Tallinn.

Within the EELC, confessional Lutheranism, interconfessional pietism, American-style → evangelism, and Roman Catholic–influenced clericalism exist side by side. In the 1990s the → Taizé Community had a notable influence on Estonian young people.

During World War II Lutheran refugees from Estonia to the West founded a church in exile — the Estonian Evangelical Lutheran Church Abroad, now based in Canada. In 1996 it included 63 congregations in the United States, Canada, Sweden, Germany, France, United Kingdom, Australia, and Argentina. Since 1991 this group and the EELC have held negotiations with regard to reunification. The two churches use the same → hymnal and prayer book (published in 1991) and are in the process of preparing a new church constitution.

2.3. Evangelical Christian and Baptist Union

Estonia's first → Baptist and → free churches were established in the 1880s in the western parts of the country, the fruits of a local evangelical revival. Important in this development were influences from Germany and Sweden (esp. the → pietism, or so-called new evangelicalism, of the Swedish lay preacher Carl Olof Rosenius [1816-68]). Later, during the Soviet period, government authorities forced the Baptist and Evangelical Christian congregations to unite with those of the → Pentecostals. With the relaxing of religious policy at the end of the Soviet era, the Union of Evangelical Christian and Baptist Churches of Estonia (ECB Union) was formed in 1989. (In 1991 the Pentecostals founded their own church.)

The ECB Union engages in organized children's and → youth work and social efforts, sponsors what is now the Theological Seminary of the ECB Union in Tartu (closed 1940-89), and publishes a newspaper and children's magazine. In 1996 it included 6,200 members in 87 congregations.

2.4. Others

Several other Christian groups are organized in Estonia, each claiming less than 1 percent of the population.

The → *Roman Catholic Church in Estonia* comprises seven congregations belonging to the Archdiocese of Lithuania. Religious → orders working with the church include → Dominicans, → Franciscans, Marianists, Brigittine Sisters, and Mother Teresa's Missionaries of Charity.

The *United → Methodist Church in Estonia* has 21 congregations and a membership of approximately 1,800. The first Methodist congregation in the country was founded in 1910, with the church organized in 1935. The UMCE sponsors the Baltic Mission Center Theological Seminary in Tallinn.

The *Estonian Conference of Seventh-day → Adventists,* founded in 1917, has 18 congregations (one in Canada), with a membership of approximately 2,000.

The *Estonian Christian Pentecostal Church,* founded in 1991 (and until 1993 known as the Estonian Christian Church), has 40 congregations and a membership of 4,000. The church operates a Bible college and maintains social work and a prison pastoral ministry.

In 1993 the → *Armenian Apostolic Church in Estonia* founded the Congregation of St. Gregory in Tallinn, which has approximately 1,500 members.

Other Christian groups registered with the government include the Estonian Charismatic Episcopal Church, Evangelical Church of the Brethren, Neo-Apostolic Church, Quakers, Union of Christian Free Churches, Union of Evangelical Charismatic Churches, Union of Full Gospel Churches, and Union of Old Believers Congregations. The largest marginal Christian groups are the Union of Jehovah's Witnesses' Assemblies in Estonia and the Mormon Church. In addition, the Estonian Bible Society, Salvation Army, Tallinn City Mission, YMCA, and YWCA — all founded (or refounded) after 1988 — are active in Estonia.

3. Interchurch Relations

The two Estonian Lutheran churches — the EELC and the EELC Abroad — are members of the → World Council of Churches. The EELC also is a member of the → Lutheran World Federation and the → Conference of European Churches (CEC). In 1996 it signed the Porvoo Declaration, which aims at promoting full communion among British and Irish Anglicans and Baltic and Nordic Lutherans. In the 1990s the EELC also established close ties with its sister churches, especially in Finland, Germany, and Sweden.

Other Estonian Protestant groups are also members of international groups: the ECB Union, with the European Baptist Federation and the Baptist World Alliance; the United Methodist Church, with the CEC, the World Methodist Council, and the North European Central Conference of United Methodist Churches; and the Seventh-day Adventists, with the Baltic Union of Seventh-Day Adventists.

The Estonian Council of Churches (ECC), active since 1989, comprises the ECB Union, EELC, Methodists, Orthodox churches (inactive since their recent dispute), Pentecostals, and Roman Catholics. The Seventh-day Adventists and the Armenian Apostolic Church are observer-members of the council. Within the framework of the ECC, the churches have agreed on religious education in the schools, pastoral care in prisons, and the work of Christian radio and TV stations.

4. Non-Christian Religions

By 1997 the following non-Christian groups had registered with the government: the Jewish Community of Estonia, the Union of Jewish Congregations and Organizations, the Islamic Community and Trust of Estonia, a Baha'i assembly, a Hare Krishna group, and the Sathya Sai Baba Association. Traditional Estonian pagan beliefs are represented by two small groups: Taarausulised (worshipers of Taara [from Thor, Norse god of thunder]) and Maausulised (worshipers of the earth).

5. Church and State

At Estonia's independence in 1918, → church and state were separated. Religious education in the schools was at first abolished but then was restored by referendum in 1923. In 1934 virtually all of the Estonian population belonged to Christian churches. The Lutheran Church (then 78 percent of the population) and the Orthodox Church (19 percent) were → people's churches.

During the Soviet period church services plus certain ecclesiastical rites and ceremonies were the only permitted church activities. Church property was na-

tionalized, and church-related organizations, including schools, were closed. Between 1958 and 1964 → atheism was actively promoted and some churches were closed. Estonia became a kind of proving ground for the atheistic rites that the Soviet Union introduced for the purpose of alienating people from Christianity. Toward the end of the 1980s, however, the Estonian church began to recover, as Soviet religious policy was liberalized and foreign contacts were allowed. Church property began to be returned.

The 1992 constitution guarantees freedom of religion, conscience, and thought, with the government neither restricting nor favoring the activities of any denomination. According to the Law on Churches and Congregations of May 1993, all religious organizations operating in Estonia must register with the Ministry of Internal Affairs in order to have legal rights, including the right to own property. By early 1997 a total of 116 religious groups had registered, in the following categories: 14 assemblies and church unions (12 of them Christian), 67 independent congregations (57 Christian), and 35 religious associations (32 Christian).

In Estonian public schools religion is taught as an optional, extra subject. The state university at Tartu has an ecumenical Faculty of Theology. In hospitals, educational establishments, penal institutions, the armed forces, and other public institutions, work of a spiritual nature can be offered, as long as it is received voluntarily. The state pays the salaries of military chaplains.

Bibliography: E. BRYNER, "Die autonomen Orthodoxen Kirchen in Finland, Estland und Lettland. Die estnische Orthodoxe Kirche," *Die Ostkirchen vom 18. bis zum 20. Jahrhundert* (Leipzig, 1996) 113-14 • *Estonian Human Development Report, 1997* (Tallinn, 1997) • J. HIDEN and P. SALMAN, *The Baltic Nations and Europe: Estonia, Latvia, and Lithuania in the Twentieth Century* (London, 1996) • J. KIIVIT JR., "Rückkehr aus dem Schweigen. Die Evangelisch-lutherische Kirche Estlands. Gedanken über die Aufgaben von morgen," *JMLB* 38 (1991) 99-118 • D. KIRBY, *The Baltic World, 1772-1993: Europe's Northern Periphery in an Age of Change* (London, 1995) • T. PAUL, *Kulturelle und kirchliche Identität mit Estland der Gegenwart. Kirchen im Kontext unterschiedlicher Kulturen auf dem Weg in das dritte Jahrtausend* (Göttingen, 1991) • T. U. RAUN, *Estonia and the Estonians* (2d ed.; Stanford, Calif., 1991) • G. SMITH, ed., *The National Self-Determination of Estonia, Latvia, and Lithuania* (New York, 1996) • *We Bless You from the House of the Lord: Estonian Evangelical Lutheran Church Today* (Tallinn, 1997).

AARNO LAHTINEN

Eternity → Time and Eternity

Ethics

Overview
1. Philosophical Ethics
    1.1. Term
    1.2. Relation of Ethics and Religion,
        and Validity of Philosophical Ethics
    1.3. The Question of the Good
        and Its Change of Form
    1.4. Questions of Legitimacy
        and Detailed Points
    1.5. Ethics, Morality, and Regional
        Moral Codes
2. OT Ethics
    2.1. Theological Influences
    2.2. The Collective Context
    2.3. Legal Codes
    2.4. Individual Modifications
    2.5. Areas of Ethical Concern
3. NT Ethics
    3.1. Basis
    3.2. Jesus
    3.3. Synoptic Gospels and Acts
    3.4. Paul
    3.5. Later Writings
    3.6. Johannine Writings
    3.7. Relevance of NT Ethics
4. Ethics in Roman Catholic Theology
5. Feminist Ethics
6. History of Christian Ethics
    6.1. Present Situation in Research
    6.2. Development
7. Tasks of Theological Ethics
    7.1. Term and Tasks
    7.2. Dogmatics and Ethics
    7.3. Bible and Ethics
    7.4. Ethics and Ecumenism
    7.5. Ethics and the Religions

Overview

One may rightly ask whether Jews and Christians really have an ethics per se. For them the law of the Lord is perfect, "reviving the soul" and "making wise the simple" (Ps. 19:7; see also Psalm 119). The Jews carefully expound and specify this law in the → Talmud, while Christians see it fulfilled in the risen Lord and find in it an offer of comprehensive freedom and direction. Theologians have made this point, especially when criticizing systems of ethics. Yet believers in every age have theorized about their conduct and formed ethical systems, often approxi-

mating to existing ethical teachings. In the Hebrew Bible we find the influence of the wisdom of Egypt and other foreign lands (→ Wisdom Literature). The NT contains selective adjustments to the rules of → Stoic ethics. In the → early church we detect considerable similarities to Platonic and Neoplatonic ethical ideals (→ Platonism). Then in the Middle Ages the rediscovered philosophy of Aristotle (→ Aristotelianism) was embraced. John → Calvin adopted Stoic ethics (→ Calvin's Theology), and later theology wrestled with the philosophical ethics and legal systems of the various epochs.

It is not surprising, then, that theological ethics has largely taken over the distinctions and divisions of philosophy, of which the following have proved useful:
1. *Descriptive ethics* is a scientific analysis, description, and comparison of ethical phenomena, problems, and solutions. The process may be historical, phenomenological, or socioethnological.
2. *Normative ethics,* in contrast, is the philosophical or theological development of guidelines, goals, orientations, and principles (→ norms) for dealing with actual ethical problems in concrete individual or social life. (The difference between descriptive and normative ethics is often overlooked in ethical arguments.)
3. *Metaethics* has been used over the past few decades for the scientific discussion of the conditions of ethical discourse. It is essential in both philosophical and theological ethics because it investigates the relation between (1) and (2) and reflects on the possibilities of (2). Insofar as it tries to replace (2), however, metaethics lays itself open to a charge of academic irresponsibility.

We may also note the following types of ethics. An ethics that rests on binding principles ("Never lie") is called *deontological* ethics (→ Deontology). An ethics that is oriented to a goal regarded as ethically good ("Always be of service to your neighbor") is called *teleological* ethics. I. Kant (1724-1804) used the term "*autonomous* ethics" for a rationally self-determined ethics (→ Autonomy), while an ethics that is dependent on something outside is *heteronomous.* (Only in appearance does all theological ethics come under this rubric.) The philosophical distinction between *formal* and *material* ethics also has limited significance in theological ethics, perhaps even in the observation that Protestant ethics inclines to the formal side and Roman Catholic ethics (→ Moral Theology) to the material side (though these fronts are becoming less distinct today).

Theological ethics also lists types according to where one locates the center of ethical argument (e.g., in values, dispositions, or → responsibility). In a complex way these centers overlap classical theological arguments for or against an ethics of rules (whether these rules be known or discernible from God's direct command or from → natural law) and also the various foundations traditionally suggested for theological ethics, including the Bible (→ Biblicism), the Ten Commandments (→ Decalogue; Parenesis), → discipleship (or imitation) of Christ, the operation of the → Holy Spirit, the teaching and → authority of the → church, and the hope of setting up God's kingdom and righteousness (→ Kingdom of God). All these are legitimate emphases in theological ethics, though when isolated and absolutized they have led to the formation of denominations, schools, and sects.

Theological ethics can no longer make much of the distinction between *personal* and → *social* ethics except for the staking out of different problems. Again, differentiation between "ethics" as reflective and "morality" as the universal determinative for action, especially in the confused discussion of the term "ethics," is no longer clear-cut and thus no longer useful in modern discussion.

Today constructive and influential work in theological ethics is done less in the books of single authors (who, apart from the German A. → Schweitzer and the American Reinhold → Niebuhr, were never very influential in Protestant discussion) and more by groups, → church conference centers, working fellowships, the commissions of the → World Council of Churches, and → base communities and protesting groups (whose work is often not published). Serious sociopolitical problems (→ Political Theology), new insights into → ecology and responsibility for the → environment, and the tasks of → medical ethics, both in industrialized nations and the so-called → Third World, pose tasks for the → church and theological ethics for which they have as yet no adequate resources.

Bibliography: F. Böckle, *Fundamental Moral Theology* (New York, 1980) • J. Fischer, *Handlungsfelder angewandter Ethik* (Stuttgart, 1998); idem, *Leben aus dem Geist. Zur Grundlegung christlicher Ethik* (Zurich, 1994) • W. K. Frankena, *Ethics* (Englewood Cliffs, N.J., 1963) • V. Guroian, *Ethics after Christendom: Toward an Ecclesial Christian Ethic* (Grand Rapids, 1994); idem, *Incarnate Love: Essays in Orthodox Ethics* (Notre Dame, Ind., 1987) • J. Gustafson, *Can Ethics Be Christian?* (Chicago, 1975) • S. S. Harakas, *Toward Transfigured Life: The Theoria of Eastern Orthodox Ethics* (Minneapolis, 1983) • J. E. Hare, *The Moral Gap* (Oxford, 1997) • S. Hauerwas, *A Community of Character: To-ward a Constructive Christian Social Ethics* (3d ed.; Notre Dame, Ind., 1983); idem, *The Peaceable Kingdom: A Primer in Christian Ethics* (Notre Dame, Ind., 1983); idem, *Truthfulness and Tragedy: Further Investigations into Christian Ethics* (Notre Dame, Ind., 1977) • A. Hertz et al., eds., *HCE* • P. L. Lehmann, *Ethics in a Christian Context* (New York, 1963) • R. Niebuhr, *An Interpretation of Christian Ethics* (2d ed.; San Francisco, 1963; orig. pub., 1935) • O. O'Donovan, *Resurrection and Moral Order* (Grand Rapids, 1986) • G. H. Outka and P. Ramsey, eds., *Norm and Context in Christian Ethics* (New York, 1968) • T. Rendtorff, *Ethics* (2 vols.; Philadelphia, 1986-89) • D. Ritschl, *The Logic of Theology* (Philadelphia, 1987) pt. 3 • H. H. Schrey, *Einführung in die Ethik* (Darmstadt, 1972).

Dietrich Ritschl

1. Philosophical Ethics
1.1. *Term*

"Ethics," which comes from Gk. *ethizō* (accustom) or *ēthos* ("disposition, character"), represents the central discipline of practical → philosophy, which also embraces law, politics, and economics. It is the doctrine of the presuppositions and conditions of moral action, with no distinction between morality and custom such as that attempted in Hegel's philosophy. Moral action is oriented to the → good and avoids → evil. Since there are many goods, "the good" is ambivalent, and there are thus many ethical positions. The specifically moral good is what ought to be done, though again this notion can be expressed materially in different ways; hence there are many moral systems (see F. → Nietzsche). Underlying them all are a relatively small number of different ethical systems (though the distinction is not a strict one and gives rise to many misunderstandings). Positional differences arise out of the choice of supreme value, as do the resultant arguments (cf. → hedonism, vitalism, → utilitarianism, and an ethics of → duty). Yet they also arise out of "regional" combinations of moral standards and regulations in various social spheres that enjoy relative autonomy, even though they are naturally subject to general ethical principles.

Law is in some sense a presupposition of morality, and → ideology a presupposition of law. Law sets up a binding order, enforceable through sanctions, among those subject to it. Its recognition presupposes a minimum of moral consent. Nonmoral behavior can be classified as illegal when it poses a common danger. Morality is thus pledged to obey the law. Since both develop historically, the moral consciousness may outstrip the law, come to oppose it as unjust, and seek to make it just. When this opposition involves the use of force, the morally motivated breaker of the law must accept its sanctions. Political ideology results from such a higher moral consciousness. It is a collective conviction concerning a more just order in the future and the means to achieve it.

1.2. Relation of Ethics and Religion, and Validity of Philosophical Ethics

As systems of spiritual orientation, most religions contain moral and ethical principles that claim to be relatively independent. European ethics (to which we shall confine ourselves) was relatively autonomous in Greece, or arose as a creation of practical → reason in conscious demarcation from the prevailing belief in the gods (→ Greek Religion). It always found sufficient secular reason for the legitimacy of ethics and morality. That is, all the foundations and arguments had to be finally clear and acceptable to individuals as rational beings.

Philosophical ethics, then, could in no way be referred back to revelations received by faith (→ Revelation) or to the → dogmas of church teaching, though the possibility was not therefore ruled out that religious ethics might contain teachings and figures of thought acceptable to secular reason. An essential part of → Greek philosophy and ethics thus incontestably supplemented, supported, and shaped Christian theology and its teachings (see 6). Other world religions — for example, → Hinduism, → Buddhism, → Confucianism, and → Taoism — also contain elements of humanistic ethics.

In the other direction, at least in Europe, philosophical ethics has been affected by Christian teachings, whose influence one may see in secularized form, for example, in Kant's ethics and religion. The following survey of the historical development of European ethics thus cannot ignore this influence.

1.3. The Question of the Good and Its Change of Form

Socrates (ca. 470-399 b.c.), as Cicero tells it, called down philosophy from heaven and brought it into the cities and houses — that is, he related questions of cosmology and → ontology in early Greek philosophy to human conduct and its standards. Socrates thus became the father of European ethics, though he merely practiced ethics and did not make a theory of it. At a time when the good had come into question, he tried to implant it by the way of self-testing in the consciousness of the new generation, though without letting it finally be equated with traditional legality.

His disciple Plato (427-347) then looked beyond all the manifestations of the good and identified it with the (perfect) world order, which one may dis-

cern as "idea" and in accordance with which one must try as far as possible to shape all human orders, that of the → state and that of the human → soul (→ Platonism). For Plato, then, the good was an idea; religiously formulated, God alone is the supreme and final measure of all things.

Aristotle (384-322), the next in line, tended back toward Socrates. He again sought the good in its worldly forms, developed a ranking of goods, and tried to construct the highest achievable good — eudaemonia, or happiness (Gk. *eudaimonia,* "well-being, happiness") — out of a synthesis of goods (→ Aristotelianism). For him happiness consisted of rational (i.e., virtuous) conduct in the form of political practice and of philosophical *theōria* (observation, reflection). The latter has the advantage that no particular means are needed to achieve it, whereas the former needs many other goods such as pleasure, the beneficial, the useful, and finally → virtue and its claim to autarky. Contemporary philosophical schools were making all of these goods into supreme values (e.g., pleasure in the case of the Cyrenaics and Epicureans, or virtue in the case of the → Cynics and → Stoics). Tradition, in contrast, made Aristotelian eudaemonia the fullest virtue. Those who have it are truly blessed *(makarios);* those who do not are not necessarily unhappy but are still unfulfilled. Along with eudaemonia in social life or philosophical thinking, there is also eudaemonia in → friendship, which with its kindly quality forms the upper limit of humanity and points already in a Christian direction.

Adopting and reappraising these definitions of the good, Christian ethics found a specific good in → love of neighbor, but also in contemplation of God, thereby maintaining but also deepening the two elements in the ethics of antiquity. At the same time, it drew clear boundaries for → humanity. The opposite of love is not moral defect but → sin, which has become our inevitable destiny through original sin. We see that we are sinful because we want to do the good but can never do it. We cannot rescue ourselves from this fate. Only the incarnation and crucifixion can accomplish what is necessary (→ Soteriology). But mediating between the divine law that the church expounds and the believing and acting conscience of the individual was a difficult problem that was not convincingly solved prior to Protestantism.

Modern ethics presupposes this → conscience. In his ethics of freedom and duties, I. Kant (1724-1804) made the individual will the principle of the good, but he balanced this subjectivity by bonding the will to the law of custom, that is, the conditions under which people who see themselves as ends may form a society (→ Kantianism). The → categorical imperative is thus the requirement for controlling the generalization of maxims. The good is achieved on the two levels of legality and morality: what duty demands, and what is done out of duty, with the conscience behind it. Morality is a personal matter. Legality, with the help of nature, has arisen almost necessarily in history and resulted ultimately in the legal forms of the republic and of the international community. Yet a moral life is finally a personal task that politics may not hinder but will not promote. In Kant the good will — that is, the will that is free (because self-determined or autonomous) — takes concrete form in the duties of law and virtue, which include the goods and virtues of antiquity and the Middle Ages in revised form. In the duties of love — as serving the happiness of others who are in any trouble through no fault of their own and need social help — we catch an echo of the love motif of Christian ethics.

For G. W. F. Hegel (1770-1831) the will is an expression of thought. The good thus moves beyond its provisional forms, which include law and morality, and becomes general — an indigenous form of the national spirit, an institutionalizing of the forms of state that develop into a growing sense of → freedom and spread abroad as such (→ Hegelianism). Hegel's freedom undoubtedly contains elements both of the voluntary (Aristotle) and of → autonomy (Kant), yet it comes to fulfillment only in the agreement of the individual will with the universal will (e.g., in the form of political patriotism) or in the dialectical union of the finite spirit and the absolute spirit (→ Dialectic).

From this lofty peak there was almost inevitably a descent into triviality. Thus L. Feuerbach (1804-72) brought back Hegel's dialectically mediated idea to the field of the sensory and of individual, natural existence. He made this notion the basis of his "positive humanism," into which there also flowed the anthropologized substance of Christianity. The good is achieved here in a concrete address to the Thou, which has no knowledge of any further tasks.

The young K. → Marx (1818-83) accepted Feuerbach's return to the "natural consciousness" and the material world, gave it an economic and social sense (→ Marxism), and thereby reduced philosophy (which according to Hegel comprehends its age in thought) to the revolutionary program of the fourth estate. This so-called class of humanity is summoned — this is the point of the designation — to break down all barriers in restoring the humanity that industrial → capitalism has destroyed. This specific postulate of revolution, comparable in its way to a situational ethics, necessarily became an economic and materialistic → philosophy of history when it was falsified by historical events, the idea being that by a necessary process of class conflicts the collective bliss of a "classless paradise" will finally be achieved. In this historical determinism there is no longer any possibility of ethical teaching.

For its part, the middle-class → liberalism criticized by Marx had long since given a utilitarian answer to the question of the good. In so doing, it tied individual hedonism (the most immediate fulfillment of the principle of utility) to a kind of social eudaemonism with the help of a figure of thought taken from the marketplace — the general welfare promoted by individual self-interest.

Materialism and Marxism on the one side, and utilitarianism on the other, were obviously trivial answers to the question of right conduct. In reply to these positions the neo-Kantians (H. Cohen, P. Natorp, J. Cohn, H. Rickert, and others) sought an escape in a philosophy of values whose formal result — ultimately of no consequence for behavior — was to provoke the reaction of an ethics of material values (M. Scheler, N. Hartmann; → Values, Ethics of). With its restitution of the older ranking of goods on a phenomenological basis, this position expected too much of the consciousness of modern ethics, which had become too sharply critical since Kant's day. The idea that we can contemplate values was a mere palliative in the face of the stringency of moral decision demanded by Kant and his successors.

The final form of the changing practical question is → metaethics. Recognizing that questions of ethical content are hard to answer, metaethics turns away from them and with a deliberate value-neutrality investigates only the concepts and vocabulary of morality and ethics.

1.4. Questions of Legitimacy and Detailed Points

From the very outset in the historical survey (see 1.3), the final goal of the good was sought on the basis of a kind of a priority of reason. This position is plain in Plato. Aristotle appealed to historical societies and traditions as means of validation, but his own theoretical constructions were an expression of reason. Christian ethicists adduced human reason as more or less illumined by God, while Kant focused finally on secularized and enlightened human reason alone, freeing itself — though not totally — from all theological ties. Neo-Kantians and value philosophers were for the most part agreed on this position. The new thing was only their final moral good, their richly varied concept of virtue. For Aristotle keeping the "proper mean" was virtue, for the Stoics it was living according to nature, for Plotinus it was dematerializing the person, for Spinoza (→ Spinozism) it was intellectual love, for Kant it was moral perfection as the overcoming of radical evil. But then in the 19th century we find advocacy of → reverence (Goethe, Schweitzer), the "will to power" (Nietzsche), showing sympathy (Schopenhauer), and rising above oneself (Jaspers). Plausible grounds were given for all these various goals.

Metaethical reflection, however, casts doubt on this plausibility. It distrusts the a priority of reason and thinks the normativity presupposed in all these moral systems is emotionally based (emotivism, e.g., A. J. Ayer, E. L. Stevenson, and in some sense R. M. Hare), may be known only intuitively (intuitionism, e.g., T. Reid, G. E. Moore, W. D. Ross, H. A. Prichard, A. C. Ewing; → Intuition), or derives ultimately from empirical insights (what is useful or pleasurable is good, e.g., D. Hume). Moore and others charge this naturalism with impermissibly moving over from descriptive to normative statements (the naturalist fallacy) and thus show it to be useless. Hare traces moral demands back to general recommendations. Thus ethical formalism relies on an analysis of the specific modes of argument in actual moral discourse.

The rules of discourse are derived from the social function of morality (S. E. Toulmin, K. Baier) or from an analysis of the meaning of moral predicates (Hare). Meeting in this analysis are Anglo-Saxon formalism and German ethics of discourse (J. Habermas), which, with principles and rules of argument taken from the ideal-language situation, intervenes to direct communication of moral standards when these have been disrupted or challenged. The Erlangen constructivists tend more strongly back to Kant by following the "principle of reason" (transsubjectivity of goal-setting) and the "principle of morality" (in every individual interest one should have regard also to the interests of those affected by the regulation; B. Lorenzen).

The problem of establishing norms leads us already to material problems that emerge at once when, in spite of their systematic antitheses, we look at the contents of the teachings of Aristotle and Kant. Aristotle developed a doctrine of goods and virtue, discussed in principle the presuppositions and conditions of moral action, talked about the formation of moral character, made justice and friendship the foundations of political and social life, and in a kind of theory of evil identified three forms of moral failure: weakness of character, indiscipline, and a perverse orientation of life through upbringing contrary to the norm. The traditional virtues of temperance, courage, justice, prudence, and wisdom were defined as the mean between two extremes, for example, courage as the mean between cowardice and foolhardiness. Action made possible by the freedom of the will follows a goal and a plan of action, and it observes the "practical syllogism" in its motivational structure. Hegel was the first to develop and differentiate this extraordinarily progressive theory of → action. In moral education insight follows practice, in express contrast to Platonic *paideia* as the direct ascent of the soul to the idea. Friendship can make justice superfluous if it truly unites all citizens.

The Copernican revolution of Kantian ethics exalted freedom, which as self-determination formed the basis of the new autonomy of philosophical ethics. All previous moral standards, including the supreme one of happiness, involved heteronomy (i.e., lack of self-determination). The happiness ethic of tradition was rejected in particular because it is oriented to a principle of inclination rather than will. For Kant the highest moral goal, and therefore virtue in the absolute sense, was a pure and selfless fulfilling of duty. There is no moral merit in such fulfillment. All that satisfies the categorical imperative can be called the content of duty. Duty itself, however, is a formal principle because its quality of goodness cannot be surpassed by any goods, no matter how valuable. Kant's ethics, then, is not an ethics of goods, like that of tradition, but an ethics of conscience. Its presupposition of absolute freedom can be justified only as freedom is removed from the determinism of the empirical world and restored to what is known as the realm of understanding.

This doctrine of two worlds with its antieudaemonism and formalism was the decisive issue in criticism of Kant, especially in the Anglo-Saxon sphere. There utilitarian ethics had already had a long tradition (T. Hobbes, D. Hume, J. Locke). It boasted of three advantages: (1) it had few normative presuppositions; (2) it was more realistic than its rivals, replacing subjective standards by the objective standard of results; and (3) by placing high value on desire and utility, it also came close to being a morality of sound common sense.

Utility, like the good, is a formal concept, and it might involve hedonistic calculation (pleasure and → joy) as well as social commitment and sympathy. Hence the English utilitarians (J. Bentham, J. S. Mill, H. Spencer) adopted as their goal the formula of C. Beccaria, "the greatest good for the greatest number," or "the greatest possible quantity of happiness." They gave it a positive sense and equated it with the common welfare of politics. This Anglo-Saxon utilitarianism also underwent several modifications and developments. One of these affects its basic structure. Nineteenth-century utilitarianism of action is now being replaced by one of rule in which maxims of the will are more prominent than individual acts and a kind of moral self-testing is recommended in the manner of Kant.

1.5. *Ethics, Morality, and Regional Moral Codes*
Morality as moral practice has its theoretical grounding in ethics and differs historically and socially according to recognized systems of values and norms or according to the claims of socially relevant spheres of action. No universally applicable or absolute morality is possible. Thus from antiquity special moral codes have been constructed that obey the basic norms and rules of the game according to the tasks of a given sphere or "region." The oldest of such regional moral systems is the → medical ethics of Hippocrates (ca. 460-ca. 377 B.C.), which still finds emotional expression in the Hippocratic oath. In the face of the pharmaceutical, biochemical, and genetic engineering problems relevant to modern health, this oath has now been developed into a bioethics.

Other regional ethics or moralities of this kind are the political, educational, economic, legal, strategic, and journalistic. One might also mention ethics of art, theological ethics (see 7), and ethics of research. Some of these have been in existence for a long time and have been the subject of lively debate (e.g., the regional moralities of theology, politics, education, and journalism). Others remain to be developed. What is called praxeology (J. Derbolav) has set itself the task of investigating and systematically presenting these regional moral systems as the expression of specific social practices.

Bibliography: K. Albert, *Ethik und Metaethik. Das Dilemma der analytischen Moralphilosophie* (Stuttgart, 1961) • A. J. Ayer, *On the Analysis of Moral Judgments: Philosophical Essays* (New York, 1954) • K. Baier, *The Moral Point of View: A Rational Basis of Ethics* (Ithaca, N.Y., 1964) • Z. Bauman, *Postmodern Ethics* (Oxford, 1993) • A. Bening, *Ethik der Erziehung. Grundlage und Konkretisierung pädagogischer Ethik* (Freiburg, 1980) • F. Böckle, *Fundamental Moral Theology* (New York, 1980) • H. Cohen, *Philosophie*, vol. 2, *Ethik des reinen Willens* (4th ed.; Berlin, 1923) • J. Cohn, *Wertwissenschaft* (Stuttgart, 1932) • J. Derbolav, *Abriß europäischer Ethik* (Würzburg, 1983); idem, *Hegels Theorie der Handlung* (Bonn, 1965); idem, *Kritik und Metakritik der Praxeologie* (Kastellaun, 1976); idem,

"Thesen zu einer pädagogischen Ethik," *Pädagogische Rundschau* 39 (1985) • A. Donagan, *The Theory of Morality* (Chicago, 1977) • J. Finnis, *Fundamentals of Ethics* (Washington, D.C., 1983) • M. Forschner, *Die stoische Ethik* (Stuttgart, 1979) • J. Habermas, "Discourse Ethics: Notes on a Program of Philosophical Justification," *Moral Consciousness and Communicative Action* (Cambridge, Mass., 1990) 43-115 • R. M. Hare, *The Language of Morals* (Oxford, 1972; orig. pub., 1952) • N. Hartmann, *Ethics* (3 vols.; New York, 1932) • O. Höffe, *Einführung in die utilitaristische Ethik. Klassische und zeitgenössische Texte* (Munich, 1975); idem, ed., *Lexikon der Ethik* (Munich, 1977) • D. Hume, *An Enquiry concerning the Principles of Morals* (Indianapolis, 1983; orig. pub., 1751) • I. Kant, *Critique of Practical Reason* (trans. M. Gregor; New York, 1997; orig. pub., 1788); idem, *Groundwork of the Metaphysics of Morals* (trans. M. Gregor; New York, 1998; orig. pub., 1785); idem, *The Idea of a Universal History on a Cosmo-political Plan* (trans. T. De- Quincey; Hanover, N.H., 1927; orig. pub., 1784); idem, *The Metaphysics of Morals* (trans. M. Gregor; New York, 1996; orig. pub., 1797) • F. Kaulbach, *Ethik und Metaethik* (Darmstadt, 1974) • W. Kluxen, *Philosophische Ethik bei Thomas von Aquin* (2d ed.; Hamburg, 1980) • H. Lenk, "The Ordinary Language Approach und die Neutralitätsthese der Metaethik," *Das Problem der Sprache* (Munich, 1967) • T. Litt, "Ethik der Neuzeit," *HPh* 3 • B. Lorenzen, *Normative Logic and Ethics* (Mannheim, 1984) • D. Lyons, *Forms and Limits of Utilitarianism* (Oxford, 1965) • A. MacIntyre, *After Virtue: A Study in Moral Theory* (Notre Dame, Ind., 1984); idem, *A Short History of Ethics* (New York, 1966); idem, *Three Rival Versions of Moral Inquiry: Encyclopedia, Genealogy, and Tradition* (Notre Dame, Ind., 1990); idem, *Whose Justice? Which Rationality?* (Notre Dame, Ind., 1988) • K. Marx, *Die Frühschriften* (1840-47) (ed. S. Landshut; Stuttgart, 1953); idem, "Preface to a Contribution to the Critique of Political Economy" (1859), *MECW* 29.261-65 • G. E. Moore, *Principia ethica* (New York, 1993; orig. pub., 1903) • I. Murdoch, *The Sovereignty of Good* (London, 1970) • P. Natorp, *Vorlesungen über praktische Philosophie* (Erlangen, 1925) • M. Nussbaum, *The Fragility of Goodness: Luck and Ethics in Greek Tragedy and Philosophy* (Cambridge, 1986) • H. Reiner, *Die philosophische Ethik. Ihre Fragen und Lehren in Geschichte und Gegenwart* (Heidelberg, 1964) • M. Riedel, *Norm und Werturteil. Grundprobleme der Ethik* (Stuttgart, 1979) • R. Reininger, *Wertphilosophie und Ethik* (2d ed.; Vienna, 1966) • W. D. Ross, *The Right and Good* (2d ed.; Oxford, 1967) • M. Scheler, *Formalism in Ethics and Non-formal Ethics of Values* (5th ed.; Evanston, Ill., 1973) • J. B. Schneewind, *The Invention of Autonomy: A History of Modern Moral Phi-*

losophy (Cambridge, 1998) • B. Spinoza, *Ethics* (London, 1996; orig. pub., 1677) • E. L. Stevenson, *Ethics and Language* (10th ed.; New Haven, 1965) • G. F. Thomas, *Christian Ethics and Moral Philosophy* (New York, 1955) • S. E. Toulmin, *An Examination of the Place of Reason in Ethics* (Cambridge, 1960) • O. Urmson, *The Emotive Theory of Ethics* (London, 1978) • B. Williams, *Ethics and the Limits of Philosophy* (Cambridge, 1985) • G. H. von Wright, *The Varieties of Goodness* (3d ed.; London, 1968).

Josef Derbolav

2. OT Ethics

2.1. *Theological Influences*

Primarily two theological influences were normative for the development of Israelite ethics. The *formation of the → covenant and its provisions* (Exod. 19:4-6; 20:3–23:33) set a base in the → Torah that remained functional and normative in varying degrees throughout the pre-Christian history of Israel. Many later ethical developments and modifications reverted to this base for a new or renewed sense of direction. And then the *doctrine of → God as Creator,* especially as universalized by P in Genesis (1:1–2:4a) and the rest of the Torah, is the main basis for making universal claims for the ethical norms in Israelite thought.

2.2. *The Collective Context*

The formation of views of ethical conduct was sharply conditioned in early Israel's experience by the collective context of its life as a people. Their roots lay first in the *heavy interdependence on family and treaty allies* in nomadic life (Numbers 20–23) as well as later in settled life (Josh. 10:1-11). It was founded on the simple fact that no one survived in the desert alone. Help in the forms of cooperative labor (Jer. 2:13), shared duties (Gen. 27:8-10), and especially shared defense efforts under external threat (Judg. 6:33-35) required others one could trust and on whom one could depend. Whether it was the labor of tending flocks (Gen. 29:1-8), moving the tents to new locations (Gen. 12:4-9), finding water in strange terrain (Exod. 15:22-27), warding off animal attacks on the livestock (Num. 32:16-17a), or keeping a secure perimeter against marauders of hostile intent (Num. 21:21-26), the interdependence of many for the life of any to survive, much less thrive, was fundamental. In these arrangements the first resource was blood kin, starting with one's immediate family (Gen. 12:1-9) and extending through marriage to embrace the entire tribe (Gen. 35:22b-29) related by blood. The mind-set

of such connections is reflected in the proverb "I and my brother against my cousin; I and my cousins against the world." Modern Middle Eastern politics is more easily understood with this collective framework in mind.

The second dimension of such a collective framework for ethics was the *binding force of treaties,* especially those envisioned as covenant agreements (Genesis 15). The use of suzerainty treaties in Hittite culture has been seen as a helpful pattern by which to understand not only much of the politics in ancient Israel's history but even the theological covenant between Israel and its delivering God as seen in Exodus 19:1-6 and following references. The "cutting" of a covenant (by means of the agreeing parties walking between the halves of an animal sacrificed as the "bonding" agent establishing the agreement) put both parties in obligatory conformity to the terms agreed upon. The → blessings (e.g., Deut. 11:26-27) and → curses (v. 28) given at the end of such agreements were citations of the benefits of keeping the agreement and the dire consequences of breaking it. As with the interdependence on family cited above, the purpose of such covenants was to support and extend the life of the people involved (Exod. 19:1-6), whether suzerain or vassal. The same purpose drove the parity covenants of the ancient Near East as well.

2.3. *Legal Codes*

Within such a framework, Israel's covenant with God established in recognition of God's deliverance of Israel's people from slavery in Egypt embraced a wide range of ethical obligations. They show up most succinctly in the provisions of the legal codes developed across Israel's history.

2.3.1. The earliest, the *Covenant Code* (Exodus 20–23) summarized in the "Ten Words" (20:2-17), gives an index to the ethical concerns uppermost in consequence of Israel's covenant with God. The premise of exclusive loyalty to the God who freed them from → slavery in Egypt (vv. 2-3) was followed by both ritual and social consequences for life to be its best. Thus the admonitions following from the newly established covenant relation included exclusive → worship and devotion to the saving God (seen in keeping him only as "their" god, vv. 4-6), honoring his name (v. 7, i.e., being true to his character), and setting aside the seventh day as devoted to him, as → "sabbath" (vv. 8-11). In addition, ethical norms were cited requiring the honoring of parents (v. 12; note family interdependence above) and forbidding murder (v. 13), adultery (v. 14; family again), theft (v. 15), deceitful witness (v. 16), and greed (v. 17). All these ethical provisions were to obtain within the bounds of the covenanted people. Dealing with outsiders was another matter.

Ethical treatment of noncovenanted folk took two forms. The tradition of hospitality to the stranger, which was current in desert experience, was embraced in provisions to care for and honor the rights of a "resident alien" (Deut. 24:17), one considered a stranger in the covenant domain. In contrast, treatment of hostile marauders or aggressive royal armies was to be without mercy and, at its most extreme, required the death of all prisoners and destruction of all booty (Joshua 7). This tradition may have had the salutary effect of diminishing any impulse toward aggressive wars of expansion or looting. If no gain was permitted, the motive for aggression was reduced.

Israel's administration of justice according to the legal norms of covenant understanding was first a family obligation, then a duty of tribal elders, and then, in the period of the judges, the responsibility of certain roving charismatic leaders charged with offering guidance as specific crises arose (e.g., Judg. 4:4-24). Formalization of a justice system took place only with the establishment of the → monarchy, especially under → David and → Solomon (1 Chr. 23:2-6). Here regularly appointed persons heard cases of complaint or reported injustice and rendered verdicts backed by the power of the monarch.

2.3.2. In the wake of the failure of the united monarchy (ca. 922 B.C.) and the loss of the northern kingdom to Assyrian forces (721), surviving Judah developed the major legal reform known as the *Deuteronomic Code* (Deuteronomy 12–26; ca. 721). In addition to accommodating certain conditions of life that had changed since the earlier "wilderness" ethic, it focused on the root of ethical motivation as being in the heart of people (Deut. 6:4-9). As such, the Deuteronomic reform under Hezekiah was aimed at crystallizing conduct anew under the covenant obligations, but seen as guided by the internal desire to do the right both to one's covenant partners and to those one faced on the outside.

2.3.3. With the loss of all monarchical government at the fall of Judah to Babylon (ca. 587 B.C.) and the devastation of deportations to Babylon, especially the leaders (beginning the period known as the exile), a major reassessment of Israel's past and redesign of its future was undertaken during captivity by the Priestly leadership as well as by some prophetic voices. This third revision of the legal expression of Israelite ethics took the form of the *P Code*, contained now primarily in Leviticus (17–26). Its goal was to define what being the holy people of the holy God meant (19:1-4).

The Priestly ethical vision involved a sharp division of life between the approved "clean" ways of behaving and the disastrous "unclean" modes of behavior (Leviticus 11). The vast majority of the provisions in this revised ethical vision are regulations for the ritual conduct appropriate to the covenant people (chap. 14). In addition, some new and updated socioethical provisions are also given (6:1-7). There is little doubt that the dominant concern was to prescribe a ritually pure life that, when followed, would engender the best and most wholesome life for all the people. The line between permitted (or obligatory) conduct and forbidden behaviors, seen as destructive, is more sharply drawn and elaborated in more detail than ever before. With the adoption of this vision and code in the postexilic community, Israel's ethical vision was given a fixed order and rigidity that in some aspects is maintained to the present day (e.g., in kosher food regulations regarding meat and dairy dishes).

2.4. *Individual Modifications*

Individual insights either at odds with the legal ethical visions or seeking to purify them by adjusting priorities appear both in Israel's prophetic corpus and in some of the → Wisdom literature. For example, Amos (northern kingdom, ca. 850 B.C.) sharply criticized the insensitivity shown by the rich members of the society toward the plight of the poor (Amos 4:1-5) and warned of the utter inadequacy of mere ritual purity if the absence of compassion and concern for the neglected and unfortunate members of the society persisted (5:18-24). He warned that God himself would throw devastation on a society thus calloused against unfair treatment (2:4-8).

Hosea (roughly contemporary to Amos) warned that Israel in its social conduct had treated the covenant obligations as shoddily as an unfaithful wife might treat her family (Hos. 1:1-7). He pleaded for the people's conduct to reflect an ethic of loving concern (6:1-6), faithful to the saving insights of their origins.

Jeremiah, living through the devastations of the final threat to the survival of the southern kingdom (Jer. 1:1-3), decried the breaches of justice and ethical conduct by all levels of leadership, from magistrates through priests to princes and kings (4:9-10). He despaired of seeing any form of salvation in his own situation (4:19-22). Rather, he looked forward to a "new covenant" (31:31-34) reminiscent of the Deuteronomic ideal of the covenant of the heart, when people would act ethically because they were led by a vision from within (vv. 33-34).

Wisdom literature shows protests against the

corruption of conduct by the masses as well. Job takes his personal experience of suffering unjustly as a template for what ailed Israel, as revealed in the conduct of his three "friends," whose comfort was no aid in their insistence that he was personally responsible for the evil he endured (Job 4–5; 8; 11). The doctrine of retribution for sinful conduct was turned on its head by Job's appeal that if life always resembles his, God himself is unjust and has turned demonic (9:15-24). A somewhat more neutral view is expressed in Ecclesiastes, where the "all is vanity" judgment (e.g., in 1:2) about what happens in history leaves little room for redemptive expectations.

2.5. Areas of Ethical Concern

From these general considerations of ethical development in Israel, a number of areas of ethical concern rose to prominence. *Family life and its protection* carried over into visions of appropriate property treatment, inheritance law, sexual ethics, and the provisions of levirate → marriage, among other concerns. Property such as livestock was communal within tribal structures but became territorial once settlement into agriculture began with the gradual but eventually complete occupation of Canaan under the Davidic monarchy. Attention was thus paid not only to communal water rights (Deut. 6:10-12) if sources were limited (whether streams, springs, wells, or cisterns) but also to boundary markers setting off fields and establishing perimeters for postharvest grazing rights (Prov. 22:28). The antitheft and antigreed provisions of the ethical concerns of the original covenant endured in this realm.

Joining the property and family considerations were the *laws of inheritance* (Num. 27:8-11). While preference was given to the eldest son's portion, inheritance law protected the rights of wives, widows, and children (Num. 27:1-7). Risk of the loss of inherited property was countered by the sabbatical return to original owning families in the 50th (jubilee) year (Lev. 27:24), and the health of the agricultural property was protected by the requirement that it be allowed to recover in a fallow state every seventh year (Exod. 23:10-11).

The *sexual integrity of the family* was supported not only by the earliest prohibitions against adultery but also by subsequent elaborations regarding incest (Lev. 18:6-18; 20 passim; Deut. 27:20, 22-23), bestiality (Lev. 18:23), and related matters.

The *status of women* is a contentious point when viewed from modern feminist ideals or standards of → equality. The relative subservience of the women to their responsible males (Gen. 19; 29:15-30) remains a potent force to this day, viewed by many as a gross weakness in Israelite ethics. On a more posi-

tive note, the rule of levirate marriage (Deut. 25:5-10), wherein a brother of a deceased husband was responsible for the welfare of the widow and fatherless children, at times through multiple marriage by the husband, emerges as a compassionate and socially enforceable welfare ethic.

Business ethics (fair pay for fair labor, Deut. 24:14; or honest weights in trading goods, Mic. 6:11), *political ethics* (despite the ambiguities involved in yielding communal political power to a monarch potentially weak or impervious to covenant standards,1 Kgs. 15:33-34 etc.), and other arenas of life in which the choices made required discernment of the best or highest good, both for individual and society's life, broadened throughout the pilgrimage of Israel in OT times.

In many of the particulars of its legal codes, Israel borrowed from common ancient Near Eastern norms (e.g., *Ludlul bel nemeqi,* the so-called Babylonian Job, or "Poem of the Righteous Sufferer"), but the distinctive core of ethical direction from its roots in the covenant eventually supported the claim that Israel's ethical insights had sufficient power to warrant universal adoption. This power is most clearly evident in the visions of the future, whether messianic (Isa. 9:2a-7; 11:1-9) or → apocalyptic (Dan. 7:9-14), in which the ideal of life reflected in the → kingdom (i.e., rule) of God would be perfectly fulfilled by universal recognition and adoption (Dan. 7:18). In the current mode of pluralistic religious insights and pressures toward situational or relativistic ethics, this vision persists with remarkable strength and popular support. It had direct influence on both Christian and Islamic ethical standards and practices.

Bibliography: S. Bernfeld, *The Teachings of Judaism,* vol. 1, *Foundations of Jewish Ethics* (New York, 1968) • B. C. Birch, *Let Justice Roll Down: The OT, Ethics, and Christian Life* (Louisville, Ky., 1991); idem, "Moral Agency, Community, and the Character of God in the Hebrew Bible," *Semeia* 66 (1994) 23-42 • W. Brueggemann, *Interpretation and Obedience: From Faithful Reading to Faithful Living* (Minneapolis, 1991) • W. Janzen, *OT Ethics: A Paradigmatic Approach* (Louisville, Ky., 1994) • W. Kaiser, *Toward OT Ethics* (Grand Rapids, 1983) • E. Otto, *Theologische Ethik des Alten Testaments* (Stuttgart, 1994) • G. D. Schwarz, "God the Stranger," *HBT* 20 (June 1998) 23-48 • H. W. Wolff, *Anthropology of the OT* (Philadelphia, 1974) • C. J. H. Wright, "The Ethical Authority of the OT: A Survey of Approaches," *TynBul* 43 (1992) 102-20, 203-31.

Roger S. Boraas

3. NT Ethics

3.1. *Basis*

In every stratum of the tradition adopted, the NT writings reflect ethical reflection and formation as the response of faith to the experience of God's saving work. This statement holds true, even though the terms "ethics" and "parenesis" do not occur in the NT itself. In many ways, by taking up materially Jewish and Hellenistic parenesis, *paraklēsis* (exhortation, encouragement, help, comfort) comes into its own in the many arguments, norms, and motivations of ethical directions and concretions. It accords with the variety of theological conceptions and also bears the clear accents of → pastoral care.

3.2. *Jesus*

Jesus teaches that the rule of God has drawn near and is already present in his own person (Luke 11:20; 17:20-21; Matt. 12:28; → Kingdom of God). This message has inherent ethical implications, for it confronts us with the God who finally prevails and with his liberating and obligating will (Luke 6:20-21; Matt. 5:21-22, 27-28, 33-37; Luke 6:36). Jesus directs us back to God's original will (→ Sermon on the Mount), frees direction and admonition from all legalism (→ Law), and excludes all calculation of reward (Luke 17:7-10). Even in what he inherited from Wisdom ethics (e.g., in Matt. 6:25-34), it is clear that for Jesus the imminent rule of God is the basis of morality, not its motivation. The two-fold command of → love (Mark 12:28-34 and par.) points beyond Jesus' earthly life, → death, and → resurrection, making ethics an inalienable obligation of love for one another before the God who is yet to come.

3.3. *Synoptic Gospels and Acts*

Ethics as claiming service before God needs exposition. In the → Synoptics, Mark stresses a → discipleship of suffering and its ethical implications (Mark 8:27–10:52), and Matthew finds discipleship in doing the higher → righteousness (Matt. 3:15; 5:20; 6:33; 21:32, 43) in its ecclesial context (8:18-22, 23-27; 18). For Luke discipleship is the Christian life plus ethical direction and equipping for the age of the → church (Luke 9:57-62 and the Lucan "travel report" in 9:51–19:27), though persistent problems like the poor and the rich in social structures cannot be simply banished (see also Acts 2:42-47; 4:32-35).

3.4. *Paul*

Pauline ethics (→ Paul) is a comprehensive development of the event of justification, which sees the baptized (→ Baptism) and justified in the mortal corporeality (→ Anthropology 2) of earthly existence (Rom. 3:21-31; 6:2-11, 12-14; 12:1-2; Gal. 5:5). According to the Pauline approach the relation between indicative and imperative (e.g., Gal. 5:25; 1 Cor. 5:7; Phil. 2:12-13; Rom. 6; 13:14; Gal. 3:27) translates the gift and task into forms, structures, and commissions of the new life, which in its eschatological orientation has a sustaining Christological reference (1 Cor. 7:29-31, 32-35; Rom. 13:11-14; Phil. 4:4-5) beyond the time-bound form of imminent expectation (→ Eschatology; Parousia). This reference leads materially to the testing of existing ethical standards (Rom. 12:2; Phil. 4:8) and *in actu* triggers the responsibility of → conscience (1 Corinthians 8; 10), which in faith, and not legalistically, is constantly to show itself afresh in love for fellow believers (1 Cor. 6:1-11; Philemon; Rom. 13:8-10; Gal. 5:6, 13-15).

3.5. *Later Writings*

Contemporaneous (2 Thessalonians) and post-Pauline (Col. 3:1-4) ethics more clearly see tasks of Christian → responsibility in the present structures of the world (Col. 3:18–4:1, → Household Rules) on the basis of the increasingly cosmic dominion of Christ (Col. 1:15-20). In Ephesians this point is further developed into a normative anchoring of ethics in the church (Eph. 4:1-16; 5:22–6:9). The later writings of early Christianity work out the abiding presence of the → gospel in practical terms of church order and offices (the Pastorals), while ethics finds in → suffering a special dimension of discipleship of Christ (1 Peter).

James offers a synergism of faith and works (2:14-26), demanding ethics as a material decision for Paul (cf. Gal. 5:6). One must, however, also consider the possible presence here of a view of ethics influenced by the Wisdom tradition.

Hebrews has its own contribution to make, one that includes not allowing for a second → repentance. In *paraklēsis* (Heb. 13:22; cf. 2:1-4), ethics is described as the discipleship of faith (13:7) in earthly pilgrimage on the way to the goal (3:7–4:13) that Jesus as the true high priest has made possible (4:14-16). Faith itself thus becomes an ethical attitude.

3.6. *Johannine Writings*

In the Johannine writings ethics has largely merged into → Christology, and in the correspondence of faith and abiding it hardly allows the new command of brotherly love to find expression in the relation of indicative and imperative (John 13:34-35; 15:12; cf. 6:29, 40, etc.). In Revelation ethical direction is often given in the traditional terminology of the connection between act and result against the background of the promise of victory in a situation of affliction (2:3; 21:7).

3.7. *Relevance of NT Ethics*

In primitive Christianity NT ethics is *paraklēsis* in the tension of ongoing time. We may have to criticize it in detail as the situation changes, but it is a sustaining center for the claim and promise of the saving work of God accomplished in Christ. In spite of every difference of time and situation, then, it is always relevant and analogically applicable (W. Schrage). This fact confirms the legitimacy both of enhanced sociohistorical research and of a renewal of a more strictly theological consideration of the material of NT ethics, as well as of a hermeneutical and systematic consideration that might continually disclose its relevance.

Bibliography: J. BECKER, "Das Problem der Schriftgemäßheit der Ethik," *HCE* 1.243-69 • V. P. FURNISH, *Theology and Ethics in Paul* (Nashville, 1968) • B. GERHARDSSON, *The Ethos of the Bible* (Philadelphia, 1981) • R. B. HAYS, *The Moral Vision of the NT: Community, Cross, New Creation. A Contemporary Introduction to NT Ethics* (San Francisco, 1996) • F. W. HORN, "Ethik des Neuen Testaments, 1982-1992," *TRu* 60 (1995) 32-60 (bibliography) • K. KERTELGE, ed., *Ethik im Neuen Testament* (Freiburg, 1984) • W. G. KÜMMEL, "Sittlichkeit V: Urchristentum," *RGG* (3d ed.) 6.70-80 • E. LOHSE, *Theological Ethics of the NT* (Minneapolis, 1991) • W. MARXSEN, *"Christliche" und christliche Ethik im Neuen Testament* (Gütersloh, 1985) • F. J. MATERA, *NT Ethics: The Legacies of Jesus and Paul* (Louisville, Ky., 1996) • W. A. MEEKS, *The Moral World of the First Christians* (Philadelphia, 1986) • O. MERK, *Handeln aus Glauben. Die Motivierungen der paulinischen Ethik* (Marburg, 1968) bibliography • H. MERKLEIN, *Die Gottesherrschaft als Handlungsprinzip. Untersuchung zur Ethik Jesu* (2d ed.; Würzburg, 1984) • K.-W. NIEBUHR, *Gesetz und Paränese. Katechismusartige Weisungsreihen in der frühjüdischen Literatur* (Tübingen, 1987) • E. REINMUTH, *Geist und Gesetz. Studien zu Voraussetzung und Inhalt paulinischer Paränese* (Berlin, 1985) • R. SCHNACKENBURG, *The Moral Teaching of the NT* (London, 1975) • W. SCHRAGE, *The Ethics of the NT* (Edinburgh, 1996); idem, "Zur Frage nach der Einheit und Mitte neutestamentlicher Ethik," *Die Mitte des Neuen Testaments. Einheit und Vielfalt neutestamentlicher Theologie* (Göttingen, 1983) 238-53 • S. SCHULZ, *Neutestamentliche Ethik* (Zurich, 1987) • G. STRECKER, "Strukturen einer neutestamentlichen Ethik," *ZTK* 75 (1978) 117-46 • H. WEDER, *Die Rede der Reden. Eine Auslegung der Bergpredigt heute* (Zurich, 1985) • E. WÜRTHWEIN and O. MERK, *Verantwortung. Biblische Konfrontationen* (Stuttgart, 1982) bibliography • J. H. YODER, *The Politics of Jesus* (Grand Rapids, 1993).

OTTO MERK

4. Ethics in Roman Catholic Theology

In Catholic theology it is only in the 16th century, in the age of the Counter-Reformation (→ Catholic Reform and Counterreformation), that we find an attempted ethics on the basis of the Christian faith in the form of moral theology. The early church and the Fathers took their urgings to a Christian lifestyle directly from the exhortations of the Bible, particularly the → Decalogue in the OT and, in the NT, the → Sermon on the Mount, the parting discourses of Jesus, and the Epistles. The event of salvation and the way of salvation were still a unity.

A change came in the 13th century with → Thomas Aquinas (ca. 1225-74), who in the second part of his great *Summa,* following Aristotelian ethics, offered an account of Christian conduct that in the following years prepared the way for the development of an independent discipline (→ Thomism). Thomas opened the ethical part of his *Summa* with the question of our chief end, which he found in happiness. His ethical essay thus has a basic teleological structure. He included our natural inclinations as a starting point for concrete ethical directions. For the part of his specifically theological ethics, he took as a principle of division the four classical cardinal virtues of prudence, justice, courage, and temperance, adding to them the three divine virtues of → faith, → hope, and → love.

This positive and essential feature of ethics was lost in the 16th century, when → moral theology emerged as a separate discipline within Counter-Reformation movements. Such theology was designed mainly to train confessors and thus found a large place for → casuistic discussions of → law, → conscience, and → obedience. The positive impulses of a Christian doctrine of salvation were handled under a separate discipline of ascetics. This restrictive tendency was reinforced by an increasingly individualistic and legalistic conception of moral casuistry. Reforming movements included the Franciscan spiritualists around Cardinal P. de Bérulle (1575-1629) and, in the 19th century, the German theologians Michael Sailer (1751-1832), Johann Baptist Hirscher (1788-1865), and Magnus Jocham (1808-93), who put their work in moral theology on a biblical footing.

Only in the second half of the 20th century, with → Vatican II, did a basic renewal of moral theology begin that reflected more strongly on biblical origins, replacing a static view of → natural law with a historical and dynamic view. A moral theology seen as theological ethics was now shaped by a responsive, dialogic, and ecclesial principle of Christian faith.

Complex → experience has a decisive role in the formation of theory. Indeed, the Bible itself is the result of a witness of experience. Moral demands are shown to be plausible according to the rationality of Christian faith; a purely authoritarian or positivist basis is not enough. What is distinctively Christian in morality does not lie in new ethical → norms but in the transcendent horizon of meaning that faith opens up for us. The message of Jesus aims more at change than at the status quo, more at personal → responsibility than at legalism. It also encourages charismatic ways (evangelical counsels — classically, poverty, chastity, and obedience).

In a Roman Catholic view, theological ethics retains its churchly character in this regard by understanding the whole → church as a fellowship of believers and the teaching office as an official medium for the communicating of Christian ethics. Traditional Catholic doctrine distinguishes between the process of finding the truth and official decision by the teaching office. Permanent significance applies to the decisions of the teaching office only for formal actions presenting truths of faith.

All believers participate in the more comprehensive and practical discovery of the truth. There can be no bypassing the testimony of committed Christians as the normative power of lived-out conviction. The church also has social responsibility as an → institution, though it is contested by what → authority and certainty it may speak and decide on concrete moral questions. Even though members may not ignore the noninfallible pronouncements of the teaching office, the responsible moral actions of adults must take place on their own responsibility and according to the decisions of their own consciences.

Bibliography: F. BÖCKLE, *Fundamental Moral Theology* (New York, 1980) • C. E. CURRAN, *The Catholic Moral Tradition Today: A Synthesis* (Washington, D.C., 1999) • K. DEMMER, *Sittlich Handeln aus Verstehen. Strukturen hermeneutisch orientierter Fundamentalmoral* (Düsseldorf, 1980) • G. GRISEZ, with J. M. BOYLE, *The Way of the Lord Jesus* (2 vols.; Chicago, 1983) • R. M. GULA, *Reason Informed by Faith: Foundations of Catholic Morality* (New York, 1989) • B. HÄRING, *Free and Faithful in Christ: Moral Theology for Clergy and Laity* (2 vols.; New York, 1982) • A. HERTZ et al., eds., *HCE* • R. A. MCCORMICK, *Corrective Vision: Explorations in Moral Theology* (Kansas City, Mo., 1994) • J. MAHONEY, *The Making of Moral Theology: A Study of the Roman Catholic Tradition* (Oxford, 1987) • S. PINCKAERS, *The Sources of Christian Ethics* (Washington, D.C., 1995) • E. SCHILLEBEECKX, *Christ: The Christian Experience in the Modern World* (New York, 1980).

JOHANNES GRÜNDEL

5. Feminist Ethics

In the United States, feminist ethics, though an academic discipline, has its recent roots in the → women's movement of the late 1960s and 1970s. More generally, feminist ethics, which is connected to the women's rights movement of the 19th century, is both a broad category identifying ethical theory by persons opposed to the subordination of → women and a more narrow category identifying the work of a subgroup of persons, primarily white women, who do not write from particular racial or ethnic standpoints. The substance of feminist ethics — which includes critically assessing traditional religious norms, especially those oppressive to women; retrieving and reconstructing traditions and practices that affirm women; and constructing new norms and paradigms of practice that liberate women — challenges systems, traditions, and practices that sustain male superiority, generally regarded as patriarchy.

Two emphases are thus central to feminist ethics: an opposition to the subordination of women and a focus on women's experiences for determining moral → norms. Developments in feminist ethics include variations on these two emphases and, at some points, quite different perspectives related to them. Earlier questions about the meaning of → feminism itself led to discussion of women's experience and of whether feminist ethics has meaning for the status of men.

While such general emphases characterized Christian feminist ethics as it originated, to define feminist ethics today involves describing its conversation with, and inclusion of, critiques brought by particular groups of women, the most significant of which calls for expanding the meaning of women's experience to include oppression because of race or ethnic identity, class, and sexual orientation. By extension, other social and physical attributes of persons (e.g., ability and age) that become bases of oppression also are included in feminist deliberation about women's experience. Feminist ethical discourse typically concentrates on four areas: moral agency, relationship, plurality, and ecology.

Moral agency. Feminist discussions of agency have centered on the nature of the self and the role of choice. In this regard, feminists often distinguish between women's traditional experience and women's feminist experience, referring respectively to perspectives and norms of practice seen in conventional roles of women and to perspectives and practices that arise from reflection on women's lives through the lens of woman-consciousness. On the basis of a qualified understanding of the Enlightenment self as a free, self-determining agent, feminist ethics calls for extending to women the → freedom asserted for universal human subjects (but reserved for men) in the → Enlightenment paradigm. At the same time, feminist ethics makes problematic any understanding of the individual as a totally self-determining agent isolated from others. Arguing that women's choices have been restricted and that women's traditional experience has been characterized by caring for others, some feminists assert that women's decision making attends to relationship as well as justice in making moral judgments.

Relationship. Other feminists see women's experience as more multifaceted and criticize normative ethical conceptions of women's agency based solely on traditional experiences of caring. Arguing that women's ability to achieve self-realization has been encumbered by traditional experiences and roles in the private sphere, some Christian feminist ethics challenges the norm of self-sacrificial love as the most appropriate way of characterizing agape → love. These feminist ethicists assert that self-realization and human flourishing must precede self-denial and lift mutuality and reciprocity in public and private life to the status of norms for realizing the meaning of agape. In this regard, agape involves relating to others in ways that recognize fragility and dependency as expressions of egalitarianism and solidarity in human relationships.

Plurality. In pursuing the goals of egalitarianism and solidarity, feminist ethicists have come to recognize complexity in women's experiences and thus put forward various approaches to the eradication of gender oppression. Interestingly, women descended from parts of the world other than Europe have challenged feminist assertions of mutuality and reciprocity, calling attention to ways in which race, class, and language have marginalized some women's consideration in feminist discourse. African American women, usually naming their perspective "womanist," and Hispanic women, often naming their perspective "mujerista," identify concerns arising from social class, racial/ethnic identity, and language as central to their experiences as women. These ethicists say that the realization of egalitarianism and solidarity means highlighting the impediments to mutuality and reciprocity among women that derive from some women's participation in, and benefit from, race and class oppression as well as noticing ways that patriarchy affects all women.

In contrast to the focus on agape, African American women emphasize the conjunction of black women's liberation with that of entire black com-

munities and lift up traditions of practice by African American women that exemplify their agency by focusing on community survival and well-being. In her pioneering work on the moral context of African American women, Katie Cannon argues that the feminist consciousness of black women arises in circumstances marked by a struggle to survive against white supremacist patriarchy, → capitalist class exploitation, and intrarace gender oppression. In exploring the moral life of Hispanic women, Ada Maria Isasi-Diaz asserts that praxis and moral agency — reflecting the significance of action, independence, and self-worth — are central to the meaning both of being moral persons and of relating to God.

In addition to racial and ethnic particularities, plurality in feminist ethics involves taking different approaches to overcoming gender inequality. Liberal feminists call attention to the need for reform to include women more fully as participants in the liberal tradition of political rights. Socialist feminists stress the need to change institutional configurations, especially economic systems, to produce material equality. Radical feminists advocate political, social, and even quasi-reproductive separation from men as the only means of ensuring autonomy and justice for women. In all of its plurality, feminist ethics offers new and renewed views of the good that move away from what has previously been identified as purely rational moral theory.

Ecology. Opposing tendencies in traditional Christian theology and ethics to objectify nature absolutely, feminist ethics seeks to overcome the mind-body split of Western philosophical and religious traditions. Feminist ethicists argue that women's bodies often have been identified with nature and therefore subjected to Western practices of conquest. They affirm that justice entails women's control of their own bodies, especially (but not only) in relation to reproductive freedom. Moreover, embodiment, human → sexuality, and the interdependence of humans and creation are seen as good gifts from God to be valued and celebrated. Healing the mind-body and nature-culture dualities means affirming human desire and the need for rest, recreation, and relationship through practices and policies that view them as social goods. Many feminists assert that affirming the human desire for relationship means broadening conceptions of appropriate sexual intimacy to include homosexuality and developing new models of family life. Furthermore, some feminists maintain that affirming human desire and the need for relationship includes noting the human connection with, and → stewardship of, all → creation.

Bibliography: B. H. ANDOLSEN, C. GUDORF, and M. D. PELLAUER, eds., *Women's Consciousness, Women's Conscience: A Reader in Feminist Ethics* (Minneapolis, 1985) • L. S. CAHILL, *Between the Sexes: Foundations for a Christian Ethic of Sexuality* (Philadelphia, 1985) • K. G. CANNON, *Black Womanist Ethics* (Atlanta, 1988); idem, *Katie's Canon: Womanism and the Soul of the Black Community* (New York, 1995) • C. E. CURRAN, M. A. FARLEY, and R. A. McCORMICK, eds., *Feminist Ethics and the Catholic Moral Tradition* (New York, 1996) • L. K. DALY, ed., *Feminist Theological Ethics: A Reader* (Louisville, Ky., 1994) • C. GILLIGAN, *In a Different Voice* (Cambridge, Mass., 1982) • A. M. ISASI-DIAZ, *En la lucha = In the Struggle: A Hispanic Women's Liberation Theology* (Minneapolis, 1993) • S. F. PARSONS, *Feminism and Christian Ethics* (New York, 1996) • A. E. PATRICK, *Liberating Conscience: Feminist Explorations in Catholic Moral Theology* (New York, 1996) • R. R. REUTHER, *Sexism and God-Talk: Toward a Feminist Theology* (Boston, 1983).

ROSETTA E. ROSS

6. History of Christian Ethics

6.1. *Present Situation in Research*

The history of the Christian church and its theology is accompanied by the development of an ethics that for its part is rooted in the many conditions of the life of the Christian community and its doctrine. The following factors have contributed to the shape of Christian ethics: maintaining Christianity over against a pagan world, delimiting → heresies, building up → church law, exercising → church discipline, developing the practice of penance (→ Penitence), and fashioning a state church and a Christian culture (→ Church and State; People's Church [Volkskirche]). Thus far there has been little research into the relation between Christian ethics and church history. Despite recent contributions involving a more limited range of historical material, the works of E. → Troeltsch still represent an important beginning and contribution in this field, especially his work *Die Soziallehren der christlichen Kirchen und Gruppen* (1911/1922) (ET *The Social Teaching of the Christian Church* [1931]).

6.2. *Development*

The tasks directing the history of Christian ethics begin, as this article has shown, with the OT and NT traditions themselves as they address the issues of life before God: Christian → perfection, life in the community, the portrayal of the Christian church to the (non-Christian) world, the related task of refashioning the world, church orders, and the social action of Christians. The NT traditions, to be properly understood, must be placed within contexts provided by the OT in respect to such concrete issues as the role of ritual in ethics for life, prophetic attitudes toward justice in society, traditions regarding the temple and the authority of the Pharisees, and the nature of such foundational social institutions as marriage and property. Consequently, it was particularly important that Christian ethics be integrated into a total biblical concept of salvation (begun by → Augustine [354-430]; Augustine's Theology). From the very beginning, Christian ethics was concerned about perfection in Christian life, the associated upbuilding of the community, and the Christian transformation of the world. In ethical teaching we thus find a depiction of the Christian life in Christian → virtues along with a listing of the various spheres of life (→ Institutions) in which Christians participate: → work, → marriage, → property, and the → state (→ Social Ethics).

6.2.1. In the → early church we also find teaching on Christian perfection and morality oriented to a monastic and ascetic ethics (thus with Basil the Great [ca. 330-79]; → Monasticism). Christian morality is contrasted, too, with that of paganism (as by → Tertullian [ca. 160-ca. 225]). The church also gives direction for life, especially in connection with penance. Ethics here takes form as → casuistry and is connected with legal thinking.

6.2.2. Christian ethics found a systematic form and basis on the path to → Scholasticism and in connection with → dogmatics. The main elements here are the doctrine of the → good, which (in Augustine) gives ethics a universal, teleological feature; the grounding of Christian conduct in the development of the will (a voluntaristic view, even in Augustine); the construction of a doctrine of virtues; and especially its teaching on Christian morality, → natural law, and → reason. Adoption of the philosophical ethics of antiquity (see 1) contributed decisively to the systematic form of Christian ethics. Yet Christian ethics basically changed the ethics of antiquity through its specifically theological elements, namely, the relating of the Christian life to the community, its embedding in salvation history, and the doctrine of → sin and → evil.

Christian ethics underwent further systematic development with the adoption of Aristotle (384-322 B.C.; → Aristotelianism) in the 13th century, specifically through various editions of his *Nicomachean Ethics* and the commentaries of Albertus Magnus (ca. 1200-1280) and Thomas Aquinas (ca.

1225-74; → Thomism; Scholasticism). Formative for ethics in this regard were the teaching on virtue and the development of → norms for moral conduct, embracing life and its reality in every aspect. A distinctive feature was the linking of moral direction to the church's mediation of salvation by penance. Incorporation of the moral → natural law, human → reason, and divine law gave ethics its authentic place in the task of universal theological learning. Other directions in the grounding of ethics, however, allowed less place for moral direction and reason (e.g., those of Duns Scotus [ca. 1265-1308]; → Scotism).

6.2.3. Reformation theology (→ Reformation) brought decisive changes to basic elements in ethics. Ethics now detached itself from the conditions of a unified Christian culture and severed its link with the church's mediation of salvation. Development of a concept of → freedom, based on ideas about freedom from works, became the presupposition of an ethics that would shape the world yet still be grounded in the Word of God. Ethics also took up the task of achieving a view of life's reality (including church orders and institutions). One may thus speak about a double origin of ethics (M. → Luther [1483-1546] and P. → Melanchthon [1497-1560]) in the modern period (T. Rendtorff). J. → Calvin (1509-64) adopted a new approach to Christian ethics and the task of reshaping the world when he oriented Christian conduct and → sanctification to the establishment of God's community in the world (→ Calvin's Theology).

6.2.4. The further development of Christian ethics in the modern period is marked by the founding of ethics on the constitution of the ethical subject, to which → Pietism and especially the critique of reason by I. Kant (1724-1804) contributed (→ Kantianism; Enlightenment). Ethics thus acquired a systematic foundation related to the formation of ethical judgment. Kant had a lasting impact on Christian ethics.

F. → Schleiermacher (1768-1834) made ethics a basic science in his encyclopedia and was influential in depicting it as a doctrine of values (e.g., see R. Rothe [1799-1867]). The idea that ethics is a basic discipline persisted into the 20th century (W. Herrmann [1846-1922]; G. Ebeling). On this view, ethics has validity as a view of reality and its constitution.

Developments in the church and in theology in the 19th century also affected theological ethics, particularly the perpetuating of a biblically oriented ethics (J. T. Beck [1804-78], the working out of a view of Christian morality related to the church as its visible locus (e.g., in the concept of calling) or to life in the middle-class world (A. Ritschl [1822-89]), the development of confessional teachings, and new attempts to deal with emergent social problems. Critical impetus to an integrated view of Christian morality came from the rediscovery of Jesus' proclamation of the kingdom of God (J. Weiss [1863-1914]) and especially from critical encounters with social change (see the → religious socialism of H. Kutter, L. Ragaz, and P. → Tillich; and the → Social Gospel of W. → Rauschenbusch).

→ Dialectical theology found a new basis for ethics in connection with its basic systematic problem: the question of the subject and the structure of reality. This basis lay in a combination of God's freedom and his Word that binds us. The result was an ethics of the biblical command (K. → Barth). At the same time, ethics as a view of reality achieved fresh validity as a doctrine of the orders of creation (esp. by E. Brunner). A necessarily broadening differentiation of problems (e.g., as regards the relation of Christian conduct and the church) may be seen significantly in D. → Bonhoeffer, whose sketch of a basis of ethics proved very provocative.

The more clearly Christian ethics has seen its place in the church and its history, the more it has been guided by insights and problems accompanying this history. Decisive in the modern age are the experiences of thought resulting from the → church struggle in Nazi Germany and from experiences of oppression in the → Third World (e.g., in relation to the political action of Christians).

Here broad theological conceptions have come up against limits where they can no longer be grasped in detail as differentiated tasks and problems of ethical investigation and judgment. They are thus accompanied by a far-reaching concern about the theory of ethics and its tradition (see 7). We may refer in this regard to the works of H.-D. Wendland, E. Wolf, A. Rich, and T. Rendtorff, and especially to a series of American contributions by P. Lehmann, J. M. Gustafson, and S. Hauerwas. Roman Catholic → moral theology has also done some decisive research in the development of a theory of ethics (see 4).

One can hardly describe the history of Christian ethics in its various specific denominational contexts, though one can see the different effects overall of Reformed or Lutheran ethics (e.g., in North America) and Roman Catholic moral theology. An obvious requirement is a study of the context of Christian ethics with a critical eye to ecumenical understanding and the linking of theological ethics to the intellectual and cultural history of the West.

7. Tasks of Theological Ethics

7.1. *Term and Tasks*

→ Theology embraces ethics in its nexus of reality, its task, its structure, and its method. It views ethics as an express → responsibility for attitude, conduct, and life (both individual and social). This responsibility may involve everyday matters, or it may deal with crisis and → conflict. As a common, rational responsibility, it has to do with the basis of life, morality, → norms, and the responsible subject. For theology, then, ethics concerns the varied fulfillment of human life. The tradition of Christian ethics has focused mainly on the structure of moral or ethical humanity (the moral person) and its reality (e.g., in the religious orders).

7.1.1. Theological ethics directs ethics to the church's action in its constitutive sense, which includes → worship. Here ethics tests the comprehensive will of God on the basis of his salvific activity and with reference to his Word in the → law and → gospel and in perception of the need of others. Theological ethics focuses on the God-given reality for which we are responsible. The scope and limits of that responsibility are defined by God's prior action and not by the limits of human possibilities in encounter with God.

7.1.2. Theological ethics, concerned about a theory of ethics embracing all such matters and grounded in theological → knowledge, thus accepts a metaethical task (→ Metaethics). This task cannot be limited to a description of Christian morals according to a particular tradition or church or to a presentation of Christian ethics understood as a reflection of traditional Christian morality. Theological ethics must thus reflect particularly on certain elements in ethical theory (e.g., the concept of → freedom).

There is no basis for distinction in principle between personal ethics and → social ethics, for individuals must be seen in their social context. Yet a distinction of spheres can be made. Greater attention is now being paid to personal ethics (e.g., in respect to the living of individual lives and individual histories). Traditionally, theological ethics has often merely put these spheres alongside one another, which has given rise to justifiable criticism.

7.1.3. Theology seeks an ethics that is commensurate with → faith yet understandable to all people. A distinction must clearly be made between (traditional) "Christian ethics" and "ethics for Christians," in which non-Christians may have a share through rational communication. This approach does not mean, however, that this ethics must be communicated in an exclusively rational way. We find reflection on this matter in theories advanced in theological ethics (esp. in the → two-kingdoms doctrine).

Theological ethics cannot base its understanding on a distinction between Christian and non-Christian ethics. It can base it only on the specific tasks of finding and establishing ethical judgments by theological reflection and analytic presentation. In particular, its theme is that which is of preeminent importance for Christians (though it must avoid a two-stage or double morality). An account of its own role is included, insofar as it must reflect theologically on its presupposition (e.g., in its concept of freedom). In this way theological ethics must construct its own particular theory.

7.1.4. Where we find the basis of theological ethics (e.g., in the view of God's reality) and what theoretical approach we adopt will depend on fundamental theological or dogmatic decisions (→ Dogmatics). Since theological ethics relates all action to that of the church, the basis of ethics cannot be made directly dependent on problems resulting from the locating of Christian faith in society or intellectual history. In this regard theological ethics will critically accept or emphasize some expositions of Christian ethics (e.g., a normative ethics of responsibility), though without excluding other levels or spheres of ethical reflection (e.g., values and basic attitudes). Important aspects of the task include perceiving the foundations of human life, considering the structures (→ Institution) of reality, reflecting on particular threats to this order, solving conflicts and contradictions, setting up norms for new possibilities of action (e.g., those opened up by → technology), and reflecting on (even revolutionary) changes in relationships.

7.1.5. The various conceptions of theological ethics rest in part on the ranking of such tasks. In particular, the different paths taken by an ethics that focuses on the structure of (social) reality and one that focuses on the responsible subject have led to different developments in the theory of ethics. We thus have various conceptions of a normative ethics (P. Ramsey, S. Hauerwas, J. H. Yoder), of an ethics that reflects on ethical orientation in the light of social change (R. → Niebuhr, G. Winter, L. Rasmussen), and of an ethical theology that tries to grasp the structure of life's reality (J. Gustafson, T. Rendtorff). These conceptual distinctions are either ethically based or rest on theological insights that arise within particular traditions. They are mostly linked to different types of problems that are again the subject of ethical reflection (e.g., the relations between faith and world, church and the public,

Christian and non-Christian ethics or morality). No comprehensive theory is conceivable that can bring all these things together.

The decisive point is that the grounding of ethics is not just a matter of individual problems but can be itself an ethical theme. Criticism of various ethical conceptions is demanded insofar as they are also linked to limited approaches, for example, the two-kingdom doctrine to a specific view of the proper relation between the church and the world or the → state, which as such cannot provide the basis for an ethics.

7.1.6. For theological ethics the distinction between theological theses and theoretical constructions is central. On this presupposition it is possible to list changes in the tasks set for ethics. Not a general attempt to shape a so-called new ethics but recognizing where ethics comes up against new basic problems is important. For example, does not responsibility for future generations or for longer periods (e.g., with regard to the disposal of atomic waste) make necessary new elements in ethical theory?

Many new issues that concern the basis of ethics have arisen in various fields and have led to the development of new spheres of ethical work (e.g., in → medical ethics with the problems of the beginning and end of life, of genetics, and of responsibility to the → Third World). These developments pose a particular demand for theological ethics. The increasing orientation to a global perspective, → peace, → disarmament, → the environment, and the shaping of the future has consequences for theological ethics that still remain to be worked out.

7.2. Dogmatics and Ethics

Theological ethics is guided by statements that belong to basic dogmatics, from which a tradition of theological ethics has developed.

7.2.1. Where important theological insights are achieved, as in Reformation theology, these have a bearing on ethics, though not directly (e.g., by the reformulation of dogmatic statements in ethical directions). It is important at this point to see and investigate the specifically theological significance of the distinction between dogmatics and ethics and the distinctive sphere of ethical learning (e.g., in the doctrine of orders or institutions), no matter what the theological approach may be. Different approaches have only a limited bearing, as, for example, the distinction between indicative and imperative, which has become a model of attaining ethical guidance with an appeal to NT modes of speech (see 3). There is danger here of misunderstanding in reformulating statements about God's action (indicative) as directions to us (imperative) without specific justification. In biblical texts and theological ethics a critical distinction exists between what God does and what humans must do on the basis of God's work and will.

7.2.2. In theological ethics dogmatics plays a large part in theoretical construction, for theological ethics acquires the elements of its theory on the basis of regulative dogmatic statements. With these statements it formulates and answers basic questions about the place of ethics, the responsible subject of conduct, and the scope and limit of responsibility. With dogmatic statements it also achieves a critical stance vis-à-vis intellectually conditioned positions (e.g., specific concepts of freedom or the knowledge of reality) and conceptual alternatives (e.g., an ethics of disposition or of responsibility) that are grounded in specific theories. This fact brings theological ethics into debate with other views of ethics. In this debate it accepts its metaethical task, more and more so in dialogue with analytic moral philosophy (→ Analytic Ethics).

7.2.3. By means of dogmatic statements theological ethics links up with dogmatics in its multifaceted development. It is also concerned, however, to adhere to dogmatic statements as regulative principles for its own theory.

7.2.3.1. One such statement is that God acts graciously toward humankind (→ Grace). This truth means that ethical knowledge cannot be restricted, for example, to an individualistic relation to God. Ethics takes its place in a total reality enclosed by God's Trinitarian work and will. Thus theological ethics must pay equal attention to what is said about → creation, → reconciliation, and the new creation, though the dogmatic basis may become increasingly narrower (e.g., limited to what is said about individual justification).

The need for a → Trinitarian basis of ethics has become increasingly clearer in the last half of the 20th century. It includes a recognition in ethics of what sustains human action and knowledge. In this connection one may see a rooting of ethics in the data of → natural law. The question is whether natural law marks only a limit of ethical grounding or whether it belongs to the theological knowledge of reality.

7.2.3.2. The concept of freedom goes along with dogmatic statements about God's work. In Reformation theology freedom is viewed as freedom from the works by which we might seek to secure the basis of life and thus lose sight of God and neighbor and the related world. Freedom, then, is bound up with recognition of the need of others and hence with knowledge in general. We must be freed, however, for this rational knowledge.

In the establishment of ethics various concepts of freedom have been developed. Thus F. Schleiermacher focused on God's fellowship with us, while K. Barth brought freedom and → obedience into dialectical relation, and R. Niebuhr adopted a Reformation view. The constitution of the free ethical subject is bound up with moral criticism in the concept of → autonomy, which has undergone a fundamental theological development in the idea of "theonomous autonomy" (F. Böckle). The concept of "theocentric ethics" is similar (J. M. Gustafson). The view of → conscience is also determined by that of freedom.

7.2.3.3. Ethics has rather a different basis when it does not focus on our being as subjects in relation to God but on God's history with us (S. Hauerwas and D. Ritschl speak of "story") and on our incorporation into the community (P. L. Lehmann). Theology thus presents us to ethics as persons in a comprehensive sense. Dogmatics has often developed this perspective in a more limited way as → sanctification. Ethics and life are thus seen as based upon God's creative work and his → faithfulness. In this regard theological ethics can speak of basic attitudes (→ Virtue) and must not rigorously reject this form of Christian morals.

7.2.3.4. What dogmatics says about sanctification shows that the theological place of ethics is eschatological (→ Eschatology) and pneumatological (→ Holy Spirit). Present reception of the promise of new → life, → righteousness, → peace, and → freedom forms the eschatological locus of ethics. It achieves here the knowledge of reality according to promise. Theological ethics thus does not merely aim at human responsibility but also seeks to establish an ethical orientation to the reality that God gives us (e.g., in the concept of the institution). This aspect might be called the pneumatological.

The relation of ethics to eschatology has been worked out in various ways, for example, as an orientation of life's relationships toward the → kingdom of God (see various forms of kingdom-of-God ethics, e.g., that of A. Ritschl) or in reflection on the commensurability or discrepancy between Christian ethics and reality. Theological ethics must test how far such conceptions correspond to the → hope based on the promise. This task is the critical one for an eschatologically oriented ethics. In this regard the theology of J. Calvin and its impact are especially important for theological ethics.

7.2.4. The construction of an ethics distinct from dogmatics, which was first attempted by Georg

Calixtus (1586-1656), had as its basis the application of the whole range of theological knowledge to ethics. Determining the task of ethics, however, was also bound up with theoretical questions, such as the epistemology of German → idealism. This approach brought ethics into the total context of learning, and it finally became a basic discipline itself. This view is still influential where ethics is seen as a discipline that must recognize the structure of reality. This idea has an impact in theological ethics when ethically viewed reality is given a hermeneutical task (→ Hermeneutics) relative to what we say about → God, or when T. Rendtorff talks about "ethical theology," which regards ethics as the science of the structure of human life. In this connection one might also refer to the idea of ethics as an integrative science of reality. In contrast is the view that ethics must be grounded in a theological concept of reality that it cannot itself produce (e.g., W. Pannenberg).

These issues are partial aspects of the distinction and unity of dogmatics and ethics. Either way, theological ethics concerns the relation between God's action and that of humans, considering not merely the scope and limit of human action but also, and primarily, God's comprehensive reality for ethics.

7.3. *Bible and Ethics*

The Bible as well as dogmatics serves as an introduction to theological ethics. The use of the Bible (→ Exegesis, Biblical) has a bearing on various tasks that biblical statements and directions set for ethics. We must consider the theological setting of biblical directions, such as the relation between the → Sermon on the Mount and the eschatological proclamation of Jesus, or that of → parenesis with statements about life in the Spirit. Ethics avoids using the Bible in a truncated and legalistic way. The designation of the → Word of God as law and gospel brings out this point theologically. In it we see how the biblical statements in their entirety comprehend faith and life.

In Christian → piety there have been different forms of a biblically based ethics, ranging from legalism to an attempt to expound the biblical statements as a comprehensive dogmatic and ethical view of reality (e.g., by K. Barth). We find a direct appeal to biblical models in conceptions that develop basic Christian attitudes (e.g., radical discipleship or a basic revolutionary attitude; → Revolution). Theological ethics will not try to rule out such attitudes but will try to give them their proper theological and ethical place.

7.4. *Ethics and Ecumenism*

In the church an ethics that accords with faith takes account of denominational factors (→ Confession).

Theological ethics, though, also has a concern for the → oikoumene (→ Ecumenism, Ecumenical Movement) and → ecumenical theology. It considers, too, how far ethics itself has an ecumenical task. In this regard the question arises whether it must formulate some theological → consensus relative to the basis of ethics or whether it can achieve consensus at the level of guidance for conduct (note the debate about the possibility of orthopraxy). Since the World Conference on Church and Society at Geneva in 1966, there has been a constant search for consensus on such issues as the participatory society, → racism, peace and justice, and responsibility for creation.

In comparing Roman Catholic → moral theology and Protestant theology, some basic insights have been achieved (e.g., in the concept of freedom) that might bring agreement in theological ethics. One decisive insight is that theological ethics too is subject to → tradition, and thus the relation of ethics to dogmatics has an ecumenical bearing. The specific ecumenical contribution of theological ethics might be that of giving specific expression to certain theological insights, such as the relation between faith and the reality of life. Ethics in an ecumenical context also includes criticism of historical foundations and of one-sided theorizings.

The link between ethics and the third article of the creed has been too little discussed. The development of ethics in relation to the church's activity, including its → liturgy, is also worth considering (as, e.g., S. Hauerwas and G. Wainwright have done). This focus is particularly important in an ecumenical ethics because it is here especially that the → Orthodox Church can make a contribution.

7.5. Ethics and the Religions

The ecumenical context in its broadest sense includes a concern for the ethics of the religions based primarily on the global perspective of ethics and the responsibility for national coexistence, which is an increasingly urgent ethical matter. New ethical research transcending the traditional problems of comparative religion forms the (also methodological) presupposition. In particular, the relation between ethics and religion must be thought out afresh. An agreement concerning ethics and morality is necessary because different religions must live together in ever closer proximity in many countries.

→ Deontology; Economic Ethics; Lifestyle; Metaethics; Motive, Ethics of; Sexual Ethics; Social Ethics; Values, Ethics of

Bibliography: M. E. ALLSOPP and J. J. O'KEEFE, eds., *Veritatis Splendor: American Responses* (Kansas City, Mo., 1995 • O. BAYER, *Freiheit als Antwort. Zur theologischen Ethik* (Tübingen, 1995) • O. BAYER and A. SUGGATE, eds., *Worship and Ethics: Lutherans and Anglicans in Dialogue* (Berlin, 1996) • K. L. BLOOMQUIST and J. R. STUMME, eds., *The Promise of Lutheran Ethics* (Minneapolis, 1998) • D. BONHOEFFER, *Ethics* (New York, 1995; orig. pub., 1949) • E. BRUNNER, *The Divine Imperative: A Study in Christian Ethics* (Philadelphia, 1947) • C. E. CURRAN, *History and Contemporary Issues: Studies in Moral Theology* (New York, 1996) • J. M. GUSTAFSON, *Ethics from a Theocentric Perspective* (2 vols.; Chicago, 1981-84); idem, *Protestant and Roman Catholic Ethics: Prospects for Rapprochement* (Chicago, 1978) • S. HAUERWAS, *The Peaceable Kingdom: A Primer in Christian Ethics* (Notre Dame, Ind., 1983); idem, *Vision and Virtue: Essays in Christian Ethical Reflection* (Notre Dame, Ind., 1974) • A. HERTZ et al., eds., *HCE* • R. HÜTTER and T. DIETER, eds., *Ecumenical Ventures in Ethics: Protestants Engage Pope John Paul II's Moral Encyclicals* (Grand Rapids, 1998) • H. KÜNG, *Global Responsibility: In Search of a New World Ethic* (New York, 1991) • J. MACQUARRIE, ed., *DCE* • J. MÍGUEZ BONINO, *Doing Theology in a Revolutionary Situation* (Philadelphia, 1975); idem, *Toward a Christian Political Ethics* (Philadelphia, 1983) • L. W. MUDGE, *The Church as Moral Community: Ecclesiology and Ethics in Ecumenical Debate* (New York, 1998) • R. NIEBUHR, *An Interpretation of Christian Ethics* (2d ed.; San Francisco, 1963; orig. pub., 1935); idem, *Moral Man and Immoral Society: A Study in Ethics and Politics* (New York, 1960; orig. pub., 1932) • T. W. OGLETREE, *The Use of the Bible in Christian Ethics: A Constructive Essay* (Philadelphia, 1983) • W. PANNENBERG, *The Church* (Philadelphia, 1983); idem, *Ethics* (Philadelphia, 1981) • R. H. PRESTON, *Confusions in Christian Social Ethics* (Grand Rapids, 1994) • P. RAMSEY, *Basic Christian Ethics* (New York, 1950) • L. L. RASMUSSEN, *Moral Fragments and Moral Community: A Proposal for Church in Society* (Minneapolis, 1993) • T. RENDTORFF, *Ethics* (2 vols.; Philadelphia, 1986-89) • A. RICH, *Wirtschaftsethik. Grundlagen in theologischer Perspektive* (Gütersloh, 1984) • H. THIELICKE, *Theological Ethics* (3 vols.; Grand Rapids, 1979) • G. WAINWRIGHT, *Doxology: The Praise of God in Worship, Doctrine, and Life. A Systematic Theology* (2d ed.; London, 1982) • J. P. WOGAMAN, *Christian Ethics: A Historical Introduction* (Louisville, Ky., 1993) • E. WOLF, *Sozialethik. Theologische Grundfragen* (Göttingen, 1975).

HANS G. ULRICH

Ethical Instruction → Parenesis

Ethiopia

	1960	1980	2000
Population (1,000s):	22,771	36,368	66,175
Annual growth rate (%):	2.30	2.46	3.06

Area: 1,133,882 sq. km. (437,794 sq. mi.)

A.D. 2000

Population density: 58/sq. km. (151/sq. mi.)
Births / deaths: 4.46 / 1.41 per 100 population
Fertility rate: 6.46 per woman
Infant mortality rate: 96 per 1,000 live births
Life expectancy: 52.4 years (m: 50.9, f: 54.1)
Religious affiliation (%): Christians 59.1 (Orthodox 36.9, Protestants 12.8, unaffiliated 7.0, indigenous 1.7, other Christians 0.8),Muslims 30.2, tribal religionists 10.4, other 0.3.

Ethiopia's population comprises some 80 distinct ethnolinguistic groups. Most numerous are the Oromo (40 percent), Amhara and Tigrean (32 percent), Sidamo (9 percent), Shankella (6 percent), Somali (6 percent), Afar (4 percent), and Gurage (2 percent). The Hadiya, Kambatta, Nuer, and Anuak are among the smaller groups.

The name of the earlier Christian kingdom situated in the northern regions of modern Ethiopia was Abyssinia, inhabited by peoples and languages of South Semitic affinity (→ Semites). It was here that the ancient kingdom of Axum flourished, becoming Christian in approximately A.D 340. Information on the first eight centuries of this venerable Christian kingdom is sketchy and shrouded in mystery. About the Zague dynasty (1137-1270), which had its capital in Lalibela (site of 11 underground rock-hewn churches), and the Solomon dynasty (1270-1974), more is known, for by then Ethiopia had become an acknowledged Christian power in the Horn of Africa. Coterminous with the ascent of the Zaguean and early Solomonic dynasties in the north were the Islamic sultanates of Hadiya, Bali, Fatagar, Dawaro, and Ifat (Adal) in the south of what is modern Ethiopia. Endemic political conflict throughout the region during the ensuing centuries was primarily defined by the rivalries between these sultanates and the Christian state, and by the emergence of the Oromo people as a vital third political force. A 30-year war from 1529 to 1559 dissipated the strength of both Christians and Muslims, paving the way for the diffusion of the Oromo throughout territories traditionally dominated by Christians and Muslims.

Modern Ethiopia traces its beginnings to Emperor Menelik II (1889-1913). His defeat of the Italians at the battle of Aduwa in 1896 gave him the distinction of being the only African ruler to defeat a modern European army, thereby legitimating his kingdom in the eyes of European colonial powers. With their political and military help, he was able to force Oromo kingdoms south of the Blue Nile and the Awash into one Greater Ethiopia. Emperor Haile Selassie (1892-1975) successfully maintained Menelik's gains until 1974, when he was deposed in a military coup that brought the Ethiopian People's Revolutionary Democratic Front (EPRDF) into power. With assistance from the former Soviet Union, the military regime pursued a Marxist-Leninist policy while at the same time continuing the Amharicizing and centralizing policy of the emperors. Throughout the 18 years of its tenure, the EPRDF was preoccupied with internal conflicts in which the Oromo, Tigrean, and Eritrean populations struggled for independence. Its repressive policies resulted in the exodus of some 1.5 million Ethiopians to neighboring countries (→ Refugees).

While Christianity, especially the → Ethiopian Orthodox Church, continues to be the dominant religious force in the highlands, adherents of Islam now constitute upwards of one-third of the total population. In the first century of the era of Muḥammad, Islam established bridgeheads on the African coast of the Red Sea (Dahlak Islands). With the help of Muslim slave traders, sultanates were then set up inland. Islamic orders (*tariqa*) established a tight network of monasteries (*zawiya*) across the whole country. Following the conquests of Menelik II, these → Islamic elements were forced underground but otherwise remained virtually intact. Following the → revolution in 1974, Muslims were invited to organize themselves democratically. Internal strife and civil war resulted in the execution and exile of leading imams, however, and the process was suspended until the overthrow of the EPRDF in 1991. With the implementation of the new constitution in December 1994, followed by national and regional popular elections in May and June 1995, Muslims once again became a political force in Ethiopia. Although at local levels qadis render judgments according to the Shari'a, Ethiopia has never had a mufti, or supreme national legal authority. Despite the demographic and growing political significance of Ethiopia's Muslims, relatively few (10 percent) find their way to → university. The reason is understandable: Amharic, a constituent part of the Abyssinian-Christian culture, is the basic language of the school system, and Muslims popularly regard it as apostasy to learn the "Christian" language and script.

Missionary work (→ Mission) has led to the formation of various Christian churches other than the Ethiopian Orthodox Church. The → Roman Catholic Church in Ethiopia, numbering approximately a half million members, traces its roots to the Portuguese expeditionary force that rescued the beleaguered Ethiopian Christians from an Islamic invasion by Aḥmad Grāñ (d. 1543). → Jesuits later secured the conversion of Emperor Susenyos (1607-32), and union with Rome followed in 1628 (→ Uniate Churches). Strong resistance by the Ethiopian Orthodox Church, expressed in the rebellion of most of the → bishops and → priests, resulted in the annulment of the union in 1632. In the 19th century Lazarists did successful missionary work in Tigray, in parts of central Ethiopia, and in Eritrea, as did Capuchins in the southern Oromo states. The churches in the North followed the Ge'ez Rite, which is parallel to that of the Ethiopian Orthodox Church, while those in the South adhered to the Latin Rite. Following the 1974-91 hiatus imposed by the short-lived EPRDF regime, Roman Catholic churches, schools, seminaries, and diaconal institutions (→ Diakonia) once again began operating freely throughout the country. The Capuchin Franciscan Institute of Philosophy and Theology, established in 1970 in Addis Ababa as the Franciscan Capuchin Friars' House of Philosophy, replaced the Stadium Philosophicum of Decamere, Eritrea. It is the only center for Catholic priestly formation in central and southern Ethiopia. Open to all religious and clergy who wish to send their candidates there for training, it enrolled some 300 students in 2000.

The earliest Protestant → missionaries to Ethiopia were the German Peter Heyling, the Swiss Samuel Gobat, and the German Johann Ludwig Krapf, arriving respectively in approximately 1634, 1830, and 1837. They each hoped to revive the Ethiopian Orthodox Church by their teaching or, failing that, to found Protestant churches. Ethiopian rulers were more interested in their industrial, military, and diplomatic services than in their religion, however, seeing in Protestant missions a potential threat to the integrity of the Ethiopian Orthodox Church and, hence, to Ethiopian cultural and political identity. Accordingly, official policy following World War I restricted Protestant missionary activity to the southern provinces — especially the Oromo territory that had been conquered and colonized by Menelik II around the turn of the century — where Orthodox churches were numerically weak and socially insignificant.

By 1935 eight mission societies were at work in southern Ethiopia: the Sudan Interior Mission, the Bible Churchmen's Missionary Society, the Seventh-day → Adventists, the United Presbyterian Mission of the U.S.A., the Church Mission to the Jews, Evangeliska Fosterlands-Stiftelsen (Sweden), Bibeltrogna Vänner (which split off from the preceeding group in 1911), and Hermannsburger Missionsanstalt. During the Italian occupation (1935-41) these mission societies had to suspend operations in the country, but since the Bible had already been translated into Oromo (by Onesimus Nesib in 1899), the few Protestant converts were able to consolidate themselves during this period, and the churches grew rapidly.

Between 1950 and 1975 these agencies were joined by numerous others, all engaged in evangelism, education, and development work. Following the very difficult period under the EPRDF, evangelical churches continue to thrive. The two numerically largest non-Orthodox denominations are the Ethiopian Evangelical Church Mekane Yesus (Lutheran, with strong Presbyterian congregations, and a member of both the → Lutheran World Federation and the → World Council of Churches), and the Kale Heywet (or "Word of Life," conservative evangelical, Baptist in orientation, with strong ties to SIM International, formerly known as the Sudan Interior Mission; → Evangelical Missions). Mekane Yesus statistics for 1998 indicate a membership of some 2.6 million, with another 1.3 million communicants, organized in 4,210 congregations and 2,416 preaching places and supporting some 1,176 evangelists. Kale Heywet numbers are equally impressive, with 1999 figures showing a membership in excess of 3.2 million, representing 4,072 congregations in 60 districts, served by 180 Bible schools and nearly 400 evangelists. Surging growth is also reported in the other nine denominations who, with the Mekane Yesus and the Kale Heywet churches, compose the Evangelical Churches Fellowship of Ethiopia.

A significant ecumenical presence in Ethiopia was radio station RVOG ("Radio Voice of the Gospel"), which from 1957 to 1977 served all of Africa (→ Christian Communication). Sponsored largely by the Lutheran World Federation with partnership from the Near East Christian Council and its successors (→ Middle East Council of Churches) and from local churches, as well as from 17 local program studios throughout Africa, the Near East, and Asia, headquarters for this station were located near Addis Ababa. The signal of RVOG extended over all of Africa and Southeast Asia. In 1977 the station was nationalized by the revolutionary government, becoming the "Voice of Revolutionary Ethiopia."

The famines that have ravaged Ethiopia, particularly that of 1984, have also been an occasion for concerted ecumenical response by the churches of the country as well as by international Christian relief agencies working alongside nonchurch and governmental relief operations (→ Relief and Development Organizations).

Bibliography: G. Arén, *Envoys of the Gospel in Ethiopia: In the Steps of the Evangelical Pioneers* (Uppsala, 1999); idem, *Evangelical Pioneers in Ethiopia* (Uppsala, 1978) • J. Bakke, *Christian Ministry Patterns and Functions within the Ethiopian Evangelical Church Mekane Yesus* (Oslo, 1987) • Ethiopian Orthodox Church, *The Church of Ethiopia: A Panorama of History and Spiritual Life* (Addis Ababa, 1997) • B. L. Fargher, *The Origins of the New Churches Movement in Southern Ethiopia, 1927-1944* (Leiden, 1996) • G. Hasselblatt, *Gespräch mit Gudina* (2d ed.; Stuttgart, 1981); idem, *Nächstes Jahr im Oromoland* (2d ed.; Stuttgart, 1984) • N. B. Hege, *Beyond Our Prayers: Anabaptist Church Growth in Ethiopia, 1948-1998* (Scottdale, Pa., 1998) • R. H. Kofi Darkwah, *Shewa, Menilek, and the Ethiopian Empire, 1813-1889* (2d ed.; London, 1978) • A. Legesse, *Gada* (New York, 1973) • I. M. Lewis, ed., *Nationalism and Self-Determination in the Horn of Africa* (London, 1983) • H. W. Lockot, *Bibliographica Aethiopica* (Wiesbaden, 1982) • M. Lundgren, *Proclaiming Christ to His World: The Experience of Radio Voice of the Gospel, 1957-1977* (Geneva, 1983) • R. Pankhurst, *A Social History of Ethiopia: The Northern and Central Highlands from Early Medieval Times to the Rise of Emperor Téwodros II* (Addis Ababa, 1990) • C. Potyka, *Haile Selassie* (Bad Honnef, 1974) • R. W. Solberg, *Miracle in Ethiopia: A Partnership Response to Famine* (New York, 1991) • J. S. Trimingham, *Islam in Ethiopia* (2d ed.; London 1965) • B. Zewde, comp., *A Short History of Ethiopia and the Horn* (Addis Ababa, 1998).

Gunnar Hasselblatt† and Jonathan J. Bonk

Ethiopian Orthodox Church

1. History and Constitution
2. Doctrines and Practices
3. Worship
4. Church and State

1. History and Constitution

The Ethiopian Orthodox Church, largest of the five non-Chalcedonian (→ Monophysite) Eastern churches (→ Oriental Orthodox Churches), traces its beginnings to the unexpected arrival of two young Syrian brothers accompanying their uncle, Meropius, on a voyage from Tyre to India in approximately A.D. 330. Putting into an Ethiopian Red Sea port for water, their ship was burned, and personnel on board were massacred in retaliation for the miscreant behavior of the crew of a vessel that had earlier visited the same port. The sole survivors were the two brothers, Frumentius and Aedesius, who were taken to Aksum, where they eventually came to occupy positions of influence in the royal court, serving as tutors to Prince ʿEzānā, whose eventual succession to the throne left them free to return to their own land. Frumentius, traveling to → Alexandria, pressed for the appointment of a → bishop to oversee the fledgling church in Ethiopia. Upon conferral with his fellow bishops, → Athanasius appointed Frumentius himself to the position. We can surmise that Frumentius enjoyed success in the exercise of his responsibilities, since Christianity soon became the official religion of the Aksumite kingdom, setting the stage for its eventual domination of the warp and woof of Ethiopian cultural and linguistic identity, a domination that continues to the present day.

In the wake of the divisive Council of → Chalcedon in 451, the Ethiopian church followed the → Coptic Orthodox Church in its adherence to non-Chalcedonian (Monophysite) doctrine. The arrival of the extraordinarily energetic "nine saints" (probably monks banished from Syria) toward the end of the fifth century further consolidated Monophysite Christianity in Ethiopia. It was they who introduced → monasticism to the country, translated the Scriptures into the Geʿez language, and laid the groundwork for the Ethiopian church's 12 centuries of successful resistance to Muslim attempts to absorb the country (→ Islam). While Muslim suzerainty over Egypt and North Africa from the seventh century onward severely hampered concourse between Egypt and Ethiopia, ties with the Patriarchate of Alexandria were nevertheless strengthened, continuing the ecclesiastical subordination of the Ethiopian Orthodox Church to the Coptic Church.

The patriarch of Alexandria selected and consecrated the church's metropolitan (*abuna*, lit. "our father") from among Egyptian monks. As a Copt, the metropolitan knew little about relations in Ethiopia and was thus largely isolated from rank-and-file clergy and church members. Three years after the death of Abuna Mattéwos in 1926, five Ethiopian monks were consecrated to serve under the newly appointed Abuna Qerillos, whose death, in turn, issued in the 1951 appointment of Basilios, the first indigenous Ethiopian abuna. Complete autonomy from → Alexandria was finally achieved in 1959, when Basilios was proclaimed → patriarch of Ethiopia, with full and duly acknowledged powers to nominate Ethiopian bishops and archbishops. The second partiarch of Ethiopia was Abuna Theopholis, who held office from 1970 to 1975. He, together with his successor, Princeton-educated Abuna Paulos, presided over the Ethiopian Orthodox Church during the country's tumultuous revolutionary years (1974-93), when the church suffered under a regime hostile to all religion generally and to the Orthodox Church in particular.

In A.D. 2000 Abuna Paulos was patriarch of Ethiopia and *echegé* (principal monk) of the See of Tekle Haimanot, presiding over 40 archbishops and archdioceses. The central office is that of → priest (*qēs*). A majority of the priests are married. Only those who are → celibate (i.e., the monks) may qualify for higher office. → Deacons and musicians (the *däbtära*s), commonly dedicated as young boys, carry out liturgical duties. In addition to strong Hebraic elements consonant with the country's Solomonic tradition, a distinguishing trait of Ethiopian Orthodox Church life is its monasticism. There are over 800 monasteries, with several houses for celibate women. Church estimates for 1997 place the number of adherents worldwide at approximately 40 million, worshiping in 30,000 churches served by 400,000 clergy, including priests, monks, deacons, and *däbtära*s.

2. Doctrines and Practices

Eleven beliefs and practices particularly characterize the Ethiopian Orthodox Church.

1. The church virtually canonizes the Ethiopic books of *Enoch* and *Jubilees,* and sometimes also *Ascension of Isaiah* (all added to the OT), and later also the *Didascalia apostolorum* and *Testamentum Domini* (added to the NT).
2. It adheres to a conciliar tradition subsequent to → Nicaea, Constantinople, and → Ephesus, resulting from the condemnation of Dioscorus (d. 454) at Chalcedon (→ Councils of the Church).
3. It holds to Monophysitism (→ Christology). (The church itself prefers the term "non-Chalcedonian," a matter of theological semantics that can never obscure an unequivocal orthodoxy.)
4. Mariology (→ Mary, Devotion to) constitutes an integral element of its → soteriology.
5. It venerates a broad panoply of → saints.
6. It practices male, and sometimes female, → circumcision.
7. It celebrates the → Eucharist both indoors (in the Holy of Holies) and outdoors.
8. It has the office of *däbtära,* specially trained musicians whose singing, dancing, and drumming constitute an integral part of Ethiopian worship.
9. It frequently observes both → Sunday and the (Saturday) → Sabbath (at least in rural areas).
10. It rejects purgatory but is officially ambivalent on the state of the dead (→ Eschatology; Hell).
11. It recognizes 250 fast days per year (→ Fasting), 180 of which are considered obligatory.

3. Worship

Modeled after the Jewish → temple, Ethiopian churches, whether round or octagonal, comprise three concentric rings. The *mäqdäs,* or innermost sanctuary, also called the *qeddastä qeddusan,* "Holy of Holies," is the liturgical center of the building, containing the *tabot,* or holy → altar slab representing the ark of the covenant, believed to have been brought to Ethiopia by Menelik I, considered the son of the biblical king → Solomon and the queen of Sheba. Only officiating priests may enter the *mäqdäs,* which is surrounded by the second ring, or *qeddast.* Worshipers receive the Eucharist in the *qeddast,* with women separated from men. The outer vestibule is the *qené mahalet* (the place of the cantors), where the *däbtära*s perform their liturgical functions, employing sistrum, drum, and harp in worship. This outer vestibule is divided into three sections by curtains, one reserved exclusively for the use of the musicians, one for laymen, and one for women. In an adjoining house, dubbed Bethlehem, a deacon prepares the sacramental unleavened bread and wine for the Eucharist. At the Eucharist 20 different formularies (→ Anaphora) are available, though only 14 are officially in print.

4. Church and State

Church and state have traditionally been closely intertwined in Christian Ethiopia, the ruler regarding himself as the defender of the faith. Following the 1974 coup d'état, which deposed Emperor Haile Selassie (ruled 1930-74), separation of → church and state was proclaimed, and the church was reduced to relative penury, losing both its privileged place and most of its revenue-generating property. Doggedly resilient throughout this period, which ended in 1993 with the restoration of religious freedom under Prime Minister Meles Zenawi, the church enters the 21st century evincing signs of renewed vitality. It continues to function as Ethiopia's cultural conservator and social catalyst throughout the highlands, where its adherents constitute a large majority of the population.

The Ethiopian Orthodox Church was a key player in the founding of the → World Council of Churches (1948) and of the → All Africa Conference of Churches (1963) and continues as an active member of both organizations. It also served as host to a meeting of the Orthodox churches in 1965, the first meeting of its kind since the ecumenical council of Ephesus in 431.

Bibliography: W. AYMRO and J. MOTOVU, eds., *The Ethiopian Orthodox Church* (Addis Ababa, 1970) • M. BELAYNESH, S. CHOJNACKI, and R. PANKHURST, eds., *The Dictionary of Ethiopian Biography* (vol. 1; Addis Ababa, 1975) • J. BONK, *An Annotated and Classified Bibliography of English Literature Pertaining to the Ethiopian Orthodox Church* (Metuchen, N.J., 1984) • E. A. W. BUDGE, *The Book of the Saints of the Ethiopian Church* (Cambridge, 1928) • ETHIOPIAN ORTHODOX CHURCH, *The Church of Ethiopia: A Panorama of History and Spiritual Life* (Addis Ababa, 1997) • E. HAMMERSCHMIDT, "Kultsymbolik der koptischen und der äthiopischen Kirche" and "Symbolik des orientalischen Christentums," *SyR* 10.212-32; 14.11-12, 15-17, 83-118 • M. E. HELDMAN, *African Zion: The Sacred Art of Ethiopia* (New Haven, 1993) • H. M. HYATT, *The Church of Ethiopia* (London, 1928) • O. A. JÄEGER, *Antiquities of North Ethiopia* (Stuttgart, 1965) • H. LUDOLF, *Ad suam historiam Aethiopicam antehac editam commentarius* (Frankfurt, 1691); idem, *Historia Aethiopica* (Frankfurt, 1681) • R. PANKHURST, *A Social History of Ethiopia: The Northern and Central Highlands from Early Medieval Times to the Rise of Emperor Téwodros II* (Addis Ababa, 1990) • S. PANKHURST, *Ethiopia: A Cultural History* (2d ed.; Essex, 1959) • C. PROUTY and E. ROSENFELD, *Historical Dictionary of Ethiopia* (Metuchen, N.J., 1981) • B. SUNDKLER and C. STEED, *A History of the Church in Africa* (Cambridge, 2000) • E. ULLENDORFF, *Ethiopia and the Bible* (Rome, 1971); idem, *The Ethiopians: An Introduction to Country and People* (London, 1965) • T. UQBIT, *Current Christological Positions of Ethiopian Orthodox Theologians* (Rome, 1973).

ERNST HAMMERSCHMIDT†, SIEGBERT UHLIG, and JONATHAN J. BONK

Ethnic Cleansing → Genocide

Ethnology

1. Terms and Tasks
2. Subject Matter
3. Methods
4. History
5. Relativizing of the European and American Monopoly of Rationality

1. Terms and Tasks

Ethnology crystallized out of older, 19th-century research into the academic discipline of describing nonliterate cultures. The Greek word *ethnos* shows that the reference is to tribes and not to nation-states. Modern ethnology no longer sees anything disparaging in this emphasis. On the contrary, anthropological relativism questions the thesis of the superiority of European and American cultures. In the German sphere ethnology has, on the one hand, a more comprehensive orientation with a strong historical accent (ethnography) and, on the other, a sociological orientation with theoretical accents (cultural and social → anthropology). The latter type goes beyond the classic restriction to nonliterate cultures and discusses literate cultures as well as theories of social change in an effort to achieve a general theory of human possibilities. Social anthropology in particular tries to understand and explain the diversity of human conduct, social organization, and cultural manifestations by comparing the widest possible variety of societies.

2. Subject Matter

In contrast to → sociology, ethnology studies the objectifications of a → culture (e.g., its art, artifacts, literature, and music). Since in nonliterate cultures the social conditions projected onto genealogies (i.e., relationships) are very important, the ethnology of relationship is a very significant field.

From the very first, the ethnology of → religion has been central to the discipline, and with the end of the colonial period, the same is also true of the ethnology of political institutions. As the peoples of the → Third World have increasingly articulated their problems of survival, interest has grown in economic anthropology, and the urgent crisis in the → environment (→ Ecology) has brought similar interest in ecological anthropology.

For a long time religious ethnology was dominated by apologetic motifs. P. W. Schmidt, for example, thought he could find everywhere an original → monotheism. B. Malinowski, E. Evans-Pritchard, and R. Horton showed the internal rationality and empirical plausibility of the be-

lief-systems of nonliterate cultures. Research into →
social movements and religious dynamics in social
crises — for example, → millenarianism and nativ-
ism (W. E. Mühlmann) — became theologically relevant (in OT studies, also the political anthropology
of tribal societies, e.g., Lang in E. W. Müller et al.).

3. Methods

Most advance has come through pioneering monographs on cultures or on aspects of a culture. Even
where no monographs exist about a given culture,
specific products or → institutions are set in relation to the general social structure. Field research,
involving observation of the life of a → society and
participation in it, is central. So is use of the language of those under study. Some part is also played
by statistical research (esp. on the economy), material inventories, cross-disciplinary studies of the
natural environment, and studies in comparative
history.

4. History

As in many other sciences, the trends that have
shaped the history of ethnology have also influenced related disciplines. These trends have included evolutionism, → functionalism, → structuralism, and neomaterialism. We know that most
societies are interested in how their customs and institutions arose and in what the differences from
neighboring societies mean. Information has been
gathered in order to understand how people adjust
to their environment, how they use economic, social, and political institutions in different ways, and
how their forms of society, always highly developed
and complex, developed from earlier forms.

In England, France, and Germany ethnology developed in the early 19th century out of attempts to
classify the human races. There were studies comparing "primitive" societies and those of antiquity,
as well as investigations focusing on the historical
development of religious and economic institutions. Finally around 1840 (before Charles Darwin),
the principle of evolution was proposed for the
study of such matters. But the insights of such
field-workers as J.-F. Lafitau and G. Forster were not
used. On the basis of these and other traveler's tales
and historical inquiries, certain cultural features —
sometimes called relics of earlier cultural epochs —
were compared. The resulting research, however, although it provided massive materials, produced no
conclusive result.

Franz Boas demanded instead that we should observe human conduct in its natural environment
and gather social facts and objects and record ob-

servable cultural processes. The individual cultures
should be seen as a whole. In the resultant functionalism (Malinowski, M. Herskowitz) the interrelation between different elements in a culture came
under investigation. Facts were explained in terms
of their actual function in a given society.

In contrast, Marcel Mauss viewed society as an
indivisible social → organism. The structuralism
based on this and on F. de Saussure's linguistics
(C. Lévi-Strauss, A. R. Radcliff-Brown) tried to
identify the elements in a culture that give it a systematic character above the fluctuations of empirical reality. The true object of study should be
the system/grammar, which, although only partially known at best to those within a society,
gives rise to both conduct and order. As was soon
recognized, inherent in such theories is a tendency to oversystematize and overharmonize.

M. Gluckman emphasized that → conflicts can
be regarded as a structuring and even a stabilizing
element in social structures. With the expansion of
economic anthropology, a surrender of the postulate of harmonization produced methodologically
different trends, all of which can be described as
neomaterialistic. We reproduce ourselves in a system of partially overlapping economic spheres that
are themselves embedded in a social structure of
power and interests.

5. Relativizing of the European and American
Monopoly of Rationality

Economic anthropologists showed that a peasant
"moral" economy follows a rationality of "safety
first," which as a survival strategy is much superior
to a principle of maximization (J. Scott). In investigations of American society that are satirical in part,
Horace Miner and W. Lloyd Warner showed that
when ethnological methods are applied to European
and American societies, we can find in core areas of
modern → everyday life the same magical thinking
as is thought to be a block to modernization in the
Third World. It has become an increasingly significant task of ethnology to decode the magical-
religious element in everyday economic belief, in
political rituals, and in the pyramidal military and
energy structures of our age.

→ Development; Evolution; Religious Studies

Bibliography: J. O. Beozzo and F. Wilfred, *Frontier Violations: The Beginnings of New Identities* (London,
1999) • F. Boas, *Race, Language, and Culture* (New
York, 1940) • E. Evans-Pritchard, *Witchcraft, Oracles,
and Magic among the Azande* (Oxford, 1937) •
H. Fischer, ed., *Ethnologie–eine Einführung* (Berlin,

1983) • M. Gluckman, *Custom and Conflict in Africa* (Oxford, 1956) • D. Groh, "Ethnologie als Universalwissenschaft," *Merkur* 36 (1982) 1217-25 • R. Horton, "African Traditional Thought and Western Science," *Africa* 37 (1967) 50-71, 155-87 • M. Klaus and M. K. Weisgrau, *Across the Boundaries of Belief: Contemporary Issues in the Anthropology of Religion* (Boulder, Colo., 1999) • R. König and A. Schmalfuss, eds., *Kulturanthropologie* (Düsseldorf, 1972) • B. Lang, *Anthropological Approaches to the OT* (Philadelphia, 1985) • C. Lévi-Strauss, *Anthropologie structurale* (Paris, 1958) • B. Malinowski, *Argonauts of the Western Pacific* (London, 1922); idem, *Coral Gardens and Their Magic* (2 vols.; London, 1935) • C. Meillassoux, *Anthropologie économique des Gouro de Côte d'Ivoire* (Paris, 1964) • W. E. Mühlmann, *Chiliasmus und Nativismus* (Berlin, 1964) • W. E. Mühlmann and E. W. Müller, eds., *Kulturanthropologie* (Cologne, 1966) • E. W. Müller et al., eds., *Ethnologie als Sozialwissenschaft* (Cologne, 1984), see esp. article by E. W. Müller • G. P. Murdoch, *Atlas of World Cultures* (Pittsburgh, 1981) • T. W. Overholt, *Cultural Anthropology and the OT* (Minneapolis, 1996) • A. R. Radcliff-Brown, *Structure and Function in Primitive Society* (London, 1959) • W. Schmied-Kowarzik and J. Stagl, eds., *Grundfragen der Ethnologie. Beiträge zur gegenwärtigen Theorie-Diskussion* (Berlin, 1981) • C. A. Schmitz, ed., *Religionsethnologie* (Frankfurt, 1964) • J. Scott, *The Moral Economy of the Peasant* (New Haven, 1976).

GEORG ELWERT

Eucharist

Overview

The Eucharist (or Holy Communion or the Lord's Supper) has had from the very beginning a place of special importance in the life of Christianity. The eating and drinking of bread and wine in obedience to the command of Jesus at his Last Supper with his disciples is a sensory representation of the spiritual reality of the Christ whom Christians believe in and confess. The celebration of the Eucharist shows clearly, and makes known, that which Christian life in praise and thanksgiving attests to (→ Worship), that which shapes it in the ministry of reconciliation (→ Diakonia), and that which Christian doctrine ponders and formulates as the work of Christ (→ Christology), as the operation of the → Holy Spirit, and as the mission of the church. As an expression of fellowship or communion, the Eucharist — along with → baptism, which incorporates into the new people of God, and the ministry, which gives structure to the Christian community (→ Offices, Ecclesiastical) — serves as a preeminent accreditation of the church of Jesus Christ. Full table fellowship is a sign of the → unity of the church. Its denial characterizes denominationally divided Christianity.

The Eucharist has been a central theme in the → ecumenical movement that began in the 19th century, as it has also been throughout church history, especially from the time of the Reformation. Theological conversations between individual churches, efforts at union in many lands (→ United and Uniting Churches), and world conferences on the topic show that agreement in the understanding and ordering of the Eucharist is regarded as absolutely essential for unity among the churches. We consider here the results of the various conversations that have been proceeding at different levels (see 1). If denominations are to come together, they must necessarily go back to the NT texts (see 2). Furthermore, they must consider the developments in the church and theology that have led to controversies about the Eucharist (see 3). We consider also the problems, trends, forms, and texts of contemporary practice (see 4), as well as the question of intercommunion (see 5), which is so important for the future of the ecumenical movement.

1. Ecumenical Discussion
In the later 20th century many Christian churches engaged in intensive discussion of the Eucharist. The results may be seen in various reports and statements of varying degrees of authority and scope, some being denominational or regional studies, others documents of convergence or consensus. The → dialogue took place, and still takes place, on three levels: (1) as a dialogue among churches of the Reformation (esp. between Lutherans and Reformed, but also involving the Anglicans), (2) bilateral conversations involving either the → Roman Catholic Church or the → Orthodox churches, and (3) conversations and statements on the level of the → World Council of Churches (WCC).

1.1. *Among Reformation Churches*
At the instigation of the Evangelical Church in Germany, conversations began in 1947 that led to the Arnoldshain Theses of 1957, with a final report in 1962. This discussion dealt with issues arising from the Lutheran-Reformed controversies of the 16th century, including the nature of Christ's presence in the Eucharist (whether a personal presence or a "substantial" presence in the elements); the mutual relation of Spirit, Word, → faith, and → sacrament; and the closely related issues of "oral eating" *(manducatio oralis)* of the Eucharist and its reception by the wicked *(manducatio impiorum)*. The answer given in thesis 4 was of decisive importance. The core of it was adopted in the → Leuenberg Agreement of 1973, and then by the participating European churches of Reformed provenance. It is to the effect that in the Eucharist the risen Jesus Christ gives himself in his vicarious body and blood through his word of promise with bread and wine (see Leuenberg no. 18). Conversations between the Lutherans and Reformed led to similar results in the Netherlands (1956), France (1960), and North America (1966).

The Lutheran World Federation and the Anglican Lambeth Conference (→ Anglican Communion) authorized conversations from 1970 to 1972 that reached a provisional conclusion in the so-called Pullach Report (1972). Though what this document says about the Eucharist primarily describes what the two churches teach and practice, it also gives evidence, especially in its comments about consecration and the eucharistic sacrifice, of attitudes to theological traditions and ways of thinking that plainly widen the horizon as compared with those in the Lutheran-Reformed documents.

1.2. *Bilateral Conversations*
1.2.1. Conversations between Anglicans and Roman Catholics about the Eucharist produced the Windsor Statement of 1971 (supplemented in 1979 by the Salisbury "Elucidations on Eucharist and Ministry"). The decisive point here is that the Eucharist is an effective representation and memorial *(anamnesis)* of the event of salvation. As such, it enables the church to participate in the movement of Christ's self-offering. In a return to biblical and early patristic paschal theology, the Eucharist is thus set in the context of a theology of salvation history and freed from a certain isolation and constriction (e.g., the Eucharist as a → means of grace). Dialogue between Methodists and Roman Catholics led to very similar results (Denver Report, 1971; Dublin Report, 1976).

1.2.2. Dialogue between the → Lutheran World Federation and the Roman Catholic Church concluded in 1978 with a statement entitled *Das Herrenmahl* (The Lord's Supper), which in its first part tries to formulate a "common witness" and in its second part mentions "common tasks." (Still open questions are the duration of Christ's eucharistic presence and the understanding of the eucharistic sacrifice and ministry.) Worth noting in the common witness is the return to liturgical tradition (the concluding doxology in the prayer of consecration has a structural function in this regard; → Eucharistic Prayer) and the emphasis, alien to the Lutheran tradition (→ Lutheranism), on the role of the Holy Spirit (including the epiclesis in the → liturgy).

The adoption of an anamnesis theology (the Eucharist as representation and memorial of the history of Christ), the positive view of a cosacrifice of Christians in the Eucharist (incorporation into Christ's sacrifice), and the development of a → eucharistic ecclesiology all led beyond traditional Lutheran teaching and also beyond the subjects and results of the Lutheran-Reformed discussions.

Conversations between Lutherans and Roman Catholics also took place at the regional level (e.g., in the United States in 1967 and 1970). Declarations in 1971 and 1972 of the Groupe des Dombes can be traced back to conversations between French-speaking Lutheran, Reformed, and Roman Catholic theologians. The jubilee of the → Augsburg Confession (→ Confessions and Creeds) in 1980 also provided opportunity to continue the dialogue, especially between Lutherans and Roman Catholics.

1.2.3. The results of conversations between the → World Alliance of Reformed Churches and the Roman Catholic Church appear in the report *The Presence of Christ in the Church and the World* (1977). This statement goes beyond the Lutheran-Reformed conversations (Arnoldshain and Leuenberg) by adopting a paschal theology and the related anamnesis theology, especially in the section on the paschal mystery of Christ and the Eucharist.

1.2.4. The Eucharist also has played an important role in conversations between the Reformation churches and the Eastern Orthodox churches. Worth noting is the Anglican-Orthodox Moscow Declaration (1976). Conversations from as early as the 1920s preceded this statement. Western points of controversy (concerning the real presence and the nature of the sacrifice) play a less important part in this declaration, and there is more stress on a pneumatologically based eucharistic ecclesiology (i.e., the Eucharist "actualizes" the church, which must constantly invoke the Holy Spirit if it is to endure).

Dialogue after 1959 between the Evangelical Church in Germany and the Russian Orthodox Church produced two reports on conversations held on the Eucharist (Zagorsk [now Sergiyev Posad, near Moscow], in 1973, on the Eucharist; and Arnoldshain, in 1976, on the sacrifice of Christ and of Christians). The Eucharist also frequently came under discussion in conversations between the Evangelical Church in Germany and the Ecumenical → Patriarchate of Constantinople (in 1975, invocation of the Holy Spirit in the Eucharist; in 1978, the Eucharist and priesthood). In conversations between the Evangelical Church in Germany and the Romanian Orthodox Church, the jubilee of the Augsburg Confession provided a chance to compare the teaching of the two churches on the sacraments.

1.3. *Lima Text*

From its very beginning, the → Faith and Order movement has addressed issues regarding the Eucharist. Almost all of its conferences have said something about it, and from Århus (1964) onward it has become a central subject. An attempt was made to summarize the agreement that the ecumenical movement had reached on → baptism, the Eucharist, and the ministry. The text of the Accra meeting

(1974), which reflected the earlier Bristol meeting (1967) and the Louvain conference (1971), was submitted to the churches for their opinions in 1975. The replies were carefully evaluated at a consultation in Crêt-Bérard, Switzerland, in 1977, and a new text was drawn up. It was approved at the Faith and Order conference held in 1982 in Lima, Peru.

The Lima text — entitled *Baptism, Eucharist, and Ministry,* and quickly nicknamed *BEM* — deals with the institution of the Eucharist, which is given to the church as a gift of the Lord and a sacramental meal. It then deals with its significance from five standpoints: thanksgiving to the Father; anamnesis, or memorial, of the Son; invocation of the Spirit; communion of the faithful; and meal of the kingdom. Of central importance are the concepts of anamnesis and epiclesis. At its core the Eucharist is a memorial of Christ and, as such, "the living and effective sign of his sacrifice" ("Eucharist," par. 5). The Christ-event is present in the power of the Spirit, and the Eucharist is thus "the foretaste of his *parousia* and of the final kingdom" (6). A final section deals with the liturgical celebration of the Eucharist. It lists the essential liturgical elements, commends frequent communion ("at least every Sunday," 31), and discusses the problem of the duration of the eucharistic presence, the possibility of the use of other elements, and who is to preside at its administration.

A kind of commentary on the Lima text, which also gives concrete form to its liturgical implications, appears in the eucharistic liturgy drawn up for Faith and Order at Lima (the Lima Liturgy of 1982). It follows in basic outline the Western type (introduction, liturgy of the Word, eucharistic celebration). The Anglican tradition has had a special influence (with its prayer of consecration), as has the revised Roman Catholic order (with its unfortunate division of the epiclesis into a transformation epiclesis and a communion epiclesis), and there are also traces of the orders of the new united churches (e.g., South India). Of special theological significance are the formulations in the eucharistic prayer that speak of an offering of the Eucharist by the church (i.e., bringing this memorial before God in unity with Christ's priesthood) or of asking God to have regard to this Eucharist that he has given the church and graciously to receive it as he receives the sacrifice of his Son.

These and similar formulations bring to light the problems that the *BEM* poses for theological thinking oriented to the → Reformers. The action of the church in the Eucharist, its "cooperation in the Spirit," receives emphasis in a way that seems to overshadow the nature of the Eucharist as a gift, though the statement does mention this aspect as well. Although Christ may indeed give himself to his people in, with, and under the action of the church in thanksgiving, praise, and anamnesis (U. Kühn), the boundary between the action of the church and the nature of the Eucharist as a gift needs to be drawn more clearly than is done in this text. The same applies to the relation between the Eucharist and the church's other acts of proclamation.

Bibliography: J. J. VON ALLMEN, The Lord's Supper (Richmond, Va., 1969) • H. DAVIES, Bread of Life and Cup of Joy: Newer Ecumenical Perspectives on the Eucharist (Grand Rapids, 1993) • R. FRIELING, "Orthodox–Evangelisch–Katholisch," MdKI 32 (1981) 94-99, 105-8; 33 (1982) 26-32 (survey of dialogue with Eastern churches) • A. I. C. HERON, Table and Tradition: Toward an Ecumenical Understanding of the Eucharist (Philadelphia, 1983) • U. KÜHN, "Abendmahl IV: Das Abendmahlgespräch in der ökumenischen Theologie der Gegenwart," TRE 1.145-212 (extensive bibliography) • H. MEYER and L. VISCHER, eds., Growth in Agreement: Reports and Agreed Statements of Ecumenical Conversations on a World Level (New York, 1984) • J. H. P. REUMANN, The Supper of the Lord: The NT, Ecumenical Dialogues, and Faith and Order on Eucharist (Philadelphia, 1985) • M. THURIAN, ed., Churches Respond to BEM (6 vols.; Geneva, 1986-88); idem, ed., Ecumenical Perspectives on Baptism, Eucharist, and Ministry (Geneva, 1983) • M. WELKER, What Happens in Holy Communion? (Grand Rapids, 2000) • WORLD COUNCIL OF CHURCHES, Baptism, Eucharist, and Ministry (Geneva, 1982).

KARL-HEINRICH BIERITZ

2. NT Texts

2.1. The Last Supper

Recollection of the last meal of Jesus on the night he was betrayed (1 Cor. 11:23) was of constitutive importance for the celebration of the Eucharist in the primitive church.

2.1.1. This conclusion emerges especially from the four NT accounts (Mark 14:22-25; Matt. 26:26-29; Luke 22:15-20; 1 Cor. 11:23-26), though they cannot be viewed as direct historical testimonies. From the standpoint of form criticism they are cultic etiologies. Their life setting is the meeting of the → congregation for a liturgical meal. Their aim is to show that Jesus founded this event and gave it its shape. The liturgical practice of the community manifested itself at many points (e.g., the command to eat and drink, the order to repeat the meal, the reference to remembrance of Jesus), as well as in the increasingly strong tendency to smooth the sayings about the bread and the cup to make them parallel to one another (→ Liturgy).

Matthew's version is the most strongly stylized. From the standpoint of the tradition, it is wholly dependent on Mark's version. Research seems to indicate that the versions of Mark and Paul are ancient and independent variants of the tradition. Although neither can claim clear priority, each has preserved original elements. In some phrases Mark 14:22-25 has some Semitic linguistic coloring, especially in the cup saying and the eschatological saying. Yet the structure and order (the parallelism of bread and cup in both word and action) give evidence of liturgical influence. The text at 1 Cor. 11:23-26 has been smoothed down linguistically and given a theological interpretation, thus making precise the relation between the → covenant and the blood, which is unclear in Mark. Again, the eschatological saying (v. 26) is freely paraphrased in adjustment to the situation of the community.

The formal divergence, however, between the two interpretive sayings (body and cup, rather than body and blood) might well be original. In the tradition behind the two versions, the sayings might have been "This is my body" and "This is my blood of the covenant that is shed for many." But in this form the cup saying can hardly be original, since the two interpretations "blood of the covenant" and "shed for many" seem to be unrelated and do not fit together too well linguistically. If we regard the covenant motif as an interpretive importation, the original could be "This cup is my blood for many." The Lukan version is close to → Paul but presupposes an independent tradition that consciously set the supper within the Passover.

2.1.2. As regards the historicity of the institution, the main point is that it harmonizes with the total picture of the work of Jesus disclosed in the Synoptic gospels. Research does not support a post-Easter origin for the institution. The same applies to a twofold origin in post-Easter feasts of the Palestinian community and in memorial feasts of the Hellenistic community (H. Lietzmann). It applies also to the theory that the → primitive Christian community continued the fellowship meals of the pre-Easter → Jesus and only secondarily gave them a Christological basis in stories of institution (W. Marxsen). The Last Supper undoubtedly stands in close relation to the meals that Jesus had with his disciples and also with tax collectors and sinners (Mark 2:16; Luke 15:2), in which he guaranteed saving fellowship with God in anticipation of the messianic banquet (→ Eschatology). Nevertheless, the

Last Supper represented a turning point in comparison with them. Whereas the presence of Jesus had previously made fellowship possible, the Last Supper now pointed to the new situation brought about by his approaching death.

The death of Jesus does not contradict his mission. On the contrary, it is its culmination. His saving intervention for others finds completion in his offering of himself for many, that is, for those who are far from God (see Isa. 53:11). Thus his death does not end fellowship but gives it a new basis. This is the point of the interpretive sayings that Jesus attaches to the benediction that normally opens the Jewish feast with the breaking of bread, and to the thanksgiving over the cup of blessing that closes it. "Body" denotes his personal, historic existence; "blood," his self-offering.

We do not have here a mere parabolic action that gives a meaningful representation of the fruit of the death of Jesus (J. Jeremias) but a real and efficacious action. As Jesus gives himself in and with the bread and wine, he brings those who are far from God into the saving fellowship with him that he makes possible and defines — namely, the fellowship in which the → kingdom of God is already present and at work. The true gift of the Eucharist to which these sayings point is the fellowship of → disciples that the intervention of Jesus in death makes possible.

A secondary question is whether the Last Supper was a → Passover meal, as the → Synoptics seem to affirm and John's presentation (John 18:28; 19:14) seems to deny. Historically, the Synoptics may well be right. The sayings, however, do not refer to specific elements in the Passover (e.g., the paschal lamb and bitter herbs) but only to the elements that the Passover had in common with other Jewish feasts. Wholly peripheral are the points of contact with the fellowship meals of → Qumran (1QS 6:2-5; 1QSa 2:17-21), for the central cultic language that we find there is completely lacking in the eucharistic traditions.

2.2. The Eucharist in Christian Worship

With → baptism, the Eucharist became a basic element in Christian → worship. It went by different names: "Lord's supper" (1 Cor. 11:20), the breaking of bread (1 Cor. 10:16; Acts 2:46; 20:7, 11), "gather[ing] together" (or synaxis, 1 Clem. 34.7). At the beginning of the second century the original term for the opening prayer (Heb. bĕrākâ, Gk. eucharistia; see 1 Cor. 11:24) became, pars pro toto, the term for the whole action, "Eucharist, thanksgiving" (Did. 9.1, 5; Ign. Eph. 13.1; Phld. 4; Smyrn. 8.1).

Paul seems to have assumed that his letters would be read at worship (see 1 Cor. 16:20-24;

2 Cor. 13:12-13), and there may be here already an allusion to fixed elements in the eucharistic liturgy; note mention of the holy → kiss (Did. 14.2), the exclusion of the unbaptized and impenitent, the cry "Marana tha" (1 Cor. 16:22; cf. Rev. 22:20), and the blessing.

The actual Eucharist was initially a real meal enframed by the solemn breaking of bread with the bread saying and by the handing round of the cup of blessing (1 Cor. 10:16) with the cup saying. Only in the second century did the real meal come to be finally separated from the sacramental meal (→ Sacrament), as anticipated in 1 Cor. 11:34.

2.3. Theological Interpretation

In the NT the theological interpretation provided powerful impulses to → Christology and ecclesiology. The motif of self-offering for many was of decisive significance for Christology. In the history of the tradition it formed the starting point for the interpretation of the death of Jesus as a vicarious → atonement for human → sin. The oldest sayings about Jesus dying "for us" are the eucharistic sayings and those rooted in the eucharistic tradition (Mark 10:45; Luke 22:27; Rom. 3:24-25; Gal. 1:4; 2:20). This tradition was also the point of departure for the development of the concept of the new covenant, the eschatological order of salvation that was established by the death of Jesus.

Decisive for ecclesiology was the concept of the → church as a fellowship established by the self-offering of Jesus. Thus in the light of the bread saying, Paul developed his understanding of the church as the body of Christ, which comes into being by participation in the gift of Jesus (1 Cor. 10:17), and in which Christ unfolds his living power as the members serve one another (12:12-27). Unloving conduct at the Lord's Table is disregard for the gift of the Eucharist (11:27-31). In keeping is the fact that Paul viewed baptism and the Eucharist as the two saving gifts with which God accompanies his people through history and by which he continually binds them to himself (10:1-13).

Bibliography: J. BETZ, Die Eucharistie in der Zeit der griechischen Väter (vol. 2/1; 2d ed.; Freiburg, 1964) • G. BORNKAMM, "Herrnmahl und Kirche bei Paulus," ZTK 53 (1956) 312-49 • G. DELLING, "Abendmahl III," TRE 1.47-58 (extensive bibliography) • J. JEREMIAS, The Eucharistic Words of Jesus (Philadelphia, 1977) • A. A. JUST JR., The Ongoing Feast: Table Fellowship and Eschatology at Emmaus (Collegeville, Minn., 1993) • B. KOLLMANN, Ursprung und Gestalten der frühchristlichen Mahlfeier (Göttingen, 1990) • X. LÉON-DUFOUR, Sharing the Eucharistic Bread: The Witness of *the NT* (New York, 1987) • H. Lietzmann, *Mass and Lord's Supper: A Study in the History of the Liturgy* (Leiden, 1979; orig. pub., 1926) • W. Marxsen, *The Beginnings of Christology, together with The Lord's Supper as a Christological Problem* (Philadelphia, 1979) • P. Neuenzeit, *Das Herrenmahl* (Munich, 1960) • E. Schweizer, *The Lord's Supper according to the NT* (Philadelphia, 1967) • D. E. Smith, "The More Original Form of the Words of Institution," *ZNW* 83 (1992) 166-86.

                                        Jürgen Roloff

3. Development in the Church and Theology

3.1. Early Church and Orthodox Churches

3.1.1. Theological Context

The Eucharist assumed central significance for the church's life in the Orthodox churches, which makes their understanding of it of decisive importance in recent ecumenical reflection on the nature of Christian → worship and the Lord's Supper.

3.1.2. Early Church

As the apostolic period shows great variety, so in the teaching of the early church about the Eucharist one can find no uniform starting point and no single line of development. Concern with practice was predominant, while interest in the underlying theological reflection was secondary. The great → Docetic, Christological, and → Donatist controversies affected the Eucharist, but it never became a specific theme of theological debate or writing. There was no set dogma until we come to the seventh ecumenical council (Nicaea II, in 787), in connection with the Iconoclastic Controversy (→ Images; Christian Art 2). This council definitively repudiated any identification of Christ's real presence in the bread and wine with his symbolic presence in → icons, which was interpreted in terms of the Platonic schema of original and copy (→ Platonism; Iconography).

The basic form of the Eucharist, which has remained binding for the great denominations today, took shape in the first four centuries. It appears in the great liturgies of the Orthodox Church, within which the doctrinal development of the early church essentially reached a culmination in the eighth century as regards the Eucharist.

3.1.3. Orthodox Churches

For the Orthodox, the Eucharist is a feast of fellowship of Christian believers at a set place, originally a house. In it they gather to remember *(anamnēsis)* with thanksgiving *(eucharistia)* and praise *(doxologia)* the saving act of God on our behalf that culminated in the crucifixion and resurrection of Jesus. In confession and concrete proclamation they also experience and bear witness to the liberating presence of the risen Lord, who forgives sins and opens up new life. They can be certain of this presence during their own future and that of the world, which is hastening to its end ("let grace come and this world perish" — *Marana tha*). The Lord and host at this feast is the exalted Christ himself. In the freedom of his grace he comes to the celebrating → congregation in the → Holy Spirit and draws it up into the redemptive fulfillment of his saving work. By his liberating work he gives it fellowship with himself and therefore fellowship within itself *(koinōnia)*. Everything takes place in the power of the Holy Spirit.

In the → liturgy, then, after a grateful glance back at → salvation history in the recitation of the words of institution, there is rapid advance to the *epiklēsis* (invocation) of the Holy Spirit, which effects the real presence of the risen Lord in the elements of bread and wine (his body and blood) that in the Great Entrance have been brought to the → altar. We see here why the epiclesis occupies such a special place in the understanding of the Eucharist in the Orthodox Church. It, not the recitation of the words of institution, has consecratory significance. Yet the process of consecration is not restricted to the epiclesis prayer, for the whole liturgy is understood in terms of epiclesis. It comes to itself, as it were, in the epiclesis prayer. Thus the Orthodox celebration is a great Spirit-effected mystery drama that enacts the saving work of God in prayer and song. Its prayer character shows that the presence of God in Christ by the Holy Spirit is solely an affair of the triune God. The epiclesis itself does not effect it, nor does the one who offers it (the priest), but only the Lord whom he invokes.

In a way that is impressive in comparison with the practice of the Roman Mass and the Protestant Eucharist (at least before the movement of liturgical renewal), this basic structure of the Eucharist accentuates especially the ecclesiologically communal, eschatological, and cosmic dimensions of the Christ who savingly re-presents himself in the liturgical action of the congregation. Already very early, however, it had undergone some profound modifications.

3.1.3.1. The detaching of the meal *(agapē)* that was originally connected with the Eucharist (1 Cor. 11:17-22) has impaired the Eucharist in all the great churches. In this meal we see the increasing dominance of the influence of the mystery religions (the elements of the Eucharist as the medicine of immortality, the antidote to death, Ign. *Eph.* 20.2) over the relationship to Jewish feasts.

3.1.3.2. The NT concept of a sacrifice of thanksgiving has been overlaid by that of an atoning →

sacrifice that the consecrating priest, and with him the church that is drawn up into the total offering of Christ, brings to God the Father. This shift results in the changing of the communion epiclesis into a consecration epiclesis and also in giving a dominant position to the cultically ordained priest, who alone makes the Eucharist possible.

3.1.3.3. A theory of transformation has developed in explanation of the process of consecration by epiclesis, and in adoption and expansion of the analogous theory of Christological assumption advanced by Justin Martyr (ca. 100-ca. 165). As the divine Logos took flesh and blood in the incarnation, so the bread and wine become Christ's flesh and blood by consecration. And as bread and wine naturally become part of the body that they nourish and are thus changed into it, so supernaturally by invocation of the Holy Spirit the elements are changed into Christ's body and blood. We are thus to worship them, though only in the context of the Eucharist; there is no sacramental cult outside it.

At the medieval councils that sought union with Rome, the theory of transubstantiation supplemented or replaced this theory of transformation, and the new theory took on a sharper profile in opposition to Lutheran and Reformed views. The eucharistic teaching of Patriarch Cyril Lucaris (1570-1638), which approximated that of Calvin, was rejected. Nevertheless, more recent Orthodox theology repudiates transubstantiation as too physical.

3.1.3.4. A commendable aspect of the Orthodox Eucharist is its emphasis on the cosmic and eschatological dimension of Christ's saving work as a new creation, in contrast to the anthropomonist restriction of this work in the West. The former, however, has come to be burdened with overphysical speculation (e.g., the idea of the impregnation of nature with powers of immortality).

3.2. Roman Catholic Church

3.2.1. Sacrifice of the Mass

The stress on the Eucharist that resulted from the Roman Catholic theory of the sacrifice of the Mass had as its decisive cause a shift in the understanding of the church that began in the early church and continued in the Middle Ages. On this view the communion of saints is a company of sinners who always need justification afresh, and the church thus becomes an institution for the dispensing of grace. The Eucharist functions as a repetition or re-presentation (which only a validly ordained → priest can effect) of the sacrificial death of Christ on the cross. As such, it is a true (*verum et proprium,*

DH 1751) expiatory offering that is brought to God and that merits salvation.

This understanding of sacrifice became totally dominant. It even penetrated into the Orthodox understanding of the Eucharist, though there the overall epicletic perspective neutralized it. In the West, however, the sacrificial emphasis prevailed. The dominance of this understanding may be seen most clearly in the delimitation over against the biblical criticism of the Reformation and in the resistance to the movement of liturgical renewal within Catholicism itself. It also manifests itself in the official, traditionalist barriers that remain in spite of the greater openness of Vatican II (e.g., see the encyclical *Mysterium fidei* of Paul VI in 1965).

The understanding of the Eucharist as a true atoning sacrifice that, in addition to Christ's one self-offering on the cross, dispenses grace and is thus to be offered as often as possible goes back originally to → Cyprian (ca. 200-258). Then by way of → Gregory I the Great (ca. 540-604) and late medieval accretions, it took written form at → Trent (irreversibly, according to the existing Roman Catholic view). Trent did make it clear that, not the priest, but Christ himself, who is present through the ministry of the priest, offers the sacrifice. Terms like *representatio, memoria,* and *applicatio* also protected words like "repetition" or "renewal" against the misunderstanding that this is an offering independent of the sacrifice of Christ on the cross. Yet it is stated just as plainly that the sacrifice of the Mass is a real, if unbloody, sacrifice and that God is reconciled by its offering. Thus reconciled, the Lord forgives. By this unbloody offering the fruits of the bloody offering on the cross are abundantly received (DH 1743). Christ may be the one who makes the offering of himself, yet in the atoning sacrifice of the Mass the church itself acts, namely, by offering Christ. Thus the new Passover that he instituted is that he himself is offered by the church (*se ipsum ab Ecclesia . . . immolandum,* DH 1741).

This aspect was fancifully developed after Trent in theories of destruction or mactation (the destruction of the offered material in a mystical immolation). The liturgical movement (see the theory of Odo Casel) has to some extent pushed these theories into the background. Yet it has not in any way overthrown them. We could say the same regarding private masses for the living and the dead.

Modern Roman Catholic interpretation of the Mass shifts the accent from a cultic expiatory offering to personal self-offering to God as a fulfillment of the true humanity that is open to God. The church's cosacrifice with Jesus is thus its self-fulfillment by appropriating participation in the total and truly human sacrifice of Jesus. This approach is interdenominationally fruitful inasmuch as it stresses in a new way the activity of the faith that is liberated for true humanity by Christ. Protestant theology ought to seize on it along the lines of a eucharistic actualization of the "new obedience" (Augs. Conf. 6) that justification makes possible as a fruit. But it must stand by the fact that this possibility and liberation have their sole basis in Christ's vicarious intervention for us and that in this vicarious work, effected not merely in his passion but in his action too, an impassable limit is set to all cooperation on the church's part. The church does not enact Christ's total offering but lives it out with joyful praise and thanksgiving.

3.2.2. *Real Presence*

Surprisingly, Trent dealt separately with the real presence and the sacrifice of the Mass. It did so, not because the former had become independent in the later Middle Ages (i.e., in the cult of the Host) but mainly because the general attack of the Reformation was directed against the Mass as an atoning sacrifice and because no dogma was available in defense, nor any theory that later Scholasticism had developed, whereas both were at hand to counter Reformation criticism of Roman Catholic views of the real presence. Dogmatically, it is self-evident that Christ's real presence under the bread and wine is a necessary presupposition of the reality of the expiatory sacrifice of the Mass. A presence of Christ's passion merely in the consciousness of believers is not enough. Thus the victory of eucharistic realism over eucharistic symbolism is the necessary consequence of a triumph of the concept of the sacrifice of the Mass.

Only the great influence of → Augustine (in his strict distinction between outward sign and inward power) delayed this victory. The medieval champions of symbolism (Ratramnus, Berengar of Tours, J. → Wycliffe, C. Honius, and then U. → Zwingli) lost the understanding of symbols that Augustine shared with the early church, namely, as power-filled copies, or real symbols. In counteraction, then, there arose a grossly materialistic realism, one that, for example, forced Berengar to confess publicly in 1059 that the body and blood of Christ are palpably, not just sacramentally, touched by the hands of the priest and crushed by the teeth of the faithful (DH 690). A later period abandoned this *manducatio capernaitica,* but the Lutheran doctrine of the real presence still had to repudiate it as a misunderstanding of *manducatio oralis,* or oral eating.

The most important step in defeating the alternative was that taken by Berengar's opponents Lanfranc and Guitmund of Aversa. With the help of → Aristotelian ontology, they worked out a philosophical explanation of the presence of Christ effected at consecration by the words of institution. The Fourth Lateran Council (1215) made the doctrine of transubstantiation a dogma (DH 802). The substances of bread and wine are changed into Christ's body and blood, but bread and wine remain as accidents. Later → Scholasticism and Roman Catholic theology in the 20th century have tried to give a more precise interpretation of this explanation (using "transignification" and "transfinalization"), seeking to replace a physical understanding in terms of natural ontology by a personal understanding in terms of relational → ontology.

With all due respect, Protestant theology must question the underlying conviction that we can rationally explain the divine miracle of the self-presentation of Christ that takes place freely by the Holy Spirit in virtue of Christ's binding promise. In this interest in the nature of Christ's presence in the Eucharist, it sees the danger of obscuring its true meaning (Leuenberg Agreement 19b). Criticism focuses especially on the restrictive fixation that diverts attention from the event of communal celebration and changes the Lord who freely meets us into a "thing" that we can materially manipulate. Such an emphasis results in a permanent (i.e., before and after communion, or *extra usum* presence of Christ, from the consecration to the final dissolution or destruction of the accidents of bread and wine.

Practices relative to the sacramental Christ (the Host) are further consequences that all other churches reject: his enclosing or reserving in the → tabernacle (§2), his exhibiting in the monstrance, and Corpus Christi processions (→ Eucharistic Spirituality). The dogma of concomitance that Trent also laid down (DH 1640-41, 1653) has as its inalienable point the presence of the whole Christ in both species. It carries decisive comfort in emergency situations, but it can also be misused as the basis of the possibility of communion in one kind for those who are mere participants (laypeople and nonconsecrating clergy), as distinct from the officiating priest, who must communicate in both kinds (DH 1726, 1732).

In the late medieval triumph of the abuse of the withholding of the cup, we undoubtedly see a trend toward the hierarchical treatment of the laity as inferior. What was at first a mere rule of the church (DH 1728) came close to becoming a universally binding prohibition of the cup in opposition to Protestantism. The question of revision, however, remained open or was left to the decision of the papacy. Only after the decline of emphatically Counter-Reformation eucharistic piety, and under the influence of the 20th-century movement of liturgical renewal, did Roman Catholics begin to raise a demand for the restoration of the cup to the laity. Such communion is now officially allowed in certain cases.

3.3. Reformation Teaching

Referring back to the Bible and the early church, and critical of dogmatic history, the Reformation doctrine of the Eucharist opposed the idea that the Eucharist is a sacrifice for sin that secures satisfaction and → indulgence for the living and the dead. It also opposed mistaken interpretations of the real presence of Christ *extra usum*. Yet within this common front against Roman Catholicism, the Reformers failed to maintain unity on the question of Christ's presence in the Eucharist.

The early Zwingli, Carlstadt (1480-1541), and the radicals viewed the presence as a purely subjective and commemorative presence in the mind. The Eucharist is an act of confession and commitment, also a common meal of believers, in commemoration of the death of Christ. Bread and wine are mere symbols or signs. The "is" of the words of institution means "signifies."

Martin → Luther also viewed the Eucharist as a sacrament of fellowship and mutual love (Eucharist sermon, 1519) but found its decisive basis in the self-giving love of the Lord, who is truly present in it. The living and exalted Lord, crucified and raised again for us, is truly among us, takes us into fellowship with himself, and thus liberates us for true human fellowship in responsibility to the world. In defending this basic presupposition of all vital faith, Luther went beyond his original thesis that by the free working of the Holy Spirit we truly have the real, personal presence of Christ, arguing for an objectively perceptible material presence of Christ's body and blood. In so doing, he brought suspicion on his defense of *manducatio oralis et impiorum* (eating with the mouth and the eating of the wicked), as though we were eating a material "something" and, in the case of the wicked, eating a heavenly substance that acts as a poison. Two supporting theories strengthened the suspicion: the doctrine of the ubiquity of Christ's human nature (→ Christology), and that of the sacramental union of the earthly elements *(materia terrestris)* of bread and wine with the heavenly realities *(materia coelestis)* of Christ's body and blood.

It is thus understandable that P. → Melanchthon and J. Calvin, although they rejected the subjectivism of the early Zwingli and the radicals, thought that Luther's true concern — real fellowship with the Christ who majestically meets us — was threatened by Luther's own overmaterial objectivism. Melanchthon, then, argued for "multivolipresence" instead of ubiquity, that is, Christ's actual presence wherever he wills to be, according to his promise, "in the Supper of our Lord under the form of bread" (Augs. Conf. 10), or "with the bread" (Concord of Wittenberg [1536], Augs. Conf. 10, var. 1540). Calvin repudiated *manducatio oralis et impiorum*, stressed the condescension of Christ and his real presence by the Spirit, and thus championed *manducatio spiritualis*, or spiritual eating. The real presence of Christ is a totally personal spiritual presence. Yet Calvin remained within the confines of traditional, Augustinian categories of thought. Calvin believed that according to his human nature Christ is at a definite point *(certo loco)* in heaven, so that real fellowship with him is possible only as, in union with the Holy Spirit, our hearts are lifted up to him *(sursum corda,* "lift up [your] hearts," from the eucharistic liturgy). He also started out with a body-soul dualism, so that in the Eucharist the spiritual feeding of our souls with Christ's body and blood runs parallel to the bodily reception of bread and wine. Understandably, his attempt at an explanation ran into the danger of restricting the truly personal, spiritual presence of Christ to the soul or spiritual nature, so that the real presence does not encounter the whole person, and it is thus curtailed if not totally denied. In opposition there was something to be said for Luther's *manducatio oralis.* The whole person, not just the soul, encounters the whole Christ. Hence Luther insisted on the bodily nature of the real presence, guaranteed in the gift of bread and wine. In the heat of controversy, however, he neglected the spiritual freedom of this presence as a personal presence.

The Lutheran Formula of Concord (art. 7) finally decided for the "in, with, and under" of bread and wine, the sacramental union, and *manducatio oralis et impiorum.* The idea of *manducatio spiritualis* was rejected as taught by Calvin but integrated into the doctrine of twofold *manducatio,* which went back to Luther. Reception is spiritual as Spirit-inspired trust in Christ's person and work, both in partaking of the Eucharist and in hearing the proclamation of the gospel. It is bodily as the oral reception of the heavenly substances of Christ's body and blood at the Eucharist alone. Polemical rigidity as regards the latter made both the Lutherans and the older Reformed orthodox blind to the possibilities of agreement in the former.

→ Calvinism had already broken away from the Roman Catholic and Lutheran fixation on the consecratory function of the words of institution and set the whole celebration under the power of the first institution by Christ. In so doing, it came closer to the Eucharist of the early church (note the Leiden Synopsis). Anglican eucharistic theology has made even more fruitful use of this trend. In its basic outline it came under the decisive influence of the Reformed (rejecting a material presence and *manducatio oralis*), yet it unmistakably emphasizes the real personal presence of Christ and hence a participation, effected by Christ himself, in his body, which was crucified for us. In contrast to the more ecclesiological understanding of communion in the early and Orthodox churches, it stresses the practical dimensions of the Eucharist in social ethics.

Through 20th-century Reformed theology (e.g., J.-J. Allmen, M. Thurian), these two perspectives — that which stresses anamnesis and epiclesis and that which stresses ethical responsibility to the world — have decisively enriched discussion of the Eucharist by the → Faith and Order Commission of the → WCC. Independently, German Lutheran and Reformed theologians have moved away from controversial formulations in the Arnoldshain Theses. The → Leuenberg Agreement makes possible a common Lutheran and Reformed understanding of the Eucharist. In the Eucharist, as in the proclamation of the gospel, Christ's self-presentation is one that takes place exclusively in the freedom of the Holy Spirit and thus involves *manducatio spiritualis*. Yet this spiritual presence is a real presence. Christ meets us really and totally, and there is thus a *manducatio oralis* "in, with, and under" the elements of bread and wine. But this encounter with Christ is an unavoidable confrontation, an invitation to both salvation and judgment. Just as the sermon is for those who hear it, so also this invitation is, for those who receive it, a fragrance either "from life to life" or "from death to death" (2 Cor. 2:16). In this sense one might speak of *manducatio impiorum*. In Reformed emphasis, however, Christ came to save, not to condemn; it is the rejecting, rather than the receiving, of Christ that brings condemnation.

The practical implication of this basic dogmatic insight is not one of completely open communion but of communion that may be open by invitation.

3.4. *Free Church Traditions*
The free churches have not developed any special doctrine of the Eucharist, since they broke with the parent churches for different reasons. Thus, simply because of origin, the view of the → Old Catholic Church is closer to the Roman Catholic teaching (with strong approximation to the Orthodox Church), while Lutheran free churches stay close to the Lutheran doctrine, and → Methodists remain within the Anglican range. In the free churches the element of communion or fellowship is strongly to the fore, and in many of them also that of commemoration, with a special emphasis on praise, thanksgiving, and total commitment. They have thus kept alive the basic elements of the Eucharist that the mainline churches have always taught fundamentally but often tended to make marginal in practice. They also rehabilitate some important aspects of Zwingli's doctrine of the Eucharist.

3.5. *Third World Churches*
It is also impossible to speak of any specific understanding of the Eucharist in → Third World churches. They have taken over the views of the Western missionary churches to which they owe their origin. From the standpoint of life and experience, however, they merit special mention. Their understanding has no special profile, but as a confession of Christ, it differentiates them publicly from those of other beliefs around them. Thus, on the one hand, the Eucharist obviously has primary importance as an act of confession and as an experience that underlies the power to build up fellowship. In this regard the eucharistic experience of forgiveness of sins and liberation from the old life comes strongly to the fore. On the other hand, there is a critical and justifiable emotional aversion to the doctrinal differences that have been imported by Western denominations. These divisions are felt to be out of place precisely with respect to the Eucharist and a vital experience of it. Also typical to a large extent is the combination of emphasis on the confessional character of the Eucharist with what is often a very powerful eucharistic realism shaped by the magical understanding of a meal deriving both from the pagan past and from contemporary pagan society.

3.6. *Sects and Religious Societies*
Among other Christian groups there seem to be wider differences in understanding the Eucharist than among the free churches. The differences range from the complete absence of ceremonies in → Christian Science to the profound and dramatic consecration-symbolism found, for example, in the Catholic → Apostolic Church. Dominant, however, is a basic spiritualizing tendency that symbolically stresses the cleansing, renewal, dedication, conversion, and transformation that we ourselves must undergo. The Eucharist is a memorial feast primarily as a sign and secondly as a renewal of the cove-

nant between us and God (and his universal rule of love and harmony), or as an act of confession on the part of those who are cleansed, worthy, and consecrated (as for → Jehovah's Witnesses; → Mormons, who use water instead of wine; and the Church of the Kingdom of God, which uses only "the bread of life"). The Catholic Apostolic Church, however, speaks also of spiritual participation in Christ's heavenly priesthood.

Bibliography: J. BETZ, *Die Eucharistie in der Zeit der griechischen Väter* (vol. 1/1-2; Freiburg, 1955-60) • O. CASEL, *Das christliche Kultmysterium* (Regensburg, 1932); idem, *Das christliche Opfermysterium* (Graz, 1968) • B. A. GERRISH, *Grace and Gratitude: The Eucharistic Theology of John Calvin* (Minneapolis, 1993) • KIRCHLICHES AUSSENAMT DER EKD, *Eucharistie. Das Sagorsker Gespräch über das Abendmahl zwischen Vertretern der EKD und der Russischen Orthodoxen Kirche* (Witten, 1974) • G. KRETSCHMAR et al., "Abendmahl III-V," *TRE* 1.58-229 • G. KRETSCHMAR, H. B. MEYER, and A. NIEBERGALL, "Abendmahlsfeier," *TRE* 1.229-328 • K. LEHMANN and E. SCHLINK, *Das Opfer Jesu Christi und seine Gegenwart in der Kirche. Kontroversen und Klärungen zum Opferverständnis* (Freiburg, 1983) • H. R. MCADOO and K. STEVENSON, *The Mystery of the Eucharist in the Anglican Tradition* (Norwich, U.K., 1997) • D. N. POWER, *The Eucharistic Mystery* (New York, 1992) • A. SCHMEMANN, *The Eucharist: Sacrament of the Kingdom* (Crestwood, N.Y., 1987) • B. D. STUHLMAN, *Eucharistic Celebration, 1789-1979* (New York, 1988) • M. THURIAN, *The Eucharistic Memorial* (2 vols.; Richmond, Va., 1960-61) • G. F. VICEDOM, *Das Abendmahl in den jungen Kirchen* (Munich, 1960) • G. WAINWRIGHT, *Eucharist and Eschatology* (2d ed.; New York, 1981).

GÜNTHER SCHNURR

4. Contemporary Practice

4.1. *Devotion*

In several Christian churches there are indications of change in eucharistic devotion and customs.

4.1.1. *Historical Survey*

From the end of the fourth century there was a rapid decline in frequency of communion. Theologically, this change had its root in anti-Arian sentiment (→ Arianism). Against the background of the ceremonial court, the → worship of the early church was changing into a public cultic act. Increasing awe at the Eucharist led to an attitude of reverent watching instead of participation. The latter became a special religious achievement that in the early Middle Ages was expected only at the three major yearly feasts. Then at the Fourth Lateran Council (1215) participation was made obligatory only once a year, at → Easter.

Increasing devotion to the → Mass characterized the Middle Ages, along with decreasing frequency of communion. Since communion often took place apart from the Mass, or from its original liturgical place in the Mass, one can even speak of two different types of devotion, that of the Mass and that of communion. The same applied to many churches in the East, where communion four times a year (mostly in connections with fasts) is still the rule. At the Reformation the Lutheran churches kept the Mass but tried to make communion once again a regular part of worship. The Reformed churches, however, took a different path. In general they celebrated the Eucharist only a few times a year, but as the communion of the whole congregation or of some classes within it.

4.1.2. *Problems*

Many contemporary problems in eucharistic practice go back to the Reformation period. Even in M. → Luther's lifetime the increased restrictions on admission (see Luther's Formula Missae et Communionis of 1523), along with other factors, made the program of weekly communion impossible. Increasing emphasis on the Eucharist as giving personal assurance of salvation, with neglect of the corporate aspects, resulted in a failure to overthrow properly the eucharistic devotion of the Middle Ages. In many ways the celebration thus seemed to be a composite private communion of individual believers. Communion as an appendix to the main service, or observed only occasionally during the → church year, was typical. The accompanying mood was one of seriousness and penitence. The obligatory coupling of (general) confession with the Eucharist strengthened this mood, as did the strong emphasis on forgiveness (→ Penitence; Sin; Confession of Sin).

Problems arose, however, even with a greater congregational stress (as in Reformed practice). The given equation of the social community with the church community could lead to the use of the Eucharist primarily as a means of social control (note the regulations about the Eucharist in older → church orders). When the equation broke down and participation in the Eucharist became a norm, not of what one must do, but of what one should do and then of what one can do, the legal character of the Eucharist, bound up with the idea of social pressure, still remained, standing in the way of any renewal of eucharistic spirituality.

Within the social framework the Eucharist also

had an important function in connection with rites of passage that are important in both church and society (confirmation, marriage, burial; cf. Good Friday as symbolic death). From these practices it took on a good deal of its significance. New eucharistic practices today usually hasten the decay of such traditional, culturally supported customs (including fixed rules about frequency, admission, preparation, clothes, and attitudes). Barriers to participation fall, and it is only at first that new ties arise (including a necessary reference to the social and cultural context).

4.1.3. *Third World*

The same kind of connection, expressed in forms that are socially and culturally significant, exists in the eucharistic practice of → Third World churches. Here the Eucharist, as an act of confession to those of other beliefs, has an unequivocal social meaning. The churches have the twofold task of setting the Eucharist in their own social context (and here the question arises of using their own foodstuffs as the elements, e.g., rice, corn, bananas, coconut juice, palm wine), and yet of also marking it off as countercultural for the sake of its theological and social meaning: the forgiveness of sins as a renewed and very concrete renunciation of the old life and constitution of a new fellowship.

The varied forms that the Eucharist takes demonstrate the vitality of the churches. Sometimes → foot washing accompanies it. There may also be spontaneous outbursts (including confessions of sin and reconciliation among members). Where the celebration takes place in the context of the struggle for liberation from unjust and repressive social structures and living conditions, eucharistic spirituality takes on new features; protest against social and racial discrimination and solidarity in sharing can express themselves in the Eucharist as a meal of unequals no less than in the embryonic anticipation of a new and liberated society.

4.1.4. *Free Churches*

Eucharistic practice in the → free churches is marked by its distinction from a sacramentalist understanding and the precedence of preaching. The proclaimed word forms the center of worship. The Eucharist is another form of the gospel and an action that reminds us of Christ's passion and death and strengthens the mutual fellowship of believers. The liturgy is simple, but the form is not uniform. All who believe in Christ are invited (open communion). Usually the Eucharist is celebrated on feast days and once or twice each quarter, though monthly in many places. → Plymouth Brethren assemblies break bread each Sunday in connection with a preaching service. On special occasions, in house churches, and at evangelistic campaigns the Eucharist serves as an expression of personal fellowship and goes hand-in-hand with testimonies, blessings, and the praise of God. Eucharistic devotion is reflected in the hymns of the churches.

4.1.5. *Reversal of Old Trends*

On the whole, only during the 20th century can one speak of a reversal of the development that began in the 4th century, though some earlier movements of renewal and awakening also had partial significance. As regards the Roman Catholic Church, a decree of Pius X in 1905 regarding frequent communion is important. The impulses behind it have achieved their full effect in the → liturgical movement. With the pulling down of specific barriers (e.g., an emphasis on fasting with communion), they have resulted in a considerable rise in frequency of communion.

In German Protestant churches similar impulses (liturgical movements after World War I, experiences during the → church struggle, and liturgical revision after World War II) have as yet produced only a partial change in eucharistic devotion. Thus far the full liturgy that revisions have sought, namely, both preaching and Eucharist, has not by any means become the rule. Some traditional practices have gone, but as yet new features resulting from biblical, liturgical, and dogmatic scholarship and the many ecumenical meetings have found only tentative acceptance in the German churches. The services have in principle disengaged the Eucharist from confession of sin, a development that has made possible an openness to neglected aspects. Thus the reference to fellowship can express itself in new forms of reception, such as communion in a circle. Development toward an ecumenical opening up of traditional eucharistic practice proceeds in much less complicated form in Protestantism elsewhere (e.g., in North American → Lutheranism)

4.2. *Eucharistic Movement*

The movement toward new forms of worship, which at first ran contrary to liturgical reforms in the 1950s, produced a new eucharistic movement at the beginning of the 1970s (note esp. the German Church Conferences at Düsseldorf in 1973 and Nürnberg in 1979). This movement has a mostly youthful base, which over the years has changed the face of the conferences. The new eucharistic spirituality combines the social involvement of the liturgical movement of the 1960s with newly aroused needs for spiritual depth and the festal, creative use of symbolic communication. From the very first, ecumenical influences have been at work (e.g., →

Taizé and its Council of Youth, with the programmatic linking of action and contemplation). These trends have led to a remarkable convergence of the movement with the results of ecumenical → dialogue, which has found expression in the new shape given to celebration of the Eucharist, including the offering of gifts with prayer and the inclusion of elements of anamnesis and epiclesis in the → eucharistic prayer.

A new eucharistic lifestyle is developing that indissolubly links communion and → communication, liturgical action and responsibility for the world. The conservation of → creation, solidarity with the poor and hungry, and action for → peace and → reconciliation (see *BEM*, "Eucharist," par. 20) are felt to be directly related to the Eucharist. Conflicts arise when this more strongly outward piety, which is oriented to the aspect of the fellowship meal, runs up against the traditional inward piety. At this point we see restructurings of communicative and social attitudes that cannot fail to have an effect on liturgical communication. The charge that the new eucharistic devotion overemphasizes the aspect of communion and neglects that of personal forgiveness hardly touches the main point, for the new attitude also has its roots in a strong need for assurance of salvation, which seems to be mediated more strongly than before by the experience of eucharistic fellowship.

4.3. Elements and Forms

Even when the two eucharistic actions of the bread and cup were detached from the festal meal and related to a liturgical text to form what is called the Mass (the earliest example in Justin Martyr [d. ca. 165]), the practice at first was still that the communicants themselves took bread and the cup from the table. But soon it became customary for the officiant and his helpers to hand out the bread and cup. Increasing awe led to the withholding of the cup in the Middle Ages. The bread was then put in the mouths of believers, communion was received kneeling, and the cup was reserved for the → priest. The East kept the cup but dipped the bread in the wine (intinction) or else mixed it in the wine and dispensed it with a spoon (in the Byzantine Rite).

Originally the members of the church brought their own ordinary bread to the service, with the leftovers used for diaconal purposes. The type of bread then made its breaking necessary as a separate liturgical act. Increasing reverence led to the use of special bread for the Eucharist. From the 9th century it was the practice in the West to use only unleavened bread. In the 12th century the practice developed of using little round wafers (the Host).

Liturgical reform in the Roman Catholic Church has brought back breadlike elements, but Lutherans still use paper-thin wafers, unlike the Reformed and the free churches. In the new eucharistic movement and under ecumenical influence, ordinary bread (mostly white) is coming into increasing use, with a stress on table fellowship, the participants sitting at a table and handing the bread and the cup to one another. Here the custom of breaking bread is also being renewed.

After Vatican II the Roman Catholic Church has extended the possibilities of cup communion. Against ancient custom it prefers white wine. In other churches red wine is customary for the sake of its symbolism. It is debated whether or how regard should be had for alcoholics (→ Substance Abuse) by the use of nonalcoholic wine or other nonalcoholic drinks. The denial of the cup to those threatened in this way is a conceivable alternative, but it raises other problems. Many churches and congregations prefer individual cups for hygienic reasons.

The use of ordinary bread, the breaking of bread, and communion at a table can help to clarify the character of the Eucharist as a meal. The same applies to efforts to set it in a full meal or to connect it with the agape (i.e., a noneucharistic love feast). When the two eucharistic actions — the bread and the cup — are related to the Last Supper, to the death and → resurrection of Jesus, then, as at the first, they can enframe the meal or open it or close it. Especially in house churches, → base communities, and retreats, one may celebrate the Eucharist in this way. Examples show that such flexibility can also be meaningful in a congregational setting.

4.4. Tasks

When along the lines of ecumenical documents the Eucharist is seen as an event that actualizes the community as the body of Christ, it is hardly possible any longer to exclude baptized children. Against this background there is need to rethink the relation between instruction and the Eucharist, also between → confirmation and the Eucharist.

Where the national or → people's church is in decay and the baptism of infants (and baptism in general) is no longer a matter of social convention, the relation between baptism and the Eucharist demands reconsideration. Are situations conceivable in which unbaptized persons might be admitted to communion for pastoral reasons?

The eucharistic movement, ecumenical dialogue, and independent theological insights demand that the Protestant churches in particular should think again about restoring the eucharistic prayer, which develops the points made in the accounts of institution: thanksgiving and praise, express remembrance of the story of Christ (anamnēsis), prayer for the Spirit (epiklēsis), and eschatological anticipation — all of which, in the language of prayer and not of teaching, bring out the various dimensions of the Eucharist.

The same applies to the matter of offering and preparing gifts (the offertory). In some circumstances restoring something like the Orthodox Great Entrance with offerings might help to connect more closely the liturgical action with social action, showing the relationship between the Eucharist and → creation as well as society.

Bibliography: Sources and text editions: A. HÄNGGI and I. PAHL, eds., Prex Eucharistica. Textus e variis liturgiis antiquioribus selecti (2d ed.; Fribourg, 1978) • R. C. D. JASPER and G. J. CUMING, eds., Prayers of the Eucharist: Early and Reformed (3d ed.; Collegeville, Minn., 1987) • I. PAHL, ed., Coena Domini, vol. 1, Die Abendmahlsliturgie der Reformationskirchen im 16./17. Jahrhundert (Fribourg, 1983).

Other literature: H. DAVIES, Bread of Life and Cup of Joy: Newer Ecumenical Perspectives on the Eucharist (Grand Rapids, 1993) • A. DAWIA, "Indigenizing Christian Worship," Christian Worship and Melanesia (Goroka, P.N.G., 1980) 13-59 (example of liturgical inculturation in New Guinea) • L. GOODWIN, "Cross-Cultural Dimensions of Eucharistie: A Reflection on African Concepts" and "Eucharist and Liminality," AfER 21 (1979) 242-50 and 348-52 • JOHN PAUL II, "Inaestimabile donum," AAS 72 (1980) 331-43 • C. JONES, G. WAINWRIGHT, and E. YARNOLD, eds., The Study of Liturgy (2d ed.; London, 1992) • A. KOOTHOTTIL, "Jesus and the Bread of Life," Vaidikamitram 14 (1981) 229-41 (on the Indian context) • G. KRETSCHMAR et al., "Abendmahl III-V," TRE 1.58-229 • G. KRETSCHMAR, H. B. MEYER, and A. NIEBERGALL, "Abendmahlsfeier," TRE 1.229-328 • E. MAZZA, The Eucharistic Prayers of the Roman Rite (New York, 1986) • F. C. SENN, Christian Liturgy: Catholic and Evangelical (Minneapolis, 1997); idem, ed., New Eucharistic Prayers: An Ecumenical Study of Their Development and Structure (Mahwah, N.J., 1987) • M. THURIAN and G. WAINWRIGHT, eds., Baptism and Eucharist: Ecumenical Convergence in Celebration (Geneva, 1983) • E. E. UZUKWU, "Food and Drink in Africa, and the Christian Eucharist: An Inquiry into the Use of African Symbols in the Eucharistic Celebration," BThA 2 (1980) 171-87 • G. F. VICEDOM, Das Abendmahl in den jungen Kirchen (Munich, 1960).

KARL-HEINRICH BIERITZ

5. Eucharistic Unity

5.1. Confessionally Characteristic Positions

The Eucharist both "signifies and effects ecclesial unity." This statement of Pope → Innocent III (1198-1216) in his treatise The Sacrament of the Altar (4.36; PL 217.879) would probably find acceptance in principle by all who celebrate the Lord's Supper: the Eucharist furthers the already existing → unity of the church. But much depends on the perceived identity and location of the church referred to, and here the various communities that claim the name of Christian differ.

5.1.1. Orthodox

The Orthodox churches stick closest to the position of → Cyprian of Carthage (ca. 200-258): there is but one catholic church and one communion; outside of it, → heretics and schismatics simply fall into an ecclesiological void; between the true church and other groups no communion is possible because the others lack the → Holy Spirit, who works in the → sacraments. While, in contemporary Orthodoxy, ecclesiological "strictness" may in practice be tempered by the exercise of "economy," the shared worship that is thereby sometimes permitted does not reach as far as "intercommunion" with non-Orthodox churches or groups. The very word "intercommunion" is rejected by the Orthodox, for whom there is either "communion" or "no communion." It remains to be seen what the effect may be of a pneumatological reading by some current Orthodox theologians of the presence of Christian faith beyond the institutional or canonical bounds of Orthodoxy.

5.1.2. Roman Catholic

Since → Vatican II the → Roman Catholic Church has somewhat moderated the exclusive position it had held on its own behalf. Thus all those "who believe in Christ and have been properly baptized are put in some, though imperfect, communion with the Catholic Church," and even the "separated churches and communities" are not "deprived of significance and importance in the mystery of salvation" (Unitatis redintegratio 3). In a perspective that remains Rome-centered, the Catholic Church is now willing in certain circumstances to accord "eucharistic hospitality" to members of other churches and communities; Roman Catholics, however, are still expected not to seek eucharistic communion from others, except in very exceptional cases, and then not from Protestants.

Pastoral provision has thus been made for rightly disposed non-Catholics whose sacramental faith is consonant with the Catholic faith to receive, upon request, the Catholic Eucharist in the emergency circumstances of mortal danger, persecution, imprisonment, or serious spiritual need (*Directory on Ecumenism* of 1967, 55; cf. the *Directory* of 1993, 129-31). According to the *Directory* of 1993 (159-60), Catholic bishops may also allow the admission of the non-Catholic partner to Catholic Communion at the celebration of a mixed marriage, provided all the other conditions are met, but such "eucharistic sharing can only be exceptional."

The Roman Catholic Church wished the Orthodox churches — and thereby made a considerable recognition of their ecclesial character — to offer reciprocal sacramental access to Catholics in exceptional circumstances (Vatican II, *Orientalium ecclesiarum* 26-29; *Directory* of 1967, 39-45; cf. the *Directory* of 1993, 122-28), but apart from the Moscow Patriarchate for some years after 1969, the Orthodox did not concur. In 1984, however, Pope John Paul II and the Syrian patriarch Ignatius Zakka I (Oriental Orthodox) signed such a mutual pastoral agreement for the sake of their faithful who had no access to their respective priests. In the case of Protestants, it is clearer that the emergency or exceptional hospitality of the Roman Catholic Church is accorded to them as individual Christians, the limited ecclesiality of their own communities being indicated by the prohibition of Catholics from receiving Communion in Protestant churches (*Directory* of 1967, 55; cf. the *Directory* of 1993, 132), since a Protestant Lord's Supper is marred by a defect at the level of ordination (*Unitatis redintegratio* 22).

5.1.3. *Protestant*

Lutherans have historically insisted on agreement in doctrine as the condition of pulpit and altar fellowship (see *Koinonia. Arbeiten des Ökumenischen Ausschusses der VELKD zur Frage der Kirchen- und Abendmahlsgemeinschaft* [Berlin, 1957]), as have also the Reformed, with in their case a stronger emphasis also on → church discipline (→ Lutheran Churches; Reformed Churches). At its Princeton Assembly in 1954, however, the → World Alliance of Reformed Churches recommended the admission to the Lord's Table of "any baptized person who loves and confesses Jesus Christ as Lord and Savior"; and in 1975 the German Lutheran churches (VELKD) adopted the position that "access to the Lord's Table is in principle open to every baptized Christian who comes trusting in Christ's word of promise as spoken in his words of institution." At a church-to-church level, the doctrinally based → Leuenberg Agreement of 1973 brought European Lutherans and Reformed into an official ecclesial and sacramental fellowship (where they were later joined by Methodists), and a similar result was achieved between some Lutheran and Reformed churches in the United States by the Formula of Agreement in 1997 (→ Consensus).

Until the 18th century, the Church of England maintained sacramental fellowship especially with the Reformed churches of the Continent, at least in the sense of mutual admission of travelers to Communion. But after the 19th-century → Oxford Movement, Anglicans insisted more and more on the need for unity in the ordained ministry, so that "episcopal succession" became practically the only condition for official churchly communion (see Church of England Archbishops' Commission on Intercommunion, *Intercommunion Today* [London, 1968]). Thus the Bonn Agreement of 1931 established full sacramental communion between → Anglicans and → Old Catholics, and negotiation of "the historic episcopate" proved essential to the Porvoo Declaration, signed in 1996 by the British Anglican churches and several Nordic and Baltic Lutheran churches. At an individual level, many Anglican churches now admit to occasional Communion any baptized member of another church.

For the stricter varieties of → Baptists, church membership and church fellowship depend on → baptism received on profession of personal → faith, and even on acceptance of the teaching and discipline of the local congregation. They thus approximate the "closed communion" characteristic of Cyprian and of the Orthodox, though with less sense perhaps of the bonds between local churches in the "church catholic."

5.2. *The Ecumenical Debate and Goal*

The question of communion in the Eucharist becomes vital only when divided Christians and churches — and always there is some implied view of the relation between the individual and the ecclesial community — are seeking unity. While communion in the Eucharist has certainly been part of the goal of the modern → ecumenical movement, opinions have differed on whether it may already be employed as a means toward the end.

5.2.1. *Intercommunion*

Until about 1970 "intercommunion" was the watchword around which the debate took place concerning the point when churches might properly enter into eucharistic fellowship with one another (see esp. the preparatory volume for the Third World Conference on → Faith and Order at Lund in 1952, entitled precisely *Intercommunion*). While the Orthodox rejected altogether the term and concept, churches with a more "federal" understanding of Christian unity used the word without any pejorative intent or sense of provisionality to describe their sacramental sharing across persisting denominational boundaries. Between those two positions stood those ecumenists who held that at some point along the road to an ever-fuller unity it became possible and desirable for churches — or their members — to practice intercommunion as both a sign of the unity they already enjoyed and an aid toward more perfect unity. Sometimes adopting an eschatological perspective (for the Lord's Supper prefigures the feast of God's final reign, where a divided fellowship is unthinkable), they argued that the goal of unity could become proleptically effective through its own active anticipation in the sacrament. T. F. Torrance spoke of the Eucharist as "the divinely given sacrament of unity, the medicine for our divisions" (*Intercommunion*, 303-50). By the time of the meeting of the → World Council of Churches (WCC) Commission on Faith and Order at Louvain in 1971, however, the need to move "beyond intercommunion" as both a concept and a reality had become apparent.

5.2.2. Toward "Unity in One Faith and in One Eucharistic Fellowship"

Since 1975 its revised constitution gives the WCC the task of helping the churches to advance to "visible unity in one faith and in one eucharistic fellowship." In this connection, the Faith and Order text from Lima in 1982 — *Baptism, Eucharist, and Ministry* — confronts the several churches with some unavoidable questions and decisions. Regarding baptism: Do "the others," by the initiatory rites practiced among them, really become Christian? Regarding the Eucharist: Is a true Eucharist, according to the Lord's institution, celebrated in the "other" communities? Regarding ministry: Are the "other" ecclesial communities genuinely "church" at all? Those are important and urgent questions because "as participants in the Eucharist," the sacrament of "the reconciling presence of God in human history," we become "inconsistent" and are even "placed under continual judgment" if we obstinately persist in "unjustifiable confessional oppositions within the body of Christ" ("Eucharist," par. 20).

While pastoral provision for exceptional admission to Communion may alleviate particular situations, and while an apparent increase in Communion by individuals in transgression of confessional boundaries or canonical discipline may perhaps function as a prophetic challenge against inertial disunity (see E. Schlink's visionary tale of a papal reception of Orthodox and Lutheran Communion in Jerusalem!), divisions have their communal dimensions, and unity in the Eucharist cannot finally be other than corporate. The need to acknowledge the facts of separation while also working to overcome them is illustrated by the continuing discussion about eucharistic practice at ecumenical meetings.

5.3. Official Practice on Ecumenical Occasions

In 1963, on the recommendation of the Fourth World Conference on Faith and Order at Montreal, the WCC Central Committee formalized a procedure whereby conferences should include both a Eucharist "according to the liturgy of a church which cannot conscientiously offer an invitation to members of all other churches to partake of the elements" and one "in which a church or group of churches can invite members of other churches to participate and partake." In the long-standing custom of an occasional "open" Communion at ecumenical events, it was the Anglicans who most often had acted as hosts, since this usually ensured a maximum number of communicants (if only because Anglicans themselves, whatever their churchmanship, were ready to receive at the hands of an Anglican celebrant, whereas they were not sure to do so in the case of a Methodist or a Presbyterian presiding).

During his time as general secretary of the WCC (1984-92), the Uruguayan Methodist Emilio Castro pressed for greater eucharistic sharing and pleaded at Canberra in 1991 that "this should be the last assembly with a divided Eucharist." Faith and Order studied the matter again in 1995-96 but concluded that "it is still not possible to move beyond the guidelines" established in 1963. Some parts of the oikoumene have expressed diminished openness toward the idea of common celebrations. In preparation for the 1998 assembly of the WCC at Harare, for example, some Orthodox churches questioned whether common prayer was possible. The Harare program included no official Eucharist, given the current impossibility of a fully common celebration. Rather, there was a penitential service in recognition of continuing divisions, and various local congregations representing the → Orthodox, → Oriental Orthodox, → Reformation, and → Roman Catholic streams of Christianity were asked to host WCC delegates at their respective celebrations of a Sunday Eucharist, with the expectation that existing denominational protocol be observed.

Bibliography: D. BAILLIE and J. MARSH, eds., *Intercommunion* (London, 1952) • W. ELERT, *Eucharist and Church Fellowship in the First Four Centuries* (St. Louis, 1966) • L. HODGSON, ed., *The Second World Conference on Faith and Order* (London, 1938) • E. SCHLINK, *Die Vision des Papstes* (1975; Karlsruhe, 1997) • G. WAINWRIGHT, "The Nature of Communion," *EcTr* 28/6 (1999) 1-8 • WORLD COUNCIL OF CHURCHES, "Beyond

Intercommunion: On the Way to Communion in Eucharist," *Faith and Order, Louvain 1971* (Geneva, 1971) 54-70; idem, *Eucharistic Hospitality* (= *ER* 44/1 [1992]); idem, *Minutes of the Meeting of the Faith and Order Board, January 1996, Bangkok* (Geneva, 1996) 54, 133-38.

GEOFFREY WAINWRIGHT

Eucharistic Congresses → Eucharistic Spirituality

Eucharistic Ecclesiology

The expression "eucharistic ecclesiology" implies a definition of the → church and, in light of that definition, the principle for studying its nature and its life. According to Orthodox doctrine, the term establishes to some extent an ontological identity between church and → Eucharist, according to the most general, substantial, and undisputed definition of the church in the Scripture: the body of Christ and the temple of the Holy Spirit. It follows that the church's actual existence, as well as its transformation into its perfect self, so as ultimately to be the → kingdom of God, depends on the measure of its "Christification" and "pneumatization," which proceed until, encompassing the whole of saved humankind and the universe, it becomes the New Jerusalem united with God, who is "all in all" (Eph. 1:23; 4:10; Col. 3:11). Given this true destiny of the church, all its thoughts, desires, and deeds should aim at reaching it, as expressly willed by God (thus the idea of universal → resurrection and → salvation; → Apocatastasis).

With this goal in view, the church prays, performs sacraments, blesses, preaches, instructs, and, in general, acts in the world. Where and when on earth does the church make its union with God actual to the highest possible degree? In its celebration of the Eucharist. "Those who eat my flesh and drink my blood abide in me, and I in them" (John 6:56); they "have eternal life" (v. 54) in the kingdom. Therefore, except for its rites, the Eucharist is not an "institution" devised and established by the church, but it is the church's own foundation and raison d'être. In its celebration the church not only asserts its very nature but indeed becomes itself, so that "we," the → people of God, may "grow up in every way into him who is the head, into Christ, from whom the whole body [is] joined and knit together" (Eph. 4:15-16).

The power thus to grow in the incarnate Word and to become his body through the Eucharist is bestowed to the church by the → Pentecost of the Holy Spirit. "For in the one Spirit we were all baptized into one body" (1 Cor. 12:13). The bread of life is the Word and the Eucharist (John 6), hence the constant epiclesis of the church, as its sacramental prayer and the descent upon it of the energy of the Spirit. According to Orthodox understanding, the church's life is entirely "epicletic": "Abide in me as I abide in you" (John 15:4), through the Spirit.

Eucharistic ecclesiology does not describe the Eucharist as merely a "production" of the church but considers the latter as actually stemming from the former. Thus the → "hierarchy," or the various functions of members of the church (bishops, preachers, laity, etc.; → Offices, Ecclesiastical), also derives from the Eucharist as the source of its life. The final criterion of all the members of the body of Christ and servants of the Holy Spirit's temple (which they are themselves, 1 Cor. 3:16; 6:19) is life in Christ through the Spirit in accomplishing the will of the Father. Since there is only one High Priest and one Eucharist, the "catholic" church is present wherever the → liturgy is celebrated because of the actual presence of Christ and of the Holy Spirit in the midst of the faithful. In that way, all the local churches identify with the universal church, which is one in its multiplicity. The catholicity of the church is but that of its High Priest and of the Pentecostal Spirit who energizes it.

Participation in the eucharistic liturgy, with receiving of Communion, was the universal practice of the → primitive Christian community, in accordance with its everlasting doctrine. Those who did not lawfully abide by it were cut off from the Holy Assembly (e.g., according to the councils of Elvira [ca. 306], Antioch [341], and Sardica [ca. 343]; the Trullan Synod [692]; and the *Apostolic Constitutions*). Finally, "What happens in the Eucharist shall take place, at the end of time, in the whole world, which is the body of humankind and hence also that of Christ" (S. Bulgakov, *Das eucharistische Dogma*), because the church of God is the eucharistic actualization of "the plan of the mystery hidden for ages in God" (Eph. 3:9), achieved in the kingdom (Rev. 21:22; 22:17). Although this doctrine has not been systematically worked out, for most Orthodox authors it is the basis of their ecclesiology.

→ Church 3.1; Economy (Orthodox Theology); Liturgy 2; Orthodox Church; Orthodoxy 3

Bibliography: P. F. BRADSHAW, *Essays on Early Eastern Eucharistic Prayers* (Collegeville, Minn., 1997) • S. BULGAKOV, "Das eucharistische Dogma," *Kyrios,* n.s.,

3 (1963) 32-57, 78-96 • D. J. Constantelos, *Understanding the Greek Orthodox Church: Its Faith, History, and Practice* (New York, 1982) • G. Florovsky, "Le corps du Christ vivant. Une interpretation orthodoxe de l'église," *La sainte église universelle. Confrontation oecumenique* (Neuchâtel, 1948) 9-57 • J. Meyendorff, "The Orthodox Concept of the Church," *SVSQ*, n.s., 6 (1962) 59-71 • A. Schmemann, *The Eucharist: Sacrament of the Kingdom* (Crestwood, N.Y., 1988); idem, *Liturgy and Tradition: Theological Reflections of Alexander Schmemann* (Crestwood, N.Y., 1990); idem, "'Unity,' 'Division,' 'Reunion' in the Light of Orthodox Eccesiology," *Theol(A)* 22 (1951) 242-54 • J. Zizioulas, *L'être ecclesial* (Geneva, 1981) 57-100, 181-94.

CONSTANTIN ANDRONIKOF†

Eucharistic Prayer

The eucharistic prayer ("canon of the Mass" in the West, → "anaphora" in the East) is the central prayer of the Lord's Supper (→ Eucharist). Its structural origins are in the Jewish table prayer *Birkat ha-Maṣōn*, which in turn represents a pattern traceable at least back to the prayer of → Abraham in *Jubilees*.

The theological origins of the eucharistic prayer are to be found in the traditions of the meal → sacrifices of Israel, and particularly in the prominence given in intertestamental → Judaism to the *zebaḥ-tôdâ*, "thanksgiving offering." The dominance of thanksgiving appears in the very name "Eucharist" (from Gk. *eucharistos*, "grateful, thankful"), which had become an important term among Greek-speaking Jews. The earliest extant eucharistic prayer, that of *Didache* 9–10, likewise gives prominence to thanksgiving, placing that section at the head of the prayer.

In the early Christian prayers that follow the pattern of *Birkat ha-Maṣōn*, praise of the Creator remains intact, but thanksgiving for the land was replaced by thanksgiving for salvation in Christ, and the supplicatory section put the → church in the place of → Jerusalem and often included an invocation (epiclesis) of → blessing upon the church, the bread and wine, and occasionally individuals. In most of the more developed prayers the Holy Spirit is invoked upon the bread and wine here, but in some it is the Word, and in some God's blessing generally. As this three-part ("West-Syrian") prayer matured, the praise section came to terminate in the Sanctus, and the thanksgiving section ended with the institution narrative, the anamnesis (memorial

of Christ's death and → resurrection), and the oblation of the bread and wine in the context of thankful remembrance, all of which entered the second section of the eucharistic prayer as a unit. The function of the institution narrative was at first warrant for the eucharistic offering. The most famous of these prayers still in use are the developed forms of the anaphorae of John → Chrysostom (ca. 347-407) and Basil (ca. 330-79). Many other variants are in use in the Eastern churches (→ Liturgy 2; Orthodox Church).

In the West a different structure made possible the growth of a different theology. In the Roman Catholic canon (→ Liturgy 1.3) and those Egyptian prayers that may well be its antecedents, we observe a two-part prayer, consisting of thanksgiving and supplication, the pattern present as early as the *Apostolic Tradition* of Hippolytus (ca. 170-ca. 236). But the difference from Hippolytus is pronounced. Hippolytus's prayer is divided into thanksgiving and supplicatory sections of about equal length, and it has a memorial and oblation that conclude the thanksgiving section. The Roman prayer has compressed praise and thanksgiving into a short variable *praefatio* (address), and the entire post-Sanctus is supplicatory, including the institution narrative and the anamnesis and oblation that accompany it. Thus in the medieval West the Roman bipartite structure made it possible to think of the eucharistic prayer as no longer the act of memorial sacrifice of praise and thanksgiving itself but as a set of supplications surrounding a material sacrifice. Finally, the idea arose that the sacrifice could effect the success of the supplications. That view, combined with the development of the theory of transubstantiation (→ Eucharist 3), made it possible to think of the eucharistic prayer as a formula in which Christ's body and blood were produced by the recitation of the institution narrative and then offered to the Father. According to the Jewish view, consecration results from sacrifice, and a Communion sacrifice is made with and by thankful memorial. Western thinkers were thus left to dwell on the mechanics of consecration and sacrifice in a way unknown in Eastern Christianity.

The 16th-century → Reformers (→ Reformation) rejected this developed Western theology and also the canon of the Mass, which had become impossible to understand apart from that theology. They had no resources to examine alternative texts for eucharistic praying but did know they wished to eliminate the late medieval doctrine of eucharistic sacrifice. Martin → Luther's (1483-1546) solution was to remove all of the post-Sanctus prayers of the Roman canon, retaining only the elements of preface, Sanctus, and institution narrative. Ulrich → Zwingli (1484-1531) replaced the canon with four much longer prayers. Many churches used an institution narrative alone, and some omitted even that narrative. Thomas → Cranmer (1489-1556) attempted to rewrite eucharistic prayers, but always in reaction to the Roman theology of the time; restoration of original patterns was not yet possible.

In the period immediately after the Reformation the texts of the ancient tripartite eucharistic prayers came to be published in the West, notably the liturgies of St. James and of the eighth book of the *Apostolic Constitutions*. Scottish Episcopalians and the Episcopal Church in the United States (1789) became the first Western churches to adopt the structure of the ancient prayers.

Reforms in the 20th century followed the explosion of liturgical research at the end of the preceding century. Three of the four eucharistic prayers of the *Missale Romanum* (1970; → Liturgical Books) are in the classical three-part pattern (although a second epiclesis of the Spirit has been added in each case). Lutheran Agendas provide a range of partial and complete eucharistic prayers, although their use is optional. Perhaps the most significant textual developments are (1) the influence of the prayer of Hippolytus on contemporary texts and (2) the ecumenical creation of "A Common Eucharistic Prayer," a modern version of the 5th-century Alexandrian prayer of St. Basil that appears in Roman Catholic and Protestant liturgies of the 1970s.

Bibliography: J.-P. AUDET, "Literary Forms and Contents of a Normal Eucharistia in the First Century," *StEv* 1.643-62 • C. CASPERS, G. LUKKEN and G. A. M. ROUWHORST, *Bread of Heaven: Customs and Practices Surrounding Holy Communion. Essays in the History of Liturgy and Culture* (Kampen, 1995) • INSTITUT SAINT-SERGE, *Eucharisties d'Orient et d'Occident* (2 vols.; Paris, 1965) • P. LARERE, *The Lord's Supper: Towards an Ecumenical Understanding of the Eucharist* (Collegeville, Minn., 1993) • R. LEDOGAR, *Acknowledgement: Praise Verbs in the Early Greek Anaphorae* (Rome, 1968) • J. McKENNA, *Eucharist and the Holy Spirit* (London, 1975) • B. SPINKS, ed., *The Sacrifice of Praise* (Rome, 1981) • T. J. TALLEY, "From Berakah to Eucharistia: A Reopening Question," *Worship* 50 (1976) 115-37 • M. THURIAN and E. CHISHOLM, *The Mystery of the Eucharist: An Ecumenical Approach* (London, 1983).

PAUL V. MARSHALL

Eucharistic Spirituality

The attitude of believers to the sacrament of Christ's body and blood (→ Eucharist) has changed greatly across the centuries. In the age of the martyrs eucharistic → spirituality found a self-evident focus in the Sunday celebration of the Eucharist. The purpose of Jesus in its institution determined the approach. The gifts of bread and wine, consecrated by the → eucharistic prayer, were distributed to those present. The deacons took them to absentees (the sick or prisoners) (Justin Martyr *Apol.* 1.67). Laity also took the bread home so as to partake of it during the week. The Eucharist was also taken on journeys so that people could receive it in moments of danger (esp. mortal danger) and also enjoy its protection (*phylaktērion*). In 325 the Council of → Nicaea made it clear that the sacrament must always be available to the dying (can. 13, concerning "those departing [this life]"). Reservation in parish churches became the general rule from the Carolingian age. The → sanctuary lamp, burning near the reserved sacrament, is attested from at least the 13th century.

A change in eucharistic spirituality came in the 4th century with a rapid decline in frequency of Communion. Excessive → reverence replaced the original respectful but relatively uninhibited handling of the Eucharist (1 Cor. 11:28-29). Especially in the sphere of the → liturgy of Antioch and Byzantium, as the celebration borrowed features from the ceremonies of the imperial court, believers came to find in the Eucharist an awe-inspiring mystery. From the 9th century there developed in the West the idea that only the hands of the priest should touch it, and receiving into the hands (folded, representing the throne of Christ) was forbidden. In the 12th and 13th centuries an exaggerated fear of desecration (*periculum effusionis*) led to the withholding of the cup from the laity. Early medieval synods, trying to deal with the low frequency of Communion, unsuccessfully pressed for reception at least at the great festivals of → Christmas, → Easter, and → Pentecost. Lateran IV in 1215 required as a minimum Communion once a year at Easter. In the → Roman Catholic sphere Communion noticeably increased only after Pius X issued his decree on frequent Communion in 1903. After → Vatican II many Roman Catholics made weekly partaking the rule (→ Mass). In the Reformation churches the late medieval inheritance worked against efforts to increase frequency, but new attempts are now being made to establish a weekly Communion. It is a → Reformation principle that Communion should be in both kinds. The liturgical reforms of Vatican II have also restored the cup in principle to Roman Catholics, though many do not avail themselves of the privilege.

In the patristic period eucharistic spirituality was primarily that of Mass and Communion, but over the years new forms developed in the West that focused on the sacrament apart from its administration. The basis of this new spirituality of adoration was emphasis on the real and abiding presence of Christ in the Eucharist that came with the attack on the teaching of Paschasius Radbertus and Berengar of Tours and opposition to the antisacramentalism of the → Cathari and Albigenses. Of decisive significance in the development of the eucharistic cult was the rite of elevation, first attested at Paris in about 1200. After reading the saying about the bread in the story of the institution, the priest lifted up the host so that believers could see and adore the Lord's body. Participants viewed the elevation of the bread, and later that of the cup (general only after → Trent), as a moving epiphany of the Son of God, who was born of Mary and offered up on the cross and who was now seated at the right hand of the Father. The ringing of bells marked this climax of the Mass, and the lighting of candles expressed veneration and also facilitated a "salvific observing" (I. Herwegen) of the sacrament. While the congregation knelt in adoration, sacramental hymns were sung (Ave verum, O salutaris hostia).

The vision-centered eucharistic spirituality of the Middle Ages found full expression in the Corpus Christi celebration on the Thursday after Trinity. This was first celebrated in Liège in 1246 on the basis of the visions of the Augustinian nun Juliana of Liège (ca. 1192-1258). The first instance of a → procession, with the Eucharist at first concealed, comes from St. Gereon in Cologne in 1277. Pope Urban IV (formerly archdeacon of Liège) introduced the observance to the whole church in 1264, and it spread quickly in the West after the publication of the bull *Transiturus* in the collection of Clementine Decretals (1317). The people greatly valued the eucharistic procession, though it was not at first prescribed. What was at first a simple perambulation round the church tended to merge in the German sphere with other pastoral processions. Under the influence of Trent (sess. 13, chap. 5), which was directed against the Reformation, the Corpus Christi procession found in → baroque its most extravagant development as an expression of a glad certainty of faith but also as a denominational demonstration. After Vatican II celebration of the Mass became more central again, and the optional procession came to be seen as a representation of the pilgrim people of God moving toward its goal with Christ.

Other expressions of Roman Catholic spirituality are → devotions before the sanctuary, blessing with the eucharistic bread reserved in the ciborium or monstrance, and hours of → worship, such as on the first Thursday evening of the month in remembrance of the institution of the Eucharist on the evening before Jesus' passion. The establishment of an "eternal prayer" came in the first half of the 16th century in Italy, first of all in the form of a 40-hour prayer (the *Quarant'ore*) inspired by an earlier 40-hour prayer vigil at the Holy Sepulchre during → Holy Week. Some dioceses have established an annual cycle for their parishes. Vatican II forbade masses before the opened → tabernacle (§2), which had previously been very popular.

In the 19th and 20th centuries special impulses toward eucharistic spirituality came from the International Eucharistic Congresses. The spur toward these great gatherings, which took place at irregular intervals and in different places, came from the French laywoman M. M. Emilie Tomissier (1844-1910). With the approval of Leo XIII, the first congress took place at Lille in 1881. Prominent at first were the eucharistic cult and the idea of Christianizing society by means of the Eucharist. Increasingly in the 20th century, however, the congresses moved toward the *Statio orbis* (Munich 1960) and a representation of the world church united in celebrating the Eucharist (→ Church 3.2). The congress at Lourdes in 1981 was marked by the reorientation of eucharistic spirituality brought about by Vatican II. This spirituality now finds its focus in active celebration and full participation, so that Communion is experienced not merely as personal salvation but as a force that establishes fellowship and changes the world.

Bibliography: J. BISHOP, *Some Bodies: The Eucharist and Its Implications* (Macon, Ga., 1993) • P. BROWE, *Die Verehrung der Eucharistie im Mittelalter* (Munich, 1933; repr., 1967) • C. CASPERS, G. LUKKEN, and G. ROUW-HORST, eds., *Bread of Heaven: Customs and Practices Surrounding Holy Communion* (Kampen, 1995) • H. DAVIES, *Bread of Life and Cup of Joy: Newer Ecumenical Perspectives on the Eucharist* (Grand Rapids, 1993) • A. HEINZ, "Schwerpunktverlagerung in der Meßfrömmigkeit. Von der Elevations- zur Kommunionfrömmigkeit," *HID* 36 (1982) 69-79 • O. NUSS-BAUM, *Die Aufbewahrung der Eucharistie* (Bonn, 1979) • K. W. STEVENSON, *Accept This Offering: The Eucharist and Sacrifice Today* (London, 1989).

ANDREAS HEINZ

Euchologion → Liturgical Books

Eugenics

First used academically by F. Galton (1883), the term "eugenics" denotes the attempt to protect the race against degeneration and damage (negative eugenics) and to achieve and, if possible, enhance its development (positive eugenics). Synonyms in various time periods have been "racial hygiene" (A. Ploetz in 1895, dropped after 1945), "propagation hygiene," and "heredity hygiene."

Means of negative eugenics are → birth control, isolation, and sterilization, while education and marriage and family → counseling are means of positive eugenics. The eugenic aims of social and population politics are dubious. W. Schallmeyer wanted the struggle of nations for existence (understood in terms of social Darwinism) to be regulated by eugenic measures rather than → war. In Indiana in the United States, compulsory sterilization on eugenic grounds was made legal in 1907. In the USSR eugenics (two institutes for which were opened in 1921) was replaced in 1930 by Marxist-Leninist social science. Under D. T. Lysenko an ideological Lamarckism held sway from 1937 to 1964.

Germany introduced sterilization for hereditary diseases (according to the then state of knowledge) in 1932-33, and between 1934 and 1936 at least 169,000 people were sterilized (only 10 percent of them voluntarily). The combination of eugenics and racial ideology had a devastating effect in the National Socialist state, with its ideas of racial inequality, white supremacy, the Aryan master race, and decline through racial mixing. Doubtful tendencies also lay behind the North American Immigration Restriction Act of 1924.

The London Ciba symposium "Man and His Future" (1962) initiated new discussion. To counteract genetic decline through advancing civilization, careful protection and selection were advocated along the lines of evolutionary humanism (J. Huxley; see also the contributions of Nobel Prize winners H. J. Muller and J. Lederberg). The proposals ran into strong criticism. Further technical advances have opened up new prospects for gene therapy but also have brought corresponding dangers.

The international Human Genome Project has now made it possible for us to understand much about the genetic makeup of human beings. While our ability to intervene in the human genetic code is still limited, we are only in the early stages of such research, and techniques for altering the genetic code will certainly advance. Many diseases, however, have various causes. Some genes can cause sickness in one environment and stabilization in another. The main task of modern eugenics is to fight against the damaging effects of civilization (mutation prophylaxis). Screening of harmful genes can help individually but is open to misuse (e.g., in discrimination in the labor market or in setting insurance rates).

People do not find meaning from their genes but from dealings with their "nature" in social, personal, and religious relations. Individuals must not be made the victims of concepts like "gene," "race," or "humanity." Such terms are abstract instruments of rational understanding. Biological knowledge makes more conscious action possible but cannot replace personal perspectives. On a Christian view, creaturely → solidarity is opposed to selectionism but will try to avoid foreseeable harm in the interests of future generations.

→ Evolution; Health and Illness; Medical Ethics; Persons with Disabilities; Racism

Bibliography: G. ALTNER, *Weltanschauliche Hintergründe der Rassenlehre des Dritten Reiches* (Zurich, 1968) • H.-M. DIETL et al., *Eugenik. Entstehung und gesellschaftliche Bedingtheit* (Jena, 1984) • A. M. HEDGECOE, "Genome Analysis," *EncAE* 2.463-70 • G. JONES, *Social Darwinism and English Thought* (Sussex, N.J., 1980) • D. J. KEVLES and L. HOOD, eds., *The Code of Codes: Scientific and Social Issues in the Human Genome Project* (Cambridge, Mass., 1992) • D. J. KEVLES and M. LAPPÉ, "Eugenics," *EncBio* 2.765-77 • J. F. KILNER, R. D. PENTZ, and F. E. YOUNG, eds., *Genetic Ethics: Do the Ends Justify the Genes?* (Grand Rapids, 1997) • P. KITCHER, *The Lives to Come: The Genetic Revolution and Human Possibilities* (New York, 1996) • K. LUDMERER, *Genetics and American Society* (Baltimore, 1972) • D. NERI, "Eugenics," *EncAE* 2.161-73 • P. T. ROWLEY, "Genetic Screening: Marvel or Menace?" *Science* 1925 (1984) 138-44 • F. VOGEL and A. G. MOTULSKY, *Human Genetics* (Berlin, 1979) • G. WOLSTENHOLME, ed., *Man and His Future* (London, 1963).

JÜRGEN HÜBNER

Eulogia

The word "eulogia" (Gk. *eulogia*, "a blessing") is used for the Heb. *bĕrākâ*, signifying both divine → blessing and human praise. In the OT only God and people are blessed, never things, but in the NT things can also be the objects of eulogia. Closely related Greek terms are *eulogeō* ("praise, bless") and *eucharisteō* ("thank"). In a significant reinterpretation, "eulogia" shifted from the praising of God for things to a blessing of the things themselves, especially bread and light.

From the third century, eulogia came to be used for the bread distributed at a common meal, in distinction from the → Eucharist as the Lord's body. In the → Orthodox churches the bread left over after celebration of the Eucharist, called the antidoron, was distributed. In the West eulogia breads became customary, especially in Gaul.

Bibliography: A. STUIBER, "Eulogia," *RAC* 6.900-928 • C. WESTERMANN, *Blessing in the Bible and the Life of the Church* (Minneapolis, 1978).

THADDEUS A. SCHNITKER

Europe

1. General Situation
    1.1. Statistics
    1.2. Political, Economic, Social, and Cultural Features
    1.3. Problem Areas
2. Religious Situation
    2.1. Statistics
    2.2. Features
    2.3. Problem Areas
3. Christian Churches
    3.1. History
    3.2. Problems and Tasks
    3.3. Christian Life, Activities, Piety
    3.4. Problems of Interdenominational and International Dialogue

1. General Situation

1.1. *Statistics*

Geographically, Europe is bounded by the Caucasus Mountains and the Mediterranean Sea in the south; by Iceland, Ireland, and the Atlantic islands of the Azores and the Canaries in the west; and by the Arctic tip of Norway in the north. In the east the conventional border has been the Ural Mountains. According to current U.N. demographic terminology, however, all of Russia is considered part of Europe, which thus extends Europe's eastern border to the Pacific Ocean. The accompanying statistics reflect this usage.

In both land area and population, Europe (with Russia) ranks third among the world's continents, or (U.N.) "major areas," behind Asia and Africa.

Alone among the continents, Europe in A.D. 2000 was estimated to have a negative annual growth rate, with 15 countries experiencing a net population decrease.

Western and central Europe present the social characteristics of a typical highly developed → industrial society. There are high standards of medical care, which tend to increase life expectancy. This factor, in conjunction with a falling birth rate, produces an aging society and a diminution of the active work force. This picture is not totally true for eastern Europe, where, since the collapse of Communism (1989-90), poverty on a large scale has been revealed, with a dramatic negative effect on life expectancy. Russia particularly has suffered in this way, having faced severe economic and social problems since the fall of Communism. There are significant ethnic and racial differences among Europeans, the intermingling of which over thousands of years has given the people a certain spiritual and intellectual standing. Today Europeans as a whole are generally regarded as energetic, skilled, and ready to take initiatives.

Opinions are divided regarding the origin of the name "Europe." According to one view it comes from Europa, a consort of the Greek god Zeus in ancient Greek mythology. Other theories locate the origin of the name in the Phoenician word for "evening" or "dusk," or perhaps as having meant "mainland" and being related to the maritime exploits of the Greeks in the Mediterranean Sea.

Europe is home to wide geographic, economic, and political differences. Most basic mineral resources can be found on this continent, together with an effective workforce, advanced scientific research, and technological capability. The discovery of oil and natural gas fields in the North Sea has helped transform the economies of the countries owning the rights (Great Britain, Germany, Netherlands, and Norway) and reduced dependence on supplies from other parts of the world. New oil and gas sources in former republics of the Soviet Union, especially Russia, are also now beginning to be exploited.

1.2. *Political, Economic, Social, and Cultural Features*

In the 20th century Europe was the source of two world wars (1914-18, 1939-45). At the Paris Peace Conference of 1919 Europe began to realize that the old order had changed and that a new player on the world stage had appeared, the United States, which had entered the war in 1917. At the same time, revolution in Russia led to the establishment of Communist rule in that country.

Europe in A.D. 2000: Demography

	Population (1,000s)	Annual Growth Rate (%)	Population Density (per sq. km. / mi.)	Births / Deaths (per 100 pop.)	Fertility Rate (per woman)	Infant Mortality Rate (per 1,000 live births)	Life Expectancy (years)
World total	**6,091,351**	**1.27**	**45 / 116**	**2.13 / 0.86**	**2.66**	**51**	**66.9**
Europe	**729,328**	**−0.08**	**32 / 82**	**1.04 / 1.19**	**1.46**	**11**	**73.5**
Eastern Europe	**306,654**	**−0.26**	**16 / 42**	**1.06 / 1.38**	**1.41**	**15**	**68.3**
Belarus	10,284	−0.23	50 / 128	1.03 / 1.28	1.40	13	70.5
Bulgaria	8,306	−0.48	75 / 194	1.02 / 1.40	1.45	14	72.1
Czech Republic	10,195	−0.13	129 / 335	1.05 / 1.19	1.40	8	73.8
Hungary	9,811	−0.56	105 / 273	1.03 / 1.49	1.40	12	70.0
Moldova	4,458	0.22	132 / 343	2.29 / 1.85	1.80	24	68.8
Poland	38,727	0.14	124 / 321	1.26 / 1.10	1.65	11	72.0
Romania	22,505	−0.23	95 / 245	1.09 / 1.22	1.40	21	70.5
Russia	146,196	−0.36	9 / 22	1.02 / 1.51	1.35	17	65.3
Slovakia	5,372	0.13	110 / 284	1.20 / 1.07	1.50	11	72.3
Ukraine	50,801	−0.36	84 / 218	0.99 / 1.40	1.38	15	70.3
Northern Europe[a]	**93,736**	**0.06**	**54 / 139**	**1.17 / 1.10**	**1.78**	**6**	**77.3**
Denmark	5,274	0.12	122 / 317	1.24 / 1.16	1.89	7	76.1
Estonia	1,418	−0.63	31 / 81	0.94 / 1.35	1.30	10	70.6
Finland	5,179	0.14	15 / 40	1.14 / 1.04	1.83	5	77.3
Iceland	282	0.88	3 / 7	1.57 / 0.69	2.19	5	79.8
Ireland	3,574	0.23	51 / 132	1.36 / 0.85	1.80	6	77.4
Latvia	2,397	−0.83	37 / 96	1.01 / 1.42	1.40	14	69.6
Lithuania	3,690	−0.24	57 / 146	1.08 / 1.21	1.50	11	71.3
Norway	4,407	0.27	14 / 35	1.29 / 1.06	1.95	5	78.1
Sweden	8,898	0.20	20 / 51	1.17 / 1.08	1.87	5	79.4
United Kingdom	58,336	0.07	239 / 619	1.16 / 1.09	1.79	6	77.9
Southern Europe[b]	**144,861**	**−0.05**	**110 / 285**	**0.98 / 1.03**	**1.35**	**9**	**77.6**
Albania	3,493	0.70	122 / 315	1.88 / 0.63	2.35	28	71.6
Bosnia and Herzegovina	4,338	0.10	85 / 220	1.04 / 0.82	1.40	12	74.0
Croatia	4,485	−0.16	79 / 205	1.09 / 1.25	1.60	9	73.1
Greece	10,597	0.09	80 / 208	1.01 / 1.06	1.45	8	78.6
Italy	57,194	−0.17	190 / 492	0.84 / 1.07	1.19	6	79.2
Macedonia	2,233	0.64	87 / 225	1.44 / 0.80	1.90	20	73.3
Malta	378	0.59	1,197 / 3,100	1.41 / 0.83	2.10	6	77.7
Portugal	9,788	−0.08	106 / 275	1.09 / 1.12	1.48	7	76.3
Slovenia	1,914	−0.20	94 / 245	0.95 / 1.15	1.30	7	74.3
Spain	39,801	−0.03	79 / 204	0.94 / 1.00	1.22	7	78.6
Yugoslavia	10,502	0.02	103 / 266	1.30 / 1.05	1.80	17	73.3
Western Europe[c]	**184,077**	**0.13**	**167 / 433**	**0.97 / 1.03**	**1.47**	**6**	**78.2**
Austria	8,292	0.30	99 / 256	0.95 / 1.02	1.42	6	77.5
Belgium	10,257	0.12	336 / 870	1.09 / 1.09	1.69	6	77.9
France	59,061	0.18	109 / 281	1.11 / 0.96	1.63	6	79.4
Germany	82,688	0.02	232 / 600	0.84 / 1.11	1.30	5	77.5
Luxembourg	430	0.74	166 / 430	1.23 / 0.98	1.83	5	77.2
Netherlands	15,871	0.25	382 / 990	1.06 / 0.91	1.55	6	78.5
Switzerland	7,412	0.43	180 / 465	1.02 / 0.92	1.53	5	79.1

Note: Because of rounding, population figures for the regions and the major area as a whole may not equal the sum of their constituent parts.
[a]Figures include Channel Islands (U.K.), Faeroe Islands (Den.), Isle of Man (U.K.). [b]Figures include Andorra, Gibraltar (U.K.), Holy See (Vatican City), San Marino. [c]Figures include Liechtenstein, Monaco.

185

Europe in A.D. 2000: Religious Affiliation (as percentage of population)

	Christians	Muslims	Hindus	Non-religious	Chinese Folk Religionists	Buddhists	Tribal Religionists	Atheists	New Religionists	Sikhs	Jews	Spiritists	Other
World total	33.1	20.0	12.8	12.7	6.3	5.9	4.1	2.4	1.6	0.4	0.2	0.2	0.3
Europe	76.8	4.5	0.2	14.7	—	0.2	0.2	3.0	—	—	0.3	—	0.1
Eastern Europe	71.9	4.5	0.3	18.7	—	0.2	0.4	3.6	—	—	0.4	—	—
Belarus	73.9	0.3	—	21.3	—	—	—	3.9	—	—	0.6	—	—
Bulgaria	80.7	12.0	—	4.8	—	—	—	2.4	—	—	0.1	—	—
Czech Republic	65.9	—	—	30.1	—	—	—	3.9	—	—	0.1	—	—
Hungary	87.0	0.7	—	7.6	—	—	—	4.2	—	—	0.5	—	—
Moldova	74.1	5.6	—	15.9	—	—	—	3.4	—	—	1.0	—	—
Poland	97.3	—	—	2.3	—	—	—	0.4	—	—	—	—	—
Romania	89.1	1.3	—	7.1	—	—	—	2.4	—	—	—	—	0.1
Russia	57.1	7.7	0.6	28.3	—	0.4	0.8	4.6	—	—	0.6	—	—
Slovakia	85.6	—	—	11.0	—	—	—	3.4	—	—	—	—	—
Ukraine	82.7	1.8	—	11.2	—	—	—	3.9	—	—	0.4	—	—
Northern Europe[a]	82.8	1.5	0.5	11.4	—	0.3	—	2.5	—	0.3	0.4	0.1	0.2
Denmark	91.5	1.4	0.1	5.3	—	—	—	1.5	—	—	0.1	—	0.1
Estonia	63.5	0.4	—	26.1	—	—	—	9.9	—	—	0.1	—	—
Finland	92.7	0.2	—	5.4	—	0.1	—	1.5	—	—	—	—	0.1
Iceland	97.5	—	0.1	1.2	—	—	0.1	0.4	—	—	—	0.5	0.2
Ireland	97.3	0.3	—	2.2	—	—	—	0.1	—	—	—	—	0.1
Latvia	67.2	0.4	—	26.4	—	—	—	5.4	—	—	0.5	—	0.1
Lithuania	87.7	0.2	—	11.1	—	—	—	0.8	—	—	0.2	—	—
Norway	94.3	1.0	—	1.8	—	1.6	—	0.6	0.5	—	—	—	0.2
Sweden	68.0	2.1	—	17.8	—	—	—	11.8	—	—	0.2	—	0.1
United Kingdom	82.3	1.9	0.8	12.0	0.1	0.3	—	1.5	—	0.4	0.5	0.1	0.1
Southern Europe[b]	83.3	5.9	—	8.2	—	0.1	—	2.4	—	—	—	—	0.1
Albania	32.3	40.4	—	17.1	—	—	—	10.0	—	—	—	—	0.2
Bosnia and Herzegovina	23.7	72.8	—	2.3	—	—	—	1.2	—	—	—	—	—
Croatia	93.4	4.4	—	1.8	—	—	—	0.5	—	—	—	—	—
Greece	94.7	3.6	—	1.4	—	—	—	0.2	—	—	—	—	0.1
Italy	82.0	1.3	—	13.0	0.1	—	—	3.6	—	—	0.1	—	—
Macedonia	63.4	29.7	—	5.6	—	—	—	1.3	—	—	0.1	—	—
Malta	98.4	0.6	—	0.8	—	—	—	0.1	—	—	—	—	0.1
Portugal	92.3	0.3	—	5.3	0.2	0.6	—	1.1	—	—	—	—	0.2
Slovenia	92.1	0.1	—	5.2	—	—	—	2.6	—	—	—	—	—
Spain	93.8	0.5	—	4.4	—	0.1	—	1.2	—	—	—	—	—
Yugoslavia	69.8	16.3	—	10.3	—	—	—	3.5	—	—	—	—	0.1
Western Europe[c]	76.6	4.7	0.1	14.7	0.1	0.4	0.1	2.6	0.1	—	0.4	—	0.2
Austria	89.8	2.4	—	6.5	—	0.1	—	0.9	—	—	0.1	—	0.2
Belgium	88.3	3.7	—	5.6	—	0.2	—	1.8	—	—	0.2	—	0.2
France	70.6	7.0	0.1	15.4	0.3	0.8	0.2	4.3	0.1	—	1.0	—	0.2
Germany	76.3	3.8	0.1	17.3	—	0.1	—	2.1	—	—	0.1	—	0.2
Luxembourg	93.8	1.1	—	3.8	—	—	—	0.8	—	—	0.2	—	0.3
Netherlands	79.9	4.1	0.7	12.7	0.1	0.5	—	1.4	0.2	—	0.2	0.1	0.1
Switzerland	88.3	2.8	0.4	6.9	—	0.1	—	1.2	—	—	0.2	—	0.1

Note: A dash represents a value of less than 0.05 percent. Because of rounding, horizontal totals may not equal 100.0.

[a]Figures include Channel Islands (U.K.), Faeroe Islands (Den.), Isle of Man (U.K.). [b]Figures include Andorra, Gibraltar (U.K.), Holy See (Vatican City), San Marino. [c]Figures include Liechtenstein, Monaco.

Europe in A.D. 2000: Church Affiliation (as percentage of population)

	Total Christians	Roman Catholics	Indigenous	Protestants	Orthodox	Unaffiliated	Anglicans	Marginal
World total	*33.1*	**17.6**	**6.2**	**5.8**	**3.7**	**1.5**	**1.0**	**0.5**
Europe	*76.8*	**39.6**	**3.3**	**10.8**	**22.1**	**2.9**	**3.4**	**0.6**
Eastern Europe	*71.9*	**20.3**	**5.6**	**3.2**	**45.0**	**0.9**	—	**0.3**
Belarus	*73.9*	14.0	1.2	1.9	50.6	6.2	—	0.1
Bulgaria	*80.7*	1.1	1.2	1.2	77.7	0.1	—	0.1
Czech Republic	*65.9*	45.4	2.2	6.9	0.8	10.3	—	0.4
Hungary	*87.0*	65.7	1.4	24.7	0.9	0.2	—	0.5
Moldova	*74.1*	2.4	19.5	2.6	48.3	0.6	—	0.8
Poland	*97.3*	93.1	0.7	0.5	2.2	0.1	—	0.7
Romania	*89.1*	15.1	1.2	11.1	84.9	0.2	—	0.8
Russia	*57.1*	0.4	4.8	1.1	52.0	0.5	—	0.1
Slovakia	*85.6*	72.0	0.4	11.2	0.5	1.0	—	0.5
Ukraine	*82.7*	11.1	15.8	2.7	55.1	0.4	—	0.2
Northern Europe[a]	*82.8*	**13.5**	**3.3**	**29.7**	**1.8**	**10.8**	**26.5**	**0.9**
Denmark	*91.5*	0.6	0.8	89.2	—	1.5	0.1	0.8
Estonia	*63.5*	0.4	0.4	17.6	22.6	21.8	—	0.6
Finland	*92.7*	0.1	0.7	91.7	1.0	5.9	—	1.0
Iceland	*97.5*	1.1	4.8	94.7	—	0.1	—	0.4
Ireland	*97.3*	89.2	0.6	0.9	—	2.3	3.9	0.4
Latvia	*67.2*	20.0	6.3	21.7	25.0	0.1	—	0.2
Lithuania	*87.7*	82.4	0.8	1.4	3.1	—	—	0.1
Norway	*94.3*	1.3	3.4	91.1	—	0.1	0.1	0.7
Sweden	*68.0*	2.0	0.7	93.3	1.6	0.6	—	0.7
United Kingdom	*82.3*	9.7	4.5	8.4	0.8	15.8	42.1	1.1
Southern Europe[b]	*83.3*	**76.5**	**0.9**	**0.7**	**13.5**	**0.2**	—	**0.7**
Albania	*32.3*	15.5	0.5	0.4	14.7	1.0	—	0.3
Bosnia and Herzegovina	*23.7*	9.2	—	0.1	14.1	0.4	—	—
Croatia	*93.4*	88.1	0.3	0.6	7.4	—	—	0.2
Greece	*94.7*	0.6	2.2	0.2	94.2	0.1	—	0.4
Italy	*82.0*	97.4	0.7	0.8	0.2	0.1	—	1.1
Macedonia	*63.4*	1.7	0.4	0.5	60.6	0.2	—	0.1
Malta	*98.4*	96.9	—	0.2	—	0.6	0.3	0.3
Portugal	*92.3*	90.9	0.9	1.5	—	0.4	—	1.3
Slovenia	*92.1*	87.7	1.8	1.5	0.6	0.2	—	0.2
Spain	*93.8*	97.2	0.8	0.4	—	0.1	—	0.5
Yugoslavia	*69.8*	3.6	1.4	1.0	63.7	0.1	—	0.1
Western Europe[c]	*76.6*	**55.9**	**1.5**	**21.6**	**0.9**	**4.1**	—	**0.8**
Austria	*89.8*	76.8	0.5	5.0	2.1	4.4	—	0.9
Belgium	*88.3*	81.9	0.5	1.3	0.5	3.3	0.1	0.8
France	*70.6*	83.0	2.3	1.6	1.2	1.4	—	0.7
Germany	*76.3*	35.7	0.9	37.2	0.9	4.7	—	0.8
Luxembourg	*93.8*	92.1	0.6	1.9	0.3	0.5	0.1	1.1
Netherlands	*79.9*	36.1	2.3	27.8	0.1	12.8	0.1	0.8
Switzerland	*88.3*	47.5	2.2	42.5	0.4	1.0	0.2	1.6

Note: A dash represents a value of less than 0.05 percent. Because of rounding, horizontal totals of the individual Christian groups may not equal the total percentage of Christians. Also, Christians in some countries are counted in more than one category, in which case the total of the individual groups may exceed the overall percentage of Christians.

[a]Figures include Channel Islands (U.K.), Faeroe Islands (Den.), Isle of Man (U.K.). [b]Figures include Andorra, Gibraltar (U.K.), Holy See (Vatican City), San Marino. [c]Figures include Liechtenstein, Monaco.

The Europe that emerged from the Second World War was shattered, divided, and exhausted — factors that largely determined developments on the continent throughout the second half of the century. Post-1945 Europe saw existing divisions based on language and nationality augmented by new ones based on political organization, economic structure, and a marked difference in standard of living and freedom of movement and expression. The postwar era (1945-89) saw the continent split East-West by what was termed an iron curtain, as it became the primary area of confrontation between the two superpowers in a period known as the cold war. The eastern half of Europe was under the influence of the Soviet Union with Communist systems of government; the western part, under American influence, was economically dynamic and politically innovative. These political divisions crystallized into two defensive pacts: the North Atlantic Treaty Organization (NATO), for western Europe plus the United States and Canada, and the Warsaw Pact, for the Communist countries of eastern Europe. Between 1989 and 1991 the eastern half of the continent experienced → revolution and the collapse of almost all the Communist regimes. East and West Germany were unified after 45 years of division. In the Soviet Union the ruling Communist party collapsed, allowing the military and economic ties with the Communist satellite states in central Europe to be broken.

In general terms, and recognizing the existence of considerable variation, Europe is highly developed both in food production and in industry. Nevertheless, within its own geographic area, Europe has its own form of North-South problems, with wealth and industry tending toward the North, leaving areas of underdevelopment in the South around the Mediterranean basin.

To stimulate economic cooperation throughout Europe and in an attempt to overcome animosities that had resulted in the world wars, a number of institutions have been created. In May 1950 the French statesman Robert Schumann proposed setting up a common authority to regulate iron and steel production in France and Germany. This step, he believed, would help to avoid further conflicts between these two great continental states. His proposal came into being in 1951. Other projects followed, such as the European Coal and Steel Community, which was set up in 1952 with six signatory states — Belgium, France, West Germany, Italy, Luxembourg, and the Netherlands. In 1955 these six nations planned further economic integration, which resulted in 1957 in the Treaty of Rome, which in turn created the European Economic Community. Membership was increased in 1973 with the accession of Great Britain, Ireland, and Denmark; Greece was added in 1981, Spain and Portugal in 1986, and Austria, Finland, and Sweden in 1994. This group today is the European Union (EU), which aims to integrate the economies, coordinate social developments, and bring about political union of the member states. The euro was launched in 1999 by 11 of the 15 member states as a common European currency. Euro notes and coins will be issued on January 1, 2002, but the new currency is already in use in noncash form by consumers, retailers, companies, and public authorities. The EU is governed by a Council of Ministers and a directly elected European Parliament. The expansion of the EU is planned with two groups of countries: Cyprus, the Czech Republic, Estonia, Hungary, Poland, and Slovenia, to be followed by Bulgaria, Latvia, Lithuania, Malta, Romania, Slovakia, and Turkey.

The Council of Europe was established in 1949 with the purpose of promoting cooperation among the member states and in order to safeguard → democratic political principles. Most of the countries of Europe, East and West, now belong to this body, which is principally known for its work in the European Court of Human → Rights.

Postwar eastern Europe, under Communist governments and the dominating influence of Russia, in 1949 set up a Council for Mutual Economic Assistance (COMECON). Its purpose was to accelerate economic → development and promote equality in levels of development of member countries. In 1991 the Soviet Union officially broke up, COMECON was disbanded, and the → Commonwealth of Independent States was formed, a loose association that eventually included 12 of the 15 former Soviet republics.

The Organization (until 1995, Conference) for Security and Cooperation in Europe (OSCE) was established in 1972 as a security organization, formed by NATO and, later, former Warsaw Pact members. It now comprises 55 states, including the United States and Canada. Aiming to further East-West relations through a commitment to nonaggression and human rights, it is the primary instrument for early warning, conflict prevention, crisis management, and postconflict rehabilitation in the European zone. It has developed cooperation not only in security issues but in economics (→ Economy), the → environment, → science and → technology, and election monitoring.

Rapid and major advances in technology, particularly cybernetics, raise the problem of the relation between employment and the distribution of wealth. Another major element in the social situation is the liberalization of personal morals, with the consequent destabilization of traditional → family life and an increase in drug abuse and in crime generally. This liberalization, however, also has its positive side with wide recognition of personal human rights and the equal status of women and men.

Social and economic changes in the last decade of the century have raised once more the complex issue of → refugees, migrants, and persons seeking asylum, a situation often provoked by economic inequality. The trafficking of women from eastern to western Europe is another widespread problem. The movement of people between the continent's countries, as well as the movement of people into Europe from other continents, is a major concern for all European countries.

The existence of a distinctive civilization in Europe may be traced to early antiquity. Today, although limited but significant exceptions exist, Europe is to a remarkable degree a cultural unity. Modern Europe benefits from a cultural inheritance that, in geographic terms, may be defined as Crete, Greece, Byzantium, and Palestine, or, in religious terms, as that of → Judaism, Christianity, and → Islam.

Linguistically, the great majority of Europeans speak in languages deriving from the Germanic, the Romance, and the Slavic families, all of which had their origin among Indo-European immigrants from the east. Probably the single most important factor historically in the development of modern European culture is the influence of the → Roman Empire, which covered a large part of the European landmass, the cultural products of which were later carried far beyond the geographic limits of the empire by Christian → missionaries.

As a result of the expansionist activities of European countries and the missionary endeavors of European churches over the past four centuries, European culture has reached all parts of the globe. Its power of attraction is abundantly evident, even though, within Europe itself, it is now experiencing a period of turbulence caused to a considerable degree by the inroads of → secularism into areas largely based on religious principles.

1.3. *Problem Areas*

Since the fall of Communism in most of Europe, historical animosities have reemerged in the Balkan region, particularly in the former Yugoslavia. This country, which had a modified Communist structure to meet its own needs and had declared itself neutral during the cold war, has been the scene of bitter ethnic hatred and war since 1991. New states emerged from the breakup of the country: Croatia, the Former Yugoslav Republic of Macedonia, and Slovenia (1991) and, after much ethnic conflict, Bosnia and Herzegovina (1992). A war in the former Yugoslav province of Kosovo (1999), involving the first use ever of NATO troops, has resulted in the de facto creation of yet another state. As a result of the war, great material destruction has taken place, and the remaining divisions of Yugoslavia — the republics of Serbia and Montenegro, plus the autonomous province of Vojvodina — are now for all practical purposes politically isolated. Strife in Chechnya and other former Soviet republics is also symptomatic of the instability that has resulted from the lifting of oppressive means of government under the Communist regime.

A deeper problem for Europe is that for centuries the reality that exercised unifying force was the Christian religion. Since the Enlightenment, however, Europe has found its confirmation and validation in scientific, cultural, and political → progress. Such a view of Europe many no longer find adequate, for European science and technology have been surpassed elsewhere. Although Europe still plays a vital role in world affairs, Eurocentricity is no longer meaningful. Nevertheless, a technological age requires strong economic, political, and technical structures, and therefore the apparent relevance of religion and its ideas and institutions has been greatly reduced.

2. Religious Situation
2.1. *Statistics*

As attendance at traditional Christian religious practice continues to decline, it is difficult to express statistically the realities of the European religious situation. Within the Christian religion, the growth of → house churches and many unregistered groupings, especially in the countries of eastern Europe, compounds the difficulty. Moreover, immigration to many western European countries of large numbers of people from Muslim, Hindu, and other religious backgrounds — many of whom do not continue to practice their religion in their new environment — serves to distort statistics on religious practice and adherence. Some idea of relative strengths may be derived from the tables on pp. 185-87, although interpretation of the numbers is hazardous and difficult. Roman Catholics form the single largest religious group, concentrated in Austria, France, Ireland, Italy, Poland, Portugal, and Spain, with large numbers also in Germany. Protestant expressions of Christianity are concentrated in northern and central Europe — Germany, Great Britain, the Netherlands, and Scandinavia. Followers of the Orthodox tradition live principally in Bulgaria, Greece, Macedonia, Romania, Russia, Ukraine, and Yugoslavia.

Concerning geographic distribution, it should be observed that because of immigration, most European countries are now regarded as → pluralistic in religious belief. While Muslim believers were once found mainly in the southern Russian republics, Turkey, and the southeastern area of the Balkans, migrations have now brought considerable numbers of Muslims, → Sikhs, → Hindus, and → Buddhists into many western European states. Examples of such immigration include many people from the Indian subcontinent into the United Kingdom, from northern Africa into France, from Indonesia into the Netherlands, and from Turkey into Germany. Moreover, the dissolution of oppressive regimes in central and eastern Europe has resulted in the public recognition there of large numbers of Christians, Muslims, and Jews (→ Judaism).

Jews were liquidated as the → Holocaust took place in Germany, Poland, and other countries under the Nazi regime during the Second World War. They were also subject to oppression during the period of Communism in central and eastern Europe. They are traditionally present in all European states, although now in far less numbers than before the war.

2.2. *Features*

As noted, most countries in the European continent now regard themselves as religiously pluralistic. This feature has been brought about by migration but also by refugee movements and asylum seekers from other continents. It is also reflected in the search for → spirituality, which is becoming characteristic of life on the continent. While attendance at traditional churches decreases, a sense of "faith" is said to be on the increase. Whether this element will have a marked effect on the life of Christianity is still not clear.

2.3. *Problem Areas*

The problem of relating the demands and practices of religion to the opportunities and achievements of the modern world is an issue for all religions in Europe. For example, the practice of self-denial — a feature of religious life — is not in the current lexicon of the secular world, where material success is the measurement by which life is judged.

The terms → "conservatism" and → "fundamentalism" are in common usage, not only in respect to Christianity. Their relevance is demonstrated both by the continuing growth and appearance of Chris-

tian sects, or sects that relate themselves to the Christian ideals, and also by the spread of Islamic fundamentalism, which now manifests itself in most areas of the continent. Ignorance of each other's beliefs, problems over ethical and social behavior, and such pervasive evils as → racism combine to create mutual hostility.

The fact that most of the non-Christian religions in western Europe were once the object of missionary efforts by the Christian churches has led to confusion and bewilderment on the part of many within the churches. Even as this issue is being faced by churches and mission agencies, however, old beliefs and activities persist in many areas.

As nationalism (→ Nation, Nationalism) has reappeared in society, so it has come to challenge the continent's churches. Many of the churches carry the name of their respective country, and some of them are now seen as identifying with extreme nationalism.

3. Christian Churches

3.1. *History*

Europe was an early mission field for the Christian faith. Its primitive ecclesial life quickly spread from its Jewish homeland across Turkey to the Mediterranean islands and the coasts of Greece and Italy. This life and its structures took root and began a remarkable and complete penetration of the whole continent. Europe, in the course of history, then became the main springboard for the diffusion of the faith and its accompanying structures throughout the world, in an ever-increasing range of expression.

From small groups of believers facing severe persecution on the northern rim of the Mediterranean, the status of Christianity changed forever in A.D. 313 with the Edict of Milan, when the Roman Emperor Constantine accorded Christianity a legal status, and in 380, in the time of the Emperor Theodosius, when it was confirmed as the religion of the Roman Empire. Deeply affected by the vicissitudes of the Roman Empire, which was politically divided between East and West from 395, ecclesiastical authority was also divided between → Rome and → Byzantium, most clearly in the dispute of 1054. This schism, which has yet to be completely healed, led to a mutual anathematization of the churches in eastern and western Europe that persisted until its lifting in 1964.

In A.D. 303, through the work of Gregory the Illuminator, the Armenian king and his court were converted to Christianity. By the end of the third century Christianity had been established in the British Isles. By the ninth century missionaries had penetrated into the Nordic lands. From 863 eastern Europe was forever influenced by the remarkable missionary work of Cyril and Methodius, which led to the conversion of the Bulgarians in 864 and the Kievan Russians in 988. The conversion of the Hungarians came at the end of the tenth century, following the preaching of Stephen.

In 1453 Byzantium was conquered by the Turks, and shortly afterward vast areas of central and southeastern Europe came under Islamic control. In some places this situation lasted until the early part of the 20th century.

In western Europe the mid-16th century saw the → Reformation movements, inspired by, among others, M. → Luther, J. → Calvin, U. → Zwingli, and Anglican Reformers under Henry VIII, Edward VI, and Elizabeth. The Counter-Reformation, solidified at the Council of → Trent (1545-63), renewed the → Roman Catholic Church with vigor and zeal. The 17th and 18th centuries in Britain saw the development of the "free churches" — the → Baptists, Congregationalists, and Methodists (→ Congregationalism; Methodist Churches).

The 18th and 19th centuries were marked by a new dimension of global missionary activity (→ Mission), spearheaded by the churches of western Europe as well as those from the United States. This activity led directly to the modern → ecumenical movement, with its aim of reconciliation between the separated churches. In 1910 the great interdenominational and world missionary conference was held in Edinburgh, Scotland. Other significant meetings followed, resulting in the 1948 founding of the → World Council of Churches and, ten years later, the regional ecumenical organization for Europe, the → Conference of European Churches.

The Second → Vatican Council was opened in 1962 by Pope → John XXIII, with advisers present from other → Christian World Communions. In 1964 Pope Paul VI met and embraced Ecumenical Patriarch Athenagoras, first among equals within the → Orthodox Church, and the anathemas of 1054 were lifted. In 1966 Michael Ramsey, the archbishop of Canterbury, primate of the Church of England, visited Pope Paul VI in Rome, and in 1983 the pope paid a reciprocal visit to Canterbury.

For the continent that saw the rise of church division and then exported that division around the world, dialogue between various Christian communions has resulted in healing agreements. A primary example is the → Leuenberg Agreement (1973), in which Lutheran and Reformed churches of continental Europe, along with some united churches and pre-Reformation churches (e.g., the →

Waldensian Church and the Church of the Czech Brethren), affirmed together a common understanding of the gospel and provided for eucharistic fellowship. Another is the Meissen Agreement, "On the Way to Visible Unity" (1988), a common statement affirming unity in faith between the Church of England and the Evangelical Church in Germany. A third is the Porvoo Common Statement (1992), a document issued by four Anglican churches and eight Nordic and Baltic Lutheran churches (later ratified by all of these bodies except the Church of Denmark). The purpose of the Porvoo statement was to draw the churches involved into a new and closer relationship for the sake of greater unity and more effective mission. Acceptance by the signatory churches meant that for the first time the Anglican churches in Britain and Ireland could move into visible communion with the Lutheran national churches of Nordic Europe and the Baltics.

Additionally, on a global level and after several decades of dialogue, Lutherans and Roman Catholics reached historic agreement on October 31, 1999, when authorized representatives of the → Lutheran World Federation and the → Vatican signed the Joint Declaration on the Doctrine of Justification. By this act, the basic theological conflict of the 16th-century Reformation was addressed, mutual condemnations over this doctrine were declared no longer applicable, and areas for intensified → dialogue were identified. Many of the key steps toward this signing were initiated in the Lutheran–Roman Catholic dialogues that have taken place since 1967.

3.2. Problems and Tasks

The problems and tasks facing European churches come from two directions: from the contemporary ecclesial developments described above, and from secular society itself. Overall, for European ecclesiastical structures, encumbered by a heritage of schism and separation, the problem and task is to rediscover and act upon the basic unity that is professed in the Christian faith itself.

→ Secularization, marked notably by the continuing decline in regular church attendance and membership, has resulted in a lessening of church influence in the structures of society. → Pluralism in faith is now a feature of most European countries. The ending of the East-West divide after the fall of the Berlin Wall at the end of 1989 presented important challenges to the churches on both sides of the fallen iron curtain. Churches in the newly free East began to rediscover their vocation in their own societies, in many countries being the only stable institutions carried over from Communist times. Overwhelmingly, however, they have shown themselves ill equipped to match the new challenges. Western churches, moreover, were tardy in responding to the new opportunities, apart from what were perhaps well-meaning but frequently misdirected mission-ary activities — which many saw as outright → proselytism. The often inflexible structures of the European churches have caused persistent prob-lems.

Other issues remain, still inadequately dealt with: the movements of populations and increasing encounters with people of other faiths, the churches' role in the resolution of social problems, their task in → disarmament and peace making, and the need of people to meet and live *with* each other, after cen-turies of living *in separation from* (though perhaps alongside of) each other. Although churches are generally no longer the leaders of public opinion, their influence, tenacity, and perspicacity are still of significance in both East and West, and their opin-ion is still often sought.

3.3. *Christian Life, Activities, Piety*

Patterns of Christian activity and → piety on the European continent present a very uneven picture. Since the end of the Communist regimes in central and eastern Europe, there has in many places been a return to the church. This upswing is, however, proving to be short lived in most central European countries, where market forces are placing great em-phasis on economic reforms in preparation for join-ing the European Union. These forces often work against the more social and communal outlook of the churches. In eastern Europe the renaissance of the Orthodox churches is clearly more visible and can be convincingly documented. With this renais-sance, however, have come sharp divisions in these churches, particularly in respect to ecumenism and relations with other churches.

Throughout Europe there is a continuing, though in some instances decreasing, drop in church membership. This fact is not always reflected in attendance at worship, where some churches point to larger congregations in spite of lower mem-bership; in these circumstances many churches are reviewing patterns and criteria for determining membership.

In recent decades the rise of the → charismatic movement has been notable throughout Europe, and churches of a more → evangelical character are also modestly on the increase. With a few notable exceptions, a decrease in vocations for various kinds of Christian ministries continues. The interest in al-ternative forms of community activity, such as house churches, seems to have peaked.

A clear mark of recent decades is the close in-volvement of many Christians and all churches in expressions of social responsibility. This feature is notable in campaigns for debt relief and aid to de-veloping countries, for disarmament, and for peace, as well as in concern for refugees, asylum seekers, and those victimized by the drug trade. Many of these concerns are being addressed on an ecumeni-cal basis.

3.4. *Problems of Interdenominational and International Dialogue*

The churches of Europe have played a major part in the initiation and continuation of the modern ecumenical movement. Numerous examples of inter-confessional dialogue are evident on the European scene, the most recent result being the 1999 Lutheran–Roman Catholic agreement on the un-derstanding of → justification.

The churches have given themselves appropriate structures for working at regional and local levels in Europe, principally through → national councils of churches, in which in many countries the → Roman Catholic Church is a full member. The main re-gional structure for the Catholics is the Consilium Conferentiarum Episcoporum Europae (CCEE, the Council of European Bishops' Conferences), and for the Anglican, Orthodox, and Protestant churches, the Conference of European Churches. These two pan-European organizations have held regular en-counters since 1978 and were the cohosts for two re-markable European ecumenical assemblies of Christians. The first, in 1989 in Basel, Switzerland, under the theme "Peace with Justice," was the first occasion since the Middle Ages when all the Chris-tians of Europe could meet together. This assembly was part of the European contribution to the world-wide conciliar process on Justice, Peace, and the In-tegrity of Creation, initiated by the World Council of Churches. A second European ecumenical assem-bly took place in 1997 in Graz, Austria, with the theme "Reconciliation: Gift of God and Source of New Life." This gathering was the largest and most significant event to have taken place among the churches since the fall of Communism at the begin-ning of the 1990s.

Changes in structures following the ending of the European divide have included the integration of the European Ecumenical Commission for Church and Society with the Conference of Euro-pean Churches (CEC). The Church and Society Commission of the CEC is now charged with moni-toring the developments and activities of European institutions, principally the European Union, the Council of Europe, and the Organization for Secu-rity and Cooperation in Europe. The Roman Catholic Church also has a body monitoring the European institutions, the Commission of the Bishops' Conferences of the European Community. The chief matters discussed in these bodies are human rights, bioethics, international relations, and → religious liberty, as well as theological problems specifically related to the European situation.

Bibliography: J. M. BAILEY, *The Spring of Nations: Churches in the Rebirth of Central and Eastern Europe* (New York, 1991) • G. BAUM, *The Church for Others: Protestant Theology in Communist East Germany* (Grand Rapids, 1996) • M. BOURDEAUX, *Gorbachev, Glasnost, and the Gospel* (London, 1990) • COMMISSION OF THE EUROPEAN COMMUNITY, *General Report on the Activities of the European Union, 1998* (Brussels, 1999) • CONFERENCE OF EUROPEAN CHURCHES, *Peace with Justice: The Official Documentation of the European Ecumenical Assembly, Basel, Switzerland, 15-21 May 1989* (Basel, 1989) • S. DAHLGREN, *Politik och Kyrka. Lutherska kyrkor i Östeuropa* (Stockholm, 1989) • U. DUCHROW, *Europe in the World System, 1492-1992: Is Justice Possible?* (Geneva, 1992) • D. L. EDWARDS, *Christians in a New Europe* (London, 1990) • D. HEDIN and V. MORTENSEN, eds., *A Just Europe: The Churches' Response to the Ethical Implications of the New Europe* (Uppsala, 1992) • D. HUBER, *A Decade Which Made History: The Council of Europe, 1989-1999* (Strasbourg, 1999) • N. NIELSEN, *Revolutions in Eastern Europe: The Religious Roots* (Maryknoll, N.Y., 1991) • R. NOLL, ed., *Reconciliation: Gift of God and Source of New Life. Documents from the Second European Ecumenical Assembly in Graz* (Graz, 1998) • G. ROBBERS, *State and Church in the European Union* (Baden-Baden, 1996) • W. SWATOS, *Politics and Religion in Central and Eastern Europe: Traditions and Transitions* (Westport, Conn., 1994) Much information is available on websites of European organizations, especially those of the CEC (http://www.cec-kek.org), the Council of Europe (http://www.coe.fr), the EU (http://europa.eu.int), and the OSCE (http://www.osce.org).

ROBIN E. GURNEY

European Theology (Modern Period)

1. Survey

1.1. Theology between Church and Academia

1.1.1. Origins

The rise of theology in Europe is intimately connected with the development of the universities. They grew out of the scholastic period, noted for its → summas, commentaries, and collections of sentences. Disputations brought scholars together, which ultimately led to the development of a transregional alliance of thinkers and writers.

The papacy granted the right to establish universities, as well as assisted them financially. Through its supranational character the papacy legitimated the university's transethnic and transnational nature (→ Pope, Papacy).

The Reformation led to renewal of the university, in part to further the education of the laity (→ Clergy and Laity). It also strengthened theological faculties, since study of theology became a prerequisite for the pastoral office. Governments exercised increased supervision over universities, making sure that the teaching corresponded with the territorial confession (→ Cuius regio eius religio).

The Council of → Trent (1545-63) mandated a reform of the education of → priests, with → bishops now being obligated to maintain diocesan seminaries. To regain territory lost through the Reformation and to educate priests, the → Jesuits became active in seminary and university education. Especially because of the → Enlightenment, Protestant theological faculties became more independent of the restrictions that the territorial confession represented. The state, however, continued to provide for the spiritual and moral education of its citizens and the academic education of its → pastors, priests, doctors, and civil servants.

1.1.2. The Present

The German government stipulates that clergy are to be academically trained, and so it maintains theological faculties in state universities. (Even under Communist rule, East Germany maintained theological faculties in state universities, although the church had no say over faculty.) Switzerland and Austria also have theological faculties in state universities. In Scandinavia the national churches are supported by theological faculties, which exist mainly in government-supported institutions.

The bitter struggle in 19th-century France between laicism and traditional Roman Catholicism resulted in legislation in 1905 to separate → church and state. This decision meant the exclusion of theological faculties from most state universities.

In the British Isles, Trinity College of the University of Dublin (founded in 1592) became the spiritual center of the → Anglicans. Once a Roman Catholic university was established (1854), however, Trinity became interdenominational. In 1853 the United Kingdom decreed that professors in Scotland need not be members of the Church of Scotland. Subsequently, in 1928, the New College in Edinburgh, created to train pastors for the Free Church of Scotland, was united with the University of Edinburgh. Other national universities such as St. Andrew's and Glasgow are also interconfessional. The same is true for England. In part, the composition of British universities, which consist of distinct colleges, facilitated this → ecumenism. There is also an increasing trend toward wider ecumenism, seen in the integration of theology and → religious studies.

European universities are typically maintained by public funds and thus largely reflect the society of which they are a part. Their status assures a mind-set that is not simply geared to the professional education of clergy and leaders of religious instruction but also is aware of itself as part of a public enterprise.

1.2. Historical and Regional Developments

1.2.1. Germany (Protestant)

In the 19th century and far into the 20th, German Protestant theology played a leading role in theological discourse. During this period many important theologians of other nationalities were either influenced by German philosophers and theologians or studied with them in Germany. In the 19th century the theological faculties in Berlin and Göttingen in particular attracted foreigners.

1.2.1.1. The church father at the turn of the 19th century was F. D. E. → Schleiermacher (1768-34), who was the first member of the theological faculty in Berlin. There he enjoyed good relations with the early representatives of → Romanticism under F. von Schlegel (1772-1829). In *Über die Religion: Reden an die Gebildeten unter ihren Verächtern* (1799; ET *On Religion: Speeches to Its Cultured Despisers* [1893]), Schleiermacher defined → religion as a relationship of the → individual with the eternal and divine, a relationship founded in one's own → experience. Schleiermacher claimed that re-

ligion is neither thought nor action but "sense and taste for the infinite."

Schleiermacher's *Glaubenslehre* (1821/22; ET *The Christian Faith* [1928]), which had an impact on the history of theology in the 19th century like no other work in Germany, paved the way for a → systematic theology that described and analyzed religion in general, then Christianity, and finally → Protestantism. → Salvation means that Jesus draws the faithful into his own God-consciousness. This movement occurs in the → congregation, where the divine work is communicated according to Scripture. → Faith ensues as a living communion with Christ.

G. F. W. Hegel (1770-1831) came to Berlin in 1818, seeking to reconcile faith and reason (→ Hegelianism). Hegel's → absolute, which he considered ahistorical and residing in the beyond, actualizes itself in human consciousness; that is, God comes into consciousness and is realized in humanity. Hegel concluded that Christianity is the ultimate religion, since it understands God as triune. Within religious history, Christianity is the completion of religion. Since the absolute spirit, God, is active in the world, history follows a reasonable course, through which God accomplishes his intentions.

The movement Hegel initiated, however, split into a left wing and a right wing. Left-wing Hegelians rejected his synthesis between idea and reality and tried to show that the origin of religion is wishful thinking, that faith in God is merely a projection into an artificial beyond. Religion therefore ought to be eliminated. This conclusion was suggested by L. Feuerbach (1804-72) and K. → Marx (1818-83). D. F. Strauss (1808-74) claimed that the divine does not appear in → Jesus as an individual, but only in humanity as a whole.

S. → Kierkegaard (1813-55) was vigorously opposed to the entire Hegelian synthesis. Decades later, however, much of German, English, and Scandinavian theology followed in Hegel's footsteps. Only the rise of empirical and historical science diminished Hegel's influence.

In philosophy, theology, and law, the right-wing Hegelians tried to show that history was a reasonable, meaningful, and God-directed course. In the mid-19th century the Hegelian right was still vigorous, as seen in F. C. Baur (1792-1860), who founded the Protestant Tübingen school. Baur judged → dogmas as time-conditioned expressions of Christian consciousness. We can trace the beginning and leading motifs of the history of dogma in the NT (→ Dogma, History of). The goal of historical development is the progress of the spirit to the freedom of self-consciousness.

Schleiermacher and Hegel influenced a strong stream of Protestant → mediating theology (*Vermittlungstheologie*) in the 19th century. Its representatives presuppose that a religious consciousness belongs to the essence of humanity. They expressed themselves in particular in the journal *Theologische Studien und Kritiken* (Theological studies and criticisms, 1828-1947). Prominent among them was R. Rothe (1799-1867), who maintained that Christianity and the → kingdom of God will evolve into a religiously grounded cultural state of nations permeated with the spirit of Christ.

In 1817 neo-Lutheranism was inaugurated when C. Harms (1778-1855), a pastor from Kiel, published Luther's 95 Theses and added 95 of his own, dealing with reviving Lutheran piety. Harms began a movement that was active in Germany and Scandinavia. He rejected rationalism and advocated an ecclesial doctrine guided by the traditional Lutheran norms of Scripture and the → confessions.

With its emphasis on Scripture, confessions, → church, and → sacrament, the decisive points of Reformation theology came to the fore. Typical for 19th-century neo-Lutheranism was its developmental thinking. Though God's revelation attested in Scripture has come to its end, → revelation can be expounded in an infinite variety of ways. The development of church doctrine, therefore, is conducted on the basis of the experience of faith and insight into its scriptural content.

W. Löhe (1808-72), who never held an academic post, was nevertheless an important teacher of the church through his sermons, writings, and training of preachers and teachers for overseas Lutherans (esp. in North America), and through his founding in 1849 of the Gesellschaft für Innere Mission im Sinne der lutherischen Kirche (Society for home mission in accordance with the Lutheran Church). In his *Drei Bücher von der Kirche* (1845; ET *Three Books about the Church* [1969]), he maintained that the Lutheran Church, which he saw as the wellspring of truth and the unifying center of all the different Christian churches, distinguishes itself from all others by having a pure confession. Since it stands guard over the pure doctrine, it cannot sacrifice any doctrinal content.

E. W. Hengstenberg (1802-69), who taught exegesis in Berlin, edited the *Evangelische Kirchenzeitung* (Protestant church magazine), which he used in a fight against → rationalism and → liberalism. His Lutheran neoconfessionalism was extremely influential in the church and the Prussian state. He provoked a reaction, especially from Reformed theologians and those who advocated → Culture Protestantism.

C. Schwarz (1812-85), who saw a threat against the scholarly status of theology, was one of the founders of the Deutsche Protestantenverein (German Association of Protestants, 1865), an organization with the stated goal of renewing the Protestant church in the spirit of freedom and in consonance with the development of → culture. T. Harnack (1817-89) from Erlangen is remembered for his warning against overestimating the confessions, since they are historically conditioned.

The most important and theologically promising direction of neo-Lutheranism was the Erlangen school, which viewed theology as an analysis of the Christian consciousness. Personal experience of faith facilitates a rediscovery and reappropriation of the doctrinal content of the Lutheran confessions. J. C. K. von Hofmann (1810-77) was a prominent representative of such theology, claiming in his influential two-volume work *Der Schriftbeweis. Ein theologischer Versuch* (The proof of Scripture: A theological attempt, 1852-56), "I, as the Christian, am for myself, the theologian, the object matter of my scholarly pursuit."

1.2.1.2. The second half of the 19th century can be characterized by an optimistic progressive mood that showed itself theologically in Culture Protestantism. This → liberal theology dissociated itself from ecclesial dogma and emphasized the relativity of historical insights and the results of the → history of religion. Especially prompted by C. Darwin's theory of → evolution, many intellectuals believed in the perfectibility of humanity with regard to intellect and moral insight. This mood was not confined to Germany or Europe in general but also characterized the American scene, as we can see in the close connections between the representatives of the → Social Gospel, such as Henry Churchill King (1858-1934) and Walter → Rauschenbusch (1861-1918), and representatives of Culture Protestantism in Germany.

A. Ritschl (1822-89), who taught more than 30 years at Göttingen, is the father of Culture Protestantism. He focused on the kingdom of God and on the individual's → vocation, calling for Christian social involvement in the affairs of the world. Ritschl's *Die Christliche Lehre von der Rechtfertigung und Versöhnung* (3 vols., 1870-74; ET vol. 3, *The Christian Doctrine of Justification and Reconciliation* [1902]) and *Geschichte des Pietismus* (3 vols., 1880-86; ET of Prolegomena in Ritschl, *Three Essays* [1972]) have enduring value. He based his dogmatics on → justification and → reconciliation, and on the NT idea of the kingdom of God, which he saw as involving both the eternal aim of God for the world and the moral task of humanity to accomplish this aim.

W. Herrmann (1846-1922), who taught systematic theology at Marburg, insisted that only two factors are important: the historical person of Jesus and the ethical demand issuing from him. In this way he furthered the emergence of neo-Reformation (i.e., dialectical) theology.

Another giant of Culture Protestantism was A. von Harnack (1851-1930), who taught successively at Leipzig, Giessen, Marburg, and Berlin. Evidencing deep piety, immense erudition, a liberal mind-set, and involvement for social betterment, Harnack in 1881 became an editor of *Theologische Literaturzeitung* (Journal of theological literature) and, in 1882, of *Texte und Untersuchungen zur Geschichte der altchristlichen Literatur* (Texts and investigations of the history of early Christian literature). His lectures during the winter semester 1899-1900, entitled *Das Wesen des Christentums* (ET *What Is Christianity?* [1957]), sold more than 100,000 copies. He asserted that Christianity is not just feeling and moral action but also a thinking religion. Itself the result of a historical process, it has changed through the centuries.

The systematician within the history-of-religions school was E. → Troeltsch (1865-1923), a student of Ritschl. His teaching career started at Göttingen, then he moved to Bonn, Heidelberg, and finally Berlin. Troeltsch saw the Enlightenment as the break between classic Protestantism and neo-Protestantism. His publications *Die Soziallehren der christlichen Kirchen und Gruppen* (2 vols., 1912; ET *The Social Teaching of the Christian Churches* [1931]) and *Die Absolutheit des Christentums und die Religionsgeschichte* (1902; ET *The Absoluteness of Christianity and the History of Religion* [1971]) made him known beyond the confines of theology.

Cultural Protestantism and liberal theology made significant scholarly contributions. Yet their trust in → progress as manifested in history and their secularized → eschatology could no longer be maintained. J. Weiß (1863-1914), professor of NT at Marburg and later at Heidelberg, emphasized the future-directed eschatological character of Jesus' proclamation of the kingdom of God. He claimed that this proclamation had nothing to do with an inner-worldly aspiration. A. → Schweitzer (1875-1965) also concluded that Jesus and his proclamation must be understood in totally eschatological terms.

1.2.1.3. The experience of World War I (1914-18) shattered 19th-century → optimism, and theological liberalism and Culture Protestantism lost their attraction. The decisive reorientation came through K. → Barth (1886-1968), who in the second edition of his commentary on Romans (1922; orig. pub., 1918; ET 1933) refuted earlier theological trends. Barth's early collaborators were E. Brunner (1889-1966), F. Gogarten (1887-1967), R. Bultmann (1884-1976), G. Merz (1892-1959), and E. Thurneysen (1888-1974). Influenced by Kierkegaard and R. Otto (1869-1937), they founded the journal *Zwischen den Zeiten* (Between the times, 1922-33). For them God is the totally other who cannot be grasped by us but who only shows himself to us.

Neo-Reformation theology had been united by a rejection of liberal and cultural theology, but it lacked a common base. This defect became evident in an exchange between Barth and Brunner. When Brunner advocated a dialogic apologetic approach to present problems and looked for a point of contact in the world to mediate Christianity, Barth retorted with an uncompromising No! (*Nein! Antwort an Emil Brunner* [1934]; ET appears in *Natural Theology: Comprising "Nature and Grace"* [1972]). God does not need any point of contact, nor does one exist. In this vein the → Confessing Church under Barth's leadership stated in the → Barmen Declaration of 1934 that it rejects the doctrine that besides the → Word of God the church needs to recognize "other happenings and powers, images and truths" (thesis 1). While this stand was certainly proper at that time, in the long run such theology tended to cut itself off from → dialogue with the world. This spirit is to a certain extent exemplified in Barth's influential and monumental *Kirchliche Dogmatik* (1932-67; ET *Church Dogmatics* [1936-69]), a 6,000-page project that Barth was ultimately unable to complete.

Rudolf Bultmann, in contrast, turned to the → existential philosophy of Martin Heidegger (1889-1976) to mediate the Christian faith. In his essay "Neues Testament und Mythologie" (1941; ET "NT and Mythology" [1984]), Bultmann maintained that the worldview of the NT is fundamentally mythological. In contrast to 19th-century liberalism, however, Bultmann pointed out that the issue is not elimination of → myth but its → interpretation. The NT addresses us with the decisive question, made possible through God's action in Jesus Christ, of whether we want to exist authentically in radical openness for God's future. Bultmann's program of → demythologization and existential interpretation of the biblical message was highly debated and often wrongly lumped together with 19th-century liberalism.

1.2.1.4. By the 1960s, neither Barth's nor Bultmann's perspectives sufficed. Much earlier, D. → Bonhoeffer (1906-45) had objected to Barth's →

positivism with regard to revelation, as well as to his neglect of ethical issues, which Barth in fact developed in later parts of his *Dogmatics*. W. Pannenberg (b. 1928) pointed out in radio lectures entitled *Was ist der Mensch?* (1962; ET *What Is Man?* [1970]) that humanity always reaches beyond that which is given, manifesting a hunger for new experience that can be interpreted as a striving toward God. Yet this God, according to Pannenberg's "Dogmatic Theses on the Doctrine of Revelation" (1961, found in *Offenbarung als Geschichte;* ET *Revelation as History* [1968]), does not disclose himself directly but only through activities in history. To this history belong Jesus' life and destiny. Its culmination is the → resurrection, which is the proleptic anticipation of the end of history. In his three-volume *Systematic Theology* (ET 1991-98; orig. pub., 1988-93), Pannenberg elaborated and refined these insights.

While Pannenberg was influenced in his universal historical approach by Hegel's philosophy, J. Moltmann's (b. 1926) main conversation partner was E. Bloch (1885-1977), with his Hegelian-Marxist philosophy. In his seminal work *Theologie der Hoffnung* (1964; ET *Theology of Hope* [1965]), Moltmann asserts that theology must be totally eschatological. Christians thus ought to be involved in efforts for justice, → peace, and stewardship in order to show their future-mindedness and their trust in God. Steeped in the Reformed tradition, he has a strong influence in ecclesiastical and ecumenical circles.

1.2.2. *Great Britain*

For T. Hobbes (1588-1679) religion derived, not from philosophy or theology, but solely from the law of the state. J. Locke (1632-1704) rejected the notion of innate ideas and paved the way for → empiricism; for D. Hume (1711-76) any experience occurs within space and time and thereby is reduced to the empirically given. With this philosophical mind-set, popularized in many ways, Great Britain took the lead in the Enlightenment movement and provided a setting in which theology had to reassert itself.

This movement, however, had its opponents. Tractarianism, also known as the → Oxford Movement, originated in an Oxford sermon entitled "National Apostasy" preached in July 1833 by J. Keble (1792-1866). J. H. → Newman (1801-90), then an Anglican, understood Keble's sermon as a divine call to defend the church in its hour of peril. The results were Newman's series Tracts for the Times, which first appeared in 1834 as small tracts but later were expanded to actual treatises. In 1845 he was received into the → Roman Catholic Church and then, after studies in Rome, was ordained as a priest (1847). In

1879 Pope → Leo XIII elevated him to cardinal. His rejection of rationalism, liberalism, and Roman centralism, as well as his insistence on the significance of the laity, has had enduring impact on the church.

C. Gore (1853-1932), with other Oxford scholars, published → *Lux Mundi* (1889), a collection of essays intended to "put the Catholic faith into its right relation to modern intellectual and moral problems." Another collection published at this time, *Essays Catholic and Critical* (1926), represents the prevailing mood of Anglican theology at the turn of the 20th century, as it sought to reinterpret Christianity in terms of contemporary → science and biblical criticism.

P. T. Forsyth (1848-1921), a Congregationalist from Scotland, studied in Göttingen under Ritschl. In two books on → atonement, *The Cruciality of the Cross* (1909) and *The Work of Christ* (1910), he insisted on the ethical power of Christian doctrine. God draws humanity to himself by Christ's example of self-sacrifice. Forsyth's sacrificial and → kenotic view of the → incarnation and → cross has been influential, as well as his polemic against the ethical naïveté of sentimental Protestantism.

The famous Cambridge trio of B. F. Westcott (1825-1901), F. J. A. Hort (1828-92), and J. B. Lightfoot (1828-89) introduced wider circles of British theology to new developments in historical and critical biblical research. They confined themselves to textual criticism and historical research in Paul, the early fathers, and the development of the ecclesial office. In 1881 Westcott and Hort issued a Greek edition of the NT (→ Bible Manuscripts and Editions 3). Their work was continued in the 20th century by C. H. Dodd (1884-1973), C. F. D. Moule (b. 1908), and D. E. Nineham (b. 1920).

Dodd, a Welsh Congregationalist, is known for his studies in John and for his "realized" eschatology, a concept developed further by J. A. T. Robinson (1919-83). Employing the methodological insights of form criticism in search of the historical Jesus, Dodd arrived at conservative results regarding the historical authenticity of the scriptural tradition. Moule continued the tradition of critical orthodoxy, again influenced by the German schools of interpretation. In his published lectures *The Use and Abuse of the Bible* (1976), Nineham emphasized the irretrievability of the NT past. Though a tentative historical outline of a reconstructed life of Jesus might be given, it does not support a contemporary Christian apologetic.

The predominance of the Anglican and Catholic tradition, with its strong influence on classical and historical training, produced a number of significant historians and patristic scholars, including G. W. H. Lampe (1912-80), an Anglican theologian and professor of theology at the University of Birmingham from 1953. He moved from a Barthian neoorthodoxy to an outspoken theological liberalism in which he argued the meaninglessness of the Trinitarian orthodoxy of the → Athanasian Creed and urged modern theologians not to be content simply to accumulate fresh insights from the past but to be prepared to modify or abandon earlier conclusions. M. F. Wiles (b. 1929), also a patristic scholar, contributed with Nineham to J. Hicks's *Myth of God Incarnate* (1977), in which he asserted that the abandonment of the incarnation as a metaphysical claim about the person of Jesus would not discard the truth of God's self-giving love.

When logical positivism became dominant in mid-20th-century England, the Metaphysicals, a group at Oxford, attempted to develop a Christian response. The group included A. M. Farrer (1904-68), M. B. Foster (1903-59), R. M. Hare (b. 1919), E. L. Mascall (1905-93), and B. Mitchell (b. 1917). They produced *Faith and Logic* (1957) as a demonstration that faith was philosophically defensible. Faith can be neither established nor refuted by empirical evidence, though it has empirical application.

Others continued to be unashamedly theological, Christ-centered, and confessional, such as T. F. Torrance (b. 1913), a Scottish Presbyterian who occupied the professorship for dogmatics in Edinburgh from 1952 to 1979. Deeply interested in the dialogue between theology and the natural sciences, Torrance strives for their synthesis to uncover what is normative to each and to relate the two dialogically.

J. Baillie (1886-1960), D. Baillie (1887-1954), and H. H. Farmer (1892-1981) sought to mediate between theology and philosophy, the gospel and contemporary culture. They emphasized the uniqueness of Christianity among the world religions and the priority of God's action in our knowing God. D. Baillie's *God Was in Christ* (1948) is a seminal work in → Christology.

J. Macquarrie (b. 1919), an Anglican theologian and professor at Oxford from 1970 to 1986, studied the specifically symbolic theology of the Christian faith. He refined Bultmann's theology in the direction of an existential ontological → theism, to replace traditional metaphysical theism.

1.2.3. *Scandinavia*

Apart from Kierkegaard, no Scandinavian theologian has decisively influenced the general European theological development. Theology in the Scandina-

vian countries has followed closely the trends observable in Europe. Until recently its closest contact has been with German theology. → Pietism greatly affected Nordic theology, led by H. N. Hauge (1771-1824) in Norway, P. Ruotsalainen (1777-1852) in Finland, C. O. Rosenius (1816-68) in Sweden, and J. V. Beck (1829-1901) in Denmark.

1.2.3.1. *Denmark.* Kierkegaard had very little influence during his lifetime but became a major voice a century later. Virtually all modern forms of → existentialism, as well as → existential theology and → dialectical theology, depend on him. Kierkegaard saw contemporary Christianity falling away from NT Christianity and called the individual to radical → discipleship. The daring decisions of faith and of existence are related to each other and must replace the compromises and half-truths of conventional Christianity. Kierkegaard's faith in Christ emphasizes incarnation, with its paradox of God coming to us in the lowly figure of a servant. Kierkegaard calls for a dialectic of existence and for existential knowing. Given the qualitative difference between God and humanity, the two can never be mediated in a speculative or reasonable way.

A contemporary of Kierkegaard was N. F. S. → Grundtvig (1783-1872), who — influenced by the Lutheran theology of the awakening, which in turn was influenced by Romanticism and → idealism — developed an ecclesial and sacramental Christianity. Grundtvig viewed the → Apostles' Creed as the full witness of the true and original faith in Christ. Since the church is invisible and a work of the → Holy Spirit, objective knowledge about Christ and the content of Christian faith is totally inadequate. He argued for complete freedom of what is taught and also a change from the confessional state church to a → people's church that should correspond to the actually present forms of religious faith and devotion to God.

The faculty of theology at Århus University has developed an independent and impressive systematic theology associated primarily with R. Prenter (1907-90), whose dogmatics, *Skabelse og genløsning* (2d ed., 1955; ET *Creation and Redemption* [1967]), is internationally known. K. E. Løgstrup (1905-81), professor of ethics and philosophy of religion, saw → nihilism as a threat to humanity. Christianity is the alternative, since its understanding of → creation provides a positive approach to life. In the context of his *Etiske fordring* (1956; ET *The Ethical Demand* [1971]), Løgstrup developed a deontological situational ethic.

1.2.3.2. *Norway.* In 1811 the University of Oslo (then Christiana) was founded, where initially a type of neoorthodoxy and Pietism prevailed, especially under G. Johnson (1812-94). At the end of the 19th century an emphasis on historicocritical exegesis and liberal systematic theology developed. This new focus led to increased internal tensions, which resulted in 1908 in the founding of a second theological faculty, the Menighetsfakultet. These two faculties now coexist peacefully, drawing their students from the different streams of piety that are deeply anchored in the Church of Norway.

1.2.3.3. *Sweden.* In the first decade of the 20th century, the University of Uppsala took the lead in Sweden, which was due to N. Söderblom (1866-1931), professor at Uppsala (1901-14) and simultaneously at Leipzig (1912-14) and archbishop of the Church of Sweden (from 1914). He was instrumental in preparing for and conducting the first conference of the → Life and Work movement, in Stockholm in 1925, as well as the inaugural conference of → Faith and Order, in Lausanne in 1927. He was convinced that the practical and ecclesial functions of theology can be obtained through a scientific view of religion.

The pioneer of Scandinavian Luther research was E. Billing (1871-1939), from 1908 professor of dogmatics and moral theology at Uppsala and then in 1920 bishop at Västerås. Emphasizing the historical character of biblical revelation, he advocated a church that does not make membership dependent on agreeing with all the teachings of the confessions.

G. Aulén (1879-1977) was professor at Lund (1913-33) and bishop in Strägnäs (1933-52). He saw theological doctrine as secondary to faith, with its only proper "object matter" the living God. He recognized the danger in emphasizing the sovereignty, divinity, and otherness of God alongside agape. Besides agape, he recognized the motifs of victory and sacrifice.

A. Nygren (1890-1978), the founder of the so-called Lundensian theology, was professor (1924-48) and bishop (1948-58) in Lund and the first president of the → Lutheran World Federation (1947-52). In his *Religiöst apriori* (1921; ET *Anders Nygren's Religious Apriori* [2000]), Nygren began his theological proposal, concluding it in *Meaning and Method: Prolegomena to a Scientific Philosophy of Religion and a Scientific Theology* (1972). He sought to provide a scientific basis for dogmatics and believed that theology has an necessary place in the sciences. Besides introducing the religious a priori, Nygren sought a foundational motif in religion. For Christianity the center is the agape motif, which focuses on the message of Christ, specifically on the incarnation and the salvific significance of the cross and resurrection.

G. Wingren (b. 1910) sought to present the content of the Christian faith by limiting himself strictly to the standpoint of Christian theology itself. Theology must start with the doctrine of God as creator and with the exposition of the → law. With this decidedly Christian apologetic, Wingren elaborates the so-called Uppsala philosophy, an analytic and antimetaphysical philosophy whose most important representative was A. Hägerström (1868-1939). This trend merged with British → analytic philosophy and formal → logic. Some representative theologians are H. Lyttkens (b. 1916), a philosopher of religion at Lund; A. Gyllenkrok (b. 1910), from Uppsala; and U. Forell (b. 1930), a systematic theologian from Copenhagen.

1.2.3.4. *Finland.* Finnish systematic theology has developed similarly to that in Sweden. It has been furthered by the theological faculty in Turku, where theology is taught in Swedish. One could mention here the Finnish Luther scholar L. Pinomaa (b. 1901) and, in philosophy of religion, S. Knuuttila (b. 1946).

1.2.4. *Netherlands*

In the Netherlands we find the Groningen school, started by H. Muntinghe (1752-1824), rector magnificus of the University of Groningen. It attempted to bridge the gap between the gospel and post-Enlightenment thought. The doctrines of original → sin and atonement were rejected, and God's revelation in Jesus Christ was understood as a means of developing a Christian personality. This kind of thinking was especially advanced through P. Hofstede de Groot (1802-86), together with his colleagues J. F. van Oordt (1794-1852) and L. G. Pareau (1800-1866).

J. H. Scholten (1811-85) first taught at Franeker and then at Leiden. Influenced by Swiss mediating theologian A. → Schweizer (1808-88) and his *Die Glaubenslehre der Evangelisch-Reformierten Kirche* (The doctrine of the Evangelical Reformed Church; 2 vols., 1844-47), Scholten endeavored to show that the Reformers and the Reformed confession found their fulfillment in idealistic thought. For him the witness of the Holy Spirit is the highest and purest form of the natural knowledge of God, though he staunchly defended Calvinistic determinism (→ Calvinism). Scholten's idealistic thinking impressed many in the Reformed Church, since they felt it was a modern and reasonable approach to the gospel.

D. Chantepie de la Saussaye (1818-74) became a representative of ethical theology. According to Chantepie, humanity has a feeling of duty and an awareness of the split between what is and what ought to be, a split that does not allow humanity to come to rest. Only Jesus Christ, the mediator between God and humanity, reconciles that which is with what ought to be and overcomes this existential anguish. One can discern in Chantepie's thoughts the influence of both Schleiermacher and Kant.

A backlash of confessional theology occurred, especially in its discussion with mediating theology. The two important representatives are A. → Kuyper (1837-1920) and H. Bavinck (1854-1921). From 1880 to 1901 Kuyper was professor of dogmatics in the Free University of Amsterdam, which he had founded, after which he became prime minister of the Netherlands. He stood for a scriptural and confessional Christianity and attempted to claim the rule of Christ even for secular areas.

Bavinck, a member of the Dutch Reformed Church and professor of dogmatics and → apologetics, succeeded Kuyper at the Free University. Bavinck was concerned with theology's specific subject. To this end he wrote *Gereformeerde dogmatiek* (4 vols., 1895-1901; ET *The Doctrine of God* [1951]). As the objective principle of knowledge, Scripture provides an objective revelation through the Holy Spirit. The subjective principle is faith, through which we can be certain that we are children of God and that Scripture is divine.

G. C. Berkouwer (1903-96), a later holder of Kuyper's chair of dogmatics, endorsed and furthered antischolastic traits present in Bavinck's theology. Berkouwer's main achievement is his 18-volume *Studies in Dogmatics* (ET Grand Rapids, 1952-75).

The influence of Barth in Reformed theology shows itself in H. Kraemer (1888-1965), professor of history of religion at Leiden. He suggested that the only sensible encounter with the world religions should be their uprooting and displacement as figments of the human mind. Another notable Leiden professor (of systematic theology) was H. Berkhof (1914-95), who was equally well acquainted with classic Reformed dogmatics and with developments in modern biblical criticism and in contemporary theology and philosophy. He is best known for his *Christelijk geloof* (1973; ET *Christian Faith* [1979]).

1.2.5. Roman Catholicism

1.2.5.1. Though there are certainly hints of regional developments in Roman Catholic theology, the centralist Roman influence makes truly regional developments unlikely. Nevertheless French and German theologians have made a lasting impact. F. R. de Lamennais (1782-1854), the founder of French Catholic liberalism, steered at first an → ultramontanist course. Claiming that the individual is unable to recognize the truth, he pointed to the significance of divine revelation embodied in the pope. Leo XII (1823-29) welcomed de Lamennais's *Essai sur l'indifférence en matière de religion* (Essay on the indifference in matters of religion; 3 vols., 1818-23).

The same trend emerged in → neoscholasticism. Its main head was the German Jesuit J. Kleutgen (1811-83), who taught in Rome. He preferred the new scholasticism but was concerned about the purity of doctrine. Mainz, one of the centers for neoscholasticism, featured J. B. Heinrich (1818-91), who taught at the diocesan seminary. Drawing on Scripture and tradition, he wrote *Dogmatische Theologie* (Dogmatic theology, 1901), which argued for a reasonable understanding of faith. The Jesuits at the theological faculty in Innsbruck also advocated neoscholasticism, as did many representatives at the Papal Theological Institutes in Rome.

The Tübingen school was attracted to idealistic philosophy but did not want to steer away from Catholic orthodoxy. J. S. von Drey (1777-1851) sought to integrate the results of Protestant historians into theology and develop a perspective of a transcendental idealism. J. A. Möhler (1796-1838) is the most significant representative of the Roman Catholic Tübingen school. His 1825 book *Die Einheit in der Kirche, oder das Prinzip des Katholizismus* (ET *Unity in the Church, or the Principle of Catholicism* [1996]) had an immense impact. His well-balanced and internally consistent theology strives for theological renewal. He emphasizes the community of the faithful but recognizes a prevalence of a → hierarchy of offices. J. B. Hirscher (1788-1865) was a reformer in → catechesis and → pastoral care. His theology was biblically oriented and strove for a realization of the kingdom of God. Trying to connect dogma and → spirituality, he was instrumental in renewing → moral theology.

1.2.5.2. An inner consolidation was especially the trend under the pontificate of → Pius IX (1846-78). Others, however, tried to reconcile the church with modern society, such as Count C. F. Montalembert (1810-70), who strove for freedom of → conscience, separation of church and state, and freedom of the press. J. J. I. von Döllinger (1799-1890), a historian and theologian, taught church history and → canon law at the newly founded University of Munich. When papal → infallibility was declared at → Vatican I (1869-70), Döllinger fought doggedly against it and finally in 1871 was → excommunicated.

K. J. von Hefele (1809-93), successor to Möhler at Tübingen in church history and bishop at Rothenburg, carefully studied the sources of dogma. He published *Conciliengeschichte* (9 vols., 1869-90; ET *History of the Councils of the Church* [1883-96]) and was one of the consultants at Vatican I. Also objecting to papal infallibility, he was the last German bishop to accept this dogma.

A. Loisy (1857-1940), instructor for biblical science at the Institut Catholique in Paris, published *L'évangile et l'église* (1902; ET *The Gospel and the Church* [1903]), which unleashed a storm unlike any other caused by a theological publication in the 20th century. This book contains the often misquoted sentence "Jesus had announced the kingdom, but what came was the church." Loisy was charged with → modernism and excommunicated in 1908. Thereafter he taught at the Collège de France.

Modernism extended beyond France into Germany and also to England and Italy. In England Baron F. von Hügel (1852-1925) and the Jesuit G. Tyrrell (1861-1909) were prominent. For Tyrell, dogma is subordinate to religious experience, and Christianity is the kernel of a universal religion of the future. In Italy modernism was connected in the social area with R. Murri (1870-1944), in the area of culture with E. Bonaiuti (1881-1946), and in the literary field with A. Fogazzaro (1842-1911).

Through a new method of apologetics, M. Blondel (1861-1949), professor of philosophy at Lille and later at Aix-en-Provence, attempted to bridge modern thought and → Catholicism, believing that tradition is Christ's activity in the church through the centuries.

In 1907 the encyclical *Pascendi* condemned modernism; also in that year a new theological school was started in Le Saulchoir, near the Belgian town of Tournai. It was run by → Dominicans with the intention of continuing the Thomistic tradition. Its first head was A. Gardeil (1859-1931). They wanted to overcome modernistic historicism by showing a continuity between revelation, dogma, and theology, while maintaining the primacy of revelation. Another center of this → *nouvelle théologie,* or new theology, was the Jesuit school in Lyon-Fourvière. It devoted itself especially to translating patristic texts under the leadership of J. Daniélou (1905-74), H. de Lubac (1896-1991), H. U. von Balthasar (1905-88), and H. Rahner (1900-1968). In 1950 Pius XII's encyclical *Humani generis* analyzed and criticized the new tendencies in theology, which meant the end of the theologians at Le Saulchoir and Fourvière, who had tried to establish a theology of renewal.

P. Teilhard de Chardin (1881-1955), a Jesuit theologian and paleontologist, tried to reconcile the doctrine of original sin with a modern evolutionary vision (→ Evolution 3.2.3). He too was dismissed from his post at the Institut Catholique in Paris. During his lifetime he was allowed to publish very little. The most important text to appear is perhaps *Le phénomène humain* (written 1938-40, published only in 1955; ET *The Phenomenon of Man* [1959]). In his *Divine milieu* (written 1926-27 and published 1957), he proposes a spirituality for Christians in the modern world. Teilhard was rehabilitated at → Vatican II.

De Lubac, a Jesuit who taught → fundamental theology and → history of religion at the Institut Catholique at Lyon, initiated and coeditored Sources Chrétiennes, a series of editions of patristic texts, which he started with Daniélou in 1942. He also began a series of theological monographs with his *Théologie* (1944). Again, *Humani generis* effectively prevented de Lubac from teaching for the next ten years, and he had to leave Lyons. His books were removed from the libraries of the Jesuits and could not be sold. Through → John XXIII he was rehabilitated and appointed as consultant working in the theological commission that prepared Vatican II. In his 1946 work *Surnaturel* (The mystery of the supernatural, 1967), he argues that humanity is drawn to God. It is the paradox of humanity that, as a finite spirit, it is opened toward the infinite. In 1982 de Lubac was finally elevated to cardinal.

Daniélou, a Jesuit and student of de Lubac, taught early Christianity at the Institut Catholique in Paris. One of his first books was banned. He maintained his teaching position after the publication of *Humani generis* and was even named dean of the Institut Catholique in 1962. In his *Essai sur le mystère de l'histoire* (1953; ET *The Lord of History: Reflections on the Inner Meaning of History* [1958]), Daniélou presents a Christian vision of history.

M.-D. Chenu (1894-1989) was professor of the history of dogma at the Dominican School at Le Saulchoir (1920-42) and head of the same school (1932-42). He wrote a small booklet in 1937 about Le Saulchoir in which he laid out a plan for a reform of theology, claiming the primacy of the revealed Word of God, acceptance of biblical and historical criticism, an open-minded → Thomism, and an openness toward the problems of the present. In 1942 this booklet was put on the index of outlawed works. Chenu was also an adviser and a theological expert concerning the → worker-priest movement in France, which had as its goal a missionary objective and solidarity with the workers. In 1954 the Vatican decided that worker-priests should no longer be allowed in factories. Chenu had to leave Paris and returned only in 1959, the year in which John XXIII announced Vatican II. He then became an adviser for the council.

Y. M. J. Congar (1904-95) was a student of Chenu at Le Saulchoir, where he taught fundamental theology and dogmatics from 1931 to 1954, interrupted only by World War II, when he was a prisoner of war in Germany. His involvement with the worker-priests meant for him exile to Israel and then to Cambridge. In 1955 he was allowed to return to France, where until 1968 he taught at the University of Strasbourg. He was rehabilitated at Vatican II and in 1994 was even elevated to cardinal. He founded the series Unam Sanctam (One holy church) in 1937, which began with his own *Chrétiens désunis* (1937; ET *Divided Christendom* [1939]). For the first time the attempt was made to define ecumenism theologically.

The Jesuits of Innsbruck attempted theological renewal with regard to a more effective → proclamation. This kerygmatic theology was especially connected with J. A. Jungmann (1889-1975) and Hugo Rahner, brother of Karl (1904-84). K. → Rahner published *Eine Theologie der Verkündigung* (1939; ET *Theology of Proclamation* [1968]) to show a way to relate theory and proclamation.

The Italian-German theologian R. Guardini (1885-1968) taught → philosophy of religion and Catholic → worldview successively at Berlin, Tübingen, and Munich. He was active in the movement for liturgical renewal and in the youth movement after World War I. He was also a popular preacher and author. He became well known through his books *Vom Geist der Liturgie* (1918; ET *The Spirit of the Liturgy* [1998]) and *Der Kreuzweg unseres Herrn und Heilandes* (1919; ET *Way of the Cross of Our Lord and Savior* [1932]).

When Guardini retired in 1964 from the University of Munich, he was succeeded by the Jesuit K. → Rahner. From 1961 Rahner was instrumental in the preparations for Vatican II. In 1967 he moved to the University of Münster. His 15 honorary doctorates show the impact he made. His *Grundkurs des Glaubens* (1976; ET *Foundations of Christian Faith: An Introduction to the Idea of Christianity* [1978]) is one of the most important texts of Catholic theology in the 20th century. Rahner proposes an anthropological method that starts below, from the human condition. Through the power of the transcendence of one's spirit, humanity lives at the shore of an infinite sea of mystery; one's categorical experience is only a tiny island in an infinite sea of the unnamed mystery (→ Immanence and Transcendence).

Balthasar, a Swiss, was a student of Lubac and Guardini who worked enthusiastically for theological renewal. In 1967 he became a member of the Papal Theological Commission and died two days before he was to be elevated cardinal. Balthasar proposes the way of → love as revealed in the absolute love of God found in the humanity of Jesus Christ. He portrays the shape of revelation in its beauty, compassion, and truth, through which it draws us into it.

1.2.5.3. While ecclesiological concerns were of prime importance immediately after Vatican II, soon a → political theology emerged in Roman Catholic and Protestant quarters. On the Catholic side the leading voice has been J. B. Metz (b. 1928), professor of fundamental theology at the University of Münster. As a student of Rahner, he published *Zur Theologie der Welt* (1968; ET *Theology of the World* [1969]), which points to the public and social consequences of the Christian message. In it he states that a new relationship between theology and praxis ought to be established because the eschatological promises of freedom, peace, justice, and reconciliation have a public dimension that must be asserted.

H. Küng (b. 1928) taught fundamental theology and dogmatics at the University of Tübingen. After Vatican II he became increasingly critical of the church, which in 1979 withdrew his authority to teach as a Catholic theologian. Subsequently, a new professorship in ecumenical theology was established especially for him at Tübingen, appropriate to an interest expressed as early as 1957 in his *Rechtfertigung. Die Lehre Karl Barths und eine katholische Besinnung* (ET *Justification: The Doctrine of Karl Barth and a Catholic Reflection* [1965]). Here he argues that one should develop a multilingual theology, acknowledging that Catholic theologians generally think and talk in scholastic terms, whereas Barth is influenced by German idealism. He then reaches the surprising conclusion that with respect to justification, there is no separation in faith between Barth and Catholicism. In his work *Unfehlbar? Eine Anfrage* (1970; ET *Infallible? An Inquiry* [1972]), Küng shows that within the church there are shepherds, teachers, leaders, and theologians who have their own charisma, their own calling and function. In *Projekt Weltethos* (1990; ET *Global Responsiblity* [1991]), he developed an ecumenical and interfaith theology for peace. Though Roman Catholic theological faculties were off-limits for Küng, he became widely read and discussed by both theologians and laypersons of all confessions.

The Belgian Dominican E. Schillebeeckx (b. 1914)

first taught at the Dominican Seminary in Louvain, and then at the Theological Faculty of the Catholic University in Nijmegen. One can distinguish two periods in his work. In the first, he followed an open-minded Thomism, while he worked on the sacraments and on a historical study of → marriage. In the second, which follows Vatican II, he abandons Thomism and picks up modern → hermeneutics to engage in dialogue with secular humanity. Schillebeeckx is convinced that Roman Catholic theology needs a new hermeneutic. His hermeneutic of experience is drawn out to a hermeneutic of praxis that concretizes the new interpretation in a radical engagement for humanity and the world, in light of the movement toward the *eschaton*. In his project on Christology — *Jezus, het verhaal van een levende* (1974; ET *Jesus: An Experiment in Christology* [1979]), *Gerechtigheid en liefde. Genade en bevrijding* (1977; ET *Christ: The Christian Experience in the Modern World* [1980]), and *Mensen als verhaal van God* (1989; ET *Church: The Human Story of God* [1993]) — he follows a radical historicocritical method to discern with certainty or a high degree of probability what we know about Jesus. He concludes that Jesus is the definitive revelation of God, who can thus show us what we actually could and should be.

1.2.6. *Orthodoxy*

1.2.6.1. Orthodox theology of eastern Europe and Greece is the theology of a → martyr church. Only in 1821 did the Greeks begin to liberate themselves from 600 years of Turkish rule. King Otto of Bavaria, the first king of the Greeks, founded the University of Athens (1837) and its theological faculty. When in the second half of the 19th century and the beginning of the 20th the Balkan states emancipated themselves from the Ottoman Empire, they founded national universities with Orthodox faculties. Originally there were three theological faculties for the Greeks — in Athens, Thessaloníki, and Chalki (near Istanbul, which the Turkish government closed in 1971).

Before the coming of Marxist rule, Orthodox theology flourished, especially in Russia. In Russia the Communists were clear about their desire to annihilate Christendom and, to that end, in December 1917 closed all theological teaching institutes. Since Stalin needed the church to support his war against the Nazis, however, two academies and eight seminaries were allowed to reopen in the 1940s under tight government control. Other Orthodox churches fared better, but the Communist goal overall was to make → theological education prohibitively difficult.

Theological faculties were usually separated from state universities and were monitored.

Philosopher of history and theologian A. S. Khomiakov (1804-60) was a systematician of → Slavophile teaching, the school that taught the unique mission of the Russian people. In his writings on a universal history, he developed a → philosophy of history that traced the dialectic between the primacy of the spirit, of freedom and love, and organic necessity based on logical laws. Khomiakov saw, on one side, the principle of the spirit and, on the other, Rome's legalism and Protestantism's rationalism. Most important was his understanding of the unity of the church, which follows necessarily from the unity of God. Significant is also his concept of *sobornost*, which means both catholicity and → conciliarity, a concept that furthered the demand for the participation of the laity in ecclesial decisions.

V. S. Solovyov (1853-1900), philosopher, theologian, and poet, also was part of the Slavophile movement. His ultimate rejection of Western Christendom was combined with advocacy of a → theocratic system. In his *Chteniya o bogochelovechestve* (1877-81; ET *Lectures on Godmanhood* [1948]), he showed that one cannot satisfy material needs once the religious foundation has been lost. Humanity is destined to be united with God and obligated to realize this unity in life.

1.2.6.2. Around the turn of the 20th century, theological work flourished throughout the Orthodox world. A key emphasis was on → salvation, especially in terms of a kenotic theology and a theology of the cross (→ Theologia crucis). An important theologian was Antony Khrapovitshy (1863-1936), for whom the suffering redeemer is the true God. Christ shows suffering love and the salvific power of this suffering. P. J. Svetlov (1861-1919), professor of apologetics at the University of Kiev, emphasized the theology of the cross in his *Krest Christov* (The cross of Christ, 1892).

Also at this time, attempts were made to dialogue with the Christian intelligentsia. The Petersburg religious philosophical meetings of 1902-3 served as a platform for these encounters. D. S. Merezhkovsky (1865-1941), a philosopher of culture, called for a new revelation and advocated an apocalyptic church in which Orthodoxy, Roman Catholicism, and Protestantism should be integrated, a call that Orthodox theologians could not accept. Those who engaged the issues, however, realized a common spiritual task and a social responsibility.

S. Bulgakov (1871-1944) showed that Orthodox theology could be progressive. Originally a Marxist and professor of political economy in Kiev, in 1903 he turned to Kantian idealism and finally to Christianity. In 1918 he was consecrated a priest, and in 1923 he was banned from the Soviet Union. He showed that → Marxism is not only an → ideology but a symptom of spiritual and intellectual decay, as well as of theological error. He therefore called for renewal through penance (→ Penitence) and a new spirituality. Bulgakov developed a → Sophiology that thematizes God's presence in the world, in terms of → grace, salvation, creation, and preservation. Humanity participates in the *sophia* (wisdom) that is effective on the boundary between cosmos and chaos. The sophia is the *natura naturans,* the feminine face of divinity, the Spirit of God, and the divine Logos as an ontological principle. His original work was cut short with the October 1917 revolution.

V. N. Lossky (1903-58) advocated a mystical theology and was opposed to Bulgakov's Sophiology. Decisive for Lossky was the connection between theology and → mysticism. The concept of mystic theology showed for him that talking about God is not only a matter of language and text but an encounter with the reality of God in this world.

After the Soviet revolution there was no longer a place for theologians in Russia. Those who survived went to France or to the United States, including the philosopher and ecumenical theologian G. Florovsky (1893-1979), the Russian-American specialist in → liturgy A. Schmemann (1921-83), and the church historian J. Meyendorff (1926-92).

The Romanian Orthodox D. Staniloae (1903-93) was lecturer at the theological academy in Sibiu but then was sent to prison for five years in 1958, charged with "attempts against the proletarian Romanian State." In 1965 he regained tenure at the Theological Institute in Bucharest. Through his *Teologia dogmatica ortodoxa* (3 vols., 1978; ET vol. 1, *The Experience of God* [1994]), Staniloae became a prominent Orthodox theologian of the second half of the 20th century. Similar to the Serbian theologian J. Popovic (1894-1979), who taught at the University of Belgrade until he was removed in 1934 and who also wrote a dogmatic theology (*Dogmatika Pravoslavne Crkve* [Orthodox Church dogmatics; 3 vols., 1932-78]), Staniloae attempted a patristic renewal and endeavored to show the relevance of the Christian doctrine for human existence.

Greek theologians could work in their own country and still maintain meaningful international relations. N. Nissiotis (1925-86) was professor at the University of Athens and director of the Ecumenical Institute in Bossey, Switzerland (1966-74), observer at Vatican II, and member of the central committee of the → World Council of Churches. While he was interested in process theology, his philosophical theology is strictly Trinitarian. J. D. Zizioulas, in his *L'être ecclésial* (1981; ET *Being as Communion: Studies in Personhood and the Church* [1985]), has developed a eucharistic theology. The → Eucharist is the center of his ecclesiology as the sacrament of unity par excellence, and therefore the expression of the mystery of the church.

1.3. *Current Trends*

Because it is no longer possible to survey theological insights from one angle, collaborative efforts are called for. The most impressive is the *Theologische Realenzyklopädie (TRE),* the first volume of which appeared in 1977. The *TRE* is international and ecumenical and, when finished, will include approximately 35 volumes. On the Roman Catholic side a third edition began appearing in 1993 of the *Lexikon für Theologie und Kirche.*

European theology is no longer exclusively the domain of men. Many women contribute to classical theological areas, such as the church historian D. Wendebourg at Tübingen, the systematician C. Axt-Piscalar at Göttingen, and S. Demel in canon law at Regensburg. In addition, women theologians advance research in areas such as spirituality, such as the German-born U. King, who teaches at Bristol, and → feminist theology, such as L. Schottroff, professor of biblical theology at Kassel.

In Germany, individual theologians are often members of an international network. I. Dalferth, a former student of E. Jüngel and professor in Zürich, is active in the European Society for the Philosophy of Religion. Since 1984 he has been an editor of *Modern Theology.* Dalferth has an abiding interest in the dialogue between theology and analytic philosophy. In that dialogue, especially prominent in Great Britain, Dalferth inquires how theologians can talk about God without being dismissed by philosophers.

O. Bayer is a professor in Tübingen and editor of the prestigious *Neue Zeitschrift für Systematische Theologie und Religionsphilosophie.* A student of E. Bizer (1904-75), his theology is discernibly Lutheran. G. Wenz in Munich is a student of and successor to Pannenberg. He is one of the editors of P. → Tillich's *Main Works / Hauptwerke* (6 vols., 1987-92) and has a theological and ecclesial interest, noticeable in his massive *Theologie der Bekenntnisschriften der Evangelisch-Lutherischen Kirche* (Theology of the confessions of the Evangelical Lutheran Church; 2 vols., 1996-97). His interest is also international, as seen in his work in the Commission of Faith and Order of the World Council of Churches. Bayer's colleague at Tübingen, E. Jüngel, is noted for his distinguished systematic work *Gott als Geheimnis der Welt* (3d ed., 1977; ET *God as the Mystery of the World* [1983]).

British theology is especially dominated by logical positivism and analytic philosophy. R. Williams, since 1999 archbishop of Wales, senses the difficulty of doing justice to the complexity and intractability of reality. While his core scholarly work has been in → patristics and the history of spirituality, he manifests a sense of the deep interpenetration of philosophy and theology, showing interest also in the relation of theology and history. R. G. Swinburne, professor of philosophy at Oxford, starts with modern natural science, analyzes it through modern philosophy, and in its light shows the meaningfulness and justification of Christian theology. C. Gunton of King's College, who is unremittingly Christocentric and Trinitarian, analyzes, restores, and restates the fundamental features of the theological tradition in an alien climate.

The new Luther research that emerged in the 1970s in Finland, especially through the dialogue between the Lutheran and the Orthodox churches, is noteworthy. Especially instrumental have been T. Mannermaa and his student R. Saarinen. Focusing on the presence of Christ in the justified, they conclude that for → Luther this justification led to the → *theōsis* of the faithful.

P. Widmann, professor of dogmatics in Århus, proposes a "thetic" theology in which humanity is dependent on God. This position stands in contrast to that of J. Glebe-Møller, professor of dogmatics at Copenhagen and proponent of a political theology according to which whatever contradicts the → autonomy of humanity and reason should not be maintained. The concept of a personal God is thus eliminated, as well as the soteriological significance of Christ's resurrection. While his colleague T. Jørgensen at Copenhagen objected, saying that Christian theology contains a certain obligatory content of knowledge, Glebe-Møller's approach is not totally un-Danish in its advocacy of a nondogmatic Christianity.

Since the science of religion became part of the regular offering in theological faculties in Sweden, theological discourse has changed. Now the study of faith and worldviews has replaced work in dogmatics and theological → ethics. Decisive for A. Jeffner of Uppsala is the idea that Jesus Christ can be experienced. What we know about the Bible must agree with what we know through science.

In Norway systematic theology has a very differ-

ent position, because theology is still a function of the church. It is not surprising, then, that I. Lønning, professor of systematic theology at the state faculty in Oslo, is critical about developments in Sweden. He argues that what looks initially like a branching out of theology into philosophy, comparative religion, and sociology is actually a narrowing down of the field, for theology now can no longer carefully attend to its own proper concerns.

Roman Catholic theology likewise shows no unilateral trend. The exuberance and creativity following Vatican II have vanished. While some rejoice in the more restrictive mood of the Vatican at the end of the century, others wait to see what a new papal configuration might bring. Nonetheless, solid works are still published, such as the *Lexikon der Katholischen Dogmatik*, edited by Wolfgang Beinert (1987; ET *Handbook of Catholic Theology* [1995]), translated into several languages.

Orthodoxy that was under Communist rule endeavors to rebuild its theological faculties, in terms of both numbers and theological acumen, and to reconnect with the rest of Europe and overseas. The Roman Catholic Church and the Protestant churches in Germany have developed special programs to further these goals. Young Greek Orthodox theologians, such as M. Begzos from Athens, maintain strong ties with Western Europe and attempt to bridge the gap between their own tradition and modernity, dealing with such topics as the reception of the Enlightenment or the significance of the Heisenberg uncertainty principle.

→ Middle Ages; Monasticism; Orthodox Church; Reformation; Scholasticism; Theology; Theology in the Nineteenth and Twentieth Centuries; University

Bibliography: K. Barth, *Protestant Theology in the Nineteenth Century: Its Background and History* (London, 1972) • M. Bauman, *Roundtable: Conversations with European Theologians* (Grand Rapids, 1990) • H. Berkhof, *Two Hundred Years of Theology: Report of a Personal Journey* (Grand Rapids, 1989) • G. C. Berkouwer, *A Half Century of Theology* (ed. L. B. Smedes; Grand Rapids, 1977) • T. Buchanan and M. Conway, eds., *Political Catholicism in Europe, 1918-1965* (New York, 1996) • D. Ford, ed., *The Modern Theologians: An Introduction to Christian Theology in the Twentieth Century* (Malden, Mass., 1977) • B. Hägglund, *History of Theology* (St. Louis, 1987) • A. Heron, *A Century of Protestant Theology* (Philadelphia, 1980) • A. E. McGrath, *The Making of Modern German Christology: From the Enlightenment to Pannenberg* (Oxford, 1986) • J. Macquarrie, *Twentieth*

Century Religious Thought: The Frontiers of Philosophy and Theology, 1900-1980 (New York, 1981) • J. MEYEN-DORFF, *Byzantine Theology: Historical Trends and Doctrinal Themes* (New York, 1974) • J. PELIKAN, *Christian Doctrine and Modern Culture (since 1700)* (Chicago, 1989) • C. READ, *Religion, Revolution, and the Russian Intelligentsia, 1900-1912* (Totowa, N.J., 1979) • R. RÉMOND, *Religion and Society in Modern Europe* (Malden, Mass., 1999) • C. WELCH, *Protestant Thought in the Nineteenth Century* (2 vols.; New Haven, 1972-85) • G. WINGREN, *Creation and Gospel: The New Situation in European Theology* (New York, 1979) • N. ZERNOV, *The Russian Religious Renaissance of the Twentieth Century* (London, 1963).

HANS SCHWARZ

2. Criticism and Distinctives

2.1. *Third World Criticism*

Third World churches (→ Third World 2) and their theologians (→ Ecumenical Association of Third World Theologians) have been critical of the dominance and universal claim of the traditional theologies of Europe and, arising by extension from them, those of North America. The customary forms and content of this so-called European theology are rooted in the Greco-Roman tradition of thought and the cultural context of Europe and North America. The criticism rests on the insight that classical, or Western, theology cannot do justice to the expression of the Christian faith in conditions of life in the Third World. It goes hand in hand with a concern to develop → contextual theologies (→ African Theology; Asian Theology; Black Theology; Latin American Theology; Liberation Theology) that are related to the cultural tradition of a nation or region and its political, social, and economic conditions (→ Third World Theology).

2.1.1. Four charges are brought against European theology: (1) that it gives normative weight to its own tradition, disregarding its cultural conditioning; (2) that it overestimates research and theory, develops faith as doctrine, and largely neglects social tasks and the concrete practicing of faith; (3) that it is linked to Western expansion (→ Acculturation; Colonialism; Colonialism and Mission; Dependence) and the technological and scientific civilization of → industrial society; and (4) that it hampers the appropriate witness needed in the face of contemporary challenges. Not merely the concepts, categories, approaches, interpretative models, modes of argument, and doctrinal forms that characterize the Western tradition of Christianity (see 2.3) are found inadequate, but so too are the biblical notions, the view of the history of → Israel (§1) held

by both the church and theology, traditional dogmatic statements (→ Christology; God; Trinity), and the various confessional documents insofar as they all are incompatible with other cultural and religious traditions and irrelevant in other social and political situations.

2.1.2. From the standpoint of critical questioning and rejection, European theology is reduced to that which contrasts with the traditions and experiences of different (i.e., non-Western) cultural and social worlds and cannot be communicated to them. In the process what is called European theology can acquire a profile corresponding to the degree to which it is provocative outside Europe, becomes conscious of the limitation and relativity of its own setting, gives expression to its contextual reference, and seeks to learn from other forms of thought, understanding, and practice. If the term "European theology" is justified in this sense, the question of the universality and/or contextuality of → theology arises (see 2.4).

2.2. *Geographic and Historical Context*

The term "European theology" loses its point once we try to identify it geographically and historically.

2.2.1. The theology that is pursued in what is geographically called Europe does not have the unity or common features that would justify describing it comprehensively as European. Thus we see formal and material distinctions that can be given the names of different countries (German, French, Dutch, Hungarian, etc.). The plurality is related partly to differing social and political situations and economic relations in the different lands (seen particularly before the recent collapse of Communism; → Church in a Socialist Society). These factors form a framework that either hampers or favors theological work, influencing it in different ways and giving it special emphases. An impact is also made by the historical experiences of a people, its national → culture and mentality, its intellectual and denominational milieu, tendencies and trends in individual and social behavior, and the resultant national characteristics. Last but not least, the provinciality and particularity of theology are a product of the structures and inner relations and possibilities and interests of the various churches in which theological work is done.

2.2.2. A historical survey must take account of the historical process of Christian theology with its two thousand years of tension-filled and richly varied development, along with the corresponding wealth of doctrinal systems and models of thought and interpretation. This whole cannot be called European because, being rooted in the history of the people of Israel, the man → Jesus of Nazareth, and the Jewish synagogue (→ Judaism), it contains essential elements from the linguistic and cultural sphere of Asia Minor that rule out a historical concept like Europe.

Whereas antiquity, in spite of all the intellectual and political differences, still sensed a kinship between East and West, this unity dissolved from the 3rd century A.D. with the division of the Roman Empire into the Western and Eastern empires. Europe then developed as the West, as a union of Western nations, comprising the spheres of Romance, Germanic, Slavic, and Celtic cultures. The → Roman Catholic Church served as an integrating force. Beginning in the 16th century, daughter cultures arose on the American continent. Europe thus differentiated itself from the East (the goal of the → Crusades), discriminated against the Jews, did missionary work among them (→ Jewish Mission), and set itself against → Byzantium, which had to resist Western usurpation. In this confrontation antiquity became a legacy of the West that had to be constantly renewed (renovatio), reawakened (renaissance), and appropriated in different ways, whether classical (→ Classicism) or → Romantic. In Byzantium, in contrast, the classical tradition was upheld continuously as an essential component of the native tradition.

The political, economic, and cultural history of the western part of the Christian world, which alone can be called European, is marked by epochal changes and manifold conflicts and has taken on worldwide significance (→ Baroque; Empire and Papacy; Enlightenment; Humanism; Marxism; Nation, Nationalism; Rationalism; Reformation; Renaissance; Restoration; Revolution; Secularization). Inseparably related to it is the development of the Roman Catholic, Anglican, and Reformation churches, and also of the → Orthodox churches of the East. Thus far all their theologies can be called Western, in spite of the differences between them, a judgment that applies also, for example, to the theology at the Orthodox academy in Leningrad. Yet the historical and cultural history of Europe has not shaped Christian thinking and action alone in this sphere, just as, conversely, the Christian orientation of life and thought has not been the only normative factor in the development of Europe.

2.3. *Distinctives*
What we now view as European theology and describe as Western combines elements from both Western and modern intellectual history. This combination produces its distinctive features.

2.3.1. European theology includes *elements that result from the original Christian witness* (→ Exegesis, Biblical; Biblical Theology). Other strands have fixed the path of Christian theology through the centuries: a reverent acceptance of → revelation, a believing investigating and teaching of Christian → truth (→ Church Fathers; Patristics), its dogmatically speculative and universal development (→ Augustine's Theology), its → scholastic rationalization, its mystical transfiguration (→ Mysticism), its confessional identification (→ Confession of Faith), and the need for communication and → apologetics in the context of debate with other religions and philosophies.

2.3.2. Furthermore, a change in the perception and apprehension of reality has led in European culture to *a tense confrontation between spirit and nature,* a setting alongside one another worldviews oriented to → language and → experience. A mark of European thinking has been the constant process of differentiating and articulating human knowledge and the desire for it (H.-G. Gadamer). This pressure is at work in European theology, stimulating and shaping theological endeavor.

2.3.3. In considering the various forms of Christian theology and their correspondence with the intentions of European thought, we come across *incompatible strands of thought* — a typical finding. Thus theological exposition uses both traditional → metaphysical terms and the principles and methods of modern science (e.g., empirical → social science). Typical are both the abstraction of → ontology and historical reflection (→ Theology of History). The preference for speculative and critical, analogical and dialectical thinking (→ Analogy; Dialectic) over → doxology and → meditation is no less surprising than theological reflection in legal categories (→ Church; Church Law; Soteriology) or the inclination to construct the theories and systems that we find in the controversial theses of the schools (→ Theology). Worth noting is the profitable use of the hermeneutical instruments (→ Hermeneutics) supplied by philosophy, linguistics, and the humanities (→ Sociology; Speech). The significant claim to be scientific finds expression not least of all in the fact that theology holds a genuine place in the academic world (→ University).

2.4. *Universality and Contextuality*
This problem does not arise merely from the standpoint of critical challenges (see 2.1). It derives no less urgently from the involvement of Christian theology with the intellectual history of antiquity and of Europe. Yet it is also posed already by the uniqueness of the saving message of Jesus and the historical

conditions for mediating and shaping Christian witness.

2.4.1. K. → Rahner has pointed out that church dogma found normative expression in European culture. Thus European theology has the task of guarding and keeping the tradition of faith. It has a mediating role among the world's theologies, which have all come from Europe.

2.4.2. T. Rendtorff points to the reality of Christianity as a historical religion whose complexity cannot be forced into uniformity of speech and expression. Thus theology must examine the truth of its cultural framework. Nevertheless, it must also take into account the "Spirit of truth" (John 14:17). From this standpoint European theology and other regional theologies must meet in a mutuality of exchange and perception.

2.4.3. D. Ritschl distinguishes *theologies*, which are related to situation-bound proclamation and practice and are thus regional, from *the one theology*, which seeks the truth about God and us. This theology must be binding and communicable, and it develops regulative principles that are transculturally valid and can be concretely tested. The task of theology is to reflect critically on one's own situation, history, claims, and concerns; to apply them constructively in a fellowship of knowledge (L. Vischer); and to seek operative principles that can secure ecumenical consensus.

2.4.4. Yet the following three points should be noted regarding the ongoing problem.

First, whereas the divine → salvation for us and the world that Jesus of Nazareth proclaimed as the → gospel and bore witness to in his deeds is *universal,* in form and content, time and place, any ecclesiastical or theological expression of this message will always be *particular.* The historical process of interpretation and communication in which the gospel is believed, accepted, confessed, narrated, expounded, and actively thought out and practiced points back in all its multiplicity and variety to the universal character of the salvation intimated.

Second, the revelation of salvation is mediated in the words and works of the Jewish man Jesus of Nazareth and thus has its own historical mode. In this sense it is subject to the conditions given with the person of the historical messenger, with his descent from the people Israel, with his contemporary experiences, and with every aspect of his concrete historical situation (intellectual, political, economic, and social). Since it seems to be impossible to detach the message of salvation from its historical mode, any transplanting of the gospel into other languages, cultures, situations, and con-

texts must relate to the original event and find its criterion there.

Finally, the universality of the message of salvation, like its dynamic, comes to expression in contextual theologies. Its claim vindicates itself as people are reached by it in their own time and place, in their own everyday life and familiar surroundings, as they bear witness to being reached by it in thought and activity corresponding to their own conditions and circumstances, and as they give it permanence in witnessing fellowships (communities, churches, and confessions) with the contextually limited means (gifts, charismata, and scholarship) and forces at their disposal.

Bibliography: Europäische Theologie herausgefordert durch die Weltökumene (Frankfurt, 1976) • E. FAHL-BUSCH, "Abscheid von der Konfessionskunde? Überlegungen zu einer Phänomenologie der universalen Christenheit," *Evangelium und Ökumene* (ed. G. Maron; Göttingen, 1986) • H.-G. GADAMER, "Die Zukunft der europäischen Geisteswissenschaft," *Europa. Horizonte der Hoffnung* (ed. F. König; Graz, 1983) 243-61 • C. GEFFRE, G. GUTIERREZ, and V. ELIZONDO, eds., *Different Theologies, Common Responsibility? Babel or Pentecost?* (Edinburgh, 1984) • J.-P. JOSSUA and J. B. METZ, eds., *Doing Theology in New Places* (Edinburgh, 1979) • K. RAHNER, "Aspects of European Theology," *Theological Investigations* (vol. 21; London, 1988) 78-98 • T. RENDTORFF, "Universalität und Kontextualität der Theologie," *ZTK* 74 (1977) 238-54; idem, ed., *Europäische Theologie, Versuche einer Ortsbestimmung* (Gütersloh, 1980) • D. RITSCHL, *The Logic of Theology* (Philadelphia, 1987); idem, "Westliche Theologie im Licht der Kritik aus der Dritten Welt," *EvT* 39 (1979) 451-65 • J. SOBRINO, "Theologisches Erkennen in der europäischen und der lateinamerikanischen Theologie," *Befreiende Theologie* (ed. K. Rahner et al.; Stuttgart, 1977) 123-43.

ERWIN FAHLBUSCH

Euthanasia

1. Active (Direct) and Passive (Indirect) Euthanasia
2. Voluntary and Nonvoluntary Euthanasia
3. Suffering
4. Withdrawing and Withholding Medical Treatment
5. Artificially Administered Nutrition and Hydration
6. Sanctity of Life, Autonomy, and Utilitarianism
7. Physician-Assisted Suicide

"Euthanasia" (Gk. *eu-*, implying "prosperity" or "ease," plus *thanatos*, "death") is often defined as "a gentle, easy → death." In current usage, however, the term involves an element of choice, so we might better define it as "choosing a gentle, easy death as a means of ending suffering."

1. Active (Direct) and Passive (Indirect) Euthanasia

Many theologians and philosophers distinguish between *active (direct)* and *passive (indirect)* euthanasia. The former involves deliberately doing something to cause the death of the suffering individual (e.g., administering a lethal drug), an action often called mercy killing in the popular media. In contrast, passive euthanasia simply involves stepping aside by withdrawing or withholding medical treatment, thereby "allowing nature to take its course."

This broad usage of the term, however, is not universal. Some limit "euthanasia" to cases involving the active sense, being sharply critical of deliberately doing anything to cause the death of the suffering individual, while allowing for the withdrawal or withholding of medical treatment under some circumstances, even if the suffering individual is likely to die as a result.

In practice, the active-passive distinction indicates the opposite ends of a far-reaching continuum, with various degrees of active involvement in the death of the suffering individual spread out along this continuum. Withholding medical treatment is at the most passive end of the continuum. Slightly more active but still toward the passive end is withdrawing medical treatment (e.g., shutting off and disconnecting artificial life support systems). Still more active is administering a painkilling medication such as morphine that, along with suppressing pain, in some cases hastens the dying process by suppressing respiratory or other vital functions. More active yet would be giving the suffering individual a lethal drug.

2. Voluntary and Nonvoluntary Euthanasia

A number of theologians and philosophers also make a distinction between *voluntary* and *nonvoluntary* euthanasia, one that pertains to the question of who makes the decision that results in the death of the suffering individual. If the sufferer makes the decision, it is voluntary, even if someone else administers the lethal drug or disconnects the artificial life-support system. If someone other than the suffering individual makes the decision to end the life, the term "nonvoluntary" applies.

The term "*in*voluntary euthanasia" has been used

for cases like the killing of → persons with handicaps during the Nazi era in Germany. Today, however, many of the situations in which the decision maker is someone other than the one suffering involve individuals who lack a decision-making capability (e.g., severely handicapped newborn infants or aged persons suffering from senile dementia). In such cases it has seemed to make little sense to talk about doing something over that person's objections (there being no ability to object), which "involuntary" might imply, and thus "nonvoluntary" has been the preferred term.

As in the case of the active-passive distinction, so here the voluntary-nonvoluntary distinction points to opposite ends of a wide-ranging continuum in which the suffering individual, to varying degrees, plays a role in the decisions that are made but is not the sole decision maker. Living wills and other advance directives extend the possibilities for the suffering individual to participate in the decision-making process, even when he or she no longer possesses a decision-making capacity sufficient to satisfy the legal requirements for competence.

A final definitional note is in order. While euthanasia is commonly defined as choosing death as a means of ending → suffering, the usage of the term is sometimes extended to situations in which the capacity for awareness either has never been present or is no longer present — for example, individuals in a persistent vegetative state (PVS). While one can argue that awareness must be present if suffering is to be experienced and that, accordingly, it is misleading to view PVS patients as suffering individuals, such finely drawn semantic distinctions probably add more confusion than clarity to the debate.

3. Suffering

In substantial measure, the way that suffering is viewed frames much of the debate about euthanasia. Historically, Christians have often believed that suffering occurs for a purpose and that → meaning and → hope are possible even in the midst of suffering. Many point to the biblical story of Jesus' crucifixion and → resurrection to give religious expression to this theme. Those who believe that meaning and hope are possible even in the midst of suffering tend to be less supportive of euthanasia than those who, reflecting the values of comfort-oriented contemporary societies, view suffering as something that ought to be avoided whenever possible.

Some take an intermediate position that distinguishes between humanizing and dehumanizing suffering. In some situations, they suggest, suffering can be humanizing by bringing families and friends closer together, by providing occasions for careful examination of questions of priority, or by providing a context for discovery or renewal of → faith. In other situations, however, suffering is so overwhelming that any humanizing aspects that might accompany suffering are obliterated. Many who take this middle approach strongly support hospice programs, which seek to make the final days, weeks, and months of life as rich and meaningful as possible for those who are terminally ill and for members of their families.

4. Withdrawing and Withholding
Medical Treatment

To speak of *the* Christian position with respect to withdrawing and withholding medical treatment would be very misleading. Here, as in many other areas, wide diversities of perspectives are to be found in various expressions of Christian traditions. The most conservative position is *vitalism,* which holds that every spark of life (esp. of human life) is precious and ought to be preserved. Vitalists typically oppose all forms of euthanasia, including withdrawing and withholding medical treatment. Many vitalists view death as a corruption of the natural created order, hence an evil that must be fought at all costs.

Slightly less conservative are those who oppose all active forms of euthanasia but allow withdrawing or withholding treatment in some circumstances. In Roman Catholic theology, a centuries-old distinction holds that some forms of medical treatment (often labeled "ordinary") are always mandatory, while others (often labeled "extraordinary") are optional. Only the latter may be withdrawn or withheld, even if doing so results in the death of the patient.

It should be added that quite apart from the definitional questions noted above, there is room for debate as to whether withdrawing or withholding extraordinary forms of medical treatment really constitutes euthanasia. Many would insist that a decision not to use extraordinary forms of treatment is nothing more than a decision to relieve the suffering individual of the burden imposed by those treatments, rather than a decision to choose death as a means of ending suffering. Though the end result might be death, it could be argued that sparing the suffering individual the additional suffering imposed by burdensome treatment is not the same as intending the death of that individual.

An increasingly common theme articulated by many contemporary Christians calls for respecting the dying process, as well as respecting all other as-

pects of the life processes. Karl → Barth asked whether doing everything possible to keep the heart beating as long as possible might be "human arrogance in the opposition direction" and whether in such situations "the fulfillment of medical duty does not threaten to become fanaticism, reason folly, and the required assisting of human life a forbidden torturing of it" (p. 427). This view is reflected in documents such as a message on end-of-life decisions issued by the Evangelical Lutheran Church in America, which asserts that "the integrity of the life processes which God has created should be respected; both birth and death are part of these life processes. . . . Medical treatment may be limited in some instances, and death allowed to occur." Those who take this approach typically view death as part of the natural created order, not an aberration of it.

5. Artificially Administered Nutrition
and Hydration

A matter of considerable debate among those who allow withdrawing or withholding medical treatment under some circumstances is the question of whether this step extends to artificially administered nutrition and hydration. Some suggest that there is a significant moral difference between withdrawing or withholding artificially administered nutrition and hydration, on the one hand, and, on the other, choosing not to use artificial life-support systems such as ventilators that support and sustain respiratory function or dialysis machines that substitute for the kidneys. In part, this distinction stems from a conviction that allowing someone to starve to death or die from dehydration is inhumane. Others, however, see no significant moral difference between discontinuing artificially administered nutrition and hydration (i.e., only where the patients are incapable of giving themselves food and water) and discontinuing the use of artificial life-support systems, since both involve artificial measures to sustain life.

6. Sanctity of Life, Autonomy, and Utilitarianism

Historically, many Christians, particularly within the Roman Catholic tradition, have advocated "an ethic of the sanctity of life" — the view that human life in all its forms, including prenatal life, ought to be treasured and preserved. Vitalism (see 4) is the most strongly stated version of this view, though many who allow withdrawing and withholding medical treatment under some circumstances would insist that they too are adhering to such an ethic.

Theologians and philosophers who place strong

emphasis on the → rights of the individual take a similar approach when they oppose some or all forms of euthanasia on the grounds that it violates the suffering individual's right to life. Rights-oriented approaches, however, do not always point in the direction of a sanctity-of-life ethic. When the emphasis is on individual autonomy, a rights-oriented approach can encompass a decision to end one's own life, should that be a deliberately chosen course of action.

By suggesting that the morality of an act is determined by its consequences, → utilitarian and other consequentialist arguments also move away from a sanctity-of-life ethic. In practice, such arguments lend themselves to extending moral sanction to far more than voluntary forms of euthanasia. If benefit to others is a factor in determining the morality of an act, there is nothing to preclude allowing those who are seriously ill or handicapped to die — or even killing them — if so doing would lessen the burden on others or otherwise would be beneficial to them. Such conclusions might be reached in cases involving nonvoluntary (or even involuntary) euthanasia, as well as in situations in which the suffering individual participates in the decision-making process.

Peter Singer applies arguments he makes in favor of abortion to infanticide as well, with particular reference to cases involving birth defects. In his widely read and much debated *Rethinking Life and Death* (1994), he argues, "Both for the sake of 'our children' . . . and for our own sake, we may not want a child to start on life's uncertain voyage if the prospects are clouded. . . . Instead of going forward and putting all our efforts into making the best of the situation, we can still say no, and start again from the beginning" (pp. 213-14).

7. Physician-Assisted Suicide

In Europe, the United States, Canada, and elsewhere, physician-assisted suicide has become a matter of considerable controversy (→ Dying, Aid for the 3). Historically, many Christians have opposed → suicide, either by asserting that it is for God and God alone to decide when life should begin and end or by arguing that we all have obligations to serve society and that ending our lives would be to default on those obligations.

In the contemporary discussion, however, individuals who share a Christian heritage can be found on all sides of the debate. Some reaffirm the traditional arguments against suicide. Others, agreeing with the position taken by organizations such as the Hemlock Society, believe that compassion and affir-

mation of human dignity point in the direction of physician-assisted suicide in some instances. Some who have deep moral reservations about physician-assisted suicide nevertheless believe that it ought to be a matter of individual → conscience, rather than subject to government regulation or prohibition. Here, as elsewhere, a good deal of pluralism characterizes Christianity, which is likely to become even more pronounced as new technological developments and changing social values reframe the debate about various forms of euthanasia.

Bibliography: K. Barth, "The Protection of Life," *CD* III/4 • T. L. Beauchamp and J. F. Childress, *Principles of Biomedical Ethics* (4th ed.; New York, 1994) • G. Dworkin, R. Frey, and S. Bok, *Euthanasia and Physician-Assisted Suicide* (New York, 1998) • R. M. Dworkin, *Life's Dominion: An Argument about Abortion, Euthanasia, and Individual Freedom* (New York, 1993) • Evangelical Lutheran Church in America, *A Message on End-of-Life Decisions* (Chicago, 1992) • E. Fox, J. J. Kamakahi, and S. M. Capek, *Come Lovely and Soothing Death: The Right to Die Movement in the United States* (New York, 1999) • M. J. Gordon, ed., *The Churches Speak on Euthanasia: Official Statements from Religious Bodies and Ecumenical Organizations* (Detroit, 1991) • C. J. Johnson and M. G. McGee, *How Different Religions View Death and Afterlife* (2d ed.; Philadelphia, 1998) • John Paul II, *The Gospel of Life = Evangelium vitae* (New York, 1995) • A. R. Jonsen, M. Siegler, and W. J. Winslade, *Clinical Ethics: A Practical Approach to Ethical Decisions in Clinical Medicine* (4th ed.; New York, 1998) • H. Küng and W. Jens, *Dying with Dignity: A Plea for Personal Responsibility* (New York, 1995) • S. E. Lammers and A. Verhey, eds., *On Moral Medicine: Theological Perspectives in Medical Ethics* (Grand Rapids, 1987) • D. C. Maguire, *Death by Choice* (Garden City, N.Y., 1984) • Pius XII, "The Prolongation of Life" (1957, in French), *AAS*, ser. 2, 24 (1957) 1027-33 • P. Ramsey, *Ethics at the Edges of Life: Medical and Legal Intersections* (New Haven, 1978) • P. Singer, *Rethinking Life and Death: The Collapse of Our Traditional Ethics* (New York, 1994) • G. Stewart and J. Kilner, *Basic Questions on Suicide and Euthanasia* (Grand Rapids, 1998) • H. Y. Vanderpool et al., "Death and Dying: Euthanasia and Sustaining Life," *EncBio* 1.554-88 • K. W. Wildes and A. C. Mitchell, eds., *Choosing Life: A Dialogue on Evangelium Vitae* (Washington, D.C., 1997).

Daniel E. Lee

Evangelical

"Evangelical" is first of all simply the adjective of "evangel" (i.e., → gospel); from the second century it has meant "relating or corresponding to the gospel" (Gk. *euangelikos, euangelikōs*; Lat. *evangelicus*). Especially a life lived according to the will of Christ might be called evangelical. In medieval religious movements *vita evangelica et apostolica* was sometimes used in criticism of the church. This use led to the idea of evangelical counsels, or counsels of perfection (i.e., poverty, chastity, and obedience). A new use arose in the later Middle Ages (J. → Wycliffe) and particularly during the → Reformation period. The → Reformers, especially M. → Luther (1483-1546), described as evangelical those insights and teachings taken from the gospel as a critical court. Soon the term came to be used for the movement of the Reformation itself and as a self-designation for its adherents. As compared with the words "Protestant" or "Lutheran," it better expressed the central concerns of the Reformation. (The implied claim aroused irritation among opponents, e.g., Erasmus, as expressed in his *Epistola contra pseudevangelicos* [1529]).

The further history of "evangelical," which was influenced by shifting church groupings, has taken a different turn in different linguistic areas. In Germany in the first decades of the 16th century it was used (alongside other adjectives such as "reformed") for states and cities that went over to the Reformation. In the following period of growing confessionalism, it increasingly came to designate collectively the → Lutheran and → Reformed churches (→ Denomination). This use, which lumped the Reformed together without distinction with adherents of the → Augsburg Confession (→ Augsburg, Peace of), became customary at imperial diets after the end of the 16th century and became officially sanctioned when in 1653 the Protestant states formed a conference called the Corpus Evangelicorum. Efforts to form a → union between Lutherans and Reformed led this conference to adopt the following resolution in 1722: "Rather than using sectarian names, both parties should call themselves 'evangelical' or 'related to the Augsburg Confession.' If they must distinguish between themselves, they should use the terms 'evangelical' or 'evangelical-reformed.' It was in this comprehensive sense that the churches arising out of the Prussian Union of 1817 claimed the term "evangelical." It bears the same sense (i.e., denoting common features) in such combinations as Evangelical-Lutheran and Evangelical-Reformed, and also in the present title of the Evangelische Kirche in Deutschland (Evangelical Church in Germany). In recent times the term "evangelical" is increasingly used to designate the whole of Protestantism. In 1992, for instance, an all-European assembly of all Protestant denominations was organized in Budapest under the title "European Evangelical Assembly."

In England, 16th-century adherents of the Reformation called themselves *evaungelicalles*. Specific groups then took over the term, and in the 18th century it took on a new use to denote revival movements (as in → Methodism and Anglican Evangelicals). Along these lines it became a general term for what are customarily regarded as evangelical views. This use is also found in North America, where evangelicals lay great stress on the evangelistic and missionary task (e.g., the → National Association of Evangelicals [1943] and the → World Evangelical Fellowship [1951]).

In France the word *évangélique* has the same narrower sense, with Fr. *protestant* corresponding to the Ger. *evangelisch*. It can acquire this narrower sense in Germany too, and for the sake of clarification *evangelikal* has now been coined to distinguish this use (→ Evangelical Movement), with *evangelisch* being retained for the broader range of meaning.

Bibliography: G. R. BALLEINE, *A History of the Evangelical Party in the Church of England* (new ed.; London, 1951; orig. pub., 1908) • D. W. BEBBINGTON, *Evangelicalism in Modern Britain: A History from the 1730s to the 1980s* (Grand Rapids, 1992) • W. BRÄNDLY, "Zur Selbstbezeichnung des Evangelischen," *Zwing.* 8 (1944-48) 471-86 • B. BRENNER, ed., *Europa und der Protestantismus* (Göttingen, 1993) • W. GEPPERT, *Das Wesen der preußischen Union* (Berlin, 1939) • A. GOETZE, "Evangelisch," *ZDW* 13/1 (1911/12) 1-24 • H. HEPPE, *Ursprung und Geschichte der Bezeichnung "reformierte" und "lutherische" Kirche* (Gotha, 1859) • D. LOTZ, "The Evangelization of the World in This Generation" (Diss., Hamburg, 1970) • *LPGL* 555 • M. NOLL, D. W. BEBBINGTON, and G. A. RAWLYK, eds., *Evangelicalism: Comparative Studies of Popular Protestantism in North America, the British Isles, and Beyond, 1700-1990* (New York, 1994) • C. SMITH, *American Evangelicalism: Embattled and Thriving* (Chicago, 1998).

LUKAS VISCHER

Evangelical Alliance → World Evangelical Fellowship

Evangelical Catholicity

"Evangelical catholicity" identifies the attempt to give specificity to *catholica,* the third of the four creedal attributes of the church. In the 19th and 20th centuries the term was used in a variety of ways in ecclesiological discussion. Sven-Erik Brodd, in his Uppsala dissertation of 1982, "Evangelisk katolicitet," distinguishes between its use in three different periods: during the 19th century, as an expression primarily used as a proposal for "the church of the future"; during the period between the two world wars, in describing the quest for sacramental and ecumenical renewal within the church; and in the period since 1960, in the churches' discussions of confessional identity in light of the ecumenical quest for visible → unity between the churches. The expression came into use within the context of German Protestantism, but it has also played a significant role in Swedish, Anglo-Saxon, and American ecclesiological reflection.

The 19th-century German discussion was brought about largely by shifts in institutional Protestantism, perhaps most notably the formation of the Prussian Church Union. Additionally, as pointed out by Klaus Penzel, "the ideal of Evangelical Catholicism was alive, though in different ways, in → romanticism (Novalis), in the philosophy of German → idealism (Schelling), in the Awakening (Neander) and in the Prussian High Orthodoxy" (pp. 91-92).

In 1845 Rudolf Smend, a German Reformed parish pastor, published *Die Zukunft der Evangelisch-Katholischen Kirche* (The future of the evangelical catholic church), in which he proposed a church with the following characteristics: it would be a fellowship of the redeemed; it would be grounded in the fullness of the → gospel, in contrast to what he labeled sectarianism; and it would be nonhierarchical. For Smend, such a church would be identical to that of apostolic times. Johan Peter Lange (1802-84), foreshadowing later debates, used evangelical catholicity as an element in the dialectics between → Catholicism and → Protestantism. Ernst Ludwig von Gerlach (1795-1877) and Heinrich Leo (1799-1878), both conservative Lutherans who looked back to the Middle Ages as the ideal period of history, supported the Prussian Church Union as an evangelical catholic church designed to withstand a Protestant confessionalism that would hinder rapprochement with Roman Catholicism. Other 19th-century scholars who made use of a concept of evangelical catholicity included Friedrich Julius Stahl (1802-61), Johann Hinrich Wichern (1808-

81), and Philip Schaff (1819-93), who upon coming to the United States made significant contributions to the development of American theology.

The two persons who were most influential during the period between the two world wars in advancing notions of evangelical catholicity to foster ecumenical and sacramental renewal within the churches were the Swedish archbishop and ecumenical pioneer Nathan Söderblom (1866-1931) and Friedrich Heiler (1892-1967), a German Roman Catholic "modernist" who in 1919 became a Lutheran. For Söderblom the concept was a component of a "branch theory" of ecclesiology (Roman, Greek, and Evangelical). His position was that priority be given to the realization of the unity that already exists between these churches by the development of sacramental fellowship and service to the world. Only then could questions of → "faith and order" be taken up in order to bring about the formal reunion of the churches. Söderblom saw the church, primarily his own Church of Sweden, as evangelical both because of its open theology in respect to church order and freedom of conscience and because of its Lutheran doctrine of → justification by grace. He saw the church as catholic when — again like the Church of Sweden — it demonstrates unbroken continuity with the universal church in respect to → liturgy and episcopal order.

Heiler used the concept of evangelical catholicity to develop an ideal synthesis of the church, not on the basis of what is "true or false" but, rather, on the basis of what is "good or bad" in church life. Examples of positive elements in such an ecclesiology are episcopal order, private confession, sacramental liturgy, and communal religious life. Negative phenomena include liturgical puritanism, Roman curialism, and forced conformity. Criteria for the positive phenomena are both a universality in time and space and a harmony with the doctrine of *sola gratia.* Heiler saw evangelical catholicity as standing against what he called Protestant reductionism and Roman Catholic → syncretism, as well as papal and curial authoritarianism.

During the 1930s and beyond, Paul → Tillich (1886-1965) developed the idea of evangelical catholicity in proposing a → dialectic between "Protestant principle" and "catholic substance," a dialectic between the principle that reveals and challenges the ambiguities of all religion and the concrete embodiment — as "Spiritual presence" — of the Christian message in the church. Jaroslav Pelikan (b. 1923) in an important work of 1964 built on Tillich's view and used it as an approach to understanding the Lutheran Reformation. "'Catholic substance' . . . means the body of → tradition, liturgy, dogma, and churchmanship developed chiefly by the ancient church. . . . 'Protestant principle' is a summary term for the criticism and reconstruction of this Catholic substance which Luther and his Reformation carried out in the name of the Christian gospel and with the authority of the Bible" (p. 13). The ecumenical movement and its dialogue has demonstrated both the Protestant need for fullness *(plērōma)* and the Catholic need for judgment and corrective (→ Ecumenism, Ecumenical Movement).

In connection with the 450th anniversary of the signing of the → Augsburg Confession, the primary Lutheran confessional document, the notion of evangelical catholicity contributed strongly to an international discussion of whether that confession could be recognized by the → Roman Catholic Church as in some sense a "catholic" statement of faith. In 1977 Cardinal Joseph Ratzinger wrote that "it might be possible to interpret [the Augsburg Confession] as a catholic confession; it was . . . drafted with inner conviction as a searching for evangelical catholicity — as a painstaking effort to filter the bubbling cauldron of the early Reformation movement in such a way that it might give it the shape of a catholic reform" (quoted in J. A. Burgess, 49). Evangelical catholicity, in giving specificity to the third creedal attribute of the church, thus proposes that the → Reformation not be seen as the establishment of new church bodies but rather as a faithful and purifying proposal to the whole church catholic concerning the gospel itself, the basic Christian message found in Scripture and tradition.

Bibliography: C. Braaten and R. Jenson, eds., *The Catholicity of the Reformation* (Grand Rapids, 1996) • S.-E. Brodd, *Evangelisk katolicitet. Ett studium av innehåll och funktion under 1800- och 1900-talen* (Lund, 1982) • J. A. Burgess, ed., *The Role of the Augsburg Confession: Catholic and Lutheran Views* (Philadelphia, 1980) • R. N. Flew and R. E. Davies, eds., *The Catholicity of Protestantism* (Philadelphia, 1950) • F. Heiler, *Evangelische Katholizität. Gesammelte Aufsätze und Vorträge* (vol. 1; Munich, 1926) • J. Pelikan, *Obedient Rebels: Catholic Substance and Protestant Principle in Luther's Reformation* (New York, 1964) • K. Penzel, "Church History and the Ecumenical Quest: A Study of the German Background and Thought of Philip Schaff" (Diss., Union Theological Seminary, New York, 1962) • N. Söderblom, *Christian Fellowship* (Chicago, 1923) • P. Tillich, *The Protestant Era* (Chicago, 1948); idem, *Systematic Theology* (vol. 3; Chicago, 1963).

Norman A. Hjelm

Evangelical Missions

1. Term
2. History
3. Organization
4. Present Significance

1. Term

The phrase "evangelical missions" refers to missions that derive their type of → piety, their theology, and their understanding of mission from → Pietism and 18th- and 19th-century → revivalism and that confess that theologically and organizationally they are part of the worldwide → evangelical movement (→ World Evangelical Fellowship). They include the evangelical → free church missions societies, independent and interdenominational → faith missions, missions with special fields or functions, and Pentecostal missions (→ Pentecostal Churches).

2. History

The rise of the → Social Gospel movement in the 1920s and the theological evaluation of non-Christian religions at the 1928 World Missionary Conference in Jerusalem led in the 1930s to the final splitting of the American missionary movement into conciliar missions, related to ecumenically oriented → national councils of churches, and evangelical missions, with no set form of organization.

For three reasons the latter made great advances in the 1940s. First, American evangelicals surged ahead and united in their own → National Association of Evangelicals (NAE) and the → fundamentalist American Council of Churches of Christ. In connection with the NAE the Evangelical Foreign Missions Association was founded in 1945.

Second, whereas older missions found themselves in a crisis after World War II because of decolonizing (→ Colonialism; Colonialism and Mission) and the achieving of independence by the churches of the → Third World, evangelical missions could develop freely because they were not tied to partner churches. They followed a principle of cooperation rather than integration.

Third, a revival movement sparked by → evangelism produced a large number of volunteers for evangelical societies. The evangelist Billy Graham was a key figure in this regard.

The new evangelical missionary movement spread quickly to Europe and the Third World churches. It acquired additional apologetic motivation when the → International Missionary Council merged into the → World Council of Churches (WCC) at New Delhi in 1961 and ecumenically oriented societies (→ Ecumenical Mission) developed a new understanding of mission. The new view arose under the influence of the → demythologization debate, the movement of social revolution, and the renaissance of world religions (→ Dialogue), the result being an apparent surrender of the goal of the historical missionary movement.

At a congress in 1966 at Wheaton, Illinois, 1,000 evangelical missionaries from the United States and other countries proclaimed their biblical understanding of mission as against social utopianism, → syncretism, and → universalism. In the same year, on the initiative of Billy Graham and Carl Henry, evangelists and evangelical theologians gathered at Berlin for the World Congress on Evangelism. After many similar Continental gatherings this movement reached its high point with the International Congress on World Evangelization at Lausanne in 1974. Here 2,700 representatives from 150 countries pledged themselves "to pray, to plan and to work together for the evangelization of the whole world" (J. Stott, 54).

3. Organization

To work out the results of Lausanne, the Lausanne Committee for World Evangelization was founded in Mexico City in January 1975. This group of 75 took up the task of coordinating and motivating evangelical forces worldwide and developing a strategy for evangelizing the non-Christians in the world (estimated in 2000 to number over 4 billion; see D. B. Barrett and T. M. Johnson, 25). This work was implemented through a series of regional congresses and consultations to develop the themes of missionary theology and methodology according to the Lausanne pledge, as well as through the use of publications. Direction for the detailed strategy adopted in 1980 at Pattaya, Thailand, was set by the principle that Donald McGavran and his disciples in the → church growth (§5) movement had developed, namely, to pay heed in missionary work to the integration of people into sociologically homogeneous units. Using webs of relationships would offer the best chance for the rapid growth of the Christian community.

A reason for evangelical separation from missions that united in the International Missionary Council was the decision of John Mott (1865-1955) to invite to the historic Edinburgh Conference (1910) only societies that were working in so-called non-Christian lands and not those working in lands where most of the people belonged to the → Roman Catholic Church or the → Orthodox Church. Because of this decision South America was not represented at Edinburgh. There, however, evangelical missions, especially from the United States, were increasingly finding an important field right at their doorstep, partly among the blacks and Indians who in their view were only nominally Christian, since many spiritist and syncretist cults flourished among them, and partly among the unreached tribes in the Amazon jungles and the Andes. The Evangelical Congress for Christian Action in Latin America, held at Panama in 1916, initiated new missionary efforts in South and Central America; in 1929 a second congress followed at Havana. Here the aim was formulated of founding an international and interdenominational union of churches in the hemisphere that would bring together the almost 350 denominations and parachurch organizations. The various Pentecostal missions and churches enjoyed the most rapid growth, and some two-thirds of the Protestant Christians in Latin America now belong to them (→ Assembleias de Deus no Brasil).

Three factors were especially important in evangelical missions in Latin America. The first was the program Evangelism-in-Depth, pioneered in the 1960s by the Latin America Mission, founded by Harry and Susan Strachan in 1921; this effort aimed to mobilize all church members for an evangelistic penetration of every area of life. The second was the development of an extensive radio mission to reach less accessible areas more quickly. HCJB, the Voice of the Andes, broadcasting from Quito, Ecuador, was especially important in this regard. The third was the work of the Wycliffe Bible Translators in reducing the languages of newly reached Indian tribes to writing. From the beginning of the 1970s criticism of this pioneering work came from both anthropologists and ecumenists on the ground that it was destructive of native cultures. In the contested Barbados Declaration of 1971, anthropologists and WCC workers demanded a halt to Indian missions in Latin America. The result was an even sharper polarization between ecumenical and evangelical missions.

4. Present Significance

Rapid growth after World War II means that about two-thirds of the 60,000 Protestant missionaries now belong to evangelical missions. By their well-equipped training centers in the West and overseas, these missions are having a great influence on churches of the Third World.

In spite of the separation between ecumenical and evangelical missions, interchanges do occur between them. Although organizational unification is unlikely, the basic theological split might be overcome if only the two sides could reach an understanding on the question of the → authority and relevance of the biblical revelation for world evangelization.

Bibliography: D. B. BARRETT and T. M. JOHNSON, "Annual Statistical Table on Global Mission: 2000," *IBMR* 24 (2000) 24-25 • R. C. BASSHAM, *Mission Theology, 1948-1975* (Pasadena, Calif., 1979) • P. BEYERHAUS, "Evangelicals, Evangelism, and Theology," *ERT* 23/2 (1987) 169-85 • A. P. JOHNSTON, *The Battle for World Evangelization* (Wheaton, Ill., 1978) • D. LOTZ, "The Evangelization of the World in This Generation" (Diss., Hamburg, 1970) • J. A. SCHERER, *Gospel, Church, and Kingdom: Comparative Studies in World Mission Theology* (Minneapolis, 1987) • J. STOTT, ed., *Making Christ Known: Historic Mission Documents from the Lausanne Movement, 1974-1989* (Grand Rapids, 1996) • P. C. WAGNER, *Look Out! The Pentecostals Are Coming* (Carol Stream, Ill., 1973) • K.-W. WESTMEIER, *Protestant Pentecostalism in Latin America: A Study in the Dynamics of Missions* (Madison, N.J., 1999) • U. WIESEMANN, *Mission und Menschenrechte* (Wuppertal, 1979) • T. YATES, *Christian Mission in the Twentieth Century* (Cambridge, 1994).

PETER BEYERHAUS

Evangelical Movement

1. Term
2. Roots
3. Theology and Organization

1. Term

Although the term "evangelical" can be used in English in the same broader sense as *evangelisch* in German, in this article it has the narrower sense for which German now uses *evangelikal*. Some definition is needed because of the theological, ecclesiastical, and practical problems associated with the word and its positive or negative aspects. On the one hand, it may be the equivalent of "pietistic," "revivalist," "confessing," or "biblical-reformational"; on the other, it may be the opposite of "liberal," "ecumenical," "progressive," or "historicocritical." It has also become a slogan in party conflicts within the church.

We need to seek its meaning in America, where it is most commonly in use. Even there, however, it covers a very wide range of not completely harmonious uses, from the → Pentecostal churches to the

→ peace churches, Missouri Synod Lutherans (→ Lutheran Churches), Southern Baptist Convention (→ Baptists), → Holiness movement (e.g., → Church of the Nazarene), charismatic groups (including Roman Catholics; → Charismatic Movement), and evangelicals in the mainline denominations. Timothy L. Smith has thus compared the evangelical movement to a mosaic. Its individual stones may be very different and far apart, but together the pieces compose a single object.

George Marsden sees three distinct senses of the term "evangelicals." First, the term denotes Christians who share common theological presuppositions. Second, it designates a movement that, in spite of great differences and undeveloped institutional ties, looks back to shared traditions, influences, and experiences, from which it derives a common direction. According to David Barrett's *World Christian Encyclopedia,* this movement includes at least 150 million Christians. Third, within this general trend there are transdenominational evangelical groups, with a complex infrastructure, that form a coalition, a fellowship, almost a denomination. The members still belong to their own churches, yet they are committed primarily to the evangelical movement. Billy Graham, for example, is more an evangelical in this sense than he is a Southern Baptist.

2. Roots

Sociological interpretation of the rise of the evangelical movement is a matter of debate. Is it a negative reaction to postmodern society (William McLoughlin), or is it an integral part of societal development, a case of symbiosis rather than reaction (Martin Marty)? If it developed in polemical differentiation from the → fundamentalism of the 1920s, and if it is also in any case a reaction to "liberal modernism" (→ Liberalism), it is clear that there are arguments for both sides. There is an element of reaction in the evangelical movement; unlike fundamentalism, however, it is open to the modern world and helps to shape it. Although the boundaries are not clear-cut, it is best to distinguish between fundamentalism and evangelicalism.

Movements persist in evangelicalism that were influential before being constricted by fundamentalism, which shows that evangelicalism has its own theological and historical significance. It is rooted in German → Pietism, → Methodism, and the Great Awakening in the 18th-century American colonies. An Evangelical ("Low Church") party developed in the → Anglican Communion, represented for example by W. → Wilberforce, Lord Shaftesbury, and W. E. Gladstone.

This party fought against social evils (e.g., → slavery) and organized Bible and missionary societies (→ Bible Societies). Similar developments took place in Scotland (T. Chalmers and the Haldanes), and the German awakening was parallel (→ Revivals), though less socially oriented. One may also mention the so-called Nonconformists (Charles H. Spurgeon), the → YMCA (George Williams), the → Salvation Army (William Booth), the → China Inland Mission (Hudson Taylor), the Keswick Movement, and the Evangelical Alliance (1846). In the United States revivalism was dominant (esp. through Charles Finney and Dwight L. Moody), with its "new measures" (→ Theology of Revivals 2). We may also refer to Pentecostal and Holiness movements, to socially active groups modeled on the → Social Gospel, to dispensationalist premillennialists represented by the *Scofield Reference Bible*, and to rationalistic biblicists in the form of the Princeton theology (E. Geldbach 1984). In a changed form one might still discern these different types in the later 20th century, such as groups for social action (Chicago Declaration of Social Concern [1973], Jim Wallis and the Sojourners Community, Evangelicals for Social Action, R. Padilla, the Shaftesbury Project), Pentecostal and neo-Pentecostal groups, the peace churches, and others.

3. Theology and Organization

Theological features are as follows:

1. Holy Scripture is the supreme → authority. Inspired by the → Holy Spirit, it is normative for the life and doctrine of the church (the congregation) and of the individual. Differences exist regarding understanding the nature of → inspiration and also the understanding of "inerrancy" and → "infallibility," but there is general agreement that Scripture discharges its normative function only through the operation of the Holy Spirit.
2. The main theme of Scripture is God's saving work. God sent his Son, who bore the sins of the world on the cross and made redemption possible.
3. Eternal salvation comes only through personal → faith in Christ, which God gives. Yet since God leaves room for freedom of decision, the experience of becoming and being a Christian assumes great importance (→ Conversion 1; Regeneration; Sanctification).
4. For this reason → evangelism and → mission tend to take precedence over social action (e.g., in the large crusades or in the work of the → faith missions).
5. Ethics is developed, not out of the situation, but out of God's → law and ordinances.
6. Christ's return is expected literally (→ Eschatology).

Since all these positions entail negations (e.g., opposition to historicocritical biblical research, to recognition of the fundamental crisis in mission, to secular ecumenism, or to threats to ethical order), evangelicals can easily differ in detail, but through the historical and theological characteristics mentioned, evangelical interdenominational groupings are easily recognizable in the modern Christian world.

In many cases Christian fellowship is refused with those persons or churches that do not share the above convictions. Evangelicals until recently remained at a critical distance from the → Roman Catholic Church and often also from the → ecumenical movement. But there are also new coalitions now, such as between conservative Catholics and evangelicals. Categorical rejection of the ecumenical movement also weakened after the WCC Assembly at Vancouver in 1983. This warming is important because the modern ecumenical movement initially owed much to evangelicals and shared their transdenominationalism. The softening of attitudes is also connected with the fact that the evangelical movement has built up a complex network of organizations and conferences that, through international exchange of experiences, has broken down many national barriers. One must add that there are many organizations that are not a direct part of the evangelical movement but still pursue evangelical aims. Finally, evangelical seminaries, colleges, and universities have produced a new generation able to rise above the old attitudes.

Evangelicals are most highly organized in North America. After the fundamentalist debacle, the → National Association of Evangelicals was founded in 1942. In 2000 it comprised a cornucopia of denominations, individual congregations, parachurch ministries, and educational institutions, in all benefiting directly or indirectly over 27 million people; its commissions deal, among other things, with publicity, education, the family, evangelization, and home mission. Many other organizations serve specific interests, such as the American Scientific Affiliation, Christian Association for Psychological Studies, Christian Businessmen's Committee, Conference on Faith and History, Evangelical Theological Society, and Fellowship of Christian Athletes. Groups at work among young people and students include Campus Crusade for Christ (Bill Bright), InterVarsity Christian Fellowship, Navigators, and Young Life (→ Student Work). Each of these groups has national staffs in many other countries as well. Among seminaries, Fuller Theological Seminary has had a significant role since its founding in 1947, and one may also point to Gordon-Conwell Seminary, Asbury Seminary, and Wheaton College with its Billy Graham Center. The National Religious Broadcasters and a large number of publishers handle publicity and publications (→ Christian Publishing).

U.S. Supreme Court rulings that eliminated prayer in the public schools (1960s) and that legalized abortion on demand (1973) contributed to a definite evangelical politicization. Many evangelicals viewed these decisions, as well as the growth of the federal government and controversies about subject matter to be part of, or excluded from, the public-school curriculum, as indicating a decline in national moral values. While evangelicals of the Billy Graham sort put no special emphasis on these issues, other leaders — including Baptist ministers Jerry Falwell and Timothy LaHaye, television broadcaster Pat Robertson, and the lay psychologist and radio host James Dobson — entered politics with a vengeance beginning in the 1970s. The latter group effectively created the "new Christian Right" and made white conservative evangelical support a key factor in the presidential campaigns of Ronald Reagan (1980 and 1984) and for much of U.S. Republican politics since Reagan.

What is true of the United States is often true of many other countries, too. Evangelicals are advancing by means of parachurch organizations, programs, conferences, fellowships, publications, and other activities, often in confrontation with the established churches and even in opposition to them. This is especially true in *Europe,* where viable alternatives to the national, → people's churches are being set up, and church and political influence is wielded through confessional movements, study groups, and the press. Use is made of modern mass media (Trans-World Radio, Evangeliumsrundfunk Wetzlar, television, newspapers, books, and publishing houses), and separate schools, seminaries, and places for study are being founded. The emphasis is different in countries with no tradition of people's churches. In *South America* the attitude to social and political efforts is less critical than in North America, where there is often a clinging to the status quo (R. Pierard). The worldwide meteoric upsurge of the Pentecostal movement has not yet been properly studied either theologically or demographically by Pentecostals or by other evangelicals. In *Africa* evangelicals are seeking to take the lead, especially in confrontation with → Islam, while in *Asia* they

must maintain the universal validity of the gospel over against the prevailing religions.

Worldwide, evangelicals are organized in the → World Evangelical Fellowship. Billy Graham and his evangelistic association have helped to pull evangelicals together and to set direction for the movement by convening the World Congress on Evangelism (Berlin, 1966) and the First and Second International Congress on World Evangelization (Lausanne, 1974, and Manila, 1989). The Lausanne Continuation Committee has organized regional consultations and cooperated with existing evangelical organizations in Africa, Asia, Latin America, and Europe, thus creating a closely woven network to promote evangelization, church growth, diaconal aid, and theological work and to make possible both a more precise differentiation of evangelical groups and a cautious approach to the ecumenical movement.

Bibliography: Periodicals: Action • *ChrTo* • *CScR* • *Evangelical Studies Bulletin* • *IDEA* • *Moody Monthly* • *The Other Side* • *Sojourners* • *ThBeitr* • *Theological News.*

Books and articles: R. M. ANDERSON, *Vision of the Disinherited: The Making of American Pentecostalism* (New York, 1979) • R. BALMER, *Mine Eyes Have Seen the Glory: A Journey into the Evangelical Subculture in America* (exp. ed.; New York, 1993) • D. W. BEBBINGTON, *Evangelicalism in Modern Britain: A History from the 1730s to the 1980s* (Grand Rapids, 1992) • D. G. BLOESCH, *The Future of Evangelical Christianity: A Call for Unity amid Diversity* (New York, 1983) • E. L. BLUMHOFER, *Restoring the Faith: The Assemblies of God, Pentecostalism, and American Culture* (Urbana, Ill., 1993) • K. BOCKMÜHL, *Evangelikale Sozialethik* (Giessen, 1975) • D. BROMLEY and A. SHUPE, *New Christian Politics* (Macon, Ill., 1984) • J. A. CARPENTER, *Revive Us Again: The Reawakening of American Fundamentalism* (New York, 1997) • D. W. DAYTON and R. K. JOHNSTON, eds., *The Variety of American Evangelicalism* (Downers Grove, Ill., 1991) • D. W. DAYTON and E. ROWE, eds., SEv • W. A. ELWELL, ed., *Evangelical Dictionary of Theology* (Grand Rapids, 1984; 2d ed., abridged, 1991) • E. FAHLBUSCH, "Evangelikal, Evangelikale Bewegung," *TRT* (4th ed.) 2.56-62 • E. GELDBACH, "Evangelikalismus. Versuch einer historischen Typologie," *Die Kirchen und ihre Konservativen* (ed. R. Frieling; Göttingen, 1984) 53-83 • E. GELDBACH et al., eds., *Evangelikales Gemeindelexikon* (Wuppertal, 1978) • J. C. GREEN, J. L. GUTH, C. SMIDT, and L. A. KELLSTEDT, *Religion and the Culture Wars: Dispatches from the Front* (Totowa, N.J., 1996) • J. A. HEDSTROM, "Evangelical Program in the United States, 1945-1980: The Morphology of Establishment, Progressive, and Radical Programs" (Diss., Vanderbilt University, 1982) bibliography • C. F. H. Henry, *God, Revelation, and Authority* (4 vols.; Waco, Tex., 1976-79) • J. D. Hunter, *American Evangelicalism: Conservative Religion and the Quandary of Modernity* (New Brunswick, N.J., 1983) • F. Laubach, *Aufbruch der Evangelikalen* (Wuppertal, 1972) • R. F. Lovelace, *Dynamics of Spiritual Life: An Evangelical Theology of Renewal* (Downers Grove, Ill., 1979) • W. G. McLoughlin, *Revivals, Awakenings, and Reform* (Chicago, 1978) • G. M. Marsden, *Fundamentalism and American Culture: The Shaping of Twentieth-Century Evangelicalism, 1870-1925* (New York, 1980); idem, ed., *Evangelicalism and Modern America* (Grand Rapids, 1984) • M. E. Marty, *The Public Church: Mainline–Evangelical–Catholic* (New York, 1981) • M. A. Noll, *Between Faith and Criticism: Evangelicals, Scholarship, and the Bible in America* (2d ed.; Grand Rapids, 1991) • M. A. Noll, D. W. Bebbington, and G. A. Rawlyk, eds., *Evangelicalism: Comparative Studies of Popular Protestantism in North America, the British Isles, and Beyond, 1700-1990* (New York, 1994) • R. V. Pierard, "From Evangelical Exclusivism to Ecumenical Openness: Billy Graham and Sociopolitical Issues," *JES* 20 (1983) 435-46; idem, "The Quest for the Historical Evangelicalism: A Bibliographical Excursus," *FiHi* 11 (1979) 60-72 • C. Smith, *Christian American Evangelicalism: Embattled and Thriving* (Chicago, 1998) • L. I. Sweet, ed., *The Evangelical Tradition in America* (Macon, Ill., 1984) • T. P. Weber, *Living in the Shadow of the Second Coming: American Premillennialism, 1875-1982* (2d ed.; Chicago, 1987) • D. F. Wells and J. D. Woodbridge, eds., *The Evangelicals* (Nashville, 1975).

Erich Geldbach

Evangelism

1. Term
2. Ecumenical Discussion
3. Modern Practices

1. Term

Evangelism means proclamation of the → gospel. As distinct from ordinary → preaching, it denotes an initial proclamation that aims at a decision for Christ by those who do not yet believe or who no longer do so. It is the communication of the whole gospel in simple form, along with a concern to address intellectual hindrances to faith or those deriving from experience.

The English language (in this respect richer than some other European languages) distinguishes between the terms "evangelism" and "evangelization." The former has wider connotations and is generally used to name the basic task of the church, which may be carried out in different ways. The latter has more practical considerations, as it is sometimes used as the title for an evangelistic rally or as the term for the Christianization of whole nations (as in the motto of the First World Missionary Conference, in Edinburgh in 1910: "evangelization of the world in this generation"). In Roman Catholic conceptual documents the term "evangelization" seems to be preferred to "evangelism."

Up to the middle of the 20th century, European churches, more sharply than they do today, tended to distinguish evangelism from → mission. On the basis of the concept of a Christian world (the *corpus Christianum*), they viewed mission as the communicating of the gospel to people outside this world (i.e., the "pagans") or to those who for vocational, moral, or social reasons were outsiders. In contrast, they reserved the term "evangelism" for efforts within Christian countries to win back negligent or lapsed church members or to kindle a new → faith in them. An important example was set for this activity by → Methodism in 18th-century England and the later Methodist circuit riders in the United States.

With the growing realization that European lands are also missionary areas, "mission" and "evangelism" have now tended to become interchangeable terms. Many Asian churches speak of evangelism in referring to their efforts to preach the gospel to their own people, while European churches use "mission" or "missionary" for the same task in their own lands. In theological discussion "mission," as participating in God's mission *(missio Dei),* is the more comprehensive concept. Within it "evangelism" represents the witnessing aspect of mission.

2. Ecumenical Discussion

2.1. Between the assemblies of the → World Council of Churches (WCC) at New Delhi in 1961 and at Uppsala in 1968, the ecumenical study "Missionary Structure of the Congregation" brought a new ferment of renewal and contributed to a broader understanding of evangelism. It also, however, aroused evangelical criticism of the WCC and its horizontal view of evangelism (maligned as "horizontalizing the gospel") and led to polarization after Uppsala (→ Evangelical Movement). Both the International Congress on World Evangelization, in Lausanne in 1974, and the WCC Assembly at Nairobi in 1975 worked to overcome this polarization and to develop a growing consensus in the understanding of evangelism, based on the assumptions in the following section.

2.2. The content of evangelism must emphasize and keep together the central facts of the faith: the life, → death, and → resurrection of Jesus Christ; the announcement of the → kingdom of God; and the call to → discipleship.

Evangelistic proclamation is an announcing of liberation and an invitation to commit oneself to serve God's kingdom. In this regard the relation between evangelism and God's promise to the poor takes on greater significance.

Evangelism demands a mental attitude of service and a readiness for → dialogue or for listening vis-à-vis the → culture and religious convictions of others.

Evangelism ties the history of Jesus Christ and the biblical message to the concrete, personal, and collective history of people. The inculturation of the church, of the evangelist, and of the message is of basic importance for a true encounter between human reality and the living Christ (→ Acculturation).

2.3. The ecumenical affirmation "Mission and Evangelism" (adopted by the WCC Central Committee in 1982), with its seven "ecumenical convictions," was the climax of these efforts to develop a consensus. It related the call for → conversion (conviction no. 1) to the proclamation of the gospel for all realms of life (conviction 2). The fifth conviction, "Good News to the Poor," states that the common challenge of the "global nature of poverty and exploitation in the world today" bursts through earlier polarizations: "Churches are learning afresh through the poor of the earth to overcome the old dichotomies between evangelism and social action. The 'spiritual Gospel' and 'material Gospel' were in Jesus one Gospel."

2.4. In essentials the findings of the → World Evangelical Fellowship at a missions conference in Wheaton, Illinois, in 1983 support this ecumenical consensus. In the evangelical concern for evangelism, however, proclamation still has priority. Its urgency is stressed in view of the billions of people who are "still unreached" by the gospel (→ Evangelical Missions).

2.5. During the same period the → Roman Catholic Church, not without contacts with the WCC, urged upon its priests and members the meaning of evangelization and the need for it. The bishops' synod discussed the theme in 1974, and in 1975 Pope Paul VI issued an apostolic letter on evangelization in the modern world in which he said that "the church must strive not only to reach greater areas and peoples with the preaching of the gospel but also by the power of the gospel to change criteria of judgment, values, interests, habits of thought, sources of inspiration, and models of life that are contrary to the Word of God and the plan of salvation" (19). The → encyclical *Slavorum apostoli* (1985) of John Paul II also gave expression to the interest in the cultural impact of the gospel that characterizes the Roman Catholic understanding of evangelization.

2.6. The seventh ecumenical conviction in the 1982 WCC affirmation (under the heading "Witness among People of Living Faiths") is also related to the open question how the salvation in Christ is available to people of diverse religious persuasions. It states, "True witness follows Jesus Christ in respecting and affirming the uniqueness and freedom of others." Section 1 ("Turning to the Living God") of the WCC World Conference on Mission and Evangelism, held in 1989 in San Antonio, Texas, further developed the idea in its §26: "We cannot point to any other way of salvation than Jesus Christ; at the same time we cannot set limits to the saving power of God."

Through the WCC program "Dialogue with People of Other Living Faiths," the controversial question was raised whether dialogue should replace witness. The concern for an attitude of dialogue toward people of other religious convictions does not replace witness, however, but underlines the idea that witness cannot be a one-way process — it implies mutual listening with the ones being addressed.

2.7. The ongoing complaints of Orthodox church leaders about proselytizing activities of Protestants and sects in eastern Europe have led to growing efforts of the WCC and other ecumenical bodies to promote "responsible relationships in mission." John Stott, an outstanding promoter of evangelical missiology and the principal author of the 1974 Lausanne Covenant, has critically noted that "when Euro-Marxism collapsed and the doors opened into the former Soviet Union and Eastern Europe," there was "a most unseemly scramble of Western missionary organizations . . . , bringing acute embarrassment to historic national church leaders, and enormous confusion" ("Twenty Years," 53).

3. Modern Practices

3.1. The agents of evangelism are fundamentally the churches and individual evangelists. The churches are agents directly by their setting up evangelistic activities and indirectly by their very being. The common life of Christians either sets forth the gospel or denies it. Thus efforts to build up the churches that seek to bring them into line with their commission are in effect a practice of evangelism. A missionary community may be known by its openness to others and by the fact that others can experience what it does as an embodiment of the gospel.

For the direct work of evangelization the church uses itinerant evangelists. Specially gifted evangelists may be invited by churches to minister in other lands (e.g., D. T. Niles, Billy Graham). Many churches sponsor training centers for evangelists. National conferences and international congresses (e.g., world congresses for itinerant evangelists launched by the Billy Graham Association in 1983 and 1986 in Amsterdam) enable evangelists to share experiences. In many African and Asian churches local church leaders with seminary training are called evangelists, in distinction from ordained pastors, who are responsible for several congregations.

3.2. There are many forms of evangelism. Being addressed to all people, evangelism must try to take into account their variety and the variety of their situations. The classic form is the campaign of several days, which makes no distinction but issues a general invitation to all. Such a campaign is usually led by a single evangelist or an evangelistic team. But there is also specialized evangelization — for example, among young people and children, in which evangelistic songs play a large part.

Examples of evangelization that do not expect people to come to a particular place are visitation, street evangelization, street theater, camping missions, literacy missions, and evangelistically oriented surveys of historical churches and cathedrals for tourists.

3.3. Evangelism is interested in the numerical growth of the churches. Special research programs, like those of the so-called church growth movement, associated with Donald McGavran (→ Church Growth 5), aim at defining methods that may lead to rapid church growth. Critics of such programs point out that methods are not neutral. Although people may "like to become Christians without crossing racial, linguistic, or class barriers" (McGavran, 198), still the gospel includes the message of the removal of barriers that separate people from each other.

Evangelistic efforts can win new members, though sometimes the total number of Christians in an area does not increase. Churches in deeply secularized or even dechristianized areas like the Czech Republic or the former East Germany have noticed that their efforts to communicate the gospel to people who have no knowledge of Christian faith may lead to conversions and some new church members. Such results, however, have not begun to counter-

balance the huge loss of membership beginning in the 1950s and 1960s. Evangelism that measures its success or justification solely by numerical growth runs the danger of degenerating into propaganda.

Bibliography: D. J. Bosch, "Mission and Evangelism: Clarifying the Concepts," *ZM* 68 (1984) 161-91 • J. D. Douglas, *Let the Earth Hear His Voice* (Minneapolis, 1975), compendium of the Lausaunne Congress • W. Hollenweger, eds., *The Church for Others* (Geneva, 1967) • John Paul II, "Slavorum apostoli," *The Encyclicals of John Paul II* (ed. J. M. Miller; Huntington, Ind., 1996) 227-53 • M. Kinnamon and B. E. Cope, eds., *The Ecumenical Movement: An Anthology of Key Texts and Voices* (Geneva, 1997) • D. McGavran, *Understanding Church Growth* (Grand Rapids, 1970) • H. J. Margull, *Theologie der missionarischen Verkündigung* (Stuttgart, 1959) • Paul VI, *Evangelii nuntiandi* (London, 1975) • J. Stott, *The Lausanne Covenant* (Wheaton, Ill., 1975); idem, "Twenty Years after Lausanne," *IBMR* 19 (1995) 50-55; idem, ed., *Making Christ Known: Historic Mission Documents from the Lausanne Movement, 1974-1989* (Grand Rapids, 1996) • D. Werner, "Missionary Structure of the Congregation," *DEM* 699-701 • T. Wieser, ed., *Planning for Mission* (New York, 1966) • F. R. Wilson, ed., *The San Antonio Report* (Geneva, 1990) • World Council of Churches, *Mission and Evangelism: An Ecumenical Affirmation* (Geneva, 1982); idem, *Toward Common Witness: A Call to Adopt Responsible Relationships in Mission and to Renounce Proselytism* (Geneva, 1997).

Emilio Castro and Gerhard Linn

Everyday Life

1. Usage
2. Sociological Perspective
3. Theological Perspective
4. Theological Problem

1. Usage

1.1. In common usage "everyday life" denotes the reality that recurs each day and that everyone experiences. It is that which in individual activity and lifestyle belongs to the daily rhythm and is repeated year by year. It applies to the people, things, institutions, and environment that we accept mechanically and instinctively, that we take for granted, that are familiar, that we treat as routine. The phrase, which has a temporal side (= what is always the same), characterizes our lifestyle and behavior (everyday food, clothes, speech, culture, duties, the daily round). It qualifies conditions and people as well as the knowledge gained in routine → experience. The many applications point to social relations and to processes. They reflect the complexity of everyday life and everyday experience, thus making definition difficult.

1.2. Because of its average and ill-defined nature (what we do each day), everyday life attracted little scientific interest before the 19th century. Writers looked at it critically and satirically and caricatured it. F. Engels and K. Marx described the misery of the everyday life of the proletariat, which led them to take up the struggle against the bourgeois master-class. They did not attempt, however, a full-scale analysis of everyday life (→ Marxism).

This topic, though, was becoming scientifically relevant once it was found that what is unquestioned and trivial constitutes a problem. Edmund Husserl, in his *Positivismuskritik* (1911) and then in his *Ideen zu einer reinen Phänomenologie* (1913; ET *Ideas: General Introduction to Pure Phenomenology* [1931]), noted the disorientation and intellectual need of the age, which he blamed on the rationalistic objectivism of natural science. He turned to prescientific life, to the world of experience, and developed a conception of life that tries to show how scientific concepts and constructs relate to reality (→ Phenomenology). With Martin Heidegger's analysis of everyday life (*Sein und Zeit* [1927; ET *Being and Time* (1962)]) and Jean-Paul Sartre's interpretation of basic anthropological situations (*L'être et le néant* [1943; ET *Being and Nothingness* [1956]]), the phenomena of everyday existence became a subject of philosophical description and reflection (→ Existentialism).

Earlier, a desire to know the techniques of everyday life had led Sigmund Freud to write *Zur Psychopathologie des Alltagslebens* (1904; ET *Psychopathology of Everyday Life* [1960]), and Max Weber had taken up the theme, characterizing → charisma as an attempt to ignore the demands of everyday life, to transcend its limitations, yet also as an attempt that can succeed only in the everyday form of domination (*Soziologische Grundbegriffe* [1918-20]). Husserl's philosophy exerted an influence on the essays of Alfred Schütz on the everyday world as a social reality (1939ff.) and also on the prominence of the question of the meaning of knowledge and its significance for life.

1.3. In the 1960s the acceptance of the idea of everyday life into sociology (see 2) brought about a paradigm shift in → pedagogy. Historical research profited from this development by paying more attention to → social history, while philosophical →

anthropology turned to the question of the world of real life, and interest in → biography became much stronger in many disciplines. "Everyday life" became a key concept in → sociology and came to be preferred to → "society" as the subject of the corresponding theories.

Jürgen Habermas called the shift to the everyday a symptom of two tendencies: first to → counterculture, then to the development of (neo-) → conservatism. Crises in everyday life had caused this shift. On his view the crisis scenario gives evidence of the deformation of everyday life by economic and → bureaucratic rationality (the colonializing of real life by the mass media, → money, and → power; the everyday person as a consumer, as clientele, etc.; the segmentation of life into partial spheres and subsystems), and evidence also of the destruction of inalienable resources of communicative practice (e.g., by the parceling out of time; the pressure to achieve and compete; the deformation of experience by the surrogates of the mass media; the exploitation of the natural environment; the loss of continuity, coherence, and meaning; and the withering of vital traditions). Everyday life is the theater and cockpit of this accumulation of crises; the subject needed to overcome them by not letting everything be reduced to the level of mere things seems not to be present.

Bibliography: G. ALLAN, ed., *Technology and Everyday Life* (Greenwich, Conn., 1994) • M. DE CERTEAU, *The Practice of Everyday Life* (Berkeley, Calif., 1988) • E. GOFFMAN, *The Presentation of Self in Everyday Life* (New York, 1973; orig. pub., 1959) • J. HABERMAS, *The Theory of Communicative Action* (2 vols.; Boston, 1984-87) esp. vol. 2 • A. KAPLAN, *Everyday Life* (New Haven, 1987) • W. LEEDS-HURWITZ, *Communication in Everyday Life: A Social Interpretation* (Norwood, N.J., 1989) • H. MACKAY, ed., *Consumption and Everyday Life* (London, 1997) • A. SCHÜTZ, *Collected Papers* (3 vols.; The Hague, 1962-66) • H. P. THURN, *Der Mensch im Alltag. Grundriß einer Anthropologie des Alltagslebens* (Stuttgart, 1980) • P. VENTURA, *History of Everyday Life* (London, 1987).

ERWIN FAHLBUSCH

2. Sociological Perspective

2.1. In sociology, "everyday life" denotes the typical ideas, convictions, and programs of social reality shared by members of a society at a given time. These factors all are activated and actualized (through planning, defining, and interpreting) in order to gain a mastery of social situations (see 1.1).

2.2. What ideas are relevant depends on what is socially and culturally normal (variously, for the group, social stratum, and cultural and denominational orientation). It also depends on the situation and on the ability to deal with these matters.

2.3. How binding the ideas become is related to how ready members of society are to obey what is supposedly normal. Developmental possibilities are acquired through interpretative interaction with what has been tacitly accepted as valid in a given historical situation.

2.4. Where the limits of everyday life are to be drawn, what is included or left out, is a question of the social claim made on the world around. In nonindustrial societies the notion of everyday life focuses on work and ignores other things. Advanced → industrial societies constantly incorporate new fields according to criteria external to everyday life, and then, so as not to overload it, they eliminate traditional things. They thus make what is alien into the everyday — secularizing, rationalizing, and normalizing it. In contrast, they abandon what is familiar — giving it up, putting it under a taboo, and criminalizing it.

2.5. The everyday must be maintained in order to safeguard its validity in this sense. Internally, symbols, ritual, and practical discourse contribute to its stability. Externally, → worldviews, mass → communication, and social interventions also contribute to such stabilization.

2.6. Modern trends in globalization and individualization have put increasing pressure on the microcosm of everyday life. The increased mobility accompanying globalization (A. Giddens) has resulted in a pluralization of everyday life and has, together with the emergence of more recent information media, generated virtual spheres of everyday life that are no longer clearly delineated in any temporal or spatial sense. Moreover, many of the more self-evident parts of everyday life are disappearing before the processes of individualization (U. Beck), so much so that the traditionally largely habitual forms and course of everyday life increasingly require active, conscious planning and orchestration. Because the inner consistency, boundaries, and support offered by everyday life have become problematic, inclinations toward delimitation have become more prevalent in the form of enclosure (the emergence of ghettos, formation of we-groups) and exclusion (violence, racism).

Everyday life has also become increasingly ethnically charged by being drawn into the vortex of global conflicts (W.-D. Bukow 1996), a situation also involving → religion. The latter, however, although not a part of everyday life in the strict sense as oriented toward practical matters, is nonetheless part of the overall nexus of practices sustaining everyday life. Religious rituals, dramatizations, and interpretations are all based on religious worldviews and exert a stabilizing influence on everyday life. In just this situation, however, they may develop increasingly fundamentalist features (R. Robertson) and, in so doing, contribute to a polarization within the microcosm of everyday life.

2.7. Academic theories have been developed largely within the framework of so-called symbolic interaction and the phenomenological tradition. In terms of the former, G. H. Mead (1863-1931) described the role of symbols in simple social systems, and then H. Blumer investigated their significance in producing ideas of everyday life. The naturalistic perspective of E. Goffman and D. Matza is similar, with its analysis of the dramaturgic aspect of the shaping of everyday life.

Within the phenomenological tradition, and building on E. Bergson and M. → Weber, A. Schütz (1899-1959) and A. Gurvitch (1894-1965) took E. Husserl's (1859-1938) later concept of real life as the presupposition of everyday and scientific understanding and elaborated a theory of the structures of real life, which T. Luckmann then reformulated. H. Garfinkel, with reference to Schütz, developed an "ethnomethodology" to understand the "deep structures" of everyday life. A. V. Cicourel and others then did further work on this paradigm under the influence of Noam Chomsky.

Everyday life became a central concept between (1) → phenomenology and → Marxism or critical theory and (2) → functionalism or the theory of systems. The one side thematized everyday life with reference to alienation (H. Lefèbvre, A. Heller, R. Barthes) or the colonializing of everyday life, while the other side used it to establish a theory of action (T. Parsons) or to achieve delimitation from the modern social system of world society (N. Luhmann). For the rest, theories of everyday life are integral parts of many praxis-oriented sociological disciplines, from the ethnology of advanced societies to pedagogy.

Bibliography: R. BARTHES, Mythen des Alltags (1957; 4th ed., Frankfurt, 1976) • U. BECK, Politik der Globalisierung (Frankfurt, 1998) • P. L. BERGER and T. LUCKMANN, The Social Construction of Reality: A Treatise in the Sociology of Knowledge (New York, 1967) • W.-D. BUKOW, Feindbild Minderheit (Opladen, 1996); idem, Kritik der Alltagsreligion (Frankfurt, 1984) • H. COX, Fire from Heaven (New York, 1995) • J. D. DOUGLAS, ed., Understanding Everyday Life (2d ed.; London, 1974) • A. GIDDENS, The Consequence of Mo-

dernity (Oxford, 1990) • E. GOFFMANN, *The Presentation of Self in Everyday Life* (New York, 1959) • A. HELLER, *Das Alltagsleben* (Frankfurt, 1978) • M. KOHLI and G. ROBERTS, eds., *Biographie und soziale Wirklichkeit* (Stuttgart, 1983) • H. LEFÈBVRE, *Everyday Life in the Modern World* (New Brunswick, N.J., 1984; orig. pub., 1968) • T. LUCKMANN, *Phenomenology and Sociology* (Harmondsworth, 1978) • H. G. PRODOEHL, *Theorie des Alltags* (Berlin, 1983) • R. ROBERTSON, *Globalization* (London, 1992) • A. SCHÜTZ, *Das Problem der Relevanz* (2d ed.; Frankfurt, 1981) • M. W. SPORONDEL and R. GRATHOFF, eds., *Alfred Schütz und die Idee des Alltags in der Sozialwissenschaft* (Stuttgart, 1979) • B. WALDENFELS, J. M. BROEKMAN, and A. PAZANIN, eds., *Phenomenology and Marxism* (London, 1984).

WOLF-DIETRICH BUKOW

3. Theological Perspective

3.1. In theology (and the church) everyday life is everywhere present as a substratum. Its complex reality has not been adequately investigated (A. Bondolfi), however, even though the problem has been taken up with varying interest and in different ways and has been worked at controversially in the context of "symptomatic signs of the times." Nontheological analyses and theories serve as an introduction.

3.2. Existential analysis, with which Heidegger thematized everydayness and pointed to existential factors in existence (e.g., → death, → anxiety, and → guilt), has inspired an existential interpretation of the Christian message (→ Hermeneutics) and an anthropological concentration in more recent theology (→ Anthropology). The question of the "meaning" of everyday life and of the truth of existence opens up the NT texts about the constitution of human existence under the call (revelation) of God and actualizes them in relation to "modern human beings." Furthermore, the question of true reality, intensified in this way, opens up an understanding of the confessional statements of Reformation theology about our human situation in the world and our personal relation to God, about the active relation between God and the world, and about the experience of God as both close and distant in the → cross and the → resurrection, in the → law and the → gospel. The ontological inquiry leaves everyday life behind it in all its multiplicity, including the concrete conditions of life and social problems. Yet the → hope remains that "being" (salvation) will eventuate in the daily "experience of nothingness."

3.3. → Phenomenology in the wider sense carries with it a basic concern to find an experience of

transcendence in everyday life (→ Immanence and Transcendence), to localize the experience of faith in that of everyday life, and to find it there as → piety (K. Rahner, B. Casper). The standpoint of salvation history is that the restoration of the human race and the whole world has begun with Christ and that by the → Holy Spirit it continues in the church up to its consummation at the end of the age. We thus may experience wholeness in the world of everyday life, where we can live it out sacramentally.

The existing agreement and remaining tension (difference) between piety and the experience of everyday life are viewed incarnationally (as at → Chalcedon, with "no confusion" and "no division"; → Incarnation). This model of thought, which is typically Roman Catholic, gives faith the wide-ranging task (see D. Wiederkehr) of making inroads on the level of everyday experience (i.e., the rooting of faith in everyday life) and of humanizing everyday life by shattering its banality (i.e., by integrating faith into the totality of the human world). In the face of the deformation and disintegration of the world of everyday life, there is little evidence for the basic theological or anthropological interpretation (see 1.3). Yet one may maintain and demand it as the spirituality of everyday life — that is, as the love of God actualized in the living of everyday life.

3.4. Sociopsychological analyses of representative questions, statistics, and investigations of various kinds bring to light denominational distinctions in the customs of everyday life and the shaping of existence. The "more general theory of denominational culture" (G. Schmidtchen) that has been developed on the basis of such findings asserts the divergence and interdependence of piety and everyday life and tries to explain specific denominational attitudes in terms of the distinctiveness of → Catholicism and → Protestantism as closed or open systems.

Yet, when we ask about the significance of the churches in the world of everyday life, the participation of their members, and the reality of their everyday life, we see that there are problems of a nondenominational type that result from manifest social, technological, and economic changes and crises in everyday life. Problems of faith that do not relate to everyday life lead to problems of personal and social orientation, while the problems of crises in everyday life — parallel to the tendencies already mentioned (see 1.3) — raise the question of a fixed point beyond the structured world of everyday life (→ Fundamentalism; Evangelical) and also bring the world of everyday life into question in the light of a reality of faith (→ Charismatic Movement; Base Community).

3.5. Theoretical access to the reality of everyday life is usually by way of symbolic interactionism (see 2.7). This approach can be used to validate → religion (the church) in the social world (religious rituals symbolize social processes, belong to human communication in everyday life, etc.; see M. Schibilsky, W. Fischer and W. Marhold), to gain a starting point for an ethical-theological program (critically considering and consistently organizing our knowledge of the everyday norm and situation, or constituting moral identity in everyday life; see A. Bondolfi), or to interpret Christian existence as the practice of messianic everyday life (everyday life as the place of gifted salvation, of God's mysterious strategy; see A. Rizzi). The aim in this approach is not to inquire into the objective constitutive conditions of everyday life but to study everyday people from within in a world of everyday life that they take for granted. Theological reflection shows that faith does not take on meaning from the experience of everyday life but that, independently of conditioned reality, it represents the basis for meaningfully shaping everyday life (i.e., as its horizon or environment).

4. Theological Problem

4.1. Thus far the concern of the church and theology with everyday life has been with the problem of communicating the → gospel and → faith as a noneveryday orientation (involving redemption, salvation, meaning, etc.) to those who live an everyday life. This issue presupposes that between (present) everyday life as a specific perspective of reality and the (sought) totality of reality there is a qualitative difference, the transcending of which can come from → God alone in virtue of his → revelation. The difference and relation between the justifying God and Savior, on the one hand, and, on the other, guilty and lost humanity set for the church the task of proclaiming the gospel (→ Mission) and thus answering the search for reality or the question of → truth.

For continuity and identity in fulfilling this task, it seems to be necessary to formulate God's self-impartation as doctrine (→ Confession of Faith) and to express it in institutionalized church activity (→ Diakonia; Pastoral Care; Worship). Relative to those who are addressed, however, this structured turning to them in their everyday life cannot rule out the fact that the → evangelism and sanctification of the world simply reproduce or enhance everyday life religiously (→ Piety). The church's efforts cannot prevent the conceptual and ecclesial objectification in → dogma and → institution from leading partly to an undesired alienation of the ev-

eryday, partly to a loss of its reality, in those who are addressed (see 3.4).

4.2. Solutions are first sought in a gracious and enduring transcendental disposition of people (→ Grace) that is mediated historically (i.e., ecclesially), which takes place in history (objectivizing), which includes everyday things and which thus brings about the being of God in the world (K. Rahner). The world of everyday life, however, resists transcendence. It restricts its reach to an achieving of plausibility or to the inner world.

Second, recourse is had to the sense of a new existence oriented to a change in practice. A gift that comes to us from outside (→ Justification) mediates a new → identity, takes an inner form when it is accepted in faith, and enables one to break through the strictures in the actions of everyday life. An individual existential decision (R. Bultmann) of this kind, however, hardly amounts to more than a change in the quality of thinking and the winning of biographical concepts. At any rate, it runs the risk of overlooking the historicalness of existence.

Third, there can be reflection on the experience of history (W. Pannenberg), with a view to escaping either spatial and temporal limitation or a narrow corner bounded by structures of plausibility, privateness, or → biography, and thus being able to grasp the totality of reality. We are pointed here to God's promised → future as an unknown condition of new → experience and an altered daily life, and we trust that with this orientation to the future there will constantly be more life in the world (J. Moltmann). This recollection and hope can take shape both individually and collectively in the practice of everyday life and in programs of engagement. An eschatological sense and programmatic anticipation of a better future, however, do not meet the demands of the critical rationality that the complications of modern life and its crises require.

4.3. Modern development shows that a Christian tradition that is reduced to → institution and organization and that is cultivated in "expert cultures" is on the whole relatively irrelevant to everyday life in the context of modern society.

4.3.1. The attempted solutions that have been mentioned (anthropological, Christological, and eschatological) always overlook or set aside in their different ways the basic question that the crises in everyday life bring to mind, namely, the question of the unsatisfactory nature of (present) reality. The theological premises given with the claim to revelation hamper the necessary paradigm shift, as does also the ontological structure that is posited with the transcendental relation between God and the world. Nevertheless, a radical change in the evaluation of transcendence is under consideration (K. Lehmann, E. Simon). Thus it might be regarded as destiny, as a pole of tension in life (stimulation, provocation), or as a process of self-fulfillment and → progress, though it can be maintained profoundly and productively only in wrestling with the problems of historicalness and active world-change (→ Revolution).

Along these lines, problems arise with the presupposed God-world relation; although it serves as a model of integration, it takes concrete shape as a structure of domination and alienation. The insight is needed that we must now think of transcendence not as an absolute in some state that is already present but in changing situations. Apart from the conditions and changes of everyday life and social reality, we can neither conceive of transcendence theoretically nor actualize it practically (not even as the revelation of God, Spirit, being, or freedom).

4.3.2. The mutual relationship compels theology to reflect on the everyday as the place of transcendence and to find in the unsatisfactory nature of (present) reality a central problem. For this task the Christian tradition already has models of interpretation and action in the → Sermon on the Mount and in → discipleship of Jesus. These models relate to the unsatisfactory nature of (present) reality and are oriented to reality as a whole. They form a basis, transcending it in a way that breaks through the limits of everyday life, relativizes our tendency to view all objects as mere things, and opens up the possibility of changing and improving everyday life. They assume paradigmatic character, however, only when we ratify and actualize them in the context and under the conditions of the concrete situation. In this regard we must consider that the experience of reality is not always and everywhere one and the same and that we cannot forestall its increasing complexity. This situation demands critical rationality and an open interpretation that is alert to the varied experiences of life. The different relations stir the church and theology to take up everyday life as a social theme under the primary aspect of human → freedom, which is threatened in so many ways.

Bibliography: A. Bondolfi et al., eds., *Ethos des Alltags* (Einsiedeln, 1983), esp. the articles by Bondolfi, A. Müller, and D. Wiederkehr • B. Casper, "Alltagserfahrung und Frömmigkeit," *CGG* 25.39-72 • W. Fischer and W. Marhold, eds., *Religionssoziologie als Wissenssoziologie* (Stuttgart, 1978) • K. Lehmann, "Transcendence," *SM(E)* 6.275-81; idem, "Ursprung und Sinn der Seinsfrage bei Heidegger I-III" (Diss., Gregoriana, Rome, 1962) • J. Moltmann, *Theology of Hope* (New York, 1967) • W. Pannenberg, *Basic Questions in Theology* (2 vols.; Philadelphia, 1971-72) • K. Rahner, *Everyday Things* (London, 1965); idem, "Revelation II: God's Self-Communication," *SM(E)* 5.353-55 • A. Rizzi, *Messianismo nelle vita quotidiana* (Turin, 1981) • J. M. Robinson and J. B. Cobb, eds., *The Later Heidegger and Theology* (New York, 1964) • J. Sabini, *Moralities of Everyday Life* (New York, 1982) • M. Schibilsky, "Theorie der Religion und Alltagswirklichkeit," *ZEE* 19 (1975) 339-62 • G. Schmidtchen, *Protestanten und Katholiken* (Bern, 1973) • E. Simon, "Transzendenz," *HPhG* 6.1540-56.

Erwin Fahlbusch

Evil

1. The Problem
2. Relevance
3. The Bible
4. Practical Significance

1. The Problem

Encounters with manifestations of evil are among the most elementary of human experiences. Both in individual and in social life, the problem of evil arises in many forms, including evil deeds, life-threatening structures, and evil as naked power. → Philosophy and → religion in particular deal with evil, and also with action aimed at overcoming its manifestations. The definition of evil varies considerably. It depends upon the anthropological premise, but especially upon the understanding of the → good that is threatened by it. If matter is thought to be fundamentally evil (as harmful to spirit), then evil will be sought especially in the material realm, in human life — especially in the bodily realm (→ Sexuality). But if healing force is found in the unrestricted expression of impulses, then ascetic repression (→ Asceticism) will seem to be evil. "Radical evil" (I. Kant) can also be located in the sphere of a self-centered free will.

In modern discussion the question of "structural evil" plays an essential part. Alienated conditions produce alienated people. → Enlightenment thinkers found such conditions in wrongly programmed mechanisms of culture and education, while Marxists found them in the rule of private property exalted as an end in itself. In such debates evil is mostly viewed as a "particular sickness" (F. Schelling). In contrast, in the history of religion evil is viewed as a destiny that is bound up with the mutability of existence and the related suffering, or as a dark cosmic force that is in conflict with the power of good (as in Parsiism and → Manichaeanism).

In general one might define evil as a threat to being and well-being, either physically or metaphysically. It is important to note that the same phenomenon may be judged more or less evil according to the higher or lower aims that it serves in the prevailing value system. A positive role can even be ascribed to evil (e.g., as an instrument of purification, or as a "lesser evil" to avert a greater).

2. Relevance

The problem of evil is acute today; its potential continually escalates. One need only note the development of → weapons of mass destruction. The presence of the media has also provided more information about the phenomena of evil. The problem has attracted scientific attention in biology (K. Lorenz), sociology (A. Plack), and philosophy (E. Fromm). Best-sellers are devoted to it. It thus poses a challenge to → theology, for which the theme of redemption from evil is constitutive. In distinction from the immediate past there is now a better understanding of the dark aspects of the Bible. However, there are also more attempts to detach modern analyses from the biblical heritage by viewing the reality of moral evil and the authenticity of the guilt experience in the light of psychological, sociological, and biological models of behavior. These models speak only of "so-called evil."

3. The Bible

The Bible, in contrast, describes evil as → sin. It thus contradicts both → moralism and → fatalism. Evil as sin is not just a specific failing but a force that threatens and rules our whole world (Ps. 14:1-3; Rom. 3:10-20). Not only does it strike marginal spheres of human life (e.g., the bodily sphere), but it affects and alienates the very center, the human heart (Jer. 17:9; Matt. 15:19). This idea of omnipresent and radical evil challenges every attempt to make it innocuous, and especially every claim to self-righteousness in human relations. Idealistic moralism misses the seriousness of the human plight. The biblical view also opposes fatalism as we find it in → Hinduism or → Buddhism or → Gnostic worldviews. Rooted in sin, evil is neither fate nor an unchangeable state of nature; the world of evil is not fatally stabilized in itself. It is set eschatologically (→ Eschatology) in the light of the coming kingdom of God, in a perspective of → hope. Hence the liberating admonition, "Do not be overcome by evil, but overcome evil with good" (Rom. 12:21). In the Bible the good lies very close to → love, which sheds a clear light on the nature of evil. It is rooted and thrives in a rejection of relationships, in egocentricity, in lovelessness ("the heart curved in upon itself").

To the classical question as to the origin of evil, the Bible offers no systematic answer. It points instead to the mystery of evil, viewing it against the background of a misuse of creaturely → freedom (Genesis 3; → Theodicy).

The biblical understanding of the mystery of evil includes recognizing the personified power of evil, a power to whose aggressive deception human beings are exposed both internally and externally. This power manifests itself as the adversary of God and of human beings — namely, as Satan, the → devil, who is "like a roaring lion" and who "prowls around, looking for someone to devour" (1 Pet. 5:8). Although the demonic power of evil is utterly superior to human beings, one need not capitulate to it within Jesus' "force field," for he "was revealed for this purpose, to destroy the works of the devil" (1 John 3:8). The resistance provided by faith is both possible and necessary (Jas. 4:7).

4. Practical Significance

Not just theoretically but above all practically, Christians encounter the challenge of evil. The way of faith, which must prove itself in personal and social involvement, avoids both an optimistic transfiguring and a pessimistic stabilizing of the human condition, knowing that on this side of God's kingdom, we have not only to work to arrest the effects of evil but also to pray, "Deliver us from evil."

Bibliography: K. Barth, *CD,* esp. §§50, 60, 65, 70 • H. Blocker, *Evil and the Cross: Christian Thought and the Problem of Evil* (Leicester, 1994) • E. Brunner, *Man in Revolt* (New York, 1939) • F. Buri, J. M. Lochman, and H. Ott, *Dogmatik im Dialog* (vol. 3; Gütersloh, 1976) • A. Delbanco, *The Death of Satan: How Americans Have Lost the Sense of Evil* (New York, 1995) • E. Fromm, *Anatomy of Human Destructiveness* (New York, 1978) • D. R. Griffin, *God, Power, and Evil: A Process Theodicy* (Lanham, Md., 1991) • J. Hick, *Evil and the God of Love* (rev. ed.; New York, 1977) • K. Lorenz, *Das sogenannte Böse* (Vienna, 1963) • R. Niebuhr, *The Nature and Destiny of Man* (2 vols.; New York, 1941-43) • S. H. T. Page, *Powers of Evil: A Biblical Study of Satan and Demons* (Grand Rapids, 1995) • T. Peters, *Sin: Radical Evil in Soul and Society* (Grand Rapids, 1994) • A. Plack, *Die Gesellschaft und das Böse* (Munich, 1967) • P. Ricoeur, *Fallible Man: Philosophy of the Will* (Bronx, N.Y., 1986) • R. Ulmer, *The Evil Eye in the Bible and in Rabbinic Literature* (Hoboken, N.J., 1994).

Jan Milič Lochman

Evolution

1. Concept

Since the term "evolution" embraces several dimensions, we cannot deal with it adequately without recognizing its various facets and clarifying precisely which of these are at issue in any given context. Four such facets are of particular importance: evolution as (1) an idea of change over time; (2) an idea of emergence, by which novelty arises from preceding entities and processes; (3) an idea that describes the origins of things, both proximate and ultimate; and (4) an idea of selection, explaining why things die or survive. Each of these facets deserves careful attention.

1.1. *Change over Time*

When evolution is described as the idea of change over time, it focuses on the study of the processes in which change is observed. This idea assumes that even though entities change, they possess an → identity that continues through the change. Although the suggestion that change is intrinsic to things is difficult for some, this aspect of the evolutionary idea is, in general, the least controversial.

1.2. *Emergence*

The idea of emergence serves to explain the idea that novelty, no matter how striking, arises from already existing components, without the need for outside intervention. Emergence has been employed to describe the origins of life from inorganic forms, as well as the emergence of human beings from primate evolution. Since a sufficiency of preexisting components is assumed here, controversy can arise from views that insist that supernatural interven-

tion is required for the most dramatic occurrences of novelty, such as → life itself or the human → soul.

1.3. *Origin*

Evolution as the idea of the origin of things is a natural step beyond the idea of emergence. If evolution is presented as only a proximate explanation of origins, it suggests the question of ultimate origins, which is in itself a metaphysical, not a scientific, question. Questions like these take such forms as, What preceded the Big Bang origin of the universe? or What caused the dramatic changes in the brain that mark the distinctiveness of human beings when compared with the other higher primates? From a theological perspective, evolution as a description of proximate origins becomes a marvelous description of what God does. In this perspective, theology and evolutionary science deal with different types of questions, the metaphysical and the material.

If, however, evolution is considered to be a description of ultimate origins, as Richard Dawkins and Daniel Dennett suppose, then the scientific description becomes the negation of theology, and → science becomes a materialist → metaphysics in its own right. Here science becomes scientism, just as evolution becomes evolutionism. At this point, the idea of evolution becomes intensely controversial.

1.4. *Selection*

Particularly in the realm of biology, the concept of selection is a central element of evolution. In this respect, evolution is about survival and extinction. Entities do not survive unless they negotiate successfully the challenges of their environment. These challenges may range from struggle with other life-forms to accidents, scarcity of food, or vulnerability to disease. Since death and extinction seem to be intrinsic to the processes of evolution, selection raises the question of evil, or → theodicy, for a theological worldview. Why is evil built-in to the process of life? Why does nature seem to favor the well-adapted organisms over those that suffer disabilities?

2. Scientific Elaborations

Just as evolution is itself a multifaceted idea, so it is expressed, both within the natural sciences and in other disciplines, in a variety of distinctive, compatible ways. It is not sufficient to relate the idea of evolution exclusively to biology and the work of Charles Darwin (1809-82). Evolutionary ideas are perennial, particularly the ideas of change and emergence, which go back to certain strands of ancient Greek philosophy and classical Christian theologians such as Gregory of Nazianzus and → Augustine. They were certainly present in the 18th century in the geological writings of James Hutton (1726-97), who propounded uniformitarian processes of change, as well in certain theories of history, literature, and culture.

A number of important and diverse contributors to evolutionary thinking antedated Darwin, some of whom influenced him, even though he fashioned his own distinctive version of evolution. These contributors include biologist Jean-Baptiste Lamarck (1744-1829), historian Thomas Malthus (1766-1834), philosopher August Comte (1798-1857), and philosopher Herbert Spencer (1820-1903), whose ideas of evolution were perhaps as influential as Darwin's in the 19th century. Darwin's contemporary Alfred Wallace (1823-1913) developed ideas similar to Darwin's, which Wallace published after the appearance of Darwin's pivotal work *On the Origin of Species* (1859).

At the risk of oversimplification, we can depict the scientific concept of evolution as a narrative with four segments: (1) cosmic evolution; (2) biological evolution on planet earth, especially the appearance of DNA; (3) the evolution of individual humans from embryo to → death (ontogenetic, or human, development); and (4) cultural evolution, which is made possible by the biology of the central nervous system. Specific sciences may focus on one or more of these segments. Increasingly, philosophers, theologians, and scientists speak of the narrative as a whole, sometimes under the term "the epic of evolution" (see 3.2.4). It is important to remember that although the term "evolution" may be applied to all of these segments, they do not all operate with the same dynamics and processes. It is particularly misleading to "biologicize" the epic of evolution, as if Darwinian ideas applied fully also to cosmology and → culture.

2.1. *Physical Sciences*
Cosmology, physics, chemistry, and geology represent physical sciences that employ evolutionary models, for example in cosmological theories of the origin and unfolding of the universe or in geophysical theories of planetary development. → Theology finds these theories significant insofar as they are relevant to understanding creation.

2.2. *Biology*
Biological evolution on the earth, to which Darwin devoted his attention, is the center of much public concern today, both in society as a whole and in religious communities, since it pertains most directly to human beings and to the pressing issues of medical science, especially genetics and the neurosciences.

Darwin dealt with both heredity and environmental natural selection in the evolution of individuals. Variability and survival, in his view, are due both to inheritance (although he was unaware of genetics) and adaptation to the environment. As Darwin observed, animal breeders exercise artificial selection of the most desirable individuals, whereas the environment exercises natural selection.

Even though Darwinian concepts continue to be of primary importance today for understanding biological evolution, they have been subjected to significant enlargement and revision since the mid-19th century. One important factor has been *the integration of genetics into Darwin's theories*. Although Gregor Mendel's (1822-84) fundamental work in genetics was contemporary to Darwin, it was largely unknown until after 1900. In the 1920s, 1930s, and 1940s, geneticists R. A. Fisher, J. B. S. Haldane, Sewall Wright, and Theodosius Dobzhansky were able to integrate genetics with Darwin's theories. Darwin provided the large theoretical explanation of evolution and described its processes at the macrolevel. Integrating genetics into his work makes it possible to give theoretical explanations of those processes, particularly with respect to inheritance, at the microlevel. Their accomplishment laid the groundwork for what is known as the neo-Darwinian, or synthetic, theory of evolution. The biogeographer Ernst Mayr, the paleontologist George Gaylord Simpson, and biologists Julian Huxley and G. Ledyard Stebbins are also considered to be architects of this synthetic theory. These developments add an emphasis on mutation and on the importance of understanding how and in what frequency any given genes are distributed in the total relevant population.

A second new element has been *molecular biology*, exemplified by the discovery in 1953 of the DNA molecule, which augments the knowledge of evolution and genetics by providing microlevel descriptions of the relevant processes. Two contrasting challenges to previous evolutionary theory arise from this research: the view that variations are grounded in molecular determinism, and the claim — known as the neutral theory — that → chance is the determinative factor.

From paleontologists Stephen Gould and Niles Eldredge comes the claim that evolution proceeds not only in small gradual steps but also in bigger jumps and starts. This claim has been developed as the theory of *punctuated equilibrium*.

Research that is often called *complexity science* adds another dimension to previous evolutionary theory. Building on theories that arose from physical chemistry — nonequilibrium thermodynamics (Ilya Prigogine), the behavior of living molecular systems (Manfred Eigen), and chaos theory — complexity has become an interdisciplinary field of study that focuses on how novelty emerges and on the relationship between order and disorder. These efforts are pertinent to every segment of the evolutionary narrative — cosmic, biological, and cultural.

There is some dispute as to whether the neo-Darwinian synthesis is unraveling or undergoing continuous dynamic revision. Most working scientists, however, seem to agree with geneticist Francisco Ayala that the various new proposals are differences of "degree and emphasis within a shared evolutionary outlook" (J. B. Miller, 184).

In 1975 the distinguished entomologist and geneticist E. O. Wilson published a landmark work entitled *Sociobiology*. Even though this work relied mainly on the work of Wilson's predecessors, it ushered in a highly significant and controversial phase of evolutionary thinking devoted to the study of the biological foundations of social behavior (hence the term "sociobiology"). One of the main emphases of this position is "inclusive fitness," the idea that survival means the survival not only of the individual but of the individual's offspring. Despite the intense criticism of this work, both on scientific grounds (arguing its insufficiency of explanation) and on sociopolitical grounds (insisting that it is a reappearance of racist genetic theories), the proposals of sociobiology have proved to be fruitful in a host of related scientific fields, in particular anthropology, neuroscience, and psychology.

2.3. Social Sciences

In some universities biologically informed anthropology is an alternative to the older cultural anthropology; in others, however, a synthesis is forming. This synthesis often presents itself as a theory of "biocultural evolution." The rapidly expanding neurosciences emphasize the role of the central nervous system in the formation of behavior and culture. Neo-Darwinian theories, coupled with molecular biology and complexity, give great force to the neurobiological interpretations of human → behavior. "Evolutionary psychology," which in some circles is replacing the term "sociobiology," brings together → psychology, cognitive science, and neuropsychology in a striking hypothesis — namely, that basic structures of human behavior, such as child rearing, social cooperation, and even religion, have formed, often in much earlier phases of human evolution, as adaptive responses that meet the test of inclusive fitness. Theoreticians are attempting to formulate the principles of cultural evolution that

can clarify this segment of evolution, seeking results that are comparable to the principles discovered by physical scientists and biologists.

2.4. Ethics

Moral behavior is one of the most debated themes of sociobiology and evolutionary psychology. Anthropology and philosophy also enter the discussion of ethical themes. Several schools of so-called evolutionary ethics have developed, each based on the thesis of inclusive fitness. Religious and other transcendence-based moral truths are not rejected but are reinterpreted. Michael Ruse, for example, respects religious moral assertions but denies any objective grounding to them. He views them as evolution's way of deceiving us so as to live in ways that promote inclusive fitness. → Ethics is gaining prominence as an evolutionary concern as genetics is allied with the practice of medicine and agriculture in genetic engineering, which includes such issues as cloning and altering both human individuals (somatic intervention) and future generations (germ line intervention).

2.5. Human Evolution

A very large field that can only be mentioned here is the history of human evolution, which studies the emergence of the human species among the other primate species. This field, which brings together primatology, paleontology, anthropology, genetics, and molecular biology, offers new ways to describe the relationship between humans and other animals.

Even this brief sketch of the range of sciences that deal with evolution indicates that evolution is today one of the most critical and fruitful ideas governing our understanding of human life and thought. Evolutionary science confronts philosophy, ethics, and theology with a formidable range of deeply significant issues.

3. Theological Issues and Engagement

Christian theology has engaged the various forms of evolutionary thinking from their first beginnings. Although the idea of evolution is not limited to the natural and social sciences (and indeed did not originate from them), this discussion focuses on the engagement between theology and these sciences. The fundamental issues raised for theology by evolution may be placed in three categories, which, at least for heuristic purposes, correspond to the three persons of the → Trinity.

3.1. Questions

First, there are the questions concerning origins, which engage the theology of → creation with particular force. Does evolutionary thinking necessarily lead to a materialistic reduction that excludes discussion of ultimate origins (i.e., of what existed before the Big Bang)? Does the scientific description of originating conditions rule out all belief in a transcendent origin of the creation? These issues relate particularly to the first person of the Trinity.

Second, the concept of natural selection underscores the fact that death is inherent in life and that life imposes an inexorable process of testing on all organisms that allows of no exceptions — the unfit (however fitness is defined) are weeded out of the process. The issue of theodicy comes to the fore here: how can a good God be reconciled with a creation in which death and evil are inherent? The theological belief in divine → providence is engaged at this point, challenged to develop a concept of God's action and guidance in the world that can come to terms with natural selection — topics traditionally associated with the third person of the Trinity. As with the issue of origins, the question of a transcendent presence in the world lies at the core of this engagement.

Third, the question of the origins and purpose of morality, as described by sociobiology and evolutionary psychology, challenges theology to speak of transcendent moral truths. Is there value — right and wrong — whose truth is sovereign over the evolutionary conditions of human origins and life-struggle? This question engages the doctrines of → revelation and of Christology and thus falls within the purview of the second person of the Trinity.

3.2. Responses

The Christian theological response to these challenges has taken four different forms: (1) opposition to the idea of evolution; (2) efforts to interpret the Christian faith in ways that take evolution into account, whether explicitly or implicitly; (3) attempts to employ evolution as a guiding motif for interpreting Christian faith; and (4) proposals to elevate the idea of evolution to the position of a creation myth, to which Christian faith (and other religious and philosophical positions) can relate its teachings and spirituality.

3.2.1. Opposition to Evolution

Opposition is expressed almost exclusively by thinkers who are identified as creationists (→ Creationism), for whom Phillip Johnson is the leading spokesperson. This school of thought assumes that the scientific theory of evolution includes an exhaustive explanation of origins, both proximate and ultimate, thereby eliminating any possibility of divine creation or transcendence. In other words, it interprets evolution as inherently a materialistic, reductionist proposal.

Since creationists do not allow for any rap-

prochement between evolution and Christian faith, they construct alternatives to evolutionary explanations. The alternatives most vigorously presented are (1) the view that the biblical stories of creation, interpreted literally, are scientifically accurate depictions of origins, and (2) theories of "intelligent design" and "irreducible complexity." The former has been brought to bear on the question of which science textbooks should be approved for U.S. public schools, as creationists have pressed in the courts for teaching the biblical narratives alongside of, or even instead of, the scientific theory of evolution. The Creation Research Institute of San Diego, California, is a leading proponent of this position.

The second alternative asserts that certain biological phenomena are so complex that they cannot be reduced to the analysis of molecular biology and hence cannot be explained by evolutionary theory. The only valid explanation is then a theory of design, which leads to the position that God has designed these features (→ God, Arguments for the Existence of). Biologist Michael Behe and philosopher William Dembke are the leading proponents of this position. Behe has argued, for example, that the ciliae of the lungs are an irreducibly complex phenomenon, while Dembke has offered sophisticated philosophical theories to substantiate the idea of design. Both of these alternatives enjoy widespread support in fundamentalist Christian groups.

3.2.2. Taking Account of Evolution

As historians have pointed out, many clergy and theologians viewed Darwin's work positively. Even before the appearance of Darwin's work, a rather impressive body of theological work had emerged that, even when not referring explicitly to evolution, interpreted Christian faith in ways that took the idea of evolution into account. The German theologian Friedrich → Schleiermacher (1768-1834) produced a monumental textbook, *Glaubenslehre* (1821/22; ET *The Christian Faith* [1928]), which presents the theology of creation and humanity in ways that do not require a literal interpretation. Adam and Eve are not viewed as a primal pair, the fall is interpreted as universally valid myth rather than as a historical event, and original sin is understood, not as the biological inheritance from an original pair, but rather as culturally transmitted sin. Schleiermacher's influential contemporary G. W. F. Hegel (1770-1831) employed a version of evolutionary thought that, though elaborated in the context of natural history, is more powerfully set forth as a theory of human history. Hegel placed a full-blown theological treatment of Christian faith within this dialectical evolutionary scheme.

In Britain an illustrious Anglican tradition of theology emerged in the 20th century, continuing traditions from the previous century that sought rapprochement with science and integrated evolutionary ideas in its presentation. John Illingworth (1848-1915) is a particularly important figure in this tradition, mainly for his contribution to the essays of → *Lux Mundi* (1889). Canon Charles Raven (1885-1964), Lionel Thornton (1884-1961), and Archbishop William Temple (1881-1944) are leading voices in this tradition, up through mid-century.

Later in the 20th century, leading theologians, although not necessarily in full agreement with each other, interpreted the Christian faith in ways that reflect full awareness of the significance of evolutionary thinking. This group includes Protestant theologians Paul → Tillich (1886-1965, who gave contemporary expression to many of Schleiermacher's ideas) and Emil Brunner (1889-1966), and Roman Catholic theologians Karl → Rahner (1904-84) and Edward Schillebeeckx (b. 1914). In addition, a papal statement to the Pontifical Academy of Sciences on October 22, 1996, seems to indicate a conditional acceptance of evolution. On this occasion John Paul II asserted that "the theory of evolution is no longer a mere hypothesis" (R. J. Russell, W. R. Stoeger, and F. J. Ayala, 4). The Vatican position has been interpreted as uncongenial to a creationist position (G. Coyne, in ibid., 11-17).

The legacy of these theologians can be related to the four dimensions of the evolutionary idea that were described at the outset. All of them understand change to be an intrinsic element of Christian faith, even as they formulated theories of how the classic tradition endures under the conditions of change. Each of them presents an interpretation of emergence, whether it is Schleiermacher's concept of the evolution of consciousness, Hegel's dialectic of negation in both nature and history, Tillich's idea of the multidimensional unity of life (which includes all of the phases of evolution), or Rahner's Christology of emergence. All of them interpret the biblical creation narratives in ways that accommodate scientific ideas. At the same time, these theologians are unanimous in rejecting reductionism. Their work represents an impressive attempt to speak of transcendence occurring under the conditions of natural, material processes, whether explicitly or implicitly; they present an interpretation of transcendence that can be present within evolutionary theories (→ Immanence and Transcendence). So-called → process theology (which is predicated on the philosophical work of Alfred North Whitehead) is the one school of theological thought that — although

not always using the terminology of evolutionary theory — has devoted massive attention to conceptualizing transcendence as an immanent presence. David Ray Griffin and John Cobb, two representatives of process theology, have dealt explicitly with the scientific concepts of evolution.

This significant legacy of 19th- and 20th-century theology does not generally receive the recognition that it deserves. It stands as evidence that theology has indeed given considerable attention to the issues raised by evolutionary thinking; as such, it deserves further elaboration. It represents an alternative to creationist thinking in its refusal to interpret evolutionary ideas as necessarily reductionistic. At the same time, it provides an alternative to materialist metaphysics and scientism.

The fourth dimension of the idea of evolution — natural selection, with its implications for theologians of theodicy — remains largely unengaged by the theological tradition of the 19th and 20th centuries. One notable exception is Ralph Wendell Burhoe (1911-97), who developed the idea that natural selection could be given metaphysical expression in ways that assigned to it attributes comparable to the Western traditional concepts of God, such as omnipotence, justice, and eternity. Employing a concept of evolution that embraced all of the sciences, as well as culture and history, he summarized this line of thinking by naming both God and natural selection "Lord of History." Since selection expresses the will of God, who in turn grants → immortality to all creatures, there is in the divine purview no evil. In this sense, Burhoe presents a liberal Protestant formulation of Teilhard de Chardin's approach to selection and theodicy (see 3.2.3).

The Center for Theology and the Natural Sciences (Berkeley, Calif.) and the Vatican Observatory have set divine providence in the context of the scientific worldview as a primary theme for a decade-long series of international symposia. Subtitled *Scientific Perspectives on Divine Action*, five volumes have appeared, copublished by the two sponsors, under the primary leadership of George Coyne, S.J., and Robert John Russell, with substantial ongoing contributions by Nancey Murphy, Ted Peters, and Philip Clayton. Although this effort focuses predominantly on the physicochemical dimensions of evolution, some attention has been given to biological and neuroscientific facets of evolution. Selection and theodicy, however, have not figured prominently in these discussions.

Gerd Theissen and Hubert Meisinger have produced two of the most important theological analyses of natural selection and morality, attempting mainly to bring NT materials to bear on the issues raised by Darwinian and sociobiological categories of selection and altruism. They conclude that the teachings of → Jesus do confront the issues raised by the sciences of evolution and that dimensions of the evolutionary processes are introduced in the NT. The sciences, however, have yet to engage this biblical legacy in an adequate fashion. Theissen couches his interpretation in an explicitly Trinitarian form. The conclusion is unavoidable that the issues of selection, theodicy, and providence — all significant for understanding the third person of Trinity — remain as pressing priorities on the agenda for future theological work.

3.2.3. *Evolution as a Guiding Motif*

The seeds of the attempt to employ evolution as a framework for interpreting Christian faith were sown in the late 19th and early 20th centuries. Worthy of mention are the Yale philosopher of natural history Newman Smyth (1843-1925), as well as Harvard biologist Asa Gray (1810-88) and the so-called first Chicago school of theology of the early 20th century, which included Shailer Mathews (1863-1941) and Henry Nelson Wieman (1884-1975).

As the 20th century moved past its midpoint, the seeds of such thinking produced much fruit and were transformed. The figures just mentioned tended in a radically revisionist direction, not considering themselves bound to the classic Christian tradition as a normative body of thought. Theologians of the mid and late 20th century in this line — notably Pierre Teilhard de Chardin (1881-1955), Karl Schmitz-Moormann (1928-96), Arthur Peacocke, and John Polkinghorne, and also John Haught, Stephen Pope, and Philip Hefner — accept the need for rethinking the Christian tradition but nevertheless show themselves beholden to its authority.

Even though it is misleading to force these figures into narrow classifications, certain broad lines of interpretation do suggest themselves. Schmitz-Moormann and Haught — both Roman Catholic thinkers — clearly stand within the tradition of French Jesuit and paleontologist Teilhard de Chardin. Teilhard draws primarily from two authorities: the classic Roman Catholic tradition of spirituality and sacramental worship, and the scientific knowledge of his day, particularly but not exclusively geology, biology, and paleontology.

Teilhard conceives of evolution in broad terms, embracing cosmology, physics, and chemistry, as well as biology, history, and culture, and he argues that this total evolutionary process is the modality of God's presence and work in the world. "Com-plexification" is his overarching concept for interpreting evolution; it is constituted by two simultaneous sets of processes — quantitative growth, termed "aggregation," and individuation, which Teilhard described as "organized multiplicity" and "centrated complexity." In physicochemical processes, molecules are thus more complex than atoms, humans more complex than other primates, the global society of the period after World War II more complex than the preceding epochs of more isolated nation-states. This process is marked by tension and conflict, even though it culminates in → love, which is defined as the increasing solidarity of persons who are growing ever more individualized. Christ is the paradigm and dynamic force of complexification; the most complex of all realities is the omega state of eternity, which is characterized as a "center of centers." Evolution as the process of complexification can therefore also be termed a process of "Christification."

Teilhard comes as close as any thinker to a Trinitarian synthesis: the origins of the cosmos lie in God, who has set evolution into motion, giving it direction and meaning in Christ; the evolutionary process is in itself the providential working of God, who brings all reality, including what we call → evil, to a divine consummation that is coincident with what is revealed in Christ. Teilhard invoked the "cosmic Christ" tradition, which is epitomized in Col. 1:17, according to which Christ himself "is before all things, and in him all things hold together." No other Christian thinker has used evolutionary ideas more powerfully and fashioned so full a Christian synthesis on the basis of evolution. Although his architectonic proposals are at points hardly more than a sketch and sometimes highly ambiguous and controversial, they rise as a monumental achievement of constructive Christian theological engagement with the idea of evolution.

Schmitz-Moormann, an editor and scholar of Teilhard's writings, stands wholly within the trajectory of his mentor but carries it in his own distinctive directions, partly to be explained by the fact that Schmitz-Moormann, unlike Teilhard, was by training a professional theologian and philosopher. He starts with the assumption that evolution has become the standard way of understanding the world process, and he believes that, since evolution moves from a static worldview to one of dynamic becoming, the traditional theology of creation and redemption should be fundamentally reconstructed in the light of evolution. He intends that this reconstruction also be a reconstruction of the theology of the Trinity. His major work, which deals with creation, encompasses a concept of evolution that includes cosmology, as well as human evolution, but is not explicitly extended to ethics, culture, or history. Within his evolutionary perspective, the history of nature is a history of increasing unity, which culminates in God's consummation. His reconstruction moves beyond the traditional concepts of creation out of nothing *(creatio ex nihilo)* and continuing creation *(creatio continua)* to a concept of "called-forth creation" *(creatio appellata)*.

Theologian John Haught is staunchly rooted in the Teilhardian tradition, but he augments it with strong influences from mathematician and philosopher Alfred North Whitehead (1861-1947) and from chemist and philosopher Michael Polanyi (1891-1976). His concept of evolution is not indifferent to cosmology, culture, and history, but it focuses much more intensely on neo-Darwinian interpretations of evolution. Beyond human evolution, his concern is largely directed toward care for the natural → environment (→ Environmental Ethics). Haught has spoken of Darwin's work as a gift that challenges the theologian to offer an interpretation of evolution that is richer and more adequate than that of the neo-Darwinian scientific materialists. He begins with the conviction that the theological tradition must be reconfigured in order to speak of "a world in evolution that is given its being, value, and meaning by God's vision for it." Materialist, reductionist formulations of evolution cannot take account of the richness of nature and human existence. Haught does not repudiate the "hierarchically construed religious traditions" but insists, in the light of evolutionary thinking, that the old hierarchies must be recast in concepts that take the future and promise into account. God becomes "the infinitely generous ground of new possibilities for world-becoming," while an evolutionary ethic carries forward "at the human level the universe's incessant impetus toward the intensification and expansion of beauty" (pp. 119, 132, 143-44).

Arthur Peacocke has also been influenced by Teilhard, but his lineage lies more significantly in the Anglican tradition of Charles Raven and William Temple. As an established scientist working on the interface of physical chemistry and molecular biology, Peacocke came to theology later in life, as part of his quest to understand the orderliness and meaningfulness of human existence in the natural world. In an unusual manner, he has combined a commitment to radical reconceptualizing of Christian faith in order to meet the intellectual challenge of the sciences with a deep involvement in the traditional liturgical and spiritual disciplines of the

church. His work has produced a comprehensive integration of evolutionary concepts within a traditional theological framework, approaching a total → systematic theology. He works with a full concept of evolution that embraces cosmology, physics, chemistry, biology, information science, and the human sciences. As the first theologian to take account of the complexity sciences, particularly the research of Prigogine and Eigen, he elaborates a particularly nuanced interpretation of evolution that takes into account theories of self-organization and so-called top-down causation. Consequently, he has been able to place the issue of origins within a theological framework. He nevertheless gives more attention to the ongoing presence and causation of God in the processes of natural evolution, specifically in human life. His theories of divine causation and of the relationship of the sciences to theology are among the most sophisticated and detailed. → Christology is a central theme in his work, in which he speaks of Christ both as the self-communication of God within the natural world and as an expression of human personal fulfillment.

John Polkinghorne was a leading theoretical physicist before his work took a theological direction. Standing in the evangelical stream of Anglicanism, his work aims to elaborate how a Christian perspective provides a richer understanding of the world than the sciences, particularly physics, describe. Indeed, he seeks to do justice both to science and to "our experience of a much wider reality than that which science could ever claim to explain." Although he deals with many traditional themes, he does so mainly on the basis of the physical and chemical dimensions of evolution, rather than Darwinian themes. He defines evolution from his stance as a physicist as a "process of development that proceeds through the interaction of contingent factors and lawful rules" ("Evolution," 1749-50). One of his most notable contributions is an extended argument to the effect that our physical understanding of the cosmos, exemplified in chaos theory, as well as in Prigogine's theories of nonlinearity and complexity, suggests that there is a "looseness" to reality, an indefiniteness and openness to the future that make it possible to bring together both the scientific understanding of nature's evolutionary processes and the Christian view that God is at work in those processes. He has said that he holds, not to a theory of gaps in the evolutionary picture of science into which God can fit, but rather to a dimension of "gappiness" in reality, to which science itself testifies and which is an aspect of God's creation.

None of the thinkers in this survey so far has

given concentrated attention to the evolutionary interpretations of human behavior and morality, as these have been set forth by sociobiology and evolutionary psychology. Two theologians, however, have attempted to take a Christian theological measure of the evolutionary ethics that has been proposed by certain scientists and philosophers, arguing that neo-Darwinian concepts of altruism and inclusive fitness can be taken into the Christian understanding, although these concepts are far from adequate to interpret the richness of moral experience. Roman Catholic moral theologian Stephen Pope works within the tradition of neo-Thomist thought. Lutheran theologian Philip Hefner has developed a concept of humans as God's "created cocreators"; they are products of natural processes but also cocreators of those processes on planet earth.

3.2.4. *Evolution as Creation Myth*

In recent years a group of thinkers has emerged that holds that evolution in its full scope, as set forth by the sciences, is itself a narrative of mythic proportions into which religious content can be placed. Some of these thinkers are Christians who bring their presuppositions to this "epic of evolution," whereas others are humanists or adherents of other religions. It is noteworthy that many proponents of this position are scientists, some very distinguished. Leading figures in this stream of thought are physical cosmologist Brian Swimme and philosopher Thomas Berry (both Roman Catholics), cell biologist Ursula Goodenough, science educator Connie Barlow, and astrophysicist Eric Chaisson. These thinkers share the view that the evolutionary narrative is inherently a witness to depth, ultimacy, and moral earnestness, and also that this witness is compatible with a reconfigured traditional religious faith, as well as with a position of → naturalism or → humanism.

4. Conclusions

The first conclusion to be drawn from the preceding discussion is that evolution is a multifaceted concept that is elaborated in a wide range of scientific fields. Without taking into account its multifaceted, interdisciplinary character, we cannot address evolution adequately.

Second, contrary to some opinions, Christian theology has been engaged with evolutionary ideas for two centuries, although that engagement has in many instances been implicit, rather than explicit. In the 20th century that engagement has reached a high level of explicitness and sophistication.

Third, and most important, even though there is a staggering variety of style and disposition among the thinkers in this survey, there is also one pervading concern and theme: that evolutionary ideas not be restricted to the materialist and reductionist interpretations that proponents of scientism tend to propound. Theologians in the main are convinced both that Christian theology can take the measure of evolution and that the idea of evolution is congenial to interpretations that bring ultimacy, transcendence, purpose, and moral earnestness into play. Scientific humanists deny this proposal, joined, ironically, by creationist thinkers; both groups insist that evolution is nothing but a materialist interpretation of the world. Interestingly, the theologians who offer a broad interpretation of evolution are joined by humanists and others of a naturalist bent who will not settle for a narrow, one-dimensional interpretation of evolution.

Finally, the issue of the engagement of theology with evolution is a major component of a broader and enduring issue: Can Christian faith take the measure of the leading knowledge of its time? Can Christian convictions about God and transcendence be integrated with full appreciation of the natural world, particularly as contemporary science describes that world? Ours is not the first era that has faced such questions. The engagement with evolution is, however, one of the distinctively contemporary forms in which these perennial questions confront the Christian community and its theologians today.

Bibliography: General: C. Darwin, *On the Origin of Species* (New York, 1993; orig. pub., 1859) • R. Dawkins, *The Blind Watchmaker* (New York, 1986) • D. C. Dennett, *Darwin's Dangerous Idea: Evolution and the Meanings of Life* (New York, 1995) • E. F. Keller and E. Lloyd, *Keywords in Evolutionary Biology* (Cambridge, Mass., 1992) • J. B. Miller, ed., *An Evolving Dialogue: Scientific, Historical, Philosophical, and Theological Perspectives on Evolution* (Washington, D.C., 1998) • M. Ruse, *The Darwinian Revolution: Science Red in Tooth and Claw* (2d ed.; Chicago, 1999).

Specific sciences: Biology: M. J. Behe, *Darwin's Black Box: The Biochemical Challenge to Evolution* (New York, 1996).

– *Complexity:* A. Peacocke, "Thermodynamics and Life," *Zygon* 19 (1994) 301-22 • M. M. Waldrop, *Complexity: The Emerging Science at the Edge of Order and Chaos* (New York, 1992).

– *Cosmology:* E. Chaisson, *Cosmic Dawn: The Origins of Matter and Life* (Boston, 1981).

– *Human evolution:* R. G. Klein, *The Human Ca-*

reer: *Human Biological and Cultural Origins* (2d ed.; Chicago, 1999).

– *Neuroscience:* T. W. DEACON, *The Symbolic Species: The Co-evolution of Language and the Brain* (New York, 1997).

– *Psychology:* J. H. BARKOW, L. COSMIDES, and J. TOOBY, eds., *The Adapted Mind: Evolutionary Psychology and the Generation of Culture* (New York, 1992).

– *Sociobiology, anthropology:* R. BOYD and P. J. RICHERSON, *Culture and the Evolutionary Process* (Chicago, 1985) • P. HEFNER, "Theological Perspectives on Morality and Human Evolution," *Religion and Science* (ed. W. M. Richardson and W. Wildman; New York, 1996) 401-24 • W. IRONS, "How Did Morality Evolve?" *Zygon* 26 (1991) 49-89; idem, "Morality, Religion, and Human Evolution," Richardson and Wildman, *Religion and Science,* 375-99 • M. RUSE, "Evolutionary Ethics: A Phoenix Arisen," *Zygon* 21 (1986) 95-112 • E. O. WILSON, *Sociobiology* (Cambridge, Mass., 1975).

Theology: Creationism: P. E. JOHNSON, *Darwin on Trial* (2d ed.; Downers Grove, Ill., 1993) • R. L. NUMBERS, *The Creationists* (Berkeley, Calif., 1992).

– *History:* I. G. BARBOUR, *Religion and Science: Historical and Contemporary Issues* (San Francisco, 1997) • J. R. MOORE, *The Post-Darwinian Controversies: A Study of the Protestant Struggle to Come to Terms with Darwin in Great Britain and America, 1870-1900* (Cambridge, 1979).

– *Mainstream theological responses:* R. BURHOE, *Toward a Scientific Theology* (Belfast, 1981) • J. F. HAUGHT, *God after Darwin: A Theology of Evolution* (Boulder, Colo., 2000) • P. HEFNER, *The Human Factor: Evolution, Culture, and Religion* (Minneapolis, 1993) • H. MEISINGER, "Christian Love and Biological Altruism," *Zygon* 35 (2000) 734-80 • A. R. PEACOCKE, *Theology for a Scientific Age: Being and Becoming–Natural, Divine, and Human* (Minneapolis, 1993) • J. C. POLKINGHORNE, *Belief in God in an Age of Science* (New Haven, 1998); idem, "Evolution. Theoriegeschichtlich und kosmologisch," *RGG* (4th ed.) 2.1749-52 • S. J. POPE, *The Evolution of Altruism and the Ordering of Love* (Washington, D.C., 1994) • R. J. RUSSELL, W. R. STOEGER, and F. J. AYALA, eds., *Evolutionary and Molecular Biology: Scientific Perspectives on Divine Action* (Berkeley, Calif., 1998) • K. SCHMITZ-MOORMANN, *Theology of Creation in an Evolutionary World* (Cleveland, 1997) • P. TEILHARD DE CHARDIN, *The Phenomenon of Man* (2d ed.; New York, 1965) • G. THEISSEN, *Biblical Faith: An Evolutionary Approach* (Philadelphia, 1985).

"Epic of evolution": U. GOODENOUGH, *The Sacred Depths of Nature* (New York, 1998) • B. SWIMME, *The Hidden Heart of the Cosmos: Humanity and the New Story* (New York, 1996) • B. SWIMME and T. BERRY, *The Universe Story: From the Primordial Flaring Forth to the Ecozoic Era–A Celebration of the Unfolding of the Cosmos* (San Francisco, 1992).

PHILIP HEFNER

Exarch → Patriarch, Patriarchate

Excommunication

1. Concept
2. History
3. Situation Today

1. Concept

In Roman Catholic → canon law, excommunication is a penalty imposed with a view to recovery. Withdrawal of the rights of → church membership is designed to lead to conversion and repentance (→ Penitence). Distinction is made between "lesser" excommunication (which relates to the sacraments and ministry) and "greater" excommunication (shunning by all other members). Besides excommunication, the interdict and the anathema are also meant to lead to recovery. The interdict forbids an individual — or even whole regions — to minister officially or to administer or receive certain sacraments. The anathema (see 1 Cor. 16:22) is a ceremonial imposition of excommunication, with ultimate consequences for the soul's salvation.

2. History

Excommunication rests on NT precedent (1 Corinthians 5; Matt. 18:15-17). Nearly all religions use similar means to protect the whole body against divine → wrath because of an individual offender. In the West excommunication was at the discretion of → bishops and the → pope until late antiquity. The secular powers increasingly honored it, and it became an important weapon of the church → hierarchy. It imposed inviolable monogamy (→ Marriage) even on kings and was also used against their attempts to control church appointments, such as in the Investiture Controversy (which saw the excommunication of Emperor Henry IV, later also King John Lackland of England).

Most efforts to stop heresies and schisms by the threat of excommunication failed. M. → Luther (1483-1546) replied to his own excommunication by burning the → bull as a sign of public rejection. The mutual excommunications of the East-West schism of 1054 were withdrawn in 1965 under the banner of ecumenism.

Excommunication as a papal weapon came into discredit when it was used excessively to try to safeguard the → Papal States politically (e.g., against the Hohenstaufens and Aragonese in Sicily in the 13th and 14th centuries; → Empire and Papacy). The development of national states and national churches further diminished its effectiveness. The → Reformation rejected the Roman system of penance and absolution (→ Church Discipline) but not excommunication as a means of purifying the church as a penitential fellowship (E. Wolf). In the Lutheran sphere the secular authorities took it over before the → Enlightenment dismantled the penitential system and forbade excommunication. Excommunication survived, however, where it was insisted that the → congregation alone can decide on penalties and impose them, as among the Taborites (→ Hussites), the followers of T. Müntzer (ca. 1489-1525), the → Anabaptists, and the radical English → Puritans, who developed it to the point of principles of revolutionary justice.

This understanding of the congregation lives on in → Congregationalism in the United Kingdom and the United States. The ministering community decides on all official actions. Public obligations and self-imposed penances as a means of discipline provide a characteristic mixture of → individualism and conformity (→ Norms).

3. Situation Today

In the → Roman Catholic Church the → Codex Iuris Canonici 1983 no longer distinguishes between grades of excommunication (cans. 1331-32, 1338). Exclusion from the → sacraments may be ended on danger of death and by "due request." Grounds of excommunication include apostasy, heresy, and schism (can. 1364), profanation of the Host (1367), attacks on the pope (1370.1), unauthorized episcopal consecration (1382), and → abortion (1398).

In Protestant Germany excommunication achieved a certain importance again after 1945 through the provision of exclusion from the Eucharist in the constitutions of some of the member churches (→ Church Orders). This penalty is decided upon by the pastors and congregational leaders after admonition and with a right of appeal, but it is hard to enforce. For a similar theoretical rule of excommunication, see canon B16 of the Church of England.

Excommunication was significant in the Middle Ages because it dissolved all relationships and allegiances. Today it is relevant only if those concerned desire to be brought back into the congregation. In Europe the widespread indifference to religion and

the church works against its significance. It is sometimes noted that excommunication is more powerful under repression. Examples may be cited from mission churches, and the experience of the → Confessing Church was similar. The greatest difficulty in applying excommunication is perhaps that fellowship may be denied to someone seeking it because of some other obstacle (e.g., in attitude or conduct). In this regard bitterness must be avoided, so that with the necessary penitence public → reconciliation will be credible.

Bibliography: F. E. Hyland, *Excommunication: Its Nature, Historical Development, and Effects* (Washington, D.C., 1928) • F. X. Lawlor and C. A. Kerin, "Excommunication" and "Excommunication, Canonical," *NCE* 5.704-7 • M. Muster, "Das Ende der Kirchenbuße" (Diss., Hannover, 1983) bibliography • R. A. Strigl, "Straftat und Strafe," *HKKR* 929ff. • E. Vodola, *Excommunication in the Middle Ages* (Berkeley, Calif., 1986) • E. Wolf, *Ordnung der Kirche* (Frankfurt, 1961) survey. For Roman Catholicism, see 1917 CIC 2259-67 and 1983 CIC 1331, 1335; for Protestantism, see the regulations of the individual churches.

Jürgen Stein

Exegesis, Biblical

1. OT
    1.1. Jewish Exegesis in Antiquity
        and the Middle Ages
    1.2. Christian Exegesis from the Early Church
        to the Enlightenment
    1.3. Exegesis in the Nineteenth
        and Twentieth Centuries
    1.4. Present Situation
2. NT
    2.1. History
        2.1.1. Early Church
        2.1.2. Middle Ages
        2.1.3. Humanism
        2.1.4. Reformation Theology
        2.1.5. Modern Period
        2.1.6. Present Situation
    2.2. Methods and Questions
        2.2.1. Textual Criticism
        2.2.2. Literary Criticism
        2.2.3. Form Criticism
        2.2.4. Redaction Criticism
        2.2.5. Linguistic and Conceptual Research
        2.2.6. Comparative Religion
        2.2.7. NT Theology

1. OT

1.1. *Jewish Exegesis in Antiquity and the Middle Ages*

Jewish exegesis of the OT precedes Christian exegesis. It had models in the OT itself, where many of the later texts refer to earlier ones, applying, varying, and extending them in a variety of ways. More or less regular exegesis arose once the texts had taken a fixed form and become canonical (→ Canon). Although true commentaries with linguistic and factual elucidations came only in the Middle Ages (such as those by Rashi, Abraham Ibn Ezra, David Kimchi, and Nachmanides), in principle and in fact much of the Talmudic literature was already exegesis, most directly so in the → Midrash. → Apocalyptic and the → Qumran texts (esp. the Habakkuk commentary) were special forms of exegesis. The starting point was usually a uniform conception of the text on the basis of the → Torah, with precise rules for detailed exposition (conclusion from the lesser to the greater, use of → analogy, etc.). Allegorizing (→ Allegory) entered from → Hellenism (Philo), and the speculative → mysticism of the → cabala gained increasing importance in the Middle Ages. More significant is the broader philological work in the translations, especially the Targums and the LXX (→ Bible Versions), and also in the fixing of the tradition by the → Masoretes, which standardized the vowel pointing, established Hebrew grammar, and gave us unquestionably the most important commentary on the OT that we possess (J. Wellhausen). We must also refer to the lexical and grammatical works of the Middle Ages, which for a long time aided Christian studies in these areas.

1.2. *Christian Exegesis from the Early Church to the Enlightenment*

Christian exegesis of the OT is very closely linked to that of the NT. Its distinctiveness arises out of the special problems that the OT posed from the very first, not only philologically and historically, but also, in the narrower sense, theologically (→ Hermeneutics 1). All of the early exegetes placed high importance on allegory, with the most significant contributions toward its understanding coming from Origen (ca. 185-ca. 254, Hexapla), Eusebius of Caesarea (ca. 260-ca. 340, *Onomasticon* and *Chronicle*), and especially Jerome (ca. 345-420, the Vg and commentaries). Among medieval commentators we might single out Nicholas of Lyra (ca. 1270-1349), whose *Postillae* [analyses] *perpetuae in Vetus et Novum Testamentum* was heavily dependent on Rashi (1040-1105) in the OT part; this work made a great impact on M. → Luther (1483-1546).

The humanist return to the sources (→ Humanism) and the → Reformation principle of Scripture led to intensive study of the OT in Hebrew and to a new definition of the extent of its validity, varying among individual → Reformers but established in → orthodoxy. In such important scholars as J. Reuchlin, S. Münster, M. Flacius, J. J. Scaliger, J. Buxtorf the Elder, H. Grotius, L. Cappel, J. Morin, S. Bochart, A. Calovius, and J. Spencer, we find a wealth of old and new material increasingly being viewed methodically. To the forefront, and hotly debated, were questions of the development of the text (involving vowel pointing and the LXX). Only gradually did the main problems of a later age (e.g., the origin of the Pentateuch) come into prominence.

The most famous studies, which go increasingly into exegetical and historical detail, are linked to a wide variety of philosophical, theological, confessional, and political programs. They include the *Leviathan* (1651), by T. Hobbes (1558-1679); the *Tractatus theologico-politicus* (1670), by B. Spinoza (1632-77); and the *Histoire critique du Vieux Testament* (1678), by R. Simon (1638-1712). J. Clericus (1657-1736), in his *Ars critica* (1696), gave rules for the comparative treatment of the Bible and other works of antiquity. The opposing, orthodox standpoint was best stated by the *Critica sacra* (1728) of J. G. Carpzov (1679-1767).

In the 18th century the critical trend gained strength steadily on the Continent, nurtured by the views of English → deism, which may be seen most convincingly in the overwhelming impression made by the *Wolfenbüttel Fragments* (7 parts, 1774-78), published by G. E. Lessing (1729-81). Two momentous works appeared in 1753. One was by J. Astruc (1684-1766): *Conjectures sur les mémoires originaux dont il paroît que Moyse s'est servi pour composer le Livre de la Genèse*. With its argument, based on the varying use of the divine names, that the present Book of Genesis represents a piecing together of earlier documents, this book prepared the way for later source criticism of the Pentateuch. The other key publication that year was by R. Lowth (1710-87): *De sacra poesi Hebraeorum*, which describes OT poetry from an aesthetic standpoint in the context of literature in general. J. G. Herder (1744-1803) took the same line in his *Vom Geist der hebräischen Poesie* (1782-83), which was an "introduction for those who love this poetry and the earliest history of the human spirit." Less brilliant but in keeping with its day was *Mosäisches Recht* (6 vols., 1770-75), by J. D. Michaelis (1717-91), an analysis of the giving of the laws of the Pentateuch as a human, historical, rational phenomenon. Soon thereafter, J. P. Gabler

(1753-1826), anticipating D. F. Strauss (1808-74), applied to the OT the concept of → myth that he took from classical philology in his *Urgeschichte* (1790-93, written with J. G. Eichhorn). Eichhorn (1752-1827) summed up the work of the 18th century in his *Einleitung ins Alte Testament* (3 vols., 1780-83).

The growing wealth of material made necessary a division of labor. Along with insight into the relativity and lack of uniformity of the canon (J. Semler, *Abhandlung von freier Untersuchung des Canon* [4 pts., 1771-75]), this increase in information increasingly detached OT exegesis from NT exegesis, though obviously many links remained.

1.3. Exegesis in the Nineteenth and Twentieth Centuries

In his *Beiträge zur Einleitung in das Alte Testament* (1806-7), W. M. L. de Wette (1780-1849) took sharp issue with Eichhorn. De Wette advanced the thesis that, in essentials, the Mosaic → law, which is the main content of the Pentateuch, does not come at the beginning of Israel's history but much later — a thesis whose establishing (and contesting!) became the main theme of all 19th-century work. In the first volume of his *Die Geschichte Israels* (1878), J. Wellhausen (1844-1918) finally won the day for this insight and in so doing radically changed the picture of ancient → Israel (§1; see also his *Israelitische und jüdische Geschichte* [1894]). One result was an enhanced importance given to → prophecy in the work of H. Ewald (1803-75, *Die Propheten des Alten Bundes* [1840-41]) and B. Duhm (1847-1928, commentaries on Isaiah [1892] and Jeremiah [1901]).

Conservative scholars like F. Delitzsch (1813-90) and A. Dillmann (1823-94) also played an influential part in exegesis, building on the lexical and grammatical foundations of exegesis that, in the context of blossoming Semitic philology, W. Gesenius (1786-1842) in particular had laid in his *Ausführliches grammatisch-kritisches Lehrgebäude der hebräischen Sprache* (1817) and his *Thesaurus philologicus criticus linguae hebraeae et chaldaeae Veteris Testamenti* (1829-58). The deciphering of hieroglyphs and cuneiform inscriptions then opened up new perspectives on the ancient Near East. It provided many different aids to understanding, but it also showed Israel to have been a latecomer among the nations and brought to light texts that are close to the OT, such as the Babylonian flood story (discovered in 1872), the code of → Hammurabi (1902), and the sayings of Amenemope (1923). The wider public was reached by works with emotional titles such as *Babel und Bibel* (2 pts., 1902-3), by Friedrich Delitzsch, or, supporting orthodoxy, *Und die*

Bibel hat doch recht (1955; Eng. ed. *Bible as History*), by W. Keller.

After the turn of the century, literary criticism advanced with the school of literary-historical criticism developed by H. Gunkel (1862-1932, commentaries on Genesis [1901] and Psalms [1926]) and H. Gressmann (1877-1927, *Mose und seine Zeit* [1913]; → History of Religions School), which focused particularly on the preliterary forms and genres. S. Mowinckel (1884-1965, *Psalmenstudien* [6 pts., 1921-24]) turned attention to an imaginatively reconstructed cult as the most important "life setting." The so-called myth and ritual school and, in a different way, the Uppsala school in Scandinavia undertook a much broader, unified traditio-historical and phenomenological study of religious tradition whose scope extends far beyond Israel and that postulates a cultic ideological pattern in which the king plays a decisive role. Two books edited by S. H. Hooke provide the best introduction to the former: *Myth and Ritual* (1933) and *The Labyrinth: Further Studies in the Relation between Myth and Ritual in the Ancient World* (1935).

A. Alt (1883-1956, *Kleine Schriften zur Geschichte des Volkes Israel* [1953-59]) and his disciples, especially M. Noth (1902-68, *Geschichte Israels* [1950]) and G. von Rad (1901-71, *Theologie des Alten Testament* [1957-60]), studied the combined history of form, tradition, and territory behind the literary works in an attempt to achieve a comprehensive view of the institutions of ancient Israel and the related traditions. Although generally conservative, by following Wellhausen in their critical handling of the biblical texts and the findings of → archaeology, they found themselves in decisive opposition to the work of the American W. F. Albright (*From the Stone Age to Christianity* [1940]) and the Israeli Y. Kaufmann (*The Religion of Israel* [1960]).

Among other things, the new theological thinking of the 1920s revived the discipline of OT theology, which in the 19th century, after such works as *Die biblische Theologie* (vol. 1, 1835), by W. Vatke (1806-82), and *De Godsdienst van Israël* (1869-70), by A. Kuenen (1828-91), had been almost completely merged into the history of Israelite religion, especially under Wellhausen's influence. There thus arose several general presentations that differ widely among themselves, notably those of W. Eichrodt (1933-39), L. Köhler (1936), T. C. Vriezen (1949), O. Procksch (1950), W. Zimmerli (1972), and C. Westermann (1978). In contrast, G. von Rad offered an account of the OT witnesses oriented to the history of the tradition.

1.4. *Present Situation*

It is difficult to give a survey of the situation at the end of the 20th century. New material continues to be discovered, including the texts from Ugarit (1928), Mari (1933), Qumran (1947), and Ebla (1975). The number of scholars and publications grows continually. There is increasing preoccupation with the history and methodology of the discipline itself. A special feature recently is that more attention is being paid to the final form of the OT texts. Various factors combine here: skepticism about often-exaggerated possibilities of getting behind existing texts and into the earlier history; interest in the later history of the original units as these were modified by emendations and redactions; analysis of the structure of the text according to a more or less pronounced literary program; and historical or theological evaluation of the canon. Since scholarly exegesis that gets behind the final form has made invaluable contributions to the understanding of this form (e.g., regarding the historical situation of the Priestly source or of Isaiah 40–55), it would be irresponsible to abandon it on the basis of a postcritical approach. Nevertheless, we must make sure that the methods of such exegesis, which largely correspond to those used for the NT (see 2.2), do not become rigid or an end in themselves. They must remain elastic and continually orient themselves to their object, which is the text of the Bible in all its diversity.

Bibliography: P. R. Ackroyd et al., eds., *The Cambridge History of the Bible* (vols. 1-3; Cambridge, 1963-70) • G. W. Anderson, ed., *Tradition and Interpretation* (Oxford, 1979). • A. Berlin, *Poetics and Interpretation of Biblical Narrative* (Winona Lake, Ind., 1994) • W. Brueggemann, *The Bible and Post-modern Imagination: Texts under Negotiations* (London, 1993) • E. A. Castelli et al., eds., *The Postmodern Bible* (New Haven, 1995) • R. E. Clements, *Century of OT Study* (Guildford, 1976) • F. W. Danker, *Multipurpose Tools for Bible Study* (Minneapolis, 1993) • J. C. Exum, ed., *The New Literary Criticism and the Hebrew Bible* (Sheffield, 1993) • J. A. Fitzmyer, *Scripture, the Soul of Theology* (New York, 1994) • G. Fohrer et al., *Exegese des Alten Testaments. Einführung in die Methodik* (3d ed.; Heidelberg, 1979) • N. K. Gottwald et al., eds., *The Bible and Liberation: Political and Social Hermeneutics* (rev. ed.; London, 1993) • H. F. Hahn, *The OT in Modern Research* (Philadelphia, 1954) • J. H. Hayes, *An Introduction to OT Study* (Nashville, 1979) • E. G. Kraeling, *The OT since the Reformation* (New York, 1955) • H.-J. Kraus, *Geschichte der historisch-kritischen Erforschung des Alten Testaments* (3d ed.; Neukirchen,

1982) • J. D. Levenson, *The Hebrew Bible, the OT, and Historical Criticism* (London, 1993) • H. W. Robinson, ed., *Record and Revelation* (Oxford, 1938) • J. Schreiner, ed., *Einführung in die Methoden der biblischen Exegese* (Würzburg, 1971) • J. Wellhausen, "Kurze Übersicht der Geschichte der alttestamentlichen Wissenschaft" (1878, 1893), *Grundrisse zum Alten Testament* (Munich, 1965) 110-19.

RUDOLF SMEND

2. NT

2.1. *History*

2.1.1. *Early Church*

Scholarly exegesis (i.e., exegesis that reflects on its methods) was already determinative for how the early church handled the NT. The catechetical school of Alexandria in the third century became a center of Christian biblical exegesis (→ Alexandrian Theology). Origen (ca. 185-ca. 254) wrote commentaries there in Greek (e.g., on Matthew) in which he dealt with questions of style and philology as well as giving a running exposition. His allegorical method of exegesis (→ Allegory), which he developed within the framework of the threefold sense of Scripture (literal, moral, and allegorical), proved very influential. Origen and his disciple Dionysius of Alexandria (ca. 200-ca. 265) sometimes made judgments on the authenticity and authorship of NT works (e.g., Hebrews and Revelation). In the main, however, early exegesis was oriented to harmonizing rather than criticism.

In the fourth century the → Antiochian school became prominent. Its most important representatives were Theodore of Mopsuestia (ca. 350-428), Theodoret of Cyrrhus (ca. 393-ca. 460), and, above all, John Chrysostom (ca. 347-407), whose many commentaries put the historical sense of Scripture at the center and yet lay stress on salvation history by means of → typology (→ Theology of History). In the Latin sphere the fame of Jerome (ca. 345-420) outshone all other significant commentators (e.g., Ambrose, Hilary of Poitiers, Augustine). By revising the Old Latin versions, he rendered the service of providing the church with a text that became normative for the West — the Vg (→ Bible Versions). In his commentaries he continued in essentials the expository tradition of the Greek fathers.

2.1.2. *Middle Ages*

The medieval theologians showed little originality in exegesis of the Bible. For the most part they simply reproduced and collected the expositions of the Fathers, working out a formal method by which to do so. In → catenae they assembled quotations, mostly in the form of glosses written in the margin, with the biblical text in the middle. Especially important were the *Glossa ordinaria* of Anselm of Laon (d. 1117) and the *Postillae perpetuae in Vetus et Novum Testamentum* of Nicholas of Lyra (ca. 1270-1349). The accepted basis of exegesis was the schema of the fourfold sense of Scripture: (1) the literal and historical, and then the spiritual, the latter in the three forms of (2) the allegorical sense (dogmatic content), (3) the moral or tropological sense (directions for moral conduct), and (4) the anagogical sense (metaphysical and eschatological mysteries). The strong emphasis on the allegorical sense and the neglect of the historical sense made it possible to find biblical support for prevailing doctrines in a way that now seems arbitrary.

2.1.3. *Humanism*

The age of humanism in the 16th century saw reawakened interest in the original text and languages. Within the span of a few years several important Bible editions appeared, beginning in 1516 with the Greek NT of Erasmus (1469?-1536), followed in 1522 by the six-volume Complutensian Polyglot, prepared by the scholars of the University of Alcalá, which contained the Greek text. Though not so well edited, the text of Erasmus established itself as the textus receptus. Luther's 1522 translation of the NT, which initiated the renderings into the vernacular, which in turn proved so decisive for the → Reformation, was based upon it. The edition of the Greek NT prepared in 1551 by Robert Stephanus added to the chapter divisions of the 13th century the verse numbering that is still accepted and that has made access to the Bible much easier.

2.1.4. *Reformation Theology*

Exposition of Scripture was central in Reformation theology. Luther gained his decisive reforming insight as a professor of biblical exegesis when he engaged in exposition of Romans. The → Reformers put Scripture above church doctrine as "the comprehensive summary, rule, and norm according to which all doctrines should be judged" (heading of the Formula of Concord, Epitome), though they did not abandon the church's → dogma (→ Reformation Principles). Their recognition that the → gospel as witness to God's saving action in Christ is the heart of Scripture (*solus Christus*) directed them to the literal and historic sense and to a basic rejection of the fourfold schema.

Also influential in Protestant exegesis was the principle that Scripture expounds itself, which brought out the need to investigate the language and thinking of Scripture on their own terms and thus implied at the same time the possibility of seeing in what way they differ from those of the present.

Protestant → orthodoxy, however, made little use of this possibility. It regarded Scripture as a self-enclosed doctrinal system that was free from all contradiction, the congruence of which with the dogmatic teaching of the → church could be presupposed, and from which proofs (*dicta probantia*, i.e., proof texts) could be drawn for the various topoi of teaching.

2.1.5. *Modern Period*

One can speak of a modern exegesis only when, without direct reference to the church's teaching tradition, one finds in the biblical writings testimonies to a very different intellectual and cultural world and tries to bring out its distinctiveness by the philosophical and historical methods that are customary in the secular world. This type of historical criticism developed exclusively in European → Protestantism apart from some abortive beginnings in the post-Tridentine → Catholicism of the 17th century (e.g., R. Simon; → Trent, Council of). English → deism provided the intellectual presuppositions in the 17th century, with its demand that the Bible should be fundamentally treated like all other human writings. The 18th century → Enlightenment helped with its criticism of the precedence accorded to church doctrine over → reason. In the 19th and 20th centuries there then followed the sometimes stormy process of materially developing the historicocritical method in close concert with general historical studies, → archaeology, the → history of religion, and philology. In the present context we can mention only a few milestones in this development.

Textual criticism, after some significant achievements in the 18th century (J. A. Bengel, J. J. Wettstein), reached an initial high point with the great critical editions of the Greek text in the 19th century (K. Tischendorf, B. F. Westcott and F. J. A. Hort). The program of a → biblical theology that was detached from → dogmatics and that presented the ideas of the individual biblical authors was formulated for the first time at the beginning of the 19th century by J. P. Gabler (1753-1826). The two-source theory greatly clarified the problem of the relation of the three Synoptic Gospels (K. Lachmann, F. Weisse). On this view Mark served as a written source for Matthew and Luke along with a collection of sayings of Jesus (→ Q). F. C. Baur (1792-1860) and the Tübingen school reconstructed primitive Christian history on the basis of Hegel's philosophy of history. A. Jülicher (1857-1938) freed the → parables of Jesus from traditional allegorical interpretations and thus opened the way for their more objective understanding in terms of the work and message of Jesus (C. H.

Dodd, J. Jeremias). Research into → Judaism (E. Schürer, P. Billerbeck, A. Schlatter) promoted an understanding of the NT in relation to its historic setting. The rise of the → history-of-religions school brought to light the involvement of primitive Christianity in the intellectual world of → Hellenism (J. Weiß, W. Bousset, A. Deissmann). The results of inquiry into the historical → Jesus were especially important. D. F. Strauss made a new evaluation of the Gospels as sources with his thesis that mythological motifs color their depiction of Jesus, so that we are not to measure them by the criteria of the modern understanding of history (→ Myth). W. Wrede (1859-1906) followed him with the argument that we are to read the Gospels primarily not as historical documents but as expressions of the faith of the community. J. Weiß (1863-1914) and A. Schweitzer (1875-1965) revolutionized the picture of Jesus by setting him against the background of contemporary Jewish → apocalyptic. The application of form criticism to the NT (K. L. Schmidt, M. Dibelius, R. Bultmann) opened up insights into the nature and development of the preliterary tradition.

2.1.6. *Present Situation*

Two factors are predominant at the turn of the 21st century. First, the historicocritical method is no longer a European-Protestant phenomenon alone but is well on the way to prevailing everywhere. It is worth noting that Roman Catholic exegesis, since the encyclical *Divino afflante Spiritu* (1943) and the dogmatic constitution *Dei Verbum* of → Vatican II lowered the barriers set up by the teaching office, has opened itself up to modern exegesis without reserve and made vital contributions to it. Ecumenical cooperation of biblical scholars is manifesting itself in numerous projects such as handbooks and commentary series.

Second, there has been a common recognition that exegesis directed solely to historical criticism cannot do justice to the central dimension of the NT texts as witnesses to faith that can also awaken → faith. This insight has led to a concern to strengthen again the relation of exegesis to faith and church doctrine that has been neglected since the Enlightenment, for example, by taking note of the patristic tradition of exegesis and the history of the actual influence of the NT.

2.2. *Methods and Questions*

2.2.1. *Textual Criticism*

Textual criticism tries to reconstruct a text that is as close as possible to the original by comparing and evaluating the ancient → Bible manuscripts. The transmission of the NT has been much better than that of the OT. One might say that it is better by far

than that of any other book of antiquity. Modern text editions (e.g., E. Nestle and K. Aland, *Novum Testamentum Graece* [27th ed., 1993]) rest upon the critical evaluation of more than 5,600 manuscripts from the period between the 2nd and the 16th centuries and must be very close to the original. Nevertheless, some details are still debatable.

2.2.2. *Literary Criticism*

Literary criticism aims to clarify the literary characteristics and structure of a text or passage, examining its composition, distinctiveness, and consistency, or, in case of inconsistency, its underlying literary sources. The final aspect, source criticism, is particularly important in NT work. It has been used especially with the → Synoptic Gospels, the Gospel of → John, and → Revelation. It has also been applied to some of Paul's epistles that many scholars do not regard as literary units. Generally, however, a shift of emphasis can be observed in literary criticism. Source criticism is more and more supplemented (or even replaced) by the application of new methods, such as discourse analysis, linguistics, and reader-response criticism.

2.2.3. *Form Criticism*

From the relation between a linguistic unit and a certain sociohistorical context, form criticism draws conclusions about the origin of a text, the history of its development, and its content. Its primary, though not exclusive, value is in providing methodological access to preliterary traditions. Basic is the fixing of the genre of a unit, that is, its placing in a group of traditions with similar features (e.g., hymns, proverbs, or miracle stories). Basic, too, is the question of the setting of this genre — the question of the social and cultural conditions and situations to which it owes its origin and within which it has its function (e.g., → worship, → catechesis, or missionary proclamation). Historical study of the tradition concerns itself with the prestages of the unit, trying to reconstruct how it began and how it reached its final stage. Form criticism also deals with the tradition in general, studying the development of ideas and groups of ideas that cannot be put in fixed genres but may be understood only in the interrelationship of certain words and concepts. At first form criticism dealt only with the Gospels, but it soon was extended to the whole of the NT. Its possibilities for research into the history of primitive Christianity have not yet been fully exhausted.

2.2.4. *Redaction Criticism*

Redaction criticism has developed during recent decades out of form criticism and literary criticism. It examines the history of a linguistic unit from its first written form to the final written version from the special standpoint of the specific forces and factors that shaped its development. Beginning with the changes that an originally isolated piece (e.g., a miracle story or a → hymn) went through when it was put in the context of a larger literary work, it proceeds to assess the contributions of authors, collectors, and redactors, as well as their various relationships. Since 1950 it has provided important insights especially into the nature of the Gospels. It has thus far been applied only in a limited way to the other NT writings. Several scholars are at work, however, on redaction criticism of the Pauline corpus. Their initial thesis is that redactors have put together the present epistles from shorter letters by the apostle himself.

2.2.5. Linguistic and Conceptual Research

Linguistic and conceptual research tries to do justice to the complex linguistic character of the NT. Its basic language is Koine, the everyday Greek of the Hellenistic age (→ Greek Language). Yet there constantly shines through a Semitic background that is partly shaped by the language of the LXX and partly by the Palestinian linguistic and conceptual world of Jesus and the → primitive Christian community. Various dictionaries, especially the monumental ten-volume *TWNT* (1933-79; ET *TDNT* [1964-76]), have made accessible the linguistic research of the middle decades of the 20th century.

2.2.6. Comparative Religion

Comparison helps us to see analogies and developmental connections between the NT texts and similar traditions in the surrounding world of religion. Three spheres have been of special interest: the Hellenistic → mystery religions; → Gnosticism, our knowledge of which the findings at → Nag Hammadi in Egypt have greatly enhanced; and the Jewish sectarian community of → Qumran, whose writings, discovered in 1947, have considerably broadened our picture of Judaism in the NT period (→ New Testament Era, History of).

2.2.7. NT Theology

NT theology offers a comprehensive view and interpretation of the theological statements and ideas of the NT. Its indispensable basis is critical reconstruction of the process of transmission and the lines of development. If it is to make good its claim to be theological, however, it must not be content to stop at this point but must press on to a convincing theological evaluation.

Bibliography: R. E. Brown, *The Critical Meaning of the Bible* (New York, 1981) • E. J. Epp and G. W. MacRae, eds., *The NT and Its Modern Interpreters* (Philadelphia, 1989) • H. J. Genthe, *Kleine Geschichte der neutesta-*

mentlichen Wissenschaft (Göttingen, 1977) • R. A. Harrisville and W. Sundberg, *The Bible in Modern Culture: Theology and Historical-Critical Method from Spinoza to Käsemann* (Grand Rapids, 1995) • A. Hilgenfeld, *Kanon und Kritik des Neuen Testaments in ihrer geschichtlichen Ausbildung und Gestaltung* (Halle, 1863) • A. M. Hunter, *Interpreting the NT, 1900-1950* (London, 1951) • K. Koch, *Was ist Formgeschichte? Methoden der Bibelexegese* (5th ed.; Neukirchen, 1989) • W. G. Kümmel, *The NT: The History of the Investigation of Its Problems* (Nashville, 1972) • O. Merk, *Biblische Theologie des Neuen Testaments in ihrer Anfangszeit* (Marburg, 1972) • S. C. Neill, *The Interpretation of the NT, 1861-1961* (London, 1964) • A. Schweitzer, *The Quest of the Historical Jesus: A Critical Study of Its Progress from Reimarus to Wrede* (New York, 1968; orig. pub., 1906).

JÜRGEN ROLOFF

Exemption

In → church law the term "exemption" denotes the exclusion of persons, corporations, or territories from the normally expected associations or structures (→ Church Government) and their placement under higher or specially appointed officials (→ Jurisdiction, Ecclesiastical).

In the Middle Ages exemptions were very important for particular → orders and congregations, for such action placed them directly under the → pope, and their heads were not subject to local → bishops. This arrangement favored the development of monasteries, protected the property of the orders, and facilitated their spread. The ramifications became one of the causes of the → Reformation. Modern states have sought to end exemptions; because of → secularization, they have been able to achieve considerable success in this effort.

Since the Council of → Trent, the → Roman Catholic Church has successively set exemptions under "pontifical right" as distinct from "diocesan right" (1983, CIC 589) or established a "particular church" within the territory of another church on the basis of personal factors (372.2; → Military Chaplaincy). The pope can still "exempt institutes of consecrated life from the governance of local ordinaries" (591), but in the future "as a rule exempt dioceses are no longer to exist" (431.2).

→ Diocese

Bibliography: R. W. Crooker, "Exemption, History of," *NCE* 5.116-17 • H. E. Feine, *Kirchliche Rechtsgeschichte*, vol. 1, *Die katholische Kirche* (4th ed.; Cologne,

1964) • J. D. O'Brien, *The Exemption of Religious in Church Law* (Milwaukee, Wis., 1943) • R. Ombres, "*Iusta Autonomia Vitae*. Religious in the Local Church," *CleR* 69 (1984) 310-19.

HEINER GROTE†

Exequies

The word "exequies" means "accompaniments." In a general sense it is used especially in the → Roman Catholic Church, the → Orthodox Church, and the → Anglican Communion (but not Protestant churches) for → funeral rites up to and including the burial.

In a narrower sense "exequies" is a musical term for the music accompanying such rites. Here we might mention particularly the many → requiems and the *Musikalische Exequien* of Heinrich Schütz (1636). Exequies in this sense mostly include pieces from the Mass for the dead, and only rarely those of the Burial Office alone.

ALBERT MAUDER†

Exercises, Spiritual → Spirituality

Existential Theology

1. Term
2. Existential Theology and
   Existential Interpretation
3. Development and Impact
4. Problems

1. Term

Existential theology is the name of a 20th-century theological movement that is informed by certain commitments within philosophical → existentialism. As such, existential theology is theological reflection on human existence and its struggle with radical freedom, alienation, anxiety, choice, and responsibility. This struggle is most evident in the human wrestling with the proclamation of Jesus as the Christ as it is described in the works of Paul, → Augustine, M. → Luther, B. → Pascal, and S. → Kierkegaard, and as it has become a feature of the intellectual history of the West.

As an independent theological trend, existential theology is apparent in the debates between K. → Barth and R. Bultmann within → dialectical theology, which rejected the syntheses of so-called → Culture Protestantism and the idealistic systems of → liberal theology. Existential theology pursued an integration of philosophical and philological methodology. Paralleling Barth's influence on Reformed theology, it also flowed over denominational boundaries as a movement of renewal in Lutheran theology, and before and after World War II it had ecumenical influence as a paradigm of German-speaking theology.

2. Existential Theology and
   Existential Interpretation

Existential theology may be presented in terms of the program of the → demythologization of the NT advocated by Rudolf Bultmann (1884-1976). Existential interpretation, a basic procedure of existential theology (→ Exegesis, Biblical), takes concrete form here as a procedure of biblical → hermeneutics. The problems posed in Bultmann's historicocritical exegesis were shaped by self-critical motifs in liberal theology (W. Herrmann [1846-1922]) and by an independent reading of Søren Kierkegaard (1813-55). The new outlook was clarified in discussion of Karl Barth's commentary on Romans (1918, 1921, and successive editions). Bultmann made the existential → ontology of Martin Heidegger's *Being and Time* (1927) the theoretical and methodological framework for his NT theology.

In existential theology, one seeks to investigate the self-understanding of the biblical authors through categories of existential analysis. These categories include "being-in-the-world," "historicity," "being-toward-death," "bad faith," "authenticity," and "thrownness." In the situation of the moment of decision, human existence can be authentic or inauthentic in its response to the → kerygma. In this situation God is historically present and active both now and in the past. The ancient → worldview of the authors of the NT, however, must be demythologized so that its truth may be manifested in modern conditions. This step makes way for the claim of the text that hearers should achieve a new understanding of existence in the light of the proclamation of Jesus. Bultmann thus called existential interpretation of the NT a consistent application of the Pauline and Lutheran doctrine of → justification to the field of → epistemology.

3. Development and Impact

3.1. Karl Jaspers (1883-1969) and other philosophers were at work at the same time as Heidegger (1889-1976), and other concepts of existential theology were present as well as those of Bultmann (e.g., that of F. Buri). Their development, interrupted by World War II, was greatly influenced by the demythologization debate. In Bultmann's own school there was fear of dissolving the saving acts (Christ's → incarnation, atoning death, and → resurrection) in the kerygma. The question of the historical Jesus reappeared — raised, for example, by Ernst Käsemann, Günther Bornkamm, and Hans Conzelmann; Bultmann had thought that only the mere fact of Jesus' existence had to be presupposed in the kerygma.

At the end of the 1950s the questions of interpretation broadened into the debate about hermeneutics and moved also into → dogmatics (E. Fuchs, G. Ebeling). There was a certain approximation to Barth (e.g., by H. Ott) and a renewed link to the later Heidegger. In one branch of the school the methodological components became less prominent in favor of direct communication (proclamation) from → revelation, while in another branch existential interpretation no longer halted at the mythological remnant of the concept of God but now offered a definition of God as the source of our security and our obligation to others (H. Braun).

Other theological systems simply took over the Heideggerian motif that the relation of existence to God (being itself) differs from its relation to the world (mere being). This distinction is less clear in Friedrich Gogarten (1887-1967; → Person, Personalism) than in, for example, Paul → Tillich (1886-1965), who, with his method of correlation, developed the basic relation to God (the ground of being, which affects us unconditionally) in a universal essence-existence schema.

3.2. Though this development of existential theology was strongly influenced by the common questions of philosophy and by Protestant theology in the German-speaking sphere, its impact was not limited to this field. Karl → Rahner (1904-84) cast a mantle of the "supernatural existential" around a → Thomistic → anthropology and an ethics of prevenient → grace. This position provided new points of contact with international Roman Catholic theology, which otherwise was more strongly influenced by French existentialism (G. Marcel [1889-1973]). An approach to French Protestantism was made by Paul Ricoeur, who continued the demythologization debate under changed conditions in a "conflict of interpretations" between hermeneutics and → structuralism. We also find the impact of existential theology in the form of similar fundamental theological reflection on Scripture, as well as in recent developments in the United States (D. Tracy, J. D. Crossan), along with independent approaches of a more strongly transcendental nature under the influence of persons as diverse as Tillich and Alfred North Whitehead (J. Macquarrie).

4. Problems

Existential theology makes a universal theological principle out of a primal Christian experience, namely, the discontinuity between believing and unbelieving existence. Some material continuities are presupposed, however, the breakdown of which constitutes the present problem. The crucial relating of exegesis to dogmatics brings to light the unclear status of the existentials and the semantic deficiency of a theology dependent on individual word-meanings, so that a theologically resigned → positivism threatens to hold sway in biblical exegesis. The exegetical poverty of existential theology brings with it the parallel development in dogmatics of a myth of radical decision that bears a striking similarity to → Gnostic views, to an interpretation of which existential theology was once attracted (H. Jonas).

We see here in theology the tendency of existentialism to handle logical distinctions as though they were things (e.g., nothingness, authenticity) instead of analyzing them at different levels (e.g., ontic/ontological, existentiell/existential). Such analyses do presuppose contents such as existential theology has undoubtedly opened up for the modern world, but they also show that asserting experienced discontinuity cannot be the end of theoretical construction but can be the beginning of a deeper theological grasp of reality in the light of this experience (cf. deconstruction and theology in the United States). Under the pressure of modern problems (e.g., the environmental crisis), the question arises whether existential theology can explicate theologically its implied witness to God the Creator (with new intentions and new possibilities of structuring) or whether such a contribution is beyond its methods and concepts.

Bibliography: T. J. J. ALTIZER et al., *Deconstruction and Theology* (New York, 1982) • K. BARTH, *CD* III/3 • H. BERKHOF, *Two Hundred Years of Theology* (Grand Rapids, 1989) • D. BONHOEFFER, *Act and Being* (Minneapolis, 1996); idem, *The Cost of Discipleship* (New York, 1995) • C. E. BROWN, *The Self in Time: Retrieving Existential Theology and Freud* (Lanham, Md., 1997) • J. D. CROSSAN, *In Parables: The Challenge of the Historical Jesus* (New York, 1973) • G. EBELING, *Dogmatik des christlichen Glaubens* (3 vols.; 2d ed.; Tübingen, 1982) • L. GILKEY, *Message and Existence* (New York, 1979) • C. D. HARDWICK, *Events of Grace: Naturalism, Existentialism, and Theology* (New York, 1996) • E. HAU-SCHILDT, *Rudolf Bultmanns Predigten. Existentiale Interpretation und lutherisches Erbe* (Marburg, 1989) • W. HERBERG, ed., *Four Existentialist Theologians: A*

Reader from the Works of Jacques Maritain, Nicolas Berdyaev, Martin Buber, and Paul Tillich (Westport, Conn., 1975) • K. Jaspers and R. Bultmann, *Myth and Christianity: An Inquiry into the Possibility of Religion without Myth* (New York, 1958) • M. Kwiran, *Index to Literature on Barth, Bonhoeffer, and Bultmann* (Basel, 1977) • J. Macquarrie, *Heidegger and Christianity* (New York, 1999); idem, *Principles of Christian Theology* (London, 1975) • P. Ricoeur, *The Conflict of Interpretations: Essays on Hermeneutics* (Evanston, Ill., 1974) • D. E. Roberts, *Existentialism and Religious Belief* (New York, 1957) • J. M. Robinson and J. B. Cobb Jr., eds., *The Later Heidegger and Theology* (New York, 1963); idem, eds., *The New Hermeneutic* (New York, 1964) • W. Schmithals, *An Introduction to the Theology of Rudolf Bultmann* (Minneapolis, 1968) • D. Soelle, *Christ the Representative: An Essay in Theology after the "Death of God"* (Philadelphia, 1967); idem, *Political Theology* (Philadelphia, 1974) • H. Thielicke, *Modern Faith and Thought* (Grand Rapids, 1990) • P. Tillich, *Systematic Theology* (3 vols.; Chicago, 1951-63).

Wolfgang Nethöfel and Scott H. Moore

Existentialism

1. Term
2. Forms and Emphases
3. Discussion and Impact

1. Term

"Existentialism" names a philosophical movement that flourished primarily on the European continent from the 1920s through the 1970s. Its direct roots, however, are to be found in the philosophical work of Søren → Kierkegaard (1813-55) and Friedrich → Nietzsche (1844-1900), and its ultimate origins in the thought of → Augustine (354-430; → Augustine's Theology). The label "existentialist" was frequently disavowed by its most characteristic proponents Martin Heidegger (1889-1976), Jean-Paul Sartre (1905-80), and Karl Jaspers (1883-1969). Its most vibrant expression was found in the response to human suffering and the experience of meaninglessness brought about by the first and second world wars.

Though never a distinct philosophical school, the term names a common philosophical commitment toward understanding the human being as an existing individual who must respond authentically to the challenges presented by lived human existence. Sartre's famous dictum "existence precedes essence" identifies a philosophical posture that embraces radical human freedom and privileges the particular existence of an individual over against preestablished norms and "essences." As such, existentialist writers reject all forms of → idealism, → rationalism, and → positivism.

2. Forms and Emphases

Existentialist authors have emphasized the dilemmas surrounding human alienation, → anxiety, choice, and → responsibility. The quest for "authentic existence" is a hallmark of existentialist thought, though its advocates differ greatly on how this commitment to authentic existence is to be understood. They may be theists (Kierkegaard) or atheists (Nietzsche, Sartre), pessimistic about human prospects (Albert Camus [1913-60]) or optimistic (Gabriel Marcel [1889-1973]; → Optimism and Pessimism). Though they predominantly focused on the problems of the individual, some, such as Jaspers, emphasized the role of the community. Some (Paul → Tillich [1886-1965]) fled from the Nazis during World War II; others (Heidegger) supported National Socialism.

In the 19th century, the works of Kierkegaard and Nietzsche stand out as exemplary investigations. Their works had a profound influence on 20th-century thought. Both Kierkegaard and Nietzsche offer strong critiques of society and conventional understandings of morality, religion, and human significance. Though Kierkegaard was a Christian and Nietzsche proclaimed "the death of God" (→ God Is Dead Theology), both men sought to overcome "the herd instinct" (Nietzsche's phrase) by urging human beings to live authentically. In this light, Russian authors such as Fyodor Dostoyevsky (1821-81) and Nicolas Berdyaev (1874-1948) can be seen as existentialists. In the 20th century Heidegger and Sartre are commonly seen as leading existentialists. In *Being and Time,* Heidegger sought to present an existential analysis of *Dasein* — the particularly human way of being human in a particular time and place. Sartre's *Being and Nothingness* is often read as a response to Heidegger.

In the 20th century existentialism has frequently been connected with → phenomenology — indeed, some of the leading figures of existentialism (Heidegger, Sartre, Maurice Merleau-Ponty [1908-61]) were also phenomenologists. Their existentialist commitment to understanding the existing individual is complemented by the phenomenological commitment to describing the intentional object of consciousness, not as what one expects to appear, but as what actually does appear.

Existentialism, however, has most often been presented through fiction, particularly through novels. Given the existentialist commitment to understanding the existent human being in his or her rooted and situated particularity, fiction is the most appropriate genre for presenting this philosophical content. Exemplary instances of existentialist fiction are Camus's *Stranger* and *Plague;* Sartre's *No Exit, The Flies,* and *Nausea;* Simone de Beauvoir's *Mandarins;* Milan Kundera's *Unbearable Lightness of Being;* and Walker Percy's *Moviegoer* and *Last Gentleman.*

3. Discussion and Impact

In the European tradition of Continental philosophy, no philosophical movement was more important for 20th-century thought than existentialism. This impact was especially felt in literature, → theology, → ontology, and → ethics. In Britain and the United States, existentialism exerted enormous influence on popular culture and thought in the post–World War II era through the 1960s. In the 1980s and 1990s, however, the appeal and influence of existentialism waned.

Several key factors may explain this decline. First, many existentialist authors (Sartre, de Beauvoir) affirmed → Marxism as a political alternative to democratic → capitalism. Through the 1960s Marxism indeed seemed a viable option for life and understanding in ways that it did not in the succeeding decades. Second, a diverse new generation of intellectuals took aim at the alleged existentialist naïveté about realism, the individual, power, language, and community. Preeminent among these critics were Michel Foucault, Jacques Derrida, Emmanuel Lévinas, Julia Kristeva, Jacques Lacan, Charles Taylor, Alasdair MacIntyre, and Jürgen Habermas. Third, in the years after Heidegger's death in 1976, the publication of much of his early books and lectures led many to reconsider the "existentialist" reading of *Being and Time.* Since this work was frequently read as the most important existentialist essay, this reconsideration has had significant implications for existentialism as a movement. Fourth, with the demise of Communism in 1989, much political and ethical philosophy has turned to focus on the questions surrounding → liberalism and communitarianism in ways that make the existentialist focus on the individual appear inadequate to meet the needs of a new day. Fifth, some attribute this decline of interest in existentialism to the relative economic prosperity of the North at the end of the 20th century and also to the passing of the generations that had an intimate memory of the world wars.

Bibliography: S. DE BEAUVOIR, *The Mandarins* (Cleveland, 1956); idem, *The Second Sex* (New York, 1993; orig. pub., 1949) • A. CAMUS, *The Myth of Sisyphus* (New York, 1991; orig. pub., 1948); idem, *The Stranger* (New York, 1993; orig. pub., 1942) • D. COOPER, *Existentialism* (2d ed.; Oxford, 1999) • F. DOSTOYEVSKY, *The Brothers Karamazov* (New York, 1999; orig. pub., 1880) • M. HEIDEGGER, *Being and Time* (Albany, N.Y., 1996; orig. pub., 1927) • S. KIERKEGAARD, *Concluding Unscientific Postscript* (Princeton, 1992; orig. pub., 1846); idem, *Fear and Trembling* (Princeton, 1983; orig. pub., 1843); idem, *Philosophical Fragments* (Princeton, 1985; orig. pub., 1844) • J. MACQUARRIE, *Existentialism* (New York, 1972) • G. MARCEL, *Being and Having: An Existentialist Diary* (New York, 1965; orig. pub., 1935); idem, *The Philosophy of Existentialism* (New York, 1965; orig. pub., 1947) • F. NIETZSCHE, *Werke* (Cologne, 1979) • W. PERCY, *The Last Gentleman* (New York, 1999; orig. pub., 1966); idem, *The Moviegoer* (New York, 1998; orig. pub., 1961) • J.-P. SARTRE, *The Age of Reason* (New York, 1992; orig. pub., 1945); idem, *Being and Nothingness* (New York, 1994; orig. pub., 1953); idem, *No Exit and Three Other Plays* (New York, 1989) • P. TILLICH, *The Courage to Be* (2d ed.; New Haven, 2000; orig. pub., 1952)..

SCOTT H. MOORE

Exodus, Book of

1. The Book
2. Sources
3. Exodus Motifs in the OT

The Book of Exodus, the second in the Bible, tells of the God who promises (chaps. 3–4; 6), saves (14–15; cf. 16–17), and commands (20ff.). It also depicts the person of → Moses, bringing together and interpreting such varied events as the exodus (1–15), the desert wanderings (16–18), and the revelation at → Sinai (19–31).

1. The Book

The family of the patriarch Jacob/Israel becomes a nation in Egypt (chap. 1), but it is forced to labor in the building of the supply cities Pithom and Rameses (v. 11, the only direct historical reference in the book, which points probably to the 13th century B.C.). Against this at best vague background the motif of infanticide forms a legendary framework for the saving of the newly born future deliverer (2:1-10). Chaps. 2–4 and 18 contain reminiscences of relations with the Midianites. Moses marries the daughter of "the priest of Midian," whose sacrificial feast the Israelites later share (18:12). Exodus 3 tells how Moses received his commission at the burning bush in the desert, insisting in this way that Yahweh is not an Egyptian god (see 5:2). With the declaration of 3:12 ("I will be with you") comes the explanation of the divine name in 3:14 — "I am who I am" (i.e., "I will be present and at work"). The parallel account of the call (6 P) is a confirmation after an initial complaint and accusation (5:21-23). The dealings with Pharaoh (5), in spite of the plagues (7–11), which culminate with the sparing of Israel on the night of the → Passover (12), are not finally successful. Israel is allowed to go (12:31-32) but is pursued as it flees (14:5; cf. 2:15). Deliverance comes only when Yahweh throws "horse and rider" "into the sea" (see the Song of Miriam, 15:21, also 14:27b J, and the Song of Moses, 15:1-18).

The Red Sea deliverance forms the transition from the Egypt tradition to the wilderness tradition (15:22–18:27; cf. 13:18), which in individual stories tells how the people were rescued from hunger, thirst, and their enemies. The meeting on the "mountain of God" (18:5), with the sacrifices and the judicial arrangements, anticipates or prepares the way for the events at Sinai. There the revelation of God with natural accompaniments (19, esp. vv. 16-18) precedes the solemn ratification of the fellowship of God and his people. The representatives of Israel are allowed to see God and to eat and drink in his presence (24:10-11, though cf. 33:20). The fellowship brought into force by a blood rite (24:6, 8a) seems only later to have been construed as a → covenant (19:3-8; 24:3, 7-8; 34).

→ Promise and deliverance precede the giving of the → law in the → Decalogue and the Book of the Covenant (20–23), along with the so-called cultic Decalogue (34). The legal statutes do not establish fellowship but result from it. After chap. 32 (with the golden calf incident) has excluded the depicting of God in terms of the second commandment, chap. 33 asks afresh about the mode of God's presence. The comprehensive priestly cultic laws (25–31) and their observance (35–40) have as their goal the presence of God among his people in a → sanctuary (29:43-46; 40:34-38).

2. Sources

Exodus gives evidence of extremely varying traditions and literary strands (→ Pentateuch). The motifs of chaps. 3 and 6 (P) are essentially parallel, with Exodus 3 itself consisting of two threads (J, E). The plague series (7–11), as well as the story of the Red Sea deliverance (14), can clearly be divided into two strata (J, P), with certain textual sections remaining uncertain (E? redaction?). The story of the → theophany (19:16-25)

also unites two different accounts (J and E, over against 24:15b-18 P). Hence the sources (J, E, with P clearly discernible from them) can be traced through the Book of Exodus, even though they are by no means equally distributed or even everywhere discernible; moreover, one must also assume the presence of extended addenda (esp. in the legal collections, also in chaps. 4; 13; 32–34, and elsewhere).

3. Exodus Motifs in the OT

The OT presents the exodus as the basic act of election (Hos. 12:9; 13:4; Exod. 20:2; Ps. 114:1-2, etc.), as "redemption" (see Exod. 6:6; Deut. 7:8, etc.). Each year at Passover it is objectified in such a way that earlier generations are identified with those of the present: He "spared *our* houses" (Exod. 12:27). The prophets can relativize the tradition (Amos 9:7; cf. Isa. 43:18-19; Jer. 23:7-8), but they can also change it into the promise of a new future surpassing all the past: "You shall not go out in haste" (Isa. 52:12, as distinct from Exod. 12:11; cf. Isa. 40:3-4, 10; 43:19-20; Mic. 2:12-13, etc.). The fellowship meal that God had with his people at Sinai (Exod. 24:11) is to be repeated in the future as a meal for all peoples (Isa. 24:23; 25:6-8).

Bibliography: Commentaries: B. CHILDS (OTL; Philadelphia, 1974) • G. W. COATS (FOTL; Grand Rapids, 1999) chaps. 1–18 • C. HOUTMAN (HCOT; Kampen, 1993-96) • B. JACOB (Hoboken, N.J., 1992) • M. NOTH (OTL; Philadelphia, 1962) • W. H. SCHMIDT (BKAT; Neukirchen, 1995-99).

Other works: G. FOHRER, *Überlieferung und Geschichte des Exodus* (Berlin, 1964) • H. GRESSMANN, *Mose und seine Zeit* (Göttingen, 1913) • E. OSSWALD, *Das Bild des Mose* (Berlin, 1962) • W. H. SCHMIDT, *Exodus, Sinai und Mose* (3d ed.; Darmstadt, 1995) • W. H. SCHMIDT, with H. DELKURT and A. GRAUPNER, *Die Zehn Gebote im Rahmen alttestamentlicher Ethik* (Darmstadt, 1993) • M. VERVENNE, ed., *Studies in the Book of Exodus* (Louvain, 1996) • P. WEIMAR and E. ZENGER, *Exodus. Geschichten und Geschichte der Befreiung Israels* (2d ed.; Stuttgart, 1979).

WERNER H. SCHMIDT

Exorcism

1. In Religious Studies
2. In Practical Theology
   2.1. Practical Development
   2.2. The Humanities
   2.3. Modern Evaluation and Practice

1. In Religious Studies

The term "exorcism" refers to a rite of healing intended to expel things or beings that supposedly have penetrated and possessed a person from the alternate reality, causing physical or spiritual → suffering. Taking place in → ecstatic trance, exorcism represents contact with the realm of the holy, and the rites thus have a sacred character.

Exorcisms occur in religions from every type of society. Among aborigines and bushmen spirit animals or other noxious beings leave objects behind in those possessed by them, and the medicine man sucks them out. According to the nomadic cattle herdsmen of Africa (e.g., Nuer and Dinka), the invaders are the unpacified spirits of the dead, the exorcism of which involves a sacrifice. Among Siberian reindeer herdsmen (e.g., Tungus [or Evenk] and Goldi), the shaman drives out the evil spirit in the setting of a clan feast, and helping spirits then take it to the underworld. The magicians of South American horticultural Indians (e.g., Sharanahua) use songs to expel harmful substances deriving from their enemies. Among peasants in Thailand and Japan, the exorcism needs to force the evil spirit to reveal its name and intention.

Although ethnographic observations confirm the success of exorcisms, psychiatry regards them as psychopathology. In a more modern view exorcism changes private conflicts therapeutically into ritually accessible symptoms by means of an ecstatic trance.

→ Demons

Bibliography: W. DAVIS, *Dojo: Magic and Exorcism in Modern Japan* (Stanford, Calif., 1980) • M. ELIADE, *Shamanism: Archaic Techniques of Ecstasy* (Princeton, 1964) • F. D. GOODMAN, *How about Demons? Possession and Exorcism in the Modern World* (Bloomington, Ind., 1988).

FELICITAS D. GOODMAN

2. In Practical Theology

Exorcism, both Christian and non-Christian, rests on the basic experience that life in its various forms and processes is often inescapably seized by evil suprahuman forces and powers. There is structural → evil (certain political relations, life-threatening social conduct of a → society, etc.) and also personal evil (→ depression, severe chronic illness, destructive and antisocial urges, etc.). The facts are undeniable. The only point is that the humanities and → theology offer different explanations and interpretations, which influence the way of dealing with them.

2.1. *Practical Development*

Part of the common tradition of the Christian churches is the confession that the work of Jesus Christ (→ Christology) brings basic liberation from evil. This liberation is given by the proclamation of the message of redemption and by → baptism, and it is accepted by → faith in Christ's redeeming work. After the model of Jesus and the → primitive Christian community, there developed in the churches of both East and West, along with the central acts of Christian faith, secondary aids to the suppression of the so-called evil forces and powers, which were often thought of personally as the → devil and → demons. Such secondary aids were blessings through the use of crosses, → relics, candles, and holy → water, as well as → prayer, penance (→ Penitence), → fasting, withdrawal from the world, → anointings, and finally exorcism.

Two basic forms of exorcism may be distinguished. The first is *deprecation,* or praying for the experience of redemption from evil in the name of Jesus; the second, *imprecation,* or commanding the devil to depart in the name of Jesus.

The official → liturgical book of the → Roman Catholic Church, the Rituale Romanum of 1999, contains an exorcism (deprecation) prayer. The petitioner asks God in prayer to deliver the person from evil, followed by an imperative (imprecation) formulation for Satan to depart before the power of faith, the prayer of the church, and the sign of the cross of Jesus Christ. This imperative part may not be spoken without the preceding petition, although it may be omitted entirely. The practice continues in the → Anglican Communion. It is also found in some Protestant churches, though not in a strict ritual or official form. Liberal Protestantism after F. → Schleiermacher (1768-1834) almost completely banished it from the churches of the Lutheran tradition. It still occurs in the → Orthodox Church, but it is not prescribed by church law or the liturgy. Exorcisms occur in the Byzantine Rite for catechumens, as also among the western Syrians (→ Syrian Orthodox Church) and Maronites. Deprecation elements appear in almost all Eastern baptismal rites.

2.2. *The Humanities*

The humanities assert that possession, or the phenomenon of possession, is neither uniform nor fully established empirically. So-called possession, or the suffering that patients experience and that many around them interpret as such, is regarded today as borderline sickness with traits of → neurosis and → psychosis. Attempts are made to analyze stories of exorcism in terms of physical traumas (e.g., brain damage), severe and untreated frustration, and early forms of mental illness. In explanation, appeal is made to split personality, to efforts by oneself and others to explain experienced evil realities (e.g., as a projection of the religious environment), or to the parapsychological abilities of the patient or exorcist. S. Freud (1856-1939) in 1922 viewed reactions of possession as the effects of rejected, repressed desires, and C. G. Jung (1875-1961) regarded them as primal collective symbols of the powerful forces that can attack and possess us.

2.3. Modern Evaluation and Practice

On a Christian view of the redeeming work of Jesus Christ, exorcism cannot be a → magical device but can only be prayer in the name of Jesus for severely suffering persons who cannot help themselves and especially feel that they are possessed by some evil reality. Furthermore, this prayer will at most involve a strengthening and a renewal of belief that in spite of the evil reality, the sick and suffering may expect redemption from evil and a fundamental restoration of health. In this religious context it may be helpful (along the lines of Lat. *benedico*, "speak well of, bless") to assure the sufferers of redemption from evil. The actual evil or concrete need should, for both theological and psychotherapeutic reasons, be addressed and articulated (rather than repressed) in such a way that it "departs." A demonic-satanic explanation may achieve momentary release, but the so-called induction or reinforcement effect is to be viewed as essentially more harmful.

For the monastic fathers and spiritual advisers of the Eastern and Western churches, the "discernment of spirits" (Gk. *diakrisis pneumatōn*, Lat. *discretio spirituum*) is the most important quality in dealing with evil, that is, the ability to distinguish and name good and evil forces. Hence qualified pastoral-psychological counseling, as well as medical psychiatric diagnosis and treatment, should always precede any liturgical and sacramental reinforcement of deliverance from evil through exorcism. Similarly, in order to protect the afflicted person, no exorcism should be carried out publicly.

Bibliography: E. BECKER, ed., *Der Exorzismus der Kirche unter Beschuss* (Stein am Rhein, 1995) • S. L. DAVIES, *Jesus the Healer: Possession, Trance, and the Origins of Christianity* (New York, 1995) • E. FIORE, *Besessenheit und Heilung. Die Befreiung der Seele* (Gülesheim, 1997) • F. GOODMAN, ed., *Ekstase, Besessenheit, Dämonen. Die geheimnisvolle Seite der Religion* (Gütersloh, 1991) • D. LINN and M. LINN, *Deliverance Prayer: Experiential, Psychological, and Theological Approaches* (New York, 1981) • M. MARTIN, *Hostage to the Devil: The Possession and Exorcism of Five Living Americans* (New York, 1976) • J. MÜLLER, ed., *Dämonen unter uns? Exorzismus heute* (Freibourg, 1997) • H. NAEGELI-OSJORD, ed., *Possession and Exorcism* (Oregon, Wis.,

1988) • J. RICHARDS, *But Deliver Us from Evil: An Introduction to the Demonic Dimension in Pastoral Care* (London, 1974) • W. SCHIEBELER, *Besessenheit und Exorzismus: Wahn oder Wirklichkeit? Aus parapsychologischer Sicht* (Ravensburg, 1985) • J. C. THOMAS, *The Devil, Disease, and Deliverance: Origins of Illness in NT Thought* (Sheffield, 1998) • G. H. TWELFTREE, *Jesus the Exorcist: A Contribution to the Study of the Historical Jesus* (Tübingen, 1993).

HEINRICH POMPEY

Experience

1. In Philosophy
2. In Theology

1. In Philosophy

In the empiricist tradition in modern philosophy, experience is contrasted with → reason as a source of knowledge. Beginning with John Locke (1632-1704), empiricists have argued that reason alone cannot provide knowledge of what actually exists in the world; for that purpose, experience is required. Rational reflection on the idea of a sphere can provide knowledge of the properties of a sphere, but only by experience can we determine whether or not something exists in the shape of a sphere. Locke held that information about things in the world comes through perception, in the form of simple ideas in the mind that are caused by the objects of perception. While rational reflection on the properties of a sphere can yield certainty, knowledge based on experience is a matter of probable belief. David Hume (1711-76) held that knowledge of objects or events in the world comes from impressions made on the mind by those objects or events. Experience, while not infallible, is "our only guide to reasoning concerning matters of fact. . . . A wise man, therefore, proportions his belief to the evidence" (*Enquiry* 10.1). In the second quarter of the 20th century, logical empiricists tried to identify basic sentences, sometimes called protocol sentences, the function of which was to report particular experiences, out of which → science could be built.

Each of these forms of → empiricism depends on the assumption that a mind is or can become passive in experience, so that objects and events can impress themselves on it by way of the senses. Experience yields data, something directly given. This assumption has been repeatedly challenged. Immanuel Kant (1724-1804; → Kantianism) argued that the mind is active in experience. We cannot conceive of or experience objects and events except as spatial and temporal. But the forms of space and time, Kant says, are imposed by the mind, as are the categories that inform our judgments about things. We cannot know whether the world apart from experience is actually spatially and temporally formed or structured in ways that correspond to our categories. What appears to be directly given is a joint product of the world affecting the senses and the shaping activity of the mind. One can no longer assume that experience provides knowledge that is unshaped and therefore unscathed by human interests.

Acknowledging that inquiry is shaped by prior beliefs and desires, William James (1842-1910) proposed a radical empiricism in which all beliefs, including those of the properties of a sphere, are subject to modification in the light of future experience. For James the assessment of a belief by experience does not mean justifying it by reference to some perceptual given but determining whether that belief is useful in solving the problem that gave rise to inquiry. Experience serves to show the consequences of holding and acting on a belief. While perception, for the classical empiricists, is a private matter, James's call for attention to consequences is public. Ludwig Wittgenstein (1889-1951) criticized the idea of a private experience and of sentences that directly report that experience. The language by which an experience is identified is public language, and it is misleading to speak of experience as prior to language. Experience is informed by language and belief.

The term "experience" is ambiguous. The meaning of "S experienced x" can vary, depending upon how x is identified. For example, consider a man out hiking who suddenly sees a bear on the trail ahead. Frightened, he climbs the nearest tree. Out of danger, he notices that the bear has not moved and realizes that it is just a clump of bushes. Did he see or experience a bear? No, because there was no bear there to be seen. Did he see or experience a clump of bushes? No, because he would not have been frightened by bushes and would not have climbed the tree. He experienced fear, but fear is always fear of something. It was not fear of bushes but fear of a bear that he experienced, even though there was no bear there.

In order to describe the experience of a subject, one must identify the object of the experience under a description that can be attributed to the subject and that is, in part, constitutive of the experience. It would make no sense to say that Socrates was afraid of dying of cancer because that particular fear, identified in those terms, was not available to him. It might be possible to say that he was afraid of dying of the disease that killed his uncle, and scholars might turn up evidence to suggest that his uncle had died of an illness with symptoms resembling those of a particular kind of cancer. But that would be a slightly different fear. An emotion, a perception, or some other kind of experience is identified under a description. An accurate descriptive account of that experience must include mention of the description under which it is identified by the subject. The hiker experienced fear of a bear. An explanation of his fear might include reference both to the clump of bushes and to the fact that he had been warned earlier in the day to watch out for bears in these woods. The experience is a product of both the object and of the description under which it is identified. One can speak of the bush as a partial cause of the hiker's fear, but the fear can be understood only with reference to his beliefs about the object of that fear. One might attribute to Socrates the fear of dying of cancer, but only with the acknowledgment that this attribution is anachronistic and does not properly describe the fear as it was experienced.

2. In Theology

So-called religious experience refers to an experience or a dimension of experience thought to be of → God, the divine, or some religious object. Theologians and theorists of religion during the past two centuries have debated whether religion is universal in human experience, taking different forms in different cultures. The answer to that question depends on how "religious experience" is understood.

→ Religion has always been an experiential matter, but the idea of religious experience is relatively new. Religion is not only a set of creedal statements and liturgical practices. A religious life is one in which beliefs and practices cohere in a pattern that expresses a character or way of life that seems more deeply entrenched for a person or community than any of the specific beliefs or practices. For this reason, scholars of religion have thought that they could provide an accurate description of religion if they could identify a distinctively religious moment in experience. Theologians have often appealed to religious experience in order to justify religious beliefs and practices, rather than to biblical and ecclesiastical authority and metaphysical argument, which were the objects of → Enlightenment critiques. These aims of description and justification have often been pursued together.

The ideas of religious experience in both theology and the study of religion have been strongly influenced by the work of Friedrich → Schleiermacher (1768-1834). In *On Religion* (1799) Schleiermacher identifies what he takes to be the distinguishing mark of religion: a feeling, specifically a "sense and taste for the infinite." He argues that the religious moment in experience is autonomous. As an immediate sense or feeling, it cannot be reduced to either thought or action, science or morality (→ Religion, Personal Sense of). Religious doctrine and practice are expressions of this sense of the infinite. When properly understood, it will be seen that statements of religious doctrine cannot conflict with statements about the world. "God created the world" as a doctrinal statement differs in meaning from "God created the world" as a scientific statement, and they can neither support nor conflict with one another. In *The Christian Faith* (1821), his → systematic theology, Schleiermacher describes the religious dimension of experience as the "feeling of absolute dependence," and he reinterprets the doctrines of Christian theology as expressions of the specifically Christian forms of this feeling. This reinterpretation establishes the autonomy of religion and precludes any conflict between science and religion.

William James's *Varieties of Religious Experience* (1902) is another classic work on the topic. Unlike Schleiermacher, James denied that there is anything psychologically distinct about religious feelings. Such feelings are common human emotions specified by their objects. Religious love is simply love directed toward God or some other religious object, as is religious joy or melancholy. James defined religious experience as "the feelings, acts, and experiences of individual men in their solitude, so far as they apprehend themselves to stand in relation to whatever they consider the divine" (p. 34). He intended this definition not to capture an essence of the experience but to circumscribe an area for study. Though James did not exploit it, his definition calls attention to something important: feelings, acts, and experiences must each be identified under a description. In describing experience, reference must be made to (1) how one apprehends oneself to stand in relation to (2) what one considers divine. The concepts and beliefs by which one who has the experience understands what is happening to oneself are themselves constitutive of the experience. The object of the experience, as well as the perceived relation to that object, must be described from the subject's point of view. This effort requires careful attention to the language, beliefs, and cultural context of the person reporting the experience or to whom the experience is ascribed.

The terms "experience" and "religious" are both ambiguous. (For the ambiguity of "experience," see 1 above.) The experience may be characterized as religious either by the person whose experience it is or by an observer. For the most part, people do not experience something as a religious experience per se. Rather, they experience fear of → Yahweh, love of Christ, conviction of → sin, hope for the → Messiah, love of Krishna, respect for ancestors, or realization of nirvana. Using the language of a specific religious tradition, people identify both the object of the experience and the ways in which they stand in relation to that object. The concepts and beliefs by which people understand what is happening to them vary from → tradition to tradition, and within traditions over time and through space. In part as a result of the influence of Schleiermacher's *On Religion* and James's *Varieties*, however, it has recently become possible to speak of a generic religious experience as well as one focused specifically on Yahweh or Christ or some other traditionally religious person or object.

An experience identified by the person whose experience it is in terms that come from a particular religious tradition might be classified by an observer as a religious experience. The observer may be an anthropologist, a historian, a theologian, or even the experiencer himself or herself reflecting on the experience. Each one might have different criteria for deciding which experiences are religious. The range of experiences classified in this way will depend on one's definition of "religion" and "religious." Experiences identified by the subject in terms of the concepts and beliefs of Christianity, → Judaism, → Islam, → Hinduism, → Buddhism, or any other major religious tradition are likely to be classified as religious. There may be disagreement, however, on which experiences are described as religious. The classification varies with the assumptions and purposes of the person doing the classifying.

A person might classify two paintings of a religious subject — one by Michelangelo and the other by Rembrandt — each as religious; in fact, the subject matter might be the same (e.g., the crucifixion of Jesus). Other viewers, however, might say that, despite the common subject matter, one is a religious artwork and the other is not. In making this judgment, they might consider the social and cultural context, the purposes the paintings were meant to serve, or their effects on viewers, both contemporary with the artist and in other times and places. Paul → Tillich (1886-1965) identified art as religious if it expresses the artist's sensitive and honest search for ultimate → meaning and significance. For example, Tillich described Picasso's *Guernica* as profoundly religious and as the best contemporary

Protestant religious picture, even though there is nothing explicitly religious or Protestant about its evident subject matter. Similarly, Tillich described as religious some experiences that are identified in terms that are without explicit religious content.

Theologians or philosophers of religion interested in showing that religious experience is universal describe that experience in very general terms, as Schleiermacher does with "sense and taste for the infinite" (p. 23). They prescind from the concepts and beliefs of specific religious traditions, and of particular times and places. This practice precludes an accurate account of a subject's experience. Such an account must include reference to the terms in which the subject understands what is happening to him or her. Here we need what anthropologist Clifford Geertz calls "thick description," the identification of an act or experience by reference to the relevant cultural context, and the concepts, beliefs, rules, and practices that would be assumed by the person to whom the experience is attributed. A vision of Christ in late 16th-century Spain during the Counter-Reformation, for example, differs from a vision of Christ in 18th-century Massachusetts during the Great Awakening. Any description that equated them would miss much of the substance of the two experiences.

Many contemporary theologians reject attempts to identify a direct or immediate religious moment in experience that could be used to ground or justify religious doctrine and practice. They recognize that all experiences are constituted, in part, by the concepts and categories that persons bring to them. In *The Nature of Doctrine* (1984) George Lindbeck criticizes Schleiermacher, rejecting what he calls the experiential/expressive way of doing theology. But William Alston, in *Perceiving God* (1991), defends the possibility of a direct experience of God and denies that the experience is constituted by the terms in which it is described. Debate over this issue is very much alive among many theologians and philosophers of religion.

Attempts to identify a core religious experience, or several types that are invariant across cultures, are unpromising. Any terms general enough to be plausible candidates for a common core are too general to capture the specifics of experiences in different traditions and at different times and places. Apologetic use of religious experience as a locus of appeal that can replace appeal to biblical or ecclesiastical authority or reference to metaphysical argument is problematic. Attention to reports of particular experiences, however, and to how people have experienced the world religiously, is essential for a proper understanding of religion. These experiences

must be described with close attention to the cultural contexts and the specific terms in which persons have understood what is happening to them. This caveat is especially relevant in a period in which Christian theology can no longer be done without careful attention to other traditions of religious belief and practice.

Bibliography: On 1: R. CHISHOLM, *Perceiving* (Ithaca, N.Y., 1957) chap. 4 • D. HUME, *An Enquiry concerning Human Understanding* (Indianapolis, 1977; orig. pub., 1748) chap. 10 • W. JAMES, *Essays in Radical Empiricism* (Cambridge, Mass., 1976; orig. pub., 1912) • I. KANT, *Critique of Pure Reason* (trans. P. Guyer; Cambridge, 1998; orig. pub., 1781; rev., 1787) • J. LOCKE, *An Essay concerning Human Understanding* (Oxford, 1975; orig. pub., 1690) bk. 4 • L. WITTGENSTEIN, *Philosophical Investigations* (3d ed.; New York, 1973; orig. pub., 1953).

On 2: W. ALSTON, *Perceiving God* (Ithaca, N.Y., 1991) • C. GEERTZ, "Thick Description," *The Interpretation of Cultures* (New York, 1973) • W. JAMES, *The Varieties of Religious Experience* (Cambridge, Mass., 1985; orig. pub., 1902) • S. KATZ, ed., *Mysticism and Philosophical Analysis* (Oxford, 1978) • G. LINDBECK, *The Nature of Religious Doctrine* (Philadelphia, 1984) • R. OTTO, *The Idea of the Holy* (2d ed.; New York, 1970; orig. pub., 1917) • W. PROUDFOOT, *Religious Experience* (Los Angeles, 1985) • F. SCHLEIERMACHER, *On Religion: Speeches to Its Cultured Despisers* (trans. R. Crouter; Cambridge, 1996; orig. pub., 1799).

WAYNE PROUDFOOT

Expressionism

1. Definition

Broadly speaking, "expressionism" refers to an artistic style flourishing in Europe in the early 20th century that emphasized → subjectivity and expression of the full range of emotions — in every medium. More narrowly, it is often used for German literature and fine arts, especially in the period 1910-24. It was part of a general European reaction to → positivism and naturalism. Parallel movements were futurism (Italy and Russia), vorticism and imagism (England), and Orphism (France). An Italian, E. Marinetti (1876-1944), was a widely translated spokesman and theoretician of the movement. Behind expressionism and its neighboring movements stood three philosophers who contributed key, nonrational concepts: H.-L. Bergson (1859-1941), with his "élan vital"; B. Croce (1866-1952), with → "intuition"; and F. Nietzsche (1844-1900), with his "Dionysian intoxication" and call for "reevaluation of all values." Expressionists also understood the "phenomenological elucidation of meaning" of E. Husserl (1859-1938) as a turning away from → rationalism. In 1917 P. Hatvani (1892-1975) defined expressionism as "a revolutionary changeover to the basic and fundamental"; in expressionism, he said, "the ego inundates the whole world."

2. Expressionist Literature
2.1. *Lyric Poetry*
In the beginning, expressionist poetry consisted of protest and satire. J. van Hoddis (1887-1942), G. Heym (1887-1912), A. Lichtenstein (1889-1914), and E. Blass (1890-1939) rejected a static world that was full of old-fashioned → taboos and that ignored existential problems. In order to shock the bourgeois, they wrote poems about decaying corpses and autopsies, made fun of the superannuated clichés of conventional poetry (e.g., Marinetti's "Death to the Moonlight"), and expressed the alienation of modern life in verses that were grotesquely cheerful or pessimistic. For expressionists, the ugly and the bizarre became the gateway to discovering social evil. Escape from the monotony of → everyday life turned into exploration of the dynamic, many-layered modern world.

The preeminent expressionist credo was "the experience of existential contradiction and of the juxtaposition of all things." W. Kandinsky (1866-1944) summarized expressionism when he commented, "Antitheses and contradictions — that is our harmony." (Cf. the significance of "simultaneity" for the futurist movement.) Expressionist journals and serials, which displayed their extreme tendencies even in their titles, included *Der Sturm* (The storm), *Die Aktion, Blast, Der Anbruch* (The beginning), *Das Ziel* (The goal), and *Umsturz und Aufbau* (Overthrow and reconstruction). The famous expressionist anthology *Menschheitsdämmerung* (Twilight [or dawn] of humanity, 1920; rev. ed., 1968) marked simultaneously the end of the world and its birth. F. Kafka (1883-1924)

saw "outstretched hands" and "convulsively clenched fists" as the emblems of the whole movement. The optimistic spiritual awakening of E. Stadler (1883-1914) and F. Werfel (1890-1945) contrasted sharply with the "black visions" of Heym and the nightmarish world of G. Trakl (1887-1914). Many lyric motifs carried contradictory evaluations: the new world of technology was idolized or condemned; big cities were considered sources of dynamism or a new Sodom and Gomorrah; the prostitute was a femme fatale or an exploited fellow human being.

The high point of many expressionist writings was the dissolution of the individual, which manifested itself in various ways. There is → ecstatic or spiritual transcending in Stadler and Werfel, androgynous visions in Trakl, merging with nature in the early B. Brecht (1898-1956), and drug-induced artificial paradises in Trakl and G. Benn (1886-1956).

2.2. *Drama*
For P. Kornfeld (1889-1942), art is "a tool of ethics and a way to religion." Expressionism thus staged "dramas of proclamation" (E. Lämmert) showing ways to salvation. The focal point was often an emotional manifesto that a seer or redeemer delivered to a community of believers. *Die Wandlung* (Change), by E. Toller (1893-1939), as well as *Der Bettler* (The beggar), by R. Sorge (1892-1916), connect the renewal of the individual with a call to a radical refashioning of reality. In the play *Der Sohn* (The son), by W. Hasenclever (1890-1940), a planned but unrealized patricide symbolizes "the murder of all fathers by their sons," that is, the total abolition of all authority and restraint. Coincidence of opposites is the key structure in *Die Erneuerung* (The renewal), by G. Kaiser (1878-1945), in which → revolution is described simultaneously in optimistic and pessimistic terms. In Sorge's *Bettler* all characters represent at the same time the antitheses of their own position, thus indicating that totality and unity can be reached only by juxtaposing contradictory tendencies.

New techniques of acting and of stage lighting also mark expressionist drama. On a purely symbolic, almost empty stage, the drama, using ecstatic gestures, is more celebrated than acted. Spotlighting and quick changes of light, shadows, and focus allow the spectator at every turn to concentrate upon the character in question.

2.3. *Expressionism and Film*
Several of the more progressive expressionists — particularly K. Pinthus (1886-1975), Hasenclever, and I. Goll (1891-1950) — analyzed the new medium of silent film. They expected the cinema to produce enriched → imagination, enhanced vitality, and the possibility of influencing → society at large.

As early as 1913 A. Döblin (1878-1957) began projecting montages. Not until the 1920s, however, through the Russian S. Eisenstein (1898-1948), did an independent → aesthetics of film arise. With projections and flashbacks, as well as with the filming of "inner images" and the changing of perspectives, he pioneered more sophisticated methods of cinematographic representation.

2.4. *Theory of Language*

Expressionism had no unified style of writing. It was by turns verbose and laconic; as Brecht observed, its style could be both pontifical and profane. Most writers believed in the immediate, world-renewing power of the word. Attempts at reform relied on the theories of Nietzsche, F. Mauthner (1849-1923), and Marinetti. Demands by Marinetti for a simplified and dynamic language, guided by "divine intuition," were very influential. H. Walden (1878-1942), L. Schreyer (1886-1966), Kandinsky, and Hatvani recommended a language free of abstract ideas and concentrated on feelings, rhythm, and sound. In the opposite direction, A. Stramm (1874-1915) created a language that is radically reduced to semantic elements, with a style related to the essentialism of G. Ungaretti (1888-1970).

2.5. *Expressionism and World War I*

Hardly any other cultural epoch was so affected by a single historicopolitical event as expressionism was by World War I. The → war was first hailed as a "redeeming abyss" (M. Scheler [1874-1928]), but its destruction soon brought a swing to → pacifism. After 1918 the bitter realization sank in of the powerlessness of → idealism. The war claimed the lives of Stadler, Stramm, Lichtenstein, Trakl, and other expressionists. After fighting for the Munich Socialist Republic, Toller and E. Mühsam (1878-1934) were incarcerated. The abandonment of all idealistic efforts finally splintered the survivors of the movement.

After the war Marinetti, H. Johst (1890-1978), Benn, and other expressionists engaged themselves politically on the Right. Others, such as H. Walden (1878-1942), J. Becher (1891-1958), L. Rubiner (1881-1920), and Brecht, turned to the dogmas of the Left or, as did Toller, replaced idealistic writing with social comedy and satire. Later, under A. Hitler, expressionism in its entirety was regarded as degenerate art.

3. Painting, Graphics, and Sculpture

Most German expressionist artists were associated with a particular geographic center. The group called Die Brücke (The bridge), located in Dresden and later Berlin, included E. Heckel (1883-1970), E. Kirchner (1880-1938), E. Nolde (1876-1956), and K. Schmidt-Rottluff (1884-1976). The second main group, in Munich, was Der Blaue Reiter (The blue rider), which included Kandinsky, P. Klee (1879-1940), and F. Marc (1880-1916). Lesser known was the Berlin group Die Pathetiker (e.g., L. Meidner [1884-1966]), and there were important individualists such as M. Beckmann (1884-1950), E. Barlach (1870-1938), O. Dix (1891-1969), G. Grosz (1893-1959), A. Kubin (1877-1959), and O. Kokoschka (1886-1980). Common to them all was a radical break with tradition.

The very name "Brücke" suggests a departure for new shores. The group members endeavored to make visible the primeval conditions of the psyche and to break through to a mythic or quasi-religious underground of existence. From E. Munch (1863-1944) they borrowed the painting of "inner images"; from H. Matisse (1869-1954) and fauvism, the garish use of color. In his *Tänzerinnen* (Dancing girls) Heckel portrays the rapture of Bacchic joys. Nolde, in the upsurges of his series *Herbstmeere* (Autumnal seas, 1913ff.), sees the absolute power of nature; Kirchner's portrait of Otto Müller (1915) expresses creative ecstasy. Next to proletarians, lunatics, and children (who are called primeval beings), expressionist painters portray prophets and visionaries. The inclusion of ugly and grotesque features in religious works often provoked condemnation from society and the → church (e.g., in the case of Nolde's *Abendmahl* [Last Supper, 1909] and Schmidt-Rottluff's *Evangelisten-Köpfe* [Heads of the Evangelists, 1912]).

From the very beginning the graphic arts had considerable influence — especially woodcuts, with their simplified black-and-white technique and easy reproduction as posters or illustrated pamphlets. Prominent between 1914 and 1918 were shocking scenes of city life, as well as religious themes, many of them expressing antiwar sentiments. Meidner's → apocalyptic visions (e.g., his *Brennende Stadt* [Burning city, 1913]) anticipate works like Beckmann's *Das Leichenhaus* (The morgue, 1916) and Barlach's *Massengrab* (Mass grave, 1915), which originated after the slaughter had started. Many of the graphics were published in the journals *Der Sturm* and *Die Aktion.*

Within Der Blaue Reiter there was also great interest in basic existential problems. In portraying them, however, the artists proceeded more methodically than did those of Die Brücke. Kandinsky, Marc, and Klee systematically investigated the problems of abstraction, that is, of the elimination of certain physical attributes. They succeeded in finding what they called "visual concepts" behind the surface of visibility (e.g., elementary geometric forms in Kandinsky's

Lyrisches [Things lyrical, 1911]). Light and color became autonomous elements of a picture. Often the attention shifted from the object to the perceptual mechanism. Similarly, the Orphist R. Delaunay (1885-1941) had discovered automatisms in the sensory process with his *sens giratoire*. According to Klee, "Art makes visible — it does not reproduce the visible." The expressionist artists experienced such "pictorial thinking" as cosmic relationships of existence and as a stimulus for the creation of total artworks. They thus discovered that dynamics expresses itself as rhythm, and rhythm can also be found in the other branches of art. The analogy of tonal oscillations to complementary colors led Kandinsky and Marc to formulate a theory of the harmony of all colors and forms. The painter Kandinsky published a "synesthetic stage-composition" entitled *Der Gelbe Klang* (The yellow sound, 1912), and in all his work we have "improvisations," "graphic counterpoints," and other musical concepts.

Only in recent years has the sculpture of the Brücke artists received much attention. Many of their sculptures are massive and larger than life. They focus the viewer's attention to the face and to the dominant gesture. One of the greatest expressionist sculptors is Barlach, whose work particularly reveals the spiritual. His *Blinder Bettler* (Blind beggar, 1906), *Schwebender Gottvater* (Hovering God the Father, 1922), *Der Todesengel* (Angel of death, 1927) on the Güstrow War Memorial, and many other works show the topics of his dramatic work in another medium. Other well-known expressionist sculptors are B. Hoetger (1874-1949), K. Kollwitz (1867-1945), and W. Lehmbruck (1881-1919).

4. Architecture

W. Gropius (1883-1969) defined the expressionist architect as "the leader and master of all artists." E. Mendelsohn (1887-1953) thought that artists conceived their work in states of ecstasy. Convinced of the social function of architecture, expressionists worked on buildings with a community orientation, like theaters and city centers. Expressionist architects, though, vacillated between glorification and condemnation of the → city. B. Taut (1880-1938), for example, the city architect of Magdeburg, called for colorful buildings; his main work, however, *Die Auflösung der Städte* (The dissolution of the cities, 1920), deals with decentralized suburbs in garden settings.

The architecture of expressionism is sculptural and tries to look like a part of nature. The tendency is either to create round plastic forms that imitate grottoes and towerlike rock formations or to work in geometric forms on glass structures that emphasize the vertical. In 1919 H. Poelzig (1869-1936) changed the inside of a Berlin theater into a cave with formations that look like stalactites. In the low, massive Einstein Tower in Potsdam (1920), Mendelsohn achieved a fusion of tower and cave. The main proponent of glass architecture was Taut, illustrated in his Cologne glass pavilion (1914). He received support from poet P. Scheerbart (1863-1915), who also was obsessed with glass. Both saw in life behind glass the foundation of a new morality and often quoted the relevant passages from the Bible (Rev. 21:18-21; 22:1) on crystal and glass.

The religious aspect in such works was no secondary motif. Taut's *Auflösung der Städte* (Dissolution of the cities) ends with a vision of dancing spheres, circumscribed with the words "Holy, holy, holy!" Taut also embraced utopian topics in *Der Weltbaumeister* (The world architect, 1920) and *Alpine Architektur* (1917). In the latter, he projected transforming the Alps in their entirety into a crystalline landscape of the Holy Grail.

Expressionist architects also created the often fantastic backdrops of famous films of the period, such as Poelzig's setting of Wegener's *Der Golem* (1920). Many of the great representatives of modernity, including Le Corbusier (1887-1965) and Mies van der Rohe (1886-1969), began as expressionists. Even the early Bauhaus is not to be considered as just a center of the Neue Sachlichkeit (new objectivity) but as a refuge of visionary expressionism.

5. Music

Vienna, with A. Schoenberg (1874-1951), A. Berg (1885-1935), and A. von Webern (1883-1945), was the capital of expressionist music. Other composers, including A. Scriabin (1872-1915), I. Stravinsky (1882-1971), and P. Hindemith (1895-1963), merely went through an expressionist phase. The goals of expressionist music were messianic and ethical. A new kind of sound was supposed to create a new humanity and to show humanity's interconnections with nature (Schoenberg's *Harmonielehre* [1911]). Musical works thus dealt with the poor and with outcasts of society (Berg's *Wozzeck* [1917-31]). They turned to myth (Stravinsky's *Rite of Spring* [1913]) or the libido (Berg's *Lulu* [1928-35]). The climax was often mystic depersonalization, seen in titles like Scriabin's *Poème de l'extase* (1908).

To express the all-encompassing role of emotion, expressionist composers tried to use the world of sound in its entirety. Schoenberg proclaimed "the emancipation of dissonance." He defined his own music (commonly called atonal) as *pan*tonal because he granted the same status to each and every sound. Unification of opposites is shown in Schoenberg's *Pierrot Lunaire* (1912) and Berg's *Wozzeck,* both of which use a form of simultaneous singing and reciting. Often the grotesque predominates, which in this medium refers to playing a melody and countermelody at the same time. Schoenberg's unfinished oratorio *Jakobsleiter* (Jacob's ladder, 1915-22) describes a vision of the interconnection of life and death.

In order to concentrate on the essential, expressionist composers eliminated all repetitions and reduced the number of orchestral instruments to a minimum. They composed microforms. For example, the second of Berg's Five Orchestra Songs, opus 4 (1912), entitled *Gewitterregen* (Thunderrain), is only 11 measures long. None of the compositions of von Webern takes more than 15 minutes to play.

Turning to what he calls the Dionysian principle of rhythm, Schoenberg uses the syncopated beat of jazz (piano arrangement of *Ragtime* [1919]). The title of Schoenberg's *Die glückliche Hand. Eine dramatische Pantomine* (The happy hand. A dramatic pantomine, 1911-13) again documents his predilection for multimedia works. The almanac of Der Blaue Reiter includes a discussion of Scriabin's color theories (1911), according to which all tones are assigned definite visual counterparts.

6. Dadaism

Dadaism was founded in Zurich in 1916 by an international group of conscientious objectors, among them H. Arp (1887-1966), H. Ball (1886-1927), and T. Tzara (1896-1963). Members of later Dada centers in New York, Paris, Barcelona, and elsewhere were M. Duchamp (1887-1968), M. Ernst (1891-1976), F. Picabia (1879-1953), and K. Schwitters (1887-1948).

Many consider Dada an iconoclastic movement directed against all of civilization, one culminating in an all-encompassing → relativism. Such characterization is true, however, only for the first two or three years. Just as the antimilitarism of the dadaists included an active commitment to world peace, so a great number of new developments emerged from originally negative positions. Duchamp, for example, sent a snow shovel and a urinal as sculptures to the New York Exhibition of 1917. These so-called objets trouvés, or ready-mades, were conscious anti-art, for Dada was against the artist as a creator of eternal values. Such prefabricated products, however, often led to the discovery of beauty in many simple objects. Art was being viewed as a product of nature, and the artist as part of forces that worked through him or her. Arp, S. Taeuber (1899-1943),

and Ernst created "artistic half-products." Selecting and shaping replaced originality and invention, the two cornerstones of traditional aesthetics. In Schwitters's collages, discarded and often ugly materials acquire a surprising beauty.

In the beginning, Dada writers protested with nonsense poems against rationalism. Soon this instinctive verbiage, under the name *écriture automatique* (automatic writing) became the officially recognized writing method of surrealism. Ball declaimed his "sound poems," which consist of nonsense syllables, like liturgical lamentations. Forster saw sound poems even connected to stammering ecstasy and "speaking in tongues" (cf. 1 Cor. 14:1-19). Playful configurations in images and words led Tzara and Arp to the recognition of the power of chance. To Arp the yellowing edges of his *papiers déchirés* (torn papers) revealed time and transiency. In later years, Arp designated as the goal of art "the dissolution of all borders" and aimed explicitly at depersonalization. In a dialectical reversal, this concept thus points no longer to alienation but to the knowledge of finding oneself embedded in the processes of a larger reality.

Bibliography: K. AMANN and A. WALLAS, eds., *Expressionismus in Österreich. Die Literatur und die Künste* (Vienna, 1994) • T. ANZ and M. STARK, eds., *Expressionismus. Manifeste und Dokumente zur deutschen Literatur, 1910-1920* (Stuttgart, 1982) • H. H. ARNASON, *History of Modern Art: Painting, Sculpture, Architecture* (rev. ed.; New York, 1978) • S. BARRON, ed., *German Expressionist Sculpture* (Chicago, 1985) • W. BECKETT, *The Mystical Now: Art and the Sacred* (New York, 1993) • P. DEMETZ, *Worte in Freiheit. Der italienische Futurismus und die deutsche literarische Avantgarde (1912-1934)* (Munich, 1990) • A. P. DIERICK, *German Expressionist Prose: Theory and Practice* (Toronto, 1987) • L. FOSTER, *The Poetry of Significant Nonsense* (Cambridge, 1962) • R. HELLER, "Expressionism," *EncA* 2.135-39 • M. S. JONES, *Der Sturm: A Focus of Expressionism* (Columbia, S.C., 1984) • H. KORTE, *Die Dadaisten* (Reinbek, 1994) • T. OTTEN, *After Innocence: Visions of the Fall in Modern Literature* (Pittsburgh, 1982) • W. PAULSEN, *Deutsche Literatur des Expressionismus* (Bern, 1983) • M. PAZI and H. D. ZIMMERMANN, eds., *Berlin und der Prager Kreis* (Würzburg, 1991) • W. PEHNT, *Die Architektur des Expressionismus* (2d ed.; Stuttgart, 1998) • P. REUTERSWÄRD, *The Visible and Invisible in Art: Essays in the History of Art* (Vienna, 1991) • H. SEDLMAYR, *Art in Crisis: The Lost Center* (Chicago, 1958) • U. WEISSTEIN, ed., *Expressionism as an International Literary Phenomenon* (Paris, 1973) • E. WILLIAMS, *The Mirror and the Word: Modernism, Literary Theory, and Georg Trakl* (Lincoln, Nebr., 1993).

GUENTHER C. RIMBACH

Extra calvinisticum

Lutheran → orthodoxy coined the term "extra calvinisticum" for the Calvinist teaching (→ Calvin's Theology; Calvinism) that the deity of Christ exists and works outside *(extra)* the spatial and historical limitations of his humanity (→ Christology 2.4). As God, he is omnipresent (→ Ubiquity); as man, however (as against the Lutheran doctrine of ubiquity), he is localized in heaven, even after his ascension to the right hand of the Father (see Calvin *Inst.* 2.13.4 and → Heidelberg Catechism q. 48).

The Christological distinction was rooted in the Protestant eucharistic controversy of the 16th century (→ Eucharist 3), in which the Reformed continued the thinking of the → Antiochian theology of the early church, along with that of the Council of → Chalcedon, whereas the Lutherans inclined more in the direction of Alexandrian Christology (→ Alexandrian Theology). The Reformed were less concerned about the metaphysical-sounding and oft-quoted axiom *finitum non capax infiniti* (the finite is incapable of the infinite) than they were about essential theological and soteriological matters, especially the unrestricted deity yet also the true and truly continuing humanity of Jesus Christ.

The Lutheran protest is justified to the extent that the unity of the person of the Son who became man might be threatened by the extra calvinisticum. This teaching, however, leaves room for the eschatological dynamic, sovereignly overarching all history, of that which took place through the incarnation, and it also blocks the danger of mere historicizing or sacramentalizing.

The → Leuenberg Agreement of 1973 achieved an ecumenical reconciling of views that had hardened in the age of orthodoxy. In shedding new light on the problem, K. Barth (1886-1968) in particular made a decisive contribution.

Bibliography: K. BARTH, *CD* I/1, 159-71; II/1, 487-90 • R. MULLER, *Dictionary of Latin and Greek Theological Terms* (Grand Rapids, 1985) 111 • W. NEUSER, "Dogma und Bekenntnis in der Reformation. Von Zwingli und Calvin bis zur Synode von Westminster," *HDThG* 2.247-50, 320-21.

ALASDAIR I. C. HERON

Exultet → Holy Week

Ezekiel, Book of

1. Book
2. Forms
3. Research
4. Theology

1. Book

Ezekiel falls into three main parts: judgments against Judah and → Jerusalem in chaps. 1–24, pronouncements against foreign nations in 25–32, and announcements of salvation for → Israel (§1) in 33–48. In contrast to the other great prophetic books, it thus gives an impression of greater cohesion. Substantive correspondences bracket the sections on judgment and salvation (cf. 2:5 and 33:33; 3:16-21 and 33:1-9; 3:26 and 33:21-22 [cf. 24:25-27]; chap. 6 and 36:1-15; 11:14-21 and 33:23-29; 11:23 and 43:4; 24:1-14 and 37:1-14).

The 14 dates mentioned (1:1-2; 3:16; 8:1; 20:1; 24:1; 26:1; 29:1, 17; 30:20; 31:1; 32:1, 17; 33:21; 40:1) — although they raise minor problems, and a bigger one in 29:17, the latest dated saying — also give an impression of an orderly temporal sequence. They span the time only from the 5th year (593 B.C., 1:2) to the 11th year (586, 33:21; see W. Zimmerli, vol. 2) after the deportation, the latter being the year in which news of the fall of Jerusalem arrives. The final temple vision is dated 14 years later (40:1).

2. Forms

The constant stylization of the book as the prophet's own first-person narrative (apart from the superscription in 1:3) finds expression — except in the four visions of 1:1-3, 15; 8–11; 37:1-14; 40–48 — in the stereotyped word-event formula that introduces the 48 remaining speeches: "The word of Yahweh came to me." Typical of the book are visions, enacted signs (4–5; 12:1-20; 21:6-7, 18-24; 24:15-24; 37:15-28), and extensive figures of speech (15; 16; 17; 23; 31), among which we may include the laments in 19 and 27.

Recurring expressions merit special attention. Along with the word-event formula we find the first-person statement "I, Yahweh, have spoken" concluding several units (5:17; 17:24; 24:14; 34:24; 37:14, etc.). There is also a knowledge formula: "they/you shall know that I, Yahweh, have spoken" (5:13; 17:21; 37:14). According to Zimmerli, these formulas mark the high point of divine self-demonstration in prophecy.

Certain individual literary and thematic contacts between Ezekiel and, for example, the → Holiness Code (cf. Ezek. 34:25-31 and Lev. 26:3-13) and also between Ezekiel and Deuteronomy (cf. Ezekiel 6 and the polemics against the high places in Deuteronomic reform) and especially Jeremiah (cf. Ezek. 3:3 and Jer. 15:16) have yet to be addressed by scholarship and should not prompt oversimplified explanations for what was historically a very complex relationship.

3. Research

Many methods have been used and many solutions proposed in dealing with the historiographic, redactional, historical, and biographical questions raised about the prophet and his book. G. Hölscher thought that the rhythmic visions and poems of the prophet that make up a good tenth of the book are the genuine core and that in the Persian period these parts were worked together editorially into a many-layered and Priestly prose work. S. Herrmann thought it just as difficult to get the genuine sayings of the prophet from the Book of Ezekiel as it is to get the ipsissima verba of Jesus from the Gospels. J. Garscha found only 21 authentic verses in Ezekiel. H. Schulz thought he saw a Deutero-Ezekiel, a "sacral stratum," while R. Liwak posited a Deutero-nomistic revision. In contrast, Zimmerli conjectured that Ezekiel himself and his school, which preserved his sayings, had put the book together, though he did not think it possible to say in detail what was the prophet's own work and what was that of the school. Finally, after analyzing redactional issues and internally discernible tendencies within the book, K.-F. Pohlmann found that one can distinguish at least between a gôlâ (captivity)-oriented and several diaspora-oriented redactional strands. The historical prophet probably worked in Babylonian exile rather than in Jerusalem (V. Herntrich).

4. Theology

Central to Ezekiel is the prophetic proclamation of the Word of God. This proclamation is served by biographical remarks about Ezekiel's silence (3:26-27; 24:27; 33:22); the death of his wife (24:15-18); his dramatic call, depicted rather drastically as the eating of a scroll on the banks of the Chebar River (2:8–3:3); and the series of physical-psychological traumas in the form of expressive and symbolic acts (4:4-15; 12:17-20; 21:6-7). Nowhere do we find a more severe message of judgment on the "rebellious house" (2:5, 7; 3:9). A historical reason for the judgment that overtakes the people of Yahweh is given in chaps. 20 and 23. Total condemnation of Jerusalem of an almost ontological character is intimated in 15 and 16. The final promises in 11, 16, 17, and 20 point ahead to the (exilic?) proclamation of salvation (after 586?) in the second part, which in the figure of resurrection refers

to the restoration of Israel as an act of new creation (37:1-14). The last chapters (40–48), which are especially difficult from the standpoint of literary criticism, contain plans for reconstruction (Zimmerli) and the drafting of a new constitution (H. Gese).

→ Prophet, Prophecy

Bibliography: History of Research: U. Feist, *Ezechiel. Das literarische Problem des Buches forschungsgeschichtlich betrachtet* (Stuttgart, 1995) • G. Fohrer, "Neuere Literatur zur alttestamentlichen Prophetie (1961-1970)," *TRu* 45 (1980) 121-29 • B. Lang, *Ezekiel. Der Prophet und das Buch* (Darmstadt, 1981) 1-18 • H. H. Rowley, "The Book of Ezekiel in Modern Study," *BJRL* 36 (1953) 146-90 • W. Zimmerli, *Ezekiel* (vol. 1; Philadelphia, 1979) xxviii-xliv, 3-8, 41-52.

Commentaries: J. Blenkinsopp (Interpretation; Louisville, Ky., 1990) • D. I. Block (2 vols.; NICOT; Grand Rapids, 1997-98) • W. Brownlee and L. Allen (WBC; Dallas, 1986-90) • G. Fohrer and K. Galling (HAT; Tübingen, 1955) • H. F. Fuhs (2 vols.; NEchtB; Würzburg, 1984-88) • M. Greenberg (AB; Garden City, N.Y., 1983) • R. W. Klein (Columbia, S.C., 1988) • B. Maarsingh (2 vols.; Nijkerk, 1985-88) • H. G. May (IB; Nashville, 1956) • K.-F. Pohlmann (ATD; Göttingen, 1996) • J. W. Wevers (CBC; Cambridge, 1969) • W. Zimmerli (Hermeneia; 2 vols.; Philadelphia, 1979-83).

Other studies: D. Baltzer, *Ezechiel und Deuterojesaja* (Berlin, 1971) • K. W. Carley, *Ezekiel among the Prophets* (Naperville, Ill., 1975) • J. Garscha, *Studien zum Ezechiel-Buch* (Frankfurt, 1974) • H. Gese, *Der Verfassungsentwurf des Ezechiel (Kap. 40–48)* (Tübingen, 1957) • V. Herntrich, *Ezechiel-Probleme* (Berlin, 1933) • S. Herrmann, *Die prophetischen Heilserwartungen im Alten Testament* (Stuttgart, 1965) • G. Hölscher, *Hesekiel. Der Dichter und das Buch* (Giessen, 1924) • T. Krüger, *Geschichtskonzepte im Ezechielbuch* (Berlin, 1989) • R. Liwak, "Überlieferungsgeschichtliche Probleme des Ezechiel-Buches" (Diss., Bochum, 1976) • J. Lust, ed., *Ezekiel and His Book: Textual and Literary Criticism and Their Interrelation* (Louvain, 1986) • K.-F. Pohlmann, *Ezechielstudien. Zur Redaktionsgeschichte des Buches und zur Frage nach den ältesten Texten* (Berlin, 1992) • H. Schulz, *Das Todesrecht im Alten Testament* (Berlin, 1969) • P. J. Swanson, *The Role of Covenant in Ezekiel's Program of Restoration* (New Orleans, 1989) • W. Zimmerli, *Ezechiel. Gestalt und Botschaft* (Neukirchen, 1962); idem, *I Am Yahweh* (Atlanta, 1982); idem, "Das Phänomen der Fortschreibung im Buche Ezechiel," *Prophecy* (ed. J. A. Emerton; Berlin, 1980) 174-91; idem, "Planungen für den Wiederaufbau nach der Katastrophe von 587" (1968), *Gesammelte Aufsätze* (vol. 2; Munich, 1974) 165-91; idem, "Das Wort des göttlichen Selbsterweises (Erweiswort), eine prophetische Gattung," *Gesammelte Aufsätze* (vol. 1; Munich, 1969) 120-32.

DIETER BALTZER

Ezra and Nehemiah, Books of

Ezra and Nehemiah form part of the Writings, the third section of the Hebrew OT. In translations they are usually counted as two books and placed among the historical books. Along with the very literal translation of Ezra and Nehemiah, the LXX has an → apocryphal 1 Esdras, which the Vg calls 3 Esdras. Apart from the story in 1 Esdras 3–4, this book corresponds essentially to 2 Chronicles 35–Ezra 10 + Neh. 7:72–8:13a; it is not a fragment of an older edition of Chronicles and Ezra-Nehemiah (without the Nehemiah memoirs) (so K. F. Pohlmann et al.) but an independent revision of the relevant canonical texts.

Ezra and Nehemiah deal with the history of Judah and Jerusalem (→ Israel 1.7) for about a century after the Babylonian exile, from 538 B.C. to the second half of the fifth century. They do not, however, form a connected narrative. Thus, for example, between Ezra 6:22 and 7:1 there is a gap of 57 years (515-458 B.C.; cf. the dates in 6:15 and 7:7), which the author hardly felt to be such (note "after this" in 7:1). Perhaps, in spite of the different kings' names, the author looked at the seventh year of 7:7 as following immediately after the sixth year of 6:15.

Here as elsewhere (note the strange sequence of Artaxerxes and Darius I in Ezra 4:8 and 4:24), it may be seen that the author's interest is not primarily historical. His basic point is that the Jerusalem community of his own day (ca. 300 B.C.?) may be traced to the returned exiles (Ezra 2 = Nehemiah 7), who kept clear of foreign influence (Ezra 9–10; Neh. 13:23-27), gathered around the → temple that was rebuilt after the destruction of 587 B.C. (Ezra 1–6) and around the law of Moses (Nehemiah 8), and made a refortified Jerusalem their capital (Nehemiah 1–7). That such steps were taken in spite of all resistance was due to God's help and the favor of the Persian kings that God secured. This concentration on essentials at the cost of historical detail, along with certain linguistic peculiarities, links Ezra and Nehemiah to 1 and 2 Chronicles, all of which many scholars regard as the work of a single Chronicler. This view is now contested (by S. Japhet and others), and the question of authorship is open.

The author used various sources: the memoirs of Nehemiah, governor of the Province of Judah under Artaxerxes I (465-425 B.C.) and builder of the wall of Jerusalem (Neh. 1:1–7:5 and parts of chaps. 12–13); the Aramaic section Ezra 4:8–6:18 with the enclosed documents, including the decree of Cyrus for the rebuilding of the temple (6:3-5); the decree, likewise in Aramaic, of Artaxerxes (I?) commissioning Ezra; and various lists, including the list of restored temple vessels (Ezra 1:9-11). The tradition going back to Ezra has at most been only indirectly used, so that Ezra is a much less distinct historical figure than Nehemiah; an official of the Persian court charged to reorganize Judah (?) emerges in tradition as a teacher of the → law. The sources are important for a reconstruction of the postexilic history of Judah (though opinions about their historical reliability differ), but objective exposition will be more concerned about what Ezra and Nehemiah are trying to say than about their historical value.

Bibliography: Commentaries: J. BECKER, (NEchtB; Würzburg, 1990) • K. GALLING (ATD; Göttingen, 1954) • A. H. J. GUNNEWEG (KAT; Gütersloh, 1985-87) • J. M. MYERS (AB; Garden City, N.Y., 1965) • W. RUDOLPH (HAT; Tübingen, 1949) • K. D. SCHUNCK (BKAT; Neukirchen, 1998-).

Other works: P. R. ACKROYD, *Exile and Restoration* (Philadelphia, 1968) • R. BACH, "Esra 1. Der Verfasser, seine 'Quellen' und sein Thema," *Gottes Recht als Lebensraum* (Neukirchen, 1993) 41-60 • J. BLENKINSOPP, "The Nehemiah Autobiographical Memoir," *Language, Theology, and the Bible* (ed. S. E. Balantine et al.; Oxford, 1993) 199-212 • A. H. J. GUNNEWEG, "Zur Interpretation der Bücher Esra-Nehemia," *VTSup* 32 (1981) 146-61 • S. JAPHET, "Sheshbazzar and Zerubbabel," *ZAW* 94 (1982) 66-98 and 95 (1983) 218-29; idem, "The Supposed Common Authorship of Chronicles and Ezra-Nehemiah Investigated Anew," *VT* 18 (1968) 330-71 • U. KELLERMANN, *Nehemia. Quellen, Überlieferung und Geschichte* (Berlin, 1967) extensive bibliography • D. KRAEMER, "On the Relationship of the Books of Ezra and Nehemiah," *JSOT* 59 (1993) 73-92 • S. MOWINCKEL, *Studien zu dem Buche Esra-Nehemia* (3 vols.; Oslo, 1964-65) • K. F. POHLMANN, *Studien zum dritten Esra* (Göttingen, 1970) • R. RENDTORFF, "Esra und das 'Gesetz,'" *ZAW* 96 (1984) 165-84; idem, "Noch einmal: Esra und das 'Gesetz,'" *ZAW* 111 (1999) 89-91 • M. SAEBØ, "Esra, Esraschriften," *TRE* 10.374-86 • W. T. IN DER SMITTEN, *Esra* (Assen, 1973) • E. UBRICH et al., eds., *Priests, Prophets, and Scribes* (Sheffield, 1992) • H. G. M. WILLIAMSON, "Ezra and Nehemiah in the Light of the Texts from Persepolis," *BBR* 1 (1991) 41-61.

ROBERT BACH

F

Faith

Overview

In the church and its milieu, the word "faith" is used with sometimes irritating generality (the English word perhaps even more crassly than its German equivalent, *Glaube*). One can distinguish at least three uses, as well as two areas of scholarly inquiry.

In one of its uses, the term "faith" is almost synonymous with → "religion"; it means essentially the basic personal disposition of individuals or communities. In analogy to "Christian faith," we can speak also of "Jewish faith" and of the "faith" of Muslims, Buddhists, and so on. Such collective terminology for characterizing a common feature in different religions, however, can be justified neither materially nor formally. Expressions such as "interfaith" dialogue, as well as the use of the plural "faiths," are thus certainly open to question.

Second, "faith" is used in the stricter sense to refer to that which is specifically Christian (or Jewish, although Jews generally perceive "faith" as an inappropriate designation) in contrast to a nonbelieving, secular, agnostic attitude toward the world and toward the meaning of life. In this second sense, a person *has* faith, can desire it, can transmit it through education, and can foster and defend it. Here "faith" can be understood as a person's disposition (similar to one's sensitivity or musicality), as a gift from one's parents and from the church, and simultaneously as a gift from God. This understanding of faith approximates the classical and medieval doctrine of the *habitus* (disposition) of believers.

Third, "faith" is understood in the strictly Reformational sense in antithesis to this understanding of *habitus*. Here Protestant theology and preaching have, however, often become rigidly fixed in negative definitions to avoid making faith into a "work," or a religious achievement. Extremely cautious and thorough distinctions must be made (see 3.4-5) if one is to avoid turning the Reformational declaration of faith in Jesus Christ into an ultimately empty series of assertoric theological formulas divorced from actual experience and concrete human reality.

With respect to scholarly inquiry, two areas are available for addressing the question of faith theologically and from the perspective of the humanities. The first is that of classic exegetical analysis of the biblical writings of the Old and New Testaments (see 1 and 2). Broader religious studies expand such analysis. Their aim is an understanding of the Bible's relationship to its surroundings and its concrete relationship today to members of other religions. The methods of exegetical study and of religious studies in the broader sense are then also applied to the history of the concept of faith itself within the Christian church (see 3.4).

A second area of inquiry is that of systematic theology as it attempts to clarify and explain faith (see 3). Today this line of investigation includes linguistic-logical as well as psycholinguistic and psychological analysis. The earlier theses of the → psychology of religion (W. James, *The Will to Believe* [1897]; E. P. Starbuck, *The Psychology of Religion* [1899]) are today partly obsolete, as are the theological attacks on their positions. Similarly, critical analyses by S. Freud (1856-1939, *Totem and Taboo* [orig. pub., 1913] and *Moses and Monotheism* [orig. pub., 1939]) are of interest today only as the basis for queries within the context of depth psychology, now replaced by the more recent → ego psychology. Reflection by systematic theology no longer excludes questions of early-childhood → socialization or of the formation and function of → symbols (P. Ricoeur, J. Scharfenberg, et al.). Moreover, any theological explanation of faith must also take into account children, the ill, and the aged so as to show that all people can be recipients of faith in God in Jesus Christ.

Bibliography: I. U. DALFERTH, ed., *Sprachlogik des Glaubens. Texte analytischer Religionsphilosophie und Theologie zur religiösen Sprache* (Munich, 1974) • H. FRIES, *Faith under Challenge* (New York, 1969) • H.-G. GADAMER, *Truth and Method* (2d ed.; New York, 1990) • J. HICK, *Faith and Knowledge* (2d ed.; Ithaca, N.Y., 1967) • P. L. HOLMER, *The Grammar of Faith* (New York, 1978) • H. O. JONES, *Die Logik theologischer Perspektiven. Eine sprachanalytische Untersuchung* (Göttingen, 1985) • J. M. LOCHMAN, *The Faith We Confess: An Ecumenical Dogmatics* (Philadelphia, 1984) • R. NEEDHAM, *Belief, Language, and Experience* (Oxford, 1972) • W. PANNENBERG, *Systematic Theology* (3 vols.; Grand Rapids, 1991-98) • H. H. PRICE, *Belief* (Bristol, 1996) • P. RICOEUR, *The Conflict of Interpretations* (Evanston, Ill., 1974); idem, *From Text to Action* (Evanston, Ill., 1991) • H. SCHÜTTE, *Glaube im ökumenischen Verständnis* (Paderborn, 1996) • G. THEISSEN, *Biblical Faith: An Evolutionary Approach* (Philadelphia, 1985) • P. TILLICH, *Systematic Theology* (3 vols.; Chicago, 1951-63).

DIETRICH RITSCHL

1. OT

The OT has no noun for faith. (In Hab. 2:4 the rendering "faith" rests on the LXX use of *pistis* for *'ĕmûnâ*, "faithfulness.") The OT speaks of faith and belief only in forms of the verb, so that whether secular or theological, it is always a process. It is expressed by he'ĕmîn (believe, rely on), which, in spite of its root relationship with → "amen" and derivatives, must be investigated on its own, since the etymology provides no help toward understanding it. Its relative infrequency is surprising, especially in relation to the NT. Other verbs are obviously better adapted to describe our relationship with God (e.g., "fear," yārē', or "praise," bērēk and tôdâ).

This use of "faith, belief" is understandable when we look at what are probably the oldest uses, which belong to the sphere of human relationships (e.g., Prov. 14:15; 26:25; Gen. 45:26; 1 Kgs. 10:7). From such passages we may pick out the following characteristics of faith: It relates to a word or to a person who speaks a word; it always demands thought and testing; it must never be given blindly; its withholding may thus be judged either positively or negatively, according to the particular circumstances. → Wisdom reflects on these matters in order to give practical help in our everyday experience of people and their words.

A faith that demands thought and careful consideration does not belong to the cultic sphere. The more surprising, then, is the occurrence of the concept in Gen. 15:6, with its cultic setting (salvation oracle in 15:1 and imputation formula in v. 6b). This passage has been traditionally ascribed to E (→ Pentateuch), but scholars now commonly regard it as late. Its closeness to early Wisdom texts, though, speaks against this assignment. Along the lines of such texts Abraham questions God's saying, and → Yahweh replies to his objections (cf. Gen. 45:26-27 E), thus enabling a genuine faith, one resting on deliberation.

Isaiah is undoubtedly an early witness to the theological use of faith (the earliest, according to R. Smend). In contrast to Gen. 15:6, Isaiah uses the verb in the absolute (Isa. 7:9; 28:16). This linguistic usage is rooted in his message proclaiming "the Holy One of Israel" (1:4 etc.). Since Isaiah presents God as father (1:2, "I reared children") and the citizens of → Jerusalem as "children" (30:9), lack of understanding and unbelief are equated with disobedience and rebellion (1:2), and the coming of judgment is the inevitable consequence (1:4-7). To "stand firm in faith" would have been the requirement of the hour (the positive version of 7:9!), closely related to "quietness" and "trust" — yet it is a vain hope in the different situations Isaiah has in mind, for no "returning" takes place (30:15; cf. 6:9-10). The Holy One of Israel is rejected by those he reared.

Confronted with this rejection from the very beginning (6:9-10; cf. Gen. 45:26), Isaiah does not give in but employs images and genres from Wisdom calling for deliberation (e.g., 1:3; 28:23-29) and consequently for acceptance of the prophetic word in which "the Holy One of Israel" speaks. Isaiah probably belonged to the Wisdom circles himself (thus J. Fichtner and I. von Loewenclau) and was therefore also familiar with discussions on believing. The prophet knew that faith enters another dimension if linked with the Holy One of Israel; this explains its linguistic usage in the absolute.

In later examples we find two different lines of development, both of which in some sense follow on from Isa. 30:15. On the one hand, "faith" loses its original relation to a person's word, becoming a matter of relying on the person, with a warning against putting any trust in human beings (Mic. 7:5). Here "belief" overlaps "trust," *bāṭaḥ*, a verb that is preferred with reference to Yahweh (Ps. 146:3; Prov. 3:5). Faith and trust are obviously not identical. On the other hand, the relation to a person's word is strengthened, as "believe" comes to be equated with "hear," *šāmaʿ* (Deut. 9:23; 2 Kgs. 17:14). The word that is to be heard is the commandment of Yahweh, the presupposition of all knowledge (Ps. 119:66) — indeed, of life as a whole (Deut. 30:15-20). Rejection of this word leads to death, and therefore one cannot question it but can only listen and obey. We readily detect here the Deuteronomistic view that in the end can see a parallel between faith in Yahweh and faith in Moses

(Exod. 14:31; 19:9), a faith that is now very close to → obedience.

The same Deuteronomistic view influences later → prophets in their call for → conversion (§1; Jer. 25:4-5; Zech. 1:4). The call is not to believe but to hear the word of God and to obey — any deliberation is futile when life is at stake. In these references we therefore miss the word "believe." In Jonah 3:5, however, we read, "The people of Nineveh believed God." Their subsequent activities underline how seriously they took his message. The prophetic word offers a chance to all people, not just to Israel. In this regard their faith forms an introduction to NT faith (see Luke 11:32).

Bibliography: B. S. Childs, *Biblical Theology of the Old and New Testaments: Theological Reflections on the Christian Bible* (London, 1992) • K. P. Donfried, "Faith in the OT," *HBD* (2d ed.) 326-27 • J. Fichtner, "Jesaja unter den Weisen," *TLZ* 74 (1949) 75-80 • A. Jepsen, "אמן *ʾāman* V," *TDOT* 1.298-309 • I. von Loewenclau, "Zur Auslegung von Jesaja 1.2-3," *EvT* 26 (1966) 294-308 • D. Lührmann, "Faith: OT," *ABD* 2.744-58 • C. Morse, "The Call to Faithful Disbelief," *USQR* 50 (1996) 1-11 • R. Smend, "Zur Geschichte von *heʾĕmîn*," *Hebräische Wortforschung* (FS W. Baumgartner; Leiden, 1967) 284-90 • H. Wildberger, "*ʾmn*," *THAT* 1.187-93; idem, "Erwägungen zu *heʾĕmîn*," FS Baumgartner, 372-86.

Ilse von Loewenclau

2. NT

2.1. *Concept*

The reason why faith became a mark of early Christian identity does not lie in the religious use of the Gk. noun *pistis* or verb *pisteuō*. Such a basis cannot be proved, nor is there proof of the thesis that in the Hellenistic period "faith" was a general religious slogan not peculiar to Christianity (contra R. Bultmann).

Primitive Christianity, rather, was adopting the usage of Greek-speaking → Judaism, which in turn points us back to Hebrew words of the root *ʾmn* that the LXX consistently translated using words of the root *pist-*. On the basis of this Jewish tradition, faith is confidence that our irritating experiences in the world can be reconciled with our confession of God as the Creator and Upholder of this world. This influence means that, subjectively, faith entails endurance and patience in difficult situations, which is close to the Greek sense of → faithfulness. Objectively, we are presented with the task of constantly integrating experience into our confession.

2.2. *Jesus*

If Matt. 18:6 and Mark 9:42 A B W (and other witnesses) are secondary as compared with Mark 9:42

א D Δ, the Synoptic Jesus did not demand faith in himself. The variously reported saying about having faith that can move mountains has as its point in the original version (Matt. 17:20 Q) the contrast between the tiniest seed and the most tremendous result. In the version in Mark 11:23 and Matt. 21:21 there is also reflection on the problem of → doubt. The power to do what seems to be impossible is also the issue when there is reference to the part of faith in the miracle stories (esp. also in Mark 9:14-29). The faith motif does not come from the → miracle stories of antiquity, comparable though these might be in other ways.

2.3. NT View of Faith

The usage of → Jesus did not itself shape the view of primitive Christianity (contra G. Ebeling). We find various spheres of usage in the NT, which are linked in different ways to the understanding of faith that developed in Judaism.

2.3.1. One line of thought appears in Hebrews and James (see also 2.3.5) that is continued in *1 Clement* and *Shepherd of Hermas*. Here faith is viewed subjectively as patience or steadfastness (par. to *hypomonē*; see Heb. 10:36-39). Hebrews 11 adduces a list of witnesses on behalf of this faith, and Jesus showed this kind of steadfastness as "the pioneer and perfecter of our faith" (12:2). The definition in 11:1 calls faith the "assurance" *(hypostasis)* and "conviction" *(elenchos)* of what is hoped for but not yet seen.

2.3.2. Heb. 6:1 uses "faith" also in the sense of "come to faith," parallel to *metanoia* as conversion. This line also is based on Judaism (see Jonah 3:5 and Jdt. 14:10). We often find it in Acts, Paul, and John (note also Mark 1:15 as a redactional summary of the preaching of Jesus). In Heb. 6:1 faith is faith in God (see 1 Thess. 1:8), but mostly the term has Christological content. It is a response to proclamation. For both Jews and Gentiles the opposite is unbelief, not false faith.

"Faith" is also a summary term to identify that to which one is converted. Thus Paul in 1 Cor. 15:1-11 reminds the Corinthians of his preaching to them, which led them to faith. This faith has a definite content, which Paul recalls, using fixed wording he has adopted (vv. 3-5). The content of this tradition points to the mission to the Jews, to whom it is not a new God that is proclaimed, but a new and definitive saving work on the part of this God. In accordance with the passive voice used relative to the resurrection, faith is faith in the God "who raised Jesus our Lord from the dead" (Rom. 4:24). To Gentiles, the true God must also be proclaimed (1 Thess. 1:9), and therefore faith seems to have a twofold object in

statements like 1 Cor. 8:6. Such a text later gave rise to the problem of holding fast the unity and uniqueness of God without making Jesus the mere proclaimer of this God. This issue is the theme of concerns in the → rule of faith *(regula fidei)* and on into the early church → confessions.

2.3.3. In 1 Cor. 15:11 Paul describes the content of faith as the common legacy of proclamation in the primitive church. A debatable matter, however, was the relation between faith and the → law, for the tradition adopted by Paul in 1 Cor. 15:3-5 left undefined the significance of "the scriptures," to which he made reference. As regards himself and his own mission, Paul concluded that the law had no positive function in giving orientation to faith. Instead, faith was independent of the law (Gal. 3:23-25), and → righteousness came, not by the law, but solely by faith, to which "the law and the prophets" attested (Rom. 3:21-26). Here faith is seen essentially in terms of its content, for what makes righteousness possible is not our own trust or steadfastness but the Christ-event as "the end of the law" (Rom. 10:4; → Justification).

With → Christology the particular experiences that seem to contradict this event most sharply, namely, → sin and → death, are taken up into the confession. Not in the law, but only in Christ, as the law itself promised (see Deuteronomy 28–30), can the confession and → experience coincide. As the embodiment of this Christ, the → congregation thus embraces such real-world polarities as Jew and Greek, slave and free, and male and female (Gal. 3:28). For the congregation, the law has not merely become impossible as a way of salvation. It must also try to find new norms of conduct in the sphere of → ethics (§2), for the law is unable to provide such primary orientation for life (see the elementary question of → dietary laws). What remains of the law is the unconditional command of love (which Gal. 5:14 and Rom. 13:9 emphatically describe as a command of the law).

2.3.4. John uses only the verb *pisteuō;* the noun *pistis* does not occur until 1 John 5:4. In the miracle stories of John faith is the result of the miracles, not what makes them possible, as it is in the Synoptics. If we trace the stories back to a "signs" source and find the original ending of this source in John 20:30-31, they are proclamation designed to awaken faith. For John himself the content of faith is defined by statements about the sending of the Son (6:29) or the relation between the Son and the Father (16:27, 30), not the cross and resurrection, as in Paul. But here again faith means → salvation. The tension between confession and experience is thus resolved as a new level of experience is introduced in contrast to the experience of the world reflected in the parting discourses. In this regard faith and knowledge are synonymous (6:69). Both carry the same promise of life and mean reception of the enacted salvation.

2.3.5. In opposition to Paul himself, not simply to a false Paulinism, James contests the antithesis of faith and works first formulated by Paul (2:14-26). On the one hand, he takes a positive view of the law (2:1-13); on the other, unlike Paul, James views faith as an attitude, for example, of steadfastness (1:3) or impartiality (2:1).

2.3.6. Among the → Synoptists we find a special usage only in Matthew, with his emphasis on the expression "little faith" (Luke 12:28/Matt. 6:30), which derives from Q. Faith here is a confidence that may be small or great.

2.4. *Theological Significance and Reception*
The NT has no single view of faith. We cannot explain the nuances in terms of historical development. Two main lines may be discerned. The first understands faith subjectively, while the second (Acts, Paul [including the Deutero-Paulines], John, and 1 John) orients it to its content. This second line finds its continuation in concerns for the rule of faith. Only with the defining of the → canon was a need felt to achieve a unitary view of faith in the NT (and the OT). This view led later to the doublet *fides quae creditur* (the faith that is believed — i.e., objective faith) and *fides qua creditur* (the faith by which [it] is believed — i.e., subjective faith), which is still influential in theological history but not really very helpful. Faith is nowhere restricted to the relation between us and God, which involves only secondarily a relation to the world. Rather, it includes the world as the setting of faith.

Bibliography: R. BULTMANN, "Πιστεύω κτλ.," *TDNT* 6.174-82, 197-228; idem, *Theology of the NT* (2 vols.; New York, 1951-55) • B. S. CHILDS, *Biblical Theology of the Old and New Testaments: Theological Reflections on the Christian Bible* (London, 1992) • G. EBELING, "Jesus and Faith," *Word and Faith* (London, 1963) 201-46 • E. GRÄSSER, *Der Glaube im Hebräerbrief* (Marburg, 1965) • K. HAACKER, "Glaube II/3," *TRE* 13.289-304 • H.-J. HERMISSON and E. LOHSE, *Glaube* (Stuttgart, 1978) • D. LÜHRMANN, "Glaube," *RAC* 11.48-122; idem, *Glaube im frühen Christentum* (Gütersloh, 1976) • A. SCHLATTER, *Der Glaube im Neuen Testament* (6th ed.; Stuttgart, 1982; orig. pub., 1885) • C. J. H. WRIGHT, "Faith of Christ, NT," *ABD* 2.758-69.

DIETER LÜHRMANN

3. Systematic Theology

3.1. *Christian Faith: Definition*
Faith, including Christian faith, is always and exclusively faith in God. As the faith of Christians, its manifestations have indeed changed through history, but as faith in Jesus Christ, it was and is always and exclusively faith in the God who according to the NT has revealed himself in Jesus Christ and through his Spirit as redemptive, compassionate, justifying love. Because, and to the extent, Christians believe in this God, their faith does differ from unbelief and superstition; yet because they too never believe only in this God, Christian faith also constantly risks being supplanted, distorted, and concealed by unbelief and superstition.

3.2. *Faith in Jesus Christ*
As faith in Jesus Christ, Christian faith is the concrete version of faith in God in the light of the gospel, rather than its complement or expansion (i.e., it is always monotheistic faith). This simple formula, "faith in Jesus Christ," unites historical, theological, and anthropological perspectives (in their reference, respectively, to Jesus, God, and humanity), along with their ecclesiological and cosmological implications. Although we may distinguish these perspectives, we cannot separate them or play them off against one another without truncating our concept of Christian faith, which can be described from various perspectives. Thus in relation to → Jesus, faith is eschatological experience of the risen Lord (Easter faith); in relation to God, it is sure trust in the promises of his saving action *(fiducia promissionis);* and in relation to believers, it is obedient acceptance of integration into God's reconciling and justifying work in Jesus Christ *(fides iustificans).*

As thus comprising faith in the resurrection, the promise, and justification, "faith" is the basic Christian term for our inclusion into the saving eschatological relation between God and us that God himself has set up (→ Salvation). It is to be distinguished not only from every kind of human relation to God (→ Piety; Religion), self (certainty, feeling), and world (experience, knowledge, action), but also from God's relation to us (creation, justification, perfection). Faith owes itself completely and exclusively to God, not to the believer (faith as *opus Dei*), yet the faith relationship between the believer and God is also to be distinguished from God's own justification of the believer, with which it substantively coincides, as its converse. That is, faith is not the human response to God's revelation, not a second human act alongside God's own act of justification. Rather, it is the abbreviation of the description of God's justifying relationship with human beings from the perspective of the justified believer, a description following the presentation and interpretation of the saving event in the gospel. Being a child is not the child's response to its parents' status as parents, nor can it be equated with such. Rather, it designates the same relation in a converse description insofar as the expression "child of" constitutes the logical converse of "parent of." Similarly, faith is not the human response to God's justification, nor simply a different way of describing it, but rather its logical converse. "I believe in God" reverses the perspective of "God has justified me"; it is not merely a different description of God's salvific activity, nor the human act accompanying and reacting to God's own actions. It is the converse description of the same event.

The two statements "I believe in God" and "God has justified me" can be spoken and confessed only in response to the gospel proclamation of Jesus Christ. Since the gospel identifies the resurrection of the crucified Jesus as God's final and absolute deliverance of the world and as the promise made to every human being *(verbum externum)*, faith expresses itself as faith in Jesus Christ and in God's justification of the sinner by faith on account of Christ *(per fidem propter Christum)*. This confession of faith is a response to the *verbum externum* of proclamation, but such an understanding does not allow the false conclusion that faith itself constitutes a response to God's justifying action. Faith *is* this divine event of justification through which God re-creates the sinner by grace alone *(sola gratia)*, but described now from the perspective of the justified sinner. The event of faith in which believers correspond to God's will and thus fulfill the first commandment is to be described theologically not as an experiential, cognitive, fiducial, habitual, or emotional qualification of the old self but as an eschatological constitution of the new self. Those who believe are justified not because of their faith *(propter fidem)* but by believing *(per fidem propter Christum)*. Moreover, this faith expresses itself as faith in Jesus Christ because, as the gospel makes clear, God justifies the sinner "outside of ourselves" *(extra nos)* in Christ; sinners are justified only gratis, rather than as the result of their own efforts (or lack thereof).

3.3. *Faith and Believing*

Because Christian faith is to be conceived wholly in terms of Jesus Christ as its basis and object, that is, God as self-defined in Jesus Christ, it can be explained only inadequately along the lines of the common use of the word "believe," which may be propositional (or doxastic) ("I believe that . . ."), fiducial ("I believe you"), or personal ("I believe in

you"). Christian faith, as faith in Jesus Christ rather than as the faith of Christians, is not a kind of acceptance expressing the certainty of subjective conviction but not the assurance of objective knowledge (I. Kant); it involves asserted certainty that precisely as such is never free of temptation. Again, it is not a kind of human trust in others ("I believe in you") or oneself ("I believe in myself") that does not weaken in the face of indications to the contrary; rather, deriving from God himself, it means being established neither on others nor on oneself but on God alone. Being so fixed on God as to realize that it is constituted by him, that is, through God's own free action, Christian faith is rendered innocuous when it is reduced to believing others or trusting oneself. It must be defined strictly in terms of its basis and object — that is, → God, as he revealed himself in the history of Israel and especially in the history and destiny of Jesus Christ. For this reason it expresses itself in elementary terms simply as "faith in Jesus Christ."

3.4. *OT and NT*

The Bible as the normative account of faith bears witness in various ways to the view sketched here. It gives us no uniform understanding of faith, however, nor even a clearly defined concept of faith. Theological reflection has thus been able to link various understandings to the different aspects of faith as we find it in the OT and the NT.

In this regard there have always been three basic problems: (1) how to define doctrinally the *object and content of faith*, that is, the knowledge of faith that by common consent the church has regarded as binding for Christians and constitutive of their identity (*regula fidei*; → Confession of Faith; Rule of Faith); (2) how to elucidate the spiritual problem of the *origin and emergence of faith*, that is, the question of its constitution, historical beginning, and subject; and (3) how to describe the *practical life of faith*, that is, the way in which faith is to be lived out and practiced in the present world, both individually and corporately. As the emphasis falls on one or another of these interrelated problems, the doctrinal, spiritual, or practical dimension of faith receives special attention, and faith is correspondingly understood primarily as doctrine, spiritual gift, or lifestyle. This irreducibly multidimensional character of faith is always a potential source of conflict in each theological tradition.

3.5. *Theological Development*
3.5.1. *Early Church*

The → early church, using an approach still methodologically typical of → European theology, tried to ward off heretical truncations of primitive resurrection faith by outlining the content of faith. In its decisions on the doctrine of the → Trinity and → Christology, it attempted to find a single theological solution to all three basic problems by developing the content of faith in such a way as to include the divine constitution of the event of faith as related to specific historical events and the divine basis of the life of faith in history, thus safeguarding its eschatological character — that is, its new beginning, deriving from God alone, in history (Jesus Christ) and in every individual life (Spirit). God was confessed at once as the eternal origin (Father), the historical basis (Jesus Christ), and the concrete mediation and empowering (Spirit) of faith. Similarly, Jesus Christ was confessed as true man and true God, in whom the object, constitution, and life of faith correspond perfectly as a grounding in God, deriving from God himself (the doctrine of enhypostasis).

3.5.2. Medieval Scholasticism

The → Orthodox Church sought to maintain this integrated approach of the early church → dogmas with its practical relevance for the life of faith both individually and in the church. It did so by linking the doctrinal content of faith and the spiritual constitution of faith in a liturgical representation of the cosmological Christ-event and by wholly anchoring the life of faith in cultic participation (→ Liturgy 2).

The West, however, took a different course. With the rise of the state church, dogmas assumed a legal character, and with their integration into an anthropologically oriented theology, they were viewed as answers only to questions of the content of faith. As the elements related to the life of faith were neglected, they became the epitome of revealed truths that surpass ordinary epistemological capabilities and demand supernatural enlightenment. Conversely, a way was opened up for the analysis of the event of faith from a purely anthropological standpoint. Augustine (354-430) distinguished between the content of faith (fides quae creditur) and the act of faith (fides qua creditur), along with describing faith as a gift of → grace that makes possible thoughtful assent to an outside witness of faith (cum assensione cogitare) but that remains dead if, through hope, it does not become → love, if it does not work by love (per dilectionem operatur) and in love become the contemplation of eternal → truth. These lines set the parameters for medieval thinking on faith (→ Augustine's Theology).

Analysis of the act of faith (Abelard, William of Auxerre) and rational reflection on the content of faith (Anselm) went together in different ways, with a stress either on understanding (Thomas Aquinas) or on will (Duns Scotus). Franciscan theology (→

Scotism) differentiated between external conviction through the authoritative witness of Scripture (fides acquisita), inner illumination through the truth of faith itself (fides informis), and faith formed by love (fides formata). Thomas Aquinas (→ Thomism) viewed faith as an infused → virtue (fides infusa) that, by way of the will, makes possible an acceptance by the intellect of the supernatural (but not antinatural) truths of faith. This habit of faith is indeed a gift of grace mediated by the church, but its infusion presupposes the human preparation of → penitence and repentance (→ Scholasticism).

3.5.3. Luther

M. → Luther (1483-1546) made a threefold attack against (1) all psychologizing analyses of faith (WA 6.84-86), (2) all attempts to explain faith epistemologically, and (3) all efforts to transfer the idea of divine-human cooperation from where it undisputedly belongs (the description of the life of faith) to where it does not belong (the analysis of the constitution, origin, and emergence of faith). Pastoral concerns (e.g., widespread uncertainty about salvation and attempts to achieve a righteousness of works) forced him to undertake a consistently theological investigation of faith. As he saw it, faith must be seen strictly in terms of its object, that is, of what God does for us in Jesus Christ. It is our comprehensive integration by God into the saving event of the crucifixion and → resurrection (sola fide–per Christum), of which we are assured through the → Holy Spirit in encountering God's word of promise. We therefore can be certain of salvation in every assault (→ Temptation; Assurance of Salvation), since it has been achieved by God alone in Christ without any cooperation on our part.

Faith as personal union with Christ (fides amplectens) is not just cognitive Christian belief (fides historica), nor is it mere credulity (fiducia without content). It is the effective eschatological division between the old self and the new, the "blessed exchange" (LW 25.188-89), in which Christ takes on himself our → sin and gives us a part in his fellowship with God. Since we thus participate in his → righteousness, we are justified. Faith is therefore not a mere condition of → justification (as Melanchthon's doctrine of imputation might seem to suggest) but is itself justification as realized in the life of the believer. If, however, believers live only insofar as they live in Christ and Christ in them, then in hearing the Word and in daily penitence they are liberated by the Holy Spirit for active involvement in the world in acts of love (→ Luther's Theology).

3.5.4. Roman Catholicism

Luther's strictly theological definition of faith as our new eschatological constitution in Christ (fides facit *personam*, WA 39/1.283.18-19), of which we have assurance only by the free ministry of the Spirit through the preaching of the → gospel, led to a breach with Rome. Rejecting the *sola fide* of the Reformation, which it (mis)understood as mere fiducial faith (→ Reformation Principles), the Councils of → Trent (→ Catholic Reform and Counterreformation) and → Vatican I saw faith as one of the three theological virtues, describing it as a supernatural virtue "by means of which, with the grace of God inspiring and assisting us, we believe to be true what he has revealed" (DH 3008; Tanner, 2.807). Faith is thus the basic virtue, though for salvation it is insufficient without → hope and → love. As a gift of divine grace, it is free and cannot be forced, but it must be focused on the divinely revealed truths that have been entrusted to the → church as an infallible deposit of faith (→ Catholicism [Roman]).

Even though Vatican II laid stronger emphasis on the personal character of faith and its relation to salvation history, which has made ecumenical approximation less difficult and led in 1999 to an official declaration that the Tridentine condemnations no longer addressed the Lutheran doctrine of justification as defined in the common declaration concerning justification, this position derived more from the decline of Lutheran theology than from any substantive move toward agreement. Debate continues not only about the presupposed understanding of revelation and the church but also about the proper theological description of the character of faith. A realization that such debates do not provide grounds for schismatic condemnations, however, was long overdue.

3.5.5. *The Protestant World*

In the Protestant world J. → Calvin (1509-64) and P. → Melanchthon (1497-1560) adopted Luther's approach but modified it for pastoral reasons. Calvin (→ Calvin's Theology) found a basis for faith in God's eternal election and stressed especially its cognitive character. Melanchthon, to make self-testing possible, analyzed the process of faith psychologically into perception (*notitia*), assent (*assensio*), and certainty (*fiducia*). The questions of faith and knowledge and of faith and → experience remained just as thorny in Reformation theology as did that of faith and works (Formula of Concord, arts. 1-6).

Taking up again the distinction between the act of faith and the content of faith, Protestant → orthodoxy tried to systematize the issues by expounding faith as an → order of salvation. In spite of efforts to preserve the Reformation legacy by differentiating special (justifying) faith from general faith, the Christological-pneumatological perspective tended constantly to be pushed into the background by an anthropological-pneumatological appropriation of scriptural truths of revelation according to the schema of → act and content. The → pietistic stress on subjective experience and the practical character of faith as decision (act) moved no less along the same lines than the demand of the → Enlightenment for a rational backing for the claim to authority and truth (content) and the resultant reactions of the dogmatism of supernatural revelation, the subjectivism of irrational faith (faith as pure feeling and experience), the theological rationalism of faith (faith as a general search for happiness and salvation apart from the → Word of God, or as a moralizing imitation of the religion of Jesus), and the speculative transformation of faith by its merging into philosophical knowledge (G. W. F. Hegel).

These efforts to understand faith as act and content, by refocusing on the basic anthropological questions of the Enlightenment (What can I know? What should I do? What may I hope?), arrived thus at the dead end characterizing the modern alternatives of subjectivism and objectivism, knowledge and action, theoretical and practical knowledge, metaphysics and morals, (natural) science and history. The resulting aporetic understandings of faith (→ Aporia) truncated or distorted it in contradictory interpretations focusing on either cognitive or fideistic, moralistic or historical, supernaturalistic or fiducial aspects, or by either dissolving faith into a general concept of religion or viewing faith from a fundamentalist biblicist perspective.

3.5.6. *Schleiermacher*

F. D. E. → Schleiermacher (1768-1834) first broke through the anthropological schema of act and content in reflection on faith by his pioneering but little understood attempt to unfold the unity of the content, event, and life of faith. In light of the conditions of the → modern period, he wanted to do justice to the divine constitution of faith (Spirit) as well as to its positive character, both historically (with respect to Jesus) and practically (with respect to the church), and without truncating faith cognitively or moralistically. Faith for Schleiermacher is not human knowledge, action, or experience but a specific determination of feeling that, as a pneumatic working of Christ through the Word, constitutes the believing subject as a specific unity of self-consciousness, world-consciousness, and God-consciousness (→ Schleiermacher's Theology).

Although every act of life includes absolute dependence on the absolute causality (origin) called "God" in symbolic religious language, such a feeling of absolute dependence does not yet constitute faith itself, since such faith, as faith in Jesus Christ, is indissolubly associated with consciousness of the distinction between sin and grace. Only as the redemption effected by Jesus validates itself in this way in the consciousness of an individual person by shaping the entire context of his or her experience can faith manifest itself in experience and be understood both reflectively in the context of knowledge and practically in that of life and action.

3.5.7. *Development since Schleiermacher*
We may summarize the main lines of discussion after Schleiermacher under the following nine headings:

3.5.7.1. *Faith and experience.* Under the many-faceted heading "experience" we are reminded that the primary theological issue is faith and unbelief, not faith and knowledge (Erlangen School; → Revivals). Here we find the beginnings of a "pisteology" of faith (I. A. Dorner), as well as exploration of the problem of faith and religion (→ Phenomenology of Religion) and investigation of the links between faith, experience, and action (→ Psychology of Religion; Sociology of Religion). Neo-Protestantism has developed an understanding of faith in terms of a theology of experience (R. Otto). It is open to the psychological analysis of faith in → pragmatism (W. James, J. Royce, G. Wobbermin) and has generalized faith as "apprehension by that which affects us unconditionally" (P. Tillich, *Werke* 11.127). These topics not only play an important role in the theory and practice of → pastoral care. By way of American culture theology (→ North American Theology), they have also helped to form a theology of religious experience in the Second and → Third Worlds (→ Third World Theology).

The richness of the concept of experience itself has prompted a variety of theological positions. In antithesis to its religious dissolution into an indefinite "courage to be," faith has been described along Reformation lines as a specific "experience with experience" (G. Ebeling, E. Jüngel), which is tied to the witness of faith mediated by the church. By contrast, concrete experiences have prompted an understanding of faith as active engagement on behalf of the poor and oppressed in the name of the gospel (liberation theology). Feminist theologies have shown that experience is always shaped by culturally dependent gender differences and by the patriarchal nexus of power. Ignoring such distinctions renders theological discussion of religious experience, the experience of faith, or mysticism abstract, and it both disregards and fosters the concrete structures of inequality.

3.5.7.2. *Faith and church.* The church mediates the witness of faith (and thus needs theology to pro-

vide critical control), but living faith also needs to be rooted in the → worship and life of the → congregation (→ Devotion, Devotions; Spirituality). From this understanding follow the importance of common → liturgy and the practice of worship (→ Anglican Communion; Ecumenism, Ecumenical Movement; Orthodoxy) for faith and the unity of faith, and also the need for a closer link between worship and life, which would make the concrete life situation of the church the main point of reference for reflection on faith (→ Contextual Theology).

Focusing on these insights, the so-called Yale school (H. Frei, G. Lindbeck, S. Hauerwas) has challenged liberal theology's attempt to understand Christian faith as (or even reduce it to) what can be explicated and justified within secular, pluralistic Western societies according to the rational standards of neutrality, universality, and the public. It is not faith that is to be understood, interpreted, and explicated before the scientific forum of the modern world, but rather quite the reverse: precisely that world is to be so examined before the forum of biblical faith. The identity of faith can be preserved and strengthened rather than undermined only if faith itself is understood theologically with reference to and on the basis of the Christian community rather than of the multireligious society of the waning modern world. It is not faith that must justify itself before history; history, rather, must justify itself before faith.

3.5.7.3. *Faith and history.* The historical point of reference of faith lies in its relation to the history of Jesus, to the historical witness to faith in Scripture, and to the historical existence of the church. The failure of the quest for the historical → Jesus and the rediscovery of the eschatological nature of faith promote insight into its linguistic surplus value compared with present reality (→ Hermeneutics) and teach us to view history as a whole as a union of historical events and divine promises (W. Pannenberg). Faith lives by God's acts not only in the past but also in the present and the → future.

Two points are important here. First, faith is always oriented toward God and thus toward a present reality; this truth needs to be said with respect to all attempts to understand the Christian faith as a historical faith or to reduce it to a Jesus-faith whose content is disappearing into an ever-receding past (Jesus Seminar). Faith is not oriented toward the past but toward the present, toward God's presence inhering in every present.

Second, a consistent distinction must be made between faith and the witnesses to faith. The latter are concretely historical; yet even though there can be no faith without witnesses to faith, neither can faith simply be equated with a specific historical witness to faith. From the outset, Christian faith has existed only in the plural and in an ongoing process of translation and transformation between persons, languages, and cultures. It has never attached itself to the witness of a specific person, group, language, or culture such that it might be understood and lived only in this particular form rather than, if required by altered circumstances, even over against that form.

Because faith is concrete and historical, it cannot be identified with any specific historical form. Christians believe in Jesus Christ, not merely as Jesus has believed; they believe in the Jesus Christ attested normatively by Scripture rather than the witness of Scripture itself. But whereas Christian faith is everywhere and always faith in Jesus Christ, it is by no means everywhere and always faith in a specific understanding of Jesus Christ or a specific teaching about Christ or a specific Christology. Just because we have no access to faith independent of all understanding of and witness to it, we must distinguish between what can be transmitted and mediated (witnesses to faith) and what only God can mediate and create (faith). Faith comes exclusively from God in Christ, concretely created and manifested through his Word and Spirit. By contrast, witnesses to faith always derive from human beings as well, and they always exhibit the temporally specific features of our own historical situation, which, in their own turn, are always in need of critique.

3.5.7.4. *Faith and life.* This specific historical reference of faith must be taken into account if we are properly to understand its character as decision and the concrete historicity of existence in faith (S. Kierkegaard, R. Bultmann; → Existential Theology) as well as the specific character of the life of faith as active → obedience in ethical, social, and political involvement in the church's present situation (→ Diakonia; Political Theology; Social Gospel). Faith not concretely lived is no faith at all, but neither does faith emerge as such merely by being lived.

In particular, the contextual theologies of the Third (though also of the First and Second) World have rediscovered the significance of the life and praxis of faith for an adequate understanding of faith and have made the necessary practical and methodological inferences (the so-called theology from below, including political theology and feminist theology). The ecumenical movement has followed up the same insight by trying to achieve a fuller material development of the common faith (laid down in its basic confession) in terms of a common practice of faith. Nor is it by accident that precisely in plural, multireligious societies we find an increasing interest in exploring new ways for fostering faith through teaching, transmission, and socialization.

3.5.7.5. *Faith and knowledge.* The rational transition from the subjective certainty of faith to the objective knowledge of faith was a central theme of theological doctrines of faith in the 19th century. But after the collapse of idealistic syntheses, the shock of Darwinism (→ Evolution), and the new theological approach of → dialectical theology, stress came to be put particularly on the incommensurability of faith and knowledge and the distinctiveness of the theological knowledge of faith.

Experiences during the second half of the 20th century, however, have clearly shown that these insights alone are not enough. First, in an increasingly multireligious world, more profound clarification is needed concerning the relationship between Christian faith and theology, on the one hand, and, on the other, the presuppositions and salvific claims of other religious traditions. Second, questions arise within theology itself concerning faith and doctrine, faith and theology, and thus also concerning the relation between theological, scientific, and other kinds of knowledge. These questions are of considerable ecumenical relevance insofar as Roman Catholics and Protestants continue to differ in precisely these areas. Third, the 20th-century analytic sensibility in the larger sense has prompted especially pragmatic, semiotic, and analytic theology and philosophy of religion to pursue a substantive, linguistic, logical, semiotic, and theoretical clarification of Christian (and other) faith assertions and truth claims. Finally, phenomenological, hermeneutical, and postanalytic theologies and philosophies of religion have studied the many cultural connections and interweavings between language, myth, faith, religion, art, science, history, and the other symbolic forms of human life. These insights have shown that more precise distinctions must be made between the various kinds of knowledge, reasoning, and rationalities, and a more precise articulation is needed of the relationship between faith and knowledge than has hitherto been the custom in either Catholic or Protestant theology. These developments have also led to a more detailed look at the relation between faith and language.

3.5.7.6. *Faith and language.* Faith manifests itself symbolically in various forms of speech, life, and praxis, forms affecting the formulation and representation of its content in witness and confession.

Theological reflection on this content goes astray if it does not pay heed to the semantic and pragmatic peculiarities of the symbolic and linguistic logic of faith and to the rhetorical and symbolic features of its imagery, metaphors, and narration. Faith does not think or articulate itself primarily in concepts, but rather in symbols, metaphors, and stories. Faith lives in rhetorically constructed imagery, and because this imagery functions according to hermeneutical rules in which indefinite, vague, or semantically open features play an important creative role, it cannot be understood or evaluated according to a reductive logic of concept, judgment, and conclusion that ignores the role of the imagination. The discussion of faith and myth and of faith and the imagination has shown that any analysis of the mythic, creative, and narrative linguistic and symbolic processes of faith must be both hermeneutically sensitive and critical. It must consider carefully the Christian "rebirth of images" (A. Farrer), that is, the poetic and hermeneutical processes of the Christian refashioning and redefinition of non-Christian forms of language, thought, and speech. But it must also critically distinguish in a fundamental way between faith itself and its symbolic manifestations, and between faith and (epistemic) belief.

3.5.7.7. *Faith and (epistemic) belief.* In distinction from faith, (epistemic) belief is a propositional attitude relative to alternatives, one of which is believed to be more probable than the other(s). The epistemic probability of a belief is a measure of the extent to which evidence renders it likely to be true, and a belief is rational if one is justified in holding it for epistemological reasons, that is, for reasons that concern the likelihood of its being true. Christian faith indeed constantly finds expression also in individual and common beliefs and systems of beliefs.

As the relation to God that God himself constitutes, however, faith is not dependent — as beliefs are — on context, time, or person, and it is thus to be distinguished from them in principle as the basis of their possibility. "I believe in God" does indeed imply "I believe that I believe in God." The epistemic belief that I believe, however, is not the faith in God about which that proposition speaks. Nor is faith in God an epistemic belief that is judged to be more or less probable. Rather, it is the opportunity for life God grants and opens up to us. Regardless of its degree of epistemic improbability, it remains the dependable soteriological basis of new life because it derives exclusively from God rather than from us. Hence the basic epistemic statement of faith is not "I believe that I believe" but, rather, "I

believe, Lord, help my unbelief." New life and the justification of sinners come about solely through that particular faith in God that God himself creates through his Word and Spirit *(per fidem propter Christum)*, not through any epistemic belief on the part of sinners that they believe in God. The same applies to faith and the consciousness of faith.

3.5.7.8. *Faith and the consciousness of faith.* Whereas faith and unbelief are mutually exclusive and total alternatives that cannot gradually merge into one another, the consciousness of faith exists only as a certainty of faith that varies individually and is always exposed to assault. The genesis of faith as the transition from lack of faith to faith and the genesis of faith-consciousness as the transition from uncertainty to certainty are thus to be described differently. Faith rests on what God has done in Christ for us once for all and in a universally valid way, and thus on God's universal justification, whose converse that faith actually is (a basis for talk about "anonymous Christians" [K. Rahner] and the hope of → apocatastasis).

The consciousness of faith, however, emerges from the event of proclamation, which must take place ever anew and is necessarily particular. In this event the Spirit of God comes freely to listeners and discloses the truth of the gospel to them. Only faith that is thus brought to consciousness can manifest itself in human life as the experience, knowledge, witness, and action of faith, though these manifestations and symbols are not to be confused with faith itself. Faith constitutes the person who witnesses to it when and in the fashion that the person apprehends faith.

3.5.7.9. *Faith and person.* The point that the constitution and manifestation of faith differ is one that W. Herrmann (1846-1922) tried to express in his distinction between "the basis of faith" and "thoughts of faith." We miss this point if we mistakenly describe faith only as a relation of personal trust (F. Gogarten, E. Brunner). In contrast, K. Barth (1886-1968) expounded emphatically the cognitive and creative character of faith by developing it as the "constitution of the Christian subject" (*CD* IV) by the Word of God. Faith is the act of God that constitutes the possibility of human works and stimulates them. It is personal, not as an attitude of the → person, but as that which constitutes the person as such.

3.6. *Typology of Theological Reflection*
In terms of the structure of the basic Christian confession ("I believe in Jesus Christ"), we may typologically distinguish three approaches in theological efforts to clarify the understanding of faith.

Although these efforts overlap at various points when they deal with common problems, their different basic perspectives lead in each case to different results.

3.6.1. *Anthropology*

The anthropocentric approach seeks to think of faith in terms of the human subject. Faith is a supernatural habit of those who are already independently constituted apart from it and who are thus enabled to perceive revealed truth that transcends reason and to live a life commensurate with that truth. Typical problems on this view concern the relation between faith and the different human capacities, such as between faith and reason, faith and will, faith and experience, faith and work, and the act of faith and the content of faith. Roman Catholicism exemplifies this approach.

3.6.2. *Pneumatology*

The pneumatocentric approach seeks to view the faith-relation between us and God as a charismatic gift of the Spirit. It thus asks how things constituted independently of faith are specifically interrelated and qualified through it. Faith is a possession of the Spirit that alters our nature (Clement of Alexandria) and perfects it (Irenaeus). Typical problems in this view center on the relations between the individual and God (henosis; → Theosis), between the individual and the church, between the church and Christ, between natural humanity and perfected humanity, between → creation and → regeneration, between natural and supernatural faith, and between faith and vision. Eastern Orthodoxy offers an example of this approach.

3.6.3. *Theology*

The theocentric approach tries to view faith in terms of the divine object of faith, which as the subject of justification is also the true subject behind the faith relation. God constitutes believers as such by bringing them into the comprehensive existential relation between himself and Jesus Christ and making them certain of this relation by his Word. Typical problems here concern the relation between the old self and the → new self, between faith and the lack of faith, between sin and righteousness, between sinners and Christ, between God and Christ, between the revealed God *(Deus revelatus)* and the hidden God *(Deus absconditus)*, between divine grace and human bondage, between person and work, between assurance and doubt, and between → law and gospel. The Reformation offers an example of this approach.

3.6.4. *"I Believe in Jesus Christ"*

Not only does each of these three approaches develop its understanding of faith from a different perspective, each also begins with a different analysis of the basic Christian confession "I believe in Jesus Christ."

3.6.4.1. The *anthropocentric approach* analyzes the structure of this confession as subject-predicate. The predicate "believe in Jesus Christ" ascribes a specific property to a human subject, namely, having faith in Jesus Christ. This proposition becomes a confession in the first-person mood when speakers ascribe this property to themselves in the act of predication, namely, as "I believe in Jesus Christ."

3.6.4.2. The *pneumatocentric approach* analyzes the structure of this confession as a bipolar relation between a human subject (I) and the divine subject (God as defined in Jesus Christ) held together by the relationship of faith ("believe in"). This relational proposition becomes a confession when persons expressly acknowledge that they do indeed stand in this relation to God.

3.6.4.3. The *theocentric approach* focuses not on the predicative or relational surface structure of the confession but on its deeper causative structure expressed as "God has brought me to believe in Jesus Christ." Here "believe" means to be integrated (passively) into the divine salvific activity. A predicative analysis of the surface structure of the confession views God as the decisive subject, not the human being. Similarly, the decisive predicate is not a human action, disposition, or attitude but God's own salvific activity in Jesus Christ. Sinful human beings who ignore God are integrated into this activity by the Holy Spirit. Faith is not a (supernatural) human characteristic, disposition, or behavioral mode but the converse of God's own salvific activity on behalf of the sinner described from the latter's perspective.

A relational analysis of the confession views faith not as an external relation between two entities that are already independent and specific (human beings and God) but rather as an internal relation without which neither God nor human beings would be what they in fact are. God is essentially he who justifies the sinner *(Deus iustificans vel salvator)*. Human beings are essentially those who have become sinners on their own initiative *(homo reus et perditus)* and now must be justified by God *(homo iustificandus fide)*. As the believers into whom God has made them, they are justified, fulfill the first commandment, and fulfill their destiny as such from creation. God himself integrates the believer into the divine life in such a way that the believer is thereby made into the created image of God, whose company God seeks. Faith is not a human activity, characteristic, disposition, or attitude; it is nothing that human beings themselves do or have, and nothing they can attain or prompt through anything they do or have. It is a mode of existence, a place at which they exist, a place to which they cannot come on their own initiative. They are there at God's initiative. He places them there, constituting them as believers by installing them in an eternal fellowship with Christ through his Spirit.

3.6.5. *Multiple Perspectives and the Trinity*

Each approach analyzes the problems of faith from a different perspective, namely, from that of the human subject, the divine object, and the relation of faith between believer and God. Each approach is inclined to absolutize itself and thus to involve some truncation and one-sidedness. The structural irreducibility of their basic perspectives, however, shows that all are theologically legitimate. Christian faith is not just irreducibly multidimensional; it also can be grasped properly only from irreducibly multiple standpoints. This analysis does not mean that a person must decide with insufficient reasons between these three perspectives, nor that they must be understood as three mutually exclusive alternatives. Although no higher position seems able to integrate them all into a single view, there are enough reasons available for deciding between them on the basis of their different offerings and theological plausibility.

It is possible, however, to understand each perspective such that the others are neither submerged nor ignored. The theological understanding of Christian faith must seek not to give one or the other perspective the preeminent position, nor to subsume all three under a (nonexistent) higher perspective. Rather, the goal of a deeper understanding of faith is to develop each position in a way that preserves and acknowledges the import and legitimacy of the others. Nor does the requisite theological concept for this task need to be invented, since it already exists in the doctrine of the Trinity. A more intensive Trinitarian analysis, reconstruction, and presentation of faith can preserve the irreducible differences between the three approaches and yet still acknowledge the points of contact between them; in so doing, it enhances our understanding not only of faith, but of the Trinitarian doctrine itself. And thus, it will be one of the important theological tasks of the future.

3.7. *Contextual Development*

Although various theological traditions have made tentative steps in this direction, none has yet succeeded in acknowledging and assessing the legitimate differences of the other approaches as essential for its own view as well. Instead, they usually merely legitimize and propagate a different order among the approaches than that entertained by the theo-

logical traditions from which they come. Reflection on faith in the contextual theologies of Asia, Africa, and America reproduces these types with characteristic changes insofar as it reverses the typical European tendency to view the faith-event and the life of faith from the perspective of the content of faith, and to understand faith from within the unity of life, experience, and confession (→ Confession of Faith). Not faith as such but the concrete consciousness of faith as a specific unity of experience, knowledge, and action is thus at the center of theological reflection. The charismatically experienced event of faith (→ Pentecostal Churches) or the concrete experiences of the common life of faith under specific social conditions (as considered by experience theology, → liberation theology, and → feminist theology) thus become the starting point for criticism and restatement of the content of faith.

Even where this reassessment takes place in considerable freedom from traditional (confessional) statements, the change in formulating the substantive issues and in focal points of faith does not involve a change in content as long as faith knows and confesses that it is faith in Jesus Christ and thus in the God who saves his creation by overcoming evil with good, unrighteousness with righteousness, and unkindness with love. It is an inalienable theological requirement, however, that this faith should develop its content with (self-)critical regard for the difference between the divine constitution of faith and its human praxis, becoming thus concretely comprehensible and capable of ecumenical consensus. Only in this way are an assertorial confession of faith and a missionary life of faith possible, and only thus will the boundaries between faith and → superstition be protected against hopeless erosion.

Bibliography: R. Aubert, *Le problème de l'acte de foi* (4th ed.; Louvain, 1970) • E. Biser, *Glaubensvollzug* (Einsiedeln, 1980) • I. U. Dalferth, *Existenz Gottes und christlicher Glaube* (Munich, 1984) • J. Diekren, *Glaube und Lehre im modernen Protestantismus. Studien zum Verhältnis von religiösem Vollzug und theologischer Bestimmtheit bei Barth und Bultmann sowie Hegel und Schleiermacher* (Tübingen, 1996) • B. Duroux, *La psychologie de la foi chez saint Thomas d'Aquin* (Tournai, 1963) • G. Ebeling, *The Nature of Faith* (London, 1961) • I. Escribano-Alberca, E. Gössmann, and H. Petri, "Glaube und Gotteserkenntnis," *HDG* 1/2 (bibliography) • J. W. Fowler, *Weaving the New Creation: Stages of Faith and the Public Church* (San Francisco, 1991) • B. A. Gerrish, *Saving and Secular Faith: An Invitation to Systematic Theology* (Minneapolis, 1999) • S. G. Hall, E. Gössmann, and

R. Slenczka, "Glaube IV-VI," *TRE* 8.305-65 (bibliography) • W. Härle and R. Preul, eds., *Glaube* (= *MJTh* 4 [1992]) • J. Hick, *Faith and Knowledge* (2d ed.; London, 1967) • G. Hoffmann, *Die Lehre von der Fides Implicita* (3 vols.; Leipzig, 1903-9) • W. Van Huyssteen, *Theology and the Justification of Faith: Constructing Theories in Systematic Theology* (Grand Rapids, 1989) • W. Joest, *Ontologie der Person bei Luther* (Göttingen, 1967) • P. Manns, *Fides absoluta–fides incarnata* (2 vols.; Münster, 1965) • U. Neuenschwander, *Glaube. Eine Besinnung über Wesen und Begriff des Glaubens* (Bern, 1957) • A. Peters, *Glaube und Werk* (2d ed.; Berlin, 1967) • W. Ries, *Glaube als Konsens* (Munich, 1979) • B. M. Seils, *Glaube* (Gütersloh, 1996) • W. C. Smith, *Faith and Belief* (Princeton, 1979) • R. Swinburne, *Faith and Reason* (Oxford, 1981) • N. P. Tanner, ed., *Decrees of the Ecumenical Councils* (2 vols.; London, 1990) • I. R. Walker, *Faith and Belief: A Philosophical Approach* (Atlanta, 1994).

INGOLF U. DALFERTH

Faith and Order Movement

1. Origins
2. Lausanne, 1927
3. Edinburgh, 1937
4. Lund, 1952
5. Montreal, 1963
6. Major Studies and Accomplishments, 1963-93
7. Santiago de Compostela, 1993
8. Prospect

1. Origins

As a central expression of the modern → ecumenical movement, the Faith and Order Movement was born in the early decades of the 20th century. Its fundamental purpose then and now is "to proclaim the oneness of the Church of Jesus Christ and to call the churches to the goal of visible → unity in one faith and one eucharistic fellowship, expressed in worship and in common life in Christ, in order that the world may believe." Inherent in this purpose — one inspired by the biblical vision of the church — are several defining dimensions of the Faith and Order vocation: (1) the goal is the *visible* unity of the church, a unity given by the triune God and therefore the inescapable calling of all churches and Christians; (2) those churches that "confess → Jesus Christ as God and Savior" resolve both to enter into theological conversations and eventual decisions about the forms that manifest their unity in faith, sacraments, ministry, mission, and common deci-

sions, and to address candidly the doctrinal, social, cultural, political, gender, and racial factors that divide the churches; and (3) the search for visible unity is empowered by the missionary calling of the church to be a sign and instrument of the unity God wills for the whole human community, in order that the world may believe the gospel of Jesus Christ.

Faith and Order came into existence in response to the modern missionary movement, made evident in the historic World Missionary Conference at Edinburgh, Scotland, in August 1910. This conference by its own decision excluded all matters of faith and order from its agenda. Charles H. Brent, a young missionary bishop of the Protestant Episcopal Church (U.S.) in the Philippines, returned from Edinburgh determined to address that omission. In October 1910 Brent inspired his church's General Convention to approve the following resolution: "That a Joint Commission be appointed to bring about a conference for the consideration of questions touching Faith and Order, and that all Christian Communions throughout the world which confess our Lord Jesus Christ as God and Saviour be asked to unite with us in arranging for and conducting such a conference."

Coincidentally, two other American churches were part of this initiative. On the day before the Protestant Episcopal action, the National Convention of the Disciples of Christ, inspired by Peter Ainslie, a friend of Bishop Brent and president of the Disciples assembly, called for "a World Conference on matters of Christian unity among all churches." The next year Ainslie launched the *Christian Union Quarterly,* an ecumenical periodical that became a primary carrier of articles and news about the early Faith and Order movement. Simultaneously, the National Council of Congregational Churches in the United States expressed its openness to any overture toward Christian unity. While the Protestant Episcopal Church played a dominant role in these early years, the founding of the Faith and Order movement was itself a collegial act.

Shortly after these initiatory actions, the appointed Joint Commission of the Episcopal Church invited churches from around the world to designate commissions committed to prepare their people for participation in the world conference. By May 1913 a total of 18 Protestant churches in the United States had named commissions, and by 1919 69 commissions were appointed. Robert Hallowell Gardiner, an influential Episcopal lawyer in Boston, became the secretary of Faith and Order. His sense of diplomacy brought confidence to the new movement as he carried on a vast correspondence in several languages with church leaders of all traditions throughout the world. Some 100,000 copies of the proposal for a world conference were mailed to the churches, and Gardiner began to publish a series of Faith and Order papers that propelled throughout the world the vision and issues related to the movement.

In order to gain the commitment of the churches outside the United States, several deputations were sent to strategic places. In June 1912 a delegation of Episcopal bishops was sent to secure the participation of → Anglican churches in Great Britain and Ireland. In January 1913 a delegation of Disciples of Christ, Congregationalists, and Presbyterians visited the Free Churches in Great Britain. After World War I, in 1919, another Episcopal delegation made a lengthy visit to Orthodox leaders in Athens, Smyrna, Constantinople, Sofia, Bucharest, Belgrade, Alexandria, Cairo, Jerusalem, and Damascus; then to Protestants in France, Norway, and Sweden; and finally to Rome for a dramatic audience with Pope Benedict XV. In every place the Orthodox unanimously affirmed their intention to attend the world conference. So did the Protestant churches visited on the Continent and Scandinavia, although tensions related to the war made communications difficult. Although the → pope received the Faith and Order representatives with genuine friendliness, he strongly rejected any possible participation in the world conference, expressing his hope instead that those who attended would "by the grace of God see the light and become reunited to the visible Head of the Church, by whom they will be received with open arms." This refusal in 1919 was reversed in 1968, however, when the → Roman Catholic Church became an official member of the Faith and Order Commission, continuing until this day as one of the most committed participating communions.

During World War I a series of gatherings of the American commissions established the method of Faith and Order dialogue and identified the issues to be considered at the world conference. In January 1916 a North American conference met in Garden City, New York, with 63 representatives, all male, of 15 churches. Strategically, this conference shaped the method of "comparative ecclesiology" and formed an advisory group of theologians to identify the central theological subjects to be considered at the projected world conference.

In August 1920 the first international preparatory conference was convened in Geneva, Switzerland. Leaders and theologians from 40 countries, representing 70 Protestant, Anglican, and Orthodox churches, made this meeting the most diverse Christian gathering in history. Significantly, this was the same year in which the → Ecumenical Patriarchate at Constantinople issued its ground-breaking → encyclical "Unto the Churches of Christ Everywhere," which committed the Orthodox churches to far-ranging ecumenical engagement with other ecclesial bodies.

Two formative decisions were made at the Geneva meeting. A widely representative Continuation Committee of over 50 members was appointed, with Bishop Brent elected chairperson and Robert Gardiner secretary. A Subjects Committee of theologians was appointed with the task to prepare the agenda for the world conference and to begin preliminary discussion of the subjects already identified. In reality the Geneva Conference of 1920 marked the official beginning of the Faith and Order movement. It was a sign of Faith and Order's intention to be truly inclusive, and it gave evidence of the new movement's capacity to face the difficult issues that divide the churches.

2. Lausanne, 1927

August 3-21, 1927, was a dramatic moment in Christian history, as 406 persons (385 men, 9 women, "a few laypersons," and 12 staff) gathered at Lausanne, Switzerland, for the First World Conference on Faith and Order. Bishop Brent was elected president of the conference, and Principal Alfred E. Garvie of the Congregational Church of England and Wales was elected deputy chairman. Because of Bishop Brent's poor health, Garvie presided at most of the sessions.

The work of the conference focused on seven subjects, largely identified a decade before: (1) the call to unity, (2) the church's message to the world — the gospel, (3) the nature of the church, (4) the church's common confession of faith, (5) the church's ministry, (6) the sacraments, and (7) the unity of Christendom and the relation thereto of existing churches. The first six reports were adopted, with no dissenting votes, for transmission to the churches. The seventh created enough tension that it was referred to the post-Lausanne Continuation Committee. Most of the delegates would have approved this report, but a few — Anglo-Catholics and Lutherans from Britain and the United States — resisted the report's call for the churches to collaborate in the work of "applied Christianity," that is, economics, social justice, and world peace. This small minority also feared that adoption of the report would commit Faith and Order to the acceptance of federation or cooperation at the expense of organic unity in faith and order. This debate illustrated the problem of differing visions of the unity that were held by the divided churches. Interestingly, it was Bishop V. S. Azariah (Church of England in India) and Professor T. T. Lew (Congregational Church of China) who protested any delay in this report's acceptance. Shortly after the conference a revised text of section 7 was approved by the Continuation Committee and sent to the churches.

In another notable intervention, Archbishop Germanos of Thyateira spoke publicly before the conference on behalf of all the Orthodox churches. While warmly affirming the purposes of the conference, he commented that except for the report of section 2, all the section reports were inconsistent with the principles of the → Orthodox Church. This statement by the Orthodox was an ominous note, typically ignored, that was to be repeated in future conferences.

3. Edinburgh, 1937

Two years after the Lausanne Conference Charles Brent died, and in August 1929 another Anglican bishop — William Temple, at the time archbishop of York and later of Canterbury — was elected chairperson of the Continuation Committee. The theological work in the intervening years produced three major reports: *The Doctrine of → Grace; The Church, Ministry, and the Sacraments;* and *The Church and the → Word of God.* In addition, the American Faith and Order Committee produced four germinal studies that pointed Faith and Order in new directions: *The Meaning of Unity, The Communion of the Saints, The Non-Theological Factors in the Making and Unmaking of Church Union,* and *Next Steps on the Road to a United Church.*

A decade after Lausanne the Second World Conference met at Edinburgh, August 3-18, 1937, attended by 414 delegates from 122 churches and 42 countries. The fact that only 95 of these participants had been at Lausanne foretold the coming of a new generation of participants. The Continuation Committee also invited 53 younger theologians to the preparatory meetings and the world conference. Edinburgh focused on five themes: (1) the grace of our Lord Jesus Christ, (2) the church of Christ and the Word of God, (3) the communion of the saints, (4) the church of Christ: ministry and → sacraments, and (5) the church's unity in life and → worship.

The theological gem at Edinburgh was a brief "Affirmation of Union in Allegiance to Our Lord Jesus Christ," which was adopted unanimously. Confessing that these churches "are one in faith in our Lord Jesus Christ, the incarnate Word of God," Edinburgh extrapolated a far-reaching conclusion:

"This unity does not consist in the agreement of our minds or the consent of our wills. It is founded in Jesus Christ himself." This document remains classic among Faith and Order documents.

At Edinburgh 1937 and at the World Conference on Life and Work, which met two weeks later at Oxford, England, there appeared a common conviction that the differing approaches of Faith and Order and Life and Work were in fact interdependent, and the interfacing of their two agendas, particularly in light of the limited resources of the member churches, called for their integration into one ecumenical body. Formal steps were therefore taken toward uniting these two movements. A handful of Faith and Order leaders, primarily British Anglicans, opposed this proposal. A series of planning conferences, however, led on the eve of World War II to the formation of "the → World Council of Churches [WCC] in Process of Formation."

When the WCC was finally constituted in 1948 in Amsterdam, the basis of Faith and Order became the basis of the new council, binding together those churches "which accept our Lord Jesus Christ as God and Saviour." The centrality of Faith and Order in this new ecumenical body was furthermore made indelible in the first function described in the WCC's constitution: "to carry on the work of the two movements for Faith and Order and Life and Work." Also clear was the promise that from Amsterdam onward, every WCC assembly would include a section on the vision and concerns of Faith and Order. Finally, the special role of Faith and Order was established by the creation of a Commission on Faith and Order, with its own constitution (later by-laws).

4. Lund, 1952

The Third World Conference on Faith and Order met in the ancient university city of Lund, Sweden, August 15-28, 1952. Almost 300 participants, including 225 delegates, came from 114 churches and 30 countries. An encouraging sign of postwar reconciliation was the presence of churches from Germany, Hungary, and Czechoslovakia. The increased number of delegates from → Third World countries, as well as the younger delegates and four observers from the Roman Catholic Church, gave evidence of widening participation in Faith and Order.

The themes at Lund reflected both the old and the new agenda confronting the movement: (1) the task of Faith and Order in a pilgrim church, (2) the indelible link between the unity of the church and the evangelization of the world, (3) the effect of social and cultural factors as causes of division among the churches, (4) the nature of the church, (5) ways of worship as signs of disunity and unity, and (6) the place of intercommunion (→ Eucharist 5.2.1), eucharistic sharing, in the ecumenical calling.

Early in the Lund conference the delegates admitted that the original Faith and Order method of comparative ecclesiology was of doubtful viability. "We can make no real advance towards unity," said the report to the churches, "if we only compare our several conceptions of the church and the traditions in which they are embodied." In order to discover the way to unity in the new era, it is necessary "to penetrate behind our divisions to a deeper and richer understanding of the mystery of the God-given union of Christ with his Church. . . . As we seek to draw closer to Christ we come closer to one another." The new methodology placed the doctrine of Christ and the → Holy Spirit at a primary place in the future work of Faith and Order.

Equally creative was the proposal made at Lund for the next steps toward unity. Some visible acts of → obedience are required along the way before the ultimate unity is won. In what has since been called the Lund Principle, the conference proposed that the churches begin to "act together in all matters except those in which deep differences of conviction compel them to act separately." This proposal of exceptional promise remains a landmark in Faith and Order history, even as it remains one of the unfulfilled promises of the churches.

5. Montreal, 1963

By the time Faith and Order convened its Fourth World Conference, the churches faced both an altered landscape in the world and the prospects of reconciliation between ecclesial bodies. Those who came confessed an awareness of "a decisive moment, a *kairos* of unity." On the campus of McGill University in Montreal, Canada, August 13-26, 1963, nearly 500 persons representing 138 churches worshiped together, listened to the Scriptures, engaged in → dialogue, and found a sense of fellowship. The ecumenical spirit of → Vatican II, which had convened in 1962, made it possible for five official Roman Catholic observers to be present and for major addresses to be given by biblical scholar Raymond E. Brown; Cardinal Paul-Emile Leger, the archbishop of Montreal; and Bishop (later Cardinal) Johannes Willebrands, secretary (later president) of the Vatican's Secretariat (later Pontifical Council) for Promoting Christian Unity. Representation of the Eastern and Oriental Orthodox churches was significantly larger than in the past because of the entrance into the membership of the

WCC at the New Delhi assembly of those Orthodox who lived in Communist countries. Particularly articulate also were delegates from transconfessional united churches and churches involved in union negotiations in Asia, the Indian subcontinent, and North America.

The conference worked in five sections: (1) the church in the purpose of God; (2) Scripture, Tradition, and traditions; (3) the redemptive work of Christ and the ministry of his church; (4) worship and the oneness of Christ's church; and (5) "all in each place": the process of growing together. The first four sections received substantial reports from theological commissions that had worked between Lund and Montreal. The fifth, on local ecumenism, became an important focus in light of the Lund Principle and the definition of visible unity proposed in 1961 at the WCC New Delhi Assembly as drawing together "all in each place." At Montreal it was prophetically affirmed that "the proving ground of unity is the local church."

Another major achievement at Montreal was the adoption of the report entitled "Scripture, Tradition, and Traditions." Differences over the authority of Scripture and of → tradition have long been a church-dividing issue, especially between Protestants, on the one hand, and Orthodox and Roman Catholics, on the other. Montreal's clarity brought hope to this dilemma. In speaking of Tradition (capital *T*), the conference meant "the → Gospel itself, transmitted from generation to generation in and by the Church, Christ himself present in the life of the Church." This Tradition is grounded in the apostolic faith and is the work of the Holy Spirit. In this sense the Tradition precedes Scripture. Christians therefore live in faithfulness to "the Tradition of the Gospel (the *paradosis* of the *kerygma*) testified in Scripture, transmitted in and by the Church through the power of the Holy Spirit." Any attempt to oppose Scripture and Tradition is illegitimate; both are authoritative.

By traditions (small *t*), then, is meant "the diversity of forms of expression and also what we call confessional traditions," for example, Anglican, Lutheran, Reformed, or Pentecostal. This theological insight gave a new way by which to evaluate diversity within the one church of Christ. The criteria for determining the content of the Tradition and how each tradition witnesses to the one Tradition remained a future issue. What has been clear since the Montreal conference is the conviction that the church's unity is found in the Tradition, that its diversity is expressed in those traditions whose authenticity is affirmed only insofar as they are rooted in the Tradition. Montreal set a new course for Faith and Order. The new Christological, or more fully Trinitarian, approach represented a gift toward a future unity.

6. Major Studies and Accomplishments, 1963-93

After Montreal no one envisioned a time lapse of three decades before a fifth world conference would be convened. This period, however, proved to be one of the most productive and wide-ranging in the history of the movement, during which substantial progress was made on a number of theological issues. Questions of methodology and the reality of more inclusive participation all required rethinking and decision, especially in order to listen to the voices and experiences of the poor, the women, the youth, and the churches in Asia, the Pacific, Africa, Latin America, and the Caribbean. Among the studies pursued in this period three especially have proved productive and promising.

The Meaning of the Visible Unity of the Church. As has been indicated, the formative purpose of the Faith and Order movement is to be an instrument of the churches in their calling to manifest the visible oneness of the church of Jesus Christ. Between 1963 and 1993 this aim found extraordinary fulfillment in three formulas defining the nature of the unity sought by the churches, each drafted by the Faith and Order Commission and approved by different assemblies of the WCC. The first and most widely acclaimed statement, approved by the New Delhi assembly (1961), envisioned a unity "made visible as all in each place are brought together by the Holy Spirit into one fully committed fellowship." The signs of such unity are praying and confessing the apostolic faith together, preaching the one gospel, sharing the → Eucharist, and having a corporate life that reaches out in witness and service to (and with) all of God's people.

The second historic statement, affirmed by the Nairobi assembly (1975), described the one church as "a conciliar fellowship of local churches which are themselves truly united." This conciliar fellowship is expressed in common witness to the apostolic faith, one baptism, the common Eucharist, recognition of each other's members and ministries, and common witness and service in the world.

The Canberra assembly (1991) restated a third vision of unity in an explication focused on unity as → koinonia (communion). The church as koinonia is a communion of all Christians drawn together by the Holy Spirit, who in → baptism confess Jesus Christ as Lord and Savior and, in all their diversity, celebrate together the eucharistic presence of the Lord. This koinonia is rooted in the triune God, who, as the perfect expression of unity and diversity, is the ultimate sign of God's love for all humankind.

Baptism, Eucharist, and Ministry. The historic divisions arising from the theology and practice of sacraments and ministry have been at the center of the Faith and Order movement from its beginning. During the 20th century, however, solid theological labor has produced promising → consensus and convergence on these church-dividing issues. This process of consensus building reached a dramatic moment after 55 years when the WCC's Faith and Order Commission, meeting in Lima, Peru, in January 1982, gave approval to a "convergence" text entitled *Baptism, Eucharist, and Ministry,* commonly referred to as the Lima text, or simply *BEM.* It is not a complete theological consensus, nor have any churches taken authoritative decisions about its reception. Nevertheless, it represents a theological convergence that could someday transform presently divided churches into a communion of common faith and sacramental life.

The meaning of baptism in *BEM* is commonly declared as "participation in Christ's death and resurrection," a sign of "conversion, pardoning, and cleansing," "the gift of the Spirit," "incorporation into the body of Christ," and "the sign of the kingdom." The baptism of infants and that of believers upon the profession of faith — both with water and the gift of the Holy Spirit — are each accepted as Christian baptism. It is a sacrament of unity. "Through baptism," says *BEM,* "Christians are brought into union with Christ, with each other and with the Church of every time and place" ("Baptism," par. 6).

In the Eucharist every Christian receives the "gift of salvation through communion in the body and blood of Christ" ("Eucharist," par. 2). The meaning of this sacrament is understood as "the great thanksgiving" to God for everything accomplished in creation, redemption, and sanctification (par. 3), and as the *anamnesis,* or memorial, of the crucified and risen Christ, that is, "the living and effective sign of his sacrifice, accomplished once and for all on the cross and still operative on behalf of all humankind" (par. 5). The Eucharist is likewise the invocation of the Spirit, who "makes the crucified and risen Christ really present to us in the eucharistic meal" (par. 14); it is the meal of the kingdom whereby God's grace is manifested and fulfilled in justice, love, and peace.

The section on the ministry represents less common ground among the churches than the first two sections, yet *BEM* offers promising agreement even on this thorny issue. The chief insight of *BEM* is the setting of the ordained ministry within the context of the ministry of the whole people of God. The ordained ministry is "constitutive for the life and witness of the Church," yet it functions not "in an exclusive way" but so as to "assemble and build up the body of Christ" ("Ministry," pars. 8, 13 comm., 13; → Ordination). While it is admitted that the NT does not reveal a single pattern of ordained ministry that might be offered as a blueprint or contemporary norm of all future ministries, nevertheless the historic threefold ministry of → bishop, presbyter (→ Elder), and → deacon — admittedly in need of reform — is commended to serve as "as an expression of the unity we seek and also a means for achieving it" (par. 22).

After its approval at Lima the *BEM* text was translated into over 40 languages, and more than 500,000 copies were printed and distributed to the member churches of the WCC for study, response, and eventual reception. Official responses were received and published in six Faith and Order volumes, representing the affirmations and questions of 190 churches (including the Roman Catholic Church), councils of churches, and theological faculties all over the world. In 1990 the Faith and Order Commission produced a response to the churches' responses in which it identified the key affirmations and issues that warrant further dialogue. The future of Faith and Order depends on this theological work and dialogue being continued and on addressing the future stages of ecumenical reception by the churches.

The Unity of the Church and the Renewal of Human Community. When the Uppsala Assembly of the WCC gathered in 1968, the churches were confronted with a new environment that would challenge and expand their understanding of the church, its mission, and unity. The world was marked by student revolts, by cries for food, justice, and human dignity, and by tragic assassinations. (The slain Martin Luther → King Jr. was to have been the preacher at the opening service.) In the midst of this human disarray the assembly's message confessed, "Torn by our diversities and tensions, we do not yet know how to live together. *But God makes new.* Christ wants his Church to foreshadow a renewed human community. Therefore, we Christians will manifest our unity in Christ by entering into full fellowship with those of other races, classes, ages, religious and political convictions, in the place where we live. Especially, we shall seek to overcome → racism wherever it appears."

At the meeting of the Faith and Order Commis-sion in Louvain, Belgium, in 1971, the main theme was "Unity of the Church — Unity of Mankind." The work of five sections involved the delegates in reflections about the unity of the church in the perspective of (1) the struggle for justice in society, (2) the encounter with living faiths, (3) the struggle against racism, (4) the handicapped in society (→ Persons with Handicaps), and (5) differences in culture. While these subthemes broke new ground at Louvain, they also caused a major controversy about the fundamental task of Faith and Order. Some theologians deeply resisted linking the search for the unity of the church with the struggles for human community, believing that the church is given its unity only through koinonia with God and with others, through Christ and as expressed in the sacramental life of the church. Others claimed that the church's unity and mission have validity only as it becomes a voice of liberation and reconciliation, identifying with the human struggles and inequities suffered by the poor and oppressed. In response to these deep differences Louvain launched an ambitious new study entitled "The Unity of the Church — the Unity of Mankind." A constructive move came when this study was broadened to include the complementary study "Giving an Account of the Hope within Us." Its design invited groups all over the world — from different churches, cultures, and social and political contexts — to affirm their hope in the gospel and to witness to the unity of all Christians. On the basis of these different accounts of Christian hope, Faith and Order drafted "A Common Account of Hope" which was adopted by the commission at Bangalore, India, in 1978.

At Lima in 1982 the same commission that unanimously transmitted *BEM* to the churches authorized a new study entitled "The Unity of the Church and the Renewal of Human Community." This study was designed to preclude any sense of the dichotomy that had developed earlier. The quest for conciliar fellowship, or visible unity, and the struggle for justice and "the renewal of human community" belong together in the ecumenical calling. Yet in its early stages this study became a lightning rod for an ecumenical polarization that existed throughout the whole ecumenical movement. Between 1982 and 1992 the Unity and Renewal Steering Group held nine international consultations in Africa, Asia, the Caribbean, Latin America, Eastern and Western Europe, and North America. In these meetings new voices and experiences of Christians not traditionally a part of Faith and Order expanded the vision and brought new insights into the quest for visible unity. This study's final report, *Church and World* (1990), became a fundamental Faith and Order document with critical clues for the tasks of Faith and Order and the ultimate unity of the church.

7. Santiago de Compostela, 1993

After a long hiatus the Fifth World Conference on Faith and Order assembled in the medieval pilgrim city of Santiago de Compostela, Spain, on August 3-14, 1993. Under the theme "Towards Koinonia in Faith, Life, and Witness" over 400 participants from churches and countries throughout the world evaluated progress made toward visible unity in recent decades, assessed the implications of the various Faith and Order studies, listened to the wider ecumenical developments among the churches, and challenged the churches to receive the signs of unity into their daily lives. Faith and Order's responsiveness to the changed ecumenical situation was positively reflected in the composition of those who took part in this event. The participation of 66 younger theologians (under age 33) was a dramatic symbol at Santiago; additionally, 30 percent of the participants were women. A greater diversity was symbolized by representatives from Pentecostal communities in the United States and from Independent Churches in Africa. For the first time a major contingency represented the Roman Catholic Church; the Orthodox Church formed the largest confessional group. Santiago truly represented a new, kaleidoscopic generation of ecumenical pilgrims.

The concept of koinonia (communion) was proposed not as a new model of unity but rather as the theological framework in which different models (e.g., "organic union," "conciliar fellowship," "a communion of communions," and "reconciled diversity") can be understood positively and evaluated appropriately. Koinonia, in Faith and Order's usage, signifies a theological relationship rooted in the nature of the triune God, marked by diversity, and made real in common faith, sacramental life, and witness and service in the world. The Santiago conference worked in four sections: (1) the understanding of koinonia and its implications, (2) confessing the one faith to God's glory, (3) sharing a common [sacramental] life in Christ, and (4) called to common witness for a renewed world.

The final days of the conference were given to critical reflections on the future of the one ecumenical movement and the role of Faith and Order within that movement. In recent years some critics had rendered dire judgments about the possibility of actual unity and the marginal commitment of the churches to such unity. Santiago was realistic about these criticisms of the ecumenical movement, Faith and Order, and particular proposals for unity before the churches. There were admissions of the need to broaden participation in Faith and Order even more and to use the gifts of a contextual methodology to encourage unity among people of difference. But the conference confirmed and celebrated the many milestones toward visible unity of the church and the renewal of human community that had been achieved in recent decades. Santiago gladly concluded: "Faith and Order has, before God, an essential service to render."

8. Prospect

The future of the Faith and Order movement is both secure and fragile. It has been observed that the Eighth Assembly of the WCC (1998), at Harare, Zimbabwe, was the first assembly in which there was no major emphasis upon Faith and Order or the calling to the visible unity of the church. Still the work of Faith and Order remains vital. Its current studies — mandated by the Fifth World Conference — deal with ecclesiology, worship and the unity of the church, ecumenical hermeneutics, ecclesiology and ethics, and the relation of national and ethnic identities to the unity of the church. After Santiago, Yemba Kekumba, a Methodist theologian teaching in Zimbabwe, was elected moderator of the Faith and Order Commission, the first so chosen from the Southern Hemisphere.

Faith and Order's witness within the ecumenical movement persists in being central and solid. Visible unity remains the constitutional goal of the ecumenical movement. Faith and Order's history proves — to enthusiasts and skeptics alike — that the ecumenical journey is always traveled in tension between the "already" and the "not yet," between the unity that God has already given to the one church and the unity that the churches are mandated to attain. In this sense the goal and work of Faith and Order is about the past, but it remains more about the future.

Bibliography: T. F. Best and G. Gassman, eds., *On the Way to Fuller Koinonia: Official Report of the Fifth World Conference on Faith and Order* (Geneva, 1994) • G. Gassmann, ed., *Documentary History of Faith and Order, 1963-1993* (Geneva, 1993) • M. B. Handspicker, "Faith and Order, 1948-1968," *A History of the Ecumenical Movement* (vol. 2; 2d ed.; ed. H. E. Fey; Geneva, 1986) 143-70 • A. Karrer, *Bekenntnis und Ökumene. Erträge aus den ersten Jahrzehnten der ökumenischen Bewegung* (Göttingen, 1996) • M. Kin-

NAMON and B. E. COPE, eds., *The Ecumenical Movement: An Anthology of Key Texts and Voices* (Grand Rapids, 1997) • G. LIMOURIS, ed., *Orthodox Visions of Ecumenism: Statements, Messages, and Reports on the Ecumenical Movement, 1902-1992* (Geneva, 1994) • H. MEYER, *That All May Be One: Perceptions and Models of Ecumenicity* (Grand Rapids, 1999) • J. E. SKOGLUND and J. R. NELSON, *Fifty Years of Faith and Order, 1910-1963* (St. Louis, 1964) • T. TATLOW, "The World Conference on Faith and Order," *A History of the Ecumenical Movement* (vol. 1; 3d ed.; ed. R. Rouse and S. C. Neill; Geneva, 1986) 403-41 • M. THURIAN, ed., *Ecumenical Perspectives on Baptism, Eucharist, and Ministry* (Geneva, 1983) • L. VISCHER, ed., *A Documentary History of the Faith and Order Movement, 1927-1963* (St. Louis, 1963) • WORLD COUNCIL OF CHURCHES, *Baptism, Eucharist, and Ministry* (Geneva, 1982); idem, *Baptism, Eucharist, and Ministry, 1982-1990: Report on the Process and Responses* (Geneva, 1990); idem, *Church and World: The Unity of the Church and the Renewal of Human Community* (Geneva, 1990); idem, *Confessing the One Faith: An Ecumenical Explication of the Apostolic Faith As It Is Confessed in the Nicene-Constantinopolitan Creed (381)* (Geneva, 1991). See also the WCC Faith and Order Papers, ser. 1, 1910-48; ser. 2, 1948-.

PAUL A. CROW JR.

Faith Missions

The term "faith missions" derives from the policy of conservative evangelical mission agencies to minimize, if not altogether avoid, public appeals for financial support; they support themselves "by faith." Pioneers of the movement in the 19th century such as George Mueller (1805-98), who operated a large orphanage in Bristol, England, and J. Hudson Taylor (1832-1905), founder of the → China Inland Mission (CIM), relied on secret prayer to "God alone" for their financial needs. While contemporary → evangelical missions continue to emphasize the faith-alone aspect of their work, many feel it is not inappropriate to make discreet public references to financial needs. Faith missions are also characterized by a return to the teaching and lifestyle of the → apostles, to worldwide missionary vision, and to a flexible openness to the guidance of the → Holy Spirit, in contrast to institutional tradition and rigidity.

When Taylor founded the CIM in 1865, he laid down the following principles: cooperation with all Protestant denominations, no guaranteed support or soliciting of funds, direction from the field rather than the home base, and the drawing up of an overall strategic plan. On this pattern other societies were formed to take the gospel to vast unevangelized areas in Africa and Latin America. In September 1917 seven faith missions joined together to form the Interdenominational Foreign Mission Association, which by 1999 represented about 100 mission groups from the United States and Canada, with over 12,000 missionaries from North America and other countries.

Distinctive of the theology of faith missions is their strict → fundamentalism, with special emphasis on salvation by Jesus Christ alone and the eternal lostness of those who die without faith in him. In keeping is their view of → mission (§§1-2). Their attention is directed to the millions throughout the world who are as yet unreached by the gospel and to whom the gospel must be preached before the return of Christ, even though → evangelism might not mean their → conversion or Christianizing. The concern is mainly for areas outside established churches. The strategy is flexible as faith missions look for unconventional ways of securing entry into closed regions and as they test new missionary methods, using all the aids now offered by modern technology (small aircraft, radio, television, correspondence courses, etc.).

The attitude of faith missions toward other churches and missions is one of reserve. They suspect theological liberalism and soteriological universalism, finding in them threats to evangelistic urgency and kerygmatic definiteness. They have thus consistently refused to join ecumenical organs of a supradenominational or denominational kind (→ Ecumenism, Ecumenical Movement; World Council of Churches). This separatist tendency, however, has not prevented them from working with other evangelical missions.

The strength of faith missions lies in the breadth of their missionary vision and their readiness for sacrifice. The weakness of some of them lies in their claim to absoluteness as they ignore the achievements of older missions and move into the territories of national churches, thus causing division and confusion. One may also ask whether they do not truncate the full content of the missionary commission by equating evangelism with a first proclamation.

Bibliography: K. FIEDLER, *The Story of Faith Missions: From Hudson Taylor to Present Day Africa* (Oxford, 1994) • A. FRANZ, *Mission ohne Grenzen: Hudson Taylor und die deutschsprachigen Glaubensmissionen* (Giessen, 1993) • H. LINDSELL, ed., *The Church's Worldwide Mis-*

sion (Waco, Tex., 1966) • R. Tucker, *From Jerusalem to Irian Jaya: A Biographical History of Christian Missions* (Grand Rapids, 1983).

PETER BEYERHAUS

Faithfulness

In opposition to an exaggerated → individualism, Christian ethics upholds a → freedom that is so free from self that it can grant space and a voice to others. Where this inclusion of the other involves unconditional commitment, we have *faithfulness*. The term denotes an unshakable commitment to someone else or to → society, of which the foundation is → trust. In a transferred sense we can also speak of faithfulness to a promise or a conviction. This virtue involves trust in its legitimacy and → obedience to what it morally demands, independently of any measurable advantage or feared disadvantage. Faithfulness finds a place in the list of → virtues. We also come across it in the → animal kingdom.

Tension can arise between freedom and faithfulness. Faithfulness can be a beguiling slogan that is misused demagogically at the expense of one's freedom. Confronted by the ideal of faithfulness, we can feel measured by standards that we do not really attain to. The insight and truth expressed by faithfulness must always be considered in a way that does not bring free people under impossible demands, so that they simply become numbers. Individuals can often feel this way as voters in the democratic process.

Ethically a long tradition stands behind faithfulness. In the OT faithfulness is a special attribute of God that often accompanies his fatherly love for the people of the → covenant. God is Israel's Rock (Deut. 32:4). He will not change (Mal. 3:6); his word stands forever (Isa. 40:8). Because he gives such assurance, God can demand faithfulness from his → people. The tragedy is that though Israel freely renews the covenant (Josh. 24:24), it fails to keep it (Ps. 78:8) and proves itself to be an unfaithful servant (Isa. 42:18-25). God's faithfulness runs through the whole of → salvation history. It is an intrinsic faithfulness, not depending on anything. Christ finally comes, the faithful witness to the truth (John 18:37; Rev. 3:14), to bring humankind → salvation, whose fullness is in him (John 1:14, 16). In the Redeemer it is plain that our trust *(pistis)* has its foundation in God's faithfulness.

On trust and faithfulness, on loyal commitment to a society and its dealings, all traditional relations depend. The → economy rests on it. So do personal relations such as → friendship, partnership, or →

marriage. Without it, no → ideology or utilitarian motivation can give lasting security to society. In spite of an unmistakable tendency to reduce faithfulness especially to a → duty for → women, it is, with trust and openness, an obligation for both partners in a Christian marriage. States as institutions lay much store by the winning and maintaining of power. To give states and → society a permanent stability, however, faithfulness — a communal trustworthiness — is needed.

Bibliography: V. AYEL, "Dynamique de la fidelité. Approches d'anthropologie spirituelle," *RDC* 33 (1983) 213-31 • H. DAVIES, *Freeing the Faith* (London, 1993) • P. DINZELBACHER, "Pour une histoire de l'amour au moyen âge," *MÂ* 93 (1987) 223-40 • J. M. GUSTAFSON, *Christ and the Moral Life* (New York, 1968) 150-87 • H. KLOMPS, *Tugenden der modernen Menschen* (4th ed.; Regensburg, 1976) • H. M. KUITERT, *I Have My Doubts* (London, 1993) • B. MITCHELL, *Faith and Criticism* (Oxford, 1994) • L. NEWBIGIN, *Prayer Confidence: Faith, Doubt, and Certainty in Christian Discipleship* (Grand Rapids, 1995) • D. NÖRR, *Die "Fides" im römischen Völkerrecht* (Cologne, 1991) • H. THIELICKE, *Modern Faith and Thought* (Grand Rapids, 1990).

PHILIPP SCHMITZ

False Decretals

The False Decretals (also known as Pseudoisidorian Decretals) are the most influential part of a comprehensive collection of church statutes that also includes the *Collectio Hispana Gallica Augustodunensis*, the Capitularies of Benedict the Levite, and the *Capitula Angilramni*. They had their origin in approximately 850 in the kingdom of the West Franks. Though naming Isidore Mercator of Seville as their author, they seem to have been written by clergy of the archbishopric of Reims.

For their historical background we must look to the growing integration of the church into the state, which began with the Carolingian reforms and increased under Louis I the Pious (emperor 814-40) and which resulted in powerful lay influence on the episcopate (→ Middle Ages 2). The immediate reason for their composition was the attempt of Hincmar of Reims (ca. 806-82) to enhance his metropolitan authority at the expense of his suffragan → bishops.

In protesting against this development, the False Decretals took the form of an appeal to the legal tradition of the → early church (papal letters, conciliar acts, etc.). To give the impression that the false or falsified documents cited (e.g., the *Constitutum Constantini;* → Donation of Constantine) were genuine, authentic writings were added. The decretals demand the freedom of the church from secular authorities and also a strengthening of the episcopate in the form of the protection of the rights of bishops against outside influence exerted by rulers, archbishops, or provincial councils. They thus made it harder to accuse or depose bishops. The → pope is viewed as the final court of appeal, who will supposedly guarantee episcopal immunity. The decretals also deal with the apostolic life, the law of → marriage, the doctrine of the → sacraments, and the → liturgy. They thus constitute a manual of church life.

The False Decretals were known in Rome as early as 864 (Nicholas I) but made little impact at first. They began to play a decisive role in the Investiture Controversy of the 11th and 12th centuries. Papal reformers such as Leo IX and → Gregory VII quoted from them in support of the jurisdictional primacy of the papacy (→ Empire and Papacy). By way of various legal collections (including those of St. Anselm of Lucca and Ivo of Chartres), they made their way into the Decretum Gratiani (CIC 1.1) and hence into medieval → canon law.

Many doubts were cast on their authenticity (e.g., by Hincmar and Nicholas of Cusa). In 1559 the Magdeburg Centuriators finally proved that they were false, a conclusion confirmed by D. Blondel (1590-1655) in 1628. Since then, it has been widely recognized that the decretals are not genuine.

→ Middle Ages 1

Bibliography: Y. CONGAR, "Les Fausses Décrétales, leur réception, leur influence," *RSPT* 59 (1975) 279-88 • H. FUHRMANN, *Einfluß und Verbreitung der pseudo-isidorischen Fälschungen* (3 vols.; Stuttgart, 1972-74); idem, "False Decretals (Pseudo-Isidorian Forgeries)," *NCE* 5.820-24; idem, "Pseudoisidor und das Constitutum Constantini," *In Jure Veritas: Studies in Canon Law in Memory of Schafer Williams* (ed. S. B. Bowman; Cincinnati, 1991) 80-84; idem, "Reflections on the Principles of Editing Texts: The Pseudo-Isidorian Decretals as an Example," *BMCL* 11 (1981) 1-7 • J. GILCHRIST, "Changing the Structure of a Canonical Collection," in Bowman, *In Jure Veritas,* 93-117 • H. HOLZE, "Ist Fälschung Lüge? Ein mittelalterliches Problem, erörtert am Beispiel der 'Konstantinischen Schenkung,' *WD* 22 (1993) 87-110 • P. R. McKEON, "A Note on Gregory I and the Pseudo-Isidore," *RBén* 89 (1979) 305-8 • R. F. REYNOLDS, "Canon Law Collections in Early Ninth-Century Salzburg," *Proceedings of the Fifth International Congress of Medieval Canon Law* (Vatican City, 1979) 15-34 • J. RUYSSCHAERT, "Les Décrétales du Ps. Isidore du Vat. Lat. 630," *Miscellanea Bibliothecae Apostolicae Vaticanae I* (Vatican City, 1987) 111-15 • S. WILLIAMS, *Codices Pseudo-Isidoriani: A Palaeographico-Historical Study* (New York, 1971) • F. YARZA, *El obispo en la organización eclesiástica de las Decretales pseudoisidorianas* (Pamplona, 1985).

HEINRICH HOLZE

Family

1. Biblical Views
2. The Family in Western Tradition
  2.1. Early Christian Norms
  2.2. The Roman Era
  2.3. The High Middle Ages
  2.4. The Reformation Era
  2.5. The Modern Era
3. Family Pastoral Care
  3.1. Family Systems Theory and Therapy
  3.2. Family Life Education and Enrichment
  3.3. Family Ministry
  3.4. The Minister's Family

1. Biblical Views

The NT allows for an ambivalence toward → marriage and the family by recognizing a place for singleness, in contrast to → Judaism and many other traditions. Salvation within Christianity is not dependent on the continuation of a biological lineage. → Jesus and → Paul, for example, were both unmarried. Yet the NT also endorses monogamous and lasting marriage as an equally valid way of life.

Jesus of Nazareth endorsed the possibility of voluntary singleness in the service of God's → kingdom, criticizing an overemphasis on the value of biological lineage in the economy of → salvation (Matt. 19:12; Mark 12:25). Paul cautions against distracting marriage obligations in light of the impending *eschaton* (1 Cor. 7:27, 31). He wishes that all could be single, as he was, but recognizes his state as "a particular gift from God" that others may not have (1 Cor. 7:7). Paul provides the Christian with two options: marriage, in which mutual and exclusive sexual intimacy is holy (vv. 3-4, 14), or singleness (v. 34), which Paul himself prefers (vv. 7, 38).

The singleness passages can be coupled with other sayings of Jesus, including those from his harsh conflict with his own family when they considered him out of his mind (Mark 3:21, 31-35). The poor and disabled are to be invited to dinner instead of relatives (Luke 14:12-14), and a follower is unfit because he would pause and bid farewell to his household (Luke 9:61-62; → Discipleship). Without question, Jesus understood all the potential spiritual pitfalls of family ties (see also Matt. 10:32-39; Luke 11:27-28; 12:49-53).

For the married, the NT lays out a profound theology of marriage that contrasts with the culture of divorce. In a key text some → Pharisees test Jesus by asking whether divorce is lawful. In his answer Jesus explains the Mosaic allowance of divorce as arising from the people's hard hearts and then appeals to the original → creation, when "God made them male and female" and when it was said, "A man shall leave his father and mother and be joined to his wife, and the two shall become one flesh." Jesus continued, "So they are no longer two, but one flesh. Therefore, what God has joined together, let no one separate." Asked later about his answer, Jesus affirms, "Whoever divorces his wife and marries another commits adultery against her; and if she divorces her husband and marries another, she commits adultery" (Mark 10:2-12).

The above text is retained in all its features in Matt. 19:3-9, although here, importantly, divorce is permitted for a wife's unchastity (a point repeated in Matt. 5:31-32). Luke 16:18 precludes divorce without exception. Paul refers back directly to the words of Jesus in reasserting the rule against divorce (1 Cor. 7:10-11). Thus does the NT deepen the family ideal, drawing out key aspects of OT thought. The writers of the Dead Sea Scrolls presented the reform of marriage in terms of a return to the single-hearted solidarity of the first couple, Adam and Eve.

Three monumental theological claims about marriage and family contained in the Hebrew Bible lie at the core of the teachings of Jesus. First, there are the exuberant and powerful statements of Genesis 1 that describe a purposeful, ordering God who pronounces that all stages of creation are "good," even "very good." He creates humankind, male and female, in his image and then commands the couple to "be fruitful and multiply" (vv. 26-28). The divine prototype was thus established: God creates, and what is created procreates, thereby ensuring the continuation of God's created good. The creation of man and woman gives God's handiwork a future.

Second, in Genesis 2 a profound, even revolutionary, → autonomy and dignity is afforded the married couple: "Therefore a man leaves his father and his mother and clings to his wife, and they become one flesh" (v. 24), suggesting intensity, fusion, and pleasure. Here is a departure from any social arrangement that would violate the integrity of this one-flesh union in the name of filial piety or honor. Consistent with the priority of one-flesh marriage over filial obligations, God sends → Abraham and his wife, Sarah, to the land of Canaan, pointedly ordering Abraham to leave "your kindred and your father's house" and to go to "the land that I will show you" (Gen. 12:1). God calls a husband and wife to begin a journey of faith, and a mark of that faith seems to be a readiness to depart from the father's house. God's → blessing, like God's creation, is bestowed on a man and a woman in the union of one flesh.

Third, the Hebrew Bible contains the prophetic assertion of the absolute spiritual integrity of marriage, most strikingly delivered in the words of Malachi: "And what does the one God desire? Godly offspring. So look to yourselves, and do not let anyone be faithless to the wife of his youth. For I hate divorce, says the LORD, the God of Israel. . . . So take heed to yourselves and do not be faithless" (2:15-16). Marriage is, then, a sacred → covenant to be honored by those in the community of covenant. In the grip of patriarchy, such an absolute is a frightening prospect; but shed of patriarchy, it promises both a loyal love and children who are socialized and acculturated with the guidance of both a mother and a father.

Malachi (and later Jesus) presents a sharp contrast to the position of Deut. 24:1-4, which allowed a man to have a certificate of divorce for even the most trivial of reasons ("she does not please him because he finds something objectionable about her"). The initiative for such divorce rested entirely with the husband. (Centuries later, → Talmudic opinion would debate the grounds for divorce.) In rejecting the permissiveness of the → Torah in allowing divorce, Malachi seems to anticipate the prophetic position taken by Jesus in Mark 10:2-12. However much polygamy and concubinage occurred among the kings, none of the prophets recognized such practices as godly, and monogamous marriage came to prevail as a divine institution given at creation. The prophet Hosea (whose activity came early in the prophetic period), by remaining faithful to his wife, Gomer, a prostitute, exemplified the monogamy and steadfast → love of which men are capable when they set aside power. This commitment contrasts with Roman culture, where divorce was commonly practiced, carried no particular stigma, and could be initiated by either the wife or the husband.

The Jewish Jesus, who claimed to have come to fulfill the law and the prophets, strongly condemned men who looked outside of marriage with even the attitude of lust (Matt. 5:28). Only when marriage and family prevented converts from following him (Matt. 10:35-39), thereby hindering the expansion of his mission, was Jesus critical of such relationships. The hard sayings, including the warning that the follower will have foes among the "members of one's own household" (Matt. 10:36), do not negate an exceptional reverence for familial ties (Mark 10:7-9) and parental love (Matt. 7:9-11).

Paul drew on the same passages from the Hebrew Bible that Jesus did when he called the unity of marriage "a great → mystery" (Eph. 5:32). Like Jesus, Paul seems to reject hierarchy in marriage (Gal. 3:28) and confers the highest honor on it by comparing it to the union of church and Christ (1 Cor. 11:3; Eph. 5:22-25). His teachings emphasize the agape love (i.e., one of serving and loyalty) that should be mutually manifested between husband and wife (1 Cor. 7:3-4). Paul's reason for ambivalence about marriage, which was misunderstood by later church ascetics, is that "the present form of this world is passing away" (1 Cor. 7:31), so familial responsibilities are not timely. But if Paul's → eschatology or philosophy of → time and history is set aside, his endorsement of permanence in marriage is clear. His personal singleness, which he did not require of others, is grounded in his historical perspective — that is, because the end is near, Christians might wisely forgo marriage, if they are able.

The teachings of Jesus on marriage and divorce are powerfully normative and do not allow departures from the principle of creation in the name of either lifestyle equality or the value of self-expression. His elevation of → women in his circle of followers, his expressed love for children, and his emphasis on a love for → neighbor that precludes cruelty and violence all point beyond the traditional patriarchal family.

Bibliography: D. S. Browning, *From Culture Wars to Common Ground: Religion and the American Family Debate* (Louisville, Ky., 1997) • A. Burguire, C. Klapisch-Zuber, M. Segalen, and F. Zonabend, eds., *A History of the Family* (2 vols.; Cambridge, Mass., 1996) • D. G. Hunter, ed. and trans., *Marriage in the Early Church* (Minneapolis, 1992) • P. K. Jewett, *Man as Male and Female: A Study in Sexual Relationships from a Theological Point of View* (Grand Rapids, 1975) • S. G. Post, *More Lasting Unions: Christianity, the Family, and Society* (Grand Rapids, 2000) • D. de Rougemont, *Love in the Western World* (New York, 1956) • J. Witte Jr., *From Sacrament to Contract: Marriage, Religion, and Law in the Western Tradition* (Louisville, Ky., 1997).

Stephen G. Post

2. The Family in Western Tradition

In the Western Christian tradition, the term "family" describes a variety of overlapping associations. The *nuclear* family consists of a married couple (or widow[er] or divorcé[e]), together with their natural or adopted children. The *blended* family consists of a married couple, living with children born or adopted of prior unions, and now called stepchildren and stepsiblings. The *extended* family consists of a nuclear or blended family plus any combination of a prior generation of parents, aunts, and uncles; a current generation of siblings as well as sons- and daughters-in law and their relatives; and a new generation of grandchildren and their eventual spouses. Historically, families of various types often included servants, slaves, students, sojourners, and other long-term household members. Historically, several families were often joined by → marriage, treaty, or contract to form clans or sibs. All these family forms were well developed in the West before Christ and have been part of the Christian church's experience and teaching from the beginning.

2.1. *Early Christian Norms*

Marriage formed the core of the Western Christian family. The ideal structure of marriage was the lifelong union of a fit man and a fit woman of the age of consent, unrelated by the blood and family ties identified in the Mosaic law. The ideal purpose of marriage was to provide mutual → love and support of husband and wife, mutual procreation and nurture of children and other dependents (→ Childhood), and mutual protection of both parties from the temptations of sexual sin. These Christian ideals were based on the biblical teaching that "a man shall leave his father and mother and be joined to his wife, and the two shall become one flesh" (Matt. 19:5, quoting Gen. 2:24; also Eph. 5:31; 1 Cor. 6:16). These ideals were further enforced by the teaching that marriage was a symbol of the enduring bond between → Yahweh and his elect, between Christ and his church (Ezekiel 16; Hosea 2; Eph. 5:32). Several biblical passages enjoin married couples to chaste love, sexual purity, and mutual respect for the sexual and physical needs of the other. These passages also speak out against intermarriage with unbelievers, unwarranted divorce, and various sexual sins, particularly fornication, adultery, concubinage, → prostitution, perversion, and immodest dress. These biblical norms on sex and marriage were amply elaborated in the constitutions of the early church and in the commentaries of the → church fathers.

The paterfamilias stood at the head of the Western Christian family. The early church idealized the patriarchal Greco-Roman household, viewing it as something of a source and symbol of the structure of the church itself. The ideal of a household with the husband, father, and master responsible for the care, education, welfare, and discipline of his wife, children, servants, and other dependents came to normative expression in later written books of the NT and in the early church constitutions. These early norms inspired the church to develop sermons, household manuals, and → catechism and confessional books to guide believers in their family relationships within the household and beyond.

These Christian ideals of sex, marriage, and the family, which were well developed by the end of the third century, have had a profound influence on the Western tradition. Three major waves of subsequent Christian influence can be distinguished, each transforming Western family law, lore, and life.

2.2. *The Roman Era*

The first transformation came with the Christianization of the → Roman Empire in the 4th century and thereafter. The Christian concept of marriage as a monogamous, heterosexual, lifelong union came to dominate Roman, and later Germanic, law and life. Biblically based concepts of marital consent and impediments to marriage, and of annulment and divorce for cause, were increasingly prescribed. Traditional Roman and Germanic practices of polygamy, concubinage, incest, → homosexuality, contraception, → abortion, and infanticide were increasingly proscribed (→ Birth Control). The Christian construction of the patriarchal household was firmly entrenched in new laws of property and inheritance, and in new legal obligations of mutual care and nurture among parents, children, and siblings. Christian clergy and monastics were prohibited from participation in sex, marriage, and family life; virginity, chastity, and → celibacy were celebrated as a high moral ideal for the Christian. This general pattern, with ample local variations, persisted throughout the Germanic era of the 5th to 11th centuries.

2.3. *The High Middle Ages*

The second transformation occurred in the 12th and 13th centuries, when a systematic Roman Catholic theology and → canon law of the family came to dominate the West. The main changes came in the lore and law of marriage. Marriage, the church now taught, was at once a natural institution of → creation, a contractual relationship between two parties, and a → sacrament of the church. First, the church taught, marriage was instituted at creation to permit persons to beget and raise children and to direct their natural passion to the service of the

community. Yet marriage was considered subordinate to celibacy, propagation less virtuous than → contemplation. Second, marriage was a → contract that prescribed an indissoluble relation of love, service, and devotion to one's spouse and children. Third, marriage was also raised to the dignity of a sacrament. It symbolized the indissoluble union between Christ and his church and thereby conferred sanctifying → grace upon the couple, their children, and the broader Christian community. Couples could perform the sacrament in private, provided they were capable of marriage and complied with rules for marriage formation.

The → Roman Catholic Church, after the 12th century, built an intricate body of family law upon this theological foundation. Since marriage was a sacrament, the church claimed exclusive → jurisdiction over it, appropriating and expanding the laws of → nature (→ Natural Law) and → Scripture as well as some of the rules in the early church constitutions and Christianized Roman law. Comprehensive new laws, called canon laws, were promulgated by the papacy and the church → councils and enforced by church courts throughout Western Christendom.

Consistent with the naturalist perspective on marriage, the church's canon law punished contraception, abortion, and child abuse as violations of the created functions of propagation and child rearing. It also proscribed unnatural sexual acts, such as sodomy and bestiality. Consistent with the contractual perspective, canon law ensured free consensual unions by dissolving marriages contracted by mistake or under duress, fraud, or coercion. It also granted husband and wife alike equal rights to enforce conjugal debts that had been voluntarily assumed and emphasized the importance of mutual love among the couple, their children, and their parents.

Consistent with the sacramental perspective, canon law protected the sanctity and sanctifying purpose of marriage by declaring valid marital bonds to be indissoluble and by annulling invalid unions between Christians and non-Christians or between parties related by various legal, spiritual, blood, or family ties. It supported celibacy by annulling unconsummated vows of marriage if one party made a vow of chastity and by prohibiting clerics or monastics from marriage and concubinage.

Earlier Christianized Roman and Germanic laws governing the relationships between husband and wife, and parent and child, were liberally appropriated by the canonists and now enforced in the church courts as well as in the confessional (→ Confession of Sins). Traditional rules and customs of arranged marriages, patriarchal restrictions on the marital estate, male-dominated inheritance laws and primogeniture, protection of the status of the paterfamilias, and restrictions on the wife's capacities to sue or be sued, to enter into contracts, to give or receive property of her own — all remained firmly in place in canon law.

2.4. *The Reformation Era*

The third transformation occurred during the Protestant → Reformation of the 16th and 17th centuries. Like Roman Catholics, Protestants treated marriage and the family as natural associations created for procreation, protection, and preservation. They also retained the traditional view of marriage as a contract formed by the mutual consent of the couple.

Unlike Roman Catholics, however, Protestants rejected the subordination of marriage to celibacy and the celebration of marriage as a sacrament. According to common Protestant lore, the person was too tempted by sinful passion to forgo God's remedy of marriage. The celibate life had no superior virtue and was no prerequisite for clerical service. It led too easily to concubinage and homosexuality and impeded too often the access and activities of the clerical office. Moreover, Protestants taught, marriage was not a sacrament. It was an independent social estate ordained by God and equal in dignity, authority, and responsibility with the church and the state. Entrance into marriage required no prerequisite faith or purity and conferred no sanctifying grace, as did true sacraments.

Calvinist Protestants (→ Calvinism) emphasized that marriage was not a sacramental institution of the church but a covenantal association of the entire community. A variety of parties played a part in the formation of the marriage covenant. The marital couple themselves swore their betrothals and espousals before each other and God, rendering all marriages tri-party agreements, with God as party, witness, and judge. The couple's parents, as God's → bishops for children, gave their consent to the union. Two witnesses, as God's → priests to their peers, served as witnesses to the marriage. The minister, holding the spiritual power of the → Word, blessed the couple and admonished them in their spiritual duties. The magistrate, holding the temporal power of the sword, registered the parties and their properties and ensured the legality of their union. This involvement of parents, peers, ministers, and magistrates in the formation of a marriage was not an idle ceremony. These four parties represented different dimensions of God's involvement in the

marriage covenant and were thus essential to the legitimacy of the marriage itself. To omit any of these parties was, in effect, to omit God from the marriage covenant.

As social estates, Protestants taught, marriage and the family were no longer subject to the church and its canon law but to the state and its civil law. To be sure, church officials should continue to communicate biblical and moral principles on sex and marriage. Church consistories could serve as state agents to register marriages and to discipline infidelity and abuse within the household. All → church members, as priests to their peers, should counsel those who seek marriage and divorce and should cultivate the moral and material welfare of baptized children, as their congregational baptismal vows required. But principal legal authority over marriage and the family, most Protestants taught, now lay with the → state.

Despite their bitter invectives against Roman canon law by the early Reformers, Protestant magistrates and jurists appropriated a good deal of traditional canon law governing sex, marriage, and the family. Traditional canon law prohibitions against unnatural sexual relations and acts and against infringements of the procreative functions of marriage remained in effect. Canon law procedures treating wife and child abuse, paternal delinquency, child custody, inheritance, and intergenerational care continued largely unchanged, but now in civil law forms. Canon law impediments that protected free consent, that implemented biblical prohibitions against the marriage of relatives, and that governed the relations of husband and wife and parent and child within the household were largely retained. These and many other time-tested canon law rules and procedures, which were as consistent with Protestant theology as with Roman Catholic theology, were transplanted directly into the new state laws of Protestant Europe.

The new Protestant theology of marriage and the family, however, also yielded critical changes in this new → civil law. Because the → Reformers rejected the subordination of marriage to celibacy, they rejected laws that forbade clerical and monastic marriage and that permitted vows of chastity to annul vows of marriage. Because they rejected the sacramental concept of marriage as an eternal, enduring bond, the Reformers introduced divorce in the modern sense, on grounds of adultery, desertion, cruelty, or frigidity, with a subsequent right to remarry, at least for the innocent party. Because persons by their lustful nature were in need of God's soothing remedy of marriage, the Reformers rejected numerous canon law impediments to marriage not countenanced by Scripture. Furthermore, because the family was such a vital social estate alongside the state and church, the Reformers gave new power and incentive to the paterfamilias to educate, nurture, and discipline the members of his household.

2.5. *The Modern Era*

From the later 16th to the early 20th centuries, these Roman Catholic and Protestant models lay at the heart of the Western family. The medieval Roman Catholic model, confirmed and elaborated by the Council of → Trent in 1563, flourished in southern Europe, Spain, Portugal, and France, as well as in their many colonies in Latin and Central America, the American South and Southwest, Quebec, and, eventually, East and West Africa. A Protestant social model rooted in the Lutheran → "two kingdoms" theory dominated portions of Germany, Austria, Switzerland, and the Nordic countries, together with their North American and later African colonies. A Protestant social model rooted in Calvinist covenant theology came to strong expression in Geneva and in portions of → Huguenot France, the → Pietist Netherlands, Presbyterian Scotland, → Puritan New England, and South Africa. A Protestant social model that treated marriage as a little commonwealth at the core of broader ecclesiastical and political commonwealths prevailed in Anglican England and its many colonies in North America and eventually in Africa and the Indian subcontinent as well.

These Roman Catholic and Protestant models of marriage and the family were not static. Particularly in the later 19th and early 20th centuries, libertarian movements within and beyond the church brought substantial reforms to the Western family. Traditional family laws had been focused on the contracting and dissolving of marriages, whereas the governance of marriages once formed and families once dissolved was left largely to the discretion of the parties and their spiritual superiors. Beginning in the 1850s, European and North American laws were dramatically reformed and expanded in order to govern much more precisely the relationship between husband and wife. Such reforms rendered marriages much easier to contract and much easier to dissolve. Wives received greater protections in their person and in their properties from their husbands, as well as greater freedoms in their relationships and activities outside the household. Children received greater protection from the abuses and neglect of their parents, plus greater access to rights to → education and welfare and freedom from oppressive rules respecting → child labor and illegitimacy.

These reform movements, from 1850 to 1950, sought to improve the traditional Western family more than to abandon it. Until 1950 most writers still accepted the traditional Western ideal of marriage as a permanent union of a fit man and a fit woman of the age of consent. Most laws accepted the traditional definition of the nuclear, blended, and extended family, reflecting those views in a series of new family-specific social benefits, tax breaks, homestead exemptions, zoning protections, evidentiary privileges, insurance and inheritance rights, and probate priorities. The primary goal of these reforms was to purge the traditional household and community of its paternalism and patriarchy and thus render the ideals of family life a greater potential reality for all.

This traditional Western lore and law of the family, as reformed, is still taught by many Christian churches throughout the world today. It is also still enforced by both church and state authorities in many parts of Latin America as well as in Christianized areas of Asia and Africa — often supplemented in these latter communities by indigenous norms and forms of clan, caste, tribe, and village.

In Europe and North America, however, this traditional lore and law of the family have come under increasing attack. Since the early 1970s much of the West has seen growing agitation for a purely private, contractual model of marriage, where each party has equal and reciprocal rights and duties and where two parties, of whatever sex or sexual preference, have full freedom and privacy to form, maintain, and dissolve their relationships as they see fit, without interference from the church, state, or other institutions.

Western states at the end of the 20th century have responded to this agitation. Privately negotiated prenuptial, marital, and separation contracts have become increasingly the norm. No-fault divorce statutes are in place in virtually every state. Legal requirements of parental consent and witnesses to marriage have largely become dead letters. The functional distinction between the rights of the married and the unmarried has been narrowed by a growing constitutional law of sexual autonomy and privacy. Homosexual, bisexual, and other intimate associations have gained increasing acceptance at large, albeit not always at law.

Although the modern Western state has largely withdrawn from attempting to govern intimate relationships between consenting adults, it has increased dramatically its protection of children.

Abused minor children are plucked from their natural homes with increasing ease. State welfare agencies, and even adolescent children themselves, are suing delinquent or abusive parents and guardians with increasing alacrity and success. The principle of "the best interests of the child" now rivals traditional principles of paternal autonomy and preservation of blood relations. As traditional family forms and functions have eroded, the state's parental role has dramatically increased.

Bibliography: W. J. BASSETT, ed., The Bond of Marriage: An Ecumenical and Interdisciplinary Study (Notre Dame, Ind., 1968) • D. S. BROWNING, et al., From Culture Wars to Common Ground: Religion and the American Family Debate (Louisville, Ky., 1997). J. A. BRUNDAGE, Law, Sex, and Christian Society in Medieval Europe (Chicago, 1987) • M. A. GLENDON, The Transformation of Family Law: State, Law, and Family in the United States and Western Europe (Chicago, 1989) • C. OSIEK and D. L. BALCH, Families in the NT World: Households and House Churches (Louisville, Ky., 1997) • S. E. OZMENT, When Fathers Ruled: Family Life in Reformation Europe (Cambridge, Mass., 1983) • P. L. REYNOLDS, Marriage in the Early Church: The Christianization of Marriage during the Patristic and Early Medieval Periods (Leiden, 1994) • L. STONE, The Family, Sex, and Marriage in England, 1500-1800 (New York, 1979) • J. WITTE JR., From Sacrament to Contract: Marriage, Religion, and Law in the Western Tradition (Louisville, Ky., 1997).

JOHN WITTE JR.

3. Family Pastoral Care

Though a concern for the well-being of families has long been a part of the church's tradition, how this interest is translated into pastoral practice is a complex matter. Public concern for the well-being and stability of the family as an institution increases in times of rapid social change. This trend is particularly true of the growing → postmodern ethos that characterized the closing decades of the 20th century, leading to sometimes contentious and highly politicized public debates about the family. The pastoral problematic can be seen against this background: what does it mean to care for families in a specifically pastoral way in an era when societal norms for the family and the moral authority of the church are increasingly uncertain? One might frame the issue in terms of the interaction of the priestly and prophetic functions of → pastoral care. The former regards how one ministers grace and hope to families in a time of social chaos, while the latter seeks to proclaim a word of truth in the midst of a → relativistic culture.

In recent decades the family as a social unit has been an increasing focus of research, therapeutic practice, and theological reflection. The literature in the first two areas far exceeds that in the third, and the manner in which pastoral care and counseling perspectives attempt to integrate these disparate domains varies greatly. In some works, theological themes predominate, while in others, theological interpretation seems either driven or justified by one's theory of the psyche. Consequently, actual pastoral-care practices frequently do not derive in a direct and necessary way from one's theological commitments.

Despite interest in the family as a subject of study, the term "family pastoral care" does not enjoy wide usage. Literature bearing directly on this subject includes such overlapping subdomains as theological treatises on family life, theoretical and practical handbooks on family ministry, Christian models of preventive family life education, and pastoral counseling monographs directed toward family-related issues such as divorce. The following sections address key ideas and sources of influence, beginning with the fields of family therapy and family life education. These provide the conceptual and practical background for a consideration of the scope of family ministry and its relationship to pastoral theology, drawing illustrations from the magisterium of the → Roman Catholic Church. A final section addresses the self-care dimension of family pastoral care by considering the dynamics of the minister's own family life.

3.1. Family Systems Theory and Therapy

In the mid-20th century, → psychotherapy professionals began to question the assumptions of their craft. Diagnostic and treatment procedures had been dominated by psychoanalytic and → behavioral perspectives, which emphasized the pathological states of individuals. Innovations in therapeutic practice converged with new research to point toward a more holistic orientation that posited the locus of pathology and treatment to reside in disordered relationship patterns. An early though simplistic view, for example, sought reasons for a child's symptomatic behavior in the dysfunctionality of the parents' → marriage. The developing movement drew its early metaphors from the fields of cybernetics and general systems theory, the latter originating in theoretical biology. The resulting perspective has come to be known broadly as family systems theory. It is this so-called systemic orientation that was held to be the unique core of the new discipline of professional marital and family therapy. Early therapeutic applications focused on changing patterns of family communication, often with the surprising result that the symptoms ceased abruptly. Since changing the system was the therapeutic goal, many therapists insisted that all members of the household were to be present in treatment.

Family therapy began as a highly directive approach, with therapists actively intervening in family interaction during sessions. More recent developments in the field, however, tend to move away from such problem-focused approaches and emphasize instead a family's basic areas of competence. → Postmodern therapists eschew the language of pathology, viewing it as an unhelpful and socially constructed form of cultural discourse. The therapist, in this view, no longer hierarchically directs the change process but works with families collaboratively to explore new ways of perceiving situations that do not result in symptomatic behavior.

While the relatively sparse literature on the pastoral care of families borrows liberally from family systems theories, it does so primarily from the earlier rather than the later literature. At a general level, families are understood as social units or systems. The system, and not each individual taken separately, is the object of care. More specific concepts, such as family rules and boundaries that govern interaction, may also be utilized.

One systems concept that is commonly cited in the family ministry literature is that of the family life-cycle. In developmental → psychology, models in which individuals progress through a predictable series of stages are common. Family life-cycle theory extends this notion to the family system, identifying the normative challenges that families face, particularly as members are added or lost. Family crises may therefore be a result of transitional stress rather than inherent pathology. This model is held as being particularly applicable to the pastoral care of families, for two reasons. First, clergy may have longer-term relationships to families than other professionals, relationships that span across developmental stages. Second, clergy already officiate at rituals that are connected with critical junctures in family development (E. Friedman). → Baptism, for example, may be an occasion to remind faithful adults of the significance of birth and parenthood. Other rituals, including → confirmation, marriage, and burial (→ Funeral), provide similar opportunities for the hortative dimensions of family pastoral care.

Thus the field of family therapy has influenced pastoral theology and practice through its systemic concepts. A parallel development can be seen in the increased legitimacy of therapy-related services in the church. Some congregations have organized → counseling ministries staffed by professionally trained psychotherapists, or host therapeutic support groups on the church campus. Other → congregations provide referrals to outside agencies in the local community. Such measures, which are commonly understood as meeting one dimension of a need for pastoral care, may be adopted more for pragmatic reasons than because of any ideological influence of family systems theory upon a pastor's theological assumptions.

3.2. *Family Life Education and Enrichment*

The preventive emphasis on educating adults for marital and family responsibilities predates the rise of the more corrective domain of family therapy. In recent years, such models have proliferated dramatically, fueled in part by concern over the stability of contemporary marriage and family life and aided by a strong tradition of self-help.

While arising out of a wide array of theoretical assumptions, these educative models generally share two characteristics in common: a positive, non-pathologizing orientation, and a focus on teaching practical relationship skills applicable to family life. Education and enrichment assume that families possess a basic level of relational health and will improve if provided appropriate information and training. Because such strategies are employed in group settings, they are a more efficient means of disseminating useful knowledge and skills to families.

Educational models offer advantages beyond therapeutic approaches, particularly with regard to the ministry of the church. The teaching office of the church is already well established, making it a natural setting for this type of intervention. Many programs are also designed in ways that require a minimum of training for group leaders and facilitators, far less than is required for the professional practice of psychotherapy. Educational programs are therefore easier to staff with available personnel. Referrals for therapy, however, may be necessary where family distress is too severe to be dealt with constructively in a group enrichment setting.

Two major subdomains of family life education are marital enrichment and parent education. Programs may teach general skills and perspectives, such as principles of human development or communication skills that apply to a variety of family relationships. They may also be more specifically oriented toward life-cycle stages pertaining to marriage and parenting. Parent education models, for example, may target specific communication and discipline issues related to various ages of children. Marital enrichment may be directed toward the premarital preparation of engaged couples, the relationship skills of current spouses, or the postmarital adjustment issues raised by divorce and separation. The Roman Catholic Church has developed ministries in each of these areas, including a comprehensive marriage preparation manual written by the National Conference of Catholic Bishops.

Recently, a multidisciplinary and ecumenical movement to strengthen marriage and family life has arisen in the United States and beyond. Educational strategies figure prominently in this movement, as does the mediating influence of churches. Because the majority of marriage ceremonies are still conducted in church settings, → pastors influence the state of marriage in their local communities through the policies they adopt, giving engaged and existing couples access to resources provided by the church. Ministers participating in a program known as Marriage Savers (M. J. McManus), for example, are encouraged to partner with other pastors in their vicinity to establish conjoint marriage policies. While such policies vary from one community to the next, three characteristics are promoted. The most central is the use of mentoring, through which established couples work directly with those with less experience. A second is the use of premarital inventories to assess potential areas of conflict. Mentor couples may themselves be trained in such assessment methods, integrating the results into the mentoring process. A third is the provision of marital enrichment events to strengthen marital relationships once established. These and other strategies are well-suited to congregational settings and hold promise for the church's civic contribution (→ Church and State).

3.3. Family Ministry

Family pastoral care encompasses a range of ministry activities, undertaken with a consistent concern for the well-being of families. Many churches already offer some form of children's ministry. In what sense, however, is this *family* ministry? It is not uncommon for adults to bring their children to church for → religious education while the adults themselves remain minimally involved, leaving the family as a unit virtually unchanged. The literature on family ministry addresses the theological and sociological rationale for ministering to the family system, as well as offering a broad array of methods for such care. The motives are diverse. For some congregations, the focus leans toward the families that compose the membership, oriented toward their health and well-being. For others, the ministry is more community oriented, conceived as a means of outreach.

Family pastoral care involves more than what families do while at church. Its goal is to strengthen family life, to affect the quality of interaction within the home. At the most general level, this effort begins with a reexamination of how current ministry policies and practices affect the lives of members' families. The question here is whether these practices promote a church-focused ministry environment that subtly undermines the coherence and stability of the families that make up the congregation. The steady proliferation of age-specific church programming, for example, may offer a wealth of options to individuals, while putting additional strain on a family's calendar. Other routines may promote the church's teaching role in a way that unintentionally subverts any expectation that parents might provide direct spiritual guidance to their children. In short, where family pastoral care is a priority, congregations must evaluate whether existing ministry habits, often taken for granted, do in fact support the spiritual vitality of the Christian home.

A thoroughgoing family ministry strategy must also consider the role and place of the laity (→ Clergy and Laity). Contemporary life leaves many families in relative isolation from each other, struggling with inadequate social resources. A church's commitment to family ministry could entail a commitment on the part of the members to family-like relationships of support with one another. In this way, family pastoral care is built upon a foundation of lay involvement, which some call congregational care (R. J. Becker).

Beyond these more general concerns, a particular congregation's programmatic ministry to families may utilize many of the therapeutic or educational concepts and strategies outlined in the sections above. It should be noted, however, that these strategies have been designed to achieve worthy but secular goals. For care to be properly pastoral, it must be oriented toward more than merely the improvement of relationships; it must be driven by a particular ecclesial calling, such as → discipleship or → evangelism. In this way, relationship enhancement becomes a means to an end, rather than an end in itself. Family pastoral care, therefore, is more than cobbling together an assemblage of programs borrowed from the secular arena, as useful as these may be. It proceeds from theological conviction regarding the mission of the church and the role that family life plays within that mission.

As a corollary, ministers should also examine carefully the philosophical assumptions that underlie any program that is proposed for use in family ministry. Therapeutic and educational models are built, implicitly or explicitly, on worldviews that may in some aspects be contrary to the Christian message. The major orientations toward parent education that arose out of the 1970s, for example, were based variously on the perspectives of behaviorism, the → humanism of Carl Rogers, or the psychology of Alfred Adler. Each gives its own explanation of → childhood misbehavior, and the terms and strategies originating from these orientations are now common coin among a variety of current programs. But how, pastors should ask, do such explanations relate to doctrines of, say, → sin and → sanctification? Christian versions of some programs exist but do not always resolve such issues, since some of these adaptations are achieved by little more than the inclusion of biblical texts, with neither a unified theology nor an examination of philosophical assumptions. The steady accumulation of research findings and intervention strategies related to the family does and will provide ample resources for a ministry of comfort. Pastoral care, however, also entails the challenge to faithful living, in ways that are not circumscribed by secular therapeutic norms. Therapeutic and enrichment resources, while valuable tools, are therefore to be used with theological discernment in the practice of family pastoral care.

The official teaching of the Roman Catholic Church with respect to the family provides an instructive example of the relationship between theology and pastoral practice. Only two key theological points will be addressed here: the concept of the family as "domestic church" *(ecclesia domestica)*, and the understanding of the marital sacrament since the Second → Vatican Council.

The family as domestic church embodies the reign of Christ as an expression of the whole church. In this respect, it supports the church's mission of evangelism by proclaiming and living out the gospel within its membership. This concept arose with early Christianity but faded in importance with the more contractual understandings of marriage promoted in the medieval period. The idea reappears, however, in the documents of Vatican II and in post–Vatican II theological reflection. Its importance lies in the priority it gives to family pastoral care. If the family is assumed to be the domestic unit where the Christian faith is nurtured and practiced, and if this functioning is intrinsic to the church's mission, then care of the family becomes a central, rather than an optional, ministry.

Parallel shifts in emphasis can also be seen in Roman Catholic writing on the marital → sacrament. Unlike → baptism or the → Eucharist, in which the sacrament is ministered by the priest, in marriage the bride and groom minister the sacrament to each other. Matrimonial consent was at the heart of the sacrament, but earlier views tended to encourage a more mechanical understanding that focused on the marriage rite through which couples entered into a contract with God. At Vatican II the notion of conjugal love is given greater emphasis, highlighting the personal covenant of self-giving between baptized believers. → Sexuality is understood as the physical expression of this self-giving, not simply the means of procreation. Children, in turn, are an extension of the gift of conjugal love, and the family is thus built up as a community in which parental love is a sign of the love of God and empowered by his grace.

This account is not to suggest that all Roman Catholic believers are in unanimous accord with the official teaching of the church. Nevertheless, the existence of this central authority and its support of the essential role of family life create the theological infrastructure for a programmatic pastoral concern for families. The emphasis on marriage as a lifelong partnership of love, and on the family as domestic church, leads to a practical concern with the actual obstacles that the family system faces in attempting to live faithfully by its covenantal commitments in contemporary society.

Several documents advance both theological and practical expressions of this pastoral concern, most notably John Paul II's apostolic exhortation *Familiaris consortio,* as well as several publications by episcopal councils. The majority of Roman Catholic dioceses in the United States have marriage policies that typically include premarital assessment and education. Various ministries for marital enrichment and postmarital intervention have also been created. Family pastoral care, however, is understood as a responsibility that extends to every level of the organized church. Family life itself is viewed as an apostolate in which married couples, receiving grace through the sacrament, collaborate with other members of the parish in the ministry of Christian formation from childhood to adulthood. Pastoral dialogue is encouraged throughout the hierarchy, the advice of family experts is welcomed, and a certain amount of conceptual pluralism is expected. The boundaries of such pluralism, however, are still defined by the authentic magisterium, with which all teaching within the church must concur.

3.4. *The Minister's Family*

Contemporary pastoral care literature includes an accent on the dimension of self-care. Applied to family pastoral care, this emphasis suggests a consideration of the quality of family life for those in the ordained ministry (→ Ordination). Empirical study of the social and psychological dimensions of ministry is a well-established discipline, but the specific emphasis on clergy family dynamics is a more recent turn.

Stressful aspects of the ministry are amply documented, and several studies examine how this stress extends to the members of the minister's family. Congregations have expectations of what kinds of people ministers and their family members should be, which may conflict with the clergy family's own goals and self-understandings. The wives of male clergy, for example, are often pressured to fulfill key roles in their congregations, even if it is not their desire to do so. The children of ministers are often expected to be inordinately mature, psychologically and spiritually, or else to fit a cultural stereotype of rebellion and prodigality. Clergy families that still live in parsonages may experience the unannounced intrusions of parishioners who consider the manse church property rather than a private residence. In such cases, the clergy family is treated with a different standard of propriety than would apply to other families in the church.

Congregations can also be supportive. Many clergy report with great affection the care they have received during times of family crisis. Ministers' children also acknowledge the benefits of growing up in a ministry environment, including the opportunity to know a variety of mature and committed Christian adults, particularly those who bring a global perspective that transcends the more limited environment of the local congregation. Overall, stress and support are but two ways in which the relationship between a minister's family and the life of the congregation can be examined. Other elements can and should be considered, including more particular variables such as personality contributions of the minister, and more comprehensive ones, including denominational polity.

Clergy are expected to be moral exemplars to their parishioners, and the quality of their family life is no exception. For this reason, many ordained ministers are tempted to adopt a facade of health and normalcy, regardless of the actual state of their relationships. Some writers have even suggested that family ministry suffers, or may even be nonexistent, in congregations where the quality of the minister's own family life would not bear public scrutiny. This comment raises questions with regard to one's theology of the ministry, particularly as it applies to family ministry. Expectations of the minister's

moral, relational, and spiritual stature, for example, may be higher in settings where clergy-congregation relationships are more hierarchical. This factor in turn may affect the extent to which family pastoral care can be based on a foundation of lay ministry.

If the members of a congregation are morally exhorted to give priority to their family relationships, does the same exhortation hold for the pastor's family? If a double standard is allowed, will it affect the viability of family pastoral care in the congregation? A strictly unilateral approach addresses only how ordained ministers care for others' families, neglecting the question of who cares for the minister's family, and how. Many clergy have left the ministry because of the negative impact it has had upon their personal and family lives. Perceived failures in the clergy family relationships, in turn, can have symbolic repercussions throughout a church. For these and other reasons, the extent to which the success of pastoral care is dependent upon the well-being of the minister's own family remains an open but important question.

Bibliography: H. ANDERSON, *The Family and Pastoral Care* (Philadelphia, 1984) • R. J. BECKER, *Family Pastoral Care* (Englewood Cliffs, N.J., 1965) • G. W. BROMILEY, *God and Marriage* (Grand Rapids, 1980) • W. J. EVERETT, *Blessed Be the Bond* (Philadelphia, 1985) • B. FREUDENBURG and R. LAWRENCE, *The Family Friendly Church* (Loveland, Colo., 1998) • E. FRIEDMAN, *Generation to Generation: Family Process in Church and Synagogue* (New York, 1985) • D. R. GARLAND, *Family Ministry: A Comprehensive Guide* (Downers Grove, Ill., 1999) • D. B. GUERNSEY, *A New Design for Family Ministry* (Elgin, Ill., 1982) • JOHN PAUL II, "Apostolic Exhortation *Familiaris consortio . . .* regarding the Role of the Christian Family in the Modern World" (November 22, 1981), *OR(E)*, December 21-28, 1981, 1-19 • M. G. LAWLER and W. P. ROBERTS, eds., *Christian Marriage and Family: Contemporary Theological and Pastoral Perspectives* (Collegeville, Minn., 1996) • K. B. LYON and A. SMITH JR., eds., *Tending the Flock: Congregations and Family Ministry* (Louisville, Ky., 1998) • M. J. MCMANUS, *Marriage Savers* (Grand Rapids, 1993) • NATIONAL CONFERENCE OF CATHOLIC BISHOPS, *Faithful to Each Other Forever: A Catholic Handbook of Pastoral Help for Marriage Preparation* (Washington, D.C., 1989); idem, *A Family Perspective in Church and Society* (Washington, D.C., 1998) • C. M. SELL, *Family Ministry* (2d ed.; Grand Rapids, 1995).

CAMERON LEE

Fascism

1. Term
2. Fascism as a Social Movement
   2.1. The Epoch of Fascism
   2.2. Profile and Explanation
3. Seizure of Power
4. Fascist Regimes
5. Fascism and Christian Culture

1. Term

Derived from It. *fascio,* "bundle, group" (from Lat. *fascis*), the term "fascism" was applied first to the regime of Mussolini. It is now used to denote right-wing political movements and nonsocialist authoritarian governments. This extension of use has led to a loss of linguistic clarity. The term ought to be restricted to the social movements that became a new political force between World War I and World War II. These movements opposed → liberalism, → socialism, Communism, and → conservatism. They combined extreme nationalism (→ Nation, Nationalism) with belief in a new epoch of collective self-affirmation through a state with a single dominant leader. They contained groups that later used → force and terror. Fascism thus produced a new political style, one also stressing manliness, youth, and purity.

Fascist movements must be distinguished from purely conservative political movements that do not glorify force, do not want a total break with the old world, and do not have a comparable concept of the "new man." Demanding absolute subordination to the leader, fascism promised a new life beyond mass society and the essential solubility of all social problems.

In the fascist party the political section stood alongside groups whose responsibilities included the exercise of force and terror when necessary. Experience with fascism is an obstacle to its possible reawakening. Economically and politically, industrialized countries are now much more stable than in the years after 1918, and the cultural traditions of the developing countries (→ Third World) favor other forms of expressing extreme protest.

2. Fascism as a Social Movement
2.1. *The Epoch of Fascism*

As a striking phenomenon between the wars, fascism was the result of unique historical circumstances. The 1917 October → Revolution in Russia had stirred up anxious opposition throughout Europe. World War I had led to many territorial, social, political, and mental changes that made entirely new demands on the economic and political system.

Nationalist, militarist, and social-Darwinist formulas joined hands with a cultural movement that opposed a militant Romanticism to what seemed to be the formalism of the modern world and extreme reason. Finally the victory of fascism in Italy promoted the rise of National Socialism in Germany and beyond.

2.2. *Profile and Explanation*

There were fascist groups in most European countries between 1919 and 1939, but mass movements developed only in central and southern Europe. Contrary to earlier views, fascist parties did not include only the middle classes, although their leadership was generally drawn from those classes. Indeed, rather than being parties of exclusively one class or another, they recall more contemporary parties that try to integrate a broader spectrum. The members of fascist groups were usually younger than those of other groups, hence fascism represented one form in which the generational conflict played itself out after 1918. Finally, fascist parties remained insignificant when they could not win over social classes that could cause permanent agitation by their activism and public influence.

In general, the rise of fascist movements must be described as a process. Sweeping generalizations that attribute their rise (1) to a moral crisis in Europe intensified by various accidents of history, (2) to a form of antiproletarian hysteria on the part of the lower middle class, or (3) to an attempt of the amorphous masses to express themselves do not do justice to the facts. We should take seriously only those theories that trace a connection to conditions of development that reach much further back.

According to W. Schieder, strong fascist movements could develop and seize power where nation building, industrialization, and democratization (→ Democracy) were simultaneous problems. In such settings antiparliamentarian, anticapitalist (→ Capitalism), and nationalist ressentiment was strongest. No accepted traditions of political culture or firm party loyalties existed. Deficient democratization opened the door to antiparliamentarian solutions for broad strata of the population and also shaped the actions of the political and social elite. Forms of authoritarian government destroyed the validity of political rule, but partial cooperation with the fascist party restored its respectability.

3. Seizure of Power

Fascism seized power independently only in Italy and Germany. In both countries middle-class forces felt hemmed in between unpredictable mass movements (→ Bourgeois, Bourgeoisie). Since the high degree of political mobilization did not permit an authoritarian solution against the wishes of the great majority of the population, fascism and National Socialism were given a part in the government in order to mollify them by the exercise of power. Hitler and Mussolini successfully offered themselves to conservatives as an alternative to a supposed revolutionary → labor movement and to extremists within their own fascist movement. In industrially less developed nations a dangerous compromise of this kind was not necessary, since there was no basic opposition to an authoritarian regime.

In Italy the idea of taming the fascists failed in part, and in Germany it was a total failure, for the middle-class partners of Mussolini and Hitler had no adequate political basis once the paramilitary groups had weakened all political and institutional opposition. Fear that failure of the new form of government would be a victory for the Left, inability to recognize the new element of fascist terror, and a skillful yielding to conservative forces in minor details by Mussolini and Hitler did the rest.

4. Fascist Regimes
In both autonomous fascist systems there were a phase of achieving power, a phase of checking party revolution, and finally a phase of radicalizing. Yet there were also clear differences. In Italy there was never a regime of terror comparable with that of National Socialism. Different worldviews, the superior military power of Germany, and different traditions of statecraft were at work in this regard. The decisive point, however, was that Mussolini never succeeded in weakening opposing conservative forces as Hitler did.

5. Fascism and Christian Culture
Fascism took over in extreme form some traditional elements of Christian culture such as processions and rituals, as well as images of a new moral order. It opposed liberalism and → Marxism, joining forces with many Christian churches in this respect. In fact, many of its theses lacked content, becoming concrete only in their rejection of the existing situation. Politically, its eschatology could ultimately have only a negative form in practice.

→ Modern Church History; Radicalism of the Right

Bibliography: S. BEHRENBECK, *Der Kult um die toten Helden. Nationalsozialistische Mythen, Riten und Symbole, 1923-1945* (Schernfeld, 1996) • R. BESSEL, ed., *Fascist Italy and Nazi Germany: Comparisons and Contrasts* (Cambridge, 1996) • A. DE GRAND, *Fascist Italy and Nazi Germany: The "Fascist" Style of Rule* (New York, 1996) • E. GENTILE, *The Sacralization of Politics in Fascist Italy* (Cambridge, Mass., 1996) • G. L. MOSSE, *Die Nationalisierung der Massen* (Frankfurt, 1976) • S. G. PAYNE, *Fascism: A Comparison and Definition* (Madison, Wis., 1980); idem, *A History of Fascism, 1914-1945* (Madison, Wis., 1995) • P. REES, *Fascism and Pre-Fascism in Europe (1890-1945): A Bibliography of the Extreme Right* (Brighton, 1984) • W. SCHIEDER, "Das Deutschland Hitlers und das Italien Mussolinis. Zum Problem faschistischer Regimebildung," *Die Große Krise der dreißiger Jahre. Vom Niedergang der Weltwirtschaft zum 2. Weltkrieg* (ed. G. Schulz; Göttingen, 1985); idem, ed., *Faschismus als soziale Bewegung. Deutschland und Italien im Vergleich* (2d ed.; Göttingen, 1983) • W. WIPPERMANN, *Europäischer Faschismus im Vergleich (1922-1982)* (Frankfurt, 1983).

ARMIN HEINEN

Fasting

1. Forms of Fasting
   1.1. Israel and Judaism
   1.2. Greece and Rome
   1.3. Christianity
   1.4. Today
2. Goals and Motives

1. Forms of Fasting
1.1. *Israel and Judaism*
In the OT → law only the Day of Atonement was a strict fast. The righteous, however, fasted also each Monday and Thursday. Fasting expressed expiation (→ Atonement) and a readiness for conversion. It intensified the prayer for help (2 Sam. 12:16; 1 Kgs. 21:27; Neh. 1:4-11) and gave force to prayer for the attainment of revelations (Dan. 9:3; 10:2-3). It was the mark of a pious life pleasing to God. Along with → prayer and almsgiving, fasting formed a triad of good works. The → prophets criticized the common practice of fasting on the ground that in many cases it did not promote inner purification (Isa. 58:1-9; Jer. 14:12; Zech. 7:5-7).

1.2. *Greece and Rome*
Fasting was practiced in the → mystery religions (in the Cybele-Attis and Isis mysteries, and in Mithraism); in divinations, as a means of seeing secret things; and in medicine, which used it against inflammations. In the philosophical schools of the → Cynics, → Stoics, Epicureans, and Pythagoreans (→ Greek Philosophy), it was a favorite ascetic tool for leading one to inner freedom, release from needs, and union with God.

1.3. *Christianity*

Very little is said about fasting in the NT. → Jesus fasted 40 days in the desert to prepare for his messianic work. He did not seek to be an ascetic, however, and in fact the → Pharisees accused him of being a glutton and a drunkard (Matt. 11:19). Yet he knew and valued fasting as an expression of → piety (Matt. 6:17). In Acts we read that missionaries were sent out with fasting, and → elders were also instituted in the same way (Acts 13:2-3; 14:23).

Fasting soon became a common practice in the early church. The devout fasted on Wednesday and Friday in remembrance of the passion of Jesus. Fasting developed as a preparation for → Easter and became a 40-day fast around 300. Fasts later became associated with Pentecost, Advent, the apostles, and Ember Days. Fasting was very important in → monasticism. Monks abstained from meat, fish, and wine; they ate only at the appointed time, and some only every second day. Fasting became one of the most important → ascetic exercises.

1.4. *Today*

Physicians recommend fasting for such typical diseases of modern civilization as rheumatism and arthritis. Fasting is also advised for the achievement of better → meditation. M. Gandhi (1869-1948) was the first to use fasting as a means of political protest. He regarded fasting as a means of identifying himself with those for whom he fasted, and as a prayer for them. The → peace movement appeals to him in its fasts for → peace.

2. Goals and Motives

For some, fasting is a means of healing body and → soul. Borrowing from Greek philosophy, the → church fathers saw it as such. Fasting purifies the mind and gives it clarity of thought and inner peace.

Fasting is also undertaken to fight the passions. In it one finds oneself; one entertains higher thoughts and feelings. It lifts up the unconscious into the conscious (C. G. Jung). It shows up one's defects and shuts out all flight to substitute satisfactions. For the monks it was a means to tame the three basic urges — gluttony, licentiousness, and avarice. They were not against themselves in fasting but wanted to develop the true self.

With prayer and almsgiving, fasting forms the triad of the devout life. It has an inner relation to the other two. It supports prayer as a prayer with body and soul that promotes the whole person.

Fasting is related to → penitence. In it we confess that we are sinners before God and declare with our bodies our readiness for conversion.

From the days of the → Gnostics, fasting has been viewed as a way of illumination, of attaining to divine secrets (→ Tertullian). It opens us to God, sharpens our sense of the supernatural, and makes mystical experiences possible (→ Mysticism).

Fasting has its dangers. It must not lead to a disparagement of the body in which one denies both the body and oneself. Nor must it become an ascetic achievement that wrongly boosts a feeling of self-worth. It is good today, however, to give our piety a physical expression. Rightly handling food and drink can have a positive effect on the mind, whereas taking too much can dull the mind and make us insensitive to others. Yet we must avoid an exaggerated focus on ourselves and our own bodies. A mark of true fasting is the inner freedom that allows us both to enjoy celebrating and to refrain with inner → joy.

Bibliography: R. Arbesmann, "Fasten," *RAC* 7.447-93; idem, *Das Fasten bei den Griechen und Römern* (Giessen, 1929) • O. Buchinger, *Das Heilfasten* (10th ed.; Stuttgart, 1960) • R. Dahlke, *Bewußt fasten* (Munich, 1983) • A. Grün, *Fasten–Beten mit Leib und Seele* (Münsterschwarzach, 1984) • J. Muddiman, "Fast, Fasting," *ABD* 2.773-76 • A. Wallis, *God's Chosen Fast: A Spiritual and Practical Guide to Fasting* (Fort Washington, Pa., 1968).

Anselm Grün

Fatalism

In general the term "fatalism" denotes the idea that whatever happens is determined and caused by an irresistible, supernatural power that leaves no room for human decision. What is ordained for individuals cannot be foreseen in advance.

The Romans gave the name *fatum* to the power that overrules birth and death (→ Roman Religion). The Greeks called it *Heimarmenē* or *Moira* (→ Greek Religion). The incalculable aspect of destiny was also known to the Greeks as *tychē* and to the Romans as *fortuna*. The → Stoics made fate the dominant principle of the universe. Yet the question of freedom of action also was raised, and Cicero (*De Fato*) rejected the concept of *fatum* because it threatened this freedom. At the same time he rejected the associated idea of prediction.

Among the Egyptians (→ Egyptian Religion) the idea of ineluctable foreordination was represented by the concept and god Šai. The Chinese thought that the will of heaven *(tien)* fixes the fate *(ming)* of dynasties. The course of things *(dao)*, the cosmic or inner path, cannot be discerned. In Indian religions the idea of → karma is characteristic in various forms. It explains in part the state of things but leaves some room for future improvement (→ Hinduism).

The Jewish tradition (→ Jewish Theology) recognizes especially the free and morally responsible action of a people or individuals in → covenant with God. Yet questions of prediction, → predestination, and → freedom of the will have constantly occupied theologians in the Jewish, Christian, and Islamic (→ Islam) traditions. Pre-Islamic ideas of fate (e.g., *manīyah,* first meaning "destiny," and then "death") were partly set aside by the Islamic stress on God's omnipotence, and partly they merged with and continued in it. In northern Europe pre-Christian ideas of fate (e.g., the Anglo-Saxon *wyrd, metod*) faded away.

Fatalism has now become a term of opprobrium in theology, but the search for a cosmically anchored understanding of the varied course of human existence is often a mark of modern religion.

Bibliography: J. HOLM, ed., *Human Nature and Destiny* (New York, 1994) • R. MAY, *Freedom and Destiny* (New York, 1999) • N. RESCHER, *Luck: The Brilliant Randomness of Everyday Life* (New York, 1995) • H. RINGGREN, ed., *Fatalistic Beliefs in Religion, Folklore, and Literature* (Stockholm, 1967) • P. TILLICH, "Philosophy and Fate," *The Protestant Era* (Chicago, 1957) 3-15.

MICHAEL PYE

Father

1. OT, NT, Early Church
2. Psychoanalysis
3. Pastoral Psychology
4. Sociology

1. OT, NT, Early Church

In the OT the father is the ancestor of a line, the protector and patriarch of the family, and has almost unlimited → authority. The → promises to the patriarchs (→ Patriarchal History) → Abraham, → Isaac, and → Jacob are central to the identity of Israel (and of the → early church; see Romans 4). → Yahweh, however, the God of the fathers, is rarely addressed as father, an attempt to avoid any proximity to the generative fertility gods in Israel's surroundings (e.g., → Ugarit; Mother Goddesses 1). Only during the postexilic period are more frequent references made to Yahweh as Father and Creator, for in → Israel's history, in election, and in → covenant (§1.2), God has shown himself to be a caring and loyal Father. Early Jewish writers address God in → prayer (§2.1) as Father, focusing not on the attendant authority that demands obedience but rather on connotations of compassion, → faithfulness, → love (§4), and provision (A. Strotmann).

→ Jesus picked up on this Jewish tradition with the form of address he used in his own prayers, simultaneously radicalizing it with the Abba address (Mark 14:36) deriving from the family. The → Lord's Prayer initiates the → disciples into the child's close relationship with the near and intimate God of Jesus. This God is at the same time the new authority relativizing all human fathers along with the structures of domination and relationships of authority deriving from them. The disciples are to call no one else on earth father, "for you have one Father — the one in heaven" (Matt. 23:9; cf. Gal. 3:29).

The early church's doctrine of the → Trinity (§1) relativizes God's position as Father by integrating him into a relationship with the Son (→ Christology 2.2) and the → Spirit (§2).

2. Psychoanalysis

The → psychoanalytic theory of S. Freud (1856-1939) and its permutations played a dominant role in 20th-century interpretations of the father. Freud's theory of the Oedipus complex describes a supposed developmental conflict typical of childhood (→ Development 2) in which the fear of castration deriving from the authoritative father prompts the boy to renounce his incestuous wishes toward his mother and ultimately to identify with the more powerful and idealized figure of the father. Freud equates this process with that of cultural appropriation (→ Culture 4), with the acceptance of the "law of the father" and with the development of the superego. Picking up on this point, A. Mitscherlich (1908-82) diagnosed a situation in which increasing industrialization (→ Industrial Society) was bringing about a fatherless society. The disintegration of patriarchal authority allegedly implies that children today remain in a static → narcissistic conflict with their mother and no longer develop any maturity through coming to terms with the patriarchal model. The leveling of any "persuasive distinctions in rank" then leads to an accommodated "mass → identity."

Feminist psychoanalysts such as C. Rohde-Dachser raise the criticism that this view presupposes, ontologizes, and prolongs an asymmetrical relationship between the genders (→ Feminism; Sexism 1), a criticism presumably also applying to more recent theory of object-relationship that replaces Freud's powerful father with the father understood as savior and liberator from the devouring mother, who threatens one's individuation, and that contrasts the "omnipotent" mother with the "impotent" father. Such images of mother and father are allegedly rooted in the social fact that in Western culture a female always functions as contact person for both genders at the beginning of life, leading to different courses of development for boys and girls and at the same time to a reproduction of the same stereotype (→ Women; Men).

3. Pastoral Psychology
→ Pastoral psychology discussed reference to God the Father largely in connection with psychoanalytic thought, assuming that the experience with one's own father shapes one's later relationship with God and, vice versa, that every religious symbol actually deals with basic human conflicts. In this sense J. Scharfenberg maintains the necessity and exclusivity of the father symbol in one's address to God because the mother symbol might pull → prayer (§3.3) into a regressive vortex that threatens to dissolve one's individuality (→ Anthropology 5).

By contrast, feminist theologians (→ Feminist Theology) emphasize that the one-sidedly male symbolism of God is no longer suitable for addressing the conflicts experienced by women, especially women whose fathers have sexually abused and mistreated them (→ Sexuality 2). They adduce gruesome father-daughter stories from the OT attesting incest and abuse and clearly articulating the ambivalence of any image of the father as omnipotent (H. Wöller; → Biblical Theology 2.6). In the search for an identity "between the father-world and feminism" (U. Wagner-Rau), gender-neutral and female symbols for the divine acquire significance by acknowledging that women are also made in God's image and by bestowing dignity and value upon their existence quite independent of fathers and sons (→ Spirituality). The father-son dominance in our image of God must thus be relativized if God genuinely is to symbolize that which transcends human relationships and also be of spiritual benefit to women.

4. Sociology
Sociologically, the dominant role of the father in family and society loses significance with the change in → modernity from a stratified, class-based social structure to one that is functionally differentiated. The image of the father no longer possesses the kind of unifying symbolic power still resonating in phrases such as "father of the country" or "holy father." Although one can describe this development as fatherlessness (Mitscherlich), such a description is not really adequate. The more complex a society becomes, the more do differentiated functional systems take over the tasks once assumed by the fathers in a segmented or stratified society. Rather than being genuinely fatherless, modern society has simply changed the framework within which one understands what it means to be a father. Only the differentiation of vocational life and family life at the beginning of modernity (→ Work 5; Family 1) established asymmetrically structured interpretations that understood the father as representing society (external) and the mother as representing the home (internal).

Only with the subsequent individualization of → women (1) (E. Beck-Gernsheim) and their inclusion in the functional systems of society, especially through vocational activity (→ Vocation 6), do these interpretations become increasingly implausible. The notion of the dominance of fathers, and those of motherly love, duty, and of the intimate mother-child symbiosis, prove to be social constructs (as in the feminist critique of patriarchalism; H. Tyrell, S. Hirschauer). Comparison with other cultures impressively illustrates this understanding and discloses the enormous variety and variability of relations between the genders and within the family structure (K. A. Rabuzzi; → Ethnology). Although the influence of popularizing developmental psychology (→ Ego Psychology) has maintained the social-emotional primacy of the mother-child relationship in society at large, more recent research into our understanding of the father and of divorce shows that from the beginning of life onward, a child is capable of enjoying equally differentiated interaction with both its father and its mother, and that the notion of a single, primary contact person who allegedly functions as a model for the relationships of an adult must be corrected (W. E. Fthenakis). Finally, research emphasizes that increased engagement on the part of fathers in a family — the "new fatherliness" (S. R. Dunde) — generally has a positive effect on all who are involved.

Bibliography: E. BECK-GERNSHEIM, "Vom 'Dasein für andere' zum Anspruch auf ein Stück 'eigenes Leben,'" *SozW* 34 (1983) 307-40 • P. BRONSTEIN and C. P. COWAN, *Fatherhood Today: Men's Changing Role in the Family* (New York, 1988) • A. D. COLMAN and L. L. COLMAN, *The Father* (New York, 1993) • M. DALY, *Beyond God the Father* (Boston, 1973) • R. DAVIS and C. DAVIS, *The Paternal Romance: Reaching God the Father in Early Western Culture* (Urbana, Ill., 1993) • S. R. DUNDE, *Neue*

Väterlichkeit (Gütersloh, 1986) • S. Freud, *Totem and Taboo* (New York, 1962; orig. pub., 1913) • W. E. Fthenakis, *Väter* (2 vols.; Munich, 1985) • S. Hirschauer, "Die soziale Fortpflanzung der Zweigeschlechtlichkeit," *KZSS* 46 (1994) 668-92 • K. Lüscher and F. Schultheis, eds., *Die "postmoderne" Familie* (Konstanz, 1988) • O. Michel, "Πατήρ," *EDNT* 3.53-57 • A. Mitscherlich, *Auf dem Weg zur vaterlosen Gesellschaft* (Munich, 1963) • J. Moltmann, "Ich glaube an Gott, der Vater. Patriarchalische oder nichtpatriarchalische Rede von Gott?" *EvT* 43 (1983) 397-415 • K. A. Rabuzzi, "Family," *EncRel(E)* 5.276-82 • H. Ringgren, "אָב *'ābh*," *TDOT* 1.1-19 • B. E. Robinson and R. L. Barrett, *The Developing Father: Emerging Roles in Contemporary Society* (New York, 1986) • C. Rohde-Dachser, *Expedition in den dunklen Kontinent. Weiblichkeit im Diskurs der Psychoanalyse* (Berlin, 1992) • K. M. Rosenthal and H. F. Keshet, *Fathers without Partners: A Study of Fathers and the Family after Marital Separation* (Totowa, N.J., 1981) • J. Scharfenberg, *Einführung in die Pastoralpsychologie* (Göttingen, 1985) 108-10 • E. Schillebeeckx and J. B. Metz, eds., *God as Father* (Edinburgh, 1981) • E. V. Stein, *Fathering, Fact or Fable?* (Nashville, 1979) • A. Strotmann, *"Mein Vater bist du!" Zur Bedeutung der Vaterschaft Gottes in kanonischen und nichtkanonischen frühjüdischen Schriften* (Frankfurt, 1991) • H. Tyrell, "Geschlechtliche Differenzierung und Geschlechterklassifikation," *KZSS* 38 (1986) 450-89; idem, "Soziologische Überlegungen zur Struktur des bürgerlichen Typus der Mutter-Kind-Beziehung," *Lebenswelt und soziale Probleme* (ed. J. Matthes; Frankfurt, 1981) 417-28 • U. Wagner-Rau, *Zwischen Vaterwelt und Feminismus* (Gütersloh, 1992) • H. Wöller, *Vom Vater verwundet. Töchter der Bibel* (Stuttgart, 1991).

Isolde Karle

Fathers → Church Fathers

Fatima

The beginnings of the Marian pilgrimage in Fatima, Portugal, are connected with six visions of Mary experienced in 1917 by the children Lucia dos Santos (b. 1907) and her cousins Francisco (1908-19) and Jacinta (1910-20) Marto. Most of the auditions related to the appearances were published, but there is debate about the so-called Third Mystery, which is preserved as a sealed document in the Vatican archives.

After many controversies the visions were officially declared to be credible by the local bishop in 1930, but by then they had already made Fatima a popular place of national pilgrimage. As many as 150,000 pilgrims had been counted by May 13, 1928. A chapel was built as early as 1925, followed later by a basilica and several convents.

Fatima soon assumed international significance with an upsurge of Marian piety, special emphasis being placed on the → rosary and → eucharistic spirituality. Like → Lourdes, Fatima became a place of international pilgrimage.

The message of Fatima, as a Roman Catholic interpretation of the events of a year that was also significant in world politics (1917), had great importance for the time that followed. It culminated with a call for → penitence, for the saying of the rosary, and for the dedication of a world threatened by war and destruction, especially the Soviet Union, to the Immaculate Heart of Mary. This dedication, made by Pius XII in 1942, is an expression of the Marian piety influenced by Fatima. The importance of the popular → piety related to Fatima has been underlined by such events as later papal visitations.

→ Mary, Devotion to

Bibliography: C. Barthas, *Fatima* (2d ed.; Freiburg, 1955) • B. Brenninkmeyer, "Zu den Erscheinungen und der Botschaft von Fatima," *ZAM* 21 (1948) 214-20 • *Der Fels* 17 (1986) 92 (on the latest discussion of the "Third Mystery") • R. Graber, *Maria. Jungfrau–Mutter–Königin* (St. Augustin, 1976) see esp. "Die Dimensionen von Fatima" • G. Jacquemet, "Fatima," *Cath.* 4 (1956) 1112-15 • V. Marion, *Eine Theologie über Fatima* (Innsbruck, [1960]) • G. M. Roschini, O.S.M., "Fatima," *Dizionario di Mariologia* (Rome, 1961) 166-67 (bibliography) • W. T. Walsh, *Our Lady of Fatima* (London, 1949).

Britta Hübener

Fear

Under the influence of S. → Kierkegaard (1813-55), later philosophers and popular authors have often distinguished "fear" from → "anxiety." The former denotes a debilitating emotion in the face of specific dangers and threats; the latter, an emotional reaction to what is unknown and indefinite. The distinction as such makes sense, but it is linguistically artificial and does not stand up to more exact analysis of academic, popular, or poetic usage. Nor do etymological findings help. Fear and anxiety are largely interchangeable.

In psychological and psychiatric literature we find a new form of distinction. In behaviorism the reactions that animals can learn to danger or punishment are usually called fear, while "anxiety" is the term for this kind of reaction in human beings. Psychiatry (→ Psychotherapy) prefers the term "anxiety" and distinguishes between different basic forms and their causes, including a free form of anxiety as distinct from a phobia.

In religious history "fear" is often used for → reverence, but also for dread of God, the holy, → punishment, → demons, → death, and certain crises in life along with the accompanying rites. Yet no uniform phenomenology of fear is possible in religious history.

In Christian usage fear is centrally oriented to OT and NT passages about fear of God. In the Bible fear of punishment, demons, sickness, shame, death, war, and judgment is set in the light of fear of God, which already implies a gracious relation between God and humans and therefore hope of → forgiveness and redemption. The biblical promise of freedom ("Fear not!") has often been played down in the church's preaching, teaching, and pastoral care, or it has been changed into the bondage of a new fear. For this reason so-called ecclesiogenic → neuroses have arisen among some people, and others have rejected the gospel.

→ Psychology of Religion

Bibliography: G. ALTNER, *Über Leben* (Düsseldorf, 1992) • K. BARTH, *CD* II/2, 597-600 • J. A. GRAY, *The Psychology of Fear and Stress* (2d ed.; Cambridge, 1987) • D. A. HOPE, *Perspectives on Anxiety, Panic, and Fear* (Lincoln, Nebr., 1996) • G. LANCZKOWSKI, K. ROMANIUK, and G. SCHNURR, "Furcht," *TRE* 2.755-67, esp. pt. 3, with comprehensive presentation and helpful bibliography • R. OTTO, *The Idea of the Holy* (New York, 1970; orig. pub., 1917) • S. TERRIEN, "Fear," *IDB* 2.256-60 • W. ZIMMERLI, *OT Theology in Outline* (Atlanta, 1978) 145-67. See also the bibliography in "Anxiety."

DIETRICH RITSCHL

Federal Theology → Covenant 3

Fellowship Movement

1. Definition
2. Distinctive Features
3. History
4. Outlook

1. Definition
The Fellowship Movement (*Gemeinschaftsbewegung*) is an umbrella concept encompassing a wide variety of pietistic and theologically → conservative groups in Germany. The term arose in the 1880s and referred essentially to the merging of vestiges of the pietistic awakening earlier in the 19th century with Holiness and revivalistic influences from Britain and North America. This blending resulted in the flowering of religious and charitable organizations, both within and outside the framework of the established regional Protestant churches.

As voluntary societies possessing the legal status of not-for-profit corporations, the organizations within the Fellowship Movement have their own officers, administrative boards, programs, and budgets, and the churches can exercise only a limited degree of control over their activities. Thus from the beginning the movement has been in tension with the churches, both over matters of membership and over the relationship of church officials and → pastors to the evangelical teachers, evangelists, and publicists of groups in the movement. No one single structure binds together the dozens of bodies grouped under this rubric, but nearly all of them participate in the Church Conference under the Word (*Gemeindetag unter dem Wort*), a biennial mass assembly at Pentecost that was initiated in 1973 as an alternative to the highly inclusive → German Evangelical Church Conference (*Kirchentag*).

2. Distinctive Features
The Fellowship Movement is characterized by an emphasis on the proclamation of the → gospel message. The Bible is God's eternal → Word and applies personally to every individual. One must respond with a clear-cut decision for Christ and experience → regeneration; there is a sharp difference between those who are reborn and those who are not. → Conversion (§1), however, is not the end but the beginning of the Christian's experience. Believers are to engage in Bible reading and → prayer and to lead an exemplary life, separate from worldly lusts. A Christian lives in Christ, who helps him or her to live in faith and have assurance of → salvation. In the true community of Christ the priesthood of all believers is the rule. According to the gifts that God has bestowed, the individual believer will engage actively in spreading the gospel, proclaiming the Word, and doing good works to help those in need. In earnest struggle and joyful hope the community looks for the day of Jesus' return (→ Parousia) and the fulfillment of his → kingdom. Christians have a part in building the kingdom and participate in its dynamic, although differences exist as to whether it is a divine-human cooperative endeavor or whether God will establish it independently of human effort.

The Fellowship Movement differs from classic →

Pietism in its use of teaching conferences to instruct laypeople in doctrinal matters and to build fellowship. Also new is the Anglo-American practice of evangelistic crusades outside the church premises, such as tent missions and large stadium rallies.

3. History

Various factors contributed to the rise of the Fellowship Movement. Revival preachers found fertile soil for their message in the areas where Pietism had been strong — Württemberg, the Upper and Lower Rhine, Hesse, Siegerland, the Wupper valley, Hamburg, Berlin, Pomerania, East Prussia, Silesia, and Thuringia. In these places the Evangelical Alliance (→ World Evangelical Fellowship) drew considerable support, a variety of city missions with → Inner Mission links and diaconal institutions were founded, and independent seminaries were established to train preachers and evangelists, the best-known of which was the Johanneum in Wuppertal-Barmen (1886).

The → Holiness movement, which spread in Germany after Robert Pearsall Smith's tour in 1875, attracted such influential personalities as theologian Theodor Christlieb (1833-89), lawyer Eduard von Pückler (1853-1924), diplomat Andreas von Bernstorff (1844-1907), Jasper von Oertzen (1833-93) of the landed gentry, and Elias Schrenk (1831-1913), the first important evangelist in Germany. The Gnadau Association (which began as a biennial conference in 1888 and became a regular organization in 1894) was the major Fellowship Movement organ. It brought together those committed to the Holiness ideas of the deeper life and entire → sanctification (perfectionism).

The rapid spread of Pentecostalism into Germany after 1907 produced serious tensions (→ Pentecostal Churches). When the leaders of the Fellowship Movement declared Pentecostalism to be heretical (in the Berlin Declaration of 1909), most → charismatics went their own way and formed separate → free churches. Walter Michaelis (1866-1953), the longtime leader of the Gnadau Association and an architect of the separation, succeeded in keeping most of the Fellowship Movement in the church. When he insisted in 1934 that the pro-Nazi German Christians were incompatible with the movement, some dropped out, while others identified with the → Confessing Church. The National Socialist regime came down hard on the movement by banning its publications and conferences.

After the trauma of World War II the Fellowship Movement renewed its activities within the territorial churches, but controversies over biblical exegesis, the pluralism of the German → people's church (Volkskirche), and → World Council of Churches' initiatives like the → Program to Combat Racism brought new tensions in the relationship. At the same time the movement experienced renewal through North American evangelistic efforts (esp. those of Billy Graham) and the new currents entering Germany through American evangelical parachurch enterprises. Another element is the annual conference sponsored by the German Evangelical Alliance in Bad Blankenburg, Thuringia, since 1886. Modeled on the English Keswick conferences with their emphasis on personal decisions for Christ, faithfulness to the Scriptures, the work of the → Holy Spirit, and anticipation of Christ's return, the conferences are interdenominational in character and do not attack the territorial churches, though Pentecostal practices are firmly rejected.

4. Outlook

With such signficant endeavors as the confessional movement No Other Gospel (*Kein anderes Evangelium*, founded in 1966 and organizer of the alternative church conferences), the evangelistic outreach of the → YMCA and the Billy Graham Evangelistic Association, new ecumenical links provided by the Lausanne Committee, and the creation of training schools for church workers outside the traditional university framework, the Fellowship Movement has taken on new life. The German evangelicals (*Evangelikale*) now have their own press service, radio work, → student ministries, and missionary societies; publishers with the Fellowship Movement or with other evangelical ties are responsible for around 60 percent of the Protestant literary output in Germany.

However, the differences between leaders of the mainline Protestants and of the Fellowship Movement as to what constitutes a → congregation and a → church are increasing, as are the tensions between those who advocate a free church and those who would remain within the national church. The process of setting up alternative institutions leads inexorably in the free church direction, and the traditional stance of the Fellowship Movement that Theodor Christlieb had articulated, "In the church and with the church but not under the church," now has a hollow ring. Whether this coming together of German pietism and Anglo-American religious organization will destroy or transform the German Protestant church remains an open question.

Bibliography: H. BURKHARDT et al., eds., *Evangelisches Gemeindelexikon* (2d ed.; Wuppertal, 1990) • J. DRECH-

SEL, *Das Gemeindeverständnis der deutschen Gemeinschaftsbewegung* (Giessen, 1984) • D. LANGE, *Eine Bewegung bricht sich Bahn. Die deutschen Gemeinschaften im ausgehenden 19. und beginnenden 20. Jahrhundert und ihre Stellung zu Kirche, Theologie und Pfingstbewegung* (3d ed.; Giessen, 1990) • J. OHLEMACHER, *Das Reich Gottes in Deutschland bauen. Ein Beitrag zur Vorgeschichte und Theologie der deutschen Gemeinschaftsbewegung* (Göttingen, 1986); idem, ed., *Die Gemeinschaftsbewegung in Deutschland. Quellen zu ihrer Geschichte, 1887-1914* (Gütersloh, 1977) • E. G. RÜPPEL, *Die Gemeinschaftsbewegung im Dritten Reich. Ein Beitrag zur Geschichte des Kirchenkampfes* (Göttingen, 1969) • P. SCHARPFF, *History of Evangelism: Three Hundred Years of Evangelism in Germany, Great Britain, and the United States of America* (Grand Rapids, 1966).

RICHARD V. PIERARD and JÖRG OHLEMACHER

Feminism

1. History
2. Global Growth
3. Differences
4. Theories and Practices
5. Feminism and the Church

Feminism as a worldwide movement is founded in women's consciousness that as a group they are, and historically have been, subordinate and that this subordination is not natural but is socially, culturally, and religiously determined. Furthermore, feminism is the conviction that → women and → men are created for full economic, political, social, and religious → equality. Finally, feminism is women's creation of alternative ways to arrange societies and institutions so that such an egalitarian future may become a reality.

1. History
Contemporary feminism, particularly in the United States and Europe, typically traces its antecedents to 18th-century → Enlightenment themes such as individual → autonomy, and to more radical traditions of → utopianism, → revolution, republicanism, sexual nonconformity, and religious → skepticism, as illustrated in Mary Wollstonecraft's *Vindication of the Rights of Woman* (1792). *Declaration of Sentiments*, written by Elizabeth Cady Stanton on the occasion of the first women's rights convention in the United States — in Seneca Falls, New York, in 1848 — expresses certain Enlightenment themes as well. Stanton's manifesto, however, also calls for societal change, not only for individual freedoms. So speaking, she reflects the formative influence of 19th-century abolition and suffrage movements on feminism in the United States. Among the leaders of these movements were Stanton, Susan B. Anthony, Matilda Joslyn Gage, and Lucretia Mott (→ Women's Movement).

All of these women were influenced by an indigenous source of lived-out feminism — the matrilineal and matrilocal society of the Iroquois. Here, as historian Sally Roesch Wagner wrote, "They caught a glimpse of the possibility of freedom because they knew women who lived liberated lives." In *History of Woman Suffrage* (1881-87), Gage spoke of the Native American cultures she knew from her Seneca neighbors as her inspiration for a "regenerated world."

2. Global Growth
Already in the 19th century, feminism was international in commitment and character. It gained this status not only through the travels of women leaders but also through organizations working for women's suffrage in various countries. At an international suffrage conference in 1902, with Anthony presiding, the International Woman Suffrage Alliance was created. This alliance was dedicated "to secure the enfranchisement of the women of all nations, and to unite the friends of women's suffrage throughout the world in organized co-operation and fraternal helpfulness." Delegates from 11 countries attended the first meeting in Berlin in 1904, including Mary Church Terrell, founder and first president of the National Association of Colored Women. (Terrell was the only U.S. delegate to address the gathering in fluent German.)

The growth of global feminism was most marked during the 1980s. This growth began with the U.N. declaration of 1975 as International Women's Year. At an attendant U.N.-sponsored conference in Mexico City, women agreed that one year was not adequate and persuaded the → United Nations to declare a Decade for Women, which was announced for 1975-85. A second international conference was held mid-decade in Copenhagen (1980), and an end-of-the-decade conference in Nairobi (1985). A fourth conference was held ten years later in Beijing.

These conferences were occasions for U.N.-related nongovernmental organizations (NGOs) to gather alongside the delegated meeting. In the wake of these NGO gatherings, which quickly grew larger than the official body, feminists increasingly worked across national borders, sharing information and resources, and standing in solidarity on issues of common concern.

3. Differences

These international gatherings surfaced significant differences among feminists. The issues brought by women from the countries of Africa, Asia, or Latin America not only were not the same as those brought by Western feminists; at times the various issues conflicted with each other. For example, Western women expressed concern for the growing → poverty of → Third World women, but they did not join in critique of multinational corporations or free trade agreements.

Stated more generally, as women's networks strengthened and interaction increased, it became clear that certain women's privileges were other women's burdens to bear. Differences defined by race, class, sexual orientation, age, geographic location, physical abilities, and so forth also define differently such matters as gender roles and expectations, as well as limitations. Feminists are therefore challenged to respect differences among women and to build coalitions that take them into account, rather than making inappropriate assumptions about what women have in common. Hope for such respect and coalition building has been encouraged in the 1990s by Latina, African, Asian, Caribbean, and Pacific feminists, who, living in their various contexts, have articulated their experiences and thoughts about being women and about social, cultural, and religious change.

4. Theories and Practices

The differences among feminists may also be defined theoretically and in terms of strategies chosen for change. Although labels for these differences are themselves debatable, it may be helpful to use adjectives such as "liberal," "socialist," "radical," and others to sketch the outlines of the vast diversity among feminists at the end of the 20th century.

Liberal feminists focus on obtaining institutional and policy changes through legislation and the courts. Issues on their agenda include the election of women to public office, equity in employment (e.g., equal pay for men and women, provision of child care and parental leave), the manner of girls' education, and defense of reproductive rights. Socialist feminists additionally argue that equity and freedom for women are possible only with the abolition of → capitalism, which they judge to create systemic injustices based on class and race as well as gender. Given the global reach of capitalism, socialist feminists are also attentive to the interconnection of women's struggles around the world. Radical femi-

nists critique sexual politics in a patriarchal system, highlighting how violence against women, pornography, and the sex industry conspire to keep women powerless.

Feminists of color have founded autonomous organizations since the 19th century. The focus of their concern is racial and economic exploitation and injustice, which multiply the gender oppression. This insight into the interconnectedness of race, class, and gender has been groundbreaking and has had theoretical significance for all feminists who are committed to systemic analysis and action.

Lesbian feminists have been among the most active in the movement since the 1970s, although some women were convinced that the presence of lesbians was a menace to the feminist movement for equal rights (→ Homosexuality). Consequently, lesbians tended to form their own groups and to engage in their own analysis of heterosexism, homophobia, and the ways these attitudes were integrally part of → sexism and the definition of traditional gender roles, which are oppressive for many women. Lesbian feminists were also culturally creative, founding bookstores, presses, women's music concerts, and record companies. Most recently, major feminist organizations in the United States and elsewhere have welcomed lesbians and recognized the unique challenges they face in societies throughout the world.

Not surprisingly, there have been bitter arguments and attendant divisions among feminists. The most controversial issues include pornography, reproductive rights, racial and ethnic identity, → class, and → sexuality. There is also controversy concerning assessments of biology — for example, whether a uniquely female biology is a potential source of strength, even a catalyst of change toward a more nurturing and less violent society, or whether any talk of female biology leads to assertions of women's "natural" roles.

5. Feminism and the Church

Radical critique of religion, particularly Christianity, has been central to the critique of patriarchy by feminists. Already in the 19th century Stanton and Gage articulated the connection between the subordinate status of women in society and women's image in Christian Scripture and tradition. In their books — Stanton's *Woman's Bible* (2 vols., 1895-98) and Gage's *Woman, Church, and the State* (1893) — the two argued that the church has been not merely the site of, but also the seedbed of, the suppression of women. Gage also spoke about prehistoric matriarchies, which she believed were egalitarian, woman-centered communities that worshiped a female deity.

Gage's book was all but erased from the histori-cal record, and not until the late 1960s and early 1970s did feminists again write about the church. Foremost among these writings were Mary Daly's *The Church and the Second Sex* (1968) and *Beyond God the Father* (1973) and Nelle Morton's essay "Women's Liberation and the Church" (1970), pub-lished in the feminist magazine *Tempo*.

The 1970s was also the decade during which many churches of the Protestant → Reformation began to ordain women, including the Lutheran Church in America (1970) and the Episcopal Church (1976). Accordingly, increasing numbers of women graduated from theological seminaries. In 1974 the → World Council of Churches sponsored a groundbreaking consultation in West Berlin, "Sex-ism in the 1970s," to consider the place of Christian women in the context of women's struggles for lib-eration around the world. One speaker at the con-sultation spoke of sexism as heresy, thereby seeking to highlight the theological significance of the issues women were raising with regard to their role in the church. From this consultation came a call for fur-ther theological study, which was taken up in "The Community of Women and Men in the Church," a study cosponsored by the Commission on Faith and Order and the Subunit on Women.

During the decades of the 1960s, 1970s, and 1980s, many feminists chose to leave the church, of-ten mourning shattered symbols of faith. A number of these feminists rejected the either/or option of patriarchal religion or no religion. Consequently, during these decades a feminist spirituality move-ment grew and flourished that took various forms. Some feature women's experiences of life, birth, nurture, and so forth. Others focus on the concept of the Goddess, the historical roots of which are much debated. New rituals, myths, and magic abound and are often interwoven with political commitments and activism.

Other feminists, who chose to stay within the church and the Christian tradition, also created al-ternative arenas in which to express their faith. One such arena is Women-Church, another Re-Imagining, in both of which women celebrate new rituals, articulate new theologies, and strengthen their determination to stand in solidarity with all women, particularly those who suffer the triple oppression of sexism, → racism, and classism.

Often feminists participate in these newly cre-ative communities of women alongside their partic-ipation in more traditional churches. In the latter, women are being ordained in increasing numbers. Moreover, women have been consecrated as bishops

in Anglican, Lutheran, and Methodist traditions, so far in Germany, Sweden, Norway, India, New Zea-land, the Philippines, and the United States. Or-dained women nonetheless face serious obstacles to their ministry, such as lower pay, difficulty finding placements and moving to more senior positions, and continuing resistance from colleagues and con-gregants. Therefore, although increasing numbers of women are being ordained, increasing numbers of women are also leaving pastoral ministry for ministry in nontraditional settings. In short, the conjunction "women and church" continues to call for critique as well as commitment. This committed critique is at the heart of → feminist theology, which has flourished since the late 1960s.

Bibliography: P. G. ALLEN, *The Sacred Hoop: Recovering the Feminine in American Indian Tradition* (Boston, 1986) • N. J. BERNKING and P. C. JOERN, eds., *Re-Membering and Re-Imagining* (Cleveland, 1995) • M. DALY, *Beyond God the Father* (Boston, 1973) • M. HUMM, ed., *Modern Feminisms: Political, Literary, Cultural* (New York, 1992) • G. LERNER, *The Creation of Feminist Consciousness: From the Middle Ages to 1870* (New York, 1993) • M. A. MAY, *Bonds of Unity: Women, Theology, and the Worldwide Church* (Atlanta, 1989) • R. RENDALL, *The Origins of Modern Feminism: Women in Britain, France, and the United States, 1780-1860* (London, 1985) • R. R. RUETHER, *Women-Church: The-ology and Practice of Feminist Liturgical Communities* (New York, 1985).

MELANIE A. MAY

Feminist Theology

1. Nineteenth-Century Traditions
2. Catalytic Insights in the Twentieth Century
3. Contributions
   3.1. Biblical Studies
   3.2. Historical Studies
   3.3. Theological Studies
4. Global and Local Contexts

Feminist theology is better referred to as feminist theologies. The theological perspectives and ways of working are as distinctive and diverse (culturally, socially, racially, ethnically, economically, geograph-ically, and sexually) as the women writing them. These theologies engage both critical and creative work undertaken within and often across what have been discrete theological disciplines, including bib-lical studies, church history, doctrinal and → sys-tematic theology, → ethics, and pastoral → counseling. In most instances, therefore, feminist theologies intend to reconceptualize these disciplines, rather than simply to offer additional insights. Feminist theologies are committed to change, including advocacy on behalf of women's personal and corporate well-being.

1. Nineteenth-Century Traditions

Although most feminist theologies have featured women's contemporary experiences, there is also a tradition of women doing theology. Strands of this tradition may be traced back at least to the Middle Ages and continued through the 18th century in the work of women such as Hildegard of Bingen (1098-1179), Margaret Askew Fell Fox (1614-1702), and Mary Astell (1666-1731). By the 19th century many more women were creating what Mary Pellauer has called a hitherto unrecognized tradition of feminist theology. Key 19th-century creators of this tradition were Sarah Grimké (1792-1873), Lucretia Mott (1793-1880), Maria Miller Stewart (1803-79), Elizabeth Cady Stanton (1815-1902), Matilda Joslyn Gage (1826-98), and Anna Julia Cooper (1858-1964).

Many, if not most, of these women were deeply influenced by 19th-century American evangelical → revivalism, whether or not they acknowledged their formation or associated themselves with → evangelical religion later in life. The interaction of evangelical religion and reform was striking. Indeed, as Keith Melder has noted with regard to the revivals of Charles Grandison Finney, "Surely it is no coincidence that the areas where Finney's revivals and women's religious education flourished — New England, upstate New York and northern Ohio — were early centers of women's reform work and → feminism" (p. 39). The preaching of Finney and other revivalists did not dwell on orthodox tenets of faith but emphasized the call to personal → perfection and a sense of moral duty. It was therefore as religious people that these women felt that the fight for their own emancipation and that of slaves was a divine calling and sacred duty.

Perhaps the most remarkable document of this 19th-century tradition of feminist theology is *The Woman's Bible,* published in two volumes in 1895 and 1898. Elizabeth Cady Stanton began the project because she saw the ways in which the Bible had been used both to justify the subordination of women and to fight against it. With a committee of women editors, she set out to ascertain just what the Bible does say about women and to produce a critical commentary on relevant passages. By the end of the project, Stanton concluded that there was very

little in the Bible that could be helpful for rational modern feminists. The problem was not merely that men have misinterpreted the true message of the Bible, as other feminists of her time argued, but that the Bible itself is androcentric and biased in the interest of men. This debate about whether the Bible and the Christian tradition, if correctly interpreted, are reformable continues among feminist theologians today.

2. Catalytic Insights in the Twentieth Century

Feminist theology burst onto the 20th-century landscape in the 1960s. More specifically, 20th-century feminist theology was catalyzed by Valerie Saiving's essay "The Human Situation: A Feminine View," published in 1960. In this essay Saiving pointed out that what theologians had called "human" experience was really men's experience, not women's. Accordingly, Saiving argued that traditional understandings of human nature — for example the understanding of sin as pride or egocentricity — typically reflect the experience of men rather than of women, whose besetting sin most often derives from the sacrifice of self through devoted service to others.

A second catalytic insight follows from the first. Not only are traditional theologies shaped by men's experiences rather than women's; these theologies reinforce — actually, sanctify — social attitudes, behaviors, conventions, and structures that privilege men and subordinate women to secondary status. A woman's status is not only secondary, it is derivative, based on her relationship with a man, whether father or husband or brother. Mary Daly captured this reality in her 1973 classic *Beyond God the Father* when she said that if God is male, then male is God.

These insights led 20th-century feminist theologians to focus on the question of theological language. Seeing the ways in which words shape the world and the place of men and women in the world, feminists critiqued the predominantly male language of theology. Some feminist theologians have retrieved female images, both human and divine, forgotten in Scripture and in Christian tradition. Some have chosen to work with nongendered, even nonpersonal, theological language. Others have attempted to recover images of the Goddess and nurture what they believe is a uniquely female → spirituality.

3. Contributions

Since the 1960s, and particularly since the early 1980s, the influence of feminist theologians and scholars has burgeoned. All the traditional theological disciplines are being reshaped as women ask new questions, explore unfamiliar themes and topics, and employ unprecedented methodologies. Feminist theologians, that is to say, are not simply adding to disciplines as already defined; they are actively reconceptualizing disciplinary perspectives, issues, and ways of working.

3.1. *Biblical Studies*

Feminist biblical scholars generally agree that the Bible, both the Hebrew Scriptures and the NT, reflects the patriarchal religion and culture in which it was written. Many feminists, however, also believe it is possible to uncover the patriarchal biases and thereby bring to light the Bible's liberating message for women as well as men. Accordingly, feminist biblical scholars often employ a "hermeneutic of suspicion," asking critical questions of texts in order to ascertain what their message about women really is. Are women to blame for there being sin in the world? Are women numbered among a man's possessions? Are women to be silent in church and obedient wives at home?

One of the major issues addressed by feminist scholars of Hebrew Scripture is the almost exclusively male presentation of God. Indeed, some scholars have portrayed → Yahweh as a jealous husband for whom fidelity was foremost and violence was the way to keep women in line. Other feminist scholars argue that, in sharp contrast to the gods of other contemporaneous peoples and religions, the God of Israel was perceived to be asexual. Still others point out that the → father concept for the God of Hebrew Scripture includes ideas and images of biological motherhood (e.g., Isa. 66:13). It is also argued that the prominence of God as father emerged quite late in the history of Israel and probably expresses a postexilic preoccupation (ca. 600/587-333 B.C.) with divine care (e.g., Isa. 63:15-16), while in earlier eras men and women may have moved rather freely between Yahweh worship and the worship of cults rooted in the countryside, which promised peace, fertility, and food and which were possibly associated with the cult of the Goddess.

Feminist research has therefore further focused on the existence of other deities, particularly female deities, that were at some point finally suppressed or forced underground. Most recently, new archaeological evidence (iconographic and epigraphic documents) offers insights other than those available in fragmented form in biblical texts. This new evidence has opened exploration of whether and how female characteristics were present in the early God of Israel, whether this God had a female consort, and how male and female deities were understood in ancient Canaan and Israel. Scholars caution, however, against naively assuming that the presence of female deities or a cult of the Goddess confirms a strong position for women in society. The study of religion, particularly of the cult of the Goddess in India, generally confirms the contrary.

Feminist scholars of Hebrew Scripture are also recovering women's stories that have sketchily survived and are often obscure. The names of Hagar, Dinah, Tamar, Zipporah, Rahab, Hannah, and Rizpah have become increasingly well known. Their fates and fortunes, as much as they can be ascertained, are presented as integral, not incidental, to the biblical narratives.

NT scholarship by feminists has focused on historical reconstruction of the early Jesus movement in order to show that it was liberating for women. Many feminist NT scholars are convinced that women are placed prominently among the marginalized people who gathered around Jesus. These feminist scholars have pointed out that it was women who were featured in narratives of the resurrection — women were the first to discover the empty tomb and the first to encounter the resurrected Jesus. Moreover, feminist scholars — Elisabeth Schüssler Fiorenza foremost among them — argue that the message of the Jesus movement was both a radical critique of the patriarchal social structures of the Greco-Roman world and an attempt to create a new and egalitarian community of women and men.

Some feminist scholars, however, think the early Jesus movement was more ambiguous and have shown ways in which gospel texts convey acceptance of the public sphere as a man's world. Accordingly, women are portrayed in serving roles and are thereby exemplars of the serving leadership witnessed to by Jesus. From this point of view, however, it is not clear whether women who were exemplars actually held leadership positions in the early Jesus movement.

Scholars also caution against the temptation to say that Christianity's liberatory message for women was a sharp break from Jewish tradition. Bernadette Brooten, for example, has shown that Jewish women were accorded official titles related to the communal life of a → synagogue, such as "head of the synagogue," "leader," and "elder." The emergence of women leaders in early Christianity was not therefore unprecedented.

Feminist scholars have researched women's leadership roles as Christianity became a missionary movement, the apostle → Paul notwithstanding. Indeed, some feminists argue that Paul's injunctions about women's proper behavior and place were made in response to the reality that women were leaders — for example, as → apostles, prophetesses (→ Prophet, Prophecy), and → deaconesses — in the early Christian communities. Some scholars argue that, as heads of households, women may also have been responsible for the oversight of local Christian communities. Others contend that, while these women were materially wealthy and able to offer hospitality and patronage to the community, it is difficult to confirm that such capacities meant that they also had authority or held positions of leadership.

3.2. *Historical Studies*

The task of reconstructing the history of women in the Christian tradition is difficult, partly because of a relative scarcity of sources and partly because debates about the place of women pervade the centuries. Indeed, during the first three centuries, debates about women's role were heated and often led to groups led by women or oriented to women being declared heretical.

Feminists have nonetheless explored, for example, the history of women in religious orders, of women preachers, of women in the Middle Ages and the witch craze, of women's mission and social reform societies in the 19th century, and of women in various ministries, including women's ordained ministry. Individual women have also been restored to a place in history, among them medieval theologians and mystics Hildegard of Bingen, Hadewijch of Antwerp (13th cent.), Beatrice of Nazareth (1200-1268), Mechthild of Magdeburg (ca. 1207-82 or somewhat later), Margaret Porette (d. 1310), and Julian of Norwich (ca. 1342-after 1416), as well as the 20th-century women who attended the Second → Vatican Council.

Women have also used the category of gender as an analytic tool for the reexamination of major events and eras in church history. For example, traditional understandings of the Protestant reformations, of Puritan New England, and of Western missions have begun to be both challenged and made more complex.

3.3. *Theological Studies*

As noted above, the distinctiveness of women's experience emerged in the 1960s as a creative source for feminist theologies and as a lens through which traditional theologies have been viewed critically. Since the late 1980s, however, "women's experience" has been a much contested category of thought. There have been attempts both to complexify and to specify "women's experience" relative to race, class, age, physical abilities, sexual orientation, geographic location, and so

on. Mujerista theology and womanist theology, articulated by Latina and African American women respectively, exemplify this attention to the diversity of women's experience. Attention to the array of women's experience has also given rise to talk of such experience as interpreted culturally or religiously or socially. There has also been relatively more talk of "representations of women" and less talk of "women's experience."

This shift to speech about women's interpreted experience and about representations of women has turned the attention of feminist theologians to creedal and doctrinal formulations, to liturgical and ritual practices, and to → symbols and → images, as well as to theoretical formulations. Feminist theologians critique articulations that privilege men and burden women; they make clear the ways in which theological discourse supports sexist societal structures and systems; they rethink the Christian theological traditions; and they create new theologies — all for the sake of creating new communities wherein women's full humanity, in mutual partnership with men, will be honored.

Feminist theologians devote various degrees of attention and impart various degrees of authority to classical Christian discourse about God. Some are convinced there is a liberating tradition to be retrieved amid the androcentric character of classical theological discourse. Similarly, some are convinced that, when women's interpreted experience is engaged together with a critical retrieval of parts of Scripture and tradition, the Christian tradition may be moved from an androcentric to a liberating view of God. Feminists are therefore reinterpreting Christian doctrines such as the → Trinity, → Christology, → sin, → atonement, and → salvation.

They are also affirming women's capacity to conceptualize, even symbolize, the divine. Seeking to reintegrate mind and spirit and body (the human body, the body of Christ, the earth's body), feminist theologians are exploring Christian anthropology and ecclesiology, as well as enunciating the theological significance of → ecological concerns. Other feminists identify themselves as post-Christian and explore new rituals and images to nurture feminist → spirituality.

Most feminist theologians are aware of the constructed and continually changing character of identities, traditions, communities, and practices. Consequently, they are increasingly inclined to work within such ambiguity rather than within abstractions drawn from complex and complicated reality.

Not surprisingly, then, the work of many feminist theologians is interdisciplinary. They employ social theories to explore newly emerging social movements. They take prostitution, the global sex trade, and sexual abuse as the subjects of their theological work, thereby affirming the presence of God in these → women and authorizing their stories of crucifixion and healing. They bring gender as an analytic category to bear on the reality of violence, → poverty, → racism, and → xenophobia in women's lives. They rethink pastoral counseling with particular regard for women's struggles and suffering.

4. Global and Local Contexts

Feminist theologies are being articulated around the world. Asian feminist theologies emerged in grassroots settings as women gathered to read the Bible in light of their experiences of poverty, sexual abuse, → colonialism, illiteracy, the exploitation of labor and environment by multinational corporations, and so forth. The relationship of gospel and → culture is among the most crucial issues, both because Christians are a small minority in most Asian contexts and because women theologians are using cultural myths, legends, and symbols to reinterpret biblical stories. Their work was encouraged as Asian feminists met other Third World women theologians at meetings of the → Ecumenical Association of Third World Theologians, beginning in 1976. Together, these women confronted the → sexism of male → Third World theologians. Subsequently, the work of Asian feminist theologians has given birth to the Asian Women's Resource Centre for Culture and Theology in Kuala Lumpur, Malaysia, and to a journal, *In God's Image*.

Feminist theology in Europe was catalyzed by the Second → Vatican Council (1962-65), by the U.N. International Year of the Woman (1975), and by the work of the → World Council of Churches (WCC), especially the study "The Community of Women and Men in the Church" (1978-83) and the ecumenical decade "Churches in Solidarity with Women" (1988-98). European women theologians have taken seriously the legacy of imperialism and racism with which they live. Most recently, European feminist theology has been in closer dialogue with many disciplines of women's studies in the universities. There is also increased commitment to interfaith dialogue with Jewish and Muslim women (→ Judaism; Islam), as well as to → dialogue with women in the Southern Hemisphere. European feminist theologians, most of whom are working in western European countries, continue long-standing attentiveness to the distinctive struggles and theologies of women in eastern Europe.

In Africa the work of women theologians is shaped by poverty, the destructive legacy of colonialism and neocolonialism, as well as by questions of Christian identity in increasingly diverse cultural and religious contexts. Here, as in Asia, the issue of the gospel and culture is crucial. Sources for theological work include traditional Christian theology, together with African cultural history and traditional religions, philosophies, spiritualities, rituals, prayers, and oracles. Most recently, leadership has been given by the Circle of Concerned African Women Theologians, whose members are teachers and pastors.

Latin American feminist theologies acknowledge the interconnections of mind, body, society, race, and culture. These theologians also stress the integrity of knowledge and practice. Accordingly, these feminists are committed to translating their theologies into work for justice and egalitarian social structures, thereby emphasizing the transformative purpose of theology. Among the different expressions of Latin American feminist theologies are indigenous theology, black feminist theology, and holistic, or ecofeminist, theology.

In each of these contexts, feminist theologies tend to be thoroughly ecumenical. Already in the 1940s women were conducting research on the role and status of women in churches around the world in preparation for the First Assembly of the WCC, in 1948. After the assembly, a permanent commission on the life and work of women in the church was established. Until the 1970s the watchword of women's participation in the ecumenical movement was "cooperation" with men. Then, at a consultation sponsored in West Berlin in 1974 by the WCC's Subunit on Women, the word "sexism" became part of the ecumenical lexicon. This consultation featured substantive theological reflection by several prominent feminist theologians and led to the study "The Community of Women and Men in the Church," which undertook theological and biblical studies on such issues as theological anthropology, biblical → hermeneutics, → Mariology, and women's ordained ministry. Central to the study process were worldwide local study groups, involving far more participants than in any previous WCC study.

The "Community" study, together with the example of the U.N. Decade for Women, led the WCC to declare the ecumenical decade mentioned above. End-of-decade evaluations in 1998 agree that the decade was a women's decade more than a decade of the churches in solidarity with women. This is to say, few men were actually involved in the conversations that took place throughout the world. Nonetheless, global networks among women were strengthened, and women's concerns worldwide were identified.

Foremost among these concerns are the global economic system and the poverty of women, racism and xenophobia, and violence against women and children. These concerns, confirmed in 1998 at the Decade Festival just before the Eighth Assembly of the WCC, in Harare, Zimbabwe, resound key issues identified for action by women at the U.N. Fourth World Conference, held in Beijing in 1996. These issues will no doubt begin to set an agenda for feminist theologians in the next decade.

Bibliography: General: L. M. RUSSELL and J. S. CLARKSON, eds., *Dictionary of Feminist Theologies* (Louisville, Ky., 1996).

On 1: N. A. HARDESTY, *Women Called to Witness: Evangelical Feminism in the Nineteenth Century* (Nashville, 1984) • K. E. MELDER, *Beginnings of Sisterhood: The American Woman's Rights Movement, 1800-1850* (New York, 1977) • M. J. SELVIDGE, *Feminist Biblical Interpretation, 1500-1920* (New York, 1996).

On 2: M. DALY, *Beyond God the Father: Toward a Philosophy of Women's Liberation* (Boston, 1973) • C. ELLER, *Living in the Lap of the Goddess: The Feminist Spirituality Movement in America* (New York, 1993) • V. SAIVING, "The Human Situation: A Feminine View," *JR* 40 (1960) 100-112 • STARHAWK, *The Spiral Dance: A Rebirth of the Ancient Religion of the Great Goddess* (2d ed.; San Francisco, 1989).

On 3.1: S. ACKERMANN, *Under Every Green Tree: Popular Religion in Sixth-Century Judah* (Atlanta, 1992) • B. BROOTEN, *Women Leaders in the Ancient Synagogue* (Chico, Calif., 1982) • E. S. GERSTENBERGER, *Yahweh–the Patriarch: Ancient Images of God and Feminist Theology* (Minneapolis, 1996) • E. PAGELS, *Adam, Eve, and the Serpent* (New York, 1988); idem, *The Gnostic Gospels* (New York, 1979) • L. SCHOTTROFF, *Lydia's Impatient Sisters: A Feminist Social History of Early Christianity* (Louisville, Ky., 1993) • E. SCHÜSSLER FIORENZA, *In Memory of Her: A Feminist Theological Reconstruction of Christian Origins* (New York, 1983); idem, ed., *Searching the Scriptures,* vol. 1, *A Feminist Introduction;* vol. 2, *A Feminist Commentary* (New York, 1993-94) • T. K. SEIM, *The Double Message: Patterns of Gender in Luke and Acts* (Nashville, 1994) • P. TRIBLE, *God and the Rhetoric of Sexuality* (Philadelphia, 1978); idem, *Texts of Terror: Literary-Feminist Readings of Biblical Narratives* (Philadelphia, 1984) • R. J. WEEMS, *Battered Love: Marriage, Sex, and Violence in the Hebrew Prophets* (Minneapolis, 1995).

On 3.2: A. L. BARSTOW, *Witchcraze: A New History of the European Witch Hunts — Our Legacy of Violence against Women* (San Francisco, 1994) • K. E. BORRESEN, ed., *The Image of God: Gender Models in Judaeo-Christian Tradition* (Minneapolis, 1991) • J. A. McNAMARA, *Sisters in Arms: Catholic Nuns through Two Millennia* (Cambridge, 1996) • M. R. MILES, *Desire and Delight: A New Reading of Augustine's Confessions* (New York, 1992); idem, *Image as Insight: Visual Understanding in Western Christianity and Secular Culture* (Boston, 1985) • R. R. RUETHER and R. S. KELLER, eds., *In Our Own Voices: Four Centuries of American Women's Religious Writing* (San Francisco, 1995).

On 3.3: R. N. BROCK, *Journeys by Heart: A Christology of Erotic Power* (New York, 1988) • R. CHOPP and S. G. DAVANEY, eds., *Horizons in Feminist Theology: Identity, Tradition, and Norms* (Minneapolis, 1997) • P. M. COOEY, *Religious Imagination and the Body: A Feminist Analysis* (New York, 1994) • M. GREY, *Feminism, Redemption, and the Christian Tradition* (Mystic, Conn., 1990) • B. W. HARRISON, *Making the Connections: Essays in Feminist Social Ethics* (Boston, 1985) • C. HEYWARD, *Touching Our Strength: The Erotic as Power and the Love of God* (San Francisco, 1989) • M. E. HUNT, *Fierce Tenderness: A Feminist Theology of Friendship* (New York, 1992) • A. M. ISASI-DIAZ, *En la lucha = In the Struggle: A Hispanic Women's Liberation Theology* (Minneapolis, 1993); idem, *Mujerista Theology: A Theology for the Twenty-first Century* (Maryknoll, N.Y., 1996) • E. A. JOHNSON, *She Who Is: The Mystery of God in Feminist Theological Discourse* (New York, 1992) • C. M. LaCUGNA, ed., *Freeing Theology: The Essentials of Theology in Feminist Perspective* (San Francisco, 1993) • S. McFAGUE, *The Body of God: An Ecological Theology* (Minneapolis, 1993) • M. A. MAY, *A Body Knows: A Theopoetics of Death and Resurrection* (New York, 1995); idem, ed., *Women and Church: The Challenge of Ecumenical Solidarity in an Age of Alienation* (Grand Rapids, 1991) • V. R. MOLLENKOTT, *Sensuous Spirituality: Out from Fundamentalism* (New York, 1992) • J. PLASKOW, *Sex, Sin, and Grace: Women's Experience and the Theologies of Reinhold Niebuhr and Paul Tillich* (Washington, D.C., 1980); idem, *Standing Again at Sinai: Judaism from a Feminist Perspective* (San Francisco, 1990) • R. R. RUETHER, *Gaia and God: An Ecofeminist Theology of Earth Healing* (San Francisco, 1992); idem, *New Heaven, New Earth: Sexist Ideologies and Human Liberation* (New York, 1975) • L. M. RUSSELL, *Church in the Round: Feminist Interpretation of the Church* (Louisville, Ky., 1993); idem, *Household of Freedom: Authority in Feminist Theology* (Philadelphia, 1987) • S. B. THISTLETHWAITE and M. P. ENGEL, eds., *Lift Every Voice: Constructing Christian Theologies from the Underside* (rev. ed.; Maryknoll, N.Y., 1998) • E. TOWNES, ed., *A Troubling in My Soul: Womanist Perspectives on Evil and Suffering* (Maryknoll, 1993) •

S. Welch, *A Feminist Ethic of Risk* (rev. ed.; Minneapolis, 1999) • D. Williams, *Sisters in the Wilderness: The Challenge of Womanist God-Talk* (Maryknoll, N.Y., 1993).

On 4: *The Beijing Declaration and Platform for Action, Fourth World Conference on Women* (New York, 1996) • V. Fabella and M. A. Oduyoye, eds., *With Passion and Compassion: Third World Women Doing Theology* (Maryknoll, N.Y., 1988) • V. Fabella and S. A. L. Park, eds., *We Dare to Dream: Doing Theology as Asian Women* (Maryknoll, N.Y., 1989) • U. King, ed., *Feminist Theology from the Third World: A Reader* (Maryknoll, N.Y., 1994) • P.-l. Kwok, *Discovering the Bible in the Non-Biblical World* (Maryknoll, N.Y., 1995) • M. A. Oduyoye, *Daughters of Anowa: African Women and Patriarchy* (Maryknoll, N.Y., 1995); idem, *Hearing and Knowing: Theological Reflections on Christianity in Africa* (Maryknoll, 1986) • C. F. Parvey, ed., *The Community of Women and Men in the Church* (Philadelphia, 1983) • J. Pobee and B. von Wartenberg, eds., *New Eyes for Reading: Biblical and Theological Reflections by Women from the Third World* (Geneva, 1986) • E. Tamez, *The Amnesty of Grace: Justification by Faith from a Latin American Perspective* (Nashville, 1993).

Melanie A. May

Fetishism

In the → religious studies and → ethnology of the 19th and early 20th centuries, the term "fetishism" was used to describe the veneration of certain objects (rocks, trees, etc. — fetishes) that were thought to possess spirits or to have special powers. Such veneration was found especially in the so-called tribal societies. On the basis of the reports of Portuguese mariners, who said that dwellers on the coast of West Africa worshiped cultic objects that the Portuguese called *feitiço* (from Lat. *factitius*, "artificially made"), C. de Brosses used the term in his study *Du culte des Dieux fétiches* (1760) to denote an original and widely spread form of religion which in human history had deviated from worship of the stars, → polytheism, and → monotheism. This early form of religious behavior arose out of fear of incomprehensible natural phenomena and corresponded to the emotional and childish spiritual situation of "primitive" or "early" people.

The evolutionary theoreticians of the 19th century (A. Comte, H. Spencer, E. B. Tylor, et al.) took up the term "fetishism" and developed it theoretically. Others also used the term quite early to describe equally "irrational" modes of conduct in our own society. Thus, for example, I. Kant (1724-1804) said that any form of → worship that consists essentially not of moral principles but of statutes, rules of faith, and observances is fetishist (AA 6.179). K. → Marx (1818-83), in criticizing political economy, spoke of a "fetishism of commodities" (*MECW* 35.81-94), inasmuch as here the products of human → work have the appearance of independent entities with a life of their own and with relations both to one another and to people. In a transferred sense the term is also used in psychoanalysis for a form of sexual aberration in which a certain part of the body or a material object becomes the sole sexual object.

The ambivalence of the terms "fetish" and "fetishism," with their linking with → evolutionary theories, has resulted in their almost complete disuse in modern studies of non-European cultures. As dubious as it is to take various phenomena out of their cultural context and subsume them under a single category, even more debatable is the idea that fetishism can be regarded as the original religion. Criticism of the term in the study of religion and ethnology also throws doubt on its usefulness as a category by which to describe certain tendencies in our own society.

→ Animism

Bibliography: E. Apter and W. Pietz, eds., *Fetishism as Cultural Discourse* (Ithaca, N.Y., 1993) • F. Eboussi Boulaga, *Christianisme sans fétiche* (Paris, 1981) • U. Erckenbrecht, *Das Geheimnis des Fetischismus* (2d ed.; Frankfurt, 1984) • K.-H. Kohl, "Fetisch, Tabu, Totem. Zur Archäologik religionswissenschaftlicher Begriffsbildung," *Neue Ansätze in der Religionswissenschaft* (ed. B. Gladigow and H. G. Kippenberg; Munich, 1983) 59-74 • W. Pietz, "The Problem of the Fetish," *Res* 9 (1985) 5-17; 13 (1987) 23-45; 16 (1988) 105-23 • J.-B. Pontalis, ed., *Objekte des Fetischismus* (Frankfurt, 1974) • P. Spyer, ed., *Border Fetishisms: Material Objects in Unstable Spaces* (New York, 1998).

Karl-Heinz Kohl

Feudalism

The word "feudalism" derives from Lat. *feudum*, "property held in fief." In the narrower sense it has to do with feudal holding, but more broadly it denotes the social system of the Middle Ages and comparable stages of → development (§1). In the Marxist view of history (→ Marxism), feudalism is one of the general constructs of human history and constitutes the stage between slavery and middle-class →

society (→ Bourgeois, Bourgeoisie). This usage, however, is now outdated. The medieval system that gave rulers vassals and also privileges of dues and dominion was not by any means so central to medieval society as to justify our describing this society as feudal. The possessions of the nobility were primarily their own and were only gradually feudalized. Unfree peasants were not in any feudal dependence, for a fief presupposed personal freedom on the part of the tenant, who had to render service rather than pay taxes to the overlord. The idea of a feudal pyramid from simple tenants to squires and then to counts, secular or ecclesiastical princes, and finally the king does not really correspond to feudal reality but reflects contemporary attempts to systematize the social structure apart from the peasantry and cities. Only in the High Middle Ages were the relations between king and princes feudally defined. In the same way the territorial magnates finally succeeded in integrating the local lords of the manor with the help of feudal law. By then, however, this law had to a great extent lost its originally personal character.

The historical use of "feudalism" comes mainly from the political vocabulary of France in the 18th century. At that time attacks on social and political conditions described them as feudal, and an antithesis was seen between the feudal and the bourgeois. The churches, too, had organized themselves feudally; since the 12th century, the → Papal States had the same organization. Innocent III (1198-1216) brought the kings of Sicily and England into feudal subjection, and some popes tried to treat the emperor (→ Empire and Papacy) as their vassal (e.g., at the imperial Diet of Besançon in 1157). In the empire the bishops and abbots were released from feudal obligations to the emperor after the Investiture Controversy. In place of → investiture with ring and staff, the emperor or king now simply bestowed on prelates the right to their territories. The bishops and abbots had their own vassals, and kings could also receive fiefs from them (→ Abbot, Abbess; Bishop, Episcopate).

Bibliography: E. A. R. BROWN, "The Tyranny of a Construct: Feudalism and Historians of Medieval Europe," *AHR* 79 (1974) 1063-88 • M. L. B. BLOCH, *Feudal Society* (Chicago, 1961) • G. DUBY, *The Three Orders: Feudal Society Imagined* (Chicago, 1980) • F. L. GANCHOF, *Feudalism* (3d ed.; New York, 1964) • L. KUCHENBUCH, *Feudalismus* (Berlin, 1977).

HARTMUT BOOCKMANN

Fideism → God

Fidelity → Faithfulness

Fiji

	1960	1980	2000
Population (1,000s):	394	634	848
Annual growth rate (%):	3.27	1.97	1.58
Area: 18,272 sq. km. (7,055 sq. mi.)			

A.D. 2000

Population density: 46/sq. km. (120/sq. mi.)
Births / deaths: 2.16 / 0.47 per 100 population
Fertility rate: 2.54 per woman
Infant mortality rate: 17 per 1,000 live births
Life expectancy: 73.7 years (m: 71.6, f: 75.9)
Religious affiliation (%): Christians 57.1 (Protestants 46.5, Roman Catholics 10.7, indigenous 9.1, marginal 2.0, other Christians 1.4), Hindus 32.9, Muslims 6.8, nonreligious 1.4, other 1.8.

1. General
2. Religion
3. The Churches and Education
4. Ecumenical Relations
5. Missions
6. The Churches and Nationalism

1. General

Fiji, an independent country since 1970, is located near the center of the South Pacific islands. Because of its location it has become the hub of South Pacific affairs. Most of the international agencies of the region, including those of religion, make their headquarters in Fiji. The country's natural beauty and tropical climate and its relatively large and varied population make it a center for agriculture, → education, → tourism, business, and some industry.

The varied population includes a few Chinese, Europeans, and people from other island countries, along with the two major groups: Indians and ethnic Fijians, who each make up nearly half the population. Starting in 1879, European planters brought over Indians for heavy labor in the fields, a type of work from which the British colonial government tried to shield the native Fijians for fear it would contribute to the decline of their numbers. The Indians have gradually come to dominate the commercial, industrial, financial, and professional life of the country.

2. Religion

The Indian population is mostly → Hindu but with a strong minority of Muslims (→ Islam) and a few

→ Sikhs. Neo-Hindu movements, started in India, are vigorous, and at least one neo-Muslim movement, the Aḥmadīyah, is active. A small group of Indians have become Christians as a result of missionary efforts led primarily by Australian Methodists.

The major Christian body is the → Methodist Church of Fiji and Rotuma. (Rotuma is a Polynesian island 300 miles distant but administratively part of Fiji.) Methodists, who arrived in 1835, were the first mission to come to Fiji, and today over 80 percent of ethnic Fijians are Methodist. Their church has been closely identified with Fijian culture and with the old social system dominated by chiefs, sometimes being called the church of the chiefs.

→ Roman Catholics were the next to arrive, in 1844. They gained footholds where the Methodists were not present, and they have grown steadily. The Marist Order has always been the chief Roman Catholic missionary body, helped in recent years by the Columban Fathers and others. The Sisters of Our Lady of Nazareth is the chief indigenous order.

→ Anglicans, coming in 1860 with the clear agreement that they would not → proselytize among Fijians, have worked mostly among Europeans, Indians, and people from other island groups. Seventh-day → Adventists, starting in 1889, have established a small but strong presence. → Mormons did not come until 1954 and then concentrated their work among Indians, since blacks, such as the Fijians, were not at that time admitted to the priesthood of their church. Several → Pentecostal bodies have become popular in recent years.

3. The Churches and Education
→ Education in Fiji was long concentrated in a network of church schools, mostly Methodist, covering every village in the country. Since about 1930 the government has been taking over primary schools, a process with which Methodists usually cooperated but which Roman Catholics have resisted. The Methodist teacher training college was taken over by the government in 1946. The Roman Catholics opposed such a takeover, and in 1954 they received permission to establish their own teachers' college. Secondary education was begun by the churches and has, in part, continued to be provided by them, although now with government aid. Tertiary education, with the exception of theological studies, has always been in the hands of the government.

There is a large Methodist theological college in Fiji, plus smaller Anglican and Seventh-day Adventist religious institutions. A higher, international faculty of theology that serves all Pacific islands is located at the Pacific Theological College in Fiji, be-

gun in 1966. Nearby a parallel Roman Catholic college, the Pacific Regional Seminary, has been established. There has always been close cooperation between these two Pacific-wide institutions.

4. Ecumenical Relations
Fiji has had a Council of Churches since 1964, with Roman Catholic participation since 1968. This council has had an uneven history, with shifting emphases and variations in leadership styles; Anglicans in particular have provided crucial personnel in some difficult times. Fiji is also the center of all-Pacific ecumenical life. The → Pacific Conference of Churches has been headquartered there since 1966, and two of its strongest secretaries, Setareki Tuilovoni and Lorini Tevi, have been Fijian Methodists. CEPAC, the Conference of Roman Catholic Bishops of the Pacific, is also centered in Fiji. Since these international bodies are located in their country, Fijians have greater regional ecumenical involvement than do the people of other islands. The Methodist Church of Fiji and Rotuma is a member of the → World Council of Churches.

5. Missions
Fiji Methodism has been a mission-minded body since 1875, when it sent its first missionaries to New Britain. Through the years most of its workers have gone to Papua New Guinea. Today, Fiji Methodist → missionaries are to be found in northern Australia, Papua New Guinea, central America, and Jamaica. A number of Fiji's Roman Catholic sisters now also serve abroad, engaging in the work of the various → orders to which they belong.

6. The Churches and Nationalism
Ethnic nationalism became a great issue in the churches of Fiji in 1987 (→ Nation, Nationalism), when a pious Methodist military officer, Sitiveni Rabuka, led a military coup that toppled the elected government. Until that year the government had been dominated by ethnic Fijians, who had been guaranteed certain rights, especially to most of the land — first by the British, and subsequently by the terms of the national constitution. Indian farmers typically worked as tenants on Fijian-owned land. The elected government that took office in 1987 shifted the balance of power toward the Indians, and as a consequence the ethnic Fijians launched mass protests, on occasion led by Methodist lay preachers. The resultant coup and a new national constitution assured domination by Fijians, especially rural Fijians and their chiefs.

At first the leadership of the Methodist Church

in Fiji, which had ecumenical and international experience, opposed the coup, although the rank and file of Methodist clergy and laity strongly supported the military move toward Fijian dominance. These nationalistic elements invaded the church headquarters, ousting the elected leaders and placing themselves in control. The Methodist Church then became more closely linked with the government, receiving favored treatment and outright gifts.

Other churches of the country, which had never had strong ties to the Fijian ethnic identity, opposed the coup and its aftermath. Consequently, the Methodists began to pull away from the other churches, ceasing their active participation in the Fiji Council of Churches and the Pacific Conference of Churches.

After a few years, however, the atmosphere began to change. Negotiations between Rabuka and Indian leaders resulted in the appointment of a Constitutional Review Commission and the adoption in 1997 of a new constitution that restored freedoms and also enlarged the place of Indians in the government. The Methodist Church also began to change, electing moderate leaders who adopted more cooperative attitudes. Participation in ecumenical bodies was gradually resumed, and the wounds within the Methodist Church began to heal. The change in the church was evident after the further coup of March 2000. The Methodist Church, like the other churches of Fiji, spoke out this time, condemning the illegal seizure of power.

Bibliography: C. W. FORMAN, *The Island Churches of the South Pacific: Emergence in the Twentieth Century* (Maryknoll, N.Y., 1982) • J. GARRETT, *Footsteps in the Sea* (Suva, 1992); idem, *To Live among the Stars* (Suva, 1982); idem, *Where Nets Were Cast* (Suva, 1997) • A. THORNLEY and T. VULAONO, eds., *Mai kea ki vei? Stories of Methodism in Fiji and Rotuma* (Suva, 1996) • A. H. WOOD, *Overseas Missions of the Australian Methodist Church* (vol. 2; Melbourne, 1978).

CHARLES W. FORMAN

Filiation

In → church law "filiation" is used for offshoots of → monasteries and parishes. Filiation was common in medieval orders and became a constitutional principle for the → Cistercians. The → abbot of the motherhouse had the right to visit (→ Visitation) daughter houses, and the "daughters" founded their own houses. Filiation of this type was later detached from the system of congregations (→ Orders and Congregations).

Filiation was a transitional stage in the forming of parishes (→ Congregation). Modern → Roman Catholic → canon law calls such offshoots quasi parishes and sets them under the pastoral care of neighboring parishes (1983 → CIC 516, 526).

In Reformation churches filiation was an auxiliary form of parish (→ Church Government). The congregation would have its own place of worship but might not have its own income or leadership and would almost never have its own minister (→ Pastor, Pastorate). Filiation might be of long standing in small places, or it might prove necessary in cases of depopulation or of growing population in areas of new settlement.

HEINER GROTE†

Filioque

The Lat. word *filioque* translates "and from the Son." It is an addition to the → Niceno-Constantinopolitan Creed that was adopted by the Western church in the Middle Ages but was emphatically rejected by the Eastern church. Along with other factors, this difference led to the schism between East and West in the 11th century, and it is still an unresolved, though ecumenically less acute, problem.

The confession made by the Council of Constantinople in 381 declared that the → Holy Spirit "proceeds from the Father." A few decades later Augustine (→ Augustine's Theology) explained that the Spirit does indeed proceed "in the first instance" *(principaliter)* from the Father but that at the same time he also proceeds from the Son in virtue of the Son's eternal begetting from the Father. Thus the Spirit is the bond of love *(vinculum caritatis)* between the Father and the Son *(De Trin.* 15.17.29). This conviction gradually permeated the Western church, as one may see, for example, at the Council of Toledo in 589. Charlemagne wanted to have the *filioque* anchored in the wording of the creed but met with opposition from Leo III (795-816), who regarded the *filioque* as theologically correct but did not think that one should tamper with a creed that had been formulated by an ecumenical council (→ Confession of Faith). Later Benedict VIII (1012-24) agreed to the addition, probably at the same time (1014) as the introduction of singing the creed into the Roman → Mass.

In the centuries that followed, theologians like → Anselm *(De processione Spiritus Sancti)* and → Thomas Aquinas *(Summa theol.* I, q. 36) set forth arguments for the correctness and necessity of the *filioque.* Attempts at reconciliation with the Eastern church at Lyons (1274) and Florence (1439) met with no lasting success. After the → Reformation the churches of the Reformation in general retained the *filioque.*

In the whole debate there have been three essential questions: (1) Does the biblical testimony justify the statement that the Spirit proceeds from the Son? (2) Is the *filioque* theologically tenable, possibly even necessary? (3) Was it right of the Western church to add to the creed on its own?

In the modern ecumenical climate of the 21st century (→ Ecumenism, Ecumenical Movement), some Western churches are ready to follow the example of the → Old Catholic Church and drop the *filioque* in order to draw closer to the Eastern church. Before a genuine solution is possible, however, the exegetical and dogmatic questions need greater clarification than has been achieved thus far.

→ Christology; Trinity

Bibliography: A. I. C. HERON, *The Holy Spirit* (London, 1983) • J. N. D. KELLY, *Early Christian Creeds* (3d ed.; London, 1972) 358-67 • A. PAPADAKIS, *Crisis in Byzantium: The Filioque Controversy in the Patriarchate of Gregory II of Cyprus (1283-1289)* (Crestwood, N.Y., 1997) • L. VISCHER, ed., *Spirit of God, Spirit of Christ: Ecumenical Reflections on the* Filioque *Controversy* (Geneva, 1981) • G. WATSON, "The Filioque–Opportunity for Debate?" *SJT* 41 (1988) 313-30.

ALASDAIR I. C. HERON

Finances → Church Finances

Finland

1. Churches
   1.1. Evangelical Lutheran Church of Finland
   1.2. Orthodox Church of Finland
   1.3. Other Churches and
        Christian Communities
2. Ecumenical and Interchurch Relations
3. Other Religions

1. Churches

The earliest influence of Christianity on Finland came from the Catholic West in the 9th and 10th centuries through tradesmen, sailors, and migrants. Organized church life emerged in the 10th and 11th centuries, mainly among the Swedish settlers in the coastal regions. The → Crusades of the 12th and 13th centuries greatly accelerated the spread of

	1960	1980	2000
Population (1,000s):	4,430	4,780	5,179
Annual growth rate (%):	0.60	0.51	0.14
Area: 338,145 sq. km. (130,559 sq. mi.)			

A.D. 2000

Population density: 15/sq. km. (40/sq. mi.)
Births / deaths: 1.14 / 1.04 per 100 population
Fertility rate: 1.83 per woman
Infant mortality rate: 5 per 1,000 live births
Life expectancy: 77.3 years (m: 73.8, f: 80.8)
Religious affiliation (%): Christians 92.7 (Protestants 91.7, unaffiliated 5.9, marginal 1.0, Orthodox 1.0, other Christians 0.8), nonreligious 5.4, atheists 1.5, other 0.4.

Christianity into the interior of the country and for several centuries consolidated the religious and political influence of the Catholic West over the whole country. Parallel to the bringing of the Finnish church under the ecclesiastical authority of the Archdiocese of Uppsala, Finland became politically annexed to the kingdom of Sweden. The episcopal see for Finland was moved to Turku (Swed. Åbo), which remains to this day the archdiocese of the Finnish church. The Roman Catholic faith was dominant until the Reformation of the 16th century, when the Finnish church became Lutheran.

Eastern Orthodoxy first came to Finland with tradesmen and migrants from the East. Extensive missionary work was launched from Novgorod, Russia, in the 11th and 12th centuries, the Orthodox faith spreading to the province of Karelia and thus to eastern Finland. Two monasteries founded on the islands of Lake Ladoga became the strongholds of the Orthodox mission in the area. The Finnish Orthodox were part of the → Russian Orthodox Church until 1923, when, after Finland had gained its independence, the church joined the → Ecumenical Patriarchate as an autonomous archbishopric. Thus from the time of the arrival of Christianity up to the present, Finland has been a meeting place for Eastern and Western cultures and church traditions.

1.1. *Evangelical Lutheran Church of Finland*

The Evangelical Lutheran Church of Finland conceives itself as being in direct continuity with the Western Catholic Church, which entered the country at the end of the first millennium A.D. The Lutheran → Reformation, which originated in Germany, brought about a major change in church life. The Bible was translated into Finnish, the vernacular was used in → worship, and a major emphasis was placed on the teaching ministry. The church became a major promoter of → literacy and the development of the Finnish language. Administratively, the Finnish church remained part of the state church of Sweden, with the king of Sweden-Finland as the head of the church. Although the tie with the Holy See of Rome was broken, the continuity of the inherited Catholic tradition was evident in the maintenance of the historic episcopate and in the liturgical structure of the → Mass.

In the following decades Lutheran teaching permeated the whole society, and the church grew in influence among the people, in spite of the extensive expropriation of church properties by the king. The Lutheran confession became part of the official ideology of the state, those not adhering to the teaching of the church becoming in practice outcasts of society. Within this framework, the first waves of spiritual renewal, stimulated by → Pietism, touched the church in the 18th century. The earliest of these indigenous pietistic movements drew their inspiration from the Lutheran → confessions (→ Confession of Faith) and from medieval → mysticism. The position of the → Lutheran Church in Finland was both spiritually and culturally very strong at the end of the 18th century.

The transfer of Finland from Swedish rule to a grand duchy of czarist Russia in 1809 seemed at first to cause very little change for the Lutheran Church. The new rulers recognized the strength and influence of the Lutheran Church. The internal structure of the church and its relation to the state remained almost unaltered when the Russian czar replaced the Swedish king as the titular head of the church. The only major change concerned the → Orthodox Church, which received a status similar to that of the Lutheran Church in relation to the state.

The long-term effect of the change of political authority nevertheless had a profound impact on both the church and the nation. The Russian rule (1809-1917) created a new political climate. The grand duchy was granted a degree of → autonomy not experienced before. New possibilities opened for the development of indigenous culture and institutions, and a new sense of Finnish national identity emerged. In 1863 the Grand Duchy of Finland was granted its own currency, different from that of imperial Russia, and the Finnish language began gradually to replace Swedish as the dominant language of the educated class. Numerous Finnish-language secondary schools were opened during the last decades of the 19th century. In 1906 the General Assembly of the Estates was replaced by a Parliament, which was elected on the basis of universal suffrage. Even as it respected the basic autonomy of the Finnish people, the mercurial Russian rule from

time to time posed serious threats to Finnish nationhood by harsh attempts to Russianize the country and to eliminate all internal autonomy.

In the 19th century the influence of indigenous spiritual renewal movements grew in strength within the Finnish Lutheran Church, deepening its life and its witness to society. Anglo-Saxon revival movements emerged alongside Continental Pietism as new sources of inspiration. From time to time these renewal movements came into tension and even conflict with church authorities, but their leaders adamantly refused to cause splits in the church. These movements have had a long-lasting influence throughout the whole Finnish church.

In the 19th century two factors arose to challenge the religious uniformity of the country. On one hand, advocates of the → Enlightenment and → liberalism began to call into question the religious foundation of the society and to attack the confessional authority of the church. On the other hand, the internal renewal movements within the church created a critical ferment that contributed to new forms of church life and to a reform both of church structure and the → church-state relationship.

The adoption of the Church Law of 1869 reflected visibly the new direction of the Finnish church. By moving toward greater independence from the state, it distanced itself from the inherited state church system that was then characteristic of all Nordic Lutheran churches. This reform became a landmark on the way toward the separation of the church from the state and toward complete religious liberty. The most visible outcome was the establishment of the Synod as the main legislative body for the church. Responsibilities for school systems and public health were transferred from the church to the state and local communities. Church finances at the parish level were separated from the communal administration. State authorities, however, still had to give their approval to decisions of the Synod.

By the beginning of the 20th century, advocacy for complete religious freedom in the country grew stronger within the Lutheran Church. This step was achieved in 1923, only after the independence of Finland from Russia, largely on the basis of church initiative. The church no longer understood itself as a state church. "Folk church" became the term of choice (cf. People's Church [Volkskirche]).

Another series of legislative changes, which pruned most of the remaining vestiges of the state church heritage, took place in the 1980s and 1990s. The constitution of the church was separated from the ecclesiastical law that governs the relationship between the state and churches. The Parliament no longer has any say on matters covered by the church constitution. The church also assumed responsibility for the costs of diocesan administration, which hitherto had been covered by the state. The perennial right of the state president to appoint → bishops was discontinued.

At the end of 1998 the Evangelical Lutheran Church had just under 4.4 million resident members, or 85.2 percent of the total national population. This percentage has declined somewhat since the Second World War, although the actual number of members has remained fairly steady (95.1 percent in 1950, down to 90.2 percent in 1980). Children baptized in the Lutheran Church in 1998 represented 88.4 percent of all children, and 89.4 percent of all young people participated in → confirmation instruction. However, only 3 percent of the members participate in the main Sunday services each week, and only 12 percent once a month. Various special worship services and congregational gatherings as well as special summer events of the church play a significant role in church life, and the audiences of regular Christian radio and TV programs rate nationally among the largest groups of hearers and viewers.

The basic unit of the church is the parish (595 at the end of 1997), each belonging to one of 79 deaneries. The church is divided into eight dioceses, of which one is Swedish speaking. The highest governing body of the church is the → Synod, which normally meets twice a year. A bishops' conference deals with all doctrinal matters. The Ecclesiastical Board is responsible for the administration of churchwide programs such as Christian education, mission, social services, counseling, hospital ministry, communication, and church finances.

Seven mission organizations, most of which were originally independent voluntary mission societies, serve as officially recognized mission agencies of the Lutheran Church. They have personnel in 35 countries. Furthermore, the church operates a separate specialized agency, FinnChurchAid, for development, relief, and interchurch assistance.

The Lutheran Church is a member of the → World Council of Churches (WCC), the → Lutheran World Federation, and the → Conference of European Churches.

1.2. *Orthodox Church of Finland*

Until 1923 the Orthodox Church of Finland was part of the Russian Orthodox Church. Traditionally the Orthodox were in the majority in the communes of the Karelian province, part of which belonged to Finland. The "folk church" character of the church in that region was officially recognized when the Russian rulers of the 19th century granted the Orthodox Church status as the second state church in predominantly Lutheran Finland. The ending of Russian rule and the gaining of national independence by Finland in 1917 brought about a major change in the situation of the Orthodox Church. It severed its ties with the Moscow Patriarchate and subsequently, in 1923, affiliated with the Ecumenical Patriarchate of Constantinople as an autonomous archbishopric. A second change resulted from the annexation of a sizable part of Finnish Karelia to the Soviet Union in 1944 and the migration of virtually all of the Finnish population from the ceded area to the Finnish side. The Orthodox Church of Finland lost the areas in which it had had its stronghold and its position as a folk church. Most of the Finnish Orthodox, once concentrated in the Karelian area, thus became scattered all over Finland. The archbishop's see was moved from the city of Sortavala in the ceded territory to Kuopio in Finland proper. The two monasteries, Valamo and Lintula, followed suit.

The Orthodox Church of Finland in 1995 included 54,000 members, about 1 percent of the total population. As a result of the displacement of the majority of Orthodox Christians into predominantly Lutheran communities after the loss of Karelian territory to the USSR, the church in the first decade after the war lost a sizable number of its members. In 1950 the Orthodox represented 1.7 percent of the total population, down in 1960 to 1.4 percent. Since 1980 the number of new members has by and large matched the number of those lost, and the percentage has remained stable. In recent decades the church has attracted a number of prominent new members, among them several intellectuals, writers, and artists.

In 1999 the Orthodox Church had three bishoprics, 25 congregations, and two monasteries. The number of ordained clergy was about 100. The training of candidates for the priesthood takes place at the Department of Orthodox Theology of the University of Joensuu and at the related Orthodox theological seminary.

The archbishop, together with the Synod, which meets every three years, leads the Orthodox Church. The church has active relationships with other members of the Orthodox world, and it participates in mission work in East Africa. It is a member of the Ecumenical Council of Finland, the WCC, and the Conference of European Churches.

1.3. *Other Churches and*
Christian Communities

At the end of 1998 the Finnish Diocese of the Roman Catholic Church had 7,300 members in seven congregations, its membership having doubled since 1980. This increase is mostly due to the arrival of refugees and other non-Finnish persons. The combined impact of the Second → Vatican Council, a papal visit to Finland in 1989, and the process of European integration has made the church more widely known in Finland. Nevertheless, in 1998 about 40 percent of its members and almost all its clergy were non-Finnish.

Among other churches and Christian communities, the largest is the latest arrival (1911), the Pentecostal movement/church, which has over 50,000 members and 260 congregations. It is the most rapidly expanding Christian group in Finland. Its foreign mission activity in 1999 involved 446 → missionaries in 37 countries. The congregations are independent, and the movement has no fixed national organization, nor is it registered nationally as a religious community.

Other churches and communities include the Finnish Free Church (14,000 members), the Seventh-day → Adventist Church (5,700 members), the Baptist Church (→ Baptists), the → Methodist Church, and the → Salvation Army. Several of these groups have independent Finnish and Swedish branches. All arrived in Finland during the latter part of the 19th century.

2. Ecumenical and Interchurch Relations

The Ecumenical Council of Finland, the origins of which go back to 1917, is the most comprehensive expression of ecumenical activity in Finland. It includes 11 church organizations as full members, 4 as observer members, and 15 ecumenically active Christian organizations. Only the Pentecostal movement remains outside. The role of the council is to deepen and expand the ecumenical commitment of its members, to involve them in ecumenical study and action programs inside the country, and to serve as a channel of communication with the World Council of Churches and other international ecumenical organizations. This communication function is especially important for those members who have little access on their own to worldwide ecumenical concerns and who are not members of the WCC. The joining of the Roman Catholic Church in 1968 increased the significance of the council, especially for the Lutheran and the Orthodox churches. The council's role in Christian activities in Finland, however, has remained very limited, largely because of the differences of size and resources of the participating churches.

Free churches in 1967 formed the Free Christian Council of Finland, which has six church communities as its members, among them the Pentecostal church. Its main objectives are to foster cooperation among its members and to protect their interests in relation to governmental authorities and in the development of national legislation.

Bilateral consultations on doctrine and church policies between the Lutheran majority church and the Finnish Orthodox Church as well as between the Lutheran Church and several members of the free church family of Finland have become a recognized part of Finnish ecumenical endeavors (→ Ecumenical Dialogue). The Finnish Lutheran Church entered a new phase in its international ecumenical relationships when in 1996 it signed the Porvoo Common Statement, which established full communion between Lutheran churches in most of the Nordic and Baltic countries and the Anglican churches in England, Ireland, Scotland, and Wales.

Another significant dimension of Finnish ecumenical relations has emerged in the framework of bilateral consultations between the Russian Orthodox Church and the Evangelical Lutheran Church of Finland. High-level talks, held about every three years since 1970, have covered a variety of topics on doctrine, → social ethics, and → mission (§§1-2), which have resulted in a series of widely circulated documents. These consultations have also opened possibilities for practical cooperation in theological education and social relief activity.

Roman Catholic–Lutheran relations have become a focal issue for the Finnish Lutheran Church through its participation in the preparation of the Joint Declaration on the Doctrine of → Justification by the Roman Catholic Church and the Lutheran World Federation, a statement signed on October 31, 1999, in Augsburg, Germany. For the Finnish Lutheran Church the process has meant a major step in the rapprochement between Catholics and Lutherans underway since the Second Vatican Council.

3. Other Religions

Muslims are on the way to becoming the largest non-Christian religious group in Finland. Their number is estimated, as of 1999, as at least 10,000 (representing some 20 different groupings), more than a tenfold increase in the last 20 years. So far they have no common national structure to link together their various groups. Most of those who have come recently do not yet appear in official statistics, which includes only the few registered → Islamic communities. The origin of Islamic communities in Finland goes back to the 19th century, when Muslim traders, mostly descendants of Tatars, migrated to the country from Russia. The rapid expansion of the last two or three decades is due to the arrival of → refugees and other Muslim immigrants, mainly from the Middle East, Somalia, Bosnia, and Kosovo.

The largest marginally Christian groups are the → Jehovah's Witnesses (17,300 members) and the Latter-day Saints, or Mormons (3,200 members).

A small but stable Jewish community has existed in Finland for several centuries (→ Judaism). It was not affected by the military alliance of the Second World War between Finland and Germany in 1941-44. In 1999 it numbered 1,100 members.

There are several other registered religious communities, including the → Baha'i community, the → Krishna movement, the → Theosophists, and the → Anthroposophists. None has as many as 1,000 members. More significant than these communities are the → "new spiritual movements" such as transcendental meditation groups and the → Church of Scientology, which either do not qualify or do not want to be registered as organized religious communities.

Bibliography: E. T. BACHMANN and M. B. BACHMANN, *Lutheran Churches in the World: A Handbook* (Minneapolis, 1989) 399-403 • EVANGELICAL LUTHERAN CHURCH OF FINLAND, *The Churches in Finland* (Helsinki, 1996); idem, *Kiev 1995: The Tenth Theological Discussions between the Evangelical Lutheran Church of Finland and the Russian Orthodox Church* (Helsinki, 1996) • N. HOPE, *German and Scandinavian Protestantism: 1700-1918* (New York, 1995) • E. JUTIKKALA and K. PIRINEN, *A History of Finland* (5th ed.; Porvoo, 1996) • L. ÖSTERLIN, *Churches of Northern Europe in Profile: A Thousand Years of Anglo-Nordic Relations* (Norwich, U.K., 1995) • K. PIRINEN, ed., *Suomen kirkon historia* (The history of the Finnish church) (4 vols.; Porvoo, 1990-93) • R. SAARINEN, *Faith and Holiness: Lutheran-Orthodox Dialogue, 1959-1994* (Göttingen, 1997).

RISTO LEHTONEN

Finney, Charles Grandison

1. Early Life and Conversion
2. Revivals in Upstate New York
3. National Evangelistic Leadership
4. Oberlin College and Later Career
5. Legacy

1. Early Life and Conversion

Charles Grandison Finney (1792-1875), pre–Civil War American evangelist and father of modern revivalism (→ Revivals), was born in Warren, Con-

necticut, to Sylvester and Rebecca Rice Finney. Like many other New England farmers, the family migrated to New York State — to Oneida County in the Mohawk River Valley in 1794 and, when Charles was 16, north to Jefferson County. Educated in common schools and perhaps Hamilton-Oneida Academy in Clinton, he taught school in Henderson before attending Warren Academy in Connecticut. Deciding against college, he taught in New Jersey until 1818, when he returned to Adams, New York, to apprentice at law.

The Second Great Awakening brought waves of revivals to the area. Finney remained aloof, although under pastor George W. Gale he served as music director in the Presbyterian Church and studied the Bible. In 1821, at age 29, he experienced a spiritual and vocational crisis, retreating on October 10 to a wooded grove outside town. Finney resolved, as he recalled in his *Memoirs*, "I will give my heart to God before I ever come down again" and "if I am ever converted, I will preach the gospel." Having seized on God's promises "with the grasp of a drowning man," in penitential prayer back in the law office he then received "a mighty baptism of the Holy Ghost" (pp. 19-23).

Finney began witnessing to the → gospel immediately. He was soon taken in care of the St. Lawrence Presbytery, which, instead of insisting on seminary training at Princeton or Andover, arranged for Gale to tutor him in theology. Although Finney criticized his pastor for Calvinist → dogmatism, Gale was instrumental in both his → conversion (§1) and his rapid acceptance into the ministry. In December 1823 Finney was licensed to preach, in March 1824 the Female Missionary Society of the Western District of New York commissioned him as an evangelist, and in July 1824 the presbytery → ordained him.

2. Revivals in Upstate New York

Finney attracted immediate attention for his extemporaneous preaching. He looked people in the eye, addressed them as "you," warned of → hell in vivid language, used everyday illustrations, and argued like a lawyer. Adopting a Methodist- and Baptist-like call for immediate conversion, his sermons sparked emotional results, with men and women weeping, shouting, falling down "in the Spirit," and testifying. He engaged in "prevailing prayer" for sinners, believing in the efficacy of specific prayers made in faith. In October 1824 he married Lydia Root Andrews, with whom he had six children and who collaborated in his ministry by leading women's prayer, missionary, and social reform groups.

Finney brought revival south to central New York State in the fall of 1825, at the call of George Gale, who had moved to Oneida County. Auspiciously, Governor De Witt Clinton had just opened the Erie Canal, linking Buffalo with Albany and New York City. Finney found his future was not in rural villages or on the frontier but in commercial cities. More than any other evangelist, Finney created revivalism as an urban phenomenon. Beginning in Rome and Utica, he transferred the northern revivals' emotional power to staid Presbyterian and Congregational churches. In 1826 he ignited revival west of Syracuse in Auburn, seat of the New School Presbyterian seminary, then responded to an invitation go to Troy, where the Mohawk River joins the Hudson, just north of Albany.

Finney was not an independent evangelist; rather, he worked in a league of New School Presbyterian → pastors, all of whom promoted the use of "new measures," including the call for immediate conversion, → prayer for sinners by name, testimony by females in mixed meetings, and emotional responses in → worship. They were opposed by more strictly Calvinist Old School Presbyterians. And they worried Lyman → Beecher, Asahel Nettleton, and other evangelical clergy of New England who were their Congregationalist partners in the 1801 Plan of Union. Defending the "western revivals," Finney branded his opponents as spiritually dead in his first publication, *A Sermon Preached in the Presbyterian Church at Troy, March 4, 1827.* Beecher organized a conference of New England and Mohawk Valley ministers at New Lebanon, New York, in July 1827, as a result of which Finney rose to national stature.

Finney and his colleagues employed the "New Haven theology" of Yale Divinity School's Nathaniel William Taylor, a progressive adaptation of → Calvinism that viewed individuals as free moral agents. Finney believed strict Calvinism denied the very possibility of salvation by removing human ability to respond to grace. Still, he insisted that the sinner "never does, and never will turn, unless God induces him to do it" (*Sermons*, 29). Inheriting a "moral government" theory of the atonement from Samuel Hopkins's New Divinity, these evangelicals felt called to broadcast God's offer of → salvation to all of sinful humanity. Defining → sin as selfishness and → sanctification as disinterested benevolence also led them to promote such moral reforms as temperance, abolition of → slavery, and women's rights (→ Women's Movement).

3. National Evangelistic Leadership

Invitations poured in for extended campaigns in major eastern cities. Finney spent 1828 in and around Wilmington, Delaware, and Philadelphia, just as the New School–Old School conflict raged in that area. A group of businessmen brought him to New York City in 1829 to preach at a "Free Presbyterian Church," and these reform-minded → evangelicals became his patrons for several years. From September 1830 to March 1831 in Rochester, New York, Finney led one of the greatest revivals in American history. Community and business leaders in Presbyterian, Baptist, Methodist, and Episcopal churches supported his work, including the additional "new measures" of the "anxious seat" (a more immediate version of traditional inquiry meetings for penitents), "protracted meetings" in nearby villages, and specific linking of conversion with temperance.

The Rochester revival made Finney America's best-known evangelist. Following an engagement in Boston in 1831-32, New York City philanthropists including Arthur and Lewis Tappan established him as pastor at the renovated Chatham Street Theater. The Tappans, who were antislavery leaders, urged him to connect revival with abolitionism. Although cautious about extremism, Finney vigorously condemned slavery as sin and refused to serve Communion to slaveholders. While antiabolition mobs vandalized his church and Old School Presbyterians renewed their attack on his theology, Finney suffered from cholera and endured a spiritual crisis. Spiritually renewed on a sea voyage, in 1835 he published *Sermons on Various Subjects* and *Lectures on Revivals of Religion.* In his view a revival is not a miracle but "a purely philosophical result of the right use of the constituted means" (*Lectures,* 13). With heresy charges likely, in 1836 he resigned his Presbyterian affiliation and became a → Congregationalist. Finney's wealthy friends, meanwhile, built Broadway Tabernacle in New York City for him as pastor.

4. Oberlin College and Later Career

Oberlin Collegiate Institute, founded with Tappan money on abolitionist and coeducation principles and with radical students and faculty exiled from Cincinnati's Lane Seminary, called Finney as professor of theology in 1835. He planned to divide his time between Ohio and New York City. Finney resigned from Broadway Tabernacle in 1837, however, and combined the pastorate of Oberlin's First Church with his professorship, positions he held for the remainder of his career.

Finney, president Asa Mahan, and other faculty

developed the doctrine of "entire sanctification" using the Wesleyan language of holiness, perfection, "higher Christian life," and "consecration of the whole being to God" (→ Holiness Movement 3.3.1). Promotion of → "perfectionism" in the *Oberlin Evangelist* and in his books *Lectures to Professing Christians* (1837) and *Views of Sanctification* (1840) led many New School Presbyterian and Congregationalist friends to turn against him. Finney developed his theology in volume 1 of *Skeletons of a Course of Theological Lectures* (1840) and volumes 2 and 3 of *Lectures on Systematic Theology* (1846-47). His beliefs were reinforced in 1847 as, during his wife's fatal illness, he experienced a "fresh baptism of the Holy Spirit."

Finney launched evangelistic campaigns, mainly in northeastern cities, during winter months away from Oberlin. With a new wife, Rochester widow Elizabeth Ford Atkinson, he undertook two successful tours of Great Britain (November 1849–April 1851; January 1859–August 1860). In August 1851 he was named president of Oberlin College, although his leadership was often largely symbolic because of such extensive travel. He was in Boston, headquartered at Park Street Church, for the 1857-58 "Businessmen's Revival." During the Civil War Finney confined himself to work in Oberlin. Following the death of Elizabeth in 1863, in 1865 he married Rebecca Allen Rayl, widowed assistant principal of Oberlin's female department. In his last years he wrote his memoirs (published posthumously in 1876) and wrote against Freemasonry. Finney retired from the college presidency in 1865 and as pastor in 1872.

5. Legacy

Charles Finney's well-organized campaigns and his preaching method, notably the immediate call for repentant sinners to come forward to accept Christ, adapted the revivalist traditions of the earlier Great Awakening and camp meetings to the cultural environment of modern cities. He influenced later generations of revivalists from Dwight L. → Moody to Billy Graham. His blend of evangelistic and academic careers exemplifies the relationship of evangelical Protestantism and higher education in America. While his social reform work anticipated the → Social Gospel, his teaching on the baptism of the Holy Spirit and entire sanctification gave expression to the → Holiness movement and set the stage for the birth of Pentecostalism.

Bibliography: Primary Sources: C. G. FINNEY, *Lectures on Revivals of Religion* (ed. W. G. McLoughlin; Cam-bridge, Mass., 1960; orig. pub., 1835); idem, *The Memoirs of Charles G. Finney* (ed. G. M. Rosell and R. A. G. Dupuis; Grand Rapids, 1989; orig. pub., 1876); idem, *Sermons on Important Subjects* (New York, 1836).

Secondary Works: C. E. HAMBRICK-STOWE, *Charles G. Finney and the Spirit of American Evangelicalism* (Grand Rapids, 1996) • K. J. HARDMAN, *Charles Grandison Finney (1792-1875): Revivalist and Reformer* (Syracuse, N.Y., 1987).

CHARLES E. HAMBRICK-STOWE

Fire

Fire has played a role in human history at least since Peking man (dated perhaps as early as 500,000 B.C.). In its use by the human race, fire can be both positive (providing light, warmth, and a means of cooking) and negative (bringing burning and destruction). It has been regarded as of heavenly origin, especially when kindled by lightning. When kindled by rubbing, it is a manifestation of human culture. When it came to be viewed as a symbol can be decided only in connection with the development of forms of religion that offer representations and → symbols, which differ from culture to culture.

In cultic usage the significance of fire lay always in its presence and then in its representative character and not its character as an object of worship. References to a fire cult and fire priests (among Indo-Europeans, Incas, and Ainus) do not imply fire worship. The earliest fire cult was at the family hearth (classically attested among the Romans). It then became a cult of the clan, tribe, people, province, and state (e.g., among the ancient Iranians). Ancient rites, often unwritten, refer to fire walking as an → ordeal. Fire is also a representation of gods (Agni in India, Atar in Iran) or of the offering burnt for them (making pyromancy possible in many cases; → Sacrifice). The natural phenomenon can also be a → theophany (as in Israel). Various interpretations of fire have arisen, both mythological (amply exemplified by the Greeks) and theological (throughout the Bible), culminating among the Iranians, Stoics, early Jews, and Germans in → eschatology (e.g., in predicting a world conflagration). At the beginning of demythologizing natural science, Empedocles and Aristotle listed fire as the first of the four elements.

In popular belief (which esp. in Europe can be traced back a long way), periodic changes in yearly climate and vegetation are marked by fire and accompanied by various customs. Fire is common in symbolic speech, especially in mystical and military experiences. Newer trends in psychoanalysis thus try to describe complexes from the psychology of illumination to pyromaniac impulses. The fascinating components of the holy in fire may still be seen in fireworks. What is not generally recognized is that the notion of a nuclear holocaust might also be related.

Bibliography: M. BOYCE, *Zoroastrianism: Its Antiquity and Constant Vigour* (Costa Mesa, Calif., 1992) • D. CANTER, ed., *Fires and Human Behavior* (New York, 1980) • C.-M. EDSMAN, "Fire," *EncRel(E)* 5.340-46 • A. HELLER, *Die Trilogie der möglichen Wunder. Roncalli, Flic Flac, Theater des Feuers* (Berlin, 1983) • N. A. HJELM, ed., *Out of the Ashes: Burned Churches and the Community of Faith* (Nashville, 1997) • J. MORGENSTERN, *The Fire upon the Altar* (Chicago, 1963) • S. A. NIGOSIAN, *The Zoroastrian Faith: Tradition and Modern Research* (Montreal, 1993) • E. SCHARANKOV, *Feuergehen. Psychologisch-physiologische und historisch-geographische Untersuchung des Nestinarentums in Bulgarien* (Stuttgart, 1980) • F. STAAL, *Agni: The Vedic Ritual of the Fire Altar* (2 vols.; Berkeley, Calif., 1983) • R. W. WEIN and D. A. MACLEAN, *The Role of Fire in Northern Circumpolar Ecosystems* (New York, 1983).

CARSTEN COLPE

Fish

The fish became a → symbol of Christ toward the end of the second century by way of the Gk. noun ἰχθύς (*ichthys*, "fish"), which was used as an acrostic for *Iēsous Christos, Theou Huios, Sōtēr* (Jesus Christ, Son of God, Savior), as well as on the basis of Luke 5:1-11 (cf. Matt. 13:47), Matt. 14:13-21 and parallels, and John 21. In dependence on rabbinic exegesis (as yet unelucidated), the → church fathers developed the following train of thought: believers as fish, Christ as fisherman, Christ as fish.

Clement of Alexandria (d. ca. 215; see *Paed.* 3) and → Tertullian (d. ca. 225; see *De bapt.* 1.3), in showing how imprecise and rich the symbol was, point back to Jewish ideas. The inscription of Abercius (2nd half of the 2nd cent.), with its concealed reference to a very large, pure fish that was conceived by a holy virgin, gives evidence of the role of the fish symbol in an arcane discipline that permits clear interpretation of the fish, especially in sepulchral areas, only when other symbols of Christ are present. As already in → Judaism the fish can stand for the believer, or it can symbolize the "elect food" of the Eucharist. The meaning is more certain when we find it in the plural with mention of bread, for then the reference is to Christ's miracle of feeding.

Around 1250 the fish symbolized the Eucharist as the body of Christ (Naumburg cathedral). Various saints have the fish as an attribute, including St. Zeno (d. ca. 375; two fish on a book); St. Benno, bishop of Meissen (1066-1106); Antony of Padua (d. 1231); and Elizabeth of Thuringia (1207-31; bowl with fish).

→ Symbolism of Animals

Bibliography: F. J. DÖLGER, *Ichthys. Die Fisch-Denkmäler in der frühchristlichen Plastik, Malerei und Kleinkunst* (4 vols.; Freiburg and Münster, 1910-43) • J. QUASTEN, "Fish, Symbolism of," *NCE* 5.943-46.

PETER MASER

Flagellants

Whipping as a religious penance or → punishment, as well as self-flagellation (Lat. *flagellum*, "whip"), are common phenomena in the history of religion. In the Christian church the scourging of Christ commended itself especially as a model for this penitential act. We find it again and again in history. As a mass movement, flagellation occurred after the middle of the 13th century and in the middle of the 14th, with small groups of flagellants persisting up to the end of the 14th.

The movement began in Perugia in 1260/61 and spread quickly to central and northern Italy, with attested incidents also in places north of the Alps, for example, Poland and Strasbourg. The movement was obviously occasioned and strengthened both by political and economic crises and by eschatological expectations (→ Millenarianism). The flagellants sought to avert the judgment of God by their public → penance. In Italy they came from all social classes, including clergy who took part in the → processions. North of the Alps the flagellants gave evidence of anticlerical and antihierarchical tendencies, going beyond the church's penitential discipline.

The processions of 1348 and 1349 were connected with the earthquakes, the Black Death, and probably also the Jewish persecutions of these years (→ Anti-Semitism, Anti-Judaism). They are attested throughout the empire and Italy. The movement ended abruptly soon thereafter, with some flagellants being persecuted as heretics (→ Heresies and Schisms). There are only a few instances of processions later, though the movement lived on in the form of small heretical groups of so-called crypto-flagellants, who differed from the earlier movements by partially adopting ideas of the → Waldenses and → freethinkers. How large numerically these groups were in the 15th century we can no more say than we can in the case of Waldensian groups. Martin → Luther (1483-1546) knew of Konrad Schmitt, a leader of flagellants in Thuringia who was executed in 1369.

Bibliography: R. AMTMANN, *Die Bußbruderschaften in Frankreich* (Wiesbaden, 1977) • P. BAILLY, "Flagellants," *DSp* 5.392-407 • N. CHON, *The Pursuit of the Millennium* (rev. ed.; New York, 1970) 127-47 • M. ERB-STÖSSER, *Sozialreligiöse Strömungen im späten Mittelalter* (Berlin, 1970) • A. HÜBNER, *Die deutschen Geißlerlieder* (Berlin, 1931) • R. KIECKHEFER, "Radical Tendencies in the Flagellant Movement of the Mid-Fourteenth Century," *JMRS* 4 (1974) 157-76 • P. SEGL, "Geißler," *TRE* 12.162-69 • P. ZIEGLER, *The Black Death* (New York, 1971).

HARTMUT BOOCKMANN

Folk Church → People's Church (Volkskirche)

Folk Religion → Popular Religion

Foot Washing

Foot washing in the Orient is a common, understood, and acceptable practice. The wearing of open sandals, the dry climate, and dusty paths make it so. In the Greco-Roman world, foot washing was done for several reasons: (1) as a ritual; (2) domestically, for reasons of personal comfort and hygiene; (3) as an expression of hospitality, a gesture of greeting, or in preparation for a banquet; and (4) as a service by servants or slaves.

Foot washing as an obligation of hospitality occurs early in the OT — in Gen. 18:4 with Abraham, and in 19:2 with Lot. Abraham's servant is provided with water to wash his feet and the feet of those with him (24:32). Similar actions are recorded in Gen. 43:24, Judg. 19:21, and 1 Sam. 25:41. Cultic references to foot washing appear in Exod. 30:19 and 40:30-32. According to Luke 7:44-46, it was customary hospitality for a host to make provision for the washing of guests' feet.

→ Jesus in John 13:1-17 lifts the act of foot washing to religious significance. From vv. 7 and 12 it is clear that Jesus' washing of his disciples' feet is sym-

bolic, with a meaning greater than that of merely hospitality or hygiene. Here the Master, in a reversal of roles, washes the feet of his → disciples. He did it during the meal instead of immediately upon entrance. The reference to washing the saints' feet in 1 Tim. 5:10 attests that the practice was taken seriously and reflects the author's acquaintance with John 13.

In the early church, Tertullian indicates a knowledge of foot washing, noting that it was a part of Christian worship (*De cor.* 8). Chrysostom encourages Christians to imitate the action of Jesus in John 13 (*In Joh. hom.* 70-71), as does Augustine (*In Evang. Iohan.* 55-57). Origen also advocates foot washing (*In Gen. hom.* 4.2). The Synod of Toledo (694) declared that foot washing should be observed on Maundy Thursday. Throughout the Middle Ages the Roman churches observed the practice on that day of → Holy Week. The Greek church recognized foot washing as a → sacrament but seldom practiced it. In the 11th and 12th centuries the Albigenses and → Waldenses observed foot washing as a religious rite. The → Bohemian Brethren also practiced it in the 16th century. Martin Luther opposed foot washing, but it was practiced by the → Anabaptists and some → Pietists.

Presently the five Brethren groups (Brethren Church, Church of the Brethren, Dunkard Brethren Church, Fellowship of Grace Brethren Churches, and Old Order German Baptist; → Brethren Churches), several of the → Mennonite groups, Primitive Baptists, Seventh-day Adventists, Brethren in Christ, and the Church of God (Anderson, Ind.) practice foot washing as an ordinance (i.e., a practice established by the example and command of Jesus). Some Mennonites practice foot washing as a preparatory service the day before receiving Communion, although most Mennonite groups that practice foot washing do so immediately following the Communion. The Brethren groups conduct a threefold service: Agape (love feast), Pedalavium (foot washing), and Eucharist (bread and cup). Foot washing is also provided for within the Maundy Thursday liturgy of the → Anglican Communion and the → Roman Catholic Church.

The practice of foot washing as an ordinance has been justified from the details of John 13, specifically on the basis of (1) Jesus' personal example (vv. 4-12), (2) his specific command ("I have set you an example, that you also should do as I have done to you," v. 15), and (3) the blessing he pronounces ("if you know these things, you are blessed if you do them," v. 17).

Foot washing has been interpreted by various

scholars and communities in sometimes contradictory ways:

It is a *courteous action of common hospitality* (Luke 7:44), but heightened by Jesus for purposes of impact. He washed his disciples' feet during the meal rather than, as customary, upon entrance, and as the Lord, not as a servant or slave.

It is an *expression of humility*, a lesson in condescension. This enacted parable teaches the importance of → humility for the disciples, who had been quarreling over who should be foremost (Luke 22:24-30). Jesus wanted them to understand that humility and exaltation go together and thus reinforced an ethical truth by a concrete example.

It is a *call to ethical action*. It expresses an inward attitude that should be perpetuated even more than the action itself. This attitude provides the moral core of the practice of the Christian life. It is an action that needs to be willingly, unselfishly, and humbly completed. The disciples need to perform the same kind of loving actions that Jesus did.

It is a *cleansing from partial defilement*. The bathing of John 13:10 refers to → baptism, which is done but once. The washing of feet follows for subsequent events in the life of the Christian that need cleansing.

It is an *encapsulation of the entire servant ministry of Jesus*. In this act he performed the work of a servant and called his disciples to continue this servant ministry. John preserves the → Synoptic tradition that "the Son of Man came not to be served but to serve" (Mark 10:45; see also Luke 22:27).

It is a *symbol of the* → *Eucharist*. The washing of the disciples' feet takes the place of the Lord's Supper in John's Gospel.

It is a *symbol of baptism*. From the variant reading of John 13:10 that omits "except for the feet" and from the Johannine practice of using two words to refer to the same thing, it is concluded that "bath" and "wash" both apply to baptism.

It is a *symbol of Jesus' death*. There is much in the passage that deals with his death, and therefore foot washing is frequently attached to → atonement.

Today there is an increased interest in foot washing — not so much as an ordinance or sacrament but as a personal experience in humility. Foot washing is being introduced on a voluntary basis in a variety of new settings. The Eucharist speaks of what God has done in Christ; foot washing brings the community of faith into the celebration.

Bibliography: R. E. Brown, *The Gospel according to John* (2 vols.; New York, 1966-70) • D. A. Carson, *The Gospel according to John* (Grand Rapids, 1990) •

O. Cullmann, *Early Christian Worship* (London, 1953) • A. J. B. Higgins, *The Lord's Supper in the NT* (London, 1952) • J. Jeremias, *The Eucharistic Words of Jesus* (London, 1966) • J. Schultz, *The Soul of the Symbols* (Grand Rapids, 1966) • D. Stoffer, ed., *The Lord's Supper: Believers Church Perspectives* (Scottdale, Pa., 1997) • J. C. Thomas, *Footwashing in John 13 and the Johannine Community* (Sheffield, 1991).

Richard E. Allison

Force, Violence, Nonviolence

1. Theology and Ethics
   1.1. Term
   1.2. Positions
2. Ecumenical Aspects

1. Theology and Ethics

1.1. *Term*

"Force" is a term with many nuances. In the sense of violence it can denote unlawful acts that threaten, harm, or destroy the → life or liberty (→ freedom) of a person (or animal), the → property of someone, or social order. It may also be used for the lawful force that a government must have in order to give stability to society. The lack of precision derives from the matter itself and is reflected in Greek and Latin as well as English, French, and German. In using the term, then, we must keep in view its history (see 1.1.1), which will make it clear that force occurs in the three spheres of nature, the political and social order, and religion (see 1.1.2).

1.1.1. The Greeks used various terms for force or violence, but not with any precision. Such words as *archē, kyros,* and *exousia* refer for the most part to the legal and official power of rule or government. *Ischys* and *bia* have in view bodily strength, superior force, violence, and physical overpowering. Sharp distinction, however, does not do justice to the facts, for legitimate force can degenerate into tyranny, but a government that lacks the physical force to maintain itself becomes the plaything of foreign powers. In Greek poetry, history, and philosophy we constantly see the ambivalence. The possibility of violence lies in our animal nature, which only a political order can restrain.

The political vocabulary of the Romans reveals a similar ambiguity. At the one end of the pole is *potestas* (based on *auctoritas*), at the other end *vis* or *violentia*. In the Latin Bible *potestas* (legal or charismatic authority) is the equivalent of *exousia*.

In modern languages English has the two words

"force" and "violence," but an unlawful or excessive use of force may itself be violence. In German the term *Gewalt* may denote legitimate government, but it may also have the sense of might as distinct from right.

1.1.2. The history of the term helps to explain its modern use. Force relates first to the working of natural (physical) forces on people and objects. Violence takes such forms as child abuse, bodily assault, rape, homicide, and murder. Whether the human capacity for violence has been sublimated over the years (as N. Elias has proposed) is doubtful. Its forms have changed with technological advances.

In the interest of human survival legal force is necessary to mitigate and restrain violence. Putting a monopoly of force in the hands of state institutions has been a common answer in different forms over the centuries. In many cases we find the theory of a social contract, according to which the citizenry hands over its sovereignty to a central body for the lawful exercise of force in its own interest. On this view the state for its part must respect the inalienable rights of all citizens (→ Rights, Human and Civil).

The link between the state's monopoly of force and law is precarious, however, for its law might simply express and protect special interests, and it might itself become the source of unlawful violence (as in National Socialism, Stalinism, and apartheid). Remembering that all natural and human force has its origin and limit in the divine will, which in the Judeo-Christian tradition is given pointed form in the first commandment of the → Decalogue, can set human force within the confines of serving the common good.

1.2. Positions

Theological and ethical evaluations of force, violence, and nonviolence part company in accordance with the aspects and relations of the phenomenon that they have in view (see 1.2.1) and the political and social perspectives that govern their formulations (see 1.2.2).

1.2.1. Most Jews and Christians are at one in rejecting arbitrary individual violence and in recognizing that "the state has the responsibility to provide for justice and peace in the yet unredeemed world, in which the church also stands, according to the measure of human insight and human possibility, by the threat and use of force" (thesis 5 of the → Barmen Declaration, 1934). M. → Luther (1483-1546) constantly stressed that the sword of secular powers is a valid divine ministry in the interests of order and → peace, but that if magistrates act on their own behalf or to help themselves, it is a de-

nial of God (Deut. 32:35; Rom. 12:19; → Luther's Theology). I. Kant (1724-1804) stood in the same tradition when he urged upon subjects the duty of → obedience to established authority (→ Kantianism). In extreme cases, at most only passive resistance, the resistance of speech, or the readiness to suffer is legitimate. Force here is viewed primarily as a means and form of action. The ethical and legal evaluation pertains to the qualifications and goals of the court that exercises force.

This type of evaluation, which stresses the connection between protection and obedience, must be seen as a reaction to medieval feudalism and the religious wars of the → modern period. It favors an authoritarian view of the state. Particularly in Western Europe and America, however, there were also attempts to limit the power of the state by an institutionalized separation of powers (J. Bodin, J. Locke, Montesquieu) and to subject it to substantive legal criteria by the guaranteeing of inalienable human rights.

Whereas these theories all agree that force as an elemental natural phenomenon can be subordinated to human, moral ends, the proponents of nonviolence more or less radically contested this assumption. The way was thus opened up to → pacifism — which often enough the church as a whole had strongly opposed — on the basis of the nonviolence of Jesus Christ as the impotent God. It took a special form in the → monastic lifestyle and was taken up again and again in protest movements that, as fellowships of radical discipleship, renounced the use of force even for the best of objectives (e.g., → Waldenses, Albigenses, → Bohemian Brethren).

The first Christian movement of the modern era whose nonviolence has endured into the present is that of the → Anabaptists. Incorporating ecclesial motifs from the NT, monasticism, and late medieval protest movements, they gave nonresistance as it is profiled in the → Sermon on the Mount *status confessionis*. In other words, they viewed a lifestyle of nonviolence as integral to Christian faithfulness. Christian humanists (→ Erasmus, J. L. Vives, R. Llull) took up the theme, as did the theologians of Spanish baroque Scholasticism who championed the rights of Indians (F. de Vitoria, B. de Las Casas).

Modern political thinking is oriented primarily to the unity or monopoly of force and responsibility for the common good, and it combines formal and material criteria of justice (→ Righteousness, Justice). If the state uses force simply to maintain its monopoly, the question arises regarding the particular interests with which public order is connected. In the name of a more comprehensive good, embracing both civil → equality and economic liberation, K. → Marx (1818-83) and his followers thus sought to justify the right to overthrow a middle-class state and → society by revolutionary violence (→ Marxism). In the classless society that he sought, the state would be superfluous. This idea is obviously an immanent, secularized version of the Christian hope of the → kingdom of God, in which the fellowship of true Christians will have no further need of force.

Although Marx stretched the concept of force beyond the traditional instrumentalist understanding to encompass every structure of political and economic repression, everything finally came together in the concept of structural violence, which entails an influencing of people in such a way as to prevent them from fully realizing their potential. The fascination that this idea has had for intellectuals is in marked contrast to a widespread indifference to the suffering and need that the banal use of force in everyday life causes in all political systems. In modern → terrorism and the contemporary attempt to justify it theoretically, the individual repugnance to the use of force seems to have decreased no less than it has for defenders of the state monopoly of force, for whom it seems to be almost an end in itself.

1.2.2. At different times the Jewish and Christian communities have taken up very different attitudes toward force and violence. In the story of Cain's fratricide the OT depicts the elemental natural potential for force. In the kingdom of → David it then reflects the pomp of political force. In the experience of the exile it finds the limit of human self-assertion in the → faithfulness of God. In Roman-occupied Palestine both Jews and Christians, far from wielding force, were the victims of force.

Not only because they were victims of state-sanctioned coercion but also because they believed the military might of the Roman empire to be idolatrous, most Christians in the second and third centuries were pacifist. With the transition to the imperial church and the possibility of assuming public responsibility, Christians found themselves in a changed situation vis-à-vis power and force. When the emperor presided at a council and gave the church imperial protection, he could also expect loyalty from Christians and their prayers for rulers. As Christians then took public office, they became entangled in the ambivalence of secular power-relationships in which, according to church teaching, they can and should serve the law and their neighbors as princes, judges, and soldiers (Augs. Conf. 16).

The renunciation of earthly power and force by

→ Jesus, as well as the injunction in the Sermon on the Mount that we should love our → enemies, led at least some Christians who were → minorities to question whether it is permissible to take part in the use of force at all. One answer lay in the renunciation of property and force as required by the monastic way of life. Another lay in the renunciation of all force by the Anabaptists; another in the → conscientious objection of the → peace churches.

The dominant position of the peace churches historically has been that in order to limit evil, the state may wield the sword. In so doing, however, it places itself outside the "perfection of Christ" (Schleitheim Confession, 1527). In the United States the peace churches faced a stiff challenge regarding their pacifism from mainline Protestants such as Reinhold → Niebuhr. John Howard Yoder's response in 1977 to Niebuhr's challenge brought the peace churches toward a position of engaged pacifism in which nonviolent participation in the institutions of society is given a role. Indeed, even members of the mainline churches, who accepted the use of force in principle, have found in Peter's statement in Acts 5:29 ("we must obey God rather than any human authority") a limit to possible participation in the use of force, though the boundary might be drawn differently at different times. Thus today the German Protestant churches have found in the long and severe suppression of human rights by the state a limit to the duty of civil obedience and a reason for claiming the right to resist. The use of force is a last resort when all efforts to improve relations have failed or have no prospect of success (Gewalt und Gewaltanwendung in der Gesellschaft).

The conviction has grown in modern mainline Christian churches in the West that in matters of force and nonviolence, there are some basic ethical principles but that each situation must be judged on its own merits. The basic principles include renunciation and prohibition of (1) → war with modern → weapons of mass destruction, (2) oppression on grounds of race (→ Racism) or sex (→ Sexism), (3) → torture, (4) the taking of hostages, and (5) the deliberate killing of innocent people. The possibilities and functions of nonviolent action on the one hand (as in → civil rights movements; → King, Martin Luther, Jr.) and of resistance that includes the use of force on the other are assessed differently according to whether there exists a legally constituted order that can be reformed or whether a legally limited state monopoly of force must still be established. All churches agree, however, in teaching that they may lay claim to no secular force in propagating the faith, for in this sphere God demonstrates his own power by emptying himself of power (see Phil. 2:6-8).

→ Authority; Disarmament and Armament; International Fellowship of Reconciliation; Peace Movement; Peace Research

Bibliography: Nonviolence bibliographies: "Bibliography on Nonviolence," *Peace Action News* (Antwerp, 1981) • A. CARTER et al., *Non-violent Action: Theory and Practise. A Selected Bibliography* (2d ed.; London, 1970). See also H. H. Schrey item below.

Other literature: P. ACKERMAN, *Strategic Nonviolent Conflict: The Dynamics of People Power in the Twentieth Century* (Westport, Conn., 1994) • R. J. BURROWES, *The Strategy of Nonviolent Defense: A Gandhian Approach* (Albany, N.Y., 1996) • J. EBACH, *Das Erbe der Gewalt. Eine biblische Realität und ihre Wirkungsgeschichte* (Gütersloh, 1980) • N. ELIAS, *Über den Prozeß der Zivilisation* (3d ed.; Frankfurt, 1977) • F. ENGEL-JANOSI et al., eds., *Gewalt und Gewaltlosigkeit. Probleme und Gestalten des 20. Jahrhunderts* (Munich, 1977) • E. H. ERIKSON, *Gandhi's Truth: On the Origins of Militant Nonviolence* (New York, 1970) • K.-G. FABER, K.-H. ILTING, and C. MEIER, "Macht, Gewalt," *Geschichtliche Grundbegriffe* (Stuttgart, 1982) 3.817-935 • J. FAHEY and R. ARMSTRONG, eds., *A Peace Reader: Essential Readings on War, Justice, Non-violence, and World Order* (New York: Paulist Press, 1987) • *Gewalt und Gewaltanwendung in der Gesellschaft. Eine theologische Thesenreihe zu sozialen Konflikten, erarbeitet von der Kammer der EKD für öffentliche Verantwortung* (Gütersloh, 1973) • T. GORRINGE, *The Sign of Love: Reflections on the Eucharist* (London, 1997) • M. KING, *Mahatma Gandhi and Martin Luther King Jr.: The Power of Nonviolent Action* (Paris [UNESCO], 1999) • M. L. KING JR., *Strength to Love* (Philadelphia, 1981) • W. LIENEMANN, *Gewalt und Gewaltverzicht. Studien zur abendländischen Vorgeschichte der gegenwärtigen Wahrnehmung von Gewalt* (Munich, 1982) • N. LOHFINK, ed., *Gewalt und Gewaltlosigkeit im Alten Testament* (Freiburg, 1983) • A. ROBERTS, ed., *Civilian Resistance as a National Defense: Non-violent Action against Aggression* (Harmondsworth, 1969) • H. H. SCHREY, "Gewalt, Gewaltlosigkeit I," *TRE* 13.168-78 • M. B. STEGER and N. S. LIND, *Violence and Its Alternatives: An Interdisciplinary Reader* (New York, 1999) • G. THEISSEN, "Gewaltverzicht und Feindesliebe," *Studien zur Soziologie des Urchristentums* (Tübingen, 1979) 160-97 • WORLD COUNCIL OF CHURCHES, "Violence, Nonviolence, and the Struggle for Social Justice," *ER* 25 (1973) 430-46 • J. H. YODER, *The Christian Witness to the State* (Newton, Kans., 1977). See also the bibliographies in "Peace" and "Peace Research."

WOLFGANG LIENEMANN

2. Ecumenical Aspects

The → ecumenical movement has addressed the issue of force, violence, and nonviolence from several angles. Early post–World War I gatherings of North Atlantic ecumenical Protestantism, such as the Stockholm Life and Work Conference of 1925, gave voice to the liberal internationalism that had led to the League of Nations. By the meeting of the Life and Work executive committee in Fanø, Denmark, in 1934, the conviction had emerged that nonviolence was an integral part of the gospel because it was inconceivable that members of the body of Christ in one country would turn on members of the body of Christ in another. On this occasion Dietrich → Bonhoeffer, who later set down his pacifistic reading of the NT in *Cost of Discipleship* (1937), called for a universal peace council of world Protestantism to promote peacemaking as the heart of the gospel. At the Life and Work Conference in Oxford in 1937, as war was approaching, there was a focus on the scandal of achieving doctrinal and liturgical unity for the body of Christ while it remained divided along hostile national lines.

Early assemblies of the → World Council of Churches (WCC) saw the matter in terms of Christian participation in → war between sovereign states. Their thinking was influenced by the just-war tradition and, to a lesser extent, by the minority witness of Christian → pacifism. In 1949 the first general secretary of the WCC, W. A. → Visser 't Hooft, invited the historic peace churches and the → International Fellowship of Reconciliation to submit a declaration on Christian pacifism to the WCC. They did so in 1951 *(War Is Contrary to the Will of God)* and again in 1953 *(Peace Is the Will of God)*. These submissions and the ensuing debate kept the peace agenda that had started between the wars before the ecumenical movement, outfitting it with an explicitly pacifist conviction.

In the 1960s the debate began to focus on situations of entrenched social injustice (→ Righteousness, Justice). The 1966 World Conference on Church and Society introduced the idea of structural violence, a concept that shifts much of the moral responsibility for → conflicts onto the shoulders of defenders of the status quo. At the same time, the U.S. → civil rights movement and the assassination, in 1968, of Martin Luther → King Jr. led the WCC to study nonviolent methods of achieving social change.

Beginning with → Vatican II, the → Roman Catholic Church became a full partner in the ecumenical search to overcome war and chauvinism. → John XXIII issued the encyclical *Pacem in terris* (1963), which began a radical shift in the Roman Catholic understanding of the just-war theory. Hereafter there was a presumption against the use of force, which has persisted in subsequent Catholic social teaching. In a historic precedent in 1965, Paul VI addressed the United Nations General Assembly on the theme of → peace. The teaching of John Paul II has continued this trend to the point where some Catholic ethicists conclude that the conditions for a just war no longer exist in the modern era.

The WCC's → Program to Combat → Racism (PCR), launched in 1970, produced sharp debate in some places about the churches' attitude toward armed struggle. Responding to the debate, the WCC Central Committee affirmed that the churches must always stand for the liberation of the oppressed and called attention to the violence often inherent in the status quo. "Nevertheless," it stated, "the WCC does not identify itself completely with any political movement, nor does it pass judgement on those victims of racism who are driven to violence as the only way left open to them to redress grievances and so open the way for a new and more just social order" (Addis Ababa, 1971)

As a further response to the PCR debate, the WCC Central Committee in 1973 commended to the member churches a major statement entitled "Violence, Nonviolence, and the Struggle for Social Justice." It urged more attention to nonviolent action, for reasons of practical effectiveness rather than pacifist principle, and challenged popular misconceptions about nonviolence. While unable to resolve the long-standing disagreement between Christian pacifists and just-war theorists, the statement argued that some forms of violence must be condemned by all Christians. Addressing questions to all sides in the debate, it called on Christians to become wiser and more courageous in translating their faith into action.

The main thrust of the 1973 statement was reaffirmed in subsequent ecumenical conferences. Gradually, however, the debate broadened. The WCC's sixth assembly (Vancouver, 1983), noting work previously done on violence and nonviolence, called for a future emphasis on the use and misuse of power. Specifically, it urged a conciliar process on justice, peace, and the integrity of creation. The subject of violence and nonviolence held a prominent place among the themes discussed in this process.

In 1992 the Central Committee of the WCC recommended a study and reflection process in which "active nonviolent action be affirmed as a clear emphasis in programmes and projects related to conflict resolution" (*Programme to Overcome Violence*, p. 7). This decision led to the creation in 1994 of the Programme to Overcome Violence (POV). The work of this body has made nonviolence as an expression of the nature of the church into a central issue on the ecumenical agenda. In December 1998 the Harare Assembly of the WCC formally declared the years 2000-2010 as "an ecumenical decade to overcome violence" (Kessler, 145).

Although the Roman Catholic Church has not formally joined the conciliar movement, it has cooperated with WCC peace and justice initiatives and, for example, supported the National Council of Churches' Faith and Order dialogues with the historic peace churches in the United States. The Orthodox Church has lessened its commitment to ecumenism and the conciliar engagement for peace in recent years, but individual Orthodox theologians of stature, such as John Breck of the United States, have actively worked with POV and parallel peace initiatives in the development of a biblically grounded peace theology.

Bibliography: L. S. CAHILL, *Love Your Enemies: Discipleship, Pacifism, and Just War Theory* (Minneapolis, 1994) • J. W. DOUGLASS, *The Non-violent Cross: A Theology of Revolution and Peace* (London, 1969) • D. KESSLER, ed., *Together on the Way: Official Report of the Eighth Assembly of the World Council of Churches* (Geneva, 1999) • M. E. MARTY and D. G. PEERMAN, eds., *New Theology No. 6* (London, 1969) • T. MERTON, *Passion for Peace: The Social Essays* (New York, 1996) • M. E. MILLER and B. N. GINGERICH, eds., *The Church's Peace Witness* (Grand Rapids, 1994) • V. MORTENSEN, ed., *War, Confession, and Conciliarity: What Does "Just War" in the Augsburg Confession Mean Today?* (Hannover, 1993) • G. STASSEN, *Just Peacemaking: Transforming Initiatives for Justice and Peace* (Louisville, Ky., 1992) • J. G. WILLIAMS, *The Bible, Violence, and the Sacred: Liberation from the Myth of Sanctioned Violence* (San Francisco, 1991) • W. WINK, *Engaging the Powers: Discernment and Resistance in a World of Domination* (Minneapolis, 1992) • WORLD COUNCIL OF CHURCHES, *Programme to Overcome Violence: An Introduction* (Geneva, 1995); idem, *Theological Perspectives on Violence and Nonviolence: A Study Process* (Geneva, 1998); idem, "Violence, Nonviolence, and the Struggle for Social Justice," *ER* 25 (1973) 430-46, with continuation in the Corrymeela Consultation of the WCC, *ÖR* 33 (1984) 257-65.

DAVID GILL and JOHN D. REMPEL

Foreigners, Aliens

1. Modern Problems and Issues
2. Church Diaconal Aid

1. Modern Problems and Issues

The term "foreigners" defines individuals or social → groups in relation to a particular state. People become foreigners when they stay in a country other than their own. Depending on the circumstances in the host country, their presence may or may not be welcome. The social problem involved in the concept is twofold: foreigners live as aliens, as those who do not belong; and they are seen by residents to be aliens, not to belong. Different situations give rise to specific differences. In states that are not ethnically uniform, the possible ethnic difference of foreigners does not have the same importance as it does in ethnically uniform states. Again, foreigners who come from the same cultural and even linguistic background are not felt to be foreigners to the same degree. If they come as individuals, the social problems are not as acute as when sizable groups of foreigners begin to affect the social life of the state. The problems also vary depending on the time dimension. Temporary stays cause few problems, but longer stays have consequences that need regulating.

In the industrial countries of western and central Europe, groups of foreigners have come especially as guest workers. As mostly unskilled workers, they have formed a new lowest class. In developing countries (→ Development; Third World) rapid industrialization (→ Industrial Society) has also brought an influx of foreign workers (e.g., in Nigeria), though here the need for experts is relatively high, and foreigners from industrialized countries have come for the most part as the technical experts. Thus the problem of dealing with foreigners is completely different in different situations. The similarity is that the conditions of the economic system have meant that foreigners have had to be sought and won and attracted. Lands with higher living standards and better employment opportunities have for the most part drained off people (including "brain drain") from less-developed neighboring states. This imbalance holds between western and southern Europe, as well as between the United States and Mexico (and other countries of Central America).

Along with economic factors, political relations have also been important in the international migration that may be observed today. → Revolutions that establish dictatorships often trigger a mass migration of people seeking → asylum (i.e., political → refugees). Both political and economic factors during World War II caused Germany to employ foreigners, with men and women being forcibly brought in from occupied European countries. In Africa (and other places) civil conflict, as well as po-

litical disagreement, has led people to flee their homes and become foreigners in other nations. For example, several times since their nations' independence Rwandans and Burundians have fled to Tanzania.

Although the phenomenon of being a foreigner is linked to many social problems, the term is primarily a legal one. Foreigners, or aliens, are those who are not citizens. All who are not citizens by birth or naturalization are foreigners. In passing laws about aliens, however, states must observe general human → rights. They also must take into account their relations with other states. Thus, for example, the European Community allows freedom of movement within member states, and the basic right to → asylum is also significant in this context.

Although laws regarding aliens are important, one should not overlook the fact that they cover only a small sector of the problem. From a broader standpoint aliens are foreigners. They are usually different, which shows itself especially in their speech. Speech is a medium of communication, but as the expression of a particular interpretation of the world, it also embodies a → culture. Foreigners are different because their nationality is different. They are shaped by a different collective history. Religion is an important part of this history. In religion, groups and individuals find their collective and individual → identity. Finally, foreigners are different because their → everyday life can be organized in a wholly different way; their techniques for living are fundamentally different from those in the new land.

All these differences are ones of degree. Some foreigners come from countries that are linguistically akin; some enjoy common historical and cultural links. A distinction should be drawn, however, between ethnicity and nationality. Some foreigners may be of the same ethnic group as their host country but technically still be foreigners. Others will come from a completely different cultural and religious background. Perhaps they move from an agricultural, preindustrial world to one that is highly technological and highly organized. In such cases the experience of foreignness on both sides is particularly vivid. The matter becomes more complex when groups with ethnic and religious ties seek to reintegrate themselves into nations with which they have these affinities, such as the Volga Germans and the Ethiopian Falashas.

In a country of immigrants like the United States, the problem is somewhat different from what it is in the European states. Here, too, the situation is different in former colonial powers like Great Britain and France from what it is in Switzerland or Germany. Great Britain accepts ethnic → minorities from Commonwealth countries. Legally, these people are often not aliens, but otherwise they have all the marks of foreigners. Their integration, if they are citizens, is a legal necessity, no matter how we understand integration. Germany, in contrast, has not been a country of immigrants. Essentially, it has been ethnically and linguistically homogeneous, and thus the integration of foreigners has been difficult. A political goal, recently being reconsidered, was that foreigners should go home in a crisis. The difficulties of reintegration of those concerned, and especially for their families, are too easily ignored by the host country as well as the country of origin.

The degree of integration of foreigners into the society can be regarded as a measure of their assimilation. M. Gordon's distinction between behavioral assimilation and structural assimilation is still useful. The former involves adopting new cultural behavior-patterns and values; the latter refers to integration into the status or class system of the new country.

Adopting cultural behavior-patterns and values can be essential if foreigners are to satisfactorily adjust their personal sense of identity. Chronologically, the process of assimilation involves three crucial steps. The first phase is that of *assimilation* of lifestyle and techniques for coping with everyday life. Then there comes *rejection* of the values of the new society. Only after this hostile phase does a final phase of *interaction* usually occur. Joining ethnic groups or societies in the host country and following the religious traditions of the home country are essential aids in the redefinition of identity, in which the different phases of one's personal → biography become the constitutive components. For host countries that were originally ethnically uniform, this process has considerable implications for the new social identity. In countries like Germany and Great Britain, for example, it is not yet clear what role → Islam will play in the publicly and legally ordered system of religion.

Economic and political crises make the problem of foreigners more difficult. They also exacerbate the problems of minorities already relatively integrated. An example is the treatment of citizens of Japanese descent by the United States during World War II. One might also consider the expulsion of guest workers from Nigeria in the early 1980s, or the policies of European countries like Germany relative to aliens and those seeking asylum. In such cases popular moods help to shape political measures. Under threat, hatred of foreigners easily leads to ethnocentrism and even racist violence (see work by G. W. Allport and T. W. Adorno; → Prejudice). Those who belong to one's own ethnic group are thought to be of higher quality than foreign groups, an attitude that can constitute a reason for rejection. Ethnocentrism can develop into ideological systems or can be an essential element in such systems (note esp. Apartheid; → Fascism).

→ Racism; Tourism

Bibliography: T. W. ADORNO, *Studien zum autoritären Charakter* (2d ed.; Frankfurt, 1996) • G. W. ALLPORT, *The Nature of Prejudice* (Reading, Mass., 1979) • P. H. ELOVITZ and C. KAHN, eds., *Immigrant Experiences: Personal Narrative and Psychological Analysis* (Madison, N.J., 1997) • M. GORDON, *Assimilation in American Life: The Role of Race, Religion, and National Origins* (New York, 1964) • N. HARRIS, *The New Untouchables: Immigration and the New World Worker* (London, 1995) • M. O. HEISLER and B. S. HEISLER, eds., *From Foreign Workers to Settlers? Transnational Migration and the Emergence of New Minorities* (Beverly Hills, Calif., 1986) • S. JENKINS, ed., *Ethnic Associations and the Welfare State: Services to Immigrants in Five Countries* (New York, 1988) • H. KURTHEN, J. FIJALKOWSKI, and G. G. WAGNER, eds., *Immigration, Citizenship, and the Welfare State in Germany and the United States* (2 vols.; Stamford, Conn., 1998) • P. R. PESSAR, ed., *When Borders Don't Divide: Labor Migration and Refugee Movements in the Americas* (New York, 1988) • A. PETERSON-ROYCE, *Ethnic Identity* (Bloomington, Ind., 1982) • P. SCHUCK and R. MÜNZ, eds., *Paths to Inclusion: The Integration of Migrants in the United States and Germany* (New York, 1997) • P. STALKER, *The Work of Strangers: A Survey of International Labour Migration* (Geneva [International Labour Office], 1994).

KARL-FRITZ DAIBER, with DENNIS W. FRADO

2. Church Diaconal Aid

Churches have been prominent among the groups that provide social assistance to aliens. They have undertaken this work as a part of their overall diaconal activities (→ Deacon, Deaconess), often citing the saying of Jesus in Matt. 25:35, "I was a stranger and you welcomed me." Usually the churches have established agencies to undertake this work — for example, Diakonisches Werk and Caritas in Germany; and in the United States, Church World Service, Episcopal Migration Ministries, Lutheran Immigration and Refugee Service in cooperation with Lutheran Services in America, and Catholic Relief Services in cooperation with Catholic Charities. These agencies work with local congregations, church groups, regional confessional and ecumenical bodies, as well as counterpart international bodies such as the → World Council of Churches, Caritas Internationalis, and the → Lutheran World Federation (→ Relief and Development Organizations).

These groups cooperate with one another regularly in various fields of activity to assist aliens. → Counseling and advocacy on behalf of individuals and families are undertaken to deal with immediate problems of a personal, communal, and legal nature. Local churches address initial issues such as integration into the new community, provision of temporary housing, enrollment of children in → kindergarten or other schools, medical care, and explanation of cultural norms. Also they can serve as a buffer against hostility that might arise in the area of settlement. In cooperation with national bodies, local churches and groups intervene with the state with regard to legal issues, including clarification of one's refugee or migrant status, employment status, and tax matters. At the national level churches advocate with national government officials for immigration and refugee laws that are humane and welcoming.

Churches often provide pastoral care to the individuals and families and offer assistance with religious matters such as finding houses of worship and making arrangements for marriages and various rites, as well as showing sensitivity to cultural traditions and helping in times of hospitalization or bereavement.

In addition to the enrollment of children, churches provide or find instruction for adults in the host country language or help in finding sources of other types of education that might assist job placement.

To provide a welcoming and respectful experience for aliens, churches often sponsor or join with others in cultural activities linked to the aliens' ethnic identity. These events may include, for example, music, traditional meals, conferences, and religious meetings.

Churches frequently make special efforts to initiate work with young immigrants and refugees or to integrate them into existing youth groups, such as clubs and athletic organizations (→ Youth Work). Attention is paid to activities for both sexes, to ensure equal opportunity as well as possibilities for girls and women, who may otherwise be marginalized or, in some cultural traditions, ignored. Some activities may be specifically directed to girls and women to respect cultural customs.

These activities are tangible demonstrations of the churches' theological understanding of the gospel expression of love for one's neighbor, just as God expressed his love for all in sending his Son to dwell among us. These expressions are made without imposing one's own beliefs on the newcomers but yet also provide a witness to the Christian faith held by members of the churches. All of these diaconal activities are undertaken as acts of solidarity and justice for the alien, a further articulation of the gospel message itself.

Bibliography: E. EGAN, *For Whom There Is No Room: Scenes from the Refugee World* (New York, 1995) • C. ELSAS, *Ausländerarbeit* (Stuttgart, 1982) • E. G. FERRIS, *Beyond Borders: Refugees, Migrants, and Human Rights in the Post–Cold War Era* (Geneva, 1993) • A. JACQUES, *The Stranger within Your Gates: Uprooted People in the World Today* (Geneva, 1986) • J. H. SCHJØRRING, P. KUMARI, and N. A. HJELM, eds., *From Federation to Communion: The History of the Lutheran World Federation* (Minneapolis, 1997) chap. 3 • R. W. SOLBERG, *Open Doors: The Story of Lutherans Resettling Refugees* (St. Louis, 1992).

DENNIS W. FRADO

Forgiveness

1. Term and Problems
2. Biblical Data
3. Doctrinal Data
4. Ecumenical Discussion and Fresh Insights
5. Ethical Importance

1. Term and Problems

Forgiveness is the readiness to pardon faults (→ Guilt). More than restitution or repayment, it seeks to restore fellowship. The fifth petition of the → Lord's Prayer refers to it as something that God does and that we ought to do in return. But what does Christian forgiveness mean when seen in the light of social, political, philosophical, psychological, and religious theories for the overcoming of guilt? Our own dealing with guilt is confronted by the external pronouncement that the guilt of → sin against God and our neighbors is forgiven on the basis of the → reconciliation that has been made by Jesus Christ.

In Protestant → worship forgiveness is proclaimed to the congregation when members confess their sins in the context of proclamation of the Word and administration of the sacrament. This context gives a strong liturgical emphasis to forgiveness. In practice, however, do the liturgical forms adequately deal with the individual and social dimensions of guilt? A much debated question is whether a place and form for penance (→ Penitence) should be found in the → liturgy.

2. Biblical Data

2.1 The OT has a technical term for forgiveness (*slḥ*, in MT Exod. 34:9; Num. 30:6, 9; Deut. 29:19, etc.). Equivalent expressions also used include the covering over of sin (piel of *kpr*, Leviticus 4–5 etc., "make atonement for"), its removing (*nś'*, Lev. 10:17 etc.), its wiping or washing away, purifying, or not remembering it. These terms are mostly cultic. More spontaneous metaphoric expressions are also used. → Yahweh sets sins far away (Ps. 103:12, "as far as the east is from the west"); he puts them behind his back (Isa. 38:17); he casts them into the depths of the sea (Mic. 7:19); he heals people in an all-embracing way that includes dealing with their sin (Isa. 57:18; Jer. 3:22; Hos. 7:1; etc.).

The one who forgives is always God. Forgiveness is experienced in → prayer (→ Psalms), in penitential exercises, and in love of → neighbors. In the story of → Joseph as a paradigm of forgiveness, it still remains a gift of → Yahweh that can be sought and received directly from him or that can be granted by one human being to another as that one is moved by Yahweh's own previous acts of forgiveness.

Objectively, divinely ordained cultic forms are the means of forgiveness: the guilt offerings of Lev. 7:7, which are accompanied by restitution and often also fines, and the sin offerings of Lev. 4:1–5:13, which may be social as well as individual. On the Day of → Atonement the → high priest as a representative of the whole people offers expiation in the ritual of the scapegoat (Lev. 16; 23:27-32; Num. 29:7-11). The forgiving and merciful God is thus not just the God who appears first only in the NT. We also find that divine actions repay human deeds (see Jer. 51:56, where the noun *gĕmûlâ*, "recompense," is used together with the piel of *šlm*, "repay"), which can have the idea of restitution, not merely revenge. Forgiveness in the OT signifies a divine act in response to believers that brings liberation from sin, the pardoning of → punishment, and comprehensive restoration and renewal (J. J. Stamm).

2.2. In the NT the Synoptics and Acts in particular prefer the words *aphiēmi* and *aphesis*. Legally these words can mean, among other things, release from office, from → marriage, or from imprisonment, as well as release from guilt and punishment (R. Bultmann). → Paul and → John seldom make use of these terms. Paul thinks of forgiveness in

terms of → righteousness *(dikaiosunē)* and reconciliation *(katallagē)*. Hebrews and the Epistles of John think of it in terms of sanctifying *(hagiazō)* and purifying *(katharizō)*. Unlike *slḥ* in the OT, forgiveness in the NT can have a human subject.

Another NT feature is that full forgiveness can be given by → Jesus (Mark 2:5-12 and par.). Some critics do not think that the historical Jesus claimed this right, but instead that the → primitive Christian community found here a basis for its own practice (P. Fiedler). The historical Jesus, though, certainly came to gather and restore the lost sheep of Israel. His conduct, as well as his → proclamation, shows that forgiveness is central and not merely peripheral to his ministry. When he suffered, died, and was raised again as the Messiah (→ Christological Titles), the forgiveness he offers acquired a deeper meaning. He gave his life as a ransom for many (Mark 10:45). He was the Lamb of God (John 1:36), the suffering Servant (1 Pet. 2:21-24; → Servant of the Lord). Paul extends the theme of the → cross and → death in Romans 3–8 and Galatians 2–4. Hebrews refers to a once-for-all sacrifice for sin that he made as both → priest and victim (10:11-14).

A debated question is whether Paul took his view of reconciliation from the postexilic OT cult (H. Gese, B. Janowski), or whether he derived it from political views in the Hellenistic world (C. Breytenbach; → Hellenism). The central point, however, is that he linked forgiveness to the crucifixion and → resurrection of Jesus. This connection gave meaning to both → baptism (Acts 2:38) and the → Eucharist (Matt. 26:28). We also see evidence of it in early penitential practice (Matt. 16:18-19; 18:15-18; John 20:23; 1 Cor. 5:9-13). Sin and forgiveness affected the community profoundly. In experiencing forgiveness, the community was moved to seek it.

The binding and loosing of Matthew (→ Keys, Power of the) has a bearing on this issue. Loosing means freeing people completely from their sins, from the powers of the world, of sin, and of death. Binding seems to mean self-binding, that is, one's refusal to accept Christ's message. Reference to the unforgivable sin against the Holy Spirit (Matt. 12:30-32; Mark 3:28-29; Luke 12:10) stresses the definitive, eschatological significance of the mission of Jesus and is not to be associated with a specific situation of guilt.

3. Doctrinal Data

3.1. The → early church took over the penitential discipline of the NT and argued that excommunicated sinners could be readmitted to the church only after giving evidence of repentance. Adult baptism was a one-time act that conferred remission of sins and admission to the → church.

From the middle of the third century the church decided, in opposition to the ethically rigorous → Montanists and Novatianists, that there could be one possibility of coming back into the church after baptism: a second repentance (Shepherd of Hermas). The aim of this "second plank after shipwreck" was → reconciliation with the church and with God. Lengthy periods of penitential discipline were imposed. Sinners would then make an open → confession, and absolution would be given in the form "God absolves you" (as distinct from the medieval indicative form "I absolve you").

Such practice, however, lost its influence in the fifth and sixth centuries. Forgiveness came to be given with the → confession of sins shortly before → death, and if this step was not sufficient or was omitted, purification would come later (i.e., in → purgatory). → Excommunication was pronounced only for exceptional offenses such as → apostasy, murder, or adultery.

In the seventh century Irish missionaries introduced a new penitential system into everyday Christianity. Forgiveness now could be received on many occasions, and penitential books laid down what penances were to be imposed. The emphasis was no longer congregational and ecclesiological but individual and private. Personal confession was now made and absolution was granted — as long as the penances were fulfilled.

3.2. In later → Scholasticism forgiveness came to be focused on the → sacrament of penance. → Thomas Aquinas (ca. 1225-74; → Thomism) regarded remorse, confession, and satisfaction as the substance of the sacrament, with the word of absolution pronounced by the priest being the form. The result was the remission of sins.

From the 11th century onward → indulgences began to develop in both theory and practice. Divine forgiveness did not deal with all the consequences of sin. For oneself or for others, these temporal penalties could be dealt with on the basis of the treasury of merits of Christ and the saints, of which the church was manager and dispenser. By the 13th century indulgences had been separated from penance. Administered only by the → popes, they became a great source of papal revenue.

3.3. For M. → Luther (1483-1546; → Luther's Theology) forgiveness was the quintessence of the → gospel, the heart of the doctrine of → justification. Its basis was the "happy exchange" that took place when Christ took our guilt and sins to himself

and gave us his righteousness. Forgiveness does not come only through penance. It is a daily occurrence that can be experienced in reading the Bible, prayer, the sacraments, and preaching (see Luther's *Kurze Vermahnung zu der Beichte* [1529]). Since forgiveness is through Christ, it follows that the penitential discipline of the Middle Ages, and especially penance, does not have the same significance. There is no compulsion to go to auricular confession. Priestly absolution is not necessary, nor is an enumeration of sins. No distinction need be made between mortal and venial sins. The pastor is not a judge but one who proclaims the → grace of God. The stress is not on attrition and confession but on remission and → faith; no human satisfaction need be offered. The universal priesthood of all believers (→ Priest 4) means that all Christians can impart forgiveness. Nevertheless, since absolution is like "God's clear voice from heaven," it is best to treat penitence as a sacrament (Apology of the Augs. Conf. 12).

The → Reformed churches link forgiveness to → church discipline. U. → Zwingli (1484-1531; → Zwingli's Theology) found no place for auricular confession, but J. → Calvin (1509-64; → Calvin's Theology) did not wholly dismiss it. The repentance and faith of penitents cannot be known with certainty, and therefore absolution can be given only with reservations. The Anglican → Book of Common Prayer, which introduced a general confession, pronounced God's absolution and remission on "all them that truly repent and unfeignedly believe his holy Gospel." All the → Reformers believed that absolution did not differ essentially from the word of forgiveness that is proclaimed in → preaching.

3.4. Problems regarding the significance and extent of forgiveness began to arise in the → modern period. I. Kant regarded a vicarious satisfaction as contrary to human → autonomy. The authoritarian structure of penance also came into discredit, since it made us dependent on a foreign court. No place was found for a divine Judge, and sin came to be seen as involving only guilt between humans. The necessary striving for moral perfection that united → Pietism and the → Enlightenment worked against the pessimism of original sin and also against a forgiveness that washed away sin and was regarded as too cheap. The humanities now looked upon sin as social and related it to the → environment, so that it did not have to be forgiven but had to be "worked through" in some form. Thus, in the terms of K. → Marx, the autonomous social process can overcome the guilt of estrangement that is caused by the ruling class. Feelings of guilt might also be seen as illusory and neurotic; they have to be dealt with medically and therapeutically (S. Freud, A. Adler).

4. Ecumenical Discussion and Fresh Insights

With his stress on individual → responsibility, D. → Bonhoeffer (1906-45) in his *Nachfolge* (1937, ET *The Cost of Discipleship*) dismissed as "cheap grace" the idea that forgiveness is a general → truth or that it can be had without penitence, without auricular confession, or without → discipleship. P. → Tillich (1886-1965) viewed sin as alienation, which did not call for forgiveness but for healing and acceptance (*Systematic Theology*, vol. 2). Others have equated forgiveness with the overcoming of guilty structures (→ Liberation Theology; Feminist Theology; Depth-Psychological Exegesis).

A further problem is the way in which the sense of sin has been detached from transcendence (→ Immanence and Transcendence) or from its relation to God. The question arises whether, if sin involves guilt only in relation to others or to nature, we may still regard it as sin that only God can forgive. What about the relation between sin and the → law (Rom. 3:20; 7:7), which concerned Luther? Some, like W. Pannenberg, have pointed out that sin is a multiple phenomenon that only God can forgive. Others have begun with the pronouncement of the gospel and the experience of forgiveness, which alone shows us what sin really is (K. → Barth).

Another question is that of relating divine and human forgiveness today, as in the fifth petition of the Lord's Prayer. We have to ask concerning the place and circumstances of forgiveness in human life, especially in the church, and to show how God's forgiveness can help promote mature human love and autonomy (C. Gestrich). It is also important not to understand Christian forgiveness simply in moral categories but to give it an → aesthetic dimension as a "recurrence of radiance" in the midst of destruction, hate, and meaningless reality.

In the closing days of the 20th century, Roman Catholics and Protestants, looking back at 16th-century divisions, saw the need for a true view of forgiveness by looking at penitence from a social and ecclesiological standpoint rather than a private standpoint. Roman Catholics found a place for public celebrations of reconciliation, and Protestants saw that forgiveness must have an ethical side. An ecumenical commission on whether doctrinal condemnations really divide the church raised the question whether new views of justification might not allow of different forms of practice that do not involve condemnation (K. Lehmann and W. Pannenberg).

5. Ethical Importance

The insight is now commonly shared that forgiveness must be given an ecclesiological and social dimension as well as an individual dimension. Opposing guilt and sin, forgiveness has a specific function in all human relationships — in → families, in churches, and among nations, cultural → minorities, and social classes. Grounded in → baptism and pronounced in preaching, absolution, penance, and the sacrament, it is now given an increasingly ethical importance by theology. Thus in social and political → ethics it finds a place in penal reform (→ Punishment 1), in culprit-victim settlements, in negotiations for amnesty, in labor questions, and in international dealings. Forgiveness plays a role as a model of human behavior by vicariously accepting human faults and failings. It coordinates the structure of human personalities in their search for maturity and identity. Ecologically, it can help overturn embedded thinking and result in simplicity and self-control (→ Environment 2). All these ramifications rest on an adequate view of the forgiveness of sins and its hermeneutical application to modern conditions.

Bibliography: K. BARTH, *CD* III, IV • D. G. BENNER and R. W. HARVEY, *Understanding and Facilitating Forgiveness* (Grand Rapids, 1996) • C. BREYTENBACH, *Versöhnung. Eine Studie zur paulinischen Soteriologie* (Neukirchen, 1989) • R. BULTMANN, "Ἀφίημι, ἄφεσις, παρίημι, πάρεσις," *TDNT* 1.509-12 • M. COLLINS and D. POWER, eds., *The Fate of Confession* (Edinburgh, 1987) • P. FIEDLER, *Jesus und der Sünder* (Bern, 1976) • C. FLORISTÁN and C. DUQUOC, eds., *Forgiveness* (Edinburgh, 1986) • H. GESE, "Die Sühne," *Zur biblischen Theologie* (Munich, 1977) 85-106 • C. GESTRICH, "Ist die Beichte erneuerungsfähig?" *BTZ* 10 (1993) 187-96; idem, *The Return of Splendor in the World: The Christian Doctrine of Sin and Forgiveness* (Grand Rapids, 1997) • M. HENGEL, *The Atonement: The Origins of the Doctrine in the NT* (London, 1981) • B. JANOWSKI, *Sühne als Heilsgeschehen. Studien zur Sühnetheologie der Priesterschrift und zur Wurzel KPR im alten Orient und im Alten Testament* (Neukirchen, 1982) • G. L. JONES, *Embodying Forgiveness: A Theological Analysis* (Grand Rapids, 1995) • J. LAFITTE, *Le pardon transfiguré* (Paris, 1995) • K. LEHMANN and W. PANNENBERG, eds., *Lehrverurteilungen–kirchentrennend?* vol. 1, *Rechtfertigung, Sakramente und Amt* (Freiburg, 1986) • K. MENNINGER, *Whatever Became of Sin?* (New York, 1974) • M. MINOW, *Between Vengeance and Forgiveness: Facing History after Genocide and Mass Violence* (Boston, 1998) • J. MUELLER, *Is Forgiveness Possible?* (Collegeville, Minn., 1998) • W. PANNENBERG, *System-*

atic Theology (vol. 2; Grand Rapids, 1994) • M. S. PEEK, *People of the Lie: The Hope for Healing Human Evil* (New York, 1983) • T. PETERS, *Radical Evil in Soul and Society* (Grand Rapids, 1994) • J. P. PINGLETON, "Why We Don't Forgive: A Biblical and Object Relations Theoretical Model for Understanding Failures in the Forgiveness Process," *JPsT* 25 (1997) 403-13 • D. W. SHRIVER, *An Ethic for Enemies: Forgiveness in Politics* (New York, 1995) • J. J. STAMM, "סלח slḥ vergeben," *THAT* 2.150-60 • J. ZEHNER, *Das Forum der Vergebung in der Kirche. Studien zum Verhältnis von Sündenvergebung und Recht* (Gütersloh, 1998).

CHRISTOF GESTRICH and JOACHIM ZEHNER

Formula of Concord

1. Background
2. Development
3. Evaluation

1. Background

The Book of Concord (1580), as a collection of the most important 16th-century Lutheran confessional writings (→ Confessions and Creeds), has formal validity to this day in most → Lutheran churches. The final text in that collection, the Formula of Concord (1577), by claiming to repeat and explain the → Augsburg Confession, using both affirmation ("we believe, teach, and confess . . .") and negation ("we reject and condemn . . ."), defines afresh the main articles of the Christian religion as M. → Luther (1483-1546), P. → Melanchthon (1497-1560), and other Reformers expounded them.

Already for Luther, the union of confession and doctrine implied a break with the papacy (→ Roman Catholic Church), with the → Anabaptists and other → "spiritualist" reformers, with humanistic reformers (→ Humanism), with the Swiss reformers, and with Upper German mediators (→ Luther's Theology; Confession of Faith). After Luther's death and the defeat of the evangelicals in the Schmalkaldic War (1547), Melanchthon's attempts at compromise with the religious policy of the empire (called the Interim) provoked resistance to perceived theological vacillation and the actual restoration of traditional ceremonies. Before the judgment seat of Christ, so all sides believed, the fight for pure doctrine was essential for the sake of → assurance of salvation. The conjoining of historical, eschatological, and doctrinal elements explains the seriousness of the conflict. Issues concerning a person being "guilty of sin and subject to death" and the fact that "God is the Justifier and Re-

deemer" (*LW* 12.311-12) needed clarification in this new situation. As a result, the end of the Interim in 1552 and the recognition of the Augsburg Confession in the Peace of Augsburg (1555; → Augsburg, Peace of) brought no real settlement to the theological debates begun after 1548.

2. Development

2.1. In the → synergistic controversy (from 1555; → Synergism), J. Pfeffinger (1493-1573), following his teacher Melanchthon, championed the part played by the human will in conversion. In the Majorist Controversy (after 1551), G. Major (1502-74) taught the necessity of good works in the process of → salvation. In opposition, N. von Amsdorf (1483-1565) pointed to the soteriological perniciousness of this teaching. In the debate about synergism V. Strigel (1524-69) interpreted original sin as an "accident" covering over a good nature, but M. Flacius (1520-75), employing Luther's language, defined it as "substantial form" *(forma substantialis)*. The Antinomians (A. Poach, A. Otho, A. Musculus) also appealed to Luther in their rejection of the third use of the → law (→ Antinomian Controversies). In the Osiandrian controversy (after 1550) Melanchthon and the → Gnesio-Lutherans set the alien → righteousness of Christ, which we grasp by → faith, and thus the → obedience of the whole person to Christ, in antithesis to A. Osiander's (1496/98-1552) separation of historical redemption on the cross and present → justification by the divine nature of Christ dwelling in us.

The eucharistic controversy (→ Eucharist 3.3) initiated by J. Westphal (ca. 1510-74) was directed against the modified Zwinglianism of J. → Calvin (1509-64) and other Reformed theologians from Germany. The Lutherans insisted on the words of institution and the concrete presence of Christ's body and blood, though successors to Melanchthon at the University of Wittenberg (→ Crypto-Calvinism) argued for an actualized presence dependent on faith. Along the lines suggested by the northern Germans J. Timann (before 1500-1557) and J. Bötker (1490-1564), J. Brenz (1499-1570) related the presence to the participation of Christ's humanity in his omnipotent and omnipresent deity (Stuttgart Confession [1559], cf. Luther). The Gnesio-Lutherans, such as M. Chemnitz (1522-86), accepted this view only hesitantly. The Strasbourg predestinarian controversy (→ Predestination), which pitted the thesis of H. Zanchi (1516-90) that grace cannot be lost against the contrary view of J. Marbach (1521-81), provisionally included the similar formula of J. Andreae (1528-90).

Questions of → anthropology, the communication of salvation, the → Eucharist, and → Christology could not be answered simply by citing the Augsburg Confession, especially as article 10 of the Variata of 1540 (→ Corpora doctrinae) had narrowed the statement about the real presence to correspond with the 1536 Wittenberg Concord. The efforts of the princes to achieve an agreed formula also failed. The Frankfurt Compact of 1558, appealing to a Melanchthonian interpretation of justification, works, Eucharist, and → adiaphora, and the attempt by the Naumburg Convention (1561) to accept the Variata along with the combined German and Latin text of Augsburg provoked opposition (the Weimar Confutation of 1559 and the Lüneburg *Confessio Saxonica* of 1561).

A later phase resulted in territorial agreements that consisted mainly of collections of texts. The *Corpus doctrinae Misnicum/Philippicum* of 1560 was accepted in Pomerania (1561) and electoral Saxony (1566). Lübeck (1560) added the Schmalkald Articles to the Augsburg Confession and the Apology, along with earlier works against the Interim, Osiander, Major, and the Sacramentarians. J. Mörlin's (1514-71) *Brunswick corpus doctrinae* (1563) and the *Prutenicum* were more strictly Gnesio-Lutheran.

2.2. J. Andreae prepared the way to a solution with his five-article "Confession and Brief Explanation" — on justification, good works, free will, adiaphora, and the Eucharist. He failed to allay the mistrust of Gnesio-Lutherans such as T. Hesshusen (1527-88), especially as Melanchthon's Wittenberg disciples gave only halfhearted approval. He thus replaced the articles with a broader agreement (1570) combining the Augsburg Confession, the Apology, the Schmalkaldic Articles, and Luther's catechisms, but when electoral Saxony wished to add the Philippicum, paralysis resulted, in spite of the readiness of southern Germany to subscribe. Andreae succeeded at his next attempt (1573), when in *Six Sermons on the Divisions* he presented the Lutheran understanding of justification, good works, original sin and synergism, → law and gospel, and the person of Christ.

Duke Julius of Wolfenbüttel (1568-89) referred Andreae to Chemnitz for advice as to revision. The result was the Swabian Concord — dealing with original sin, free will, law and gospel, the third use of the law, adiaphora, the Eucharist, the person of Christ, and God's eternal providence and election — which was sent to Julius in 1574. Chemnitz then initiated in northern Germany a process of further consultation and revision in which the Rostock faculty played a leading part. He himself put the articles in scholarly form, while D. Chyträus

(1531-1600) of Rostock wrote the articles on free will and the Eucharist, giving them an ethical and personal accent, extending the eucharistic presence to the whole eucharistic act, and positing voluntary limitation of the communication of attributes between divinity and humanity in Christ.

Sent to Württemberg in 1575, the Swabian-Saxon Concord came into a changed theological and political situation. The Philippist Crypto-Calvinism had collapsed in 1574, and electoral Saxony was more ready for compromise. Würtemberg did, however, draw up its own Maulbronn Formula, with emphasis on the third use of the law and less place for synergism in anthropology and → soteriology, though still with references in the preface to Melanchthon. Andreae himself preferred this statement, but he commended the Swabian-Saxon Concord to Elector Augustus (1553-86) as a basis for further conversations.

Andreae, Chemnitz, Chyträus, N. Selnecker (1530-92), C. Korner (1518-94), and A. Musculus (1514-81) took part in the decisive Torgau negotiations of 1576. Musculus successfully opposed the third use of the law, Chyträus defended the slightly synergistic trend in free will, two Luther quotations strengthened the Christology, and a stricter Lutheranism was accentuated by use of the Maulbronn introduction. When conflict arose in Hamburg regarding J. Aepin's (1499-1553) view of the → descent into hell, an article was added that included reference to M. → Luther's Torgau sermon of 1533 (WA 37.62.30–67.2), which described the descent as a victory over → hell, → death, and the → devil.

Discussions in Bergen Abbey (1577) involved exchanges on the Torgau Book. In article 7 on the Eucharist, Chyträus unsuccessfully opposed linking the eucharistic presence to the ubiquity of Christ's humanity. He also had to accept the reduction of Melanchthonian expressions in the articles on original sin (art. 1), free will (2), justification (3), and good works (4). Musculus still had doubts about article 2, though the independent cooperation of the human will was now denied. On May 29, 1577, all six signed the 12 articles of what came to be the Formula of Concord's Solid Declaration; the Epitome, which had been prepared by Andreae, was also accepted as the first part of the formula.

Andreae's preface, in accordance with the irenic wishes of Ludwig VI of the Palatinate (1576-83), was designed to win over hesitant rulers and theologians and to allay imperial suspicion that this was a new confession involving change from the Augsburg Confession itself. The full Book of Concord was ready for the 50th anniversary of the Augsburg Confession in 1580. As the *corpus doctrinae* of most Protestant churches of the empire, it contained the three early, "ecumenical" creeds (Apostles', Nicene, and Athanasian), the Augsburg Confession (1530), the Apology of the Augsburg Confession (1531), Luther's Schmalkaldic Articles (1537), Melanchthon's *Treatise on the Power and Primacy of the Pope* (1537), Luther's Small and Large Catechisms (1529), and the Formula of Concord.

In response to Calvinizing opposition (e.g., in *Admonitio neostadiana*) and Philippist resistance (centered in Anhalt, Bremen, Hesse, and Holstein), and in debate with followers of Flacius, T. Kirchner (1533-87), Selnecker, and Chemnitz defended the Formula of Concord in a 15-chapter apology (Heidelberg, 1583; Dresden, 1584). On the basis of work by L. Osiander (1534-1604) and H. Heerbrand (1521-1600), the Formula of Concord was translated into Latin by Selnecker in 1580 and more fully by Chemnitz in 1584.

3. Evaluation

The Formula of Concord sums up the results of the Lutheran → Reformation (§3) with theological precision, even though it limits the wealth of Luther's own experience and moderates the antithetical dynamic of his theology (e.g., his doctrine of the *Deus absconditus*). Without the ecclesial shape and the cultural force that the Lutheran Reformation received from the Formula of Concord, it would have devolved into warring territorial churches and would have been lost in the wake of the → Thirty Years' War, the resurgence of Roman Catholicism (→ Catholic Reform and Counterreformation), and the "second reformation" of German Calvinism. To that extent, we may say that the ecumenical presence of the Lutheran Reformation today is due to the Formula of Concord.

Bibliography: Primary sources: BSLK 735-1100 • R. KOLB and T. J. WENGERT, eds., *The Book of Concord: The Confessions of the Evangelical Lutheran Church* (Minneapolis, 2000) 481-660.

Secondary works: J. BAUR, "Christologie und Subjektivität. Geschichtlicher Ort und dogmatischer Rang der Christologie der Konkordienformel," *Einsicht und Glaube* (Göttingen, 1978) 189-205; idem, *Wahrheit der Väter–Hilfe für morgen, 400 Jahre Konkordienformel* (Stuttgart, 1977) • H. C. BRANDY, "J. Andreaes Fünf Artikel von 1568/69," *ZKG* 98 (1987) 338-51 • M. BRECHT and R. SCHWARZ, eds., *Bekenntnis und Einheit der Kirche. Studien zum Konkordienbuch* (Stuttgart, 1980) • J. B. CARPZOV, *Isagoge in libros ecclesiarum lutheranorum symbolicos* (Leipzig, 1665; 2d ed., 1675) • I. DINGEL, *Concordia controversa. Die öffentlichen Diskussionen um das lutherische Konkordienwerk am Ende des 16. Jahrhunderts* (Gütersloh, 1996) • J. C. EBEL, *Wort und Geist bei den Verfassern der Konkordienformel* (Munich, 1981) • L. C. GREEN, *The Formula of Concord: An Historiographical and Bibliographical Guide* (St. Louis, 1977) • A. J. KOELPIN, ed., *No Other Gospel: Essays in Commemoration of the 400th Anniversary of the Formula of Concord, 1580-1980* (Milwaukee, Wis., 1980) • R. KOLB, *Andreae and the Formula of Concord: Six Sermons on the Way to Lutheran Unity* (St. Louis, 1977); idem, *Confessing the Faith: Reformers Define the Church, 1530-1580* (St. Louis, 1991) • B. LOHSE, "Das Konkordienbuch," *HDThG* 2.138-64 • I. MAGER, "J. Andreaes lateinische Unionsartikel von 1568," *ZKG* 98 (1987) 70-86 • L. W. SPITZ and W. LOHFF, eds., *Discord, Dialogue, and Concord: Studies in the Lutheran Reformation's Formula of Concord* (Philadelphia, 1977) • G. WENZ, *Theologie der Bekenntnisschriften der evangelisch-lutherischen Kirche* (2 vols.; Berlin, 1996-98) vol. 2, *Einführung in das Konkordienbuch*.

JÖRG BAUR, with TIMOTHY J. WENGERT

Fortune-Telling → Divination

France

1. The Church in France
    1.1. Roman Catholic Church
    1.2. Protestant Church
    1.3. Free Churches
    1.4. Orthodox Church
2. Interchurch Relations and Cooperation
    2.1. Inter-Protestant
    2.2. Protestant and Catholic
    2.3. National Council of Churches
3. State and Church
    3.1. General
    3.2. Alsace-Lorraine
4. Non-Christian Religions
    4.1. Islam
    4.2. Judaism

1. The Church in France

It is hard to say how many of the nearly 60 million people in France belong to a church, for official statistics do not list church membership. The largest church, the Roman Catholic, is uncertain of its own precise membership. There are no church taxes (→ Church Finances), nor is there legal membership (→ Church Membership). If we take → baptism as a standard, then most people (80 percent) belong to

	1960	1980	2000
Population (1,000s):	45,684	53,880	59,061
Annual growth rate (%):	1.30	0.47	0.18

Area: 543,965 sq. km. (210,026 sq. mi.)

A.D. 2000

Population density: 109/sq. km. (281/sq. mi.)
Births / deaths: 1.11 / 0.96 per 100 population
Fertility rate: 1.63 per woman
Infant mortality rate: 6 per 1,000 live births
Life expectancy: 79.4 years (m: 75.4, f: 83.3)
Religious affiliation (%): Christians 70.6 (Roman Catholics 83.0, indigenous 2.3, Protestants 1.6, unaffiliated 1.4, Orthodox 1.2, other Christians 0.7), nonreligious 15.4, Muslims 7.0, atheists 4.3, Jews 1.0, other 1.7.

the church. Even anticlericalists want their children baptized, and the church does not refuse them. Otherwise, however, only about 50 percent of the people make use of the church's ministry and maintain their allegiance to it, while only a small portion of this 50 percent (variously estimated between 5 and 30 percent) takes an active part in church life. The modern wave of → secularism is less immediately obvious than in other European countries, since the process of → secularization began in France many years before it became a fact in other countries.

In describing the state of Christianity in France today, geography is important. The churches are still strong in the west and east of France (Brittany and Alsace-Lorraine), claiming the allegiance of about 80 percent of the local population. An area from Switzerland to Spain (the Jura range, northern Alps, Rhone valley, Cévennes, and Pyrenees) is mostly Christian in observance. Many other parts of the country are indifferent to the Christian tradition, with Christians constituting less than 30 percent of the population in some districts.

A new interest in religion and religious questions has been growing for some time in France, stirred up by the economic crisis, anxiety about the future, and the loss of traditional values. Evangelical and Pentecostal churches (see 1.3) have shown a lively growth. So have other religious movements (including the → Church of Scientology, the → Unification Church, and Asian religions) and such parareligious activities as astrology. France is now home to more fortune-tellers than Christian priests and pastors.

1.1. Roman Catholic Church

The Christian presence in France began in the first century with a church founded in the Roman port of Massilia (Marseilles). The French Roman Catholic Church, which rightly has been called the eldest daughter of the church, has written decisive chapters on church history as a whole and even today continues as an important social force. By nature (→ Catholicism [Roman]), it is strictly hierarchical in structure, with 28 archbishops, 180 bishops, 28,000 priests, and many catechists serving the church's more than 30,000 parishes (1999). As in other countries, there is a national bishops' conference, which meets annually in Lourdes. Since the church depends on gifts from its members, stipends are small, and there are few assistants.

The French Roman Catholic Church has always been closely linked to → Rome. This relationship has led to a generally conservative attitude, which is apparent in the more recent position statements (e.g., regarding disarmament in 1985) and in → popular religion (e.g., → Lourdes as a place of pilgrimage). Yet the church has also always shown its independence, from the Middle Ages (e.g., in → Gallicanism) to the modern period. In the 19th century the Ultramontane party got the upper hand. In the 20th century many pioneering initiatives took place: lay movements arose that sought to bring laity to take their full share in the life of the church and nation; the often-noted "worker-priests" attempted to reach out to the working class, which was lost to the Christian faith in the 19th century; and new ground was broken in the fields of biblical studies and theology. Some French theologians were experts (periti) at → Vatican II. Nevertheless, a conservative movement, drawing in part on discontent caused by the enforcement of liturgical reforms decided upon by Vatican II, is growing in strength. The younger generation of priests is identified largely with this trend.

In the late 1990s the religious orders had 80,000 members (15,000 men and 65,000 women). Nuns who are not confined to life in their monasteries serve in hospitals, engage in social work, or take up catechetical tasks. Men and women, lay and ordained, control the church's educational work, including schools and universities, which train approximately 20 percent of the nation's young people. The more intellectual orders (esp. → Jesuits and → Dominicans) also engage in theological research. Young people have shown a new interest in the monastic life (to which 1,600 men and 8,000 women have devoted themselves), especially as inspired by the charismatic movement.

1.2. Protestant Church

The Protestant churches encompass only a small minority of France's population (less than one million). For the Lutheran and the Reformed communities (→ Lutheran Churches; Reformed and Presbyterian Churches), distinctions follow confessional, geographic, and cultural lines.

1.2.1. The Reformed churches go back to John Calvin (1509-64; → Calvinism). Before they were outlawed in 1685, they were territorial churches in certain areas of the southeast, the southwest and west, and the east of France. After a century of life underground (1685-1789), the Reformed believers had, by the 19th century, become the majority in rural areas such as the Cévennes and the Rhone valley, as well as in the southwest (Béarn, Tarn, Poitou) and in Normandy. With the flow of population from the countryside to the towns, the Reformed have mainly become middle class and are largely scattered throughout the whole of France. Life in diaspora is common, even though there remain some significant territorial churches in districts where the Reformed presence has been unbroken since the Reformation.

For historical reasons that go back to the 19th and 20th centuries, there are now three Reformed churches. The Église Réformée de France (ERF) is the largest Protestant church in France (400,000 members, 580 pastors, 1,000 places of worship). It was formed in 1938 by the union of several churches and covers the whole country except for Alsace-Lorraine. Throughout the country many departments contain one or two ERF churches. The church is divided into eight regions and is governed by a synod, a national council, and a president.

A second church is the Église Réformée d'Alsace et de Lorraine (ERAL, 30,000 members, 53 pastors, 70 places of worship). The ERAL is de facto the ninth region of the ERF, but it is an established church (see 3.2). Its members come partly from the old Reformed tradition of eastern France, but there are also newcomers from central France (typically in industry and the professions). Links to the ERF are close.

A third Reformed church is the Églises Réformées Évangéliques Indépendantes (EREI, 15,000 members in 45 congregations). After the union that produced the ERF, the EREI arose as a conservative group in southern France that wanted to retain unchanged the statement of faith of 1872. → Union with liberal Reformed who did not feel bound by any confession (→ Confessions and Creeds) was found to be impossible. The EREI maintains a theological faculty of the Reformed tradition at Aix-en-Provence.

1.2.2. The Lutheran churches are territorial and are closely linked to the large Lutheran churches of Europe. Almost all the Lutherans (95 percent) live in eastern France. The various Lutheran churches work together in the Alliance Nationale des Églises Luthériennes de France (ANELF). The Église de la Confession d'Augsbourg d'Alsace et de Lorraine (ECAAL), a union of various churches from the time of Napoléon (1802), has 200,000 members, 248 pastors, and 500 places of worship. This church is an established church (see 3.2). It consists of seven inspectorates led by spiritual inspectors, who have a right to ordain. The synod is the chief court. Administrative leadership falls to the directory and its president (usually lay). The general picture resembles that of the Protestant → people's churches of central Europe. The language of worship used to be mainly German but now, in 80 percent of the churches, is French. The state pays the ministers' stipends, but the church must finance everything else. Many → church employees serve without compensation. The church does a good deal of diaconal work; in missions, it works closely with mission organizations in Germany (Hermannsburg) and Switzerland (Basel; → French Missions).

Lutherans outside Alsace and Lorraine belong to the Église Évangélique Luthérienne de France (EELF, 40,000 members, 48 pastors, 70 places of worship). This group has two inspectorates. The first is that of Montbéliard, an area once in Württemberg south of Alsace. The church is in a difficult situation here and has few resources. The economic crisis of the late 20th century hit the district and the church hard (most of the members being workers for Peugeot). The second inspectorate, Paris, has 10,000 members. This church was founded by immigrants, first in the 17th century from Sweden, then from Germany and Alsace. It has 13 pastors. It lays great stress on missionary work and on its Lutheran identity (→ Evangelism; Inner Mission; Lutheranism). Two small congregations in Lyons and Nice were founded from Paris.

1.2.3. Various communities have been founded by the Reformed and Lutheran churches (→ Communities, Spiritual). The best known is that of → Taizé, which is now interdenominational and maintains little contact with the Protestant church. The women's community of Pomeyrol (Arles) is an important spiritual center for the whole church. The same is true of communities that arose out of deaconess houses (Reuilly-Versailles, Erckartswiller-Neuenberg, Hohrodberg) or that are small, new foundations (Caulmont, Charme, Valleraugue).

1.3. *Free Churches*

The Protestant → free churches are becoming more important. They are called free because, in the 19th century, they were not established churches. Now, apart from the departments of Alsace and Moselle, all churches share the same status in France and could therefore also be described as free.

1.3.1. Some of these free churches belong to the Protestant federation (see 2.1), including the → Baptists (72 congregations), Gypsy Mission (50 congregations), Apostolic Church (10 congregations), and Église de Dieu en France (10 congregations). The vibrant congregational life of these groups, marked as it is by → pietistic spirituality, attracts young people from traditional Protestant churches, but especially from Roman Catholic and secular circles.

1.3.2. The same is true of free churches that do not belong to the federation. Some of these have a long history (→ Friends, Society of; Mennonites; Methodist Churches; Salvation Army). Others are new and are growing rapidly (e.g., the Pentecostals, from 50 groups in 1942 to 1,500 in 1998; → Pentecostal Churches). Many are divided, and some develop into sects. Since there are no official statistics, it is hard to be precise.

1.4. *Orthodox Church*

The Orthodox Church (180,000 total members, plus a higher number of those affiliated with it) belongs to the worldwide Orthodox Communion, though in France it is divided among the various national Orthodox churches. The Patriarchate of Constantinople is represented by a Greek Orthodox metropolitan church (Paris and Marseilles). In Paris there is also an autocephalous Ukrainian church and a Serbian church (→ Autocephaly). The largest group is the Russian Orthodox, most of whom belong to the former Russian exarchate of the Patriarchate of Constantinople. Others are affiliated with the Moscow exarchate for western Europe, the Orthodox Church with Western Rite (Russian synod), or the Romanian Orthodox Church. The Orthodox center St. Serge (Paris) gives theological instruction to students from all the churches.

2. Interchurch Relations and Cooperation

2.1. *Inter-Protestant*

The Fédération Protestante de France (FPF) is the meeting ground of the Lutheran, Reformed, and other Protestant churches in France, as well as of the charities, adult and youth movements, and (what is now fairly significant in France) the varous societies and communities that claim to be Protestant. Founded in 1905, the FPF was led by Marc Boegner from 1929 to 1961. In spite of its scattered nature and financial weakness, Protestantism does a good deal of diaconal work (e.g., Mission Populaire Évangélique, CIMADE, Fondation John Bost). The

federation's positions on social and political issues attract considerable national attention (e.g., with its *Église et pouvoirs* [1972] and *Commerce des armes et force de frappe* [1973]). The federation is not a doctrinal union, but its member churches have agreed to share the Eucharist with one another. The FPF now has the overall responsibility for representing the Protestant churches in their relationships with the other churches in France as well as with international church organizations.

The Lutheran and Reformed churches (apart from those in EREI; see 1.2) have set up a common standing council, the Conseil Permanent Luthéro-Réformé (CPLR). Theological conversations led in 1964 to the Thèses de Lyon (which included agreement on Scripture, baptism, and the Lord's Supper), which was a precursor to the far broader → Leuenberg Agreement, accepted in 1973. Between these churches there is pulpit and table fellowship (→ Eucharist 5). In 1996 these churches declared ecclesiastical fellowship with the European Methodists, and in 1999 they subscribed to the Reuilly Agreement, which establishes fellowship in both Word and sacrament with the British Anglicans. The CPLR engages in ecumenical → dialogue with the Roman Catholic Church (see 2.2).

Theology is taught in the state Theological Faculty of the University of Strasbourg and in the two free faculties of Paris and Montpellier under the control of the Institut Protestant de Théologie, which is itself directly responsible to the EELF and the ERF. The evangelical churches and the Mennonites share the Free Theological Faculty of Vaux-sur-Seine. The Theological Faculty of Aix-en-Provence, linked to the EREI, claims to be strictly faithful to orthodox Calvinism.

The Lutheran and Reformed churches (including those in EREI) and the Baptist churches share a common missionary service and belong to the Communauté Évangélique d'Action Apostolique (CEVAA), a worldwide fellowship of mainly, but not exclusively, French- and English-speaking churches generally related historically to the Paris Mission.

Several free churches (including Baptists, Mennonites, and Methodists) have formed the Association d'Églises de Professants des Pays Francophones (including Belgium and Switzerland). This union maintains a free theological faculty in Vaux-sur-Seine.

2.2. *Protestant and Catholic*

Ecumenical contacts have been growing in significance (→ Ecumenism, Ecumenical Movement; Local Ecumenism) and in some places have led to common activities between Protestant and Roman Catholic parishes. The Bible is often an effective meeting ground. Realities of the quite uneven majority-minority relation between Catholics and Protestants, however, do not make things easy, even though in some areas all the Christians together form but a minority of the population. The Roman Catholic bishops appoint a full-time priest to oversee ecumenical relations on the national level; the FPF appoints his counterpart. An ecumenical theological dialogue takes place in a so-called Mixed Committee, the members of which are appointed by the Roman Catholic bishops and the CPLR.

The noninstitutional Groupe des Dombes (including Roman Catholic, Reformed, and Lutheran theologians) has an international reputation for its research and discussions on the Eucharist, orders, the episcopal office, the Holy Spirit, Mary, the sacraments, and the Petrine office.

2.3. *National Council of Churches*
In 1985 the Roman Catholic Church proposed the founding of a → National Council of Churches. It was formed and today includes all Christian churches at the national level.

3. State and Church
3.1. *General*
France, with its king, was a Roman Catholic country linked to the Roman See by the Concordat of Bologna (1516), a reality that was accentuated after the revocation of the Edict of Nantes in 1685. This situation persisted up to the French Revolution, at the end of the 18th century. A few years later, after Napoléon had seized power, a new concordat was signed with Rome (1801), but Roman Catholicism then had to share the status of recognized religion with the Reformed and Lutheran churches and with Judaism. All four bodies were governed by the Organic Articles of 1802.

A movement opposed to all links between religious organizations and the state, including schools, as well as social and medical institutions (the *mouvement laïc*), claimed that religion was a private matter and that the state itself should remain strictly neutral in all matters concerning personal belief and worship. This movement also asserted that such neutrality did not apply to ethics, which should be taught in schools. The outcome of the political victory of the "laics" at the end of the 19th century was the disestablishment of all religious organizations in 1905. Since then, the law prohibits the state from recognizing or subsidizing any religion.

There was strong opposition by the Roman Catholic Church to the whole idea of a neutral state. The common effort to win the war of 1914-18, however, reconciled Roman Catholicism and republican France. Since that time there has been general agreement concerning neutrality on the part of the state in respect to all matters of religion.

The churches, however, are not without influence. They speak out on public issues, and the voice of the Roman Catholic Church especially is of some importance in the life of the nation. Church schools are highly rated, and an attempt in 1984 to nationalize them was generally understood to be a threat to the freedom of education, leading to public demonstrations and the ultimate withdrawal of the proposal.

3.2. *Alsace-Lorraine*
In Alsace-Lorraine the church remains linked to the state by the Napoleonic Concordat, for this area was in German hands in 1905, and the situation was not adjusted after 1918. An attempt to do so in 1924 led to the fall of the government, and the status quo has continued unchanged. Pastors and priests are appointed by the state (through the prime minister on the advice of the church) and are paid as state officials. The churches have access to public services (education in the school, hospital chaplaincies, etc.). At Strasbourg the state supports Roman Catholic and Protestant faculties of theology. The church has varying amounts of freedom according to the will of the government in power.

4. Non-Christian Religions
4.1. *Islam*
With somewhat over 4 million adherents → Islam is the second largest religious group in France. Most Muslims have immigrated from the former French colonies in North Africa. Also many Asian groups (esp. from Iran) have sought asylum in France. A quarter of these have connections with the main body of Islam. The Christian churches are concerned to establish relations with Islam (→ Islam and Christianity).

4.2. *Judaism*
There are over 500,000 adherents of → Judaism in Paris, northeastern France, and the Mediterranean area. They typically belong to higher social strata (commerce, banking, etc.). In the cities they have their own schools. The concordat in Alsace-Lorraine applies not only to Christians but also to the Jewish community. Many new → synagogues were founded after 1945. Paris is the seat of the General Council of French Jews.

Bibliography: Y. M. BERCÉ, *The Birth of Absolutism: A History of France, 1598-1661* (New York, 1996) • S. A. CURTIS, *Educating the Faithful: Religion, Schooling, and*

Society in Nineteenth-Century France (DeKalb, Ill., 2000) • *Deux mille ans de christianisme* (10 vols.; Paris, 1975-1976) • C. ELWOOD, *The Body Broken: The Calvinist Doctrine of the Eucharist and the Symbolization of Power in Sixteenth-Century France* (New York, 1999) • *Histoire des protestants de France* (Toulouse, 1977) • M. P. HOLT, *The French Wars of Religion, 1562-1629* (New York, 1995) • D. K. VAN KLEY, *The Religious Origins of the French Revolution: From Calvin to the Civil Constitution* (New Haven, 1996) • M. LARKIN, *Religion, Politics, and Preferment in France since 1890: La Belle Epoque and Its Legacy* (New York, 1995) • F. LEBRUN, ed., *Histoire des catholiques en France* (Toulouse, 1980) • K. McQUILLAN, *Culture, Religion, and Demographic Behaviour: Catholics and Lutherans in Alsace, 1750-1870* (Liverpool, 1999) • A. MITCHELL, *Victors and Vanquished: The German Influence on Army and Church in France after 1870* (Chapel Hill, N.C., 1984) • E. RAPLEY, *The Dévotes: Women and Church in Seventeenth-Century France* (Montreal, 1990) • N. L. ROELKER, *One King, One Faith: The Parlement of Paris and the Religious Reformations of the Sixteenth Century* (Berkeley, Calif., 1996).

ANDRÉ BIRMELÉ and JEAN-PIERRE MONSARRAT†

Francis of Assisi

Francis of Assisi (1181/82-1226), baptized Giovanni Bernardone, was the founder of the → Franciscan Order. The son of a wealthy cloth merchant, Peter Bernardone, and his French wife, Pica, Francis experienced the kind of wild youth appropriate for a later saint. After participating in a war between his hometown Assisi and Perugia in 1202 and being held captive for a year, and after a lengthy illness, he underwent a → conversion (§1) during the years 1204-7, the details of which are difficult to understand. In his testament Francis recounts an ascetically motivated encounter with lepers that was extremely unpleasant and repugnant to him. When he left the lepers, God transformed that bitter disgust into a sweetness filling both body and soul, after which Francis felt himself to be a new person free of sinfulness (→ New Self). Later vitae and legends speak of a conversion process accompanied by → visions. The witness of St. Clare (founder of the Poor Clares) is also of significance, for beginning in 1212 she and several female companions tried to live a life according to Francis's model. She recounts the story of the speaking crucifix of the church of St. Damiano, which charged Francis with rebuilding the church.

Francis quarreled with his father and, choosing the → ascetic way of life, placed himself under the protection of the church authorities. In 1207, at the invitation of the → bishop, Francis broke publicly and dramatically with his father (taking off his clothes and giving them to his father). He then was able to begin his life of → penitence, apparently with the bishop's permission. Francis and his companions wandered around barefoot and shabbily clothed, trying in this way to live the apostolic life according to the Gospels. In about 1209 he went to Rome and received the → pope's confirmation of the *Regula primitiva* of his society. Close association with the → curia, which Francis did not oppose, also resulted in his order having a → cardinal as protector from 1220 — Ugolino of Segni, the future Pope Gregory IX.

Francis's society quickly grew beyond the boundaries of both Umbria and Italy, albeit not without problems and tensions. In 1219, after a failed attempt in 1212-13, Francis followed the → crusader army to Egypt, where he allegedly preached before the sultan, apparently without success. He returned in 1220. A serious eye ailment was a factor in his handing over day-to-day leadership of the brothers to Peter Cathanii (d. 1221) and then Elias of Cortona. In 1221 Francis had a second version of the rule drawn up and confirmed by the pope, the *Regula non bullata*. In 1223 Pope Honorius III confirmed by a papal → bull the final revision of the rule, the *Regula bullata*. Toward the end of his life, Francis was increasingly marginalized within his order, ultimately withdrawing into seclusion on the mountain retreat of La Verna (Alvernia). There in 1224 occurred the mysterious → stigmatization, with Francis receiving in his body a reproduction of the wounds of the passion of Christ (the first known such experience). Francis died on October 3, 1226 (feast day: October 4).

In his final testament, Francis charged his companions and successors with following literally and without change in interpretation the rule given him by God, though he did not distinguish between the various versions of his rule. In 1230 Gregory IX declared this testament invalid in the bull *Quo elongati*.

Francis wanted to live in the → discipleship of Christ according to the Gospels. In its various versions, his rule serves to articulate this form of life in the sense of dramatic ascetic poverty and → humility, with which he associated an unconditional demand for → obedience. As revealed in various letters, prayers, and hymns (e.g., "Song of the Sun"), the center of Francis's piety includes the joyous praise of God by all creatures, worship of Christ, and a strongly accentuated veneration of the → sacraments.

Bibliography: H. Feld, *Franziskus von Assisi und seine Bewegung* (Darmstadt, 1994) • A. Haase, *Swimming in the Sun: Discovering the Lord's Prayer with Francis of Assisi and Thomas Merton* (Cincinnati, 1993) • A. M. Kleinberg, *Prophets in Their Own Country* (Chicago, 1992) • J. M. McNamara, *In the Presence of the Wise and Gentle Christ* (New York, 1993) • R. Manselli, *St. Francis of Assisi* (Chicago, 1988) • G. Wendelborn, *Franziskus von Assisi. Eine historische Darstellung* (Leipzig, 1977).

          Winrich A. Löhr

Franciscans

1. Francis and Beginnings
2. Developments in the 13th and 14th Centuries
3. The Order in the Reformation Period
4. The Franciscans after Trent

1. Francis and Beginnings

Francis of Assisi was born in 1181/82, died on October 3, 1226, and was canonized on July 15, 1228; his feast day is October 4. Baptized Giovanni, he was the son of a cloth merchant, Pietro Bernardone, who knew France well through business journeys and thus called his son Francesco. He was expected to carry on his father's trade but preferred to seek social advancement. A crisis in his life led him to renounce the world in 1206 and to gather a brotherhood around him. Innocent III recognized and promoted this brotherhood in 1209/10, and with its astonishing growth it quickly came to occupy a central place in church history for all of Latin Christendom. The situation can be explained only in terms of the combination of an ecclesiastical and social crisis with an obviously extraordinary personality.

This combination solved the immediate crisis but later brought on crises of its own. At the center was a lay brotherhood within the church that renounced any fixed abode, → property, or legal status after the model of the life of Jesus depicted in the Gospels (→ Discipleship). It involved an understanding of the relevance of the gospel that went back 150 years and had led to the formation of similar groups already in the second half of the 12th century. Because of tensions with a clericalized church that had been inherited from antiquity, and because of the → Investiture Controversy, which was dominated by the nobility, these groups had been declared heretical (e.g., the reformer Arnold of

Brescia, who was hanged; → Cathari; Heresies and Schisms; Waldenses). But now this understanding established itself afresh in Catholic Christianity in a society that was shaped by the development of the middle class and urbanization (→ Bourgeois, Bourgeoisie; City). Harmony with the hierarchical church was achieved by way of the concept of → poverty, which entailed the renunciation of legal status after the pattern of the Son of God, who had humbled himself.

→ Francis also shared in the developing eucharistic → piety of the church (→ Eucharist; Eucharistic Spirituality). For him the Eucharist was the only visible manifestation of the incarnate Lord. Unconditional reverence was thus due to the → priest who dispensed this sacrament of the otherwise invisible Son of God, even though the whole lifestyle of the first Franciscans was a visible criticism (by implication) of the bad example set by a → clergy that neglected its pastoral duties. In this regard one may also note a sensory and aesthetic feature of the Franciscans. The nature of Francis was alien to abstraction and to the contemporary development of theology. It wanted to represent tangibly the life of Christ and his disciples and thus focused on deed, → prayer, and witness. With such an emphasis Francis made a lasting impression in what was at first the predominantly nonclerical and nonintellectual milieu of his society. He thus developed capacities suited to middle-class, communal, and commerical circles in the 12th and 13th centuries and made a home for them in religion and the church. Sociologically, the type of the wandering friar differs fundamentally from that of the liturgical monk (→ Monasticism) of the Benedictine tradition (→ Benedictines; Cistercians) and also from that of the ordained canon.

The basic witness to the uniqueness of Francis may be found in his Testament, his "Song of the Sun," his various letters and admonitions, and his so-called First Rule *(Regula non bullata)* — a compilation of sayings and resolutions from the first great decade of growth (1210 to 1221). We may also consider later anecdotal recollections of his immediate associates. The official records of the order have preserved much of this material, but on the whole they are the testimony of a different ecclesiastical and clerical world that gratefully seized on the figure of Francis, stylized him as a new type of saint, and thus refashioned his essential historical features according to a liturgical and hagiographic ideal (→ Saints, Veneration of). The Franciscans came to see in their founder-saint an agent of church renewal in his day (a "second Christ"), as evidenced in his stigmata, which occurred in 1224, the revelation of which came only after his death two years later.

2. Developments in the 13th and 14th Centuries

The hierarchical church of priests, bishops, and pope managed to clericalize the order, adapting it to older patterns. With the final form of the rule (the *Regula bullata*, 1223), it became a huge mendicant order of Little Brothers (*fratres minores*, a name chosen by Francis himself), the *Ordo fratrum minorum* (OFM). With its help the church was able to offer pastoral care to the rising population in the cities, to compete with similar-looking heretical movements that had been successful there, and in this way to win back the cities for the church. Other orders such as the → Dominicans and the Humiliati worked in much the same way. After 1231 the → Inquisition was entrusted to these orders — first to the Dominicans and then to the Franciscans.

The Franciscans and Dominicans commended themselves to the wealthier classes in the cities, who in the traditional manner gave them endowments (for the health of the souls of the givers). For the Franciscans, who have a basic and novel principle of poverty — the renunciation not merely of private possessions in the monastic manner but also of communal property — such gifts led to all kinds of legal problems and fictions. Procurators, and later the curia, held endowments for the order, allowing it (in theory) only a very modest use of them according to need.

As the order gained recruits among educated people, students, and masters of theology, it moved into the world of → Scholasticism, which Francis had respected but not regarded as a proper field of activity for his mostly not well educated brothers. From the 1220s the Franciscans had their own schools and their own teaching chairs at the universities. Among the various trends in Scholasticism we may distinguish a Franciscan school. It included an older form, illustrated chiefly by Alexander of Hales (ca. 1185-1245) and Bonaventura (ca. 1217-74), and a middle and later Franciscan school, by Duns Scotus (ca. 1265-1308; → Scotism). Theologically, the most significant and influential theologian of the order was William of Ockham (ca. 1285-1347).

The Franciscan character of these forms of theology cannot be brought under a single concept and perhaps does not even exist in any consistent way. Yet within the trends of Scholasticism one may distinguish certain specific features that mark the theology of the order. For example, it differs from the theology of the Dominicans in its doctrine of the freedom of the will (→ Predestination) and its late medieval → Mariology (defending the immaculate conception; → Mary, Devotion to). The most Franciscan of these theologians — Bonaventura, the general of the order, who wrote the official and definitive account of the life of Francis (*Legenda maior, minor*) — also took up a position of his own, consciously differing from the → Aristotelianism of Thomas Aquinas (ca. 1225-74; → Thomism), and was distinctive even within the order, with his mystical theology. Another very significant Franciscan theologian, who was suspected of being a Spiritual but who followed Bonaventura (and Joachim of Fiore) ecclesiastically, was Petrus Johannis Olivi (ca. 1248-98). In the midst of controversies in the order, Olivi helped develop the doctrine of papal → infallibility.

The artistic depiction of the story of Francis from the middle of the 13th century (San Francesco in Assisi, the tomb basilica with its frescoes by Cimabue [ca. 1240-ca. 1302] and Giotto [ca. 1266-1337] and others as a prototype of the whole line of iconographic development up to the high renaissance ca. 1500) follows not the original and "authentic" picture of Francis but the official church picture.

The tension between Francis's original aims and lifestyle, on the one hand, and, on the other, the further development of the order led soon after the death of Francis to a movement of protest within the order. The opposition, led especially by brothers living as hermits in central Italy, was strengthened after the 1270s by the formation of the Spirituals, whose ideal of a "spiritual" church and brotherhood was nourished by the original picture of Francis (mythically transfigured) and also, from the 1240s, by the influence of elements of expectation of a renewed, true "church of the Holy Spirit" (Joachim of Fiore; → Millenarianism). The struggles of the majority and the papacy (→ Pope, Papacy) against the Spirituals and their successors lasted over half a century (till about 1330). At the climax John XXII in 1323 condemned as heretical the exaggerated thesis, seen as a criticism of the church, that Christ and the apostles had neither personal nor communal property (a view that would have made the radical Franciscans the only true disciples of Christ). (For this reason the Lutheran theologian Matthias Flacius in 1556 listed John XXII in his *Catalogus Testium Veritatis* [List of witnesses to the truth].)

In a moderated form the order took up the concerns of the Spirituals, who had authored legends about Francis critical of the order, in the form of Observant movements, that is, reforming movements stressing stricter adherence to the rule. The whole of the 15th century was taken up by the struggle concerning observance. Finally in 1517 Leo X separated the Observants from the Conventuals, a branch allowing adaptations and modifications of Francis's rule.

There is a paradox in the fact that a movement founded by Francis, a rich man who embraced poverty, became the main institution offering pastoral care to the rich. As the nobility had formerly sought salvation from the Benedictines, the middle class now sought it from the mendicants. But we must not press this paradox any more than that of Francis and the papal church which adopted him and made him serve its own purposes. The paradox certainly ought not to be the antithetical principle of our whole presentation. There is in fact a historical continuity, though not harmony, and Francis, for all his sense of mission and his determination to live what he took to be a divinely imposed form of life, was loyal to the church in principle. Cardinal Ugolino, the first sponsor of the order, was Francis's confidant and friend, and when he became Gregory IX, he canonized Francis in 1228. Paul Sabatier's *Vie de Saint François* (1893), which is built on that overstressed antithesis, remains the most brilliant account of Francis, though it should not be read without the balance of a more reliable historical depiction (R. Manselli, G. Wendelborn).

As in the whole poverty movement of the 12th century, so among the Franciscans women played a part corresponding to the growth of the population. In 1212 after the conversion of Clare (d. 1253, canonized 1255), who belonged to the nobility of Assisi, a sisterhood quickly developed around her under church influence and became a second order pledged to poverty (the Poor Clares) — in this case a conventual order, rather than one of itinerants and preachers. With the support of princesses, some of whom took the veil (e.g., Agnes of Prague in 1233), this order kept pace with the expansion of the Franciscans.

The urban laity that was the particular target of the movement also enthusiastically aligned itself with the pre-Franciscan brotherhood movement, later the so-called → Tertiaries, or Third Order, a name first used after 1201 for lay supporters of the Lombardian Humiliati.

3. The Order in the Reformation Period

From the standpoint of the renewal of the church accomplished by the → Reformation, interest lies in the origins and development (or false development, as the Reformers saw it) in the 13th century. Development of the order followed conditions laid down by the papal church, although we cannot ignore the

significance at a popular level of the great Franciscan preaching and pastoral care of the later Middle Ages.

Late medieval legends so elevated the figure of St. Francis himself to the likeness of Christ that the order came under severe Protestant criticism. During the Reformation it lost most of its provinces in central and northern Europe. At the same time, the Capuchins arose in Italy from 1525 (→ Orders and Congregations) as a third branch of the order, along with the Observants and Conventuals (separated in 1517). The Capuchins grew out of the reforming movement within Roman Catholicism and strengthened the ascetic elements in the Franciscan lifestyle. Reformation ideas infiltrated it, and in 1541 its general, Bernardino Ochino, a popular preacher, went over to the Reformation, though he did not find a home in any of the main Reformation churches. The order then became a main champion of Tridentine reform and the Counter-Reformation (→ Catholic Reform and Counterreformation).

4. The Franciscans after Trent

The three branches of Franciscans have shared in many ways in the history and culture of modern → Catholicism. In the 19th and 20th centuries → neoscholasticism edited works by the great 13th-century Franciscan theologians (Bonaventura, Duns Scotus) and enriched the tradition of the order by editing early sources (at Bonaventura College in Florence from 1877, in Rome after the flood of 1966 at Grottaferrata). The debate about the original ideals of St. Francis is reflected in lengthy internal Franciscan discussions of present-day tasks. The crisis after → Vatican II affected the order. Many members left, but there was also a strong movement of renewal. The tradition of poverty led to missionary and social involvement and to contributions that are disputed in official circles, such as to Latin American → liberation theology (L. Boff).

The Papal Yearbook of 1999 lists 2,807 houses and 17,763 brothers, 11,760 of whom were priests (a laicizing trend may be seen here). The Conventuals had 672 houses and 4,574 brothers (2,746 priests), the Capuchins 1,648 houses and 11,323 brothers (7,352 priests). There was also a smaller Third Order, which contrary to its name included mostly ordained brothers. Listed, too, were many congregations of Franciscan women (mostly sisters). In many countries there were also various congregations of clergy and laity that appealed to Francis.

Bibliography: Primary source: C. ESSER, *Opuscula Sancti Patris Francisci Assisiensis* (Grottaferrata, 1978).

General: W. Dettloff, "Franziskanerschule," *TRE* 11.397-401 • *FQS* • K. S. Frank, "Franziskaner," *LTK* (3d ed.) 4.30-35 • *FS* • Gratien de Paris, *Histoire de la fondation et de l'évolution de l'Ordre des Frères Mineurs au XIII siècle* (Paris, 1928; repr., with newer bibliography, Rome, 1982) • H. Holzapfel, *Handbuch der Geschichte des Franziskanerordens* (Freiburg, 1909) • J. Moorman, *A History of the Franciscan Order from Its Origins to the Year 1517* (Oxford, 1968) • K. B. Osborne, ed., *The History of Franciscan Theology* (New York, 1994) • J. Schlageter, "Franziskaner," *TRE* 11.389-97 • *WiWei.*

On 1: K. Esser, *Anfänge und ursprüngliche Zielsetzungen des Ordens der Minderbrüder* (Leiden, 1966) • U. Köpf, "Franz von Assisi," *Gestalten der Kirchengeschichte,* vol. 3, *Mittelalter I* (Stuttgart, 1983) 282-302 • R. Manselli, *St. Francis of Assisi* (Chicago, 1988) • G. Wendelborn, *Franziskus von Assisi* (2d ed.; Vienna, 1982).

On 2: K. Balthasar, *Geschichte des Armutsstreites im Franziskanerorden bis zum Konzil von Vienne* (Münster, 1911) • H. Belting, *Die Oberkirche von San Francesco in Assisi. Ihre Dekoration als Aufgabe und die Genese einer neuen Wandmalerei* (Berlin, 1977) • D. Berg, *Armut und Wissenschaft. Beiträge zur Geschichte des Studienwesens der Bettelorden im 13. Jahrhundert* (Düsseldorf, 1977) • J. B. Freed, *The Friars and German Society in the Thirteenth Century* (Cambridge, Mass., 1977) • M. D. Lambert, *Franciscan Poverty . . . (1210-1323)* (London, 1961) • L. K. Little, *Religious Poverty and the Profit Economy in Medieval Europe* (London, 1978) • P. Normile, "Secular Franciscans: A Vibrant Part of the Franciscan Family," *SAnM* 101 (1993) 36-41.

On 3: J. Halvorson, "Franciscan Theology and Predestinarian Pluralism in Late-Medieval Thought," *Spec.* 70 (1995) 1-26 • E. Kurten, *Franz Lambert von Avignon und Nikolaus Herborn in ihrer Stellung zum Ordensgedanken und zum Franziskanertum* (Münster, 1950) • K.-V. Selge, "Franziskus von Assisi in der protestantischen Geschichtsschreibung des 16. Jahrhunderts," *L'immagine di Francesco nella storiografia . . .* (Assisi, 1983) 169-98 • H.-M. Stamm, *Luthers Stellung zum Ordensleben* (Wiesbaden, 1980).

On 4: Annuario Pontificio per l'anno 1985 • L. Boff, *Zärtlichkeit und Kraft. Franz von Assisi, mit den Augen der Armen gesehen* (Düsseldorf, 1983; Portuguese original, 1981) • L. Boff et al., *Bedrohte Befreiung. Zur lateinamerikanischen und katholischen Kontroverse um politische Praxis im Christentum* (Rheinfelden, 1985) • J. Malone, "What St. Francis Would Do in These Times," *Origins* 22 (1992) 65-70 • W. Short, *The Franciscans* (Wilmington, Del., 1989).

Kurt-Victor Selge

Francke, August Hermann

August Hermann Francke (1663-1727) was a Lutheran-Pietist theologian, pedagogue, and social reformer. Francke, the son of a jurist, was born in Lübeck and spent his childhood in Gotha. He was early destined for spiritual office, as well as for scholarship, studying in Erfurt and Kiel (1679-82), Hamburg (1682), and Leipzig (from 1684). In 1685 he received his master of philosophy degree on the basis of a work on Hebrew grammar and acquired authorization to teach. As a counter to instructional theology that was reduced largely to → dogmatics, in 1686 he founded the *Collegium philobiblicum,* focused on reading and interpreting biblical pericopes in the original languages. In 1687 Francke translated two writings by the Spanish mystic M. Molinos, though only partially did he identify with the content of these writings. In the same year Francke went through a severe crisis of faith, leading him to doubt the existence of God. This crisis, which he later interpreted as the result of his previous intellectualism, was resolved through a direct experience of → conversion (§1). Thereafter Francke distanced himself from Lutheran → orthodoxy.

Influenced by P. J. Spener (1635-1705), who had attended the *Collegium philobiblicum* in 1687 and yet had criticized it as being too remote and scholarly, Francke conducted *Collegia biblica* for edification in Leipzig homes beginning in 1689. Although these *collegia* resulted in an awakening among students and the city's inhabitants, they also raised suspicions on the part of orthodox professors and clergy. After an investigation instigated by J. B. Carpzov II, in which the → Enlightenment thinker C. Thomasius came to his defense, Francke was dismissed from his teaching post in 1690. Although he accepted a pastorate in Erfurt, this too was soon taken from him because of, among other things, his contacts with radical-pietistic and church-reform groups in the vicinity. Through Spener's contacts, he received a pastorate in Glaucha, Brandenburg, at the end of 1691 and a professorship for Greek and Oriental languages in nearby Halle. Through → catechism instruction and → church discipline, Francke began to renew the neglected → congregation, combining instruction in faith with social and educational reforms.

In 1695 Francke founded a school for the poor, followed quickly by a citizen's school, a boarding school with a higher school for sons of the nobility, a Latin school for sons of the citizenry, and also a school for daughters of the upper classes (which did not last long). In the same year, Francke began to take in foster children, also establishing a house for them. From this house an orphanage ultimately developed, the cornerstone for its new edifice being laid in 1698. Here Francke engaged students as caretakers and teachers in order to expand their faith and life experiences and to focus their studies on actual practice; from 1698, Francke was also professor of theology, in which capacity he also became engaged in reforming the course of theological studies (→ Theological Education).

From the beginning, Francke's → pedagogical thinking was both admired and criticized. It included such concepts as support of the gifted, the combination of theory and practical work, life experiences, instruction in modern foreign languages, comprehensive behavioral control (involving "breaking the individual will"), the discrediting of leisure, the dominance of the utilitarian, and methodological rigorism in both faith and education (so the criticism of Thomasius). It was, however, quite successful, and found support in none other than Frederick William I, king of Prussia, who, influenced by Francke, announced universal compulsory education in 1717. The *Seminarium selectum praeceptorum*, which Francke assembled from gifted teacher-students, is generally viewed as the beginning of organized teacher training in Germany.

By establishing a bookstore with its own printing press and publishing company, as well as a pharmaceutical business, Francke was able to make the Glaucha Institutes, which were initially dependent on donations, to a large extent economically independent. He understood the Halle Institutes as the germ cell of a "general reformation of the world." This idea contains the inner basis of Francke's extensive writing and ecumenical activity (writings for → edification, Bible publications, correspondence, dispatch of students, and support for foreign missions, esp. in India).

Despite a certain measure of conceptual and personal proximity, the Enlightenment remained alien to Francke, and in 1723 he supported the expulsion of the → rationalist philosopher C. Wolff from Halle. Francke's comprehensive life work exerted immeasurable influence, especially on the understanding of schools and → education, Christian social welfare, → mission, and devotional styles.

Bibliography: Primary sources: E. PESCHKE, ed., *Schriften und Predigten* (Berlin, 1981ff.); idem, ed., *Werke in Auswahl* (Berlin, 1969).

Secondary works: M. BRECHT, "August Hermann Francke und der Hallesche Pietismus," *Geschichte des Pietismus* (ed. M. Brecht et al.; Göttingen, 1993) 1.439-539 • D. L. BRUNNER, *Halle Priests in England: Anthony William Boehm and the Society for Promoting Christian Knowledge* (Göttingen, 1993) • E. PESCHKE, *Studien zur Theologie August Hermann Franckes* (2 vols.; Berlin, 1964-66) • T. D. THOMPSON, "God's Special Way: August Hermann Francke, Friedrich Wilhelm I, and the Consolidation of Prussian Absolutism" (Diss., Ohio State University, 1996) • R. WILSON, ed., *Eighteenth-Century Traffic in Medicines and Medical Ideas* (= *Caduceus: A Humanities Journal for Medicine and the Health Sciences* 13/1 [1997]).

BERND OBERDORFER

Frankfurt School → Critical Theory

Free Church

The term "free church" dates from 1843, when Thomas Chalmers (1780-1847) led 474 like-minded ministers out of the Church of Scotland to found the Free Church. They were protesting against state control of the church. In 1892 English Nonconformists ventured to adopt the term when Presbyterians, Congregationalists (→ Congregationalism), → Baptists, and Methodists (→ Methodism) formed the National Free Church Council, claiming to be no less a church than the established Church of England (→ Anglican Communion). In both cases the adjective points to a basic feature. As compared with a state church, a national church, or a territorial church, the free church is structurally a type of church that rejects any equation of the civil and Christian community, any marriage of throne and altar (→ Church and State), any related religious uniformity imposed by ecclesiastical or governmental compulsion (→ Inquisition). In the conditions prevailing in Italy, Conte di Cavour's (1810-61) goal of a free church in a free state still served the intertwining of church and state. The free church world is divided into several denominations, which is a consequence of taking freedom of conscience and belief seriously.

The free church really began in modern times with the → Anabaptists (Mennonites) and the formative conviction that the church must be composed only of confessing, regenerate believers. Membership in such a church comes through voluntary, adult decision, and a church composed of such members could be governed by the → Holy Spirit, free of historical → creeds, normative liturgies, and government control. In the 17th century

→ Puritanism was a decisive factor. Nor should we overlook the influence of John → Wycliffe (ca. 1330-84) as a pre-Reformation source. (Note Wycliffe's influence on Jan → Hus and the contacts of the → Hussites with the → Waldenses.) The Puritans included Congregationalists, Baptists, Presbyterians, and Quakers (→ Society of → Friends). The Act of Toleration in 1689 allowed these groups to expand, although it did impose restrictions on entrance to the universities, which shut members out of influential professions until the removal of religious tests in 1871.

In the 18th century the Methodist revival (→ Revivalism), contrary to the original aim of John → Wesley (1703-91), led to the formation of a new church. The Moravian Brethren also formed their own → Moravian Church. The 19th century saw the emergence of the → Salvation Army, the Free Evangelical Churches, the → Pentecostals, and the → Adventists.

America became the land of the free church through the immigration of → Dissenters and the persistent advocacy of → religious liberty, especially by the Baptists. Roger Williams in Rhode Island (1644) and William Penn in Pennsylvania (1682) were champions of religious freedom, which the First Amendment to the Constitution guaranteed with the founding of the Republic. This step opened a new chapter in church history, since the federal government — and, later, individual state governments — were restrained from supervising → denominations or favoring any one of them (disestablishment).

The establishment of religious liberty is an essential contribution of the free church to the formation of modern → pluralistic society. The idea is neither to promote religious indifference nor to hasten the decline of religion (in spite of the → Enlightenment and modern criticism of religion). Even in lands where → ideology does envision the withering away of religion (e.g., China and, formerly, the USSR), the free churches are steadily growing.

The free church demands a decision for → church membership and thus strengthens the members' sense of responsibility, even financially (→ Stewardship), for the congregation. To a surprising degree it also fosters lay cooperation (expressing the priesthood of all believers) and more effective → church discipline. Constant renewal takes place according to the pattern of the life of the primitive community. Voluntarism and evangelistic and missionary zeal are two sides of the same coin. Great importance is attached to educational work (e.g., → Sunday school, Bible school, Vacation Bible School) and → youth work.

Free churches were historically attractive because of their participatory polity and the intimate → piety of their small, family-like congregations (→ House Church). Members could have intensive contacts with one another and with the → pastor, though intimacy could also lead to tensions. These features remain characteristic of many free churches, though their polity has also proved conducive to the growth of huge individual congregations, the increasingly well-known "megachurches."

For sociological reasons the free church is often the church of the lower middle class, so that in the United States we find an upward social movement to respectable churches (e.g., Pentecostals to Methodists, or Baptists to Episcopalians). Very significant ecumenically is the missionary work of the free churches (→ Mission; Evangelical Missions). In the 19th and 20th centuries this effort has led to a swift spread of Protestantism in countries of the → Third World. Most of the younger churches are structured as free churches.

The beginnings of the → ecumenical movement, both in the Evangelical Alliance (→ World Evangelical Fellowship) and in the → World Council of Churches, may be explained essentially in terms of free church initiatives (e.g., by John Mott). Of the larger free churches only the Southern Baptist Convention refuses to work with the WCC, though it does not totally reject all ecumenism.

→ Church 3.6; Church Growth

Bibliography: S. E. AHLSTROM, *A Religious History of the American People* (New Haven, 1972) • H. BRANDENBURG, *The Meek and the Mighty: The Emergence of the Evangelical Movement in Russia* (London, 1976) • D. F. DURNBAUGH, *The Believers' Church: The History and Character of Radical Protestantism* (Scottdale, Pa., 1985; orig. pub., 1968) • J. L. GARRET, ed., *The Concept of the Believers' Church* (Scottdale, Pa., 1969) • E. GELDBACH, *Freikirchen–Erbe, Gestalt und Wirkung* (Göttingen, 1989) • U. KUNZ, ed., *Viele Glieder–ein Leib* (Stuttgart, 1963) • F. H. LITTELL, *The Free Church* (Boston, 1957); idem, *From State Church to Pluralism: A Protestant Interpretation of Religion in American History* (New York, 1971) • W. G. McLOUGHLIN, *New England Dissent, 1630-1833: The Baptists and the Separation of Church and State* (2 vols.; Cambridge, Mass., 1982) • H.-B. MOTEL, ed., *Glieder an einem Leib. Die Freikirchen in Selbstdarstellung* (Constance, 1975) • E. A. PAINE, *The Free Church Tradition in the Life of England* (rev. ed.; London, 1965) • G. WESTIN, *Geschichte des Freikirchentums* (Kassel, 1956). See also the bibliography in "Ecumenical Theology" 4.

ERICH GELDBACH and S. MARK HEIM

Free Religion (Freireligiöse)

1. So-called Free Religion is a concern of groups, especially in Germany, that want → freedom *in* religion, not freedom *from* religion, which for them means no dogmatic or organizational commitments in their religion. Although rejecting → dogmas and hierarchical structures, they form a union with special features and its own history.

Free Religion has both Catholic and Protestant roots in → German Catholicism and Protestant free churches (the so-called Friends of Light, or Protestant Friends). German Catholicism was an early liberal movement started as a reaction to restoration trends in Roman → Catholicism in the first half of the 19th century. The Silesian Johannes Ronge (1813-87), an opponent of → Ultramontanism, formed the movement into the German Catholic Church when he was suspended from the Roman Catholic Church in 1845. The first council of the church met in Leipzig in the same year; by 1847 the Berlin synod had 259 congregations.

The other root of Free Religion, the German Protestant free churches, was led by liberal pastors as early as 1841 in protest against the → revival movement, which sought a return to orthodoxy and an alliance with the idea of a Christian state promoted by Frederick William IV. They joined forces with German Catholicism in 1859 to found the Union of Free Religious Congregations of Germany. They had already had some political influence in the revolution of 1848 and suffered severe persecution as a result. Gradually, however, their liberal revolutionary zeal abated. Some of the Free Religion societies were dissolved in 1933.

After World War II there were Free Religion federations in northern and southern Germany. A working fellowship was established at Offenbach in 1948, and a federation in 1950 (the Bund Freireligiöser Gemeinden Deutschlands [BFGD]), with the legal status of a corporation. The latter united with the German Union for Freedom of Spirit, which had been dissolved in 1933 and reconstituted in 1949, and which sought to bring together all those who wanted freedom of religion, belief, and spirit.

2. The BFGD claims 70,000 members and some 175,000 adherents if families are counted. The center of religious life is the corporate devotional hour, which is focused on an address by the preacher. Important rites are those associated with birth, youth dedication, marriage, and death. The symbols are non-Christian and vary from congregation to congregation. The piety of Free Religion carries an element of → reverence for the unfathomability and mysterious richness of being, but also a rationalistic confidence in → reason and in the compatibility of religion with → evolution and a scientific → worldview. Other features are nature mysticism, a sense of the solidarity of life, and rationalistic morality. Special concerns are human equality, freedom of spirit and conscience, and → peace between all nations and races.

The adherents of the BFGD see themselves no longer as a Christian → sect but as a nonecclesiastical and non-Christian society with a distinct worldview, hence they seldom seek → dialogue with the churches. For their part, the churches regard them as an insignificant minority.

Bibliography: Die freireligiöse Bewegung. Wesen und Auftrag (Mainz, 1959) • A. GOODMAN and A. MACKAY, eds., *The Impact of Humanism on Western Europe* (London, 1990) • F. HERMANN, *Freie Religion* (N.p., 1968) • F. HEYER, ed., *Religion ohne Kirche. Die Bewegung der Freireligiöse* (Stuttgart, 1977) • H. MYNAREK, *Religion–Möglichkeit oder Grenze der Freiheit?* (Cologne, 1977); idem, *Religiös ohne Gott?* (Düsseldorf, 1983).

HUBERTUS MYNAREK

Freedom

1. Philosophical
    1.1. Etymology and Concept
    1.2. History and Systematics
        1.2.1. Antiquity
        1.2.2. Middle Ages
        1.2.3. Modern Period
    1.3. Development
2. Theological
    2.1. Biblical Tradition
    2.2. Early Church and Orthodox Tradition
    2.3. Middle Ages
    2.4. Luther
    2.5. Calvin
    2.6. Calvinism
    2.7. Modern Theories
    2.8. Roman Catholic Church
    2.9. Modern Protestantism

1. Philosophical

1.1. *Etymology and Concept*

With related terms in other languages, the word "free" derives from the Indo-European root **prai-*, meaning "protect, spare, like, love." The Latin word

for "freedom" is *libertas,* the Greek, *eleutheria* (esp.
in the sense of political freedom). The latter occurred for the first time in Pindar (ca. 522-ca. 438),
who said of Hieron I (ca. 540-467/466), founder of
the city of Etna, that he founded it "with ordered
freedom" (*Pyth.* 1.61). The *eleutheroi* were free persons who, as distinct from slaves, lived in their fa-
therland with their own kind.

1.2. History and Systematics
1.2.1. Antiquity
1.2.1.1. In Greek thought, social and political
freedom was to the fore at first, being viewed negatively as freedom from domination by others. It became a philosophical problem when the laws of the
polis were no longer felt to be a natural expression
of freedom and when *physis* (nature; i.e., that which
is developed without external compulsion) was opposed to *nomos* (law; → Greek Philosophy). With
Socrates (ca. 470-399 B.C.) and Plato (427-347), the
definition of freedom became a theme in → ethics.

Following legal practice and starting with the
question of moral accounting, Aristotle (384-322
B.C.) defined an action as voluntary *(hekōn)* as long
as the person who performs it is not under external
constraint and is aware of what he or she is doing —
that is, as long as the person is the cause of the act
(*Eth. Nic.* 1110ff.). At the heart of the discussion are
freedom of action and freedom of choice. The question of freedom of the will as an inner indetermi-
nacy is raised only insofar as what is done is done
responsibly in pursuit of what seems to be a worthy
goal. Thus choice *(proairesis),* although primarily
restricted to choice of means, relates finally to the
goal as a basic decision of conduct in general.

The supreme form of freedom is autarky, a
theme in ethics from the time of Democritus. Literally meaning self-sufficiency, autarky was for
Plato the highest and divine form of being and the
basis of the → good (*Phlb.* 67A). For Aristotle it was
a mark of *eudaimonia* (→ happiness; *Eth. Nic.*
1097a-b) to the degree that it means not only external independence but the ability to self-exist and to
lead a full life commensurate with one's nature.

1.2.1.2. In → Stoicism (esp. Zeno [ca. 335-ca.
263 B.C.] and Chrysippus [ca. 280-ca. 206]), the
problem of freedom was radicalized in the light of
divine providence and the resultant permeation of
the whole cosmos with meaning. The thought of
freedom lost its political dimension and was
interiorized. It was seen as the possibility of subjection to a world process that proceeds with necessity
and independent of humanity. Freedom means recognizing what is known to be a law.

In opposition to this determinism Epicurus

(341-270 B.C.) and his school, rejecting the concept
of providence and the universal validity of causal
law, defined freedom as "having no cause." Freedom
is thus the freedom of the will, a choice between various possibilities that is determined by no cause. If
for Stoics autarky thus lay in a self-subjecting indifference and impassibility in the face of cosmic
change, for Epicurus the greatest happiness as
summa voluptas lay in abstraction from the world
and the ignoring of needs.

In Neoplatonism (→ Platonism) Plotinus (ca.
A.D. 205-70) for the first time gave the concept of
freedom a metaphysical basis. For him only the One
is absolutely free, since it is in itself its own work
(*Enn.* 6.8.20).

1.2.2. Middle Ages
The decisive impulse toward a new view of freedom
came from → Augustine (354-430; → Augustine's
Theology). He integrated into his thinking the
Christian acknowledgment of the individual as a
person and thus sought to conceive of the supreme
good in terms of freedom, not in terms of a perfection of nature that must be achieved. This absolutizing made a new concept of → evil necessary.
Since evil was thought to arise out of individual free
will, the phenomenon of → conscience came to the
fore as that in which individuals transcend themselves in their self-relation.

Later, freedom aroused interest as the problem of
the free will, a question being whether one must accord primacy to → reason or to the will (→ Voluntarism). → Thomas Aquinas (ca. 1225-74) argued
that freedom lies in the will and that the role of the
intellect is simply to place objects before it, though
he also stressed that the goal of action is not subject
to the free will (→ Scholasticism; Thomism). William of Ockham (ca. 1285-1347) raised again a
question that had come up in debate with the
Averroists (→ Islamic Philosophy 4.6), namely, how
far one can prove the reality of freedom.

1.2.3. Modern Period
1.2.3.1. In modern philosophy the problem of
freedom, though always present, received no new
treatment before I. Kant (1724-1804). Adopting
motifs from the 17th and 18th centuries, Kant advanced a *transcendental view* that in essentials is still
normative (→ Kantianism).

For Kant, freedom is not a quality of the will but
→ autonomy. It is the character of reason insofar as
it prescribes the law of its own acts (→ Categorical
Imperative). More precisely defined as a transcendental practical idea, as thinking oneself free, freedom expresses itself in the "thou shalt!" of the moral
law. It is the presupposition of observance of this

law. In this sense it can be seen as a kind of → causality opposing the causality of nature. This opposition and the theoretical nondemonstrability of freedom are dealt with in the doctrine of antinomies in the *Critique of Pure Reason*. Defining the relation between freedom and nature is still at issue, however, the question being how to make freedom concrete in the world of phenomena. This theme is developed in post-Kantian philosophy.

Following up on Kant, G. W. F. Hegel (1770-1831; → Hegelianism) pointed out, on the one hand, that we must understand freedom in the light of its origin and, on the other hand, that freedom takes concrete form in historical → institutions. According to Hegel, we are destined for supreme freedom. K. → Marx (1818-83; → Marxism), however, thought we could reach this goal only in the true society, for he did not find it in irrational and unfree early history. As J. Habermas rightly pointed out, on these presuppositions the freedom that Kant's categorical imperative demands does not exist. The concept of a "kingdom of freedom," which derives from F. Schiller and German → idealism and which Marx also uses, necessitates a leap out of the "kingdom of necessity" (thus F. Engels and V. Lenin), though this idea needs closer definition.

In the train of Hegel and his concept of freedom, the question of needs, interests, and wishes, which serve as motivation and goal orientation, takes on great significance. So too does the reference to the field of social and political action. Hence the rational and normative structures of action come under discussion. By means of an analysis of the field of action and the relationships of life, the sphere of possible freedom is staked out. Evidence of this approach may be seen in existential philosophy, which in M. Heidegger (1889-1976) upholds Kant's concept of freedom as an essential determination of humanity, equates existence and freedom, and stresses the fact that the ethical dimension lies in finite freedom and must be realized in self-choice. This view expressly entails mastering actual existence in the structural context of reference to self and the world. Typical of the existential philosophy of K. Jaspers (1883-1969) and J.-P. Sartre (1905-80) in particular is the fact that it begins with a factual appeal to the experience of freedom and inquires into the concrete responsibility of those who act.

1.2.3.2. Under the slogan → *emancipation,* freedom is often dealt with as the problem of liberation from alien rule. Thus T. Adorno (1903-69) speaks about the fiction of positive freedom and thinks that in the last resort we can understand freedom only as negation.

1.3. *Development*
As freedom takes many forms, so we can distinguish between the freedoms of conscience, belief, opinion, information, doctrine, education, and so forth. The democratic states (→ Democracy; State) guarantee various forms of freedom. One of the tasks of law is to ensure that there is room for freedom of action in both the individual and the social spheres.

Bibliography: M. ADLER, *The Idea of Freedom* (New York, 1958) • A. FAHRER, *The Freedom of the Will* (London, 1958) • R. GARAUDY, *Die Freiheit als philosophische und historische Kategorie* (Berlin, 1959) • J. HABERMAS, *Knowledge and Human Interests* (Boston, 1971) • R. M. HARE, *Freedom and Reason* (Oxford, 1966) • M. HORKHEIMER, "On the Concept of Freedom," in *Diogenes* (Paris, 1966) • D. MILLER, ed., *Liberty* (Oxford, 1991) • J. SIMON, ed., *Freiheit* (Freiburg, 1977).

HEIMO HOFMEISTER

2. Theological
The biblical tradition has influenced the understanding of freedom in Western culture. There has been tension and synthesis with Greek, Roman, Jewish, Germanic, humanist, and modern views.

2.1. *Biblical Tradition*
The OT has no word for freedom as an individual or social quality. Yet the story of the liberation of → Israel (§1) from bondage in Egypt had a decisive impact. The relevant verbs here are "save," "redeem," "rescue," and "lead out." The normative subject appears in Exod. 20:2: "I am YHWH your God, who brought you out of the land of Egypt, out of the house of slavery." Israel was brought out. Thus in the biblical and Christian tradition freedom is seen to have its true basis in God. The reference back to Israel's own enslavement had great significance for the status of slaves in Israel (→ Slavery).

According to Luke 4:18, → Jesus in his preaching in Nazareth declared that Isa. 61:1-2a was now being fulfilled. His mission was "to proclaim release to the captives and recovery of sight to the blind, to let the oppressed go free." The → kingdom of God that Jesus proclaimed is a comprehensive event of liberation that breaks the power of Satan (→ Devil) and → demons, servile obedience to the → law, and the violence of rulers.

→ Paul so transformed the Greek concept of *eleutheria* (freedom) that the term became central in his understanding of the liberating lordship of Jesus (Rom. 7:23–8:4; Gal. 5:1, 13). Freedom and maturity were for him characteristics of believers, the children of God, who for this reason could follow their → conscience, deciding and living with regard for that of others (1 Cor. 10:28-29; Rom. 12:2). This freedom is not autarky but empowering by God's saving act in Christ for independence and service.

2.2. Early Church and Orthodox Tradition
Although the → early church used Greek and Latin terms, it did not understand freedom in human terms alone. For → Irenaeus (ca. 130-ca. 200) God alone is absolutely free and in this sense good (*Adv. haer.* 4.20.2; 4.38.4). Humanity is created by God in orientation to the freedom of God (3.23.1) and therefore is on the way to freedom. → Augustine (354-430) thought of us as beings made for freedom and transcending nature (see 1.2.2). For him "free choice" *(liberum arbitrium)* was a choice between greater being and less; an unfree evil will, in a corruption of the order of being, prefers the lower to the higher, which ultimately is fellowship with God (→ Augustine's Theology).

In the mystical theology of the East (→ Orthodoxy 3), in which → *theōsis* is central, freedom (e.g., in Maximus the Confessor [ca. 580-662]) is the authentic (divinized) mode of being a person.

2.3. Middle Ages
In the West, *libertas* and *liberum arbitrium* remained theologically central during the Middle Ages, but they came under wider discussion from philosophical, psychological, and ethical angles. The moderate → voluntarism of → Thomas Aquinas (ca. 1225-74; see 1.2.2) was radicalized epistemologically in later → Scholasticism, for example, by William of Ockham (ca. 1285-1347) and G. Biel (ca. 1420-95). The will is free to create presuppositions for God's giving of → grace: it is reliable but not compulsory. Erasmus of Rotterdam (1469?-1536; → Humanism) accepted this conclusion when he argued that "by 'free will' [*liberum arbitrium*] . . . we understand a power of the human will by which man may be able to direct himself towards, or turn away from, what leads to eternal salvation" (21).

2.4. Luther
Martin → Luther (1483-1546) disputed this thesis of Erasmus from an early date, and most fully in his *Bondage of the Will* (1525, *LW* 33). In relation to God, he claimed, we can only receive. We can do nothing to achieve our own → salvation. Decisive here is the focus on the doctrines of → sin and → justification and a corresponding understanding of → predestination. Those who speak about free will deny that we have salvation only by the merits of Christ in → faith. To the lack of freedom to win salvation by works there corresponds a freeing from → sin, → death, and the devil, all of which confers incomparable power. Luther's primary work *The Free-*

dom of a Christian (1520) develops a twofold thesis: "A Christian is a perfectly free lord of all, subject to none. A Christian is a perfectly dutiful servant of all, subject to all" (*LW* 31.344). In 1525, during the → Peasants' War, Luther sharply opposed the misuse of evangelical freedom in the pressing of one's own rights in the form of self-help and revolt. In so doing, he sought to overcome certain older German legal notions that were still exerting some influence.

Already in the Invocavit sermons in Wittenberg in 1523, Luther had resisted the unloving freedom of self-help that proceeds without regard for the consciences of other Christians. Yet the widespread view that Luther's talk about the bondage of the will led to a passive and → quietistic understanding of Christianity is mistaken. God in fact "does not work in us without us, because it is for this he has created and preserved us, that he might work in us and we might cooperate with him" (*LW* 33.243). This situation applies in the kingdom of God's omnipotence and, to an even greater extent, for the believer in the kingdom of the spirit, since there the relationship is additionally bound up with knowing and willing. This human cooperation with God does not rest on human autarky or → autonomy but on divine empowering. Thus it is a matter of a subsequent freedom that Christians find in themselves a joyful response to God's Word.

2.5. Calvin
Agreeing for the most part with Luther, John → Calvin (1509-64) deals with Christian freedom from the compulsion of the → law in book 3 of his *Institutes.* This freedom alone makes cheerful → obedience possible. The liberated conscience of believers is not subject to human power but must be distinguished from libertinistic and anarchic misuse. In the renowned 20th chapter of book 4, Calvin appeals to 1 Cor. 7:21 and observes that spiritual freedom might well coexist with civil bondage. He thus defends the superiority of divinely given freedom over all secular relations. The authorities indeed ought to be guardians of the freedom of the people according to the ordinance of God.

2.6. Calvinism
In western Europe and the Anglo-Saxon world, the tension in Calvin's understanding of freedom made → Calvinism a powerful influence upon modern developments in the direction of freedom and finally of → secularization. The thought of the covenant (in federal theology; → Covenant 3) linked up with Calvin's concept of the mutual obligations of rulers and people and developed into the doctrine of the twofold covenant between God and people and between ruler and people. This step led in turn

to the modern development of the social contract and the constitutional state that guarantees civil → rights (see W. Förster, *Thomas Hobbes und der Puritanismus* [Berlin, 1969] 74-126).

Calvin's doctrine of double predestination — some to salvation and some to perdition — emphasized the → responsibility of isolated individuals and thus had the effect of promoting an individualistic view of freedom. In the face of uncertainty about their election, individuals were to look for marks of divine grace in their own goodness or success in life (the so-called practical syllogism). They were thus spurred on to unceasing activity by way of demonstration. In his *Protestant Ethic and the Spirit of Capitalism* (1904/5), Max → Weber found here the decisive condition for the rise of modern → capitalism, with its combination of personal restraint in → consumption and free productivity.

C. B. Macpherson in *Political Theory of Possessive Individualism* (1962) described the new understanding of freedom as a power of control, whether over one's labor (Levellers) or over one's business capital according to rules of the market oriented to self-interest (→ Property). If early → Puritans still set the enterprises of Christians under the strict discipline of love of neighbor, later Puritans replaced this framework with the free power of an economic individualism corresponding to the nonconformism of the Independents.

The Virginia Declaration of Rights (1776) gave constitutional formulation for the first time to the principle that all people "are by nature equally free and independent." This was the starting point for the freedoms mentioned in standard lists of human or basic rights up to the present day.

2.7. Modern Theories

Modern concentration on the subjectivity and autonomy of human beings, who are free "by nature," has wrongly seen itself in antithesis to a theonomous understanding of freedom. In Germany the → Enlightenment, → Kantianism, and → idealism found themselves in opposition to western European and American → individualism because of the latter's association with → deism, → materialism, and → liberalism.

Karl → Marx (1818-83) opposed both a theonomous basis for freedom and the real existence of freedom for most people in a middle-class capitalistic society. In communism human beings supposedly gain control of their own history by their knowledge of scientific laws and for the first time create freedom for all (→ Marxism).

The victorious march of natural science favored (at least until the fundamental crisis in physics in the 1920s) a deterministic → worldview that accepted freedom only as a subjective phenomenon of consciousness. Today the alternatives of freedom and determinism seem to be theoretical and abstract, and we cannot answer the question regarding their relation when it is put in this form. Undoubtedly, every decision is influenced by physical, psychological, social, political, and cultural ties. As we are to some extent aware of these factors and use them selectively, however, there is room for our own reactions and responses to the influences that press in upon us. For this reason alone can legal codes assess guilt (→ Punishment).

Sigmund Freud (1856-1939), who was still tightly linked with the scientific view of the 19th century, pointed out that in our dependence on the unconscious we are only too seldom "in charge of our own house." His therapy (→ psychoanalysis) aimed at increasing spiritual freedom in such a way as to make a distinction between conscious and unconscious activity (*Gesammelte Werke* 10.319-20). This program provokes the counterquestion whether the unconscious activity of the → soul restricts freedom or helps to make it possible (thus C. G. Jung).

2.8. Roman Catholic Church

Up to World War II the → Roman Catholic Church fought a bitter war against the modernist, autonomous view of freedom and equality (→ Anti-Modernist Oath; Modernism). → Leo XIII (1878-1903), the leader in developing the social teaching of the church (→ Social Ethics), traced the French → Revolution, "unbridled license," and wrongful ideas about freedom to their ultimate source in the "so-called Reformation" (*Diuturnum* [1881]). A cautious revision of antimodernism followed, especially at → Vatican II. → Moral theology then sought a middle way between the Christian ethos, on the one side, and, on the other, autonomous reason, self-discovery, and freedom (e.g., Franz Böckle, *Fundamental Moral Theology* [1980]; → Ethics 4).

2.9. Modern Protestantism

In modern → Protestantism the Reformation ethos of freedom, mostly secularized, has entered into many alliances. In Germany after 1815, and especially after 1871, a national Protestantism arose that ultimately offered little resistance to nationalism and National Socialism (→ Fascism). It lost power after 1945. Protestant social ethics, triggered by social questions and founded in 1868 by A. von Oettingen, was often viewed as an attack on the ideal of the free Christian personality, since many people did not want to accept the dependence of moral decisions on the social situation and perceived a threat to a theonomous view of freedom. This tendency was still influential, if for other reasons, in the time of → dialectical theology, and it condemned social ethics to impotence. The freedom of God and his Word was the main theme introduced by Karl → Barth (1886-1968). The → Confessing Church defended the freedom of the gospel and of the church against National Socialism.

Experiences under Hitler, the choice for the "free West," and the rejection of Communism made freedom a leading theme after 1945 even in theology, completely suppressing the already feeble theme of equality. Leaning on the early philosophy of M. Heidegger (→ Existentialism), R. Bultmann (1884-1976) developed an existential, ontological view of freedom (→ Existential Theology) that left little room for its social and communicative dimensions and gave a place to existential experiences of solitariness. Completely omitted were other basic values that were of supreme importance in drawing up a constitution for West Germany (e.g., equality and social sharing). Thus a Christian social ethics seemed to be impossible. The same tendency may still be seen in the linguistic, hermeneutical theology (→ Hermeneutics) of, say, G. Ebeling, who in his *Dogmatik des christlichen Glaubens* (3 vols.; 1979) developed freedom thematically along the lines of Luther but did not set it in the dimension of concrete → ethics or relate it to the ethos of equality. Nor did Barth, although he did develop his ethics in terms of the freedom that is made possible by God's turning to us and that is therefore eminently active and communicative (*CD* II/2, §§36-38, and III/4).

Only with difficulty did Protestant social ethics develop in West Germany, and along with it an appropriate view of freedom in correlation with obligation. The understanding of freedom as a basic right and as a self-designation of the political constitution made it necessary for theologians to take up material positions and led to fundamental discussions on how to relate secular and theological views of freedom. The law allowed freedom of personal development, the inviolable freedom of the person, and freedom of belief, conscience, and confession; also it provided for the freedom of conscientious objection, freedom of research, teaching, and media, freedom of assembly, freedom in the choice of residence, and freedom of vocation and work. Yet there was still considerable debate about the relationship of these freedoms to other basic rights such as equality. In this debate Protestant social ethics had to assert its own view of freedom. It is not merely an issue of freedoms codified as basic rights but of the whole of life in the dialectic of de-

pendence and freedom, of obedience and freedom, in society and the world.

In the context of social ethics, the freedom that believers owe to God's turning to us in Christ is marked by its communicative character. It finds actualization in a prompt turning to other people and other creatures. It is not subject to human caprice but empowers believers for mature independence of all perverted ties and for mutual "being for others" (D. → Bonhoeffer). To be sure, this freedom neither can nor should be made a general social norm, but it offers a perspective for the expounding of all secular freedom. When freedom is thus developed as communicative, reciprocal → solidarity, it does not come into competition with equality and sharing but is complementary to them. If Christian social ethics can bring to light in this way the meaning of freedom, which is only partially reached in secular expositions but which is their final goal, then it can point to a universal meaning of freedom that is now disclosed to faith. Aiming at the same goal in very different contexts are → feminist theologies and African American, Hispanic, Latin American, and Asian → liberation theologies. Written from the point of view of the oppressed and marginalized, these theologies offer radically different perspectives on the meaning of freedom.

→ Anthropology 3

Bibliography: H. ARENDT, *The Human Condition* (2d ed.; Chicago, 1998; orig. pub., 1958); idem, *On Revolution* (Harmondsworth, 1990; orig. pub., 1963) • O. BAYER, *Freiheit als Antwort. Zur theologischen Ethik* (Tübingen, 1995) • R. BULTMANN, "The Significance of the Idea of Freedom for Western Civilization," *Essays Philosophical and Theological* (New York, 1955) 305-25 • J. H. CONE, *A Black Theology of Liberation* (Philadelphia, 1970) • W. CONZE et al., "Freiheit," *GGB* 425-543 • L. D. EASTON and K. H. GUDDAT, eds., *Writings of the Young Marx on Philosophy and Society* (New York, 1967) • ERASMUS, "A Discussion of Free Will" (1524), *Collected Works of Erasmus* (vol. 76; Toronto, 1999) 1-89 • W. FÖRSTER, *Thomas Hobbes und der Puritanismus. Grundlagen und Grundfragen seiner Staatslehre* (Berlin, 1969) • G. GUTIÉRREZ, *A Theology of Liberation* (rev. ed., Maryknoll, N.Y., 1988) • P. C. HODGSON, *New Birth of Freedom: A Theology of Bondage and Liberation* (Philadelphia, 1976) • W. HUBER and H. E. TÖDT, *Menschenrechte. Perspektiven einer menschlichen Welt* (Munich, 1988) • P. LEHMANN, *The Transfiguration of Politics* (New York, 1975) • LEO XIII, "Diuturnum" (1881), *The Papal Encyclicals* (5 vols.; ed. C. Carlen; Raleigh, N.C., 1981) 2.51-61 • C. B. MACPHERSON, *Political Theory of Possessive Individual-*

ism: Hobbes to Locke (Oxford, 1988; orig. pub., 1962) •
D. L. MIGLIORE, *Called to Freedom* (Philadelphia, 1980)
• H. J. MULLER, *Freedom in the Ancient World* (New
York, 1961) • K. NIEDERWIMMER, *Der Begriff der Frei-
heit im Neuen Testament* (Berlin, 1966) • M. POHLENZ,
*Freedom in Greek Life and Thought: The History of an
Ideal* (Dordrecht, 1966) • R. R. RUETHER, *Sexism and
God-Talk: Toward a Feminist Theology* (Boston, 1983) •
M. WEBER, *The Protestant Ethic and the Spirit of Capi-
talism* (Los Angeles, 1998; orig. pub., 1904-5).

HEINZ EDUARD TÖDT†

Freemasons → Masons

Freethinkers

1. Goals
2. History
3. Relations with the Churches

1. Goals

Freethinkers represent a cultural, political, and philosophical movement, atheistic in belief and made up of
various groupings that seek to rid people of religious
and scientific errors and prejudices. This movement
rejects the teachings and ties of religious institutions.

The various groups stress the separation of →
church and state, oppose the traditional influence of
the Christian church on public life, advocate cremation instead of church burial (→ Funeral), oppose
church-sanctioned → war, seek the legal recognition of their societies as corporations alongside the
churches, and promote freethinking ceremonies as a
replacement for the church ceremonies associated
with birth, maturity, marriage, and death.

2. History

The freethinking movement arose out of the British
and French → Enlightenment. The term "freethinker" was first used in 1697 by W. Molineux, who
saw in J. Toland (1670-1722) a "candid freethinker."
It came into philosophy with *A Discourse of Freethinking* (1713), by A. Collins. The term first denoted those who subjected Christian faith to the
judgment of → reason and who held the epistemological principle of noncontradiction. Then it
came to be used for those who oriented thought
solely to the evidence of the object, apart from all →
authority. Later the term came to be erroneously
equated with the English → deists, and in the 19th
and 20th centuries it covered all atheistic thinkers.

The radical French rationalists D. Diderot
(1713-84), C.-A. Helvétius (1715-71), and P.-H.-D.
d'Holbach (1723-89) gave the term *libres penseurs*
an atheistic and materialistic accent. In Germany
freethinkers were first called *Freigeister* and, with
few exceptions, were wrongly seen as religious sec-
tarians. In the 19th century they influenced the liberal middle class in the form of a natural philosophy
that was partly materialistic and partly anti-
materialistic (→ Monism). The movement was
strongly oriented to natural science (K. Vogt,
L. Büchner, I. Moleschott, E. Haeckel) and to the
criticism of religion by L. Feuerbach (1804-72) and
D. F. Strauss (1808-74; → Religion, Criticism of). It
began to influence the working class by way of the
dialectical → materialism of K. → Marx (1818-83;
→ Marxism). In the middle of the 19th century,
middle-class → atheism was replaced by a socialist
atheism, which was a development of the philosophy and ideology of Marx and Engels (e.g., by
A. Bebel, K. Kautsky, F. Mehring, and V. I. Lenin).

At the end of the 19th century and the beginning
of the 20th, various federations were formed in several countries, reaching a peak between 1930 and
1940. The *Fédération Internationale de la Libre
Pensée* was formed in 1880. In 1905 the Union of
Freethinkers for Cremation was founded, and in
1908 the Central Union of German Proletariat Freethinkers, who published the paper *Der Atheist*.
These groups merged in 1927, becoming the Union
for Freethinking and Cremation (after 1930, the
German Freethinking Association). Before the
emergency decree of 1932 the proletarian Communist freethinking movement had its headquarters in
Berlin. Communist members of the merged group
withdrew to form the Union of Proletariat Freethinkers. After the Nazis banned the union, it was
reconstituted in 1951. In 1958 it split into two
unions, one in Dortmund and one in Berlin.

In Russia a union of atheists was founded in
1925, called the Union of Militant Atheists from
1929. It was dissolved in 1942. After World War II its
tasks and functions were assumed by the United Society for the Propagation of Scientific Knowledge.

Freethinkers are sometimes confused with →
Freemasons. This mistake overlooks the fact that
Freemasonry demands of its members a recognition
of "the supreme master builder of the universe."

3. Relations with the Churches

Prominent for freethinkers in their battle with the
churches is an overcoming of the ideology of obedience and of a sense of destiny. They oppose especially the glorifying of supposedly divinely ap-

pointed authorities. For their part, the churches challenge the Marxist criticism of religion and the scientific atheism that they find in freethinkers.

Bibliography: J. A. I. CHAMPION, *The Pillars of Priest-craft Shaken: The Church of England and Its Enemies, 1660-1730* (Cambridge, 1992) • J. E. H. COURTNEY, *Freethinkers of the Nineteenth Century* (New York, 1967) • A. L. GAYLOR, ed., *Women without Superstition: "No Gods–No Masters." The Collected Writings of Women Freethinkers of the Nineteenth and Twentieth Centuries* (Madison, Wis., 1997) • O. P. LARSON, *American Infidel: Robert G. Ingersoll* (New York, 1962) • J. MARSH, *Word Crimes: Blasphemy, Culture, and Literature in Nineteenth-Century England* (Chicago, 1998) • M. PRIESTMAN, *Romantic Atheism: Poetry and Freethought, 1780-1830* (New York, 1999) • S. WARREN, *American Freethought, 1860-1914* (New York, 1966).

HELMUT·REINALTER

French Missions

A sense of responsibility for foreign mission developed in France after the great upheavals of the French → Revolution of 1789 (→ Mission 3). After many years of mistrust and indeed persecution, the → Lutheran and → Reformed churches now had a guaranteed right to existence. They used their new freedom of action to found the Société des Missions Évangéliques de Paris chez des Peuples Non-chrétiens (SMEP), which could take part in the missionary movement without official restriction. The birthday of this society was November 4, 1822, in Paris.

Originally the SMEP did not plan to send its own → missionaries abroad but to place missionaries at the disposal of other societies. Only in 1827 did it consider the possibility of supervising its own overseas work. Areas discussed were the Near East, Mauritius, Canada, Louisiana, and Guyana, all lands in which work could be done in French.

Finally in 1829, in conjunction with the London Missionary Society (→ British Missions), which was already at work in southern Africa, the SMEP sent missionaries to the Cape. Some of these established the first mission station in what is now Botswana, but they soon moved to the area of the present-day state of Lesotho and began a work that later gave rise to the Evangelical Church of Lesotho. Lesotho was also the starting point for François Coillard (1834-1904), who moved north and in 1887 founded the Evangelical Zambesi Mission in what is now Zambia.

At the end of the 19th century the SMEP opened up new fields, including Senegal (St. Louis and Dakar) and Tahiti. In 1890 it took over the work of an American Presbyterian missionary society in Gabon. As a result of French colonizing (→ Colonialism; Colonialism and Mission), English missionary societies at work in Madagascar invited the SMEP to help them in 1896. At the same time and for the same reason, French missionaries went to New Caledonia, especially to assist in educational work. After World War I political circumstances made work possible in Cameroon, where the Protestant church had lost its missionaries from the Basel Mission. A similar thing happened in Togo, which the Bremen Mission had to abandon. The first missionaries of SMEP arrived there in 1928.

From the outset the SMEP had Lutherans as members, and the work went ahead with no denominational preconditions. French Lutherans became increasingly interested also in Lutheran missionary societies (Scandinavian, American, and German), which were active in lands that had become francophone as a result of colonizing (e.g., Madagascar). After World War II there was also cooperation with the Norwegian and American Lutherans at work in northern Cameroon.

The end of missionary activity was in sight, however, in terms of the classic movement of evangelism from north to south. The SMEP recognized this change in the first years after World War II. It took the initiative to promote the founding of autonomous churches (→ Independent Churches; Third World 2): Cameroon in 1957, Madagascar in 1958, Togo in 1959, New Caledonia in 1960, Gabon and Tahiti in 1961, and finally Zambia and Lesotho in 1964. In concert with these churches and with the other Protestant churches of Europe that shared in its work, the SMEP sought a new form of cooperation that would transcend national, denominational, racial, and cultural boundaries. It found a solution in the creation of a federation of churches resolved to support one another and to work together in evangelization and the giving of Christian instruction to their people. Thus the Communauté Évangélique d'Action Apostolique (CEVAA) came into being in 1971, with member churches in Europe, Africa, and the Pacific, all pledged to give each other mutual help.

When the SMEP finally ended its work after 150 years of existence, the Lutheran and Reformed churches in France decided to integrate missionary work into their own organization, and for this purpose they formed the Département Évangélique Français d'Action Apostolique (DEFAP). In parallel with this move, the Lutheran churches formed their own commission for relating to churches of the Third World (the Commission Luthérienne des Relations avec les Églises d'Outremer), which is attached to the Alliance Nationale des Églises Luthériennes de France (ANELF).

Bibliography: R. BLANC, J. BLOCHER, and E. KRUGER, *Histoire des Missions protestantes françaises* (Flavion, 1970) • J. M. MOHAPELOA, *From Mission to Church: Fifty Years of the Work of the Paris Evangelical Missionary Society and the Lesotho Evangelical Church, 1933-1983* (Morija, Lesotho, 1985) • *ParMiss,* January 1965, containing R. Blanc, "L'œuvre missionnaire des Églises luthériennes," and M.-A. Ledoux, "Les missions réformées" • H. ROUX, *Église et mission* (Paris, 1956) • SOCIÉTÉ DES MISSIONS ÉVANGÉLIQUES DE PARIS, *Voie nouvelle* (Paris, 1961) • J.-F. ZORN, *Le grand siècle d'une mission protestante. La Mission de Paris de 1822 à 1914* (Paris, 1993).

RENÉ BLANC

Friends, Society of

1. Definition
2. Origins
3. Early Theology
4. Polity
5. Three Hundred Years of Activity

1. Definition

The Society of Friends — whose members are popularly known as Quakers, a name now acknowledged proudly, although it was originally pejorative — originated in 17th-century England. In 1999 there were members in 43 countries, totaling approximately 280,000. The countries with the five largest memberships are Kenya (93,000), the United States (92,000), Bolivia (31,000), the United Kingdom (17,000), and Burundi (10,000).

Known particularly for their relief and diplomatic work during and after the two world wars, Quakers have been awarded three Nobel Peace Prizes: Emily Greene Balch (1867-1961) in 1946, the Friends Service Council in Britain (predecessor of Quaker Peace and Service) and the American Friends Service Committee jointly in 1947, and Philip J. Noel-Baker (1889-1982) in 1959.

2. Origins

Although Quakerism began in the period following the English civil wars (1642-51), it is debatable whether the movement should be seen as a manifes-

tation of → Puritanism. Beginning under the guidance and inspiration of George Fox (1624-91), Quakerism contained some Puritan elements, but there were also mystical and → Anabaptist features. Quakerism most adequately views itself as a fresh flowering of the NT church, which the Friends believed to have been in apostasy since apostolic times (see 2 Tim. 3:1-5).

Fox was soon joined in itinerant preaching by those known as the Valiant Sixty, who spread out in pairs, like the 70 sent out in Luke 10. They proclaimed the day of the Lord and the spiritual return of Christ. In 1652, while preaching in northwestern England, Fox secured the protection of a local judge and his wife, Thomas and Margaret Fell. Their home, Swarthmore Hall, became an organizational center. Within six years the movement had spread as far as Rome and Constantinople, as well as the settlements in America and all parts of Great Britain. Margaret Fell became one of the leaders of the movement; in 1669, after a decade of widowhood, she married George Fox.

Under the Puritans 3,000 Friends were imprisoned one or more times, and when the monarchy was restored in 1660, another 4,000 were jailed at a single time. Between 300 and 500 died in prison, largely from unsanitary conditions. In addition to this suffering in England, four "Boston Martyrs" — one a woman — were hanged for daring to preach in the Congregationalist Commonwealth of Massachusetts.

3. Early Theology

While George Fox was the principal formulator of Friends doctrine, he was but one of six outstanding theologians within early Quakerism (and the only one who lacked higher education). Samuel Fisher (1605-65), holder of an Oxford M.A. and an Anglican priest before his → conversion (§2) to Quakerism, was one of the leading Scripture scholars of any denomination in 17th-century England. Isaac Penington (1616-79) studied at Catherine Hall, Cambridge. George Keith (ca. 1638-1716), who earned an M.A. from Marischal College, Aberdeen, was a Presbyterian minister before joining the Friends. William Penn (1644-1718), a follower of the Congregationalist John Owen at Cambridge, later studied at Saumur, a French Reformed institution. Robert Barclay (1648-90) was educated at the Roman Catholic Scots College in Paris under its rector, his uncle (also named Robert Barclay). Barclay's *Catechism and Confession of Faith* (1673) and his *Apology* (Lat. 1676, Eng. 1678) have never been displaced as the principal systematic statements of Quaker beliefs.

Friends believed that through his inward Light, Christ not only leads Christians into → unity and continues to reveal truth (John 1:9-18; 16:13-14) but is savingly active even for non-Christians. Although the substance of the ecumenical creeds was accepted, the → creeds themselves were rejected as wrongly used to enforce doctrinal conformity. Both the creeds and Trinitarian doctrine were also rejected because they contained philosophical terminology and concepts not found in Scripture. Nonetheless, God's tri-unity was accepted, and → Unitarianism was opposed. Interpreting the new covenant as being wholly inward (Jer. 31:31-34), the Friends rejected sacraments such as → baptism and the → Eucharist, refused to swear oaths or use honorific titles and forms of address, and practiced nonviolence (→ Peace Churches).

To understand how these beliefs fit together for Quakerism, one must begin with → Christology and be aware of the constant and indispensable dependence of both the individual and the group on Christ's presence through the Spirit. This spiritual return of Christ represents a more adequate interpretation of the Gk. term → *parousia,* which, in broadest terms, means simply "presence" or "coming." Fox saw this continuing of Christ's "presence in the midst" of his followers (Matt. 18:20) as being in the succession of the numerous accounts of his apparitions to the disciples through the Holy Spirit, the Paraclete, particularly in the Gospel of John (esp. 16:7, 12-15).

This fundamental Quaker doctrine "is the basis for the Quaker approach to voteless decision-making, and to worship, and has profound effects on many other aspects of their community life" (W. Roberts, 37). In Fox's words, "Christ is come again to teach his people himself." The salvific effect of personal and corporate attention to the Light of Christ and the guidance and direction he provides constitute a vast theology of grace in which the terms are often fluid and interchangeable but nevertheless create an indissoluble link between belief and practice.

Quaker worship, based on silent and expectant waiting, hinges on the belief that Christ will inspire anyone he chooses to speak and that he will provide the substance of the message. Although the majority of Friends now worship in a "programmed" way — with a standard Protestant-like sequence of call to worship, Scripture readings, hymns, and sermon — a period of silence after the sermon, in which anyone is free to speak as led, is still normally provided.

4. Polity
Quakerism at times appears to be a way of worship with a loose religious organization attached. Such characterization, however, is far from accurate. Both "programmed" and "unprogrammed" Friends have the same process for decision making, in which the church is seen to be "a gospel fellowship, a gospel order, a holy community." Within it the indwelling Christ is heard and obeyed by individuals and as *the* head of the community. At the meeting for business ("for church affairs," in British terminology) a clerk — not the pastor, if one exists — chairs the meeting. His or her function is to maintain an orderly agenda and to record "the sense of the meeting." The latter is periodically read aloud and amended until everyone present is satisfied that the "sense" has been caught accurately. Neither clerk nor pastor enjoys privileged address; both must ask permission to express their views (J. Punshon 1987, 94, 96).

A willingness to be persuaded is essential for the proper functioning of this method of decision making, in which no votes are taken. Only then can it be discerned how faith can be applied to new circumstances and individual leadings tested against the common understanding of Scripture and collective experience. The discipline of silent waiting is essential for this process, which cannot be equated with consensus building or merely an exercise in pure democracy; such an interpretation "disregards these theological underpinnings" (ibid., 97).

This "gospel order" is replicated in geographically widening associations known as Monthly, Quarterly (in England, "General"), and Yearly Meetings. These are named for the frequency with which they meet to conduct business, not for the frequency of worship, which is weekly. Each of these associations has a committee structure designed to carry out the mandates of the plenary sessions. The authority is neither hierarchical nor congregational. Monthly Meetings alone decide who can become members, be married, or be buried under Friends care. Monthly Meetings are, in turn, expected to abide by the rules — originally described, undogmatically, as advices — set forth by their Yearly Meeting. In more recent times, Testimonies and a Discipline have been added; except in property matters, these terms are not legal requirements.

5. Three Hundred Years of Activity
In the 18th and 19th centuries, Friends turned inward. They expelled ("disowned") those among them who brought discredit to the Society by bankruptcy, joining the militia, or marrying nonmembers. This era has been described as a time of →

quietism, but the emphasis was still on "a clearly defined way of life with a spiritual basis" (H. H. Brinton 1952, 184).

A major concern, building on 17th-century precedents, continued to be the improvement of the social order. The equal treatment of all people, including native inhabitants, characteristic of Pennsylvania ever since its charter was granted in 1681, thus continued to be in the center of Quaker life. At Germantown in Pennsylvania (named for Palatinate settlers, who included Lutherans, Mennonites and Brethren) the Friends in 1688 issued the first declaration against → slavery. By 1776 Pennsylvania Quakers had freed all their own slaves under the leadership of John Woolman (1720-72), Anthony Benezet (1713-84), and others, all of whom were also active in the international antislavery movement.

In early 19th-century England Elizabeth Fry (1780-1845) began work for penal reform, concentrating especially on the betterment of women prisoners. Under William Tuke (1732-1822) the York Retreat in England in 1796 became the world's first hospital for the treatment, and not merely the custody, of the mentally ill. In 1813 Friends Hospital in Philadelphia became the first hospital in the United States to abolish the chaining of patients.

From the beginning, women occupied a position of equal partnership in Quakerism. Women as well as men undertook individual journeys on behalf of the movement that often lasted for years, frequently crossing the Atlantic. For example, Martha Routh, an English schoolteacher in poor health, traveled 11,000 miles in America (1794-96), and Catherine Phillips traveled 8,750 miles on horseback (1753-56). Quaker women, particularly Susan B. Anthony (1820-1906) and Lucretia Mott (1793-1880), were active in the women's suffrage movement after the Seneca Falls Conference of 1848. More recently the Quaker Alice Paul (1885-1977) was a leader in the long but unsuccessful campaign for an Equal Rights Amendment to the U.S. Constitution.

In addition to this concern for social improvement, Friends have been creatively active in → education, having established 82 schools in the United States, 2 of which have been in continuous operation since 1689. Only rarely has Quaker presence in a country not resulted in the establishment of schools, as illustrated by the more than 400 Quaker schools in Kenya. In the 19th century Friends began to establish colleges in the United States, where they now sponsor ten colleges, two universities, and seven seminary-level programs or institutions. Quakers now also have seminaries in Kenya and Guatemala and are involved, with evangelicals, in similar institutions in Taiwan, Bolivia, and India (in Yavatmal, Maharashtra).

Since World War I Friends have been internationally involved in → relief work. This activity has been accompanied by efforts to uncover and deal with the causes of → war (→ Peace Research). Together with several Roman Catholic and Jewish groups and agencies, Friends were the original group to be accredited by the → United Nations as nongovernmental organizations. The first standing national religious lobby to the U.S. government was the Friends Committee on National Legislation, established in 1943. As significant as these activities are, however, Friends do not see themselves primarily as a social or humanitarian agency but as a "compelling form of New Testament society" (Lon Fendall).

The 20th century has also seen the formation in the United States of overarching national bodies. Among such largely "unprogrammed" bodies are the Friends General Conference (FGC) and the Conservative Friends; "programmed" bodies include the Friends United Meeting (FUM) and Evangelical Friends International (EFI). Both the FUM and the EFI, headquartered in the United States, are international groups involved in extensive mission work. It is to be noted, however, that none of the bodies has authority to compel its Yearly Meetings in any matter; they merely advise, where appropriate, and engage in joint ventures. The Friends World Committee for Consultation is a → "Christian world communion," in ecumenical terms, with its small staff located in London; it has regional sections in key parts of the world.

Publications by the Quakers are disproportionately many. There are three Quaker publishing houses and bookstores in the United States, and two of each in the United Kingdom. The 77 Quaker periodicals include historical and theological journals in the two countries.

Patterns of ecumenical involvement vary. Friends historically have had a certain impatience with much ecumenical work, since their life has always been marked by a rejection of both an ordained ministry and sacramental worship and, positively, by an emphasis on the equality of women. Nevertheless, the FGC, FUM, and the Canadian Yearly Meeting were founding members of the → World Council of Churches, and many Yearly Meetings belong to national Christian councils.

In spite of being numerically small, Quakers have taken their place within the world of theological scholarship, particularly in biblical studies. Henry Joel Cadbury, whose work centered largely on the study of Luke-Acts, in 1919 became the first non-Congregationalist professor at the Divinity School of Harvard University; he was also an important member of the team of scholars that produced the Revised Standard Version of the Bible in 1952. Other Friends who have made important contributions to biblical studies have included H. G. Wood, George Boobyer, and Paul Anderson.

Bibliography: M. P. ABBOTT, *A Certain Kind of Perfection* (Wallingford, Pa., 1997) • H. S. BARBOUR and J. FROST, *The Quakers* (New York, 1994) • H. H. BRINTON, *Friends for Three Hundred Years* (New York, 1952); idem, *Quaker Journals* (Philadelphia, 1972) • E. P. BROWN and S. M. STUARD, eds., *Witnesses for Change: Quaker Women over Three Centuries* (New Brunswick, N.J., 1989) • H. J. CADBURY, *A Quaker Approach to the Bible* (Guilford, N.C., 1953) • W. A. COOPER, *A Living Faith* (Richmond, Ind., 1990) • G. FOX, *The Journal of George Fox* (ed. J. L. Nickalls; London, 1975); idem, *"The Power of the Lord Is over All": The Pastoral Letters of George Fox* (ed. T. Canby Jones; Richmond, Ind., 1989) • D. FREIDAY, *Speaking as a Friend* (Newberg, Oreg., 1995); idem, ed., *Barclay's "Apology" in Modern English* (Newberg, Oreg., 1967) • O. GREENWOOD, *Quaker Encounters* (3 vols.; York, 1975-78) • D. GWYN, *Apocalypse of the Word* (Richmond, Ind., 1986) • D. NEWMAN, *A Procession of Friends* (New York, 1972) • J. PUNSHON, *Encounter with Silence* (London, 1987); idem, *Portrait in Grey: A Short History of the Quakers* (London, 1984) • A. O. ROBERTS, *Through Flaming Sword: A Spiritual Biography of George Fox* (Portland, Oreg., 1959) • A. O. ROBERTS and H. BARBOUR, eds., *Early Quaker Writings* (Grand Rapids, 1973) • W. P. ROBERTS, *The Quakers as Type of the Spirit-Centered Community* (Pittsburgh, 1972) • M. J. SHEERAN, S.J., *Beyond Majority Rule: Voteless Decisions in the Religious Society of Friends* (Philadelphia, 1983) • D. V. STEERE, *Quaker Spirituality* (New York, 1984) • *To Lima with Love: A Quaker Response to "Baptism, Eucharist, and Ministry"* (London, 1987) • J. WILLCUTS, *Why Friends Are Friends* (Newberg, Oreg., 1984) • W. R. WILLIAMS, *The Rich Heritage of Quakerism* (rev. ed.; Newberg, Oreg., 1987) • L. L. WILSON, *Quaker Vision of Gospel Order* (Burnsville, N.C., 1993).

DEAN FREIDAY

Friendship

In wrestling with the concept of friendship, theology and the church must do some rethinking. They must begin at the point where, in the tension between isolation with limited contacts (→ Anonymity) and self-alienating life in the mass (→ Masses, The), the question arises afresh concerning what forms of relationship can both promote fellowship and establish identity. The paradigm of friendship can help us understand how the following relations condition each other and can become less moralistic: those between → love of God and the liking for others, between altruistic and egoistic strivings, and between acts of outreach and feelings of rivalry. In this sense the possibility or obligation of friendship is a task that demands attention not only in an educational setting but also in a pastoral context (→ Counseling; Pastoral Care).

If a problem arises for Christians in relation to the concept and experience of friendship, it is against the background of the conversation between theology and the humanities. It is no accident that from antiquity to the present, friendship has repeatedly been the object of philosophical reflection. Because different epochs ascribe different social value to friendship, it has similarly prompted both historical and sociological studies. Finally, given its function as an element affecting behavior within interpersonal relationships, it can be subjected in any given context also to psychological examination. A hermeneutical key might be provided by the question how the experience of friendship is developed and shaped in basic tension with the opposing experience of competition (which only in exaggerated form becomes enmity; → Enemy). To achieve a proper attitude in the social nexus, all of us must learn how to handle other people and things. In the process of learning, we unavoidably come into rivalry (with parents, siblings, and neighbors), which will also be the case in later spheres of development on various fronts. At the same time, the world around us, which shares our work and enforces roles, demands that we live and work together. Harmony and competition are natural antitheses, and it is a constant struggle to relate them.

At the various stages of life the resultant capacity for friendship functions to bring → emancipation and personal → identity. The friendship of children helps them in the necessary task of breaking free from parents and → family. Friendship among adults not only leads to marriage but also helps to differentiate loving relationships and avoid symbiotic relationships. Friendship in old age brings support when there is mourning for the loss of loved ones (→ Grief). These effects make it plain why the inability to make friends (by remaining stuck in one-sided competitiveness, being afraid of closeness to others, or an anxiety about tabooed homosexual tendencies) can express a fundamental feeling of incompetence and can even be a symptom of deeper problems.

Bibliography: K. Adomeit, *Aristoteles über die Freundschaft* (Heidelberg, 1992) • N. K. Badhwar, ed., *Friendship: A Philosophical Reader* (Ithaca, N.Y., 1993) • J. F. Fitzgerald, ed., *Greco-Roman Perspectives on Friendship* (Atlanta, 1997) • C. Gremmels and W. Huber, eds., *Theologie und Freundschaft. Wechselwirkungen: Eberhard Bethge und Dietrich Bonhoeffer* (Gütersloh, 1994) • J. W. Lynes, *Themes in the Current Reformation in Religious Thinking: The Covenantal Friendship of God* (Lewiston, N.Y., 1997) • A. C. Mitchell, "Friendship," *MCE* 330-34 • A. Nygren, *Agape and Eros* (Chicago, 1982; orig. pub., 1930) • F. Ortega, *Michel Foucault. Rekonstruktion der Freundschaft* (Munich, 1997) • H. H. Schrey, "Freundschaft," *TRE* 11.590-99 (bibliography) • L. Thomas, "Friendship," *EncAE* 2.323-33 • K. Winkler, *Emanzipation in der Familie* (Munich, 1976).

Klaus Winkler†

Fulfillment → Promise and Fulfillment

Functionalism

1. Definition
2. Functionalism and Psychology
3. Functionalism and Sociology

1. Definition
In medieval usage "function" simply denoted the public tasks of individuals or institutions. Following C. Darwin, F. Galton, and H. Spencer, however, it assumed increasing importance for → psychology and sociology. What is generally understood by "function" now is the contribution that some element, event, or process makes to the maintaining of a given structure.

2. Functionalism and Psychology
In close relation to → pragmatism and behaviorism, and along the lines of Darwin and Spencer, functionalist psychology primarily inquires into the suitability of describing natural and social settings in terms of psychological processes. In this respect it differs from a structurally oriented psychology (cf. the experimental psychology of W. Wundt) that finds its task in expounding the ultimate elements in the consciousness and their relations to one another. The main proponents of a functionalist psychology include W. James, J. R. Angell, J. M. Baldwin, and S. T. Hall.

3. Functionalism and Sociology
The idea of function takes on basic sociological significance in the work of É. Durkheim (1858-1917) and in Anglo-Saxon cultural → anthropology. According to Durkheim, the function of an → institution is the social value that it has objectively, that is, apart from the will of those active in it. As R. K. Merton showed in a criticism of the cultural anthropological functionalism of B. Malinowski and A. R. Radcliffe-Brown, it cannot be deduced from this thesis that every institution must have a social function, that it should be functional for → society as a whole, or that because of its functional significance it might not be changed or replaced without harm.

Functional statements are valid only in relation to a specific structure or problem. Both factors in the relation may change. If there is a relational change, various functional or dysfunctional effects may follow for an element, event, or process. Thus far, no convincing methods have been found to achieve a functional balance in estimating such effects. If we consider different elements, events, and processes in the same context, comparison among them is possible. If they can achieve the same results, they are functionally equivalent. The contextual relativity of functional statements, however, opens up an unforeseeable field of possible assertions about functionalities, dysfunctionalities, and functional equivalences, whose theoretical integration causes problems.

A reaction to this situation is the *structural-functional theory* of T. Parsons, which relates the concept of function to the universal, analytically derived problems of action systems and thus provides a fixed theoretical framework for functional analyses. Most recently, neofunctionalism especially (Jeffrey Alexander, Richard Munch) has picked up on Parsons's work.

In contrast to the Parsonian strand of functionalism, Niklas Luhmann's *theory of social systems* tries to free the concept of function from its dependence on a presupposed structure by means of a radicalization of functional analysis. Luhmann inquires concerning the function of structures themselves and understands their function as the delimitation of an otherwise unlimited space of indefinite possibilities. This procedure thus introduces the reduction of complexity as the ultimate problem of functional analysis, one that replaces the universal problems of self-preservation of action systems or social systems in structural-functionalistic theory. Taking this ultimate problem as the point of departure, this approach is to develop a universal functionalistic theory in the form of a descending hierarchy of relational problems and related classes of equivalent solutions, thus combining the technique of functional analysis with the concept of the "autopoietic" (self-reproducing) system.

Bibliography: J. C. ALEXANDER, *Neofunctionalism and After* (Malden, Mass., 1998); idem, *Twenty Lectures* (New York, 1987) • J. R. ANGELL, "The Promise of Functional Psychology," *PsRev* 14 (1907) 61ff. • A. J. BLASI, "Functionalism," *EncRS* 193-97 • P. COLOMY, *Neofunctionalist Sociology* (Brookfield, Vt., 1990); idem, ed., *Functionalist Sociology* (Brookfield, Vt., 1990) • É. DURKHEIM, *The Rules of Sociological Method* (New York, 1982; orig. pub., 1895) • W. JAMES, *The Principles of Psychology* (Cambridge, Mass., 1983; orig. pub., 1890) • N. LUHMANN, "Funktion und Kausalität," *Soziologische Aufklärung* (vol. 1; 5th ed.; Opladen, 1984) 9-30; idem, "Gesellschaft als soziales System," *Die Gesellschaft der Gesellschaft* (Frankfurt, 1997); idem, "System and Function," *Social Systems* (Stanford, Calif., 1995) chap. 1 • M. H. MARX and W. A. HILLIX, "Functionalism," *Systems and Theories in Psychology* (3d ed.; New York, 1979) chap. 5 • R. K. MERTON, "Manifest and Latent Functions," *Social Theory and Social Structure* (8th ed.; Glencoe, Ill., 1963) 19-84 • R. MUNCH, *Theory of Action* (London, 1987) • T. PARSONS, *The Social System* (London, 1991; orig. pub., 1951).

BERNHARD GIESEN and WOLFGANG SCHNEIDER

Fundamental Theology

1. Concept
2. Development of the Discipline
3. In Roman Catholic Theology
4. In Protestant Theology

1. Concept

"Fundamental theology" is a comprehensive term used to describe reflection that is basic to → theology as a whole. The term has been used in a variety of ways, and the shape and scope of this theology often depend on the specific theological conception or issue under discussion at the time. Some theologians employ the term "foundational theology" and "philosophical theology" interchangeably with "fundamental theology," while others make a distinction between these terms. Fundamental theology provides elements for the development of → systematic theology by expounding on the possibility and reality of revelation. As → apologetics, it provides a basis for faith's claim to → truth. In the form of the German → encyclopedia, it deals with the unity and academic character of theology in all its branches.

2. Development of the Discipline

The first example of fundamental theology as a modern theological discipline may be found in J. F. Kleuker of Kiel, whose *Grundriß einer Encyklopädie der Theologie* appeared in 1800-1801. For Kleuker, the task of fundamental theology is prior to that of systematic, practical, and historical theology and, as such, is a critical, exegetical, and apologetic science, showing how the Bible can function as the foundational principle of all theology. A. F. L. Pelt, also of Kiel, adopted Kleuker's term in his *Theologische Encyklopädie* of 1843, which itself was heavily influenced by F. D. E. → Schleiermacher's *Kurze Darstellung des theologischen Studiums* (1810; 2d ed., 1830). Here fundamental theology is the first part of systematic theology, followed by substantive teachings on faith and morals.

J. S. Drey developed the field of apologetics into an independent field in his *Apologetik* (3 vols., 1843-47), in which he defended the concept of revelation in light of the challenges to it from → Enlightenment rationality. His methods continued the tripartite division within Roman Catholic fundamental theology that found their origins in the 17th-century works of H. Grotius and P. Charron and the 18th-century works of L.-J. Hooke and P. M. Gazzaniga, which focused on the activity of divine revelation. In this schema fundamental theology was divided into the defense of Christian revelation, revelation in the resurrection of Jesus Christ, and Catholic revelation in the foundation of the church. This threefold division became the central feature of subsequent Roman Catholic handbooks of fundamental theology.

Although fundamental theology attracted increasing attention in Protestant theology around the middle of the 19th century, the concept increasingly found a home in Roman Catholic theology but tended to be forgotten in the Protestant sphere. The Roman Catholic theologian J. N. Ehrlich wrote the first monograph on fundamental theology as such (Prague, 1859-62), in which he tried to demonstrate the possibility, necessity, and historical reality of revelation.

3. In Roman Catholic Theology

In 1870 → Vatican I (sess. 3, chap. 4, DH 3019) recognized the term "fundamental theology" and gave the discipline a determinative Roman Catholic content. In its view → faith and → reason assist one another, as right reason demonstrates the truth of the foundations of faith *(fidei fundamenta)*.

The successful execution of this task required an objective apologetics that tries to show the credibility of Christian teaching apart from the believing subject. Faith, it argued, is rational; Christian doctrine has a divine origin; the Catholic Church is the only true church (→ Church 3.2; Teaching Office); and as the one true church, it guards true doctrine (*demonstratio religiosa, christiana,* and *catholica*). Since the objectivity of this apologetic seemed to be open to historical criticism, and since faith was put on too much of an intellectual level, an "apologetic of immanence" also arose in France (under the stimulus of M. Blondel [1861-1949]) and in Germany. In his transcendental → anthropology K. → Rahner (1904-84) showed how human beings are open to revelation, thus finding a point of contact for faith (→ Immanence and Transcendence). The objective and immanent modes of proof could now be combined in an "integral apologetics" (A. Lang).

→ Vatican II strengthened these concerns, making possible a broad discussion with Protestant theology, and thus greatly widened the themes with which fundamental theology concerned itself. The ever-present danger was that fundamental theology might absorb the tasks of all other theological disciplines. The council's Declaration on Religious Freedom *(Dignitatis humanae),* together with hermeneutical and correlational promptings from Protestant theology, gave vitality to the *demonstratio religiosa.* The preconciliar *demonstratio catholica,* however, ran into difficulties because the new ecumenical openness permitted a use of the word → "church" in the plural. The historical thinking that had found a place in Roman Catholic biblical scholarship demanded a rethinking of the doctrine of revelation and of the nature of Christianity.

After Vatican II, Roman Catholic theologians began working out a new theological consensus that took into account newer methodological and anthropological approaches, employed relevant themes from the Bible and ecclesiastical tradition, and paid careful attention to the relation between the church and the world (see the overview by R. Latourelle and G. O'Collins). H. Stirnimann's arrangement of fundamental theology under four central categories — dealing with the relation of faith to reason, understanding, practice, and experience — is an example of this emerging consensus.

According to one's particular philosophical, theological, political, or ideological commitments or interests, a particular theological theme can become central to a theologian's method. As the influence of existential philosophy and the "critical social theory" of the Frankfurt School (→ Critical Theory) began to wane, J. B. Metz formulated a practical fundamental theology based on the premise that all theological themes can be known and assessed only on the basis of "orthopraxy," or "right practice" (→ Political Theology). In this view, fundamental theology offers a changed form of the *demonstratio catholica:* the church as the defender of doctrine is now replaced by the suffering → people of God, who are on their way to redemptive freedom.

Employing contemporary hermeneutical methods, F. S. Fiorenza returned to some of the classic themes in Roman Catholic fundamental theology. His "foundational theology" reexamined the traditional themes of the tripartite structure of Roman Catholic fundamental theology: the resurrection of Jesus, the foundation of the church, and the mission of the church. David Tracy, also employing hermeneutical methods, developed a theological anthropology that focused on transcendental reflection on human → experience.

4. In Protestant Theology

Toward the end of the 19th century, the influence of A. Ritschl (1822-89) weakened Protestant interest in fundamental theology. The rejection of metaphysics and natural theology, as well as the idea of a theology that in principle is based in the church, ruled out investigation of the transition from existence before faith to existence in faith. This basic → biblicism was strengthened after World War I in → dialectical theology. This approach confirmed the misunderstanding that fundamental theology, not merely in terminology but also in substance, was specifically a Roman Catholic discipline.

P. → Tillich (1886-1965) was one of the few Protestant theologians who refused to follow Ritschl in making theology solely a concern of the church. Using philosophy, he devoted himself to a renewal of apologetics by working out a "method of correlation." When he was forced into exile from Germany in 1933, he developed his theological approach in the United States, where his influence has been the most extensive. In a further development of this method of correlation, G. D. Kaufman related Christian inner history (the Bible and church history) to the present-day experience of faith. E. Farley juxtaposed the phenomenologically described world of faith with the criteria of theological assessment.

Once the question in Germany — raised most acutely in the → church struggle of the Nazi era — of the relationship of fundamental theology to the church had eased, unsolved problems in fundamental theology reared their heads again. The question of revelation, which formerly had been dealt with doctrinally, now took the form of → hermeneutics, and in this form it raised issues that the fundamental theology of the 19th century had shelved.

Pursuing his hermeneutical inquiries, G. Ebeling sketched a Protestant fundamental theology, giving it the task of expounding the unity and truth of theology. He put fundamental theology at the end of the theological encyclopedia (outline of studies) and not at the beginning. For Ebeling, fundamental theology must first reflect on theology as a presentation of what is essentially Christian in the Bible and church history. It must also show the basic theological significance of the event behind the → tradition of the church and the Word of God (hermeneutics). Finally, it must investigate the truth of theology in three areas: the certainty of the experience of faith, the academic nature of theology, and the task of the theologian.

Ebeling's view somewhat lessened the fear of the use of the term "fundamental theology" among Protestant theologians. W. Joest gave his handbook, which discusses revelation as a foundation of theology and theological methodology, the title *Fundamentaltheologie.* (H. Beintker took a similar approach). E. Jüngel proposed a foundational theology situated in the "dispute between theism and atheism" and grounded in the "Crucified One." More common in contemporary German theology is the treatment of the themes of fundamental theology in terms of the → philosophy of science or with the question of the integration of the humanities into theology.

→ Dogmatics; Epistemology

Bibliography: H. BEINTKER, "Verstehen und Glauben. Grundlinien einer evangelischen Fundamentaltheologie," *KuD* 22 (1976) 22-40 • G. EBELING, "Erwägungen zu einer evangelischen Fundamentaltheologie," *ZTK* 67 (1970) 479-524; idem, *The Study of Theology* (London, 1979) • E. FARLEY, *Ecclesial Man* (Philadelphia, 1975); idem, *Ecclesial Reflection* (Philadelphia, 1982) • F. S. FIORENZA, *Foundational Theology: Jesus and the Church* (New York, 1984) • W. JOEST, *Fundamentaltheologie. Theologische Grundlagen- und Methodenprobleme* (Stuttgart, 1988) • E. JÜNGEL, *God as the Mystery of the World* (Grand Rapids, 1983) • G. D. KAUFMAN, *Systematic Theology* (2d ed.; New York, 1978) • W. KERN et al., eds., *HFTh* • A. LANG, *Fundamentaltheologie* (4th ed.; 2 vols.; Munich, 1967) • R. LATOURELLE and R. FISICHELLA, eds., *Dictionary of Fundamental Theology* (New York, 1994) • R. LATOURELLE and G. O'COLLINS, *Problems and Perspectives of Fundamental Theology* (New York, 1982) • J. B. METZ, *Glaube in Geschichte und Gesellschaft* (5th ed.; Mainz, 1992) • H. PEUKERT, *Science, Action, and Fundamental Theology* (Cambridge, Mass., 1984) • K. RAHNER, *Hearer of the Word* (New York, 1994; orig. pub., 1940) • J. RATZINGER, *Theologische Prinzipienlehre. Bausteine zur Fundamentaltheologie* (Munich, 1982) • J. SCHMITZ, "Die Fundamentaltheologie im 20. Jahrhundert," *Bilanz der Theologie im 20. Jahrhundert* (ed. H. Vorgrimler; Freiburg, 1969-70) 2.197-245 • H. STIRNIMANN, "Erwägungen zur Fundamentaltheologie," *FZPhTh* 24 (1977) 291-365 • J. E. THIEL, *Nonfoundationalism* (Minneapolis, 1994) • P. TILLICH, *Systematic Theology* (vol. 1; Chicago, 1951) • D. TRACY, *The Analogical Imagination* (New York, 1981); idem, *Blessed Rage for Order* (New York, 1975) • H. WAGNER, *Einführung in die Fundamentaltheologie* (2d ed.; Darmstadt, 1996); idem, "Fundamentaltheologie," *TRE* 11.738-52 (bibliography) • H. WALDENFELS, *Kontextuelle Fundamentaltheologie* (2d ed.; Paderborn, 1988).

ROLF SCHÄFER and CRAIG A. PHILLIPS

Fundamentalism

The term "fundamentalism" is said to derive from a series of tracts, *The Fundamentals* (1910-15), though not everything in these writings was fully "fundamentalist." As generally used, the term "fundamentalism" designates a form of conservative evangelical → Protestantism (→ Evangelical Movement) that, along with other traditional doctrines such as the → Trinity, → incarnation, deity of Christ (→ Christology), original → sin, human depravity, and justification by faith, lays an exceptional stress on the inerrancy and infallibility of the Bible as the absolutely essential foundation and criterion of → truth. Along with this emphasis goes the stress on personal → faith, the sense of sin and need for salvation, and personal involvement and appropriation of the → grace of God. Though it affirms many older doctrines, the real spiritual affiliation of fundamentalism is less with the Reformation or the older church and more with the tradition of → Pietism and → revivalism.

According to fundamentalism, the basis of faith is something given. This given does not lie in the → church as → institution, and in this respect fundamentalism is opposed to the → Roman Catholic conception. Equally is it opposed to "moderate" or "enlightened" conceptions: faith is not a matter of reasoned or dispassionate discussion, not something to be worked out or discovered, but is something already known and to be proclaimed without uncertainty. This given character of the basis of faith is most clearly exemplified in the Bible, which must be accepted without question or qualification. Like the character of faith itself, the nature of the Bible is not an open question. The radical opposition of fundamentalism to biblical criticism may be explained as objection to the latter's implication that the nature and the meaning of the Bible become an open question.

The term "fundamentalism" is often felt as pejorative, and its adherents would commonly describe themselves rather as "evangelical" or "orthodox." Fundamentalism is not one unitary viewpoint but has various strands within it. A central element is the doctrine of Scripture inherited from Protestant → orthodoxy but modified, notably through dilution of the dictation theory. In the 19th century this view was developed particularly by the Princeton theology, best exemplified by B. B. Warfield (1851-1921), with considerable finesse and logical acuity.

Much fundamentalism, however, is populist, ignorant, and hostile to intellectual theology. Many fundamentalist leaders have been popular preachers, ill educated in theology and ignorant of biblical studies, only loosely connected with institutional churches, and effectively working through individual organizations of their own. Modern technical developments (radio and television) made this kind of independent fundamentalism more influential, especially in the United States and through the worldwide influence of its culture. Another strand is the "prophetic" → millenarianism, disseminated particularly through the Scofield annotated edition of the English Bible; yet another is the "charismatic" emphasis on direct experience of God.

For much fundamentalism, the Bible acts as central symbol of a worldview. Thus the theory of → evolution is perceived as a challenge to the naive physical worldview believed to be founded on the Bible. This approach can develop toward → creationism. It was often thought that fundamentalism would disappear with the increasing influence of education and science; recent experience suggests that this is not so and that fundamentalism is well adapted to the modern world and well able to survive and increase within it.

The Christology of fundamentalism lays great stress on the deity of Christ, his → virgin birth, and the infallibility of his teachings. Atonement is by penal substitution: God's own Son is made the substitute for guilty humanity. → Justification is closely linked with the → conversion (§1) experience, to which most fundamentalist praxis is directed.

Central to all fundamentalist doctrine is the infallibility of Scripture. Interpretation is literal, but only at those points where it is important to funda-

mentalist religion that it should be literal; where literal interpretation would be dangerous to fundamentalist religion (e.g., through questioning the unity or inerrancy of the Bible), literality is abandoned and nonliteral meanings are accepted. Although *all* Scripture is infallible and authoritative, fundamentalism actually works through the ordering and ranking of various strands within the Bible, the preference being dictated by the past history of the evangelical tradition and its present needs. Philosophically, fundamentalism goes back to a naive realism and a *Weltbild* of fixed character. Development within history has little significance: the world remains the same until God's direct action brings about catastrophic change.

Fundamentalism is not institutionally identical with any particular → denomination. Though some confessional groups are basically fundamentalist in nature, fundamentalism commonly exists as a stratum within a wider confession (→ Confession of Faith). But it also has informal organizations of its own — including missionary societies, societies for work among students, and publishing houses — which are usually doctrinally strict and polemical against nonfundamentalist viewpoints. Some of the matters that divided the older confessions, such as questions of polity or sacraments, are often considered nonessential, and fundamentalism has a certain kind of interdenominationalism about it.

Toward other types of Christianity, however, and especially what is supposed to be "liberalism," fundamentalism shows marked hostility. Toward the → ecumenical movement it is also rather negative, considering that questions of → unity between the churches are not very important unless priority is given to the issues as seen by fundamentalism itself and especially to its view of Scripture.

Fundamentalism is particularly strong and widespread in the English-speaking lands and in the Christianity of regions culturally affected by them. It is also often characteristic of Protestantism in lands that are dominantly Roman Catholic, the infallibility of the Bible contrasting with that of the church. It has much in common with traditions deriving from Protestant orthodoxy (e.g., Dutch → Calvinism as seen in South Africa, or → Lutheranism as seen in America). It has reflections in → Third World lands also but seldom assumes there the hard ideological form seen in the English-speaking world.

In politics and social matters, although fundamentalism is not entirely homogeneous and has at times included certain progressive aspects, the overwhelmingly dominant tendency is to favor the →

conservative far right. Only the second coming of Christ will overcome the tensions of human existence; → socialism, reformism, and radicalism are revolts against the true purpose and plan of God. The 1970s and 1980s witnessed, especially in the United States, increasing attempts by fundamentalist groups to organize their political power and bend society as a whole toward the pattern favored by them.

The term "fundamentalism," first used within Protestant Christianity, has been applied increasingly to phenomena found in other religions, notably → Islam, but also → Judaism, → Hinduism, and aspects of Roman Catholicism. The viability of this extension of meaning has still to be proved by scholarly analysis.

→ Biblicism

Bibliography: J. BARR, *Escaping from Fundamentalism* (London, 1984); idem, *Fundamentalism* (2d ed.; London, 1995) • H. A. HARRIS, *Fundamentalism and Evangelicals* (Oxford, 1998) • W. JOEST, "Fundamentalismus," *TRE* 11.732-38 • B. B. LAWRENCE, *Defenders of God: The Fundamentalist Revolt against the Modern Age* (Columbia, S.C., 1995) • M. E. MARTY and R. S. APPLEBY, eds., *The Fundamentalism Project* (5 vols.; Chicago, 1991-95) • B. B. WARFIELD, *The Inspiration and Authority of the Bible* (ed. C. van Til; Phillipsburg, N.J., 1948).

JAMES BARR

Funeral

1. General
2. Historical Development
   2.1. Biblical
   2.2. Early Church
   2.3. Middle Ages
   2.4. Reformation
   2.5. Modern Times
3. Orthodox Church
4. Christian Africa
5. Contemporary Western Examples
   5.1. Roman Catholic Church
   5.2. Protestants in North America
      5.2.1. Traditional Funeral Rites
      5.2.2. American Funeral Practices
      5.2.3. Reform and Revision

1. General

In human life the funeral is the ritual by which a → society, clan, or → family reconstitutes itself after the → death of a member. It is the → rite of passage

in which a community marks and sometimes actually effects the transition both of a living person to the realm of the dead and of bereaved persons through mourning to reestablished life. The funeral accomplishes the reintegration of the affected group by dramatizing the positive and negative elements in death and in this specific dead person. Its ritual and symbolic forms give evidence of love and respect for the dead, of → anxiety in the face of death, and of defense against the spirits of the dead. Practices that destroy the corpse frequently go hand in hand with ritual actions that seek to preserve it. The appropriate place for the dead is sought. Psychologically, the funeral is to be regarded as an essential element in mourning. It definitively records the loss of a loved one. It also gives status to the mourners and puts them in fellowship with others with new bonds. It serves to recognize both the loss and the overcoming of the loss (→ Grief).

WOLFGANG STECK

2. Historical Development
2.1. *Biblical*

Along with mourning by the family or a special class of mourners (Jer. 9:17, 20; 2 Sam. 1:19-27), the OT mentions various customs at the observance of a person's death: tearing clothes (Gen. 37:34; Josh. 7:6), wearing special clothing (2 Kgs. 6:30), covering the face (2 Sam. 19:4), scattering dust on the head (Josh. 7:6), and especially keeping various food rites, including a seven-day → fast (1 Sam. 31:13) and eating a funeral meal (Jer. 16:7; → Cultic Meal). There is a biblical concern for decent burial of both Israelites and non-Israelites (Josh. 8:29; 10:26). The deuterocanonical book Tobit tells a story about the extraordinary efforts taken by one devout Jew to bury the dead (Tob. 1:17-19; 2:4-8; 12:13). In the forefront of such funeral rites is defense against the threatening aspects of death: the spirits of the dead and the uncleanness of the corpse. Links with the non-Israelite cult of the dead and → ancestor veneration are clear. Positively, the grave is regarded as the locus of honor for, and remembrance of, the dead (Eccl. 12:5; Ps. 49:11).

NT accounts give evidence of both OT and nonbiblical forms of preparation and burial. The body of Dorcas is washed (Acts 9:37). The grave of → Jesus is a cave closed by a stone (Mark 15:46; see also John 11:38), where he is placed after being wrapped in a clean linen cloth (Matt. 27:59). Use of spices is mentioned (e.g., Mark 16:1). According to archaeological discoveries, long-term care for the place of burial and long-term honor for the dead frequently involved the later bundling of the bones of the dead and their preservation in ossuaries.

The NT attaches theological meaning to the tomb of Jesus. It is linked to the Easter tradition (Mark 16:2; Luke 24:1); the empty tomb points to the resurrection hope.   WOLFGANG STECK

2.2. Early Church

Although ritual care for the dead and optimistic interest in the next life were something that Christians shared with the world around them, early Christian → eschatology and funeral practices were distinctive. While, initially, Christians and pagans were buried side by side in public cemeteries, Christian graves were distinguished by decorations depicting Jesus as tending sheep or presiding over the heavenly banquet. Later, however, as the paschal nature of death was accentuated, depictions of Jesus' miracles, such as the raising of Lazarus, came to dominate. All of these images suggest that the dead were no mere shades to be remembered with sadness and resignation. Rather, these images signified that the new life entered at → baptism and nourished through the → Eucharist is not affected by physical death but continues in the → paradise of the Good Shepherd, the place of refreshment, light, and peace. The epitome of participation in the paschal mystery of Christ's death and resurrection was martyrdom, and thus the tombs of the → martyrs became places of vigil and devotion.

There are also records of funeral meals (refrigeria), which probably had their origin in the Roman belief that the dead needed nourishment. What we know of these feasts is derived from archaeological remains of dining rooms at Christian places of burial as well as from condemnations issued by various bishops who, concerned about unruly behavior and resulting scandal, encouraged prayer vigils, fasting, and gifts to the poor as more appropriate customs.

Another custom that drew the corrective influence of bishops involved communing the dead. It was the custom of the Romans to put a coin into the mouth of the deceased to pay Charon, the ferryman who was to carry the dead across the river Styx. The reception of the Eucharist for the dying person (food for the journey, or viaticum) was regarded as so crucial for the journey to the next life — Ignatius of Antioch (ca. 35-ca. 107) referred to the Eucharist as "the medicine of immortality and the antidote preventing death . . . leading to life in Jesus Christ forever" (Eph. 20:3) — that it was inevitable that some would abuse this practice by placing Communion in the mouth of the dead. The councils of Hippo (393), Carthage (397

and 525), Auxerre (578), and Trullo (692) condemned this practice, noting that the dead could neither take nor eat the Eucharist.

A final distinctive Christian practice was the transformation of the mourning ceremonies. In particular, Christians replaced lamentations and dirges sung in alternation with the antiphonal singing of the Psalms, underscoring their belief that the dead have not met with total death (→ Augustine, Conf. 9.12.29-31; Chrys. In Heb. hom. 4). In praying for the deceased and for the consolation of the bereaved, grief was acknowledged (Serapion, Sacra. 18), but it led not to despair but to hope for the rest, light, refreshment, and peace that the deceased would enjoy until the resurrection on the last day.

2.3. Middle Ages

The oldest Roman funeral rite is found in Ordo Romanus 49, a seventh-century order devoted to the preparation for death, waking, and burial of the body. This liturgical order was totally focused on the resurrection on the last day. Communion was to be given to the dying person as the defense and help against death, and for assurance of resurrection. The reading of the → passion of the Lord, which was to accompany the dying person to death, served to provide hope and confidence that, united with the Lord, the deceased would pass from this world to eternal life. The response at the moment of death, consistent with other elements that dealt with the preparation, waking, and burial of the body, requested welcome into paradise and rest in the bosom of Abraham, in anticipation of the resurrection on the last day, when the fullness of the person would be restored.

Gradually, however, a shift occurred in the expressed attitude of Christians, so that the liturgy of the dead became increasingly somber in tone. Concerns about the dangers of the lower world, the snares of punishment, and all the tribulations of death in the interim period of the afterlife began to dominate. In addition, the focus of entering peacefully into the joy of the Lord shifted to escaping the terrible and pitiless judgment that was embodied in the 13th-century funeral text Dies irae (Day of wrath), an imaginative and apocalyptic meditation on the last judgment as seen from an individual's standpoint. The funeral liturgy in the 1614 Rituale Romanum, the normative liturgical sacramentary that sought to bring order to disparate monastic and diocesan rites that preceded it, and which was used in Latin-Rite Roman Catholic communities until the reforms of the Second → Vatican Council (1962-65), continued to emphasize God's mercy in its funeral texts but also repeatedly begged God to spare the sinner from the pains of → hell.

JAMES DONOHUE, C.R.

2.4. Reformation

The → Reformation rejected the idea that the living can influence the destiny of the dead and discarded the late medieval Offices and Masses for the dead (→ Mass). Burial was viewed as a duty of love that the living owe the dead and that they discharge by giving them respectful burial. M. → Luther thus provided no order for burial, and early Protestant burials were frequently regarded as civil and familial affairs with little relationship to the church. Nonetheless, Luther did urge that → hymns of comfort, resurrection, and trust in → forgiveness should be sung in the funeral procession and at the burial. And Luther as well as other reformers argued that the funeral also offered a significant opportunity to proclaim the resurrection and to issue a reminder that death comes to all. The rituals that slowly began to develop in diverse Protestant churches thus were intended to serve the faith of the living rather than the salvation of the dead. The positive aspects of the observance of death thus came to the fore, sometimes to the neglect of the negative aspects.

2.5. Modern Times

Awareness of death in the modern Western world is ambivalent. On the one hand, the relation to it is more abstract. Only few die where they have lived, and only few experience the actual dying of loved ones. Death is less visible. It has been eliminated from the living world, and the experience of it has been repressed. On the other hand, in keeping with the cultural orientation of modern society, there are many symptoms of the repression of death. These become constitutive elements in the funeral ritual and are particularly noticeable in the United States. They go hand in hand with the commercializing of the funeral to meet the supposed needs of mourners. A funeral creates an illusion of death that is the counterpart of an illusory life. With the help of embalming and use of the dead person's clothing, the corpse is made to seem asleep rather than dead. The funeral parlor becomes a "slumber room," and the coffin a showcase. The stern sense of death of Puritan New England yields to an aesthetic denial of death dominated by → civil religion. At the same time, in what seems to be a → countercultural move, many of the Christian churches have been undertaking a modern revision of the liturgies celebrated at death with the goal of exhibiting both the reality of dying and the strength of a baptismal the-

ology; that is, those who have been immersed into Christ are also raised with him to hope.

Bibliography: A. VAN GENNEP, *The Rites of Passage* (Chicago, 1961) • F. S. PAXTON, *Christianizing Death: The Creation of a Ritual Process in Early Medieval Europe* (Ithaca, N.Y., 1990) • G. ROWELL, *The Liturgy of Christian Burial: An Introductory Survey of the Historical Development of Christian Burial Rites* (London, 1977) • A. C. RUSH, *Death and Burial in Christian Antiquity* (Washington, D.C., 1941) • J. M. C. TOYNBEE, *Death and Burial in the Roman World* (Ithaca, N.Y., 1971) • J. UPTON, "Christian Burial," *The New Dictionary of Sacramental Worship* (ed. P. Fink; Collegeville, Minn., 1990).

WOLFGANG STECK

3. Orthodox Church

The Orthodox Church accompanies people at their death with many liturgical acts. Some of these are in preparation for a peaceful death, others are in remembrance of the dead and in intercession for them. There are five types of services: for adult laity, for children up to about seven years old, for married clergy, for monks and members of the hierarchy, and for those who die in the first week of Easter.

The dying are given the sacraments of → penance, Communion, and unction. For those who are incurably ill but cannot die, there is a liturgical act at the heart of which stands a prayer for death. The dead are washed (Acts 9:37) — the clergy simply anointed — then clad in new, clean clothes signifying the new and incorruptible state of the body after the resurrection of the dead (1 Cor. 15:42-44). Clergy are buried with appropriate robes and a copy of the Gospels on their breasts. As a sign that the dead are Christ's and are entrusted to him in death, an → icon or a → cross is laid on their breast as a symbol of victory. By the open coffin in the house of the deceased occurs the ritual of *pannychida* (from Gk. *pan nyx ǭdō*, "sing all night"), a short form of the burial service that recalls the songs and prayers that were in earlier times sung and prayed all night at the coffin, especially in times of the → persecution of Christians when the dead were buried by night. The actual funeral service takes place in church. There the life in Christ begins with → baptism, and there its earthly end is celebrated.

Along with many readings from the OT and the NT, the Orthodox burial service consists of a great number of hymns, prayers, and odes. Holy Scripture is the source for these texts; they both reflect on the meaning of life in the face of the mystery of death and express fundamental doctrines as they point to human frailty, to infinite love and mercy, and also to the approaching divine judgment. The sustaining note is → faith in the resurrection of Jesus Christ. The service as a whole can be viewed as an urgent request to God to forgive the sins of the deceased and to grant rest to the soul at the place of light and life. Belief in the immortality of the → soul is evident throughout the service. A final prayer and the singing of "Eternal Remembrance" take place at the grave, and the priest then sprinkles the corpse or coffin with oil and wine, saying, "Purge me with hyssop, and I shall be clean; wash me, and I shall be whiter than snow" (Ps. 51:7). The priest then throws earth on the coffin and says, "The earth is the LORD's and all that is in it; the world, and those who live in it" (Ps. 24:1). Interment is the rule. The agape meal follows, recalling the funeral feasts (convivia funebralia) of Greek and Roman religions. Acts of charity are enjoined as a mark of remembrance for the deceased.

The care of the Orthodox Church for the dead reaches beyond the grave. It comes to expression in services of remembrance (parastasis) for those who sleep. These services are not to be seen in terms of the living making satisfaction on behalf of the dead. Rather, they are the church's prayers that God will have mercy on the dead. They also express the fact that, in the Orthodox view, the living and the dead form one fellowship in the church.

Bibliography: I. F. HAPGOOD, Service Book of the Holy Orthodox–Catholic Apostolic Church (New York, 1956) 360-453 • M. O'CONNELL, trans., Temple of the Holy Spirit: Sickness and Death of the Christian in the Liturgy (New York, 1983) esp. articles by C. Andronikof, A. Kniazeff, P. Kovalevsky, E. Melia, A. Nelidow, and G. Wagner • G. ROWELL, The Liturgy of Christian Burial (London, 1977) esp. 31-56 • A. SCHMEMANN, For the Life of the World (Crestwood, N.Y., 1973) esp. 95-106 • SIMEON OF THESSALONIKA, "De fine et exitu nostro e vita et de sacro ordine sepulturae," PG 155.670-96.

VIOREL MEHEDINŢU

4. Christian Africa

In traditional African religions the burial of adults is a lengthy affair. Naturally there are also places where burial is simple and short, as it is among nomadic herdsmen. African Christians combine various traditional rites with biblical ideas and Western customs.

Burial usually takes place in the grounds or village where the dead person lived. Those who die in → cities are brought back home to the country for burial by friends and relatives. Some are also buried

in → cemeteries when it is impossible to "take them home." Relatives, friends, neighbors, and the → congregation take part in the funeral. Mourners may number in the hundreds or even thousands.

Burial takes place on the day of death or one to two days later. In some places the body is placed in a funeral parlor so that relatives from a distance have enough time to come. Saturday and Sunday are the preferred days for burial, which often takes place after Sunday worship. Men dig the grave some distance from the house if the burial is not in the common churchyard or cemetery.

In many places the corpse is washed, anointed, or embalmed. A new robe, or the best robe, is then put on the corpse. Traditionally, it is wrapped in a mat or, in Uganda and elsewhere, a bark cloth. In other places (e.g., South Africa) it is wrapped in a white garment, white being the color of → death. Often the mourners view the corpse to say farewell. The corpse is then put in the grave either directly or in a coffin. In some places a wake takes place right up to the time of burial. During such a wake there are songs and prayers, and in some places candles are lit at the head and feet of the corpse. In South Africa the wake is viewed as a way of accompanying the dead.

The funeral service most usually takes place at the grave, although in some cases the service takes place in church with a short service at the grave. Songs and prayers are interspersed with biblical texts. Roman Catholic churches celebrate → Mass. A choir will often sing songs of mourning. "Fellowships of the dead" take part in these services in Ethiopia, and burial societies elsewhere. At the grave participants speak about the life of the deceased, what the departed one has meant and done. At the end they throw a handful of earth into the grave. Sermons, meditations, songs, and prayers stress the fact that the deceased still lives in → heaven with God, emphasizing the hope of → resurrection. These acts thus give comfort to those left behind, strengthening their faith that death is simply a door that leads to everlasting life with God through Jesus Christ. It is thus presupposed that the dead and those who are left will see one another again. Often the mourners will take a collection for the bereaved as a concrete sign of comfort and support. When the family is in special need, the congregation will try to give further help, especially in the Independent Churches.

After a period of time the family or congregation will set up a solid cover over the grave, put up a stone or statue or photograph of the deceased, or plant a tree on the grave. In many places another rite will follow some weeks or months later in remembrance of the dead. In various ways the family will keep the memory of the deceased alive — through descendants, deeds, prayers, care of the grave, honoring, → dreams in which the deceased appear, observance of the day of death, and hope of the resurrection to eternal life in Jesus Christ.

Bibliography: H.-J. Bekken, *Theologie und Heilung* (Hermannsburg, 1972) • M. D. Biyela, "Funeral Rites in the South African Cultural Context," *Baptism, Rites of Passage, and Culture* (ed. S. A. Stauffer; Geneva, 1998) 153-64 • T. Christensen, *An African Tree of Life* (Maryknoll, N.Y., 1990) • J. S. Mbiti, *African Religions and Philosophy* (London, 1989) • H. Sawyerr, "Graveside Libations in and near Freetown," *Sierra Leone Bulletin of Religion* 7 (1965) 48-55; idem, "More Graveside Libations in and near Freetown," ibid. 8 (1966) 57-59; idem, "A Sunday Graveside Libation in Freetown after a Bereavement," ibid. 9 (1967) 41-55.

John Mbiti

5. Contemporary Western Examples

5.1. *Roman Catholic Church*

The Second → Vatican Council (1962-65), in its Constitution on the Sacred Liturgy (*Sacrosanctum concilium*), called for the reform of all liturgical rites in the → Roman Catholic Church (→ Liturgical Books). Specifically, it directed that funeral rites be revised in such a way that they would "express more clearly the paschal character of Christian death" and would "correspond more closely to the circumstances and traditions found in various regions" (81). The reforms also called for the revision of the rite for the burial of infants and for the provision of a special Mass for this occasion (82). The initial reform of the funeral rites, *Ordo exsequiarum,* was authorized for use in 1969. The vernacular edition of the *Ordo exsequiarum* for the dioceses of the United States, entitled the Order of Christian Funerals (OCF), was approved by the National Conference of Catholic Bishops in November 1985, was confirmed by the Apostolic See in April 1987, and was published for use in October 1989. The OCF contains a general introduction that expands on the Latin original, rearranges the rites in a way that will be of greater use to ministers in preaching and presiding, provides pastoral notes before each of the funeral rites, and includes newly composed prayers to provide for situations not addressed in the Latin original.

Although cremation was prohibited for Catholics for centuries because of the fact that belief in the → resurrection of the body could be denied by the choice, it is a practice now permitted in some circumstances. In its *Reflections on the Body, Cremation, and Catholic Funeral Rites* (1997), the Committee on the Liturgy of the National Conference of Catholics Bishops recognized that the disposition of the bodies of Roman Catholic Christians by means of cremation is a fairly recent development that, however, is becoming more widespread. The instruction *Piam et constantem* (May 1963), issued by the Vatican's Holy Office (now the Congregation for the Doctrine of the Faith), made allowance for cremation. This concession is provided for in the *Ordo exsequiarum* and has been incorporated into the 1983 CIC 1176.

The OCF was prepared by the International Commission on English in the Liturgy, a joint commission of Catholic Bishops' Conferences, and was subsequently approved for use in the dioceses of the United States in 1989. When the rites of the OCF are fully celebrated, they ritualize the paschal exodus of one of the Lord's disciples in his or her journey from life through death to fullness of life in God. The threefold intent of the Roman Catholic funeral liturgy is outlined in OCF 129, where it states: "At the funeral liturgy the community gathers with the family and friends of the deceased to give praise and thanks to God for Christ's victory over → sin and → death, to commend the deceased to God's tender mercy and compassion, and to seek strength in the proclamation of the paschal → mystery." To this end, the OCF provides rites for adults, as well as adapted rites for children, which are divided into three groups of rites that correspond in general to the three principal ritual moments in Christian funerals: "Vigil and Related Rites and Prayers," "Funeral Liturgy," and "Rites of Committal."

The first section includes rites that are celebrated between the time of death and the funeral liturgy. Through these rites the church accompanies and ministers to the mourners in their initial adjustment to the fact of death and to the bewilderment, shock, and grief this experience may entail. The second section, "Funeral Liturgy," provides two forms of the central celebration of the Christian community for the deceased: the Funeral Mass and the Funeral Liturgy outside Mass. In this liturgy, the community is joined together by the → Holy Spirit as one body of Christ to reaffirm in → sign and → symbol, word and gesture, that each believer through → baptism shares in Christ's death and resurrection and can look to the day when all the elect will be raised up and united in the kingdom of light and peace. The third section, "Rites of Committal," includes two forms of the concluding rite of the funeral order.

Through the committal of the body to its resting place, the community expresses the hope that, with all who have gone before marked with the sign of faith, the deceased awaits the glory of the resurrection.

An important liturgical element for each funeral rite is the reading of the → Word of God. These readings proclaim to the assembly the paschal mystery, teach remembrance of the dead, convey the hope of being gathered together in God's kingdom, encourage the witness of Christian life, and, above all, tell of God's designs for a world in which suffering and death will relinquish their hold on all whom God has called. Liturgical symbols, such as the Easter (or paschal) candle, holy → water, the pall, and the → cross, remind the faithful of Christ's victory over sin and death and of their share in this victory by virtue of baptism. → Incense honors the body of the deceased, which through baptism has become the temple of the Holy Spirit.

While the → priest is expected to preside at the funeral rites, especially the mass, a → deacon or a layperson may lead the vigil and related rites or the rite of committal. That said, the OCF clearly states that the ministry of consolation rests with the whole believing community, with each Christian sharing in this ministry according to various gifts and offices in the church: pastoral care, acts of kindness, prayer, mutual comfort, as well as the various liturgical ministries.

JAMES DONOHUE, C.R.

5.2. Protestants in North America
5.2.1. Traditional Funeral Rites

Christians brought to North America funeral rites and customs they had known in Europe. Among Protestants this tradition included less attention to the body of the deceased and more attention to the comfort of the living.

Some orders for the burial of the dead developed on American soil. Preeminent among these was the order in the → Book of Common Prayer (BCP) adopted by the Episcopal Church in 1790. The Burial Office included the reading of Scripture sentences as the body was brought into the church building, a cento of Psalms 39 and 90, the reading of 1 Cor. 15:1-20, the optional use of a hymn or anthem and → Apostles' Creed, and prayers. At the graveside there were Scripture sentences, the committal of the body, a reading of Rev. 14:13, the threefold Kyrie, the → Lord's Prayer and collects, and a → benediction. This order was amended in 1892 by the addition of more optional psalms, readings, and prayers, so that the Burial Office took on the form of the daily Prayer Offices. In the 1928 BCP a statement that "this Office is appropriate to be used only for the faithful departed in Christ" was substituted for the older rubric "that the Office ensuing is not to be used for any unbaptized adults, any who die excommunicate, or who have laid violent hands upon themselves." This change recognized religious pluralism in the United States and the need for pastoral discretion. Included among the prayers were specific petitions for the faithful departed, which had long been advocated by Anglo-Catholics. John → Wesley had kept the Burial Office of the 1662 BCP for the use of Methodists, though omitting Psalm 39 and the committal. Methodists added the singing of hymns of hope.

Funeral services were not always printed in the hymnals of American Lutherans but were in the Agendas used by pastors (→ Liturgical Books). This meant that pastoral discretion could dictate the content of the service. The Order for the Burial of the Dead was included in the Church Book of the General Council (1892 ed.), the Common Service Book (1917), the Service Book and Hymnal (1958), and the present Lutheran Book of Worship (1978). As this order evolved, it included the Kyrie, Psalms 130 and 90 and others with appropriate antiphons, lessons, a responsory or hymn, an address, a canticle with antiphon (Nunc Dimittis, Benedictus, Song of Hezekiah, or Beatitudes), the short litany, the Lord's Prayer, and other prayers. All four books provide full musical settings, mostly → Anglican chant, that were not always, however, used in practice.

In the Reformed tradition, burial was conducted "without any ceremony" but was often followed in the church by a service of psalms, readings, sermon, and prayers. Even funeral sermons became controversial among → Puritans because they often degenerated into eulogies extolling the virtues of the deceased rather than proclamations of the → Word of God addressed to the congregation. Some in the Puritan and free-church tradition regarded burial as purely a secular matter and conducted no services. This practice undoubtedly contributed to the development of the institution of the funeral home.

5.2.2. American Funeral Practices

In the atmosphere of the American funeral home, the reality of death is typically denied, with assurance of → immortality substituted for the proclamation of the → resurrection of the dead. Corpses are turned into mannequins to make them look as lifelike as possible. Sentimental music, excessive flowers, exorbitant expenditures on coffins and vaults, and even delay of interment are commonplace. Often funeral services are held in the funeral home chapel, where minimal participation in the service by the mourners is expected. Exactly what the Puritans objected to has occurred: the dead are eulogized not only by officiating ministers but also by relatives and friends. In a countermove, clergy increasingly encourage families to have the body transported to the church for the funeral service in order that they might exercise more control over the content and style of the service.

5.2.3. Reform and Revision

The reform of the Roman Catholic Order of Christian Funerals (OCF) after the Second → Vatican Council emphasized the paschal character of Christian life and faith. This change also influenced the Episcopal, Lutheran, Methodist, and Presbyterian orders, which consist of an opening sentence and entrance hymn, readings and homily, intercessory prayers, the optional celebration of the → Eucharist (for which proper prefaces and post-Communion prayers are provided), and an optional commendation of the deceased, followed by a rite of committal in the place of interment. In these revisions there is an effort to include a ministry to the departed as well as to the living in terms of the lighting of the paschal candle (recalling Easter and baptism, when the newly baptized receive the light of Christ), the commendation of the faithful departed to God, and the reverent disposal of the body through burial or cremation — all within the context of a caring and celebrating Christian community that lays hold of the promises of God.

Bibliography: Liturgical books: The Book of Common Prayer [Episcopal] (New York, 1977) 469-510 • *Book of Common Worship* [Presbyterian] (Louisville, Ky., 1993) 905-47 • *Book of Worship: United Church of Christ* (New York, 1986) 357-90 • *Lutheran Book of Worship* [Evangelical Lutheran Church in America] (Minneapolis, 1978) 206-14 • *Lutheran Worship–Agenda* [Lutheran Church–Missouri Synod] (St. Louis, 1982) 169-96 • *Order of Christian Funerals* [Roman Catholic] (Collegeville, Minn., 1989) • *The Rites of the Catholic Church* (vol. 1; New York, 1983) • *The United Methodist Book of Worship* (Nashville, 1992) 139-72.

Other works: M. HATCHETT, *Commentary on the American Prayer Book* (New York, 1981) • J. F. HENDERSON, ed., *The Christian Funeral* (= NBLi 119 [1989]) • L. MITCHELL, *Praying Shapes Believing* (Minneapolis, 1985) • J. MITFORD, *The American Way of Death* (New York, 1963) • P. PFATTEICHER, *Commentary on the Lutheran Book of Worship* (Minneapolis, 1990) • *RefW* 24 (June 1992) • R. RUTHERFORD, *The Order of Christian Funerals: An Invitation to Pastoral Care* (Collegeville, Minn., 1990) • R. RUTHERFORD,
with T. BARR, *The Death of a Christian: The Order of Christian Funerals* (rev. ed.; New York, 1990) • S. A. STAUFFER, ed., *Baptism, Rites of Passage, and Culture* (Geneva, 1999).

FRANK C. SENN

Future

1. The future is the → time that is not yet. Increasingly, however, it is viewed as a dimension of human beings and of the world. The Latin terms *futurum* and *adventus* express both the connection and the distinction. Scholars have come to speak of an → "ontology of not-yet-being" (E. Bloch), addressing both the identity and the distinctions attaching to the notions of "being and time" (M. Heidegger). Insight into "that which is" then leads less into a time of human beings and of the world that must be energetically produced than it does to the "advent of being" (Heidegger). The Christian tradition views the future as arrival (advent), as the return of Christ, which includes the → last judgment but leads on to the coming glory (Rom. 5:2; → Eschatology). This salvific experience shapes the disposition of believers.

The advent of being, of the sort that Heidegger (1889-1976; → Existential Philosophy) claimed could be experienced from within the philosophical dimension of thought and especially of the early Greek beginnings of philosophy itself (→ Greek Philosophy), was originally cast as history. Initially, the → myth reflects an understanding that one tries to transcend today. Whereas gods know the future, it is inaccessible to human beings. Even if the myth seeks to mediate between the two, → philosophy has revealed the boundaries articulated in what was said about the distinctions between being and nonbeing, between being and time, as well as about knowing and not knowing (esp. Plato; → Platonism).

The step beyond this philosophy begins when human beings themselves try to decide what is and what is not, what it means to know and not to know. Thus does modern philosophy begin, along with one of its principles: "Ubi ergo generatio nulla . . . ibi philosophia nulla intelligitur" (T. Hobbes); that is, human beings understand only that which they themselves make, a principle that ends with K. → Marx (1818-83; → Marxism), with whom one can say that human beings are only that which they manufacture and produce, a statement applicable to every cultural sphere. Within this "productive" mode of thought and life, the will determining all consideration of the future begins increasingly to dominate. The will has → power over time, and precisely therein do we see the "will to power" (F. → Nietzsche) and its "hatred" of "time and its 'what was.'" This will overcomes all faith in some advent, the expectation of something ultimate (the *eschaton*), and any life and interpretation of time and history in an "eschatology"; thus it leads to a "recurrence of the same" (Nietzsche; → Nihilism).

2. According to Hobbes (1588-1679; → Philosophy of Nature 5), human beings are not only hungry, they also hunger for future hunger *(fame futura famelicus)*. This comment, which is ultimately about desire in the larger sense, we find expanded in Heidegger's principle that "the essence of Being there [Dasein] resides in its existence." In both instances, human beings are related to the future, since existence for Heidegger (an understanding of existence that had been developing at least since F. Schelling [1775-1854; → Idealism 5]) means standing out ("ex-istence"), possibility, and also "care, worry," "draft, plan."

Early modernity produced some extremely broad drafts of this sort, namely, in the concept of → utopia, which initially maps out a quite distant future, but then increasingly seeks its arrival here and now in the social utopias of the 18th and 19th centuries. Writers of the 20th century finally spoke about a "concrete utopia" (Bloch). The future is present — indeed, it resides in the past, which has left "traces," on the basis of which we may hope (Bloch's "principle of hope") that some things, or even many if not all things, can be changed. We are human beings of the future, with the "future of the past" (Bloch).

3. Here future is viewed together with → freedom, and freedom understood more precisely as → autonomy, meaning that human beings are able to take control of their own destinies. Freedom in the sense of autonomy has become a popular theme in modernity. The assertion is that the themes of praxis (i.e., freedom), future, and → language are actually the three basic themes of philosophy.

The notion of future shapes the modern development of the → sciences, which with the natural sciences can become knowledge of laws and thus prognoses concerning the course of natural events, just as later both → sociology (A. Comte) and historical science (Marx) similarly tried to be sciences of laws capable of competing with the natural sciences. The → philosophy of history from G. B. Vico (1668-1744) to I. Kant (1724-1804), G. W. F. Hegel

(1770-1831), and Marx is essentially a philosophy that considers history within the entirety of time and thus draws the future itself into the present (of thought). Such thinking includes the modern idea of system (→ Social Systems); history (future) and system belong together.

The philosophy of history as a philosophy of the future is gradually developing into a *science* of the future (futurology), a process beginning already in the 19th century with the principle of Comte (1798-1857; → Positivism) *voir pour prévoir* (see in order to foresee). In the possibility of prediction resides positive knowledge, the positive spirit. Because the future has in the meantime increasingly become a matter of concern precisely because of scientific-technological developments, we see today the emergence of an *ethics* of the future, namely, the notion that we must act with responsibility for coming generations and for the future of the world itself.

4. Modern autonomy has led ultimately to contemporary → philosophy of science. Constructivism (→ Cognition 1) can be traced back directly to Hobbes's principle, aiming at a future improvement of both knowledge and action by constructing an exact language ("ortholanguage"). Commensurate with critical → rationalism (§2), the future itself becomes the criterion of every theory, which, as a universal statement, will be "falsified" the moment a single individual case contradicts it (empirically). → Critical theory, especially in its final form as discourse theory, is wholly concerned with a better future. The evolutive *movimento* is reflected especially in system theory. This theory systematically addresses the basic question of the contemporary age, namely, "How will things go? What will happen?" Systems focus on the future.

→ Hope; Modernity; Postmodernism; Process Philosophy; Process Theology; Worldview

Bibliography: E. BLOCH, *The Principle of Hope* (3 vols.; Cambridge, Mass.; 1995; orig. pub., 1959) • D. BÖHLER and R. NEUBERTH, eds., *Herausforderung Zukunftserwartung* (2d ed.; Münster, 1993) • W. H. CAPPS, *Time Invades the Cathedral: Tensions in the School of Hope* (Philadelphia, 1972) • E. CORNISH et al., *The Study of the Future* (Washington, D.C., 1977) • O. K. FLECHTHEIM, *Der Kampf um die Zukunft. Grundlagen der Futurologie* (Bonn, 1980) • M. HEIDEGGER, *Being and Time* (New York, 1962; orig. pub., 1927) • G. T. KURIAN and G. T. T. MOLITOR, eds., *Encyclopedia of the Future* (2 vols.; New York, 1996) • W. MITTELSTAEDT, *Zukunftsgestaltung und Chaostheorie. Grundlagen einer neuen Zukunftsgestaltung unter Einbeziehung der*

Chaostheorie (Frankfurt, 1993) • J. MOLTMANN, "The Future as a New Paradigm of Transcendence," *The Future of Creation* (Philadelphia, 1979); idem, *Theology of Hope: On the Ground and the Implications of a Christian Eschatology* (London, 1967) • R. B. NORRIS, *God, Marx, and the Future: Dialogue with Roger Garaudy* (Philadelphia, 1974) • K. RAHNER, "Marxist Utopia and the Christian Future of Man," *Theological Investigations* (vol. 6; New York, 1982) 59-68 • G. STENGER and M. RÖHRIG, eds., *Philosophie der Struktur. Fahrzeug der Zukunft?* (Freiburg, 1995) • H. WISSMANN, ed., *Zur Erschließung von Zukunft in den Religionen. Zukunftserwartung und Gegenwartsbewältigung in der Religionsgeschichte* (Würzburg, 1991).

ARNO BARUZZI

G

Gabon

	1960	1980	2000
Population (1,000s):	486	691	1,235
Annual growth rate (%):	0.36	2.98	2.45

Area: 267,667 sq. km. (103,347 sq. mi.)

A.D. 2000

Population density: 5/sq. km. (12/sq. mi.)
Births / deaths: 3.50 / 1.28 per 100 population
Fertility rate: 4.99 per woman
Infant mortality rate: 77 per 1,000 live births
Life expectancy: 57.5 years (m: 55.9, f: 59.2)
Religious affiliation (%): Christians 90.8 (Roman Catholics 70.0, Protestants 21.9, indigenous 17.0, unaffiliated 2.1, other Christians 0.7), Muslims 4.7, tribal religionists 3.0, other 1.5.

1. General Situation
2. Religious Situation

1. General Situation

Gabon straddles the equator on the west coast of central Africa. It is bounded on the north by Cameroon, on the east and south by Congo (Brazzaville), and on the north and west by Equatorial Guinea. Its population includes about 68 distinct ethnic groups, the largest being the Bantu family (esp. the Fang, Eshira, Bapounou, and Bateke peoples). French is the official language, with 40 other languages also spoken in the country. In 1995 the literacy rate of Gabon was 63 percent.

Gabon's per capita income is four times that of most other nations in Africa. Extreme poverty has been reduced, but a wide disparity in incomes means that much of the population remains poor. Oil, which was discovered offshore in the early 1970s, accounts for 50 percent of the gross domestic product. Despite considerable natural wealth (esp. timber and minerals such as manganese and uranium), the → economy has been hobbled by fiscal mismanagement and by fluctuating oil prices.

Earliest encounters between Europe and what is now Gabon date back to the arrival of the Portuguese Duarte Lopez in 1497; in time the Portuguese initiated slave trade (→ Colonialism). In 1839 the French signed a treaty with King Denis of Gabon, and in 1850 it was established as a French colony. Between 1897 and 1910 it was part of the French Congo, and after 1910 it became French Equatorial Africa. Gabon became independent in August 1960. Léon Mba, who had been mayor of Libreville, was elected the nation's first president in 1961. After a failed coup and Mba's subsequent death in 1967, Albert-Bernard Bongo was elected president. In 1968 Bongo initiated a one-party system in Gabon, an expression of an authoritarian regime from which many are excluded. For clearly economic reasons that center on the petroleum industry, France has continued to support this authoritarian regime in spite of its breach of many human rights.

Out of political expediency, Bongo converted to → Islam, changing his first name to Omar in 1974. Although only a small minority of the population is Muslim, Omar led the country into the Islamic Conference in 1974. A new constitution was enacted in May 1991 that allowed for multiparty elections. Bongo, however, was reelected head of state in 1993 and 1998, both times amid a series of alleged election irregularities.

2. Religious Situation

The traditional religion of the Gabonese is practiced by many who otherwise consider themselves Christian. Since culture is the solvent of religion, the religion is manifest particularly at the cultural rites of passage, including birth, initiation, marriage, sickness, and death.

President Bongo's conversion to Islam seems not to have led to significant gains for Islam. It has grown somewhat, though, through immigration of West African Muslims and an infusion of Middle Eastern oil money.

By far, the largest religion is Christianity. Roman Catholicism came with the Portuguese in the late 15th century. In the 17th century Italian Capuchins did considerable missionary work in Gabon, but the Portuguese expelled them in 1777. In their place came → missionaries of the Congregation of the Sacred Heart (1841) and Holy Ghost Mission (1848). In 1900 there were approximately 15,000 Roman Catholics. The hierarchy was established in 1955.

Protestant missions began in 1842, when the American Board of Commissioners for Foreign Mission established a station at Barake. In 1870 the Presbyterian Church in the U.S.A. took over this work, and subsequently it was transferred in 1892 to the Paris Missionary Society, which established stations at Angouma, Lambaréné, and Telagouga (→ French Missions). Gabon's most well-known missionary was Albert → Schweitzer (1875-1965), who worked at his hospital at Lambaréné until his death. The Paris Mission asked the Christian and Missionary Alliance in the Congo to undertake evangelistic work in southern Gabon in 1934.

Notably, indigenous Protestant churches grew out of the work of the Paris Mission. Personal issues rather than theological or ecclesiological considerations caused certain divisions within Protestantism. The Église Évangélique de Pentecôte was an outgrowth of the Paris Mission's work in 1936, and the Église Évangélique du Sud Gabon was established in 1956, stemming from the work of the Paris Mission as carried on by the → Christian and Missionary Alliance (→ Evangelical Missions; Evangeli-

cal Movement). The Église Évangélique du Gabon, the largest Protestant church, grew out of the work of the same Paris Mission in 1961.

There are other independent religious movements in Gabon, such as the Église des Banzie (Church of the initiates), a syncretistic group that grew out of a Bwiti secret movement about 1890. Over time this group has become more specifically Christian and is increasingly active and aggressive, now having more than 20 churches in Libreville.

Bibliography: M. Aicardi de Saint-Paul, *Gabon: The Development of a Nation* (New York, 1989) • J. F. Barnes, *Gabon: Beyond the Colonial Legacy* (Boulder, Colo., 1992) • J. Bentley, *Albert Schweitzer: The Enigma* (New York, 1992) • D. E. Gardinier, *Historical Dictionary of Gabon* (2d ed.; Metuchen, N.J., 1994) • P. Stoecklin et al., *L'Église Évangélique du Gabon, 1842-1961* (Alençon, 1962) • D. A. Yates, *The Rentier State in Africa: Oil Rent Dependency and Neocolonialism in the Republic of Gabon* (Trenton, N.J., 1996).

John Mbiti

Galatians, Epistle to the

1. Contents
2. Problems
3. Theology

1. Contents

After an introduction (Gal. 1:1-5), Paul omits the usual thanksgiving and refers at once to the reason for writing, which is the appearance of those who preach "a different gospel" (vv. 6-10). He then develops the theme of the letter (1:11–5:12): the gospel — faith or the law? In accordance with the thesis of 1:11-12, he describes to his readers his own path from Damascus to Galatia as the path of the → gospel (1:13–2:21). He then presents the gospel in 3:1–5:12, especially in its relation to the → law. In 5:13–6:10 comes the → parenesis, in which he shows what it means ethically to achieve → freedom from the law in terms of → love and spirit. The letter ends with a postscript in his own hand (6:11-18), without the customary greetings.

2. Problems

Paul composed Galatians during the time of his missionary work around the Aegean (A.D. 50-56), before Romans but after 1 Corinthians, since in 1 Cor. 16:1 the Galatian churches were still taking part in the collection for Jerusalem, whereas they are no longer mentioned in 2 Corinthians 8–9 or Rom. 15:26. Perhaps the letter did not have the success that Paul hoped for, with contacts between the apostle and the Galatians being severed. The letter was probably written around 52 or 53 at Ephesus or at one of the cities to which Paul went from his main location at Ephesus.

Paul came to Galatia after leaving the congregation at Antioch. This schedule in 2:11-14 and 3:1 fits in with Acts 16:6 (though it rules out any actual mission) and 18:23 (which presupposes churches in Galatia). The reference is to a thinly populated area in the vicinity of modern Ankara. Celtic tribes had settled there in the second century B.C. Gal. 4:13-14 shows that sickness forced Paul to stop in Galatia for a time on his way west. The older thesis that the churches at issue are those in the south, mentioned in Acts 13–14, no longer commends itself. Some scholars question whether Paul visited Galatia a second time according to the report in Acts 18:23, since Paul never mentions this journey clearly in his letters, not even in 4:13-14.

Soon after Paul left, opponents found an entry into the Galatian churches. These were Christians, for they do not seem to have contested → baptism (3:27). What they required was the → circumcision of Gentile Christians (5:2-12; 6:12-13) and the observance of times set by the stars (4:10). Such practice raised for Paul the basic question of the significance of the law. Although one might call his opponents Judaizers, we learn from the counterthesis of W. Schmithals, who thinks that all Paul's opponents were → Gnostics, that their teaching contained features that were inconsistent with a Pharisaic (→ Pharisees) understanding of the law. We should perhaps describe them as Jewish-Christian missionaries to the Gentiles (→ Jewish Christians) who were trying to combine circumcision and the law with → Christology.

3. Theology

Galatians is characterized by emphatic reflection on the relation between → faith and the law in the context of → justification. A special attempt is made to show that the law itself poses this alternative (4:21). The law is given for a set period (3:17, 23-25), and in contrast to faith, it cannot bring the promised → righteousness (3:21). Faith, Christologically defined, brings the age of law to an end, makes righteousness possible, and is marked by possession of the Spirit (3:2). With no reference to a particular situation, Paul later develops the same theme in Romans, including there the themes of → anthropology (Romans 5–8) and the relation to → Israel (chaps. 9–11), which he does not deal with in Galatians.

Bibliography: Commentaries: J. BECKER (NTD 8; 2d ed.; Göttingen, 1981) 1-85 • H. D. BETZ (Philadelphia, 1979) • U. BORSE (RNT 6; Regensburg, 1984) • E. D. BURTON (ICC; New York, 1920) • D. LÜHRMANN (ZBK; Zurich, 1978) • J. L. MARTYN (AB; New York, 1997) • F. MUSSNER (HTKNT 9; 4th ed.; Freiburg, 1981) • H. SCHLIER (KEK 7; 4th ed.; Göttingen, 1971) • P. N. TARAZI (Crestwood, N.Y., 1994).

Other works: D. BOYARIN, Galatians and Gender Trouble: Primal Androgyny and the First-Century Origins of a Feminist Dilemma (Berkeley, Calif., 1995) • J. D. G. DUNN, The Theology of Paul's Letter to the Galatians (Cambridge, 1993) • J. ECKERT, Die urchristliche Verkündigung im Streit zwischen Paulus und seinen Gegnern nach dem Galaterbrief (Regensburg, 1971) • K. A. MORLAND, The Rhetoric of Curse in Galatians: Paul Confronts Another Gospel (Atlanta, 1995) • W. SCHMITHALS, "Judaisten in Galatien?" ZNW 74 (1983) 27-58; idem, "Paulus und die Gnostiker," TF 35 (1965) 9-46 • J. M. SCOTT, Paul and the Nations: The OT and Jewish Background of Paul's Mission to the Nations, with Special Reference to the Destination of Galatians (Tübingen, 1995).

DIETER LÜHRMANN

Gallicanism

Since the debate about papal → infallibility in the 19th century, the term "Gallicanism" has been used for the theological doctrines and political practice of the state church in France (→ Church and State). In the late Middle Ages national and ecclesiastical interests (→ Conciliarism), joining forces in opposition to the universal claims of the papacy and curial centralism, had secured a wide measure of autonomy for the French church. Les libertés de l'Église gallicane (The freedoms of the Gallican church; 1594), compiled by P. Pithou, and the Preuves (Evidences; 1639) of P. Dupuy gained official status as a statement of the right the church had traditionally claimed. The University of Paris and the clergy became staunch supporters of Gallicanism.

Gallicanism reached its climax in the 17th century under the absolutism of Louis XIV (ruled 1643-1715). The conflict with Rome over the royal appointment of bishops led to the classic formulation of Gallicanism by J.-B. Bossuet (1627-1704) in his Four Gallican Articles (1682):

1. Kings and princes are not subject to ecclesiastical authority in temporal and civil matters.
2. Papal powers are limited by the decrees of the Council of Constance (1414-18; → Reform

Councils), thus asserting the authority of general councils over the pope.

3. The use of papal apostolic power must be in accordance with the traditions of the French church.

4. Papal decisions in matters of faith need the consent of the whole church (i.e., meeting in general council).

Though the papacy condemned Gallicanism, it was defended in many theological and historical works and influenced other → national church movements (e.g., Febronianism, in 18th-cent. Germany; → Josephinism).

Napoléon (1804-15) abandoned Gallicanism in the Concordat of 1801 but not in his Organic Articles (1802), in which he enforced the articles of 1682.

→ Ultramontanism could not fully suppress Gallicanism. It finally played a part in French opposition before and also at → Vatican I, though the definition of universal primacy (which Gallicanism had prevented at → Trent) and also of intrinsic papal → infallibility (in opposition to the fourth article) rendered it dogmatically obsolete.

Bibliography: G. Adriányi, "Gallikanismus," *TRE* 12.17-21 (bibliography) • C. Berthelot du Chesnay, "Gallicanism," *NCE* 6.262-67 • DH 2281-85, 3059-75 • A. Gough, *Paris and Rome: The Gallican Church and the Ultramontane Campaign, 1848-1853* (Oxford, 1986) • J. N. Moody, "Gallicanism," *EncRel(E)* 5.467-68 • M. O'Gara, *Triumph in Defeat: Infallibility, Vatican I, and the French Minority Bishops* (Washington, D.C., 1988) • *QGPRK* (5th ed.) 419, 445, 466-67 • H. Schneider, *Der Konziliarismus als Problem der neueren katholischen Theologie* (Berlin, 1976) • D. K. Van Kley, *The Jansenists and the Expulsion of the Jesuits from France, 1757-1765* (New Haven, 1975).

Hans Schneider

Gambia

The West African Republic of Gambia was a British colony until 1965, when it gained its independence (→ Colonialism). As a country, it is one of the smallest in population, one of the most artificial colonial creations, and among the least developed countries in Africa. It consists of a strip of land on both sides of the Gambia River, 320 km. (200 mi.) long but never more than 45 km. (30 mi.) wide.

As a political entity, Gambia has roots going back to the medieval empire of Mali, of which it formed

	1960	1980	2000
Population (1,000s):	352	641	1,244
Annual growth rate (%):	2.72	3.01	2.07
Area: 10,689 sq. km. (4,127 sq. mi.)			

A.D. 2000

Population density: 116/sq. km. (301/sq. mi.)
Births / deaths: 3.65 / 1.58 per 100 population
Fertility rate: 4.81 per woman
Infant mortality rate: 112 per 1,000 live births
Life expectancy: 49.0 years (m: 47.4, f: 50.7)
Religious affiliation (%): Muslims 87.0, tribal religionists 7.5, Christians 4.1 (Roman Catholics 2.6, other Christians 1.5), other 1.4.

the extreme western point. Records attesting to its history reach much further back, however, to 500 B.C., when Hanno the Carthaginian settled the west coast, leaving observations on the country and its culture. The French scholar Raymond Mauny, in his work *Tableau géographique* (1961), proposed a bold and novel hypothesis that sailors from the Senegambian/Mauritanian coast crossed the Atlantic centuries before Columbus. The Senegambian region is thus full of history preserved in documentary, archaeological, and oral forms. A good deal of that history is enacted in local musical traditions.

The Gambia River was the most navigable waterway in premodern West Africa. At the headwaters of the river are soils rich in gold, which made its way down the river to European trading ships. Coffee, ebony, hides, wax, ivory, and spices were also brought down the river, which thus became an essential artery of the regional economic trade. The major point from which trade might be controlled was Fort James, built on an island in an estuary, 20 miles from the sea. This fort, originally built by Baltic Germans, was acquired by the English in 1661 and then named after James II. After several changes in control it was accidentally blown up in 1725 and, after some restoration, was finally destroyed by the French in 1778.

With a population of just over a million and few natural resources, the country has been bypassed by modern communication routes. Historically, however, Gambia was at the crossroads of attempts to open up Africa, an indispensable coordinate in geographic knowledge and exploration of the continent. The river brought the traveler virtually to the doorstep of the great trans-Saharan routes that dissected and knitted the grain- and gold-producing regions of the area. Today, however, the country languishes in relative political obscurity (→ Development; Third World).

In July 1994 a group of junior army officers seized power in a bloodless coup d'état. President Dawda K. Jawara and his family fled to a visiting U.S. frigate berthed in the harbor, fleeing subsequently to Senegal and eventually, and permanently, to London. Jawara had ruled Gambia for over 30 uneventful years. Subsequent discussions have been held to return the country to democratic civilian rule, but they have not been productive, and all local political activity has remained suppressed.

In terms of culture, ethnic groupings (45 percent Mandingo), and above all in the character and religious intercommunication of the Muslim majority (over 85 percent of the population), Gambia can be distinguished only by its use of English from Senegal, the much larger francophone state that surrounds it on every side. Alex Haley, author of the renowned *Roots* (1976), believed that his ancestors were sold into slavery from this area and brought to America.

Gambia's historical ties to Britain have been of importance in the history of its churches. The Anglicans and British Methodists began mission work in 1816 and 1821 respectively (→ British Missions). Christians, however, account for less than 5 percent of the total population, and most of them are from traditionally Christian Creole families, whose time of settlement dates from the early 19th century, when the British navy brought them to Gambia after freeing them from slave ships.

Although the churches are not inactive in providing social services and some newer Protestant mission work is carried out by radio, it is hard to see any strong signs of their expansion, either in numbers or in influence. The → Roman Catholic Church appointed a papal pro-nuncio to Gambia in 1978 and is represented in the Gambia Christian Council (1963; → National Christian Councils).

Gambia is home to more than 9,000 → Baha'is.

→ Islam is centuries old in Gambia. In the Marabout Wars of the 19th century, an Islamic puritan movement had lasting influence on popular belief and practice. All Gambian Muslims follow the Malikite school of law, and most of them are attached to the Kadiriya or Tijaniya orders of → Sufism. Muslims in Gambia follow the orders of the Prophet with mild disposition and gentle means, which fosters amicable relations with its pagan and minority Christian neighbors. Christians, in their turn, have settled into the easygoing ways of the larger population, offering education to Muslims without expecting or wanting converts among their pupils, as if instinctively surrendering a policy of active evangelism in return for the Muslim rejection of militant jihad. The two traditions of a pacifist Islam and an accommodating Christianity have created an ethos of religious and political moderation that has fitted in well with the country's → pluralist makeup. Gambia is one of the few Muslim countries that observes as national holidays Christian feasts such as Good Friday and the Feast of the Assumption of the Blessed Virgin.

Bibliography: H. A. Gailey, *Historical Dictionary of the Gambia* (Metuchen, N.J., 1987) • M. Hudson, *Our Grandmother's Drums* (New York, 1991) • M. F. McPherson and S. C. Radelet, eds., *Economic Recovery in the Gambia: Insights for Adjustment in Sub-Saharan Africa* (Cambridge, Mass., 1995) • D. E. Maranz, *Peace Is Everything: World View of Muslims in the Senegambia* (Dallas, 1993) • B. Prickett, *Island Base: A History of the Methodist Church in the Gambia* (Bo, Sierra Leone, 1969) • L. Sanneh, *Piety and Power: Muslims and Christians in West Africa* (Maryknoll, N.Y., 1996) • R. A. Schroeder, *Shady Practices: Agroforestry and Gender Politics in the Gambia* (Berkeley, Calif., 1999).

Paul Jenkins and Lamin Sanneh

Genesis, Book of

1. Name
2. Contents and Structure
3. Literary-Critical and Theological Problems

1. Name

In the Hebrew Bible the first book of the → Pentateuch is named for its first word: *bĕrēʾšît,* "in the beginning." "Genesis" is a Latinized form of Gk. *genesis,* "origin," which is the title in the LXX. This word describes the contents, whereas "First Book of Moses" has reference to the early traditional author.

2. Contents and Structure

Genesis forms part of the longer Pentateuchal narrative, but it is also a relatively self-contained whole. It tells the story from the beginning of the world to the Egyptian sojourn of the sons of → Jacob, the ancestors of the 12 → tribes of Israel.

Genesis falls into three main parts: the → primeval history of chaps. 1–11, the patriarchal stories of 12–36 and 38, and the stories of Joseph in 37 and 39–50 (→ Patriarchal History). The first part is the story of the human race as a whole from the beginnings to the rise of the nations. A genealogy from → Noah to → Abraham connects this part with the history of the patriarchs. After the pervasive and worsening → sin that brings the flood on the whole race, God gives Abraham the promise of a new blessing, nation, and land. The traditions of Abraham that follow tell of the delay in the fulfillment of the promise, the birth of the promised son, and the difficult test of Abraham's obedience when he is told to offer up this son. Except in chap. 24 (his marriage), the stories about → Isaac are short and run parallel to those of Abraham, especially in 26:7-11 and in 12:10-20 and chap. 20.

The Jacob traditions are more colorful. The events take place partly in Aram (Syria) and partly in Canaan. Jacob's stealing the birthright (chap. 27) sets things in motion. For fear of Esau Jacob flees to Aram and marries Leah and Rachel. He has 11 sons and a daughter, and then a 12th son (Benjamin) after his return. The story of the ladder (28:10-22) and that of his night wrestling with a spirit (32:22-32) form the framework of the events in East Jordan.

The Joseph story is very different. It is a unified short story and represents a link between Genesis and Exodus. Sold into Egypt by his brothers, Joseph becomes the right-hand man of Pharaoh and makes it possible for Jacob's family to settle in Egypt when they are threatened by famine.

3. Literary-Critical and Theological Problems

The main problems of this first book of the Hebrew canon and of the → Torah are the same as those of the Pentateuch as a whole. They concern the identification and dating of sources (documents) along with their origin and the peculiarities of the redacted material. A broad consensus acknowledges the presence of a basic Priestly writing, dating from the exile or the postexilic period (primarily 1:1–2:4a; parts of the flood narrative, esp. 9:1-17; 17:1-27; 23:1-20), into which materials from older sources (J and E; primal history and the main corpus of the patriarchal narratives) have been worked. The theological weight of Genesis is considerable, and its virtually inexhaustible motifs include → creation, the fall, → curse, the promise of blessing (→ Promise and Fulfillment), and divine guidance in faith.

Bibliography: Commentaries: W. Brueggemann (IBC; Atlanta, 1982) • T. E. Fretheim (NIB; Nashville, 1994) • G. von Rad (OTL; rev. ed.; Philadelphia, 1973; orig. pub., 1953) • N. M. Sarna (JPSV; Philadelphia, 1989) • E. A. Speiser (AB; Garden City, N.Y., 1964) • C. Westermann, *Genesis* (3 vols.; Minneapolis, 1984-86; orig. pub., 1974-82).

Other works: A. Brenner, ed., *A Feminist Companion to Genesis* (Sheffield, 1993) • J. S. Kselman, "The Book of Genesis: A Decade of Scholarly Research," *Int* 45 (1991) 380-92. See also the bibliographies in "Patriarchal History," "Pentateuch," and "Primeval History (Genesis 1–11)."

Antonius H. J. Gunneweg†

Genetic Counseling

Many thousands of hereditary human ailments and characteristics are now known to be due to changes in specific genes. Human genetics studies their causes and transmission. Prognosis is possible on the basis of diagnosis and family histories. Under certain conditions the probability of gene and chromosome distribution and thus of genetic sickness in the next generation may be calculated. During pregnancy prenatal diagnosis (e.g., by amniocentesis in the 16th to the 17th week, by analysis of the chorionic villi during the 8th to 11th weeks, or by other procedures such as ultrasound or fetoscopy) may determine whether the child has a specific illness. In the case of Down's syndrome there is a superfluous chromosome 21, whereas in other cases there may be a gene defect. Genetic technology is constantly bringing to light other genetic abnormalities.

Genetic → counseling is usually offered in university clinics or institutes. It provides information about heightened risks (hereditary illnesses in the family, several miscarriages, age over 35, harmful influences during pregnancy, etc.). It thus helps people to make decisions about marriage and parenthood and offers support during pregnancy. If there are signs of serious sickness or anything less than perfection in the fetus, → abortion is legally permissible up to a certain point in many countries, though ethically controversial. In such cases counseling should simply communicate the results of prenatal diagnosis and not become merely a matter of → birth control. Throughout, a dedicated concern for those affected is urgently needed and ethically demanded.

Prenatal diagnosis may be misused for the selection of sex or the avoiding of minor ailments (metabolic diseases, harelip, hemophilia). Special ethical problems arise when diagnosis is only statistical, when the severity of an affliction cannot be measured (e.g., Down's syndrome or Huntington's chorea, which emerges only after the age of 40), or when the attempt must be made to consider how a family can cope with a problem. All social discrimination against the handicapped and their parents and doctors must be resolutely opposed, along with suits in the case of neglected abortions.

Specific problems are raised by genomic analysis and screening procedures to pinpoint dangers at the place of work or to eliminate defective genes (e.g., spina bifida). These have social value but may lead to discrimination or promote a kind of progressive → eugenics. Freedom of individual decision must be safeguarded and even the right not to know.

→ Medical Ethics

Bibliography: J. C. FLETCHER, ed., *Ethics and Human Genetics: A Cross-Cultural Perspective* (Heidelberg, 1987) • W. FUHRMANN and F. VOGEL, *Genetische Familienberatung* (3d ed.; Berlin, 1982) • J. HÜBNER, *Die neue Verantwortung für das Leben* (Munich, 1986) 27-40; idem, "Zur Ethik genetischer Beratung," *ZEE* 25 (1981) 102-8 • J. F. KILNER, R. D. PENTZ, and F. E. YOUNG, eds., *Genetic Ethics: Do the Ends Justify the Genes?* (Grand Rapids, 1997) • C. LINK, "Die Herausforderung der Ethik durch die Humangenetik," *ZEE* 25 (1981) 84-101 • I.-H. PAWLOWITZKI, J. H. EDWARDS, and E. A. THOMPSON, *Genetic Mapping of Disease Genes* (San Diego, Calif., 1997) • K. A. QUAID, D. H. SMITH, J. A. GRANBOIS, and G. P. GRAMELSPACHER, *Early Warning: Cases and Ethical Guidance for Presymptomatic Testing in Genetic Diseases (Medical Ethics)* (Bloomington, Ind., 1998) • J. REITER and U. THEILE, eds., *Genetik und Moral* (Mainz, 1985) • W. SCHLOOT, ed., *Möglichkeiten und Grenzen der Humangenetik* (Frankfurt, 1984).

JÜRGEN HÜBNER

Genetic Engineering → Medical Ethics

Genizah

From the Heb. verb *gnz*, "keep, enclose," the genizah is a side room in a → synagogue (usually a cellar or attic) in which to keep old, discarded, damaged, or in some way unserviceable MSS. Because these writings contain the name of God, they are not to be destroyed. Older → Judaism also placed heretical texts in the genizah. Most of the older synagogues had a genizah.

The most famous genizah was found in Old Cairo, on the second floor of the Ezra Synagogue, built in A.D. 882. Discovered as early as 1753 by Simon of Geldern, it was made famous by Solomon Schechter, who in May 1896 found there 140,000 biblical, liturgical, rabbinic, and exegetical fragments, among them (1) most of the Hebrew original of Sirach (→ Apocrypha), (2) extracts from Aquila's Greek translation of the OT, (3) fragments

of the Jerusalem and Palestinian → Talmud, (4) parts of the *Damascus Document* (→ Qumran), and (5) a Jewish life of Jesus. The oldest datable MS there is Zikron-Edut, from A.D. 750.

Among these discoveries the Hebrew Sirach was very important for biblical scholarship, since this book had previously been known only in its Greek version. Also important were materials illustrating the history of the Hebrew text of the Bible and translations, those relating to the history of the Jews in Egypt and Palestine between 640 and 1100, those relating to the Essene movement in Palestine, and those shedding light on traditions outside the mainstream of Judaism.

Bibliography: W. Z. FALK, "A New Fragment of the Jewish 'Life of Jesus,'" *Imm.* 8 (1978) 72-79 • N. GOLB, "Sixty Years of Genizah Research," *Jdm* 6 (1957) 3-16 • A. M. HABERMANN, "Genizah," *EncJud* 7.404-7 • P. E. KAHLE, *The Cairo Genizah* (2d ed.; Oxford, 1959) • S. C. REIF, ed., *Published Material from the Cambridge Genizah Collection: A Bibliography, 1896-1980* (Cambridge, 1988) • S. SHAKED, *A Tentative Bibliography of Genizah Documents* (Paris, 1964). Cairo Genizah texts and research appear also in *JAOS, JNES, JQR,* and *RevQ.*

JAMES R. BUTTS

Genocide

1. Definition
2. Explanation
3. Prevention

1. Definition

During the Second World War, the eminent jurist Raphael Lemkin coined the term "genocide," by which he meant "a coordinated plan of different actions aiming at the destruction of essential foundations of the life of national groups, with the aim of annihilating the groups themselves." By "destruction" he meant to include not only the biological aspects of a group's existence but also its cultural and social institutions. In 1948, in the wake of the Nazi genocide, the → United Nations formulated its own definition, relying on Lemkin's but also departing from it. According to the widely accepted U.N. formulation, genocide means actions "committed with intent to destroy in whole or in part a national, ethnic, racial, or religious group as such."

The U.N. definition has been criticized for being both too broad and too narrow. On the one hand, it is too broad in not discriminating sharply enough among a pogrom or massacre, a policy of mass murder whose aim is the repression of a group, and the extermination or total destruction of a collectivity. For example, the U.N. definition cannot discriminate between the massacre of some 10,000 Ibos in northern Nigeria in 1966 and the → Holocaust. In the former case the intent of the killers was to drive the Ibos out of northern Nigeria, not to exterminate them as a collectivity. In the latter instance, nearly six million people were murdered following the intent of the Nazis to exterminate the Jews.

On the other hand, Kuper has criticized the U.N. definition for being too narrow because, unlike the Lemkin definition, it does not include cultural and social aspects of group destruction, and because it excludes social classes and other collectivities that are not ethnic or communal groups. Thus without amendment the U.N. definition could not be applied to the destruction of the Kulaks during the collectivization period under Stalin, nor could it be extended to the destruction of the Cambodian upper and middle classes, who were for the most part ethnically identical to their Khmer Rouge killers.

For these reasons Melson has suggested that genocide be defined as a "public policy mainly carried out by the state whose intent is the destruction in whole or in part of a social collectivity or category, usually a communal group, a class, or a political faction." He goes on to distinguish between "massacre," "partial genocide," "total genocide," and "the Holocaust." In this formulation, the Holocaust is seen as an extreme case of total genocide in which the Jewish people were to be exterminated not only in Germany but the world over and their cultural institutions and influence (their "spirit") destroyed and banished.

It should be noted that the above definitions of genocide explicitly stress the intent and the policies of the → state. There are instances, however, of mass destruction and systematic mass murder where the intentions and policies of the state are not clearly involved. For example, it has been estimated that millions of native Americans ("Indians") perished from disease following the arrival of Europeans to the New World. Similarly, settlers in Australia and New Zealand and those following on the heels of the industrialization of virgin forest areas in Brazil, Paraguay, and Venezuela have committed mass murder against native peoples. There is a debate in the literature, therefore, whether an explicit statement of intent, especially by the state, is a necessary condition for genocide, or whether a pattern of systematic mass murder implying intent suffices.

2. Explanation

A number of factors have been advanced to account for genocide, including the dehumanization of the victims, the → ideology of the perpetrators, the needs of the bureaucracies and agencies that are given the task to solve a human "problem," the inner dynamics of totalitarian regimes, national crises, → revolutions, and → wars. It should be apparent that genocide is unlikely without the prior dehumanization of the victims, who are viewed as racially inferior (→ Racism) or as national or class enemies or as savages. Similarly, the perpetrators of genocide are usually motivated by an ideology that justifies their actions in terms of racial, national, or class conflict. Moreover, in the modern world → bureaucracies or other organized agencies are given the task of "solving" ethnic, racial, or class "problems." Indeed, some writers have argued that genocide as a policy initiative is formulated at the lower levels of the regime and then is justified by the ideology of the national decision makers. A number of writers have also pointed out that genocide is most likely to take place under conditions of crisis for the state and stress for society. Revolutionary conditions and wars thus can become occasions for genocide.

An older view first posited by Hannah Arendt suggested that genocide is inherent in totalitarian regimes like the Nazi and the Soviet states. The internal dynamics of such states may indeed have driven them to genocide, but we cannot say that genocide is committed only by totalitarian states. For example, the genocide of the Armenians from 1915 to 1922 was committed by the Ottoman Empire, governed by the Young Turks, but that regime cannot easily be identified with → totalitarianism.

3. Prevention

Following the Second World War and the Nürnberg trials of the Nazi war criminals, it was hoped that the United Nations would become an institution that would protect the world from the scourge of genocide. To this point, however, the United Nations has not been able to play an active role in the prevention of genocide mainly because its members are sovereign states that in times of crisis are willing to use extreme means, including genocide, while the United Nations itself does not have the power to stop them.

In recent years the world community has been able to prevent genocide against the Kurds in Iraq following the Gulf War, but only because the international alliance against Iraq had the military power and the will to act in that crisis. By way of contrast, the United Nations was powerless in the Yugoslav civil war and in the Rwanda genocide of 1994. In former Yugoslavia the United Nations sent in observers and monitors, but they were explicitly told not to intervene in cases of massacre. Only NATO was able to act in Bosnia and Kosovo in 1999, albeit late in the day after thousands had been killed or expelled from their homes. In Rwanda, neither the United Nations nor any of its member states, including the United States, had the will to prevent or to stop genocide, despite ample knowledge and appeals for help.

A number of nongovernmental organizations such as Human Rights Watch, the International Federation of Human Rights, International Alert, and the International Commission of Jurists are trying to predict genocidal situations and to monitor acts of genocide. Without power, however, they can do little to prevent such destructions from occurring.

Bibliography: H. ARENDT, *The Origins of Totalitarianism* (New York, 1958) • F. CHALK and K. JONASSOHN, *The History and Sociology of Genocide* (New Haven, 1990) • I. CHARNY, *Genocide: A Critical Bibliographic Review* (2 vols.; New York, 1988-92) • A. L. DES FORGES, *"Leave None to Tell the Story": Genocide in Rwanda* (New York, 1999) • H. FEIN, ed., *Genocide: A Sociological Perspective* (= *CuSoc* 38/1 [1990]) • L. KUPER, *Genocide: Its Political Uses in the Twentieth Century* (New Haven, 1981); idem, *The Prevention of Genocide* (New Haven, 1985) • R. LEMKIN, *Axis Rule in Occupied Europe* (New York, 1973; orig. pub., 1944) • R. MELSON, *Revolution and Genocide: On the Origins of the Armenian Genocide and the Holocaust* (Chicago, 1992) • D. RIEFF, *Slaughterhouse: Bosnia and the Failure of the West* (New York, 1996) • E. STAUB, *The Roots of Evil: The Origins of Genocide and Other Group Violence* (New York, 1989).

ROBERT MELSON

Gentiles, Gentile Christianity

1. Usage
2. OT
3. NT
4. Modern Problems

1. Usage

Gentile Christianity takes on its meaning in antithesis to Jewish Christianity. The reference is to all non-Jewish Christians. Another term often used for non-Jews before Christian conversion is "heathen," as in "missions to the heathen." In the modern understanding of → mission, however, this terminol-

ogy is usually regarded as either too militant or too patronizing, and it is thus thought better to speak of non-Christians and to describe heathen religions as non-Christian religions, though this is perhaps more in keeping with modern ideas than with the views of Scripture (see 2 and 3).

2. OT

Heb. *goy* means "people [as a national unit]" and can thus refer also to → Israel (§1); in the plural (*goyim*, "the nations; peoples"), however, it denotes non-Israelite peoples and, by extension, increasingly the adherents of non-Jewish religions. The usage is basically political, but because Israel as a people is identical with the worshipers of → Yahweh, other peoples can be called Gentiles. In Deuteronomy the basis of enmity toward other peoples is that God is displeased with their idolatry, which is a temptation to Israel. The singular *goy* for a Gentile does not occur in the OT but occurs first only in the → Talmud. In various prophets there are sayings about foreign peoples (Amos 1:3–2:3; Isaiah 13–23; Zeph. 2:4-15; Jeremiah 46–51; Ezekiel 25–32, 35; Joel 3; Obadiah; Nahum; Mic. 4:1-4), which are mostly pronouncements of judgment against these peoples (i.e., foreign nations) and imply a claim to the lordship of Yahweh. It is significant that in Isaiah 40–55 the expected new → salvation for Israel is so glorious that alien peoples will be attracted to it and will have a share in it. The non-Jewish king Cyrus can even be called messiah (Isa. 44:28–45:1).

3. NT

All the Gospels carefully avoid directly linking what is said about → Jesus to a Gentile mission or even to the church. This avoidance is historically apposite, but there is in it also the apologetic desire to present Jesus as Israel's Messiah who has come for all Israel, including its sinners, and who cannot be accused of careless dealings with Gentiles or of a program of Gentile mission. We find various types of statements:

1. If Israel rejects Jesus' message, there is a threat of turning to the other peoples and Israel's loss of its uniqueness (Matt. 3:9 and par.; Luke 13:22-30; probably also Matt. 21:33-46 [esp. v. 43]).
2. In analogy to Isa. 49:12; 59:19, Jesus reckons on a future ingathering of other peoples (Matt. 8:11; see also John 10:16). The use of Deutero-Isaiah in the NT rests largely on the idea of an eschatological ingathering of the nations.
3. Jesus performs miracles for non-Jews by remote healing (Mark 7:24-30 and par.; Luke 7:1b-9 and par.; John 4:46b-53; cf. John 12:20-26).

4. Some signs are recorded precisely because they symbolize the removing of Gentile need and impurity (see Mark 5:1-20, with, according to v. 20, the ensuing proclamatory activity of the healed person in the Decapolis).

5. Only the risen Lord gives the commission for mission to all nations (Matt. 28:19, in contrast to 10:5b; Mark 16:15; Luke 24:47; John 20:21; Acts 1:8; Gal. 1:16).

Hellenists apparently led the way in mission to non-Jews without demanding circumcision (Acts 11:20), and → Paul took up the challenge, with Peter also playing a big part, according to Acts 10. It was the gift of the Spirit (→ Holy Spirit) that made this mission possible, according to Acts 10:44 and Paul. Only the Spirit of God, in whom the risen Lord is at work, can bring people to God and make them his children (Gal. 4:6-7), thus making circumcision unnecessary in the case of Gentile Christians.

But the Spirit is none other than the promise to Abraham (Gal. 3:8, 14), and thus Gentile Christians are conceivable only if they are taken up into Israel (see the olive tree illustration in Rom. 11:15-24). They are not second-class Christians, but they achieve their being in Christ, from Israel's standpoint, only as Jesus sets them in God's history with Israel. Non-Christian Jews are still God's chosen people, though this fact does not guarantee the salvation of individuals.

In general we may say that the NT comes from missionary churches whose whole aim is to impart the joy of salvation to as many people as possible. Statements still occur, however, about the possible perdition of those who do not believe (John 3:18; Mark 16:16). These texts are not to be taken dogmatically or categorically. Form-critical considerations advise against making too much systematically of texts of appellation. No NT statements function as definitive statements about the salvation or perdition of non-Christians. The "if . . . then" relation functions (only) as an appeal.

4. Modern Problems

In contrast to NT authors, a crisis has now developed in circles that seek new models to explain both theoretically and practically the relation of Christianity to other religions (→ Theology of Religions). The older model of *scattered germs of* → *truth in other religions* has been replaced in part by the following approaches.

First, we find *practical cooperation* in humanitarian affairs and ongoing → dialogue about common features in the face of the threat of → materialism and the new paganism.

Then there is the model of *anonymous Christians* (K. Rahner), even as individuals who do not believe in Christ seek to be the best they can be according to the light they have and thus manifest something incarnational, being called Christian in this sense. A question here is whether we do justice to the way other religions view themselves. A further question is whether we do not at the same time sell Christianity itself short.

Another model is that of *concentric circles*. Some religions and worldviews, it is argued, are especially close (e.g., → Islam, → anthroposophy, or → Judaism, which is hardly separable from Christianity) and form an inner "ring" with many things in common. Other religions are a little more distant (→ Buddhism and those of the Far East), but mission can do little among them, and they agree in important matters (e.g., religious practice; → Buddhism and Christianity; Hinduism and Christianity). Finally, others are more remote and can gain most from Christianity's innovative power. On this model mission should be directed only to those whom Christianity can help most, and Matt. 5:13-17 should be its basic principle.

Distinction between the *new paganism among Christians, foreign religions*, and *the irreligious* underlines the solidarity of religions but also the fact that the new pagans who are baptized and who belong to the church are different from adults who make no religious profession at all. New Christian paganism is a product of national churches.

All definitions of the relation to other religions should reflect the fact that the hands of Christians are tied to some extent by the fact that they have been incorporated into the history of the Jewish people of God. Hence they also must always take into account the relation of Israel to other religions.

Many Christians and Christian bodies, of course, still adhere more strictly to the biblical understanding and, although they may differ in detail, take seriously the truth of revelation and reconciliation in Christ alone and the implied task of Gentile mission, that is, the proclamation of the gospel to all nations (→ Evangelism).

→ Agnosticism; Apologetics; Atheism; Neo-Germanic Paganism

Bibliography: K. BERGER, "Almosen für Israel. Zum historischen Kontext der paulinischen Kollekte," *NTS* 23 (1976/77) 180-204 • W. S. CAMPBELL, *Paul's Gospel in an Intercultural Context: Jew and Gentile in the Letter to the Romans* (Frankfurt, 1992) • C. COLPE, *Theologie, Ideologie, Religionswissenschaft* (Munich, 1980) • R. DABELSTEIN, *Die Beurteilung der "Heiden" bei*

Paulus (Frankfurt, 1981) • T. L. DONALDSON, *Paul and the Gentiles: Remapping Paul's Convictional World* (Minneapolis, 1997) • W. W. FIELDS, *Sodom and Gomorrah: History and Motif in Biblical Narrative* (Sheffield, 1997) • H.-W. GENSICHEN, *Glaube für die Welt. Theologische Aspekte der Mission* (Gütersloh, 1971) • H. KRAEMER, *The Christian Message in a Non-Christian World* (Grand Rapids, 1961; orig. pub., 1938) • M. PALDIEL, *Sheltering the Jews: Stories of Holocaust Rescuers* (Minneapolis, 1996) • G. G. PORTON, *The Stranger within Your Gates: Converts and Conversion in Rabbinic Literature* (Chicago, 1994) • C. W. STENSCHKE, *Luke's Portrait of the Gentiles prior to Their Coming to Faith* (Tübingen, 1999) • S. STERN, *Jewish Identity in Early Rabbinic Writings* (Leiden, 1994) • W. A. VISSER 'T HOOFT, "Evangelism among Europe," *IRM* 264 (1977) 349-60; idem, "Gläubiges neues Heidentum," *LM* 11/12 (1977) 634-37, 699-701 • M. WEINFELD, *The Promise of the Land: The Inheritance of the Land of Canaan by the Israelites* (Berkeley, Calif., 1993) • D. ZELLER, *Juden und Heiden in der Mission des Paulus. Studien zur Römerbrief* (2d ed.; Stuttgart, 1976).

KLAUS BERGER

Geography → History, Auxiliary Sciences to, 8

Geography of Religion

1. The geography of religion may be variously viewed as a department in → religious studies (G. Lanczkowski), a branch of cultural geography (H.-G. Zimpel; → Culture), or an interdisciplinary field involving geography and religious studies (M. Büttner). Most broadly, its concern is with the relations between → religions and space, or landscapes.

2. Up to the → Enlightenment, geography (like most other disciplines) was put in the service of → theology and had the task of giving academic support to God's world sovereignty. Theologian B. Keckermann (1571-1609; → Orthodoxy 2.3) and philosopher I. Kant (1724-1804; → Kantianism) paved the way for the freeing of geography from theology. C. Ritter (1779-1859) and others helped to establish modern geography in the 19th century, though his teleological outlook (which included the view that the earth is our schoolhouse) recalled the early days of the discipline. *Physical geography* was dominant at first, stressing natural geofactors such as relief, soil, vegetation, and climate. Only as *human* or *cultural geography* became more prominent

toward the end of the 19th century did religion come into view as something that is bound to places and influenced by them.

At the beginning of the 20th century, the modes of thought and explanation of *environmental determinism* were common in German human geography. Their impact on the understanding of religions is illustrated by the title "Islam, the Religion of the Desert," in which W. Gebel argued that religions not only are predominantly influenced by their → environment but must be seen as dependent on it.

The *ecology of religion* (A. Hultkranz) may be regarded as a later, purified addition to this deterministic type of study. After the phase of environmental determinism, the *landscape paradigm* followed in the development of geography. The question here was how religion, or the chief religions in given areas, or even minority religions, affect the physical landscape. The focus was on physiognomy — that is, structures, → pilgrimage sites, and so forth. The attempt by P. Fickeler to find a theoretical place for the geography of religion as a department of geography was strongly influenced by this way of thinking, although here, and even more clearly so in the work of P. Deffontaines, we also find approaches to a functional view that has since shaped the whole discipline and produced *social geography*.

3. On the basis of the studies of the sociology of religion, especially by M. Weber (1864-1920), inquiries are made into the impact of religious communities as social groups on population, settlement, economics, and politics (note esp. the important contributions in a volume edited by M. Schwind; → Sociology of Religion). In this way, limitation of research to visible phenomena is overcome. Geography has become a spatial science, and this development has also influenced the geography of religion. Especially important has been the work of Büttner (e.g., in *GRel*) in seeing a "religious body" or group or communion as a mediating force between religion and the world around. Influenced by its environment, a religious body influences the world geographically in various ways. E. Isaac distinguished between the geography of religion and *religious geography*, by which he meant investigation of the earth, or of some part of it, and of the factors that influence it, from the standpoint of a specific religion.

Before the Enlightenment (see 2), geography might be called *Christian geography* on this view. D. Sopher set the geography of religion within the context of a general cultural geography that, on the one hand, inquires into the interaction between a culture and its area's geography and, on the other, investigates the spatial interaction between different cultures. Later studies broadened the field and sought to develop a *geography of ideologies* that would also include the impact of different views and world pictures on spatial structures and processes, even though they might not be religious in the narrow sense. (Büttner 1976). Religious scholars (J.-F. Sprockhoff, K. Hoheisel) have produced few works on the relations between religion and space written from a religious standpoint, but there are many important contributions from the side of geography, whose common theme is the impact of the religions on places.

Another subject that has again attracted attention is the geographic distribution of the religions and its causes (J. D. Gay). These studies include the investigation of the mixing or segregation of religious groups and the related conflicts. The expansion of religions by → mission and its impact (R. Henkel), settlements on a religious basis (H. Schempp; → Perfectionists), and "religious tourism" (S. M. Bhardwaj and G. Rinschede) have also called for more intensive study. At the same time, although the relation between humans and their environment has always been a central subject in geography, geography has surprisingly taken part only marginally in the discussion of the complex of → environmental ethics and ecological theology (→ Ecology).

Bibliography: S. M. Bhardwaj and G. Rinschede, eds., *Pilgrimage in World Religions* (Berlin, 1988) • M. Büttner, "Von der Religionsgeographie zur Geographie der Geisteshaltung?" *Die Erde* 107 (1976) 300-329; idem, "Zur Geschichte und Systematik der Religionsgeographie," *GRel* 1.13-121 (bibliography) • P. Deffontaines, *Géographie et Religions* (Paris, 1948) • P. Fickeler, "Fundamental Questions in the Geography of Religions," *Readings in Cultural Geography* (ed. P. L. Wagner and M. W. Mikesell; Chicago, 1962) 94-117; idem, "Grundfragen der Religionsgeographie," *Erdkunde* 1 (1947) 121-44 • *GRel* • J. D. Gay, *The Geography of Religion in England* (London, 1971) • W. Gebel, "Der Islam–die Religion der Wüste," *JSGVK*, Beiheft, 1922, 104-33 • R. Henkel, *Christian Missions in Africa* (Berlin, 1989) • K. Hoheisel, "Geographische Umwelt und Religion in der Religionswissenschaft," *GRel* 1.123-64 • A. Hultkrantz, "An Ecological Approach to Religion," *Ethnos* 31 (1966) 131-50 • E. Isaac, "Religious Geography and the Geography of Religion, Man, and the Earth," *University of Colorado Studies, Series in Earth Sciences* 3 (1965) 1-13 • G. Lanczkowski, *Einführung in die Religionswissenschaft* (Darmstadt, 1980) • C. C. Park, *Sacred Worlds: An Introduction to Geography and Religion* (London, 1994) • H. Schempp, *Gemeinschaftssiedlungen auf religiöser und weltanschaulicher Grundlage* (Tübingen, 1969) • M. Schwind, ed., *Religionsgeographie* (Darmstadt, 1975) • D. Sopher, *Geography of Religions* (Englewood Cliffs, N.J., 1967) • J.-F. Sprockhoff, "Religiöse Lebensformen und Gestalt der Lebensräume," *Numen* 11 (1964) 85-146 • H.-G. Zimpel, "Religionsgeographie," *Westermann Lexikon der Geographie* 3.1000-1002.

Reinhard Henkel

Georgia

	1960	1980	2000
Population (1,000s):	4,160	5,073	5,418
Annual growth rate (%):	1.47	0.83	0.02

Area: 69,700 sq. km. (26,900 sq. mi.)

A.D. 2000

Population density: 78/sq. km. (201/sq. mi.)
Births / deaths: 1.38 / 0.99 per 100 population
Fertility rate: 1.90 per woman
Infant mortality rate: 21 per 1,000 live births
Life expectancy: 73.6 years (m: 69.5, f: 77.6)
Religious affiliation (%): Christians 60.5 (Orthodox 56.9, unaffiliated 1.4, other Christians 2.1), Muslims 19.4, nonreligious 16.9, atheists 2.8, other 0.4.

1. Christian History
2. Present Situation
3. Ecumenical Tensions

Situated at the crossroads of empires on the plateau south of the Caucasian mountain range, eastern and western Georgia, as well as Armenia, has experienced a long and dramatic Christian history. Having managed to maintain, over against the Roman and Persian empires, a distinctive identity since the 5th century, Georgian culture after the 11th century was further shaped by the influence of → Byzantium and the Arab caliphates. Then, as the united Georgian kingdom at its apogee in the 12th and 13th centuries, it sustained a national-religious identity thereafter when surrounded by the Muslim world of the Ottoman Empire. Georgia was then incorporated into the expanding Russian Empire in 1801, the Georgian Orthodox Church also being absorbed (as an exarch with Russian leadership) into the Russian Orthodox Church in 1811. After 1917 the Georgian church regained its autocephaly. After 1921, however, when Georgia became a Soviet republic, the Stalinist purges — carried out by three Georgians: J. Stalin, G. K. Ordzhonikidze, and L. P. Beria — decimated the church far more than had been the case with the earlier Russian absorption. Since 1990 the new independent Georgian state has been described as controlled chaos, with church life recovering but having nowhere near as pervasive an influence as when Georgia first emerged as a nation.

1. Christian History

Christianity in Georgia began in 326 when Nino, a female prisoner of war, won over the Georgian king Mirian. Christian faith quickly took root, at first closely related to the Patriarchate of Antioch and its Greek → liturgy. In the sixth century a vernacular translation of Scripture and the liturgy accounted for the lasting cultural independence of Georgia. The → conversion (§1) was a conscious rejection of the Zoroastrianism of its Persian neighbors (→ Iranian Religions 7). Unlike neighboring Persian and Armenian Christians, however, the Georgian church (western Georgia) in the 600s recognized the Council of → Chalcedon (451) and sustained ties to the Ecumenical Patriarchate. The Georgian church became → autocephalous in the eighth century. Between 1100 and 1300, when the Georgian kingdom reached its greatest expanse — particularly under David II (1089-1125) and Queen Tamara (1184-1213) — intermarriage with the Byzantine dynasties ensured friendly ties. Members of the Georgian aristocracy also held high office in the Byzantine administration.

→ Monasteries contributed to the growth of Christianity in Georgia at the beginning, Georgian monasteries being among the first to establish foundations in Jerusalem (5th cent.). The country's literary flowering in the 11th and 12th centuries especially is inconceivable without monasticism. The monastery of Iveron (meaning "of the Iberians," referring to the ancient region of Iberia, roughly coextensive with modern Georgia) is the third oldest monastery at Mount → Athos in Greece, where Georgian monks resided until the 1950s. Under David II there was a strong effort to send monastics to Mount Athos to translate ecclesiastical texts. It is also worthy of note that 85 Georgian MSS are preserved at Mount → Sinai.

In pursuing a vigorous campaign against abuses in church life, David II facilitated the deepening of monastic life and the translation of Greek texts into Georgian. The Synod of Ruisi-Urbnisi of 1103, over which the king presided, produced church legislation to eliminate numerous manifestations of simony and nepotism within the monastic and ecclesiastical administrations. The synod also regulated the religious life of the laity by specifying that girls in church marriages must be at least 12 years old and by forbidding → marriage with infidels or heretics.

At the time of the absorption of the Georgian Orthodox Church into the Russian church in 1811, Czar Alexander I at first relied on a Georgian, Metropolitan Varlam Eristavi, to serve as exarch of church. Six years later Metropolitan Feofilakt Rusanov, a Russian, was appointed exarch. Feofilakt belonged to the very small, educated elite on whom the czar had relied to design a major reform of the theological education system in Russia, and he was expected to extend that reform to Georgia. On the positive side, this move marked another systematic effort to deal with abuses inside the church, although it was done by means of Russification. By the end of the 19th century the secular streams of nationalism were making an impact on the Georgian church (→ Nation, Nationalism). With the collapse of the Russian Empire in early 1917, the Georgian Orthodox Church regained its autocephaly, and its head became the → patriarch of Georgia.

In 1917 there were nearly 2,500 → Orthodox churches in Georgia. After the Communist purges had ended, however, only 40 remained open. Proportionately more churches, by a factor of eight, were forcibly closed in Georgia than was true for Russian Orthodoxy. Only 5 percent of the Georgian intelligentsia survived the purges of the 1930s, and control over intellectuals was such that doctoral theses could be approved only upon prior approval of the Russian translation sent to Moscow. It was therefore most fitting that a Georgian film by Tengiz Abuladze, *Pokoiane* (Repentance), shown across the Soviet Union in 1987, became a turning point for perestroika, the moment when the Soviet Union began to recover history, speak publicly about atrocities, and acknowledge the reality of Soviet-Russian domination of Georgia.

2. Present Situation

The recent recovery of Georgian Orthodoxy involved another difficult period of exposing and eliminating abuses that extended deep into the church structure that had survived the Communist onslaught. Zviad Gamsakhurdia, son of the famous nationalist writer and poet Konstantin Gamsakhurdia, became well known for human → rights activism, including a series of samizdat documents published in the West in 1974 that exposed the corruption within the church hierarchy. These accusations included an expose of the homosexuality of some bishops and of the financial corruption for which Metropolitan Gaioz was imprisoned in 1979. Patriarch David V, who had succeeded Patriarch Efrem in 1972 (in place of Ilia, whom Efrem had named as his successor), had no theological qualifications for the position, and his short reign marked the height of corruption and of KGB involvement in the affairs of the Georgian church. In 1977 Ilia II was elected patriarch, and he began a course of reforms, following similar actions being undertaken within the Communist Party by Eduard Shevardnadze, then party secretary. In 1988 there were 180 priests, 40 monks, and 15 nuns for the faithful, who were variously estimated as being from one to five million. There were 200 churches, one seminary, three convents, and four monasteries.

A moment of high drama came in 1989 as the rival nationalist forces within Georgia reached a critical level, along with pervasive anti-Russian sentiments among the populace. Patriarch Ilia had issued an edict that anyone using armed force against compatriots would be → excommunicated. The moment of test came on April 9, when several hundred thousand demonstrators came to the capital, Tbilisi, in peaceful demonstration asking the Communist Soviet government to leave Georgia. The patriarch joined the people and urged them to withdraw to the church to avoid bloodshed. The nationalist political leaders failed to respect this call, and Soviet tanks using poison gas moved in, leaving behind 22 dead and hundreds injured. A television documentary showing the mass funeral was shown across the Soviet Union and further cast shame on the Communist Party of the USSR, which soon lost its power. Not long afterward Georgia became a sovereign state.

A further period of trouble ensued when in 1990 Zviad Gamsakhurdia became head of state, for he set out to institute a → theocratic program. Using a curious interpretation of John 11 in which Lazarus was seen as identical with John the Evangelist, "the beloved disciple," Gamsakhurdia spoke of the Georgian language as the Lazarus among languages (i.e., primordial). The resurrected Georgia, like the resurrected Lazarus-John, was under the special protection of the Theotokos, since John had become the adopted son of Mary at the cross. The resulting political program was an attempt to marry church and state and to equate the nation with Orthodoxy.

By 1992 Gamsakhurdia had been driven from office, and Eduard Shevardnadze, who had contributed so much to Soviet perestroika as foreign minister, returned to Georgia and was elected its president. The political role of the church was weakened, even though Shevardnadze publicly converted to Christianity by → baptism (1992). After the death of Gamsakhurdia in January 1994, his supporters continued to foster a civil war by means of attempts on the life of the president, disruptions of Parliament, and other acts of civil disorder.

There had long been a Jewish community in Georgia that had amicable relations with the Christians, in large part because of the strong national tradition of pilgrimage to the Holy Land. Georgia had also served as a place of refuge for Russians fleeing the czar's wrath. Russian evangelical Protestants regard the baptism of Nikita Vornonin near Tbilisi (Georgia) in 1867 as their official beginning. By 1917 there was a thriving → Baptist congregation in Tbilisi, and a separate Georgian-speaking congregation began to form.

Following the reopening of churches in the USSR after 1944, an ethnically mixed Evangelical Christian Baptist Union was led by Russians until 1973, when N. Z. Kvirikashvili became the senior presbyter, or bishop. The current president and bishop of the Baptist Union, V. S. Songulashvili, has the distinction of having completed a doctorate in Semitic languages under a professor of Jewish origins during the Soviet era. He subsequently played a very active role in the translation of the NT into modern Georgian (→ Bible Versions), a project that was completed in partnership with the United → Bible Societies, with Songulashvili working closely with a committee of Georgian Orthodox scholars.

3. Ecumenical Tensions

The impact of the monasteries, including especially the ties to the Mount Athos monastic foundation, led to an extremely precipitate action in May 1997. Following an emergency meeting of the Holy Synod of the Orthodox Church of Georgia on May 20, the church announced its withdrawal from the → World Council of Churches (WCC), an ecumenical organization it had joined together with other Soviet churches in 1962. The stated complaint against the WCC was that it is dominated by a Protestant ethos that fails to take Orthodox interests into account. Archimandrite Georgi, father superior of a leading monastery, had sent an open letter to Patriarch Ilia II announcing that the monastery was suspending communion with the patriarch because of his "ecumenical heresy." Ilia II had been a WCC president from 1979 to 1983.

Behind this action lay the vigorous fundamentalistic reaction of the Mount Athos Federation of Monasteries against the decision of the Chalcedonian Orthodox and the → Monophysite Orthodox churches to withdraw the mutual anathemas of 451 and to give full recognition to each other, to be put into effect in September 1989. To the monks of Mount Athos this decision seemed to be calling into question the infallibility of Chalcedon, an ecumenical → council. Furthermore, this split between the Orthodox Church of Georgia and the → ecumenical movement as expressed in both the WCC and the → Conference of European Churches involved renewed isolation over against the Western churches also in reaction to perceived → proselytism of Orthodox Christians by Western "missionaries."

Efforts to restrict the freedoms of non-Orthodox religious in Georgia have continued to increase. In early 2000 numerous Baptist congregations in Georgia experienced harassment in efforts to close their places of worship. Lengthy court appeals by the → Jehovah's Witnesses, a sect that has been present in Georgia for several decades, ended in a denial of their right to function.

Bibliography: J. F. BADDELEY, *The Russian Conquest of the Caucasus* (Richmond, Eng., 1999) • "Can Georgia Achieve National Reconciliation?" RFE/RL *Caucusus Report,* 3/29 (July 20, 2000) [www.rferl.org] • F. CORLEY, "Georgian Police Break Up Evangelistic Meeting," *Keston News Service,* June 12, 1999; idem, "Trial against the Jehovah's Witnesses Begins in Georgia," *Keston News Service,* June 16, 1999 • P. CREGO, "Religion and Nationalism in Georgia," *REEu* 14/3 (June 1994) 1-9 • "Istoriia evangel'skikh khristian-baptistov v SSSR," *Vsesoiuznogo soveta EkhB* (Moscow, 1989) 496-97 • F. VON LILIENFELD, "Reflections on the Current State of the Georgian Church and Nation," *Seeking God: The Recovery of Religious Identity in Orthodox Russia, Ukraine, and Georgia* (ed. S. K. Batalden; Dekalb, Ill., 1993) 220-31 • "An Orthodox Church Leaves the WCC," *CCen,* June 4/11, 1997, 554-55 • A. PAPADAKIS, "The Christian East and the Rise of the Papacy," *The Church in History* (Crestwood, N.Y., 1994) 2.136-50 • C. J. PETERS, "The Georgian Orthodox Church," *Eastern Christianity and Politics in the Twentieth Century* (ed. P. Ramet; Durham, N.C., 1988) 286-308 • P. REDDAWAY, "The Georgian Orthodox Church: Corruption and Renewal," *RCL* 3/4-5 (1975) 14-23 • "Split Widens between Orthodox, WCC," *CCen,* October 8, 1997, 868 • R. G. SUNY, *The Making of the Georgian Nation* (Bloomington, Ind., 1988) • P. WALTERS, ed., *World Christianity: Eastern Europe* (Monrovia, Calif., 1988) 49-52.

WALTER SAWATSKY

German Christians

1. Definition
2. Origins
3. Ascendancy in 1933
4. Later History
5. Theological Evaluation

1. Definition

The German Christians (GCs) were clergy and laypeople in the Protestant church of Nazi Germany who believed that the National Socialist revolution would restore the church to its rightful place at the heart of German culture and society. Distinguishing between the "invisible" and the "visible" church, they argued that the church on earth was based on divinely ordained distinctions of race and ethnicity (→ Racism). The GCs set out to build a heroic, manly, doctrinally free → "people's church" (Volkskirche) composed solely of individuals of German "blood" and "race." Excluded would be those regarded as impure (e.g., baptized Christians of Jewish ancestry). GCs numbered around 600,000 and occupied influential positions at every level within the Protestant church during the Third Reich. They were actually a complex grouping of people who ranged from enthusiastic Hitler nationalists who were willing to make compromises to align the church with the new order to extreme radicals who rejected the biblical and theological foundations of German Protestantism. Countering GC power was the primary focus of the → church struggle.

2. Origins

GC roots lay in Christian → anti-Semitism and in racialist *(völkisch)* → ideology, which were promoted by the German Church League (founded 1921), the Church Movement of German Christians (formed in the late 1920s by the Thuringian pastors Siegfried Leffler [1900-1983] and Julius Leutheuser [1900-1942]), the conservative nationalist Christian German Movement (founded 1930), and other small Protestant associations dedicated to renewing church life by emphasizing ethnicity. In the spring of 1932 Wilhelm Kube (1887-1943), a prominent Nazi politician who was active in church politics in Berlin, formed the Evangelical National Socialists to enlist Protestant support for the party. When Adolf Hitler vetoed use of "Evangelical," Kube renamed it the Faith Movement of German Christians and placed activist pastor Joachim Hossenfelder (1899-1976) in charge.

Earlier Hossenfelder had prepared a list of guidelines for the fall church elections calling for the merger of the more than two dozen territorial churches into one national church (the *Reichskirche*), racial purity in the church, and the repudiation of internationalism. In September 1932 he created a national organization and in October began a newspaper, *Evangelium im Dritten Reich* (Gospel in the Third Reich). In November the GCs made a respectable showing in the Old Prussian Union Church elections.

3. Ascendancy in 1933

When Hitler came to power on January 30, 1933, Hossenfelder's GCs had little influence in the church, but they eagerly sought Nazi party backing. At a national conference on April 3-4, they demanded a unified Protestant national church corresponding to the political mission of the new Germany, one that would merge all → confessions and effect the integration of → church and state. The church authorities protested against this agenda, but Hitler supported the move and on April 25 appointed the unknown military chaplain Ludwig Müller (1883-1945), a GC and devoted Nazi, as his representative for Protestant church affairs. Müller pushed ahead for church → union and made a bid to become bishop of this to-be-united church. A group known as the Young Reformers, led by Martin → Niemöller (1892-1984), opposed the GC efforts, especially their attempt to impose the civil service's Aryan Paragraph on the church. This ruling would require the dismissal of all church staff of Jewish racial ancestry. The Young Reformers and other moderates encouraged Friedrich von Bodelschwingh (1877-1946) of the Bethel Institution in Westphalia to enter the race for *Reichsbischof,* and the majority of church leaders gave him their support at a meeting on May 27.

As this action was a setback to his program to coordinate all Germany's institutions under Nazi rule, Hitler threw his weight behind Müller. The Prussian churches were placed under a state commissioner, while the Lutheran bishops wavered in their support of Bodelschwingh, who resigned on June 24. Turmoil now reigned in the church, but a constitution for a confessionally united and centralized German Evangelical Church was adopted on July 14 and elections set for July 23. The Young Reformers entered a list of candidates under the name "Gospel and Church," but Hitler's endorsement enabled the GC to win two-thirds of the synodic seats. On September 5-6 the Old Prussian Union Church general synod named Müller its bishop and enacted the Aryan Paragraph. This move so alarmed the Young Reformers that on September 21 they formed the Pastor's Emergency League, whose members pledged to oppose the Aryan Paragraph and to support persecuted pastors. At the GC-controlled national synod in Wittenberg on September 27, the league protested in vain against these actions. Müller was appointed Reichsbischof, but implementation of the Aryan Paragraph was deferred because of embarrassing international criticism.

Müller tried to win Nazi party members back to the church, but Hitler made it clear that he had no interest in the internal life of the church, and party officials consistently avoided church functions. A lull in the conflict set in, but then at a GC rally in the Berlin Sportpalast on November 13, Reinhold Krause (1893-1980), a schoolteacher serving in the Berlin GC leadership, called for the dismissal of those pastors not behind the National Socialist revolution, immediate implementation of the Aryan Paragraph, and the liberation of the church from everything un-German, especially the Jewish OT and what he labeled the scapegoat mentality and inferiority complex of the rabbi Paul. The crowd of 20,000 then approved resolutions affirming Krause's demands. The Sportpalast affair aroused such indignation that many churchmen cut their GC ties, the GC leaders began fighting among themselves (which led to the dismissal of both Krause and Hossenfelder), and Hitler withdrew any backing for the group. Even as GC influence seemed to wane, Müller imposed still more restrictions on the church, and the opposition rapidly coalesced into the → Confessing Church.

4. Later History

In December 1933 Christian Kinder (1897-1972) gained control of the main GC organization, but the movement disintegrated into a dozen or more splinter groups with constantly changing names. In its → Barmen Declaration (adopted unanimously on May 31, 1934), the Confessing Church took direct aim at the errors perpetrated by the GCs and Reichsbischof Müller regarding revelation, Scripture, the church, and confession, and it rejected the power politics of the GC.

After Hanns Kerrl (1887-1941) formed the Ministry for Church Affairs in July 1935, the GC regrouped, with the main elements being a radical Thuringian body led by Leffler and Leutheuser and the successor Reich organization under Werner Rehm (1900-1948) and Werner Petersmann (1901-88). Kerrl's appointment of "church committees" to supervise church affairs and the call for new church elections in 1937 enhanced GC legitimacy. In their campaign to regain influence, the scattered GC groups rejected ecumenism and portrayed Christianity as the foe of → Judaism in their Godesberg Declaration of April 1939. The war brought fulfillment of some GC goals, including an aggressive Christianity uniting the people and exclusion of Jewish influence from the religious community, but the GCs and their publications were muzzled because of the Nazis' open hostility toward Christianity. After the war most GCs were rehabilitated (denazified) or simply overlooked and were quietly received back into the church.

5. Theological Evaluation

As the foremost modern example of the compromised church, the GCs take on enormous significance. They longed to be a vital part of the new order and to provide the spiritual foundations for the National Socialist state. In so doing, they inculcated the idea of race and *Volk* in the church and its message, called for the de-Judaizing of Christianity, detached the theology of creation and salvation from → Christology, and exalted the political realm. By placing the German nation and people above the universal claims of the Christian faith, they deceived themselves into believing that their earthly rulers — whom they assumed to be ordained by God — deserved their unquestioned respect and obedience. By holding a weak view of Scripture, the GCs easily jettisoned the parts of the Bible that they took as Jewish or as containing teachings contrary to their ideology. Because they emphasized action instead of doctrinal beliefs, they accepted all too uncritically the Nazi views on manliness, struggle, and racial nationalism. The GCs demonstrate that compromising Christian beliefs with the totalitarian demands of the modern → state destroys the integrity and witness of the church.

Bibliography: H. BAIER, *Die Deutschen Christen Bayerns im Rahmen des bayerischen Kirchenkampfes* (Nürnberg, 1968) • D. L. BERGEN, *Twisted Cross: The German Christians in the Third Reich* (Chapel Hill, N.C., 1996) • R. P. ERICKSEN and S. HESCHEL, *Betrayal: German Churches and the Holocaust* (Minneapolis, 1999) • R. GUTTERIDGE, *Open Thy Mouth for the Dumb! The German Evangelical Church and the Jews, 1879-1950* (Oxford, 1976) • R. E. HEINONEN, *Anpassung und Identität. Theologie und Kirchenpolitik der Bremer Deutschen Christen* (Göttingen, 1978) • E. C. HELMREICH, *The German Churches under Hitler: Background, Struggle, and Epilogue* (Detroit, 1979) • K. MEIER, *Die Deutschen Christen* (3d ed.; Göttingen, 1967) • T. M. SCHNEIDER, *Reichsbischof Ludwig Müller. Eine Untersuchung zu Leben, Werk und Persönlichkeit* (Göttingen, 1993) • K. SCHOLDER, *The Churches and the Third Reich* (2 vols.; Philadelphia, 1987-88) • H.-J. SONNE, *Die politische Theologie der Deutschen Christen* (Göttingen, 1982) • C. WEILING, *Die christlich-deutsche Bewegung* (Göttingen, 1998) • J. A. ZABEL, *Nazism and the Pastors: A Study of the Ideas of Three Deutsche Christen Groups* (Missoula, Mont., 1976).

RICHARD V. PIERARD

German Missions

1. Historical Development of German Protestant Missions
2. Present Situation and Future Prospects

Although spreading the → gospel message to all peoples has been a hallmark of the Christian faith from the very beginning, the identification of → missionary work with individuals from a specific nationality is a post-Reformation and primarily → Protestant phenomenon. Because the → Roman Catholic Church was an international body, individuals who served in religious or missionary → orders were theoretically part of the larger community, although many of these bodies actually had a national basis. Examples of distinguished German-born figures include the → Jesuit missionaries Johann Adam Schall von Bell (1592-1666) and Johannes B. Hoffmann (1857-1928), who worked in China and India respectively, the great historian of Catholic missions Heinrich Hahn (1800-1882), and Joseph Schmidlin (1876-1944), the father of Catholic → missiology. A noteworthy missionary order founded by a German was the Society of the Divine Word, formed in 1875 by Arnold Janssen (1837-1909) largely in response to the growing Protestant → mission effort, but its personnel and constituency are now quite international in character. Since → Vatican II individual dioceses have increasingly taken responsibility for mission work, especially in its diaconal forms (→ Catholic Missions; Relief and Development Organizations).

1. Historical Development of German Protestant Missions

Although Martin → Luther did not actively promote missions, the universality of the message was clearly evident in his preaching. In 1596 Philipp Nicolai (1556-1608) published *The Reign of Christ*, a theoretical work calling on the → Lutheran Church to be involved in missions because it had recovered the full gospel and made the divine → Word accessible to all. Nicolai's advice, however, went unheeded. The philosopher Gottfried Leibnitz (1646-1716), who was impressed with the Dutch colonial mission and Jesuit achievements in China, wanted to see an interchange of scientific and cultural knowledge between East and West. He included in the purpose statement of the Prussian Academy of Sciences (1700) a provision calling for the spreading of the Christian faith among other peoples. The earliest German-born missionaries, however, were individuals, such as Peter Heyling (1607/8-ca. 1652), who served in Egypt and Ethiopia without institutional support and eventually died in Africa, and Justinian von Welz (1621-ca. 1668), who called for Protestants to engage in world mission, developed a scheme for a missionary society, and went on his own to Surinam in South America, where he died unnoticed.

→ Pietism was the major force in 18th-century missions, with Halle and Herrnhut as centers of the movement. August Hermann → Francke's institution trained and sent missionaries, and in 1706 the first workers went to Tranquebar, South India, under the auspices of the Danish church mission. Ultimately over 50 men went to India from Halle, the most noteworthy being Bartholomäus Ziegenbalg (1682-1719), J. P. Fabricius (1711-91), and C. F. Schwartz (1726-98). The missionary letters published in the Halle magazine and the extensive correspondence carried on by Francke and his successors did much to foster missionary interest throughout Protestant Europe.

The Moravian Brethren (Unitas Fratrum) church of Count N. L. von → Zinzendorf (1700-1760), whose center was at Herrnhut (Saxony) and had close ties with Halle, undertook the most extensive missionary operation in the century. In 1732 the first Moravians went to the Danish West Indies, and soon thereafter workers were dispatched to Estonia, West and South Africa, Greenland, Labrador, frontier North America, and Surinam. By 1782 the Moravians had 175 missionaries working in 27 places, supported by branches in the Netherlands, Denmark, England, and North America. Even today the extraordinary → Moravian community, with its international character and ecumenical vision, maintains mission enterprises in Africa, Asia, and the Americas.

The evangelical awakening, or revival (Erweckung), provided a new impulse for Protestant missions. Johannes Jänicke (1748-1827), a key figure in the movement in Berlin, opened a missionary training school in his church, and British and kindred mission boards employed his graduates (→ British Missions). In 1815 a mission school and society was founded in Basel that drew support from neopietistic "awakened" circles in southwestern Germany. The graduates served under British boards and then in the mission's own fields in the Gold Coast (now Ghana), Cameroon, India, China, and Borneo.

Other voluntary societies to foster missions quickly sprang up throughout Germany, above all the Berlin Mission (1824), Rhenish Mission (1828), Gossner Mission (1836), and North German Mis-

sion (1836). Regarding themselves as the free outgrowth of the spirit of missions in the church as a whole, they had no organic connection with the territorial churches and thus were not "program boards" as such. The churches allowed them to exist as legal entities, however, and to solicit support from the congregations. A local organization formed a society, sought donations, and eventually built a regional or national organization tied together through its publication. A society often took its name from the city where its seat was located. They cooperated together in conferences and finally in 1885 formed a Standing Committee (Ausschuß) of German Protestant Missions to coordinate their efforts, mediate differences among the societies, and interact with the government. They also created special mission seminaries to train workers, since their position was that anyone whom God had called should be sent out to the foreign field.

By the early 1930s over 35 societies were formed, falling roughly into three categories: ecumenical, Lutheran confessionalist, and faith missions. The ecumenical agencies tended to downplay differences and stressed the importance of cooperative efforts to spread the Word of God. This group included the Basel (to some extent, although, as a Swiss-based group, it saw building Christian communities as its primary task), Berlin, Rhenish (also known as Barmen), North German (later Bremen), and Gossner (later another Berlin) Missions, as well as two foundations created during the colonial era: the German East Asia Mission (1884) and the Bethel (1886) Mission. The Berlin Mission operated in South Africa, China, and Tanganyika, while the Rhenish Mission's major fields were Southwest Africa (Namibia) and Sumatra; the North German Mission focused on Togo and Dahomey; and the Gossner Mission had a thriving work in North India. The German East Asia Mission (originally the General Protestant Mission Association) was the creation of liberal "Cultural Protestants," who promoted education and the idea of a universal world civilization in their fields in China and Japan. The Bethel Mission, founded by colonial enthusiasts as the Protestant Missionary Society for German East Africa, at first went bankrupt because of mismanagement. Friedrich von Bodelschwingh (1831-1910) rescued it by moving the seat from Berlin to his Bethel institution at Bielefeld and refocusing its efforts on medical work.

The Lutheran confessionalists were uneasy about cooperating with Anglicans and Reformed. The most important of their societies was the Leipzig Mission (1836), which brought together Lutheran mission initiatives, carried on the legacy of the

Danish-Halle Mission in India, and opened a fruitful field in East Africa. The Hermannburg Mission (1849) was the foundation of Ludwig Harms (1808-65), a strong-willed confessionalist from Hannover, and it promoted peasant settlement colonies in South Africa and a work in South India. The Neuendettelsau Mission of Wilhelm Löhe (1808-72) originally worked among Lutheran settlers in the United States, but in the 1880s it embarked on a major work in Papua New Guinea. The Schleswig-Holstein Evangelical Lutheran Mission at Breklum (1876) sent missionaries to China and South India, while the Bleckmar Mission (1892) in Hannover had a field in South Africa.

The most recent creations were the faith missions, modeled on the Bristol orphanages of George Mueller (1805-98) and the China Inland Mission (CIM) of J. Hudson Taylor (1832-1905). The Neukirchen Mission (1882) was the only Reformed society. Inspired by Mueller, it began with an orphanage and later added other works in Kenya and Java. The CIM was replicated in the Alliance Mission of Barmen (1889) and the Marburg Mission (1909), each of which sent workers to China, while its German branch, the Liebenzell Mission (1899), initiated a notable work in the Pacific islands that Germany acquired from Spain in 1899.

Some faith groups, many of which were charitable endeavors, focused on the Near East. Thanks to the influence of Samuel Gobat (1799-1879), a Basel-trained Lutheran who served in Ethiopia with the Church Missionary Society and was consecrated bishop of Jerusalem in 1846 under the joint British-Prussian missionary episcopacy, several groups could initiate works in the Holy Land, including the Kaiserwerth Deaconesses (1851), the Berlin Jerusalem Society (1852), the Syrian Orphanage in Jerusalem (1860), and the St. Chrischona Pilgrim Mission. The last mission was founded in 1840 by C. F. Spittler (1782-1867) and sent lay workers to the East. Its most memorable venture was an effort in the 1860s (ultimately unsuccessful) to establish a chain of mission stations from Jerusalem to Ethiopia. Other groups in the East included two relief bodies formed in 1896 that started out aiding Armenian refugees — the German Orient Mission, founded by Johannes Lepsius (1858-1926), and the German Christian Aid for the Orient, started by Ernst Lohmann (1860-1936) — and also the Sudan Pioneer Mission, later Protestant Mission in Upper Egypt (1900), which evangelized Muslims; the convalescent facility of the Protestant Carmel Mission (1904); and the Mission to the Blind of Ernst Christoffel (1876-1955), which began in Turkish Kurdistan and today has a worldwide ministry.

There were a variety of other enterprises. Along with the customary women's auxiliaries that the regional societies sponsored were the Oriental Women's Mission (1842), Hildesheim Mission to the Blind (1890), Malche Women's Mission (1898), Women's Missionary Prayer League (1900), and the Mission of the Women's and Girls' Bible Circles (1925). The German Institute for Medical Missions was founded in Tübingen in 1906, and after World War II the Educational Assistance for Young Christians in Asia and Africa (1960) and the Children's Emergency Relief Agency (1961) were created. The German Baptists formed their own society in 1890 and sent missionaries to Cameroon, then a Germany colony, and today still an active Baptist field. The Seventh-day Adventists in 1930, the Methodists in 1930, and some smaller free churches also created mission agencies.

Worldwide, the Germans took the lead in developing the scientific study of missions (*Missionswissenschaft*), or what today is called missiology. The leading figures in this were Karl Graul (1814-64), a Leipzig Mission leader and scholar of Tamil; Carl Plath (1829-1901), director of the Gossner Mission and a visiting lecturer at Berlin University, who fought to have missions recognized as a discipline in the theological curriculum; Gustav Warneck (1834-1910), pastor and professor at Halle, author of important books in mission history and theory, and founding editor of the first scholarly journal devoted to missions, the *Allgemeine Missions-Zeitschrift*; and Julius Richter (1862-1940), Warneck's successor as editor of the *AMZ*, an author of 30 books, the first professor of missions at Berlin, and a leading ecumenist. Contemporary with them were several other missions scholars who distinguished themselves in such fields as linguistics, geography, ethnology, and anthropology. Among the 20th-century luminaries in German missiology were Martin Schlunk (1874-1958), Karl Hartenstein (1894-1952), Walter Freytag (1899-1959), Georg Vicedom (1903-74), and Hans-Werner Gensichen (1915-99). A large endowment for mission studies, the German Protestant Evangelical Missions Assistance Fund (*Missionshilfe*), was raised in 1913, and the German Society for Missiology, the first scholarly society devoted to the field of missions, was formed in 1918.

2. Present Situation and Future Prospects

World War I had a devastating impact on the German foreign mission enterprise, from which it has never fully recovered. The ecumenical relationships that had developed in the prewar years were shattered, the missionaries were cut off from funds, in areas under Allied control they were removed from their stations and interned or repatriated, and their properties were confiscated. Mission leaders in the Allied countries, however, managed to obtain a provision in the 1919 Paris peace treaty that permitted these properties to be held in trust by other missions. Although misunderstood at the time, this action saved the mission holdings, and over the next decade the Germans were allowed to return to their fields. At the same time, the ecumenical ties were gradually restored, and Germans took part in the various international missionary conclaves. The umbrella agency for the societies was renamed the German Protestant Missionary Conference (*Missions-Tag*), with the Missionary Council (*Missionsrat*) as its standing executive.

Although the missionaries failed to grasp the threat of National Socialism and made many grievous compromises with the Nazi order, the experience led to inner renewal. At a conference in Tübingen in October 1934, in what has been called the → Barmen of German missions, the missionaries overwhelmingly identified with the → Confessing Church. Since the Nazis had no use for missions, they cut off the flow of money to the fields, and the Second World War resulted in a complete disruption of overseas ties. The → International Missionary Council (IMC) mounted a massive campaign to save the German enterprises (the Orphaned Missions Program), and the Germans were able to enter into an ecumenical "partnership in obedience" (a slogan prominent at the 1947 IMC conference in Whitby, Canada) that would preserve the Christian witness in a changing world. Western missions were transformed into world missions, and the Germans embarked on a new relationship with the "mission churches," where partnership replaced paternalism. Expatriate church personnel were now coworkers with indigenous leaders.

Just as significant was the internal change the new relationship between church and mission brought about. The unity of the *missio Dei* (or, as Freytag put it, "mission as God's reality in this world") called for the whole church to witness by word and deed in real brotherhood and sacrificial service. The desired integration did not come about, however, and the division of Germany merely exacerbated the tensions within the church. In the 1960s the mission agencies drew closer to the territorial churches, and the regional missions now came to be seen as appropriate organizations in which the church organs could participate. The Protestant Council for World Mission, formed in 1963, was the first organization that formally linked the churches and the societies. The creation of the Protestant Mission Work in 1975, an agency concerned with development, further strengthened ties between church and mission.

A parallel development occurred among the theological conservatives (the *Evangelikale*), who possessed a wide network of Bible schools, mission societies, and evangelistic organizations and who formed a separate Conference of Evangelical Missions (1969). The existence of the rival bodies indicates that the tensions between conciliar Protestants and → evangelicals existing on the global scene are present and even exacerbated at the local level. Moreover, mission boards of some American denominations have founded works in Germany, such as Baptist Mid-Missions (1950, of the General Association of Regular Baptist Churches), the Southern Baptists (1961), and the Grace Brethren (1969). They share the view of the conservative evangelicals that today Germany itself is a mission field.

Bibliography: J. Aagaard, *Mission–Konfession–Kirche. Die Problematik ihrer Integration im 19. Jahrhundert in Deutschland* (Lund, 1967) • G. H. Anderson, ed., *Biographical Dictionary of Christian Missions* (New York, 1998) • K. J. Bade, ed., *Imperialismus und Kolonialmission. Kaiserliches Deutschland und koloniales Imperium* (Wiesbaden, 1982) • H.-W. Gensichen, *Missionsgeschichte der neueren Zeit* (3d ed.; Göttingen, 1976) • H. Gründer, *Christliche Mission und deutscher Imperialismus, 1884-1914* (Paderborn, 1982) • J. A. B. Jongeneel, *Philosophy, Science, and Theology of Mission in the 19th and 20th Centuries* (2 vols.; New York, 1995-97) • H. Kasdorf, *Gustav Warnecks missiologisches Erbe* (Giessen, 1990) • N.-P. Moritzen, "Aus deutscher Sicht," *Geschichte der christlichen Mission* (ed. S. Neill; Erlangen, 1974) • W. Oehler, *Geschichte der Deutschen Evangelischen Mission* (2 vols.; Baden-Baden, 1949-51) • R. V. Pierard, "Shaking the Foundations: World War I, the Western Allies, and German Protestant Missions," *IBMR* 22 (1998) 13-19 • W. Raupp, ed., *Mission in Quellentexten. Geschichte der Deutschen Evangelischen Mission von der Reformation bis zur Weltmissionskonferenz Edinburgh 1910* (Bad Liebenzell, 1990) • W. Ustorf, "Anti-Americanism in German Missiology," *MisSt* 6/1 (1989) 23-34.

Richard V. Pierard

Germanic Mission

The Germanic Mission was a complex process extending over almost a millennium. In about 180 Irenaeus of Lyons mentions churches in Germania (*Adv. haer.* 1.10.2); in the 12th century, the Germanic mission ended in Sweden. Geographically, too, the overall process was extremely broad and encompassed quite varied phenomena.

1. Individual Witnesses in Southeastern Europe (3d-4th Centuries)

In the beginning of the great migration of peoples in Europe (the *Völkerwanderung*), Goths in about A.D. 264 carried off Christians from Asia Minor into slavery in Dacia, north of the Lower Danube (present-day Romania). These Christians held fast to their faith and eventually exerted influence on individual Goths. We know the most about Ulfilas (largely through church historian Philostorgius and Milanese bishop Auxentius), who grew up in the Christian tradition, though one of his parents was a Goth. Probably in 337 he was consecrated as bishop of Gothic Christians in Constantinople, perhaps as the direct successor of the Gothic bishop Theophilus, whose name occurs in the acts of the Council of → Nicaea (325). A → persecution of Christians forced Ulfilas and his circle to flee south (probably in 344) to the → Roman Empire. Their descendants are described around 560 as a peaceful people in the southern Balkans (*Gothi minores,* according to Gothic historian Jordanes). Ulfilas, who died in 383, translated parts of the Bible and liturgy into Gothic (→ Bible Versions 2.4), for which purpose he created a written Gothic language.

The → mission emanating from the circle around Ulfilas is clearly discernible because it was separated dogmatically from the Catholic Church of the Roman Empire. Contrary to the Council of Constantinople in 381, Ulfilas maintained the → confession of faith (→ Christology 2) that was valid in the mid-fourth century, according to which

Christ is similar *(homoios)* to God the Father. According to Auxentius, shortly before his death Ulfilas identified himself as a "Homoean." This Homoean theology became known historically as Germanic Arianism, to be distinguished from original → Arianism. Gothic → martyrs included Innas, Rhemas, and Pinnas, all of whose → relics were preserved by a Bishop Goddas. There are 22 names mentioned as victims of a church burning; the Gothic princess Gaatha tried to salvage the relics, and her companion was stoned. Martyrs also included the missionary Nicetas and the Goth Sabas because he took the side of the Christians. The nascent Germanic mission thus attests the confessional engagement of individual Christians who were also willing to suffer martyrdom.

2. Homoean Mission (4th-6th Centuries)

Because of pressure from the Huns, King Fritigern (ca. 370-83) of the *Visigoths* (i.e., the western Goths) tried around 370 to form an alliance with the Roman Empire, one that included Christian mission. Emperor Valens (364-78) thus sent Homoean missionaries who spoke Gothic, that is, adherents of Ulfilas. The majority of Visigoths were Christianized, which explains their sparing the churches in Rome when they conquered it in 410. Within the following decade they had found a new home in southern France and Spain.

Another Germanic people was the *Vandals,* who embraced Arian Christianity in the Balkans before 400. Also under pressure from the Huns, the Vandals migrated to Spain in 409 and then, in 429 under their king Gaiseric, left Spain for North Africa. There they promoted their Homoean confession, at times through military means. Shortly after 500, the Arian Vandal king Thrasamund debated with the Catholic bishop Fulgentius.

The *Ostrogoths,* or eastern Goths, also adopted Homoean Christianity in the Balkans before 400. Under Theodoric the Great (471-526) the Ostrogoths conquered Italy, beginning in 490. Theodoric had the Ulfilas Bible copied; parts of a splendid copy written in gold and silver letters are preserved in Uppsala (the *Codex argenteus*). Theodoric's policies extended as far as Thuringia, where one of his nieces married the local king; a golden helmet of Ostrogothic origin found there carries Christian emblems.

Around 500, the Arian Germanic peoples around the western Mediterranean rim were united in an alliance that ended with the defeat of the Vandals and Ostrogoths by Byzantium in the sixth century, as reported by the Byzantine historian Procopius. The church of the Visigoths under King Recared (586-601) joined the Catholic Church in Spain in 589.

In the late fifth century, the *Life of St. Severinus* (the "Apostle of Austria"), by his companion Eugippius, mentions the *Rugi* and *Sciri* people as in part a Homoean tribe. In the Balkans, the mission of Ulfilas's circle reached the *Gepidae* and perhaps also the *Heruli*. The *Burgundians* in the Rhein-Main region and the *Suebi* in Portugal were also influenced by Arian Christianity. Homoean missions to Bavaria, Saxony, or indeed England are less certain (see K. Schäferdiek, *RAC* 10.519-22).

The last Germanic tribe affected by this Arian mission was the *Lombards,* who from 568 continued the Ostrogoth tradition in Italy. After contact with Pope Gregory I (590-604), they joined the Catholic Church during the course of the seventh century. In 774 they were absorbed into the empire of Charlemagne.

3. Christianization of the Franks
(5th-8th Centuries)

The Catholic Church in Gaul was severely affected by the great migrations. Salvian of Marseilles (ca. 400-ca. 480) presented the Germanic peoples as ethical models to the Christians, though he was also familiar with Christian Germanic peoples. He mentions only peripherally the most important tribe, the Franks, who conquered or settled Gaul from the northwest. Individual Franks then became Christians.

The decisive event was the baptism of King Clovis (ruled 481-511) around 500 by Bishop Remigius of Reims, sealing Clovis's relationship with the Catholic Church, the most important organization in Gaul. His Catholic wife, Clothide, also influenced him. In his *Historia Francorum* (History of the Franks) 2.30-31, Gregory of Tours (538/39-94) also mentions a battle in which Clovis invoked and received Christ's help. Writing around 590, Gregory was admittedly already presupposing the existence of a Frankish Catholic Church. Although Bishop Avitus of Vienne (ca. 490-518) immediately anticipated great things from Clovis's baptism, the actual Christianization of the Franks proceeded only slowly.

In the mid-sixth century, Queen Radegunde, who had been captured in Thuringia and enslaved, destroyed a pagan shrine of the Franks (Venantius Fortunatus, *Life of Radegunde* 2.2). The expansion of the Franks to southern Gaul was aided by their alliance with the church, although Bishop Caesarius of Arles (ca. 470-542) remained somewhat reserved toward them.

The prologue to the Salic Law, an early version of which was drawn up during the reign of Clovis, claims Christ as the Frankish national God: "Long live Christ, who loves the Franks. May he keep their empire and fill their princes with the light of his grace. May he protect their army and defend their faith."

The thwarting of the Muslims (→ Islam) in 732 by Charles Martel (ruled 717-41) and the crowning of Pepin III (741-68) as Frankish king — with anointing by Frankish bishops in 751, repeated in 754 by Pope Stephen II — provide a line from the Germanic mission to the empire of Charlemagne.

4. The Anglo-Saxons in Mission History
(5th-8th Centuries)

The church in Britain underwent significant trauma in the fifth century, especially as a result of Anglo-Saxon conquests (according to Gildas, British monk and historian of the 5th cent.). Pope Gregory I sent monks to engage in missionary activity among them, which led in 597 to the baptism of Ethelbert, king of Kent. Gregory wanted to preserve pagan temples and turn them into churches, and he had plans for establishing bishoprics and archbishoprics. In his church history of the English people, the monk Bede ("The Venerable," ca. 673-735) describes this process after 700. Over time, the mission suffered setbacks, and the attitudes of the various kings changed. The Christianization of the Anglo-Saxons ultimately influenced poetry.

Wilfrid (634-709), an English prelate, intensively advocated the Christian faith and sought contact with Peter's successor in Rome. At the Synod of Whitby (664) he succeeded in asserting the Roman mission against Irish competition, adducing Peter's role as the keeper of the gate, able to open or close heaven to the deceased. The influence of this devotion to Peter had a long history.

The English were soon engaging in missionary activities on the Continent as well. Bede mentions Egbert, Wigbert, and Willibrord ("Apostle of Frisia"), who previously had been in Irish monasteries, where the notion of discipleship of Christ actualized in foreign missions had already been fostered. Willibrord died in 739 as archbishop of Utrecht.

The most important figure for the Germanic mission, however, was Winfrid ("Apostle of Germany," ca. 675-754), who in 719, during his first visit to Rome, received the name Boniface. He later was active in Hesse, Thuringia, Bavaria, and Frisia, where he was martyred in 754. He felt related by blood to the Saxons (*Ep.* 46). His correspondence describes the situation in German regions as well as his relationships with Rome and with his home church in England, especially its monasteries.

5. Christianization of the Saxons (6th-10th Centuries)

Anglo-Saxon Christians engaged in missionary activities among their tribal kin on the Continent. After Boniface, Lebuinus (d. 780) continued missionary work, often in the face of great danger (according to the anonymous *Vita Lebuini*). The Franks frequently waged war against the Saxons, and the religious question acquired increasing significance. In 777 the Saxon lands were divided into mission regions, and the Saxon nobility included a party friendly to the Christians. In 782 the mission was considered concluded. Although it was to be secured through law (in the *Capitulatio de partibus Saxoniae*), revolts still arose, first under Saxon duke Widukind, who in 785 submitted to Charlemagne and was baptized. His descendants later became German kings and emperors.

The Germanic mission continued, in spite of these wars between Franks and Saxons. The Anglo-Saxon Willehad (730-89) became bishop of Bremen in 787, the Frisian Liudger bishop of Münster in 805. The Anglo-Saxon Alcuin (ca. 732-804) congratulated Charlemagne (ruled 768-814) on his missionary successes while simultaneously criticizing his violent methods, asserting that faith must be accepted voluntarily.

The Old Saxon biblical poem → *Heliand* (Savior; 830s) presents Christ in a Saxon environment. Although a Germanization of Christianity did indeed come about, the severity of the → Sermon on the Mount was fully preserved.

The Saxon monk Gottschalk (ca. 804-ca. 869) propounded an extreme form of Augustine's doctrine of predestination (→ Augustine's Theology), which brought him into conflict with the archbishops of Mainz and Reims. Despite being beaten and imprisoned in a monastery, he held fast to his theology. Shortly after 900 the so-called Poeta Saxo viewed the Christianization of the Saxons as one of Charlemagne's good works, for which one ought to be grateful. In about 970 the Saxon historian Widukind of Corvey understood himself as representing Christianity to the backward pagan Slavs east of the Elbe.

6. Conclusion of the Germanic Mission in Scandinavia (8th-12th Centuries)

The Germanic mission in Scandinavia began through contacts with merchants. Willibrord came to Denmark after 700, and Ebbo of Reims, appointed apostolic legate by Pope Paschal I, led a Frankish mission into Denmark in 822-23. A clearer picture emerges of Anskar (801-65), who came to Sweden first in 829, where he took Birka on Lake Mälaren as his base of operations. There a nobleman underwrote the construction of a church. Anskar became bishop of Hamburg in about 832, and after the destruction of the city in 845 was finally able to continue his work as archbishop of Hamburg-Bremen from about 848. He received a call from King Horik I in Denmark, where there were already Christians, and later again to Sweden. His successor, Rimbert (author of *Life of Anskar*), similarly spent time in the North.

A second line of influence came from England, which in the ninth century was partially conquered by Danish Vikings. The encounter of Danish King Sigifrid III (= Godefrid?) with the English church moved him to be baptized in 885.

Haakon I the Good (935-ca. 961), the first Christian king of Norway, was brought up at the court of the English king, and two of his successors — Harold II Gråfell (Gray Cloak) and Olaf I Tryggvason — became Christians in England while it was occupied by the Danes. The Christianization of Norway came to its conclusion under St. Olaf (= King Olaf II Haraldsson, d. 1030).

By the year 1000 Iceland had become Christian. Politically, Norway had attempted to control Iceland since the ninth century. A high point was Danish king Canute I the Great (d. 1035), who for a time united Denmark, England, and Norway.

Although English bishops were appointed for new bishoprics, the legal and ecclesiastical influence of Hamburg-Bremen predominated. In the 10th century it established the bishoprics of Schleswig, Ribe, and Århus.

Unwan, archbishop of Hamburg-Bremen, ordained the first bishop in Sweden, Thurgot of Skara (ca. 1013/14). Adalbert of Bremen, a later archbishop, sought to establish himself as Patriarch of the North; Adam of Bremen recounted the events after the collapse of Adalbert's archbishopric in 1066. The North became independent with the establishment of the archbishopric of Lund in 1104, from which additional archbishoprics then emerged: Trondheim (Nidaros) in 1153 for Norway, Uppsala in 1164 for Sweden. Nordic sources make clear the inner appropriation of Christianity.

Conclusions concerning the earlier religion of the Germanic peoples are a matter of debate, since the written sources are already colored by Christian influence. Generalizations regarding the Germanic missions are ill advised because the events were much too varied. Romantic notions about a particular "predisposition" of the Germanic peoples for Christianity are clearly obsolete, even though the

Germanic mission itself was doubtless more than merely a socioeconomic process (→ Acculturation).

→ Middle Ages 2; Mission 3

Bibliography: Primary sources: M. Erbe, *Quellen zur germanischen Bekehrungsgeschichte* (Gütersloh, 1971) • G. Haendler, *Das Christentum und die Germanen* (Berlin, 1961) • W. Lange, *Texte zur germanischen Bekehrungsgeschichte* (Tübingen, 1962).

Secondary works: A. Angenendt, *Das Frühmittelalter. Die abendländische Christenheit von 400 bis 900* (2d ed.; Stuttgart, 1995) • C. M. Cusak, *Conversion among the Germanic Peoples* (London, 1998) • G. Haendler, *Die abendländische Kirche im Zeitalter der Völkerwanderung* (Berlin, 1980); idem, *Geschichte des Frühmittelalters und der Germanenmission* (2d ed.; Göttingen, 1976) • Y. Hen, *Culture and Religion in Merovingian Gaul, A.D. 481-751* (Leiden, 1995) • J. N. Hillgarth, *Christianity and Paganism, 350-750: The Conversion of Western Europe* (London, 1986) • H. Jedin, ed., *HKG(J)*, 2/1 and 2/2 • L. Milis, *De Heidense Middeleuwen* (Brussels, 1991) • C. Nolte, *Conversio und Christianitas. Frauen in der Christianisierung vom 5. bis 8. Jahrhundert* (Stuttgart, 1995) • T. Nyberg, *Die Kirche in Skandinavien* (Sigmaringen, 1986) • L. E. von Padberg, *Mission und Christianisierung. Formen und Folgen bei Angelsachsen und Franken im 7. und 8. Jahrhundert* (Stuttgart, 1995) • K. Schäferdiek, "Germanenmission," *RAC* 10.492-548; idem, *Die Kirche des frühen Mittelalters* (Munich, 1978); idem, "Wulfila — vom Bischof in Gothien zum Gotenbischof," *ZKG* 90 (1979) 107-46 • S. Schipperges, *Bonifatius ac socii eius. Eine sozialgeschichtliche Untersuchung* (Mainz, 1996) • F. Staab, *Zur Kontinuität zwischen Antike und Mittelalter am Oberrhein* (Sigmaringen, 1994) • R. E. Sullivan, *Christian Missionary Activity in the Early Middle Ages* (Aldershot, 1994) • I. Wood, *The Merovingian Kingdoms, 450-751* (London, 1994).

Gert Haendler

Germany

	1960	1980	2000
Population (1,000s):	72,673	78,304	82,688
Annual growth rate (%):	0.90	−0.16	0.02

Area: 356,974 sq. km. (137,828 sq. mi.)

A.D. 2000

Population density: 232/sq. km. (600/sq. mi.)
Births / deaths: 0.84 / 1.11 per 100 population
Fertility rate: 1.30 per woman
Infant mortality rate: 5 per 1,000 live births
Life expectancy: 77.5 years (m: 74.2, f: 80.7)
Religious affiliation (%): Christians 76.3 (Protestants 37.2, Roman Catholics 35.7, unaffiliated 4.7, other Christians 2.6), nonreligious 17.3, Muslims 3.8, atheists 2.1, other 0.5.

1. Political Background

The political history of Germany in the 20th century has seen a series of revolutionary, traumatic changes that have profoundly affected the lives of its citizens and their social institutions. In 1918, on Germany's defeat in the First World War, the Hohenzollern Empire was overthrown and a new parliamentary → democracy established, commonly called the Weimar Republic. Because of strong opposition from many leading circles in the nation, however, this unprecedented experiment with democratic ideas and institutions proved unstable. Further factors undermining the Weimar Republic were the almost universal refusal to accept the terms of the 1919 Versailles Treaty, the ambition to restore Germany's international position, and the desire to return to the familiar pattern of authoritarian government. Such trends played into the hands of political extremists, especially those of the National Socialist Party, led by Adolf Hitler, which came to power on January 30, 1933.

Contrary to the illusions of those who welcomed Hitler as a conservative leader and a bulwark against the danger of Communist revolution, the Nazis soon embarked on a radical program of seizing control over all existing policies and institutions. All social groups that might prove resistant to Nazi ambitions were to be "coordinated" or suppressed. The response of the churches to this incipient threat was remarkably naive.

The majority of Protestants enthusiastically endorsed Hitler's plans and wanted to align their churches closely to the state in a joint act of national renewal. A minority, later to be called the → Confessing Church, resisted any state interference in their affairs but otherwise supported the Nazis' secular goals. The Roman Catholic leaders, similarly deluded, urged the Vatican to conclude a Reich Concordat with the new regime, which was signed during the summer of 1933. The illusion that this treaty would safeguard Catholic interests was only reluctantly abandoned. The Catholic → bishops never admitted their mistake. They were thus unable to mobilize their followers to resist the Nazi crimes and atrocities. The consequent → church struggle was therefore always an ambivalent affair as the churches sought to reconcile their nationalist and ecclesiastical loyalties, never daring to recognize that these loyalties were incompatible.

Far more ominous were the Nazis' ever-escalating racial and expansionist goals (→ Racism). The → anti-Semitic campaign designed to purge Germany and, later, Europe of its entire Jewish population led by successive stages to the organization of mass-murder centers in concentration camps and to the killing of at least six million Jews. At the same time, Hitler's provocative goal of nationalist and military expansion led to war in 1939. His defeat was achieved not by his opponents in Germany but solely by the massed military power of his foreign enemies.

The victory of the Allies in 1945 brought about the extinction of German sovereignty, the military occupation of the whole country, and the cession of territories to Poland, Czechoslovakia, and the Soviet Union. Consequent disagreements between the Western allies and the Soviet Union resulted in the division of the country along the line of the so-called Iron Curtain. There followed the creation of mutually rival German governments, the Federal Republic (FRG) in the west, and the German Democratic Republic (GDR) in the east. Both claimed to be the true legislative authority for the whole country and drew support, both military and economic, from their respective partners.

In the 1950s, during the onset of the cold war, hopes faded for a compromise that would enable reunification on the basis of a neutralized and nonaligned Germany, as desired by some of the church groups. Instead, both German governments indulged in ideological attacks on the other. After the building of the Berlin Wall in 1961, the citizens of East Germany were physically prevented from Western contacts. During the 1960s and 1970s the division of the country came to be accepted as unavoidable, and the separate populations grew apart.

In the 1980s the contrast between the political and economic success of the Federal Republic and the lackluster performance of East Germany under the → totalitarian control of the Socialist Unity Party (SED) led to increasing dissatisfaction in the GDR. In 1989 this movement resulted in a sharp increase in protest rallies, often sponsored by churches, luckily nonviolent, and in the eventual capitulation of the SED authorities. The dismantling of the Berlin Wall in November 1989 symbolized the collapse of the Communist regime and prompted desires for reunification with the FRG.

The speedy demise of the entire GDR system followed. Thanks to West German chancellor Helmut Kohl and his leadership in negotiation with the former occupation powers, this goal was achieved in October 1990.

The subsequent years have been spent in trying to assimilate and mold together the two separate populations, a task that has proved to be much more demanding and expensive than was envisaged. The absence of any foreign intervention, as well as the relative success of the German economy, has allowed the attempt to succeed. Despite continuing disparities in income levels between west and east, the whole country now enjoys a stable democratic form of government, offering all social institutions, including the churches, the opportunity to forge their own destinies.

2. The Churches
2.1. *Political and Social Stance*

Over the past 100 years the German churches have shared a common experience of living through the above-described succession of political disasters and totalitarian rule. In no other country, except Russia, have the churches been forced to face such striking challenges from hostile governments. At the same time, they have been obliged to confront vital questions about their own self-understanding. A large part of the churches' intellectual witness in recent decades has been preoccupied with the attempt to come to terms with their experiences under these antagonistic conditions. The resulting controversies, which range from defensive self-justification to lacerating self-criticism, have been a notable feature of church life.

Especially for the two major churches — the Roman Catholics and the German Evangelical Church (Evangelische Kirche in Deutschland, EKD) — the major concern over the past 80 years has been the relations between church, state, and society. Successive political regimes have enacted or imposed legislative ordinances, not necessarily for the churches' benefit, but usually stemming from political expediency. The churches, in turn, have responded by seeking constitutional guarantees of their privileges, as in the terms of the 1919 Weimar constitution. This settlement was largely repeated in the West German constitution of 1949, which was extended to cover the whole country in 1990. The Catholics, for their part, sought the same security, through a series of provincial and national → concordats, in particular the 1933 Reich Concordat, an official treaty between the German state and the Vatican.

These constitutional safeguards, however, proved ineffective against the onslaughts of both the Nazi authorities in the 1930s and the Communists in East Germany in the 1950s. Many critics have asserted that the churches failed in their task to prevent or to mitigate the totalitarian criminality of these dictatorships. Others have pointed to the widespread readiness of church members to indulge in illusions about the political character of these regimes. For the Nazi period, such failings can be seen in the early acclaim given to Hitler in 1933, the enthusiastic support for his aggressive foreign policy, the applause for Germany's military victories in 1940, and, most shamefully of all, the silence at the Nazis' ruthless degradation and later annihilation of the Jewish people. For the period of Communist domination in the GDR, criticism has been expressed at the readiness of the church leaders, especially the Protestants, to seek a constructive relationship with this regime, despite its visible system of repression.

Defenders of the churches, in return, have argued that they were faced with unprecedented attacks by these totalitarian regimes, using the extraordinarily powerful force of propaganda and deliberately determined to overthrow the religious traditions of many centuries. Such confrontations were not initiated by the churches. They remained throughout on the defensive, seeking to protect their autonomy and the purity of their theologies, as well as to preserve the opportunities for pastoral care of their followers.

These as-yet-unresolved controversies have meant that debates about what role the churches should play in the official national or provincial legislatures, and the methods to ensure their continuing social significance, have been continuous and often heated. The 1919 constitution resulted in a practical, if peculiar, compromise. The two major churches were no longer to be part of the official state structures, as before 1918. They were free to govern themselves outside the tutelage of the civil service or political parties. They were accorded the status of corporations within the public law and hence were entitled to special financial privileges. After 1933 the Nazi authorities sought to reimpose the state's domination, through a new Ministry for Church Affairs. In 1945 this body was abolished. Afterward, in the absence of any form of German self-government, the churches sought to take the

lead in the re-Christianizing of the → nation. They believed they should be entrusted with a wide range of social activities in order to serve all classes and ages of people. In West Germany, such initiatives were welcomed after 1949 by the governments of the FRG, which were anxious to negate the Nazis' centralist policies. As a result, large numbers of educational, medical, and social welfare institutions came to be established or reestablished under church auspices (→ Relief and Development Organizations).

By contrast, in the GDR the religious policies of its new rulers were deliberately designed to diminish the influence of the churches and of their social outreach. Only after 1970 did this government begin to recognize that such charitable works could be of assistance, especially in the field of mental health, care of derelicts or drug addicts, or old age and nursing homes. After reunification, the West German system of church-sponsored social welfare activities was extended to the whole country.

These activities are largely financed by the church tax. This money is collected from adherents of those churches considered as corporations under the public law, as a percentage (8-10 percent) of each individual's income tax. Members of the various free churches are exempt; these churches depend wholly on voluntary contributions. Because of the economic successes of the (West) German society in the past 50 years, the churches' resources have vastly expanded. Both major churches use such revenues to maintain their historic buildings, to cover the costs of their public activities, to pay the salaries of their clergy and lay professional staff, and even to organize programs of foreign aid (→ Church Finances).

Such practical achievements must be offset by the undoubted fact of the diminution of the churches' influence in the general population. As in other western European countries, the spread of secular humanism has led to widespread abandonment of church attendance, especially in the cities, such as Berlin, where the percentage of the population attending church services was already notably low 100 years ago. Debate continues as to the extent to which this crisis of belief was caused by rejection of traditional Christian orthodox doctrines, or how far it was the result of external factors, such as the repressive actions of both the Nazi and Communist dictatorships. It is notable, however, that the overthrow of these repressive systems did not lead to a re-Christianization of German society, despite vigorous efforts by church authorities to achieve that end. A more durable explanation for the churches' striking decline in prestige and credibility must be

seen in the political behavior of the churches themselves, such as their overenthusiastic endorsement
of extreme German nationalism and their misuse of
theology to justify German war aims. So too the
readiness of some church leaders to give approval to
both the Nazi and Communist systems has induced
a sense of disillusionment among a more skeptical
population.

In this situation, the churches' traditional claims
to be the moral and spiritual guardians of the nation
have been, and still are, challenged, especially in the
areas of public policy. This legacy, however, drawn
from the centuries when the churches enjoyed both
power and prestige, cannot be lightly abandoned, all
the more since the attempts by political ideologies
to usurp this role have proved so disastrous. The dilemma for the churches is apparent: how to mobilize their followers to witness against dangerous
concentrations of political power, against dehumanizing ideologies, or against the erosion of moral and
religious values in contemporary society; but also
how to avoid the kind of triumphalism and
establishmentarianism of earlier years. Some radical
Protestant theologians, following the teachings of
Dietrich Bonhoeffer, have argued in favor of a voluntary renunciation of the churches' privileges and
status. Others have called for a return to the more
traditional pastoral witness and abstention from
political engagement. All are agreed, however, that
the churches should now support a pluralistic democracy that emphasizes the defense of individual
worth and freedom as the best defense against any
reversion to totalitarianism (→ Pluralism; Individualism).

After 1945 the readiness of Catholics and Protestants in West Germany to unite in forming a national
political force, the Christian Democratic Union
(CDU), as a moderate conservative party, was, and
has remained, a source of political stability and continuity. In contrast to the 1920s the CDU, which has
held office during most of the period since 1949, has
succeeded in maintaining the churches' commitment
to parliamentary democracy and private enterprise.
The impressive economic results in West Germany
and the resulting spread of wealth through enhanced
systems of social welfare bore witness to the pressure
exercised by churches for a fair and equitable distribution. By contrast, the failure of the GDR's brand of
Communism to produce similar results can be ascribed in part to the refusal of ideological support
from the majority of the population, including
church members.

In the post-1945 period the need to build barriers against any repetition of the Nazis' extreme na-

tionalism, and at the same time to create a bulwark
against the threat of Soviet expansion, led many
thoughtful Germans to advocate the unprecedented
plan of a new federal Europe. Particularly to German Catholics, the idea was appealing of a federated
western Europe with those countries — Italy,
France, Belgium, and possibly Spain and Portugal
— that shared a common Catholic culture and heritage. The first West German chancellor, the Catholic
Konrad Adenauer, promoted this cause and drew
support from other Catholic leaders abroad. A small
minority of German Protestants, to be sure, opposed such a plan, on the grounds that it would preclude any possible reunification of the country,
when Protestants would again become the largest
denomination. The intransigence of the GDR, however, put an end to such hopes, at least temporarily.

By the 1960s most West German Protestants
came to agree with German Catholics in accepting
the value of such a gradualist approach to western
European unity. The Vatican encouraged such developments for the sake of strengthening the international community. After the Second → Vatican
Council, no one resented the pope's sage advice.
Neither nationalist Catholics nor militant Protestants objected. It was a significant step forward both
politically and ecumenically. Nor was this policy altered with the 1990 reunification of the whole country. Church commentators have followed closely the
debate as to how the rival pressures of national
identity and regional integration can be reconciled.

2.2. Protestants

The present situation of the Protestants in Germany
can be understood only in light of the 40 years of
separation imposed by the political division of the
country after 1945 and the postunification legacy in
the most recent years.

In 1945 control of the German Evangelical
Church was taken over by the surviving leaders of the
anti-Nazi Confessing Church, leaders such as
Theophil Wurm, bishop of Württemberg; Otto
Dibelius, bishop of Berlin-Brandenburg; and Martin
Niemöller, later church president of Hessen-Nassau.
They saw their task as exercising pastoral responsibility for the whole country, especially vis-à-vis the military occupation forces. In October 1945 the new Executive Council of the church issued the famous
Stuttgart Declaration of Guilt, admitting the church's
shortcomings in not having more vigorously opposed the Nazi regime. In order to seek maximum
unity and support, however, no thorough purging of
former Nazis in the church was carried out along
such lines as followed by other institutions. So too no
radical reforms of the church's structures were un-

dertaken. The central administration of each provincial church remained intact. Similarly, a convenient interpretation of the church's experience during the Nazi years was propagated, stressing ecclesiastical and spiritual resistance to Nazi encroachments but keeping silent as to (1) the extent of the complicity and compromises with Nazi crimes of aggression and racial persecution and (2) the failure to speak out except when the church itself was under attack.

During the 1950s the EKD sought to act as a bridge for the then increasingly divided country. As inheritors of the → Reformation, they believed the church had a national mandate for all Germans. They therefore opposed both the clerical Catholicism of the west and the godless Communism of the east. The building of the Berlin Wall in 1961, however, made this strategy inoperative. As a result, the churches east and west were obliged to establish separate administrations, though professing to be still spiritually united. For nearly 30 years the exigencies of their very different settings led to divergent church policies, which were in turn backed by contrasting theologies (→ Church Government 5.1).

2.2.1. Evangelical Church (EKD)

In West Germany the 1949 constitution restored the provisions of the Weimar Republic, establishing the EKD as one of the corporations operating under public law, with attendant advantages. Freedom of expression was guaranteed. Each branch of the church was entitled to self-government without outside political interference. This restored continuity enabled the church to maintain Martin Luther's heritage, while tacitly abandoning the predilection for authoritarianism, anti-Catholicism, and anti-Semitism. This strategy could be described as seeking the re-Christianization of Germany from the top downward. In the 1950s two significant developments helped this process: the establishment of evangelical academies in most of the provincial churches, with extensive programs for lay education, and the holding of biennial church rallies (Kirchentage) as large-scale efforts to draw together different sections of the church. The popularity and success of these institutions has continued.

In the late 1940s and 1950s the priority of the EKD's efforts was given to the task of binding up the wounds of war, and especially of assimilating the several million Germans expelled from their homes in eastern Europe, most of whom were Protestants. Considerable assistance in these efforts was provided by the → Lutheran World Federation and by the → World Council of Churches' Reconstruction Department. This project involved a very extensive building program. The establishment or extension

of a large number of social institutions was called for. Schools, hospitals, old-age homes, and facilities catering to a wide range of needs were created, often in partnership with or under contract to government agencies. The major church agency for this task was the → Inner Mission, with many branches across the FRG, while a vigorous church foreign assistance program was organized by Bread for the World. So too the rebuilding of the theological faculties in the universities was part of a stabilizing and normalizing strategy (→ Theological Education). The resulting establishmentarianism was only heightened by the large-scale church bureaucracies created to implement these projects.

Criticism of this pastoral emphasis came from a small minority found particularly in the ranks of the Protestant university parishes (Studentengemeinde), who stressed the need for the church to take up a more prophetic role in society, deriving their inspiration from the Swiss theologian Karl Barth. Largely drawn from the more radical wing of the Confessing Church, and still led until the 1980s by its often controversial champion, Martin Niemöller, these theologians kept alive the hope that the lessons of the church struggle would be learned, and they acted as the conscience of the church. The church is now called, they affirmed, to embark on a more direct and prophetic condemnation of the misuse of state power. The church should make an explicit commitment to the victims of oppression and injustice. In political terms, this group launched protests against the West German alignment with NATO, against the remilitarization of the country, and against the stationing of nuclear weapons on German soil. They formed the core of a significant → peace movement and sought to build bridges to Germany's former enemies. Their witness included (1) the → Darmstadt Declaration of 1947, which unequivocally condemned the desire for national aggrandizement, (2) the 1965 pronouncement on the need to recognize the permanency of Germany's eastern borders, and (3) the 1980 Rhineland Synod's statement affirming the place of Israel among the nations. One important initiative was the founding of the Aktion Sühnezeichen as an opportunity for young Germans to participate in reconstruction programs in eastern Europe and Israel. So too the strong and continuing support given by the EKD to the radical initiatives of the World Council of Churches can be seen as a fulfillment of the church's prophetic role.

Particularly notable has been the EKD's support for a new beginning in Christian-Jewish relations. It was principally sponsored by the generation of pastors and theologians who lived through the Nazi era, men and women who were acutely conscious of the church's failure to seek to prevent or mitigate the persecution of the Jews. As a result, beginning in the 1960s, and parallel to similar efforts undertaken by the Vatican, the EKD has devoted considerable resources to this theme. First, the → prejudices and theological stereotypes of previous centuries — including those perpetrated by Luther — have been rejected and purged. Second, a new era of → partnership in theological discussion and discovery has been sought, often with positive results. The sin of anti-Semitism has been combated and condemned, especially the long-established teaching of contempt for the Jews as nourished by the church for centuries. At the same time, the Christian triumphalist and → dispensationalist stance toward Judaism has been discarded. The Rhineland Synod's 1980 declaration calling for an end of mission to the Jews set a precedent for German and other churches to make similar professions of support. Difficulties, however, were experienced when theological justifications for Judaism seemed to give approval to the secular policies of the government of Israel. Over the last few decades, however, a totally new and much more vibrant chapter in Christian-Jewish relations has been ushered in.

2.2.2. In East Germany

The situation of the church in the German Democratic Republic during the 45 years of Communist domination constituted a striking contrast. After its establishment in 1949, the ruling Socialist Unity Party made no secret of its hostility to the churches. They were regarded as survivals of a presocialist culture, due to be replaced by the historically destined victory of → atheistic Communism. The subsequent strategy of propaganda and → persecution aimed to eliminate Christianity both institutionally and personally. The repressive measures taken against the churches in the 1950s were reminiscent of the actions suffered at the hands of the Nazis. In particular, the GDR regime sought to control all aspects of youth education and indoctrination. Its imposition of the Youth Dedication Ceremony, which became mandatory for all teenagers seeking advanced education, presented a strong challenge to the churches, which in effect they failed to meet. The churches adopted a defensive strategy designed to prevent encroachments while maintaining the hope that they would be rescued from their beleaguered situation by the West.

By the early 1960s this policy was seen to be unrealistic. Under incessant pressure from the GDR government, church leaders reluctantly relinquished

many of their ties to the West German churches. In 1969 the Union of Evangelical Churches in the GDR was established as a separate administrative unit in order to refute the regime's charge that the church was acting as an agent of Western interests.

In the subsequent two decades the East German Protestant church took a new path. For the first time in Lutheran history, it was obliged to wrestle with the unprecedented challenge of how to serve God in a Marxist land. It also had to reflect upon the loss of its long-held position as the upholder of the nation's morality and identity. Younger church leaders, such as Albrecht Schönherr, who became bishop of Berlin-Brandenburg, sought a more positive response to the new situation, being much influenced by the ideas of Bonhoeffer. In particular, they were attracted by his call for the abandonment of traditional privileges, including the church's former role as provider of theological justifications for militarism and nationalism. In its place, the church should now become the "church for others," as a community of witness and service within the socialist society, not beside it, and not against it. The short slogan *Kirche im Sozialismus* became the benchmark of this movement as the basis upon which a more constructive relationship with the Communist state could be built.

These theologians and church leaders recognized that in a Marxist-dominated society — at least for the foreseeable future — their position would be marginal. They nevertheless refused to withdraw into a pietistic sect, concerned only with their own personal salvation. Instead, they affirmed that the church's task in society was one of "critical solidarity." Such ideas, however, met with suspicion from the ruling Communists and with skepticism from traditionalists in their own ranks. They were obliged to tread a thin dividing line between accommodation and opposition to the regime, seeking to steer a course that would offer them as much freedom as possible.

By the end of the 1970s this strategy seemed to be successful. The SED regime had abandoned its objective of rooting out all Christian influences from public life and instead acknowledged the contributions of church institutions to social welfare. The church was allowed relative freedom to control its own affairs, though still within revocable limits. For their part the church leaders were prepared to recognize the continuing existence of the GDR and its policies. Critics, however, accused the church authorities of giving the regime an undeserved approval and legitimacy. At the time no one knew the extent to which the church leadership was being infiltrated by the notorious secret police (Stasi). Suspicions were rife; proof was absent. Only in the aftermath did documentary evidence appear, though heavily slanted. In summary, church policies were only marginally affected by such seductions. Far more potent was the desire to pioneer a new role for the church, distinctive from both the past and the Western partners.

In the 1980s this impulse became evident at parish levels. New initiatives to boost the church's freedom of action were begun. The peace movement, locally led and fueled by genuine fears, sought to mobilize the public against all destructive weapons on either side of the Iron Curtain. The response was gratifying and led to similar moves to protect the → environment and to advocate human → rights.

This network of activities helped to strengthen the church's sense of autonomy and independence as a social force. The churches provided not only physical facilities but, more important, the organizational space for an increasing range of popular initiatives, particularly those that drew attention to the defects and oppressive character of the regime. In church halls and basements in Leipzig, Dresden, Magdeburg, and East Berlin, the churches put themselves in the forefront of popular pressures for reform.

The church leaders never promoted open resistance. They were at pains to refute any charges that they were agents of political subversion, working hand in glove with West Germans seeking the regime's downfall. Resisting demands from more strident supporters for a sweeping and revolutionary overthrow, they instead demonstrated their determination to preach peace and → reconciliation. By the summer of 1989 weekly church-led peace prayer meetings attracted larger crowds than ever and spilled over into street demonstrations. It was largely due to the influence of the church authorities that violence was avoided.

The sudden collapse of the SED's authority and the spectacular breaching of the Berlin Wall on November 9, 1989, unleashed an enormous wave of public jubilation and relief. It also, however, revealed the ambivalences of the church's position. It became clear that most of those who had participated in the church-based rallies and meetings had done so for opportunist reasons, because of the lack of legitimate alternatives. In the long run, the churches received no extra support. So too the church leaders' hopes that the radical changes would open the way for a reformed → socialism based on a biblical vision of → righteousness and → peace were to be disappointed. Instead, the vast majority of the population voted for amalgamation with West Germany. By October 1990 this unification took place and was ratified in the following December elections. Within a few months, the separate East German Union of Evangelical Churches was dissolved, and the eight eastern provincial churches were reintegrated with their western counterparts.

2.2.3. *The Postunification Period*

As was the case with all social institutions, the reunification of the churches meant in fact the absorption of the east by the west, with its far greater resources of money and personnel. Disillusionment and disappointment were felt on both sides. The GDR church leaders found that their experiences were dismissed as deviant, their theology as misguided, and their witness as wrongheaded. The revelations of how far the Stasi had succeeded in gaining collaborators in the churches only increased the feelings of animosity. For their part, the West German church authorities were obliged to count the cost of having to subsidize their eastern partners in order to achieve a parity of status throughout the whole church. So too they were dismayed by the obvious unwillingness of their eastern colleagues to acknowledge any regret for their mistaken policies towards the dictatorship they had so readily served, let alone any willingness to make a gesture similar to the 1945 Stuttgart Declaration of Guilt. The GDR proponents of *Kirche im Sozialismus* were only with difficulty reconciled to having to live in the new state dominated by Western-style capitalism. From time to time, they issued prophetic protests but were ignored. The work of reconciliation between the two sides has been arduous and time consuming.

Among the issues that have proved problematic has been the churches' role in the provision of → religious education in schools in the new eastern provinces, after decades of exclusion. So too the place of theological faculties in the universities, as well as the role of military chaplains, has required extensive discussions and the negotiation of new concordat-like agreements for both major churches. Such attempts to reinforce the churches' position with legally binding regulations have not, however, been widely popular, and it is questionable whether this procedure has advanced the churches' cause in the new provinces.

The basic administrative structure of the EKD is the provincial church, or *Landeskirche*. There are currently 24 of these provincial churches, most of whose boundaries coincide with those of secular jurisdictions, though some smaller enclaves survive for historical reasons. Each provincial church is administered by an Executive Council (*Evangelisches*

Oberkirchenrat), one of whose clerical members is the elected bishop or church president. The legislative body is the Provincial Synod, consisting of both clergy and lay delegates, elected from each constituent parish. The day-to-day business is conducted by a mainly legally trained staff. Each provincial church enjoys complete doctrinal autonomy. All are linked in a federation, the EKD, which has its own council but no powers to control the local churches' doctrinal or internal policies. The EKD is principally responsible for relations with other churches and with such bodies as the World Council of Churches. In fact, over the years, the EKD has come to be the principal financial support of the World Council of Churches, despite considerable differences in outlook and some major disagreements with WCC projects, such as the → Program to Combat Racism. Since Germany's unification, this support has been notably decreased in order to provide more assistance to the churches in the so-called new provinces, formerly in East Germany.

Theologically these 24 provincial churches reflect the different emphases of the Reformation tradition, either → Lutheran, → Reformed (Calvinist), or → United. The last tradition is represented by the churches formerly in the kingdom of Prussia, whose monarch in 1817 ordered a compulsory amalgamation. Those churches following strictly the teachings of Martin Luther formed themselves, with the exception of Württemberg and Oldenburg, into the Union of Evangelical-Lutheran Churches in Germany (VELKD). All of these churches — those in the VELKD, Württemberg, and Oldenburg — are members of the Lutheran World Federation and assist in its programs. On the Reformed or Calvinist side, there exists a Reformed Union, which has similar world links abroad, most notably with the → World Alliance of Reformed Churches.

Thanks to recent ecumenical agreements, such as the 1973 → Leuenberg Agreement, there is now in effect a substantial measure of "full communion" between all of these churches. In addition, the impetus in favor of reconciliation between the churches can be seen in such agreements as the 1988 Meissen Agreement between the EKD and the Church of England, or the even more significant Joint Declaration on the Doctrine of Justification between the Roman Catholics and Lutherans of October 1999. This latter document affirms that the condemnations regarding the doctrine of → justification issued in the 16th century should no longer be regarded as applicable or a cause of division between the churches. Thus it is a notable step forward, which may well help the integration of Catholics

and Protestants in Germany after many centuries of hostility and antagonism.

A notable feature in recent years has been the increased interest in "spirituality." However the term is defined, this development can be seen as one aspect of the privatization of religious sentiments, much induced by new technologies and by the influence of secular media. The churches face, not for the first time, a special dilemma. To insist on the rightness of traditional orthodoxy would open the way to charges of being behind the times, or even of obscurantism. If their followers were encouraged to conform to every whim of contemporary fashion, however, there would soon not be much of a church left — and all the more so when many such radical or tendentious ideas have been put forward primarily in order to shock and scandalize the faithful. Pastors and laity alike have thus come to suspect those theologians who, like Adolf Harnack a century ago, reduce the faith of their fathers to the kind of belief they assume modern persons will accept. To be sure, the EKD has no central controlling body to determine doctrinal truth, but this liberty can lead to incompatible positions being advanced without contradiction. Reformation theology surely emphasizes the need for redemption and → salvation for each individual, but this teaching does not mean that one can achieve this goal by one's own efforts. The proliferation of unsubstantiated radical theories can confuse the faithful irrevocably. Bonhoeffer's denunciation of "cheap grace" still needs to be heard.

2.3. Roman Catholic Church

After German unification in 1870, the → Roman Catholic Church was placed in a minority position and subject to continuous discrimination at the hands of the dominant Prussian Protestant majority. The subsequent → Kulturkampf led to a defensive mentality on the part of the Catholic leaders that was not overcome until after the Second World War. The 1919 Weimar Constitution removed almost all the earlier discriminatory legislation. Despite the signing of the Reich Concordat in July 1933, the Nazis undertook a systematic persecution of Catholic institutions and personnel. In these circumstances the Catholic hierarchy sought to prove its national loyalty by refraining from open conflict. There were only a few notable but limited exceptions, such as the bishop of Münster's protest against → euthanasia. After the defeat of Nazism and the subsequent political division of the country, Catholics in West Germany gave strong support to the founding of the Federal Republic. Catholic laymen played a leading role in rebuilding the nation on Christian lines. In the Soviet zone of occupation, which in 1949 became the GDR, Catholics formed a small minority of less than 7 percent of the population, since the largest number of Catholics had formerly resided in those areas of Silesia that were ceded to Poland. Such populations may be presumed to have resettled in West Germany.

The traditional heartland of German Catholicism lay in Bavaria and along the river Rhine. Support from these areas was crucial in the establishment of the FRG in 1949. Having successfully weathered the storms of the Nazi years, the Catholic leaders adopted a pastoral and defensive strategy designed to preserve and protect their interests. Such a policy was reinforced by the fear of atheistic Communism and the knowledge of the repressive policies imposed on Catholics in the GDR. A large network of social institutions was reestablished to provide for the needs of the Catholic population. In the 1950s vigorous and successful efforts were made, despite a lengthy legal battle, to ensure that the provisions of the 1933 concordat were maintained in the FRG. This settlement restored substantial benefits, especially in the field of education. Until the end of the 1960s social and political → conservatism prevailed.

In the GDR, the Catholics were from the first suspected as being agents of the Vatican and its alleged Western capitalist backers. The parishes were soon brought, and remained, under surveillance from the secret police. Conscious of their being in such a minority position, the GDR Catholics adopted a very low profile, were entirely absorbed in their own pastoral concerns, and did not seek to play any public role. Of necessity, the bishops established their own conference in East Berlin. They thus avoided giving any open sign of support for the regime, and only in the last few years of the 1980s began to join with active Protestants in protest groups seeking a more open form of government. Following reunification in 1990, the bishops' conferences in west and east were again joined, and now they meet annually as the Fulda Bishops' Conference.

There are currently 27 Catholic dioceses, grouped in 7 archdioceses. Some of these are very ancient and small, and for historical reasons their boundaries do not coincide with those of present-day secular jurisdictions. There are somewhat under 30 million Catholics, served by 14,000 priests. The dioceses are linked to the Vatican through the papal → nuncio, resident in the nation's capital, formerly Bonn, now Berlin. There is also a senior clergyman, usually a bishop, whose office deals with all branches of the government. The holders of the two largest → dioceses, Cologne and Munich-

Freising, are frequently promoted to the rank of → cardinal.

In more recent decades, the former pattern of Catholic separate identity has been dissipated because of the → technological revolutions, the increase in mobility, the spread of secular ideas (→ Secularism), and the reality of religious and political pluralism. Fewer Catholics attend church, individualistic social behavior has challenged traditional morality, and a better educated population is less willing to accept clerical leadership as directors of their social and political lives. Politically, however, especially in such heartlands as rural Bavaria, Catholics form the anchor of the conservative Christian Democratic Union. They approved reunification as a victory over Communism. They support closer ties with western Europe because of the Catholic connection. They agree with Vatican positions on private and public morality.

In the wake of the reforms introduced by the Second Vatican Council, German Catholics have now left behind the authoritarian and hierarchical patterns of the past and are prepared to enter into dialogue with the more pluralist and secular settings in which they live. So too German Catholicism has adopted a more ecumenical and open stance, leading, for instance, to a marked improvement in relations with both Protestants and Jews. Such developments, however, have led to increased tensions between the conservative and liberal wings of the church, as can be seen for example in the Vatican's refusal to approve the Catholic bishops' proposal to allow their adherents to take part in → abortion counseling, which is now required by law for all women seeking an abortion in Germany.

The postunification years have seen resolute steps taken to reintegrate the eastern provinces and to restore the level of church activities and institutions there. This task has been made all the more difficult by the highly secularized state of the former GDR and has been only accentuated by the already existing shortage of → priests throughout the whole country. Numerous priests from Poland, Latin America, and East Asia have been sent to Germany both for training and for active service in local parishes. A similar decline in numbers is to be seen in the religious → orders of monks and nuns. Nevertheless, these orders carry out their traditional roles and are assisted by new forms of spiritual renewal, such as the cursillo movement. The church continues to play a significant role in education, since religious instruction is mandatory under the constitution as a normal part of each school's curriculum. Catholic theological faculties are established at 12 major universities, and over 30 subsidiary colleges exist for the training of religious education teachers and church social workers.

2.4. *Other Churches*

Religious freedom came to Germany in the wake of the Napoleonic invasion. Successive governments, however, as well as the two major established churches, discouraged the principle and impeded the practice. The continued presence of other churches was held to be a source of religious and political disunity. Both Nazis and Communists persecuted recalcitrant groups and sects suspected of national disloyalty.

Germany's position in the heart of Europe, however, meant that adherents of other churches, both east and west, settled there and had to be allowed to worship in their own fashion. If they found converts, these too demanded the same freedom (→ Religious Liberty). The result has been the proliferation of small churches and sects, but few have become large enough to establish sizable national organizations. When persecuted by the state, almost all compromised — with the notable exception of the → Jehovah's Witnesses. Even in more peaceful times, however, such groups are not encouraged. Although they should be in favor of religious pluralism, in fact the struggle to preserve their own identity is all-engrossing.

The → Orthodox Church is represented by emigrants or exiles from eastern Europe. All doctrinal authority and church policy is decided from their home constituencies in Russia, Serbia, Greece, Romania, or the Ukraine. Orthodox services are celebrated regularly in 282 centers, though some hold services only monthly. Approximately half share the buildings of other denominations. The strongest concentrations are in North Rhine–Westphalia, Baden-Württemberg, and Munich. The congregants are largely so-called guest workers, especially from Greece. They are ministered to by 160 priests.

The Federation of Evangelical Free Church Parishes in Germany is a loose association linking a number of groups, of which the Baptist Church is the largest, having some 60,000 members. Arriving from England in 1834, the → Baptists take pride in their freedom from state control or state support. Other groups coming from England include the → Methodists, → (Plymouth) Brethren, → Salvation Army, and Quakers (→ Friends, Society of).

From the United States have come such energetically missionizing groups as Jehovah's Witnesses, → Mormons, Seventh-day → Adventists, and, of a different character, → Christian Scientists and → Pentecostals. More recently the → Church of Scientology has received attention as the only group or cult accused by the FRG government of being a public

danger, since it allegedly uses a religious disguise for financial manipulation of individuals.

The → Moravian Brethren, first established in southern Saxony at the end of the 17th century, have their headquarters in Herrnhut and are heirs to a remarkable worldwide missionary tradition. Originally German were the followers of Menno Simons, or → Mennonites. In the 16th century they were expelled as radical → anabaptists. Later they were invited to settle in imperial Russia, where they retained their language and liturgy. In more recent years they suffered under Communist rule and have now sought refuge in Germany, where several thousands are now settled. In addition there are several churches that broke off from major denominations, such as the → Old Catholic Church and the Free Lutheran Church. Numerous smaller sects exist only on the local level.

3. Non-Christian Religions

The Jewish communities in Germany currently number 73, and now include close to 100,000 members. Despite the appalling crimes of the Nazi Holocaust, some Jews survived in Germany after the Second World War and have since been joined by those who returned from exile or who have fled from continued oppression, especially from the former Soviet Union. All branches of Jewish observance are represented in Germany. The Central Council for Jews in Germany acts as a meeting ground for all Jews and is very active is guarding against any repetition of anti-Semitic outbursts, although recent activities by neo-Nazi "skinheads" give serious reason for apprehension.

In recent years approximately 2 million adherents of → Islam have come to Germany, mainly coming from Turkey as guest workers. Until 1998 governmental policy refused to consider these immigrants as eligible for citizenship. → Xenophobic attacks against them, however, have led to widespread support from church groups, prompting new efforts to try to assimilate these families in schools and social institutions. Numerous mosques have now been built, but the difficulties of religious dialogue are still paramount, principally because, as yet, neither governments nor the general public as a whole accept the idea of religious pluralism or integration as a desirable goal. Instead, the belief is still widely held that Germany is a Christian country, even if host to millions of non-Christians.

This situation, however, is likely to change under pressure from these minority groups in the direction of a more open society. In 1999, for example, a constitutional court ruled that crucifixes should no longer be hung in Catholic schools in Bavaria, for they were seen as discriminatory against the numerous non-Catholic children. Similarly, in the interests of pluralism, the court also sanctioned the provision of Islamic instruction within the state school system. In the short term, such developments will probably produce increased tension. In the long run, however, they may eventually lead to Germany's following other democratic countries toward a more pluralistic society.

Bibliography: G. BAUM, *The Church for Others: Protestant Theology in Communist East Germany* (Grand Rapids, 1996) • T. BEESON, *Discretion and Valour: Religious Conditions in Russia and Eastern Europe* (rev. ed.; Philadelphia, 1982) • J. BENTLEY, *Martin Niemöller* (New York, 1984) • G. BESIER, "Pfarrer, Christen und Katholiken," *Das Ministerium für Staatssicherheit der ehemaligen DDR und die Kirchen* (Neukirchen, 1991); idem, *Der SED-Staat und die Kirche* (3 vols.; Munich, 1993-95) • G. BESIER and G. SAUTER, *Wie Christen ihre Schuld bekennen. Die Stuttgarter Erklärung 1945* (Göttingen, 1985) • E. BETHGE, *Dietrich Bonhoeffer: A Biography* (London, 1970; orig. pub., 1967) • J. BURGESS, *The East German Church and the End of Communism* (Oxford, 1997) • K. CLEMENTS, *Patriotism for Today: Dialogue with Dietrich Bonhoeffer* (Bristol, 1984) • J. S. CONWAY, *The Nazi Persecution of the Churches, 1933-1945* (London 1968; repr., Vancouver, 1997) • K. ENGELHART et al., eds., *Fremde Heimat Kirche. Die dritte EKD-Erhebung über Kirchenmitgliedschaft* (Gütersloh, 1997) • J. FORSTMANN, *Christian Faith in Dark Times: Theological Conflicts in the Shadow of Hitler* (Lousiville, Ky., 1992) • R. GOECKEL, *The Lutheran Church and the East German State* (Ithaca, N.Y., 1990) • M. GRESCHAT, *Protestanten in der Zeit. Kirche und Gesellschaft in Deutschland vom Kaiserreich bis zur Gegenwart* (Stuttgart, 1994) • J. HAMEL, *Christenheit unter Marxistischer Herrschaft* (Berlin, 1959) • R. HENKYS, ed., *Die evangelische Kirche in der DDR* (Munich, 1982) • S. HERMAN, *The Rebirth of the German Churches* (New York, 1948) • F. LITTELL, *The German Phoenix* (New York, 1960) • R. J. NEUHAUS, ed., *Confession, Conflict, and Community* (Grand Rapids, 1986) • E. H. ROBERTSON, *Christians against Hitler* (London, 1967) • J. H. SCHJØRRING, P. KUMARI, and N. A. HJELM, eds., *From Federation to Communion: The History of the Lutheran World Federation* (Minneapolis, 1997) • K. SCHOLDER, *The Churches and the Third Reich* (2 vols.; Philadelphia, 1988; orig. pub., 1977) • R. SOLBERG, *God and Caesar in East Germany* (New York, 1961) • F. SPOTTS, *The Churches and Politics in Germany* (Middletown, Conn., 1974) • J. SWOBODA, *The Revolution of the Candles* (Macon, Ga., 1996).

JOHN S. CONWAY

Gerontology → Old Age

Gestalt Psychology

The term "Gestalt psychology" denotes a movement in → psychology that began at the turn of the 20th century as the Berlin School. Christian von Ehrenfels, who in 1890 introduced the term "Gestalt" into psychology, was its founder; Max Wertheimer, Wolfgang Köhler, and Kurt Koffka were its chief representatives (all of whom emigrated after 1933). Wolfgang Metzger summarized its teachings in Germany.

Gestalt psychology arose in opposition to the mechanistic views of association psychology and psychophysics. Its main thesis was the old one that the whole is greater than the sum of its parts, that the whole cannot be explained by the working of these parts, but only by its inner nature. Ehrenfels used the example of a melody that we can recognize in a different key. From this comparison he derived the principles of totality and transposability. Over 100 laws were worked out in some brilliant experimental research (e.g., on the seeing of movement and on optical illusions).

Theoretically, Gestalt psychology rests on → phenomenology, and in some cases (e.g., for Metzger) it is related to an → idealist position that finds no exact correspondence between the reality of physics and human feelings, the phenomena of personal experience being organized independently on the basis of innate (given) structural forms (the laws of Gestalt), though in specific analogy to physical relations in the structures of the brain (see Köhler's principle of the functional, but not anatomical, isomorphy between psychological and neurophysiological phenomena). It is thus maintained that the laws of Gestalt apply not only in the sphere of perception but also in relation to the processes of learning, memory, thought, speech, and action. Koffka applied a similar approach to problems in the psychology of → development (§2), while Kurt Lewin extended it to → social psychology, and Fritz Perls was inspired thereby to formulate the principles of Gestalt therapy.

Ideas about the self-organization of matter (H. Haken and others) found rapid, intuitive correspondence in the thinking of Gestalt psychology about the dynamic self-affirmation of life. The theories of Gestalt psychology have all been refuted in detail, but by way of Karl Duncker their impulses have been followed up in cognitive psychology (→ Cognition), in which, divested of their idealistic components, they have undergone fruitful development.

In the intellectual heirs of Gestalt psychology we find two ancient and antithetical views of humanity. Within → humanistic psychology the stress is on the Gestalt laws of individual dynamic, especially "Become what you are," while along the lines of cognitive psychology it falls on the demand "Let go; you are free for creative correspondence with the world."

Bibliography: M. G. Ash, Gestalt Psychology in German Culture, 1890-1967: Holism and the Quest for Objectivity (New York, 1995) • A. J. Frankel, Four Therapies Integrated: A Behavioral Analysis of Gestalt, T.A., and Ego Psychology (Englewood Cliffs, N.J., 1984) • W. Köhler, The Task of Gestalt Psychology (Princeton, 1969) • R. G. Lee and G. Wheeler, The Voice of Shame: Silence and Connection in Psychology (San Francisco, 1996) • K. Lewin, Resolving Social Conflicts and Field Theory in Social Science (Washington, D.C., 1997) • W. Metzger, Gestalt-Psychologie. Ausgewählte Werke aus den Jahren 1950-1982 (ed. M. Stadler; Frankfurt, 1999) • D. J. Murray, Gestalt Psychology and the Cognitive Revolution (New York, 1995) • M. Wertheimer, Drei Abhandlungen zur Gestalttheorie (Darmstadt, 1967; orig. pub., 1925).

Susanne Bosse

Ghana

	1960	1980	2000
Population (1,000s):	6,775	10,808	19,928
Annual growth rate (%):	2.90	3.44	2.71
Area: 238,533 sq. km. (92,098 sq. mi.)			

A.D. 2000

Population density: 84/sq. km. (216/sq. mi.)
Births / deaths: 3.64 / 0.94 per 100 population
Fertility rate: 4.85 per woman
Infant mortality rate: 65 per 1,000 live births
Life expectancy: 60.0 years (m: 58.2, f: 61.9)
Religious affiliation (%): Christians 57.7 (Protestants 20.3, indigenous 14.8, Roman Catholics 12.8, unaffiliated 7.1, marginal 1.6, Anglicans 1.1), tribal religionists 21.8, Muslims 20.1, other 0.4.

1. Political Situation
2. Church Situation
3. The State and the Churches

1. Political Situation

Ghana, known until 1957 as the Gold Coast, is a West African nation being welded out of congeries of loosely knit tribes. Ethnic pluralism and its encirclement by francophone Africa cause tensions for this former British colony, raising issues of national unity and security that have preoccupied successive governments. Its religions include African traditional religions (→ Guinea 2), Christianity, and → Islam (mostly the school of the Malikites and the Aḥmadīyah sect).

Since independence from British → colonial rule in 1957, Ghana has had five civilian administrations (1957-66, 1969-72, 1979-81, 1992-99) and three military administrations (1966-69 1972-79, 1981-92). At issue in this seeming political instability are matters of ideological orientation, worsening economic circumstances, corruption (esp. in political circles), and disappointing efforts to satisfy the heightened aspirations of the people regarding jobs, decent living standards, and security for the future.

2. Church Situation

Christianity came to Ghana in the era of Vasco da Gama (ca. 1460-1524). Its story was linked to the forts that guarded trading posts of the Portuguese, Dutch, Danish, and finally the British. In 1948, the beginning of the era of African nationalism, Christians represented 30 percent of the population, as compared with 66 percent belonging to traditional religions and 4 percent to Islam. Since that time, the percentage of Christians has approximately doubled, that of Islam quintupled, both at the expense of the traditional religions. These religions, however, do not exist as water-tight compartments but flow into each other.

Since the churches engage heavily in → education, → health care, and → linguistic research, their influence has spread to many fields other than their own. In the public arena they enjoy much goodwill, many politicians having been educated in church institutions. Through their teaching and social achievements they are a kind of guardian angel of African nationalism and thus highly influential in society.

At the same time, because of Christianity's link with the European forts, → mission practices that assumed a tabula rasa view of the indigenous people, a certain paternalism, and a rather careless identification of → missionary with trader-colonialist, Christianity in Ghana has sometimes been seen as yet another aspect of the colonial invasion of Africa (→ Colonialism and Mission).

There are four streams of Christianity in Ghana: three "historical" and one "indigenous." → Roman Catholicism was introduced in 1482 by way of the Portuguese fort Elmina. Its official organ is the Ghana Bishops' Conference (GBC), the executive arm of which is the National Catholic Secretariat (NCS).

The Orthodox stream is present in small numbers in two traditions (→ Orthodox Church). The Greek Orthodox were often sojourners in Ghana from Greece and were in the first instance traders and industrialists. The other is the Alexandrian tradition, which is vigorously missionary and fast becoming indigenized in the Ghanaian context. It belongs to the Christian Council of Ghana (CCG).

Protestants are represented by the CCG, founded in 1929 and comprising the African Methodist Episcopal Church (1933; → Black Churches), African Methodist Episcopal Zion Church (1896), the → Baptist churches (1946, 1962), Christian Methodist Episcopal Church (1950), Church of the Province of West Africa (→ Anglican, 1752), Evangelical → Lutheran Church (1950), Evangelical Presbyterian Church (1830, from the work of the Bremen Mission; → German Missions), the → Mennonite Church (1956), the Presbyterian Church of Ghana (1828, from the Basel Mission; → Reformed and Presbyterian Churches), the → Salvation Army (1922), the Society of → Friends (1927), the Wesleyan → Methodist Church (1835), and the → YMCA and YWCA.

The → Independent Churches take part in three groupings: (1) the Pentecostal Association of Ghana, including, for example, the Nigritian Episcopal Church and the Musama Disco Christo; (2) the Ghana Pentecostal Council (e.g., the Gold Coast Apostolic Church and the Christ Apostolic Church); and (3) the Association of Spiritual Churches (e.g., the F'Eden Church, or Eden Revival Church, which also belongs to the CCG). These groups and churches represent cultural revivalism, pragmatic religion, and a protest against the imported forms of Christianity to which the "historic" churches are beholden. The Independent Churches reflect the felt needs and values of Africans, claiming to solve people's problems by the Spirit (→ Holy Spirit). Some of these churches are products of African nationalism.

3. The State and the Churches

The churches enjoy a considerable partnership, even if it is sometimes rocky, with the state, receiving government subventions for social services (→ Church and State). The churches have also become the conscience of society, challenging successive governments through sermons, quiet diplomacy, memoranda, and pastoral letters of the GBC, NCS, and CCG on issues of human → rights, in light of the fact that any government tends to become dictatorial and thus to neglect the well-being of the people. The response of the state to such intervention has been to accuse the churches of abandoning the pulpit for politics and to castigate them as imperialist lackeys. The real issues in such cases, however, have been those of power and jealousy, along with the question of whether the conscience of society resides in the church or in the party or the government itself. Intervention by the churches has been seen as an affront to the party in power. The very extensive influence of the church, even in the remotest areas of the country, has also aroused considerable jealousy on the part of politicians.

Another response by politicians has been to resort to "divide and conquer" tactics. Although President Kwame Nkrumah (1960-66), for example, complained that the divisions of the church exacerbated the difficulties of uniting the nation, politicians on occasion played off the African Independent Churches against the historic churches. Such tensions highlight the ecumenical imperative of the gospel.

The historic churches have not been blameless in these tensions. They have sometimes chosen to do battle for the wrong causes, as, for example, in opposing efforts of the state to take over the nation's schools (1951) and in opposing plans to legalize polygamy (1960). They have also often displayed a pathological fear of → socialism and its ideology. In such cases, though, sound and critical theology has been at stake, requiring, among other things, a sensitivity to the fact that the state of Ghana is pluralist. The resultant clashes have sometimes been bitter, but bloodless.

Bibliography: E. O. Addo, Kwame Nkrumah: A Case Study of Religion and Politics in Ghana (Lanham, Md., 1997) • K. Donkor, Structural Adjustment and Mass Poverty in Ghana (Brookfield, Vt., 1997) • A. Ephirim-Donkor, African Spirituality: On Becoming Ancestors (Trenton, N.J., 1997) • S. E. Greene, Gender, Ethnicity, and Social Change on the Upper Slave Coast: A History of the Anlo-Ewe (Portsmouth, N.H., 1996) • J. P. Obeng, Asante Catholicism: Religious and Cultural Reproduction among the Akan of Ghana (Leiden, 1996) • A. P. Osei, Ghana: Recurrence and Change in a Postindependence African State (New York, 1998) • J. S. Pobee, "Church and State in Ghana, 1949-60," Religion in a Pluralistic Society (ed. J. S. Pobee; Leiden, 1976) 121-44; idem, "Church and State in the Gold Coast in the Vasco da Gama Era," JChS 17 (1975) 217-37; idem, Kwame Nkrumah and the Church in Ghana, 1949-66 (Accra, 1987); idem, Politics and Religion in Ghana (Accra, 1991); idem, Toward an African Theology (Nashville, 1979); idem, West Africa: Christ Would Be an African Too (Geneva, 1996) • J. S. Pobee and G. Ositelu II, African Initiatives in Christianity (Geneva, 1998).

John S. Pobee

Ghetto

"Ghetto" was the name of a quarter of the city of Venice that in 1516 was set aside exclusively for Jews. It lay on the site of a former cannon foundry, from which it derived its name (It. *getto* means "throwing" or "casting [bronze or iron]"). The segregation was decreed out of a desire to avert the wrath of God, which seemed to hang over the city because of lack of success in the war against the League of Cambrai. The thinking was that God's anger had been kindled because thus far, in defiance of canonical rulings, Jews had been allowed to mingle freely with Christians, even during Holy Week. Fully in the tradition of the 15th century, Franciscan preachers of repentance had stirred up this anxiety.

The name of this Venetian city ward became a general term, first for segregated Jewish areas, then for areas inhabited by other religious or ethnic → minorities. As a rule (the Venetian ghetto was an exception), these sections, apart from a small elite, were characterized by great poverty and misery and, as a result of overcrowding, dirt and lack of hygiene.

The idea of separate ethnic quarters in cities is actually very old. Thus in → Alexandria in the pre-Christian era there was a special Jewish quarter, into which all Jews were forced in A.D. 38, when crowded living conditions produced riots. For something similar in another culture, one might also mention the separate areas in Japanese cities set apart for the Etas (a social class whose name means "extremely defiled" or "untouchable").

Such quarters were not always forced on their inhabitants by superior authority. For example, the Amsterdam Jewish quarter (until the German occupation in 1940 made it a ghetto in the narrower sense) and many ghettos for blacks and Chinatowns in the United States show that separate quarters have often developed for economic or religious reasons but then are often perpetuated through discrimination or social pressure. In some instances laws were then passed that made such Jewish streets or ethnic areas into true ghettos. The Frankfurt ghetto is a familiar example. From it came the Rothschilds, whose name comes from the red *(rot)* shield *(schild)* that used to mark the houses in the ghetto.

Various causes underlie the growth of noncompulsory Jewish ghettos. The ruling that orthodox Jews may go only a short distance on foot on the → Sabbath encouraged them to live as near as possible to a → synagogue. Jews were also restricted in the work they could do. Being excluded from certain → vocations, they were forced to specialize in lending and secondhand trading. In medieval cities there was often a physical concentration of trades in specific streets or districts (streets for smiths, for rope dealers, etc.). The Jewish quarter, then, contained the streets for moneylenders, pawnbrokers, and rag-and-bone merchants, plus those who catered particularly to the Jewish market, such as Torah scribes and kosher butchers and bakers.

The need for a certain secrecy, for mutual support and solidarity in a hostile world, also favored the tendency to live in a special district. The same is true regarding black ghettos, Chinatowns, and other ethnic areas (Greek, Italian, Polish, etc.) common in North American cities.

Because the church forbade → usury (though not interest), Jewish moneylending was hated and despised. Thus the → Franciscans, for example, tried to break the power of pawnbrokers by their own *monti di pietà* (pawnshops). The idea was spread abroad that ghetto work involved "pariah vocations," or at any rate jobs of little social worth. The Chalcoprateia (later the Pera), the Jewish quarter in Constantinople (→ Byzantium), was also an area where many Jews did evil-smelling — and therefore despised — tanning and dyeing. In the ghetto in → Rome, established by the bull *Cum nimis absurdum,* issued by Paul IV in 1555, Jewish economic activity was restricted to the rag-and-bone trade and the making of mattresses, which was very unhealthy, causing diseases of the lungs. In Japan the Etas were engaged in garbage removal and in doing the necessary work on dead animals (butchering, tanning, shoemaking), which was forbidden for the Japanese and despised by them. After working on completing the American railroads, the Chinese were almost totally restricted to despised "women's work" — cooking, laundry work, and domestic service. In the black ghettos of the United States most of the inhabitants are unskilled workers or unemployed, though this situation has not prevented independent cultural development (e.g., in New York's Harlem district; note also the Yiddish theater in the poor Jewish quarter of the London East End). In South Africa, particularly under apartheid, black work was by definition unskilled and contemptible "kaffir work," and therefore those who lived in the sections for blacks and colored had jobs with lesser prestige. Everywhere, there is a natural, direct connection between low prestige and → poverty.

A gruesome form of the ghetto was the National Socialist Jewish quarter, a hermetically sealed section of a city in which Jews were gathered and in which, if they were not deported to the gas chambers (→ Holocaust), they starved to death. The most infamous was the Warsaw ghetto, set up in 1939.

→ Anti-Semitism, Anti-Judaism; Judaism; Racism

Bibliography: D. Corcos, "Jewish Quarter," *EncJud* 10.81-88 • R. P.-C. Hsia and H. Lehmann, eds., *In and out of the Ghetto: Jewish-Gentile Relations in Late Medieval and Early Modern Germany* (Washington, D.C., 1995) • J. Michman, "Ghetto," *EncJud* 7.543-46 • C. G. Roland, *Courage under Siege: Starvation, Disease, and Death in the Warsaw Ghetto* (New York, 1992) • C. J. Vergara, *The New American Ghetto* (New Brunswick, N.J., 1995) • D. Ward, *Poverty, Ethnicity, and the American City, 1840-1925: Changing Conceptions of the Slum and the Ghetto* (New York, 1989) • L. Wirth, *The Ghetto* (2d ed.; New Brunswick, N.J., 1998; orig. pub., 1928).

Dirk van Arkel

Gloria in excelsis → Mass

Glory

1. The Hebrew term for "glory" (*kābôd,* also "weight") has its basis in secular usage. Human glory consists of the "weight" carried in a community; that is, regard. → Yahweh's glory expresses power, loftiness, and beauty. It accompanies his revelation (Exod. 24:16; Isaiah 6; Ezekiel 1), indicating both proximity and inaccessibility (→ God; Revelation). It seals the → faithfulness manifested in the → covenant between God and humankind. Thus the concluding of the covenant at → Sinai is crowned by the revelation of God's glory (Exod. 24:15-17). Eschatologically this glory is manifested to all peoples and illumines the whole earth (Isa. 40:5; Ezek. 39:21).

The NT takes up the essential themes of the OT and applies them Christologically. The doxological statement about God — "Glory to God in the highest heaven" (Luke 2:14; also Luke 19:38; Rev. 4:9) — is referred to Christ as well (Heb. 13:21; 1 Pet. 4:11; Rev. 5:12-14). The NT can speak of "the God of glory" (Acts 7:2), but the heart of its message is the confession of "the Lord of glory" (1 Cor. 2:8; Jas. 2:1). The glory of God accompanies the whole person and history of → Jesus. Conversely, this person and history show forth God's glory. Glory encircles the risen Lord (Rom. 6:4; 1 Pet. 1:21; 1 Tim. 3:16; Acts 7:55). Yet glory may be seen also in his earthly course, not merely in mysterious anticipations, as in

the story of the transfiguration (Mark 9:2-10 and par.), but supremely in the NT climax of the passion story, in which the Crucified is "the Lord of glory" (1 Cor. 2:8), and his way of exaltation (as esp. in John) is the way of the cross. Glory in the NT is the glory of the cross.

In this sense glory is a mark of the Christian life, not as an expression of triumphalism *(theologia gloriae),* but as a liberating promise of God's faithfulness precisely in situations of → suffering. The whole existence of Christians is set in the light of Christ's glory (2 Cor. 3:18), especially when they are "afflicted . . . but not crushed; perplexed, but not driven to despair; persecuted, but not forsaken" (2 Cor. 4:8-9).

2. Dogmatics has adopted some of the richness of the biblical concepts and developed it in different ways. Irenaeus (d. ca. 200) stated that "the glory of God is man." A. Polanus (1561-1610) added that "the glory of man is God." Both theses state the one → gospel, the message of the → incarnation and our divine destiny (→ Theosis). Doxological and ethical impulses have also been at work. In Reformation piety, glorifying God is the aim of life. Part of this response is → doxology as liturgical adoration. Part, too, is the political service of God, as "to God alone be the glory" serves a demythologizing function vis-à-vis earthly authorities. Part again is concern for → creation as "the theater of God's glory" (J. Calvin).

3. The → aesthetic dimension of glory has claimed relatively less attention, though the motif of beauty is unmistakably present. According to the Bible, glory expresses God's pleasure in human beings (Luke 2:14) and his kindness toward them (Titus 3:4). Thus the response of a faith that corresponds to God doxologically is hardly conceivable without the element of delight or even joy in beauty. Glorifying God and enjoying him — the ethical and aesthetic dimensions — belong together inseparably in the polyphony of life. There is good ecumenical reason for the program of working out Christian theology in the light of the third transcendental, of supplementing the vision of the true and the good by that of the beautiful (H. U. von Balthasar, vol. 1).

Bibliography: H. U. von Balthasar, *The Glory of the Lord: A Theological Aesthetics* (7 vols.; San Francisco, 1982-91) • K. Barth, *CD* II/1 • G. Kittel, "Δοκέω κτλ.," *TDNT* 2.242-55 • A. Laurentin, *Doxa* (Paris, 1972) • J. M. Lochman, *The Theology of Praise* (Atlanta, 1982) • J. Moltmann, *The Church in the Power of the Spirit* (New York, 1977); idem, *God in Creation: A New Theology of Creation and the Spirit of God* (New York, 1985) • A. M. RAMSEY, *The Glory of God and the Transfiguration of Christ* (London, 1949) • G. WAIN-WRIGHT, *Doxology* (London, 1980).

JAN MILIČ LOCHMAN

Glossolalia

1. Definition and Terminology
2. Glossolalia in the NT
3. Historical Overview
4. Twentieth-Century Explanations
5. Theological Reflections

1. Definition and Terminology

Glossolalia, or "speaking in tongues" (or simply "tongues"), refers to the religious phenomenon of persons speaking languages not known to them. The term "glossolalia" derives from *glōssais lalō*, a Greek phrase used in the NT meaning "speak in, with, or by tongues [i.e., other languages]." The related term "xenolalia" is used to describe glossolalia when the language being spoken is an identifiable language never learned by the speaker.

2. Glossolalia in the NT

Glossolalia in the NT, generally considered to be a language → miracle, played a unique role in the witness and → prayer life of first-century Christians. → Paul considered such inspired utterances to have been fairly common in the churches with which he was familiar (1 Cor. 11:5, 16), and Luke traces tongues to the earliest Jewish converts to Christianity (Acts 2:4-11). For Luke, the outpouring of the Spirit on the Day of Pentecost was followed by miraculous tongues, which were understood by → diaspora Jews as the languages of their foreign homelands.

On one view, these tongues signaled the increasingly expansive work of the → Holy Spirit through the public witness of the church in crossing cultural and linguistic boundaries with the → gospel. At → Pentecost the God of the Hebrews was revealed through the outpouring of the Spirit as also being the God of the nations. The Spirit's expanding witness to the gospel included men and women, rich and poor, young and old (Acts 2:17-21, quoting Joel 2:28-32). Barriers were broken down between the Jewish followers of Jesus and the Samaritans (Acts 8), the Gentiles (chap. 10), and the followers of → John the Baptist among Greek-speaking Jews (chap. 19). At

decisive points during this ecumenical journey, tongues speaking occurred, which can be seen as a prophetic sign of this → reconciling work of the Spirit (Acts 2:4-13; 10:44-48; 19:6). One can contrast the tongues of Pentecost with the tower of Babel, which divided humans through language diversification (Gen. 11:1-9). One is also reminded of Philo's reference to the voice of God manifested in a flame and understood near and abroad (*Decal.* 35, 46).

For Paul, tongues spoke "mysteries in the Spirit" that cannot be understood by anyone and are therefore primarily meant for the believers' private prayers for self-edification (1 Cor. 14:2-4, 13-19). Consequently, Paul favored prophecy in the public meetings of the church. Tongues speaking as unintelligible speech was allowed to edify the entire congregation if followed by an inspired interpretation, the responsibility for which Paul lays primarily on the shoulders of the speaker, who was to pray for the interpretation of a tongue that he or she did not understand (1 Cor. 14:13-14). Tongues have thus been viewed as ecstatic utterances similar in nature to the unintelligible sacred languages of several ancient religions of Asia Minor.

Some have argued that Paul may have viewed tongues as the language of → angels (1 Cor. 13:1; cf. 2 Cor. 12:4), as in the first-century Jewish writing *Testament of Job* 48–50. A more probable connection is in Paul's reference to "sighs too deep for words" (Rom. 8:26; cf. 1 Cor. 14:14), of finding strength in weakness, which implies a form of prayer beyond the boundary of human understanding. That Paul understood tongues speaking as xenolalia seems unlikely, since in 1 Corinthians 14 he nowhere assumes that a natural understanding of the gift is possible. It is crucial for Paul that tongues speaking, as with all inspired speech, serves to point to Christ's lordship (1 Cor. 12:1-3), to build up the church in the love of God (chaps. 13-14), and to conform in its use to apostolic instruction and proper church order (14:27-38).

Much of the biblical research into glossolalia in the NT has focused on the apparent difficulty in reconciling Luke's understanding of tongues as a public witness with Paul's view of tongues as private prayer for self-edification. Even Paul's enigmatic reference to the sign value of tongues among unbelievers (1 Cor. 14:21-25) points to a negative sign, since the implication is that unbelievers will have no more success at understanding such language than the Israelites had of understanding the strange tongues of their Assyrian captors (cf. Isa. 28:11-12). Why, then, does Luke make tongues understandable among the unbelievers at Pentecost? Certain source-critical studies of Acts 2 have speculated that Luke had transformed an earlier account of ecstatic and unintelligible tongues into an understandable language-event of prophetic significance in order to symbolize the future mission of the church to the → Gentiles. One is tempted, however, to view the tongues of Pentecost as unintelligible but as miraculously interpreted in the languages of the nations for the hearing of the audience, since each one present heard "them" (presumably the entire company of believers) speak in his or her own particular language (Acts 2:6). Thus the unutterable sighs for the new creation mentioned by Paul (Rom. 8:26) become symbolic for Luke of the power of the Spirit to reconcile divided communities and to bring the goodness of God to all nations.

3. Historical Overview

While glossolalia is identified closely with modern-day Pentecostalism (→ Pentecostal Churches), its practice has been a recurrent phenomena throughout history. It is most clearly associated with attempts to restore the dynamics of apostolic Christianity. Glossolalia was associated with the → Montanists, a second-century renewal movement. → Tertullian (d. ca. 225), himself a Montanist, wrote of the practice of tongues speaking as being common practice in their gatherings. The phenomenon, however, was already present in groups more closely associated with mainstream Christianity. → Irenaeus made references to prophetic gifts and persons who "through the Spirit speak all kinds of languages, and bring to light for the general benefit the hidden things of men, and declare the mysteries of God" (*Adv. haer.* 5.6.1). Furthermore, Irenaeus associated tongues with the "last days" prophecy of Joel 2:28-29.

References to glossolalia are found in the writings of Hilary of Poitiers (d. ca. 367) and of Ambrose of Milan (d. 397). → Chrysostom (d. 407) wrote of glossolalia occurring in earlier times at the → baptism of adult converts but warned that because tongues could be confused with the work of an evil spirit, they should be discouraged in the church. It was → Augustine of Hippo (d. 430) who gave to the church the view that tongues were given to the church to indicate the coming spread of the gospel over the whole earth. He thus saw the accounts in Acts as symbolic of the church, which would one day exist throughout the world. Glossolalia was for Augustine something that had vanished and would not return to the church. Pope → Leo I (d. 461) took up Augustine's thought and in a Pentecost sermon wrote of "the Spirit of Truth" giving to

the church the languages peculiar to each nation. The Augustinian explanation thus became accepted by the church and continues to be held by many Christians today.

Church history, however, includes scattered reports of glossolalia occurring in individuals (e.g., St. Vincent Ferrer [1350-1413]) and in movements (e.g., the → Huguenots and the → Jansenists [mid-17th cent.]). References are also made to the experience of tongues among the → Moravian Church (from 1722).

Although there is no indication that tongues speaking occurred among the early → Methodists, there were unusual manifestations of the Spirit that J. → Wesley felt necessary to defend. In so doing, he referred to the Montanists as "real scriptural Christians," noting that the disappearance of the charismatic gifts from the church was due to "dry formal orthodox men," who had begun to ridicule what they themselves did not possess (*Journal*, 3.496; *Works*, 6.556).

Tongues speaking was reported during the revivals of the Second Great Awakening both in the United States and in Europe. The most famous of these reports is found in the ministry of Edward Irving (1792-1834), a Scottish Presbyterian minister. Tongues and interpretations occurred at his prayer meetings in London, which became so controversial that Irving was investigated and expelled by his presbytery in Scotland. Writing in 1859, the American Horace Bushnell defended Irving's ministry and experiences. He went on to defend the practice of tongues speaking and suggested in his book *Nature and the Supernatural* (1858) that glossolalia was found more among the lower classes because among them "the conventionalities and carnal judgements of the world have less power."

The Wesleyan-Holiness revivals of the late 19th century were characterized by overt physical responses to the Spirit's presence (→ Holiness Movement). The movement promoted → sanctification, a second crisis experience following an experiential → conversion (§1). Some within the movement came to associate this second experience with scriptural references to "the baptism with the Holy Spirit." Thus the experience came to signify either a second blessing of sanctification or one of empowerment. Glossolalia was not associated with this experience, although it was a known occurrence among many scattered groups. For instance, the Welsh Revival (from 1904) was accompanied by many manifestations of the Spirit, including glossolalia.

Most Pentecostals understand glossolalia to be a

gift of the Holy Spirit that serves as the initial evidence of the baptism of the Holy Spirit. This teaching may be traced to the ministry of Charles Fox Parham (1873-1929) and his Bible School in Topeka, Kansas. Parham had concluded that sanctification and baptism with the Holy Spirit were distinct experiences, the former addressing freedom from → sin, the latter, power for Christian service, especially world → evangelism. This understanding brought a new dimension to the Holiness teaching on the baptism with the Holy Spirit. Parham and his students searched the Bible for "indisputable proof" of this religious experience. They concluded that tongues were the evidence of the baptism with the Holy Spirit and began to seek such an → experience (§2). One after another of Parham's students experienced the baptism of the Holy Spirit with the accompanying sign of glossolalia. News of the events at the Topeka Bible School was quickly spread by Parham and his students, who became evangelists of the "full gospel."

While in Houston, Texas, where he had moved his headquarters, Parham came into contact with William Seymour (1870-1922), an African-American Baptist-Holiness preacher. Seymour took from Parham the teaching that the baptism of the Holy Spirit was not the blessing of sanctification but rather a third work of grace that was accompanied by the experience of tongues. In 1906 Seymour traveled to Los Angeles to speak at a small mission church. Seymour's message — that the tongues experience of the disciples in Acts 2 should happen today — was rejected by the mission. He was consequently invited to hold meetings in a home, where he and members of the home Bible study group experienced speaking in tongues. Soon the house was filled with people anxious to hear Seymour's message, and crowds filled the residential avenue. The group moved to a livery stable on Azuza Street that had been converted to a church building. Reports of the frenzied meetings, which included the innovation of interracial worship, were published in major newspapers. The Azuza Street Revival drew people from all over the country and the world, many of whom took back to their homes and spread the message of the baptism of the Holy Spirit and the experience of speaking in tongues. In many ways this revival signaled the birth of the modern Pentecostal movement.

In the century since the revival, Pentecostalism has grown rapidly, especially among the disenfranchised of the Two-Thirds World. For the most part, the traditional churches of the Protestant → Reformation rejected tongues speaking, seeing it as an ex-

cessive emotional experience associated with the religion of the disenfranchised. Holiness groups also typically denounced it as excessive. During the 1960s, however, with the advent of the → charismatic movement, glossolalia was experienced by many in mainline and Roman Catholic circles. Responses of these churches have ranged from overt hostility and rejection to attempts to incorporate glossolalia into full church life.

Persons who claim to have experienced glossolalia number well over 450 million. At the dawning of the 21st century, the phenomenon of tongues is found in every branch of Christianity. Some view it as a divisive practice, others as a unifying force.

4. Twentieth-Century Explanations

During most of the 20th century, research on glossolalia focused on the psychological and sociocultural dynamics of the phenomenon. For the most part, psychological descriptions of persons who speak in tongues have been uncomplimentary, coming from the assumption that tongues speaking represents aberrant behavior, a form of psychopathology. Before the mid-20th century, explanations were given that tongues were a form of hysteria and schizophrenia. Several studies in the 1960s focused on the unconscious needs of persons associated with glossolalia, explanations ranging from tongues as an escape from inner conflict to tongues arising from deep personality needs that in turn may have arisen from contemporary culture.

These sociocultural studies of glossolalia focused on the → marginal socioeconomic position of Pentecostals. As a result, glossolalia was understood as part of the "vision of the disinherited," serving as an outlet for repressed conflicts and as a means of overcoming the lack of social power with spiritual power. With the advent of the charismatic movement, however, explanations shifted to include tongues as meeting the deep-felt needs of persons facing rapid social change.

As the Pentecostal-charismatic movement has grown in numbers, the focus on tongues speaking as aberrant behavior has all but disappeared. Instead, the emphasis has shifted to glossolalia as the normal behavior of some Christians. Today, tongues speaking is viewed by researchers on Pentecostalism as a liberating and revolutionary practice that dismantles the privileges of the educated and literate, allowing the poor and uneducated to have a voice (e.g., W. Hollenweger in *The Pentecostals*). In his work *Fire from Heaven*, Harvey Cox explains tongues as a form of "primal speech" that responds to the "ecstasy deficit" of contemporary society.

5. Theological Reflections

Until very recently theological reflection on the practice of glossolalia has been limited to its relationship to Spirit baptism. Most Pentecostals hold the assumption that tongues speaking is the necessary evidence of Spirit baptism. Many Pentecostals and Charismatics now, however, see tongues as a unique gift not immediately associated with the baptism of Holy Spirit.

Early Pentecostals viewed tongues as signs of the eschatological inbreaking of the → kingdom of God, signaling the imminent return of Christ. While this understanding is still present in the movement, newer theological reflections on glossolalia focus on developing a more fully elaborated theology of glossolalia. This work, still in its early development, is generating an increasing amount of publications and research.

Such reflection ranges from an understanding that tongues are part of the theophanic signs and wonders of divine self-disclosure (F. Macchia) to viewing glossolalia as the remaking of language as a sign that God is remaking history and transforming social relationships (M. Dempster). The sacramental dimensions of glossolalia are being explored, according to which tongues are seen to mediate a context for divine-human encounter (Macchia).

Additional studies on glossolalia focus on the ability of Pentecost to reverse the curse of Babel, providing a lowest common denominator between people that cuts through differences of class, gender, and race, themes also found in the writings of early Pentecostals.

Finally, tongues are being studied in relation to the → postmodern understanding of deconstruction. In this sense glossolalia serves as a dismantling of language as power (C. Johns).

Bibliography: J. Behm, "Γλῶσσα κτλ.," TDNT 1.719-27 • H. Cox, Fire from Heaven: The Rise of Pentecostal Spirituality and the Reshaping of Religion in the Twenty-first Century (Reading, Mass., 1995) • M. Dempster, "The Church's Moral Witness: A Study of Glossolalia in Luke's Theology of Acts," Paraclete 23/1 (1989) 1-7 • R. A. Harrisville, "Speaking in Tongues: A Lexicographical Study," CBQ 38 (1976) 35-48 • W. Hollenweger, The Pentecostals (London, 1972) • B. C. Johanson, "Tongues, a Sign for Unbelievers? A Structural and Exegetical Study of 1 Corinthians XIV.20-25," NTS 25 (1979) 180-203 • C. B. Johns, "Meeting God in the Margins: Ministry among Modernity's Refugees," The Papers of the Henry Luce III Fellows in Theology (vol. 3; ed. J. Strom; Atlanta, 1999) • E. Käsemann, "The Cry for Liberty in the Worship of the Church," Perspectives on Paul (Philadelphia, 1971) 122-37 • M. T. Kelsey, Tongue Speaking: An Experiment in Spiritual Experience (New York, 1964) • F. Macchia, "Sighs Too Deep for Words," JPentT 1 (1992) 47-73; idem, "Tongues as a Sign: Towards a Sacramental Understanding of Pentecostal Experience," Pneuma 15/1 (1993) 61-76 • W. Mills, ed., Speaking in Tongues: A Guide to Research on Glossolalia (Grand Rapids, 1986) • W. J. Samarin, Tongues of Men and Angels (New York, 1972) • K. Stendahl, "Glossolalia and the Charismatic Movement," God's Christ and His People (ed. J. Jervell and W. A. Meeks; Oslo, 1977) 122-31; idem, "The NT Evidence," The Charismatic Movement (ed. M. P. Hamilton; Grand Rapids, 1975) • C. G. Williams, Tongues of the Spirit: A Study of Pentecostal Glossolalia and Related Phenomena (Cardiff, 1981) • G. H. Williams and E. Waldvogel, "A History of Speaking in Tongues and Related Gifts," Hamilton, Charismatic Movement.

CHERYL BRIDGES JOHNS and FRANK MACCHIA

Gnesio-Lutherans

1. Term
2. Melanchthon's Role
3. The Disputes
4. Significance

1. Term

In the history of dogma (→ Dogma, History of), "Gnesio-Lutherans" (or "authentic Lutherans") refers to a group of theologians who, in the internal Protestant debates between the Augsburg Interim (1548) and the → Formula of Concord (1577; → Confessions and Creeds), argued against Philippism that they were the true guardians of the heritage of Martin → Luther (1483-1546; → Luther's Theology) and who thus described themselves as (true) Lutherans. The center of this strongly Lutheran movement was first Magdeburg and then the University of Jena. One of its most important representatives, renowned for his academic achievements, was Matthias Flacius (1520-75) — the opponents of the Gnesio-Lutherans called them Flacians. Other leaders were Nikolaus von Amsdorf (1483-1565), Kaspar Aquila (1488-1560), Joachim Mörlin (1514-71), Nikolaus Gallus (1516-70), Johann Wigand (1523-87), Tilemann Heßhusen (1527-88), Matthäus Judex (1528-64), and Timotheus Kirchner (1533-87).

2. Melanchthon's Role

Although the Gnesio-Lutherans sharply criticized their opponents for their attitude to → tradition and → humanism and firmly stressed the → authority of the biblical message, in their views of the → church and → theology they largely followed the same line as Philipp → Melanchthon (1497–1560; → Reformers). Thus in the debates about Philippism, which related primarily to questions of → salvation and its appropriation, there were many fronts, just as there were also considerable differences of opinion among the Gnesio-Lutherans.

3. The Disputes
The controversies arose against the background of the Augsburg Interim, the weak reaction of the Wittenbergers, especially Melanchthon, and the resultant crisis in early → Lutheranism. The Philippist concept of the function of the authorities immediately became a stone of offense for the Gnesio-Lutherans (→ Two Kingdoms Doctrine).

3.1. The battle about → adiaphora (i.e., things indifferent) has come to be known as the first adiaphora controversy. At issue was the reintroduction of Catholic rites. Amsdorf took the initiative against Melanchthon, and Flacius formulated the main thesis that in matters of confession and offense, there is no adiaphoron.

3.2. Georg Major (1502-74) started the Majoristic Controversy with his view that good works are necessary for salvation. The Gnesio-Lutherans saw here a denial of → justification by faith alone and attacked the view fiercely.

3.3. The antinomian controversy was closely related. It concerned the so-called third use of the → law (§3) — that is, the validity and significance of the law in the life of the regenerate (*usus in renatis;* → Regeneration). In this matter the Gnesio-Lutherans were divided. Flacius and Mörlin defended the third use, but Andreas Poach (1516-85), Anton Otho (1505-83), Michael Neander (1525-95), and Andreas Musculus (1514-81) rejected it. At a different level of the discussion, the whole Melanchthon school was suspected of antinomianism.

3.4. The synergistic controversy began with statements by Johannes Pfeffinger (1493-1573) that, in agreement with Melanchthon, taught the cooperation of the human will in → conversion. Amsdorf and Flacius opposed Pfeffinger and the "Synergists," emphasizing in the Weimar Confutation (1559) that by nature we can do nothing to save ourselves. Viktorin Strigel (1524-69) then came into conflict with Flacius, and Flacius was driven to make his extreme statement that original sin is the substance of humanity (→ Anthropology 3).

3.5. The Osiandrian controversy touched on the very heart of Reformation theology. Andreas Osiander

(1496/98-1552) rejected Melanchthon's doctrine of justification and taught the essential → righteousness of the new self. The Philippists and Gnesio-Lutherans joined forces against this view and emphatically upheld an alien, imputed righteousness.

3.6. In the so-called second eucharistic controversy the Gnesio-Lutherans rejected what they regarded as crypto-Calvinistic Philippism and stood firm by the real presence of Christ's body and blood in the → Eucharist (→ Crypto-Calvinism). In this connection questions of → Christology (e.g., the doctrine of ubiquity) also became a subject of debate.

4. Significance
By way of the "political crisis of Philippism" (B. Lohse), the eucharistic controversy made possible the unifying work of the Formula of Concord. This statement certainly rejected the extreme positions of the Gnesio-Lutherans, but in many details it vindicated their often fervently waged protest against Philippism.

Bibliography: H.-W. GENSICHEN, *Damnamus* (Berlin, 1955) • R. KELLER, "Gnesiolutheraner," *TRE* 13.512-19 (bibliography) • R. KOLB, *Nikolaus von Amsdorf (1483-1565): Popular Polemics in the Preservation of Luther's Legacy* (Nieuwkoop, 1978) • B. LOHSE, "Dogma und Bekenntnis in der Reformation," *HDThG* 2 (bibliography) 64-166 • W. PREGER, *Matthias Flacius Illyricus und seine Zeit* (Hildesheim, 1964; orig. pub., 1859-61) • H. E. WEBER, *Reformation, Orthodoxie und Rationalismus* (Darmstadt, 1966; orig. pub., 1937-51).

STEFFEN KJELDGAARD-PEDERSEN

Gnosis, Gnosticism

1. Term, History, and Definition
2. Phenomenology
 2.1. Main External Features
 2.2. Worldview, Myth, Redemption
 2.3. Limits
3. Origins
4. Types and Trends
5. Sources
6. Ethics and Cult
7. Relation to NT and Christianity
 7.1. NT
 7.2. Early Church

1. Term, History, and Definition
The Gk. noun *gnōsis* originally meant knowledge of things and objects that the knower could apprehend

by understanding *(nous)* and → reason *(logos)* — that is, rationally (→ Epistemology).

Along with the basic epistemological sense a qualitatively new meaning developed from the first century B.C. that separated the object and act of knowledge from rational → experience and transferred it to the religious level. "Gnosis" now came to mean knowledge of divine mysteries, this knowledge being reserved for a select circle and disclosed only to those who were identical with the object of imparted or revealed knowledge. Gnosis of this kind presupposes an original identity of being between God and human beings that has been disrupted but that can now be regained by Gnosis (i.e., by this redeeming knowledge). This fundamental idea is given expression in the Gnostic myths, systems, and individual teachings. These items explain our human origin and destiny, describe our life, and define its goal (see Clement of Alexandria *Exc. Theod.* 78.2). The Gnostic myths are thus etiologically and soteriologically motivated.

Their themes are cosmogony, anthropogenesis, → soteriology, and → eschatology. These four basic themes are only seldom present as a whole in a myth (e.g., *Ap. John; Orig. World, NHC* 2.5). Yet in various settings one may find partial Gnostic statements about God, humanity, the cosmos, or redemption.

2. Phenomenology

2.1. *Main External Features*

Gnosis arose in the Mediterranean world and the Near East at the same time as primitive Christianity but independently of it. Reaching its high point in the second and third centuries, it interacted in various ways with Christianity. In a broad sense it included the Hermetic books, Marcion (→ Marcionites), → Manichaeanism, and the religious fellowship of the → Mandaeans.

It is hard to classify Gnosis religiously. Apart from Manichaeanism, it was not an institutional religion, yet it did not develop anonymously. It was not a book religion, having no normative scripture, yet it had many religious writings. It was not a cult religion referring to an etiological cult legend or central cultic event, yet it had many cultic rites and practices (see 6). It was not a national religion, yet it was also not a universal religion, for it excluded from its message and from all possibility of redemption those whom it termed hylics (from Gk. *hylē,* "wood, matter") or choics (Gk. *choïkos,* "of earth, of clay").

Gnosis was *an esoteric religion of redemption and revelation* (→ Esotericism) whose members grouped themselves around particular teachers and gathered in conventicles. The distinction between "Gnosis" as redeeming wisdom and "Gnosticism" as a term for the systems developed in the second and third centuries has not gone uncontested and cannot be made in a wholly logical manner.

2.2. *Worldview, Myth, Redemption*

Gnosticism is characterized by a radical anticosmic → dualism that distinguishes between an infinitely lofty and transcendent world of light, remote from everything earthly, and this present material and evil world of darkness. Corresponding to the world of light is an acosmic, spiritual deity with its aeons and light essences, while an inferior creator of the world (the Demiurge, often equated with the creator God of the OT) and its helpers (the archons) correspond to the world of darkness. The latter constitute a rebellious and ungodly antiworld.

Human beings, by nature the imitation of a light essence, have been doubly entombed: in this material world, and in their bodily husk. → Myth describes how humankind, or rather the spark of light within (the *pneuma,* "spirit"), has come into this material husk and how it can be freed. Only the *pneuma* is by nature inclined to accept the divine message and therefore capable of redemption, whereas the hylic components of humankind are under condemnation. In tripartite → anthropological systems, which postulate *psychē* as well as *pneuma* and *hylē* (e.g., the Carpocratians and Valentinians), the *psychē* can also be redeemed if it opens itself up to the Gnostic message. This message is imparted by the Gnostic redeemer, who at root is merely a proclaimer. Christianized Gnosis transfers this function to Christ.

2.3. *Limits*

The anticosmic dualism, the radical separation in the view of God and humanity, and the call to redemption are basic features of Gnosis that condition one another and assume mythographic form. By these criteria Marcion (d. ca. 160) and early Jewish mystical esotericism are not part of Gnosis. However, structural elements of Gnosis (e.g., the flesh/spirit dualism and speculation about the primal man and Sophia) may be found both before and outside Gnosis. One must always ask how far such elements are constitutive of the total developed system or merely part of its presuppositions. One must also ask how we are to evaluate them (note the use of such vague terms as "pre-Gnostic," "proto-Gnostic," and "gnosticizing").

3. Origins

In contrast to preceding and contemporary philosophical and religious movements, Gnosis was readily adapted to the systems contemporary with it. The diversity of such relations raises the question of its origins, to which different answers have been given. The only consensus is that no single origin can be shown, whether a degenerate form of → Greek philosophy, an acute Hellenizing of Christianity (A. Harnack), Babylonian astral mythology, reconstructed Iranian redemption mysteries, or heretical Hellenistic or dualistic → Judaism. We can say that the role of Jewish Hellenistic Wisdom traditions was important. Hans Jonas succeeded in breaking with the affiliation method and, by existential ontological interpretation of Gnostic myths, reached an understanding of the structure and nature of Gnosis. The problem of a true interpretation has been set in perspective with further research into the philosophical and religious antecedents of these myths, with the help of historical, sociological, and psychological questions and methods.

Gnosis in its various forms reflects the experience of a profound human crisis and is an attempt to overcome it. Viewing the Creator, the cosmic order, and both secular and religious institutions (the rabbinate and church → hierarchy) all as ungodly, Gnostics turn away from them with lofty contempt. Their own answer to the crisis is to project the crisis of humanity upon a crisis of deity. A divine disruption and apostasy explain earthly phenomena. Gnostics accept no guilt for their experience of weakness, homelessness, and alienation; rather, they are the victims of persecution by archons and ultimately of the primal fall, to which they and the world owe their origin.

4. Types and Trends

Contemporaries were already aware of the multiplicity of Gnostic teachings and systems. Irenaeus (*Adv. haer.* 1.30.15) compared them to the many-headed Hydra and traced them all back to Simon Magus of Samaria (1.23.2). The → church fathers listed Gnostic systems according to their leaders (Simon, Menander, Dositheus, Basilides, Valentinus, etc.), the figures in their myths (Seth, Cain, Barbelo, the Ophites and Naassenes), or their derivation (the Peratae).

Since H. Jonas, two basic types have been distinguished: the Syro-Egyptian and the Iranian. Systems of the former type (Gnosis in the strict sense) postulate the fall of a (usually female) deity from the world of light and the graded → emanation of aeons down to the earthly world. The Iranian type (Manichaeanism) postulates a primal dualism of light and darkness and their mingling by the voluntary descent of a light-deity. Genetically we can distinguish pagan Gnosis (the Hermetic books; *NHC* 7.5, 8.1, 9.2, 11.3-4; Simonian Gnosis), Christianized Gnosis (→ Nag Hammadi), and Christian Gnostic systems (beginning with Cerinthus and Carpocrates).

Basilides and even more so Valentinus (both fl. 2d cent.) were particularly successful in founding schools. Both engaged in extensive speculation about aeons, and Valentinus took a relatively mild view of the Demiurge and psychics, for whom he found a measure of → salvation (see Irenaeus *Adv. haer.* 1.5.1-6). From the Nag Hammadi texts we see that Sethian Gnosis, which displays a sharp → anti-Judaism, formed another important group (H.-M. Schenke).

5. Sources

Gnostic sources fall into two groups, secondary and primary. Secondary sources, the only ones available up to the 19th century, include the anti-Gnostic polemic writings of the Fathers from Irenaeus to Epiphanius and the criticisms of Neoplatonic philosophy (Plotinus *Enn.* 2.9 and, to a lesser extent, Porphyry *Plot.* 16; → Platonism).

Primary sources are the Hermetic books (treatises 1, 7, 13), Coptic Gnostic texts, *Pistis Sophia,* two books of Jeu, an anonymous work, the Berlin Codex 8502 (*Gospel of Mary, Ap. John, Soph. Jes. Chr.,* and the non-Gnostic *Acts of Peter*), and, since their discovery in 1945, the Nag Hammadi texts, not all of which are Gnostic, but which opened a new chapter in Gnostic research. Note should also be taken of the Gnostic passages in the *Acts of Thomas.* There is as yet no literary history of Gnostic writings.

6. Ethics and Cult

In keeping with the Gnostic view of the world and humanity, Gnostic ethics is marked by hostility to the body and striving to escape from the world. In patristic attacks the Gnostics are constantly accused of → libertinism, and especially of sexual excess and dissipation. This criticism finds no support in the original texts, which point rather to a strongly → ascetic lifestyle and which contain sharp attacks on the legalistic morality of the Fathers.

Gnosis found a place for the following cultic acts: baptism, the Eucharist, anointing, extreme unction, spiritual marriage, the ritual kiss, dancing, and prayer. All these acts tend to reinterpret, reappraise, or replace the church's → sacraments. Gnosis strongly condemned the variety of orgiastic cults (Epiphanius *Pan.* 25-26), as we see from *Pistis Sophia* 147. We find rich testimony to the sacraments of the Valentinians in *Gos. Phil.* These have a strong eschatological orientation as anticipation of reunion with the heavenly original (the Eucharist, marriage). The dead were furnished with water and oil to protect the *pneuma* from the attacks of archons. This motif recurs in burial prayers (Irenaeus *Adv. haer.* 1.21.5; *Acts of Thomas* 147; *2 Ap. Jas.* 62-63; *Pistis Sophia* 35; *Manichaean Psalter* 49-113; and esp. the Mandaean rites).

7. Relation to NT and Christianity
7.1. *NT*
The problem of the relation between Gnosis and the NT is extremely complex, and various answers have been given. The Synoptics (apart perhaps from Matt. 11:27) and Acts show no trace of either relationship or polemic. The Pastorals reject Gnosis as false teaching (esp. 1 Timothy). The problem is more acute in the Pauline and Deutero-Pauline epistles and the Johannine writings (esp. John). Developed Gnostic systems can hardly be assumed in NT days, but Paul and John knew Gnostic concepts, structures of thought, and early literary units, and we thus find parallels in them — for example, the fall of → Adam and creation (Rom. 5:12-17; 8:19-22), the antitheses of light and darkness (Rom. 13:11-13; 1 Thess. 5:5-6, and commonly in John) and of psychics and pneumatics (1 Cor. 2:14-15), the demonic ruler of this aeon (1 Cor. 2:6-8; John 12:31), our enslavement to the powers of the cosmos (Eph. 1:21; Col. 1:16), the descent and ascension of the Redeemer (Phil. 2:6-11; Eph. 4:8-10), the body of Christ as cosmic body (Eph. 5:23), the Gnostic Sophia myth (John 1:1-18), and the Gnostic summons to awake (Eph. 5:14). No matter whether we explain these motifs genetically or in some other way, the question how they are interpreted in the NT always arises.

Standing apart from Gnosis are the biblical antithesis of → sin and → grace, God's historical act of salvation through the crucifixion of Jesus, and creation's longing for redemption (Rom. 8:19-22), none of which are compatible with Gnostic positions.

7.2. *Early Church*
The relation between Gnosis and the early church was consistently polemic on both sides. From the church's standpoint Gnosis threatened to absorb the NT message and to dissolve it in speculation. From the Gnostic standpoint the church was subject to the ruler of the cosmos and took part in the persecution of pneumatics. The anti-Gnostic polemic of the church fathers did not succeed in quenching Gnosis. Only the development of the episcopal office (→ Bishop, Episcopate), the church's confession (→ Confession of Faith), and the biblical → canon made it possible for the church to deal with Gnosis

effectively, which finally in the Byzantine Empire came under the legislation passed against heresies.

→ Hellenism; Hellenistic-Roman Religion; Heresies and Schisms

Bibliography: Primary sources: B. P. COPENHAVER, *Hermetica: The Greek Corpus Hermeticum and the Latin Asclepius in a New English Translation* (Cambridge, 1995) • W. FÖRSTER, *Die Gnosis* (2 vols.; Zurich, 1969-71) • R. HAARDT, *Gnosis: Character and Testimony* (Leiden, 1971) bibliography • H.-J. KLIMKEIT, ed., *Gnosis on the Silk Road: Gnostic Texts from Central Asia* (San Francisco, 1993) • J. M. ROBINSON, ed., *The Nag Hammadi Library in English* (3d ed.; Leiden, 1988) • C. SCHMIDT, *Koptisch-gnostische Schriften* (vol. 1; 4th ed.; ed. V. H.-M. Schenke; Berlin, 1981) • W. TILL, *Die gnostischen Schriften des koptischen Papyrus Berolinensis 8502* (2d ed.; Berlin, 1972) • W. VÖLKER, *Quellen zur Geschichte der christlichen Gnosis* (Tübingen, 1932). See also the bibliography in "Nag Hammadi."

On 1-6: R. VAN DEN BROEK and W. J. HANEGRAAFF, *Gnosis and Hermeticism from Antiquity to Modern Times* (Albany, N.Y., 1998) • R. VAN DEN BROEK and M. J. VERMASEREN, eds., *Studies in Gnosticism and Hellenistic Religion* (Leiden, 1981) • R. BULTMANN, "Γινώσκω κτλ.," *TDNT* 1.689-719 • C. COLPE, "Gnosis II (Gnostizismus)," *RAC* 11.537-659 • G. FILORAMO, *A History of Gnosticism* (Oxford, 1990) • W. S. FLORY, *The Gnostic Concept of Authority and the Nag Hammadi Documents* (Lewiston, N.Y., 1995) • H. JONAS, *Gnosis und spätantiker Geist* (vol. 1; 3d ed.; Göttingen, 1964; orig. pub., 1934) • B. LAYTON, ed., *The Rediscovery of Gnosticism* (2 vols.; Leiden, 1980-81) • D. MERKUR, *Gnosis: An Esoteric Tradition of Mystical Visions and Unions* (Albany, N.Y., 1993) • P. NAGEL, ed., *Studien zum Menschenbild in Gnostizismus und Manichäismus* (Halle, 1979) • B. PEARSON, *Gnosticism, Judaism, and Egyptian Christianity* (Minneapolis, 1990) • G. QUISPEL, *Gnostic Studies* (2 vols.; Leiden, 1974-75) • K. RUDOLPH, *Gnosis: The Nature and History of an Ancient Religion* (Edinburgh, 1983) bibliography; idem, ed., *Gnosis und Gnostizismus* (Darmstadt, 1975) • H.-M. SCHENKE, *Der Gott "Mensch" in der Gnosis* (Berlin, 1962) • R. T. WALLIS, ed., *Neoplatonism and Gnosticism* (Albany, N.Y., 1992) • W. WINK, *Cracking the Gnostic Code* (Atlanta, 1993).

On 7: J. P. COULIANO, *The Tree of Gnosis: Mythology from Early Christianity to Modern Nihilism* (San Francisco, 1992) • K. KOSCHORKE, *Die Polemik der Gnostiker gegen das kirchliche Christentum* (Leiden, 1978) • A. H. LOGAN and A. WEDDERBORN, eds., *The NT and Gnosis* (Edinburgh, 1983) • J. MAGNE, *From Christianity to Gnosis and from Gnosis to Christianity* (Atlanta, 1993) •

M. Meyer, *The Gospel of Thomas: The Hidden Sayings of Jesus* (San Francisco, 1992) • S. J. Patterson, *The Gospel of Thomas and Jesus* (Sonoma, Calif., 1993) • P. Perkins, *Gnosticism and the NT* (Minneapolis, 1993) • D. M. Scholar, ed., *Gnosticism in the Early Church* (New York, 1993) • R. A. Segal, *The Gnostic Jung* (Princeton, 1992) • A. Welburn, *Gnosis: The Mysteries and Christianity. An Anthology of Essene, Gnostic, and Christian Writings* (Edinburgh, 1994) • R. M. Wilson, *Gnosis and the NT* (Oxford, 1968).

Peter Nagel

God

1. Ideas of God in the Religions

Ideas are phenomena. We may interpret them in broader social and intellectual contexts, but they also speak for themselves in images, words, names, and texts. Even when deity is their content, they can display only themselves, not show whether → revelation or merely human imagination underlies them, though this observation does not mean that we can rule out divine revelation.

To speak of an idea of God tacitly presupposes horizontal comparison between societies and cultures. We set different ideas of God on different levels, though not necessarily on an evolutionary ladder. Using terms taken from Hebrew, Greek, and Latin, we do so in a way that is to some degree Eurocentric. In reality we have no reason to use such terms indiscriminately for the beings worshiped in the ancient Germanic or → Egyptian religions, or among Hindus (→ Hinduism) or → Buddhists, or for personifications of natural forces or hypostatizations of ethical values. In more or less autonomous cultures we can discern only qualitative changes — for example, from thing to person, from attributes to total being, from hypostasis to name, from → experience to the other that may be addressed, contemplated, and worshiped. In interrelated cultures — even to the point of → syncretism — we can assess the results of earlier change and study the arrival of new change.

Our task is to relate qualitative change to the point when there is a leap to an idea of God or from one such idea to another. Since we cannot escape Eurocentric academic language, which overlaps popular language and has come into global use, we make a virtue of necessity and orient ourselves (nonjudgmentally) to the ideas of God in → Judaism, Christianity, and → Islam, along with those in pagan antiquity. In so doing, we find some broad features. Anything that corresponds in other religions may then count as an idea of God. Everything else must either be excluded and related to other concepts (e.g., fortune or → force), or it must be viewed as an idea of God only within its own system, and only to the degree that it is analogous to the Mediterranean systems.

2. Concept of God and Social Development

Pre-Christian and non-Christian religion, including that of pagan antiquity, did not express itself in a concept of God, though it did recognize God, and even did so conceptually. Christian → theology was the first to use classical → ontology to construct a concept of God — one still used by nontheological scholarship and the → science of religion. A concept of this kind must use statements about deities, relations to them, and beliefs in them that have no concept of their own if it is to be able to make comprehensive utterances about socially relevant ideas that are comparable to theorems about → society and → development.

The question how far social developments relate to specific concepts of God is both theoretical and sociological. It involves the difficult issue of reflecting and representing, which is the crucial point in dealings between → religion and society.

There is little of substance to say about the historical origins of religions with a concept of God. We can show when and where, but not under what conditions, higher beings assumed the quality of deity. We can show in what social units they were polytheistic or more monotheistic or henotheistic. It is hard to say, however, whether a specific deity stood for a specific social structure. Thus a great goddess (mother or huntress) might stand for a matriarchy, but it also might be an object of male worship in a patriarchy. There is no universal rule.

Once beyond prehistory, we find that concepts of God are in such harmony with social forms or partial forms that we can establish laws of development. Thus when a segmented society precedes one that is centralized, → polytheism precedes → henotheism. In a functionally ordered society (e.g., Indo-European societies), deities correspond to the functions (e.g., the Roman Jupiter, Mars, and Quirinus, or the Indo-Iranian Vayu, Indra, and the two Nāsatyas). The creative activity of the gods will also resemble earthly reproduction or the human making or ordering of things. Fertility gods and goddesses occur in archaic societies suffering hunger or fear. Gods of war go with destruction, and gods of wrath and grace with a developed sense of → sin. A static concept is found in a stable society; thus in late antiquity monotheism evolved into cosmic monarchy to validate political monarchy. The idea of a living, moving, and changing deity relates to movements of liberation and revolution (→ Theology of Revolution). Nevertheless, changes in the concept of God do not always accompany social changes. The concept of God is basically more tenacious than a social structure and is not simply shaped by it, as though it were merely an external symbol of the society. Furthermore, a concept of God represents individuals as well as collectives, such as outsiders in an archaic society, the → prophets, and those who engage in protest today.

For accurate information we may use the sociological method of scalogram analysis. Its aim is to clarify the attitudes of selected individuals or small groups (→ Congregation; Family) to deity (e.g., love, hate, fear, denial, obedience, sense of nearness or distance, ambivalent and multiple attitudes). It takes samples from different age-groups. When sorted, the cumulative findings tell us something (though not causally) about the relation between the form of society and the concept of God, allowing for differences in social class and age. The results show that we must view the concept of God as a factor in social development. With modern questionnaires the procedure is quite feasible, though always with a 10 percent margin of error. Applying the method to the history of religion is harder. In principle, scholarship can supply the data, with variations from culture to culture, but we always face the potential absence of rich materials through historical accident.

→ Everyday Life; Evolution; Immanence and Transcendence; Mother Goddesses; Progress

Bibliography: On 1: K. ARMSTRONG, *A History of God: From Abraham to the Present. The 4,000-Year Quest for God* (London, 1993) • B. GLADIGOW, "Präsenz der Bilder–Präsenz der Götter," *VisRel* 4 (1986) 114-33 • W. K. C. GUTHRIE, *The Greeks and Their Gods* (Boston, 1950) • H.-W. HAUSSIG, ed., *WM* • E. A. JOHNSON, *She Who Is: The Mystery of God in Feminist Theological Discourse* (New York, 1992) • E. RAE, *Woman, the Earth, the Divine* (Maryknoll, N.Y., 1994) • N. SÖDERBLOM, *The Living God: Basal Forms of Personal Religion* (London, 1933); idem, *Das Werden des Gottesglaubens* (2d ed.; Hildesheim, 1979; orig. pub., 1916) • A. J. WENSINCK, *The Muslim Creed* (2d ed.; Cambridge, 1965; orig. pub., 1932). See also the series IoR.

On 2: F. J. VAN BEECK, *God Encountered: A Contemporary Catholic Systematic Theology* (Collegeville, Minn., 1994) • C. COLPE, "Muttergöttinnen und keltisch-germanische Matronen. Ein historisches-psychologisches Problem," *BoJ.B* 44 (1987) 229-39 • P. EICHER, ed., *Gottesvorstellung und Gesellschaftsentwicklung* (Munich, 1979) • R. E. FRIEDMAN, *The Disappearance of God: A Divine Mystery* (Boston, 1995) • H. GÖTTNER-ABENDROTH, "Matriarchale Spiritualität," *Sachkunde Religion* (vol. 2; ed. J. Lott; Stuttgart, 1985) 231-43 • L. GUTTMAN, "The Basis for Scalogram Analysis," *Measurement and Prediction* (ed. S. Stouffer et al.; Princeton, 1950) 60-90 • T. JACOBSEN, "Ancient Mesopotamian Religion: The Central Concerns," *PAPS* 107 (1963) 473-84 • P. RADIN, *Primitive Man as Philosopher* (New York, 1927) • H. SCHULZ, "Religion in Stammesgesellschaften," in Lott, *Sachkunde Religion,* 11-41 • P. WINZELER, *Widerstehende Theologie. Karl Barth, 1920-35* (Stuttgart, 1982).

CARSTEN COLPE

3. Philosophy
3.1. Origins of the Western Philosophical Concept of God

The movement toward a philosophical concept of God in the West began with the Greek philosophers, who gradually turned away from mythological ideas and stories about the gods gathered on Mount Olympus (→ Greek Philosophy; Greek Religion). On the one hand, reflection on the nature of the basic stuff and how it changes opened the way for more naturalistic and rationalist understandings of the cosmos and humans, which in some philosophers resulted in skepticism about God. Xenophanes (ca. 570-ca. 478), for example, rejected the popular explanation of natural events like the rainbow as caused by the gods and viewed the idea of the immorality of the gods as a scandal. Indeed, he said, by projecting human traits, humans create the gods ("Men suppose that gods are brought to birth, and have clothes and voice and shape like their own"). On the other hand, the movement away from myth led to sustained philosophical discourse about a more abstract notion of a supreme being in Plato (427-347 B.C.) and Aristotle (384-322).

The divorce of reason from myth was incomplete, however; myth lived on in the mystery cults (→ Mystery Religions), which in turn influenced Christian theology, especially in the → church fathers, and through them Christian esoterics (→ Esotericism) and the theology of → symbol. In philosophy (e.g., Plato) → myth served to express themes that were difficult to convey conceptually, requiring a degree of abstraction in thought and language not yet available. Greek poetry from Homer to the tragic dramatists was also important in philosophical development, having an impact on the formation of the concept of humanity (often in antithesis to the religions). The tragic motif of fate that even the gods cannot control led to the concept of providence in → Stoicism and its opposite in Epicurus (341-270 B.C.), who contested the influence of the gods on the human world, then to a similar idea in Christianity and → Islam.

3.2. Beginnings of a Philosophical Concept

The Logos concept of Heraclitus greatly influenced the Stoics and became theologically influential through the Johannine Prologue. Of greater significance was the thinking of the Eleatics, especially Parmenides (ca. 540-after 480 B.C.). Four themes would affect all future development: (1) the reference to the need in knowledge to transcend the sensory world (where sensory reality is considered the epitome of phenomena; → Epistemology); (2) the struggle for a concept of → unity in the relation of the one and the many; (3) the refusal to apply sensory predicates to the One and instead the characterization of it as unchanging, uncreated, eternal, and nonspatial, thus commencing a movement toward → negative theology and → mysticism (the fullest development of the philosophy and theology of the One coming in → Neoplatonism; see Plotinus *Enn.* 1.5-6; → Platonism); and (4) the relating of the One to thought, with the resultant defining of God in terms of the thinking of thought *(noēsis noēseōs)* in Aristotle and, finally, of Spirit in G. W. F. Hegel (1770-1831; → Hegelianism).

3.3. Socrates

The distinctive uniting of enlightenment and religion found embodiment in Socrates (ca. 470-399 B.C.). Although Socrates set all that he did under a divine commission, the Athenians condemned him to drink poisonous hemlock on the ambiguous charge of introducing new gods of his own. It is possible that Socrates' *daimōn* who provided individual guidance was a revolutionary concept in Greece. Plato in his *Euthyphro* (10A) had Socrates put the thorny question whether the gods turn to those who are devout or whether the turning of the gods to them makes them devout. The question of the meeting of God and humans in religion (or faith) is here formulated in a preliminary way. It occupied Plato when, as over against the thesis of Protagoras (ca. 483-ca. 410) that humans are the measure of all things, he set the thesis that God is the measure of all things (*Leg.* 716C).

3.4. Plato and Aristotle

The divine (spoken of in both singular and plural) is good, the source of all good things (*Rep.* 379B) and related to the form or idea of the → good that, giving existence and essence to the other forms, determines the meaning of true knowledge and the moral character of the individual and the → state. Eros *(Phdr.)* leads us to the good by way of the idea of the beautiful. Plato's system, more than any, influenced subsequent philosophical thinking. In particular, his doctrine of the forms or ideas anticipated the medieval doctrine of → transcendentals in which the One, as the supreme ruler or being, is defined as represented by the true, the good, and the beautiful (→ Scholasticism). On it rested the medieval concept of order and of European → ontology in general *(ens et unum et verum et bonum convertuntur,* "being is interchangeable with one, true, and good"). Plato's mythological god, the Demiurge (*Ti.* 28Aff.), shaped the cosmos from preexisting matter like a craftsman, with guidance from the realm of ideas, and hence is to be distinguished from the Christian Creator-God, who created out of nothing. Although here we see a difference between the Greek view of the cosmos and the Christian concept of the → creation, yet the idea as the formative ideal of creation in God, as thought in the mind of God or in the Logos, and finally the Christian Logos as the second person of the → Trinity had a normative influence on the age that followed.

Aristotle called the first philosophy theology (*Metaph.* 1026a13). He became a foremost influence in Europe through his special doctrine of God as the prime mover and *noēsis noēseōs* (1071bff.) and by his works on → metaphysics, → logic, the soul, →

ethics, and statecraft (→ Aristotelianism). His metaphysics of act and potency and his formulation of the four causes influenced the construction of theistic arguments (→ God, Arguments for the Existence of) by both the Islamic philosophers and → Thomas Aquinas (ca. 1225-74).

3.5. *Philosophy and Theology*

The coming of monotheistic religions (→ Monotheism), especially Christianity, into world history brought a profound change in the conception of God, for philosophy and theology now found themselves in a relation of mutual referral that neither could escape (→ Philosophy and Theology). In working out its → confessions and → dogmatics, theology had to use philosophical terms, while philosophy could not overlook the fact that there were independent doctrines of God of religious derivation.

Between the poles of (1) a philosophical knowledge of God apart from any specific religion and (2) philosophy as the handmaid of theology, there were various ways of speaking about God. On the one hand some were critical of religion almost by necessity; on the other hand, some held religion aloof from philosophy and worldly wisdom in view of our inability to comprehend rationally God's saving action. In this regard one might say that there were two distinct theologies. One referred in basic philosophical fashion to the → absolute, the other (e.g., that of → Judaism, Christianity, and → Islam) based itself on a historical faith that is presupposed positively. Mediating philosophy and theology were thinkers like Aquinas (→ Thomism), who, seeking a synthesis of → faith and → reason, put forth the doctrine of the twofold truth that held theology and philosophy together by emphasizing both their respective competency to know and their complementarity. Others, like Siger of Brabant (ca. 1240-ca. 1284), affirmed competency without requiring complementarity.

Already in the Middle Ages the difficulty and singularity of authoritative talk about God inevitably became apparent. The special nature of such talk found significant formulation at Lateran IV (1215), when the council stated that we cannot speak of likeness between Creator and creature without also speaking about their greater unlikeness. In spite of every distinction this thesis lies behind the analogy of being *(analogia entis)* of Thomas Aquinas and the later theories of the → analogy of faith *(analogia fidei)* and analogy of the Word *(analogia Verbi)*.

3.6. *Modern Period*

With the beginning of the → modern period the relation between philosophy and theology underwent significant change. The theological → nominalism of the late Middle Ages shattered the medieval concepts of order and to a large extent became normative for the modern philosophical view of knowledge. The development of natural science, especially with Galileo's (1564-1642) employment of the hypothetical deductive method, raised the question of the relation between God and the universe, religion and science. I. Newton (1642-1727), R. Boyle (1627-91), and others provided a theological rationale for their conception of a mechanical universe when they contended that since → chance inadequately explained the mechanism of the universe, the laws of → nature were of God's making. Gradually, however, → empiricism and an emphasis on the investigative power of reason, combined with attacks on the church, led → Enlightenment theists to find a place for faith by separating it from philosophical and scientific → truth.

The modern period also reflects a radical shift in the role assigned to God. Whereas the medievals held that God was the highest good *(summum bonum)* at which humans aimed, R. Descartes (1596-1650), in treating God as the nondeceiving guarantor of our knowledge that extended substances existed, viewed God more as a means than an end *(Meditations; → Cartesianism)*. Subsequent thinkers like N. Malebranche (1638-1715) with his occasionalism, B. Spinoza (1632-77) with his → pantheism *(Ethics)*, and G. W. Leibniz (1646-1716) with his doctrine of preestablished harmony *(Monadology)* also tended to see God in a philosophical role mediating attributes, modes, or monads. Ultimately, rationalistic thought, which led to → skepticism about → revelation, → providence, and → miracles, reduced God's interaction with the world to that of → creator (→ Deism). Despite the attempt of G. Berkeley (1685-1783) to make God essential to sustaining the world by insisting that we can be sure things exist apart from our perception of them only because they are perceived by God *(Three Dialogues between Hylas and Philonous)*, the crushing blow came from D. Hume (1711-76), whose critique of traditional views of causation and analyses of belief and knowledge led him to conclude that we have no justification for rational theology and its claims about God's existence and nature.

Leibniz and his school largely maintained the traditional doctrine of God, but development in Europe led to a theological Enlightenment that was close to that in England (→ Deism). In opposition to the → Enlightenment and to all philosophy, J. G. Hamann (1730-88) and F. H. Jacobi (1743-1819) stressed the particularity of faith. I. Kant (→ Kantianism), in his specific → philosophy of religion *(Religion within the Limits of Reason Alone)*, belonged to the Enlightenment, for he interpreted the historical religion of revelation in essentially moral terms as a religion of reason, even though his doctrine of postulates included elements that opened up other possible ways of relating philosophy and theology. J. G. Fichte (1762-1814) at first followed Kant but then modified his position in essential ways as his thinking developed (→ Idealism), yet he always insisted that philosophy can achieve on its own a doctrine of God that is in material harmony with Christianity. He never fully grasped the importance of the problem posed by → positivism to the Christian faith.

Hegel, however, was quickly aware of the problem *(Theologische Jugendschriften* [ed. H. Nohl; 1907]; → Hegelianism). His later aim was to conceptualize Christianity. His final position *(Philosophy of Religion)* finds expression in the statement that in faith God is known only in conception, while in philosophy he is known in concept. One might take this distinction to mean that the former is the necessary mode of knowledge of faith (as F. D. E. → Schleiermacher did), or one might take it that the true claim of faith is fulfilled when Christianity arrives at concept, and that in this way the historical religion of revelation reaches its goal. The older F. W. J. von Schelling (1775-1854) brought to light some serious objections to this gnosis of Hegel (the putting of God in the coffin of → dialectic), but his own positive philosophy *(Werke* [ed. M. Schröter; 1926] vols. 5-6) did not resolve the tension between traditional philosophy and theology. Under totally different conditions M. Heidegger (1889-1976) took up similar themes. S. → Kierkegaard (1813-55) stressed against Hegel the paradoxical nature of faith (→ Existentialism). L. Feuerbach (1804-72) appealed to Hegel in an obviously untenable interpretation (letter to Hegel of November 22, 1828; Esence of Christianity [1841]). This approach laid the foundation of the ensuing criticism of religion in K. → Marx and → Marxism, F. → Nietzsche, S. Freud, and → analytic philosophy (→ Religion, Criticism of).

British and American idealists developed the notion of the absolute in important ways. F. H. Bradley (1846-1924, *Appearance and Reality* [1893]) held that since reality is fundamentally nonrelational, the absolute is not a plurality of individual realities but the unity of which everything else is an aspect. The absolute is suprarational and suprapersonal, of which the personal is only an appearance. In contrast, J. Royce (1855-1916, *The World and the Individual* [1900-1901]) held that the absolute was personal — an eternal, infinite consciousness. At the same time he rejected a → dualism that separates God from the world, struggling to hold together the one and the many.

3.7. *The Influence of Kant*

In the light of 19th-century development, some philosophers and theologians tend to take up and develop some insights from Kant. For Kant, God could neither be demonstrated empirically nor be proved logically. Yet Kant still saw some questions of supreme concern to humanity that philosophy could not neglect, since the answers that we give to them motivate human action. In general what is at issue is a ranking of goals, that is, of interests and claims over the whole range of human existence. On his own presuppositions the task for Kant could be achieved only by way of a well-founded insight into our ignorance (i.e., in the analogous speech of *docta ignorantia,* "instructed ignorance"). Some efforts in modern philosophy and theology are now being made along these lines. As regards their relationship, the result is that for all the importance of basic philosophical questions, it is best not to speak of God in connection with the absolute (whether we regard this concept as attainable or not). All the same, in the necessary rational appropriation of faith, a procedure is required in which theology not only is still referred to philosophy but can hardly be separated from it because of their common concern.

3.8. *Contemporary Views of God*

With the demise of positivism, the late 20th century saw a flowering of diverse concepts of God and renewed attention to → language about God. A rejuvenated but nonreductionist analytic tradition reconsidered the arguments for God's existence, on the one hand applying the techniques of modern logic, including modal logic, to the traditional arguments, while on the other hand suggesting and developing stronger inductive formulations. Often in the context of → Anselm's perfect-being theology, analytic philosophy also focused on discussing the meaning and coherence of God's attributes and the logical problems they create, for example, problems having to do with understanding God and other minds, the paradox of omnipotence, divine goodness and the existence of evil, divine foreknowledge and human → freedom, and God's action in the world (e.g., in atonement, miracles, and response to petitionary prayer). Theists in the analytic tradition often seem less concerned with establishing the truth of claims about God's nature than exploring their intelligibility and compatibility.

Taking up the insights of A. N. Whitehead

(1861-1947), → process theology developed a dipolar, panentheistic view of God who is in the world (God's primordial nature) and in whom the world is (God's consequent nature). The world is composed of energy events (actual occasions) that in each instant constitute themselves by combining the evaluation of their past with the best possibility that God provides to each event. God relates reciprocally to the world, changing as the world changes, while maintaining the relational processes. Rejecting the traditional understanding of creation, process theology sees God in his primordial nature persuasively rather than coercively creating the world; God is not before but with the world. In his consequent nature, God influences all actual occasions by luring them by his vision of truth, beauty, and goodness to new possibilities of self-actualization, thereby saving all that can be saved insofar as God synthesizes actual occasions into the immediacy of God's own life.

Mary Daly's claim that "if God is male, then the male is God" (*Beyond God the Father* [1973] 19) has shaped much recent feminist reflection on the nature of God. Sallie McFague followed up on Daly's point by evaluating the influence of traditional language about God as Father, King, and Lord and by proposing alternative models of God as Mother, Lover, and Friend. Feminists contend that the language we predicate of God shapes the way we conceive of God, ourselves, and indeed the whole world, and they consequently argue for a personal, relational understanding of God that recognizes women as well as men as created in God's image (→ Feminism; Feminist Theology).

→ Postmodern philosophers see in the end of → metaphysics the end of God as being — as *causa sui,* the ground of being — and instead look to the God beyond being: "the God who reveals himself with nothing withheld has nothing in common (at least in principle, and provided that he not condescend to it) with the 'God' of the philosophers, of the learned, and eventually, of the poet" (Jean-Luc Marion, 52). To say that God is dead in a postmodern, Nietzschean perspective refers to the various "regional" understandings of "God," each of which expresses a particular conceptual approach (e.g., Aquinas's self-caused cause or Kant's ground of the moral law) that limits God and thus makes the concept of God an idol. To think of God outside metaphysics/ontology is not a negative theology; it is to experience God as given phenomenologically under an → icon such as agape.

One can anticipate that the new century will see → Third World philosophers creating new concep-

tions of God from their perspectives in the same way as, for example, → liberation theologians have done with their emphasis on the God who is concerned for the poor and takes on human suffering. Philosophical ideas derived from other world religions, including nonmonotheistic religions, will also have a significant impact on future philosophical conceptions of God.

→ Atheism; Emanation; Immanence and Transcendence; Theism

Bibliography: J. B. Cobb Jr. and D. R. Griffin, *Process Theology: An Introductory Exposition* (Philadelphia, 1976) • C. Hartshorne, *The Divine Relativity: A Social Conception of God* (New Haven, 1948) • E. Heintel, *Grundriß der Dialektik* (2 vols.; Darmstadt, 1984); idem, *Mündiger Mensch und christlicher Glaube* (Darmstadt, 1988) • H. Hofmeister, *Truth and Belief* (Dordrecht, 1990) • E. A. Johnson, *She Who Is: The Mystery of God in Feminist Theological Discourse* (New York, 1992) • S. McFague, *Models of God: Theology for an Ecological, Nuclear Age* (Philadelphia, 1987) • J.-L. Marion, *God without Being* (Chicago, 1991) • A. Plantinga, *God and Other Minds* (Ithaca, N.Y., 1967) • K. Rahner, *Foundations of Christian Faith: An Introduction to the Idea of Christianity* (New York, 1978) • W. Röd, *Der Gott der reinen Vernunft. Die Auseinandersetzungen um den ontologischen Gottesbeweis von Anselm bis Hegel* (Munich, 1992) • R. Swinburne, *The Coherence of Theism* (Oxford, 1977) • G. Ward, ed., *The Postmodern God* (Oxford, 1997) • W. Weischedel, *Der Gott der Philosophen* (3d ed.; Darmstadt, 1998) • A. N. Whitehead, *Process and Reality* (New York, 1929) • E. R. Wierenga, *The Nature of God* (Ithaca, N.Y., 1989).

Erich Heintel and Bruce R. Reichenbach

4. OT

In theology and piety the special importance of the OT is that it speaks about God under the name of Yahweh (W. H. Schmidt). Because readers and listeners find the multilayered experiences of God in the OT relatively easily accessible, and also because essential parts of the OT testimony were adopted by the NT and the church, the OT made an imposing contribution to the Christian doctrine of God.

4.1. Development of OT Statements

4.1.1. The OT speaks about God in different ways (see merely Exod. 15:1-18) and uses various names and descriptions (→ Yahweh, Yahweh ṣĕbā'ôt [Lord of hosts], 'ēl, 'ĕlōhîm, 'ĕlôah, 'ēl šadday, 'ādôn/ 'ădōnāy [Lord]), which is due to the differences and development of the OT belief in God. The OT is a collection of many different texts and works. Thus Amos and the Chronicler, for example, do not talk about God in exactly the same way.

4.1.2. Yahweh was probably not the God of (all) → Israel (§1) from the very outset (Josh. 24:2; the question in Exod. 3:13; Gen. 31:53-54). Yahweh had forerunners. The groups around the patriarchs (→ Patriarchal History) seemed to have known and worshiped other deities (Gen. 31:42, 53; 49:24; also 15:1?) or other versions of El (Gen. 16:13; 17:1; 21:14-34; 28:10-17; 35:7; 49:25; cf. 33:20; 46:3; Exod. 6:3; also Gen. 14:18-23; Num. 24:4, 16) as the "God of my/your/their father," the "God of → Abraham, → Isaac, and → Jacob" (Gen. 26:24; 31:5, 42, 53, etc.) and therefore as the personal God who went with them (Gen. 26:24, 28; 28:20-21, etc.), the God of the clan. Each group probably worshiped only the one particular God, with whom it had its own personal encounter (Gen. 12:7; 13:14, etc.), while still recognizing the gods of other groups. The promise of the land, of guidance, and of posterity was constitutive, while at first priests, temple, and feasts played no part.

4.1.3. It is not by accident that both the Elohist and the Priestly writing introduce the name Yahweh only through and from the time of → Moses (Exod. 3:14; 6:2-3; → Pentateuch). If we would dispute the role of Moses (as the one who announced and interpreted the Red Sea deliverance?) in establishing the OT belief in God, then we must find someone else who performed an analogous function, for the word of interpretation and the personal element of individual belief are part of the development as well as the historical event.

Along with the accounts of deliverance by Yahweh (Exodus 13–14; 15:21), there is also that of his → theophany (chap. 19). The Savior God pledges his people to himself (chap. 20) and himself to this people (34:10). He also keeps faith with a grumbling people during the desert wanderings.

4.1.4. That Yahweh, the God of Israel (Judg. 5:3-5) as the Giver of the land (Joshua), was also the God of fertility became clear only with the further development of Israel's religious history (Hosea), which was mostly polemical but which expanded faith in Yahweh. With the more nomadic groups (the patriarchs and the Moses groups), there now came to be associated more rural groups who had a different view of life (focusing on rain, → creation, monarchy, etc.). In the conflict with neighbors who threatened Israel's settling of the land, the Yahweh who at the exodus had been known as a warlike liberator (Exod. 14:13-14; 15:3, 21) was experienced afresh as a "man of war" (Judges 4–5 etc.). He came

from the South (Judg. 5:4-5; Deut. 33:2, etc. = Sinai? Seir? the land of the Midianites?) and displayed again his military power (see Num. 21:14; Psalm 68, etc.).

After the days of → David and → Solomon, a strongly personal popular piety developed (M. Rose) alongside the official state religion. We see this development from archaeological findings, the polemic of the → prophets, and the position of the Deuteronomic/Deuteronomistic school. Yet the influence of Yahweh was all-pervasive (see arts. by O. Keel, F. Stolz, and H.-P. Müller in the vol. ed. by O. Keel). To ignore Yahweh or to engage in subjective evaluations is to explain nothing. The Deuteronomic school with its "Yahweh is one" (Deut. 6:4) had and needed forerunners (→ Elijah and Hosea; see the vol. ed. by E. Haag).

4.1.5. With the adoption of the (Syrian-Canaanite) predicates of El, Yahweh came to be seen as the holy and most high God with his own court, the world ruler in glory (Isaiah 6; Psalms 96–99), the living God who never dies but is always mightily at work, the Creator. Conflict with surrounding beliefs that took the form of either rejection or critical adaptation (e.g., the creation story and the battle against chaos) broadened what was said about Yahweh.

4.1.6. The → prophets declared that the God who, from the days in Egypt (Hos. 12:10; 13:4; Amos 9:7), had been believed to be with Israel and in the midst of it (Amos 5:15; Mic. 3:11) would come again to his people, this time to punish them (Amos 4:12, etc.). Yahweh himself speaks in the prophetic word. His relationship with his people (seen in anthropomorphisms that refer to Yahweh's repentance, hand, eye, etc.) now turns against the people, since they no longer do his will nor live as his people (Amos 3:2). His day, then, will be darkness and not light (Amos 5:18-20). Israel must recognize afresh that "I am Yahweh" (Ezek. 6:7-14, etc.), for he is not as people would wish him or think of him (Jer. 15:10-14; Job). He is not dependent on us (Psalm 50). He can reject as well as elect (→ Saul; Jer. 7:29; Lam. 5:22, etc.).

4.1.7. Precisely when the exile forced Israel to reflect on the power and impotence of its God as compared to other (victorious?) gods, Deutero-Isaiah dared to put on the lips of Yahweh the words "I am the first and I am the last; besides me there is no God" (Isa. 44:6) and in judgment scenes to discover with mockery not merely the impotence but the nonexistence of all other gods (40:25, 28; 43:11; 44:6-8, etc.; cf. Deut. 4:32-40). Here and in Deuteronomy and the Priestly writing, we have the most mature statements about God. Although earlier there had been no particular disputing of the existence of other gods (Judg. 11:24; 1 Sam. 26:18-19; 2 Kgs. 3:27; 5:17-18; Psalm 82; Ruth 1:15-16; Deut. 32:8-9, 43 text. em.), Yahweh nonetheless had been "a jealous God" (Exod. 20:5 and par.) who would not tolerate any other gods in and for Israel (Exod. 20:3 and par.; cf. Mic. 4:5). This idea was not just a later postulate (see the later texts Exod. 22:20; 34:14). The OT offers no unequivocal evidence in favor of a temporary → monolatry in times of crisis (A. van Selms; cf. B. Lang).

4.1.8. If older → Wisdom spoke of God as the founder and guarantor of the act-consequence nexus (Prov. 10:24; 11:18; see also Ps. 37:25 etc.), this theology, probably associated with particular classes, ran into a crisis that contested its ideology of a connection between God and world harmony (Ecclesiastes; Job). God speaks and wants trust. He is not destiny or a principle of cosmic interpretation. The critique probably also addresses some parts of Chronicles, which gives more precise indications of God's individual retributive acts.

4.2. Uniqueness of OT Statements

4.2.1. Unlike the world around it the OT cannot speak of an origin of God (Ps. 90:2). Yahweh declares his name and may be invoked, but one must not misuse his name in → magic or necromancy (Exod. 20:7 and par.). The prohibition of images (Exod. 20:4-5 and par.; 20:22-23; 34:17) protects his freedom. He reveals himself but does not surrender himself. The prohibition of → images is closely tied to that of false gods, for images of Yahweh would be idols (Hos. 11:2; 13:2, etc.). The world is God's creation but not a part of him. He keeps his distance from it, even though human beings are his image and partner (Gen. 1:27). Religious criticism of foreign gods and their idols is nourished by the assurance of his majesty.

4.2.2. Even as the God of Israel, Yahweh is transcendent (Jer. 23:23). He remains the Holy One, even as the Holy One of Israel. He fights for his people but also against them. He can be contemplated in the temple but not tied to it (Jeremiah 7). He is present for his people in freedom, and his reference is to the → future and → faith. He wants to be feared as well as loved. Toward his people and the world he acts in various ways (as Spirit, wisdom, → angel, → glory, word, countenance). Yet always he is also hidden (Ecclesiastes; Job; Jeremiah; Genesis 22). He is known mainly as he works in history, but he cannot be calculated on this basis. He grants his people a king, but the → monarchy is constantly an object of his critical speech and action.

To this tension the limited OT statements about

his attributes bear testimony (Exod. 34:6-7; Ps. 103:8; 106:1; 116:5; 139; Job 7; cf. Psalm 8 etc.). His → righteousness is predominantly his saving act (Judg. 5:11; Isa. 41:2, etc.), but it may also be experienced as punishment (Ps. 7:9, 11). He is praised (Psalm 113), yet both people (Psalm 80) and individuals (Psalms 13; 22) complain to him, calling him "my God," even though feeling forsaken by him (Ps. 22:1). The prophets proclaim his judgment, yet the question arises (and not just for present scholarship) whether this word means the end of his ways with his people. For Yahweh is a sympathetic God (Jeremiah) who struggles with himself (Hosea 11). Only his "I" (Isa. 54:7 etc.) can disclose a new future. The OT does not think in terms of immutability (see his repenting) but in terms of → faithfulness (Isa. 65:16; Ps. 143:1; Deut. 7:9).

4.2.3. The OT speaks of experiences of God on the part of individuals, then especially of groups, then through the cult (Psalms; → Prayer). These experiences focus on the necessary connection that the OT faith in God makes between history, the people of God, law, and ethos, as well as between election and commitment, fellowship and transcendence. They show that and how God was and is and will be present for his people, yet in such a way as to preserve his mystery and majesty. His word brought creation into being, shapes history, and saves and judges devout individuals who respond to him. What the OT has to say about God lies within the relation of a personal I-thou. To engage in discussions *about* God is not really to speak of him at all (Job 42:7).

According to the OT, it is only the fool who tries to live out a practical → atheism (Ps. 14:1; cf. Zeph. 1:12, etc.). A basic theoretical atheism was impossible in OT Israel.

Bibliography: E. Bosetti, *Yahweh, Shepherd of the People: Pastoral Symbolism in the OT* (Slough, Berkshire, 1993) • W. Brueggemann, *OT Theology* (Minneapolis, 1992) • F. M. Cross, "אל *'ēl*," *TDOT* 1.242-61 • D. N. Freedman, M. P. O'Connor, and H. Ringgren, "יהוה YHWH," *TDOT* 5.500-521 • E. Haag, ed., *Gott, der einzige* (Freiburg, 1985) • O. Keel, ed., *Monotheismus im Alten Israel und seiner Umwelt* (Fribourg, 1980) • B. Lang, "Vor einer Wende im Verständnis des israelitischen Gottesglaubens?" *Wie wird man Prophet in Israel?* (Düsseldorf, 1980) 149-61; idem, ed., *Der einzige Gott* (Munich, 1981) • N. Lohfink et al., eds., "*Ich will euer Gott werden." Beispiele biblischen Redens von Gott* (2d ed.; Stuttgart, 1982) • J. Marböck, "Anfänge der Rede von Gott," *Anfänge der Theologie* (Graz, 1987) 1-24 • R. Mason, *OT Pictures of God* (London, 1993) •

J. Miles, *God: A Biography* (New York, 1995) • H. Ringgren, "אֱלֹהִים *ᵉlōhîm*," *TDOT* 1.267-84 • M. Rose, *Der Ausschließlichkeitsanspruch Jahwes* (Stuttgart, 1975) • W. H. Schmidt, "Gotteslehre II: Altes Testament," *TRE* 13.608-26 (bibliography) • C. Schwölel, *God: Action and Revelation* (Kampen, 1992) • R. L. Smith, *OT Theology: Its History, Method, and Message* (Nashville, 1991).

Horst Dietrich Preuss†

5. NT

5.1. *General Characteristics*

In general, one might say that the NT teaching about God is marked by the tension of two tendencies. On the one hand, it adopts and develops the OT view of God (see 4). It bears witness to the definitive → revelation of the one God, who has already declared himself to → Israel (§1). It thus stresses a strict → monotheism — the creative work of God (→ Creation), which sets him in sharp antithesis to everything created, and his control of history, which shows itself in his dealings with his people. On the other hand, it goes beyond the OT by linking what it says about God exclusively to statements about the message, destiny, and person of Jesus, thus making → Christology the key to its doctrine of God.

5.2. *Jesus*

Both strands are present already in the message and ministry of → Jesus. Jesus confirms expressly the central idea of the Jewish doctrine of God when, in answer to the question concerning the chief commandment, he names the basic confession of the one God (*šĕmaʿ yiśrāʾēl*, Deut. 6:4; Mark 12:28-34). He does not abolish the → law but radicalizes it by stressing the unconditional will of God the Creator that lies behind it (Mark 10:1-9), which distinguishes it from the human statutes and casuistic compromises of the Mosaic → Torah (Mark 10:4-5; Matt. 5:21-22). The framework for this teaching is Jesus' message of the imminence of God's kingdom (Mark 1:15; → Kingdom of God). God will visibly establish his saving lordship over his world and his people; Jesus, on his part, is thus aware that he has been sent for the eschatological gathering of Israel (Matt. 19:28) — not just the righteous, but specifically "the lost sheep of the house of Israel" (Matt. 10:6), which are far from God's commandment.

The nearness of God and his rule is not to be understood merely in the chronological sense of a → future that is distinct from the present but in the sense of something that is directly at hand. Jesus demands that we count on the saving and judging nearness of God already in the present, that we count on acts of God that will change all relationships. The healings of Jesus are signs in which one may detect already the eschatological new creation that is expected (Matt. 12:28; Luke 11:20; → Healing). The bold anthropomorphic speech of his → parables shows that God is near, making the motives for this action clear to human understanding (Luke 15:1-10) and challenging the hearers to recognize how different this action is from all human expectations and calculations (e.g., Luke 15:11-32; Matt. 20:1-16). In particular, the prayers of Jesus (→ Prayer), for which he adopts the familiar *abba* of the child (Mark 14:36; see also Rom. 8:15) and which are characterized by an absolute certainty of being heard (Luke 11:9-13), express this closeness of God. In this light we can understand his demands that we should not be anxious but should have confidence in the goodness of the Creator (Matt. 6:25-34). We do not have here a naive creation faith that is blind to experience of its negative side. Instead, we have an assurance of the nearness of God and his eschatological creative work, in the light of which one may see in the old world that now is, in and under all its negative features, traces of the original good and perfect will of the Creator.

The decisive point, however, is that Jesus does not just talk about this nearness of God but powerfully represents and activates it in his message and works. In spite of the protests of Pharisaic scribes (→ Pharisees), he exemplifies God's unconditional turning to those who are far from him by forgiving their → sin (Luke 7:48) and gathering them for table fellowship as a sign of God's immanence (Mark 2:15-17). He promises salvation to those who justify God in his acts (Mark 5:34; Matt. 8:10-13). He claims that he declares the original will of the Creator, even when he seems to be in opposition to the sacred word of the Mosaic → Torah (Matt. 5:17-48), and that the divinely established meaning of the → Sabbath is actually fulfilled by his breaking it (Mark 3:4). This claim brought upon Jesus the charge of blasphemy and led to his violent death.

5.3. *New Post-Easter Accents*

For primitive Christianity the message of the → resurrection of Jesus was the crucial point in the doctrine of God. It meant that God expressly recognized the claim and ministry of Jesus and therefore that salvation and the knowledge of God for all people were linked to acceptance of the exposition of God by Jesus and God's dealings with him (Acts 2:22-24; 4:10-12). The dealings of God with Jesus were the beginning of the eschatological raising of the dead and therefore a declaration of God's plan for an eschatological new creation. It is God who gives life to the dead (Rom. 4:17; 2 Cor. 1:9). By exalting Jesus to his right hand and making him Lord (Ps. 110:1 = Acts 2:34-35 etc.) — that is, the one who finally executes his eschatological plan of salvation (Revelation 5; → Eschatology) — he definitively demonstrates his control of history.

Early liturgical formulas like 1 Cor. 8:6 and 1 Tim. 2:5-6, which set the one God alongside the one Lord, seek to relate God and Jesus personally and historically along these lines rather than to make them ontologically parallel. The proclamation of the Gentile mission contains a central motif of Jewish monotheism when it condemns the exchanging of Creator for creature as the basic sin of the Gentile world and demands a return to the one God, who confronts the creature at a distance that cannot be bridged (Acts 14:15-17; 17:23-31). This return, which is not possible merely by reverting to the natural knowledge of God that is accessible to all people, can happen only on the basis of God's end-time acts in Jesus (1 Thess. 1:9-10). Here is God's final word, a promise of forgiveness for past alienation from God (Rom. 3:25) but also a declaration of judgment on the unbelief that rejects the present offer of fellowship.

Along different lines, the statements of Hellenistic Christianity regarding preexistence also bring about a close bracketing of the doctrine of God and Christology (Phil. 2:6; Col. 1:15-20; John 1:1-18). Here creation and eschatological salvation are seen to be closely linked. Because the God who saves us in Jesus is none other than the Creator, the world is not far from God. It is not a sphere that lies under the control of → demons and the powers of fate. It is an expression of the saving and loving will of God that has come to fulfillment in Jesus Christ.

5.4. Paul
Characteristic of the doctrine of God in → Paul is the tension between God's → wrath and his → love. All people, Gentiles and Jews alike, have rejected the Creator's offer of fellowship with his creatures and have tried to live on their own and for themselves alone. Because this choice violates God's honor, his wrath at them has been revealed (Rom. 1:18). God himself holds them in the sphere of perdition, to which they have consigned themselves. Hence they cannot escape from it by themselves (Rom. 1:24). In Jesus Christ, however, God has revealed his → righteousness, his faithfulness in fellowship. This characteristic is imparted as a gift, by → grace, to those who come to Christ in → faith, giving up their former attempt to live autonomously.

Paul thinks of the Christ-event strictly as an act of God. The cross is for him the decisive mode of God's self-declaration. God reveals himself here in a way that is diametrically opposed to all human values or ideas of God — that is, in the deepest humiliation and shame, but also in a radical love for sinners that knows no bounds (1 Cor. 1:18-31).

In spite of the heavy stress on God's justifying and reconciling of individuals, Paul never loses sight of the cosmic aspect of God's action, nor does he fail to see it from the standpoint of → salvation history. God wills to reconcile the world to himself (2 Cor. 5:19). He will show his covenant faithfulness to all Israel by opening to it the way of salvation (Rom. 11:28-32), and finally he will visibly overcome all opposing powers and forces, thus demonstrating his faithfulness to all creation (1 Cor. 15:28).

5.5. John
In the Johannine writings there is a narrowing down of the doctrine of God and Christology that has no parallel elsewhere in the NT. This feature is connected, on the one hand, with the view of Jesus as the Revealer (John 1:18) and, on the other, with the identification of the gift of salvation with the Giver. Jesus does not give specific gifts; he gives himself (John 6:26-35; 10:11; 15:5). Similarly, his revelation of God is not objective speech about God but a confrontation with God himself. Those who encounter Jesus have to do with the Giver of salvation and therefore with God himself. He is not just the way to salvation but is its goal and content, namely, truth and life (John 14:6). In this sense those who see him see the Father (John 14:9).

Furthermore, John explains the work of Jesus in terms of his essential fellowship with the Father (John 5:17-23), which is grounded in the mutual love of Father and Son (John 3:35; 5:20; 15:9). The Father's sending of the Son discloses their oneness in the fellowship of love (John 10:30, 38). The statement "God is love" (1 John 4:8, 16) is not, then, an abstract definition but a way of describing the mission of the Son, which originates in the love of God.

Bibliography: A. W. ARGYLE, God in the NT (London, 1965) • R. E. BROWN, Studies in Early Christology (Edinburgh, 1994) • B. J. COOKE, God's Beloved: Jesus' Experience of the Transcendent (Philadelphia, 1992) • J. COPPENS, ed., La notion biblique de Dieu. Le Dieu de la Bible et le Dieu des philosophes (Gembloux, 1976) • C. DEMKE, "Gott IV," TRE 13.645-52 • M. J. HARRIS, Jesus as God: The New Testament Use of theós in Reference to Jesus (Grand Rapids, 1992) • M. HENGEL, Studies in Early Christology (Edinburgh, 1993) • H. MERKLEIN and E. ZENGER, eds., "Ich will euer Gott werden." Beispiele biblischen Redens von Gott (Stuttgart, 1981) 177-205 • W. C. PLACHER, Narratives of a Vulnerable God: Christ, Theology, and Scripture (Louisville, Ky.,

1994) • G. Ramshaw, *God Beyond Gender: Feminist Christian God-Language* (Minneapolis, 1995) • W. Schrage, "Theologie und Christologie bei Paulus und Jesus auf dem Hintergrund der modernen Gottesfrage," *EvT* 36 (1976) 121-54 • E. Schweizer, *Beiträge zur Theologie des Neuen Testaments* (Zurich, 1970) 207-18 • G. Vermes, *The Religion of Jesus, the Jew* (London, 1993) • N. T. Wright, *The NT and the People of God: Christian Origins and the Question of God* (Minneapolis, 1992).

JÜRGEN ROLOFF

6. Orthodox Tradition

In the → Orthodox Church the doctrine of God as the basis of Christian faith has two inseparable and complementary aspects: the dogmatic teaching, and the experiencing of it in → liturgy and → mysticism. One could thus say that the whole of Orthodox theology is devoted to the doctrine of God and the relation of God to us and the world.

→ Dogma is what God reveals about himself. We know from the OT that God is being, the One, the eternal source of all existence as its Creator, and that he is holy and personal. We cannot conceive of him, yet he reveals himself, declaring himself in us in the *imago Dei*, which we bear from the beginning of his creation and which he must bring to full divine likeness. On the Orthodox view God reveals himself in all the cosmos by his providence, by his → grace and energies (→ Palamism), and also by his → angels. → Creation itself and created existence bear witness to the doctrine of God, as is indicated in Romans and Hebrews.

Furthermore, we learn from the NT that God is spirit, love, and light (John). It is also testified that as the One he is also three, making himself known as Father, Son, and Holy Spirit (Matt. 28:19), the one name "God" in his three persons (→ Trinity). Finally — and this is basic to the doctrine of God — the second hypostasis of this Holy Trinity of the one God became man (→ Incarnation). He became the new → Adam. He became in history what he is in the eternity to which he returns in his → ascension (→ Christology 3). There thus follow the dogmas of → salvation by redemption, the → resurrection, the → last judgment, the → *theōsis* of humanity and the transfiguration of the cosmos, and eternal life from eternity to eternity. The whole → gospel is proclamation of the → kingdom of God, the New Jerusalem, in which Christ will recapitulate all people in his bride, the church (→ Church 3.1), and God will then be "all in all" (1 Cor. 15:28; → Apocatastasis).

Because of God's → love for his creatures, his profound mercy and grace, and his incarnation, fallen humans (→ Anthropology) can freely do God's will and thus attain to a transfigured dignity, in accordance with God's original plan, as the image receives the likeness of God that → sin had distorted. The whole relation between God and us derives from the revelation of his primal and most proper nature and is thus a development of the doctrine of God as this is applied.

Yet theology and the cult are oriented more strongly to the divine persons than to the divine nature. Theological access to the doctrine of God is based on the fact that the Son of God, conceived by the Father through the Holy Spirit, incarnate Word and Son of Man, defines himself as "the way, and the truth, and the life" (John 14:6). The other Advocate, who will always be with us, the → Holy Spirit of truth, who proceeds from the Father and whom the Father sends in the name of Christ, makes it possible for the church to remember and to understand all the acts and words and instructions of Christ — that is, the real doctrine of God (John 14:16, 26; 15:26). The Spirit works this insight from creation as he is unceasingly poured out upon humanity and the world, and then by his → pentecost in history as the church seeks and secures his outpouring by unbroken → prayer and the → sacraments.

Ontologically and eschatologically, then, the church is rooted in the most proper nature of God as it describes this nature in its teaching. In heart and mind it relates itself to the three persons of the sacred Trinity in accordance with the will of the triune Creator that we should be united with him as his adopted children. → Paul sums up this point when he defines the church as the body of Christ and the temple of the Holy Spirit, and individual members as children of God and joint heirs with Christ (Rom. 8:16-17; Eph. 1:11; Gal. 3:29; 4:7, etc.). The church's liturgy, which sanctifies humanity and the world, is simply an expression and actualization of this teaching. The daily life of Christians in the world ought normally to correspond to it, for God shows his nature by ordering us to be holy as he is holy (Lev. 11:44; 1 Pet. 1:16).

In spite of all the mysteries that it contains, this doctrine of God has never been questioned in the Orthodox Church from the very beginnings of Christianity. Hence, with just one exception, it has not been the subject of special treatment. In his dogmatics Panagiotis N. Trempelas follows the example of Western authors by dealing with the doctrine of God separately. In contrast, Sergius Bulgakov, the most important Orthodox theologian of the 20th century, does not take this course in his dogmatic trilogy.

Theologically, the doctrine of God rests on the → Niceno-Constantinopolitan Creed, the ecumenical councils, and the Fathers (e.g., Gregory of Nazianzus *Or. theol.* 27-31 [*PG* 36], John Chrysostom, *Homilies on the Incomprehensible Nature of God* [*PG* 48]). The liturgy, which culminates in the → Eucharist (a representation of the chief principle of ecclesiology), may be regarded as a commentary on the doctrine of the Trinity, Christology, and pneumatology.

→ Apophatic Theology; Orthodoxy 3

Bibliography: S. BIGHAM, *The Image of God the Father in Orthodox Theology and Iconography* (Torrance, Calif., 1995) • S. BULGAKOV, *Die Braut des Lammes* (Lausanne, 1984; orig. pub., 1945); idem, *Das Lamm Gottes* (Lausanne, 1982; orig. pub., 1933); idem, *Le Paraclet* (Paris, 1946; orig. pub., 1936) • P. CREMER, *Baptism and Change in the Early Middle Ages* (Cambridge, 1993) • L. D. DAVIS, *The First Seven Ecumenical Councils (325-787): Their History and Theology* (Wilmington, Del., 1987) • P. EVDOKIMOV, *Gotteserleben und Atheismus* (Vienna, 1967) • F. GAVIN, *Some Aspects of Contemporary Greek Orthodox Thought* (London, 1923) 57-144 • J. N. D. KELLEY, *Golden Mouth, the Story of John Chrysostom–Ascetic, Preacher, Bishop* (London, 1995) • V. LOSSKY, *The Mystical Theology of the Eastern Church* (2d ed.; Crestwood, N.Y., 1976) • G. L. PRESTIGE, *God in Patristic Thought* (2d ed.; London, 1952) • P. TREMPELAS, *Dogmatique de l'Église orthodoxe catholique* (vol. 1; Chevetogne, 1966) 168-361.

CONSTANTIN ANDRONIKOF†

7. Historical Development and Modern Discussion

7.1. *Themes and Tendencies*

In considering God, we must distinguish strictly theological doctrines of God and the → Trinity from the biblical witness, from early creeds (→ Confession of Faith), and from statements about God in liturgies and church art (→ Church Music; Iconography). Analytic, systematic reflection on belief in God, however, is naturally (e.g., in the → early church) very closely connected with → prayer (→ Doxology) and → liturgy. Doctrine is found in the → church (→ Theology) when existential and congregational confession of God and talk about him, including what is said to him in prayer, are subjected to linguistic analysis. Such study may be needed to achieve inner clarification, to resist inappropriate foreign influences (→ Apologetics), or to reformulate insights of faith in crisis situations.

Though we may applaud 19th-century Protes-

tant theology (→ Liberal Theology) for its criticism of the early church for allowing the Christian message to be permeated by Greek philosophy in the interests of doctrinal construction, with hindsight we now understand the urgent need to test ideas and concepts of God with the means and methods of modern → philosophy and → epistemology. The question how far criticism of the philosophical forms of classical doctrines (including the Trinity and → Christology) is appropriate forms today an important element in ecumenical discussion with the → Roman Catholic Church and especially the → Orthodox Church. On the Protestant side a corresponding revision of evaluation of the medieval doctrines of God is also ecumenically necessary.

7.1.1. We may summarize the development of the idea of God from the early church to the → Reformation in terms of the following themes.

7.1.1.1. *The unity of God* had to be a subject of reflection in the early church because (1) the biblical witness stressed the centrality of God's uniqueness; (2) → polytheistic ideas, though vague, exerted pressure on early Christians from the world around them; (3) → Platonism promoted this concept and found a corresponding unity and simplicity in the → soul; and (4) → Stoicism regarded the link between the one God and the one cosmos as of central importance. Whether "simplicity" required reduction to one basic idea of God, and how one might think of a multiplicity of thoughts in God, remained largely an open question, as did that of the origin of → evil and its compatibility with God's omnipotence. The second-century → apologists — Justin Martyr (d. ca. 165); Irenaeus, active after 177; and Tertullian, active from 190 to 207 — raised such reflection to a relatively high level. The true development of the concept of unity, though, came only after Origen (d. ca. 254) with → Alexandrian theology and the three great → Cappadocians: Basil (d. 379), his brother Gregory of Nyssa (d. ca. 395), and their friend Gregory of Nazianzus (d. 389/90). It did so in the context of the doctrine of the Trinity.

7.1.1.2. The issue of *the identity of God with the God of the OT* poses the question of God's unity in historical terms and relates also to the problem of evil. Is the God who sends → Jesus the Savior identical with the Creator, the OT God? Marcion (→ Marcionites) of Asia Minor (excommunicated in 144) answered no. The fact that the church decided against him weakens the charge sometimes made that it greatly Hellenized the biblical message and its concept of God. The apologist Theophilus of Antioch and, after him, Irenaeus so clearly linked God to the history of → Israel (§1), the church, and the world that it became possible to develop the so-called economic doctrine of the Trinity (i.e., history structured in accordance with the "economy" of God).

7.1.1.3. According to its logical presupposition, *the doctrine of the Trinity* is the "economic" doctrine. Extremely helpful to believers, this teaching relates the God of Israel (the Creator and the electing God) to the God who sent Jesus, was present in him, and in him suffered with us, and then again to the God who in the Spirit is present in the churches. The true unity of God is the unity that is thus understood in Trinitarian terms and that is worshiped in the → doxology.

This is the doctrine of God that Athanasius (ca. 297-373) and the Cappadocian Fathers made it their theological lifework to formulate. The movement was from the three ways in which God manifests himself (the hypostases) to his unity. In his unity God is the source *(pēgē)*, root *(rhiza)*, and ground *(aitia)* of all being, → love, and → grace. Believers cannot penetrate to his true mystery, his essence (the ousia). They can experience his energies *(energeiai)*, however, and "through the Son in the Spirit" they can learn to understand that the whole cosmos would collapse were it not sustained by these divine energies in grace. The doctrine of the "immanent" Trinity (i.e., how God is "in himself") found expression in the creed in the language of prayer. There then developed negative theology (→ Apophatic Theology) and the mysticism of Dionysius the Pseudo-Areopagite (ca. 500), which also influenced the West.

7.1.1.4. *The development of the idea of God in the West* took a different course. It hardly went through the preliminary stages of the doctrine of the Trinity but accepted the rulings of the Councils of Nicaea (325) and Constantinople (381; → Niceno-Constantinopolitan Creed). The movement now was from the one God to the three persons.

Augustine (354-430; → Augustine's Theology) had a high regard for many of the concerns of the apologists and the later Greek fathers (→ Church Fathers): God's unity and uniqueness, his apathy (i.e., immunity from suffering and passion), his immutability, his mystery (though with a different epistemology from that of the Cappadocians), and the orthodox formulas of Trinitarian doctrine. Yet his concept of God was not the same, for Augustine linked God to historical movements. Thus the occasion of his *City of God* was the fall of Rome in 410. Augustine's God, however, was timeless and therefore, in the last resort, alien to human history. → Dualistic concepts from his → Manichaean period

also shaped his view of God, not just his idea of the two cities. His doctrine of the Trinity did not really have the function of deepening or constituting his knowledge of God. Along the lines of Plotinus (→ Platonism) he made it a doctrine of the relations between the Father (eternity), the Son (wisdom), and the Spirit (beatitude). These elements find reflection in the human soul (image of God) as the trinity of memory, rational knowledge, and will (or the lover, the beloved, and the power of loving). The decisive element in this "psychological" interpretation was not the explaining of God but our personal relation to him. For all the assurances that God is pure being, he was really seen as will. In Augustine's understanding, with its emphasis on will, the energies of the Eastern teaching were replaced by → predestination. The door was thus opened for non-Trinitarian ideas, for questions as to the being and will of God in "himself."

7.1.1.5. Whether we are to think of God as being or as will, and how he is to be known in his relation to the world, dominated *the medieval doctrines of God*. The decisions of the councils were recognized, but the Greek fathers were known only in a few texts or in collections. The influence of Augustine was powerful. In → piety and → liturgy the ascent of the soul to God was a constant goal. Erigena of Ireland (ca. 810-ca. 877), the translator of Dionysius the Pseudo-Areopagite, found a speculative basis and possibility for such an ascent in the → emanation (descent) from God of a mighty → revelation through and in all creation. The later theologians of → Scholasticism proceeded by rational analysis, but → mysticism remained alive and could also appeal to Augustine.

The central question was still that of God's relation to the world and its order. Another issue, in the interests of the knowledge of God, was that of the mediation between revelation, → faith, and → tradition, on the one side, and, on the other, human → reason. Grace and → nature constituted the poles of mediation. In accordance with the approach adopted (Platonic or Aristotelian), God was either the starting point (→ Realism) or the end point (→ Nominalism) of theologicophilosophical deduction or conceptualizing construction. The path of knowledge itself, however, was circular. Anselm of Canterbury (1033-1109) made faith the presupposition of his proofs of God.

Thomas Aquinas (ca. 1225-74) certainly thought that natural reason can know God's existence and unity, but only by revelation can one know the Trinity, the essence of God, the love of God, and God as personal. Revelation thus elucidates what is known by natural reason. (In his *Summa contra Gentiles,* written for missionaries to pagans, the presupposition of faith is clearer.) Everything, including the course of knowledge (→ Epistemology), is set in motion by God as first cause or prime mover *(actus purus)* in creation. For all the dissimilarity between God and the world, the world is still in → analogy to God and thus makes possible in principle an inferring of God from it (→ Thomism).

Some 500 years later there were strange parallels in Protestant Scholasticism (→ Orthodoxy 1-2) and in → physicotheology, the only difference being that in the Middle Ages the protest against such thinking took place within the Christian faith, whereas in the 18th and 19th centuries it resulted in → atheism.

In the Middle Ages the protest came from the Franciscan Duns Scotus (ca. 1265-1308) and his followers (→ Scotism). Along Augustinian lines Scotus viewed God directly as omnipotent and infinite will *(potentia absoluta,* "absolute power"). As such, God is hidden from us. He may be known only as he limits himself in the multiplicity of his possibilities and ties himself to his work of creating and ordering *(potentia ordinata,* "ordained power"). Epigrammatically, one might say that what God wills is good, not that God wills what is good. In William of Ockham (ca. 1285-1347) this approach finally led to a crass separation of reason and revelation, in the position that there can be no knowledge of God through reason. With the detaching of the doctrine of God from → Aristotelianism, human reason was conferred an → autonomy that foreshadowed the modern → renaissance individual.

At the same time, we must take medieval mysticism seriously as regards the doctrine of God. It too produced intellectual fruits that influenced contemporary and later teachings. In Meister Eckhart (ca. 1260-ca. 1328) and others we find a reversal of the notion that God is being. Being is God, but we cannot master him. He is pure, self-thinking thought. Such concepts are not unlike the doctrines of God in Zen Buddhism (→ Buddhism; Zen).

7.1.2. The doctrines of God from the Reformation to the → Enlightenment may be grouped as follows.

7.1.2.1. As in Christology, so in the doctrine of God, the Bohemian, German, and Swiss-French Reformations produced nothing new. This observation is interesting, for although the Reformation offered completely new teachings on grace, → justification, biblical understanding, the → sacraments, and the church's teaching authority, it obviously did not necessitate a total revision of classical Christology and doctrines of God.

In the writings of Jan Hus (ca. 1372-1415) and the Four Articles of Prague (1420, on God's Word, the sacraments, the church, and the Christian life), one finds nothing in the doctrine of God that goes beyond what we find in later Scholasticism (→ Hussites). The social impulses have their basis in an eschatological consciousness rather than in the doctrine of God. What is new is believers' access to God rather than the doctrine of God as such. The same is true a hundred years later in the Reformation works of Ulrich Zwingli (1484-1531), in which the concept of God is fully oriented to the supreme good *(summum bonum;* → Zwingli's Theology).

Martin Luther (1483-1546), like the Lutheran confessional writings, accepted the rulings of the early councils and condemned all heretical teachers and → anti-Trinitarians, past and present (→ Luther's Theology). The doctrine of the Trinity, however, played no decisive role in his theology. The kind and gracious God who grants us → righteousness, coming to us in Jesus Christ and making himself known in him, can be known by reason at most only theoretically. It is only by the witness of the Holy Spirit, with no merit of works or piety, that he comes into the heart as the forgiving and gracious God. Luther's roots are unmistakably in the Franciscan, Ockhamistic tradition, which holds that philosophy can give us no real knowledge of God. Nevertheless Luther, reflecting his Augustinian legacy, could allow a dualistic concept to enter into his doctrine of God. On the one hand, God is the *Deus absconditus,* the hidden, mysterious, and fearful God, who undoubtedly sustains the world but whose "work on the left hand," an "alien work" *(opus alienum),* we do not know as → gospel but can perceive only through the admonitions of the → law (→ Law and Gospel). On the other hand, God is the *Deus revelatus,* the revealed, gracious, and pardoning God, whom we know through Jesus Christ in Scripture and the preaching of the church, and whose "work on the right hand" is his "proper work" *(opus proprium).*

Although John Calvin (1509-64) also had a doctrine of two kingdoms (*Inst.* 3.19 and 4.20), we do not find in him any such → dualism (→ Calvin's Theology). He is more in the tradition of medieval realism, with its question of God's being and intellect and a monistic rather than a dualistic view. For this reason, even in textbooks constant attention has been paid to the emphasis on God's sovereignty, although it is doubtful whether one may find in Calvin himself any key concept along these lines, such as predestination, the majestic ruler-God, or God's glory. Of central importance in both Luther and

Calvin is Christ's mediatorship between God and us, God's presence in the world, and his suffering along with us.

7.1.2.2. From the end of the 16th to the early 18th century, Protestant orthodoxy found itself forced by confessional debates into an analysis of the Reformation ideas of God, with special regard for the relation between natural and revealed knowledge of God, and also for the attributes of God. The resultant ossification, particularly in the use of the Reformation Scripture principle (→ Biblicism; Reformation Principles), came acutely to light in contact with the Enlightenment theologians and their orientation to reason and → experience. Nature and God were seen together, with God as the epitome of all stability and order. The starry heaven was a revelation of God. "Physicotheology" is a general term to describe the various attempts to arrive at God from a consideration of purpose in nature.

At the Enlightenment, philosophical and theological doctrines of God parted company. The separation became complete in England and Scotland with the → deists, at the latest with David Hume (1711-76), in Germany with Christian Wolff (1679-1754) and Immanuel Kant (1724-1804; → Kantianism), who banished classical → metaphysics with his critiques, and in France already with René Descartes (1596-1650; → Cartesianism), Charles de Montesquieu (1689-1775), and Voltaire (1694-1778). In America a new and imposing synthesis was achieved by Jonathan Edwards (1703-58).

7.1.2.3. The reaction of Protestant theology can hardly be described as uniform, since many important writers saw themselves as both theologians and philosophers, notably Friedrich D. E. Schleiermacher (1768-1834; → Schleiermacher's Theology) and Georg W. F. Hegel (1770-1831; → Hegelianism). If we set aside the special situation in England, we find that especially in Germany the choice for a theological doctrine of God lay between (1) a radical restriction of what may be said metaphysically about God, in view of Kant's work, and (2), along the lines of Hegel's philosophy of history, a linking of God and the world by an overarching concept of history that, as a model to defeat → atheism, even included God's self-negation and self-alienation on the path to his own self-actualization. Schleiermacher and Albrecht Ritschl (1822-99) chose the first way, while the theological Hegelians, mostly historians, chose the second.

The criticism leveled at the first choice, namely, that it ignores God's → wrath and reduces him to love and finally to a point of orientation for → ethics, is too simplistic. To say that statements about God are value judgments is not to reduce the doctrine of God to ethics. Today English → philosophy of religion is asking again whether statements about God are not by their very nature moral. It is right to observe, however, that theologies at the turn of the 20th century that amount to little more than social ethics (→ Religious Socialism; Social Gospel) arose from this tradition of a comprehensive conception oriented toward the "goal" of the → kingdom of God.

The Hegelian way left both clear and hidden traces throughout the 19th century. Some have even wanted to set K. Barth (1886-1968) on this path, although his concept of history is not above God but is grounded in the Trinitarian God (in his history with himself). The → history-of-religions school undoubtedly took this course, with its great exegetes at the turn of the century and its systematic theologians Rudolf Otto (1869-1937) and Ernst Troeltsch (1865-1923). Otto's rediscovery of Luther's *Deus absconditus* and God's awe-inspiring transcendence (→ Immanence and Transcendence), the *tremendum* (*The Idea of the Holy* [1917; ET 1923, 1970], kept theology from being simply philosophy or ethics (see Schleiermacher). God as the Wholly Other is like the God of Barth's early concern (→ Dialectical Theology).

In Barth, however, talk about God, on the basis of his exegetical works, his rejection of Schleiermacher, and his study of Anselm (1931), found its basis and possibility only in a strict reference to God's revelation in his Word (Jesus Christ). His *Church Dogmatics* develops what is to be said about God along these lines and in II/1 and II/2 (1957) offers an explicit doctrine of God that — in opposition to Kant's restrictions, Hegel's historicizing, and Schleiermacher's reconstruction in terms of the believing consciousness — deals with God's being, his perfections, his electing, and the basis of ethics in the doctrine of God. The influence of this doctrine of God was profound. Dietrich Bonhoeffer had received these volumes before his death, and for all his agreement, he voiced the first objection (regarding the "positivism of revelation"). The great questions raised against classical doctrines of God by 18th- and 19th-century theologians still remained and, in constant debate with Barth, became a theme again in English-speaking and more recent German-speaking theology.

7.1.2.4. The reaction of Roman Catholic theology to 18th-century criticism of the Christian doctrine of God took shape in the Catholic Tübingen School (after 1817) in a strong commitment to philosophical → idealism and to Schleiermacher(!). Syntheses of → Romanticism, church tradition, and historical research made possible speculative ideas of God along similar lines to the seeking of truth in history in the → Oxford Movement (John H. Newman [1801-90]). There was also theological debate with Kant.

After the middle of the 19th century, however, neo-Thomism (→ Neoscholasticism), confirmed in 1879 in Leo XIII's → encyclical *Aeterni Patris*, attempted a revival of timeless theological truth and a safeguarding of tradition. Thomistic teaching was deployed against every form of → modernism. Against this background we are to evaluate the liturgical movement and the biblical movement of the first half of the 20th century, which found a place for personalism (→ Person) and → existentialism in the doctrine of God.

Already before → Vatican II there were new syntheses of philosophical metaphysics and the Christian doctrine of God, but with some attention to situational questions and the political and cultural problems of the age. With Karl Rahner's "transcendental anthropology" (i.e., the linking of our destiny, as beings oriented to God's absolute transcendence, with the knowledge of God), these matters have now become a theme in the doctrine of God, so that theocentricity and anthropocentricity are no longer polar opposites. Rahner himself, however, did not draw out the implications in the sense of → political theology (J. B. Metz; → Liberation Theology).

7.2. Problems and New Approaches

Agreements and differences in the theological question of talk about God cut across the (Western) confessions today. As regards schools, one might think primarily of Barth, not of Paul Tillich (1886-1965) and his complementary relating of a metaphysics of being and the biblically revealed God, or of Rahner and his transcendental theology. Almost without exception the churches and their teachers have had to face the question of → theodicy, in view of two shattering world wars, the → Holocaust, and the millions of lives lost around the world in countless savage wars and disturbances. It is no longer possible to talk so naively of God's action as the Lord of history. God's condescension is a closer and more comforting theme than his omnipotence or transcendence. Above all, no one any longer finds it so easy to claim God for national and cultural goals. Liberation theology should not be too hastily criticized as a fresh example of the misuse found in older generations. (There were in fact some new versions of the claiming of God for political goals, such as the claim that the advent of Marxism-Leninism in eastern Europe was God's doing.)

The following ten problems and new approaches have arisen in modern theological and ecumenical discussion.

7.2.1. The first question is *whether we can talk and think about God at all*, or whether we are driven back to feeling and mysticism. The theology of the Word of God insists that we can conceive of God and speak about him (K. Barth, E. Jüngel). But is the God of human formulation the same as the living God? Gordon Kaufman, Langdon Gilkey, Joachim Track, Ingolf U. Dalferth, and others are working on this problem with the instruments of classical theology and → analytic philosophy.

7.2.2. A second question is *whether the human inquiry into meaning and history is not unavoidably referred back to God* (W. Pannenberg, K. Rahner, G. Ebeling). Tillich's question regarding our ultimate concern points in the same direction.

7.2.3. Another issue is that of *rediscovering and reformulating the doctrine of the Trinity* as the most appropriate way of talking about God, about his relation to history, and about his fellow-suffering with us (J. Moltmann, D. Ritschl, C. Gunton).

7.2.4. The fourth question is that of *God's omnipotence*. Is it causal, or is it an omnipotence of love (E. Jüngel)? How does the stress on God's impotence differ from the errors of classic patripassianism, from an absolutized theology of the cross? Does contesting the classical idea of omnipotence bring comfort or discouragement? The various liberation theologies insist that God takes the side of the oppressed, but do they understand the resurrection in their own political interest as their liberation (minjung theology; → Asian Theology 4.2)?

7.2.5. In *Jewish-Christian dialogue* it is asked whether we can talk of God at all after Auschwitz, what right Christians have for critical theological → dialogue, and what forms Christology must take in order to speak with Jews about God in Trinitarian terms with reference to Jesus and the Holy Spirit (H. Gollwitzer, F. W. Marquardt, P. von der Osten-Sacken, R. Rendtorff, P. M. van Buren, M. Stöhr, et al.).

7.2.6. The *question of God and → nature, a new "natural theology,"* and not simply the ecological crisis (→ Ecology), has initiated a testing of the classical concepts of God and creation. Furthermore, awareness of the philosophical implications of modern science (J. Polkinghorne) has raised the question of an ultimate identity between the rationality of God and the world (T. F. Torrance), though no one is taking the path to a knowledge of God that was suggested by classical → natural theology (→ Science and Theology).

7.2.7. In → *process theology* the classical way of knowledge finds renewed interest on the basis of the metaphysics of A. N. Whitehead (1861-1947), as developed theologically by American process theologians (Schubert M. Ogden, John B. Cobb). In his own experience and self-creation, God is supposedly synthesizing the process of completed and not yet actualized reality. In God there is a distinction between his primal nature and the process that triggers reality. This view seems particularly difficult to harmonize with classical doctrines of God.

7.2.8. The → World Council of Churches, the Roman Catholic Church, numerous churches in Asia and Africa (→ African Theology; Asian Theology), and individual authors still champion *the God of the Bible in debate with other concepts of God* held by representatives and writings of non-Jewish and non-Christian religions (see 1). The search for synthesis or for a common denominator, which began with the Enlightenment, tries to find a place for insight into the truth of the particular "story" of confessional traditions.

7.2.9. *Feminists' questioning* of the classical way of talking about God brings up the problem of whether the male attributes of God are an integral part of the biblical testimony or a projection of earlier patriarchal structures in church and society (→ Feminist Theology).

7.2.10. Finally, in *the debate with* → *atheism* the question arises how far Jews and Christians in this discussion must cling to classical → theism. Is the theistic thesis a meaningful and legitimate compendium of the creed of biblically oriented believers (→ God Is Dead Theology)?

→ Absolute, The; Anthropology; Black Theology; Language; Monotheism; Philosophy of Religion; Theology of History; Word of God

Bibliography: J. Baur, "Gott," *HST* 6 • R. Bernhardt, *Was heißt "Handeln Gottes"?* (Gütersloh, 1999) • G. van den Brink, *Almighty God: A Study of the Doctrine of Divine Omnipotence* (Kampen, 1993) • V. Brümmer, *Speaking of a Personal God: An Essay in Philosophical Theology* (Cambridge, 1992) • J. M. Byrne, ed., *The Christian Understanding of God Today* (Dublin, 1993) • I. U. Dalferth, *Gott. Philosophisch-theologische Denkversuche* (Tübingen, 1992); idem, *Religiöse Rede von Gott* (Munich, 1981) • P. Davies, *God, Cosmos, Nature, and Creativity* (Edinburgh, 1995) • N. Fischer, *Die philosophische Frage nach Gott. Ein Gang durch ihre Stationen* (Paderborn, 1995) • H. Gollwitzer, *The Existence of God, as Confessed by Faith* (London, 1965) • D. W. Hardy, *God's Ways with the World* (Edinburgh, 1996) • T. W. Jennings Jr., *Beyond Theism: A Grammar of God-Language* (Oxford, 1985) • R. W. Jenson, *Systematic Theology* (New York,

1997) • E. Jüngel, *God as the Mystery of the World: On the Foundation of the Theology of the Crucified One in the Dispute between Theism and Atheism* (Grand Rapids, 1983) • W. Kasper, *The God of Jesus Christ* (London, 1984) • G. D. Kaufman, *God the Problem* (Cambridge, Mass., 1972); idem, *The Theological Imagination: Constructing the Concept of God* (Philadelphia, 1981) • T. A. Kelly, *Language, World, and God* (Dublin, 1996) • H. Küng, *Does God Exist? An Answer for Today* (New York, 1980) • S. McFague, *Models of God: Theology for an Ecological Nuclear Age* (London, 1987) • J. Moltmann, *The Trinity and the Kingdom of God* (London, 1981) • G. Newlands, *God in Christian Perspective* (Edinburgh, 1994) • E. Osborn, *The Beginning of Christian Philosophy* (Cambridge, 1981) • W. Pannenberg, *Basic Questions in Theology* (2 vols.; Philadelphia, 1970-71) 2.119-83 • G. L. Prestige, *God in Patristic Thought* (London, 1952) • K. Rahner, *Foundations of Christian Faith* (New York, 1978) • D. Ritschl, *The Logic of Theology* (Philadelphia, 1987) • E. Schlink, *Ökumenische Dogmatik* (2d ed.; Göttingen, 1993) pt. 4 • D. Staniloae, *Orthodoxe Dogmatik* (vol. 1; Gütersloh, 1985) • T. F. Torrance, *The Christian Doctrine of God: One Being, Three Persons* (Edinburgh, 1996); idem, *God and Rationality* (London, 1971); idem, *Transformation and Convergence in the Frame of Knowledge* (Grand Rapids, 1984) • J. Werbick, *Bilder sind Wege. Eine Gotteslehre* (Munich, 1992) • N. Wolterstorff, *Divine Discourse* (Cambridge, 1995). See also the bibliography in "God Is Dead Theology" and "Trinity."

Dietrich Ritschl and Reinhold Bernhardt

God, Arguments for the Existence of

1. General
  1.1. Arguments, Proofs, and Basic Beliefs
  1.2. Essence and Existence
  1.3. Argument Forms
2. Logical Structures
  2.1. Ontological Arguments
  2.2. Axiological Arguments
  2.3. Epistemic Arguments
  2.4. Cosmological Arguments
  2.5. Teleological Argument
3. Assessment

1. General

1.1. Arguments, Proofs, and Basic Beliefs

William Clifford (1845-79) wrote that "it is wrong always, everywhere, and for anyone, to believe anything upon insufficient evidence" ("The Ethics of

Belief"). This evidentialist position reflects the view, common in the modern era after R. Descartes (1596-1650; → Cartesianism), that belief in God should be justified by arguments. This strong evidentialism contrasts somewhat with the prior Augustinian tradition (→ Augustine's Theology), which viewed the arguments for God's existence as arising from faith seeking understanding. → Anselm (1033-1109), for example, couches his argument in the context of a prayer to God, who is properly understood as the greatest conceivable being (*Pros.* 1). Traditionally, arguments for God's existence were treated deductively as proofs deriving from premises more readily knowable by us; thus → Thomas Aquinas (ca. 1225-74; → Thomism; Scholasticism) reasons deductively from effect to cause. He holds that such reasoning is proper and not contrary to faith, for although one cannot have both faith and demonstration concerning the same article of faith, the existence of God is a preamble to the articles of faith.

Within the last century theists like F. R. Tennant (1866-1957, *Philosophical Theology* [vol. 2; 1968]) and Richard Swinburne have placed greater emphasis on inductive or probabilistic reasoning on the grounds that not only are the deductive theistic proofs or arguments flawed but proofs are not required for everything we know. Indeed, proofs play a minor role in our intellectual life, for little is provable, and what is provable is often uninteresting. Other contemporary theists such as Alvin Plantinga have proceeded further, contending that we can be justified in believing in God's existence without arguments, that belief in God can be properly basic (Plantinga and N. Wolterstorff).

1.2. *Essence and Existence*

Anselm, Descartes (*Med.* 5), and others believe that when we truly understand God, we see that existence belongs necessarily to God's essence. Descartes argues that God has all perfections, and existence is a perfection. Aquinas contends that although God's being does not differ from God's essence, God's existence is not derivable merely from God's essence, since the self-evidence of this truth is not known to all (*Summa theol.* I, q. 2, art. 1). This feature differentiates the claim that God necessarily exists from necessarily true claims that are self-evident both in themselves and to us.

1.3. *Argument Forms*

Arguments for God's existence may be classified as either a priori or a posteriori, depending on whether the premises are deemed true prior to → experience or on the basis of experience. The most common form of the a priori argument is the onto-

logical argument, which commences from a claim about the nature of God (Anselm, Charles Hartshorne, Plantinga) or our conception of God's nature (Descartes). The axiological argument holds that because the moral law requires that the highest good be attainable, we must postulate (I. Kant; R. Adams, *The Virtue of Faith* [1987]) or infer (H. Rashdall, *The Theory of Good and Evil* [vol. 2; 1924; repr., 1971]; C. S. Lewis, *Mere Christianity* [1952; repr., 1997]) that God exists. Augustine's epistemic argument also falls in this category.

A posteriori arguments derive from Aristotle's (384-322 b.c.; → Aristotelianism) analysis of → causality (*Ph.* 2) and → metaphysics. According to the cosmological argument, whatever is moved must be moved by something already actual, and since the series of intermediate movers cannot continue to infinity, a logically first mover must exist (*Ph.* 7-8; *Metaph.* 12). The cosmological argument takes on a more temporal tone in the Islamic *kalam* argument (→ Islam 5), where the first cause is not merely logically but temporally prior. In the modern era the cosmological argument eventually loses a particularly Aristotelian causal frame while maintaining the emphasis that contingent beings, individually or in totality, must be grounded in a necessary being, appealing rather to versions of G. W. Leibniz's (1646-1716) principle of sufficient → reason (W. L. Rowe). The teleological argument (→ Teleology) is also traced back to Aristotle, who invokes the notion of a final cause, according to which all things act for an end, to account for how the unmoved mover moves everything else.

2. Logical Structures

The demise of → positivism and the verification theory in the second half of the 20th century gave rise to renewed interest in the theistic arguments. The criticisms advanced by D. Hume (1711-76) and Kant (1724-1804) were revisited, new forms of the arguments were developed employing modal logic (Plantinga, *Nature of Necessity,* x), and deductive forms of reasoning frequently were replaced by inductive reasoning.

2.1. *Ontological Arguments*

This argument form deduces the existence of God from certain concepts or an analysis of God's essence. Anselm's argument (*Pros.* 2-4) may be recast as follows:

Presuppositions:

(a) A being than which no greater can be thought is conceivable (i.e., it exists in the mind); we call this being *A*.

(b) A being than which no greater can be thought

can be thought of as existing (i.e., it exists in reality); we call this being *B*.

(c) If *A* and *B* are the same in every respect except that *B* actually exists and *A* does not, then *B* is greater than *A*.

Proof:

(1) Suppose *A* does not exist in reality (initial hypothesis).

(2) *B* is greater than *A*, given (c).

(3) But what is said in (2) contradicts (a); that is, the claim that *A* is a being than which none greater can be thought.

(4) Thus the hypothesis of (1) is false and must be rejected.

(5) *A* exists in reality.

Formally, as a reductio ad absurdum, this argument is valid. To reject the argument one must reject one of the presuppositions (→ Axioms). Gaunilo (11th cent.), for example, argued against (a) that such a being is inconceivable. For example, a highest number is inconceivable. Anselm replied that we can know enough about God to know that, at the very least, God must be the greatest conceivable being; more recent defenders argue that God must be conceived as exemplifying "necessarily a maximally perfect set of compossible great-making properties" (T. V. Morris, *Anselmian Explorations* [1987] 12). Objections to (c) are even stronger, for one may doubt that existence is a great-making property. Whereas Kant argued that existence is not a real predicate and hence adds nothing to the concept, Hartshorne, in discovering a so-called second Anselmian argument, contended that necessary existence is a great-making property (*Anselm's Discovery* [1991]), such that if God's necessary existence is possible, God necessarily exists. The soundness of the ontological argument clearly hinges on the status of existence and necessary existence as proper predicates, on distinguishing different kinds of existence, and on whether ultimately one can move from the conceptual to the ontological.

2.2. Axiological Arguments

Thomas Aquinas proposed an axiological argument based on the concept of maximums that cause the values in their respective genus. The best-known version, however, was produced by Kant, who, though he critiqued the traditional arguments, proposed an argument of his own. He contended that attainment of the highest good, which is virtue and happiness, is both necessary for us and unattainable because we cannot control nature to harmonize it with our ends. Hence, we must postulate a cause of all nature that is distinct from nature and is the ground for reconciling happiness with morality

(*Critique of Practical Reason*). Consequently, although God's existence cannot be the subject of proof, it can be postulated as a necessary prerequisite of an adequate conception of the moral law.

2.3. Epistemic Argument

In the context of showing the rationality of what one already accepts, → Augustine offered an interesting but little-regarded epistemic argument. The mind apprehends eternal → truths that are superior to it because they are unalterable by the mind, for we make judgments not about the truth but according to it. Truth is either ultimate, in which case truth is God, or there is something higher than truth, which is God (*De lib. arb.* 2.25).

2.4. Cosmological Arguments

This argument form is older than the ontological argument, being found in Plato (427-347 B.C.; → Platonism), Aristotle, and the → Islamic philosophers. The argument begins by invoking an alleged empirical fact about the universe (contingent beings exist; something is in motion; the universe began to exist) and proceeds to determine the cause or explanation of this fact. If the immediate cause is itself contingent, then another cause or explanation is sought. We must either postulate an infinite series of causes or assume that there is a first, noncontingent cause to the series. But since an infinite series of contingent causal conditions cannot provide an adequate explanation or sufficient reason, a first cause or necessary being must exist.

Two importantly different versions of this argument can be discerned. One, advanced by Thomas Aquinas (*Summa theol.* I, q. 2, art. 3), S. Clarke (1675-1729), F. Copleston (in J. Hick, *The Existence of God* [1985]), and R. Taylor (*Metaphysics* [4th ed.; 1992]), considers the explanatory causal conditions in terms of their logical, rather than their temporal, relation to the effect, so that the first cause to which the argument concludes is not necessarily a first cause in time but a sustaining cause — a necessary being on which all else depends for its continued existence. The other version, advanced by the Arabic philosophers al-Kindī (d. ca. 870) and al-Ghazālī (1058-1111) and by William Craig (*The Kalam Cosmological Argument*), argues for a first cause in time.

Swinburne has accused defenders of the first version of the completist fallacy. He holds that an explanation is provided once we derive the existence of the contingent thing from some relevant theory plus the existence of what is necessary for its existence (*The Existence of God*). Recent objections to the second form of the argument have rejected the causal principle, contending that it is possible that the universe can come into existence without a cause from a vacuum state. Kant rejected the cosmological argument for being grounded on the ontological argument. More fundamentally, he held that since the domain of human reason is limited, the idea of God cannot be a constitutive, but only a regulative, idea.

2.5. Teleological Arguments

Although both the teleological and cosmological arguments are causal arguments reasoning from effect to cause, the starting point of the latter is the ordered structure of the universe, not its mere existence. Because the universe contains evidences of means-ends ordering, it is believed to have an intelligent designer (→ Physicotheology). We find this reasoning in the Bible in the form of hymns in praise of the glories of the world (→ Doxology) that point to its Creator. Wisdom 13 (→ Apocrypha) contains a formally correct logical argument to which → Paul obviously alludes in Rom. 1:18-20.

The teleological argument has a long history of formulations that reflect the prevailing → worldviews of the time. Thomas Aquinas developed a deductive version utilizing Aristotle's notion of final causation. The demise of final causation prior to the → Enlightenment led to the reformulation of the argument by Hume (*Dialogues,* eventually to be rebutted) and William Paley (1743-1805) as an analogical argument. The means-ends ordering of the universe and its components approximates that of a watch; since the latter requires an intelligent maker, so does the former. Charles Darwin's proposal that natural selection provides an adequate, nonteleological explanation for means-ends ordering brought about the demise of the analogical versions of the argument in the 19th and 20th centuries.

Recently, however, the argument has been revived in post-Darwinian forms, such as the anthropic argument, whose defenders hold that the universe contains a vast complex of seemingly unrelated conditions, any of which have a very low antecedent probability. Had any of these initial conditions been different from what they were, there would be no observers of those conditions. Hence, the existence of such observers argues for a teleological account as the best explanation.

3. Assessment

Assessment of the theistic arguments can proceed on three fronts. The first evaluates the soundness or cogency of the individual arguments, taking account especially of their metaphysical framework. For example, Hume's critique both of the traditional view of causation and of the causal principle itself led to serious criticism of the a posteriori arguments framed in terms of causation (*Enquiry* 7-8).

The second approach evaluates the function of the arguments. Many theists contend that it is a mistake to base the belief that God exists simply on one argument; instead, the arguments function as part of a cumulative case that may be constructed for God's existence. This approach resembles reasoning in → science and → jurisprudence. Critics contend that conjoining unsound arguments cannot establish a true conclusion.

The third kind of assessment concerns whether the arguments are relevant to → religion. In particular, is the being to which the arguments conclude (necessary being, greatest conceivable being, intelligent being) to be identified with the God of religion? That these diverse concepts have the same referent is not immediately apparent; some sort of method of correlation must be invoked to determine which concept of God espoused by the various religions best correlates with that put forth by the philosophical arguments.

Bibliography: F. Bertoli and U. Curi, *The Conditions for the Existence of Mankind in the Universe* (Cambridge, 1991) • W. L. Craig, *The Cosmological Argument from Plato to Leibniz* (New York, 1980); idem, *The Kalam Cosmological Argument* (London, 1979) • S. T. Davis, *God, Reason, and Theistic Proofs* (Grand Rapids, 1997) • C. Hartshorne, *A Natural Theology for Our Time* (La Salle, Ill., 1967) • J. Hick and A. C. McGill, eds., *The Many Faced Argument* (New York, 1967) • A. Kenny, *The Five Ways* (New York, 1969) • M. Martin, *Atheism: A Philosophical Justification* (Philadelphia, 1990) • R. Messer, *Does God's Existence Need Proof?* (New York, 1993) • T. L. Miethe, "The Cosmological Argument: A Research Bibliography," *NSchol* 52 (1978) 285-305 • G. Oppy, *Ontological Arguments and Belief in God* (Cambridge, 1995) • H. P. Owen, *The Moral Argument for Christian Theism* (London, 1965) • A. Plantinga, *God, Freedom, and Evil* (New York, 1974); idem, *The Nature of Necessity* (Oxford, 1974) • A. Plantinga and N. Wolterstorff, eds., *Faith and Rationality* (Notre Dame, Ind., 1983) • R. Prevost, *Probability and Theistic Explanation* (Oxford, 1990) • B. R. Reichenbach, *The Cosmological Argument: A Reassessment* (Springfield, Ill., 1972) • J. M. Robson, ed., *Origin and Evolution of the Universe: Evidence for Design?* (Kingston, Ont., 1987) • W. L. Rowe, *The Cosmological Argument* (Princeton, 1975) • R. Swinburne, *The Existence of God* (Oxford, 1979) • M. Wynn, *God and Goodness: A Natural Theological Perspective* (London, 1999).

BRUCE R. REICHENBACH

God Is Dead Theology

David Hume's formulation and defense of empiricist nontheism in *Dialogues concerning Natural Religion* (1779) initiated the modern effort to write God's death certificate. Derived mostly from philosophical, sociological, political, scientific, and literary contexts, such writings have contributed significantly to the texture of the last 200 years of theological history. They have contained protests and refinements to doctrines of → God as Necessary Being, Transcendent → Mystery, and even "acting in history." In the two centuries following the → Enlightenment, God is not seen as Ultimacy or Ground of Being so much as a fascinating and inescapable *problem*. Theology as usually understood is rendered an obfuscating discipline or a tangle of incredible uncertainties or annoying evasions. The "God problem" looms large in the antitheological literary artistry of such writers as Thomas Carlyle, Matthew Arnold, Thomas Hardy, Edward Gibbon, and George Eliot; in eminent and persuasive philosophical luminaries such as Ludwig Feuerbach, Auguste Comte, and Friedrich → Nietzsche; and in political and psychological movements initiated by Karl → Marx, Sigmund Freud, and Thomas Huxley. It is obvious that the God-is-dead theology (or, perhaps more commonly, the "death-of-God movement") is a clear and influential theme in the history of modern religious and theological life and letters.

In sharp contrast to these remarkably creative 18th- and 19th-century affirmations of God's mortality has been the largely American death-of-God movement of the 1960s. Current critical responses to the few theologians who energized this short-lived and now largely forgotten protest insist that these theological diagnoses were largely overblown, sensationalized, and seriously mistaken. The prediction that → atheism and → naturalism would finally reign after the unsettling sixties has been proved either unlikely or clearly wrong. Instead of the divine death, what has come to pass — quite unexpectedly in light of the → cynicism of that decade, with its traumas of cold war and Vietnam War — has been a pluralistic rebirth of religion and the vitalizing of theological symbols, both traditional and popular.

The earliest published statement of what came to be a controversial and popular literature was *The Death of God* (1957), by Gabriel Vahanian. Hardly a theological manifesto, it was an iconoclastic cultural analysis claiming that God was no longer a factor or a presence that means anything in the spiritual dryness of modern life. Somewhat in the mode of Søren → Kierkegaard, Vahanian blamed facile and conventional religiosity for God's death as the Transcendent Other. This opening salvo was a widely read rejection of → theism as compatible with human → experience. What can be said to distinguish God as *Totaliter Aliter* from the experience that God is dead? Vahanian made his case energetically, though after the book appeared, he dissociated himself from like-minded writers because their efforts to define a godless faith turned into one more of the conventional idolatries he had rejected.

Vahanian's book was followed a few years later by *Honest to God* (1963), a widely discussed best-seller by the bishop of Woolwich, John A. T. Robinson. The best-known English work on the subject, it was a livelier version of work by Ronald Gregor Smith of Glasgow (e.g., *The Doctrine of God* [1970]), who affirmed the primacy of → secularization in a way similar to the later work of Harvey Cox. Robinson's book — an analysis and interpretation of Paul → Tillich, Rudolf Bultmann, and Dietrich → Bonhoeffer — offered a restatement of God in panentheistic and somewhat mystical terms that a secular culture, with its post-Enlightenment views of Ultimacy, might find congenial. These efforts of Vahanian and Robinson to reconstruct a critical nontheism for modernity and its "cultured despisers" endeavored to go beyond the dense doctrines of closed theological systems in favor of the clarity of the "ordinary language" of → analytic philosophy.

Paul van Buren's work *The Secular Meaning of the Gospel* (1963) continued what by then was the discernible momentum of this movement. Van Buren used the methods of logical → empiricism to correct traditional God-language that could not meet the standards of verifiability required by analytic philosophy. Van Buren, as well as other like-minded sympathizers with British empiricism, was vigorously responded to by Langdon Gilkey in *Naming the Whirlwind* (1969). (In his later work van Buren turned to other issues, notably the relation of → Judaism to Christianity, which brought him back more closely to Karl → Barth, his original teacher.)

Thomas Altizer, another contributor to the death-of-God movement, proposed an even more radical view in his *Gospel of Christian Atheism* (1966). According to his theory (as in classical → Buddhism), what is ultimate is what is discovered only in the fullness and passion of human life. In that passion, the very act of denying God actualizes the liberation of human beings.

William Hamilton, trained in theology and ethics by Paul Tillich and Reinhold → Niebuhr, held that the need for a modern atheism is inspired by the great creativeness of classical literature. Through a kind of Nietzschean hermeneutics of protest, Hamilton argued that the genius of the art of great literature affirmed and inspired human (and humane) greatness throughout all history. In his "Orestean theology," religious mythology was stood on its head so that an all-too-human world in all its squalor and meanness would define the great divine absence, which was to be filled by the purpose and order of humanity itself.

Richard Rubenstein in *After Auschwitz* (1966) defended an essential pessimism that construes the → Holocaust as the paradigmatic event requiring a thoroughly tragic vision of human life without God. How can God's death not be acknowledged "after Auschwitz" — and, by extension, after all the unspeakable evil in the post-Holocaust world?

By the middle of the 1960s, when this protest movement was being popularly debated, Harvey Cox published *The Secular City* (1965), refined in 1970 in a notable article in *Playboy* magazine. A scholar who derived his views both from constructive interpretations of classical biblical motifs and the history of theology and philosophy rather than from the vigors of atheistic protest, Cox relied on an interpretation of Dietrich Bonhoeffer and Friedrich Gogarten and their conviction that reliance on the secular is a sign of humanity's having "come of age." Secularization was in; it was not, however, religion's enemy. The modern locus of theological vision was seen to be immediate and empirical. The essential model and symbol was the → city, whether polis, town, or metropolis — or, by extension, this world (i.e., cosmo*polis*). Such symbolizing contained a modern understanding of the human and the divine, because the human is the unique *Homo symbolicus*, or "the man at the giant switchboard" capable of denoting and naming. For Cox, Bonhoeffer was accurate in his claim that God is not a problematic concept vulnerable to denial. God is, for Cox, the name that is mysterious, beyond speech, meaning absolutely nothing. Moderns will say that God is the name that indicates the omnipresence that vitalizes such an omnipresence as urban civilization itself. Cox's view was not atheistic or nontheistic; it was an effort at describing the secular model as an alternative to theological and metaphysical idolatries.

This recent and modest movement of religious and theological radical criticism, briefly energized by a company of American theologians, is at best a pale reflection of creative modern atheistic thought. It will be remembered as one of the many features of a turbulent decade that decried transcendence and ultimate mystery as well as the traditions that carried them. By attempting to name new symbols and

fresh religious attitudes, it tried to define and actualize the denouement of modern theology — specifically, deicide.

Bibliography: T. J. J. ALTIZER, *The Gospel of Christian Atheism* (Philadelphia, 1966) • T. J. J. ALTIZER and W. HAMILTON, *Radical Theology and the Death of God* (Indianapolis, 1966) • J. BOWDEN, ed., *Thirty Years of Honesty: Honest to God Then and Now* (London, 1993) • P. M. VAN BUREN, *The Secular Meaning of the Gospel: Based on an Analysis of Its Language* (New York, 1963) • H. COX, *The Secular City: Secularization and Urbanization in Theological Perspective* (New York, 1965) • L. GILKEY, *Naming the Whirlwind: The Renewal of God-Language* (Indianapolis, 1969) • W. HAMILTON, *The New Essence of Christianity* (New York, 1961) • J. A. T. ROBINSON, *Honest to God* (Philadelphia, 1963) • R. RUBENSTEIN, *After Auschwitz: Radical Theology and Contemporary Judaism* (Indianapolis, 1966) • G. VAHANIAN, *The Death of God* (New York, 1957; 4th ed., 1961) • A. N. WILSON, *God's Funeral* (New York, 1999).

RALPH HJELM

Godparent

1. Historical Development
2. Suggested Reinterpretation

1. Historical Development

Research into the ecclesial role of godparents has revealed many different legal, social, liturgical, pastoral, and educational dimensions of the practice. Little, however, has as yet been done regarding many sociological and popular religious aspects (→ Piety: Social History). Borrowing from non-Christian practice, the church used godparents (Lat. *sponsor, patrinus,* Ger. *Vadder,* It. *padrino,* Sp. *compadre*) as early as the second century to vouch for adults in baptism and to be responsible companions for them in their catechumenate (→ Catechesis). The parents of those baptized had primary responsibility, but with the rise of infant → baptism, godparents assumed the task of asking for baptism on the children's behalf, in their stead promising renunciation of sin and making → confession of faith. In the Middle Ages a demand for more responsible Christian nurture resulted in both the establishment of a spiritual relationship between godparents and children and the exclusion of parents from the office. In the eighth century an examination of godparents was initiated, focusing on their knowledge of basic Christian texts in order to establish at least minimal fitness for their responsibilities.

The Reformation churches took over essential parts of earlier practice. In particular, the baptismal theology of Martin → Luther gave godparents the responsibility of acting as aides at baptism who would offer special prayers for the candidates. The → Reformation strengthened civil and familial piety and, in the process, enhanced the social tasks of godparents. Subsequent criticism of the practice often overlooks the important practical functions taken up by godparents in the traditional social structures of village and rural life (e.g., helping materially, contributing to education and nurture, becoming adoptive parents) where they helped to create for children an → identity independent of that of the biological parents.

Godparents still have important functions in the countries of southern Europe and Latin America where the influence of Roman Catholic and Orthodox churches has been strong (M. E. Kenna, J. Pitt-Rivers, H. V. C. Harris). A progressive loss of teaching functions can be judged only in the context of broader developments. Relevant in this regard are the loss of many people to the churches (→ Secularism), the tendency to make religion a private family affair, and the development of more specialized and institutionalized forms of religious education (→ Confirmation; Religious Education). The role of godparents in → Third World churches depends largely on the traditions of the earlier mission churches as well as local social structures.

Protestant churches generally regulate the practice of baptismal sponsorship by their understanding of the rite itself. The special responsibility assumed by godparents for prayer, assistance, and Christian upbringing is derived from the basic responsibility of the whole → congregation. Sponsorship as such normally ends with confirmation. In most cases the practice of accepting godparents from other churches is accepted. Some churches record the names of godparents in a baptismal register, not allowing later deletions or additions. Under certain circumstances baptism without godparents is allowed.

In the Roman Catholic Church rules regarding godparents are more comprehensive (1983 CIC, 762-69), although there is a growing tendency to allow variations (K. Baumgartner). Reform of the practice on the basis of church discipline has been rejected on theological grounds (M. Metzger).

2. Suggested Reinterpretation

Two main concerns have guided attempts in the Protestant world at reform of the practice of baptismal sponsorship by godparents: (1) a concern to strengthen congregational involvement in sponsorship, though without neglecting irrevocable family responsibilities; and, (2) a desire for a fresh integration of liturgical, pastoral, and pedagogic functions. With the relative diminution of the role of parents, such reappraisal began in relation to the liturgical dimensions of the baptismal rite.

In the process of relating the → occasional services of the church to the human life cycle, the participation of godparents in the baptismal catechumenate, a practice extending over all of life and spanning the generations, seems to make good sense. This catechumenate begins at baptism and then relates lessons regarding Christian faith to the actual life experiences of the baptized persons and their parents. Only thus can a foundation be laid for a later relation with the baptized that will allow godparents to play a continuing role that fosters trust without ceasing to be critical.

The relativizing of parental authority by dedication of the child to God, which baptism symbolizes, is given a social dimension in this view of sponsorship. The actualization of this understanding depends on how successful the congregation is in freeing the selection of godparents from purely family considerations. The education of the entire congregation is, in this context, necessary — not only in traditional ways such as baptismal services, classes regarding baptism, or in communications to godparents, but at all occasions of worship and all occasions for the education of children and adults (→ Continuing Education).

→ Initiation Rites

Bibliography: G. ANDERSON, "Il Comparragio: The Italian God-Parenthood Complex," *SWJA* 13 (1957) 32-53 • K. BAUMGARTNER, "Neue Wege des Taufpastoral," in *Glauben lernen, Leben lernen* (ed. K. Baumgartner et al.; St. Ottilien, 1985) 439-71 • H. V. C. HARRIS, "Human Sexuality as a Religious Phenomenon" (Diss., Lancaster, 1982) • H.-G. HEIMBROCK, "Taufpaten," *Handbuch Religiöser Erziehung* (ed. W. Böcker, H.-G. Heimbrock, and E. Kerkhoff; Düsseldorf, 1986) 82-92 • M. E. JOHNSON, ed., *Living Water, Sealing Spirit: Readings on Christian Initiation* (Collegeville, Minn., 1995) • B. JUSSEN, *Patenschaft und Adoption im frühen Mittelalter* (Göttingen, 1991) • M. E. KENNA, "The Idiom of Family," in *Mediterranean Family Structures* (ed. J. G. Peristiany; Cambridge, 1976) 347-62 • G. W. LATHROP, *Holy People: A Liturgical Ecclesiology* (Minneapolis, 1999); idem, *Holy Things: A Liturgical Theology* (Minneapolis, 1993) • J. H. LYNCH, *Godparents and Kinship in Early Medieval Europe* (Princeton, 1986) • M. METZGER, *Die Amtshandlungen der Kirche* (vol. 1;

2d ed.; Munich, 1963) • J. Pitt-Rivers, "Ritual Kinship in the Mediterranean: Spain and Balkans," in Peristiany, *Mediterranean Family Structures*, 317-34 • S. A. Stauffer, ed., *Baptism, Rites of Passage, and Culture* (Geneva, 1999).

HANS-GÜNTER HEIMBROCK

Golden Age

In his epic poem *Works and Days* (lines 109-201), the Greek poet Hesiod (fl. ca. 800 B.C.) tells the story of a golden age in which humans lived like gods with no cares, illnesses, or wickedness. This period was followed by successive declines into the silver age and then the bronze. A heroic age arrested the decline but was followed finally by the iron age, which was full of plague and evil.

To the ancient idea of an ideal primitive age there correspond the myths in different cultures concerning an ideal place, → paradise (an Iranian word), a garden (Eden, see Gen. 2:4–3:24), the mountain of God (see Ezek. 28:11-19), the island of the blessed, the Elysian fields, and, in Greek comedy and fairy tales, lotusland and other places. Often these places are present not merely at the beginning of the world but, as something perfect, coexisting with our imperfect time and world in a sphere beyond, as in Jewish and Islamic piety and doctrine. Later Jewish and Christian piety has this notion, though with no biblical support.

Theologically important questions are whether Hesiod's vision of decay, which strongly influenced Greek and Roman literature, indicated a pessimistic view of history typical of antiquity, and whether the OT and later Christian → hope of the → kingdom of God contradicts the Greek and Roman understanding, as is often maintained. It is striking that the OT and NT seldom refer back to Genesis 2 or to a happy primal age. Instead, they contain many promises of → peace, divine justice, and a new → heaven and new earth. The Greeks and Romans, though, also had a concept of → progress and perhaps of a golden age in the → future, mentioned, for example, in the Fourth Eclogue of Virgil (70-19 B.C.). Nor was the Christian view of history wholly oriented to the future, especially as it extolled Jesus Christ as the fulfillment and center of time (O. Cullmann; → Time and Eternity).

→ Paul also spoke about aeons, and later Christian doctrine about *saecula* (generations, ages). In accordance with early church concepts of → salvation history, Joachim of Fiore (ca. 1135-1202) divided the ages into three (→ Millenarianism). There have always been divisions and end-time calculations of this kind, especially to some extent under the influence of → apocalyptic.

→ Historiography; Philosophy of History; Theology of History; Worldview

Bibliography: O. CULLMANN, *Christ and Time* (New York, 1977; orig. pub., 1946) • K. LÖWITH, *Meaning in History* (Chicago, 1964) • E. ROHDE, *Psyche, Seelencult und Unsterblichkeitsglaube der Griechen* (vol. 1; 1893; 10th ed., 1925) • H. STRACK and P. BILLERBECK, Str-B IV/2, 1016-1165 • C. WESTERMANN, *Genesis 1–11* (Minneapolis, 1994) excursus "Eden."

DIETRICH RITSCHL

Golden Rule

The "Golden Rule" (a phrase not used before the 16th cent.) identifies the principle formulated in Matt. 7:12a and its parallel Luke 6:31, with either positive or negative parallels also among the Greeks (though hardly in philosophical → ethics), the Romans, and the Jews (from the Hellenistic period), as well as in China, India, and elsewhere. It rests on the insight that life in society demands regulated giving and receiving, acting and reacting. It is thus a formal statement of what is generally demanded by way of social conduct, with no attempt to state the related values. It is a kind of universal ethical rule that is not specifically Christian. It may be used in very different ways, even opportunistically and subjectively.

With the Golden Rule, Luke 6:31 universalizes love of → enemies. It thus has in view how to behave in → conflicts. When fellowship is disrupted, it must be restored unilaterally. It is hoped that, because both opponents are human, they will respond to one another.

According to Matt. 7:12 the Golden Rule sums up the → law expounded in the → Sermon on the Mount (see 5:17-20); it functions analogously for the Jews and the Greeks. It is thus a form of the command to love one's neighbor "as yourself" (Matt. 22:34-40).

Matthew and Luke were both using → Q (→ Synoptics); Luke is perhaps closer to the original and possibly to → Jesus. Both have been very influential, among other things as a bridge between Christian and non-Christian ethics.

Bibliography: W. D. DAVIES and D. C. ALLISON, *The Gospel according to St. Matthew* (vol. 1; Edinburgh, 1988) • A. DIHLE, "Goldene Regel," *RAC* 11.930-40;

idem, *Die Goldene Regel* (Göttingen, 1962) • H.-P. MATHYS, R. HEILIGENTHAL, and H.-H. SCHREY, "Goldene Regel," *TRE* 13.570-83.

CHRISTOPH BURCHARD

Good, The

1. Definition and Terminology
2. The Good in the History of Philosophy
3. The Good in the Philosophy of Religion

1. Definition and Terminology

The good (Gk. *agathon,* Lat. *bonum*) is that which contributes to the perfection of something or constitutes it. Distinction is made between the absolute good and the relative good. The former involves the actualizing of every innate possibility of perfection (Gk. *entelecheia,* Lat. *bonum honestum*). The latter, along the lines of utility *(bonum utile)* or satisfaction *(bonum delectabile),* contributes to the fulfillment of another and produces a hierarchy of goods, at the head of which is the supreme good *(summum bonum).*

2. The Good in the History of Philosophy

For Plato (427-347 B.C.) it was only in the light of the "idea of the good" *(idea tou agathou)* that the ideas acquire their real being as a being-known (*Resp.* 503E-509D; → Platonism). Aristotle (384-322) defined the good as "that for which everything strives"; among human beings it is → happiness *(eudaimonia),* which is achieved in philosophical → contemplation (*Eth. Nic.* 1094a-1103a, 1176a-1179a; → Aristotelianism). With his → hedonism Epicurus (341-270) linked the good to desire *(hēdonē).* For Augustine (354-430) God was the supreme good, and since all creatures have a share in his goodness, → evil could be seen only as a diminution of good (*De nat. boni;* → Augustine's Theology). On this basis → Scholasticism distinguished between God as *bonum per essentiam* and the creation as *bonum per participationem,* this participation being the basis of the doctrine of transcendentals (Thomas Aquinas *Summa theol.* I, q. 1, arts. 3-4).

In the modern period the ontological and theological understanding of the good has given way to an ethical understanding. The → utilitarianism of T. Hobbes (1588-1679) defined the good as that which satisfies needs according to particular place, time, and person. I. Kant (1724-1804) rejected a material definition in terms of an ethics of → values and proposed the → "categorical imperative" as a formal interpretation of the good (→ Kantianism). Action according to this imperative makes us worthy of happiness as the supreme good but does not achieve happiness as the consummated good. For G. W. F. Hegel (1770-1831) Kant's formalism was not enough, and he gave it concrete content in the → institutions of morality (i.e., → family, → society, and the → state; → Hegelianism). F. Nietzsche (1844-1900) argued that the superman must replace the notion of the good by the law of might. G. E. Moore (1873-1958) understood the good as an indefinable "simple notion" (→ Analytic Philosophy). From the nonverifiability of the concept A. J. Ayer (1910-89) concluded that it was meaningless, but R. M. Hare (b. 1919) thought that it might find meaningful use in value judgments (→ Analytic Ethics).

3. The Good in the Philosophy of Religion

The moral good (in the sense of Kant's ethics of → motive) never replaces the ontological good (as perfection of being) because action under the sign of the good is always implicated in → guilt and is helpless when confronted by → death. The final inability of the good to solve the question of the → meaning of human existence can be overcome only on the level of → faith.

Bibliography: A. C. EWING, *The Definition of the Good* (New York, 1947) • E. FARLEY, *Good and Evil: Interpreting the Human Condition* (Minneapolis, 1990) • R. M. HARE, *The Language of Morals* (Oxford, 1952) • G. W. F. HEGEL, *Elements of the Philosophy of Right* (Cambridge, 1991; orig. pub., 1821) §§129ff. • I. KANT, *Critique of Practical Reason* (trans. M. Gregor; New York, 1997; orig. pub., 1788) A54ff. and A198ff. • M. E. MARTY, *The One and the Many: America's Struggle for the Common Good* (Cambridge, Mass., 1997) • G. E. MOORE, *Principia ethica* (Cambridge, 1903) • F. NIETZSCHE, *Beyond Good and Evil* (New York, 1974; orig. pub., 1886) • W. NIKOLAUS, "Ist Religionsphilosophie möglich?" *WJP* 16 (1984) 61-80 • W. W. POWELL and E. S. CLEMENS, *Private Action and the Common Good* (New Haven, 1998) • J. G. STACKHOUSE, *Can God Be Trusted? Faith and the Challenge of Evil* (New York, 1998) • C. SWEIG and S. WOLF, *Romancing the Shadow: Illuminating the Dark Side of the Soul* (New York, 1997).

WOLFGANG NIKOLAUS

Gospel

1. Biblical

1.1. *Greek Usage*

The word "gospel" is a translation of Gk. *euangelion*. Often found in the plural and attested from Homer, this word means "that which is proper to an *euangelos,* or messenger of good news." The verb *euangelizomai* (mid. and pass.) means "speak as an *euangelos*," that is, "bring (good) news."

The verb and noun have religious significance in the Greco-Roman world only in the emperor cult, in which *ta euangelia* is used for the good news of the birth or benevolence of the emperor. This usage has only background importance; it is not the source of the NT vocabulary of proclamation, which goes back to → Jesus, to early Judaism, and to the OT.

1.2. *OT and LXX*

The OT uses the verb *bśr* (Pi. and Hithp.) in the sense "spread (good) news" (e.g., Ps. 40:10 [40:9]; Isa. 60:6). The related noun *bĕśōrâ* means "(good) news" (e.g., 2 Sam. 18:27; 2 Kgs. 7:9) or "reward for (good) news" (e.g., 2 Sam. 4:10).

In Deutero-Isaiah (and Ps. 96:2) the verb can also relate to news of the dawn of God's rule. The messenger of good news (*mĕbaśśēr,* Nah. 1:15) proclaims to → Israel (and the world) the coming of God (Isa. 40:9; 52:7). The one who bears this message that promises liberation to the poor is, according to Trito-Isaiah (Isa. 61:1-4), anointed by the Spirit (i.e., is a → prophet). The noun *bĕśōrâ,* however, is not yet used in a specific sense in the Hebrew OT.

The LXX makes no actual use of *euangelion.* Yet the use of the *euangel-* stem for the Hebrew root *bśr* alerts Greek readers to the fact that messages of salvation are at issue (e.g., Ps. 95:2 [96:2]; Isa. 40:9; 52:7; 61:1).

1.3. *Early Judaism*

In early Jewish and rabbinic sources *bśr* and *bĕśōrâ* occur along with other words for "proclaim" (e.g., *šm'* Hiph.) and "message" (e.g., *šĕmû'â*). Especially in the older and later Targums, *bĕśōrâ* is used for the message of the prophets, whether good or threatening. The early text of *Tg. Isa.* 53:1 also has *bĕśōrâ* rather than *šĕmû'â.* We now find a specific use of *bĕśōrâ,* which helps us to understand NT examples like Rev. 14:6 and Mark 1:15.

Early Judaism offers an interpretation of Isa. 52:7 (Nah. 1:15) and 61:1. From Qumran, 1QH 23:14 refers Isa. 61:1 to the message of the "teacher of righteousness," 4QMessApoc 12 refers it to the message of God's salvation, and 11QMelch 2:15-25 refers both verses to Melchizedek as a heavenly deliverer. In the → rabbis the *mĕbaśśēr* of Isa. 52:7 is God himself (as also Acts 10:36) or Elijah as the precursor of the Messiah or the Messiah (→ Messianism) or (as in Rom. 10:15) one of the many evangelists in the end time (see *Midr. Ps.* on 147:1 §2; see also Joel 3:5 LXX [2:32]). Isa. 61:1 is understood messianically.

1.4. *Jesus*

How Jesus understood and described his message may be seen from the → Q traditions in Luke 7:18-23 and parallel; 16:16 and parallel; Mark 1:14-15; 8:35; 10:39; 14:9. Viewed with "critical sympathy" (W. G. Kümmel), the sources invite the following reconstruction. Jesus worked as a messianic evangelist to the poor (cf. Luke 4:16-21; 6:20-26; 7:18-23 and par. with Isa. 61:1-4); we catch echoes of Isa. 52:7 and *Targ. Isa.* 53:1 in Mark 1:14-15. Whether the message was called *bĕśōrâ* (Aram. *bĕśōrtâ*) before → Easter, though quite possible in view of the traditional wording of Mark 1:15, must be left open because of the influence of early missionary vocabulary on Mark 1:14, 8:25, 10:39, and 14:9. The Matthean expression "good news of the kingdom" (Matt. 4:23; 9:35; 24:14) is a good historical characterization of the proclamation of Jesus.

From time to time Jesus sent out his → disciples "to proclaim the → kingdom of God" (Luke 9:1-6 and par.). The message, though, was firmly linked to Jesus' person and work (cf. Luke 16:16 with 11:20; 17:21). His work culminated in his vicarious self-offering (Mark 10:45 and par.; 14:22-25 and par.).

1.5. *Primitive Community*

Following the mission command of the Resurrected (Matt. 28:18-20), the → apostles after → Pentecost preached that God had elevated Jesus as both "Lord and Messiah" (Acts 2:36; 5:42). Jesus' message of God's rule thus became the gospel of Jesus Christ (→ Christology). The translation of the root *bśr* by *euangelizomai/euangelion* followed in → Jerusalem with the → mission to Greek-speaking Jews.

Acts 10:36-43 and Mark 14:9 and parallels show that in this mission the story of Jesus was told as the gospel (of God). Early formulas like those in 1 Cor. 15:3-5 helped to preserve the recollection of the heart of the gospel — namely, the death and resurrection of Jesus "for our sins." This tradition came to Paul.

1.6. Paul

Called to be an apostle instead of a persecutor (Gal. 1:15-16), → Paul stands or falls with the proclamation of the gospel. The word occurs in his universally accepted epistles 48 times. The "gospel of God" (1 Thess. 2:2, 8; Rom. 1:1), as Christ's commanding word, is for Paul a salvific power (Rom. 1:16), to which he owes → obedience (1 Cor. 9:16).

According to his calling, the gospel is for Paul (1) *the preaching of Christ.* God caused the true knowledge of Christ to shine upon him outside Damascus (2 Cor. 4:6; 5:16), and from that time on, Paul proclaimed the Crucified as the power and wisdom of God (1 Cor. 1:23-24, 30; 2:2).

The gospel is then (2) *the word of reconciliation* (2 Cor. 5:17-21), surpassing the → law. The revelation of Christ put an end to Paul's zeal for the law (Gal. 1:13-14) and set him in the service of Christ. He thus preached Christ as "the end of the law . . . for everyone who believes" (Rom. 10:4). "His gospel" (1 Thess. 1:5; Gal. 1:11; Rom. 2:16) stands in eschatological contrast to the law.

The gospel is also (3) *the message of justification.* Taken up into service by Christ even as a sinner (1 Cor. 15:8-10), Paul found in the atoning death of Christ the basis of → justification of the sinner by faith alone, without the works of the law. This justification stood at the heart of the gospel (Phil. 3:7-10; Rom. 3:21-30). Thus Paul could proclaim "the message about the cross" (1 Cor. 1:18) as the gospel of the righteousness of God in Christ (Rom. 1:16-17).

Because of this gospel, Paul was an "apostle to the Gentiles" for the sake of Israel (Rom. 11:13-15) and was involved in controversies all his life (Gal. 2:11-14; 2 Cor. 11:24-28; Romans). Since the gospel was inalienable for him, he could not preach "another Jesus" (Gal. 1:6-9; 2 Cor. 11:4), nor could he tolerate a deemphasis of Christ's authority as judge (Rom. 2:16).

For Paul the gospel was an oral word of promise still concealed from unbelievers (1 Cor. 2:6-16; 2 Cor. 4:3-4). Its origin lay in God's → promise in the OT (Rom. 1:1-2); its goal was the parousia of Christ and the salvation of "all Israel," which would follow the mission to the → Gentiles (Rom. 11:25-31; 15:16).

1.7. Post-Pauline Witnesses

For Paul's school (Colossians, Ephesians, 2 Thessalonians, 1-2 Timothy, and Titus), the legacy of Paul is normative. As in Rom. 16:25-26, the gospel reveals the "mystery" of God's saving plan in Christ (Eph. 1:9-14; 6:19), and it is thus the mighty "word of (the) truth" (Eph. 1:13; Col. 1:5) that promises deliverance.

The → Pastoral Epistles also emphasize that the gospel handed down by Paul is a trust and must be kept unfalsified in the face of → Gnostic error (1 Tim. 6:20-21; see also 2 Tim. 1:14; 2:8-14, etc.). Here, as in 1 Cor. 15:1-4 and Rom. 6:17-18, the gospel is the doctrinal tradition.

In 1 Peter also, the gospel is the word of God that abides for ever (1:23-25). Those who do not believe it will fall under the judgment of death (4:17). In Revelation we find an older Jewish-Christian use. The "eternal gospel" (14:6) is the message of imminent divine judgment (→ Last Judgment).

1.8. Synoptics

On the basis of the → Midrash pattern in Acts 10:36-43 (G. N. Stanton), (John) Mark (mentioned in Acts 12:12; 1 Pet. 5:13) shortly before A.D. 70 combined the passion story with the essential Petrine → tradition (→ Peter) to form the first written Gospel. According to the heading in 1:1 and the summary in 1:14-15, the message and history of Jesus are the origin and normative content of the gospel, which is to be universally proclaimed (13:10). Mark 8:35, 10:39, and 14:9 confirm this program.

Following Mark, Matthew emphasizes that Jesus preached the "good news of the kingdom" (Matt. 4:23; 9:35; 24:14). In Matt. 24:14 and 26:13 "this good news" refers to the Gospel of Matthew itself. Luke in his Gospel uses only the verb *euangelizomai* for the message of the angels (1:19; 2:10), John the Baptist (3:18), and Jesus (4:18; 7:22, etc.). In Acts it denotes missionary proclamation (5:42; 8:4, 12, etc.), and *euangelion* is used for the preaching of Peter and Paul (15:7; 20:24). The absence of the stem *euangel-* from John and the Johannine Epistles points to an independent tradition.

The titles and colophons added to the Gospels already in the first century were meant to distinguish them in the congregational archives and to give indication of the contents when they were read (e.g., see Mark 13:14). "The gospel according to . . ." does not simply identify the author but has the force of "the one (revealed) gospel according to the witness of . . ." (M. Hengel).

1.9. *Luther*

Luther felicitously summed up the biblical meaning of "gospel" when he said that it "signifies nothing else than a sermon or report concerning the grace and mercy of God merited and acquired through the Lord Jesus Christ with his death. . . . [It] is not what one finds in books and what is written in letters of the alphabet; it is rather an oral sermon and a living Word, a voice that resounds throughout the world and is proclaimed publicly, so that one hears it everywhere" (*LW* 30.3).   PETER STUHLMACHER

2. Dogmatic

2.1. *Concept*

The term *euangelion* was taken over from secular speech, in which it was used, for example, for bringing news of a victory. It acquired a religious nuance in the emperor cult, in which good news focused on the ruler as a divine person. NT usage (see 1) is based primarily on the OT and early Jewish understanding of the messenger of joy (Matt. 11:5; Rom. 10:15). The term is rare in the → Synoptics. Yet in Mark 1:14-15 and par., the whole work of Jesus is set under this guiding motif. The one who brings the message of eschatological salvation is identical with the coming of divine → salvation. Whether → Jesus himself used the concept cannot be decided from the sources. In → Paul, to proclaim (*euangelizomai*, 1 Cor. 1:17) the eschatological message of the coming of Christ is part of the office of the → apostle. Paul's vocabulary gave the concept its normative use. In the apostolic tradition "gospel" became a technical term embracing the proclamation of Jesus, his person as the one proclaimed, and his destiny of → cross and → resurrection as God's eschatological act of salvation.

2.2. *Genre*

In the second century the term "gospel" came to be used for an authentically Christian literary genre in which the sayings of Jesus and accounts of his life and work were presented as the result of bringing together and editing original fragments, both oral and written. In this sense the word can be used in the plural, and in the first Christian generations there were evidently many gospels (note the Gospels of Thomas and Philip, discovered in 1945). In his → canon Marcion (d. ca. 160; → Marcionites) accepted only the Gospel of Luke, but in opposition to → Gnosis and → Montanism the → early church fixed on the Gospels *kata* (according to) Matthew, Mark, Luke, and John. Matthew was viewed as particularly authentic in light of the incident and words recorded in Matt. 9:9-13.

2.3. *Controversies*

A mutual tension and ordering of → law and gospel is latent already in the Pauline writings (Gal. 4:8-31). Marcion made of this tension a radical antithesis, which the → church fathers tried in different ways to relieve. Along the same lines → Thomas Aquinas (ca. 1225-74) followed → Augustine in referring to the *nova lex evangelii* (*Summa theol.* I of II, q. 106, arts. 1-2). The Council of → Trent (1545-63), in opposition to the → Reformation, did not make the problem an independent theme. All the more plainly Vatican II (1962-65) made the decisive statement that the gospel "always offers itself as a leaven with regard to brotherhood, → unity, and peace" (*Ad gentes* 8).

The centrality of the problem goes back to the Reformers' doctrine of → justification. In M. → Luther's theology the gospel is, next to the law, God's other word, his promise, in which all → grace, → righteousness, → peace, and freedom are vouchsafed to believers in Christ (WA 7.24). Penitence flees from the commands, faith flees to the promise, and hence through faith we are justified by the divine words (WA 7.34). There are detailed debates within Protestant theology, especially regarding the third use of the law (i.e., the command for Christians, who are under the gospel).

2.4. *Ethical and Political Aspects*

The problem assumed an ethical and political dimension in Luther's controversy with the left wing of the Reformation. New inquiry into the social relevance of the gospel came with the "social question" of the 19th century. Not just religious socialists (→ Religious Socialism) like A. Stoekker, C. F. Blumhardt, L. Ragaz, and H. Kutter put this question, but A. von Harnack (1851-1930) could also say that the gospel is a social message — that is, the proclamation of solidarity and brotherhood on behalf of the poor (see his *What Is Christianity?*).

The controversy reached a climax in the debate between K. → Barth (1886-1968) and neo-Lutheranism (→ Lutheranism) when he reversed the formula "law and gospel," arguing that the law is nothing other than the necessary form of the gospel, whose content is grace. This thesis had dogmatic and ethicopolitical implications that emerged in theses 1 and 2 of the → Barmen Declaration. The ethicopolitical aspect may also be seen in the contextual → liberation theology of the → Third World.

Always a central issue is the problem of the scope of the Protestant freedom of Christians (Luther) in relation to the world, which tendentiously claims autonomy for itself (F. Naumann).

Bibliography: Biblical materials: C. H. DODD, *Gospel and Law: The Relation of Faith and Ethics in Early Christian-*

ity (New York, 1951) • H. Frankemölle, *Evangelium. Begriff und Gattung. Ein Forschungsbericht* (Stuttgart, 1988) • G. Friedrich, "Εὐαγγελίζομαι κτλ.," *TDNT* 2.707-37 • M. Hengel, *Die Evangelienüberschriften* (Heidelberg, 1984); idem, *Studies in the Gospel of Mark* (London, 1985) • W. H. Kelber, *The Oral and the Written Gospel* (Philadelphia, 1983) • H. Koester, *Ancient Christian Gospels: Their History and Development* (London, 1990) • J. H. Reumann, *Righteousness in the NT* (Philadelphia, 1982) • J. Schniewind, *Die Begriffe Wort und Evangelium bei Paulus* (Bonn, 1910); idem, *Evangelion. Ursprung und erste Gestalt des Begriffs Evangelium* (2 vols.; Gütersloh, 1927-31) • G. N. Stanton, *Jesus of Nazareth in NT Preaching* (Cambridge, 1974) 70ff. • G. Strecker, "Εὐαγγέλιον," *EDNT* 2.70-74 • P. Stuhlmacher, *Gerechtigkeit Gottes bei Paulus* (2d ed.; Göttingen, 1966); idem, *Das paulinische Evangelium* (vol. 1; Göttingen, 1968); idem, *Reconciliation, Law, Righteousness: Essays in Biblical Theology* (Philadelphia, 1986); idem, ed., *The Gospel and the Gospels* (Grand Rapids, 1991).

Martin Luther's theology: G. Ebeling, *Luther: An Introduction to His Thought* (Philadelphia, 1960) • B. Lohse, *Martin Luther's Theology: Its Historical and Systematic Development* (Minneapolis, 1999) • G. Rupp, *The Righteousness of God: Luther Studies* (London, 1953) • P. S. Watson, *Let God Be God! An Interpretation of the Theology of Martin Luther* (London, 1947).

Dogmatic questions: P. Althaus, *The Divine Command* (Philadelphia, 1966) • K. Barth, "Gospel and Law," *God, Grace, and Gospel* (Garden City, N.Y., 1960) • R. Bultmann, "Christ the End of the Law" (1940), *Essays: Philosophical and Theological* (London, 1955) 36-66 • G. Ebeling, *Dogmatik des christlichen Glaubens* (vols. 2-3; Tübingen, 1979); idem, "On the Doctrine of the *Triplex usus legis* in the Theology of the Reformation" and "Reflexions on the Doctrine of the Law," *Word and Faith* (London, 1963) 62-78, 247-81 • W. Elert, *Law and Gospel* (Philadelphia, 1967) • W. van Gemeren, *The Law, the Gospel, and the Modern Christian: Five Views* (Grand Rapids, 1993) • F. Gogarten, *Der Mensch zwischen Gott und Welt* (Stuttgart, 1956) • A. von Harnack, *What Is Christianity?* (New York, 1957; orig. pub., 1900) • W. Pannenberg, *Systematic Theology* (vol. 2; Grand Rapids, 1994) chap. 11 • E. Schlink, "Gesetz und Evangelium als kontroverstheologisches Problem," *KuD* 7 (1961) 1-35 • S. Sykes, *The Identity of Christianity: Theologians and the Essence of Christianity from Schleiermacher to Barth* (London, 1984) • T. J. Wengert, *Law and Gospel: Philip Melanchthon's Debate with John Agricola of Eisleben over Poenitentia* (Grand Rapids, 1997).

Alfred Jäger

Gospel Song

The term "gospel song" refers to a particular kind of religious song that flourished in the United States during the religious → revivals of the Reconstruction era (1865-77) following the Civil War. Its texts are generally characterized by simple, direct words describing the condition of sinners and of their "being saved," joined with music rooted in various European, British, and Afro-American folk traditions.

The musical origins of the gospel song are found in the camp-meeting song (from 1800), one of the most important of its antecedents, together with the later songs associated with the → Sunday school movement, the → YMCA, "prayer and praise" meetings, the → Salvation Army, the temperance movement, and the patriotic songs of the Civil War.

Philip P. Bliss (1838-76) was the first to use the term in his *Gospel Songs* (1874). Bliss, together with evangelist D. W. Whittle, was among the first in a line of songwriter-publisher-evangelists who used these simple, popular songs in the evangelistic meetings of the late 19th and early 20th centuries (→ Evangelism). Other such teams included, among many, Dwight L. → Moody and Ira Sankey, Billy Sunday and Homer Rodeheaver, and, more recently, Billy Graham and George Beverly Shea. The establishment of the U.S. Copyright Office in 1870 effectively centralized copyright registration of many gospel songs, allowing only their owners to print and copy these materials for their exclusive use in their own revival meetings.

Other writers of gospel songs in the days of Reconstruction include Fanny Crosby (1820-1915), Annie S. Hawks (1835-1918), Will L. Thompson (1847-1909), Joseph M. Scriven (1819-86), and Joseph H. Gilmore (1834-1918). A continuing line of writers still produces songs in this genre to the present day, and there has also been a development of new kinds of gospel songs in improvisatory style with piano, guitar, and percussion.

Though viewed by many as America's unique religious song, the gospel song has been criticized as being inadequate in expressing the social demands of the Christian → gospel and as providing "much too friendly musical settings for words that describe the life, death, and resurrection of Jesus Christ" (C. Young). Its close connection with exclusive copyright ownership, mass printing, and distribution in both printed form and through recordings has also incurred the criticism of bringing an unhealthy commercial grounding to this form of religious song.

→ Hymn; Hymnal; Hymnody

Bibliography: L. F. BENSON, *The English Hymn* (rev. ed.; New York, 1962; orig. pub., 1915) • P. P. BLISS, *Gospel Songs: A Choice Collection of Hymns and Tunes, New and Old, for Gospel Meetings, Sunday Schools* (Cincinnati, 1874) • J. H. HALL, *Biography of Gospel Song and Hymn Writers* (New York, 1914) • E. J. LORENZ, *Glory, Hallelujah! The Story of the Camp Meeting Spiritual* (Nashville, 1980) • E. H. PIERCE, "Gospel Hymns and Their Tunes," *MQ* 26 (1940) 355ff. • W. J. REYNOLDS, *Hymns of Our Faith* (Nashville, 1964) • C. YOUNG, "Gospel Song," *Key Words in Church Music* (ed. C. Schalk; St. Louis, 1978) 173-77.

CARL SCHALK

Gothic → Middle Ages

Government Ethics → State Ethics

Grace

Overview
1. Bible
    1.1. OT and Judaism
    1.2. Paul
    1.3. Other NT Writings
2. Orthodox Teaching
    2.1. Grace as God's Self-Communication
    2.2. Theological Development of the Concept
    2.3. Human Action and the Work of Grace
3. Roman Catholic Teaching
    3.1. Augustine and His Influence
    3.2. Middle Ages
    3.3. Molinism
    3.4. New Tendencies
4. Reformation Teaching
    4.1. Reformation Breakthrough
    4.2. Protestant Orthodoxy
    4.3. Methodism, Awakening,
        and Enlightenment
    4.4. New Approaches

Overview

In common parlance the words "grace" and "gracious" denote a human attitude. A gracious person is kind, well-disposed, considerate, gentle, and ready to show favor, to pardon, or to show clemency. The terms also occur in courtly formulas. In a legal setting grace is shown by the authorities when a reprieve or amnesty is granted. The language of religion (cf. ideas of redemption in → Buddhism, →

Hinduism, → Islam, and → Jainism) understands grace as divine assistance, the unmerited mercy of God, though also the mercy that may be expected on the basis of sacrifices or works.

Grace is a central expression in Christian faith and → piety and a basic concept in theological reflection and church activity. It concerns the relation between God and us (or the world) and has as its content God's loving and saving address to his creatures, his favor, and his act of deliverance that is manifest in the Christ-event (→ Christology) and that has in view our → salvation. The grace of God discloses itself only to → faith, which is a gift of God that we again owe to grace.

In the context of a multiplicity of divergent religious understandings (→ Meaning; Religion), grace as a total theological concept seems to have been relativized, individualized, and restricted to a partial sphere (→ Subculture). In the same vein is the attempt in religious sociology to characterize grace as a concept of → identity and to link the traditional dogmatic substance to the → everyday world. Grace here means liberation from biographical and socioeconomic determinations, which can be overcome by fundamental acceptance and love (M. Schibilsky).

A juridical view (W. Grewe) draws attention to the rise of the canonical idea of a → dispensation and its dependence on a theological understanding of grace. The dispensation is the legal form of a decision that has grace as its motive and meaning. As the idea of grace influenced the development of law (see the formula "by the grace of God," found from the 5th cent. for spiritual, later also for secular, rulers), so human sinfulness (→ Sin), which was the target of divine grace, stimulated medieval political thinking; that is, the fall validates secular → power and → force (W. Stürner).

The legal structure of grace that defines it as the restitution of a broken legal relation, or as the reconstitution of an earlier one, can be used to show that → church law is a law of grace (H. S. Dombois). In the process it may be seen how far theological reflection has neglected to its own detriment the legal character of its basic concepts, for example, → righteousness, → law, and → justification (grace being understood as a purely nonlegal process in salvation history). Here such reflection is closely linked with the changing course of legal ideas and contributes to that change.

The presentation of the Christian doctrines of grace in the history of dogma and theology (note the following partial contributions) focuses not only on biblical findings but also on various theological options and initiatives. In the largely typological view (Orthodox, Roman Catholic, Reformational), key elements include, in addition to theological motifs and questions and church interests and considerations, also the cultural and biographical conditions affecting the various concepts.

The references provided in the sections below give some indication of the outstanding problems and tasks. The ecumenical context, which includes not only the various Christian churches but also the Jewish tradition and other religions and worldviews, might offer theological reflection and church practice a chance to take up the reality denoted by grace as a leading theme (at the expense of questions of ecclesiastical structure and specific theological and pastoral problems). With a view to the urgent present-day situation of human existence, such a context could look anew at the implications of divine grace and show its practical relevance.

Bibliography: H. S. DOMBOIS, *Das Recht der Gnade* (3 vols.; Bielefeld, 1961-75) • W. GREWE, *Gnade und Recht* (Hamburg, 1936) • M. SCHIBILSKY, "Gnade 1," *TRT* (4th ed.) 2.208-10 • W. STÜRNER, *Peccatum und Potestas* (Sigmaringen, 1987).

ERWIN FAHLBUSCH

1. Bible

1.1. *OT and Judaism*

The closest Hebrew equivalent of "grace" is the noun *ḥēn* (or verb *ḥnn*), a word that probably comes from court usage. The king (1 Sam. 16:22; 27:5; 2 Sam. 14:22, etc.) or someone highly placed (Gen. 39:21; Exod. 3:21; 11:3) shows *ḥēn*. There is also reference to the *ḥēn* of Yahweh (Gen. 6:8; Exod. 33:12-17; Ps. 84:11), but this use has no theological precision. For this reason the LXX rendering *charis* plays no role in postbiblical → Judaism.

Far more common and theologically much more important is *ḥesed* (originally "kindness, friendship"; LXX *eleos*). This word does not describe the attitude of a greater to a smaller but a partnership within which people show kindness to one another and help one another (Gen. 21:23; Josh. 2:12, 14; 2 Sam. 2:5-6, etc.). It is debated whether *ḥesed* presupposes a prior relationship between the partners (in the case of Yahweh and Israel, the → covenant; N. Glueck) or whether it simply constitutes such a relationship (H. Reventlow). In any case, steadfastness is of the essence of *ḥesed*. It is not just a spontaneous act but a characteristic attitude on which one can rely (1 Kgs. 20:31; Prov. 11:17, etc.).

The many references to the *ḥesed* of Yahweh are structured accordingly. Because → Abraham and the other patriarchs have already experienced Yahweh's *ḥesed* (Genesis 24; 32), Israel can count upon it that he will act according to his *ḥesed* (Ps. 25:7; 51:1; 109:26). At the same time, *ḥesed* is for Israel the fruit of God's gracious acts, his salvation, as such parallel terms as "salvation" (Ps. 85:7), "faithfulness" (Ps. 85:10; 98:3), "life" (Job 10:12), and "redemption" (Ps. 130:7 RSV) show.

The term occurs supremely in praise of God (Exod. 34:6). In the liturgy of the postexilic temple we find the recurrent phrase "for his *ḥesed* endures forever" (K. Koch). The element of relationship may be seen in the fact that an answering of Yahweh's *ḥesed* by human *ḥesed* is presupposed (Hos. 4:1; 6:4, 6; Jer. 2:2, etc.). The latter shows itself in → obedience to God's gracious, saving will, to the → Torah. → Law and grace thus correspond to one another in meaning; no conceivable tension is possible between them.

That these meanings hold true also for postbiblical Judaism may be seen paradigmatically in the → Qumran writings, in which a rigorous legalism accompanies an emphatic theology of divine grace. The Qumran community is aware that humanity has fallen into sin and therefore sets its hope solely on the grace of God, which it extols in forms that are ever new (1QS 4:4; 10:4, 16; 1QH 5:17-18, etc.). It views this grace as a fulfillment of the counsel in virtue of which God ordained them to be sons of light. "He will draw me near in his mercies, and by *ḥesed* set in motion my judgment; he will judge me in the justice of his truth, and in his plentiful goodness always atone for all my sins" (1QS 11:13-14). This encompassing by grace proves itself in radical obedience to the Torah. Grace thus does not close the path of salvation by law; rather, it directs us to it.

1.2. *Paul*

We owe it to Paul that grace became a leading concept in Christian theology. Paul took the word *charis*, which in secular Greek meant "charm, favor, thanks" and which had not been a specifically theological word in the biblical tradition, and brought it into the theological vocabulary, primarily within the message of → justification, as the heavy concentration of instances in Romans 3–6 makes clear.

Grace is God's free and loving turning to sinners in the atoning death of Jesus Christ. "They are now justified by his grace as a gift, through the redemption that is in Christ Jesus" (Rom. 3:24). By his choice of *charis* Paul obviously wants to stress the fact that God's saving act has the character of a gift and is not tied up with any human presuppositions. God's grace is closely linked to his love as an act and not just as an attribute. God gives up his Son to declare his love to those who are hostile to him, in this way reconciling them and opening up for them fellowship with himself (5:1-11). This act is a powerful event and is superior to the power of → sin, which, coming into the world with the first man's disobedience, has set us in bondage. Grace disarms this power (vv. 12-17). All this has taken place in Jesus Christ, the man who followed the way of obedience and suffering even unto death (→ Christology 1), so that in him, weak and powerless though he may be by human standards, the power of God is manifest.

Paul, however, does not merely contrast sin and grace. In a most important deviation from the OT and Jewish view of grace, he also contrasts law and grace (Rom. 6:14-15; Gal. 2:21; 5:4). The dominion of sin results from our failure to tread the saving path of law. Because all of us defy God's good and holy will in the law and because, in an attempt at autonomy, we are betrayed into enmity against God, the law has become an accusing and judging power of condemnation (Rom. 3:20). It can no longer be a way of salvation; none can now be justified by its works. → Salvation can come only by the act of God in Christ. Grace, then, is the way of salvation, having definitively replaced the way of salvation by law (Rom. 3:21-31; 4:16).

It does not contradict this understanding of grace as act and event that Paul can see it also as a sphere of force in which believers "stand" (Rom. 5:2; 6:14; 2 Cor. 6:1). Expressed hereby is the fact that grace is not just a single event that we appropriate in an act of subjective understanding but a transsubjective reality that determines believers, just as sin is a similar reality. The possibility, then, of leaving room for sin where grace reigns is quite absurd for Paul (Rom. 6:14). By the working of the → Holy Spirit there is manifested in the sphere of the rule of grace the eschatological reality of salvation. Grace, then, takes concrete form in the many gifts of grace (the charismata, e.g., 1 Cor. 2:12; 12:4-11; Rom. 12:6; → Charisma). Grace, to be sure, is not a fixed possession. Those who do not subject themselves consistently to it in → faith run the risk of falling from it (Gal. 5:4; cf. Rom. 3:28).

A special, concrete form of grace is Paul's own apostleship (→ Apostle). He can describe both his calling (1 Cor. 15:10) and the office itself (Rom. 1:5) as grace because he realizes that he is a messenger and instrument of grace (2 Cor. 5:11–6:1). Grace encounters the churches through his presence (2 Cor. 1:15) but also through his letters, as may be seen from the liturgical ascription of grace in the greetings and the closing blessings.

1.3. Other NT Writings

In the rest of the NT the term "grace" stands largely under Paul's influence and, for the most part, tends to be more weakly formal. Closest to Paul are 2 Tim. 1:9 and Titus 3:4-7, which take up the link between grace and justification and the antithesis of grace and works (see also Eph. 2:5-9).

In 1 Pet. 2:19-20; 5:12 grace is a gift with the appropriate form of the Christian life (i.e., → suffering) as its content. Luke gives us to understand that he is aware of the relevance of grace for Paul's message (e.g., Acts 14:3; 15:11; 20:24). Elsewhere, however, he either uses the term *charis* (in the OT sense of *hēn*) for God's condescension to us (Luke 1:30; 2:40; Acts 7:46) or uses it formally for the state of grace that is granted to the church and its members (Acts 13:43; 14:26; 15:40). Secular usage ("grace" as an official favor) occurs in Acts 24:27; 25:3, 9. In John 1:14, 16-17 grace is a result of the working of the Logos among us, probably in the sense of a state of grace.

Bibliography: V. Brümmer, *The Model of Love: A Study in Philosophical Theology* (Cambridge, 1993) • R. Bultmann, *Theology of the NT* (2 vols.; New York, 1951-55) 1.292-98 • B. S. Childs, *Biblical Theology of the Old and New Testaments: Theological Reflection on the Christian Bible* (London, 1992) • H. Conzelmann and W. Zimmerli, "Χαίρω κτλ.," *TDNT* 9.359-415 • D. J. Doughty, "The Priority of χάρις: An Investigation of the Theological Language of Paul," *NTS* 19 (1972/73) 163-80 • D. N. Freedman, J. Lundbom, and H.-J. Fabry, "חָנַן *hānan*" etc., *TDOT* 5.22-36 • N. Glueck, *Das Wort ḥesed im alttestamentlichen Sprachgebrauch als menschliche und göttliche gemeinschaftsgemäße Verhaltensweise* (Berlin, 1927) • K. Koch, "Denn seine Güte währet ewiglich," *EvT* 21 (1961) 531-44 • N. Lohfink and E. Zenger, *The God of Israel and the Nations: Studies in Isaiah and the Psalms* (Collegeville, Minn., 2000) • A. E. McGrath, *Christian Theology: An Introduction* (Oxford, 1994) • W. A. Meeks, "Law versus Grace and the Problem of Ethics," *The Writings of St. Paul* (New York, 1972) 215-72 • H. Reventlow, R. Goldenberg, and E. Ruckstuhl, "Gnade I-III," *TRE* 13.459-76 (bibliography).

Jürgen Roloff

2. Orthodox Teaching

2.1. Grace as God's Self-Communication

Patristic thinking about grace always has a → Trinitarian reference. To receive grace is thus to receive the Trinitarian God. By his grace God does not give something of himself; he gives *himself.* The inseparability of grace from God's essence and the perichoretic mode of existence of the divine hypostases explain why the presence of the one person includes that of the others (Athanasius *Ep. Serap.* 3.6; cf. John 14:23). Grace is not monistically related to one person of the Trinity. There is only one grace; the one God and each of the divine hypostases is its source and giver (Rom. 1:7; 5:5; 1 Cor. 15:10).

Patristic theology (→ Church Fathers; Patristics) understands by "grace" the almighty, unconditioned, undeserved, free, and loving divine act of the → creation of the world and humanity, of redemption in Christ (→ Soteriology), of the appropriation of redemption in the → church in the power of the → Holy Spirit, of our liberation from the dominion of → sin, and of our renewal up to the eschatological consummation (→ Eschatology 4). Hence the term "grace" stands for *the whole act of God's creation, redemption, and providence in Jesus Christ by the Holy Spirit* (→ Salvation 2).

We ourselves are less prominent in this view of God's saving acts (→ God 6). We can bring to God only the "sacrifice of praise" (Heb. 13:15) and prayers for mercy. Yet statements about grace are also statements about humanity (→ Anthropology). The power of grace is infinitely stronger than that of → sin (Rom. 5:20). The Son of God came because we were totally unable to achieve salvation on our own. With his → incarnation and the redemption that was achieved by his death and → resurrection (→ Christology 2) and that becomes a present reality in the church by the Holy Spirit, the term "grace" is Christologically and pneumatologically defined.

Since grace and → truth came by Jesus Christ (John 1:17), → salvation history in Christ becomes a present event in → faith through the Spirit whom Christ sent (John 16:7). Christ and the Holy Spirit are inseparably linked in their working in the economy of salvation. The grace of the Holy Spirit relates to Christ's redeeming work (John 15:26; 16:14), which does not mean that it is in any way subordinate to the grace of the Son (V. Lossky). Christ sends the Spirit to us, and the Spirit sets us in relation to Christ, yet not merely as an instrumental mediator. The grace of the Holy Spirit is itself a hypostatic force. Cyril of Jerusalem (ca. 315-?386) speaks of the personal, sanctifying, and efficacious power of the Holy Spirit (*Cat.* 17.34). Only thus can it enable us to participate in the divine persons. Cyril of Alexandria (ca. 375-444) does not view the Spirit's grace as ministerial but as a grace that makes possible our participation in God (*Dial. Trin.* 7 [*PG* 75.1089B]).

Although the stream of grace flows everywhere, having a rich source in Christ, we receive it particularly through the → means of grace in the church, where we find a variety of gifts of grace (1 Cor. 12:27-31; → Charisma). As the Spirit gives all his grace to all who have a share in him (Basil *De Spir. S.* 9.45), they become through him the children of God (Rom. 8:14-15). This biblical thought of adoption is an important theme in patristic theology. Whereas Irenaeus (ca. 130-ca. 200) refers only to the Christological aspect (*Adv. haer.* 3.19.1), Athanasius (ca. 297-373) in his discussions about the adoption of Christians as God's children points to the function of the Spirit. Sonship is a gift of the Spirit (*Ep. Serap.* 1.19; *Contra Arian.* 3.19).

Essential to supernatural sonship, says Gregory of Nyssa (ca. 330-ca. 395), is participation by grace. To become a child of God is a grace that far transcends our human nature (*De beat.* 7). We attain to divine likeness, or → *theōsis* (Athanasius *De incar.* 54.3), with the help of divine grace. Basil (ca. 330-79) ascribes to grace, as the operation of the Spirit, a new formative power. It fashions our divine likeness, making us conformable to the image of the Son of God (*De Spir. S.* 26.93). Among the results of baptismal grace Basil mentions the forgiveness of sins, life-giving power, a new beginning of life, and being born again from above (15.60). According to John Chrysostom (ca. 347-407), grace also gives → righteousness, → sanctification, sonship (*In Joh. hom.* 14.2 [*PG* 59.94]), → regeneration, and new creation (not merely cleansing; see *Cat.* 1.3 [*PG* 49.227]).

2.2. Theological Development of the Concept

Development of the concept of grace proceeded differently in the East than it did in the West (see 3). Although the term "grace" is fairly common in most of the Greek fathers, no specific doctrine of grace emerged. Instead of dogmatic definitions or theological treatises, we find many early statements mentioning grace that deal with the doctrines of God and salvation. In discussion of the saving work of Father, Son, and Holy Spirit, the function of grace emerges clearly. The dogmatic decisions made in the fourth century concerning the Trinity and Christology must not be overlooked as the background of the understanding of grace. It is in this light that we are to view the relation of grace to the Trinity and the soteriological and Christological framework of statements about the function of grace. Grace is not a power divorced from the divine persons but their own direct and personal operation, an insight that tends to check the development of a special doctrine of grace. That which is inseparable in the reality of faith — namely, the operation of grace on the one side and the divine persons on the other — may not be presented separately in theological reflection.

The result of this personal understanding of grace (i.e., that grace cannot reach human beings independently of the divine persons) was that the doctrine of grace was unable to extricate itself from Christology and pneumatology, or that grace itself was understood in a material sense. In Orthodox worship, grace is experienced as the immediate effect of a Trinitarian person, something evident in a prayer from the liturgy of St. Chrysostom: "May your good Spirit of grace descend upon us, upon the gifts here, and upon your people."

Just as God's compassion and love, both of which count as grace, are not something God sends to human beings without communicating himself to them as well, so also is grace God's immediate personal effect on human beings. God does not *have* an "inventory of grace" from which he distributes grace to human beings; rather, he *is* himself gracious and thus is himself present and active when he sends his grace. The reality of grace becomes the experience of grace. God's graciousness is not a transcendent characteristic of his essence. Rather, he is communicating or mediating himself to human beings, and only for that reason can they experience him as the gracious God.

Leaning on this early understanding, Gregory Palamas (ca. 1296-1359) offered a more precise theological definition of grace in the Byzantine Middle Ages (→ Palamism). Grace for him is an uncreated energy that emanates from the one essence of God that is common to all the persons. It is not distinct from God but is present in the operation of the persons. This teaching, which does justice both to God's transcendence (in his essence) and to his immanence (in his work in the economy of salvation; → Immanence and Transcendence), has benefited all of Orthodox theology. It put a concern for pneumatology at the center of theology and liturgy. Thus the doctrine of grace developed particularly in the context of pneumatology and also of sacramental teaching. Attention has also been directed recently to an understanding of the word of proclamation as a means of grace.

2.3. Human Action and the Work of Grace

Patristic theology did not regard human action and the work of grace as antithetical. Attention and expectation focus on God's action. For our part, we are seen as recipients of grace, but not from the standpoint of achievement or cooperation. Our deeds are a response, a gift in virtue of the gifts of grace that are received.

The antithesis of our work and God's (cf. the controversy between Augustine and Pelagius; see 3) never bothered the Eastern church. Concentration on God's work in the church, which experiences and extols him as the only Savior, did not lead Eastern theology, with its strong liturgical links, to theoretical reflection on a precise definition of the relationship between our work and God's. In modern Orthodox theology the relationship is even deeper. Grace does not rule out human cooperation (→ Synergism) but includes it. Underlying discussion of the relationship are the fundamental presuppositions that grace is decisive and an absolute necessity for salvation, that it is not given on the ground of human achievement but is granted freely, that it is a merciful initiative of God, and that we are totally unable to achieve salvation on our own. The only question is whether, as coworkers with God after receiving grace, we contribute in any way to our salvation. The problem of synergism arises if a positive answer is given to this question.

Synergism, however, is not a wholly negative concept. Cooperation between God and us is a common thought in the Fathers. It is of decisive importance that in them the absolute necessity of works in no way obscures the absolute necessity of grace. We must not misunderstand our cooperation with grace as though it made of the believer a coredeemer. The believer is a recipient of grace, yet not passively, but is also a coworker with God. God wills and brings it about that the believer is a coworker.

To the deepening and development of the understanding of grace belong discussions of pneumatological Christology and ecclesiology (N. A. Nissiotis) as a correction of Christomonistic tendencies and as insight into the need for an ongoing renewal of the church as the source of impulses for the renewal of the world and all creation. Orthodox theology views grace as oriented to the cosmos, as may be seen in the → worship (§3) of the → Orthodox Church (→ Liturgy 2). It views grace not merely as a unifying bond in the church but also as the basis of synodal, Catholic → unity. The free working of grace finds expression, then, in the fact that this unity rests on a plenitude of varied gifts of grace (D. Staniloae).

→ Orthodoxy 3

Bibliography: T. B. BARNES, *Athanasius and Constantius: Theology and Politics in the Constantinian Empire* (Cambridge, Mass., 1993) • C. BAUMGARTNER and P. TIHON, "Grâce," *DSp* 6.701-50 • C. DRATSELLAS, "Questions of the Soteriological Teaching of the Greek Fathers," *Theol(A)* 39 (1968) 621-43 • A. FRANGOPOULOS, *Our Orthodox Christian Faith* (Athens, 1984)

172-85 • N. N. Gloubokovsky, "Grace in the Greek Fathers (to St. John of Damascus) and Inter-Church Union," *The Doctrine of Grace* (ed. W. T. Whitley; London, 1932) 61-105 • V. E. F. Harrison, *Grace and Human Freedom according to St. Gregory of Nyssa* (Lewiston, N.Y., 1992) • V. Lossky, *The Mystical Theology of the Eastern Church* (2d ed.; Crestwood, N.Y., 1976) • A. Nichols, *Byzantine Gospel: Maximus the Confessor in Modern Scholarship* (Edinburgh, 1993) • N. A. Nissiotis, *Die Theologie der Ostkirche im ökumenischen Dialog. Kirche und Welt in orthodoxer Sicht* (Stuttgart, 1968) • E. Osborn, *The Emergence of Christian Theology* (Cambridge, 1993) • D. Staniloae, *Orthodoxe Dogmatik* (Zurich, 1985) • T. F. Torrance, *The Doctrine of Grace in the Apostolic Fathers* (Grand Rapids, 1960) • C. N. Tsirpanlis, *Introduction to Eastern Patristic Thought and Orthodox Theology* (Collegeville, Minn., 1991).

Viorel Mehedințu

3. Roman Catholic Teaching

3.1. *Augustine and His Influence*

Theologically, East and West took different paths, especially in → anthropology. For the → apologists and Greek fathers redemption meant *paideia* — that is, example, teaching, instruction (education) — by Jesus Christ, with → theosis as the goal (see 2). The West, however, tended to lay more stress on the subjective, human side of redemption (in close connection with the humanity and mediatorship of Jesus Christ). Thus in the East human beings were seen from the very first more in their anchoring in God, the image of God being manifested in the teaching activity of the Logos. In the West, however, attention focused on human beings in their subjectivity and autonomy (though not in the full modern sense).

The reasons for this difference may be briefly stated. On the one side is the role of Plato (427-347 B.C.), with his teaching on ideas (→ Platonism). On the other is the priority of political and legal thinking. The approach in terms of the → incarnation differs from the approach in terms of redemption, the restoration of the broken order by expiation. With logical historical consistency, then, it follows that very early (beginning with Tertullian) the West worked out the difference between subjective and objective redemption. Grace comes into play as a specific divine power by which we who are independent by nature attain to → salvation. On a larger canvas this emphasis led to an extensive coupling of the teaching on grace with → Christology.

The development that is briefly sketched here is profiled in Augustine (354-430), especially in his controversy with Pelagius (→ Pelagianism). Pelagius (d. after 418) is misunderstood if he is thought primarily to have championed a theory of natural self-redemption. In his view grace is mediated concretely through → salvation history and its continuation in church history. We cannot take for granted, however, a divinely given working within us. Face to face with the moral decadence of the age, Pelagius, for predominantly pastoral reasons, contended for the goodness of creation and natural human → freedom.

In opposition, Augustine, relying especially on insights from Holy Scripture and the practice of infant baptism and influenced by his own personal experiences, argued for the absolute primacy of the work of divine grace (→ Augustine's Theology). Through the mediation of Christ and his → church (*totus Christus* — the whole person of Christ), God grants salvation in pure mercy. Profoundly unfree and enslaved, humankind cannot be liberated from without (e.g., by examples from history, by education, or the like). Instead, we are radically thrown back on the God who saves. Not illogically from this standpoint, Augustine introduced the ambivalent concept of → predestination.

Augustine's basic options and leading ideas are hard to discern plainly in his powerful work and are set out in many versions, even stylistically. The history of the Western teaching on grace is largely identical with that of the reception or interpretation of Augustine. A first point is that various councils, especially the Synod of Carthage in 418, dealt with Pelagianism. In the spirit of Augustine, Carthage opposed Pelagius and described grace as *adiutorium* — that is, absolutely necessary for action oriented to salvation.

The semi-Pelagianism of the fifth and sixth centuries is characterized more by a refusal to follow Augustine than by any systematic view of grace. As was noted, the underlying concern was more pastoral than doctrinal. The theological core was that, in protection of human freedom, a prayer for grace stands at the beginning of the salvation-event. This prayer is the first step on the way to the → faith that leads to salvation *(initium fidei)*, though God's grace is unconditionally necessary for any further steps. The Second Council of Orange (529) adopted a radical Augustinianism in opposition to semi-Pelagianism, arguing that we of ourselves have nothing but sin and falsehood (DH 392).

3.2. *Middle Ages*

In the Middle Ages the teaching on grace continued in a constant dialogue with Augustine, though it followed different directions and models (→ Scholasticism). The ninth century saw another debate about predestination, which reminds us of the earlier semi-Pelagian controversies. Gottschalk, Ratramnus, and Remigius of Lyons were strong supporters of Augustine; Rabanus Maurus and Hincmar of Reims took a moderate position but in obvious relation to Augustine.

From the 12th century onward the problem was that of describing the preparation for grace. It was unfortunate that various important documents from the Pelagian and semi-Pelagian conflicts were not then known (e.g., the statement of the Second Council of Orange). Hence many important theologians (e.g., Thomas Aquinas) sometimes said things that sound semi-Pelagian. But step by step under the influence of Aristotelian philosophy and Thomas (ca. 1225-74; → Aristotelianism; Thomism), the terms and categories of a full treatise on grace were worked out, including *dispositio* (disposition), *dispositio ultima* (final disposition), *habitus infusa* (infused disposition), *gratia gratis data* (grace given undeservedly) and *gratia gratum facens* (grace making gracious).

The theology of the → Franciscans, especially Bonaventura, remained more dynamic, existential, and concrete. Important medieval scholars have agreed that beyond all the controversies, the uncontested core of the theology of grace was God's presence in us by grace *(Deus per gratia inhabitans)* — the presence of the God who is the one God in three persons. There was thus a link between the theology of grace and the doctrine of the → Trinity.

Later medieval → nominalist trends, especially among the Franciscans, deserve mention because under some conditions they are important for the positions of the Reformers. As regards the Augustinian Martin Luther (1483-1546), we must note not only the influence of Scripture and of the father of his order but also that of mystical tendencies (→ Mysticism; Luther's Theology).

In its decree on justification the Council of → Trent represented in some sense a break and conclusion when it established the following convictions about grace: we can achieve salvation only by God's grace; God respects our freedom; we can thus cooperate in the work of grace; we become active as we are awakened, helped, and preceded by grace; and God's grace has an effect in us, since it is not merely a mode of the presence of the acting God himself *(gratia increata)* but a new reality in and upon us *(gratia creata)*.

3.3. Molinism

In post-Reformation thinking (→ Catholic Reform and Counterreformation) we again find positions for and against Augustine. This struggle is especially palpable in the so-called Molinist controversy, which was not just a theological debate but a battle between two orders, the → Dominicans and the → Jesuits. On the one side stood the Dominican Domingo Báñez (1528-1604), who sought to preserve God's absolute transcendence (→ Immanence and Transcendence) in describing the cooperation of divine grace and human freedom. God first gives us grace to enable us to decide, in which grace we are given the possibility of free saving action, but we can still make it a reality only by a fresh divine initiative *(praemotio physica)*. On the other side the Jesuit Luis de Molina (1535-1600) championed a stronger emphasis on human freedom (→ Molinism), contending that divine and human actions are in "simultaneous concursus."

The Dominicans, who viewed themselves as the true representatives of Augustine, decried the Pelagian → heresy they saw in their opponents. The Jesuits thought that they were the proper interpreters of the church father and that the other side had radicalized him. No official judgment was passed on the controversy.

3.4. *New Tendencies*

The Roman Catholic teaching on grace has experienced serious upheavals in the modern age and has adopted a series of new approaches. The so-called personalist thinking that increasingly began to penetrate Roman Catholic theology in the middle of the 20th century (esp. through Hans Urs von Balthasar, Henri de Lubac, Otto Semmelroth, and Karl Rahner) had a special impact on the doctrine of grace by way of its thesis that God himself gives himself to us. This approach put "uncreated grace" at the center. It set the distinctions of → neoscholasticism, and therefore many distinctions in the doctrine of grace, firmly in the background, giving center stage instead to biblical perspectives and the perspectives of salvation history.

→ Vatican II did not focus explicitly on grace. Yet this dimension is everywhere present in the texts, whether in traditional formulations or in new perspectives and formulas. Grace as participation in the divine life, as sonship, and as the indwelling of the Holy Spirit is totally unearned. This principle is old. What is new is that the grace of God finds a partner, particularly in ecclesial encounter (*Lumen gentium* 12, 19; *Presbyterorum ordinis* 16).

A truly new approach is the linking of the modern idea of freedom with what is said about grace (see esp. Gisbert Greshake and Karl Rahner). Christ is the place of human freedom. God's turning to us in Jesus Christ frees us for service of God and neighbor. From this point it is only a small step to the understanding of grace as liberation and therefore to interaction with sociopolitical processes. → Liberation theology believes that grace (quite apart from its sin-destroying character) has to do with human self-fulfillment and → identity and thus that we must take into account the horizontal, social aspects of this truth.

→ Catholicism (Roman); Soteriology

Bibliography: S. DUFFY, *The Dynamics of Grace: Perspectives in Theological Anthropology* (Collegeville, Minn., 1993) • A. D. FITZGERALD, ed., *Augustine through the Ages: An Encyclopedia* (Grand Rapids, 1999) • G. GRESHAKE, *Geschenkte Freiheit. Einführung in die Gnadenlehre* (Freiburg, 1977); idem, *Gnade als konkrete Freiheit. Eine Untersuchung zur Gnadenlehre des Pelagius* (Mainz, 1972) • H. GROSS, P. FRANSEN, et al., "Gottes Gnadenhandeln," *MySal* 4/2.595-982 (bibliography) • M. C. HILKERT, *Naming Grace: Preaching and the Sacramental Imagination* (New York, 1997) • H. DE LUBAC, *Die Freiheit der Gnade* (2 vols.; Einsiedeln, 1971) • L. J. O'DONOVAN, *A World of Grace: An Introduction to the Themes and Foundations of Karl Rahner's Theology* (Washington, D.C., 1995) • K. RAHNER, *Foundations of Christian Faith: An Introduction to the Idea of Christianity* (New York, 1978) • T. A. SMITH, *De Gratia: Faustus of Riez's Treatise on Grace and Its Place in the History of Theology* (Notre Dame, Ind., 1990) • H. WAGNER, "Báñez" and "Molina," *Theologen-Lexikon* (Munich, 1987) 21-22 and 166-67 (bibliography).

HARALD WAGNER

4. Reformation Teaching
4.1. *Reformation Breakthrough*

The → Reformation brought a far-reaching turn in the evaluating and profiling of the doctrine of grace by going back directly to → Paul, by viewing grace especially in the light of → soteriology, and by making the → justification of the sinner "by grace alone" the predominant theological motif. Thus the Augsburg Confession, for example, states: "It is also taught among us that we cannot obtain forgiveness of sin and righteousness before God by our own merits, works, or satisfactions, but that we receive forgiveness of sin and become righteous before God by grace, for Christ's sake, through faith, when we believe that Christ suffered for us and that for his sake our sin is forgiven and righteousness and eternal life are given to us. For God will regard and reckon this faith as righteousness" (art. 4). John Calvin taught similarly that justification is simply "the acceptance with which God receives us into his favor

as righteous men. . . . It consists in the remission of sins and the imputation of Christ's righteousness" (*Inst.* 3.11.2).

Statements of this kind present the grace of God primarily as that of the Judge who for Christ's sake pardons and justifies those who are accused and guilty. Grace as taught by the Reformers can be understood only in the framework of justification. The doctrine is not an abstract one of grace in itself; it is the doctrine of God's grace *in Jesus Christ.* Accordingly, as in the NT itself, grace is seen as an attribute of God himself, not as a mediating substance between God and the world that works quasi-mechanically, let alone as a quality of the creature.

In this way the Reformation doctrine about grace took on a different coloring and orientation from that of the scholastic theology of the high and late Middle Ages (→ Scholasticism; see 3). In fact the teaching of Thomas Aquinas (ca. 1225-74) about grace, forgiveness, and justification was not miles apart from that of the Reformation. The church father Augustine (354-430) lay behind both (→ Augustine's Theology; Thomism). Yet the Reformation emphasis on soteriology was stronger, whereas in Thomas the schema of → nature and grace held the field.

Much greater were the differences between the Reformation doctrine of grace and that of later Scholasticism, with its tendency to objectify grace, to divide it into various *gratiae creatae* (created graces), with which it linked very closely the concept of merit. For this reason Martin Luther in his "Disputation against Scholastic Theology" (1517) protested, "It is dangerous to say that the law teaches that its performance takes place in the grace of God" (thesis 57; *LW* 31.13). Such a formulation means that having the grace of God is a new demand beyond that of the law, and consequently grace becomes more hateful to us than the law itself. In other words, the late scholastic teaching on grace fails to perceive the distinction between → law and gospel, and hence grace can no longer be recognized as grace.

In contrast, as P. Melanchthon (1497-1560) noted in his *Loci* (1559), the doctrine of grace and justification (*Locus de gratia et de iustificatione*) contains the sum of the gospel, and it is thus closely related to many others, that is, to → predestination, → sin, → reconciliation, and → eschatology. Even the doctrine of God cannot be excluded, and for this reason K. Barth in *CD* II/2 dealt with predestination as the election of grace within the context of the doctrine of → God.

Many questions that had arisen before the Reformation in connection with the doctrine of grace came up again in Reformation theology and, in some cases, were put even more radically. Does grace work infallibly, or can we successfully resist it? How does divine grace relate to human → freedom? Must we deny the freedom of the will with Luther's *De servo arbitrio* (Concerning the bondage of the will, 1525; → Luther's Theology)? Must we accept the final logic of double predestination with Calvin (→ Calvin's Theology)? Or can we, like Melanchthon, evade conclusions of that kind? What place is there for "good works" or for → obedience to the → law of God if → salvation finally depends solely on God's grace? Is justification purely forensic, or does it bring about a real change in us? These and similar questions were hotly debated in the 16th century. → Lutheranism arrived at a provisional conclusion in the → Formula of Concord (1577), which taught that although grace does it all, it is not irresistible. The Reformed arrived at their own conclusion in the Canons of Dort (1619; → Arminianism), which in the context of a consistent doctrine of predestination stressed the irresistibility of grace (→ Calvinism).

4.2. *Protestant Orthodoxy*
In Protestant → orthodoxy there was a fresh development of the doctrine of grace in two areas. On the one side, Reformed federal theology (→ Covenant 3) found the true driving force of → salvation history in the covenant of grace in tension with the covenant of works. On the other side, Reformed → Puritans, like the Lutherans, developed an interest in coordinating the practical outworkings of grace in an orderly sequence. The term *ordo salutis* (→ order of salvation) soon came into use for the resulting schemata, which were very numerous. An example was that of Theodore Beza (1519-1605), which made a great impact (also in Germany) when it was republished in expanded form in W. Perkins's *A Golden Chaine* (1592). This schema depicted the whole life of the elect and the reprobate in the setting of all salvation history from the eternal decree of the triune God to the → last judgment. The Westminster Confession (1647) follows a similar path in its central articles 10 through 18 (effectual calling, justification, adoption, sanctification, saving faith, repentance unto life, good works, the perseverance of the saints, and assurance of grace and salvation; → Westminster Assembly and Confession).

The last proponent of Lutheran orthodoxy, D. Hollaz (1648-1713), distinguished nine stages in the working of the "applicative grace of the Holy Spirit" *(gratia Spiritus Sancti applicatrix):* calling, illumination, conversion, regeneration, justification,

mystical union, renewal, confirmation and preservation in faith, and glory (cited in K. Barth, *CD* IV/3, 505-6). In this development the question of → assurance of salvation and the "practical syllogism" (*syllogismus practicus* — a logical construction to establish the certainty of a person's election) undoubtedly played a great part, but so too did the concern to link → faith and doctrine concretely to → experience. This concern later became very important in → Pietism.

4.3. *Methodism, Awakening, and Enlightenment*
Not only in Pietism was there a widespread desire in the 18th century to relate grace and justification in a new way to experience, → piety, and → sanctification of life. Alongside N. L. von Zinzendorf (1700-1760) and the → Moravian Brethren, who found renewal at Herrnhut and who were characterized by a fervent devotion to Christ, Methodism, which was vitally influenced by them, and the associated movement of awakening in the second third of the 18th century were also of significance for both church and theology.

J. Wesley (1703-91) called himself an Arminian and viewed with scorn the Calvinist doctrine of predestination. His concern so bore witness to the power of grace as he himself had experienced it that others also were gripped by it and began a striving for Christian perfection. Among his most important allies, however, were Calvinists, who regarded predestination as guaranteeing the power of grace. Thus J. Edwards (1703-58), the most significant Reformed theologian of his generation, wrote *Religious Affections* (1746) on the basis of his experiences in → revivals in New England. Long before F. D. E. Schleiermacher (1768-1834), this work was a first pioneering investigation of the links between doctrine, → preaching, personal experience, and the Christian life.

The → Enlightenment, however, could hardly understand the Reformation doctrine of grace, whether in its rationalistic first phase, which was marked by → deism, or later in the profounder moral phase introduced by I. Kant (1724-1804). To the Enlightenment the idea of justification seemed to be morally untenable, and the idea of supernatural intervention dubious except in the sense of ethical influence. (Typical are the general observations at the end of the fourth part of Kant's *Religion within the Limits of Reason Alone* [1793], e.g., the observation that the concept of supernatural intervention to aid our moral but deficient capacity is transcendental and is a mere idea, of which experience can give us no guarantee.)

4.4. *New Approaches*

→ Romanticism and → idealism soon brought new views of the relation between God and the world that burst through the dualism of Kant. J. G. Fichte (1762-1814) believed that the emergence of the moral will, which we cannot explain in terms of the sensory nature, has a religious character. It is therefore grace, to the degree that it participates in the will of God, though Fichte's approach had the disadvantage of forcing him to give up the doctrine of God as Creator. For the theology influenced by G. W. F. Hegel (1770-1831), the self-revelation of the absolute spirit in the finite spirit was itself grace (→ Hegelianism; cf. A. E. Biedermann [1819-85]).

The treatment of the theme by Schleiermacher deserves special notice (→ Schleiermacher's Theology). The whole second part of his *Christian Faith* (2d ed., 1830/31) is based on the thesis that "the distinctive feature of Christian piety lies in the fact that whatever alienation from God there is in the phases of our experience, we are conscious of it as an action originating in ourselves, which we call Sin; but whatever fellowship with God there is, we are conscious of it as resting upon a communication from the Redeemer, which we call Grace" (§63). A primary question that we must still put to Schleiermacher is whether he does not here think of grace too horizontally and not vertically enough.

This question was raised by the → dialectical theology of the 20th century and led to pregnant discussions between E. Brunner (*Nature and Grace* [1934, ET 1960]) and K. Barth (*No! Answer to Emil Brunner* [1934]). Among other 20th-century contributions we may refer here only to J. W. Oman's *Grace and Personality* (1917), an important work for Anglo-Saxon theology.

Bibliography: Works with bibliographies: W.-D. HAUSCHILD and K. OTTE, "Gnade IV-V," *TRE* 13.476-511 • A. I. C. HERON, ed., *The Westminster Confession in the Church Today* (Edinburgh, 1982) • R. T. KENDALL, *Calvin and English Calvinism to 1649* (Oxford, 1979) • O. H. PESCH and A. PETERS, *Einführung in die Lehre von Gnade und Rechtfertigung* (Darmstadt, 1981) • G. WAINWRIGHT, *Geoffrey Wainwright on Wesley and Calvin* (Melbourne, 1987) • G. WENZ, *Geschichte der Versöhnungslehre in der evangelischen Theologie der Neuzeit* (2 vols.; Munich, 1984-86).

Dogmatic development and the Reformed reception: W. BOGGS, *Sin Boldly: But Trust God More Boldly Still* (Nashville, 1990) • K. A. DAVID, *Sacrament and Struggle: Signs and Instruments of Grace from the Downtrodden* (Geneva: 1994) • EVANGELICAL LUTHERAN CHURCH IN AMERICA, *The Use of the Means of Grace: A Statement on the Practice of Word and Sacrament* (Minneapolis, 1997) • S. KIERKEGAARD, *Practice in Christianity* (Princeton, 1991; orig. pub., 1850) • F. VON LILIENFELD and E. MÜHLENBERG, eds., *Gnadenwahl und Entscheidungsfreiheit in der Theologie der Alten Kirche* (Erlangen, 1980) • E. MÜHLENBERG, "Synergism in Gregory of Nyssa," *ZNW* 68 (1977) 93-122 • J. RUTHVEN, *On the Cessation of the Charismata: The Protestant Polemic in Postbiblical Miracles* (Sheffield, 1993) • A. SCHINDLER, "Gnade," *RAC* 11.382-446 • H. H. SCHMITT, *Many Gifts, One Lord* (Minneapolis, 1993) • T. R. SCHREINER and B. A. WARE, eds., *The Grace of God, the Bondage of the Will* (Grand Rapids, 1995).

ALASDAIR I. C. HERON

Gradual

In the medieval Roman → Mass, the gradual, a structure of psalmodic material usually sung from the ambo, or reading desk, came between the Epistle and Gospel readings. In the early centuries of the church, this chant was a simple psalm sung by a solo voice, with the → congregation singing a recurring refrain. In the later development of the Mass, the gradual became one of its most elaborate and melismatic chants.

The Lutheran → Reformation replaced the gradual with a congregational hymn. M. → Luther's *Formula Missae* (1523) first suggested a congregational hymn immediately following the gradual, then his *Deutsche Messe* (1526) replaced the gradual with a congregational hymn. In either case the hymn was to be *de tempore* (i.e., appropriate to the character of the day, or at least related in meaning and content to the psalmodic material that it replaced). Thus this psalmodic song, which in the early church was the response of the people and which gradually became the province of cantors and choirs in the Middle Ages, was restored to the people in a new and significantly different form: the gradual hymn (the *de tempore* hymn, or "hymn of the day"), around which an important choral and organ literature developed.

In the period of liturgical decline in the 17th and 18th centuries, the close connection between the gradual hymn and the lessons was lost. Instead, the hymn became attached to the sermon and was increasingly referred to as the sermon hymn, a practice and terminology that continues in much of American Protestant nonliturgical worship.

The period of liturgical renewal in 19th-century Germany saw a revived interest in the *de tempore* hymn largely because of the work of such men as Rochus von Liliencron and Ludwig Schoeberlein and, in the 20th century, Christhard Mahrenholz, Wilhelm Thomas, and Konrad Ameln. Its introduction into America can be credited largely to the pioneering work of men like Ralph Gehrke and Edward Klammer in the middle of the 20th century. With the publication of *Lutheran Book of Worship* (1978), *Lutheran Worship* (1982), and *Christian Worship: A Lutheran Hymnal* (1993), the hymn of the day for the first time achieved official recognition in the → liturgies of North American → Lutheranism, its placement occurring either after the Gospel reading or following the sermon. In recent liturgical revisions the → Anglican churches have also largely reintroduced the gradual hymn prior to the Gospel reading.

Bibliography: F. BLUME, *Protestant Church Music: A History* (New York, 1974) • E. KLAMMER, "The Hymn of the Day," *Lutheran Worship: History and Practice* (ed. F. Precht; St. Louis, 1993) 559-65 • P. PFATTEICHER and C. R. MESSERLI, *Manual on the Liturgy: Lutheran Book of Worship* (Minneapolis, 1979) • C. SCHALK, *The Hymn of the Day and Its Use in Lutheran Worship* (St. Louis, 1983).

CARL SCHALK

Great Britain → United Kingdom

Greece

	1960	*1980*	*2000*
Population (1,000s):	8,327	9,643	10,597
Annual growth rate (%):	0.53	0.60	0.09
Area: 131,957 sq. km. (50,949 sq. mi.)			

A.D. *2000*

Population density: 80/sq. km. (208/sq. mi.)
Births / deaths: 1.01 / 1.06 per 100 population
Fertility rate: 1.45 per woman
Infant mortality rate: 8 per 1,000 live births
Life expectancy: 78.6 years (m: 76.0, f: 81.1)
Religious affiliation (%): Christians 94.7 (Orthodox 94.2, indigenous 2.2, other Christians 1.3), Muslims 3.6, nonreligious 1.4, other 0.3.

1. Churches
2. Ecumenism
3. Church and State
4. Other Religious Groups

1. Churches

Greece is a unidenominational country, with the vast majority of citizens belonging to the Orthodox Church of Greece. Constitutionally, this church represents the "dominant," established religion. The church is divided into some 80 bishoprics. The number fluctuates as provinces are divided when the population increases. Control is exercised by the → Synod of the Hierarchy, comprising the members of the Holy → Hierarchy, or all the metropolitans. The 12-member Permanent Holy Synod, consisting of metropolitans who serve in a one-year rotation under the presidency of the archbishop of Athens and all Greece. This synod deals with the church's ongoing business.

1.1. The Autocephalous Church of Greece came into being when the national Greek church gained its independence from the → Ecumenical Patriarchate of Constantinople in 1833 on the initiative of T. Farmakides (1784-1860), who already in 1826 had founded an autocephalous (i.e., independent) church. In 1850 the ecumenical patriarch confirmed → autocephaly. Some territories that later joined the Greek state are still under the ecumenical patriarch's → jurisdiction, including Crete and the Dodecanese islands. The 20 monasteries on Mount → Athos also come under the ecumenical patriarch, as do several dioceses in northern Greece (which, however, are administered by the Church of Greece).

1.2. The church's work is done by the approximately 80 metropolitans and 8,000 parish priests, who, unlike the bishops, are mostly married. For the most part, the clergy simply meet the elementary religious needs of the people, celebrating the liturgy and handing on a Greek Christian tradition, which is a mixture of classical elements and the Byzantine spirit of → Orthodoxy (§3), along the lines of the Eastern church. After 1936, with the founding of the church organization Apostoliki Diakonia, there has been an intensification of nonparochial church activities, bringing a great advance to → diakonia and → mission.

1.3. The laity are still the most essential factor in the renewal of church and society in terms of the gospel. Christian movements, especially the Zoe Fraternity, filled the gap prior to 1936. Lay theologians, who play the most important part in academic theology, are also vital. Most of the more recent Greek Orthodox theology has been done by lay theologians. For Greek theology, → dogma, → canon law, and → liturgy are still the most significant elements.

1.4. Roman Catholics and Protestants each claim less than 1 percent of the population. The churches represented are the Catholic Church of the Latin Rite, the Greek Church in Union with Rome, the Greek Evangelical Church, the German-speaking Evangelical Church, the Anglican St. Paul's Church, and the interdenominational American St. Andrew's Church. The last three are all in Athens and are extensions of a home church of the respective countries. Finally, note should be taken of the Oriental Orthodox → Armenian Apostolic Church, with its 10,000 members.

2. Ecumenism

In Greece interchurch relations are very weak. In particular, the relation between Orthodox and Roman Catholics (especially Uniate) is very unsettled. Since the → Uniate Church uses the same rite as the Orthodox, it is regarded as a Trojan horse whose aim is → proselytism. Savas Agouridis mentions a "Roman Catholic neurosis" that impedes logical discussion.

Another manifestation of this neurosis came with the decision of the Greek government to enter into diplomatic relations with the → Vatican. For the first time since Greek independence in 1821, there is a Greek representative at the Holy See and a → nuncio in Athens. This development has not been a positive element in the → dialogue between the churches because it is the work of the government and aroused stiff opposition in ecclesiastical and religious circles.

2.1. Furthermore, we cannot say that relations between the Church of Greece and the → ecumenical movement, including the → World Council of Churches, are positive. Conservative groups within Greece still call ecumenism a superheresy and defame the late Ecumenical Patriarch Athenagoras (d. 1972) for his contribution to ecumenical openness in the Orthodox Church.

This sphere also includes laypeople who do the main theological work (→ Lay Movements). All that the Orthodox Church contributes to the → ecumenical movement, and any openness it expresses, is due to the work of the laity. After World War II the Greek church was the only free Orthodox church, and it had to assume the whole burden of representing Orthodoxy in the ecumenical movement.

2.2. The monks help to perpetuate resistance to ecumenism (→ Monasticism). Their true sociological importance is very slight, though there are still 200 monasteries and 12,000 monks in Greece. These monks (esp. those of Athos), however, embody an extremely conservative Orthodox spirit. This spirit undoubtedly influences the religious life of Greece,

and the antiecumenical efforts of the monks significantly hamper the attempts of the → Ecumenical Patriarchate to foster interchurch relations.

Supporters of the Old Style calendar aid the monks. Some 200,000 believers under the leadership of a schismatic hierarchy continue to resist the transition made by the Ecumenical Patriarchate in 1923 to change from the Julian calendar to the Gregorian.

3. Church and State

The antiecumenism of the Greek church is linked, among other factors, to its ethnocentrism, which in turn is explained by the church's relation to the state. Already in → Byzantium, on the theory of an imitation (*mimēsis*) of the → kingdom of God in the state of Constantine the Great, a link was forged between → church and state that was to the detriment of each other. The question who would be supreme — the patriarch or the emperor — is now seen to have been decided in favor of the emperor.

3.1. The dominance of the state was possible only because the church and theologians in Byzantium believed that the conflicts resulting from the two roles of serving God and serving the emperor could finally be resolved by sacralizing the emperor (i.e., in Caesaropapism; → Empire and Papacy). The most important contributor to this line of thinking was Eusebius of Caesarea (ca. 260-ca. 340), who integrated the emperor into a theological system that related the empire and the gospel in such a way that imperial absolutism corresponded to Christian → monotheism.

3.2. The collapse of Byzantium led to the development of an incipient national consciousness in the Orthodox churches. These churches entered into close relations with the newly emerging national states, a development that was clearest in Russia before the revolution (→ Nation, Nationalism). But it has also been a factor in Greece, where to the present the political arm guarantees the church economic support; in return, religion legitimizes and sacralizes political power.

3.3. The coup in Greece in April 1967 offers an illustration of the church-state relation. It confirmed the fact that church and society are two different and alien worlds in Greece, but also that they are united by common national interests. The leaders of this revolt, ostensibly protecting these interests against the "enemy," had to bring about a minirevolution in the church so as to make the church a worthy bearer of their Greco-Christian → ideology and thus to show that the revolt was a sacred event. Some church circles were ready at once to lend their active support. With the help of the military they seized power in the church and legitimated the ideology of the new government, declaring it to be necessary for the protection of the country.

3.4. At that time A. Papandreou brought in a → socialist government, the first in Greek history, winning the election with the slogan *Allagē* (Change). The change initiated by the new government also affected the church. Article 3 of the new constitution of June 9, 1975, stated (as before) that the "Eastern Orthodox Church of Christ" is the "prevalent" religion. A separation between the two was planned, however, and relations between church and state have become more difficult.

Furthermore, most of the younger supporters of the new government were against the church because it symbolized the conservative and reactionary forces that had thus far shaped the destiny of Greece. Greece, then, began a process of secularizing that, in contrast to similar processes in the West, might well destroy the church. Greece is repeating a phenomenon that was so decisive in Russia. As Ernst Benz has shown, most sociopolitical impulses in Russia did not arise from Orthodox believers, whereas in Anglo-Saxon countries it was believers, especially in the → free churches, who took the lead in social renewal.

Nevertheless, the Greek people are still religious, and Greek socialists are not against religion, though they may be against the church. Thus the church may well escape the dangers that threaten it. Whether it does so or not depends primarily on whether it is ready to accept social change — not merely to develop a social teaching and ethics in keeping with political demands but to put these ideas into dynamic practice.

4. Other Religious Groups

The church in Greece, now for the first time in its history, must reckon with → religious liberty and → tolerance, that is, pluralism. It is thus forced to coexist with other religious groups. The new constitution grants all "recognized religions" full freedom of practice. The result is that the Orthodox Church can no longer count on the help of the government, the judiciary, or the police to prevent competition.

4.1. Groups regarded as sects, especially → Jehovah's Witnesses, profit the most by this change. The number of Witnesses is still small, but they do very intensive and widespread work among the people. For this reason the Church of Greece, with help from the state, persecuted them for so long. Under the new constitution in 1975, however, it was unable

to stop the Witnesses from organizing an international congress in Greece to which 20,000 members came. In view of the religious neutrality of the socialists, the church is also helpless to block the entrance of foreign → sects and religious movements that appeal especially to the younger generation.

4.2. Though the Orthodox Church is hostile to sects, it coexists peacefully with the few Muslims (→ Islam) and Jews (→ Judaism). In all Greece there are well below a half million Muslims (mostly in Rhodes or in northern Greece). The number of Jews has been very small since the German occupation in World War II.

4.3. The following reason from the → sociology of religion might be advanced for the failure of the Greek church to come to terms with religious liberty and tolerance. Although Greece is part of highly developed and industrialized Europe, its social system is strongly oriented to a tradition whose religious and national elements are united against all the forces that seek an overturn of traditional values. Until now, this focus has been possible only because the church's own values, norms, and traditions could be mobilized (with the backing of the government) to reject any competing value system.

Bibliography: E. BENZ, *The Eastern Orthodox Church: Its Thought and Life* (Garden City, N.Y., 1963) • P. BRATSIOTIS, *The Greek Orthodox Church* (Notre Dame, Ind., 1968) • J. CAMPBELL and P. SHERRARD, *Modern Greece* (New York, 1969) • C. CAVARNOS, *Modern Greek Thought* (Belmont, Mass., 1986) • R. CLOGG, *A Concise History of Greece* (Cambridge, 1997) • A. M. CONIARIS, *Introducing the Orthodox Church: Its Faith and Life* (Minneapolis, 1998) • D. J. CONSTANTELOS, *Understanding the Greek Orthodox Church: Its Faith, History, and Life* (Brookline, Mass., 1998) • P. EVDOKIMOV, *The Art of the Icon: A Theology of Beauty* (Redondo Beach, Calif., 1990) • D. J. GEANAKOPOULOS, *A Short History of the Ecumenical Patriarchate, 330-1990* (Brookline, Mass., 1990) • S. S. HARAKAS, *The Orthodox Church: 455 Questions and Answers* (Minneapolis, 1988) • F. LITSAS, ed., *A Companion to the Greek Orthodox Church* (2d ed.; New York, 1988) • J. MEYENDORFF, *The Orthodox Church: Its Past and Its Role in the World Today* (Crestwood, N.Y., 1996) • T. WARE, *The Orthodox Church* (rev. ed.; London, 1993).

DEMOSTHENES SAVRAMIS†
and GEORGE C. PAPADEMETRIOU

Greek Language

Ancient Greek, a daughter language of Indo-European, was the language of the tribes that in the second millennium B.C. pushed into various areas of the mainland of Greece, into the Aegean Islands, and onto the west coast of Asia Minor. At this time there were only two dialects, Northern Greek and Southern Greek, which did not differ so greatly as the dialects of the historical period. From Southern Greek there developed Old Ionic, Mycenaean, Ionic (with Attic), Arcadian, and Cypriot. From Northern Greek arose Aeolic (Lesbian, East Hessalian, Boeotian) and Doric-Northwest Greek, which gradually became more and more distinct from Ionic.

Of literary significance were the heroic poems of Asia Minor written in Ionic (with some Aeolic features). A literary language came into being in which the *Iliad* and the *Odyssey* have come down to us. These epics are the end result of a long tradition that is not wholly exhausted by them.

Since the first prose writers wrote Ionic, this was the language of prose up to the fifth century B.C. From the middle of the fifth century Attic extended its range because of the cultural eminence of Athens. It became the basis of a Mediterranean lingua franca, the Koine, and although individual peculiarities were eliminated, the structure and vocabulary remained Attic, and up to the imperial period the style of Attic authors of around 400 B.C. was imitated. When the Romans conquered the eastern Mediterranean (→ Roman Empire), they used Koine as an official language. Greek syntax, with its wealth of nuances, served as a model for Latin, on which the syntax of many European languages is based (although Latin itself lacks the range of semantic and syntactic forms present in Greek).

As Koine achieved dominance in the Mediterranean lands, it inevitably became the form of Greek into which the OT was translated. The LXX, however, tried to follow the original in its choice of words and sentence structure, often at the cost of intelligibility (→ Bible Versions). The NT books were written in the first century A.D. in the Koine of the day and under LXX influence. The stylistic range covers Luke at one end (with occasional Atticisms) and Mark at the other. Greek remained the language of the Western church until Latin replaced it after Tertullian (d. ca. 225) and Minucius Felix (d. ca. 250).

Bibliography: W. BAUER, W. F. ARNDT, F. W. GINGRICH, and F. W. DANKER, *A Greek-English Lexicon of the NT and Other Early Christian Literature* (5th ed.; Chicago, 1979) • F. BLASS, A. DEBRUNNER, and R. W. FUNK, *A Greek Grammar of the NT and Other Early Christian Literature* (Chicago, 1973; orig. pub., 1896) • P. CHANTRAINE, *Dictionnaire étymologique de la langue Grecque* (Paris, 1968) • G. W. H. LAMPE, *A Patristic Greek Lexicon* (Oxford, 1961) • H. G. LIDDELL and R. SCOTT, *A Greek-English Lexicon* (9th ed.; Oxford, 1940; repr., 1996; orig. pub., 1843) • H. RIX, *Historische Grammatik des Griechischen* (Darmstadt, 1976) • E. SCHWYZER, *Griechische Grammatik* (6 vols.; Munich, 1968-94).

HELMUT DÜRBECK

Greek Orthodox Church → Orthodox Church

Greek Philosophy

1. Epochs
2. Pre-Socratics
3. Sophists
4. Socrates
5. Plato
6. Aristotle
7. Postclassical Philosophy
    7.1. Epicureans
    7.2. Stoics
    7.3. Skeptics

1. Epochs

Greek philosophy was developing from the sixth century B.C. to the first century A.D. Within this period we may distinguish the archaic or preclassical, classical, and postclassical epochs.

The archaic period is essentially characterized by questions that the so-called pre-Socratics (thinkers preceding Socrates and his followers) posed in the sphere of the → philosophy of nature. These questions served the interests of rational explanation and involved a breaking free from → myth and its approaches. The classical period, represented in particular by Plato's dialogues and Aristotle's treatises, opened up a view of reality in general and reflected on the position of humanity *sub specie aeternitatis.* In the postclassical period there was a narrower focus on matters of individual lifestyle in a world that was increasingly felt to be threatening.

2. Pre-Socratics

The thinking of the pre-Socratics made the step from myth to Logos and in so doing laid down the conditions necessary for the development of philosophical reflection. We see this step clearly in the use of such terms as *kosmos* and *physis*.

2.1. The word *kosmos* came from everyday speech, where it referred to any kind of order or adornment, and also was used in ethical and political connections. With its application to what we now call the world, there opened up for early thinking a new dimension of comprehensive order within which things and events have their place. In particular, the use of *kosmos* for the world as a whole brought out a normative element, namely, the idea that all that is, is well ordered as it is. This normative element found expression in the concept of right (*dikē*). Becoming and perishing are happenings that obey a specific order and follow the principle of compensatory → righteousness. Above all, the normative significance applies to the concept of origin. The *archē* is the starting point, the beginning, the genesis, the basis — and it can also be used for political government. It is not surprising, then, that the origin of all things (e.g., air or → fire or, in Anaximander [610-546/45 B.C.], the boundless) is also that which directs and governs all the things that arise from it.

No less significant was the concept of *physis*. This word, usually translated "nature" (Lat. "place of birth"), etymologically suggests in its root *phy-* the idea of seeding, bearing, and growth, with the suffix *-sis* indicating a process. Thus when the word was applied to the world of → experience in general, the early philosophers depicted in terms of growth that which we now call reality and think of in terms of action. The term *physis* is a first term for reality. Also worth noting is the fact that reality, in this depiction, is self-controlling. This thought finds particular expression in Empedocles (ca. 490-430 B.C.), who described the four basic elements of earth, air, fire, and water as the roots (*rizōmata*) of all being (*Frg.* 6.1) and thus anchored reality, as it were, in itself. But reality was also seen as something that may be meaningfully and adequately described in terms like growth. We find this thought in Anaxagoras (ca. 500-ca. 428), who postulated that seeds (*spermata*) and aggregates (*panspermia*) of seeds were the basic qualities (*Frg.* 4), and in Anaximander, who postulated a generative potential (*gonimon*). There are close connections here with the physiological theories of medical writers.

2.2. The development of philosophical inquiry was determined further by reflection on the conceptual implications of the above ideas. The Pythagorean school was interested in such matters as measure, proportion, and harmony. Especially Philolaus (fl. ca. 475 B.C.) seems to have applied such concepts

to cosmological matters. His discussion of the definite (*peras*) and the indefinite (*apeiron*) influenced speculations on the conditions that are posed for the objects of real knowledge.

Heraclitus (ca. 540-ca. 480 B.C.), who attracted Hegel, pondered the question of unity and stressed that things and forces that everyday thinking regards as polarities are to be properly understood as expressions of a universal → reason (Logos). Nor is the reference merely to the becoming and perishing of individual things, for the perishing of one thing corresponds to the genesis of another, and vice versa; terms like "stability" and "change" go together. This thought gave rise to the metaphor of the river ("one cannot step twice into the same river," for new currents are constantly flowing by; *Frg.* 12). This metaphor shows that the identity of a thing involves movement and change. Here is the root of the thinking that would later be called dialectical (→ Dialectic). Everyday thought isolates and separates, whereas in reality there is unity and integration.

Early philosophical thought entered another dimension with the question of being, which was raised in particular by Parmenides (d. after 480 B.C.), the founder of Western → metaphysics and → ontology. In a didactic poem stylized as the revelation of an unnamed goddess, Parmenides espoused the thesis that the sensory world of multiplicity and change is a product of the erroneous conception of human thought. In what seems to be an anticipation of Spinoza, he argued that we may think truly and coherently only of the one eternal being. His distinction between an unreal world of *physis* and a true world of being inspired the two-world teaching of Plato. Above all, his deliberations on the → logic of being forced all subsequent philosophers to reflect in a new way on the phenomenon of becoming, perishing, and change. They did so by viewing the processes of change as a mixing or unmixing of previously existing and eternal elements (Empedocles); as a reordering of eternal, physically autonomous atoms (Leucippus, Democritus); or as an unmixing and mixing of seedlike particles (Anaxagoras).

3. Sophists

In the fifth and fourth centuries B.C. there was also a trend of thought that is usually known as Sophistry, which can be viewed as an anthropological development in philosophy. It quickly gained ground, for a change in political structures highlighted the need for skill in argument and for abilities that could be put to practical use. This need was met by men like Gorgias (ca. 483-ca. 376 B.C.) and Protagoras (ca. 485-ca. 410). Among the themes of the day was the question whether values exist in nature or are a matter of mere agreement. There is especially impressive witness to such discussions in Plato's early dialogues. Thus Callicles in *Gorgias* argues for the right of the stronger — a thought that influenced F. Nietzsche. Antiphon, another Sophist, attempted to see in legal norms a perversion of our true nature. Protagoras's most famous principle (Humans are the measure of all things — of things that are, that they are, of things that are not, that they are not) is the manifesto of a mode of thinking traditionally regarded as → relativism.

4. Socrates

Socrates (ca. 470-399 B.C.) comes into the story as the opponent and opposite of the Sophists. This evaluation of a person about whom we know next to nothing historically derives from Plato's dialogues. They depict Socrates as the thinker who pressed the Sophists with questions such as What is virtue? and What is bravery? Looking for general definitions, he entangled his opponents in contradictions. To a desire to be successful in politics he opposed the need to reflect on the health of one's soul. The → soul alone counts, for it is the true person. In this light we can understand what are sometimes felt to be the paradoxical Socratic theses that doing wrong is worse than suffering wrong, and that no one does wrong voluntarily. Socrates, the victim of a politically motivated accusation, was the first philosopher to be put to death for his views.

5. Plato

Plato (427-347 B.C.) transformed the initiatives of Socrates into a broad net of deliberations. In him → philosophy reached its full range and developed all its special themes (→ Platonism). With good reason, A. N. Whitehead once described the philosophical tradition of Europe as merely a series of footnotes on Plato. In his dialogues Plato dealt with all the themes he regarded as worth discussing. This literary form prevents us from making an overly strict systematization and sets a certain distance between what Plato was really thinking and what he presented.

The main figure in the debates is Socrates. The early dialogues discuss primarily themes that arose in discussion with the Sophists. In the so-called middle dialogues the literary Socrates goes beyond destroying the claims of others to set forth his own theses, and here Plato's own views find expression. He gives his thoughts about the true nature of reality, about knowledge, about his soul, and about the task of living as a philosopher. In the later dialogues Plato seems to think out many of his views afresh. In *Parmenides,* for example, he discusses difficulties of understanding that some of his disciples had experienced. Sometimes these so-called critical dialogues are interpreted as evidence of Platonic self-criticism.

5.1. At the heart of Plato's philosophy is the doctrine of the two worlds, a development of the ideas of Heraclitus and Parmenides. Plato shares with the former the view that the world of experience is in constant flux, offering no firm foothold for thought. He shares with the latter the idea that this world is one of appearance. In contrast, as we see in *Phaedo* and the *Republic,* there is the world of unchangeable being, the realm of the ideas. Gk. *idea* means strictly a visible form, which Plato uses to describe that which the mental eye sees and which irreversibly influences us. The ideas are thus objects of mental knowledge. They are models or archetypes (see Plotinus, whom C. G. Jung read sporadically). They serve as → norms of thought and as models for the world and the things in it (thus esp. *Timaeus,* which is of central importance for an understanding of medieval philosophy).

The ideas — for example, beauty in itself — are the purest form of what we know in the empirical world only as an aspect (e.g., the beauty of this statue or of that music), which, however, is not to be confused with the thing itself. Things share in the ideas, but they are not that for which the ideas alone stand. If we want to know the true nature of virtue, for example, we must turn to the idea itself.

5.2. Human beings (→ Anthropology 4) or their souls are citizens of two worlds. In virtue of its relation to the ideas, however, the soul really belongs to the world of being. In fact Plato, like Pythagoras, seems to have assumed that after physical → death the soul must answer for all the deeds done in life. We thus have the task of living with a view to eternity and in this way finally escaping the cycle of birth and rebirth (→ Reincarnation). It is thus in our best interest to know how to order life's conditions, in the broadest sense, in such a way as to achieve this eternal perspective to the greatest possible extent. To this end Plato, in the *Republic,* constructs an ideal → state that takes into account our objective interests.

6. Aristotle

Aristotle (384-322 B.C.), from Macedonia, joined the school of Plato when he was 18 years old. Relatively early in his stay there, Aristotle seems to have argued against many of the views of his teacher (esp. regarding the concept of transcendental ideas). His own thinking first found expression in dialogues, which are now lost, and then especially in didactic writings that were later revised and put in their present form and sequence (→ Aristotelianism). His works show a definite system, and his own systematic interest may have contributed to the distinguishing of various philosophical disciplines and the corresponding separation of subjects. Along with logic, which he founded, we have such purely theoretical disciplines as mathematics, natural philosophy, and metaphysics (lit. "[books] after physics"), and then practical or action-oriented disciplines like → ethics and politics.

6.1. Belonging to logic in the broader sense is the inquiry into the structures of statement and thought, which are treated together along the lines of → realism. In this connection Aristotle speaks also about → categories (originally "accusations"), which he regarded as natural divisions of → language and reality.

To logic in the narrower sense of logical theory belong the teaching on syllogisms and then, on that basis, → epistemology. In this connection we find a theory of explanations and an inquiry into claims to knowledge. Like Plato, Aristotle had a strict concept of knowledge. To know something is to be able to say *why* it is. Claims to knowledge thus are justified only by *explanations* of the things at issue.

6.2. Like Plato, Aristotle criticized previous thinkers who in their explanations simply referred to immanent structures and took no account of metaphysical structures. Unlike Plato, however, he did not postulate the existence of ideas outside time and space. For him, the forms of things were immanent in the things themselves. He distinguished material cause (the physical stuff of the thing in question), formal cause (the plan or idea of the thing), efficient (or moving) cause (the agent actually producing the thing), and final cause (the end or purpose of the thing).

Consideration of these concepts led Aristotle to the postulating of an eternal, unmoved mover beyond time and space who exists without matter and without change (→ God 3). Of central importance in his explanation of natural processes was also his distinction between possible being *(dynamis)* and actual being *(energeia)*, along with his distinction between the being of substance *(ousia)* and the being of properties.

6.3. In ethics Aristotle focused primarily on an analysis and description of moral phenomena as they offer themselves for reflection. In this sense he was the first to conceptualize that which in some sense we know. We see this accomplishment especially in the discussion of actions as actions, in the description of voluntariness and involuntariness, and in the description of → virtue as the mean between two negative extremes. Crucially important are his discussions of desire and of human well-being *(eudaimonia;* → Happiness). The supreme form of human life consists of the contemplation *(theōria)* of eternal truths.

7. Postclassical Philosophy

Greek philosophy after Aristotle is characterized by the Epicureans, Stoics, and Skeptics. Political changes and menacing personal conditions gave philosophy new priorities. All philosophers expressed trust in Socrates, adopting his concern for human welfare.

7.1. *Epicureans*

Epicurus (341-270 B.C.) taught that the immediate task of philosophy is to free the soul from unfounded anxieties (e.g., fear of death or fear of the gods). The atomism that he championed (and tried to justify with what were at times complicated arguments) can be understood as a way to make the world seem to be a product of → chance. Empirical reality has no meaning; there is nothing metaphysical. Chance — the free, unmotivated, inexplicable variation of atoms — is the answer to all questions. The only meaning is that which we ourselves posit. Learning from experience, Epicurus found this meaning in the natural striving of all living creatures for pleasure. Humans alone can achieve true well-being. Surprisingly, Epicurus defined pleasure primarily as the state of freedom from pain (which suggests that he himself had a painful life). This definition, though, is hard to justify, and the general thesis of → hedonism, with its equation of the desirable and the good, suffers from the fact that a thing is not worth striving for simply because we do strive for it.

7.2. *Stoics*

→ Stoicism, named after the Athenian *stoa* (colonnade) in which it was taught, was in direct rivalry with the school of Epicurus. The older Stoics — Zeno (ca. 335-ca. 263 B.C.), Cleanthes (331/30-232/31), and Chrysippus (ca. 280-ca. 206) — were rigorous moralists who found the ideal of life in freedom from passions, which intellectually they either regarded as the result of wrong judgments (Zeno) or equated with such judgments (Chrysippus). A life of virtue was for them a life of reason. They viewed reason as a part of the rational structure of the whole. The world itself was permeated by a firelike *pneuma* and was a providentially ordered unity. Philosophy thus had the task of recognizing that the totality is a rationally governed structure of meaning to which we must fatalistically adjust. If we see ourselves as parts of the whole, we also live in harmony with ourselves.

Later Stoics like Panaetius (ca. 180-109 B.C.) and Poseidonius (ca. 135-ca. 51) seemed to have softened much of Stoic teaching. The Stoicism of the empire (esp. that of Marcus Aurelius) displays many contacts with the Platonic tradition.

7.3. Skeptics

→ Skepticism (Gk. *skeptikos,* "thoughtful, reflective") derived from Pyrrho of Elis (ca. 360-ca. 272 B.C.), who regarded the relativizing of all claims to knowledge as the way to peace of soul. The developed skeptical arguments of Sextus Empiricus (fl. early 3d cent. A.D.) display the basic undogmatic attitude of such thinkers. Exaggerated claims to knowledge seemed to him to be dangerous.

A competing skeptical tradition arose temporarily in the Platonic Academy. Arcesilaus (316/15-ca. 241 B.C.) and even more so Carneades (ca. 213-129) attacked the dogmatism of the Stoics. At times for them the principle that nothing is knowable even seems to take the form of a negative → dogmatism. There is a difference here from the followers of Pyrrho, who did not seek to advance any claims to knowledge at all but, within the limits of the present state ("we are still seeking"), left things hanging in the air.

→ Hellenism

Bibliography: T. COLE, *Democritus and the Sources of Greek Anthropology* (Atlanta, 1990) • F. M. CORNFORD, *From Religion to Philosophy: A Study in the Origins of Western Speculation* (Princeton, 1991) • A. GRAESER, *Die Philosophie der Antike,* vol. 2, *Sophistik und Sokratik, Plato und Aristoteles* (Munich, 1983) • G. W. F. HEGEL, *Lectures on the History of Philosophy* (3 vols.; trans. E. S. Haldane; Lincoln, Nebr., 1995) • M. HOSSENFELDER, *Die Philosophie der Antike,* vol. 3, *Stoa, Epikureismus und Skepsis* (Munich, 1985) • W. RÖD, *Die Philosophie der Antike,* vol. 1, *Von Thales bis Demokrit* (Munich, 1976) • C. STEAD, *Philosophy in Christian Antiquity* (Cambridge, 1999).

ANDREAS GRAESER

Greek Religion

1. General Character
2. Historical Development

1. General Character

As a product of the → polytheism of pagan antiquity, Greek religion had no concept of a transcendent → God or of an omnipotent Creator and Ruler of the world. Its pantheon is a hierarchically and, in part, genealogically integrated system of immanent, functionally limited deities of various types who represent natural forces (→ Nature Religion) and cosmic phenomena (Poseidon as god of the sea, Helios and Selene as astral gods, Boreas as a wind demon) or terrestrial, agrarian powers (Demeter as goddess of the harvest, Dionysus [Bacchus] as god of wine, Hades [Pluto] as lord of the underworld) or forces that are important for human existence in an uncertain environment (Artemis as goddess of the chase, Aphrodite as goddess of love, Ares as god of war, Hermes as god of commerce and travel, Hecate as mistress of the underworld). In some deities, too, the aptitude of the Greeks for technical and artistic creativity comes to light (Athena as goddess of handicraft and practical wisdom; Apollo as god of poetry, healing, and prophecy; Hephaestus as god of fire and metalworking).

To the distinctiveness of these figures as specific potencies with anthropomorphic or anthropopathic qualities, and with activities oriented to spheres of human life, there corresponds a formally established canon of cultic rites and practices with → prayer, → sacrifice, and feasts. There was, however, no written or oral confession, no religious proclamation or instruction, and no revealed content of belief.

2. Historical Development

Because of the lack of political unity and the formation of only regional states, there was never any homogeneous Greek religion. Instead, we find cultic centers with transregional significance (e.g., Delos, Delphi, Dodona, Eleusis, and Olympia). The Olympian circle came together before the time of the Greeks, when the religious ideas of an indigenous Mediterranean population, already of varied cultural status, were influenced by the traditions of Indo-European migrants into the Balkan peninsula, along with marginal elements from Pontus and other Near Eastern regions.

Among the deities attested by Mycenean Linear B tablets is Zeus (Myc. Diwo), the original Indo-European god of sky and weather, but later partially infiltrated by a childish numen of Cretan-Mediterranean provenance (Zeus Kretagenes) and Anatolian West Semitic weather gods (Zeus Labrayndos, Zeus Kasios). Ares, the god of war (Myc. Are), has on the one side Thracian Indo-European roots but might also be compared to the Carian battle demon Enyalios (Myc. Enuwarijo). Behind the armed daughter of Zeus Athena (Myc. Atana Potinija) may be seen an old Minoan goddess of shield and palace whose position as ruler (Potnia) finally made her

Athena Polias (i.e., guardian of the city). Hera (Myc. Era), the spouse of Zeus and patroness of marriage, gives evidence of Aegean influence, as may be seen from traditional wooden statues *(xoana)* in Argos and Samos that display her genealogical relation to Eileithyia (Myc. Ereutija), the pre-Hellenic goddess of childbirth. Artemis (Myc. Atimite), who with her brother Apollo is a bow-carrying twin-numen with roots in Asia Minor, has the features of a Near Eastern–Anatolian mistress of animals. Even by name Hermes is related to a heap of stones such as was used to mark highways (Gk. *herma*) or to phallic pillar idols (Myc. Emaa) of an aniconic stone cult of a Mediterranean type. Dionysus (Myc. Diwonusojo), with an ancient sanctuary on Chios, took on features of Thrace and Phrygia (sometime being identified with the god Sabazius) and of Lydia (from association with Semele). Similarly, Hephaestus displays Tyrrhenian features (esp. from Lemnos), as Aphrodite does Semitic-Oriental features (of Ishtar-Astarte). In contrast, the hippomorphic Poseidon (Myc. Posedaone), the counterpart to Zeus, is related to the horselike Demeter and is Indo-European in origin, though possibly incorporating Minoan prefigurations of an animal-like god of the sea and of earthquakes (the Cretan bull).

The mythology of the Homeric epics unites these genetically disparate gods into an Olympian family modeled on the early Greek feudal nobility and oriented to a world of heroes living by a knightly code. The relating of this world to similar but immortal gods (Hesiod *Theog.* and *Cat.*) fixed also the religious practice and experience of the Homeric period (which involved sacrifices, individual veneration, oaths, visions, and direction through dreams). It also influenced its eschatological vision (which included Elysium and the veneration of heroes).

In contrast, the religion of the polis in the post-Homeric age stressed the official worship of locally significant numina from a patriotic standpoint and the respecting of personified communal values (e.g., Dike, Themis, Nike, and Aidos, the goddesses of justice, wisdom and good counsel, victory, and shame). It also emphasized the unifying factor of Pan-Hellenic festivals and games (including the Olympic games every fourth summer beside the Alpheus River, Isthmian games at Corinth, biennial games at Nemea), which take up older features of extralocal significance (the Eleusinian mysteries, the ecstatic cult of Dionysus, the Orphic doctrine of transmigration; → Mystery Religions). Two aspects of religious life in the later archaic and classical periods — the questioning of divine-human relations in Attic tragedy, and reflection on the ideas and mani-

festation of the divine in → Greek philosophy (by pre-Socratics, Sophists, and → Platonism) — are landmarks on the way to the postclassical religion of → Hellenism (→ Hellenistic-Roman Religion).

→ Myth, Mythology

Bibliography: C. M. Antonaccio, "Contesting the Past: Hero Cult, Tomb Cult, and Epic in Early Greece," *AJA* 98 (1994) 389-410 • H. D. Betz, ed., *The Greek Magical Papyri in Translation, Including the Demotic Spells* (2d ed.; Chicago, 1992) • J. N. Bremmer, *Greek Religion* (Oxford, 1994) • W. Burkert, *Griechische Religion der archaischen und klassischen Epoche* (Stuttgart, 1977) • R. G. A. Buxton, *Imaginary Greece: The Contexts of Mythology* (Cambridge, 1994) • E. Des Places, *La religion grecque* (Paris, 1969) • K. Dowden, *The Uses of Greek Mythology: Approaching the Ancient World* (London, 1992) • R. Garland, *Religion and the Greeks* (London, 1994) • M. Gerard-Rousseau, *Les mentions religieuses dans les tablettes mycéniennes* (Rome, 1968) • P. J. Jensen, "Die griechische Religion," *HRG* 3.135-216 • M. C. Nussbaum, *The Therapy of Desire: Theory and Practice in Hellenistic Ethics* (Princeton, 1994) • R. Parker, *Athenian Religion: A History* (Oxford, 1996).

Wolfgang Fauth

Gregorian Chant

1. Term
2. Historical Development
3. Repertory
   3.1. Genres
   3.2. Musical-Aesthetic Description
4. Liturgical Function
   4.1. Roman Catholic Church
   4.2. Lutheran Church

1. Term

"Gregorian chant" is the collective name and stylistic designation for the (medieval) tradition and repertory collected in liturgical books of the monodic, originally unaccompanied chant of the → liturgy of Roman Catholic ritual. The designation derives from a legend arising in connection with the Frankish reception of the Roman liturgy in the eighth and ninth centuries, one identifying Pope Gregory I (590-604) as the author or editor first of the texts, then also of the melodies of the *cantus gregorianus* (first in the 9th cent.). Although no historical proof has been adduced for Gregory as the initiator either of the texts or of the melodies, his efforts at organizing the liturgy itself may well have indirectly affected the emergence or editing of the choral repertory.

Gregorian chant, an expression concerned with a linguistically appropriate choral development of liturgical texts based on a spiritual understanding of the words, continues to influence musical developments in → worship today. It represents a potential, specific genre of irreplaceable significance for liturgical music in general even today, one that cannot be replaced, for example, by the hymnic form (→ Church Music; Hymnody).

2. Historical Development

The transition from Greek to Latin in the Roman liturgy (3d-4th cent.) was accompanied by a corresponding adaptation of choral elements. The beginnings of this musical development are as complex as they are obscure. The earliest sources of the choral tradition initially called *cantilena romana* (by Paul the Deacon [d. ca. 800]) or *cantus romanus* are manuscripts from the eighth and ninth centuries, primarily from the Frankish sphere, containing liturgical texts as yet without any musical notation.

The first manuscripts with complete repertory and with the neumatic notation date from the early 10th century. Although these manuscripts do not yet provide information regarding tonal intervals, they do contain extremely detailed instructions for the interpretation of the melodies and melodic models the singers already knew by heart. The earliest manuscripts fixing the melodic intervals by means of notation lines appear a century later.

Beginning in the 11th/12th centuries, regional choral traditions can be discerned, including what is known as the ancient Roman tradition. Distinct choral traditions have also been identified for Milan ("Ambrosian chant"), Spain ("Mozarabic chant"), and Benevento. Scholars also speak of a Germanic and East Frankish choral dialect that spread from Germany to eastern Europe and Scandinavia. Musicologists in this area try to determine how changes in the (oral) tradition caused by certain elements being committed to writing (Frankish redaction) and the subsequent modifications (tropes, → motets) then interact within the context of altered liturgical conditions. Recasting of Gregorian chants for new feast days (of saints) and the blossoming of polyphony support the weakening, already evident beginning in the 10th century, of the Gregorian tradition.

Efforts to restore the authentic tradition began in the mid-19th century. Commensurate with the order of Pius X (1903-14) to reproduce the Gregorian chant according to the earliest manuscripts, the most important chants were published between 1905 and 1912 in connection with research conducted at the abbey at Solesmes. Insufficient scientific grounding, the influence of "living choral traditions," and an interest in solutions capable of immediate pastoral-liturgical implementation, however, resulted in faulty compromises in melodic reconstruction and in the theoretically inappropriate transposition of modern or Greek-influenced metrical rhythmic systems to Gregorian melodies, even though the theory of oratory choral rhythms advanced by Dom J. Pothier (1835-1923) had already pointed in a different direction.

Semiology, emerging in the mid-20th century and founded by Dom E. Cardine (1905-88), marks a new stage in restoration efforts. A paleographically based study of sources has attempted to reconstruct the melodies behind the earliest manuscripts and to establish a choral interpretation as authentic as possible by determining the exact meaning of the neumatic signs. The results of these efforts, ecclesiastically confirmed at Vatican II (*Sacrosanctum concilium* [SC] 117), have included works from *Graduel neumé* (1966) to *Benediktinisches Antiphonale*, vol. 4, *Vorsängerbuch* (1997).

3. Repertory

3.1. *Genres*

Gregorian repertory consists essentially of songs for the → Mass and for the canonical → hours, the former of which can be classified according to liturgical recitatives and songs of the proper and the ordinary of the Mass (the *Proprium missae* and *Ordinarium missae*). The cantillation (i.e., solemn recitation with musical tones of prayer or scriptural texts) by the leader, lector, or → congregation draws from recitational models underscoring a text's syntactic structure with an emphasis on meaning.

Songs of the proper include antiphonal (introit, originally the offertory, communion) and responsorial (→ Gradual) types. Commensurate with their various liturgical functions, the former are cast as songs for accompanying a rite within a more simplified (oligotonic) compositional style, while the latter, as liturgical actions, have a pronounced meditative or proclamatory character and, with their melismatic compositional style (several tones per syllable), make higher demands on the singers. In the tract (the song preceding the Gospel during Lent), Psalm verses are sung one after another, without any interceding repetition pieces. During the 9th and 10th centuries, the strophic sequence arose, a song providing the foundation in both music and liturgical history for the vernacular → hymn in the Roman liturgy.

The songs of the ordinary, in contrast to those of the proper, do not exhibit any fixed musical forms. Depending on their liturgical function and textual form, they exhibit either a basic acclamative or hymnic character (Kyrie, Sanctus, Agnus Dei) or (more often) a recitative character (Gloria, Credo). Early on, the song of the → Psalms (§2) and → canticles of the canonical hours developed recitative models (Psalm melodies) whose structure corresponded to the literary structure typical of the Psalter and other biblical canticles. The various intervals between the basic tone (the *finalis* of the antiphon) and psalm tone with the accompanying location of half-steps yields the characteristic key ("tuning") of the various choral modes and simultaneously the criterion for classifying the psalm tones into an eight-tone schema.

3.2. Musical-Aesthetic Description

The basis for melodic construction in (non-recitative) Gregorian chant is both modally and rhythmically the sound of the (Latin) word and the semantic structure of the text itself. As a given word's dynamic center, its accented syllable supplies the impulse for the movement of melodic tension and release, and in the final word, the melodic movement itself serves an important function of either release (architectonic) or buildup (rhetorical). Choral chant thus does not mean that "music is added to the word or the word made into music," but that "the resonance or sounding of the word itself is the music" (G. Joppich).

4. Liturgical Function

Given its inclination to generate a uniformity and "objectivity" of musical expression, Gregorian chant functions specifically as a musical expression of word proclamation and of its response in the form of → meditation, → prayer, confession, and praise as the basic acts of the communal celebration of the liturgy.

4.1. Roman Catholic Church

The admittance of the vernacular into the Roman Catholic liturgy by → Vatican II does not eliminate the acknowledgment of Latin Gregorian chant as the proper choral style of the Roman liturgy (*SC* 116). The council, however, expressly approved of using all musical forms of true art in structuring a worship service commensurate with the liturgy (*SC* 112.3). Such statements signaled a willingness to structure worship in a way that considers the needs of the participants and allows a critical review of the traditional Gregorian repertory (uneven in its quality) with regard to liturgical function and musicological qualities.

4.2. Lutheran Church

The Lutheran tradition edited large portions of the Gregorian repertory in anthologies for worship (e.g., by M. Luther and T. Müntzer; → Lutheranism). German reworkings of the Latin choral tradition emerged first in the liturgical recitatives of the Mass (from 1521), then also among the other parts of the Latin repertory for the Mass and the canonical hours. These reworkings involved several different approaches. Either the German text was set to unaltered melodies (maintaining the melismata), or the melismata were eliminated in order to adapt the melodies to the syllabic structure of the text. Luther was very critical of both procedures, pointing out the necessity of maintaining a strict correspondence between melody and language ("Against the Heavenly Prophets" [1525], *LW* 40.141). He therefore reworked only the psalmody and lectionary models for the German text, fitted the melody to the German text in other songs, or created new, linguistically appropriate compositions following motifs and structures of original melodies. Latin Gregorian chant now began to lose significance in Protestant services, and the tension between a more ornamental, "musically oriented" style and a direct structuring of German hymnic modes based more rigorously on the sound of the language itself now shaped the development of the repertory.

Bibliography: Journals: Beiträge zur Gregorianik (Regensburg, 1985-) • *Études grégoriennes* (Solesmes, 1954-) • *Studi gregoriani* (Cremona, 1985-) • *Tijdschrift voor Gregoriaans* (Breda, 1975-).

Other works: L. AGUSTONI and J. B. GÖSCHL, *Einführung in die Interpretation des Gregorianischen Chorals* (2 vols.; Regensburg, 1987-92) • L. AGUSTONI et al., "Gregorianischer Choral," *Musik im Gottesdienst* (ed. H. Musch; 2d ed.; Regensburg, 1983) 1.203-374 • W. APEL, *Gregorian Chant* (3d ed.; Bloomington, Ind., 1966) • E. CARDINE, *Gregorian Semiology* (Solesmes, 1982) • G. J. CUMING, *The Liturgy of St. Mark Edited from the Manuscripts, with a Commentary* (Rome, 1990) • S. J. P. VAN DIJK, "Recent Developments in the Study of the Old-Roman Rite," *StPatr* 8.299-319 • B. HÖCKER, *Lateinische Gregorianik im Lutherischen Gottesdienst?* (St. Ottilien, 1994) • H. HUCKE, "Gregorian and Old Roman Chant," *NGDMM* 7.693-97 (bibliography); idem, "Toward a New Historical View of Gregorian Chant," *JAMS* 33 (1980) 437-67 • A. HUGHES, *Medieval Manuscripts for Mass and Office* (Toronto, 1995) • K. W. HUMPHRIES, ed., *The Friars' Libraries: Corpus of British Medieval Library Catalogues* (London, 1990) • C. S. JAEGER, *The Envy of Angels: Cathedral Schools and Social Ideals in Medieval Europe,*

950-1200 (Philadelphia, 1995) • S. KLÖCKNER, "Semiologie," *MGG* (2d ed.) 8.1241-50 • M. PFAFF and J. STALMANN, "Gregorianik," *TRE* 14.191-99 (bibliography) • B. STÄBLEIN, "Gregorianik," *MGG* 5.786-96 • R. STEINER, "Gregorian Chant," *NGDMM* 7.697-98.

MARKUS EHAM

Gregory I

Pope Gregory I (ca. 540-604), known as Gregory the Great, was the last of the traditional Latin "Doctors of the Church." Little is known of his life apart from a letter he attached to his work on the Book of Job *(Magna moralia in Iob)* and scattered references in his other letters and writings. Unlike some other figures of the → patristic church, there is no contemporary biography. Most medieval accounts of his life are dependent upon the same sources available to modern scholarship.

The son of a senator, Gregory in 573 occupied the highest civil position in → Rome *(praefectus urbi)*. Shortly after this date, in an act not unusual for his time, Gregory sold his considerable holdings, provided assistance to the poor, and established the monastery of St. Andrew in Rome and six others in Sicily. He became a monk at St. Andrew and at some point around the year 579 was ordained one of the seven → deacons of Rome *(regionarius)*, either by Benedict I or by Pelagius II.

In the following year the same pope sent him to Constantinople as episcopal representative *(apocrisarius)*. Gregory remained as representative at the Imperial Court of the Eastern Empire for about seven years. There he knew Leander, who later became bishop of Seville, and engaged in theological discussions with Patriarch Eutyches. The degree to which Gregory knew Greek is subject to disagreement among experts. By 586 Gregory was back in Rome and again at St. Andrew's monastery. It is uncertain whether at this time he became → abbot of the community, but as a monastic he assisted the next pope, Pelagius II, with his papal duties. Upon Pelagius's death in 590, Gregory was the overwhelming choice of the people of Rome to become their bishop. He resisted, however, genuinely not desiring the office, even to the extent of urging Emperor Maurice not to approve of his election. Finally Gregory accepted election and entered into the papal office on September 3, 590.

He was the first monk chosen bishop of the Roman church. As a person skilled in administration, Gregory quickly moved on a number of fronts. The wars of Justinian I to reestablish control over Italy and the invasion of the Lombards had placed Italy in distressing circumstances. In 592 or 593 Gregory established peace with the Lombards, setting aside the authority of the emperor's representative. Gregory encouraged friendly relations with the Franks and Visigoths. He sought to alleviate shortages of food and help the many refugees entering Rome. The mission of Augustine, later of Canterbury, was promoted by Gregory, along with → Benedictine → monasticism. He provided for the efficient administration of the estates of the Roman church. Gregory, as pope, insisted on the supreme authority of the Roman See and rejected the claim of the patriarch of Constantinople to the title "ecumenical patriarch." His relations with the East were often strained.

After an eventful pontificate of 14 years, Gregory died on March 12, 604. He was canonized by popular acclaim immediately after his death. The appellation "the Great" indicates his contributions to the church of Rome. Contemporary scholarship sees Gregory as an educated late Roman aristocrat who converted to the ascetic ideal and was caught in a tension between his monastic vocation and papal ministry at a time of profound change for the western Roman world.

Throughout his life Gregory applied himself to writing. Not a speculator of original intellect, his works reflect pastoral and practical concerns. There is a vast number of Gregory's letters, collected in a work known as *Registrum epistolarum*. Two additional collections of letters are extant. Together these groupings contain 854 letters and provide a detailed picture of this period.

Regula pastoralis, dating from the early years of Gregory's pontificate, is a set of instructions for bishops in the discharge of their responsibilities. Its popularity was immediate and immense. *Dialogi de vita et miraculis patrum Italicorum* describes the lives and miracles of the saints of Italy. Its purpose was to offer comfort and encouragement to the people of Italy in this time of wars and famine.

Moralia in Iob is Gregory's major exegetical work. He began it during his days in Constantinople and continued to work on it with interruptions until July of 595. Gregory interpreted the biblical text of Job in a threefold manner: historical, typological, and moral. In this work of 35 books his preference was decidedly for the moral meaning. There is also a commentary on 1 Kings 1-16, which only within the past 50 years has been identified as Gregory's.

Several series of Gregory's sermons survive. They include those on the liturgical cycle of gospel lessons and on sections of the Book of Ezekiel and the Song of Solomon.

Gregory has also been identified with a sacramentary and a form of liturgical chant. His relationship to both developments is slight at best. He certainly wrote some prayers, but beyond this observation it is difficult to assign him with certainty a role in the evolution of the Western → liturgy.

Bibliography: Primary sources in English: Book of Pastoral Rule and Selected Epistles, NPNF (ser. 2) 12-13 • *Dialogues*, FC 39 • *Forty Gospel Homilies* (trans. D. Hurst; Kalamazoo, Mich., 1990) • *Pastoral Rule*, ACW 11.

Secondary works: J. C. CAVADINI, ed., *Gregory the Great: A Symposium* (South Bend, Ind., 1996) • F. H. DUDDEN, *Gregory the Great* (2 vols.; London, 1905) • E. DUFFY, *Saints and Sinners: A History of the Popes* (New Haven, 1997) esp. 45-57 • G. R. EVANS, *The Thought of Gregory the Great* (Cambridge, 1986) • R. A. MARKUS, *Gregory the Great and His World* (Cambridge, 1997) • C. STRAW, *Gregory the Great: Perfection in Imperfection* (Berkeley, Calif., 1988) with valuable bibliographic essay.

WILLIAM G. RUSCH

Gregory VII

Gregory VII (ca. 1018-85), whose baptized name was Hildebrand, was a pope and reformer of the church in the 11th century and one of the major figures in the struggle of that time between → church and state. The exact date of Hildebrand's birth is unknown. It was certainly before 1034, and a date around 1018 is probably quite accurate. He was born in Tuscany, probably in the vicinity of the modern city of Savona. Early in his life he went to → Rome and was educated there, presumably in the monastery of St. Mary on the Aventine. By the year 1047 or 1049 he had taken his monastic vows.

In 1046 Hildebrand was with Gregory VI when the latter was exiled to Germany. Even at this time Hildebrand was known for his concern to reform the church. By 1049 he had returned to Rome, Pope Leo IX having selected him to be the administrator of the patrimony of St. Peter. During the ensuing years Hildebrand played a major role in the affairs of the Roman church. He was involved during the pontificate of Nicholas II in the production of a decree that assigned the election of → popes to the cardinals. In 1059 Hildebrand became the archdeacon of the church of Rome, a position that he held until 1073.

That year saw the death of Pope Alexander II, under whom Hildebrand had served as chancellor of the Apostolic See. Immediately after his death a heated and disputed election took place to select his successor. The person finally chosen was the Archdeacon Hildebrand, who upon his election took the name of Gregory VII. It was recognized by many that the proceedings were irregular; even the decree of Nicholas II, in which Hildebrand had a hand, was ignored. The dubious nature of this election cast a shadow over Gregory VII's pontificate and more than once was used by his enemies to discredit him.

Quite soon after his election, in a Lenten synod of 1074, the new pope issued decrees against clerical incontinence, → simony, and lay → investiture. Gregory clearly saw the reform of the church as his highest priority, and here he could argue that he was continuing the activities of his predecessors. He saw his responsibility as being the restoration to the perfection of the apostolic church and sought models in the NT, → canon law, and → monasticism. Unfortunately, many of the sources to which he gave credence were Carolingian forgeries. His view of the apostolic church was a collection of history, legend, and even misunderstanding.

In 1074 Gregory's efforts to mount a campaign against the Turks failed. Also his efforts to bring about a reconciliation between the Western and Eastern churches had no success. In 1078 and 1079 Gregory condemned the opinions of Berengar of Tours, who denied that the bread and wine really changed into the body and blood of Christ in the liturgy of the → Mass.

Papal legates, especially in Germany and France but also elsewhere, had difficulty in enforcing the new, reforming decrees of 1074. In Germany this situation led to the famous confrontation between the German emperor Henry IV and Gregory VII. Henry had threatened Gregory with a ban and deposition and held two synods in 1076, at Worms and Piacenza, which declared the pope deposed. Gregory replied in kind by deposing and banning Henry. At the castle of Canossa near Reggio nell'Emilia in northern Italy, Henry in 1077 submitted to Gregory and was absolved. Some authorities have seen too much attention given to the events at Canossa. Yet this collision with Henry is a significant example of Gregory's will to implement his policy of reform, and its effects on the papacy were profound.

The peace of Canossa did not endure for long. In 1080 Henry was again → excommunicated. During the next three years the emperor built up his position in northern and central Italy. This strategy had the result of opening up the split between Gregory and a large group of discontented persons within the church at Rome. By 1084 some 13 cardinals and much of the papal staff dropped their alliance to

Gregory. In the same year a council at Brixen selected Clement III as the new pope, who was soon enthroned in Rome. This antipope crowned Henry emperor, for the second time, in the same year.

Neither Gregory nor Clement, claimants to the papacy, could hold the city of Rome. Gregory left the city under the protection of the Normans and spent the remainder of his life under their protection. He first went to Monte Cassino and later Salerno, where he died on May 25, 1085. Gregory VII was canonized in 1606; his feast day is May 25.

There has been considerable disagreement concerning how Gregory and his papacy should be assessed. Past scholarship has tended to view him as an unbridled tyrant. Recently this view has shifted, with Gregory's intentions being seen in a more positive light. He is viewed as committed to righteousness *(iustitia)* and genuine reform of the church.

A final evaluation of Gregory depends upon the interpretation of his *Registrum,* or *Dictatus papae,* the fundamental statement of the "Gregorian reform." This document, consisting of 27 statements compiled by Gregory probably at the beginning of his papacy, emphasized the position of the Roman church in the church universal, drew conclusions for the authority of the pope as universal leader, and specified the privileges of the pope as the head of the *sacerdotium* over against *regnum* and *imperium.* Does this document convey Gregory's response to his dispute with German bishops and Henry, or is it a broad statement of policy that clarifies Gregory's future actions? No final answer seems possible to this question, but much recent research tends to see the document not as a statement of papal absolutism but of emergency powers so that the Roman See can reform the church.

Bibliography: Primary sources in English: H. E. J. COWDREY, trans., *The Epistolae vagantes of Pope Gregory VII* (Oxford, 1972) • E. EMERTON, trans., *The Correspondence of Pope Gregory VII: Selected Letters from the Registrum* (New York, 1990).

Secondary works: E. DUFFY, *Saints and Sinners: A History of the Popes* (New Haven, 1997) esp. 94-99 • I. W. FRANK, *A Concise History of the Mediaeval Church* (New York, 1995) • M. J. MACDONALD, *Hildebrand: Life of Gregory VII* (London, 1932) • R. MORGHEN, *Gregorio VII e la riforma della chiesa nel secolo XI* (Palermo, 1975) • C. MORRIS, *The Papal Monarchy: The Western Church from 1050 to 1250* (Oxford, 1989) esp. 109-21, 597-99.

WILLIAM G. RUSCH

Gregory the Great → Gregory I

Grief

1. Symptoms
2. The Grief Process
3. Support

Grief is the reaction to a loss. It is caused especially by the death of a loved one, but also by divorce (→ Marriage and Divorce 4), moving, the loss of a job, sickness, the loss of cultural elements, destruction of the normal conditions of life, and so forth. → Animals can also experience grief.

1. Symptoms

Those who grieve experience a profound shattering of their understanding of themselves and of their world (→ Identity). Each type of grief has its own form. In many cases it involves preoccupation with a former loved one who has died and withdrawal from other relations and tasks. It may involve a feeling of meaninglessness (→ Meaning), pressure on life even to the point of → suicide, restlessness, insomnia, tears (→ Laughing and Crying), → aggression, feelings of → guilt, psychosomatic reactions (e.g., asthma, heartbeat disturbances, greater risks of infection, headaches), changes in attitudes, differences in perception even to the point of delusions, or drug dependence (→ Substance Abuse). Socially, grief often involves isolation through withdrawal from daily activities (→ Everyday Life).

Grief is a difficult → experience that can be a threat even to one's personality. This experience, however, is a necessary part of life. To repress it brings sickness to the → soul. A conscious acceptance of loss in an "existence of partings" (V. Kast) can give depth to → life and prepare us for → death. Though their symptoms may be similar, → depression differs from grief (S. Freud, 1917). Freud called depression melancholy, borrowing from the four basic temperaments of Hippocrates (ca. 460-ca. 377 B.C.).

2. The Grief Process

Dealing with grief consists of accepting loss and seeking to loosen ties to the departed, thus becoming free for a new orientation. Literature dealing with death lists a multiphasic grief process (see Y. Spiegel). First, a usually short phase of *shock* comes with news of the loss. The bereaved reacts with numbness and cannot really believe what has happened.

Next is the phase of *control.* → Funeral arrangements and calls have to be made. These tasks claim the attention of the bereaved and have a controlling effect upon their feelings and attitudes.

After the burial a phase of *repression* comes as the reality of the loss sinks in. Grief now involves intense feelings. Earlier experiences of loss come again to mind. Grief takes hold with thoughts of the relation to the departed. The one grieving feels → despair, → anxiety, helplessness, aggression, and feelings of guilt. He or she may seek the loved one in → dreams, in fantasies (→ Imagination), in other people, and elsewhere. It is a time for wrestling with the history that has been shared and its conclusion.

The phase of *adaptation* is finally reached when we know the departed only inwardly and the loss has been so well integrated that a new perspective on life can be reached (→ Lifestyle). We must apply these four phases very cautiously, since individual grief may take different forms.

3. Support

The bereaved need others to stand by them and support them. For Christians, such sharing of grief is an important pastoral duty (→ Pastoral Care). At the burial, pastors come into very close contact with the bereaved. They can show human understanding, help them to express their grief as they listen to them, carefully interpret this grief with traditional Christian → symbols, and engage in → prayer. The ritual of burial is an important pastoral help.

Problems with the grieving process can arise especially when the relation to the departed has been ambivalent, when the loss is that of a child, or when death is sudden and unexpected. In such cases professional help may be needed. Emotional numbness, the threat of severe self-injury, persistent grief, or serious psychosomatic disturbances are all indications of the need for therapy (→ Crisis Intervention).

Therapy will usually be short, helping the bereaved through the process of grief. They must accept their feelings, even the forbidden ones of aggression. They must learn about the process in a way that reduces anxiety and must work through their feelings of guilt. Therapy must pay special attention to anger at the loss and to any attempt to cling on in some way to the departed. The different schools of psychology (→ Psychology 4; Psychotherapy) have their own forms of therapy, and there are also therapeutic grief-groups under professional leadership or the leadership of bereaved who themselves have undergone training. As far as therapy is concerned, purely self-help groups that have had no grief training have not proved to be of great value (→ Consolation, Comfort; Counseling).

Bibliography: J. Bowlby, *Attachment and Loss,* vol. 1, *Attachment;* vol. 2, *Separation: Anxiety and Anger;* vol. 3, *Loss: Sadness and Depression* (New York, 1969-81) • S. Freud, *Trauer und Melancholie* (Berlin, 1982; orig. pub., 1917) • V. Kast, *Trauern* (Stuttgart, 1982) • E. Lindemann, *Jenseits von Trauer* (Göttingen, 1985) • C. M. Parkes and R. S. Weiss, *Recovery from Bereavement* (Northvale, N.J., 1995) • B. Raphael, *The Anatomy of Bereavement: A Handbook for the Caring Professions* (London, 1989) • Y. Spiegel, *Der Prozeß des Trauerns* (8th ed.; Munich, 1995) • W. S. Stroebe and M. Stroebe, *Bereavement and Health* (New York, 1987) • M. S. Stroebe et al., eds., *Handbook of Bereavement* (Cambridge, Mass., 1993) • W. J. Worden, *Grief Counseling and Grief Therapy: A Handbook for the Mental Health Practitioner* (2d ed.; New York, 1991).

Ulrike Wagner-Rau

Group and Group Dynamics

1. Group
2. Group Dynamics
    2.1. Psychodynamic Perspectives
    2.2. Sociopsychological Perspectives
    2.3. Systems Perspectives
    2.4. Implications for Churches
        2.4.1. Theology and Piety
        2.4.2. Pastoral Leadership
        2.4.3. Congregational Participation
        2.4.4. Pastoral Care

1. Group

A group is a number of individuals organized to fulfill a common purpose or purposes. Thus, as Wilfred Bion has commented, a crowd of sunbathers lying on a beach is not yet a group. If, though, they are aroused by the cries of a girl who is drowning and begin to cooperate in her rescue, they become a rudimentary group. All groups have purpose, structure, and dynamics. Their complexity lies in the variability and interaction of these aspects.

A group's *purposes* may be few or many. They may also be explicit or tacit, conscious or unconscious. Even a temporary, spontaneously formed group like the crowd of sunbathers now trying to effect a rescue can have a complicated array of primary and secondary goals (e.g., saving a drowning child, allaying primal anxieties stimulated by the child's cry, fulfilling unconscious rescue fantasies on the part of some members, gratifying curiosity, and discharging excited impulses). Most organized groups are motivated by an amalgam of competing purposes, many of which are emotionally charged. For this reason staying oriented to a primary mission or work goal proves challenging at times for most groups and → organizations.

A group's *structure* includes such aspects as its size, boundaries, functional roles, decision-making formats, and leadership structure. It also includes formal and informal → norms that regulate group behavior, patterns of → communication that regulate → information flow, and recurring feedback processes that stabilize and destabilize the group's overall structure. Most groups have both a visible structure based on conscious designs and an invisible structure based on unconscious or tacit assumptions.

Finally, a group's *dynamics* include the political and emotional forces that shape its purposes and structure and that affect its attempts to live them out. It also includes the developmental processes by which groups mature over time.

Churches are complex groups that vary greatly in purpose, structure, and dynamics. Since the primary purposes of a → church are religious and involve matters of ultimate concern, they are apt to be charged with high levels of emotional investment. Because they are often broad and visionary, a church's purposes are also subject to idiosyncratic interpretation by its members. Structurally, churches may be influenced by traditional denominational patterns and still evolve into unique congregational cultures. Because of the felt ultimacy of congregational commitments, church dynamics often involve primal emotional processes with deep unconscious roots.

2. Group Dynamics

Groups are living systems that interact with their environments and develop over time. Their behavior, while purposive, is also fluid and unpredictable, for at any given time it is influenced by multiple social, psychological, and systemic forces of which it is only partially aware.

Since the end of World War I the subject of group dynamics has occupied theorists and professionals, ranging from → psychoanalysts to economists (→ Economy), sociologists, marketers, therapists, and managers. Overall, three perspectives have contributed most to our understanding of this important field, those of psychodynamics, → social psychology, and systems.

2.1. *Psychodynamic Perspectives*

Psychodynamic perspectives focus on the deep and often unconscious psychological currents that influence groups and their members. S. Freud focused on the irrational expectations groups have of their leaders and the emotionally charged bonds of loyalty that hold groups together. According to Freud, these bonds and expectations have their source in unconscious wishes for a father-protector who can guard the group and its members from danger and uncertainty. Such a leader must be at once powerful, caring, omniscient, and morally incorruptible. He must also be strong and fair enough to subdue the competitive, incestuous, and aggressive currents in group life. To secure and protect such a leader, Freud argued, group members regularly sacrifice their own intelligence, freedom, and even moral integrity.

Later psychoanalytic theorists emphasized the deeper maternal longings and dependencies that influence members' expectations of leaders. These longings are even more primal and emotionally charged than those Freud described. Both male and female leaders are targets of *both* maternal and paternal transferences. These transferences are responsible for many of the strong reactions members have toward group leaders and the group as a whole. Often unconsciously, these dynamics exert powerful psychological pressure on group leaders.

The pioneering work of Wilfred Bion continues to be influential among psychodynamically oriented group theorists. Bion distinguished between two levels of group life that occur simultaneously. The "work group" describes the rational, task-oriented level of group life. The "basic assumption group" describes the unconscious emotional life of the group that tends to manifest itself in "as if" behavior. For example, a church finance committee might behave as if its real task were to place the whole burden for solving the congregation's budget problems on the minister's shoulders (→ "dependency"). At another time the group might act as if its purpose were to find someone to blame or do battle with over the issue of finances ("fight-flight"). According to Bion, primal hopes and fears originating in infancy are activated by the vicissitudes of group life and lie at the source of such behavior.

Modern psychoanalytic thinkers have continued to study the mental processes that affect the behavior of group members, leaders, and the group as a whole. For example, Otto Kernberg emphasized the role that innate → aggression and fears about aggression play in the emotional life of groups and their members. Kernberg also emphasized the psychological pressures groups exert on their leaders, as well as the effects a leader's character disturbances can have on a group. Heinz Kohut and Robert Randall emphasized the role that groups, including churches, play in supporting or undermining the healthy self-cohesion and self-esteem of their members. They also argued that groups have a *group self* that can be nurtured or injured in its relations with leaders, members, and the environment. According to Kohut and Randall, group violence and destructiveness often result from some real or felt injury to the core self of the group or its members. In his *Psychodynamics of Work and Organizations* (1993), on the psychology of the workplace, William Czander presented a comprehensive review of the major psychodynamic theories of group dynamics.

2.2. *Sociopsychological Perspectives*

While psychoanalytic thinkers focus on hidden psychological forces in group life, social psychologists emphasize the study of observable patterns of social behavior in groups. The development and application of sophisticated research methods have been important in shaping social psychology as a science. Such methods include both quantitative studies that focus on measuring → behavior and qualitative methods that emphasize learning from → experience and participant-observation.

In the decades following World War II, many social psychologists focused on problematic social behavior like authoritarianism, conformity, classism (→ Class and Social Stratum), crime, intolerance, and racial → prejudice. Their studies helped clarify common features, precursors, and effects of such behavior and suggested strategies for progressive change.

Indeed, promoting positive social change has been a common concern among social psychologists. In 1947 the National Education Association in the United States sponsored the establishment of the National Training Laboratories to help train teachers, business leaders, and other professionals how to study and apply group-dynamic insights to help create more effective and democratic learning and work environments. Their training events focus on increasing participants' awareness of group dynamics as well as their own participation in them.

An early shaper of this perspective was Kurt Lewin, who argued that groups can best be understood by studying their here-and-now relationship to primary goals of survival and mastery. In pursuit of these goals, groups are motivated by "driving forces," frustrated by "opposing forces," and held back by "restraining forces." Their dynamics are determined by the alignments among these forces at any point in time. Thus, for example, a → congregation struggling to increase its membership might be helped by analyzing the extent to which this goal is one of survival or of taking its next step as a community of faith. It might then examine the current configuration of driving, opposing, and restraining forces related to the goal of increased membership.

This effort, in turn, might clarify the current mix of factors keeping the congregation from meeting its goals and suggest new strategies for progress. For Lewin, there is never one cause or one cure for group dysfunction. Groups must be viewed as whole social entities. Focusing on relationships instead of single factors or individuals is thus the most effective way to bring about change.

Today, topics studied by social psychologists continue to be rich and far-ranging in scope. Interpersonal and intergroup relations, communication processes, cognitive functioning, power relations, → conflict, multicultural diversity, and organizational culture are some of the themes frequently revisited.

2.3. *Systems Perspectives*

Before the mid-20th century the prestige of the social sciences suffered from comparisons to the physical → sciences, where experimental methods of observation and prediction were thought to be more objective and reliable. Classic scientific models assumed that all dynamics, even human dynamics, were ultimately mechanical and deterministic. In this view, → social science deserved respect only to the extent that it could approximate the experimental rigor of the physical sciences and reveal the deterministic rules that govern its subject matter.

This view was challenged by Kurt Lewin, but even more profoundly by Ludwig Bertalanffy. Bertalanffy was a biologist who argued that living systems differ in essential ways from classic mechanical systems. Mechanical systems are *closed* in that they operate independently of their environments. They behave like clocks that "wind down" when they run out of stored-up energy. Living systems, in contrast, are *open* in that they are constantly exchanging energy with their environments. This feature gives them the ability to sustain themselves and to evolve complex forms that are neither mechanical nor deterministic in the classic sense.

Bertalanffy's theory of general systems emphasized the independence between open systems and their environments. It also emphasized the interdependence between parts of complex systems. According to this perspective the whole is always greater than the sum of its parts. Thus ministers trying to understand the dynamics of their congregation should not focus only on the dynamics of individual members. Rather, they should focus on the way members influence and are influenced by the whole system and its relationship to its various environments. They should not look for simple causes of behavior but study broad patterns of interaction and performance, especially those that reoccur over time. Finally, they should observe the way the group is structuring itself both to maintain balance and to develop new adaptations.

Drawing on Lewin and Bertalanffy, Yvonne Agazarian has developed an approach to working with groups and organizations that focuses on helping individuals take up their roles as group members and cooperate in building a group that matures as a whole while simultaneously fostering the maturation of its individual members. According to Agazarian, groups mature through predictable phases of → development that pose challenges both to its members and to the whole group. Leadership focuses on reducing restraining forces that prevent member and group from meeting these challenges.

One of Agazarian's most important contributions has been her emphasis on functional subgroups. There is a tendency in all groups for members to seek security by aligning with others they perceive as similar to them and distancing from those they perceive as different. These spontaneously formed subgroups tend to be based on stereotypes that hinder group cooperation. Rather than oppose subgrouping, Agazarian encourages leaders to train subgroups to explore similarities and differences in more conscious and realistic ways. The formation of *functional* versus *stereotypical* subgroups is the way healthy groups contain and explore the different emotional positions that inevitably arise when groups face developmental hurdles. By encouraging functional communication within and between subgroups, leaders can help prevent scapegoating, avoidance, polarization, and other defensive behaviors that impede progress.

Systems theory has gained increasing influence among students of family, group, and organizational dynamics over the past two decades. Murray Bowen studied the ways families structure themselves to maintain togetherness while providing for the individuation of their members. E. H. Friedman applied Bowen's family system theory to congregational dynamics. P. M. Senge focused on the complex systemic dynamics that characterize modern business organizations. W. N. Fletcher has emphasized ways religious congregations function more like specialized organizations than like families.

The most recent developments in systems theory are emerging from a new rapprochement between the social and the physical sciences. Over the last 50 years physicists have increasingly left the classic model of dynamics behind. → Relativity, → quantum mechanics, nonlinear mathematics, chaos theory, and complexity theory have created a picture of the physical world that looks in ways as "messy" as the one social scientists have always

inhabited. In the last decade a number of these developments in the physical sciences have been published in works for nonphysicists and nonmathematicians. Of special relevance to group theorists is the emphasis on defining complexity and the impact complexity has on group dynamics. Physicists and social scientists are now cooperating in the study of complex adaptive systems that are able to evolve in changing environments by exploiting the tension between order and chaos.

Depth psychology, social psychology, and systems theory provide a broad range of perspectives on group dynamics. While there is tension between these views, Ronald Heifetz is one of a growing number of theorists who believe that good leadership requires integrating insights from all three. In particular, Heifetz argues that leaders must strike a balance between focusing on emotional and on systemic dynamics. The subjectivity of members and of the group as a whole must be considered along with broad systemic patterns and challenges. The work of the leader should be that of "facilitating adaptive work." This task requires a delicate mix of emotional support, sensitive timing, confrontation, and respect for dissenters.

2.4. *Implications for Churches*

A congregation is a group, and thus group dynamics pervade every aspect of congregational life. Ministry is essentially group work, from leading worship to teaching Sunday school to conducting administrative meetings. Even the most private and confidential of pastoral encounters occurs within this group context. Indeed, the definitions of "private and confidential" often reflect tacit group norms that vary considerably from congregation to congregation.

Taking seriously the implications of group dynamics for the church requires considering their relevance in at least these four categories: → theology and → piety, pastoral leadership, congregational participation, and → pastoral care.

2.4.1. *Theology and Piety*

Group theory favors approaches to theology and piety that view life and faith as essentially social and dynamic. It is simultaneously critical of individualistic and static tendencies in theology and piety. Paul → Tillich argued, for example, that human fulfillment requires both individuation and participation. Because these two potentialities pull in different directions, anxiety, conflict, and faulty choices are inevitable parts of life. → Process theology emphasizes interconnection and unfolding as essential features of → creation. Human and divine nature are thus created through the ongoing and often

477

messy processes of social and cultural → evolution (§4). Social-justice theologies emphasize the necessity of → covenant in human and divine-human relationships. Accordingly, group dynamics are inherently ethical. Finally, → postmodern theologies emphasize the embeddedness of all human acts in the particularity of group/cultural contexts. There is no other reality than social reality. In each of these perspectives, therefore, group life points to matters of ultimate concern for the theology and piety of the church.

2.4.2. *Pastoral Leadership*

Congregations are living systems. They have many goals and expressions, but their deepest purposes derive from the greatest commandment (Mark 12:28-34) and can be fulfilled only in and through living communities of faith. Because congregations are living systems, they cannot remain static or insular. They are meant to develop and evolve progressively mature expressions of their faith in response to new environments and new calls to ministry. The primary responsibility of pastoral leadership is to facilitate this maturational work.

Congregations, like their members, do not grow smoothly without fear, resistance, interruption, or conflict. The main purposes of pastoral leadership are to help congregations discern and stay oriented to their missions, face developmental challenges, and resolve issues that impede congregations from fulfilling their unique potential as missional communities.

For a number of reasons, emotional forces, vulnerabilities, and conflicts operate closer to the surface in religious groups than they do in other types of organizations. First, religious communities involve matters of ultimate concern to their members. Therefore, commitments are often passionate and viewed in either/or terms. Second, religion addresses ultimate human dependence and thus arouses primal longings, fears, and conflicts originating in childhood dependence. Third, some congregations have ethical commitments to welcoming racial, ethnic, gender, and religious diversity. Dealing with diversity is difficult, however, and often exposes deep-rooted fears and prejudices. Fourth, many congregations operate under conditions of real or felt scarcity. Such conditions are inherently frustrating and stimulate anxieties about survival or annihilation. Finally, modern congregations are increasingly bound by voluntary commitments. Such bonds can be fragile in times of stress or conflict. They also place limits on authority, which make it difficult to lead decisively in times of crisis.

For all of these reasons, congregations are highly vulnerable to emotional upheaval and to defensive operations like wishful thinking and fight-flight. These conditions impose great psychological and spiritual demands on leaders, who must deal very sensitively with emotional dynamics while keeping groups oriented to their mission, work goals, and adaptive challenges. Meeting such demands requires high capacities for self-awareness, knowledge about group dynamics, interpersonal skills, ability to exercise → authority without abusing it, skills in managing conflict, and → empathy for group struggle. It also requires keen abilities to discern and articulate the deep religious and theological dimensions of group process and development.

Despite the importance of these disciplines, most clergy and lay leaders have received little formal training in group dynamics and congregational leadership. Though some American seminaries include elective courses and some denominations require → Clinical Pastoral Education for ordination, the study of group and congregational dynamics remains a neglected topic in → theological education.

2.4.3. *Congregational Participation*

Early theories of group dynamics emphasized relations between leaders and followers. Modern thinkers and trainers tend to view leadership as a number of functions that can and should be shared widely among group members. They point out the dangers of overdependence on individual leaders and emphasize the responsibility of all group members for helping the congregation meet its purposes and goals.

According to this viewpoint, most churches remain too pastor- or priest-centered in their expectations and performance. Healthy congregations do not look to pastors to fulfill all their leadership needs; rather, pastors should help congregations discern their maturational work and mobilize the leadership resources within the group to accomplish it. Such congregations devote resources to leadership and discipleship training throughout the congregation. They understand and rely on the specialized leadership functions of clergy and lay leaders while encouraging all members to share responsibility for the mission and maturation of the group.

2.4.4. *Pastoral Care*

Finally, understanding group dynamics has broad implications for pastoral care. First, pastoral care focuses not only on the emotional and spiritual needs of individuals but also on those of the whole group. Congregations experience crisis, trauma, and growing pains just as their members do. Pastors who are able to tune in and minister to the needs and wounds of the group as a whole are less likely to collude in making individual members function as symptom-bearers for the congregation.

Second, pastors who understand systems thinking are better equipped to understand and respond to individual members in crisis. Even when they are working one-on-one, they are able to take into account the complex familial, group, and cultural contexts in which their parishioners' struggles are embedded. They are aware that the most private act of pastoral caregiving occurs within a communal religious context that greatly determines its meaning and efficacy. Viewing parishioners' struggles in this more holistic way can significantly enhance the resources pastors have to offer.

Congregational expectations of pastoral care tend to be highly personalized and emotionally charged. In most congregations, these expectations are pastor focused and emphasize one-to-one interactions. Group dynamics theory suggests wider possibilities, including the use of small- and large-group pastoral interventions as well as greater congregational participation in pastoral caregiving. Optimally, pastoral care is viewed as a ministry of the whole church, with pastor and lay members collaborating. Such a situation cannot be accomplished by decree, however. Because of the emotional expectations and vulnerabilities connected with pastoral caregiving, congregations must be carefully prepared for any changes in focus or approach.

Bibliography: Y. M. Agazarian, Systems-Centered Therapy for Groups (New York, 1997) • C. E. Bennison Jr., with K. Davis, A. Lummis, and P. Nesbit, In Praise of Congregations: Leadership in the Local Church Today (Cambridge, Mass., 1999) • W. R. Bion, Experiences in Groups, and Other Papers (London, 1961) • W. M. Czander, The Psychodynamics of Work and Organizations: Theory and Practice (New York, 1993) • W. N. Fletcher, "The Congregation and the Sphinx: Group Dynamics in Religious Congregations" (Diss., Lutheran Theological Seminary, Philadelphia, 1995) • S. Freud, Group Psychology and the Analysis of the Ego (New York, 1959) • R. T. Golembiekwski and A. Blumberg, eds., Sensitivity Training and the Laboratory Approach: Readings about Concepts and Applications (Itasca, Ill., 1970) • R. A. Heifetz, Leadership without Easy Answers (Cambridge, Mass., 1994) • O. F. Kernberg, Ideology, Conflict, and Leadership in Groups and Organizations (New Haven, 1998) • R. L. Randall, Pastor and Parish: The Psychological Core of Ecclesiastical Conflicts (New York, 1988) • P. Tillich, The Courage to Be (2d ed.; New Haven, 2000; orig. pub., 1952) • M. J. Wheatley, Leadership and the New Science: Learning about Organization from an Orderly Universe (San Francisco, 1994).

Wallace N. Fletcher

Grundtvig, Nikolai Fredrik Severin

Nikolai Fredrik Severin Grundtvig (1783-1872) was a Danish theologian, philosopher, historian, pedagogue, and writer. His accomplishments ranged from the development of a distinctive view of Christianity to ground-breaking studies in Anglo-Saxon poetry, the composition of more than 1,500 hymns (→ Hymnal 1.3), leadership in the establishment of the Danish system of parliamentary → democracy, and the formation of a philosophy of education that has had global influence.

Grundtvig grew up in an orthodox Lutheran, pietistic parsonage in Udby on southern Sjælland. While studying theology in Copenhagen between 1800 and 1803, he broke with the traditional Christianity of his parents and embraced a → rationalistic theistic faith. From 1805 through 1808 he worked as a private tutor on the Egeløkke estate on the island of Langeland. Here, his hopeless love for Constance Steensen de Leth, the wife of the landowner, plunged him into a profound crisis from which he was able to emerge only by losing himself in the study of German → Romanticism and Nordic mythology. Between 1808 and 1811 Grundtvig worked as a secondary school teacher in Copenhagen, in 1810 undergoing another crisis of faith, this one prompting him to turn away from Romanticism and back to the Christianity of his parents. He also returned to his parents physically insofar as he accepted his father's invitation to return to Udby in 1811 as an assistant pastor. After his father's death in 1813 he returned to Copenhagen, trying unsuccessfully to find a permanent position as a → pastor. From 1816 to 1821 he lived exclusively as a writer.

In 1821 Grundtvig became pastor in the small town of Præstø in southern Sjælland. In 1822 he returned to Copenhagen as curate at Our Savior's Church, where in 1824 he composed his two great visionary poems "De levendes Land" (Land of the living) and "Nyårs-Morgen" (New Year's morning). In this and other works of the same period, Grundtvig began to articulate a new view of Christianity, rooted in the early church but still nourished by Romanticism. In this view, frequently described as Grundtvig's "matchless discovery," the church's foundation is not the Bible but the living Christ himself as present in the marks of the church that have remained the same through the centuries, namely, the → Apostles' Creed, → baptism, and the → Eucharist. He also developed this sacramental understanding of Christianity in 1825 in Kirkens gienmæle (The church's rejoinder), a writing directed against Henrik Nikolai Clausen, a theologian at the University of Copenhagen who was a disciple of Friedrich → Schleiermacher,. Unfortunately, this writing resulted in Grundtvig's being censured for life; he thus resigned his post in 1826 and lived until 1831 again as a freelance writer.

Between 1829 and 1831 Grundtvig made three trips to England, with financial support from the Danish crown, in order to study medieval Anglo-Saxon MSS, notably *Beowulf*, the tenth-century Exeter Book, and others. English liberalism, including its views on freedom of faith and confession, made a considerable impression on him. A later visit, in 1843, was meant to provide contacts for Grundtvig with leaders of the → Oxford Movement of the Church of England.

After 1832 Grundtvig's → censure, in an exceptional act, was lifted, and in 1839 he accepted the position of pastor at the Spital Church in Vartov, Copenhagen. Between 1848 and 1858 he was also a member of Parliament, in which capacity he was able strongly to influence Denmark's first democratic legislation. He summarized his own theology in 1868 in *Den christelige Børnelærdom* (a title variously translated "Elementary Christian Doctrine" and "Christian Children's Teachings").

One characteristic feature of Grundtvig's basic theological and philosophical position was his differentiation between *the human* and *the Christian*. To be a Christian, Grundtvig thought that one must of necessity reflect on the unique value of human existence as created by God; "human first and then Christian," he wrote with reference to John 1:4. This position enabled him to exchange views openly and to cooperate even with those who were not of his persuasion, without having to focus on specifically Christian goals. Grundtvig did not mean that human living has primacy over Christian living, but rather that the humanity of individual living and of the indigenous life of a people, created in the image of God, has a primary influence upon Christian experience and fellowship in the church.

Grundtvig was a prodigious writer and editor. He was an acknowledged scholar of Anglo-Saxon poetry as well as of Nordic mythology, producing popular Danish translations of medieval Nordic works as well as of the great Anglo-Saxon poem *Beowulf*. He also published interpretations of world history and edited, from 1816 to 1819, the periodical *Danne-Virke*, which contained his own historical and philosophical essays. In 1848 he started a small weekly, *Danskeren* (The Dane), chiefly in order to promote his democratic and political ideas. Finally, he composed his own church hymns and reworked hymns from the early church and medieval periods.

Grundtvig occupies a major position in respect to sociopedagogical issues, having instigated and supported free education for both children and adults on the basis of the language, myths, poetry, and history of *folket* (the people). He envisioned *skolen for livet* (the school for life) as preparation for participation in all aspects of social, cultural, and political life. Such education was to be marked by lively interaction between teachers and students. As an educator, Grundtvig became a pioneer in the *Folkehøjskoler* (folk high school) movement. These schools appeared between 1840 and 1850 in Denmark and have given inspiration to the importance of such schools in present-day Denmark as well as in many other parts of the world, not least increasingly in certain → Third World countries.

Grundtvig's influence has persevered long after his death. His work remains a lively source of insight for theological, ecclesial, cultural, and educational life.

Bibliography: Primary sources: Selected Writings (trans. J. Knudsen; Philadelphia, 1976) • *Udvalgte skrifter* (10 vols.; ed. H. Begtrup; Copenhagen, 1904-9) • *Værker i udvalg* (10 vols.; ed. G. Christensen and H. Koch; Copenhagen, 1940-49) • *What Constitutes Authentic Christianity?* (trans. E. D. Nielsen; Philadelphia, 1985).

Secondary works: A. M. ALLCHIN, *N. F. S. Grundtvig: An Introduction to His Life and Work* (Århus, 1997) • A. M. ALLCHIN, S. A. J. BRADLEY, N. A. HJELM, and J. H. SCHJØRRING, eds., *Grundtvig in International Perspective: Studies in the Creativity of Interaction* (Århus, 2000) • A. M. ALLCHIN, D. JASPER, J. H. SCHJØRRING, and K. STEVENSON, eds., *Heritage and Prophecy: Grundtvig and the English-Speaking World* (Århus, 1994) • S. M. BORISH, *The Land of the Living: The Danish Folk High Schools and Denmark's Non-violent Path to Modernization* (Nevada City, Calif., 1991) • N. DAVIES, *Education for Life: A Danish Pioneer* (London, 1931) • J. KNUDSEN, *Danish Rebel: A Study of N. F. S. Grundtvig* (Philadelphia, 1955) • H. KOCH, *Grundtvig* (Yellow Springs, Ohio, 1952) • E. D. NIELSEN, *N. F. S. Grundtvig: An American Study* (Rock Island, Ill., 1955) • K. THANING, *N. F. S. Grundtvig* (Copenhagen, 1972) • C. THODBERG and A. P. THYSSEN, eds., *N. F. S. Grundtvig, Tradition and Renewal: Grundtvig's Vision of Man and People, Education and Church, in Relation to World Issues Today* (Copenhagen, 1983).

THEODOR JØRGENSEN and NORMAN A. HJELM

Guatemala

	1960	1980	2000
Population (1,000s):	3,964	6,917	12,222
Annual growth rate (%):	2.84	2.82	2.68

Area: 108,889 sq. km. (42,042 sq. mi.)

A.D. *2000*

Population density: 112/sq. km. (291/sq. mi.)
Births / deaths: 3.39 / 0.60 per 100 population
Fertility rate: 4.43 per woman
Infant mortality rate: 34 per 1,000 live births
Life expectancy: 69.0 years (m: 66.5, f: 71.7)
Religious affiliation (%): Christians 98.0 (Roman Catholics 79.4, Protestants 17.4, unaffiliated 12.0, indigenous 9.9, marginal 2.0), nonreligious 1.0, other 1.0.

1. The Land
   1.1. Geography
   1.2. Population
   1.3. Political Development
   1.4. Economic Development
2. The Churches
   2.1. Roman Catholic Church
   2.2. Protestant Churches
   2.3. Ecumenism

1. The Land

1.1. *Geography*

Among the eight nations in Central America, Guatemala is the fourth largest in area. It has a narrow access to the Caribbean and a long coastline along the Pacific. It is traversed by the Cordillera, a mountain chain that stretches from Alaska to Patagonia. Two-thirds of the country is mountainous. Along the Pacific coast there is a range of 33 partly active volcanoes. One of these, Tajumulco (4,220 m. / 13,845 ft.), is the highest mountain in Central America outside of Mexico. Several geological faults cause frequent earthquakes. To the north there is a large, flat rain-forest region, the sparsely populated Petén.

1.2. *Population*

In 2000 the estimated population of Guatemala made it the second most populous country in Central America (after Mexico). The capital is Guatemala City, 1,525 m. (5,000 ft.) high, with an estimated population of 2.2 million. The proportion of Indians is variously estimated at between 45 percent and 60 percent, according to whether physical features or sociocultural allegiance is emphasized. Ladinos, of mixed Indian and Spanish descent, are the second largest group (also called mestizos in other countries). Blacks, mulattoes, and whites form only a small percentage of the population. The official language is Spanish, but over 50 others are spoken, the most important being Quiché, Cakchiquel, Mam, and Kekchí. Descendants of the Maya-Quiché peoples, who live mostly in the high country of the North and West, still preserve their traditional customs.

1.3. *Political Development*

In the second half of the 19th century, Guatemala was opened up to outside economic interests, first from central Europe, then also from the United States. Early exports included indigo, then coffee and bananas. After 1901 the United Fruit Company was active in Guatemala. Along with its plantations it developed a railway and a harbor, key elements of the country's transportation system. Under the dictators Manuel Estrada Cabrera (1898-1920) and Jorge Ubico (1931-44), the large plantations prospered.

After the revolution of October 20, 1944, limited reforms under the presidency of Juan José Arévalo (1945-51) led to the development of political parties, factories, agricultural diversification, and the beginnings of national industry. Further reforms came under Jacobo Arbenz (1951-54), as the privileges of landowners were reduced and agrarian reforms redistributed underutilized estates, compensating the owners. The amount of compensation for the United Fruit Company led to a dispute with the United States, whose secretary of state, John Foster Dulles, had been a legal adviser for the company. Isolation and the charge of Communism led to a coup. In July 1957 Colonel Carlos Castillo Armas, with air support from the United States, ended the reforming period. Subsequently, civilian presidents drawn from the oligarchy alternated with generals, who achieved power by assassination, coups, or electoral fraud.

Guerrilla groups with close ties to Cuba started operations in the 1960s. By the eighties they had found much support among the Indians, and the military regime under General Efraín José Ríos Montt (1982-83) reacted with harsh repression. The nation returned to civilian rule in 1986 with the election of President Vinicio Cerezo (1986-90).

In 1996 President Alvaro Arzú Irigoyen concluded peace negotiations with the leftist rebels, thus ending more than 35 years of armed conflict, in which as many as 200,000 people were killed or simply disappeared. Presidential elections in 1999 were won by reform-minded Alfonso Portillo.

1.4. *Economic Development*

The economy of Guatemala is to a large extent dependent on expensive imports of industrial products, motor vehicles, iron and steel, and oil. Agriculture is largely oriented to exports — coffee, sugar, bananas, vegetables, flowers and plants, timber, rice, and rubber — which in 1999 represented only 55 percent of the value of the imports. There is some mining of nickel and drilling for oil, but these resources are not significant.

Though the country is rich in natural resources, → poverty is rampant. As much as 40 percent of the people are unemployed or underemployed (e.g., migrant workers on the large plantations). The result is that people leave the land and move into city slums. Illiteracy stands at around 45 percent (much higher among the Indians).

2. The Churches

Like almost all Latin American countries, Guatemala is predominantly Roman Catholic. Protestant missions, however, have been especially effective here.

2.1. *Roman Catholic Church*

In Guatemala the → Roman Catholic Church in 1996 had ten → dioceses, one prelature, and two vicariates apostolic. Of the 916 priests active in Guatemala in 1996, only a small minority were Guatemalan.

At the time of the Spanish conquest in 1524 (→ Colonialism), the Mayas lived in theocratically governed tribes mainly in the highlands. Agriculture and trade were well developed, although the high point of cultural development (A.D. 200-900) had passed. With the conquerors came the → Franciscans, soon after the → Dominicans and Mercedarians, and later the → Jesuits. In 1537 Bartolomé de Las Casas (1474-1566), a Dominican, launched a nonviolent missionary effort in the Province of Vera Paz. He defended the human rights of the Indians (→ Mission 3). From 1543 to 1547 Las Cases was bishop of Chiapas, which has belonged to Mexico since 1823.

From the second half of the 18th century, the colonial rule of the Spanish crown and of the Roman Catholic Church began to weaken. Political independence was declared in 1821. After 1870 conflicts increased between liberals and the church, which wanted to retain its privileges. In 1871 the archbishop and the Jesuits were expelled, and in 1879 came constitutional separation of → church and state, the dissolving of the orders, and the appropriation of church property. In 1884 a new → concordat was concluded that gave the church legal status, although tensions continued for another 50 years.

Christianity came as the religion of the conquerors (→ Colonialism and Mission), and by 1610

two-thirds of the original population had been wiped out. The few priests could not do extensive missionary work, and thus pre-Christian Mayan religious elements survived, to an increasing degree as a distinct religion, but to some extent also syncretistically. Such syncretism was helped by aspects of the Christian faith being easily integrated into Mayan religion — for example, the → cross, which might be seen as a symbol of the four quarters of heaven or the universe. Features that have been retained are the mythical understanding of nature, the land, and the harvest; ceremonies of sacrifice and prayer on the steps of the church of Santo Tomás in Chichicastenango; and veneration of the Black Christ of Esquipulas. Some elements of older traditions have gained new vitality in the → base communities.

Inspired by → Vatican II and the second → Latin American Bishops' Conference (at Medellín in 1968), Roman Catholics have engaged in → Catholic Action, in base communities, and in social projects. Bible study in basic groups led by → catechists (→ Catechesis) has had a formative effect (→ Biblical Theology 2.5). Sociopolitical clashes between various interest groups culminated in 1978-83 in civil disorders, which included military repression, death squads, popular resistance, and guerrilla fighting. Persecution and massacres (→ Persecutions of Christians 4.2) forced many Christians underground or into armed conflict. From 1976 to 1983, a total of 13 priests were murdered, and another 5 disappeared.

Since 1990 the number of Catholics in Guatemala has remained steady or actually declined. One factor has been the disciplining of the large charismatic renewal movement, which has led many Catholic charismatics to join evangelical churches of Pentecostal persuasion.

2.2. *Protestant Churches*

According to the Alianza Evangélica de Guatemala (Evangelical Alliance of Guatemala), there were 318,000 active, baptized members of Protestant churches in 1980 (about 5 percent of the population). In 2000 the number of Guatemalans who regard themselves as *evangélico* was estimated to be as high as 30 percent. Strongest are the → Pentecostal churches (some two-thirds of all evangelicals and growing). Other groups include the Evangelical Church of Central America, → Adventists, Christian Brethren, → Baptists, and Presbyterians (→ Reformed and Presbyterian Churches).

Protestant work began in 1824, when English merchants distributed Bibles and tracts. The Anglican F. Crowe started educational work in 1845, but the next year the Roman Catholic archbishop secured his expulsion. With the rise of the liberal anti-Catholic movement, Protestantism gained influence in Guatemala. The first Protestant missionary from the United States (John Hill, a Presbyterian) came to Guatemala in 1882 at the express invitation of President Justo Rufino Barrios, who gave the Presbyterians land adjacent to the national palace for a church building. After 1900 other missions from the United States started work (→ North American Missions): the Central American Mission (Congregationalists from Texas), the Society of Friends and the → Nazarenes (both from California), and the Primitive Methodists (from Pennsylvania). The Synod of the Evangelical Church of Guatemala was founded in 1935, but only as a vehicle of cooperation. It was renamed the Evangelical Alliance in 1951. Between 1931 and 1938 the NT was translated into the four most important Indian languages (→ Bible Versions), and in 1978 the → Bible Society of Guatemala came into being.

Guatemala was the birthplace of the Theological Education by Extension (TEE) movement, which was launched in 1963. Also it was the site of the Bible translation and "people movement" emphasis generated during the 1930s by William Cameron Townsend (1896-1982), founder of the Wycliffe Bible Translators. These two thrusts have reverberated throughout the global missions movement.

The period of Protestant work in Guatemala has been divided into *founding* (1882-1923, with about 5,000 members), *spread* (1923-44, up to 15,000 members), and *explosion* (1944 to the present, with numbers in the millions). Different reasons are given for this significant growth: the work of the → Holy Spirit (as the movement understands itself), the contrast to a weak → Catholicism and the combination of → millennial elements with the striving for social betterment. A special impact was made by North American → evangelical missions with a → fundamentalist and anti-Communist thrust. The aim of making Guatemala the first Latin American country with a Protestant majority was supported by the coup that made Ríos Montt the first Protestant president in 1982. He had been converted through the El Verbo denomination in 1978. He was replaced by another coup, however, 16 months later. A papal visit in March 1983 was in part a reaction to radical evangelical mission.

2.3. Ecumenism

Little ecumenical cooperation is evident in Guatemala, as the interdenominational climate is marked by competition and hostility. Among themselves, the evangelical denominations have cooperated in major united → evangelism efforts, such as Evangelism in Depth (1960s) and the movement Discipling a Whole Nation (DAWN, 1980s). They also work together in the Protestant university Mariano Gálvez and in Protestant schools and hospitals.

The Protestant churches have not joined the → World Council of Churches or the → Latin America Council of Churches (CLAI). Some belong to the Latin American Evangelical Fellowship (CONELA; → World Evangelical Fellowship). A few congregations or groups also engage in some common projects with the World Council of Churches or its member churches. After 1980 the work for human → rights done by the Comité Pro Justicia y Paz de Guatemala was represented abroad by the → liberation theologian Julia Esquivél, living in exile in Switzerland.

Bibliography: C. ALVAREZ, *People of Hope: The Protestant Movement in Central America* (New York, 1990) • P. BERRYMAN, *Stubborn Hope: Religion, Politics, and Revolution in Central America* (Maryknoll, N.Y., 1994) • B. DÍAZ DEL CASTILLO, *The Conquest of New Spain* (trans. M. Cohen; Baltimore, 1963; orig. pub., 1632) • J. ESQUIVÉL, *Paradies und Babylon* (Wuppertal, 1985) • *Guatemala, Never Again!* [official report of the Human Rights Office, Archdiocese of Guatemala] (Maryknoll, N.Y., 1999) • S. JONAS, *Of Centaurs and Doves: Guatemala's Peace Process* (Boulder, Colo., 1999) • B. DE LAS CASAS, *History of the Indies* (trans. A. Collard; New York, 1971) • D. M. NELSON, *A Finger in the Wound: Body Politics in Quincentennial Guatemala* (Berkeley, Calif., 1999) • S. C. SCHLESINGER and S. KINZER, *Bitter Fruit: The Untold Story of the American Coup in Guatemala* (New York, 1982) • D. SULLIVAN-GONZÁLEZ, *Piety, Power, and Politics: Religion and Nation Formation in Guatemala, 1821-1871* (Pittsburgh, 1998).

BRANKO NIKOLITSCH and EKKEHARD ZIPSER

Guest Workers → Foreigners, Aliens

Guilt

1. Definition and Phenomenon
2. Theological Aspects
3. In Religious History
4. Philosophical Aspects
5. Psychological Aspects
6. Legal Aspects
7. Theological Demarcation

1. Definition and Phenomenon

Guilt is to be understood in relation to the violation of a fixed → norm or ideal, or to the failure to live up to it. It presupposes some authority that calls us to account, such as → God, → reason, → nature, or human law (→ Rights, Human and Civil). In content it is hard to distinguish among criminal, political, moral, metaphysical, and religious guilt. Today guilt is also felt in geoeconomic, ecological, social, and technological matters.

2. Theological Aspects

In the Bible it is hard to differentiate guilt from → sin (§§1, 2; see Luke 15:18; 18:13). Guilt stresses the individual aspect more strongly; in sin we see a more generalizing trend.

In → Augustine (354-430; → Augustine's Theology) the understanding of sin as pride, self-love, and concupiscence emphasizes the element of guilt in sin. The teaching of the → Reformers defines → sin (§3) in terms of a basically perverted orientation in relation to God. The Reformers questioned the classifying of sins as mortal, cardinal, and venial. In distinction from → Scholasticism, they viewed original sin as real guilt along the lines of radical or essential sin. Actual sins result from it. In this context the → justification of sinners (Romans 1–3) is solely a work of divine → grace in Christ that overcomes the power of sin (Romans 6) and brings → reconciliation to God (2 Cor. 5:18-21), thus eliminating guilt.

In the post-Reformation era an ethical view of sin developed (→ Ethics 4.2) that was described in terms of → anthropology (§3.2). → Pietism ran the risk of trying to explain sin psychologically and to overcome it almost along perfectionist lines.

3. In Religious History

In the history of religion guilt involves the breaking of a God-given → taboo or the violating of a divinely given social order. It has cultic and ethical aspects; attempts are made to → atone for it by various expiatory acts.

4. Philosophical Aspects

In the ancient Greek and Roman world, guilt arose from the breaking of laws that it was the task of the → state to enforce. On the scholastic view (→ Thomas Aquinas; → Thomism) guilt results from disobeying the → conscience as the voice of God, and it is meant to lead to → repentance (→ Trent, Council of). For I. Kant (1724-1804; → Kantianism) guilt arises out of a deficient sense of → responsibility before "the voice of the inner judge."

In the → Enlightenment and the → modern period, however, increasing questions have been put to the concept of guilt. Often we can no longer say clearly what guilt is, for there is a conflict between obedience to → authority and preserving our → human dignity. Radically causal thinking also probes into the origin of guilty behavior. Evolutionary thought (→ Evolution) and sociological determinism argue that the concept is merely a social product. Theorems that claim to unmask guilt (K. → Marx, F. → Nietzsche, S. Freud) raise the issue of a morality without guilt. Behavioral research, social philosophy (→ Critical Theory 2.1), and → sociology note the close connections that guilt has with both inborn impulses and social influences (A. Plack, K. Z. Lorenz, H. Marcuse).

The modern age has seen the development of the concept of an individual experience and assigning of guilt (W. Oelmuller). To the fore is discussion of tendencies to eliminate guilt (B. F. Skinner, N. Luhmann, G. Kaufmann) or to restrict it to actions in intrapersonal relations and social institutions for which we know we are responsible (Oelmüller). Since what we do affects all humanity (→ Action Theory 3), we need a broader sense of guilt, an ethic for the age of → science (K. O. Apel), and an orientation to the principle of responsibility (M. Jonas) that embraces humanity and → nature.

5. Psychological Aspects

Various schools of psychology — behaviorist, developmental (J. Piaget), structuralist (R. Wellek), and psychoanalytic (Freud, C. G. Jung, A. Adler) — have addressed the problem of guilt (→ Psychology 4; Development 2; Sin 4; Behavior, Behavioral Psychology). → Psychoanalysis suggests a close relation between feelings of guilt and the emergence of the superego. According to Freud (1856-1939), the social feeling of guilt associated with the conscience (as it feels guilty for breaking a taboo) is followed by the feeling of guilt resulting from the inner conflict between the superego and those impulses opposed to it. Jung (1875-1961) argued that guilt occurs when the voice of conscience, not the same as the superego (E. Fromm), is not followed as the voice of the → self, and thus the path of individuation that it indicates is not taken (→ Development 2). Under the influence of M. Heidegger (1889-1976; → Existential Philosophy), an anthropological psychiatry and psychotherapy developed (W. von Siebenthal, G. Condrau) that viewed psychological sickness as a form of defective existence, defined as a flight from the personal → conscience (§2.4).

Disruption of spiritual development can involve

the suppression of guilt feelings and the denying of guilt in principle. Relief might be sought in projection, excessive → narcissism, intellectualizing, anonymity, depersonalizing, identification with a collective, or expiatory acts. In such approaches, however, real dealing with the phenomenon is hardly possible (H. Häfner, L. Wurmser).

Pathological guilt feelings are often part of misguided efforts to subject the ego to excessive demands of the superego. The result may be → neuroses or → psychoses, with a domination by either compulsion or melancholy (Freud, Häfner, Wurmser).

Psychotherapy tries to distinguish between psychologically analyzable feelings of guilt and real guilt. It aims to identify elements of the personality that have been harmed and deformed by overly strict superego structures, freeing them from automatic impulses, and promoting responsibility and a true sense of guilt. Somatic therapy may be needed in the case of psychotic guilt feelings.

6. Legal Aspects

Legally we must differentiate guilt in civil law from guilt in criminal law. Penalties (→ Punishment 1) still rest on the principle of guilt but now aim more at prevention. No consensus exists regarding the nature and content of guilt. Empirically and pragmatically it is defined as failure to live up to the standards of conduct expected of ordinary citizens (H. L. Schreiber). Legislators presume that we are responsible for our acts and thus that we enjoy ethical and legal → freedom.

Legal systems allow that there may be diminished guilt or no real guilt at all in cases of mental or emotional disturbance, weakness of mind, or other psychological impairment. Such conclusions require evaluation of the psychological state, personality, motivation, situation, and biographical development.

7. Theological Demarcation

The humanities can bring to light pathological guilt feelings, a defective sense of guilt, or special circumstances. Such insights are important, and in both → proclamation and → pastoral care we need to use them relative to various presuppositions and situations of → suffering. Even if one understands sin as the essential conduct human beings display toward God, as conduct completely shaped and determined by the power of sin and by the accompanying sense of guilt, one still cannot reduce sin simply to psychological or moral concepts and terminology. We must differentiate the moral view of guilt, that of

autonomous persons, from the theological concept of sin. We cannot define sin solely on the basis of a phenomenology of guilt. We can know it truly only as we hear the → Word of God. Knowledge of sin comes only in → faith and is the work of divine → grace. Sin manifests itself as lack of faith (Rom. 14:23) and failure to meet the claim of God's love (Matt. 5:43-48). In → forgiveness (Matt. 6:12) the gift of new life in fellowship with Christ is conferred (Gal. 2:20; 2 Cor. 5:17). Sin, which is a false orientation of human life that has lost contact with God, can be forgiven only with restoration of fellowship with God.

The decisive point is the distinction between *guilty conduct*, which can be analyzed and clarified and perhaps corrected, and *sin*, which needs forgiveness. Involved is a new ability to distinguish between wickedness and evil (C. Gestrich). Wickedness must be forgiven, but in all spheres of human life there are also evils that can be tackled and perhaps set aside by human efforts in → counseling, psychotherapy, and involvement in the struggle for justice, → freedom, and the responsible handling of → science and → technology.

→ Ego Psychology; Humanistic Psychology; Identity; Pastoral Psychology; Psychology of Religion; Shame

Bibliography: B. Bron, "Schuld und Freiheit–psychiatrisch-psychotherapeutische und anthropologische Aspekte," *Psychotherapie, Psychosomatik, medizinische Psychologie* 40 (1990) 480-87 • G. Condrau, *Angst und Schuld als Grundprobleme der Psychotherapie* (Bern, 1962) • S. Freud, "Trauer und Melancholie" (1917), *Gesammelte Werke* (London, 1946) 10.428-46 • C. Gestrich, *The Return of Splendor in the World: The Christian Doctrine of Sin and Forgiveness* (Grand Rapids, 1997) • H. Häfner, *Schulderleben und Gewissen* (Stuttgart, 1956) • M. Heidegger, *Being and Time* (Albany, N.Y., 1996; orig. pub., 1927) • K. Jaspers, *The Question of German Guilt* (New York, 1961; orig. pub., 1946) • G. Kaufmann, ed., *Schulderfahrung und Schuldbewältigung. Christen im Umgang mit der Schuld* (Paderborn, 1982) • H. S. Kushner, *How Good Do We Have to Be? A New Understanding of Guilt and Forgiveness* (Boston, 1996) • A. P. Morrison, *The Culture of Shame* (New York, 1996) • W. Oelmüller, "Schwierigkeiten mit dem Schuldbegriff," *Schuld und Verantwortung* (ed. H. M. Baumgartner and A. Eser; Tübingen, 1983) 9-30 • H.-L. Schreiber, "Was heißt strafrechtliche Schuld und wie kann die Psychiater bei ihrer Feststellung mitwirken?" *Nervenarzt* 48 (1977) 242-47 • W. von Siebenthal, *Schuldgefühl und Schuld bei psychiatrischen Erkrankungen* (Zurich, 1956) •

P. TOURNIER, *Guilt and Grace: A Psychological Study* (New York, 1962) • A. VERGOTE, *Guilt and Desire: Religious Attitudes and Their Pathological Derivatives* (New Haven, 1988) • M. WESTPHAL, *God, Guilt, and Death: An Existential Phenomenology of Religion* (Bloomington, Ind., 1984) • L. WURMSER, *The Mask of Shame* (Baltimore, 1981).

BERNHARD BRON

Guinea

	1960	1980	2000
Population (1,000s):	3,136	4,461	7,861
Annual growth rate (%):	2.13	2.23	2.86
Area: 245,857 sq. km. (94,926 sq. mi.)			

A.D. 2000

Population density: 32/sq. km. (83/sq. mi.)
Births / deaths: 4.53 / 1.65 per 100 population
Fertility rate: 6.07 per woman
Infant mortality rate: 114 per 1,000 live births
Life expectancy: 48.5 years (m: 48.0, f: 49.0)
Religious affiliation (%): Muslims 67.4, tribal religionists 28.0, Christians 4.4 (unaffiliated 1.8, Roman Catholics 1.3, other Christians 1.3), other 0.2.

1. General Situation
2. Religious Situation

1. General Situation

The Republic of Guinea, on the west coast of Africa, was a French colony from 1904 until it gained independence in 1958 under the leadership of the Parti Démocratique de Guinée, the Guinea branch of the Reassemblement Démocratique Africaine (→ Colonialism). The constitution of 1958 declared Guinea a secular state, with equal rights guaranteed to all citizens, regardless of religion (art. 39). The independence struggle was led by Sékou Touré, who in 1952 became the party's secretary-general. Although a potentially rich country with abundant land, rich soil, plenty of water and sunshine, and abundant mineral resources (esp. gold, diamonds, bauxite, and rubber), francophone Guinea has been poor. In 1998 the per capita gross domestic product was estimated at only $1,180; furthermore, the country has great imbalance in its distribution of wealth, poor medical development, and a literacy rate of only 36 percent (1995 est.).

Part of Guinea's difficult situation results from the corruption and mismanagement of the country's affairs by its first president, Sékou Touré (1958-84). After breaking with the French community in 1958, even though the French maintained their interests and investment, he adopted → socialism as the ideology of the state and, in consequence of that decision, forged links with the Eastern bloc. Curiously, he also maintained economic links with North America, especially with its bauxite industry. The economic sector of Guinea was subjected to state control and collectivization. Any criticism of government policy was met with violence and incarceration. In light of this situation, many went into exile.

The collapse of the economy and the abuse of human → rights led the army under Colonel Lansana Conté to stage a coup d'état in 1984, just days after the death of Sékou Touré. The ensuing military government, led by military officers, lasted until 1993, when Lansana Conté changed hats to head a civilian government, leading the Parti de l'Unité et du Progrès. Under this dispensation there was political reform and a legalization of political parties, which were most often ethnic parties.

2. Religious Situation

African religion has been the traditional religion of Guinea from time immemorial. It evolved without a founder and developed strong roots in Guinea as in other African countries (→ Tribal Religions). It acknowledges God as Creator and Sustainer of all things. Each African people or language has a name for God, such as Hala (Kissi), Hununga (Tenda), and Gala, Guele, and Jalang (Malinke). Prayers are usually made to God. People believe that life continues after death, and the spirits of the dead are said to be in close contact with their families for up to four or five generations (→ Ancestor Worship). Communal shrines are important centers of such religious activities as → prayer, → sacrifice, rituals, and festivals. → Priests and priestesses are responsible for communal religious activities and sacred places. African traditional religion permeates all life and culture; it has been the country's cultural solvent, making it difficult, if not impossible, to draw a division between sacred and secular realms of life.

Guinea is a predominantly Muslim country, with → Islam claiming the vast majority of the population. Tribal religionists represent the second largest number of adherents, with only a small minority claiming to be Christians. A Muslim holy war (*jihād*) was proclaimed in 1725, initiating the process of Islamization among the indigenous peoples.

Christianity came to Guinea with the Portuguese in 1462 during the reign of King John II. From 1481, largely in connection with the establishment of trading ports along the West African coast, he pursued a policy of using the influence of African rulers to advance the cause of Christianity. Those earliest attempts at → evangelism, led by Capuchin monks, did not, however, yield much fruit. Much later, in 1877, the Holy Ghost Fathers resumed this mission, which yielded results, even though it encountered stiff Muslim opposition.

The → Christian and Missionary Alliance came from the United States to Boro in the Niger Valley in 1918. The Église Évangélique Protestante, a grouping of Protestant denominations and the Church of the Province of West Africa (Anglican), is also present. Radio ELWA, an organ of the SIM mission (→ Evangelical Missions) broadcasting from Ivory Coast, carries regular programs of Christian teaching and preaching in local languages.

The Christian presence in Guinea is small, virtually lost in a sea of Islam. Of the Christian population, the → Roman Catholics are predominant, with a large number of unaffiliated. Its first African archbishop, Raymond Tchidimbo, was consecrated in 1962; later he suffered a period of imprisonment (1970-79; → Persecution of Christians). In 1967 all foreign missionaries were expelled except 11 from the Christian and Missionary Alliance. Even African priests and pastors from other African countries were expatriated. There are no independent churches. Although there is no ecumenical council, the church is gradually assuming a significant role in the country.

Bibliography: L. Adamolekum, *Sékou Touré's Guinea* (London, 1976) • J. Arulpragasam, *Economic Transition in Guinea: Implications for Growth and Poverty* (New York, 1997) • M. A. Klein, *Slavery and Colonial Rule in French West Africa* (New York, 1998) • T. E. O'Toole, *Historical Dictionary of Guinea* (Metuchen, N.J., 1995) • L. Sanneh, *Piety and Power: Muslims and Christians in West Africa* (Maryknoll, N.Y., 1996).

JOHN MBITI

Guinea-Bissau

1. General Situation
2. Religious Situation

1. General Situation

Guinea-Bissau, a republic on the west coast of Africa, is bounded to the west and south by the Atlantic Ocean, by Senegal to the north, and by Guinea to the east and south. This small country contains over 27 ethnic groups speaking 22 languages. The official language is Portuguese, and Creole is the language of trade.

	1960	1980	2000
Population (1,000s):	542	795	1,180
Annual growth rate (%):	−0.68	1.87	1.98
Area: 36,125 sq. km. (13,948 sq. mi.)			

A.D. 2000

Population density: 33/sq. km. (85/sq. mi.)
Births / deaths: 3.89 / 1.91 per 100 population
Fertility rate: 5.05 per woman
Infant mortality rate: 123 per 1,000 live births
Life expectancy: 45.3 years (m: 43.8, f: 46.8)
Religious affiliation (%): tribal religionists 45.5, Muslims 41.6, Christians 11.1 (Roman Catholics 8.1, indigenous 2.9, Protestants 1.1, other Christians 0.3), nonreligious 1.6, other 0.2.

Guinea-Bissau's first encounters with Europe came when Portuguese traders arrived in 1446 and → Roman Catholic → missionaries followed in 1462. More striking was the → slave trade, which the Portuguese carried out in the 17th century. In 1879 Guinea-Bissau become a Portuguese colony (→ Colonialism).

In that period there was a rather ambivalent relationship between Guinea-Bissau and the Cape Verde Islands, lying 620 km. (385 mi.) off the coast of West Africa. Between 1446 and 1870 the Portuguese ruled as a dependency of Cape Verde. Consequently, the mixed settlers *(mestiço)* from Cape Verde and their descendants in Guinea-Bissau constituted a privileged class that controlled all trade. This history explains the rather frosty subsequent relationship between Cape Verde and Guinea-Bissau, a growing enmity that came to its culmination in the coup d'état of 1980 and the subsequent suspension of all plans for unification of the two countries. Relations thus reverted to the situation at independence, when the two were governed as nonaligned socialist states under the African Independence Party of Guinea and Cape Verde (PAIGC).

The story of Guinea-Bissau is often remembered because of the 11-year people's war (1962-73) under the leadership of the celebrated socialist theoretician Amílcar Cabral, which culminated in the independence of Guinea-Bissau in 1974. That war was costly and ruined the country. The leader of the war of independence died just at independence, and Luiz Cabral became head of a civilian government (1974-80). The military government that seized power in 1980, led by João Bernard Vieira, was socialist. As avowed socialists, the leaders were initially oriented toward the socialist countries of Eastern Europe.

Guinea-Bissau changed its constitution in 1984, and there were further revisions in 1991 and 1993.

The last constitution contained provisions for multiparty democracy. In the meantime the country, in bondage to rigid and blind ideology, was reduced to poverty. The gross domestic product was estimated at $1,000 per capita in 1998. Compounding the plight of the country, there was a civil war in 1999, which led to the flight of Vieira.

2. Religious Situation

In spite of the avowal of → socialism, religion has continued. The Sunni tradition of → Islam is represented among the peoples of the east and south, especially the Soninke, Susu, Jola, and Fula. In the 1973 state constitution, and in subsequent revisions, all persons are recognized as equal before the law and possessing religious liberty.

The first to bring Christianity to the area were Roman Catholic → Franciscans, who arrived in 1462. In 1532 the diocese of St. James of Cape Verde was created, and it was given responsibility for doing missionary work on the mainland. The → Jesuits joined in this mission. → Evangelism, however, was slow. With the 1940 concordat between the Holy See and Portugal, Guinea-Bissau became a mission independent of Cape Verde. In 1955 it became a prefecture apostolic, in 1977 a diocese.

On the Protestant side, the World Evangelical Crusade came to Guinea-Bissau in 1939. Its work continues in the Evangelical Church of Guinea-Bissau, the largest Protestant group. The Church of the Province of West Africa's Diocese of the Gambia (Anglican) also has a small community.

The civil war of 1999 destroyed much of the work of the missions in the interior, forcing the workers to retreat to the western part of Guinea-Bissau. The complete Bible has been translated into one indigenous language, the NT into three languages, and other portions of Scripture into four additional languages (→ Bible Versions). There is no central or ecumenical organization of churches in the country.

Bibliography: M. DHADA, *Warriors at Work: How Guinea Was Really Set Free* (Niwot, Colo., 1993) • J. B. FORREST, *Guinea-Bissau: Power, Conflict, and Renewal in a West African Nation* (Boulder, Colo., 1992) • R. E. GALLI and L. J. JONES, *Guinea-Bissau: Politics, Economics, and Society* (London, 1987) • R. LOBBAN and J. FORREST, *Historical Dictionary of the Republic of Guinea-Bissau* (Metuchen, N.J., 1988) • C. LOPES, *Guinea Bissau, from Liberation Struggle to Independent Statehood* (Boulder, Colo., 1987) • S. URDANG, *Fighting Two Colonialisms: Women in Guinea-Bissau* (New York, 1979).

JOHN S. POBEE

Guru Movement → Ānanda Mārga; Bhagwan Shree Rajneesh; Divine Light Mission; Krishna Consciousness, International Society for; Transcendental Meditation

Guyana

	1960	1980	2000
Population (1,000s):	569	759	874
Annual growth rate (%):	2.52	0.87	0.98
Area: 215,083 sq. km. (83,044 sq. mi.)			

A.D. 2000

Population density: 4/sq. km. (11/sq. mi.)
Births / deaths: 1.88 / 0.70 per 100 population
Fertility rate: 2.10 per woman
Infant mortality rate: 52 per 1,000 live births
Life expectancy: 66.2 years (m: 63.1, f: 69.4)
Religious affiliation (%): Christians 51.3 (Protestants 22.6, Roman Catholics 9.5, Anglicans 7.8, unaffiliated 6.0, indigenous 3.3, Orthodox 1.1, marginal 1.0), Hindus 32.4, Muslims 8.0, tribal religionists 2.1, Baha'is 2.0, spiritists 1.7, nonreligious 1.5, other 1.1.

1. History, Society, Economy, and State
2. Churches
3. Church and State
4. Non-Christian Religions and Cults

1. History, Society, Economy, and State

Guyana (officially The Co-operative Republic of Guyana), on the north coast of South America, is the only English-speaking country in the continent. Its capital is Georgetown, which in 1995 had an estimated population of 254,000.

European settlement began in 1616-21 with the arrival of the Dutch West India Company. England took possession for the first time in 1796 but then returned the land to Holland in 1802. In 1814 it was partitioned among contending powers, with a commission awarding one part to Britain and the rest to the Netherlands (present-day Suriname) and France (Cayenne, in French Guiana).

By 1830 over 100,000 black slaves had been shipped to Guyana to work on the plantations. Following the abolition of → slavery in 1834, the blacks spread out over Guyana, some of them becoming small landowners. The plantation owners now had to look for other sources of labor, a need filled by Indians from India, a smaller number of Chinese, and also Portuguese from the Azores and Madeira. Up to 1917 some 239,000 workers had come from India alone. Though 76,000 (32 percent) returned home when their contracts expired, by 1949 the number of Indians in Guyana had risen to 185,000 (out of a total population of 460,000).

This complex history of settlement has produced a population that is greatly divided racially. In the interior are Amerindians (6.8 percent in 1992-93), mostly Caribs and Arawaks. On the coast we find Indians (49.4 percent), the descendants of the slaves and the so-called Bush Negroes (i.e., descendants of those who fled from the plantations into the interior, 35.6 percent), mixed (7.1 percent), Europeans (mostly of Portuguese descent, 0.7 percent), and Chinese (0.4 percent).

After 1949 the People's Progressive Party (PPP), under the leadership of Cheddi Jagan, fought for self-government and social revolution. Britain granted a constitution in 1953, and independence in internal affairs began in 1961 with a PPP government under a British governor. Violent unrest in 1962-64 brought elections in 1964 by proportional representation, which enabled the two opposition parties, the People's National Congress (PNC) and the United Force, to form a coalition government with Forbes Burnham (PNC) as prime minister. In 1966 Guyana became an independent member of the Commonwealth. In 1970 a republic was proclaimed with Raymond Arthur Chung as the first president and Burnham as prime minister. Burnham, who enjoyed American aid and had campaigned on a strict anti-Communist line, quickly emerged as a reformist who entered into diplomatic relations with states in the socialist camp, adopted a policy of cooperatives, and, following a referendum in 1978, pushed through a constitution in 1980 that declared Guyana to be a "cooperative republic . . . in transition from capitalism to socialism." Under this constitution, Burnham became executive president with considerably expanded power.

In the 1970s key industries were nationalized with the help of advisers from Cuba, China, and East Germany. Nevertheless, Guyana remained in the international organizations of the West. Strong tensions between Indo-Guyanese and Afro-Guyanese caused constant political instability. A sharp rise in population and rapid urbanization created severe social and economic problems for the new state, in which there have been no local elections since 1970. The large-scale abandonment of cooperatives and a fall in world prices of sugar and bauxite, which with rice are Guyana's main exports, led to a steady worsening of the economic situation after 1978, exacerbated by a serious brain drain. In

1982 the currency reserves were completely exhausted, which left Guyana able only to barter.

When Forbes Burnham died in 1985, his successor, Desmond Hoyte, tried to follow a neutral line, avoiding anti-American rhetoric in order to draw closer to the West and also improving conditions in the private sector so as to attract investment and secure credits for the large foreign debt, which is three times the gross national product. The later, general collapse of socialism in Eastern Europe and the Soviet Union allayed United States' fears of a possible leftist regime in Guyana, with the result that in 1992 it supported free and fair elections, from which the Marxist-Leninist Cheddi Jagan (PPP/Civic), the representative of the largely rural Indo-Guyanese, emerged victoriously as the third president.

With a per capita income of $330/year and a national debt that consumes 90 percent of the country's income, this impoverished country finds itself in an almost hopeless situation. The Bretton Woods Reform Organization developed an alternative program for "structural accommodation" in 1995. After Jagan's death in March 1997, however, the implementation of this program seemed increasingly doubtful. Jagan's widow, the 77-year-old Janet Jagan, won the subsequent, well-organized election, in the face of which former president Desmond Hoyte (PNC) announced that he would do everything in his power to "make the country ungovernable." Even though Janet Jagan has long been politically active, the fact that her origins were in a U.S. Jewish-American family suffices for many Afro-Guyanese to consider her unqualified. As the representative of the largely urban Afro-Guyanese, the PNC controlled the government between 1964 and 1992 by means of election fraud and is now having a difficult time giving up power. Ethnic tensions also contribute to making any genuinely rational policy-making impossible.

2. Churches

Capuchins began missionary work in 1657 ($\rightarrow$ Catholic Missions). In the colonial era there was little penetration into the interior and only superficial work among some of the Amerindians, much of which was reversed under the Dutch. The $\rightarrow$ Moravians began work in the Dutch period, but this work suffered serious setbacks after a rebellion by blacks in 1763; by 1962 the Moravians counted less than 3,000 members. In 1743 Dutch settlers founded a Lutheran congregation that, at the beginning of the 20th century, received help from the United States. By 1999, as the Lutheran Church in Guyana, it had grown to 11,000 members. After

1766 Scottish settlers started what is now the Presbytery of Guyana. Anglicans began work in 1826 with the help of British missionary societies (→ British Missions). In 1842 an independent diocese was founded under William Pierce Austin, who worked there for 50 years and became primate of the West Indies Church. The Anglicans and Scottish Presbyterians both enjoyed state recognition, but the former were more active. The Anglican Church numbered 76,000 members by 1900, or about one-quarter of the population; by 2000 its percentage of the total population had shrunk dramatically.

The → Roman Catholic Church, which at first recruited mainly from the Portuguese section, by 1985 had become larger than the Anglican Church and is today the largest church body in the country. The first Roman Catholic priest of recent times came in 1826, a vicariate apostolic was established in 1837, and later a diocese. Of the 78 priests in 1971, however, only 15 were born in Guyana. In 1967 the church was made up of 60 percent Afro-Americans, 20 percent Amerindians, 5 percent Portuguese, and 15 percent Indians, Chinese, and non-Portuguese Europeans.

The Methodists (→ Methodist Churches) began work among blacks in 1892. They enjoyed success among freed slaves who had come from the island of Nevis, but they also numbered some 5,600 Hindus. After the abolition of slavery in 1834, the planters and the government took a more favorable view of work among blacks, subsidizing education and even encouraging the missionaries to give religious instruction. By the end of the 19th century not only the descendants of Europeans but most of the blacks and Chinese were Christians.

Beginning in 1887 the Seventh-day → Adventists and the → Salvation Army established a presence in Guyana. Other Christian groups came after World War II, including the Southern → Baptists, Baptist Mid-Missions, Pentecostals (→ Pentecostal Churches), three → Churches of God, Assemblies of God, and Congregationalists (→ Congregationalism). The Unevangelized Fields Mission works among various Indian tribes close to the Brazilian border. National churches began to form in the 19th century, such as the Hallelujah Church, an Amerindian prophetic movement that attempts a synthesis of Amerindian religion and Christianity, and, in the 1920s, the Jordanites. Several African American denominations from the United States are active among Afro-Guyanese, including the African Methodist Episcopal and African Methodist Episcopal Zion Churches.

In 1937 an Anglican layman founded the Christian Social Council, which included Roman Catholics and Protestants. In 1967 this group merged with the Evangelical Council (which had been established in 1960) to form the present Guyana Council of Churches. The council includes the 2 U.S.-based black churches, plus 13 others, and is organized in four autonomous regional councils. In cooperation with government departments it maintains the Davis Rose Centre, a self-help project, in the poorest parts of Georgetown. The member churches cover five different strata of the population, with seven of the churches serving mainly Afro-Guyanese, and two mainly Indo-Guyanese.

3. Church and State

The preamble to the Guyanese constitution of 1966 declares that the people of Guyana find in the worship of the deity "the basis of freedom, justice, and peace in society." → Religious liberty is guaranteed (→ Church and State). In September 1976 the Christian Social Council mounted vigorous protests against the nationalizing of schools, which were then almost all church schools.

The Roman Catholic and Anglican bishops met with leaders of the opposition and expressed their deep disillusionment over the elections of 1985. The result was an attack on the churches by the controlled press, searches of the residences of the bishops and Moravian leaders for weapons, the banning of English Jesuits, and the intimidation of other clergy — all of which led to a visit by a delegation of Caribbean archbishops in December 1986. When Anthony Dickson, the Roman Catholic bishop of Barbados, was detained for 17 hours at the airport and then expelled from the country, protests arose from statesmen of the Caribbean Community (Caricom).

4. Non-Christian Religions and Cults

In November 1978 the mass suicide-execution of 911 members of the U.S. People's Temple sect in Jonestown captured international headlines.

About one-third of the people of Guyana (some 70 percent of the Indo-Guyanese) are → Hindus, whose organizations range from the American Aryan League, representing reformed Hinduism, to the traditionalist Hindu Orthodox Guyana Sanathan Maha Sabba.

Another 9 percent overall are Muslims, but 18 percent of the Indo-Guyanese people, especially those engaged in agriculture, adhere to → Islam. Some are orthodox Sunnites (→ Sunna), and others belong to heterodox Aḥmadīya sects.

Finally, 4 percent of the people, largely Tarumas

and Arawaks, follow Amerindian religions or are adherents of the → voodoo cult (mostly persons of Afro-Guyanese descent; → Afro-American Cults), though at the same time maintaining a nominal identity as Christians. Only a few Afro-Guyanese have adopted Hinduism or Islam.

Bibliography: C. BARBER and H. JEFFREY, *Guyana: Politics, Economics, and Society* (London, 1985) • P. BEATTY JR., *A History of the Lutheran Church in Guyana* (South Pasadena, Calif., 1972) • A. J. BUTT, "The Birth of a Religion: The Origins of Hallelujah, the Semi-Christian Religion of the Carib-Speaking People of the Borderlands of British Guayana, Venezuela, and Brazil," *Time*, September 1959, 37-48 • M. COLCHESTER, *Guyana: Fragile Frontier. Loggers, Miners, and Forest Peoples* (London, 1997) • K. S. LATOURETTE, *A History of the Expansion of Christianity*, vol. 5, *The Great Century in the Americas, Australia, and Africa*, A.D. 1800–A.D. 1914 (London, 1945) • T. MERRILL, ed., *Guyana and Belize: Country Studies* (Washington, D.C., 1993) • R. PRICE, *The Guiana Maroons: A Historical and Bibliographical Introduction* (Baltimore, 1976) • C. SEECHARAN, *Tiger in the Stars: The Anatomy of Indian Achievement in British Guiana, 1919-29* (London, 1997) • A. THOMPSON, *Colonialism and Underdevelopment in Guyana, 1580-1803* (Bridgetown, Barbados, 1987).

HANS-JÜRGEN PRIEN and WINSTON D. PERSAUD

Gypsies → Roma

H

Habakkuk, Book of

The Book of Habakkuk has a liturgical form. A complaint by the prophet in 1:2-4 is followed by God's reply (vv. 5-11), which announces the coming of the Chaldeans (v. 6). When the prophet objects (vv. 12-17), Yahweh gives a fresh answer (2:1-5), to which a series of woes is appended (6-20). Chap. 3 contains a prayer, the heart of which is the depiction of a → theophany. This chapter is structured in such a way that it can be used in → worship.

The presence of social criticism, which in the present context is directed at international events and especially at the Babylonians, creates something of a discrepancy, which has led some scholars to postulate a process of redaction. Habakkuk was supposedly a prophet of judgment who addressed domestic evils (the oppression of the weak and the perversion of justice) and expected divine punishment at the hands of the Babylonians. During the exile, however, redactors turned the threat of judgment against the Babylonians and gave the book its liturgical form (J. Jeremias, cf. E. Otto).

Little is known about the person of Habakkuk. He was presumably a cult prophet at the Jerusalem → temple at the time of early Babylonian expansion, perhaps after the battle of Carchemish (605 B.C.) and certainly before the first capture of Jerusalem (597). His sayings were probably handed down and edited in prophetic circles.

The earliest exposition of Habakkuk is the Qumran commentary 1QpHab, which deals only with the first two chapters and relates the text to contemporary events.

→ Prophet, Prophecy

Bibliography: Commentaries: K. L. BARKER, W. BAILEY, and D. W. BAILEY (NAC; Nashville, 1997) • A. DEISSLER (NEchtB; Würzburg, 1984) • K. ELLIGER (ATD; 8th ed.; Göttingen, 1982) • J. J. M. ROBERTS (OTL; Philadelphia, 1991) • O. P. ROBINSON (NICOT; Grand Rapids, 1990) • K. SEYBOLD (ZBK; Zurich, 1991) • R. L. SMITH (WBC; Dallas, 1984).

Other works: J. JEREMIAS, *Kultprophetie und Gerichtsverkündigung in der späten Königszeit Israels* (Neukirchen, 1970) • E. LOHSE, ed., *Die Texte aus Qumran* (3d ed.; Darmstadt, 1981) • E. OTTO, "Habakuk / Habakukbuch," *TRE* 14.300-306 (bibliography) • M. A. SWEENEY, "Habakkuk, Book of," *ABD* 3.1-6 (bibliography) • A. VAN DER WAL, *Nahum, Habakkuk: A Classified Bibliography* (Amsterdam, 1988).

WINFRIED THIEL

Hadith → Sunna

Haggadah

Haggadah (Heb. for "story") is the narrative form of Jewish rabbinic literature. It embraces all the forms and themes that do not count as → Halakah, or legal texts. Small forms of Haggadah are the parable, the exemplary tale, the case, exegesis (insofar as it does not serve Halakic purposes), the legend, the sermon, and biographical, ethical, and historical notes. Larger forms are commentaries (→ Midrash) on the biblical books, which most clearly demonstrate the tendency of Haggadah to relate Israel's → salvation history to the given present. There is thus a distinction between Haggadic literature and the individual Haggadah as a literary unit and form.

The Haggadah may be linked to a purpose and may thus illustrate a Halakah, but one may not derive a Halakah from a Haggadah or base it on a Haggadah. The Haggadah can be an end in itself and may simply present playful or associative narrative fancy. Its significance depends on the sphere of reference in which the Haggadic tradition now stands or from which it arose.

The paschal Haggadah deserves special attention, for it reflects the decisive event in Israel's salvation history (the exodus from Egypt; → Passover). The counterpart of Haggadah in → Judaism is Halakah.

→ Jewish Theology

Bibliography: A. R. E. AGUR, *Hermeneutic Biography in Rabbinic Midrash: The Body of This Death and Life* (Berlin, 1996) • R. AUS, *Samuel, Saul, and Jesus: Three Early Palestinian Jewish Christian Gospel Haggadoth* (Atlanta, 1994) • S. H. DERNER, *Rachel* (Minneapolis, 1994) • A. KAMESAR, "The Narrative Aggada As Seen from the Graeco-Latin Perspective," *JJS* 45 (1994) 52-70 • S. E. KARFF, *Agada: The Language of Jewish Faith* (Cincinnati, 1979) • M. LATTKE, "Haggadah," *RAC* 13.328-60 • H. L. STRACK and G. STERNBURGER, *Introduction to Talmud and Midrash* (Edinburgh, 1991) • G. VERMÈS, *Scripture and Tradition in Judaism: Haggadic Studies* (2d ed.; Leiden, 1973).

GERD A. WEWERS†

Haggai, Book of

The Book of Haggai contains sayings of the prophet woven into a narrative and set in a chronological framework. Haggai emerged in Jerusalem in 520 B.C., the second year of the Persian monarch Darius I, and served there for only four months. Economic difficulties stemming from poor harvests were troubling the community, and reconstruction of the temple had come to a halt. This setting provided the occasion of Haggai's (and Zechariah's) ministry.

The → temple stood at the heart of Haggai's message. The distress of the day, he taught, was the result of breaking off the rebuilding of the temple. He admonished the people to resume the work, and his plea found a hearing among the leaders. Zerubbabel, a descendant of David, and Joshua, the → high priest, whom the Persian court had sent back to Palestine with a group of returning exiles, again took up the work of reconstruction and carried it through to the end. Haggai evidently did not live to see the dedication of the temple (in 515 B.C.).

Along with his demand for the rebuilding of the temple, Haggai proclaimed a positive hope for the future. A divine shaking of the nations and a redistribution of power would bring the wealth of the nations to Jerusalem (2:6-9), where Zerubbabel would reign as God's anointed (vv. 20-23). This hope of deliverance was perhaps kindled by unrest on the accession of Darius to the throne of Persia. Darius, however, was able to consolidate his kingdom. Zerubbabel disappeared, and Judah continued to form part of the Persian empire as a community centered on the temple.

→ Prophet, Prophecy

Bibliography: Commentaries: K. ELLIGER (ATD; 8th ed.; Göttingen, 1982) • C. L. MEYERS and E. M. MEYERS (AB; Garden City, N.Y., 1987) • D. L. PETERSON (OTL; Philadelphia, 1984) • H. GRAF REVENTLOW (ATD; Göttingen, 1993) • R. L. SMITH (WBC; Dallas, 1984) • P. A. VERHOEF (NICOT; Grand Rapids, 1987) • H. W. WOLFF (BKAT; Neukirchen, 1986).

Other works: W. A. M. BEUKEN, *Haggai-Sacharja 1– 8* (Assen, 1967) • K.-M. BEYSE, *Serubbabel und die Königserwartungen der Propheten Haggai und Sacharja* (Berlin, 1971) • K. KOCH, "Haggais unreines Volk," *ZAW* 79 (1967) 52-66 • C. MEYERS and E. M. MEYERS, "Haggai, Book of," *ABD* 3.20-23.

WINFRIED THIEL

Hagiography → Lives of the Saints

Hail Mary → Ave Maria

Haiti

1. General Situation
2. Religious Situation
   2.1. Roman Catholicism
   2.2. Protestantism
   2.3. Voodoo
   2.4. Ecumenical Relations

	1960	1980	2000
Population (1,000s):	3,804	5,353	7,817
Annual growth rate (%):	1.71	1.81	1.84

Area: 27,700 sq. km. (10,695 sq. mi.)

A.D. *2000*

Population density: 282/sq. km. (731/sq. mi.)
Births / deaths: 3.29 / 1.19 per 100 population
Fertility rate: 4.40 per woman
Infant mortality rate: 73 per 1,000 live births
Life expectancy: 55.7 years (m: 54.0, f: 57.3)
Religious affiliation (%): Christians 95.9 (Roman
Catholics 83.2, Protestants 21.1, indigenous 5.5,
unaffiliated 2.9, Anglicans 1.5, other Christians 0.7),
spiritists 2.6, nonreligious 1.3, other 0.2.

1. General Situation

The Republic of Haiti is located in the western third of the Caribbean island of Hispaniola. The country is mostly mountainous; the population of almost 8 million has a black majority and a mulatto minority. The great majority of Haitians are descendants of African slaves who, brought as a labor force by the Spaniards or (from 1659) the French (→ Slavery), replaced the original indigenous Indian inhabitants, who had been largely exterminated by the 16th century because of the cruelty of slavery and epidemics of European diseases.

Hispaniola was discovered by Columbus in 1492 and was the first part of the New World colonized by Spain. Spain ceded the western third of Hispaniola to France in 1697. The struggle for independence began in 1791 with an uprising of the 450,000 slaves on the sugar and cocoa plantations against the approximately 40,000 whites (there were also 28,000 freed slaves). Led by Toussaint Louverture, the rebellion involved a period of almost constant battles, accompanied by horrific massacres. After winning control over the whole island, Louverture was deceived by the French and died in a French dungeon. Napoléon's Third Army under his brother-in-law General LeClerc regained Haiti for France, but Jean-Jacques Dessalines, with his general Henri Christophe, liberated the country again in 1803 and declared its independence from France on January 1, 1804, the second country in the New World to win its freedom from a colonial power. After independence Christophe ruled in the North and A. S. Pétion, a mulatto leader against Dessalines, in the South. Pétion divided the land among the people, but the socioeconomic oppression experienced in the colonial period ultimately continued.

Anarchic conditions in 1915 caused the United States under the Monroe Doctrine to send marines to Haiti, which they occupied until recalled by President Franklin D. Roosevelt in 1934. The political influence of the United States remained dominant. Dr. François Duvalier ("Papa Doc") won election in 1957 as a champion of black interests. After the revolution in Cuba in 1958, François and his son Jean-Claude ("Baby Doc") won support from the United States because of their firm opposition to Communism. F. Duvalier, however, established a reign of terror that ultimately claimed some 50,000 victims. At the same time, the stable government and the "Duvalier Revolution" encouraged a new rising educated middle class of blacks and a rapid increase in light industry and a large migration to Port-au-Prince, the capital. Under J.-C. Duvalier the repression subsided somewhat, but plundering the country for personal gain continued, causing further deterioration of an already weak → economy. The regime fell in February 1986, leaving Haiti the poorest country in the Western hemisphere, with an undernourished population, a literacy rate of only 15 percent, an unemployment rate of 60 percent, the highest infant mortality rate in the → Third World (20 percent), and over a million → refugees in neighboring lands. Drastic social reform was urgently needed.

After J.-C. Duvalier's fall the country was ruled by army generals except for Leslie Manigat's six-month presidency. General Avril was forced to resign in March 1990 because of massive antigovernment protest. Supreme Court Justice Ertha Pascal-Trouillot became the acting president, the first woman to lead the country. In December 1990 a Catholic priest, Jean-Bertrand Aristide, won the election fairly, a process that was more democratic than any previous election in Haiti. President Aristide took office in February 1990 and started to investigate all former officials. His followers who were impatient for reform reacted with acts of violence. Artistides' followers forced the Assembly to adjourn while they were debating a vote of no confidence. Many were killed during this time of instability. Rebel troops in September 1991 seeking to end the excessive acts of the president's supporters put Aristide out of office. This bloody military coup forced Aristide, whom the masses viewed as a bearer of hope, to leave the country that month.

The rightest Progressive Front (FRAPH) was a paramilitary unit that was responsible for the murder and → torture of hundreds of people during the three-year military dictatorship. The 2 percent of the population that controls 44 percent of gross domestic production, also the majority of the Catholic hierarchy, supported the military regime. A trade embargo imposed by the United Nations drove Haiti even further into misery, destroying Haiti's fragile economic infrastructure, causing almost all industry to close or move to other countries and intensified its economic dependency. Industry eliminated some 100,000 jobs. The fuel shortage caused by the embargo resulted in enormous environmental damage in the form of forest destruction.

Backed by the threat of U.S. military intervention as approved by the U.N. Security Council, U.S. mediator Jimmy Carter managed to extract an agreement from the military to step down in 1994. After intervention by U.S., and then U.N., troops, Aristide returned as president in 1996 but at the end of his legal mandate handed over the office to his colleague, the former Maoist René Préval, who had been elected with 88 percent of the votes. Préval dissolved Parliament in January 1999. Foreign aid has been frozen because no budget has been passed since 1996.

Conditions within Haiti at the turn of the century are dismal: the average annual income is only $250 (1998), 80 percent of the population live in extreme poverty, and the unemployment rate stands at perhaps more than 65 percent. Inflation remains high, and 40 percent of the national budget depends on foreign aid (1996). Since Haitians have confidence only in real estate as a long-term investment, there is major new building construction throughout the country; money is coming primarily from family members residing abroad and from drug trafficking. Haiti has the highest rate of AIDS infection in the Western hemisphere. Although 66 percent of the population derives its living from agriculture, almost half of all foodstuffs must be imported, including even sugar. Clear-cutting and erosion have decimated the countryside. In this, the poorest country in the Americas, women bear the main burden and yet have few opportunities.

2. Religious Situation
The religious life of the people is characterized by Christianity and the syncretistic → voodoo cult.

2.1. *Roman Catholicism*
Even after two centuries of a presence in Haiti, the → Roman Catholic Church had not been able to establish its own → hierarchy there. Two prefectures apostolic were set up only in 1705 under the supervision of the → Dominicans and → Jesuits. Because of the lack of → missionaries and the colonists' failure to support → evangelism, the effect of Christianity on the African masses, who regarded it as the religion of the slaveowners, was very small (→ Mis-

sion 3). The → priests, though, must have shown greater concern for the blacks in the 18th century, for most of them survived when plantation-owner whites were massacred in the struggle for independence. After the conclusion of a → concordat in 1860, Haiti was divided into five → dioceses, including the Archdiocese of Port-au-Prince.

Two small seminaries were founded in the second half of the 19th century, and the resultant emergence of a native clergy entered upon a decisive phase with the establishment of a large seminary by the Jesuits in 1942. The pastoral work of the church was hindered by the interference of the government, especially after 1959, when it forcibly nationalized the church, banned many missionaries and priests, including the archbishop, and closed the seminary, the result being that for a time the Vatican broke off diplomatic relations with Haiti.

The church has long struggled against the role of voodoo in Haitian society, which Haitians have used as a means of establishing their identity. In 1941 church and state together attempted finally to destroy the voodoo temples. Every baptized person had to take a vow to renounce the practices and teachings of voodoo, which was condemned as a Satanic cult. Papa Doc Duvalier, however, who was close to voodoo, ended the persecution and used voodoo as a political instrument.

When John Paul II visited Haiti in 1983, he encouraged the official church to oppose the brutal regime of Duvalier. Already by 1980 Roman Catholic young people had increasingly assumed the role of a political opposition and were building up political awareness among the oppressed people, many of whom were nominal church members. To be sure, the 11-member episcopate included only one voice opposed to the country's dictatorship, namely Willy Romélus, bishop of Jérémie (in southwestern Haiti). Moreover, because of Aristide's political activity in the spirit of the unpopular → liberation theology, the Vatican excluded him from his Salesian Order. Earlier, Archbishop François Wolff Ligonde, with the support of the military, actively opposed this message of liberation theology. For his own part, Aristide, who was also dismissed from the priesthood in 1994, upon his return demonstratively embraced the conservative bishop François Gayot; three bishops received him at his return, offering a glimmer of hope for reconciliation in the church and among Haiti's inhabitants.

2.2. *Protestantism*
In 1807 two British Methodist missionaries began work among black slaves who had fled from the United States to Haiti. But later the → Methodist

Church, like the Anglican (→ Anglican Communion), became more a church of the ruling caste. The → Baptists began work in the 19th century, but Protestant missions made a noticeable impact only from the time of the American occupation. According to sociologist Charles-Poisset Romain, Protestants grew from only 1.5 percent of the population in 1930 to 20 percent in 1978.

Today the Baptists are the largest Protestant church, followed by the → Adventists and two → Pentecostal churches. A sizable proportion of Protestants are organized in native churches that are independent of missions from abroad. Because many Haitian pastors are poorly trained and financial resources are small, many of the Haitian church groups are still greatly dependent on U.S. missionaries and their money (→ North American Missions).

2.3. Voodoo

The majority of Haitians practice an animistic cult called voodoo, which is a mixture of African → animism and a distorted understanding of Roman Catholic beliefs and rites. It is not viewed as a religion but simply as a way of life. (When asked about religious preference, most Haitians identify themselves as either Roman Catholic or → "Evangelical.")

Voodoo is → monotheistic in that the Great Master's permission is asked before almost every ceremony. Practically, however, it is → polytheistic, with many loas (identified as local gods, deified ancestors, or Catholic saints). Priests of voodoo are either male (houngan) or female (mambo). They function also as fortune-tellers, magicians, medicine men and women, and very often as heads of an extended family. While there are collective → altars, voodoo is primarily a family religion, giving greater importance to the family altar (houmfo). There are many ceremonies, with the climax being the possession (or "mounting") of a worshiper by a loa. Each loa has its own symbol, ritual, drumbeat, and often a Catholic saint counterpart.

Although voodoo has many taboos, it does not foster a sense of → guilt. Its practitioners thus typically show little interest in the Christian message of → forgiveness. What interest there is in the → gospel usually arises from a → dream or from a wish to be delivered from a → curse.

2.4. Ecumenical Relations

Many of the Protestant groups participate in the Council of Evangelical Churches of Haiti (comprising 11 conservative denominations and affiliated with the World Evangelical Fellowship) and also in the broader based Protestant Federation. The Roman Catholic Church cooperates in the Ecumenical Research Group (1968) and the Commission of Haitian Churches for Development. Some believe that there cannot be a full → acculturation of Christianity in Haiti until there is serious → dialogue with the representatives of voodoo.

→ Afro-American Cults

Bibliography: E. Abbott, *The Duvaliers and Their Legacy* (New York, 1991); idem, *Haiti* (New York, 1991) • J.-B. Aristide, *In the Parish of the Poor: Writings from Haiti* (Maryknoll, N.Y., 1990) • D. B. Barrett, ed., *WCE* 348-51 • J. M. Dash, *Haiti and the United States: National Stereotypes and the Literary Imagination* (2d ed.; New York, 1997) • J. Dayan, *Haiti, History, and the Gods* (Berkeley, Calif., 1995) • A. Dupuy, *Haiti in the New World Order: The Limits of the Democratic Revolution* (Boulder, Colo., 1997) • J. L. González, *The Development of Christianity in the Latin Caribbean* (Grand Rapids, 1969) • L. E. Harrison, "Voodoo Politics," *Atlantic Monthly,* June 1993, 101-7 • R. D. Heinl, *Written in Blood: The Story of the Haitian People, 1492-1995* (2d ed.; Lanham, Md., 1996) • C. Kumar, *Building Peace in Haiti* (Boulder, Colo., 1998) • M. Lundhals, *Peasants and Poverty: A Study of Haiti* (London, 1979) • A. Metraux, *Voodoo in Haiti* (New York, 1972) • E. H. Preeg, *The Haitian Crisis: Two Perspectives* (Coral Gables, Fla., 1988); idem, *The Haitian Dilemma: A Case Study in Demographics, Development, and U.S. Foreign Policy* (Washington, D.C., 1996).

Hans-Jürgen Prien, Laënnec Hurbon,
and Edwin S. Walker

Halakah

Halakah (Heb. for "going" or "way") is a postbiblical norm or rule in rabbinic → Judaism that applies the legal judgments of the → Torah to existing situations. As far as rabbinic practice and the rabbinic understanding of tradition are concerned, Halakah effectively can count just as much as the Torah (i.e., as the → revelation to → Moses from → Sinai). It is oral torah. It decides (often by specific cases) what is clean or unclean, innocent or guilty, permitted or forbidden. In an actual case the decision is binding, but later it forms a basis for discussion with support and refutation. In cases of doubt the majority decides, though on occasion the authority of the champion of a single view might prevail.

From the discussions of Halakah there developed Halakah as a literary genre. The various works fall into two classes: compendiums (→ Mishnah,

Tosepta, → Talmud, and medieval and modern collections) and commentaries (→ Midrash). The compendiums arrange the materials in tractate form or thematically. The biblical commentaries base Halakah directly on the Bible, compare it with the Bible, and thus give the Bible regulative relevance. The counterpart of Halakah in Judaism is → Haggadah.

Bibliography: N. Danzig, *Introduction to Halakhot Pesuqot* (New York, 1993) • M. Fishbane, ed., *The Midrashic Imagination: Jewish Exegesis, Thought, and History* (Albany, N.Y., 1993) • R. Hammer, *The Classic Midrash: Tannaitic Commentaries on the Bible* (Mahwah, N.J., 1995) • M. Lattke, "Halakah," *RAC* 13.372-402 • J. Neusner, *The Components of the Rabbinic Documents* (12 vols.; Atlanta, 1997-98); idem, *Introduction to Rabbinic Literature* (New York, 1994) • J. Neusner and W. S. Green, *Writing with Scripture: The Authority and Uses of the Hebrew Bible in the Torah of Formative Judaism* (Minneapolis, 1989) • J. Roth, *The Halakhic Process: A Systematic Analysis* (New York, 1986) • A. Sagi, "'Both Are the Words of the Living God': A Typological Analysis of Halakhic Pluralism," *HUCA* 65 (1994) 105-36 • L. H. Schiffman, *From Text to Tradition: A History of Second Temple and Rabbinic Judaism* (Hoboken, N.J., 1991) • H. L. Strack and G. Sternburger, *Introduction to Talmud and Midrash* (Edinburgh, 1991) • E. E. Urbach, *The Halakhah: Its Sources and Development* (Jerusalem, 1986).

Gerd A. Wewers†

Hamartiology → Sin

Hammurabi, Code of

The Code of Hammurabi is one of the oldest and best-known cuneiform law codes in Akkadian. It appears on a stele over 2 m. (6 ft.) high (now in the Louvre; there are many copies). It was promulgated by Hammurabi, king of the first dynasty of Babylon (1792-1750 B.C.), in an attempt at legal reform. In 282 casuistically formulated legal rulings, selected cases from various branches of law (trial, property, family, and inheritance) are dealt with, along with judgments concerning bodily injuries, various occupations, the hiring of cattle and servants, and the holding of slaves.

Worth noting is the severity of the punishments with which Hammurabi hoped to put an end to the people's widespread ignoring of the law. In over 30

cases a capital sentence is imposed, and there are also maimings (§§192ff.) and talionic penalties (§§196ff.). For the latter there are parallels in the OT (Exod. 21:23-25 and par.), as also for many laws, though there are also differences (cf. §14 with Exod. 21:16 and par., §129 with Lev. 20:10 and par., §132 with Num. 5:11-22, §§195-214 with Exod. 21:12-27, §§250-52 with Exod. 21:28-32, etc.). A direct link with the OT is certainly improbable.

→ Babylonian and Assyrian Religion

Bibliography: R. Borger, "Der Codex Hammurapi," *TUAT* 1/1.39-80 • C. H. Gordon, *Hammurabi's Code: Quaint or Forward-Looking?* (New York, 1957) • V. Korošec, "Keilschriftrecht," *HO* 1.E.3.94-118 (bibliography) • B. M. Levinson, ed., *Theory and Method in Biblical and Cuneiform Law: Revision, Interpolation, and Development* (Sheffield, 1994) • T. J. Meek, "The Code of Hammurabi," *ANET* 163-80 • S. M. Paul, *Studies in the Book of the Covenant, in the Light of Cuneiform and Biblical Law* (Leiden, 1970) • H. Petschow, "Gesetze A §3.6," *RLA* 3.255-69 (bibliography) • M. T. Roth, *Law Collections from Mesopotamia and Asia Minor* (Atlanta, 1995) • S. A. West, "The Lex Talionis in the Torah," *JBQ* 21/3 (1993) 183-88.

Hermann Spieckermann

Happiness

1. Definition
2. Judeo-Christian Tradition
   2.1. Biblical Macarism
   2.2. Augustine
   2.3. Scholasticism
   2.4. Luther
3. Modern View
4. Transcultural Aspects

1. Definition
Both linguistically and materially, it is hard to define "happiness" and related terms such as "(good) fortune," as many interdisciplinary attempts show (e.g., *Was ist Glück? Ein Symposion*). Some have emphasized that, while happiness may fulfill desires and longings, it is not at the disposal of the will and cannot be attained by us (U. Hommes, in F. G. Jünger et al., 242). A. Gehlen finds happiness only in acquisition, not in possession (ibid., 29). We can grasp it plainly in terms neither of past nor of future. As M. Freund says, we are all the semantic forgers of our own fortune. But none of these descriptions is really felicitous.

2. Judeo-Christian Tradition

2.1. *Biblical Macarism*

The biblical macarism ("Blessed [i.e., happy] are those who . . .") ascribes to us an ability to achieve happiness and shows both how to achieve it and what to expect by way of it. In the OT, material and spiritual blessings constitute happiness, which is not blind fate but is at God's disposal. Such → blessings include a "sensible wife" (Sir. 25:8), children (Gen. 30:13), beauty (Cant. 6:9), well-being, riches, honor, and wisdom (Job 29), also divine reproof and discipline (Job 5:17) and even martyrdom (4 Macc. 7:15).

The NT macarism is regulated by the Christ-event and is more comprehensive than in the OT, though statistically rare (D. Ritschl). In expansion of the Jewish tradition happiness is eschatological and spiritual, and in contrast to what we find in → Greek philosophy, it is fundamentally Christological. Not the whim of fate but the new reality disclosed in Christ's cross and → resurrection is the source of good fortune for believers (→ Christology). Macarisms thus do not apply to the gods, as in Aristotle (*Eth. Nic.* 1178b25), but paradoxically to living people (Matt. 5:1-12). The blessing is → salvation (→ Assurance of Salvation), participation in the → kingdom of God (Matt. 13:16-17), belonging to the Lord in life and death (Rev. 19:9; 22:14), or being in Christ (Rom. 4:7-8). The new creation lives by the blessing of illumination (2 Cor. 4:5-6); enjoys total blessing in spirit, → soul, and body (1 Thess. 5:23); clings to it eschatologically, even in misfortune (2 Cor. 4:7-10); and experiences it dialectically (1 Cor. 4:7).

2.2. *Augustine*

In *The City of God* (19.1) Augustine (354-430) finds 288 forms of happiness in antiquity, distinguishing between pagan *felicitas* and Christian *beatitudo*. Defining happiness as having all that we want (*De Trin.* 13.5), he thinks that "having" reaches its climax in "knowing" or "seeing" in the beatific vision (J. Pieper, in Jünger et al., 47-48), the alternatives of having and not having being fixed by → predestination (→ Augustine's Theology). Along with the beatific vision, the enjoyment of God *(frui Deo)* plays an important role in Augustine's theology (see *De doc. christ.* 1.22.33; *Enarr. in Ps.* 121.3). This concept had an important influence on the Scholastic tradition, the later Reformation catechisms (Westminster Shorter and Larger in 1647), and English-speaking Protestant piety in general.

2.3. *Scholasticism*

On the basis of the beatific vision, borrowing from 1 Tim. 1:11 and 6:15, and in analogy to the theology of happiness in antiquity, → Scholasticism found in the vision of God the supreme blessing. A debate arose between → Thomism and → Scotism whether we achieve this vision by an act of mind or by an act of will.

2.4. *Luther*

In his Romans commentary of 1515-16 M. Luther (1483-1546) cut the ground from under the whole theology of beatitude with the idea of resignation to hell. He viewed humankind rather from the standpoint of → law and → gospel. This approach, however, could lead to a dialectical understanding of the concept of happiness such as we find today in a radical version of the doctrine of → justification.

3. Modern View

The modern age has taken up the question of what happiness is and whether it is for all or only for the individual. In "foreseen effects" (see T. Hobbes, 9) the → Enlightenment counts on the kindness to others that is necessary for the happiness of all (A. Smith, 382-83). B. Pascal (1623-62), however, drew attention to the incompatibility of earthly and eternal felicity (W. E. Mühlmann, in Jünger et al., 207).

At the same time, the right to the pursuit of happiness was stated especially to be one of the "unalienable rights" of all people (U.S. Declaration of Independence, July 4, 1776). Enjoying the benefits of nature is happiness, according to P. T. d'Holbach (p. 13). Individual conditions make the happy seem to be "outside the theater of world history" (G. W. F. Hegel, 56-58).

For this reason K. Marx (1818-83), protesting against individual privilege, demands a situation that will reconcile universal reason with individual claims to happiness (A. Schmidt, in Jünger et al., 93; → Marxism). F. Nietzsche (1844-1900), in contrast, argues that "man has discovered happiness" (p. 11), while S. Freud (1856-1939) is resigned to the view that happiness is "not included in the plan of creation" (p. 434). Happiness is substantially understood, even though it is projected nostalgically or along utopian lines in time. The absence of it is tedium (Gehlen, in Jünger, 34-35).

F. Engels (1820-95) made the breakthrough to a dialectical view of happiness with his statement that "living is dying" (p. 554). The weighting of happiness with unhappiness is itself happiness, according to O. Marquard (p. 32). As lived out self-transcendence, happiness can transform a hopeless situation into an achievement. "Out of the Calvary of Auschwitz has come our Easter sunrise" (V. E. Frankl, in Jünger et al., 121-22).

4. Transcultural Aspects

The basic dialectical structure of happiness corresponds also to modern experience in the humanities and can appeal to → Paul and the → Reformation inasmuch as it finds a place for existential dying and rising again with Christ. In Eastern religions the question arises whether happiness is the removal of antitheses (W. Bauer, in Jünger et al., 200). If the impossibility of deciding whether happiness exists leads to the belief that perfect happiness is precisely the absence of happiness (R. Wilhelm, 135-36), an appeal is made to a nothing that makes possible the power of a dialectical being (cf. K. Nishitani). Happiness is the experienced identity of what is not truly identical (R. Okochi and K. Otte, 63-64). If Islamic (H. Ritter) and Judeo-Christian thinking about happiness is still under the influence of a substantial concept (I. Maybaum), enlightenment by divine dialectic can become real happiness in vibration over nothingness.

→ Zen argues that those who seek happiness must venture the primal leap (Ur-Sprung), which is its origin. According to Paul, they must believe as → Abraham did that God "calls into existence the things that do not exist" (Rom. 4:17). "If they survive this venture, their destiny is to meet unbroken truth . . . , the formless origin of all origins, the nothing that is all things, being engulfed by it and born again out of it" (Herrigel, 94). May it be that the "forge of happiness" lies in the transcultural act?

→ Blessing; Curse; Fatalism; Joy; Life; Meaning; Suffering; Worldview

Bibliography: R. F. Capon, Health, Money, and Love— and Why We Don't Enjoy Them (Grand Rapids, 1990) • J. Delumeau, History of Paradise: The Garden of Eden in Myth and Tradition (Urbana, Ill., 2000) • R. A. Emmons, The Psychology of Ultimate Concerns: Motivation and Spirituality in Personality (New York, 1999) • F. Engels, "Dialektik der Natur," MEW 20 (= MECW 25.311-587) • S. Freud, "Das Unbehagen in der Kultur" (1930), Gesammelte Werke (London, 1948; ET Civilization and Its Discontents [New York, 1994]) • M. Freund, "Glück — das unfaßbare Gefühl," Psychologie heute 11 (1984) 26-29 • G. W. F. Hegel, Vorlesung über die Philosophie der Geschichte (Stuttgart, 1961; ET Lectures on the Philosophy of World History [Cambridge, 1975]) • E. Herrigel, Zen in der Kunst des Bogenschießens (N.p., 1979) • T. Hobbes, De corpore (1655; Leipzig, 1949) • P. T. d'Holbach, System der Natur oder von den Gesetzen der physischen und moralischen Welt (Berlin, 1960) • F. G. Jünger et al., Was ist Glück? Ein Symposion (3d ed.; Munich, 1980) • A. H. Khan, "Salighed" as Happiness? Kierkegaard on the Concept "Salighed" (Waterloo, Ont., 1985) • O. Marquard, Glück im Unglück. Philosophische Überlegungen (Munich, 1995) • I. Maybaum, Happiness outside the State (London, 1980) • F. Nietzsche, Also sprach Zarathustra (Wiesbaden, n.d.; ET Thus Spake Zarathustra [London, 1960]) • K. Nishitani, Was ist Religion? (Frankfurt, 1982) • R. Okochi and K. Otte, Tan-Ni-Sho. Die Gunst des Reinen Landes (Bern, 1979) • D. Ritschl, The Logic of Theology (Philadelphia, 1987) • H. Ritter, Al Ghasali. Das Elexier der Glückseligkeit (Jena, 1923) • L. S. Rouner, ed., In Pursuit of Happiness (Notre Dame, Ind., 1995) • F. Schleiermacher, On What Gives Value to Life (1792; Lewiston, N.Y., 1995) • A. Smith, Theory of Moral Sentiments (Amherst, N.Y., 2000; orig. pub., 1759) • R. Wilhelm, ed., Zhuang Zhou. Das wahre Buch vom südlichen Blütenland (Jena, 1920).

Klaus Otte

Hare Krishna → Krishna Consciousness, International Society for

Harvest Festivals

The harvest festival is one of the oldest of religious feasts. Because of the different times of harvest we naturally find that there is no single date. In the OT there were two such feasts, Weeks and Tabernacles (Exod. 23:16). In the Roman sphere there were four feasts. The Middle Ages continued these in the context of the ember seasons (→ Church Year), but only the one in September bore reference to the harvest. Masses of thanksgiving, with blessing of the fruits, were also held, commonly on the last Sunday in September in central Europe.

The → church orders of the 16th century set aside days for sermons or → worship services after harvest, often on the Sunday after St. Michael's Day (September 29). In 1773 Prussia officially instituted a common harvest festival on this Sunday, and the first Sunday in October is now the usual day in the Protestant churches and Roman Catholic dioceses of Germany. The Catholic services often include the blessing of the produce and local observances. In other countries, such as England, there is more flexibility, the town parishes often taking a Sunday in September, rural parishes tending to prefer early October, when the harvest is complete. The Eastern churches have no special harvest festival.

In the United States the Pilgrim Fathers celebrated a harvest feast some time between September 21 and November 11. In the 18th century its character as a holy day vanished in favor of an emotional and family occasion. The Continental Congress proclaimed the first national Thanksgiving Day as a "solemn" occasion in 1777; later it evolved into state observances. In 1863, in the midst of the U.S. Civil War, Thanksgiving Day was proclaimed as a national holiday by President Abraham Lincoln, to be held on the last Thursday in November. The date was changed and fixed by the Congress in 1941 as the fourth Thursday in November. It has become a shopping as well as a family event, with little reference to the harvesting season.

In Canada the English navigator Martin Frobisher held a formal ceremony of thanksgiving in present-day Newfoundland for the journey to America. Other settlers continued this practice. The French settlers, under the leadership of Samuel de Champlain, also held huge thanksgiving feasts. In 1879 the Canadian Parliament declared November 6 a day of Thanksgiving. After World War I, Armistice Day and Thanksgiving Day were joined commemorations until 1931. In 1957 Parliament proclaimed the second Monday of October to be the permanent "Day of General Thanksgiving to Almighty God for the bountiful harvest with which Canada has been blessed."

The dilemma of celebrating a festival due to the bounty of nature and the work of humans, by Christianity, a religion based on God's revelation not in nature but history, has never been satisfactorily solved. These two completely different approaches may be irreconcilable, with an ensuing unease about a harvest festival proper. Nowadays, however, with a growing concern for the → environment (→ Ecology) and world → hunger, the harvest festival has increasingly become an important occasion for instruction on Christian → responsibility in the handling of → nature.

Bibliography: O. Bischofberger et al., "Feste und Feiertage," *TRE* 11.93-143 • R. N. McMichael Jr., ed., *Creation and Liturgy* (Washington, D.C., 1993) • T. A. Schnitker, "Erntedankfest," *RGG* (4th ed.) 2.1464-65.

Thaddeus A. Schnitker

Hasidism

The term "Hasidism" (from Heb. *ḥāsîd,* "devout, pious") is a general one for various popular movements in → Judaism that historically bore no relation to one another.

1. There was first the "assembly of the devout" (*synagogē asidaiōn),* which came on the scene at the beginning of the Maccabean revolt (1 Macc. 2:42) and was distinguished for strict adherence to the Torah (vv. 29-38). It is conjectured that the Essenes (→ Qumran) and → Pharisees had their roots here.

2. There was then Ashkenazic Hasidism, in Germany in the 12th and 13th centuries. Perhaps influenced by the → Crusades, this group developed an ascetic-pietistic theology of penitence (the chief work being *Sefer Ḥasidim* [Book of the pious], presenting the teaching of Judah the Ḥasid and others), which helped shape early Jewish → esotericism (Elazar of Worms).

3. Eastern European Hasidism arose in southern Poland in the first half of the 18th century and soon became a mass movement among all eastern European Jews. Its founder was the charismatic healer Israel ben Eliezer (ca. 1700-1760), later called Baʿal Shem Tov (Master of the Good Name), which was shortened to Besht. His pupils Jacob Josef of Polonne, and especially Dov Baer of Mezhirichi (both towns in present-day Ukraine), the Great Maggid (= Preacher; d. 1773), laid the theoretical foundations of Hasidism. Also important were Naḥman of Bratslav (ca. 1800) and Shneur Zalman of Lyady (before 1800, both towns then Russian), the founder of Ḥabad Hasidism.

The teaching of Hasidism popularized the → cabala and is strongly individualistic (stressing the → immanence of God, inwardness, and suppression of collective messianic expectation). The → piety of the group contains ecstatic features, and song and → dance play a major role. At the heart of the religious life is the Ṣaddiq (the righteous one), who vicariously links himself to the deity on behalf of his followers and can later have messianic qualities. Increasing stress on the Ṣaddiq led to hereditary Ṣaddiq dynasties, which sometimes held court in great style and competed with one another.

Hasidism produced a considerable and as yet little-known literature. M. Buber (1878-1965) published narratives taken from this literature that in particular have facilitated the modern reception of Hasidism. His popularizing and in part inaccurate renderings, however, obstruct adequate religious and historical evaluation of Hasidism.

After the destruction of eastern European Judaism, new fellowships arose in the United States and Israel, mostly in the direction of Ḥabad Hasidism, which attempts a synthesis between the traditional and the modern. These fellowships are now enjoying a renaissance and are playing a decisive part in the religious renewal of Judaism.

Bibliography: M. BUBER, "Die Erzählungen des Chassidismus," *Werke* (vol. 3; Munich, 1963) 69-712 • J. DAN, "Chassidismus, aschkenasischer," *TRE* 7.705-10 • S. DUBNOW, *Geschichte des Chassidismus* (2 vols.; Jerusalem, 1969; orig. pub., Berlin, 1921-32) • R. ELIOR, *The Paradoxical Ascent to God: The Kabbalistic Theosophy of Habad Hasidism* (Albany, N.Y., 1993) • A. GREEN, *Tormented Master: A Life of Rabbi Nahman of Bratslav* (University, Ala., 1979) • L. GULKOWITSCH, *Der Hasidmus religionswissenschaftlich untersucht* (Leipzig, 1927) • M. IDEL, *Hasidism: Between Ecstasy and Magic* (Albany, N.Y., 1995) • I. MARCUS, *Piety and Society* (Leiden, 1981) • G. SCHOLEM, "Martin Bubers Deutung des Chassidismus," *Judaica* (vol. 1; Frankfurt, 1963) 165-206.

PETER SCHÄFER

Hasmonaeans

The Hasmonaeans (also sometimes called the Maccabees) were the last Jewish ruling family. Under the Hasmonaeans the Jews in Palestine enjoyed a period of political independence in the second and first centuries B.C. The Hasmonaean name occurs for the first time in Josephus (*Asamonaioi*), and later it is common in the rabbinic writings *(beth/běnê ḥašmonai)*. The derivation is uncertain. Josephus (*Ant.* 12.265; *J.W.* 1.36) refers to an ancestor of the same name, but more likely it arises from an association with the place Heshmon (Josh. 15:27) or Hashmonah (Num. 33:29-30).

The family was of priestly origin. It did not originally belong to the priestly aristocracy (→ Priest, Priesthood) but to a simple priestly group (the family of Joarib, 1 Macc. 2:1-5; cf. Joiarib in Neh. 11:10; 12:6, 19). It owed its rise to power to the leading role played by the Hasmonaean Mattathias (1 Macc. 2:15-28, 42-48) and his sons Judas ("who was called Maccabeus," 166-160 B.C., 1 Macc. 3:1–9:23; 2 Macc. 8–15), Jonathan (160-143, 1 Macc. 9:31–12:52), and Simon (143-135, 1 Macc. 13:1–16:16) in the war against the Seleucids.

The Hasmonaeans became dynastically established in 140 B.C. with the recognition of Simon as ethnarch, commander-in-chief, and → high priest (1 Macc. 14:25-48). His descendants developed their rule in the style of Hellenistic potentates (→ Hellenism) and thus came into conflict with the original goals of the Maccabean revolt. John Hyrcanus I (135-104) extended his kingdom beyond the borders of the Judean heartland. Aristobulus (104-103) took the title of king. Alexander Jannaeus (103-76) combined external expansion with internal repression (e.g., of the → Pharisees). His widow, Salome Alexandra (76-67), attempted a policy of moderation but with no lasting success.

The way was prepared for the collapse of Hasmonaean rule by the struggle for the succession between Salome's sons Aristobulus II (67-63 B.C.) and John Hyrcanus II (67, 63-40). Its fate was finally sealed by the penetration of the Romans into Syria and Palestine. First the Romans restricted the dominion of the Hasmonaeans to Judea, then they removed the last Hasmonaeans, Hyrcanus and Antigonos (40-37), from office and set up → Herod the Great as a client king. Herod ended the Hasmonaean dynasty both politically and, to a large extent, physically.

→ Israel 1

Bibliography: B. BAR-KOCHVA, *Judas Maccabeus* (Cambridge, 1989) • J. G. BUNGE, "Zur Geschichte und Chronologie des Untergangs der Oniaden und des Aufstiegs der Hasmonäer," *JSJ* 6 (1975) 1-46 • J. A. GOLDSTEIN, "The Hasmoneans: The Dynasty of God Resisters," *HTR* 68 (1975) 53-58 • T. RAJAK, "Hasmonean Dynasty," *ABD* 3.67-76 • E. SCHÜRER, *The History of the Jewish People in the Age of Jesus Christ* (trans. G. Vermes and F. Millar; vol. 1; Edinburgh, 1973) 125-286. • J. SIEVERS, *The Hasmoneans and Their Supporters: From Mattathias to the Death of John Hyrcanus I* (Atlanta, 1990).

BERNDT SCHALLER

Haustafeln → Household Rules

Healing

Healing deals therapeutically with sicknesses or injuries, whether of body or soul, in a living organism (→ Health and Illness). It does so in at least four ways:

(1) It may be *self-healing.* The organism reachieves stability, the balance of all bodily and psychological functions and cycles. The aggression of infection, injury, sickness, and so forth is warded off, resolved, set aside, or addressed. Self-healing is also an important aspect of psychotherapy, though percentages are hard to ascertain. "Time heals" many ills.

(2) Healing takes the form of *restoration.* The ideal state prior to the onset of sickness or injury is reached again. Sickness was a disruption of the norm; it interrupted the ability to work and to enjoy. By healing, the disrupted state of the patient's

life story is dismissed, and the old capacities are fully restored. Modern medicine, in spite of criticism on various sides, orients itself largely by this model.

(3) Healing may also be *acceptance of limitations*. In it the sick go through a learning experience. They will not be as they were before. Healing shows them that → life, sickness, and → suffering go together, and ultimately also → old age and → death. The sick (even sick children) grow by means of their sickness. They learn to understand themselves afresh. This broad and less precise concept of healing also has a pedagogical place in learning how to find a full life in spite of physical and psychological disabilities (→ Persons with Disabilities), and also in rehabilitation.

(4) Healing also involves *renewal of relations,* not merely to the self, as in (3), but to others. In relation to the self, one is healed when one has learned how to be sick in a healthy way (instead of healthy in a sick way). In relation to others, true healing shows itself in orientation to life rather than sickness. This view leads us closest to the Judeo-Christian understanding of → salvation.

The four concepts of healing point to different views of illness and of the meaning of life. An absolutizing of (1) can lead to the renouncing of medical help and, in a religious exaggeration, to the identification of God and natural processes. → Christian Science, which in the last resort sees only spirit and not matter, will not accept medical help. The spirit alone brings healing. An overvaluing of (2) rests on a nonhistorical and hedonistic view of humanity and the world (→ Ethics; Hedonism; Worldview). Human beings are ultimately thought of as functioning like machines. Even a fully psychosomatic standpoint offers no automatic protection against this kind of exaggeration. Concepts (3) and (4), in contrast with the idealizing of the strong and victorious sick in (1) and (2), include the danger of putting sickness, suffering, and inescapable death at the center of life and thus distorting the profound biblical significance of these views of healing.

Undoubtedly the postbiblical and modern Jewish view of the great importance of life finds full support in the OT. It does not escape the ambivalence, however, that suffering is part of life (as in the Book of Job) and that the God of Israel is to be found among the weak and not the strong. The NT develops this theme with a powerful focus on the suffering of → Jesus and the first churches. The healings of Jesus were not the beginning of a great work of healing or even the model for a new health system. They were signs, visible sermons, pointing to the dawning of the new and imminent → king-

dom of God (→ Miracle). A therapist could never justify singling out one person for healing out of "five porticoes" full of the sick, blind, lame, and consumptive, as Jesus actually did (John 5:1-29). Yet he summoned his disciples to acts of healing (Matt. 10:8), and the accounts in Acts and the lists of charismatic gifts (1 Cor. 12:9) include healing by the → congregation (→ Charisma).

Over the centuries the church has discharged the commission to heal in different ways but has never forgotten it. Miraculous healings still take place today, with → prayer and → laying on of hands. It is hard to draw a line between responsible Christian practices and esoteric practices. In the United States, Australia, and New Zealand, congregations have been divided and even destroyed over this issue. We also read of services of healing in Africa, though, that are more generally accepted. To this context also belong → Fatima and → Lourdes (→ Pilgrimage) in the Roman Catholic sphere. The Vancouver Assembly of the → World Council of Churches (1983) made the church's ministry of healing one of its themes.

The diaconal task of the church (→ Diakonia) is undoubtedly therapeutic, at least in the sense of (4). The central theological problem of healing is that of the relation between medical and psychotherapeutic/pastoral healings and the biblical promise of the new creation. Do healings reflect the new creation?

→ Medical Ethics; Pastoral Care

Bibliography: N. Cousins, *Anatomy of an Illness as Perceived by the Patient* (New York, 1979) • D. M. Feldman, *Health and Medicine in the Jewish Tradition* (New York, 1986) • H. Kohut, *The Restoration of the Self* (Independence, Mo., 1977) • L. LeShan, *You Can Fight for Your Life: Emotional Factors in the Causation of Cancer* (New York, 1977) • M. Maddocks, *The Christian Healing Ministry* (2d ed.; London, 1985) • M. E. Marty and K. L. Vaux, eds., *Health/Medicine and the Faith Traditions: An Inquiry into Religion and Medicine* (Philadelphia, 1982) • H. Remus, *Jesus as Healer* (Cambridge, 1997) • F. Rosner, *Medicine in the Bible and Talmud* (New York, 1977) • K. W. Schmidt, *Therapieziel und Menschenbild* (Münster, 1995) • H.-H. Stricker, *Krankheit und Heilung* (Stuttgart, 1994).

In conjunction with the volume edited by Marty and Vaux, note G. F. Snyder, *Health and Medicine in the Anabaptist Tradition* (Valley Forge, Pa., 1995), with similar volumes on 13 other traditions: Anglican, by D. H. Smith (New York, 1986); Catholic, by R. A. McCormick (New York, 1984); Christian Science, by R. Peel (New York, 1988); Eastern Orthodox, by S. S.

Harakas (New York, 1990); evangelical, by L. I. Sweet (Valley Forge, Pa., 1994); Hindu, by P. N. Desai (New York, 1989); Islamic, by F. Rahman (Chicago, 1998); Jewish, by D. M. Feldman (New York, 1986); Latter-day Saints, by L. E. Bush Jr. (New York, 1993); Lutheran, by M. E. Marty (New York, 1983); Methodist, by E. B. Holifield (New York, 1986); native North American, by Å. Hultkrantz (New York, 1992); and Reformed, by K. L. Vaux (New York, 1984).

See also the bibliography in "Health and Illness."

DIETRICH RITSCHL

Health and Illness

The terms "health" and "illness" denote a variety of conditions — individual and institutional — that are variously perceived and understood from one culture to another, as well as within cultures. Common to all is a perception of health as a sense of well-being — physical, mental, social, and societal — and of illness as a lack thereof.

Common to all is also the premium placed on health, however defined. In the ancient Greek and Roman worlds, where illness often led to poverty or an early death, health was a supreme good. In the Hippocratic oath, to which physicians still subscribe in principle if not verbatim, Hygeia — "Health" personified — follows the name of Asclepius, the Greek god of healing. The frequent references in the Bible to illness manifest a similar concern, as do the enormous sums spent on health care today.

Responses to illness show some common patterns. Home remedies, a traditional first response, are attested in the Bible (2 Kgs. 20:1, 7; Isa. 1:6; Mark 6:13; Luke 10:34; 1 Tim. 5:23; Jas. 5:14) and described in Roman agricultural treatises (Cato, Varro). Persisting or severe illness or trauma commonly leads to seeking out a physician. So too in the ancient world. Though physicians are mentioned frequently in the Bible (Jer. 8:22; Matt. 9:12 and par.) and in ancient Jewish literature (Sir. 38:1-15; Josephus *Ant.* 17.171; 20.46; *J.W.* 1.246; *Life* 420-21), little is said of their lore. That information is imparted in Greek and Roman medical treatises. Medical works ascribed to or associated with the name of Hippocrates (ca. 460-ca. 377 B.C.), which were influential into the modern period, offer both case studies and theory (e.g., health is the normal state and the true "nature" of an individual, illness a disturbance of it, → healing a return to it, and "nature" one of the means the physician employs to effect that return; H. Remus 1983; R. Jackson).

Consulting a physician can be costly as well as futile (Mark 5:25-26). The many shrines and temples of Asclepius in the ancient Mediterranean world show both how common illness was and how inadequate were the theory and practice of medicine to deal with it (E. J. Edelstein and L. Edelstein). The many recipes, incantations, and spells in the "magical" papyri (1st-11th/12th centuries) calling on deities and powers to maintain or restore health (H. D. Betz; M. Meyer and R. Smith) offer further evidence of the same, as do the many healing accounts in early Christian literature and other writings of the same period (S. Davies, H. Remus 1997).

With the rise of modern scientific medicine, "health" and "illness" have come to refer primarily to physical and, more recently, also mental states, with corresponding diagnosis and treatment. Religious traditions have commonly offered understandings and explanations of health and illness that place them, and human → life generally, in a wider context of relations between humans and the divine. When these relations are askew, illness may result (Lev. 26:14-16; Num. 21:4-7; 2 Kgs. 5; 1 Cor. 11:27-30). If some malign agent is causing an illness, a benign power should be mustered against it (1 Sam. 16:14-23; Mark 1:32, 34; 3:11; 5:1-20; magical papyri in Betz and in Meyer and Smith). One of the Hippocratic treatises, *The Sacred Disease*, disparages such diagnosis and treatment. The so-called sacred disease is epilepsy; it has diagnosable, natural causes, and will respond to medical treatment. The treatise is not antireligious, nor were (or are) physicians necessarily or generally. Tensions between the two approaches to illness and health were (and are) inevitable, however, given the often divergent presuppositions of each.

Sometimes medical and religious views of illness are seen as antithetical. Relying on physicians rather than God for healing is seen as reprehensible in one passage in the Hebrew Bible (2 Chr. 16:12), for God is the great Healer (Gen. 20:17; Exod. 15:26; 2 Kgs. 20:5; Ps. 6:2; 30:2; 103:3; Isa. 19:22; 30:26). Tatian, a second-century convert to Christianity, portrays recourse to medicine as manifesting lack of trust in God (*Orat.* 18). More common today is inclusion of medicine in a religious view of health and illness, a tradition with ancient antecedents: physicians and their art and medicines are gifts "from the Most High" (Sir. 38.2); Asclepius, famed as a physician, becomes the god of healing, and physicians were present at his temples.

Alongside medicine, or when it falters or fails, → prayer and healing rituals — individual and communal — have been common responses to illness, from ancient times (2 Cor. 12:7-9; Acts 9:40; Jas. 5:13-16; Irenaeus *Adv. haer.* 3.31.2) to the present. Prayer and ritual may fail, too, however, posing questions about the source of illness and the suffering it causes. Religions such as → Judaism and Christianity, which stress human responsibility, have often ascribed illness and → death to → sin (Numbers 12; 16:41-50; Deuteronomy 28; 2 Sam. 12:1-15; 2 Kgs. 5:19-27; 1 Cor. 11:29-30; Acts 5:1-11; 12:21-23). Such a cause-and-effect relationship does not go unchallenged, however (Job; John 9:1-3). The "wintry" psalms (M. Marty) of the Hebrew Bible bewail → suffering and puzzle over the reason for affliction, even as they also look to God for deliverance.

Illness is also corporate. The Hebrew prophets decry "sick" societies that inflict suffering and that will in turn suffer at the hand of a just God. The → prophets sometimes dramatized such impending suffering through symbolic actions (Isaiah 20; Jeremiah 19; 27; Ezek. 4:4-8), even to the point of invoking physical trauma on themselves (1 Kgs. 20:35-43). Today an individual's illness can "voice" society's illness (A. Siirala); for example, Alice James sickens into invalidism in a society and culture that discouraged full self-expression of women (J. Strouse).

In recent decades the relation between mind and body and the implications for health and illness have received increasing attention, both in religion and medicine (W. B. Cannon, N. Cousins, T. Harpur, M. E. Marty and K. L. Vaux, B. Moyers). That health and illness have to do with the whole person is implicit in the NT gospel traditions. While illness or suffering as divine punishment is denied (Luke 13:1-5; John 9:2-3), yet the one healing story in which Jesus first proclaims forgiveness of a man's sin before healing him (Mark 2:5 and par.) implies that more than healing of the physical body is involved. The restoration to health in the many gospel healing accounts is also a restoration of the person *to* society, and thus also a restoring of health *in* that society. The various assertions of → forgiveness for, and acceptance of, the → marginalized (Matt. 18:27; Luke 7:42; 15) and Jesus' association with "sinners" function similarly.

The story of the physician who comes to call the sick (Mark 2:17), heals the sick, and then himself suffers death on a cross has been significant for Christian interpretation of health and illness in several ways. Jesus' acceptance of suffering has been taken as modeling patience for those in pain and suffering, or these experiences have been interpreted as a way of participating in Christ's suffering; conversely, Christ is seen as suffering with the sufferer. Furthermore, Jesus' healing of illness has

served as incentive to strive against illness, both individually and institutionally (e.g., in hospitals).

Aging as illness (→ Old Age) — ineluctable infirmity and senility — is increasingly disputed (B. Friedan). Along with many other literatures, the Bible honors age (Lev. 19:32; Job 32:6; Prov. 23:22; 1 Tim. 5:1) and promises long life to the faithful (Deut. 5:33; 11:20-21; Psalm 91; Prov. 10:27). Also, however, it contemplates the fragility of life and the inevitability of death (Psalm 90; Isa. 40:6-8; Jas. 1:10; 1 Pet. 1:24) and envisages continuity between life before and after death, between deeds done or left undone and life hereafter (Luke 16:19-31; Rom. 2:1-13; 2 Cor. 5:10; Rev. 14:13). In Christianity, forsaking or dying to an old way of life and embracing or rising to a new are prominent, promising "salvation" — health — now and hereafter (Luke 15:11-32; Mark 8:34-35 and par.; Rom. 6:1-11; Gal. 2:20). Similarly, the "healthy" society, in which "justice roll[s] down like waters, and righteousness like an everflowing stream" (Amos 5:24) and peace and justice reign (Isa. 11:1-9), stands in continuity with visions of a final, eschatological deliverance of both creation and creatures (Rom. 8:20-23), an ultimate reconstitution of what is, with God and humanity reconciled, privation and suffering banished, and all tears wiped away (Rev. 7:13-17; 21:1-5).

Bibliography: H. D. BETZ, ed., *The Greek Magical Papyri in Translation* (Chicago, 1992) • W. B. CANNON, "Voodoo Death," *AmA* 44 (1942) 169-81 (repr., abridged, *Reader in Comparative Religion* [ed. W. Lessa and E. Z. Vogt; 3d ed.; New York, 1972]) • N. COUSINS, *Head First: The Biology of Hope and the Healing Power of the Human Spirit* (London, 1989) • S. DAVIES, *Jesus the Healer* (New York, 1995) • E. J. EDELSTEIN and L. EDELSTEIN, *Asclepius* (Baltimore, 1945) • B. FRIEDAN, *The Fountain of Age* (New York, 1993) • T. HARPUR, *The Uncommon Touch* (Toronto, 1994) • R. JACKSON, *Doctors and Diseases in the Roman Empire* (Norman, Okla., 1988) • H. G. KOENIG, *The Healing Power of Faith: Science Explores Medicine's Last Great Frontier* (New York, 1999) • M. E. MARTY, *A Cry of Absence* (San Francisco, 1983) • M. E. MARTY and K. L. VAUX, eds., *Health/Medicine and the Faith Traditions: An Inquiry into Religion and Medicine* (Philadelphia, 1982) • M. MEYER and R. SMITH, eds., *Ancient Christian Magic* (San Francisco, 1994) • B. MOYERS, *Healing and the Mind* (New York, 1993) • H. REMUS, *Jesus as Healer* (Cambridge, 1997); idem, *Pagan-Christian Conflict over Miracle in the Second Century* (Cambridge, Mass., 1983) • A. SIIRALA, *The Voice of Illness* (Philadelphia, 1964) • J. STROUSE, *Alice James: A Biography* (London, 1980).

HAROLD REMUS

Heaven

1. Meaning
2. Biblical Traditions
3. Theological and Scientific Cosmologies

1. Meaning

From antiquity onward, across various cultures, the concept of heaven unites and distinguishes several notions and systems of reference.

1.1. Heaven is what people see above the earth, marking it off or securing it (i.e., the firmament). It is sometimes regarded as a material half-globe or a disk arching over the earth.

1.2. Heaven is also a syndrome of powers and uncontrollable forces. We cannot directly measure or manipulate it. It has a decisive impact on life on earth by granting or withholding life and water, also by sending storms, hail, and so forth.

1.3. Heaven is the place of the gods, the home of the Supreme Being or various supernatural forces, to which many orders, including social orders, ascribe their coherence.

1.4. Heaven can be equated with → God, the Godhead, or his manifestation and thus gives rise to many more or less figurative and nuanced concepts of the transcendent or transcendence (→ Immanence and Transcendence).

1.5. Finally, heaven is the place of life after → death, in which a more perfect and indestructible → life is possible and from which standards for the orientation of this present life are derived (e.g., → hope).

2. Biblical Traditions

In the biblical traditions we find elucidation and systematization.

2.1. The deifying of heaven is resisted (see 1.4). Heaven is created by God (e.g., Gen. 1:1; 14:19, 22; Ps. 8:3; 33:6; Prov. 3:19; 8:27; Isa. 42:5; 45:18; Acts 4:24; Rev. 10:6). Its stability is under threat, and although it typifies endurance (Deut. 11:21; Ps. 89:29; Sir. 45:15), it will perish or be destroyed in the → last judgment (Job 14:12; Ps. 102:25-26; Isa. 34:4; 51:6; Jer. 4:23-28; Amos 8:9; Matt. 5:18; Mark 13:31 and par.; 2 Pet. 3:7-10). Heaven and earth must be perfected or created anew (Isa. 65:17; 66:22; 2 Pet. 3:13; Rev. 21:1). Being created, heaven is part of the world, which is made up of heaven and earth (e.g., Gen. 2:4a; Matt. 11:25) or of heaven, earth, and sea (Exod. 20:11).

On this basis the demonizing of cosmic entities can be challenged, and cosmological theorizing can begin (e.g., Genesis 1; Job 36:27-33; 38:33; Isa.

55:10; see *THAT* 2.967-68). Especially noteworthy in this regard is the doctrine of seven heavens (oriented to the seven constellations). It is hardly possible today to trace other numberings.

2.2. Although created by God and part of the world, heaven is also the dwelling place of God (Deut. 26:15; 1 Kgs. 8:30-51; 2 Macc. 3:39; Ps. 2:4; Matt. 5:34; 23:22; Acts 7:49; Rev. 4:2) and the sphere of God's rule (Deut. 4:39; Judg. 5:20; 1 Kgs. 22:19-23; Job 1:6-12; Ps. 11:4; Eph. 1:20; Heb. 1:3). God comes down or looks down from it, especially on humans (Ps. 14:2 etc.). God speaks from heaven, blessing and punishing (e.g., Gen. 11:5; 19:24; 49:25; Exod. 20:22; Deut. 26:15). In a special way God's reign there is uncontested.

2.3. As the place of God's uncontested lordship (Matt. 6:10), heaven is the dwelling place of the "heavenly hosts," or the → angels who surround, worship, and serve God (Neh. 9:6; Ps. 103:20-22; 148:1-6; Matt. 18:10b; Luke 2:13, 15; 22:43). Heaven, then, is not just the point of departure for natural forces (see 1.2) but also the sphere of social forces that direct history.

Nevertheless, although heaven is the location of great powers, the Bible clearly maintains the distinction between it and God (Deut. 10:14; 1 Kgs. 8:27; 2 Chr. 2:5-6; 6:18; Heb. 7:26). In the NT it is from heaven that the triune God does his work for us as the "Father in heaven" (Matt. 5:16, 45; 6:1, 9; 23:9, etc.; cf. Mark 1:11 and par.) through the Christ-event (see 2.4) and the sending of the → Holy Spirit from heaven (Mark 1:10 and par.; Acts 2; 1 Pet. 1:12).

2.4. Through the Christ-event (→ Christology) there is communion (J. Moltmann) between heaven, the sphere of the undisputed lordship of the God who is distant from us and relatively inaccessible to us, and earth. This communion is set forth in the descent of Christ from heaven (John 3:13; 6:38, 42; Eph. 4:9), the opening of heaven at his → baptism (Matt. 3:16-17 and par.), his → ascension (Mark 16:19 and par.; Acts 1:9), his session at the right hand of the Father (Eph. 1:20; Heb. 1:3; 8:1), his awaited coming again as Kyrios (Matt. 24:30; 26:64; Mark 14:62; 1 Thess. 1:10; 4:16-17), and his being given all power in heaven and on earth (Matt. 28:18; cf. Eph. 1:10; Col. 1:16). The coming → kingdom of God can also be called the kingdom of heaven (almost always in Matthew).

2.5. Heaven is the place where the dead are either close to God or distant from him. It is also the place where believers experience their definitive personal (Matt. 16:19; Luke 10:20; Heb. 12:23) and public (2 Cor. 5:1; Phil. 3:20; Heb. 3:1; 13:14) calling and the fulfillment of their hope (Col. 1:5).

3. Theological and Scientific Cosmologies

Direct conflicts between theological and scientific cosmologies have led both to escape in the deifying of heaven — strengthened and attacked by the philosophical criticism of religion (L. Feuerbach; → Religion, Criticism of) — and to a suppression of the doctrine of heaven. Rehabilitation of the doctrine is possible on the basis of a multisystemic thinking, which shows that different reference systems combine in different ways in what is said about heaven as cultures and perspectives change (J. Moltmann, largely following M. Welker 1981). In modern Western culture temporal ideas predominate (heaven as the future), or modal-theoretical concepts (heaven as the reign of possibilities) prevail.

A developed doctrine of heaven can help give us a better grasp of the political and cosmic dimensions of the Christ-event and the differentiated unity of the work of the triune God. Serious theological and conceptual difficulties stand in the way of such a development, however, especially unresolved conceptions of eternity (see Aristotle's *De caelo* 283b29: heaven containing and enclosing immeasurable time) and problems in fixing the relations between creatures of nature and those of culture.

→ Eschatology; Worldview

Bibliography: K. BARTH, *CD* III/3, §51.2 • H. BIETENHARD, *Die himmlische Welt im Urchristentum und Spätjudentum* (Tübingen, 1951) • L. BRÉMOND, *Le ciel, ses joies et ses splendeurs* (Paris, 1925) • L. FEUERBACH, *The Essence of Christianity* (New York, 1957; orig. pub., 1841) chap. 19 • T. FLÜGGE, "Die Vorstellung über den Himmel im Alten Testament" (Diss., Borna-Leipzig, 1937) • J. HAEKEL, J. SCHMID, and J. RATZINGER, "Himmel," *LTK* 5.352-58 • C. HOUTMAN, *Der Himmel im Alten Testament* (Leiden, 1993) • J. MOLTMANN, *God in Creation: A New Theology of Creation and the Spirit of God* (New York, 1985) 158-84 • S. MORENZ and G. GLOEGE, "Himmel," *RGG* (3d ed.) 3.328-33 • U. E. SIMON, *Heaven in the Christian Tradition* (London, 1958) • J. A. SOGGIN, "שָׁמַיִם šamájim Himmel," *THAT* 2.965-70 • H. TRAUB and G. VON RAD, "Οὐρανός κτλ.," *TDNT* 5.497-543 • M. WELKER, *Creation and Reality* (Philadelphia, 1999) chap. 3; idem, *Universalität Gottes und Relativität der Welt* (Neukirchen, 1981) esp. 203ff.

MICHAEL WELKER

Hebrew Language

1. Apart from some Aramaic sections, the OT is written in Hebrew. The word "Hebrew," absent from the OT, occurs first in the prologue to Sirach, and then among the → rabbis, who stressed the dignity of the language of the canonical Scriptures by calling it a holy language.

2. Hebrew represents a dialect group whose local idioms (see Judg. 12:6; 2 Kgs. 18:26) the Israelites adopted. Like the South Canaanite of the Amarna Letters, Phoenician Punic, Moabite, Ammonite, Ugaritic, and Amorite, Hebrew is a Canaanite language (see Isa. 19:18). Canaanite and Aramaic (→ Arameans) form the Northwest Semitic branch of Semitic languages.

3. Three linguistic stages may be distinguished. *Ancient Hebrew* (lasting ca. 1,000 years) runs from the earliest parts of the OT (e.g., Judges 5) by way of the classical Hebrew of the monarchy to the late postexilic period. Sources apart from the OT include the farming calendar of Gezer, the ostraca of Arad and Samaria, the Siloam tunnel inscription, the Lachish Letters, seals, coins, vessels, and inscribed weights.

Middle Hebrew occurs in an older stage (Ecclesiastes, Tobit, Sirach, nonbiblical → Qumran texts) and a later scholarly stage (→ Mishnah and other rabbinic works).

Modern Hebrew is the form revived in the 19th century under the influence of the Jewish enlightenment and → Zionism, greatly enriched lexically, and syntactically influenced in part by European languages. Hebrew (along with Arabic for the Arab minority) is the official language of the State of Israel.

4. As a Semitic language, Hebrew has the following features:
- gutturals and emphatic sounds;
- two genders, masculine and feminine;
- roots mostly with three consonants and carrying the general sense, with more specific meanings and grammatical forms being indicated by the vocalic pattern or by a prefix, infix, or suffix;
- an attributive relation between two nouns whereby the governing noun comes first in the so-called construct state and the governed noun comes second in the absolute state;
- frequent parataxis in sentence construction;
- distinction between a nominal statement (with no "to be"), which says something about the state of a subject, and a verbal statement, which usually puts the verb first and can describe an act, a process, or a state.

Historically, Hebrew went through a series of stages. Thus an originally long $\bar{a}$ became $\bar{o}$, and diphthongs were contracted (*ay* to *ê*, and *aw* to *ô*).

Nouns lost their early case endings. An originally more complex system of verbs was simplified to result in (1) a durative (or continuative) *yiqṭōl* (< *yaqṭulu*), with a mainly present-future function; (2) past tense *wayyiqṭōl* (< *yaqṭul*); (3) a constative *qāṭal*, with a mainly past function; and (4) a *wĕqāṭal*, with a future, imperative, or iterative function.

Gradually replaced by Aramaic as the language of the people from the sixth century B.C., Hebrew developed under the influence of Aramaic into Middle Hebrew.

Biblical Hebrew took its present shape in the long and complex process of standardizing, which finally fixed the consonantal text (ca. A.D. 100) and ended with the adding of vowel points by the Tiberian Masoretes (8th to 10th cent.; → Masorah, Masoretes).

Bibliography: W. JOHNSTONE et al., *Computerized Introductory Hebrew Grammar* (4 disks; Edinburgh, 1993) • P. JOÜON, *A Grammar of Biblical Hebrew* (Rome, 1991) • P. H. KELLEY, *Biblical Hebrew: An Introductory Grammar* (Grand Rapids, 1992) • L. KOEHLER et al., *The Hebrew and Aramaic Lexicon of the OT* (Leiden, 1994-96) • E. Y. KUTSCHER, *A History of the Hebrew Language* (Jerusalem, 1982) • W. RICHTER, *Grundlagen einer althebräischen Grammatik* (3 vols.; St. Ottilien, 1978-80) bibliography • A. SÁEZ-BADILLOS, *A History of the Hebrew Language* (Cambridge, 1993) • H.-P. STÄHLI, *Hebräisch-Kurzgrammatik* (3d ed.; Göttingen, 1992) • E. ULLENDORFF, "A History of the Hebrew Language," *JJS* 46 (1995) 283-92.

HANS-PETER STÄHLI

Hebrews

The term "Hebrews" — in Hebrew *'ibrî* (pl. *'ibrîm*), in Ugaritic *'pr* (pl. *'prm*), in Egyptian *'pr* (pl. *'pr.w*), in Akkadian *ḫab/piru* (pl. *ḫab/pirū*, ideogram *lú*SA.GAZ, with the broader reading *ḫabbātu* = robbers), in Greek *Hebraios* — common in the ancient Near East from the late third millennium B.C., designated people who had lost their position in society through war, debt, criminal acts, and so forth, who were organized in loose bands, and who offered their labor to foreign masters in return for recompense. Not by accident in the second half of the second millennium, a time of political and social disintegration and migration, there is a great increase in records of such groups.

The OT examples begin at this period, and though the dating is hotly contested, a connection is rightly seen with the parallel constitution of the people of Israel. The name now acquired a new accent. It was still in the first instance a foreign designation used by Egyptians and → Philistines, but it was now applied to the groups out of which → Israel (§1) was composed. This pejorative sociological term was deliberately adopted by those concerned and made into a proud, ethnically understood self-description.

When the Israelites are called Hebrews in the conflict with the Philistines (1 Sam. 4:6, 9; 13:3, 7, 19; 14:11; 29:3), we can see that the Hebrews have become a people. The exodus tradition, though more literary, embodies an authentic recollection when it calls the people of → Moses Hebrews (Exod. 1:15-16, 19; 2:6-7, 11, 13; 3:18; 5:3; 7:16; 9:1). It is natural, then, that we should find the term also in the Joseph cycle (Gen. 39:14, 17; 40:15; 41:12; 43:32).

Finally, in the law concerning slaves in Exod. 21:2-11, the emphatic characterization of slaves as Hebrews (v. 2) is probably following theological considerations, recalling thereby the people's own perilous beginnings in the Egyptian "house of → slavery" (20:2 etc.; note amendment of the law concerning slaves in Deut. 15:12[-18], as a → Deuteronomistic citation in Jer. 34:14, and as a Deuteronomistic commentary in 34:9).

Genealogical speculations deriving the ancestral father Eber (*'ēber*) from the gentilic *'ibrî* represent a relatively recent phenomenon in the history of transmission (Gen. 10:21, 24-25; 11:14-17; 1 Chr. 1:18-19, 25; cf. Num. 24:24). The *'ibrî* themselves derived from the same tradition within which during the exilic-postexilic period the term "Hebrew" became a historically unburdened, ethnic-religious honorific name (Gen. 14:13; Jonah 1:9; similarly in the NT: 2 Cor. 11:22; Phil. 3:5 [alongside the designation of the Aramaic-speaking Jews as Hebrews, Acts 6:1; cf. 21:40; 22:2; 26:14]).

Bibliography: G. W. AHLSTRÖM, *The History of Ancient Palestine from the Palaeolithic Period to Alexander's Conquest* (Sheffield, 1993) • R. B. COOTE, *Early Israel: A New Horizon* (Minneapolis, 1990) • F. M. CROSS, "An Interview I: Israelite Origins," *BibRev* 8 (1992) 20-32, 61-62 • O. LORETZ, *Habiru–Hebräer* (Berlin, 1984) bibliography • D. B. REDFORD, *Egypt, Canaan, and Israel in Ancient Times* (Princeton, 1992) • M. WEIPPERT, *Die Landnahme der israelitischen Stämme* (Göttingen, 1967) 66-102.

HERMANN SPIECKERMANN

Hebrews, Epistle to the

1. Structure and Contents
2. Historical Questions
3. Literary and Theological Character
4. Place in the History of Primitive
   Christian Theology

1. Structure and Contents
The Epistle to the Hebrews, which begins like a theological tractate (1:1-4) and ends like a Pauline congregational letter (13:22-25), is an artistic construct that uses many literary and rhetorical devices. A constant interchange of teaching and admonition marks its structure. At its heart, as an address to the mature (5:11–6:20), is the development of a high-priestly → Christology (7:1–10:18). The preceding section leads up by several detours (2:5-18; 4:14–5:10; 6:19-20) to this main Christological theme but also shows that the development of the doctrine aims at the consoling, admonishing, and warning of the recipients (2:1-4; 3:1-6; 3:7–4:13; 5:11–6:20). Along similar lines an expansive conclusion follows the central teaching section (10:19–12:29; 13:1-21). Here the admonition reaches its climax as faith → parenesis, again on the Christological basis (10:19-25; 12:2-3; 13:8-17).

2. Historical Questions
The author of Hebrews is unknown. Probably he was an early Christian teacher in the Pauline tradition (13:22-25) who used the exegetical method developed in the Hellenistic synagogue (preeminently by Philo). Since the traditional title ("The Letter to the Hebrews," i.e., Jewish Christians) seems to derive secondarily from the material, the original recipients are also unknown. Their situation seems to be the typical one of a postapostolic Gentile church that, under pressure, was growing slack in faith and afraid of suffering, so that there was the danger of apostasy (2:1-4; 3:12; 10:25, 32-39; 12:12-13) rather than of relapse into Judaism. If we agree that Hebrews is quoted in 1 Clement (17.1; 36.3-5), then it must have been written by at least between A.D. 80 and 100.

3. Literary and Theological Character
The presupposed church situation corresponds to the literary character and theological concern of Hebrews as a work of comfort and admonition after the manner of the Hellenistic synagogue (13:22), the aim of the author being to motivate the pressured community to hold fast to the confession (3:1; 4:14; 10:23) and to remain steadfast in → faith

(10:35–12:3). The specific means used is an exposition of the confession oriented to the OT (LXX), using a high-priestly Christology that interprets the death and exaltation of Jesus as a once-for-all and definitive self-offering. The offering of Jesus shows the cultic and sacrificial order of the OT to have been earthly and provisional, and it constitutes entry into the heavenly sanctuary. This Christology, which is oriented to the antithesis of the earthly and the heavenly, is applied to the specific situation of the assaulted church by means of the motif of the pioneer, or forerunner. The exalted → high priest is the one who himself learned → obedience by suffering (5:7-10; cf. 2:10-18) and who thus became the church's "forerunner" (6:19-20; 12:2-3; 13:12-13).

4. Place in the History of Primitive
   Christian Theology
Although Hebrews formulates its own answer to the trial of the church separately from → Paul, in its exposition of the confession with reference to the church situation, it stands in continuity with the history of primitive Christian theology. Doubts about its authorship were current already in the → early church, but its final acceptance into the NT → canon rested not merely on its mistaken ascription to Paul but also on the self-contained kerygmatic conception that is found in it.

Bibliography: Commentaries: H. W. ATTRIDGE (Hermeneia; Philadelphia, 1989) • P. ELLINGWORTH (NIGTC; Grand Rapids, 1993) • E. GRÄSSER (EKKNT; Neukirchen, 1997) • H.-F. WEISS (KEK; Göttingen, 1991).

Other works: E. GRÄSSER, "Der Hebräerbrief, 1938-1963," *TRu* 30 (1964) 138-236 • G. HUGHES, *Hebrews and Hermeneutics: The Epistle to the Hebrews as a NT Example of Biblical Interpretation* (Cambridge, 1979) • E. KÄSEMANN, *Das wandernde Gottesvolk* (2d ed.; Göttingen, 1975) • F. LAUB, *Bekenntnis und Auslegung. Die paränetische Funktion der Christologie im Hebräerbrief* (Regensburg, 1980) • A. VANHOYE, *La structure littéraire de l'épître aux Hébreux* (2d ed.; Paris, 1976).

HANS-FRIEDRICH WEISS

Hedonism

Deriving from Gk. *hēdonē* (pleasure, joy), hedonism is an ethical theory that is close to → utilitarianism. It regards → happiness as the goal of human action (so generally eudaemonism; → Ethics), equating this happiness positively with the achieving of the greatest possible pleasure and negatively with the avoiding of unhappiness or pain. The term has been used since the 19th century to describe the ethical theories of the Cyrenaics (Aristippus, Euhemerus), the Epicureans, the philosophers of the → Renaissance (L. Valla), those of the → Enlightenment (C.-A. Helvétius, P.-H. D. d'Holbach), and some moderns (J. S. Mill, H. Sidgwick; → Modernity).

Besides *practical hedonism,* an unthinking readiness for enjoyment found among many people, two types of hedonism are distinguished. First is *psychological hedonism.* As a psychological description, this position makes a statement about the final motivation of human action, finding it oriented exclusively or chiefly to the attainment of as much pleasure as possible and the avoidance of pain. The pleasure principle of S. Freud (1856-1939) is close to this concept. Second, *ethical hedonism* at the normative level finds the basis of all ethics in pleasure as the only or supreme good, whether it be momentary pleasure or a more lasting pleasure that includes some renunciation.

It is beyond question that people seek happiness. It may be doubted, however, whether pleasure is all that is desired, or whether it may not be simply the accompaniment of a striving for something else, and whether hedonism does not make an empirical fact — the experience of pleasure — into a starting point for normative ethics. In so doing, it commits the naturalistic fallacy (→ Analytic Ethics).

Bibliography: R. B. BRANDT, "Hedonism," *EncPh* 3.432-35 • J. W. DRANE, "Christians, New Agers, and Changing Cultural Paradigms," *ExpTim* 116 (1994) 172-76 • W. K. FRANKENA, *Ethics* (Englewood Cliffs, N.J., 1963) • J. GOLLNICK, *Love and the Soul: Psychological Interpretations of the Eros and Psyche Myth* (Waterloo, Ont., 1992) • I. KASSORIA, *Nice Girls Do—and Now You Can Too* (Los Angeles, 1980) • D. KINSLEY, *The Goddesses' Mirror* (Albany, N.Y., 1989) • M. E. MARTY, ed., *Modern American Protestantism and Its World* (Munich, 1993) • G. E. MOORE, *Principia ethica* (Cambridge, 1903).

WERNER SCHWARTZ

Hegelianism

A definition of Hegelianism is hardly possible. Various positions in modern thought appeal to the phi-

losophy of G. W. F. Hegel (1770-1831), both those of his direct and indirect followers, as well as those of thinkers who had nothing directly to do with the Hegel school. We can achieve an adequate concept of Hegelianism only by reconstructing its development.

1. The Hegel School

Hegel's philosophy took up an idea that influenced modern thought from the time of R. Descartes (1596-1650; → Cartesianism); namely, it tried to present the totality of secular thought and knowledge insofar as it could be ascertained without recourse to the truths of faith. The result was a circular system in three divisions (→ logic, → philosophy of nature, and philosophy of spirit), each of which itself had three parts. The philosophy of spirit is of particular interest as it divides into the philosophy of subjective, objective, and absolute spirit. In turn the last is divided into the philosophy of art, religion, and → philosophy itself, with which the system returns to its starting point, logic. The method that made the system possible was Hegel's developed → dialectic.

This conception, which from Hegel's Heidelberg period (1816-18) went under the title *Encyclopedia of Philosophical Science,* and the dialectical method (→ Dialectic), which made systematic use of the operation of negation, soon brought Hegel many followers. Already from the Jena years (1801-7) came G. A. Gabler (1786-1853), who was called to Berlin as Hegel's successor in the chair of philosophy. Among the Heidelberg disciples were F. W. Carové (1789-1852), F. W. Hinrichs (1794-1861), and K. Daub (1765-1836), a professor of theology in Heidelberg. Hegel's work in Berlin (1818-31) attracted the greatest number of followers, the Hegel school in the narrower sense. This school included the theologian P. K. Marheineke (1780-1846), the philosopher L. von Hennecken (1791-1866), the historical theologian F. C. Baur (1792-1860), the jurist E. Gans (1798-1839), the jurist and philosopher K. L. Michelet (1801-93), and the aestheticians G. Hotho (1802-73) and H. T. Rötscher (1803-71), to mention only the most important.

As one may see from the composition of the school, → law, the → state, and → religion were the main themes that made Hegel's teachings attractive to students. Against the attacks of the *Evangelische Kirchenzeitung* (1829) on Hegel's philosophy as pantheistic and atheistic, K. F. Göschel (1781-1861), also in 1829, published a work in which he expounded Hegel's attempt to reconcile → faith and knowledge. His ideas were the starting point for the

Hegelian right wing. The left wing can be traced back by way of L. A. Feuerbach (1804-72) to the time when Hegel taught in Berlin.

Along with religious questions Hegel's disciples gravitated to the politically relevant themes of law and state. From the Bern period (1793-96) Hegel was interested in political matters; in particular, thinking about → revolution was central for him. His *Philosophy of Right* (1821), published at a politically explosive time, represented his attempt to defend liberal advances against both foes and false friends. For Hegel, contradictory elements in the early stages of modernity found reconciliation in the state.

2. Decline of the School

Hegel's school did not divide into two hostile camps immediately upon his death. Instead Marheineke, Gans, L. von Henning (1791-1866), Hotho, and others, along with Hegel's biographer K. F. Rosenkranz (1805-79), formed a society to produce an edition of the writings of their late teacher.

The work that is usually regarded as making the split apparent is *The Life of Jesus* (1835), by D. F. Strauss (1808-74). Strauss adopted the Enlightenment biblical criticism that Hegel had himself used in his early writings and made a theological attack upon both supernaturalism and → rationalism. He expounded the NT narratives as → myths, which "do not stand on a historical basis or ground." Understandably this view provoked strong reactions. In a polemical defense of the work (1837), Strauss distinguished between left-wing and right-wing Hegelians and a middle group between them. Contrary to a widespread but mistaken interpretation, the difference was not exclusively or even primarily politically motivated but concerned different positions in the controversy about → Christology. For Strauss, the right wing holds the position of the Gospels, whereby Christ unites in himself a divine and human nature; the left wing doubts the truth of the gospel accounts; and the center seeks a middle course between the two. Strauss put himself on the left wing, Rosenkranz in the center, and Göschel, Gabler, and B. Bauer (1809-82) on the right.

3. Left and Right Wings

In hindsight the left-wing Hegelians, or Young Hegelians, were rather differently constituted than in the sketch by Strauss. According to K. Löwith, it included not only Feuerbach and Bauer but also H. Heine (1797-1856), A. Ruge (1803-80), M. Stirner (1806-56), M. Hess (1812-75), S. → Kierkegaard (1813-55), and K. → Marx (1818-83). What united these men, in spite of their different positions, was their common interest in applying philosophy, that is, in translating into practice Hegel's theoretical proposals for reconciliation.

This reconciliation did not take place independently of the question of the criticism of religion (→ Religion Criticism of), which was central for the direct followers of Hegel. We see this connection most clearly from the role played by Feuerbach's philosophy, which had a decisive influence on German thought in the mid-19th century. Feuerbach's criticism of religion led to the same point as his criticism of Hegel, namely, that our sensory nature may be seen in both. Philosophy derives from this tie, for as religion is a mere projection of defective human reality, so true philosophy is a genetically critical reduction of all thoughts to "natural grounds and causes."

This reversal of Hegel's idealistic mode of thinking into a materialistic mode impressed Marx among others. He and F. Engels (1820-95), however, missed in the anthropological → materialism of Feuerbach both the concrete politicoeconomic expression of human nature and the dialectical method. If we add these factors, the result is that the social relations that constitute human nature develop in the context of a history whose dialectic is the real history of class conflict (→ Marxism). The Christological → salvation history of the self-manifesting God has taken the secular form of political → economy, and the eschatological element has become the idea of a classless society linked to expectation of the "parousia" of the imminent and final → proletarian revolution.

According to H. Lübbe the right wing, or Old Hegelians, included the historians of philosophy J. E. Erdmann (1805-92) and K. Fischer (1824-1907), the biographer Rosenkranz, followers like Carové, Gans, Hinrichs, and Michelet, the liberal publicist and politician H. B. Oppenheim (1819-80), and the publicist and philosopher of law and society C. Rössler (1820-96). The strongest impact of Hegel's philosophy may be seen in this group. Up to the middle of the century this philosophy in its right-wing form was the background against which individualists could appear like A. Schopenhauer (1788-1860), Kierkegaard, and F. W. → Nietzsche (1844-1900), as well as the thinkers of historical and dialectical materialism.

Along with upholding the idea of a personal God (→ Theism) and the → immortality of the → soul, what united this group was a liberal, middle-class consciousness. They adopted the clear-cut but pragmatic position of the → liberalism of the period 1815-48 and of the 1848 revolution itself.

4. Impact of Hegel's Philosophy

In the second half of the 19th century there was a spread of thinking oriented to Hegel outward from Germany — to France, Russia, Britain, Italy, Scandinavia, and the United States.

V. Cousin (1792-1867) introduced Hegel's philosophy to France in lectures (1828-29) on the history of philosophy. More important was the → positivist H. Taine (1828-93), who admired Hegel's philosophy and tried to combine it with the → empiricism of É. Condillac and J. S. Mill. Yet one can hardly speak of a Hegelian Taine. The theologian J.-E. Renan (1823-92) could hardly find a place for the God of the theologians in his eclectic → pantheism, in which a self-generating God evolves in the → progress of humanity to the rule of the spirit.

The first to bring Hegel to Moscow was the → anarchist theoretician M. Bakunin (1814-76). Bakunin also made Hegel known to the philosopher and aesthetician V. G. Belinsky (1811-48), who was already inclined to a left-wing Hegelian standpoint. A. I. Herzen (1812-70) tended in the same direction, as did N. G. Chernyshevsky (1828-89), with whom he opposed the czarist regime after 1860.

The beginning of acquaintance with Hegel's philosophy in Great Britain is usually connected with the publication of the book *The Secret of Hegel* (1865) by J. H. Stirling (1820-1909), the first British monograph on Hegel. Other important British thinkers influenced by Hegel were the Oxford Hegelians — for example, T. H. Green (1836-82) — who were motivated by their studies of classical antiquity. Green found in German → idealism a way to combat → atheism and empiricism with a rehabilitation of spirit and the idea of a personal God.

In Italy Hegelianism was welcomed for its liberating effect after the risorgimento as almost a cult or a substitute for religion. At first oriented in a radically democratic direction, it interested B. Spaventa (1817-83) and F. De Sanctis (1817-83) by way of Hegel's political works, but then interest spread to his other writings as well. In the 20th century the neo-Hegelians B. Croce (1866-1952) and G. Gentile (1875-1944) adopted this Neapolitan Hegelianism.

In Denmark Hegel's thinking had a strong influence on theology and, through J. L. Heiberg (1791-1860), also on literature and → aesthetics. Kierkegaard sharply criticized Hegel's pure theory of absolute spirit as totally out of touch with real human existence, but even his opposition helped make Hegel known. In Sweden J. J. Borelius (1823-1909), in Norway M. J. Monrad (1816-97), and in Finland J. V. Snellman (1806-81) contributed to the spread of Hegelian ideas, though more along the lines of the right wing.

Hegelianism made a very early entry into the United States. F. A. Rauch (1806-41), who had been a student of Hegel's, went to the United States in 1831 and in 1836 became president of Marshall College in Pennsylvania. The first pages of Hegel appeared in English in *German Prose Writers* (1832), by F. H. Hedge. From this work W. T. Harris (1835-1909), the most zealous American Hegelian, learned Hegel. His teacher was H. C. Brokmeyer (1826-1906), translator of Hegel and founder of the St. Louis school, which also included T. Davidson (1840-1900), D. J. Snider (1841-1925), and others. This school, through the *Journal of Speculative Philosophy* (1867-93), which Harris founded and edited, plus his career as U.S. commissioner of education (1889-1906), influenced directly the American system of schools and → kindergartens.

5. Hegel Renaissance

In the 20th century Hegel's philosophy was been taken up again in various places and for various reasons. Neo-Hegelianism in Italy was a continuation of existing trends, but a genuine Hegel renaissance occurred in Germany with W. Dilthey (1833-1911) and H. Nohl (1879-1960). In particular, Nohl's edition of *Hegels theologische Jugendschriften* (The theological writings of Hegel's youth, 1907) stimulated discussion of the philosophy of religion. A first phase of philological and critical debate with Hegel now began.

In an advance on neo-Kantianism, Hegel was set in some proximity to early National Socialism. In opposition to this development H. Simon, A. Kojève, A. Koyré, and others in France developed a realistic historical interpretation of Hegel that was strongly affected by French philosophy after 1940 and that followed Kojève's lectures on Hegel's *Phenomenology*. These lectures influenced many, including J.-P. Sartre (1905-80).

Also in opposition to the National Socialist usurping of Hegel there was at the same time a revival of left-wing Hegelianism in a critical movement that deviated from orthodox Marxism and that ranged from explicit Marxist approaches (G. Lukács and E. Bloch) to middle and later → critical theory (M. Horkheimer, T. Adorno, and J. Habermas). This movement especially took over from the left wing the emancipatory motif of reflection and engaged in criticism of the preoccupation of orthodox Marxism with economics.

The nationalist interpretation of Hegel faded out completely after World War II, but the left-wing movement of social criticism and the hermeneutical approach (→ Hermeneutics) persisted. From the mid-1950s these two interests came together in an International Hegel Society and a closely related society for the publication of a critical edition of Hegel's works. In 1981 they spawned an International Society for Dialectical Philosophy (Societas Hegeliana), whose main aim is to promote dialectical philosophy and its relations with the development of learning. There are also various national Hegel societies.

New theological interpretations and appropriations of Hegel have appeared in the past quarter century, and a critical edition of the *Lectures on the Philosophy of Religion*, edited by W. Jaeschke and translated by P. C. Hodgson and others, appeared in 1983-85. Hegel is viewed as providing to theology a postmetaphysical ontology that stresses the processive, relational character of absolute spirit and the interaction of God and the world.

→ Absolute, The; Philosophy of History; Philosophy of Religion

Bibliography: W. J. Brazill, *The Young Hegelians* (New Haven, 1970) • E. L. Fackenheim, *The Religious Dimension in Hegel's Thought* (Bloomington, Ind., 1967) • P. C. Hodgson, ed., *G. W. F. Hegel: Theologian of the Spirit* (Minneapolis, 1997) • W. Jaeschke, *Reason in Religion: The Foundations of Hegel's Philosophy of Religion* (Berkeley and Los Angeles, 1990) • C. O'Regan, *The Heterodox Hegel* (Albany, N.Y., 1994) • L. Stepelevich, ed., *The Young Hegelians: An Anthology* (Cambridge, 1983) • J. E. Toews, *Hegelianism: The Path toward Dialectical Humanism, 1805-1841* (Cambridge, 1980) • R. R. Williams, *Recognition: Fichte and Hegel on the Other* (Albany, N.Y., 1992) • R. K. Williamson, *Introduction to Hegel's Philosophy of Religion* (Albany, N.Y., 1984).

WALTHER C. ZIMMERLI

Heidelberg Catechism

1. Occasion
2. Composition and Author
3. Contents
4. History, Spread, and Significance

The Heidelberg Catechism (1563), which was originally the catechism of the Palatinate (*Catechismus oder christlicher Unterricht, wie der in Kirchen und Schulen der kurfürstlichen Pfalz getrieben wird),* took its name from the city in which it was first printed. Its wide dispersal finally made it the Reformed equivalent of Martin Luther's Small → Catechism.

1. Occasion

The Palatinate, though it went over only late to the → Reformation under Elector Ottheinrich (1556-59), achieved no stability. When Frederick III (1559-76) became ruler, forces devoted to M. Luther, P. Melanchthon, and Reformed teaching were struggling for mastery in the university, church, and government. A Heidelberg eucharistic controversy and competing orders of worship and catechisms polarized the territorial church. Elector Frederick turned step by step to the Reformed confession, and in December 1561 he introduced the Reformed rite of breaking bread (→ Eucharist) to Heidelberg. A new and unifying catechism that would also serve as a standard for pastors was the first act in a wider movement for liturgical and ecclesiastical reform along Reformed lines.

2. Composition and Author

We have only a few scattered accounts of the development of the Heidelberg Catechism. Among the theologians and church councillors of Heidelberg, the main author seems to have been Melanchthon's disciple Zacharias Ursinus (1534-83), who had become professor of dogmatics in Heidelberg in 1562. From him we have a Latin draft with 108 questions dating to 1562. He used Lutheran and Reformed catechisms of the period along with → confessions and doctrinal writings. The elector took a personal interest, adding supporting biblical texts. The project was put before a conference of superintendents in January 1563. On January 19 the elector signed the preface, and on March 5 the first printed copies were available. At the suggestion of church councillor Caspar Olevianus (1536-87), another question (80) was added to the second edition concerning the difference between the Lord's Supper and the → Mass. The final form came in April 1563 in a corrected German copy and a Latin translation for use in schools (now with 129 questions). In November 1563 the text was added to the new church order, and along with this order it was everywhere made definitive in a visitation (→ Church Orders).

3. Contents

The Heidelberg Catechism used the Geneva Catechism of John Calvin (1509-64) as a model, but in its much-quoted first question concerning our "only comfort in life and in death," and throughout the series, it gives precedence to personal → assurance of salvation. To have knowledge of → salvation three things are necessary: (1) knowledge of sin (qq. 3-11, on the human plight), (2) knowledge and appropriation of redemption (12-85, on human redemption, with the creed and sacraments to vouch for salvation in Christ), and (3) living for God (86-129, on gratitude, according to the → Decalogue and in → prayer). The definitions of faith (21), the church (54), and justification (60) have become classic. Reformed features may be seen in the → Christology, in the emphasis on pneumatology (→ Holy Spirit) and the → sacraments, especially the Eucharist, and also in the puritanical thrust in the exposition of the Ten Commandments. There is sharp differentiation from Roman Catholicism.

4. History, Spread, and Significance

Continuous reading on each of ten Sundays before worship, along with regular catechetical preaching (→ Worship) in 52 sections on Sunday afternoons, helped to make the Heidelberg Catechism part of the congregational heritage. In scope and nature it was more a book for the congregation as a whole than a catechism for children. From 1576 there were shorter versions for the instruction of children and first communicants. Netherlanders in the Palatinate adopted it in 1563, as did the Netherlands as a whole in 1571 and Hungary in 1567. With Nassau-Dillenburg in 1581 it began to be accepted in German Reformed churches (esp. Lower Rhine and Westphalia), and the Swiss Reformed adopted it in 1614. It achieved confessional status when the Synod of Dort (1618-19) made it a formula of unity. Emigrants and missionaries took it to South Africa, Indonesia, and the United States. In the 1990s some branches of the Reformed Church in America and the Christian Reformed Church continued to make direct use of the Heidelberg Catechism, in some cases basing the regular Sunday preaching on its questions and answers.

Many important Reformed theologians have expounded the catechism, including G. Voetius (1589-1676) in a methodology of the spiritual life, J. Cocceius (1603-69) along the lines of federal theology (→ Covenant 3), F. A. Lampe (1683-1729) in terms of Pietism, H. F. Kohlbrügge (1803-75) in opposition to sanctification-synergism (→ Sanctification), and K. Barth (1886-1968) in the interests of Reformed reconstruction. The → Enlightenment took no interest in it, but the Awakening rediscovered it. Its twofold nature as a confession and a congregational book forms a link between theology and the congregation. An ecumenical explanation was added in 1976 to the rejection of the Mass in q. 80. Its widespread and distinctive character have made it a classic document of the Reformed understanding of the faith.

→ Calvinism; Calvin's Theology; Reformed and Presbyterian Churches

Bibliography: K. Barth, *Learning Jesus Christ through the Heidelberg Catechism* (Grand Rapids, 1982) • *The Commentary of Dr. Zacharias Ursinus on the Heidelberg Catechism* (trans. G. W. Willard; Columbus, Ohio, 1851) • *The Heidelberg Confession* (trans. A. O. Miller and M. E. Osterhaven; Philadelphia, 1962) • *Der Heidelberger Katechismus* (ed. V. O. Weber; 2d ed.; Gütersloh, 1983) • H. Hoeksema, *The Triple Knowledge: An Exposition of the Heidelberg Catechism* (3d ed.; Grand Rapids, 1990) • M. Noll, ed., *Confessions and Catechisms of the Reformation* (Grand Rapids, 1991) 133-64 • C. Olevian and L. D. Bierma, *A Firm Foundation: An Aid to Interpreting the Heidelberg Catechism* (Grand Rapids, 1995) • C. Plantinga Jr., *A Place to Stand: A Reformed Study of Creeds and Confessions* (Grand Rapids, 1979) • D. Visser, ed., *Controversy and Conciliation: The Reformation and the Palatinate, 1559-1583* (Allison Park, Pa., 1986) 73-100 and 197-225.

J. F. Gerhard Goeters†

Heilsgeschichte → Salvation History

Heliand

Heliand (from an Old English word meaning "Savior"; Ger. *Heiland*) is an Anglo-Saxon poem in various related sections, consisting originally of more than 6,000 alliterative verses. Combining the tradition of later Latin Bible poetry and the Anglo-Saxon Christian epic, it is by an unknown author and dates to the second half of the ninth century. Using Tatian's Diatessaron and various contemporary commentaries (by the Venerable Bede, Alcuin, Rabanus Maurus, and others), it narrates the life, teaching, suffering, death, and resurrection of the Savior.

The distinctive use of the language and style of Germanic epic for the gospel story raises a problem in Christian literary aesthetics and is not an expression of → syncretism. The dogmatic orthodoxy and the propagation of the → Sermon on the Mount push pagan connotations (esp. the language of fate) into the background. The general avoidance of → allegory in favor of elemental catechetical additions has led to erroneous interpretations (e.g., as missionary literature, as forerunner of Protestant Bible piety).

M. Luther (1483-1546) and P. Melanchthon (1497-1560) knew the work, and M. Flacius (1520-75), in the second edition of his *Catalogus testium veritatis* (1562), published a Latin preface that introduced a (lost) codex of *Heliand* and a later Anglo-Saxon Genesis. To Flacius's work we owe the only direct references to the author and the time of composition.

→ Literature, Biblical and Early Christian 3

Bibliography: Primary sources: O. BEHAGHEL, ed., *Heliand und Genesis* (9th ed.; ed. B. Taeger; Tübingen, 1984) • J. E. CATHEY, *Hêliand: Text and Commentary* (Amherst, Mass., 1996) • G. R. MURPHY, *The Heliand: The Saxon Gospel. A Translation and Commentary* (New York, 1992).

Secondary works: K. GANTERT, *Akkommodation und eingeschriebener Kommentar. Untersuchungen zur Übertragungsstrategie des Helianddichters* (Tübingen, 1998) • A. HAGENLOCHER, *Schicksal im Heliand. Verwendung und Bedeutung der nominalen Bezeichnungen* (Cologne, 1975) • G. R. MURPHY, *The Saxon Savior: The German Transformation of the Gospel in the Ninth-Century Heliand* (New York, 1989) • B. SOWINSKI, *Darstellungsstil und Sprachstil im Heliand* (Cologne, 1985) • B. TAEGER, "Heliand," *VL* 3.958-71.

DIETER KARTSCHOKE

Hell

1. Religious History
2. The Bible and Dogma

1. Religious History

The word "hell" comes from Old Ice. *hel,* the term in Nordic mythology for the place of the dead in the underworld and for its female ruler. All the dead are there or under her rule except for those killed in battle. The idea was not negative from the outset, as the etymology also shows, for the meaning of the root is "hide, conceal."

The concept became a negative one only with the demonization of virtually all pre-Christian material by the repressive methods of missionaries and by those who after conversion engaged in committing German myths to writing. Although the term became the Germanic designation for the world of the → dead in popular Christian belief, one now evoking fear and focusing on rescue from postmortem punishment, a neutral, scientific use remained admissible as well, one that, in lieu of the terms "underworld" or "realm of the dead," does cover a large number of extremely disparate ideas about a more or less concretely subterranean "beyond." In our own cultural sphere, the most important ideas alongside hell as an underworld, one not simultaneously a place of punishment, include Israelite Sheol, Greek Hades or Tartarus, and Roman *orcus.*

Among ancient peoples, according to the relevant → worldview, the underworld lies where known land or sea moves into the unknown, or below the grave of the deceased, who have been interred beneath the surface of the earth and now live a diminished life. The two ideas sometimes merge. Ideas deriving from the cultural sphere of the Aegean allude historically to conceptionally similar though geographically different notions of the underworld in Mesopotamia and Egypt. Beginning in the middle of the second millennium B.C., the latter acquire → dualistic features, whereby the conditions of life in the beyond also exhibit features of torture, burning, beating, and butchering. The interpretation of these features as repayment for torments the deceased inflicted upon others while alive — that is, as actually → punishment — represents a basic human notion with parallels especially in Mahayana → Buddhism and among Central American Indians.

The closest concept in the Aegean sphere was the Orphic view of the underworld reflected in the (Christian) *Apocalypse of Peter* (→ Apocrypha 2.4). A synthesis of this kind, which included Jewish ideas of the → last judgment, converged from the third century A.D. onward with other, diverse notions. The clearest of these ideas were localized hypostatizations of the rule of → evil from Iranian tradition (→ Iranian Religions) as altered when mediated through Hellenized magicians (→ magic) and → Manichaeans. We must also refer to concepts of Gehenna (originally the Hinnom Valley at → Jerusalem, known from the time of Isaiah and Jeremiah as the site of every abomination because of the human sacrifices to Molech offered there during the Israelite monarchy in the eighth and seventh centuries). In the first century A.D. hell came to designate the place of punishment reserved for the ungodly in the intermediate state. In the Arab world, Muḥammad further developed and updated this idea in the seventh century (→ Islam).

The various concepts all came together in grandiose form in the inferno of Dante's (1265-1321) *Divine Comedy,* including influences from the visionary literature of Islam, itself nourished only in part by the → Koran. The fear of hell in the West, which culminated probably in the 13th century, has entered into associations with the utterly independent demonizing of the pagan underworld (see above) such that, given the possibility of a nuclear inferno in today's world, these associations will for the foreseeable future continue to entangle both historical-psychological and therapeutic-psychological enlightenment.

Bibliography: P. Arnold, *Das Totenbuch der Maya* (Bern, 1980) • M. Asin Palacios, *Islam and the Divine Comedy* (London, 1926) • A. E. Bernstein, *The Formation of Hell: Death and Retribution in the Ancient and Early Christian Worlds* (Ithaca, N.Y., 1993) • S. G. F. Brandon, *The Judgment of the Dead* (London, 1967) • P. Camporesi, *The Fear of Hell: Images of Damnation and Salvation in Early Modern Europe* (University Park, Pa., 1991) • J. Jeremias, "Ἅδης" and "Γέεννα," *TDNT* 1.146-49 and 657-58 • H. Kees, *Totenglauben und Jenseitsvorstellungen der alten Ägypter* (3d ed.; Berlin, 1977; orig. pub., 1926) • J. Kroll, *Gott und Hölle. Der Mythos von Descensuskampfe* (Darmstadt, 1963) • A. Masters, *The Devil's Dominion: The Complete Story of Hell and Satanism in the Modern World* (New York, 1978) • E. Pagels, "The Social History of Satan, the Intimate Enemy: A Preliminary Sketch," *HTR* 84 (1991) 105-28 • Str-B 4/2.1016-165 • P. Thieme, "Hades," *BSAW* 98/5 (1952) 35-55 • K. van der Toorn, B. Becking, and P. W. van der Horst, eds., *Dictionary of Deities and Demons in the Bible* (2d ed.; Grand Rapids, 1999).

Carsten Colpe

2. The Bible and Dogma

The OT does not refer to hell in the later sense but speaks only of a shadowy existence in the realm of the dead (in Sheol, or LXX Hades). This existence, which includes neither enjoyment of life nor praise of God, is a state of remoteness from God. In later → Judaism ideas of → resurrection and retribution developed under Iranian and Hellenistic influence, and there was some discussion of the nature of the hereafter (→ Apocalyptic; Pharisees). Up to the → last judgment the realm of the dead will be divided into separate sections for the wicked and the righteous. In Josephus (ca. 37-ca. 100) the → souls of the righteous go straight to → heaven at death (see Luke 16:19-22), so that hell is simply a place of punishment for the damned. Finally, the school of Hillel (1st cent. B.C.–1st cent. A.D.) found in hell a place of purification.

In the NT we find various identifications. Hades is the realm of the dead, Tartarus the prison for disobedient → angels (2 Pet. 2:4). In Revelation hell is the abyss (11:7) or the lake of fire (19:20; 20:10). Gehenna, the Hinnom Valley south of Jerusalem (Mark 9:45-48), is the place of lurking → evil. It will be an eschatological prison and the place of punishment for the damned after the last judgment (though cf. Luke 16:19-26). In general the NT shows little interest in the geography of the realm of the dead. Even Christ's → descent into hell is only alluded to very indirectly. What is said about hell does not give us a cosmic → worldview as much as it sharpens the message of → salvation in Jesus Christ.

In 543 a synod meeting in Constantinople proclaimed nine anathemas against the teachings of Origen, the last of which (DH 411) specifically rejected the doctrine of → apocatastasis, according to which ultimately even the → devil would be redeemed. During the Middle Ages the West came to distinguish between the *limbus patrum* (borderland of the patriarchs), which has allegedly been empty since Christ's descent into hell; the *limbus infantium* (borderland of infants), where the souls of infants burdened only with original → sin are kept; → purgatory, through which those are purified who did not die in mortal sin; and finally hell in the narrower sense, the place of eternal punishment for the damned (DH 925-26), who are sent there immediately after death (DH 1002).

From the eighth and ninth centuries onward, impressive depictions of hell began to appear in both East and West (e.g., in Dante's *Divine Comedy,* the frescoes of Michelangelo, and Milton's *Paradise Lost*). One could speak of hell as a component of an entire worldview (→ Iconography). These concepts are still influential today, though less in theology than in literary fancy, which (largely in detachment from Christian faith) is fascinated by the idea of a hellish hierarchy, of Satanism, and of black magic and which accepts → faith at most only as a means of → exorcism.

On biblical and theological grounds, the → Reformation rejected the ideas of limbo and purgatory but not the usual concepts of hell. Only with the → Enlightenment did the opinion gain ground that hell is not a place but a state of distance from God and consequent dereliction. Thus F. M. Dostoyevsky (1821-81) declared that hell is the pain of no longer being able to love, and J.-P. Sartre (1905-80), pressing the same concept atheistically, said that other people are hell. It may well be that descriptions of hell, both ancient and modern, are to a large extent the projection of human horrors (e.g., Auschwitz). Theologically, however, we must cling to the fact that Jesus Christ bore distance from God and dereliction on the cross and that he overcame them there — indeed, for all humanity — so that we have to ask whether there is not some truth in apocatastasis, at least in hope (see F. D. E. Schleiermacher, *The Christian Faith,* §163) or de jure, though not in every case necessarily de facto (K. Barth, *CD* IV/3a, §70.3).

→ Eschatology

Bibliography: R. Bauckham, "Hades, Hell," *ABD* 3.14-15 • A. Brenk and A. Brulhart, "Hölle," *LCI* 2.313-21 • F. F. Church, *The Devil and Dr. Church: A Guide to Hell for Atheists and True Believers* (San Francisco, 1986) • N. Cohn, *Cosmos, Chaos, and the World to Come* (New Haven, 1993) • J. Gnilka, J. Ratzinger, and K. Beitl, "Hölle," *LTK* (2d ed.) 5.445-50 • F. C. Grant et al., "Hölle," *RGG* (3d ed.) 5.400-407 • F. Heer, *Abschied von Hölle und Himmeln* (Munich, 1970) • M. Himmelfarb, *Tours of Hell: An Apocalyptic Form in Jewish and Christian Literature* (Philadelphia, 1983) • T. Rasmussen, "Hölle II," *TRE* 15.449-55 (bibliography) • J. L. Walls, *Hell: The Logic of Damnation* (Notre Dame, Ind., 1992).

Alasdair I. C. Heron

Hellenism

1. Problems
2. Development
   2.1. Politics
   2.2. Economy
   2.3. Education, Science, Culture
   2.4. Philosophy
   2.5. Religion
3. Judaism and Christianity

1. Problems

In the days of J. G. Droysen (1808-84), "Hellenism" was a term used for Greek culture and thought, and more specifically for nonclassical biblical Greek. Droysen, however, applied it to the epoch of the fusion of Greek and Near Eastern patterns, which began with Alexander the Great (336-323 b.c.). For him the postclassical age was no longer one of decay but a time of transition from Greek to Christian → culture. He also saw a development in the Greek world itself to a rational view of things and a rationalistic replacement of pagan religion as a driving force in the historical process.

These contradictory evaluations have confused the debate ever since. The idea of fusion has also proved to be inappropriate. Yet one can accept the beginning of a new era with the campaigns of Alexander, for his conquests made Greece the dominant and unifying force — politically, economically, and culturally — from Sicily to the Indian peninsula, and from the Caspian Sea to Nubia. The end came in 31 b.c., when the last Hellenistic kingdom, Egypt, became a Roman province. Even then, however, there was a marked impact on the Roman world, so that one might speak of a Hellenistic Roman culture, which for its part affected the Byzantine Empire.

2. Development

2.1. *Politics*

Alexander's vision of an empire that would unite Greece and Persia remained unfulfilled. The conflicts of his successors gave rise to the system of Hellenistic territorial states. The most important of these were Antigonid Macedonia, Ptolemaic Egypt, and the kingdom of the Seleucids, which embraced Syria and parts of Asia Minor. These dynasties were all rivals. There were also several medium-sized and smaller states, all of which were absolute monarchies. The rulers viewed the countries as private property won by the spear.

Power was maintained primarily by the Greek-Macedonian army and by Greek bureaucracy. The costs of the court, the army, and the administration were borne by the native populations through an ingenious system of direct and indirect taxation. Absolutism found its clearest expression in → emperor worship, the basis of which was the veneration of city founders, lawgivers, and warriors in the Greek cities.

2.2. *Economy*

Alexander opened up Asia to Greek trade. The introduction of Attic coinage as the imperial currency made international commerce possible. → Alexandria was the main port for Egyptian goods (grain, papyrus, glass, cosmetics). Goods from the north coast of the Black Sea (grain, hides, wood) were marketed in Sinope, Byzantium, and Rhodes. Raw materials from Asia and India were manufactured in → Antioch on the Orontes. Banking and a system of credit were developed. Greek science aided the domestic economy, for example, with inventions to aid agriculture. The working class did not share the profits, which resulted in social conflicts, especially in Egypt. → Slave labor prevailed in agriculture and industry.

2.3. *Education, Science, Culture*

Since the army, administration, and economy were mostly in Greek hands, Greek in the form of Koine (→ Greek Language) soon became the lingua franca of the Hellenistic world. In the many cities that the Seleucids founded to protect their far-flung and heterogeneous kingdom and that the Ptolemies set up in their extensive possessions, but also in the many Egyptian villages that were inhabited by Greeks, there were Greek primary schools and gymnasiums. The gymnasium was the school of Hellenistic urban culture (teaching sports, music, and literature). The graduates kept up contacts in clubs, just as societies played a lively part in other aspects of Greek life. Social advance was linked to adoption of the Greek language and education in the gymnasium. In Egypt non-Greek aliens (Persians, Jews) could more easily move up to the class of Hellenes than could native Egyptians.

The exact sciences blossomed in Hellenism, with major contributions from Euclid (fl. ca. 300 B.C., geometry), Archimedes (d. 212, π, infinitesimal calculus, the principle of buoyancy, and the Archimedean screw), Aristarchus of Samos (ca. 310-230, the heliocentric system), Eratosthenes (ca. 276-ca. 194, mathematical geography), and Herophilus (d. ca. 280, the function of the brain, the circulation of the blood, and the nervous system). The Hellenistic kings promoted science and literature.

Ptolemy I (king 323-285 B.C.) founded the Museion at Alexandria, which financially supported poets and scholars and provided excellent opportunities for work (including the library, observatory, and zoological garden). Alexandria was a center of philology (textual criticism, commentaries, lexicography) and also of the new literature and its pursuit of formal excellence, notably Callimachus in the short epic, Theocritus in pastoral poetry, and Aratus in didactic poems on astronomy and meteorology. → City culture included the theater. The new comedy of Hellenism presented neither mythology nor politics but general human problems. Prominent was Menander (ca. 342-ca. 292) with his character delineation, translated into Latin and adapted by the Roman comic poets Plautus (250-184) and Terence (186/85-?159).

2.4. Philosophy

The philosophy of Hellenism (→ Greek Philosophy) was marked by a turning to the individual and an attempt to find a center of meaning for an extended world with no orderly outward structure or sheltering conventions. Epicurus (341-270 B.C.), appealing to the atomic theory of Democritus, sought to free his contemporaries from fear of the gods, from unrest, and from sorrow and to lead them to a joyous life in a circle of like-minded people.

The founder of the Athenian Stoa, Zeno of Citium (ca. 335-ca. 263 B.C.; → Stoicism), viewed the world and humanity as overruled by the purposeful creative world spirit, the Logos, and urged a life in harmony with this Logos. The masses venerated this universal deity (which represented a monotheistic thrust) under various names. The supreme goal was individual moral perfection. Later, Panaetius (ca. 180-109) regarded the fulfilling of → duty in society as the chief goal and made Stoicism acceptable to the Roman world. His disciple Poseidonius (ca. 135-ca. 51), called the Leibniz of antiquity, brought religious elements to Stoicism (including belief in the afterlife, demonology, astrology, and divination).

The movement of the anticultural Cynics was started by Diogenes of Sinope (d. ca. 320 B.C.); their popular didactic address, the diatribe, was adopted by the Stoics. → Platonism focused on problems of knowledge (→ Epistemology) and fell victim to skepticism. Neoplatonism, preeminently through Plotinus (ca. A.D. 205-70) and Porphyry (ca. 232-ca. 303), restored a religious dimension.

2.5. Religion

→ Greek religion, which was traditionally oriented to society, lost significance with the decay of the polis, to which also the religious criticism of the philosophers, sophists, and poets contributed. In keeping with the mood of the age, a large following attached to the cults of deities that taught a personal relation with adherents, including Asclepius, Dionysus, and the mystery gods (→ Hellenistic-Roman Religion). Mysteries (→ Mystery Religions) had long existed in Greece, but in Hellenism Near Eastern cults (e.g., Isis, the Great Mother; see Lucian's De Dea Syria) also assumed a mystery character. Here was the closest fusion of East and West (→ Syncretism). By their exclusive nature, their individual claim on believers, and their promise of immortality to initiates, these cults gave security to many who would otherwise have thought themselves the playthings of capricious → chance (tychē) or the victims of the iron laws of fate (Heimarmenē).

From the second century B.C., → astrology, which came originally from Babylon, became increasingly important. Starting with an ancient philosophical belief in the deity of the stars and with the axiom of a strict → causality that determines all that takes place, and with the added influence of Stoic concepts, there arose a closed system of scientific explanation. Elements of astrology found their way into many forms of religion, including the mysteries.

3. Judaism and Christianity

Judaism encountered Hellenism at home as well as in the → diaspora, for there were traces of Hellenistic influence in Palestine from the middle of the third century B.C. Ecclesiastes reflects the rationalistic spirit of early Hellenism. Even the conservative Jesus, son of Sirach (→ Apocrypha 1), adopts popular philosophical presuppositions when he equates the divine world reason with wisdom and the → Torah. Indeed, the groups that arose out of opposition to Hellenism were also under Hellenistic influence, including → Qumran (→ Dualism) and the → Pharisees (in their educational system, chain of tradition, exegetical methodology, and general cosmological, anthropological, and eschatological ideas). Dispersion Judaism, linked to → Jerusalem by pilgrimages and the temple tax, had a closer encounter with Hellenism, as the translation of the OT into Greek (the LXX; → Bible Versions) demonstrates. Alexandrian Judaism produced a good deal of literature around 200 B.C. Jewish history was glorified in the form of novels and verse. Around 160 Aristobulus of Paneas expounded the Torah allegorically in order to make it acceptable to Greek scholars. Philo of Alexandria (15-10 B.C.–A.D. 45-50) tried to show the harmony between the Torah and both the Platonic doctrine of ideas and Stoic ethics.

Primitive Christianity thus arose out of a Judaism that was permeated by Hellenistic thought. → Paul linked up with the monotheistically and eschatologically oriented preaching of the Hellenistic synagogue but set Christ in place of the → law (1 Thess. 1:9-10; 1 Cor. 8:5-6). The Logos Christology of → John had roots in Hellenistic Judaism; it was Justin Martyr (d. ca. A.D. 165) who brought in the concept of the Stoic Logos. From the time of the → apologists an explicit debate with Greek → metaphysics was an unavoidable task that, according to modern research, resulted not so much in the Hellenizing of Christianity as in the Christianizing of Hellenism.

→ New Testament Era, History of; Roman Empire

Bibliography: R. BICHLER, "Hellenismus." Geschichte und Problematik eines Epochenbegriffs (Darmstadt, 1983) • G. W. BOWERSOCK, Hellenism in Late Antiquity (Cambridge, 1990) • J. G. DROYSEN, Geschichte des Hellenismus (2 vols.; Darmstadt, 1952-53; orig. pub., 1836-43) • J. H. ELLENS, Alexander the Great and Hellenistic Culture: The Impact of Political and Military Achievements upon the Life of the Mind and Spirit (Claremont, Calif., 1997) • P. GREEN, Alexander to Actium: The Historical Evolution of the Hellenistic Age (Berkeley, Calif., 1990); idem, ed., Hellenistic History and Culture (Berkeley, Calif., 1993) • M. HENGEL, Judaism and Hellenism: Studies in Their Encounter in Palestine during the Early Hellenistic Period (2 vols.; Philadelphia, 1981) • H. LAUTER, Die Architektur des Hellenismus (Darmstadt, 1986).

HELMUT MERKEL

Hellenistic-Roman Religion

1. Basis in Hellenism after Alexander

The Hellenistic-Roman period embraces many centuries. "Hellenistic" is used for the time from the conquests and alliances of Alexander the Great (336-323 B.C.) to the incorporating of the last great Hellenistic state into the → Roman empire, namely, the seizure of Egypt by Augustus in 31 B.C. "Roman" is used for the time when → Rome, Italy, and the western provinces adopted Greek and Near Eastern ideas and practices, and on to the final stages of antiquity. For all the differences in detail the → history of religion finds certain common features that justify our speaking about Hellenistic-Roman religion during the period of the development and decay of Roman rule.

1.1. Spread

The conquests of Alexander (→ Hellenism) led to the collapse of the earlier Greek city-state (the polis) and eroded belief in the ancient gods (→ Greek Religion), leaving this belief to linger on only by habit. At the same time, the extension of the horizon of philosophers propagated a cosmopolitan understanding of people as world citizens. As the Greeks who spread across the Near East were concerned to maintain themselves, belief in fortune (tychē) gained currency, and along with it city cults of political personages, the founders and benefactors upon whom so much depended.

The worship of the Greek gods rested solely on the upper classes, who kept it alive by literary instruction and the official cult. Although poorer people took part in the feasts, the gods were alien to them. Their allegiance was to the smaller local deities and heroes, whom they could not take with them when they moved and who lost much of their significance with the devastation of their motherland. As the empire of Alexander was broken up, the political background of a world religion vanished, but the question had been raised and was tackled in the Hellenistic dominions of Alexander's successors.

1.2. *Urbanization*

The rural population played little part in the development of religion. The masses of little people who gathered in the cities were the engine of change. They had been uprooted, had little political influence, were on their own, and made their own choices about contacts and marriages with Greeks or natives. They also decided upon their gods. To promote their religious interests they had to form a new mode of community by way of private societies or mass movements, in which women also became important and which posed a task of integration for statecraft.

The many new Greek cities in Asia Minor, the Semitic Near East, and Egypt became the focal point as centers of political life and Greek culture. Since this culture claimed leadership and was not immediately accessible to the natives, it tried to make itself attractive, and as a result Greek religion had a palpable impact on native religions in the Greek interpretation of these religions and in the fusion of traditions in religious → syncretism. This process began with theocrasy, the linking of formerly separate gods on the assumption that the name of a god may be translated like any other word. This development overcame the elements of different origin (Greek among the educated, non-Greek among the ordinary people), first by setting them alongside one another, then by a process of admixture. At the same time, political inequality provoked national reactions, which strengthened the native religious elements. This process occurred especially when Greek power began to wane about 200 B.C. and the Hellenistic states were unable to resist the rise of Rome.

2. Main Ideas

Characteristic of Hellenistic-Roman religion is its orientation to demonstrations of divine power rather than to divine personages.

2.1. *Philosophy*

From the time of the Sophist criticism of religion about 400 B.C. (→ Greek Philosophy), philosophy replaced religion in educated circles. It increasingly offered a criterion for life and protection against the vacillations of fortune, dispensing comfort and summoning to repentance and conversion in order that people might achieve redemption in their own strength. The gods of mythology were lost in physical and often related allegorical explanations such as we find especially in → Stoicism. They thus became at most only semipersonal. Euhemeristic interpretation found in them human beings who were honored as deities because of their great deeds.

2.2. *Worldview*

At the same time, the firmly established ancient → worldview underwent tremendous extension as it came to be believed that the earth floats in a void, surrounded by an atmosphere that reaches as far as the moon and that is peopled by semispiritual souls and → demons. Beyond the atmosphere are the seven spheres of the planets, where the gods are discerned in their regularity, and then the starry heaven as the eighth and highest sphere. The doctrine of power as very real emanation or breath gave consistency to this worldview and determined the religious ideas. Along with belief in fortune there was also belief in the destiny of individuals, which is directed by the demon or genius assigned to each.

Philosophy also discussed the supreme god, while → astrology regarded the stars as the entities whose forces shape cosmic destinies. Similar forces were also found in rocks, rings, amulets, and parts of bodies or plants on the basis of the idea of a sympathetic working together of the world as macrocosm and the human being as microcosm. In both → philosophy and → magic or → divination, the traditions of good and bad demons were linked to this cooperation.

2.3. *Divine Overcoming of Fate*

People turned to a deity primarily because of the demonstration of its superior power by → healing, → exorcisms, and so forth. The deity was honored with titles like Absolute Ruler (→ Emperor Worship) and also furnished with stellar powers and omnipotence to determine human fate. Astrologers argued that people could not obviate what is foreordained by → prayer and → sacrifice, yet Near Eastern deities like Isis were attractive specifically in the promise to those initiated into their mysteries that they could overcome fate. Once Greek astronomy had constructed the astrological system (on the basis of Babylonian belief in the power of the stars; → Babylonian and Assyrian Religion), the inevitability of occurrence in the world (= Gk. *Heimarmenē*) was felt to be an oppressive burden that people tried to escape.

2.4. *Liberation for Divine Life*

In ecstatic exaltation above the earthly, people found an experience of regeneration and even deification. If they did not think they could save the earthly body, they left it confidently to the fate that controls the material world and concentrated on the → soul or inner self as the divine part of humanity, seeking its absorption into the spiritual or transcendent realm that is beyond the reach of determinism. The decisive aspect could not be put in words but was an irrefutable certainty for initiates into the mysteries (→ Mystery Religions) and for philosophers. Life, they believed, would find a happy continuation. The key concept in all the new movements was *redemption,* that is, deliverance from danger in a world that had become too big, and increasing assurance of a positive afterlife in the world to come.

2.5. *Dualistic Tendencies*

Religious experience of ecstatic mystical union with the divine as the sublimely spiritual, through which people knew liberation from the body and a rising above the sensory world, produced a disparagement and even a despising of the corporeal as an obstacle to this state of divine communion that is our true being. As Near Eastern religions encountered Greek Orphic teaching and the Platonic doctrine of → dualism between the eternal world of ideas and the transitory world of physical phenomena (→ Platonism), the feeling grew stronger that a sinful soul is imprisoned in the body. Asceticism and search for knowledge of the divine would make it possible for the soul to attain a place of bliss instead of remaining in the underworld of punishments. In accordance with the current cosmology, this place was localized in the air. In literary and philosophical circles the writings of the Hellenized magi of Iran (→ Iranian Religions) claimed great attention, and frequently the Iranian dualism of → good and → evil sharpened the Greek dualism of soul and body.

2.6. *General View of the Divine*

Since divine power in general captured the people's interest, there was no exclusive god. Offerings were made to all the gods, and the attributes of one god could be attributed to another in order to express the fullness of divine powers. One god could be regarded as ontically one with the others whose attributes it had, and along the lines of → henotheism it could be invoked under the most effective name as the god of all peoples, going under different names among the different peoples.

Philosophy and astrology constructed a system at the head of which stood the god of heaven — not the abstract Greek god, but the Near Eastern sun god. Or in the interest of mediation the transcendent god was accompanied by a second god as mediator, as in the doctrine of the Demiurge as creator of the lower world, or of the Logos as the divine word that is responsible for creation and redemption (→ Gnosis, Gnosticism). Faith and hope against the background of a gloomy fear of annihilation were thus typical concepts in Hellenistic-Roman religion. Love of the deity was uncommon, however. When love did appear, it was as striving love, *erōs,* and not the love of human interrelationship.

3. Official and Popular Forms

3.1. *The Cult as a Bond*

As individuals sought to gain divine power, they had also to seek it for the ruler insofar as their own well-being depended on his. Thus alongside honor given for specific benefactions from the ruler, an emperor cult was propagated from above.

As a religious bond, the Ptolemies in Egypt promoted the cult of Alexander and their own predecessors, and finally that of living rulers. To increase religious allegiance, they propagated in this connection the worship of Sarapis, a deity half Egyptian and half Greek, through links to the Demeter mysteries of Eleusis. Other Near Eastern religions spread among the Greeks as their deities were strongly Hellenized in presentation and operation, and especially their views of the afterlife, notwithstanding their exotic appearance. As Greek culture took deep root and exerted a major influence in the great centers of Ptolemaic Egypt, this country became the most significant melting pot.

3.2. *Astrology, Magic, and Belief in the Underworld and Miracles*

Bolos of Mendes gave the concept of power its predominant occult form in about 200 B.C. The Babylonian doctrine of the stars then developed into the astrological constructs of Nechepso-Petosiris and Hermes Trismegistos. As in other → occult teachings, the authors used pseudonyms designed to give their writings greater authority among the Greeks.

Magic appeared at the same time as astrology. It sought to modify for personal advantage the laws of nature and their normal operation. The use of amulets aimed to satisfy the demand for security, especially against the hostile powers to which magic was oriented. As the power of the god could be invoked into his image by certain rites, so → demons possessed powers that could be directed by the use of exact formulas as we know them best from the many Greek magic papyri found in Egypt.

With the magic on execration tablets and the Orphic gold texts, we also find a belief in the underworld that gave instructions to the deceased in the tomb on how to reach the place of blessedness. For the living there was a similar belief in miracles, which could link up with Greek traditions in the case of helper-gods like Asclepius, but which also turned to Near Eastern deities.

4. Development in the Roman Empire

4.1. *Impact of the Hellenized Near East*

In the course of the third century B.C., the Hellenization of all spheres of culture, intensive acquaintance with other civilizations, and destructive and often precarious wars led even Rome, now quickly becoming an empire rather than a city, to uncertainty regarding its own → identity and to a search for new certainties (→ Roman Religion). Greek rites were adopted by ruling circles for political reasons, usually on the recommendation of the *Sibylline Oracles.* The new cult was meant to guarantee the stability of the state.

In 205 B.C. an official delegation brought the cult of the Great Mother Cybele from Asia Minor to Rome. In Rome the goddess had to put off all the features that were dangerous for state and people, and there could be no question of personal veneration or a mystery cult. These elements, for which there was intense yearning, were suppressed in 186 B.C. with the bloody crushing of the Dionysian mysteries, which were setting up what was almost a countergovernment in Italy and Rome.

The introduction of the cult from Asia Minor opened a gap through which the Hellenized Near East could finally make an entry. Near Eastern cults offered people fellowship in the veneration of a god for whom they had made a conscious decision, and also fellowship with this god. This nearness also gave added glory to the power of the god and caused adherents to dedicate themselves to it. When the related orgiastic rites could no longer be celebrated, the state preserved the Roman character of the Cybele Attis mysteries by setting up a Roman as high priest and by instituting the sacrifice of a bull as the new main rite. This Romanizing did not happen, however, in the case of the worship of Isis. Only the emperor cult, which was officially designed to perpetuate the old religion, and worship of the sun as the ideological basis of the divinity of the emperor remained as pillars of a single empire-wide religion.

Special cults, however, refused to be excluded, and like the Mithra cult or that of Jupiter Dolichenus as the religion of soldiers, they could have important functions in integrating social groups and upholding Roman power. Along with the mysteries, which flourished in the imperial period, wonder-workers like Apollonius of Tyana (fl. 1st cent. A.D.) gained many followers and came to be honored as *theios anēr* (a divine man).

4.2. Hermetic and Neoplatonic Synthesis

Small circles of educated people met to study edifying works deriving from the revelations of Hermes Trismegistos as the Egyptian god Thoth. These works, which have come down to us mainly in versions from the second and third centuries A.D., contain the core of Platonic philosophy in the language of religious revelation in an Egyptian dress, along with many other elements of Greek popular philosophy and mythology, astrological speculations, and ideas from the Jewish creation story. → Alchemy, which developed in Egypt, also came to be linked to this type of piety. In its variety, which is not very well systematized and even admits of contradictions in individual works, Hermetism is typical of the age and of the integrative power of small syncretistic groups of a mystical type. These groups regarded themselves as the elect, for unlike the ignorant world around them, they had Gnosis, the knowledge of the true nature of God, the world, and humanity. In part this basic attitude, as we see it especially in "Poimandres," the introductory tractate of the *Corpus Hermeticum,* involved dualistic trains of thought and became Gnosis in the narrower sense as we know it also from Christian Gnosticism.

Like Hermetism, Neoplatonic religious philosophy was a later product of Hellenistic-Roman religion, which was most influential in passing on the traditions of antiquity. In connection with the theurgy of Chaldean oracles, which showed how to evoke revelations from gods and demons, this philosophy achieved a monistic systematizing of the legacy of Hellenistic-Roman religion. Beginning with the Supreme One, it set up a → hierarchy of all the things that, as more immediate or more distant reflections of the One, have more or less being and worth. In Rome this idea meant recognition of the emperor as head, and all traditional forms of national religion were regarded as truth imparted by knowledge of the one supreme god. It thus became an apt basis for the reform by Emperor Julian (360-63) of Hellenistic-Roman religion as a counterblast to Christianity.

Bibliography: M. M. AUSTIN, ed., *The Hellenistic World from Alexander to the Roman Conquest: A Selection of Ancient Sources, in Translation* (Cambridge, 1981) • G. W. BOWERSOCK, *Hellenism in Late Antiquity* (Ann Arbor, Mich., 1990) • R. BULTMANN, *Primitive Christianity in Its Contemporary Setting* (New York, 1956; orig. pub., 1949) • W. BURKERT, *Ancient Mystery Cults* (Cambridge, 1987) • H. CANCIK and J. RÜPKE, eds., *Römische Reichsreligion und Provinzialreligion* (Tübingen, 1997) • F. CUMONT, *The Oriental Religions in Roman Paganism* (New York, 1956; orig. pub., 1906) • M. DZIELSKA, *Apollonius of Tyana in Legend and History* (Rome, 1986) • C. ELSAS, *Neuplatonische und gnostische Weltablehnung in der Schule Plotins* (Berlin, 1975) • G. FOWDEN, *The Egyptian Hermes* (Cambridge, 1986) • L. R. Fox, *Pagans and Christians* (London, 1986) • J. G. GRIFFITH, "Hellenistic Religions," *EncRel(E)* 6.252-66 • H.-J. KLAUCK, *Die religiöse*

Umwelt des Urchristentums (2 vols.; Stuttgart, 1995-96) • L. H. Martin, *Hellenistic Religions: An Introduction* (New York, 1987) • M. W. Meyer and P. A. Mirecki, eds., *Ancient Magic and Ritual Power* (Leiden, 1995) • A. D. Nock, *Essays on Religion and the Ancient World* (2 vols.; Oxford, 1972).

CHRISTOPH ELSAS

Helvetic Confession

With the *Confessio et expositio simplex orthodoxae fidei* of 1566, the so-called Second Helvetic Confession, the Reformed churches in German-speaking Switzerland achieved a definitive, common, and lasting confession (→ Confessions and Creeds). The original principle of the sole authority of Scripture, which had been argued against the → Roman Catholic Church, contained no spur to the formulation of a confession. The impulse came with the introduction of the → Reformation to individual cities. Thus we have the Berne Theses in 1528, the Berne Synod in 1532, and the → Basel Confession in 1534.

The announcement of a council and negotiations for agreement with Martin Luther (1483-1546) then forced the German Reformed churches at a conference in Basel in February 1536 to adopt a short, common confession of faith, usually known as the First Helvetic Confession or sometimes as the Second Basel Confession, since it followed the Basel model. The main themes of the confession are the doctrines of Holy Scripture, of Christ's person and reconciling work (→ Christology), and of the → church and its ministry. Martin Bucer (1491-1551) helped to draw up the article on the → Eucharist, and at his urging the confession was not published at once. A copy was sent to Luther, who expressed his delight at the Christian character of the work and promised to do what he could to promote unity. Leo Jud translated the Latin into Swiss German, and he and Bullinger were in favor of a rider subjecting the confession to the primary authority of Scripture.

The hope that the Swiss might be brought into the Wittenberg Concord of 1536 proved illusory. Instead, in May 1549 John Calvin (1509-64) and the Zurich theologians concluded the Consensus Tigurinus (Zurich Agreement), which defined it as the chief purpose of the Eucharist to attest and seal the → grace of God to believers.

The drafting of a Second Helvetic Confession was first of all a private enterprise of Heinrich Bullinger (1504-75) in Zurich in 1561. He completed it as his personal theological testament when sick of the plague in 1564. Prior to the Augsburg Diet in 1566 the Reformed elector Frederick III of the Palatinate (1559-76) requested a confession. Bullinger's text was proposed, and it received its final form in consultation with Theodore Beza (1519-1605) and Bern. It was published in 1566 in the names of the churches of Zurich, Bern, Schaffhausen, St. Gall, Chur, Mühlhausen, Biel, and Geneva. Basel at first declined to accept it, since it already had its own confession, but it later consented. Beza prepared a French version. The confession later found approval not only in St. Gall, Appenzell, and Neuchâtel but also as far afield as Scotland (1566) and France (1571). It was adopted by the Reformed church in Hungary (1567) and Poland (1570). Beginning in 1781 all Reformed churches under the Hapsburgs were officially known as churches of the Helvetic Confession. The Second Helvetic still retains its validity in Switzerland, though subscription to it ceased to be demanded in the 19th century.

The most comprehensive of the Reformed confessions, the Second Helvetic takes up the main theses of the First Helvetic and deals with almost all the articles of faith on a broad biblical and historical basis. Primary emphases are the doctrine of the → Word of God, the rejection of → images in the churches, a doctrine of → predestination that carefully amends Calvin's teaching (→ Calvin's Theology), the Reformed understanding of → law and gospel, justification by → faith and its fruits, the church under Christ as its sole Head, the Reformed understanding of the sacraments, and a Reformed concept of the church's ministry and → worship. A point that merits special attention is Bullinger's insistence that Reformed teaching is in full concert with that of the creeds and early councils and Fathers. He also maintains that agreement in essentials can go hand in hand with differences in nonessentials.

→ Calvinism; Heidelberg Catechism; Reformed and Presbyterian Churches; Reformers; Zwingli's Theology

Bibliography: Primary sources: BSRK 26.101-9; 29-30. 159-63; 31-32.170-221 • A. C. Cochrane, ed., *Reformed Confessions of the Sixteenth Century* (1966) 97-111 and 220-301 • P. Schaff, ed., *The Creeds of Christendom* (6th ed.; 3 vols.; New York, 1931) 3.211-31 and 233-306.

Secondary works: E. Koch, *Die Theologie der Confessio Helvetica Posterior* (Neukirchen, 1968) • R. Pfister, *Kirchengeschichte der Schweiz* (vol. 2; Zurich, 1974) 196-99, 211-14, 298-312 • J. Staedtke, ed., *Glauben und Bekennen. 400 Jahre Confessio Helvetica Posterior* (Zurich, 1966) • E. Zsindely, "Confessio Helvetica Posterior," *TRE* 8.169-73 (bibliography).

J. F. GERHARD GOETERS†

Henotheism

"Henotheism" (or "kathenotheism") refers to veneration of a single god as the true deity (→ God). It is a relative → monotheism that does not rule out the existence of other gods (→ Polytheism) and that finds cultic expression in the subjective monolatry of individual deities, which in turn may emerge as supreme. Inspired by the distinction made by F. W. J. von Schelling (1775-1854) between henotheism (Gk. *heis, henos,* "one") and monotheism (Gk. *monos,* "only"), Orientalist Max Müller (1823-1900) developed the concept, pointing out that the singer of the Vedas, invoking a particular god, was turning simply to the one god (Gk. *kath' hena theon*), the other gods retreating into the background and their mighty acts and attributes being ascribed to this one god. This form of religion, which makes it possible for one god to be invoked after another, each having the attributes of a supreme being not transcended by the others, Müller regarded as a transitional stage between polytheism and monotheism. Other scholars found similar thinking in the hymns of other religions, especially those of → Babylonian, → Egyptian, and → Greek religions.

Today, however, henotheism no longer ranks as a stage in the → evolution of → religion, nor is the term used to describe any special religion. Instead, it comes into use in the → phenomenology of religion inasmuch as religious people find special manifestations of power and love and wrath in their encounters with the particular deity that seems to be especially important for their lives. Historically speaking, henotheism might be regarded as an essential element in the movement of → syncretism that was promoted by the extension of the early kingdoms and that came to full flower in the empire of late antiquity.

Bibliography: H. VON GLASENAPP, *Die Religionen Indiens* (2d ed.; Stuttgart, 1956) 73-74 • F. HEILER, *Erscheinungsformen und Wesen der Religion* (2d ed.; Stuttgart, 1979) 460; idem, *Das Gebet* (5th ed.; Munich, 1923) 171ff. • G. VAN DER LEEUW, *Phänomenologie der Religion* (2d ed.; Tübingen, 1956; orig. pub., 1933) 189 • F. M. MÜLLER, *Vorlesungen über den Ursprung und die Entwicklung der Religion* (2d ed.; Strasbourg, 1881) 6th lect. • F. W. J. von SCHELLING, *Philosophie der Mythologie* (Stuttgart, 1857; repr., 1966) 4th lect. • W. SCHMIDT, *Der Ursprung der Gottesidee* (vol. 1; 2d ed.; Münster, 1926) 87, 94ff. • M. YUSA, "Henotheism," *EncRel(E)* 6.266-67.

CHRISTOPH ELSAS

Herder, Johann Gottfried

Johann Gottfried Herder (1744-1803), Lutheran theologian and philosopher, was born in Mohrungen in East Prussia. He began his study of → theology and → philosophy in 1762 in Königsberg, being strongly influenced there by the pre-Critique I. Kant and by J. G. Hamann, with the latter of whom Herder developed a lifelong friendship. Herder's studies included historical-critical biblical scholarship, the philosophy of G. W. Leibniz and C. Wolff, and so-called rational orthodoxy (e.g., S. J. Baumgarten). In 1764 Herder became a teacher at the cathedral school in Riga, serving also as a preacher. A sea journey led him to Nantes and Paris in 1769, where he studied French literature and historical philosophy. In 1770 Herder visited M. Claudius and G. E. Lessing. In Darmstadt he met Caroline Flachsland, whom he married in 1773.

Herder's *Essay on the Origin of Language* was awarded first prize by the Berlin Academy in 1771. Herder's thesis, prompting severe criticism from J. G. Hamann, was that human → language arose neither through supernatural instruction from God nor on the basis of pure convention; rather, it is rooted in the intellectual nature of human beings themselves. Also in 1771 Herder became a member of the consistory in Bückeburg, where he studied primeval history (writing *Oldest Documentation of the Human Race*). Developing influences from Hamann and combining these with his own understanding of history as God's planned revelatory activity, Herder discovered the language of the book of nature, that is, of creation's own glorification of God. Herder's mode of → exegesis is characterized by his interest in interpreting biblical texts in the context of Near Eastern and Eastern religions, in the light of, for example, the Zend-Avesta, and also by his poetic-literary assessment of the → Hebrew language (*On the Spirit of Hebrew Poetry,* 1782-83), a work that influenced later form-critical studies.

In 1776, on J. W. von Goethe's initiative, Herder became general → superintendent in Weimar, where he spent the rest of his life. In 1801 he became president of the High Consistory there. He supervised the establishment of a teacher's seminary and worked on reforming the → liturgy and → hymnal, opposing any → rationalist reworking of chorales. In 1788 he was offered and declined a professorship in theology in Göttingen.

This period in Weimar was Herder's most productive. In his *Letters concerning the Study of Theology* (1780-81), he drafted a plan of study circumscribing the entirety of theological science, responded to Lessing's (and Reimarus's) *Wolfenbüttel Fragments* (1774-78), and drew on Reformation-hermeneutical principles in defending the → canonical status of the Holy Scriptures as witness to God's revelation. In contrast to enlightened → rationalism, Herder sensed no contradiction between → reason and → revelation, subscribing instead to Lessing's notion as outlined in *The Education of the Human Race* that it was through revelation that the truths of reason became such in the first place.

→ Christology receded in Herder's thinking, and he distanced himself from the classical doctrine of → reconciliation. With a theory of the revivification of the Crucified resembling C. F. Bahrdt's thesis of Jesus' merely apparent death, Herder tried to assert at once both the historical credibility and the revelatory character of the Holy Scriptures.

During 1778-79 Herder edited a collection of folksongs *(Volkslieder)* and developed a draft of → salvation history in his *Outlines of a Philosophy of Human History* (1784-91). In the latter work Herder defined God as the origin and goal of all events, a view that exerted considerable influence all the way to Teilhard de Chardin.

In a synthesis of world history and anthropology, Herder understood history as a progressive development and education of the human genius in God's image, the human form of existence then culminating eschatologically in eternal life. I. Kant rejected this notion as the kind of metaphysical speculation that he had already overcome. In 1799 and 1800, and under the renewed influence of Hamann, Herder published two "metacritiques" of Kant, signaling at the same time his break with the Fichtean philosophy of → identity. This quarrel with Kant isolated Herder, a situation made even worse through his break with F. Schiller and Goethe. Herder died on December 18, 1803.

Bibliography: Primary sources: M. Bunge, ed., *Against Pure Reason: Writings on Religion, Language, and History* (Minneapolis, 1993) • J. G. Herder, *On the Origin of Language* (Chicago, 1986); idem, *The Spirit of Hebrew Poetry* (Naperville, Ill., 1971) • B. Suphan, ed., *Sämtliche Werke* (33 vols.; Berlin, 1877-1913).

Secondary works: P. Gardiner, "Herder, Johann Gottfried," *EncPh* 3.486-89 • G. Günther, A. A. Volgina, and S. Seifert, *Herder-Bibliographie* (Berlin, 1978) • R. Häfner, *Herders Kulturentstehungslehre* (Hamburg, 1995) • R. Haym, *Herder nach seinem Leben und Werken* (2 vols.; 2d ed.; Berlin, 1958; orig. pub., 1877-85) • F. W. Kantzenbach, *Johann Gottfried Herder mit Selbstzeugnissen und Bilddokumenten* (6th ed.; Reinbek, 1996; orig. pub., 1970) • W. Koepke, ed.,

Johann Gottfried Herder: Innovator through the Ages (Bonn, 1982) • D. Kuhles, *Herder-Bibliographie, 1977-1992* (Stuttgart, 1994) • M. Morton, *The Critical Turn: Studies in Kant, Herder, Wittgenstein, and Contemporary Theory* (Detroit, 1993) • R. E. Norton, *Herder's Aesthetics and the European Enlightenment* (Ithaca, N.Y., 1991) • T. Zippert, *Bildung durch Offenbarung* (Marburg, 1994).

Johann Anselm Steiger

Heresies and Schisms

1. Dogmatic Aspects
2. Historical Data
   2.1. Primitive Christianity
   2.2. Early Church
   2.3. Middle Ages
   2.4. Reformation
   2.5. Modern Period
   2.6. Ecumenical Discussion
   2.7. Roman Catholic Church
3. Historical Schisms

1. Dogmatic Aspects

Heresy is the opposite of pure doctrine (→ Orthodoxy). As schismatic deviation from the unity of faith, it belongs to the doctrine of the → church. It presupposes (1) the idea of a pure doctrine that, at least in demarcation, formulates → truth in doctrinal statements and thus defines the church's → unity. A verdict of heresy, however, also points to (2) criteria by which to distinguish redeeming faith in → Jesus Christ from sinful falsification. Finally, to establish heresy there is needed (3) a court that, in the name of the faithful, can name and lawfully exclude falsification.

1.1. All three criteria are necessary if the church is to be able to constitute itself as a community that achieves unity of → faith and publicly preserves and communicates the true message of the → gospel. On a Protestant view, however, the three criteria cannot be institutionalized but are open to constant theological reflection, with the result that heresy lies on the outer edge of the church's theological discipline. A zeal to confess should not lead us astray at this point, for it can work out in practice only in the form of an appeal to freedom of → conscience. The → Roman Catholic Church has put the problem in the hands of the → teaching office and thus decided what is orthodox for the church as an → institution. Since an evaluation of what is heresy belongs to the *esse* of the church in its unity of faith, by means of this papal teaching office the church has given itself a self-definition whose claim the members of the → World Council of Churches cannot accept and the Protestant churches of the → Reformation period condemned as itself heresy. The Reformation argument that no earthly institution can have the → authority to bind consciences is still convincing. A compelling slogan in this regard is that no one has control over the → Word of God.

1.2. The concept of pure truth gives rise to the opposing concept of heresy, which either falsifies truth or deviates from it by reduction. Since the Christian faith is not without content, it may be formulated, and its content may be taught in dogmatic theology (→ Dogmatics). Elements of truth are enumerated in the formulas of → confessions, which state positively what must be held and negatively what must be ruled out or even condemned. The demarcation of what is distinctively Christian from an arbitrary multiplicity of formulations rests on the fact that truth can only be one, and also on the fact that faith can have assurance of → salvation and that the content of such faith can also come to expression.

Such an approach also raises the whole problem of heresy, for, as a life of trust, faith is more than can be stated in doctrine; formulations in the form of theological teaching and confessional statements cannot fully and adequately express the truth that is believed. The exclusion of heresy is thus related to the joint inquiry into truth; a single person cannot be condemned as a heretic. We can thus understand why the path to unity in faith is one of convergence rather than full → consensus. In the process separations will occur, for attempts at the persuasion of others run up against limits at which it is impossible to find agreement.

1.3. On a Protestant view the most common criterion is the Word of God as we have it in the Holy Scriptures, the biblical → canon. Although *sola Scriptura* (→ Reformation Principles) is the unconditional norm, the canon itself has many voices, so that we also need to seek beyond its center. The church historically has decided for various expositions, which have then served as a basis for unity of faith. Protestants believe that the Reformation confessions correspond to the center of Scripture, which must be constantly established afresh by a combination of biblical → exegesis, church history, and dogmatics. In the Lutheran tradition (→ Lutheranism) there was a definitive collection in the Book of Concord (1580). In the Reformed tradition (→ Calvinism) each confession is a testimony that can be expanded. Hence the Lutherans debated whether the Barmen Declaration (1934) could be

accepted as a no less binding confession than those already endorsed, though there was no dispute concerning the declaration's repudiations as heresy.

1.4. A court that can pronounce anathema upon a doctrine runs contrary to the truth of the priesthood of all believers. On a Protestant view individuals can judge any doctrine. They cannot delegate their freedom of conscience, not even to a democratic process of discussion or the majority vote of a synod. The only possible authority is an obligation (albeit institutionalized) to the responsibility of understanding aright the Word of God as we have it in the Bible. This understanding is a special responsibility of those whom the church calls to public preaching and teaching. In extreme cases these persons may be removed from office, though not → excommunicated.

2. Historical Data

"Heresy" is derived from a Greek word. It denoted the various philosophical schools (→ Greek Philosophy) and, in the Jewish sphere, religious groups. In Christian usage it took on a negative connotation (1 Cor. 11:19). In the sense of → heterodoxy, it came to mean erroneous teaching (2 Pet. 2:1; see also 1 Tim. 6:3-5). It implied moral disqualification (see Gal. 5:20). Tertullian (ca. 160–ca. 225), linking it to the basic Greek idea of choice, found in it something arbitrary. Ephesians sums up the basic idea in a formula: "There is one body and one Spirit, just as you were called to the one hope of your calling, one Lord, one faith, one baptism, one God and Father of all" (4:4-6).

2.1. *Primitive Christianity*

The earliest sources show that (1) Christians were conscious of a claim to → truth, (2) belonging to the fellowship was dependent on agreement with the message, and (3) the person of Jesus was the basis of the common proclamation. The absolute claim to truth rested on direct divine → revelation, as one may see, for example, in → Paul (see Galatians 1–2). Human communication, which Paul himself allows (1 Cor. 15:1-3), is limited at first to the imparting of historical information concerning the life of Jesus, though it successively came to include insights deriving from this information. We see this process in the Gospels in their concealed redaction history and also in the Pauline Epistles up to the → Pastoral Epistles, in which preservation of the tradition is openly a basic principle (e.g., 1 Tim. 1:18-20). The Johannine writings also show interest in preserving a tradition that traces back to contemporaries of Jesus (1 John 1:1-4), but here the process of expansion is not simply reflected (v. 10) but is related to basic elements in the tradition of Jesus (2:22; 4:1-4).

It was an unusual thing in antiquity to contend so exclusively for the possession of truth that deviations were rejected as heterodox and the existence of schools like the philosophical schools was condemned as disruptive of fellowship. There were two reasons for it, both unique to Christianity and both alien to the philosophical spirit. The first was the tracing back of all doctrines to the person of Jesus, and the second was the religious certainty of possessing in the → confession of Jesus (→ Confession of Faith) as God's revelation the truth that links us to God. Insofar as faith in Jesus as Christ and Lord gave assurance of eternal → salvation, it created an exclusive fellowship in confessional formulations (see Ignatius). Those who in their preaching did not adopt the basic elements (e.g., among the itinerant preachers and teachers) were said to be led astray by the → devil. In the earliest documents there is no toleration of competing forms of belief except in the apostolic decree of Galatians 2 and Acts 15 (echoed in Justin Martyr *Dial.* 47). In the → canon, however, different traditions were left unreconciled side by side.

2.2. Early Church
In the middle of the second century the rise of Christian → Gnosticism made the distinguishing of correct belief from heresy a main theme of theology and a main problem for the church. Perhaps it was not by chance that this issue arose at the time when the → apologists were speaking in the name of Christianity and the application of the name "Christian" also became problematic because of external considerations (see also the views of the pagan philosopher Celsus, in Origen *C. Cels.* 3.10-12). The case of Marcion (d. ca. 160) was plain at once, even without theological deliberation. His hatred of the Creator, his rejection of Scripture (the Jewish Bible), and his revision of the canon made his irreconcilability apparent. Two churches resulted (→ Marcionites).

The Christian Gnostics (e.g., Basilides and Valentinus) founded schools that, on the basis of exposition of the Gospels and Paul, tried to elevate simple Christians to higher knowledge and greater separation from the world. Accordingly, they were credible and even attractive, in spite of coming under suspicion of harboring a sense of superiority. The first generation could apparently indulge only in futile denunciations of individuals, but Irenaeus (d. ca. 200) unmasked their system and, in spite of similarities of confession, pointed out the differences, namely, the doctrine of the Creator and the identity of Christ and Jesus (*Adv. haer.* 4 pref.). In

addition to illogicalities in the system, Irenaeus found as his formal basis for refutation the fact that all that we know about Jesus Christ was written by the → apostles and is publicly known and preserved in the church's → tradition. Since the Christian Gnostics began with biblical interpretation and built on the canon, teachers like Irenaeus and Tertullian also set forth a → rule of faith *(regula fidei)* as a doctrinal summary.

Broader theological debate came first with the Alexandrians Clement (ca. 150-ca. 215) and Origen (ca. 185-ca. 254), who, quoting 1 Cor. 11:19, realized that orthodox theology is formed only in controversy with heresies (→ Alexandrian Theology; Origenism). At the end of the second century we also hear that Roman bishops were removing heretics, and in Asia Minor a synod took action against the → Montanists. The decisions of regional bishops in condemnation and exclusion of heresy found general recognition inasmuch as the → church was universal and was regarded as → catholic.

The rulings of the → synods that Emperor Constantine (306-37) and his Christian successors called could be regarded as accepted by the whole church. The → bishops formulated orthodoxy as a confession and rejected heretical teachings in the form of anathemas. Those who refused to subscribe were deprived of office and banished by the emperor. Heretical books were burned, and their possession was forbidden. The laity had to do penance (→ Penitence) for heresy in accordance with the church's regulations. Nevertheless, although the confession of Nicaea (endorsed at the First Council of Constantinople, 381; → Niceno-Constantinopolitan Creed) prevailed against → Arianism, and the church had imperial support against heretical deviations from orthodoxy, heresy remained a constant threat. Churches still exist (→ Oriental Orthodox Churches) that arose out of the heresies condemned at the Councils of → Ephesus (431) and → Chalcedon (451).

Clarity was sought by the compiling of lists of heresies (notably by Epiphanius and Philaster), but even in regard to past heresies it had to be conceded that these were incomplete. Even Augustine (354-430) regarded the definition of heresy as very difficult, and the simple formula was adopted that everything that differs from the catholic faith is heretical. (Cf. the canon of Vincent of Lérins, which defines catholicity as "what has been believed everywhere, always, and by all.")

2.3. Middle Ages
Inasmuch as medieval theologians simply collected the teachings of the Fathers and unified them in new systems (→ Scholasticism), they could regard

agreement with tradition as the criterion of orthodoxy and disagreement with it as the mark of heresy.
The new element in the Middle Ages, apart from
doctrinal controversy, was the rise of the → Cathari
and the → Waldenses, who in opposing ways contested the sacramental way of salvation in the papal
church. In the Investiture Controversy (→ Empire
and Papacy) church office had been tied to the papal
→ hierarchy. Laity who made church appointments
were declared to be heretics (→ Simony), with excommunication as the penalty for disobedience; ongoing excommunication with no sign of penitence
raised the suspicion of heresy. Measures against the
new deviations were thus simply a logical attempt
by the new official sacramental hierarchy to assert
itself (→ Clergy and Laity). The → Inquisition was
set up against them, against their adherents, and
against those who protected them by failing to de-
nounce them. The secular arm punished the guilty
by burning, for despising the church counted as a
form of lèse-majesté. The long-simmering conflict
between Pope Gregory IX (1227-41) and Emperor
Frederick II (1215-50) typifies these tensions.

2.4. Reformation

The papal church condemned the → Reformation
as heresy, excommunicating M. → Luther (1483-
1546) in 1521 (for details, see the proceedings of →
Trent, Council of). The → Reformers then had to
defend themselves against the charge of heresy. Luther called for a general council, but he still insisted
that he be refuted by the → Word of God ("the testimony of the Scriptures or by clear reason," as he said
at Worms [LW 32.112]). Zwingli took the same
view, claiming in article 1 of his Sixty-seven Theses
(1523), "All those who say that the gospel is nothing
without the confirmation of the church make a mistake and blaspheme God." Calvin, too, justified separation from the church by the fact that the unity of
the church rests on pure doctrine according to
God's Word (see Inst. 4.2.5). They all maintained
this position in considerable deviation from traditional modes of exposition (→ Calvin's Theology;
Luther's Theology; Zwingli's Theology). By making
loyalty to the Bible the only criterion of orthodoxy
as distinct from heresy, they set up in principle an
institutional court that could decide concerning
heresy (see 1), equating personal trust in God's
Word with the understanding of the Bible.

The Reformation churches defended themselves
against individual caprice by laying down pure doctrine in confessions for the public (for both church
and school) and appealing to the fact that these presentations and rejections are established by the
Word of God in Holy Scripture. The Reformers

charged the → Anabaptists and enthusiasts with not
keeping to the written ("external") Word of God.
They were thus heretics, and by setting up conventicles they incurred secular punishment for rebellion.
The new imperial law of 1532 contained no sections
on heretics.

2.5. Modern Period

The Reformation churches believed that the secular
powers had a duty to provide for true worship of
God (the first table of the → Decalogue). By the
Peace of Augsburg in 1555 (→ Augsburg, Peace of)
the states had responsibility in this sphere. Although
→ orthodoxy almost equated theology with the
faith that is necessary to salvation, and polemical
demarcation resulted in increasingly comprehensive
statement, some — especially among Lutherans (→
Lutheranism) and Calvinists (→ Calvinism) —
wanted to transcend mutual condemnation; theological argument was to be a recourse to fundamental articles of faith (G. Calixtus [1586-1656]).

From the → Enlightenment and → Pietism came
a demand to end heresy-hunting on the ground that
true faith does not consist of agreement with doctrines and that state law can provide religious tolerance (freedom of conscience) without in any way
damaging community. Where theology took a historical path in the 18th century, a history of religious
parties and teachings resulted, as did the history of
dogma, which divested historical confessions of their
binding → authority and charged fanatics and enthusiasts with heresy (→ Dogma, History of).

Demonstration of the historical emergence of
the biblical books (→ Exegesis, Biblical) seemed to
eliminate any objective reference point to which
dogmaticians might appeal (→ Dogmatics). The
unavoidable result would have been to make heresy
the heteronomy of authority as opposed to autonomous → reason. It was recognized, however, that
faith as the pious consciousness has a concern to
promote itself, so that doctrines of the faith could
also speak of heresies. Yet there should be no condemnation, for the pious mind is a bond of fellowship, and a fellowship of mind is canceled where
there is defective → Christology or → soteriology
(F. Schleiermacher). The → theology of revivals
sought the required objectivity in confessionalism
(→ Denomination) and fervently denounced heresies in its own church.

F. C. Baur (1792-1860) viewed the history of theology according to the dialectical principle of
G. W. F. Hegel (→ Dialectic; Hegelianism) and tried
to understand the historical heresies as steps to a
synthesis that still had to be found. In this regard he
saw it as the inalienable task of church history to

give a fresh hearing to the heresies that had been condemned but, in so doing, to appropriate critically the nexus of tradition.

2.6. Ecumenical Discussion

Ecumenical discussion of heresy is deeply characterized by a relativity of dogmatic claims, which are differentiated not so much by historical priorities (see W. Bauer, 1934) as by consideration of the arguments. The experience of encounter in ecumenical conversations (esp. in the world conferences of → Faith and Order, beginning at Lausanne in 1927; → Ecumenism, Ecumenical Movement) has taught, on the one hand, that the division of Christianity is to be felt as a burden and, on the other, that there can be no → unity without common doctrinal formulation. The Third World Conference of Faith and Order, at Lund in 1952, discussed the terms "schism," "heresy," and → "apostasy" and determined that heresy can arise only in relation to certain essential articles, though orders and structures are not exempt inasmuch as they are grounded in the concept of the church (Edinburgh, 1937).

In keeping with the increasing attention to the world responsibility of Christians, → koinonia is expounded as a "fully committed fellowship" (Third Assembly of the → World Council of Churches, at New Delhi in 1961). The idea of moral heresy has been introduced relative to the practical conduct of church members (W. A. Visser t' Hooft at the fourth assembly, at Uppsala in 1968).

German church history under A. Hitler showed the need for condemnation, and follow-up is needed in the ethical field in such matters as → racism and → peace.

2.7. Roman Catholic Church

Since the Reformation the Roman Catholic Church has maintained an impressive identity in an institutionalized self-consciousness (→ Catholicism [Roman]). Against the Reformation churches it appealed to the Bible and also to unwritten apostolic teachings that had either been given orally by Christ or dictated by the Holy Spirit and preserved in unbroken succession in the church. It gave highest place to "holy mother church, whose function is to pass judgment on the true meaning and interpretation of the sacred scriptures" (Trent sess. 4; DH 1507; Tanner, 2.664).

What the Reformation churches claimed for the invisible church, the Catholic Church claimed for the papacy. "When the Roman pontiff speaks *ex cathedra,* that is, when, in the exercise of his office as shepherd and teacher of all Christians, in virtue of his supreme apostolic authority, he defines a doctrine concerning faith or morals to be held by the whole church, he

possesses, by the divine assistance promised to him in blessed Peter, that infallibility which the divine Redeemer willed his church to enjoy in defining doctrine concerning faith or morals" (DH 3074; Tanner, 2.816; → Vatican I; → Infallibility; Teaching Office). The corresponding legal definition of heresy is thus obvious: "Heresy is the obstinate post-baptismal denial of some truth which must be believed with divine and catholic faith, or it is likewise an obstinate doubt concerning the same" (1983 CIC 751).

There is lively debate among theologians on how to apply this definition. → Vatican II recognized "an order or 'hierarchy' of truths" (*Unitatis redintegratio* 11) but did not offer a closed list. It is also allowed that churches deriving from heresies share in the fundamentals of the faith, so that → dialogue with them can be profitable to both sides. Theologians argue for a legitimate → pluralism in the church. Since this feature involves the risk of error, the question of heresy and its demarcation from orthodoxy is raised within the church. How is the discipline of theology to be related to the church's teaching office?

3. Historical Schisms

The term "schism," like "heresy," denotes separation from the one church. A schism is a division that breaks the bond of love. The idea that a schism relates only to order and not, like heresy, to dogma, goes back to Origen (→ Origenism). By way of a canonical letter of Basil the Great of Caesarea (ca. 330-79, *Ep.* 188), it made its way into church law in the East. Because Cyprian (ca. 200-258) judged that separation from a valid → bishop was an offense against belief in the unity of the church, he regarded the opposing church of Novatian (ca. 200-257/58) as heresy (→ Heretical Baptism). Jerome (ca. 345-420) claimed that every schism thinks up a heresy to justify the split. Augustine, after initial hesitation, finally denied to the → Donatists the status of schismatics, since their separation amounted to stubborn rebellion.

Dogmatic differences caused (e.g., the Acacian schism, 484-519) or accompanied (e.g., the Photian schism, from 867; mutual excommunications by the bishop of Rome and the → patriarch of Constantinople in 1054; → Byzantium) the schisms between the Eastern and Western churches. This split has not yet been healed. In the West differences brought about schisms that reached a climax in the Great Schism (1378-1417; → Conciliarism; Pope, Papacy; Reform Councils).

These historic experiences produced a canonical definition in the Roman Catholic Church: "Schism is the refusal of submission to the Roman Pontiff or of communion with the members of the Church subject to him" (1983 CIC 751, cf. 1364). Since the primacy of papal → jurisdiction is a dogma, the definition of schism hardly differs from that of heresy.

Given their understanding of the church, the Protestant churches have found it hard to develop a doctrine of schism, either canonically or theologically.

→ Church; Ecumenical Theology; Hussites; Legitimation; Monophysites; Pelagianism; Religion, Legal Protection of; Religious Liberty; Teaching Office

Bibliography: C. A. F. ALLISON, The Cruelty of Heresy: An Affirmation of Christian Orthodoxy (Harrisburg, Pa., 1994) • D. BAKER, ed., Schism, Heresy, and Religious Protest (London, 1972) • W. BAUER, Rechtgläubigkeit und Ketzerei im ältesten Christentum (Tübingen, 1934; 2d ed., 1964) • P. L. BERGER, Der Zwang zur Häresie. Religion in der pluralistischen Gesellschaft (Frankfurt, 1992) • H. D. BETZ, A. SCHINDLER, and W. HUBER, "Häresie," TRE 14.313-41 (bibliography) • P. BILLER and R. B. DOBSON, eds., The Medieval Church: Universities, Heresy, and the Religious Life (Woodbridge, Suffolk, 1999) • D. J. BINGHAM, Irenaeus' Use of Matthew's Gospel in Adversus Haereses (Louvain, 1998) • N. BROX, "Häresie," RAC 13.248-97 • M.-J. CONGAR, "Schisme," DTC 14/1.1286-1312 • Y. CONGAR, "Abspaltungen von der Einheit der Kirche," MySal 4/1.411-57 • B. D. EHRMAN, The Orthodox Corruption of Scripture: The Effect of Early Christological Controversies on the Text of the NT (New York, 1993) • R. M. GRANT, Heresy and Criticism: The Search for Authenticity in Early Christian Literature (Louisville, Ky., 1993) • M. D. LAMBERT, Medieval Heresy: Popular Movements from Bogomil to Hus (2d ed.; Oxford, 1992) • G. LEFF, Heresy in the Later Middle Ages: The Relation of Heterodoxy to Dissent (2 vols.; Manchester, 1967) • W. LOURDAUX and D. VERHELST, eds., The Concept of Heresy in the Middle Ages (11th-13th Cent.) (Louvain, 1976) • G. LÜDEMANN, Heretics: The Other Side of Early Christianity (Louisville, Ky., 1996) • A. MICHEL, "Hérésie. Hérétique," DTC 6.2208-57 • K. RAHNER, "Häresien in der Kirche heute?" Schriften zur Theologie (vol. 9; Cologne, 1970) 453-78; idem, "Was ist Häresie?" ibid. (vol. 5; Cologne, 1962) 527-76 • E. SEHLING, "Schisma," RE 17.575-80 • N. P. TANNER, ed., Decrees of the Ecumenical Councils (2 vols.; London, 1990) • H. E. W. TURNER, The Pattern of Christian Truth: A Study in the Relations between Orthodoxy and Heresy in the Early Church (1907; New York, 1978) • S. L. WAUGH and P. D. DIEHL, Christendom and Its Discontents: Exclusion, Persecution, and Rebellion, 1000-1500 (Cambridge, 1996) • K. WENGST, Häresie und Orthodoxie im Spiegel des 1 Johannesbriefs (Gütersloh, 1986).

EKKEHARD MÜHLENBERG

Heretical Baptism

1. In the third century the question arose for the first time how to treat believers returning to the → church from dissident groups. Was the → baptism that they had received outside the church valid or not? In North Africa (perhaps under the influence of Tertullian's De bapt. 15) and also in Asia Minor, synods were held between A.D. 220 and 230 that ruled that heretical baptism was invalid and hence that believers who came over to the church had to receive the church's baptism (as their first baptism; see Cyprian Ep. 73.3.1, 75.7.5; Eusebius Hist. eccl. 7.5.5, 7.7.5). As regards Rome, there is no record of any synodal decision, but Stephen I (254-57) appealed to the Roman tradition of receiving returning baptized converts in the same way as returning Catholics, namely, by the mere → laying on of hands (Cyprian Ep. 74.1).

Conflict arose between the two different practices only in 255, when for the first time Novatianists in North Africa wished to join the Catholic Church. The Novatianists seem themselves to have rebaptized the baptized Catholics who joined them (see Cyprian Ep. 73.2). Cyprian of Carthage (ca. 200-258) became a strong champion of the African tradition (Ep. 69). As he saw it, it made no difference that the Novatianists were just schismatics and not heretics (→ Heresies and Schisms). They had founded their own church, and the African confession that they used in baptism was against them, namely, the confession of faith in the remission of sins and eternal life through the holy church (Ep. 69.7.2). The Council of Carthage in 255 supported Cyprian (Ep. 70).

In answer to the question whether this ruling did not go against the Roman tradition, Cyprian drew attention to the difference between the two kinds of converts. Those baptized in the Catholic Church did not need baptism, but those baptized by dissidents did (Ep. 71.2). Early in 256 another Carthaginian council ruled in Cyprian's favor. The decision was sent with an accompanying letter to Stephen (Ep. 72), but the latter would not receive the African delegation and threatened → excommunication (see Ep. 75.25).

When Firmilian of Caesarea in Cappadocia (d. 268), in a letter to Cyprian (Ep. 75) at the end of 256, assured his colleague of the full support of the churches of Asia Minor on the issue and complained vehemently of Stephen's lack of collegiality, Stephen threatened these churches as well with excommunication (Eusebius Hist. eccl. 7.5.4). With the death of both Stephen and Cyprian, however, the dispute ended with no further consequences. Possibly Dionysius of Alexandria (d. ca. 265) acted as a mediator shortly afterward, though his own position is not clear.

2. In the fourth and fifth centuries, during the → Donatist controversy in North Africa, the issue arose again. The Council of Arles in 314 (can. 8) had ruled against the Donatists in favor of the Roman practice, as long as the heretics had been "baptized into the Father, the Son, and the Holy Spirit." The Donatists, however, cited Cyprian as their main witness. Augustine (354-430) was at great pains to whitewash Cyprian *(De bapt.)*. He himself accepted the Roman view and gave it an ecclesiological basis (→ Augustine's Theology). In spite of its toleration of dissident baptism, the Catholic Church could take very intolerant measures against heresy and schism.

Augustine wanted the → state to force the Donatists back into the church for their own → salvation (appealing to Luke 14:23; see also his *Ep.* 93, 185). His practice shows that the question of the relation between baptism and ecclesiology, or baptism and the gift of the Spirit as the Reformation would see it, had not been solved by his interpretation of the rite and the resultant recognition of heretical baptism.

→ Early Church

Bibliography: Primary source: C. MIRBT and A. ALAND, *Quellen zur Geschichte des Papsttums und des römischen Katholizismus* (vol. 1; 6th ed.; Tübingen, 1967) 182-207.

Secondary works: G. VON BAREILLE, "Baptême des hérétiques," *DTC* 2.219-33 • A. BENOÎT and C. MUNIER, *Le baptême dans l'église ancienne* (Bern, 1994) • W. C. FREND, *The Donatist Church: A Movement of Protest in Roman North Africa* (Oxford, 1985) • P. B. HINCHLIFF, *Cyprian of Carthage and the Unity of the Christian Church* (London, 1974) • G. KRETSCHMAR, "Die Geschichte des Taufgottesdienstes," *Leit.* 5/1.1-346 • G. W. H. LAMPE, *The Seal of the Spirit* (2d ed.; London, 1967; orig. pub., 1951) • C. MUNIER, *Le baptême dans l'église ancienne* (Bern, 1994) • J. J. SEBASTIAN, ". . . *Baptisma unum in sancta ecclesia . . .": A Theological Appraisal of the Baptismal Controversy in the Work and Writings of Cyprian of Carthage* (Delhi, 1997) • G. S. M. WALKER, *The Churchmanship of St. Cyprian* (Richmond, Va., 1969) • G. G. WILLIS, *St. Augustine and the Donatist Controversy* (London, 1950).

WILLY RORDORF

Hermeneutics

1. OT
    1.1. Significance
    1.2. Approach
    1.3. Task
2. NT
    2.1. Concept and Task
    2.2. History
    2.3. Modern Problems
3. Philosophy and Theology
    3.1. Concept and Task
    3.2. Hermeneutical Philosophy
    3.3. Hermeneutical Theology
    3.4. Results and Criticism

The original meaning of "hermeneutics" is "translation" in the broadest sense: the authoritative → communication of a message (e.g., from God) that needs a mediator, the rendering of a text from one language into another, and the exposition of something said or written with a view to bringing out its → meaning. The term is derived from the Greek *hermēneuō,* "interpret, explain, translate." The root derives from the name of the Greek god Hermes, the mediator of meaning between the realm of gods and that of human beings. In the NT the term (including its use with the prefixes *dia-* and *meta-*) is translated "interpret" (Luke 24:27; see also 1 Cor. 12:10), "explain" (Luke 24:27 NEB), "translate" (John 1:38, 42), and "mean" (Heb. 7:2). In Acts 14:12 Paul, taken to be a god in human form, is "called Hermes, because he was the chief speaker."

1. OT

1.1. *Significance*

The Hebrew Bible, known to Christians as the Old Testament, has status as Holy Scripture for both → Judaism and Christianity and is also important to the Koran of → Islam as a source of information and tradition for that faith. Its vitality to Judaism began early in the formation of the community of → Israel (§1), when parts of its present form were considered authoritative for faith and practice, such as core statutes and summaries of law, ritual prescriptions, poetic outcries of both pain and celebration, and collections of sayings of prophets and wise thinkers.

Its vitality to Christian faith began with the use of parts of it by → Jesus, → Paul, the gospel authors, and writers of other NT books. The argument over its necessity for Christian guidance, raised by Marcion (d. ca. 160), was answered by the church with a decisive Yes in its march toward establishing a → canon of Scripture.

Its importance to Islam is seen both in the Koran's dependence on various narratives, characters, and events (e.g., Hagar's exile [Genesis 16; 21:8-21; cf. Koran 14:35-39]) and in the prominence of some ideas in Islamic theology, such as the apocalyptic vision of the end times and the judgment of the human race (Dan. 11:40–12:13; cf. Koran 12; 81; 82).

1.2. Approach

Even with the development of various aspects of biblical research (from earliest scribal corrections to canonical criticism) over 3,000 years, each of which contributes its part to the total understanding and → interpretation of the OT, still the most basic hermeneutical encounter is with an individual textual unit, or pericope. In seeking to interpret a given story, song, law, poem, or other segment of the material now enclosed in the OT, a sound hermeneutical approach includes the elements and perspectives outlined in the following paragraphs. The overall approach applies for any version of the OT, → Apocrypha and → pseudepigrapha included.

The first task is to ascertain the state of the *text* itself. Are all the words clear? Are there different readings or different witnesses to what the text says? Use of the various language options, the textual variants, the changes in vocabulary, and all related materials are basic to ascertaining just what sentences have been produced in the unit under consideration.

The second step is to discern the *form* of the unit. Is it poetry of a particular sort, a special type of prophetic speech, a conditional or absolute law, a new or unique form of expression without parallel elsewhere in Scripture? The form itself sometimes has a certain meaning, including its use in a given context, with implications for the overall application of the pericope.

Once the text and form are clear, one should look for any *pre- or extrabiblical use* of such a unit in other ancient Near Eastern texts. Israel borrowed materials from Canaan as well as other surrounding countries. Light from such sources can occasionally illuminate what biblical writers had in mind by using material that reflected the "common knowledge" of the times. The prohibition against cooking a kid in its mother's milk (Exod. 23:19; 34:26), for example, makes more sense when it is seen as proscribing Israel's participation in a common Canaanite ritual (see J. C. Rylaarsdam, "Exodus: Text, Exegesis," *IB* 1.1013-14).

Given the centuries-old enterprise of examining physical remains for evidence of the biblical people and the events they report, one should ask whether there are → *archaeological data* that shed light on

the unit, and if so, what they suggest. Arguments persist about the value of such connections. To see the actual size of ancient defensive and other walls, however, and to know the location of old travel routes can enable one to gain new insight into "the shade of a great rock" (Isa. 32:2), both as refuge from the midday heat and as a dangerous place where robbers or others of ill will might be hiding, or even a place from which to spring a military ambush (Josh. 8:1-23). References to water jars, broken pots, and the hazards of cisterns all beg for the light of archaeology to be shed on them. Jeremiah's teaching about how the Lord would break rebellious Judah "as one breaks a potter's vessel" by smashing it on the ground (Jer. 19:11) reflected a real slice of everyday life then, just as it remains vivid to this day.

At this point one may ask about the *first OT use* of the unit and what its meaning or meanings may have been in that literary setting. Given the long period of oral transmission of most units before they were put into writing, however, it is sometimes impossible to trace back the original meanings to the community out of whose travels and experiences, faith and practices, the utterance was first coined. To begin with, the best we can do is to approximate its apparent use and meaning in its present context, unless there are clear extrabiblical evidences of its earlier functions.

It is appropriate to ask, beyond the immediate impressions the unit gives, whether it appears in *later OT contexts*, how it may have been revised, and what use and meaning(s) each revision suggests. That is, the OT itself is the first "hermeneutical workshop" for OT texts. This feature is apparent in the → Pentateuch, for examination of the stories of Israel's beginnings shows that the earliest ones were first systematically collected and edited about 950 B.C. (commonly referred to as the J source, for its association with Judah and its use of YHWH [Yahweh, Ger. *Jahwe*] for God's name). A century later the earliest texts were reexamined, sometimes revised, supplemented with new material, and sometimes rearranged (by the so-called E source, for its northern association [tribe of Ephraim] and its use of Elohim for the name of God). Then in the eighth century Deuteronomic reformers produced another revision (the D source, for the new material in Deuteronomy), and later again, between the sixth and fourth centuries, by scribes with priestly and ritual interests (P source, mainly in Leviticus) trying to reconstitute a pure Israelite community in place of the one destroyed by Assyrian and → Babylonian aggression (ca. 721 and 597-586 B.C.). In each stage, new circumstances saw new meanings and new emphases take shape in the treatment of the stories. Just as in our own time, the meaning was searched for its relevance to the new situations encountered in life, and the interpretive process was continued for each successive audience. The same process occurred when early Christian writers took basic prophetic texts and reapplied them to their understandings in the wake of Jesus' life among them.

It is also vital to examine the *various OT literary settings* in which the unit may appear. Events are sometimes celebrated poetically as well as reported in a prose form. Major examples here are the celebration of Israel's deliverance from Egyptian slavery to freedom as a people. The story and event described in Exodus 12–14 are also celebrated and interpreted poetically in the Song of Moses (Exod. 15:1-18) and the Song of Miriam (vv. 20-21). Similarly, the Song of Deborah (Judges 5) puts the memories of the slaying of the Canaanite commander Sisera (Judges 4) in a different literary form. The aids to remembering, such as summaries of law as ten commandments (e.g., in Exod. 20:1-17; Deut. 5:6-21; lit. "the Ten Words," Exod. 34:28 NEB), or repetitive phrases citing the same idea in a prophet's speech (Jer. 25:30) or a psalm (Ps. 92:12), reflect what it was like to keep important things in mind while living without available written records, or without libraries for storing important materials for managing life. The literary forms of a curse, of a lament over loss at death, or of an obligation conditional on some combination of circumstances all speak of regular patterns of utterance used and considered transportable for use in various times and places judged appropriate. They help us understand the life situation in which a form took shape, to which it was intended to speak with particular power.

It is now possible to ask what role or meaning the unit has for Israel's *theology,* that is, Israel's sense of God, God's presence, God's character, God's will. Israel's pilgrimage worked its way theologically from multiple gods in the religions of its neighboring cultures to hints of multiple gods worshiped and served by its ancestors (e.g., "the gods [that] your ancestors served," Josh. 24:14-15). First clearly cited by the prophet of the exile commonly called Second Isaiah, Israel's belief that besides YHWH "there is no other" (Isa. 45:5-6) became normative in the exilic period as the → monotheism that characterizes Judaic, Christian, and Islamic theology to this day. While some changes in the characterization of God occur, each biblical unit reflects its place in the process of theological formation occurring throughout the OT. Variations in theological aspects of the meaning of a pericope will occur within each of the religious communities devoted to these texts, as well as from one community to the others. Serious effort to find what the text may mean in today's life requires that we determine, if possible, what role it has played in the growing awarenesses of God, both God's character and will.

At this stage one should ascertain, as relevant, the *first use in the NT.* Writers of the NT use OT passages in a variety of ways. Both the criteria of selection and the specific application to the "new" situation will shed light especially on what meaning the NT writer intended to convey. One of many illustrations of this point appears in Joel Marcus's discussion of uses made of OT material by the author of the Gospel of Mark in the very first verses of the gospel. Here the writer conflates OT material and applies it in the context of "proclamation" to a Christian community under stress in the agitation of the Jewish revolt against Rome in A.D. 66-70 (J. Marcus, *Mark 1–8* [New York, 2000] Introduction and 141-49). As the "beginning of the good news," it is intended to interpret Jesus and his proclamations in a context of stress and suffering, giving aid and hope to the audience the writer addressed in the mid-first century. That setting suggests clues to its possible meaning for modern people, also suffering stress, if not political persecution or the devastations of war.

As with the OT, so also with the NT, units are sometimes used in more than one place or by more than one author; in the process, the use and meaning may change. Thus it is incumbent to search for *other NT uses* of the unit. The writer of the Gospel of Matthew clearly intends to employ as many OT references as possible to support his claim that Jesus fulfilled OT expectations in all aspects of his life and death (e.g., Matt. 1:22; 2:5, 17; 3:3, etc.). OT apocalyptic expectations are "translated" in the speech attributed to Jesus in Matt. 24:3-8, as they are in Paul's first letter to the Thessalonians (4:13-18), Mark's chapter 13, and the bulk of the book of Revelation. Tracking a single unit or a pattern of ideas is important in determining the use and meaning the early Christians found in the OT material.

In addition to insights gained from the NT canonical material, it is often helpful in understanding an OT pericope to examine its *use by other groups.* A first choice might be the → Gnostics, given the abundance of materials from → Nag Hammadi. Marcion and his arguments could also be explored. Attention should also be paid to the differences between the emerging Christian churches and their Jewish neighbors. Christians borrowed heavily from

Jewish hermeneutical methods (esp. in their attention to texts, translations, and methods of historical and allegorical interpretation; → Bible Versions), and the emergence of a Christian theology that accommodated not only the God of the OT but the person of Jesus and the continuing felt presence of God's activities in their communal life was itself a process that continues into modern life.

It is also important to examine the place of a pericope in *the history of doctrine and the life of the church* — liturgical, devotional, and even organizational. Some units have become firmly planted in Judaic, Christian, and Islamic thought. Deut. 6:4, for example, claiming that God is one, is an example of a biblical text that has become central to all three bodies of believers. An implication of this belief is that all activity involving human devotion to, worship of, or obedience to any other power, reality, or ideal is what defines idolatry, unfaithfulness, misguided behavior, and mistaken thinking. Islam goes so far as to cite forgetfulness of God as the primary sin of humans (hence the requirement to pray five times every day). Ritual life in Judaism, Christianity, and Islam (→ Rite) reflects in common the obligation to remember God's gracious acts, thus keeping life focused where its center belongs.

The purpose of all these explorations is to interpret the biblical text for modern human life. What are the *contemporary applications* of this pericope in daily life? For some units there may not be any clearly in view. Conditions change, and some admonitions no longer apply in today's largely urban setting (→ City). Furthermore, with the changing conditions of life in the digital age, only extrapolated or analogous applications may be possible. Yet basic human questions about what life is, what it can become, how the self may interact in various social formats from family to the global village, and related questions of how to treat one's fellow humans in all their conditions and locations are always relevant. The limitation of → death still needs to be understood and interpreted within the theology given in biblical forms. Theological, intellectual, ritual, social, and global concerns call for translating biblical insights into the stuff of daily life for ordinary people. Such translation is the primary task of → preaching as biblical → proclamation. Patterns of organization to allow it must be explored in the ever-changing social scene, and the fellowship of believers must be nourished by the best proclamatory and educational insights believers can muster.

Third World perspectives need to be explored for the riches they can provide and for the insights that Western intellectual history may have missed in its affluence, power, and gross self-absorption. Westerners need to listen to their brothers and sisters in other cultures. The relative lack of sophisticated technological distractions in the → Third World (however short-lived such lack may be) may allow a different focus and sensitivity and, most important, a differently stirred imagination by which to hear and speak the will of God conveyed through Scripture.

Interest in unfolding biblical insights continues to draw *new voices* into the discussion. We have had about 30 years of genuine help from women's work on interpreting biblical texts (→ Feminist Theology). Voices added from Latin American perspectives (→ Liberation Theology), as well as from African and African American participants (→ African Theology), complement the evolution of subspecialties such as rhetorical criticism, linguistic analysis (→ Linguistics), storytelling, and many others that explore the pericopes from new angles and perspectives.

1.3. Task

If the center of the OT is the interaction of → Yahweh with the people of Israel, its goal is surely the creation and support of human life at its maximum potential for mutual support and excellence in achievements — from → healing the sick to all forms of nourishing wholeness and richness of human expression.

The hermeneutical task is to proclaim the biblical content in the face of all misguided human standards and endeavors. Then can begin a creation of new life that not only well serves the human communities but endures far beyond the span of any given society or time. Such is God's gift of life in a universe in which, viewed both temporally and spatially, the natural condition is death. Such is the biblical message of → grace, which comes from God alone.

→ Exegesis, Biblical

Bibliography: J. Barton, *Reading the OT: Method in Biblical Study* (Louisville, Ky., 1996); idem, ed., *The Cambridge Companion to Biblical Interpretation* (Cambridge, 1998) • A. Brenner et al., eds., *A Feminine Companion to Reading the Bible: Approaches, Methods, and Strategies* (Sheffield, 1997) • W. Brueggemann, *Interpretation and Obedience: From Faithful Reading to Faithful Living* (Minneapolis, 1991) • R. Carroll and M. Daniel, *Contexts for Amos: Prophetic Poetics in Latin American Perspective* (Sheffield, 1992) • M. Fishbane, *The Garments of Torah: Essays in Biblical Hermeneutics* (Bloomington, Ind., 1989) • F. C. Holmgren, *The OT and the Significance of Jesus: Em-*

bracing Change–Maintaining Christian Identity. The Emerging Center in Biblical Scholarship (Grand Rapids, 1999) • J. KALTNER, *The Use of Arabic in Biblical Hebrew Lexicography* (Washington, D.C., 1996) • A. LACOCQUE and P. RICOEUR, *Thinking Biblically: Exegetical and Hermeneutical Studies* (Chicago, 1998) • J. D. LEVENSON, *The Hebrew Bible, the OT, and Historical Criticism: Jews and Christians in Biblical Studies* (Louisville, Ky., 1993) • S. SEKINE, *Transcendency and Symbols in the OT: A Genealogy of Hermeneutical Experiences* (Berlin, 1999) • R. S. SUQIRTHARAJAH, *Voices from the Margin: Interpreting the Bible in the Third World* (Maryknoll, N.Y., 1991).

ROGER S. BORAAS

2. NT

2.1. *Concept and Task*

The task of biblical hermeneutics to make the Bible, as the canon of the church, intelligible so that the church is equipped to make an "accounting [*apologia*]" (1 Pet. 3:15) for faith in → Jesus Christ and its proclamation (→ Canon). The NT itself offers clear standards for this process. The object of interpretation is the biblical witness to the revelation of God in Jesus Christ.

The center of Christian theology is the Christevent (→ Christology). This event can be understood only within the totality of the OT and the NT (1 Cor. 15:3-5; 2 Cor. 1:20; Luke 24:25-27; John 5:39). The → gospel of Jesus Christ is a divine gift demanding obedient reflection and response (1 Cor. 1:30; 2:6-16; 2 Cor. 4:5-6). Exposition, therefore, must orient itself to the tradition of the apostolic faith (1 Cor. 15:1-11; Rom. 6:17; 2 Tim. 3:14-17; 2 Pet. 1:20-21; → Exegesis, Biblical). These criteria place biblical hermeneutics in fruitful tension with any exposition that would set up its own criteria apart from them.

2.2. *History*

The Christian exposition of the NT (and OT) arose in the second century in opposition to → Gnostic theosophy, the anti-Jewish reduction of the tradition to (a misunderstood) → Paul in → Marcion, and the fanaticism of → Montanism. Its framework was the → rule of faith (→ Irenaeus *Adv. haer.* 1.10.1-3). It moved from a focus on the literal sense of a text to its spiritual sense, the goal being to advance love of God and neighbor (→ Augustine *De doc. christ.* 3.10.15). By the time of the Scholastics, Scripture was interpreted according to its four major senses: (1) the literal sense, and then various figurative senses relating to (2) faith, (3) ethics, and (4) hope. According to → Thomas Aquinas (ca. 1225-74), the literal sense alone is decisive in theological argumentation (*Summa theol.* I, q. 1, art. 10). According to the medieval church, the normative authority for the interpretation of Scripture, therefore, rested solely within the church.

Faced with what they felt to be an abuse of this authority, the → Reformers argued that it was possible to expound on the meaning of Scripture (in the original Hebrew and Greek) apart from the authority of the church and that Scripture alone is the measure of faith. M. → Luther's principle of *sola Scriptura* was itself a hermeneutical thesis, maintaining that the meaning of Scripture is not obscure and thus that its interpretation does not necessitate a tradition to understand it. Scripture, Luther maintained, possesses a certain clarity *(claritas)*, and he further maintained that the light shining from Scripture illumines the tradition of the church. Luther and the Protestant reformers who followed him asserted that there is a literal sense to every passage of Scripture *(sensus literalis unus est)* and that Scripture can function as its own interpreter. Jesus Christ alone, they affirmed, is the basis of → salvation and is at the center of all Scripture. Faith in him alone leads to salvation in the form of → justification. This hermeneutical reorientation gave the task of biblical exposition enormous importance and enforced the practice of the continual testing of tradition by Scripture.

In reply, the Council of → Trent (1546) asserted that both Scripture and → tradition were the norms of Christian faith and declared the canon and text of the Vulgate to be officially normative for the church (DH 1506-7; → Bible Versions). Trent argued that the revelation testified to in Scripture could not be correctly understood without the hermeneutical assistance of the traditions of the church. The insistence on the Vg as the authoritative Scripture of the church, and not the Greek or Hebrew, also served to preserve the cogency and authority of the traditional doctrines and theological formulations as developed and maintained within the Latin language.

In the theological controversies of the 17th century, Protestant → orthodoxy appealed to the authority of the verbally inspired canon and as a result lost any influence it might have had on the developing (rationalistic) historicocritical understanding of Scripture. → Pietism's separation of biblical hermeneutics into critical and noncritical components offered no protection against this development.

At the beginning of the 19th century F. → Schleiermacher (1768-1834) achieved a forwardlooking synthesis of biblical criticism and the Christian faith (see 3.1.2). Because everyone did not follow the path Schleiermacher took, the 19th century witnessed a polarization between historicocritical exposition (e.g., J. C. Baur) and → biblicist exposition of Scripture that still exists today (e.g., J. T. Beck). A. Ritschl and A. Schlatter could do nothing to bridge this gap. Overall during the 18th and 19th centuries, realist interpretation of biblical texts steadily declined with the rise of historicocritical methods of interpretation.

A more fruitful hermeneutical polarity between historicocritical and biblicist methods of exposition came into play in → dialectical theology. K. → Barth (1886-1968) worked out his hermeneutics dogmatically from Scripture, demanding that exposition always be faithful to the scriptural texts. He found historical criticism to be only an aid in expressing the biblical witness to revelation.

R. Bultmann (1884-1976), in contrast, placed historicocritical exposition at the center of his theological and hermeneutical method. For him, exposition (of the NT) must penetrate to the → kerygma so that it might have critical validity within a modern scientific and rationalist worldview. In cooperation with M. Heidegger (1889-1976) and H. Jonas (1903-93), Bultmann developed his program of the → demythologization of the NT proclamation, which he saw as a consistent application of the doctrine of justification to the field of biblical hermeneutics. Taking Bultmann and Luther as their point of departure, G. Ebeling (b. 1912) and E. Fuchs (1903-83) further developed hermeneutics into a "language of faith," at whose beginning and end stands Jesus himself.

Beginning in the 1960s, the criticism of Bultmann's program and of the theological understanding of language and the limitations of historical biblical criticism led to the development of new, competing hermeneutical paradigms (political, materialistic, psychological, linguistic, feminist, etc.). Characteristic of this development was the well-known claim made by W. Wink, in advancing a psychological hermeneutic for biblical study, that "historical biblical criticism is bankrupt" (see below 3.2.3, 3.3.3, 3.4).

2.3. Modern Problems

If biblical hermeneutics (of the NT) accepts the criteria mentioned under 2.1, it comes into tension with contemporary hermeneutical theory, which often centers on a "hermeneutic of suspicion" (P. Ricoeur). In the interpretation of Scripture, however, a hermeneutics of historical → doubt or suspicion must give way to a hermeneutical procedure that, out of interest in the original witness of Scripture, leaves room not only for the insights of biblical criticism but also for their dogmatic exposition. The understanding and interest that lie behind

the exposition of Scripture must not be that of critical doubt but that of critical sympathy with the textual tradition (W. G. Kümmel). Because of the central role of Scripture within the life of the church, historical criticism must make room for the possibility of nondeducible historical events as they are recorded in Scripture. Since there are no originally objectifying myths in the NT (and OT), → myth should be viewed primarily as the means that religious → language uses to make things understandable.

The criterion for a theologically sound and material criticism therefore cannot be located with the culturally variable horizon of modern understanding. Rather, it must be located within the gospel of Christ and the criteria of true and false, of free and unfree, and of good and bad posited by it (1 Thess. 5:21). The task of the theological explication of the NT is to interpret the inspired biblical texts in connection with the canon of the Old and New Testaments "through faith for faith" (Rom. 1:17). The center of Scripture is the gospel witness to the definitive saving work of the one God in and through his Son Jesus Christ (Rom. 1:1-6, 16-17). In its history, exposition always engages in (critical) dialogue with → confessions of faith, the normative summaries of the expositions of faith by previous generations of Christians.

Finally, it should be noted that the given truth of the gospel seeks not only to be known by the mind but also to be acknowledged by the will. Only then is the gospel truly understood in the biblical sense (John 7:16-17). Biblical hermeneutics therefore not only assists in the interpretation of the faith of the church; it also points to it.

Bibliography: K. Barth, *CD* I/2, III/2 • C. E. Braaten and R. W. Jenson, eds., *Reclaiming the Bible for the Church* (Grand Rapids, 1995) • R. Bultmann, *Jesus Christ and Mythology* (New York, 1958); idem, *NT and Mythology, and Other Basic Writings* (ed. S. M. Ogden; Philadelphia, 1984) • G. Ebeling, "Hermeneutik," *RGG* (3d ed.) 3.242-62; idem, *Word and Faith* (Philadelphia, 1963) • H. Frei, *The Eclipse of Biblical Narrative: A Study in Eighteenth and Nineteenth Century Hermeneutics* (New Haven, 1974) • K. Froehlich, *Biblical Interpretation in the Early Church* (Philadelphia, 1984) • R. A. Harrisville and W. Sundberg, *The Bible in Modern Culture: Theology and Historical Critical Method from Spinoza to Käsemann* (Grand Rapids, 1995) • P. Ricoeur, *Essays on Biblical Interpretation* (Philadelphia, 1980) • P. Stuhlmacher, "'Aus Glauben zum Glauben'–zur geistlichen Schriftauslegung," *ZTK.B* 9 (1995) 133-50; idem, *Historical Criticism and*

Theological Interpretation of Scripture (Philadelphia, 1977); idem, *Vom Verstehen des Neuen Testaments* (2d ed.; Göttingen, 1986) • A. C. THISELTON, *New Horizons in Hermeneutics* (London, 1992); idem, *The Two Horizons: NT Hermeneutics and Philosophical Description* (Grand Rapids, 1980) • H. WEDER, *Neutestamentliche Hermeneutik* (Zurich, 1986) • W. WINK, *The Bible in Human Transformation: Toward a New Paradigm for Biblical Study* (Philadelphia, 1973).

PETER STUHLMACHER and CRAIG A. PHILLIPS

3. Philosophy and Theology
3.1. *Concept and Task*
3.1.1. Hermeneutics, as the art of interpretation, is central both to Christian theology and to Western philosophical and legal traditions (→ Philosophy; Jurisprudence). Recognizing the distance between the reader (or interpreter) and the text (or object of interpretation), hermeneutics seeks to develop criteria for the interpretations of texts or aesthetic objects. Biblical hermeneutics addresses the question of how the meaning of biblical texts can be interpreted and communicated. The assumption that interpretation is always historically rooted and grounded in specific temporal and spatial contexts is central to modern hermeneutics (→ Interpretation).

The interpretation of the Bible is still an important task of hermeneutics (see 1, 2). The literal translation of a biblical text alone is often not enough to convey its meaning or import, as the history of Christian → mission teaches. Even when translation from a foreign language is not involved, Christian → preaching always faces the problem of conveying the meaning of a text written in another place and time in the context of what is now being experienced in the life of the local congregation. What is said may sound strange, even if the words themselves are familiar. What is meant in the Bible can often be communicated only by giving the words a new twist. Hermeneutics confronts its limit at this point. The expositor or preacher has to trust that the Word of God can be put into human language and that the preconceptions or prejudgments found in every human expression and in every act of comprehension are nevertheless unable to control what God wants to communicate in his way.

In the NT, hermeneutics is understood to be the art of exposition or translation. Paul regarded the hermeneutical task as a → charisma (1 Cor. 12:10). Ecstatic utterances needed interpretation if what was said to God alone was to be opened up for the congregation (14:9-13).

3.1.2. The definition of hermeneutics by F. → Schleiermacher (1768-1834) as the art or doctrine of understanding was a turning point in the history of this discipline. As a theologian, he was concerned primarily with the interpretation of traditional texts, particularly the Scriptures. If one is to understand these writings, one must enter into the world in which they were produced and so open oneself to them that they become fresh and lose their strangeness. → Tradition represents a problem that can be resolved only as interpreters delve into the situation out of which the traditions arose. They must see what is handed down as a medium of historical life so that it can help to illuminate the present. Understanding takes place in the creative repetition of an original perception of humanity, world, and God that, although expressed at first in one way, now takes a new linguistic form.

The philosophy of I. Kant (→ Kantianism; Philosophy of History) and other philosophers of the Enlightenment provided the impetus for the development of a philosophy of interpretation freed from the constraints of dogmatism. Texts now could be interpreted according to a set of rationally defined principles or rules and not according to any preexisting dogmatic formulations. The emerging discipline of hermeneutics sought to provide such rules and methodologies.

Schleiermacher, enriched by → Romanticism, developed his hermeneutical methods in debate with the issues raised by the → Enlightenment and German → idealism. His hermeneutics employed both grammatical and psychological methods to arrive at an "understanding" of the text being interpreted. Where the grammatical methods examined the structure, terminology, and literary form of the text, the psychological methods sought the divination of the author's immediate intentions.

Building on the work of Schleiermacher, W. Dilthey (1833-1911) developed a method of hermeneutics in which the interpreter attempted to reconstruct the subjective life-world of the author of the text under investigation. Romantic hermeneutics sought the retrieval of meaning *(Verstehen)* by means of an imaginative identification with the author's intention. Dilthey maintained that everything within the life-world of human beings is historical, and therefore all human persons are included within the ongoing process of the adoption, appropriation, and alteration of traditions. These traditions, freed from the constraints of external → institutions (i.e., state, church, law), now could be seen to have their own autonomy. They formed the basis of the discipline of the humanities (or human sciences), which, in contrast to the natural sciences of the Enlightenment, were oriented to the question of human understanding and meaning.

Hermeneutics thus became a theory that sought to provide scientific validation for human sciences (*Geisteswissenschaften*). After the two world wars, especially in Germany, hermeneutics began to be understood as the philosophical method by which a person might come to a sense of his or her own historical situation. From this point on, hermeneutics as the task of exposition, particularly in the areas of theology, philology, and jurisprudence, must be distinguished from hermeneutics as a method of basic philosophical reflection, a revision of → ontology, with attempts to replace → metaphysics.

3.2. *Hermeneutical Philosophy*
M. Heidegger (1889-1976) traced all actions (including thought) to the existence that unfolds in time and that is oriented to one's own → death as the ultimate possibility of understanding (→ Existentialism). Because human beings are always situated within a particular time or history and within traditions that they are not able to see as an object, they are unable to break free of this historical situatedness and understand themselves apart from this history or these traditions. All attempts at human understanding are thus trapped within a hermeneutical circle. To the question of the apparent subjectivism that this hermeneutical circle might imply for the interpretation of a text, Heidegger answered that whenever persons consult a text, they must be so challenged by it that in reply they can only ask further questions of it. In this way subjectivism is avoided.

H.-G. Gadamer (b. 1900) has shown in an exemplary fashion that part of the universal claim of hermeneutics is its constant reevaluation of its own claims as they have developed throughout its history. Hermeneutics is a theory of real → experience, that is, a way of thinking or reflecting on human experiences situated within particular live and historical traditions so that they cast light on present-day life. The horizon of the present can never exist apart from the influence of tradition. Whenever a human being attempts to understand a text or cultural object from the past, there can only be a convergence of the horizons of the past and present and never a fusion of them.

According to contemporary hermeneutical theory after Heidegger and Gadamer, human beings meet the world only in the medium of language. Hermeneutics thus becomes a world-hermeneutics, in the course of which the possibilities and difficulties inherent in every communication are made more visible. The act of putting something into words (e.g., experiences in → psychotherapy) is already a hermeneutical achievement. In the interpretation of texts and other forms of communication, the need is to press on to the language-event, in which reality identifies and expresses itself. In this respect the attention of hermeneutics is directed to the narrative process, to the relation of story to history (e.g., by P. Ricoeur). Experience is therefore always communicated in narrative form. Knowledge (→ Epistemology) remains embedded in a linguistic nexus and can never be exhaustively developed or explicated by concepts (M. Polanyi).

3.3. *Hermeneutical Theology*
The development of historical biblical criticism and biblical → exegesis and the question of the place of tradition within theological discourses opened Protestant theologians to the need for basic hermeneutical reflection. Only after → Vatican II were hermeneutical principles generally employed within Roman Catholic theology. We must distinguish, however, between an integration of hermeneutical methods into theology and an understanding of theology as applied hermeneutics that was thus named as human science (→ Philosophy of Science).

3.3.1. R. Bultmann (1884-1976), like Heidegger, concentrated on the issue of human self-understanding and tried theologically to extend the possibilities of Heidegger's philosophy into biblical theology. → Faith, Bultmann argued, gives rise to a new self-understanding when a person is called to the cross of Jesus Christ and thus finds liberation from every sort of bondage, whether to self or others. Those who have faith are freed from the world by the → grace of God, which calls them to decision in the word of the cross, the → kerygma (1 Cor. 1:18). The program of the → demythologization of the NT seeks a hearing for this message (see 2.2). The picture of the world that is presented in the biblical texts, it argues, must always be interpreted existentially, that is, it must be expounded as the expression of the experience of existential change (→ Existential Theology).

3.3.2. G. Ebeling (b. 1912) and E. Fuchs (1903-83) placed more stress on language as an exposition of reality and called the salvation that is communicated in faith in Jesus a word-act or language-event. Ebeling also linked the doctrine of the → Word of God, which both kills and makes alive, to the experience of successful or unsuccessful communication, whether between God and the world or among human neighbors. At this point hermeneutics became a form of → fundamental theology. A Roman Catholic version of this view also took the form of a hermeneutics. This position is evident in the work of E. Biser (b. 1918), for whom faith is understood in terms of God's promise of salvation, which helps human beings regain wholeness in their lives.

3.3.3. The claim of hermeneutics to offer a deeper and more comprehensive understanding of history has been attacked by many scholars, including those who wish to return to an idealistic conception of world history (e.g., W. Pannenberg). One particular question addressed to hermeneutics concerns the concept of tradition: Is tradition a continuum of imparted insights that forms an objective fact, or is tradition a series of comparative and integrative investigations and ongoing textual interpretations?

The question of the relationship between the philosophy of language and hermeneutics is also important. Hermeneutics has made us aware of how ambivalent language is and how easy it is to exploit the ambiguity of words and become lost in word games when precision is demanded. It also reminds us that a fixation on language as a self-acting and self-contained entity is questionable.

3.4. Results and Criticism

The development of hermeneutics brought an integrative attitude and style of thinking to philosophy and theology. It reminded these disciplines of their common roots in the Western tradition. It also reiterated many of the historical points of contact between Protestant and Roman Catholic theology. In hermeneutical theology the boundaries of historical research, dogmatic theology, and preaching merge into one another.

3.4.1. This unifying view of hermeneutics (within which there are still many tensions) primarily describes the hermeneutics of central Europe. At the same time, given the very real differences in human understanding of existence and activity in the world, a hermeneutical view of the world, language, and history cannot be given worldwide translation. A universal hermeneutics could not of itself be achieved.

3.4.2. From its outset, the program of hermeneutics was advanced as an alternative to empirical and analytic modes of operation and therefore was opposed to any kind of intellectual constructivism. The growing influence of empirical and analytic approaches to → linguistics and → sociology poses a dilemma for hermeneutics. On the one hand, hermeneutics might pay more attention to human society and the forces of social conditioning and control employed within it; in this regard → critical theory might be viewed as a further development of hermeneutics (J. Habermas). On the other hand,

it might investigate its own historical, social, and political presuppositions and ideological commitments (H. Albert).

3.4.3. Whereas analytic thinking concerns itself with regularity within observable limits (e.g., with usage and changes of meaning within linguistics), hermeneutics addresses that which already seems to be valid or that which seems to have become quite commonplace (even if it is not!). To this degree Anglo-Saxon analytic philosophy is in competition with hermeneutics. The analytic observation of common conditions and the hermeneutical observation of historically diachronous developments, however, can fruitfully supplement one another.

Comprehensive explanatory concepts (in theology, → feminist theology, and → political theology; see also materialistic exegesis) have contested the claim of conventional hermeneutics to offer a total understanding of the world. This conflict is most pointed in contextual theology. At its core this theology argues hermeneutically in its understanding and exposition of the social and political milieu of the church and its theology as a textual nexus. Nevertheless, because it sees texts as the product of an attempt to master the world, contextual theology scrutinizes textual traditions, especially the Bible and → dogma, so that they can be made to address the complex demands of the present situation.

Bibliography: I. BALDERMANN et al., eds., *Biblische Hermeneutik* (Neukirchen, 1997) • H.-G. GADAMER, *Truth and Method* (2d ed.; New York, 1994) • W. JEANROND, *Theological Hermeneutics: Development and Significance* (London, 1991) • A. LACOCQUE and P. RICOEUR, *Thinking Biblically: Exegetical and Hermeneutical Studies* (Chicago, 1998) • R. LUNDIN, C. WALHOUT, and A. C. THISELTON, *The Promise of Hermeneutics* (Grand Rapids, 1999) • K. MUELLER-VOLLMER, ed., *The Hermeneutics Reader: Texts of the German Tradition from the Enlightenment to the Present* (New York, 1985) • M. OEMING, *Biblische Hermeneutik* (Darmstadt, 1998) • F. F. SEGOVIA and M. A. TOLBERT, eds., *Readings from This Place* (Minneapolis, 1995) • A. C. THISELTON, *New Horizons in Hermeneutics: The Theory and Practice of Transforming Biblical Reading* (Grand Rapids, 1993); idem, *The Two Horizons: NT Hermeneutics and Philosophical Description* (Grand Rapids, 1980) • G. WARNKE, *Gadamer: Hermeneutics, Tradition, and Reason* (Stanford, Calif., 1987).

GERHARD SAUTER and CRAIG A. PHILLIPS

Hermits → Anchorites

Herod, Herodians

1. Herod the Great ("the Elder," according to Josephus *Ant.* 18.130), the founder of the last Jewish dynasty, derived on his father's side from Idumeans, who had been forcibly Judaized, and on his mother's side from Nabateans. He was born in 73 B.C. Already in his youth he was given political appointments by his father Antipater, one of the highest officials in the → Hasmonaean kingdom. In 47 B.C. he became military commander in Judea. Like his father, he exploited power struggles between the Hasmonaean brothers Hyrcanus II and Aristobulus II, who were under Roman protection, for the advancement of his own power.

In 40 B.C. the Parthians, who had invaded Palestine, helped Antigonus II, the son of Aristobulus, to the throne. Herod fled to Rome and there was made king of Judea, Samaria, and Idumea. Returning to Palestine with a Roman army, he conquered it in 37 B.C. after hard fighting.

As a client king of Rome, Herod had little scope in foreign policy, but thanks to good relations with Octavian (later the emperor Augustus), his kingdom soon became as large as → David's had been. At home he acted as an absolute monarch. With the support of a standing army, he enforced his rule everywhere, removing opponents by force, even in his own family (probably the basis of the legend of the slaughter of the innocents at Bethlehem in Matthew 2).

The establishment of a central government enabled Herod to control the economy, priming it by a vigorous building program (including the new cities of Caesarea and Samaria, plus the rebuilding of the temple at Jerusalem; see John 2:20). He also promoted culture. His relationship with → Judaism was mixed, for he both observed and scorned Jewish customs. On the whole, apart from personal ambition, his policies were pro-Jewish but with a cosmopolitan concern to bridge the gulf between the Jewish people and the Hellenistic world (→ Hellenism).

2. After the death of Herod the Great in 4 B.C., the kingdom was divided among his three surviving sons.

2.1. *Herod Archelaus* became ethnarch of Judea, Samaria, and Idumea. The Romans terminated his unbridled rule (see Matt. 2:22) in A.D. 6.

2.2. *Herod Antipas* became tetrarch of Galilee and Perea. Jesus of Nazareth was his subject (Luke 13:31; 23:7-12), and he was responsible for the death of → John the Baptist (Mark 6:14-29). Antipas was deposed in A.D. 39.

2.3. *Philip* took over the non-Jewish territories of Gaulanitis, Batanea, Trachonitis, and Auranitis, northeast of the Sea of Galilee (see Luke 3:1). He was succeeded in A.D. 33/34 by Agrippa I, a grandson of Herod the Great (also called Herod in Acts 12). The whole kingdom of Herod was briefly reunited under Agrippa (41-44), but finally it became a Roman province apart from Philip's former tetrarchy, which was assigned to Agrippa II (ruled ca. 50 to ca. 93 or 100; see Acts 25:13–26:32), a son of Agrippa I and the last Herodian.

Bibliography: G. Baumbach, "Herodes / Herodeshaus," *TRE* 15.159-62 (bibliography) • D. C. Braund, "Herodian Dynasty," *ABD* 3.173-74 • R. K. Fenn, *The Death of Herod* (New York, 1992) • M. Grant, *Herod the Great* (New York, 1971) • H. W. Hoehner, *Herod Antipas: A Contemporary of Jesus Christ* (rev. ed.; Grand Rapids, 1980) • A. H. M. Jones, *The Herods of Judea* (2d ed.; London, 1967; orig. pub., 1938) • L. I. Levine, "Herod the Great," *ABD* 3.161-69 • P. Richardson, *Herod: King of the Jews and Friend of the Romans* (Minneapolis, 1999) • S. Sandmel, *Herod: Profile of a Tyrant* (Philadelphia, 1971). • D. R. Schwarz, *Agrippa I: The Last King of Judaea* (Tübingen, 1990).

BERNDT SCHALLER

Hesychasm

In the → Orthodox Church, Hesychasm (from Gk. *hēsychia,* "quietness, stillness") is the tradition of quiet, inner, prayerful contemplation of God. The early monks (→ Monasticism) of the 3d and 4th centuries sought this stillness in their ascetic program by outward flight from the world and the combating of inner unrest (→ Anchorites). Simeon the New Theologian (949-1022), who described his encounters with God as visions of light, must be regarded as the pioneer of Hesychasm. Tractates of the 12th to the 14th centuries (esp. by Nicephorus of Athos and Gregory of Sinai) show that on Mount → Athos a form of intellectual → prayer was used that was linked to breathing exercises and that had as its goal the vision of divine light (→ Light; Mysticism).

In the Hesychast controversy Gregory → Palamas (ca. 1296-1359), an Athos monk and later archbishop of Thessalonica, championed Hesychasm, and Barlaam the Calabrian (ca. 1290-ca. 1350) emerged as its opponent. Starting with the mystical experience of the monks (who claimed to see the transfiguration light of Mount Tabor), theological discussion focused on whether the essence of the triune God is accessible to us. Palamas, who distinguished between essence and energies, regarded the light as one of the energies with which the divine Trinity turns to us. Formal acceptance of Hesychasm occurred at three councils of Constantinople (1341, 1347, and 1351), ending the controversy and opening the door for its acceptance as a basic pillar of Eastern → spirituality.

The collection of mystical Hesychastic texts assembled by Nicodemus the Hagiorite (1748-1809) known as the → Philocalia (Love of what is beautiful; published in Vienna in 1782) helped to spread Hesychasm, right up to the present day, even beyond the borders of the Eastern church.

→ Starets

Bibliography: H. BACHT, "Das Jesusgebet. Seine Geschichte und Problematik," *GuL* 24 (1951) 326-38 • H.-G. BECK, "Kirche und theologische Literatur im byzantinischen Reich," *Byzantinisches Handbuch* (vol. 2/1; Munich, 1959) 344-68, 780-85 • M. DIETZ and I. SMOLITSCH, *Kleine Philokalie. Belehrungen der Mönchsväter der Ostkirche über das Gebet* (2d ed.; Zurich, 1981; orig. pub., 1956) • K. HOLL, *Enthusiasmus und Bußgewalt beim griechischen Mönchtum. Eine Studie zu Symeon dem Neuen Theologen* (Hildesheim, 1969; orig. pub., 1898) • F. VON LILIENFELD, "Hesychasmus," *TRE* 15.282-89 • J. MEYENDORFF, *Byzantine Hesychasm: Historical, Theological, and Social Problems* (London, 1974) • G. PALAMAS, *Apology for the Holy Hesychasts* (ed. J. Meyendorff; New York, 1983) • *The Philokalia: The Complete Text* (3 vols.; ed. G. E. H. Palmer, P. Sherrard, and K. Ware; London, 1979-84) • G. PODSKALSKY, *Theologie und Philosophie in Byzanz* (Munich, 1977) • I. SMOLITSCH, *Lehre und Leben der Starzen* (2d ed.; Cologne, 1952; orig. pub., 1936) • D. WENDEBOURG, *Geist oder Energie. Zur Frage der innergöttlichen Verankerung des christlichen Lebens in der byzantinischen Theologie* (Munich, 1980).

RUTH ALBRECHT

Heterodoxy

"Heterodoxy" (Gk. *heterodoxia,* "other opinion"), in a theological and ecclesiastical context, denotes teaching that diverges from official church doctrine. In the → early church it meant the same as → heresy (Ignatius). Today, however, especially for Roman Catholics, it means formal divergence from → orthodoxy, with "heresy" used for outright denial of the truths of the faith (see 1983 CIC 1364).

→ Dogma   THE EDITORS

Hierarchy

1. Church Law
2. Criticism

1. Church Law

1.1. Hierarchy derives from Gk. *hiera archē,* denoting holy origin or rule. Dionysius the Pseudo-Areopagite seems to have been the first to use the term in theology to expound and rank the ministry. His works *The Celestial Hierarchy* and *The Ecclesiastical Hierarchy* at the end of the fifth century give clear evidence of a Neoplatonic origin, which he tries to fuse with Christian doctrine. For him the ecclesiastical hierarchy is a reflection of the celestial hierarchy. As the latter comprises three "triads" with three "choirs" each, so the former comprises three triads, each with three members: three sacraments (baptism, Eucharist, confirmation), three orders (bishop, elder, deacon), and three lesser ranks (monks, members, and those not fully members — i.e., catechumens and penitents). God is the author of the hierarchy, and participation in it is participation in God. Hierarchy is both a task and a state.

Theology and → canon law adopted this arrangement as far as the second two triads are concerned. Hierarchy thus became a central concept in church law.

1.2. From about the 18th century (→ Enlightenment), "hierarchy" has also been used for the ranking in religious organizations (as also the priesthood in Egypt and → Judaism). It then came into secular use (→ Bureaucracy).

In one text of → Vatican II we also find the phrase "hierarchy of truths" (*Unitatis redintegratio* 11.3). This wording implies that the revealed truths of Christian faith differ in weight and significance according to their relation to → salvation history and the mystery of Christ. The ranking of truths arises out of their connection with the basis or center of the faith.

1.3. As a result of the separation between ordination and office, there arose in canon law after the 12th century the concepts of *hierarchia ordinis* and *hierarchia iurisdictionis,* which according to the teaching of the → Roman Catholic Church are given by sacramental → ordination and canonical sending (→ Missio canonica; Codex Iuris Canonici; see 1917 CIC 109). The hierarchy of ordination is that of → bishop, elder (→ Priest, Priesthood), and deacon; the hierarchy of jurisdiction is that of → pope and bishop. According to Catholic teaching, both are based on divine law (see 1983 CIC 330-41,

375-411, 1008-9). As R. Sohm (1841-1917) insightfully points out, it would be a theological misunderstanding to regard the two as separable and independent.

Vatican II (see *Lumen gentium*) and the 1983 CIC that followed worked out ever more clearly the unity of powers, though without neglecting the primacy of the pope (see 1983 CIC 331-36) or the difference between spiritual officeholders (i.e., the hierarchy) and other believers (can. 207.1; → Clergy and Laity). The 1983 CIC avoids the term "hierarchy," speaking instead of "sacred authority" *(potestas sacra)*, which is conferred by ordination. Nevertheless it uses the adjectival form "hierarchical" to describe the structure of the church (can. 207.2), its constitution (bk. 2, pt. 2), and the nature of the episcopal college (cans. 336, 375.2; → Church 3.2).

1.4. The → Orthodox Church and the → Anglican Communion have also used the term "hierarchy" for the threefold ministry (bishops, priests, and deacons) and in this way established a distinction from the nonordained (the laity). The Reformation churches, on the basis of the doctrine of the priesthood of all believers, do not recognize orders *(ordo)* in the Roman Catholic sense and make no legal distinction between hierarchy of ordination and hierarchy of jurisdiction.

→ Church Government; Jurisdiction, Ecclesiastical; Offices, Ecclesiastical

Bibliography: J. T. BURTCHAELL, *From Synagogue to Church: Public Services and Offices in the Earliest Christian Communities* (Cambridge, 1992) • R. A. CAMPBELL, *The Elders: Seniority within Earliest Christianity* (Edinburgh, 1994) • G. DIX, *Jurisdiction in the Early Church: Episcopal and Papal* (London, 1975) • P. EICHER, "Hierarchie," *NHThG* 2.177-96 • R. F. HATHAWAY, *Hierarchy and the Definition of Order in the Letters of Pseudo-Dionysius* (The Hague, 1969) • P. KRÄMER, *Dienst und Vollmacht in der Kirche. Eine rechtstheologische Untersuchung zur Sacra-Potestas-Lehre des II. Vatikanischen Konzils* (Trier, 1973).

HERIBERT HEINEMANN

2. Criticism

In → sociology the term "hierarchy" denotes the pyramid of relations within an → organization. The vertical ranking of responsibility and authority structures the modes of command and communication and makes possible the execution of a unified, highest-ranking will (→ Bureaucracy; Power). Criticism in structural sociology, system theory, and social psychology has noted the limited efficiency of hierarchical organizations in dynamic socioeconomic development and its ambivalent effects,

since it favors the abuse of authority and works against → emancipation. Theological criticism is aimed primarily at the → clergy-laity distinction, which has been historically and materially a feature in church hierarchy.

2.1. In the climate and ideology of the reforms of Gregory VII (1073-85), a hierarchical order was stabilized that committed the execution of Christ's saving work in the world exclusively to those whom the → pope, as the successor of Peter, either directly or indirectly called and commissioned for the purpose. With the rejection of the claims and powers of secular rulers (→ Empire and Papacy; Middle Ages 2), all influence of the laity on the church was rejected (→ Investiture; Proprietary Church; Simony).

In his *Defensor pacis* (Defender of the peace; 1324), Marsilius of Padua opposed the papal hierarchical system, which divided the church into rulers (clergy) and ruled (laity; see the bull *Unam sanctam* [1302]). Legislative power, he argued, belongs to the people in council; → congregations should choose their → priests, and there is no biblical basis for papal primacy.

Religious movements from the 11th century onward resisted the primacy of the priestly office and normative papal authority. For them the evangelical counsels (e.g., voluntary → poverty) and the *vita apostolica* were the rule. At first limited to monasticism (Cluny) and church reform and thus only to monks and the clergy, these movements began to shape the lives of all Christians and to engage them in the apostolate without ordination or → missio canonica (including preaching on the basis of Mark 16:15). The discrepancy between hierarchical-sacramental orders and an apostolic lifestyle according to the law of Christ led the → Cathari and → Waldenses into heresy and forced John Wycliffe (*Tractatus de ecclesia* [1378]) and Jan Hus (→ Bohemian Brethren; Hussites) into an enduring movement of reform that branded the papacy and the hierarchy as → antichrist (→ Reformation).

The criticism of hierarchy in → conciliarism, which gives power to the congregation of the faithful *(congregatio fidelium)*, is not consistent, for it retains the priestly office *(sacerdotium)* as an essential mark of the church, commits representation to the clergy alone, and thus restricts active lay rights (Nicholas of Cusa, *De concordantia catholica* [1431-33]). Criticism of hierarchy as the structural principle of the sociopolitical order of the Middle Ages (a hierarchically guaranteed unity of the priesthood and the monarchy [*regnum*] and a ranking on the model of body and soul; → Organism) continued with the disintegration of the medieval worldview (→ Middle Ages 1) and the rise of nationalism. The sovereignty of the people as a principle and the representative constitutional state required no theological validation by the concept of a celestial and ecclesiastical hierarchy.

2.2. Reformation polemics took up the medieval criticism of the pope as antichrist and his institution as founded by the devil (e.g., M. Luther, "Against the Roman Papacy, an Institution of the Devil," *LW* 41.263-376; Calvin *Inst.* 4.7.24-30). It was not just a matter of papal abuses. The primacy of the pope and his claim to be Christ's vicar on earth were contested on biblical and theological grounds, as was the distinction between → bishop and → pastor by reason of ordination (Melanchthon, *Treatise* [1537]). Criticism of the hierarchical-sacramental priestly office went hand in hand with this rejection.

For the Reformers there could be no question of a separate spiritual office. Within the priesthood of all believers that is given at baptism, the only difference is in work, not in status (*LW* 13.331, 44.129-30). The distinction among believers is functional, not qualitative (*Inst.* 4.19.28). All church offices (→ Offices, Ecclesiastical) have a pneumatic character (*Inst.* 4.3.1-9); in principle they are equal (*LW* 39.74; *WA* 8.426). Pastor and congregation *(clerus et plebs)* are mutually committed to one another, bound to God's Word and to Christ as Head and Lord of the → church. Relations between them are according to the law of brotherliness *(ius fraternae coniunctionis)*. Regulated in this way, the relation between public office and universal priesthood was for Calvin the principle that shapes the church's constitution (see J. Bohatec, 417ff.). The term "hierarchy" became no more than an anti-Romanist slogan.

2.3. Criticism of the hierarchy within Roman Catholicism is pastorally, ecclesiologically, and socially an enormous problem that still hangs over the church (P. Eicher). It reflects the tension between → church law and alternative practice and projects perspectives for the structuring of what E. Schillebeeckx called "the church to come."

The → teaching office, however, insists on the essential distinction between "the common priesthood of the faithful" and "the ministerial or hierarchical priesthood" (*Lumen gentium* 10.2). This distinction comes to light in the celebration of the Eucharist (the "summit toward which the activity of the Church is directed," as well as "the fount from which all her power flows," *Sacrosanctum concilium* 10.1; → Mass). Only an ordained priest may officiate at the liturgy (which includes the sermon and homily, *Lumen gentium* 28.1; lay preaching is also forbidden, 1983 CIC 766, 767.1). This sacramental order, which relativizes functional structures of ministry and in some cases sets them aside, gives lay ministries their standing (see *Zur bischöflichen Verantwortung*, 132-33).

2.4. In ecumenical → dialogue (→ Ecumenism, Ecumenical Movement) the threefold ministry of bishops, priests, and → deacons is contested to the degree that it involves hierarchical ranking, excludes other offices, and is viewed as obligatory for all churches. Also controversial are the ontological description of it (hierarchy as the reflection of an order of being; see 1.1), its binding dogmatic and canonical nature in church order, and the sacramental element as an essential mark of spiritual office and a condition of the mediation of salvation, as though there could be no "eucharistic mystery" in "the absence of the sacrament of Orders" (*Unitatis redintegratio* 22.3). Any theoretical or practical alteration of the ordained priesthood as the church's infrastructure seems to be utopian if it does not also change the overarching hierarchical system of the church (according to a protest statement at the 1971 Synod of Bishops on "the crisis in the priesthood").

Bibliography: J. BOHATEC, *Calvins Lehre von Staat und Kirche* (Aalen, 1968; orig. pub., 1937) • P. EICHER, "Priester und Laien–im Wesen verschieden?" *Priester für heute* (ed. G. Denzler; Munich, 1980) 34-51 • E. GELDBACH, *Ökumene in Gegensätzen* (Göttingen, 1987) • J. S. GRAY and J. C. TUCKER, *Presbyterian Policy for Church Officers* (2d ed.; Louisville, Ky., 1990) • M. HARRIS, *Organizing God's Work: Challenges for Churches and Synagogues* (New York, 1998) • W. MAURER, *Luthers Lehre von den drei Hierarchien und ihr mittelalterlicher Hintergrund* (Munich, 1970) • PONTIFICAL COUNCIL FOR THE LAITY, *Zur bischöflichen Verantwortung für die Laienapostolat* (Vatican City, 1982) • J. H. PROVOST and K. WALF, eds., *The Tabu of Democracy within the Church* (London, 1992) • E. SCHILLEBEECKX, *Christliche Identität und kirchliches Amt* (Düsseldorf, 1985); idem, *Das kirchliche Amt* (Düsseldorf, 1981) • A. C. TURNQUIST, *A Lutheran-Episcopal Vision and Practicum* (St. Paul, Minn., 1997).

ERWIN FAHLBUSCH

Hierarchy of Truths → Hierarchy 1

High Priest

The office of high priest, directing the cult and its personnel, was one of the religious institutions of → Israel (§1), as it was of most ancient societies.

1. We have no documentation from the earliest period. The oldest references come from the age of the → monarchy (Amos 7:10-15; 1 Sam. 14:3; 21:1-9; 2 Kgs. 12:7; 16:10-16), but with no specific description of the office. Postexilic texts first include the titles *hakkōhēn haggādôl* (Lev. 21:10; Num. 35:25-28; Hag. 1:1) and *kōhēn hārō'š* (2 Chr. 19:11 etc.). The tasks are set forth (atonement of the whole congregation, Lev. 4:16-20), along with the rights (entering the holy of holies, chap. 16). Details also appear regarding the insignia (breastplate, ephod, robe, tunic, turban, and sash, Exodus 28–29), institution (anointing, Lev. 8:10-13; 21:10), tenure (for life, Num. 20:26-28), and qualification (descendant of Aaronic Zadok, 1 Chr. 6:50-53; Sir. 51:12 Heb.).

2. Historically we know little about the function of the high priest at the → temple in Jerusalem before the Hellenistic period. Some names have come down to us (e.g., 1 Chr. 6:15; Zech. 3:1; 6:11). At the end of the monarchy the high priest took over political functions as leader of the people (Sir. 50:1-21).

More is known from the beginning of the second century B.C. The legitimate Zadokite high priesthood came to an end in 176/175 B.C., when Antiochus IV deposed Onias III (2 Macc. 4:7-22). Political and economic interests then determined the choice. The → Hasmonaeans again created a dynasty but on no valid basis. → Herod the Great and the Romans appointed and removed high priests at will. The office finally came to an end with the destruction of the temple in A.D. 70.

3. Despite the historical developments, the office of the high priest stood in high regard in → Judaism. The high priest was the symbol of atonement, and the office was given a cosmic dimension. Expectation of a coming heavenly high priest was common in many circles (e.g., Qumran and the Essenes). Christian theology took up this theme and found the office of high priest fulfilled in Christ (Heb. 4:16; 7:11-28; 9:11-12).

→ Priest, Priesthood

Bibliography: I. GAFNI, "High Priest," *EncJud* 8.470-74 • J. JEREMIAS, *Jerusalem zur Zeit Jesu* (2d ed.; Göttingen, 1962) 167-81 • W. C. KAISER JR., "Leviticus," *NIB* 1.983-1191 • K. KOCH, "Ezra and Memeroth: Remarks on the History of the High Priesthood," *Sha'arei Talmon: Studies in the Bible, Qumran, and the Ancient Near East* (ed. M. Fishbane and E. Tov; Winona Lake, Ind., 1992) 105-10 • E. SCHÜRER, G. VERMÈS, F. MILLAR, and M. BLACK, *The History of the Jewish People in the Age of Jesus Christ* (vol. 2; Edinburgh, 1979) 226-36.

BERNDT SCHALLER

Hildegard of Bingen

Hildegard of Bingen (1098-1179) was a theologian, pastoral adviser, poet, monastic administrator, composer, preacher, and scientific and medical encyclopedist. Born into a noble family in Bermersheim in the Rhineland, at the age of 8 she was dedicated by her parents to the religious life. When she was 14 her parents formally bound her to the Benedictine community of St. Disibod, under the care of Jutta, a 20-year-old kinswoman who became the mistress of the small community of female recluses attached to that monastery (→ Orders and Congregations). After Jutta's death in 1136 Hildegard became her successor as mistress, and five years later, in 1141, Hildegard began her literary activity. The impetus for this transition was, according to her testimony, divine: she describes herself as being overcome by a fiery light coming from the opened heavens and as "suddenly tasting the understanding of the exposition of Scripture." Then she heard a voice from heaven identified as the Living Light, commanding her to write down what she saw and heard.

Hildegard claimed that she had had unusual visionary powers since her early childhood, but the experience of 1141 marked a significant turning point, crystallizing her sense of being mandated by God to communicate her → visions for the → edification of the faithful. From this point until her death, Hildegard spoke, wrote, and acted in the voice of the "Living Light." Although she asserted that it was not with normal eyesight and hearing that she learned God's will, her physical well-being was intimately connected to her sense of receiving divine → revelation. She interpreted her physical maladies — diagnosed in modern times as migraine — and her much rarer physical exuberance as part of her overall → experience (§2) of "divine invasion." Hildegard's claims that her words came from the Living Light have unduly vexed modern analysis of her education and the influences on her thought. These claims should not be construed as a denial of any normal form of human learning. In fact Hildegard seems to have absorbed much of the intellectual traditions available to a 12th-century monastic, whether through direct study or mediated through → liturgy, while she remained critical of newer styles of scholastic education that did not directly serve pastoral ends.

Progress on the *Scivias,* her first major work, brought Hildegard into a wider circle of attention. She sought and received encouragement from → Bernard of Clairvaux, who also directed the attention of Pope Eugenius III to her activities. Her growing fame benefited the → monastery at Disibodenberg, but in 1148 she announced a divine mandate to move the women's community to Rupertsberg. As mistress of this new convent, Hildegard diversified her literary endeavors, composing music for the nuns' liturgy, writing hundreds of letters to a wide range of correspondents, and synthesizing what she read and observed concerning the natural world around her. Her correspondence attests to the spread of her reputation; she responded to letters from nuns and laywomen, → bishops and → priests, kings and princes, most of whom sought her insight about the troubles vexing them.

Letter writing was also one of Hildegard's means for intervening in situations she thought demanded her prophetic attention. Many of her letters, as well as her major theological works, were expressions of her commitment to the moral regeneration of the Christian society that she saw crumbling around her, largely because of clerical corruption and the greed of ecclesiastical as well as political leaders. The threat of → heresy, for example, particularly the appeal of the radically → dualistic → Cathari, not only elicited Hildegard's theological critique of Cathar perspectives but inspired even more fervent condemnation of the clergy for their pastoral failure. Such urgent pastoral convictions inspired Hildegard to move beyond the written word and leave her convent to undertake preaching tours in which she addressed audiences of clergy, laypeople, and monastics, in ecclesiastical settings, warning them of imminent apocalyptic judgment.

Hildegard's major theological works — *Scivias* (Know the ways), *Liber vitae meritorum* (The book of life's merits), and *Liber divinorum operum* (The book of divine works) — are constructed as records of her visions. The visions, often painted in vivid detail, are also described verbally as experiences usually including movements and sound, and invariably with long sections in which a voice from heaven is said to explain the meaning of the images seen. The *Scivias* is a wide-ranging compendium of Christian theology treating → salvation history from → creation to → apocalypse and final judg-

ment, with particular attention to Ecclesia, the divinely established institution that supersedes Synagoga as the embodiment of the eternal counsel (Caritas and Sapientia) of God. As these Latin nouns indicate, Hildegard envisioned various feminine entities as expressions of divine manifestation in this world, even as she affirmed the male Son of God as the fullest divine → incarnation in history. In the *Liber vitae meritorum* Hildegard contributes to the promotion of the → sacrament of penance by exploring the nature of → sin, the virtues that correspond to particular human failings, and the penitential means of atoning for sin. The *Liber divinorum operum* offers a grand theological vision of the harmonies between Creator and creation, permeated by the fiery force of Caritas. Hildegard also wrote a long musical play, several minor theological, pastoral, and hagiographic works, and a glossary of her own neologisms.

Hildegard gathered her liturgical music into a collection entitled *Symphonia armonie celestium revelationum* (Symphonia of the harmony of celestial revelations). This collection contains over 70 pieces, including sequences, hymns, antiphons, and responsories. These pieces were largely intended for use in the Divine Office, the one service of → worship for which most contemporary liturgical music was composed, since texts for the → Mass were already largely fixed by her time. The compressed poetic images of these poems are set to haunting music that her contemporaries recognized as different from the traditional chants of the Office (→ Hymnody 2.5).

Two scientific texts are attributed to Hildegard, although their MS transmission and place in the chronology of Hildegard's works have yet to be clarified. The *Physica,* or *Liber simplicis medicinae* (The book of simple medicine), is an encyclopedia of natural history, including works on the properties of plants, animals, stones, and other elements of nature. *Liber compositae medicinae,* or *Causae et curae* (Book of compound medicine, or Causes and cures), is a treatise describing diseases and their cures.

Although Hildegard was well known and respected in her day, her immediate influence seems to have been limited to two major directions. On the one hand, her works were combed for apocalyptic prophecies by Gebeno of Eberbach, a Cistercian monk, who in 1220 produced a compilation of extracts entitled *Speculum futurorum temporum* (The mirror of future times). This was the form in which later medieval generations came to know Hildegard and interpret her as a prophet — variously, as a prophet of the rise of the mendicant orders, prophet of the Protestant → Reformation, or prophet of the apocalypse. On the other hand, she was known to other women as a model of visionary experience and writing. Her contemporary Elisabeth of Schönau knew the *Scivias* and had a personal and epistolary relationship with Hildegard. It is not surprising that the genre Hildegard developed for her theological writing — the record of visionary experience — became the most important vehicle for women's religious expression in the Middle Ages.

In our own day, Hildegard has been the focus of a new flowering of attention. The early music movement has rediscovered her liturgical compositions, and thus through performances and recordings Hildegard has been introduced to a nonscholarly, Anglophone audience. Also, feminist scholars have turned their attention to Hildegard's complex life and works. While it is still possible to find simplistic views of Hildegard as protofeminist, feminist scholarship has in general sketched a much more nuanced picture. Most salient in these analyses is a recognition that Hildegard dealt extensively with questions of gender. She struggled to articulate her sense of herself as a woman empowered to act in untraditional ways because of the failure of men who wielded power granted in traditional ways. This empowerment was not something totally unique to her and unavailable to other women. Although she articulated one of the earliest theological arguments prohibiting women from priestly ordination, she developed a view of women's virginal life as exalted beyond priestly status and unencumbered by the strictures of the subordination to male authority that marked the lives of married women. Her repeated meditations on the story of Eve, the fall from divine favor, the divine feminine power of Sapientia, and the role of the Virgin → Mary in the redemption of the human race, all developed in the context of her life within a community of women committed to virginity, suggest how profoundly Hildegard dealt with gender as a theological and pastoral issue. Although 20th-century commentators have been disappointed by Hildegard's typically 12th-century views about class hierarchy, the richness of her theological vision is only beginning to be appreciated.

Bibliography: Primary sources: Causae et curae (ed. P. Kaiser; Leipzig, 1903) • "Ordo virtutum," *Nine Medieval Latin Plays* (ed. P. Dronke; Cambridge, 1994) 147-84 • *Physica*, PL 197 • *Symphonia: A Critical Edition of the Symphonia armonie celestium revelationum* (ed. B. Newman; Ithaca, N.Y., 1998). In addition, the major visionary works and the letters have been newly edited and published by Brepols, Louvain, in the series CChr.CM.

Primary sources in English translation: J. L. Baird and R. K. Ehrman, trans., *The Letters of Hildegard of Bingen* (2 vols.; New York, 1994-98) • M. Berger, trans., *Hildegard of Bingen: On Natural Philosophy and Medicine. Selections from "Causae et curae"* (Cambridge, 1999) • M. Fox, *Hildegard of Bingen's Book of Divine Works, with Letters and Songs* (Santa Fe, N.M., 1987) • C. Hart and J. Bishop, trans., *Scivias* (New York, 1990) • B. W. Hozeski, trans., *Hildegard of Bingen: The Book of the Rewards of Life (Liber vitae meritorum)* (New York, 1994) • P. Throop, trans., *Hildegard von Bingen's Physica* (Rochester, Vt., 1998).

Secondary works: P. Dronke, *Women Writers of the Middle Ages* (Cambridge, 1984) • S. Flanagan, *Hildegard of Bingen, 1098-1179: A Visionary Life* (2d ed.; London, 1998) • K. Kerby-Fulton, *Reformist Apocalypticism and Piers Plowman* (Cambridge, 1990) • M. B. McInerney, ed., *Hildegard of Bingen: A Book of Essays* (New York, 1998) • B. Newman, *Sister of Wisdom: St. Hildegard's Theology of the Feminine* (Berkeley, Calif., 1997); idem, ed., *Voice of the Living Light: Hildegard of Bingen and Her World* (Berkeley, 1998).

Anne L. Clark

Hinduism

1. Characteristics
2. Spread
3. Historical Development
    3.1. Vedic Period
    3.2. Classical Hinduism
    3.3. Hindu Middle Ages
    3.4. Modern Period
4. Present Situation

1. Characteristics

Hinduism is a very complex, contradictory, yet coherent nexus of writings, rites, and ways of life. It is not an organized → religion stabilized by dogmatic unity but an order that is believed and lived out as supratemporal and cosmic (as *sanātana dharma*, "traditional duty" or "traditional practices") and that regulates precisely all the spheres of individual life and the arrangement of social groups (→ Caste). It unites in itself widely divergent religious types, from personalistic → theism to a doctrine of transpersonal isolation, from magical rites to objectless → meditation. It regards all these forms as different ways, suited to varying human abilities, to the one goal of liberation *(mokṣa)* from entanglement in the conditioning factors and situations that resist the full development of being or truth *(satya)*.

Between the Hinduism of the higher castes, which has produced philosophical systems, and that of the common people, which expresses itself in innumerable rites and cults (honoring the village deity [*grāmadevatā*], snake cults, animistic forms of belief, etc.), there are both differences and similarities. Popular Hinduism seems externally to be only a form of → polytheism. Each god *(deva)* is a personified force *(śakti)* of the one primal force experienced in the multiplicity of the cosmic and human drama. Reality is a hierarchy of levels of existence. Each level relates to the whole and gives it relative expression. By means of this model Hinduism can integrate all religious forms and values.

Typical of almost every manifestation of Hinduism are (1) belief in an eternal order *(ṛta)* that rules events as well as the moral and intellectual spheres *(dharma)* and that, as → karma, relates individuals' responsibility for their own destiny to a universal nexus, thus guaranteeing a temporal-eternal continuum that is not limited to this one life but manifests itself in the life-stream of many existences (→ Reincarnation); (2) an intuition of the unity of reality that sees all things as manifestations of the primal ground or personal God, that can honor God in every creature, and that culminates in the doctrine of the nonduality *(advaita)* of the human self *(ātman)* and the basis of the world *(Brahman)*; and (3) the desire for a direct experience of the mystery of the spirit *(anubhava)*, which as transrational knowledge can be achieved either by shamanistic extension of consciousness, the concentration of all mental energies (e.g., in loving dedication to God, or *bhakti*), or systematic training of the body-consciousness continuum (→ Yoga).

2. Spread

From the subcontinent of India, Hinduism spread by migration to Indonesia (esp. Bali), Malaysia, Oceania (esp. Fiji), Mauritius and East Africa, South Africa, the Caribbean, and South America. Through Indian immigrants it has also gained a foothold in Great Britain, Canada, and the United States. The conversion of non-Indians (esp. in western Europe, the United States, and Australia) is a new phenomenon that is changing Hinduism itself.

3. Historical Development

The beginnings of Hinduism are lost in prehistory. Incontestably, many cultures came together to produce that which emerged as Hinduism during the first millennium B.C., which has continued to develop in new combinations ever since. These cultures were (1) the Indus culture (3500?-2000 B.C.), which had female deities, phallic symbols, and a seal of the god who, enthroned in heaven *(yogāsana)* with a trident *(triśūla)*, perhaps became a model for the later god Siva; (2) the Dravidian cultures of the south, which provided a basis for the main worship ritual *(pūjā)* and also for, among others, temple architecture, most of the gods, food and dress, and pilgrimages (i.e., for most of the essential practices of Hinduism); (3) tribal cultures, with elements such as → shamanism; and (4) the culture of the Indo-European tribes that after 1500 B.C. gradually subdued the subcontinent, bringing with them the hymns of the Veda, composed in archaic Sanskrit, and rituals of sacrifice. The Indo-Europeans came under Dravidian cultural and religious influences but escaped racial assimilation by means of the caste system. Dravidizing and Sanskritizing processes went constantly hand in hand. The stages of cultural fusion may be seen in the various historical epochs.

3.1. *Vedic Period*

The Vedic period (1500-500 B.C.) rests on the four Vedas (the Rig-, Sama-, Yajur-, and Atharva-Veda) brought by the Indo-Europeans. The oldest of these was the Rig-Veda, hymns to gods and cosmic forces. They are in the Indo-European Vedic (Sanskrit) language, with Dravidian borrowings. The central cultic action is → sacrifice *(yajña)*, which requires very complicated rituals carried out by the highest, priestly caste (the Brahmans) and laid down in the Sama-Veda and Yajur-Veda. Other rites are domestic, including the responsibility of the father in the household. The Atharva-Veda contains magical sayings and represents an assimilation of indigenous cults.

Later ritual commentaries — the Brahmanas — were added to the Vedas that, in practical and mythological detail, relate sacrifice to the central position of the priestly caste. There followed the Aranyakas and the → Upanishads, whose theme, developed at ever deeper philosophical levels, is experience of the One *(ekam)* behind the manifestations, or the identity of the self *(ātman)* with the All *(Brahman)*.

3.2. *Classical Hinduism*

Classical Hinduism emerged from 500 B.C. to about A.D. 600. The Upanishads led the way from a religion of sacrifice to a more inward religion of spirit (cf. parallel developments in → Buddhism and → Jainism). They reflected a new feeling for life. The multiplicity of the cosmic drama had awakened awe in the Vedic period, but now an attempt was made to find the mystery of the world inwardly. Metaphysical and psychological parallels were drawn that could reinterpret sacrifice and lay a foundation for psychosomatic teaching on the development of the spirit (through Yoga), which was designed to lead to a liberating experience of unity.

The division of Vedic literature into Mantra (sayings of the Rig-Veda), Brahmana, Aranyaka, and Upanishad corresponds to the ideal of the four ages of life: the state of being a celibate student *(brahmacarya)*, then that of being a householder *(gṛhastha)*, that of a forest-dwelling hermit *(vanaprastha)*, and finally that of a wandering, mendicant ascetic *(sannyāsa)*. The celibate student *(brahmacārin)* learns the sayings and their philosophical implications and applies them in household life, with an obligation to maintain the sacrificial flame as studied in the Brahmanas. Later he returns to a hermit fellowship in the forest *(vānapraha)*, where study of the Aranyakas (forest books) prepares him for philosophical insight into the unity of atman and Brahman, which, according to the Upanishads, he actually enjoys as an itinerant monk *(sannyāsin)*, along with liberation, or moksha, from the cycle of births *(saṁsāra)*. These ideals are laid down in the books of law (the *dharmaśāstra*s), which regulate every sphere of life *(dharma*, "duty," here the earning of religious merit; *artha*, "wealth, property," here the goal of honest commercial success; and *kāma*, "love, desire," here the moderate satisfaction of sensual desire), and are finally oriented to moksha.

Sanskrit literature came to full flower in the six orthodox systems *(darśana)* of philosophy — that is, Nyaya, Vaisheshika, Sankhya, Yoga, Mimamsa, and Vedanta — which are systematized in the sutras and set forth with great logical precision in the later commentaries. The two epics → Ramayana and → Mahabharata also belong to this period.

The → Bhagavad Gita (part of the Mahabharata) influenced the religious history of India more than almost any other text by relating the unity of the three aspects of spiritual striving *(sādhana)* — namely, selfless action *(karmayoga)*, love of God *(bhaktiyoga)*, and knowledge *(jñānayoga)* — to a religion of grace centered on dedication to the one God. Even uneducated Hindus know parts of the Gita by heart and recite certain mantras (along with some of the Rig-Veda) in daily → prayer. Non-Vedic cults were already common in the classical age and blossomed in that which followed.

3.3. *Hindu Middle Ages*
The Hindu middle ages (from ca. A.D. 700 to the 18th cent.) were marked by the spread of → Bhakti religion, which dissolved Vedic sacrifice *(yajña)* in puja, or worship. Dravidian deities were now equated with the Vedic deities and replaced them. Three groups of cults became influential and still dominate Hinduism: Saivism, Vaishnavism (with the Krishna mysticism of the North), and Shaktism. Grouped around the main deities were divine families that comprised local gods. In the Puranas (6th-16th centuries) we read about these families in creation myths, genealogies, and so forth. The literature of the Agamas might be regarded as theological speculation explaining liturgical rules.

Saivaism, Vaishnavism, and Shaktism based their teachings and practices on the relevant Agamas. Southern Saivaism, which culminated in the philosophical system of Saiva Siddhanta (which taught a realist, dualistic doctrine of grace), and Kashmir Saivism (which taught an idealistic monism, viewing the world's unity in differentiation, and, esp. through the brilliant Abhinavagupta [11th cent.], made an impact and integrated Tantric elements) each regarded their Agamas as having revelatory authority *(śrūti)* like the Vedas.

Siva is the transcendent, one God. He is gracious and yet destroys all created things. He is located at places of burning but is also enthroned, sunk in eternal meditation, on Mount Kailas. Now he is lord of animals, now the epitome of the desire of love and the regeneration of the world. Vishnu comes to earth in different forms in times of trouble. There are ten classical forms of descent *(avatāra)*, which theologically may be viewed as docetic → incarnations. The most important are the seventh (Rama) and the eighth (Krishna).

Vishnu's consort, Lakshmi, is the goddess of fortune and riches, while Siva stands related to the female deities Durga (the wrathful aspect) and Parvati (the kindly aspect). These two represent old mother cults and are venerated in Shaktism, or in Tantric movements, which are always present in India's religious history. The primal energy of becoming is represented in the great mother (Kali, a fierce aspect of Devi, the supreme goddess), in whose power *(śakti)* there may be ritual participation and who plays an important saving role by controlling the forces that bring redemption through the uniting of polarities. Tantrism is a universal sacramentalism that awakens spiritual powers by sublimation *(kuṇḍalinī-yoga)* and that may be used to give actualization to the spiritual in material form.

The Siva and Vishnu cults have at times been exclusive (though not everywhere), but the choice of a favorite deity *(iṣṭadevatā)* does not depend on considerations of caste or cult. In later Hinduism the god Brahma (now seldom worshipped) is the Creator, Vishnu the Sustainer, and Siva the Destroyer.

They are thus three aspects (*trimurtī*, "three forms") of the one god.

The Hindu middle ages saw struggles with Buddhism and → Islam. There thus arose philosophical schools with an apologetic aim. In the battle with Buddhism we find the three schools of the Vedanta. First is the nondualism (*advaita*) of Śankara (700?-750?), who in his nondualistic theory (*vivartavāda*) viewed the variety of the world as a deception or illusion (*māyā*) of the consciousness. Then there is the qualified nondualism (*viśiṣṭādvaita*) of Rāmānuja (ca. 1017-1137), who depicted the relation of God and world in terms of the unity of soul and body, which permeate one another but are eternally distinct. Finally there is the dualism (*dvaita*) of Madhva (ca. 1199-ca. 1278), who strictly separated God, world, and individual souls.

The bhakti movements brought together elements that were otherwise hard to unite socially and historically. This unifying trend is plain in mystics and singers like Kabīr (1440-1518), Mīrā Bāī (1450?-1547?), and Caitanya (1485-1533). Puja, feasts, pilgrimages, and → astrology (which controls everything, including politics and economics) all helped to give piety its shape. Tradition was handed down by priest (*purohita*), scholar (*paṇḍita*), and sannyasin, who often served as a personal teacher (*guru*) of individuals or families, guiding their study of the writings, initiating them into methods of mediation, and offering them counsel. *Pujārī*s serve as religious functionaries at temples.

3.4. *Modern Period*

The modern period (from the 18th cent.) has seen a renaissance of Hinduism through the experience of British rule (→ Colonialism), the challenge of Christianity, and modern means of communication and printing. These factors and others are changing Hinduism as its power of assimilation deals with the legacy and forms of life of Western civilization.

The first impulses came from Bengal. There Rammohan Ray (1772-1833) was influenced by Christian ethics and in 1828 founded Brahmo Samaj (Society of Brahma), which taught → theism and rationality against the background of Indian mysticism and which made an impact on the elite that had received English schooling. It turned away from the magical rites of popular Hinduism and sought reform. Debendranath Tagore (1817-1905), the father of a famous Bengali poet, joined the society in 1842 and added the dimension of prayer.

In 1857 the young Keshub Chunder Sen (1838-84) joined the society and stressed social Christianity. Later he formed a new group, the Brahmo Samaj of India, which adopted some Christian teachings, championed the emancipation of women, and favored marriage between people of different castes.

With the Arya Samaj (Society of Aryans [i.e., nobles]), founded by Dayananda Sarasvati (1824-83) in 1875, Hinduism, which had achieved greater self-awareness through the enthusiasm of European Orientalists and a developing sense of nationality, went on the offensive against Christianity. A ceremony of reconversion (*shuddi*) to Hinduism was initiated, and colleges were founded on a Hindi basis.

Neo-Vedantic movements began with Ramakrishna (1836-86), who in glowing love for God was often taken up for days into altered states of consciousness, and who also had a vision of Christ. He is considered one of India's most significant holy men.

Ramakrishna's disciple Swami Vivekenanda (1863-1902) united Ramakrishna mysticism with the Vedanta and believed that he could integrate the noblest teachings of other religions into this universal Vedanta. With a message of worldwide unity and love, he came before the World's Parliament of Religions at Chicago in 1893, where he enjoyed great success. He claimed that all religions are true, that India is the mother of religions, that the Vedanta does not contradict natural science, and that he could free the materialistic West with the spiritual message of India. In 1897 he founded the Ramakrishna Mission, which is organized like a Roman Catholic order. It runs schools and hospitals, publishes classical texts in popular editions, and promotes dialogue with the academic world.

Mohandas K. Gandhi (1869-1948) applied the love of God that is taught in the Bhagavad Gita and the ethics of the → Sermon on the Mount to India's social and political fight for liberation, with special emphasis on the ideal of nonresistance and nonviolence (*ahiṁsa*, "noninjury"; → Force, Violence, Nonviolence) and on the method of *satyāgraha* (devotion to truth), or sticking to the truth at all costs. He linked these ideals to the serving of all people and the promoting of the common good. Living a simple lifestyle, Gandhi believed in village industries, which would be ecologically sound and would bring social integration and a modest prosperity to India. He wanted to end untouchability (but not the caste system) and to reconcile Hindus and Muslims. These efforts earned him the enmity of radical Hindus and led to his assassination.

Aurobindo Ghose (1872-1950), who combined Western doctrines of → evolution with eastern Yoga in an integral Yoga covering all spheres of life, was also at first a political revolutionary. Later, however, he founded an ashram at Pondicherry. In → Theosophy, too, we find a tendency to integrate elements of religion from Hinduism and Christianity.

Ramana Maharishi (1879-1950) was not affected by modern trends. As a "living Upanishad," he taught an uncompromising ideal of the wandering, ascetic life *(sannyāsa)* and of a self-pondering inquiry *(vicāra),* a contemplative method of self-examination. He had great influence in India and became one of the first gurus to attract seekers from the West.

In 1953 Swami Chinmayananda (1916-93) began to teach an easily intelligible Vedanta adapted to the modern world and designed to protect educated people against secularism and materialism. He attracted millions of followers, including many from abroad. He sometimes attacked Christianity, unlike other gurus, who sought → dialogue. Swami Chidananda Saraswati (b. 1916), called the St. Francis of Rishikesh, especially illustrates the latter strategy, for he has many important Indian Christians among his friends and pupils.

Sri Satya Sai Baba (b. 1926) gained fame through spectacular healings and materializations and attracted millions of adherents, especially among the Indian middle classes. He used vast sums of money to build his own center of healing and education, which combines modern studies with classical Hindu courses. He causes much controversy in India, which only increases his popularity.

Maharishi Mahesh Yogi (b. 1911), with his popularization of a method of → transcendental meditation (a form of *japa,* or constant repetition of a mantra as an aid to concentration), has made little impact on traditional Hindus but has had more of a following abroad.

Shree Rajneesh (1931-90), who let himself be called → Bhagwan (i.e., "god"), espoused an eclectic Tantric philosophy that supposedly leads to peace of spirit through sexual emancipation and the experience of creative joy. Hindus rejected him, but he gained about one million followers among estranged Christians.

Swami Muktananda (1908-82) taught a form of *kuṇḍalinī-yoga* against the background of the philosophy of Kashmir Saivism. He founded over 100 centers worldwide and has followers among → New Age scholars. Some Christians are among his pupils.

The Hare Krishna movement (from 1965) has its roots in the ecstatic Vaishnavism of Bengal and has enjoyed great success in both India and the West (→ Krishna Consciousness, International Society for). Millions gather for its feasts in Mathura and Delhi.

4. Present Situation

Hinduism in the modern era has shown remarkable resiliency and adaptability in response to forces of modernization and secularization. Through encounter with Christianity (→ Hinduism and Christianity), Hindu intellectuals and leaders have come to emphasize social responsibility and the need to eliminate the caste-based social discrimination of people. The growing revolt of the outcaste, tribal, and other economically backward communities, often inspired by impulses from Christianity and Buddhism, has forced Hinduism to be open to social change. Traditional caste structure has been co-opted by political forces for democratic mobilization of people (in electoral politics), which thus positively empowers people but also, negatively, perpetuates the traditional caste structure in society.

The politicization of Hinduism during the last quarter of the 20th century through the ideology of *hindutva* (the Hindu way of life) has given birth to an intense Hindu nationalism, or "fundamentalism," that is hostile toward other religious communities in India. The Hindu-Muslim conflict in the aftermath of the destruction of a medieval mosque in 1992 and subsequent persecution of Christian communities by fanatic Hindus in India are examples of an emerging attitude of intolerance that has tarnished the image of Hinduism and its purported openness toward other religions. A corollary development is the emergence of a historically unprecedented "Pan-Hindu ecumenism," with an emphasis on a unity that blurs traditional Hindu sectarian divisions. The growth of the Hindu diaspora, especially in the West, with more than 120 Hindu temples in the United States alone, and the use of modern communication technology and media (video, audio, websites, etc.) have contributed both to the expansion of Hinduism beyond its traditional boundaries and to the development of a more strident posture for the movement.

The future of Hinduism depends on its continued ability to accommodate forces of modernization and social change without a perversion of its spiritual values into a nationalistic ideology. Put differently, its future depends on its openness to dialogue with other social forces and religions in India and elsewhere.

Bibliography: D. R. KINSLEY, *Hinduism: A Cultural Perspective* (Englewood Cliffs, N.J., 1982) • K. K. KLOSTERMAIER, *A Survey of Hinduism* (Albany, N.Y., 1988) • J. LIPNER, *Hindus: Their Religious Beliefs and Practices* (London, 1994) • T. M. P. MAHADEVAN, *Outlines of Hinduism* (2d ed.; Bombay, 1984) • G. OBERHAMMER, ed., *Studies in Hinduism: Vedism and Hinduism* (2 vols.; Vienna, 1997-98) • W. D. O'FLAHERTY, ed., *Textual Sources for the Study of Hinduism* (Totowa, N.J., 1988) •

R. Panikkar, *The Vedic Experience* (2d ed.; London, 1979) • R. Pramesh, *Hinduism* (New Delhi, 1996) • G.-D. Sontheimer, ed., *Hinduism Reconsidered* (New Delhi, 1997) • B. M. Sullivan, *Historical Dictionary of Hinduism* (Lanham, Md., 1997) • D. Vashuda, ed., *Representing Hinduism: The Construction of Religious Traditions and National Identity* (New Delhi, 1995) • B. Walker, *The Hindu World: An Encyclopedic Survey of Hinduism* (2 vols.; New York, 1968).

Michael von Brück and J. Paul Rajashekar

Hinduism and Christianity

A first attempt at communication between Hinduism and Christianity was made by Robert de Nobili (1577-1656), who, with a view to missionary effectiveness (→ Mission 3), adopted the lifestyle of a sannyasin, or itinerant ascetic, in order to understand Hinduism better. Only with the Hindu renaissance in the 18th and 19th centuries (through Rammohan Ray and others; → Hinduism 3.4) did a dialogic exchange begin. Hindu reformers found in → Jesus a divine → incarnation, gained inspiration from him, and made his → ethics a criterion for reforming Hinduism. They rejected the church, however, as an → institution alien to Indian culture. At the same time, 19th-century Western linguists (e.g., Max Müller) were enthusiastic about Indian culture, and 20th-century Westerners who practiced Hindu → meditation found in Hinduism spiritual depth, a universal symbolism, and a channel of Christian renewal.

Already at the beginning of the 20th century (e.g., through the teaching of Brahmabandhav Upadhyaya, V. Chakkarai, P. Chenchiah, and A. J. Appasamy), and especially after independence in 1947, Christians began to adapt Hindu spirituality and to find it in Jesus and his experience of God (e.g., as taught by P. D. Devanandan, R. Panikkar, Swami Abhishiktananda, Bede Griffiths, and Sister Vandana). The Christian ashram movement belongs in this context, especially Christukula Ashram, in Tirupattur (founded in 1921); Christa Prema Seva Sangha Ashram, in Pune (1927); Shantivanam, near Tiruchchirappalli (1950); and later almost 100 other Christian or interreligious ashrams. After the 1960s there were conferences initiated by Christians (→ Dialogue) with a view to overcoming prejudices on both sides. Disenchantment followed when there was not the courage to engage in common → prayer and meditation or to undertake practical social work together.

Only a few groups make a place for dialogue. The Christian Institute for the Study of Religion and Society (1956), in Bangalore, pursues it from the standpoint of an Indian → liberation theology. Catholic institutes (ashrams; Vidyajyoti, Institute of Religious Studies, in Delhi; National Biblical, Catechetical, and Liturgical Center, in Bangalore; and Inter-Faith Dialogue Center, Aikiya Alayam, in Madras) add the → contemplative dimension. Education for dialogue occurs primarily in theological colleges and seminaries but is seldom promoted at the level of churches and congregations.

The plurality of religions and their values (→ Theology of Religions) and the complementarity of Hindus and Christians find increasing recognition. Hindus have displayed respect and reverence to Jesus Christ, and some consider him to be an avatar (i.e., an incarnation). Christians and Hindus work together in economic and other spheres, though such partnership hardly leads to a conscious religious encounter. Hindus are aware of the social commitment of Christians but complain of their lack of → spirituality and their foreign dependence. This climate creates problems of identity for the Indian Christian minority. The evangelistic impulse of Christianity (→ Evangelical Movement) does not make cooperation easy, nor does the intolerance of Hinduism.

Two recent developments have considerably derailed Hindu-Christian encounter. One is the emergence of politicized Hinduism, under the ideology of *hindutva* (the Hindu way of life), as promoted by Viswa Hindu Parishad, Rashtria Swayam Sevaks, Siva Sena, and the Bharatiya Janata Party, which has precipitated considerable anti-Christian and anti-Muslim sentiment among Hindu masses. Sporadic persecution of Christians in some northern Indian states, including destruction of churches, murder of missionaries, and forced reconversion of Christians who had converted to Hinduism, has poisoned the atmosphere for Hindu-Christian interaction.

The second development concerns the Indian Christian community, 65 percent of whom are converts or descendants of outcaste or *dalit* (oppressed) communities. Overall, they have come to experience a resurgence of *dalit* consciousness, which is overtly antagonistic toward Brahmanic Hinduism, since the latter has oppressed them for centuries. As a result, there is a growing interest in the recovery of *dalit* symbols in the development of a *dalit* theology that is concerned with issues of justice and social change. Dalit Christians have little interest in dialogue with the religion of their Brahmanic oppressors.

Bibliography: K. P. Aleaz, *Jesus in Neo-Vedanta: A Meeting of Hinduism and Christianity* (Delhi, 1995) • W. Ariarajah, *Hindus and Christians* (Grand Rapids, 1991) • J. L. Brockington, *Hinduism and Christianity* (New York, 1992) • M. von Brück, *The Unity of Reality: God, God-Experience, and Meditation in the Hindu-Christian Dialogue* (New York, 1990); idem, ed., *Emerging Consciousness for a New Humankind* (Bangalore, 1985) • B. Griffiths, *The Marriage of East and West* (London, 1982) • R. Panikkar, *The Unknown Christ in Hinduism* (London, 1981) • S. Samartha, *The Hindu Response to the Unbound Christ* (Madras, 1974) • V. F. Vineeth, *Self and Salvation in Hinduism and Christianity: An Inter-religious Approach* (New Delhi, 1997).

Michael von Brück and J. Paul Rajashekar

Historicism

1. The term "historicism," now used mostly in a critical sense, still had positive significance in the mid-19th century. Thus it could denote a philosophy that, following G. W. F. Hegel (1770-1831; → Hegelianism), viewed world history as a realization of the absolute (C. J. Braniss). It then soon became a polemical title for Hegel's own → philosophy of history (R. Haym), for the historical school of law (I. H. Fichte), and finally for a concept of human life oriented primarily to historical facts and contexts.

Critics of historicism did not dispute the historicity of this life but stressed that human nature cannot be viewed as merely the object of academic study. Thus F. Nietzsche (1844-1900), in part 2 of his *Unzeitgemässe Betrachtungen* (1873-76; ET *Thoughts out of Season* [1909]), criticized the dominion of history as that of an objectifying and relativizing outlook that threatens the survival and enhancement of life by setting it in artificial political and cultural constructs. For H. Cohen (1842-1918) and G. Simmel (1858-1918), historicism constituted a danger analogous to the naturalizing of humanity in natural science. In opposition Cohen posited an ethics of pure will, and Simmel countered it with the insight that history is sovereignly created by → categories proper only to those who study it.

Working out these categories and thus overcoming historicism was the task of W. Dilthey (1833-1911), though Dilthey finally achieved an understanding of history only on an aesthetic and relativizing level. Hence E. Husserl (1859-1938) complained that only a strictly scientific phenomenological approach could offer an alternative to

historicism, namely, orientation to the factual sphere of the empirical intellectual life (→ Phenomenology).

Historicism came under criticism in → theology as well as → philosophy. Thus P. Tillich (1886-1965) described it as the name for an irresponsible attitude to history and tried to block any attempt to propagate the relativity of historical perspectives or to overcome it by maintaining supposedly valid standpoints, pointing instead to the experience of the "prophetic spirit" and the model of "prophetic interpretation."

2. E. Troeltsch (1865-1923) adopted a position that was not merely critical of historicism. He tried to develop a concept of historicism that would avoid the objectifying and relativizing of human life yet do justice to the movement of this life from the past into the → future. Thanks to Troeltsch historicism came increasingly to bear a neutral or positive sense, and as in F. Meinecke (1862-1954), it could become a general term for historical thinking from the days of the → Enlightenment. This use has been influential in later theological discussion, as in the systematic theology of G. D. Kaufman.

3. The various efforts to rehabilitate historicism have not been able fully to eliminate its polemical connotation. Even when M. Heidegger (1889-1976) in *Being and Time* (1927) described human existence as fundamentally historical, he could still say that the problem of historicism is a very clear indication that history as a discipline tends to rob existence of its true historicity. The → hermeneutics of H.-G. Gadamer, following Heidegger, then undertook to demonstrate the truth of the historical consciousness as distinct from historical research that is oriented to the ideal of method. The influence of Heidegger and Gadamer helped to make the problem of historicism a historiographical problem.

4. K. R. Popper spoke of historicism in what was still a polemical yet also a different sense. Nietzsche and Husserl had prepared the ground for this usage, in which historicism describes attempts to find the laws of historical development, especially in opposition to → Marxism.

Bibliography: K. Arasola, *The End of Historicism: Millerite Hermeneutic of Time and Prophecies in the OT* (Uppsala, 1990) • C. R. Bambach, *Heidegger, Dilthey, and the Crisis of Historicism* (Ithaca, N.Y., 1995) • W. D. Dean, *History Making History: The New Historicism in American Religion* (Albany, N.Y., 1988) • *Essays on*

Historicism (Middletown, Conn., 1975) • H.-G. GADAMER, *Truth and Method* (2d ed.; New York, 1990) • E. HUSSERL, *Philosophie als strenge Wissenschaft* (ed. W. Szilasi; Frankfurt, 1965; orig. pub., 1910-11) • G. D. KAUFMAN, *Systematic Theology: A Historicist Perspective* (New York, 1968) • K. R. POPPER, *The Poverty of Historicism* (London, 1957) • M. RIEDEL, *Erklären oder Verstehen? Zur Theorie der Geschichte der hermeneutischen Wissenschaft* (Stuttgart, 1978) • H. SCHNÄDELBACH, *Geschichtsphilosophie nach Hegel. Probleme des Historismus* (Freiburg, 1974) • G. SIMMEL, *Die Probleme der Geschichtsphilosophie* (Leipzig, 1892) • P. TILLICH, *Gesammelte Werke*, vol. 6, *Der Widerstreit von Raum und Zeit. Schriften zur Geschichtsphilosophie* (Stuttgart, 1963) • E. TROELTSCH, *Der Historismus und seine Probleme* (Tübingen, 1922; repr., 1961) • M. H. VOGEL, *Rosenzweig on Profane/Secular History* (Atlanta, 1996).

GÜNTER FIGAL

Historicocritical Method → Exegesis, Biblical

Historiography

1. OT

1.1. *Historiography and Historical Thinking*

To a greater extent than is sometimes realized, ancient → Israel (§1) shared in the very diverse "mythical" historical thinking of the surrounding world. It read present events in the light of past events, beginning in a distant primal period, which would both explain and if necessary validate them. It thus narrated, established, and handed down the stories of the past, not least of all in the cult. The course of history was determined by human conduct in response to divine ordinances. Presenting this history, either in detailed episodes or in larger frameworks, had a paradigmatic function, offering warning and admonition by means of actual examples.

The uniqueness of OT historical thinking arose out of the historical experiences of Israel, and even more so out of their interpretation. The basic event was the exodus from Egypt, probably historically the successful escape from Egyptian rule of a small people group that was later interpreted as the miraculous liberation of Israel's forefathers by God, → Yahweh of → Sinai, whom henceforth Israel knew and confessed as God.

Another crisis then came in the eighth–sixth centuries B.C., during which Israel in several stages lost the national independence that had been magnificently established by King → David and became permanently integrated into alien world empires. → Prophetic proclamation intimated the end of Israel in this crisis, but the prophets did not interpret such a development as blind fate or as the withdrawal of Yahweh, who had shown himself to be Israel's God at the exodus. Instead, they found in it a judgment of this God, besides whom there neither is nor can be any other, upon a disobedient people — a judgment that could be followed by a redemptive new beginning only in virtue of a gracious, miraculous act on God's part.

From this point onward Israel engaged in constant reflection on its past and put together several major sketches that make up more than half of the OT. In the process it used various older traditions (stories, poems, lists, and annals) that can now be reconstructed only with varying degrees of probability, the dates of which are contested.

Another debatable question is whether what we have here is real history. E. Meyer (1855-1930), trained in Greco-Roman historiography, believed that the history goes back as far as the period of the early monarchy, but he was dubious as regards anything earlier. The boundaries of "saga" are undoubtedly fluid, and religious pragmatism is far more important here than world politics, yet the realism of the depiction of individual events and characters, and the power with which disparate elements are forged into comprehensive accounts in the various works, are totally without parallel in the surrounding world.

1.2. *Main Works*

The story of the succession to David's throne (2 Samuel 9–20; 1 Kings 1-2) might well be contemporary. It is a masterly account of the complicated happenings as a result of which → Solomon became king. The few passages (2 Sam. 11:27; 12:24; 17:14) referring to God's part in these events are probably later additions, so that some scholars rightly see here political rather than theological history, if so sharp a distinction is drawn at all (E. Würthwein).

The collection and redaction of the traditions of Israel's pre-Palestinian period culminates in the work of the Yahwist (J) and is by contrast eminently religious (→ Pentateuch 1). Yet even if the term "historiography" in the modern sense is not appropriate, it must be emphasized that Israel saw here the story of its true beginnings and that this fact alone had great historical force.

The half millennium from the conquest to the exile is the subject of the → Deuteronomistic history. Interest focuses here almost exclusively on God's relation to Israel and its kings (→ Monarchy in Israel), but many ancient sources are used that would otherwise have been lost, and we are also given a fairly reliable chronology of the period of the monarchy.

On the basis of the works of the Yahwist and Deuteronomist (which in the meantime had been substantially expanded), the Priestly writing (P) and the Books of Chronicles offer a fresh presentation of the same period. Any differences rest on shifts in theological emphases rather than on new sources. The more original work Ezra and Nehemiah is appended to Chronicles.

The victorious struggle of the Maccabees in the second century B.C. provided the occasion for the final engagement in historiography during the OT period (→ Apocrypha 1).

Bibliography: B. ALBREKTSON, *History and the Gods* (Lund, 1967) • R. E. COLLINGWOOD, *The Idea of History* (New York, 1956) • H. GESE, "Geschichtliches Denken im Alten Orient und im Alten Testament" (1958), *Vom Sinai zum Zion* (Munich, 1974) 81-98 • A. K. GRAYSON, D. LATEINER, and T. L. THOMPSON, "Historiography," *ABD* 3.205-19 • K. KOCH, "Geschichte / Geschichtsschreibung / Geschichtsphilosophie II," *TRE* 12.569-86 (bibliography) • P. W. LAPP, *Biblical Archaeology and History* (New York, 1969) • B. PECKHAM, *History and Prophecy: The Development of Late Judean Literary Traditions* (New York, 1993) • G. VON RAD, "Der Anfang der Geschichtsschreibung im alten Israel" (1944), *Gesammelte Studien zum Alten Testament* (4th ed.; Munich, 1971) 148-88 • H. H. SCHMID, "Das alttestamentliche Verständnis von Geschichte in seinem Verhältnis zum gemeinorientalischen Denken," *WD* 13 (1975) 9-21 • R. SMEND, "Elemente alttestamentlichen Geschichtsdenkens" (1968), *Die Mitte des Alten Testaments* (Munich, 1986) 160-85 • R. DE VAUX, *The Early History of Israel* (Philadelphia, 1978) • M. WEIPPERT, "Fragen des israelitischen Geschichtsbewußtseins," *VT* 23 (1973) 415-42 (bibliography) • E. WÜRTHWEIN, *Die Erzählung von der Thronfolge Davids–theologische oder politische Geschichtsschreibung?* (Zurich, 1974).

RUDOLF SMEND

2. NT

In antiquity historiography often served specific purposes (see Thucydides *Hist.* 1.22.4; Polybius *Hist.* 1.1), which is true also of 1-3 Maccabees and Josephus (*J.W.* 1.2-3, 6; *Ant.* 1.4-14) as Jewish historiography in the milieu of the NT. The listing of the OT historical books as "former prophets" shows that written history was seen as an unfolding of God's revelation to Moses, with relevance for both the present and the future (see 1).

2.1. Acts

We find true historiography in the NT only in Acts. This book depicts the spread of the → gospel from → Jerusalem to → Rome and is thus a historical monograph. Its aim is to present the spread of the gospel as a universal way of salvation and thus to establish assurance of faith. The method used — connected episodes, along with key speeches — is consistent with the historiography of antiquity.

When we consider the purpose and the state of the sources, the depiction is astonishingly accurate, in spite of minor problems and simplifications in detail. The educated author must have had some acquaintance with pagan historiography, though in content the main impact comes from OT Jewish historiography. Since God is to be in action, he discloses himself in history. Acts shows how the witness to God's definitive act of salvation works itself out in history. The Gospel of Luke is presupposed. Sources probably include lists of places at which Paul stopped on his journeys and reports of the mission of the Hellenists, with → Antioch as the focus.

There can hardly have been true historiography before Acts. Yet 1 Cor. 9:5-6; 15:32; 2 Cor. 11:23-27, 32-33; Gal. 1:13–2:14; Phil. 3:5-6, along with 1 Thess. 1:9 and Gal. 1:23, show that biographical data had already been given as testimony to the life of faith.

2.2. Synoptics

The link between Luke and Acts (see Acts 1:1-2), together with Luke 1:1-4, gives evidence that also Luke is meant to be in some respect true history. Though faithful to its predecessors, Luke develops the gospel genre as historiography. Yet Mark had already shown an interest in history. The biographical tradition of OT Jewish historiography influenced the writing of the Gospels. In Matthew the biography of Moses had an impact in various ways.

All the Gospels present the story of Jesus because it has decisive present significance as the story of God. In Christ God has acted definitively and yet historically, and therefore the account of this act may and must be applied to each new situation and reinterpreted. The nature of historiography emerges clearly here.

2.3. Revelation

The Book of Revelation represents a special kind of historiography — the → apocalyptic (§3.5). By means of concealing symbols it presents and predicts world history in its relation to the history of God and his community.

Bibliography: R. BULTMANN, *The History of the Synoptic Tradition* (2d ed.; Oxford, 1972) • O. CULLMANN, "Geschichtsschreibung II," *RGG* (3d ed.) 2.1501-3; idem, *Heil als Geschichte* (Tübingen, 1965) • M. HENGEL, *Zur urchristlichen Geschichtsschreibung* (Stuttgart, 1979) • H. KOESTER, *Introduction to the NT,* vol. 1, *History, Culture, and Religion of the Hellenistic Age;* vol. 2, *History and Literature of Early Christianity* (2d ed.; New York, 1995-2000) • J. KREMER, ed., *Les Actes des Apôtres* (Gembloux, 1979) esp. arts. by W. C. van Unnik (pp. 37-60) and E. Plümacher (457-66) • U. LUZ, "Geschichte / Geschichtsschreibung / Geschichtsphilosophie IV," *TRE* 12.595-604 (bibliography) • R. MADDOX, *The Purpose of Luke-Acts* (Göttingen, 1982) • J. NEUSNER, *The Christian and Jewish Invention of History* (Atlanta, 1990) • E. PLÜMACHER, "Lukas als griechischer Historiker," PWSup 14.235-64; idem, "Wirklichkeitserfahrung und Geschichtsschreibung bei Lukas," *ZNW* 68 (1977) 2-22 • J. ROLOFF, *Das Kerygma und der irdische Jesus* (Göttingen, 1970) • H. STEICHELE, "Vergleich der Apostelgeschichte mit der antiken Geschichtsschreibung" (Diss., Munich, 1971) • H. STRASBURGER, *Die Wesensbestimmung der Geschichte durch die antike Geschichtsschreibung* (3d ed.; Wiesbaden, 1975). See also the bibliographies in "Acts of the Apostles" and "Theology of History."

TRAUGOTT HOLTZ

3. Church History

3.1. General

The separation of the discipline of church history from general or universal history in academic teaching and research took place in the 17th and 18th centuries (see 3.6 and → Theology of History 3.8). Yet from the 1st century to the 21st there has been a continuity between the writing of church history and general historical writing.

3.1.1. Concentration on the → institution of the church has meant, and still means, that the setting must also be taken into account. Naturally as regards the reciprocal influence, interdependence, and overlapping of church and world, there have been enormous fluctuations from the black-and-white depiction of the first three centuries in Eusebius and the stories of ancient heresies (see the principle of M. Flacius's *Catalogus testium veritatis*) to Otto of Freising (d. 1158) and modern sociological studies (→ Social History), which present the interaction in very different ways.

3.1.2. As regards the temporal framework of history, there was for many centuries a claim to absoluteness that has now largely vanished. Church history used to regard its theme as the central event between → creation and the → last judgment (→ Eschatology). Hence a universalist claim persisted up to the 19th century (seen particularly in the historiography of G. W. F. Hegel and F. C. Baur; see 3.6) and on into the 20th century (note the history of → mission [§3] in its relation to the coming → kingdom of God). Besides the claim regarding creation and eschatology, division into epochs (e.g., the evaluation of the → Reformation) has also served to link church history to world history. For centuries the idea of the four monarchies was dominant (see 3.3). Then a threefold division into antiquity, Middle Ages, and the modern period characterized both church history and secular history. Today this question has been reopened, especially by the self-understanding of the countries and churches of the → Third World.

3.1.3. A usually unwanted and often unrecognized effect of the interaction between the world and the church was the formation of divergent traditions that partly coexist peacefully but also partly condemn each other and in this way divide the church. Up to the → modern period the typical reaction of each group was simply to assume that it alone had preserved the true apostolic heritage and that all the rest were heretics. Individualistic spirituality and the transvaluation of all (orthodox) values, most clearly and influentially seen in G. Arnold's *Unparteiischer Kirchen-und Ketzer-Historie* (1699/1700), brought about a change and led among other things to strivings for visible → unity (i.e., the → ecumenical movement).

With the recognition of legitimate ecclesiastical → pluralism (§2), the way became clear for every church to have its own historical understanding and for the orthodox to have a proper estimation of the church history written by earlier heretics (→ Heresies and Schisms). Thus the classic church history of the great denominations is brought into ecumenical tension and can close its eyes neither to its alleged heretical siblings of the past nor to the indigenous historical sketches that will come from the Third World in the future.

3.2. *Beginnings of Christian Historiography*

The fact that the NT → canon (§2) includes a unique type of church history is no accident. Since the church is the fellowship in which the risen Lord is at work by the → Holy Spirit (see Acts 1:1-8), and since it is thus an object of → faith and yet also a secular phenomenon subject to temporal change, a thoughtful faith inevitably must face the question of where and how the church that is the object of faith can be seen in the documents and events of the past. Failure to face this question always means either that continuity between the Christ-event and the present-day church is (naively) thought to be self-evident or that it is (skeptically and resignedly) rejected as incomprehensible. The latter course, however, runs into conflict with belief in the historical → incarnation of the Son of God (→ Christology).

The Book of Acts is thus the first work of Christian historiography inasmuch as it presents the events of the first decades in terms of the acts and journeys of the → apostles (see 2.1). The temporal claim to universality rests, on the one hand, on continuity with the OT and → Judaism and, on the other, on expectation of the end. The spatial claim, as in → Paul, is indicated by the journeyings of the apostle from east to west (Acts 1:8). So far, however, it has not been possible to detect a fully thought out purpose on the part of the author, or one that gives historiographical unity to the material.

In contrast, both are achieved to a high degree by Eusebius of Caesarea (ca. 260-ca. 340), whose church history cannot be detached from his world chronicle. The universalist claim of the works of Eusebius is plain both horizontally and vertically. As he saw it, world history had now taken a decisive turn, for now pagan wisdom, the divine wisdom revealed in Scripture, and the many earlier kingdoms had all come together in the rule of Constantine. There is no sense of crisis here, no anticipation of the end, and no expectation of further cataclysms. The continuation of Eusebian history led through later Greek historians without fundamental break to Byzantine history (esp. as written by Socrates Scholasticus, Sozomen, Theodoret of Cyrrhus, Evagrius Scholasticus, Nicephorus Callistus Xanthopoulos, and, as the historians of heretical churches, Philostorgius and John of Ephesus).

3.3. *Augustine and Orosius*

Although *The City of God* by Augustine (354-430) does not represent historiography in the strict sense, since it is an apology, the historical argument dominates, especially in books 11-22, to such an extent that it is legitimate to regard the work as a history of the two cities (*civitates;* → Augustine's Theology). For Augustine, strongly affected by the sack of Rome in 410, what is to the fore is the distinction between all who love God above all things (*civitas Dei*) and those who love themselves, loving God at most only in their own interests (*civitas terrena* or *diaboli*). This emphasis leaves no place for the division of history into epochs or for identifying the "cities" with church and state. Even though the worldwide spread of Christianity is regarded as a fulfillment of biblical prophecies, history as a whole shows no progress, nor does it legitimate a Christian empire, as in Eusebius.

In contrast, Orosius (early 5th cent.), whose view almost became dogma in the Middle Ages, believed that we are now in the fourth and last monarchy (Daniel 7), which is identical with the Roman Empire, and that the breakup of this kingdom will herald the approach of → antichrist (Revelation 17). His influential *Historia adversus paganos* is also a true world history in terms of Augustine's task, though not his spirit.

3.4. *Middle Ages*

This concept of the fourth monarchy in different ways affected both East and West. After the collapse of the Roman Empire in the West, historians there could not adopt it without modification. But when the papacy made alliance with the Franks and Charlemagne was crowned emperor (800), belief in it revived and it was accepted for hundreds of years. This framework explains the type of history that developed later, especially in the Holy Roman Empire, with its universalist claim and perspective but also with its Germanocentric conviction that the Holy Roman Empire had to maintain its identity and could not perish, undergo division, or forsake its roots, which were traced back to biblical times and late antiquity.

At the same time, the ideology of the Byzantine Empire and — from the time of George Hamartolos (9th cent.) — its historiography clung to its claim that the Roman Empire, or, now that the first Rome had fallen, → Byzantium (the second Rome), was to be equated with the fourth kingdom of Daniel. When Constantinople itself fell in 1453, the Russian state and Russian → Orthodoxy declared Moscow to be the third Rome (attested from 1540).

Apart from national and local histories, the world history of western Europe remained dedicated to the same schema. Differing views had little effect on historiography. Yet the interpretation of

Abbot Joachim of Fiore (ca. 1135-1202) offered a counterproposal that would have an incomparable influence on the future. On his view the first age, that of the OT, was the age of the Father, the present age is that of the Son, and the age of the Spirit is to follow (→ Millenarianism). This conception introduced the idea of progress into medieval historical thinking. When dissident groups applied this idea to themselves (e.g., the → Franciscan Spirituals as pioneers of the third kingdom), it became discredited in the eyes of official authorities in both church and state. But according to the understanding of history found in sects condemned as heretical (→ Cathari; Waldenses; Wycliffe, John; Hus, Jan), the official church itself had to be denounced and opposed as the result or victim of decadence.

3.5. *The Reformation and Its Opponents*

The decadence model became dominant wherever the Reformation triumphed (its way having been prepared by → humanism). As this model had it, the first centuries were largely free of decline, but under the rule of the papacy the church had been laid waste and pure doctrine was corrupted. The historiography corresponding to this view found monumental expression in the *Historia ecclesiae Christi* (1559-74) produced by the Centuriators of Magdeburg, under the direction of Flacius. The indispensable presupposition of this concept was the conviction that biblical teaching and the true form of the church had now been rediscovered and that isolated witnesses to the truth could be found even in the "dark centuries." Even more extreme examples of the decadence model may be seen in dissident and heretical groups (e.g., the → Anabaptists and → Anti-Trinitarians) and a few Joachimist elements. It figures most broadly in Sebastian Franck's *Chronica* (3 vols., 1531), which dates the decline to the age of the apostles and does not identify itself with any of the newly arisen confessions.

Roman Catholic historiography, which developed alongside that of Protestantism, had the declared aim of showing continuity between the true church and the visible church, especially during the centuries under the papacy (→ Pope, Papacy). It did so by presenting the result of massive research into Vatican sources. Thus the *Annales ecclesiastici* (12 folio vols., 1588-1607) of Casare Baronius served implicitly to refute the Centuriators of Magdeburg. In the 17th century came the impressive editions of sources by the Bollandists (hagiography) and the Maurists (church fathers). By relying on critically evaluated sources, Gottfried Arnold (see 3.1.3) achieved a high degree of scholarship on the non-

conformist side. All these approaches saw God at work in history.

3.6. *Enlightenment and Nineteenth Century*

The Protestant Enlightenment, classically represented by Johann Lorenz von Mosheim (1694-1755) and, earlier, by some Humanist scholars of the 16th and 17th centuries (e.g., Jean Bodin [1530-96]), viewed history from the standpoint of human activities, though not deliberately trying to exclude God. For the first time, the church history of the → Enlightenment interpreted the churches programmatically and consistently as human societies, with their → dogmas as variable human opinions. Integration of the past in terms of → salvation history now yielded partly to its contingency (→ Chance) and partly to God's general → providence. Belief in → progress emerged as a basic concept related both to rational knowledge of God and to culture and science (e.g., G. B. Vico, Voltaire, G. E. Lessing, J. S. Semler, I. Kant). With the rationality of true religion (and its individualizing, esp. as in → Pietism) and with the resultant relativizing of dogmatism, the 18th century was confident that it had transcended the older Protestant orthodoxy.

→ Romanticism, however, developed a feeling for past peoples and religions as individualities with their own intrinsic value (J. G. → Herder). Individuality, however, cannot stand alone and needs a universal setting. The "idea" thus became a unifying concept (already in W. von Humboldt and F. D. E. Schleiermacher), especially in → Hegelianism and the application of it by F. C. Baur (1792-1860) to church history and the history of → dogma, though on different presuppositions. For the first time it was now possible to read the antitheses in ecclesiastical and doctrinal history as the development of the idea, the inner process of the spirit, and hence to interpret them in terms of the synthesis that transcends the thesis and antithesis — that is, in terms of the future (→ Dialectic).

The great historians of the 19th and early 20th centuries abandoned these speculative presuppositions in favor of strict adherence to what is historically documented and positively proved. Yet a basic religious character was still normative in L. von Ranke (who said that each epoch was immediate to God) and A. von Harnack (who described a synthesis of Christianity and culture). These generations of historians ran into the dangers of → historicism, that is, of the relativism that inevitably results from a historicizing of all our thinking about humanity and human culture and values, as E. Troeltsch (1865-1923) put it. Troeltsch himself, though, could offer no tenable alternative to historicism.

3.7. *Twentieth Century*

New thinking under the banner of → dialectical theology put an end to the dominance of historicism in German-speaking Protestant theology. K. Barth (1886-1968) energetically demanded theology's return to talk about God as the exclusive theme of theology and gave to history, and especially church history, only the servant function of an auxiliary discipline, since even church history "answers, from the point of view of Christian language about God, to no question that need be put independently, and is therefore not to be regarded as an independent theological discipline" (*CD* I/1, 3).

Since World War II there have been various approaches aimed at reinstating church history as a theological discipline and describing it more positively. Much debated and amended has been G. Ebeling's treatment of church history as the history of the exposition of the Bible. If this position is not understood too narrowly but embraces all that flows from the → gospel, it would seem to ensure the theological character of the discipline and yet achieve openness to universal history. If there can never be a corresponding comprehensive presentation, this limitation is connected with the changed state of theoretical discussion that also characterizes these later developments.

The traditional definition of history as an intellectual discipline has thus been partly abandoned in favor of various attempts to see it as a social discipline (related to anthropological structuralism, critical sociological theology, or historical sociology). The significance of this debate for church history lies in the tools provided for an analysis of the interdependence of church, → state, → society, economy, and culture, this interrelationship being studied methodically and not just sporadically.

Changed ecclesiastical conditions are another essential feature of modern development. Prominent here is the advanced ecumenical process. For church historiography this development poses a challenge to overcome traditional national church or denominational barriers. Often proclaimed, this task has been partly achieved only in individual sectors (e.g., K. S. Latourette's history of mission) or joint presentations (e.g., the work of Roman Catholic, Protestant, and Orthodox historians published by R. Kottje and B. Moeller). As regards the history of → Third World churches, the implication is an approach oriented to context (→ Contextual Theology) rather than mission. Since the early 1970s various attempts at a contextual church history have been made in Latin America, Asia, and Africa. With their interest in the independent development of Christianity in the context of different regions, these attempts raise the question of a global church history with new urgency.

→ Culture; Philosophy of History; Teleology; Theology of History; Worldview

Bibliography: M. ADAS, *Islamic and European Expansion: The Forging of a Global Order* (Philadelphia, 1993) • M. BAUMAN and M. I. KLAUBER, *Historians of the Christian Tradition: Their Methodology and Influence on Western Thought* (Nashville, 1995) • K. BORNKAMM, "Kirchenbegriff und Kirchengeschichte," *ZTK* 75 (1978) 436ff. • J. E. BRADLEY and R. A. MULLER, *Church History: An Introduction to Research, Reference Works, and Methods* (Grand Rapids, 1995) • G. CHESNUT, *The First Christian Histories: Eusebius, Socrates, Sozomen, Theodoret, and Evagrius* (Paris, 1978) • J. COLEMAN, *Ancient and Medieval Memories: Studies in the Reconstruction of the Past* (Cambridge, 1992) • E. DUSSEL, *A History of the Church in Latin America* (Grand Rapids, 1981) • C. GINSBURG, *History, Rhetoric, and Proof* (Hanover, N.H., 1999) • H.-W. GOETZ, *Die Geschichtstheologie des Orosius* (Darmstadt, 1980) • H. GRUNDMANN, *Geschichtsschreibung im Mittelalter. Gattungen–Epochen–Eigenart* (Göttingen, 1965) • W. KÖHLER, *Luther und die Kirchengeschichte* (vol. 1; Erlangen, 1900) • R. KOTTJE and B. MOELLER, *Ökumenische Kirchengeschichte* (3 vols.; Mainz, 1979-83) • K. S. LATOURETTE, *A History of the Expansion of Christianity* (7 vols.; New York, 1937-45) • P. MEINHOLD, *Geschichte der kirchlichen Historiographie* (2 vols.; Freiburg, 1967) • G. PODSKALSKY, *Byzantinische Reichseschatologie* (Munich, 1972) • F.-J. SCHMALE, *Funktion und Formen mittelalterlicher Geschichtsschreibung* (Darmstadt, 1985) • H. R. SEELIGER, *Kirchengeschichte–Geschichtstheologie–Geschichtswissenschaft* (Düsseldorf, 1981) • C. UHLIG, *Funktion und Situation der Kirchengeschichte als theologische Disziplin* (Frankfurt, 1985) • S. L. VERHEUS, *Zeugnis und Gericht. Kirchengeschichtliche Betrachtungen bei Sebastian Franck und Matthias Flacius* (Nieuwkoop, 1971) • L. VISCHER, *Towards a History of the Church in the Third World* (Bern, 1985) • T. J. WENGERT, *Telling the Churches' Stories: Ecumenical Perspectives on Writing Christian History* (Grand Rapids, 1995) • K. WETZEL, *Theologische Kirchengeschichtsschreibung im deutschen Protestantismus, 1660-1760* (Giessen, 1983) • M. WICHELHAUS, *Kirchengeschichtsschreibung und Soziologie im 19. Jahrhundert und bei E. Troeltsch* (Heidelberg, 1965) • H. ZIMMERMANN, *Ecclesia als Objekt der Historiographie* (Vienna, 1960).

ALFRED SCHINDLER and KLAUS KOSCHORKE

History, Auxiliary Sciences to

1. Survey

Of great importance in the writing of church history (→ Historiography 3) are a comprehensive knowledge, critical evaluation, and reliable assessment of the extant sources. Writings that were once unknown and materials that have been neglected can bring to light new facts and open up new perspectives. A scientific discussion of existing opinions rests on such endeavors. Reliable accounts of historical events often must be reconstructions. In depicting the views, goals, and motives of historical personages, subjective judgments, intentional propaganda, and time-bound or confession-bound appraisals must be differentiated from actual facts. The date and authenticity of traditions must be clarified, as must also the facts concerning those who start them. An original tradition cannot always be understood at once, which is where the need for the auxiliary sciences arises.

Some of these sciences — philology, paleology, and diplomatics — deal mainly with written or printed sources, while others — epigraphy, numismatics, heraldry, and sphragistics — deal with artifacts or monuments. The auxiliary sciences move on from the external sources to their content and thus also involve philology, chronology, geography, and genealogy. They have undergone increasing development from → humanism and the → Renaissance, especially during the 19th century, and there is now specialization in specific epochs or areas. Historians can consult them individually or in combination. To the extent that they can still yield results, independent work must still incorporate the appropriate methods.

2. Philology

The science of philology deals with the history of languages and the critical analysis and exposition of literary texts. A knowledge of older languages makes possible a better understanding of the sources. Research into vocabulary and the resultant etymological dictionaries, glossaries, and accounts of intellectual and linguistic influences all add their con-

tribution, making possible a better appreciation of the thoughts behind the writing. Philology also clarifies the textual history by bringing to light alterations, dependencies, and various strands of tradition. It offers guidelines for the establishment of an authentic text and thus permits evaluation of available editions.

Ancillary to philology and the history of art is emblematics. By consulting contemporary handbooks and collections, one finds that this field can open up a treasury of images. Emblems served to objectify abstractions, for example, in sermons, spiritual lyrics, and genealogies, as well as on signets, books, coins, badges, and flags. They can allude to the character, feelings, and aims of individuals or to historical situations, and they shed light on intellectual relations. Emblematics is especially important with regard to many written and nonwritten sources of the period from the 14th to the 17th century.

3. Paleography

Paleography investigates a work in terms of time-related features, classifies it by genre and purpose, clarifies materially conditioned and technical presuppositions, and examines factors affecting style and tradition (e.g., chancelry customs, writing schools). Graphological studies are also undertaken relative to individual practices. Tables are made of alphabets and their development, plus handbooks of the development of writing, codes and shorthand, and abbreviations. These various branches make possible the deciphering of texts and an estimation of date and place of composition. If features do not correspond to the supposed date, fraud may be present.

Paleography also brings to light later emendations and helps to unravel deleted passages that may be read with technical means. It examines writing materials and, by means of them, can establish the authenticity and age of a text (e.g., by identifying watermarks). It is especially valuable in the study of undated and anonymous works or in correcting erroneous assumptions about authorship. Bringing to light earlier misreadings often results in wholly new insights.

4. Epigraphy

The science of epigraphy deals with inscriptions on buildings, sculptures, monuments, pictures, and other places. Its most important task is to assemble, describe, catalog, and publish the texts. It solves questions of date and origin with the help of the history of art, philology, and paleography. With its study of decorative writing on ornaments and monuments, it helps to integrate and interpret unpublished inscriptions. When other written sources are not available for an era, locality, or social stratum, the study of inscriptions can be very rewarding. So too can be the study of the inscription tradition (e.g., in intellectual or religious centers) as well as the use of inscriptions in biographical research. Evaluation of inscriptions can often correct traditional historical judgments. Religious inscriptions on tombs are a rich source in studying the history of religion.

5. Numismatics

Numismatics deals with coins and medals. Their form, writing technique, inscriptions, marks, and figures (e.g., with weapons) shed light on their date, place of origin, those who issued them, and other historical factors. The titles, devices, and allegorical or symbolic figures give evidence of religious views or political claims. In deciphering abbreviations and interpreting figures, paleography, the history of art, and the study of weapons and seals are all helpful. Comparative research relies on catalogs and publications, and general histories of coinage and economics play a part. Church history uses numismatics to trace the extent of ecclesiastical jurisdictions and the course of religious and political change. Numismatics is of special value when written sources are defective or when coins and medals were valued as means of propaganda, as in the period leading up to and just before the 17th century.

6. Diplomatics

The science of diplomatics originally had the task of testing the authenticity of documents in the advancing or defending of legal claims. It then applied these methods to history in the evaluation and correct interpretation of sources. It is helpful in dealing with documents relating to the rights, finances, and property of churches and in understanding political aims and power relations. It differentiates documents according to those who issue them (e.g., pope, emperor, king, or private person). By style and structure it distinguishes solemn documents establishing lasting rights and privileges from everyday documents of transitory significance. Examples and collections help in this regard. There are also specific means of accreditation. By establishing regular patterns, diplomatics can spot deviations and thus unmask fraud or falsification.

Earlier church histories can be supplemented by diplomatics. From studying the composition of documents, diplomatics has now gone on to study the records of chancelleries and their personnel, of-

fering new insights of general significance. Many documents of the later Middle Ages and early modern period still await investigation.

7. Chronology

Chronology helps in the dating and interrelating of events. Different peoples and churches have used different dating systems. Christian dating rested at first on the Julian calendar, introduced into the → Roman Empire in 46 B.C.

Along with dates from the founding of → Rome or the regnant years of the emperor and high officials, dating by popes and bishops came in during the Middle Ages. Because it helped in fixing movable feasts (→ Easter), dating from Christ's birth began sometime between the 6th century and the 11th. From the 12th century to the 15th the cycle of the → church year and holy days increasingly affected secular dating. Up to the late Middle Ages there were various ways of relating the new year to church festivals.

In 1582 the Roman Catholic Church introduced the Gregorian calendar to solve the problem of deviations between the Julian calendar and astronomical calculations. The Protestant world adopted it after 1700. To keep straight the calendar used for a given date, it was sometimes necessary to specify "New Style" or "Old Style." The French Revolution established its own dating between 1792 and 1805. The Eastern church kept its own system up to the 18th century (in some places, even up to the 20th cent.).

Chronology uses comparative handbooks, tables, surveys, and lists of the names of days and months, by the help of which it can interpret dating contradictions in documents. It harmonizes church history with modern dating and corrects errors in older works.

8. Geography/Cartography

Historical geography provides aids for identifying and describing historical locations. Using archaeology, natural science, and written and artistic sources, it reconstructs landscapes, dwellings, and towns. It may work comparatively or in isolation, either looking at longer processes or studying conditions at a particular time. The facts in reference works and atlases often stand in need of correction. Geography is essential in studying the church's administration, property, and history of → mission (§3). Cartography provides the means to put the results on maps.

Bibliography: On 1: F. Beck and E. Henning, eds., *Die archivalischen Quellen. Eine Einführung in ihre Benutzung* (Weimar, 1994) • A. von Brandt, *Werkzeug des*

Historikers (9th ed.; Stuttgart, 1980; orig. pub., 1958) • S. B. CHILD and D. P. HOLMES, *Checklist of Historical Records Survey Publications: Bibliography of Research Projects Reports* (rev. ed.; Washington, D.C., 1943) • F. M. CROSS, "How the Alphabet Democratized Civilization," *BibRev* 8/6 (1992) 18-31 • R. DELORT, *Introduction aux sciences auxiliaires de l'histoire* (Paris, 1969) • L.-F. GÉNICOT, *Introduction aux sciences auxilières traditionelles de l'histoire de l'art. Diplomatique, héraldique, sigillographie, chronologie, paléographie* (Louvain-la-Neuve, 1984) • B. KRUITWAGEN, *Laatmiddeleuwsche paleografia, paleotypica, liturgica, kalendalia, grammaticalia* (The Hague, 1942) • J. MAZZOLENI, *Paleografia e diplomatica e scienze ausiliare* (2d ed.; Naples, 1970).

On 2: A. BÖCKH and R. KLUSSMANN, *Encyklopädie und Methodologie der philologischen Wissenschaft* (2d ed.; Leipzig, 1886) • P. M. DALY, *Emblem Theory: Recent German Contributions to the Characterization of the Emblem Genre* (Nendeln, 1979) • F. W. DANKER, *A Century of Greco-Roman Philology: Featuring the American Philological Association and the Society of Biblical Literature* (Atlanta, 1988) • Y. GIRAUD, ed., *L'emblème à la renaissance* (Paris, 1982) • A. HENKEL and A. SCHÖNE, *Emblemata. Handbuch der Sinnbildkunst des 16. und 17. Jahrhunderts* (Stuttgart, 1967; supp. vol., 1976) • K. J. HÖLTGEN, *Aspects of the Emblem: Studies in the English Emblem Tradition and the European Context* (Kassel, 1986) • M.-T. JONES-DAVIES, ed., *Emblèmes et devises aux temps de la renaissance* (Paris, 1981) • J. LANDWEHR, ed., *Bibliotheca emblematica* (vols. 1, 3, 5-6; Utrecht, 1970, 1972, 1976) • P. MAAS, *Textkritik* (3d ed.; Leipzig, 1957; orig. pub., 1927) • S. PEUKERT, *Emblem und Emblematikrezeption* (Darmstadt, 1978) • M. PRAZ, *Studies in Seventeenth-Century Imagery* (2d ed.; Rome, 1964; addenda and corrigenda added 1974; orig. pub., 1939) • J. E. SANDYS, *A History of Classical Scholarship* (3 vols.; Cambridge, 1906-8) • *SBO* • P. VERNEUIL, *Dictionnaire des symboles, emblèmes et attributs* (Paris, 1897) • H. WALTHER, *Die Namenforschung als historische Hilfswissenschaft. Eigennamen als Geschichtsquelle* (Potsdam, 1990) • U. VON WILAMOWITZ-MOELLENDORFF and H. LLOYD-JONES, *History of Classical Scholarship* (Baltimore, 1982).

On 3: J. AUTENRIETH, ed., *Renaissance- und Humanistenschriften* (Munich, 1988) • R. BARBOUR, *Greek Literary Hands, A.D. 400-1600* (Oxford, 1982) • B. BISCHOFF, G. J. LIEFTINCK, and G. BATTELLI, *Nomenclature des écrits livresques du IX au XVI siècle* (Paris, 1954) • M. P. BROWN, *A Guide to Western Historical Scripts from Antiquity to 1600* (Toronto, 1990) • G. CENCETTI, *Scritti di paleografia* (2d ed.; ed. G. Nicolai; Dietikon, 1993) • J. P. DEVOS and H. SELIGMAN, eds., *L'art de déchiffrer* (Louvain, 1967) for the 17th

cent. • V. FEDERICI, *La scrittura delle cancellerie italiane. Dal secolo 12 al 17* (2d ed.; Rome, 1964; orig. pub., 1934) • J. G. FÉVRIER, *Histoire de l'écriture* (Paris, 1948) • H. FOERSTER, *Abriß der lateinischen Paläographie* (2d ed.; Bern, 1963; orig. pub., 1949) • W. FRANZ, *Kryptologie. Konstruktion und Entzifferung von Geheimschriften* (Stuttgart, 1988) • H. HAARMANN, *Universalgeschichte der Schrift* (2d ed.; Frankfurt, 1991) • L. C. HECTOR, *The Handwriting of English Documents* (London, 1958) • H. HUNGER et al., eds., *Geschichte der Textüberlieferung der antiken und mittelalterlichen Literatur* (vol. 1; 2d ed.; Zurich, 1975; orig. pub., 1961) • H. JENSEN, *Die Schrift in Vergangenheit und Gegenwart* (3d ed.; East Berlin, 1969; orig. pub., 1935) • B. M. METZGER, *Manuscripts of the Greek Bible: An Introduction to Paleography* (New York, 1981) • M. B. PARKES, *English Cursive Book Hands, 1250-1500* (Berkeley, Calif., 1980) • J. RÖMER, *Geschichte der Kürzungen (dt. Texte)* (Göppingen, 1997) • E.-D. STIEBNER and W. LEONHARD, *Bruckmanns Handbuch der Schrift* (Munich, 1977) • J. STIENNON, *L'écriture* (Turnhout, 1995).

On 4: J. L. VAN DER GOUW, "Epigrafica," *NAB* 70 (1966) 37ff. • R. M. KLOOS, *Einführung in die Epigraphik des Mittelalters und der frühen Neuzeit* (Darmstadt, 1980) • W. KOCH, "Epigraphica," *UH* 46 (1975) 69-94 • A. LEMAIRE, "Writing and Writing Materials," *ABD* 6.999-1008 • R. J. WILLIAMS, "Writing and Writing Materials," *IDB* 4.909-21.

On 5: A. BLANCHET and A. DIEUDONNÉ, *Manuel de numismatique française* (Paris, 1912-36) • G. DEPEYROT, *Histoire de la monnaie des origines au 18 siècle* (3 vols.; Wetteren, 1995-96) • H. FENGLER, G. GIEROW, and W. UNGER, *Lexikon der Numismatik* (3d ed.; Berlin, 1982) • H. FRÈRE, *Numismatique. Initiations aux méthodes et aux classements* (Louvain-la-Neuve, 1982) • F. FRIEDENSBURG, *Münzkunde und Geldgeschichte der Einzelstaaten des Mittelalters und der Neuzeit* (Munich, 1926) • P. GRIERSON and A. R. FREY, *Dictionary of Numismatic Names* (New York, 1973) • W. HOLZ, *Lexikon der Münzabkürzungen* (Munich, 1981) • F. W. MADDEN, *History of Jewish Coinage, and of Money in the Old and New Testament* (New York, [1967]) • L. A. MAYER and M. AVI-YONAH, *A Bibliography of Jewish Numismatics* (Jerusalem, 1966) • M. PRICE, *Coins and the Bible* (London, 1975) • B. PROKISCH, *Grunddaten zur europäischen Münzprägung der Neuzeit ca. 1500-1990* (Vienna, 1993) • B. SPRENGER, *Das Geld der Deutschen (bis zur Gegenwart)* (2d ed.; Paderborn, 1995) • P. SPUFFORD, *Handbook of Medieval Exchange* (London, 1986) • C. H. SUTHERLAND, *Art in Coinage* (London, 1955).

On 6: A. DE BOÜARD, *Manuel de diplomatique française et pontificale* (Paris, 1948) • H. BRESLAU and

H.-W. Klewitz, *Handbuch der Urkundenlehre für Deutschland und Italien* (4th ed.; Berlin, 1968) • C. Brühl, "Derzeitige Lage und künftige Aufgaben der Diplomatik," *MBM* 35/1 (1984) 37ff. • A. Giry, *Manuel de diplomatique* (2d ed.; Paris, 1925; repr., 1972) • E. J. Polak, *Medieval and Renaissance Letter Treatises and Form Letters* (2 vols.; Leiden, 1993-94) • L. Santifaller, *Urkundenforschung* (2d ed.; Darmstadt, 1968; orig. pub., 1937).

On 7: L. Basnitzky, *Der jüdische Kalender. Entstehung und Aufbau* (Königstein, 1986) • W. G. Dever, "The Chronology of Syria-Palestine in the Second Millennium b.c.e.: A Review of Current Issues," *BASOR* 288 (1992) 1-22 • R. W. Ehrich, *Chronologies in Old World Archaeology* (Chicago, 1965) • O. Fambach, *Kalendarium der Jahre 1700 bis 2080* (Bonn, 1982) • H. Grotefend, *Taschenbuch der Zeitrechnung des deutschen Mittelalters und der Neuzeit* (11th ed.; Hannover 1971; orig. pub., 1898) • H. Lietzmann, *Zeitrechnung der römischen Kaiserzeit, des Mittelalters und der Neuzeit* (4th ed.; Leipzig, 1984; orig. pub., 1934) • F. Maiello, *Storia del calendario. La misurazione del tempo, 1450-1800* (Turin, 1996) • F. M. Powicke and E. B. Fryde, *Handbook of British Chronology* (2d ed.; London, 1961; orig. pub., 1939) • A. E. Samuel, *Greek and Roman Chronology: Calendars and Years in Classical Antiquity* (Munich, 1972) • H. Zemanek, *Kalender und Chronologie* (6th ed.; Munich, 1990).

On 8: A. R. H. Baker and M. Billunge, eds., *Period and Place: Research Methods in Historical Geography* (Cambridge, 1982) • R. H. Baker, ed., *Progress in Historical Geography* (Newton Abbot, 1972) • P. Claval, *La géographie culturelle* (Paris, 1995) • S. Courville, *Introduction à la géographie historique* (Quebec, 1995) • K. Fehn et al., eds., *Siedlungsforschung. Archäologie, Geschichte, Geographie* (Bonn, 1988) • S. Franz, *Historische Kartographie* (2d ed.; Bremen, 1962) • A. Hüttermann, *Karteninterpretation in Stichworten*, vol. 1, *Geographische Interpretation topographischer Karten* (3d ed.; Berlin, 1993) • H. Jaeger, *Historische Geographie* (Wiesbaden, 1969) • H. Jedin et al., eds., *Atlas zur Kirchengeschichte* (Freiburg, 1970) • V. H. Matthews and J. C. Moyer, "Bible Atlases: Which Ones Are Best?" *BA* 53 (1990) 220-31 • K. Neberzahl, *Maps of the Holy Lands: Images of Terra Sancta through Two Millennia* (New York, 1986) • R. Ogrissek, *Die Karte als Hilfsmittel des Historikers* (Gotha, 1968) • N. J. G. Pounds, *An Historical Geography of Europe* (Cambridge, 1990) • G. Tanner, E. Schulz, and R. Jäcker, *Einführung in die Kartographie und Luftbildinterpretation* (2d ed.; Gotha, 1983).

Eva Giessler-Wirsig

History of Religion

1. According to the view one takes of → religious studies, the history of religion is either one department of such studies or it is the main discipline itself. In about 1694 G. W. Leibniz (1646-1716) became the first to differentiate the *histoire des religions* from church history. In his *Natural History of Religion* (1757), D. Hume (1711-76) became probably the first to juxtapose critically religion's "natural history" (terminology adopted by the whole Enlightenment) with the → salvation history represented by the church. In French and Italian, for example, the use of the plural "history of religions" recognizes that many historical religions must be investigated. English and German use the singular to maintain focus on the one religion in all of them.

In what follows, for the sake of clarity (which only academic study and not practice allows), we will presuppose that religious studies in the larger sense (the "study of religion" that can refer to the singular or plural form of "religion(s)," depending on the given case) can be divided into the separate disciplines of the history of religion(s), the → phenomenology of religion, the → sociology of religion, and the → psychology of religion. Even when we limit the field in this way, however, the problems that are now raised differ from those dealt with in the past.

2. We may distinguish four different approaches to the research and writing of the history of religion. They are based not on terms or definitions or types of religion(s) but on the facts and data and phenomena that go beyond those definitions as found in the history of everyday or private life, of societies, of peoples, and of states. Historians can successfully investigate the history of religion only if they do not just survey the whole chronologically but divide it into several historical classifications, which in principle can be mastered only one at a time. We thus must consider the following four approaches, in each case raising the question of comparable factors.

First we have the history of religion as it has a place in the life of societies and individuals (what up to the Enlightenment was called *religio naturalis*, "natural religion"), the focus here being largely on regions and periods, with little account taken of → acculturation.

Then we have the history of religion(s) as represented positively through prophets, seers, → priests, founders, and reformers. It thus stands independently within or over against the secular, largely in times in which stable ethnic groups developed along with their religions, even though some may now have perished.

Then we have the history of religions as they have become institutionalized in their own organizations, cults, → temples (§1), and so on, largely in times in which conflicts played a dominant role. These conflicts might be between the more widespread or world religions, often linked to states, in Asia from the beginning of the third century B.C. to the end of the European, Byzantine, and Islamic Middle Ages (though noncontemporaneously!), with parallel phenomena in South and East Asia. Or the conflicts might be between states that had confessionalized world religions within their borders, that is, situations obtaining largely in modern times and before industrialization.

Finally, we have the history of religion and of religions that in a secularized form play a part in general history or take elements of this history into (or back into) themselves and thus represent the dialectic of secularization, largely in periods inclined toward an economic and technological worldview (→ Modern Church History; Technology).

3. The history of religion is not a theological discipline (→ Theology), and we must not view it in the light of theological issues. Nevertheless, we may in principle have new cause to reconsider theology as the history of religion (H. W. Schütte).

Furthermore, historical theology can also use the methods of the history of religion if it offers a history of the Israelite religion instead of a historical theology of the OT; or if it presents a comprehensive history of religions — one including early Christianity — focusing on Hellenism (→ Hellenistic-Roman Religion), ancient Judaism, and the Roman Empire (→ Roman Religion; History of Religions School) instead of simply juxtaposing the theology of the NT and the surrounding world, in a fashion dictated by an existentially focused hermeneutic; or if it prepares a critical history of the church instead of a history of dogma and theology prepared for use by systematic theology.

Systematic theology can take up the problem of the absoluteness of Christianity and the history of religion (E. Troeltsch) in a theology of religions, directing special attention precisely to the history of religion.

The → theology of history (§3) may also deal with all these issues, with additional attention given the history of religion.

4. History as event cannot be separated from the writing of history, from historians, and from all those who view themselves historically. History thus has an additional dimension that is constituted by the self-understanding of the nonreligious as well as of the religious person. We can view what has taken place in the history of religion as the past of religion or religions only to the extent that it offers answers to the questions posed by both believers and atheists.

Bibliography: C. J. BLEEKER and G. WIDENGREN, eds., *Historia religionum: Handbook for the History of Religions* (2 vols.; Leiden, 1969-71) • J. BOTHAMLEY, *Dictionary of Theories* (London, 1993) • P. D. CHANTEPIE DE LA SAUSSAYE, *Lehrbuch der Religionsgeschichte* (4th ed.; 2 vols.; ed. A. Bertholet and E. Lehmann; Tübingen, 1925; orig. pub., 1887-89) • *CRE* • *EAR* • M. ELIADE, *A History of Religious Ideas* (3 vols.; Chicago, 1978-85) • C. ELSAS, H. G. KIPPENBERG, et al., eds., *Loyalitätskonflikte in der Religionsgeschichte* (Würzburg, 1990) • N. GOTTWALD, *The Hebrew Bible in Its Social World and in Ours* (Atlanta, 1993) • *HR* • *HRG* • H.-I. MARROU, *De la connaissance historique* (4th ed.; Paris, 1960) • J. PELIKAN, *The Christian Tradition: A History of the Development of Doctrine* (5 vols.; Chicago, 1971-89) • *RM* • H. W. SCHÜTTE, "Theologie als Religionsgeschichte. Das Reformprogramm Paul de Lagardes," *NZSTh* 8 (1966) 111-20 • E. TROELTSCH, *Die Absolutheit des Christentums und die Religionsgeschichte* (Tübingen, 1912) • H. ZINSER, ed., *Der Untergang von Religionen* (Berlin, 1986).

CARSTEN COLPE

History of Religions School

The history-of-religions school was a group of young theologians who, in the late 1880s, influenced → theology and the → church first at Göttingen and then over wider circles, handling exegesis and church history in a way that made an impact not only on Protestant but also on Roman Catholic theology (→ Modernism) and on the dialogue with the world religions. In OT and NT scholarship the history-of-religions school helped to prepare the way for form criticism and redaction criticism and made methodological demands today that only a sociologically concerned theology and → historiography can meet.

1. The group, whose main proponents were A. Eichhorn (1856-1926), W. Wrede (1859-1906), H. Gunkel (1862-1932), J. Weiß (1863-1914), W. Bousset (1865-1920), E. → Troeltsch (1865-1923), and the religion historian H. Hackmann (1864-1935), did not form a school in the strict sense, but its leaders

shared common academic interests and methods. They had in common with historically oriented 19th-century theology (→ Theology in the Nineteenth and Twentieth Centuries) the ethos of autonomous historicocritical research, but they attempted more deliberately than that theology, and especially at a critical distance from A. Ritschl (1822-89) and their other liberal teachers (→ Liberal Theology 3.4), to exclude theological and practical church interests and presuppositions from their historical inquiries, thus incurring criticism from the theological opponents of → historicism.

2. The history-of-religions school aimed to achieve an objective understanding of the → religion underlying the documents of primitive Christianity and → Judaism (→ Hellenism), which they tried to unlock and understand in terms of psychological and sociological questions and categories. In their historical work → eschatology (Weiß), the cult (Eichhorn, Bousset), and pneumatology (Gunkel; → Holy Spirit) played a prominent part as loci and principles of interpretation experientially understood. Under → Romantic influences, they viewed religion not primarily as an ethical matter but instead as something psychological and even, in many cases, nonrational.

In their portrait of Jesus, however, the history-of-religions school was still captive to liberal ethical value judgments. Characteristic for the methodology was the renewed adoption of the literary interests of the 18th century, as suggested by Eichhorn. Wrede in his *Messiasgeheimnis in den Evangelien* (1901, ET *Messianic Secret* [1972]) engaged in study of the history of → traditions, showing how motifs and ideas might undergo shifts in meaning in the course of their history and viewing the changes in understanding as expressions of specific religious needs in the → congregations. In relation to contemporary biblical theology opposition arose especially against a historically improper fixing of the → canon on the basis of → inspiration, the role of exegetical work as subservient to practical theology, and a doctrinal concept method that isolates religious life.

Wrede envisioned a replacement of NT theology by a history of the religion of primitive Christianity (→ History of Religion) that would be purely historically oriented and that would take into account the broader history of religion and the social context. He was never able to execute his plan, but thematically limited monographs such as Bousset's *Kyrios Christos* followed his methodological suggestions and ranged far beyond the canon.

A historical understanding of Christianity, viewed as a syncretistic religion (→ Syncretism), sought to define it primarily in terms of the religious history of what was then called later Judaism. The next generation of the history-of-religions school focused more on Hellenism and → Gnosticism. Many people assumed that the academic study and theological handling of Gnosticism and its redeemer myth were the chief concern of the history-of-religions school, a misunderstanding that retained a certain influence throughout the century.

3. The attempt of the history-of-religions school to give an objective depiction of the religion of Judaism and early Christianity resulted in some striking theological antitheses — for example, between Jesus and Paul (Wrede) or between the radically eschatological experience of early Christianity and modern cultural Christianity (Weiß).

When we contextualize the history-of-religions school, we are struck by the generation gap between its advocates and their liberal teachers, as also by the definite rejection of historical work in the service of the institutional church in favor of a concept of academic autonomy. Even though Ritschl and A. von Harnack (1851-1930) are indeed to be reckoned among the fathers of the history-of-religions school, the school itself differed from liberal theologians insofar as it was not inclined to press its scientific work and findings precipitously into the service of → denominations or of → culture (→ Culture Protestantism), although it was certainly willing to place those same findings at the disposal of the quest for human self-understanding.

The influence on the school of teachers like B. Duhm (1847-1928), P. de Lagarde (1827-1891), and U. Wilamowitz-Moellendorf (1848-1931), who were nondenominational or hard to place denominationally or even hostile to the church and theology, is typical as regards the interdisciplinary work that was demanded. The popularizing of the history-of-religions school in lectures and publications (e.g., the RV series, the *RGG,* and *Lebensfragen*) sharpened the tensions with denominationally oriented theologians and church authorities but made the findings more widely known.

The history-of-religions school did more than stimulate Protestant exegesis, systematics (e.g., the question of the absoluteness of Christianity; → Systematic Theology), and missiology (e.g., the legitimacy of → mission). Its congregationally oriented and experiential understanding of early Christianity found an echo in Roman Catholic modernism and produced a new → apologetic against Protestant theological liberalism that was profoundly misunderstood in its own church (A. F. Loisy, G. Tyrrell). In the second generation a further stimulus was given to dialogue with world religions and with the → phenomenology of religion and the → history of religion (R. Otto, F. Heiler).

Bibliography: Works by members of the school: W. BOUSSET, *Kyrios Christos. Geschichte des Christusglaubens von den Anfängen des Christentums bis Irenaeus* (6th ed.; Göttingen, 1967; orig. pub., 1913) • A. EICHHORN, *Das Abendmahl im Neuen Testament* (Leipzig, 1898) • H. GUNKEL, *Schöpfung und Chaos in Urzeit und Endzeit. Eine religionsgeschichtliche Untersuchung über Gen 1 und Apk. Joh. 12* (Göttingen, 1895); idem, *Die Wirkungen des heiligen Geistes nach der populären Anschauung der apostolischen Zeit und die Lehre des Apostels Paulus* (2d ed.; Göttingen, 1899); idem, *Zum religionsgeschichtlichen Verständnis des Neuen Testaments* (Göttingen, 1903) • E. TROELTSCH, *Die Absolutheit des Christentums und die Religionsgeschichte* (2d ed.; Tübingen, 1912; orig. pub., 1902); idem, "Die Dogmatik der Religionsgeschichtlichen Schule" (1913), *Gesammelte Schriften* (vol. 2; 2d ed.; Tübingen, 1922; repr., 1962) 500-524 • J. WEISS, *Die Predigt Jesu vom Reiche Gottes* (3d ed.; Göttingen, 1964; orig. pub., 1892) • W. WREDE, *Das Messiasgeheimnis in den Evangelien. Zugleich ein Beitrag zum Verständnis des Markusevangeliums* (Göttingen, 1901); idem, *Über Aufgabe und Methode der sogenannten Neutestamentlichen Theologie* (Göttingen, 1897).

Other works: E. BARNIKOL, "Albert Eichhorn (1856-1926). Sein 'Lebenslauf,' seine Thesen 1886, seine Abendmahlsthese 1898 und seine Leidensbriefe an seinen Schüler Erich Franz (1913-1919) nebst seinen Bekenntnissen über Heilige Geschichte und Evangelium, über Orthodoxie und Liberalismus," *WZ(H).GS* 9 (1960) 141-52 • H. BOERS, *What Is NT Theology?* (Philadelphia, 1979) • C. COLPE, *Die Religionsgeschichtliche Schule. Darstellung und Kritik ihres Bildes vom gnostischen Erlösermythus* (Göttingen, 1961) • H. GRESSMANN, *Albert Eichhorn und die Religionsgeschichtliche Schule* (Göttingen, 1914) • J. S. HELFER, ed., *On Method in the History of Religions* (Middletown, Conn., 1968) • W. KLATT, *Hermann Gunkel. Zu seiner Theologie der Religionsgeschichte und zur Entstehung der formgeschichtlichen Methode* (Göttingen, 1969) • B. LANNERT, *Die Wiederentdeckung der neutestamentlichen Eschatologie durch Johannes Weiß* (Tübingen, 1989) • G. LÜDEMANN, "Die Religionsgeschichtliche Schule," *Theologie in Göttingen. Eine Vorlesungsreihe* (ed. B. Voeller; Göttingen, 1987) 325-61 • G. LÜDEMANN and M. SCHRÖDER, *Die Religionsgeschichtliche Schule in Göttingen. Eine Dokumentation* (Göttingen, 1987) • H. RENZ and F. W. GRAF, *Troeltsch-Studien. Untersuchungen zur Biographie und Werkgeschichte* (Gütersloh, 1982) • H. ROLLMANN, "From Baur to Wrede: The Quest for a Historical Method," *SR* 17 (1988) 443-54; idem, "Theologie und Religionsgeschichte. Zeitgenössische Stimmen zur Diskussion um die religionsgeschichtliche Methode und die Einführung religionsgeschichtlicher Lehrstühle in die theologische Fakultäten um die Jahrhundertwende," *ZTK* 80 (1983) 69-84 • G. STRECKER, "William Wrede. Zur hundertsten Wiederkehr seines Geburtstages," *ZTK* 57 (1960) 67-91 • A. VERHEULE, *Wilhelm Bousset. Leben und Werk: Ein theologiegeschichtlicher Versuch* (Amsterdam, 1973).

HANS ROLLMANN

Holiness Code

The Holiness Code, which is found in Leviticus 17–26, is the earliest book of law that forms part of the → Pentateuch. A. Klostermann coined the name with an eye to the significance of the concept of holiness in this section (see 19:2; 20:26; 21:8). God's holiness is here the basis of the demand for holiness that is addressed to → Israel (§1).

The Holiness Code opens in chap. 17 with rules of → sacrifice, which particularly regulate the contact with blood, and closes in chap. 26 with statements about → blessing and → cursing. In between are various legal regulations, for example, about sex (18), rules for the priests (21:1–22:16), the quality of animals used for sacrifice (22:17-33), feasts (23), and the land (25). At the heart of the code are laws oriented to social ethics (19).

Various theories have been advanced as to the origin of this code. It is thought by most to be an independent entity that was integrated into P (K. Grünwaldt), though K. Elliger, V. Wagner, and A. Ruwe do not agree. It is also debated whether different parts were put together to make up the code (C. Feucht) or additions were made to an original text (R. Kilian). In any case there seems to have been some editing. W. Thiel thinks the work dates from the exile, which would explain the similarity that many find to Ezekiel. Such provenance, however, would not rule out the use of much older legal materials.

Bibliography: A. S. DARLING, "The Levitical Code: Hygiene or Holiness?" *Medicine and the Bible* (2d ed.; ed. B. Palmer; Carlisle, Cumbria, 1992) 85-99 • K. ELLIGER, *Leviticus* (Tübingen, 1966) • C. FEUCHT, *Untersuchungen* zum Heiligkeitsgesetz (Berlin, 1964) • K. GRÜNWALDT, Das Heiligkeitsgesetz Leviticus 17–26 (Berlin, 1999) • H. K. HARRINGTON, The Impurity Systems of Qumran and the Rabbis: Biblical Foundations (Atlanta, 1993) • J. E. HARTLEY, Leviticus (Dallas, 1992) • J. JOOSTEN, People and Land in the Holiness Code: An Exegetical Study of the Ideational Framework of the Law in Leviticus 17–26 (Brussels, 1994) • R. KILIAN, Literarkritische und formgeschichtliche Untersuchung des Heiligkeitsgesetzes (Bonn, 1963) • B. A. LEVINE, Leviticus (Philadelphia, 1989) • A. RUWE, "Heiligkeitsgesetz" und "Priesterschrift." Literaturgeschichtliche und rechtssystematische Untersuchungen zu Leviticus 17,1–26,2 (Tübingen, 1999) • H. T. C. SUN, "Holiness Code," ABD 3.254-57 • W. THIEL, "Erwägungen zum Alter des Heiligkeitsgesetzes," ZAW 81 (1969) 40-73 • V. WAGNER, "Zur Existenz des sogenannten 'Heiligkeitsgesetzes,'" ZAW 86 (1974) 307-16 • W. ZIMMERLI, "'Heiligkeit' nach dem sogenannten Heiligkeitsgesetz," VT 30 (1980) 493-512.

                                    HANS JOCHEN BOECKER

Holiness Movement

1. General Description
2. Distinguishing Doctrine
3. History
  3.1. Phoebe Palmer and the Shorter Way
  3.2. Dissenting Methodism
  3.3. Revivalism and the Camp Meeting
    3.3.1. Finney and Oberlin Perfectionism
    3.3.2. National Camp Meeting Association
    3.3.3. Conflict
  3.4. Denominations and Associations
    3.4.1. Holiness Church
    3.4.2. Church of God (Anderson, Ind.)
    3.4.3. Church of God (Holiness)
    3.4.4. Salvation Army
    3.4.5. Church of the Nazarene
    3.4.6. Wesleyan Church
    3.4.7. International Holiness Convention
    3.4.8. Cooperation

1. General Description

The Holiness movement is a worldwide aggregation of evangelical Protestant individuals, congregations, and denominations whose distinguishing mark is adherence to John → Wesley's teaching concerning Christian → perfection. Somewhat fewer than half of the 9 million who would identify with the Holiness movement belong to the various mainline Methodist denominations; most of the rest belong to denominations, associations, and congregations that identify themselves primarily as Holiness bodies. Many of this latter group recognize strong Methodist roots and maintain ties of varying strength to mainline Methodism. About 70 percent of the Holiness movement is represented in the → World Methodist Council.

Most of the Holiness groups bear other Methodist characteristics along with their commitment to Wesley's doctrine of scriptural holiness. Such beliefs and personal traits include their commitment to historic Trinitarian → orthodoxy; a commitment to Protestant understandings of → justification by → grace alone through → faith alone; the sufficiency and ultimate authority of the Old and New Testaments for faith and practice; the priesthood of all believers; → Arminianism; an emphasis upon evangelical experience; evangelistic zeal; and a tendency to organize with → evangelism and social action as priorities.

The largest of the Holiness denominations are the → Church of the Nazarene (1.3 million members worldwide) and the → Salvation Army (1 million officers and soldiers worldwide). Together, the Church of God (Anderson, Ind.; → Churches of God), the Wesleyan Methodist Church, a worldwide federation of autonomous denominations, and the Free Methodist Church, also a global federation, account for approximately another 1.5 million persons worldwide. Another half million or more belong to about 60 smaller Holiness denominations and a dozen missionary associations (→ Methodist Churches).

Most Holiness bodies carry on active evangelizing efforts in fields far from their home bases — for example, the Church of the Nazarene has congregations in about 70 nations; the Salvation Army has corps (i.e., congregations) in about 90 nations; and the Wesleyan Church in about 20. A global figure of 4.5 million members of Holiness churches would be conservative and realistic, and it is noteworthy that more than half of that figure are citizens of countries other than the United States.

There is, however, an anomaly in connection with these statistics: it is estimated that some 9 to 10 million persons are in attendance in the → Sunday schools and → worship services in Holiness churches on a given Sunday. This anomaly arises from the fact that while the Holiness bodies' doctrinal and behavioral requirements for membership are almost universally stringent, those same bodies almost universally encourage attendance and participation in their services by "all sorts and conditions," insofar as the conscience of the given community and the given nonmember allow. Communion is open to all who believe in Jesus Christ as personal savior. Few of the Holiness bodies require one to be "in the experience" of Christian perfection for membership; most require members at least to be seeking and expecting it. Neither fidelity to the doctrinal standards nor adherence to the behavioral requirements is taken as a sign of either justification or entire → sanctification, except in some of the "folk theology."

In addition to its intense evangelistic activities, the Holiness movement has since its earliest days established schools at all levels in its home countries and in its missions areas. At present in the United States 34 fully accredited liberal arts colleges and universities identify with the Holiness movement, as do 7 fully accredited graduate-level theological schools; also identifying with the movement in the United States are several dozen Bible colleges and junior colleges and about a dozen liberal arts institutions not regionally accredited. As a specific denominational example, the Church of the Nazarene operates one liberal arts college, seven universities, a graduate-professional theological seminary, and a Bible college in the United States; universities in Kenya and Korea; five university-level theological schools, some 30 baccalaureate-level theological institutions, and a handful of nurses' training schools (all residential) outside of the United States (most of the U.S. universities have schools of nursing); and close to 100 theological institutes and extension programs (→ Religious Education).

All of the larger Holiness → denominations maintain extensive programs of ministry to social needs and provide disaster → relief in cooperation with other national and international relief bodies, ecclesiastical and secular, around the world. Such work is indeed the special vocation of the Salvation Army.

Camp and revival meetings are still quite common among Holiness people. And most of the larger Holiness bodies publish at least one periodical, a hymnbook, and literature for Christian education at all age levels. Five of the larger denominations have developed the Aldersgate Group and publish Sunday School and Vacation Bible School materials cooperatively. The publishing houses of the Church of the Nazarene, Salvation Army, Church of God (Anderson), Wesleyan Church, and Free Methodist Church develop and print materials in several languages.

2. Distinguishing Doctrine

The Holiness movement claims John Wesley (1703-91), Church of England priest, Oxford don, and a principal founder of → Methodism, as its ma-

jor mentor and as the source of its distinguishing doctrine. Wesley said that God had raised up the Methodists "to spread scriptural holiness over these lands and to reform the nation [i.e., Great Britain]." For Wesley, "scriptural holiness" referred to what he believed was biblical teaching, confirmed by significant Christian tradition, reason, and evangelical experience, namely, that Christ's atoning work makes available to the justified and regenerate believer the grace fully, or "perfectly," to keep the Great Commandment — to love God and → neighbor unconditionally.

Wesley taught that subsequent to justification and → regeneration, the → Holy Spirit perfects the believer in holiness in an instantaneously granted second work of grace, "entire sanctification," which purifies the heart so that we may "perfectly love [God] and worthily magnify [his] name" (e.g., see *Plain Account of Christian Perfection* and sermon 43, "The Scripture Way of Salvation"). Grace is understood to be the unmerited favor of God. As a work of grace, this evangelical experience of entire sanctification, or Christian perfection, is receivable only through faith in the provisions of the atoning work of Christ, not through works. Faith, from God's side, is a divine gift. Humanly, it is grace-driven active assent to the promises, commands, and work of God. The Holy Spirit assures the believer that entire sanctification has been granted, but assurance too comes independent of works, and as a gift of grace it is received by faith.

Wesley referred to the biblical, theological, and experiential dimensions of this gift of divine grace with such terms as "scriptural holiness," "Christian perfection," "perfect → love," and "entire sanctification." His followers have expanded the vocabulary to include a number of synonyms, synecdochic terms, and abbreviations. These include "holiness," "full salvation," "freedom from sin," "perfect cleansing (from sin)," "fullness of the Spirit," "fullness of the blessing," and "the second blessing."

The Holiness movement has generally followed Wesley's teaching, but it has emphasized more than he did the instantaneous character of entire sanctification and of its attendant → assurance. It has also emphasized somewhat more than he did the definiteness of the experience. Holiness people have often referred to it as a crisis experience to distinguish it from an → experience (§2) that is solely progressive. The movement has always struggled, primarily against strong currents of folk theology, to retain Wesley's insistence that → salvation, including entire sanctification (or Christian perfection), is all of grace.

Except for some theologically careless adherents, the Holiness movement, with Wesley, absolutely rejects the notion of sinless perfection in this life. Rather, it teaches that the experience of entire sanctification, or Christian perfection, always entails the need for Christ's atoning work and continuing growth in grace. It always entails participation in the life of the church, for the church provides the means of grace for nurturing and sustaining it, and likewise provides avenues for its expression. Works do not save, but the expression of Christian perfection appears in works of compassion in the church and in the world as well as in personal piety. Hence, the great majority of the movement agrees with Wesley's dictum: "There is no holiness but social holiness."

Some elements of the movement, such as the Salvation Army, have persisted in keeping a strong social conscience. Other elements, wanting to avoid the very appearance of supporting the theologically liberal → Social Gospel, especially in the period from about 1940 to the early 1970s, closed or reduced their support of orphanages, homes for unwed mothers, hospitals, and other social service agencies, tended to accept uncritically the social values of their surrounding cultures, and emphasized personal piety alone. Since the early 1970s, however, the whole movement has experienced a strong resurgence of social action rooted in the same Wesleyan theological base that had led the movement to social activism in its earlier days.

Wesley did not require his Methodists to be "in the experience [of Christian perfection]," but he did require his preachers to be "groaning after [or 'going on to'] perfection," expecting to be "made perfect in this life" (*Large Minutes,* q. 51). Contrary to this openness, most Holiness denominations require definite testimonies to entire sanctification from candidates for → ordination. Some require such testimonies from those holding significant congregational responsibilities (e.g., Sunday School teachers and members of official church boards).

3. History

Wesley's Methodists came to America in the late 1760s and brought the Wesleyan doctrine of Christian perfection with them. Their perfectionist teaching, if not their organization itself, attracted followers in other traditions almost immediately. Examples are the German Reformed pietists and → Mennonites, who united in 1800 to form the United Brethren denomination, and those Lutheran pietists who joined in the founding of the Evangelical As-

sociation in 1807 (from 1822, the Evangelical Church).

From the early 1900s, however, mainline Methodist bodies tended to mute Wesleyan perfectionism, and only since the 1970s have they begun again to give serious attention to the Holiness people among them. Ironically, until the mid-1900s, the largest concentrations of those deliberately advocating Wesley's doctrine of Christian perfection were still be found in the mainline British and British-originated American Methodist denominations, both in their indigenous settings and in their missionary enterprises. Only since about 1970 could it be said with some certainty that the majority of the Holiness movement are to be found outside of those denominations.

The preaching of the doctrine of Christian perfection, usually under the terms "entire sanctification" or "holiness," was prominent in American Methodism's first century, with some flagging of interest immediately following the death of Bishop Francis Asbury in 1816. The late 1830s saw an intense renewal of the doctrine and experience, especially in the northern and border states in the United States and in Great Britain. This renewal carried on for another 60 years or so.

Three linked elements played the primary roles in this renewal. Of principal importance at first was an intensely loyal, articulate, ecclesiastically well-placed, and financially well-fixed urban minority in the Methodist Episcopal Church (MEC) in the United States (together with some in the Methodist Episcopal Church, South [MECS], after the division of 1845), matched, as it were, by a significant minority of intensely loyal, articulate, evangelistically energetic British Wesleyan and Primitive Methodists who "spread scriptural holiness" at home and abroad. Of some importance at first and of greater importance after the 1860s were the activities of two, and after 1860 three, dissident Methodist denominations in the United States. Of great importance on both sides of the Atlantic was the development of camp and revival meetings as instruments for propagating Holiness.

3.1. *Phoebe Palmer and the Shorter Way*

The renewal that became clearly visible in the MEC by the late 1830s was deeply influenced by Phoebe Worrell → Palmer (d. 1874) and the Tuesday Meeting for the Promotion of Holiness in New York City. Founded in 1836, by Phoebe's sister, Sarah Worrell Lankford, the Tuesday Meeting met in the commodious home shared by the Palmer and Lankford families. A typical session included hymn singing, various "seasons" of → prayer, and a "talk" by

Phoebe Palmer. By 1840 all recognized "Sister Phoebe" as the Tuesday Meeting's natural leader. She directed it from that year until her death, except for the years 1861-64, when she and her husband, Walter, a physician, evangelized in Britain. There they built upon the work done by American evangelists, especially James Caughey (d. 1891) and Asa Mahan (d. 1889). And they left a strong foundation for the further work of Robert Pearsall Smith (d. 1898) and his spouse, Hannah Whitall Smith (d. 1910) and others.

Rather rapidly, the Tuesday Meeting for the Promotion of Holiness became a gathering place for prayer and → Bible study for religious leaders across the spectrum of Protestantism, but especially for Methodists. Its tone was clearly urban, upper-middle class, and professional. The theme of the meetings — "holiness of heart and life" — was applied to the needs of both those "in the experience" and those seeking it.

In addition to leading the Tuesday Meeting, Phoebe Palmer wrote nine highly popular books and many articles, especially appearing in the *Guide to Holiness,* which she edited from 1864 to 1874. She actively engaged in several significant humanitarian projects in New York City, including the founding and management of the Five Points Mission. And at least 317 times she spoke at revival and camp meetings in the United States, Canada, and Great Britain. She herself did not seek ordination and would not allow her "talks" to be referred to as sermons, but she did argue very strongly for the women's right to preach. Phoebe Palmer's principal legacy within the Holiness movement is her "altar theology," or "shorter way." She had come into the experience of entire sanctification after a long struggle for assurance, during which she was relieved to find what she called the shorter way.

Wesley had insisted that God granted the grace of perfect love definitely and instantaneously, but in God's own good time, and that the gift of assurance would also come in God's good time. Phoebe Palmer, fusing Romans 12:1 and Matthew 23:19, believed that a justified, regenerate person, by consecrating (giving or surrendering) himself or herself — that is, by "placing oneself on the altar" — met the single qualification necessary for the reception of the second blessing (entire sanctification, perfect love). Having consecrated oneself (i.e., placed oneself on Christ, who is our altar), one could receive the blessing and the assurance of having received it, simply by trusting in the biblical promises and declarations (for "the altar sanctifies the gift").

A number of Methodist theologians, including some who generally supported her work, especially Nathan Bangs and Randolph Sinks Foster, opposed this altar theology. Besides offering sharp exegetical critique, they insisted that in spite of her disclaimers, it made → consecration a meritorious work, thereby making entire sanctification a consequence of a good work rather than a work of grace. Palmer's doctrine of assurance, they said, made one dependent upon personal appropriations of biblical texts rather than the internal witness of the Holy Spirit. They urged her to retain Wesley's less rigid delineation of the experience in order to avert attempts to force God to follow human calendars, as it were; to fend off any kind of works-righteousness; and to ensure that assurance itself be understood as a gift of grace and not as a product of human appeals to biblical texts.

Generally, these theological and experiential warnings went unheeded. Phoebe Palmer's shorter way, which was eminently suited for revivalism, became almost immediately dominant and all but absolute in the Holiness movement. The great majority of Holiness people, deeply influenced by the emphases of revivalism on immediate decision, instantaneous divine response, and vivid evangelical experience, found the shorter way sure and empirically satisfying. And they were fully convinced that Palmer's view in no way contradicted Wesley's. Those holding the older understanding tended to tolerate, sometimes only barely, the majority view, believing, in typical Methodist fashion, that the cause of "spreading scriptural holiness" outweighed the problems inherent in Palmer's teaching.

By the 1920s Holiness people almost universally accepted the shorter way and now identified the altar theology as Wesley's own. More than a half century of marked success in spreading scriptural holiness, largely through camp meetings and revival campaigns, had convinced them of its correctness. The Church of the Nazarene alone, for example, grew from 10,000 members in 1908 to 136,000 by 1936.

The New York City Tuesday Meeting, ecumenical in spirit and in fact, was imitated across the country. But Mrs. Palmer and her closer associates remained strictly and loyally MEC. Mrs. Palmer's ministry had led a significant proportion of MEC (and a few MECS) leaders, some of whom would become bishops, into the experience of Christian perfection. This fact, together with the social location of the Palmers and Lankfords, made the Tuesday Meeting quite sensitive to the concerns of MEC leadership. Supporters of the Tuesday Meeting consistently declared that it existed solely to "spread scriptural holiness." This understanding clearly placed discussion of several roiling issues out of bounds, including ecclesiastical polity, slavery, and festering debates about personal piety (e.g., regarding styles of dress, forms of entertainment, and use of leisure time). Ironically, most supporters of the Tuesday Meeting were abolitionists and held very conservative views regarding issues of personal piety. To them, charges leveled by radical abolitionist MEC Holiness loyalists — of being disloyal to earlier MEC polity regarding slavery and personal piety, moral cowardice, and spiritual weakness — seemed ignorant at best, if not impertinent.

By 1860 the dissonance had created two camps within the young Holiness movement: on one side, those aligned with Mrs. Palmer and her friends, mostly MEC and some MECS adherents, along with a scattering of non-Methodists; on the other, the radical abolitionists and the critics of behavioral issues and ecclesiology, mostly dissident Methodists, including some MEC radicals. Between them stood MEC Holiness people whose ideology matched the latter group but whose primary desire was ecclesiastical peace and unity, especially after the wrenching division into the MEC and MECS in 1844-46. The social location of the Tuesday Meeting exacerbated the division. Those who looked to Mrs. Palmer and her friends tended to be, or aspired to be, urban and middle or upper-middle class — in perspective, if not also in fact.

3.2. Dissenting Methodism
It is here that dissenting Methodism enters the picture as the second of the three elements critical to the formation of an identifiable Holiness movement. Between the mid-1820s and 1860, four distinctly Wesleyan perfectionist, anti-MEC bodies arose in the United States. The *Primitive Methodist Church* came to the United States with British immigrants in 1826. It had arisen in Britain as a revivalist and Wesleyan perfectionist protest against the middle-class pretensions of of mainline Methodism. In America it retained its emphases on revivalism and Holiness. The *Methodist Protestant Church* (MPC), founded in 1830, arose primarily in dissent from within the MEC over issues of episcopal control. It generally retained the earlier MEC emphasis on Christian perfection. In 1877 it added to its articles of faith an article, "Of Sanctification," in the style of the Holiness movement. (The MPC rejoined the episcopal Methodists in 1939, bringing with it its article of faith on [entire] sanctification.) The *Wesleyan Methodist Connection* (WMC; later, Wesleyan Methodist Church and, since 1968, the Wesleyan Church) and the *Free Methodist Church*

(FMC), radical abolitionist Wesleyan perfectionists, were founded in 1843 and 1860 respectively, in protest against the heavy-handedness and temporizing of MEC bishops, primarily on the question of the abolition of → slavery. Both bodies also charged the MEC with worldliness, especially in matters of dress, entertainment, use of leisure, association (esp. membership in oath-bound secret societies or lodges), formality in worship, and catering to the tastes of the well-to-do at the expense of the poor. They generally supported Mrs. Palmer in her concern to spread scriptural holiness but freely criticized her silences as self-contradictions, furthering the division within Holiness ranks.

These four groups pointedly wrote Christian perfection into their basic articles of faith and consistently proclaimed it. Each of the four saw itself as a reradicalizing of Methodism and linked Holiness with their more democratic polities and their enforcement of behavioral rules. Each tended to view the eddy of the Holiness movement that swirled about Mrs. Palmer as inconsistently Wesleyan.

Since the 1840s, when the MPC sought to unite with the WMC, these dissident Methodist bodies have occasionally talked about merger in varying combinations, but generally it has evaded them. Differences in polity and → piety, born of experience rather than theology, have seemed insuperable.

After the Civil War many WMC and FMC clergy and laity returned to the MEC, not a few of them still bearing their criticisms of MEC laxity and middle-class status. This number would eventually serve as bridges between the Holiness people in the MEC, the WMC, and the FMC, which now self-consciously preached Wesleyan perfectionism as amended by altar theology.

3.3. Revivalism and the Camp Meeting
The third element in the development of a clearly definable Holiness movement in the United States was the quasi-Wesleyan revivalism, along with its offspring: the revival meeting and the camp meeting. Especially important here is the influence of Oberlin perfectionism, which abetted the love of revivalism manifested in all branches of Methodism for their first hundred years, longer for most Holiness branches.

3.3.1. Finney and Oberlin Perfectionism
By the mid-1820s Charles Grandison → Finney (1792-1875) had risen to prominence as an innovative and astoundingly effective evangelist and pastor. Deeply influenced by the modified → Calvinism of Yale's Nathaniel Taylor, Finney developed a voluntaristic (some said Pelagian) understanding of justification. By the early 1830s the unacceptably

high rate of "backsliding" he was seeing among converts at his → revivals led him to undergird that doctrine of justification with an equally voluntaristic doctrine of entire sanctification.

Finney's Holiness language sounded quite Wesleyan to many Holiness people. He taught that God promises believers grace to love God and neighbor unconditionally in this life and that this grace, given subsequent to regeneration, is instantaneously received by faith and cleanses the heart of all sin. In contrast to the antebellum Wesleyan Holiness people, Finney declared the human will to be naturally free. Grace necessarily aided such decisions but was not their sole ground. Wesleyans of both Wesley's way and Palmer's shorter way taught that prevenient grace is the source of such → freedom (§2). Finney taught that faith is a conscious decision to appropriate the justifying and sanctifying provisions of the → atonement. Wesleyans of both sorts understood that faith is a grace-driven trust in the justifying and sanctifying provisions of the atonement.

From 1851 to his death Finney served as president and professor of theology at the new, radical abolitionist, coeducational college at Oberlin, Ohio. There, he and his friend and colleague Asa Mahan (a Congregationalist deeply affected by Wesleyan teaching) matured their long-developing doctrines of sanctification into what became known as Oberlin perfectionism. While many Holiness people rejoiced in believing that in Oberlin perfectionism a form of Calvinism had become Arminian, they did not see that they themselves were increasingly trading their Arminian doctrine of prevenient grace for → Pelagianism's naturally free will. By the late 1870s Holiness people generally saw the theological differences between the Oberlin and Wesleyan perfectionisms as niceties for classroom debate but without practical consequences.

Both the Oberlin and the Wesleyan perfectionists reveled in the revivalistic milieu that they supported, and sometimes dominated. Finney, Mahan, and the Palmers, among others, evangelized in the United States, Canada, and Great Britain even before the American Civil War. Especially effective in Victorian Great Britain and in Germany were the "transatlantic Smiths," Hannah and her husband, Robert, wealthy American → Friends. Also significant as Holiness evangelists and writers on both sides of the Atlantic were William Arthur (d. 1901), an Irish clergyman-author in the British Wesleyan Methodist Church, and William Boardman (d. 1886), a U.S. Presbyterian.

From the 1860s British and American Wesleyan perfectionist advocates evangelized with no little success in what was becoming a united German state and with limited success in Scandinavia. More important still was the activity of Wesleyan perfectionists in the burgeoning missionary enterprises of British and American Methodism — episcopal and dissenting — especially in Latin America and in British colonies. Two peripatetic examples are William Taylor (d. 1902), an MEC missionary and bishop firmly committed to the doctrine and experience of Christian perfection, who evangelized tirelessly on every continent but Australia and Antarctica, and Vivian Dake (d. 1892), an FMC missionary and founder of the Pentecost Bands, who evangelized in Europe and Africa. The Salvation Army, founded in 1865 East London as the Christian Mission, and building on a perfectionist foundation, developed a radical Wesleyan combination of revivalism, missionary enterprise, and social action.

3.3.2. *National Camp Meeting Association*

The critical moment for what is now called the Holiness movement came in July 1867. John Inskip, William McDonald, George Hughes, John A. Wood, and several other ever-loyal MEC pastors conducted a camp meeting at Vineland, New Jersey, with two stated purposes: reviving the doctrine and experience of "holiness of heart and life," principally among Methodists, and recovering the camp meeting, lately plagued by emotional excesses, as an instrument for reviving holiness within Methodism.

The Vineland camp meeting exceeded expectations and gained the informal blessing of the MEC bishops. Immediately about a dozen of the Vineland preachers formed the National Camp Meeting Association for the Promotion of Holiness, with John Inskip, New York City pastor, as president. (From 1893 it was known both as the National Association for the Promotion of Holiness and as the National Holiness Association; in 1971 it became the Christian Holiness Association and, in 1997, the Christian Holiness Partnership. Another direct descendant is the smaller Interdenominational Holiness Convention, an ultraconservative association formed in 1947 by persons who believed that the National Holiness Association was succumbing to worldliness.)

The National, as it came to be called, held about 60 ten-day camp meetings across the United States, in India, and in Australia between 1867 and 1894, always on invitation from local committees. These events usually attracted thousands (e.g., in 1869, at Round Lake, near Troy, N.Y., over 20,000 attended). They were public news, and the press noted their clarity of purpose and their decorum. Those held near urban areas often drew wealthy urban Methodists who used them to combine spiritual edification and physical rest.

Throughout this time the National itself remained a slowly growing, relatively small group of denominationally loyal MEC pastor-evangelists (e.g., in 1869 there were only 19). In its first 52 years, it had only three presidents: John Inskip (1867-84), William McDonald (1884-93), and Charles Fowler (1893-1919). Only in the late 1880s did it begin to admit non-MEC clergy to membership, and only in 1942 did it elect its first non-MEC president.

The National's successful camp meetings spawned scores of local, state, and regional Holiness camp meeting associations that, by the 1880s, were sponsoring scores of camp meetings and hundreds of revival campaigns per year with considerable success. The National increasingly became a rallying, consultative, and advisory body. The smaller associations courted support and leadership from outside the MEC and MECS, tended to be less urban and middle-class in perspective than the National, and more directly criticized the MEC and MECS for alleged compromises with sin and worldliness.

3.3.3. *Conflict*

By the mid-1870s, thanks in part to the success of the local, state, and regional associations, the Holiness movement faced stiff opposition in both the MEC and MECS. By the late 1870s this opposition was actively negating the doctrine of Christian perfection itself in both its classically Wesleyan and shorter-way forms. It objected to several demands that the movement was making, such as that the MEC and MECS make Holiness revivalism the denominations' priority, that the MEC and MECS firmly enforce their behavioral standards, and that Holiness evangelists be free to preach when and where they saw fit, without having to gain permission first from → bishops, presiding → elders, or → pastors. The National, loyally MEC, sought to mediate, only to face criticism from both sides.

Within the MEC and the MECS the Holiness cause had become "the Holiness question." The bishops publicly declared official allegiance to the Holiness cause, but in both denominations they sought to stave off the division that they saw coming. The MEC General Conference of 1872 had elected eight new bishops, six of them self-identified "Holiness men." Holiness voters had hoped for a denominational Holiness revival; other voters had hoped to corral the Holiness people institutionally. The Bishops' Address to the MECS General Conference of 1874 lamented the divisiveness of the Holiness people, and the conference called for the Holiness evangelists to work by invitation only. Some

MECS leadership looked upon the Holiness movement as an MEC doctrinal and experiential exaggeration and as one more of the MEC's continuing attempts to establish itself in the South. In addition, a significant body of leaders in both the MEC and the MECS saw the Holiness movement, the National excepted, as an obstacle in the way of their march to social power and respectability. They responded with an emphasis on ecclesiastical discipline. In response, the movement, except for the National, became even more strident in its criticisms, demands, claims, and free-lancing practices.

From the early 1870s Holiness laity in the MEC and MECS began to find anti-Holiness pastors being assigned them, and Holiness pastors began to find themselves assigned to anti-Holiness congregations, or so-called hardscrabble circuits. MEC and MECS Holiness evangelists found themselves unable to commend new converts or the newly entirely sanctified to MEC or MECS congregations.

By the early 1880s the Holiness question had become the church question: Should Holiness people remain with the MEC or MECS? Should they join existing Holiness bodies, or should they form new Holiness churches? The leadership of the National urged denominational loyalty, insisting that the Holiness cause could still carry the day in the MEC, if not in the MECS. To do so, it needed the support of the non-MEC/MECS adherents to the Holiness movement. To encourage the cause and to keep the flame burning brightly within episcopal Methodism (→ Episcopacy), the National issued official calls for four conferences of Holiness people between 1877 and 1901. The first two, in 1877, were essentially MEC gatherings. The last two, in 1885 and 1901, called for accredited delegates from all Holiness bodies, and each was attended by persons from at least two dozen denominations and other bodies. Leaders from at least a dozen Holiness and mainline bodies endorsed the call to the meeting of 1901, including bishops of the MEC and representatives of its German conferences in the United States, bishops of the United Brethren Church, several yearly meetings of Friends, and the African Methodist Episcopal and African Methodist Episcopal, Zion, churches. Altogether 229 persons registered as delegates.

In these assemblies, all agreed that fanatics — including especially the advocates of sinless perfection — were heretical. All opposed, however, any understanding that asserted that "entire sanctification is sin under control, and not sin exterminated," or that "entire sanctification is holiness imputed and not holiness imparted." But the really controversial issue, the church question, could not be resolved. Nor could they resolve the issue of ecclesiastical control over itinerant evangelists.

Both clergy and laity tended to see opposition to the Holiness movement anywhere as opposition to the Holiness movement everywhere. In regional, state, and local Holiness associations, sentiment grew in favor of new ecclesiastical arrangements. Holiness people began to identify themselves as "come-outers" (or "pushed-outers") with reference to their decisions to leave established denominations, especially the MEC and, to a lesser degree, the MECS.

3.4. Denominations and Associations

In the 1870s, largely on personal rather than on denominational bases, and in spite of misgivings over its allegiance to the MEC, some members of the distinctly Holiness WMC and FMC had established fraternal if not formal ties with the National. And WMC and FMC clergy found welcome and places of leadership in the local, state, and regional associations, if not (at least not for a quarter-century) in the National. An anomaly lies in the fact that the majority of Holiness people disaffected by the MEC and MECS did not join the WMC or the FMC. Instead, from about 1880 to 1914, they established some 50 new distinctly Holiness denominations or associations in Canada, the United Kingdom, and the United States. And between 1896 and 1914 they formed another 20 in Bolivia, Brazil, Mexico, and Japan. Some of these groups were schisms from older bodies, but most were fresh starts. From about 1900 to 1920 roughly half of these 70 groups engaged in partial or complete mergers, reducing the total number of denominations and associations to about 50. At the same time, however, large numbers of Holiness congregations remained independent, and new Holiness denominations and associations continued to form. Few Holiness congregations, denominations, or associations simply disbanded, and none went back into the MEC or MECS.

3.4.1. Holiness Church

To no one's surprise, the first associations of independent, distinctly Holiness congregations (apart from the WMC, FMC, and ethnically originated Wesleyan Holiness denominations) arose in 1880 — one in Great Britain, one in the United States. The Holiness Church in Britain seems not to have survived organizationally past the mid-1890s. The American group arose out of the Southern California and Arizona Holiness Association and was predominantly, but by no means solely, MEC and MECS in origin. It called itself the Holiness Bands until 1896, when it took the name "Holiness Church." Its ecclesiology was congregational with elements of primitivism, and it required all members to be in the experience of entire sanctification. In 1946 it merged with the Pilgrim Holiness Church.

3.4.2. Church of God (Anderson, Ind.)

Between 1880 and 1883 two more distinctly Holiness bodies formed, both of which survive at present. Probably the first was the association now known as the Church of God (Anderson, Ind.). In 1877 Daniel S. Warner (d. 1895), a minister in a small German pietist denomination with a basically primitivist or → restorationist ecclesiology, influenced by some workers from the National, experienced entire sanctification.

By January 1878 Warner was preaching the necessity of both Holiness and Christian (ecclesiastical) unity. He and his people asserted that denominations (which they called churches of sect) are biblically untenable. Even terms such as "Wesleyan" and "Protestant" have validity only as they meet biblical criteria. This body has always been intensely primitivist in polity, refusing even to keep membership lists, but its congregations have a keen sense of association. Adherents celebrate three "ordinances" (they reject sacramental terminology): believer's baptism by immersion, the Lord's Supper, and → foot washing. The Lord's Table is open to all believers. Most adherents are amillennial.

Early on called the Gospel Trumpet people (after a publishing company that Warner started), it is now, more formally, the Church of God Reformation movement. Popularly, it is the Church of God (Anderson, Ind.). The parentheses indicate the location, since 1906, of its publishing house and its first and principal training school (now Anderson University). It has congregations in some 60 countries.

3.4.3. Church of God (Holiness)

The third association of independent Holiness congregations in the United States resulted from a dissident takeover of the Southwestern Holiness Association, which had been established in 1880 in the wake of a National camp meeting held that summer near Lawrence, Kansas. The dissidents, mostly MEC and MECS pastors and people, sought to establish a truly NT church. The first congregation of this body, which called itself the Church of God (Holiness), was "set in order" in Centralia, Missouri, in 1883, and eight were ordained to ministry as elders. By 1897 a debate over representation to its General Convention brought division, but by 1922 the two groups had reconciled to re-form the Church of God (Holiness). Its principal offices, publishing house, a camp meeting ground, and its largest Bible college are in Overland Park, Kansas. It has congregations in seven countries.

3.4.4. *Salvation Army*

In 1879 the Salvation Army arrived in the United States (in Philadelphia) to stay, an effort in Cleveland, Ohio, in 1869 having been aborted. It unhesitatingly became an integral part of the Holiness movement. The Salvation Army, however, is atypical of the movement in four of its features: its unique military ecclesiology, its indifference to → sacraments or ordinances, its indifference to the establishment institutions of higher education, and its steadfast commitment to remaining physically near the urban poor and needy. By the end of the 19th century, still largely under the command of various members of the Booth family, the Salvation Army was well established almost everywhere where there were North Atlantic commercial interests. It currently has corps in some two-thirds of the world's countries.

3.4.5. *Church of the Nazarene*

The process of merger in the period 1896-1914, together with the exit of a significant number of clergy and laity from the MEC and MECS into the Holiness bodies, gave rise to the Church of the Nazarene (CN) and to the more radical, but still quite Methodistic, Pilgrim Holiness Church (PHC), among others.

A group of predominantly MEC laity and clergy led by Phineas Bresee (d. 1915), a prominent MEC minister associated with the National, established the First Church of the Nazarene in Los Angeles, California, late in 1895. By 1907 this congregation had quickly become the nucleus of a denomination, with congregations as far east as Iowa. In that year the Church of the Nazarene joined forces with the rather more loosely organized (and more loosely Methodist) Association of Pentecostal Churches of America, itself the product of a number of mergers that began in 1895 in New York and New England. The oldest congregation in this group, the People's Evangelical Church in Providence, Rhode Island, founded in 1894, originated among disaffected members of the MEC. The newly merged denomination took the name Pentecostal Church of the Nazarene (PCN). A year later, 1908, the Holiness Church of Christ, another product of a series of mergers in the old Southwest, with a few congregations in Tennessee and Georgia, joined forces with, and took the name of, the new PCN. This step made the PCN the first distinctly Holiness denomination to become nationwide. In fact, by 1908 missionaries of the various groups in the mergers were already working in the Cape Verde Islands, Mexico, and In-

dia, and the Nazarenes had established Chinese congregations on the West Coast.

Between 1899 and 1901, in Nashville, Tennessee, J. O. McClurkan, a Cumberland Presbyterian minister, had formed the Pentecostal Mission, with considerable support of laity and clergy from both the MEC and the MECS. This organization, at first more → mission than congregation, soon gave birth to mission congregations in several of the large cities in the old South and border states. In 1915, upon his death, as McClurkan wished, the Pentecostal Mission merged with the PCN. Also in 1915 George Sharpe, a former Methodist and Congregationalist pastor and now leader of the Pentecostal Church of Scotland, centered in Glasgow, brought his congregations into the PCN. In 1919 the PCN became simply the Church of the Nazarene (CN), seeking to distance itself from the rapidly growing "tongues movement," as early Pentecostalism was called.

As early as 1910 many Holiness people, including several of the leaders of the National, opined — some happily, some with foreboding — that the PCN would soon unify the entire Holiness movement. By 1920, however, it was clear that the CN was insufficiently Methodist to win away from the MEC and MECS more than a minority of their Holiness people; it was too flaccid in both doctrine and ethic to attract many of the more doctrinally and behaviorally conservative Holiness people, and it was too denominational to win over the primitivists. Most of the MPC, FMC, and WMC, as well as the ethnically originated Wesleyan denominations that still held to Holiness teaching, saw the Nazarenes offering nothing that they did not already have, including, especially, formative tradition.

In the course of the mergers, the (P)CN accepted the views of both Wesley and Palmer regarding entire sanctification and assurance, but it leaned in practice toward Palmer's position. It received baptism and the Lord's Supper as sacraments while not disparaging foot washing as a pious practice; and it also practiced both infant baptism and infant dedication (according to the desire of the parents). Its prescribed sacramental rituals are essentially those of Methodism. It has practiced rebaptism, especially outside of North Atlantic cultures, but its theology clearly runs against the practice, and Nazarenes are slowly abandoning it. Until the 1990s, when it added the order of deacon, the CN, with the great majority of Holiness bodies, held to one order of ordained ministry. Ordination is "ordination to ministry in the Church of God." The (P)CN has not required reordination of ministers transferring credentials, as is typical of the Holiness denominations. In principle, the (P)CN has had no objection to ordaining women to ministry since its founding, but principle yielded to practice in the period 1925-80, when the proportion of ordained women dropped from 20 percent in 1908 to 3 percent in 1980. Principle has again begun to rule, and the proportion is rising. The story of the relationship between principle and practice in the (P)CN is typical of that of almost all other Holiness denominations. The Salvation Army, with its military ecclesiology, has been the consistent exception.

Ecclesiologically, following a path of compromise in the course of its many mergers, the CN has sought a middle ground between episcopalianism and → congregationalism. Its quadrennial General Assembly, which is theoretically half lay and half → clergy, is its highest legislative body. Executive authority lies with quadrennially (re-)elected general superintendents, who itinerate. On many narrower issues of concern to evangelicals — including millennialism, mode of baptism, the nature of the inspiration and authority of Scripture, and divine healing — the CN has generally taken no specific stance.

3.4.6. Wesleyan Church

The PHC began in 1897 as the International Apostolic Holiness Union and Prayer League. In 1905 it became the International Apostolic Holiness Union and Churches; in 1913, the International Apostolic Holiness Church; and in 1919, the International Holiness Church. In 1919 it became the PHC, which merged in 1968 with the WMC to form the Wesleyan Church.

At its outset, it was led by Martin Wells Knapp (d. 1901) and George Kulp (d. 1939), both MEC clergy, and from the 1910s by Seth C. Rees (d. 1933), a former Friends and PCN minister. Knapp and Kulp were both closely associated with the National and with God's Bible School, which Knapp had founded in Cincinnati in 1900. At first they intended their group to serve as a nonecclesial prayer gathering, not altogether unlike the Tuesday Meeting. But the general resistance of urban MEC congregations to Holiness preaching and the absence of a strong, united Holiness voice in the northern cities between the Alleghenies and the Mississippi, in the mill towns and furniture manufacturing towns in North Carolina, and in urban California, especially in the inner cities among the recent arrivals, led to the development of congregations and the formation of a denomination.

At least six mergers have marked the development of this denomination, which was characterized by deep commitment to revivalism, seen best in its vigorous missionary and inner-city ministries and in its style of worship. Only in the strength of its commitment to a camp meeting style of worship, its rather more rigorous behavioral requirements for membership, its stronger tendency toward a → fundamentalist understanding of Scripture, and its insistence on premillennialism did it differ from the Nazarenes. Both denominations practiced pedobaptism and also offered believer's baptism in the mode requested by the one baptized; both required personal acceptance of Christ as Savior for membership; both opened the Lord's Supper to all who personally accepted Christ as Savior; and their forms of → church government were similar. The PHC brought to its 1968 merger with the WMC a very strong tradition of giving and a deep interest in world evangelization — with missionaries in some 30 countries and two-thirds of its membership outside of the United States. It also had one liberal arts college and several Bible colleges. The WMC also brought a tradition of strong financial support and a deep interest in both liberal arts education (four colleges) and world evangelization (missionaries in eight countries and among North American indigenes). And while it had on several occasions turned away merger overtures from the FMC, fearing a too-strong centralization, the WMC, over the years, had experienced about the same number of mergers as had formed the PHC.

Neither the WMC nor the PHC could bring all of their congregations into their 1968 merger. Already in 1963 the New York District of the PHC voted to become the independent PHC of New York, which now has congregations in five states and two Canadian provinces; and a majority of the Allegheny Conference of the WMC withdrew from the denomination and formed the Allegheny Wesleyan Methodist Connection in 1966, in advance of the 1968 merger. In the previous decade, the CN had suffered the secession of three groups, largely over the general issue of worldliness, and more specifically over centralization of denominational power, television, apparel, amusements, and jewelry, including wedding bands. All of these denominations have Bible colleges and vigorous overseas missionary programs.

3.4.7. International Holiness Convention

These denominations and associations and others like them — about 25 in all — are the heart of the Interdenominational Holiness Convention (IHC). H. E. Schmul (d. 1998), a Wesleyan Methodist minister who later was a principal in the formation of the Allegheny Wesleyan Methodist Connection, founded the IHC in 1947 as a source of fellowship for the more conservative Holiness individuals, congregations, denominations, and associations and as a conscience for the Holiness movement as a whole. The *Convention Herald,* official paper of the IHC, has carried out this latter role with important effect. The IHC does not have a membership list, as the Christian Holiness Partnership (CHP) does.

3.4.8. *Cooperation*

Relationships between affiliates of the IHC and members of the much larger CHP are not always cordial, but they are seldom acerbic. Cooperation across the lines of these umbrella organizations is quite common. Some denominations, such as the Churches of Christ in Christian Union, belong to the CHP but also have strong ties with the IHC. This body separated from the Christian Union Movement in 1909 in response to strong anti-Holiness movement sentiment in the older movement. It has retained much of the primitivist polity of its originating movement and, like the PHC, has held to a revivalistic style of worship as the ideal. Most of its 200 congregations are in southern Ohio and neighboring states. It maintains a Bible college and has a strong missionary interest in about a dozen countries and among North American indigenous peoples.

In addition to the CHP and IHC, both descendants of the National, the Wesleyan Theological Society (WTS) has served as a locus of cooperation within the Holiness movement. Officially the theological commission of the CHP, the WTS has increasingly served as a formative and influential forum for theological discussion among the movement's English-speaking scholars and teachers since its founding in 1966. The *Wesleyan Theological Journal* is the society's official periodical.

Generally, the → World Council of Churches and the → National Council of Churches of Christ in the U.S.A. have proved unattractive to Holiness bodies because of the latter's view of the councils' political commitments and involvement. Holiness bodies have cooperated with both councils in disaster relief, however, and Holiness movement adherents have sat on the councils' respective commissions on Faith and Order. The five largest Holiness bodies and others belong to the → National Association of Evangelicals but, with their own extensive missionary enterprises, do not formally cooperate with the →World Evangelical Fellowship. Most Holiness bodies encourage their pastors to participate in local ministeriums.

Bibliography: M. E. DIETER, *The Holiness Revival of the Nineteenth Century* (Metuchen, N.J., 1980) • C. E. JONES, *Black Holiness: A Guide to the Study of Black Participation in Wesleyan Perfectionist and Glossolalic Pentecostal Movements* (Metuchen, N.J., 1987); idem, *A Guide to the Study of the Holiness Movement* (rev. ed.; Metuchen, N.J., 2000); idem, *Perfectionist Persuasion: The Holiness Movement and American Methodism* (Metuchen, N.J., 1974) • T. L. SMITH, *Revivalism and Social Reform: American Protestantism on the Eve of the Civil War* (Baltimore, 1980; orig. pub., 1957) • V. SYNAN, *The Holiness-Pentecostal Tradition: Charismatic Movements in the Twentieth Century* (2d ed.; Grand Rapids, 1997; orig. pub., 1971).

PAUL BASSETT

Holland → Netherlands

Holocaust

During the second half of the 20th century, "Holocaust" became the usual term for the mass extermination of Jews during World War II. Seldom used at first, the word gained ground in the 1960s, especially in the United States, and finally found universal acceptance, though it is often misused analogically for any forms of mass murder and not merely for the National Socialist → genocide.

The Vg uses *holocaustum* for Gk. *holokautōma* and *holokautōsis,* which in the LXX, and later in Philo and Josephus, are mostly translations of Heb. *ʿōlâ* (burnt offering), less commonly *kālîl* (whole burnt offering). The Greek terms derive from *holokauteō* (also *-tizō*), another derivate being *holokautos* (occasionally *-stos*). They signify "what is wholly burnt" (*-tōma*) and "incineration" (*-tōsis*). The biblical whole offering (→ Sacrifice) led to the further sense of the complete destruction of people or animals, total annihilation or slaughter, when "Holocaust" became a loan word, particularly at first in English.

When the mass murder of the Jews in occupied Europe after 1939 came to be known in Palestine, it was first described in the 1940s by the Hebrew-Yiddish word *ḥurban* (destruction) or by *šōʾâ* (catastrophe). Then as awareness of the historical significance of the mass murder developed in the 1960s and 1970s, especially in the United States, "Holocaust" became the common term for National Socialism's "final solution of the Jewish question." The related term "genocide" was coined by Raphael Lemkin in 1944.

Of all the above words *šōʾâ* might well be the best

to describe what happened. But all of them, especially "Holocaust," reflect both abhorrence of the Nazi concept of a final solution and the helplessness of language before the Nazi policy of extermination. Historical analysis shows that the attack on the Jews involved more than mass murder. Step by step the German Jews were singled out, isolated, and deprived of civil rights from 1933 onward. Early in World War II came Hitler's call for racial and political "purification," which led to mass murder. Jews were systematically destroyed in the conquered and occupied countries of Europe. There also was an equally systematic expurgation, unparalleled in history, of the psychologically ill (→ Euthanasia), an attempted extirpation of the leading classes (e.g., in Poland and Russia), and a killing of Gypsies (→ Roma). The Nazi aim was a new biological order for Europe. We must see the Holocaust against the background of this total vision of the Hitler government.

Traditional → anti-Semitism, the establishment of a pseudoscientific doctrine of race, and imperialistic plans for a National Socialist Europe were all features of Hitler's policy. The different stages of the Jewish policy saturated German society with anti-Semitic propaganda and increasingly brought the apparatus of state and society into the assault upon the Jews. When, therefore, at the height of the expectation of victory in 1941, the "final solution" was adopted, the various institutions, bureaucracies, and units that had had a direct or indirect part in the campaign, being now accustomed over many years to defaming the Jews and denying them their rights, became the executors. The exploiting of national aspirations and the linking of supposed racial superiority with racially motivated imperialism (→ Racism) made it possible for the mass murder to be carried out without a serious hitch. Many of Hitler's plans had to be abandoned as impracticable, but the policy of persecuting and exterminating the Jews was one of the policies of the regime that was most consistently adopted and executed.

The religions have thus far found it hard to offer any interpretation of these events. For Christianity they raise the question of → guilt and → responsibility, and especially also that of the relation to → Judaism in the mirror of history and religion (→ Jewish-Christian Dialogue). In → Jewish theology, after long hesitation, the question of → theodicy has again come under discussion, though no answers have been found that shed light on the events. Historical interpretations and explanations of the mass murder under National Socialism may be discerned in outline, but theological explanations of some-

thing so incomprehensible can be sought only in the strength of → faith.

Bibliography: A. Bein, *Die Judenfrage* (Stuttgart, 1980) • H. J. Cargas, *Shadows of Auschwitz: A Christian Response to the Holocaust* (rev. ed.; New York, 1990) • A. T. Davies and M. T. Nefsky, *How Silent Were the Churches? Canadian Protestantism and the Jewish Plight during the Nazi Era* (Waterloo, Ont., 1997) • K. P. Fischer, *The History of an Obsession: German Judeophobia and the Holocaust* (New York, 1998) • R. S. Gottlieb, *Thinking the Unthinkable: Meanings of the Holocaust* (New York, 1990) • S. R. Haynes, *Prospects for Holocaust Theology* (Atlanta, 1991) • R. Hilberg, *Die Vernichtung der europäischen Juden* (Berlin, 1982) • S. T. Katz, "Holocaust: Jewish Theological Responses," *EncRel(E)* 6.423-31 • D. E. Lipstadt, *Denying the Holocaust: The Growing Assault on Truth and Memory* (New York, 1993) • J. Robinson, J. Litrack, G. Lewy, and J. M. Snoeck, "Holocaust etc.," *EncJud* 8.828-916 • E. Schuster and R. Boschert-Kimmig, *Hope against Hope: Johann Baptist Metz and Elie Wiesel Speak Out on the Holocaust* (New York, 1999) • L. Thomas, *Vessels of Evil: American Slavery and the Holocaust* (Philadelphia, 1993) • R. G. Weisbord and W. P. Sillanpoa, *The Chief Rabbi, the Pope, and the Holocaust: An Era in Vatican-Jewish Relations* (New Brunswick, N.J., 1992).

Wolfgang Scheffler

Holy Communion → Eucharist

Holy Kiss → Kiss of Peace

Holy Spirit

1. Biblical Data
   1.1. OT and Early Judaism
   1.2. NT
       1.2.1. Mark and Matthew
       1.2.2. Luke and Acts
       1.2.3. Paul
       1.2.4. John
       1.2.5. Later Writings
2. Theological Data
   2.1. Problems
   2.2. NT Variety
   2.3. Resultant Problems
   2.4. Trinity and Filioque
   2.5. Open Questions in Modern
         Ecumenical Theology

1. Biblical Data
1.1. *OT and Early Judaism*

Statements about the *rûaḥ* (spirit) of Yahweh are of direct pneumatological interest. The working of the *rûaḥ* is at first ecstatic, equipping charismatic leaders (Judg. 3:10; 6:34; 1 Sam. 10:6; → Charisma) and → prophets (1 Sam. 10:6; 19:20-24) for their tasks. Time and again those concerned are gripped by the Spirit. More permanent endowment first appears in the case of → David (1 Sam. 16:13). The great preexilic prophets appeal to the Word of Yahweh rather than to his Spirit (though see Hos. 9:7 and Mic. 3:8; → Word of God). Perhaps they wished to stay at a distance from the traditional ecstatic prophets of deliverance. After the exile the ecstatic element was less prominent, and the Spirit became more important theologically as the force behind prophetic proclamation and a moral → lifestyle (Isa. 59:21; 61:1; Ezek. 36:27; Joel 2:28-29; Hag. 2:5, etc.). At this period too the Spirit was viewed as a creative power to which we owe → life (Job 34:14-15; Ps. 104:30) and which, especially in eschatological expectation (→ Eschatology 1), accomplishes the new creation and thus establishes the reign of Yahweh in the world. The Messiah in particular (→ Messianism) would be permanently endowed with the Spirit (Isa. 11:2), but all God's people would also share in the Spirit (Joel 2:28-29; Ezek. 39:29). This gift was understood as the steadfast promise of Yahweh, not as a possession (Ps. 51:10-11).

In early → Judaism Gk. *pneuma* (wind, spirit, breath) is an expression of the divine being and activity, present especially in prophecy and wisdom (Isa. 61:1; Wis. 1:6; 7:22; → Wisdom Literature). In this way a link exists between the transcendent God and → creation (Philo *De opif. mun.* 135, 144). As the → rabbis saw it, the Spirit was at work particularly in the prophets. Sometimes we find the idea that the Spirit left → Israel (§1) after the last prophets Haggai, Zechariah, and Malachi and will be given again only in the end time (*t. Soṭa* 13.2; → Apocalyptic 2). Elsewhere, however, the ongoing work of the Spirit is in view, whether in the rewarding of lives pleasing to God or in outstanding acts of rabbis (*Lev. Rab.* 35:7, on 26:3). At → Qumran the spirit of → truth was seen opposing the spirit of deceit (1QS 3:18-19). A striking point, and an important one relative to what Christians would later say about the Spirit, is that already in early Judaism the Spirit was seen as a separate entity that represents God but is not the same as God.

1.2. *NT*

Along with the tradition of the earthly → Jesus and the appearances of the risen Lord, the experience of the Spirit was the third essential element in the constituting of the first Christian congregation (see esp. Acts 2:1-21; → Primitive Christian Community). The giving of the Spirit shows the church that it is an eschatological fellowship that is equipped in all respects for the life it must lead (→ Worship; Lifestyle; Mission).

1.2.1. *Mark and Matthew*

The understanding of the Spirit in Mark and Matthew is strongly rooted in the tradition of the OT and Judaism (see Mark 1:12 and par.). Jesus is endowed with the Spirit from his → baptism (Mark 1:10) and even from birth (Matt. 1:18-20), and he drives out → demons through the Spirit (Matt. 12:28). Such presence of the Spirit shows that the → kingdom of God is at hand. Blasphemy against the Spirit is thus the unforgivable sin (Mark 3:28-30 and par.). That is, those who do not perceive that in Jesus God himself is present and who interpret his power as devilish (→ Devil) exclude themselves from the new aeon that is dawning.

Jesus not only bears the Spirit as a prophet but also gives the Spirit as the risen Lord. We may surely see in Mark 1:8-9 and parallel a link to early Christian experience of the Spirit and, perhaps, indirectly to water baptism. The same applies to the so-called Great Commission in Matt. 28:18-20, now with a direct reference to a triadic formulation of baptism in the name of Father, Son, and Holy Spirit. Mark and Matthew do not speak of an ongoing work of the Spirit in believers, but they do say that the Spirit, as the power of God sovereignly at work, enables believers to say the right thing at the right time (Mark 13:11 and par.).

1.2.2. *Luke and Acts*

The Spirit has a much larger role in the Lukan writings. Here the ecclesiological aspect, closely linked to the Christological (→ Christology 1), is central. The endowing of Jesus with the Spirit plainly goes hand in hand from the outset with his ministry (Luke 4:18-19, quoting Isa. 61:1-2). Similarly, when the risen Lord imparts to his → disciples the Spirit, whom he has received from the Father (Acts 2:33), he is equipping them for global witness by this baptism of the Spirit (1:4-8). In keeping with his theology of history, Luke sees the Spirit as typifying the age of the → church (§2.1). The Spirit is given permanently to all members of the church and is at work especially in the worldwide → proclamation to those outside (8:29; 13:4; 16:7). The problem of the relation of the Spirit to ministry arises in 20:28 (cf. 6:3; → Offices, Ecclesiastical).

We also find in Luke at least the beginnings of a pneumatology, though only in the form of hints and leaving many gaps. The relation to baptism is plain

(Acts 2:38) but not its nature. The giving of the Spirit may precede baptism (10:44-47), or it may follow baptism with the → laying on of hands (8:17; 19:6). Nothing is said about the relation of the Spirit to → faith (§2), to sonship, or to the deeds of believers. In Luke the Spirit is often seen as a force that makes extraordinary deeds of power possible.

1.2.3. *Paul*
→ Paul does more than other NT authors to think through in its different aspects what is said about the Spirit of God. He takes the common view that the Spirit is God's gift that shows believers to be standing in the *eschaton* (Rom. 8:1-30). Not the law *(nomos)* as letter but the law of the Spirit *(nomos tou pneumatos)* characterizes this life (→ Law 2). The latter law alone leads to life (8:2). In the Spirit, that which is intended in the law but not achieved by it finds fulfillment (2 Cor. 3:14-18). Paul's formula for the enthusiastic claim of primitive Christianity is that those who are "in Christ" *(en Christō)* are a "new creation" (5:17; cf. "in the Spirit" [*en pneumati*], Rom. 8:9 etc.; → New Self). The Spirit of God as the "spirit of faith" *(pneuma tēs pisteōs,* 2 Cor. 4:13) fully defines believers. Less prominent here is the idea of the OT and early Judaism that the Spirit is a sovereign power that masters us; instead we find the more Hellenistic idea of continuous filling and controlling. By describing the Spirit as *arrabōn* (first installment, guarantee, 2 Cor. 1:22; 5:5) or *aparchē* (first fruits, Rom. 8:23), Paul guards against a negatively enthusiastic misunderstanding of this new being (→ Gnosis, Gnosticism).

Believers are temples of the Holy Spirit (1 Cor. 3:16). The classic formulation of the problem of indicative and imperative — "if we live by the Spirit, let us also be guided by the Spirit" *(ei zōmen pneumati, pneumati kai stoichōmen,* Gal. 5:25) — means that the Spirit who has been given produces fruit consisting especially of → love *(agapē,* Gal. 5:22; 1 Corinthians 13). The Spirit, as in Luke, is thus the power that constitutes the assembly of the church. The understanding of the church as the "body of Christ" *(sōma Christou)* brings out the ecclesiological dimension of what Paul has to say about the Spirit (1 Cor. 12:13, 27). Each member of this *sōma* has a particular spiritual gift whose use must serve to build up the → congregation, as the view of → glossolalia demonstrates (chap. 14). In this regard the Spirit-directed distinction of spirits by means of the confession that Jesus is *Kyrios* (Lord) is very important (12:3).

Many sayings closely link God, Christ, and Spirit. In 2 Cor. 3:17 Lord *(kyrios)* and Spirit *(pneuma)* are equated, and then there is immediate reference to "the Spirit of the Lord" *(pneuma kyriou,* see Gal. 4:6; Phil. 1:19). The formulas "in Christ" *(en Christō)* and "in the Spirit" *(en pneumati)* are interchangeable (Rom. 8:1, 9). We read similarly of the presence of both Christ and the Spirit in believers (Rom. 8:9-10). In Rom. 8:9 we find both "the Spirit of God" *(pneuma theou)* and "the Spirit of Christ" *(pneuma Christou).* In Gal. 4:6 God sends forth the Spirit of his Son. In 1 Cor. 12:4-5 the many spiritual gifts are related to the one God, the one Christ, and the one Spirit; also note the triadic formula in 2 Cor. 13:13. An inner Trinitarian process is also present in the Spirit's prayer in Rom. 8:26-27. All these sayings promote, if they do not actually present, an explicit doctrine of the → Trinity.

1.2.4. *John*
John typically sets "spirit" *(pneuma)* in antithesis to "flesh" *(sarx,* 3:1-8). Being born "of the Spirit" (3:6; or "of God," 1:13; or "from above," 3:3, 7) describes the new life of believers, who are no longer governed by the flesh but incorporated into the life of the Spirit and thus belong to the sphere of God, for God is spirit (4:24). There will be a future consummation (see 14:2-3; 17:24), but the present aspect of this new being is especially strongly emphasized. John does not describe the Spirit as an ecstatic phenomenon but as the life-giving power of God that summons to new and true life (6:63).

In John the Spirit is more personal than elsewhere in the NT and is endowed with loftier titles (→ Christological Titles): He is "another Advocate" (or "Helper," *allos paraklētos*), who will abide with the community after Jesus has returned to the Father (14:16). In five Paraclete sayings Jesus announces what the Spirit will do in the community (14:16-17, 26; 15:26; 16:7b-11, 13-15). He will teach the disciples all things, remind them of the sayings of Jesus (14:26), and thus lead them into all truth (16:13). This promise does not imply supplementing inadequate proclamation but suggests giving it eschatological force, since Jesus only now is seen as the exalted Lord. John most consistently, then, linked the Spirit to Christ as the former is present in proclamation. We find similar-sounding statements about both — sending by the Father (14:24, 26), teaching (7:14; 14:26), bearing witness (8:14; 15:26), convicting the world *(kosmos)* of sin (3:18-21; 16:8-11), and so forth — yet there is no identity, for the risen Lord sends the Paraclete (15:26; 16:7; 20:22), as the Father also does (14:16, 26; 15:26). Here again the doctrine of the Trinity is needed to explain such statements. The Paraclete shows what is the true eschatological significance of the history of Jesus. It is not just a record but a present reality.

He thus adequately continues that history after Easter.

1.2.5. *Later Writings*

The later NT writings contain many relevant pneumatological sayings. In Ephesians the understanding of the Spirit is very eschatologically oriented as the power of → revelation through → apostles and prophets (1:17; 3:5) and also of the growth of the church by inner renewal (3:16). In the Pastorals the Spirit effects the resurrection of Jesus (1 Tim. 3:16), authoritative prophetic utterance (4:1), the safekeeping of the deposit of faith (2 Tim. 1:14), and a responsible lifestyle (2 Tim. 1:7; Titus 3:5). In Hebrews the Spirit signifies the → grace of God (10:29), speaks through Scripture (3:7; 9:8), and works → miracles (2:4).

Similar statements in the Catholic Epistles and Revelation relate the Spirit to prophecy (1 Pet. 1:11-12; 2 Pet. 1:21; 1 John 5:6-7; Rev. 19:10), sanctification (1 Pet. 1:2), and Christ's abiding in believers (1 John 3:24; 4:13). What we find is for the most part traditional, and because of the brevity and the situational nature of the writings, there is no systematizing. That development would come later.

Bibliography: H.-D. Betz, "Geist, Freiheit und Gesetz," *ZTK* 71 (1974) 78-93 • U. Brockhaus, *Charisma und Amt. Die paulinische Charismenlehre auf dem Hintergrund der frühchristlichen Gemeindefunktion* (Wuppertal, 1987) • Y. Congar, *I Believe in the Holy Spirit* (New York, 1997) • M. Green, *I Believe in the Holy Spirit* (Grand Rapids, 1989) • K. S. Hemphill, *Spiritual Gifts* (Nashville, 1988) • A. Holl, *The Left Hand of God: A Biography of the Holy Spirit* (New York, 1988) • H. Hübner, "Der Heilige Geist in der Heiligen Schrift," *KuD* 36 (1990) 181-208 • B. J. Jahnke and C. M. Keller, *How Does the Spirit Lead? Questions of Faith* (2 vols.; Minneapolis, 1992) • H. Küng and J. Moltmann, *Conflicts about the Holy Spirit* (New York, 1979) • G. W. H. Lampe, *God as Spirit* (Oxford, 1977) • M. E. Lodahl, *Shekinah/Spirit: Divine Presence in Jewish and Christian Religion* (New York, 1992) • F. Martin, "Le baptème dans l'Esprit," *NRT* 106 (1984) 23-58 • J. Moltmann, *The Source of Life: The Holy Spirit and the Theology of Life* (Minneapolis, 1997) • C. F. D. Moule, *The Holy Spirit* (Oxford, 1978) • P. Schäfer, *Die Vorstellung vom Heiligen Geist in der rabbinischen Literatur* (Munich, 1972) • E. Schweizer, *Heiliger Geist* (Stuttgart, 1978) • A. E. Sekki, *The Meaning of Ruaḥ at Qumran* (Atlanta, 1989) • M. Turner, *The Holy Spirit and Spiritual Gifts, Then and Now* (Carlisle, Cumbria, 1996) • J. S. Vos, *Traditionsgeschichtliche Untersuchungen zur paulinischen Pneumatologie* (Assen, 1973) • M. Welker, *God the Spirit* (Minneaplis, 1994) • R. M. Wilson, "The Spirit in Gnostic Literature," *Christ and Spirit in the NT* (ed. B. Lindars and S. S. Smalley; Cambridge, 1973) 345-55 • M. Winter, *Pneumatiker und Psychiker in Korinth* (Marburg, 1975).

Wilhelm Pratscher

2. Theological Data

2.1. *Problems*

The rather clumsy word "pneumatology" itself raises a basic problem. It is used for the attempt to clarify theologically the function and work of the living Spirit of God in the hearts of believers, in the church, in the world, and in all → creation. But can one make the living Spirit of God a doctrinal theme? There is a widespread call for the development of an independent pneumatology in Europe (→ European Theology), and especially in the English-speaking churches and in the → Third World, and this interest is not merely in the increasingly numerous charismatic groups and churches (→ Charismatic Movement; Pentecostal Churches). It often goes hand in hand with the complaint that there is no specific doctrine of the Spirit in most classical or even modern Christian theologies. This concern has been prompted in similar ways and almost independently by traditional believers wanting clarification about the basic significance of the Holy Spirit, by more recent charismatic movements, and by the → Orthodox Church (→ Orthodoxy 3), with its longtime criticism that the West has neglected pneumatology in both → faith and doctrine.

In both → piety and theology the Western churches have indeed little to offer by way of pneumatology that is original, concrete, or intelligible. One may ask, however, whether anything of that kind is possible, whether we can make an independent theme of the Spirit of God (the Father and the Son) as though it were something separate, a concretely definable "it," graspable by definitions. It might be objected that the Spirit is not separate from God the Father and Creator or from Jesus, in whom God is present, and not even from believers, for faith itself is called a work of the Holy Spirit. Nor can we really lay hold of the Spirit if he is truly Spirit and moves where he wills (John 3:8). As for understanding, he is himself the understanding of that which we understand in faith. It seems, then, that the call for a new and understandable pneumatology is an unrealizable wish.

Nevertheless, the modest resignation or excused neglect on this topic that typifies the West is out of place. For one thing, the Western tradition in both church and theology is not in fact so poor in profound insights into the work of the Holy Spirit, whether in → prayer or in clarifying texts, as modern criticism asserts. For another, the biblical basis, insights from the history of theology, and observation of the survival crises of humanity make possible the development of new and profound and helpful theological thoughts contributing to an understanding of what is said about the Holy Spirit.

Nevertheless, complaint of a gap at this point is valid. In the West the Holy Spirit has been largely detached from an understanding of the Trinity or linked only formally with it. Unhappy polarizations have hampered the theological explication of the Spirit over long periods — for example, the contrast between spirit and matter (→ Platonism), between the individual (→ Individualism) and the → institution (both in Roman Catholic theology), as well as that between the divine and the human spirit. That is, there has been an emphasis on radical separation and a criticism of spiritual experience apart from the Word of God (both in Reformation and esp. in → dialectical theology). A new and ecumenically responsible pneumatology must overcome these antitheses.

2.2. *NT Variety*

The biblical material, which is rich and yet simultaneously quite disparate, demands a new look. Scholarly studies have analyzed this material with philological, historical, and religiohistorical tools (see the bibliography in M. Welker), and over the past few decades the noticeable lack of unity within the Bible materials — compared with the ancient Oriental and Greek understanding of the spirit — has once more yielded at least a relative sense of unity.

Negatively, at least we can say what most of the biblical passages do not say about the Spirit: There is no automatic endowment of all people, or of special dignities such as kings, with the Spirit of God; there is no idea of a rising up of the human spirit to the height of the divine Spirit; there is no permanent hostility between spirit and body, but also there is no crass embodying or "materializing" of the divine Spirit (→ Materialism). Varied though the biblical sayings about the Spirit may be (the decisive distinctions are not so much between the OT and NT but between Paul and John, on the one side, and, on the other, Luke and Acts), doctrines of the above type are not present at all in the Bible or are so only on the margin.

Positively — and here a suitable summary is more difficult — the biblical writings always present the Spirit as God's Spirit; indeed, God himself is Spirit, and we must worship him in the Spirit. The Spirit is God at work among us to bring → life, →

truth, → righteousness, and → mercy. Death is the opposite of the Spirit. The Spirit, who does new things, is in fact the Creator Spirit.

2.2.1. In early → Israel (§1) certain people had the gift of the Spirit. The judges were led by the Spirit, as were later the kings, though not automatically (→ Monarchy in Israel). The same was true of the → prophets, often in opposition to the kings. The Spirit of the Lord will rest on the Messiah King — "the spirit of wisdom and understanding, the spirit of counsel and might, the spirit of knowledge and the fear of the Lord" (Isa. 11:2; → Messianism). He receives the Spirit, and in the Spirit the → covenant (§1) is actualized. The end time will bear the marks of the Spirit, who will be poured out "on all flesh" (Joel 2:28).

2.2.2. These and similar OT passages are often quoted in the NT and are seen to be fulfilled or on the point of fulfillment. The NT does not really transcend them or give them new content but makes them concrete and historical by relating them directly to Jesus and to the → Pentecost-event in the community, in which the Holy Spirit does things that are in accord with the recollections and promises of Israel. New features are the relating to the coming and sending of Jesus and the strong accentuating of the link between the Holy Spirit and the work of the risen (and in John also the glorified) Lord.

2.3. *Resultant Problems*

2.3.1. The relating of the Holy Spirit to the coming of Jesus and to his ongoing ministry after his death and → resurrection also raised serious problems (→ Eschatology). Paul and especially John stressed the sending of the Spirit by Jesus, but in the Synoptic gospels Christ himself is endowed with the Spirit. Luke sees in the Holy Spirit a continuation of the work of Jesus, but Paul and John emphasize the bringing of believers by the Spirit into the fellowship of the Father and the Son. We see here the beginning of later confessional distinctives (→ Denomination), that is, of the differences between (1) Eastern theology and piety and (2) the theology of Western Catholicism and the Reformation. These distinctives can often justify themselves exegetically — an important insight for ecumenism.

The relating of the Spirit to Jesus gave the doctrine of the → Trinity its true theme. Another possibility might have been a "binity" — God the Father and Creator reaching his creation, especially his human creation, through a Mediator. This Mediator would then have been the Spirit-filled Jesus, the Messiah, whose earthly work after his death is continued by the Spirit of God, who once dwelled in him. This approach might have yielded an ideal, simple doctrine that Jewish believers could have accepted (→ Jewish Christians) and interested Greeks would have found intelligible (→ Hellenistic-Roman Religion).

It was not so much the Trinitarian formulas in the NT (the blessings, the missionary command in Matt. 28:19) as the Johannine Prologue that blocked this kind of development. There the Logos and not the Spirit was that in God that became incarnate. At a deeper level Spirit and Logos, for all the intimate relation between Word and Spirit, are not one and the same. Jesus, the true Son, calls out "Abba!" in his passion and dereliction, and that is the Spirit's cry. Romans 8:1-8 especially tells us that only because we have been adopted in the Spirit, in the place of the Son, because we too have become children of God, are we able to cry "Abba!" amid the sufferings of the present time.

The Spirit is the Spirit of adoption who takes us up into the fellowship of the Father and the Son and in authentic humanity enables us to maintain the tension between → suffering and → hope. He is the Spirit of → freedom, the Comforter (→ Consolation, Comfort). Believers greet and bless one another in the Spirit (→ Blessing). He heals infirmities (→ Health and Illness) and manifests God's mercy to the weak. As he thus makes God present to us, we see him to be personal and pray to him as a → person.

2.3.2. The fact of the Spirit's personhood was not always perceived in church history. (A "new pneumatology" would have to begin here.) Attention first centered on God and Christ, Father and Son. The Spirit was valued for his work in the church, but he was a problematic third in the doctrine of the Trinity, within which he was "officially" recognized only at Constantinople in 381 (→ Niceno-Constantinopolitan Creed). He had mostly been viewed only as a bridge between God and creation, between the Word and believers. This approach could involve trivializing, for in fact the Spirit is not just a mediating something, a divine phenomenon between the Father and the Son, or a mere representation of the Father in the Son or of Jesus Christ to the church. The promises of Jesus that he would send the Paraclete after going away (John 14:16-17; 16:7-15) might suggest this kind of interpretation, which for the rest entails a reading of historical Trinitarian ideas into the "immanent Trinity," the source of many misunderstandings.

2.4. Trinity and Filioque

The doctrine of the Trinity must be seen as a help to believers, not an obstacle. It links Israel and the Creator God to the coming of Jesus the Logos and the

functioning of the church in the Spirit. The Eastern church has kept this role in mind better than the Western, in which the three persons in God have been hard to differentiate and hence the Spirit has been handled in theology largely in terms of "mediation," for example, with reference to creation, the church, charisms, offices, justification, and so forth.

By adding *filioque* (lit. "and the Son") to the Nicene Creed (→ Nicaea, Councils of), the West has stated that the Spirit proceeds from both Father and Son, as though he were a continuation of Christ or his representative. This idea was attractive because it could be used to validate the church's ministry (→ Pope, Papacy) and its exclusive claim to grant salvation (→ Order of Salvation) or, later, the Word-monopolism of Protestantism (i.e., the total linking of the Spirit to the biblical Word; → Word of God).

To this day the East has maintained its strong protest against the *filioque* and has upheld the strict differentiation of the Son and the Spirit, who both proceed from the Father. This belief makes it possible to think of the Spirit as also operating outside the church (see examples in Russian piety and literature). The Eastern teaching, though, is not without its dangers. Its advantage is that it makes room for a freer and richer doctrine of the Holy Spirit.

Some churches of the West (e.g., the → Anglican Communion) are prepared to delete the *filioque*, and John Paul II omitted it at a joint mass with the Orthodox to celebrate the 1,600th anniversary of the Council of Constantinople. These churches still assert, however, that the Spirit be understood as the Spirit of Christ and not as a spirit floating in the void (esp. as we recall the 1934 → Barmen Declaration, with its rejection of ideological appeals to a new "spirit").

2.5. Open Questions in Modern Ecumenical Theology

Ecumenical theology has new tasks in this area (→ Ecumenical Theology). It must still deal with the *filioque*, which is not simply a matter of theological quibbling but implies different understandings of the Trinity in East and West. It also must deal with the ongoing tension between the classic Roman doctrine of infused grace, which seems to replace the direct work of the Spirit with a habitual capacity for faith (by grace), and the Reformation emphasis on the actual working of the Spirit in the proclamation of the Word. Fresh theological thinking might help to bridge these gulfs (see esp. the works listed below by K. Blaser, A. Heron, J. Moltmann, and M. Welker). Related are questions regarding the understanding of the sacraments, the question of the Spirit and the institution (much debated within

Protestantism), and that of the relation between the freedom the Spirit gives and political freedom (→ Liberation Theology; Political Theology). The simple reduction of the Spirit to intrahuman → communication hardly calls for serious discussion.

New work focuses on the Trinitarian anchoring of pneumatology, the concrete experience of the Spirit, and his liberating work in believers and also in the threatened world (→ Ecology). The Trinitarian God and the working of the living God might perhaps be described in analogy to dynamic fields of force in the new physics (W. Pannenberg, D. Ritschl).

→ Christology; Dogmatics; God; Spirituality

Bibliography: K. BARTH, CD IV/1-3, §§62-63, 67-68, 72-73 • H. BERKHOF, The Doctrine of the Holy Spirit (Atlanta, 1982) • K. BLASER, Vorstoß zur Pneumatologie (Zurich, 1977) • E. BRUNNER, Dogmatics, vol. 3, The Christian Doctrine of the Church, Faith, and the Consummation (Philadelphia, 1978; orig. pub., 1946) • Y. CONGAR, I Believe in the Holy Spirit (New York, 1997) • C. HEITMANN and H. MÜHLEN, eds., Erfahrung und Theologie des Heiligen Geistes (Hamburg, 1974) • G. S. HENDRY, The Holy Spirit in Christian Theology (Philadelphia, 1956) • A. HERON, The Holy Spirit (London, 1983) • H. KREMKAU, ed., Das religiöse Bewußtsein und der Heilige Geist in der Kirche (Frankfurt, 1980), see esp. the part by R. Williams • G. H. W. LAMPE, God as Spirit (Oxford, 1977) • J. McINTYRE, The Shape of Pneumatology (Edinburgh, 1997) • J. MOLTMANN, The Spirit of Life: A Universal Affirmation (London, 1992) • O. NOORDMANS, Das Evangelium des Geistes (Zurich, 1960) • C. SCHÜTZ, Einführung in die Pneumatologie (Darmstadt, 1985) • P. TILLICH, Systematic Theology (vol. 3; Chicago, 1963) • L. VISCHER, ed., Spirit of God-Spirit of Christ: Ecumenical Reflections on the Filioque Controversy (Geneva, 1981) • O. WEBER, Foundations of Dogmatics (2 vols.; Grand Rapids, 1981-83; orig. pub. 1955) 2.227-407 • M. WELKER, God the Spirit (Minneapolis, 1994).

DIETRICH RITSCHL

Holy War

→ War as the resistance of one's orderly world to an alien and dangerous nonworld has always been integrated into religion. It is only recently that there have been real "secular" wars, and the term "holy war" raises problems not merely in relation to → Israel (§1). Warlike acts are often accompanied by ritual acts, and in many religions (e.g., → Islam) war is also the theme of theoretical religious reflection. In fact, wars are seldom exclusively or even predominantly religiously motivated. In Israel, where war could be differentiated from ordinary marauding (see 1 Sam. 21:5), it was self-evidently encompassed with ritual, as in other lands in its day.

As regards Israel, certain literary strata present a relatively unified picture of the "war of Yahweh" (see esp. Deuteronomistic works). At a summons the people of Yahweh gather, and after certain preliminaries (→ Sanctification) they go out to battle with the promise of victory, → Yahweh being the leader and fighting for them. Linked to victory there is often a ban (see esp. Joshua 6–12; Judges 4; 6-7; the introductory speeches of Deuteronomy). This theology of war articulates Yahweh's claim to exclusiveness and the corresponding fact that Israel is not to make treaties with other nations.

Behind this conception lies a cultic and political ideology common to the Near East. On this view the authority of one's own gods must be asserted against alien disorder. Historical experiences also shaped the religion of Israel from the earliest times. These events are echoed in the traditions behind the stories of the judges and in songs like the Song of Deborah in Judges 5 (see also the Book of the Wars of Yahweh, Num. 21:14). In the epoch of the formation of state and people, the wars of Yahweh were elementary experiences that fashioned Israel's consciousness of being one people, the people of Yahweh. The theory that an institution like the amphictyony (→ Tribes of Israel) waged these wars is unnecessary.

→ Peace

Bibliography: I. CORNELIUS, "The Iconography of Divine War in the Pre-Islamic Near East: A Survey," JNSL 21 (1995) 15-36 • P. C. CRAIGIE, The Problem of War in the OT (Grand Rapids, 1978) • G. H. JONES, "The Concept of Holy War," The World of Ancient Israel (ed. R. E. Clements; Cambridge, 1991) 299-321 • S. M. KANG, Divine War in the OT and in the Ancient Near East (Berlin, 1989) • H. G. KIPPENBERG, "'Pflugscharen zu Schwertern.' Krieg und Erlösung in der vorderasiatischen Religionsgeschichte," Töten im Krieg (ed. H. von Stietencron and J. Rüpke; Munich, 1995) 99-123 • M. C. LIND, Yahweh Is a Warrior (Scottdale, Pa., 1980) • A. VAN DER LINGEN, Les guerres de Yahvé. L'implication de YHWH dans les guerres d'Israël selon les livres historiques de l'Ancien Testament (Paris, 1990) • P. D. MILLER, The Divine Warrior in Early Israel (Cambridge, Mass., 1973) • S. NIDITCH, War in the Hebrew Bible: A Study of the Ethics of Violence (Oxford, 1994).

FRITZ STOLZ

Holy Water → Water, Consecrated

Holy Week

1. Origins of Holy Week
2. Palm (Passion) Sunday
3. Monday, Tuesday, Wednesday
4. Holy (Maundy) Thursday
5. Good Friday
6. Easter Vigil

1. Origins of Holy Week

Did. 7.4 calls for a fast of one or two days before → baptism (§2.2). When baptism came to be celebrated at the paschal (Easter) celebration, this tradition applied to the two days before the Pasch (Friday and Saturday). Third-century sources from Alexandria and Syria (the festival letters of Bishop Dionysius of Alexandria and the Syrian *Did. apos.* 21) indicate that this fast was extended to six days before → Easter. References to the commemorations of the events of the last week of Jesus' life in the third century were greatly expanded in the fourth century. Especially influential on the development of "Holy Week" (or, in the East, "Great Week") were the pilgrimage sites and offices developed by the Jerusalem church during and after the reign of Constantine I (306-37). Descriptions of these sites and offices appear in the diary of the Spanish pilgrim-nun Egeria, narrating a journey she took to holy sites (ca. 381-84).

2. Palm (Passion) Sunday

Egeria describes the reading of Matthew 21 and a → procession down the Mount of Olives to Jerusalem led by the bishop "in that manner in which our Lord was then led," with all carrying palm branches and singing → hymns. This dramatic reenactment was introduced in Spain in the 5th century, in Gaul in the 7th century, and in England by the 8th century, but in Rome not before the 12th century. The earliest blessing of palms is found in the Spanish *Liber ordinum* (6th cent.) and is attested in the Gallic Bobbio Missal (8th cent.). The procession typically began outside the church building. The hymn of Theodulf of Orléans (ca. 750-821) *Gloria, laus, et honor* (All glory, laud, and honor) came to be widely sung.

The → Reformation typically suppressed the blessing of palms, but the procession was retained in some places (e.g., Brandenburg). In the 20th century the distribution of palms has been restored in Protestant practice, for example, after the service as a memento of attendance. In 1955 the → Roman Catholic Church greatly revised its Holy Week rites to make them more accessible to the people. The *Book of Offices* (1960) of the Episcopal Church restored the blessing of palms and procession, and Lutherans in North America followed suit in the 1970s (*Contemporary Worship-6* [1973]; *Lutheran Book of Worship* [ministers ed., 1978]).

The unique feature of the medieval Palm Sunday → Mass was the dramatic chanting of the entire passion according to Matthew by three voices: a tenor for the Evangelist, a bass for Jesus, and an alto for all other roles. This practice was expanded with a role for the chorus in the passion oratorios of Lutheran composers in the 17th and 18th centuries (e.g., the *St. Matthew* and *St. John* passions of J. S. Bach; → Passion Music). In the revised Roman → lectionary (1969) and its adaptation in the Episcopal, Lutheran, Common, and Revised Common lectionaries, the Matthew, Mark, and Luke passions are read over the course of three years (→ Passion, Accounts of the).

3. Monday, Tuesday, Wednesday

There are no special liturgies for the first three days of Holy Week, although traditionally the passions according to Mark and Luke were read on Tuesday and Wednesday respectively. These are now replaced by gospel readings that portray the betrayal of Jesus. The medieval Roman → liturgy for Wednesday in Holy Week included the Solemn Prayers, also known as the Bidding Prayers, which were repeated in the Good Friday liturgy. This element probably reflected the desire to pray for the candidates who would be baptized at the Easter Vigil.

In the practice of the → Orthodox Church, the → Eucharist is not celebrated on a → fast day, so the main liturgy of these three days is that of the presanctified (a liturgy of the Word followed by the distribution of Communion from elements consecrated on Sunday). In some Orthodox churches the Matins of Holy Wednesday is replaced with a communal form of anointing of the sick, perhaps inspired by the gospel episode of the anointing of Jesus at Bethany before his passion.

4. Holy (Maundy) Thursday

"Maundy" is an Old English corruption of the Lat. *mandatum* (commandment) of John 13:34. Holy Thursday is one of the most crowded liturgical days in the → church year. The Gelasian Sacramentary (8th cent.) provided propers for three masses: the Reconciliation of Public Penitents, the Blessing of the Chrism, and the Evening Mass of the Lord's Supper.

Tenebrae (Lat. "darkness, shadows") is the morning Office of Lauds anticipated on the evenings before Maundy Thursday, Good Friday, and Holy Saturday. Hence it includes psalmody, the Benedictus as the proper → canticle, and the Lauds psalms (148-50). Its unique feature is the progressive extinguishing of candles until the last candle is removed and the church is in darkness. A loud noise is made, said to symbolize the earthquake that opened the tomb of Christ, and the candle is brought back into view. The rationale for the extinguishing of candles is debated: it either was utilitarian as dawn approached, or else it was conceived purely as a dramatic device. Many Protestant congregations have a service of shadows on the evening of Good Friday with the gradual extinguishing of lights, but it is not usually the historic Office of Tenebrae.

In the fourth century Lent became a time during which the church prayed for the *reconciliation of its public* → *penitents* as well as for its catechumens. In his letter to Decentius (416), Pope Innocent I (402-17) mentions the custom of absolving the penitents on the Thursday before Easter. The penitents were led into the church before the bishop, who prayed for their forgiveness and received them back into the communion of the church with the → kiss of peace. This Mass remained in the sacramentaries long after the institution of the order of public penitents had effectively died out. In Lutheran practice the Order for Corporate Confession with individual absolution and the → laying on of hands had been used on Wednesday night during Holy Week and is now incorporated into the Maundy Thursday liturgy. Where the reconciliation of penitents is being practiced in the Roman Catholic Church today, the rite of reconciliation is also being integrated into the Mass of the Lord's Supper.

The Gregorian Sacramentary, unlike the Gelasian, has only the Chrism Mass for Holy Thursday. This Mass is for the *blessing of the oils* that will be used in the → initiation (§2) of the baptized at the Easter Vigil, in → exorcisms performed on the catechumens, and for the anointing of the sick. This custom is being revived today in non–Roman Catholic churches as an opportunity to emphasize the bishop's pastoral role.

The most important liturgy of Maundy Thursday is the *Evening Mass of the Lord's Supper,* which begins the continuous three-day paschal period *(Triduum Paschali)* that includes the Good Friday liturgy and the Easter Vigil. The unified liturgical rites of these days commemorate the passion, death, and resurrection of Christ. The noteworthy features of the Maundy Thursday liturgy include the → foot washing after the homily in imitation of the servant action of Jesus in the upper room (John 13), the removal of the Communion elements and vessels after the Communion during the singing of Thomas Aquinas's hymn *Pange lingua corporis* (Sing, my tongue, of the glorious body), and the stripping of the → altar and chancel during the chanting of Psalm 22.

5. Good Friday

Good Friday is a day of devotion to the life-giving sacrifice of Christ on which, except in some Lutheran and Protestant practice, the Eucharist is not celebrated.

The popular late-medieval devotion known as the *Way of the Cross* with its 14 stations has been revived for use on Good Friday mornings, especially in Hispanic communities, in which the events in the passion of our Lord are acted out in the streets and parks of cities. Meditations at the stations frequently include homiletic application to current events.

The *Three-Hours' Service* originated in Lima, Peru, in the 17th century and has become popular throughout the Americas. It lasts between noon and 3:00 P.M., the hours Jesus was on the cross, and often focuses on the so-called seven last words of Jesus from the cross. This devotional service has lent itself to ecumenical use in which clergy from different churches give homilies on the seven last words.

The *Good Friday liturgy,* which is part of the *Triduum Paschali,* is usually celebrated after 3:00 P.M. It includes an ancient form of the liturgy of the Word, the center of which is the reading of the passion according to John, and concludes with the Solemn, or Bidding, Prayers. To these elements is added the Veneration of the Cross, which includes the Reproaches that originated in sixth-century Gaul and the adoration hymn of Venantius Fortunatus *Pange lingua gloriosi* (Sing, my tongue, the glorious battle). In the Roman Rite Holy Communion is distributed from the presanctified elements. A popular practice in Eastern → Orthodoxy is reenactment of the burial of Christ at Vespers. The devout prostrate themselves before the winding cloth on Good Friday evening and Holy Saturday up until the beginning of the Paschal Vigil.

6. Easter Vigil

The Great Vigil of Easter, which is the climax of the *Triduum Paschali,* is regarded as the most significant liturgy of the church year. The earliest references to the Paschal Vigil are from the Quartodeciman practice in Asia Minor in the second century, which was the Jewish Passover transcended and Christianized (see the *Peri Pascha* of Melito of Sardis). The vigil has been considered the premier time of the year for Christian initiation since the third century. During the Middle Ages in the West the vigil decreased in importance, probably because of the prevalence of the separation of baptism from the paschal celebration, and it came to be celebrated on Saturday morning. This arrangement was made obligatory in the Missal of Pope Pius V (1570). In 1951 the decree *Dominicae resurrectionis vigiliam* from the Roman Congregation of Rites (→ Curia) allowed the vigil to be restored to the night before Easter "by way of experiment." The night vigil was completely restored in 1955 with the general restoration of Holy Week liturgies (in *Maxima redemptionis nostrae mysteria*). → Anglican and → Lutheran churches also experimented with the restoration of the Easter Vigil in the 1960s.

The structure of the vigil includes a service of light, a service of readings, the liturgy of Holy Baptism, and the first Eucharist of Easter. In Western practice the vigil begins around a new → fire lighted outside the church building, at which the paschal candle is lighted and carried into the darkened church as the deacon sings "The Light of Christ." There are various forms of the paschal blessing in early medieval sacramentaries, but the Gallican form known as the Exsultet is the one most widely used today. The service of readings includes up to 12 OT readings. The Gloria in Excelsis is sung at the start of the paschal Eucharist, and it has become popular to ring bells and to decorate the altar with Easter flowers during this dramatic beginning of the Easter celebration.

It is not considered appropriate to begin the vigil before sundown. In Eastern Orthodox churches the paschal celebration does not begin until midnight; it lasts all night, ends with the Eucharist at dawn, and is concluded with Easter breakfast. Attempts to use the vigil as a form of the Easter sunrise service so popular in Protestant practice have not proved to be successful precisely because the service of light requires darkness for effectiveness and a vigil is, by definition, nocturnal.

Bibliography: A. ADAM, *Das Kirchenjahr mitfeiern* (Freiburg, 1979) • J. F. BALDOVIN, "Holy Week, Liturgies of," *NDSW* 542-52 • K.-H. BIERITZ, *Das Kirchenjahr* (Munich, 1987) • P. F. BRADSHAW and L. A. HOFFMAN, eds., *Passover and Easter: Two Liturgical Traditions* (vol. 6; Notre Dame, Ind., 1999) • J. G. DAVIES, *Holy Week: A Short History* (Richmond, Va., 1963) • P. PFATTEICHER, *Manual on the Liturgy: Lutheran Book of Worship* (Minneapolis, 1979) • K. STEVENSON, *Jerusalem Revisited: The Liturgy of Holy Week* (Washington, D.C., 1988) • T. TALLEY, *The Origins of the Liturgical Year* (New York, 1986) • J. W. TYRER, *Historical Survey of Holy Week: Its Services and Ceremonial* (Oxford, 1932).

FRANK C. SENN

Holy Year

The holy year is a year in which → Roman Catholics are invited to make a special → pilgrimage to Rome, for which the → pope grants a special jubilee → indulgence. The practice began in 1300, and since 1400 a holy year has been proclaimed every 25 years, with special proclamations in 1933 and 1983 commemorating the 1,900th and 1,950th anniversaries of Christ's act of redemption. The special indulgence is hardly the attraction for pilgrims when so many others are available; rather, it is the chance of gaining a stronger sense of religious fellowship, especially at the great papal masses (→ Eucharist). The year opens and closes with the opening and closing of the Holy Door of St. Peter's by the pope on the eve of → Christmas (originally the beginning of the new year).

In contrast to previous custom, at midnight on December 24, 1999, Pope John Paul II pronounced the blessing "Urbi et Orbi" (to the city [i.e., Rome] and for the world). For the first time, the pope himself opened the three additional Holy Doors in December and January, namely, St. John Lateran, Santa Maria Maggiore, and St. Paul's outside the Walls. Moreover, representatives from other churches participated in opening the fourth door in St. Paul's on January 25, 2000, thereby making this act an ecumenical one for the first time.

Bibliography: A. GIANNINI, ed., *Holy Year: The Jubilee of 1950* (2 vols.; Milan, 1950) • W. LURZ, "Heiliges Jahr II: In der Kirche," *LTK* 5.125-26 (bibliography with works in several languages) • D. O'GRADY, *Rome Reshaped: Jubilees, 1300-2000* (New York, 1999) • H. THURSTON, *The Holy Year of Jubilee: An Account of the History and Ceremony of the Roman Jubilee* (St. Louis, 1900).

BALTHASAR FISCHER

Home Mission → Inner Mission

Homiletics → Preaching

Homosexuality

1. Definitions
2. Debates
3. Dialogue

In the years leading up to the 21st century, one of the topics most heatedly debated by the churches was homosexuality. Some are convinced that homosexuality is forbidden by Scripture. Some see homosexuality as a sign of Western moral decadence. Some focus on it as a threat to → marriage and the → family. Others, however, believe that the dignity and worth of each person created in the image of God is at stake. Informing these divergent views are varied interpretations of Scripture and diverse understandings of theological anthropology, as well as of → sin and → salvation. Different beliefs about the nature of God (esp. regarding God's love and mercy and judgment) are also at issue.

1. Definitions
The definition of "homosexuality" is difficult to clarify. Many scholars today argue that the term is best understood in the context of western European societies in the late 19th and early 20th century. "Homosexuality" is derived from the Gk. *homos,* "the same," and referred to both men and women. Historically speaking, the term is first attested in writing in a letter from Hungarian-German writer and translator Karoly Maria Kertbeny to Prussian "Uranian" (i.e., gay) activist Karl Heinrich Ulrichs, on May 6, 1868. "Homosexuality" was first widely used in Germany at the kaiser's court in 1907, with reference to an espionage scandal that implicated, at least according to the press, a "homosexual clique."

Linguists argue that "homosexual" became the term with the most common currency at this time both because it could be transposed into an abstract noun, "homosexuality" (thereby facilitating the increasing medical and scientific interest in the topic), and because it had a convenient binary opposite, "heterosexuality." Given the Western cultural proclivity toward binary oppositions and → dualisms, it is noteworthy that many contemporary terms for same-gender sexual relations come in pairs, for example, "heterosexual/homosexual" and "gay/straight."

Although "homosexuality," etymologically speaking, refers to both → men and → women, already in the late 19th century, in Western societies, distinct terms for sexual relations between men and for those between women were emerging. These terms include "sodomite" for men and "sapphist" or "lesbian" for women. Interestingly, these are terms whose geographic specificity has been metaphorically extended. "Sodomite" is the proper name for the inhabitant of a historical city, whose story is told in Genesis 19. As an extended metaphor, it refers to all who are associated with the sexual practice (considered by later interpreters as "against nature") of the residents of that city. "Sapphist" and "lesbian" both derived from Sappho, the first known poet to make love for other women the subject of her writing. So doing, already 2,500 years ago, she put her home, the Aegean island of Lesbos, on the linguistic map. At different times, many other terms have been used to refer to persons who desire same-gender sexual relations, including "bugger," "dyke," "faggot," "fairy," "grinder," "molly," "queen," "queer," and "tribade."

Although this discussion of definition has so far focused on Western societies, most anthropologists agree that in nearly all times and places there have been, and are, persons who desire sexual relations with persons of the same gender. This reality is easily overlooked, since in nearly all cultures around the world, → marriage and children are definitive of full → adulthood. Anthropologists argue, however, that the apparent absence of terminology says more about Western cultural bias about → sexuality than about the reality of sexual relations in the rest of the world, past and present. Anthropologists, in collaboration with the accounts of Western missionaries, have identified at least three forms of same-gender sexual relations that are globally widespread and significant: (1) *transgenerational,* in which partners are of different ages; (2) *transgenderal,* in which same-sex partners take on different gender roles; and (3) *egalitarian,* in which partners are socially similar. In each instance, it is clear that this same-gender sexual behavior cannot be construed apart from the whole social and cosmological scheme of things, including kinship, marriage, and family, and the sacred.

2. Debates
The most heated debates about homosexuality are focused on the interpretation of Scripture. For those who read the Bible rather literalistically, there is considerable clarity: homosexuality is a sin, an abomination. Passages such as Lev. 18:22, Rom. 1:24-32, and 1 Cor. 6:9-10, as well as the Genesis narratives (18:20-21; 19:4-7), are cited as definitive condemnations. For those who read the Bible less literalistically, these passages are set in the wider narrative of God's → salvation history, which is a history of liberation for those who are oppressed, including gay and lesbian liberation from oppressive systems of gender.

Another arena of debate is Christian → tradition. Early Christian writings of the first and second centuries, such as the *Didache* and the *Epistle of Barnabas,* were unequivocally opposed to male → prostitution and pederasty. In the early third century, Clement of Alexandria also condemned homosexuality in his *Paedagogus.* He condemned homosexuality more generally because it was nonprocreative and therefore unnatural. Because Clement also believed that patriarchal gender roles were natural, he specifically judged lesbians for acting contrary to nature (i.e., acting like men). In nature's gendered order, according to Clement, men were active and women were passive; therefore, women who took an active role sexually were unnatural. Clement's near contemporary Tertullian wrote that those who engaged in "all the other frenzies of passions [other than adultery and fornication] . . . beyond the laws of nature" should be banished "not only from the threshold, but from all the shelter of the Church, because they are not sins, but monstrosities" (*De pud.* 4).

Some scholars, however, note that in the early church homosexuality was not a primary category for distinguishing acceptable sex from unacceptable; the primary distinction, rather, related to procreation. Homosexuality was a derivative category of nonreproductive sexual activity. Nonetheless, by the 12th century, homosexuality was closely associated with → heresy. In the late medieval and early modern eras, the church played an active role in the persecution of homosexuality. Until quite recently, there has been little change in the church's condemnation and persecution of homosexuality.

By the late 20th century churches had adopted various positions on homosexuality. Especially since the early 1970s, many churches, at least in the United States and Canada, have conducted studies, held debates, and voted on position statements. These statements address issues such as Scripture and traditional Christian teaching, civil and human rights for gays and lesbians, as well as the ordination of gays and lesbians. The United Church of Canada, for example, has said that all persons, "regardless of sexual orientation," can be received as members and be considered as candidates for ordained ministry. Gay or lesbian persons can be ordained in congregations of the United Church of Christ (U.S.A.), but the national church cannot impose this policy on its congregations.

Most Baptist, Lutheran, Methodist, and Presbyterian churches have declared that homosexuality is incompatible with Christian teaching, and they therefore argue that ordination of noncelibate gays and lesbians is impossible; some of these churches have, however, affirmed gays and lesbians as persons of sacred worth. An analogous distinction between the person and the behavior, or orientation and → lifestyle, is made in recent statements by the → Roman Catholic Church. While these statements reiterate the teaching that homosexual activity or a homosexual lifestyle is sinful, there is also recognition that some persons have an orientation that is unchosen, the origin of which remains a mystery. Such persons, viewed from this perspective, are worthy of the → pastoral care of the church. Other churches maintain that homosexuality is a disease or a sort of sexual dysfunction and advocate therapeutic treatment.

The contemporary controversy about homosexuality, at least in the United States and Canada, also focuses on whether clergy may perform same-sex union ceremonies. In the United Methodist Church, for example, clergy who have presided at such "holy unions" have been brought to trial, convicted, and stripped of holy orders.

3. Dialogue

Although churches and other religious bodies have most often chosen to speak about homosexuality abstractly, the actual lives of gays and lesbians have become increasingly visible. This visibility has been occasioned by the formation of gay and lesbian support and advocacy groups in many churches and religious bodies, as well as in secular societies. Such organizations include Hindus, Buddhists, Muslims, and Jews, as well as Christians of various ecclesial traditions. Most of these groups are independent of, and not formally endorsed or funded by, their respective religious bodies. Groups exist in most North Atlantic countries, as well as in countries such as Argentina, Brazil, Greece, South Africa, and Zimbabwe.

The lives of gays and lesbians have also become more visible through the theologies being written from the perspectives of gays and lesbians. An early, and by now classic, text is John McNeill's *The Church and the Homosexual.* Other theologies include Elizabeth Stuart's *Just Good Friends: Towards a Lesbian and Gay Theology of Relationships* and Richard Cleaver's *Know My Name: A Gay Liberation Theology.*

The → World Council of Churches has not directly addressed ethical, theological, and ecclesiological issues related to homosexuality. The sixth assembly (Vancouver, 1983) encouraged churches "to examine and study for themselves and with one another the question of homosexuality, with special stress on the pastoral responsibility of the churches everywhere for those who are homosexual." Most recently, homosexuality was the subject of discussion at the eighth assembly (Harare, 1998). The assembly further called for the council to conduct a study of human sexuality, most especially homosexuality.

Bibliography: D. L. Balch, ed., *Homosexuality, Science, and the "Plain Sense" of Scripture* (Grand Rapids, 2000) • J. Boswell, *Christianity, Social Tolerance, and Homosexuality* (Chicago, 1980) • A. A. Brash, *Facing Our Differences: The Churches and Their Gay and Lesbian Members* (Geneva, 1995) • B. J. Brooten, *Love between Women: Early Christian Responses to Female Homoeroticism* (Chicago, 1996) • R. Cleaver, *Know My Name: A Gay Liberation Theology* (Louisville, Ky., 1995) • G. D. Comstock, *Unrepentant, Self-Affirming, Practicing: Lesbian/Bisexual/Gay People within Organized Religion* (New York, 1996) • L. W. Countryman, *Dirt, Greed, and Sex: Sexual Ethics in the NT and Their Implications for Today* (Philadelphia, 1988) • P. Germond and S. de Gruchy, ed., *Aliens in the Household of God: Homosexuality and Christian Faith in South Africa* (Cape Town, 1997) • D. F. Greenberg, *The Construction of Homosexuality* (Chicago, 1988) • G. Herdt, *Same Sex, Different Cultures: Gays and Lesbians across Cultures* (New York, 1997) • *Homosexuality: Some Elements for an Ecumenical Discussion* (= *ER* 50/1 [1998]) • J. McNeill, *The Church and the Homosexual* (Boston, 1976) • M. Nissinen, *Homoeroticism in the Biblical World: A Historical Perspective* (Minneapolis, 1998) • S. M. Olyan and M. C. Nussbaum, eds., *Sexual Orientation and Human Rights in American Religious Discourse* (Oxford, 1998) • K. Rudy, *Sex and the Church: Gender, Homosexuality, and the Transformation of Christian Ethics* (Boston, 1997) • R. Scroggs, *The NT and Homosexuality: Contextual Background for Contemporary Debate* (Philadelphia, 1983) • C.-L. Seow, ed., *Homosexuality and Christian Community* (Louisville, Ky., 1996) • J. S. Siker, ed., *Homosexuality and the Church: Both Sides of the Debate* (Louisville, Ky., 1994) • E. Stuart, *Just Good Friends: Towards a Lesbian and Gay Theology of Relationships* (London, 1995) • W. Wink, ed., *Homosexuality and Christian Faith: Questions of Conscience for the Churches* (Minneapolis, 1999).

Melanie A. May

Honduras

	1960	*1980*	*2000*
Population (1,000s):	1,894	3,569	6,485
Annual growth rate (%):	3.39	3.19	2.49
Area: 112,492 sq. km. (43,433 sq. mi.)			

A.D. 2000

Population density: 58/sq. km. (149/sq. mi.)
Births / deaths: 3.00 / 0.51 per 100 population
Fertility rate: 3.72 per woman
Infant mortality rate: 31 per 1,000 live births
Life expectancy: 71.0 years (m: 68.6, f: 73.4)
Religious affiliation (%): Christians 97.2 (Roman Catholics 91.3, Protestants 8.6, indigenous 3.4, marginal 1.5, unaffiliated 1.1, other Christians 0.2), spiritists 1.1, other 1.7.

1. History, Society, Economy, State

Honduras, a Central American republic, was first sighted by Columbus in 1502. It shares borders with Guatemala, El Salvador, and Nicaragua. Its coasts touch both the Caribbean Sea, often referred to as its Atlantic coast, and the Pacific Ocean.

From the first millennium A.D. the western part of Honduras was inhabited by the Maya, who built Copán as one of their most impressive cult cities. The site of that city, however, had already decayed by the time the territory of the modern republic of Honduras became part of the Spanish Captaincy General of Guatemala in 1538. As part of the United Provinces of Central America, Honduras gained independence from Spain in 1821. In 1838, after the dissolution of that federation, the country became politically independent.

The population of Honduras, which reached its pre-Spanish level of 1.2 million only in 1945, shows much Indian influence among its mestizos. Honduras became the prototype of a so-called banana republic, as three banana companies dominated virtually the whole Atlantic coast up to World War I. Those companies had decisive influence on the country, a role consolidated by the political and military actions of the United States. Economic independence was achieved in Honduras after the depression of the 1930s, and at the end of the 20th century only the United Fruit Companies remained in a position of influence.

The fall in the prices of coffee, cotton, and sugar after 1980 brought economic crisis. → Industrialization in accord with capitalist ideology, the importation of → technology, and attendant socioeconomic → development together served only to increase geographic imbalance, with undue concentration on Tegucigalpa and San Pedro Sula. Monopolization and domination by foreign capital resulted. After the United States withdrew its support from the ruling conservative forces in 1980, the Liberal Party took power in 1982, signaling the end of the de facto military dictatorship. Until the end of the Contra war, however, the Liberals' range of activity remained severely restricted because of both the massive U.S. military presence and the country's enormous dependence on American economic aid. With the end of the Contra war, however, Honduras lost its geopolitical significance for the United States, and the country thus lost America's financial aid. In consequence of these developments, Honduras became marked by economic stagnation, a high crime rate, bombings and assassinations, and increasing corruption in public life.

In 1997 over 70 percent of Hondurans lived below the → poverty line. Although almost 60 percent of the population work in agriculture, a 1992 law of agricultural modernization has increasingly curtailed people's access to credit. Although 125,000 families are waiting for land grants, citizens have been forbidden to use the forests for hunting or gathering, since they have been sold to firms engaged in the export of tropical wood. Even though the production of basic foods (e.g., corn and black beans) has decreased since 1992, the state has encouraged the export of foodstuffs as a means of acquiring foreign currency. The Ministry of Health estimates that 80 percent of all Hondurans exhibit symptoms of malnourishment. Roman Catholic leaders have repeatedly criticized the government of Honduras, next to Haiti the poorest country in the Americas, for engaging in excessive economic repression at the expense of the poor as well as for diverting, in accord with neoliberal ideology, almost half of the country's export income to external debt payment.

In order to implement comprehensive changes in the structure of the national police and to remove the police from the control of the military, Parliament in 1997 named Archbishop Oscar Andrés Rodríguez Maradiaga to oversee a board for police reform. In this position the archbishop also has responsibility for the investigation of 184 instances of the suspicious disappearances of persons, dating from the 1980s.

In January 1998, in the fifth national election since the ending of the military dictatorship in 1982, Carlos Flores of the ruling Liberal Party, and one of the wealthiest persons in Honduras, was elected president of the country. The → Roman Catholic Church decried the election campaign as a "dialogue of deaf-mutes," since none of the five candidates for the presidency discussed the country's economic problems or the impoverishment of the country's inhabitants. The devastating effects of Hurricane Mitch in October 1998 only exacerbated an already desperate situation, causing the socioeconomic development of Honduras to become completely uncertain.

2. Churches

In 1531 the Roman Catholic Diocese of Honduras was established, first based in the Caribbean port of Trujillo and then, from 1539, in Valladolid in the Comayagua Valley. Spanish → Franciscans began intensive missionary work in 1550.

Most of the people of Honduras belong to the Roman Catholic Church, which itself forms a province with an archbishopric and six bishoprics (1996). Its main organs are the Bishops' Conference (nine bishops), a National Pastoral Commission, a Council of Parish Churches, and a Council of Members of Orders (→ Latin American Council of Bishops). There are 327 priests, only a small minority of whom are nationals. In light of this shortage of ordained clergy, the work of ten apostolic → lay movements is extremely important, not least in the leadership of Services of the Word, in which some 10,000 persons are involved. The church is at work in evangelization, → catechizing, → liturgy, and → pastoral care.

Most Protestant → missionary work did not begin in Honduras until the late 19th century. By 1859 → Anglicans were working on the Bay Islands off the northern coast, at that time under English control. By 1891 the Seventh-day → Adventists had established work, and in July 1896 the Central American Mission became the first Protestant group to initiate organized missionary activity on the mainland. The → Plymouth Brethren established work in San Pedro Sula in 1898, and by 1911 the → Friends were at work in the country. The first denominational mission in Honduras was the Evangelical Synod of North America, which arrived in 1921; the Evangelical and Reformed Church of Honduras emerged from this work. In 1931 the → Moravians began work among the Miskito Indians, and in 1937 the first missionaries from the → Assemblies of God entered Honduras from nearby El Salvador.

No fewer than 110 Protestant denominations are now active in Honduras. Rapid growth came to these groups in the 1960s, with increases averaging four times greater per year than that of the population at large. Groups with a large membership are the → Baptists (which began their efforts in 1954), Seventh-day Adventists (1887), the Central American Mission, Evangelical Church of the Brethren (1930), and the Assemblies of God (1937). Pentecostal church growth — which includes the Assemblies of God, the Church of God (Cleveland, Tenn.), the Foursquare Gospel Church, the Church of God of Prophecy, and several Pentecostal groups indigenous to Mesoamerica, as well as many independent charismatic churches — has accelerated so rapidly since the 1950s that this movement now constitutes the largest sector of Honduran Protestantism.

Protestants engage primarily in → evangelism and church establishment. Mass evangelism campaigns as well as radio and television ministries and the translation and distribution of the Bible contribute to this thrust. Leaders receive biblical and theological instruction through institutions that employ a variety of delivery systems. Protestants also engage in extensive cultural and educational work, including the operation of schools and → literacy programs.

In addition, small communities of Orthodox believers are present in Honduras, the result of immigration from Middle Eastern nations.

3. Ecumenical Relations

Relationships between Roman Catholics and Protestants are marked by tension as a result of doctrinal differences and vigorous evangelistic efforts by Protestants among nominal Roman Catholics. Also, many Protestants have supported government repression of Roman Catholics working in organizations to support the poorest classes, in the belief that these organizations were pursuing a → Marxist agenda.

In Honduras, Protestant ecumenism is relatively weak, mainly because most Protestant churches and movements are very conservative theologically, and many are not only independent in spirit but ecclesiologically separatistic. Yet there are some common efforts, notably the Evangelical Committee for Development and National Emergency (comprising 30 groups and organizations), the Commission for Development and National Emergency (9 local organizations and churches with a readiness for cooperation and coordination with Roman Catholic parishes), and the National Alliance of Evangelical Pastors. Other organizations that cross denominational lines include World Relief, the Alliance of Evangelical Institutions, the Christian Fraternity of Businessmen, and some regional clergy associations.

4. Church and State

Relations between the Roman Catholic Church and the state began to deteriorate in the 1980s because of an increasing alienation of the church from the overall social system (→ Church and State). For reasons the church attributed to institutionalized injustice, the system became less and less able to deal with the national social, political, and economic crisis.

Protestant churches enjoy good relations with the state, in spite of a constitutional separation between the two. Most of the Protestant denominations and organizations are politically conservative and are uncritically obedient in principle to the establishment, which makes them easy for the state to favor.

5. Non-Christian Religions

Christianity, even though often nominal, is part of the cultural identity of Honduras. Non-Christian religions that include Christian elements are therefore more important than those that do not. Honduras includes pseudo-Christian groups (e.g., → Jehovah's Witnesses, → Mormons), Gnostic groups (e.g., Universal Movement of Christian Gnostics), Afro-American animists (marked by a surprising → syncretism between the blacks of the Caribbean and those of the Honduran Atlantic coast; → Afro-American Cults), indigenous → animists in the isolated communities of Paya, Sumo, and Jicaque; and other, smaller religious groups (e.g., → Judaism and → Baha'i).

Bibliography: C. ALVAREZ, *People of Hope: The Protestant Movement in Central America* (New York, 1990) • G. BLANCO and J. VALVERDE, *Honduras. Iglesia y cambio social* (San José, C.R., 1990) • K. BRAUNGART, *Heiliger Geist und politische Herrschaft bei den Neo-Pfingstlern in Honduras* (Frankfurt, 1995) • M. CARIAS, *La Iglesia Católica en Honduras, 1492-1975* (Tegucigalpa, 1991) • D. A. EURAQUE, *Reinterpreting the Banana Republic: Region and State in Honduras, 1870-1972* (Chapel Hill, N.C., 1996) • H. K. MEYER and J. H. MEYER, *Historical Dictionary of Honduras* (Metuchen, N.J., 1994) • J. A. MORRIS, *Honduras: Caudillo Politics and Military Rulers* (Boulder, Colo., 1984) • D. E. SCHULZ, *The United States, Honduras, and the Crisis in Central America* (Boulder, Colo., 1994) • R. SIERRA FONSECA, *Fuentes y bibliografía para el estudio de la historia de la iglesia de Honduras* (Choluteca, 1993).

HANS-JÜRGEN PRIEN, EDWIN AGUILUZ,
and KENNETH MULHOLLAND

Hong Kong and Macao

1. Hong Kong
2. Macao

1. Hong Kong

Hong Kong, an enclave of southeastern China now comprising over 200 islands plus part of the Chinese mainland, was occupied by the British in 1839 and ceded to them in 1842 by the Treaty of Nanking. Boasting one of the world's busiest ports, Hong Kong became an important commercial and financial center. By terms of a joint declaration between China and Great Britain in 1984, Hong Kong reverted to the People's Republic of China on July 1, 1997, when it became a special administrative region of China. It occupies an area of 1,075 sq. km. (415 sq. mi.). In 1999 its estimated population was 6.85 million, 95 percent of whom were ethnic Chinese. At least 10 percent of the people are Christian.

Following World War II the population of Hong Kong expanded quickly because of the → revolution and civil war in China. Cheap labor and foreign investment soon brought strong industrial development to Hong Kong, and it became one of the most productive areas in the Far East. While many industrial enterprises have been transferred to other parts of China, the service sector has gained increased importance. Although Hong Kong overall is affluent, there continue to be sharp social and economic contrasts within the population.

Various church groups and organizations engage in social ministry. The Industrial Committee of the Hong Kong Christian Council, the Hong Kong Christian Institute, and other Christian initiatives attempt to meet the challenges underlying a highly divergent society. Besides medical work, the churches carry on comprehensive educational programs, an effort that relies heavily on government grants. In Hong Kong 16 theological seminaries and Bible schools provide theological training not only for Hong Kong but also for other areas of Asia.

The → Roman Catholic population is gathered in the Diocese of Hong Kong, established in 1946. There is a wide range of Protestant → denominations, including → Anglican, → Methodist churches, the Church of Christ in China, → Baptists, → Christian and Missionary Alliance, Presbyterians (→ Reformed and Presbyterian Churches), and → Lutherans. Anglo-Saxon and continental European missionary activity, which started in 1842 (→ British Missions; German Missions), played an important and influential role in the development of this Christian community. When → missionaries were forced to leave mainland China in 1949, many mission groups and organizations settled in Hong Kong.

The Hong Kong Chinese Christian Churches Union includes over 225 congregations. With so many different church groups and denominations, the Hong Kong Christian Council, founded in 1954, has a challenging ecumenical task. In the Roman Catholic community, there are many congregations, social service agencies, schools, and orders of clergy and laity.

The Tao Fong Shan Ecumenical Centre and the Christian Study Centre on Chinese Religion and Culture (founded in 1957, and having become an institute within the Chinese University of Hong Kong) help the churches to interpret the intellectual, social, and religious context in which the tradition of China (→ Buddhism, → Confucianism, → Taoism, and other traditional Chinese religions) converges with Western → secularism and the emerging ideological challenges of the People's Republic of China.

The transition to Chinese rule, under the principle of "one country, two systems," was smooth and has had little impact on public life, although there have been currents objecting to perceived infringements on democratic proceedings. With the reversion of Hong Kong to China, churches are being required to rethink their discipleship, witness, mission, and ministry, including the fundamental question of their role in a country that now has brought together two different political systems.

2. Macao

Macao, also an enclave of southeastern China, situated roughly 65 km. (40 mi.) west of Hong Kong, consists of a peninsula and two small islands in the Pearl River delta. It was founded in 1557 as a Portuguese trading colony. By the terms of a 1987 agreement, Portugal returned Macao to the People's Republic of China on December 20, 1999, under terms similar to those in Hong Kong. Its area of 18 sq. km. (7 sq. mi.) is home to 435,000 people (1999 est.). Ethnically, 95 percent of the people are Chinese and 3 percent Portuguese.

In its early days, Macao was a center of Christian → mission in East Asia. After the founding of Hong Kong in 1842, this small colony lost its importance. The majority of Christians in Macao are Roman Catholic (est. 65,000 persons). The much smaller Protestant community (ca. 1,500 persons) is linked very closely with the church bodies and congregations in Hong Kong.

Bibliography: D. H. Bays, *Christianity in China: From*

the Eighteenth Century to the Present (Stanford, Calif., 1996) • G. T. Brown, *Christianity in the People's Republic of China* (Atlanta, 1986) • C. L. Chiou and L. H. Liew, eds., *Uncertain Future: Taiwan–Hong Kong–China Relations after Hong Kong's Return to Chinese Sovereignty* (Aldershot, 2000) • Y. P. Ghai, *Hong Kong's New Constitutional Order: The Resumption of Chinese Sovereignty and the Basic Law* (2d ed.; Hong Kong, 1999) • T. Lambert, *The Resurrection of the Chinese Church* (London, 1991) • P.-K. Li, *Hong Kong from Britain to China: Political Cleavages, Electoral Dynamics, and Institutional Changes* (Aldershot, 2000) • J. McGivering, *Macao Remembers* (New York, 1999) • S. Shipp, *Macau, China: A Political History of the Portuguese Colony's Transition to Chinese Rule* (Jefferson, N.C., 1997) • C. T. Smith, *Chinese Christians: Elites, Middlemen, and the Church in Hong Kong* (Hong Kong, 1985) • A. Y. So, *Hong Kong's Embattled Democracy: A Societal Analysis* (Baltimore, 1999) • J. Spence, *The Search for Modern China* (New York, 1996).

Winfried Glüer and Thomas F. Schaeffer

Hope

1. The Bible
    1.1. Usage
    1.2. OT
    1.3. NT
2. Theology and Ethics
    2.1. The Phenomenon
    2.2. Development of the Christian Doctrine
    2.3. Determinants of the Christian View
3. Present-Day Discussion

1. The Bible

1.1. *Usage*

The biblical vocabulary of hope includes also important terms that are rendered "expect," "wait," "trust," and "rely."

1.2. *OT*

Eccl. 9:4 states a general truth in saying that "whoever is joined with all the living has hope." What is hoped for is something positive (e.g., marriage and children, Ruth 1:9, 12). Hope can be disappointed, such as that of the owner of the vineyard in Isa. 5:2, 4, 7. Those who suffer can be without hope or have only a distant object of hope (Job 6:19-20); they can complain to God, who has "uprooted" their hope (Job 19:10). Hope reaches only up to → death and not beyond. → Suffering may be so severe that only death is hoped for (Job 6:8). For the righteous, loss of hope means ungodliness (Job 8:20; 11:13-20). →

Israel (§1) as a whole may also lose hope or have its hope destroyed (Ezek. 37:11).

In the OT hope is not set on people but on → salvation, deliverance, light, an end of distress, and so forth. It must not be set on riches (Ps. 52:7; Job 31:24), one's own → righteousness (Ezek. 33:13), other people (Jer. 17:5), human thoughts (Ps. 94:11; 33:10; Isa. 19:3), religious centers like the → temple (Jer. 7:4) or Bethel (Jer. 48:13), idols (Hab. 2:18), or power and alliances (Hos. 10:13; Isa. 31:1) — indeed, on anything that one might think to count on or control. Rather, hope is to be set on → Yahweh and his free → grace, which is not at our disposal but which will never disappoint us, since it is rooted in his → covenant (§1) faithfulness (Hos. 12:6; Jer. 31:17; Ps. 40:1). This hope is God's gift (Ps. 62:5; Jer. 29:11). Believers obediently bow to his rule (Ps. 33:18; 147:11) without allowing anxiety (Isa. 7:4; 12:2).

This kind of hope in God is new in Israel and typifies its relation to God. No worshipers in Babylon ever called one of their gods "my hope." Hope in Yahweh and waiting upon him are rooted in the confession of trust in Yahweh as we find it especially in the Psalms. In prayer believers can say that they hope in the word of Yahweh (Ps. 130:5) or his arm (Isa. 51:5) or his salvation (Mic. 7:7). In place of something that is hoped for stands the one from whom it is hoped. Yahweh is he whose very being is help and salvation. He is thus hope for Israel.

The goal of hope is Yahweh's kingdom, his reign on the new earth, the conversion of Israel and the peoples, the new covenant (Isa. 25:9; 49:6; 65:17-25; Jer. 31:31-34; Hos. 3:5). "Those who wait for the Lord" (Ps. 31:24; 37:9, etc.) characterizes the righteous. We find a new turn in Isa. 42:4: "The coastlands wait for his teaching," that is, the → Gentiles wait for his salvation. The confession of confidence becomes an address to the self (Ps. 42:5; 43:5). Complaint can end with a confession of trust and a call to the community to hope (Ps. 27:13-14). Believers move on from → prayer to admonition and devout wisdom.

1.3. *NT*

In the NT hope is theologically important, especially in the Epistles. It is motivated by its object, for which it waits, leading to patience and endurance. For → Paul, → Abraham is a model of hope. When, humanly speaking, Abraham had nothing to hope for, he still hoped. This response showed his → faith, for he put his trust in God alone (Rom. 4:18).

NT faith is essentially hope. Especially for Paul triadic formulas are important: faith, hope, and → love (1 Cor. 13:13; 1 Thess. 5:8; linked to work, labor, and steadfastness in 1 Thess. 1:3). The Christian life is described in terms of the faith and love of those who hope for the eschatological consummation (1 Thess. 3:6; Gal. 5:5-6). A mark of love is that it hopes all things (1 Cor. 13:7). In distinction from Christians, pagans have no hope (1 Thess. 4:13; Eph. 2:12). Faith and hope belong together (Rom. 6:8; 8:38-39). Hope rests on the act of God in the → resurrection of Jesus (1 Cor. 15:20-23). Not based on anything human, earthly, or calculable, it reaches beyond death and has a universal goal (1 Cor. 15:28). The hope of Christians is that of every creature (Rom. 8:22-25): deliverance, righteousness, resurrection, eternal life, and the vision of God. It is personalized, for Christ himself is our hope (1 Cor. 15:19; Col. 1:27; 3:1-4; 1 Tim. 1:1).

Christians hope in the future of him who came and who is now exalted (Phil. 2:9; Eph. 1:22; 1 Thess. 1:3, 10). They live in the tension of the Now and the Then (Rom. 8:23-24; 1 John 3:2). Like faith, hope is a gift of the Father in heaven (2 Thess. 2:16), of the one who is the God of hope (Rom. 15:13). Being a Christian means being born again to a living hope (1 Pet. 1:3). This hope is that of being saved in the judgment (1 Thess. 5:9), of experiencing sonship and the redemption of the body (Rom. 8:23), righteousness (Gal. 5:5), and life with Christ (1 Thess. 5:10). Hope is bound up with reception of the → gospel and entrance into the → church (Eph. 1:18; 4:4).

The work of the → apostle is governed by hope (2 Cor. 1:10; 3:11-12; Titus 1:2), and Christians themselves are his hope (1 Thess. 2:19). In Acts hope also has a place in apologetics, for Paul is brought to judgment for his hope of the resurrection (Acts 23:6; 28:20). Hope of the resurrection is a motive for a devout life (Acts 24:15-16). The resurrection is the hope of Israel (Acts 24:15; 26:7; 28:20).

According to Heb. 11:1, faith is "the assurance of things hoped for," and the community endures as it holds fast its confidence in hope, which assures access to God (3:6; 7:18-19). Hope is the anchor of the soul (6:19). It derives from Christ's appointment as → high priest (10:23). In 1 Peter hope is central (1:3-9; 3:5, 15): we are born again to a living hope based on Christ's resurrection. Faith in Christ, who was raised from the dead, becomes hope.

→ Eschatology; Kingdom of God; Promise and Fulfillment; Soteriology

Bibliography: J. BARR, The Garden of Eden and the Hope of Immortality (London, 1992) • G. R. BEASLEY-MURRAY, Jesus and the Last Days (Peabody, Mass., 1993) • A. E. BERNSTEIN, The Formation of Hell: Death and Retribution in the Ancient and Early Christian Worlds (London, 1993) • R. BULTMANN and K. H. RENGSTORF, "'Ελπίς κτλ.," TDNT 2.517-35 • N. COHN, Cosmos, Chaos, and the World to Come: The Ancient Roots of Apocalyptic (New Haven, 1993) • W. J. DUMBRELL, The Search for Order: Biblical Eschatology in Focus (Grand Rapids, 1994) • W. C. KAISER, The Messiah in the OT (Grand Rapids, 1995) • F. LANG, Die Briefe an die Korinther (Göttingen, 1986) • B. MAYER, "'Ελπίς κτλ.," EDNT 1.437-41 • G. VON NEBE and J. GÖTZMANN, "Hoffnung / Furcht / Sorge," TBLNT 1.993-1015 • G. J. RILEY, Resurrection Reconsidered: Thomas and John in Controversy (Minneapolis, 1995).

HANS BIETENHARD

2. Theology and Ethics

2.1. The Phenomenon

Hope is a feature of the emotional life. It is rooted in the sense of time, which gives us an awareness of change. We can imagine future events and relate to them. This relation to future events affects the present, for it presupposes a view of reality and of existence in the future. The NT witness shows that being a Christian includes hope (see 1.3). The task of a dogmatic and ethical theology of hope is to reflect on the relation between → faith and hope and therewith on the relation between what is hoped for and the → act of hope. It must seek to conceptualize and categorize these relations.

2.2. Development of the Christian Doctrine

2.2.1. After early beginnings in Augustine (354-430), we find a thorough discussion of the concept of Christian hope first in → Scholasticism, especially in Thomas Aquinas (ca. 1225-74; → Thomism). Thomas set Christian hope within the Aristotelian theory of the emotions (→ Aristotelianism). Hope is an emotional orientation to a future good that is hard to obtain but that may be reached under certain conditions (Summa theol. I of II, q. 40, art. 1). Thomas modified this general view, however, by relating hope to eternal life in fellowship with God (the beatific vision as the final goal of creaturely life) and by linking the attainability of this good, in line with the doctrine of → grace, to the help given by God's power and goodness (ibid. II of II, q. 17, art. 2). Hope is thus the emotional side of the certainty of faith, and like faith, it is a theological and supernatural → virtue that derives from God's gracious action. The orientation of hope to the reality of God is the ground of Thomas's criticism of the speculative theology of history advanced by Joachim of Fiore (ca. 1135-1202; → Theology of History).

2.2.2. Reformation theology protested against the philosophical framework of this teaching regarding hope and also against the dominant role that the idea of merit played in it. In its strict doctrine of → sin and the forensic implication of its concept of → justification, hope was an essential element of the relation to God governed by trust. The object of hope is the → righteousness of humankind before God. This gift is promised in the → gospel of Jesus Christ and grasped in faith, but it is deeply hidden by the assaults of sin, the → law, and → death (→ Temptation). In the precise formula of M. Luther (1483-1546), Christian hope is "purest hope in the purest God" (WA 5.166.18). The point is that the hope that is of the essence of faith is confidence relative to God's work (→ Luther's Theology). This eschatological orientation of the Christian life, precisely in its expectation of the imminent end of the world, meant decided rejection of → apocalyptic and chiliastic (→ Millenarianism) transformations of Christian hope.

2.2.3.

From the beginning of the → modern period complex intellectual and social changes brought a far-reaching shift in the objects of possible hope. The → philosophy of history that arose with G. B. Vico (1668-1744) and Voltaire (1694-1778), using models from the theology of history, developed the idea of a fulfillment of history within history, all prior historical periods being considered prehistory (R. Koselleck). Within this concept hope thus assumes the character of a → utopian consciousness, its certainty being based on the postulates of historical or evolutionary regularity (→ Evolution).

F. D. E. Schleiermacher (1768-1834) did not make Christian hope a special theme, but in his doctrine of the perfecting of the → church, he carefully expounded the object of individual and collective hope. He also gave an eschatological orientation to his teaching on → prayer (→ Schleiermacher's Theology). He initiated attempts to reconcile hope in God's eschatological future with creative historical action.

The mediating trends in neo-Protestantism were opposed by → dialectical theology, which defined the Christian life exclusively as life in hope. K. Barth (1886-1968) moved beyond this criticism with his doctrine of the glorifying of here-and-now existence (*CD* III/2, §47.5). The various attempts at → political theology also try to formulate theologically a tenable reconciling of human historical action with God's redemptive action.

2.3. *Determinants of the Christian View*

Dealing with hope is an urgent task today both internally in worldwide Christianity and externally in general → culture. We must avoid both the apocalyptic visions of → fundamentalism and the determinism of historical → materialism. The assurance of hope must be described in such a way that its practical value is clear and also its difference from prognostic guesses, illusory wishes (→ Illusion), or a "principle of hope" (E. Bloch) with no clear certainty. As Christian hope is conceivable only in a nondeterministic view of reality, its emotional power is significant for action only under contingent conditions.

According to Christian teaching, the object of hope is the fulfillment of the newness of → life in which → baptism into the death of Christ places us (cf. Rom. 6:3-5 with 8:17-25). Its object, then, is the completion of what begins in encounter with the word of the gospel through the Holy Spirit but that stands in need of a constant renewal and preservation of → faith and → love. The statements that express this object of hope are grounded in the life with Christ (see Gal. 2:20). The life that is lived in faith and love is referred to hope, not only because sin is still a determinative factor right up to death, but also because God's action is deeply hidden under the sufferings of time. By its origin, then, the hope of the church in the world is always hope for the world. Statements about hope can be credible only if it is possible for God to create conditions for participation in his eternal life beyond the space-time experiences of today. Christian hope is thus an implication of the doctrine of → God, but the eschatological perspective of Christianity also has ontological ramifications.

The assurance of hope is ethically significant, but not because the object of hope might involve practical, normative knowledge. Hope is objectified if the unconditionality of the imperative or the end that is constitutive for action is declared to be its object. In terms of a theory of → action, hope has to do neither with the genesis of moral insight nor with its voluntary affirmation. It relates instead to the realizing of ends under natural and interpersonal conditions. The assurance of hope becomes important in the crisis of expectations (see Rom. 4:18). It can overcome the resignation and despair that come when our own acts encounter superior opposition or when the test of → conscience shows them to be defective or a failure. It gives us the power to persevere. A test of the viability of a church doctrine of hope is whether we can quietly hope in God even in the existentially worst situations of incurable → suffering or dying. This hope is exercised in prayer.

In the present theological situation it may be doubted whether we can deal with hope in the purely objective language of religion. Theology, rather, has the duty of expounding rationally the relation between the object of hope and the assurance of hope and thus making possible a → hermeneutics of eschatological statements. The term of reference of such an exposition cannot be an arbitrarily chosen theory that contradicts the elementary content of a description of Christian existence. A theory is demanded that does justice to our creaturely being-in-the-world. Such a theory might be sketched on the ground of a material concept of → freedom. Freedom is the condition in which it is possible to engage individually in theoretical and practical action. As such, it is given by God, the ground of freedom, but in the situation of unbelief it is perverted into lying and wickedness. Christian hope can be effective as the power of endurance because it is not oriented to what is beyond our being-in-the world. It is longing for fellowship with the basis of freedom, in which the conflicts that we now experience and suffer between truth and falsehood, good and evil, life and death, will be transcended and overcome.

→ Eschatology; Ethics; Future; Immanence and Transcendence; Progress; Resurrection; Salvation; Salvation History

Bibliography: R. ALVES, A Theology of Human Hope (Washington, D.C., 1969) • P. BADHAM, Christian Beliefs about Life after Death (London, 1981) • K. BARTH, CD III/2, §47; IV/3, §73 • E. BLOCH,The Principle of Hope (Cambridge, Mass., 1995; orig. pub., 1954) • S. T. DAVIS, ed., Death and Afterlife (London, 1989) • G. FLOROVSKY, "The 'Immortality' of the Soul," Collected Works (vol. 3; Belmont, Mass., 1976) 213-40 • A. A. HOEKEMA, The Bible and the Future (Grand Rapids, 1979) • G. MARCEL, Philosophie der Hoffnung (Munich, 1957) • J. MOLTMANN, Theology of Hope (Minneapolis, 1993) • W. PANNENBERG, Theology and the Kingdom of God (Philadelphia, 1969) • F. D. E. SCHLEIERMACHER, The Christian Faith (2 vols.; New York, 1963; orig. pub., 1821-22) • K. STOCK, "Hoffnung als Dimension der Freiheit," Gottes Zukunft–Zukunft der Welt (Munich, 1986) 14-22 • T. P. WEBER, Living in the Shadow of the Second Coming: American Premillennialism, 1875-1982 (Chicago, 1987) • B. WITHERINGTON III, Jesus, Paul, and the End of the World: A Comparative Study in NT Eschatology (Downers Grove, Ill., 1992).

KONRAD STOCK

3. Present-Day Discussion

During the 1960s the theme of hope assumed great importance. This prominence was due in part to the growing relevance of the idea of the future in a situation of increased tension between the threat to humanity and the possibility of its development, but also in part to the intellectual tendency to view humanity in its temporality in terms of the future, or of the "principle of hope" (E. Bloch). Thus → ecumenical theology (enriched by the rediscovery of biblical → eschatology) became a "theology of hope" (P. Teilhard de Chardin, J. Moltmann, J. B. Metz; → Liberation Theology).

The Second Assembly of the →World Council of Churches, in Evanston (1954), took as its overriding theme "Jesus Christ, the Hope of the World," and the fourth assembly, in Uppsala (1968), focused on the theme "See, I Am Making All Things New" (Rev. 21:5). This ecumenical focus on hope reflected the feeling of new beginnings regnant in both the industrial world and, to a certain extent, also in developing countries at that time. The 1970s and 1980s, however, were marked by a noticeable change. Too many efforts at renewal in all "three worlds" had failed, thus eroding confidence in any universal principle of hope. Still, the biblical theme of hope was not abandoned, and especially the ecumenical commission on → Faith and Order worked intensively between 1971 and 1978 on rendering an account of hope that was both biblically grounded and oriented toward contemporary life.

A theology of hope does justice to the biblical basis only when it bears comprehensive witness to the theme. In this regard three dimensions must be kept in mind. The first is the *political dimension*. We need to recognize and activate this dimension in view of the strong tendency to make hope private and spiritual. The central concepts and motifs of biblical hope are (in an elementary sense) political concepts: the kingdom and the city of God (→ Kingdom of God). Eschatological hope is never a matter of human politics. It is God-oriented, but still it reflects the *politics* of God. The divine promises relate to political relations. None of our cities will be the New Jerusalem. Hope for the New Jerusalem, however, affects us in our earthly cities. Hope that would ignore political relations is shortsighted and truncated.

Second, there is a *personal dimension*. Christian hope is also truncated if it undervalues the personal element. It has in view the kingdom and city, but not in the sense of anonymous collectives. It concerns unique people with their own names, their personal present and future in life and in death. Augustine, the Schoolmen, the Pietists, and the existentialists were all right to link hope to the personal concerns of the human soul and human life.

No human tears (Rev. 21:4) or human dreams are insignificant on this view.

Finally, there is the *theological dimension.* Christian hope is inseparably bound up with a name: God. Here is its beginning, even historically. The entrance of biblical hope into history is related to the Easter-event. The NT knows no other basis, and this accent is still relevant today. If God is erased, the only carrier of hope is the cosmic process or human achievement. Experience and the modern situation teach us not to rest our final hope in either of these. Biblical hope frees us from any transfiguring of the human world or ideology of achievement. Confessing God, it gives us → freedom over against the world, not as *beati possidentes,* those who have "already reached the goal" (Phil. 3:12), but as those who in solidarity with the world seek to practice hope in the world and for it.

→ Immanence and Transcendence; Political Theology; Salvation History

Bibliography: K. Barth, *CD* IV/3, §73 • J. Bowker, *The Meanings of Death* (Cambridge, 1991) • M. Bull, ed., *Apocalypse Theory and the Ends of the World* (Oxford, 1995) • C. W. Bynum, *The Resurrection of the Body in Western Christianity* (New York, 1995) • D. Cohn-Sherbok and C. Lewis, eds., *Beyond Death: Theological and Philosophical Reflections on Life After Death* (London, 1995) • W. Crockett, ed., *Four Views on Hell* (Grand Rapids, 1992) • F. M. Kamm, *Morality, Mortality,* vol. 1, *Death and Whom to Save from It* (New York, 1993) • H. Küng and W. Jens, *A Dignified Dying* (London, 1995) • A. L. Lester, *Hope in Pastoral Care and Counselling* (Louisville, Ky., 1995) • J. M. Lochman, *Christ and Prometheus? A Quest for Theological Identity* (Geneva, 1988) • J. Macquarrie, *Christian Hope* (London, 1978) • P. Teilhard de Chardin, *The Phenomenon of Man* (New York, 1959) • F. J. Tipler, *The Physics of Immortality* (New York, 1994) • W. A. Visser 't Hooft, *The Evanston Report: The Second Assembly of the World Council of Churches, 1954* (New York, 1955) • World Council of Churches, *Sharing in One Hope: Reports and Documents from the Meeting of the Faith and Order Commission . . . Bangalore, 15-30 August, 1978* (Geneva, 1979).

Jan Milič Lochman

Hosea, Book of

1. Hosea was the only native writing prophet of the northern kingdom. He was active between 755/50 and 725 B.C., a period that saw the last years of peace for → Israel (§1) under Jeroboam II, the so-called Syro-Ephraimite war of 733, and the successive dismantling of the northern kingdom by the Assyrian king Shalmaneser V. The defeat of Samaria and deportation of Israel by the Assyrians are not yet reflected in the book. Hosea worked in Samaria but probably also in Bethel and Gilgal. He differs from Amos in that his message contains less social complaint and more criticism of the cult.

2. The book is made up of three complexes. Chaps. 4–11 contain sayings of Hosea, probably composed by disciples, that are well thought out and well arranged, both chronologically and substantively. The lack of insertions or framework formulas shows that the aim was to present the original sayings as a literary and material unity that would embody Hosea's total message (J. Jeremias). In chaps. 12–14 we have another complex of Hosea's late sayings relating especially to Israel's historical guilt. Chaps. 1–3 contain traditions about Hosea's marriage. After the collapse of the northern kingdom in 722, the Hosea traditions came to Judah and underwent some revision as they were applied to the Judean situation.

3. Hosea's message goes to the root of Israel's → faith and → worship and shows it to be perverted. Israel has responded to God's loving attention and gifts of salvation, not with commitment, but with → apostasy. It has fallen away to the fertility gods of Canaan, equating Yahweh with Baal. It has violated both the first and the second commandments and has adopted wrong policies that are detached from God. The → priests and → monarchy come under special criticism. God's reaction to apostasy is judgment. He withdraws his favor and hands over the land and its products to destruction.

Hosea, however, also expects salvation on the basis of God's mercy. From the zero point of judgment God will begin a new history with his people, lead them back from the wilderness to the land, and establish a state of unbroken fellowship.

4. There has been debate about Hosea's → marriage. Various materials come together in chaps. 1–3, where third-person (chap. 1) and first-person (chap. 3) narratives frame a sequence of sayings (chap. 2). The stress in chap. 1 is on the ominous names of Hosea's children, in chap. 3 on dealings with his unfaithful wife. What happens symbolizes Yahweh's relation to Israel and the people's destiny.

Hardly in keeping with this intention is the view that Hosea's wife was a normal Israelite woman who had submitted (as was common) to Canaanite rites of initiation (H. W. Wolff). Chap. 3 points to adultery rather than temple prostitution. Another view is that the condemnation of Hosea's wife in chap. 1 is redactional (W. Rudolph). Hosea at any rate vividly describes the broken relation between Israel and Yahweh in terms of marriage — a daring comparison inasmuch as it derives from the myth of divine marriage.

Hosea's message found followers in the Deuteronomic movement and in Jeremiah.

→ Prophet, Prophecy

Bibliography: Commentaries: F. I. ANDERSEN and D. N. FREEDMAN (AB; Garden City, N.Y., 1980) • D. A. GARRETT (NAC; Nashville, 1998) • J. JEREMIAS (ATD; Göttingen, 1983) • A. A. MACINTOSH (ICC; Edinburgh, 1997) • W. RUDOLPH (KAT; Gütersloh, 1966) • D. STUART (WBC; Dallas, 1987) • H. W. WOLFF (BKAT; 3d ed.; Neukirchen, 1976).

Other works: D. R. DANIELS, *Hosea and Salvation History* (Berlin, 1990) • G. I. EMMERSON, *Hosea: An Israelite Prophet in Judean Perspective* (Sheffield, 1984) • J. JEREMIAS, "Hosea / Hoseabuch," *TRE* 15.586-98 (bibliography) • C. L. SEOW, "Hosea, Book of," *ABD* 3.291-97 (bibliography) • H. UTZSCHNEIDER, *Hosea. Prophet vor dem Ende* (Fribourg, 1980) • G. A. YEE, *Composition and Tradition in the Book of Hosea* (Atlanta, 1987).

WINFRIED THIEL

Hours, Canonical

1. Term
2. Elements
3. History

1. Term

The canonical hours are the regular → worship service of the → church based on the change of hours, especially in the morning and evening, through which the church in the → Holy Spirit hears the → Word of God and responds in praise and petition. The → congregation celebrating the canonical hours picks up the daily rhythm, especially the sunrise and the commencement of night, understands it as symbolizing God's central salvific deed in the death and → resurrection of Christ. As the voice of all → creation, the church offers to God *expressis verbis* the veneration and worship due him (→ Prayer). All those who are baptized are called to this service of worship.

2. Elements

Certain elements are present in every celebration of the canonical hours. It is God's Word that is being proclaimed, though for centuries this particular feature was missing from some canonical hours. The church's response includes → psalms, → hymns, and prayers as praise and petition.

3. History

At least in the two most important times of prayer, morning and evening, the Christian canonical hours pick up on features long known to religious phenomenologists, namely, the numinous quality of sunrise and sunset, and the impulse to offer thanksgiving for light. In this natural context, the canonical hours arose as a product of Christianity in its emergence from paganism rather than from → Judaism, however much the Jewish prayer times were still scrupulously observed by the early Christians. Alongside the morning and evening prayers, brief times of prayer also arose during the second century for the third, sixth, and ninth hours of the day, since in the larger cities these hours were publicly announced and at the same time could be associated with the remembrance of the passion of Christ and events of → Pentecost. A prayer at midnight was also advised, exemplifying the Christian's watchfulness and anticipation of the → parousia.

At the end of the fourth century, this schema then became fixed as the classic system of daily prayer for all Christians, and in the middle of the same century the fundamental distinction developed between the *cathedral* and the *monastic* canonical hours, a development of crucial significance. Especially at sunrise and sunset all the members of the congregation assembled in church to give thanks and praise and to pray for protection, in what later became Morning Prayer and Evensong. These two prayer times were specifically obligatory for everyone and included the full participation of all services and offices (→ Bishop, Episcopate; Deacon, Deaconess; Elder; Lector; Ordination).

In fourth-century Egypt, nascent → monasticism focused on Luke 18:1 in taking a different path. Here the morning and evening assemblies served not the celebration of communal → liturgy but → meditation on the Holy Scriptures, which is also communal. This action involves personal prayer, which is performed sometimes communally, sometimes individually, though the important factor here is not when, where, and with whom one prays but the idea that the monk's entire life should become prayer.

A mixed form of the canonical hours developed in the East, with Egyptian monasticism still providing the standard. In the West, Benedict (ca. 480-ca. 547; → Benedictines) fixed this schema of hours as

Lauds, Prime, Terce, Sext, None, Vespers, and Compline, as well as the vigils positioned before the Lauds as a night service. In his rule for monks, he fixed also the structure of the individual hours themselves, the admixture of cathedral and purely monastic elements already being historically self-evident for him.

In the church of the West, the cathedral offices were abandoned in the early → Middle Ages, since monasticism had in the meantime come to represent the ideal embodiment of Christian life. Whereas earlier the entire Christian congregation was obligated to offer this praise during the canonical hours, it now became the commission of the cleric as an individual (→ Clergy and Laity).

Beginning in the 11th century, breviaries emerged summarizing the various books for the canonical hours (→ Liturgical Books), and in 1568 the first unified Roman breviary was published for clerics. Private recitation continues to be the point of departure, the books constituting prayer books for clerics and members of orders, while the congregation itself is permitted to join within this framework.

The → Reformers followed the same path in the 16th century by starting with the monastic form. Martin Luther (1483-1546; → Luther's Theology) wanted to recast morning and evening hours into services of the Word serving instructional purposes, but he failed because his suggestions were unsystematic and incapable of implementation. The → Book of Common Prayer of the → Anglican Church succeeded in reviving the morning and evening hours as congregational worship, although here too the monastic form has provided the point of departure, with the reading of the entire Psalter being spread out over several weeks, and the Old and New Testaments being read in (almost) every service.

Bibliography: J.-J. VON ALLMEN, "The Theological Meaning of Common Prayer," StLi 10 (1974) 125-36 • H. GOLTZEN, "Der tägliche Gottesdienst," Leit. 3.99-294 • C. JONES, G. WAINWRIGHT, E. YARNOLD, and P. BRADSHAW, eds., The Study of Liturgy (rev. ed.; New York, 1992) 399-454 • M. KLÖCKENER and H. RENNINGS, eds., Lebendiges Stundengebet (Freiburg, 1989) bibliography • F. KOHLSCHEIN, "Den täglichen Gottesdienst der Gemeinden retten," LJ 34 (1984) 195-234 • A. G. MARTIMORT, ed., The Church at Prayer: An Introduction to the Liturgy (Collegeville, Minn., 1992) • P. SALMON, L'office divin (Paris, 1959) • T. A. SCHNITKER, "The Liturgy of the Hours and the History of Salvation: Towards the Theological Penetration of 'The Public and Communal Prayer of God,' StLi 15 (1983) 145-57; idem, "Morgen- und Abendlob. Prolegomena zu einer aus dem Geist der Alten Kirche erneuerten Tagzeitenliturgie," Christus spes. Liturgie und Glaube im ökumenischen Kontext (ed. A. Berlis and K.-D. Gerth; Frankfurt, 1994) 265-75 • H.-J. SCHULZ, In deinem Licht schauen wir das Licht (Mainz, 1980) • R. TAFT, The Liturgy of the Hours in East and West (Collegeville, Minn., 1986) bibliography.

THADDEUS A. SCHNITKER

House Church

The term "house church" refers to a group of Christians meeting in a private house for mutual pastoral support, for celebration and fellowship, and for common ministry to others. Such groups traditionally engage in → Bible study, → prayer, and → meditation (→ Devotion, Devotions). They may be linked to traditional churches, although many function as small independent churches, especially in cases of persecution or isolation (→ Diaspora). Especially in China since 1949, when the government ended foreign missionary involvement, several types of house churches have flourished, representing in 2000 approximately two-thirds of all Chinese Christians.

In many respects (esp. in size, structure, and orientation), house churches follow early Christian models (see Rom. 16:3-5; 1 Cor. 16:19; Col. 4:15; Phlm. 2). They also reflect the influence of such groups as the → Waldenses, → Bohemian Brethren, Society of → Friends, Methodists (esp. their class meetings; → Methodism), → Moravians, and (Zurich) → Anabaptists. M. Luther considered the idea of a kind of house church (see "Third Way," in the preface to his German Mass [1526]). The most direct influence was that of German → Pietism, especially of P. J. Spener and A. H. Francke (with the idea of the ecclesiola in ecclesia, "a little church within the church"). More recently the → Oxford Movement and the Marburg circle adopted the same model.

Today two types of house church may be discerned. There is the more traditional base community movement similar to the Roman Catholic → base communities, but more ecumenical. Then there is the movement of intentional communities in the United States and elsewhere, particularly from the 1970s and 1980s. The latter are trying to recapture the vitality, fellowship, and simple → lifestyle of the early church; stress personal religion; commit themselves more fully to the gospel and to their fellows; grant equal roles to men and women; maintain a critical loyalty to the church and the

Christian tradition; relate faith to the world; and place more value on deepening of faith and life than on numerical growth.

According to A. L. Foster, house churches fall into seven types on the basis of their relation to the established churches: (1) the supplemental house church; (2) the substitute house church, which offers all that a church does; (3) the ecumenical house church, with members from various denominations; (4) the satellite house church, which sees itself as a responsible part of some larger church; (5) group house churches, composed of several groups; (6) the solo house church, which is independent, may or may not be linked to a denomination, and may at times be underground; and (7) the house church that is part of a network of house churches.

Under the influence of the human potential movement, recent house churches are characterized by (1) commitment for a set time; (2) free, face-to-face interactions; (3) self-understanding as ministering fellowships on the basis of the priesthood of all believers; and (4) a great variety of forms of communication (discussion, exchanges, sharing of feelings, dancing, etc.). Defects that might occur are elitism and self-centeredness, difficulties because of intimacy or distance, too great demands placed on a small group by problems that arise, and hostility or manipulation on the part of a larger church. The house church has great ecumenical and educational possibilities, especially through the experience of deep personal membership in a supporting group.

→ Church Growth; Congregation

Bibliography: P. ANDERSON, *The House Church* (Philadelphia, 1975) • R. BANKS, *Paul's Idea of Community: The Early House Churches in Their Historical Setting* (Grand Rapids, 1980) • L. BARRETT, *Building the House Church* (Scottdale, Pa., 1986) • V. BRANICK, *The House Church in the Writings of Paul* (Wilmington, Del., 1989) • J. S. CAMPBELL, "The Translatability of Christian Community: Ecclesiology for Postmodern Cultures and Beyond" (Diss., Fuller Theological Seminary, Pasadena, Calif., 1999) • J. CHAO, ed., "Independent House Church Movement," *The China Mission Handbook* (Hong Kong, 1989) 44-49 • S. B. CLARK, *Building Christian Communities: Strategy for Renewing the Church* (Notre Dame, Ind., 1972) • A. L. FOSTER, ed., *The House Church Evolving* (Chicago, 1976) • R. FUNG, *Households of God on China's Soil* (Geneva, 1982) • H.-J. KLAUCK, *Hausgemeinde und Hauskirche im frühen Christentum* (Stuttgart, 1981) • G. LANCZKOWSKI, F. WERNER, K.-H. BIERITZ, and C. KÄHLER, "Haus," *TRE* 14.474-92 (bibliography) • T. ODEN, *The Intensive*

Group Experience (Philadelphia, 1972) • O. SCHWEITZER, *Werkbuch Hauskreis* (Wuppertal, 1986) • E. TROELTSCH, *The Social Teaching of the Christian Churches* (2 vols.; Louisville, Ky., 1992; orig. pub., 1912) • J. VANIER, *Community and Growth: Our Pilgrimage Together* (New York, 1979).

G. KEITH PARKER

Household Rules

The so-called household rules are NT → parenetic lists describing the duties of the members of Christian households (the *oikos*, which included wives and husbands, children and parents, slaves and masters). In the strict sense they occur in the NT only in Col. 3:18–4:1 and Eph. 5:22–6:9. Closely related are the passage on socioethical duties in 1 Pet. 2:13–3:9 and various unstructured statements (1 Tim. 2:8-15; 6:1-2; Titus 2:1-10; 3:1-2; 1 John 2:12-14; *1 Clem.* 1.3; 21.6-9; Ign. *Pol.* 4–6; Pol. *Phil.* 4.1–6.1; *Did.* 4.9-11; *Barn.* 19.5-7). The household rules set Christians in the framework of the household as the smallest social unit in the social structure of antiquity and thus introduce a fixed schema into Christian exhortation that corresponds to the more developed situation in the later NT church.

The problems relating to religious history and the history of the tradition have been intensively discussed. A Stoic background to the rules (M. Dibelius, K. Weidinger) has been largely accepted. Yet so have links to Jewish tradition (E. Lohmeyer), to the authentically Christian household (K. H. Rengstorf), to the Jesus tradition and Pauline theology (L. Goppelt, D. Schroeder), and to Hellenistic Jewish propaganda (J. E. Crouch).

The schema of household rules is shaped by threefold division, by pairs or reciprocal structure, by apodictic form, and by the household situation. The main elements occur in pre-Christian Greek and Jewish-Hellenistic tradition. The origins lie in the unwritten laws of Greek folk tradition, which had influenced the ethical systems of the philosophy of antiquity, especially the → Stoics, and which had linked up with Jewish elements in Hellenistic → Judaism. Christian instruction was probably the connecting link to the NT Christian household rules.

The distinctively Christian element is the Christological, ecclesiological, and futurist-eschatological setting. Thus the relations between married couples (→ Marriage 3.2) are to be controlled by mutual subjection to the lordship of the Kyrios (Eph. 5:21-30). Being respected as a partner results from integration into the church (§2) as the body of Christ, whose members belong to each other (Eph. 5:30). The relations between slaves and masters (→ Slavery) are shaped by common brotherly responsibility before the world Judge (Col. 3:22–4:1). The NT household rules thus regulate the household with reference to being in Christ, which is understood as the key principle.

→ Ethics 3

Bibliography: M. Barth and H. Blanke, Colossians (New York, 1994) • J. E. Crouch, The Origin and Intention of the Colossian Haustafeln (Göttingen, 1972) • M. Dibelius, "Exkurs zu Kol 4,1," An die Kolosser, Epheser, An Philemon (Tübingen, 1953) 48-50 • L. Goppelt, Der erste Petrusbrief (8th ed.; Göttingen, 1978); idem, "Jesus und die Haustafeln-Tradition," Orientierung an Jesus (Freiburg, 1973) 93-106 • A. E. Harvey, Strenuous Commands: The Ethic of Jesus (London, 1990) • B. Hoose, Received Wisdom? Reviewing the Role of Tradition in Christian Ethics (London, 1994) • E. Lohmeyer, Kolosserbrief (8th ed.; Göttingen, 1930) • E. Lohse, Colossians and Philemon (Philadelphia, 1971) • W. A. Meeks, The Origins of Christian Morality: The First Two Christian Centuries (New Haven, 1993) • S. Pinckaers, The Sources of Christian Ethics (3d ed.; Washington, D.C., 1995) • K. H. Rengstorf, Mann und Frau im Urchristentum (Cologne, 1954) • D. Schroeder, "Die Haustafeln des Neuen Testaments" (Diss., Hamburg, 1959) • K. Weidinger, Die Haustafeln (Leipzig, 1928).

Georg Strecker†

Huguenots

The name "Huguenots" for French Protestants at home and abroad derives from the transferring of a local story from Tours concerning Hugh Capet (d. 996) to the Protestants who met by night. It does not derive etymologically from Iguenots (= Eidgenossen, "confederates," i.e., part of the Swiss Confederation) but is a diminutive of Hugo. It was used by others from about 1555 and adopted by the Protestants, especially emigrants, as a term for themselves after 1685.

The rise of the party name marks the transition from the Protestant movement to a church that, under the influence of → Calvinism, was formed in 1559 out of its organized congregations. It held its first national synod at Paris, where it adopted its own confession (the Gallican Confession, which is a statement of J. Calvin's theology; → Calvin's Theology) and own → constitution. The latter also shows evidence of Calvinism in its decentralized synodal and presbyterial structure (→ Confessions and Creeds).

Besides their church, the Huguenots also developed their own social profile of → Gallicanism. Sociologically, their strength lay among the urban middle class and the landed nobility. Some of the higher aristocracy (e.g., the Navarre, Condé, and Coligny families) were also Huguenots. Both religiously and politically they opposed royal absolutism, a position that led to open conflict in eight religious wars between 1562 and 1598. When the fighting ended, leadership passed from the nobility to the middle class, and though its members were largely excluded from office, the Huguenots enjoyed a period of expansion, their main centers being in the trading cities and manufacturing areas of southwest, southeast, and northwest France.

The intellectual centers of Huguenot life were the academies of Nîmes, Orthez, Montauban, Sedan, and Saumur. In the theological controversies within Calvinism they firmly resisted → Arminianism. They engaged especially in → polemics and → apologetics. Saumur played a leading role, making an important contribution to Reformed → orthodoxy (§2).

When Henry IV of Navarre (1589-1610) was converted, his Edict of Nantes (1598) granted limited toleration to the Huguenots as a politically privileged minority. From the beginning of the 17th century, however, their unity suffered, and the new religious wars of 1620-29 failed to restore it. The recatholicizing policy of Louis XIV (1643-1715), at first concealed but constantly becoming more forceful, aimed at ending what was seen as a state within a state. It reached a climax with the revocation of the Edict of Nantes by the Edict of Fontainebleau in 1685. Ultimately over 200,000 Huguenots fled the country, which represented a severe economic setback for France. In England, Holland, Switzerland, Germany (esp. Prussia and Hesse-Cassel), and the United States, they and their descendants played an important economic, academic, and artistic role. After the French → Revolution and the Napoleonic era, the Huguenots were ultimately integrated into the countries in which they had sought refuge.

In France a new phase began for the Huguenots after 1685. Under brutal persecution apocalyptic prophecy arose in the Cévennes, and there was armed resistance. As a "wilderness church" (Rev. 12:6), the Huguenots lived on illegally until they were finally granted equal rights by the Edict of Versailles (1787) and the Napoleonic Code (1804).

→ France; Reformed and Presbyterian Churches

Bibliography: H. Dubief, "Hugenotten," *TRE* 15.618-31 (bibliography) • R. P. Gagg, *Hugenotten. Profil ihres Glaubens* (Basel, 1984) • R. M. Golden, ed., *The Huguenot Connection: The Edict of Nantes, Its Revocation, and Early French Migration to South Carolina* (Dordrecht, 1988) • J. G. Gray, "The Origin of the Word 'Huguenot,'" *SCJ* 14 (1983) 349-59 • O. Reverdin et al., *Genève et la révocation de l'Édit de Nantes* (Geneva, 1985) • O. E. Strasser-Bertrand, *Die evangelische Kirche in Frankreich* (Göttingen, 1975) • G. S. Sunshine, "From French Protestantism to the French Reformed Churches: The Development of Huguenot Ecclesiastical Institutions, 1559-1598" (Diss., University of Wisconsin-Madison, 1992) • N. M. Sutherland, *The Huguenot Struggle for Recognition* (New Haven, 1980) • R. von Thadden and M. Magdelaine, eds., *Die Hugenotten, 1685-1985* (2d ed.; Munich, 1986) • K.-H. Wegner, *Dreihundert Jahre Hugenotten in Hessen* (Kassel, 1985).

Hans Schneider

Human Being → Adam; Anthropology; Men; Women

Human Dignity

1. Term
2. Theological Aspects
    2.1. Roman Catholic View
    2.2. Protestant Approaches
    2.3. Ecumenical Discussion
3. Non-Christian Ideas
4. Philosophical Concepts
5. Questions and Problems

1. Term

In the → modern period the concept of human dignity has been inseparably related to human and civil → rights. Human dignity is generally seen as the inner basis of these rights, and it thus serves as a moral term that legally states and politically ensures the independence and inviolability of the → person. It finds constitutional expression in article 1 of the U.N. Universal Declaration of Human Rights (1948): "All human beings are born free and equal in dignity and rights. They are endowed with → reason and → conscience and should act towards one another in a spirit of brotherhood." On the basis of human dignity, human rights involve at their heart the inalienable rights to → life, physical security, → freedom, and → equality (W. Lienemann, 191).

In the 20th century human dignity found a place in the constitutions of many countries of different and even contrary political composition, including Afghanistan (1987, art. 41), Brazil (1988, art. 1; cf. art. 5), Costa Rica (1949, art. 33), Federal Republic of Germany (1949, art. 1), Greece (1975, art. 2), Guatemala (1985, art. 4), Ireland (1937 and 1987, preamble), Nicaragua (1986, art. 26), Peru (1979, preamble), Portugal (1982, art. 1), South Korea (1987, art. 10), Spain (1978, art. 12), and Turkey (1961 and 1972, art. 14). (On international law, see P. Häberle, 818-19).

2. Theological Aspects

2.1. Roman Catholic View

The theological tradition derives human dignity from the divine likeness (→ Anthropology 3.4.3). Thus for Roman Catholics it is a common opinion that "all things on earth should be ordained to man as to their center and summit" (*Gaudium et spes* 12). This supreme position of humanity in the cosmos serves as a basis and origin for the claim to dominion over → nature. Human dignity manifests itself in → reason, with which we seek → truth and → wisdom (15). Conscience is another element of human dignity, for "by conscience, in a wonderful way, that → law is made known which is fulfilled in the → love of God and of one's → neighbor" (16). This transcendental constitution of conscience (→ Transcendental Theology) is the basis of the possibility that we cannot lose human dignity, even though conscience may err "through ignorance which it is unable to avoid" (16, though cf. the stricter position of Thomas Aquinas, who links error to human reason, which ought to know God's law, *Summa theol.* I of II, q. 10, arts. 5-6; → Thomism).

The fact of → sin calls into question this understanding of human dignity based on a theology of creation. It obscures but does not completely destroy our ability to live and act in accordance with the will of God. In recognition of the brokenness and ambivalence of human reason, recourse is thus had to the divine likeness in the light of the NT eschatological motif of the relation between Adam and Christ. Christ is the → new self, and Adam represents the old and sinful self (→ Christology 2), who needs redemption but who is also capable of it (→ Soteriology). This qualification in understanding human dignity serves to correct any unjustified optimism deriving from our natural capacities.

2.2. Protestant Approaches

Protestants have no uniform view of human dignity. For all the differences, however, they share the view that we must give much greater significance to (original) sin than Roman Catholics do. Already in his 1517 "Disputation against Scholastic Theology" (*LW* 31.9-16; → Scholasticism), M. Luther (1483-1546; → Luther's Theology) formulated the thesis "There is no moral virtue without either pride or sorrow, that is, without sin" (thesis 38), and "We are never lords of our actions, but servants" (thesis 39).

Since no place in the world has not seen the invasion of sin, there is no → autonomy of reason or conscience. All need the → grace of God, which does not perfect nature (as Thomas claimed) but creates anew. The divine likeness and human dignity are not, then, self-evident. They are a matter of eschatological → promise (→ Eschatology).

Taking up this problem, K. Barth (1886-1968) tried to find a Christological basis for human dignity and to understand its practice as an implication of God's reconciling the world (2 Corinthians 5; cf. E. Jüngel, 239-45; → Christology 6.4).

In a contemporary proposal J. Moltmann set human dignity within the dimensions of → politics (pp. 20-23), cohumanity (23-25), cocreatureliness (25-27), and → responsibility for the → future (27-28). An unmistakably modern concern is not primarily to derive dominion over → creation from the divine likeness that underlies human dignity but to determine the limits of this dominion and to stress instead such parameters as care or responsibility (C. Link, 17-26, 32-45, and the legal discussion in O. Kimminich, 291-95).

2.3. Ecumenical Discussion

Ecumenical discussion deals with human dignity especially in the context of human and civil rights. In the battle for racial equality (both political and social) in the United States (M. L. King Jr.) and South Africa (D. Tutu), in the rise of → liberation theologies in Latin America or of the minjung theology in Asia (→ Asian Theology), which fight for political conditions that are indispensable to a life of human dignity, we see many international efforts to practice human dignity and not merely to discuss its theological basis.

An interesting test case was the → Program to Combat Racism, begun by the → World Council of Churches in 1970. In discussing this program, it became clear that precisely the churches and theologians that most vehemently demanded human rights and human dignity in the then socialist states had the most reservations and criticisms about the program. The context was the debate about the "politicizing" or "individualizing" of the gospel and its social and political implications (→ Political Theology).

3. Non-Christian Ideas

The common thesis that the idea of human dignity derives most clearly from the Christian tradition proves to be only partially correct. A consideration of (non-Christian) → Stoicism and of the constitutions of non-Christian countries (see 1) relativizes such a connection. → Buddhism, for example, whose doctrine of → reincarnation prevents it from recognizing the singularity or one-time nature of human existence, takes seriously the notion of practical responsibility for all creatures. It shows that human dignity relative to that of the rest of creation does not require derivation from a relationship of opposition or of dominion.

4. Philosophical Concepts

Human dignity plays an important role also in philosophical approaches. We find the issue itself, if not the term, in the Stoic idea of human equality. Some centuries later it occurs again in the Italian humanists (→ Humanism). It then assumes central importance in the philosophy of I. Kant (1724-1804; → Kantianism). According to Kant, "Humanity itself is a dignity; for a human being cannot be used merely as a means by any human being . . . but must always be used at the same time as an end. It is just in this that his dignity (personality) consists, by which he raises himself above all other beings in the world that are not human beings and yet can be used, and so over all *things*." As Kant saw it, a person "is under obligation to acknowledge, in a practical way, the dignity of humanity in every other human being" (*Metaphysics of Morals,* "The Doctrine of Virtue," §38 = A 140). As ourselves ends (*Kritik* 210 = A 156), we have clear precedence in creation in virtue of our reason and the autonomy of our freedom (*Grundlegung* 69 = BA 79).

By deriving human dignity from freedom, German → idealism followed a similar course. A. Schopenhauer and S. Kierkegaard, however, disagreed, and this motif came under radical questioning at the end of the 19th century by F. Nietzsche, and in literature by É. Zola, G. Hauptmann, H. Ibsen, and others. In the English (J. Locke, T. Hobbes) and French (B. Pascal, J.-J. Rousseau) traditions, we find attempts to base rights in society on contract theories derived in different ways from → natural law. Discussion of human dignity, however, was not at the center of interest, as it was not in the American tradition.

Human dignity acquired a fresh orientation with K. Marx (1818-83; → Marxism 3), who focused on real material and political relations and opposed "all relations in which man is a debased, enslaved, forsaken, and despicable being" (*MECW* 3.182). Yet even this approach remained idealistic in the sense that it proclaims "man to be the highest being for man" (189). E. Bloch (1885-1977) took up the same line of thinking in an attempt to reconcile human dignity with classical natural law and to see in it something that still must be achieved and that has utopian potential in the shaping of social relations (→ Utopia). The 20th century recognized the ambivalence of such overemphasis (→ Critical Theory). In a later attempt to detach human dignity from Promethean anthropocentrism, R. Spaemann tried to reclaim dignity for all creation and to extend Kant's dictum to acting in such a way as to use nothing in creation as merely a means, but to use all things also as ends (302).

5. Questions and Problems

The idea of human dignity proves to be a lofty theoretical claim that reality often contradicts. Putting it in a constitution offers no safeguards against abuses, particularly as it has in the main a defensive purpose and does not underlie any positive actions on the part of the state. The legal understanding of human dignity is inclined to view it as intrinsic to human nature as such and thus as a human characteristic; that is, it views human dignity as the intrinsic value of a person.

In many situations indeed, a legal understanding of human dignity may be affronted (e.g., in cases involving → women, children (→ Childhood), elderly, the sick, or → persons with disabilities; → Medical Ethics). Difficulties can also arise at the level of systems. In → socialism individuals are under the tutelage of the party and the → state (→ Political Parties), and there is a massive curtailment of human rights (e.g., freedom). In → capitalism various economic decisions and the concentration of productive capacity in the hands of a few mean other losses (e.g., sharing resources). In the so-called developing countries of the → Third World much of the population does not even have a minimal means of subsistence and thus effectively loses the right to → life (see 1).

The positive link between human dignity and human freedom and conscience is unmistakable and inalienable (→ State Ethics). Nevertheless, when human dignity serves to validate an unlimited human claim to dominion over creation, it loses the link to freedom. Even when it is used, as on the mission of John Paul II to Africa in 1990, to buttress the prohibition of contraception in an age of → hunger, overpopulation, and AIDS, it degenerates into an ideological mask (→ Ideology) for heteronomy, → suffering, and mass poverty.

→ Jurisprudence

Bibliography: G. Baker-Fletcher, Somebodyness: Martin Luther King and the Theory of Dignity (Minneapolis, 1993) • K. Bayertz, ed., Sanctity of Life and Human Dignity (Dordrecht, 1996) • M. Bednár, ed., Human Dignity: Values and Justice (Washington, D.C., 1999) • E. Bloch, Gesamtausgabe, vol. 6, Naturrecht und menschliche Würde (Frankfurt, 1977) • D. Egonsson, Dimensions of Dignity: The Moral Importance of Being Human (Dordrecht, 1998) • P. Häberle, "Die Menschenwürde als Grundlage der staatlichen Gemeinschaft," Handbuch des Staatsrechts der Bundesrepublik Deutschland (vol. 1; ed. J. Isensee and P. Kirchhof; Heidelberg, 1987) 815-61 • M. Harmin, Inspiring Discipline: A Practical Guide for Today's Schools (West Haven, Conn., 1995) • E. Jüngel, "Der königliche Mensch. Eine christologische Reflexion auf die Würde des Menschen in der Theologie Karl Barths," Barth-Studien (Gütersloh, 1982) 233-45 • I. Kant, Critique of Practical Reason (trans. M. Gregor; New York, 1997; orig. pub., 1788); idem, Groundwork of the Metaphysics of Morals (trans. M. Gregor; New York, 1998; orig. pub., 1785) • O. Kimminich, "Die Verantwortung für die Umwelt in der Wertordnung des Grundgesetzes," Verantwortlichkeit und Freiheit (ed. H. J. Faller, P. Kirchhof, and E. Träger; Tübingen, 1989) 277-95 • W. Lienemann, "Die Zerstörung der Menschlichkeit im Nationalsozialismus und das Ethos der Menschenrechte," Ethik in der europäischen Geschichte, vol. 2, Reformation und Neuzeit (ed. S. H. Pfürtner; Stuttgart, 1988) 148-65 • C. Link, "Der Mensch als Geschöpf und als Schöpfer," Versöhnung mit der Natur? (ed. J. Moltmann; Munich, 1986) 15-47 • G. Marcel, The Existential Background of Human Dignity (Cambridge, Mass., 1962) • M. J. Meyer and W. A. Parent, eds., The Constitution of Rights: Human Dignity and American Values (Ithaca, N.Y., 1992) • J. Moltmann, Menschenwürde, Recht und Freiheit (Stuttgart, 1979) • D. Ritschl, "Der Beitrag des Calvinismus für die Entwicklung des Menschenrechtsgedankens in Europa und Nordamerika," EvT 40 (1980) 333-45 • M. A. Smith, Human Dignity and the Common Good in the Aristotelian-Thomistic Tradition (Lewiston, N.Y., 1995) • R. Spaemann, "Über den Begriff der Menschenwürde," Menschenrechte und Menschenwürde (ed. E.-W. Böckenförde and R. Spaemann; Stuttgart, 1987) • D. Tutu, "God Intervening in Human Affairs," Missionalia 5 (1977) 111-17.

Ekkehard Starke

Human Sacrifice

1. Almost all religions include reports of people sacrificing the dearest thing they have, even → life. Only in rare cases, however, do we find accounts of the regular killing of people as → sacrifices, as among the Mayans and Aztecs. Human sacrifice usually took place in times of extraordinary danger such as prolonged drought, with expiation being attempted in the face of serious pestilence, disaster, or other emergencies. Reports of the practice almost always reflect distaste for the horror.

In its aims human sacrifice differs in principle from other forms of sacrifice. It serves the end of purification (→ Cultic Purity), expiation (the scapegoat, Gk. *pharmakon*), offering to affirm the deity and gain its support, payment or compensation for infringements on what belongs to the deity (e.g., one's firstborn), more rarely → communication with the gods or spirits, and finally the maintaining or ensuring of the fertility of fields or of the life cycle (see *ERE* for examples).

Whether an execution is to be seen as a human sacrifice to restore the divinely instituted social order is hard to decide. It may have no religious significance, but in some tribal societies religion, → law, and → culture are closely intertwined (→ Tribal Religions). Another debated issue is whether the killing of Christians in the → persecutions or the autos-da-fé and burnings of witches (→ Inquisition 3; Witchcraft) for the glory of God and the purging of the → devil should be regarded as an extreme form of capital punishment (→ Death Penalty) or as human sacrifice for the upholding of the religious order. In any case human sacrifice is contrary to Christian teaching.

2. The OT expressly abhors and forbids human sacrifice (Lev. 18:21; 20:2-5; Deut. 12:31-32; 18:10; 1 Kgs. 16:30-34). In particular, sacrificing children is seen as an atrocity and an offense against God's commands (e.g., Jer. 7:31; Ezek. 16:20-21; 20:31). There are, however, some neutral accounts of such offerings (Judg. 11:30-40; cf. also 1 Kgs. 16:34; 2 Kgs. 16:3; 17:17; 21:6; 23:10; Ezek. 20:26; Mic. 6:7). Even though these accounts are mostly critical and offer no proof of the regular offering of children, they show how widespread was the idea. Whether God's command "the firstborn of your sons you shall give to me" (Exod. 22:29; cf. 13:2) meant the actual offering of all firstborn is contested. Other passages refer to an equivalent payment (Exod. 34:20; Num. 18:15-16), such as we find in the story of the sacrifice of → Isaac (Genesis 22).

3. The substituting of an animal for Isaac supports the theory that in the course of the → history of religion, sacrificial customs underwent humanization (first → animals, then straw figures). This theory is not solid, however, for apart from a few poorly attested exceptions, we do not find human sacrifice among hunters and gatherers, only at later agricultural stages.

→ Cannibalism; Cultic Meal; Dead, Cult of the; Magic

Bibliography: W. Burkert, *Anthropologie des religiösen Opfers* (Munich, 1984) • A. E. Crawley et al., "Human Sacrifice," *ERE* 6.840-67 • J. Day, *Molech: A God of Human Sacrifice in the OT* (Cambridge, 1989) • E. S. Gerstenberger, "'... He/They Shall Be Put to Death': Life-preserving Divine Threats in OT Law," *ExAu* 11 (1995) 43-61 • J. D. Levenson, *The Death and Resurrection of the Beloved Son: The Transformation of Child Sacrifice in Judaism and Christianity* (New Haven, 1993) • R. J. Quinones, *The Changes of Cain: Violence and the Lost Brother in Cain and Abel Literature* (Princeton, 1991) • A. Wendel, *Das Opfer in der altisraelitischen Religion* (Leipzig, 1927) • E. Westermarck, *The Origin and Development of the Moral Ideas* (2 vols.; London, 1906-8).

Hartmut Zinser

Humanism

1. History
2. Content
3. Modern Discussion

1. History
Several stages of humanism may be distinguished: (1) the Renaissance humanism of the 15th and 16th centuries; (2) the new humanism of German classicism; (3) the "third humanism," or attempted revival of idealism after 1900; (4) the anti-idealistic humanism of the 19th century; and (5) modern movements that are critical of classical humanism (including existential philosophy, dialectical theology, → critical theory, and practical realism).

1.1. In the first instance, humanism is the literary and intellectual movement that arose with the Italian → Renaissance and that represents free and independent human development in conscious opposition to → Scholasticism. Liberation from the church's → authority and from dogmatic ties went hand in hand with adherence to a classical view of culture and humanity. Parallel to the revival of ancient art, learning, and culture was the discovery of the national element, which led humanists, especially Germans, to study their own past.

In Italy from the time of the poet Petrarch (1304-74), this idea of culture also assumed significance as a philosophy of religion (G. Gemistus Plethon, Bessarion, M. Ficino, Pico della Mirandola). Criticism of tradition was accompanied by a revival of especially Platonic ideals (P. Ramus, J. L. Vives; → Platonism). The *uomo universale* (Renaissance man) stood above all groupings.

In Germany humanism developed specifically nationalistic components (J. Agricola, Celtes, U. von Hutten, J. Reuchlin). It soon came into conflict with the church (Reuchlin, D. Erasmus). → Erasmus (1469?-1536) in particular stressed a concept of culture that would lead to true humanity and thus resisted the danger posed by an overemphasis on poetry and rhetoric.

The stress on → human dignity, → freedom, and → autonomy was fundamentally Christian, but although the → Reformation at first adopted some of the motifs, humanism could not easily be reconciled with M. Luther's (1483-1546) central concern for the soul's salvation and the relation to God (→ Luther's Theology). Through P. Melanchthon (1497-1560) and his valuation of the idea of culture, humanism certainly made an important contribution to the Reformation. In general, however, the connections between the two did not have too great an impact.

1.2. Melanchthon's ideas about education, which later earned for him the title *praeceptor Germaniae,* were adopted again at the beginning of the 19th century in connection with the ideals of German → classicism. J. Winckelmann's (1717-68) enthusiasm for Greece and some elements in the philosophy of German → idealism contributed to this new humanism, as did also the → Enlightenment concept of toleration and general opposition to an idea of → education that relied mainly on utility and profitability. Along these lines the Bavarian educational reformer F. I. von Niethammer (1766-1848) used the term "humanism" to differentiate our *humanitas* from our *animalitas.*

The ideal of a human individuality that is fully developed both aesthetically and morally and that covers every sphere of human learning and action signifies also an ideal of humanity as such. This ideal is prefigured in the Enlightenment, which viewed autonomy, reason, freedom, and tolerance as key elements of humanism. Similarly, the Enlightenment considered one essential goal of humanism to be an emancipation from the idea of creation and from the theologically given order of things. These goals are articulated in the English tradition (J. Locke, D. Hume) as well as among the French (J.-J. Rousseau, Montesquieu, Voltaire) and in I. Kant.

1.3. The reform of personality, above all by a return to antiquity as classical guide, was the main point for the so-called third humanism, which arose out of dissatisfaction with the positivist and materialistic atmosphere of the first half of the 20th century. It stressed the need to revive classical culture (W. Jaeger) and to reassert the ethical and political element in antiquity.

1.4. Already in the 19th century, following G. W. F. Hegel but also in reaction to him, there was criticism of idealistic humanism and the postulating of a concrete, or real, humanism. A. Ruge (1803-80) promoted the dialectical historical principle that the spirit overcomes nature (→ Dialectic; Philosophy of History). L. Feuerbach (1804-72) advocated human unity as the basic principle of his "new philosophy," which he defined as → anthropology. K. Marx (1818-83) demanded "true human emancipation," which posits communism as perfected naturalism (i.e., humanism) and perfected humanism as naturalism, and which is derived from the basic concept of → labor (→ Marxism).

The humanism demanded by the early Marx was revived from different standpoints by the neo-Marxism of the 20th century (H. Marcuse, H. Léfebre, L. Kolakowski, A. Schaff, P. Vranicki, G. Petrovič, M. Machoveč, etc.). In Marx himself, however, further development led to a modification, if not an abandonment, of his original humanistic approach.

1.5. In opposition to prior forms of humanism, various modern philosophers have entered the debate. M. Heidegger (1889-1976) was most comprehensive, believing that humanism of every type is tied to → metaphysics and, in his thought about being, rejecting every material definition of humanism and every attempt to find a basis for *humanitas.* Human nature, he thought, cannot be fixed and must be thought out and defined afresh in terms of new historical events (→ Existentialism).

→ Dialectical theology shared this turning aside from ego-related autonomy, setting God's creative and gracious act to the fore. We thus can speak somewhat as did K. Barth (1886-1968) about God's humanity and about the → love of God, which enables us to see ourselves as God's creatures by → grace.

From another angle J.-P. Sartre (1905-80) called his existentialism a humanism precisely because he did not begin with a metaphysically or theologically preconceived human nature. For Sartre the dimension of selfhood and humanity, understood existentially and in freedom, derives from situational conditioning and the free possibility of projecting human existence, and he accused the humanism that builds on a given human nature of an alienating and ontologically inadequate view of humanity. A. Camus (1913-60), in early parallelism with Sartre, began with the basic absurdity of the "human condition." Later, however, he came closer to acknowledging or subscribing to the notion of "human nature," which, rather than being fixed or presupposed, abides in a permanent state of human revolt and rebellion. As such, it is precisely history, for which it prescribes a boundary shaped by just this nature.

M. Merleau-Ponty (1908-61) thought along similar lines, beginning with the basic ambiguity of meaning and history. He thus posited a humanism that is against any preconceived interpretation of the person and that defines → humanity as an ethical and social claim.

In the United States the → pragmatism of W. James (1842-1910) and F. C. S. Schiller (1864-1937) called itself humanism; it judged human conduct, not by an absolute supernatural standard, but by its social and individual consequences. Schiller also argued that "rehumanizing" can begin only when we cease to overrate the intellect at the expense of the totality and fullness of our humanity. For him, human nature as a whole, along the lines of Protagoras, was the axis of "pragmatic" humanism. Humanism might be a historical movement, but it could also be a philosophy concerned about human nature and → human dignity.

2. Content

Closely related to the self-understanding of humanism is the metaphysical-ontological or theological basis of the view of humanity. Modern thought has increasingly moved beyond the Enlightenment, idealism, and the related reactions and on to a secularized discussion that is guided largely by the individual disciplines and in which, for example, comparative studies, sociobiology, and social science openly or implicitly reject any views of humanity that raise normative claims.

Philosophical anthropology raises the question of the "special place" of humanity in and over against nature, and it is in this light that most philosophical and anthropological approaches today regard themselves as humanist (→ Anthropology 4). Beginning with the work by M. Scheler (1874-1928) on the structure of the biophysical world and the differentiating of human beings in terms of spirit, there are various biologically controlled theories such as those of A. Gehlen (1904-76) and A. Portmann (1897-1982), but also that of H. Plessner (1892-1985), who in opposition to → racism draws attention to the specifically biological conditions of human existence. Meeting biological defects and achieving culture by way of compensation are viewed here as signs of human openness to the world, which alone forms humanism. The fact that humans cannot be pinned down makes of humanism a constant demand that lies in the very nature of humanity and that is part of our biological conditioning.

The tie back to philosophy or to philosophical anthropology that emerges in this context is often understood as a criticism of humanism, one that in its own turn imputes ideological features to the (metaphysically) derived ideal of a balanced, harmonious development of humanity, its spirituality, or its divine likeness. The antianthropocentric trend discernible in this context is of special significance, a trend emerging especially in the present and also manifesting itself in ecological themes or in criticism of society and science.

3. Modern Discussion

The present discussion of humanism contains many of these elements and is characterized by a polarity between, on the one hand, clinging to a traditional ideal of humanity and, on the other, destroying the special status accorded human beings. The "decentralizing" of human beings has been advocated especially as a result of poststructuralist debates, thus robbing human beings of their modern status as autonomous, self-controlling subjects. At the same time, the debate concerning the universality of human rights as well as concerning the dignity of human beings postulates a form of humanity that is essentially accepted by almost all the countries of the world, even though it remains rather vague and cannot be defined with any real precision. This debate concerning human dignity has been prompted not least by the rapid development of science and technology and is particularly volatile in the sphere of medicine (e.g., genetics).

By contrast, postmodern thinking views humanism as a specific accomplishment of modernity and goes on to criticize the attendant logocentrism as well as the special status accorded human beings as subjects (M. Foucault, J. Derrida, J. F. Lyotard). Computer and information technology allegedly presents yet another threat to humanism, where contemporary debate concerning humanism focuses on the tension between subject-oriented autonomy, on the one hand, and, on the other, an objectifying material view of human beings.

Bibliography: R. ABEL, *The Pragmatic Humanism of F. C. S. Schiller* (New York, 1955) • K. BARTH, *Humanismus* (Zurich, 1950) • G. BÖHME, *Humanismus zwischen Aufklärung und Postmoderne* (Idstein, 1994) • A. BULLOCK, *The Humanist Tradition in the West* (New York, 1985) • R. BULTMANN, "Humanismus und Christentum," *StGen* 1.70-77 • J. BURCKHARDT, *The Civilization of the Renaissance in Italy* (London, 1960; orig. pub., 1860) • A. CAMUS, *The Rebel: An Essay on Man in Revolt* (New York, 1991) • T. DAVIS, *Humanism* (London, 1997) • P. DESAN, ed., *Humanism in Crisis* (Ann Arbor, Mich., 1991) • R. A. ETLIN, *In Defence of Humanism* (Cambridge, 1996) • M. FOUCAULT, *The Order of Things: An Archaeology of the Human Sciences* (New York, 1971) • E. GARIN, *Italian Humanism: Philosophy and Civic Life in the Renaissance* (Oxford, 1966) • F. GEERK, *2000 Jahre Humanismus* (Basel, 1998) • A. GEHLEN, *Anthropologische Forschungen* (Hamburg, 1961) • E. GRASSI, *Humanismus und Marxismus* (Hamburg, 1973); idem, *Renaissance Humanism: Studies in Philosophy and Poetics* (Binghamton, N.Y., 1988) • M. HEIDEGGER, *Platons Lehre von der Wahrheit. Mit einem Brief über den "Humanismus"* (4th ed.; Frankfurt, 1997; orig. pub., 1947) • U. HORSTMANN, *Das Untier* (Frankfurt, 1983) • P. KAMPITS, *Der Mythos vom Menschen. Zum Atheismus und Humanismus Albert Camus'* (Salzburg, 1968) • L. KOLAKOWSKI, *Traktat über die Sterblichkeit der Vernunft* (Munich, 1967) • E. LÉVINAS, *Humanisme de l'autre homme* (Montpellier, 1972) • C. LÉVI-STRAUSS, *Structural Anthropology* (2 vols.; New York, 1963-76) • J. M. LOCHMAN, "Bilanz des europäischen Humanismus," *Das radikale Erbe* (Zurich, 1972) 55-68 • H. MARCUSE, *Kultur und Gesellschaft* (Frankfurt, 1965) • K. MARX, "On the Jewish Question" (1844) and "Contributions to the Critique of Hegel's Philosophy of Law" (1843/44), *MECW* 3.146-74 and 175-874 • M. MERLEAU-PONTY, *Humanism and Terror: An Essay on the Communist Problem* (Boston, 1969) • J.-P. SARTRE, *Existentialism* (New York, 1946) • M. SCHELER, *Man's Place in Nature* (Boston, 1961) • F. C. S. SCHILLER, *Humanisme* (London, 1903) • E. STEELWATER, "Humanism," *EncAE* 2.641-49.

PETER KAMPITS

Humanistic Psychology

1. Source

Humanistic psychology was started in the 1960s by A. Maslow, C. Bühler, C. Rogers, R. May, A. Koestler, J. Bugental, and others. Without the pioneering work of K. Goldstein, O. Rank, K. Horney, and V. Frankl in → psychology, plus the → group methods of K. Lewin and J. Moreno and the "totality psychology" of the Würzburg school, humanistic psychology would not have been conceivable. It has firmly established itself as a possible third alternative to behaviorism (→ Behavior, Behavioral Psychology) and orthodox → psychoanalysis.

2. Theoretical Presuppositions

For its theoretical presuppositions humanistic psychology draws on three philosophical sources: (1) the humanist tradition (J. G. → Herder, K. → Marx; → Humanism), (2) → existentialism (H. Bergson, M. Buber, G. Marcel), and (3) → phenomenology (E. Husserl, M. Merleau-Ponty). Humanistic psychology sets the human → person at the center as a totality, key aspects of which are corporeality, history, values, → norms, social relations, and the → ecological setting (→ Anthropology).

People are both active and positive. They live consciously and are fundamentally oriented to → meaning. Understanding among human beings results from mutual acceptance and encounter; growth comes as self-fulfillment. → Creativity enables people to compensate for defects and to integrate tensions. The ability to decide makes possible an independence of external control and acceptance of → responsibility for acts. The idea of self-responsibility contains the polarity of → autonomy and interdependence.

3. Content and Objectives

As a dialogic science, humanistic psychology does not isolate individuals or merely collect data. It finds interdependence between the subjects and objects of research (i.e., between therapists and patients), for it thinks in terms of interdependence and process. Its goal is the living out of the reality of one's own existence. Negative experiences, sorrows, → sufferings, and → conflicts are part of life and merit attention.

Important goals in humanistic → psychotherapy are the ability to meet people, the ability to decide, self-consciousness, self-responsibility, meaning, activity, and creativity. The accent throughout is on the here and now. In a climate of mutual appreciation and partnership, clients learn to accept themselves, including conflicts in their → identity. Techniques include → Rogerian psychotherapy, → Gestalt psychotherapy, psychodrama, transactional analysis, logotherapy, body therapy, therapeutic community, and bonding psychotherapy.

4. Significance for Psychology

Humanistic psychology is not just descriptive and academic but attempts to work out a positive anthropological concept oriented to the healthy person. It tries to overcome both the mechanistic concept of behaviorism and the pessimistic concept of psychoanalysis. The danger here is that of anthropological truncation. Humanistic psychology thinks it can replace spirituality (→ Immanence and Transcendence) by belief in the self. Will, the ability to decide, responsibility, activity, creativity, meaning, self-fulfillment, and readiness for encounter are the only pillars of human → freedom.

A. Maslow saw this danger and demanded a fourth psychology that would not put human beings alone at the center but rather would be transhuman and suprapersonal, looking beyond human needs, interests, identity, and self-fulfillment. According to Maslow, without transcendence we become sick, hyperactive, nihilistic, hopeless, and apathetic; we need something greater than ourselves to venerate.

→ Ego Psychology

Bibliography: C. Bühler and M. Allen, *Einführung in die humanistische Psychologie* (Stuttgart, 1974) • J. Cohen, *Humanistic Psychology* (Louisville, Ky., 1958) • H. G. Coward, *Jung and Eastern Thought* (Albany, N.Y., 1985) • R. J. DeCarvalho, *The Founders of Humanistic Psychology* (New York, 1991) • W. J. Lowe, *Evil and the Unconscious* (Chico, Calif., 1983) • A. Maslow, *Toward a Psychology of Being* (3d ed.; Princeton, 1998) • R. May, *The Courage to Create* (New York, 1994) • D. Moss, ed., *Humanistic and Transpersonal Psychology: A Historical and Biographical Sourcebook* (Westport, Conn., 1999) • R. D. Nye, *Three Psychologies: Perspectives from Freud, Skinner, and Rogers* (Monterey, Calif., 1986) • C. Rogers, *On Becoming a Person: A Therapist's View of Psychotherapy* (Boston, 1995) • J. B. P. Shaffer, *Humanistic Psychology* (New York, 1978) • T. A. Wallach, *Psychology's Sanction for Selfishness: The Error of Egoism in Theory and Therapy* (San Francisco, 1983) • F. J. Wertz, "The Role of the Humanistic Movement in the History of Psychology," *JHPs* 38 (1998) 42-70.

KONRAD STAUSS

Humanity

1. The term "humanity" is used in different ways: (1) in distinction from animality, (2) as a collective term for the human race (humankind), and (3) as a norm of human existence — for example, in distinguishing the person from the → animals, as in (1), or relating the individual to humankind, as in (2). In the third sense it relates both to everyday activities and to ethical reflection on human enterprises. Such things change, which makes it always necessary to test them against Christian belief.

2. *Humanitas* was a fixed term in the Ciceronian rhetorical tradition. Rhetoricians refused to leave → truth (as wisdom) only to the logicians. They devoted themselves to topics such as the art of finding truth in linguistic disclosure rather than merely to the analytics of Aristotle, the source of Western → logic. Humanity for them was not a matter of correct statement but of knowledge related to life (→ Epistemology). Cicero (106-43 B.C.) stressed both the distinction from animals and also aesthetic-intellectual education, which was to form the ruler-ideal. Early and medieval Christianity was interested more in the humanity of Christ and stressed the distinction from his deity (→ Christology 2).

With the arrival of the → Renaissance, humanity came to involve a distinctive lifestyle. Education was an aid to true humanity (→ Humanism), and the humanities replaced theology as the core. "Humanity" came to mean certain qualities of a lifestyle. For M. Luther, it was mercy; in aristocratic circles, it was honesty, civility, and courtesy. Johann Zedler's *Universal-Lexikon* (1732-50) equated humanity with politeness and affability.

A conception tied in this way to social strata and historical developments inevitably reflected social restructuring. Such changes occurred with the → Enlightenment and the middle class that sponsored it (→ Bourgeois, Bourgeoisie). I. Kant (1724-1804) stressed rational self-determination in → freedom (→ Autonomy; Kantianism); his *homo noumenon* would not follow outward inclination but in relation to self and others would view humanity as an end, not a means. While Kant was among those who seek the universally human in terms of a logical idea of unity, J. G. Herder (1744-1803) stood more in the topical-rhetorical tradition. He viewed humanity as a disposition that must be unfolded according to nature, spirit, and soul. In the course of their life, people will develop their humanity through speech and education.

Around 1800 the term "humanism" came into vogue to denote the cultural ideal. A subject of debate in German → idealism and among its later critics was the relation between rational self-determination, natural history, and social influences. J. G. Fichte (1762-1814) found in the division between → reason and life an imperfect autonomy. G. W. F. Hegel (1770-1831) located the ideal of humanity in the abstract freedom of middle-class society (→ Hegelianism), arguing that the morality of the → state must give substance to the ideal concept. Critics saw the problems in such mediation. L. Feuerbach (1804-72) wanted to give to humanity the greatness attributed to an imaginary deity. The young K. Marx (1818-83) regarded true naturalism (appropriation of nature by → work) as true humanism (the finding of the human self).

In the Anglo-Saxon sphere two contributions helped to promote the idea of humanity. On the one hand, ideas of → natural law and the principles of moral philosophy combined with a fading → theism to promote the idea of human rights, that is, the belief that "all men are by nature equally free and independent and have certain inherent rights" (art. 1 of the 1776 Virginia Declaration of Rights), or the conviction that there is in all people an innate compassion that will help to control the egoism that rules in the economic marketplace (Adam Smith). On the other hand, → pragmatism brought together the two ways of thinking mentioned earlier: the analytic-logical tradition in the theory of signs and the rhetorical tradition in pragmatic concern for meaningful conduct (C. Peirce). In this context, coexistence (with others; see G. H. Mead) and communication (or a community based on communication) oriented toward the → future become constitutive for human existence as such.

3. New problems and questions have been added to the old in modern discussion, concerning:

- education (What contents and lifestyles are appropriate for a humane → society?)
- psychology (What work on the outer and inner conditions of life will make self-discovery possible? → Identity)
- human and civil → rights
- economic foundations and the response to the various human needs
- the shape of a world that will make humane life possible (→ Culture; Ecology; Technology).

These questions involve the various perspectives of human biology. Anthropology in the narrower sense defines human beings, in distinction from animals, as defective creatures (A. Gehlen) that compensate for their defects in institutions (including → speech). The idea of the development of humanity is less prominent here. New developments such as sociobiology (the cultural effects of genetic mate-

rials) and biological epistemology (thinking as a strategy for survival in → evolution) act in the same way as biological anthropology to minimize the question of the future and the human antithesis to nature.

4. Seeking human dignity and the human norm is a central theme in → ethics. In spite of Kant, Hegel, and Marx, it constantly raises the question of the coordination of reason both individually and ecologically, that is, in relation to nature and society. To coordinate the two perspectives it is not enough merely to begin with the *humanum*, for this concept is always mediated socially and historically. The theology of the Word of God (→ Dialectical Theology) opposed humanism, having in view the presuppositions — not yet discussed — of the unquestioned ideals of humanity. But it knew well enough that an abstract → Word of God does not allow debate with dubious assertions, especially of an ideological nature. Such theology thus turned to the *man* → Jesus Christ and did not classify individuals a priori according to any overriding universal concept of "humanity." For the humanity of individuals lies also in their diversity and therefore in the vulnerability and need that are experienced concretely by each and every individual.

This Christological insight, however, needs translation into the more general questions of our humanity. Personal ethics and social ethics belong together. The former deals with people who are reconciled to God within their creaturely limits; instead of virtues or values it seeks to offer them life perspectives. The NT looks in different directions: to the blessedness of the needy whom God has accepted (→ Sermon on the Mount), to → justification for → freedom to test the → good and to live it out (Paul), to life in → love and truth (John). → Social ethics finds in economic and social processes concurrent and often unconsciously practiced or enforced pictures of humanity (as lifestyles). These views entangle people in a social and economic nexus (with needs and ideals of achievement etc.), but they may be politically limited or changed in such a way as to achieve penultimately (so D. Bonhoeffer) the freedom of those who are reconciled to God.

Bibliography: I. Asheim, ed., *Humanität und Herrschaft Christi* (Göttingen, 1968) • K. Barth, *The Humanity of God* (Richmond, Va., 1970) • E. Bloch, *Natural Law and Human Dignity* (Cambridge, 1986) • H. E. Bödeker, "Menschheit, Humanismus," *GGB* 3.1063-1128 • I. Eibl-Eibesfeldt, *Human Ethology* (New York, 1989) •

L. FEUERBACH, *The Essence of Christianity* (London, 1854) • E. FROMM, *The Nature of Man* (ed. E. Fromm and R. Xirau; New York, 1968) • P. GAY, *The Party of Humanity* (New York, 1959) • A. GEHLEN, *Man, His Nature and Place in the World* (New York, 1988) • J. H. HALLOWELL and J. M. PORTER, *Political Philosophy to Search for Humanity and Order* (Scarborough, Ont., 1997) • G. W. F. HEGEL, *Elements of the Philosophy of Right* (Cambridge, 1991; orig. pub., 1821); idem, *Phenomenology of Spirit* (Oxford, 1977; orig. pub., 1807) • J. G. HERDER, *Briefe zur Beförderung der Humanität* (1794), *Sämtliche Werke* (33 vols.; ed. B. Suphan; Berlin, 1877-1913) vol. 17; idem, *Ideen zur Philosophie der Geschichte der Menschheit* (1784), ibid., vol. 13 • T. HOBBES, *Leviathan* (Harmondsworth, 1968; orig. pub., 1651) • O. HÖFFE, *Strategien der Humanität* (Freiburg, 1975) • I. KANT, *Anthropology from a Pragmatic Point of View* (The Hague, 1974; orig. pub., 1799); idem, *The Metaphysical Elements of Justice* (Indianapolis, 1999; orig. pub., 1797) • D. KRIES, ed., *Piety and Humanity: Essays on Religion and Early Modern Political Philosophy* (Lanham, Md., 1997) • P. O. KRISTELLER, *Renaissance Thought* (2 vols.; New York, 1961-65) • J. LOCKE, *Essays on the Law of Nature* (Oxford, 1958; orig. pub., 1664) • K. MARX, *Economic and Philosophic Manuscripts* (1844) (Moscow, 1959) • T. G. MASARYK, *The Ideals of Humanity* (London, 1937) • R. NIEBUHR, *The Nature and Destiny of Man* (New York, 1953) • I. PAPE, "Humanismus, Humanität," *HWP* 3.1218-30 • C. S. PEIRCE, W. JAMES, C. LEWIS, J. DEWEY, and G. H. MEAD, *Pragmatism: The Classical Writings* (Indianapolis, 1982) • T. RENDTORFF and A. RICH, eds., *Humane Gesellschaft* (Zurich, 1970) • J.-J. ROUSSEAU, *The First and Second Discourses* (New York, 1964; orig. pub., 1750, 1753) • J. R. SACHS, *The Christian Vision of Humanity: Basic Christian Anthropology* (Collegeville, Minn., 1991) • F. SCHILLER, *On the Aesthetic Education of Man, in a Series of Letters* (Oxford, 1967) • O. ŠIK, *For a Humane Economic Democracy* (New York, 1985) • H. E. TÖDT, ed., *Das Humanum als Kriterium der Gesellschaftsgestaltung* (Tübingen, 1972).

CHRISTOFER FREY

Humility

1. History of the Term
2. Development as a Christian Virtue
3. Relevance
4. Theology

1. History of the Term

Humility is the → virtue of respect and true self-evaluation. Antiquity rejected it but demanded a sense of one's own limitations in fear of the envy of the gods. The OT finds in it an expression of basic dependence as we realize that existence is a gift of God, not a necessity. Humility arises out of astonishment and unconditional trust and is less a trait of character than a lifestyle (Ps. 51:17; Prov. 15:33; Isa. 57:15). The NT links it to childlikeness and poverty of spirit. → Jesus was a model as he humbled himself in self-giving to God's loving action (Phil. 2:2-8; Matt. 11:29; 18:4 and par.; Luke 14:11). Paul admonished us to subject ourselves to one another and to avoid boasting (1 Cor. 1:29, 31; Rom. 12:10, 16).

2. Development as a Christian Virtue

For Augustine (354-430) humility was a disposition in which we seek out humanity. Thomas Aquinas (ca. 1225-74) related humility to the cardinal virtue of temperance (moderation and discipline). J. Calvin (1509-64) called it the chief virtue for → faith. M. Luther (1483-1546) called for a preaching of sin that would lead to humility (Heidelberg Disputation [1518], thesis 17; WA 55.203). As he saw it, God definitely promises his → grace to the humble, that is, to those who have despaired of themselves and given up on themselves (*LW* 33.61-62).

The history of humility is also one of its perversions. Often to the fore is not a recognition of limitations but self-repudiation, self-abasement, resentment (Nietzsche), and → dogmatism. The preaching of humility has been an instrument that those in power have used against weaker groups (in a patriarchy esp. to keep women in order). In this regard it helped to lessen conflicts in feudal relations (in chivalry, the troubadours in their relations with noble women; → Feudalism). It also helped to motivate unselfish action in → orders and religious communities.

3. Relevance

Ethics and pastoral psychology have given us good reasons for speaking about humility today. With reference to the world, humility is respect for the world, especially for living creatures, as we see ourselves as part of → creation with a responsibility to conserve it and protect it against destruction.

With reference to the self, we need the humility with which we can affirm ourselves in a balanced manner, knowing the self and being true to it.

With reference to politics, humility is underdeveloped in Western culture, or it would not have crushed other cultures in the belief that its form of life and religion were superior. Humility springs from regard for the → human dignity of others, binds to the duty of justice, and frees from envy at the situation of others. This kind of humility constitutes the lifestyle of "reciprocity" (H. Stierlin) and includes → dialogue with others, a preservation of the → autonomy of every individual, and an appreciation of differences.

With reference to mystery (→ Mysticism), humility is a surprised feeling of being taken under God's protection, rests on a readiness for values higher than one's own life, and results in love as recognition.

4. Theology

Theologically, humility must be understood as (1) a readiness to accept being directed to God and to → justification, (2) a concern to be true to one's self, and (3) a social virtue, insofar as the → discipleship of Christ that is sought in humility leads to service on behalf of one's neighbor.

Bibliography: P. Adnès, "Humilité," DSp 7.1136-87 (bibliography) • S. R. Dunde, "Neid," IKZ 4 (1984) 233-46 • R. J. Furey, So I'm Not Perfect: A Psychology of Humility (Staten Island, N.Y., 1986) • F. Nietzsche, On the Genealogy of Morality (Indianapolis, 1998; orig. pub., 1987) • H. Stierlin, Das Tun des Einen ist das Tun des Anderen: Eine Dynamik menschlicher Beziehungen (7th ed.; Frankfurt, 1995).

Siegfried Rudolf Dunde

Humor

The idea that humor is laughing in spite of one's circumstances carries an essential point. Dealing humorously with difficult inner or outer realities is a way of controlling life. As distinct from wit, mockery, or irony, humor deals nonaggressively with circumstances of trouble or conflict. Its affinity to grinning or → laughing finds clearest expression where such forms of psychological release are found to relieve tension or bring liberation and where they can be an "infectious" aid to communication.

The modern use of the term must be seen against a significant change in meaning. It first had a physical connotation, then came to denote a quality, and was then increasingly viewed as one of the most powerful forces of the human spirit. Ancient Greek → philosophy of nature had a doctrine of four humors (i.e., fluids; Lat. umor means "sap, juice, moisture"). By way of medicine (Hippocrates and his school), a so-called humoral pathology developed in the last centuries B.C. (Galen, 2d cent. B.C.), which influenced the medieval doctrine of the temperaments.

With the changed view of humanity in the → Renaissance, the idea of humor, especially as influ-

enced by the → Enlightenment and idealistic philosophy (→ Idealism) and in the context of an increasingly independent → anthropology, now became an essential element in the structure of human behavior. By way of definitions in Jean Paul, I. Kant, G. W. F. Hegel, S. Kierkegaard, and also S. Freud, it served as a way of illuminating and mastering existence. Deliberate exercise of humor came to be regarded as a signal of inner freedom, for it distances individuals from things that they cannot change or from psychological → anxiety. The element of the comic relativizes tragic destiny. In opposition to apparently unavoidable doubt about the meaning of events, the self, and others, one can meet life under the banner of wisdom and humor (H. Kohut). It is not surprising, then, that from antiquity humor has been used creatively in literature and the plastic arts to express and mediate → joy in life, in spite of all the contrarieties of human existence.

A theological definition of the relation between humor and → faith must begin at the point where both alleviate difficult, real-life situations. Humor, like an illusory faith, might perhaps negate reality. Thinking eschatologically, we should define it positively as a provisional possibility of experiencing reality that will finally be transcended in the event of reconciliation that embraces all reality, thus interpreting it Christologically (so best K. Barth). In → everyday human interactions, humor needs to be cultivated and strengthened to where it clarifies the human (esp. the all-too-human) and offers a better understanding of it. At that point it can fulfill the hermeneutical principle of truly human conduct, that is, conduct characterized by love of neighbor.

Bibliography: J. P. Albert, "Humor als Autonomie und Christonomie" (Diss., Erlangen, 1975) • K. Barth, CD III/4 • J. Bremmer and H. Roodenburg, A Cultural History of Humor: From Antiquity to the Present Day (Cambridge, 1997) • S. Freud, Studienausgabe, vol. 4, Psychologische Schriften (ed. A. Mitscherlich; Frankfurt, 1982) • W. Frings, Humor in der Psychoanalyse (Stuttgart, 1996) • C.-R. Gruner, The Game of Humor: A Comprehensive Theory of Why We Laugh (New Brunswick, N.J., 1997) • S. Kierkegaard, The Concept of Irony, with Continual Reference to Socrates (Princeton, 1989) • H. Kohut, The Analysis of the Self: A Systematic Approach to the Psychoanalytic Treatment of Narcissistic Personality Disorders (New York, 1971) • H. Kotthoff, ed., Das Gelächter der Geschlechter (Constance, 1996) • D. L. F. Nilsen, Humor Scholarship: A Research Bibliography (Westport, Conn., 1993) • W. Thiede, Das verheißene Lachen (Göttingen, 1986).

Klaus Winkler†

Hungary

	1960	1980	2000
Population (1,000s):	9,984	10,707	9,811
Annual growth rate (%):	0.33	−0.24	−0.56
Area: 93,033 sq. km. (35,920 sq. mi.)			

A.D. 2000

Population density: 105/sq. km. (273/sq. mi.)
Births / deaths: 1.03 / 1.49 per 100 population
Fertility rate: 1.40 per woman
Infant mortality rate: 12 per 1,000 live births
Life expectancy: 70.0 years (m: 65.4, f: 74.7)
Religious affiliation (%): Christians 87.0 (Roman Catholics 65.7, Protestants 24.7, indigenous 1.4, other Christians 1.5), nonreligious 7.6, atheists 4.2, other 1.2.

1. Historical Survey
2. History of the Church
3. Contemporary Churches
   3.1. Roman Catholic Church
   3.2. Reformed Church in Hungary
   3.3. Lutheran Church
   3.4. Unitarian Church
   3.5. Free Churches
   3.6. Orthodox Church
4. Interchurch Relations
5. Non-Christian Religions

1. Historical Survey

During their migration in the fifth to the eighth centuries, the Finno-Ugric Magyars came into contact with → Byzantine missions (→ Mission 3). Toward the end of the ninth century they settled in the Carpathians and Alps and by the Danube. After decades of fighting (esp. after the battle of Lechfeld, in 955), St. Stephen I (prince 997-1000, king 1000-1038) established Christianity; he called missionaries from Rome, received a royal crown from Rome, and organized ten dioceses. When the Mongols invaded in the 13th century, King Béla IV (1235-70) and Hungary acted as the bulwark of Christianity. Hungary played the same role in the time of the Turkish wars. In 1526 Sultan Süleyman I the Magnificent (1520-66), allying himself with the papacy (→ Pope, Papacy), France, England, Florence, and Venice in the League of Cognac, declared war. Hungary was decisively defeated by the Turks at the battle of Mohács in 1526. The kingdom was divided into three parts, with Buda, the capital, under Turkish rule from 1541 to 1686. Turkey occupied the middle of the country. In the East was the princedom of Transylvania, and the rest of the kingdom of

Hungary was to the north and west under the rule of the Hapsburgs.

After 1686, when Hungary was liberated from the Turks, it became part of the Hapsburg Empire. In 1867 it regained its internal independence under the Austro-Hungarian monarchy, under which it continued until after World War I, when, by the Treaty of Trianon (1920), Hungary lost more than two-thirds of its former possessions. The policies and social relations of the divided states increased Hungarian emigration, and there is today a large-scale Hungarian → diaspora.

Hungary became a "people's republic" after World War II (→ Socialism 2.1). Domestic problems in 1956, 1968, and 1987/88 brought political and economic reforms. The Republic of Hungary was proclaimed in October 1989, beginning a political and economic transformation (including a multiparty system and a market economy), though not without difficulties.

2. History of the Church

Church life in the Middle Ages was much the same as in other Western countries (→ Middle Ages 3): the church organization was built up, one in ten villages built a church, and religious orders appeared throughout the country. The → Reformation at first followed the Wittenberg pattern (→ Luther's Theology; Reformation 2.10), but it quickly came under Swiss influence (→ Calvin's Theology; Zwingli's Theology). The Hungarian reformers (esp. János Sylvester, Mátyś Biró Dévai, István Szegedi Kis, Michael Sztárai, Gallus Huszár, Péter Melius, Johannes Honterus, Caspar Heltai, and Gáspár Károlyi) displayed a certain independence in their teaching, though they wished to incorporate the various emphases into a unified system. By the beginning of the 17th century, two trends were evident, with support both for the church of the → Augsburg Confession and for the church of the → Helvetic Confession. In the 16th century Transylvania adopted a policy of → toleration for four religions: Roman Catholicism (→ Catholicism [Roman]), → Lutheranism, → Calvinism, and → Unitarianism (→ Religious Liberty). Such granting of equal recognition to four → confessions was unique in its time (→ Augsburg, Peace of; Cuius regio eius religio).

Roman Catholics under Hapsburg leadership attempted counterreformation (→ Catholic Reform and Counterreformation). The princes of Transylvania — I. Bocskay (1557-1606), G. Bethlen (1580-1629), and G. Rákóczi I (1593-1648) — resisted the state and its agents, the → Jesuits. By the second half of the 17th century, however, the princes had lost their power, and counterreformation proceeded in the kingdom of Hungary. Hundreds of Protestant pastors and teachers were arrested and condemned to death, then "graciously" pardoned — but only to be sold as galley slaves. International action eventually freed those who did not find a → martyr's death.

In the 18th century the Counter-Reformation continued more quietly. In 1781, however, Joseph II (1764-90) issued an edict of toleration (→ Josephinism 4). The situation now improved, more than 1,000 congregations were reestablished, and Protestants were now able to set up their own church organization. By this time, because of the influence of the 200-year-long Counter-Reformation, more than two-thirds of the population again belonged to the Roman Catholic Church.

After World War I and the dismemberment of Hungary, the churches had to organize themselves afresh. They ran into difficulties under socialism after 1948. In that year the Protestants came to terms with the state, as did the Roman Catholics in 1950 and 1964. The state provided financial support and granted relative freedom for worship, religious instruction, publishing, and printing and distributing Bibles. → Evangelism, however, was forbidden outside the church, and economic activities remained restricted. The churches regained full freedom in 1989.

3. Contemporary Churches

Statistical data on the various churches today are based on partly conflicting sociological surveys or church records. In 1989 there were 14 registered religious groups in Hungary; by 1999 the number had risen to 92. The so-called historical churches exist somewhat in the framework of a → people's church (Volkskirche). These churches practice infant baptism, and their membership is based on the number of baptized people, although they also make a distinction between membership in name only and active membership. The smaller → denominations typically record active membership only.

3.1. Roman Catholic Church

The → Roman Catholic Church in Hungary is divided into four archbishoprics and eight dioceses. For ministry in the more than 3,500 parishes there are only approximately 2,400 → priests. Before 1989 four religious orders were permitted to maintain only eight schools, none higher than high school. In 1999 there were 55 sisterhoods and 25 brotherhoods, plus over 200 Roman Catholic educational institutions from → kindergarten through university. In 1997 the Hungarian state signed a → concordat with the Vatican, according to which the govern-

ment began funding the schools and charitable institutions run by the church.

The → uniate Greek Catholic Church has one bishop, 160 parishes, and 230,000 members. It maintains a seminary in Nyíregyháza.

3.2. Reformed Church in Hungary

The Hungarian Reformed Church has 4 districts and 27 presbyteries (→ Reformed and Presbyterian Churches), each of which is led by a double presidency — a church president (bishop or senior) and a lay president (a chief elder). In 1999 there were 1.9 million church members in 1,200 congregations, served by 1,300 pastors. Training for ministry is offered at four seminaries: in Budapest, Debrecen, Pápa, and Sárospatak.

Similar to the concordat with the Vatican, the Hungarian government in 1998 reached an agreement with the Reformed Church in Hungary. The state now supports the schools and charity institutions run by the church. Whereas in 1989 the church had only one high school and two seminaries, plus about 20 charitable institutions, in 1999 it supported more than 100 educational institutions, with another 40 institutions engaged in charity or mission work. The latter efforts included homes for those with mental and physical handicaps, plus facilities for the elderly, homeless, alcoholics, and drug addicts (→ Diakonia).

3.3. Lutheran Church

The Lutheran Church was divided into two districts in 1999 (and will become three in 2001). Each district is led by a bishop and a lay district inspector. The church has approximately 410,000 members in 350 congregations, under the care of 400 pastors. Training for ministry is offered at the Lutheran University in Budapest. Altogether, the church sponsors more than 50 educational institutions.

3.4. Unitarian Church

Only in pre-Trianon Hungary did the → anti-Trinitarian movement develop into an organized Unitarian church. Most of the adherents now live in Transylvania (Romania), with only 12,000 members left in Hungary.

3.5. Free Churches

The majority of the 75 registered Christian groups in Hungary are small, free churches, together totaling approximately 100,000 members. The largest are the → Baptists (30,000 members), followed by the Nazarenes, → Assembly of God, Seventh-day → Adventists, → Apostolic Church, Methodists (→ Methodist Churches), and Christian Brethren. Under socialism, many of the free churches belonged to the Council of → Free Churches, an association that disbanded after the political change in 1989.

3.6. *Orthodox Churches*

The → Orthodox Church in Hungary has about 40,000 members in four groups. Altogether there are 50 congregations served by 30 priests and under the → Patriarchates of Moscow, Belgrade, Bucharest, and Sofia.

4. Interchurch Relations

The Protestant and Orthodox churches belong to the Ecumenical Council of Churches in Hungary (since 1943), which is a member of the → World Council of Churches, the → Conference of European Churches, and the Leuenberger Church Fellowship (→ National Councils of Churches). They are also part of their respective international organizations. For some years Protestants and Roman Catholics have drawn closer together, talking about → mixed marriage and also about common translations of the → Lord's Prayer and the → Apostles' Creed (→ Confessions and Creeds). In 1998 discussions began regarding the preparation of a joint Roman Catholic–Protestant translation of the Bible.

5. Non-Christian Religions

In 1894 → Judaism was granted → religious freedom. It suffered persecution during the years 1938-44 (→ Holocaust), although in Budapest, unlike in the other cities of Europe, the Jews survived as a community. An institute for the training of → rabbis is located at Budapest, the only one in eastern and central Europe. The Christian churches engage in → Jewish-Christian dialogue.

In 1999 there were 17 non-Christian religious groups among the 92 registered. Of this number, 12 had a Buddhist background, 3 Hindu, and 1 Muslim.

Bibliography: On 1: S. R. Burant, ed., *Hungary: A Country Study* (Washington, D.C., 1990) • T. Cox, ed., *Hungary: The Politics of Transition* (London, 1995) • G. Csepeli, *National Identity in Contemporary Hungary* (New York, 1997) • P. Hanák, ed., *Die Geschichte Ungarns* (Budapest, 1988) • E. Lengyel, *One Thousand Years of Hungary* (New York, 1958) • J. Nanay, *Transylvania: The Hungarian Minority in Romania* (New York, 1976) • L. Nëhäm, *The Cultural Aspirations of Hungary from 896 to 1935* (Budapest, 1935) • G. Ránki, ed., *Hungary and European Civilization* (Budapest, 1989) • J. Szücs, *Nation und Geschichte* (Budapest, 1981).

On 2-5: J. Barcza et al., eds., *Geschichte und Gegenwart der Reformierten Kirche in Ungarn* (Budapest, 1986) • M. Bucsay, *Der Protestantismus in Ungarn, 1521-1979* (2 vols.; Vienna, 1977-79) • B. Dercsényi, *Lutheran Churches in Hungary* (Budapest, 1992) • F. Dusicza, ed., *Egyházunk, a Magyarországi Református Egyház — Our Church: The Reformed Church in Hungary* (bilingual, Hungarian and English) (Budapest, 1997) • G. Gombos, *The Lean Years: Hungarian Calvinism in Crisis* (New York, 1960) • I. Kádár, *The Church in the Storm of Time: The History of the Hungarian Reformed Church during the Two World Wars, Revolutions, and Counter-Revolutions* (Budapest, 1958) • Lutheran World Federation, *The Hungarian Lutheran Church of Today* (Lund, 1947) • K. Marton, *Wallenberg* (New York, 1985) • M. Tomka, *Religion und Kirche in Ungarn. Ergebnisse religionssoziologischer Forschung* (Vienna, 1990) • A. S. Unghváry, *The Hungarian Protestant Reformation in the Sixteenth Century under the Ottoman Impact: Essays and Profiles* (Lewiston, N.Y., 1989).

Mihály Márkus

Hunger

The term "hunger" denotes a shortage of nourishment that, if it lasts, can lead to → death. Hunger crises persist in the Third World, even with all the socioeconomic → development of the recent decades (of which crises the public seems now generally more aware). Natural causes of hunger like drought are overestimated. In the past, farming structures and systems were better able to cope with cyclic changes in natural conditions. At the beginning of the 21st century, Bread for the World estimates the number of hungry in the world to be 800 million, or one-sixth of the population of the world's developing nations.

In the monetary sphere (→ Money) and the sphere of subsistence production, the structures that we have now created seem to make famines more likely and more severe. First, the market mechanism is partly to blame. In some cases production for export hampers the growing of food for home consumption; often the money gained is not enough to make good the deficiency. Second, the widespread cutting down of rain forests can also be a threat to food production. The remaining small groups of hunters and gatherers, those who live in the vicinity, and coming generations can all suffer from the so-called external effects of ecological mismanagement.

The needs of a wealthy minority can control production much more strongly than do those of the destitute, a pattern found also in developed countries. Lack of purchasing power is plainly a cause of hunger. If there is no possibility of increasing the purchasing power of the poor, their better nourishment is often attempted by political intervention to regulate the market, an approach that often leads to other forms of imbalance.

A striking feature of policies of development is their urban bias (→ City), which shows a preference for urban populations that is not economically justified. The effect is to promote an antiagrarian policy, where the fixing of prices and food aid from abroad govern farming prices. Instead of encouraging farmers to raise more food by offering higher prices, governments often try to dissuade them with subsidies.

Subsistence farming is production for individual needs, for immediate neighbors, and for barter. If it is a constituent of a farming economy along with the production of goods, it can maintain cycles of production in a controlled system. In most strategic planning it is forgotten that subsistence farming is declining and that rural → solidarity is being weakened by the dissolution of traditional social structures. Yet subsistence farming and the traditional social solidarity are still buffers that prevent the worst from happening when natural conditions change and agrarian policies fail. Today, however, global realignments and changes in rainfall patterns are injuring the very poorest in an unprecedented way.

To produce enough for emergencies social structures are needed that make possible and even demand an output above what is normally needed. Production thus needs to be geared to the worst circumstances that can be expected. So many fields are thus worked and are so carefully weeded that even part of the crops that may normally be expected will be enough. If the surplus cannot be sold, in a long series of good years it makes such efforts seem unnecessary. To encourage farmers there must be financial and moral inducements.

Networks of economic solidarity and distribution systems make it possible to support households with a high proportion of children and older or sick people. Even in normal years such households can survive only if they are brought into a network of traditional economic solidarity that makes up the deficit. The network involves complicated relationship of relatives and friends in which individuals have qualitatively different rights and duties.

Famines show that the household cannot always be regarded as the unit of reproduction. All members of a household do not always have adequate means for physical reproduction. In some places malnutrition of children has served as a means of population control. The malnutrition of older people or married women is often also a phenomenon of social disintegration.

Linked to each social mode of production is a specific form of social control. Today, however, the link between production and control has disappeared in many forms of agricultural economy. Village and family authorities used to organize social control, and those who would not participate in the production and storing of surpluses lost regard or came under sanctions. The expansion of the colonial and postcolonial state, however, broke the power of these authorities, rendering religious, social, and political systems unable to stabilize the storing of surpluses. When marriage contracts became so loose that the extended family was weakened, there was no longer any social control, and new families could no longer protect the married women against neglect and undernourishment (→ Family 1.7; Sexism).

In South America especially, the processes of land acquisition promote famine. Small farmers are led into debt, pressure may be brought to bear on them, or political influence may be exerted, and big landowners take over the land of the poor without any obligation to feed those who are left landless.

After periods of high yield, agrarian and ecological change can also result in environmental degradation or lead to great fluctuations in production, both of which favor famine.

Developmental organizations have programs of famine relief. With their own logistics governmental agencies can distribute the agricultural surplus from industrialized countries. Church programs (e.g., Bread for the World, Misereor, Oxfam, World Vision) make use of partner organization (e.g., Caritas, Action by Churches Together, Lutheran World Service) in developed states. Gifts of food, however, depress producer prices in the same regions. Social anthropologists are thus asking that gifts of food be brought into traditional forms of distribution and aid; with the churches, they want more emphasis on preventive projects.

→ Colonialism; Dependence; Ecology; Fasting; Poverty

Bibliography: S. Barbour, ed., *Hunger* (San Diego, Calif., 1995) • D. M. Beckmann, *Grace at the Table: Ending Hunger in God's World* (New York, 1999) • D. M. Boucher, ed., *The Paradox of Plenty: Hunger in a Bountiful World* (Oakland, Calif., 1999) • L. F. DeRose, E. Messer, and S. Millman, *Who's Hungry? And How Do We Know? Food Shortage, Poverty, and Deprivation* (New York, 1998) • J. Drèze and A. Sen, eds., *The Political Economy of Hunger* (3 vols.; New York, 1990-91) •

R. GALER-UNTI, *Hunger and Food Assistance Policy in the United States* (New York, 1995) • L. JIMÉNEZ SÁNCHEZ, R. S. MORGENTHAU, and B. PEÑA OLVERA, eds., *Fighting Rural Hunger in a World Full of Grain: South-South Transfer of Village-Level Experience* (Pueblo, Mex., 1988) • P. L. KUTZNER, *World Hunger: A Reference Handbook* (Santa Barbara, Calif., 1991) • L. F. NEWMAN and W. C. CROSSGROVE, *Hunger in History: Food Shortage, Poverty, and Deprivation* (Cambridge, Mass., 1990) • G. RICHES, ed., *First World Hunger: Food Security and Welfare Politics* (New York, 1997) • R. SIDER, *Rich Christians in an Age of Hunger: Moving from Affluence to Generosity* (rev. ed.; Waco, Tex., 1999) • L. YOUNG, *World Hunger* (London, 1997). See also recent annual hunger reports of Bread for the World (Washington, D.C.): *A Program to End Hunger* (2000); *The Changing Politics of Hunger* (1999); *Hunger in a Global Economy* (1998); *What Governments Can Do* (1997); *Countries in Crisis* (1996); *Causes of Hunger* (1995).

GEORG ELWERT

Hus, Jan

Born into poverty in Husinec in southern Bohemia, Jan Hus (ca. 1372-1415) became a significant leader in what has been called the First Reformation. Upon receiving his master of arts degree in 1396, he became professor at Charles University in Prague. In 1402 he began a ten-year pastorate at Bethlehem Chapel, center of the growing reform movement within Bohemia and the symbol of expanding nationalism against the → Roman Catholic Church and the Germans, who exerted the major control at Charles University. This situation inspired a lifelong passion in Hus for moral purity and → truth. His → preaching in the vernacular attracted large crowds to hear sermons that predominately explored the need for morality, especially in reforming the → corruption of the church, urged increased spiritual zeal, and searched the Scriptures for truth. Hus consistently asserted that it was more important to follow Christ and the Scriptures than the pope or tradition. He was responsible for modest liturgical reforms in introducing and expanding congregational participation, translating and writing → hymns in Czech, and a sung mass. The inscription on the Hus monument in Prague's Old Town square bears these words from his *Exposition of the Faith:* "Therefore, O faithful Christian, search for truth, hear truth, learn truth, love truth, speak the truth, hold the truth, defend the truth till death." This passion for uncovering the truth led Hus to make major improvements in the Czech language and to publish the *Orthographia Bohemica.*

Philosophically, Hus favored the → realism of Wycliffe over the prevailing approach of → nominalism. Some 19th-century scholarship, notably of German origin, has erroneously derided Hus as being little more than a carbon copy of the English reformer. Hus expressed greater admiration for Wycliffe's philosophical works than for his works of theology. It is a grievous misunderstanding to see Wycliffe as the sole or even major formative influence upon Hus. Parallel developments within Bohemia had been formulating a national reform movement. While Wycliffe obviously shaped Hus's thinking, Hus was equally inspired by the Czech leaders Jan Milič of Kroměříž (ca. 1325-74), the acknowledged father of the Czech Reformation, and by Matthew of Janov (1355-93), a brilliant NT scholar.

Morally, Hus was incensed by the growing corruption among the clergy. Pope John XXIII's decision in 1412 to fund his war with King Ladislas of Naples through the sale of → indulgences only exacerbated this situation and increased the need for church reform. Drawing upon Pauline and Augustinian principles, Hus understood the church to be a body of those predestined in heaven and earth who believe by faith in Jesus Christ, not a corporation governed by the → pope or councils. For Hus the central focus was internal conviction, not mere outward display. It was for his doctrine of the church more than anything else that Hus was branded a heretic.

After his fourth → excommunication Hus withdrew into exile in southern Bohemia (1412-14), thus allowing the interdict to be lifted from Prague. This heightened crisis led to his most prolific period of writing, as he produced 15 books, including his most mature and radical work, *De ecclesia.* Among his other major writings were "On Simony"; expositions on the → Apostles' Creed, the → Decalogue, and the → Lord's Prayer; plus *Postilla,* a collection of sermons. Hus agreed to attend the Council of Constance (1414-18) once Emperor Sigismund promised safe passage and the opportunity to defend his position. This council was convened to deal with the growing Bohemian heresy and the Great Schism aggravated by the Council of Pisa (1409). Upon arriving, however, Hus was thrown into prison and relocated only when it appeared he would die before the council could consider his case. The trial repeatedly sought for Hus's recantation, which he refused, for to abjure statements falsely credited to him would have been perjury. On July 6, 1415, Hus was convicted as a heretic, degraded from the priesthood, and burned at the stake, singing to his last breath a hymn of praise to God (→ Martyrs).

Hus was a significant reformer and inspirational leader of the First Reformation. Yet he never became a → Protestant, nor was the theological divide as narrow as Luther had assumed between the two reformers. While Hus held to the supreme authority of Scripture and encouraged the practice of Utraquism (from the Lat. phrase *sub utraque specie*, "under each kind"), or receiving both the bread and wine in the Lord's Supper, he maintained the doctrine of transubstantiation and of → purgatory throughout his ministry, as well as encouraging proper veneration of the Virgin → Mary and the saying of special masses for departed souls. Furthermore, for Hus salvation was forged on the anvil of love and necessitated good works, contrary to Luther's emphasis upon divine grace. Additionally, while Hus asserted that one must obey Christ rather than custom or human leaders, he encouraged obedience to the pope and other authorities, provided they were faithful to Scripture. The reforming flame ignited at Constance immediately spread to the nascent Hussite movement as well as inspiring the later Unitas Fratrum, or → Moravian Church.

Bibliography: Primary sources: De ecclesia (trans. D. S. Schaff; Westport, Conn., 1974) • *John Hus at the Council of Constance* (trans. M. Spinka; New York, 1965), an eyewitness acccount • *The Letters of John Hus* (trans. M. Spinka; Totowa, N.J., 1972) • "On Simony" (trans. M. Spinka), *Advocates of Reform from Wyclif to Erasmus* (Philadelphia, 1953) 187-278.

Secondary works: T. FUDGE, "'Ansellus dei' and the Bethlehem Chapel in Prague," *CV* 35 (1993) 127-61 • M. SPINKA, *John Hus: A Biography* (Princeton, 1968) • P. DE VOOGHT, *L'hérésie de Jean Huss* (2d ed.; Louvain, 1975) • E. WERNER, *Jan Hus: Welt und Umwelt eines Prager Frühreformators* (Weimar, 1991) • J. ZEMAN, *The Hussite Movement and the Reformation in Bohemia, Moravia, and Slovakia, 1350-1650: A Bibliographic Study Guide* (Ann Arbor, Mich., 1977).

TOM SCHWANDA

Hussites

1. Background
2. The Four Articles of Prague
3. Legacy

1. Background

Like the → Waldenses, the Hussites were a medieval movement summoning the church back to its original Christian form. The condemnation and burning of Jan Hus (ca. 1372-1415) at the Council of Constance (→ Reform Councils) on July 6, 1415, provoked a national protest in Bohemia that led to the adoption of reforming ideas and the rise of the Hussites.

In 1414 Jacob of Mies, with the approval of Hus, had given the cup to the laity in Prague (→ Eucharist), a departure from custom that became a symbol of the Hussites. The moderate Hussites of Prague thus came to be known as Utraquists (from Lat. *sub utraque specie*, "under each kind") or Calixtines (from their demand for the *calix*, "cup"). The Utraquists found support especially among the nobles and middle class.

South of Prague at Tábor, however, a fellowship arose in 1420 among the lower classes under the leadership of Jan Žižka (ca. 1376-1424) that attempted to live out the primitive Christian model in → poverty and → community of goods. This extreme party of Hussites, which became known as the Taborites, rejected all ecclesiastical customs that were not commanded in God's law (→ fasting, veneration of → saints, → monasticism, → relics, etc.). With their revolutionary social ideas the Taborites combined → apocalyptic tendencies.

2. The Four Articles of Prague

In July 1420 the Utraquists and the Taborites accepted the Four Articles of Prague, a statement formulated by Jacob of Mies (d. 1429) that reflects the essential themes of the Hussites. It would have been accepted by Hus himself.

The first article calls for *freedom of preaching the Word of God*. This point addresses the origin and foundation of the Czech Reformation — Scripture — along with the Hussites' belief that centuries of tradition had layered human accretions over the core doctrines of Christianity. The instrument of renewal was the free preaching of God's Word, from which followed the central concern to translate the Bible, sermons, and hymns into the language of the people. This desire to speak from the Scriptures brought a renewed emphasis upon → truth, which required those who had eyes to see and ears to hear to speak out against the rampant abuses.

The next article defends *Communion in both kinds* (hence "Utraquism"). The Hussites returned the chalice to the laity. While previously the average layperson communicated only once a year, the Hussites stressed a more frequent, even weekly, celebration as more biblical. This second principle reflects many key Hussite concerns.

In withdrawing the chalice, the church authorities had dared to manipulate even the sacramental memory of the death and resurrection of Jesus Christ. The realization that the actual church practice in effect ignored Christ's command to "do this in remembrance of me" scandalized the Hussites. According to Jacob of Mies, "All priests are actually the thieves of the blood of Christ" (Lochman, 81). Furthermore, since Christ's blood is the basis of salvation for all the people of God, it must not become a privilege of a select group of church officials. In the presence of God, all distinctions and barriers collapse. The Hussites took the priesthood of the laity seriously in believing that all are priests at the Lord's Table. For them, the chalice signifies the community of all Christians. Also, eschatological awareness was particularly strong among the Hussites, who celebrated the sacrament as an anticipation and representation of the coming of God's kingdom. Frequently the Eucharist was celebrated on mountaintops (esp. by the Taborites), which further heightened this eschatological sense.

The third article argues for *poverty of the clergy and expropriation of church property.* Priests should live an obedient life based on the apostolic model. Such an attack on the privileged lifestyle of the institutional church was, not surprisingly, staunchly resisted. Hus had often sharply contrasted the life of Jesus as the "poor King of the poor" to the power and wealth of the pope and his church bureaucracy.

The final article demands *punishment of all public sinners;* moral discipline and purity of lifestyle were to be practiced by all citizens, regardless of social class. All Christians need to reflect the law of God in loving God and one's neighbor.

3. Legacy

In 1420 Emperor Sigismund (king of Bohemia 1419-37) initiated a military crusade against the Hussites. Under the brilliant military leadership of Žižka and Prokop Holý (or Procopius the Great, ca. 1380-1434), the Hussites were able to repel all attacks by emperor and pope. As a result the Hussites negotiated with the Roman Catholics on equal terms at the Council of Basel (1431-49), which devised a peaceful solution to the dispute, granting the cup to the Hussites as well as meeting several other demands (in the council's "Compactata"). This agreement divided the Utraquists from the Taborites (who did not agree to the terms reached), which led to the battle of Lipany in 1434, where the moderates decisively defeated the Taborites.

In connection with the work of the radical pacifist Hussite Peter Chelčický (ca. 1390-ca. 1460), the → Bohemian Brethren continued the reforming efforts of the Hussites. Martin Luther (1483-1546) and Thomas Müntzer (ca. 1489-1525), who each looked up the remnants of the Hussites in Bohemia itself, found in the Hussites forerunners of their own attempts to reform the church.

→ Middle Ages 2; Moravian Church; Reformation

Bibliography: Primary sources: J. ERŠIL, ed., *Acta summorum pontificum res gestas Bohemicas aevi praehussitici et hussitici illustrantia* (2 pts.; Prague, 1980) • J. HUS, *Opera omnia* (3 vols.; ed. W. Flajshans; Osnabrück, 1966; orig. pub., 1903-5); idem, *Tractatus de ecclesia* (ed. S. H. Thomson; Prague, 1958) • *Hus in Konstanz. Der Bericht des Peter von Mladenowitz* (trans. J. Bujnoch; Graz, 1963).

Secondary works: W. R. COOK, "The Eucharist in Hussite Theology," *ARG* 66 (1975) 23-35 • R. FRIEDENTHAL, *Ketzer und Rebell. Jan Hus und das Jahrhundert der Revolutionskriege* (Munich, 1972) • T. FUDGE, *The Magnificent Ride: The First Reformation in Hussite Bohemia* (Brookfield, Vt., 1998) • F. HEYMANN, *John Žižka and the Hussite Revolution* (Princeton, 1955) • H. KAMINSKY, *A History of the Hussite Revolution* (Berkeley and Los Angeles, 1967) • J. M. LOCHMAN, *Living Roots of Reformation* (Minneapolis, 1979) • J. MACEK, "Die böhmische und die deutsche Radikale Reformation bis zum Jahre 1525," *ZKG* 85 (1974) 149-73; idem, *The Hussite Movement in Bohemia* (New York, 1958) • A. MOLNÁR, "Die eschatologische Hoffnung der böhmischen Reformation," *Von der Reformation zum Morgen* (ed. J.-L. Hromádka; Leipzig, 1959); idem, *Jean Hus, témoin de la verité* (Paris, 1978) • F. SEIBT, *Hussitica. Zur Struktur einer Revolution* (Cologne, 1965) • F. ŠMAHEL, *Husitská revoluce* (4 vols.; Prague, 1993) • M. SPINKA, *John Hus: A Biography* (Princeton, 1968) • J. ZEMAN, *The Hussite Movement and the Reformation in Bohemia, Moravia, and Slovakia, 1350-1650: A Bibliographical Study Guide* (Ann Arbor, Mich., 1977).

RUTH ALBRECHT and TOM SCHWANDA

Hutterites

The founder of the Hutterites, or the Hutterian Brethren, was Jacob Hutter, an → Anabaptist who was burned at the stake as a heretic in Innsbruck in 1536. He had led a group that practiced the → community of goods along the lines of Acts 2:44.

The Hutterites enjoyed a golden age of development from 1565 to 1592. Every community had a minister of the word, a minister to the needy, and also a → kindergarten and school — all of which continue as features of Hutterite communities. A leader or elder directs the whole community.

Plundering by the Turks and by various armies during the → Thirty Years' War, along with persecutions by the → Jesuits, caused the decimated Hutterites to move to Hungary and later, by way of Transylvania and Walachia, to Russia (1770). When a general draft was introduced in 1871, they moved to North America in three groups between 1874 and 1879. The "Darius people" arrived in 1874, led by Darius Walter; the "*Schmiede* [blacksmith] people," in 1877, led by Michael Waldner, a blacksmith; and the "*Lehrer* [teacher] people," in 1879, led by Jacob Wipf, a teacher.

The Hutterites engage in agriculture with the most modern machinery. The size of their farms averages 3,000 ha. (7,400 acres). Individual members, who are admitted by → baptism between 14 and 18, receive only pocket money. The community as a whole is wealthy. Once the number of members in a community rises above 130, a daughter community is founded, which poses a need for capital.

For the Hutterites, German functions as a religious language, which reduces their contacts with the outside world. In daily devotions and Sunday services they read the addresses and teachings of their 16th- and 17th-century leaders. In their clothes, furniture, and indeed whole lifestyle, simplicity reigns; theologically, they call this value *Gelassenheit* (calmness). Their community is "a pure and holy people separate from the abominations of the world," the ark of God "in which each gives according to ability and receives according to need."

There are now more than 25,000 Hutterites, who live in approximately 200 communities, or "colonies," in the prairie states and provinces of northwest United States and Canada.

In Germany, Eberhard Arnold (1883-1935) adopted the Hutterite tradition when he founded the Rhön-Bruderhof (1927). His community, or Bruderhof, was expelled from Nazi Germany in 1937, with members moving to England, Paraguay, and the United States. In 2000 there were six Bruderhofs in the United States, two in England, and one in Australia. The U.S. group publishes the works of Arnold and like-minded authors under the imprint of the Plough Publishing House.

Bibliography: E. ARNOLD, *Eberhard Arnold: A Testimony to Church Community from His Life and Writings* (2d ed.; Farmington, Pa., 1998) • M. BAUM, *Against the Wind: Eberhard Arnold and the Bruderhof* (Farmington, Pa., 1998) • J. W. BENNETT, *Hutterian Brethren: The Agricultural Economy and Social Organization of a Communal People* (Stanford, Calif., 1967) • *Brothers Unite: An Account of the Uniting of Eberhard Arnold and the Rhön Bruderhof with the Hutterian Church* (Ulster Park, N.Y., 1988) • D. F. DURNBAUGH, *The Believers' Church: The History and Character of Radical Protestantism* (Scottdale, Pa., 1985) • R. FRIEDMANN, *Hutterite Studies* (Goshen, Ind., 1961) • E. GELDBACH, "Der reiche Mann und der arme Lazarus. Kanadisch-japanische Begegnung auf Hutter-Deutsch," *ZRGG* 34 (1982) 347-63 • L. GROSS, *The Golden Years of the Hutterites* (Scottdale, Pa., 1980) • S. HOFER, *Hutterites: Lives, Histories, and Images of a Communal People* (Saskatoon, 1998) • B. S. HOSTETLER and J. A. HOSTETLER, *The Hutterites in North America* (New York, 1995) • W. S. F. PICKERING, *The Hutterites* (London, 1982) • M. K. TOWNE, *Jacob Hutter's Friends: Twelve Narrative Voices from Switzerland to South Dakota over Four Centuries* (Indianapolis, 1999).

ERICH GELDBACH

Hymn

1. OT
2. NT

1. OT

From the time of W. M. L. de Wette and H. Gunkel, the term "hymn" (Gk. *hymnos*, corresponding in part to Heb. *tĕhillâ*) has been used in studies of the Psalms for psalms of praise such as Psalms 8, 19, 29, 33, 46–48, 65, 67–68, 76, 84, 87, 93, 96–100, 103–5, 111, 113–14, 117, 135–36, 145–50, as well as Exodus 15, 1 Samuel 2, Deuteronomy 33, Judges 5, Habakkuk 3, and texts from Amos 4–9 and Isaiah 40–66. Insofar as these passages are not just portions of a larger text but independent texts themselves, a threefold structure may be discerned: (1) introduction or introit, (2) main section or predication, and (3) conclusion or epilogue. There are many variations on this structure.

Special forms and characteristics define a subgroup of "imperative hymns," with the typical *kî* statement in the main part, which is more affirmative than causal (e.g., Exod. 15:21; Psalm 136). As Gunkel saw it, this type arose out of *hallĕlû-yāh* ("praise Yahweh"), the "primary cell of the hymn." Another type is a psalm with a "hymnic participle," a feature common throughout the ancient Near East (e.g., Psalms 104 and 146; F. Crüsemann). Other subgroups include the Yahweh-kingship hymns (47; 93; 96–99) and the Zion hymns (46; 48; 76; 84; 87).

For other groupings, see works by Gunkel and Crüsemann.

Typical stylistic features and forms probably go back to unknown but undoubtedly very varied rhythmic and musical presentations, including choral and solo works (e.g., → litanies like Psalms 29 and 136), liturgies (100), instrumental accompaniment (150), and other types. Such forms correspond to the liturgical needs of the worshiping community. The general function of these psalms is that of invocation and praise. In appellative speech there is a call to respond to the action of God set forth in basic statements and an invitation to participate in celebrating these events (→ liturgy as response). In predicative speech God's → glory (Heb. *kābôd*, Gk. *doxa*) is descriptively represented (C. Westermann's "descriptive praise"). These hymnic statements thus have the character of confession (→ Confession of Faith) and even credo as they set forth the objective side of religion (note the creation hymns Psalms 8; 19; 104; cf. Job 38–39). The widespread recitative use of such hymnic pieces confirms this confessional function.

There are many such hymns in the Psalter, and they are very varied. Thus Psalm 8 hymns the order of creation and humanity's high destiny, while Psalm 19 praises God's majesty in his work and word; Psalm 29 celebrates the epiphany of the Almighty, Psalm 104 expresses astonishment at the system of preservation based on the primal element of water, and Psalm 150 summons to praise of God in a multiplicity of voices: "Let everything that breathes praise Yahweh." The texts all have their own history, but little is known about the history of → hymnody overall in Israel.

→ Literature, Biblical and Early Christian 1

Bibliography: W. Brueggemann, *Israel's Praise* (Philadelphia, 1988) • W. Burkert and F. Stolz, eds., *Hymnen der Alten Welt im Kulturvergleich* (Freiburg, 1994) • F. Crüsemann, *Studien zur Formgeschichte von Hymnus und Danklied in Israel* (Neukirchen, 1969) • E. S. Gerstenberger, *Psalms, Part 1, with an Introduction to Cultic Poetry* (Grand Rapids, 1988) • H. Gunkel and J. Begrich, *Einleitung in die Psalmen* (4th ed.; Göttingen, 1984; orig. pub., 1933) • C. Westermann, *The Praise of God in the Psalms* (Richmond, Va., 1965; orig. pub., 1953).

KLAUS SEYBOLD

2. NT

2.1. In the → worship of the → primitive Christian churches, jubilation at God's gift of end-time → salvation found its clearest expression in praise. In

1 Cor. 14:26 (cf. 14:15) Paul puts the *psalmos* (psalm) first among the elements of worship in the Spirit. In Col. 3:16 (par. Eph. 5:19) we find the two other important LXX terms for spiritual songs used for Christian praise: *hymnos* and *ōdē* (song [of praise]). Acts 2:46-47 and Heb. 13:15 both affirm the central function of praise and thanksgiving, as does also Pliny's account of Christian worship to Emperor Trajan: "They met regularly before dawn on a certain day to chant verses antiphonally among themselves in honor of Christ as if to a god" (*Ep.* 10.96.7). Nor were hymns used only in worship, as may be seen clearly from Acts 16:25 and Jas. 5:13.

2.2. NT hymns were modeled on the praise songs of the OT and later → Judaism. The NT congregations show dependence on both the Psalter and Jewish hymns, such as the Magnificat in Luke 1:46-55. In the case of the Benedictus (Luke 1:68-79), it is debated whether a whole psalm has been adapted, a Jewish hymn (vv. 68-75) has been combined with a Christian part (vv. 76-79), or both parts are Christian in origin.

2.3. Apart from these psalms in the Lukan infancy narrative and the hymnic portions in Revelation, which are literary compositions (K.-P. Jörns), we also find hymns in the narrower sense as independent larger units in John 1:1-18 and the Epistles. They are used here in argument and → parenesis but are not identified as such. Thus it is often uncertain whether larger or smaller hymn fragments are present or to what extent they have been altered in their new context. There is virtual consensus that hymns may be discerned in Phil. 2:6-11; 1 Tim. 3:16; Col. 1:15-20; 1 Pet. 2:21-24; Heb. 1:3(-4), all of which are hymns to Christ. There is also a hymn to God in Rom. 11:33-36, where → Paul rounds off with adoration and praise his account of the mercy of God, which leads Gentiles and Jews to → salvation in spite of their disobedience.

2.4. The hymns to Christ, which were especially important in the development of primitive → Christology (M. Hengel), depict and praise Christ's saving work. The most influential were those that hymned the history of his way as Savior (Phil. 2:6-11 and John 1:1-18; see also Heb. 1:3-4 and 1 Tim. 3:16). Literarily the oldest is the pre-Pauline hymn in Philippians 2. In two strophes (vv. 6-8 and 9-11) the hymn contrasts the self-humbling of the pre-existent Jesus to the lowest depths (→ Kenosis) with his exaltation as Lord over all creatures. We catch a glimpse here of the three modes of Christ's being that made the greatest impact on later Christology, though with differing accents: as he who comes from God, he is the Revealer; as he who became man, he is the Redeemer; and as the exalted, he is the Kyrios, whom all creatures will worship in the final consummation.

Prose insertions conspicuously interrupt the artistic form of John 1:1-18 (see vv. 6-8, 12c-13, 15, 17, 18). The culmination and endpoint of the underlying hymn is the gift of becoming children of God, a gift constituting the goal of the Logos's work in creation and redemption (12b). The congregation responds with the confession in vv. 14, 16: "The Word became flesh and lived among us, and we have seen his glory . . . [and] we have all received, grace upon grace."

→ Benediction; Canticle; Doxology; Literature, Biblical and Early Christian 2

Bibliography: R. DEICHGRÄBER, *Gotteshymnus und Christushymnus in der frühen Christenheit* (Göttingen, 1967) • C. DEMKE, "Der sogenannte Logos-Hymnus im johanneischen Prolog," *ZNW* 58 (1967) 45-68 • M. HENGEL, "Hymnus und Christologie," *Wort in der Zeit* (Leiden, 1980) 1-23 • O. HOFIUS, *Der Christushymnus Philipper 2,6-11* (2d ed.; Tübingen, 1991); idem, "Struktur und Gedankengang des Logos-Hymnus in Joh 1,1-18," *ZNW* 78 (1987) 1-25 • K.-P. JÖRNS, *Das hymnische Evangelium* (Gütersloh, 1971) • R. J. KARRIS, *A Symphony of NT Hymns: Commentary on Philippians 2:5-11, Colossians 1:15-20, Ephesians 2:14-16, 1 Timothy 3:16, Titus 3:4-7, 1 Peter 3:18-22, and 2 Timothy 2:11-13* (Collegeville, Minn., 1996) • R. P. MARTIN, *A Hymn of Christ: Philippians 2:5-11 in Recent Interpretation and in the Setting of Early Christian Worship* (Downers Grove, Ill., 1997); idem, "Hymns in the NT," *ISBE* 2.788-90 • J. T. SANDERS, *The NT Christological Hymns* (Cambridge, 1971) • G. SCHILLE, *Frühchristliche Hymnen* (Berlin, 1965) • K. WENGST, *Christologische Formeln und Lieder des Urchristentums* (2d ed.; Gütersloh, 1973).

GERT JEREMIAS

Hymnal

1. Europe
   1.1. Germany, Lutheran
   1.2. Calvinism and Western Europe
   1.3. Scandinavia and Eastern Europe
   1.4. Roman Catholic Church
2. Anglo-American Sphere
3. New Hymnals

Today, the term "hymnal" refers in general to any collection of congregational songs intended primarily for use in the public → worship service. Such collections are the creation of reforming movements, especially in the early 16th century. In the → Reformation period hymnals frequently bore such titles as Enchiridion, Spiritual Songs, or (in the Calvinist tradition) Psalter or Psalms of David. Since the mid-18th century "hymnal" has been the common designation in both Roman Catholic and Protestant circles. Hymnals employ one of three basic formats: melody with text, text only, or full music edition (i.e., text plus parts for several voices).

1. Europe

1.1. *Germany, Lutheran*

1.1.1. We find the beginnings of hymnals in the lay brotherhoods of the late 15th century. The St. Ursula Brotherhood printed a first song in Strasbourg in 1481, and the (Bohemian) → Moravian Brethren published the first hymnal in 1501. The → Reformation, too, began with individual pieces that were then collected (*Achtliederbuch* [Nürnberg, 1524]).

The move toward collections with a specific orientation (often described in the preface) led to the hymnal. Thus two Erfurt enchiridions (handbooks), with almost the same contents, appeared in 1524 as the first hymnals designed to be carried by "every Christian so that these spiritual songs and psalms can be practiced and meditated upon at any time" (from the title page). Wittenberg produced a choral hymnal in 1524 (J. Walter, preface by M. → Luther) and a congregational hymnal in 1526 (H. Lufft).

1.1.2. Luther (1483-1546) helped in the development of hymnals up to 1545, with hymnals appearing in many different places beginning in 1525. Most of them copied the first Erfurt and Wittenberg hymnals in structure and contents, which were themselves basically alike. Often, however, the texts and tunes were not authentic, with doubtful material being added. In J. Klug's Wittenberg hymnal of 1529, for which he wrote a new preface, Luther attempted to set a new direction in selection, version, and arrangement, all of which, in the Wittenberg sphere of influence, was largely successful. V. Schumann added an appendix (Leipzig, 1545), which became a common way of cautiously expanding the tradition. The hymnal of V. Babst (also published in Leipzig in 1545), with "a new preface" by Luther himself, was the climax of the Wittenberg tradition during Luther's own lifetime.

Beginning with the 1529 Klug edition, the arrangement in these hymnals was always the same: first Luther's hymns (arranged according to the → church year, → catechism, metrical psalms, other hymns and liturgical pieces), then other Reformation hymns, pre-Reformation hymns, biblical psalms, and other spiritual hymns "composed by devout Christians." Additions included Luther's burial hymns (1542), then also (similarly since 1529) collects, versicles, → psalms, and → canticles (some for several voices) for family and congregational worship. Most hymnals thus far usually also contained melodies or indicated previous or familiar tunes. G. Rhau of Wittenberg brought out a new choral book in 1544 closely related to that of Babst. Newer types developed such as the Strasbourg and Constance hymnals, as well as the German hymnals of the Bohemian Brethren (the first by M. Weisse in 1531).

1.1.3. From the middle of the 16th century to the end of the 17th, Babst's arrangement and contents pointed the way. Territorial churches now took the initiative instead of publishers (who had often worked with theologians), now granting publishing licenses and controlling the official introduction of new hymnals. Private initiative concentrated on collections of individual authors (e.g., J. Heermann in 1630, J. Rist from 1641) or composers (e.g., J. H. Schein in 1627, J. Crüger in 1640), who from the end of the 16th century published simple choral works in *Cantionalia,* to which they later added a harmonic key (figured bass).

The next step was hymnals with figured bass for home use that complemented the text with melodies and bass lines. J. Crüger (1598-1662) of Berlin did pioneering work with his new hymnal of 1640. His *Praxis pietatis melica* of 1647, which went through several expanded editions, was a primary source for most of the hymns of P. Gerhardt (1607-76).

1.1.4. From the end of the 17th century on, → Pietism and its "springtime of hymns" introduced a new and enduring type that made the older family hymnal a book of devotion for individuals and groups. To be noted here are a hymnal by J. A. Freylinghausen (1704), one for the Moravians by N. L. → Zinzendorf (1700-1760) and C. Gregor (1723-1801), and a hymnal by J. Porst (published anonymously in 1708, reprinted from 1711 to 1908). The last hymnal had no musical notation — a common practice from the middle of the 17th century. At this time organists began using special choral books as sources for melodies.

1.1.5. To a large extent, even officially, → rationalism led to the replacement of the traditional orthodox hymnal by a pedagogical hymnal that engaged in ruthless modernization with new versions and compositions. Its loss of biblical substance and tradition sharply altered → piety and the character

of worship, most radically perhaps in S. Diterich's *Lieder für den öffentlichen Gottesdienst* (Berlin, 1765).

1.1.6. The 19th-century restoration sought to hold the line by reverting to the pre-Pietist hymnal. E. M. Arndt (1769-1860) showed the way in his programmatic work *Von dem Wort und dem Kirchenliede* (1819). With the striving for national unification came the call for a united interconfessional German hymnal. The draft at a conference at Eisenach was not followed up, however, and it was only after World War I that some territorial churches moved in this direction, using a foreign hymnal from 1915 as the basis.

In 1937 a completely new hymnal was planned, under the direction of C. Mahrenholz (1900-1980) and O. Söhngen (1900-1983). This hymnal was completed after World War II and since 1950 has been in use in most German and Austrian churches. It follows clearly the Reformation pattern in both contents and structure. It emerged from movements of musical renewal between the wars, but both the modern period and material from ecumenical sources are underrepresented.

1.1.7. Beginning in 1994 and after years of preparation, a new standard hymnal replaced the older one in the Evangelical Church in Germany. This new hymnal addresses the devotional needs of individual Christians and house churches as well as traditional worship services and other parts of congregational life. It contains not only church hymns but also shorter songs (often in canon form), liturgical songs, prayers, and confessions (including one for the Psalter arranged for call and response), as well as considerably more hymns from the 19th and 20th centuries. Similarly, foreign hymns from the global → oikoumene have also finally been incorporated into the German Protestant hymnal (in German translation, often with the addition of the text in the original language). As did the earlier hymnal, so also this new one consists of a basic section applicable to all territorial churches as well as regionally specific sections.

1.2. *Calvinism and Western Europe*
Up to the end of the 16th century the hymnals in German-speaking Switzerland were based on the Constance hymnal of 1540 and followed the traditions of German Lutheranism. J. → Calvin (1509-64), however, took a completely different path in Geneva. Because he allowed only biblical texts, especially the Psalms, the Reformed hymnal became a Psalter. The first such hymnal, which appeared in 1539 during Calvin's exile, contained 18 psalms as well as the Nunc Dimittis, the → Decalogue, and the

creed, all in verse form. In later editions (from 1542 in Geneva) there were more psalms, and all the psalms by 1562. The French texts of C. Marot and T. → Beza, with tunes by G. Franc, L. Bourgeois, and P. Dagues, became canonical and the standard on which other translations were based. The German hymnal of the Lutheran A. Lobwasser (1573) became the standard until it was replaced in 1793 by the work of M. Jorissen with new psalms.

Dathen's Dutch translation of the Geneva Psalter similarly replaced W. van Nievelt's *Souterliedekens* and was itself replaced in 1773. The *Gesangbundel*, with some free compositions (usually from the German), appeared in 1807. After a revision in 1938 the interconfessional *Liedboek voor de Kerken* was introduced in 1973, which contained mostly revised texts and new compositions.

In German-speaking Switzerland the hymnal of 1952 revived the independent local tradition. In 1998 a new hymnal for the Reformed Churches of German-speaking Switzerland was introduced, closely related to the contemporaneous Catholic hymnal for the German-speaking Catholic Church of Switzerland and to the hymnal for the Swiss Old Catholic Church. It represented the fruits of the Study Group for Ecumenical Hymns (AÖL).

In French Protestantism a Psalter from 1938 was reintroduced in 1979 with psalms and hymns *(Louange et Prière)*.

From Reformed Pietism came J. Neander's *Bundeslieder* (1680) and G. Tersteegen's *Geistliches Blumengärtlein* (1727).

1.3. *Scandinavia and Eastern Europe*

The first hymnal in northern and eastern Europe was that of the Danish reformer H. Tausen (1494-1561) in 1544. H. Thomisson's *Danske Psalmebog* of 1569 was later supplemented by liturgical and devotional materials (note T. Kingo's *Aandeligt sjunge kor* of 1674 and 1681). In 1699 Kingo's *Gradual* replaced Thomisson's hymnal and pursued a style modeled on the spiritual aria. A Pietist hymnal appeared in 1740, and in 1852 N. F. S. → Grundtvig (1783-1872), Denmark's greatest hymnal reformer, published *Psalmebog*. In 1953 the reforming efforts of T. Laub resulted in a thorough revision.

In Sweden the brothers Claus and Lorenz Petri made the first collection, and Lorenz published a full hymnal in 1569. Other important hymnals included a Pietist hymnal in 1695, a rationalist hymnal in 1819, one in 1937, and an interconfessional hymnal in 1986.

Norway had its own hymnal only after separating from Denmark (from 1869). In Finland the Latin *Piae cantiones* came out in Greifswald (1582).

Sweden published a proposal for a new hymnal in 1983, as did Finland in 1984. Iceland has had its own hymnal since 1972. Poland published a Protestant hymnal abroad in Königsberg around 1544. A Reformed Psalter came out in Kraków in 1558, and a Lutheran hymnal in a new edition in 1976. In the Czech Republic and Slovakia there have been various hymnals since the Reformation. In Hungary Reformed and Lutherans share a common hymnal.

1.4. *Roman Catholic Church*

Whereas one can hardly speak of a hymnal in the → Orthodox Church, the → Roman Catholic Church since the 16th century has tried to promote popular singing by regional hymnals. The first was that of M. Vehe (Leipzig, 1537). A notable achievement was the hymnal of J. Leisentritt in 1567. The German-speaking bishops produced *Gebet- und Gesangbuch* in 1975. *Gotteslob* reveals a new Catholic understanding of the hymnal, from the fostering of popular piety (→ Popular Religion) to a congregational "role book" in keeping with the reforming impulses of → Vatican II. Similar developments may be noted in other countries (concerning Switzerland, see 1.2 above).

→ Calvinism; Choir; Gradual; Hymn; Hymnology; Liturgical Books; Liturgy; Mass; Prayer 4

Bibliography: General: C. ALBRECHT, *Einführung in die Hymnologie* (pt. C; 2d ed.; Berlin, 1984) • *JLH* (1955-).

Bibliographies: K. AMELN, M. JENNY, and W. LIPPHARDT, eds., *Das deutsche Kirchenlied. Kritische Gesamtausgabe der Melodien* (2 vols.; Kassel, 1975-80) • W. BÄUMKER, *Das katholische deutsche Kirchenlied in seinen Singweisen* (4 vols.; Hildesheim, 1962; orig. pub., 1886-1911) • A. FISCHER, *Das deutsche evangelische Kirchenlied des 17. Jahrhunderts* (vol. 6; Hildesheim, 1964; orig. pub., 1916) • P. WACKERNAGEL, *Bibliographie zur Geschichte des deutschen Kirchenliedes im 16. Jahrhundert* (Hildesheim, 1961; orig. pub., 1855) • J. ZAHN, *Die Melodien der deutschen evangelischen Kirchenlieder aus den Quellen geschöpft und mitgeteilt*, vol. 6, *Chronologisches Verzeichnis der benutzten Gesang-, Melodien- und Choralbücher* (Hildesheim, 1963; orig. pub., 1893).

Articles and monographs: H. C. DRÖMANN, "Grundsätze für die Arbeit an einem neuen Gesangbuch," *MuK* 50 (1980) 166-75 • H. GLAHN, "Melodistudier til den lutherske Salmesangshistorie fra 1524 til ca. 1600" (2 vols.; Copenhaven, 1954) • K. HLAWICZKA, "Zur Geschichte der polnischen evangelischen Gesangbücher," *JLH* 15 (1970) 169-91 • M. HOBERG, *Die Gesangbuchillustration des 16. Jahrhunderts* (2d ed.; Baden-Baden, 1982; orig. pub., 1933) • M. JENNY, *Geschichte des deutschschweizerischen evangelischen*

Gesangbuches im 16. Jahrhundert (Basel, 1962) • C. Mah-
renholz, Das evangelische Kirchengesangbuch. Ein
Bericht über seine Vorgeschichte (Kassel, 1950); idem,
"Gesangbuch," MGG 4.1876-89 • T. Schulek, "Kurzer
Abriß der Geschichte des ungarischen Kirchengesang-
buchs und des Standes hymnologischer Forschung in
Ungarn," JLH 14 (1968) 130-40 • J. Stalmann,
"Gotteslob evangelisch. Zur Frage einer Theologie des
neuen Gesangbuchs," MuK 65 (1995) 246-55 • A. Wan-
tula, "Das neue polnisch-lutherische Kirchen-
Gesangbuch," JLH 16 (1970) 199-201.

JOACHIM STALMANN

2. Anglo-American Sphere

The first English hymnal was Miles Coverdale's
Goostly Psalmes and Spirituall Songes (ca. 1535),
which included the first attempt to introduce the
German chorales in English translation. Soon
banned by Henry VIII (1509-47), English congregational song continued to draw almost exclusively on
T. Sternhold and J. Hopkins's Psalter (1562) and
later the "New Version" of N. Tate and N. Brady
(1696). By the turn of the 18th century a new epoch
of congregational song arose, principally through
the influence of Isaac Watts, an English → Dissenter,
who was instrumental in loosing the ties of congregational song to psalmody. His Horae lyrica (1705)
but especially his Hymns and Spiritual Songs (1707)
and The Psalms of David Imitated (1719) remain
monuments to the man who is called the father of
English → hymnody.

The work of John → Wesley and Charles Wesley,
especially their hymnals A Collection of Psalms and
Hymns (Charlestown, S.C., 1737; another under the
same name published in London in 1738) and
Hymns and Sacred Poems (1739), were important
contributions to the Evangelical hymnody of the
day, as was John Newton and William Cowper's
Olney Hymns (1779), the last of a group of hymns
that sought to bring Evangelical hymnody within
the Church of England without any accommodation to the → Book of Common Prayer.

The 1830s saw the beginning of the so-called →
Oxford (or Tractarian) Movement in England,
which decisively affected the future development of
hymnody. John Keble's Christian Year (1827) and
John Mason Neale's many translations from the
Greek and Latin Office hymns and sequences that
appeared in The Hymnal Noted (1851) were joined
by other translations by Edward Caswall (Lyra
Catholica [1851]) and Catherine Winkworth (Lyra
Germanica [1855]), greatly enriching the English
repertoire from the early church and from Reforma-

tion times. This movement reached further fruition
with the publication of Hymns Ancient and Modern
(1861), a landmark collection in the history of English hymnals. The early 20th century saw the publication of several important English hymnals, the
most important of which were The English Hymnal
(1906) and Songs of Praise (1925).

The first book of any kind published in America
was the Bay Psalm Book (1640). Early American
hymnody was shaped primarily by the Psalter tradition, including the Psalters that the early settlers
brought with them from their homelands, such as
the Ainsworth Psalter (Amsterdam, 1612). Early
American "singing schools" produced many important collections, among them James Lyon's Urania
(1761) and the various publications of William Billings, including The New England Psalm Singer
(1770), The Singing Master's Assistant (1778), The
Psalm Singer's Amusement (1781), Suffolk Harmony
(1786), and Continental Harmony (1794).

American hymnody in the 19th century was significantly affected by the development of the
camp-meeting song in numerous collections and by
the southern "shape-note" tradition, which produced such collections as Kentucky Harmony
(1817), Southern Harmony (1835), and Sacred Harp
(1844). The → gospel song tradition, which is associated with the revivals of the later 19th and early
20th centuries, also contributed countless collections to American hymnody.

In general, the immigrants who came to the
United States in the 18th and 19th centuries
brought with them the hymnals of their homelands
in their native languages — German, Norwegian,
Swedish, Danish, and other languages. By the 20th
century, however, most groups had made the transition to an English-language hymnody. The 1960s in
both England and America saw the beginning of the
rise of popular musical styles in hymnody, much of
it criticized as deficient in both texts and music; this
development has had relatively little effect on the
contents of denominational hymnals published in
the intervening years.

From the 1960s to the present, most → denominations in North America have issued new or newly
revised hymnals for their constituencies. Among the
more important of these recent collections are Lutheran Book of Worship (1978), Lutheran Worship
(1982), The Hymnal 1982 (Episcopalian), Worship
(Roman Catholic; 3d ed., 1986), The United Methodist Hymnal (1989), and Presbyterian Hymnal
(1990). In addition, significant books have been
produced by → Moravians, → Mennonites, the

United Church of Christ, and a number of other churches in both the United States and Canada.

Bibliography: L. F. BENSON, *The English Hymn: Its Development and Use in Worship* (New York, 1915; rev. ed., 1962) • F. BLUME, *Protestant Church Music: A History* (New York, 1974; orig. pub., 1965) • L. ELLINWOOD, ed., *Bibliography of American Hymnals* (New York, 1984) • H. ESKEW and H. T. MCELRATH, *Sing with Understanding* (Nashville, 1980) • J. JULIAN, *A Dictionary of Hymnology* (2 vols.; New York, 1937; orig. pub., 1907) • W. REYNOLDS and M. PRICE, *A Joyful Sound: Christian Hymnody* (New York, 1978).

CARL SCHALK

3. New Hymnals

An explosion of new hymns and songs has resulted in the production of many new hymnals. The hymns come in all styles, although the main influence is still the traditional → hymnody of the West. Poets have created new texts using familiar hymn meters and using familiar tunes for congregational singing accompanied by a keyboard. New melodies, often with popular rhythms, are transforming old words. Most often new words are put to new tunes, with guitars, synthesizers, and drums providing the instrumental support. In places that can afford them, hymnals remain the most common means for congregational participation in singing its faith.

Although the predominance of Western → missionary hymns is not broken, increasingly hymns in styles appropriate for their own culture are being created and sung. Particularly lively are the songs from Africa, with their vibrant and often complicated rhythms. The pattern of leader-response is common, which encourages improvisation by both the leader and the assembly. The Africans have led the way in bringing → dance into worship, not as an art form but as an expression of community. Unfortunately, most hymnals are lacking the basic instructions necessary to help congregations and congregational leaders know how to move. In some cases companions to the hymnals and audio tapes have filled this gap.

The popularity of the African → Independent Churches, the struggle toward independence from → colonialism, and the fight against apartheid have brought African music into the former missionary churches. A first attempt to put some of this music into notation was a collection in 1987 called *Africa Sings* (vol. 2), produced by the → All Africa Conference of Churches. A badly needed new version of this hymnal has long been in the planning but not yet produced. Much has now been notated, however, and become available in the North, even if not so much in Africa itself. One major difficulty is that the notation freezes a song, which in its original African context is often passed on orally with great fluidity. Another is the difficulty of transcribing the complexity of African rhythms in a way that is not daunting for congregational use. A third problem is the need to produce materials in Africa in tonic sol-fa notation, the method used there.

With all the new songs available now in Latin America, new hymnals are kept from being produced only by the lack of funds. The liturgy network of the → Latin American Council of Churches keeps encouraging the production of new songs. Each Assembly of that ecumenical organization brings out a new worship book complete with new songs. With its mixtures of cultures (indigenous, African, and European), the music appears with a variety of rhythms and instruments. This series builds on the work that for many years has come out of Instituto Superior Evangélico de Estudios Teológicos (ISEDET), the ecumenical seminary in Buenos Aires. Their series *Cancionero abierto* broke new ground. In Brazil a collection edited by Jaci Maraschin, *O novo canto da terra* (1987), brought many new rhythmic Brazilian songs into a hymnal with a simplified piano accompaniment to give a hint at the rhythm.

In the Caribbean, the → Caribbean Conference of Churches produced *Sing a New Song* (1981). This hymnal appeared with a version with piano accompaniment and, for some hymns, four-part harmony, and also a words-only edition. Unfortunately, with the exception of a couple of very popular Caribbean hymns, this hymnal has not become widely used in the Caribbean churches themselves. Lois Kroehler has edited a hymnbook in Spanish for Cuba, *Toda la iglesia canta* (1989), combining traditional Western hymns with new hymns from Cuba and the rest of Latin America.

The → Christian Conference of Asia, in cooperation with the Asian Institute for Liturgy and Music (Manila), has produced *Sound the Bamboo* (1990), edited by I-to Loh and others. It is the largest and most comprehensive compilation of songs in the wide variety of Asian musical languages. The use of ornaments, microtones, and differently tuned scales marks much of the music. There is an extensive introduction to help the uninitiated into the correct style, as well as an accompanying tape. Most of the songs have transliterated lyrics with a guide to pronunciation. Although Asian churches continue to look to the West for the bulk of their singing, composers are providing alternatives that increasingly find a place. Gongs, all kinds of drums, *ching* (a kind of finger cymbal), and marimbas accompany and give character to the music, much of which is sung without harmony. (A common Western distortion of this music is to add Western harmony.) New hymnals have been produced by the Lutherans in Hong Kong (1992) and by the Kyodan, the United Church of Christ in Japan (1997). The latter has a fine collection of new Japanese hymns, many moving outside traditional Western patterns.

Two particular places in Europe have had a profound influence on the use of music in worship, and both have produced music books. The → Iona Community in Scotland has often put new words to Celtic folk songs. Iona demonstrates that musical inculturation in worship was also useful in the West. The → Taizé Community in France has developed a whole body of short repetitive pieces, many in Latin or in a range of translations. Jacques Bertier, who wrote much of this music, was a master of finding simplicity that does not yield to boredom even after the 30th repeat. Taizé brought a new mysticism to church music. Both Iona and Taizé are widely represented in the new hymnals around the world.

In both North America and Europe many denominations have developed new hymnals within the last 20 years. Of particular note are those in Sweden and Scotland, which have been produced ecumenically. The Scottish book, *Common Ground* (1998), is accepted for use by the major confessions, including the Roman Catholics. In Sweden two-thirds of the basic hymnal, *Den svenska psalmboken* (1986), contains common songs. Separate editions fill the remaining third with music particular to each confession. In Germany each of the Landeskirchen has produced a new hymnal, although most share a common core. The edition by the Evangelical Lutheran Church in Bavaria and Thuringia is particularly innovative, for it is designed for private or family devotion as well as for congregational use. It includes many → prayers, but also notably many pages of art. The sections are color coded for easy use.

The influence of the → women's movement has provided one of the greatest impulses for new hymnals in North America. If new images of God were going to enter the human consciousness, they needed to be sung. The *New Century Hymnal*, produced in the United States by the United Church of Christ (1995), is the hymnal that has taken this challenge most seriously.

Other issues or needs have produced new texts and tunes in the major new hymnals. The common lectionary has inspired some songs connected to the biblical lessons of the day. New concerns for justice and the → environment, along with a new sense of community, have found their place in hymnals. More choices for weddings, baptisms, healing services, and Communion have been included. Almost all the major denominations have produced new hymnals since the 1980s. The *Lutheran Book of Worship* served as a uniting factor in the creation of the Evangelical Lutheran Church of America (1988). A Spanish-language hymnal, *Libro de liturgia y cántico*, produced for the same church in 1998, is one of the first to have an appendix with notes on Latin American rhythms along with notation for a variety of instruments appropriate for each style. *Voices United* (1996), the hymnal of the United Church of Canada, includes many new Canadian hymns.

Most new hymnals have at least a few songs that cross cultural and stylistic boundaries, and many include significant contributions from other parts of the world. This change in content proclaims the wonder and gift of the diversity of music that God has given the church. The global meetings of the → World Council of Churches (WCC) with their worship books and also those of international church groups have furthered the use of music from many cultures and languages and have demonstrated their potential utility within the liturgy. These hymnals build on the initial work in *Cantate Domino* (1974), produced by the WCC, and *Laudamus* (the most recent edition in 1984), by the Lutheran World Federation. Mission agencies of larger churches have begun publishing songs from a variety of cultures as part of mission education, most of them being accompanied by CDs. The largest compilation of songs from around the world, *Thuma mina: Singing with our Partner Churches. An International Ecumenical Hymnbook* (1995), has been edited by Dieter Trautwein, Beatrice Aebi, Johanna Linz, and Dietrich Werner. Although it was produced for Germany and Switzerland, it keeps the original language and often other translations as well.

Many parts of the church do not use hymnals. In some traditions the music for the congregation is so well known that books are unnecessary. Orthodox churches would be an example, as well as those churches in predominantly oral cultures. In many settings, books are too expensive for mass use. In the West another phenomenon leads to the disuse of hymnals. New technology allows words or sometimes words and music to be flashed on screens in front of the congregation. This change signals more than just a stylistic trend, for in this format songs for worship do not come from a bound repository of collected musical faith but arrive for the congregation according to current need and local taste.

The influence of the → charismatic movement and Pentecostal churches with their choruses and gospel songs, and with their connection to the music industry, have made this practice a powerful (although in some circles an unwelcome) force. It remains to be seen whether modern technology will lead to the demise of hymnals as we have known them for the last four centuries.

Bibliography: Hymnals mentioned: *Africa Sings / L'Afrique chante* (Nairobi, 1987) • *Cancionero abierto* (Buenos Aires, 1982) • J. C. MARASCHIN, ed., *O novo canto da terra* (São Paulo, 1987) • P. PRESCOD, ed., *Sing a New Song* (Bridgetown, Barbados, 1981) • L. C. KROEHLER, ed., *Todo la iglesia canta* (Havana, 1989) • F. FELICIANO, I. LOH, and J. MINCHIN, eds., *Sound the Bamboo* (Manila, 1990) • *Hymns of Praise* (Hong Kong, 1994) • *Hymnbook 21* (Tokyo, 1997) • *Common Ground: A Song Book for All the Churches* (Edinburgh, 1998) • *Den svenska psalmboken* (Stockholm, 1986) • *Evangelisches Gesangbuch–für Gottesdienst, Gebet, Glaube, Lehre* (Munich, n.d.) • *New Century Hymnal* (Cleveland, 1995) • *Lutheran Book of Worship* (Philadelphia and Minneapolis, 1978) • *Libro de liturgia y cántico* (Minneapolis, 1998) • *Voices United: Hymn and Worship Book of the United Church of Canada* (Etobicoke, Ont., 1996) • *Cantate Domino* (Geneva, 1974) • *Laudamus: Hymnal for the Lutheran World Federation* (Geneva, 1984; orig. pub., 1952) • D. TRAUTWEIN, B. AEBI, J. LINZ, and D. WERNER, eds., *Thuma mina: Singing with Our Partner Churches. An Intnal Ecumenical Hymnbook* (Basel and Hamburg, 1995).

Additional hymnals and other sources: Alleluia *Aotearoa: Hymns and Songs for All Churches* (Christchurch, N.Z., 1993) • *A.M.E.C. Hymnal* (African Methodist Episcopal Church) (Nashville, 1984) • *The Book of Praise* (Presbyterian Church in Canada) (Don Mills, Ont., 1997) • *Cantate all'eterno un cantico nuovo* (Federation of Evangelical Churches in Italy) (Rome, 1994) • *The Chalice Hymnal* (Christian Church–Disciples of Christ) (St. Louis, 1995) • *The Divine Liturgy* (Orthodox Church in America) (Crestwood, N.Y., 1982) • *Ghana Praise: Tunes from Ghana, Africa, and the World* (Accra, 1979) • P. HARLING, *Hela världen sjunger* (Stockholm, 1997) • *Holy Cross Liturgical Hymnal* (Greek Orthodox Archdiocese of America) (Brookline, Mass., 1988) • *Hymnal: A Worship Book, prepared by Churches in the Believers Church Tradition* (Elgin, Ill., Newton, Kans., and Scottdale, Pa., 1992) • *Hymns Ancient and Modern: Revised* (Norwich, 1981; 1st ed., 1861) • *Hymns and Psalms* (Baptist Union, British Methodist Conference, Church of England, Churches of Christ, Congregational Federation, Methodist Church in Ireland, United Reformed Church, Wesleyan Reform Union) (London, 1983) • *Ina Pepese la* (Apia, Western Samoa, 1986) • *The Presbyterian Hymnal: Hymns, Psalms, and Spiritual Songs* (Louisville, Ky., 1990) • *Psaumes. Cantiques et textes pour le culte* (Swiss Reformed Churches, French) (Monthey, Switz., 1976) • *Rejoice and Sing* (United Reformed Church) (London, 1991) • *Sing Alleluia: A Supplement to the Australian Hymn Book* (Blackburn, Victoria, 1987) • *Songs for a Gospel People: A Supplement to the Hymn Book of 1971* (Winfield, B.C., 1987) • *Songs of Zion* (United Methodist Church) (Nashville, 1981) • *Teimbiitezimbuka* (Evangelical Lutheran Church in Namibia) (Ondangwa, 1993) • *Tuomaslauluja* (Helsinki, 1991) an ecumenical hymnal • *United Methodist Hymnal–Book of United Methodist Worship* (Nashville, 1989) • *With One Voice: A Lutheran Resource for Worship* (Minneapolis, 1995) • *World Praise: Jubilate Hymns* (London, 1993).

TERRY MACARTHUR

Hymnody

1. Antiquity
   1.1. Hellenism
   1.2. Non-European Cultures
   1.3. OT
2. Early Church
   2.1. NT
   2.2. Early Christian Worship
   2.3. Syriac and Armenian Hymns
   2.4. Greek Hymns
   2.5. Latin Hymns
3. Roman Catholic Hymns
4. German Hymns
5. Scandinavian Hymns
6. Reformed Hymns
7. Britain
8. United States
9. Canada
10. Other Places
   10.1. China and Southeast Asia
   10.2. Australia and New Zealand
   10.3. Africa
   10.4. Caribbean, Central and South America
   10.5. Eastern Europe
11. Ecumenical Aspects
12. Recent Developments

1. Antiquity
1.1. *Hellenism*

→ Hellenism produced a variety of monodic and choral songs in honor of gods and heroes, as well as individual and group epic narratives, incantations, and marriage songs, sometimes combined with → dance when in a liturgical context. Later refinement led to hymns in three forms: paean (e.g., a hymn to Apollo), dithyramb (e.g., a hymn to Dionysus), and liturgical → processions. The tripartite form of the Homeric hymn greatly influenced the development of classical Greek poetry and is also reflected in the hymns in the Hebrew Psalms. Until Proclus (5th cent. B.C.) the instrumental accompaniment was by kithara (stringed instrument), aulos (woodwind), syrinx (panpipe), or kalamos (reed-pipe, flute). Hymns functioned in old and new cultic → rites and in the revival of festivals in the second century B.C., which were replete with libation and sacrifice.

1.2. Non-European Cultures

A significant repertory of hymns and hymnic performance practice have come from non-Western sources, including (1) Mesopotamian hymns dating from 1200 B.C.; (2) ancient Indian Vedic hymns of offering and sacrifice from the Rig-Veda (modified in Sama-Veda performance practice) that some date as early as 4000 B.C., though most date them about 1500 B.C. (→ Hinduism); (3) Buddhist hymns (→ Buddhism); (4) the Gatha songs or hymns in the Zoroastrian Avesta (→ Iranian Religions 7); (5) Egyptian hymns to Amon-Re and Akhenaton's Great Hymn to Aton (ca. 1300 B.C.); (6) Islamic liturgical chanting of the Koran, the teachings of Muḥammad (ca. 570-632; → Islam); (7) Chinese hymns extant as early as the T'ang dynasty (618-907) and imitated in the 13th-century Chin Twelve Hymns; and (8) a Korean hymn of thanks to Confucius dating from the 14th century A.D.

1.3. OT

Important OT hymns include the tripartite hymn in Exodus 15:1-18 and the great collection of hymns in the Psalter (e.g., Psalm 100 or 117), an opening festival hymn of praise quoted by → Paul in Rom. 15:11 (→ Hymn 1), and the Hallel (Psalms 113-18), sung or recited at the Passover meal, one of which may have been sung by Jesus and the disciples as they left the Last Supper (Mark 14:26 and par.).

2. Early Church

2.1. NT

The psalmody of Jewish synagogue and household worship is thought to be linked with Christian → worship.

2.2. Early Christian Worship

NT hymns contain Christological and → apocalyptic descriptions and → metaphors, whose overall style maintains both Hellenistic poetic form (e.g., 1 Tim. 3:16) and Semitic/Hebrew characteristics of parallelism and accentual rhythm (→ Hymn 2).

Many writers consider these hymns to have formed part of the earliest catechetical instruction. Hymns and hymn-singing with the Psalms, particularly those with messianic content, became the essential components of early Christian worship and → proclamation.

2.3. Syriac and Armenian Hymns

The Eastern worship-song is the precious link (cf. Eric Werner's [1901-88] Sacred Bridge) between Jewish and Christian traditions of Scripture-song, prayer, and praise. Creating and singing hymns to teach doctrine and celebrate the incarnation of God in Christ are a distinctive feature of Eastern worship, which began in NT and patristic times and culminated in the elaborate, varied, and complex repertory of Byzantine classic hymnody.

Syrian hymnody has recently been identified and evaluated as a distinct body of literature. Ephraem Syrus (ca. 306-73), author of "The Pearl: Seven Hymns on the Faith," is considered the father of Eastern hymnody. The hymnody of the Armenian church probably stems from Syriac sources beginning in the 5th century. Most of the 1,200 hymns written since the 12th century are arranged chronologically in the Sharakan (Hymns), the traditional collection of Armenian hymns.

2.4. Greek Hymns

Four periods of Greek hymnody have been identified.

2.4.1. The first is the Gnostic-Hellenistic, beginning with the Paedagogus of Clement of Alexandria (ca. 150-ca. 215) and the second-century Didache (→ Apostolic Fathers 2.1). Greek hymns of this period often reflect preaching and teaching to converts against the excesses and contradictions of apocalyptic and → Gnostic teaching.

2.4.2. The Judeo-Hellenistic period (late 3rd through 5th cent.) saw a return to Hebrew metaphor and biblical story. The Apostolic Constitutions (late 4th cent.) includes many hymns of this period. One example is the anonymous third-century evening hymn Phos hilaron, "O gladsome light, pure brightness." The fifth-century Codex Alexandrinus lists 14 canticles that were performed by a soloist, the congregation responding. Other forms of Greek hymnody of the period are the troparion, short prayers troped between verses of a psalm, later composed in strophic form, and the kontakion, made up of between 18 and 30 troparia connected by an acrostic. During this period the Coptic and Ethiopian churches, their unique oral chant repertory, and instruments such as the sistrum (a kind of rattle), still used in Ethiopian Orthodox churches and Fellasha synagogues, were separated from the Eastern church.

2.4.3. Next was the *Syrian-Hellenistic* period, which saw the flowering of Greek hymnody with the development of the contrapuntal canon.

2.4.4. Finally was the period of *iconoclasm and schism* (9th to 14th cent.; → Heresies and Schisms), an unproductive time marked by the decline of the empire. The iconoclasts destroyed many ancient hymn MSS.

The 1,500-year proliferation, development, and expansion of this body of hymnody in the many languages of Eastern liturgies, and their prominence in those liturgies, is unprecedented in pre-Reformation hymnody. Two aspects of its repertory and performance practices — Christological hymns and responsory psalmody — were taken into early Western hymnody and are perpetuated in its worship song and hymnic literature.

2.5. *Latin Hymns*

Early Latin hymns were composed in defense of orthodoxy against the preaching and hymn singing of the Arians (→ Arianism). The encyclopedist Isidore of Seville (ca. 560-636) considered Hilary of Poitiers (ca. 315-ca. 367) the first significant hymn writer, followed by his prominent and influential contemporary Ambrose of Milan (ca. 339-97), who is thought to have incorporated the style of the simple and direct Syrian doctrinal hymns in the 18 iambic Office hymns often attributed to him. Hymns came into use in monastic worship centered on the seven canonical hours. → Benedict of Nursia (ca. 480-ca. 547; → Benedictines) made the practice compulsory, and it spread to other → orders. The monastic worship-song included Office hymns and other early doctrinal hymns (e.g., the *Te Deum*), plus the Psalter, which was usually recited or sung in one week. The musical settings of early Western hymns and the Psalms are thought to be some form of chant.

By the 9th century the growth of → monasticism, combined with the Carolingian liturgical reforms, increased the need for hymns reflecting the monks' contemplative, otherworldly, and often mystical lifestyle (→ Contemplation; Mysticism), culminating in the 12th century in the writings of Bernard of Cluny, Bernard of Clairvaux, and Peter Abelard. In Germany → Hildegard of Bingen (1098-1179) wrote hymns and sequences for the worship of her communities. Other contributions of Latin hymnody are the topical hymns for feasts, festivals, processionals, saints days, feasts of the Virgin Mary, and the sequence. Hymns were admitted into the → Mass in the 12th century. Medieval and Renaissance composers made polyphonic settings of chant hymns; the earliest source with several settings is Codex Apt (ca. 1400). Italians composed *Laudi*, popular songs in the vernacular, including Francis of Assisi's (1181/82-1226) "Cantico de le creature comunemente de lo frate Sole" (Canticle of the sun).

3. Roman Catholic Hymns

→ Roman Catholicism, responding to the popular appeal of → Reformation hymnody, published two hymnals, M. Vehe's (ca. 1480-1539) *Ein neue Gesangbuchlein Geistlicher Lieder* (1537) and J. Leisentritt's (1527-86) *Geistliche Lieder und Psalmen* (1567). Efforts toward simplicity and singability resulted in diocesan hymnals (e.g., the *Paris antiphoner* of 1681). At a later time in England, following the reestablishment of the Roman → hierarchy in 1850, the needs of parish worship and the influence of the Anglican Tractarians initiated a distinctively Anglo-Roman hymnody (illustrated by F. W. Faber's [1814-63] hymn "Faith of Our Fathers"; → Hymnal 1.4).

4. German Hymns

Martin → Luther (1483-1546; → Luther's Theology), musician and articulate writer, translator, and preacher, in shaping the chorale used (1) the sequence and Office hymn, such as "Veni, Creator Spiritus" ("Komm, Gott Schöpfer"); (2) the *Leisen*, which integrated, for example, the pre-Reformation folk hymn "Christ ist erstanden" and the Latin sequence "Victimae paschali laudes" to form "Christ lag in Todesbanden"; (3) Latin songs such as "In dulci jubilo"; (4) contrafacts, for example using the melody of "Aus fremden Landen" for the setting of "Vom Himmel hoch da komm ich her"; and (5) original texts (hymns and psalms in metrical paraphrase) and tunes. Poets and composers of this period, influenced by the Meistersingers, used the bar form "Stollen, Stollen, Abgesang" (essentially AAB), as in "Ein' feste Burg ist unser Gott," to enhance the memorable qualities of the texts. Rhythmic, vigorous, and memorable unison tunes were composed to be sung without accompaniment, sometimes alternately by choir and congregation. Johann Walter (1496-1570), Luther's musical colleague who served as compiler and editor of early collections of chorales, contributed both original melodies and adaptations of old tunes.

Two decades after Luther's death a second generation of poets turned toward a more devotional and reflective style, illustrated by P. Nicolai's (1556-1608) "Wachet auf, ruft uns die Stimme" and "Wie schön leuchtet der Morgenstern." L. Osiander (1534-1604) simplified the earlier vocal style, *con-*

trapunctum simplex, into the popular song style by placing the principal melody in the upper voice and, in performance, allowing all possible combinations for choir, → organ, instruments, and congregation.

In the period 1618-48 hymns of the cross and of consolation were composed, many of which became masterpieces of devotional poetry, such as P. Gerhardt's (1607-76) "Befiehl du deine Wege." Major and minor keys replaced the earlier church modes, and the rhythmic chorale was replaced by the isometric chorale. In the baroque period, hymnody drew new impulses from Pietists J. Neander (1650-80), G. Tersteegen (1697-1769), and N. L. von → Zinzendorf (1700-1760), among others. Important collections of this period are J. A. Freylinghausen's (1670-1739) *Geistreiches Gesangbuch* (1704) and *Neues Geistreiches Gesangbuch* (1714) and G. C. Schemelli's (1680-1762) *Musikalisches Gesangbuch* (1738), with J. S. Bach (1685-1750) as music editor. Orthodoxy was championed by B. Schmolck (1672-1737) and E. Neumeister (1671-1756), the latter a cantata lyricist for Bach. Melody was increasingly influenced by the more lively solo-aria.

Hymns and chorales from 18th-century → rationalism include M. Claudius's (1740-1815) "Wir pflügen und wir streuen" and C. F. Gellert's (1715-69) "So jemand spricht: Ich liebe Gott." This hymnody featured the rational-religious recasting of classic hymns, isometric melodies, and melodic reworking.

The confessional revival of the 19th century (→ Confession of Faith) expanded the hymnic repertoire through the influence of the awakening movement, mission, and retrospective confessional reflections (e.g., K. J. P. Spitta [1801-59], "O komm, du Geist der Wahrheit," and A. Knapp) (1798-1864), through the initial adoption within the German-speaking sphere of hymns deriving from the Anglo-Saxon movement of awakening, hymns that in their own turn were being spread worldwide, and through the tradition of free church hymnody. Efforts also were being made to unify the collection of hymns (e.g., by E. M. Arndt [1769-1860]) and to recover the original versions. J. Zahn's (1817-95) six-volume *Melodien der deutscher evangelischen Kirchenlieder* (1889-93) traces nearly 9,000 tunes and their variants. Hymnic research in the 20th century was advanced by K. Ameln (1899-1994), M. Jenny, and P. Harnoncourt. German-language hymns in North American hymnody are discussed in A. Haeussler (1891-1967), *The Story of Our Hymns,* and in M. Stulken, *Hymnal Companion to the Lutheran Book of Worship.*

Hymnic renewal in the 20th century affirmed the choral movement of the period between the 1920s and 1940s with its retrospective on Reformation hymns, melodies, and structures of the 16th and 17th centuries, and newer hymns that in their own turn drew from these and earlier traditions (e.g., J. Klepper's [1903-45] *Geistliche*). This development led to the strict selection and restoration of hymns in the Protestant hymnal of the 1950s. Hymns from the Kirchentag (church conference) movement, including D. Trautwein's pop and folk-derived songs, provide the first really viable alternatives to the classic hymn. The melodies of H. W. Zimmermann and R. Schweitzer represent learned, academic counterparts to this lighter music. On the whole, the texts depart from the traditions of → Pietism and turn instead to concern for the earth, the → environment, and to nonviolent alternatives to → conflict (→ Force, Violence, Nonviolence). The Protestant hymnals of the 1990s, for example, the Swiss *Evangelisch-reformiertes Gesangbuch* (1998), are increasingly pluralistic and ecumenical, yet maintain a core of traditional hymns and chorales. Translations of recent British, American, and global hymns have been added to the repertory, including those of H. Handt.

5. Scandinavian Hymns

In the 19th and 20th centuries Scandinavian hymnody, which was profoundly influenced by the Lutheran chorale tradition, developed into two distinct streams: (1) Danish, Norwegian, and Icelandic; and (2) Swedish and Finnish, each with remarkably unique features. The revitalization of Scandinavian hymnody is reflected in the recent hymnals of Norway (*Norsk salmebok* [1980]), Iceland (*Sálmabók* [1997]), Sweden (*Den svenska psalmboken* [1986]), and Finland (*Virsikirja* [1986]). The supplements *Salmer* (Norway, 1997) and *Psalmer i 90-talet* (Sweden, 1994) include a wider range of music from many cultures around the world. Important contributions have been made by composers S.-E. Bäck (1919-94) and E. Hovland (b. 1924); poets O. Hartmann (1906-82), B. G. Hallqvist (1914-97), A. Frostenson (b. 1906), and S. Ellingsen (b. 1929); and contemporary composer/poets P. Harling and T. Boström.

6. Reformed Hymns

A second stream of Reformation hymnody — metrical psalmody, a by-product of the reforms of M. Bucer (1491-1551) and others — emerged in the 1520s in Strasbourg, Basel, Zurich, and parts of Germany and became identified with the Genevan liturgy of John → Calvin (1509-64), who limited congregational song to the unaccompanied, unison singing of metrical paraphrases of the Psalms, the Lord's Prayer, the Song of Simeon (Nunc Dimittis), and the → Decalogue (→ Calvin's Theology). Calvin enlisted the services of poets C. Marot (ca. 1497-1544) and T. → Beza (1519-1605), who composed metrical paraphrases in a variety of meters. Composers L. Bourgeois (ca. 1510-after 1561) and C. Goudimel (ca. 1510-72) carefully crafted modal and rhythmic tunes for Calvin's Psalters with no apparent reference to plainsong, the chorale, or folk melodies. Calvin published five Psalters from 1539 to 1562, culminating with *Les Psaumes mis en rime, françoise, par Clement Marot et Théodore Bèz* (the so-called Genevan Psalter), which included 150 psalms, the Ten Commandments, and the Song of Simeon composed in 110 meters and set to 125 different tunes.

In France and the southern areas of the Low Countries, psalm singing was identified with religious descent; in the latter a Spanish royal decree banned their singing. In the northern provinces, where Calvinism flourished, the Genevan texts were translated into Dutch and sung to the original tunes. Goudimel and others in France and the Netherlands composed thousands of arrangements of Genevan psalm tunes for voices and instruments, and later for organ, intended to be performed outside the church. These efforts culminated in Jan Sweelinck's (1562-1621) florid motet-style settings of all the Genevan psalms in four volumes (1604-21). Metrical psalm singing was brought to southeast Europe by the spread of Calvinism, especially to Hungary. Dutch traders and settlers brought it to Australia, Indonesia, South Africa, Canada, and to the area of the later United States, where it was introduced by four groups: French Huguenots who settled in Florida, Dutch Reformed settlers in New York, English colonists in Jamestown, and English separatists (Pilgrims) who, after some time in exile in the Netherlands, settled in Massachusetts. The last group produced the *Bay Psalm Book* (1640), the first book of any kind published in British North America.

7. Britain

English metrical psalmody began with translations of Lutheran psalms in M. Coverdale's (1488?-1569) *Goostly Psalmes and Spirituall Songes* (ca. 1535), probably used as devotional reading. The first attempt at English-style metrical psalms, perhaps influenced by Reformed exiles from France and the Low Countries, was by T. Sternhold (d. 1549), who included 19 in his *Certayne Psalmes chosen out of the Psalter of David . . .* (London, ca. 1547), whose work was expanded by J. Hopkins (d. 1570) in *Al such*

psalmes of David . . . (London, 1549). Their texts were set in ballad meter, called common meter (8.6.8.6), which distinguished them from multi-metered Genevan Psalters. Clergy exiled during the reign of Mary Tudor (1553-58) issued a complete Psalter in Geneva, *One and fiftie Psalmes of David in Englishe metre . . .* (1556), called the Anglo-Genevan Psalter. At the beginning of the reign of Elizabeth (queen 1558-1603), the exiles returned and, after much debate, published a basic Psalter that was unrivaled for nearly a century and a half, *The Whole Book of Psalmes . . .* (1562), popularly known as the Old Version.

Within a century the extensive publication of Psalters for public worship had established psalm singing as the norm of English congregational song. The repertory and performance practice of psalm singing developed in very dissimilar places and circumstances, including the Chapel Royal, → cathedrals, parish churches, abbeys, and college chapels.

Genevan-style psalmody was brought to Scotland by J. → Knox (ca. 1513-72). The Anglo-Genevan Psalter was reprinted and revised in Edinburgh in 1564, with additional psalms added from the 1562 English Psalter. The definitive *Psalmes of David in Prose and Meeter* was published in 1635.

By the mid 17th century the Book of Common Prayer (BCP) and the King James Version (1611) of the Bible (→ Bible Versions) constituted the language base for future hymn writing. T. Ken (1637-1711) and S. Crossman (1624-83) both wrote hymns, J. Cosin (1594-1672) translated *Veni, Creator Spiritus,* and in 1623 O. Gibbons (1583-1625) composed tunes for *Hymnes and Songs of the Church,* the metrical paraphrases of Scripture and the hymns of G. Whither (1588-1667). N. Tate (1652-1715) and N. Brady (1659-1726) published *New Version of the Psalms of David* (1696), including in its *Supplement* (1710) six hymns for Christmas, Easter, and Holy Communion. Isaac Watts (1674-1748) transformed English Protestant congregational song from strictly psalmody to a mixture of psalmody and hymnody. Watts Christianized the Psalms, wrote them in the language of the day, and established the practice, common among English Evangelicals in the early 18th century, of paraphrasing sermons and key biblical words, phrases, and images into congregational hymns that were easily learned and sung.

The greatest figure in English hymnody of the mid and late 18th century was John → Wesley (1703-91), who translated, compiled, edited, and distributed hymns and hymn tune collections. While serving in the American colony of Georgia as a missionary priest, John compiled his *Collection of Psalms and Hymns* (1737), the prototype of the modern English hymnal, which included translations from Freylinghausen's *Geistreiches Gesangbuch* and *Neues Geistreiches Gesangbuch,* English metrical psalms, and devotional poetry. John's brother Charles (1707-88), the most prominent hymn writer of the 18th century as a whole, lyrically expressed in hymns the revival's themes of salvation, universal love, perfection, justification by faith, and assurance. In the Wesleyan interplay of preaching and song, hymn singing was at once the confession of → dogma and an act of → piety, → prayer, and → liturgy. Variants of Wesleyan-style hymn singing developed in urban hospital chapels (e.g., in foundling hospitals), where it was led by choirs, keyboard, and instruments. Also there were recitals of operatic-style solo settings with keyboard (e.g., J. F. Lampe's [ca. 1703-51] *Hymns on the Great Festivals and Other Occasions* [1746]).

Not until 1821 was hymn singing officially sanctioned for Anglican worship (→ Anglican Communion), but already in the previous century Evangelical hymns had made inroads into parish worship by way of the Anglican hymn writers J. Newton (1725-1807) and W. Cowper (1731-1800) and the Moravian J. Montgomery (1771-1854). R. Heber (1783-1826), in his *Hymns Written and Adapted to the Weekly Services of the Year* (1827), prepared the first Evangelical hymnal that was arranged topically and doctrinally. In other settings, urban reform and charity missions, temperance societies, the YMCA, and the Salvation Army sang cause-oriented marching songs and choruses that are precursors of the gospel song.

In its search for the "Catholic roots" of the Anglican Church, the → Oxford Movement posed the first significant challenge to almost a century of Evangelical hymnody. Hymns were written about the → church, its → mission, and its → sacraments. Also many Greek and Latin hymns were translated, for example, by J. M. Neale (1818-66), and plainsong melody was introduced, albeit in four-part harmony. During this period German hymns were translated as well, notably by Christina Rossetti (1830-94). *Hymns Ancient and Modern* (1861; ed. H. W. Baker, musical ed. J. Barnby) was the culmination of Anglican hymnic activity and became the most popular English-language hymnal.

The English Hymnal (1906) is the most important literary and musical reaction to the inbred popular and comfortable Victorian worship practice, and the most influential single volume of English hymns for use in Anglo-Catholic worship. Its content of plainsong, Roman Catholic hymn tunes, carols, folk tunes, and hymn tunes by R. Vaughan Williams (1872-1958), who was musical editor and author of the remarkable preface, C. H. Parry (1848-1918), C. V. Stanford (1852-1924), C. Wood (1866-1926), G. Holst (1874-1934), and J. N. Ireland (1879-1962), with new texts and translations by M. Bridges (1800-1894) and general editor P. Dearmer (1867-1936), was imitated by *Songs of Praise* (1925) and mainly similar denominational hymnals appearing during the next half century in Great Britain and the United States. Important commentators on English hymnody include J. Julian (1839-1913), L. Benson (1855-1930), P. Dearmer, M. Frost (1888-1961), J. Wilson (1905-92), and E. Routley (1917-82), also R. A. Leaver, A. Luff, N. Temperley, and J. R. Watson.

The mid-1960s saw a hymnic explosion whose texts demonstrate the shift in the language base away from the KJV and BCP toward the metaphors and descriptions contained in recent translations of the Bible and revisions of the language of liturgy. They reflect also the impact of 20th-century science and technology. They name the church as servant and its people as pilgrims in a world whose environment as well as the human family faced extinction. They show the influence of → Vatican II and other gestures of Christian → unity depicting the → sacraments, particularly the → Eucharist, in a global and ecumenical setting. Geoffrey Beaumont's (1903-70) *Twentieth Century Folk Mass* (1957), Sydney Carter's (b. 1915) quasi-folk hymns such as "Lord of the Dance," and the Light Church Music Group's *Eleven Hymn Tunes* (1957) made pop-style music a viable alternative to traditional worship music. The Dunblane Consultations and Workshops (1962-67) identified and developed multistyle hymn writers and composers who fashioned a modest but influential repertory of texts and tunes. Evangelical Anglicans such as M. A. Baughen (b. 1930) and M. A. Perry (1942-96) formed the Jubilate Hymns Trust, a group of writers and composers. The Church of Scotland and the → Iona Community produce ecumenical and global hymnals and recordings. Roman Catholic hymnals also reflected the explosion, beginning with *New Catholic Hymnal* (1970) and *Sing a New Song to the Lord* (1970).

The period's most important and articulate influences were J. Wilson and E. Routley, who linked the "hymnic explosion" in Great Britain with the "hymnbook explosion" of the 1980s in North America. Representative hymn and song writers of the explosion were A. Bayly (1901-84), F. P. Green (b. 1903), T. Dudley-Smith, F. Kaan, and B. Wren.

Composers of hymn tunes such as P. Cutts and M. Williamson have used traditional as well as 20th-century compositional technique.

8. United States

African American spirituals and other religious songs, the gospel hymn, and the Social Gospel hymn are the unique contributions of the United States. Early U.S. hymnody falls into three periods. The first covers 1620-1721, from the Pilgrims' earliest settlement to the *Bay Psalm Book,* the publication of the first standard tune book. The second, 1721-93, saw the rise of the singing schools, shape-note notation, the fuguing tune, and finally the publication of the earliest U.S. tune still in common use, "Coronation." William Billings (1746-1800) was the foremost composer of this period. The third runs from 1793 to 1861, an era that saw the widespread use of precursors of the gospel hymn: spiritual songs and choruses from the camp meetings of the Great Awakening, folk and shape-note hymnody, and the songs and songbooks of the → Sunday school, → Salvation Army, → YMCA and YWCA, and temperance movement.

Over a period of 250 years African American slaves in colonial America and the rural South developed a variety of work and freedom songs and spirituals. W. F. Allen, C. P. Ware, and L. M. Garrison's *Slave Songs of the United States* (1867) was one of the first attempts to transcribe the melodies of this oral tradition into standard musical notation. Many of the 113 texts are rendered in dialect, with commentary and sources. The bulk of this distinctive religious song remained in the oral tradition, expressed and taught in African American worship; only recently have African American denominational hymnals included them in any great number. In the 1870s spirituals plus freedom and work songs were arranged for the Fisk Jubilee Singers, who performed this music around the world. In the mid-20th century arranged spirituals entered the standard vocal and choral repertory.

Early in the 20th century the urban black gospel hymn was originated by the Philadelphia Methodist preacher C. A. Tindley (1851-1933) and by composer T. A. Dorsey (1899-1993), who pioneered a distinctive gospel performance style. Liberation themes and improvised style set it apart from the 19th-century "white" gospel hymn. The black spiritual and gospel hymn were sung by blacks and whites in the antiwar and → civil rights movements of the 1960s. Roman Catholic and Protestant publishers have produced African American supplements to their hymnals, including *Songs of Zion* (1981), edited by J. Cleveland (1937-86) and V. Nix

(b. 1933), whose work W. F. Smith (1941-97) continued in *The United Methodist Hymnal* (1989).

In the era of Reconstruction (ca. 1870) P. P. Bliss (1838-76) and I. Sankey (1840-1908) styled the gospel song with its repetitive music and words to complement the urban revival preaching, in the United States and Great Britain, of D. L. → Moody (1837-99; → Revivals 2.1). Many of the simple, singable, and memorable harmonies, rhythms, and melodies are styled after the military march, the waltz and other dance steps, the popular parlor ballads and minstrel songs of S. C. Foster (1826-64), and the camp-meeting choruses, folk hymns, and traditional melodies of the expanding American frontier. The most prolific writers and composers of gospel songs include F. Crosby (1820-1915), W. Bradbury (1816-68), and W. Doane (1832-1915). Western missionaries brought the gospel song to Asia and the Americas, where it remains the most characteristic and popular congregational song of evangelical Protestantism.

The third contribution of American hymnody is the Social Gospel hymn, whose precursors are abolitionist hymns and hymns formed from the works of poets such as J. G. Whittier (1807-92) (e.g., "Dear Lord and Father of Mankind"), hymns of pastor-poet Unitarians such as E. H. Sears (1810-76) ("It Came upon the Midnight Clear" and S. Longfellow (1819-92) ("Holy Spirit, Truth Divine"), Congregationalist W. Gladden (1836-1918) ("O Master, Let Me Walk with Thee"), Methodist F. M. North (1850-1935) ("Where Cross the Crowded Ways of Life"), and Episcopalian W. R. Bowie (1882-1969) ("O Holy City, Seen of John"). The 20th-century Social Gospel hymn is grounded in the writings and teachings of W. Rauschenbusch (1861-1918), whose book *Christianity and the Social Crisis* (1907) was the manifesto for the theological reconstruction of the mainline church, including its worship, mission, education, and hymnody. Social Gospel hymns by W. P. Merrill (1867-1954) ("Rise Up, O Men of God"), H. E. Fosdick (1878-1969) ("God of Grace and God of Glory"), and H. H. Tweedy (1868-1953) ("O Spirit of the Living God") became the marching songs of liberal Protestantism.

The hymnic explosion in Great Britain tended to obscure the work of less prolific but skilled U.S. writers such as F. B. Tucker (1895-1984), C. Daw, R. Duck, G. Grindal, and J. Vajda; hymn tunes by D. Damon, W. Dirksen, C. Doran, C. Hampton, M. Haugen, R. Hillert, D. Hurd, J. Marshall, R. Proulx, W. Rowan, and C. Schalk; pop-style ballads and songs by R. Avery and D. Marsh; and neogospel songs by W. Gaither, J. Peterson, and D. Rambo. A recent development in mainline hymnals is a significant increase in Anglo-American frontier folk hymns and spirituals, the Reconstruction era and African American gospel hymns, the charismatic chorus and Scripture song, praise and worship hymns, and songs and hymns from African American, Hispanic, Native American, and Asian American sources. During the past two decades nearly all denominations have produced new or revised hymnals, and in some instances their supplements.

The People's Mass Book (1964) was the first Roman Catholic hymnal to reflect the liturgical and language changes initiated at the Second Vatican Council. Among recent hymnals that reflect an increased ecumenical hymnic repertory and breadth of musical styles — including, for example, the rounds and choruses sung in the → Taizé Community and the psalm settings of J. Gelineau (b. 1920) — we should note *Worship* (1985), *Gather* (1988, 1994), and *Glory and Praise* (3d ed.; 1997).

Principal commentators on U.S. hymnody include R. McCutchan (1877-1958), A. Haeussler, F. Gealy (1894-1976), J. V. Higginson (1896-1994), and L. Ellinwood (1905-94), plus E. Brink, A. Clyde, M. Costen, H. Eskew, R. Glover, D. Hustad, A. Lovelace, D. Music, M. Oyer, W. Reynolds, P. Richardson, J. Spencer, M. Stulken, P. Westermeyer, D. Yoder, and C. Young.

9. Canada

Canadian hymnody has undergone a transformation in style and content beginning roughly in the 1980s, as well as demonstrating an increasing confidence and self-reliance, coupled with an ability to produce significant congregational song. This development is due in part to the rise of Canadian writers such as M. Clarkson (1915-98) and T. H. O'Driscoll, plus composers, including H. B. Cabena, who are well represented in major hymnals in North America and the United Kingdom. Recent Canadian hymnals include *The Catholic Book of Worship* (1994), *Voices United* (1996), and *Common Praise* (1998). *If Such Holy Song: The Story of the Hymns in the Hymn Book* (1971), by Stanley Osborne (1907-98), and Lionel Adey's *Class and Idol in the English Hymn* (1988) rank with the best hymnological research and commentary.

10. Other Places

10.1. *China and Southeast Asia*

The first pandenominational Chinese hymnal was *Putian songzan* (Hymns of universal praise, 1936; rev. ed., 1977; Eng. ed., 1981), with music editor B. Wiant (1895-1975). It contains 678 selections, including 62 indigenous hymns and 72 Asian melodies with Western harmonies. In 1983 the Three-Self Patriotic Movement of Protestant Churches (→ China 2), Shanghai, published *Zanmei shi ximbian* (New hymns of praise; Chinese-English ed., 1998), which by 2000 had distributed 22 million copies. Many hymnals are published in Hong Kong by denominations and private presses to be distributed in Chinese-language communities throughout the world, such as *Huaren shengsong* (Chinese praise, 1992). The first representative source for pan-Asian hymns was the *EACC Hymnal* (Tokyo, 1964), compiled by D. T. Niles (1908-70) and J. M. Kelly. Its successor, *Sound the Bamboo* (Manila, 1990, rev. 2000), edited by I-to Loh, includes a greatly expanded repertory and instructions for performance practices.

Other recent South Asia hymnals include Cambodian collections in Khmer; examples are *Christian Missionary Alliance Hymnal* (1993), with 229 translations of Western hymns with their tunes and 298 indigenous hymns and melodies, many composed by Sarin Sam; *CCM Hymnal* (1986), for Malaysian churches; *Laotian Hymns* (1985); *Thai Indigenous Hymns* (1984); *Madah bakti* (1982), an Indonesian Roman Catholic hymnal; and *Mazmur dan kidung jemaat* (1995), with 478 selections, including 100 indigenous hymns and 150 psalm settings, many by Louis Bourgeois. I-to Loh has compiled and edited a number of collections of indigenous and global hymns for Taiwanese churches, including *Hoan-lok ko-siong 1* (Rejoice and sing 1, 1992) and *Ban-bin siong-chan* (All peoples praise, 1995). Filipino hymnals include *Alawiton sa pagtao* (Songs of faith; ed. E. Maquiso), *Imnaryong pilipino* (Filipino hymnal, 1990), and *Ang pilipino himnal* (The Filipino hymnal, 1995). Indian hymnals include *Sacred Hymns in Marathi* (1930) and *Tamil Christian Lyrics* (1932), both with recent tune editions, and the recent *Christian Lyrics and Songs of Life* (1988).

The Korean/English Hymnal (1989), prepared by Methodists, is widely used elsewhere in Korean-language communities, including those in the United States. Recent collections include *Chanyong chanyong* (Praise, praise, 1991) and *Heenyonul uihan norae* (Songs for Jubilee, 1991, texts by Goh Jung-hee, music by Lee Geonyong). U.S. Korean Methodists produced a Korean/English hymnal in 2000. In Japan the United Church hymnal *Sambika 21* (The hymnal 21, 1997), with 580 selections, is the successor to previous editions in 1954 and 1967, and to *Tomo ni utaoo* (Let's sing together, 1976) and the children's *Sambika* (Songs of praise, 1987).

10.2. *Australia and New Zealand*

The hymnals of mainline churches in Australia and New Zealand, once dominated by Anglican-style words, music, and performance practice, now include a variety of musical styles as well as indigenous hymns. Recent Australian hymnals include the ecumenical *Australian Hymn Book* (1977), published elsewhere as *With One Voice* (1978-79), and its supplement, *Sing Alleluia* (1987), each with noteworthy companions by Wesley Milgate (1918-99); the Presbyterian *Rejoice!* (1987) and *Reformed Book of Worship* (1990); and from New Zealand, *With One Voice, New Zealand Supplement* (1982) and the indigenous *Alleluia Aotearoa: Hymns and Songs for All Churches* (ed. J. Murray). New Zealand composer C. A. Gibson and hymn writer S. E. Murray have made significant contributions to Australian, New Zealand, U.S., Canadian, and U.K. hymnals. The predominately Western hymnals of Pacific Rim churches (e.g., in Fiji and Samoa) include some indigenous hymns with folk performance practices.

10.3. *Africa*

The hymnals and hymnic performance practices of African churches were basically Anglo-European until the 1960s and 1970s, when Western missionaries, ethnomusicologists, and their African students encouraged the use of indigenous music in African-style liturgies. Among the first collections from the mid-continent were *Tamale Orders and Hymns* (ed. T. Colvin), *Tunes of Nyasaland* (comp. H. Taylor), and *Africa Praise* (1969). African independence movements sang and danced call-and-response pan-African liberation songs and Christian hymns accompanied by traditional instruments, hand clapping, and body movement. A significant number of indigenous hymns and hymnals have appeared, and congregational song is increasingly styled after tribal practices. The first ecumenical hymnal was *Africa Sings* (1987). Other recent collections include *Sing Freedom! Songs of South African Life* (comp. M. Hamilton), *Let Us Walk This Road Together* (comp. T. Colvin), and *Africa Praise Songbook* (comp. P. Matsikenyiri).

10.4. *Caribbean, Central and South America*

In the 16th and 17th centuries Roman Catholic missionary priests in the Caribbean and in Central and South America taught native Indians the Roman-Spanish liturgy and Western musical notation, style, form, and vocal technique. Some encouraged the collecting and performance of their indigenous religious folk expressions, including dance instruments. Typical of indigenous religious folk hymns are the *alabados* (songs of praise), sung in village churches, and the *corito* (praise and Scripture chorus), often accompanied by tambourine, maracas, drums, and guitar. While gospel hymns and choruses brought by Protestant missionaries remain the most characteristic song of Haitian-, Portuguese-, and Spanish-speaking evangelical Protestants, new songs have been composed in these languages to be sung using indigenous instruments and performance practices.

Roman Catholic and Protestant hymn writers from the Caribbean, the Americas, and Spain have recently composed hymns of liberation and hope, including W. Soto (1935-96); P. Sosa, compiler of the six-volume *Cancionero abierto* (Open Songster, 1974-90), S. Monteiro, and S. Chávez-Melo (1944-92); and C. Gabaraín (1936-91). Recent Caribbean collections include *Caribbean Hymnal* (1980), *Responsorial Psalms* (1984), *Sing a New Song 3* (1981), and *Caribbean Praise* (1999, ed. G. Mulrain, featuring calypso-style melodies). Latin American hymnals include *Cantemos, Hermanos, con Amor* (1985), *Canções de rua* (1992), and *Abierto* (1993). A number of U.S. publishers have produced collections of Spanish-language hymnals and supplements, such as *Flor y canto* (1989), *Mil voces para celebrar* (1996, ed. R. M. Martínez), and *Himnario y libro de adoración* (1999, ed. R. Gutiérrez-Achon).

Songs from Asia, Africa, the Caribbean, and Latin America are included in ecumenical collections such as *Cantate Domino* (1974), *Many and Great: Songs of the World Church* (vol. 1, 1990), *Worshipping Ecumenically* (1994), *Thuma mina* (1995), and *Global Praise 1 & 2* (1996-2000).

10.5. *Eastern Europe*

After the end of the cold war, most Eastern European churches began to reprint hymnals published in the early 20th century. Others have published new hymnals, including Baptists (ca. 1991), Korean Methodists (1993), and Lutherans (1995). Methodists in Russia and Lithuania are completing work on their first hymnals since early in the 20th century.

11. Ecumenical Aspects

Research in indigenous hymns is expressed in recent companions to hymnals, the work of the three hymn societies, Hymn Society in the United States and Canada, Hymn Society in Great Britain and Ireland, and Internationale Arbeitsgemeinschaft für Hymnologie (→ Hymnology), and → World Council of Churches consultations and workshops on indigenous hymnody that precede their assemblies. Prominent leaders of global song include J. Bell, C. M. Hawn, S. T. Kimbrough Jr., I-to Loh, T. MacArthur, P. Matsikenyiri, and P. Sosa.

12. Recent Developments

An increasing effort is being made by hymnal editors and revision committees to modify archaic expressions and traditional descriptions and forms of address to both people and deity. We also find a much broader selection of themes, now including liberation, → ecology, → peace, justice (→ Righteousness, Justice), the human → family, and the world Christian church as servant in the world (→ Ecumenism, Ecumenical Movement). Hymnic research, for example *The Hymn Tune Index* (comp. N. Temperley, 1998), and *HymnQuest* (project chair A. Luff, 2000), is increasingly produced on CD-ROM, and accessible from Internet Websites. Licensing local churches to allow copying of copyrighted hymns has expanded authors' and publishers' income with no apparent letup of churches' insatiable appetite for (and the ability to purchase) new hymnic products. In many places the traditional performance practice of singing thick didactic texts from hand-held hymnals has given way to choruses and Broadway-style songs voiced from throw-away word sheets and fleeting images on screens.

→ Cantata; Canticle; Church Year

Bibliography: L. F. BENSON, *The English Hymn: Its Development and Use in Worship* (Richmond, Va., 1962; orig. pub., 1915) • W. BLANKENBURG, *Der gottesdienstliche Liedgesang der Gemeinde* (vol. 4; Kassel, 1961) • E. R. BRINK, ed., *Psalter Hymnal Handbook* (Grand Rapids, 1998) • M. W. COSTEN, *African American Christian Worship* (Nashville, 1993) • F. FORMAN, ed., *The New Century Hymnal Companion* • M. FROST, *English and Scottish Psalm and Hymn Tunes, ca. 1543-1677* (London, 1953); idem, ed., *Historical Companion to Hymns Ancient and Modern* (London, 1962) • R. GLOVER, *The Hymnal 1982 Companion* (4 vols.; New York, 1990-96) • C. M. HAWN, "The Tie That Binds: A List of Ecumenical Hymns in English Language Hymnals Published in Canada and the United States since 1976," *Hymn* 48/3 (1997) 25 • J. JULIAN, *A Dictionary of Hymnology* (2d ed.; 2 vols.; New York, 1907) • R. LEAVER, *"Goostly Psalmes and Spiritual Songes": English and Dutch Metrical Psalms from Coverdale to Utenhove, 1535-1566* (London, 1991) • G. F. LOCKWOOD, "Recent Developments in U.S. Hispanic and Latin American Protestant Church Music" (Diss., Claremont, Calif., 1981) • I-TO LOH, *Asian Resources on Music, Worship, and the Arts* (T'ai-nan, 1997) • C. McCONNELL, *Comentario sobre los himnos que cantamos* (El Paso, Tex., 1985); idem, *La historia del himno en Castellano* (3d ed.; El Paso, Tex., 1987) • J. A. McGUCKIN, *At the Lighting of the Lamps: Hymns of the Ancient Church* (Harrisburg, Pa., 1995) • C. MAHRENHOLZ and O. SÖHNGEN, eds., *Handbuch zum evangelischen Kirchengesangbuch* (3 vols.; Göttingen, 1956-70) • W. MILGATE, ed., *A Companion to "Sing Alleluia"* (rev. ed.; Sydney, 1988); idem, ed., *Songs of the People of God: A Companion to "The Australian Hymn Book/With One Voice"* (rev. ed.; Sydney, 1985) • J. M. NEALE, *Hymns of the Eastern Church* (London, 1862) • *New Oxford History of Music*, vol. 1, *Ancient and Oriental Music* (London, 1957) • W. J. REYNOLDS, M. PRICE, and D. MUSIC, *A Survey of Christian Hymnody* (Carol Stream, Ill., 1999) • E. ROUTLEY, *The Music of Christian Hymns* (Chicago, 1981); idem, *A Panorama of Christian Hymnody* (Collegeville, Pa., 1979) • E. SOUTHERN, *The Music of Black Americans: A History* (3d ed.; New York, 1997) • M. STULKEN, *Hymnal Companion to the Lutheran Book of Worship* (Philadelphia, 1981) • N. TEMPERLEY, *The Music of the English Parish Church* (2 vols.; Cambridge, 1979) • P. WACKERNAGEL, *Das deutsche Kirchenlied von der ältesten Zeit bis zum Anfang des 17. Jahrhunderts* (5 vols.; Leipzig, 1864-77) • J. R. WATSON, *The English Hymn* (London, 1997) • R. WATSON and K. TRICKETT, *Companion to Hymns and Psalms* (London, 1988) • E. WELLESZ, *History of Byzantine Music and Hymnography* (London, 1949) • E. WERNER, *The Sacred Bridge* (2 vols.; 2d ed.; London, 1960) • V. WICKER, ed., *The Hymnology Annual* (vols. 1-5; Berrien Springs, Mich., 1992-97) • A. WILSON-DICKSON, *A Brief History of Christian Music* (Oxford, 1997) • C. R. YOUNG, *Companion to the United Methodist Hymnal* (1989) (Nashville, 1993); idem, *Music of the Heart: John and Charles Wesley on Music and Musicians* (London, 1995); idem, *My Great Redeemer's Praise: An Introduction to Christian Hymns* (Akron, Ohio, 1995).

CARLTON R. YOUNG

Hymnology

Hymnology (from Gk. *hymnos*) is the study of → hymns, a science that is both pure and applied. Hymnology intersects with the disciplines of biblical studies (→ Exegesis, Biblical), → theology, literature, history, → biography, → anthropology, musicology, and → liturgy. Hymnology is connected with the mission of the church, including its → worship, → evangelism, and → education. A related term is → "hymnody," which refers to the hymns of a particular time, place, or group. In its broadest scope, hymnology is the study of all the particular hymnodies.

Hymnology includes the history and bibliography of the sources of hymns. This discipline encompasses the life and work of poets and composers, as well as the study of → hymnals and collections of hymn texts and tunes. Hymnology also contributes toward understanding the form and meaning of hymns, including their cultural contexts and functions.

Hymnology is concerned with applying the knowledge of various hymnodies to the practice of congregational singing, as in the editing of hymns for current use, the teaching of unfamiliar hymns to a congregation, and the selection of appropriate hymns for public worship. Hymnologists have researched the development of hymns in each age of the church from the early Greek and Latin hymns to current hymnic expressions.

Three contemporary organizations that support hymnology are the Hymn Society in the United States and Canada (founded 1922), the Hymn Society of Great Britain and Ireland (1936), and the Internationale Arbeitsgemeinschaft für Hymnologie (1957).

Bibliography: L. F. BENSON, *The English Hymn: Its Development and Use in Worship* (New York, 1915; rev. ed., 1962) • L. ELLINWOOD, ed., *Bibliography of American Hymnals* (New York, 1984); idem, ed., *Dictionary of American Hymnology: First-Line Index* (New York, 1984) • H. ESKEW and H. T. MCELRATH, *Sing with Understanding: An Introduction to Christian Hymnology* (2d ed.; Nashville, 1995) • M. FROST, ed., *Historical Companion to Hymns Ancient and Modern* (London, 1962) • J. JULIAN, *A Dictionary of Hymnology* (2 vols.; New York, 1937; orig. pub., 1907) • D. W. MUSIC, *Hymnology: A Collection of Source Readings* (Lanham, Md., 1996) • E. ROUTLEY, *The Music of Christian Hymns* (Chicago, 1981) • S. P. SCHILLING, *The Faith We Sing* (Philadelphia, 1983) • J. R. WATSON, *The English Hymn: A Critical and Historical Study* (Oxford, 1997).

HARRY ESKEW

I

Iceland

	1960	1980	2000
Population (1,000s):	176	228	282
Annual growth rate (%):	1.74	1.13	0.88

Area: 102,819 sq. km. (39,699 sq. mi.)

A.D. 2000

Population density: 3/sq. km. (7/sq. mi.)
Births / deaths: 1.57 / 0.69 per 100 population
Fertility rate: 2.19 per woman
Infant mortality rate: 5 per 1,000 live births
Life expectancy: 79.8 years (m: 77.9, f: 81.7)
Religious affiliation (%): Christians 97.5 (Protestants 94.7, indigenous 4.8, Roman Catholics 1.1, other Christians 0.5), nonreligious 1.2, other 1.3.

Overview
1. From Earliest Settlement
2. The Modern Era
3. Evangelical Lutheran Church
4. Other Religious Groups
5. Church and State

Overview

Iceland is one of the least-populated countries in Europe. It has nevertheless preserved a vigorous culture and a distinct national identity. The Evangelical Lutheran Church of Iceland (ELCI) is an integral part of this identity and of the way of life of the Icelandic people (→ Lutheran Churches; Lutheranism).

Iceland was an independent republic from 930 until 1262, when civil war and anarchy allowed it to come under the rule of the kings of Norway. In 1380 it passed, with Norway, under the Danish crown. Not until 1944 did Iceland regain its status as a fully independent republic.

In the year 2000 the Icelandic people celebrated the millennium of Christianity in their country.

1. From Earliest Settlement

The first people setting foot on Icelandic soil, perhaps in the early ninth century, were Celtic hermits seeking refuge to worship Christ. They were driven out by later Norse settlers, some of them Christian, but most worshiping the old Norse gods. When Iceland was constituted as a republic in the year 930, it was based on the heathen religion. Beginning in the late 900s, missionaries from the Continent sought to spread Christianity among the population (→ Germanic Mission).

Soon the nation was deeply divided between the adherents of the two different religions, which refused to tolerate each other. In the legislative assembly (the Althing, at Thingvellir, the world's oldest surviving parliament) in the year 1000, the country stood on the brink of' civil war. The leaders of the two groups realized the danger and found a solution. They chose a person whom everyone respected for his wisdom, the heathen priest and chieftain Thorgeir of Ljosavatn, to decide which way the peo-

639

ple should go. Thorgeir retired to his dwelling, where he spent the day in meditation. On the next day he called forth the assembly and made known his decision: "If we put aside the law, we will put aside the peace. Let it be the foundation of our law that everyone in this land shall be Christian and believe in one God — Father, Son, and Holy Spirit." The people agreed and were subsequently baptized. This remarkable story, which marks the beginning of the church in Iceland, continues to be an important part of Icelandic culture and identity.

Missionary bishops and priests from Germany, England, and eastern Europe worked among the population to organize the church. The first Icelandic bishop was Ísleifur, who was consecrated in Bremen in 1056. He established his episcopal see at Skálholt, which became the center of Christian learning and spirituality in the country up through the 18th century. The church was originally part of the Province of Bremen, later came under the archbishop of Lund, and in 1153 became part of the Province of Nidaros (Trondheim), Norway.

There was great literary activity between the 11th and 13th centuries, producing extensive religious literature in the Icelandic language as well as the well-known sagas (most of which were doubtless written by clergy). By the 13th century parts of the Bible had been translated into Icelandic. This powerful and enduring literary tradition, with its strong national character, has shaped the Icelandic language and inspired literary activity. Icelandic has had a continuity that makes it the oldest living language in Europe. Icelanders can easily read texts dating from the 13th century.

In 1540 the Lutheran Reformation was established in Iceland, enforced by the Danish crown. Monasteries were dissolved, and much of the property of the episcopal sees was confiscated by the king of Denmark, who became the supreme head of the church. A dark spot in the history of Iceland was the execution in 1550 of Catholic bishop Jón Arason of Hólar, along with his two sons.

The Reformation began a period of renewed literary activity in the country. The publishing of the Icelandic translation of the NT in 1540 and the whole Bible in 1584 was an important step in the history of the language and a major factor in its preservation. *Passíusálmar* (Hymns of the passion; 1666), 50 meditations on the cross by the poet and pastor Hallgrímur Pétursson (1614-74), were for generations the most important instruction in prayer and wisdom. The same can be said of *Húss-Postilla* (Sermons for the home), by Jón Vídalín, bishop of Skálholt (1698-1720).

The 19th century saw the beginning of a national → revival in Iceland and a movement toward political independence. Many churchmen played an important part in this effort.

2. The Modern Era

Around the turn of the 20th century church legislation was reformed, parish councils were established, and → congregations gained the right to elect their → pastors. A new translation of the Bible was printed in 1912, revised in 1981.

In the early 1900s → liberal theology was introduced in Iceland, which led to great theological strife between liberals and conservatives. Textual criticism of the Scriptures and radical theological liberalism were quite influential in the newly founded Department of Theology of the University of Iceland. Spiritism and theosophical writings were also influential in intellectual circles. Opposing this trend were the → inner mission, the → YMCA and → YWCA, and missionary societies with orthodox pietistic leadership. This conflict marred church life in the country well into the 1960s.

At the turn of the century a couple of Lutheran → free churches were founded, based on the same confession as the national church and using the same liturgy and hymnal, but structurally and financially independent. Earlier, → Roman Catholic priests and nuns established missions and founded hospitals. In the early decades of the 20th century, Seventh-day → Adventists and Pentecostal missions were quite successful (→ Pentecostal Churches).

Until the 20th century the population of the country was predominantly rural farmers and fishermen, whose lifestyle was traditional. Modern social upheavals have brought with them problems for the church in Iceland, as Iceland has become a modern and highly urbanized society, highly secularized (→ Secularism), with increasing → pluralism of belief.

3. Evangelical Lutheran Church

Even though Iceland is becoming increasingly multicultural, with a variety of faiths, 90 percent of the population belong to the ELCI. More than 90 percent of the children are baptized and later confirmed; 75 percent of the people are married in the church, and 99 percent are buried in the church. A recent Gallup poll shows that only 12 percent of adults in Iceland attend at least one church service a month. The state broadcasting system transmits worship services every Sunday morning and daily devotions morning and night.

Iceland is one diocese under the bishop of Iceland, whose office is in Reykjavík. There are about 300 Lutheran parishes nationwide, served by approximately 150 priests and 10 ordained deacons, with 10 other priests working in specialized ministries in hospitals and other institutions. The ELCI also has priests serving Icelandic congregations abroad. Women have been ordained since 1974 (→ Ordination); in 1999 about one-quarter of the pastors were women.

The theological faculty of the University of Iceland, founded in 1911, educates the clergy and deacons of the church. Many theologians go abroad for further studies in seminaries and universities on both sides of the Atlantic. The church, far from being isolated, is subject to all influences of the times, including theological trends.

The ELCI is a member of the → Lutheran World Federation and the → World Council of Churches. It signed the Porvoo Declaration between the Anglican churches of the British Isles and the Nordic and Baltic Lutheran churches.

The Missionary Societies of Iceland, in cooperation with the Norwegian Lutheran Mission, has operated missions in China, Ethiopia, and Kenya (→ Scandinavian Missions), with the African missions still active. The Icelandic Church Aid has worked in cooperation with foreign relief and developmental agencies in development work and emergency aid in various parts of the world.

4. Other Religious Groups

According to the census of 1999, just under 90 percent of the population belongs to the Evangelical Lutheran Church of Iceland (247,245 people), 4 percent to the Evangelical Lutheran Free Churches (10,622), and 1 percent each to the Roman Catholic Church (3,827) and to Pentecostal and charismatic congregations (2,999).

Several other groups have less than 1,000 members each: Seventh-day Adventists, → Jehovah's Witnesses, and → Mormons; also → Baha'is, → Buddhists, Old-Norse Asa-cultists, and Muslims (→ Islam).

5. Church and State

The constitution of 1874, which guaranteed → religious liberty, declared that the "Evangelical Lutheran Church is a national church, and as such it is protected and supported by the State." This provision continued in the constitution of the Republic of Iceland of 1944. Although the church is established by law, it is autonomous in internal matters. The state is pledged to support the church, and it also collects membership dues for the church and

other denominations and religious communities in the country.

On January 1, 1998, a new law came into effect defining the status of the ELCI and its relations with the government. Most → church law, which previously had been enacted by the Althing, is now made by the annual Kirkjuthing (Church assembly), which is the highest legislative authority of the church. The highest executive authority is the Kirkjurad (Church council), with two clergy and two laymen elected by the Kirkjuthing and presided over by the bishop of Iceland. In addition, the bishop annually summons all the pastors and theologians of the church to the pastors' meeting, the Synod, to discuss the affairs of the church and society.

Bibliography: J. H. ADALSTEINSSON, *Under the Cloak: The Acceptance of Christianity in Iceland* (Uppsala, 1978) • M. FELL, *And Some Fell into Good Soil: A History of Christianity in Iceland* (New York, 1999) • K. HASTRUP, *A Place Apart: An Anthropological Study of the Icelandic World* (Oxford, 1998) • M. M. LÁRUSSON and S. EINAARSSON, "The Church in Iceland," *Scandinavian Churches* (ed. L. S. Hunter; London, 1965) 104-11 • P. PÉTURSSON, *Church and Social Change: A Study of the Secularization Process in Iceland, 1830-1930* (Vänersborg, 1983).

BERNHARÐUR GUÐMUNDSSON

Icon

1. Term and Definition
2. Rise
3. Philosophical and Cultural Context
4. Theological Basis
5. Aesthetics and Typology
6. Place and Function

1. *Term and Definition*

The term "icon" denotes a sacred picture *(eikōn)* in the Eastern church. On the Orthodox view (→ Orthodox Church) it points to the suprasensory original, presenting it in realistic symbolism.

As distinct from religious pictures in the West, which are aesthetic tools of instruction ("art for the sake of religion"), → devotion, and → meditation, the icon is a → revelation of the transcendent in the immanent (→ Immanence and Transcendence). The metaphysical → ontology of the icon as a manifestation of heavenly realities, or their → identity and existential vindication, lies in the mystical presentation of the invisible original.

2. *Rise*

The pre-Nicene → church fathers, out of regard for their pagan setting, still related the Christian faith to the prohibition of images in the → Decalogue (Exod. 20:4-5). After the toleration of Christianity and its recognition as the state religion at the end of the fourth century, however, the Fathers integrated the Greek cultural legacy (→ Hellenism) into Christian culture and thus adopted a more favorable attitude toward images. By the early seventh century the icon no longer came under suspicion of idolatry, although there were still some critical voices. Apart from the latter and the superstitious abuses associated with the growing cult of icons, we cannot explain the iconoclasm (→ Images) that shook the → Byzantine Empire for a century and a half until the seventh ecumenical council — Nicaea II (787) — ratified a theologically based veneration of icons and related icon and word.

3. *Philosophical and Cultural Context*

It was not by accident that the veneration and theology of icons developed in a sphere shaped by Greek culture. Images played a dominant role in the everyday life of the Greeks. Their poetry and philosophy (→ Greek Philosophy) are characterized by a plastic thinking that closely relates presentation to what is presented, or image to original. Plato (427-347 B.C.) underlined the transcending function of images, providing a classical basis for the venerating of images in antiquity (*Leg.* 930E-F). His doctrine of the ideas (→ Platonism) as it was developed in Neoplatonism and especially the writings of Dionysius the Pseudo-Areopagite (A.D. ca. 500) forms the philosophical background to the patristic theology of icons, in which the ancient Greek idea of the close relation between content and visible form, or idea and phenomenal reality, survives (see A. Kallis art. in D. Papandreou, *L'icône*).

4. *Theological Basis*

Although the theology of icons borrows from Platonic thinking, in content it has a biblical and Christological basis. It thus overcomes the Platonic → dualism of the intelligible and the sensory world. Christ's assumption of flesh (→ Incarnation) denotes the ontological unity of the intelligible and the sensory.

In defense of the icon the Fathers used biblical, ethical, religious, anthropological, didactic, cosmological, and epistemological arguments, along with the argument from tradition. The decisive argument, however, was from → Christology. The veneration of icons was for them a logical consequence of belief in the reality of the incarnation of the Logos, who in his human form is "the image of the invisible God" (Col. 1:15). Dogmatically the victory of veneration meant a consistent acceptance of the Council of → Chalcedon (451), while intellectually it meant the triumph of Greek Orthodox thinking (→ Orthodoxy 3) over the formlessness of the East.

5. *Aesthetics and Typology*

As a symbol expressing inexpressible metaphysical realities, the icon has its own → aesthetic, depicting neither an idealistic nor an objective reality of earthly naturalism but a spiritual reality. This reality constitutes its strangeness and its distinctive inner beauty, the beauty of the → truth that is God himself.

The iconographic types that went hand in hand with dogmatic development form a supratemporal language that is common to all Orthodox churches and that is not the work or achievement of individual artistic skill. Proof of this commonality lies in the anonymity of the Hagiographa, the signature "by the hand," and especially the tradition of the *acheiropoiētoi* (not made by [human] hands), which points to the heavenly and spiritual dimension (see Mark 14:58; 2 Cor. 5:1; Col. 2:11).

Limits are thus set to the arbitrary imagination of the *hagiographa,* though without restricting their creative powers; note the icons of Manouel Panselinos (first half of the 14th cent.), Theophanes the Greek (ca. 1330/40-1405), Andrey Rublyov (ca. 1360/70-1430), Theophanes the Cretan (ca. 1500-1559), and Michael Damaskinos (16th cent.). The development of → iconography proves this dynamic, for the icons bear the specific imprint of the different periods. Models for iconic art arose relatively late (16th cent.) and were not canonized by the church but simply served as aids. A slavish imitation of old icons gives evidence of an imitation mentality that wrongly seeks its justification in → dogmatics.

6. *Place and Function*

The inner link between icon and → liturgy protects the icon against superstitious misuse (→ Magic). Whether in church or at home, the icon has a liturgical function, namely, encounter with the heavenly world. It bears witness to the presence of the original, not ontically, but in mystical hypostasis that gives access to the original. Hence Nicaea II distinguished between simple veneration (*timētikē proskynēsis*) and true worship (*alēthinē latreia*), which must be offered to God alone. It quotes Basil's famous saying that the honor paid to the icon transfers to the original (*De Spir. S.* 18.45).

The icon is seen as the visible ray of the invisible → absolute, which reveals itself in the icon but remains hidden in essence. Its shining enhances sense perception and understanding and demands a special liturgical contemplation so that through the visible there may be access to the invisible, the true reality of the icon. This *theognōsia* (knowledge of God) comes in the process of *theōria* (contemplation) of that which is beyond logic as participation in invisible transcendence. The icon shatters the idolatrous images of the understanding (→ Apophatic Theology) and frees us for encounter with the ineffable.

→ Christian Art; Iconostasis; Liturgy 2; Piety; Saints, Veneration of; Worship 3

Bibliography: H. BELTING, *Likeness and Presence: A History of the Image before the Era of Art* (Chicago, 1994) • "Bild und Glaube (Nikaia II 787-1987–Ringvorlesung der Universität Munich im SS 1987)," *OrthFor* 1 (1987) 131-267 • F. BOESPFLUG and N. LOSSKY, eds., *Nicée II, 787-1987. Douze siècles d'images religieuses* (Paris, 1987) • P. EVDOKIMOV, *The Art of the Icon: A Theology of Beauty* (Redondo Beach, Calif., 1990) • W. FELICETTI-LIEBENFELS, *Geschichte der byzantinischen Ikonenmalerei* (Olten, 1956); idem, *Geschichte der russischen Ikonenmalerei in den Grundzügen dargestellt* (Graz, 1972) • H. P. GERHARD, *The World of Icons* (London, 1971; orig. pub., 1957) • *L'icône dans la théologie et l'art* (Geneva, 1990) • A. KALLIS, "Nikaia II (787). Aktualität und ökumenische Relevanz des letzten ökumenischen Konzils," *Hermeneia* 3 (1987) 186-92; idem, "Der philosophisch-kulturelle Kontext der Ikonenverehrung und -theologie," *L'icône dans la théologie et l'art* (Geneva, 1990) • K. KALOKYRIS, *Orthodox Iconography* (Brookline, Mass., 1985) • T. NIKOLAOU, "Die Ikonenverehrung als Beispiel ostkirchlicher Theologie und Frömmigkeit nach Johannes von Damaskus," *OS* 25 (1976) 138-65 • K. ONASCH, *Icons* (London, 1963); idem, *Ikonen. Faszination und Wirklichkeit* (Freiburg, 1995) • L. OUSPENSKY, *Theology of the Icon* (rev. ed.; 2 vols.; New York, 1992) • L. OUSPENSKY and V. LOSSKY, *The Meaning of Icons* (rev. ed.; New York, 1982) • C. VON SCHÖNBORN, *L'icône du Christ* (Paris, 1986) • P. SHERRARD, *The Sacred in Life and Art* (Ipswich, 1990) • N. THON, *Ikone und Liturgie* (Trier, 1979).

ANASTASIOS KALLIS

Iconoclasm, Iconoclasts → Images

Iconography

1. The Study of Images
2. The Body of Christian Imagery
   2.1. Early Church
   2.2. Middle Ages
   2.3. Reformation to Modern Times
3. Christian Iconography in Architecture

In the context of Christian art the term "iconography" (Gk. *eikonographia*, "description, sketch," from *eikōn*, "image," and *graphia*, "writing") has three possible meanings: (1) the production and study of icons, those images of holy figures or narratives devoutly prepared and venerated as possessing a special sanctity through which the faithful may pray to the original of the image; (2) the identification and analysis of → images and their meanings; and (3) the repertory of images included and employed in → Christian art. The first has been discussed elsewhere (→ Icon); this entry treats the second and third meanings.

1. The Study of Images

At its simplest level, iconography may be a description of a visual image, either basic or, as in the ancient literary form of *ekphrasis* (description), embellished with commentary or (usually laudatory) critical judgment. At its most complex, iconography may involve not only the identification of subject matter or theme but also an investigation of possible meaning(s), sources (visual, literary, theological, philosophical, etc.), and reasons for the artist's and/or patron's choices; this intensive approach is often termed "iconology."

Cultures become adept at constructing and deciphering → meaning in their own use of imagery, especially the imagery of substitution, such as → symbols, emblems, and → allegorical figures and episodes. In the history of art, over time certain images or combinations of images (often called programs) were sanctioned and even codified by religious or secular authorities and, by virtue of widespread circulation and commonality of form and presentation, were fully legible even to the uneducated and illiterate over a much larger geographic area than their point of origin and a much longer period of time. Christianity constructed its imagery gradually, but the cumulative effect was prodigious: once in the repertory of images, very little ever disappeared. Even now, what is not still actively employed is usually remembered and understood.

The recognition of Christian imagery in its earliest periods was aided by the fact that most of the images were reflected or reiterated in → prayers, Scripture and biblical commentaries, liturgical texts, sermons, apologia, hymn texts and poetry, and hagiographic and theological works. It was in fact the clerics, theologians, and philosophers producing such literature who dictated the content and form of Christian images to the largely nameless artists of the first 1,500 years of the faith. In the late Middle Ages and the → Renaissance, the construction of religious images was often achieved not only with the collaboration of erudite theologians, humanists, and poets but also in combination with motifs and subjects from Greek and Roman literature and history. The results were complicated and intricate, meant to be completely unraveled only by a small group of cognoscenti, but it was not unusual for detailed commentaries and exegeses to be circulated, at least by word of mouth.

The dissemination throughout Europe of printed books such as Andrea Alciati's *Emblemata* (Augsburg, 1531) and the even more influential *Iconologia* by Cesare Ripa (Rome, 1593; first illustrated ed., 1603) signal the first works of iconography, in which symbols, emblems, narratives, and the physical appearance and attributes of allegorical figures and designs were minutely described and often illustrated, providing patrons and artists with a common vocabulary. Ripa's work was utilized by artists until nearly the end of the 18th century, and following his usage the term "iconology" was employed for what we now call iconography, whereas the latter term was restricted to the description of portraiture.

With the progression of history and the destruction or temporary loss of pertinent documents, both visual and written, successive generations lost the clues needed to decipher many visual images, and speculation and subjectivity were rife. In the 18th century Johann Joachim Winckelmann advocated the careful study of works of art in order to perceive and understand their meanings; this program set the stage for the formal art-historical approach known as iconography, established and given form in the later 19th and earlier 20th centuries primarily by French and German scholars such as Adolphe-Napoléon Didron, Fernand Cabrol and Henri Leclerq, Émile Mâle, Anton Springer, Karl Künstle, Raymond van Marle, Aby Warburg, and Erwin Panofsky.

During the first two-thirds of the 20th century, iconography was, with the study of form and of context, one of the major art-historical methodologies. If not mutually exclusive, these three neverthe-less existed in separate realms: practitioners of iconography rarely dealt with style and included only what context was necessary for the identification of sources. In more recent scholarship, iconography as an approach often incorporates a consideration of both the form that conveys meaning and the historical and cultural context from which the image emerges. In the last three decades of the century, many of the critical approaches to art adopted from literary theory are in fact iconographic in nature, such as semiotics, the study of the assignment and perception of meaning, and deconstruction, the detachment of meaning from the concept of original intention. Because of the human desire for order and meaning, iconography is unlikely to vanish from the scholar's repertoire of tools.

2. The Body of Christian Imagery
2.1. *Early Church*

As noted above, very few motifs that ever became part of the repertoire of Christian imagery ever completely disappeared. A number of the oldest symbols are still in use, and many more have survived in only slightly altered form. The iconography of scenes from the OT, of the life of Christ, and of many episodes depicting the Virgin → Mary and other saints is as recognizable to the modern Christian as it was to those who first invented it in the early centuries of the church (although reference works on iconography must sometimes be relied upon).

From extant evidence, the earliest perceptibly Christian images were simple or complex symbols, many derived from the cultures from which the Christians came (and of which they were still a part) and transformed in meaning through scriptural or theological justification. These images included the fish, anchor, ship, plow, star, tree, and → cross, as well as letters or combinations of letters such as the Chi-Rho (the → monogram of Christ), scratched on a stone ossuary or traced in plaster over a sealed tomb.

Christians in the East employed figural imagery, even representations of Christ, as early as the middle of the third century. For example, the → baptistery of the → house church at Dura-Europos, on the Euphrates River at the eastern edge of the → Roman Empire, included the temptation of Adam and Eve, David and Goliath, the Good Shepherd and his flock, the Samaritan woman at the well, Christ healing a paralytic and walking on water (pulling Peter up, watched by a shipful of apostles), and a procession of ten women divided into two groups of five at a door, a scene that was probably a conflation of the holy women coming to the tomb on Easter morning and the parable of the wise and foolish virgins. Such a combination of Old and New Testament themes, including some taken from gospels and other writings excluded from the NT → canon, was common in funerary art in both East and West and demonstrated an important concept in Christian art: visual typology, in which a figure or event from the OT is read as a prefiguration of an event from the life of Christ or another NT figure.

A chronology of motifs in Rome and the Western Empire is difficult to establish because of the paucity of dated or datable evidence. In → catacomb paintings and carved sarcophagi, scenes of OT patriarchs and prophets in dire peril proclaimed the → salvation that comes from God alone; especially popular was Jonah, whose three days in the belly of the fish corresponded to Christ's three days in the tomb (Matt. 12:40). Many catacomb figures were shown orans (lit. praying), with arms raised, a prayer posture dating from the most ancient religions. Also found in Western funerary art in the same period were pagan substitutes for Christ, including Orpheus for his resurrection-like return from the underworld, Hercules for his strength and good deeds, and a brace of sun gods, Apollo and Helios or Sol Invictus (the Invincible Sun), for their power and splendor. There were also transitional images that might be read as either pagan or Christian, depending on their context, such as the philosopher (Christ with his disciples) or the herdsman, a figure going back at least to the seventh century B.C. in Greece, which was perceived as a good luck charm by pagan Romans and as the Good Shepherd by Christians.

→ Images of Christ himself appeared in the West by the end of the third century. He is distinguished not by distinct facial features but by his → baptism and → miracles, scenes in which he appears as one of several short-haired, togaed Romans, distinguished only by a "magic" wand or gesture of power. Sculptural representations, especially on marble sarcophagi, depict him as a young man distinguished from his companions by his long, curly hair and lack of beard, in possible reference to pagan gods he was replacing. The dark, bearded Christ that has become the most familiar representation in Christian art seems to have come from Syria and Palestine in the fourth century. Also in the fourth century, with the imperial sanction of Christianity, comes the image of Christ enthroned as god or emperor, the passion of Christ (in which he is never seen to suffer), the lamb as a sacrificial substitute, and the earliest images of saints (esp. → martyrs) as holy helpers, by

whom the recently deceased are led to eternal life, the saints here taking over the role of Hermes/Mercury in Greco-Roman religion.

Other themes were gradually added, such as extended cycles of the life and passion of Christ and scenes from the life of the Virgin Mary, particularly after the Council of Ephesus in 431 that declared her *theotokos* (God-bearer). As the company of saints grew, they were featured more prominently, as single figures, in episodes from their lives, or in company with Christ and the Virgin in icons, church frescoes, or codices and scrolls.

Just as theological and liturgical rifts occurred between the Christians of the East and West, so did iconographic motifs diverge. The → resurrection was at first universally indicated by the encounter of the holy women with the angel at the empty tomb; then, in the sixth century, the East began to favor a warrior Christ standing on a serpent and a lion, later followed by an image of Christ descending to the underworld (the *Anastasis*) to pull his faithful forebears from the jaws of death, while the West shifted in the Middle Ages (by the 9th cent.) to Christ stepping from the tomb.

2.2. Middle Ages

Despite a long period of iconoclasm in the East (726-843) and a few outbursts in the West, Christian iconography, while retaining the body of images mentioned above, was enriched with new saints, new legends, and new extensions and refinements of previous narratives. Images in the East (including Greece and, later, Russia) remained static in type and style out of a reverence for ancient representations possibly created by divine intervention, such as the Mandylion of Abgar, believed to have been created when Christ wiped his face on a linen napkin. Important developments in the West include a gradual shift, beginning shortly before 1000, from an "imperial" Christ enthroned in the heavens to the suffering Savior hanging on the cross, lying dead across his sorrowing mother's lap (the Pietà), or displaying his broken body as a sacrifice (the Man of Sorrows), motifs that sprang from popular piety and proliferated in the penitential atmosphere of the Middle Ages. It was also customary for huge representations of the last judgment or other apocalyptic themes in stone, mosaic, or fresco to be prominently displayed on the interior or exterior entrance wall of churches to encourage the faithful in a holy life on this earth.

Symbolic and allegorical figures from the classical past often reappeared in medieval Christian art, particularly personifications of the liberal arts, virtues, and vices, as well as the zodiac and a popular calendar of agricultural scenes known as the labors of the months; often the last two are combined with an image of Christ to suggest that the endless cycle of time is broken once and for all by the unique event of the → incarnation (e.g., in the Church of Mary Magdalene, Vézelay). The sibyls, prophetic women of ancient Greece and Rome, were absorbed into Christian iconography as companions for the OT prophets because their ambiguous predictions seemed to encompass the birth of Christ. OT imagery remained important: stone carvings of prophets and patriarchs, biblical kings and queens encrusted the exterior of medieval churches, and stained-glass windows told their stories.

In the 14th century the church itself sanctioned a typological iconography in which each episode from the life of Christ (*sub gratia,* "under grace") was accompanied by two OT scenes, one from before the time of Moses (*ante legem,* "before the law") and one from his life or later (*sub lege,* "under the law"). This *Biblia pauperum,* or "Bible of the poor," was intended both to educate the clergy, many of whom were too illiterate to read works of theology or even the Bible, and to combat the Albigensians and other heretics who insisted the OT had no validity after the coming of Christ.

In the 15th century, popular piety, → humanism, and the rebirth of interest in the classical past introduced new elements into Christian iconography. In the northern countries, in the work of artists such as Robert Campin and Jan van Eyck, biblical scenes took place in contemporary domestic interiors furnished with minutely depicted household objects, but these ordinary elements were suffused with hidden meaning: a ray of light passing through a glass of water, for example, represented the conception of Christ in the womb of the Virgin. A new appreciation of humanity and human achievement prompted an increase in depictions of living men and women in Christian art, as donors or participants in holy mysteries; images of the saints, those once-flawed mortals who rose to glory, outnumbered images of the adult Christ. In Italy especially, sophisticated visual "programs" were developed for artists such as Sandro Botticelli and their patrons by humanists who strove to reconcile the Christian and classical worlds. For example, tales of Greek and Roman morality were conflated with good works of the saints, characteristics of Venus with those of the Virgin Mary.

2.3. *Reformation to Modern Times*
The period of the Protestant and Catholic → Reformations in the 16th century saw great changes in religious imagery. In Protestant areas where imagery was not prohibited altogether, the number of acceptable themes was considerably decreased, primarily to the Last Supper, the crucifixion, and often convoluted theological allegories; even in iconoclastic areas such as Zurich and Geneva, however, newly translated and printed German Bibles were illustrated with woodcuts. A few artists such as Albrecht Dürer and the Lucas Cranachs (father and son) attempted to develop a Protestant iconography, Lucas the Elder introducing some new or rarely depicted themes to illustrate the → grace and accessibility of Christ, such as the woman taken in adultery or Christ with the children, but no artists continued their work. Not until a century later did Christian imagery revive in Protestant cultures, some of it disguised as moral messages in the symbolism of still lifes, landscapes, or genre scenes. Biblical narratives became a common subject for prestigious history paintings; a few artists such as Rembrandt chose scenes from Scripture for the opportunity to study the human condition.

In Roman Catholic countries imagery became, if anything, more effusive, but also more carefully controlled by the church and the rulings of the Council of → Trent (1545-63); artists were permitted to depict only what was scriptural and morally edifying. Violations could be addressed by the → Inquisition itself, before which the Venetian artist Paolo Veronese was brought in 1573 for the inclusion of "frivolous" elements in a vast painting depicting the Last Supper. Despite the church's call for restraint and moderation, vast exploding church ceilings and saints of remarkable physical beauty writhing in exquisite torments or ecstasies were calculated to awe the faithful and win back the schismatics by the glory and splendor of the faith. Religious art became high theater, with the traditional themes enhanced and at times overwhelmed by the elaborate set designs of Gian Lorenzo Bernini or the dramatic lighting of Caravaggio or the multimedia spectacle of pilgrimage churches of Bavaria and Austria, where architecture, sculpture, and painting are inseparably linked.

In the increasingly secular culture of the → Enlightenment, as → religion became a more private concern and the beleaguered church devoted its decreasing resources to more pressing needs than the patronage of art, traditional Christian iconography was depicted less and less frequently. "Christian values," however, were communicated by seemingly secular subject matter in the 18th century, such as William Hogarth's *The Rake's Progress,* a popular transformation of the parable of the prodigal son, and historical figures were shown in poses and situations resonant with Christian meaning, such as Jacques-Louis David's assassinated revolutionary Marat in the pose of the dead Christ or John Singleton Copley's harpoonist in *Watson and the Shark* in the pose of the militant archangel Michael.

In the age of → Romanticism and → realism in the 19th century, artists in movements such as the Pre-Raphaelite Brotherhood in England and the Nazarener in Germany, and even self-proclaimed anticlerical artists throughout Europe, chose to depict narratives from the Old and New Testaments, seeing the protagonists as the epitome of romantic heroes or heroines, in moments of high drama and pathos; not the least of the heroic figures were Christ himself, dying young for a noble cause, and Mary Magdalene, the redeemed sinner, faithful to the end. The realists often depicted Christ and his apostles as poor working men of great dignity and presence or as authentic Palestinians. Landscape artists from the American Thomas Cole to the German Caspar David Friedrich incorporated religious scenes and images or simply imbued their panoramic works with a sense of the Creator, who had formed such wonders. Even the new art form of photography posed men and women as biblical characters or saints.

The 20th century saw two significant developments in Christian iconography: the readoption of traditional imagery, and the increasing abstraction of art, often simultaneously encompassed in the same work. Developments in the 19th and earlier 20th century, from the → impressionists to the abstract → expressionists, gave artists new vocabularies of color and form imbued with a potential for not only expressing content but enlisting the composition itself in the expression of religious feeling. The titles of many abstract or nonrepresentational works suggest religious content, but it is not an easy matter to judge whether Christian subject matter has been employed purely for its associations or whether an artist is expressing deeply felt personal faith. Was the reappearance of traditional Christian imagery among the German expressionists — for the most part a hard-bitten, cynical lot — when faced with a disintegrating society and personal angst in the 1920s and 1930s, an ingrained cultural impulse or a personal choice? Artists who professed no faith were sometimes enlisted by clergy who decried the declining quality of Christian art and felt that Christian imagery executed by great artists who were not believers was more meaningful than bad art executed by Christian artists. Christian themes and concepts have now been widely appropriated by artists of every persuasion, for nearly as many reasons: deliberately, in order to express personal faith,

comment upon or criticize Christianity and its practitioners, or challenge the viewer; unconsciously, because Christian imagery is part of the culture in which the artist lives; ultimately, because of the recognizability of such themes and their ability to carry meaning to many people.

3. Christian Iconography in Architecture

Architecture has its own iconography, for shapes, sizes, materials, and even construction methods may deliberately convey meaning (→ Church Architecture). For centuries the circle, a perfect and eternal form, was considered the ideal shape for a church. Octagonal baptisteries were derived from the mystical meaning of the number 8, referring to the survivors of the great flood and the day of resurrection. Circles and the shapes that could be inscribed in them also carried into Christian architecture a reference to the tombs of ancient kings and heroes, just as the form of the dome suggested the heavens and was often decorated as such. The shape of most medieval, Renaissance, and baroque churches was that of a cross, and the elaborately ornamented Gothic cathedrals were intended to be earthly configurations of the heavenly Jerusalem as described in the Book of Revelation.

Throughout the history of architecture the revival of earlier styles suggested a return to the values and meanings of earlier cultures; certain supporters of the Gothic revival in Great Britain and Ireland in the 19th century, such as A. W. N. Pugin, believed that the style exercised a moral imperative, a call to return to the orthodoxy of an age when God governed human affairs, and that it was the only possible style for Christian architecture. The early → Puritan meetinghouses in the New World were built without central aisles in a rejection of the processional pomp of the High Anglican churches; the pulpit was centrally placed to symbolize the primacy of the Word. In contemporary church architecture there are many interpretations of older motifs and referential or symbolic configurations of the sanctuary, such as the use of a semicircular arrangement of pews to remind worshipers of the Christian community and the placement of the baptismal font at the doorway of the sanctuary to symbolize entrance into Christian life.

Bibliography: J. DRURY, *Painting the Word: Christian Pictures and Their Meanings* (New Haven, 1999) • G. FINALDI et al., *The Image of Christ* (London, 2000) • A. GRABAR, *Christian Iconography: A Study of Its Origins* (Princeton, 1968) • S. KOSTOF, *A History of Architecture: Settings and Rituals* (2d ed.; rev. G. Castillo;

New York, 1995) • É. Mâle, *Art religieux après le Concile de Trent* (Paris, 1972); idem, *Religious Art in France* (3 vols.; ed. H. Bober; Princeton, 1978-86) • T. F. Mathews, *The Clash of Gods: A Reinterpretation of Early Christian Art* (rev. ed.; Princeton, 1999) • D. Morgan, *Visual Piety: A History and Theory of Popular Religious Images* (Berkeley, Calif., 1998) • L. Murray and P. Murray, *The Oxford Companion to Christian Art and Architecture* (Oxford, 1996) • H. van Os et al., *The Art of Devotion in the Late Middle Ages in Europe, 1300-1500* (Princeton, 1994) • L. Réau, *Iconographie de l'art chrétien* (3 vols.; Paris, 1955-59) • G. Schiller, *Iconography of Christian Art* (2 vols.; Greenwich, N.Y., 1971).

Susanna Bede Caroselli, S.S.G.

Iconostasis

The iconostasis, or *templon,* is a lattice screen of marble or wood that is decorated with → icons and that, in Byzantine churches, separates the sanctuary (→ Altar) from the main body of the church. The two parts are linked by three doors: two side doors and the so-called Beautiful Gate, or Holy Door, in the middle. In the early period of the church this barrier was very low and undecorated. In the Byzantine period small pillars were then added, with an architrave above. Curtains were put between the pillars, as were, from the end of the 13th century, the so-called great, or despotic, icons: those of Christ, the divine mother (→ Mary, Devotion to), and the patron saint. To these were added the 12 images of the great festivals (the *dōdekaorton*).

According to one theory, the proscenium of the ancient Greek theater was the model for the iconostasis. Obviously the curtain in the Jewish temple had an influence. The iconostasis gradually increased in height, and it now separates a special area that has mystical significance. The various prayers of the priests at → worship, as well as the → iconography on the walls of this area, which relates to the mystical offering of the Lamb, give evidence of this significance. The fathers of the Orthodox Church, and its painting, confirm that the sanctuary is regarded as a symbol of the heavenly Jerusalem, a place of → reverence and respect. Those who do not have the grace of the priestly office (→ Priest, Priesthood) are denied access to it. This division, however, does not imply an ideological separation based on the distinction between → clergy and laity. Such a separation is unknown in the Orthodox Church.

→ Images

Bibliography: M. Chatzidakis, "Ikonostas," *RBK* 3.326-52 • P. Florenskij, "Ikonostas," *BoTr* 9 (1972) 80-148 • K. Holl, "Die Entstehung der Bilderwand in der griechischen Kirche," *ARW* 9.365-84; idem, *Gesammelte Aufsätze zur Kirchengeschichte* (vol. 2; Tübingen, 1928) 225-37 • J. B. Konstantinowicz, *Ikonostasis. Studien und Forschungen* (vol. 1; Lvov, 1939) • J. Walter, "The Origins of the Iconostasis," *ECR* 3 (1971) 251-67.

Konstantinos D. Kalokyris

Idealism

1. Meanings of "Idealism"
2. Platonism
3. Descartes to Berkeley
4. Kant
5. Fichte
6. The Early Schelling
7. Hegel
8. The Later Schelling
9. Critics of German Idealism
10. Later Idealism
11. Idealism and Christian Theology

1. Meanings of "Idealism"

Idealism in the philosophical sense embraces a range of positions affirming that ultimate reality consists of mind(s), thought(s), or a domain of nonphysical, mental, or spiritual entities. Some idealists hold that minds and their thoughts are all there is, that physical or phenomenal objects are illusory if taken to be more than just thoughts. Others hold the less extreme view that physical or phenomenal objects actually exist as such, but their existence and natures are understood to be the self-actualization of a spiritual or mental realm, that what makes them what they are is not matter in motion but their mind-given, intelligible natures. *Absolute* idealists affirm a single mind behind the phenomenal universe. *Personal* idealists speak of a number of finite minds (persons) that collectively engender the world of known objects. These and other varieties of philosophical idealism have exerted great influence on religion, including Christian thought and practice.

2. Platonism

Plato (427-347 b.c.; → Platonism) held that the metaphysical objects he called ideas (perfect, unchangeable, and eternal objects) are the ultimate foundation of the kinds of sensible objects that exist in space and time. Each concept (and its definition) has its correlative idea, accessible to thought alone and fully "real" (genuine, substantial) in a way that its phenomenal exemplifications are not. The term "idealism" has its historical roots in Plato's theory of ideas. Though these ideas have affinities with our minds or → souls, Plato regarded them not as thoughts or thinking but as the objects that minds think about. His Neoplatonic heirs, such as Plotinus (ca. A.D. 205-70), speak of them as an array in a supersensible mind (nous), but not, as such, a thinking process as we know it. In scholastic debates of the Middle Ages this Platonic philosophy was called → realism (in contrast to → nominalism), an indication that it differs considerably from what is meant by idealism in the modern era.

3. Descartes to Berkeley

René Descartes (1596-1650; → Cartesianism) changed the philosophical landscape with his focus on the ego, or subject, as knower and on clarity and distinctness as criteria of the truth of our ideas. But with his → dualistic segregation of extended substance from thinking substance and his mechanistic view of nature, he cannot be called an idealist. Likewise Baruch Spinoza (1632-77), whose → pantheistic → metaphysics treats the mode of extension (body) as parallel and irreducible to the mode of thought. Only Gottfried Wilhelm Leibniz (1646-1716) among the great rationalists could be termed an idealist in a limited sense, in that his "monads," the fundamental and immaterial entities, exist in a noninteractive, preestablished harmony, each being a unique perception of, or perspective on, all the others.

Oddly enough, we find the only full-fledged idealist in this period among the British empiricists, namely, George Berkeley (1685-1753), who held that "to be is to be perceived," that matter and physical objects as such are not real, that all our perceptions of the ostensibly physical world are actually thoughts given to our minds by the mind of God. (Samuel Johnson sought to refute him by kicking a stone, but the pain in his foot was likewise a sensation placed in his mind by God.) It is the brand of idealism most often discussed and criticized in Anglo-American philosophy.

4. Kant

Immanuel Kant (1724-1804) set the agenda for subsequent German idealism. In his *Critique of Pure Reason* (1781; rev. 1787) synthetic a priori knowledge configures the sensible manifold into our world of experienced objects. This doctrine weds → rationalism and → empiricism so that the knowing subject's constitutive activity predominates, but without making the given or phenomenal aspect of experience itself into thought. A brief "refutation of idealism" criticizes Descartes and Berkeley and argues that "consciousness of my own existence proves the existence of objects in space outside me." → Reason errs in forming pure concepts (transcendental ideas) with no empirical component, namely, the ideas of the thinking subject as soul or substance, of the world as a whole, and of God. Kant's *Critique of Practical Reason* (1788) expounds the noumenal domain of moral obligation, deriving from it the certainty (though not the knowledge) of our free will, of God, and of our → immortality. Kant's *Critique of Judgment* (1790) treats aesthetic and teleological judgment, the last part showing how regulative (not constitutive) employment of reason usefully organizes our knowledge of the world hierarchically, as if it were purposively ordered by a higher intelligence. The principal German idealists can be approached according to the particular facet of Kant's philosophy on which each chiefly dwells.

5. Fichte

Johann Gottlieb Fichte (1762-1814) sought to unify the theoretical and practical domains of → Kantianism by giving primacy to practical reason and human → freedom. In his *Science of Knowledge* (1798) the self-positing by the subject, or I, of theoretical knowing directly involves its positing of its other, the not-I, which is both constituted by it and a limit to it. This complex dialectic underlies both the objective world as known by theoretical reason and the realm of natural necessity that opposes our free moral striving. This I, common to both domains, is Kant's noumenal self, now said to be absolute and the originator of all knowing and doing. (Kant repudiated this effort to unite the two distinct domains, with the I producing the very manifold of perception itself.) Elevating the free, noumenal I to this absolute, originative standpoint makes Fichte an idealist. He kept his main focus on ethics throughout his career and developed from it a social and political philosophy that recognizes some limits to the freedom of the individual I, limits set by its inescapable coexistence with other free selves. His version of Kantian → ethics led him to deny that the moral order needs a personal God as its overseer, for which stance he was accused of atheism. This position, together with his derivation of all philosophy from individual self-consciousness, makes his brand of idealism of limited interest to Christian thought.

6. The Early Schelling

Although at first enamored of Fichte's preoccupation with self-conscious freedom, Friedrich Schelling (1775-1854) soon moved on to a wider vision, embracing knower and known in a system transcending the limits of a dialectic of self-consciousness. We can view him as transforming Kant's third critique so that systematic reasoning about reality as a whole now has a constitutive, not just a regulative, status. One aspect, explicated in his *System of Transcendental Idealism* (1800), depicts the known world as the product of the constructive activity of the knower. Its correlative, his → philosophy of nature, depicts the world as disclosing its real structures to empirical, scientific investigation. For the two taken together, what we know is both our knowing self's construct and a knowable structure existing apart from us.

There is an "absolute identity" between these parallel domains of mind (subject) and physical, organic world (object), an identity indifferent to, but also the source of, this ideal-real distinction and the many finite constituents of each of its poles. This identity, both ontological and noetic, is accessible to our minds if we abstract from particular instances of thinking. Here "absolute idealism" means that the ultimate principle and source of all is rational, that all reality (subjective and objective) derivative from it has rational structure, and that the finite knower has direct, intuitive access to this all-pervasive rationality. Schelling's correlative philosophy of art holds that, in aesthetic intuition, the → absolute unifies the inspired artist's intention with the unconscious properties of the artist's medium, so as to resolve the tension between the two and result in a beautiful object expressing the perfection of the whole.

7. Hegel

For G. W. F. Hegel (1770-1831) every possible object for consciousness is in principle knowable. Kant was mistaken in positing noumenal objects and so setting indefensible limits to knowing. Knowledge of particulars is contextual, and knowledge is complete only as a system, with everything comprehended in an interrelated way. In his logic Hegel delineates in a hierarchy the general concepts employed in thinking anything whatsoever (not just in experiencing phenomenal objects). These concepts structure our knowing and all its objects, including the very being of concrete existents. ("The rational is the real; the real is the rational.")

Hegel's absolute is → reason; finite thinkers and the objects of their thought are actualizations of this universal reason. Hegel thus resembles Schelling, ex-

cept that for him the movement of thinking proceeds through contradiction or opposition. Furthermore, its development (and that of its objects) is from implicit to explicit phases and grasps concrete actualities, not mere abstractions. Hegel's principal mentor in this respect is Aristotle, whereas Schelling's is Plato. Hegel derides Schelling's absolute identity as "the night in which all cows are black," an abstraction presupposed, not a concept constructed from careful distinctions. Hegel calls his own absolute "spirit" as well as "reason," indicating thereby that it is a motive power and not just a principle of knowing. His *Phenomenology of Spirit* (1807) exhibits the layers of spirit's operation from the simplest (matter, sensation) to the highest (art, religion, philosophy).

The realization of absolute spirit in thinking and being is thoroughly historical. Hegel's lectures on world history chart the twists and turns of spirit through historical epochs, culminating in the modern consciousness that human beings as such are free. His lectures on the history of philosophy present the sequence of philosophies as spirit's self-correcting labor of coming to full self-consciousness in the domain of thought as such. Hegel's philosophy of spirit is the most well-articulated and influential instance of absolute idealism.

In the religious domain, Hegel's early essays take up such themes as positive religion, Christianity in comparison to → Judaism and to → Greek religion, the divine and the human in → Jesus, and the spirit in the church as successor to the historical presence of Jesus. In *Phenomenology* religion conveys, in the form of representations, the higher, conceptual truths of philosophy. The later lectures on the → philosophy of religion construct historical-conceptual sequences of the world religions, culminating in their fulfillment in Christianity, the "consummate" religion. The incarnation — absolute spirit's self-actualization in a concrete being in historical time — marks the complete conjunction of the divine with humanity. Christ's dying and rising (the "Golgotha of spirit") is the cost of reconciliation and, for Hegel, concrete proof that spirit must suffer contradiction to emerge as fully self-knowing, fully reconciled with itself.

But is Hegel's speculative interpretation of the → Trinity a proper elucidation of the theological doctrine? Is his absolute spirit a suitable conception of a personal, Christian God? Is his spirit indeed the → Holy Spirit? Does he give undue primacy to spirit in the Trinity? Opinions on such issues varied widely in his day and afterward. The "right wing" among his Christian disciples favored his absolute idealism as the correct religious philosophy. Others did not. Some on the "left wing" rejected a theistic reading entirely, going as far as to hold that "spirit" denotes nothing transcendent but stands only for progressive developments in human thought and culture.

8. The Later Schelling

Influenced by the heterodox speculation of Jakob Böhme (1575-1624), Schelling, beginning in 1809, conceived cosmic evil as grounded in a pole of nonbeing (*mē on*) in God. By subordinating nonbeing to his will, God establishes his own being and then freely wills a creation mirroring him, but one vulnerable to evil when creaturely will freely actualizes the possibility of nonbeing within itself. On this view, radical contingency and → irrationality are features of reality. Schelling then portrays → Hegelianism and his own earlier idealism as "negative philosophy" (rational speculation) that needs confirmation and completion by a "positive philosophy," an "empirical" account of God's self-manifestation in history, of what God actually wills to be and do — Schelling's "philosophy of mythology" and "philosophy of revelation."

As with Hegel, the culmination of humanity's religious history comes with Christianity. In Schelling's case, however, it is not the concrete realization of absolute spirit as rational, but instead God's freely willed activity in overcoming evil, one neither foreseeable nor comprehensible by reason alone. The larger framework of idealism survives, namely, that underlying all reality, both knowing and being, is a single principle or power that is fundamentally spiritual, not material, in nature. Yet this self-conscious, spiritual foundation is ultimately will more than reason.

9. Critics of German Idealism

Hegel's absolute idealism remained a powerful force through the mid-1800s, though incisive critiques soon followed his death. Søren → Kierkegaard (1813-55), in attacking the Danish Hegelian H. L. Martensen (1808-84), championed the subjectivity of the existing individual over against an absolute idealism that seems to swallow it up by subordinating personal faith to abstract reason. On the antireligious side, Ludwig Feuerbach (1804-72) depicted Hegel's philosophy as a transposing of religious consciousness into an abstract logical system (he is "the modern Proclus"), whereas the correct philosophy is → materialism ("man is what he eats"), and religious beliefs are simply mental projections on the part of finite individuals and their culture. His follower and fellow materialist

Karl → Marx (1818-83) accused Hegel of making philosophy "walk on its head," while borrowing his seminal analysis of the master-slave relation and also distorting his method into the wooden "thesis-antithesis-synthesis" apparatus of dialectical materialism. Nearly all of the philosophy of Friedrich → Nietzsche (1844-1900) conflicts with idealism's view of God, the world, reason, and human existence.

10. Later Idealism

In Britain the most influential idealists were Bernard Bosanquet (1848-1923) and F. H. Bradley (1846-1924). Each regarded reality as a comprehensive whole, the absolute, and wrestled with the connections of human thoughts and judgments to this absolute, Bosanquet doing so in a way somewhat closer to Hegel. Bradley, more of a monist in the ancient sense, treated relations and thoughts about them as contradictory, as appearance and not reality. G. E. Moore (1873-1958), a realist, published an article "Refutation of Idealism" in 1903 that many Anglo-American philosophers took to be definitive, although it addresses only Berkeleyan or Bradleyan types of idealism. Other notable idealists include the Englishmen J. M. E. McTaggart (1866-1925) and the early R. G. Collingwood (1889-1943), as well as the Italians Benedetto Croce (1866-1952) and Giovanni Gentile (1875-1944). The American idealist philosopher Josiah Royce (1855-1916) dealt explicitly with Christian themes of → the church, → sin, and → atonement in several of his major works. None of these later idealists, however, had an impact on Christian theology comparable to that of the German idealists.

11. Idealism and Christian Theology

The romantic idealism of Schelling's early writings influenced mainly the Roman Catholic theologians of Bavaria and of the Tübingen school, including Franz von Baader (1765-1841) and J. J. von Görres (1776-1848). Hegel's chief disciples on the theological side were Ferdinand Christian Baur (1792-1860) and David Friedrich Strauss (1808-74), who wrestled with the relation of the Hegelian idea to historical facts, in particular with the relation of Christ and the Spirit to the historical Jesus and the church. I. A. Dorner (1809-84), a prominent historian of Christian doctrine, constructed a ground-breaking treatise on divine immutability with elements drawn not only from Friedrich → Schleiermacher but also from Hegel and Schelling.

In the 20th century the theme, from the later Schelling, of a *mē-onic* basis in God for the being and freedom of the creation was revived by Nikolai

Berdyaev (1874-1948) and by Paul → Tillich (1886-1965), whose *Systematic Theology* (1951-63) also shows Hegel's influence in its structure and in its treatment of spirit. Theologians of the late 20th century whose works incorporate elements drawn from Hegel include Jürgen Moltmann and Peter C. Hodgson.

Bibliography: Primary sources: G. W. F. HEGEL, *Lectures on the Philosophy of Religion* (3 vols.; ed. P. C. Hodgson; Berkeley, Calif., 1984-87) • P. C. HODGSON, ed., *G. W. F. Hegel: Theologian of the Spirit* (Minneapolis, 1997).

Secondary works: H. ALLISON, *Kant's Transcendental Idealism* (New Haven, 1983) • E. BEACH, *The Potencies of Gods: Schelling's Philosophy of Mythology* (Albany, N.Y., 1994) • A. BOWIE, *Schelling and Modern European Philosophy: An Introduction* (London, 1993) • R. BROWN, *The Later Philosophy of Schelling* (Lewisburg, Pa., 1977) • W. JAESCHKE, *Reason in Religion: The Foundations of Hegel's Philosophy of Religion* (Berkeley, Calif., 1990) • K. LÖWITH, *From Hegel to Nietzsche* (Garden City, N.Y., 1967) • N. SMART et al., *Nineteenth Century Religious Thought in the West* (3 vols.; Cambridge, 1985) • C. TAYLOR, *Hegel* (Cambridge, 1975) • G. VESEY, ed., *Idealism, Past and Present* (Cambridge, 1982) • A. WHITE, *Schelling: An Introduction to the System of Freedom* (New Haven, 1983).

ROBERT F. BROWN

Identity

The question of how the → self and the world maintain their identity in the midst of apparent change and flux has been a perennial issue debated throughout the history of Western → philosophy. Since the time of Parmenides (ca. 540–after 480 B.C.), the idea of being as an infinite and changeless substance undergirding and guaranteeing the permanence of both the world and the self has been a major answer to the problem of how a sense of identity is sustained in the midst of change and flux. The Parmenidian answer influenced the philosophies of Socrates, Plato, and Aristotle (→ Greek Philosophy) and, through these figures, much of Western philosophical and religious thought. In German → idealism G. W. F. Hegel (1770-1831) used his triad in the → philosophy of history to describe the coming of the human spirit to itself.

On the whole, modern philosophy and psychology have been dissatisfied with the classical answer, especially as it was applied to account for the identity of the self. The American psychologist and phi-

losopher William James (1842-1910) advanced a complex critique of the substance theory of the self's identity. The subsequent history of concern by psychology with the problem of identity has followed only half of his solution, and the modern post-James psychological theories of identity have had a major influence on 20th-century discussions of the problem. In chap. 10 of his monumental *Principles of Psychology,* James developed a theory of the self that addressed the problem of identity in two ways. First, he developed a theory of the empirical self that viewed the self as an object in the world identified with the sum total of all that a person can call his or her own. Although James subdivided the empirical self into the material, social, and spiritual selves, his followers, especially George Herbert Mead (1863-1931), primarily developed his theory of the social self. In his theory of the social self, James taught how the gestures and attitudes of significant individuals in our social worlds build our sense of identity and self-definition. This building occurs when we take attitudes toward ourselves that reflect the attitude that significant others have toward us.

But James was also interested in a second perspective on the problem of identity, which he addressed in his doctrine of the "pure ego." Indeed, James admitted, identity was partially a product of social recognition. But there was also an internal sense of identity — an inner sense of "I" — for which socially mediated identity did not account. James explicitly repudiated the classical doctrine, which claimed that our sense of inner identity comes from the transhistorical and unchangeable substantial → soul with which all humans are born. He proposed instead a complicated theory of the "I" as born anew in separate pulses of experience that communicate continuity and identity through the sense of familiar feelings that they transmit to one another.

James's interest in explaining the continuity of the "I" was basically dropped in later developments in both American → social psychology and → psychoanalysis. Mead accounted for the sense of identity through an amplification of James's theory of the social self. This view, in turn, was influential on American → psychiatry in the work of both Harry Stack Sullivan (1892-1949) and Erik Erikson (1902-94).

In the work of Erikson, the concept of the self and the concept of identity are virtually identical. Erikson introduced and popularized the concept of identity in American psychiatry and psychoanalysis. Yet he built his concept on both Mead's idea of the social self and Heinz Hartmann's theory of self-representation. Hartmann (1894-1969) was the first psychoanalyst to suggest that there was a fourth structure of the personality, namely, the "self-representation," which could be distinguished from the id, superego, and ego. Without explicitly building on the American tradition of James and Mead, Hartmann did indeed introduce into psychoanalysis a rudimentary but analogous concept of the social self.

Erikson amplified insights from both Hartmann and Mead into the concept of identity. Erikson defined identity as "the accrued confidence that the inner sameness and continuity prepared in the past are matched by the sameness and continuity of one's meaning for others" (p. 261). In another place Erikson says that identity is the child's sense "that his individual way of mastering experience (his ego synthesis) is a successful variant of a group identity and is in accord with its space-time and life plan" (235; → Childhood). This last quotation points out that Erikson believed that → groups can have identity just as can individuals. Furthermore, Hans Mol in his *Identity and the Sacred* has argued that it is precisely the function of religion to protect and enhance the fragile sense of group and individual identity. In fact, Mol defines religion as sacralized identity or sacralized → ideology. This insight became important in Europe after World War II as → nation and → vocation seemed to lose significance. To help young people find identity became a task of → religious education.

The concept of identity has sensitized ecumenical theological discussions to the psychological infrastructures underneath all religious identity. Religious identity is a source of psychological cohesion and is not easily changed or disrupted. In the area of → proclamation and → mission, this insight has sensitized Christians to the need to take the identity of others seriously and to work to change the identity of others only when the new, perhaps Christian, identity being offered in its place has a genuine chance of becoming sufficiently deep to provide a durable and cohesive self-definition.

→ Acculturation; Contextual Theology; Culture; Development 2; Dialogue; Ecumenical Theology; Ego Psychology

Bibliography: E. ERIKSON, *Childhood and Society* (New York, 1963) • H. J. FRAAS, *Glaube und Identität* (Göttingen, 1983) • H. HARTMANN, *Essays on Ego Psychology* (New York, 1964) • E. HERMS, *Radical Empiricism* (Gütersloh, 1977) • W. JAMES, *The Principles of Psychology* (3 vols.; Cambridge, Mass., 1981; orig. pub., 1890) • G. H. MEAD, *Mind, Self, and Society* (Chicago, 1962; orig. pub., 1934) • H. J. MOL, *Identity and the Sacred* (New York, 1976) • H. REISER, *Identität und religiöse Einstellung* (Hamburg, 1927).

DON S. BROWNING

Ideology

1. Term
2. Ideologies in Relation to Theology and Religion

1. Term

1.1. An early history of the concept of ideology might be reconstructed from F. Bacon (1561-1626). The actual word itself, however, goes back to A.-L.-C. Destutt de Tracy (1754-1836), who first used it in a talk in 1796 to refer to the strictly scientific study of ideas. In the tradition of sensationalist epistemology, sense perception was for him the source of perceptions *(idées)*, by an exact analysis of which we may attain to sure knowledge and proper rules for politics, morality, and education.

The philosophical school of the Idéologues adopted the principles that Destutt de Tracy formulated and had a great impact on the French educational system. This fact, along with their political claims, brought Napoléon (1804-15) into the picture. After initial agreement he ridiculed them as hair-splitting metaphysicians and thus gave the term a new and negative content. In 19th-century Germany, with no direct connection to the French Idéologues, the term became a general one used to defame liberal tendencies.

1.2. Modern use of the word "ideology" derives primarily from K. Marx (1818-83), who developed it in his critical adoption of the philosophy of G. W. F. Hegel (1770-1831) and along the lines of L. Feuerbach (1804-72; → Religion, Criticism of; Marxism; Hegelianism). In his *Wesen des Christentums* (1841; ET *The Essence of Christianity* [New York, 1957]) Feuerbach described God as the inner self whom we project and worship externally before finding him within. Rightly, according to Marx, Feuerbach thus traced back the apparent independence of religion, morality, and → metaphysics to human nature itself but unfortunately understood this "self" abstractly, thus missing the social character of the process of becoming independent (see Marx's critique in "Theses on Feuerbach").

According to Marx and F. Engels (1820-95) in their long essay "The German Ideology," material life is objectively beyond our grasp. In form, that nontransparent nature has its basis in the social contradictions that are immanent in the present historical stage. These social relations seem to people to be naturally given, and people's thinking seems to be something different from a simple awareness of current praxis. As ideological thinking provides a basis for the current world in thoughts and ideas and independent conceptual expression, it hypostatizes the present stage of social development as historically and epistemologically universal, masks the underlying reality, and offers an apparent mediation between the universal and the particular.

In Marx's day, however, the hypostatized universality also favored in practice the particular interests of the ruling class, whose ideas were the historically dominant ones (→ Class and Social Stratum). Criticism of ideology can thus show that the mediation is a sham one and attack in practice the apologetic interpretation of the world. In Marx, at least, this criticism was always conducted implicitly against the background of self-evident universality as the basis of criticism. This universality would increasingly become a problem after Marx (E. Bloch) and can ultimately be defined only as the negation of bad universality (T. W. Adorno). In a different nuance that was a great help in popular interpretation, Marx also called ideologies forms of consciousness that correspond to the political superstructure erected on an economic basis and in which we struggle with our social → conflicts. In a positive reformulation V. I. Lenin (1870-1924) could even use the term to denote the class interests of the workers that the party must communicate to them, since these interests are not immediately apparent.

1.3. Outside the Marxist tradition the term "ideology" became an important one in the → sociology of knowledge, which tried to make it neutral in differentiation from Marxist criticism. K. Mannheim (1893-1947) in particular radicalized the tendency already present in M. Scheler (1874-1928) to generalize the concept by showing the essential relationship of all thinking to its structural features in their historical and social context. As Mannheim put it, the content of thinking is dependent on its social setting, so thinking itself always posits being at some point and thus posits some sphere as absolute, thereby pointing beyond given reality. In contrast to a → utopia, whose realization can admittedly be ascertained only retrospectively, ideology is without consequence and conceals existing social relations (→ Society). The task of the sociology of knowledge is to work out the relation between the social situation and perspective and to relate the content of consciousness to the social situations in which it arises.

1.4. The critique of ideology and the sociology of knowledge represent the most important stations on the path along which the concept of ideology acquired in part extremely different meanings during the second half of the 20th century. The critique of totalitarianism articulated by critical theory as well as attempts at expanding the concept of ideology psychoanalytically (initiated esp. by E. Fromm [1900-1980]) also understand themselves as a critique of ideology. By contrast, the neutralization of the concept by the sociology of knowledge led to its psychological treatment in a multiplicity of monographs and finally resulted in skeptical relativism.

After the collapse of "real socialism" in 1989 and the attendant end of what was also a competition at the level of worldview between the two blocs, the significance of the concept of ideology was greatly diminished, and the area it formerly covered seems to have shifted in two directions. On the one hand, debates on economic and technological globalization — corresponding, as well, to a "globalization" of culture and thus of worldview — have implicitly adopted elements of the Marxist critique of ideology. On the other hand, themes formerly covered by the concept of ideology itself are now increasingly reflected at the level of cultural differences.

2. Ideologies in Relation to Theology and Religion

2.1. Forms of ideology undoubtedly existed before the modern period and, in their hypostatized universalizing, had an influence by supporting established power by means of art, → religion, → theology, and → philosophy. Yet they could hardly be distinguished from the latter as separate forms. When external dependence on power and systems cannot be broken, and where power and system instead are converted into the source of order and rule and take intellectual form in theology and philosophy, ideology is necessarily intermingled with the latter two.

Such forms of ideology for the mere perpetuation of power still exist, but Christian theology comes up against the fact that the incarnation, the concept of salvation, and the implications for freedom make totally impossible any transcendental grounding of social order. Working out the antitheses of human → freedom and the divine will results in a theological system in which we "control" the concept of → God by proofs (→ God, Arguments for the Existence of). Theologicophilosophical speculation thus contributes indirectly to the → secularization of religion, and finally ideology takes an independent form differing from philosophy and theology.

2.2. In the → modern period this secularization came to a head as the economic constraints were breached and as actions, orders, and systems found their justification in the being of humanity. Ideology came to differ from theology by reason of its practical claim, and from religion by the principle of rationality, which asserts that it can derive views of the world and actions from basic logical and axiomatic principles (→ Axiom; Logic). At first taking on a progressive bridge function, ideology soon came to posit one absolute form of human existence that is characterized by mastery over nature, by applied science, and by meeting human needs and conflicts with economically organized production and the resultant → consumption. The bridge function thus gave way to an appearance function. That is to say, ideological systems tried to give the appearance of solving the riddle of history by absolutizing one form of human existence. They thus could advance an apparent end of history or a discernible meaning for the future, one that is under human control and can be incorporated into human planning as something genuinely attainable. Finally, they could offer the appearance of a nexus in which we are assured that action within a certain rational system is good and will bring with it a better → future. With a practical purpose they thus can select the "truths" that serve the current political system and then absolutize them as the only possible form of human existence. In this regard the great ideologies of East and West are alike for all their material differences.

2.3. Modern ideologies, however, have run up against their limits as the limits of the economic basis to which they are politically committed have come to light. Structurally, they constantly simulate the future, but they have to infer from the present situation in order to offer guidelines for action. Their projections of the future become problematic when current limitations are seen that throw doubt on their basis. They have thus fallen into disrepute.

2.4. In theological discussions the concept of ideology undoubtedly involves in many cases overhasty rejections as the form in which some problems are stated arouses the suspicion of ideology. A consideration of the problems of ideology, however, can provide meaningful criteria relative to especially sensitive problems that confront Christians today. The concept has particular critical relevance to the problem of Christian → unity (→ Ecumenism, Ecumenical Movement) when the dialectic of unity and contradiction is threatened by a claim to absoluteness. In the discussion of the various → social systems and the related worldviews, we must also see that ideologies bring to light the problems and con-

traditions of human existence, in tandem with which ideological systems can develop their practical potential (→ Capitalism; Marxism and Christianity; Socialism). Finally, when it is a matter of the practical implications of the gospel for human action, the concept of ideology cannot be adduced in favor of limiting the social practice of the individual to the private sphere. All action takes place in the context of social practice and increasingly globally connected systems. For this reason it is *eo ipso* political. Thus the problems of the → Third World demand positions that must not be overhastily suspected of ideology (→ Liberation Theology).

In general, religion and theology can learn important lessons from the decay of the dominant modern ideologies. Negatively, they can avoid the idea that motivations result directly from theoretical and rational insights, the frightful consequences of self-dogmatizing when it is linked to power, and the ideological justification of a single principle of existence that is oriented solely to the mastering of nature and that ranks all other needs accordingly. Positively, they can learn to look at problems as a whole and not at isolated problem areas, to be more actively engaged, and to seek an economy that does not relate all needs to the principle of a technological mastering of nature and that can genuinely transcend the older ideologies.

→ Conservatism; Criticism; Ecumenical Theology; Fascism; Prejudice

Bibliography: T. W. ADORNO, *Negative Dialectics* (New York, 1973) • F. BACON, *The New Organon and Related Writings* (Indianapolis, 1960; orig. pub., 1620) • E. BLOCH, *Erbschaft dieser Zeit* (2d ed.; Frankfurt, 1962) • C. DAVIS, *Religion and the Making of Society: Essays in Social Theology* (New York, 1994) • A. DESTUTT DE TRACY, *Éléments d'idéologie* (5 vols.; Paris, 1801-15) • L. FEUERBACH, *The Essence of Christianity* (New York, 1957; orig. pub., 1841) • E. FROMM, *Psychoanalysis and Religion* (New Haven, 1950) • C. GEERTZ, "Ideology as a Cultural System," *Ideology and Discontent* (ed. D. E. Apter; New York, 1964) 47-76 • A. F. GEYER, *Ideology in America: Challenges to Faith* (Louisville, Ky., 1997) • P. HEINTEL, *System und Ideologie* (Vienna, 1967) • K. LEHMANN, "Die Herausforderung der Kirche durch die Ideologien," *HPTh* 2/2.148-202 • J. M. LOCHMAN, "Ideologie und Toleranz," *Das radikale Erbe* (Zurich, 1972) 84-96 • N. S. LOVE, *Dogmas and Dreams: Political Ideologies in the Modern World* (Chatham, N.J., 1991) • K. MANNHEIM, *Ideologie und Utopie* (3d ed.; Frankfurt, 1952) • K. MARX, "Theses on Feuerbach," *MECW* 5.3-8 • K. MARX and F. ENGELS, "The German Ideology" (1846), *MEW* 5.19-539 • K. RAHNER, "Christianity and Ideology," *The Church and the World* (ed. J. B. Metz; New York, 1965) 41-58 • M. SCHELER, *Die Wissensformen und die Gesellschaft* (2d ed.; Bern, 1960) • P. SCOTT, *Theology, Ideology, and Liberation: Towards a Liberative Theology* (Cambridge, 1994) • C. E. SHENK, *When Kingdoms Clash: The Christian and Ideologies* (Scottdale, Pa., 1988) • N. SMART, *Worldviews: Cross-cultural Explorations of Human Beliefs* (New York, 1983) • P. D. STEEVES, *Keeping the Faith: Religion and Ideology in the Soviet Union* (New York, 1989) • L. J. SWIDLER, *The Meaning of Life at the Edge of the Third Millennium* (New York, 1992) • J. B. THOMPSON, *Studies in the Theory of Ideology* (Oxford, 1984).

PETER HEINTEL and WILHELM BERGER

Ignatius of Loyola

Iñigo López de Oñaz y Loyola (1491-1556) was the founder and first general of the Society of Jesus (1541-56), the → Jesuits. As a Basque nobleman, Ignatius underwent a courtly-knightly education (1506-16), then served from 1518 as an officer of the viceroy of Navarre. On May 20, 1521, his leg was shattered during the French siege of Pamplona, and while recovering at Castle Loyola, he read religious writings (esp. the *Vita Christi* by Ludolf of Saxony, also → biographies of saints) and experienced the initial religious turn of mind that would lead him to his future calling. Probably during a visit to the monastery at Montserrat in 1522, he became acquainted with the *Exercises of the Spiritual Life* of the abbot Francisco Ximénez de Cisneros, who stressed purification, illumination, and → union with God. In Manresa in 1522-23 Ignatius experienced a mystical illumination from which his new life plan and the basic concept of his "spiritual exercises" arose, which continued to develop until 1540. They focused on cultivation of the personality through contemplative training for exclusive, active service on behalf of Christ, who lives on in the visible church, the goal being "to help souls."

For 15 years Ignatius's goal was to work in → Jerusalem, and to this end he undertook a → pilgrimage there in 1523/24. From 1524 to 1526 he became a student of Latin in Barcelona and also studied in Alcalá and Salamanca. As a mystic (*alumbrado,* "enlightened one") suspected of heresy and as a propagandist, Ignatius was brought before the → Inquisition but was found not guilty. He took his studies to Paris (1528), where in 1535 he received his master of arts degree. By way of guidance in spiritual exercises, he acquired six Spanish companions who united with him on August 15, 1534, on Montmartre as "friends in the Lord," taking a vow of poverty and service to others in Jerusalem.

By way of Spain, Ignatius traveled to Venice in 1535/36, where his six Parisian companions joined him in 1537, and together they were ordained priests. Because the military situation with the Turks prevented them from continuing on to Palestine, they went to → Rome in 1537 and chose the name "Society of Jesus." This step was preceded by a renewed vision (according to tradition, in La Storta, just outside Rome) in which Ignatius experienced God placing him at Christ's side. Despite disputes concerning their orthodoxy, in November 1538 they petitioned Paul III (1534-49) to grant them a commission commensurate with their vows and decided to preserve their collective by establishing an order. The order would vow obedience to both the general and the pope, who would send the members out in his educational service and according to his judgment, for the salvation of souls, to "Turks, Indians, heretics, other believers, or nonbelievers." The pope confirmed the order on September 27, 1540.

In 1541 Ignatius himself accepted his election as general and, until his death in 1556 in Rome, executed the duties of that office together with several secretaries in the form of an expanded but tight administration. Ignatius's initial six companions included Pierre Favre, who in 1540 was sent to the imperial diet in Worms; Francis Xavier, who from 1541 was a missionary to India and the Far East; and conciliar theologian Diego Laínez. In 1549 the society began its mission in Brazil as well as its counterreformational activity in Germany (most effectively under Jesuit Peter Canisius). These pan-European and worldwide activities spanning the next 150 years were initiated by Ignatius himself, who in his spiritual exercises, in his order's constitution, and in his administration, together with highly trained colleagues, was able to create an enduring form for his order.

Ignatius's *Spiritual Exercises* is a text for training the soul in which, for over four weeks and under the guidance of a spiritual director, one works at attaining self-cognition and trains one's will. Only those who in the future will become full members (limited to 60) are to be admitted to the entire course of exercises, while the others complete only part of them. Ignatius sought to train his members to the point of a spiritual "either-or" in the service of an endangered church in transition to a new era of defensive struggle and world proselytizing through pedagogy and mission among the population at large. On its medieval-monastic foundation, the radical nature of the decision he demanded is structurally analogous to the Reformational alternative between serving God or serving idols and the devil. The order's success in education, preaching, mission, recruiting (at Ignatius's death, the order had 38 full members and 1,000 additional members), and longevity attests to its founder's spiritual and organizational energy, his ability to establish tradition, and his contemporaneity. Ignatius was canonized in 1622; his feast day is July 31.

Bibliography: Primary sources: IGNATIUS OF LOYOLA, *Personal Writings: Reminiscences, Spiritual Diary, Select Letters, Including the Text of "The Spiritual Exercises"* (trans. J. A. Munitiz and P. Endean; New York, 1996) • J. N. TYLENDA, *A Pilgrim's Journey: The Autobiography of Ignatius of Loyola* (Wilmington, Del., 1985).

Secondary works: D. LONSDALE, *Eyes to See, Ears to Hear: An Introduction to Ignatian Spirituality* (Chicago, 1990) • G. MARON, "Ignatius von Loyola in evangelischer Sicht," *Ignacio de Loyola y su tiempo* (ed. J. Plazaola; Bilbao, 1992) 819-36 • L. VON MATT, *St. Ignatius of Loyola* (New York, 1963) • W. W. MEISSNER, *Ignatius of Loyola: The Psychology of a Saint* (New Haven, 1992); idem, *To the Greater Glory: A Psychological Study of Ignatian Spirituality* (Milwaukee, Wis., 1999) • K. RAHNER, *Spiritual Exercises* (New York, 1965) • K. RAHNER, P. IMHOF, and H. N. LOOSE, *Ignatius von Loyola* (Freiburg, 1978) • R. SCHWAGER, *Das dramatische Kirchenverständnis bei Ignatius von Loyola* (Zurich, 1970) • J. I. TELLECHEA IDÍGORAS, *Ignatius of Loyola: The Pilgrim Saint* (trans. C. M. Buckley; Chicago, 1994).

KURT-VICTOR SELGE

Illness → Health and Illness

Illusion

1. Aesthetics
2. Metaphysics and Criticism of Religion

The word "illusion" derives from Lat. *illusio* (action of mocking) and *illudo* (mock at, play with). In common usage it denotes "self-deception," "false idea," "misleading perception," or "fantasy," but it also has more specific senses in → aesthetics, → metaphysics, and criticism of religion (→ Religion, Criticism of).

1. Aesthetics

In aesthetics illusion is the term for a state of perception induced by a work of art (plastic, literary, or rhetorical) in which those who see, read, or hear the work are voluntarily carried into the relation to its object that the work effects. The 18th century saw important discussions (by J. B. Dubos, M. Mendelssohn, et al.) focusing on the pleasure or moral value of artistic illusion and the degree of deception involved.

2. Metaphysics and Criticism of Religion

In the field of metaphysics and the criticism of religion, the → empiricism of D. Hume (1711-76) and the → criticism of I. Kant (1724-1804) describe all dogmatic metaphysical notions as illusory. Kant (→ Kantianism) points to the transcendental illusion, namely, the fact that in → epistemology there are basic rules in the use of → reason that seem to be objective principles. Hence the subjective necessity of a certain linking of concepts is viewed as an objective necessity in defining "things in themselves" — a process that we can detect but cannot avoid.

The idea of illusion in L. Feuerbach (1804-72) is more directly critical of religion. Feuerbach tries to show that the antithesis that → theology posits between God and humanity is an illusion, being a cleavage in humanity itself. K. Marx (1818-83) gives Feuerbach's criticism a typical twist when he finds in religion an illusory comfort for comfortless reality (→ Marxism).

F. Nietzsche (1844-1900) calls all striving for truth or for solid concepts an illusion; destroying such illusions, however, leads us nowhere. In the → psychoanalysis of S. Freud (1856-1939), religion is merely wishful thinking and its strength is that of wishful thinking, a view that comes to pervade the academy. In the tradition of → positivism E. Topitsch (b. 1919) attempts to unmask as illusions all metaphysical, theological, and ideological thought forms (→ Ideology), and especially attempts to find some overarching and total → meaning.

The term "illusionism" is used for views that hold the external world of time and space to be mere appearance.

→ Imagination; Solipsism; Subjectivism and Objectivism

Bibliography: A. S. ABBOTT, *The Vital Lie: Reality and Illusion in Modern Drama* (Tuscaloosa, Ala., 1989) • J. C. EXUM and D. J. A. CLINES, *The New Literary Criticism and the Hebrew Bible* (Sheffield, 1993) • L. FEUERBACH, *The Essence of Christianity* (New York, 1957; orig. pub., 1841) • S. FREUD, *The Future of an Illusion* (ed. J. Strachey; New York, 1989; orig. pub., 1927) • I. KANT, *Critique of Pure Reason* (trans. N. K. Smith; New York, 1987; orig. pub., 1781; rev., 1787) • W. A. KORT, *Take, Read: Scripture, Textuality, and Cultural Practice* (University Park, Pa., 1996) • B. D. PALMER, *Descent into Discourse: The Reification of Lan-*

guage and the Writing of Social History (Philadelphia, 1990) • W. STRUBE, "Illusion," *HWP* 4.204-15 (bibliography) • E. TOPITSCH, *Erkenntnis und Illusion* (Hamburg, 1979).

FRANK OTFRIED JULY

Image of God, Imago Dei → Anthropology

Images

1. Early Religion
2. Judaism
   2.1. OT
   2.2. Late Antiquity
3. Christianity
   3.1. Early Period
   3.2. Byzantine Iconoclastic Controversy
   3.3. Reformation Churches
   3.4. Present Situation and
        Theological Evaluation

1. Early Religion

Even in prehistoric times it was thought that images have power. By drawing objects, one could achieve control of them, for example, in the picturing of animals that were to be slain (such as in the cave paintings at Altamira, Spain, ca. 15,000 B.C.; → Magic). The divine was encountered at first in objects that had not been fashioned or in natural phenomena (stones, trees, etc.). Higher religions then had cultic images in animal or human form. These figures were always three-dimensional, were the focus of care and ceremony, and were clothed, anointed, provided with food, put to death, and destroyed. The cult required a priesthood, an → altar, and a → temple (§1). The point of images was to give visibility to the holy and to bring it under control (→ Sacred and Profane).

The Egyptians and Greeks made images that told the myths of the gods. These narrative images were fundamentally different from cultic images, for only the latter demanded veneration. In the assessment of images we may note a religious pluralism that ranges from acceptance (Egyptians and Greeks) to toleration to strict rejection (→ Judaism and → Islam). Already in classical antiquity we find criticism of images and their veneration. Xenophanes and Heraclitus (6th cent. B.C.) argued that images were incompatible with the dignity of God. In the Roman period Lucian (d. after A.D. 180) ridiculed elaborate images of God as the dwelling place of worms and mice. Despite this criticism the world into which the early church came was full of temples, images, and centers of pilgrimage that localized divine power.

2. Judaism
2.1. OT

Judaism was a religion fundamentally without images. When images did occur, they were regarded as an error and a breach of God's command. The basis of the prohibition of images is the second commandment (Exod. 20:4-5; → Decalogue). If originally this law forbade only images of God, in the Deuteronomic version (Deut. 4:15-19) it forbids *any* artistic depiction. We often find this commandment linked to the abhorrence of foreign gods (Exod. 34:14; Lev. 19:4; Hos. 11:2), at times with the requirement to put away images (Gen. 35:2-4; Exod. 23:24). God's → wrath is appeased when idolatrous images are put away (Judg. 10:6-16; Isa. 27:9). Yahweh sends faithful kings to do this removal (1 Kgs. 15:12) or stirs up the people to do it (2 Kgs. 11:18). There is debate as to the origin of the prohibition and its sphere of validity.

2.2. *Late Antiquity*

In the period of late antiquity there were two opposing trends in Judaism. The strict orthodox condemned the making and possessing of images. Those under Hellenistic influence, however, were open to them. Dispersion Judaism, which became increasingly important, could not avoid some adjustment to a world that affirmed images. An independent Jewish art thus developed that reached its climax in the third century A.D. We find an extensive artistic imagery both in the Jewish heartland (Beth-Alpha synagogue) and in the → diaspora (Dura-Europos synagogue).

3. Christianity
3.1. *Early Period*

Up to the end of the second century neither literary nor archaeological sources give any evidence of the existence of → Christian art. The NT says nothing about the use of images. One may infer from this silence a lack of interest due to many causes. One was that primitive Christianity lived in tense expectation of the → parousia. Another was that in the struggle against paganism (→ Gentiles, Gentile Christianity), images were regarded as idolatrous and magical signs. Finally, the small number of Christians, and their lowly social status, prevented them from building their own places of worship, which might have functioned as centers of Christian art. Furthermore, the church, which saw itself as the new and true Israel, viewed the OT commandment as binding.

The oldest record of the existence of an image of Christ comes from Irenaeus (d. ca. 200), who tells us that the → Gnostic sect of the Carpocratians set up and venerated an image of Christ, along with the images they maintained of great philosophers (*Adv. haer.* 1.25.6). In nonheretical churches voices against images increased toward the end of the second century, from which we may infer that such images were now present. Tertullian (d. ca. 225) denounced all images, but Clement of Alexandria (d. ca. 215) thought that neutral motifs might be used on seal rings. Origen (d. ca. 254) rejected images on the ground that they are a hindrance to spiritual knowledge. The Council of Elvira (ca. 306) decisively condemned images in the church.

Since, in spite of these negative voices of the theologians, we find Christian images at the latest by 220 (in the → catacombs in Rome and in the Dura-Europos → house church), we may assume that in assimilation to pagan customs, Christians had images in defiance of official church teaching. These images, which revolved around the themes of → sin, → death, and redemption, arose at the same time in different parts of the Roman Empire, both in funerary and in liturgical settings.

In the Constantinian age criticism declined or focused on portraits or → images of Christ. Eusebius of Caesarea (d. ca. 340) did not oppose symbolic images or those that depicted scenes, but he sharply rejected the request of the emperor's sister Constantia for an image of Christ on the ground that the divinely transfigured Christ cannot be depicted.

Although Epiphanius of Salamis (d. 403) still rejected images, the monuments of the fourth century show that, as distinct from the naive lay art of the third century, there had now developed a theologically shaped church art. Especially after the Council of → Nicaea (325), an attempt was made to express in art the dogmatically asserted coessentiality of the Son with the Father by making images of Christ similar to those of the all-powerful and divine emperor and by decorating churches more heavily with biblical and dogmatic cycles. Third-century images were influenced by the desire of lay piety for deliverance and preservation in death, in contrast to those of the fourth century, which became the expression of theological speculation. Obviously significant for private → devotion were souvenirs from → pilgrimages and the → relics of saints (→ Saints, Veneration of), which were regarded as worthy of veneration and were thought to bring good fortune.

3.2. *Byzantine Iconoclastic Controversy*

The story of images in Christianity became that of the dialectic between joyful acceptance and strict rejection. The chief example is the Iconoclastic Controversy, which lasted almost one and a half centuries, from 726 to 843. As in all such controversies, the motivation was not just religious. The struggle took place against the background of a monastic and imperial fight for precedence. In 726 Byzantine emperor Leo III (717-41) ordered the destruction of an image of Christ on the gate of the imperial palace in Constantinople. The enemies of images (iconoclasts, "destroyers of images") used as arguments the OT commandment and our inability to portray the divine nature of the Son. Those who favored images (iconodules, "slaves of images") were charged with Nestorianism and Monophysitism. John of Damascus (d. ca. 749) supplied the latter with their theological justification, namely, that the visible is an image of the invisible, and that the veneration of images is transferred to that of which they are images. The → incarnation provided Christological justification.

The seventh ecumenical council, Nicaea II (787), tried to mediate the controversy by distinguishing between the forbidden adoration of images (*latreia*) and the permitted veneration (*timētikē proskynēsis*). Those who favored images eventually prevailed, but they took steps to establish strict church supervision for the regulation and systematization of → Byzantine art.

3.3. *Reformation Churches*

It is against the background of a developed image-centered devotion and even bondage that we must see the → Reformers' criticism of images. Certainly from the time of Augustine (354-430), the Roman church had made the usual distinction in principle between images and what they depict. They had thus accorded to images, not adoration, but only didactic and moral value. During the Middle Ages, however, popular → piety had increasingly seized upon images. The veneration addressed to them had increasingly come to resemble cultic adoration. This development was closely related to the emergence of a new, previously disparaged type of sculpture in the round (the cult of relics). Finally, new types of images were produced for veneration — → devotional and wonder-working images.

Criticism of images had already arisen both within the church (→ Cistercians) and outside it (→ Cathari; Hussites). The arguments of Protestant image-breakers were the same as those already expressed in the → early church and during the Iconoclastic Controversy. The position of M. Luther (1483-1546) toward images was extremely subtle and in part situational. He could use the same vehemence against both the superstitious veneration of images and the vandalism of images by the so-called left-wing of the → Reformation (e.g., Carlstadt). Rejecting images in principle, he could also justify their educational use. We can plainly establish neither their rejection nor their use from Luther.

The Swiss reformers U. Zwingli (1484-1531) and J. Calvin (1509-64) were more consistent and more radical. Their absolute concept of God did not leave any place for an artistic depiction of Christ. They forbade even a didactic use of images on the ground that images always lead to idolatry. The Reformed Church thus instituted a worship without images, whereas the Lutheran Church still values images highly.

The → baroque brought rich decoration even to Protestant churches. Only in the age of the → Enlightenment did rationalistic tendencies and the desire for denominational differentiation lead to a → Protestantism without images.

3.4. Present Situation and Theological Evaluation

The renunciation of images in Protestant churches, reflected in present-day → church architecture, has its basis in the → Renaissance and → secularization as well as the → Reformation. It has brought some impoverishment to Christian piety. By its particular insistence that the church must be the church of the Word, Protestantism has made faith a matter of the head in a way that does not do justice to the full dimension of human beings as creatures of feeling as well as intellect. The attempts of Protestant Romantics (C. D. Friedrich, P. O. Runge) and the Catholic Nazarenes to revive religious art in opposition to Enlightenment trends must be regarded as a failure.

The mass production of sweetly pious images for private devotions on into the 20th century has had considerable influence, but Christian art has not been able to secure a place in the church. Religious images have not disappeared completely, but they have freed themselves from official church control and led to critical and often destructive complaints against established Christianity. Now that art has become autonomous, it will be difficult indeed to bring it back into the church.

Bibliography: On 1: F. HEILER, Erscheinungsform und Wesen der Religion (Stuttgart, 1961) • H. SCHRADE, Der verborgene Gott. Gottesbilder und Gottesvorstellungen in Israel und im Alten Orient (Stuttgart, 1949).

On 2.1: O. KEEL and C. UELINGER, God, Goddesses, and Images of God in Ancient Israel (Minneapolis, 1998) • T. N. D. METTINGER, No Graven Image? Israelite Aniconism in Its Ancient Near East Context (Stockholm, 1995) • H. SCHÜNGEL-STRAUMANN, Gottesbilder und Kultkritik vorexilischer Propheten (Stuttgart, 1972) •

K. VAN DER TOORN, The Image and the Book: Iconic Cults, Aniconism, and the Rise of Book Religion in Israel and the Ancient Near East (Leuven, 1997) • W. ZIMMERLI, "Das Bilderverbot in der Geschichte des Alten Israels," Studien zur alttestamentlichen Theologie und Prophetie (Munich, 1974) 247-60.

On 2.2: C. ROTH, Die Kunst der Juden (2 vols.; Frankfurt, 1963) • K. SCHUBERT, "Das Problem der Entstehung einer jüdischen Kunst im Lichte der literarischen Quellen des Judentums," Kairos 16 (1974) 1-13; idem, "Spätantikes Judentum und frühchristliche Kunst," SJudA 2 (1974) 1-86.

On 3.1: H. BECK and P. C. BOL, eds., Spätantike und frühes Christentum. Ausstellung im Liebighaus (Frankfurt, 1983) • F. W. DEICHMANN, Einführung in die christliche Archäologie (Darmstadt, 1983) • W. ELLIGER, Die Stellung der alten Christen zum Bilder in den ersten vier Jahrhunderten (Leipzig, 1930).

On 3.2: M. CAMILLE, The Gothic Idol: Ideology and Image-Making in Medieval Art (Cambridge, 1989) • J. IRMSCHER, ed., Der byzantinische Bilderstreit (Leipzig, 1980) • K. A. KNAPPE, "Bilderstürmerei. Byzanz–Reformation–Französische Revolution," Kunstspiegel 3 (1981) 265-85 • G. LIMOURIS, ed., Icons, Windows on Eternity: Theology and Spirituality in Colour (Geneva, 1990) • S. MICHALSKI, The Reformation and the Visual Arts: The Protestant Image Question in Western and Eastern Europe (London, 1993).

On 3.3: H. BELTING, Likeness and Presence: A History of the Image before the Era of Art (Chicago, 1994) • J. ROHLS, "'. . . unser Knie beugen wir doch nicht mehr.' Bilderverbot und bildende Kunst im Zeitalter der Reformation," ZTK 81 (1984) 322-51 • G. SCAVIZZI, The Controversy on Images from Calvin to Baronius (New York, 1992) • M. STIRM, Die Bilderfrage in der Reformation (Heidelberg, 1977).

On 3.4: L. ALEXANDER, Images of Empire (Sheffield, 1991) • W. HOFMANN, ed., Luther und die Folgen für die Kunst. Katalog der Ausstellung in der Hamburger Kunsthalle (Munich, 1983) • A. B. MOORJANI, The Aesthetics of Loss and Lessness (New York, 1992) • H. SCHWEBEL, Das Christusbild in der bildenden Kunst der Gegenwart (Giessen, 1980) • R. SÖRRIES, Die Evangelischen und die Bilder (Erlangen, 1983).

REINER SÖRRIES

Images of Christ

1. Theoretical Basis
2. Historical Trends
3. Eastern Church
4. Outside Europe

1. Theoretical Basis

The term "images of Christ" refers to the visual substitutes that art finds for the person of Jesus Christ (→ Jesus), which primarily and authentically has come down to us, and may be identified, only in verbal form. Since there are no original pictures of Christ and the NT tradition tells us nothing about the outward appearance of Jesus of Nazareth, all images of Christ are works of religious imagination. As such, they are important but also debatable in the history of devotion and theology.

As regards the origin and development of these images, the productive impulse came from writings (biblical, apocryphal, legendary, doctrinal, and spiritual) and from artistic models (→ iconography, types, use of various techniques, etc.). The status of images of Christ can be understood in analogy either to the Word (as having a kerygmatic or didactic function) or to the sacrament (as a mode of divine presence for veneration as a cultic image or for dialogic contemplation as a devotional image).

As an iconographic group, images of Christ are hard to classify. Cultic and devotional images demand that Christ be either isolated or dominant. When the function is kerygmatic or didactic, however, pictures that make any reference to Christ may be read as statements about him. (On theriomorphic or material symbols of Christ, see the articles "Cross," "Fish," "Monogram of Christ," and "Symbolism of Animals.")

2. Historical Trends

2.1. The earliest images of Christ in the third century (using symbols of the Good Shepherd and Teacher, with narratives of the baptism and miracles) were a kerygmatic presentation of his saving significance, his teaching, and his power over death. In iconographic form Christ appeared first as a young, beardless, Apollonian bringer of salvation. From the Constantinian age the dignified figure of an older, bearded man became increasingly dominant.

Then the → dogma of his deity and humanity (→ Christology 2) and the adoption of the imperial insignia created the new figure of Christ as the heavenly Basileus (king), the cosmic Pantocrator (almighty ruler), with scenes of homage and lawgiving. With the development of veneration of images in the sixth century came the first independent images of Christ linked to interest in the *acheiropoiētoi*, "those not made with hands" (in the East, the Abgar legend; in the West, esp. in medieval devotion, the *vera icona* [true icon], or Veronica legend).

2.2. Images of Christ in the age of Charlemagne and Otto and the Romanesque period (→ Middle Ages 1) developed the basic imperial model, depicting the divine majesty, with Christ as world judge or crowned on the cross. Soteriological and Christological teaching shaped the image cycles that came with early Romanesque.

From the 12th century a visual differentiation in the depiction of God developed, with the Father now being a separate figure in human form alongside Christ (at the mercy seat). This arrangement provided scope for Gothic to make humankind and the humanity of Christ a dominant theme (e.g., Christ as a child, Christ triumphant, and esp. the Christ of the passion). In the history of devotion this emphasis is connected with the spirituality of the mendicant → orders (→ Dominicans; Franciscans), the literature of mystical visions (→ Mysticism), and the mystery plays (→ Religious Drama).

2.3. Renaissance art tried to bring out the deity in the figure of Christ by depicting perfect bodily beauty. Scenes picturing the transfigured Christ predominated.

The → Reformation brought a decisive break either by stopping any further development of images of Christ (esp. where the influence of → Calvinism was strong) or by focusing interest on the painting of preaching and teaching. The selection and execution of scenes were meant to bring to light the Protestant understanding of the grace and → justification manifested in Christ. In Catholic → baroque (→ Catholic Reform and Counterreformation) the stress lay on images of Christ, on dramatic passion scenes infused with passion mysticism, and then on scenes of triumph that were given visual form with all the means available of spatial illusionism and handling of light. From the humanist tradition came also an interest in emblems and allegories of Christ.

The Christ images of Rembrandt (1606-69) are denominationally an isolated phenomenon. The artist depicted the incarnation in the human mystery of everyday situations and faces on which the light of the knowledge of God shines.

2.4. In images of Christ in the 19th and 20th centuries, one may see divergence between the Christian art that followed traditional Christian iconography and Christian art that pursued the avant-garde, which developed apart from the sacral tradition and made Christ a theme only occasionally or incidentally. Without being able to classify individual artists and their works unequivocally or exclusively, one may note some basic trends from the beginning of the 19th century. The church tradition promulgated and propagated by the Nazarenes and

Pre-Raphaelites, following early medieval models (up to Raphael), sought to produce historical and devotional pictures that would establish cultural continuity with the ideal medieval world and a mood of subjective piety.

On the margin of the church, or outside it, two families of Christ images have emerged. One has produced images of Christ with private mythological and mystical features, which we could classify as:

- *nature-mystical* — C. D. Friedrich (1774-1840), P. O. Runge (1777-1810), J. Beuys (1921-86);
- *syncretist-surrealist* — W. Blake (1757-1827), M. Klinger (1857-1920), S. Dali (1904-89);
- *symbolist* — O. Redon (1840-1916), P. Gauguin (1848-1903), M. Denis (1870-1943);
- *expressionist* — E. Nolde (1867-1956), E. Barlach (1870-1938; → Expressionism); and
- *meditative* — A. Jawlensky (1864-1941), K. Malevich (1878-1935), A. Rainer (b. 1929).

In this context, the possibility of nonrepresentational images of Christ has been discussed by M. Rothko (1903-70), B. Newman (1905-70), and others.

The second family of Christ images are those that articulate the significance of Christ by putting his figure in individual situations (as the artist-Christ) or in social situations of contemporary suffering and conflict. Artists here include H. Daumier (1808-79), L. Corinth (1858-1925), J. Ensor (1860-1949), E. Munch (1863-1944), G. Rouault (1871-1958), A. Kubin (1877-1959), M. Beckmann (1884-1950), K. Schmitt-Rottluff (1884-1976), M. Chagall (1887-1985), O. Dix (1891-1969), G. Grosz (1893-1959), G. Sutherland (1903-80), and A. Hrdlicka (b. 1928).

Up to the middle of the 20th century, the church and theology adopted an attitude of reserve or even rejection toward these trends. They have now been accepted and adapted to church art and architecture, but there has still been too little theological reflection on the historical dimensions and demands of the plastic arts in the 19th and 20th centuries.

3. Eastern Church

The concept of artistic depiction that emerged from the Iconoclastic Controversy — a combination of the doctrine of the incarnation with prototypes (→ Images 3.2) — characterized images of Christ through the centuries. The relation of original and copy in terms of physiognomy was maintained, as was that of the grouping of narrative and representative themes. Within this framework, however, especially today, there are variations in piety and style. Iconographically worth noting are special types that

diverge from the Western repertoire (e.g., the unsleeping eye and Christ as angel). The Eastern veneration based on the relation of original and copy gives images of Christ a central place in churches (→ Iconostasis; Icon) and liturgy.

4. Outside Europe

Thus far, images of Christ in churches outside European culture have been inadequately studied from a Eurocentric perspective. In a proper investigation of images of Christ in a developing polycentric world culture, these images would need to be set in a history of art of the individual cultures, with a discussion of their relation to the development of the European art (and its avant-garde), which has been dominant for centuries.

→ Devotional Images; Symbol

Bibliography: H. AURENHAMMER, "Christusbilder," *LCI* 1.454-638 • C. CARVARNOS, *A Guide to Byzantine Iconography: Detailed Explanation of the Distinctive Characteristics of Byzantine Iconography* (Boston, 1993) • J. H. FOREST, *Praying with Icons* (Maryknoll, N.Y., 1997) • P. HINZ, *Deus Homo* (2 vols.; Berlin, 1973-81) • M. JONES-FRANK, *Iconography and Liturgy* (Chicago, 1994) • J. KOLLWITZ et al., "Christus, Christusbild," *LCI* 1.355-454 • L. OUSPENSKY, *Theology of the Icon* (Crestwood, N.Y., 1992) • M. QUENOT, *The Resurrection and the Icon* (Crestwood, N.Y., 1997) • G. ROMBOLD and H. SCHWEBEL, *Christus in der Kunst des 20. Jahrhunderts* (Freiburg, 1983) • H. SCHWEBEL, *Das Christusbild in der bildenden Kunst der Gegenwart* (Giessen, 1980) • N. P. ŠENČENKO, "Types of Christ," *ODB* 1.437-39.

ALEX STOCK

Imagination

In its primary sense, the imagination (Lat. *imaginari*, "picture to oneself") is the power to form mental images, or "likenesses," of the objects that appear in the external world. Its function is to reproduce or represent these objects, even when they are not immediately present to the senses. Imagination complements perception by presenting to the rational faculty the images originating in the senses. It is thus a kind of bridge between the world of the senses and the world of conceptual thought.

A secondary power of the imagination is its ability to fantasize, that is, to envision pictures of things or events that do not actually exist in the natural world. The dual powers of representation and fantasy are related because fantasy depends on images that are already present in the mind. Whether imaging objects of the external world or composing new images via fantasy or → dream, the imagination is representing or manipulating impressions originating from the sensory world.

These powers of the mind are included in what → Augustine called spiritual vision, "the kind of vision by which we represent in thought the images of bodies even in their absence." For Augustine the weakness of the imagination (spiritual vision) was that it, like the senses, could be deceived, which happens when it "judges the objects of its vision to be real bodies, or when it attaches some property of its own fancy and false conjecture to bodies that it has not seen but merely conjures up in imagination." The imagination escapes deception, however, "in the intuitions of the intellect" (*De Gen. ad litt.* 12.25)

The likelihood of sinful conjectures is what made the imagination suspect to many in the Christian tradition. John → Calvin, for example, thought that paying heed to fantasies would lead believers away from clear understanding of the natural laws of God's creation: "As then vain men weary themselves with speculations, which have not in them, so to speak, any practical knowledge, it is no wonder that they run headlong into many delirious things" (*Comm. Jer.*, at 51:19). The tendency to view imagination as the locus of natural depravity in the mind is enhanced by the use of the word "imagination" in the KJV and other translations of Gen. 6:5 and 8:21 ("the imagination of man's heart is evil from his youth"). The disparagement of → images and → icons in Protestant churches is related to this distrust of imagination, as is the occasional suspicion of fiction, theater, and the arts generally.

An expanded view of the imagination emerges in what is commonly called the → Romantic era. Samuel Taylor Coleridge, following Immanuel Kant, ascribes to the imagination a new role that makes it an equal to, and a companion of, discursive or scientific reason. For Coleridge the imagination is not just a bridge to higher mental functions but is itself one of those functions. In developing his view, Coleridge distinguishes between primary and secondary imagination. The former embraces the two powers described above, whereas the latter goes beyond the powers of representation and fancy. Primary imagination is limited to the representation and manipulation of the images gleaned from perception, but secondary imagination is creative. Using the images given to it by the primary imagination, the secondary imagination creates new combinations of im-

ages that are produced only in the imagination, and thereby it brings about new forms of understanding. Understanding thus includes not only analytic and scientific processes of thought but also those that are intuitive or imaginative. The latter consist of seeing relationships among the constituent elements of observation and experience and integrating them into unified and truthful conceptions or visions of reality. → Reason is analytic, scientific, and discriminating, whereas imagination is integrative, poetic, and unifying. Reason predominates in the sciences, and imagination predominates in the arts, but both are necessary for the development of true understanding.

Many Romantic thinkers after Kant and Coleridge regard the imagination as the superior power of the mind, since it has the power to integrate disparate experiences and forms of knowledge into a cohesive unity. It is often seen as a power opposed to → science because it creates, primarily through the arts, a vision of the world that transcends the empirical limitations of science. Imagination, in this view, explores the universal conditions of all of reality, whereas science is limited to the universal conditions of the empirical world.

The elevation of, and faith in, the imagination that occurred in Romantic → aesthetics extended into the 20th century (e.g., J. Derrida, M. Foucault, J. Kristeva). It was brought into question, however, by the → postmodernists of the later 20th century. Much recent literary and historical scholarship concentrates on showing how the power of the imagination is tied to cultural and linguistic institutions. The imagination, in this view, cannot explore the universal conditions of experience, since it is necessarily conditioned by cultural environments.

Nevertheless, the imagination is still an agent of freedom; it can explore all of the new possibilities of → experience and thought that are continually opened up by the processes of history. And since it is concerned with cultural and historical rather than absolute → norms, it thrives in an intellectual environment characterized by unpredictability, → pluralism, and relativity. It seeks out what is unexpected, unusual, arbitrary, shocking, and often rebellious rather than what is universal, normative, or traditional. In the postmodern view, the imagination enables us to "play" with possibilities without requiring us to make commitments to any view of ultimate truth.

Bibliography: E. T. H. Brann, *The World of the Imagination* (Totowa, N.J., 1991) • J. M. Cocking, *Imagination: A Study in the History of Ideas* (London, 1991) • J.

Derrida, *Dissemination* (Chicago, 1988; orig. pub., 1972) • M. FOUCAULT, *The Order of Things* (New York, 1973) • R. KEARNEY, *Poetics of Imagining: Modern to Post-Modern* (2d ed.; New York, 1998) • J. KRISTEVA, *In the Beginning Was Love: Psychoanalysis and Faith* (New York, 1987).

CLARENCE WALHOUT

Immanence and Transcendence

1. The Terms
2. Antiquity
3. Christian Theology
4. Modern Philosophy
5. Modern Theological Discussion

1. The Terms
In antiquity the terms "immanence" and "transcendence" (from Lat. *immaneo,* "remain in place," and *transcendo,* "step over, pass over or beyond") do not occur in their later metaphoric sense as substantive constructions for an all-encompassing relationship or for that to which the notion of "passing over or beyond" is referring. The metaphoric meanings seem to occur for the first time in the work of Duns Scotus (ca. 1265-1308) and William of Ockham (ca. 1285-1347).

2. Antiquity
If not the term itself, at least the metaphoric point of transcendence is undoubtedly present in the pre-Socratics (→ Greek Philosophy) when they base all being in a principle, although this principle admittedly still cannot be essentially distinguished from what is based on it. Parmenides (ca. 540-after 480 B.C.) and Plato (427-347), with his doctrine of the ideas (→ Platonism), find a more radical basis for being in which there is an ontological distinction between the basis and what is based on it. Thus in his comparison with the sun, Plato describes the idea of the → good as the epistemological and ontological basis of all being (*Resp.* 509B), though not itself of the quality of what is attested or known.

Aristotle (384-322), who views all being as motion initiated by an unmoved mover, does approach the notion of something transcendent to being (→ Aristotelianism). As the unmoved mover (*Metaph.* 1074b34, the *noēsis noēseōs*) directly effects and sustains cosmic order, however, its activity finds fulfillment in this function. The order of the cosmos is grounded in it and, as the aim of pure activity, is immanent to it (→ God 3).

3. Christian Theology
With the coming of the Judeo-Christian doctrine of God, the idea of transcendence, which has always received more emphasis in the history of Christianity than immanence, was decisively radicalized. In the philosophy of antiquity the ideal order of the cosmos had an origin that more or less transcended the phenomenological world but that could be perceived by philosophical effort. In contrast, the biblical understanding of God and the resultant Christian teaching developed a view of transcendence in which God is wholly other and is hidden from human knowledge (→ Epistemology); the existence of God absolutely transcends human existence. This Christian view of God thus brought a new stress on transcendence and consequently gave the terms "immanence" and "transcendence" a new significance.

At the same time, the ancient view of the world as one of statically cyclic occurrence yielded to an eschatological and historically defined view (→ Eschatology; Theology of History). This shift led to a desecularizing of the world that radically exposed humanity to divine → grace. God's plan of salvation, which is beyond our comprehension, transcends history (→ Salvation History).

The new meanings of transcendence thus introduced have determined the usage right up to the → modern period. It should be noted, however, that from the first century A.D. antiquity's view of transcendence began to mingle with the biblical understanding of God, resulting in the adoption of philosophical positions that led to a concealing of the authentic Christian concept. The idea of transcendence was not so radical in the resultant systems of thought and ran increasingly into the danger of being weakened by metaphysical conceptions according to the definition of the divine-human relation or the knowability of the divine. Finally, the question of God's transcendence became an epistemological question. Either (as for Plotinus) God is infinite and nothing positive can be said about him (God's transcendence), or (as for Thomas Aquinas) the nature of God discloses itself by analogy (God's immanence).

4. Modern Philosophy
Knowledge of God's total unknowability, which found its most impressive expression in Anselm (1033-1109), Nicholas of Cusa (1401-64), and M. Luther (1483-1546), lost its epistemological relevance with the rise of modern → philosophy. God's transcendent being and qualities ceased to be a central theme as there developed a greater awareness of

→ reason, which increasingly focused on what it may know. For R. Descartes (1596-1650; → Cartesianism) God existed ultimately as governor of the mathematically determinable order of the world, and his existence could be deduced by pure reason. As reason was deified, divine and human knowledge came to be merged, thus weakening God's transcendence. The idea of divine immanence penetrated instead into philosophical systems, reaching a climax in the doctrines of B. Spinoza (1632-77) and G. W. Leibniz (1646-1716).

With I. Kant (1724-1804) immanence and transcendence lost their exclusive link to the question of God (→ Kantianism). The distinction runs through all Kant's works on theoretical philosophy but must be differentiated from the concept of the transcendental, which he introduced into German philosophy. This term describes a specific way of knowing objects insofar as it is possible a priori (*Critique of Pure Reason*, B25) and thus denotes a philosophical method. In contrast, an immanent method relates to the use of the categories of the understanding insofar as the latter derive exclusively from perception presented to → experience, and insofar as knowledge remains focused exclusively on such perception. If knowledge is to be commensurate with the criterion of scientifically certain knowledge, it will always derive from this immanent method. This criterion of scientific knowledge can be filled out, however, by the constant possibility of passing over the limits of experience and becoming transcendent (*Prol.* §40). In this way we view the synthesized multiplicity of what we observe in its totality, though not as an object of experience. For Kant the epistemological field is always open to a transcendence that makes possible an extension of knowledge.

J. G. Fichte (1762-1814) rejected epistemologically any form of transcendence, since it does not arise from the ego itself. For Fichte the concept of the act, which defines the ego as self-originating, made possible the deduction of the reality of the ego as both acting and knowing its action. In his view only this stage of knowledge as intellectual perception reached the level of true philosophy or criticism (→ Idealism).

Already the young G. W. F. Hegel (1770-1831), in his criticism of Kant and Fichte, hit upon the idea of the identity of reason with itself, with no place for any world "outside" (→ Hegelianism). Mediation was the central category in the positing of this identity. Philosophy cannot begin, as in Fichte, with an absolute first principle, for it is mediated or defined by something else, which is opposed to that basic principle. Hegel's whole system is thus rationally structured in stages, in which it reflects the degrees of mediation. For Hegel, then, the transcendent is the next stage of reason that has not yet reflected on its relation to the other that conditions it. From the standpoint of the → absolute (i.e., unceasing mediation), transcendence is immanent to the absolute.

The later F. W. J. Schelling (1775-1854) took up the problem of the self-mediation of reason. For him the central question was how reason, which takes all the steps of mediation, can establish its own existence. He had to admit that its being is thus transcendent for thought. The being of reason is absolutely transcendent being (*SW* 13.127). Its self-limitation, which he proposed in order to give the proper rank to its being and to its basis in God, brings to light the dilemma in all his later philosophy. By positing itself ecstatically outside its grounding impulse, reason grants transcendence its rights, as it were; these rights, however, are sanctioned only by the self-communication of reason itself.

"Self-transcendence in relation to origin" (W. Schulz) is also constitutive of the philosophy of S. Kierkegaard (1813-55) in the ethical demand that the subject should determine itself, in spite of the contrary experience of its being determined by its origin in God. Kierkegaard makes this situation a positive one as existence, by accepting mediation through transcendence, relieves itself of despair of the world and by this very fact establishes a relation that opens up new possibilities.

Less in terms of Kierkegaard's existential questioning and more in terms of what he thought was his own more basic existentialist approach, M. Heidegger (1889-1976) said, in relation to transcendence, that "being is the transcendens pure and simple" (*On Being and Time*, 62). This understanding is the ontological basis of his philosophy, for ontologically he saw a distinction between that which exists *(das Seiende)* and being as such *(das Sein)*, which is the basis of the former. That which exists can be truly grasped only on the basis of transcendence. Transcendence, then, is the basis of the possibility of → truth, because "there is Being [*Sein*] (not being [*Seiende*]) only in transcendence as world-projecting and situated grounding" (p. 123). Existence as the special being that alone understands being as such consists of the possibility of transcending the distinction (→ Existentialism). In this regard Heidegger parted company with his teacher E. Husserl (1859-1938), who argued that the world is a world only for the consciousness and that the question of transcendence is thus linked to subjective philosophy. Transcendence in every form is a meaning of being that constitutes itself in the ego.

In → Marxism there was a complete change in the approach to the question of transcendence. The interest of K. Marx (1818-83) focused not on the spiritual basis but on the concrete social relations that underlie it and their historical development, which Marx regarded as the cause of human self-alienation. For him, therefore, → ethics, → metaphysics, and → religion, in which transcendence is the theme, could be unmasked as an ideological superstructure, since they reflect a nonhistorical autonomy and have been made dispensable by revolutionary practice (→ Ideology). One might view Marxist philosophy as a way of setting aside the problem of transcendence.

T. W. Adorno (1903-69) took a different course, for although he advocated the social dimension in opposition to traditional subjectivism, he gave new significance to the problem of transcendence. Noting the basic disunion of the activities of thinking that establish identity and unity, on the one hand, and, on the other, a world that is totally alienated from this thinking, a world whose deformity cannot be grasped through thought, he found for philosophy the task of leaving open within and, as it were, over against thought itself a sphere of the nonconceptualized, the particular, the individual, or the nonidentical, which transcends the closed circle of thinking. By means of the concept, philosophy must reach beyond the concept.

English-speaking philosophy, unlike its German counterpart, has tended not to distinguish between "transcendental" and "transcendent" and generally uses the former term. This usage can be observed, for example, in the lively and still ongoing debate regarding "transcendental arguments," triggered by P. F. Strawson's rejection of skepticism in the late 1950s. The ambiguous use of the term "transcendent" can be also found in the early philosophy of L. Wittgenstein (1889-1951). In his *Tractatus Logico-Philosophicus* (1919), he describes logic and ethics as "transcendental" (6.13 and 6.421 respectively), whereas the analogous passages of his pre-*Tractatus* notebooks use the term "transcendent" (see entry for July 30, 1916). At this early stage of his work Wittgenstein explicitly designed philosophy as an instrument that sets the limits of meaningful language. Ethics and logic were considered to be beyond these limits, thus transcendent.

The reception of Wittgenstein's philosophy entailed two major reactions. On the one hand, a positivist reaction eliminated all nonverifiable subjects (e.g., metaphysics) from serious (i.e., scientific)

thinking, a view adopted by the Vienna Circle and neopositivism. On the other hand, a neopragmatic approach (→ Pragmatism) advocated dealing with metaphysical problems such as transcendence solely within their social contexts. Language was no longer considered to be a medium of world representation but rather an exchange of signs for specific purposes. So while for a positivist a philosophical consideration of "transcendence" was simply nonsense, for a pragmatist such an idea was of no philosophical interest. Both philosophical streams were influenced by the linguistic turn which replaced the mind-world relation with the language-world relation as a major paradigm of modern philosophy. The transcendent becomes the unspeakable.

So-called New England → transcendentalism was a philosophical and social movement in the northeastern United States in the middle of the 19th century. It used pantheistic, antiempiricist, and metaphysical ideas to express the spiritual unity of the world (thus highlighting immanence) and argued for "another reason" besides understanding that is better equipped to intuit metaphysical truths.

5. Modern Theological Discussion

→ Dialectical theology, or theology of the Word of God, which arose in the 1920s, borrowed from Heidegger's analysis of being. Thus R. Bultmann (1884-1976) found in the concrete, nonobjectifiable processes of existence and in the existential framework of historicity a possibility of transcending ontic existence in a movement to our true origin. In this regard the same applies to P. Tillich (1886-1965), who tried to find a new meaning for transcendence in our ability, with a new perspective, to move beyond unsatisfactory reality to → hope.

This realization of → faith, which in Bultmann and Tillich was put in concrete existential acts, was linked by K. Barth (1886-1968) to an essentially more radical insight, namely, that only God himself in his → revelation posits the basis of knowledge of God (i.e., God is known only by God, *CD* II/1). In this way Barth could uphold God's otherness from the world and humanity and protect himself against interpretations that link knowledge of the biblical message to a specific immanent experience. In this regard D. Bonhoeffer (1906-45) was akin, stressing the openness of the question of God and our being claimed by God in a way that no religion can match: "God is he who comes; that is his transcendence." In contrast, J. Moltmann (b. 1926) proposed that immanence and transcendence are not alternatives but perspectives woven into history (a "forward-looking transcendence").

In Roman Catholic theology K. Rahner (1904-84) brought transcendental considerations into his discussion of transcendence. To finite subjects God's ineffability and sovereignty are known as the conditions of knowledge and contingency. God is the a priori presupposition of the world and our knowledge of it. He is an essentially spiritual being and in this way transcendent. He is present as a holy mystery.

H. Küng (b. 1928) also began with our experience of contingency, our imperfection, our hopes and expectations and longings. We confront these experiences with our capability of transcendence beyond our one-dimensional existence. On a similar basis E. Bloch (1885-1977) found here a critical urge to restructure society (transcending without transcendence). Küng, however, was interested in the ground of the divine. Encounter with God's knowledge and action as an absolutely necessary and incontestable claim (K. Lehmann) points finally to something more, the precise definition of which can do justice to the various theological positions.

→ Future; Transcendental Philosophy; Transcendental Theology; Worldview

Bibliography: T. W. Adorno, *Negative Dialectics* (trans. E. B. Ashton; New York, 1973) • K. Barth, *The Epistle to the Romans* (London, 1957; orig. pub., 1919; 2d ed., 1922) • E. Bloch, *Atheismus im Christentum* (Frankfurt, 1968) • P. F. Boller Jr., *American Transcendentalism, 1830-1860: An Intellectual Inquiry* (New York, 1974) • D. Bonhoeffer, *Gesammelte Schriften* (vol. 5; Munich, 1972) • R. Bultmann, "What Does It Mean to Speak of God?" *Faith and Understanding* (vol. 1; New York, 1969; orig. pub., 1933) 53-65 • D. Chidester, *Patterns of Transcendence: Religion, Death, and Dying* (Belmont, Calif., 1990) • Y. Congar and R. F. Trevett, *The Mystery of the Temple; or, The Manner of God's Presence to His Creatures from Genesis to the Apocalypse* (Westminster, Md., 1962) • J. G. Fichte, *Grundlage der gesamten Wissenschaftslehre* (Leipzig 1794) • G. W. F. Hegel, "Glauben und Wissen," *Kritisches Journal der Philosophie* (Jena, 1802) • M. Heidegger, *The Essence of Reasons* (Evanston, Ill., 1969; orig. pub., 1929); idem, *On Being and Time* (London, 1962; orig. pub., 1927) • E. Husserl, *Cartesian Meditations* (The Hague, 1965; orig. pub., 1931) • J. W. Jones, *Contemporary Psychoanalysis and Religion: Transference and Transcendence* (New Haven, 1991) • I. Kant, *Prolegomena to Any Future Metaphysics That Will Be Able to Come Forward as Science* (trans. G. Hatfield; New York, 1997; orig. pub., 1783) • S. Kierkegaard, *The Sickness unto Death: A Christian Psychological Exposition for Upbuilding and Awakening* (trans. H. V. Hong and E. H. Hong; Princeton, 1980) • H. Küng, *Vierundzwanzig Thesen zur Gottesfrage* (5th ed.; Munich, 1993) • K. Lehmann, "Transzendenz," *LTK* (2d ed.) 10.316-19 • E. Lévinas, *Alterity and Transcendence* (New York, 1999) • J. Moltmann, "Die Zukunft als neues Paradigma der Transzendenz," *IDZ* 2 (1969) 2-13 • L. Oeing-Hanhoff, "Immanenz," *HWP* 4.230-37 • W. Pannenberg, "Gott V," *RGG* (3d ed.) 2.1717-32 • K. Rahner, *Schriften zur Theologie* (vol. 3; Einsiedeln, 1957) • R. R. Reno, *The Ordinary Transformed: Karl Rahner and the Christian Vision of Transcendence* (Grand Rapids, 1995) • R. Rorty, "Verificationism and Transcendental Arguments," *Noûs* 5 (1971) 3-14 • F. W. J. Schelling, *Philosophie der Offenbarung* (2 vols.; Stuttgart, 1858-59) • W. Schulz, *Die Vollendung des deutschen Idealismus in der Spätphilosophie Schellings* (Stuttgart, 1955) • F. Schuon, *Logic and Transcendence* (New York, 1975) • P. F. Strawson, *Individuals* (London, 1959) • B. Stroud, "Transcendental Arguments," *JPh* 65 (1968) 241-56 • P. Tillich, *The Courage to Be* (New Haven, 1952).

Herbert Hanreich

Immortality

1. Term
2. Early Non-Christian Views
3. Christian Views
4. Post-Christian Views

1. Term

The word "immortal," from Lat. *immortalis,* means "not susceptible to death" or "not going to die." Like its Greek synonym, *athanasia,* the term explicitly negates → death, the apparently inevitable fate of all living things. The NT predicates *athanasia* of → God (1 Tim. 6:15) and also of resurrected humans (1 Cor. 15:53-54). All Christians affirm "the → resurrection of the body and the life everlasting" (Apostles' Creed), yet some disagree about the immortality of the → soul and the nature of the resurrection. While the Christian understanding of immortality shares similarities with some other religions and philosophies, it is different from most and, in the final analysis, unique.

2. Early Non-Christian Views

The notion of immortality, both divine and human, is found in primal → animistic and → polytheistic religions, but it is neither universal nor uniform. While the high god or gods typically exist without end, lesser deities and spiritual beings may be killed or periodically die and be reborn. In → Babylonian mythology the god Marduk creates the world from the body of the goddess Tiamat, whom he has slain in combat. Beliefs about human immortality vary widely in primal religions. Some apparently do not affirm any kind of afterlife, as in the Gilgamesh epic. Others, such as the underworld in the ancient Near East and Greece, envision a shadowy, sleepy remnant of earthly life. In some primal religions important persons become immortal demigods after death, whereas the shades of commoners fade into oblivion. In others the dead are spirits who perpetually help or harm the living. Still others believe that their tribe is a permanent group of souls who are periodically reincarnated throughout the generations. Common to all these notions of immortality is belief that an essential part of earthly humans — a soul, spirit, or ethereal body — continues to exist beyond physical death and acquires the characteristics suited for the next life. In some religions (e.g., that of the Egyptian Book of the Dead; → Egyptian Religion), immortality is determined by divine judgment of the individual's earthly life.

The great Oriental religions, → Hinduism and → Buddhism, also include a variety of beliefs about immortality. Most traditions affirm → reincarnation, the idea that individuals are part of the cosmic cycle of life (saṁsāra) and continually return as other living things until they generate enough good moral-spiritual energy (→ karma) to transcend the wheel of life. These traditions differ, however, concerning the ultimate destiny of the soul and its immortality. In monistic Hinduism the individual soul (jīva) is regarded as a temporary manifestation of Atman, the immortal cosmic consciousness, also called Brahman, God, or Ultimate Reality. When the individual transcends reincarnation, its identity with Atman/Brahman is realized, attaining immortality but losing its individuality. In nonmonistic branches of Hinduism and in Mahayana Buddhism, the individual soul retains its existence and is able to achieve immortality beyond reincarnation in the perpetual bliss of pure consciousness (samādhi, nirvāṇa). More austere Hinayana and → Zen Buddhist traditions are agnostic about what transcends earthly experience and affirm only that the goal of life is full awareness and oneness with Reality, which is neither mortal nor immortal.

A similar variety of views is found in → Greek philosophy. → Materialists, such as Democritus, held that the soul is generated by the body and thus ceases to exist when the body dies. Aristotle held that human individuals are constituted of matter and a "soul," which he viewed as individuated, immaterial, rational-animal form. At death the two el-

ements are separated, matter decomposing into more simple forms, and the form losing its individuality. Aristotle thus could affirm the immortality of the universal Active Intellect, but not of individual human souls. It was Plato whom later Christian thinkers found most useful. He held that individual humans consist of an eternal, uncreated rational soul and a naturally mortal material body. At death the soul is freed from the body for another incarnation or perhaps for eternal freedom from the impediments of material existence. The → Gnostics and some → mystery cults in the Roman Empire also believed in the immortality of the individual soul liberated from the material world.

3. Christian Views

All Christians believe in immortality, understood as a final resurrection to everlasting life. The majority have held that immortality also includes continuing existence of the soul or person between death and resurrection. Almost every detail of this general confession and its biblical basis, however, has been disputed.

The debate has been fueled by the development of beliefs about the afterlife within the Bible itself and the variety of language in which they are expressed. The Hebrew Bible does not present the human soul (nepeš) or spirit (rûaḥ) as an immortal substance, and for the most part it envisions the dead as ghosts in Sheol, the dark, sleepy underworld. Nevertheless it expresses hope beyond death (see Pss. 23 and 49:15) and eventually asserts physical resurrection (see Isa. 26:19; Dan. 12:2).

Intertestamental Judaism includes several accounts. The → Sadducees emphasized the dissipation of life in Sheol and sometimes adopted Greek materialism, which denied the afterlife altogether. Others, such as Philo, were strongly influenced by Plato and stressed the immortality of the soul rather than physical bodily resurrection. The → Pharisees embraced both the Sheol and the resurrection texts of the OT, affirming an intermediate state, a future bodily resurrection at the coming of the Messiah, and immortality in his kingdom.

The NT develops a position most like the Pharisees (see Acts 23:6-8). While its greatest stress is on the resurrection of the body, which is explicitly identified as "immortal" (see 1 Cor. 15:53-54), it also envisions personal communion with Christ immediately upon death (Luke 23:43, 46; 2 Cor. 5:1-10; Phil. 1:20-24). It uses "soul" (psychē) and "spirit" (pneuma) in largely synonymous, nontechnical senses and does not explicitly describe either as "immortal." On the basis of this reading of Scripture, most Christians have understood immortality as "everlasting life," a gift of God to the individual believer that is given already in this life (John 6:47), continues after death in an "intermediate state" until bodily resurrection, and endures forever with God in his eternal kingdom, the new heaven and new earth.

Two minority interpretations have challenged the majority reading of Scripture. One reflects → Platonism, the other materialism. The first view, as with Plato and Philo, focuses on the soul or spiritual dimension as the immortal essence of human nature, regarding bodily life as incidental or even as an impediment. It understands resurrection as transformation of the earthly human into a spiritual being (see 1 Cor. 15:44) and immortality as eternal communion with God in heaven. It tends to read the NT and even the OT texts about human nature and the afterlife as though they taught Platonism. This view has been defended by some theologians but has been more widespread in popular piety. It was challenged by Cullmann's famous essay "Immortality of the Soul or Resurrection of the Dead?" (1956).

The other minority view is implicitly materialistic. It is found mainly among 16th-century → Anabaptists and later sects, such as Seventh-day → Adventists. Held in England by Thomas Hobbes and John Milton, it has gained popularity among intellectuals in the 20th century. It holds that a person cannot exist without a body and denies the immortality of the soul. It thus rules out the intermediate state, although it may speak of "soul sleep," and affirms only the resurrection of the body to immortality at Christ's second coming. It denies that the OT envisions an afterlife and that the NT teaches an intermediate state. It believes that the majority Christian view results mainly from Platonism, not the Bible. Both the Platonist and materialist minorities agree with the majority that the resurrection will occur at Christ's return. There is another minority, including philosopher John Hick, who believe that resurrection, whether spiritual or physical, occurs at the instant of death. In spite of these disagreements, however, traditional Christians all believe that they will undergo resurrection and receive eternal life imparted by Jesus Christ on the basis of his own resurrection (1 Corinthians 15; Phil. 3:20-21).

Christian thinkers have affirmed the immortality of the soul in several ways. Some, like Augustine and Thomas Aquinas (who differ in their views of the nature of the soul and its relation to the body), held that the immortality of the soul is a biblical teaching but also offered philosophical reasons for it, such as its simple, indivisible nature: what is noncomposite cannot decompose. They disagreed with Plato in asserting that the soul's immortality is conferred by God when created. Others, such as Duns Scotus, doubted that the immortality of the soul can be established philosophically. René Descartes, too, although he was rationally certain that the mind is a substance distinct from the body and thus can exist without it, came to doubt that he could prove its immortality but accepted it as a teaching of Scripture. Theologians have also debated whether the soul is immortal intrinsically or only because God perpetually maintains its existence.

4. Post-Christian Views

→ Deistic thinkers such as Voltaire, J.-J. Rousseau, and I. Kant continued to affirm the immortality of the soul as a rationally justified belief apart from → revelation. Kant considered it a postulate of moral reason: the unconditional obligations of morality justify belief in an unending afterlife necessary to fulfill them. Other non-Christian thinkers came to different conclusions. Some redefined immortality to mean the termination and transformation of personal existence into something else that endures. B. Spinoza, a → pantheist, believed that humans are immortal only in the sense that they are part of the eternal divine mind that endures beyond their individual lives. This view is similar to Aristotle's Active Intellect and the Hindu Atman. Immortality by means of assimilation into a greater reality is also found among German and English → Romantics (J. W. Goethe, A. Tennyson), New England transcendentalists (R. W. Emerson, H. D. Thoreau; → Transcendentalism), and → idealistic philosophers (G. W. F. Hegel, F. H. Bradley). The → process philosopher A. N. Whitehead spoke of "objective immortality," the view that individuals "live on" in the continuing effects of their lives in the world. In neopagan and naturalistic worldviews "immortality" is attained by reassimilation into the "life force," or the perpetual life cycle of nature, or by "living on" in the memory or genes of one's progeny. All these definitions of immortality are figurative and paradoxically affirm the extinction of individual persons at death.

More tough-minded, the 18th-century agnostic D. Hume stated that there is no reason to think that humans survive death any more than other physical objects and living things. This view is held by most materialists and scientific → rationalists. These thinkers simply deny human immortality and dismiss Romantic and idealistic notions of "living on" as sentimental nonsense. In contrast, spiritists, appealing to parapsychological phenomena and near-death experiences, have continued to assert immortality understood literally as personal survival of death.

Christians who find modern idealism, romanticism, naturalism, → spiritism, or reincarnationism more compelling than the traditional biblical worldview often replace the historic Christian view of immortality or attempt to harmonize it with another notion. However, the majority view of the Christian tradition — that personal immortality is a gift of God in Christ already in this life, continues between death and resurrection, and is completed with the resurrection of the body to life in God's everlasting kingdom — remains the teaching of most churches and the belief of most Christians worldwide, whether Orthodox, Roman Catholic (see *Catechism of the Catholic Church* [1994]), or traditional Protestant.

Bibliography: AUGUSTINE, *De immortalitate animae* (On the immortality of the soul), CSEL 89 (1986) 101-28 • J. CALVIN, *Inst.* 3.25 ("The Final Resurrection") • O. CULLMANN, *Immortality of the Soul or Resurrection of the Dead?* (London, 1958) • M. ELIADE, "Death, Afterlife, Eschatology," *From Primitives to Zen: A Thematic Sourcebook of the History of Religions* (New York, 1967) chap. 4 • J. HICK, *Death and Eternal Life* (New York, 1976) • J. RATZINGER, *Eschatology: Death and Eternal Life* (Washington, D.C., 1988; orig. pub., 1977) • S. D. F. SALMOND, *The Christian Doctrine of Immortality* (5th ed.; Edinburgh, 1903) • F. SCHLEIERMACHER, *The Christian Faith* (2 vols.; New York, 1963; orig. pub., 1821–22) §161 ("The Resurrection of the Flesh") and §163 ("Eternal Blessedness") • THOMAS AQUINAS, *Summa theol.* I, qq. 75-76, 89-90 (on the soul, body, and intermediate state), and III supp., qq. 69-93 (on the intermediate state and final resurrection).

JOHN W. COOPER

Immunity

Immunity is exemption from prevailing rules. It gives persons, things, and places a privileged position involving rights of both freedom and authority.

1. The concept of immunity derives from Roman law. It related first to relief from various public burdens. Under Constantine (306-37) the clergy (→ Clergy and Laity) and church property enjoyed relief from taxation. In Frankish law immunity included judicial immunity as well as freedom from taxes and duties. Modern constitutions have added new forms such as parliamentary immunity. A common practice is to grant immunity from prosecution to important witnesses.

2. Medieval → canon law used immunity for the comprehensive legal claims of the church in opposition to secular power, including the right of the clergy to be tried only in church courts. As → church and state drew apart in the 19th century and as the state suppressed ecclesiastical → jurisdiction, the church found it increasingly difficult to press its claim, in spite of the condemnations in the → Syllabus of 1864. The development of → Roman Catholic → church law corresponds to the loss of immunity. The 1917 → Corpus Iuris Canonici could still claim broad privileges for the clergy and → exemption for sacred places, but the 1983 CIC refrains from bringing such matters under church law.

3. The church's claims to immunity are in many cases protected by → concordats that form part of state constitutions or by the de facto granting of the rights of self-determination and protection and other privileges. Churches and church buildings, however, seldom enjoy a legal immunity from police entry, although students in even secular universities often claim this privilege on the basis of the fact that universities originally enjoyed immunity as church institutions (and their members as clergy).

A much-debated issue in this field is that of → asylum, which has traditionally been an important aspect of church immunity. Thus some churches in the United States claim immunity on behalf of certain illegal aliens. The claim has no very clear legal basis, but probably in view of a proclaimed separation of church and state, plus the lingering impact of medieval → tradition, the authorities have shown no great enthusiasm to intervene.

→ Jurisprudence

Bibliography: R. DANIELI, P. S. LEICHT, and P. PALAZZINI, "Immunità ecclesiastica," *EC* 6.1696-1700 • J. E. DOWNS, *The Concept of Clerical Immunity* (Washington, D.C., 1941) • F. MEEHAN, "Immunity," *NCE* 7.391-93 • O. VOLK, "Immunität," *TRE* 16.84-91 • D. WILLOWEIT, "Immunität," *HDRG* 2.312-30 (bibliography).

BERND T. DRÖSSLER

Impressionism

1. Term

Impressionism is a stylistically uniform orientation in the history of art. It finds manifestation especially in paintings and graphics, but also in sculpture, literature, and music.

2. Development

The beginning of impressionism is usually traced to 1874, when a group of young artists who had been barred from an exhibition exhibited their works privately in Paris. At the time the impressionistic method had already reached a peak, and the showing did not enjoy any great success. Instead, the artists were subjected to scorn and contempt. Their pictures were said to give evidence of madness. In 1874 the famous journalist Louis Leroy, in reaction to Monet's *Sunrise,* coined the ironically contemptuous term "impressionism," which would come to characterize the whole movement.

3. Painting

The impressionists were almost all born between 1830 and 1840: C. Pissarro in 1830, É. Manet in 1832, E. Degas in 1834, A. Sisley in 1839, C. Monet in 1840, P.-A. Renoir and B. Morisot in 1841. They were often viewed as a group, but they rejected being called such, stressing their individual methods of work and modes of depiction.

3.1. *Technique*

What viewers missed in 1874 was the usual realism. While impressionism does seek a realistic portrayal, a significant change from tradition lies in the representation of light not merely as brightness but as illumination, strengthened by complementary con-

trasts. The comma technique (pointillism) with its short, spontaneous, undirected strokes brings complementary colors into inner, sparkling contact. In a light-filled atmosphere landscape, buildings, and people are then presented as the reflection of a moment. This technique makes demands on viewers, since their eyes must mix the colors from a distance to get the effect of illumination. With their freedom of form and coloring and brushwork, combined with objectivity, the artists achieve a high level of → illusion. For this reason impressionism is often seen as the beginning of abstract painting. It certainly abandons naturalism and shows that art has its own means of expression independent of nature.

Even before the famous 1874 exhibition the French artists had taken a revolutionary course. With the study of nature then in the forefront, impressionism came in 1874 in the form of landscape painting. Other pictures then depicted novelties in the developing cities, with paintings from the spheres of art, entertainment, the theater, the boulevards, and the restaurants. We also find still-life pictures, portraits, and nudes. The painters who used oils are the most famous; watercolorists are often unknown.

3.2. *Criticism*

Even before the first exhibition contemporaries charged that the new style of art was offensive. The public regarded many of Manet's works, such as *Luncheon on the Grass* (1863), as scandalous. His *Olympia* (1863) deliberately avoids giving the impression of a statue. By contours and half-tones he gave a light-filled atmosphere distinctive expression. Young and independent artists who did not belong to any school soon recognized the typical character of the new style.

3.3. *Models*

Impressionism itself found its models in landscape and open-air paintings and in the Dutch painting of the 17th century. Already in 1834 J. Turner in England had painted a fire as an optical event with completely new methods. It would be a whole generation before young French painters adopted similar techniques.

3.4. *Impact*

The French painters made an impact beyond the borders of France. Painters in Germany such as M. Liebermann (1847-1935), F. Uhde (1848-1911), L. Corinth (1858-1925), and M. Slevogt (1868-1932); in England such as C. S. Keene (1823-91) and P. W. Steer (1860-1942); in the United States such as T. Eakins (1844-1916); in Holland such as J. Israëls (1824-1911), J. Maris (1837-99), A. Mauve (1838-88), and M. Maris (1839-1917); as well as artists in Poland, Scandinavia, and Russia all came under the influence of impressionism and neo-impressionism as the principles of the impressionistic use of color were systematized in a seemingly scientific fashion (e.g., in separation of colors and pointillism).

4. Sculpture

In sculpture, too, artists burst through the limits of convention and abandoned smooth, static works in favor of works with a dynamic interplay of light and shade. Particular attention was attracted by the bronze *Citizens of Calais* (1884-86), in which A. Rodin (1840-1917) presented the collective sacrifice as a secular version of the crucifixion. The painter E. Degas (1834-1917) also gave a new impulse to sculpture in Europe with his *Little Dancer* (1880).

5. Literature

Impressionism also invaded the world of literature. Influenced by French criticism of É. Zola (1840-1902), the literary critic H. Bahr (1863-1934) forecast in 1891 a new art and literature that would impress sensations, images of the moment, and fleeting events upon the nerves.

5.1. *Literary Technique*

Writers in Vienna especially devised a new technique while avoiding novelty in content. They dismissed attempts at seeing the world as it is as naive faith. For them the essential element in literature is constituted by sense impressions and momentary reflections of things in the ego. Authors experience with their nerves and grasp things as creative individualists who withdraw from society into an isolated artistic existence. The new work was in sharp contrast to naturalistic writing.

As in the case of painting and drawing, this literature needs a reader for the decisive step in the creation of art. In painting, the viewers have to mix the colors. In literature, they must make the associations that are consciously not stated, or only hinted at, in the work. Sound imitations, speech rhythms, and speech tempos characterize the style. The sentences are in part short and snappy, at other times syntactically incomplete.

Naturalistic principles of style were still dominant in the early days of impressionistic writing, so that the founders of consistent naturalism, A. Holz (1863-1929) and J. Schlaf (1862-1941), could be ranked as impressionists. Other important impressionist writers were D. Liliencron (1844-1909), A. Schnitzler (1862-1931), R. Dehmel (1863-1920), S. George (1868-1933), the early H. Hofmannsthal (1874-1929), R. M. Rilke (1875-1926), and especially P. Altenberg (1859-1919), also C.-P. Baudelaire (1821-67) and K. Hamsun [Pedersen] (1859-1952).

5.2. *Criticism*

This new direction in literature was called either symbolism (because of the symbolic style) or impressionism. The group was also given the name "decadent" because of (as critics saw it) the moral degeneracy and weaknesses of the authors. This term denotes the writers' rejection of middle-class values, a luxuriating in sensory beauty through exaggerated subjectivism, and a repudiation of belief in → progress. Bahr called the poetry of the decadents pathological — a new form of madness. F. Nietzsche (1844-1900) found in it an unavoidable manifestation of European exhaustion but also the possibility of a new beginning. For him it was as necessary as any other step forward in life, and there was no way of avoiding it.

6. Music

Difficulties arise when we try to apply the term "impressionism" to music, but scholarship since the turn of the last century has used the word to describe the compositions of C. Debussy (1862-1918), though he himself did not like the term because of its originally pejorative use.

6.1. *Musical Technique*

Debussy's style, which betrays some influence of the Far East, is marked by static, nonfunctional harmonies and circular themes with ornamental motifs. A warmth and softness evocative of the moods of nature predominates. The music tries to capture the open air, and by refined coloring Debussy manages to create an analogy to painting. It seems to be the task of his music to mediate the charm of multiple coloring, but it can be done only through synaesthesis on the part of the listeners. The harmonic devices (juxtaposition of dissonant chords, stacked thirds, etc.) are for the most part of → Romantic derivation.

6.2. *Definition*

Only in relation to Debussy is it possible to define an impressionistic style in music, so that one might just as well speak of Debussy's style rather than that of impressionism. This style strongly influenced other composers such as E. MacDowell (1860-1908), R. Strauss (1864-1949), A. Roussell (1869-1937), the early M. Ravel (1875-1937), M. de Falla (1876-1946), O. Respighi (1879-1936), and C. M. Scott (1879-1971).

7. Theory

Common to all three artistic forms are psychologistic and → solipsistic features. Bahr traced the underlying theory to the work of the physicist and theoretician E. Mach (1838-1916), who found in objects only a relative consistency. Matter for him was simply a collection of elements, tones, and colors — a shifting impact of features that exist only as they are perceived. We can make objective statements about them because individuals have similar sensations. The receptive ego sifts the various impressions. Bahr seemed to think that for Mach each of us perceives the world differently and that all of us ourselves are in constant change. The effect of the moment becomes the fundamental feature.

8. Feeling for Life

The impressionistic feeling for life had ethical and religious implications (→ Ethics). The artists of impressionism took up Christian themes (→ Christian Art) and thus cast a religious aura, but they reinterpreted traditional Christian contents and thus created a contemporary → faith with human creativity at the root. This understanding is clear in Rilke's *Book of Hours*. The God of this modern prayer book does not exist but must be created subjectively (W. Falk).

Ethically, the egocentricity of this view of life is clear in the exaltation of life. Painters prefer the feminine nude as a means of expressing the element of enjoyment and intoxication. Writers like F. Wedekind (1864-1918) in his play *Hidalla* (1905) expound the duty of love and tear down the barriers of middle-class convention. We see this trend especially in the decadent movement. A naturalistic ethic of compassion is replaced in impressionism by an ethic of enjoyment (R. Hamann and J. Hermand) in a new form of → hedonism.

9. Movement

Like other periods, that of impressionism does not form a historical unity. Impressionism is more a category in artistic history. The fact that there is a gap of more than two decades between the first impressionistic painting and the first impressionistic literature shows that we are dealing more with a movement of impressionism than with an epoch. One might say that the only common feature is the break with tradition. In place of social confession and depiction of the milieu, we find a harmony parallel to nature and a subjective transcending of the given. This development leads on to cubism and prepares the ground for → expressionism.

Bibliography: H. Albrecht, "Impressionismus," *MGG* 6.1046-90 • H. Bahr, *Die Überwindung des Naturalismus* (Dresden, 1891) • J. Clay, ed., *Impressionism* (Secaucus, N. J., 1973) • W. Falk, "Auswirkungen des epochalen Wandels auf Formen der Religiosität," *Religion und Zeitgeist im 20. Jahrhundert* (Stuttgart, 1982) 179-220 • T. Garb, *Die Frauen des Impressionismus* (Stuttgart, 1987) • P. Gay, *Art and Act: On Causes in History–Manet, Gropius, Mondrian* (New York, 1976) • R. Hamann, *Impressionismus in Leben und Kunst* (Marburg, 1907) • R. Hamann and J. Hermand, *Impressionismus* (Berlin, 1977) • J. D. Herbert, "Impressionism," *EncA* 2.473-77 • R. L. Herbert, *Impressionism: Art, Leisure, and Parisian Society* (New Haven, 1998) • D. F. Hoopes, *The American Impressionists* (New York, 1972) • D. Kullmann, ed., *Erlebte Rede und impressionistischer Stil. Europäische Erzählprosa im Vergleich mit ihren deutschen Übersetzungen* (Göttingen, 1995) • E. Mach, *Erkenntnis und Irrtum* (Leipzig, 1905) • F. W. Nietzsche, *Aus dem Nachlaß der Achtzigerjahre* (9th ed.; ed. K. Schlechta; Munich, 1969) • J. Renoir, *Renoir, My Father* (Boston, 1962) • R. M. Rilke, *Poems, 1906-1926* (Norfolk, Conn., 1957) • M. Schapiro, *Impressionism: Reflections and Perceptions* (New York, 1997) • P. Smith, *Impressionism: Beneath the Surface* (New York, 1995) • S. Strumper-Krobb, *Impressionistische Erzählverfahren im Spiegel der Übersetzung* (Göttingen, 1997).

Helmut Bernsmeier

Imprisonment → Punishment

Incarnation

1. Religious Aspect
   1.1. Term
   1.2. Non-Christian Examples
2. Theological Aspects
   2.1. Concept
   2.2. Development in Christian Theology
   2.3. Significance
3. Controversial Aspects
   3.1. Chalcedonian Definition
   3.2. Orthodox Theology
   3.3. Roman Catholic Theology
   3.4. Reformation Theology
   3.5. Modern Discussion

1. Religious Aspect

1.1. *Term*

The term "incarnation," which is now used in religious discussion as well as Christian theology, is not always plainly distinct from related terms like "manifestation" or "epiphany." There is thus no uniform usage, and the employment of the word is much debated. It seems best to limit its use to the idea that *a divine being has embodied itself in human form and in this form lived on earth.* A distinction might be made between continuous incarnation in an → institution or dynasty and a discontinuous incarnation in single individuals.

1.2. Non-Christian Examples

In → Egyptian religion, at least in the early period up to the Fourth Dynasty, the idea of a continuous incarnation occurs. The name of Horus, the god of heaven, is put before that of Pharaoh, signifying that Pharaoh is an incarnation of this god.

In Tibetan → Buddhism the idea of a continuous incarnation is central. The Dalai Lama is supposedly an incarnation of Bodhisattva Avalokiteśvara. Yet the use of "incarnation" here is open to question, since it is not clear that the idea of Buddha or the bodhisattva is the same as that of God.

In the Vishnu strand of → Hinduism the idea of a discontinuous incarnation arose. The descent *(avatāra)* of the god into the world brings disruption of cosmic order. The sources disagree on the number of avatars. Usually there are ten, the last of which is awaited in the future. Apart from avatars in human form, of which Krishna is the best known, there are also avatars in animal or mixed form. The divine being may also be either wholly or partially present in an avatar. In the 20th century Hindus and Indian Christians have discussed the similarity between this teaching and the Christian doctrine of the incarnation (→ Hinduism and Christianity).

In some extreme → Shia → sects various ideas of incarnation occur. The Druze regard the caliph al-Ḥākim (985-1021?) as the final incarnation of deity. The Nusayris of northern Syria find an incarnation of deity in ʿAlī (ca. 600-661), the fourth caliph.

Bibliography: S. Akhilananda, *Hindu View of Christ* (New York, 1949) • A. J. Appasamy, *The Gospel and India's Heritage* (London, 1942) • M. Elze et al., "Inkarnation," *HWP* 4.368-82 • D. E. Bassuk, *Incarnation in Hinduism and Christianity: The Myth of the God-Man* (London, 1987) • J. B. Cobb Jr. and C. Ives, eds., *The Emptying God: A Buddhist-Jewish-Christian Conversation* (Maryknoll, N.Y., 1990) • F. Frankfort, *Kingship and the Gods* (Chicago, 1948) • M. H. Harper, *Gurus, Swamis, and Avataras: Spiritual Masters and Their American Disciples* (Philadelphia, 1972) • M. Mutahhari, *Fundamentals of Islamic Thought* (Berkeley, Calif., 1985) • G. Parrinder, *Avatar and Incarnation* (London, 1970).

Ulrich Berner

2. Theological Aspects

2.1. Concept

The notion of a preexistent heavenly or angelic being (→ Angel) appearing on earth in the last days is by no means totally foreign to the Jewish world of the first century A.D. → Qumran knew of and developed traditions about Melchizedek returning as judge and king, and of Michael the archangel descending to defend or lead the people of God in the → eschatological battle. Likewise, both → Judaism and → Hellenism were familiar with the idea of historical figures representing or mediating the rational structures of the universe. Philo (b. 15-10 B.C.–A.D. 45-50) takes various OT figures as living symbols of the divine Logos (i.e., God revealing and sharing his eternal creative reason), and Hellenistic culture often described a king or sage as *logos* (or *nomos*) *empsychos* — the Logos (or law) of the cosmos clothed in a human → soul (→ Hellenistic-Roman Religion).

What is striking about early Christian belief is the combination of the following themes:

- → Jesus has a specific (and recent) human identity;
- he is not an angel or a resurrected patriarch;
- the Logos he embodies is not a general and impersonal principle.

John 1:1-14 *could* be read in a "Philonic" way, yet the rest of the gospel assumes that whatever preexists the historical life of Jesus is in some sense a subject of knowing and loving (17:1-5). Likewise, the famous Christological hymn of Phil. 2:5-11 seems to assume (though there is some debate on this point among critical scholars) that the subject of the experiences of Jesus of Nazareth is continuous with a preexisting being capable of choice and purpose.

2.2. Development in Christian Theology

2.2.1. Incarnational language is only one of several options in the NT for describing or discussing Jesus' nature and significance. As theology develops, however, such language is increasingly seen as an indispensable tool for asserting that, in Jesus Christ, human nature is radically transformed by union with the divine life (Ignatius, Irenaeus). If Jesus is — as the NT overall suggests — more than a teacher of enlightenment, if the history of his acts and sufferings is an essential component of Christian belief (→ Faith) in the changing of the world, there is a need to say of the presence and agency at work in him that it is not to be reduced simply to the ordinary dimensions of created activity. Jesus has God's own authority and power to "re-create," to reconstitute the bounds of the human world — yet he does so *within* that world (Irenaeus again).

2.2.2. Incarnational language constantly faces the risk of dissolving back into its original components. Those disposed to see Jesus as offering primarily enlightenment, liberation from darkness and ignorance, have no difficulty in thinking of his earthly form as phantasmal; for them his real identity is as a heavenly power (→ Christology 2). Human experience, especially suffering, is at best irrelevant to his work, at worst degrading and compromising. Such a position leads to classical → Docetism. Various forms of → Gnosticism either espoused this picture or distinguished sharply between an earthly figure (not necessarily fully human) who has a purely instrumental role and a heavenly spirit descending on this materially tangible individual (Basilides).

Other Christians, concerned equally about compromising the divine Logos's immutability and impassibility, tended to minimize the distinct individuality of the Word and to see it as a power inspiring and exalting the man Jesus (Paul of Samosata [d. after 272]). Origen (ca. 185-ca. 254) attempted an ingenious solution in which the real subject of incarnation was the preexistent soul of Jesus. Being perfectly united with the Logos, this soul, on entering the flesh, transmits the power and life of the Logos to that flesh, so that Jesus of Nazareth is indeed "transparent" to the eternal Word (→ Origenism).

2.2.3. With the rejection first of Origen's doctrine of preexistent souls, and then of Paul of Samosata's view of the Word inspiring a complete and distinct human individual, some theologians tended to assume that a human soul was lacking in Jesus, being replaced directly by the Word. Arius (ca. 280-336) thus concluded that the Word, as subject to limitation and suffering, could not strictly speaking be divine (→ Arianism). The reaffirmation at → Nicaea of the Word's full divinity (→ Niceno-Constantinopolitan Creed) guaranteed that the Word could not now be thought of as becoming *part* of a human being — and so, indirectly, guaranteed a recognition of Jesus' full humanity and a rejection of the teaching of Apollinaris of Laodicea (ca. 310-ca. 390) that the Word replaced the *nous* or *hēgemonikon* (the ruling intellectual principle) in Jesus.

2.2.4. The insistence, however, of the Antiochene theologians (→ Antiochian Theology) on a sharp disjunction between the passible human Jesus and the unchanging Logos awakened memories of the teaching of Paul of Samosata. Alexandrian writers (→ Alexandrian Theology) accused their opponents of "teaching two Christs" — a charge whose origins

lie ultimately in the struggle against Gnosticism. In reaction to Antiochene theology Cyril (ca. 375-444) developed the concept of *hypostatic union:* Word and man are uniquely related in such a way that the individuation and actuality of the particular human nature belonging to Jesus are wholly dependent on the presence of the Word as a kind of substratum, the *hypostasis* (foundation, substance) that sustains the natural predicates of Jesus' humanity.

2.2.5. The language of hypostatic union was canonized at the Council of → Chalcedon in 451 (though not in a way that satisfied more consistent supporters of Cyril). The history of much subsequent Christology is a history of the refinement of this language. In the sixth and seventh centuries there was a refusal to merge either the human will of Jesus or his human *energeia* (his distinctively human "mode of operation") in the divine will and activity. The hypostatic union continues to serve as a conceptual device for securing the total humanity of Jesus and the transcendence of the Word.

In the theology of → Scholasticism debates arose as to whether the divine Word "adds" anything to the particular human nature of Jesus. Thomas Aquinas (ca. 1225-74) considered that the Word provides the active principle by which Jesus' humanity exists as something that itself has active and historical form (→ Thomism), while Duns Scotus (ca. 1265-1308) insisted that the presence of the Word is a purely negative determination — that which constitutes the individual humanity a non-dependent, self-determining reality (→ Scotism). The two great doctors also disagreed over whether the incarnation was intelligible only as a response to the fall (Aquinas) or could have occurred simply as a gift consummating the human calling given in creation (Scotus).

2.2.6. The Reformation period was dominated at first by the problem of the *communicatio idiomatum* (the communication [i.e., interchange] of properties in the unity of the person) — M. → Luther's (1483-1546) defense of the omnipresence of Christ's glorified humanity and J. → Calvin's (1509-64) insistence on the distinction between even glorified humanity (which remains limited and created) and the divinity of the Word. Later came the debate between Giessen and Tübingen theologians over the exercise of divine power by the Word in his incarnate and humbled condition (*status exinanitionis*, "state of self-emptying"), Giessen arguing for a real abandonment of this power (→ kenōsis), Tübingen for a concealment (*krypsis*). The question thus raised recurred still more forcibly in the 19th and early 20th centuries, when it was asked how a historically and psychologically plausible picture of the incarnate Word can be presented, especially when the evidential value of John's gospel as testimony to Jesus' self-consciousness was increasingly denied. In England C. Gore (1853-1932) and F. Weston (1871-1924) attempted reconstructions of a kenotic Christology, but with limited appeal and success.

The doctrine of the incarnation became increasingly significant for ecclesiology (→ Church) in Roman Catholic, Anglican, and Orthodox circles from the middle of the 19th century (see 3.3). These traditions have each sometimes called the church an extension of the incarnation, an eternal reality of the Son in time, especially in their sacramental life (→ Sacrament). In Roman Catholic theology during the last century much was made of the church as an organization. In the later 19th and 20th centuries some Anglican theology often used similar language and was inclined to view the incarnation as the climax of a general principle of the divine presence in creation and solidarity with it as it is now symbolized by the church's sacramental life. Orthodox theology, especially in the 20th century, regarded the Christological → dogma of Chalcedon as providing a structure for reflection on the church, with the church, like Christ, being a human entity that is transformed into a divine entity without being denied or swallowed up thereby.

D. Bonhoeffer (1906-45) took up similar themes in his early conception of the church as Christ existing as a fellowship, although we also see here the themes and influences of → idealism and early sociological theories. Later this kind of model became much less popular. It has been increasingly recognized that it obscures the dialectical and challenging relation between Christ and the church and leaves little room for Christological criticism of the church in its existing form. Yet the Chalcedonian → analogy is still relevant in orthodox ecclesiology and has shown itself to be capable of nuanced development, thus avoiding some of the above dangers.

2.2.7. The 20th century has seen vigorous attacks on the "mythological" notion of preexistence (R. Bultmann); a sophisticated restatement of the → *extra calvinisticum*, qualified by a powerful account of the virtual identity of the Son's eternal → obedience and Jesus' historical obedience (K. Barth); a defense of preexistence imagery as something generated and validated by the eschatological event of the → resurrection (W. Pannenberg); a rejection of traditional doctrines of impassibility in a theology of divine → solidarity with human suffering (J. Moltmann); and a wholesale repudiation of incarnational language as such by several English writers (M. Wiles,

J. Hick, D. Nineham). Outside the Protestant traditions, Roman Catholic theologians (esp. K. Rahner) have seen the incarnation as revealing the intrinsic orientation of human nature to the divine life (the "supernatural existential"), thus reviving the ancient Irenaean and Athanasian view that the purpose of the incarnation is to impart → *theōsis,* or deification. This understanding is closely paralleled in modern Eastern → Orthodox writing (G. Florovsky, V. Lossky).

2.3. *Significance*
Incarnation has increasingly been used to validate Christian options for solidarity, involvement, and vulnerability (Bonhoeffer, the Roman Catholic → worker-priest movement, etc.). Yet we need to be aware that such a theological → ethics uses the language of incarnation in a highly mythological way, as if the Word and Jesus were one psychological subject. A similar point, however, could be made in these terms: incarnation, seen from the already fairly demythologized perspective of "hypostatic union," affirms that *human* meaning, dignity, and → hope are shown in Jesus to be capable of identification with *God's* meaning; he made our cause his own (E. Schillebeeckx). God as responsive → love, as Son or Word, can be fully and unequivocally expressed in a human → identity, in a life of → poverty and a criminal's death. On this basis it is possible to reconstruct a theology of *theōsis* as the fruit of incarnation. God's → freedom for relationship, his eternal Trinitarian life, remains as a gift, a challenge, and a possibility for human beings over and above the apparent triumphs of oppression and dehumanization. Incarnation is still potentially a disturbing and a transforming doctrine.

→ Immanence and Transcendence; Soteriology; Trinity

Bibliography: D. M. BAILLIE, *God Was in Christ: An Essay on Incarnation and Atonement* (New York, 1948) • H. U. VON BALTHASAR, *The Scandal of the Incarnation: Irenaeus against the Heresies* (San Francisco, 1990) • J. D. G. DUNN, *Christology in the Making: A NT Inquiry into the Origins of the Doctrine of the Incarnation* (Grand Rapids, 1996) • M. GOULDER, ed., *Incarnation and Myth: The Debate Continued* (London, 1979) • A. E. HARVEY, ed., *God Incarnate: Story and Belief* (London, 1981) • B. HEBBLETHWAITE, *The Incarnation* (Cambridge, 1987) • G. S. HENDRY, *The Gospel of the Incarnation* (Philadelphia, 1958) • J. HICK, ed., *The Myth of God Incarnate* (London, 1977) • J. MOLTMANN, *The Crucified God: The Cross of Christ as the Foundation and Criticism of Christian Theology* (New York, 1974) • W. PANNENBERG, *Jesus, God and Man* (2d ed.;

Philadelphia, 1977) • W. L. PORTER, *Tradition and Incarnation: Foundations of Christian Theology* (New York, 1994) • K. RAHNER, "Theology as a Science," *Theological Investigations* (vol. 13; London, 1975) pt. 1, 1-102 • K. RAHNER, *Schriften zur Theologie* (vol. 10/1; Einsiedeln, 1972) • H. STICKELBERGER, *Ipsa assumptione creatur* (Bern, 1979) on the development of K. Barth's doctrine of incarnation • V. WHITE, *Atonement and Incarnation: An Essay in Universalism and Particularity* (Cambridge, 1991).

ROWAN D. WILLIAMS

3. Controversial Aspects

3.1. *Chalcedonian Definition*

The Chalcedonian Definition (→ Chalcedon) offered an authoritative interpretation of → Jesus of Nazareth and confirmed dogmatically his uniqueness as the bringer of salvation and of God's redeeming → love to all humanity (→ Christology). The central statements of the Christian → faith regarding God's presence in the man Jesus (John 1:14) and the → salvation that is given in him (Acts 4:12) found here a conceptual form. The Definition involved first the Christological affirmation that Jesus is "truly God and truly man" and that in this divine-human person deity and humanity conjoin with "no confusion" and "no separation" as two distinct essences, each of which retains its distinctive qualities. This statement also embraced the reality of a saving relation between the Holy One and human existence as this relation is experienced in encounter with Jesus and attested to in faith. The soteriological aspect of the event (→ Soteriology) was thus upheld, and the idea of incarnation with its specific terminology could have more than a Christological thrust.

To later interpreters it seemed, on the one hand, that the Definition could answer the basic question of the relation between God and us (Creator and creature) and, on the other, that it structures our participation in salvation and therefore individual and collective faith. Orthodoxy, Roman Catholicism, and the Reformation all accepted Chalcedon in principle. They have used it in different ways, however, so that its interpretation and paradigmatic use belong properly to controversial theology.

3.2. *Orthodox Theology*

Orthodox theology regards the incarnation as the immeasurable and inexpressible divine mystery of salvation (→ Christology 3). It links that incarnation of Christ to his → resurrection, views both as the work of the Holy Spirit, and finds in them the reality of → theophany. The victory of the God-man over → death and corruptibility shapes the whole world of Orthodox belief.

3.2.1. The divinizing of human nature, which is accomplished in the incarnation, reveals the → reconciliation of the creaturely reality that had fallen into → sin and indicates the inner relation of God to the world, which is fulfilled in fellowship between Creator and creature. The incarnation, then, opens the way to our own deification (→ Order of Salvation 1.1; Theosis) and to the restoration of all things, the consummation of → creation.

3.2.2. The incarnation continues and is extended as the God-man Christ unites believers to himself and to one another in his mystical body, the church (→ Church 3.1), which is thus a divine-human → organism. God and humanity meet in the liturgical and sacramental life of the church. In this life believers experience the energies (modes) of the incarnation (→ Eucharistic Ecclesiology). In the divine liturgy (→ Liturgy 2; Worship 3) believers experience the mystical presence of Christ. The → icon leads them to the original, and they are taken up into mystical union. Divine forces permeate their nature and reason and give their lives quality and orientation.

3.3. *Roman Catholic Theology*

In Roman Catholic theology the incarnation serves as a basic principle of reflection on the faith and as a conceptual model for a whole series of relationships (→ Catholicism [Roman] 3.4). The mystery of the incarnation has this basic significance because the absolute and infinite God revealed himself in the incarnation of the Logos to what is creaturely and nondivine (humanity and the world) and accomplished salvation for it. Transcendence becomes here a this-worldly (saving) event, and the love of God becomes historically concrete (→ Immanence and Transcendence). An answer is given in principle to the question of the relation between God and humanity (the world), for as the Logos assumes human form, the absolute finds correspondence in the finite (in the *analogia entis* [→ analogy of being]), and there is a real relation between God and us. This interpretation carries with it further insights and permits the use of the incarnation as a paradigm.

3.3.1. The self-objectification of God's saving will in history (→ Revelation) enables us to see that God is the basis of the world and its consummation, and consequently to see the inner connection between creation and redemption. It gives evidence of the supreme worth of humanity and its final destiny to share in the divine life. It reveals to us the unity and distinction between God and the world.

3.3.2. With its dynamic the incarnation embraces the whole cosmos. The work of the → Holy Spirit has an eschatological goal and is not limited to a once-for-all historical event. The incarnation thus involves the interrelationship of all reality, human dignity, temporal order, and all human talents, tasks, and activities (→ Everyday Life). In this permeation of the whole cosmos by the → grace of God, both natures retain their distinctiveness. God assumes and adopts temporal things and spheres and activities, but he does not take from them their self-determination. → Freedom and → autonomy are possible.

3.3.3. What the incarnation discloses and seeks is further "revealed to us and continued in the church" (*Lumen gentium* 52; → Church 3.2), the mystical body of Christ. The church is the "real symbolic working form of the Holy Spirit" (K. Rahner). It has a part in the mystery of the incarnation as the gracious and enduringly effective self-impartation of God takes place in the dimensions of the visible and palpable (→ Sacrament) and of the social and communal (→ Institution). The church owes its existence to the event of incarnation. This event, however, also constitutes the church's nature (as a "theandric," or divine-human, structure), qualifies its institution and discipline (→ Church Government; Church Law), defines its historical destiny (as giving ontic reality to the salvation-event), gives it its task (the sacrament that mediates salvation), regulates its functioning, and structures its work in the world. In short, the incarnation is a guiding concept in → pastoral theology, sociology, and → Catholic missions.

3.3.4. The incarnational principle of Chalcedon's "no confusion" and "no separation" lives on in the theological reflection on qualitative differences and relations (e.g., between the crucifixion and resurrection, the church and Christ, nature and grace, reason and faith, law and love, world and church, universal and hierarchical priesthood). The principle also is relevant for the recognition of unity and truth — for example, in conjoining concrete plurality and universal totality (→ Catholic, Catholicity 2.2), → representation and what is represented (e.g., organ of salvation and presence of Christ), and sign and thing signified (e.g., as regards the understanding of the sacrament).

This conceptual model provides for interdependence in the Roman Catholic structure of doctrine, so that a new interpretation or accent in one sphere affects every other and threatens the integrity of the system. Thus to emphasize and bestow normative significance on what we might call the cause of Jesus as a principle instead of the incarnation has implications for the understanding of the church and pastoral practice (→ Liberation Theology; Political Theology).

3.4. *Reformation Theology*

Reformation theology avoids objective or ontological statements about Christ "in himself" and stresses instead his mediatorship (→ Christology 2.4 and 6.1-5). It regards the relation between God and us not as something incarnationally given and sacramentally mediated but as an ongoing personal event (of Word and proclamation) between God and us (→ Justification). The so-called → *extra calvinisticum* has this dynamic in view.

3.4.1. Christ's mediatorship presupposes the incarnation of the Logos. In the incarnation the omnipotent God conceals himself in weakness, the Holy One in the accursed; the Son of God is made sin that is not his own sin but ours (by nature we do not want God to be God; see thesis 17 of Luther's "Disputation against Scholastic Theology" [*LW* 31.10]). Hence the incarnation is not a sanctifying qualification of human nature. Taking the places of sinners, the Son of God can vicariously bear the divine judgment (the cross) and experience divine grace (the resurrection). What takes place in the cross and resurrection (i.e., the death of the old self and the creation of the new) becomes ours in faith, which trusts God's promise and lays hold of the new life. In the → union with Christ that is ours in faith, Christ's mediatorship reaches its goal, thus achieving the aim of the incarnation.

3.4.2. Believers, who are sinners in fact but righteous by God's saving intervention (*simul iustus et peccator*), live by hearing the gospel (→ Word of God) and are always in the process of being forgiven (→ Forgiveness; Reconciliation). This relation alone (*sola fide;* → Reformation Principles) determines the divine-human relation, characterizes the fellowship of believers (→ Church 3.3-4), defines the church's structure and task (→ Catholic, Catholicity 2.3.1), and is the norm of action in secular spheres (→ Social Ethics). Believers are called out of profane and ungodly relations and sent out to serve the fallen world in a union of gift and task, of being righteous and doing what is right.

3.5. *Modern Discussion*

Modern discussion of the form, content, and significance of the incarnation, insofar as it does not involve a total questioning of traditional doctrines and concepts, involves Christological, soteriological, anthropological, and ethical issues (see 2.2.7 and 2.3; → Christology).

The interpretation and application of dogmatic statements in the various Christian traditions show how tenaciously the incarnation and its vocabulary affect the thinking, → spirituality, devotional forms, and self-understanding of the churches concerned and provide for their continuity and stability. This phenomenon is hardly changed in any way, in spite of appearances, by new approaches in exposition of the history of Jesus or in understanding God, humanity, and the world in the context of modern experiences and insights and related practical efforts in everyday church life. The reasons for this continuity are in part anthropological, theological, psychological, and sociological.

It should also be noted that the relevance of this fact is often missed in ecumenical ventures and church conversations, or at least too little attention is paid to it. In the task of clarifying controverted issues between confessions and bringing to light the church's → unity (→ Ecumenism, Ecumenical Movement), interest focuses on themes and practices that seem to serve an ecumenical purpose (esp. baptism, the Eucharist, the ministry, or common problems, programs, and activities). The point is thus neglected that behind ecclesiology in the various Christian traditions lies (implicitly or explicitly) the incarnation, the → reception of which — no matter in what interpretation or form — is a basic factor. Any comprehensive ecclesiology must take this constant element into account.

In answering the question of the significance of the incarnation, we first must decide whether the incarnation is to be viewed as a retrospective theological concept (D. Ritschl) or whether the message of Jesus, of his life and destiny in the context of the history of his people → Israel (§1), can be understood and interpreted in some other way. We then must consider what the impulses and implications of this basic decision are for Christian self-understanding and action, for the ecumenical process, and for the fellowship of the churches. In any case, the Christological problem is an ecclesiological problem, and vice versa.

Bibliography: M. AMBROSE, ed., *Zimbabwe: The Risk of Incarnation* (Geneva, 1996) • ATHANASIUS, *On the Incarnation* (Crestwood, N.Y., 1996) • A. CORN, *Incarnation: Contemporary Writers on the NT* (New York, 1990) • E. FAHLBUSCH, *Kirchenkunde der Gegenwart* (Stuttgart, 1979) esp. 26-104, 114-19, 274-84 • N. A. NISSIOTIS, *Die Theologie der Ostkirche im ökumenischen Dialog* (Stuttgart, 1968) • M. A. RAE, *Kierkegaard's Vision of the Incarnation: By Faith Transformed* (Oxford, 1997) • K. RAHNER, "Incarnation," *SM(E)* 3.110-18 (bibliography) • B. C. RAW, *Trinity and Incarnation in Anglo-Saxon Art and Thought* (Cambridge, 1997) • D. RITSCHL, *The Logic of Theology* (Philadelphia, 1987) • T. SAWARD, *The Mysteries of March: Hans Urs von Balthasar on the Incarnation and Easter* (Wash-

ington, D.C., 1990) • T. SCHNEIDER, ed., *Handbuch der Dogmatik* (2 vols.; Düsseldorf, 1992) • O. SKARSAUNE, *Incarnation, Myth or Fact?* (St. Louis, Mo., 1991). See also the bibliography in §2.

ERWIN FAHLBUSCH

Incense

Incense (from the Latin for "burning") is made of woods and resins that, when burned or heated, give off a fragrant odor. Frankincense, a pure incense (also called olibanum), was given as a gift to the Christ child by the Magi (Matt. 2:11). Incense is burned in a bowl or a thurible. It is stored in a vessel called an incense boat, from which it is spooned into the thurible.

Incense is widely used in world religions. In the OT it symbolized the presence of → Yahweh in the temple (Isa. 6:4); it was a pleasing offering; it had a purificatory significance, not only hygienically (→ Cultic Purity), but also as a sign of redemption (Num. 16:46-50; → Atonement); and it became a figure of the prayers of the faithful (Ps. 141:2; Rev. 5:8; 8:3-4). There is no evidence that it had a practical use as an agent to counter the odor of burnt sacrifices.

There was no ceremonial use of incense in the first three centuries of Christian → worship because of its association with emperor worship and use in pagan cults. In the fourth century incense came into widespread honorific use in association with the dignity granted to → bishops by the emperor (→ Roman Empire 3-4), as well as with the relics of saints and the dedication of altars and holy places. It also came into use in the prayer Offices. John Chrysostom interpreted its use in Vespers as a penitential rite. In the Western church it has been primarily a symbol of prayer (→ Symbol 4).

Incense has been used in an honorific sense in the eucharistic liturgy at the entrance procession (censing of the → altar), at the gospel procession (censing of the book), at the offertory (censing of the gifts, the ministers, and the people), and at the consecration (censing of the elevated Host and chalice). In the prayer Offices both East and West, it has been used at the gospel canticle and at Psalm 141 in Vespers.

Bibliography: E. G. C. F. ATCHLEY, *A History of the Use of Incense in Divine Worship* (London, 1909) • W. J. GRISBROOKE, "Incense," *NWDLW* 265-66 • K. NIELSEN, *Incense in Ancient Israel* (Leiden, 1986).

FRANK C. SENN

Inculturation → Acculturation; Mission 1

Independent Churches

1. Term
2. Causes
3. History
4. Theology
5. Spirituality
6. Organization
7. Ecumenism

1. Term

In the broader sense, the term "independent churches" denotes simply churches that are independent (e.g., those belonging to the → International Council of Community Churches) or indigenous (e.g., → Pentecostal churches). More commonly, it applies especially to independent Christian churches that in the last century have been formed simultaneously in Africa south of the Sahara but have no organizational attachment to one another (in this usage, the term is often capitalized). Because these churches are biblically oriented, they are not → new religions and are not syncretistic (→ Syncretism), as often charged. Just as the gospel has been contextualized (→ Acculturation) in → European theology, so we find in them what might be described as an African Reformation. Of the more than 300 million Christians in Africa, approximately one-fourth of them belong to the Independent Churches, of which there are about 10,000. Their number is also growing rapidly as the search for African identity continues (→ African Theology 3).

2. Causes

Several features account for the development and spread of the Independent Churches. Politics played a part, especially the links between → missionaries and the colonial powers (→ Colonialism and Mission). The Independent Churches were often viewed as movements of emancipation and were in places suppressed, often through the use of force. Social and economic changes also caused an uncertainty that prompted new initiatives, one indicator being that the Independent Churches are strongest in industrialized countries such as Nigeria and South Africa (→ Industrial Society). Apartheid was also a contributory factor (→ Racism 2.7).

Though we must take account of these various factors, religious motivation was clearly the primary cause. Religion has always had a primary place in the everyday life of the people (→ Africa 2). Al-though the Christian message was gladly received, disputes arose concerning its Western form, which did not seem to accord with African ethical norms (→ Ancestor Worship; Marriage 2.7; Social Ethics 4). The North Atlantic missionaries were concerned to adapt their message to tribal religions and cultures (indigenization).

Bible translation into the various tribal languages, however, a work undertaken by the → Bible societies and fostered particularly by Protestant missions, made Africans directly aware of the sources of their faith and helped them to think things through for themselves. Statistically there is congruity between Bible translations and the rise of Independent Churches among the tribes of Africa. As these tribes want to preserve the valuable elements in their own traditions within their faith, innumerable groups in the mission churches have determined to think out afresh and articulate their faith within their own culture and environment (→ Contextual Theology) in order to live the Christian life.

Christians usually stayed within their churches, but if they ran into misunderstandings and patronization, they soon left the mother churches. Thus in Sierra Leone, for example, as early as 1819 a group of Creoles (the Settler's Meeting) separated from the Wesleyans (→ Methodist Churches 2); in 1862 on the Gold Coast (present-day Ghana), the Methodist Society, a group of abstainers, also left the Methodist Church; and in 1872 in Basutoland (now Lesotho), the Hermon Community separated from the Paris Mission (→ French Missions). The acquisition of independence by such congregations was always only the tip of the iceberg of attitudes that were — and are — still widespread in the missionary churches.

3. History

The history of Independent Churches really begins with the separatist Ethiopian movement (a process having no connection with the → Ethiopian Orthodox Church). As the only African country independent of the colonial powers at that time, Ethiopia was a symbol of redemption for the peoples of color (see Ps. 68:31). In 1888 the Native Baptist Church in Nigeria split away from the mission of the American Baptists. Then in 1889 the Lutheran Bapedi Church, with their missionary J. A. Winter (1847-1921), left the South African church that had been established by the Berlin Mission (→ German Missions 1.3). In 1892 dissatisfied Wesleyans in South Africa took the name "Ethiopian Church." With other secessions this movement developed into a group of tribal churches that later connected with an African American church, the African Methodist Episcopal Church (→ Methodist Churches 2.3). The aim was both ecclesiastical and political independence from whites, but political independence became secondary once independence movements started around 1910.

A new wave of ecclesiastical independence known as the Zionist movement was more strongly influenced by African → spirituality (§2). The name of this movement, which has nothing to do with Jewish → Zionism, indicates the influence that another African American church, the Christian Catholic Apostolic Church in Zion, had on the Independent Churches in Africa. On this wave came a great number of mostly smaller churches that usually have "Zion," "Jerusalem," "Apostolic," or "Faith" in their names. The borders between the two waves were not fixed, with both types found in this movement and also in the traditional mission churches.

Larger African churches formed a third group of independents, a group bound together only loosely. Founded by charismatic → prophets, they have kept themselves free of foreign influences and are not tied down to particular tribes. Three of the most important are the Church of Christ on Earth called the → Kimbanguist Church), founded by the prophet Simon Kimbangu (1889?-1951) in Zaire; the Nazareth Church of the prophet Isaiah Shembe (1870-1935) in Zululand; and the Zion Christian Church of the prophet Engenas Lekganyane (1885-1948) in North Transvaal. The central position of the prophets, which carried with it the notion of a royal priesthood, meant that these churches could initially be seen as part of a messianic movement (→ Messianism 2). It is now understood that the prophets do not replace Christ but help believers to experience him. They are, as it were, icons, and their groups are known as Iconic churches.

This history is based on field studies by outsiders. The communities themselves know it only in the memories of believers, as is the rule among peoples without written culture. It is told at worship or around the fires. There are no historical tables or dates. Events and stories are recounted, as in the Gospels, and are seen to be witnesses to the faith. To preserve these valuable traditions, the Independent Churches have now begun to assemble this → narrative theology in cooperation with ecumenical historians, and to translate and evaluate it.

4. Theology

The Independent Churches have developed a → contextual theology that corresponds to African questions and needs (→ African Theology). The Africans think, as the Bible does, of the whole person as part of a collective, and so they find it easier to deal with the gospel (→ Biblical Theology 2.3) than with individualistic Western theology. Fellowship is important to these churches, for it sustains and is sustained by individuals. A holistic view of the person means that the → salvation (§6.3) anticipated from God covers body, mind, and soul. Worship in Independent Churches is in keeping with this view, drawing as it does from the members' earlier experiences and from what it also finds in the Bible. A strong orientation toward Scripture acts as a barrier against → syncretism. The plurality of these churches, which is much greater than in centrally controlled denominational churches, can still, however, manifest common concerns.

As churches of the poor (→ Poverty), the Independent Churches do not have much money. They mostly use collections to help those in need. Similarly, few of the churches are architecturally imposing. Usually a circle of whitewashed stones around a tall tree serves as a → temple for → worship. The ministers (→ Bishop; Pastor) and congregation dress colorfully in garments that are adorned with → symbols expressing their identity. They use horns and drums instead of organs to accompany native chorales. They clap their hands and → dance gracefully to the glory of God. Each congregation has its own → liturgy, which includes → prayer and → preaching. Room is left, however, for spontaneous testimonies and in some cases for → glossolalia (§2).

The → sacraments are administered at the climax of feast days. Strong missionary activity means that baptism by immersion, preferably in flowing water, the river, or the sea, often involves many new members. Only mediums enjoy similar rites of → initiation in the tribal religions, but all Christians have access to God. The → Eucharist is usually celebrated at night and with native elements. It is linked to meals that demonstrate the fellowship of the living with deceased ancestors (→ Ancestor Worship) in the form of union with the exalted Lord and with the deceased. Preparation is made for reception of the sacrament by → fasting and confession of sins.

5. Spirituality

The Independent Churches follow Matt. 10:7-8 and Jas. 5:13-16 in praying for the sick. In older African religions the → priest (§1) was also the medicine man. Renunciation of his medicines comes with → conversion (§1). This aversion also serves as protection against the flood of modern pharmaceutical products. Trusting in God for full salvation, the congregation prays for those who suffer. The Independent Churches, however, do not believe in faith healing per se. As part of their concern and care, the members talk with God. → Suffering includes not only bodily and psychosomatic illnesses but also hunger, family disruption, → unemployment, accidents, and homelessness. Prayer is made, but also help is given. Childless women turn for help to the Independent Churches, for in Africa the blessing of children also provides for the women's care in old age. The Independent Churches are caring communities in a world of rapid change.

What the Bible says about spirits and → demons is not strange to these churches. They are familiar with such destructive powers and use → exorcism in the name of Jesus to liberate those who are possessed. The ones who are healed are integrated into the churches as a safeguard against relapse. The ethics of the Independent Churches calls for a healthy life. They typically shun tobacco, hemp, and alcohol, and they stress hard work, purity, and peacefulness (→ Social Ethics 4). They have various attitudes toward polygamy (→ Marriage), but they consistently oppose divorce and premarital sex, which were taboo in tribal religions, and against which there is rigorous → church discipline in order to avert the detrimental influences of modern society.

Festivals help draw the larger churches together. They are held at the bishops' headquarters, by the seashore, or on holy mountains. Often spending weeks at these festivals in grass huts or tents, the people find opportunity there for → Bible study, → meditation, discussion, and worship, which includes singing and dancing together.

6. Organization

As is the custom in Africa, the ministers (→ Offices, Ecclesiastical) need the approval of the churches. They are not trained theologically, for no faculties teach African theology, a fact that often brings them condemnation. Some take correspondence courses at Bible schools and afterward hang up their diplomas to win a measure of respect. Recently, individual candidates for the ministry have also been sent to attend training courses at institutions of mainline churches that are willing to accept the students without alienating them from the character of their particular Independent Church, for example at the Lutheran Theological College Umpumulo, Natal, South Africa.

The bishops of neighboring churches take part in → ordinations and thus confer a greater unity on the movement, an African version of apostolic succession (→ Bishop, Episcopate 1) that does not demand an organization. In smaller congregations the leader acts as a father who knows and cares for all his people. In larger churches the minister has the position of a chieftain and is respected and honored accordingly. Although these positions have emerged from tradition, a new development has come with the ordination of → women. Women bishops are now quite common in the Independent Churches.

7. Ecumenism

Ecumenical structures are a problem for the Independent Churches. Many attempts have been made to organize the churches, but membership tends to be haphazard. Personal friendship and informal contacts fit in better with the thinking of Africans, and such relationships are fostered through mutual visitations, as in the early church. Relations with the mission churches are strained by the fact that the latter are constantly losing members to the Independent Churches. The → national councils of churches understand the independents' concerns, but the independents' lack of structure does not mesh well with the organizational demands of the councils. The Independent Churches see themselves as churches of the people, but they desire ecumenical fellowship and cooperation. Some of them are represented on the → All Africa Conference of Churches, and a few have been welcomed into the → World Council of Churches (e.g., the Kimbanguist Church in 1969, and the African Israel Nineveh Church in 1975). The Organization of African Instituted Churches, founded at Nairobi in 1978, is concerned to bring together Independent Churches throughout the continent.

Rapid growth can be expected for these churches in the near future. A longer view sees the various open or latent streams converging into a people's church in an African context. The path of division will perhaps lead ultimately to unity.

Bibliography: D. B. BARRETT, *Schism and Renewal in Africa: An Analysis of 6,000 Contemporary Religious Movements* (Nairobi, 1968) • D. B. BARRETT and T. J. PADWICK, *Rise Up and Walk!* (Nairobi, 1989) • H.-J. BECKEN, "Schrift und Tradition in den Afrikanischen Unabhängigen Kirchen," *Sola Scriptura* (ed. H. H. Schmid and J. Mehlhausen; Gütersloh, 1991) 337-47; idem, *Theologie der Heilung. Das Heilen in den Afrikanischen Unabhängigen Kirchen in Südafrika* (Hermannsburg, 1972); idem, *Wo der Glaube noch jung ist. Afrikanische Unabhängige Kirchen im Südlichen Afrika* (Erlangen, 1985) • I. HEXHAM, ed., *The Scriptures of the AmaNazaretha of EKuphaKameni* (Calgary,

1994) • I. Hexham and G. C. Oosthuizen, eds., *The Story of Isaiah Shembe*, vol. 1, *History and Traditions Centered on EKuphaKameni and Mount Nhlangakazi*; vol. 2, *Early Regional Traditions of the Acts of the Nazarites*; vol. 3, *The Sun and the Moon: Oral Testimony and Sacred History of the AmaNazaretha under the Leadership of Johannes Galilee Shembe and Amos Shembe* (trans. H.-J. Becken; Lewiston, N.Y., 1996-2000) • E. Kamphausen, *Anfänge der kirchlichen Unabhängigkeitsbewegung in Südafrika* (Frankfurt, 1976) • G. Lademann-Priemer, ed., *Traditional Religion and Christian Faith: Cultural Clash and Cultural Change* (Hamburg, 1993) • G. C. Oosthuizen, *The Healer-Prophet in Afro-Christian Churches* (Leiden, 1992); idem, *The Theology of a South African Messiah: An Analysis of the Hymnal of "The Church of the Nazarites"* (2d ed.; Leiden, 1976) • G. C. Oosthuizen et al., eds., *Afro-Christian Religion and Healing in Southern Africa* (Lewiston, N.Y., 1989) • J. S. Pobee and G. Ositelu II, *African Initiatives in Christianity: The Growth, Gifts, and Diversities of Indigenous African Churches* (Geneva, 1998) • B. G. M. Sundkler, *Bantu Prophets in South Africa* (2d ed.; London, 1961); idem, *Zulu Zion and Some Swazi Zionists* (London, 1976) • B. Tembe, *Integrationismus und Afrikanismus* (Frankfurt, 1985) • H. W. Turner, *Bibliography of New Religious Movements in Primal Societies*, vol. 1, *Black Africa* (Boston, 1977).

HANS-JÜRGEN BECKEN

India

1. General Situation
2. Religions
    2.1. Hinduism
    2.2. Islam
    2.3. Sikhs
    2.4. Jainism
    2.5. Buddhism
    2.6. Zoroastrians
    2.7. Jews
3. Christian Churches
    3.1. Orthodox Churches
    3.2. Roman Catholic Church
    3.3. Protestant Churches and Ecumenism
4. Church and Society

1. General Situation

India, consisting of 26 states and 6 union territories, became an independent nation-state in 1947, when British rule ended and the subcontinent was partitioned into India and Pakistan. Little is known about its early inhabitants. Advanced civilization

	1960	1980	2000
Population (1,000s):	442,344	688,856	1,006,770
Annual growth rate (%):	2.26	2.17	1.45

Area: 3,165,596 sq. km. (1,222,243 sq. mi.)

A.D. *2000*

Population density: 318/sq. km. (824/sq. mi.)
Births / deaths: 2.29 / 0.85 per 100 population
Fertility rate: 2.74 per woman
Infant mortality rate: 65 per 1,000 live births
Life expectancy: 64.1 years (m: 63.4, f: 64.8)
Religious affiliation (%): Hindus 72.1, Muslims 11.9, tribal religionists 5.5, Christians 5.3 (indigenous 1.9, Protestants 1.7, Roman Catholics 1.7, other Christians 0.3), Sikhs 2.2, nonreligious 1.4, other 1.6.

has existed in India since 3000 B.C. but has undergone much change and destruction as successive waves of immigrants invaded from the northwest. Indo-European groups entered in the second millennium B.C., and from their intermingling with Dravidian, Proto-Australoid, and perhaps also Semitic cultures, → Hinduism resulted.

Six main races now live together in India, speaking over 1,600 languages and dialects, although only 19 of these are officially recognized — Hindi (the official language), English (the "associate official" language), and 17 regional languages. According to the 1991 census 75 percent of the population live in rural areas. The literacy rate for men is 81 percent and for women, 64 percent. It is estimated that nearly 40 percent of the population live below the poverty line; in spite of significant industrial, economic, and technological progress since independence, the elimination of mass → poverty, especially among the lower strata of society, has remained an elusive goal. India is the seventh largest and second most populous country in the world, and the per capita annual income is about $1,600. By the end of the 20th century, the population of India had exceeded one billion persons.

Despite its plurality of cultures, religions, languages, and races, India, since independence, has functioned as a secular democratic state, the largest in the world. The Congress Party has ruled independent India for the most part, but as the century ended, the country was going through a period of political instability because of frequent changes of government and the ascendency in 1998 of the Hindu nationalist Bharatiya Janata Party (BJP) to power. Economic reforms initiated by successive governments in the 1990s have led to a rapidly developing economy.

2. Religions

Modern India comprises four major religious groups: (1) Hinduism, which evolved out of the interaction between indigenous religions with those of early immigrants; (2) religions that resulted from Hindu reform movements (→ Jainism, → Buddhism, and → Sikhism); (3) religions that entered by way of conquest and colonialism (→ Islam and Christianity); and (4) religions brought by isolated groups of immigrants (→ Judaism, → Zoroastrianism, and → Baha'i). In addition to these four groupings, one can add the continued existence of native tribal religions, whose adherents have been influenced by Hinduism and are counted as Hindus, even though their practice accords neither with Hinduism's self-understanding nor with its social reality.

2.1. *Hinduism*

Hinduism is the dominant tradition of India. It represents an evolving tradition and therefore can not be regarded as a single, separate "religion" in the sense that this term is often understood. Hinduism has no founder or agreed-upon creedal system. It embraces with tolerance diverse philosophical, theological, and ideological viewpoints, on the one hand, and, on the other, socioethical discrimination and intolerance (→ Caste). Because of its pluralistic outlook, Hinduism has to some degree accepted or accommodated other religions within its framework. In the same spirit, the modern constitution of India, a secular state, accords the freedom to profess, practice, and propagate to all religions (→ Religious Liberty).

With the rise of religious and cultural nationalism in the postindependence period, however, some orthodox or radical Hindu groups (esp. Rashtria Swayam Sevaks [RSS], Vivekananda Kendra, Viswa Hindu Parishad [VHP], and Siva Sena) have politicized Hindu identity to the detriment of religious minorities in India. The most influential of these groups is RSS, which was founded in 1925 and was partly responsible for the murder of Mohandas K. Gandhi (1869-1948), the pioneer of Indian independence. In recent years, pressure has been brought upon the national government and some state governments to restrict the right of Islam and Christianity to seek converts (→ Conversion 1). There have been sporadic persecution, violence, and the destruction of Christian and Muslim places of worship. While the chronic antagonism between India and Pakistan (nations that have fought three wars) over the disputed territory of Kashmir and the display of nuclear strength by both nations has indeed exacerbated Hindu-Muslim relations, the link

between Christian missions and India's colonial history has made Hindu-Christian relations difficult (→ Colonialism and Mission; Mission 3; Hinduism and Christianity). The Christian involvement in overcoming social exploitation in India has contributed to the negative reaction of the ruling castes toward Christianity.

2.2. *Islam*

Islam developed in India in four periods: (1) Arab invaders and the first trading settlements (711-1206); (2) the Islamic sultanate, first in the North, then pushing South (1206-1526); (3) the Mogul Empire, which at its height covered the whole of India apart from the extreme South and culminated in the attempt of Akbar (emperor 1556-1605) to integrate Hindu values and lifestyles into the Islamic state but declined as the Marathas gained power, the Persians mounted their campaigns (Delhi falling to Nāder Shāh in 1739), and the colonial power of Britain increased (from the first settlements in 1601 to all India coming under the British crown in 1858); and (4) the decay of Islamic influence, with independence and partition in 1947 into predominantly Hindu India and Islamic Pakistan.

The memory of more than 1,000 years of hostility between native Hindus and invading Muslims still poisons the atmosphere. The resurgence of Islam in the Muslim world has invigorated some Muslim groups to extend their influence by economic expansion and conversion. Since Islam to a large extent breaks down caste barriers, it is an attractive alternative for the untouchables. Mass conversions to Islam (such as in 1981 at Minakshipuram, Tamil Nadu) for political and social reasons have provoked violent reactions on the part of Hindus. Although the Muslims do not have castes, they do have religiously sanctioned → hierarchies, with sheikhs and sayyids at the top. Islam has taken over various ideas of purification and also Hindu → astrology. Muslims also participate in the Hindu → temple cult. Conversely, Hindus go on pilgrimage to the graves of Muslim saints (e.g., to a famous tomb in Ajmer in Northwest India) to find → blessing.

→ Sufism flourishes in India. It is close to Hinduism in its nondualistic → worldview and its practice of meditation. From medieval times in India → Bhakti Hinduism has embraced both Hinduism and Islam, with the result that some figures (e.g., Kabīr [1440-1518]) are claimed by both religions.

Hindu-Muslim relations in India have deteriorated considerably in recent times in light both of the ongoing territorial dispute between India and Pakistan in Kashmir and of the destruction of the

Babri Mosque at Ajodhya in 1992 by radical Hindus who claim that the site was the birthplace of the Hindu god Rama. Hindus have claimed that Mogul rulers built some mosques in India over the site of destroyed Hindu temples and have sought to reclaim such sites for the rebuilding of those temples. This situation militates against Hindu-Muslim → dialogue.

Christians, however, do seek dialogue with Islam (→ Islam and Christianity). The Anglican Henry Martyn (1781-1812) and the Lutheran Karl Gottlieb Pfander (1803-65) each sought to engage in theological conversation, with a view to conversion. The reformer Sayyid Ahmad Khan (1817-98) tried to prepare the ground for a Muslim-Christian ecumenism. The Belgian Jesuit Victor Courtois (1907-60) published *Notes on Islam* (Calcutta) over a 14-year period. In 1959 the Henry Martyn Institute was founded at Hyderabad as a center for dialogue between Islam and Christianity.

2.3. Sikhs

The rise and importance of the Sikh religion are closely tied to the political history of the Punjab in India's Northwest. Because of the presence there of many races and religions, it was the site of severe tensions between Hindus and Muslims in the 15th century. The result was the politicizing of the Sufis and also conflicts after the death of Akbar (1605). Guru Nānak (1469-1539) founded a new type of devotion on the basis of visions, going beyond both Hinduism and Islam. Nine other gurus followed him. The tenth (and last), Gobind Singh (1666-1708), organized the Khālsā (lit. "pure"), a religiopolitical, military brotherhood that helped give the Sikhs military significance.

In religious practice the Sikhs never wholly broke loose from Hinduism, borrowing rituals and feasts from it, yet they are persecuted by both Hindus and Muslims because of their political significance. There are still tensions in the Punjab, the breadbasket of India, which was particularly affected by the 1947 partition. The Sikhs feel that they are threatened both politically and economically — that is, that they are being robbed of their identity — since they are often subsumed under Hindu culture.

A radical Sikh movement in the 1980s sought to reassert Sikh identity through the establishment of a separate Sikh state. This effort resulted in a violent conflict between the radicals and the Indian army at the Golden Temple in the city of Amritsar, the most sacred Sikh religious center. The perceived sacrilege to the temple by the army led to the assassination of Indira Gandhi (1917-84), who was then prime minister of India, by two of her Sikh bodyguards.

2.4. Jainism

Compared with the other religious groups, Jainism is numerically small, and less powerful ideologically and economically, although still quite important. Its doctrine of *ahiṁsā* (nonviolence), which M. K. Gandhi reinterpreted, the strict → asceticism of its monks and nuns, and its lay asceticism inspired well-to-do circles in Bombay (now known as Mumbai) and Gujarat to found student centers, publishing houses, and benevolent institutions during the 20th century. Although Jainism repudiates the caste system, it fosters groupings that give family and economic stability. It maintains hardly any relations with other religions.

2.5. Buddhism

Siddhārtha Gautama, the Buddha (ca. 563-ca. 483 B.C.), founded the religion of Buddhism, which has practically died out in India in its original form. Contributing to its decline have been its strict repudiation of the caste system, its lofty spiritual and moral claims, the resultant discrepancy between its monks and others, the partial integration of Buddhist concerns into Hinduism (e.g., Śankara's system), and the destruction of the great Buddhist centers in the North by Muslims.

After independence in 1947 R. B. Ambedkar (1893-1956) recommended and effected the conversion of about 200,000 Hindu untouchables to Buddhism, which rejects caste but is still a native religion. Several million people, especially in Maharashtra and Madhya Pradesh, but increasingly also in the slums of the big cities like New Delhi and Bombay, have now officially gone over to Buddhism.

Since 1959 about 100,000 Tibetan Buddhists have been in exile in India. They have a relatively important role in India because of the high religious and moral influence of the Dalai Lama. They maintain cultural centers and share actively in religious dialogue for → peace and justice (→ Righteousness, Justice).

2.6. Zoroastrians

The Zoroastrian community (i.e., the Parsis) derives from immigrants who came from Persia in the seventh and eighth centuries, when it was conquered by Islam. Zoroastrian piety is based on an ideological → dualism but with a strong this-worldly orientation. This fact gives it a consistent → social ethics, which plays a role in leading economic and judicial circles. Since the Zoroastrians do not mix with other groups, they are threatened with extinction. They are open to dialogue with other religions but try to protect themselves from any outside influence that might threaten their identity.

2.7. *Jews*

Jews, who emigrated to India perhaps as early as pre-Christian times, founded colonies on the Malabar Coast under the protection of the Hindu kings. Today there are only a few Jewish families in Cochin and Bombay. Since the formation of the State of Israel, a large portion of the Indian Jewish community have migrated to Israel.

3. Christian Churches

The long history of the Christian presence in India has seen the establishment of all major Christian denominations or churches in the country. The Syrian Orthodox tradition represents the earliest Christian presence, with Roman Catholicism being established during the period of mercantile colonialism. Modern colonialism under Protestant powers led to the formation of Protestant churches. In the postindependence era, independent evangelical and Pentecostal churches have also flourished. As a former "mission field" of Western churches, India provided the necessary setting for the development of ecumenical cooperation and dialogue between Protestant churches. The most significant achievement in connection with ecumenism was the formation of the → Church of South India (CSI) in 1947 and the Church of North India (CNI) in 1970.

3.1. *Orthodox Churches*

All the Orthodox churches in India belong to the → Oriental Orthodox and derive from (Eastern) Syrian traditions (→ Syrian Orthodox Churches in India). In many cases they are under the corresponding → jurisdiction, which has led to numerous conflicts and splits that still persist. Overall, the Orthodox Indian churches are held in high regard. They often form a part of the caste system. They have only recently developed an interest in mission and are active in ecumenical fellowship with other Christians worldwide, and also in dialogue with Hindus.

It is asserted, but cannot be proved, that the apostle Thomas founded the first churches on the Malabar Coast and later the Coromandel Coast and then in A.D. 72 suffered martyrdom and was buried in Madras (now known as Mylapur). For many Indian Christians this tradition is the source of an irreplaceable sense of identity. By the 3rd century at the latest, a church was certainly in existence in India. What language it spoke, how far it spread, how much → autonomy it had, and whether it was → Nestorian are all debated questions. When the Portuguese came in the 15th century, they found a unified church that was using Syriac as its ecclesiastical language. There is a sure link to Persia, which proba-

bly goes back to the first Sassanid persecution under Shāpūr II (309-79) and the associated emigration. Persian sources bear witness to the autonomy of this church in the 7th and 8th centuries, since they mention an Indian metropolitan. Around the year 800 Timotheos I (780-823) put the Indian church under direct Persian-Nestorian jurisdiction.

In 1292 the Franciscan John of Monte Corvino (1247-1328), in the course of his → Mongolian mission (as an envoy from Pope Nicholas IV to the court of Kublai Khan), made contact with the Indian church. In 1329 John XXII founded the → Diocese of Quilon under the Dominican bishop Jordanus of Severac, but without accusing native Indian Christians of taking part in the Nestorian → heresy.

Only with Portuguese colonization (Vasco da Gama arrived in 1498) did the dogmatically based Romanizing of non-Catholic Christians begin. An attempt was then made to bring the Indian church under papal jurisdiction, and a history of division followed when the Syrian → patriarchs resisted. Under the Portuguese *padroado* (patronage), there were three groups: the Latins, the Syrians who were under Rome but kept the Syrian liturgy, and the independent Thomas Christians. The last group supported the Coonen Cross revolt of 1653 against the rulings of the Synod of Diamper (1599), at which the Portuguese archbishop of Goa, Alexis Menezes (1559-1617), ordered the Indian churches to take an oath of loyalty to the → pope, recognize the seven sacraments, and abandon many native customs.

Today Indian Christianity of the Syrian tradition is split into no fewer than 15 churches. The following eight are the most important.

3.1.1. The *Syro-Malabar Church,* or Syrian Catholic Church, is a Roman Catholic church with an Eastern Syrian liturgy (→ Uniate Churches). It has some two million members and 13 bishops.

3.1.2. The *Syro-Malankara Church,* or Malankara Syrian Catholic Church, is also a Roman Catholic church. It came into being with the split of Mar Ivanios from the Syrian Orthodox Church in 1930. It uses the Western Syrian liturgical tradition and has about 200,000 members.

3.1.3. The *Syrian Orthodox (Jacobite) Church* is the largest Indian Oriental Orthodox church. With 1.5. million members it is independent under the → catholicos of the East (whose seat is at Kottayam).

3.1.4. The *Mar Thoma Syrian Church* resulted from an evangelical reforming movement in the Syrian Orthodox Church around 1843. It has about 600,000 members and is now in communion with the CSI and the CNI, though distinct from the "Anglican Syrians," who are also part of the CSI.

3.1.5. The *Church of the East,* with only 10,000 members, resulted from a split in 1874 when the Nestorian patriarch of Iran, Mar Elias Mellus, tried to claim jurisdiction over the Malabar Christians.

3.1.6. The *Malabar Independent Syrian Church of Thozhiyur,* with fewer than 1,000 members, arose for the same reason early in the 19th century. It is close to the Mar Thoma Church.

3.1.7. The *St. Thomas Evangelical Church of India* separated from the Mar Thoma Church in 1961 as a result of the work of American evangelicals. It has about 2,500 members (→ Proselytism).

3.1.8. The *Travancore-Cochin Anglican Church* (→ Anglican Communion) resulted from a split from the Kerala diocese of the CSI, essentially in a revolt of former untouchables against the caste mentality of Syrian Christians.

3.2. *Roman Catholic Church*

The → Roman Catholic Church is spread all across India and numbers about one-third of all Indian Christians. It runs many nationally recognized schools and hospitals, has an educated clergy (→ Clergy and Laity), and finds much support in influential → orders. There are tensions in the area of politics, since some socially committed → priests tend toward → Marxism as a political weapon.

The church owes its origin to Portuguese missionaries who came from 1502 onward, along with traders and colonizing soldiers. First to arrive were the → Franciscans and → Dominicans, then the → Jesuits, → Augustinians, and others (→ Roman Catholic Missions). One of the most significant missionaries was Francis Xavier (1506-52), who came to India in 1542. His grave in Goa is an important place of pilgrimage. The Diocese of Goa was founded in 1533, with Cochin following in 1557 and Madras in 1606. The → Inquisition came to Goa in 1560 and led to a mass exodus. The Carmelites worked in the South in the 17th century.

There has been accommodation to Indian culture in theology (e.g., R. Panikkar, Swami Abhishiktananda), in liturgy (an Indian Rite, now mostly withdrawn under pressure), and in lifestyle (the ashram movement). Robert de Nobili (1577-1656) made the first approaches in this direction. In Madurai in 1605 he became a "Christian Brahmin," which meant a recognition of caste in the church. The result was a conflict with Rome. His method was approved in 1623, but later (1744) Rome decided against the introduction of Hindu customs into the church.

Since the end of the 19th century the church has systematically trained Indian → priests and appointed Indian → bishops. It is more active than other churches in dialogue with Hindus.

3.3. *Protestant Churches and Ecumenism*

Almost all Protestant churches belong to the CSI or the CNI, though the Lutherans (→ Lutheran Churches) and some → Baptists remain separate, along with several smaller groups.

Protestant missions began with the German theologians Bartholomäus Ziegenbalg (1682-1719) and Heinrich Plütschau (1677-1752), who landed at Tranquebar on the Coromandel Coast in 1706 as "royal Danish missionaries." They learned the language, published a Tamil translation of the NT in 1714, founded schools and orphanages, and made common cause with the Indian people, which won them high regard and much success. Their mission was supported by the Society for Promoting Christian Knowledge (SPCK, founded 1698; → British Missions 1). The English Baptist William Carey (1761-1834) did successful work in the North from 1793 to 1834 and founded Serampore College, under whose charter the theological education and training of Protestant clergy continues to this day. After 1833 the British missions were supplemented by American societies (→ North American Missions), the Basel Mission around Mangalore (1834), the Gossner Mission in the North (1839), and the Leipzig Mission in the South (1841). The Hermannsburg Mission followed in the Telugu area (1865), followed by the Breklum Mission in Orissa (1882), along with various American and Scandinavian Lutheran missions.

The Northeast has had a largely separate missionary history. In the 17th and 18th centuries Portuguese Roman Catholics set up settlements in Assam and the neighboring hill country as way stations to Tibet, and even in 1850 Assam was still under the apostolic vicariate in Lhasa. In the early 19th century Baptists from Serampore founded two small mission stations. At the request of the British government in 1836, American Baptists from Burma founded a mission station in Sadiya (in Assam). In 1841 Methodists (later Welsh Presbyterians) began work among hill tribes, with the first larger churches being formed among the Khasi from 1875. The number of Christians grew rapidly from then on. Work had begun among the Garo tribes in 1860. In 1862 Anglicans came on the scene, continuing the work begun by two Basel missionaries at Tezpur. The Welsh Presbyterians by 1895 had set up central indigenous structures among tribes that were formerly hostile to one another.

After World War I the American Baptists made great efforts and achieved much success through a well-organized school system (over 250,000 Christians by 1941). The defeat of the Kuki revolt against Britain in Manipur; the replacement of tribal cultures (1917-19); the enhanced economic and educational influence of the British administration; the suppression of → slavery, headhunting, and tribal wars; and increasing communication with the outside world all contributed to the destruction of the tribal system. Christianity meant the cultivation of tribal identity in a new form that would fit in with the new political and economic relations. The attention to local languages by the missionaries and their reduction to writing played an important role in this regard. The North East India Christian Council was formed in 1926 to prevent splits. A vast majority of the tribal population in Northeast India is Christian. After World War II Roman Catholics enjoyed much success with their fine system of schools and colleges. The Indian government for the most part does not allow Protestant missionaries from abroad; the Roman Catholics use priests and teachers from South India. Conflicts of interest have arisen between Protestant and Catholic churches.

After independence the earlier hostility to the British (the Kuki revolt, the Naga resistance from 1929 to 1931, the revival of the Kampai cult) was now directed against the central Indian government. Economic neglect by the government of Assam led to open rebellion by the Mizos in 1966. Guerrilla groups in Mizoram and Nagaland had to be suppressed by the army. The political revolt was linked to a sense of Christian identity in the face of Hindu superiority, which often gave the conflict religious features. The churches officially declared their loyalty to India, but most of the rebel leaders were Christians who had been educated in Christian schools. For political reasons there has been news censorship on both sides, so that accurate statistics are not available. In Nagaland over 66 percent of the people are Christian, in Mizoram as many as 90 percent, about three-fourths of them Baptists. The Council of Baptist Churches in North India numbers some 800,000 members.

In southern and central India Vedanayagam Samuel Azariah (1874-1945), later the first Indian bishop of Dornakal, founded the National Missionary Society in 1905 to prevent Protestant splits and missionary competition. As a result of developing Indian nationalism, and under the inspiration of John R. Mott (1865-1955), the National Missionary Council was founded in 1912 to give advice to missions. It was the forerunner of the National Christian Council of India (NCCI; → National Christian Councils), which was formed in 1922 and to which

almost all non–Roman Catholic churches now belong. The council's studies of missionary and social questions and its initiatives on educational and social problems in concert with the Roman Catholics have made this an important body. Its work includes the founding of student centers, refugee work among Bengalis and Tibetans, radio → evangelism, and social services through the Church's Auxiliary for Social Action, to which 26 churches belong, and which engages in relief, education, well-drilling, rehabilitation, and other projects in some 130 agricultural centers. The council also sends Indian missionaries overseas, including (since 1976) to Europe and America. It is an important means of contact between Christians and the state.

Of even greater ecumenical importance was the formation of the CSI and the CNI. As early as 1908, Congregationalists, Presbyterians, and Dutch Reformed groups had formed a union of churches, which in 1919 the Basel Malabar Mission also joined, forming the South India United Church (SIUC). In 1947 the Anglican dioceses in India, including those in Myanmar and Sri Lanka, the Methodist Church of South India (British Wesleyan), and the SIUC merged in the formation of the Church of South India. This church was considered a model for church union movements around the world, especially in its adoption of the Anglican doctrine of episcopal succession, which it reconciled with the views of other denominations. The CSI Book of Common Worship is also considered an ecumenical achievement for its utilization of the resources of several denominations. In 1991 the CSI had a membership of 1.6 million persons. Inspired by the union in the south, the CNI was formed on the same model in 1970; it also numbered Baptists within its membership. A common council of the CSI, the CNI, and the Mar Thoma Church was formed in 1978.

In 1928 eight Lutheran churches formed the Federation of Evangelical Lutheran Churches in India, and in 1975 these churches, joined by one founded by the Lutheran Church–Missouri Synod, came together to form the United Evangelical Lutheran Churches in India (UELCI). Unlike the CSI and the CNI, the UELCI serves as an umbrella organization, under which the member churches retain their autonomy and divergent polities. Negotiations between the CSI and the UELCI began in 1948, and theological agreements were reached in 1959, but for the most part nontheological factors have prevented greater unity. The Baptist and Methodist churches that are not part of the CSI or the CNI have also organized themselves into regional or national conferences of their own. The growth of evangelical, Pentecostal, and nondenominational churches has similarly led to the formation of new organizations or networks of relationship.

Besides the NCCI, there are also a number of regional Christian councils. Other important ecumenical bodies are the Bishops' Council of Kerala, on which all the episcopal churches (→ Episcopalianism) in the area are represented; the Christian Council of Kerala, comprising non–Roman Catholic and non-Orthodox churches; and the Commission for Higher Education (1969) and the Commission of Ecumenical Questions (1973), with which Roman Catholics also cooperate. The → YMCA and YWCA are also active ecumenically.

The caste system is present in church life down to the very roots. This anomaly leads to tensions in the various institutions and the leadership. A striving for economic power and social recognition is an obstacle to → unity. An intensive education of both laypeople and theologians against the background of social commitment and the rooting of the faith in Indian → spirituality, as well as the strengthening of ecumenical cooperation in promoting unitary models of development, is urgently necessary.

Impulses toward ecumenism have come from dialogue with → Hinduism, the resultant ashram movement (with its Roman Catholic and Protestant wings), and some 1,200 social action groups that, independently for the most part of the established churches and religions, have tried to be symbols of hope for human liberation in the slums and villages. These groups work for human rights by means of new forms of community, political analysis of situations, and the mobilizing of the disenfranchised. They are partly supported and partly opposed by the church organizations. They are often interreligious and, in some cases, antireligious. The denominational question does not arise in most of them. The emergence of *dalit* (oppressed) movements across religious lines against high-caste dominance and social exploitation has added a new dimension to Christian identity, unity, and involvement in society.

4. Church and Society

The relation of Christians to the nation (→ State and Church) is complicated by the link between Western Christianity and colonial history. Few Christians played an active role in the battle against colonialism. Christians are regarded as a foreign body by the Hindus, and their rights (e.g., in social legislation) are not fully respected.

In 1954 the government of Madhya Pradesh set up a commission of inquiry (the Niyogi Commit-

tee) that recommended the expulsion of missionaries because they destroy "traditional social structures and values." Arunachal Pradesh followed suit in 1978. The same year representative O. P. Tyagi in New Delhi proposed legislation that would forbid conversion by improper means and would prevent the conversion of untouchables to Islam or Christianity for social reasons. The Roman Catholic Bishops' Conference and the NCCI in 1979 called for public demonstrations against the proposal, which some Hindus, Sikhs, and Buddhists joined, as well as Muslims. The government did not pursue the matter.

The emergence of the Hindu nationalist BJP as the ruling party, with the support of the RSS and VHP, has led to more pronounced and strident antiminority sentiments among Hindus. Under the ideology of *hindutva* (the Hindu way of life), radical groups have promoted anti-Christian propaganda and policies. The threat of persecution by Hindu groups has, to some degree, galvanized the Christian churches, regardless of denominational affiliation, to organize and protest in solidarity against atrocities committed against Christian institutions, workers, and missionaries. There has been an intense debate about conversion to Islam or Christianity in recent years.

The question of conversion is complex. Hindus complain of Christian intolerance, exclusivism, and false propaganda against Hinduism. Ecumenical connections with Western churches have also been regarded with suspicion. Hindus view Christian educational and service institutions, which have provided yeoman service to the Indian society, as proselytizing agencies. Historically, conversion to Christianity has taken place largely among oppressed, or *dalit*, communities seeking to escape exploitative caste structures, which has aroused Hindu fears over the continued Hindu identity of India. Experience shows, however, that *dalit* communities cannot attain emancipation except by becoming Buddhist, Muslim, or Christian. Conversion as a purely spiritual experience with no social ramifications is an abstraction. This intertwining of motivation makes trust among various religious communities very hard to achieve. The crusading spirit of certain Christian groups, often sponsored by independent North American churches, has not been helpful in promoting dialogue and harmony among the various religious communities in India. A Christian commitment to dialogue with a strong focus on the social emancipation of the oppressed will determine the future growth of Christianity in India.

→ Asia; Asian Theology

Bibliography: S. K. CHAUBE, *Hill Politics in North-East India* (Bombay, 1973) • G. EICHINGER FERRO-LUZZI, ed., *Rites and Beliefs in Modern India* (New Delhi, 1990) • C. B. FIRTH, *An Introduction to Indian Church History* (3d ed.; Madras, 1990) • F. HARDY, *The Religious Culture of India: Power, Love, and Wisdom* (Cambridge, 1994) • S. B. HARPER, *In the Shadow of the Mahatma: Bishop V. S. Azariah and the Travails of Christianity in British India* (Grand Rapids, 2000) • H. KULKE and D. ROTHERMUND, *A History of India* (3d ed.; London, 1997) • G. J. LARSON, *India's Agony over Religion* (Albany, N.Y., 1995) • D. S. LOPEZ, ed., *Religions of India in Practice* (Princeton, 1995) • D. LUDDEN, ed., *Contesting the Nation: Religion, Community, and the Politics of Democracy in India* (Philadelphia, 1996) • A. M. MUNDADAN, *History of Christianity in India,* vol. 1, *From the Beginning up to the Middle of the Sixteenth Century* (Bangalore, 1984) • V. S. NARAVANE, *A Cultural History of Modern India: Nineteenth Century* (New Delhi, 1991) • S. C. NEILL, *A History of Christianity in India,* vol. 1, *The Beginnings to* A.D. *1707;* vol. 2, *1707-1858* (Cambridge, 1984-85) • J. THEKKEDATH, *History of Christianity in India,* vol. 2, *From the Middle of the Sixteenth to the End of the Seventeenth Century* (Bangalore, 1982) • P. VERGHESE, ed., *Die Syrische Kirchen in Indien* (Stuttgart, 1974) • H. ZIMMER, *Philosophie und Religion Indiens* (9th ed.; Frankfurt, 1998).

MICHAEL VON BRÜCK and J. PAUL RAJASHEKAR

Indian Settlements → Reductions

Individualism

1. Term
2. History
3. Modern Development
4. Questions

1. Term

Literally, individualism is a view that gives precedence to the individual (Lat. *individuum,* "what cannot be divided"). The type of individualism depends on what the individual has precedence over — → society in the case of *social individualism,* the → state in the case of *political individualism,* the economy as a whole in that of *economic individualism,* or the moral collective in that of *ethical individualism.* Other criteria might lead to emphasis on either the level of intensity or the function. Thus there are radical and moderate forms of individualism in each of the four cases, and each of these might function theoretically, methodologically, or existentially.

2. History

The term "individualism" first came into use in the 19th century, but the idea itself goes back much further. The framework for every sense is the logico-ontological distinction between the general concept and the proper name, which in antiquity (Plato, Aristotle) and the Middle Ages (Thomas Aquinas, William of Ockham) governed the discussion of the *atoma* (the ultimate elements) and the *individua.* In this form (note S. Kripke's "rigid denominators"), and in the form of the nominalist debate and the strife about universals (→ Nominalism; Scholasticism), the discussion continues today. The statement *individuum est ineffabile,* which is mistakenly ascribed to → Thomism, denotes the central insight that what can be expressed is not the individual but the universal concept.

3. Modern Development

The attempt undertaken in the → modern period to address the question of individualism in practical philosophy, including doing so through the notion of a transcendent creator God (though without validating such a step), has taken place in three stages: the *theoretical contractual individualism* of the 17th and 18th centuries, the *economically oriented ethical individualism* of the late 18th and early 19th centuries, and finally the radical *existential individualism* of the late 19th and early 20th centuries, which renounces systematic thinking. In general we must say that all three forms developed in constant debate with various forms of collectivism, → socialism, and Communism and have always contained an element of ethical individualism.

3.1. The goal of the various contract theories of the 17th and 18th centuries was to show that we can deduce the rights and principles of life in society only from an analysis of the qualities of the individual. At root there were two ways of explaining the formation of the state and society from the characteristics of the individual in the natural state: the doctrine of power and the doctrine of right.

The English statesman and philosopher T. Hobbes (1588-1679) championed the doctrine of power. He began with the idea that the natural state is a constant battle of all against all, each being an → enemy of the other. In the interests of the weak this feature in individuals forces a concentration of power in the hands of an absolute prince who can protect the weak against the attacks of the strong.

The English philosopher and psychologist

J. Locke (1632-1704), following the Dutch jurist H. Grotius (1583-1645), championed the doctrine of right, as did to some degree J.-J. Rousseau (1712-78). Before the existence of any contract, individuals have by nature rights and duties. It is not the warring urge for power but a natural social impulse that causes the individual to make a contract with other individuals. It is a legitimate natural → duty to protect the positive natural qualities of the human individual against their perverted reduction by the state.

3.2. From the basic assumptions of contractual individualism, which lead from absolutism to constitutionalism, it is a small but logical step to the enrichment of individualism with economic ideas. The individual must have both economic and political power to enjoy economic as well as logical, ontological, social, or political priority. Hence with the principle of a sharing of political power (Montesquieu [1689-1755]), the 18th and 19th centuries brought what is in effect an individualistic restriction of the power of government in economic matters. For the Scottish moral philosopher and economist A. Smith (1723-90), each individual is clearly an end, and the state and its economy are simply means to serve this end. Self-interest is the engine of economic prosperity.

→ Utilitarianism developed the logic of this economic form of ethical individualism. The English philosophers J. Bentham (1748-1832) and J. S. Mill (1806-73), with their "utilitarian calculus," advocated the greatest happiness of the greatest number as an ethical antithesis to the nonindividualistic ethics of I. Kant (1724-1804; → Kantianism).

3.3. The end of the 19th century brought great individualistic reactions to the systematician G. W. F. Hegel (1770-1831). M. Stirner (1806-56) championed a kind of egotistic materialism; S. Kierkegaard (1813-55) developed a Christian existentialism; F. Nietzsche (1844-1900) revived the doctrine of power. The existential surrender of the torn individual → self to the → absolute in a rejection of all official churchly Christianity (Kierkegaard) was just as influential for 20th-century → existentialism as the idea of a powerful individual that must shun weak Christian altruism and stride on to the next evolutionary stage, that of the superman (Nietzsche).

Aware of the difficulties and problems that beset this radicalizing of individualism to the point of → solipsism, M. Heidegger (1889-1976) — contrary to his own declared intention — aided existential individualism with his doctrine of the authenticity of existence as a movement toward death and his radical isolation of existence. Above all, the French existentialists around the early J.-P. Sartre (1905-80) and A. Camus (1913-60) linked existential individualism to an ethical individualism, in this way deriving from their idea of the meaninglessness and absurdity of human life a doctrine of human responsibility for others and for the whole world.

4. Questions

The present situation might be called one of reindividualizing in reaction to the dominance of the collectivist interpretations of neo-Marxism in the 1960s. With its more pronounced theoretical and methodological orientation, this reindividualizing focuses on the basic problem of individualism in the larger sense, a problem whose mirror image can be found in the analogous basic problem of all collectivism. Put briefly, the society is always more than the sum of individuals, while the individual is always more than merely a part of that society.

Politicoeconomic theories of order such as we find in F. A. von Hayek and J. M. Buchanan may be viewed as theories that measure the functioning of social regulation and well-being in terms of individual well-being according to the criterion of human → freedom.

The individualistic program that figures in many sociological approaches also proves to be an explicit methodological individualism. Such a program explains sociological events and generalizations by hypotheses about individual → behavior. The problem known as that of the individual and society appears here in the form that synergistic effects or higher linkages in social processes do not admit of explanation. The practical results may be seen in new and predominantly Eastern forms of religion, whose religious character consists of a radical individualism that aims at the elimination of the individual element by bodily exercise.

→ Anthropology 3-4; Autonomy; Ethics; Liberalism; Person; Subjectivism and Objectivism

Bibliography: R. N. Bellah, *Individualism and Commitment in American Life: Readings on the Themes and Habits of the Heart* (New York, 1987) • A. Béteille, "Individualism and Equality," *CA* 27 (1986) 121-34 • T. Doi, *The Anatomy of Self: The Individual versus Society* (Tokyo, 1986) • E. Fox-Genovese, *Feminism without Illusions: A Critique of Individualism* (Chapel Hill, N.C., 1991) • D. L. Gelpi, *Beyond Individualism: Toward a Retrieval of Moral Discourse in America* (Notre Dame, Ind., 1989) • F. A. von Hayek, *Individualism and Economic Order* (London, 1946) • A. I. McFadyen, *The Call to Personhood: A Christian Theory of the Indi-*

vidual in Social Relationships (Cambridge, 1990) • D. L. MILLER, *Individualism: Personal Achievement and the Open Society* (Austin, Tex., 1964) • W. RAUB and T. VOSS, *Individuelles Handeln und gesellschaftliche Folgen* (Darmstadt, 1981) • B. A. SHAIN, *The Myth of American Individualism: The Protestant Origins of American Political Thought* (Princeton, 1994) • D. SHANAHAN, *Toward a Genealogy of Individualism* (Amherst, Mass., 1992) • R. ZINTL, *Individualistische Theorien und die Ordnung der Gesellschaft* (Berlin, 1983).

WALTHER C. ZIMMERLI

Indonesia

	1960	1980	2000
Population (1,000s):	96,194	150,958	212,565
Annual growth rate (%):	2.14	2.06	1.31
Area: 1,919,317 sq. km. (741,052 sq. mi.)			

A.D. 2000

Population density: 111/sq. km. (287/sq. mi.)
Births / deaths: 2.09 / 0.71 per 100 population
Fertility rate: 2.37 per woman
Infant mortality rate: 39 per 1,000 live births
Life expectancy: 67.3 years (m: 65.3, f: 69.3)
Religious affiliation (%): Muslims 55.4, new religionists 20.6, Christians 13.6 (Protestants 6.2, indigenous 4.3, Roman Catholics 3.0, other Christians 0.2), Hindus 3.5, tribal religionists 2.3, nonreligious 2.2, Chinese folk religionists 1.4, other 1.0.
Note: Figures do not include Timor.

1. Religions
2. Churches
   2.1. Protestants
   2.2. Roman Catholic
3. Society and Christianity
4. Islam and Christianity

The Republic of Indonesia, which covers the territory of the former Dutch East Indies, comprises over 13,500 islands, 6,000 of which are inhabited. Among over 100 ethnic groups, the dominant two are the Javanese (45 percent of the population) and the Sundanese (14 percent).

1. Religions
Most of the native Indonesians originally had only unwritten forms of belief and worship (→ Tribal Religions), and many of them have found a new identity in → Islam or Christianity. Small ethnic groups, as in Irian Jaya, retain their traditional tribal beliefs.

Mahayana → Buddhists have been in Indonesia from before the 5th century, reaching their high point in the 8th to the 11th centuries. By 1965 eight groups of different traditions and ethnic origins had gained recognition by the state as religious fellowships; 6,271 new adherents in the years 1970 to 1980 (*WCE* 382) give evidence of a revived interest.

Indian influence from around A.D. 200 resulted in a mixed religious culture, part Hindu and part Javanese, which is still influential today (→ Syncretism). → Hinduism established itself especially on Bali, and Indonesian independence in 1945 also gave impetus to Hinduism on Java. In 1958 it received government recognition.

Islam ultimately became more prominent than Hinduism. Merchants from India brought → Sunni Islam to Indonesia in the 13th century, where its → acculturation led to different forms. There is a traditional and strongly orthodox form in Sumatra, West Java, South Sulawesi, and the northern Moluccas. In Central and East Java, Islam has combined with Hindu-Javanese mysticism in a religious practice known as Kebatinan, a set of religious practices that enables a practitioner to experience the inner reality of being *(batin)*. Since 1966 there has been a missionary-oriented movement known as Dakwah (or Da'wah, "summons"), which arose in reaction to foreign influences and seeks an active upholding of Islamic beliefs. A basic problem for Islam is the development in many areas throughout Indonesia of tensions between native lifestyles and Islamic Shari'a. Some conservative Muslim groups press politically for the formation of an Islamic state. For the time being, however, the government and the military have successfully resisted these demands.

2. Churches
2.1. *Protestants*
Among the 270 Protestant denominations we can distinguish (1) smaller regional churches; (2) the Union of Protestant Churches of Indonesia (1970), which is close to the Far Eastern Council of Christian Churches at Singapore and also to the → World Evangelical Fellowship, most of whose member churches result mainly from the work of → fundamentalist or conservative Anglo-Saxon missions since 1945; and (3) the Communion of Churches in Indonesia (Persekutuan Gereja-Gereja di Indonesia [PGI], founded in 1950), which has 75 member churches and represents 85 percent of the Protestants in Indonesia. In their effort to achieve unity, the member churches in 1984 reorganized the PGI structure to combine as a fellowship or communion rather than as a council.

The history of the Protestant churches goes back to the change in colonial rule, when the Reformed Dutch drove the Catholic Portuguese out of the Moluccas in 1601-5. The result was the founding of the oldest Protestant church in Asia. With the support of the Dutch Reformed Church, the Dutch East India Company provided for pastoral and missionary work in its settlements in the territory. This church, which for nearly three centuries was the dominant Christian body, became a state church when the Dutch government took over the company in 1816.

In the 19th century several missionary societies from the Netherlands, Germany, and Switzerland founded many Christian congregations and institutions in what was then the Dutch East Indies. In the late 19th and early 20th century, a number of American mission societies also took up work in the archipelago. In the 1930s and during the aftermath of the Second World War, the Protestant Church in the Dutch Indies and other mission churches became autonomous. In many cases relations with Western missionary societies changed into partnerships, as promoted and coordinated especially by the European Working Group for Ecumenical Relations with Indonesia. North American churches developed bilateral relationships with churches in Indonesia and also pursued coordinated work through the National Council of the Churches of Christ in the U.S.A.

Most of the larger churches in the PGI developed among ethnic (tribal) groups. Thus the work of Rhineland Missionary Fellowship, for example, gave rise to several church groups in North Sumatra, the largest being the Batak Christian Protestant Church (HKBP, 1861), which in 1998 had 1.6 million members. The Christian Evangelical Church in Minahassa, North Sulawesi (1568), includes over 90 percent of the people of the area (555,000 members) and is notable for diaconal and educational work. The Evangelical Christian Church in Timor (1612), with 525,000 members, enjoyed revival and renewal in the latter part of the 20th century. The Moluccan Protestant Church (1534), with 505,000 members, is strongly traditional. In the Evangelical Christian Church in Irian Jaya (1855), with 400,000 members, there is ethnically and geographically varied work in parish development, education, and highland missions among the Jali tribes. The Nias Christian Protestant Church (1865), founded by the Rhenish Mission and with 280,000 members, has become the territorial church on the island of the same name. The Evangelical Christian Church in Sangihe-Talaud (1568), with 185,000 members, has a pro-

gram of parish development and education supported by Dutch partners. The Toraja Church Rantepao of Sulawesi (1913), which resulted from the work of the Nederlandsch Zendelinggenootschap and has 175,000 members, is famous for its rapid growth and its martyrs. The Christian Church in Central Sulewesi (1893), with 125,000 members, does work among → marginal groups and migrants from Bali and Java. The Evangelical Church in Kalimantan in the Dayak region (1836) has 90,000 members and resulted from work by the Rhenish and Basel Missions.

The Christian Churches of Java (Jogjakarta, 1858), the product of Reformed missions, is also important and has a notable attraction for Islam (121,500 members). The Christian Church in Indonesia on Java (1934), with 65,000 members, is the largest church among native and immigrant Chinese.

In eastern Indonesia the percentage of Christians is relatively high (42 percent), but Christians are weakest in the most highly populated and fully developed regions, Java and Bali (at most, 1 percent). Over half of the member churches of the PGI are numerically small and are for the most part ethnic and rural.

Denominationally, 62 percent of the PGI member churches belong to the Reformed tradition (→ World Alliance of Reformed Churches). Those that resulted from the work of the Rhenish and Basel Missions are → union churches. Of this number, the Batak churches, though not Lutheran by name, joined the → Lutheran World Federation, having had its confession of faith accepted as conforming to the Lutheran confessional tradition, beginning in 1952. Pentecostals (→ Pentecostal Churches), Methodists (→ Methodist Churches), and → Mennonites are also found in Indonesia. Of the churches in Indonesia, 29 belong to the → Christian Conference of Asia, 26 to the → World Council of Churches. The PGI and its churches participate in many development projects on behalf of rural and coastal areas. The PGI also cooperates with the Roman Catholic Bishops' Conference in matters of common concern vis-à-vis the government.

2.2. Roman Catholic

The → Roman Catholic Church was established in the 16th century by → Franciscans, → Jesuits, and → Dominicans in the course of Portuguese conquest. In the 19th century these orders laid great stress on education and the building up of a native structure. The first native Indonesian priest was ordained in 1926, and an Indonesian hierarchy was set up in 1961. Before 1974 there were 9 Indonesian bishops out of 31, and half the clergy were Indonesian. By 1980 there were 7 archbishoprics, 24 dioceses, and 2 apostolic prefectures. An active Roman Catholic consciousness may be seen in lay fellowships. The Roman Church strengthens itself by a variety of teaching and instructional activities, as well as through welfare institutions. It also has a remarkable outreach in businesses, in the press (e.g., at the Gramedia complex in Jakarta), and in hotels. Noteworthy is its dedication to the younger generation. Apart from its presence on the island of Flores, it manifests an urban character.

3. Society and Christianity

The relationship of the churches to state and society is marked by their participation in the national movement. In 1945 President Sukarno (1901-70) established Pancasila ("five pillars") as the "soul" of the constitution, comprising belief in one Deity, human dignity, national unity, democracy, and social justice (→ Civil Religion 5). This worldview, as he saw it, guaranteed religious → pluralism (→ Religious Liberty) and therefore leaves room for churches to live, even as minorities. In 1985 the government adopted Pancasila as a binding norm for all social and political organizations, including religious groups.

Christians made a contribution to Pancasila with their own interpretation of its meaning and force. In article 3 of its constitution the PGI maintained that it is based on Jesus Christ as Lord and Savior (Matt. 16:18; 1 Cor. 3:11). It also stated (art. 5), however, that it is ready to share in efforts to practice Pancasila as the only basis for the life of society, the nation, and the state. The Roman Catholic Church affirms Pancasila, not because it sees in it a practical law, but on account of its lofty values, which are in accord with the striving of humanity for God and the view of humanity held in the Christian faith (National Conference of Catholic Fellowships in Jakarta, 1984).

4. Islam and Christianity

Relations between → Islam and Christianity alternate between neighborliness and aversion. The Fourth Seminar of Religions held by the PGI in 1984 laid a basis for understanding between central institutions. Representatives of both religions discussed the theme of education in religion and society from the standpoint of renewal by schools, Kebatinan, the gospel, and Pancasila.

Events in recent years following the fall of the 36-year rule of President Suharto have led to uncertainty concerning the path of future developments in Indonesia. There are signs that Indonesia is advancing toward further democratization, as evidenced by the holding of national elections in 1999, the selection of a new president, and the acceptance by the Indonesian government of the separation of East Timor from Indonesia. Nonetheless, the violence perpetrated in East Timor by military-backed militias and the demands for autonomy or independence from other areas such as Atyeh and Irian Jaya have given rise to questions concerning the ultimate viability of Indonesia as a unified nation state.

Such a climate of uncertainty has led to increased strains in relationships between Islam and Christianity, as well as in relations between Islam and the other recognized religions in Indonesia. Ongoing unrest between the Muslim and Christian communities in the Moluccan Islands as well as scattered acts of violence in other areas of Indonesian does not bode well. Yet voices from the Muslim community, as well as other faith communities, have been in the forefront of those calling for → peace. In a democratic state, Islam, as the majority religion, will clearly have great influence. The role of the other religious communities, including Christianity, still remains to be clarified.

→ Asian Theology

Bibliography: J. CAMPBELL-NELSON, *Indonesia in Shadow and Light* (New York, 1998) • F. COOLEY, *The Growing Seed: The Christian Church in Indonesia* (Jakarta, 1982) • R. CRIBB and C. BROWN, *Modern Indonesia: A History since 1945* (London, 1995) • E. DARMAPUTRA, *Pancasila and the Search for Identity and Modernity in Indonesian Society* (Leiden, 1988) • T. VAN DEN END, *Ragi Carita. Sejarah Gereja di Indonesia* (vol. 1, 5th ed.; Jakarta, 1993; vol. 2; Jakarta, 1989) • T. VAN DEN END et al., eds., *Indonesische Geloofsbelijdenissen* (Leiden, 1986) • R. M. KOENTJARANINGRAT, *Introduction to the Peoples and Cultures of Indonesia and Malaysia* (Menlo Park, Calif., 1986) • M. P. M. MUSKENS, *Partner in Nation Building: The Catholic Church in Indonesia* (Aachen, 1979) • P. B. PEDERSEN, *Batak Blood and Protestant Soul* (Grand Rapids, 1970) • D. E. RAMAGE, *Politics in Indonesia: Democracy, Islam, and the Ideology of Tolerance* (London, 1995) • *Report of the Bishops' Conference of Indonesia to the Holy See* (Jakarta, 1989) • L. SCHREINER, *Adat und Evangelium* (Gütersloh, 1972) • A. SCHWARZ, *A Nation in Waiting: Indonesia in the 1990s* (Sydney, 1994) • *Sejarah Gereja Katolik Indonesia* (5 vols.; Jakarta, 1974) • T. B. SIMATUPANG, *Gelebte Theologie in Indonesia* (Göttingen, 1992) • A. A. YEWANGOE, *Theologie Crucis in Asia* (Amsterdam, 1987) • A. G. ZAINU'DDIN, *A Short History of Indonesia* (New York, 1970).

LOTHAR SCHREINER and WARNER LUOMA

Indulgence

1. Definition
2. History
3. Modern Understanding

1. Definition

On the basis of the new order for penance in the apostolic constitution *Indulgentiarum doctrina* of Paul VI (1963-78), issued on January 1, 1967, and revised in 1968 in *Enchiridion indulgentiarum,* the 1983 → Codex Iuris Canonici defines an indulgence as "a remission before God of the temporal punishment for sin the guilt of which is already forgiven, which a properly disposed member of the Christian faithful obtains under certain and definite conditions with the help of the Church which, as the minister of redemption, dispenses and applies authoritatively [*auctoritative dispensat et applicat*] the treasury of the satisfactions of Christ and the saints" (can. 992). According to canon 994, "The faithful can gain partial or plenary indulgences [*indulgentias sive partiales sive plenarias*] for themselves or apply them for the dead by way of suffrage [*ad modum suffragii*]." Finally, "No authority beneath the Roman Pontiff can commit to others the power to grant indulgences unless it was expressly given to him by the Apostolic See" (can. 995).

2. History

In the early Middle Ages public penance gave way to private penance (→ Penitence), and acts of penance to offset the temporal penalties of sin became part of reconciliation. This change opened the door for an increasing regulation of such acts. In this connection early ideas of commutation and redemption (deriving from Germanic law) led in France in the 11th century to the concept of the indulgence as the remission of temporal penalties through the official assurance of the all-powerful intercession of the church, the guilt of → sin and its eternal penalties having already been remitted by absolution in penance.

In 1095 Urban II (1088-99) proclaimed full indulgence for taking part in a crusade. In 1187 Gregory VIII (1187) granted an indulgence to those who helped to finance a crusade. In 1230 Hugh of St. Cher (d. 1263) worked out the doctrine of the "treasury of the church" *(thesaurus ecclesiae);* on this view the → pope can grant an indulgence out of the treasury of the superfluous merits of Christ and the saints. In the jubilee year 1300 Boniface VIII (1294-1303) declared a plenary indulgence for visiting the apostolic churches in Rome (→ Holy Year).

The indulgence, which had thus far been a subject of the church's authoritative intercession, had now come under its jurisdiction. In 1343 Clement VI (1342-52) made the doctrine of the *thesaurus ecclesiae* official in the bull *Unigenitus.* Peter Abelard (1079-1142) had totally rejected indulgences, but Albertus Magnus (ca. 1200-1280), Bonaventure (ca. 1217-74), and Thomas Aquinas (ca. 1225-74, *Summa theol.* III supp., qq. 25-26) gave them a theological definition and basis.

In the 14th and 15th centuries the indulgence came to be increasingly commercialized in the form of letters of penance and indulgence (the latter for the dead). The resultant weakening of penance came under sharp criticism from John Wycliffe (ca. 1330-84), Jan Hus (ca. 1372-1415), John of Wesel (ca. 1400-1481), Wessel (ca. 1419-89), and then Martin Luther (1483-1546) in his 95 Theses (*LW* 31.25-33). According to Luther, "The entire life of believers [is] to be one of repentence" (thesis 1), and "any truly repentant Christian has a right to full remission of penalty and → guilt, even without indulgence letters" (thesis 36).

The Council of → Trent (sess. 25) checked the commercialization of indulgences but refined and renewed the theory. In its basic elements it remains valid in the → Roman Catholic Church.

3. Modern Understanding

Especially K. Rahner (1904-84), following B. Poschmann (1878-1955), attempted a spiritual and personal interpretation of indulgence that sees in it not merely an amnesty for the temporal penalties of sin but a qualified (because infallible) act of intercession by the → church. This act helps to make penitence more intensive and therefore more swift and salvific, so that the growth of → love will set aside the temporal penalties of sin, which govern human nature as a whole. The indulgence, then, is not a substitute for penitential acts but their gracious intensification.

A somewhat different position set before → Vatican II in 1965 and promoted by Cardinal Charles Journet (Fribourg) found its way into the apostolic constitution *Indulgentiarum doctrina* of 1967. Although this position avoids some of the traditional mistaken developments, it enshrines the understanding of the indulgence as an authoritative jurisdictional act on the part of the papacy and the church.

Bibliography: G. A. Benrath, "Ablaß," *TRE* 1.347-64 • F. Beringer, *Die Ablässe, ihr Wesen und Gebrauch* (15th ed.; Paderborn, 1930; orig. pub., 1906) •

H. Bornkamm, *Thesen und Thesenanschlag Luthers* (Berlin, 1967) • J. E. Campbell, *Indulgences* (Ottawa, 1953) • K. Rahner, "On the Official Teaching of the Church Today on the Subject of Indulgences," *Theological Investigations* (vol. 10; New York, 1973) 166-98; idem, "Remarks on the Theology of Indulgences," ibid. (vol. 2; New York, 1963) 175-201 • R. W. Southern, *Western Society and the Church in the Middle Ages* (Harmondsworth, 1970) 136-43.

Karl-Heinz zur Mühlen

Industrial Society

1. Definitions
2. Capitalism, Industrial Society, Modern Age
3. Chief Problems

1. Definitions

We must distinguish between a narrower and a broader definition of "industrial society." In the narrower sense the term indicates that a specifically industrial technology of production controls a country's economy. The industrial element in this → technology is principally the use of machines in the mass production of goods (i.e., mechanization of production). K. Marx (1818-83) thought that the new thing in industrial technology was the profound change in the relation of people and machines (→ Marxism). "In handicrafts and manufacture, the workman makes use of a tool, in the factory, the machine makes use of him" (*Capital*, vol. 1, *MECW* 35.425).

Societies change from agrarian to industrial when the industrial sector (manufacturing), in which goods are made by machines, becomes economically dominant. In preindustrial, agrarian societies agriculture is the most important branch of the economy. In postindustrial → service societies the service sector (commerce, banking, business, the state) is central. C. Clark and others have called this distinguishing of societies by the dominant economic sector, and the postulating of a movement from the agrarian via the industrial to the service society, the three-sectors hypothesis.

The proportion of workers in a sector indicates whether that sector is dominant. A century or so ago it was common for over half of a country's labor force to work on the land. Now, however, things have changed. In the mid-1990s in Germany, for example, only 6 percent of the labor force was engaged in agriculture, compared with 41 percent in industry and the majority in the service sector. In the nar-

rower sense, German society has long since changed from industrial to service.

On a broader definition, however, which pays attention to the structural and cultural developments related to new production technology and the rise of big industry, Germany is still an industrial society. According to R. Aron these developments include the separation (materially as well as in space and time) between home and job (M. Weber), the technologically demanded division of labor, the concentration of labor in places of → work, the accumulation of capital, economic growth, and economic rationalization by making investment decisions on the basis of forecasts of profitability. In the literature (K. Kumar), changes brought about by the development of industrial societies are described in terms of population growth, urbanization, the decline of society, → secularization, rationalization (according to Weber, the debunking of religious worldviews by modern science), and democratization (→ Democracy). Judged by these criteria, a country like Germany is still an industrial society. Transition to a postindustrial stage does not reverse trends like increasing rationalization and bureaucratization. By standards of this kind the postindustrial society is simply a continuation of the industrial society.

2. Capitalism, Industrial Society, Modern Age

Whereas the narrower definition raises the question of the relation to → capitalism, the problem on the broader definition is that of the unity of the industrial society within the multiplicity of the features characterizing it.

2.1. An economy is organized capitalistically when the direct producers (the workers) are distinct from the means of production, when there is thus a market for labor, when decisions about production are based on profitability, and when these privately made decisions are decentrally coordinated with the market. On a Marxist view this capitalistic organization is the main thing, the basis on which industrial technology and the other qualities of industrial societies can develop. An argument in favor of this theory is that the capitalistic mode of production is older than industrialization. Its beginnings are in the 16th century (I. Wallerstein), whereas the industrial revolution dates only from about 1760. Since the work of Aron, it has become customary to view capitalism as one main form of the industrial society; → socialism is the other.

In socialist societies, too, home and job are separate (perhaps not so fully as in capitalist societies), a technological division of labor holds sway, and industrial methods of production are demanded. The relevant differences relate to the question of → property (private or collective) and the way of directing the economy (market planning).

2.2. American → sociology prefers the term "modern → society" to "industrial society," which in the narrower sense is related too closely to industrialization and in the broader sense is simply a conglomerate of the typical features of industrial societies. In the sociology of modern societies an attempt is made to work out the basic structure of such societies in contrast to premodern, traditional societies (R. Bendix, T. Parsons). Functional differentiation is the key. In modern societies functional spheres such as the economy and → politics are distinct. Each sphere has its own basis and operates by its own rules. The primary presupposition is freedom from the shackles of tradition. For example, without free trade and the freedom to transfer property and labor rights, a capitalistic economy could never have arisen. → Religion is implicated in the process of differentiation. In modern society it is assigned specific tasks and loses its comprehensive social function as a "bracket" (→ Sociology of Religion).

Liberation from traditional bonds is demanded by the dynamic that typifies the functional systems of modern societies. This dynamic takes different directions according to the sphere in which it is at work. *Socially,* differentiation means the loss of traditional ties and increasing individualization. *Culturally,* it means the universalizing of social values and science's dethroning of religion as a central point of orientation. *Politically,* the result is constitutional democracy. *Economically,* there is an unparalleled increase in productivity.

3. Chief Problems

The debate whether forces unleased by the development of industrial societies primarily are destructive or civilizing has not yet been laid to rest. A first point of discussion relates to *the consequences of industrialization for workers.* An argument that can be traced back to Adam Smith (1723-90) is that industrialization involves the degradation of labor. Today this negative view is thought to hold true only for specific branches and periods. The same applies to the basic law of Marx that capitalistic accumulation results in poverty.

Also discussed are *the consequences for society.* One important thesis is that industrial development is uneven both in specific spheres (as illustrated by economic crises) and as a whole. Social inequalities arise because behavior that might be economically

appropriate (commercialization) invades other spheres. As A. Ferguson said as early as 1767, "The commercial arts may continue to prosper, but they gain an ascendant at the expense of other pursuits. The desire of profit stifles the love of perfection" (p. 217). In the sociological theory of society (e.g., of Parsons), failure to relate the different spheres (disintegration) is a primary problem in differentiated societies. There are then *the consequences for the relation between the individual and society.* Both conservatives (e.g., A. Gehlen) and radicals (e.g., H. Marcuse) have described the problems of alienation, such as treating people in the mass (→ Masses, The), → anonymity, rootlessness, bureaucratization, and individual experiences of powerlessness. One detects in many diagnoses of this type nostalgic lamentations for a past, lost world.

Next are *the consequences for developing countries.* Well over half a billion people in the → Third World suffer from → hunger. Next to avoiding nuclear → war the overcoming of → poverty and hunger is perhaps the greatest international problem. It seems natural to relate the poverty of nonindustrialized countries causally to the wealth of industrialized countries (→ Dependence), but the causal relation of the rising discrepancy between the poor South and the rich North to their respective industrial structures is far too general to be convincing. A more plausible theory is that the discrepancy involves the marginalizing of developing countries (D. Senghaas) when they are integrated into the world market. No less important than the study of mechanisms like markets, economic systems, and population growth is an analysis of the part that governments, leaders, banks, and so forth can play in fighting Third World poverty.

Finally, there are *the consequences for the relation between society and → nature,* that is, the polluting of the → environment with industrial waste and the using up of nonrenewable resources, both of which contribute to the destroying of nature on a global scale (→ Ecology). Although the harmful effects of industrialization on nature have been known for a long time, the limiting of growth became a widely influential theme only in the mid-1970s. Criticism of environmental degradation took a practical turn in new social movements (→ Counterculture). The future of the industrial society depends decisively on whether ecological problems are recognized and mastered.

→ Achievement and Competition; Consumption; Development 1; Economic Ethics; Social Partnership; Sociology of Churches; Unemployment; Worker-Priests

Bibliography: R. Aron, *Die industrielle Gesellschaft* (Frankfurt, 1962) • R. Badham, ed., *The Sociology of Industrial and Post-Industrial Societies* (= *CuSoc* 32/1 [1984]) • D. Bell, *Die postindustrielle Gesellschaft* (Frankfurt, 1975) • R. Bendix, "Tradition and Modernity Reconsidered," *CSSH* 9 (1967) 292-346 • M. L. Blackburn, ed., *Comparing Poverty: The United States and Other Industrial Nations* (Washington, D.C., 1997) • S. P. Burggraf, *The Feminine Economy and Economic Man: Reviving the Role of Family in the Post-industrial Age* (Reading, Mass., 1997) • C. Clark, *The Conditions of Economic Progress* (3d ed.; New York, 1957) • A. Ferguson, *An Essay on the History of Civil Society* (Edinburgh, 1966; orig. pub., 1767) • J. K. Galbraith, *The New Industrial State* (New York, 1967) • K. Kumar, *Prophecy and Progress: The Sociology of Industrial and Post-Industrial Society* (Harmondsworth, 1978) • D. Nohlen and F. Nuscheler, eds., *Handbuch der Dritten Welt* (vol. 1; 2d ed.; Hamburg, 1982) • T. Parsons, *The System of Modern Societies* (Englewood Cliffs, N.J., 1971) • D. Senghaas, *Von Europa lernen. Entwicklungsgeschichtliche Betrachtungen* (Frankfurt, 1982) • L. Tiger, *The Manufacturing of Evil; Ethics, Evolution, and the Industrial System* (New York, 1987) • I. Wallerstein, *The Modern World-System: Capitalist Agriculture and the Origins of the European World-Economy in the Sixteenth Century* (New York, 1974) • M. Weber, *Gesammelte Aufsätze zur Religionssoziologie* (vol. 1; Tübingen, 1920).

JOHANNES BERGER

Infallibility

1. "Infallibility" is a term common in the Christian tradition. It was first used for God and the truth of the → gospel (→ Dogma 2). Then by the 14th century it came to be used for the → church, its → councils, and the papal magisterium (→ Pope 1.3). Alternative words are "inerrancy" (*inerrantia*) and "indefectibility" (*indefectibilitas*).

2. The → church (§3.2) is infallible as long as it upholds the → truth of the gospel with the assistance of the Holy Spirit (e.g., see John 14:16-17; 16:13; 1 Tim. 3:15). In common with most Christians, Roman Catholicism teaches that the books of the Bible "firmly, faithfully and without error, teach that truth which God, for the sake of our salvation, wished to see confided to the sacred Scriptures" (*Dei Verbum* 11; → Vatican II).

The Reformers and their successors made much of this point. Though the early confessions used the word "infallible" only rarely, the Belgic Confession could call Scripture "this infallible rule" (art. 7), equivalent to the "sure rule" of the Gallican (art. 4). Later the Westminster Confession stated that "assurance of the infallible truth" derives from "the inward work of the Holy Spirit bearing witness by and with the Word" (1.5). Scripture is also "the infallible rule of interpretation of Scripture" (1.9), though with a further reference to "the Holy Spirit speaking in the Scripture" (1.10). Authority rather than infallibility was the Reformers' key concern. Calvin insisted that the authority of the church, even though it claims guidance by the Spirit, is inseparably "attached to" the Word, for the Spirit cannot contradict himself (*Inst.* 4.8.13). The infallible authority of Scripture is set in opposition to the infallible authority of the church.

Within the → Roman Catholic Church itself, disagreement arose concerning which witnesses of the → Word of God are able to deserve the unwavering loyalty of the church and claim infallibility themselves. Both the → Orthodox Church and the Roman Catholic Church agree with the → early church that this promised guidance applies first of all to the → faith (§3.5.2) of the church as attested by the → consensus of faith in the church as a whole (→ Faith 3.5.7.2). This consensus is diachronous consensus by tradition and synchronous consensus by councils and their → reception. Vatican II says that "the whole body of the faithful who have an anointing that comes from the holy one (cf. 1 Jn. 2:20 and 27) cannot err in matters of belief" (*Lumen gentium* 12). These churches thus believe that a statement of the → teaching office cannot claim authority when it is contrary either to Scripture or to the witness of the faith of the whole church.

3. As church doctrine was developed and doctrinal decisions had to be made, the episcopal (→ Bishop, Episcopate) and papal offices (→ Offices, Ecclesiastical 2) gained, beside the authority of leadership (→ Hierarchy 1.3), also that of preserving tradition by making doctrinal decisions. Scripture and tradition were still the material criterion of truth, but the decisions of councils and popes as well as the consensus of the whole church were now the formal criterion and binding on all believers. Infallibility thus came to mean the binding nature of solemn dogmatic decisions (→ Dogma 3.3). The Roman Catholic Church bases this claim on the fact that bishops and popes now have the commission of the → apostles to proclaim and preserve the gospel in the name of Christ. They can be confident that this ministry will still enjoy the assistance that will protect the church from error.

This conviction caused → Vatican I to define the infallibility of the papal teaching office. The more general features of earlier development may be seen here. From the preeminence of the church at Rome as the place where the apostles → Peter and → Paul preached arose the teaching authority of the bishop of Rome, as Peter's successor (→ Roman Catholic Church 1). According to Vatican I, when the pope speaks ex cathedra — that is, when he, exercising his supreme apostolic authority, defines a doctrine concerning faith and morals to be held by the whole church — he has the infallibility that Christ promised the church (DH 3074). It is added that the pope does not need the formal approval of the church, though in fact he does need this consensus if his decisions are to be received by the church. Vatican II linked papal infallibility more plainly to the infallibility of the church's faith and the authority of Scripture.

The definition of papal infallibility raised a storm of protest from the Protestant churches and also a Roman Catholic minority. It also gave impetus, however, to a new emphasis on the infallibility or inerrancy of the Bible, which was developing in any case in reaction against both 19th-century secularism and the new and critical approach to Scripture. In the debates and controversies that followed, the issues tended to become confused. Opposing modernism, Roman Catholicism itself also contended strongly for the infallibility or inerrancy of the Bible. In this regard it fought a common battle with conservative Protestants. The infallibility of the papal office, however, was seen by Protestants to be contrary to the infallibility and authority of Scripture. The question of infallibility was thus a cause of division. Vatican II declared also that even outside the council setting as such, the college of bishops proclaims the doctrine of Christ with infallibility when, "in their authoritative teaching concerning matters of faith and morals, they are in agreement that a particular teaching is to be held definitively and absolutely" (*Lumen gentium* 25).

Bibliography: L. M. BERMEJO, *Infallibility on Trial: Church, Conciliarity, and Communio* (Westminster, Md., 1992) • J. P. BOYLE, *Church Teaching Authority: Historical and Theological Studies* (Notre Dame, Ind., 1995) • D. A. CARSON and J. D. WOODBRIDGE, eds., *Scripture and Truth* (Leicester, 1983) • R. R. GAILLARDETZ, *Witness to the Faith: Community, Infallibility, and the Ordinary Magisterium* (New York, 1992) • N. L. GEISLER, ed., *Inerrancy* (Grand Rapids, 1979) • *Infallibility in the Church: An Anglican-Catholic Dialogue* (London, 1968) • J. J. KIRVAN, ed., *The Infallibility Debate* (New York, 1971) • H. KÜNG, *Infallible? An Inquiry* (Garden City, N.Y., 1971) • J. W. MONTGOMERY, ed., *God's Inerrant Word* (Minneapolis, 1973) • M. O'GARA, *Triumph in Defeat: Infallibility, Vatican I, and the French Minority Bishops* (Washington, D.C., 1988) • H. J. POTTMEYER, *Towards a Papacy in Communion: Perspectives from Vatican Councils I and II* (New York, 1998) • B. TIERNEY, *Origins of Papal Infallibility, 1150-1350* (Leiden, 1972).

HERMANN J. POTTMEYER

Infant Baptism → Baptism

Information

1. Definition
2. Historical Background
3. Information Theory
4. Information, Creativity, Access, and Analysis
5. Information Explosion, Information Revolution, Information Processing
6. Information Overload
7. Information Rich and Information Poor
8. Information and the Church

1. Definition

"Information" is not "communication." The former refers to a message transmitted by a code, over a channel, to a receiving device at a particular destination. → Communication, in contrast, is the sharing of meaning between individuals, through a common system of → symbols. Information in itself, therefore, is not determined by any particular meaning.

A simple dictionary definition of "information" specifies "something told, news, intelligence, word," plus, probably, "knowledge acquired in any manner, facts, learning, data." The dictionary would then explain that the term applies to data gathered in any way, as by reading, observation, hearsay, and so forth, and does not necessarily connote validity. Relevant phrases are "information agency," "information desk," "information center," and, more recently, "information highway." The last example, with its connotations of Internet and the World Wide Web, provides the direction that must be taken in exploring the notion of information at the beginning of the 21st century.

2. Historical Background

The level of ability of individuals and the consequent means of presenting and storing information have always had an impact on the functioning of societies. The possession of information is a key to power over those who do not have that information, usually because they lack the means to obtain it. Historically this defect could have been as simple as not being in the circle where information was exchanged; in other words, one's position in society dictated access. From the position of having access to information, one would then hope to gain skills of presentation and persuasion in order to become (e.g., in predominantly oral cultures) an effective orator. An orator would attempt to use information in a communicative process. An eloquent orator not only would provide information but also would use the power of oratory to persuade, to change the thoughts, hopes, or expectations of listeners.

This model could be extended in the following manner. With the invention of the printing press, information could more easily be transmitted. Again, however, only the people with access to the printed word — those who had both financial access and the skill of reading — could benefit from the results of the new technology. The gifted writer would be able to utilize the technology of printing and thus not only provide information but also convert or even subvert the minds and opinions of readers.

In both of these scenarios, oral and literary, the information available would be only what the presenter decided to pass on. Society, at the end of the 20th century, has undreamed of opportunity to be selective from virtually limitless information repositories. The skills now needed are not only those of listening, looking, or reading but those attendant upon organized analysis and wide-ranging, technically competent searching and recording. Great machines are already available; even greater minds are now needed to deal with the information age.

3. Information Theory
One major approach to understanding the concept of information has come from the study of the electronic sciences. In his *Theories of Human Communication* Stephen Littlejohn describes information theory as involving the quantitative study of signals and as having "practical applications in the electronic sciences that design transmitters, receivers, and codes [which] facilitate efficient handling of information" (p. 45).

Claude Shannon and Warren Weaver in *The Mathematical Theory of Communication* have examined the organization of events from the perspective of engineers and mathematicians. These authors' model of communication was a starting point for many later attempts to construct theoretical models related to both information and communication.

For Shannon and Weaver, information theory is not involved with the meaning of messages but only with their transmission and reception. Thus the elements of their model are source, transmitter, channel, receiver, and destination, with special attention to the implications of noise within the channel. For Donald MacKay, furthermore, information theory is concerned with the meaning of representations, that is, with symbolism in its most general sense.

Many forms of information theory have been severely criticized, mainly on the grounds of not dealing with standards of appropriateness. Some of the philosophical assumptions of these theories do not seem readily compatible with the human process of communication. Early work on information theory and the organization of events seems often to have been linked to the concept of entropy and its impact. Entropy in some situations causes uncertainty; the more entropy, the more unpredictability and thus less control over the organization of events and consequent information. The continuing link is that information is the measure of the uncertainty (entropy) in a situation. As Littlejohn points out, "The more information in a situation, the more choices you can make within that situation" (p. 46).

4. Information, Creativity, Access, and Analysis
Edward De Bono, who is celebrated for his work on so-called lateral thinking, claims that "if we had perfect information in a particular situation then thinking would be unnecessary. But our chances of getting perfect information are low." Thus modern society faces an increasing dilemma of effectively handling the wealth of information now available. De Bono asserts that creativity comes into play when consideration is given to what exactly is wanted by way of information. How is what is desired best obtained? And how should what is discovered be analyzed and synthesized? And how should what has been found be shaped and used in order to be communicated as shared meaning? De Bono answers that, in order to "understand" acquired information, it is necessary to propose a hypothesis, which provides a framework in terms of which to look at information so that we begin to notice things that we have not noticed; it "gives us something to work towards in proving or disproving it" (pp. 13, 47).

5. Information Explosion, Information Revolution, Information Processing
The last decade of the 20th century has seen the multiplication of phrases and sloganed claims including the word "information." We thus hear about

the information explosion, the information revolution, "information rich" and "information poor," the information superhighway, and, perhaps most important, information acquisition and information handling.

It is universally accepted that skills for information handling are necessary for success in today's developed world. Of great relevance is the search for understanding with regard to the way individuals interpret or make sense of all the information with which they are bombarded. Information processing theory attempts to deal with the way in which individuals handle information.

Various researchers, particularly those devoted to the development of theories of → education, have argued that the main concern with regard to information should now be how information is processed. In their *Mass Communication Theory — Foundations, Ferment, and Future*, Stanley Baran and Dennis Davis provide a succinct outline of this process and also raise important issues concerning the complexity of the cognitive process itself. They stress the need to "routinely scan our environment, taking in, identifying and routinely structuring the most useful stimuli and screening out irrelevant stimuli." This process and how to develop the abilities needed for its utilization may well be at the heart of what educators attempt to achieve: "We must be able to process the structured stimuli that we take in, hold these structures in memory long enough so that we can sort out the most useful ones, put the useful ones into the right categories (schemas), and then store them in long term memory" (pp. 273-74). Persuaders in such fields as advertising, public relations, and politics seek to structure (i.e., "spin") their information in such a way that it fits readily into these processes.

For information providers or seekers who have access to modern technology, the Internet and the Web have become the source to which one turns. The danger is that this source contains an ever increasing, often bewildering torrent of information. Current offerings on the Web related to the concept, for example, of religious information illustrate the astounding number of sites and the range of information available. A few instances are instructive.

As of early November 1999 the website "BELIEVE Religious DataBase Program" (www.mb-soft.com/believe) had over 700 topics, ranging from "Amish" through "Bible," "Book of Baruch," "Christian Humanism," "Hinduism," "Martin Luther," and "Reincarnation" to "Transubstantiation." The website "ReligiousTolerance.org" provided some 780 essays on various topics relating to religion and religious tolerance, including the major categories "Christianity," "64 Other Religions and Ethical Systems," and "Religious Hatred and Other Not So Spiritual Topics," with subcategories including "Medical Treatment vs. Prayer," "Separation of Church and State," and "Common Signs of Destructive Cults." Also on this date the website of the Internet Christian Library — ICLnet, at www.iclnet.org — had several massively large categories, including "Guide to Christian Resources on the Internet" (subcategories "Christian College Web Sites," "Periodicals," etc.) and "Guide to Christian Literature on the Internet" (subcategories "Bibles," "Sermons," "Creeds/Confessions," "News Sources," etc.). A final example is "Finding God in Cyberspace," a Web guide to religious studies resources that provides information on "Print Resources" (libraries, publishers, etc.), "Digital Resources" (e-texts, multimedia and graphics, etc.), and "Academic Disciplines" (archaeology, church-state studies, sociology of religion, and 11 others).

Browsing even briefly through sources of information such as these can unearth gems of information in electronic documents. To consult such documents has hitherto often involved long searches and subsequent delays in obtaining printed copies from libraries or other repositories. Readily accessible now are materials as diverse as the sermons of John Wesley, the canons of the Council of Orange from 529, the anathemas of the Second Council of Constantinople of 553, and reflections on the → spirituality of the → New Age.

Similarly, the coming together of news and information sources is growing rapidly. It is of considerable interest that newspapers, newsletters, and journals frequently no longer claim to provide full information in their stories and articles. Rather, they normally provide Internet and Web addresses that can give additional and relevant information on the topics they address.

6. Information Overload

Questions concerning information that face society at the start of the 21st century include: Can there be too much information? Will society be able to adapt and function effectively and happily in situations marked by increasing information overload? How is information that never becomes hard copy to be discovered and utilized?

The new technologies have enabled human beings to indulge in an obsessive development of information systems and information banks. Virtual mountains of processed information now tower over society, exponentially growing higher and higher, with few limits in sight. Stark questions concerning this development must be addressed: What shadows are cast by these mountains of information? What effect do such shadows have on life in the valleys beneath the mountains? What are the skills needed to climb these mountains? Finally, what will have been achieved when the mountains have been mastered, or will the horizon reveal only more and higher mountains?

7. Information Rich and Information Poor

Issues concerning the haves and the have-nots have marked the whole of human history in respect to wealth, food, housing, and water, as they now do with respect to information, particularly given the exponential growth of information systems. Access to such systems continues to demand higher and higher levels of wealth and education. Without access to new technologies and the wider world of information, individuals and countries too poor to join the information highway suffer in terms of societal, corporate, economic, and personal growth and development. Various aspects of this issue have always been a concern of those willing to cross global boundaries in their concern for the welfare of others. Many who have such concern have pointed out that the information → revolution is only a distant dream in large parts of the world, particularly in the Southern Hemisphere. Marshall McLuhan may have foreseen a global village, but did he anticipate one that contained so many informationless ghettos?

In recent years global initiatives taken by several groups have focused on these economic, technological, ideological, and structural imbalances in free access to, and use of, information throughout the world. Leading the way have been the London-based World Association for Christian Communication, the → Vatican, the → Lutheran World Federation, and the → World Council of Churches, largely in concert with, though sometimes in critical response to, the celebrated New World Information and Communication Order proposed by UNESCO and its MacBride Commission.

8. Information and the Church

It is commonly accepted that the invention of the printing press in the 15th century and subsequent increased opportunities for access to information were instrumental in the shaping of Christianity over the past five centuries. It is often claimed that the information revolution began with the change from script to print, which in turn hastened the → Renaissance, the → Reformation, and the scientific revolution.

Churches are presently marked by increasing and rapidly changing sophistication in their use of information technologies in → evangelism, education, journalism, and public relations. Professional journalists working within church frameworks — as publishers and editors of periodicals, journals, books, and audiovisual materials — are increasingly being required to deal with complexities hitherto seen as the exclusive province of secular journalism. Thoughtful journalists (e.g., those involved in professional organizations such as the Associated Church Press) and others concerned with the role of information in church life now must deal as a matter of course with an increasing range of professional, technical, ideological, and ethical questions: To what extent can impersonal, technologically determined conveyors of information be used for the support of authentic Christian community? Are there justified structural limitations that can be imposed by religious bodies on the spread of information — for example, does a journalist employed by a church body actually possess a fundamental right to free and responsible expression, or do perceived institutional needs of the denomination, which may often conflict with free expression, take precedence? How is information directed toward the religious community to be shared with the society at large? That is, how can the product of religious journalism be heard in the secular world?

The development of clear understandings of what is really at stake in the ongoing information revolution — for church, societies, and the world — seems to lag. The current development of an information economy within an information society has often led the church, like many other institutions, to accept the view that information and its messages are basically commodities, or consumer items. With this acceptance, even "God" is sometimes indiscernible in the midst of a plethora of information. To use information as a means of communication is one thing; to offer a critical analysis of that use is another thing. It is now incumbent on the church to offer new and prophetic views of the human use of information in our present technological age.

Bibliography: S. J. BARAN and D. K. DAVIS, *Mass Communication Theory–Foundations, Ferment, and Future* (Belmont, Calif., 1995) • E. DE BONO, *De Bono's Thinking Course* (New York, 1994); idem, *Serious Creativity: Using the Power of Lateral Thinking to Create New Ideas* (New York, 1992) • E. KATZ and P. F. LAZERSFELD, *Personal Influence: The Part Played by People in the Flow of Communication* (New York, 1955) • S. W. LITTLEJOHN, *Theories of Human Communica-*

tion (6th ed.; Belmont, Calif., 1999) • D. LOCHHEAD, *Shifting Realities: Information Technology and the Church* (Geneva, 1997) • S. MACBRIDE, *Many Voices, One World: Toward a New, More Just, and More Efficient World Information and Communication Order* (London, 1988) • D. M. MACKAY, *Information, Mechanism, and Meaning* (Cambridge, Mass., 1969) • M. MC-LUHAN, *Understanding Media: The Extensions of Man* (New York, 1964) • D. MCQUAIL, *Mass Communication Theory: An Introduction* (Beverly Hills, Calif., 1987) • W. J. ONG, "Information and/or Communication Interactions," *Communication Research Trends* 16/3 (1966) 3-16 • W. SCHRAMM, *Mass Media and National Development: The Role of Information in the Developing Countries* (Paris, 1964) • C. SHANNON and W. WEAVER, *The Mathematical Theory of Communication* (Urbana, Ill., 1949) • M. TRABER, ed., *The Myth of the Information Revolution: Social and Ethical Implications of Communication Technology* (Beverly Hills, Calif., 1986) • M. TRABER and K. NORDENSTRENG, eds., *Few Voices, Many Worlds: Towards a Media Reform Movement* (London, 1992).

JAMES KEEGAN

Infralapsarianism → Predestination

Initiation Rites

1. Religious
   1.1. Term
   1.2. Categories
   1.3. Significance
2. Christian
   2.1. Term
   2.2. Basic Statement and Primary Order: Restoration and Renewal of the Catechumenate
   2.3. Development of a Secondary Form: Confirmation
   2.4. Relation of Baptism and Confirmation
   2.5 Third World

1. Religious

1.1. *Term*

Deriving from Lat. *initium,* the term "initiation" denotes the ceremony of joining a mystery fellowship. *Initium* means "entry"; its use in the plural became linked with the concept of the sacred or holy (→ Sacred and Profane), which had much the same sense as "mysteries" had in late antiquity. At the same time, in a play on words, the Greek *teletē* for initiation into the mysteries came to be associated with

teleutaō (finish, die). In an extension of usage the term then denoted various phenomena that laid claim to a qualitative change of social and/or religious life on the part of the initiate, along with secrecy vis-à-vis noninitiates.

1.2. *Categories*

Collective rites incumbent on all members of a society are a form of such "rites of passage." These rites mark the end of → childhood and entry upon the status of a responsible, adult member of society. Such ceremonies include puberty rites (→ Youth), maturity rites, tribal rites, and age rites. An example is the Hindu *upanayana* ritual, which is obligatory for the three upper → castes in → Hinduism. Initiates adopt the behavior, techniques, and institutions of adults along with the sacred traditions. In tribal groups that practice such rites, that which constitutes the new life — independence, → sexuality, and spiritual values — is basically traced back to the work of supernatural beings in primal antiquity. Rather drastic tests are part of the initiation and may include separation from one's mother, isolation under a supervisor, special dieting, and physical measures such as blows, teeth extraction, and → circumcision, which symbolize death. These tests often precede a symbolic resurrection and the giving of a new name.

A second form of initiation is reception into a special group within the larger society. The introduction now is to a higher stage of mysteries, and the tests are more demanding. The examples include men's and women's fellowships, mystery groups, war bands like the ancient Nordic berserkers, → mystery religions, → orders, brotherhoods, lodges, guilds, and student unions and clubs.

A third form of initiation, with even more exacting tests, is the initiation that qualifies one for a specialized religious function. Ordination to → priesthood is an example, or initiation as a shaman (→ Shamanism), which is marked by specific → ecstatic elements that are also found in other categories of initiation. Among North American Indians responsible tribal membership is based on → dreams and → visions (→ Tribal Religions); similar are the stages of → meditation in India and Tibet and the Islamic dervish order.

1.3. *Significance*

From a humanitarian standpoint many of the initiation tests must be rejected as humiliating tortures. Yet we should not forget the important content of initiation in religion and culture. Nothing expresses more clearly the definitive end of something than the symbolism of death, which is common in initiation. Significantly, too, the symbols of death — cosmic night, the womb of the earth, the belly of a

monster — and such things as isolation and naked-
ness and dealing with ghosts do not denote annihilation but the return to an unformed embryonic
state corresponding to precosmic chaos. New and
stronger life is made possible by going back to the
forces that originally imparted themselves in a special way to the human world and imposed order on
chaos, or by going back to ancestors as representatives of this time of origin.

→ Baptism; Confirmation; Youth Dedication

Bibliography: A. DROOGERS, *The Dangerous Journey:
Symbolic Aspects of Boys' Initiation among the Wagenia
of Kisangani, Zaire* (The Hague, 1980) • L. EILE, *Jando:
The Rite of Circumcision and Initiation in East African
Islam* (Lund, 1990) • M. ELIADE, *Birth and Rebirth: The
Religious Meaning of Initiation in Human Culture* (New
York, 1958) • M. ELIADE, W. O. KAELBER, and B. LIN-
COLN, "Initiation," *EncRel(E)* 7.224-38 • J. S. LA FON-
TAINE, *Initiation* (Manchester, 1986) • T. A. LEEMON,
*The Rites of Passage in a Student Culture: A Study of the
Dynamics of Transition* (New York, 1972) • B. LINCOLN,
*Emerging from the Chrysalis: Studies in Rituals of
Women's Initiation* (Cambridge, Mass., 1981) • L. C.
MAHDI, S. FOSTER, and M. LITTLE, *Betwixt and Be-
tween: Patterns of Masculine and Feminine Initiation*
(La Salle, Ill., 1987) • M. NTETEM, *Die Negro-
Afrikanische Stammesinitiation* (Münsterschwarzach,
1983) • S. OTTENBERG, *Boyhood Rituals in an African
Society* (Seattle, 1989) • R. TURCAN, "Initiation," *RAC*
18.87-159.

CHRISTOPH ELSAS

2. Christian

2.1. *Term*

In ecumenical use, without the more general religious connotation (see 1), "initiation" denotes the
acts associated with incorporation into the church
— that is, → baptism, → confirmation, and the →
Eucharist (First Communion). The usage seems to
go back to L. Duchesne (*Origines du culte chrétien*
[1889]), though his formulation was adopted only
hesitantly. → Vatican II (*Sacrosanctum concilium*
[*SC*] 65, 71) uses the term *initiatio (christiana)* in
Duchesne's sense (see also 1983 → CIC 879). The
Lima Declaration (1982), *Baptism, Eucharist, and
Ministry,* avoided the term but affirmed the idea of
incorporation by baptism and admission to communion.

2.2. *Basic Statement and Primary Order:
Restoration and Renewal of the
Catechumenate*

The term "initiation" reflects a basic biblical and patristic understanding of what it means to become a

Christian. In Acts 2:38 Christians are those who are
baptized in Christ's name and who receive the gift of
the → Holy Spirit. By the middle of the second century (as reported by Justin Martyr), initiation culminates with First Communion. → Tertullian (ca.
160-ca. 225) testifies that we become Christians by
baptism, confirmation, and the Eucharist of Christ
(*De res. car.* 8). Only those who in the Eucharist partake of Christ's body and blood in the sense of
1 Cor. 10:16 are fully incorporated into his body.
Here initiation is completed, and since by nature the
Eucharist may be repeated (unlike baptism or confirmation), it is also continually renewed.

In the first centuries baptism and confirmation
preceded communion in a single liturgical act.
Hippolytus of Rome gives the earliest detailed description (ca. 220). After washing and a first anointing come the laying on of hands and anointing on
the forehead by the → bishop, with an accompanying prayer for the descent of the Holy Spirit on the
candidate. In the Latin West the latter act came to be
called *confirmatio.* The Eastern Orthodox Church
and the → Uniate churches in chrismation still retain this original order. At infant baptism the →
priest after the baptism confirms by anointing and
offers the Eucharist (the wine alone in the case of
infants). A bishop or → patriarch must consecrate
the anointing oil. This provision ensures an ongoing
place for episcopal participation.

Rome after Vatican II restored the primary order
in the case of adults (1971). Previously confirmation often had to be postponed because it was reserved for the bishop, but now the priest who bap-
tizes may also confirm (1983 CIC 883.2). Normally
the original triad of baptism, confirmation, and Eucharist now stands again at the beginning of the
Christian life. But the isolation of baptism, customary since the Middle Ages, continues in the new rite
for infant baptism (see 2.3.1). The English (Anglican) Alternative Service Book of 1980 also combines
the three for adults in a single liturgical act, though
the bishop must officiate.

With the restoration of the primary form of initiation for adult candidates, the → Roman Catholic
Church revived the adult catechumenate, no longer
restricting it to the missionary situation but seeing
in it a preparation for initiation, accompanied at
each stage by liturgical rites. Both in → mission and
at home, reception of the renewed catechumenate
has been mixed. It has functioned in the United
States but has hardly begun to do so in Germany. A
new stage of → reception began when it became
part of canon law (in 1983 CIC 788).

Other churches have also acted to restore the

catechumenate. The English Alternative Service Book did not do so, but American Episcopalians (→ Anglican Communion) included it among their occasional services in 1979. Also in 1979 Lutheran churches in the United States and Canada took similar steps.

2.3. Development of a Secondary Form: Confirmation

2.3.1. Unlike the East, the Roman Catholic (and Anglican) West reserved confirmation for the bishop and thus laid such stress on its ecclesial value that it had to be postponed if the bishop was absent or could not be reached. Separation of the bishop from baptism (which began with → emergency baptisms) became unavoidable when regional bishops replaced city bishops. When Lateran IV (1215) made 7 the age of First Communion (the so-called age of discretion), the same age also often became the age of confirmation. The Council of → Trent stated that infant communion (still widely practiced) was unnecessary (DH 1730, 1734). Early in the 19th century the age of First Communion was raised to between 10 and 14, but Pius X (1903-14) restored the earlier custom with his *Quam singulari* (1910), and so also 1983 CIC 914.

The 19th-century idea was that the age of leaving school was a suitable one for confirmation, which could then serve as a → sacrament of passage from → childhood to → youth. By putting confirmation after the age of discretion and First Communion between baptism and confirmation, the original order was lost, and the notion was strengthened that confirmation is independent of baptism. Today advocates of a very early confirmation want to maintain the connection with baptism and the original order, but they are in the minority.

2.3.2. The Reformation churches (→ Lutheran Churches; Reformed and Presbyterian Churches) no longer recognized the sacramental character of confirmation but gave it initiatory significance by linking it to admission to communion. There have now been many changes in this regard.

In the ecumenical world a cry is heard for the admission of unconfirmed children to communion (Lima Declaration, "Baptism," par. 14, comm. *b*). Lutherans in the United States and Canada accept a more or less informal admission of unconfirmed children to the Lord's Supper. In 1985 Episcopalians issued their Boston Statement "Children and Communion," which viewed baptism as giving a right to communion without any intervening ceremony of admission. When pressed, this position leads to a demand for infant confirmation and communion, as in the Orthodox Church (see the 1979 Book of

Common Prayer and the 1985 Canadian Book of Alternative Services). G. Austin advocates a similar course in the Roman Catholic world.

The primary order of initiation would be restored along such lines, but one has to ask whether the wheel of Western liturgical history can be turned so radically without damage. Primary solutions are not always the best. Yet outright condemnations of the development hardly do justice to a very complex situation (see J. Brosseder; H. A. J. Wegman, 178).

2.4. Relation of Baptism and Confirmation

Confirmation is often called a completion (*perficere*) of baptism. Laying on of hands and anointing of the forehead supplement and complete the act of baptizing. The question naturally arises, though, in what sense, in view of Paul's theology of baptism, one can say that baptism needs completing, as though the Spirit were given only in the second act. The point can hardly be that baptism merely has the negative task of cleansing from original → sin and personal → guilt, while confirmation brings filling with the Holy Spirit. On the basis of the NT doctrine of baptism (John 3:5), the conviction has been growing in ecumenical circles that baptism itself is related to the outpouring of the Spirit in the full sense.

In recent decades Roman Catholic theology has engaged in incessant discussion of confirmation and the Holy Spirit — a sacrament, some have said, in search of a theology. The debate has shown that confirmation can be viewed only in very close relation to baptism. The fullness of what takes place in baptism cannot be put in a single sign. Coming up out of the water expresses the gift of the Spirit insofar as it denotes life from Christ's death. It cannot denote, however, the horizontal, ecclesial, Pentecostal dimension of the gift of the → Holy Spirit. Formulations like "passing on the message," "public confession," and "the priestly task of the baptized vis-à-vis the world" do not find expression in it. The sign of confirmation, however, embraces exactly this dimension. Laying on of hands and anointing address the horizontal dimension of the baptism-event. The baptized are sent out and are to spread the savor of Christ everywhere. They have a prophetic task. Baptism and confirmation are related in the same way as → Easter and → Pentecost, the two feasts of redemption: Easter inasmuch as life flows to believers from Christ's death (cf. John 7:37-39 with 19:34) and is breathed into them (John 20:22), Pentecost inasmuch as this life is given to the redeemed in order that they might proclaim it (the sign of tongues) and kindle it (the sign of fire).

2.5. *Third World*

Only in the 20th century has it been discussed how the Christian rite of initiation, which developed in the Mediterranean area, can preserve this essential character while fitting in to other cultures. In *SC* 65, Vatican II encouraged missionary churches to include elements from their countries' own rites of initiation (→ Acculturation). Not surprisingly, there have thus far been only the first beginnings in this direction. Specialists still must be trained; Vatican II expressed a wish for their cooperation in liturgical reform (*SC* 40.3). In the Reformation churches stronger theological reservations regarding contextualization slow down the process.

In sum, one might say that what we see today in the field of initiation is advance on an unparalleled scale since the Reformation. For all the present confusion, it may finally be said that the movement is a hopeful one from an ecumenical standpoint.

→ Liturgics; Liturgy; Mass; Occasional Services; Worship

Bibliography: On 2.1: T. F. BEST and D. HELLER, *Becoming a Christian: The Ecumenical Implications of Our Common Baptism* (Geneva, 1999) • O. CULLMANN, *Baptism in the NT* (London, 1950) • A. KAVANAGH, *The Shape of Baptism: The Rite of Christian Initiation* (New York, 1978) • WORLD COUNCIL OF CHURCHES, *Baptism, Eucharist, and Ministry* (Geneva, 1982).

On 2.2: C. ARGENTI, "Die Chrismation," *Ökumenische Perspektiven von Taufe, Eucharistie und Amt* (ed. M. Thurian; Frankfurt, 1983) 64-87 • C. BRUSSELMANS, ed., *Becoming a Catholic Christian: A Symposium on Christian Initiation* (New York, 1979) • C. O. BUCHANAN and M. VACEY, *New Initiation Rites: A Commentary on Initiation Services Authorized as Alternative Services in the Church of England from Easter, 1998* (Cambridge, 1998) • L. DELLA TORRE, "Implementation of the *Ordo Initiationis Christianae Adultorum:* A Survey," in *Structures of Initiation in Crisis* (ed. L. Maldonado and D. Power; New York, 1979) 47-56 • M. E. JOHNSON, *Living Water, Sealing Spirit: Readings on Christian Initiation* (Collegeville, Minn., 1995); idem, *The Rites of Christian Initiation: Their Evolution and Interpretation* (Collegeville, Minn., 1999) • A. KAVANAGH, "Christian Initiation in Post-conciliar Roman Catholicism," *StLi* 12 (1977) 107-15 • S. MADIGAN, *Liturgical Spirituality and the Rite of Christian Initiation of Adults* (Chicago, 1997) • C. VINCIE, *The Role of the Assembly in Christian Initiation* (Chicago, 1993) • R. WEBBER, *Liturgical Evangelism* (Harrisburg, Pa., 1992).

On 2.3 and 2.4: J. AMOUGOU ATANGANA, "Ein Sakrament des Geistempfangs? Zum Verhältnis von Taufe und Firmung," *OF* 3/1 • G. AUSTIN, *The Rite of Confirmation: Anointing with the Spirit* (New York, 1985) • J. BROSSEDER, "Taufe/Firmung," *NHThG* 4.169-82 • C. BUCHANAN, ed., *Nurturing Children in Communion: Essay from the Boston Consultation* (Bramcote, Nottingham, 1985) • G. DIX, *The Theology of Confirmation in Relation to Baptism* (London, 1946) • P. FRANSEN, "Firmung," *SM* 2.33-45 (bibliography) • P. J. JAGGER, *Christian Initiation, 1552-1969: Rites of Baptism and Confirmation since the Reformation Period* (London, 1970) • A. JILEK, "Die Diskussion um das rechte Firmalter. Eine Übersicht über die deutschsprachige Literatur der letzten Jahrzehnte," *LJ* 24 (1974) 31-51 • G. KRETSCHMAR, "Firmung," *TRE* 11.192-204 • G. W. H. LAMPE, *The Seal of the Spirit: A Study in the Doctrine of Baptism and Confirmation in the NT and in the Fathers* (London, 1967) • B. NEUNHEUSER, "Taufe und Firmung," *HDG* 4/2 • H. RELLER, ed., *HRGem* (with information on the baptismal practice of the various Protestant denominations) • F. SENN, *The Witness of the Worshiping Community: Liturgy and the Practice of Evangelism* (Mahwah, N.J., 1993) • H. A. J. WEGMAN, *Geschichte der Liturgie im Westen und Osten* (Regensburg, 1979).

On 2.5: M. DUJARIER, "Developments in Christian Initiation in West Africa," *Structures of Initiation in Crisis* (ed. L. Maldonado and D. Power; New York, 1979) 57-64 • A. T. SANON and R. LUNEAU, *Enraciner l'évangile. Initiations africaines et pédagogie de la foi* (Paris, 1982) • S. A. STAUFFER, ed., *Baptism, Rites of Passage, and Culture* (Geneva, 1999); idem, ed., *Christian Worship: Unity in Cultural Diversity* (Geneva, 1996); idem, ed., *Worship and Culture in Dialogue* (Geneva, 1994).

BALTHASAR FISCHER

Inner Mission

The term "Inner Mission" *(Innere Mission)* refers generally to the organized charitable endeavors of the German Protestant churches. It is often conflated into the larger conception of charitable or social service (→ Diakonia), and some writers even refer to it as a → social gospel. Essentially a conservative concept, Inner Mission (IM) included conscious efforts (1) to cope with the harmful effects of the industrial system, which caused the masses to fall victim to the power of → sin; (2) to bring about the moral and spiritual → regeneration of both the individual person and the church; and (3) to advance the → kingdom of God through the spread of Christian → piety and morals. The IM sought to renew the ideal of Christian → charity within the German *Volk,* or nation, and by this means to revitalize the two major orders of creation, → church and state. Both would then cooperate peacefully within God's kingdom and thereby extend its boundaries on earth.

The movement's founder was Johann Hinrich Wichern (1808-81), who was born into a petty → bourgeois family of limited means in the port city of Hamburg. As a youth, he was sensitized to the → poverty and misery of the working classes and was affected by the piety of the early 19th-century awakening (the *Erweckungsbewegung*). He studied theology at Göttingen and Berlin under Friedrich Lücke (1791-1855), August Neander (1789-1850), and Friedrich → Schleiermacher (1768-1843), who sharpened his understanding of Christian → ethics, the priesthood of all believers, and the kingdom of God. His association with the circle around Baron Hans Ernst von Kottwitz (1757-1843), the founder of workshops for impoverished laborers, introduced him to the pietistic ideal of a life spent in service.

After returning to Hamburg in 1831, the youthful Wichern worked as a teacher until a wealthy person helped him in 1833 to establish a residential shelter for destitute children in the suburb of Horn in an old building known as the Rauhe Haus (Rough house). Here he linked education, work, and faith in a communal effort to nurture the human spirit and to transform delinquent children into devout Christians. He also trained lay brothers (assistants) to serve as teachers, many of whom found employment in orphanages elsewhere. His enterprise operated independently of the other charities in the city, and he sought to extend this principle of voluntary organized charity, which in 1843 he first called the Inner Mission, throughout the Protestant church. In 1844 Wichern began publishing the *Fliegende Blätter aus dem Rauhen Hause,* a religious periodical in which he spread the message that Christian love expressed in deeds could save humankind. Reaffirming the faith of baptized Christians through charitable activity would be the moral counterweight to the irreligious forces of the age. This movement would bind together all social classes and the various segments of German Protestant life and assure the tranquility of Christendom.

At the first → German Evangelical Church Conference *(Kirchentag),* in Wittenberg in September 1848, Wichern called on German Protestants to deal with the social question by establishing city missions and sending preachers into the streets to reach the working class. Since public charities could not cope with the moral issues of poverty, he asked that the IM be given responsibility for them. The confer-

ence failed to achieve any semblance of church unity in Germany, but Wichern did proceed with his intention to form a Central Committee of the IM. Founded in early 1849, it was marked with political and social → conservatism from the outset and was seen as a bulwark against revolutionary disorders and communist schemes. At the same time, confessionalist critics of the emphasis upon lay resources mobilized in voluntary associations feared that the Inner Mission would undermine clerical authority and become a "church within the church." Several regional churches showed little interest in the IM because of its close ties with the Prussian state.

Wichern fostered the formation of IM associations and committees in the various territorial churches to coordinate their charitable works, but the Central Committee had no power to direct these activities. Its task was largely that of holding regular conferences and providing a forum for discussion of social problems. The IM's influence increased with the growing professionalization of social welfare, and by the early 20th century it had become one of the highest-profile church associations. The Central Committee now encouraged activism in the churches on such matters as drunkenness, → prostitution, honoring the Lord's Day, literature distribution, and caring for seamen, migrants, and foreign laborers.

During World War I the IM was heavily involved in → social service work, and after the war it unsuccessfully sought formal integration into the new Protestant church structure. The welfare-state policies of the Weimar Republic that addressed the social needs of the immediate postwar years had a profound impact on philanthropic societies like the IM. Whereas before they had been dependent on private contributions, now public funds flowed into their coffers. Bureaucratic pressures increased, and the traditional emphasis on mission was pushed aside while the Central Committee's new welfare department ballooned in size. The trauma of the Great Depression, along with outright mismanagement, led to the virtual financial demise of the Central Committee in the so-called Devaheim Scandal. The mood among the IM leaders was one of deep crisis, and they turned against the democratic republic that they had only grudgingly accepted and placed their faith in a strong, authoritarian → state.

Like most pastors and church members, the IM welcomed Hitler's accession to power as the country's salvation, but soon they were faced with the sober reality of what had happened. A new "state commissioner" was appointed to supervise the Prussian church, and he abruptly replaced two top IM officials with → German Christian pastors. The action was rescinded in 1934 only under pressure from the → Confessing Church's task force for diaconal and missionary works. From that point on there were ongoing struggles with the regime's public welfare program and social service entities like → kindergartens and nursing stations; ultimately, the only area in which the IM was allowed a free hand was care of the "unproductive" and those incapable of rehabilitation. The mission took the pragmatic approach of avoiding open confrontation with the authorities and negotiating quietly, in hopes of protecting as many areas of operation as possible from state intervention.

The IM's greatest failure during the Nazi era was its stance on → eugenics and sterilization. In 1931 it set up a eugenics division and later one for racial hygiene, and it also accepted voluntary sterilization for the incurably mental ill in its institutions, but it would not extend the policy to the physically handicapped. That decision brought the IM institutions into collision with Nazi legislation, but they avoided compulsory sterilization and eugenic → abortions by referring such cases to state institutions. Eventually, however, they caved in to state pressures, which weakened their power to resist, and many patients in Protestant institutions were victims of → euthanasia. Although some individual doctors resisted, the leaders did not openly protest the policy. They felt that such actions would be of no use and would have severely hampered the IM's other works.

In 1945 the new Evangelical Church in Germany (EKD) decided to create its own Relief Organization *(Hilfswerk),* which assumed some of the responsibilities of the IM Central Committee. However, a renewed Inner Mission soon was active again in both parts of the divided Germany. In 1957 an organizational merger of the IM and Hilfswerk occurred, although the conceptual differences between the two were not fully smoothed over. In 1965 the new title "Diaconal Work of the EKD" was introduced, which made it clear that charitable and social service work would be the task of the church itself and not merely of parachurch voluntary societies.

Bibliography: E. Beyreuther, *Geschichte der Diakonie und Inneren Mission in der Neuzeit* (3d ed.; Berlin, 1983) • M. Gerhardt, *Ein Jahrhundert Jahre Innere Mission* (2 vols.; Gütersloh, 1948) • J. E. Groh, *Nineteenth Century German Protestantism* (Washington, D.C., 1982) • H.-V. Herntrich, *Im Feuer der Kritik. Johann Hinrich und der Sozialismus* (Hamburg, 1969) • J.-C. Kaiser, *Sozialer Protestantismus im 20. Jahrhundert. Beiträge zur Geschichte der Inneren Mission* (Munich, 1989) • J.-C. Kaiser and M. Greschat, eds., *Sozialer Protestantismus und Sozialstaat. Diakonie und Wohlfahrtspflege in Deutschland, 1890 bis 1918* (Stuttgart, 1996) • U. Röper and C. Jüllig, *Die Macht der Nächstenliebe. 150 Jahre Innere Mission und Diakonie, 1848-1998* (Berlin, 1998) • W. O. Shanahan, *German Protestants Face the Social Question* (Notre Dame, Ind., 1954) • T. Strohm and J. Thierfelder, eds., *Diakonie im "Dritten Reich"* (Heidelberg, 1990) • W. R. Ward, *Theology, Sociology, and Politics: The German Protestant Social Conscience, 1890-1933* (Bern, 1979) • J. H. Wichern, *Sämtliche Werke* (10 vols.; ed. P. Meinhold; Göttingen, 1958-88) • J. M. Wischnath, *Kirche in Aktion. Das Evangelische Hilfswerk, 1945-1957* (Göttingen, 1985).

RICHARD V. PIERARD

Innocence, State of

1. Biblical
2. Church History
3. Modern Period

1. Biblical

The dogma of the state of innocence represents an attempt to develop systematically what the Bible has to say about the creation of humanity according to (or "in") the image of God (Gen. 1:26-27; 1 Cor. 11:7). It shows that the emergence of → sin was the decisive event in human history that triggered the events of → salvation history (Rom. 5:12-21). It also presents the standards set up with → creation that enable us to interpret both sin and → regeneration or renewal (Eph. 4:24).

Despite their dissimilarity, the two motifs — the historical and the anthropological (→ Anthropology 1-3) — come together in church tradition with the assumption of an original perfection in paradise of (the first) human beings. The theological problem put by the doctrine of this first estate has thus always focused on the sense in which one can say that the divine destiny of human beings established at creation was lost — that is, on what being created in the image of God might mean.

2. Church History

2.1. Development of the doctrine may be traced back to two exegetical decisions that today are still a matter of dispute. From the time of Irenaeus (d. ca. 200, *Adv. haer.* 5.6.1), a distinction was made between (1) the way in which we correspond to God by nature or condition, that is, the reflection of the divine original (the "image": Gk. *eikōn*, Lat. *imago*), which never realizes the prototype itself, and (2) our ongoing relationship with that original (the "likeness": Gk. *homoiōsis*, Lat. *similitudo*). These motifs were interpreted as our habitual states. The *imago* is the inner light of → reason, self-determinative → freedom for → good or → evil. The *similitudo*, as a superadded gift, is the gift of moral perfection enabling us to live in the original → righteousness (*iustitia originalis*).

The pseudo-Augustine Alcherus Claraevallensis (→ Augustine's Theology) coined the pregnant formula that normatively determined Roman Catholic doctrinal development: *imago, quia rationalis; et similitudo, quia spiritualis* ("image," because [human beings are] rational; and "likeness," because spiritual; *De spir. et an.* 10, *PL* 40.786; see *PL* 194.1895). By supernatural → grace (*prima gratia*) → Adam enjoyed the ability not to sin (*posse non peccare*) and even not to die (*posse non mori*). He could know God without concealment, could fully harmonize his intellect and his free will, and could effortlessly reign over the → animal world. The Council of → Trent (sess. 5, can. 1) speaks of the holiness and righteousness with which Adam was equipped (*constitutus* [constituted], not *creatus* [created]!).

2.2. The theology of the → Reformers deviated considerably from the mainstream of tradition. It surrendered the distinction between *imago* and *similitudo* and thus equated the original righteousness with God (*iustitia originalis*) as realized in the primal state of innocence with original, natural human conduct, that is, with the ongoing relationship to God. It thus no longer found in this *imago Dei* any special, supernatural capacity but a basic orientation of human life (the knowledge, fear, trust of God [*notitia, timor, fiducia Dei*]).

Later definitions, both Lutheran and Reformed, identify the state of integrity with *natural* character. It is a natural gift, not supernatural (a *habitus concreatus*). This deviation raised serious problems of its own, for if the *iustitia originalis* was lost as a result of Adam's transgression, the unavoidable consequence is that one must deny human beings now the *imago Dei*, which remained in Irenaeus's distinction (along with free will; Trent, sess. 6, can. 5), even though the supernatural endowment had been lost.

The two positions are equally problematic, however, and as a result the renewal of the *imago Dei* (see 2 Cor. 3:18) was then expected from the justification and rebirth of the sinner. Justification, however, now came into unresolvable tension with the thesis of an original likeness. That is, the substance of the traditional doctrine of innocence is essentially surrendered if a *new* human being (→ New Self), Jesus Christ, had to arise in order that we humans might correspond to God, as is our destiny.

3. Modern Period

The modern age has brought revisions of the doctrine that amount almost to a new formulation. Viewing the Genesis story itself as legendary removed any foundation for the assumption of a historical condition of initial perfection. F. D. E. Schleiermacher (1768-1834; → Schleiermacher's Theology) was the first to reject any temporally identifiable original state as an article of faith and to understand this tradition as a reference to the enduring and original perfection of nature that comes to fulfillment in a universal consciousness of God (and thus in ultimate perfection in Christ; *The Christian Faith*, §61.5).

The objection by S. Kierkegaard (1813-55) to the "fantastical" attempt to understand the figure of Adam as an exception to human history was no less influential. The turning point was his maxim — one adopted by P. Tillich (1886-1965), among others — that "that which explains Adam also explains the race and vice versa" (*The Concept of Dread*, 1.1; → Anxiety). Instead of searching for specific gifts possessed by some "first" human being, gifts that were subsequently lost, theologians focused on the inalienable measure whose actualization does indeed identify human beings as God's creation, that is, on the question of human character or destiny as such (W. Pannenberg, with reference to J. G. Herder).

Instead of looking back at a historically inaccessible prepast, one should look forward to the promised → future, in which human nature will first "attain its full splendor" (Calvin *Inst.* 1.15.4). Only in this way can one overcome the objection to the idea of → evolution (addressed esp. by → process theology) and especially the tension with the doctrine of justification. In this light, the notion of an original condition emerges as our → hope, projected back into the past, for approximating the being and behavior of him who in his own character is our prototype (K. Barth, *CD* III/2). Understood in this way, the state of innocence is the critical standard revealing how we have failed in our own present task of shaping the world. Above all, however, it reminds us that human beings enter history not as lost sinners but under the auspices of the divine Yes (C. Gestrich).

Bibliography: K. BARTH, *CD* III/1 • E. BRUNNER, *Man in Revolt: A Christian Anthropology* (London, 1939) • J. COMBLIN, *Retrieving the Human: A Christian Anthro-*

pology (Maryknoll, N.Y., 1990) • C. Gestrich, Die Wiederkehr des Glanzes in der Welt (Tübingen, 1989) • M. P. Hogan, The Biblical Vision of the Human Person: Implications for a Philosophical Anthropology (Frankfurt, 1994) • S. Kierkegaard, The Concept of Dread (2d ed.; Princeton, 1957; orig. pub., 1844) • H. D. McDonald, The Christian View of Man: Foundations for Faith (Westchester, Ill., 1988) • B. L. Mack, Innocence and Power in the Christian Imagination (Claremont, Calif., 1989) • R. Niebuhr, The Nature and Destiny of Man: A Christian Interpretation (2 vols.; Louisville, Ky., 1996; orig. pub., 1941-43) • T. Otten, After Innocence: Visions of the Fall in Modern Literature (Pittsburgh, 1982) • W. Pannenberg, Anthropology in Theological Perspective (Philadelphia, 1985); idem, Systematic Theology (vol. 2; Grand Rapids, 1994) • F. D. E. Schleiermacher, The Christian Faith (2 vols.; New York, 1963; orig. pub., 1821–22) • U. Schnelle, The Human Condition: Anthropology in the Teachings of Jesus, Paul, and John (Edinburgh, 1995) • P. Tillich, Systematic Theology (vol. 1; Chicago, 1951) • T. F. Torrance, Calvin's Doctrine of Man (Edinburgh, 1948) • O. Weber, Foundations of Dogmatics (2 vols.; Grand Rapids, 1981-83; orig. pub., 1955).

Christian Link

Innocent III

Innocent III (1160/61-1216), whose baptized name was Lothario de' Conti di Segni, was pope in the early 13th century. His pontificate represented the apex of the medieval papacy, as it attained unrivaled powers in church and state. Son of a noble family, the Scotti, Lothario was born in Anagni and was brought up and received his early education in → Rome. He later studied theology in Paris under Peter of Corbeil until 1187 and possibly → canon law in Bologna, although this latter phase of his education is less certain. His instruction in Paris was significant for him, and he always recalled it with a certain fondness.

By 1189 or 1190, when Lothario was barely 30, he was made a → cardinal and became active in the affairs of the pontificate of Celestine III. Within the next five years he wrote two works, one on contempt of the world (De contemptu mundi), and the other on the → Mass (De missarum mysteriis). Both works, though not representing original thinking, enjoyed great popularity during the Middle Ages.

On January 8, 1198, while not yet a priest and at the age of 37 years, Lothario was elected the successor of Celestine III. He received a majority on the first ballot at the conclave and the necessary two-thirds on the next vote. Upon his election Lothario took the name of Innocent III. From the outset of his pontificate Innocent displayed an exalted opinion of the papal office and a determination to strengthen, expand, and continue to define the "plenitude of power" of the church of Rome. He regularly began to employ for himself the title "vicar of Christ."

At the collapse of German rule in Italy, the exceptional abilities of Innocent provided the papacy with a unique opportunity, and Innocent did not hesitate to seize the occasion. He insisted upon a role for the pope in the election process of any emperor of the Holy Roman Empire. His policies and actions were based both on the notion of the right of the papacy to interfere in secular matters in order to control the moral behavior of rulers, and on the concept of papal → feudal lordship.

Innocent actively involved himself in the politics of Europe whenever he felt the interests of the church were at stake. He removed German mercenaries from Sicily and elsewhere in Italy, and he established papal control in Campagna and Tuscany. Through a papal bull, Venerabilem (1203), Innocent insisted that the pope had the right and authority to examine the suitability of the person to be elected emperor. In 1214 Innocent supported successfully the French king Philip II Augustus against Emperor Otto IV at Bouvines. In a dispute over the selection of Stephen Langton as archbishop of Canterbury, Innocent in March of 1213 secured the submission of King John of England, who acknowledged Innocent as his feudal lord. Innocent's influence was felt in Scandinavia, Spain, the Balkans, and even Cyprus and Armenia. He did not confuse church and state, but he saw the exercise of his power as appropriate whenever there were problems among Christian rulers or quarrels requiring arbitration.

A major concern of Innocent was the recovery of the Holy Land. As early as 1198 he began to lay plans for the Fourth Crusade, which he planned to direct personally. This crusade did not get underway until 1202, however, and by that time Innocent had lost control of the venture to the doge of Venice. The crusade never reached the Holy Land but instead was diverted to Constantinople, the capital of the Eastern empire. The crusaders stormed the city, which fell on April 13, 1204. The fall of Constantinople was a disaster and, to the Greeks, an unforgettable insult. The Greek patriarch and Byzantine emperor were replaced by Latins.

Throughout his pontificate Innocent was concerned about → heresy. He promoted a series of preaching missions against the Albigenses and finally authorized a crusade against them. The pope also gave considerable support to the new orders of friars, both the → Franciscans and → Dominicans.

To encourage his goals of reform in the church and resistance to heresy, Innocent convened the Fourth Lateran Council in 1215, which in many ways was the high point of his reign. The council condemned heresy, especially the Albigenses, formulated doctrine, encouraged the establishment of schools, required higher standards of conduct by the clergy, endeavored to regulate several political issues, and suspended Archbishop Langton from office. The implementation of this council's decisions, however, was not to be Innocent's. One year later, on July 16, 1216, he died. After his lengthy pontificate one can see in Innocent a major figure who succeeded in changing the Roman church and its relations with the world.

Throughout his active career Innocent was also a voluminous writer. Before becoming pope, he wrote the two works mentioned above, as well as *De miseria humanae conditionis,* on the misery of the human condition. Over 6,000 of his letters survive. His correspondence concerning the selection of an emperor after the death of Henry VI is contained in the *Registrum super negotio Romani imperii.*

Bibliography: Primary sources in English: C. R. CHENEY and W. H. SEMPLE, eds., *Selected Letters of Pope Innocent III concerning England, 1198-1216* (Oxford, 1953) • R. E. LEWIS, ed. and trans., *De miseria humanae conditionis* (Athens, Ga., 1978).

Secondary works: J. CLAYTON, *Pope Innocent III and His Times* (Milwaukee, Wis., 1941) • E. DUFFY, *Saints and Sinners: A History of the Popes* (New Haven, 1997) 110-15 • C. MORRIS, *The Papal Monarchy: The Western Church from 1050-1250* (Oxford, 1989) esp. 417-51, 636-639 • J. M. POWELL, ed., *Innocent III: Vicar of Christ or Lord of the World?* (2d ed.; Washington, D.C., 1994) • J. E. SAYERS, *Innocent III: Leader of Europe, 1198-1216* (London, 1994) • H. TILLMAN, *Pope Innocent III* (Amsterdam, 1980).

WILLIAM G. RUSCH

Inquisition

1. Presuppositions
2. History
3. Process

The Inquisition (13th-19th cent.) was a process developed by the Latin church to detect and judge baptized heretics and their supporters so as to protect the divine world order and the eternal → salva-

tion of believers. It was a typical manifestation of medieval church history (→ Middle Ages 2) and came under criticism in principle from → humanism, the → Reformation, and the → Enlightenment, which was later accepted by the → Roman Catholic Church itself. Efforts focused on → torture to secure "voluntary" confessions and on the death penalty (burning at the stake; → Punishment) for obstinate and relapsed heretics; the general assumption was that belief, once accepted, could be made compulsory.

1. Presuppositions

The remote presuppositions of the Inquisition lie in the → early church and the enforcing of church unity (→ Church 2), which resulted from the alliance with the → Roman Empire from the fourth century onward. Thus the later Augustine (354-430; → Augustine's Theology) defended the compulsory conversion of the → Donatists, and Roman law threatened death for heretics, especially the → Manichaeans.

The more direct presuppositions lay in medieval developments. From the 11th century the Latin church centralized itself under hierarchical papal leadership (note esp. the Gregorian reforms and the Investiture Controversy). In the 12th and 13th centuries economic and social development, population shifts, and the growth of → cities formed a basis for popular → heresies. Revision of the law of the Holy Roman Empire came at the same time. Around 1200 the Roman church saw a moral threat to the divine world order and to the salvation of the members committed to its care.

Historically, one might view what took place as part of a crisis in adjustment. A church institution based on ancient foundations had to respond to a process of growth and differentiation in the High Middle Ages that was leading to the national and social pluralism of the later → Middle Ages and the → modern period. It saw a need to enforce uniformity of belief with new weapons. Its premises of thought could not allow any challenge to this uniformity, which was increasingly viewed in legal terms.

2. History

When heresies and divisive religious movements (esp. the → Cathari and → Waldenses) began to flourish in Upper Italy and southern France, the Roman church and Frederick I Barbarossa (1152-90) reacted at Verona in 1184 by ordering regular episcopal → visitations to spy out suspicious persons. This step was a departure from previous procedure, which allowed investigation only on accusation.

Since a → bishop was not able to carry out the order thoroughly, and since heresies continued to spread, Gregory IX (1227-41) decided in 1231 to entrust the execution of the order to the new mendicant orders, especially the → Dominicans and, soon after, the → Franciscans. After a disorderly start, which included attacks and spotty persecution that stirred up widespread resistance in France (e.g., against Robert le Bougre), Germany, and Italy (including the murders of papal inquisitors Conrad of Marburg and Peter Martyr of Verona), a more detailed judicial procedure was established. Bishops and inquisitors appointed by the orders now shared in the task, though not without friction.

The Inquisition was not a universal medieval institution but functioned only in areas that were under suspicion of heresy (southern and western Europe and, from the 13th and 14th cent., Germany and eastern Europe — but not, for example, Scandinavia; in England ordinary courts of church and state dealt with heretics from 1401 onward). Under a grand inquisitor appointed by the king, a centralized Inquisition came into Spain in 1487 and into Portugal in 1536 that spread to baptized → Jews (→ Anti-Semitism, Anti-Judaism) and later the Moors. The Portuguese Inquisition ended only in 1821, and the Spanish between 1808 and 1834. A special type of state and church Inquisition that controlled church work was set up in Venice in 1550.

Because of the threat of → Protestantism, which extended also to Italy, Paul III (1534-49) established a central authority in Rome in 1542, the Sacra Congregatio Universalis Inquisitionis, which was also put in charge of the Index of Forbidden Books drawn up in 1559 (→ Catholic Reform and Counterreformation; Censorship). When the classic Inquisition was abandoned, this authority received the new name "Congregation of the Holy Office" at the beginning of the 20th century, and then in 1965 it was again renamed as the Congregation for the Doctrine of the Faith. The medieval inquisition was thus reduced to a matter of → church discipline, such as occurs also in premodern Protestantism.

In the Middle Ages those who were the targets of the Inquisition criticized it in terms of the → Sermon on the Mount, charging also that the Roman Catholic Church's hands were stained with the blood of martyrs. Later, humanism, the Reformation, and the Enlightenment took up the attack. In 1518 M. Luther claimed that burning heretics is against the will of the Holy Spirit. The Roman Catholic Church accepted the criticism in the 19th and 20th centuries.

Evaluations in church history, however, suffer in some cases from apologetic bias. The universal claim of Christianity and the supposedly necessary uniformity of belief, which could hardly be achieved in practice, were both real problems for the Middle Ages. The Inquisition was thus a time-bound mistake in how it attempted to fulfill an intrinsically legitimate task. The questions that remain for our own century are what form church unity should take in keeping with the nature of Christianity and the present situation, and what appropriate and legitimate means we should adopt to achieve this unity.

3. Process

The classic Inquisition of the 13th to the 15th centuries opened with a "time of grace," when those charged with heresy might give themselves up and escape punishment by recanting. Any confession of heresy, though, had to be done publicly, which was a momentous step, for any later (even external) association with heresy would then rank as relapse and be threatened with the most severe punishment. After the expiration of the grace period, those under suspicion were personally cited and forced to appear by secular officials or church laypeople (→ Clergy and Laity). Those who fled were tracked down by spies. The cooperation of the secular arm was essential, but it was often refused, even though such an action itself might involve suspicion of heresy.

The goal of the church-law trial — in which the judge was usually both prosecutor and sentencer, witnesses were heard in secret, and defense was difficult by modern standards for lack of lawyers willing to help the defendants — was always recantation and repentance (→ Penitence). Penances ranged from → pilgrimages (which had to be vouched for) to the feared carrying of a large yellow cross on the breast and back and finally to "perpetual" (usually multiyear) imprisonment on bread and water. Reductions might be granted later by the inquisitors.

The obstinate and apostate were handed over to the secular arm for execution (first generally ordered in 1231 but only gradually applied). Execution was by burning at the stake (which in Germanic law was reserved for witchcraft and poisoning; in Roman law it had been introduced against the Manichaeans). A few heretics were executed in the 11th and 12th centuries. Burning at the stake first became legal in Aragon in 1197. Frederick II (1215-50) ordered it in Lombardy in 1224; the papacy adopted it in 1231.

Recantation did not necessarily spare apostates (see Thomas Aquinas [ca. 1225-74]). Its genuineness might not be certain, and there was always the sense of having to forestall a renewed spread of heresy. Decisive for the intensification of punishments was a comparison with lèse-majesté, first used by Innocent III (1198-1216) in 1199. He initiated other penalties, such as the exclusion of even orthodox-believing children from inheritance (in addition to the original confiscation) and the destruction of homes. The same punishments were inflicted posthumously on heretics already dead.

Heresy must be put in its social context. As a deterrent, sentences were solemnly pronounced within the liturgy as "acts of faith" (or "auto-da-fé," according to the Spanish term). At the same time, the church took pains to protect public penitents against social hostility. To force confessions Innocent IV (1243-54) in 1252 adopted tortures (the rack, the strappado, and singeing of the feet) from secular law and put secular officials in charge. The confessions exacted were valid only if later repeated without torture. In the 14th century, and especially the 15th, the procedure was extended to many other offenses (e.g., witchcraft as a relapse into idolatry; → Magic; Witchcraft). The persecution of witches increased in the 15th century and reached a peak in the 16th century. It took place in Protestant countries as well, where with the end of the Inquisition, as also in France, it was a matter for the secular courts.

In principle the Inquisition applied only to Christians. It was a church court that needed the secular arm when using force (→ Church and State), for the church itself technically shed no blood. The moral requirements for inquisitors were high. Inner contradictions arise at this point. They result from the fiction of the freedom of decision of faith and of the purely spiritual character of church measures in a uniformly Christian society, based on infant → baptism, in which governments should wield the secular sword under the direction of the spiritual authority, and both spiritual and secular courts demanded loyalty to a decision of faith once made. In fact this arrangement was merely the decision of the whole Christian society, in which illiterate individuals often never learned the doctrines or adopted them for themselves. Since this order was regarded as sacred and divinely established, there was no opposing it; the procedure of Inquisition seemed logical. Only with the demise of the presuppositions did (and could) it end.

→ Beguines; Empire and Papacy; Excommunication

Bibliography: A. ALCALÁ, ed., *The Spanish Inquisition and the Inquisitorial Mind* (Boulder, Colo., 1987) • A. BRÜCK, "Hexen II," *RGG* (3d ed.) 3.308-10 • J. COHEN, *The Friars and the Jews* (Ithaca, N.Y., 1982) • H. A. F. KAMEN, *The Spanish Inquisition: A Historical Revision* (New Haven, 1998) • H. C. LEA, *A History of the Inquisition of the Middle Ages* (3 vols.; London, 1888) • B. NETANYAHU, *The Origins of the Inquisition in Fifteenth-Century Spain* (New York, 1995) • M. E. PERRY and A. J. CRUZ, eds., *Cultural Encounters: The Impact of the Inquisition in Spain and the New World* (Berkeley, Calif., 1991) • K.-V. SELGE, *Texte zur Inquisition* (Gütersloh, 1967) • E. VAN DER VEKENÉ, *Bibliotheca bibliographica historiae sanctae inquisitionis* (2 vols.; Vaduz, 1982-83).

KURT-VICTOR SELGE

Inspiration

1. Jewish and Early Christian Understanding
2. Early Church
3. Since the Middle Ages
4. Significance

1. Jewish and Early Christian Understanding

The belief that the Jewish and Christian Scriptures are "inspired" by God — that is, that their language and imagery are directly willed by God and committed to writing under his direction — is ancient and influential. Yet the notion of a *text* whose production is directed by God belongs more to the world of Hellenistic/Jewish culture than to the earlier strata of Israel's traditions, in which → Torah and prophecy are indeed the *direct speech* of God to his people, but are so primarily in the context of the Israelite community's liturgical and imaginative reflection on its own identity. Torah (esp. in Deuteronomy) has its place as a set of formulas recited in ceremonies of → covenant (§1) renewal; prophecy (ecstatic and shamanistic at first, more literary and controlled later) often arises in response to the unreality of such ceremonies against a general background of injustice and of refusal to hear in society at large. There is no suggestion that the formulas that "speak for" God can be seen in abstraction from their performance in the public life and ritual of Israel.

The legend of the divine inspiration of the LXX (→ Bible Versions) illustrates the shift to the view that the text, as a closed and determinate document, is the utterance of God. This understanding may be what is reflected in 2 Tim. 3:16 (where the word *theopneustos*, "breathed out by God," recalls classical language about oracular dreams). Although the Christian communities were familiar both with ecstatic prophecy and with the authoritative teaching of the Lord through the ministry of the → apostles, they rapidly came to share the prevailing view of textual inspiration, particularly in reaction to the private "inspirations" of → Gnostic teachers and the ecstatic proclamations of → Montanist charismatics. In this context, the inspired text serves as a tangible and common bond in "catholic" Christian groups over against the arbitrary Schwärmerei of the sects (→ Canon 2).

2. Early Church

The early church at first used the image of the inspired author as an instrument (harp or flute) "played" by the Spirit. However, since the Montanists used such language and were thought to mean by it that the divine Spirit wholly suppressed the human personality, Catholic authors tended to prefer images of inspiration that allow a real place to the human mind (→ Reason). Even the idea of divine "dictation" (first in Irenaeus) was designed for this purpose. The ancient amanuensis was not a slavish copyist but often played an active role in giving final form to a composition. Such language underlies Theodore of Mopsuestia's account of inspiration (late 4th cent.), in which the Spirit provides the inner structure of ideas and understanding, and the human author determines the detail of the final expression.

Earlier, Origen (ca. 185-ca. 254) had seen scriptural inspiration as a supreme case of human understanding raised to its full power as *logikos* (i.e., perfectly attuned to the eternal Logos). Origen saw Scripture as inspired throughout but did not see this quality as involving the inerrancy of the *literal* meaning of the text. Nor did he think that all Scripture is equally transparent to God. The → gospel is the heart of Scripture and controls the interpretation of other parts (like the epistles of → Paul), in which authors speak, not directly in the person of the Logos, but in their own → authority as holy men.

Augustine (354-430) qualifies the imagery of dictation, preferring *suggestio*, which allows him a certain latitude in regard to the literal sense of the text. No text can be held to provide, at the surface level, information about doctrine or practice independently of the doctrine and practice of the Catholic Church — an important point in the → Donatist controversy, where Augustine had to combat an exegesis both superficially literalist and arbitrarily fanciful (→ Augustine's Theology).

3. Since the Middle Ages

3.1. High → Scholasticism challenged some features of traditional exegesis by stressing the primacy of the literal sense, thus laying the foundations for a strong doctrine of verbal inspiration in the later Middle Ages. In Thomas Aquinas (ca. 1225-74) the primacy of the literal has to do with God's ability to speak first in the events underlying Scripture, not simply in the words of an isolated text. If God speaks through narrative, it is because he first speaks in the life of persons and communities (→ Thomism).

3.2. Outside this context, the doctrine of verbal inspiration changes its character noticeably. In the post-Reformation period we encounter the unprecedentedly rigorous doctrine of the inspiration of every detail of the original text, including vowel points in the Hebrew (e.g., the 1675 Swiss Formula of Consensus).

M. Luther (1483-1546) himself seems less consistent. All of Scripture — "every syllable" — is inspired, yet parts of it (the Books of Revelation, Second Peter, and, most famously, James, the "epistle of straw") are of little or limited Christian use. Essentially, though, he was consistent in seeing Scripture *in its wholeness* as inspired, which also allows him to affirm that there are principles internal to Scripture (above all the doctrine of → justification) that enable us to see other portions in right perspective (→ Luther's Theology). Scripture is given to lead us to unconditional dependence on divine → grace. The text is not, so to speak, a flat and uniform surface but a landscape.

So too with J. Calvin (1509-64), who speaks of the writers of Scripture as amanuenses of the Holy Spirit but does not assume that each portion of it is equally authoritative. The unifying pattern of true interpretation comes from the testimony of the Spirit in the believer's heart (→ Calvin's Theology).

3.3. Reaction to the Council of → Trent's emphasis on Scriptural authority within the context of the church's authoritative → tradition of interpretation helped to strengthen the Protestant doctrine of Scripture as its own interpreter and, ultimately, the more extreme doctrines of verbal inspiration common in the 17th century. The alliance of this view with a thoroughgoing rationalist philosophy pervaded a good deal of Continental orthodox theology (→ Orthodoxy 1-2) in the century following and reappeared in 19th-century America. There, under the influence of Scottish "common sense" philosophy (→ Empiricism), the Princeton school defended verbal inspiration against the questionings of incipient biblical criticism, assuming the identity of inspiration and factual inerrancy. B. B. Warfield (1851-1921) provided the fullest statement of this view in the last decades of the century, establishing the intellectual basis for modern → fundamentalism.

Alternatives to this approach appeared in the theories of "real inspiration," developed by Richard Rothe and others in the 19th century, and "personal inspiration," particularly in F. D. E. Schleiermacher (1768-1834), also, in rather different form, in W. Sanday in England at the beginning of the 19th century. For Rothe, Scripture is bound up with the revealing acts of God in the consciousness of the author. The focus is not the words written but the psychology of the writer, who for a fleeting moment has true insight into God's work in history. → Revelation lies in this union of the subjectivity of the author and the objectivity of history, not in the words of the Bible. For Schleiermacher, inspiration must be a category that is used only of the human person. Scriptural inspiration means that the person and consciousness of an author, representing the "common spirit" of the community, become normative witnesses to it. It thus lies prior to the text and outside it.

3.4. Reaction in the 20th century against subjectivism led to heavy criticism of "personal inspiration." For K. Barth (1886-1968), God's utterance is not to be tied either to the state of a human consciousness or to a written text; it occurs where there is → obedience and self-yielding. Scripture is *Holy* Scripture because and insofar as it witnesses to God's incarnate Word in Jesus Christ and the Holy Spirit speaks in and through it, so that faith hears and obeys God himself speaking, triumphing over human self-sufficiency and establishing himself as the ground of our speaking and our knowing (→ Dialectical Theology). Hence Scripture cannot properly be treated as an oracle in itself. It is a model of obedient speech, summoning us to the same obedience. In this transparency to God's summons, its authority is God's authority, not its own impeccability.

Roman Catholic theology in the 19th century (esp. J. H. Newman, influenced by the 17th-cent. H. Holden) considered the notion of grades of inspiration, which was compatible with some human error. Such views were condemned in the antimodernist encyclicals of Pius X (1903-14) but have been retrieved and partially vindicated since → Vatican II. A reaction against propositional doctrines of revelation has led to greater stress on the work of the → Holy Spirit in the whole experience of the believing community (K. Rahner, G. Moran). This focus has also been part of the → consensus emerging in the discussions of the → Faith and Order consultations on scriptural authority (→ World Council of Churches). The Word is really heard as such only in the community of the Spirit. It is "Word" not in virtue of its inerrancy or "inspirational" character for individuals but because it recalls the church to the confrontation with God's summons in Jesus that is its origin and center. It is "Word" because it is part of the Spirit's work of forming Christ in the community by bringing to mind (John 14:26; 15:26; 16:13-15) the work of Christ (→ Congregation).

Eastern → Orthodoxy (§3) has not developed many theories of inspiration since the patristic age. When it discusses the theme, it relates the inspiration of Scripture very closely to the Holy Spirit's work in the church. A. S. Khomiakov (1804-60) insists that Scripture is a Spirit-inspired Word of the → church to its children. G. V. Florovsky argues that because the Bible is a book of the → covenant and because a covenant implies a covenant community, the Bible is read aright only where the history of the encounter between God and humanity continues — that is, in the sacramental assembly, in which the union of God and humanity is celebrated without disruption (→ Liturgy 2; Worship 3). The language of Scripture is a paradigm of the undisrupted union of divine initiative and human response.

4. Significance

Inspiration has thus increasingly been seen in relation to the Bible's role in the worshiping church. As in the OT, God's Word is heard when the people of God "narrate," in word and act, the story of God's commitment of himself to his creation in the making of a covenant for the church, the new covenant in Jesus Christ, constantly activated by the Spirit. In this light, room can be made for biblical criticism, and its frequent agnosticism about historical accuracy in the text, without denying that Scripture, in its overall pointing away from itself to God, is indeed a "Word from elsewhere."

→ Biblicism; Exegesis, Biblical; Hermeneutics; Legitimation; Scriptural Proof; Word of God

Bibliography: J. Barr, *The Bible in the Modern World* (London, 1973) • K. Barth, *CD* I/2, §19 • P. Benoit, *Aspects of Biblical Inspiration* (Chicago, 1965) • D. G. Bloesch, *Holy Scripture: Revelation, Inspiration, and Interpretation* (Carlisle, Cumbria, 1994) • J. T. Burchaell, *Catholic Theories of Biblical Inspiration since 1810* (Cambridge, 1969) • *The Cambridge History of the Bible* (3 vols.; Cambridge, 1963-70) • E. Flesseman–van Leer, *The Bible: Its Authority and Interpretation in the Ecumenical Movement* (Geneva, 1980) • G. V. Florovsky, *Bible, Church, Tradition: An Eastern Orthodox View* (Belmont, Mass., 1972) • T. E. Fretheim and K. Froehlich, *The Bible as Word of God: In a Postmodern Age* (Minneapolis, 1998) • A. R. Hunt, *The Inspired Body: Paul, the Corinthians, and Divine Inspiration* (Macon, Ga., 1996) • G. Moran, *Scripture and Tradition* (New York, 1963) • K. Rahner, "Über die Schriftinspiration," *ZKT* 78 (1956) 137-68 • W. M. Schniederwind, *The Word of God in Transition: The Second Temple Period* (Sheffield, 1995) • K. R. Trenbath, *Evangelical Theories of Inspiration: A Review and Proposal* (New York, 1987) • B. B. Warfield, *The Inspiration and Authority of the Bible* (London, 1951) • O. Weber, *Foundations of Dogmatics* (vol. 1; Grand Rapids, 1981; orig. pub., 1955) • O. Weber and W. Philipp, "Inspiration," *RGG* (3d ed.) 3.773-82.

Rowan D. Williams

Institution

1. Meaning
2. Nontheological Usage
3. Theological Usage

1. Meaning

1.1. The term "institution" derives etymologically from the Latin group *instituo/institutio,* which originally had the broad sense of making or establishing or of its result (i.e., what is made or established). The term first took on a precise sense in Roman law, from which it passed into Latin → church law and then into the → apologetics and → dogmatics of the Western tradition. Here it mainly denotes an act of divine foundation or its effects, though it occasionally also has the sense of instruction (in the Christian life).

In common use today the word denotes what modern → sociology calls → organizations — that is, the large constructs that increasingly mark social life, including school, military, → state, justice system, church, business corporations, insurance companies, and so forth. Academically, it is so ambivalent that there is serious doubt as to its value. Yet it is gradually establishing itself as a basic concept in social science, and also recently it has been making its way into politics and social psychology. Its ambivalence is due in part to its use in various disciplines but also to its dependence on the various approaches within each discipline. One particular sociological semantic variation might function as a kind of common denominator. On this view, the concept of institution refers to *generally inculcated patterns of behavior and relationships that in their own turn are characterized by longevity and by an of-*

ten relatively diffuse matrix of validating acts, including various customs and traditions.

1.2. Connected to the concept are many sociophilosophical and sociopolitical problems that in part are highly abstract but still have great practical consequences. These matters are related both to the peculiar nature of the social phenomenon in question and to the context of the discussion. Theoretically, the various approaches rest on different definitions of the relation between the → individual and → society, → subjectivity and objectivity, the general and the particular, → freedom and commitment, or, more generally, → nature and → culture. At issue are principial anthropological ideas, personal experiences, and concrete political goals. Differences here make objective agreement difficult.

The polarizing impact of an attractive term like "institution" undoubtedly finds an important basis in the growing dependence of individuals on institutions like church and state that seem to be both characteristic of modern societies and unavoidable in them (→ Bureaucracy). An anti-institutional result is noticeable in many places. This reaction is occasionally connected with older spiritualist and → anarchist motifs, and in the churches it often expresses itself in a basic repudiation of the "official church," whose enduring, suprapersonal, and obligatory qualities are seen very negatively as immobility, → anonymity, and coercion. This tension explains the rise of opposing movements in both church and state that aim and claim to suppress, or at least restrict, the formation of institutions in both personal and impersonal relationships.

2. Nontheological Usage

2.1. As a technical term in law, "institution" goes back to the *Corpus iuris civilis,* which the Roman emperor Justinian published in 533 as a binding basis for practical jurisprudence and the training of attorneys. The first book of the code is entitled *Institutiones* and contains a distinctive mixture of general and theoretical considerations and concrete legal principles on matters of private or civil law (e.g., family issues and civil offenses; → Jurisprudence).

Against this background European law that was oriented to Roman law developed in the 19th century a concept of the law of institutions covering the rules and → norms in a legal relationship (e.g., → marriage or → property ownership). As regards the founding of such institutions, from the standpoint of social theory recourse was often had to the contract doctrine of J.-J. Rousseau (1712-78), and stress was laid on the primacy of the will in the rise of institutions. In contrast, the so-called institutional view of law saw in institutions social constructs that are an organic product of the life and spirit of a people, that gradually come to expression in a general legal consciousness, and that are then translated into positive law and legal pronouncements. The idea of law that is immanent in institutions supposedly acts as a creative norm and inspiration in legal development.

The French jurist and sociologist M. Hauriou (1856-1929) similarly viewed the institution as an objective entity that does not derive from individual subjective decisions, that does not necessarily arise out of a legal norm, and that does not have itself a legal character, but one that still must take legal form and that thus always develops in specific legal relations. He distinguished between objective institutions *(institutions-choses)* and corporate or personal institutions *(institutions-corps)*. Analyzing the latter, Hauriou found that an essential element in them was a "work idea" *(l'idée de l'œuvre)* or a governing idea *(l'idée directrice)*, which a group accepts collectively as the basic inspiration for its activities and which it must declare to be its organizing principle if it is to achieve social reality and legal permanence.

Common to both the above positions is criticism of will and contract theories and also of mechanistic explanations in social theory that intentionally or in fact bring it close to neo-Thomist ideas of → natural law or a theology of orders.

2.2. The English scholar H. Spencer (1820-1903) was a pioneer, and in spite of many later modifications, he provided a model for an approach along the lines of cultural anthropology and sociology. He viewed all societies as natural → organisms and saw institutions as their organs. Like organs, institutions differ in form and function, and as in a biological organism, growth demands of society an increasing differentiation of organs (i.e., institutions) and their functions, but also their integration into a harmonious common process. Here already the way was prepared for the lively modern debate regarding the relation of the institution to social change.

For B. Malinowski (1884-1942) institutions as a nexus of successful adjustments of individuals or → groups serve to satisfy vital biological and culturally mediated needs. In so doing, they may have several functions. Considering a hierarchy of needs, Malinowski saw the development of institutions, through a self-induced dynamic, as meeting secondary needs.

In the institution theory of A. Gehlen (1904-76), human beings are biologically defective. Lacking an-

imal instincts, they must be open to the world but, at the same time, must forge substitutes (→ Anthropology 5). Institutions as cultural creations are a kind of second nature and they take over the task of stabilizing and orienting human relations, which must be relieved of the constant need to master new situations. Institutions are thus absolutely essential to our "humanizing" as natural creatures, and in the context of our wrestling with nature, they form autonomous sediments of rational → behavior quite apart from any individual goals.

2.3. Functional analysis, pioneered by Spencer, became the dominant methodology in the modern sociology of T. Parsons (1902-79). Parsons combined the perspectives of clinical psychology and social anthropology with the problem of social order — that is, the constitution of society in general. He noted that every social → system must meet four functional prerequisites in its environment if it is to survive: appropriateness, attainment of goals, integration, and structural stability. Since individuals and social systems constitute each other's environment and thus are functionally dependent, harmony between (1) individual needs and interests and (2) social demands must be established by mechanisms of institutionalizing or role formation (the problem of order).

Parsons found the vital significance of institutionalizing and institutions in their ensuring of social → consensus and conformity and coordination of behavior. N. Luhmann, however, with his theory of systems found the core of the process in the binding adoption of what is in part a fiction. Since we can never establish consent or presuppose interaction with all other persons, we must accept it as given, and temporally, materially, and socially we generalize this acceptance. On this view institutions rest primarily on trust, which minimizes uncertainty.

P. Berger and T. Luckmann adopt an interactionist approach, which views the process of institutionalizing as a reciprocal stereotyping of people's habitualized actions. As a process of objectivation (i.e., of objectifying the results of human creativity), this stereotyping mediates between externalizing and internalizing, so that individuals and society coexist.

3. Theological Usage
3.1. The theological struggle for an appropriate doctrine of institutions has focused with shifting emphases on three problems: the correct understanding of social institutions, the church as institution, and institutions in the church. Along with

philosophical influences, the way in which the relation between the order of creation and that of redemption is defined has traditionally played a decisive role. Thus institutions may be viewed either as in principle an expression of our social nature by creation or as divinely willed emergency orders that exist only in virtue of the corruption of human nature.

Confessionally influenced controversies of this kind affect ecclesiology and sacramental theology (→ Sacrament), but especially they affect dogmatic views regarding the correct form of the church and its life, which, as may be seen in the debate about → early Catholicism and the history of → Reformation research, influence the evaluation of historical processes. Ecclesiological conceptions that invalidate institutions as such can describe the process of institutionalizing the Christian religion only as a decline, while a high dogmatic estimation of institutions leads from the outset to skepticism in principle regarding spiritualizing and individualizing tendencies. Within Protestant theology, such an estimation leads to the revival of R. Sohm's antithesis of the church of law and the church of love in millenarian ideas that nondialectically oppose event and institution, → charisma and office, the basic church and the official church.

Criticism of such positions has three bases. In traditional apologetics it rests on the historical proof of the formal founding of the church by Jesus Christ. In the theology of law it rests on a reference to the legal nature of the divinely instituted fundamental institutions of the old and new → covenants. Finally, in → fundamental theology it rests on a sociological reference to the impossibility of understanding the church theologically and empirically as a unique construct that lies totally outside the ordinary institutionalizing of human existence.

3.2. In → ecumenical theology the problem of institutions involves their controversial character and the insight that church disunity is institutionalized by the formation of separate bodies and the favoring of institutionalizing by other institutions (the state, social groups, etc.). Along these lines the Second World Conference on Faith and Order, at Edinburgh in 1937, listed institutionalism as one of the nontheological factors in disunity. The third conference, at Lund in 1952, then tried to analyze its actual impact on the basis of a document on the significance for division of social and cultural factors. The resulting commission published a report in 1961 that, based on comprehensive studies, was presented at the fourth conference (Montreal, 1963) under the title *Institutionalism and Church Unity*

(N. Ehrenstrom and W. G. Muelder). In the course of discussion its predominantly negative orientation was corrected by stress on the part that social factors play in promoting ecumenism and by serious recognition that, in analogy to church division, ecumenical relations also need institutionalizing. Since then the view has frequently been advanced that institutionalizing and "ecclesiasticizing" in reality bring a regrettable stagnation to the → ecumenical movement.

→ Base Community; Charismatic Movement; Church 4; Church Government; Democracy; Free Church; Functionalism; Hierarchy; House Church; People's Church (Volkskirche); Social Movements; Sociology of Religion; Spirituality

Bibliography: H. U. VON BALTHASAR, *Pneuma and Institution* (Einsiedeln, 1974) • G. BAUM and A. M. GREELEY, *The Church as an Institution* (New York, 1974) • P. BERGER and T. LUCKMANN, *The Social Construction of Reality: A Treatise in the Sociology of Knowledge* (Garden City, N.Y., 1966) • J. F. DRANE, *Authority and Institution: A Study in Church Crisis* (Milwaukee, Wis., 1969) • N. EHRENSTROM and W. G. MUELDER, eds., *Institutionalism and Church Unity: A Symposium* (New York, 1963) • A. GEHLEN, *Urmensch und Spätkultur. Philosophische Aussagen und Ergebnisse* (2d ed.; Bonn, 1964) • M. HAURIOU, *Die Theorie der Institution und der Gründung* (Berlin, 1965; orig. pub., 1925) • N. LUHMANN, "Institutionalisierung. Funktion und Mechanismus im sozialen System," *Zur Theorie der Institution* (ed. H. Schelsky; Düsseldorf, 1970) 28-41; idem, *Vertrauen. Ein Mechanismus zur Reduktion von Komplexität* (2d ed.; Stuttgart, 1973) • D. O. MOBERG, *The Church as a Social Institution: The Sociology of American Religion* (Englewood Cliffs, N.J., 1962) • T. PARSONS, *The Social System* (New York, 1964) • J. A. SCHÜLEIN, *Theorie der Institution. Eine dogmengeschichtliche und konzeptionelle Analyse* (Opladen, 1987) • G. STRAUSS, *Enacting the Reformation in Germany: Essays on Institution and Reception* (Brookfield, Vt., 1993).

HEINZ-GÜNTHER STOBBE

Intercommunion → Eucharist 5

Interest → Usury

International Association for Religious Freedom

The International Association for Religious Freedom (IARF) is a "world community of religions," an → oikoumene of world religions, and a world association of religiously liberal individuals and groups. It was founded in Boston in 1900 by American → Unitarians. In 1999 it had member groups in 30 countries, with chapters in Bangladesh, Canada, Germany, Great Britain, India, Japan, Netherlands, Philippines, and the United States. Overall, it had 10 million members. Represented in it are "free Christians," → free religionists, religious humanists, Unitarians and Universalists, and liberal movements in → Buddhism, → Shinto, → Hinduism, and → Islam. Included are Unitarian churches from Romania and Hungary. The largest group is the lay Buddhist organization Rissho Kosei-kai from Japan, with about two million members. The Japanese Shinto group Tsubaki Grand Shrine also belongs, as does the Shinto group Misogi-Kyo. A member in India is the Hindu reform movement Sadharan Brahmo Samaj. In Germany free religious groups, Unitarians, and free Christians all belong, though their combined numbers amount to only 10,000 members. In the United States the Unitarian Universalist Association is a member, as is the International Association of Liberal Religious Fellowship, a liberal religious youth organization set up in 1923 as the Leyden International Bureau.

The IARF accepts both individual and group membership. At its head is a president, who is elected at a congress from the International Council of Ministers, the governing body of the IARF. The main activity is the congress, which is held every three years (most recently, in India in 1993, Korea in 1996, and Canada in 1999). Regional conferences are held annually in North America, Europe, and Asia. IARF is accredited as a nongovernmental organization by the → United Nations, the Economic and Social Council (ECOSOC), and UNESCO, and it shares in the work of the United Nations through a permanent representative in New York. In 1974 the seat of its general secretariat moved from The Hague to Frankfurt.

The IARF, which has no direct control over its member groups, rejects the idea of a super- or metadogmatics. Its program does not include the creation of a religious synthesis that might serve as a common denominator for all the member organizations. It sees itself, rather, as embodying a practical philosophy of → pluralism and → freedom with the aim of deepening internationally the sense of the importance of spiritual and religious values. Specifically, it seeks to give religious force to international movements for → peace, social justice, and human → rights, along with a sense of ecological responsibility (→ Ecology; Environment).

Bibliography: IARF publications: IARF Member Group Profiles (Frankfurt, 1985) • IARF News • Introduction to Our Association: Its Purposes, History, Programs, and Vision (Frankfurt, 1985).

Other works: F. HEYER and V. PFITZER, eds., Religion ohne Kirche (Stuttgart, 1977) • H. MYNAREK, Religiös ohne Gott? Neue Religiosität der Gegenwart in Selbstzeugnissen (Düsseldorf, 1983) • J. NEWMAN, On Religious Freedom (Ottawa, 1991) • H. RELLER, ed., HRGem.

HUBERTUS MYNAREK

International Church Conferences → Ecumenical Movement

International Council of Christian Churches

The International Council of Christian Churches (ICCC) regards itself as a worldwide movement of → fundamentalism. Its founder and president, Carl McIntyre (b. 1906), belongs to the fundamentalist wing of the Presbyterian church (→ Reformed and Presbyterian Churches). Soon after taking a pastorate in Collingswood, New Jersey, he founded the Bible Presbyterian Church. To counter the → Social Gospel and the → liberal theology of the Federal Council of Churches, he founded the American Council of Christian Churches (ACCC) in 1940. Then, with antiecumenical objectives, the ICCC set up headquarters in Amsterdam and held its first assembly there in 1948, a few days before the founding of the → World Council of Churches (WCC) in the same city.

The ICCC, which was violently anti-Communist, accused the ecumenical movement in general of being servants of Communism. It publicly denounced church leaders from Communist countries who participated in ecumenical meetings. With the demise of Communism, the relevance of the ICCC has decreased. In 1998 it reported comprising 700 denominations from over 100 countries, many of these groups being the result of splits and divisions caused by the ICCC.

The doctrinal basis of the ICCC is the → Apostles' Creed and a statement stressing the divine → inspiration and → infallibility of the Bible, the → Trinity, the deity and sinless humanity of Jesus, the

→ virgin birth, the substitutionary death and passion of Jesus, his bodily → resurrection and return, total corruption through the fall, → salvation by → grace alone through → faith and → regeneration, the eternal bliss of the saved and eternal torment of the lost, the spiritual unity of the saved, and church purity in life and doctrine according to the → Word of God. Historically the ICCC combines Reformed → orthodoxy with premillennialism, Darby-type → dispensationalism, and "fighting fundamentalism." Against the WCC and its search for → unity (→ Ecumenical Theology), which it views as signs of apostasy and preparation for a world church, its weapons are separation, → apologetics, and → mission.

The ICCC is to be distinguished from the → evangelical movement, which does not find a solid basis for association in the negative motifs of criticism and rejection of the → ecumenical movement. The ICCC charges evangelicals with a readiness for compromise.

The organ of the ICCC is the *Reformation Review.* There is also the weekly *Christian Beacon,* which McIntyre founded. Regional and global conferences, often openly parallel to ecumenical gatherings, keep it in public view. The 16th World Congress is scheduled to take place in Jerusalem in November 2000.

Bibliography: G. K. CLABAUGH, "Carl McIntire's Twentieth Century Reformation," *Thunder on the Right: The Protestant Fundamentalists* (Chicago, 1974) 69-97 • G. W. DOLLAR, *A History of Fundamentalism in America* (Greenville, S.C., 1973) • "International Council of Christian Churches (ICCC)," *EAR* (6th ed.) no. 13 • E. JORSTAD, *The Politics of Doomsday: Fundamentalists of the Far Right* (Nashville, 1970) • J. REICH, *Twentieth Century Reformation* (Marburg, 1969) • B. SHELLEY, *Evangelicalism in America* (Grand Rapids, 1967).

LUDWIG ROTT

International Council of Christians and Jews

Starting in the 1920s in Great Britain and the United States, and then especially after World War II, organizations were set up in various countries for promoting cooperation and mutual understanding between Christians and Jews. Gradually, international coordination between these organizations was sought. After almost three decades of looser organizational structures, the International Council of Christians and Jews (ICCJ) in its present form was established in 1974. In 1979 the former home of Martin Buber (1878-1965) in Heppenheim became its headquarters, so that the international coordination of joint Christian and Jewish work is now directed from Germany, the center of the atrocities against Jews under National Socialism.

The aim of the ICCJ is to promote mutual respect and cooperation between Christians and Jews, to give them a clearer insight into their distinctive historical and religious relations, to combat discrimination and prejudice in their dealings with one another and with others, and to give force to the religious and moral principles that underlie their traditions in the relations of religions, peoples, and states. Through annual colloquia in different countries the ICCJ promotes an exchange of experiences and insights among its member organizations and beyond. Special emphasis is laid, on the one hand, on the presentation of → Judaism and the Jewish people in non-Jewish instruction (i.e., in religious education and the teaching of history) and, on the other, on the presentation of Christianity in Jewish instruction. As distinct from Christian and church groups that deal with Judaism and → Jewish-Christian dialogue, in the ICCJ Jews and Christians work as equal partners.

The ICCJ unites people and groups from very different backgrounds, including North America, where there is a strong Jewish community; Latin America, with long-established Jewish communities; western, central, and eastern Europe, where relations between Jews and Christians still bear the marks of the → Holocaust and of the impact of Communist rule; and → Israel (§§2-3), with its specific relevance to the three Abrahamic faith communities. To bring together these different experiences, and in this way to deepen Jewish-Christian dialogue, has throughout been the declared aim of the ICCJ.

At present, the ICCJ has member organizations in 29 countries. In view of more recent developments relating to the growth of Islam, the council in 1995 formally decided to develop a trilateral dialogue involving also Muslims. To this end it created the Abrahamic Forum Council, which held its first conference in Berlin in October 1999.

→ Anti-Semitism, Anti-Judaism

Bibliography: M. BRAYBROOKE, *Children of One God: A History of the Council of Christians and Jews* (London, 1991) • *ICCJ News* • INTERNATIONAL COUNCIL OF CHRISTIANS AND JEWS, "Guidelines on the Portrayal of Jews and Judaism in Education and in Teaching Materials," *JES* 21 (1984) 523-30 • J. SCHONEVELD, "De 'International Council of Christians and Jews'–een overzicht," *Ter Herkenning-Tijdschrift voor Christen en Juden* 15/2 (1987) 109-19 • W. W. SIMPSON and R. WEYL, *The Story of the International Council of Christians and Jews* (Heppenheim, 1995).

FRIEDHELM PIEPER

International Council of Community Churches

The International Council of Community Churches (ICCC) is a national organization of independent churches in the United States. It works particularly to foster a sense of Christian loyalty to a church's own community, instead of primary loyalty going to a denomination or other organization outside that community. Its fourfold stated vision is to "affirm individual freedom of conscience; protect and promote church self-determination; proclaim that the love of God, which unites, can overcome any division; and be an integral partner in the worldwide ecumenical movement." The ICCC insists on the absolute → autonomy of the local → congregation and rejects any supracongregational structure with doctrinal or teaching authority.

The council was formed in 1950 through a merger of the International Council of Community Churches (founded 1946), dominated by largely white congregations, and the Biennial Council of Community Churches, formed in the 1930s out of largely black congregations. In 1994 it encompassed 250,000 members in 398 churches. Within its wider sphere the ICCC serves over 1,500 Community Churches in all 50 U.S. states plus several nations.

The council stands in direct contact with each individual congregation, whose membership is renewed annually. The member churches send delegates to the annual conference, which chooses a Board of Trustees for overseeing the council's ongoing business and appoints an executive director who oversees the work in the various council commissions (Ecumenical Relations, Men's Work, Missions, Rural Church Work, Study Commission, Women's Christian Fellowship, Youth Work).

The tasks and authority of the council are strictly limited by the principle of congregational autonomy. Its task is first to advise congregations, to supply them with informational materials, and to encourage them to participate in ecumenical, missionary (→ Mission), social, and political activities. In so doing, the council does not conduct any programs of its own but simply recommends participation in local and regional interconfessional activities or actions of other confessions. Commensurate with the council's own origin, particular importance attaches to activities aimed at overcoming racial barriers (→ Racism); other important concerns include disarmament (→ Peace; Disarmament and Armament) and the problem of → poverty.

Second, the council offers aid and advice for congregations that have become independent from larger confessional bodies. Third, through its executive director the council represents its member congregations in the → National Council of the Churches of Christ in the U.S.A. (→ National Councils of Churches), as well as in the → World Council of Churches. In both organizations, the council is a member with an advisory vote.

The council's annual full assemblies provide mutual counseling and support, discussion of substantive questions (esp. ecumenical concerns; → Ecumenism, Ecumenical Movement), and the continuing education of pastors and laity.

Bibliography: A. J. VAN DER BENT, ed., *Handbook, Member Churches: World Council of Churches* (rev. ed.; Geneva, 1985) 222-23 • *Christian Community* (monthly) • F. S. MEAD and S. S. HILL, *Handbook of Denominations in the United States* (10th ed.; Nashville, 1995) 122-23 • *Pastor's Journal* (quarterly) • J. R. SHOTWELL, *Unity without Uniformity* (Homewood, Ill., 1984).

NOTGER SLENCZKA

International Ecumenical Fellowship

The International Ecumenical Fellowship (IEF) is an association with the religious and educational aim of "seeking to hear the Word of God, to do the will of God, to help the people of God to be perfectly one in God, breaking the bread of God to the glory of God, Father, Son, and Holy Spirit." Historically, the beginnings of this movement may be traced to the Anglo-Roman Unity Campaign, which was started in 1889 by Viscount Halifax and Père Étienne Fernand Portal and which reached a remarkable high point in the "Malines Conversations" (1921-26) through Cardinal D.-J. Mercier, who wrote in his ecumenical "Testament": "In order to unite with one another, we must love one another; in order to love one another, we must know another; in order to know one another, we must go and meet one another."

Other important roots of the IEF can be found in the High Church movements in the European churches of the Reformation, the → Faith and Order movement, the Hochkirchliche Bewegung, the Evangelische Michaelsbruderschaft, the Hilversum Convent of the Dutch Reformed Church, and the → Old Catholic Church in Germany. All these mostly clerical circles consisted of non–Roman Catholics who saw the heartbeat of → ecumenism in the catholicity of the church as a worshiping body (→ Catholic, Catholicity).

In the 1950s these groups organized themselves — outside the → World Council of Churches and outside the → Roman Catholic Church — in the International League of Apostolic Faith and Order (ILAFO). When, after the ecumenism of → Vatican II, Roman Catholics could and would no longer be excluded, the ILAFO became too narrow for many. At their meeting in Fribourg in 1967, they decided to open their ranks to theologically educated and charismatically motivated laypeople (→ Charismatic Movement) from all mainline churches and formally organized themselves into a new body, called the IEF. They established an Executive Committee consisting of 11 members (4 → clergy and 7 lay, of whom 4 were women) representing Anglican, Lutheran, Orthodox, Reformed, and Roman Catholic traditions in Great Britain, Holland, and North America (→ Anglican Communion; Lutheranism; Orthodox Church; Reformed and Presbyterian Churches). Their inaugural conference took place in Gwatt, Switzerland, where the IEF presented itself as a fellowship of Christians from different nations daily worshiping together with members of other churches, thus taking over the principle of daily shared → Eucharist as developed by the ILAFO at Lund in 1952.

In 1999 the IEF could be described as a body of ecumenically spirited Christians from all mainline churches in the North Atlantic area that — for at least one week each year — tries to "live today as the church of tomorrow." It is organized, independently of any church body, through a council based in Brussels as a representative body of 11 national regions, of which 2 in southeastern Europe are in the process of formation. Besides regional activities, the council holds an International Conference annually, with an attendance of about 300 members, who assemble for one week, mostly in a traditional pilgrimage center such as Canterbury or Vierzehnheiligen, in order to discuss, study and pray together, and especially to celebrate the Eucharist daily according to the different orders of the churches represented through their members.

→ Ecumenism, Ecumenical Movement; Liturgical Movements; Spirituality

Bibliography: J. BURLEY, "How IEF Began," *Newsletter of British Region of IEF* (January 1993) • G. CURTIS, *The Malines Conversations, 1921-1926* (London, 1976) • F. GLENDON-HILL, "Worshipping Witness–the IEF," *JES* 15 (1978) 395-96 • W. VON LUPIN, "Im Dienste der Einheit aller Christen. Die Internationale Ökumenische Gemeinschaft (IEF)," *MDÖC,* no. 20 (December 1982).

ERNST L. SCHNELLBÄCHER

International Evangelical Church

The International Evangelical Church (IEC), originally called the International Evangelical Church and Missionary Association, was founded in 1959 by John McTernan in order to meet the needs of a missionary ministry in Italy. It was legally recognized in the United States in 1965. In addition to Italy, expansion of the church has extended largely to Brazil and Nigeria. The Nigerian constituency is now the largest regional group. In 1985 the IEC had 168,000 members in 459 congregations.

Holy Scripture is the basis of its church work, the only rule of faith, doctrine, and practice. It values the historic → confessions, but the → Word of God is above every interpretation of the faith (→ Biblicism). Behind its propagation stands the biblical conviction that all true believers are members of the one body of Christ. It views individual → conversion (§1) as very important. Along with → evangelism (esp. through the → mass media), → edification by → pastoral care and → diakonia are important goals. The emphasis varies with each region — for example, education and literacy programs are more prominent in Nigeria, social projects in Brazil, help for the homeless in the United States.

From 1972 to 1975, under McTernan, the IEC took an active part in → dialogue between the → Roman Catholic Church and the → Pentecostal churches, but it is now represented only by an observer. It is a member of the → World Council of Churches. Leadership of the IEC is placed in a three-person presidium, with members representing Nigeria, Brazil, and the United States. In 2000 headquarters of the church were in Upper Marlboro, Maryland.

SILVANO LILLI

International Fellowship of Reconciliation

The International Fellowship of Reconciliation (IFOR) is an international, spiritually based movement composed of people who, from the basis of a belief in the power of love and truth to create justice and restore community, commit themselves to active nonviolence as a way of life and as a means of personal, social, economic, and political transformation. Membership is open to all who are grounded in an absolute respect for human life and dignity. IFOR respects religious and cultural diversity.

The impulse toward the formation of the IFOR came in 1914, on the eve of World War I, from a conference in Constance of the World Alliance for Promoting Friendship through the Churches. The German Lutheran F. Siegmund-Schultze (1885-1969) and the English Quaker H. Hodgkin (1877-1933) pledged themselves to work against growing hatred, increasing militarization, and bellicosity in their respective countries, no matter what their governments might do.

IFOR was founded in 1919 at a conference at Bilthoven, Netherlands. Its basis was the common conviction that → discipleship of Jesus Christ sets us in the service of social justice and peace among the nations and summons us to vanquish war, to reject every form of violence (whether direct or structural; → Force, Violence, Nonviolence), and to espouse a principle of nonviolence in both the personal and the sociopolitical sphere. Traveling secretaries and active members formed local groups, which combined at the regional and national levels.

IFOR supported M. Gandhi (1869-1948) in India in his struggle for national liberation. During World War II many members were arrested for → conscientious objection, two of whom were executed in Germany. It gave aid to Jewish refugees and, in the United States, led the struggle against the internment of Japanese-Americans. It was the first nonviolent movement to establish East-West dialogue during the cold war period. In South Africa A. Luthuli (1898-1967), first president of the African National Congress, was a member. With M. Luther King Jr. (1929-68) as IFOR vice-president, the fellowship was active on behalf of → civil rights. It was influential in the founding of Servicio Paz y Justicia in 1975, a Latin American network for peace and justice. In 1983 it began work in South Africa against apartheid, and in 1986 in the Philippines against the Marcos regime. IFOR was influential in Chile in the toppling of General Pinochet in 1989, and in 1990-91 it was active in working to prevent war between Iraq and the U.S.-led alliance and then in giving relief to Iraq. It took various actions against the East-West arms race (→ Peace Movement). Individual members — among them five winners of the Nobel Peace Prize — have given the work its distinctive stamp.

Rejecting the theory of a just → war, IFOR supports → conscientious objection. Its members are active in initiatives against armaments (including demonstrations, mass meetings, and petitions). They also engage in civil disobedience (e.g., P. and D. Berrigan). They espouse an alternative concept of security (G. Sharp, T. Ebert). In the struggle for justice the IFOR seeks liberation from oppression, exploitation, and → racism and thinks that those responsible, as well as the victims, must be freed from the inhuman laws of unjust structures. By various acts of solidarity IFOR opposes capital punishment and → torture and advocates human → rights. Along the lines of the → Sermon on the Mount, it works for reconciliation among peoples and for open dialogue between those of opposite views, with a view to mutual agreement. It is at work in Northern Ireland, in the Middle East, and also among refugees (→ Asylum) and guest workers.

IFOR now has an international office at Alkmaar, Netherlands, which links the national branches. Every four years an International Council determines a common direction. An International Steering Committee makes all the necessary decisions in the intervening years. In 1999 there were branches in more than 40 countries in all continents.

IFOR is now a multireligious organization. Its membership includes adherents of all the major spiritual traditions, as well as those who have other spiritual sources for their commitment to nonviolence.

→ Disarmament and Armament; Pacifism; Peace; Peace Research; Weapons

Bibliography: G. Baum and H. Wells, The Reconciliation of Peoples: Challenge to the Churches (Geneva, 1997) • D. Berrigan, No Bars to Manhood (Garden City, N.Y., 1970); idem, Ten Commandments for the Long Haul (Nashville, 1981) • T. Ebert, Gewaltfreier Aufstand. Alternative zum Bürgerkrieg (Waldkirch, 1979); idem, Ziviler Ungehorsam (Waldkirch, 1984); idem, ed., Ziviler Widerstand (Düsseldorf, 1970) • A. H. Friedlander, A Thread of Gold: Journeys towards Reconciliation (Philadelphia, 1990) • H. Gressel, ed., Fünfzig Jahre IVB, Versöhnung und Friede (Dortmund, 1964) • G. Jochheim, Soziale Verteidigung (Düsseldorf, 1988) • W. E. Pannell, The Coming Race Wars? A Cry for Reconciliation (Grand Rapids, 1993) • R. J. Schreiter, Reconciliation: Mission and Ministry in a Changing Social Order (Cambridge, Mass., 1992) • S. N. Williams, Revelation and Reconciliation: A Window on Modernity (Cambridge, 1995) • W. Wink, When the Powers Fall: Reconciliation in the Healing of Nations (Minneapolis, 1998)

Konrad Lübbert†

International Law

1. History
2. Subjects
3. Sources
4. Relation to National Law
5. Regulatory Spheres

1. History

Antiquity knew no international law, though early forms might be found in the relations among the Greek city-states. Even when the → Roman Empire collapsed, 1,000 years passed before the development of an international order. When the concept of the unity of Christendom was abandoned, it came to be seen as both necessary and possible that a legal system should be set up to regulate relations between powers that were both equal and independent. The theory of a law that should regulate the dealings of sovereign states was put forward in the 16th century. The Peace of Westphalia (1648; → Thirty Years' War 1.4), with its recognition of state sovereignty, was the first stage in the practical application of international law. International law has now established itself as a way of handling the dealings of sovereign states with one another. It has never been a people's law.

2. Subjects

The subjects of international law are sovereign states and alliances and confederations of such states. Historically the only exceptions are the → Vatican, the International Committee of the Red Cross, and the sovereign Maltese Order. Increasingly from the late 19th century and especially since the end of World War II, international organizations have to some degree become subjects of international law, deriving this legal position from the will of their members (i.e., the sovereign states) as it finds expression in their statutes.

Nongovernmental organizations (e.g., international umbrella organizations of alliances, associations, or other bodies) cannot be the subjects of international law. They come under the laws of the countries in which they have their headquarters. Some of them enjoy consultative status in the → United Nations. The → World Council of Churches, for example, is a nongovernmental organization headquartered in Geneva. Individuals are not covered by international law except indirectly through the states of which they are citizens. The 20th century, however, considered changes that would extend international law also to individuals (→

Rights, Human and Civil) and to peoples (e.g., the right of self-determination).

3. Sources

The sources of international law are treaties, customs, and general legal principles (see art. 38 of the International Court of Justice; → Jurisprudence). Treaties both are legal affairs and establish objective laws for the signatory states, whether they are bilateral or multilateral (i.e., in conventions). To some degree they perform the same function as legislators. Law based on custom emerges when it is established by long-lasting or at least repeated usage on the part of several subjects sharing the same legal conviction. It may be global or regional, according to the nature of the participating states. General legal principles can be recognized as international law only if they have a worldwide reference and are in keeping with legal cultures.

4. Relation to National Law

International law is a closed system claiming no precedence over domestic law. Each state must see to it that by domestic law its own organs and representatives measure up to the norms of international law. The custom is that no state should be able to escape its international responsibilities by appealing to domestic law. It is in the interests of each state to incorporate the norms of international law in its domestic law.

5. Regulatory Spheres

From the very outset → war and → peace have been at the center of international law both in theory and in practice. The first major discussion was about just war with reference to Spanish conquests in the New World. A just war demanded authority, cause, and legal form, but only the first of these conditions was met. Sovereign states alone could wage war. Since by definition they could be subject to no higher power, there was no way of subjecting their decisions to wage war to any legal test. All decisions of sovereigns or sovereign states to wage war were justified. This right to wage war (ius ad bellum) has dominated all classic international law, which has left sovereigns with only two legal possibilities for dealing with other states: war or peace. In 1920, however, the League of Nations established a partial prohibition of war. In 1928 the Kellogg-Briand Pact was meant to put an end to war. In 1945 a decree of the United Nations forbade the general use of force. The states are now pledged to seek peace instead of insisting on their right to wage war. Armed defense against aggression, however, is still permitted.

Classic international law already contained not only the right to wage war but also rights in war *(ius in bello)*, that is, rights of war and neutrality. Those dealing with war as such regulate the conduct of war (means and methods), on the one hand, and, on the other, address humanitarian concerns for the protection of both participants and civilians. Despite the prohibition against war, this convention is still valid, applying in the case of armed conflict to all participants regardless of who the aggressor is; nor does punishing those responsible for the aggression run counter to such application. A first effort was made in this direction by the Nürnberg Trials of 1945-46.

Peacetime dealings between nations come under laws that govern diplomatic and consular modes of conduct as codified under the 1961 and 1963 conventions. Questions dealing with treaties (entering, fulfilling, and ending them) are regulated by a 1969 convention. In all these matters, however, international custom also still rules. The United Nations has given increasing importance to civil rights. International law has also been refined regarding international spheres such as the high seas, the ocean floor, the Antarctic, and space. Attention is being paid as well to the → environment (→ Ecology). In such matters, however, the task of actually implementing international norms is still basically under the jurisdiction of the individual sovereign states. U.N. executives also need the help of the member states.

The International Court of Justice has no obligatory legal jurisdiction, relying instead on the voluntary subjection of the subject states to its jurisdiction. Nevertheless, a principle of mutuality and a system of limited self-help ensure that international law functions efficiently. The U.N. charter stipulates that flagrant violations be addressed as a priority issue by the collective action of its members.

Bibliography: C. HERMAN, ed., *International Law and Institutions: Some Current Problems* (New York, 1970) • S. HOFFMANN, R. C. JOHANSEN, J. P. STERBA, and R. VÄYRYNEN, *The Ethics and Politics of Humanitarian Intervention* (Notre Dame, Ind., 1996) • K. IPSEN, *Völkerrecht* (Munich, 1990) • M. KHADDURI, *War and Peace in the Law of Islam* (New York, 1979) • O. KIMMINICH, *Einführung in das Völkerrecht* (5th ed.; Munich, 1993; orig. pub., 1975) • I. SEIDL-HOHENVELDERN, *Völkerrecht* (8th ed.; Cologne, 1994; orig. pub., 1965) • J. D. VAN DER VYVER and J. WITTE, *Religious Human Rights in Global Perspective: Legal Perspectives* (Boston, 1996) • B. WICKER and F. VAN IERSEL, *Humanitarian Intervention and the Pursuit of Justice: A Pax Christi Contribution to the Contemporary Debate* (Kampen, 1995) • R. K. WOETZEL, *The Nuremberg Trials in International Law, with a Postlude on the Eichmann Case* (Boston, 1962).

OTTO KIMMINICH

International Lutheran Council

The International Lutheran Council (ILC) is a worldwide association of established confessional → Lutheran church bodies that possess an unconditional commitment to the Bible as the inspired and → infallible Word of God and to the Lutheran confessions contained in the Book of Concord (→ Confessions and Creeds) as the true and faithful exposition of the → Word of God.

The origins of the ILC can be traced to a meeting of leaders of confessional Lutheran churches in Uelzen, West Germany, in July 1952. At a meeting in Cambridge, England, in 1963 the name "International Lutheran Theological Conference" was chosen for periodic informal gatherings. The ILC as a council of church bodies officially came into existence in 1993 with the adoption of a constitution.

The ILC exists to encourage, strengthen, and promote confessional Lutheran theology and practice, both among member churches and throughout the world. It seeks to accomplish these goals by providing opportunities for the joint study of contemporary theological issues, by encouraging member churches in mission outreach, by strengthening → theological education, and by stimulating and facilitating the publishing of literature. Its official publication is *ILC News,* a quarterly.

The executive committee of the ILC includes representatives from six world areas: Africa, East Asia, Europe, Latin America, North America, and Southeast Asia and Australia. An executive secretary, presently located in St. Louis, Missouri, is responsible for providing administrative and technical support. Member churches provide financial support for the ILC on the basis of their total baptized membership. The council, which meets every two years, had 28 participating church bodies as of August 1999 (the largest is the Lutheran Church–Missouri Synod), together representing 3.3 million members.

The ILC is not a church, nor does it exercise churchly functions or prescribe any course of action for its member churches. Membership of church bodies in the ILC does not imply formally declared altar and pulpit fellowship between those churches, but they are pledged to mutual respect and to the preserving and strengthening of confessional agreement, which manifest themselves at the altar and in the pulpit. A few churches within the ILC are also members of the → Lutheran World Federation.

SAMUEL NAFZGER

International Missionary Council

1. Formation
2. World Conferences
3. Integration with the WCC

The International Missionary Council (IMC) was the most significant and effective planning organization for international Protestant → missionary cooperation of the 20th century. Its formal organization in 1921 came about as a direct outcome of the Edinburgh World Missionary Conference of 1910. In its brief 40-year history it was an important expression of the movement toward Christian unity, especially in the dimension of world mission, and a forerunner of the modern → ecumenical movement.

1. Formation

The Edinburgh World Missionary Conference of 1910 — itself the successor to landmark 19th-century missionary conferences and to the New York Ecumenical Missionary Conference (1900) — created a Continuation Committee (CC) to carry out the mandates of that conference and to establish an agency for international missionary cooperation. John R. Mott, chairman of the conference, was designated CC chair, and Joseph H. Oldham, its secretary. The outbreak of World War I delayed the formal organization of the IMC but did not prevent the CC from carrying out important functions related to the formation of local mission councils and the response to wartime emergencies. In 1912 it began publication of the scholarly quarterly *International Review of Missions.*

The peripatetic Mott met with church and mission leaders in Asian countries, urging the organization of national missionary councils. Similar councils already existed in European countries and in North America and were planned in Africa. In 1918 an Emergency Committee of Cooperating Missions was formed under the leadership of Mott and Oldham. Oldham himself was active at the Paris Peace Conference of 1919, working to protect German and other missions threatened with seizure by the Allied nations as wartime reparations. Oldham's draft for article 438 of the Versailles Treaty accorded

all missions "supranational" status and protected them from expropriation as wartime booty. These interim achievements underscored the need for a permanent organization for international missionary cooperation.

In October 1921 the IMC was formally constituted at Lake Mohonk, New York, uniting 17 Protestant national missionary councils or councils of churches, of which 13 were Western and the remainder from Asia, Africa, and Latin America. The Germans at first held back but within six months joined the council. Joint IMC offices were opened in New York and London. Immediate concerns included securing the rights of German missions, work among Jews and Muslims, mission work in Latin America and Africa, and the production of Christian literature. As an international council of national mission councils, the IMC began its work of coordinating activities, initiating common studies, and planning consultations and global conferences.

2. World Conferences

2.1. During the Easter season of 1928 the IMC convened its first major world missionary assembly, on the Mount of Olives in Jerusalem. One-quarter of the delegates represented the new and growing "younger churches." At Jerusalem the IMC set forth its consistent missiological conviction that the indigenous churches of Asia, Africa, and Latin America, rather than Western mission societies, were the responsible agents for mission in their respective areas. The message from Jerusalem in relation to non-Christian systems of thought, including → secularism, was "Jesus Christ . . . the revelation of what God is and of what man through him may become." Furthermore, "Christ is our motive and Christ is our end. We must give nothing less, and we can give nothing more." During the late 1920s the IMC set up a Department of Social and Economic Research, headed by J. Merle Davis, who prepared field studies on the social and economic environment of younger churches and the need for creative approaches to local self-support. The International Committee on Christian Literature for Africa was also created. Focus on rural mission led to the establishment of the Agricultural Missions Foundation. Emergency assistance to orphaned missions continued and was later intensified in the Hitler period.

2.2. Late in 1938 the Tambaram (India) World Missionary Conference was convened on the campus of Madras Christian College. More globally representative than the Jerusalem conference, the gathering at Tambaram drew half of its delegates from

→ Third World nations. Overshadowing the meeting were the threats of World War II, which underscored the urgency of maintaining ties of → solidarity, mutual support, and → prayer among churches on all six continents. Tambaram stressed that local churches, not foreign missions or parachurch groups, must become the principal agents in world → evangelism: "We summon the churches to unite in the supreme task of world evangelization until the kingdoms of this world become the kingdom of our Lord."

The Tambaram theological message was strongly Christocentric, as expressed in Hendrik Kraemer's monumental study *The Christian Message in a Non-Christian World*, prepared for Tambaram at the request of the IMC. Kraemer called for "biblical realism" and asserted a total discontinuity between the gospel message and non-Christian cultures and systems of salvation. The relativistic theology of William Ernest Hocking, chairman of the American Laymen's Foreign Missions Inquiry of the early 1930s, was also sharply criticized.

In 1938 the IMC began forging closer links with the incipient → World Council of Churches (WCC), then already "in process of formation," following a joint meeting that year at Utrecht of committees from the → Life and Work and the → Faith and Order movements. Joint committees of the IMC and the WCC functioned from that time on "in association with" each other, a concrete embodiment of this arrangement being the Joint East Asia Secretariat of the IMC/WCC.

2.3. As World War II ended, it was discovered that many churches in Asia, Africa, and Oceania had grown and matured without benefit of foreign missionaries or mission support, including some that had been orphaned by war from parent mission societies. Former "receiving" churches were becoming mission-sending bodies. Decolonization and movements for independence in Asian and African countries increased pressure on Western mission boards and societies to hasten devolution and grant full independence to daughter churches. In 1947, under the theme "Partnership in Obedience," the IMC convened a meeting at Whitby, near Toronto, Canada. Delegates from six continents rejoiced that their fellowship had survived the war and the years of separation, only to emerge with "an even deeper vision of the reality and fullness of the universal church." Churches everywhere, older and younger, were asked to engage in a global partnership in which "all churches alike are called to the total evangelistic task." The recovery of vast areas that had fallen prey to → atheism, as well as the conversion of nominal Western church members, was seen as part of the same global task as converting nonbelievers to faith in Christ.

2.4. The decade of the 1950s confronted the IMC with decisive challenges that could no longer be postponed, including (1) clarifying the theological basis of → mission and (2) determining the structural relation of mission(s) to the church. The Willingen Conference of 1952, the first IMC meeting to be held in Germany, set itself the tasks of reformulating the church's missionary mandate and revising mission policies in conformity with a deeper theological understanding of mission. The world mission movement was being drained by powerful revolutionary forces in China and North Korea, and its response was weakened by hesitancy, defensiveness, and lack of unity. Theologically, Willingen could speak of a single calling of the church to mission and unity — "to be one family in Him and to make known to the whole world, in word and deed, His Gospel of the Kingdom." Mission was the task of the whole church, of every baptized believer.

The church-centered concept of mission that had marked IMC thinking at Jerusalem and Tambaram, however, was now criticized as being too narrow. Rather, a Trinitarian understanding of mission as God's own activity *(missio Dei)* — with the world as locus of mission, the kingdom as its goal, and the church as privileged agent and foretaste of the kingdom — began to replace the older thesis of the church as the starting point and goal of mission. The displacement of the church from its place at the center of mission activity would have far-reaching consequences, both positive and negative, in years to come.

3. Integration with the WCC

In 1948 the new World Council of Churches came into being at Amsterdam as a global fellowship of churches. Newly independent Third World churches wished to have direct church-to-church relationships with other churches throughout the world, not simply with representatives of Western mission societies or church mission boards. The Second Assembly of the WCC, held in 1954 at Evanston, Illinois, set up a joint committee with the IMC to study integration. The last full meeting of the IMC — in Accra, Ghana, in 1958 — is remembered for having launched the Theological Education Fund, a major global initiative to upgrade training for ministry in the Third World, but the issue of integration with the WCC was also a crucial item of business. In Accra integration seemed a foregone conclusion, having been vigorously advocated by WCC general secretary W. A. → Visser 't Hooft, who believed that integration would compel all churches "to rethink the meaning of the missionary and apostolic calling of the church." Lesslie Newbigin, last general secretary of the IMC, supported integration on the basis that "the missionary task is no less central to the life of the church than the pursuit of renewal and unity."

There were important opposing arguments. Eastern Orthodox churches, which generally equated mission and evangelism with the proselytizing of their members, opposed integration. Some IMC supporters contended that mission was a special charism of voluntary groups, particularly mission societies, and that large bureaucratic state churches with no previous mission experience were not suited to carry it forward. The unique calling to mission across frontiers would be lost, they feared, in programs of interchurch aid. Many Latin American evangelicals remained cool toward the WCC, and conservative → evangelicals generally did not relish identification with liberal WCC programs. Yet the overwhelming support of Third World member councils in favor of integration won the day.

Thus in late 1961 in New Delhi, at the closing meeting of the Third Assembly of the WCC, the IMC approved integration with the WCC, with but two lone dissenting voices (the Norwegian Missionary Council and the Congo Christian Council). In a formal act of integration, the former IMC became the WCC Commission on World Mission and Evangelism.

The new WCC mission unit, itself now four decades old, has undergone many structural changes but has continued the tradition of world mission conferences, sponsoring gatherings in Mexico City (1963), Bangkok (1973), Melbourne (1980), San Antonio, Texas (1989), and Salvador (Bahia), Brazil (1996).

Bibliography: W. R. HOGG, *Ecumenical Foundations: A History of the International Missionary Council and Its Nineteenth Century Foundations* (New York, 1952); idem, "International Missionary Council," *CDCWM* 289-91 • L. NEWBIGIN, "Mission to Six Continents," *A History of the Ecumenical Movement*, vol. 2, *The Ecumenical Advance, 1948-1968* (2d ed.; Geneva, 1986; 1st ed., 1970) 171-97 • T. STRANSKY, "International Missionary Council," *DEM* 526-29.

JAMES A. SCHERER

Interpretation

In the history of the human sciences the distinction is often made between the *interpretation* of an event, object, or text and its *meaning*. In antiquity people turned to objects in the natural order to find the → meaning of the world around them. The entire cosmos seemed to be connected and interrelated in one comprehensive nexus of meaning. The interpretation of one object potentially might reveal larger meanings in the cosmos. For this reason the entrails of animals, marks on the human body, objects in the sky, or tea leaves, for example, might be consulted. While various forms of → divination are prohibited in the OT, the interpretation of → dreams is frequently attested to. We see this practice, for example, in the accounts of the dreams of Jacob (Gen. 28:12-15), Joseph (Gen. 37:5-10), and Daniel (Dan. 7:1-27) and, in the NT, in the dreams of Joseph, the husband of Mary (Matt. 1:20; 2:12-13, 19-20).

Borrowing methods employed in the Hellenistic exegesis of Homer, Jewish and Christian exegetes of the Holy Scriptures, including Philo of Alexandria, Clement of Alexandria, and → Origen, often made use of → allegory. By the time of the Scholastics, four approaches were commonly employed in the interpretation of Scripture. The first, literal interpretation, was augmented by three spiritual methods, the allegorical, the moral or tropological, and the anagogical or mystical.

The questioning of the relation between the subject and the object of interpretation by René Descartes (1596-1650) shattered the idea of a comprehensive nexus of meaning in the cosmos. Natural phenomena no longer needed to be interpreted; they now needed to be explained according to human → reason and scientific methods of observance.

With the → Enlightenment the search for meaning shifted from religious traditions, including → magic and other superstitions, to human reason and scientific methodologies. This change is what Max → Weber (1864-1920) called the disenchantment of the world. Immanuel Kant (1724-1804) urged others to think rationally on their own, without external constraints of force or any heteronomous authority, such as might be exercised by the state or by religious institutions. Kant's focus on the central role of the human subject in the construction of the meaning of the sensible world around it forcibly raised the question of → subjectivity and objectivity in interpretation.

This emphasis on reason did not go unchallenged. Romantics investigated human experience and works of art (aesthetics) to find a way around the one-sided tyranny of reason in the rationalist philosophy of their day.

Following the Enlightenment, new fields of academic inquiry emerged to interpret the activity and meaning of human life. The disciplines of → sociology, → anthropology, → psychology, and the study of literature took their places alongside → philosophy and → theology in this task.

The depth psychology of Sigmund Freud (1856-1939) sought to explain human beings and their behaviors both singularly and collectively. Freud introduced the concept of the overdetermination of meaning — when an action or behavior is brought about by a multiplicity of causes, it is often difficult, if not impossible, to determine the sole cause of that action. Freud focused his interpretive methods on the symbolic interpretation of → myths and → rites, seeking to interpret dreams and other hitherto unexplored activities of the singular human psyche and the larger collective society in which it lives.

Walter Benjamin (1892-1940) argued that the conceptual violence of philosophy often merely imposed subjective meanings on the objects being interpreted. His philosophy, taking up the issues raised and methods employed by the Romantics, looked to find a constellation of meanings in even the most disparaged or marginalized object of interpretation. His philosophical methods sought the larger nexus of meaning absent in positivist Kantian and neo-Kantian philosophy.

In the later part of the 20th century a variety of philosophical and theological methods have been employed in the area of interpretation. Hans-Georg Gadamer (b. 1900) expanded on the earlier → hermeneutics of Friedrich → Schleiermacher (1768-1834) and Wilhelm Dilthey (1833-1911). Challenging → Cartesian epistemological foundationalism, Gadamer argued that every text or cultural object that is interpreted is already an interpretation itself. The horizon of the interpreter and the horizon of the object that is being interpreted do not fuse in the act of interpretation; rather, they form a new and ever-receding horizon of meaning. In its fullest sense, hermeneutics is not confined solely to the interpretation of texts or objects; it also describes the activity of the production and reproduction of all human knowledge. The speech-act theory formulated by J. L. Austin (1911-60) distinguished "linguistic meaning" from "speaker meaning" and examined how spoken and written discourses communicate meaning.

In *Knowledge and Human Interests,* Jürgen Habermas (b. 1929) proposed a nonfoundational and universal method of interpretation that sought to challenge the inherent conservatism of tradition and allow for the development of emancipatory practices. In *The Theory of Communicative Action* Habermas sought to develop the conceptual foundations for a critical theory of society. Where structuralists sought to describe the overarching totalities that seem to operate independently from the awareness of human persons, poststructuralists rejected the possibility of totalities and the power implicit in the "master narratives" of Western philosophical and theological discourses, pointing to the dispersal and multiplicity of meanings in everything that is interpreted.

Christian theology has employed a wide range of academic disciplines to interpret its message. Pastoral theology, for example, employing methods developed in the fields of psychology, sociology, and anthropology, has emerged as a theological discipline in which the questions of human meaning and purpose, including phenomena and ideas often ignored by scientific methodologies, are allowed to come to expression.

Bibliography: J. L. AUSTIN, *How to Do Things with Words* (2d ed.; Cambridge, Mass., 1975) • W. BENJAMIN, *Selected Writings* (2 vols.; Cambridge, Mass., 1996-99) • H. G. GADAMER, *Truth and Method* (2d ed.; New York, 1993) • J. HABERMAS, *Knowledge and Human Interests* (Boston, 1971); idem, *The Theory of Communicative Action,* vol. 1, *Reason and the Rationalization of Society;* vol. 2, *Lifeworld and System: A Critique of Functionalist Reason* (Boston, 1984-87) • I. KANT, "What Is Enlightenment?" (1783), *Foundations of the Metaphysics of Morals and What Is Enlightenment?* (trans. L. W. Beck; Indianapolis, 1959) 85-92 • H. DE LUBAC, *Medieval Exegesis,* vol. 2, *The Four Senses of Scripture* (Grand Rapids, 2000) • G. WARNKE, *Gadamer: Hermeneutics, Tradition, and Reason* (Stanford, Calif., 1987) • M. WEBER, "Science as a Vocation," *Max Weber: Essays in Sociology* (New York, 1974) 129-56.

CRAIG A. PHILLIPS

InterVarsity Christian Fellowship → Student Work; Youth Work

Intuition

Based on the Lat. *intuitio, intuitus,* and coined by
W. von Moerbeke (ca. 1215-86) as a philosophical
term, "intuition" in the sense of inspiration or an
intuitive grasp of something belongs to a philosophical tradition that goes back to Epicureanism (→
Greek Philosophy), which used *epibolē* for a sudden,
total, and immediate understanding of the whole
object of knowledge. More broadly, "intuition" can
denote the direct knowledge that carries within itself its own conditioning and justification. In →
mysticism it relates to an intuitive → experience
(§2) of God. In → epistemology it contrasts with
discursive knowledge, which claims methodologically mediated validity.

The breadth of definition of "intuition" may be
seen from the fact that it may be located purely in
the intellect (Plotinus) or related to given objects
(Duns Scotus). Terms such as "perception" (I. Kant),
"intellectual perception" (F. W. J. Schelling), or "essential vision" (E. Husserl) also come close to it. Intuition is a basic concept in the philosophy of H.-L.
Bergson (1859-1941). In modern epistemological
discussion basic principles are often called intuitive.
C. G. Jung (1875-1961) regarded the function of intuition as a primary psychological function by
which we have unconscious perception of the
world.

Bibliography: B. J. F. LONERGAN, *Insight: A Study of Hu-
man Understanding* (London, 1957) • I. MARCOULESCO,
"Intuition," *EncRel(E)* 7.269-70 • R. RORTY, "Intuition,"
EncPh 4.204-12 • E. ROTHACKER and J. THYSSEN,
Intuition und Begriff (Bonn, 1963).

FRANK OTFRIED JULY

Investiture

The term "investiture," in the sense of the ceremonial conferral of symbols of office or honor, comes
from the law of property under the Carolingian Empire, where it referred to a purchaser's acquisition of
authority over a piece of real estate in the form of a
concrete vesting order or by the transference of representative symbols (e.g., a stalk). In the secular
world investiture with the property later became a
constitutive part of feudal law. In → church law
similar symbolic acts of investiture occurred when a
patron appointed a minister to a → proprietary
church. From around 900 secular rulers invested
imperial bishops with an episcopal staff as a symbol
of their religious authority. The → bishop had to
swear an oath of fealty to the king and to do homage. The investiture of bishops and → abbots became the general practice in Ottonian Germany.

The Gregorian reformers opposed the practice of
investiture by secular rulers. Humbert of Silva
Candida took the lead in his *Adversus simoniacos*
(1057), but it was only after the November Synod at
Rome in 1078 that the papacy prohibited investiture
by emperors, kings, or any laypersons. The question
of lay investiture now became a leading issue in the
so-called Investiture Controversy between → empire and papacy (→ Middle Ages 2; Simony).

With the elimination of investiture by secular
rulers, the term became equivalent to induction into
ecclesiastical office by the proper authorities, and it
occurs in this sense in the classic canon law of the
12th and 13th centuries (→ Corpus Iuris Canonici).
From the middle of the 13th century a distinction
was made between *transfer of office,* which conferred
full right to the benefice, and a subsequent *solemn
institution,* which was now called investiture. This
distinction rested on the separation of the concept
of office from the idea of legal possession, investiture being *missio in possessionem* (sending forth in
possession). Along these lines the term lives on in
the 1983 CIC, where in canon 527.2 it deals with the
institution of a priest into his office by the ordinary
or a → priest whom he delegates for this purpose.

In Protestant churches we occasionally find "investiture" used for the installation of ministers (→
Pastor, Pastorate) into their spiritual office. Investiture into a specific ministry is distinguished from →
ordination.

Bibliography: R. BENSON, *The Bishop-Elect: A Study in
Medieval Ecclesiastical Office* (Princeton, 1968) •
S. BEULERTZ, *Das Verbot der Laieninvestitur im
Investiturstreit* (Hannover, 1991) • U.-R. BLUMENTHAL,
*The Investiture Controversy: Church and Monarchy
from the Ninth to the Twelfth Century* (Philadelphia,
1988) • N. F. CANTOR, *Church, Kingship, and Lay Investiture in England, 1089-1135* (Princeton, 1958) •
W. HARTMANN, "Der Investiturstreit," *Enzyklopädie
deutscher Geschichte* (Munich, 1993) • "Investiture
Controversy," *ODCC* 842-43 • J. LAUDAGE, *Gre-
gorianische Reform und Investiturstreit* (Darmstadt,
1993) • R. SCHIEFFER, *Die Entstehung des päpstlichen
Investiturverbots für den deutschen König* (Stuttgart,
1981).

PETER LANDAU

Iona Community

1. Origin
2. Aims
3. Contemporary Expression

1. Origin

The Iona Community, an ecumenical Christian community, was founded in 1938 when George F. MacLeod (later MacLeod of Fuinary) gathered a group of Church of Scotland ministers in training and unemployed craftsmen to rebuild the monastic quarters of an ancient Benedictine monastery on the island of Iona off the west coast of Scotland. Iona had been the base for the Celtic mission from the sixth century A.D.

2. Aims

The aims of the Iona Community have been to engage in mission, particularly in relation to industry (→ Industrial Society), to the great new housing schemes of Scotland, and to areas of → poverty both within and without that land. Central to the life of the community is corporate → worship and the search for the renewal of → liturgy. The community seeks to bring insights from the Christian faith to bear upon the politics and economics of the nations, which will lead to → peace and justice (→ Righteousness, Justice), → healing (both corporate and individual), the relating of worship to → everyday life, and local community development. To this end the community early began to promote work with young people and has established youth centers on Iona and the Ross of Mull. A house was also acquired in Glasgow for the furthering of its purposes on the mainland.

3. Contemporary Expression

The abbey, completed in 1967, has become a focus for the renewal of worship and for a permanent community of men and women, married and single, with their children. It offers hospitality to many visitors to the island. In 1999 the community, which is drawn from Protestant and Roman Catholic Churches, numbered over 200 people, with 1,500 associate members and 1,700 friends. The members (most of whom are in Great Britain) are committed to a common rule of daily prayer and Bible study, sharing and accounting for their use of time and money, and regular meeting and action for justice and peace. Members meet monthly in local "family groups" and in plenary gatherings three times a year on the mainland and for a week during the summer on Iona.

→ Communities, Spiritual

Bibliography: G. F. MacLeod, *Only One Way Left* (Glasgow, 1956); idem, *We Shall Rebuild: The Work of the Iona Community on Island and Mainland* (Glasgow, 1944; repr., 1962) • T. R. Morton, *The Iona Community: Personal Impressions of the Early Years* (Edinburgh, 1977).

Graeme Brown

Iran

	1960	1980	2000
Population (1,000s):	21,552	39,254	76,429
Annual growth rate (%):	2.70	4.40	2.60

Area: 1,638,057 sq. km. (632,457 sq. mi.)

A.D. 2000

Population density: 47/sq. km. (121/sq. mi.)
Births / deaths: 3.13 / 0.54 per 100 population
Fertility rate: 4.23 per woman
Infant mortality rate: 35 per 1,000 live births
Life expectancy: 70.8 years (m: 69.7, f: 72.0)
Religious affiliation (%): Muslims 97.9, other 2.1.

1. Geography and Recent History
2. Christians in Iran
   2.1. Groups
   2.2. Bible Translation
   2.3. Muslim-Christian Relations

1. Geography and Recent History

Iran, lying between the 25th and 40th northern latitudes, borders on Turkey and Iraq to the west; Pakistan and Afghanistan to the east; Armenia, Azerbaijan, Turkmenistan, and the Caspian Sea to the north; and the Persian Gulf and the Gulf of Oman to the south. It includes a number of Persian Gulf islands in its territory. Iran is a land bridge between Asia Minor and central Asia. Its high country consists of mountains, steppes, and deserts. Iran's main economic activities are petroleum, agriculture, and manufacturing, with its crafts especially notable for fine carpets. Some 90 percent of the population are Shiite Muslims (→ Islam; Shia, Shiites), with → Sunnites also present. The 1996 census showed Christians as less than 1 percent of the population, Jews and Zoroastrians as less than 0.1 percent, with → Baha'is and others also present. Persian is the main linguistic group, but there are also speakers of Kurdish, Luri, Arabic, Baluchi, and Turkic languages. Iran is home to the largest refugee population in the world, the greatest number coming from Afghanistan.

Present-day Iran is the heartland of the ancient

Persian empire. Until 1979 it was ruled by monarchs, with the exceptional powers of the *shah* (king) continuing within the constitutional monarchy declared in 1906. With the "White Revolution," Moḥammad Reza Pahlavi (1919-80, shah 1941-79) forced modernization and industrialization on Iran from 1963, making it a threshold country of the → Third World, with all the associated problems, including flight to the cities, especially Tehran (a hub in which about 10 percent of the population lives), the rise of an impoverished → proletariat, and a wealthy class with a Western lifestyle and the slackening of religious ties. As a result, the influence of the clergy (ayatollahs and mullahs) grew among the embittered poor, and even many intellectuals and the developing middle class turned against the police state.

An opposition alliance that ranged from religious Muslims to Communists made possible the revolution of 1979 that overthrew the regime of the shah and, with it, the monarchy. Under the leadership of Ayatollah Ruhollah Khomeini (1900?-1989), the Islamic Republic of Iran was founded, and a new constitution was adopted by popular vote in 1979 (with revisions in 1989). The constitution (art. 4) states that "all civil, penal, financial, economic, administrative, cultural, military, political, and other laws and regulations must be based on Islamic criteria." The form of government provides for ongoing guidance and interpretation of religious sources to ensure this orientation (see art. 2; cf. arts. 107-12 on the role of the Leader). After the initial stages of the revolution, power was consolidated, and some forces were ousted that were initially involved. The Islamic Republic has achieved basic stability; internal struggles, however, have involved questions of property, civic and civil rights, and ties with foreign nations. The leaders of the revolution have sought new self-understanding in culture, education, science, and finance. They have expected a degree of uniformity in language and public lifestyle (including Islamic standards of attire, gender segregation, and prohibition of alcohol). This expectation affects different Islamic and Christian groups, including Armenians and Assyrians, who have nonetheless been able to preserve their own language and culture. War with Iraq, beginning in 1980, had major impact upon Iranian life for a decade and has left its economic consequences. The population has more than doubled since the beginning of the revolution, also creating problems.

Ayatollah Ali Khamenei succeeded Khomeini as Leader, the supreme political and religious authority, upon Khomeini's death in 1989. In 1997 Mohammad Khatami, a moderate, was elected president by a substantial majority of the electorate. General elections in early 2000 supported the moderate policies of Khatami, with the newly elected Parliament largely comprising supporters of moderation. The impact of this shift in political leadership, for Iran and its international relations, remains to be seen.

2. Christians in Iran

Christianity has been present in Persia since the early days of the church and, in spite of tribulations, has never ceased its existence there. Persian Christian missionaries journeyed beyond their own region, as witnessed by an eighth-century inscription found in Xian, China; Armenians and Assyrians, however, have not understood Iran to be an area they entered in mission.

Today Christians, together with Jews and Zoroastrians — all adherents of "religions of the book" — are recognized by the constitution of the Islamic Republic of Iran as official religious minorities with rights to perform their own religious ceremonies, follow their own canons in personal affairs, and engage in religious education (art. 13; cf. 26, 64, 67). Minorities must not engage in "conspiracy or activity against Islam and the Islamic Republic of Iran" (art. 14). Most of the Christians in Iran belong to the traditional Armenian and Assyrian/Chaldean churches (→ Oriental Orthodox Churches). Armenians and Assyrians are recognized according to the commands of the → Koran and have representation in Parliament. Their clergy and ecclesiastical bodies maintain their religious communities' own personal status laws, and their church leaders are recognized. No special recognition is granted other Christians. In the Islamic Republic, as distinct from the caliphate or Ottoman regime, Christians do military service. Armenians have their own schools, which follow the government syllabus, according to which Persian is the primary language of instruction. Government-commissioned Islamic authors have prepared textbooks in religion for the minorities.

As distinct from members of the traditional Christian churches, those who have been won by missionary work (→ Mission) — that is, Protestants and Roman Catholics of the Latin Rite — find life more difficult in the Islamic Republic of Iran, in part because of persistent Iranian suspicions concerning perceived Christian links to the West and, in the case of Protestants especially, because of their mission to Muslims. (Historically, persecution of Persian Christians broke out in the sixth century after the Roman Empire, enemy of the Persian Empire, embraced Christianity.)

A disproportionate number of Christians have emigrated to North America, Europe, and Australia. Within the milieu of the Islamic Republic, Christians cannot expect full access in public life, but they have played an important role in the economy, trade, the oil industry, and transport. They can generally live their private lives as freely as do Muslims.

2.1. Groups

2.1.1. In 1990 there were somewhat over 10,000 Assyrian Christians in Iran. Frequently labeled → Nestorian by others, their traditional church is the ancient apostolic Church of the East. In pre-Islamic Persia they influenced culture, scholarship, medicine, and the economy. Even under Islamic rule they flourished up to the Tatar invasion around 1400. A few then lived on in the Kurdish highlands and around Lake Urmia in northwest Iran. In World War I the Assyrians, like the Armenians, fell victim to world politics. They lost their homeland in southeast Turkey and a third of their members. They revived in Iran under Shah Moḥammad Reza Pahlavi, and the bishopric of Tehran was founded in 1962.

After losing many members to other churches, the Church of the East is now growing again, along with the development of a sense of its culture and language. The church is a member of the → World Council of Churches, has close ties to the Church of England (→ Anglican Communion), and has achieved significant agreements with the → Vatican through a series of dialogues.

Partly because ecclesiastical leadership is hereditary among Assyrians, some groups left their ancient church in the 16th century and joined Rome (→ Uniate Churches). Those Assyrians who became Catholic have been known as Chaldeans. Chaldeans in Iran belong to the Patriarchate of Babylon, which was founded in 1830 and located in Baghdad from 1850. Most Iranian Chaldeans live in Tehran, where their bishop has his seat. Emigration steadily reduces their numbers.

2.1.2. Most of the Armenians in Iran belong to the → Armenian Apostolic Church, whose bishops in New Julfa/Eṣfahān, Tabrīz, and Tehran are under the Cilician catholicos (whose seat is Antelias, Lebanon). Their church has provided significant ecumenical leadership within the World Council of Churches and the → Middle East Council of Churches. Armenians honor St. Thomas and St. Thaddeus as the founders of their church and Gregory the Illuminator (ca. 240-332, the "Apostle of Armenia") as converting their king and nation to Christianity in about A.D. 300. The Armenians' brief

independent kingdoms were destroyed by powerful neighbors, and they were scattered. In 1604 the Ṣafavid shah Abbas the Great (1588-1629) forcibly removed thousands of Armenians from the area around the Araks River to the New Julfa quarter of Eṣfahān (named for the city of Julfa in Azerbaijan, their former home) in order to help with the construction of his new capital. In World War I many Armenians fled from eastern Turkey to Iran, and from there many later emigrated to the Republic of Armenia (which was a part of the U.S.S.R.). In spite of long years of persecution, the Armenian people and culture still persist in the Armenian Apostolic Church.

The Armenian Catholic Church, which came into being in the 18th century, has members in Iran. The church's hierarchical structure was reorganized in 1928 with the patriarch of Cilicia in Lebanon and a diocese in Iran.

The Armenians live for the most part in Tehran, in New Julfa, around Eṣfahān, in northwest Iran, and in the petroleum-industry areas. Many of them who achieved prosperity and status under the late shah in industry, learning, culture, and state service left Iran after the revolution. Left-wing intellectuals who had opposed the shah remained, however, along with small farmers and manual workers. Today, thanks to their ongoing church life, the Armenians have their own culture, manifested in schools, clubs, and educational institutions in Tehran, and they have been able to maintain a right to their own language. Many of them fell during the war with Iraq and are honored as national martyrs.

2.1.3. The Protestant churches in Iran are small. North American Presbyterians did successful missionary work among the Nestorians around Lake Urmia in the 19th century, where they built schools, hospitals, and mission stations and where modern Eastern Aramaic emerged out of the Christian dialect spoken around Lake Urmia. The Anglican Church, also active in Iran, and Presbyterians made many attempts to unite but were unsuccessful. The two missions divided their efforts so that Presbyterians worked in the North and Anglicans in the South. Major early Presbyterian work was among Assyrians; most Anglican work was among Armenians, Jews, and Muslims. After World War I the Anglicans founded the Episcopal Church of Iran, which is now a part of the Anglican Province of Jerusalem and the Middle East. Eṣfahān is the Episcopal bishop's seat, where the first national bishop was consecrated in 1961. Presbyterian-related congregations formed the Evangelical Church of Iran, a fully independent church as of 1934, centered in

Tehran, with membership in the World Alliance of Reformed Churches. The Evangelical Church reported in 1971 that 55 percent of its membership was Assyrian, and this segment of its church life is now regarded by some as the most viable Protestant Christian expression in Iran today.

Other Protestant church bodies exist, notably Pentecostal congregations that affiliated with the General Council of the Assemblies of God in 1965.

Some half dozen church leaders in the Episcopal, Assemblies of God (Philadelphia), and Presbyterian churches died between 1979 and 1985 through assassination or execution. This number includes two men who had been presidents of the council of Protestant churches.

2.1.4. → Roman Catholic missions have left some Latin Christians (→ Roman Catholic Church). The → Dominicans, → Franciscans, Capuchins, Carmelites, and Lazarists set up schools, but since the time of the late shah, these have been nationalized together with other schools.

2.2. Bible Translation

In order to further education among ordinary people, a printing press was developed by Armenians in New Julfa. In Armenian history, the idea of printing a whole Bible in Armenian translation was first conceived in New Julfa, though the actual printing occurred in Amsterdam because of technological needs. The first widely circulated translation of Christian Scripture into Persian was the NT, published in 1815 through the work of Henry Martyn, an Anglican priest who came to Shīrāz by way of India. The Bible Society of Iran was established in 1967 for translation and distribution of Christian Scripture, but its work was closed by the government in 1990.

2.3. Muslim-Christian Relations

The relation between Christians and Muslims varies according to political relations (→ Islam and Christianity). Social relationships between people of various groupings are not extensive. In the period before and just after the revolution, there were more contacts, especially in the younger generation, but today groups mostly keep to themselves, the more so as the state demands a religiously governed life even from non-Muslim minorities.

In recent years several → dialogues have been held between Iranian religious and cultural leaders and Christians from the West.

Bibliography: S. BAKHASH, The Reign of the Ayatollahs: Iran and the Islamic Revolution (rev. ed.; New York, 1990) • F. HEILER, Die Ostkirchen (Munich, 1971) • N. HORNER, "A Guide to Christian Churches in the Middle East," Present-Day Christianity in the Middle East and North Africa (ed. W. R. Shenk et al.; Elkhart, Ind., 1989) • J. JOSEPH, The Nestorians and Their Muslim Neighbors (Princeton, 1961) • N. R. KEDDIE, ed., The Iranian Revolution and the Islamic Republic (Syracuse, N.Y., 1986) • D. LYKO, Gründung, Wachstum und Leben der evangelischen christlichen Kirchen in Iran (Cologne, 1964) • S. MACKEY, The Iranians: Persia, Islam, and the Soul of a Nation (New York, 1996) • R. MOTTAHEDEH, The Mantle of the Prophet: Religion and Politics in Iran (New York, 1985) • K. SARKISSIAN, The Armenian Christian Tradition in Iran (Eṣfahān, 1973) • B. SPULER, "Religionsgeschichte des Orients in der Zeit der Weltreligionen," HO 8/2 • K. J. THOMAS and F. BAHMAN, "Persian Translations of the Bible," Encyclopedia Iranica (London, 1990) 4/2.209-14 • R. WATERFIELD, Christians in Persia (London, 1973) • R. WRIGHT, The Last Great Revolution: Turmoil and Transformation in Iran (New York, 2000). The website "Iran: Virtual Library — Social, Political, and Economic Studies," at http://www2. prestel.co.uk/neman/, provides Internet access to the constitution of the Islamic Republic of Iran and to a commentary on the political structure of the state.

HELGA ANSCHÜTZ

Iranian Religions

1. Definitions
2. Original Iranians
3. Western Iranians
4. Northern Iranians
5. Eastern Iranians
6. Zoroaster
7. Zoroastrianism
8. Hellenism and Syncretism
9. Ancient Judaism and Early Christianity
10. Gnosticism
11. Shiite Islam

1. Definitions

Iranian religions are the authentic religions of peoples and tribes that spoke or speak Iranian languages. One may also refer to other religions whose features appear in Iranian religions and are material variants of them. We do not include religions in non-Iranian languages that are native to territories that came under the rule of Iran (e.g., the Elamites) or that came to Iran later and in so doing underwent changes (e.g., the many Turkic tribes) or that are regarded as their own only by a few Iranian speakers (e.g., the → Buddhism of the Sakas and Sogdians).

The Iranian languages are the western branch of

the Aryan Indo-European family, whose speakers apparently lived in central Asia north of the Tian Shan Mountains. We assume that a people speaking Irano-Aryan, as distinct from Indo-Aryan, moved to the Aral Sea area by the rivers Oxus and Iaxartes (modern Amu Dar'ya and Syr Dar'ya) and to the northwest of modern Afghanistan (→ Nomads). The ethnogenesis and progress of the movement of this Iranian people, which began about 2000 b.c., are unknown. The only certainty is that around 1500 they spread west and south in several thrusts.

2. Original Iranians

Statements, names, and practices that are common to more or less all Iranian religions and the Vedic religions (→ Hinduism 3) permit certain hypotheses regarding the religions of the ancient Iranian people. Around 1500 b.c. a non-Iranian people lived in northern Mesopotamia, the Hurrites, whose dynasty had an Aryan name, the Mitanni. This group might have been simply an exclave of the ancient Iranian people. Here in the 14th century we find common features and Indo-Aryan or Indian developments that enable us to reconstruct a religious system that included a sun god (Sūrya), lords that guarantee → oath and treaty (Varuṇa, with a tendency to become the god of the rainy → heaven; Mitra, with a tendency to become the god of the starry heaven), a cosmic moral law (the *rita*, or *rta*), a war god (Indra), two horsemen who appear at dawn for a daily → sacrifice (the Nāsatyas), a nobility, charioteers, and peasants. Included are myths of the first man, early kings, and the Oxus goddess Ardvī Sūrā Anāhitā (a variant of a pre-Aryan → mother goddess), also the first cattle stealing from non-Aryan neighbors, who are represented as a three-headed → serpent. In the cult a continual → fire was kept burning that was partly a medium and partly an object of worship. Libations were brought. The use of a hallucinogenic drink (Iranian *haoma*, Indian *soma*) points to → shamanism, from which derive the gift of → visions and the experience of having multiple souls, which are found among all later Iranians. Several of the elements discussed below (see 3-8) were present already, though many details are hotly contested.

3. Western Iranians

3.1. The most important migrations were those of peoples that later played a historical role. At the end of movements around the Caspian Sea, through the valleys of the Caucasus and Zagros Mountains, and through the Caspian Gates between the Damāvand peak in the Elburz Mountains and the uninhabitable salt desert, there appeared the Medes and Persians as the conclusion of the expansion of the Parthians to the area southeast of the Caspian Sea. In the ninth century the Persians came into contact with the Assyrians south of Lake Urmia. They then came into the southwest of modern Iran in the seventh century. For the previous thousand years Iran had been occupied by the culturally and linguistically independent Elamites.

The Medes moved into the northwest of modern Iran, where around 620 b.c. they founded a state that included the Urartians (a people related to the Hurrites) and a Persian subkingdom. The Mede Cyrus II the Great (ruled 558-529 b.c.) laid the foundation for a great empire under his own dynasty, the Achaemenian. He himself incorporated Lydia (547/546) and Babylon (539) by conquest, and his successors ruled over all the territory east to the Indus, including that of the original Iranian peoples, as well as over Egypt and Asia Minor. This first world empire lasted until it fell to Alexander the Great (336-323) in 333-323.

3.2. Among the Persians we find the "lords" (the *ahura*s), which were important along with cosmic forces like wind (Vayu) and fire (Ātar). But Indra and the Nāsatyas and others, which were gods for the Indians, were now denigrated as evil spirits. A mythological → dualism was constructed that found social expression in the antithesis of order or truth (Asha, for *rita*) versus deceit or falsehood (Druj). All slaughtering was sacrificial (→ Sacrifice), and like haoma, it served to renew life for both earthly and heavenly beings.

Among the Medes a special priestly office (→ Priest, Priesthood) was delegated to the magi, one of the six orders under the king, which the successors of Cyrus took over. The magi of Media created their own dualism. In their ritual practice they treated the earthly world in terms of two diametrically opposed spheres: the clean and the unclean. To the unclean sphere belonged human corpses, the burial of which became a central religious and social concern (→ Funeral). Since interment or cremation would make the two pure elements of earth and fire unclean, there remained only exposure in special places, where unclean birds would eat the corpses and thus limit the defiling of the air.

The religion of the Parthians can be reconstructed only from a few later attested words and from the archaeology of the early steppe peoples. We know the names of cultic places (including graves), along with priestly offices, rites, and gods. In their worship, components with an orientation to nature were more important than the social components. Relics of western Iranian religion appear in the folklore of the → Kurds.

4. Northern Iranians
Several nomadic peoples, breaking out from the original Iranian homeland in the steppes both westward and eastward, clung to their nomadic lifestyle. Greek writers from the time of Herodotus (ca. 484–between 430 and 420 B.C.) call them Scythians. In the eighth century B.C. they were scattered across southern Russia, and from the sixth century they lived in symbiosis with non-Iranian peoples of similar culture from the Ukraine to China. Shamanism was common to all of them and was probably more important structurally than the Iranian version of its → mythology.

5. Eastern Iranians
Ethnically we must regard as eastern Iranians the inhabitants of the vast area from Transoxiana across the Hindu Kush to around Hamun-i-Mashkel. These peoples spoke Khwarazmian, the dialect of Zoroaster, Bactrian, and Sogdian. The common Iranian tradition may be found especially in poems and epics about kings and heroes. The three-headed serpent is actualized from now on as a foreign usurper (Azī Dahāka) from whom a hero must wrest back the kingdom. Gods of fertility, water, stars, destiny, and victory are also extolled in hymns. Relics of the Iranian religions (original, northern, and eastern) may still be found in the folklore of peoples between Nuristan and Dardistan.

6. Zoroaster
In eastern Iran, first around Balkh (now Wazirābād in northwest Afghanistan), Zoroaster lived for more than 75 years in the sixth century B.C. (or perhaps as early as the 10th cent.). Half his life he performed a priestly ritual (Yasna), and half he was the → prophet of a new relation to God. He consistently opposed an orgiastic nomadic religion and was the reformer of a farming religion that cherished plants and animals. He based the → truth on an ethos bound up with cattle raising and related falsehood to the → ecstasy induced by drinking the blood of beasts and haoma. In this way he established the strongest of all Iranian dualisms.

The relating of the truth to the most powerful of the traditional lords robbed this lord of the ambivalence that produced a milder dualism and made him unequivocally the Wise Lord (Ahura Mazda). To slacken the opposition to the new dualism, which was also generalized as that of good and evil, and which had an evil spirit (Angra Mainyu) on the bad side, a holy spirit (Spenta Mainyu) was set in dialectical relation to Ahura Mazda, partly identical and partly independent. Life as conflict between truth and falsehood and their two gods, or the principles of → good and → evil, brought for the first time a historical dimension to what had previously been a timeless worldview. Elements were spiritualized as "holy immortals" (Amesha Spentas), and ethical actions were related to them. God and humans could act by the same Good Mind (Vohu Manah). Zoroaster also had earthly "helpers" (Saoshyants) in the conflict, whose work he discerned in a kind of realized → eschatology. After death the truthful and liars would be separated at the "bridge of decision," the good (i.e., Zoroaster's followers) being able to cross the bridge, the bad being afraid to do so.

The strictness of decision that Zoroaster demanded seems to have stirred up the hatred of his contemporaries, so that he had to flee. His new protector, Vishtaspa, was king of northern Khwārizm (south of the Aral Sea). The message of Zoroaster spread there, and then in his original homeland.

7. Zoroastrianism
Soon after Zoroaster's death his teaching spread west by way of central Afghanistan, not by conscious mission but because the Iranians found in his new unambiguously ethical interpretation an essential completion of their own religion. Later the Persian emperors accepted Zoroastrianism, relating truth to their own legitimacy and falsehood to the position of their political opponents. The cultic practices of the Median magi were integrated into Zoroastrianism, leading to the exposure of the dead on special towers. The message of Zoroaster was reinterpreted. Gods that had become irrelevant with the worship of Ahura Mazda were given a new meaning (as Mithra or Anahita). The dualism was not just that of the two chief gods but also of demons and the saving immortals and other good spirits. The "bridge of decision" now led to a sphere of perfect life, or endless lights. The wicked could also cross it but would fall into → hell.

In the period of the Sassanids (224-651), Zoroastrianism became a state religion. The power of Ohrmuzd (= earlier Ahura Mazda) and that of the king were the same, as were also the rebellions of the king's opponents and of Ahriman (= earlier Angra Mainyu). A network of burial towers (the *dakhma*, "tower of silence") and hierarchically graded fire-temples covered the land. Haoma was drunk again, but now for purification. The religious system became a cosmology with a cosmic year of 12,000 years. The religious tradition that had developed since Zoroaster was assembled and given a form corresponding to the cult (Avesta).

Zoroastrianism still lives on among the so-called Iranis in Yazd, Kermān, and Tehran, and among the Parsis who moved to Gujarat, India, in the 8th century and organized themselves in the 13th century.

8. Hellenism and Syncretism

After Alexander the Seleucids (from 312 B.C.), the Diodotids (from 239 B.C.), and several Indo-Scythian states (up to the 3rd cent. A.D.) made the Iranian territories and peoples quantitatively the most important agents of → Hellenism. They were culturally strong and pure Greek only in these areas and neighboring satrapies (i.e., Bactria, Aria, and Gandhara — today the Persian province Khorāsān, Afghanistan, and northern Pakistan), while between them and the Hellenized areas that linked the Semitic and Hellenistic worlds in the West, their presence seems to have been very minimal. Politically, the Parthians were its liquidators; culturally, while leaving it in the cities, they restored Iranian beliefs and Zoroastrianism in rural areas from the third century B.C. For various reasons Hellenistic religion adopted so many Iranian elements in zones of contact (→ Syncretism) that their transmission to Mediterranean Hellenism has left proportionately small, although discernible, traces.

The royal ideology of many Hellenistic rulers and several whole dynasties (→ Emperor Worship) were influenced by Iranian ruler charisma, or royal glory (the *khvarnah*). The phenomenon of → magic received its normative representatives, its theory, and its name from the magi, who by symbiosis with neo-Babylonian Chaldeans and the subsequent Hellenization had become a mobile guild of diviners, experts in nature and healing, everyday ritualists, rainmakers, and astrologers. Many demonologies (→ Demons) took on new forms and a dualistic character. Iranian speculation about infinite time (Zurvān Akarana, "Eternal Lord") gave a new dimension to aeon theology. Iranian-Greek theocracies changed the nature of the gods in many mythologies, among them those that became the teaching of the Mithra mysteries (→ Hellenistic-Roman Religion) in Asia Minor and later in Rome.

9. Ancient Judaism and Early Christianity

By the second century B.C. futurist eschatology in conflict with foreign Hellenistic rule had developed into national Iranian → apocalyptic. Structural similarities with Jewish apocalyptic are explained by similar conditions of origin. In the first century A.D. the two traditions converged even in details (e.g., in

angelology, demonology, world conflagration, resurrection, though not the Messiah). The exegesis of the Book of Daniel and the tradition of the Oracle of Hystaspes give evidence of the convergence. In the eschatology of the early church and the West as a whole, the idea of a millennium (the final millennium in the Zoroastrian cosmic year) came in by way of Rev. 20:2-10, where we also find the serpent in the form of a cosmic monster.

10. Gnosticism

→ Gnostic Sethianism contained a doctrine of cosmic ages that → Manichaeanism developed as a cosmogony after the Zoroastrian model, using peripheral older Iranian traditions in Middle Persian, Parthian, and Sogdian forms. For three generations there has been scholarly debate about an Iranian background for Gnosticism. The question is a good one as concerns the *salvator-salvandus* idea, the heavenly journey of the → soul, anticosmic dualism, and the dualism of light and darkness. Iranian influence would be on the nonhistorical surface, but Iranian (mostly Zoroastrian or Zurvanite) structures of thought played a role in dialectical historical processes that in many places led to central Gnostic statements.

11. Shiite Islam

→ Shia, which has been dominant in Iran since 1501 and which expects the hidden twelfth imam, or Mahdi, had its center in Arab countries (Iraq and Lebanon) and became the confession of the dominant Safawids in Anatolia. It was thus as non-Iranian as → Islam in general. Yet the local coloring that it was given by the neo-Persian that is spoken and written by the majority of Shiites, and by all of them in Iran, raises the question whether the many Iranian traditions (religious, legal, etc.) have not had an impact in modern as well as medieval Iran. Has the returning imam something to do with the Saoshyants, the → mysticism with Zoroastrian idealism? Is there a link between the orders and the former male guilds? Continuities of this kind are not certain, but popular belief suggests many common motifs and symbols, and the → esotericism suggests pre-Islamic illuminative or metaphysical movements.

One might speak of a kinship between Iranian → spirituality and Neoplatonic (→ Platonism) or Gnostic thought. In many forms it produced an independent → theosophy (e.g., in Suhrawardī in the 12th cent.), though this association would always be regarded as an exaggeration and result in inner conflicts. Thus Shiite insistence on the link between divine inspiration *(hulūl)* and the genealogy of the imams might be regarded as an institutional reaction to the free inspiration of "zealots" *(ghulāt)*, which leads to intellectual and political → anarchy. Paradoxically the Twelver Shiites in this way endowed their imams with a halo of legitimacy (the *khvarnah,* or *farr)* that they themselves never claimed and that had already been conferred on ancient Iranian rulers. The truly righteous scholar *(faqīh)*, who represents the hidden imam on earth, profits from this legitimacy (see arts. 107-12 of the constitution of November 15, 1979). Thus an incontestably national self-consciousness can shine, even through the new institutions of the Islamic Republic of Iran.

→ Mystery Religions

Bibliography: K. BARR, C. COLPE, and M. BOYCE, "Die Religion der alten Iranier / Zarathustra und der frühe Zoroastrismus / Der spätere Zoroastrismus," *HRG* 2.265-372 • M. BOYCE, *A Persian Stronghold of Zoroastrianism* (Lanham, Md., 1989); idem, *Zoroastrianism: Its Antiquity and Constant Vigour* (Costa Mesa, Calif., 1992) • *The Cambridge History of Iran* (6 vols.; Cambridge, 1968-86) • C. COLPE, "Historische und religiös-politische Konfliktpositionen im iranisch-irakischen Krieg," *Praxis der Unwelt- und Friedenserziehung* (vol. 3; ed. J. Calließ and R. E. Lob; Düsseldorf, 1988) 671-94 • P. GIGNOUX, *Recurrent Patterns in Iranian Religions: From Mazdaism to Sufism* (Paris, 1992) • G. GNOLI, "Iranian Religions," *EncRel(E)* 7.277-80 • K. GREUSSING, ed., *Religion und Politik im Iran* (Berlin, 1981) • H. W. HAUSSIG, ed., *Götter und Mythen der kaukasischen und iranischen Völker* (Stuttgart, 1986) • J. NEUSNER, *Judaism and Zoroastrianism at the Dusk of Late Antiquity* (Atlanta, 1993); idem, *Judaism, Christianity, and Zoroastrianism in Talmudic Babylonia* (Lanham, Md., 1986) • S. A. NIGOSIAN, *The Zoroastrian Faith: Tradition and Modern Research* (Montreal, 1993) • S. SHAKED, *Dualism in Transformation: Varieties of Religion in Sassanian Iran* (London, 1994); idem, *From Zoroastrian Iran to Islam: Studies in Religious History and Intercultural Contacts* (Brookfield, Vt., 1995).

CARSTEN COLPE

Iraq

1. Geography and Economy
2. Political Development
3. Religion
4. Religious Policy
5. Shiite Role
6. Position of Christians

	1960	1980	2000
Population (1,000s):	6,847	13,007	23,109
Annual growth rate (%):	3.05	3.27	2.86

Area: 435,052 sq. km. (167,975 sq. mi.)

A.D. *2000*

Population density: 53/sq. km. (138/sq. mi.)
Births / deaths: 3.40 / 0.54 per 100 population
Fertility rate: 4.80 per woman
Infant mortality rate: 39 per 1,000 live births
Life expectancy: 69.4 years (m: 68.0, f: 70.9)
Religious affiliation (%): Muslims 96.0, Christians 3.2 (indigenous 1.4, Roman Catholics 1.1, other Christians 0.7), other 0.8.

1. Geography and Economy

Iraq's population is mostly Arabs, with about 23 percent → Kurds. The Tigris and Euphrates Rivers create favorable conditions for agriculture, which is but poorly developed. Oil is the most important economic factor. It brought in 26 billion dollars in 1980 and is the basis of a large-scale development program. As a result of the Gulf Wars and the economic boycott imposed by the United Nations since 1990, however, this program largely came to a standstill.

2. Political Development

With the fall of the Ottoman Empire at the end of World War I, Iraq came under British mandate and then achieved independence in 1932. The 1958 revolution put an end to the monarchy and eliminated British influence. The Arab Socialist Ba'th Party took over in 1968. The party, which promotes an → ideology of Arab → socialism, is attempting a comprehensive transformation of the economy and the society. It views itself as a progressive party shaping the sociopolitical process.

The long Kurdish War ended in 1975 when an arrangement with the shah of Iran stopped Iranian aid to the Kurds. In 1979 Saddam Hussein assumed all more important state and party offices (including president and general secretary of the Ba'th Party). He tried to counter the danger emanating from Ayatollah Khomeini's Islamic revolution in Iran by waging a preventative war with Iran between 1980 and 1988, when this Gulf War ended in a cease-fire. The occupation of Kuwait by Iraqi troops on August 2, 1990, resulted in the second Gulf War (January 17–February 27, 1991) in which the anti-Iraq coalition, led by the United States, forced Iraq to withdraw. The social situation of the Iraqi people deteriorated as a result of the economic blockade imposed by the U.N. Security Council. In March 1997 the first transports of foodstuffs arrived in Iraq within the framework of the program "Oil for Food." Attempts by the Iraqi leadership to prevent U.N. representatives from inspecting and destroying Iraqi chemical and bacteriological weapons programs were met by repeated air strikes carried out by the United States and Great Britain.

3. Religion

Among Iraqi Muslims, the Shiites are the largest religious group (55 percent; → Shia, Shiites). Other religions are represented by relatively small numbers of Yezidis, Mandaeans, Jews (→ Judaism), and → Baha'is.

The most significant Christian group is the Chaldeans, numbering between 500,000 and 600,000 and having been united with Rome since the 16th century (→ Uniate Churches). Its → patriarch resides in Baghdad. The next largest groups are the Catholic Syrian Church and the → Syrian Orthodox (Jacobite) Church, each with less than one-tenth as many adherents. Armenians in Iraq mostly belong to the → Armenian Apostolic (Gregorian) Church, but a minority to the Catholic Armenian Church. Other, even smaller Christian groups include → Nestorians (the Apostolic Catholic Assyrian Church of the East), → Roman Catholics, Greek Orthodox (→ Orthodox Church), → Anglicans, and various Protestant groups.

4. Religious Policy

In the interests of maintaining internal stability, the Ba'th Party follows a secular policy with strict separation of religion and the state. From the Islamic side charges have been made that the party wants to replace Islam by its own ideology. The party respects Islam as a significant part of the Arab legacy but will not accept it as the state religion. Since the war with Iran, and even more so since the Gulf War in 1991, Saddam Hussein has tried to use Islam to lend legitimacy to his regime by portraying himself as a pious Muslim, including the reintroduction of the *basmala* formula in speeches (*Bismillāhi rahmāni rahīm*, "In the name of God, the Merciful, the Compassionate") and the addition of the words "Allahu akbar" (God is great) to the Iraqi flag.

5. Shiite Role

The Shiites have always felt repressed by the Sunnites (→ Sunna) and oppose the policies of the Ba'th Sunnites. There has been periodic unrest, for example, in 1979 after Khomeini returned to Iran

from exile. The general revolt for which Iran called, however, did not take place. In 1980 a secret organization (ad-Da'wa) was discovered, and about 60 leading Shiites, including their head, Ayatollah Baqir as-Sadr, were executed. An uprising of the Shiites after the end of the Gulf War was brutally put down in 1991.

Already in 1978 the government had put the Shiite clergy under its own control, supervising the income from religious endowments. But Saddam Hussein also sought better relations with the Shiites, stressing the compatibility of his policy with the principles of Islam and increasing government subsidies for → mosques.

6. Position of Christians

With its secular policy the regime grants toleration to the Christian → minorities. Legally, there is no discrimination against Christians; they can hold the highest offices. In 1999 the foreign minister, Tariq Aziz, was a Chaldean Christian. Christians generally have a better education and are especially well represented in the urban middle class, particularly as physicians and lawyers. Because of the opposition of Shiites and Kurds, the government increasingly seeks the support of the Christians, especially the Chaldeans, who have largely remained loyal. The situation is more difficult for non-Arabic minorities, such as the Assyrians and Armenians, who feel their identity threatened by the totalitarian claims of the Arabic nationalism attaching to Ba'th ideology.

→ Islam and Christianity

Bibliography: H. ANSCHÜTZ and P. HARB, *Christen im Vorderen Orient. Kirchen, Ursprünge, Verbreitung. Eine Dokumentation* (Hamburg, 1985) • L. CHABRY and A. CHABRY, *Politique et minorités au Proche-Orient* (Paris, 1984) • J. JOSEPH, *Muslim-Christian Relations and Inter-Christian Rivalries in the Middle East* (New York, 1983) • R. LAFITTE, "Chrétiens d'Irak. Rien n'est jamais acquis," *Cahiers de l'Orient* 48 (1997) 73-79 • B. LANDRON, *Chrétiens et musulmans en Irak* (Paris, 1994) • R. LE COZ, *L'église d'Orient. Chrétiens d'Irak, d'Iran et de Turquie* (Paris, 1995) • J. YACOUB, *The Assyrian Question* (Chicago, 1986) • G. YONAN, *Assyrer heute. Kultur, Sprache, Nationalbewegung der Aramäisch sprechenden Christen im Nahen Osten. Verfolgung und Exil* (Hamburg, 1978).

THOMAS KOSZINOWSKI

Ireland

	1960	*1980*	*2000*
Population (1,000s):	2,834	3,401	3,574
Annual growth rate (%):	0.29	0.87	0.23

Area: 70,285 sq. km. (27,137 sq. mi.)

A.D. *2000*

Population density: 51/sq. km. (132/sq. mi.)
Births / deaths: 1.36 / 0.85 per 100 population
Fertility rate: 1.80 per woman
Infant mortality rate: 6 per 1,000 live births
Life expectancy: 77.4 years (m: 74.7, f: 80.2)
Religious affiliation (%): Christians 97.3 (Roman Catholics 89.2, Anglicans 3.9, unaffiliated 2.3, other Christians 1.9), nonreligious 2.2, other 0.5.

1. Churches
  1.1. Roman Catholic Church
  1.2. Church of Ireland
  1.3. Presbyterian Church in Ireland
  1.4. Methodist Church in Ireland
  1.5. Other Churches
2. Interdenominational and
  Ecumenical Organizations
3. Church and State
4. Other Religions

Although Ireland became two states in 1922 — with the establishment of the Irish Free State, which became the Republic of Ireland in 1949, and Northern Ireland, which remained part of the United Kingdom — the churches remained organized on an all-island basis. The pattern of membership distribution of the various churches on the island, however, is not uniform in the two states.

1. Churches

1.1. *Roman Catholic Church*

The Irish Catholic Church, which traces its roots in Ireland to at least the beginning of the fifth century, is the largest church on the island. The 1996 *Irish Catholic Directory* gives the Roman Catholic population in Ireland in 1994 as 3,919,568, which is 75 percent of the total population of the island. The church is served by 3,714 diocesan clergy in 26 → dioceses; the primate is the archbishop of Armagh. The membership of the church represents 92.5 percent of the population of the Republic of Ireland and 38.5 percent of the population in Northern Ireland.

In 1937 the Catholic Church was accorded a special place in the constitution of the Republic of Ireland, which was subsequently abolished by referendum in 1972. With a high average attendance at → mass, however, the church retains great influence in the Republic of Ireland and is associated with Gaelic nationalist culture throughout the land.

From the earliest days of Christianity in Ireland, a strong missionary movement to other countries was evident. This impulse has continued through the work of a variety of religious → orders that have been active above all in the educational and medical spheres.

The church in both states is heavily involved in → education, with primary and secondary schools and teacher training; though funded by the different governments, it is under the direct control of the church authorities. A wide range of social and medical services have also been provided by the church, though these are increasingly being brought under state control. Because of the high incidence of urban deprivation, a number of informal Catholic organizations have emerged to focus on the issues of justice (→ Righteousness, Justice) and → peace and to try to tackle → unemployment.

1.2. *Church of Ireland*

With the establishing of the Church of England in the 16th century, the government of Ireland passed into the hands of Anglicans (→ Anglican Communion). The Church of Ireland emerged in a manner parallel to that of the Church of England. Reinforced by the "planting" of English people who were faithful to the government in England, and who also provided the economic substructure for that government in Ireland, Anglicanism became associated with the establishment and the "ascendancy," and with the Anglo-Irish section of the population on the island. In law the Church of Ireland was the established church until 1870.

Statistics of 1991 showed the membership of the Church of Ireland as 371,150, serviced by 484 clergy in 10 dioceses and 2 archdioceses. The primate is the archbishop of Armagh. The membership comprised 2.5 percent of the population in the Republic of Ireland and 18 percent of the population in Northern Ireland.

In the past the Church of Ireland was associated with the main institutions of the state and with the universities. Since disestablishment, however, this relationship has ended, and membership has been showing a gradual decline in the Republic of Ireland. The church has been involved in overseas missionary work.

1.3. *Presbyterian Church in Ireland*

The Presbyterian Church in Ireland (→ Reformed and Presbyterian Churches) emerged as part of the process of settlement, as did the Church of Ireland.

The majority of the settlers came from Scotland and the church is regarded as having developed the "psychology of colonial frontiersmen." This community, which was largely based in what is now known as Northern Ireland, became identified as Ulster-Scots. In 1997 there were 297,205 members in the church, supported by 430 ministers and organized in 21 presbyteries. The membership of the church comprised 23 percent of the population in Northern Ireland and 0.4 percent in the Republic of Ireland. For much of its history the church was regarded as being → "dissenter" and was subject to penal laws in the same way as the Catholic Church. This situation led to a large emigration to America, where Irish Presbyterians were very influential in the founding of the state and its institutions, especially universities.

The Presbyterian Church in Ireland has engaged in missionary work outside Ireland. In 1873 it became the first Presbyterian church to seek the foundation of the World Presbyterian Alliance, now the → World Alliance of Reformed Churches. Members of this church tend to be associated with the business and professional worlds, though its influence throughout the population of Northern Ireland is evident.

1.4. *Methodist Church in Ireland*

In 1996 the Methodist Church in Ireland (→ Methodist Churches) had 58,659 members, supported by 120 ministers and composing some 2 percent of the population of the whole island and 0.14 percent of the Republic of Ireland. Formed as a result of frequent visits to Ireland by John → Wesley (1703-91), it has been very active in overseas missionary work.

1.5. *Other Churches*

A number of other churches and communities exist in Ireland with much smaller memberships, including the Non-Subscribing Presbyterian Church (mainly in Northern Ireland), → Moravian Church, Religious Society of → Friends (two-thirds of whom live in Northern Ireland), → Lutheran Church (organized as one congregation throughout Ireland), → Salvation Army (mainly in Northern Ireland), Baptist Union (→ Baptists), and Free Presbyterian Church (the church of Ian Paisley).

2. Interdenominational and Ecumenical Organizations

The *Irish InterChurch Process* (Ballymascanlon), established in 1972, brought together representatives of the Roman Catholic Church and member churches of the Irish Council of Churches to discuss divisive theological questions and questions of common social concern. Since 1986 this process has

been serviced by two advisory committees — on theological questions and on social questions — in the attempt to develop common theological perspectives and action throughout Ireland.

In 1923 the United Council of Christian Churches and Religious Communions in Ireland was established. Its member churches were the Protestant churches in Ireland, and it undertook a wide range of interchurch and social activities. This body was superseded in 1966 by the *Irish Council of Churches* (→ National Council of Churches), which is serviced by a full-time secretariat. The main member churches of the council are also member churches of the British Council of Churches, since Northern Ireland is part of the United Kingdom. The Irish Council of Churches reflects the concerns of similar councils throughout the world.

In 1999 a proposal was discussed by each church in Ireland to establish a conference of churches in Ireland that would formally recognize and legally institutionalize the *Irish Inter-church Meeting* and that would have the effect of merging the Irish Council of Churches with it. At the time of writing, the discussions are continuing.

Tripartite conversations began in 1968, sponsored by the Church of Ireland, Presbyterians, and Methodists, after various bilateral conversations involving different combinations of these churches failed to bring the churches into → unity. The conversations came to an inconclusive end in 1988.

In the past 20 years a wide variety of interchurch bodies (about 65) have emerged to promote specific issues (e.g., interchurch families and community work). A number of reconciliation centres have also been established to promote ecumenism and peace (→ Ecumenism, Ecumenical Movement; Local Ecumenism), including the Corrymeela Community and the Glencree Centre for Reconciliation. Many of these groups have arisen as a response to the current conflict in Northern Ireland.

Both formal and informal contacts have transformed a situation in which the churches had tended to define themselves over against each other. Now, however, although the churches are still to a large extent associated with their respective cultural communities, no church is able to make a statement without its being sensitive to the reaction of the other churches.

3. Church and State

No Irish church is established in either the Republic of Ireland or Northern Ireland. All churches feel free to be critical of the governments and the institutions of state while enjoying state support for some of their activities (e.g., education; → Church and State). The Catholic Church, however, does wield considerable influence in the Republic of Ireland and has tried to ensure that the law of the state reflects Roman Catholic moral teaching (e.g., in matters of divorce and → abortion).

4. Other Religions

Muslim and Jewish communities exist in the Republic of Ireland and in Northern Ireland (→ Islam; Judaism). The Muslim community has 10,000 members in the Republic of Ireland and 5,000 in Northern Ireland, according to figures published in 1999. The Jewish community, largely Orthodox, was established in the 19th century and participates in the Irish Council of Christians and Jews, founded in 1981 (→ Jewish-Christian Dialogue). In 1996 there were 1,000 members each in the Republic of Ireland and in Northern Ireland. A number of → new religions have begun to appear in the Republic of Ireland in recent years, but as yet it is difficult to assess their size or importance.

Bibliography: D. Bowen, *History and the Shaping of Irish Protestantism* (New York, 1995) • P. J. Corish, *The Irish Catholic Experience: A Historical Survey* (Dublin, 1985) • I. Ellis, *Vision and Reality: A Survey of Twentieth Century Irish Inter-church Relations* (Belfast, 1992) • G. A. Ford, *The Protestant Reformation in Ireland, 1590-1641* (Frankfurt, 1985) • E. Gallagher and S. Worrall, *Christians in Ulster 1968-80* (London, 1982) • J. A. Watt, *The Church and the Two Nations in Medieval Ireland* (Cambridge, 1970) • J. H. Whyte, *Church and State in Modern Ireland, 1923-1970* (2d ed.; Dublin, 1980)

Alan D. Falconer

Irenaeus of Lyons

Irenaeus of Lyons (fl. 180) was a second-century → bishop whose work shaped the Scriptures, → exegesis, institutions, theology, and → spirituality of early Christianity so profoundly that his imprint remains discernible almost two millennia later. Through his teacher, Polycarp, Irenaeus retained a link to the first Christian generation, since Polycarp had talked "with John and with others who had seen the Lord" (Eusebius *Hist. eccl.* 5.20.6). Eusebius preserved part of the letter in which Irenaeus described his early years with Polycarp in Smyrna (modern-day Turkish İzmir). When Irenaeus traveled from his home in Asia Minor to the Rhone River town of Lugdunum (modern Lyons), he found compatriots set-

tled there. Some formed part of the church in which he was a presbyter and whose emissary he was to Eleutherius, bishop of Rome, after the martyrdoms of 177 (5.4.1-2). When Pothinus, head of the church of Lyons, died in prison, Irenaeus succeeded him (5.5.8).

Two complete works of Irenaeus have survived: *Eis tēn epideixin tou apostolikou kērygmatos* (Proof/ Demonstration of the apostolic preaching) and *Adversus haereses* (Against → heresies). The former, recovered in 1904, is a brief apologetic work couched in catechetical form. The latter is an extended reply to the → Gnostics (esp. the Valentinians) in which he describes those known to him (bk. 1), rebuts them rhetorically (bk. 2), and proclaims the Christian positions through the → interpretation of Scripture (bks. 3-4).

Fundamental to Irenaean thought is the → Rule of Faith, or Rule of Truth (see proof 3, *Adv. haer.* 1.9.5–1.10.2). It governs right exegesis, and the Scriptures (the object of the exegesis) in turn explain the Rule of Faith. The relationship here may seem circular, but in practice Irenaeus understands the connection between the Rule of Faith and the Scriptures primarily as dialogic. Text and interpretation, Scripture and tradition, word and experience are less mirror images of one another than conversation partners, each amplifying and correcting the insights of the other.

The Bible known to Irenaeus certainly included the Jewish Scriptures, the four Gospels, a collection of Paul's letters, Acts, Revelation, 1 Peter, 1 and 2 John, and possibly also *Shepherd of Hermas*. Not only did Irenaeus first name the collection of Christian documents the "New Testament" (*Adv. haer.* 4.9.1), but he was the first to reflect thematically on biblical interpretation. In a prior step Christians had already effected a transformation of the sacred writings of the Jews by reading them as witnesses to Christ. At each stage what was involved was a theological reading of the Scriptures. Irenaeus asserted that the Scriptures belong to the church in such a way that *any valid reading must be congruent with the faith of that community* (e.g., 1.3.6). The question then becomes who enunciates the faith of the community.

Irenaeus contributed a theory of → authority that correlated the right of teaching (and thus of interpretation) with succession in office. In essence, he argues as follows: Jesus taught → truth to his disciples, all the truth necessary for salvation, intending that they hand it on in its entirety to their successors. These successors are the bishops, whence the importance Irenaeus attached to the apostolic lineage of any see. The process of → tradition is thus linked to a process of apostolic succession. He buttressed his argument by referring to the "succession lists" maintained by the churches, enumerating that of the church of → Rome (*Adv. haer.* 3.3.2-3).

Irenaeus stood for → faith in one God revealed by the one Son, → Jesus Christ, whose teaching was preserved in the one church through the one authoritative episcopal succession. In his view, the bishops succeed the → apostles through the gift of the Spirit. Thus for him the faith is ordinarily validated by the church's authoritative teachers, the bishops; even his strongest passages on this topic, however, refer also to those whose belief seems to have been more immediately under the action of the Spirit of God (see *Adv. haer.* 3.4.2 and 3.24.1–3.25.7). Ultimately faith rests on the Jesus of the church, and allowance must always be made for the role of the Spirit. The situation undoubtedly was somewhat more ambiguous than Irenaeus's analysis of the doctrine of succession would suggest.

Irenaeus held an economic Trinitarianism, maintaining that there is one God (the Father), who is revealed by the one Son, Jesus Christ. The strong emphasis on the oneness of God and of Christ counters any literal reading of the Gnostic myths of the pleroma. His rudimentary Trinitarian references (e.g., *Adv. haer.* 3.16.3) assign roles to each of the three persons in the divine economy. In other places (e.g., 4.20.1) he refers to the Son and the Spirit as "the hands of God," who form and adorn the → creation.

Irenaean Christological emphases include Jesus as the recapitulation of Adam (from his reading of Rom. 5:12-19) and insight into the relation between → incarnation and → salvation. He insists that "it was necessary for the Mediator between God and humanity, through his own being at home in both, to lead both back to friendship and concord" (*Adv. haer.* 3.18.7). Here we have an early enunciation of what is today termed the soteriological principle, namely, that in the incarnation what Christ took to himself is what was saved. This principle, which remained influential in the Christological controversies through the Council of → Chalcedon (451), was applied to such questions as whether the Incarnate One had a human soul.

Concern for the reality of Christ's human body finds an appropriate parallel in Irenaeus's understanding of the → Eucharist. Irenaeus maintained that the consecrated elements are indeed the body and blood of Christ. In reflections wholly compatible with the thought of John 6, he writes, "Just as the bread which is from the earth, receiving the invocation of God, is now not common bread but Eucha-

rist, constituted from two things, earthly and heavenly, so our bodies receiving the Eucharist are no longer corruptible, having the hope of → resurrection" (*Adv. haer.* 4.18.5). The parallel is clear: as bread receives word to become Eucharist, so through the medium of the Eucharist flesh receives spirit to enable humans to share in the risen life. This conception of the Eucharist, while still theologically somewhat naive, is dynamic and respectful of the diverse elements joined sacramentally. It exerted immense influence in shaping patristic sacramental theology from the second century through the time of → Augustine.

In the Irenaean perspective, the human person is what God became in order that humans might be drawn into God's family. The nourishment for that process is the Eucharist, and the completion of the process will come in resurrection. As to the here and now, humans are in the image and likeness of God. The image, being in the flesh, was not lost in the fall. An aspect of the likeness to God is human → freedom, which is also retained after the fall. Irenaeus holds that humans use free will to taste good and evil, learning by experience to choose the good and reject the bad. Ultimately, through God's vivifying gift of grace, humans are called to grow into the fullness of life, the vision of God: "The glory of God is the human person fully alive, and the life of the human person is the vision of God" (*Adv. haer.* 4.20.7).

Bibliography: D. L. BALÁS, "The Use and Interpretation of Paul in Irenaeus's Five Books *Adversus haereses*," *SecCent* 9 (1992) 27-39 • D. J. BINGHAM, *Irenaeus's Use of Matthew's Gospel in "Adversus haereses"* (Louvain, 1998) • Y. M. BLANCHARD, *Aux sources du canon, le témoignage d'Irénée* (Paris, 1993) • M. A. DONOVAN, *One Right Reading? A Guide to Irenaeus* (Collegeville, Minn., 1997) • J. FANTINO, *La théologie d'Irénée. Lecture des Écritures en réponse à exégèse gnostique: Une approche trinitaire* (Paris, 1994) • R. M. GRANT, *Irenaeus of Lyons* (New York, 1997) • D. L. HOFFMAN, *Women and Gnosticism in Irenaeus and Tertullian* (Lewiston, N.Y., 1995) • D. MINN, *Irenaeus* (Washington, D.C., 1994) • R. A. NORRIS JR., "Theology and Language in Irenaeus of Lyon," *ATR* 76 (1994) 285-95 • T. L. TIESSEN, *Irenaeus on the Salvation of the Unevangelized* (Metuchen, N.J., 1993).

MARY ANN DONOVAN, S.C.

Irrationalism

1. The term "irrationalism" comes from the Lat. *irrationalis,* which ranges in meaning from the opposite of *rationalis* (i.e., "incomprehensible" or "illogical") to the opposite of "reasonable" (i.e., an attitude that is not subject to the universal and subjectively communicable laws and structures of thought but determined by illogical forces). According to the position vis-à-vis the rational and the related evaluation, there are two forms of irrationality: that which is above the rational (i.e., the suprarational or transintelligible) and that which is below it (i.e., the pre- or sublogical). If by "rationality" we mean the necessary regularity of the analytic and discursive understanding, then ontologically the former relates to the rational totality that is beyond the understanding, the → absolute, the divine sphere; the latter, then, relates to the individual, particular, or unique that is below the understanding. In → psychology, this subrational takes the form of the emotional, the impulsive life, the dark forces of the mind and soul; in history, the form of the contingently historical, of vital creative forces; and in → nature, the form of the accidental. Epistemologically, the former comprises abilities that transcend the understanding: → reason, intellectual intuition, → faith, and → revelation; the latter, those that are subordinate to the understanding: sensory perception, → intuition, feeling, emotion, and → empathy.

Unlike → rationalism, irrationalism has produced no philosophical positions or trends of its own; it arises only within other philosophical theories. The point is usually to clarify the relation between the rational and the irrational, showing either how they counterbalance one another or how one dominates the other.

2. According to the epistemological approach taken, irrationalism can assume many forms. It may be → *agnosticism,* which claims that we cannot know the suprarational. It may have the form of *believing because absurd,* that is, religious → paradox that accepts the suprarational because it is against our understanding. It may be → *negative theology,* which in the *docta ignorantia* (learned ignorance) teaching of Nicholas of Cusa (1401-64) begins with the rational but then thinks we can indicate what lies beyond it only by the *via negativa* (negative way) by renouncing finite rational predicates or, paradoxically, by a coincidence of opposites. It may be → *mysticism,* which embraces the other world by illumination or inner vision. It may be a *theology of revelation* that goes beyond theory to ontic revelation, as in the case of F. H. Jacobi (1743-1819) or S. Kierkegaard (1813-55).

3. When there is equation with the subrational — → life, instinct, impulse, emotion, feeling, → love, immediacy, individuality, historical forces, → chance, and so forth — irrationalism may be historically viewed as *emotionalism,* as in the Sturm und Drang movement or in → Romanticism. Or it may be viewed methodologically as → *historicism* (esp. in 19th-cent. discussions). Or it may be viewed philosophically as *life philosophy* (→ Philosophy of Life) or → *existentialism* according to W. Dilthey (1833-1911), M. Heidegger (1889-1976), and J.-P. Sartre (1905-80).

Whereas these positions recognize the irrational as the unavoidable basis of the rational, extreme rationalistic positions reject the irrational as unreasonable. → Marxism pronounced the sharpest and most unequivocal verdict, viewing irrationalism as the opposite of scientific thought and → progress, as a disparagement of reason and understanding, and as an uncritical glorification of intuition. As such, it represents an aristocratic epistemology, a repudiation of social and historical progress, and a forging of myths (G. Lukács, 10).

4. The discussion of irrationalism achieved new relevance in the latter part of the 20th century. It did so in the field of *politics* in the form of a moral judgment on totalitarian systems like National Socialism, Stalinism, → fascism, and others, along with their irrational foundations and their inadmissible consequences, including → racism, the elimination of the Jews (→ Holocaust), the Soviet gulags, and myths such as that of blood and soil often underlying them. It did so also in the field of *philosophy,* where from the time of the provocative theses of the Paris avant-gardists (M. Foucault, J. Baudrillard, and J.-F. Lyotard) modern → philosophy has been brought under appraisal and a reversal is in process.

In philosophy the antithesis of rationalism and irrationalism — often under the symbols of Sarastro and the queen of the night, from Mozart's *Magic Flute* — is discussed in terms of the modern (→ Modernity) and the → postmodern. The modern is equated with → enlightenment, → freedom, → autonomy, → emancipation, subjectivity, but also systematization, a thrust toward unity, and a desire to generalize and equate concepts (T. W. Adorno; → Critical Theory). In contrast, the postmodern — which some decry as regression, while others laud it as modernity — is seen in complexity (of the world), heterogeneity, multiplicity of forms of life and speech, particularity, minority, also myth construction and irrationality.

Politically, irrationalism is negative. It is equated with lack of thought, reason, or responsibility, as well as with capricious action and an uncontrolled lust for power, uncritical ideologizing (→ Ideology), stereotypes of → enemies, and hate-filled → prejudices.

Philosophically, irrationalism is ambivalent. It has its supporters (as the modern euphoria for myth shows), who think that irrational emotional or mental forces complement more precise, abstract thinking, or who even rate mythical experience of the world above the scientific. It also has its critics, who see in it the dangers of anarchic → pluralism à la P. Feyerabend, of uncommitted → play and mere appearance, of a lack of any will for unity, and of apocalyptic visions.

→ Epistemology; Kantianism; Logic; Metaphysics

Bibliography: W. Barrett, *Irrational Man: A Study in Existential Philosophy* (New York, 1958) • G. R. Dodds, *The Greeks and the Irrational* (Berkeley, Calif., 1963) • H. P. Duerr, ed., *Die Wissenschaftler und das Irrationale* (2 vols.; Frankfurt, 1981) • E. Feil, *Antithetik neuzeitlicher Vernunft. "Autonomie-Heteronomie" und "rational-irrational"* (Göttingen, 1987) • G. Lukács, *Die Zerstörung der Vernunft* (Berlin, 1953) • R. L. Patterson, *Irrationalism and Rationalism in Religion* (Durham, N.C., 1954) • P. G. Swingle, *The Structure of Conflict* (New York, 1970).

Karen Gloy

Isaac

1. Biblical Tradition
2. History of Scholarship
3. Isaac in the NT

1. Biblical Tradition

Stories about Isaac appear in Genesis 17–28. Although they are largely to be ascribed to J, P is represented at the beginning (17:15-27) and end (27:46–28:9), and E in 21:1-7 and 22:1-19 (→ Pentateuch). Chap. 26 elaborates most fully on Isaac's life, including his adventures and quarrels in Gerar, God's theophany in Beer-sheba with the promise to bless Isaac, and his covenant with Abimelech.

2. History of Scholarship

Isaac has been described as a legendary figure (H. Gunkel; → Abraham), as a figure representing tribal history (O. Eißfeldt), though also as a histori-

cal individual, as a seminomadic leader, or as the founder of a cult (A. Alt). The Isaac narratives belong to an older cultural stage than do the West-Jordanian Jacob narratives (M. Noth) and reflect an era in which the Israelite tribes were not yet sedentary (→ Tribes of Israel) and had, in the course of seeking grazing areas, come into contact in southern → Palestine with the inhabitants of the settled countryside. A. Jepsen maintains the connection between the Isaac tradition and the North, adducing in support especially Amos 7:9 ("the high places of Isaac").

The figure of Isaac was enhanced when the theme of the → promise, previously bound to the cults of the "God of the Fathers" (Alt, Noth), was incorporated into the Israelite creed during the southern-Palestinian stage of the growth of the Pentateuch tradition. Although Isaac as the successor of → Jacob became established as one of Israel's patriarchs (→ Patriarchal History), his tradition receded in favor of that of Abraham (Noth).

3. Isaac in the NT

The most interesting occurrences of Isaac in the NT are Gal. 4:28-31 and Jas. 2:21-24. The former associates Hagar with the Sinai covenant and Sarah with the → covenant of → grace, into which her son, Isaac, enters. The latter adduces Abraham's sacrifice of Isaac as proof that → justification requires works as well as → faith.

→ Israel 1

Bibliography: A. Jepsen, "Zur Überlieferungsgeschichte der Vätergestalten," *WZ(L).GS* 2/3 (1983) 265-81 • R. Martin-Achard, "Isaac," *ABD* 3.461-70 • H.-J. Ritz, "Ισαάκ," *EDNT* 2.199-200. See also the bibliography in "Abraham."

William McKane

Isaiah, Book of

1. Overall Structure
2. Trito-Isaiah
3. Deutero-Isaiah
    3.1. Suffering Servant Songs
    3.2. Other Themes
4. First Isaiah

1. Overall Structure

Ever since B. Duhm's epochal commentary (1892), scholars have generally divided the Book of Isaiah into three parts:

- Isaiah I, chaps. 1–39, according to the dating in 1:1; 6:1; 36:1, the testament of the → prophet Isaiah from the eighth century B.C.;
- Isaiah II (Deutero-Isaiah), chaps. 40–55, which the reference to Babylon (43:14; 47) and the election of the Persian king Cyrus (558-29; Isa. 44:28; 45:1) identify as an exilic prophecy; and
- Isaiah III (Trito-Isaiah), chaps. 56–66, which the mention of the second → temple (§1) and of the rebuilding of → Jerusalem (60:7, 10) identifies as prophetic literature from the (early) postexilic period.

Faith in the presence and dominance of Israel's God permeates all three parts, with self-criticism in times of hope, consolation in times of despair, and guidance in times of rebuilding among wretched circumstances.

That witnesses from such disparate periods coalesced into a single book derives both from external factors (the usual length of ancient scrolls, plus the possibility that several prophets bore the name *yĕša'yāhû*, "Yahweh helps") and from the inner cohesion of the Isaiah tradition itself. The same comment applies also to the part added last, namely, the so-called Apocalypse of Isaiah (24–27). This small writing apparently grew in sequence from a series of late-prophetic oracles and responsory songs such that a kind of liturgy emerged. With its anticipation of a catastrophic final judgment (24:17-23; → Last Judgment) and a universal resurrection of the dead (25:8; 26:19), it recalls the kind of → apocalyptic articulated in Daniel.

Chaps. 33–35 provide virtually a key to understanding the Book of Isaiah as a whole. The dreadful Edom prophecy in chap. 34 transfers the catchword "[measuring] line," which in 28:13, 17 appears in a threat against Judah, first to Edom (34:11) and then into a salvific promise for Judah (34:17). Reversals of oracles of disaster into oracles of salvation are also found in 35:5 over against 6:9-10, and in 33:7 over against 29:1. Furthermore, Deutero-Isaiah comes into view in the divine predicate "king" ("the LORD is our king," 33:22; cf. 43:15; 52:7) and in the promise of miraculous profusion of water (35:7; cf. 41:17-19; 43:19-20). Finally, the sociocritical passage 33:7-8 points back to First Isaiah (e.g., chap. 5) as well as forward to Trito-Isaiah (e.g., 59:1-15; cf. also 33:14-22 with 10:20-23 and 65).

What are known as the Isaiah legends (chaps. 36–39) function as a bridge between the three parts of the book. The patriotic Isaiah portrayed here does not really fit with the Isaiah who comes to expression in 31:1-3 or 22:1-14, though he does admittedly harmonize well with the Zion theology in First Isaiah, whether that theology is (probably) authentic (1:21-26; 14:24-27) or appended (e.g., 2:2-5; 30:27-33). Chapter 39 points to Deutero-Isaiah with his fully developed Zion theology (40:9-10; 49:14-21; 54:11-17). The legends have been appropriated from 2 Kgs. 18:17–20:19, from the → Deuteronomistic history. The structure and appropriation of tradition in Isaiah 33–39 thus suggest a postexilic author living in Judah with access to both Deuteronomistic and exilic literature.

2. Trito-Isaiah

Trito-Isaiah combines themes that permeate the entire Book of Isaiah, for example, the notion of obduracy, blindness, and deafness, as well as the promise of healing these defects (cf. 6:9-10; 42:18-20; 43:8; 44:18; 59:9-10 with 29:18; 30:19-21; 42:7; 64:3-4), the critique of sacrifices (1:10-17; 43:22-28; 58), worship of foreign deities (cf. 57:3-13; 65:1-7 with 2:8; 17:7-11; 30:22; 44:9-20), and destruction and rebuilding (6:11; 44:26; 58:12; 60:10, 17-22; 61:4). These features identify the historical locus. The exile is past, but its wounds remain; the preexilic prophecy of doom must still be overcome; and the exilic prophecy of salvation offers the needed guidance and motivation.

These common features suggest that the linking of First Isaiah with Deutero-Isaiah possibly took place at the level of Trito-Isaiah. Statements from the two initial parts can be found in 57:14-20 in an extremely concentrated and independent reformulation. Strikingly, both 57:17b and 59:15 show a typically Deuteronomistic language. Because both this penitential confession as well as the lament in 63:7–64:12 and in the prophetic interrogation in chapter 58 attest elements from a worship context, the question arises whether the composition of the Book of Isaiah as a whole as well as its individual parts are not perhaps addressing liturgical needs. Other features suggesting a liturgical focus might include the sequence of disaster in First Isaiah and → salvation in Deutero-Isaiah/Trito-Isaiah, or the structure of chaps. 28–32, or even the interwoven accusations and laments in Deutero-Isaiah (e.g., 42:18-25; 43:22-28; 45:9-17; 46:8-13). The role of the → Sabbath (56:2; 58:13-14) and of the temple (60:7, 13; 66:20-21) might also suggest liturgical concerns. Isa. 56:7 even opens the temple cult to non-Jews, and 56:1-6 encourages the acceptance of → proselytes.

In contrast, we find efforts to delimit all non-Jews from the community (63:1-6; 66:15-16, 24; → Congregation) and to distinguish between the righteous and the unrighteous within it (57:19-21; 65). Such tensions suggest that the book was put together from various parts and that it also includes subsequent expansions in Trito-Isaiah. The vital energy of the Isaianic tradition even during the postexilic period is evoked by the ethical depth of 58:6-9a (expanded in 9b-12) and by the liberating power of 61:1-2 (incorporated in Luke 4:18-19).

3. Deutero-Isaiah

3.1. *Suffering Servant Songs*

Perhaps it was the basic author of Trito-Isaiah who edited Deutero-Isaiah and in the process inserted the Suffering Servant Songs (42:1-4; 49:1-6; 50:4-9; 52:13–53:12; with expansions in 42:5-9; 49:7-13; 50:10-11). The identity of the Suffering Servant is uncertain (→ Servant of the Lord). In Deutero-Isaiah, → Israel — in particular, those in exile — bears this title (41:8; 44:1 and elsewhere). The redactors probably also had this interpretation in mind, perhaps also inserting it into 49:3. The commission to engage in service *to* Israel in 49:5-6, however, and the juxtaposition of the "servant" and the community in the fourth song point to an individual rather than to a collective.

Whether the reference is to a → messianic figure, a ruler, or a past or present prophet, however, is uncertain. Much suggests that the Suffering Servant is the prophet from whom the core of Deutero-Isaiah ultimately derives. The other parts of Deutero-Isaiah may contain hints of the personality and biography of the prophet, but this conclusion depends on the respective interpretation of the texts. The Servant Songs, however, for one prepared to view them biographically, provide a sharp outline of the prophetic author himself.

3.2. *Other Themes*

Even apart from these songs, Deutero-Isaiah has been consciously composed and structured through a framework in 40:8, 10-11 and 55:10-13 (the power of God's word and the promise of return), through an organizing of its 50-70 textual units according to themes, contrast, and keyword resonance, and through various expansions (e.g., 45:9-10; 48:22, probably also the polemic against idols such as that in 44:9-20). The structuring, however, does not eliminate the distinct individual profile of the prophet standing behind Deutero-Isaiah.

Precisely the demonstration of → Yahweh's superiority over all other gods was especially important to the author, which he presented in disputation (40:27-31) or in judgment oracles (43:22-28; 44:6-8). Yahweh, whom the course of history had apparently repudiated, was nonetheless now, and would remain in the future, the master who can and would indeed guide history as he planned to a posi-

tive conclusion for Israel and to a disastrous end for Israel's oppressors. Accordingly, Deutero-Isaiah is dominated by genres such as predictions and oracles of salvation, imitating (or perhaps even exercising) thus the function of the cultic prophets in the → worship service, namely, to respond to laments and petitions with the assurance of divine aid (a conclusion one may draw in Psalm 6, for example, from the juxtaposition of vv. 1-7 and vv. 8-10).

The content of this promise, though variously altered, is always the same in Deutero-Isaiah: the → suffering of the exile has atoned for Israel's sin, and the exiles' return is imminent. This → hope is so ambitious that the earlier exodus seems but a weak reflection of the new one (43:16-21); indeed, even → creation itself seems a mere preparation for Israel's redemption (44:24-28). This message takes its cue from the political reality of the victorious campaigns by the Persian Cyrus (558-529 B.C.; cf. 44:28–45:7), which ultimately did indeed result in the fall of Babylon and the return to Judah, even though the former was not quite as catastrophic, and the latter not quite as triumphal, as the unknown exilic prophet anticipated.

The designation "Deutero-Isaiah" is justified by its various and clearly not merely redactionally appended connections with First Isaiah. The call scene before the heavenly council in 40:3-11 picks up on chap. 6; the concept of the witnesses in 43:10, 12; 44:8 on 8:2, 16; the reference to God's plan in 46:11 on 14:24-27; the reference to Israel's refinement in 48:10 on 1:22, 25; and so on. The tradition of First Isaiah seems to have traveled the path through the Babylonian exile and was thus not subject to Deuteronomistic redaction. During the exile, it elicited the quite contrary and yet congenial prophecy of Deutero-Isaiah. Then, having doubtless already been recast and expanded (for use in worship?), it was combined with Deutero-Isaiah at the level of Trito-Isaiah after the return home.

4. First Isaiah

Scholarship is uncertain about the form and the stages of growth of First Isaiah up to the exile and about the scope of later addenda. Various theories have been presented. O. Kaiser (in his OTL commentary) represents an extremely critical position, suggesting 11 developmental stages, the oldest being chaps. 36–39(!). A few others came from the sixth century, the 7 most important from the fifth century, and the rest later. U. Becker attributes some 20 verses — all of them oracles of salvation! — to the real Isaiah and postulates a growing Isaiah tradition from exilic times onward containing prophecies of doom and of salvation in a sequence of several stages. J. Barthel, however, assigns a considerable quantity of text material to the prophet of the eighth century.

H. Barth represents a mediating position, suggesting the presence in chaps. 2–32 of larger collections of authentic material put together in part by Isaiah himself, then a broad "Assyrian redaction" from the end of the seventh century, and finally a framework consisting of chaps. 1 and 33-39 from the (post)exilic period. In a similar vein, R. Kilian finds the presence of only a few pure oracles of disaster from Isaiah himself, with all oracles involving the Messiah, the remnant, Zion, anti-Assyrian sentiment, and repentance coming after the exile. H. Wildberger (in his BKAT commentary) represents a conventional position, finding a considerable basic collection of original Isaiah material, including oracles of salvation, in chaps. 1–12 and 28–32, also in 13–23; larger expansion did not take place until the exilic period, and then partly under the aspect of "salvation," partly under that of "disaster"; a final postexilic redaction occurs only in chaps. 11-12, 13-20, 24-27, 33-35, and 36-39. The closest scholars have come to a consensus regards the cycle involving the foreign nations, chaps. 13–23; here the view is that a postexilic redactor constructed this section after the model of other prophetic books (Jeremiah 46–51; Ezekiel 25–32), also using Isaianic material (in chaps. 17-18, 20, 22, and probably also 14).

For the rest, scholars observe a growth pattern not in linear strata but through the sequential addition of partial collections. The first (1:1–2:5) offers a cross-section through Isaiah's message, the second (2:6–5:30 and 9:8–12:6) especially his early proclamation, the third (6:1–9:7) oracles concerning the Syro-Ephraimite War (734/733), the fourth (28–32) concerning the Assyrian crisis (before 701 B.C.). All four, however, also contain non-Isaianic material largely of a salvific-consoling nature, especially the great concluding prophecies in 2:2-4(5); 9:2-7; 11:1-10 (and vv. 11-16); 32:15-20. This does not mean, however, that Isaiah proclaimed only disaster. Although the call account (6:9-10) might suggest as much, it was probably formulated later, nor does it exclude the possibility that it was an attempt to preserve Israel from judgment. Precisely such an attempt surfaces clearly in explicit admonitions (1:5, 16-17; 7:3-4; 28:12; 30:15) and reserved promises (1:21-26; 8:1-4; 10:5-15; 14:24-27; also 17:12-14 and 29:1-8?). Words of disaster, however, do clearly predominate (see merely 1:2-3; 5:1-7 [also vv. 8-25]; 8:11-14; 20; 28; 30).

Although these two aspects are difficult to harmonize, the extreme solutions mentioned above are of no help. The Isaianic borrowing from earlier salvific traditions is too concentrated and plausible (esp. from the tradition of Zion), the Isaianic language too multifaceted, and the multilinearity of the entire Isaianic tradition too obvious for one to conclude credibly that Isaiah himself was a one-sided prophet of doom (or of salvation). One can leave open the question whether he conceived judgment and → grace dialectically together or saw them coming one after the other, or whether his efforts at rescuing his doom-threatened people were repeatedly disappointed, prompting him to move from the proclamation of salvation to that of disaster. In any event, his final word is a biting No (22:1-14). Especially in the political sphere, Isaiah saw Israel and Judah fail its God, or its God fail his people. That precisely this God and this people, despite everything, had held to one another was to be brought to expression anew in the collections of First Isaiah and in Deutero-Isaiah and Trito-Isaiah, partly following and partly countering Isaiah himself.

→ Monarchy in Israel; Monotheism

Bibliography: Commentaries: B. DUHM (HKAT; 5th ed.; Göttingen, 1968; orig. pub., 1892) • K. ELLIGER (BKAT; Neukirchen, 1978) • G. FOHRER (ZBK; Zurich, 1966-67) • O. KAISER (OTL; Philadelphia, 1972-74) • J. L. MCKENZIE, *Second Isaiah* (AB; Garden City, N.Y., 1968) • C. WESTERMANN (OTL; Philadelphia, 1969) • H. WILDBERGER (BKAT; Neukirchen, 1978-82).

On 1-2: W. A. M. BEUKEN, "Isaiah Chapters lxv–lxvi: Trito-Isaiah and the Closure of the Book of Isaiah," *Congress Volume Leuven 1989* (ed. J. A. Emerton; Leiden, 1991) 204-21 • R. CLEMENTS, "The Unity of the Book of Isaiah," *Int* 36 (1982) 117-29 • G. I. EMMERSON, *Isaiah 56–66: OT Guides* (Sheffield, 1992) • C. A. EVANS, *To See and Not Perceive: Isaiah 6.9-10 in Early Jewish and Christian Interpretation* (Sheffield, 1989) • M. H. GOSHEN-GETSTEIN, ed., *The Book of Isaiah* (Jerusalem, 1995) • C. HARDMEIER, *Prophetie im Streit vor dem Untergang Judas* (Berlin, 1990) • K. KOENEN, *Ethik und Eschatologie im Tritojesajabuch* (Neukirchen, 1990) • R. MELUGIN and M. A. SWEENEY, eds., *New Visions of Isaiah* (Sheffield, 1996) • R. H. O'CONNELL, *Concentricity and Continuity: The Literary Structure of Isaiah* (Sheffield, 1994) • O. H. STECK, *Bereitete Heimkehr. Jesaja 35 als redaktionelle Brücke zwischen dem Ersten und dem Zweiten Jesaja* (Stuttgart, 1985) • M. A. SWEENEY, "The Book of Isaiah in Recent Research," *CR.BS* 1 (1993) 141-62 • H. G. M. WILLIAMSON, "Sound, Sense, and Language in Isaiah 24–27," *JJS* 46 (1995) 1-9.

On 3: R. E. Clements, "Beyond Tradition-History: Deutero-Isaianic Development of First Isaiah's Themes," *JSOT* 31 (1985) 95-113 • H. Haag, *Der Gottesknecht bei Deuterojesaja* (Darmstadt, 1985) • P. D. Hanson, *Isaiah 40–66* (Louisville, Ky., 1995) • H.-J. Hermisson, "Israel und der Gottesknecht bei Deuterojesaja," *ZTK* 79 (1982) 1-24 • R. G. Kratz, *Kyros im Deuterojesaja-Buch* (Tübingen, 1991) • C. G. Kruse, "The Servant Songs: Interpretive Trends since C. R. North," *SBT* 8 (1978) 3-27 • A. Labahn, *Wort Gottes und Schuld Israels. Untersuchungen zu Motiven deuteronomistischer Theologie im Deuterojesajabuch* (Stuttgart, 1999) • R. F. Melugin, *The Formation of Isaiah 40–55* (Berlin, 1976) • C. R. North, *The Suffering Servant in Deutero-Isaiah* (2d ed.; Oxford, 1956) • H. D. Preuss, *Deuterojesaja. Eine Einführung in seine Botschaft* (Neukirchen, 1976) • O. H. Steck, *Gottesknecht und Zion. Gesammelte Aufsätze zu Deuterojesaja* (Tübingen, 1992) • C. Westermann, "Sprache und Struktur der Prophetie Deuterojesajas," *Gesammelte Studien* (vol. 1; Munich, 1964) 92-170 • H. G. M. Williamson, *The Book Called Isaiah: Deutero-Isaiah's Role in Composition and Redaction* (Oxford, 1994) • W. Zimmerli, "Jahwes Wort bei Deuterojesaja," *VT* 32 (1982) 104-24. See also the bibliography in "Servant of the Lord."

On 4: H. Barth, *Die Jesaja-Worte in der Assyrerzeit* (Neukirchen, 1977) • J. Barthel, *Prophetenwort und Geschichte. Die Jesajaüberlieferung in Jes 6–8 und 28–31* (Tübingen, 1997) • U. Becker, *Jesaja–von der Botschaft zum Buch* (Göttingen, 1997) • E. W. Davies, *Prophecy and Ethics: Isaiah and the Ethical Tradition of Israel* (Sheffield, 1981) • W. Dietrich, *Jesaja und die Politik* (Munich, 1976) • W. J. Doorly, *Isaiah of Jerusalem: An Introduction* (New York, 1992) • J. C. Exum, "Isaiah 28–32: A Literary Approach," *SBLSP* 17/2 (1979) 123-51 • Y. Gitay, *Isaiah and His Audience: The Structure and Meaning of Isaiah 1–12* (Assen, 1991) • R. Kilian, *Jesaja 1–39* (Darmstadt, 1983) • O. Loretz, *Der Prolog des Jesaja-Buches (1,1–2,5)* (Altenberge, 1984) • W. H. Schmidt, "Die Einheit der Verkündigung Jesajas. Versuch einer Zusammenschau," *EvT* 37 (1977) 260-72 • C. R. Seitz, *Isaiah 1–39: Interpretation Commentary for Teaching and Preaching* (Louisville, Ky., 1993) • J. Vermeylen, *Du prophète Isaïe à l'apocalyptique* (2 vols.; Paris, 1977-78) • W. Werner, *Eschatologische Texte in Jesaja 1–39* (Würzburg, 1982) • H. G. M. Williamson, "Relocating Isaiah 1:2-9," *Writing and Reading the Scroll of Isaiah* (ed. D. D. Broyles and C. A. Evans; Leiden, 1997) 263-77.

Walter Dietrich

Islam

1. Muḥammad and the Prophetic Revelation
2. Spread
3. Cult and Ritual
4. Tradition and Law
5. Theology
6. Confessions and Movements
7. The Hereafter and Eschatology
8. Popular Customs, Cult of the Saints
9. Modern Developments, Organizations
10. Islam in America

Islam is the monotheistic, revealed religion founded by the → prophet Muḥammad. From its original home in the Arabian Peninsula, Islam spread over the Near East, North Africa, central Asia, India, and Indonesia, and it is still winning new adherents in Africa and around the world. In A.D. 2000 approximately 1.2 billion people are Muslims, some 20 percent of the world population. The countries that are home to the largest numbers of Muslims are Pakistan (150 million), India and Indonesia (120 million each), Bangladesh (110 million), Iran (75 million), Turkey (65 million), and Egypt and Nigeria (55 million each). About 90 percent of Muslims are Sunnites, the rest mainly Shiites.

1. Muḥammad and the Prophetic Revelation

Muḥammad, born in about A.D. 570, emerged in his home town of Mecca around 610 as the preacher of a divine revelation that he felt called upon to pass on to his pagan Arab fellow tribespeople. Although the form of the revelations — a strongly rhythmic, rhyming prose (→ Koran) — derived from the pronouncements of older Arab seers *(kāhin)*, Muḥammad denied belonging to their number. As he saw it, God (Arab. *Allāh,* a contraction of *al-Ilāh,* "the God") wanted to impart through him — in Arabic (Koran 16:103) and to Arabs — the same revelation God had given to the first man → Adam, then through → Abraham and → Moses to the Jews, then through → Jesus to Christians.

In Arabia the way had long since been prepared for → monotheism by Jewish and Christian communities along the Incense Road from Yemen to Syria. Islam respected the recipients of these older revelations as "people of the book" *(ahl al-kitāb).* Accepting monotheism — even that of the older revelations — is denoted by the Arabic verb *aslama* (submit to [God's will]), from which come the noun *islām* (submission) and the participle *muslim* (one who submits). The main content of the oldest revelations was proclamation of the one Creator God

(→ Creation) and the threat of judgment for unbelievers and wrongdoers (→ Last Judgment).

The first followers of Islam were close relatives of the Prophet, including his wife Khadījah and his cousin and son-in-law ʿAlī. The pagan merchant oligarchy of Mecca, however, saw in the revelation a threat to their privilege of controlling the pagan pilgrim centers in the city, and Muḥammad was forced to leave Mecca. He was accepted by two rural tribes at the oasis Yathrib (modern Medina, formerly Madīnat an-Nabī, "city of the prophet"). From this so-called hegira (hijrah, "flight") and his arrival on September 20, 622, begins the Islamic calendar.

In Medina Muḥammad, with the support of emigrants (muhājirūn) who followed him and locals who joined him (anṣār, "helpers"), founded a theocratic community whose laws were the divine revelations that steadily came from his lips. These proclamations increasingly contained laws in the strict sense (e.g., criminal law and laws of inheritance). The community (ummah) in Medina grew as both → nomads and settled tribes in Arabia accepted Islam.

After attacks on the caravans of pagan Mecca and military clashes, Muḥammad was able to seize Mecca in 630. He removed the idols and changed the pagan pilgrim rites at the city → sanctuary, the Kaaba (kaʿba, "cube"), into a pilgrimage in honor of the one God, ascribing its institution to the prophet Abraham and his son Ishmael. Mecca thus became the religious center of Arabia, which made it easier for the pagan aristocracy there to go over to Islam. Soon after his last participation in the Mecca rites, Muḥammad died on June 8, 632, at Medina.

Since Muḥammad had not named a successor (khalīfah, whence "caliph"), the Medina community rallied around his fellow refugee Abū Bakr, who, as "caliph of the messenger of God" (khalīfat rasūl Allāh), was the leader of the community in all secular and religious matters, although he could claim no prophetic → inspiration. Prophets arose in many Arabian tribes, but Abū Bakr during his brief caliphate (632-34) succeeded in overcoming external independence movements, suppressing false prophets, and establishing the hegemony of the original Medina community.

After Abū Bakr's death ʿUmar became the second caliph (634-44), again with no prophetic inspiration but still able to lead the community, which provided the model for future organization. Under the next caliph, ʿUthmān (644-56), the proclamations of the Prophet, which had been handed down orally or in writing, were collected in a canon. The Koran (qurʾan, "reading, recitation") thus received its final form and became the community's most important standard.

2. Spread

Under Caliph ʿUmar the Islamic community began to expand by force beyond Arabia and to subjugate great portions of the → Byzantine and Sassanid Persian empires (gaining Damascus in 635; → Jerusalem in 638; Mesopotamia, with the founding of Basra and Al-Kufa in 638; Egypt from 640, with the founding of Al-Fustāt, or Old Cairo; Caesarea in 641; Iran from 642). With the cities, usually represented by their → bishops or local princes, the Islamic generals concluded treaties of surrender that guaranteed the safety of the persons and property of the inhabitants, the unhindered practice of their religion (→ Religious Liberty), and the possession of their houses of worship. In return they had to pay tribute, a practice based on the Koran (9:29). The protective treaty (dhimma) was a fixed part of Islamic law that governed the relations between, for example, the Turkish Ottomans and the Christians in the Balkans up to the 19th century. All adherents of monotheistic, revealed religions — "people of the book" (i.e., Jews and Christians, later also Zoroastrians [→ Iranian Religions 6-7] and Hindus) — enjoyed this treaty protection. The tribute of those under protection, or dhimmis (sing. dhimmīy, pl. ahl adh-dhimma), was soon changed into a regular poll tax (jizyah).

After the murder of the third caliph ʿUthman in 656, and during the confusion under his successor ʿAlī (656-61), the conquests came to a halt, but they were resumed under the Umayyad Caliphate (661-750). The Umayyads made Damascus their capital, and they continued to spread both west and east (siege of Constantinople in 674-78; founding of Kairouan [al-Qayrawān] in 670; capture of Carthage in 696; conquest of West Gothic Spain in 711, Bukhara in 709-10, Samarqand in 712, and the area of modern-day Pakistan in 711-13). The attack on France (the battle of Tours and Poitiers in 732), the conquest of Tashkent, and the clash with a Chinese army at the Talas River in central Asia (751) marked the limits of Islamic expansion in the eighth century.

The Abbasid Caliphate (750-1258), which descended from Muḥammad's uncle ʿAbbās and which founded the new capital of Baghdad in 762, did not extend the frontiers any further. At the same time, Islamic kingdoms on the borders began to set up more or less autonomous states as the military rulers of the provinces, the emirs (amīr, "commander"), refused to pay homage to the caliph (thus

Spain in 756 and Morocco in 790) or were recognized as separate dynasties by the caliph (Tunisia under the Aghlabids in 800, Egypt under the Tulunids in 868, central Asia under the Samanids in 875). When the Turk Maḥmūd of Ghazna (998-1030), who had been a military slave, received recognition from the caliph as ruler over eastern Iran, the title "sultan" (*sulṭān,* "authority [moral or spiritual]") became established for local rulers.

The conquests in central Asia brought Islam to Turkic peoples in the central Asian steppes. Turkish nomads under the leadership of the Seljuk clan then pushed into Iran, made Baghdad a protectorate (1055), and, in the battle of Manzikert (1071), conquered what had hitherto been Byzantine Asia Minor. This development led to a new phase of Islamic expansion headed by the Turks. Later the kingdom of the Ottoman sultans, based on a Turkish frontier emirate in Bursa in northwest Asia Minor, penetrated the Balkans and central Europe from 1357 (capturing Serbia in the battle of Kosovo in 1389, Constantinople in 1453, and Hungary in 1526; laying siege to Vienna in 1529 and 1683). When the Abbasid Caliphate in Baghdad fell to an invasion of Mongols in 1258, the Ottoman sultan became the leading Islamic power. After occupying Syria and Egypt in 1517, the sultans in Constantinople (now known as Istanbul) took also the title "caliph," which continued until its abolishment by the first Turkish National Assembly on March 3, 1924.

The Islamic conquests spread Islamic rule over non-Muslims, but not with a view to their → conversion (§1) by force. The practice of protective treaties was still the model for relations with non-Muslim subjects. For a jihad (*jihād,* "striving [in the way of Allah]," 2:218]), or the holy war against unbelievers, there were strict rules. Over against the sphere of Islam (*dār al-islām*) stood that of war (*dār al-ḥarb*), with which in theory there could be only short armistices but no lasting → peace. In practice, ghazis (*ghāzī*), or volunteer fighters for the faith, gathered every year on the frontiers for plundering forays, which, if organized on behalf of the state, would result in permanent conquests.

With the failure of the Ottomans at Vienna in 1683, the classic jihad lost its meaning. The Islamic world now had to defend itself against European incursions. During European → colonialism the jihad could take on new meaning as anticolonial conflict. In the 20th century it was directed variously against → Zionism, American influence, and the Soviet invasion of Afghanistan. It is also often used for the fight against social injustice, economic backwardness, and illiteracy.

Since Islam has no missionary command or churchlike organization, there has never been any systematic → mission, especially to other higher religions. Mission to pagans in, for example, central Asia or Africa is always only the work of individuals or small groups such as the Sufis (*ṣūfīy,* "mystic"; → Sufism) or dervishes (Pers. *darviish,* "beggar"), or efforts of heterodox groups like the Pakistani Aḥmadīya, which are trying to increase their own membership in this way.

3. Cult and Ritual

To distinguish themselves from the adherents of other monotheistic religions, Muslims call themselves "the people of direction in prayer" (*ahl al-qibla*). Practicing prescribed rituals (→ Rite) is more important in Islam than confession of doctrines; orthopraxis takes precedence over orthodoxy. Heretical deviation (→ Heresies and Schisms) is more commonly in terms of uncanonical innovation in applying the law than it is in terms of dogmatic error. The ritual of Islam goes back essentially to Muḥammad and is embedded in the Koran. Along with the transformed pagan pilgrim rites of Arabia and pre-Islamic → circumcision, we find practices that suggest Judeo-Christian models, such as ritual prayer and the Ramadan fast.

3.1. The rites of the *pilgrimage to Mecca,* which derive from pagan times, became in Islam a monotheistic cult that Abraham, Hagar, and Ishmael supposedly instituted (2:124-27). Legends connected the rites with the three and explained them. The Kaaba in the center of the sacred sector (the *ḥaram,* "sanctuary") of Mecca originally contained statues of the oracle-god Hubal and other old Arabian gods. Another sacred object built into the east corner of the building was the Black Stone, perhaps a meteorite (the best-known example of a baetyl). The pilgrimage ritual is restricted to Mecca. The "lesser pilgrimage" (*'umrah*) can be made throughout the year. It consists of a sevenfold circling (*ṭawāf*) of the Kaaba and then a sevenfold running (*sa'y*) between the two hills Safa and Marwa (2:158), which were once crowned with stone idols but have now been leveled and are connected by a covered corridor.

The great pilgrimage, or hajj (*ḥajj,* related to Heb. *ḥāg,* "make a circle"), can be made only during the pilgrimage month Dhu'l-Hijja, the 12th month in the Islamic lunar calendar (which loses 11 days a year relative to the solar calendar). The hajj connects the Mecca rites with a visit to the hill of Arafat, 24 km. (15 mi.) southeast of Mecca, which involves a ritual that stretches over several days. The pilgrims first enter into a consecrated state (*iḥrām*) by washing and putting on the pilgrim robe, made of two white pieces of cloth. After the individual *'umrah* rites the common rites begin on the seventh of the month with a sermon at the Kaaba. On the eighth day the pilgrims go to Arafat, where they spend the night and the following day devoutly standing *(wuqūf)* on the slopes of the Mount of Mercy (Jabal ar-Raḥma). After sunset they go in pilgrim procession to Muzdalifah (with another *wuqūf*) and Minā, where on the 10th day they all throw seven little stones on a stone monument (the so-called stoning of the → devil). On this same day the slaughtering of sacrificial animals (→ Sacrifice) takes place throughout the Islamic world. It is the main feast of Islam (*al-'Īd al-Kabīr,* "greater feast," or *'Īd al-Aḍḥā,* "sacrifice feast"). After three festal days the pilgrims then cut their hair and nails. A procession seven times round the Kaaba concludes the ceremonies.

The hajj is required at least once for all Muslims who are able to undertake it (3:97). Those who make the pilgrimage gain for themselves the honorary title "hajji" *(ḥajjī,* Turk. *hacı).* Islamic law permits the sending of a substitute and regulates dispensations, for example, in the case of women with no male relatives to accompany them.

The sacred sites at Mecca are maintained by an endowment *(waqf).* The Islamic authorities — specifically, the caliph as the leader *(imām)* of the community — bore responsibility for the safety of pilgrims and the welfare of pilgrim caravans. From the 10th century this role was taken over by the dynasties that ruled the Hejaz (i.e., the western region of Arabia) from Egypt, the area that includes Mecca and Medina. It was they who set up the black and gold–flecked cover *(kiswah),* renewed every year, which lies over the Kaaba except at times of pilgrimage, when it is replaced by a white one. After 1517 the Ottoman sultans in Istanbul, as rulers of Egypt, became protectors of the holy places. In the 20th century the Kingdom of Saudi Arabia assumed this function.

3.2. The salat *(ṣalāt,* from Aram. *ṣĕlōtā,* "prostration"), or *ritual prayer five times a day,* is a duty for all Muslims. The times, calculated astronomically, are roughly dawn, midday, afternoon, sundown, and evening. A call to prayer *(adhān)* is given by the muezzin *(mu'adhdhin,* Turk. *müezzin)* and by optical signals (a flag or lantern on the mosque). Certain preparatory ablutions must be made to put one in a state of ritual cleanness *(ṭahārah).* A place of assembly (→ Mosque) can serve as the site of prayer, but individuals can also pray at home or in the open (e.g., while on a journey). The ground must be clean, which can be achieved by spreading a cover,

usually a rug. Prayer must be made in the proper direction *(qiblah).* Muḥammad originally prescribed Jerusalem, but a revelation (2:136-50) changed the qibla to the Kaaba at Mecca. The salat proper consists of rak'a *(rak'ah),* a fixed series of ritual movements and formulas, such as standing, bowing down, and touching the forehead to the ground. When there is a group, one person serves as leader. At the Friday midday prayer *(ẓuhr),* a sermon *(khuṭbah)* by the preacher *(khaṭīb)* precedes the prayers. Large mosques, often with courtyards, are built for Friday worship, for which, ideally, the whole community of a city should gather.

3.3. The month-long → *fast (ṣaum,* cf. Heb. *ṣôm)* during Ramadan, the ninth Islamic month and the month of the first Koranic revelation, is obligatory for all Muslims except those who are sick or traveling. Days that are missed can be made up (2:185). All eating, drinking, and sexual intercourse are forbidden (→ Asceticism) from morning (i.e., when "the whiteness of the day becomes distinct from the blackness of the night at dawn," 2:187) until sunset. The month of fasting is ended by a feast (*'Īd al-Fiṭr,* "lesser festival"; Turk. *Şeker Bayramı,* "sugar festival"), the second most important Islamic feast.

3.4. These community rites give all Muslims a strong sense of unity and strengthen egalitarianism, for all Muslims are equally slaves (*'abīd*) of the divine Lord *(rabb).* Pilgrimage, prayer, fasting, as well as the confession *(shahādah;* see 5) and almsgiving *(zakāt* or *ṣadaqah),* are the five "pillars" *(arkān)* of Islam that unite all Muslims, no matter what their sect.

4. Tradition and Law

Along with the commands and prohibitions of the Koran, the sunna *(sunnah,* "custom, habit"), or words and deeds, of the first community soon became important. The hadith *(ḥadīth,* "speech, report") — the traditional rules, decisions, and standards of the Prophet and his companions (his *ṣaḥābah)* — became binding on all Muslims. They were increasingly ascribed to the Prophet alone and at first handed down orally in the form of many dicta and anecdotes. The number of these hadith increased in the party struggles of the seventh and eighth centuries. Opposing opinions quoted alleged sayings of the Prophet, so that a critical sifting of the tradition became necessary. Six great collections were thus made in the ninth and early tenth centuries in which materials that were regarded as authentic were assembled, with the names of those who had handed them down, going back to the original earwitnesses and eyewitnesses. The best-known collections are those of al-Bukhārī (d. 870) and Muslim ibn al-Ḥajjāj (d. 875), both entitled *aṣ-Ṣaḥīḥ* (The authentic).

The sunnas collected in these materials regulate Muslim life in detail from religious and cultic duties to everyday matters of clothing and hygiene. Islamic law (*fiqh*, "understanding") rests on them. From the eighth century onward, local legal traditions developed that were linked to the names of famous jurists and soon took on the character of schools. Four of these schools are regarded as legitimate in Sunnite Islam (→ Sunna).

The Koran, sunna, and jurisprudence constitute Islamic law, or Shariʿa (*sharīʿa*, "path"), which no longer has the original sense of the divinely revealed religion but now denotes the divinely willed earthly legal and social order embracing every sphere of life. The Shariʿa is handed down by a professional class that, since Islam has neither a hierarchical priesthood (→ Priest, Priesthood) nor a central teaching office, acts as the collective guardian of tradition and the bearer of authority. This group is the class of jurists (*fuqahāʾ*, sing. *faqīh*) or scholars (*ʿulamāʾ*, sing. *ʿālim*).

The traditional place of training for these professional jurists is the madrasa (*madrasah*, "place of study"), a kind of legal and theological seminary. The madrasa developed in eastern Iran in the 10th century and spread to the whole Islamic world (e.g., reaching Egypt by the 12th cent.). Islamic rulers choose a judge, or qadi (*qāḍī*), from the ranks of the ʿulamāʾ, but the qadis' authority rests on the expert opinions (*fatwā*) that the muftis (*muftī*), or experts, give on all questions of religion, → law, and → everyday life. In principle these opinions are not binding, and they thus depend on the personal authority of the mufti, who acts in place of the missing central authority. For Sunnites the rulings of the professors of al-Azhar University in Cairo — at its head the *shaykh al-Azhar* — have more than regional importance. In many countries the office of mufti has been regionally institutionalized (e.g., the mufti of Tashkent, for the central Asian Muslim republics of the former Soviet Union).

The Shiites (→ Shia, Shiites) of Iran address the ʿulamāʾ as mullah (Pers. *mulla*, from Arab. *mawlā*, "lord"). Especially important in Iran is a jurist (*mujtahid*), who can give independent legal decisions (*ijtihād*) and who is frequently given the honorary title "ayatollah" (Pers. for "sign of God," from Arab. *āya*, "sign, miracle," plus *allāh*).

The Koran allows a man to marry up to four wives as long as he can treat them equally well (4:3). The legal position of wives is dealt with specifically in sura 4. The Koranic rulings were meant to give women rights and protection against caprice in the Arab tribal society of the seventh century. But women do not have equal rights with men (4:34). Wives have a right of divorce only when their husbands can no longer support them or when their husbands mistreat them. They then keep their dowry, as do widows, and may also remarry (→ Marriage and Divorce). The social restrictions imposed on women in Islamic countries (e.g., arranging of marriages by male relatives, restriction to the home, veiling) are rooted in the patriarchal tradition of Near Eastern societies rather than in Islamic law, and Islamic modernizers now oppose them as outdated.

5. Theology

The confession (*shahādah*, "witness") formulates the central belief of Islam: "There is no god but God, and Muḥammad is his prophet" (*ashhadu an lā ilāha illa 'llāh, wa-anna Muḥammadan rasūl Allāh*). Over against this confession of God's radical oneness, or tawhid (*tawḥīd*, a verbal noun of *waḥḥadah*, "declare as one"), the main sin is *shirk* (lit. making a partner [of someone]), or associating other gods with God. For those who do so (the *mushrik*, i.e., → polytheists), Islam has no tolerance. The → dogma of the tawhid was originally aimed at ancient Arab paganism but also at the Christian doctrine of the → Trinity (Koran 112).

The tawhid raised the two problems of → theodicy and the nature of the divine attributes (eternal or created?). Reflection on these problems gave rise to kalam (*kalām*, "word, speech, dialectic"), or Muslim scholastic theology. From around 670, different answers were given to the question whether God is also responsible for → evil. In the eighth century those who held that we are responsible for our own acts, that these were not foreordained by God's creative word, formed in Syria and Iraq (Basra) the oldest theological school, the Qadarites (from *qadar*, "power, ability").

The second question was whether the attributes (*ṣifāt*) that the Koran ascribes to God — omniscience, omnipotence, and goodness, plus anthropomorphic features such as eyes, mouth, and hands — are intrinsic to his nature and thus eternal, or whether they are independent entities (→ God 1). The danger in the latter view is that of associating divinelike entities with God and thus denying the tawhid. In the theological school of the Muʿtazilites (*muʿtazilah*, separatist), whose main representatives worked in Basra (esp. Wāṣil ibn ʿAṭāʾ [d. 748]) and Baghdad from the late eighth century, exemplary answers were given to both questions. Their main points were that we have the capacity (qudra) for responsible action and that the word of God, the Koran, and the other attributes are created.

The doctrine that the Koran is not eternal was declared binding by Caliph al-Ma'mūn (813-33) and remained state dogma until Caliph al-Muta-wakkil in 849 came out for the eternity of the Koran and strict determinism. The predestinarian tradition finally consolidated itself in the hadith tradition of the ninth and tenth centuries and has since been part of Sunnite theology.

6. Confessions and Movements

The division of the Islamic community into different groups or schools (firqah, "part, section," or madhhab, "way, method") goes back to the seventh century. Differences of opinion (ikhtilāf) flared up less over doctrinal differences than over the question who was the imam (imām), or legal head, of the community. Two great religious and political parties, the Shiites and the Kharijites (khārijī, one that departs, dissenter), formed after the third caliph, 'Uthman, fell victim to his Islamic rivals in 656. The Shiites argued that only 'Alī, the Prophet's son-in-law, and his physical successors had a right to the imamate or caliphate. Against them the Kharijites contended that only the morally best person, no matter of what origin or descent, was qualified to lead the community, and they thus argued for an elective imamate. Shia, which in the tenth century dominated much of the Muslim world but which is now split up into many → sects and movements, is still the most significant Islamic grouping next to the Sunnites. The Kharijite view, which had its roots in Iraq, established itself as the national religion of the Berbers of North Africa and still exists in small pockets in this area (e.g., Tiaret and Ghardaïa in Algeria, the Tunisian island of Jerba) and in Oman.

Along with the three main groupings, which go back to division in the early community, Islam from time to time has seen movements of renewal that seek to restore the one pure Islam of the earliest days and to do away with all innovations. These movements have often resulted in the founding of separatistic, puritanical states, such as the movement of the Almohads (al-muwaḥḥidūn, "confessors of the tawhid") in Morocco in the 12th century, or that of the Wahhabis in Arabia (led by reformer Muḥammad ibn 'Abd al-Wahhāb [1703-92]), which led ultimately to the founding of the Kingdom of Saudi Arabia in 1932. Not infrequently these movements have had → eschatological traits and awaited the unifying of Islam by the coming of the Mahdi

(mahdī, "divinely guided one"), a charismatic ruler figure (→ Charisma; Messianism). The reform movement of the Salafiyya at the end of the 19th century has had great influence on modern Islam. By a return to the spirit of the original Islam of the ancestors (salaf), it hoped for victory over the legal tradition that had led to sterility in the Middle Ages (note esp. the work of Egyptian Muḥammad 'Abduh [d. 1905] and his Syrian disciple Muḥammad Rashīd Riḍā [d. 1935]).

Mystical trends (→ Mysticism), which may be detected from the ninth century, disparaged the outward cultic practices and legal regulations based on the Shari'a and put personal experience of the vision of God beside them or in place of them. The jurists long suspected and opposed these trends, but Sunni Islam came to recognize them in a modified form through the work of the theologian al-Ghazālī (d. 1111). The mystic congregation, or tariqa (ṭarīqah, "way, path," later the mystic order itself), with its collective devotional exercises (dhikr), became a vital element in Islamic popular piety and, in the main, a stronghold of traditional conservatism.

7. The Hereafter and Eschatology

God is the Lord of heaven and earth (2:107). By hadith tradition his throne is in the highest of the seven heavens. Angels (malak) dwell in the heavens and praise God. Popular tradition gives some of them special functions: Jibrīl (Gabriel) brings the Koranic revelation, Riḍwān and Mālik are the gatekeepers of → heaven and → hell, 'Azrā'īl is the angel of death, Munkar and Nakīr question the dead in the grave, and Isrāfīl blows the trumpet on the last day. The disobedient angel Iblīs (from Gk. diabolos, "slanderer, the devil") is the devil. He refused to bow down with the other angels before Adam, God's representative, as God commanded (2:30-34; 7:11-18). Iblīs, who entices human beings into evil, is the same as Shayṭān (Satan) in 2:36, the one who persuaded Adam and Eve to eat of the forbidden tree.

The → resurrection (qiyāmah) of the dead and the day of judgment (yawm ad-dīn) are themes of Muhammad's earliest preaching. By God's righteous judgment the righteous are set in a fertile garden (jannah), while the wicked are punished with terrible torments in an eternal → fire (nār).

8. Popular Customs, Cult of the Saints

Besides the two main feasts (see 3) the Prophet's birthday (mawlid an-Nabī) is celebrated by tradition on the 12th day of the month Rabi I, and the birthdays of local mystics and saints are also observed. The Shiites have their own calendar of celebrations. The turning points of human life — birth, circumcision, marriage, and death — are marked by rituals and feasts, though with great regional differences. The circumcision *(khitān)* of boys is a fixed rite for Sunnis, since the Prophet was circumcised. Female circumcision *(khafḍ, khifāḍ)*, which is customary especially in African countries and Arabia, is not an Islamic practice per se and is sanctioned only by some legal experts (e.g., Aḥmad ibn Ḥanbal [d. 855]; → Sexism).

The local veneration of the tombs of saints is found everywhere in Islam, especially in North Africa, where ascetics and contenders for the faith are called *murābiṭ* ("one who is garrisoned," whence the Eng. and Fr. "marabout"). Among Shiites, visiting the graves of imams and their relatives *(imāmzādeh)* plays an important role. Puritanical renewal movements like that of the Wahhabis reject the veneration of → saints as an inappropriate *bidʿah,* or innovation.

9. Modern Developments, Organizations

Since the Islamic movement took a political form even under the Prophet, it did not have to develop anything like an ecclesiastical organization. The Islamic → state had the task of guaranteeing the validity of the Shariʿa for every sphere of life. The traditional unity of the civil and religious community was broken by European colonialism. The colonial rulers — and after them the governments in independent states — limited the scope of the validity of the Shariʿa or completely ended it, thus breaking the cultural and legal monopoly of the ʿulamā' (e.g., through the reforms of Kemal Atatürk in Turkey, Reza Shah Pahlavi in Iran, and Habib Bourguiba in Tunisia). Only in a few countries (e.g., Saudi Arabia) has the Shariʿa remained in full force.

Against secularizing European influence (→ Secularization) organizations were founded after World War I with the aim of again making Islam the determinative force in state and society. The Muslim Brotherhood (al-Ikhwān al-Muslimūn), founded in 1928 by Ḥasan al-Bannā', is a conservative, traditionalist, and fundamentalist opposition in Arab countries such as Egypt and the Sudan that seeks political influence. The Jamaʿat-i Islami, founded in British India in 1941 by Sayyid Abul Aʿla al-Mawdudi, gradually changed Pakistan into an Islamic republic since 1947, with the introduction of an Islamic system in 1979 and the formation of a league of Shariʿa law in 1980. In Iran the Shia revolution of 1979 led to the founding of the Islamic Republic of Iran, with a constitution that gives a leading position to Islamic jurists *(vilāyet-i faqīh).*

Since the caliphate of the Turkish sultan was abolished in 1924, pan-Islamic ideas have fueled efforts to overcome the particularism of the national states that the colonial powers left behind and that are in many cases artificial. A permanent Muslim World Congress was founded in Karachi in 1949, which lost its importance with the formation of the Muslim World League at Mecca in 1962. Members of the league are individuals and organizations, not states. There is a permanent office at Mecca, and the league enjoys observer status at the → United Nations. Its aim is to strengthen and spread Islam worldwide. At the country level there is the Organization of the Islamic Conference, the charter of which was accepted in 1972 at Jidda by 30 states at the third conference of Islamic foreign ministers. Now numbering over 40 member countries, it organizes summits of heads of state and conferences of foreign ministers.

→ Baha'i; Islam and Christianity; Islamic Philosophy

Bibliography: C. Cahen, *Der Islam,* vol. 1, *Vom Ursprung bis zu die Anfängen des Osmanenreiches* (Frankfurt, 1968) • *CHIs* • N. J. Coulson, *A History of Islamic Law* (Edinburgh, 1964) • *EI* • W. Ende and U. Steinbach, eds., *Der Islam in der Gegenwart* (Munich, 1984) • G. Endress, *Einführung in die islamische Geschichte* (Munich, 1983) • C. Glassé, *The Concise Encyclopedia of Islam* (San Francisco, 1991) • G. E. von Grunebaum, *Der Islam im Mittelalter* (Zurich, 1963); idem, *Der Islam in seiner klassischen Epoche* (Zurich, 1966); idem, ed., *Der Islam,* vol. 2, *Die islamische Reiche nach dem Fall von Konstantinopel* (Frankfurt, 1971) • T. Nagel, *Staat und Glaubensgemeinschaft im Islam* (2 vols.; Zurich, 1981) • R. Paret, *Mohammed und der Koran. Geschichte und Verkündigung des arabischen Propheten* (Stuttgart, 1957) • *The Qur'an* (trans. M. H. Shakir; 10th U.S. ed.; Elmhurst, N.Y., 1997) • W. M. Watt, *Islamic Philosophy and Theology* (Edinburgh, 1962); idem, *Muhammed at Mecca* (Oxford, 1953); idem, *Muhammed at Medina* (Oxford, 1977); idem, *A Short History of Islam* (Oxford, 1996).

Heinz Halm

10. Islam in America

Muslims in the United States and Canada represent a great many movements and identities: immigrant and indigenous, Sunni and Shiite, conservative and liberal, orthodox and hererodox. While exact numbers are difficult to determine, most estimates at the end of the 20th century assume that there are over four million, perhaps as many as six million, Muslims in North America.

The majority of American Muslims are themselves immigrants or are the descendants of those who first began to arrive in the West in the latter part of the 19th century. The early arrivals, primarily laborers and merchants, settled in the East, the Midwest, and the Pacific coast. Other waves of immigration occurred as a direct result of political and economic circumstances in the Arab and Muslim world, including the breakup of the Ottoman Empire, the partition of India, Israeli defeat of the Palestinians, the Iranian revolution, and uprisings in Africa and Asia. Initially coming mainly from the Middle East, immigrants in the last decades of the 20th century represent all Islamic nations of the world. While the first arrivals generally were not well trained or economically advantaged, today they are often among the most highly educated and professionally successful Americans.

In earlier decades, because their numbers were relatively small, immigrant Muslims were forced to come together in mixed groups for → worship and social interaction. As more arrived and settled in various parts of the country, national and ethnic groups were able to meet and worship separately. These associations continue, although with the rise in consciousness of being Muslim in the North American context, more immigrant Muslims of differing nationalities are living in proximity and worshiping together. Shiites, who account for about one-fifth of the American Muslim community, observe some rites and holidays distinct from Sunnis and usually worship separately.

Growing numbers of Muslims in the United States are African American. In the early decades of the 20th century, several black nationalist movements began to claim Islamic roots and identity. The Nation of Islam became the most prominent African American freedom movement to identify with Islam, beginning in Detroit in the 1930s under the leadership of the Honorable Elijah Muhammad. Many of the teachings of the Nation are irreconcilable with traditional Islam, including recognition of the prophethood of Elijah and the promotion of racial separatism. The prominent and popular minister Malcolm X, one of the Nation's most influential spokesmen, left the organization after experiencing the brotherhood of all Muslims while on pilgrimage. He was assassinated in 1965.

Meanwhile the Nation continued to grow. When Elijah Muhammad died in 1975, he was succeeded by his son Wallace. The new leadership brought momentous changes as the political → millenarianism of the earlier Nation gave way to a visible move toward orthodox Islam. Wallace, who changed his name to Warith Deen Mohammed, played down the nationalism that had characterized the preaching of both his father and Malcolm, focusing on Islam as a spiritual force rather than a political tool. His organization, whose name has evolved a number of times, is now called the Muslim American Society, and its members no longer consider themselves part of the Nation but simply Sunni Muslims. African Americans, including those belonging to other Sunni groups as well as a number of heterodox movements, constitute some 40 percent of the Muslim community in America.

The Nation of Islam itself is now under the leadership of Minister Louis Farrakhan, who first came to prominence as minister of a → mosque in Harlem, where he succeeded Malcolm X when the latter left the Nation in 1964. In 1977 Farrakhan broke with Warith Deen Mohammed, leader of what was then called the World Community of Islam, in order to rebuild Elijah Muhammad's Lost-Found Nation of Islam in the Wilderness of America. Since then, Minister Farrakhan has become a celebrated and controversial figure within American society, largely as a result of his perceived → racism and → anti-Semitism. He has, however, succeeded in reconstructing the Nation of Islam and in recent years has shown an ability to bring various segments of the African American Islamic community together and thus has helped that community find a place within the pluralistic world of American religion.

A third grouping of American Muslims, far smaller than the immigrants or African Americans, is made up of others who have decided to adopt Islam as a faith and an identity. These Muslims include people associated with Sufi movements, women who change their faith on marriage, some who find Islam intellectually persuasive, and growing numbers of Hispanics and Native Americans. The *da'wa*, or Islamic missionary movement, is strong in America, and Muslims are active in making conversions in prisons, in the academic world, and in various minority communities.

For many decades Muslims in America functioned with little or no trained leadership and without their own designated space for meeting and worship. Several places claim to be the site of the first American mosque, most notably Cedar Rapids, Iowa. Other mosques were built in New York, Massachusetts, and the Midwest in the 1920s and 1930s. The mosque movement began to gain momentum by the middle of the century, highlighted by the completion of the Islamic Center in Washington, D.C., in 1957. Toward the end of the 20th century much of the funding for building

Islamic establishments, as well as for providing trained leadership for Muslim congregations, came from oil-producing countries of the Middle East. Flourishing Islamic communities are now found in most major cities of the United States, and the number of mosques and Islamic centers has grown enormously. They provide a range of activities aside from worship, including after-school education, libraries, gymnasiums, facilities for the elderly, and contexts for social engagement. Many Muslim groups, especially African American congregations, for whom finances remain a major consideration, continue to worship and meet in much smaller facilities such as converted houses or storefronts.

While some imams trained overseas provide leadership to American mosques, their numbers are insufficient, and their training often is inadequate to meet the concerns of life in America. Significant efforts are underway to educate indigenous leadership. American imams are called on to function in capacities well beyond what is expected in Islamic societies. Paralleling the roles of Christian and Jewish clergy, imams not only preach and teach but also provide counseling, raise funds, perform weddings and → funerals, educate the public about Islam, and participate in community projects. Trained imams are increasingly present in the armed services, in the prison system, and as college chaplains.

Beginning in the 1960s with the establishment of the Muslim Student Association, America has seen a steady growth of Muslim organizations at the local and national levels. Some are specific to professions and interests, while others serve as umbrella organizations. Of the latter the two largest are the Islamic Society of North America and the somewhat smaller and more conservative Islamic Circle of North America. Organizations exist to advance the political presence of Muslims in America, to support women's rights, and to spread accurate information about Islam in the effort to combat anti-Muslim → prejudice. The national Muslim Youth of North America and many local groups sponsor summer gatherings and work opportunities for teenagers.

Some of the Muslim organizations publish journals with articles designed to help Muslims live Islamically in the context of what they see as an essentially secular society. These journals, along with growing resources on the Internet, services provided by mosques and local communities, and the large amount of literature and media information available on Islam, offer a range of solutions to the concerns of → everyday life. These concerns include raising and educating children, dating and → marriage, women in the workplace, appropriate dress for both men and women, participation in the American economic system, observing daily prayer rituals in the public sphere, and maintaining proper Islamic diet. Some Muslims feel that the best way to maintain their Islamic identity in America is to avoid contact as much as possible with those who are not Muslim, while others are equally convinced that full participation and involvement are not only appropriate but necessary.

Muslims in America are in the process of determining the nature and validity of an indigenous American Islam. Immigrant Muslim communities are subject to a range of international influences, and they are struggling to determine when interpretations of Islam from different political and cultural contexts are appropriate to the practice of the faith in the West. Muslims who traditionally have not been active in American politics are increasingly aware of the potential for political power, and many are working to build coalitions and political action committees to sponsor Muslim candidates and support Muslim causes. As the children and grandchildren of immigrant Muslims find themselves increasingly distant from their international cultural heritage, they are engaging in the task of emphasizing commonality over distinctiveness. They also acknowledge that the creation of an American *ummah,* or community, must result in bringing together immigrant and indigenous Muslims, converts and those with a long heritage of Islam. To the extent to which they succeed, American Muslims believe that they will be able to contribute significantly to the international discourse about Islam in the contemporary world and the role to be played in it by Muslims in → diaspora.

Bibliography: C. L. ANWAY, *Daughters of Another Path: Experiences of American Women Choosing Islam* (Lee's Summit, Mo., 1996) • L. BAKHTIAR, *Sufi Women of America: Angels in the Making* (Chicago, 1996) • S. BARBOZA, *American Jihad: Islam after Malcolm X* (New York, 1994) • L. FARRAKHAN, *A Torchlight for America* (Chicago, 1993) • M. GARDELL, *In the Name of Elijah Muhammad: Louis Farrakhan and the Nation of Islam* (Durham, N.C., 1996) • Y. Y. HADDAD, ed., *The Muslims of America* (New York, 1991) • Y. Y. HADDAD and J. L. ESPOSITO, eds., *Muslims on the Americanization Path?* (Atlanta, 1998) • Y. Y. HADDAD and A. T. LUMMIS, *Islamic Values in the United States: A Comparative Study* (New York, 1987) • Y. Y. HADDAD and J. I. SMITH, *Mission to America: Five Islamic Sectarian Communities in North America* (Gainesville, Fla., 1993); idem, eds., *Muslim Communities in North America* (Albany, N.Y., 1994) • G. KEPEL, *Allah in the West: Islamic Movements in America and Europe* (Stanford, Calif., 1997) • M. A. KOSZEGI and J. G. MELTON, eds., *Islam in North America: A Source-book* (New York, 1992) • M. F. LEE, *The Nation of Islam: An American Millenarian Movement* (Syracuse, N.Y., 1996) • C. E. LINCOLN, *The Black Muslims in America* (3d ed.; Grand Rapids, 1994; orig. pub., 1961) • A. B. McCLOUD, *African American Islam* (New York, 1995) • C. E. MARSH, *From Black Muslims to Muslims: The Transition from Separatism to Islam, 1930-1980* (Metuchen, N.J., 1984) • B. D. METCALF, ed., *Making Muslim Space in North America and Europe* (Berkeley, Calif., 1996) • L. POSTON, *Islamic Da'wah in the West: Muslim Missionary Activity and the Dynamics of Conversion to Islam* (New York, 1992) • A. SHAHID, *Reflections of an American Muslim* (Chicago, 1994) • J. I. SMITH, *Islam in America* (New York, 1999) • R. B. TURNER, *Islam in the African-American Experience* (Bloomington, Ind., 1997) • E. H. WAUGH, S. M. ABU-LABAN, and R. B. QURESHI, eds., *Muslim Families in North America* (Edmonton, 1991) • R. WORMSER, *American Islam: Growing Up Muslim in America* (New York, 1994).

JANE I. SMITH

Islam and Christianity

1. Context and Historical Sketch
2. Islam as a Challenge to Christian Theology and Practice of Mission
3. Christian-Muslim Engagement Today

1. Context and Historical Sketch

1.1. As the 20th century drew to its close, many Christians sensed both the urgency and the promise of new developments in the 1,400-year-old history of Christian-Muslim relations. Dramatic gestures such as the visits of Pope John Paul II to Muslim leaders throughout the world communicated the widely felt sense that new Christian attitudes toward → Islam were developing and that new conversation and cooperation between Christian and Muslim theologians and institutions were possible. In Europe and North America, due in part to the increasing presence of Muslim guest workers, immigrants (including → refugees), and converts, interest in Islam has increased by leaps and bounds. Even in places where Muslims had long been seen as exotic outsiders, Christians began to encounter Muslims in their neighborhoods, their workplaces, and — through marriage — their own families.

Christian churches have turned their attention to → Islam at denominational and ecumenical levels,

and specialized institutes for the study of Christian-Muslim relations have flourished, for example, those at the University of Birmingham (U.K.), Hartford Seminary (U.S.), Georgetown University (U.S.), and the Pontificio Istituto di Studi Arabi e d'Islamistica (Rome). Such interest is by no means limited to the West. Some of the most moving testimonies of the possibilities for Christian-Muslim understanding and common work come from the churches of the non-Western world and from institutions such as the Christian Study Centre in Rawalpindi, Pakistan, the Henry Martyn Institute in Hyderabad, India, and the Program for Christian-Muslim Relations in Africa (formerly the Islam in Africa Project).

1.2. The sense of urgency in these new developments in Christian-Muslim relations can be understood only against the background of a long history of hostility and estrangement (→ Force, Violence, Nonviolence). Even at the end of the 20th century, violence involving Christian and Muslim communities continued to be all too common in many parts of the world, including the Sudan, Nigeria, the Balkan states, and parts of Indonesia. While each case is complex and resists classification merely as a religious → conflict, each adds its own sad load to the burden of history that continues to weigh down individuals and communities seeking harmonious relations between Christians and Muslims.

1.3. Competition between the two faiths was present from the very beginning. Within a decade of the death of Muḥammad (in A.D. 632), the Prophet of Islam, Muslim armies had conquered a huge part of the ancient Christian heartland, including Palestine, Syria, and Egypt. For centuries, Islam and Christianity were the faiths of competing, expansionistic power blocs, each of which saw military success as a sign of divine favor. Therefore, in spite of intensive cultural exchanges, the prevalent attitude was one of hostility. Muslim armies conquered North Africa and Spain, and by 711 they had crossed into France; centuries later, the Ottoman Turks captured Constantinople (1453) and reached the walls of Vienna (1529).

Echoes of the fears of Christendom may be found even today in Christian → worship. The celebration of the Feast of the Transfiguration on August 6 commemorates the lifting of the Turkish siege of Belgrade on that day in 1456, and many continue to sing M. → Luther's hymn "Lord, keep us steadfast in thy Word / And curb the Turks' and papists' sword" (written after the Christians' defeat at Budapest in 1541), with only slight revisions.

On the other side, Christians launched the →

Crusades (in the Holy Land, 1095-1291) and the *reconquista* of Spain (completed in 1492). Aggression by Christians continued in the modern period with → colonialism, which brought about British rule in parts of the Near East, Egypt, the Sudan, and India, as well as Dutch rule in Indonesia and French rule in North Africa. The establishment of the modern state of Israel (1948) has been understood by many Muslims to be merely a continuation of this Western "crusading" history.

2. Islam as a Challenge to Christian Theology and Practice of Mission

2.1. As well as posing geopolitical challenges to Christian empires, Islam has posed theological challenges to Christian faith. The new faith arose in a region where → Judaism and Christianity were known, and it claimed to be the culmination of a → salvation history in which the older faiths figured: → Moses and → Jesus were prophets and apostles in a line that came to its climax in Muḥammad, "the Seal of the Prophets," while the scripture revealed to Muḥammad, the → Koran, confirmed previous revelations, including the → Torah *(Tawrāt)* sent down to Moses and the Gospel *(Injīl)* sent down to Jesus. The Islamic revelation thus allowed a certain legitimacy to the Jewish and Christian communities (they were "people of the Book"), although the Koran and the developing Islamic tradition were also sharply critical of Jewish and Christian "distortions" in their beliefs, including the Christian worship of Jesus as Lord and God. In the light of Islam's passionate → monotheism *(tawḥīd)*, Christian teachings about the triunity of God and the → incarnation of the Son of God were immediately suspect, as were Christian practices such as the veneration of the → cross and → images. Furthermore, the portrait of Jesus that emerges from the Koran — an apostle of Islam whom, it appears, God took up into heaven in order to save him from an ignominious death by crucifixion — is obviously at odds with the portrait of Jesus in the NT Gospels.

2.2. While the fact of the rapid Islamic conquest of so much of the historical heartland of the Christian movement posed a theological problem to the church of the seventh and eighth centuries, resulting in much soul-searching and finger-pointing at → sins and → heresies that might have provoked God's wrath, Christian thinkers were slow to grasp Islam itself as a challenge to Christian thought. Thus the church father → John of Damascus (d. ca. 750) was able to classify Islam as merely a recent Christian heresy. John's casual and contemptuous dismissal of "the still-prevailing deceptive superstition

of the Ishmaelites, the forerunner of the Antichrist" (Sahas's translation) was characteristic of many early Greek and Latin writings on the subject, some of which amounted to little more than war propaganda. These works often treated Islam as merely a form of idolatry; indeed, until 1180, converts from Islam to Christianity in → Byzantium were required to anathematize "the god of Muḥammad." Islam was frequently explained in apocalyptic terms; for example, in the late 12th century Joachim of Fiore (d. 1202) identified the fourth head of the dragon of the Book of Revelation with Muḥammad, and the sixth head as Ṣalāḥ al-Dīn al-Ayyūbī (Saladin), who had recently (1187) recaptured Jerusalem from the Crusaders. In the Latin West wild stories about Muḥammad and the genesis of Islam were eagerly related without examination, since "it is safe to speak evil of one whose malignity exceeds whatever ill can be spoken" (Guibert of Nogent, writing before 1112; Southern's translation).

Although the West's knowledge of Islam grew in the centuries that followed (see 2.5), sharp antitheses between Christianity and Islam continued to be drawn by many of the → Reformers (see Luther's remarks about Muḥammad and the Koran), by early Protestant → mission (§§1-2) theology (for which Islam, being post-Christian, was seen as anti-Christian), and by some currents of → dialectical theology (in which Islam is to be respected but is still judged to be mere → religion in contrast to the biblical → revelation, a view held by Hendrik Kraemer). The antitheses are still very strongly stressed by some contemporary Christians, especially some conservative Protestants (not only in the West but now throughout the world), who continue to hold very negative assessments of Islam in general, and in particular of its God *(Allāh)*, its Prophet (Muḥammad), and its Book (the *Qurʾān*).

2.3. A somewhat different attitude was found among Arabic-speaking Christian theologians, who, in writings from the late eighth century onward, attempted to convince Muslims of the intellectual respectability of Christian faith (i.e., that Christian doctrines of the Trinity and of the incarnation were not merely forms of tritheism and idolatry), and even more to persuade Christians to remain within the Christian community (a task in which they were only partially successful, to judge from the wave of → conversions to Islam that marked the ninth and tenth centuries in many parts of the Islamic caliphate). These arabophone theologians diligently sought out common ground upon which apologies for Christian faith could be built. They all used the word *"Allāh"* without reservation to refer to the Christian God.

A church leader such as the Nestorian catholicos Timothy (d. 823) could make a carefully nuanced affirmation that Muḥammad had "walked in the path of the prophets." Writers such as Theodore Abū Qurrah, Ḥabīb Abū Rā'iṭah, and 'Ammār al-Baṣrī (all active early in the 9th cent.) were skilled in making use of Koranic vocabulary and content and were able to address Muslim dialectical theologians (mutakallimūn) in their own idiom. To these names may be added those of Ḥunayn ibn Isḥāq (d. 873) and Yaḥyā ibn 'Adī (d. 974) as examples of participants in the great projects of translating → Greek philosophy and science into Arabic and the creation of a tradition of Arabic philosophy (falsafah), as a result of which Arabic-speaking intellectuals came to share a common language and a common canon of philosophical and scientific literature to which an → apologist might make appeal. Thus was established an Arabic Christian apologetic tradition that has continued to our own day, one that may continue to give inspiration to Middle Eastern Christian communities that have survived over the centuries, coexisting with Muslims and making major cultural contributions, despite the vicissitudes of life under Islamic rule (see 3.1).

2.4. Contemporary with the development of an Arabic Christian apologetic tradition is the development of an Islamic "refutation of the Christians" literature, which developed the Koranic critique of Christian teaching and practice mentioned above (see 2.1). This literature fulfilled a variety of functions: it warned against trends in Islamic teaching and practice that could be considered Christianizing, it played a role in the making and "catechizing" of converts, and in its early decades it assured Muslims of the superiority of their faith, despite what at first was the greater intellectual sophistication of their Christian subjects. Some of this literature displays a very good grasp of Christian teachings (and Christian divisions!) and responds to them with impressive dialectic (e.g., by al-Warrāq [d. ca. 861], al-Nāshi' al-Akbar [d. 906], al-Bāqillānī [d. 1013], and Ibn Taymiyyah [d. 1328]). The literature is also interesting for its varied treatments of Christian scripture, which is sometimes utilized although transposed into an Islamic key (e.g., by al-Qāsim ibn Ibrāhīm [d. ca. 860] and 'Alī ibn Rabbān al-Ṭabarī [d. ca. 860]), and sometimes attacked for its internal contradictions and general unreliability (e.g., by Ibn Ḥazm [d. 1064]).

2.5. A number of issues that would be important for the subsequent history of Christian-Muslim relations were raised in the medieval Christian West. The need for a greater understanding of Islam was perceived and addressed, a notable example being the translation project of Peter the Venerable, abbot of Cluny, which included the Latin Koran translation of Robert Ketton (in 1143). Similar ventures grace the following centuries and are dramatically illustrated by Luther's defense of Theodore Bibliander's publication of a Latin translation of the Koran in Basel in 1543.

St. → Francis of Assisi (d. 1226) and the Franciscans pioneered a nonviolent → missionary approach to the Muslims (→ Mission); a weirdly brilliant → Franciscan tertiary, Ramon Llull (d. ca. 1315), was a champion of noncoercive rational apologetic. The → Benedictine monk Uthred of Boldon (at Oxford in the 1360s) explored possibilities for the salvation of non-Christians; although his opinions on the matter were censured, his idea that an individual's destiny-deciding encounter with God takes place at the moment of death was picked up by others, such as John → Wycliffe (d. 1384).

After the fall of Constantinople, Nicholas of Cusa (d. 1464) imagined a heavenly Christian-Muslim dialogue through which Christians could explain their faith; his friend John of Segovia (d. 1458) did his utmost to make such a → dialogue (contraferentia) an earthly reality. It was the same Nicholas who, in his Sifting of the Koran, affirmed that the Koran contains → truth. All of these issues would be revisited by Christian Islamicists and missionary thinkers in the 20th century.

2.6. The great age of Protestant Christian missions is marked by a number of initiatives aimed at bringing the → gospel of Jesus Christ to Muslims throughout the world. It should be noted from the outset that neither Catholic nor Protestant missionary work among Muslims has led any great number to → baptism, partly because of the Islamic "law of apostasy" prohibiting conversion out of the Islamic community (see 3.1). However, the missionaries' work in countries throughout the world — frequently under colonial protection — enabled Christian values, philosophy, and culture to exert an indirect influence. In particular, extensive educational work has been very significant in the formation of Muslim elites.

Some individual figures who must be mentioned include missionaries to Muslims in South Asia such as Henry Martyn (d. 1812), Karl Gottlieb Pfander (d. 1865), Thomas Valpy French (d. 1891), and Lewis Bevan Jones (d. 1960). While adorned from the beginning with great linguistic and intellectual gifts and love for individuals, the work of such persons has moved from a reliance on the controversial method (esp. marked in the case of Pfander) to a dialogic approach that takes Islam seriously as a context within which to pursue the Christian theological task (esp. Jones and the Henry Martyn School/Institute, of which he was first principal). The American Reformed missionary Samuel M. Zwemer (d. 1952) may have done more than any other individual to generate the interest of Western Protestant churchgoers in the Muslim world. Anglican missions in the Near East contributed a special character of thoughtfulness and a desire to understand Islam "from the inside," a tradition graced by figures such as Temple Gairdner (d. 1928) and Constance Padwick (d. 1968) and also producing Kenneth Cragg. Cragg, whose seminal work *The Call of the Minaret* (1956) has been followed by dozens of other elegantly written books, has exerted an enormous influence on Protestant missionary thinking and practice with respect to Islam in the second half of the 20th century. Many other Protestant theologians have made major contributions to the → theology of religions, the respectful Christian study of Islam, and the practice of Christian-Muslim dialogue, including Wilfred Cantwell Smith (d. 2000), W. Montgomery Watt, and Willem A. Bijlefeld.

2.7. The towering figure in the development of Catholic attitudes toward Islam in the 20th century is the French Islamicist Louis Massignon (d. 1962), who in his teaching, hundreds of publications, and a life full of activity on behalf of Muslims explored the spiritual kinship between the two faiths and probed the mystery of Islam's place in God's providence. His influence is plain to see in the large number of Catholic thinkers who have drawn inspiration from him, and especially in documents of the Second → Vatican Council (1962-65). *Lumen gentium* 16 explicitly states that the Muslims are included in "the plan of salvation," while *Nostra aetate* 3 begins with the deceptively simple yet revolutionary statement that the church "looks with esteem upon" the Muslims and ends with a call for Christians and Muslims to strive for mutual understanding and to work together on behalf of all humankind. Other names that should be mentioned here include Massignon's disciples Youakim Mubarac (d. 1994) and Guilio Basetti-Sani, the → Dominicans Jacques Jomier and Georges Anawati (d. 1994), the Père Blanc Robert Caspar, and the academic theologian Hans Küng.

3. Christian-Muslim Engagement Today

3.1. Islamic history is in general characterized by → tolerance toward communities of Christians and Jews, communities that have enjoyed → freedom of worship and that have ordered their affairs according to their own laws of "personal status." At certain times and places there have been creative interaction and cooperation, and even theological discussion, between communities. This tolerance is dictated by the Koran itself, which not only prohibits coercion in matters of religion but positively enjoins respect for Jews and Christians as "people of the Book" — even though, as we have seen, the Koran also criticizes what it views as Christian and Jewish exaggerations or excesses in their beliefs.

A practical difficulty in intercommunal relations is the fact that Islamic tolerance does not in theory allow for the possibility of → conversion from Islam to any other religious community (see the Islamic Declaration of Human Rights of 1981). In contrast, conversion to Islam is encouraged and welcomed, with demographic results that are obvious in the (once Christian) Middle East and North Africa. Another pressing issue in some nations where Islam is dominant is the place of non-Muslims in an Islamic state. Can Christians, for example, be full co-citizens of such a state, or will they have the status of dhimmis (*dhimmīy,* "protected people")? Muslim minorities in Western countries have analogous concerns: can their members live as Muslims and pass their faith on to their children in secularized Western societies?

3.2. During the final third of the 20th century, "dialogue" has been a key concept for thinking about new and renewed approaches in Christian-Muslim relations. Building on the developments adumbrated in 2.6 and 2.7 above, possibilities for dialogue have been explored by the → Roman Catholic Church's Secretariat for Non-Christians (established in 1964), which in 1988 became the Pontifical Council on Interreligious Dialogue (PCID), and by the → World Council of Churches, which sponsored its first formal Christian-Muslim dialogue in 1969 in Cartigny, Switzerland, and two years later established a program subunit Dialogue with People of Living Faiths and Ideologies. These efforts have helped to establish a new climate for dealing with both theological and practical problems. In frequent formal meetings between Muslim and Christian leaders, theological and spiritual issues have been discussed as well as common concerns about human → rights and dignity (the protection of minorities, → religious liberty, peacemaking, justice for oppressed peoples, etc.) and the practice of Christian mission and Islamic *da'wah* ("summons," including issues concerning → proselytism, diaconal work, and the entanglement of Christian mission with Western imperialism).

3.3. The present situation is full of complexity. Muslim communities continue to grow in once-predominantly Christian countries; clashes involving Christians and Muslims continue to occur with sad regularity in various parts of the world; the vigorous revival of Islam in many parts of the Islamic world brings an increasingly self-confident and assertive presence to Christian-Muslim relations; and Christians continue to hold widely divergent views on the proper "approach" to Muslims. Dialogue is here to stay, the reality and risk of conflict in some parts of the world making it a critical component of building both community and nation.

It has gradually become apparent that the most effective dialogue is not that carried on at major international conferences but that which takes place at the local level and which focuses on very concrete challenges and problems. In many places (e.g., Egypt, Pakistan, and Indonesia) there has been fruitful interaction between Christian and Muslim intellectuals in matters of human rights, the development of the civil society, and other areas, while at the grass roots Christians and Muslims have worked together to promote health, literacy, and economic development.

3.4. Another area for Christian reflection and dialogue involves a recognition of the continuing theological and ethical challenges of Islam (see 2.1). A growing number of Western Christian theologians in the current postmodern situation are realizing the importance of other faith traditions such as Islam — and not just Western philosophies — as major dialogue partners for Christian theology. As Christian theologians in the Islamic world gain a voice, they too (in continuity with the arabophone theologians mentioned in 2.3) point to new possibilities for elaborating a Christian dialogic theology in relation to Islam.

3.5. Intense interest in Christian-Muslim dialogue does not mean that traditional Christian concerns for the → proclamation of the gospel have been forgotten. Evangelical Protestants, many of them associated with the Lausanne Covenant (1974), have pressed to keep → evangelism at the top of the international Christian agenda, and the end of the 20th century witnessed intense activity aimed at the evangelization of peoples within the so-called 10/40 Window (i.e., the parts of Africa and Asia lying between 10 and 40 degrees North), many of them Muslim. (This activity is mirrored by that of Muslim groups that see the de-Christianized West as a field ripe for the harvest of Islam.)

Ecumenical Protestant and Roman Catholic theologians and missiologists have devoted much energy to the harmonizing of the twin imperatives of (1) genuine dialogue with people of other faiths and (2) faithful witness to the gospel of Jesus Christ (note the publication on this issue by the PCID in

1991). Christians of the post-Constantinian West may well have much to learn about these matters from the experience of those Christians who have lived as minority communities in Muslim lands and who have learned from long experience the practice of humble yet confident and joyful Christian witness in a context dominated by Islam.

→ Islamic Philosophy; Shia, Shiites; Sufism; Sunna

Bibliography: W. A. BIJLEFELD, ed., *Christian-Muslim Relations* (= *MW* 88/3-4 [1998]) • M. BORRMANS, *Guidelines for Dialogue between Christians and Muslims* (New York, 1990) • K. CRAGG, *The Call of the Minaret* (2d ed.; Maryknoll, N.Y., 1985) • N. DANIEL, *Islam and the West: The Making of an Image* (Edinburgh, 1960) • J.-M. GAUDEUL, *Encounters and Clashes: Islam and Christianity in History* (2 vols.; Rome, 1990) • Y. Y. HADDAD and W. Z. HADDAD, eds., *Christian-Muslim Encounters* (Gainesville, Fla., 1995) • R. G. HOYLAND, *Seeing Islam As Others Saw It: A Survey and Evaluation of Christian, Jewish, and Zoroastrian Writings on Early Islam* (Princeton, 1997) • J. C. LAMOREAUX, "Christianity's Earliest Encounters with Islam," *Touchstone* 5 (1992) 26-31 • T. MICHEL and M. FITZGERALD, eds., *Recognizing the Spiritual Bonds Which Unite Us: Sixteen Years of Christian-Muslim Dialogue* (Vatican City, 1994) • R. E. MILLER, ed., *Islam* (= *WW* 16/2 [1996]) • R. E. MILLER and H. A. O. MWAKABANA, eds., *Christian-Muslim Dialogue: Theological and Practical Issues* (Geneva, 1998) • G. D. NICKEL, *Peaceable Witness among Muslims* (Scottdale, Pa., 1999) • PONTIFICAL COUNCIL FOR INTERRELIGIOUS DIALOGUE AND THE CONGREGATION FOR THE EVANGELIZATION OF PEOPLES, *Dialogue and Proclamation: Reflections and Orientations on Interreligious Dialogue and the Proclamation of the Gospel of Jesus Christ* (Vatican City, 1991) • D. J. SAHAS, *John of Damascus on Islam: The "Heresy of the Ishmaelites"* (Leiden, 1972) • S. K. SAMIR and J. S. NIELSEN, eds., *Christian Arabic Apologetics during the Abbasid Period (750-1258)* (Leiden, 1994) • J. I. SMITH, "Islam and Christendom: Historical, Cultural, and Religious Interactions from the Seventh to the Fifteenth Centuries," *The Oxford History of Islam* (ed. J. L. Esposito; Oxford, 1999) 305-45 • R. W. SOUTHERN, *Western Views of Islam in the Middle Ages* (Cambridge, Mass., 1962) • L. L. VANDER WERFF, *Christian Mission to Muslims–the Record: Anglican and Reformed Approaches in India and the Near East, 1800-1938* (South Pasadena, Calif., 1977) • J. D. WOODBERRY, ed., *Muslims and Christians on the Emmaus Road* (Monrovia, Calif., 1989) • K. ZEBIRI, *Muslims and Christians Face to Face* (Oxford, 1997).

PAUL LÖFFLER and MARK N. SWANSON

Islamic Philosophy

1. Basis and the Various Approaches
   to Theology and Law

The → Koran is the basis for the development of Islam, providing obligatory guidelines for its expression. In contrast, the tradition of the Prophet Muḥammad (ca. 570-632), with his sayings and deeds, gives Islam its practical side. The relation between the Koran and the tradition (sunnah) is like that between an architect's master plan and the detailed instructions of the builder. When Islam spread outside Arabia, social and political issues arose that were not covered by the religious statutes. A way of giving religiously satisfactory answers to the various questions had to be found, for which jurists developed four categories: (1) qiyās (analogy), which used known cases to deal with similar ones; (2) ijmā' (agreement), which would ideally be full consensus; (3) ra'y (expert private opinion); and (4) istiḥsān (discretion, or what seems to be right and good, even though it differs from what might logically be deduced from revealed law or analogy).

Traditionalists rejected the independent use of → reason and preferred to build on the Koran and the tradition of the Prophet. Some of them even rejected qiyās and ra'y.

The mutakallimūn (Lat. loquentes), whom we might call the theologians of Islam, attempted to confirm the Koranic revelation by rational arguments alone, simply quoting the relevant verses from the Koran, followed by the relevant supporting points of tradition. They believed that God's actions are in accordance with reason and that → good and → evil are not just arbitrary or conventional terms with a validity rooted in the divine commands but rational concepts that may be communicated with the help of reason alone.

Advocates of a middle way between theology and philosophy, such as al-Ghazālī (Lat. Algazel, d. 1111), regarded philosophy as reliable but only when developed on a solid basis of faith. The Koran, al-Ghazālī thought, shows us convincingly what is good and what is bad. Reason is subordinate to → revelation and does not have the unshakable certainty of → faith. Such certainty can be achieved only with the help of inspiration, a superior power that God alone can give. Human effort cannot achieve certainty.

The philosophers championed pure reason. They laid down rational premises and worked out the logical implications. If the results of their deliberations conflicted with revelation, they tried to achieve a reconciliation by a suitable interpretation of revelation.

2. First Movements of Political
   and Theological Dissent

The first notable conflict in the history of Islam that led to controversial speculations was the debate between 'Alī (the 4th caliph) and Mu'āwiyah (later the 5th caliph). The struggle for leadership of the Islamic community produced the Kharijites (khārijī, "dissenter, seceder"), who opposed both men and who first raised the problem of the basis and limitation of political authority and also the thorny question of what constitutes a grave → sin, that is, one of such a nature that those who commit it must be banned from the fellowship of the faithful or, in the case of a caliph, must abdicate or be put to death. The Murji'ites (murji'ah, "postponer, believer in suspension of judgment") thought that even this kind of sin should not necessarily involve a loss of membership and preferred to leave such matters to the judgment of God. The Shiites (→ Shia, Shiites) gave unconditional loyalty to 'Alī and, in dealing with the legal question, followed formal rather than material considerations.

Discussion of the nature of a grave sin led to the question of free will and predestination. The Qadarites (from qadar, "fate, destiny") held to the doctrine of free will, arguing that only free sinners had to suffer the consequences of their sins and be banished from the community. Opposing them were the Jabarites (from jabr, "power, force"), who denied free will, viewing all acts as having their origin in God.

Wāṣil ibn 'Aṭā' (d. 748) tried to solve this problem by postulating an intermediate state between belief and unbelief. Wāṣil and Abū al-Hudhayl al-'Allāf (d. ca. 841) systematized for the first time the teaching that would later be known as the school of the Mu'tazilites (mu'tazilah, "those who stand apart"), who stressed the absolute unity and justice of God. The Mu'tazilites, the rationalists of Islam,

focused on the decisive concepts of the divine →
righteousness and unity. They expounded their
teaching in five principles of faith that are the core
of their confession: (1) the unity and uniqueness of
God, (2) his righteousness, (3) the intermediate
state of the grave sinner, (4) the inevitability of the
divine threats and promises, and (5) the demand for
good and the warning against evil.

3. Other Influences

In al-Rāzī (Lat. Rhazes, d. 923/32) we can see some
Indian influence deriving from al-Irānshahrī, especially his atomism. Some important differences between this teaching and its Greek predecessors —
including the atomistic nature of time, space, and
accidents, or the perishability of atoms and their accidents — reflect this influence.

Persian influence affected mostly the moralistic
or aphoristic tradition and focused on the religious
and philosophical implications of → Manichaean
→ dualism.

The encounter between → Greek philosophy and
Islam provoked an ambivalent reaction in Islamic
thought. One party tried to submit the foundations
of religious revelation to critical investigation by
philosophical thinking, Another, however, saw philosophy as audacious and refused to be engaged
with it.

Progress came through constant interaction with
reform movements such as that of al-Ashʿari (d.
935/36), for whom the final and basic source of
good and evil is simply the command or prohibition
of God, or Ibn Taymīyah (d. 1328), who attacked
theologians (the *mutakallimūn*) as well as philosophers. This thought sought to validate the traditionalist concepts and presuppositions of the early protagonists of Islam, the so-called pious ancestors
(al-salaf al-ṣāliḥ) of the Islamic fellowship.

4. Individual Philosophers

4.1. *Al-Kindī*

Yaʿqūb ibn Isḥāq al-Ṣabāḥ al-Kindī (d. ca. 870),
called the Philosopher of the Arabs, was the first to
make use of the Greek legacy. Influenced by Aristotle (384-322 B.C.; → Aristotelianism), al-Kindī
had knowledge of a mixture of legendary and historical sayings of Socrates (ca. 470-399). He also had
a secondhand knowledge of Plato (427-347; → Platonism), whose views about the → soul he shared.
He had a basic knowledge of Aristotle's theology derived from Plotinus *Enn.* 4-6. The theology of Aristotle and the anonymous *Liber de causis* (Book of
causes, by way of Proclus's *Stoicheiōsis theologikē*
[Elements of theology]), which had been translated

into Arabic by Syrian Christians and ascribed to Aristotle, formed the main starting point for Islamic
Neoplatonism.

Although following Aristotle's insights for the
most part, al-Kindī deviated from Aristotle's teaching at many points and was imbued with the spirit
of Islamic dogma. Resisting the idea that the truth
of Islamic revelation might be proved by syllogisms,
he upheld the superiority of revealed → truth to human knowledge. With the theologians, he defended
many Islamic beliefs against materialists, dualists,
and others. He championed the creation of the
world ex nihilo, the → resurrection of the body, the
possibility of → miracles, the validity of prophetic
revelation (→ Prophet, Prophecy), and the origin
and final destruction of the world by God.

4.2. *Al-Fārābī*

Abū Naṣr Muḥammad al-Fārābī (Lat. Alpharabius or
Avennasar, d. ca. 950), known as the "second teacher"
(after Aristotle), noted the antitheses between philosophical schools and made great efforts to reconcile
the teachings of Plato with those of Aristotle. Following Simplicius of Cilicia (fl. ca. 530), al-Fārābī wrote a
treatise on the theme. In the problem of the eternity
of the world and Plato's doctrine of the ideas,
al-Fārābī came close to throwing doubt on the authenticity of Aristotle's theology. He made many contributions to philosophy and political theology and
had a varied influence on later Muslim philosophers.

Al-Fārābī's system of emanations was original,
though essentially he borrowed his images, terms,
and ideas from Plotinus (ca. 205-70). Starting with
the thought that from one, only one can come (not
taken from Plotinus), he argued that from the first
one comes only one being: immaterial and insub-
stantial intelligence. Then comes → emanation in a
process of twofold regress to self-being and to the
first one. This emanation is a natural and automatic
process that brings forth ten distinct and totally immaterial intelligences. The first being is above the
highest of the distinct intelligences. The tenth intelligence is the active intellect. Al-Fārābī thus made a
sharp distinction between God and the first impulse.

This distinction was the basis of the teaching of
Avicenna that it is impossible to establish God's existence by natural proofs. Both ideas would have a
decisive influence on the Latin European Middle
Ages by way of Avicenna (→ God, Arguments for
the Existence of). Al-Fārābī was the first to distinguish between existence and essence, a distinction
that Avicenna adopted and developed in ontological
terms. This insight was regarded as one of the great
achievements of the Middle Ages.

4.3. *Ibn Sīnā (Avicenna)*

The *Rasā'il ikhwān al-ṣafā'* (Discourses of the pure brothers, 10th cent.) and the works of al-Fārābī, along with the works of Aristotle and his Greek commentators, had a decisive impact on the thinking of Ibn Sīnā (Lat. Avicenna, d. 1037), a Persian physician who has been called the most famous Islamic philosopher-scientist. This work consists of 52 pamphlets dealing with the current knowledge in every field, from mathematics, physics, and psychology to epistemology, law, and theology. It outlines three kinds of faith: one for the elect, one for the → masses, and one that combines the two. The last is to be most extolled, for, rooted in knowledge, it is also based on revelation and is available to all, no matter how they seek the truth. Philosophy, → dogma, → metaphysics, and science are thus accessible to all. In many Islamic philosophers like al-Fārābī, Avicenna, al-Ghazālī, and Averroës (see 4.6), we find a classifying of people according to their intellectual abilities, with philosophers first, followed by theologians, then the common folk.

Avicenna, like al-Fārābī, developed a Neoplatonic, though strictly monotheistic, philosophy. Yet both were regarded by Muslim scholars as heretics because they believed in the eternity of the world as distinct from its creation ex nihilo. Avicenna had a great influence on → Scholasticism. Besides his distinction between existence and essence, which became a pillar of → Thomism, he introduced the idea of the person who is free from all external influences, who has no contact with the external world, but to whom it is revealed by individual thought that he or she both is and thinks. This → allegory shows much similarity to the *cogito, ergo sum* of R. Descartes (1596-1650; → Cartesianism).

At this point in philosophical development the political and theological situation in the Islamic world in the East blocked most further progress. An exception was the illuminationist philosophy Avicenna expressed in his Oriental writings, which was espoused and developed in Iran by such luminaries as Shihāb al-Dīn Yaḥyā al-Suhrawardī (d. 1191) and Mullā Sadrā (also called Ṣadr al-Dīn al-Shīrāzī, ca. 1571-1640), whose long line of disciples have maintained the tradition to the present day.

Philosophy developed further in Islamic Spain, where it blossomed under Ibn Gabirol and the three philosophers considered in the following subsections. During the lifetime of Averroës, a great translation enterprise was launched under Archbishop Raymond of Toledo. Along with the works of Aristotle the philosophical and medical writings of

Avicenna, al-Ghazālī, Averroës, and many others were translated into Latin.

The unbridgeable gulf that al-Fārābī put between the first being and the highest of the distinct intelligences and his stress on the divine aspect of the active intellect *(intellectus agens)* prepared the way for the uniting of the human soul with this intellect. Avicenna's God, too, was inaccessible, and the union that was sought may be ascribed to the mystical element in his philosophy, an element not wholly absent from that of al-Fārābī.

4.4. *Ibn Bājjah (Avempace)*

Ibn Bājjah, or Abū Bakr Muḥammad ibn al-Sāyigh (Lat. Avempace, d. 1139), a confessed pupil of al-Fārābī, was a Spanish Arab philosopher, physician, astronomer, mathematician, and poet. He espoused the theory of union between the soul and the active intellect, to achieve which a person must become ruled by will and reason and then increasingly strip off materiality in an upward movement toward the active intellect itself. His psychological and moral insights were his main contribution to philosophy.

4.5. *Ibn Ṭufayl*

Ibn Ṭufayl, or Abū Bakr Muḥammad ibn Ṭufayl (d. 1185/86), Moorish philosopher and physician, is best known for his book *Ḥayy ibn yaqẓān* (Alive son of awake). This parabolic work tells the story of Ḥayy, who grows up alone on a deserted island. Through private → contemplation he attains to wisdom and achieves knowledge of nature and God. In this state he comes across Asāl, a member of a religious community on a nearby island. After learning how to speak with Asāl, Ḥayy discovers that his philosophy and Asāl's religion are two versions of the same truth. The basic theses of the → parable are that there is no contradiction between philosophy and religion; there is only one truth, which may be attained by different paths; union with the active intellect may be achieved by the persistent effort of philosophers; and there are various solutions to metaphysical problems.

→ Islam and Christianity; Middle Ages; Sufism; Sunna

Bibliography: G. C. ANAWATI, "Philosophie, Theologie und Mystik," *Das Vermächtnis des Islams* (ed. J. Schacht and C. E. Bosworth; vol. 2; Zurich, 1980) 119-65 • A. J. ARBERY, *Reason and Revelation in Islam* (London, 1957) • A. BADAWI, *Histoire de la philosophie en Islam* (2 vols.; Paris, 1972) • T. J. DE BOER, *Geschichte der Philosophie im Islam* (Stuttgart, 1901) • H. CORBIN, *Historie de la philosophie islamique* (vol. 1; Paris, 1964); idem, "La philosophie islamique depuis la mort d'Averroes jusqu'à nos jours," *Histoire de la philosophie* (vol. 3; Paris, 1974) 1067-1188 • M. CRUZ HERNÁNDEZ, *Historia de la filosofía española, filosofía hispano-musulmana* (2 vols.; Madrid, 1957) • M. FAKHRY, *A History of Islamic Philosophy* (New York, 1970) • *Mélanges de philosophie juive et arabe* (Paris, 1859; repr., 1927) • J. P. DE MENASCE, *Arabische Philosophie* (Bern, 1948) • S. MUNK, *De principaux philosophes arabes et de leur doctrine* (Paris, 1955; repr., 1982) 309-458 • M. M. SHARIF, ed., *A History of Muslim Philosophy* (2 vols.; Wiesbaden, 1963-66) • R. WALZER, "Islamic Philosophy," *History of Philosophy, Eastern and Western* (ed. S. Radhakrishnan; vol. 2; London, 1953) 120-48 • W. M. WATT, *Islamic Philosophy and Theology* (Edinburgh, 1962) • W. M. WATT and M. MARMURA, eds., *Der Islam,* vol. 2, *Politische Entwicklungen und theologische Konzepte* (Stuttgart, 1985) • H. A. WOLFSON, *The Philosophy of the Kalām* (Cambridge, Mass., 1976). Also see the articles "Falsafa," "Kalām," and "Taṣawwuf," *Enzyklopädie des Islams* (Eng., Leiden, 1960ff.).

SAMIR VOUWZEE

4.6. *Ibn Rushd (Averroës), Averroism*

4.6.1. Abū al-Walīd Muḥammad ibn Rushd (Lat. Averroës, 1126-98) integrated Islamic traditions and Greek thought. In 1169 Ibn Ṭufayl himself introduced Averroës to Caliph Abū Yaʿqūb Yūsuf, who asked Averroës to write a commentary on the Aristotelian corpus. He set about this task with great zeal, developing a detailed interpretation of Aristotle's system that remained very influential for centuries.

The term "Averroism" denotes various philosophical movements in Italy from the mid-13th to the 17th century. These movements began with the reception of Aristotle (→ Aristotelianism) by way of the commentary of Averroës. Common to all of them was the scholastic method of dealing with the teaching of Aristotle sentence by sentence with the help of the commentary. Often the views would find only their starting point in Averroës. Averroism served as a stimulus to independent secular thinking, which produced various schools appealing to it. It was repeatedly condemned on the basis of its supposed denial of human freedom and personal immortality.

4.6.2. The thought of Averroës must be seen in conjunction with his total work as an Islamic jurist and theologian and must not be viewed solely from the perspective of his commentary on Greek philosophy. For him matter and the world were eternal, and their development was necessary. God is part of the world, its first cause or prime mover. Creation is a constant movement, not a static creation ex nihilo.

As regards the intellect, Averroës saw a passive as well as an active intellect. The real intellect is the functional union of the two, which is dissolved at death. The → immortality of the → soul and the → resurrection cannot be proved philosophically but may be known by → revelation. The nuanced position of Averroës became in Averroism a monopsychism that denied the soul's individual immortality.

Averroës is remembered also as the author of the theory of double truth, which holds that philosophical thinking can sometimes lead to results that specifically contradict revealed truth. For Averroës, however, this contradiction had no material impact because, using the methods of Islamic jurisprudence, he resolved it in favor of philosophy by an → allegorical exposition of Koranic revelation. Philosophical learning is esoteric and beyond the masses, though philosophers also must follow religious orthodoxy outwardly. The contradiction became materially significant in the Latin Middle Ages. At first the doctrine of double truth was meant to protect philosophers (through mental reservation), who could recognize religious truth and present philosophy as merely mental play. Such teaching, though, ultimately produced and claimed knowledge that was independent of religious presuppositions, which introduced material conflict with orthodoxy.

4.6.3. The commentary of Averroës was known in the West from 1230. It played an important role for Albertus Magnus and → Thomas Aquinas (→ Scholasticism; Thomism); Boethius of Dacia took up Averroism as a scientific method. Paris synods in 1270 and 1277 under Bishop Stephan Tempier condemned the main teachings of Averroism and other tenets of the philosophers of the Paris faculty (esp. Siger of Brabant). This censure, however, did not end discussion of its method and teaching, which found critical adherents and developers in John of Jandun, Marsilius of Padua, Thomas Wilton, Walter Burleigh, Angelo of Arezzo, Taddeo of Parma, and others.

In Italy from 1320 Averroist schools arose in Bologna and Padua that recognized the teachings of the commentary as authoritative and developed them in a closed, rationalistic system. Here we might mention Pietro d'Abano, Cajetan of Thiene, and Pietro Pomponazzi, whose doctrine of double truth was contested by Nicholas Taurellus and Philipp → Melanchthon.

Averroism has many implications for social ethics. The idea that we must follow a natural way to → happiness and knowledge was popularized by wandering clerics (Goliards) and was taken up as a theme in literature. The rejection of individuality and the immortality of the soul, bound up with a psychological determinism that ruled out personal responsibility, became a weapon against the direction of conscience by the church. Philosophy's claim to be a source of knowledge and truth independently of religious presuppositions was in keeping with the social situation in Italy after the 14th century, for the middle and merchant classes were now freeing themselves from clerical and feudal tutelage and laying the foundations of a modern understanding of the world (→ Renaissance).

Averroism eventually hardened into a closed doctrine, "learning nothing and forgetting nothing" (É. Gilson); in a world that it had originally changed, it became a reaction that rejected the modern scientific → worldview. This development, however, should not cause us to minimize the contribution of Averroism to the development of thought in the West. One of its main ideas, that of a single world intelligence, has gained a surprising new relevance today as the Darwinian theory of → evolution is being replaced by a cybernetic view that postulates a cosmic plan.

Bibliography: L'averroismo in Italia (Rome, 1979) • L. V. Berman, *Ibn Rushd's Middle Commentary on the Nicomachean Ethics in Medieval Hebrew Literature* (Paris, 1978) • E. Gilson, *History of Christian Philosophy in the Middle Ages* (New York, 1955) • *Multiple Averroes. Acte du Colloque international organise a l'occasion du 850e anniversaire de la naissance d'Averroes* (Paris, 1978) • B. Nardi, *Studi di filosofia medievale* (Rome, 1960) • F. von Steenberghen, *Die Philosophie im 13. Jahrhundert* (Munich, 1977).

Manfred Kropp

Israel

1. Historical Israel
    1.1. Name
    1.2. Prenational Period
    1.3. Nation Building
    1.4. David and Solomon
    1.5. Northern Kingdom until 722
    1.6. Judah until 586
    1.7. Exile and Restoration
    1.8. Hellenism
    1.9. Roman Rule
2. Modern State of Israel
    2.1. History

	1960	1980	2000
Population (1,000s):	1,777	3,233	4,982
Annual growth rate (%):	3.85	1.75	1.56

Area: 20,400 sq. km. (7,876 sq. mi.)

A.D. *2000*

Population density: 244/sq. km. (633/sq. mi.)
Births / deaths: 1.88 / 0.64 per 100 population
Fertility rate: 2.53 per woman
Infant mortality rate: 6 per 1,000 live births
Life expectancy: 78.3 years (m: 76.3, f: 80.3)
Religious affiliation (%): Jews 76.2, Muslims 12.5, Christians 6.1 (Roman Catholics 3.0, indigenous 2.1, other Christians 1.0), nonreligious 4.2, other 1.0.
Note: Figures exclude the West Bank, East Jerusalem, the Gaza Strip, and the Golan Heights.

    2.2. Society
    2.3. Economy and Culture
    2.4. Constitution
    2.5. Religions
3. Christian Groups in Israel and Palestine
    3.1. Orthodox Churches
    3.2. Roman Catholic Churches
    3.3. Oriental Orthodox Churches
    3.4. Protestant Churches
    3.5. Other Christian Bodies and Ecumenism

1. Historical Israel

1.1. *Name*

"Israel" is a theophorous name in which the proper name "El" (God) is combined with the verb *śrh* as its subject. The OT gives this verb the sense of striving. The patriarch → Jacob is called Israel because he had "striven with God" (Gen. 32:28, see also Hos. 12:3-4). This popular etymology, however, is not a reliable witness for the original meaning of the verb, and it also misunderstands the theophoric element "El" as an object.

In the OT, the name "Israel" refers to different, albeit related, entities: the early tribes, the united kingdom of → David and → Solomon, the northern kingdom after the disruption, Judah when the North collapsed, and finally, from a religious standpoint, the Jews as a whole (→ Judaism).

1.2. *Prenational Period*

The first historical occurrence of the name "Israel" is found in about 1225 B.C. in an extrabiblical witness, namely, the "Israel Stele" of Pharaoh Merneptah, which reads in part, "Israel is laid waste, his seed is not" (*TGI* [3d ed.] 40; *ANET* 378; *AOT* 24-25). The hieroglyphic orthography with the determinative "people" and the accompanying context make it likely that the reference is to a group of people rather than to a city or some other locale, and it proves that this particular Israel was already settled in precisely the area in which the biblical Israel did indeed find its homeland. Although some connection must thus obtain between the Israel of the stele and that of the OT, the connection itself is difficult to articulate, just as the history of Israel's pre-state period in the larger sense can at best only be hypothetically disclosed.

The OT states that in its earliest period, Israel was a confederation of 12 tribes (Judges 5) genealogically descended from the patriarch Jacob-Israel and through him from → Isaac and → Abraham. That the genealogical line Abraham-Jacob-Israel is just as much a fiction as the notion of the 12 → tribes emerging from Jacob's 12 sons does not necessarily mean that this richly developed OT tradition has no basis in historical fact. Rather, the patriarchal traditions (→ Patriarchal History) have been fused through genealogical references with authentic Israel traditions. Jacob becomes Israel, and the 12 tribes are viewed as descendants of Jacob's sons. So even though the traditional historical combinations may be fictitious and secondary, the patriarchal traditions themselves, along with the (independent) traditions about a tribal confederation called Israel, do indeed contain the basic core of Israel's prehistory.

The original core of the patriarchal stories betrays an early stage at which seminomadic groups became sedentary (→ Nomads) and, over the course of their seasonal moves to different pastures, acquired the right of domicile on the periphery of cultivated areas. Various considerations — including the meaning of the patriarchs' names, the seminomadic backdrop, legal customs, and locales — make this understanding more probable than other attempts that understand the patriarchs as fictitious figures created by the pious exilic-postexilic imagination. Similarly, and despite its overlayering by legends and later attempts at standardization and idealization, the notion of a confederation of 12 tribes of Israel is certainly no mere fiction. No cogent reason can be adduced that might have prompted the later invention of this sort of fiction, particularly given Israel's own profound and enduring attachment to the notion of tribe within its own identity, though the character and organization of such a confederation called Israel, a confederation apparently already presupposed by the Merneptah stele, can be described only hypothetically, and even then only in rough outline.

The hypothesis developed especially by Martin Noth regarding Israel's pre-state identity in analogy

to Greek and Italian amphictyonies has recently been subjected to justified criticism. That analogy was actually taken too far, drawing from in part more recent texts and from notions not actually attested until much later (e.g., the → covenant, making a covenant, the central sanctuary, amphictyonic law) in presenting an overly detailed picture of Israel's prehistory and early history, one that cannot stand up to serious scrutiny. Nonetheless, one can still assert with some certainty that in the second half of the 13th century B.C., a tribal confederation existed that worshiped the God El and thus called itself Israel. Israel's "religious" name as well as its religiously oriented traditions concerning that pre-state period do allow the assumption that especially shared religious beliefs and cultic ties were constitutive for its early history; these elements then found expression in fictitious kinship relations that for those affected did nonetheless manifest themselves in very real ways, and thus also in the idea of an amphictyony of 12 tribes.

Because this confederation did not, however, have any constant central authority with political and military powers, one can with F. Crüsemann also call Israel in its pre-state form an *acephalous segmentary society*. Although almost the only thing reported about the officeholders scholars describe as "lesser judges" — in contradistinction to the charismatic leaders (→ Charisma) described as "greater judges" — is that they "judged Israel" (Judg. 10:1-5; 12:7-15), which does not allow reference to a seamless succession of leaders, their tasks obviously did involve Israel as a whole. Formulas used almost as technical terms such as "such a thing ought not to be done," "a disgraceful act in Israel," or "such a thing is not done in Israel" (Gen. 34:7; Deut. 22:21; Judg. 20:6; 2 Sam. 13:12; Jer. 29:23) demonstrate that in the meantime, the pan-Israelite ties were not merely ideal but were also at least minimally institutionalized in binding → laws. These formulas refer to sexual transgressions prohibited in Israel, and the expression "in Israel" makes it clear that the situation is reflecting a specific law applicable to all of Israel rather than clan ethos.

A more difficult task is reconstructing Israel's emergence in Canaan. The OT portrayal, which seems to be historically inaccurate, says that the tribes left Egypt under → Moses' leadership, spent 40 years in the wilderness, conquered the land of Canaan in a unified campaign under Moses' successor Joshua, and then divided the land among themselves. The traditions recounting this version are perhaps legends. Tradition criticism has also shown that the tradition complexes out of which the →

Pentateuch and Joshua derive — namely, the patriarchal narratives, exodus, wilderness wanderings, →
Sinai, and the conquest — were originally unrelated
and reflect the experiences of different groups; only
later did these groups fuse into the entity Israel. This
insight, however, also caused the narrative framework extending from Abraham to Joshua to collapse, such that the framework itself can no longer
be employed directly for any historical reconstruction, which must instead begin with the original individual traditions, critique them for historical accuracy, and then combine them with both
archaeological (→ Archaeology 1) and extrabiblical
findings. The following four hypothetical reconstruction attempts are currently on the table:

1.2.1. *The biblical portrayal is essentially reliable;*
contradictions between Joshua 1–12 (conquest of
Canaan in a single, pan-Israelite campaign) and
Judges 1 (conquest by individual tribes) are only apparent, since Judges 1 is referring only to later area
adjustments among the tribes (Y. Kaufmann, W. F.
Albright, G. E. Wright). This activity thus constituted
a conquest in the stricter sense whose traces archaeol-
ogists can discern in the destruction of Canaanite cities (e.g., Hazor) during the transition from the Late
Bronze to the Iron Age (ca. 1200).

This view, however, overlooks the contradictions
of the biblical portrayal and underestimates the legendary character of most of the traditions themselves. The actual cause of the destruction of cities
can be surmised only with uncertainty, and precisely the cities of Jericho and Ai, whose conquest is
traced back to Joshua himself (Joshua 7–8), had already become ruins during an earlier period.

1.2.2. *The "conquest" was actually a gradual and
peaceful process.* During the course of seasonal
changes of pastures, individual clans settled on the
periphery of the cultivated land and on the as yet
uninhabited mountains; only later did military
clashes develop between the emergent Israelite
tribes and the Canaanites, who controlled the cities
(A. Alt, M. Noth).

This thesis remains problematic insofar as it
maintains the untested presupposition that the wilderness was always the homeland of nomads and
seminomads who repeatedly intruded into the cultivated areas and displaced or were absorbed into the
earlier inhabitants.

1.2.3. *The "conquest" actually represented a shift
in social stratification.* This shift, which took place
only very gradually, caused the position of power
that the internally divided Canaanite cities originally held to collapse and recede in the face of
broader Israelite territorial organization. Israelite

tribes of → Hebrews, persons of less rank attested
elsewhere during this same period, extracted themselves from the previous feudal system of the cities
and assumed power peacefully (G. E. Mendenhall)
or seized it through revolution (N. Gottwald).

This view correctly recognizes that the traditional notion of a nomadic origin of the Israelites is
highly unlikely, according to which they either entered from the wilderness or even intruded into Canaan in military campaigns. The hypothesis does
not, however, do justice to the deeply rooted and
widespread tradition of Israel's receiving Canaan as
a gift from its God or to the fact that → Yahweh,
who is identified with El and whom Israel worshiped, does not represent a Canaanite deity.

1.2.4. The contradictory multiple strata of the
various traditions correspond best to the assumption that *the "conquest" was largely an in-
ner-Canaanite process involving a shift in social stratification accompanied by an influx of nomadic and
seminomadic elements* from outside the cultivated
regions who imported from Sinai the worship of
Yahweh — a zealous, jealous, bellicose God. The
identification of this God with the El of Israel must
probably also be understood as taking place only
gradually and contemporaneous with the transition
from the initial, peaceful "conquest" to the second,
military stage.

The so-called conquest narratives reflect these
events (Num. 21:21-35; 32; Joshua 11; Judg. 1:1-26).
Although they take place in their present context
during the period of Moses and Joshua, or immediately after Joshua's death, historically they date to
the period during which Israel's tribes were consoli-
dating themselves. Israel itself became stronger and
involved in disputes not only with Canaanite cities
but also with neighboring peoples. The Book of
Judges shows that it was individual tribes or smaller
groups that were led into war (→ Holy War) by
charismatic "judges," though the → Deuteronomistic redaction does portray a continuity in the
history of Israel as a whole between Joshua and →
Saul's accession by construing a succession of judges
interrupted by interim periods of oppression "without judges" prompted by Israel's apostasy from
Yahweh.

Individual traditions, however, show that actual
events took place with much less continuity. Apart
from Ehud (Judg. 3:12-30), a Benjaminite who
came into conflict with Moab, it is especially
Jephthah of Gilead (10:17–12:7) and his battle with
the Ammonites, and then also Gideon from Man-
asseh (6–8), who thwarted the Midianites, whose
histories acquire sharper contours. The most im-

portant event, however, was the battle of Megiddo (4–5) against a coalition of Canaanite cities. Under the leadership of Barak of Naphtali and the Ephraimite charismatic Deborah, several Israelite tribes from Galilee fought together and defeated the superior opposing forces.

One of the leaders of that opposition, Sisera, bears an Illyrian name, showing him to be a member of the sea peoples (→ Philistines), whose emergence can be dated to approximately 1300 B.C. This movement was part of the Doric migrations and included non-Semitic elements ("the uncircumcised") who also settled in the coastal regions of northern Syria and in southern Philistia, apparently with the permission of Egypt, resulting in the development of the Pentapolis of Gaza, Ashdod, Ashkelon, Gath, and Ekron. Whereas the name "Sisera" shows that the Philistines had acquired power in the North at the expense of the Canaanites by the time of the battle of Megiddo, the Samson stories (Judges 13–16) show that the Philistines had already come to rule virtually the entire southern part of the country. This Philistine threat prompted the emergence of the state of Israel itself.

1.3. *Nation Building*
Certain witnesses suggest that steps were taken to form a state earlier as well. Although the traditions concerning Abimelech (Judges 8–9) are legendary and somewhat muddled, it is clear that Abimelech did try to establish a state with its capital at Shechem to force a symbiotic relationship between Israel and Canaan, though this attempt ended with Abimelech's own violent death. Traditions surrounding Gideon also reveal attempts to establish a more stable center of power. Gideon himself allegedly founded a sanctuary to Yahweh in his hometown of Ophrah, probably as a sacred center, and was asked to be king (8:22-23). His alleged rejection of this offer is, however, narrated with formulations from a later period (v. 23), presumably concealing the true course of events.

Whereas the OT views Abimelech as a usurper and Gideon as a devout judge who did not wish to challenge Yahweh's own rule, traditions concerning the Benjaminite Saul openly proclaim not only that Saul affirmed the notion of kingship but that Yahweh himself bestowed kingship upon Saul. These traditions also show that threats from external enemies, namely, the Ammonites and especially the Philistines, made it necessary to establish a more tightly organized system of leadership, since the Israelite army was no match for the superior military power of the Philistines. After Saul proved himself as a charismatic leader in a war against Ammon, the people made him king (1 Samuel 11).

Saul's kingship was above all a military kingship representing the highest military leaders of the tribal confederation, though it remains uncertain just which tribes acknowledged him as king. In any event, the judge Samuel, representing the tribal confederation, legalized this innovation, as shown by 1 Sam. 10:25, which mentions a book outlining the duties of the kingship. Under his own and his son Jonathan's command, Saul organized a standing army (14:52) and established an ongoing leadership office in the person of the "commander of his army," as the first of which he appointed his cousin Abner (14:50). These measures as well as the fact that his son Ishbaal was considered to be his successor after his death (2 Sam. 2:8-10) show that a dynasty was to be established, though it did not come about. After initial successes, Saul failed in his defeat at the hands of the Philistines on Mount Gilboa (1 Samuel 31).

1.4. *David and Solomon*
It seems almost miraculous that soon after the disastrous fall of Saul, David was able to defeat the Philistines, found a state, and expand it into a kingdom that, in more modest form, survived the vicissitudes of history up to 586 B.C. David had first served under Saul, then with the Philistines. He had formed his own force, and with its help he had himself proclaimed king of Judah (2 Sam. 2:1-4a). He then extended his rule to all Israel (5:1-3). He captured the Canaanite city of → Jerusalem in the neutral area between the southern and northern tribes and made it his capital (5:6-7). He took over any remaining independent Canaanite towns and in various forms integrated Moab, Ammon, Aram-Damascus, and Edom into his kingdom.

David's empire was thus made up of (1) Judah, together with the southern confederated groups; (2) the territory of the northern tribes; (3) the city of Jerusalem; (4) Canaanite towns; (5) the territory of Philistine vassal princes; and (6) relatively autonomous neighboring states. Israel had now become multinational. The people did not wholly welcome this development, however, as may be seen from the revolts against David (Absalom in 2 Samuel 15–19, Sheba in 20:1-22). Contemporary → historiography also confirms this view in its free criticism of the → monarchy (see the history of David's succession, 2 Samuel 9–20; 1 Kings 1–2).

The reign of Solomon (965-926), although it saw crumbling on the frontiers, was a time of consolidation and glory. Solomon extended the capital and built a palace complex with a → temple (§1) that had the dignity of a royal state → sanctuary. Tyre, with whose king (Hiram) David had established friendly relations, provided the model and the materials for the temple. As an Oriental king, Solomon was God's own son, dwelling in his palace as God's neighbor. Jerusalem became the entry point for foreign ideas such as the notion of Yahweh as a God reigning on Zion who makes his dwelling place impregnable (Psalm 46) and as the supreme God and Creator (Gen. 14:18-20). For the purposes of administration and taxation, the kingdom was divided into 12 districts (1 Kgs. 4:7-19). For security a force of chariots was established (4:26-28), with stalls and garrisons at Hazor, Megiddo, Gezer, and Beth-Horon (9:15-17). Trade flourished, and a fleet was built at Ezion-geber. The new state, however, brought with it the violation of many native freedoms and crushing taxation. Conservative resistance developed in the North, and after Solomon's death disruption quickly followed.

1.5. *Northern Kingdom until 722*

The break became final when the northern tribes refused to accept Rehoboam, Solomon's son, and chose as king instead Jeroboam, a former official under Solomon (1 Kgs. 12:20). The northern kingdom now came to be known as Israel. This shows that the name "Israel" had already become more firmly established here than in the south and that Judah too had already become a relatively independent entity. Nonetheless, the division of the kingdom was more than the dissolution of a mere personal union, since despite any establishment of independence, Judah and Benjamin and the rest of Israel did belong together as a result of their prehistory and worship of Yahweh. The histories of the two kingdoms, though, took different paths.

The Davidic dynasty was firmly established in Judah, but Israel had no such stability. Jeroboam gave it two sanctuaries in Bethel and Dan but did not build a capital. Shechem served first as the royal residence, then Tirzah. Bloody coups ended any hope of a dynasty. Throughout the period up to 722, only two of the ten houses lasted for any length of time: that of Omri (Omri, Ahab, Ahaziah, Joram/Jehoram, 881-845), and that of Jehu (Jehu, Jehoahaz, Joash, Jeroboam II, 845-746).

Omri gave the state a fortified capital at Samaria. He also ended border disputes with Judah, realizing that the two states had to stand together against the → Arameans of Damascus and the expansive, aggressive Assyrians. His son Ahab followed the same policy. According to an inscription of the Assyrian king Shalmaneser III (859-824), Ahab joined the coalition that defeated Assyria at the battle of Karkar in the Orontes valley in 854/853 (*ANET* 278-79; *TGI*

[3d ed.] 49-50). The house of Omri attempted fusion with the Canaanites and the coexistence of Yahweh and Baal. This blending was the point of Ahab's marriage with Princess Jezebel of Tyre, which the → prophets of Yahweh → Elijah, → Elisha, and their circle condemned and contested as apostasy. The bloody revolt of Jehu put an end to this policy. As recorded on the Black Obelisk (*AOB* [2d ed.] 121-25), Jehu paid tribute to Assyria.

A lull in Assyrian expansion after 838 ushered in the period of the worst Aramean crisis (see Amos 1:3-5). Only when Assyrian pressure on the Arameans brought relief could Israel blossom again (ca. 800-750). The prophets Amos and Hosea threatened judgment on the people's lack of → righteousness and knowledge of God, and this judgment fell when bloody internal conflict followed the death of Jeroboam II in 746.

Around 733 Assyrian aggression provoked resistance on the part of Israel and other small states. When Asa of Judah prudently remained neutral, the allied Israelites and Syrians tried to topple him. This war (Isaiah 7–8; Hos. 5:8-11) was the beginning of the end for Israel. The Assyrians attacked and reduced it to Samaria and Mount Ephraim, dividing the rest among three Assyrian provinces. A last attempt at resistance on the part of Hoshea ended in 722 with the long siege and capture of Samaria. As happened ten years earlier, many leaders were deported, and a foreign upper class settled in Israel (*ANET* 284; *TGI* [3d ed.] 60-61; 2 Kings 17).

1.6. *Judah until 586*

Judah up to 586 enjoyed several stabilizing factors: the Davidic dynasty, Jerusalem as its capital and site of the temple, Zion as the place of the divine presence, and the smallness of the state after the loss of the associated territories. As Assyria expanded, Judah became a tributary state pledged to loyalty. Revolts in association with other small states, and with the hope of help from Egypt, worsened the situation in 723-711 and 705-701, and Jerusalem barely escaped capture in 701. Isaiah, who had warned Judah about seeking help from Egypt instead of from Yahweh (Isa. 30:1-5; 31:1-3), complained that the land had become a desert and that the cities had been burned with fire (1:4-9). Such a picture vividly portrayed the situation.

Like Israel 100 years earlier, Judah enjoyed another brief blossoming when Assyrian power declined at the end of the seventh century. The reform of → Josiah (639-608) was an expression of the new independence. Josiah was even able to annex territory in the North, including Galilee. It almost seemed as though the kingdom of David and Solomon might be restored. When the power vacuum was filled again, however, Judah inevitably came under new foreign subjection. Josiah's death in fact meant the end of national independence.

Josiah's successor, Jehoiakim, was named by Pharaoh in place of another son called Jehoahaz. At first an Egyptian vassal, Jehoiakim became a tributary of Babylon after the Babylonians (Chaldeans) defeated the Egyptians at Carchemish on the Euphrates (605). Jeremiah preached unmistakably that subjection to Babylon was the will of Yahweh, his judgment on his disobedient people. Attempts to break free from Babylon brought down disaster. In 598 Jehoiachin, son of Jehoiakim, had to capitulate to save Jerusalem from destruction. He and some of the upper class, probably including Ezekiel, went into exile. Jeremiah sent them a letter in Babylon in which he told them to prepare for a long captivity, to see in the well-being of the city their own → salvation, and to seek it from Yahweh (Jeremiah 29). When Judah's last king, Zedekiah, attempted a new revolt against Jeremiah's advice, Jerusalem was captured and destroyed in 586. More of the people were then deported.

1.7. *Exile and Restoration*

The biblical account, according to which the entire population had gone into exile (2 Kgs. 25:11, 21b; 2 Chr. 36:20-21), is not historically accurate; its intention is to point out that God's judgment was total. Although they too diverge, the numbers reported in 2 Kgs. 24:14-16 and Jer. 52:28-30 are a bit more reliable. According to Jeremiah, 4,600 inhabitants were already deported in 598, and according to 2 Kings it was 10,000. Although it is clear enough that this deportation did deplete the population somewhat, especially since the leading classes were particularly affected, it did not decimate the Judean population. Gedaliah, a Judean, was made governor over those who remained. He lived at Mizpah in the north of Judah, which was now a province. He was assassinated, however, and it seems that Judah then became part of the Province of Samaria.

Although we speak of the Babylonian captivity, the exiles were not prisoners. They formed a semifree subject people on the Lower Euphrates and Tigris. As we see from Ezekiel, they practiced their religion as far as it was possible in exile. → Circumcision and keeping of the → Sabbath, which were not tied to the Holy Land, became very important as acts of confession. For many, however, the "land of their fathers" was the goal of their hope, as may be seen especially in the promises of a new exodus (see Isaiah 46–55).

When the Persians took over the Babylonian em-

pire (538), pursuant to their policy of restoration the new rulers promoted the return of the exiles and the rebuilding of the temple. There was no united or otherwise miraculous return; as we see from Ezra and Nehemiah, groups of exiles went back in several stages. The second temple was dedicated in 515. Of the greatest significance for the future was the Persian revision of Israel's legal status. The recognition of Israel's own law forms the background of the accounts in Ezra and Nehemiah (Ezra 7:25-26). The Israelites and Judeans had now become Jews in the sense of a legally recognized and autonomous religious society on the basis of descent and nationality. At the latest by the time of Nehemiah (445-432), Judah became a separate province with its own governor, a status it maintained up to the Roman period.

1.8. *Hellenism*

Alexander the Great's march through Palestine to Egypt (333/332) ended Persian rule and began Hellenistic domination. After the conflicts between his successors were concluded, Israel and Judah became part of the Egyptian state of the Ptolemies up to 198. In keeping with the tolerant spirit of → Hellenism, we may assume that the autonomy and privileges of the Jews were left intact. The highest official was the → high priest, alongside whom was a council of notables, the Gerousia, later the Sanhedrin.

A Greek-speaking Jewish colony lived in → Alexandria, the capital, where it developed a rich cultural life. A Greek translation of the OT was made there (→ Bible Versions 2), the LXX, which later became Holy Scripture of the → early church. Jewish families also settled in Asia Minor, Lydia, Phrygia, Damascus, on Delos, and in Sparta. A worldwide Judaism arose that spoke Greek and was open to Hellenistic culture. The Hellenization of Samaria, where a military colony was settled, led conservative circles to build a temple of their own at Shechem (→ Samaritans). The way was thus prepared for the Samaritan schism, though it did not become final until after the destruction of the Gerizim temple by the Hasmonaean John Hyrcanus I (135-104).

In 198 B.C. Phoenicia and southern Palestine, including Judea, became part of the Seleucid kingdom. This change of power at first brought extended privileges, but it then ended the positive relationship with the foreign rulers. Antiochus IV Epiphanes (175-164) interfered with the inner affairs of the cultic community in Jerusalem, where a Hellenized and a conservative party were feuding, acting in favor of the Hellenists. He plundered the city, forbade the Jewish cult, including circumcision and the Sabbath, and in 167 made the temple into a sanctuary for Zeus Olympios (see Dan. 11:31; 12:11:

"the abomination that desolates"). This forced Hellenization provoked a violent reaction in conservative Jewish circles. The priestly family of the Hasmonaeans-Maccabees took the lead, including Judas (166-160), Jonathan (160-143), Simon (143-135), and John Hyrcanus I, who like Simon was also high priest.

With the decline of the Seleucids the monarchy was restored: Aristobulus I (104-103), Alexander Jannaeus (103-76), Alexander's wife, Salome Alexandra (76-67), John Hyrcanus II (67, 63-40), and Aristobulus II (67-63). The revolt of Judas and his brothers was so successful that resistance came from the devout groups known as the Hasidim (→ Hasidism), who only wanted a restoration of → religious liberty. The seizure of the office of high priest by the Hasmonaeans, who were not Zadokites, was illegal in conservative eyes and led to the secession of the Essenes (→ Qumran). The uniting of the high priestly and the kingly offices from the time of Aristobulus I was inevitably resisted as a sign of Hellenistic secularization.

Hasmonaean policies were rejected by the → Pharisees, who came into being at this time as a lay group. For them the expounding and practicing of the → law in everyday life was the essence of true religion and the mark of true Israel. They gained great influence over the people and were behind a revolt against Alexander Jannaeus. Salome in particular had to take their demands into account.

1.9. *Roman Rule*

When Salome's death in 67 B.C. led to strife over the succession, Pompey in 63 saw a good reason to intervene, confirming Hyrcanus II as high priest but stripping him of the kingship. Judea now became part of the Province of Syria and lost the coastal cities and the cities in East Jordan (Decapolis) that the → Hasmonaeans had annexed. Samaria, conquered in 107, was also detached from Judea. Judea still included southern Idumea, which John Hyrcanus had Judaized by force, Perea east of the Jordan, and Galilee. With religious freedoms and privileges being upheld, the people in all these areas took part in worship at Jerusalem.

The situation changed when the Idumean → Herod the Great, son of the procurator Antipas (whom Rome had favored), became king with the blessing and assistance of Rome (ruled 37-4 B.C.). Along with Judea and Samaria, Augustus placed under his rule Jericho, Gaza, Anthedon, and Strato's Tower on the coast, plus Gadara and Hippus east of the Jordan. Herod's inclinations were Hellenistic and Roman, but he took into account the religious sensibilities of the people. He built the Jerusalem temple in

the style of the day and more than doubled the size of the temple precincts. The surviving wall of this temple, the so-called Western Wall, once part of the city walls, is a testimony to his building activity. Fortresses were also built or extended, including Herodeion near Bethlehem, Macherus east of the Dead Sea, and Masada just west of the Dead Sea.

In spite of his services in strengthening the state, Herod, as a vassal of Rome, had no popular base. Believing that he was surrounded by enemies, he defended himself by merciless cruelty. After his death his territories were divided among his sons. Judea went to Archelaus (4 B.C.–A.D. 6), Galilee and Perea to Herod Antipas (4 B.C.–A.D. 39), and Trachonitis, Batanea, and Auranitis to Philip (4 B.C.–A.D. 34). In A.D. 6 Judea came under a procurator, with Caesarea as the seat of government. This would remain its status apart from a break in 41-44, when Herod Agrippa ruled as king over Judea and almost all Palestine.

Anti-Roman unrest began already with the death of Herod the Great. The most important leaders of resistance were the → Zealots, who directed their zeal against the Romans and all who did not accept their radicalism. Revolt came in 66 and ended in 70 with the capture and destruction of Jerusalem by Titus. Masada held out until 73, when the Romans took it after desperate resistance.

A later revolt of Simeon bar Kokhba (i.e., "Simeon, Son of the Star," afterward changed to bar Koziba, "Son of the Liar," d. 135) enjoyed only initial successes, though coins were minted that, with fragments of authentic writings of the period found in 1951/52, suggest that the revolt had an eschatological character (→ Messianism). The revolt ended with defeat, devastation, and the decimation of the people. Many → rabbis were martyred, among them Akiba ben Joseph, who supposedly viewed Simeon as the Messiah. Jerusalem was now renamed Aelia Capitolina, and Jews were forbidden to enter the city. The province was named Syria-Palestina (→ Palestine), after Israel's former enemies, the Philistines.

→ Monotheism; New Testament Era, History of; Roman Empire; Semites

Bibliography: General Histories: G. W. AHLSTRÖM, *The History of Ancient Palestine from the Palaeolithic Period to Alexander's Conquest* (Sheffield, 1993) • R. B. COOTE, *Early Israel: A New Horizon* (Minneapolis, 1990) • F. M. CROSS, *From Epic to Canon: History and Literature in Ancient Israel* (Baltimore, 1998) • L. L. GRABBE, ed., *Can a "History of Israel" Be Written?* (Sheffield, 1997) • A. H. J. GUNNEWEG, *Geschichte Israels bis Bar Kochba* (5th ed.; Stuttgart, 1984) • J. M. MILLER, "Introduction to the History of Ancient Israel," NIB 1.244-71 •

M. Noth, *Geschichte Israels* (9th ed.; Göttingen, 1981; orig. pub., 1950) • J. Pedersen, *Israel: Its Life and Culture* (Atlanta, 1991) • J. B. Pixley, *Biblical Israel: A People's History* (Minneapolis, 1992) • J. A. Soggin, *An Introduction to the History of Israel and Judah* (London, 1993) • R. de Vaux, *The Early History of Israel* (Philadelphia, 1978).

Ancient texts: W. Beyerlin, ed., *Near Eastern Religious Texts Relating to the OT* (Philadelphia, 1978) • K. Galling, ed., *TGI* • H. Gressmann, ed., *AOB;* idem, ed., *AOT* • O. Kaiser, ed., *TUAT* • J. B. Pritchard, ed., *ANEP;* idem, ed., *ANESTP;* idem, ed., *ANET.*

On 1.1: H.-J. Zobel, "יִשְׂרָאֵל *yiśrā'ēl*," *TDOT* 6.397-420 (bibliography).

On 1.2: G. Ahlström, *The History of Ancient Palestine from the Palaeolithic Period to Alexander's Conquest* (Sheffield, 1993) • A. Alt, "Erwägungen über die Landnahme der Israeliten in Palästina" (1939), *Kleine Schriften* (vol. 1; 4th ed.; Munich, 1968) 126-75 • D. Edelman, ed., *The Fabric of History* (Sheffield, 1991) • I. Finkelstein, *The Archaeology of the Israelite Settlement* (Jerusalem, 1988) • N. K. Gottwald, "Recent Studies of the Social World of Premonarchic Israel," *CR.BS* 1 (1993) 163-89; idem, *The Tribes of Yahweh* (Maryknoll, N.Y., 1979) • Y. Kaufmann, *The Biblical Account of the Conquest of Palestine* (Jerusalem, 1953) • T. E. Levy, ed., *The Archaeology of Society in the Holy Land* (London, 1995) • G. E. Mendenhall, *The Hebrew Conquest of Palestine* (New Haven, 1962) • H. M. Niemann, *Die Daniten* (Göttingen, 1985) • M. Noth, *Das System der zwölf Stämme Israels* (Darmstadt, 1980; orig. pub., 1930) • G. A. Rendsburg, "The Date of the Exodus and the Conquest/Settlement: The Case for the 1100s," *VT* 42 (1992) 510-27 • R. Smend, *Zur ältesten Geschichte Israels* (Munich, 1987) • T. L. Thompson, *Early History of the Israelite People: From the Written and Archaeological Records* (Leiden, 1992) • K. W. Whitelam, "Sociology or History: Towards a (Human) History of Ancient Palestine?" *Words Remembered, Texts Renewed* (ed. J. Davies, G. Harvey, and W. G. E. Watson; Sheffield, 1995) 149-66.

On 1.3: A. Alt, "Die Staatenbildung der Israeliten in Palästina" (1930), *Kleine Schriften* (vol. 2; 4th ed.; Munich, 1978) 1-65 • R. B. Coote, *Early Israel: A New Horizon* (Minneapolis, 1990) • F. Crüsemann, *Der Widerstand gegen das Königtum* (Neukirchen, 1978) bibliography • J. A. Soggin, *Das Königtum in Israel* (Berlin, 1967) also relates to 1.4–1.6 • K. van der Toorn, "Saul and the Rise of Israelite State Religion," *VT* 43 (1993) 519-42.

On 1.4: A. Alt, "Das Großreich Davids" (1950), *Kleine Schriften* 2.66-75 • A. Malamat, *Das davidische und salomonische Königreich und seine Beziehungen zu Ägypten und Syrien* (Vienna, 1983) • E. Würthwein, *Die Erzählung von der Thronfolge Davids* (Zurich, 1974).

On 1.5: A. Alt, "Das Königtum in dem Reichen Israel und Juda" (1951), *Kleine Schriften* 2.116-34 • W. H. Barnes, *Studies in the Chronology of the Divided Monarchy of Israel* (Atlanta, 1991) • B. Becking, *The Fall of Samaria: A Historical and Archaeological Study* (Leiden, 1992) • J. S. Holladay, "The Kingdoms of Israel and Judah: Political and Economic Centralization in the Iron IIA-B (ca. 1000-750 B.C.E.)," *The Archaeology of Society in the Holy Land* (ed. T. E. Levy; London, 1995) 368-98 • S. A. Irvine, *Isaiah, Ahaz, and the Syro-Ephraimitic Crisis* (Atlanta, 1990) • J. A. Soggin, *An Introduction to the History of Israel and Judah* (Sheffield, 1993) • S. Timm, *Die Dynastie Omri* (Göttingen, 1982) • W. I. Toews, *Monarchy and Religious Institution in Israel under Jeroboam I* (Atlanta, 1993).

On 1.6: W. H. Barnes, *Studies in the Chronology of the Divided Monarchy of Israel* (Atlanta, 1991) • A. Malamat, "The Kingdom of Judah between Egypt and Babylon: A Small State within a Great Power Confrontation," *StTh* 44 (1990) 65-77 • H. Spieckermann, *Juda unter Assur in der Sargonidenzeit* (Göttingen, 1982) • E. Würthwein, "Die Josianische Reform und das Deuteronomisch," *ZTK* 73 (1976) 395-423.

On 1.7: P. R. Ackroyd, *Exile and Restoration* (London, 1968) • L. L. Grabbe, *Judaism from Cyrus to Hadrian* (2 vols.; Minneapolis, 1992) • K. C. Hoglund, *Achaemenid Imperial Administration in Syria-Palestine and the Missions of Ezra and Nehemiah* (Atlanta, 1992) • W. T. In der Smitten, *Esra* (Assen, 1973) • U. Kellermann, *Nehemia* (Berlin, 1967).

On 1.8: R. J. Coggins, *Samaritans and Jews* (Oxford, 1975) • H. Koester, *History, Culture, and Religion of the Hellenistic Age* (Berlin, 1995) • J. D. Purvis, *The Samaritan Pentateuch and the Origin of the Samaritan Sect* (Cambridge, Mass., 1968) • P. Schäfer, *Geschichte der Juden in der Antike* (Neukirchen, 1983) bibliography (also relates to 1.9).

On 1.9: M. Hengel, *The Zealots: Investigations into the Jewish Freedom Movement in the Period from Herod I until 70 A.D.* (Edinburgh, 1989) • P. Schäfer, *Der Bar Kokhba-Aufstand* (Tübingen, 1981) • A. Schalit, *König Herodes* (Berlin, 1969) • A. Schlatter, *Geschichte Israels von Alexander dem Großen bis Hadrian* (3d ed.; Stuttgart, 1925; repr., 1972).

Antonius H. J. Gunneweg†

2. Modern State of Israel

2.1. *History*

The State of Israel is named after the patriarch → Jacob-Israel, whose descendants were promised the Holy Land (see 1.1). From the time of Joshua until today, the land has had a continuous Jewish presence, with the size of the population in direct proportion to the friendliness toward Jews of the regime in power.

The modern name "Israel" expresses the claim and self-understanding of the state. Its founding is seen as the realization of a political goal that was formulated in the Basel Program of the first Zionist Congress (1897), namely, a "publicly guaranteed homeland for the Jewish people in the land of Israel" (i.e., → Palestine), which found political recognition in the Balfour Declaration of 1917. Politically, "Palestine" meant only land west of the Jordan River. In 1921 Transjordan was closed to Jewish settlement and was made the Emirate, later the Kingdom, of Jordan.

On November 29, 1947, the U.N. General Assembly voted to divide Palestine into a Jewish state and an Arab state. Most Jews of the time welcomed this decision. The Palestinian Arabs, however, resisted. As the Jewish population grew, so did the nationalism of the Palestinian Arabs, who regarded the land as their own and saw their rights threatened by the Jewish immigrants. They attacked Jewish settlements, which had increased greatly between 1936 and the outbreak of World War II.

That same month saw the beginning of the Israeli War of Independence. With help from the Arab states, the Palestinian Arabs attacked and isolated Jewish settlements and cut off → Jerusalem from the rest of the country. On May 14, 1948, when Prime Minister David Ben-Gurion (1886-1973) proclaimed the State of Israel in Tel Aviv on the departure of the British troops, all the states bordering Israel had already taken up arms against Israel. The war, however, led to an extension of the Israeli boundaries set by the United Nations. Galilee, the Negev, the coastal strip, and the new part of Jerusalem all came within the new state. The old city of Jerusalem and the West Bank (comprising the traditional Jewish "Judea and Samaria") were annexed by Jordan (an action recognized internationally by only the United Kingdom and Pakistan), and the Gaza Strip was occupied by Egypt. In 1949 separate armistices were signed with the various Arab nations.

The various armistices contained the seeds of future hostilities, especially as numerous camps of Palestinian refugees remained on Israel's eastern borders, which increasingly became bases for Palestinian resistance. Israeli-Palestinian antagonism dominated the political, economic, and social life of Israel from 1948 onward, even as the state had arisen in the shadow of the → Holocaust. Its citizens, who were striving to build a normal life as a nation, felt the pressure of this trauma as they came up against the stubborn resistance of the Palestinian Arabs and the Arab states, which challenged Israel's right to exist. The fronts hardened.

When Arab guerrillas again atacked Jewish settlements, and when Egypt, Jordan, and Syria formed a joint command in 1956, Israeli troops invaded the Sinai peninsula in order to forestall further attack. Under pressure from the United Nations and especially the United States, led by Secretary of State John Foster Dulles, Israel withdrew from Sinai and the Gaza Strip four months later. General G. A. Nasser (1918-70), the president of Egypt, vehemently proclaimed a state of war between Egypt and Israel, in spite of the armistice. An uneasy truce prevailed on the border for the next ten years, with numerous attacks by Arab fedayeen between 1957 and 1967. Jewish settlements near the Golan Heights in the North were within the range of Syrian guns, and Palestinian attacks across the Jordan were the order of the day.

War appeared to be a certainty at the end of May 1967, when Nasser ordered a blockade of the Gulf of Aqaba, made a military alliance with Jordan and Iraq, and sent troops to the Sinai. In response Israel launched what became known as the Six-Day War, which ended with drastic boundary changes. Israel occupied the Golan Heights, the West Bank, and the Gaza Strip; until 1982 it also occupied the Sinai peninsula. East Jerusalem and the old city were under the same administration as the new section and later annexed. The question of the future of the occupied areas has remained a thorny issue in Israeli politics ever since, for Israel won the war but not the peace. "No peace with Israel" was the slogan of the Arab states; "no negotiations without recognizing the State of Israel" was Israel's response. A key event was the surprise attack on Yom Kippur in October 1973 by Egypt and Syria. Egypt enjoyed initial successes with its drive on the Sinai peninsula, but Israel's counterattack brought it to the west bank of the Nile. A U.N. peacekeeping force later oversaw the return of Sinai to Egypt.

In November 1977 Egyptian president Anwar Sadat (1918-81) took an unconventional and bold peace initiative, traveling personally to Jerusalem for peace talks. After secret negotiations between Sadat, Prime Minister Menachem Begin of Israel, and U.S. president Jimmy Carter at Camp David, Maryland, Israel and Egypt signed a formal peace treaty. The main points were the handing back of the Sinai peninsula to Egypt, an agreement to enter into negotiations on the future of the occupied territories, and the establishment of diplomatic relations. Tensions mounted, though, on Israel's other borders. Israel's settlement policies in the occupied areas have been a constant source of friction. The leftist labor parties support these policies for security reasons, while the rightist national and religious parties favor them because of a historical claim to all the land of Israel.

The religious and national side of the argument, which won support from the settlers and the government of the national parties, aggravated the situation. The military authorities in the occupied territories reacted to partisan attacks by Palestinians with repression. Bombings, airline hijackings, and armed attacks by the Palestine Liberation Organization (PLO) and other resistance groups similarly met with reprisals from Israel.

In June 1982 Israel invaded southern Lebanon with the stated aim of pacifying Galil (northern Israel) by destroying resistance bases. This action led to the besieging and shelling of Beirut and thus took on dimensions that overshadowed the importance of pacifying Galil as a military goal. Israel, however, seemed to lose more by this war than it gained. Pressure from abroad, civil war in Lebanon, and new thinking at home, stimulated by a new → peace movement that demanded "peace now," caused Israel to withdraw from Lebanon in the summer of 1985.

Widespread discontent among Palestinian Arabs led in December 1987 to a three-year period of defiance and revolt known as the intifada (Arab. "shaking"). Peace negotiations with the PLO eventually led in 1993 to the Oslo accords, in which for the first time the PLO recognized Israel's right to exist and Israel recognized the PLO as the Palestinians' representative. Other significant events in recent years include the establishment of formal diplomatic relations between the Vatican and the State of Israel (1993-94), the assassination of Prime Minister Yitzhak Rabin (1995), and repeated efforts by U.S. president Bill Clinton to mediate a settlement between the two sides (1998-2000).

Since its founding, the State of Israel has had to deal with 50 years of conflict with its Arab neighbors. Peace treaties have been signed only with Egypt (1979) and Jordan (1994); in 2000 Syria, Iraq, and Lebanon remained officially at war with Israel. The tension results from the ideology of an inalienable Jewish state, which is a main element in the unbroken historical thinking of the dispersion lands, deepened by the inextinguishable longing for Zion and the messianic hope (→ Messianism) of religious Jews. In the gathering together of the scattered (Qibuz Galuyot), Israel sees its most noble task; only in a state in the Holy Land can Israel work out its own history, promised in the Bible.

2.2. Society

Although the conception of the Jewish state was influenced by secular notions, the religious sense became stronger among the people and helped to justify Israeli policy, for example, in the "occupied territories." The basic secular idea of the first generation of settlers was sustained by the attempted social renewal of the Jews in their own land on the basis of social justice and solidarity. The halutz (pioneer) was the ideal human type, actualized in the kibbutz. The kibbutz knows no distinction between different kinds of jobs. It raises the children in community houses, achieves complete freedom from poverty, and rejects the idea of wages. It runs its affairs after the model of parliamentary democracy. Although only a small part of the total population actually lives or has lived on kibbutzim, many influential people in public life have come from it, and it typifies the national social ideal.

A pioneering and community spirit also motivated the founders of the Israeli labor movement, Histadrut, which since 1920 has been the center of the economic, social, and political life of the workers. It promoted the kibbutz, founded many enterprises and cooperatives, and provided Israel with most of its labor. It created an autonomous Jewish labor market and developed a health insurance system that today protects most of Israel's workers. For many decades it operated an egalitarian wage policy, but eventually the more highly skilled groups forced it to accept a wage differential. It has helped to absorb and integrate different waves of immigrants from the most diverse countries into the life of Israel.

2.3. Economy and Culture

For all its many achievements (e.g., in agriculture and technology) and for all its successes in developing natural resources (e.g., potash, phosphates, salts), Israel is still far from enjoying economic independence. Its economy is hampered by its large defense budget, social programs, and a negative balance of trade. The support of friendly states (esp. the United States) is of decisive economic importance.

In the spirit of its previous history as a "developing Jewish state" (T. Herzl), Israel has been sustained by an ideology of utopian → socialism, which has borne fruit in the fields of culture and education. Basic schooling for eight years, with one school for students from all social classes, has the aim of training the rising generation in a sense of solidarity with the founders.

One of the greatest cultural achievements of the first generation of settlers was the revival of Hebrew as a written and spoken language (→ Hebrew Language). Orthodox → Judaism might regard Hebrew as a sacred tongue that should not be used in → everyday life, but the settlers viewed it as a source for the renaissance of Jewish creativity.

Although the basic schools and high schools are divided into religious and general schools, Bible study is a central discipline in both. The language and history of the biblical books, as the common cultural heritage of every ethnic group, is an important factor in cultural integration. Israel has universities in all the large cities. The oldest and most important is Hebrew University (1925) in Jerusalem. Tel Aviv University (1953) followed the founding of the state. The Technion at Haifa (1912) and the Weizmann Institute of Science (1934) at Reḥovot enjoy international renown.

Although the founders had the vision of a future peaceful state and, at least in some cases, closed their eyes to the reality of the Arab population, pressure from the Arabs, and later from neighboring states, forced Israel to become heavily militarized. Its defensive army, the Zva Haganah l'Israel (Israel defense forces), commonly shortened to Zahal, is a people's army. It consists of a professional core, men and women conscripts, and reservists. The principle of short service for the highest officers and frequent replacements prevent the development of a military caste distinct from society as a whole. Serious tension arose between the army, the minister of defense, and society only during the campaign into Lebanon in 1982. This was the first war that was not regarded as wholly defensive and necessary to sustain national existence. Criticism of its goal and conduct was the basis of a broad peace movement.

The interplay of a political need for security, an ethnic wish to ensure Jewish continuity, and a territorial claim based on biblical history, deepened and overshadowed by the Holocaust, influences social life and thinking in Israel. The settlement policy in the occupied territories must be seen against this background. The interweaving of religious and national elements in Israel's self-image has an impact on the role of the religious parties in the government and Parliament. Although most of the people want a modern, secular society, they tolerate — often reluctantly — the dominance of the religious parties.

In family and inheritance cases Jews are subject to the rabbinic courts, and Christians and Muslims are under their own religious institutions. Israel has neither civil → marriage nor civil divorce. The Ministry of Religious Affairs is responsible to Parliament for the proper functioning of religious courts. It also sees to the observance of → dietary laws and feast days in public life (→ Jewish Practices). Although the boundaries of civil and religious → law are not closely defined, Israel is not a theocratic state. Individuals make their own decisions regarding individual lifestyle; religion is a private matter. The pressure of the minority religious parties in shaping public life (e.g., on the → Sabbath and on feast days, banning public transportation and prohibiting trade, theaters, and concerts) is the result of political pragmatism and of toleration on the part of the nonreligious majority, which views religious law as a factor in the integration of ethnic groups and as a link with Jews in other countries.

2.4. Constitution

Israel, a parliamentary → democracy, has no written constitution (similar to the United Kingdom). After its founding, however, some basic laws were passed, including the law of return, which establishes the right of any Jew to come to Israel and become a citizen.

The names of government institutions bear witness to the link with history: *nassi* (president), *ssar* (minister), and *Knesset* (Parliament) all come from the history of biblical and rabbinic Judaism. The nassi is elected by the Knesset for five years; his office is representative. The Knesset, a unicameral parliament, consists of 120 deputies; elections take place every four years. The government is chosen by the nassi with the Knesset's consent. It is responsible to the Knesset and may be overthrown by a vote of no confidence. The justice system consists of magistrates' courts, district courts, and a supreme court. The law contains elements from Ottoman and British law, along with laws passed by the Knesset. There are three main party groupings, though these are divided into many smaller parties: the socialist labor parties, the religious parties, and the coalition of liberal middle-class parties with the conservative Likud Party. In addition, there are smaller Communist and Arab parties.

2.5. Religions

Jerusalem, which Israel has proclaimed as its capital, is the "holy city" of three world religions. Each has its own groups of faithful and own holy places (notably the Western Wall, the Church of the Holy Sepulchre, and the Dome of the Rock, with other places sacred alike to Jews, Christians, and Muslims), making the city a little world in itself. About three-quarters of the population is Jewish, mainly represented by Orthodox Jews. The administration and workers of the Hebrew University are centered there, as well as the offices of the Israeli government. (Most countries, however, maintain their embassies in Tel Aviv.)

The largest non-Jewish group consists of Muslims (→ Islam). The oldest Christian church is the Greek Orthodox (see 3.2). Other Christian communions include Greek Catholic, Roman Catholic, Maronite, and Protestant (Anglican, Presbyterian, Lutheran, and Baptist). The heads of the various religious groups (the → patriarchs, archbishops, and → bishops) live in Jerusalem. Overall, for all the political tension, there is normally little disruption of daily life within the city, which some see as a sign of hope for Israel as a whole.

Bibliography: M. Buber, Israel and Palestine: The History of an Idea (London, 1952) • K. Cragg, Palestine: The Prize and Price of Zion (London, 1997) • M. Gilbert, Israel: A History (New York, 1998) • E. Karsh, ed., Israel: The First Hundred Years (London, 2000) • M. N. Penkower, The Holocaust and Israel Reborn: From Catastrophe to Sovereignty (Urbana, Ill., 1994) • M. Prior, Zionism and the State of Israel: A Moral Inquiry (London, 1999) • H. M. Sachar, A History of Israel: From the Rise of Zionism to Our Time (2d ed.; New York, 1996) • B. Thomas, How Israel Was Won: A Concise History of the Arab-Israeli Conflict (Lanham, Md., 1999).

Marianne Awerbuch

3. Christian Groups in Israel and Palestine

Followers of → Jesus have been present in Israel and Palestine since the birth of Christianity. The size and diversity of the various Christian groups have fluctuated for 2,000 years. At the beginning of the 21st century, approximately 150,000 Arabic-speaking Christians represent some 40 different churches and → denominations present in → Jerusalem and throughout Israel. (For the remainder of this section I use "Israel" only as a geographic term that includes the present State of Israel and the wider area of Palestine. This designation implies no prejudice to the ultimate political settlement involving both Israel and Palestine. Furthermore, it is recognized that determining the exact number and breakdown of Christians in modern Israel is particularly difficult, given the often conflicting claims and inconsistencies reported for the various groups.)

The importance of these Christians and churches extends well beyond numbers and statistics. The communities represent a continuing link to the larger community of Middle Eastern Christians as well as various churches around the world that have an ongoing connection to the historic lands of the Bible.

Many Middle Eastern churches trace their origins to the apostolic era. The NT portrays → Paul as a zealous missionary whose extensive travels helped establish churches in the northern and eastern lands of the Mediterranean basin. Long-standing traditions associate various disciples with the spread of Christian churches: Peter (and Paul) ventured west to Rome; Mark is revered in Egypt as the founder of the Coptic Church; Thomas is believed to have gone east and established churches in ancient Mesopotamia (present-day Iraq) as well as in India.

The NT Epistles and late first-century documents depict the formative stages of ecclesiastical structures. During the second and third centuries the authority of → bishops was gradually extended. The most important changes, however, took place in the fourth and fifth centuries, when the bishops of the larger churches in the larger cities exercised their authority over bishops in smaller towns and villages. The former were also the ones who convened and led local councils (synods) of bishops. They came to be known as metropolitan archbishops.

By the time of the Council of → Chalcedon in 451, the metropolitan archbishops in the five largest and most influential cities had become heads of regional synods that encompassed large territories. Their status was recognized and codified at the council. They were also accorded the title → "patriarch," with their areas of jurisdiction becoming known as patriarchates. The order of the five patriarchs was (1) → Rome, recognized as first among equals; (2) Constantinople (modern Istanbul), the second capital of the empire; (3) → Alexandria (in Egypt); (4) → Antioch (in Syria); and (5) Jerusalem. Jerusalem was recognized not because of its stature as a city, which then was minor, but because of its status as "the mother of churches" and the site of Jesus' earthly life, crucifixion, and resurrection.

The churches in the contemporary Middle East continue to relate to the structures of these ancient patriarchates. Most of these ancient communities of faith have maintained a presence in Jerusalem and Israel.

It is difficult to characterize this diverse Christian community. Today, as has been the case throughout their history, relationships within and among these communities of faith have been complicated by doctrinal differences, internal disputes, and sometimes by turbulent political dynamics. Some contemporary Middle Eastern Christians are deeply involved with and committed to Christian ecumenism as well as Jewish-Christian and Muslim-Christian dialogue; others display little interest in ecumenical or interfaith initiatives.

Since the vast majority of indigenous Christians

are Arabs, their experiences and perspectives have been shaped by the larger political and religious dynamics dominating the region, including the birth and spread of the churches under Roman rule, the coming of Islam, the great schism (1054) between the Western and Eastern churches, the → Crusades, the Ottoman Empire, the era of → colonialism, the emergence of modern Israel, the rise of Arab nationalism (→ Nation, Nationalism), the Arab-Israeli conflict, and political upheaval associated with various contemporary Islamist movements. To understand a particular community in a particular setting today requires thoughtful historical and contextual analysis.

The churches in the Middle East can be grouped into four "families": Eastern Orthodox (→ Orthodox Church), → Roman Catholic, → Oriental Orthodox, and Protestant. The two largest groupings are among the Orthodox churches. Approximately 85 percent of the indigenous, Arabic-speaking Christians throughout the Middle East belong to Oriental (Coptic, Syrian, and Armenian) or Eastern (Greek) Orthodox Churches. The Roman Catholic and Eastern Rite Catholic Churches comprise some 12 percent of the region's 15 million Christians, while the Protestant churches include roughly 3 percent of the total. A fifth distinctive community, the Assyrian Church of the East, now dispersed around the world, continues to have worshiping communities in Iraq, Turkey, Syria, and Iran.

In Jerusalem and Israel the proportional size of the various communities is somewhat different. The Eastern Orthodox and various Catholic Christians represent the largest communities, followed by the Oriental Orthodox and then the Protestant churches.

3.1. Orthodox Churches

The *Greek Orthodox Church* is one of the largest (26,000) in Israel. The patriarch of Jerusalem dates his authority to A.D. 451. His primacy is reflected in the title; the other patriarchates are merely "in" Jerusalem. He presides over 18 archbishops and archimandrites in the Holy Synod, which includes churches in neighboring Jordan and a special Brotherhood of the Holy Sepulchre. Western pilgrims and tourists frequently encounter this community because it has a major role and responsibility for the care and maintenance of holy places. Traditionally, the leadership of this church has come from Greece. The community reflects a blend of Arabic and Greek heritage, including the use of both languages in worship.

Two *Russian Orthodox* churches are visibly present in Jerusalem: The Russian Orthodox Church of the Patriarchate of Moscow and the Russian Orthodox Church outside Russia (headquarters in New York). Russian Orthodox missionary activity began in 1841. The Russian Ecclesiastical Mission was established in 1857, and the missionary Orthodox Palestine Society in 1881.

The *Romanian Orthodox Church* acquired land for a church, a monastery, and a hospice for Romanian pilgrims shortly before World War I. A congregation and a building were established in 1935. Under the leadership of an archimandrite, supported by a deacon and a community of nuns, this church cares for Christians of Romanian origin and the steady stream of Romanian pilgrims who visit the Holy Land.

3.2. Roman Catholic Churches

The Roman Catholic Church (or Latin Church, approximately 15,000 members) supports some 180 religious institutions and is represented by 24 orders. The Latin Patriarchate in Jerusalem was established initially in 1099. It was discontinued about a century later and then reestablished in the middle of the 19th century. Over the centuries this church has shared in the upheavals and changing fortunes of the sacred city. It has also provided the framework for a wide variety of → mission efforts, including the establishment of various Eastern Rite churches. In an unprecedented move to affirm the Jerusalem Patriarchate as an indigenous church, Pope John Paul II named Michel Sabbah the first Palestinian Arab patriarch in 1988.

The *Greek Catholic Church* traces its origins to the early 18th century. This Eastern Rite community was formed out of the Eastern Orthodox churches within the Patriarchates of Alexandria, Antioch, and Jerusalem. The term → "Melchite" is often used in relation to Greek Catholics. It derives from a fifth-century term meaning "the king's men" and originally designated those Christians who embraced the theological formulations put forth at the Council of Chalcedon in 451. Following the establishment of this Eastern Rite church, the designation shifted to the Greek Catholics. While the patriarch of the church resides in Damascus, the archdiocese in Jerusalem (founded in 1833) has been under the leadership of an archbishop. There are more than 400,000 Arabic-speaking → Melchites in the region. The large majority in Israel (over 40,000) reside in the Galilee region, where there are 27 parishes.

The *Maronites,* the Lebanon-based Catholic community, count more than 5 million members in the Middle East, Europe, and North and South America. Formally uniting with Rome in 1181, the Maronite Church includes some 6,000 members in

Israel today. Most of the Maronites live in northern Galilee, near the border with Lebanon.

The *Armenian Catholics* are the most recent members of this family of churches. Although some Armenian Orthodox converted to Catholicism as early as the 14th century, the Armenian Catholic Patriarchate was not established until 1840. The large majority of this 35,000-person community lives in Syria and Lebanon today. The church in Jerusalem includes some 500 adherents under the care of a prelate.

The *Syrian Catholic Church* began in 1662 when part of the Syrian Orthodox Church sought union with Rome. The Patriarchate in Jerusalem, created in 1890, today cares for small congregations (about 300 members) in Jerusalem and Bethlehem.

The *Coptic Catholic Church* traces its origin to 1824. Though formally united with Rome, its more than 100,000 members in Egypt continue to relate closely with the → Coptic Orthodox Church. This church includes a patriarchate in Jerusalem (dating from 1955) and a small congregation of some 35 members.

The *Chaldean Catholic Church* (formed in 1551) emerged from the Assyrian Church of the East. Approximately half of the 250,000 members of this church remain in the Middle East today, with the large majority (over 100,000) in Iraq. The patriarchate-vicariate was established in Jerusalem in 1908. The community in Jerusalem today includes about 35 members.

3.3. Oriental Orthodox Churches

For many centuries the → *Armenian Apostolic Church* has played a major role in caring for the sacred sites in the Holy Land. The Armenian patriarch has resided in Jerusalem since 1311. This Oriental Orthodox community has two churches, a monastery, a retirement home, and the residence of the patriarch in the Armenian Quarter of the old city of Jerusalem. Approximately 2,150 adherents live in Israel, most in Jerusalem and small numbers in Jaffa, Ramla, Haifa, and Nazareth.

The *Syrian Orthodox Church* (also known as the Jacobites) has a long history in the region. St. Mark's Cathedral in Jerusalem has been the seat of their bishop since 1471. The community today includes approximately 1,000 members.

The *Coptic Orthodox Church* is, by far, the largest community of Christians in the Middle East, with some 6-7 million members in Egypt. Although Copts have been present in Jerusalem for many centuries, their first bishop was not installed until 1853. The church today includes monks and nuns, along with a few laypeople. It has many rights and responsibilities related to the holy places in Jerusalem.

3.4. Protestant Churches

The *Anglican Church* (→ Anglican Communion) installed its first bishop of Jerusalem in 1841. This archbishopric included five dioceses covering the lands between Iran and Arabic-speaking North Africa. In 1975 the name Evangelical Episcopal Church was adopted. The church today has over 2,000 members in its congregations in Jerusalem, Rām Allāh, Ābūd, Nazareth, and ʿAkko. It also supports a home for handicapped children, two colleges, and two hospitals.

The *Lutheran Church* set up a joint bishopric with the Anglicans in 1841. In subsequent decades, the Lutherans supported a variety of medical and educational mission programs. The Evangelical Lutheran Foundation was established in 1899 to provide support for several schools, an orphanage, and hospital care. In 1910 the Carmel Hospice and Augusta-Victoria Hospital were built on the Mount of Olives with the assistance of Kaiser Wilhelm II of Germany. The → Lutheran World Federation has taken the lead in supporting these and other ministries in Israel since the 1950s. Today there are four Lutheran congregations in Jerusalem, serving speakers of Arabic (approximately 1,600 members), German (160 members), English (60 members), and Danish (30 members). The bishop of the Evangelical Lutheran Church in Jordan, a body that in 1998 had 2,000 members, is at the heart of the various Lutheran ministries, including worshiping congregations in Rām Allāh, Beit Sahur, Beit Jala, Bethlehem, and Amman.

The *Church of Scotland* (Reformed) provides support for a hospital in Tiberias, a college in Jaffa, and an active church in Jerusalem.

3.5. Other Christian Bodies and Ecumenism

A wide variety of other Protestant and evangelical churches are also present in Israel today. The Southern Baptist Convention, the largest Protestant community in the United States, operates several schools and supports small → congregations in several towns within Israel. The Baptist Convention in Israel (American Baptists) dates to 1923. Their work today includes a Baptist Center and the First Bible Church. Smaller Protestant communities include various → Pentecostal churches, → Churches of God, the → Mennonites, the Society of → Friends (Quakers), the → Church of the Nazarene, the Seventh-day → Adventists, and the Church of Christ. Other prominent churches, such as the United Methodist Church, are also actively involved in Israel. In some cases, these churches prefer to support and work through indigenous churches as part of their commitment to Christian ecumenism.

The → ecumenical movement among indigenous churches has grown stronger over the second half of the 20th century. Within Israel the International Christian Committee has been at the center of development and has done work among Palestinian Christians and Muslims since the 1950s. All of the indigenous churches in Israel now participate in the various ministries coordinated by the regional → Middle East Council of Churches (MECC). The Catholic churches, which are not formal members of ecumenical bodies in most parts of the world, joined the MECC in the mid-1980s. This cooperation is visible in the work of the Jerusalem office of the MECC.

Israel is also home to a wide range of nondenominational and parachurch Christian organizations. The → YMCA and YWCA, for example, have been present and active in the region for over 100 years. More recently, many small, independent groups have been visible and active. Most such groups or parachurch organizations are motivated by a theological frame of reference focused on → eschatology. Convinced that the end of the world is near, some appear eager to have a front-row seat for the apocalypse. Some such groups, like the International Christian Embassy, frequently associated with the Christian Right in the United States, have become fixtures in Jerusalem in recent decades. Others come and go, the latter particularly when the government of Israel perceives the groups or their adherents to present significant security risks.

The Christian landscape in Israel also includes a number of → organizations and institutes that are dedicated to ecumenical and interreligious cooperation. The Ecumenical Institute for Theological Research at Tantur (on the outskirts of Jerusalem and bordering Bethlehem), for instance, includes short-term and long-term programs, seminars, and conferences related to ecumenism and Jewish-Christian and Muslim-Christian dialogue. Other initiatives include Ness Amim (1961), a Christian guest house in western Galilee concentrating on Jewish-Christian relations, and the American Institute of Holy Land Studies, a group focused on the history of Israel and Jewish-Christian relations. These and a vast array of other groups have diverse theological orientations and goals.

Bibliography: N. S. Ateek, Justice and Only Justice: A Palestinian Theology of Liberation (Maryknoll, N.Y., 1989) • E. Chacour and M. E. Jensen, We Belong to the Land: The Story of a Palestinian Israeli Who Lives for Peace and Reconciliation (San Francisco, 1990) • K. Cragg, The Arab Christian: A History in the Middle East (Louisville, Ky., 1991) • W. D. Dalrymple, From the Holy Mountain: A Journey among the Christians of the Middle East (New York, 1998) • A. Hilliard and B. J. Bailey, Living Stones Pilgrimage: With the Christians of the Holy Land (South Bend, Ind., 1999) • C. A. Kimball, Angle of Vision: Christians and the Middle East (New York, 1992). Much helpful information appears in the website www.christusrex.org/www1/ofm/cic/CICmain.html.

Charles A. Kimball

Italy

	1960	1980	2000
Population (1,000s):	50,200	56,434	57,194
Annual growth rate (%):	0.75	0.12	−0.17

Area: 301,309 sq. km. (116,336 sq. mi.)

A.D. 2000

Population density: 190/sq. km. (492/sq. mi.)
Births / deaths: 0.84 / 1.07 per 100 population
Fertility rate: 1.19 per woman
Infant mortality rate: 6 per 1,000 live births
Life expectancy: 79.2 years (m: 76.0, f: 82.2)
Religious affiliation (%): Christians 82.0 (Roman Catholics 97.4, marginal 1.1, other Christians 1.9), nonreligious 13.0, atheists 3.6, Muslims 1.3, other 0.1.

1. Roman Catholic Church
   1.1. Roman Empire
   1.2. Papal States
   1.3. Teaching and Culture
   1.4. Secularism and Renewal
   1.5. Hierarchy
2. Protestant Churches
3. Foreign Churches
4. Ecumenism
5. Other Religious Groups

1. Roman Catholic Church

As Raffaele Pettazzoni has stated, the history of Italian religion may be seen in terms of the creative tension between the institutionalized, dogmatic religion of the state (religione dello stato) and the personalized, voluntaristic religion of the individual (religione dell'uomo).

1.1. Roman Empire

The → Roman Empire, in which the Christian message first spread, had a religion that sought the perpetuity and "salvation" of social and political institutions (→ Hellenistic-Roman Religion). The Edict of Milan (313) ended the illegal status of Christianity and the → persecution of Christians (§2). The progressive organization of the church of the Roman Empire from the fourth century onward involved an intertwining of ecclesiastical and temporal order and power, mainly on the basis of the church receiving gifts of property throughout Italy.

The financial and political power of the church gave geographic and political esteem and influence to the → bishop of Rome. As the "patrimony of St. Peter," the lands given to the church became a kind of independent state (→ Papal States); from the eighth century the church claimed the right to govern → Rome and Italy (→ Donation of Constantine). Already in the sixth century the Roman bishop had taken the titles *papa* and *summus pontifex* (supreme pontiff). The term "pope" is from the ancient Greek colloquialism *papas,* a respectful address for fathers, adopted by Gregory VII in his *Dictatus papae* (1075) as the official, singular title of the successors of the apostle Peter.

1.2. *Papal States*

The Roman Catholic Church and Italian Catholicism were deeply influenced by the vicissitudes of the Papal States, their relations with other dynastic states in the peninsula and the island regimes in Sardinia and Sicily, and relations also with foreign powers. Following favorable plebiscites, the Papal States were annexed to the emergent kingdom of Italy (1859-60). The pope's temporal power ended when Rome was seized, was annexed by plebiscite, and became the capital of a united Italy (1870-71).

Having opposed the nationalist movement, the papacy reacted to the territorial losses by excommunication of the vocal exponents of Italian unification, rejection of the Cavourian formula "a free church in a free state," and repudiation of the Papal Law of Guarantees (1871), which represented liberal Italy's attempt to codify church-state relations in light of the new realities. Roman Catholic participation in the political process was prohibited by the decree of Pius IX *Non expedit* (1868). Earlier the same pope had issued *Syllabus of Errors* (1864), a virtual declaration of war on liberalism, nationalism, and evolving modern society, which together were held responsible for the alienation of the Papal States. Papal infallibility, first proclaimed in *Pastor aeternus,* issued on July 18, 1870, at the concluding session of the First Vatican Council, was not only conceived as an express statement of Catholic dogma; it was also designed to bolster the prestige of the supreme pontiff, thought to have been seriously undermined by the loss of his temporal sovereignty. Protesting that he had no choice, Pius IX relegated himself to the Vatican offices in Rome, where he ruled the church as the self-described "prisoner of the Vatican."

By means of concordats with European states, the papacy sought also to defend its prerogatives by strengthening diplomatic ties, reinforcing the church's role in education, protecting the religious liberties of its members, and confirming its concern for social welfare. It also countered with all possible means the aggressive anticlerical campaigns periodically unleashed by liberal and radical elements in Italy and other countries.

With the advance of socialism and secularism, a different approach was soon deemed essential by both church and state. Isolation and confrontation benefited only the enemies of both orders. Leo XIII's *Rerum novarum* (1891), disavowing class struggle and the extreme utopias of the Left, endorsed the principle of labor-management collaboration in solving the problems of industrial society. Unions and employers were to engage in genuine collective bargaining for the establishment of safer and more congenial workplaces, viable wage standards, and the introduction of health and retirement assistance. Because of this newer outlook, and also the labor shortages caused by the demands of World War I, Roman Catholic laity and clerics, where permitted by the civil authorities, entrenched themselves in local administration, the national bureaucracy, private and public education, charitable institutions, chaplaincies (hospitals, prisons, armed forces), and health care institutions.

Between 1904 and 1918 a gradual relaxation of *Non expedit* occurred, to the point where Roman Catholics voted and, in increasing numbers, ran for public office. In 1919 the Italian Popular Party was formed by the prelate Don Luigi Sturzo under the watchful eye of the papacy and the Catholic Church. As a result of the elections of 1919, the "Popolari" won 100 seats out of 508 in the Chamber of Deputies, second only to the Socialists' 150. By the general elections of 1922, although its parliamentary delegation had risen to 115, the party was in disarray, with the Left (the "Clerico-Moderates") oriented toward Marxism, and the Right (the "Clerico-Fascists") sympathetic toward fascism. The Popular Party rapidly lost favor with Pius XI, Catholics in general, and all voters; it was finally driven from the scene by the passage of the fascist state's Exceptional Decrees (1926). The party was reborn in 1943, however, as the Christian Democratic Party, and it subsequently has had a commanding position in local and national governments of republican Italy, in spite of corruption and scandals.

As the fascist movement gained momentum, the church's leadership increasingly viewed it positively as an authoritative, corporatist, youthful, patriotic, and spiritual antidote — a middle way between atheistic, collectivist Communism/socialism and militant, materialist, statist liberalism/social democracy. Roman Catholicism, in turn, appealed to Mussolini and his chieftains as a valuable instrument for the mobilization of the Italian masses in support of the fascist takeover of the government, which had occurred on October 28, 1922.

This incipient mutuality bore fruit in the Lateran Accords of 1929, secretly negotiated between the fascist state and the Holy See. The accords included the Conciliar Treaty, which settled the question of Rome, as the Holy See recognized the kingdom of Italy under the House of Savoy, with Rome as its capital, while the Italian state reaffirmed Roman Catholicism as the sole religion of Italy. Vatican City was at this time created from a section of Rome; there the papacy and church were free to conduct their activities without pressure or interference from civic or political bodies. In this concordat, Italy guaranteed the Roman Catholic Church complete independence in jurisdictional and ecclesiastical matters. According to the Financial Convention, Italy promised the church 750 million lire in cash and one billion lire in government bonds as partial indemnity for the papal territories, which had earlier been annexed to Italy.

Embedded pockets of racism and anti-Semitism in the Roman Catholic Church hierarchy, its administrative curia, and among rank-and-file Catholics prevented the papacy from articulating an unequivocal stand against the racist and anti-Jewish laws and restrictions propagated by the fascist government in Italy and in its African empire.

After World War II the Lateran Accords were incorporated into the constitution of the Italian republic, adopted in 1948. Beginning in 1975, Italy contemplated changes in church-state relations, which were completed in 1984. These changes, formalized in a revised concordat, terminated the "one faith" confessional state, thus rescinding Roman Catholicism's status as the only religion of the state.

1.3. *Teaching and Culture*
The presence of the Roman Catholic Church in Italian society may be seen in → religious instruction in both primary and secondary schools, chaplaincies (in hospitals, prisons, and military barracks), social work, and church schools.

Roman Catholic teaching and culture were much affected by the Counter-Reformation (→ Catholic Reform and Counterreformation; Trent, Council of), which tied worship to a fixed → liturgy in Latin (→ Worship 2.2). New impulses came only in the 20th century. The church's opposition to → mod-

ernism hampered the development of biblical → exegesis and theological research. Only with the liturgical reforms of → Vatican II did Catholic believers secure more participation in worship and more access to Bible study.

→ Popular piety is esteemed and promoted. The veneration of → Mary and the → saints has been given liturgical form. Room is left for popular practices that are significant in → everyday life and that promote personal piety.

1.4. *Secularism and Renewal*
The process of increasing → secularism and renewal marked the latter part of the 20th century. The number of practicing Roman Catholics who follow the ethical and sociopolitical directions of their bishops has steadily declined. Although the church claims virtually 100 percent of the population, still (in 1983) 2 percent were not baptized, 18-20 percent were not confirmed, 8-11 percent of the → marriages were not church marriages, and 15-20 percent were not buried by a priest. Legislation regarding divorce (May 12, 1974) and → abortion (May 17, 1981) is no longer in conformity with the wishes of the church.

In the early 1970s the bishops and militant Catholic movements proclaimed a "condition of mission." → Evangelism was to be the main sphere of the church's work in society. This decision may be clearly seen in the pastoral program Evangelizzazione e Sacramenti (Proclamation and sacraments, 1973-75) and in the congresses Evangelizzazione e Promozione Humana (Proclamation and the promotion of humanity, 1976) and Riconciliazione Cristiana e Communità degli Uomini (Christian reconciliation and society, 1985). The → base communities, although marginal, are helping to put this basic emphasis into effect. Also working for renewal are spiritual movements like Communione e Liberazione and the Focolare movement (→ New Spiritual Movements).

1.5. *Hierarchy*
The Roman Catholic Church has 227 → dioceses in Italy. The bishops' conference has 269 members, the largest in Europe. The number of → priests is declining. In 1982 there were only 355 ordinations, as compared with 708 priests lost by death or resignation. The seminaries were modernized in the late 20th century.

2. Protestant Churches
Less than a million people in Italy belong to Protestant or indigenous Christian churches. With the exception of the Waldensian churches, none of these groups was in Italy before the 19th century.

The renewal movement of the → *Waldenses* dates back to the 12th century. They made common cause with the → Reformation in 1532, were persecuted by the Inquisition, and faced attempts to exterminate them in the 16th and 17th centuries. They survived, nevertheless, in the Alpine valleys and in the 19th century spread across the whole country. A royal edict in 1848 lifted the ban on their work. They formed a theological faculty in 1855, moving it to Rome in 1921. With their historical tradition, territorial roots, and ecclesiastical structures, the Waldenses form the vital core of Italian Protestantism. In the climate of the risorgimento after 1830, when political ideas combined with hopes for religious revival in the struggle for Italian unity, other churches came on the scene, followed by yet others in the course of the → revival movement at the end of the 19th century.

The → *Methodist Church* (Chiesa Evangelica Metodista) goes back to the missionary activity of the Englishmen Henry Pigott in the North (from 1861, in Piedmont, Veneto, and Emilia-Romagna) and Thomas Salvator Jones in the South (from 1864, in Naples). In 1871 Leroy Vernon came from the Episcopal Methodist Church of the United States and did work in Milan, Florence, and Rome. The missionary work from London resulted in the founding of the Chiesa Metodista Wesleyana, that from the United States in the founding of the Chiesa Metodista Episcopale. The two united in 1946 as the Chiesa Evangelica Metodista d'Italia and then, during 1975-79, formed a new church body with the Waldenses. In 1990 approximately 30,000 people were affiliated with this Waldensian-Methodist Church.

The → *Pentecostal churches* (Le Chiese Pentecostali Italiane) trace their origin to Giacomo Lombardi, who embraced the Pentecostal experience as a member of the First Italian Presbyterian Church of Chicago, Illinois. Between 1908 and 1923 he undertook six visits to Italy to preach the Pentecostal message. The first congregation was formed in Rome in 1908, the second at La Spezia in 1909, and the third in Milan in 1914. Some of the congregations came together in 1947 as the Assemblee di Dio in Italia (ADI), but others remained independent. The free congregations (Congregazioni Pentecostali) are linked by a correspondence center. Other, much smaller Pentecostal groups include the missionary movement Fiumi di Potenza (Streams of power), the Missione del Pieno Evangelo (Full Gospel Mission), and the Chiesa del Nazareno Puglia (Church of the Nazarene). The various Pentecostal groups together included some 425,000 adherents in 1990,

A group around Count Piero Guicciardini formed the *Plymouth Brethren* (Chiesa Cristiana dei Fratelli) in Florence around 1835. In exile in London, the count, with other evangelicals, had come into contact with the revival associated with John Darby (→ Plymouth Brethren). The fellowship that he founded on returning to Italy was the starting point for a wider spread across the country. In 1990 there were approximately 225 meetings with some 25,000 total adherents. Pledged to God's Word as the only rule of faith and conduct, they have no organizational structure and shun ecumenical contacts.

The → *Baptists* (Chiesa Evangeliche Battiste) gained a foothold in Italy through the work of the English pastors John Wall in Bologna and Edward Clarke of the Baptist Missionary Society in La Spezia (from 1866). Other Baptist missionaries came from the United States and Canada in the 19th and 20th centuries. The majority of Baptists belong to Unione Cristiana Evangelica Battista d'Italia (10,000 adherents in 1990).

The → *Apostolic Church* (Chiesa Apostolica) came to Italy in 1927 through a delegation of English pastors. The Communità Evangelica Apostolica split off from it in 1978. The Chiesa Apostolica Italiana was founded in Florence in 1979. In 1990 it had approximately 10,000 adherents in 50 places of worship.

There are many smaller Italian Protestant groups. The → *Adventists* (Unione Italiana Cristiana delle Chiese Avventiste) formed small groups in 1864 as a result of the missionary work of the Pole M. B. Czechowski in Torre Pellice near Turin. They have members now also in Rome and the South. The → *Salvation Army* (L'Esercito della Salvezza) was introduced by Captain G. B. Vint of England in 1883. It began work in the North, then spread to the South. Banned by the Fascists in 1940, it resumed work, especially in the social sector, after World War II. The *Chiesa di Cristo* began work in 1949 under an American missionary. Italian Protestantism also includes many *free churches* (Chiese Libere) and missionary groups that are mostly → fundamentalist. These bodies usually have foreign contacts (mostly in the United States).

3. Foreign Churches

From the middle of the 17th century there have been foreign congregations in many cities, usually connected with diplomatic delegations. The → Lutheran churches, which have existed in various places for two centuries, came together in 1948 as the Evangelical Lutheran Church in Italy (Chiesa Evangelica Luterana in Italia). Other foreign churches are the American Episcopal Church, the Church of England, and the Église Évangélique Réformée Suisse.

The community of → Orthodox churches included approximately 20 congregations and nearly 40,000 adherents in 1990. Most congregations were attached to the Ecumenical Patriarchate of Constantinople, with others belonging to the Russian Orthodox Church outside Russia and to the Orthodox Churches of Russia, Romania, and Serbia.

4. Ecumenism

In the 1960s many parts of the Italian Protestant world heard a summons to unity on the basis of the gospel and common evangelical witness in Italy (Second Evangelical Congress, Rome, May 1965). As a result, the Baptists, Lutherans, Methodists, and Waldenses founded the Federazione delle Chiese Evangeliche in Italia (FCEI) at Milan in November 1967. Most of the Protestant churches participate in this organization, whose statement of faith member churches subscribe to. The FCEI holds assemblies every three years and publishes the monthly bulletin *Notizie evangeliche* and the ecumenical weekly *Com–Nuovi tempi*.

The Protestant churches engage in → proclamation, → education, and → diakonia. They sponsor several institutions for biblical and theological training (including the Waldensian seminary in Rome), plus cultural institutions (libraries, museums, etc.), Bible societies, publishing houses, bookshops and presses, evangelistic organizations, newspapers and church papers, radio and television stations (many run by the Assemblee di Dio), youth and culture centers, hospitals, retirement communities, and various other social institutions.

→ Ecumenism is both a task within Protestantism and a matter of relations with Roman Catholicism (→ Local Ecumenism). Of the approximately two dozen ecumenical centers, most are under Roman Catholic direction. The Segretariato Attività Ecumeniche has run study leaves since the 1960s. The youth village Agape (in Prali, near Turin), dedicated in 1951, is a fruit of the ecumenical movement. It is a center for meetings and study conferences. Promoting ecumenical contacts is one of the main tasks of the FCEI, which is also concerned to make approaches to Protestant churches and groups that are hostile to the → World Council of Churches.

5. Other Religious Groups

The many other religious groups in Italy include → Jehovah's Witnesses (close to 2,500 congregations and 400,000 adherents in 1990), → Mormons (14,000 adherents), → Christian Science, → Baha'i, and the International Society for → Krishna Consciousness.

By A.D. 2000 there were approximately 750,000 Muslims living in Italy (→ Islam), mostly guest workers from Arab lands. The numbers continue to increase with the flood of immigrants.

Jews (→ Judaism) have been in Italy since the second century B.C. Until modern times they were forced to live in → ghettos. Only with King Charles Albert's edict of toleration in 1848 were they allowed to leave the ghetto — at first only in Sardinia, then throughout Italy in 1861. During World War II 8,000 Jews were deported for annihilation (→ Holocaust). In 1990 there were approximately 30,000 Jews in Italy.

The Italian state constitutionally guarantees minorities the right of assembly and grants them legal recognition. Historically, most Protestant and all evangelical churches in Italy, as almost always elsewhere, have refused to agree to concordats that, in effect, would make them religions of the state. The Assembly of the Federation of Evangelical Churches, meeting in Florence on November 4, 1970 — and subsequently reaffirmed on October 28, 1976 — by official letter to the Italian government adamantly refused to participate in a concordat strategy designed to stabilize church-state relations. Concordats were seen by the Assembly as invasive and morally untenable in a genuinely liberal national environment. The state was finally compelled to sign an unprecedented *intesa* (agreement) with the Waldensian-Methodist Church (February 21, 1984) which lifted all lingering restrictions preventing the free exercise of the privileges and responsibilities normally identified with organized religion. A similar agreement was negotiated by the government with the Assemblies of God in Italy in 1986, thus granting juridical recognition to the Pentecostal faith in Italy. It was expected that this precedent would become a model for all church-state understandings in Italy.

Bibliography: M. Bunson, *The Pope Encyclopedia: An A to Z of the Holy See* (New York, 1995) • F. J. Coppa, ed., *Controversial Concordats: The Vatican Relations with Napoleon, Mussolini, and Hitler* (Washington, D.C., 1998); idem, ed., *Encyclopedia of the Vatican and Papacy* (Westport, Conn., 1999) • R. Davis, trans., *The Book of Popes: Liber Pontificalis* (Liverpool, 1989) • E. Duffy, *Saints and Sinners: A History of the Popes* (New Haven, 1997) • E. Habson, *The Catholic Church in World Politics* (Princeton, 1987) • S. W. Halperin,

Italy and the Vatican at War (Chicago, 1939); idem, *The Separation of Church and State in Italian Thought from Cavour to Mussolini* (Chicago, 1937) • J. Hubert and J. Dolan, eds., *History of the Church* (10 vols., New York, 1980-82) • A. C. Jemolo, *Church and State in Italy, 1850-1950* (Oxford, 1960) • P. Nichols, *The Politics of the Vatican* (New York, 1968) • G. Tourn et al., *You Are My Witnesses: The Waldensians across 800 Years* (Turin, 1989).

Cesare Milaneschi and Ronald S. Cunsolo

Ivory Coast

	1960	1980	2000
Population (1,000s):	3,799	8,194	15,144
Annual growth rate (%):	3.51	3.75	2.32

Area: 322,463 sq. km. (124,504 sq. mi.)

A.D. *2000*

Population density: 47/sq. km. (122/sq. mi.)
Births / deaths: 3.57 / 1.29 per 100 population
Fertility rate: 4.55 per woman
Infant mortality rate: 78 per 1,000 live births
Life expectancy: 52.3 years (m: 51.3, f: 53.4)
Religious affiliation (%): tribal religionists 37.1, Christians 31.7 (Roman Catholics 14.5, indigenous 10.8, Protestants 5.6, other Christians 0.8), Muslims 30.6, other 0.6.

1. General Situation
2. Religious Situation

1. General Situation

The Ivory Coast (or, its preferred form, Côte d'Ivoire), a West African republic, became a French protectorate in 1842, a French colony in 1893, and in 1960 gained its independence. Its first contacts with Europe were with the Portuguese in the 15th century, followed by the Danes and French, who traded in ivory and → slaves (→ Colonialism). The country has been created out of more than 60 ethnic groups speaking as many native languages. The largest groups are the Baoulé (23 percent), Bété (18 percent), Senoufou (15 percent), and Malinké (11 percent); the most widely spoken language is Dioula (Jula). Ivory Coast is among the largest French-speaking countries in Africa.

Politically, the Ivory Coast has been relatively stable, in spite of attempts in the 1960s by Kwame Nkrumah's Ghanaian government on its eastern border to subvert it and, more recently, the social and political chaos of neighboring Liberia and Sierra Leone. At independence the government of

President Félix Houphouët-Boigny built good and collaborative relationships with the Ivory Coast's erstwhile colonial ruler, France. This policy was both insurance for political security and security for economic success.

Economically, the Ivory Coast is predominantly an agricultural country. It is one of the world's largest exporters of coffee, cocoa beans, and palm oil. Its economy is therefore highly sensitive both to weather conditions and to international price fluctuations.

The economy has been hurt by the country's highly centralized national presidential system, in which the resources of the nation were used for the president's own political and personal benefit. These developments coincided with governmental loss of control over public expenditure and, in 1976-77, with an increase in world oil prices. The result was a considerable foreign exchange debt for Ivory Coast. In 1981 it thus adopted the World Bank's recipe of a "structural adjustment" program. This effort failed, however, being frustrated by a collapse in world prices for cocoa and coffee. In 1986 a second dose of the structural adjustment program was administered. The drastic consequences of this program for salaries, employment, and so forth were predictable: strife became a mark of Ivorian society.

Houphouët-Boigny died in 1993. Henri Konan Bédié was elected to complete Boigny's unfinished term and then in October 1995 was elected in his own right as the president of Ivory Coast. Bédié pursued a policy of "regulated openness," by which political changes were made, including deregulation, liberalization, and privatization. In 1994 there were signs of improvement in the economy. The intensification of nontraditional agriculture and the improvement in the world cocoa and coffee prices led to this improvement. The net effect was that there was real economic growth of 6-7 percent.

On Christmas Eve 1999, just a year before scheduled elections, Konan Bédié was ousted by a junta led by retired General Robert Guei. A military government took control, and in July 2000 a new national constitution, supported by all political parties, was approved by 87 percent of the voting public.

2. Religious Situation

Religion is a major feature of Ivorian society. The principal religions include African traditional religions, which represented 94 percent of the population in 1900 but less than half in 2000 (→ Tribal Religions; Guinea 2). → Islam grew from 5 percent in

1900 to six times that percentage in 2000. Christianity, which represented only 1 percent of the population in 1900, has grown to slightly more than the current level of Islam.

One might take these figures as indicating that Islam and Christianity have grown at the expense of traditional religion. African religion, however, is also part of the culture, so that Christians at the crisis points of life continue to practice something of traditional religion. Also, because of the church's involvement in social services, the influence of the Christian faith may go beyond the official statistics.

The Christian → missionary presence in the Ivory Coast dates back to about 1637, when six Capuchin priests from France came to Abiany. In spite of the goodwill of the king, the mission did not go far because of the death of four of the six priests within a year, and the two remaining had to depart to Axim in Ghana. Not until 1893, when Ivory Coast became a French colony, was there renewal of Roman Catholic work. In 1895 the Société des Missions Africaines de Lyon (SMA) also sent missionaries to Ivory Coast. In 1898 Religieuses de Notre Dame des Apôtres (Sisters of Our Lady of the Apostles) also sent missionaries. It took until 1934 before the first African was ordained. Roman Catholicism is mostly in the South and in the cities, but urbanization often goes with some de-Christianization. In other words, the church has yet to define its mission in the urban centers. In 1922 the Église Déimateste separated from the → Roman Catholic Church.

Roman Catholicism in the Ivory Coast has become globally celebrated through the erection by President Houphouët-Boigny (1986-89) of the Basilica of Our Lady of Peace, advertised as the largest church in the world. Situated in Yamoussoukro, the official capital of Ivory Coast, the church was consecrated by John Paul II (1990) and remains a highly controversial structure.

Protestants came to the Ivory Coast after World War I. The British Methodist Missionary Society, arriving in 1924, was followed by Missions Biblique (→ French Missions), the → Christian and Missionary Alliance (CMA, United States), the Worldwide Evangelization Crusade (WEC), and → Baptist groups. These groups, guided by a principle of comity, settled in different areas, in consequence of which the various Protestant denominations today look like tribal churches. Other Protestant denominations found in the Ivory Coast include → Methodists and Seventh-day → Adventists.

While there is no national Christian council, the Evangelical Federation of the Ivory Coast brings together churches that have grown out of the CMA, the WEC, the Unevangelized Fields Mission, Conservative and Freewill Baptists, and Missions Biblique. The Taizé Community of France promotes dialogue between Protestant and Roman Catholic Churches.

One of the most significant factors in the Ivory Coast church scene is the movement of indigenous churches (→ Independent Churches). The most widely known is the Harris Movement. It takes its name from William Wadé Harris (ca. 1860-1929), a charismatic leader from Liberia who appeared in the Ivory Coast in 1913 as a preacher of the gospel whose ministry was marked by the driving out of evil spirits (→ Exorcism), witchcraft, and → magic. Harris's outstanding success caused considerable attention within the government and also created some tension with the Roman Catholics. After his imprisonment some of his followers joined the Roman Catholic Church and others the → Methodist Church. A remnant Harrist Church continues today, though there have been several schisms.

Bibliography: R. W. L. ALPINE, Agriculture, Liberalisation, and Economic Growth in Ghana and Côte d'Ivoire: 1960-1990 (Paris, 1993) • M. A. COHEN, Urban Policy and Political Conflict in Africa: A Study of the Ivory Coast (Chicago, 1974) • A. GOTTLIEB, Parallel Worlds: An Anthropologist and a Writer Encounter Africa (Chicago, 1994) • C. GROOTAERT, Analyzing Poverty and Policy Reform: The Experience of Côte d'Ivoire (Aldershot, 1996) • G. M. HALIBURTON, The Prophet Harris: A Study of an African Prophet and His Mass-Movement in the Ivory Coast and the Gold Coast, 1913-1915 (London, 1971) • R. LAUNAY, Beyond the Stream: Islam and Society in a West African Town (Berkeley, Calif., 1992) • J. RAPLEY, Ivoirien Capitalism: African Entrepreneurs in Côte d'Ivoire (Boulder, Colo., 1993) • D. A. SHANK, "The Legacy of William Wadé Harris," IBMR 10 (1986) 170-76 • S. S. WALKER, Religious Revolution in the Ivory Coast: The Prophet Harris and the Harrist Church (Chapel Hill, N.C., 1983).

JOHN S. POBEE